Carmichael's
MANUAL OF CHILD PSYCHOLOGY

Carmichael's

MANUAL OF CHILD PSYCHOLOGY

Third Edition

PAUL H. MUSSEN, *Editor*

VOLUME I

JOHN WILEY & SONS, INC.   New York · London · Sydney · Toronto

Copyright © 1946, 1954, 1970, by John Wiley & Sons, Inc.

All rights reserved.

20 19 18 17 16 15 14 13 12 11

Library of Congress Catalogue Card Number: 69–16127

SBN 471   62695   3

Printed in the United States of America

Contributors to Volume I

Nancy Bayley
D. E. Berlyne
Leonard Carmichael
Dorothy Eichorn
John H. Flavell
Joan Grusec
Marshall M. Haith
Eckhard H. Hess
Jerome Kagan
Nathan Kogan
William Kessen
Jonas Langer
Robert B. McCall
Gerald E. McClearn
David McNeill
Jean Piaget
Anne D. Pick
Herbert L. Pick, Jr.
William D. Rohwer, Jr.
Philip H. Salapatek
Harold W. Stevenson
J. M. Tanner
William R. Thompson
Michael A. Wallach
Sheldon White

Preface

This is the third edition of the *Manual of Child Psychology*. The first and second editions, edited by Leonard Carmichael, were published in 1946 and 1954 respectively. It should be clear from the outset, however, that the present volumes are not, in any real sense, a *revision* of the earlier editions; this is a completely new *Manual*.

The general purpose of this edition, like that of the previous ones, is to provide a comprehensive and accurate picture of the current state of knowledge—the major systematic thinking and research—in the most important research areas of the psychology of human development. But developmental psychology has been radically transformed, in numerous and complex ways, in the last two decades. While some features of the discipline—its goals, approaches, and research foci—have not changed much, its overall "look" in 1970 is vastly different from what it was in 1950. Complete specifications and analyses of all the changes, which are intimately connected with one another, and of the reasons for them, would require a long essay on the history of the field and the social forces that shaped it. However, a brief survey of some of the enduring characteristics and major shifts may help to provide a broader perspective and to clarify the contrasts between the 1954 edition and the present one.

Many crucial contemporary problems were apparent even in antiquity and have recurred repeatedly throughout the history of developmental psychology; however, they remain unresolved and continue to be the impetus for much research. An example is the problem of whether the individual's development and attainments are primarily determined by his genetic makeup or by environmental conditions, by nature or by nurture? Generally speaking, the basic objectives or tasks of present-day developmental psychology, which are interrelated, are the same ones that characterized the field 20 years ago—description of the genesis of behavior and of age changes; explanation of these (the mechanisms, processes, and determinants of change); delineation of the relationships between early and later behavior. But the distribution of scientific resources and publications devoted to the various goals has changed markedly. Until approximately 25 years ago, developmental psychologists were primarily concerned with precise descriptions of children's capabilities at various ages and reliable determination of age changes in psychological functions such as psychomotor performance, problem solving, and aggressive reactions. And there are continuing needs for more accurate, detailed descriptions of the transformations, continuities, stages, and discontinuities in many aspects of development, particularly in cognitive functions and in social and emotional behavior.

The major contemporary empirical and theoretical emphases in the field of developmental psychology, however, seem to be on *explanations* of the psychological changes that occur, the mechanisms and processes accounting for growth and development. Hypotheses dealing with the beginnings of behavior, and with the determinants of change have been tested experimentally and in naturalistic settings. Investigations of factors correlated with individual differences in psychological functions, traits, and abilities as well as longitudinal research, also yield valuable data bearing on the problems of stability and continuities in development and the mechanisms of change. Compared with the last edition, this one includes many more accounts of studies of these kinds.

Increased interest in mechanisms of change stimulated more theory-building and, consequently, theory seems to be generally more prominent in the literature of developmental psychology today than it was in 1950, often playing a much more critical role in determining the direction of empirical research. This is particularly true in the area of cognitive development, where the theories of Piaget and of Werner have been major sources of research hypotheses and further conceptualizations relating to the nature of perception, thought, and problem solving.

The 1954 edition of this *Manual* had only one theoretical chapter and that was concerned with Levinian theory which, so far as we can see, has not had a significant lasting impact on developmental psychology. Volume I of the present edition includes four chapters exclusively devoted to theory and, in addition, relevant theoretical issues are discussed in some detail in most of the substantive chapters. Psychoanalytic theory is probably not as powerful an intellectual force in child psychology today as it was 20 years ago but it is still important in stimulating and guiding research in personality and social development. Unfortunately, the chapter on psychoanalysis as a developmental theory, originally planned for this edition, was not completed. However, a number of chapters in this volume discuss aspects of this theory and two recent books offer excellent discussions and critiques of psychoanalytic developmental theory.[1]

Like all scientific fields, developmental psychology has experienced its own "knowledge explosion." The sheer number of revelant articles and books has increased, and continues to increase, at an awe-inspiring rate, and the newer literature is broader in scope and more varied in content than that of 20 years ago. Theoretical and empirical analyses of fundamental problems have become more penetrating, refined, and sophisticated. At the same time, the invention of ingenious new methods and techniques of investigation in

developmental psychology and related fields, together with modifications and improvements in older ones, paved the way for more adequate, reliable, and meaningful research into complex problems of long standing (or variations of these) and into more recently formulated questions. As a result of these advances, many new facts have been accumulated and many previously "accepted" findings have been reconsidered and discarded. Some established theories have been revised and abandoned while alternative theoretical approaches have been proposed and systematized. Whole areas of research and theory such as behavior genetics, ethology, and large segments of developmental physiology, hardly existed 20 years ago but, by 1970, they have achieved scientific maturity and contribute substantially to the field of developmental psychology. Largely because of this kind of knowledge explosion and its consequences, this edition of the *Manual* is in two volumes, rather than the one-volume previous edition, and has twice as many pages.

Recent social and historical events have also generated more active concern with the potential practical contributions of the systematic study of developmental psychology. Responding to critical social needs, many developmental and educational psychologists have turned their research attention to applied problems such as promoting cognitive abilities, improving teaching techniques, raising the educational and intellectual status of the culturally disadvantaged, understanding the etiology and treatment of mental retardation and psychopathology, and preventing juvenile delinquency. The findings of empirical investigations in these problem areas have both practical and theoretical significance, as several of the chapters in this volume demonstrate. (See, for example, the chapters in Volumes I and II on early experience, creativity, implications of cognitive development for education, social class and ethnic group influences on socialization, moral values and behavior, mental retardation, behavior disorders, and psychosis in childhood.)

Inevitably, the knowledge explosion and the continuous, if modest, advance in theory and application in developmental psychology have resulted in greater specialization within the field. The organization of the present volume and the contents of the chapters are

---

[1] See Baldwin, Alfred L., *Theories of child development*. New York: Wiley, 1967, and Langer, Jonas, *Theories of development*. New York: Holt, Rinehart, and Winston, 1969.

testimony of this. While the 1954 edition of the *Manual* had only one chapter on emotional development and another on social psychology, Volume I of the present edition has a major section on socialization, consisting of seven chapters. These deal with the following topics: sex typing and identification, affiliative behavior and dependency, aggression, moral values and behavior, peer interaction, and social organization. Two chapters of the second edition were devoted to mental growth and development, and one dealt with psychopathology. The present edition contains ten chapters on cognitive development (Volume I), and three on abnormal behavior in children (Volume II).

The enormous growth in quantity of relevant literature, the high degree of specialization, and the changing tone of developmental psychology make it exceedingly difficult to produce a full, balanced, accurate, and up-to-date representation of the state of the discipline. In trying to achieve this, I was most fortunate to have the help of five distinguished developmental psychologists who served as an Advisory Committee: Professors Jerome Kagan of Harvard University, William Kessen of Yale University, Eleanor Maccoby of Stanford University, Harold Stevenson of the University of Minnesota, and Sheldon White of Harvard University. We worked together in every phase of planning and organizing this *Manual*, from original conceptualization to final editing.

As we conceived it, the *Manual* is a comprehensive textbook or sourcebook for advanced undergraduate and graduate students as well as for specialists in many areas of psychology and in related fields such as ed-ucation, psychiatry, and pediatrics. Hence, it must represent, as far as possible and in abbreviated form, all the established and influential theories, as well as the reliable accumulated knowledge, in developmental psychology. But it should not consist simply of organized summaries of the literature. Instead, great stress should be given to critical analyses and evaluations; major gaps in theory and data should be illuminated. In brief, the *Manual* should foster the development of new perspectives and insights and, ultimately, it may stimulate some readers to formulate hypotheses and to conduct research.

With this in mind, we made many difficult, critical decisions about the table of contents, essentially pooling our judgments about the areas that are currently most productive of theory and investigation. Obviously, specialized areas of interest could not be fully covered. We collaborated in selecting and inviting recognized authorities who could write stimulating, comprehensive, and integrated chapters, and fortunately, almost all our invitations were enthusiastically accepted. Every "working outline" and final manuscript was reviewed by the editor and at least one member of the Advisory Committee who made suggestions for revisions.

Without the diligent and painstaking work of the authors and the invaluable assistance of the members of the Advisory Committee, this book could not have been completed. I gratefully acknowledge my vast indebtedness to all of them. Whatever success these volumes achieve is due as much to their efforts as to my own.

Paul Mussen

Berkeley, California, January, 1970

Contents

VOLUME I

PART I

BIOLOGICAL BASIS
OF DEVELOPMENT

1. Ethology and Developmental Psychology

ECKHARD H. HESS

Man is an animal. He is a biological organism with an evolutionary history. Nevertheless, when it is suggested that, in common with other animals, man may manifest inherited, or genetically programmed behaviors, dissent often comes quickly from behavioral scientists. Indeed, it is unfashionable these days to investigate such genetically determined behavior in humans. For example, Spuhler and Lindzey (1967) complete a recent summary of human behavior genetics with respect to possible racial differences by stating that it is "an area of research that is procedurally difficult, politically dangerous, and personally repugnant to most psychologists, sociologists, and anthropologists."

If we look at the behavior of *all* animals on this earth we reach three inescapable conclusions.

1. Innate behavior is the necessary and *sufficient* condition for the survival of most organisms.

2. Learned behavior, alone, is the necessary and *sufficient* condition for the survival of none. Those few organisms most interesting to us, as psychologists, undoubtedly are heavily influenced by learning. This, however, does not alter the truth of these two conclusions.

3. Innate, or genetically programmed behavior is necessary for the survival of *all* animals.

Even the effectiveness of learning or conditioning has to depend on the genetically determined *positive* or *negative* value of whatever reinforcement takes place. Reward and punishment are meaningless concepts when used without reference to the conditions that make them work. These conditions must already be present, that is, innately possessed, or else they must be built up by environmental or learning processes which ultimately *rest on some innate response*. In other words, learning cannot be shaped by reward or punishment unless the organism is already structured so that reward and punishment *will* have positive and negative values, respectively: the survival value of specific consequences of behavior has, through the course of evolution, formed organisms that are innately constituted to act to attain reward and to avoid punishment. The "consummatory acts" of learning experiments are innately fixed behavior patterns which serve to reinforce preceding behavior acts. It is particularly in the human infant that we have an opportunity to observe behaviors that *must be there* for the infant to survive. Learning cannot come along quickly enough to assure its survival.

We shall not enter into the argument regarding the "usefulness" of distinguishing between innate and learned behavior, which has been brought up by numerous psychologists. "Innate behavior" is used here to mean genetically programmed behavior, just as we have genetically programmed morphology. Morphology, as is well known, is based upon genetically stored information possessed by the species and the individual. The sequential development of the body form during ontogeny, beginning with fertilization and following through to the mature shape, is programmed by this genetic information. Innate behavior is programmed in the same way, and in this sense specific innate behaviors may be regarded as individual organs

1

possessed by the organism (Lorenz, 1937). Beginning with the section on Innate Behavior we shall discuss how ethologists have utilized this concept.

"Learning" here refers to what the learning psychologists call learning. Miller (1967) has listed a set of criteria for determining instances of learning. Environmental components such as temperature, oxygen, and water are excluded from learning. Such components can have an effect on behavior, just as they can have an effect on morphology, and thus they should be regarded as factors that can alter the expression of genetic potential rather than as learning.

With this frame of reference, then, let us turn to a description of the ethological approach to the study of behavior and to the concepts and theoretical viewpoints characteristic of most of those scientists who can be called "ethologists."

BASIC CONCEPTS IN ETHOLOGY

The Ethological Approach to the Study of Behavior

Behavior is so multiform that innumerable theories have been developed in the attempt to explain it on the basis of partial knowledge. Indeed, the facets of behavior are such that it is possible to glean supporting evidence for any theory of behavior, even one that is capriciously constructed. The fable of the blind men and the elephant is completely applicable to this situation: theories of behavior are usually extrapolations based upon only some segment of all the behavioral phenomena that exist.

Recently the discipline of ethology has gained increasing attention from students of behavior, principally because ethologists have taken theoretical positions very different from those maintained by traditional behavioristic theories, which sought principally to examine the influence of the environment upon behavior. However, the theoretical positions of ethologists are not their only distinguishing characteristics, for the very data that they gather are also different.

It must be said, nevertheless, that the ethologists' theory does not determine what kind of facts they search for and which ones they will discard. Rather, it is the philosophy of ethologists that facts come first; after they have been gathered, a theory to accommodate *all* facts may be attempted. Any theories so constructed are limited to the particular set of facts upon which they were founded. And ethologists tend to have an almost compulsive passion for collecting *all* the facts.

Even so, the facts that ethologists initially collect are those of a particular universe. This is because ethology has as its major premise the notion that the study of behavior begins through the compilation of as complete an inventory as possible of all the behaviors of the organisms in, and in relation to, its natural environment, throughout its entire life cycle. A collection of such observations on a single species is called an "ethogram." An ethogram is purely descriptive, cataloguing as exhaustively as possible what an animal does without any concurrent concern regarding the causal bases of such behavior. However, ethograms do go beyond the usual naturalistic approach because the behaviors are then classified and compared with those of many other species, particularly related ones.

Ethology first developed from the work of zoologists, who were interested in the study of the natural behavior of animals. Faced with the mass of facts they had garnered, these zoologists soon saw several conceptual similarities between morphology and innate behavior. In fact, modern ethology really began with the discovery of the taxonomic value of the innate behaviors known as fixed action patterns (Heinroth, 1910, Whitman, 1898). Today we can see a rather thorough application of concepts derived from morphology, evolution, and embryology to the analysis of innate behavior.

From the outset ethologists have emphasized the importance of the natural behavior of animals in their own habitats as the fundamental basis upon which any subsequent analysis of behavior must build before formulating any hypotheses regarding behavior. This initial approach was intended as a corrective to an earlier, prevailing tendency of environmentally oriented animal psychologists to confine their attention to a limited number of phenomena observed in a few species maintained in impoverished and artificial laboratory surroundings since birth. Such circumscribed and unnatural observations nevertheless led these psychologists to formulate extremely wide-ranging theories, which proposed to encompass all behavior phenomena, even those in man.

The importance of the natural environment in studying the behavior of animals has been emphasized because it is much more difficult to maintain animals in an optimum state of health in conditions of captivity. Captivity may thus result in the failure of animals to manifest some aspects of their behavior capabilities. In addition, captive animals frequently engage in abnormal stereotyped behaviors, as is evident to most zoo-goers.

There is an intimate relationship between the behavior of animals and the characteristics of their wild habitat, according to ethologists. Certainly it is obvious that there is a relationship between what an animal needs, in the way of shelter or food, for example, the environment in which these are naturally found, and the animal's behavior in relation to that environment. Unlike laboratory conditions, which place restrictions and artificial conditions on the animal, the animal's behavior in the wild significantly fits the natural environment.

The ethologists have concentrated initially on naturally occurring behavior rather than solely on learning processes, as many animal psychologists have done. It is their conviction that the basic material already present in an animal must be known before changes in this substratum through learning or any unusual environmental exposure can be studied. This emphasis has led some psychologists to mistakenly assume that ethologists do not regard learning as very important. On the contrary, they regard learning as of the highest importance, and as one of the many mechanisms that produce behavior in animals. They do not hold the belief that a given behavior is either wholly learned or wholly innate—only the basic components or units are one or the other; this aspect of ethological theory will be discussed later.

Although the starting point is always the collection of ethograms, the ethologists naturally go much farther than this. Subsequent to the cataloguing of the animal's behavior into an ethogram is the analysis of the behaviors with respect to the factors that enter into or influence the behaviors. At this point it is considered permissible to change the environment experimentally because we can then know with greater certainty in what ways these changes influence the animal's behavior. Deprivation experiments, in which animals are deprived of certain environmental factors such as social experience, auditory experience, or visual experience, constitute a technique as familiar to the ethologists as to animal psychologists.

Consonant with their biological training, the ethologists not only study animal behaviors with respect to environmental factors but also attempt to assay their probable evolution, ontogenetic development, survival value or function, and physiological bases. All of these are extremely important aspects of present-day ethological theory and research.

Innate Behavior

Early workers such as the German zoologist Baron von Pernau (1707), the French naturalist Réaumur (1734–1742), Charles Darwin (1872), the English naturalist Spalding (1873), and later the American zoologists Jennings (1904), Craig (1918), and Whitman (1898), and the German zoologist von Uexküll (1909) had all studied unlearned behavior in animals scientifically. But the blatantly promiscuous use of the term "instinct" during the late nineteenth and early twentieth centuries by many psychologists in the United States and elsewhere had reduced it to a catch-all explanation for behaviors which were not readily understood. The reaction to this inappropriate use of the term was like "throwing out the baby with the bath water," for the concept of instinct or innate behavior was completely denied by psychologists who were attracted to Watson's (1922, 1928) behavioristic theory, which promised to explain behavior on the basis of simple relationships between the individual and his environment.

The work of the ethologists has provided a substantial scientific and renewed theoretical basis for the use of the concept of innate behavior. The ethological concept of innate behavior is that it is relatively complex animal activity, which generally involves the whole organism rather than merely an isolated part. Such behavior is a characteristic of the species to which the animal belongs rather than of the individual, whereas learned behavior is *individually* acquired during ontogeny. Since the behavior is a species characteristic, it originates without previous experience or modification caused by experience: it is genetically programmed, as are many morphological features. Environmental factors, of course, can alter the expressions of innate behavior or morphology. Inheritance, or phylogenetic adaptation of the species recorded in the genome (set of chromosomes with constituent genes), is considered the ultimate criterion of innate behavior. Stereotypy is not the criterion of innate behavior, since it can also occur in many individually acquired learned behaviors. Furthermore, innate behavior has an end or purpose; but many experiments have shown that the animal does not perform the behavior for this purpose. To cite only one example, prey hunting by dogs and cats that are well fed is performed for its own sake. In other words, the animal appears to need to perform the movements involved in hunting, and not solely for the purpose of obtaining food, although the fact that under wild conditions such behavior does have this utility indicates the survival value which tends to preserve this behavior in the species. Finally, species-specific behavior is itself composed of several elements: reflexes, taxes (directed orientations), and fixed action patterns.

Ethologists maintain that it is sometimes difficult to distinguish between innate behavior and behavior learned early in the life of the animal because there are some innate behaviors that are not apparent until after certain developmental stages in the life cycle have been achieved. This is the problem of ontogeny, which sometimes still presents an impasse between most ethologically oriented researchers and certain animal psychologists. Just as did Erasmus Darwin (1794) or Kuo (1932a–d), the latter proposed that the presence of a given behavior at the moment of birth could mean that it was *learned before birth*, whereas ethological researchers were vigorous proponents of the view that innate behaviors could be regarded as possessed by animals as are organs or other morphological features. Furthermore, the ethologists pointed out that there are morphological features that are not present at birth.

Charles Darwin (1883) viewed innate behaviors as being just as subject to modification by natural selection as are morphological characters. In fact, Darwin applied exactly the same principles of morphological evolution—convergent, divergent evolution, natural selection pressure, and variation between individuals—to the evolution of innate behavior. Before Darwin it had been generally believed that the "knowledge" animals displayed in their innate behavior was implanted in them by the Creator. With Darwin's theory came the notion of the transmission of such innate behavior from one generation to another through heredity, evolving in response to the forces of natural selection. The evolutionary view of behavior was supported and expanded on by Spalding (1873), Morgan (1896), Wesley Mills (1896), Romanes (1881, 1883), Whitman (1898), Thorndike (1899), and Heinroth (1910).

The biological and evolutionary viewpoint on innate behavior remains the bulwark of ethological philosophy and theory. A recent definition of innate behavior by an ethologically oriented neurophysiologist, for example, is: "actions of an individual animal that are inevitable expressions of a neural organization determined and unfolded in ontogenesis in the same way as is the body form characteristic of the species" (Roeder, 1963). The genotype, according to Roeder, expresses itself in the entire morphological make-up of the individual organisms, including the nervous system down to fine details of sense organs, nerves, and neuronal connections. Innate behavior is regarded as the expression of this neural organization.

Today many psychologists in the United States have what is called an "epigenetic" view toward behavior; the main proponents of this view are Schneirla (1946, 1956, 1957; also Schneirla and Rosenblatt, 1961), Hebb (1953), Lehrman (1953, 1956), and Moltz (1965). The epigenetic viewpoint, according to Moltz (1965), "considers gene effects as capable of entering into different classes of relationships depending on the prevailing complex." Essentially, this epigenetic viewpoint appears to be one that arose out of the growing conviction that the traditional heredity-environment dualism served only to obscure the problem of the origin of behavior. This viewpoint apparently has its roots as long ago as 1925 when Carmichael pointed out that it was not possible on the basis of the then-current knowledge to differentiate between that which is native and that which is acquired, once the fertilized egg has begun to develop. "The so-called hereditary factors can only be acquired in response to the environment and likewise the so-called acquired factors can only be secured by a modification of already existing structure, which in the last analysis is hereditary structure," Carmichael (1925) declared.

Thus it is that psychologists such as Schneirla (1946, 1956) have postulated that species-typical behaviors do exist, while denying that there are separate (and/or unitary) entities such as learning or instinct, which produce behavior. Learned behavior and innate behavior, although usually regarded as distinct by many ethologists, are not necessarily antithetical, as we shall soon see.

The Functions of Innate Behavior

Although ethologists use the terms innate and learned, they do not conceive of two parallel, independent neural mechanisms determining behavior. Learning processes may possibly constitute a natural unit, from the ethological point of view, and they may possibly have similar physiological processes in common with each other. But it is an error to think that ethologists postulate only *one* neural behavior-determining process into which learning does not enter. Rather, they say that *many* physiological processes innately determine behavior and that these processes are as different from each other as they are from learning. Not only do they have different origins, but they also are completely distinct from each other in their functions. Such mechanisms as the "innate releaser mechanism," "fixed action pattern," "orientation reactions," and "optomotoric reactions" are examples. Their only common property, according to the ethologists, is a negative one: the lack of learning processes, a criterion as useless as the lack of dental enamel in an anatomic group composed of knees, hands, and nose. All of the preceding behavior mechanisms, both learning processes and innately based behavior processes, are considered distinct rather than antithetical. Basic components or units of behavior rather than entire behaviors are determined by one or another of these mechanisms, so that any instance of gross behavior may be seen to consist of a unit-by-unit *intercalation* (interpolation or interweaving) of learned and various innate behavior mechanisms, an important concept which shall be discussed shortly.

One of the overriding interests of the ethologists in the analysis of behavior is the consideration of its *survival value* (defined as utility in the struggle for existence). In some cases the survival value of a behavior is so apparent that it hardly requires experimental investigation, (e.g., incubation behavior in broody hens), yet there are several other cases where this is far from true, and with these instances considerable study and analysis are required to elucidate their survival value. As Tinbergen (1963) pointed out, why do certain cryptic insects (those that escape predation by resembling leaves, bark, or twigs) perform rocking movements? Movement is a stimulus to which predators commonly react. Nevertheless, the rocking movement occurs in a large number of cryptic animals, which indicates that this movement has a survival value that is in some way related to camouflage.

The difficulty in immediately ascertaining survival value also exists with respect to morphological and certainly physiological features. As an example consider man's unfurred skin in stark contrast to the abundant fur of all other primates. Because any given behavior or bodily character has been subjected to the forces of evolution, it has therefore served as a means for survival, either in the past or at present. It does not, of course, necessarily have the most survival value for the particular animal in comparison with other alternatives. This is illustrated by the fact that male argus pheasants possess tremendous feathers, which have the function of sexually attracting the female. However, these feathers are detrimental to escape from predators, and thus conflict with that survival need. Nevertheless, the attendant survival value of their sexual attractiveness is such that the argus pheasant does not evolve shorter feathers in the male (Lorenz, 1966).

Although the past evolution of a species' behavior cannot be subjected to experimental proof and must be traced by indirect means, ethologists maintain that it is certainly possible in many cases to examine the question of how the present-day behavior of animals serves to promote survival. The fact that animals do survive in their natural environment is a problem that is related to every detail of behavior and structure, no matter how self-evident or insignificant it may seem to be. For example, as Tinbergen (1963) stated, there are adaptive reasons for the differences in the walking behavior of the godwit and the lapwing, as Klompf (1954) has shown. Godwits lift and fold their feet much more than do lapwings and thus avoid getting their toes caught in the tall grass in which they breed. Lapwings, however, avoid habitats with tall vegetation. Tinbergen (1963) has demonstrated that the question of the survival value of behavior is in itself a vast field for experimental study that has great potential.

Regardless of whether a behavior is a learned or a phenotypic expression, its ultimate value is, as we have stressed, assumed to be in the service of the survival of the individual or species. Learned behavior aids in the survival of the individual only, whereas other behavior mechanisms insure the survival of the species. Lorenz (1961, 1965) has developed a theoretical position with this notion at its core. He maintains that there are really two and only two entirely independent (but not antithetical) mechanisms that effect the *adaptation* of behavior. If an organism shows adaptive behavior, this means that it has been molded to fit the environment in a way that will achieve survival; according to Lorenz, there are only two ways in which this molding may be achieved. The first is the process of phylogeny, which evolves behavior mechanisms just as much as any morphological feature or physiological function. The second is the process of ontogeny, which involves adaptive modification of behavior during the individual's life. Lorenz has emphasized that although mutation and individual learning, are two entirely distinct processes, both have the very important function of creating and/ or adaptively changing the structure of the neural apparatus determining behavior. In fact, Lorenz's position goes to the extent of postulating that there is selection for learning ability during the process of phylogeny, and this ability has been fixated in the genetic constitution of the species. The increase in survival value effected by learning processes is, in Lorenz's opinion, the ultimate proof that learning processes in themselves are the product of adaptive evolution.

Therefore, Lorenz deduced, learning is a *specific* survival-achieving function of the organism. Modifiability of behavior through learning processes, he suggested, occurs at specific, evolutionarily preformed places where inbuilt learning mechanisms wait to perform just that function. Very often these inbuilt learning mechanisms are unable to modify any but *one* very circumscribed system of behavior mechanisms. For example, Lorenz points out, honeybees can use irregular forms such as trees and rocks as landmarks to find their way to the hive. But they are unable to use these forms as signals indicating the presence or absence of food. The types of forms that bees *can* learn to use as food signals are those that are geometrically regular, preferably radially symmetrical.

Examples of coexistent learned and innate components in behavior are numerous in ethological literature. It has been observed in many bird species that innate nest-building movements may be made but the individuals must learn which materials to use for this purpose. Eibl-Eibesfeldt (1956a) has shown that in the prey-killing technique of the polecat, the killing bite, that is, the sinking of the teeth into the animal and shaking at the same time, is innate, whereas the directing of the killing bite to the prey's neck is learned in a few trials. Eibl-Eibesfeldt (1956b) also showed that nut-cracking in squirrels consists of a number of acts—manipulating, gnawing, cracking—which develop in naive individuals without the benefit of practice; however, the integration of these individual acts into an adaptive sequence must be learned.

Further examples are found in the classical social "imprinting" phenomenon in which newly hatched nidifugous (not remaining in the nest, motorically precocious) birds such as ducklings and chicks show an innate drive for contact with a parent object during a genetically determined "sensitive period" in the early hours of life with the result that under normal conditions the characteristics of the parent object are learned. In all these examples of learning a *genetic program* that limits the range of items that may be involved or the time of learning, or both, is present.

The notion of the intercalation or interweaving of different behavior mechanisms in a sequence of actions is a primary mainstay of the ethological approach to the analysis of behavior. Lorenz's term for this, coined in 1937, is *Instinkt-Dressur-Vershränkung*, translated as *instinct-training-interlocking*. It implies that behavior is a continuous process of smooth integration of chunks of learned behaviors with innate ones. The learned components are considered to lend a flexibility to behavior and to promote greater adaptability in various environmental conditions. The innate components insure that certain reactions to specific stimuli will be made without the necessity of learning. These innate components, Lorenz stressed, can be seen most clearly in cases where, if learning were required, the possibility of survival would be greatly diminished.

Innate Behavior Mechanisms

We previously mentioned that the ethologists have postulated the existence of several innately determined (genetically programmed) behavior mechanisms. We shall now discuss a few of the most important of these mechanisms and show how these concepts are used to deal with motivation and reinforcement.

The *fixed action pattern*, or, more simply, fixed pattern, is one of the most fundamental concepts. In fact, modern ethology was founded on the independent discoveries of this phenomenon by Heinroth (1910) and Whitman (1898).

The fixed action pattern is defined as a genetically programmed sequence of coordinated motor actions. The animal can perform it without antecedent learning or previous exercise and without having seen another species member perform it. The fixed action pattern is *constant in form*, which means that the sequence of motor elements never varies. The form constancy is the same as that which occurs in the case of morphological features possessed by members of the same species.

These patterns are not equivalent to the well-known reflexes, nor are they chain reflexes. There is neurophysiological evidence (e.g., von Holst, 1935, 1937) which has been interpreted as supporting this contention. We cannot adequately discuss within the limits of this chapter the many and complex differences between the fixed action patterns and the reflexes which the ethologists have pointed out, but one of the most important of these differences is the fact that the frequency with which the fixed action pattern is performed depends in part on how long it has been since it was last performed; this is not the case with reflexes. This factor, involving the concept of *action specific energy*, will

be discussed later. Furthermore, the fixed action pattern can serve as a consummatory act that ends a sequence of appetitive behavior (also discussed later). No such appetitive behavior ending in the discharge of a reflex has been found.

Ethologists maintain that the notion of the genetic fixedness of fixed action patterns is supported by their appearance in animals isolated from other members of their own species. For example, Eibl-Eibesfeldt (1956b) has observed that squirrels reared in isolation and never given any objects to handle nevertheless attempted to bury nuts or nutlike objects in a bare floor upon their first encounter with them, making scratching movements as if to dig out earth, tamping the object in the floor with the nose, and, finally, making complete covering movements in the air. Thus fixed action patterns are presumed to be based on specific inherited central nervous system mechanisms. As we mentioned earlier, ethologists stress *inheritance*, or genetic coding, and not stereotypy, as the ultimate criterion of fixed action patterns if they are truly to be considered as taxonomic, species-specific characteristics.

As with other morphological and physiological characters, fixed action patterns have been found to be characteristics not only of species but also of genera and orders right up to the highest taxonomic categories. Fixed action patterns, as Whitman (1898) and Heinroth (1910) observed, have value in assaying the taxonomic relationships between species. Furthermore, evolutionary changes that occur in fixed action patterns are similar to those that may be seen in morphological or physiological characters. It is postulated that selection may favor the development of a fixed action pattern that has much survival value or cause it to die away or atrophy when it has no survival value. Ethologists have found behavioral rudiments (or vestigal behaviors) which remain even though they have little survival value. An example of this is the fact that mutant *Drosophila* with no wings still perform the wing-preening movements typical of the species (Heinz, 1949). It is possible to find a kind of ontogenetic development similar to Haeckel's (1866) well known "phylogenetic recapitulation" of organs: a primitive behavior pattern may be seen to precede a more recently acquired one during the ontogeny of the species. Thus, as Lorenz (1937) observed, there are some species of birds (the lark, the raven, and the starling) belonging to the *Passeres* whose original form of ground locomotion was hopping (as postulated on the basis of comparison with other species) but that now live on the ground and run. The juveniles of these species hop in biped fashion before they run.

Ethologists have recently extended their work from the study of the probable phylogenesis of fixed action patterns to their physiological bases, and have obtained evidence strongly indicating that these are indeed based on inherited and structured neurophysiological mechanisms. However, the fixed action pattern is still generally defined in purely functional terms.

The *innate releasing mechanism* is another very fundamental concept. It is fundamental because it recognizes the fact that an animal, like man, does not give a particular response to *all* of the stimuli it perceives; most stimuli are only *potential* ones. The animal may learn to respond to some of these. The fixed action patterns, in particular, are elicited by only a few of the stimuli in an animal's environment. These eliciting stimuli are called *sign stimuli,* or *releasers* of the behaviors they evoke. Corresponding to these releasers are the innate releasing mechanisms within the animal, which respond to these sign stimuli by permitting the discharge of internally produced energy for the performance of the relevant fixed action patterns. These innate releasing mechanisms are abbreviated as IRMs.

The simplicity of the stimuli that elicit innately fixed behavior in animals may be illustrated by innumerable examples. One is the case of the carnivorous water beetle *Dysticus marginalis.* It does not react to the sight of prey, even though it has perfectly well developed compound eyes, but it does respond to the chemical stimuli emanating through the water from the prey. If it is presented a tadpole in a glass tube, the beetle will not attack, but if a meat extract solution is put into the water, the beetle engages in frantic searching behavior, clasping inanimate objects (Tinbergen, 1951).

Still another example of sign stimuli and innate releaser mechanisms is provided by the work of von Uexküll (1909). The common tick apparently responds to only three environmental stimuli during the greater part of its adult life. First, photoreceptors in its skin guide the tick's movements to the brightest part of its environment, which usually results in the tick climbing up a bush or tree. Second, the tick responds to the scent of butyric acid, which is given off by warm-blooded animals, by releasing its hold on the twig upon which it has been resting and thus dropping downward. Third, when it encounters a temperature of approximately 37°C, usually on a skin area of a mammal, it attaches itself and begins to drink blood. The relationship between these three stimuli and these responses is innate in origin and certainly each of them ensures survival of the species.

The reactions of animals to sign stimuli is automatic. For example, a hen will fail to rescue a chick that it can see struggling under a glass bell, but that it cannot hear. On the other hand, it comes to the chick's rescue immediately if it does not see it but can hear its distress cries (Brückner, 1933).

Although sign stimuli often consist of a simple quality such as butyric acid, they usually consist of relational characteristics between stimuli. For example, Koehler and Zagarus (1937) found that the ringed plover reacts more strongly to an egg having black spots on a white background than to one having dark brown spots on a light brown background because the spots contrast more strongly with the background in the case of the preferred eggs. More remarkably, they prefer abnormally large eggs, even ones they cannot sit upon. Such stimuli that release a response stronger than that released by the natural stimuli are called *superoptimal,* or supernormal sign stimuli by ethologists. There are many instances of superoptimal sign stimuli.

Sign stimuli are considered particularly important in intraspecies and interspecies communication. Striking examples of this can be seen in the courtship behavior of many animals, particularly the showy displays of some bird species. The IRMs which respond to these sign stimuli are regarded as *organs* possessed by the animal, with special functions in the service of survival. The IRM is thought to operate as a receptor of key stimuli and by necessity adapted to the world as it exists, so that it will respond only to stimuli that unfailingly characterize a particular biological situation, and no other. If a particular response is elicited by several sign stimuli belonging to a certain biological situation, then the presence of most of these stimuli in that situation guarantees the elicitation of the response in question. A pike cannot attach any releaser or sign stimulus to the fish on which it preys in order to differentiate it from a fisherman's lure; therefore the species must adapt the IRM accordingly. Otherwise, for lack of the ability to discriminate prey from a lure, the fish may be caught. Furthermore, it is obvious that the pike might not get enough to eat if it is unable to discriminate between prey and nonprey. Thus survival needs necessitate maximum discrimination capacities on the part of the IRM.

However, within a species or where interspecies communication takes place, natural selection can quickly result in the evolution of special sign stimuli or releasers that will be understood easily by the reacting animal. Ethologists have stressed that similar movements or behaviors performed by unrelated species for communication purposes have completely different meanings, for example, tail-wagging by the dog and by the cat. In related species the same movement is more likely to have the same social releaser value and meaning as well as the same genetic basis.

Further important concepts of ethologists can be seen in their treatment of the organization of behavior. Lorenz (1937, 1950) and Craig (1918) distinguished between two types of behavior: the *appetitive* and *aversive behaviors,* and the *consummatory act.* Appetitive behavior consists of initially variable searching behavior that becomes more and more specific until the simpler and more stereotyped consummatory act, in response to a releasing stimulus situation, is performed. Aversive behavior has some similarity with appetitive behavior, but it continues until a disturbing situation is removed and the animal reaches a state of equilibrium. Here the goal is not the discharge of any specific behavior patterns (consummatory acts) but the cutting off of aversive-appetitive behavior,

which normally consists of undirected locomotion.

Ethologists do not make an absolute distinction between appetitive behaviors and consummatory acts but postulate that there are many intermediate forms. These concepts, in effect, merely serve to mark extremes, with appetitive behavior being variable and plastic in character and the consummatory act being relatively fixed and stereotyped. The consummatory act, in fact, is the same as the fixed action pattern and is usually oriented toward specific directions by a *taxis.* Taxes, it may be briefly noted, are oriented locomotory movements steered to a certain direction by stimulation. An example is the movement of an animal toward a source of heat or light, the direction of the movement being determined by the intensity of the stimuli. In most cases the consummatory act is at the end of a long chain of behavior patterns involved in the appetitive behavior. In some cases, however, the consummatory act occurs so quickly that the appetitive stage is not readily apparent unless the opportunity to perform the consummatory act is withheld through the imposition of some obstacle. In this case appetitive behavior becomes plainly evident as the animal makes persistent attempts to perform the consummatory act in question.

Craig (1918) emphasized the notion that appetitive behavior is accompanied by a certain *readiness to act* and that many of the behavior patterns performed during the appetitive act are not innate but are learned. For example, a thirsty animal may go to a particular location for water because it has previously encountered water there. But the end action—the consummatory act—in itself is always innate, as is the actual drinking behavior. Further evidence of the innateness of the consummatory act is found in the occurrence of incipient consummatory acts or *intention movements* during the appetitive sequence, when the adequate stimulus for the consummatory action has not yet been received. In other words, we may observe incipient drinking movements in the thirsty animal searching for water.

Lorenz (1937, 1950) further enlarged upon this conceptualization of behavior by noting that there were observable fluctuations in the animal's readiness to perform fixed action patterns. The ease with which a given sign stimulus elicits or releases the corresponding fixed pattern through the innate releasing mechanism (IRM) apparently is dependent upon how long it has been since the animal has last given that response and not on the animal's general fatigue. Lorenz thus developed the notion of *action-specific energy* to describe this phenomenon. According to his conceptualization, action-specific energy, that is, energy for a particular action, is produced continuously in an animal's central nervous system. At the same time, this energy is held in check by some inhibitory mechanism until the appropriate stimulus releases it to certain muscular systems and the reaction takes place. The longer the animal has gone without performing the action in question, the more easily this behavior can be triggered off or released. In fact, in the case of a very prolonged absence of relevant stimulation during an appetitive behavior sequence this behavior can go off without there being any observable stimulus present. This special case Lorenz called the *Leerlaufreaktion*, or *vacuum activity*. This phenomenon is very readily seen in captive animals deprived of their natural environment.

Lorenz (1966) cited as an instance of vacuum activity a hand-reared starling that had always been well fed from a dish but that nevertheless would take off suddenly from its perch, fly to the ceiling to catch an invisible insect, return to the perch, and "eat" the insect. Likewise, dogs that are well fed will not lose their inclination to hunt and kill prey.

On the other hand, if the relevant stimulation is repeatedly given, the animal's response can decrease to the point where there is no response at all. A jumping spider (*Salticidae* family) catches prey by leaping at it rather than by building a web (Drees, 1952). A life-sized picture of a prey can be presented to this spider 30 to 40 successive times to elicit the attack response before it will cease responding in this way. If the spider is placed in a dark box for 2 hours, 10 to 20 more attack responses may then be elicited. Muscular fatigue is not the reason for the spider giving fewer attack responses than before, because if in the two-hour interval the spider is kept in a long runway with lights at each end alternately turning on and off, causing the

spider to run back and forth constantly, it will, at the end of this period, still make 10 to 20 attack responses to the picture of a prey.

It should be noted that Lorenz's notions of the building up and dissipation of the "reservoir" of the readiness to react are an extension of Craig's notions of appetitive behavior seeking the discharge of the consummatory act, especially as seen in the presence of incipient consummatory acts before the actual releasing situation has been encountered.

Tinbergen (1951) has further enlarged the Craig-Lorenz behavior scheme by proposing that there is a *hierarchical ordering of appetitive behaviors and consummatory acts* in animal behavior. Tinbergen explained that a particular appetitive behavior does not usually end in a consummatory act but, rather, leads to a stimulus situation that initiates other, more specific appetitive behavior. A chain of appetitive behaviors gives rise to a temporal sequence of *moods (Stimmung)*, that is, readiness to act, thought to be anchored in the central nervous system. Thus different levels of integration in behavior were seen by Tinbergen to be organized into a hierarchical system.

An illustration of this is the reproductive behavior of the male stickleback, as described by Tinbergen (1951). In spring the gradual increase in length of day brings the fish into a reproductive state. The males first begin migration into shallow fresh water with the females. The rise in water temperature as the fish go further inland, together with the visual stimulation arising from suitable territory consisting of heavily vegetated sites, is then the instigator of the entire reproductive behavior sequence in individual fish.

After a male has established his own territory his belly becomes red. This red belly, a nuptial coloration, is a characteristic of a male stickleback under a reproductive drive and serves a communication function, having an effect on both males and females of the species. At this point the male in the nuptial coloration begins to react to particular stimuli that previously had no effect on it. This can be shown by the fact that if males caught during migration are put together in a bathtub they will all remain together in a school with the exception of one, who establishes a territory by the drain plug chain.

This chain is the only structured element in the bathtub, and it is for this reason that a territory is established there. Furthermore, it provides enough territory for only one male.

This male will now fight at the appearance of a stranger, begin to build a nest with any possible suitable material, and court passing females. Since the male's behavior depends principally on the stimulus situation, it is difficult to predict precisely what he will do. Fighting, for example, is released by the stimulus *red belly* on a male intruding into the fish's territory. But it is not possible to predict which of five known fighting movements will occur, since each is dependent on still further, highly specific stimuli. If the stranger bites, the territory owner will bite in turn; or if the stranger beats with its tail, the owner makes the same response. Fleeing will elicit chasing, and threatening will elicit threatening in turn. In summary, the stimuli emanating from an established territory will activate the fighting, building, and mating

drives. The more specific stimulus *red-bellied male* activates only a general readiness to fight; the specific movements made are dependent on even more specific stimuli.

Thus the ethologists conceptualize chains of behavior tendencies that are connected in higher and lower levels of integration. As Tinbergen postulated, the adaptive advantages of having a mood hierarchy rather than a stereotyped series of single, fixed action patterns lie in its flexibility in response to several situations. To Tinbergen and other ethologists it appears that there must be a structural organization within the central nervous system which parallels the lawfulness of behavior as indicated by the mood hierarchy. As a matter of fact, much neurophysiological work has lent strong support to such a notion. Weiss (1941) has shown a similar hierarchical organization of the central nervous system mechanism in motor processes. This hierarchical organization is almost exclusively below the level of the integration

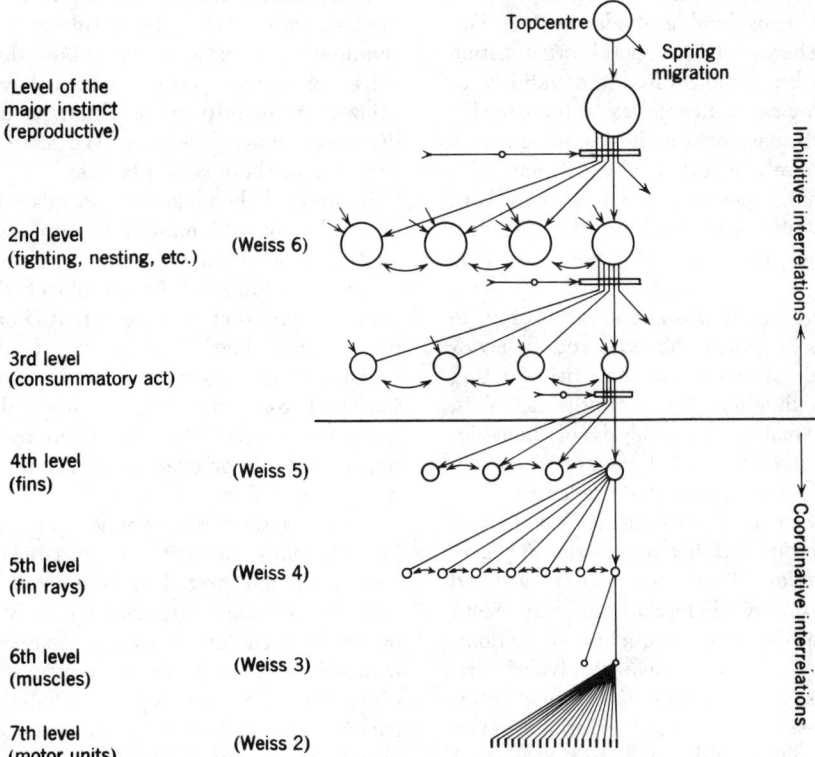

Fig. 1. Tinbergen's diagram of the hierarchical organization of instincts, superimposed on Weiss' diagram of the hierarchical organization of central nervous mechanisms. Weiss' highest level incorporates the same phenomena as those placed in Tinbergen's hierarchy. (From Tinbergen, 1951.)

of the goal-forming fixed action patterns. A diagram integrating the hierarchical theory of Tinbergen with Weiss's organization is shown in Fig. 1.

Tinbergen's hypotheses, of course, were intended as a simplifying scheme and do not cover all the possible complications that exist in the organization of behavior. For example, some of the behavior patterns present at the lower level, such as locomotion, can also be among the final effecting links in several different hierarchical organizations. Tinbergen's notions and findings are particularly valued by ethologists because they link physiology of the central nervous system to behavior, an area of research which even at its very beginning represented a task of immense magnitude.

The neurophysiology of behavior is currently an area being worked on with great fervor. Such ethophysiological studies as those of W. R. Hess (1943, 1944; also Hess and Brügger, 1943 a, b; Brügger, 1943), and especially those of von Holst and von St. Paul (1958, 1960, 1962), have not merely served to provide considerable evidence for Tinbergen's schema of behavioral organization but have also demonstrated the validity of such ethological concepts as action-specific energy or displacement activities, which were originally purely hypothetical constructs. Also of very great importance in von Holst's work are the investigations involving the electrical elicitation of different drives at the same time.

There are many instances, according to ethologists, in which the observed behavior is the result of more than one drive acting upon the individual at the same time. This, of course, makes the analysis of behavior quite complex. Several types of such behaviors have been postulated: *successive ambivalent behavior, simultaneous ambivalent behavior, redirected behavior, and displacement behavior.* These are not considered mutually exclusive behaviors and can occur together in the same sequence of actions.

In the case of successive ambivalent behavior it is observed that the animal alternates between incompletely performed movements associated with conflicting drives. A classic example of successive ambivalent behavior is that of the male stickleback's "zigzag" dance in the courtship of the female

(Tinbergen, 1951). Tinbergen described the dance as an expression of two conflicting tendencies: to attack the female and to lead her to the nest. The "zig" toward her is actually incipient attack; the "zag" leading her toward the nest reflects sexual motivation. Van Iersel (Lorenz, 1966) confirmed this and showed by experimentation that the lengths of the zigs and zags indicate the relative strengths of the aggressive and sexual motives. Furthermore, the alternation of the motivations has actually become ritualized in the stickleback, according to Lorenz (1966), so that a rhythmical zig-zagging occurs in the courtship sequence.

Simultaneous ambivalent behavior is apparent when both of the conflicting drives are performed at the same time. For example, the "Halloween" threat posture of the cat, according to Leyhausen (1956), results from the animal retreating more rapidly with the front paws than with the rear ones, or by his advancing with the rear paws while retreating with the front ones.

Redirected behavior and displacement behaviors, two other types resulting from the simultaneous presence of more than one drive, are two concepts which have been utilized frequently by psychiatrists and students of human behavior. We shall discuss their use of these concepts later.

Redirected behavior is postulated when one behavior is inhibited or suppressed by another motivation with the result that this behavior is directed to an object different from the one that really elicits it. For example, a male black-headed gull feeling aggressive toward its mate is at the same time inhibited from actual attack. Hence the male gull may redirect the aggression by attacking other birds or even an object if no third party is available.

This is a relatively common phenomenon; in fact, many elements of courtship display have been interpreted as redirected aggression. Several animal species normally do not have close contact between members, and courtship activity serves as a means of handling the aggressive responses that the close contact entailed by sexual reproduction elicits. As Baerends (1958) has shown, redirection of aggression in the male cichlid fish *Cichlasoma meeki* during courtship appears in incipient attacks toward plants.

Courtship behavior, of course, performs other functions, such as the synchronization of the physiological cycles of the male and female.

Moreover, aggression is one of the factors promoting sex recognition in a wide segment of the animal kingdom, especially where there is no distinctive sexual dimorphism. Oehlert (1958) demonstrated that in both of the two cichlid species he studied, *Cichlasoma biocellatum* and *Geophagus brasiliensis,* when two strange fish meet, three drives—sex, aggression, and fear—are always aroused simultaneously. However, the mixture of these three drives is very different for the male and female sexes in both species. In the males the sexual drive mixes with aggressive behavior very easily but becomes suppressed by even the most minimal flight drive. In the female, on the other hand, the sexual drive superimposes with the flight drive with no difficulty, but aggression immediately inhibits sexuality. In this way the formation of male-female pairs is guaranteed and the avoidance of homosexual pairs is accomplished. In several other species it has been observed that fear dampens male sex drive, while aggression does the same for female sex drive.

Hinde (1959) has suggested that in closely related sympatric species the sole differences in courtship behavior may be in the strengths and relative intensities of the three drives of aggression, flight, and sex. It is these differences that can have the effect of preventing the occurrence of hybridization between these closely related species.

The final type of mixed drive behavior to be discussed is displacement activity. This is seen in conflict situations in which the animal shows behavior patterns that do not belong to *either* of two conflicting drives. At first such "irrelevant behavior" appears anomalous, but it has been observed that a particular irrelevant act is often typical of a particular set of conditions. For example, fighting cocks may suddenly peck at the ground as if they were feeding (Lorenz, 1935, Tinbergen, 1939) and similar instances have been seen in other birds. The "irrelevant feeding" in this case, according to ethologists, results from a conflict between aggressiveness and fear. It appears to some ethologists that the neurological activity generated by the two conflicting behavior patterns "sparks over" into the third inappropriate behavior when these behaviors are blocked. Thus when an animal faces an opponent which it is motivated to attack but which it is afraid of, it may decide instead to peck at nonexisting food, according to Tinbergen (1952).

Many types of displacement activities have been observed and described by ethologists. Such activities often occur when fighting and escape drives appear to be simultaneously aroused. They are also very common in sexual situations. They can, of course, be aroused by combinations of other drives as well. Finally, they are apparently more likely to take place when the conflicting drives are relatively intense.

The validity of the displacement activity construct has been considerably supported by the neurological work of von Holst and von St. Paul (1960, 1962), who studied the effects of arousing different drives simultaneously in an animal by means of electrode implants in the brains of chickens. At any time that two specific motivations were stimulated simultaneously, these researchers always observed the same specific ambivalent, redirected, or displacement response by the animal. This indicates the same type of lawfulness found in nature wherein specific ambivalent, redirected, or displacement actions are typically elicited by highly particular sets of conditions for each.

THE DEVELOPMENT OF BEHAVIOR

The Problem of the Phylogenetic Scale

For many years comparative psychologists and other investigators of animal behavior in this country utilized the laboratory rat almost exclusively in their experimental studies. The many experiments on learning using rats as subjects were carried out with the assumption that the results of such studies were directly applicable to learning processes in all other animals, including human beings, since it was believed that learning processes are qualitatively similar for all species. With such a premise it appeared patently obvious that it would be unnecessary to study these processes in several different species. The rat was considered representative of all animals.

Today, no one is this naive; nevertheless, there is considerable need for sounding cautionary notes in interpreting the behavior of one species on the basis of experimental results obtained with another species. By virtue of their emphasis upon the genetic transmission of behavior characteristics, ethologists have shown from the first a strong awareness that it is necessary to distinguish carefully not only among species but also breeds within species and even strains within breeds. It has been only recently that behavior geneticists in this country have begun to appreciate the fact long stressed by ethologists that experimental results must either be considered as restricted to the animals from which they were obtained, or else tested on many species before they are used as the basis for any generalization.

Yet there is sometimes an unwarranted tendency among seemingly hard-headed scientists to think in terms of explaining human behavior on the basis of animal behavior. This does not in any way imply that the notion of behavioral continuity between species should be denied. What is meant is that just because something is known about the effects of early social experiences on the later adult behavior of geese, for example, we cannot make inferences about the nature of the effects of early life experiences on the adult behavior of human beings. Even if experiments on the effects of early social experience are carried out using primate species, we cannot necessarily make generalizations applicable to human beings. Just as inferences cannot be made regarding human visual perception on the basis of experiments carried out on lemurs, which lack color vision, we cannot make extrapolations regarding the social or intellectual behavior of man from data obtained on monkeys or apes.

An extreme case of unjustified anthropomorphism is given by the writings of Monboddo (1774). Monboddo, in attempting to prove that speech and language were not original attributes of man's behavioral capacities, argued that the orangutan and man belong to the same animal species on the basis of anatomy and behavior. The name "orangutan," in fact, comes from the aboriginal native word meaning "wild man," and there were attempts to call this animal Homo sylvestris, thus placing it in the same genus as man. So evidently anthropomorphism is nothing new!

Not even extrapolation from one lower primate species to another is justifiable. For ex-

ample, there is a very wide variety of social systems among different primate species. South American howling monkeys have clans with no dominant male; spider monkeys have a similar structure, but contrary to most ape or monkey groups the female is emancipated and takes an important role in social activities. Rhesus monkeys have, generally speaking, a harem-type social structure, with a dominant male heading a group. The baboon, on the other hand, may have aggregations of harems. With the gorilla we find a social structure in which there may be a single male and some females and young. The only primate that seems to fits at least some of our own notions of "proper" human social structure is the Lar gibbon, an animal that is supposedly monogamous with two parents raising the young and keeping their infants with them.

Although infant-infant social experience can overcome the deleterious effects of three months of total social deprivation in the case of the rhesus monkey (Harlow and Harlow, 1962), we cannot necessarily draw the conclusion that the same would be true for another primate species such as the Lar gibbon in which there is apparently little infant-infant interaction under normal conditions. Furthermore, there is certainly no justification for making any suggestion that a similar phenomenon may be found in man, particularly since rhesus monkeys apparently can overcome the effects of total social deprivation for the first three months of life, whereas all the evidence to date appears to indicate the rather drastic effects of only *partial* social deprivation during the first six months of life in human beings (e. g., Bowlby, 1951).

Thus it is apparent that there is a need, through an exhaustive and comparative study of several species, to determine the relationship between social structure and normal behavior. Then and only then is it possible to set up experiments in the laboratory that can take advantage of this information, and permit us to make some accurate predictions about specific effects of early social experience on later social behavior in other primates and human beings.

It certainly has been implied often enough that along all intellectual lines the monkey is the animal closest to man. But there is one capacity in which an animal other than a monkey (or ape) comes closer to man: the ability to pick out the correct stimulus in terms of the number of discrete components it contains. Koehler (1943) showed individual birds a small box having a lid with a number of irregular black blotches randomly distributed on it. Then the birds were shown a group of several boxes, each having a different number of blotches on their lids. Although these boxes were all present simultaneously, the birds were able to select the one that had the same *number* of blotches on it as did the sample, even though the sizes and arrangement of the blotches were different. This box contained a food reward. These birds could do this with any number of blotches up to six or seven, the same level as that achieved by people. Kühn (1953) and Hicks (1956) have shown that such a task is more difficult for the rhesus monkey to do since stimulus characteristics such as density, size, color, and shape interfere with their ability to use purely numerical cues; their maximum discriminable number was three or four spots. It may be mentioned that Kellogg (1961) suggests that it is entirely possible that the intelligence of the dolphin is more like man's than is the intelligence of any lower primate, since the dolphin has an absolute brain weight and a brain weight–body weight ratio that are closer to the corresponding values in man than those of any other animal.

All these considerations regarding the phylogenetic relationships of behavior are entirely consistent with the ethological standpoint. Both continuity of behavior as seen in closely related species and taxonomic groups as well as behavioral differentiation between species occupy prominent positions in ethological thinking.

Ritualized Behavior and Evolution

Fixed action patterns, as we stated earlier, are subject to evolutionary forces, with the evolutionary changes mentioned being the same as those that are known to occur with morphological or physiological features.

The ethologists have postulated that there are two stages in the evolution of motor patterns. In the first stage there is a quantitative increase or decrease in the basic motor elements, perhaps actual disappearance in some cases. In the second stage the basic motor units, almost unalterable in themselves, are coupled to or disengaged from each other.

This coupling of previously independent basic motor elements into a new fixed sequence is part of the phylogenetic process that Huxley, an English naturalist, called *ritualization* in 1914.

Another part of the postulated ritualization process is the phenomenon in which a recently formed fixed action pattern may become motivationally autonomous of the situation that originally aroused it, or dependent upon another motivation. An example of this phenomenon has been described by Lorenz (1941) on the basis of the different forms of the female's "inciting" movement during courtship in the different species of swimming ducks (*Anatinae* family). In the original form of this behavior (as it still exists in some species) the female attempts to separate the male from the group by inciting fights between her partner and other males. To do this she runs toward the strange male, but at a certain point fear overtakes her, and she runs back toward her mate. When she is close enough to him, however, aggressiveness again takes hold of her, and she stops and turns toward the strange male. This, Lorenz interpreted, results in her standing at the point of equilibrium, near her mate, but stretching her neck toward the other male, making inciting movements. Here the angle between her body and her stretched-out neck is a function of her position and those of the two males. This behavior constitutes the unritualized form of incitement.

In some other species the behavior has become fixed to the point that the female simply stands near her mate and moves her head back over the shoulder, regardless of where the strange male is. In this case it appears that the movement is performed solely as a courtship act by the female. Lorenz considers the interpretation of this behavior as ritualized incitement to be further justified by the fact that still other species perform actions which are intermediate between these two extremes when in a similar situation (Lorenz, 1941).

In a third, less common phenomenon postulated in the ritualization process, the fixed action pattern ceases to be performed in different degrees of intensity and is executed in one intensity only. In such cases the degree of motivation is not expressed in the intensity of the behavior but in how often the behavior is repeated, much as the urgency of a telephone call may be recognized by the persistence of ringing rather than in loudness. All fixed patterns with a single or typical intensity function as means of communication between species members. Selection pressure would in these cases operate to enforce a quite simple and unmistakeable form of the movement, according to Morris (1957).

The comparison of different species is the principal means by which the evolution of certain behavior patterns is deduced by ethologists. During the course of ritualization original behavior patterns are very often changed into mimetically exaggerated performances through the increase of their amplitudes and frequencies. In addition, these behavior patterns are thought in some instances to be transformed by the evolution of additional structures. For example, the ceremonial feeding seen in the courtship behavior of many *Gallica* birds and pheasants often appears to have been transformed and accentuated by additional shaking movements, feather spreading, swelling of exposed vascularized skin structures, and sounds in one or another of these species.

Since behavior patterns are regarded as species characteristics, they can be considered homologous in related species, as the preceding example of the female duck's "inciting" movement during courtship indicates. As a matter of fact, ethologists use the very same kind of criteria for determining behavior homologies that comparative morphologists use for bodily features (Remane, 1956). The three criteria they rely most heavily upon are (1) *similarity in structure,* that is, similarity in the spatiotemporal pattern of muscle contractions or movement, (2) *similarity in order of occurrence of movements,* and (3) *linkage by intermediate stages in different species.*

Thus the more fixed action patterns of different species correspond with each other in their special characteristics—such as internal causal factors and releasing situations—as well as in the coordinations themselves, and the more complex these characters are, the more likely they are to be classified as homologies. Sometimes, of course, ethologists caution, similar structures, bodily or behavioral, can evolve independently of phylogenetic relationship in different groups of animals as a result of adaptation to the same environmental conditions,

and in such cases they would be *analogies.* For example, food hiding in very different species may at first look homologous, but the similarity would actually be due to function and not to common history, since there are only a few ways in which food can be stored.

Two somewhat different movements, however, may be considered homologous to each other if they occur in the same place in a specific sequence of movements performed by the two related species in question. The courtship of the female by the males of the species *Tilapia mossambica* and *Tilapia nilotica* consists of the same sequence of movements, *a, b, c, d, e, f, g, . . .,* but at one point in the sequence the tail-wagging movements are comparable but different in the two species (Baerends, 1958). Furthermore, two different movements performed by different species may be considered homologies if intermediate stages of these movements are found to be performed by other related species of the taxonomic group. It is considered necessary in such cases to have enough instances of intermediate stages between disparate forms for comparison as a cautionary measure to prevent the mistaken homologizing of similar-appearing but different activities in two related species. An illustration of this kind of homology has been provided by Lorenz (1941). Males of many duck species perform an up-down movement with the head and bill while courting the female. Some species, however, do not perform this action; in its place they make a drinking response. Not only do these two different movements have some similarity, but other duck species show a range of forms intermediate to these two behaviors, leading all the more forcefully to the conclusion that these two different behaviors constitute homologies of the different species in question.

An interesting example of homologous behavior is a specific movement that is now thought to be phylogenetically very old and extremely widespread among four-limbed vertebrates. This is the scratching movement. Thorndike (1899) observed that "the frog, lizard, chick, and cat all react to irritation of the head by scratching with the hind leg with a quick, repetitive motion that is startlingly alike in the last three. Here we have an instinct which apparently ranges over a subkingdom." This scratching movement, made by the hind limb raised over the front limb in the majority of these species, was subsequently discussed in some detail by Heinroth (1930) and more recently by Lorenz (1958). Many birds have been observed to lower their wings in a rather peculiar way and reach forward in front of the shoulder with the leg, in spite of the fact that it would seem to be less clumsy for the bird to move its claw directly to its head without moving its wing, which is normally folded on its back and out of the way. Apparently the bird reconstructs the spatial relationship of the body that was possessed by its four-legged reptilian ancestor and thus behaves as if it had an obstructing front leg. A few bird species such as stork, heron, and pigeon have developed the habit of scratching the easier way, but most have retained the original technique. There is even one species, according to Lorenz (1958), which has learned to eat with its claws and brings them directly to the head. But when scratching, it still brings its claw over its lowered wing and cannot be trained to do otherwise.

Other very clear examples of homologous behavior patterns are found in the courtship behaviors of ducks, as studied by Heinroth (1910) and Lorenz (1941) and in the same behaviors of pheasants and related fowl (Schenckel, 1956, 1958).

Ethologists also believe that the concept of *homonomies* applies just as well to behavior patterns as to morphological forms. Morphological homonomies refer to a series of organs possessed by the same species which have undergone differential modification. For example, the feeding legs of crustaceans have been found to be in actuality modified walking legs, because there are a series of other limbs between the feeding legs and the walking legs which represent intermediate forms between these two types. Behavioral homonomies are postulated when animals perform both ritualized movements and the original ones from which they have been derived. An illustration of behavioral homonomies is given by grooming movements, which are used in social interactions as an expression of friendliness and peaceful intentions. A friendly dog, as is well known, greets by licking and nibbling. In some other animals movements exactly like those used in grooming are also used as a greeting ceremony to a member of

the same species before any actual physical contact has been made.

While in many cases there appear to be extremely close similarities between highly ritualized movements, movements that appear obviously ascribable to homology, ethologists exercise caution in applying the concept. This is because expressive movements often serve the function of conventional signals in a given species. Thus it is postulated that what a given movement signals is a phylogenetically evolved convention, just as the meanings of individual words in human languages are conventions. Hence different meanings may be expressed by similar movements in different species—such as tail-wagging in the dog and cat—depending on the motivational situation from which they have derived. Also, in cases where similar movements appear in entirely unrelated species and there is no spread of these movements among other species in the same taxonomic groupings to provide evidence of phylogenetic progression, such movements are considered to have been acquired independently and are certainly analogous. The rattling of the tail by the rattlesnake and the porcupine is such a case, for two different taxonomic classes, reptilian and mammalian, are involved, and we do not find numerous instances of tail-rattling among other species of the vertebrate subphyla to which they both belong.

At the present time ethological research on the genetics of behavior is still in its infancy, but it has every promise of becoming increasingly important and many theoretical implications concerning the mode of genetic transmission and the origin of behavior have already been made. Ramsay (1961), for example, reported on studies of the transmission of courtship behavior patterns in crossbred progeny of different species of ducks which he had observed since 1956. He crossed a male black duck and a female mallard. The courtship displays of the two parent species are essentially identical, but the F_1 generation hybrid performed several sequences that were characteristic of neither parent species. In one case there was an elimination of one movement in a sequence; it never gave the nod-swimming following the head-up tail-up display. This display is omitted in the mallard only 7% of the time and in the black duck 20% of the time in the typical sequence.

These percentages were based on approximately 75 recorded observations for each animal. In the hybrid the movement sequence of bill-shaking, grunt-whistle is reversed. Sometimes in the parent species this sequence is tail-shaking, bill-shaking, grunt-whistle. In the hybrid this is reversed to grunt-whistle, tail-shaking, bill-shaking. This hybrid also showed other occasional deviations from pattern such as head-up-tail-up, down-up.

Von de Wall (unpublished study) has also made studies of the genetic basis of courtship behavior in hybrid ducks. His hybrids performed motor elements in courtship that, even if not present in either of the different parent species, were distributed in the *Anatinae* family (swimming ducks) to which these species belong. Some hybrids performed integrations and coordinations that, again, were not present in any of the parent species but were present in certain other species of the *Anatinae* group.

These studies have supported the ethological postulation, originally based on comparative studies, that certain complete series of fixed action patterns were primary, or original, in a taxonomic group, but that the absence of some of these fixed patterns in any member species of that taxonomic group is a more recent phenomenon. Although the basic components, or fixed action patterns, do not change their character as a result of crossing, their sequence can be rearranged.

Courtship behavior is not the only behavior to which ethologists have applied their concepts of genetic transmission of behavior. Dilger (1962) has investigated nest material carrying behavior in F_1 hybrids of a male *Agapornis roseicollis* and a female *Agapornis personata fischeri*. Both of these species cut strips of paper or leaves and take them to the nest to be used for building. *Fischeri* carries the strips to its nest in its bill. *Roseicollis*, however, tucks the strips under the lower back and rump feathers, with their plumage erect while the material is being tucked, and then flies off to the nest. The remarkable thing about this difference in behavior between these two closely related species is that both have body feathers modified with tiny hooks whose function is to bind the feathers more closely to the body, but *roseicollis* also uses them for holding strips of material under the feathers.

The sequence of the *roseicollis* female's behavior is composed of the following elements: the cutting of the strip, grasping of the strip, bringing the head back over the shoulder, erecting the lower back and rump feathers, tucking the strips between these feathers, bringing the head into the normal position, and lowering the back and rump feathers. This sequence is an innate pattern, the only changes due to experience being the subsequent standardization of the size and shape of the strips. Strips that are accidently dropped are not picked up, but new ones are cut to take their place. *Fischeri*, which carries the cut strips in its bill, however, will pick up strips that lie on the ground.

The nest-building behavior of the F_1 hybrids resulting from a cross between these species is most interesting. They cut the leaves and tried to tuck them under their feathers, but their attempts never succeeded, for a variety of reasons. Sometimes the birds would tuck the strip under the feathers but be unable to let go of it. In such cases, after repeated attempts had been made, the strip would be abandoned and a new one cut. In some other cases the hybrid might be able to let go of the strip, but the feathers would fail to hold the material, probably from not being pressed against it. Sometimes the hybrids would try to put the strips in inappropriate locations such as the breast, belly, flanks, or wings. Quite commonly, the tucking behavior would change into preening behavior. It was very clear that the hybrids were displaying a conflict between the tendency to carry the material in the feathers and the tendency to carry it in the bill. They were successful in getting material to their nests only when they carried it in the bill. But even when they carried the strip in the bill, which happened very rarely during their first attempts at nest building, they engaged in tucking movements.

After two months of experience the hybrids made fewer tucking attempts before carrying leaf strips in the bill to the nest. Nevertheless, two years passed before their behavior became more efficient and more like their *fischeri* parent's. Even so, they continued to perform tucking movements. These movements themselves were performed better but were never successful as a means of carrying leaf strips to the nest.

Among other behaviors that have been studied with respect to genetic transmission are exploratory tendencies, temperature preferences, and even cocoon-spinning. Ethologists maintain that it is already evident that behavior patterns or their components are genetically transmitted from generation to generation in a fashion similar to that for physiological or morphological characteristics.

Intraspecific Aggression

Although we have touched upon the role of aggression in mixed drive behavior and especially in courtship behavior, we shall briefly consider specifically the function of aggression between members of the same species because of the recent attention given by Lorenz (1966) and others to aggression in human behavior.

As with other behaviors, ethologists have studied aggression as it occurs in different animal species in terms of its function and survival value for the species concerned. Under natural conditions aggression has been always found to have a positive function: the optimal spacing of the individuals of the species about the available habitat of that species. In fact, all species require territorial spacing unless the special interests of a social organization demand close aggregation of its members. Otherwise the ecological niche of the area that serves a particular species will not have sufficient supplies to support all resident members of this species. The same area, of course, can support different species utilizing different niches. Lorenz (1966) has remarked that this is analogous to the fact that it is generally disadvantageous to society and to mechanics for all mechanics to live and ply their trade in the same area, but a grocer and a mechanic do not take trade away from each other.

Other positive functions of aggression have been known since Darwin (1859) asserted that it was always favorable to the future of a species if the stronger of two rivals takes possession of either the territory or the desired female. These, however, are special cases, subordinate to the principal value found in the proper spacing of the species. Defense of the young is another positive feature of aggression. Lorenz (1966) has suggested that in such animals as bisons and baboons family defense has evolved the rival fight which in turn has selected for males more powerful and stronger than the females.

A particularly interesting feature of aggression has been pointed out by Lorenz. This is the fact that strong and faithful individual bonds (e.g., enduring pair formation in mating) are found only in species in which there is measurable aggression. Whereas aggression can be found without personal bond formation, or "love," Lorenz asserted that there is no love without aggression. The differentiation between family, friends, and strangers as individuals appears most strongly manifested in aggressive behavior: this occurs in both humans and other animals.

Innate Behavior in Man

For several decades behavioristic psychologists in the United States have strongly resisted the very notion of innate behavior in man. There seems to be some tolerance toward the notion of innate behavior in animals, perhaps because for so many centuries the notion of instinctive behavior was applied only to animals on the basis of theologically derived concepts of the distinctiveness of man and his superiority over all lower animals. Man, according to these concepts, could guide his actions by reason, whereas animals had only instincts to lead them to act.

However, ethologists believe that it is possible to apply many of the same concepts they have developed with respect to the study of animal behavior to human beings. Darwin (1872), of course, had an ethological approach to human behavior. Craig (1918), one of the first modern ethologists, in discussing appetitive and consummatory behaviors, remarked, "all human behavior runs in cycles which are of the same fundamental character as cycles of avian behavior."

Certainly human behavior is extremely complex and plastic. The degree of learning in the determination of behavior is probably higher in man than in most other animals. But in many instances ethologists have drawn parallels between human and animal behavior, particularly from a phylogenetic viewpoint. Such parallels, of course, are made with the understanding that in no case do they necessarily imply anything more than an illustration of how ethological concepts may be applied as tools for the analysis of human behavior. At present studies of animal behavior can provide only *ideas* regarding human behavior. Ultimately, we must, if we are interested in the behavior of the human animal, do research with the human being as a subject. This, of course, is not a simple matter, since if the human is both experimenter and subject, numerous biases inimical to objectivity are present. We must guard against such biases as well as against anthropomorphism.

Lorenz (1943) has postulated that there is a releaser which is very widespread in the animal kingdom. This releaser is the quality we call "babyishness." If the young and adults of several species are compared for differences in bodily and facial features, it will be seen readily that the nature of the differences is apparently the same almost throughout the phylogenetic scale. Limbs are shorter and much heavier in proportion to the torso in babies than in adults. Also, the head is proportionately much larger in relation to the body than is the case with adults. On the face itself, the forehead is

Fig. 2. Comparison of visual features provided by morphological characteristics of infantile and adult forms of four different species: human, rabbit, dog, and bird. While the infantile characteristics release parental responses, the adult ones do not. (From Lorenz, 1943.)

more prominent and bulbous; the eyes large and perhaps located as far down as below the middle of the face, because of the large forehead. In addition, the cheeks may be round and protruding. In many species there is also a greater degree of overall fatness in contrast to normal adult bodies. Figure 2 shows a group of heads of young and adult humans, dogs, rabbits, and birds. Lorenz (1943) also remarked that the doll industry has conspicuously utilized these physical characteristics and, in fact, make dolls and other toys function as superoptimal releasers of man's mothering response.

In the light of Lorenz's suggestions Cann (1953) conducted a study that gauged the positive responsiveness of men and women, single and married, parents or childless, to pictures of infant young and adults of several different animal species. These pictures were shown as a series of 53 pairs, each pair consisting of one baby and one adult of the same species, both printed in the same size. It was found that significantly more of the "baby" pictures were preferred over the adult pictures by single women and by childless married women than by single men and childless married men. While women at different ages and marital and parental states tended to show about the same high degree of responsiveness to the pictures of the babies, the responses shown by men tended to increase as a function of marriage and parenthood. The men whose wives were expecting for the first time showed greater responsiveness than did single men; those who had children showed even greater responsiveness. However, the men never exceeded the women in responsiveness.

The status of "babyishness" as a releaser in human beings has been further studied by Hess and Polt (1960) and by Hess (1967). In the earlier study it was found that when people look at pictures which arouse their interest their eye pupils enlarge significantly. There was also a difference between men and women in their pupil responses to pictures of babies. All these results were independent of illumination conditions. Women's pupils enlarged considerably when they looked at such pictures, whereas men's pupils showed very little change in size. This result, of course, substantiates Cann's earlier results.

Subsequently Hess (1967) reported on the

results of showing people progressively stylized drawings of human or animal faces. This stylization was in a trend toward greater and greater babyishness in the appearance of the faces, culminating in the Walt Disney-type portrayal of infant and animal babies. Correspondingly greater pupil responses are elicited by greater babyishness, a result which appears to support the ethological notion that the quality of babyishness definitely has positive appeal to people. This shows also that in man, as in other animals, social prescriptions and customs are not the sole or even primary factors that guarantee the rearing and protection of babies. This seems to indicate that the biologically rooted releaser of "babyishness" may have promoted infant care in primitive man before societies were ever formed, just as it appears to do in many animal species. Thus this releaser may have a high survival value for the species of man.

Not only the quality of babyishness but also the apparently unconscious perception of the pupil size of other people during interpersonal contact appears to influence pupil size and other behaviors of people. Studies by Hess (1965), Stass and Willis (1967), and Simms (1967) have confirmed that pupil dilation itself functions as a signal in interpersonal communication, especially in heterosexual confrontations. In other words, the perception, even if not on the conscious level, of increased pupil size in a person of a different sex acts as a releaser and triggers off a pupil size increase. This phenomenon is analogous to the "social releasers" which ethologists have observed in the social behavior of animal species. In ethological studies it has been found in very many instances that movements or specific behaviors of one animal act as "releasers" eliciting certain responses in the other animal perceiving these behaviors. Such responses can elicit still further behaviors in the original partner of the interacting pair.

Not only the concept of releasers but also that of fixed action patterns is applicable to human behavior. In this connection it is interesting to note that Piaget, the Swiss child psychologist, has postulated that the child and infant have organized dispositions to perform certain invariant action sequences, or "schemas," as he has termed them (see Piaget's chapter 5 in this book). Piaget's concept of schemas, as discussed by Flavell (1963) has certain similarities to the fixed action patterns; however, there are very fundamental differences in that Piaget includes learned action sequences and specifies that they need not be overt. Thus innateness is not a criterion for the schema, although the true fixed action pattern would in all probability be regarded as a schema by Piaget, since reflex acts are considered schemas. Piaget further postulates that experience in the use of schemas results in their differentiation; hence it does not appear that he directly considers endogenous maturation as a factor in the ontogeny of schemas.

Nevertheless, the principal similarity between Piaget's schemas and the fixed action patterns is a striking one: a single schema constitutes a class of *similar action sequences,* these sequences of necessity being strong, bounded totalities in which the constituent behavioral elements are tightly interrelated. Piaget himself wrote: "every schema of assimilation constitutes a true totality, that is to say, an ensemble of sensorimotor elements mutually dependent or unable to function without each other" (Flavell, 1963, p. 54). Of further and considerable interest is the fact that Piaget considers the child to evidence functionally invariant, *organized* behavior totalities from birth onward, with these totalities set in motion again and again. Although the child's use of schemas does have a corrective function in the apprehension of reality, the child's behavior toward the environment definitely is not considered random or fortuitous. The child has strategies, or tools, that is, *psychological organs,* in the form of schemas, to deal with aspects of the environment which are responded to selectively and specifically. It is particularly evident early in development that the elementary schemas such as grasping tend to run off whenever an appropriate stimulus is presented to the child. The belief in the lack of randomness in behavior elicitation is similar to the ethological viewpoint on animal behavior. While the schemas are defined as *cognitive* functions, Piaget considers that they have underlying action systems in the brain and, according to Flavell, has made some speculations on these.

The smiling behavior of small babies is both a fixed action pattern in the ethological sense and a schema in Piaget's sense. Smiling therefore can be analyzed by ethological methods and in fact exhibits many of the phenomena which we have described for innate behaviors of animals. Eibl-Eibesfeldt (1967) is one ethologist currently studying smiling behavior in human beings, both children and adults.

We have discussed the quality of babyishness as an elicitor of responses in people; it also seems that people elicit responses in babies, mostly those of smiling. Such smiling responses normally serve to further increase the appeal of babies to people and therefore serve a definite survival function in that both the babies and their caretakers are bound to each other. (See Maccoby, Chapter 23, and Kessen, Chapter 10, both in this book, regarding the social value of smiling behavior.)

The earliest studies of the smiling response of babies dealt with the qualities of the stimuli which elicit smiling and the ontogeny of the response itself. It now appears, according to ethological thinking, that the human face constitutes an innate releaser of the smiling response. The investigations of Spitz and Wolf (1946), Wolff (1963) and Wilson (1963) have shown that the face has an innate positive value in eliciting smiling in babies. Wilson (1963), in particular, showed that assocation with food during nursing is not the factor that promotes the effectiveness of the face as an evocator of smiling. Food itself therefore is not the major factor in the socialization of human babies as reflected by the smiling response. This is analogous to the observation that during the primary socialization of newly hatched precocial birds, the young will follow the parent long before it has any need for food; as a result of this initial social experience the young bird becomes socialized to its own species. This is the phenomenon of imprinting, one of the areas in which ethologists and psychologists have done a great deal of investigation. Later we shall briefly discuss the relevance of the social imprinting phenomenon for the study of human development.

It is of great interest that as long ago as 1872 the phenomenon of smiling as a universal characteristic of the human species was observed by Charles Darwin, one of the early forerunners of present-day ethology. Darwin noted that smiling could be seen in babies of every literate and preliterate culture with which he had come into contact. The ubiquity of this behavior has been expressed well by Wolff (1963), who termed smiling a "congenitally present expressive movement."

One of the strongest supporters of ethological concepts in application to human development, especially in the sphere of social behavior, has been John Bowlby (1957, 1958), who views smiling in the human infant as an instinctive behavior pattern and has drawn certain analogies between imprinting and the human mother-child relationship (discussed later). In outlining the similarity between smiling in the infant and innate behavior patterns found at the animal level, Bowlby (1957) presented the hypothesis that smiling behavior increases the infant's chances of survival since it makes the infant more appealing to the mother. Bowlby further suggested the possibility that during evolution there has been a selection factor favoring smiling behavior in man and that infants without this behavior pattern had a much higher mortality rate. Bowlby also noted that there is a specific stimulus which will elicit smiling in the infant. Ths stimulus consists of the schema of the human face and this can, of course, be considered a releaser in the ethological sense.

Wolff (1963) reported a great many concepts regarding the smiling response of babies which are completely consistent with concepts that have been proposed by ethologists with respect to fixed action patterns, even though Wolff himself is not an ethologist and he declines any commitment as to whether he regards smiling as an innate behavior. Nevertheless, Wolff has strongly posited that "the infant is congenitally equipped . . . to smile." He also observed smiling by premature babies, and on the basis of this concluded that the morphological mechanism for smiling is present extremely early in development: "the smile is not a contortion due to gas pains," Wolff affirmed.

Wolff, like Freedman (1966), noted that smiling occurs in newborn babies and those less than a month old in the absence of any external stimulation. This observation indicates that smiling at that time is aroused by central factors, not solely by peripheral stimulation, a notion which ethologists have vigorously championed with respect to innate fixed action patterns. Although this fact and the fact that blind babies also smile (Freedman, 1966; Eibl-Eibesfeldt, 1967) mean that smiling is not released solely by an external facelike visual stimulus, such facts are not at all incongruent with ethological thinking. One reason is that another important ethological concept, that of the "vacuum reaction," is demonstrated. As may be recalled, the vacuum reaction occurs when centrally produced action-specific energy builds up to the point where the action is run off by the organism even though the normally relevant stimulus is not observable. Thus blind babies may smile, because they are morphologically and neurologically constituted to smile; when the specific energy for smiling builds up to a certain level it is then discharged through spontaneous smiling. This spontaneous smiling, however, is relatively fleeting. And, of course, with blind babies smiling never comes to be elicited by visual, social stimuli during the second month of life, as happens with normally seeing infants (Freedman, 1966). It can, however, come to be released through stimulation in other sensory modalities (Eibl-Eibesfeldt, 1967).

The existence of more than one releaser of the smiling response, as shown by Wolff (1963) and by Freedman (1966), constitutes a phenomenon which resembles that for many fixed action patterns of lower animals. The fighting response of the male of a tropical fish, *Astatotilapia strigigena* (Pfeffer), to pick only one such case, can be elicited by several different stimuli, all of which are characteristics of an intruding and attacking male (Seitz, 1940). Any single characteristic is about as effective as any other in eliciting fighting; however, if two are present, then the elicited fighting response is twice as great. The more stimuli simultaneously present, the more intense the fighting response of the fish. Thus the intensity of an innate fixed action pattern's performance can depend not only on what sign stimuli are present, but also on how many are present. Analogously, Wolff (1963) reported that month-old babies smiled more to a nodding, talking head than to either a merely nodding or merely talking head.

However, unlike the stimuli that elicit

fighting behavior in Seitz's fish, it was found by Wolff that different stimuli had different effectiveness in eliciting the smiling response. This is also the case with many other fixed action patterns, an example being the egg-retrieving behavior of the ringed plover (Koehler and Zagarus, 1937), as mentioned earlier. Wolff observed that the bare face is more effective than a mask, a face with sunglasses, or a mask with sunglasses.

Wolff (1963) also reported evidence suggesting that the ethological concept of action-specific energy can apply to the smiling response in ways other than the existence of the "vacuum reaction." The baby, Wolff noted, must be in the proper "mood" or readiness for smiling. The smiling behavior is exhaustible by sufficiently repeated presentations of a single stimulus and then may be elicited anew either after a period of no smiling or by a new stimulus. For example, a face may be presented from seven to ten times before smiling is depressed. Then, if a mask is presented, smiling can once more be elicited, but for fewer times, perhaps five. Then, if sunglasses are added, smiling may be elicited about three more times.

The applicability of the ethological concept of action-specific energy to smiling behavior is even more clearly seen in the observed presocial smiling of babies less than one week old (Wolff, 1963). During this age period, spontaneous smiling is seen only during states of irregular sleep or drowsiness. When smiling occurs under such conditions, there is a refractory period of five minutes or more before the baby smiles again. At this age the performance of the smiling response also has a definite relationship in interaction with the performance of other behavior patterns. For example, there is an inverse relationship between the frequency of smiling and frequency of other spontaneous behavior patterns in which the baby may engage, such as startling, rhythmical mouthing, sobbing inspirations, or stirring, according to Wolff. Similar frequency relationships between different fixed actions have also been observed in chickens by von Holst and von St. Paul (1960, 1962) in their neurophysiological investigations.

The change in the character of smiling behavior as an expression of spontaneous neurological discharge to one elicited by definite stimuli, as noted by Wolff (1963) and by

Freedman (1966), is another phenomenon that ethologists have noted in animal behavior. This is that the innate releasing mechanism (IRM) may become increasingly selective toward sign stimuli during the life of the individual. Such a process is postulated to occur in all members of the species, not in just one individual. The increased selectivity may be of either of two types: (1) narrowing of the range of stimuli evoking a particular response through the dropping out of individual stimuli; and (2) selection and strengthening of a few releasers out of a large range of potential releasers, with the result that only these and not any of the others elicit the response. The second is the phenomenon seen in social imprinting of precocial bird species; the first is the phenomenon seen when habituation to specific stimuli of the innate behavior pattern occurs or when strong negative conditioning of aversive stimuli occurs. For example, the fright behavior to predators drops out with respect to moving leaves and twigs. Or, a toad will at first snap at all small objects, but after a single unhappy experience it will avoid bees and wasps.

Hence we see that the human face becomes increasingly effective as an elicitor of the smiling response in human babies; at the same time the response becomes increasingly selective as a function of age. This is because whereas eyes alone are initially effective, greater and greater approximation to the natural human face becomes required in order to properly elicit smiling behavior, according to Ahrens (1954). Similarly, Wolff (1963) found that touching the infant's hands with his own and then patting his hands together three times in succession failed to elicit smiling until the infant was around the age of four to six weeks, when it suddenly became effective (precautions were taken to ensure practice effects were not responsible) and thereafter was effective even when the baby was fussy.

The notion of increased selectivity of the innate releaser mechanism as a consequence of the experience of the individuals of the species appears to also be applicable to smiling behavior. Ambrose (1963) pointed out that there seems to be an early sensitive period for smiling, and this sensitive period appears to be terminated by wariness of

strangers. Ambrose regards the situation as analogous to the social imprinting phenomenon found in precocial animals wherein following tendencies are terminated at the appearance of fear of strange objects. The notion of the temporal coincidence of the appearance of the fear of strangers by human babies with the ending of the sensitivity for learning primary social responses to people was proposed even earlier by Hess (1959b).

The Value of Ethology to the Study of Human Behavior

Fundamentally, it is the ethological *attitude* which is most valuable in the analysis of human behavior, rather than merely the use of the particular *terms* used by ethologists. An investigator does not need to be an ethologist or even to have had any direct contact with ethology to make behavior analyses which are congruent with ethological thinking. He merely must approach his subject with a concern for the *complete* context in which observed behaviors occur, including biological bases and adaptive function.

Ethologists have made a great many speculations on human behavior, and there have been several actual experimental investigations. For example, von Holst (1938) demonstrated that relative coordination of movement occurs in man just as it does in other animals: if two arms are moving at different speeds, one twice as fast as the other, the faster arm will make alternate long and short sweeps in coincidence with the down and up strokes of the slower arm. And, of course, psychologists have known for some time that locomotion matures in human beings (Gesell, 1947, McGraw, 1947) just as it does in animals (Carmichael, 1926, 1927; Grohmann, 1939).

Lorenz (1943) has described a relatively stereotyped motor response which occurs in humans. The touch stimuli from an insect crawling on the skin release the action of throwing it off quickly with the hand. There is both a fixed pattern component and an orientation component in this reaction. Hence it is not simply a reflex. Tinbergen (1951) has suggested that this action, though maturing relatively late, is probably innate.

The application of ethological concepts appears particularly apropos to problems of human development in both the ontogenetic and phylogenetic sense. The behavior stereotypies of captive animals, for example, have been observed to be akin to the behavior stereotypies that can be seen in orphaned children, as reported by Klimpfinger (1950a, b). The reiteration or perseveration of certain movements by hospitalized children can also be seen in home-reared children whose mother has no child care helper and is very busy with her housework or her profession (Lorenz, 1955). Maternal deprivation thus appears as a factor in the etiology of this behavior in children, just as social deprivation appears in the etiology of the cage stereotypies of captive animals.

Several ethological concepts currently are becoming increasingly important in application to human development. One such concept is that of "sensitive periods." The notion of sensitive periods in development has been utilized since 1900 by Europeans in many different fields. Even before this there were several beginnings of the sensitive period notion in the work of the early embryologists, notably Geoffroy-St. Hilaire (1822) and Dareste (1869, 1877). In biology, the Dutchman de Vries (1899, 1901, 1905) applied it to the growth of plants. He found that there was a time during which environmental conditions could influence the form taken by poppy flowers of a particular variety; after this particular developmentally linked sensitive period had passed, such environmental conditions could no longer influence subsequent morphological development, even though the development in question had not yet even occurred. In fact, de Vries himself used the term "sensitive period" to denote this phenomenon, which he also observed in the development of many other plants.

In the beginning of the development of psychoanalysis Sigmund Freud (1905) stated the notion that there are sensitive periods in the early development of children. Freud postulated that injurious events during these periods had relatively lasting effects on adult behavior. In education, the Italian Maria Montessori (1936, 1949) applied the concept of sensitive periods fully to the mental development of children. At the same time Lorenz (1935), an Austrian, applied the notion to the imprinting phenomenon in the social behavior of precocial birds.

Lorenz observed the behavior of newly hatched geese, both in the company of the natural parents and when he presented himself to the young animals as a parental object before they had an opportunity to associate with their own parents. Because the latter animals later in life treated other human beings as fellow species members and the former animals remained with their own species as a result of having first associated with their own parents, Lorenz (1935) concluded that species recognition was "imprinted" (*Prägung*) onto the nervous system of these young during the first period of exposure after hatching.

Under natural conditions imprinting serves its purpose quite well: the first object seen is, of course, the natural parent. Furthermore, the rapid attachment of the young to the parent is necessary for the survival of the young animal. During the first days of life, the parent broods the young, protects it from predators, leads it away from dangerous situations, and takes it to food objects in the environment.

Since the early 1950s imprinting has been extensively studied in the laboratory, particularly in the United States. This work has been reviewed in papers by Moltz (1960, 1963), by Hess (1959, 1964), by Sluckin (1964), and by Bateson (1966). The results of laboratory investigation on imprinting carried out by Hess (1964) can be stated in five main points, each of which appears to make imprinting a phenomenon quite different from the association learning commonly studied by experimental psychologists.

1. In waterfowls there was a sharp and distinct critical period found by Hess. In the case of wild mallard ducks there is a peak of sensitivity to the imprinting process at about 16 hours after hatching in socially isolated birds, after which time the sensitivity drops rapidly. By 32 or 48 hours of age the increased fear response of the young animal appears to interfere with further imprinting capability. Similar critical periods have been found for imprinting in other birds as well. Although they are not necessarily within the first day, all of them are in the very early life of the organism.

2. The use of certain drugs, particularly muscle relaxants, interferes completely with the acquisition of the imprinting effect. These

same drugs do not interfere at all with the normal acquisition of a discrimination habit such as would be experimentally studied in a psychology laboratory.

3. Massed practice is more effective than spaced practice. In addition, Hess discovered the *law of effort,* which states that the strength of imprinting is positively related to the amount of energy expended by the precocial hatchling bird in going to or in attempting to go to the imprinting object.

4. Primacy and recency work in a way completely different from association learning. In imprinting it is clearly the first thing that is "learned" which is retained, whereas in association learning a primacy-recency experiment will show that the animal tends to respond to the last meaningful stimulus.

5. The effect of punishment, or painful stimulation, is the opposite of what occurs in an association learning situation. This notion is of particular interest in the field of child psychology and in psychiatry. A study on this phenomenon was published by Kovach and Hess (1963).

In Kovach and Hess's investigation there are data on groups of chicks at an age close to the critical period peak of 13–16 hours after hatching, 18 hours, and at an age well beyond the critical period for imprinting, 48 hours. At each age the experimental animals were given electrical shocks while in an imprinting apparatus with a model (a "parent" object), while others received no shock in this situation. However, the animals that were shocked during the optimum period for imprinting actually followed the parent model significantly more than the control animals that did not receive any shock. The reverse was true for the chicks exposed at the age of 48 hours.

Although these results would be perplexing from the standpoint of association learning, they are not unreasonable from the standpoint of instinctive behavior and the normal survival value of such behavior, in ethological terms. If, for example, in the natural situation the young animal were to be stepped on by the parent before it leaves the nest, it would not be biologically useful to have the young avoid the parent, leave the nest, and die. If anything, there seems to be an overcompensation for any punishment associated with the parental object since the animals receiving shock did follow better than the control animals when the initial exposure occurred during the critical period. Anthropomorphically, it is as though the animal in a painful situation depends at that moment on the parent to a tremendous degree insofar as survival is concerned, and will then seek to get even closer to the parent object.

At least one paper published in the psychiatric literature seems to tie this phenomenon to behavior in young children. Menaker (1956) relates submissive behavior in a child with an unloving, powerful, exploitative, and dominating mother to innate mechanisms of submission which prevent species members from killing each other. However, it would appear that, in the light of the research involving imprinting and shock, the child who is in an essentially punishing relationship with the parent and reacts by idealizing the parent and picturing this parent as all-powerful and loving is doing much the same thing that a chick does during the critical period when it follows a model even more closely when punished in its presence. The motor patterns involved in the two cases, of course, are different and therefore not in any sense homologous. It is not impossible that both submission and intensified affiliation can operate innately in the human child and be vital to survival. Just as there is a selection pressure for a chick or a duckling to stay with the parent under the most adverse conditions, a similar selection pressure must operate with the human child who obviously could not survive alone.

The fact that most modern societies have made provisions to give children adequate physical care may obscure the functioning of a mechanism which would bind the child to the parent during his period of dependency even when he is physically punished. As Polt (1966) suggests, it almost seems as though the normal parent-child relationship implicitly assumes that something of this sort operates. Whereas association learning would predict that when a child is chastised by the parent for an undesirable act, the child will associate the punishment with the parent as the agent of the punishment, the child in fact associates the punishment with the misdemeanor.

Numerous theoretical papers have attempted to delineate the relationship between socialization in human infants and the imprinting phenomenon. Bowlby (1953, 1958, 1960), for example, has pointed out several congruent features between the ethological findings regarding imprinting and psychoanalytic principles on the development of social attachments in human babies: the innate drive to make a "love" relationship with a parent figure, the strong influence of the individual's early love object on the selection of a love object (both sexual and parental) in adult life (a process which in abnormal cases in human beings may be carried to the point of pathological fixation), and the critical or sensitive phases of development with reference to both the organization of the motor patterns adopted and the nature of the object selected.

With regard to the notion of sensitive periods for the establishment of emotional bonds between mother and infant, several writers have postulated specific ages for primary social development to occur. Gray (1958) proposed the period of six weeks to six months, Hess (1959b) the first five and one-half months of age, Rollman-Branch (1960) the first six months, and Ambrose (1963) the age period from five to twelve weeks.

Ambrose (1963) has contended that there are good grounds for drawing an analogy between social imprinting and primary socialization in humans. On the basis of his own earlier research with the smiling response (Ambrose, 1961), he suggested that the sensitive period for supra-individual learning of the human face starts at approximately the fifth week of life and ends at approximately 12 weeks of age for family-reared infants and at approximately 18 weeks of age for institutionalized infants. The postulation by Ambrose that the location of the sensitive period depends upon the nature of the caretaking to which the child has been exposed is congruent with the idea that the end of the sensitive period for social imprinting is delayed when the sensory-social input to the organism is below normal, a notion found in some other studies of social imprinting (e.g., Klopfer, Adams, and Klopfer, 1964). The supra-individual learning of the human face, furthermore, was proposed by Ambrose as the human analogue of supra-individual learning of the species in precocial birds.

The question of whether social imprinting exists in man has been a perennial one. This issue is certainly difficult and complex. One of the principal difficulties is that the baby cannot actually follow the parent at an early age, as is the case with precocial species which have demonstrated imprinting in primary socialization. Furthermore, it appears to many writers that primary socialization occurs in the human child before it is able to crawl.

Gray (1958) has suggested that the smiling response is homologous to the following response of young precocial birds, particularly since it ends when a fear response to strangers appears, as we mentioned earlier. The comparison between the fear response of young infants to strangers and that shown by young birds has also been made by Freedman (1961). However, it certainly is not permissible to *homologize* between avian and human species: the motor patterns of following and smiling are not the same. Besides, there is an insufficiency of cases of social imprinting in intermediate species. Also, just because there is a period of positive responsiveness and positive attachment followed by the fear reaction, this does not establish the existence of a social imprinting phenomenon in human beings, as Ambrose (1963) has rightly contended. The distress behavior evident in young chicks or ducklings already imprinted to their siblings or to another parent object may possibly reflect a searching for the lost companionship rather than fear of the new situation per se. Thus, while fear may cause incompatible response in birds which have been completely isolated socially since hatching, this may not be the case in socially maintained ones.

Other comparisons between social imprinting in birds and primary socialization in humans, however, have been suggested by Ambrose (1963). He pointed out the broad similarity between the nature of the innate releasing situations for smiling in babies and following in chicks and ducks, which are both releasing situations that involve mother objects. Not only are there close similarities in causation, in his opinion, but there is also a close similarity in function. This function is keeping the young organism close to the mother object. Whereas the young chick or duckling can follow, the human infant is utterly incapable of doing so for several months. However, the human baby's crying normally does serve to bring his mother to him from a distance and his smiling serves to keep her present when she is already nearby. Ambrose also pointed out that another similarity between smiling in human babies and following in chicks and ducks is that both gain in response strength in the period of supra-individual learning of the species without any conventional reward such as food.

Lastly, Ambrose also postulated that the time at which fixation upon an object is possible is a better criterion for the beginning of social imprinting and the beginning of supra-individual learning of the species in human babies than is the time when learning is first evident, which Gray (1958) had proposed. This is because, as Ambrose pointed out, a bird cannot learn its parent unless it can follow, and following of the parent is impossible unless the young bird can keep it fixated. Thus commencement of visual learning, he suggested, is conditional upon the achievement of the ability to fixate an object. In line with this notion Ambrose suggested that the mother's eyes are the first object to consistently elicit visual fixation by the infant, particularly since the studies of Ahrens (1954) and others have indicated that the smiling response is initially elicited by the eyes alone. It is of interest that Caldwell (1962) has also suggested that *visual pursuit* constitutes the "following" of the parent figure by the infant.

However, the existence of these several similarities does not necessarily force the conclusion that there is actually a phylogenetic connection between the imprinting phenomenon in birds and filial attachments to parents in human infants, as Hinde (1961) has pointed out. The synapsid and diapsid reptiles, from which mammals and birds arose, have been distinct since at least the Permian period of the Paleozoic era. Therefore parental care and infant-to-mother attachment behaviors probably have evolved independently in the two groups. Hence the similarities would more accurately indicate that these behaviors constitute analogies rather than homologies, and they originate from similar selective forces in the evolutionary process.

Hinde is undoubtedly correct with respect to the development of social attachment. However, it must be pointed out that if *imprinting* is a type of learning process which, as Hess (1964) has proposed, can be applied

to a variety of situations in which specific behavior patterns are attached to a class of stimulus objects, such as food imprinting in chicks (Hess, 1962) and turtles (Burghardt and Hess, 1966), maternal imprinting in goats (Klopfer, Adams, and Klopfer, 1964), or environmental imprinting in a variety of species (as reviewed by Hess, in preparation), then imprinting is a genetically programmed learning mechanism which probably is very old phylogenetically. Indeed it seems likely that the imprinting process could have been independently seized upon by both mammals and birds for use in the development of social behavior systems, as well as in other object-response relationships. Therefore the homology, if it exists at all, would be through the phylogenetic transmission of the imprinting phenomenon and not through the phylogenetic transmission of parental care and filial attachment systems.

It can be seen that the implications regarding the effect of environmental influences during early life on the later behavior of an animal are now, and will become, increasingly important in the study of human development. Certainly the notion of stages or phases in psychological development in human beings is a very old one. The stages of babyhood, childhood, adolescence, adulthood, and old age have been enumerated for centuries. Froebel (1826) long ago declared that events in each of these stages had consequences very important for succeeding ones, a notion which has assumed since then considerable importance in the investigation of the ontogeny of behavior. To date very many sensitive periods have been suggested in the literature (reviewed by Hess, in preparation), particularly in the spheres of social-emotional behaviors and intellectual activities. The very variety of these proposed sensitive periods shows that this will continue to be a fertile field of investigation for several decades to come.

The concept of displacement activity, an extremely widespread phenomenon in the animal kingdom, has proven to be another notion of considerable interest to psychiatrists and other scholars in the area of human behavior and development. The ethological concepts of ambivalent behavior and redirected activity have already been foreshadowed for some time in the case of human behavior. Freud (e.g., 1905) clearly enunciated the concept of ambivalent motivation in normal and disturbed persons. Simultaneous love and hate is the best known case of such ambivalence. Redirected behavior, particularly in the form of scapegoating, has indeed been folklore. Banging tables or desks in anger and throwing crockery are some of the most common instances of this, as is also kicking the dog or scolding the wife after a harrowing day at the office. Lorenz (1966) has described several specific examples of scapegoating as instances of redirected aggression.

Still other indications regarding displacement activities in human behavior may be found in remarks by Tinbergen (1951) and Morris (1967a). Tinbergen noted that learned activities as well as innate ones can function in this context. Examples of such learned activities include cigarette lighting and handling of handkerchief or keys; examples of innate activities having this function include head scratching and preening, often manifested in mild conflict situations. Women, for example, can often be seen adjusting nonexistent disorder in their coiffure, while men handle their beards and mustaches or cheeks and chins if clean shaven. Morris (1967a) has added to this list of human displacement activities drinking, eating, nose scratching, nose picking, ear lobe pulling, lip licking, and hand rubbing.

Makkink (1936) some time ago discovered sleep functioning as a displacement activity in the avocet when in a conflict between aggression and escape. It has since then been found in several wading birds. It is interesting in this connection that there is a widespread belief among many people, including college counselors, that fatigue commonly occurs as a response to frustration, anxiety, or boredom, rather than solely as a consequence of overexertion. Tinbergen (1951) pointed out that yawning is a low intensity manifestation of sleep and is very commonly seen in moderate conflict conditions. Yawning, as most of us know from personal observation, is "catching" and it is rather amusing to find that the same phenomenon should occur in the ostrich, as reported by Sauer (1967).

Contemporary psychiatrists have used the displacement activity concept in at least three ways as a tool for approaching human behavior. Although each approach is somewhat different, each seems to provide a valid working *hypothesis* at the human level. Naturally, these comparisons between human and animal behaviors, just as with any comparison between different animal species, must be tested by appropriate means. This is the case even when behavior phenomena are as ubiquitous as are displacement activities: considerable caution must be taken in regarding the human examples as actual cases of displacement activities.

The fact that many displacement activities at the animal level do not serve to maximize the survival of the individual or the species has been emphasized by Weigert (1956). She has related displacement activity to neurotic anxiety, which Freud considered to be the result of a frustrated libidinal impulse and which is, of course, basically detrimental to the individual. This interpretation of displacement activity emphasizes the nonfunctional aspect of neurotic behavior. At the same time it should be kept in mind that the conflict situation experienced by the individual may, under certain circumstances, result in the sublimation of libidinal energy into activities condoned by society, a point which was strongly made by Freud.

Another way of viewing displacement activity is that taken by Ostow (1957). After drawing some parallels between the psychoanalytic and ethological concepts of instinct, he used displacement activity as an illustration of a logical progression of development in man. Taking only the sexual instincts as an example, Ostow has hypothesized that the gratification of these instincts takes different forms during different periods of development and that the mechanism which leads from one form to another functions in the same way that displacement activity functions in lower animals. As one mode of gratification is inhibited, the instinct accepts another mode of gratification. In this way Ostow traced the sexual aims in the psychic development of humans through oral, anal, phallic, and genital stages.

The third view is that of Kaufman (1960 a, b), who suggested, on the basis of his study of ethology, that in addition to the sexual and aggressive instincts in man, there might also be an instinct for flight. Kaufman has drawn heavily on work with displacement activities since many of them are the result of a conflict between aggression and fear. He pointed out that with most infrahuman animals components of sexual behavior, aggression, and flight are all built-in tendencies and that the same is likely to be true of man. Further, he has advanced the notion of the usefulness of this theoretical paradigm in the treatment of patients where shyness and timidity would not have to be construed as a reaction to hostile or sexual impulses, but as a drive in its own right, that is, as a low intensity manifestation of a flight tendency.

Whereas the members of the human species have generally considered intraspecific aggression among themselves as antisocial and undesirable since it can be highly destructive, Lorenz (1966) has taken the position that it has the same positive functions as it does in infrahuman animal species and, in fact, has had an important role in the formation of human society from the beginning of mankind's existence. "Aggression, far from being the diabolical, destructive principle that classical psychoanalysis makes it out to be, is really an essential part of the life-preserving organization of instinct. Though by accident it may function in the wrong way and cause destruction, the same is true of practically any functional part of any system" (Lorenz, 1966, Chap. 3, p. 48).

The observation of the various means by which aggression is dealt with in animal behavior during interactions between congeners (members of the same species) prompted Lorenz to point out the existence of several similarities in human behavior. The aggression drive, being primarily a species-preserving instinct, arises spontaneously in the organism and is subject to the same building up of specific energy and discharge that we discussed earlier for other instincts. The very same process can be seen in human beings, and Lorenz cited several instances of it. Redirection of the aggression to other objects, superstitions, and ritual ceremonies are all among the means utilized by both lower animals and human beings to deal with intra-specific aggression. Culturally derived "manners," Lorenz pointed out, have an aggression-appeasement function which immediately becomes apparent through the reaction of hostility when a person fails to observe

them. This can readily occur when people from different countries or even from different regions of the same country come into contact and are unaware that there are differences in what are considered "good manners." Similar observations have been made by a sociologist, Hall (1959, 1966).

Our discussions of aggression, smiling behavior, responses to babyishness, pupil responses (as indicators of differences between males and females in biological reaction to specific pictorial stimuli, of personality differences, and as social-communicative signals in specific situations), and displacement activities have covered only a small range of ethology's great potential in making theoretical and substantive contribution to the study of normal and abnormal human behavior. The large body of experimental data on the effects of early experience and imprinting has made it possible to draw parallels, though with considerable caution, and, in at least some respects, to test hypotheses generated by the animal work in relation to human early behavior.

Of considerable importance is the application of the methods and techniques developed by ethologists to the analysis of human behavior. For example, knowledge of the normal behavior and the normal development of behavior are cases in point. The use of schematic representations to determine whether or not sign stimuli or releasers are operating at the human level, such as in the case of the smiling response to schematic representations of the human face, allow us to come to grips with certain aspects of early human behavior.

The use of still other techniques which do not involve verbal responses may allow us to gain information regarding the development of attitudes and perceptions in the infant and growing child, either before verbal responses may be obtained or where verbal responses may not be trustworthy. Two examples of such techniques are the recording of changes in the size of the eye pupil (Hess, 1965), which has been used in a preliminary study of psychosexual development in boys and girls from the age of 5 to 18 years by Bernick (1966) and the recording of the length of visual fixation of different objects by human infants (Fantz, 1965). Both of these techniques are clearly ethological methods.

In the same vein, several studies on proxemic behavior by sociologists and anthropologists (e.g., Hall, 1959, 1966; Somer, 1959; Goffman, 1963) bear strong similarities to the ethological method of behavior study. Both emphasize the communicative (but nonverbal) function of such behavior, that is, the reaction of other individuals to specific actions that are performed. The use of space and the effects of population density are also allied to the ethological approach. In fact, Leyhausen (1965), an ethologist, is studying the effects of population density on behavior.

However, it is not only the ethological tradition of objectivity in behavior study that has importance for the study of human development. Of even greater importance are the twin concepts of the phylogenetic context of human behavior and the biological bases of this behavior. There are now many cases in which these have been or currently are applied to human behavior.

One such is the investigation of actions expressive of emotions. Indeed, Darwin (1872) was among the first to investigate this from a phylogenetic viewpoint. Other investigators, ethologists or not, have studied the form and function of expressive actions in human beings from a functional and objective viewpoint, and this area of investigation has considerable promise. Scheflen (1964, 1965), a psychiatrist, has observed the existence of various "quasi-courtship" gestures functioning as communicative signals in interactions with others and apparently on an unconscious level. These gestures were discovered through the objective recording of the motor actions and body postures of participants in interpersonal situations and not through introspection or verbal interviewing. Leg crossing, preening movements, sitting back or leaning forward, and arm folding were found to be among such movements and to be useful in establishing rapport and communication in psychotherapeutic situations. Blurton Jones (1967) has studied three- to five-year-old nursery school children with respect to facial and bodily motor expressions and the specific responses which these elicit from others. Wickler (1967) has made a preliminary comparison of sociosexual signals in man and other primates.

A frankly biological approach to human behavior may be found in genetics. This is a very young field that promises to become extremely fertile, particularly when the ethological premise of the biological bases of behavior is accepted without racist handicaps. In my own unpublished research I have found a strong and highly consistent correlation between eye color and modes of perception and personality. Blue eyes were associated with form dominance in perception and a scientific attitude, whereas brown eyes were associated with color dominance in perception and a nonscientific attitude. The genetic bases of this obviously could be studied.

The significance of the phylogenetic viewpoint in the consideration of human behavior is highly apparent in Lorenz's *On Aggression* (1966): "all specifically human faculties, the power of speech, cultural tradition, moral responsibility, could have evolved only in a being which, before the very dawn of conceptual thinking, lived in well-organized communities. Our prehuman ancestor was indubitably as true a friend to his friend as a chimpanzee or even a dog, as tender and solicitous to the young of his community and as self-sacrificing in its defense, aeons before he developed conceptual thought and became aware of the consequences of his action" (Chap. 13 p. 245). Also, Lorenz asserted, "if, in the Greylag Goose and in man, highly complex norms of behavior, such as falling in love, strife for ranking order, jealousy, grieving, etc., are not only similar but down to the most absurd details the same, we can be sure that every one of these instincts has a very special survival value, in each case almost or quite the same in the Greylag and in man. Only in this way can the conformity of behavior have developed" (Chap. 11 p. 218). These similar behaviors in the Greylag Goose and in man, Lorenz emphatically stressed, arose through convergence and not through common inheritance. Such convergence supports even more strongly the notion that these behaviors have highly important species-survival functions.

In closing, it would seem that the most significant contribution of ethology to the study of human development, in both the phylogenetic and ontogenetic senses, is the recognition that man is a biological organism, and that he has an evolutionary history. The present-day members of the species of man have an ancient repertoire of behaviors.

From the ethological point of view, the human infant is not a completely naive being, but possesses a legacy of potential behavior patterns which at one time assured the survival of the organism even without the aid of social learning or customs. Some of these innate behavior patterns involve elements of sexual behavior, aggressive behavior, and innate social responses. Recognition of these as part of our heritage is important because, in terms of man's evolutionary history, we are not at all far from the time when there were no widespread cultural influences upon our behavior. Without our built-in behaviors, we, as a species, simply could not have managed to survive for a million years.

Indeed, as Desmond Morris (1967a) has suggested, man needs to face up to the accumulated genetic legacy of his whole evolutionary past, and as a result he may be "less worried and more fulfilled." It is the realization that these potential, genetically programmed behaviors are present and that many of them must be channeled into quite different directions in our present-day civilized world, which may make the greatest contribution toward an approach to the problems of the human species and may have a tremendous impact on the search for mental health as well as a fuller understanding of human behavioral development. In this connection Morris (1967a), in stating that basic biological changes rather than simply acculturation have been primarily responsible for the development of uniquely human behavior from its original primate form (one example is the incest taboo), has stressed his belief that "our unbelievably complicated civilizations will be able to prosper only if we design them in such a way that they do not clash with or tend to suppress our basic animal demands."

This, of course, presupposes that we actually do succeed in knowing just what our basic animal needs are. To assume, for example, that aggression is solely the result of bad training and environment is to close one's eyes to the evolutionary usefulness and possible biological survival value of aggression, factors which surely must have a place in the make-up of man, as they do in all other animal organisms. If in this case alone the theoretical viewpoint becomes one in which aggression, when properly directed, is recognized as a useful biological consequence of man's inherent constitution, it would seem that ethology will have made a major contribution to the field of human behavior.

References

Ahrens, R. Beitrag zur Entwicklung der Physiognomie- und Mimikerkennens. Z. exp. angew. Psychol., 1954, 2, 414–454, 599–633.

Ambrose, J. A. The development of the smiling response in early infancy. In B. M. Foss (Ed.), Determinants of infant behaviour. First Tavistock Seminar on Mother-Infant Interaction, London, 1959. New York: Wiley, 1961. Pp. 179–201.

Ambrose, J. A. The concept of a critical period for the development of social responsiveness in early human infancy. In B. M. Foss (Ed.), Determinants of infant behaviour II. Second Tavistock Seminar on Mother-Infant Interaction, London, 1961. New York: Wiley, 1963. Pp. 201–225.

Baerends, G. P. Comparative methods and the concept of homology in the study of behaviour. Archs. néerl. Zool. 1958, 13, Suppl. 1, 401–407.

Bateson, P. P. G. The characteristics and context of imprinting. Biol. Rev. 1966, 41, 177–220.

Bernick, N. The development of children's preferences for social objects as evidenced by their pupil responses. Unpublished doctoral dissertation, University of Chicago, 1966.

Blurton Jones, N. G. An ethological study of some aspects of social behavior in nursery school. In D. Morris (Ed.), Primate ethology. Chicago, Ill.: Aldine, 1967. Pp. 347–368.

Bowlby, J. A. *Maternal care and mental health*. Geneva: World Health Organization, 1951.

Bowlby, J. A. (Remarks) In J. M. Tanner (Ed.), *Prospects in psychiatric research*. Proceedings of Oxford Conference of Mental Health Research Fund, 1952. Oxford: Blackwell Scientific Publications, 1953. Pp. 80–86.

Bowlby, J. A. A symposium on the contribution of current theories to an understanding of child development. I. An ethological approach to research in child development. *Br. J. med. Psychol.*, 1957, **30**, 230–240.

Bowlby, J. A. The nature of the child's tie to his mother. *Int. J. Psychoanal.*, 1958, **39**, 350–373.

Bowlby, J. A. Separation anxiety. *Int. J. Psychoanal.*, 1960, **41**, 89–113.

Brückner, G. H. Untersuchungen zur Tiersoziologie, insbesondere der Auflösung der Familie. *Z. Psychol.*, 1933, **128**, 1–120.

Brügger, M. Fresstrieb als hypothalamisches Symptom. *Helv. physiol. Pharmac. Acta*, 1943, **1**, 183–198.

Burghardt, G. M., and Hess, E. H. Food imprinting in the snapping turtle, *Chelydra serpentina*. *Science*, 1966, **151**, 108–109.

Caldwell, B. M. The usefulness of the critical period hypothesis in the study of filiative behavior. *Merrill-Palmer quart.*, 1962, **8**, 229–242.

Cann, M. A. An investigation of a component of parental behavior in humans. Unpublished masters thesis, University of Chicago, 1953.

Carmichael, L. B. Heredity and environment: are they antithetical? *J. abnorm. soc. Psychol.*, 1925, **20**, 245–260.

Carmichael, L. The development of behavior in vertebrates experimentally removed from the influence of external stimulation. *Psychol. Rev.* 1926, **33**, 51–58.

Carmichael, L. A further study of the development of behavior in vertebrates experimentally removed from the influence of external stimulation. *Psychol. Rev.*, 1927, **34**, 34–47.

Craig, W. Appetites and aversions as constituents of instincts. *Biol. Bull.*, 1918, **34**, 91–107.

Dareste, C. Sur l'arrêt de développement considéré comme la cause prochaine de la plupart des monstruosités simples. *C. r. Acad. Sci.*, 1869, **69**, 963–966.

Dareste, C. *Recherches sur la production artificielle des monstruosités*. Paris: C. Reinwald, 1877, 1891.

Darwin, C. *Origin of species*. London: John Murray, 1859.

Darwin, C. *The expression of the emotions in man and animals*. London: Murray, 1872.

Darwin, C. Instinct. In G. J. Romanes, *Mental evolution in animals*. London: Kegan Paul, Trench, & Co., 1883.

Darwin, E. *Zoonomia*. 1794.

Dilger, W. C. The behavior of lovebirds. *Scient. Am.*, 1962, **206**(1), 88–98.

Drees, O. Untersuchungen über die angeborenen Verhaltensweisen bei Springspinnen (*Salticidae*). *Z. Tierpsychol.*, 1952, **9**, 169–207.

Eibl-Eibesfeldt, I. Angeborenes und Erworbenes in der Technik des Beutetötens (Versuche am Iltis, *Putorius putorius* L.). *Z. Säugetierk.*, 1956, **21**, 135–137. (a)

Eibl-Eibesfeldt, I. Über die ontogenetische Entwicklung der Technik des Nüsseöffnens vom Eichhörnchen (*Sciurus vulgaris* L.) *Z. Säugetierk.*, 1956, **21**, 132–134. (b)

Eibl-Eibesfeldt, I. Neue Wege der Humanethologie. *Homo*, 1967, **18**, 13–23.

Fantz, R. L. Ontogeny of perception. In A. M. Schrier, H. F. Harlow, and F. Stollnitz (Eds.), *Behavior of non-human primates*. New York: Academic Press, 1965. Vol. 2 pp. 265–403.

Flavell, J. H. *The developmental psychology of Piaget.* Princeton, N. J.: Van Nostrand, 1963.

Freedman, D. G. Hereditary control of early social behavior. In B. M. Foss (Ed.), *Determinants of infant behaviour III.* Proceedings of the third Tavistock Study Group on Mother-Infant Interaction, 1963. New York: Wiley, 1966. Pp. 149–159.

Freud, S. Three essays on the theory of sexuality. 1905. In *The standard edition of the complete psychological works of Sigmund Freud.* London: Hogarth, 1953. Vol. 7, pp. 125–248.

Froebel, F. W. A. *Die Menschenerziehung, d. Erziehungsunterrichts u. Lehrkunst.* Leipzig: Weinbrack, 1826.

Geoffroy-St. Hilaire, E. *Philosophie anatomique. III. Des monstruosites humaines.* Paris: Author, 1822.

Gesell, A. The ontogenesis of infant behavior. In L. Carmichael (Ed.), *Manual of child psychology.* New York: Wiley, 1946. Pp. 295–331.

Goffman, E. *Behavior in public places.* New York: Free Press, 1963.

Gray, P. H. Theory and evidence of imprinting in human infants. *J. Psychol.*, 1958, **46**, 155–166.

Grohmann, J. Modifikation oder Funktionsreifung? *Z. Tierpsychol.*, 1939, **2**, 132–144.

Haeckel, E. *Generelle Morphologie der Organismen.* Berlin: 1866.

Hall, E. T. *The silent language.* Garden City, N. Y.: Doubleday, 1959.

Hall, E. T. *The hidden dimension.* Garden City, N. Y.: Doubleday, 1966.

Harlow, H. F., and Harlow, M. K. Social deprivation in monkeys. *Scient. Am.*, 1962, **207**, 137–146.

Hebb, D. O. Heredity and environment in mammalian behaviour. *Br. J. Anim. Behav.*, 1953, **1**, 43–47.

Heinroth, O. Beitrage zur Biologie, namentlich Ethologie und Psychologie der Anatiden. *Verhandlungen des V. Internationalen Ornithologenkongresses in Berlin*, 1910, 589–702.

Heinroth, O. Über bestimmte Bewegungensweisen der Wirbeltiere. *Sitzungsberichte gesamte Naturforsch Freunde* (Berlin), 1930, 333–342.

Heinz, H.-J. Vergleichende Beobachtungen über die Putzhandlungen bei Dipteren im allgemeinen und bei *Sarcophaga carnaria* L. im besonderen. *Z. Tierpsychol.*, 1949, **6**, 330–371.

Hess, E. H. Imprinting. *Science*, 1959, **130**, 133–141. (a)

Hess, E. H. The relationship between imprinting and motivation. In M. R. Jones (Ed.), *Nebraska Symposium on Motivation, 1959.* Lincoln: University of Nebraska Press, 1959. Pp. 44–77. (b)

Hess, E. H. Imprinting in birds. *Science*, 1964, **146**, 1129–1139.

Hess, E. H. Attitude and pupil size. *Scient. Am.*, 1965, **212**(4), 46–54.

Hess, E. H. Ethology. In A. M. Freedman, and H. I. Kaplan (Eds.), *Comprehensive Textbook of Psychiatry.* Baltimore, Md.: Williams and Wilkins, 1967. Pp. 180–189.

Hess, E. H. *Effects of early experience.* In preparation.

Hess, E. H., and Polt, J. M. Pupil size as related to interest value of visual stimuli. *Science*, 1960, **132**, 349–350.

Hess, W. R. Das Zwischenhirn als Koordinationsorgan. *Helv. physiol. pharmac. Acta*, 1943, **1**, 549–565.

Hess, W. R. Das Schlafsyndrom als Folge dienzephaler Reizung. *Helv. physiol. pharmac. Acta*, 1944, **2**, 304–344.

Hess, W. R., and Brügger, M. Das subkortikale Zentrum der affektiven Abwehrreaktion. *Helv. physiol. pharmac. Acta*, 1943, **1**, 33–52. (a)

Hess, W. R., and Brügger, M. Der Miktions- und der Defäkationsakt als zentraler Reizung. *Helv. physiol. pharmac. Acta*, 1943, **1**, 511–533. (b)

Hicks, L. H. An analysis of number-concept formation in the rhesus monkey. *J. comp. physiol. Psychol.*, 1956, **49**, 212–218.

Hinde, R. A. Behavior and speciation in birds and lower vertebrates. *Biol. Rev.*, 1959, **34**, 85–128.

Hinde, R. A. The establishment of the parent-offspring relation in birds with some mammalian analogies. In W. H. Thorpe and O. L. Zangwill (Eds.), *Current problems in animal behaviour*. London: Cambridge University Press, 1961. Pp. 175–193.

Holst, E. von. Über den Prozess der zentralnervösen Koordination. *Pflügers Arch. ges. Physiol.*, 1935, **236**, 149–158.

Holst, E. von. Vom Wesen der Ordnung im Zentralnervensystem. *Naturwissenschaften*, 1937, **25**, 625–631, 641–647.

Holst, E. von. Über relative Koordination bei Säugern und beim Menschen. *Pflügers Arch. ges. Physiol.*, 1938, **240**, 44–59.

Holst, E. von. Die Auslösung von Stimmungen bei wirbeltieren durch "Punktförmige" electrische Errengung des Stammhirns. *Naturwissenschaften*, 1957, **44**, 549–551.

Holst, E. von, and St. Paul, U. von. Das Mischen von Trieben (Instinktbewegungen) durch mehrfache Stammhirnreizung beim Huhn. *Naturwissenschaften*, 1958, **45**, 579.

Holst, E. von, and St. Paul, U. von. Vom Wirkungsgefüge der Triebe. *Naturwissenschaften*, 1960, **18**, 409–422.

Holst, E. von, and St. Paul, U. von. Electrically controlled behavior. *Scient. Am.*, 1962, **206**(3), 50–59.

Huxley, J. S. The courtship habits of the great crested Grebe (*Podiceps cristatus*); with an addition to the theory of sexual selection. *Proc. zool. Soc. Lond.*, 1914, 491–562.

Jennings, H. S. *Contributions to the study of the behavior of lower organisms*. Carnegie Institution of Washington Publication No. 16, 1904.

Kaila, E. Die Reaktionen des Säuglings auf das menschliche Gesicht. *Annls Univ. fenn. åbo.* Series B., 1932, **17**, 1–114.

Kaufman, C. Some ethological studies of social relationships and conflict situations. *J. Am. psychoanal. Ass.*, 1960, **8**, 671–685. (a)

Kaufman, C. Symposium on psychoanalysis and ethology. III. Some theoretical implications from animal behavior studies for the psychoanalytic concepts of instinct, energy, and drive. *Int. J. Psychoanal.*, 1960, **41**, 318–326. (b)

Kellogg, W. N. *Porpoises and sonar*. Chicago, Ill.: University of Chicago Press, 1961.

Klimpfinger, S. *Zur Psychologie des Kleinkindalters. Gegenwartsfragen d. Kindererziehung*. Wein: Osterr. Bundesverlag, 1950. (a)

Klimpfinger, S. *Der Kindergarten als familiensoziologisches Problem*. Wein: Osterr. Bundesverlag, 1950. (b)

Klompf, H. Die terreinkeus van de Kievit, *Vanellus vanellus* (L.). *Ardea*, 1954, **42**, 11–40.

Klopfer, P. H., Adams, D. K., and Klopfer, M. S. Maternal "imprinting" in goats. *Proc. natn. Acad. Sci.*, 1964, **52**, 911–914.

Koehler, O. Zahl-versuche an einem Kohlraben und vergleichsversuche an Menschen. *Z. Tierpsychol.*, 1943, **5**, 575–712.

Koehler, O. and Zagarus, A. Beitrage zum brutverhalten des Halsbandregenpfeifers (*Charadrius h. hiaticula* L.). *Beitr. Fortpfl Biol. Vogel*, 1937, **13**, 1–9.

Kovach, J. K., and Hess, E. H. Imprinting: effects of painful stimulation upon the following response. *J. comp. physiol. Psychol.*, 1963, **56**, 461–464.

Kühn, E. Simultanvergleich gesehener Mengen beim Rhesusaffen. Z. Tierpsychol., 1953, **10**, 268-296.

Kuo, Z. Y. Ontogeny of embryonic behavior in Aves. I. The chronology and general nature of the behavior of the chick embryo. J. exp. Zool., 1932, **61**, 295–430. (a)

Kuo, Z. Y. Ontogeny of embryonic behavior in Aves. II. The mechanical factors in the various stages leading to hatching. J. exp. Zool., 1932, **62**, 453–489. (b)

Kuo, Z. Y. Ontogeny of embryonic behavior in Aves. III. The structures and environmental factors in embryonic behavior. J. comp. Psychol., 1932, **13**, 245–272. (c)

Kuo, Z. Y. Ontogeny of embryonic behavior in Aves. IV. The influence of embryonic movements upon the behavior after hatching. J. comp. Psychol., 1932, **14**, 109–122. (d)

Lehrman, D. S. A critique of Konrad Lorenz's theory of instinctive behavior. Q. Rev. Biol., 1953, **28**, 337–363.

Lehrman, D. S. On the organization of maternal behavior and the problem of instinct. In P. P. Grassé (Ed.), L'instinct dans le comportement des animaux et de l'homme. Paris: Masson et Cie., 1956. Pp. 475–520.

Leyhausen, P. Verhaltensstudien an Katzen. Z. Tierpsychol., 1956, Beiheft 2.

Leyhausen, P. The same community—a density problem? Discovery, 1965, **9**, 27–33.

Lorenz, K. Z. Der Kumpan in der Umwelt des Vogels; die Artgenosse als auslösendes Moment sozialer Verhaltungsweisen. J. Orn., 1935, **83**, 137–213, 289–413.

Lorenz, K. Z. Über die Bildung des Instinkbegriffes. Naturwissenschaften, 1937, **25**, 289–300, 307–318, 324–331.

Lorenz, K. Z. Vergleichende Bewegungsstudien an Anatiden. J. Orn., 1941, **89**, 194–294.

Lorenz, K. Z. Die angeborenen Formen möglicher Erfahrung. Z. Tierpsychol., 1943, **5**, 235–409.

Lorenz, K. Z. The comparative method in studying innate behavior patterns. Symp. Soc. exp. Biol., 1950, **4**, 221–268.

Lorenz, K. Z. (Remarks) In B., Schaffner (Ed.), Group processes. Transactions of the first conference, 1954. New York: Josiah Macy, Jr., Foundation, 1955. Pp. 63–64.

Lorenz, K. Z. The evolution of behavior. Scient. Am., 1958, **199**(6), 67–78.

Lorenz, K. Z. Phylogenetische Anpassung und adaptive Modifikation des Verhaltens. Z. Tierpsychol., 1961, **18**, 139–187.

Lorenz, K. Z. Evolution and modification of behavior. Chicago, Ill.: University of Chicago Press, 1965.

Lorenz, K. Z. On aggression. New York: Harcourt, 1966.

McGraw, M. Maturation of behavior. In L. Carmichael (Ed.), Manual of child psychology. New York: Wiley, 1946. Pp. 332–369.

Makkink, G. F. An attempt at an ethogram of the European Avocet (Recurvirostra avosetta L.) with ethological and psychological remarks. Ardea, 1936, **25**, 1–62.

Menaker, E. A note on some biologic parallels between certain innate animal behavior and moral masochism. Psychoanal. Rev., 1956, **43**, 31–41.

Miller, N. Laws of learning relevant to its biological basis. Proc. Am. phil. Soc., 1967, **111**(6), 315–325.

Mills, T. W. The nature and development of animal intelligence. New York: Macmillan, 1896.

Moltz, H. Imprinting: empirical bases and theoretical significance. *Psychol. Bull.*, 1960, **57**, 291–314.

Moltz, H. Imprinting: an epigenetic approach. *Psychol. Rev.*, 1963, **70**, 123–138.

Moltz, H. Contemporary instinct theory and the fixed action pattern. *Psychol. Rev.*, 1965, **72**, 27–47.

Monboddo, J. B. *Of the origin and progress of language.* (2nd ed.) Edinburgh: Balfour, 1774. Volume I.

Montessori, M. *The secret of childhood.* Translated by B. Carter. New York: Longmans, Green, & Co., 1936.

Montessori, M. *The absorbent mind.* Translated by C. Claremont. Adyar and Madras: The Theosophical Publishing House, 1949.

Morgan, C. L. *Habit and instinct.* London: Edward Arnold, 1896.

Morris, D. "Typical intensity" and its relation to the problems of ritualisation. *Behaviour*, 1957, **11**, 1–13.

Morris, D. *The naked ape.* New York: McGraw-Hill, 1967. (a)

Morris, D. (Ed.), *Primate ethology.* Chicago, Ill.: Aldine, 1967. (b)

Oehlert, B. Kampf und Paarbildung einiger Cichliden. Z. *Tierpsychol.*, 1958, **15**, 141–174.

Ostow, M. The erotic instincts—a contribution to the study of instincts. *Int. J. Psychoanal.*, 1957, **38**, 305–324.

Pernau, F. A. von. *Unterricht/ Was mit dem lieblichen Geschopff denen Vogeln/ auch ausser dem Fang/ Nur durch die Ergrundung Deren Eigenschafften/ und Zahmmachung/ oder anderer Abrichtung/ Man sich vor Lust und Zeit-Vertrieb machen konnen: gestellt.* Coburg: 1707.

Polt, J. M. The effects of social experience on imprinting. Unpublished doctoral dissertation, University of Chicago, 1966.

Ramsey, A. O. Behavior of some hybrids in the mallard group. *Anim. Behav.*, 1961, **9**, 104–105.

Réaumur, R. A. F. *Mémoires pour servir à l'histoire des insectes* I–IV. Paris: Impr. Royale, 1734-1742.

Remane, A. *Die Grundlagen des natürlichen Suptems der vergleichenden Anatomie und der Phylogenetik.* Leipzig: Akad. Verlag, 1956.

Roeder, K. D. Ethology and neurophysiology. Z. *Tierpsychol.*, 1963, **20**, 434–440.

Rollman-Branch, H. S. On the question of primary need. *J. psychoanal. ass.*, 1960, **8**, 686–702.

Romanes, G. J. *Animal intelligence.* (1st ed.) London: 1881.

Romanes, G. J. *Mental evolution in animals.* London: Kegan Paul, Trench, & Co., 1883.

Sauer, E. G. F. Yawning and other maintenance activities in the South African ostrich. *Auk*, 1967, **84**, 571–587.

Scheflen, A. The significance of posture in communication systems. *Psychiatry*, 1964, **27**, 316–331.

Scheflen, A. Quasi-courtship behavior in psychotherapy. *Psychiatry*, 1965, **28**, 245–257.

Schenckel, R. Zur Deutung der Balzleistungen einiger Phasianiden und Tetraoniden I. *Ornithologische Beobachter*, 1956, **53**, 182–201.

Schenckel, R. Zur Deutung der Balzleistungen einiger Phasianiden und Tetraonidin II. *Orn. Beob.*, 1958, **55**, 65–95.

Schneirla, T. C. Problems in the biopsychology of social organization. *J. abnorm. soc. Psychol.*, 1946, **41**, 385–402.

Schneirla, T. C. Interrelationships of the "innate" and the "acquired" in instinctive behavior. In P. P. Grassé (Ed.), *L'instinct dans le comportement des animaux et de l'homme.* Paris: Masson et Cie., 1956. Pp. 387–439.

Schneirla, T. C. The concept of development in comparative psychology. In D.

B. Harris (Ed.), *The concept of development: an issue in the study of human behavior*. Minneapolis: University of Minnesota Press, 1957. Pp. 78–108.

Schneirla, T. C. and Rosenblatt, J. S. Behavioral organization and genesis of the social bond in insects and mammals. *Am. J. Orthopsychiat.*, 1961, **31**, 223–253.

Seitz, A. Die Paarbildung bei einigen Cichliden. I. Die Paarbildung bei *Astatotilapia strigigena* (Pfeffer). *Z. Tierpsychol.*, 1940, **4**, 40–84.

Simms, T. M. Pupillary response of male and female subjects to pupillary difference in male and female pictures. *Perception and Psychophysics*, 1967, **2**, 553–555.

Sluckin, W. *Imprinting and early learning*. London: Methuen, 1964.

Somer, R. Studies in personal space. *Sociometry*, 1959, **22**, 247–260.

Spalding, D. A. Instinct, with original observations on young animals. *Macmillan's Magazine*, 1873, **27**, 282–293. Reprinted in *Br. J. Anim. Behav.*, 1954, **2**, 2–11.

Spalding, D. A. Instinct and acquisition. *Nature*, 1875, **12**, 507–508.

Spitz, R. A., and Wolf, K. M. The smiling response: a contribution to the ontogenesis of social relations. *Genet. Psychol. Monogr.*, 1946, **34**, 57–125.

Spuhler, J. N., and Lindzey, G. Racial differences in behavior. In J. Hirsch (Ed.), *Behavior-genetic analysis*. New York: McGraw-Hill, 1967. Pp. 366–414.

Stass, J. W., and Willis, F. N. Eye contact, pupil dilation, and personal preference. *Psychonomic Sci.*, 1967, **7**, 375–376.

Thorndike, E. L. Instinct. *Biological Lectures, Woods Hole*, 1899, **7**, 57–68.

Tinbergen, N. On the analysis of social organization among vertebrates, with special reference to birds. *Am. Midl. Nat.*, 1939, **21**, 210–234.

Tinbergen, N. *The study of instinct*. London: Oxford University Press. 1951.

Tinbergen, N. "Derived" activities: their causation, biological significance, origin, and emancipation during evolution. *Q. Rev. Biol.*, 1952, **27**, 1–32.

Tinbergen, N. On aims and methods of ethology. *Z. Tierpsychol.*, 1963, **20**, 410–433.

Uexküll, J. von. *Umwelt und Innenwelt der Tiere*. Jena: 1909.

Vries, H. de. Alimentation et sélection. In *Cinquantenaire de la Societé de Biologie*. Vol. Jubilaire. Paris: Masson et Cie., 1899. Pp. 17–38.

Vries, H. de. *Die Mutationstheorie*. Leipzig: 1901.

Vries, H. de. *Species and varieties*. Chicago, Ill.: Open Court Publishing Company, 1905.

Watson, J. B. *Behaviorism*. New York: The People's Institute Publishing Co., 1922.

Watson, J. B. *The ways of behaviorism*. New York: Harper's, 1928.

Weigert, E. Human ego functions in the light of animal behavior. *Psychiatry*, 1956, **19**, 325–332.

Wickler, W. Socio-sexual signals and their intraspecific imitation among primates. In D., Morris (Ed.), *Primate ethology*. Chicago, Ill.: Aldine, 1967. Pp. 69–147.

Weiss, P. Self-differentiation of the basic patterns of co-ordination. *Comp. Psychol. Monogr.*, 1941, **17**, 1–96.

Whitman, C. O. Animal behavior. *Biological Lectures, Woods Hole, Mass.*, 1898, **6**, 285–338.

Wilson, J. P. Nursing experience and the social smile. Unpublished doctoral dissertation, University of Chicago, 1963.

Wolff, P. H. Observations on the early development of smiling. In B. M. Foss (Ed.), *Determinants of infant behaviour II*. Second Tavistock Seminar on Mother-Infant Interaction, London, 1961. New York: Wiley, 1963. Pp. 113–138.

2. Genetic Influences on Behavior and Development

GERALD E. McCLEARN

The genetic data and principles most obviously relevant to problems of behavioral development are those that constitute the area of developmental genetics. The purpose of this chapter is to outline developmental genetics in general terms and to describe research that explicitly demonstrates genetic influence on behavioral development. However, the discussion of developmental genetics requires some acquaintance with concepts from the areas of transmission, quantitative, molecular, and physiological genetics. The first portion of the chapter constitutes a brief presentation of basic principles from these fields that are important for later discussion.

MENDELIAN RULES AND CONCEPTS

The origin of the modern field of genetics is generally traced to the discovery by Gregor Mendel in 1865 of certain "laws" that seemed to characterize the mode of action of hereditary factors, and the manner in which they are transmitted from one generation to the next. The publication of these laws in 1866 caused no immediate stir in the biological world, and it was not until 1900 that Mendel's work was "rediscovered" and a period of intensive research was initiated. In the early years, much research was devoted to assessing the generality of the Mendelian laws. This generality was found to be very great indeed, with respect to both the variety of characteristics that could be shown to be describable in Mendelian terms and the variety of organisms in which the laws could be demonstrated.

Transmission Genetics

It was not until some time later that evidence concerning the physical nature of the hereditary material became available, so Mendel's laws were formulated in terms of hypothetical elements. These elements were named "genes." Each individual organism was assumed to have two of each gene, with one member of this pair of genes contributed by the maternal parent, and the other by the paternal parent. A gene can exist in two (or more) alternative states, called *alleles*. Two types of conditions can be described for any given individual with respect to a particular gene pair. Given the allelic state of the gene from one parent, that from the other parent must be either the same or different. If the two allelic states are the same, the individual is described as *homozygous*; if the two allelic states are different, the individual is described as *heterozygous*. Now, if we characterize one possible allelic state of a gene as A and the other as A', it can be seen that there are two homozygous states, AA and A'A', and one heterozygous state, AA'. These are descriptions of the *genotype* of the individual with respect to this particular gene pair.

A major conceptual development was the distinction between genotype and phenotype, or the observed characteristics of the individual. There is a relationship, causal and directional, from genotype to phenotype, but the relationship is not perfectly isomorphic. In different cases, different relationships of phenotype to genotype were discovered. Figure 1 illustrates several of the relationships that may occur. Genotypes are shown along the abscissa with the ordering of the genotypes and the spacing between them based upon the number of A' alleles present. The ordinate displays the phenotype under consideration. If the phenotypic value of the heterozygote AA' is exactly halfway between

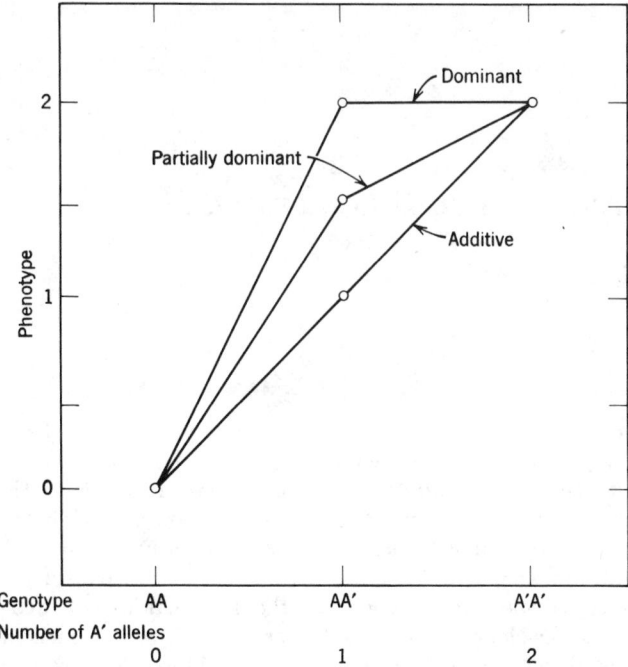

Fig. 1. Several different types of relationships of phenotype to genotype.

the values of the two homozygotes, the system is *additive*. If the heterozygote has a phenotypic value indistinguishable from that of one of the homozygotes, *dominance* is said to exist, and the allele of the homozygous parent from which the heterozygote is not distinguishable is described as being *dominant* over the alternative allele. Intermediate situations, in which one allele is partially dominant over the other, are also possible. In such cases the heterozygote lies somewhere between the halfway point and one of the homozygotes.

Each individual begins life as a single cell, which is formed by the union of two gametes, the ovum, supplied by the mother, and the sperm, provided by the father. In the process of formation of the gametes, only one of each gene pair is included. In Fig. 2 three individuals are represented. Each individual is shown as a square, with the genotype written within the square. The phenotype is represented by the presence or absence of hachures. The A' allele is shown as dominant over the A allele. The process of gamete formation is indicated by the dashed lines and the resultant gametes are shown as small circles, each with a single allele designated. (Each gamete will actually receive many genes—one from each autosomal gene pair the parent organism contains—but our present discussion concerns only a single locus.) AA individuals can produce only A gametes, and A'A' individuals can produce only A' gametes. The heterozygote AA', however, can generate both A and A' gametes.

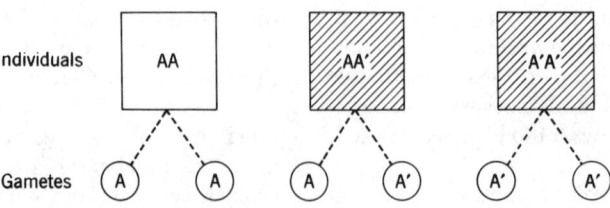

Fig. 2. Gamete formation.

The process by which these alternative alleles are distributed to gametes appears to be a random one, with equal numbers of each type of gamete being produced. Note that two individuals that are alike phenotypically, A'A' and AA', differ in the types of gametes that they are capable of producing.

Now let us assume a mating between two of the heterozygous AA' individuals. Each will produce equal numbers of A and A' gametes, which will unite at random. The situation is represented in Fig. 3. Gametes from parent 1 are shown in the columns; gametes from parent 2 are shown in rows. The four cells of the table represent the four possible genotypes that can arise from such a mating. In genotypic terms, there are three possibilities: AA, AA', or A'A'. Phenotypically, there are only two outcomes: "hachured" and "nonhachured." The ratio of stippled to non-stippled is three to one. This is the classic Mendelian ratio to be expected in offspring between two heterozygous individuals when there is complete dominance.

Other matings would provide other results. Consider, for example, the mating of an AA with an AA' individual. Figure 4 shows the possible outcomes. The outcome of yet other matings can be easily described. Matings of AA with AA will yield only AA offspring. Matings of A'A' with A'A' will give only A'A' offspring. Now, in three of the mating types mentioned, AA offspring can result. An AA

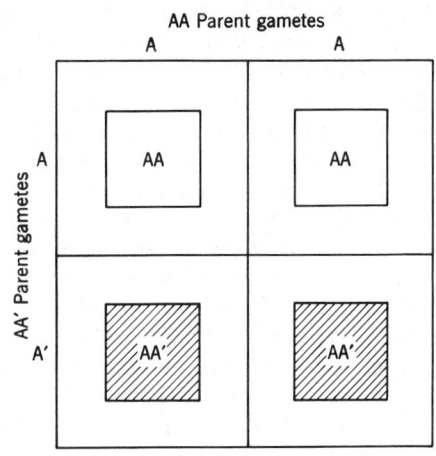

AA Parent gametes

Fig. 4. Possible offspring genotypes resulting from random union of gametes from one homozygous (AA) and one heterozygous (AA') parent.

offspring of mating AA with AA' individuals will necessarily have received one of its A alleles from the AA' parent. That A allele has been in residence with an A' allele during the life of this heterozygous parent. On the other hand, an AA offspring of a mating of an AA with an AA individual will receive A alleles that have only been in the company of other A alleles in the previous generation. Yet these two types of AA offspring are indistinguishable phenotypically, as well as genotypically. The alleles are not influenced by association with a partner of a different type.

Another extremely important Mendelian principle involves the consideration of the segregation of more than one gene pair at a time. Assume that, in addition to the gene pair A-A', we have another gene pair B-B'. The rule of independent assortment refers to the fact that in gamete production the "selection" of a particular member of one gene pair does not influence the (random) selection from another gene pair for inclusion in the same gamete. A double heterozygote individual, AA'BB', would therefore produce gametes AB, A'B, AB' and A'B' in equal quantities. Operation of this rule is subject to some restrictions, which will be described later.

The traits to which the simple and basic Mendelian rules can be applied most directly are dichotomous traits, in which the individual may be unambiguously assigned to one

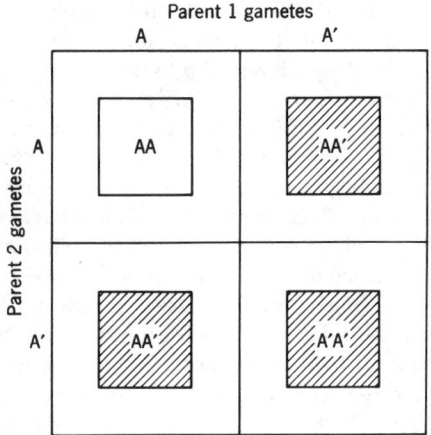

Parent 1 gametes

Fig. 3. Possible offspring genotypes resulting from random union of gametes from two heterozygous (AA') parents.

or another group. This situation is most frequently encountered in the case of rare abnormalities, although some "single-gene" conditions determine traits which fall in the normal range of variability. With human subjects, the classical method of studying such situations involves examination of family pedigrees. Clear-cut dominance or recessivity is frequently revealed by the pattern of transmission from one generation to the next. If a rare trait is determined by an allele that is dominant over its partner, affected individuals appear in each generation, and about half of the offspring show the characteristics. There is an easily understood explanation of this typical pattern. In the case of a rare condition, the affected individual probably will be heterozygous because, if the condition is rare, the alleles will be rare, and the liklehood of two such rare alleles combining in one individual will be remote. The affected individual, usually married to a phenotypically normal partner, can produce only two types of gametes with respect to this gene pair: one-half of his gametes will contain the dominant, trait-producing allele; the other half will contain the "normal" recessive allele. All of the alleles provided by the normal parent will be of the normal "recessive" variety. Therefore half of the offspring of one affected individual will receive only recessive alleles from each parent, whereas half will receive a recessive allele from the normal parent but the dominant allele from the affected parent.

In case of a recessive characteristic, the individual who displays the characteristic must be homozygous for the recessive alleles. An affected individual may appear in the progeny of the mating of two normal parents because in each of them the effects of the recessive allele are masked by the presence of the dominant "normal" allele. Since each of the parents can produce two types of gametes in equal number, the probability of the recessive alleles uniting is equal to $\frac{1}{2} \times \frac{1}{2} = \frac{1}{4}$.

The principles that yield these outcomes are, of course, probabilistic ones, and pedigrees departing considerably from these "ideal" types are encountered in practice. Thus, simply by chance, some families consisting of four children from the mating of two heterozygous parents will have no affected individuals; others may have one, two, three, or four.

Single Genes and Behavior

A number of traits are known, both in animals and human beings, in which single genes have important influence over behavioral characteristics. Probably the best known of these conditions is phenylketonuria, or phenylpyruvic idiocy. This condition was first described as an etiological entity by Fölling in 1934. Individuals homozygous for the recessive alleles suffer from a metabolic abnormality, to be described in more detail later; and, often but not always, they suffer from a severe degree of mental retardation.

A condition known as Huntington's chorea provides an example of a trait inherited as a dominant. This condition is characterized by the onset of neural degeneration in adulthood and the development of psychotic behavior.

Ability to taste a substance called phenylthiocarbamide is also dependent upon a single gene pair. Individuals possessing one or two of the dominant alleles find the substance to be extremely bitter. Individuals homozygous for the recessive allele find it to be tasteless.

Animal research provides many examples of single gene pair influence on behavior. A whole series of conditions bearing names such as Shaker, Jerker, Pirouette, Fidget, Jittery, Trembler, and Reeler have been described in mice. These conditions variously involve vestibular or neural defect, and they are characterized by head shaking, body trembling, and difficulties in locomotion and maintaining balance (see Grüneberg, 1952). The albino gene in the mouse, which can be easily studied because of its obvious effect upon coat color, has been shown also to have effects upon performance in water escape learning (Winston and Lindzey, 1964), activity, and emotional responses (DeFries et al., 1966).

A single gene pair in fruit flies has been shown to affect mating behavior (Bastock, 1956), and a complicated series of behavioral responses involved in removal of diseased larvae by honeybees has been shown to be under the influence of two gene pairs (Rothenbuhler, 1964). Worker bees homozygous for the recessive alleles of each of these gene pairs will both uncap the cells of the diseased larvae and remove them from the nest. The presence of a dominant allele of one of the gene pairs results in the failure to remove the diseased larvae after uncapping; a dominant

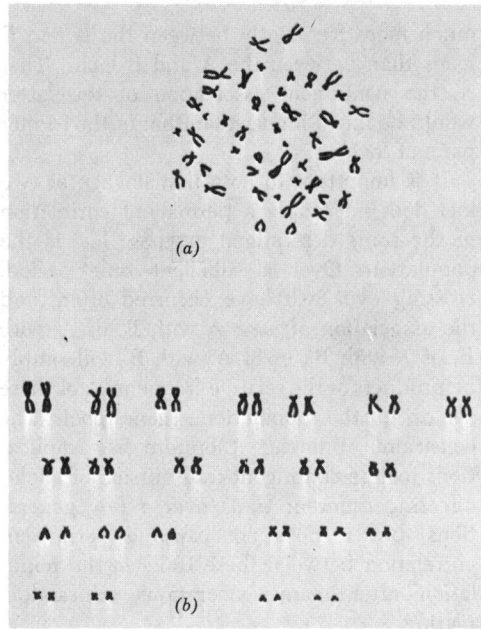

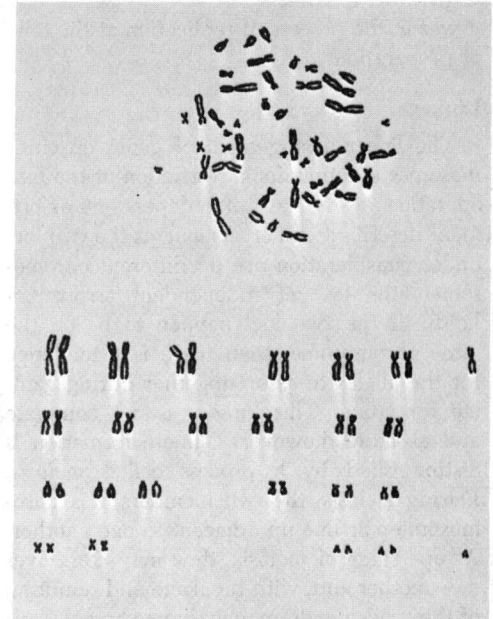

Fig. 5. Normal human chromosome complement. Female on left; male on right. (*a*) Photomicrograph. (*b*) Arrangement of chromosomes into standard karyotype arrangement. The sex chromosomes are shown in the right-hand column of each karyotype display. The two X chromosomes of the female are shown in the top row; the single X of the male is also shown in the top row, and the small Y chromosome is shown below it in the bottom row. The other chromosomes, the autosomes, are arranged by pairs in order of descending size. (Furnished by Professor A. Robinson.)

allele of the other pair results in the failure to uncap.

The preceding are examples of major gene effects on behavioral phenotypes. As we shall see later, more complicated models are required to account for many quantitatively distributed traits of particular interest to behavioral scientists where major gene effects are not present. Nevertheless, the demonstration of the operation of the basic laws in behavioral phenotypes permits us to proceed to the more complex formulations with confidence.

CHROMOSOMES: PHYSICAL VEHICLES OF THE HEREDITARY MATERIAL

The first insight into the physical nature of the genes came through observations of parallels between the rules governing Mendel's hypothetical elements and the actions of small bodies within the nucleus of cells. These small bodies were found to stain selectively under certain conditions and were therefore named chromosomes. Like Mendel's elements, the chromosomes exist as paired entities. During gamete formation, each gamete receives only half of the total number of chromosomes, one of each pair. Ingenious researches provided evidence that the chromosomes were indeed the physical vehicles of the genes, and that the genes were linearly arranged along the length of the chromosomes. Each gene pair has a relatively fixed position, or *locus*, on a particular chromosome. The number of chromosomes is generally constant within the cells of an organism and across organisms within a species. Species differ from one another in chromosome number; however, the number provides no clue to phyletic status. Mice possess 20 pairs, crayfish 100 pairs, fruit flies (*Drosophila*) 4 pairs, and man 23 pairs. Figure 5 shows a normal human chromosome complement. Figure 5*a* shows the chromosomes as seen in the microscopic preparation; part *b* presents the same chromosomes arranged in groupings according to size and other characteristics. Because of the stage at which the cells were prepared for examination, each individual member of the chromosome pair appears doubled. This is because it was in the process of replication at the time of preparation.

Linkage

The linear arrangement of genes on chromosomes accounts for a restriction of the free operation of the law of independent assortment described earlier. As long as the two loci under consideration are on different chromosomes, the law of independent assortment holds. If the two loci happen to be on the same chromosome, then there is a tendency for the alleles to assort together during gamete formation. This *linkage* is not complete and absolute, however. Gamete formation is distinguished by a process called *meiosis*. During meiosis, the two members of a chromosome pair line up adjacent to one another. At one stage of meiosis, they may cross over one another and, with breakage and reuniting of the broken ends, may exchange homologous portions. For example, let us suppose that we are concerned with three particular loci out of the very many loci that will occupy the length of the chromosome. Let us assume that an individual received a chromosome from his father which contained an A′, B, and C′ allele, whose loci are arranged as shown in Fig. 6. Assume further that the maternal chromosome contained alleles A, B′, C, at these loci. The individual in question is therefore heterozygous for the three loci. The alleles will not randomly and independently appear in the gametes formed by this individual. If a gamete contains A′, the probability is greater than one-half that it will also contain B. Crossing over, and the exchange of genetic material, is a function of the linear distance between loci. Therefore crossing over would, in our hypothetical example, occur much more frequently between the B and C locus than between the A and B locus. That is, the contingent association of the latter would be much higher than that of the former pairs of loci.

It is important to note that linkage of two loci does not imply a permanent correlation of the traits determined by these loci in the population. Over a sufficient time period, crossing over will have occurred often, and the association of, say, A with B, of A′ with B, of A with B′, or of A′ with B′ will simply be products of the relative frequencies of these alleles in the population's gene pool. The constraint of linkage therefore has implications for the contingent transmission of alleles affecting different traits over a few generations, but it does not cause a permanent correlation between these traits in the population after many generations of random mating.

Sex Linkage. A special kind of linkage relationship is attributable to the chromosomal basis of sex determination. Two kinds of chromosomes may be distinguished. In the *autosomes,* which in man number 22 pairs, the individual members of the pairs appear to be equal, both in terms of microscopic appearance and also in terms of having the same loci arranged in the same order. In the males of man, mouse, fruit fly, and many other organisms, there is an inequality of the members of one chromosome pair, the *sex chromosomes.* The longer of the sex chromosomes is called the X chromosome, and the shorter one the Y chromosome. Females possess two X chromosomes. Males, on the other hand, possess one X and one Y chromosome. It appears that the small Y chromosome contains no or very few loci homologous to those on the X chromosome. Thus a recessive allele on the X chromosome of a man cannot have its effects masked by the presence of a dominant allele on the Y chromosome. In other words, the concepts of homozygosity and heterozygosity do not apply to sex linked loci in males. This situation produces some interesting patterns of transmission. Note that females can only produce X bearing ova. Males can produce both X bearing and Y bearing sperm. A male will therefore have received his only X chromosome from his mother, and he cannot transmit it to any son.

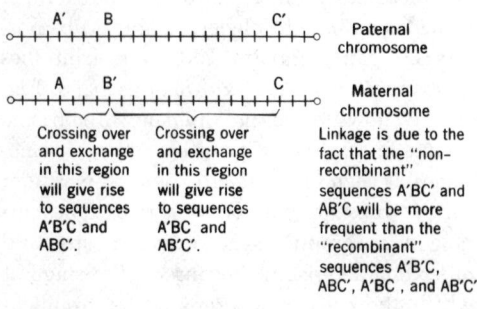

Fig. 6.   Gene linkage and crossing over.

GENETIC INFLUENCES ON BEHAVIOR AND DEVELOPMENT 45

Red-green color blindness is a classic example of a sex linked trait in man. Women who are homozygous for the recessive alleles cannot distinguish the two colors readily or at all. Heterozygous women or those homozygous for the dominant allele have normal color vision. A male has only one allele, and if it be the dominant, color vision will be normal; if recessive, color vision will be defective. As a consequence of these relationships, certain regularities ensue. All normal visioned daughters of color blind men must be heterozygotes. If they marry normal color visioned men, one-half of their sons, on the average, will be color blind. A color blind woman will have received one recessive allele from her father, who must therefore be color blind, and one from her mother.

One characteristic of sex linked conditions is that the frequency of occurrence is much greater in males than in females. The reason for this inequality in incidence can be readily understood. Let p represent the proportion of the dominant allele in the population, and q represent the proportion of the recessive allele. If mating is at random, the probability of a recessive allele combining with another recessive allele in a female child is $q \times q = q^2$. For males, however, the frequency will simply be equal to the population frequency, or q. Since these values are stated as proportions, q^2 is much smaller than q. An extension of this reasoning permits the estimation of the number of heterozygotes or "carrier" women in the population. The probability of two dominant alleles uniting is p^2, and the probability of heterozygote combinations is equal to $2pq$. The frequency of color blind males in the population, which, as we have seen, estimates q directly, is approximately .08. By subtraction, p must equal .92, and p^2 therefore is equal to .85, which represents the number of homozygous normal females; $2pq$ is equal to .15, which is the frequency of "carriers," and q^2, the frequency of color blind women, is less than .01.

Chromosome Anomalies and Behavior

Ordinarily, in the process of gametogenesis, the duplication of chromosomes in a cell, and their subsequent allocation to daughter cells, is accomplished with great precision. Occasionally, however, mistakes occur which result in the formation of gametes with ab-

normal chromosomes or an abnormal number of chromosomes. One such error is *nondisjunction*. In nondisjunction, both chromosomes of a given pair go to the same daughter cell, with the result that one of the gametes formed will have the normal complement plus one extra chromosome, whereas the other gamete will have the normal complement minus one chromosome. If an egg which has an extra chromosome due to nondisjunction is fertilized by a normal sperm, the resulting zygote will have the normal pair of chromosomes for all except one, which will be present in triplicate. This condition is known as trisomy. Similarly, an egg lacking one chromosome, fertilized by a normal sperm, will give rise to a condition known as monosomy in which one chromosome is present only in a singlet. Similar results occur, of course, when abnormal sperm fertilize normal eggs.

Autosomal Trisomy. The well-known and intensively studied syndrome of mental retardation known as Mongolism or Down's syndrome was one of the first human syndromes in which a chromosomal anomaly was described. Lejeune et al. (1959) and Jacobs et al. (1959) almost simultaneously reported that mongoloid individuals possessed 47 instead of the usual number of 46 chromosomes. Detailed analysis revealed that the extra chromosome was a small one with cytological features that identified it as number 21. This discovery illuminated greatly the etiological picture of Down's syndrome, which had become a confusing assemblage of contradictory evidence concerning various genetic hypotheses and hypotheses about environmental causal factors. The "accidental" nature of nondisjunction renders irrelevant speculation over whether the trait is inherited as a dominant or as a recessive. Similarly, since the critical event has occurred during gametogenesis, theories implicating environmental factors which occur during gestation are also seen to be beside the point. However, there are two links in the etiological sequence that remain to be clarified. The first is the circumstance or circumstances that cause the "accident" of nondisjunction; the second concerns the reason why excess genetic material causes the developmental abnormalities.

Regarding nondisjunction, it has been well

established that the risk of bearing a child with mongolism increases markedly with maternal age. Since the sex cells of the human female are partially formed before birth, rather than being continuously produced throughout life, it seems reasonable to speculate that the age dependent risk function reflects the fact that the gametes of older females have been exposed to environmental forces, as yet unknown, for a longer period of time than have those of younger females, with a corresponding increased likelihood of aberration. The nature of the relevant environmental factor is as yet unknown, although some recent work (Nichols et al., 1962) has suggested the possibility of a viral infection being an important factor in chromosome breakage. The possibility of an infectious determinant of nondisjunction is also suggested by the epidemiological studies that have shown Down's syndrome births to occur more closely in space and time than would be expected on the basis of a random occurrence hypothesis (Collman and Stoller, 1960; Heinrichs et al., 1963).

With respect to the problem of the mechanism whereby extra hereditary material causes abnormality of development, it has been proposed that overproduction of enzymes is the critical factor, and research on this point is actively in progress (Herring et al., 1967; also see Lejeune review, 1964), but without definitive results at present.

Trisomy probably occurs with respect to all autosomes, but it is evidently lethal in most cases. For example, one recent study (Carr, 1967) examined 227 spontaneous abortions for evidence of chromosome anomaly. Fifty of the abortuses were found to have an anomaly, and 27 of these were trisomics. This incidence of chromosome abnormality in abortuses is more than 50 times as high as that in infants born alive.

Two other autosomal trisomic conditions, trisomy D and trisomy E, have been described in live-born infants. Both of these conditions involve extensive abnormalities and poor prognosis for survival. Trisomy D (the triplet chromosome is not exactly identifiable, but is one of group D, nos. 13-15) involves deficient telencephalic development, absence of the olfactory tracts, and small or absent eyes. Trisomy E involves cardiac and kidney defects and hypertonicity. See Smith

(1963) for a review of these conditions.

Autosomal monosomics have not been described in man, suggesting that the absence of one member of an autosomal pair is highly lethal. The absence of autosomal monosomics in the study of abortuses already cited (Carr, 1967) suggests that the lethality of the condition is manifested at a very early stage of development.

Other Autosomal Anomalies. Another type of chromosomal accident arises from the occasional exchange of material between nonhomologous chromosomes. Through this means, a chromosome is sometimes formed with extra material from another chromosome pair or with part of its original material exchanged with material from a different chromosome pair. When a gamete possessing such an abnormal chromosome is fertilized by a normal gamete, the resulting zygote will be deficient with respect to some hereditary material and will possess an excess of other hereditary material. A translocation of this nature was suspected when a patient with Down's syndrome was shown to have the normal number of 46 chromosomes, rather than 47 (Polani et al., 1960). Detailed study of the chromosome complement showed that one chromosome was longer than usual. The interpretation was that this larger chromosome had extra chromosomal material from chromosome number 21 attached to it. It therefore appears that Down's syndrome may be caused by an excess of a portion of chromosome number 21.

Still another type of chromosome anomaly involves the deletion of some chromosomal material. Such a condition appears to underlie the clinical syndrome known as "cri-du-chat." This syndrome involves quite severe mental retardation, and the affected children are characterized by a cry that is very similar to that of a cat or kitten—thus the name. A number of cases have been reported since the original observation by Lejeune and co-workers (Lejeune et al., 1963; Macintyre et al., 1964; Schmid and Vischer, 1967; Itoh and Gotoh, 1967; Schlegel et al., 1967).

Affected individuals have been found to lack one end of one member of the chromosome number 5 pair.

Sex Chromosome Trisomy. Klinefelter's syndrome is a condition of incomplete sexual development in ostensible males which is very often associated with mental defect. The syndrome is probably a heterogeneous one composed of different etiological entities. Many of the affected individuals have been shown to have 47 chromosomes, with the normal number of paired autosomes and a sex chromosome constitution of XXY.

Another trisomy involving the X and Y chromosomes has recently been found to have interesting behavioral implications. Hauschka et al. (1962) described a case of an XYY male who was asymptomatic. A short while later Ricci and Malacarne (1964) described an XYY individual with deficient mental development. Jacobs et al. (1965) conducted a survey of mentally retarded male patients who had violent, dangerous, or criminal propensities, in a maximum security prison hospital. They found 7 of the 197 examined patients to have an XYY sex chromosome complement. This incidence is greatly in excess of that to be found in the normal population, and suggests that the presence of the extra Y may relate to the degree of mental retardation and to the aggressiveness characteristic of these inmates. These individuals are also unusually tall. Price and Whatmore (1967) performed follow-up observations on these patients and found them to differ from control inmates who had a normal sex chromosome complement in the following ways.

1. The record of XYY males revealed considerably fewer crimes of violence against persons than did those of the XY males. The XYY violence was evidently more directed against property than persons.

2. The behavior disturbance of the XYY inmates had an earlier onset than that of the XY inmates.

3. Siblings of XYY inmates were significantly less likely to have antisocial records than siblings of XY inmates.

Another recently reported case (Forssman, 1967) conforms to the general picture in that extreme aggression became apparent at about age 10, and Stanford Binet IQ was 69 at age 15. This child was also unusually tall and suffered from epileptic seizures.

XXX individuals have also been described, but as yet no consistent clinical picture has emerged (Day et al., 1964).

Sex Chromosome Monosomy. Although monosomy of autosomes appears to be incompatible with life, one of the possible sex chromosome monosomies is found. Individuals with only a single Y have not been found, but the single X condition (symbolized XO) gives rise to Turner's syndrome, which involves sexual infantilism in presumptive females. In addition to the abnormalities of sexual development, Turner's syndrome patients have been found to suffer from a specific form of perceptual-cognitive deficiency. Money (1963, 1966) has described a series of tests measuring spatial ability in which Turner's patients are strikingly inferior to normal control individuals.

Other Chromosome Anomalies. Polysomies of higher order than trisomy have been identified with respect to the sex chromosomes. XXX, XXXY, XXXYYY, and XXXY individuals have been described, for example. Mosaics have also been identified in which some of the body cells have one chromosome complement, others have a different one. For example, XO/XX, XO/XY, XX/XY and even the triple mosaic of XO/XY/XXY have been described with respect to the sex chromosomes. Mosaicism has also been implicated in Down's syndrome in a case (Clarke et al., 1963) in which some cells were found to be trisomic and others normal. Other mosaics for Down's syndrome have been described; and, in some but not all, the mosaic cases have been shown to have higher IQs than the typical case (Polani, 1963).

QUANTITATIVE GENETICS

It is very important to appreciate the fact that the demonstration of a single locus effect, as in phenylketonuria, does not imply that the normal allele for that locus is exclusively responsible for determining the normal expression of the character. It is appropriate to regard the defect as due to the occurrence of the genetic block at one of the many possible crucial points in a multiplex system. In the absence of a block of this kind, the normal expression of variability in a population is attributable to the joint action of a number of loci, each of which makes a small contribution to the total phenotype. Investigation of these complexly determined phenotypes constitutes the field of genetics called polygenic, multiple factor, or quanti-

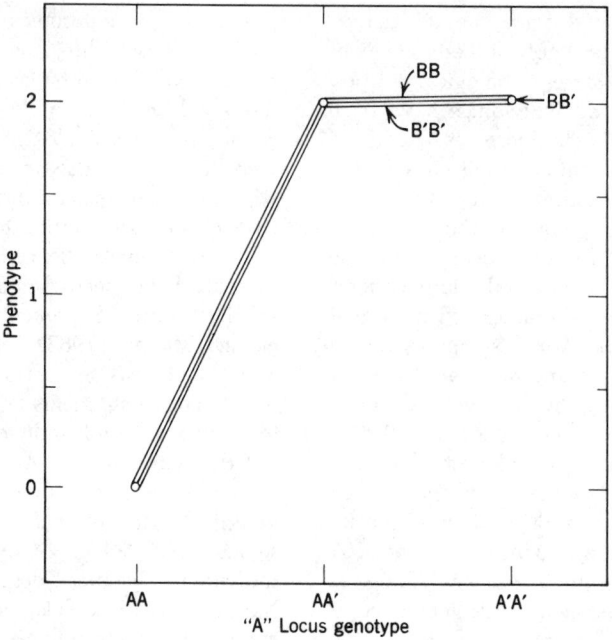

Fig. 7. Absence of epistasis. Effect of A locus genotype on phenotype is independent of B locus genotype.

tative genetics. It is easy to see that the basic applicable model is a binomial one, since each (autosomal) locus is present in duplicate. If we then assume a number of loci, each with two allelic states, each with an equal small individual effect, each acting additively, the distribution of the phenotype under consideration would be simply $(A + A')^{2n}$ where $n =$ the number of loci.

This very simple picture becomes complicated, of course, if dominance exists at any of the loci. In addition to dominance, which may be regarded as a form of intralocus interaction, in polygenic systems we must be concerned with interlocus interaction, usually termed in this context *epistasis*. Essentially, epistasis refers to a situation in which the relationship of the phenotype to the genotype at one locus is dependent upon the genotype at a different locus. Consider Fig. 7, for example. Phenotype is plotted against locus A genotype, with locus B genotype as a parameter. With the lines separated only for graphic convenience, this hypothetical example shows that the effectiveness of the A locus in influencing the phenotype is independent of the genetic condition at the B

locus. Figure 8 represents a situation in which the effect of the A locus is unaffected by the B locus if the genotype is B'B' or BB', but the A locus has no influence at all if the genotype is BB. A specific illustration of this type of interlocus interaction is the effect of the albino gene in mice. A number of coat color loci have been described, some of which determine the type of pigment, some of which determine the location of the pigment along the hair, and so on. None of these loci have any phenotypic effect, however, in the presence of a homozygous recessive condition at the albino locus.

The analysis of a polygenically determined system cannot be accomplished by the classical methods of pedigree analysis, since the effects of the individual genes are assumed to be small. Statistical analysis is therefore required, and a number of models and techniques have been developed to estimate various genetic parameters from statistics. A key concept in quantitative genetics is *heritability* (Lush, 1940), which is defined in terms of various ratios.

If we may assume that genotype and environment are uncorrelated, the total phenotypic variance (V_P) in a population may be regarded as the sum of genetic variance (V_G) plus environmental variance (V_E). For only one locus,

$$V_P = V_G + V_E$$

where the genetic variance itself may be subdivided into an additive portion, arising from the average effects of genes, and a dominance portion. When more than one locus is involved, another source of genetic variance, arising from epistatic interactions among loci, must be considered:

$$V_P = V_A + V_D + V_I + V_E$$

where V_A is the additive genetic variance, V_D represents intralocus interaction, and V_I represents interlocus interaction. It is often convenient to combine intralocus and interlocus interaction in a nonadditive variance term:

$$V_P = V_A + V_{NA} + V_E$$

In a broad sense, heritability is sometimes defined as the proportion of total phenotypic variation which is ascribable to genetic sources: V_G/V_P. However, for many purposes, both in description and prediction, a more narrowly defined ratio, V_A/V_P, is employed. To distinguish these two, Falconer (1960) proposed a usage that describes the second as heritability and the first as degree of genetic determination.

It is worth repeating and emphasizing at this point that the key concept of heritability explicitly and necessarily involves the simultaneous consideration of both genetic and environmental determinants. With this formulation, an attempt to describe a trait as being "genetic" or "environmental" in origin is seen to be meaningless. It is also important to know that the heritability estimate obtained from a particular set of operations, such as those to be described shortly, is not an eternal, fixed value of the trait. Depending simultaneously upon environmental and genetic variance sources, the heritability will change as a given population is subjected to different environmental circumstances, or as its genetic composition changes. Thus a heritability value refers to a given trait in a given population at a given time in a given environment.

Human Research

In research on quantitative inheritance in man, the principal techniques have involved studies of the resemblance of relatives, including twins, and of foster children.

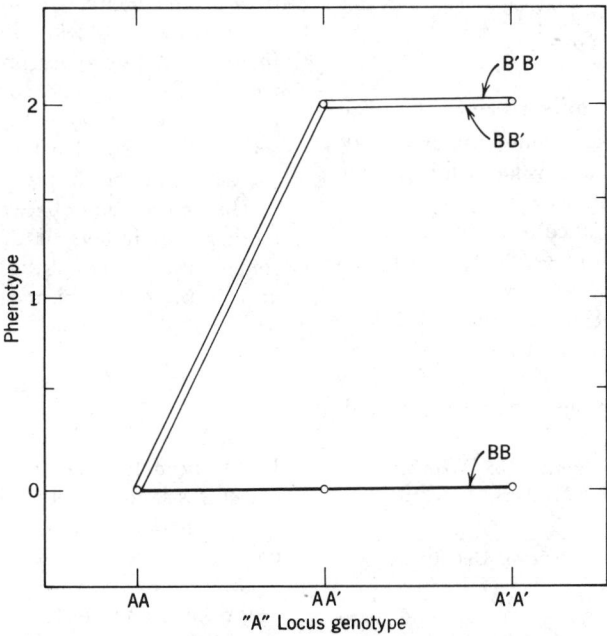

Fig. 8. Epistasis. Effect of A locus genotype on phenotype is dependent upon B locus genotype.

Resemblance of Relatives. The assessment of the phenotypic correlation that exists among relatives provides certain estimates of the genetic determinants underlying the phenotype. In a population which is in a "Hardy-Weinberg" equilibrium, the relative proportion of A'A', AA', and AA genotypes will be p^2, $2pq$, and q^2. Essentially, the conditions that must be satisfied for the population to be in this equilibrium state are that mating be random with respect to the traits influenced by the genes under consideration, that there be no differential reproductive advantage to any of the genotypes of the locus under consideration, and no significant migration into or out of the population. Admittedly, these requirements are likely to be violated in real populations, but a consideration of the ideal case forms a basis for the discussion. If we assume furthermore that the alleles of the locus act additively, and that there is no environmental effect on the trait in question, we may arbitrarily set the phenotypic values of the genotypes as

$$AA = 0, \quad AA' = 1, \quad A'A' = 2.$$

Then, since our frequencies are in terms of proportions, the mean of any generation will be equal to

$$p^2(2) + 2pq(1) + q^2(0)$$
$$2p^2 + 2pq$$
$$2p(p+q)$$

but

$$p + q = 1, \quad \text{so the mean} = 2p.$$

If the population is in equilibrium, as we have assumed, then this mean value will be characteristic of all generations.

Similarly, the variance of a generation will equal $p^2(4) + 2pq(1) - (2p)^2$, which simplifies to $2pq$.

The covariance can be obtained by the following consideration. Table 1 gives frequencies of association of one parental (say, maternal) and offspring genotypes, and indi-

cates the arbitrarily assigned cross-product values. The frequency values in the body of the table were derived from considerations of the mating frequencies and of the relative proportion of the genotype of children from the different mating types. For example, A'A' women, who are p^2 of the population of women may marry either A'A', AA', or AA men who are present in the population in the frequencies $p^2 : 2pq : q^2$. Then, if mating is at random with respect to this locus, the matings of A'A' women with A'A' men will occur with a frequency of $(p^2) (p^2) = p^4$. Similarly, A'A' by AA' matings will occur with a frequency of $(p^2) (2pq) = 2p^3q$, and that of A'A' by AA with a frequency of $(p^2) (q^2) = p^2q^2$. If we assume that all matings are equally fertile, and that all children are equally viable, the proportion of children from each mating type will equal the frequency of the mating type. Thus A'A' by A'A' matings will produce p^4 of the next generation. All p^4 of the children will be A'A'. Of the mating type A'A' by AA', one-half, or p^3q, of the children will be A'A' and the other p^3q will be AA'. Of the mating type A'A' by AA, all p^2q^2 children will be AA'. Thus A'A' mothers will have A'A' children in the relative frequencies of $p^4 + p^3q = p^3(p + q) = p^3$; and AA' children in the relative frequencies of $p^3q + p^2 q^2 = p^2q (p + q = p^2q$. Similar computations for other mating types provide the other entries in Table 1. The covariance will equal $p^3 (4) + 4p^2q + pq - (2p)^2$ where the last term is the correction for the mean. This expression simplifies to pq.

The correlation between offspring and mothers (or fathers, if the locus is an autosomal one) will equal the ratio of the covariance to the geometric mean of the variances, or

$$\frac{pq}{\sqrt{(2pq)\ (2pq)}} = \frac{pq}{2pq} = \frac{1}{2}.$$

It may be noted that this formulation is only correct as long as both alleles are present in the population; that is, when p and $q > 0$. If only one allele is present, the ratio is undefined.

We have now dealt with a single locus. If no epistatic interactions occur, the same will hold for the summated effects of many loci. Complications arise if there is any dominance

Table 1. Relative Frequencies of Offspring Genotypes for Mothers of Different Genotypes

Maternal Genotype	Offspring Genotype		
	A'A'	AA'	AA
A'A'	$p^3(4)$	$p^2q(2)$	—
AA'	$p^2q(2)$	$pq(1)$	$pq^2(0)$
AA	—	$pq^2(0)$	$q^3(0)$

in the system. Consider again a single locus. Following Li (1955), it is algebraically more convenient to assign the phenotypic value of 1 to the homozygous recessive condition (AA in our present notation) and the value of 0 to the heterozygote AA' and the homozygote A'A'. The mean of a generation under these circumstances will be equal to $p^2 (0) + 2pq (0) + q^2(1) = q^2$. The variance will equal $p^2(0) + 2pq(0) + q^2 - (q^2)^2$. The covariance is equal to $q^3 - (q^2)^2$, and the correlation then will equal

$$\frac{q^3 - q^4}{\sqrt{(q^2 - q^4)(q^2 - q^4)}} = \frac{q^3 - q^4}{q^2 - q^4} = \frac{q}{1 + q}$$

Thus, in the situations where dominance exists, the expected value of the correlation is dependent upon gene frequencies. In the case of the different alleles being equally frequent ($p = q = .5$), the correlation would be expected to be .333. As the frequency of the recessive allele approaches 1, the expected correlation coefficient will approach .5. Similar considerations show that the expected correlation of siblings, given dominance and the other conditions assumed, will be .416 for $p = q = .5$, and approaches .5 as the frequency of recessive alleles increases.

A relatively large amount of research has been conducted on the correlations between parents and offspring and between siblings with respect to both anatomical and intellectual characteristics. The outcome is very often surprisingly close to the theoretically expected value of .5. Considerable caution must be urged, however, that this outcome not be accepted as demonstrating the existence of the restrictive conditions assumed in generating the model. Assortative mating, for example, is known to exist with respect to many of the traits in question. In some cases, the correlation of mates itself approaches the value of .5. In general this could be expected to raise the correlation coefficients.

Environmental factors, which have to this point been assumed to be negligible, may have a wide variety of effects. Perhaps a most common one would be the increase in variance, which would tend to reduce the correlation coefficient. Many other problems of a statistical nature are also encountered, such as those pertaining to the adequacy of the sampling procedures, or reliability of the measuring de-

vice. From the point of view of the behavioral scientist, the most interesting and relevant results have been those that pertain to measures of intelligence. Erlenmeyer-Kimling and Jarvik (1963) have recently reviewed the relevant literature. Twelve studies of parent-child resemblance on intelligence test scores provided correlation coefficients ranging from about .2 to about .8 with the median being at about .5. Thirty-five cases of correlation coefficients of siblings reared together gave values ranging from about .3 to about .75 with the median result, again, being at about .5. A difficulty of interpreting these results is that it is often not made clear if the correlation is between single offspring and single parent, to which case the preceding discussion pertains, or between sibship means and parent means, for which case there are different expectations.

Correlations among relatives may be related to the concepts of heritability. Actually, regression coefficients are more useful than correlation coffecients. The regression of offspring on one parent can be shown to estimate $\frac{1}{2} V_A/V_P$, or $\frac{1}{2}h^2$, where the symbol h^2 refers to heritability in the narrow sense described above. The regression of offspring on midparent estimates V_A/V_P and thus directly estimates h^2. The intraclass correlation of full sibs is more complicated, yielding an estimate of $(\frac{1}{2}V_A + \frac{1}{4}V_D + V_E)/V_P$, where V_{EC} refers to that part of the environmental variance which is common to siblings. The study of sibs thus provides an "upper-limit" estimate of heritability.

Twin Research. The techniques of correlational or regressional analysis are pertinent to the entire population, and their proper execution requires very careful representative sampling of the population under consideration. The next techniques to be discussed are applicable only to "special cases." One of the best known and most widely employed methods for this study of human genetics has been twin comparisons. There are actually several twin study methods which serve different research purposes. The basic twin method is the comparison of identical with fraternal twins. Identical twins (*monozygotic* or *MZ*) are individuals with identical genotypes, having arisen from the same fertilized egg. Fraternal twins (*dizygotic* or *DZ*), on the other hand, are no more alike genetically than are ordinary siblings. Any difference that appears between members of an MZ twin pair must be attributed to differences in environment. Differences between members of DZ pairs, however, will reflect both environmental and genetic influence.

It is worth emphasizing that the primary datum in twin studies is a difference score. Now, if we may safely assume that environmental forces contribute no more to variability of the DZ than to the variability of the MZ twin pairs, a simple subtraction of the mean intrapair differences of a sample of MZ twins from the mean intrapair difference of DZ twin pairs should give an index of the genetic contribution to the differences between twins. More elegantly, the variances of the twin differences can be computed, and F ratios or intraclass correlations can be computed. The straightforward application of twin study results to the population at large is prevented by two features of the twin situation. The magnitude of the genetic effect is assessed by comparing differences between genetically identical individuals to the differences between genetically diverse individuals; the genetic diversity, however, is only that which can exist among progeny of the same parents. This will be much less variability than exists in the population as a whole. Similarly, the environmental forces whose impact is assessed by MZ pair differences are only those environmental differences that exist within a family. Again, this must certainly underestimate the range of environmental forces at work in the population.

Numerous criticisms have been leveled at the MZ-DZ comparison method. Perhaps the most serious of these is the likelihood that the range of environmental forces generating DZ intrapair differences is greater than that of the environmental forces contributing to MZ intrapair differences. If the environmental sources are not equal for the two types of twin pairs, we are left in a position of having two equations with two unknowns. Nevertheless, used properly, the twin method is useful in providing information about areas for future profitable research and also for setting limits. Furthermore, it should be noted that the objection concerning differences in environmental effects on MZ and DZ twin pairs is relevant only if these environmental differences are influential on the

trait under study. In some circumstances it may be possible to provide empirical data concerning the importance of differences in environmental effect between the two types of twins for a particular trait. Vandenberg (1965, 1966) has considered many of these criticisms in recent reviews. .

The classical work involving comparison of MZ and DZ twin pairs typically employed more or less global measures of intelligence or personality traits (see McClearn, 1962, for review). Recently the trend has been toward the utilization of more specific tests, in keeping with new developments in psychometrics and test construction. A most important result of the application of specific factor tests is that the evidence for hereditary determinants differs from factor to factor. This is not only a valuable finding from the point of view of genetic interpretation, but it also offers the prospect of a model for experimental verification of the existence and identity of specific factors. Vandenberg (1966) presented data from two of his own large-scale twin studies and compared these results with those of two earlier investigators, Blewett (1954) and Thurstone et al. (1955). Table 2 gives the values of the F ratio be-

Table 2. F Ratios between DZ and MZ within Pair Variance

Primary Mental Abilities Subtest	Michigan	Kentucky
Verbal	2.65[a]	1.74[b]
Space	1.77[b]	3.51[a]
Number	2.58[a]	2.26[a]
Reasoning	140	1.10
Word fluency	2.57[a]	2.24[a]
Memory	1.26	Not used

[a] $p < .01$.
[b] $p < .05$.

tween DZ and MZ within pair variances for six Primary Mental Ability subtests from the two Vandenberg studies, one conducted in Michigan, the other in Kentucky. The F ratios are significant, indicating a significant hereditary determinant, for verbal, space, number, and fluency. There is no evidence of hereditary determination for reasoning or for memory. An interesting suggestion in this connection has been made by Roberts (1967), who points out that a lack of evidence for genetic determination of a trait in a contemporary population may be interpreted as evidence for a high selective advantage of the trait in earlier evolutionary time, with natural selection having "used up" the additive genetic variance.

The twin study methodology has also been brought to bear upon inheritance of normal personality traits. Gottesman (1963, 1965) has made extensive use of the Minnesota Multiphasic Personality Inventory and has found consistent evidence for hereditary influence in depression, psychopathic deviate, and social introversion. These and other researches, including many of his own, have recently been reviewed by Vandenberg (1967) in a summary of the accumulated evidence. Vandenberg concluded that there is clear evidence of a strong hereditary component for the personality dimension of extroversion-introversion, for emotionality, and for activity.

Another early use of MZ-DZ twin comparisons is in the study of the inheritance of psychosis. In dealing with quantitatively defined traits, such as presence or absence of schizophrenia, the results are usually considered in terms of *concordance*. The research design frequently involves screening of affected individuals resident in, or admitted to, an institution, determining those who have twins, and ascertaining whether the twin also has the condition. If so, the twin pair is scored as concordant; if not, they are discordant. Kallman (1953) reported that 86.2% of the MZ co-twins of schizophrenic patients were also or had been schizophrenic, whereas only 14.5% of the DZ co-twins of schizophrenics were also or had been schizophrenic. This has been a very active research area, and it cannot be adequately summarized here. A good recent review is provided by Gottesman and Shields (1966), who also present new data of their own. A particularly interesting feature of these data pertains to the hypothesis of biological heterogeneity in schizophrenia.

Rosenthal (1959) has suggested that the schizophrenia of concordant MZ twin pairs might differ from the schizophrenia of a member of a discordant MZ twin pair, with the latter more likely to be of environmental origin. Studies of other family members of concordant and discordant cases may then provide an approach to etiological distinctions. In analyzing some data obtained by Slater, Rosenthal found that the condition was more severe in the case of concordant than discordant twins, and that there was a higher frequency of schizoid relatives in the families of concordant than in the families of discordant twins. The results of Gottesman and Shields (1966) confirmed the findings concerning a differential in severity. Defining severe schizophrenia as requiring more than one year of hospitalization, and mild as requiring less, MZ concordance for the severe schizophrenics was 67% compared with a concordance rate of 20% for mild MZ schizophrenics. These authors point out that if the predisposition to schizophrenia is a polygenically determined characteristic, possession of a number of alleles making for increased susceptibility to schizophrenia would probably at the same time make for greater severity and for an increased likelihood of a co-twin developing similar symptoms.

Another variant of the twin study method involves the comparison of MZ twins reared together and MZ twins reared apart. It should be noted that in this paradigm, there is no genetic variance. Such comparisons therefore provide no evidence concerning the heritability of a trait, although they are useful in assessing the impact of various environmental factors and are useful as adjuncts in a MZ-DZ comparison. The classical work of this type is that of Newman et al. (1937). More recent examples are provided by Shields (1962) and Burt (1966). In the intelligence measure employed by Shields (1962) the intraclass correlation for MZ twins reared apart was .77 and for MZ twins reared together was .76. By comparison, the value for DZ twins reared together was .51. On the basis of these values, the environmental differences of upbringing appear to have had but little influence on the intelligence of the MZ twins. In an extensive study Burt (1966) included observations on a variety of biological relationships among twins reared together and apart. The correlations for MZ twins reared together and MZ twins reared apart was .92 and .87, respectively. DZ twins reared together gave a value of .53, as did siblings reared together. The intraclass correlations of siblings reared apart was .44 and for unrelated children reared together was .27. These results are clearly consistent with a genetic interpretation.

The co-twin control procedure is essentially a controlled variant of the method of comparing MZ twins reared apart to MZ twins reared together. Instead of a prolonged environmental difference persisting over a long developmental period, a specific and well controlled environment, usually special training, is given to one of an MZ twin pair, with the other being untreated for control comparison.

A method complementary to twin studies involves the observation of adopted children. The basic logic is that any resemblance between an adopted child and his adopted parent will be of environmental origin. Comparisons of correlations of this kind with correlations of children living with their biological parents should then provide some estimate of the relative influence of genetic and environmental factors on the trait in question. Honzik (1957) presented data on correlations between child's IQ and education of mother and of father and compared these values to those obtained by Skodak and Skeels (1949) in a study of the relationship of adopted child's IQ to true mother's education and also to foster mother's education. In brief, the finding was that the relationship of adopted child's IQ to true parent education followed the same course over time as that of a child reared by its own parent, with the correlation leveling off at about .35. The relationship of the adopted child's IQ to the foster mother's education never exceeded a value of .10, and in the case of the relationship of the adopted child's IQ to foster father's educational level, the correlation never exceeded .05.

Other variants of studies of adopted children have involved comparison of children's IQ scores before and after placement, or the comparison of groups placed in homes of different socioeconomic level. These approaches provide valuable information concerning the influence of environmental factors, but they are not really relevant to genetic study.

Other Methods. Although the described methods have been those most widely employed in human behavioral genetics, other approaches are possible. Cattell (1953), for example, has proposed a multiple variance analysis system that would estimate genetic parameters from a series of equations relating observed variance of particular family groupings to theoretical environmental and genetic components and their interactions. In another paper, Cattell (1963) reviewed some research that had been conducted using the multiple variance analysis system on the inheritance of personality. The evidence currently indicates that there is high heritability of the cyclothyme-schizothyme, excitable-phlegmatic, and superego strength factors. Environment appears to be the principal determinant of the dimensions of *tender* versus *tough minded* and *fatiguability* versus *will responsiveness*, however.

A novel approach to the study of hereditary determination of components of intelligence was provided by Schull and Neel (1965), who assessed the effects of inbreeding in a Japanese population upon performance on a version of the Wechsler Intelligence Scale for Children. Various degrees of inbreeding were investigated, including offspring of second cousins, of first cousins, and of first cousins once removed. As we shall see later in the discussion of animal research, the effect of inbreeding is to increase homozygosity. The offspring of consanguineous matings will tend to be homozygous at more loci than will members of the general population. Homozygosity for the recessive alleles at many loci appears to be detrimental. It was therefore of great interest to examine the effect of this relatively modest degree of inbreeding upon intelligence. Using the mean of a control, "outbred," group of children as a reference point, depression of the various WISC subtest scores was consistently found for the children of the consanguineous matings.

Animal Research

In animal research it is, of course, possible to control matings of the experimental subjects, and thus several methods for the study of behavioral inheritance are possible which cannot be utilized in studies on man. One of the most widely used of these has been comparison of inbred strains.

Inbred Strains. Inbreeding, or the mating of related individuals, leads to an increase in homozygosity of the offspring. This is basically due to the fact that relatives are more likely to share alleles by virtue of their common ancestry. In animal research, close inbreeding, usually brother by sister, is employed. If this procedure is repeated over generations, with each generation derived from the mating of a single sibling pair, the result will theoretically be an asymptotic approach to a condition of homozygosity at all loci. This state of "purity" for practical purposes can be regarded as being attained after 20 consecutive sib-mated generations. Several factors prevent the attainment of this ideal (see McClearn, 1967), but as an approximation and a working model, strains bred in this fashion may be regarded as genetically homogeneous. A number of inbred strains of mice exist. In the main, these strains were developed for cancer research, but many also differ widely with respect to various behavior patterns.

The logic of strain comparisons is essentially as follows. The likelihood of any two separately developed inbred strains coming to be homozygous for the same alleles at all their (perhaps 100,000) loci is vanishingly small. Therefore, if two or more strains are reared and maintained under the same environmental conditions, and if differences in behavior are manifested between any of them, the difference must be attributed to genotype differences. The discovery of the strain difference in behavior therefore serves as a demonstration that there is an important genetic component in the behavior. Such demonstrations have now become commonplace, with differences in activity (Thompson, 1953; McClearn, 1959; Bruell, 1962; DeFries, 1964), learning (Lindzey and Winston, 1962; Carran et al., 1964), hoarding (Manosevitz and Lindzey, 1967), sexual behavior (McGill, 1962), alcohol perference (McClearn and Rodgers, 1959; Fuller, 1964), aggressiveness (Scott, 1942; Ginsburg and Allee, 1942), dominance (Lindzey et al., 1961), and others.

Such demonstrations of genetic influence on behavior patterns provide little evidence concerning the nature of the genetic system, and they should be regarded primarily as entering wedges for subsequent research oriented toward analysis of the quantitative aspects of the genetic system or the physiological mechanisms through which the genes are expressed. Examples of the latter type of research will be discussed later. The assessment of quantitative parameters of the genetic system utilizing inbred strains depends

upon the fact that the inbred strains themselves are genetically uniform, as are the first generation hybrids between them, but that subsequent generations are genetically heterogeneous. Consider, for example, one strain that is homozygous AABBC'C' . . . and another that has the genotype A'A'B'B'C'C'. . . . If these two strains are crossed, each can make only one kind of gamete. The first-named strain can produce only ABC' . . . gametes, and the second-named strain can produce only A'B'C' . . . gametes. When these gametes unite the offspring will be AA'BB'C'C' . . . . Thus the offspring will be heterozygous at all loci at which the parent strains differ but will still be homozygous at those loci at which the parent strains were homozygous in like state. Although heterozygous at many loci, all individuals within an F_1 generation will be identical genotypically. When matings are made among individuals from within this F_1 generation, segregation occurs and the F_2 generation will be genetically heterogeneous. Variability within the inbred parent strains or their derived F_1 must be attributed to environmental factors, since there is no genetic variability within these groups. Phenotypic variability of the F_2 group, however, will be due to both genetic and environmental factors. These relationships permit the estimation of the degree of genetic determination of a trait. For example, using closely related inbred mouse strains as parent strains, two different investigations (Fuller and Thompson, 1960; McClearn, 1961) provided estimates that the degree of genetic determination for open field activity was about .6. That is, about 60% of the variance of the F_2 generation was due to genetic activity differences.

Selective Breeding. Another research methodology available to the animal researcher that is not possible for human research is selective breeding. In this procedure, a sample of animals is measured with respect to some trait, and the ones showing an extreme manifestation of the trait are chosen to be the parents of the next generation; the extreme individuals of this offspring generation are again chosen to become parents of the succeeding generation, and so on. Providing that there is a genetic contribution to the variance of a trait in the initial population, this procedure will result in a systematic increase in the mean of the trait over the succeeding generations. The amount by which the mean will shift is dependent upon the relationship $R = h^2 S$ where R refers to selection response, S refers to selection differential, and h^2 refers to heritability in the narrow sense. The selection differential is the difference between the mean of those selected to be parents of the next generation and the mean for the entire generation of which the parents were members. The selection response is the difference between the mean of the parent's generation and the mean of the offspring generation. Thus, when heritability is high, selection response will be rapid. When heritabilty is low, selection response will be slow. A successful selective breeding study thus demonstrates that the trait in question had a significant additive genetic component.

A number of selective breeding studies with rats have followed the pioneering effort of Tolman (1924). Probably the best known is Tryon's work (1940) in which one strain of rats was selected for superior performance in a 17-unit multiple T maze and another strain, from the same foundation population, was selected for poor performance in the same maze. This procedure of selecting bidirectionally is necessary because of the shifts in mean within any single strain that can occur because of environmental fluctuations. The critical information therefore becomes that of the difference between the two lines selected in opposite directions.

A study contemporaneous with Tryon's was that of Heron (1941), who also was successful in selectively breeding for maze dullness and maze brightness in rats. Yet another successful maze learning selection study with rats employed the Hebb-Williams maze (Thompson, 1954), and more recently, successful selection for conditioned avoidance responses has been described (Bignami, 1964). Selection for high and low emotionality, as measured by defecation in a brightly illuminated open field, was undertaken by Hall (1938). This work was replicated by Broadhurst (1958). Rundquist (1933) selectively bred for high and low activity in rats. With mice, there has been successful selection for aggressiveness (Lagerspetz, 1961), alcohol preference (McClearn, unpublished), open-field activity (DeFries and Hegmann,

in press), and audiogenic seizure susceptibility (Frings and Frings, 1953). Sex drive (Wood-Gush, 1960) and aggressiveness (Guhl et al., 1960) have been successfully bred for in chickens. In insects, with a short generation interval, selection studies may be carried out over many generations in a relatively short period of time. Hirsch and Boudreau (1958) selected for phototaxis in *Drosophila*. Subsequently, Erlenmeyer-Kimling et al. (1962) selectively bred for high and low manifestation of geotaxis in *Drosophila*. Manning (1961) has selectively bred for mating speed in *Drosophila*, and has provided an example of the technique of estimating heritability from the selection response; since $R = h^2 S$, $h^2 = R/S$. In Manning's case, "realized" heritability calculated in this fashion was .30.

After a behavioral difference has been established between two inbred strains, or after a selective breeding program has generated strains of animals highly different on some behavioral trait, these animals become valuable research material for testing hypotheses about correlated traits at the behavioral level of analysis, or about physiological mechanisms underlying the traits. Several examples of the utility of selected animals in exploring related behavioral variables may be cited. Singh (1959) sought to determine the generality of the "emotional" response of the rats selected by Broadhurst for "reactivity" and "nonreactivity" as measured by defecation in the open field situation. Rats of the reactive strain were found to acquire a conditioned emotional response more rapidly than did animals of the nonreactive strain. Insights into the nature of the performance difference between the Tryon "maze bright" and "maze dull" rats were provided by Krechevsky (1933) who found that bright rats responded more in terms of spatial stimuli, and the dull rats responded more in terms of visual stimuli. Searle's (1949) work implicated motivational and emotional factors in determining the performance differences of these two strains. In descendants of the Tryon strains, McGaugh et al. (1962) have shown that the strain differences are most pronounced with very short intertrial intervals. As the distribution of practice was increased the differential between the strains diminished; and, at a

24-hour intertrial interval, the difference vanished entirely. These results suggest a difference in the consolidation mechanism in the two groups of animals. Examples of the use of inbred and selectively bred animals for the study of physiological mechanisms will be given later.

THE CHEMISTRY OF GENETICS

During the last 15 years there have been enormous advances in the understanding of the biochemical and physiological mechanisms through which the effects of genes are manifested. Fundamental to these developments has been the clarification of the chemical nature of the gene itself. The fundamental component of hereditary material is deoxyribonucleic acid (DNA). A DNA molecule has a double helical structure as shown in the schematic representation in Fig. 9. The two strands are composed of sequences of phosphate and deoxyribose sugar groups and they are held a fixed distance apart by pairs of bases on the interior of the helix. The stereochemical limitations of this molecular structure are such that the four bases involved (adenine, thymine, guanine, cytosine) can only pair in two combinations. Adenine always pairs with thymine, and guanine always pairs with cytosine. The doubled nature of the DNA molecule and the restrictions on base pairing make possible one of the essential features of hereditary material, that of self-duplication. Obviously, the genetic material must be duplicated many times over in the process of development from a single fertilized cell into a complex, multicellular organism. Evidently, in the process of cell division, the helices of the DNA molecule unwind, with the base pairs separating and one of each pair going with each strand. The raw materials from which the DNA molecule is formed appear to be plentiful in the nucleus of the cell. These raw materials occur in the form of nucleotides, consisting of one of the four bases, a deoxyribose sugar, and a phosphate. The bases of these nucleotides come to pair with the exposed bases of the unwound strands, and in this way complementary strands are formed against the originals. Eventually two DNA molecules exist where there had been but one.

The chromosomes containing DNA are

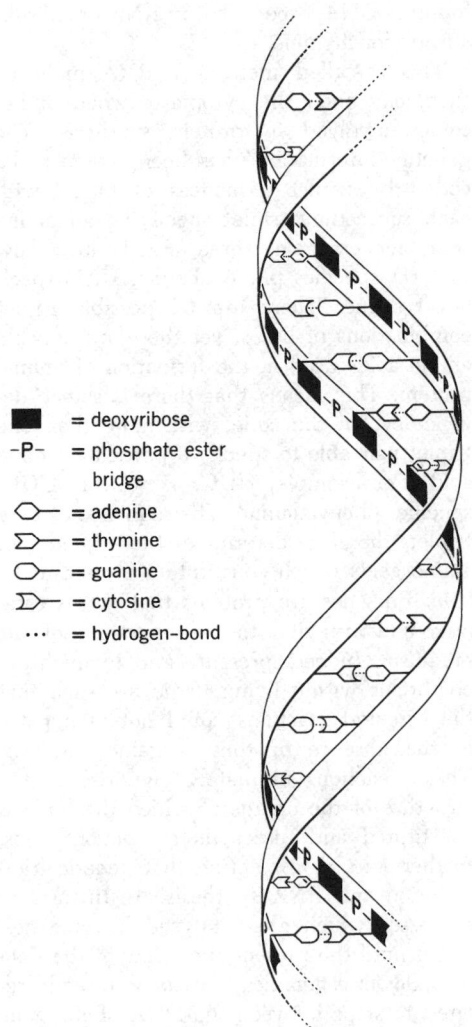

= deoxyribose
-P- = phosphate ester bridge
○— = adenine
Ↄ— = thymine
○— = guanine
Ↄ— = cytosine
··· = hydrogen-bond

Fig. 9. Schematic representation of a DNA double helix.

located in the nucleus of the cell, yet much of the biochemical work of the cells takes place in the cytoplasm. It is therefore necessary that the "information" that is coded in the DNA molecule be transmitted to the cytoplasm. This is accomplished in two steps. The first step is a transcription of the information from the DNA molecule onto a single-stranded ribonucleic acid (RNA) molecule. In reactions similar to those involved in the duplication of DNA strands, RNA can be formed in a specified sequence against one of the DNA strands. RNA is composed of a ribose sugar, phosphate, and the same bases found in DNA, except that in RNA uracil substitutes for thymine.

This so-called messenger RNA molecule then may enter the cytoplasm where it becomes involved in protein synthesis. The genetic "information" has been shown to be coded by triplet sequences of bases, with each succeeding triplet specifying an amino acid; for example, three uracils in a row (UUU) specifies phenylalanine, UAU specifies tyrosine. There are 64 possible triplet combinations of bases, yet there are only 20 amino acids used in the formation of animal protein. This means that there is some "degeneracy" in the code, with more than one triplet pair able to specify a particular amino acid. For example, UUC, as well as UUU, specifies phenylalanine. The sequence of base triplets therefore determines the sequence of amino acids which constitute a protein molecule. Enzymes are proteins that act as catalysts and are vital to the operation of the organism. Indeed, pressure and temperature conditions within living tissue are such that the essential reactions could not take place in the absence of these organic catalysts. These reactions ultimately give rise to the structure of the organs of which the body is constituted and direct their function. It is, furthermore, worth noting that genetic transcription and RNA synthesis are themselves processes which are catalyzed by enzymes.

Up until the present time, few of the data of behavioral genetics have been directly related to steps between the DNA of the gene and the formation of enzymes. Beginning at this point, however, there is an accumulating body of evidence relating genetically determined enzyme differences to behavioral consequences. The classical example is phenylketonuria. In 1934 Fölling described a biochemical defect in a particular type of mental retardation now known as phenylketonuria, phenylpyruvic oligophrenia, phenylpyruvic idiocy, or Fölling's disease. Shortly thereafter this condition was shown to be inherited in a simple Mendelian recessive manner (Jervis, 1937). The clinical picture of phenylketonuria involves a generally reduced stature, light pigmentation, microcephaly, hand posturing, rhythmic rocking back and forward, temper tantrums, and, frequently, abnormal EEG patterns (Hsia, 1967). The distribution of intelligence scores

in the institutionalized and untreated cases of phenylketonuria is markedly positively skewed, with approximately 50% of the cases falling below an IQ of 20 and with over 90% of the cases falling below an IQ of 50 (Jervis, 1954). Some untreated individuals have been found to have intelligence within the normal range, however.

The biochemical difficulty arises from an inability of the affected individuals to convert phenylalanine, an essential amino acid, into tyrosine. This inability is due to a deficiency of the liver enzyme phenylalanine hydroxylase. In fact, it has been shown (Mitoma et al., 1957; Wallace et al., 1957) that the enzyme has two fractions, one of which is labile and found only in the liver, whereas the other is stable and found in several tissues. Phenylketonuric patients are deficient with respect to the labile fraction only. Biochemical inadequacy at this single step has widespread consequences, as described in recent reviews by Hsia (1967) and Menkes (1967). Figure 10 shows some of the relationships of the involved metabolites. The inability to convert phenylalanine to tyrosine results in an accumulation of phenylalanine, which is converted to phenylacetylglutamine. The presence of an excessive amount of phenylalanine inhibits the conversion of tryptophan to 5-hydroxytryptamine with a consequent reduction in the blood level of the last-named substance. Excessive phenylalanine also inhibits conversion of tyrosine to melanin, thus accounting for the reduced pigmentation of affected individuals.

An understanding of the metabolic lesion naturally suggests therapies. Since it is not yet possible to supply intracellular enzymes, the therapeutic aproach has been to reduce the dietary intake of phenylalanine. This was first done by Bickel et al. (1954), and a number of reports are now available on the effectiveness of the treatment. It seems quite apparent that a normalcy of the chemical milieu can be maintained by the dietary therapy. It is also generally agreed that there is an improvement in intellectual functioning, although disagreement persists as to its extent. One of the principal problems in assessing the extent of improvement is in the selection of a control group. Properly, such a control comparison group should be all of

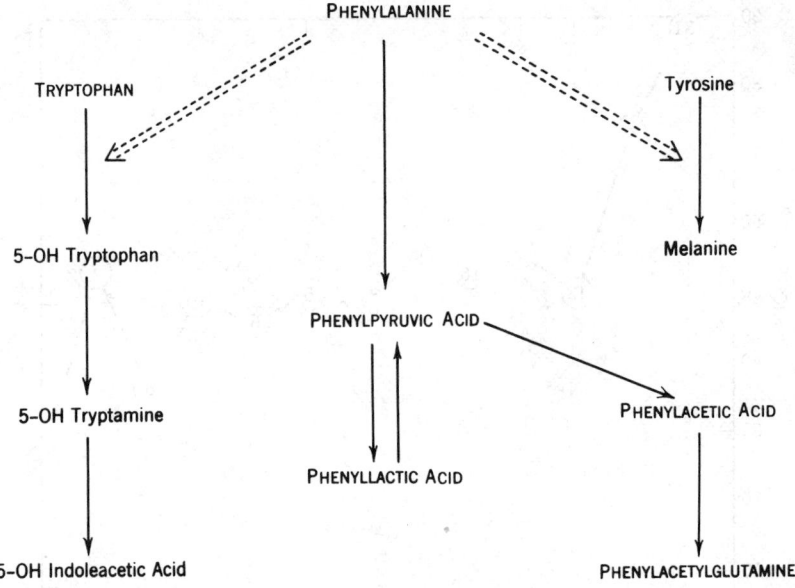

Fig. 10.   Metabolic pathways in phenylketonuria.

the untreated individuals with the biochemical lesion. A number of these individuals, however, are of normal intellectual competence, and are therefore not available in institutional settings. Hsia (1967) has summarized several studies, including his own, on the IQ level attained by patients who were given therapy beginning at different ages. There is a general decline in attained IQ level as the age of beginning of treatment increases. It is furthermore noteworthy that the highest IQ levels attained were around 100. Sutherland et al., (1967) has reported a somewhat more favorable outcome in a study of the intelligence of 7 patients for whom treatment was begun prior to 11 weeks of age. The mean IQ of these 7 was 110, as compared to an IQ of 106 for 10 of their unaffected siblings. However, 5 siblings who were affected and either untreated or treated beginning at a late age had a mean IQ of 68. The mean IQ of 5 treated patients, whose treatment began from 9 to 12 months of age, was 78. The necessity of early treatment is indicated by these data, and it is further emphasized by the results of Baumeister (1967), who studied the effects of dietary treatment in 162 phenylketonuric patients. The results are shown in Fig. 11.

Many states now require the testing of newborn children for phenylketonuria. The frequency of the condition appears to be about 1 in 10,000 live births.

For purposes of genetic counselling, as well as for research purposes, an ability to identify heterozygotes is important. Hsia et al. (1956) provided a method for detecting heterozygotes for phenylketonuria by means of a phenylalanine tolerance test. After a given dose of L-phenylalanine is administered orally, blood levels of phenylalanine are found to be higher in heterozygotes than in normal controls. This finding illustrates the fact that the mode of gene action is not always the same at all levels of analysis. At the level of mental defect, phenylketonuria appears to be a "good" recessive with no manifestation in the heterozygote. At the level of biochemical functioning, however, the heterozygotes are seen to be affected to some extent.

Numerous other conditions involving abnormal metabolism of an amino acid have been described; and, with the investigation of phenylketonuria serving as a model, research oriented toward detailed description of the metabolic consequences, and possible rational therapy, is proceeding rapidly. (See Nyhan, 1963, for a review of some of these conditions.)

Other types of metabolic disturbance have also been identified in genetically determined

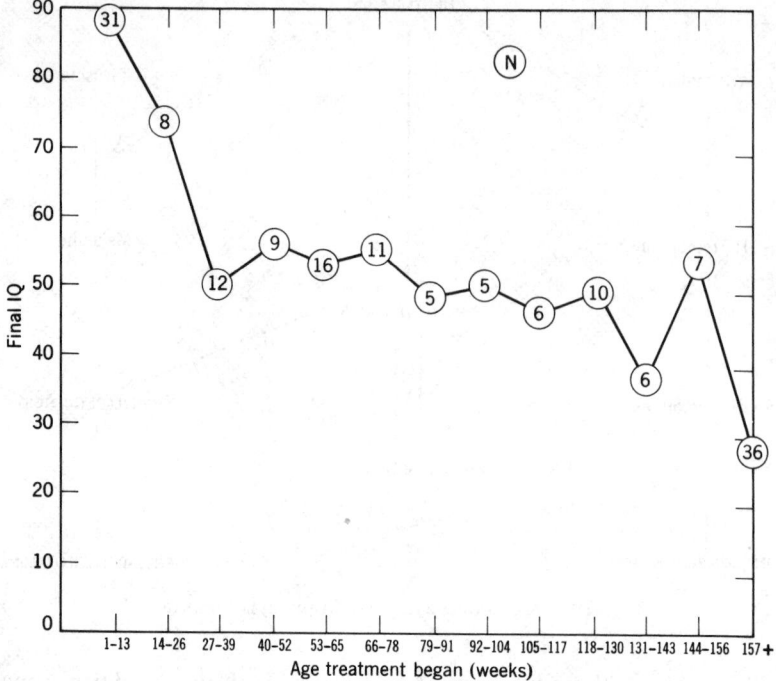

Fig. 11. Relationship between age at beginning of treatment and attained IQ in phenylketonuric patients. (Data from Blumeister, 1967.)

conditions involving mental retardation. Two types of amaurotic idiocy, for example, have been described which involve accumulation of abnormal quantities of lipoid substances in the nervous system. The first of these conditions, Tay-Sachs disease, or infantile amaurotic idiocy, involves mental deterioration which proceeds rapidly to complete idiocy. The onset of symptoms is typically at 5 or 6 months, and the average age of death of these patients is about 18 months. Juvenile amaurotic idiocy, which is also referred to as Spielemeyer-Vogt disease, has an onset at about 6 years of age with progressive degeneration extending over a period of 5 to 10 years, during which intelligence level falls from normal to profound idiocy. Both of these conditions are inherited in a recessive manner. The reader interested in discussions of these and other similar conditions is referred to Penrose (1963).

Although this chapter is particularly oriented toward evidence derived from studies on man, it is appropriate to mention briefly some of the studies with experimental animals that have identified anatomical, bio-

chemical, or physiological intermediates between genes and behavior.

A systematic attempt to describe relationships between learning ability, brain biochemistry, and brain morphology has been made by Rosenzweig and co-workers (1960). The starting point of their research was the exploration of differences in brain acetylcholinesterase between the S_1 and S_3 rat strains, which were descendants of Tryon's maze bright and maze dull strains, respectively. Selective breeding has also been employed to alter the enzyme activity with subsequent examination of behavioral differences. Thus four lines have been selectively bred for high and low brain acetylcholinesterase activity, and two lines have been selectively bred for high and low acetylcholine concentration in the brain. The conclusion of these studies has been that the critical factor is the ratio of the substrate acetylcholine to acetylcholinesterase.

Another example of research into mechanisms of gene action is the work of Ginsburg (1967). Ginsburg found audiogenic seizure susceptibility in mice was associated with the activity of the enzyme nucleotide triphosphatase in the grandular cell layer of the dentate fascia of the hippocampus. Other research on causal dynamics of audiogenic seizure susceptibility (Schlesinger et al., 1964) has shown that deficiency of serotonin and norepinephrine in the brain may be responsible for the differences in seizure susceptibility in different strains of mice.

DEVELOPMENTAL GENETICS

It is most important to appreciate that the influence of genes is not manifested only at conception or at birth or at any other single time in the individual's life history. Developmental processes are subject to continuing genetic influence, and different genes are effective at different times. Several examples of Mendelian inheritance in man may illustrate this point. The timing of gene action, for example, is shown by the late age of onset of Huntington's chorea, to which reference has already been made. The genes responsible for determining blood groups, on the other hand, appear to have their effect early in the development of the fetus, and the phenotype remains unaltered throughout life. Yet another characteristic, hemoglobin type, changes very dramatically early in life but remains stabilized thereafter. In a more complex case, presumably subject to the influence of a number of loci, Vandenberg and Falkner (1965) performed a twin study on human growth and found evidence for genetic control of growth rate and of deceleration of growth rate, but not for length at birth.

Other examples may be drawn from research with animals. Hrubant (1964) investigated the effects on longevity of different alleles at a single locus in the inbred mouse strain designated C57BL/6. This strain is usually homozygous for an allele (a) that renders the coat color nonagouti. By various mating procedures it is possible to substitute other alleles at this locus, and it was found that the substitution of either A or a^t resulted in a significant decrease in life span of animals.

The genetic control of a developmental anomaly in mice is illustrated by the condition known as Kreisler. Kreisler is inherited as a recessive, and the homozygous recessive animals at 10 to 14 days of age begin crawling in circles, become rigid when placed on the back, and are subject to head shaking and tossing and running in small circles. Some survive and reach sexual maturity. The affected individuals have one or two liquid-filled cysts under the pons which compress the adjacent brain structures. This results in a gross deformation of the telencephalon in general. The condition is identifiable in embryos at about 9 days of age, due to the fact that the otic pit is situated at some distance from the neural folds in the homozygous recessive animals. The embryological interactions in the development of Kreisler animals is described by Deol (1964).

A demonstration of presumably polygenic influence on developmental processes in rats is provided by Stone and Barker (1940), who selectively bred for early and late puberty. In the sixth generation the mean age of onset of puberty for the early and late strains, respectively, were, for males, 47.6 and 61.2 days and for females, 43.0 and 56.9 days.

Fraser and co-workers have demonstrated a genetic difference in susceptibility to the teratogenic effect of injected cortisone during embryological development. Fraser et al. (1954) showed that the administration of cortisone to pregnant A strain mice resulted in cleft palates in 100% of the offspring. Similar treatment to C57 mice resulted in the cleft palate abnormality only in 17% of the offspring. In later research they (Walker and Fraser, 1957) traced the embryology of the palate in the two strains under the experimental and control conditions. They concluded that the strain difference in susceptibility to the teratogenic action of cortisone is attributable, at least in part, to the normally earlier closing of the palate in the C57 embryos under control conditions.

Models of Control of Gene Action

The preceding examples, of only marginal behavioral interest, should serve to document the fact that genes exert influence over developmental processes. Important progress in understanding the means by which genes may be "turned on" or "turned off" has been made recently. The operon model of gene action (Jacob and Monod, 1961) has been particularly valuable. Although the basic data were obtained from research with microorganisms, it now seems a reasonable working hypothesis that similar mechanisms may occur in higher organisms (Ursprung, 1965).

The operon model postulates two different types of genes, regulator genes and structural genes. The discussion up until this time has been concerned with what under this model would be described as structural genes, whose function is to produce messenger RNA, which will in turn eventually result in enzyme formulation. A structural gene has an operator adjacent to it. The operator is a segment of DNA which is apparently the critical starting point for the molecular transcription of RNA and DNA. A regulator gene, which may or may not be physically adjacent to the operator or the structural gene, produces a repressor substance that attaches to the operator and thus inhibits transcription of RNA molecules from that particular structural gene.

These features of the model are represented in the top part of Fig. 12. An "inducer" may enter the system by, for example, diffusion from adjacent cells or from the external environment. This inducer combines with the repressor, and the compound is now unable to occupy the strategic site on the operator. RNA transcription and the consequent enzyme production can then proceed. The gene has been "turned on." This situation is represented in the bottom part of Fig. 12. If one

of the metabolic products that results from the reactions initiated by the enzyme is the inducer or a similar molecule, the effect is to keep the gene locked on. A similar mechanism can turn off or lock off a gene that is initially on. Although this mechanism has not been demonstrated in mammalian systems, it provides a useful conceptual framework for viewing processes of growth and differentiation. By this mechanism or similar mechanisms, genes may be turned on or off at different times and in different parts of the developing organism. That systematic, genetically controlled differences in enzyme activity over time and in different organ systems do occur in mammals is shown by the research of Paigen (1961). Animals of the C3H strain have much lower activity of the enzyme β-glucuronidase than animals of the DBA/2 strain. The relative specific activity of the various organs of the C3H animals as compared with DBA animals is shown as a function of age in Fig. 13. The differences of the age function for the different organs and the strain differences are obvious.

Chromosome Puffs

Another type of evidence that relates developmental processes to differential gene ac-

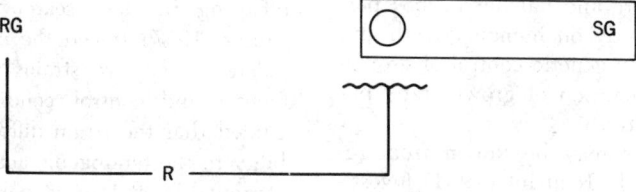

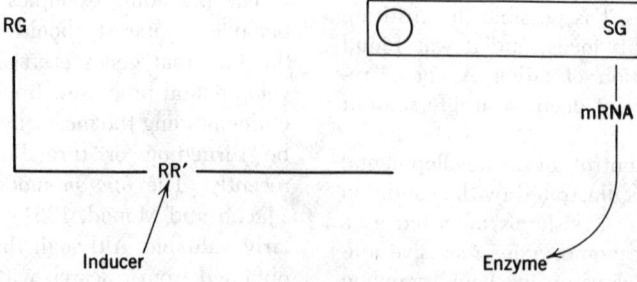

Fig. 12.   The operon model.

tivity is provided by research on chromosome puffing (Beerman, 1963). In some tissues of the larvae of certain insects, giant chromosomes exist which are visible under the ordinary light microscope. Because of their size these chromosomes have been intensively studied, and one phenomenon that has been described is the "puffing" of different regions of the chromosomes. Puffing is reversible; the puffs show signs of intensive RNA production; only a small percentage of the chromosomal loci puff in any given cell; and the pattern is different for different tissues and within any one tissue during different developmental phases. These features strongly suggest that the chromosome puff is a physical manifestation of the activity of one or a few gene loci. In *Chironomus*, further research has provided evidence that hormones may be effective in control of gene activity. The hormone ecdysone is normally found in the larvae during the molt. When ecdysone is administered to a larva not yet old enough for spontaneous molting, a series of events is initiated which is typical in the untreated animal at the normal molting time. Thirty minutes after the injection, a puff appears on one chromosome and this puff persists until the molt is complete. Thirty minutes after the first puff appears, there appears on a different chromosome another puff which lasts for two days and then recedes.

Quantitative Models

The operon model and the evidence of sequential gene action in chromosome puffs, derived from research on microorganisms and insects, are useful concepts for guiding theory and research in the genetics of mammalian development. Nevertheless, in complex systems involving many loci, theories that can account for developmental phenomena in terms of statistical descriptions of the aggregate actions of the separate loci and the complexities of interactions among the loci would be useful. Unfortunately, completely satisfactory theories of this type have not yet been developed. Waddington (1962) has pointed out the need for formulations that bridge the gap between the rapidly increasing knowledge of molecular genetics and the phenomena of metazoan embryology. It appears likely that this type of theory will be most pertinent to

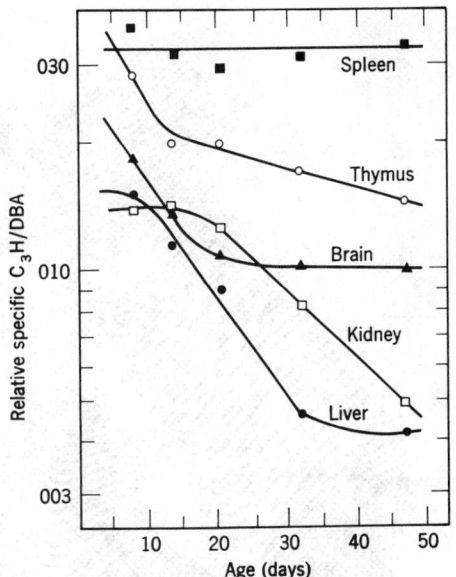

Fig. 13. Relative specific enzyme activities in various organs of mice as a function of age.

many of the problems of developmental psychology.

Waddington (1962) has provided valuable contributions to this theoretical development. The basic elements of developmental theory, he maintains, are stabilized or buffered pathways of change, which he terms "creodes," from Greek roots meaning, essentially, necessary path. A system with a multiplicity of genetic determinants can be described as a point in n-dimensional space, and, geometrically, the creode may be envisioned as a trajectory of this point through the n-space, toward some specified endpoint. The buffering characteristics of a creode are such that, when deviations from the trajectory occur as the result of some disturbance, there is a tendency for the system not simply to adopt a new path to the old endpoint, but to return to the original pathway leading toward the endpoint (Waddington, 1957). Tanner (1963) has provided empirical data on this "catch-up" process in the growth curves of children whose growth is disturbed by illness.

Such a system must obviously involve feedback loops, probably of great variety and complexity. Waddington (1962) describes various contributions toward the development of mathematical formulations of control systems in developmental genetics, the details

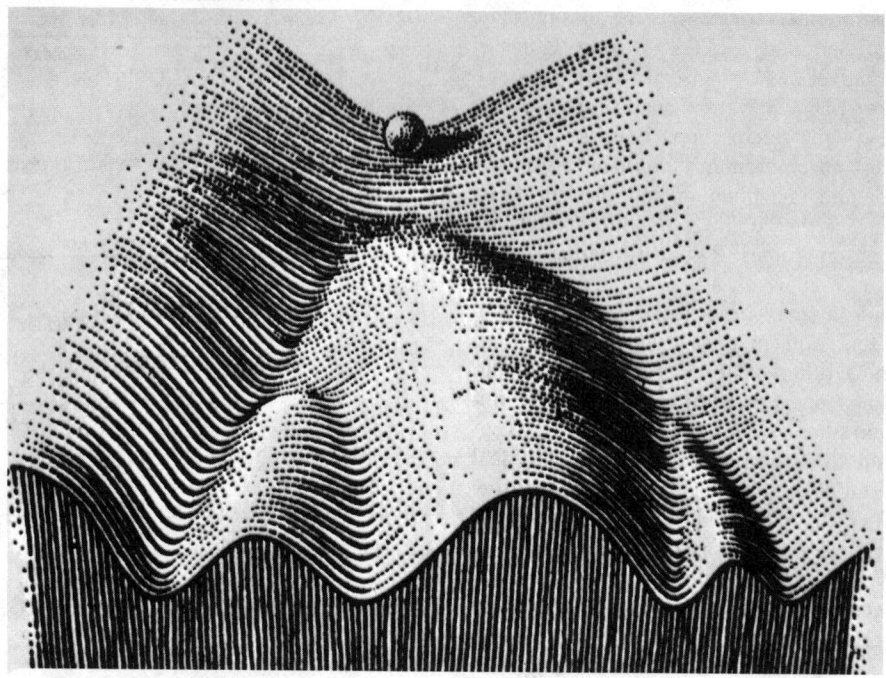

Fig. 14. Waddington's "epigenetic landscape."

of which cannot be reviewed here. A three-dimensional physical analogy serves to convey some of the essential points of creodic functioning, however. Figure 14 shows Waddington's "epigenetic landscape," which he warns is only suggestive and not to be interpreted in any literal sense. Briefly, the contour of the landscape is determined by genotype, and the position of the ball represents the value of the developing phenotype. In the developmental process, represented by the ball rolling forward, environmental forces may act laterally upon the ball and displace it from its path. At crucial moments such a displacement can shift the system into a new channel of development. An important property of creodes is represented in this schema by the cross section of a valley in the epigenetic landscape. A wide valley floor with gradually sloping sides represents a developmental pathway that is not well buffered, and permits environmental forces to displace the phenotype considerably. A narrow floor with steep walls, on the other hand, represents a highly buffered or canalized pathway.

Both the genetic control of growth trajectories and the relative degree of canaliza-

tion of these trajectories are shown in research on mice by Roberts (1961). Animals of six different genetic groups were weighed at regular intervals through their entire life span. The RCL and NF stocks had been selectively bred for high six-week weight; the MS and NS were selected for low six-week weight; the M × R was the F_1 generation of a cross between MS and RCL, and the NC was an unselected control stock. The mean growth curves of the males of the different stocks are shown in Fig. 15. Not only are there clear differences in highest body weight attained but, in the large strains, there are obvious declines which occur at different ages. Clear strain differences are apparent also in longevity, indicated in the figure by the point of termination of the lines. In Fig. 16 the growth curves of individual animals are shown. These results show differences in canalization of the growth process in the various strains.

Again, it should be emphasized that the epigenetic landscape is offered as a simplified model only; it may serve, however, to indicate the sort of theoretical formulation that may be required to account for the inter-

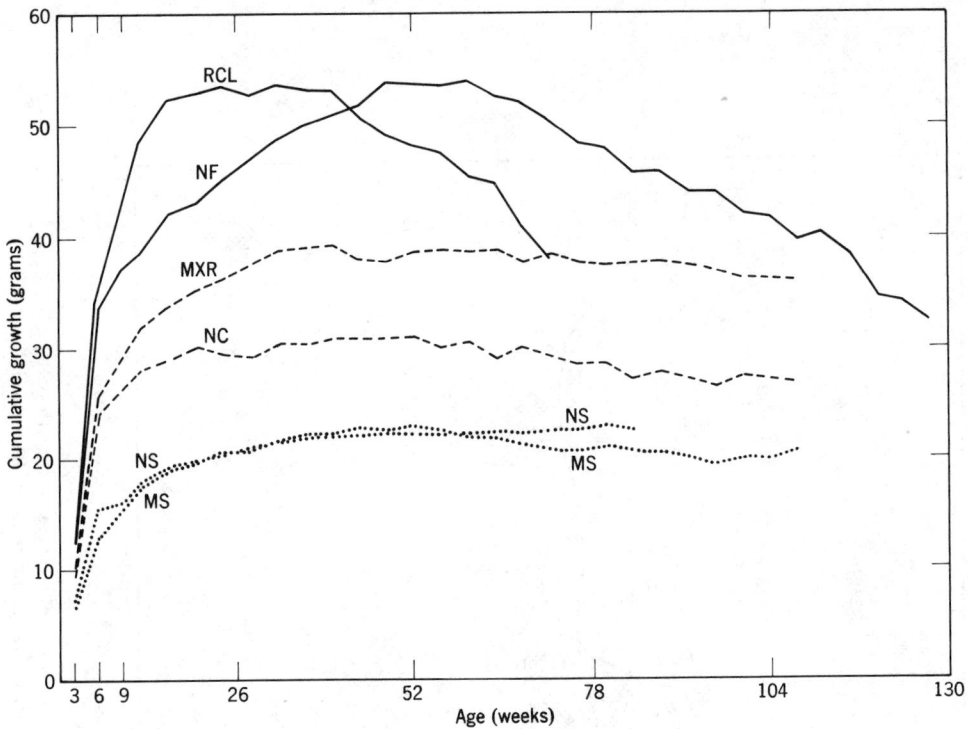

Fig. 15. Cumulative growth curves of male mice for each stock.

actions of genotype and environment in behavioral development.

Undoubtedly, as research progresses, translations may be made from one theoretical level to another. Tanner (1963), for example, in discussing the cases of "catch-up" growth in children, proceeds from control system notions to molecular speculations. The key elements necessary in an automatic closed-loop control system are an output signal, a command signal, and the error signal that results from a discrepancy between these two (Wilkins, 1966). The command signal in this case is the size the organism "ought" to be if the developmental trajectory had not been disturbed. The output signal is the size actually attained. Tanner proposes that the output signal is the concentration of some substance that is an inevitable consequence of protein synthesis. Thus the mass of the body would be directly proportional to the concentration of this substance, which he calls "inhibitor." The command signal may be the number of molecules of some other substance that has a receptive site for "in-

hibitor" and which increases directly with elapsed time. The error signal would be the number of unoccupied sites, and would result in the release of a growth-promoting substance. When, as a consequence of accelerated growth, the number of inhibitor molecules equals the number of receptive sites, no more growth-promoting substance would be released until the passage of time provided yet more receptive sites. Tanner speculates further that the rate of accumulation of receptive sites, and the rate of change of that rate, may be an inherited characteristic.

Developmental Genetics and Behavior

In a very real sense it is the case that any demonstrated genetic control over an adult characteristic is, at the same time, an implication of genetic control over the developmental processes that culminate in that characteristic. Research aimed explicitly at studying the genetic control of behavioral development unfortunately has been rare, particularly with respect to man. The re-

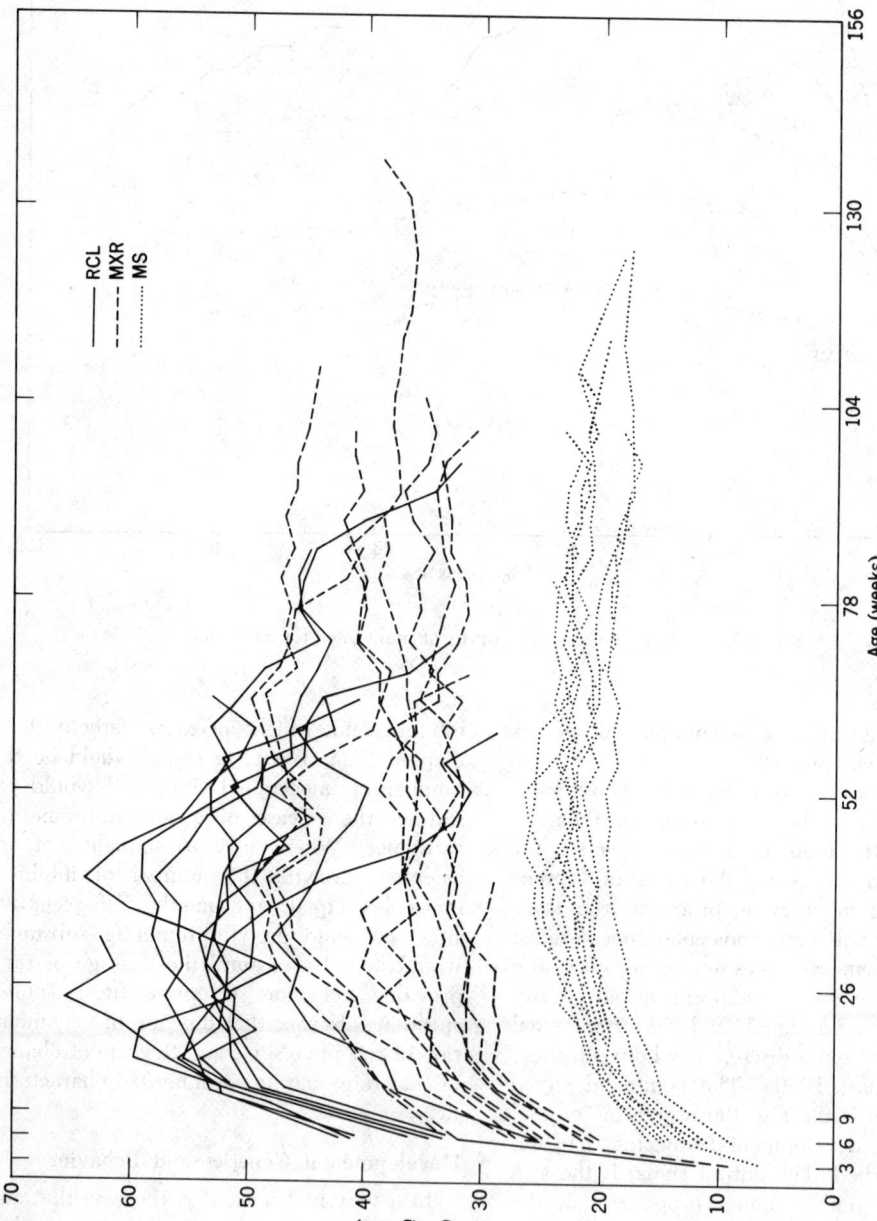

Fig. 16. Individual growth curves of male mice, showing differences in growth pattern between stocks. (Five NS males lived longer than shown, but some of their weights inadvertently were not recorded.)

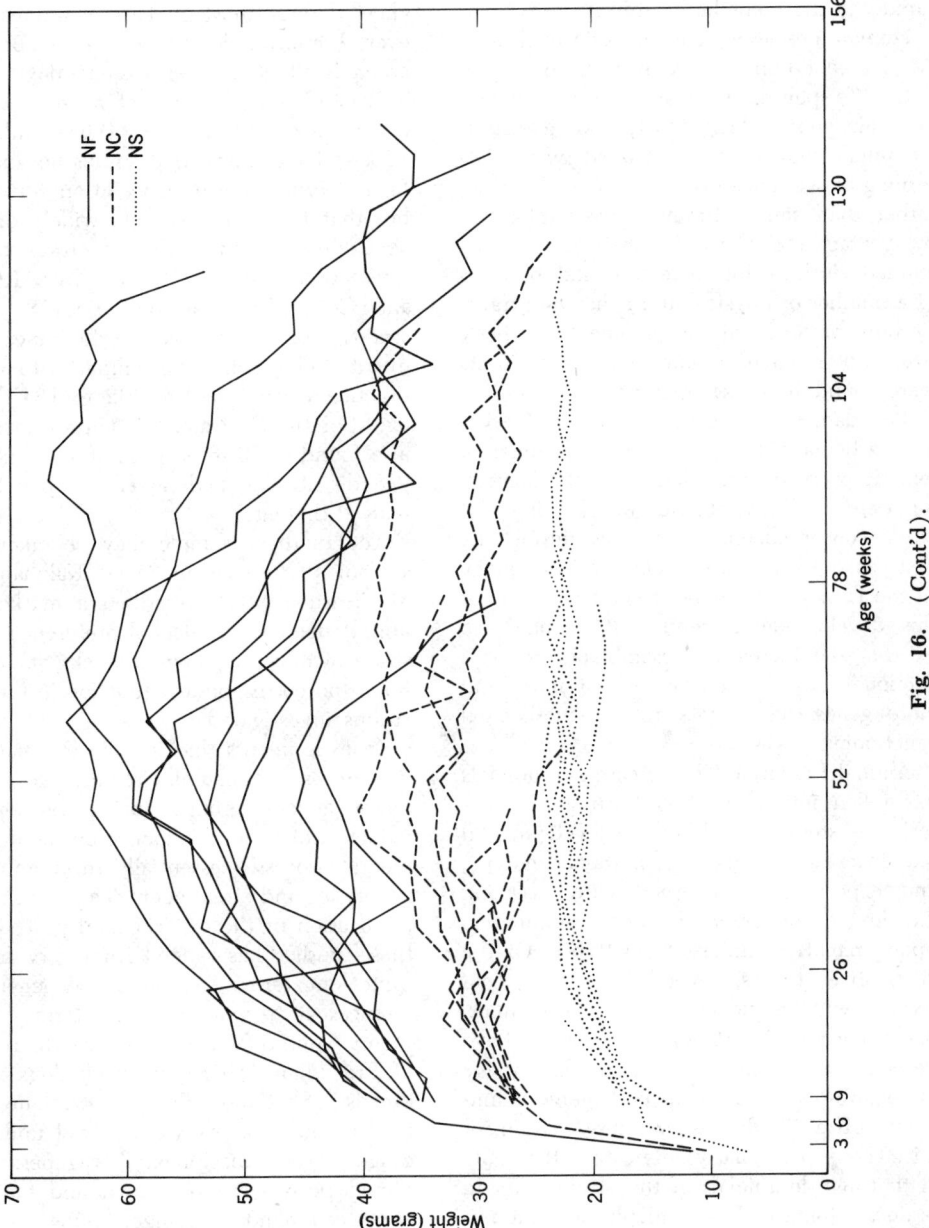

Fig. 16. (Cont'd).

67

search that has been conducted, however, has demonstrated well the advantages of the developmental genetic approach to behavioral processes, and it appears to be a safe prediction that work in this area will increase rapidly in the immediate future.

Human Research. That genetic control of developmental processes persists over the entire life span has been shown by Jarvik and her colleagues (1957, 1962), who have studied intellectual functions in aged twins. Patterning or sequence of developmental events, rather than simple timing, was emphasized by Sontag and Garn (1956/57), who examined sibships for developmental patterns of a number of physical and behavioral traits. Certain patterns of development of body size, motor coordination, and other traits were found to be characteristic of families.

The data summarized by Honzik (1957) are particularly suggestive of developmental genetic processes that determine the increasing degree of resemblance of offspring and parent on intellectual measures during the first years of life. Problems of test inadequacy in the earlier years may account for some of this developmental trend, but it may also be that the increasing resemblance is a reflection of the "switching on" of more and more genes that play a role in intellectual functioning.

Animal Research. The research on animals has fallen into two general categories: descriptive studies of different developmental sequences in groups of different genotype, and experiments concerned with assessing the impact of environmental manipulation upon animals of different genotypes. Of the descriptive studies, several have been concerned with audiogenic seizures in mice. Schlesinger et al. (1964), for example, have described a very sharp peak at 21 days of age in seizure-susceptibility to audiogenic stimulation of a "high susceptibility" strain of mice. It is particularly interesting that only at that age do animals of this strain differ in brain serotonin and norepinephrine from animals of the "low susceptibility" strains. Fuller and Sjursen (1967) have reported many different patterns of convulsive risk and of death risk in 11 different inbred strains exposed to audiogenic stimulation.

Thiessen (1965) investigated behavioral aspects of the "wabbler" lethal condition in mice. Homozygous recessive animals display hind limb incoordination and paralysis, with accompanying myelin degeneration, beginning at about 14 days of age. Developmental changes are under way prior to the appearance of these most obvious symptoms, however. For example, activity in an open field arena is affected as early as 10 days of age.

In studies of learning of mice in a water maze, Meier and Foshee (1963) and Meier (1964) have shown that strains not only differ in learning performance at any given age, but that there are, as well, widely different developmental functions. A strain by age interaction was also shown by McGaugh and Cole (1965) in rats. Both S_1 and S_3 strains showed improved performance under distributed practice as compared to massed practice when tested at 142 to 164 days of age. For the S_1 strain, this improvement was also found at 29 to 33 days of age, but practice distribution had no effect upon S_3 animals at that age.

Yet another example may be taken from alcohol preference in mice. Kakihana and McClearn (1963) described a marked and abrupt decrease in alcohol preference of one strain of mice, at about 9 weeks of age, but found no corresponding function in the other strains investigated.

In experiments that involve the manipulation of environmental circumstances of different genetic groups during development, evidence of genetic influence on the developmental process is essentially an interaction of genotype and treatment. The duration of application of the experimental procedure in these studies has ranged from very brief to quite long term. An example of genetic differences in response to long-term environmental conditions is provided by the research of Freedman (1958) in which dogs of four breeds (Shetland, Basenji, wirehaired fox terrier, and beagle) were reared under "indulgent" or "disciplinary" regimes. Disciplined pups were restrained and taught to obey commands. Indulged pups were encouraged to undertake all manner of activity and were never punished. These conditions persisted from the third to the seventh week of life, at which time each dog was tested in the following manner. When the dog ate from a food bowl in the center of the room, he was punished by a swat and shout from the experimenter. After three minutes the experimenter left the room and the time until the animal returned to eating was recorded. Mode of rearing was found to have a large effect on beagles and terriers, with disciplined animals returning to eat much sooner than the indulged animals. For the other breeds, mode of rearing had no effect. The Basenjis of both groups ate quickly, suggesting that they were relatively unaffected by the treatment. The Shetlands of both groups, on the other hand, were so affected by the punishment in the test situation that they avoided the food entirely.

Another experiment on the effects of long-term rearing conditions is that of Dixon and DeFries (in press). Mice of two inbred strains (BALB/c and C57BL/6) were reared under high illumination or low illumination conditions from birth until 40 days of age, at which time they were tested for activity in an open field apparatus. BALB/c mice reared under high illumination had higher activity and lower defecation scores than those reared under low illumination, whereas C57BL/6 mice were not affected by rearing illumination.

Different sublines of these strains were studied by Ressler (1963) in an experiment on the effects of foster rearing on panel press manipulation, and panel press for illumination. BALB/c mice were more manipulatory than C57BL/10 mice whether they were reared by BALB/c parents or by C57BL/10 parents. These results indicate that the developmental processes that lead to greater manipulatory behavior by adult BALB/c mice were not subject to influence by parents during the period from birth until weaning at 23 days of age. That parental influence during this period can be important is demonstrated by the results on visual exploration. There was no significant difference between the strains, but animals of both strains engaged in more visual exploration if reared by BALB/c than by C57BL/10 parents.

Much shorter experimental intervention was employed by Lindzey and co-workers (1960, 1963), who subjected mice of four inbred strains to the trauma of a loud, high-frequency auditory stimulus from the fourth through the seventh day of life. Animals were later tested in situations designed to assess emotionality, activity, and timidity. Their conclusion (1963) was that animals of

the C57BL strain have a very high sensitivity to noxious infantile stimulation, relative to the other strains investigated.

Levine and Wetzel (1963) studied the effects of manipulation during infancy on adult avoidance-learning performance in rats. The manipulation involved removal from the nest, three-minute detention in a compartment, and return to the nest. This treatment was administered once daily from birth through 21 days of age. Two different substrains of Long Evans rats showed an effect of treatment, with the manipulated animals making higher avoidance scores during the learning test. Another strain, Sprague-Dawley, showed no similar effect.

Application of the experimental condition was moved forward into the prenatal period by Thompson and Olian (1961). They studied the effects of injections of adrenalin to pregnant mice during the second or third trimester upon the adult activity of the offspring. The activity test was performed under normal conditions, and also under the stress of electrical foot-shock. In the A strain, offspring of injected mothers were more active under both normal and stress conditions of testing. BALB/c animals were unaffected by the treatment, and C57BL/6 mice showed only marginal effects when tested under the stress condition.

DeFries and his colleagues have explored further the role of prenatal stress in influencing adult behavior. The prenatal stress administered to the mothers consisted of daily exposure for three minutes to each of three stress conditions, beginning with the tenth postmating day and continuing throughout pregnancy. The stress conditions were forced swimming, exposure to intense white noise, and placement of the cage on a reciprocating shaker. In two reports (Weir and DeFries, 1964; DeFries, 1964) the effects of this treatment upon the adult open-field activity and emotional defecation of the fetuses were assessed. BALB/c and C57BL/6 mice were employed, and highly significant strain by treatment interaction was demonstrated. Subsequently, DeFries et al. (1967) have shown that the differential effects of the stress treatment are a function of both the maternal genotype and the fetal genotype. It was further demonstrated that injections of adrenalin did not have the same effect as did the administration of the physical stress.

One means of assessing the importance of maternal environment on development is to compare reciprocal F_1 hybrids between two strains of mice. Thus hybrids between the strains C57BL/6 and BALB/c have the same autosomal genotype regardless of whether their mother was a BALB/c and the father a C57BL/6 or the converse. In the one case, however, the fetuses will have developed in a BALB/c uterine environment, and in the other case in a C57BL/6 environment. DeFries (1964) studied reciprocal F_1s of this kind, and the results illustrate the complexity of interactions that may occur. The prenatal maternal stress was found to result in a decrease in activity of F_1 hybrid offspring carried by C57BL mothers, which is an effect similar to that on inbred BALB/c offspring. On the other hand, the effect on F_1 hybrids carried by BALB/c females was similar to that on the C57BL strain.

The comparison of reciprocal F_1 hybrid litters is by definition constrained to hybrid groups. An assessment of maternal uterine environment effects on inbred strains may also be accomplished by the use of ovary transplant techniques. DeFries et al. (1967) transplanted ovaries from donors of the inbred strains BALB/c and C57BL/6 into F_1 hybrid recipients. Appropriate matings provided inbred offspring carried by either hybrid or inbred mothers. The very large differences in the adult activity levels of the BALB/c and C57BL animals were found, regardless of whether the animals had developed in the uterine environment of a mother of identical genotype or in a hybrid.

SUMMARY AND CONCLUSIONS

The intent of this chapter has been to provide an introduction to the empirical data and theoretical perspectives of the field of genetics, and to provide, where possible, examples that demonstrate the effect of genetic variables on behavior. Behavioral phenotypes appear to be in no qualitative way distinct from the anatomical or physiological traits that constitute the bulk of the empirical data upon which the science of genetics is based. Examples of single locus influence have been shown; the methods of quantitative genetics have been examined and their application to continuously distributed behavioral traits has been reviewed; examples have been provided of the physiological and biochemical route through which the genes are expressed; and the role of genes in determining developmental sequence has been discussed.

Developmental behavioral genetics is of very recent origin, and there is yet to emerge a coherent body of knowledge. The work that has been done by the pioneering workers in this area, however, has demonstrated beyond question the importance of heredity in processes of behavioral development. It is extremely important that the future progress in this specialty be communicated to the general field of developmental psychology, and become an integral part of the empirical knowledge and theoretical framework of that field.

References

Bastock, M. A gene mutation which changes a behavior pattern. *Evolution*, 1956, **10**, 421–439.

Baumeister, A. A. The effects of dietary control on intelligence in phenylketonuria. *Am. J. ment. Defic.*, 1967, **71**, 840–847.

Beerman, W. Cytological aspects of information transfer in cellular differentiation. *Amer. Zool.*, 1963, **3**, 23–32.

Bickel, H., Garrard, J., and Hickmans, E. M. The influence of phenylalanine intake on the chemistry and behavior of a phenylketonuric child. *Acta paediat. Upps.*, 1954, **43**, 64–77.

Bignami, G. Selection for fast and slow avoidance conditioning in the rat. *Bull. Br. psychol. Soc.*, 1964, **17**, 5A (Abstract).

Blewett, D. B. An experimental study of the inheritance of intelligence. *J. ment. Sci.*, 1954, **100**, 922–933.

Broadhurst, P. L. Studies in psychogenetics: the quantitative inheritance of behaviour in rats investigated by selective and cross-breeding. *Bull. Br. psychol. Soc.*, 1958, **34**, 2A (Abstract).

Bruell, J. H. Dominance and segregation in the inheritance of quantitative behavior in mice. In E. L. Bliss (Ed.), *Roots of behavior*. New York: Harper, 1962, Pp. 48–67.

Burt, C. The genetic determination of differences in intelligence: a study of monozygotic twins reared together and apart. *Br. J. Psychol.*, 1966, **57**, 137–153.

Carr, D. H. Chromosome anomalies as a cause of spontaneous abortion. *Am. J. Obstet. Gynec.*, 1967, **97**, 283–293.

Carran, A. B., Yeudall, L. T., and Royce, J. R. Voltage level and skin resistance in avoidance conditioning of inbred strains of mice. *J. comp. physiol. Psychol.*, 1964, **58**, 427–430.

Cattell, R. B. Research designs in psychological genetics with special reference to the multiple variance method. *Am. J. hum. Genet.*, 1953, **5**, 76–93.

Cattell, R. B. Statistical methods and logical considerations in investigating inheritance. *Proc. Int. Congr. Hum. Genet.*, 1963, **3**, 1712–1717.

Clarke, C., Ford, C. E., Edwards, J. H., and Smallpiece, V. 21-Trisomy-normal mosaicism in an intelligent child with some mongoloid characters. *Lancet*, 1963, **2**, 1229.

Collman, R. D., and Stroller, A. A survey of mongoloid births in Victoria, Australia, 1942–1957. *Am. J. publ. Hlth.*, 1960, **52**, 813–829.

Day, R. W., Larson, W., and Wright, S. A. Clinical and cytogenetic studies on a group of females with XXX sex chromosome complements. *J. Pediat.*, 1964, **64**, 24–33.

DeFries, J. C. Prenatal maternal stress in mice: differential effects on behavior. *J. Hered.*, 1964, **55**, 289–295.

DeFries, J. C., and Hegmann, J. P. Genetic analysis of open-field behavior. In G. Lindzey and D. D. Thiessen (Eds.), *Contributions to behavior-genetic analysis: the mouse as a prototype*. In press.

DeFries, J. C., Hegmann, J. P., and Weir, M. W. Open-field behavior in mice: evidence for a major gene effect mediated by the visual system. *Science*, 1966, **154**, 1577–1579.

DeFries, J. C., Thomas, E. A., Hegmann, J. P., and Weir, M. W. Open-field behavior in mice: analysis of maternal effects by means of ovarian transplantation. *Psychon. Sci.*, 1967, **8**, 207–208.

DeFries, J. C., Weir, M. W., and Hegmann, J. P. Differential effects of prenatal maternal stress on offspring behavior in mice as a function of genotype and stress *J. comp. physiol. Psychol.*, 1967, **63**, 332–334.

Deol, M. S. The abnormalities of the inner ear in *kreisler* mice. *J. Embryol. exp. Morph.*, 1964, **12**, 475–490.

Dixon, L. K., and DeFries, J. C. Effects of illumination on open-field behavior in mice. *J. comp. physiol. Psychol.*, in press.

Erlenmeyer-Kimling, L., Hirsch, J., and Weiss, J. M. Studies in experimental behavior genetics: III. Selection and hybridization analyses of individual differences in the sign of geotaxis. *J. comp. physiol. Psychol.*, 1962, **55**, 722–731.

Erlenmeyer-Kimling, L., and Jarvik, L. F. Genetics and intelligence: a review. *Science*, 1963, **142**, 1477–1479.

Falconer, D. S. *Introduction to quantitative genetics*. Edinburgh: Oliver and Boyd, 1960.

Fölling, A. Über Ausscheidung von Phenylbrenztraubensäure in den Harn als Stoffweekselanomalie in Verbindung mit Imbezillitat. *Z. physiol. Chem.*, 1934, **227**, 169–176.

Forssman, H. Epilepsy in an XYY man. *Lancet*, 1967, **1**, 1389.

Fraser, F. C., Kalter, H., Walker, B. E., and Fainstat, T. D. The experimental production of cleft palate with cortisone and other hormones. *J. cell. comp. Physiol.*, 1954, **43**, 237–259.

Freedman, D. G. Constitutional and environmental interactions in rearing of four breeds of dogs. *Science*, 1958, **127**, 585–586.

Frings, H., and Frings, M. The production of stocks of albino mice with predictable susceptibilities to audiogenic seizures. *Behaviour*, 1953, **5**, 305–319.

Fuller, J. L. Measurement of alcohol preference in genetic experiments. *J. comp. physiol. Psychol.*, 1964, **57**, 85–88.

Fuller, J. L., and Sjursen, F. H., Jr. Audiogenic seizures in eleven mouse strains. *J. Hered.*, 1967, **58**, 135–140.

Fuller, J. L., and Thompson, W. R. *Behavior genetics*. New York: Wiley, 1960.

Ginsburg, B. E. Genetic parameters in behavioral research. In J. Hirsch (Ed.), *Behavior-genetic analysis*. New York: McGraw-Hill, 1967. Pp. 135–153.

Ginsburg, B. E., and Allee, W. C. Some effects of conditioning on social dominance and subordination in inbred strains of mice. *Physiol. Zool.*, 1942, **15**, 485–506.

Gottesman, I. I. Heritability of personality: a demonstration. *Psychol. Monogr.*, 1963, **77(9)**, No. 572.

Gottesman, I. I. Personality and natural selection. In S. G. Vandenberg (Ed.), *Methods and goals in human behavior genetics*. New York: Academic Press, 1965. Pp. 63–80.

Gottesman, I. I., and Shields, J. Schizophrenia in twins: 16 years' consecutive admissions to a psychiatric clinic. *Dis. nerv. Syst.*, 1966, **27**, 11–19.

Grüneberg, H. *The genetics of the mouse*. The Hague: Martinus Nijhoff, 1952.

Guhl, A. M., Craig, J. V., and Mueller, C. D. Selective breeding for aggressiveness in chickens. *Poultry Sci.*, 1960, **39**, 970–980.

Hall, C. S. The inheritance of emotionality. *Sigma Xi Q.*, 1938, **26**, 17–27.

Hauschka, R. S., Hasson, J. E., Goldstein, M. N., Koepf, G. F., and Sandberg, A. A. An XYY man with progeny indicating familial tendency to nondisjunction. *Am. J. hum. Genet.* 1962, **14**, 22–30

Heinrichs, E. H., Allen, S. W., Jr., and Nelson, P. S. Simultaneous 18-trisomy and 21-trisomy cluster. *Lancet*, 1963, **2**, 468.

Heron, W. T. The inheritance of brightness and dullness in maze learning ability in the rat. *J. genet. Psychol.*, 1941, **59**, 41–49.

Herring, R. M., Phillips, J., Goodman, H. O., and King, J. S., Jr. Enzymes in Down's syndrome. *Lancet*, 1967, **1**, 1157.

Hirsch, Jr., and Boudreau, J. C. Studies in experimental behavior genetics: I. The heritability of phototaxis in a population of *Drosophila melanogaster*. *J. comp. physiol. Psychol.*, 1958, **51**, 647–651.

Honzik, M. P. Developmental studies of parent-child resemblance in intelligence. *Child Dev.*, 1957, **28**, 215–228.

Hrubant, H. E. Specific genetic control of life span. *J. Geront.*, 1964, **19**, 451–452.

Hsia, D. Y. The hereditary metabolic diseases. In J. Hirsch (Ed.), *Behavior-genetic analysis*. New York: McGraw-Hill, 1967. Pp. 176–193.

Hsia, D. Y., Driscoll, K. W., Troll, W., and Knox, W. E. Detection by phenylalanine tolerance tests of heterozygous carriers of phenylketonuria. *Nature*, 1956, **178**, 1239–1240.

Itoh, Y., and Gotoh, H. Cat cry syndrome. *Tohoku J. exp. Med.*, 1967, **91**, 349–354.

Jacob, F., and Monod, J. On the regulation of gene activity. *Cold Spring Harb. Symp. quant. Biol.*, 1961, **26**, 193–209.

Jacobs, P. A., Baikie, A. G., Court Brown, W. M., and Strong, J. A. The somatic chromosomes in mongolism. *Lancet*, 1959, **1**, 710.

Jacobs, P. A., Brunton, M., and Melville, M. M. Aggressive behaviour, mental subnormality and the XYY male. *Nature*, 1965, **208**, 1351–1352.

Jarvik, L. F., Kallmann, F. J., and Falek, A. Intellectual changes in aged twins. *J. Geront.*, 1962, **17**, 289–294.

Jarvik, L. F., Kallmann, F. J., Falek, A., and Klaber, M. M. Changing intellectual functions in senescent twins. *Acta Genetica et Statistica Medica*, 1957, Separatum Vol. 7, No. 2, 421–430.

Jervis, G. A. Introductory study of fifty cases of mental deficiency associated with excretion of phenylpyruvic acid. *Archs. Neurol. Psychiat.*, 1937, **38**, 944–963.

Jervis, G. A. Phenylpyruvic oligophrenia (phenylketonuria). *Proc. Ass. Res. nerv. ment. Dis.*, 1954, **33**, 259–282.

Kakihana, R., and McClearn, G. E. Development of alcohol preference in BALB/c mice. *Nature*, 1963, **199**, 511–512.

Kallmann, F. J. *Heredity in health and mental disorder.* New York: Norton, 1953.

Krechevsky, I. Hereditary nature of "hypotheses." *J. comp. Psychol.*, 1933, **16**, 99–116.

Lagarspetz, K. Genetics and social causes of aggressive behavior in mice. *Scand. J. Psychol.*, 1961, **2**, 167–173.

Lejeune, J. The 21-trisomy—current stage of chromosomal research. In A. G. Steinberg and A. G. Bearn (Eds.), *Progress in medical genetics.* New York: Grune and Stratton, 1964. Pp. 144–177.

Lejeune, J., Gautier, M., and Turpin, R. Etude des chromosomes somatiques de neuf enfants mongoliens. *C. r. Acad. Sci.*, Paris, 1959, **248**, 1721–1722.

Lejeune, J., LaFourcade, J., Berger, R., Vialatte, J., Boeswillwald, M., Seringe, P., and Turpin, R. Trois cas de deletion partielle du bras court d'un chromosome 5. *C. r. Acad. Sci.*, Paris, 1963, **257**, 3098–3102.

Levine, S., and Wetzel, A. Infantile experiences, strain differences, and avoidance learning. *J. comp. physiol. Psychol.*, 1963, **56**, 879–881.

Li, C. C. *Population genetics.* Chicago, Ill.: University of Chicago Press, 1955.

Lindzey, G., Lykken, D. T., and Winston, H. D. Infantile trauma, genetic factors, and adult temperament. *J. abnorm. soc. Psychol.*, 1960, **61**, 7–14.

Lindzey, G., and Winston, H. Maze learning and effect of pretraining in inbred strains of mice. *J. comp. physiol. Psychol.*, 1962, **55**, 748–752.

Lindzey, G., Winston, H., and Manosevitz, M. Social dominance in inbred mouse strains. *Nature*, 1961, **191**, 474–476.

Lindzey, G., Winston, H. E., and Manosevitz, M. Early experience, genotype, and temperament in *mus musculus. J. comp. physiol. Psychol.*, 1963, **56**, 622–629.

Lush, J. L. Intra-sire correlations or regressions of offspring on dam as a method of estimating heritability of characteristics. *Thirty-third Ann. Proc. Amer. Soc. Anim. Prod.*, 1940, 293–301.

McClearn, G. E. The genetics of mouse behavior in novel situations. *J. comp. physiol. Psychol.*, 1959, **52**, 62–67.

McClearn, G. E. Genotype and mouse activity. *J. comp. physiol. Psychol.*, 1961, **54**, 674–676.

McClearn, G. E. The inheritance of behavior. In L. Postman (Ed.), *Psychology in the making.* New York: Knopf, 1962. Pp. 144–252.

McClearn, G. E. Genes, generality, and behavioral research. In J. Hirsch (Ed.), *Behavior-genetic analysis.* New York: McGraw-Hill, 1967. Pp. 307–321.

McClearn, G. E., and Rodgers, D. A. Differences in alcohol preference among inbred strains of mice. *Q. J. Stud. Alcohol*, 1959, **20**, 691–695.

McGaugh, J. L., and Cole, J. M. Age and strain differences in the effect of distribution of practice on maze learning. *Psychon. Sci.*, 1965, **2**, 253–254.

McGaugh, J. L., Jennings, R. D., and Thomson, C. W. Effect of distribution of practice on the maze learning of descendants of the Tryon maze bright and maze dull strains. *Psychol. Rep.*, 1962, **10**, 147–150.

McGill, T. E. Sexual behavior in three inbred strains of mice. *Behavior*, 1962, **19**, 341–350.

Macintyre, M. N., Staples, W. I., LaPolla, J. J., and Hempel, J. M. The "cat cry" syndrome. *Am. J. Dis. Child.*, 1964, **108**, 538–542.

Manning, A. The effects of artificial selection for mating speed in *Drosophila melanogaster. Anim. Behav.*, 1961, **9**, 82–92.

Manosevitz, M., and Lindzey, G. Genetics of hoarding: a biometrical analysis. *J. comp. physiol. Psychol.*, 1967, **63**, 142–144.

Meier, G. W. Differences in maze performances as a function of age and strain of housemice. *J. comp. physiol. Psychol.*, 1964, **58**, 418–422.

Meier, G. W., and Foshee, D. P. Genetics, age, and the variability of learning performances. *J. genet. Psychol.*, 1963, **102**, 267–275.

Menkes, J. H. The pathogenesis of mental retardation in phenylketonuria and other inborn errors of amino acid metabolism. *Pediatrics*, 1967, **39**, 297–308.

Mitoma, C., Auld, R. M., and Udenfriend, S. On the nature of enzymatic defect in phenylpyruvic oligophrenia. *Proc. Soc. exp. Biol. Med.*, 1957, **94**, 634–635.

Money, J. Cytogenetic and psychosexual incongruities with a note on space-form blindness. *Am. J. Psychiat.*, 1963, **119**, 820–827.

Money, J. Cognitive defects in Turner's syndrome. *Second invitational conference on human behavior genetics*. Louisville, 1966.

Newman, H. H., Freeman, F. N., and Holzinger, K. J. *Twins: a study of heredity and environment*. Chicago: University of Chicago Press, 1937.

Nichols, W. W., Levan, A., Hall, B., and Östergren, G. Measles-associated chromosome breakage: preliminary communication. *Hereditas*, 1962, **48**, 367–370.

Nyhan, W. L. Genetic defects of amino acid metabolism. *Pediat. Clins. N. Am.*, 1963, **10**, 339–368.

Paigen, K. The genetic control of enzyme activity during differentiation. *Proc. Nat. Acad. Sci.*, 1961, **47**, 1641–1649.

Penrose, L. S. *The biology of mental defect.* (Rev. Ed.) New York: Grune and Stratton, 1963.

Polani, P. E. Cytogenetics of Down's syndrome. *Pediat. Clins. N. Am.*, 1963, **10**, 443–448.

Polani, P. E., Briggs, J. H., Ford, C. E., Clarke, C. M., and Berg, J. M. A mongoloid girl with 46 chromosomes. *Lancet*, 1960, **1**, 721–724.

Price, W. H., and Whatmore, P. B. Criminal behavior and the XYY male. *Nature*, 1967, **213**, 815.

Ressler, R. H. Genotype-correlated parental influences in two strains of mice. *J. comp. physiol. Psychol.*, 1963, **56**, 882–886.

Ricci, N., and Malacarne, P. An XYY human male. *Lancet*, 1964, **1**, 721.

Roberts, R. C. The lifetime growth and reproduction of selected strains of mice. *Heredity*, 1961, **16**, 369–381.

Roberts, R. C. Implications of behavior genetics for genetics. In J. Hirsch (Ed.), *Behavior-genetic analysis*. New York: McGraw-Hill, 1967. Pp. 340–343.

Rosenthal, D. Some factors associated with concordance and discordance with respect to schizophrenia in monozygotic twins. *J. nerv. ment. Dis.*, 1959, **129**, 1–10.

Rosenzweig, M. R., Krech, D., and Bennett, E. L. A search for relations between brain chemistry and behavior. *Psychol. Bull.*, 1960, **57**, 476–492.

Rothenbuhler, W. C. Behavior genetics of nest cleaning in honey bees: IV. Responses of F1 and backcross generations to disease-killed brood. *Am. Zool.*, 1964, **4**, 111–123.

Rundquist, E. A. Inheritance of spontaneous activity in rats. *J. comp. Psychol.*, 1933, **16**, 415–438.

Schlegel, R. J., Neu, R. L., Leão, J. C., Reiss, J. A., Nolan, T. B., and Gardner, L. I. Cri-du-chat syndrome in a 10 year old girl with deletion of the short arms of chromosome number 5. *Helv. paediat. Acta*, 1967, **22**, 2–12.

Schlesinger, K., Boggan, W., and Freedman, D. X. Genetics of audiogenic seizures: I. Relation to brain serotonin and norepinephrine in mice. *Life Sci.*, 1964, **4**, 2435–2351.

Schmid, W., and Vischer, D. Cri-du-chat syndrome. *Helv. paediat. Acta*, 1967, **22**, 22–27.

Schull, W. J., and Neel, J. V. *The effects of inbreeding on Japanese children*. New York: Harper and Row, 1965.

Scott, J. P. Genetic differences in the social behavior of inbred strains of mice. *J. Hered.*, 1942, **33**, 11–15.

Searle, L. V. The organization of hereditary maze-brightness and maze-dullness. *Genet. Psychol. Monogr.*, 1949, **39**, 279–325.

Shields, J. *Monozygotic twins*. London: Oxford University Press, 1962.

Singh, S. D. Conditioned emotional response in the rat. I. Constitutional and situational determinants. *J. comp. physiol. Psychol.*, 1959, **52**, 574–578.

Skodak, M., and Skeels, H. M. A final follow-up of one hundred adopted children. *J. genet. Psychol.*, 1949, **75**, 85–125.

Smith, D. W. The No. 18 trisomy and D1 trisomy syndromes. *Pediat. Clins. N. Am.*, 1963, **10**, 389–407.

Sontag, L. W., and Garn, S. M. Human heredity studies of the Fels Research Institute. *Acta genet. Statist. med.*, 1956/57, **6**, 494–502.

Stone, C. P., and Barker, R. G. Change of the age of puberty in albino rats by selective mating. *Proc. Soc. exp. Biol. Med.*, 1940, **44**, 48–50.

Sutherland, B. S., Umbarger, B., and Berry, H. K. The clinical management of phenylketonuria. *Gen. Pract.*, 1967, **35**, 93–98.

Tanner, J. M. Regulation of growth in size in mammals. *Nature*, 1963, **199**, 845–850.

Thiessen, D. D. The Wabbler-Lethal mouse: a study in development. *Anim. Behav.*, 1965, **13**, 87–100.

Thompson, W. R. The inheritance of behaviour: behavioural differences in fifteen mouse strains. *Can. J. Psychol.*, 1953, **7**, 145–155.

Thompson, W. R. The inheritance and development of intelligence. *Proc. Ass. Res. nerv. ment. Dis.*, 1954, **33**, 209–231.

Thompson, W. R., and Olian, S. Some effects on offspring behavior of maternal adrenalin injection during pregnancy in three inbred mouse strains. *Psychol. Rep.*, 1961, **8**, 87–90.

Thurstone, T. G., Thurstone, L. L., and Strandskov, H. H. *A psychological study of twins*. Chapel Hill, N. C. Report No. 4 from the Psychometric Laboratory, University of North Carolina, 1955.

Tolman, E. C. The inheritance of maze-learning ability in rats. *J. comp. Psychol.*, 1924, **4**, 1–18.

Tryon, R. C. Genetic differences in maze-learning ability in rats. *Yb. nat. Soc. Stud. Educ.*, 1940, **39**(1), 111–119.

Ursprung, H. Genes and development. In R. L. DeHaan and H. Ursprung (Eds.), *Organogenesis*. New York: Holt, Rinehart and Winston, 1965. Pp. 3–27.

Vandenberg, S. G. Multivariate analysis of twin differences. In S. G. Vandenberg

(Ed.), *Methods and goals in human behavior genetics.* New York: Academic Press, 1965.

Vandenberg, S. G. The nature and nurture of intelligence. Paper presented at Conference on Biology and Behavior, Rockefeller University, New York, 1966.

Vandenberg, S. G. Hereditary factors in normal personality traits (as measured by inventories). In J. Wortis (Ed.), *Recent advances in biological psychiatry.* Vol. 9, New York: Plenum Press, 1967. Pp. 65–104.

Vandenberg, S. G., and Falkner, F. Hereditary factors in human growth. *Hum. Biol.*, 1965, **37**, 357–365.

Waddington, C. H. *The strategy of the genes.* New York: Macmillan, 1957.

Waddington, C. H. *New patterns in genetics and development.* New York and London: Columbia University Press, 1962.

Walker, B. E., and Fraser, F. C. The embryology of cortisone-induced cleft palate. *J. Embryol. exp. Morph.*, 1957, **5**, 281–289.

Wallace, W. W., Moldave, K., and Meister, A. Studies on conversion of phenylalanine to tyrosine in phenylpyruvic oligophrenia. *Proc. Soc. exp. Biol. Med.*, 1957, **94**, 632–633.

Weir, M. W., and DeFries, J. C. Prenatal maternal influence on behavior in mice: evidence of a genetic basis. *J. comp. physiol. Psychol.*, 1964, **58**, 412–417.

Wilkins, B. R. Basic mathematics of control. In H. Kalmus (Ed.), *Regulation and control in living systems.* London: Wiley, 1966. Pp. 29–58.

Winston, H. D., and Lindzey, G. Albinism and water escape performance in the mouse. *Science*, 1964, **144**, 189–191.

Wood-Gush, D. G. M. A study of sex drive of two strains of cockerels through three generations. *Anim. Behav.*, 1960, **8**, 43–53.

3. Physical Growth

J. M. TANNER

All the skills, aptitudes and emotions of the growing child are rooted in or conditioned by his bodily structure. Behind each stage of learning lies the development of essential cell assemblies in the brain; behind each social interaction lies a body image conditioned by the facts of size and early or late sexual maturation. It needs no arguing that a child psychologist should have some knowledge of the facts of physical growth, and especially of those facts which particularly affect the child's feeling and behavior. That girls mature earlier physically than boys is known by every schoolteacher; but that boys of 14 may be completely prepubescent or completely physically mature is unknown or forgotten by many. Both facts have profound effects on the psychology of the children and the sociology of the school.

The growth of the brain is, of course, of paramount importance to the psychologist, but unfortunately we know less about this than about any other organ. This is due to technical difficulties, at last slowly being overcome. One section of this chapter is devoted to brain growth; another to growth of the endocrine system.

A third section is called "the organization of the growth process." In it are discussed general problems such as the regulation of growth, the catch-up after a period of malnutrition or disease, the existence of critical or sensitive periods, the existence of discrete stages of growth, the importance of invariant sequences of events occurring at varying ages. These problems are important to the psychologist not only in themselves, but because the situation in physical growth is a model for similar situations believed or known to occur in psychological development. The facts of physical growth are easier to be sure of than those of mental development; hence the models from this field have a concreteness and certainty that the mental equivalents may still lack. Thus this chapter has both factual and theoretical importance for the psychologist-reader.

I. THE HUMAN GROWTH CURVE

Figure 1 shows the most famous of all records of human growth. It concerns the height of a single boy, measured every six months from birth to 18 years. This is the oldest longitudinal record in existence, and it remains, for our purposes of illustration, one of the best. It was made during the years 1759-1777 by Count Philibert de Montbeillard on his son and it was published by Buffon in a supplement to the *Histoire Naturelle*.

In Fig. 1a is plotted the height attained at successive ages; in 1b are shown the increments in height from one age to the next expressed as the rate of growth per year. If we think of growth as a form of motion, then the upper curve is one of distance traveled, the lower curve one of velocity. The velocity or rate of growth naturally reflects the child's state at any particular time better than does the distance achieved, which depends largely on how much the child has grown in all the preceding years. The blood and tissue concentrations of those substances whose amounts change with age are thus more likely to run parallel to the velocity rather than to the distance curve. In some circumstances, indeed, it is the acceleration rather than the velocity curve which best reflects physiological events;

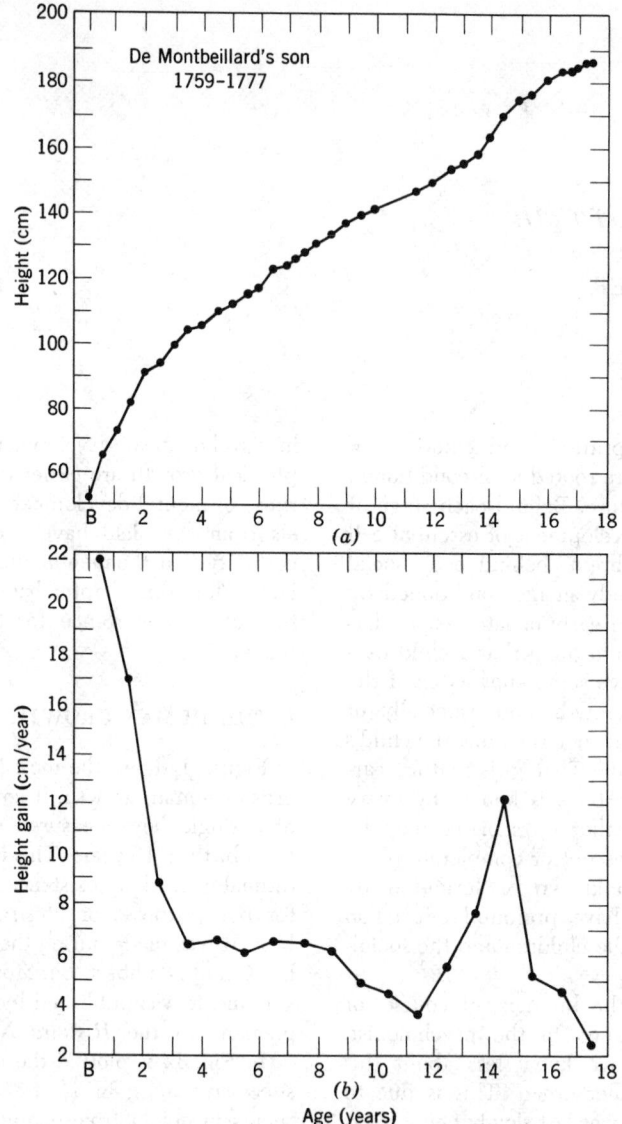

Fig. 1. Growth in height of de Montbeillard's son from birth to 18 years, 1759–1777. (*a*) Distance curve, height attained at each age. (*b*) Velocity curve, increments in height from year to year. (From Tanner, 1962; data from Scammon, 1927.)

it is probable, for example, that the great increase in secretion of the endocrine glands at adolescence is manifested most clearly in acceleration of growth (see Fig. 18).

Figure 1*b* shows that in general the velocity of growth decreases from birth (and actually from as early as the fourth month of fetal life; see Section II), but that this decrease is interrupted shortly before the end of the growth period. At this time, from 13 to 15 years in

this particular boy, there is a marked acceleration of growth, called the adolescent growth spurt. (Also, horribly, called the circumpuberal growth spurt. Some writers distinguish sharply the terms "adolescence" and "puberty," though not all who do so agree in their distinctions. Some use puberty to refer to physical changes, adolescence to refer to psychosocial ones. I have used the terms interchangeably in this chapter.) From birth until age 4 or 5 the rate of growth in height declines rapidly, and then the decline, or deceleration, gets gradually less, so that in some children the velocity is practically constant from 5 or 6 up to the beginning of the adolescent spurt. A slight increase in velocity is sometimes said to occur between about 6 and 8 years, providing a second wave on the general velocity curve. Although Fig. 1 seems to show its presence, examination of many other individual records from age 3 to 13 fails to reveal it in the great majority; if it occurs at all, it is only in a minority of children.

As the points of Fig. 1 show, growth is in general a very regular process. Contrary to opinions still sometimes met, growth in height does not proceed by fits and starts, nor does growth in upward dimensions alternate with growth in transverse or, more ominously, anteroposterior ones. The more carefully these measurements are taken, with precautions, for example, to minimize the decrease in height that occurs during the day for postural reasons, the more regular does the succession of points in the graph become. Figure 2 shows the fit of a smooth mathematical curve to a series of measurements taken on a child by the same observer every 6 months from age 3½ to 10. None of the points deviates from the line by an amount more than measuring error. This is generally

true, although in some children regular seasonal variations (discussed later) superimpose an added 6-month rhythm about the curve. There is no evidence for "stages" of growth in height (or any other physical measurement) except for the spurt associated with adolescence. Perhaps increments of growth at the cellular level are discontinuous; but at the level of bodily measurements, even of single bones measured by X-rays, we can only discern complete continuity, with a velocity that changes gradually from one age to another.

Many attempts have been made to find mathematical curves which fit, and thus summarize, human and animal growth data. Most have ended in disillusion or fantasy; disillusion because fresh data failed to conform to them, or fantasy because the system eventually contained so many parameters that it became impossible to interpret them biologically. What is needed is a curve or curves with relatively few constants, each capable of being interpreted in a biologically meaningful way. The fit to empirical data must be adequate, of course, within the limits of measuring error. Part of the difficulty arises because the measurements usually taken are themselves biologically complex. Stature, for example, consists of leg length and trunk length and head height, all of which have rather different growth curves. Even with such relatively

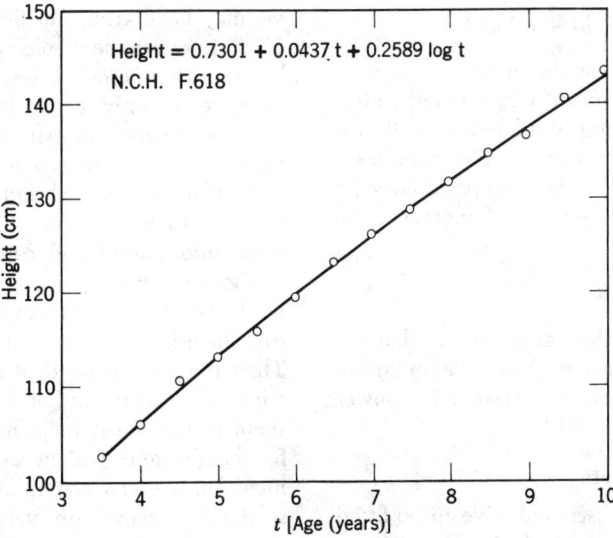

Fig. 2. Curve of form $y = a + bt + c \log t$ fitted to stature measurements taken every 6 months by R. H. Whitehouse on a girl from age 3½ to 10. Harpenden Growth Study. (From Israelsohn, 1960.)

homogeneous measurements as humerus length or calf-muscle width, it is not clear what purely biological assumptions should be made as the basis for the form of the curve. The assumption that cells are continuously dividing leads to a different formulation from the assumption that cells are adding constant amounts of nondividing material, or amounts of material at rates varying from one age period to another.

But fitting a curve to the individual values is the only way of extracting the maximum information about an individual's growth from the measurement data. This fact becomes increasingly inescapable when the effect of environmental circumstances on growth rate (e.g., illness on height growth) is investigated, or when two different measurements are being compared for the consistency of each as the child grows up. The individual's consistency can only be measured by deviations from his own growth curve. A change of rank order of two individuals from one age to another in a measurement may represent not inconsistency but consistently differing rates of change, one individual having a small velocity in the measurement, and the other individual a larger one.

More than one curve is needed to fit the postnatal age range. It seems that two curves may suffice, at least for many measurements such as height and weight. A curve of the form

$$y = a + bt + c \log t$$

where y is the measurement at age t, appears to fit well from a few months after birth to the beginning of adolescence. This is the curve shown in Fig. 2. The adolescent spurt is fitted well by the Gompertz curve, a skew S-shaped exponential, of mathematical form

$$y = Ke^{-e^{1+mt}}$$

which expresses the assumption that in equal small intervals of time the organism loses equal proportions of its remaining power to grow.

Types of Growth Data

The curves just discussed have to be fitted to data on single individuals. Yearly averages derived from different children each measured once only do not, in general, give the same curve. Thus the distinction between the two sorts of investigation is very important. The method of study using the same child at each age is called *longitudinal;* that using different children at each age is called *cross-sectional*. In a cross-sectional study each child is measured once only and all the children at age 10, for example, are different from those at age 9. A study may be longitudinal over any number of years; there are short-term longitudinal studies extending from age 3 to 5, for instance, and full birth-to-maturity longitudinal studies in which the children may be examined once, twice, or even more times every year from birth until 20 or over.

In practice it is always impossible to measure exactly the same group of children every year for a prolonged period; inevitably some children leave the study and others, if that is desired, join it. A study in which this happens is called a *mixed longitudinal* study, and special statistical techniques are needed to get the maximum information out of its data. In the past this has not always been understood, with the result that three-quarters and more of the useful information of mixed studies has been thrown away; or, to put it differently, that twenty times more children have been used to establish a mean velocity to within certain statistical limits than were actually required. One particular type of mixed study is that in which a number of relatively short-term longitudinal groups are interlocked; here we may have groups of 0-6, 5-11, 10-16, and 15-20 to cover the whole age range. Problems arise at the "joins" unless the sampling has been remarkably good, but the whole age range is covered for estimates of mean yearly velocity in the research time of five years.

Both cross-sectional and longitudinal studies have their uses, but they do not give the same information and cannot be dealt with in the same way. Cross-sectional surveys are obviously cheaper and more quickly done, and can include far larger numbers of children. They tell us a good deal about the distance curve of growth and it is essential to have them as part-basis for constructing standards for height and weight and other measurements in a given community. Periodic cross-sectional surveys are valuable in assessing the nutritional progress of a country or a socioeconomic group and the health of the child population as a whole. But they have one great drawback: they can never reveal individual differences in rate of growth or in the timing of particular phases such as the adolescent growth spurt. It is these individual rate differences which chiefly throw light on the genetical control of growth and on the correlation of growth with psychological development, educational achievement, and social behavior. Longitudinal studies are laborious and time consuming; they demand great perseverance on the part of those who make them and those who take part in them; and they demand very high technical standards, since in the calculation of a growth increment

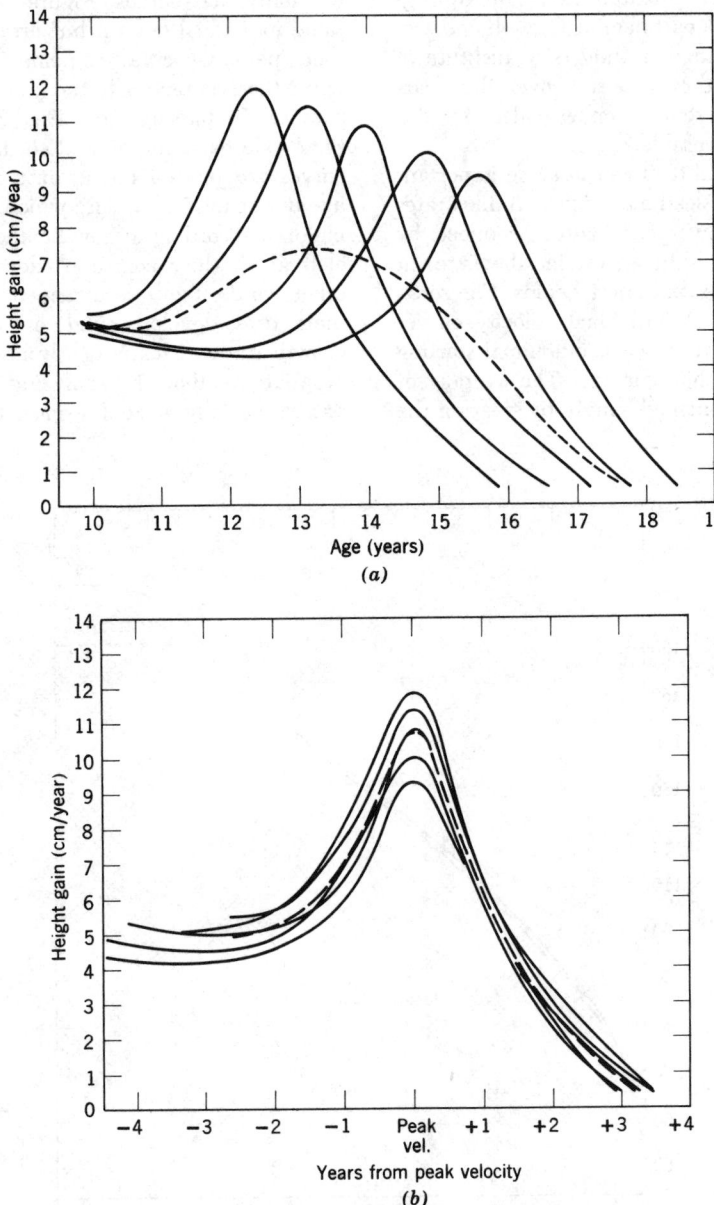

Fig. 3. The relation between individual and mean velocities during the adolescent spurt. (*a*) The individual height velocity curves of five boys of the Harpenden Growth Study (solid lines) with the mean curve (dashed) constructed by averaging their values at each age. (*b*) The same curves all plotted according to their peak height velocity. (From Tanner, Whitehouse, and Takaishi, 1966).

from one occasion to the next two errors of measurement occur. They demand also a sequential approach to problems, with all past data fully computerized and available for analysis in relation to a specific question at any time. The evidence of the past suggests that unless accompanied by cross-sectional surveys and animal experimentation, as they are at the Fels Research Institute in Yellow Springs Ohio and the Department of Growth and Development at London University Institute of Child Health, they can sink over the years into sterile deserts of number-collecting. But they are indispensable.

Cross-sectional data can in some important respects be misleading. Figure 3 illustrates the effect on "average" figures produced by the individual differences in the age at which the adolescent spurt begins. Figure 3a shows a series of individual velocity curves from 10 to 18 years, each individual starting his spurt at a different age. The average of these curves, obtained simply by treating the

values cross-sectionally and adding them up at age 10, 11, 12, etc., and dividing by 5, is shown by the dashed line. This line in no way characterizes the "average" velocity curve; on the contrary, it is a travesty of it. It smoothes out the adolescent spurt, spreading it along the time axis. It does not take account of the "phase-differences" between the individual curves. Figure 3b shows the same individual curves, but arranged so that their peak velocities coincide; the average curve then characterizes the group in a proper manner. In passing from Fig. 3a to 3b the time-scale has been altered so that in 3b the curves are plotted not against chronological age but against a measure which arranges the children according to how far they have traveled along their course of development; in other words, they are arranged according to their true developmental or physiological growth status. This is nearly always the appropriate method in analyzing longitudinal data, especially at adolescence. It is just this

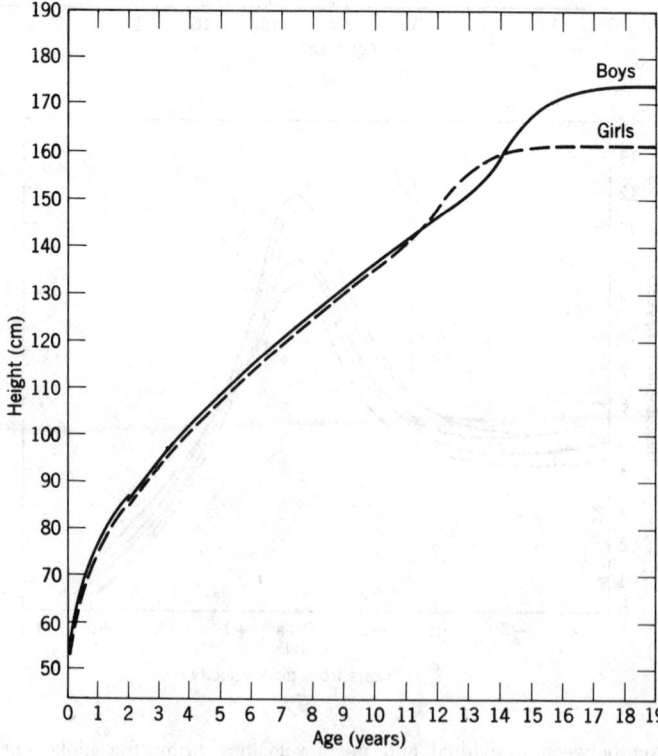

Fig. 4. Typical-individual height-attained curves for boys and girls. (Supine length to the age of 2.) Integrated curves of Fig. 5. (From Tanner, Whitehouse, and Takaishi, 1966).

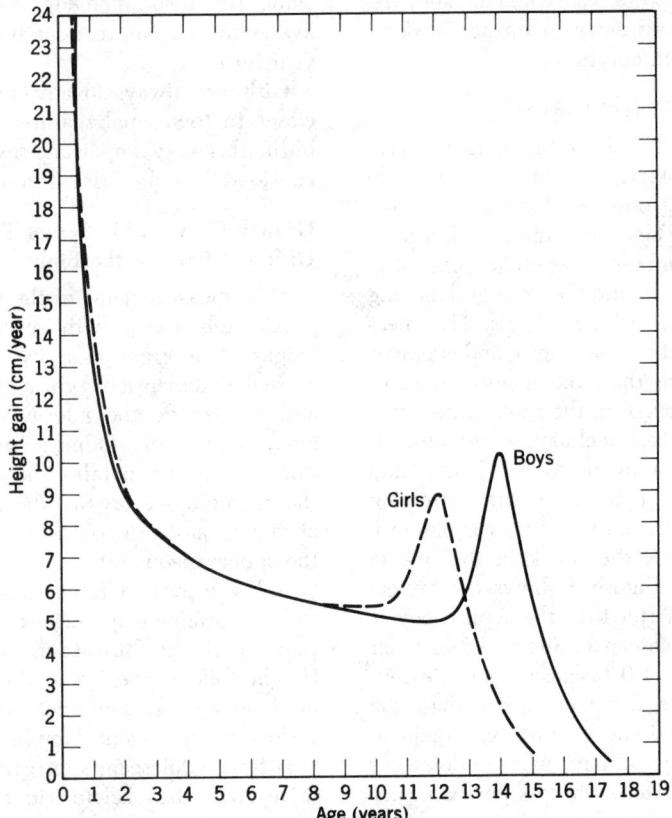

Fig. 5. Typical-individual velocity curves for supine length or height in boys and girls. These curves represent the velocity of the typical boy and girl at any given instant. (From Tanner, Whitehouse, and Takaishi, 1966.)

sort of difficulty that curve-fitting overcomes so well, one parameter representing the peak velocity reached, another the age at which it occurred, and so on.

Averages computed from cross-sectional data, however, inevitably produce velocity curves of this flattened, distorted type; and, equally, distance curves show the distortion by not rising sufficiently rapidly at adolescence.

Until recently all the published height and weight standards used in hospitals and schools incorporated this distortion. However, it is possible to construct curves whose fiftieth percentile represents the actual growth of a typical individual by taking the shape of the curve from individual longitudinal data, and the absolute values for the beginning and end from large cross-sectional surveys (Tanner, Whitehouse, and Takaishi, 1966). Figures 4

and 5 show height-attained and height-velocity curves for the "typical" boy and girl in Britain in 1965, determined in this way. By "typical" is meant that boy or girl who has the mean birth length, grows always at the mean velocity, has the peak of the adolescent growth spurt at the mean age, and, finally, reaches the mean adult height at the mean age of cessation of growth. There is of course a certain danger in showing such a smooth, average curve, for measurements on a single individual are naturally less regular, however expert the measurer. Practically no individual follows the fiftieth percentile curve of Figs. 4 and 5; but most have the same shaped curve. Some individuals, mostly late-maturing boys, however, seem to have a slight dip in the velocity curve just before the adolescent spurt starts. These are such a small minority that they have been ignored when the typical-individual curves were constructed. They remain an interesting entry to further work on the human growth curve.

Boys' and Girls' Height Curves

Figures 4 and 5 show the height curves from birth to maturity. Up to age 2 the child is measured lying down on his back. One examiner holds his head in contact with a fixed board and a second person stretches him out to his maximum length and then brings a moving board into contact with his heels. This measurement is called supine length, and averages about 1 cm more than the measurement of standing height taken in the same child, even when, as in the best techniques, the child is urged to stretch upward to full height and is aided in doing so by a measurer applying gentle upward pressure to his mastoid processes. This causes the break in the line in Fig. 4 at age 2. Figure 4 shows the typical girl as slightly shorter than the typical boy at all ages until adolescence. She becomes taller shortly after age 11.0 because her adolescent spurt takes place 2 years earlier than the boy's. At age 14.0 she is surpassed again in height by the typical boy, whose adolescent spurt has now started, whereas hers is nearly finished. In the same way, the typical girl weighs a little less than the boy at birth, equals him at age 8, becomes heavier at age 9 or 10, and remains so till about age 14½.

The velocity curves given in Fig. 5 show these processes more clearly. At birth the typical boy is growing very slightly faster than the typical girl, but the velocities become equal at about 7 months and then the girl grows faster to 4 years. From then till adolescence no difference in velocity can be detected. The sex difference is best thought of, perhaps, in terms of acceleration, the boy decelerating harder than the girl over the first 4 years (see also Deming, 1957; Deming and Washburn, 1963). In Britain in 1965 the typical girl begins the adolescent height spurt at about age 10.5 and reaches peak height velocity at approximately 12.0. The boy begins his spurt and reaches his peak just 2 years later. The boys' peak is higher than the girls, averaging in our data 10.3 ± 0.2 cm/year compared with the girls 9.0 ± 0.2 cm/year (as "instantaneous" peaks, i.e., peaks obtained by fitting smoothed curves to the observations; the velocities over the whole years which include the peak moment are naturally less, averaging 9.5 cm/year for boys and 8.4 cm/year for girls).

Girls are always in advance of boys (i.e., closer to their final mature status), even at birth; this very important sex dimorphism is considered in more detail in Section IV.

Growth Curves of Different Tissues and Different Parts of the Body

Most measurements of the body follow approximately the growth curve described for height. The great majority of skeletal and muscular dimensions grow in this manner, and so also do the internal organs such as liver, spleen, and kidneys. But some exceptions exist, most notably the brain and skull, the reproductive organs, the lymphoid tissue of the tonsils, adenoids, and intestines, and the subcutaneous fat.

In Fig. 6 these differences are shown, using the size attained by various tissues as a percentage of the birth-to-maturity increment. Height follows the "general" curve. The reproductive organs, internal and external, have a slow prepubescent growth, followed by a very large adolescent spurt; they are less sensitive than the skeleton to one set of hormones and more sensitive to another.

The brain, together with the skull covering it and the eyes and ears, develops earlier than any other part of the body and thus has a characteristic postnatal curve. (Brain growth is further discussed in Section VI.) If the brain has any adolescent spurt at all, it is a very small one. A small but definite spurt occurs in head length and breadth, but all or most of this is due to thickening of the skull bones and the scalp and development of the air sinuses. The dimensions of the face follow a path somewhat closer to the general curve. There is a considerable adolescent spurt, especially in the mandible, resulting in the jaw becoming longer and more projecting, the profile straighter, and the chin more pointed. But, as always in growth, there are considerable individual differences, to the point that a few children have no detectable spurt at all in some face measurements.

The eye probably has a slight adolescent spurt, although present data are not sufficiently accurate to make this certain. Very likely it is this that is responsible for the

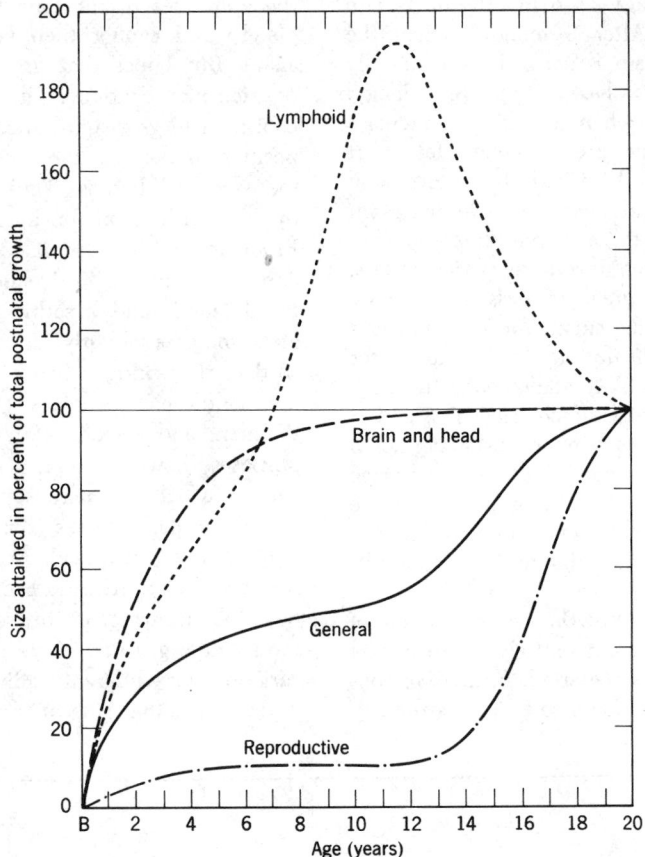

Fig. 6. Growth curves of different parts and tissues of the body, showing the four chief types. All the curves are of size attained, and plotted as percent of total gain from birth to 20 years, so that size at age 20 is 100 on the vertical scale. (From Tanner, 1962, redrawn from Scammon, 1930.)

Lymphoid type: thymus, lymph nodes, intestinal lymph masses. *Brain and head type:* brain and its parts, dura, spinal cord, optic apparatus, cranial dimensions. *General type:* body as a whole, external dimensions (except head) respiratory and digestive organs, kidneys, aortic and pulmonary trunks, musculature, blood volume. *Reproductive type:* testis, ovary, epididymis, prostate, seminal vesicles, Fallopian tubes.

increase in frequency of short-sightedness in children which occurs at the time of puberty. Although the degree of myopia increases continuously from at least age 6 to maturity, a particularly rapid rate of change occurs at about 11 to 12 in girls and 13 to 14 in boys, and this would be expected if there was a rather greater spurt in the axial dimension of the eye than in its vertical dimension (for references see Tanner, 1962).

The lymphoid tissue has quite a different growth curve from the rest of the body (see Fig. 6). It reaches its maximum amount before adolescence and then, probably under the direct influence of sex hormones, declines to its adult value.

The subcutaneous fat layer also has a curve of its own, of a slightly complicated sort. Its thickness can be measured either by X-rays or, more simply, at certain sites in the body, by picking up a fold of skin and fat between the thumb and forefinger and measuring its thickness with a special, constant-pressure caliper. Figure 7 shows the distance curves of skinfolds taken halfway down the back of the arm (triceps) and at the back of the chest, just below the shoulder blade (subscapular). Subcutaneous fat begins to be laid down in the fetus at about 34 weeks postmenstrual age, increases from then till birth and from birth to about 9 months. (This is in the average child; the peak may be reached as early as 6 months or as late as 12 or 15.) After 9 months, when the velocity of fat gain is zero, the fat actually decreases, that is, has a negative velocity, until age 6 to 8 when it begins to increase once more, in the pre-adolescent fat spurt comprehensively described by Stolz and Stolz (1951). Girls have a little more fat than boys at birth, and the difference becomes more marked during the period of loss, which is not so great in girls as in boys. From 8 years on the curves for girls and boys diverge more radically, as do the curves for limb and body fat. At adolescence the limb fat in boys decreases (see triceps, Fig. 7); the body fat shows a temporary slowing down of gain, but no actual loss in the average boy. In girls there is a slight halting of the limb-fat gain at adolescence, but no loss; the trunk-fat shows only a steady rise until adulthood.

Postadolescent Growth. Growth, even of the skeleton, does not entirely cease at the end of the adolescent period. In man, in contrast to some other mammals such as the rat,

the epiphyses of the long bones close completely and cannot then be made to grow again. But bones that grow by surface deposition may continue. The vertebral column continues to grow until about age 30, by apposition of bone to the tops and bottoms of the vertebral bodies. Thus height increases by a small amount, on average 3 to 5 mm. From about 30 to 45 it remains stationary, and then it begins to decline (Büchi, 1950). Head length and breadth and facial diameters increase slightly throughout life; and so does the width of bones in the leg and in the hand, in both sexes (Garn, Rohmann, Wagner, and Ascoli, 1967). For practical purposes, however, it is useful to have an age at which we may say that growth in stature virtually ceases, that is, after which only some 2% is added. At present in North America and northwest Europe the average boy stops growing, in this sense, at 17.5 and the average girl at 15.5 years, with a normal variation for different individuals of about 2 years on either side of these averages.

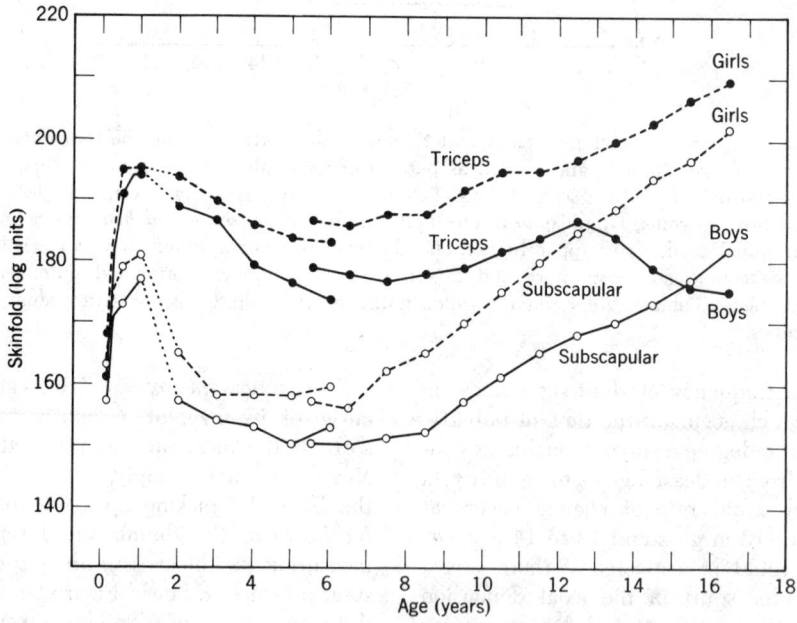

Fig. 7. Distance curve of subcutaneous tissue measured by Harpenden skinfold calipers over triceps and under scapula. Logarithmic transformation units. Data 0–1 year, pure longitudinal, 74 boys and 65 girls (Brussels Child Study, Graffar, Asiel and Corbier, unpub.); 2–6 years, London Child Study Center (Tanner, unpub.) with pure longitudinal core 4–6 years of 59 boys and 57 girls, actual mean increments subtracted or added to get means at 2 and 3; 5–16 years, London County Council (Scott, 1961) cross-sectional, 1000 to 1600 of each sex at each year of age from 5 to 14; 500 at 15; 250 at 16. (From Tanner, 1962.)

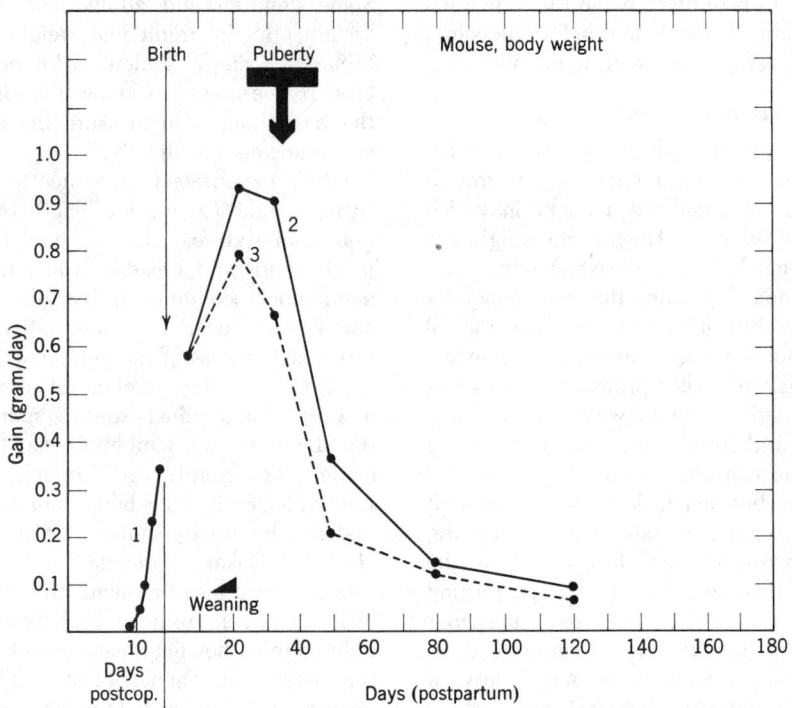

Fig. 8. Weight velocity curve for the mouse. Curve 1 sexes combined, cross-sectional, from Mac-Dowell, Allen, and MacDowell (1927). Curves 2 and 3, males (18) and females (18), pure longitudinal, MacArthur large strain (Butler and Metrakos, 1950). Time of puberty from Engle and Rosasco (1927) and Flux (1954). (From Tanner, 1962.)

The Human Growth Curve as a Primate Characteristic

The characteristic shape of the human growth curve is shared by apes and monkeys (or at least by chimpanzees and rhesus, the only species for which we have adequate data). But it is apparently a distinctive primate characteristic, for neither rodents nor cattle have curves resembling it.

In Figs. 8 and 9 are shown the velocity curves for body weight of mice and chimpanzees (weight has to be used, since so few data on length exist). In the mouse, as in the rat, there is little interval between weaning and puberty, and no visible adolescent spurt because there is no period of low velocity between birth and maturity. In terms of the maturation of their organs, mouse and rat are born earlier in development than is man. The peak velocity of the mouse's weight curve occurs at a time that corresponds closely, by this organ-maturation calendar, with birth in man, which is when

the first peak of man's weight velocity curve occurs. In the chimpanzee (Fig. 9), on the other hand, the curve resembles entirely that of man. The first peak velocity of weight must be shortly before or at birth, but this is followed by a gradual decrease of velocity during the long interval between weaning and puberty. The rhesus monkey has a similar curve, though with less time intervening between weaning and puberty. The magnitude of the adolescent spurt, and in particular the degree of sex dimorphism occurring during it, varies in primates from species to species.

The prolongation of the time between weaning and puberty appears to be an evolutionary step among the mammals, taken by the primates, and reaching its most pronounced development in man. The increased time necessary for the maturing of the primate brain has been sandwiched into this period. At least some of the evolutionary reasons for this are not hard to find. It is probably advantageous for learning, and especially learning to cooperate in group or family life, to take place while the individual remains relatively docile and before he comes into sexual competition with adult males.

Measurements and Methods

This is not the place to discuss what measurements are most important in growth studies, nor to detail the manner in which they should be made. Height and weight are the traditional basic measurements, and height is indeed perhaps the most generally useful one. But it is not the best for all purposes, for if we are interested in comparing humans with other primates or with less closely related mammals, we must dissociate the limb and trunk and compare sitting height or crown-rump length. Weight is easier to measure but much less useful, since it consists of a conglomerate of all the tissues, which, as we have seen, do not all have the same growth curves. Thus if a child is putting on weight, this may be because of muscular and skeletal growth or fat growth only. Failure to gain weight, or actual loss of weight in an older child, may signify nothing except a better attention to diet and exercise, whereas failure to gain height or muscle would call for an immediate investigation.

Some children and adults who are "overweight" by the traditional weight-for-height tables are simply athletes with heavy muscles. If one wants to know if a child is fat, the best thing is to measure the amount of subcutaneous fat directly.

Other measurements frequently made are sitting height (giving leg length by subtraction from stature), shoulder and hip width, head length and breadth, arm and calf circumference, skinfolds, and widths across the elbow and knee. Two internationally used series or batteries of measurements are available. One is the baseline of the birth-to-maturity longitudinal studies sponsored by the International Children's Center, Paris, made concurrently in Brussels, London, Louisville, Paris, Stockholm, and Zurich, and matched by exactly similar studies in Prague, Helsinki, Dakar, Kampala, and elsewhere. The 13 basic measurements and the manner of making each are given in Falkner (1960). Photographs showing measurement technique can be seen in Tanner (1964). The second international battery is the rather more ambitious measurement schedule laid down for use of all studies of growth and physique made in association with the International Bio-

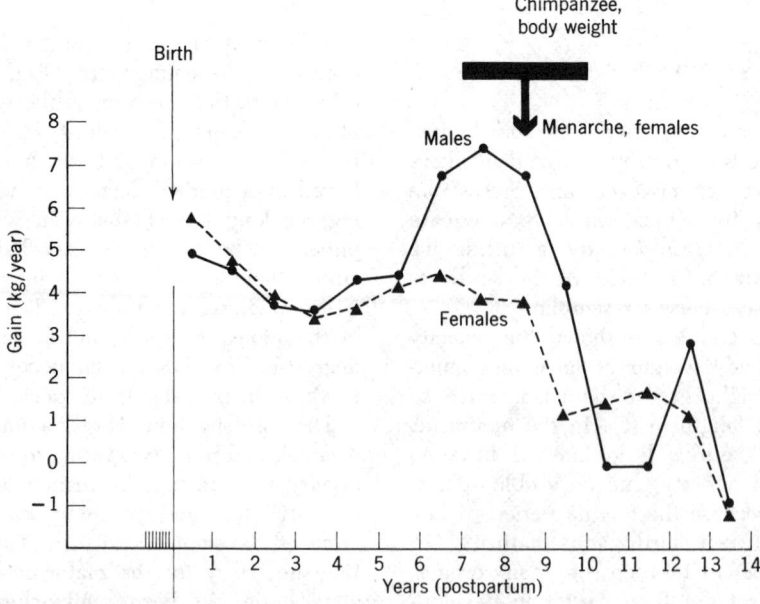

Fig. 9.   Weight velocity curve for the chimpanzee. Actual increments from Grether and Yerkes (1940). Menarche from Young and Yerkes (1943) and Gavan (1953), average 8.8 years, range 7.0 to 10.8 (From Tanner, 1952.)

logical Program. Two schedules are given, one comprising 21 measurements, the other 37 (Tanner, Hiernaux, and Jarman, 1968). This I.B.P. Handbook also gives details of radiographic techniques for demonstrating bone muscle and fat. These are also illustrated and described in Tanner (1964).

The International Children's Center Studies are designed longitudinally and call for the children to be examined at 1, 3, 6, 9, 12, 18, and 24 months and yearly thereafter. Age limits are laid down for these examinations; thus at 3 to 18 months the child should be within ± 7 days of the required date and at later ages within ± 14 days. In practice the use of such limits turns out to be more important for cross-sectional surveys than for longitudinal studies where individual curve-fitting may be done whatever the dates of examination. There is, however, an apparently small but significant technical point. Calculating velocities for individual children examined at varying intervals is intolerably difficult if the usual system of age in years and months is used. It is much simpler to use *decimal age,* that is, a calendar which operates in decimals of a year. In such a calendar June 1, 1968 is 68.414, for example. If a child's birth date is August 16, 1961 (61.622), his age on June 1, 1968 would be simply 68.414 − 61.622 = 6.79 (rounded). Increments of age from one examination to the next are easily calculated by subtraction and rates of growth are calculated by simple division. A table of decimals of a year can be found in the IBP Handbook or in Tanner, Whitehouse, and Takaishi (1966).

A last point concerns the reporting of growth data. Confusion still arises between means referring to, say, children all aged exactly 6.0, children aged 6.0 to 6.99, and children aged 5.5 to 6.49. The best terminology is to label the means of these age groups as 6.0, 6+, and 6±, respectively.

II. PRENATAL GROWTH

The period of prenatal growth is vitally important to the child's future well-being; yet it is the period about which, inevitably, we know least. For the first two-thirds of pregnancy we have to rely on cross-sectional studies, and to a large extent on embryos and fetuses expelled from the uterus because one or the other was abnormal. For later fetal life we can study infants born prematurely, making the assumption that these children have grown before birth and will grow after it in exactly the same way as children who remain in the uterus the average length of time. Though this seems to be a hazardous assumption, it is probably justified, if children with certain abnormalities are excluded.

Our ignorance begins at the beginning, for we do not know what forces are responsible for selecting out of the millions of sperm the one which fertilizes the ovum. Fertilization takes place in one of the tubes which lead from the ovaries to the uterus. The fertilized egg spends about seven days drifting down the tube and floating in the uterine cavity before implantation into the wall of the uterus takes place. During this time the cells divide steadily, so that when it is ready for implantation, the blastocyst, as it is called, consists of several dozen cells. Blastocysts can be washed out of the tube and implanted in a foster-mother, and in animals this technique has been used both for examining the effect of different kinds of uterine environment on development (McLaren and Michie, 1956) and for transporting by air the fetuses of large animals packaged, temporarily, in the uteri of small ones.

After implantation the outer layer of the blastocyst undergoes a series of changes culminating in the formation of the placenta, and a small portion of the inner layer develops into the embryo. The period of the embryo is considered to begin two weeks after fertilization and ends eight weeks after fertilization, when the child, now recognizably human, with arms and legs, a heart that beats, and a nervous system that shows the beginnings of reflex responses to tactile stimuli, is called a fetus. At this age it is about 3 cm long.

This is a hazardous period, and considerably more ova are fertilized than come to fruition. Probably about 30% of embryos are aborted, usually without the mothers' knowledge. This is due in most cases to abnormalities of development, either of the embryo or of its protective and nutritive surrounding structures. For example, chromosomal abnormalities are present in between 3 and 4% of fertilized ova, but in only ¼% of newborns. Thus about 90% of all conceptuses with these abnormalities are rejected as early spontaneous abortions. Lesser degrees of abnormality may result in a viable fetus and child, but one which grows less than normal. An example of this is the child with the chromosomal disorder of triple-21, discussed in Chapter 2 of this book.

The reckoning of age in the prenatal period presents a problem. Traditionally and because we have no better way, age is counted from the first day of the last menstrual period. This occurs on average two weeks before fertilization. Thus the most frequent age at birth is 280 days or 40.0 weeks, reckoned as "postmenstrual age," but it represents only 38 weeks of true fetal age. There are difficulties in individual cases, however; the interval from menstruation to fertilization varies considerably; and worse, menstrual bleeding, or something like it, may continue in some women for one or even two months after fertilization.

Thus reliable growth curves of the fetus are hard to come by. Figure 10 shows the distance and velocity curves of body length, so far as it may be measured, in prenatal life and for 2 years after birth. The peak velocity

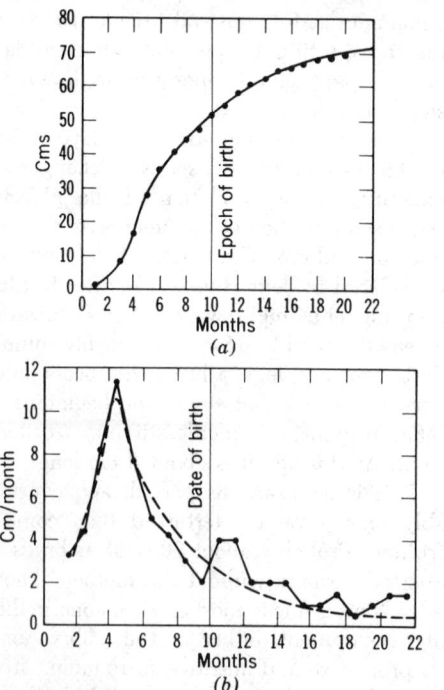

Fig. 10. Distance (*a*) and velocity (*b*) curves for growth in body length in prenatal and early postnatal period. Cross-sectional data of His and Russow. (Redrawn from Thompson, 1942.)

is reached at about 4 months postmenstrual age. In the embryonic period the velocity is not very great. During these first 2 months differentiation of the originally homogeneous whole into regions, such as head, arm, and so forth, occurs, as does histogenesis, the differentiation of cells into specialized tissues such as muscle or nerve. At the same time each region is molded, by differential growth of cells or by cell migration, into a definite shape. This process, known as morphogenesis, continues right up to adulthood and, indeed, in some parts of the body, into old age. But the major part of it is completed by the eighth postmenstrual week.

The great rate of growth of the fetus compared with that of the child is largely due to the fact that cells are still multiplying. The proportion of cells undergoing mitosis in any tissue becomes progressively less as the fetus gets older, and it is generally thought that few if any new nerve cells (apart from neuroglia) and only a small proportion of new muscle cells appear after 6 fetal months, the time when the velocity in linear dimensions is sharply dropping. The muscle and nerve cells of the fetus are considerably different in appearance from those of the child or adult. Both have little cytoplasm around the nucleus. In the muscle there is a great amount of intercellular substance and a much higher proportion of water than in mature muscle. The later fetal and the postnatal growth of muscle consists chiefly of building up the cytoplasm of the muscle cells; salts are incorporated and the contractile proteins are formed. The cells become bigger, the intercellular substance largely disappears, the concentration of water decreases. This process continues quite actively up to about 3 years of age and slowly thereafter; at adolescence it briefly speeds up again, particularly in boys, under the influence of androgenic hormones. In the nerve cells cytoplasm is added, nucleoprotein bodies appear, and axons and dendrites grow. Thus postnatal growth is, for at least some tissues, chiefly a period of development and enlargement of existing cells, whereas early fetal life is a period of the division and addition of new cells.

The Effect of the Uterine Environment

Growth in weight of the fetus follows the same general pattern as growth in length, ex-

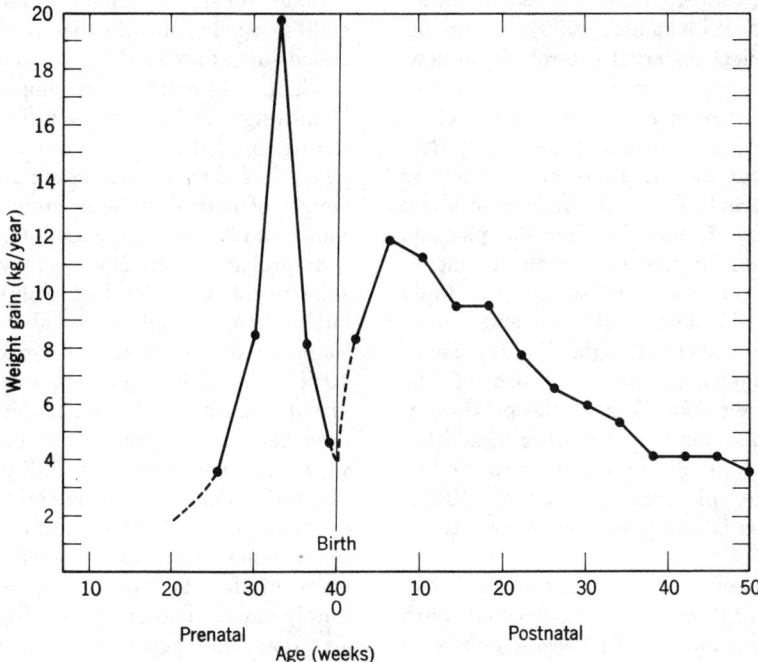

Fig. 11. Velocity of growth in weight of singleton children. Prenatal curve from data of McKeown and Record (1952) on birth-weights of live-born children delivered before 40 weeks of gestation. Postnatal data from Ministry of Health (1959); mixed longitudinal data (their Table VII). Dashed line shows estimate of velocity immediately before and after birth, showing catch-up. (From Tanner, 1963.)

cept that the peak velocity is reached much later, at approximately 34.0 weeks postmenstrual (Gruenwald, 1967). There is considerable evidence that from about 34 or 36 weeks on the rate of growth of the fetus slows down due to the influence of the maternal uterus, whose available space is by then becoming fully occupied. Twins slow down earlier, when their combined weight is approximately the 36-week weight of the singleton fetus (McKeown and Record, 1952, 1953; Naeye, Benirschke, Hagstrom, and Marcus, 1966). In Fig. 11 is plotted the velocity curve for mean weight of live-born singletons of gestation period 24 to 40 weeks, with a postnatal curve from a large-scale mixed longitudinal study of a similar population (Ministry of Health, 1959). The velocity rises in the immediate postbirth period to make a peak which would quite naturally join with the prebirth peak to make a smooth velocity curve without the dip in the last few weeks before birth. The increase in velocity after birth represents a catch-up (see Section

VII) on the part of those newborns who have been most held up in the uterus. Thus there is a significant negative correlation between length at birth and length increment during the first year, and also between weight and weight increment.

This slowing-down mechanism enables a genetically large child developing in the uterus of a small mother to be successfully delivered. It operates in many species of animal; the most dramatic demonstration was made by crossing reciprocally a large Shire horse and a small Shetland pony. The pair in which the mother was a Shire had a large newborn foal, and the pair in which the mother was Shetland had a small foal. But both foals were the same size after a few months, and both ended about halfway between their parents. The same has been shown in cattle crosses (Dickinson, 1960). In man the correlation between length at birth and adult height is only about .3; but it rises sharply during the first year and between length at age 2 and adult height is nearly .8 (Tanner, Healy, Lockhart, Mac-Kenzie, and Whitehouse, 1956). These figures also reflect maternal control of the newborn size.

How this control is exercised is not clear. The placenta grows at first more rapidly than the fetus, but then it grows more slowly so that the placenta/fetus ratio falls from about 30 weeks on. It may be that the placenta simply cannot increase its capacity to supply nutriments sufficiently to sustain the rapid 34-week fetal velocity. In mice and guinea pigs it seems likely that the limiting factor is a hemodynamic one, the size of the placenta being dependent on the pressure at which the maternal blood reaches it, and the size of the fetus depending, in turn, on the size of the placenta (McLaren, 1965). Whether this is also important in man is not yet known.

Poor environmental circumstances, especially of nutrition, result in lowered birth weight in the human. This seems chiefly to be due to a reduced rate of growth in the last 2 to 4 weeks of fetal life, for weights of babies born at 36 or 38 weeks in various parts of the world under various circumstances are rather similar (Gruenwald, 1967). Mothers who due to adverse circumstances in their own childhood have not achieved their full growth potential may produce smaller fetuses than they would have had they grown up under better circumstances. Thus two generations or even more may be needed to undo the effect of poor environmental circumstances on birth weight.

So-Called "Premature" Babies

Some babies are born earlier than others and they naturally tend to be smaller. Until recently all babies under the birth weight of 2500 grams (5½ pounds) were designated "premature" whatever in fact their physiological state or gestation period. This definition (promulgated by WHO in 1948) did a lot of harm and has now been dropped; the word premature has gone out of scientific use. Babies less than 2500 grams at birth (WHO 1961; but a better usage is 2000 grams) are called low-birth-weight infants; babies born after a shorter than usual period in the uterus are called short-gestation-period infants. Standards exist for comparing the birth weight of a short-gestation child with that of others of similar gestation. If the child's weight on this basis is low, he is called small-for-dates.

These distinctions are important. Low-birth-weight children grow faster than others during the first two years, catching up somewhat; but they do not reach the height or weight of normal children growing up under similar environmental circumstances by age 5 or probably ever. Nor do they on average achieve the same level of ability in tests of intelligence, though here also they show catch-up in the first two years (Drillien, 1964). The deficits in both size and ability increase as the birth weight decreases; children between 2000 and 2500 grams at birth show little impairment of ability and only a slight size deficit. A considerable proportion of those under 2000 grams, however, have some mental or neurological defect. Evidently many of the 2000 to 2500-gram babies are simply small babies born after a normal gestation to genetically small mothers, whereas most of those below 2000 grams have suffered some developmental difficulty. It is interesting that mothers of these babies have a higher proportion of abnormal outcomes in other conceptions also than do mothers of larger infants.

Clearly the prognosis for a small child born after the normal length gestation and an equally small child born after a shortened gestation may be very different. Leaving the uterus early is not in itself necessarily deleterious, whereas growing less than normally during a full uterine stay implies pathology of fetus, placenta, or mother.

Birth as a Happening

For some physiological functions birth signifies upheaval and change, often associated with a particular vulnerability. But it is important to realize that for very many others birth is an incident without much significance in a steadily maturing and changing program of events.

The respiratory and the cardiovascular systems are the ones most altered by the fact of birth. Failure to establish satisfactory respiration during the crucial period just after birth is a common cause of neonatal death and of brain injury among survivors. The newborn infant, however, has a much greater capacity to survive straightforward anoxia undamaged than do children or adults, and we are moving toward the view that in many cases it is pre-existing brain damage, of developmental or uterine origin, which is the reason for failure to initiate respiration, or failure apparently to survive a period of anoxia. "Almost all medical literature still equates failure to breathe at birth with 'birth injury' placing the damage at the time of delivery. The evidence suggests that pre-existing brain damage interferes with the ability to adjust to extra-uterine life and to initiate respiration" (Knobloch and Pasamanick, 1962). Drillien (1964) remarks of her own comprehensive study that the more severe defects originate usually at an early stage of fetal development rather than from damage to a potentially normal nervous system occurring in the last three months of pregnancy or during delivery. Differences in later behavior are found between children who have been subjected to certain obstetric hazards and those who have not, however, and these may be wholly or partly due to minimal brain damage occurring at the time of delivery.

Some enzyme systems are equally sharply affected by the fact of birth. Thus in rabbits there is a sudden rise in glucose-6-phosphatase in the liver at birth and not before, whether birth is induced early, occurs normally, or is late (Dawkins, 1961). Other animals also show a rise in this enzyme at birth. This is readily accounted for. The enzyme catalyzes the breakdown of glycogen to glucose, and during the last part of fetal life many mammals store a lot of glycogen in the liver. Just after birth there is great need of glucose in the blood and tissues, pending the full establishment of lactation, and the enzymic events are adjusted in a way which brings this about.

On the other hand, numerous enzymes exist with time courses of development which are quite independent of birth (see Sereni and Principi, 1965). A well-known example is the switch from production of fetal hemoglobin to adult hemoglobin. These are forms of hemoglobin with slightly different molecular structures. A gradual switch in production occurs, so that the percentage of fetal hemoglobin begins dropping from about the thirty-sixth postmenstrual week. The switch is not due to birth, however, because the fetal percentage remains high in prematurely born babies and is low in those who are postmaturely born (Jonxis, 1965). Thus in this, as in other respects, the prematurely born has to await the striking of some differently regulated biological clock.

Most importantly, the maturation of the nervous system seems to be little affected by the fact of birth. The electroencephalogram of an infant born prematurely at 28 weeks will 6 weeks later be much the same as that of an infant born at 34 weeks (Dreyfus-Brisac, 1966; Minkowski, 1966). Birth also does not influence the date of appearance of conditioned reflexes (Papousek, 1961) nor the stages of motor behavior elicited by detailed neurological examination. According to Dargassies (1966) the development of this behavior occurs in a prematurely born infant just "as if birth before term did not perceptibly alter the course of neurological maturation. [(The schedule)] is adhered to just as closely in an incubator as in utero."

III. GROWTH AND DEVELOPMENT AT ADOLESCENCE

After birth the growth rate of most body tissues falls steadily, the fall being swift in the first two or three years and slower thereafter. The rate of growth in height decreases slowly from an average of 6.5 cm/year at age 5.0 to about 5.0 cm/year just before the adolescent spurt begins. Weight velocity is almost constant from age 3 to puberty (rising from an average of 2.0 kg/year to about 2.7 kg/year), since the increase in fat velocity balances the drop in velocity of muscular and skeletal dimensions. Body shape continues to change, since the rate of growth of some parts, such as the legs and arms, is greater than the rate of growth of others, such as the trunk. But the change is a steady one, a smoothly continuous development of the final prepubescent physique rather than any passage through a series of separate stages.

The Adolescent Growth Spurt

At puberty, a very considerable change in growth rate occurs. For a year or more the velocity of growth approximately doubles: a boy is likely to be growing at a rate he last experienced at about age 2. During the year which includes the moment of peak height velocity a boy usually grows between 7 and 12 cm and a girl between 6 and 11 cm. Children who have their peak early reach a higher peak than those who have it late, the correlation between peak height velocity and the age at which it is reached being about —.45 (this is visible in the lines of Fig. 3). The average age at which the peak occurs varies more from one population to another than does the magnitude of the peak, depending on environmental and perhaps genetic circumstances. In moderately well-off children in West Europe the peak is reached on average at about 14.0 in boys and 12.0 in girls; in the United States it is reached about 6 months earlier in the corresponding socioeconomic group.

The adolescent spurt is at least partly under different hormonal control from growth in the preceding period (see Section V). Probably as a consequence of this the amount of height added during the spurt is to a considerable degree independent of the amount attained before it. Most children who have grown steadily up, say, the thirtieth percentile line on a height chart till adolescence, end up at the thirtieth percentile as adults, it is true; but a number end as high as the fiftieth or as low as the tenth, and a very few end at the fifty-fifth or fifth. The correlation between adult height and height just before the spurt starts is about .8. This leaves some 30% of the variability in adult height as due to differences in the magnitude of the adolescent spurt.

Practically all skeletal and muscular dimensions take part in the spurt, though not to an equal degree. Most of the spurt in height is due to acceleration of trunk length rather than length of legs. There is a fairly regular order in which the dimensions accelerate; leg length as a rule reaches its peak first, followed by the body breadths, with shoulder width last (Stolz and Stolz, 1951). Thus a boy stops growing out of his trousers (at least in length) a year before he stops growing out of his jackets. The earliest structures to reach their adult status are the head, hands, and feet. At adolescence, children, particularly girls, sometimes complain of having large hands and feet. They can be reassured that by the time they are fully grown their hands and feet will be a little smaller in proportion to their arms and

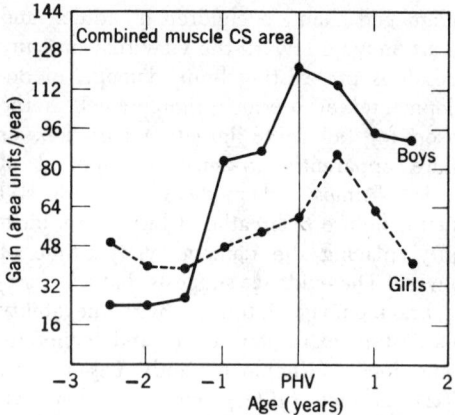

Fig. 12. Mean velocity of combined muscle cross-sectional area (calf, arm, and thigh). Longitudinal data, individual curves aligned on peak height velocity (PHV). (From Tanner, 1965.)

legs, and considerably smaller in proportion to their trunk.

Changes in Body Composition at Adolescence

The relative changes in bone muscle and fat can be followed in radiographs of the limbs, taken in a standardized way (Tanner, 1964). The marked spurt in muscle is illustrated in Fig. 12 and the simultaneous loss of fat in Fig. 13. These curves are derived from 28 boys and 21 girls in the Harpenden Growth Study measured each 6 months during puberty (for details see Tanner, 1965). The resulting individual curves have been aligned according to the child's point of peak height velocity (PHV) instead of according to chronological age. This technique, introduced into growth studies by Boas (see Tanner, 1959) some 80 years ago, and furthered by Shuttleworth (1937) and Stolz and Stolz (1951), overcomes the difficulty caused by some children having an early adolescent spurt and some a late one. When chronological age is used as a base the mixture of preadolescent, midadolescent, and postadolescent children at each age obscures the course of events in the manner illustrated in Fig. 3.

Figures 12 and 13 represent a summary of radiographic measurements of calf, thigh, and upper arm. In each case the widths of the bone, muscle, and fat were measured at a standard level, and the cross-sectional areas

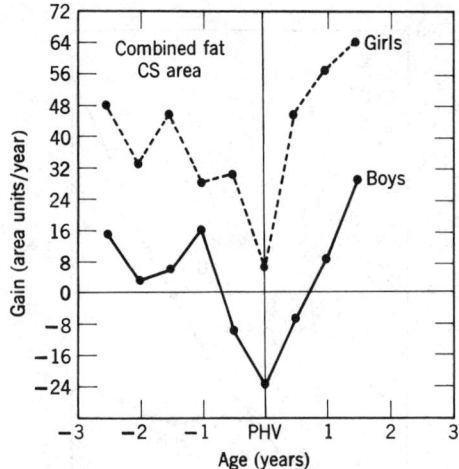

Fig. 13. Mean velocity of combined subcutaneous fat cross-sectional area (calf, arm, and thigh). Longitudinal data, individual curves aligned on peak height velocity (PHV). (From Tanner, 1965.)

of each were calculated on the assumptions that the limb was circular, and that, at the level measured, the three tissues were distributed in concentric rings. (Simple muscle and fat widths, however, give very similar curves.) The values for muscle cross-sections in calf, arm, and thigh were summed, but with the thigh value halved first, since it was about twice that of the other regions. The same procedure was followed with the fat.

These figures give the velocity curves. Both boys' and girls' muscle cross-sections (Fig. 12) show large increases in velocity, reaching peaks a trifle after the points of maximal height velocity (when the boys' curve is smoothed). The boys reach a considerably greater velocity than the girls. From infancy to adolescence boys have on average somewhat larger muscles than girls, but the girls' adolescent spurt, beginning two years earlier than the boys', carries them beyond the boys temporarily. Thus from about 12½ to 13½ girls on average actually have larger muscles than boys. Then the boys' spurt begins and the adult sex difference comes to be established.

The curve for limb bone width resembles that for muscle, but with its peak coincident with peak height velocity. The adolescent spurt is wholly or largely attributable to in-crease in width of the dense bony cortex; the size of the marrow cavity on the inside of the bone seems to change little if at all (Tanner, 1968).

Figure 13 shows the curve for fat. Boys on average actually lose fat at adolescence, with maximum rate of loss coincident with peak height velocity. Girls show an identically shaped curve, but the decrease in velocity is not sufficiently great to carry the mean below zero, that is, to give an absolute loss. Most girls have to content themselves with a temporary go-slow in fat accumulation. Fat on the body shows a much smaller decrease of velocity than fat on the limbs (see Fig. 7).

Strength and Exercise Tolerance

The increase in muscle size is naturally accompanied by an increase in strength, illustrated in Fig. 14, drawn from the mixed longitudinal data of Jones (1949). Arm pull refers to the movement of pulling apart clasped hands held up in front of the chest, the hands each holding a dynamometer handle; arm thrust refers to the reverse movement of pushing the hands together. Each individual test represents the best of three trials made in competition with a class mate of similar ability and against the individual's own figure of six months before. Only with such precautions can maximal values be approached. The boys show a very marked strength increase, whereas the girls have little real spurt; by the age of menarche their strength has reached its maximum. Other data indicate that, except in hands and forearms, girls and boys are similar in strength for a given body size and shape until puberty begins.

After adolescence, however, boys are much stronger, chiefly by virtue of having larger muscles, and partly, probably, by being able to develop more force per gram of muscle tissue. They also develop larger hearts and lungs relative to their size, a higher systolic blood pressure, a lower resting heart rate, a greater capacity for carrying oxygen in the blood, and a greater power for neutralizing the chemical products of muscular exercise such as lactic acid (see Tanner, 1962, p. 168). In short, the male becomes at adolescence more adapted for the tasks of hunting, fighting, and manipulating all sorts of heavy objects, as is necessary in some forms of food-gathering.

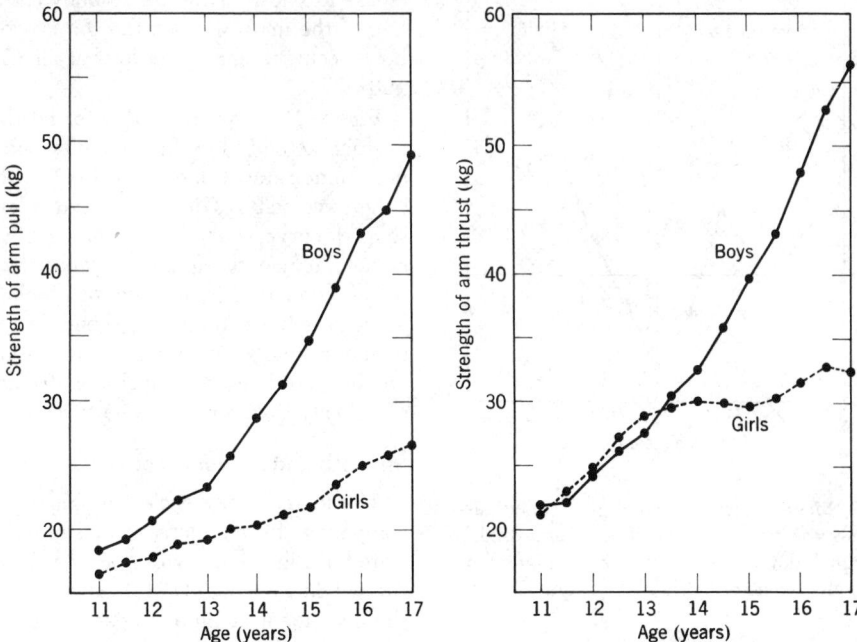

Fig. 14.   Strength of arm pull and arm thrust from age 11 to 17. Mixed longitudinal data, 65–93 boys and 66–93 girls in each group. (From Tanner, 1962; data from Jones, 1949.)

The increase in hemoglobin, associated with a parallel increase in the number of red blood cells, is illustrated in Fig. 15, drawn from the data of Young (1963). The hemoglobin concentration is plotted in relation to the development of secondary sex characters instead of chronological age, for the same reason as the muscle and fat cross-sections were previously plotted in relation to peak height velocity. Girls lack the rise in red cells and hemoglobin, which is brought about by the action of testosterone.

It is as a direct result of these anatomical and physiological changes that athletic ability increases so much in boys at adolescence. The popular notion of a boy "outgrowing his strength" at this time has little scientific support. It is true that the peak velocity of strength is reached a year or so later than that of height, so that a short period may exist when the adolescent, having completed his skeletal and probably also muscular growth, still does not have the strength of a young adult of the same body size and shape. But this is a temporary phase; considered absolutely, power, athletic skill, and physical endurance all increase progressively and rapidly throughout

adolescence. It is certainly not true that the changes accompanying adolescence enfeeble, even temporarily. If the adolescent becomes

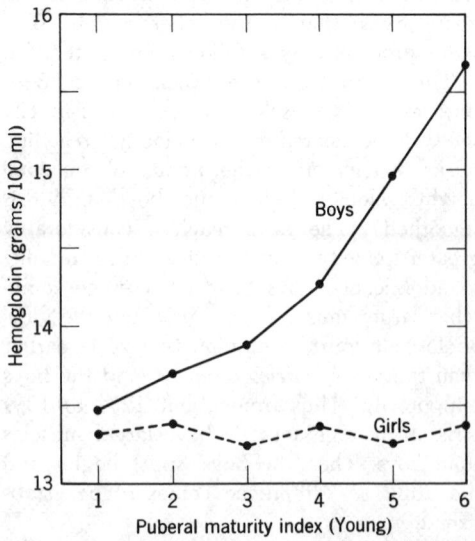

Fig. 15.   Blood hemoglobin level in girls and boys acording to stage of puberty. Cross-sectional data. (From Young, 1963.)

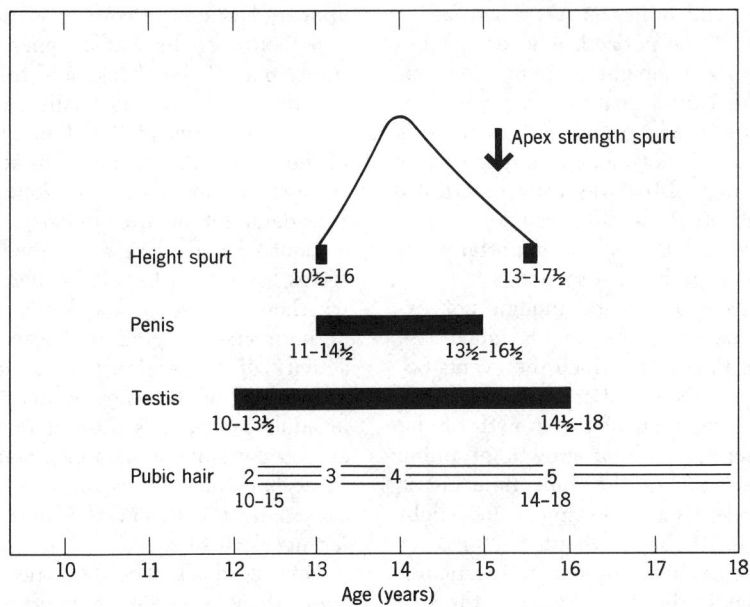

Fig. 16. Diagram of sequence of events at adolescence in boys. An average boy is represented; the range of ages within which each event charted may begin and end is given by the figures placed directly below its start and finish. (From Tanner, 1962.)

weak and easily exhausted it is for psychological reasons and not physiological ones.

Development of the Reproductive System

The adolescent spurt in skeletal and muscular dimensions is closely related to the rapid development of the reproductive system which takes place at this time. In the older literature the word puberty was used to denote the appearance of the pubic hair, but more recently it has been taken to refer to the period of time at which the testes or ovaries and such organs as the uterus, prostate, and seminal vesicles suddenly enlarge. In this way it is possible to talk about puberty in mammals in general, for in most mammals the growth curves of these reproductive organs differ from the growth curves of other parts of the body by being nearly flat at first and then suddenly steeply rising (see Fig. 6).

The sequence of events in man is shown diagrammatically in Figs. 16 and 17. Figure 16 is largely based on the classic study by Herbert and Lois Stolz (1951) of the growth of 67 boys in Oakland, California, followed over seven years of adolescence. This study is remarkable both for the detail in which individual differences in growth rates were analyzed and for the introduction of carefully posed serial photographs as an integral part of the descriptive technique, a method later copied and made more quantifiable in the Harpenden Growth Study (Tanner, 1962). Figure 17 is chiefly based on Reynolds' and Wines' (1951) data from the Fels Research Institute, and also the data of Nicholson and Hanley (1953) and Tanner, Whitehouse, and Takaishi (1966). The solid areas in Fig. 16 marked *penis* and *testis* represent the period of accelerated growth of these organs, and the horizontal lines and the rating numbers marked *pubic hair* stand for its advent and development. The sequence and timings given represent in each case an average value for West European boys; North Americans may average a few months earlier. To give an idea of the individual departures from the average, figures for the range of ages at which the spurts for height, penis growth, and testis growth begin and end are inserted under the first and last point of the curves or bars. The acceleration of penis growth, for example, begins on average at about age 13, but sometimes as early as 11 and sometimes as late as 14½. The completion of penis development usually occurs at about age 15 but in some boys at 13½ and others at 17. There are a few boys, it will be noticed, who do not begin their spurts in height or penis development until the earliest maturers have entirely completed theirs. At ages 13 and 14 there is an enormous variability among any group of boys, who range all the way from practically complete maturity to absolute pre-adolescence. The psychological and social importance of this is discussed in the next section.

The *sequence* of events, though not exactly the same for each boy, is much less variable than the age at which the events occur. The first sign of puberty in the boy is usually an acceleration of the growth of the testes and scrotum. Slight growth of pubic hair may begin about the same time but is usually a trifle later. The spurts in height and penis growth begin about a year after the first testicular acceleration. The testicular growth is mainly due to increase in the size of the sperm-producing structures. The Leydig cells, which secrete male sex hormone, take up little space; they are present at birth but regress rapidly and from one month till puberty are few, inconspicuous, and inactive. At puberty they reappear and their full development, judged by histological criteria, is only reached late in puberty, at about the time when active sperm are being produced and the testes have reached near-adult size.

Some designation of how far a child has progressed through puberty is often required in clinical, educational, and anthropological work, and pictorial rating scales from 1 (prepubescent) to 5 for genital development in boys, breast development in girls, and pubic hair development in both sexes will be found in texts of adolescent development (e.g., Tanner, 1962, 1969). Some systems use a combination of genital and pubic hair growth for the male, but since some degree of dissociation between these two developments may occur, it is better to keep them separate. In this way also the same standards can be used for pubic hair in males and females. The size of the testes can be approximately determined by comparison with a string of standard plastic models of the same shape as the testis, known as the Prader orchidometer.

Axillary and facial hair both appear on average some two years after the beginning of pubic hair growth. There is a definite order in which the hairs of mustache and beard appear; first at the corners of the upper lip, and then over the whole upper lip, then the upper part of the cheeks and the midline below the lower lip, and finally along the sides and lower border of the chin. The remainder of the body hair appears from about the time of first axillary hair development until a considerable time after puberty. The ultimate amount of body hair an individual develops seems to depend largely on heredity, though whether because of the kinds and amounts of hormones secreted or because of the reactivity of the end-organs is not known.

Breaking of the voice occurs relatively late in adolescence; it is often a gradual process and so not suitable as a criterion of puberty. It accompanies enlargement of the larynx, caused by the action of testosterone on the laryngeal cartilages.

During adolescence the male breast undergoes changes, some temporary and some permanent. The diameter of the areola, which is equal in both sexes before puberty, increases considerably, although less than it does in girls. Representative figures are 12.5 mm before puberty, 21.5 mm in mature men, and 35.5 mm in mature women (Garn, 1952). In some boys (between a fifth and a third of most groups studied) there is a distinct enlargement of the breast about midway through adolescence. This usually regresses again after about one year.

Concomitantly with growth of the penis, and under the same influence, the prostate gland and seminal vesicles enlarge. The time of the first ejaculation of seminal fluid is to some extent culturally as well as biologically determined, but as a rule it is during adolescence and about a year after the beginning of accelerated penis growth.

The sequence of events in girls is shown in Fig. 17. The appearance of the "breast bud" (stage 2 in breast development) is as a rule the first sign of puberty in girls, though the appearance of pubic hair sometimes precedes it. The uterus and vagina develop simultaneously with the breast. As in boys, there is a large variation in the age at which the various events occur. Menarche, the first menstrual period, is a late event in the sequence. It occurs almost invariably after the peak of the height spurt has been passed.

In Fig. 18 a Gompertz curve has been fitted to the height measurements of a girl

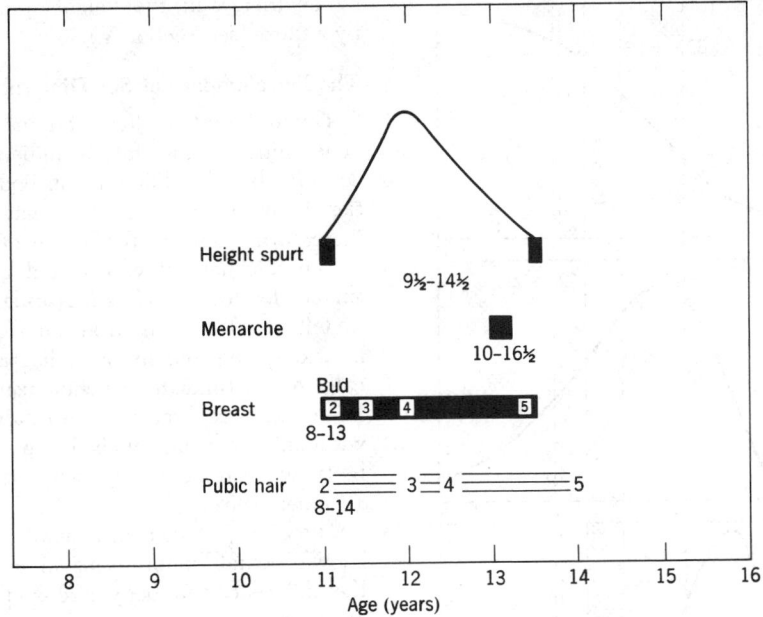

Fig. 17. Diagram of sequence of events at adolescence in girls. An average girl is represented; the range of ages within which some of the events may occur is given by the figures placed directly below them. (From Tanner, 1962.)

from 10½ to 16, and differentiated to give the smoothed velocity (middle) and acceleration (lower) curves. The acceleration begins by rising to a peak, then falls progressively, crosses the zero line at the point of maximal velocity, reaches its own maximum deceleration, and then returns to zero. B2 represents the first appearance of breast bud and B5 the time at which a more or less adult breast form was reached. The first appearance of pubic hair could not be determined since only photographs were available, but P3 and P5 give the intermediate and completed pubic hair points. Menarche is also given. This particular girl's menarche took place some seven months later than average, but its relationship with the height curve is typical. Menarche occurred at the moment when deceleration was maximal, as is usually the case. This relationship makes the point that some hormonal forces may be better reflected in acceleration rather than velocity or distance curves.

Menarche marks a definitive and probably mature stage of uterine development, but it does not usually signify the attainment of full reproductive function. The early menstrual

cycles, which in some girls are more irregular than later ones, often occur without an ovum being shed. There is frequently a period of adolescent sterility, lasting a year or 18 months after menarche. The same occurs in apes and monkeys. Similar considerations may apply to the male, but there is no reliable information on this. On average girls grow about 6 cm more after menarche, although gains of up to twice this amount may occur. The gain is practically independent of whether menarche occurs early or late.

The diagrams of Figs. 16, 17, and 18 must not be allowed to obscure the fact that children vary a good deal in the relative closeness with which the various events of puberty are linked together. At one extreme we may find a girl who has not yet menstruated, though she has reached adult breast and pubic hair ratings and is already two years past her peak height velocity; at the other we may find a girl who has passed all the stages of puberty within the space of two years. In Fig. 19 the relations between events in a series of girls in the Harpenden Growth Study are charted (Marshall and Tanner, unpublished). The variability between in-

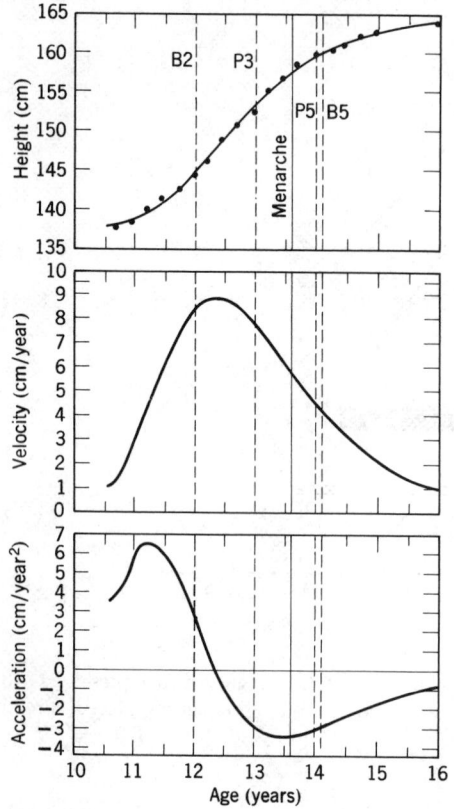

Fig. 18. Height attained, height velocity, and height acceleration curves of a girl at adolescence. B2 marks beginning of breast development, B5 adult form. P3 marks intermediate stage of pubic hair development, P5 adult form. M marks menarche. (From Tanner, 1967.)

by another, and the height spurt probably by a third (see Section V).

The Development of Sex Dimorphism

The differential effects on the growth of bone, muscle, and fat at puberty increase considerably the difference in body composition between the sexes. Boys have a greater increase not only in the length of bones but in the thickness of cortex, and girls have a smaller loss of fat. Thus it is usually possible to tell an adult man from an adult woman by examining merely a radiograph of the calf. A discriminant function using fat and bone widths separates the sexes after puberty with only 5% misclassified. But before puberty we can do barely better than chance (Tanner, 1962).

There are, of course, a number of better-known sexual dimorphisms in man. Among the differences in body size and shape the most striking ones are the man's greater stature and breadth of shoulders and the woman's wider hips. These dimorphisms are produced chiefly by the changes and timing of puberty. Boys and girls are almost the same height before puberty, but boys have a greater adolescent height spurt. Furthermore, they have two more years of pre-adolescent growth than girls; thus when their spurt

dividuals is equally marked in boys. The average boy takes about two years to pass from genital stage 2 to stage 4, but exceptional boys may take as long as five years. In both sexes the acceleration in skeletal development and the development of genitalia and breasts are rather closely linked. The growth of pubic hair is a little less closely bound up with skeletal and reproductive events (see Reynolds and Wines, 1951).

The basis for some children having loose and some tight linkages between pubertal events is not known. Probably the linkage reflects the degree of integration of various processes in the hypothalamus and the pituitary gland, for breast growth is controlled by one group of hormones, pubic hair growth

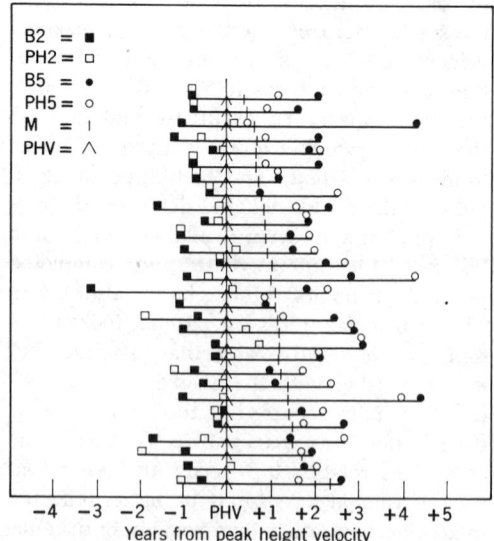

Fig. 19. Intervals between different events of puberty in a series of 29 girls. Girls are aligned by peak height velocity. (From Marshall and Tanner, unpub.)

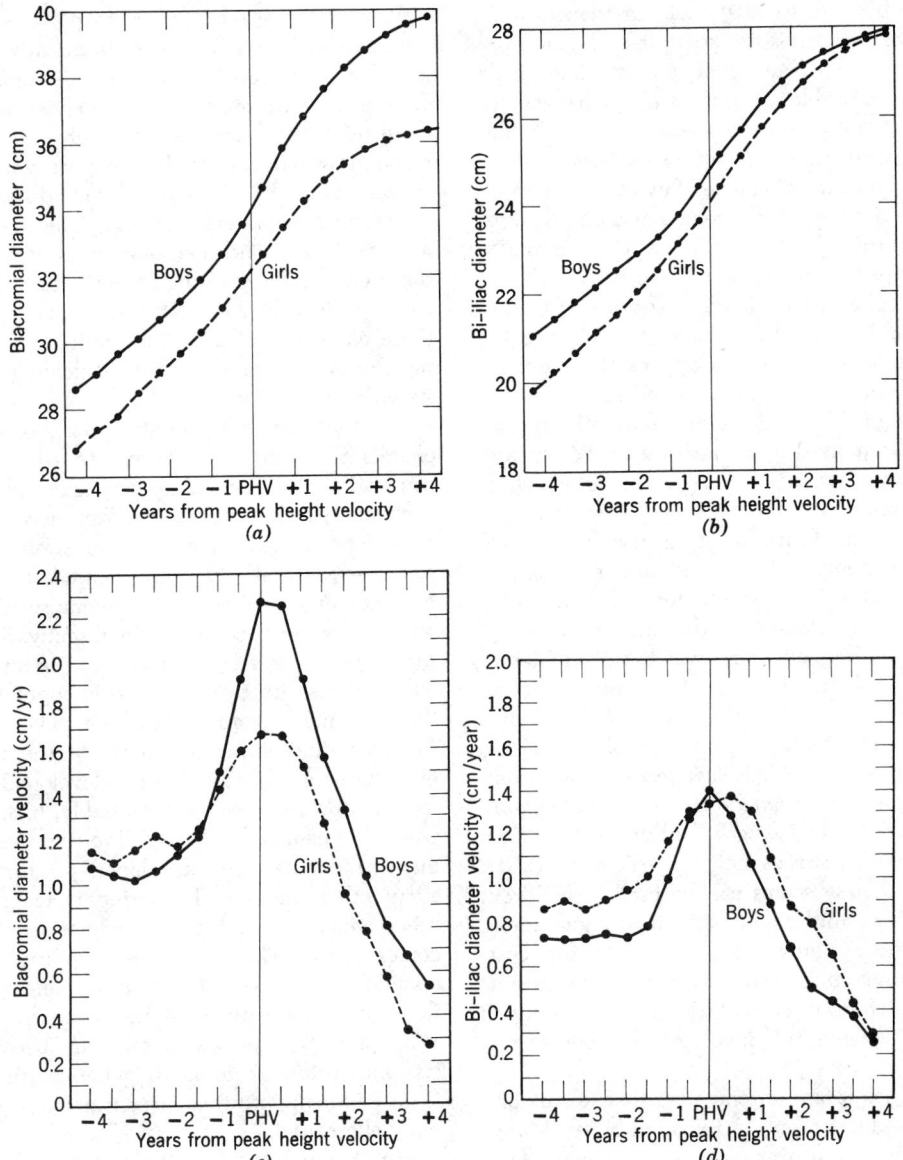

Fig. 20. Distance (*a* and *b*) and velocity (*c* and *d*) curves of shoulder width and hip breadth in boys and girls at puberty, plotted against peak height velocity "age." Mixed longitudinal data of Harpenden Growth Study.

starts they are on average about 10 cm taller than were the girls when their spurt began. This difference in tempo of growth, as Boas called it, is also to a large extent responsible for mens' legs being longer than womens' relative to their body length. During the immediately pre-adolescent years the legs are growing relatively faster than the trunk, and boys spend longer in this phase of growth.

The manner in which the shoulder/hip distinction arises is illustrated in Fig. 20. Girls have a particularly large adolescent spurt in hip width, a spurt which is quantitively as great as that of the boys' despite the girls' spurt being in most other dimensions a good deal less. The shoulder width spurt, on the other hand, is particularly marked in boys. These differences in growth occur because cartilage cells in the hip joint area of the pelvis are specialized to multiply in response to estrogens, and cartilage cells in the shoulder region are specialized to respond to androgens such as testosterone. Such specializations can be lost as well as gained during the course of evolution. In most apes and monkeys the male has a large canine tooth, suitable for fighting. This normally develops at puberty, but it can be induced to grow before then by administration of testosterone. In man the canine, though slightly bigger in the male, has apparently lost most of its ability to respond to androgens.

The shoulder-hip width dimorphism has long been used as a measure of bodily androgyny, that is, of the degree to which a male resembles a female and vice versa. A discriminant function using just these two measurements misclassifies about 10% of young adults. It has the form *3 Biacromial diam.—1 Bi-iliac diam.* and this may be used as an androgyny score which is less biased by sheer body size than the simple ratio of shoulder to hip widths. The trunk-leg difference can be taken into account also, leading to only 6% misclassification, by using the score *3 Biacromial diam.—1 Bi-iliac diam. + 0.5 Subischial length* (subischial length is stature less sitting height) (Tanner, 1951; 1962). These scores can be used in children as well as adults, but without any guarantee that the weights are appropriate for best separating pubescent boys and pubescent girls. Before puberty little discrimination is possible; separation increases as puberty progresses.

It is important to remember that sex dimorphisms do not only arise at puberty. Many dimorphisms appear much earlier. Some, like the external genital difference itself, develop during fetal life. Others develop continuously throughout the whole growth period by a sustained differential growth rate rather than a differential growth rate operating only at a particular time such as puberty. An example of this is the greater relative length and breadth of the forearm in the male when compared with whole arm length or whole body length (see Tanner, 1962; Hiernaux, 1968 for further discussion). A major dimorphism, and one which leads to others, is the difference in rate of maturing, discussed in the next section.

Part of the sex difference in pelvis shape antedates puberty. Girls at birth already have a wider pelvic outlet, that is, a wider opening at the bottom of the bony pelvis, which constitutes the narrowest part of the canal through which a baby has to pass when it is born. Thus the adaptation for child-bearing is present from a very early age. The changes at puberty are concerned more with widening the pelvic inlet and broadening the much more noticeable hips. It seems likely that these changes are more important in attracting the males' attention than in dealing with its ultimate product.

For these sex-differentiated morphological characters arising at puberty—to which we can add the corresponding physiological and perhaps psychological ones as well—are secondary sex characters in the straightforward sense that they are caused by sex hormone or sex-differential hormone secretion and serve reproductive activity directly. Some serve more directly than others, naturally. The penis is directly concerned in copulation, the mammary gland in lactation. The wide shoulders and muscular power of the male may perhaps also have been developed for use in copulation, or more probably, together with the canine teeth and brow ridges in mans' ancestors, they developed for driving away other males and insuring peace from other animals, an adaptation which soon becomes social. The dimorphism is originally maintained by sexual selection, since the fighting involves males of the same species. When this type of sexual selection becomes less important, as in man, genetical theory leads us to suppose that these traits are gradually eliminated.

But a number of traits persist, perhaps through another mechanism known to the ethologists as ritualization. In the course of evolution a morphological character or a piece of behavior may lose its original function and, becoming further elaborated, complicated, or simplified, may serve as a sign stimulus to other members of the same species, releasing behavior that is in some way advantageous to the spread or survival of the species. It requires little insight into human erotics to suppose that the shoulders, the hips and buttocks, and the breasts (at least in a number of widespread cultures) serve as releasers of mating behavior. The pubic hair (about whose function the medical textbooks have always preserved a cautious silence) probably survives as a ritualized stimulus for sexual activity, developed by simplification from the hair remaining in the inguinal and axillary regions for the infant to cling to when still transported, as in present apes and monkeys, under the mothers' body. Similar considerations may apply to axillary hair, which is associated with special apocrine glands which themselves only develop at puberty and are related histologically to scent glands in other mammals. The beard, on the other hand, may still be more frightening to other males than enticing to females.

At least ritual use in past communities suggests this is the case; but perhaps there are two sorts of beards.

IV. DEVELOPMENTAL AGE: EARLY AND LATE MATURERS

Children vary greatly in the rate at which they develop, in their tempo of growth. The effects are most dramatically seen at adolescence. In Fig. 21 are three boys all aged exactly 14.75 years and three girls all aged exactly 12.75. All are entirely normal and healthy. At ages 13, 14, and 15 in boys and 11, 12, 13 in girls there is an enormous range

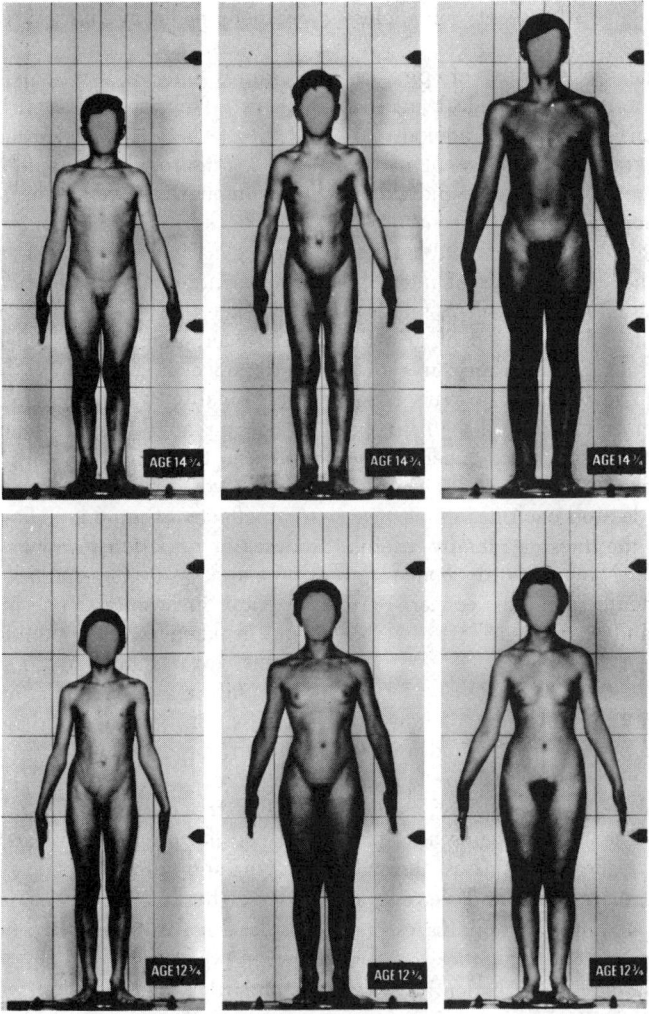

Fig. 21. Differing degrees of pubertal development at the same chronological age. Upper row three boys all aged 14.75 years. Lower row three girls all aged 12.75 years. (From Tanner, 1969.)

of development, running all the way from complete maturity to absolute pre-adolescence. The boy on the left in the figure is small, with childish muscles and no development of reproductive organs or pubic hair; the boy on the right is practically a grown man, with broad shoulders, strong muscles, adult genitalia, and a bass voice; he could easily be mistaken for a 17- or 18-year-old.

Manifestly it is ridiculous to consider all these three boys as equally grown up either physically, or, since much behavior at this age is conditioned by physical status, in their social relations. The statement that a boy is 14 is in most contexts hopelessly vague; all depends, morphologically, physiologically, and to a considerable extent sociologically too, on whether he is pre-adolescent, midadolescent or postadolescent.

Evidently some designation of physical maturity, apart from chronological age, is needed, and in this instance the obvious one would be the degree of development of the reproductive system. But the same individual differences in tempo of growth occur at all ages, even if not so obviously as at adolescence. Thus we need a measure of *developmental age* or *physiological maturity* applicable throughout the whole period of growth. There are numerous possible measures that meet this criterion in whole or in part, ranging from the number of erupted teeth to the percentage of water in muscle cells. The various developmental "age" scales do not necessarily coincide, and each has its particular use. By far the most generally useful, however, is skeletal maturity or *bone age*. Others of potentially general concern are dental maturity and shape age.

Skeletal Maturity

Skeletal maturity is a measure of how far the bones of an area have progressed toward maturity, not in size, but in shape and in their relative positions one to another, as seen in a radiograph. Each bone begins as a primary center of ossification, passes through various stages of enlargement and shaping of the ossified area, acquires in some cases one or more epiphyses, that is, other centers where ossification begins independently of the main center, and finally reaches adult form when these epiphyses fuse with the main body of the bone. All these changes can be

easily seen in a radiograph, which distinguishes the ossified area, whose calcium content renders it opaque to the X-rays, from the areas of cartilage where ossification has not yet begun. The *sequence* of changes of shape through which each of the bone centers and epiphyses pass is the same in all individuals. Skeletal maturity is judged both from the number of centers present and the stage of development of each.

In principle any or all parts of the skeleton could be used to give an assessment of skeletal maturity, but in practice the hand and wrist form the most convenient area and the one generally used. The hand is an area where a large number of bones and epiphyses develop, and an X-ray of it is easily made without exposing the remainder of the body to measurable doses of radiation. It itself requires only a very small dose of X-rays (Garn, Helmrich, Flaherty, and Silverman, 1967). This is of the order of 4 milliroentgens, a figure which should be compared with the amount received from unavoidable everyday background radiation, which is 100 milliroentgens per year at sea level rising to 300 milliroentgens at 2000 meters. There is no evidence that 4 milliroentgens does any harm whatever; indeed it would be surprising if it did, since it represents the dose obtained unavoidably by every child who spends a week on holiday in the mountains. We emphasize this now because the public is justifiably worried about the medical and genetical effects of atomic fallout and about the doses of radiation given in diagnostic radiology and, to a far greater degree, in radiotherapy in hospitals. The matter can only be put in perspective by thinking in quantitative terms; even simple diagnostic procedures in hospitals may involve a hundred times the dose of a bone-age radiograph, and radiotherapy procedures run up to a million times the dose.

For the radiograph the left hand is used, placed flat on an X-ray casette with the palm down and the tube positioned 30 inches above the knuckle of the middle finger. The skeletal maturity assessment is made by comparing the given radiograph with a set of standards. There are two ways in which this may be done. In the older, "atlas" method, the radiograph is matched successively with the standard Greulich-Pyle (1959) plates representing ages 5.0, 6.0, and so on. The age of the standard with which the radiograph most nearly coincides is recorded as the skeletal "age," interpolation between standards being made if it is thought to be justifiable. In the more recently developed "maturity points" method (see Acheson, 1966) a series of standard stages are given for each individual bone, independent of age, and each bone of the radiograph is assigned a score corresponding to the stage it has reached. The scores are mathematically weighted to produce the best overall estimate of total maturity. The scores for the individual bones are added; thus the whole hand radiograph scores a total of so many weighted maturity points. This score is then compared with the range of scores of a standard group at the same age and a percentile status is assigned, just as it would be for height. A skeletal age may also be assigned, this being simply the age at which the given score lies at the fiftieth percentile. This method is somewhat finer in gradation and easier to use than the atlas method, although it is slightly more time-consuming. The standards are those of Tanner, Whitehouse, and Healy (1962), and it must be remembered that they are based on a large random sample of Scottish urban and rural children, who are six to nine months less advanced than the North American well-off middle-class children on whom the Greulich-Pyle method was standardized. Thus the two methods do not lead to the same result in terms of bone age, unless a correction is made.

In the Greulich-Pyle standard boys and girls have a different series of plates, since the girls are more advanced. The Tanner-Whitehouse stages for each individual bone are common to both sexes, and the sequence of appearance and development of one bone relative to another in the hand is also closely similar. Hence in this method only one set of standards is used. The skeletal maturity score at any given chronological age is simply higher for girls than for boys. This is illustrated in Fig. 22, which shows the standard percentile chart for boys, with the fiftieth percentile line for girls of the same chronological age plotted upon it. The early- and late-maturing boys seen in Fig. 21 are also shown. It is noteworthy that this measure of skeletal maturity has a marked adolescent spurt. There is evidence that the hormonal control of skeletal maturation is different before and during the spurt. The maturity score can itself be used as a scale of developmental age common to boys and girls, against which hormone excretions and other functions may be plotted (Tanner, 1969).

Skeletal maturity provides a true common scale of development, which measures such as "height age," sometimes used by paediatricians, and indeed IQ fails to do. This is because every healthy individual reaches the same skeletal maturity eventually. The skeletal score represents a "per cent of maturity attained"; thus a low score for age can be unequivocally taken to signify retardation in the true sense of delay in skeletal maturing. Final adult height or final IQ, on the other hand, varies from individual to individual. For this reason height age and mental age are more closely related to final height and final IQ than to advancement/retardation. Hence height ages cannot be validly compared from one individual to another as a measure of maturity status.

Standards are available for skeletal development of the pelvis and knee and ankle, besides the hand and wrist. Indeed, at ages under 1 year the knee and ankle provide better estimates of maturity than the hand, and in work upon infants and newborns the stages described by Vincent and Hugon (1962) should be used with locally derived norms.

Dental Maturity

Dental maturity can be obtained by counting the number of teeth erupted and relating this to standard figures in much the same way as skeletal maturity. The deciduous dentition erupts from about 6 months to 2 years of age and can be used during this period. The permanent or second dentition provides a measure from about 6 to 13 years. From 2 to 6 and from 13 on little information is obtainable from the teeth by simple counting, but stages of calcification of teeth as seen in jaw radiographs can be used in just the same way as calcification in the bones of the hand and wrist.

Shape Age

As the child grows older his shape changes because different parts of the body grow at

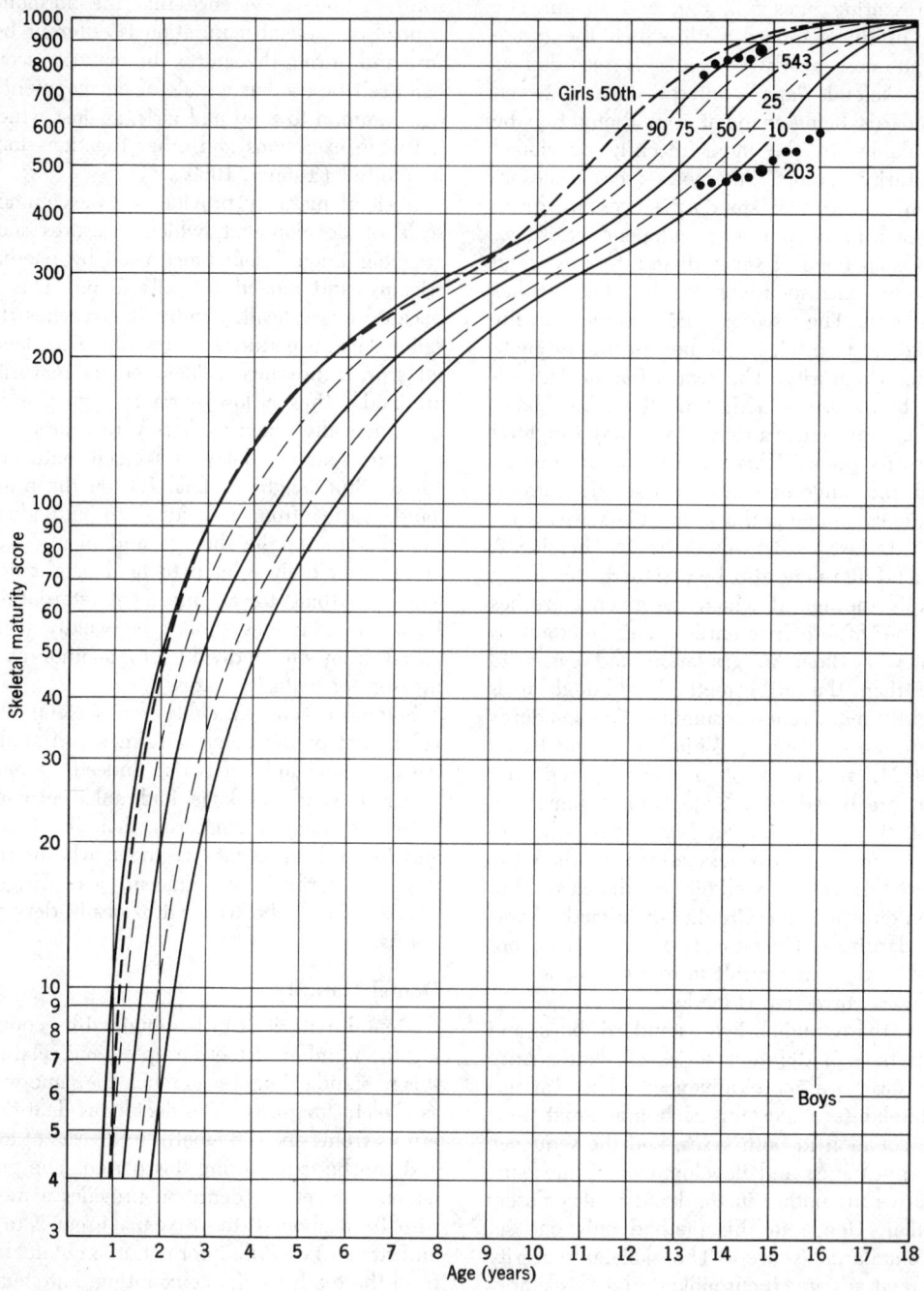

Fig. 22. Tanner-Whitehouse skeletal maturity standards for boys. Heavy dashed line shows the fiftieth percentile for girls. The dots show skeletal maturity scores from 13½ onwards of the early- and late-maturing boys represented in Fig. 21 at age 14.75. The larger dots represent the age illustrated in Fig. 21.

different rates. The legs and arms get relatively longer and the head relatively smaller, for example. In a culture where birth date is unknown a remarkably crude but reputedly effective way of judging whether a child is old enough to work, attend school, or carry out some other task is to see if he can touch his left ear with his right hand, the arm pass-

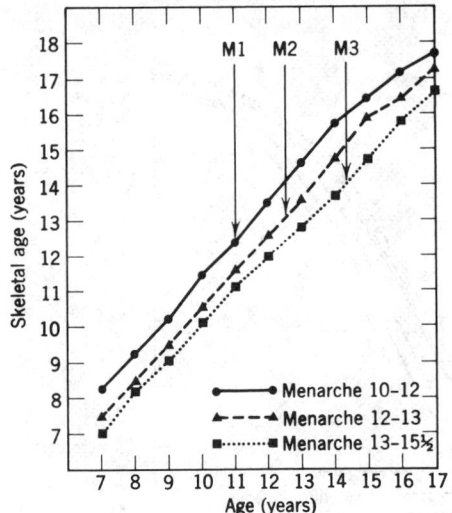

Fig. 23. Relation of skeletal maturity and age at menarche. Skeletal development ages (Todd Standards) for early-, average-, and late-menarche groups of girls, from age 7 to maturity. M1, M2, M3 represent average age of menarche for each group. Mixed longitudinal data. (From Tanner, 1962, redrawn from Simmons and Greulich, 1943.)

ing over the top of the head. In Europe it was formerly (and is sometimes actually) proposed that children should begin to attend school only when a certain "form-change" (*gestaltwandel*) has occurred and should only go on from one type of school to another at a second "form-change" (Zeller, 1952).

In principle the degree of shape change achieved could be made a measure, and a very convenient one, of developmental maturity. But it would only be useful if a measure could be devised which is independent of the final shape reached. Otherwise it would be subject to the same criticism as height age. To find such a measure is a mathematically complex and difficult task, not yet accomplished.

Relations between Different Measures of Maturity

Skeletal maturity is closely related to the age at which adolescence occurs, that is, to maturity measured by secondary sex character development. Thus the range of chronological age within which menarche may normally fall is about 10 to 16½, but the corresponding

range of skeletal age is only 12 to 14½. Evidently the physiological processes controlling progression of skeletal development are in most instances closely linked with those that initiate the events of adolescence. This is illustrated in Fig. 23. Three groups of girls are plotted; those with an early, those with a middling, and those with a late menarche. The points M1, M2, and M3 represent the average age of menarche in each group. Those with an early menarche have an advanced skeletal age, those with a late menarche a retarded skeletal age. The linkage, however, is not complete; menarche occurs at a slightly greater skeletal age in the successive groups, not at precisely the same one.

Figure 23 illustrates another important point. Children tend to be consistently advanced or retarded in maturity during their whole growth period, or at any rate after about age 3. The early-menarche girls are skeletally advanced not only at the age at which menarche takes place, but at all ages back to 7. The late-menarche group is consistently retarded. The correlation between menarcheal age and skeletal age at menarche itself is about .85, and between menarcheal age and skeletal age at chronological age 5 or 6 is about .55. The correlation becomes less the further back in growth one goes. The children's velocity curves are steeper then and they cross each other more, bringing reassortment of growth status; and the same is true of their skeletal maturity curves. By and large, however, there is a consistency in acceleration or retardation of skeletal and general bodily maturity.

Dental maturity partly shares in this general skeletal and bodily maturation. At all ages from 6 to 13 children who are advanced skeletally have on average more erupted teeth than those who are skeletally retarded. Likewise those who have an early adolescence on average erupt their teeth early, as shown in Fig. 24 (see also Garn, Lewis and Kerewsky, 1965a). Girls on average have more erupted teeth than boys of the same age.

But this relationship is not a very close one, as the figure also implies: even with only three maturity groups in each sex some crossing of the lines takes place. Quantitatively it is the relative independence of teeth and general skeletal development which should be emphasized. This is not surprising, in that the teeth are part of the head of the organism, and as

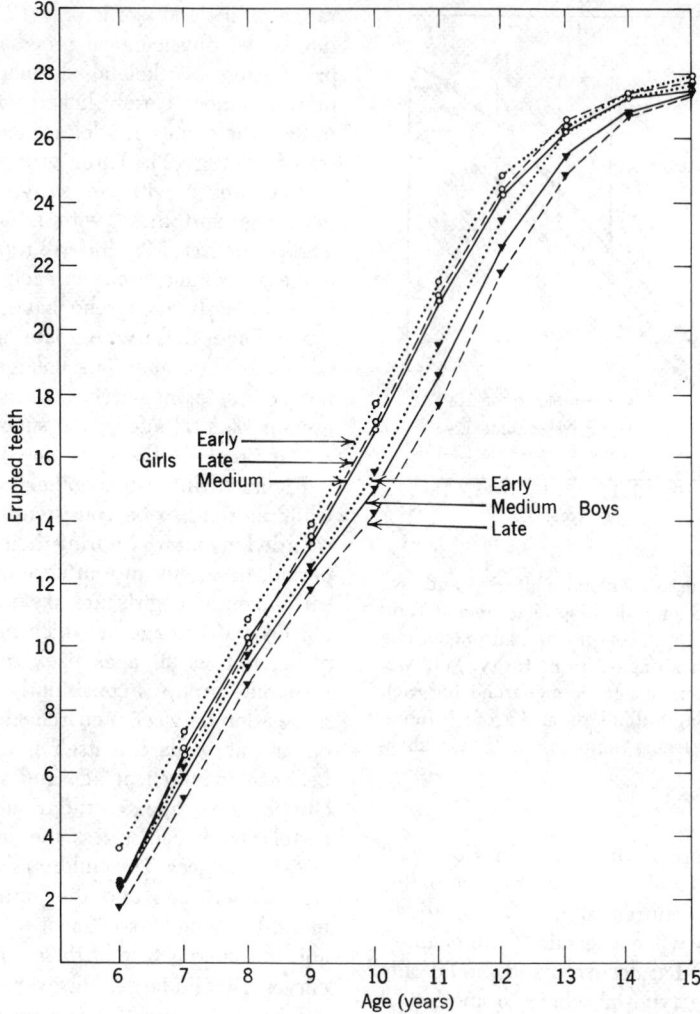

Fig. 24. Total number of erupted teeth at each age for early-, medium-, and late-maturing girls and boys. Maturity groups defined by age at peak height velocity. Mixed longitudinal data, reported longitudinally. (From Tanner, 1962, redrawn from Shuttleworth, 1939.)

we have already seen, the head is advanced over the rest of the body and for this reason its growth curve and growth control differ somewhat from the general growth curve.

Evidently there is some general factor of bodily maturity throughout growth, creating a tendency for a child to be advanced or retarded as a whole; in his skeletal ossification, in the percentage attained of his eventual size, in his permanent dentition, doubtless in his physiological reactions, and possibly in his intelligence test results also. But not too much should be made of this general factor. It should be especially noted how very limited

is the loading, so to speak, of brain growth in it. There is little justification in the facts of physical growth and development for the concept of "organismic age" in which almost wholly disparate measures of developmental maturity are lumped together.

Set under this general tendency are groups of more limited maturities, which vary independently of it and of each other. The teeth constitute two of these limited areas (primary and secondary dentition being largely independent of each other); the ossification centers another; the brain at least one more. Some of the mechanisms behind these relations can be dimly seen. In children who lack adequate thyroid gland secretion, for example, tooth eruption, skeletal development, and brain organization are all retarded; whereas in children with precocious puberty, whether due to a brain disorder or a disease of the adrenal gland, there is advancement of skeletal and genital maturity without any corresponding effect upon the teeth or, as far as we can tell, upon the progression of organization of the brain.

Sex Differences in Developmental Age

Girls are on average ahead of boys in skeletal maturity form birth till adulthood, and in dental maturity also during the whole of the permanent dentition eruption (though not, curiously, in primary dentition). It would seem therefore that the sex difference lies in the general maturity factor (as well as in various more detailed factors). Girls are usually ahead of boys in motor development also and in certain forms of aptitude tests.

The skeletal age difference begins during fetal life, the male retardation being due, probably indirectly, to the action of genes on the Y chromosome. Children with the abnormal chromosome constitution XXY (Klinefelter's syndrome) have a skeletal maturity indistinguishable from the normal XY male, and children with the chromosome constitution XO (Turner's syndrome) have skeletal maturities approximating to the normal female XX, at least until puberty. The male retardation may be established as early as the differentiation of testis or ovary, or, more probably, it may be caused by the secretion by the fetal gonads or adrenals of sex-specific hormones. At birth boys are about four weeks behind girls in skeletal age, and from then till adulthood they remain about 80% of the skeletal age of girls of the same chronological age. The percentage difference in dental age is not so great, boys being about 95% of the dental age of girls.

The sex difference is not precisely the same for all bones, nor for all teeth. There is a sex-bone and sex-tooth interaction. Thus in girls the canines erupt on average 11 months earlier than in boys, whereas the first molars erupt only two months earlier. Similar effects are seen in skeletal ossification, particularly in knee and elbow (Garn, Rohmann, and Blumenthal, 1966).

The sex difference in skeletal maturity is not confined to man but occurs in chimpanzees, gorillas, and rhesus monkeys, and in rats also. It may be characteristic of all or most mammals. Its full biological significance is not at present obvious.

Developmental Age and the Prediction of Adult Height

The age at which growth ceases is related much more closely to the age at which adolescence occurs than to chronological age. After the age of 9 the amount of growth left to occur, and hence final adult stature, can be predicted better by reference to skeletal age than to chronological age. This can sometimes be of practical educational or social importance. For example, girls usually enter the Royal Ballet School at 9 or 10 years old, and thereafter they undergo a very rigorous and specialized training and are vocationally oriented to becoming dancers. But the exigencies of the *corps de ballet* require that the dancers shall all be within certain rather narrow height limits. If a girl grows up to be too short or too tall her career may be over. We cannot as yet control the extent to which children grow —and perhaps we should not when we can— but we can at least warn on entry those whose chances of ending between the required height limits are statistically rather small. The prediction of adult height requires knowledge of chronological age, bone age, and present height. We use either the Greulich-Pyle atlas for bone age and then the Bayley-Pinneau (1952) tables, or the Tanner-Whitehouse skeletal maturity and an associated multiple regression equation. The accuracy is such that 90% of predictions from age 9 on lie within ± 1½ inches of true final height. This is rather better than predictions based on height of parents.

Physical Maturation, Mental Ability, and Emotional Development

Clearly the occurrence of tempo differences in human growth may have profound implications for educational theory and practice. This would especially be so if advancement in physical growth were linked to any significant degree with advancement in intellectual ability and in emotional maturity.

There is good evidence that in the European and North American school systems children, who are physically advanced toward maturity, score on average slightly higher in most tests of mental ability than children of the same age who are physically less mature. The difference is not great, but it is consistent and it occurs at all ages that have been studied, going back as far as 6½ years. Similarly, the intelligence test score of postmenarcheal girls is higher than the score of premenarcheal girls of the same age (see references in Tanner, 1962, 1966c). Thus in age-linked examinations physically fast-maturing children have a significantly better chance than slow-maturing children.

It is also true that physically large children score higher than small ones, at all ages from 6 on. In a random sample of all Scottish 11-year-old children, comprising 6940 pupils, the correlation between height and score in the Moray House group test was .25 ± .01, allowing for the effect of age difference from 11.0 to 11.9 (Scottish Council, 1953). An approximate conversion of these test scores to Terman-Merrill IQ leads to an average increase of .67 points for each centimeter of stature, or roughly 1½ points per inch. A similar correlation was found in London children. The effects can be very significant for individual children. In 10-year-old girls there was a 9-point difference in IQ between those whose height was above the seventy-fifth percentile and those whose height was below the fifteenth. This is two-thirds of the standard deviation of the test score.

Children with many sibs are shorter in stature and score less in intelligence tests than children with few sibs. About half of the correlation above is associated with differences in sib number; but about half remains when number of sibs is allowed for (Scott, 1962).

It was usually thought that both the relationships between test score and height and between test score and early maturing would disappear in adulthood. If the correlations represented only the effects of co-advancement both of mental ability and physical growth, this might be expected to happen. There is indeed no difference in height between early- and late-maturing boys when both have finished growing. But it is now clear that, curiously, at least part of the height-IQ correlation persists in adults (Tanner, 1966c). It is not clear in what proportion genetical and envir-

onmental factors are responsible for this (see Section VIII).

There is little doubt that being an early or a late maturer may have repercussions on behavior, and that in some children these repercussions may be considerable. There is little enough solid information on the relation between emotional and physiological development, but what there is supports the common-sense notion that emotional attitudes are clearly related to physiological events.

The world of the small boy is one where physical prowess brings prestige as well as success, where the body is very much an instrument of the person. Boys who are advanced in development, not only at puberty but before as well, are more likely than others to be leaders. Indeed this is reinforced by the fact that muscular, powerful boys on average mature earlier than others and have an early adolescent growth-spurt. The athletically built boy not only tends to dominate his fellows before puberty, but by getting an early start he is in a good position to continue that domination. The unathletic, lanky boy, unable, perhaps, to hold his own in the pre-adolescent rough and tumble, gets still further pushed to the wall at adolescence, as he sees others shoot up while he remains nearly stationary in growth. Even boys several years younger now suddenly surpass him in size and athletic skill, and perhaps, too, in social graces. Figure 25 shows the height curves of two boys, the first an early-maturing, muscular boy, the other a late-maturing, lanky one. Although both boys are of average height at age 11, and are together again at average height at age 17, the early maturer is 4 inches taller during the peak of adolescence.

The late developer at adolescence may sometimes have doubts about whether he will ever develop his body properly and whether he will be as well endowed sexually as those others he has seen developing around him. At a deeper level the lack of development may act as a trigger to reverberate fears accumulated deeper in the mind during the early years of life.

It may seem as though early maturers have things all their own way. But early maturers have their difficulties also, and particularly the girls in some societies. Though some glory in their new possessions, others are embarrassed by them. The early maturer has a longer

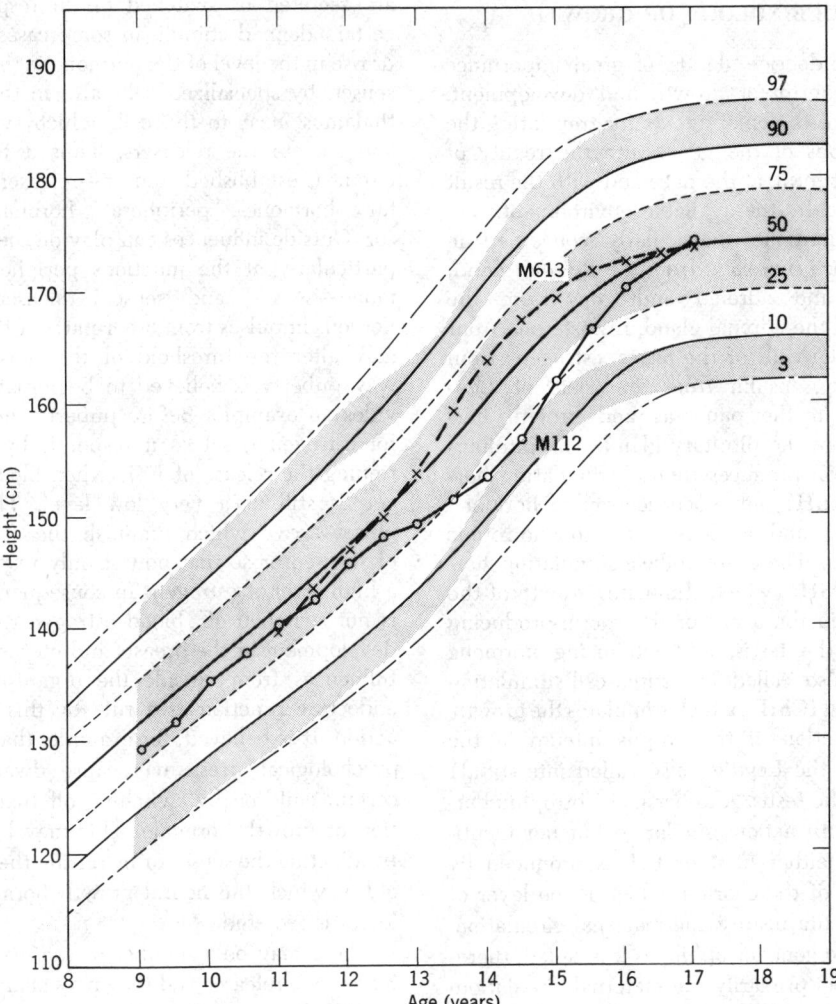

Fig. 25. Height attained from age 11 to 17 of two boys of Harpenden Growth Study, one (M613) with an early and the other (M112) with a later adolescent spurt. The plots are made against the Tanner-Whitehouse 1965 British Standards. (Redrawn from Tanner, 1961.)

period of frustration of sex drive and of drive toward independence and the establishment of vocational orientation. Studies at the University of California have given evidence of the psychological consequence of early and late maturing. Late-maturing boys showed more attention-getting behavior and were rated by their age peers and trained observers as more restless, talkative, and bossy. They were less popular and had lower social status. In contrast, the outstanding leaders came from the early-maturing group. Projective techniques revealed in the late maturers deeper feelings of inadequacy, greater anxiety, and

greater anticipation of rejection by the group. Follow-up studies in young adulthood showed that, at least in the society of the United States, the early-maturing boys became more sociable and less neurotic (Jones, 1957; Mussen and Jones, 1957 and 1958).

Little can be done to diminish the individual differences in children's tempo of growth, for they are biologically rooted and not significantly reducible by any social steps we may take. It therefore behooves all teachers, psychologists, and pediatricians to be fully aware of the facts and alert to the individual problems they raise.

V. ENDOCRINOLOGY OF GROWTH

The endocrine glands, of great importance in the control of growth and development, are one of the chief agents for translating the instructions of the genes into the reality of the adult form, at the pace and with the result permitted by the available environment.

The hormones particularly concerned in growth are thyroxine from the thyroid gland, cortisol and adrenal androgens from the cortex of the adrenal gland, testosterone from the Leydig cells of the testes, estrogens from the ovary, insulin from the islets of Langerhans in the pancreas and growth hormone from the pituitary gland. The pituitary in addition produces thyroid-stimulating hormone (TSH), adrenocorticotrophic hormone (ACTH), and at least two gonadotrophic hormones. These are follicle-stimulating hormone (FSH), which stimulates growth of the follicles in the ovary or the sperm-producing cells in the testis, and luteinizing hormone (LH), also called interstitial-cell-stimulating hormone (ICSH), which stimulates the growth and secretion of the corpus luteum in the ovary or the Leydig (also called interstitial) cells in the testis. Another gonadotrophic hormone, with actions similar to but not identical with either FSH or LH, is produced by the cells of the chorion, which is the layer of the placenta nearest the maternal circulation. Chorionic gonadotrophin, as it is called, therefore enters primarily the maternal circulation. Lactogenic hormone, produced by the pituitary and necessary for lactation (also called prolactin) is very similar to growth hormone. Some animals have also a pituitary mammogenic hormone, essential for development of the mammary glands.

Control of Endocrine Secretions

Most endocrine glands secrete their hormones in response to the stimulus of an activating hormone from the pituitary gland. Thus thyroxine is secreted in response to pituitary thyroid-stimulating hormone, cortisol in response to adrenocorticotrophic hormone, and so on. The pituitary hormones are themselves secreted in response to the arrival of releaser substances originating in nearby areas of the brain, chiefly the median eminence of the hypothalamus. The releaser substances, in turn, are secreted or switched off in response to certain defined stimuli, in some cases a drop or rise in the level of the hormone in the blood, sensed by specialized cells also in the hypothalamus, near to the cells which synthesize and secrete the releasers. Thus a feedback circuit is established: sensor—releaser—pituitary hormone—"peripheral" hormone—sensor. Outside influences can play on the circuit, particularly at the junctions peripheral hormone—sensor, and sensor—releaser. Thus nervous impulses from other parts of the brain may alter the threshold of the sensor. The way puberty is believed to be initiated provides an example. Before puberty the sensor for estrogen is set so it responds by discontinuing the release of FSH when blood estrogen is still at a very low level. Then impulses arrive which diminish the sensitivity of the sensor so that now it only responds to a high level of estrogen. In consequence FSH is not switched off, blood estrogen rises, and development of the breasts and uterus occurs. Influences from outside the organism affect endocrine function as a rule by this type of action. It is believed, for example, that severe psychological stress may cause dwarfism in certain children by switching off their secretion of growth hormone. This may be either by affecting the sensor or by raising the threshold at which the neural growth hormone releaser is secreted.

There may be a number of sensors all acting on one releaser and they may change their relative importance at different times of life or under different circumstances. Thus there is probably one sensor for growth hormone releaser which responds to a drop in blood sugar and another which responds to a rise in certain amino acids; one may be more important in fetal life and another in childhood. Certainly there are many sensors of which we are still ignorant; and probably there are some releasers and even some pituitary hormones (e.g., the stimulus to adrenal androgen secretion at puberty) that are still unknown.

Some hormones are released usually or sometimes without the full circuit being involved. There is good evidence that a rise in the level of blood thyroxine is sensed usually directly at the pituitary level, switching off the secretion of TSH immediately, rather than at the level of the hypothalamus.

Prenatal Period

Most of the endocrine glands begin to function relatively early in fetal life and are clearly of importance in the healthy development of the fetus. However, the immense technical difficulty of investigating endocrine function at this time of life has so far precluded much detailed knowledge of the situation in the human. For several hormones we do not even know to what extent the fetus, at various ages, has itself to secrete the compound and to what extent it can rely on transfer across the placenta of the hormone secreted by the mother.

We have very little knowledge about the maturation of the hypothalamus-pituitary feedback system in the fetus. For one thing, we are grossly ignorant of the development of the human hypothalamus in terms of histochemistry, ultrastructure, and even conventional cytology. Neurosecretory material, presumed to be releasing substances, is first seen at about 20 weeks postmenstrual age in the nerve cells near the capillary loops of the hypophysial-portal system of blood vessels which carry the releasers from brain to pituitary. Thus it appears that this part of the system starts to function about halfway through pregnancy (Raiha and Hjelt, 1957). Various hormones are present in the pituitary gland before this, but we cannot take their presense to imply they are secreted, only that they are synthesized.

Thyroid hormone (thyroxine) is necessary for the normal development of the brain. It begins to be secreted by the fetal pituitary around the fifteenth to twentieth postmenstrual week, probably under the stimulus of TSH from the fetal pituitary. Maternal TSH does not cross the placenta, and maternal thyroid hormone does so only in insignificantly small amounts (French and van Wyke, 1964). Thyroid hormone affects protein synthesis in the brain of the fetus and the very young child. As the brain matures this action diminishes. In the absence of adequate thyroid hormone, the nerve cell bodies and their dendrites and axons are all reduced in size; the dendrites branch less and the connectivity (see Section VI) is decreased (Eayrs, 1964). These changes are irreversible if they persist for very long.

The adrenal gland in the human fetus consists of the inner medulla and the function-ally and structurally quite different outer cortex, as in the adult. But the cortex in the fetus differs in appearance, and presumably in function, from the adult cortex. There is a special fetal zone of cells, constituting 80% of the cortex, lying between the medulla and the outer 20% of cells, which resemble the adult tissue. This "fetal cortex" grows steadily from about 12 postmenstrual weeks till birth or a little before, when it atrophies rapidly, the weight of the two adrenals falling from around 6 gm at birth to around 3 gm a month later. There is no appreciable sex difference. The fetal cortex is not incorporated into the permanent cortex, which develops separately, for the most part after the fetal cortex has disappeared. The fetal cortex is characteristic of primates, it seems, though a somewhat analogous zone arises about 2 weeks after birth in mice. It is not yet clear whether ACTH from the fetal pituitary is the factor responsible for its growth in man or whether chorionic gonadotrophin is the stimulus (Lauritzen and Lehmann, 1967). Nor is it clear what causes it to secrete whatever it does secrete. Fetal ACTH secretion is itself probably caused by the secretion of corticotrophin-releasing factor (CRF) by the hypothalamus (see Jost, 1966).

In the adult the adrenal cortex secretes mainly three groups of hormones.

1. *Mineralocorticoids.* Aldosterone and to a lesser extent 11-deoxy-corticosterone, which maintain within acceptable limits the concentrations of sodium and potassium in the tissue fluids, are thus essential to life. The secretion is not controlled by a pituitary hormone but directly by alterations in blood volume and composition.

2. *Glucocorticoids (or Corticoids).* Cortisol and to a lesser extent corticosterone, which increase the formation of glucose from protein, and have an antiinflammatory or antistress action. Their secretion rate is raised in response to the stress of infection, extreme exercise, or severe emotion. The administration of cortisol, or its near relative cortisone, to a person whose pituitary is destroyed is essential if they are to lead anything approaching a normal life. The secretion is controlled by a feedback running through the hypothalamus and involving CRF; a shorter feedback of cortisol acting directly on the pituitary to

inhibit ACTH secretion may also occur. The role of cortisol in normal growth is not known; at normally encountered levels it may have little effect. But excess amounts of cortisol or cortisol-like substances (cortisone, prednisone, etc.) either secreted in response to chronic stress, or given by a pediatrician for intractable asthma or other disease, have a powerful growth-retarding effect. This is manifested by small size and delayed bone age. It appears to represent a direct effect on cellular metabolism.

3. *Androgens.*   Dehydroepiandrosterone (DHA), DHA sulphate, 11β-hydroxyandrosterone, and, in smaller quantities, androstenedione are secreted by the adrenal. In peripheral blood the main substances found are DHA sulphate and androsterone sulphate. In urine the adrenal androgens are excreted as a number of substances collectively known as 17-oxosteroids (formerly 17-ketosteroids). Their function is apparently to cause some of the changes of puberty (discussed later) and perhaps to maintain some secondary sex characters, including muscle bulk. The stimulus to their production is not clear; ACTH does stimulate their secretion a little, but not to the extent it stimulates cortisol production. Lack of androgens is not fatal.

Whether the special fetal cortex secretes any of these substances is doubtful. It may perhaps secrete androgens, since blood levels of these are high for the first few days after birth, and at birth the level in the umbilical cord is above that in the mother's blood, signifying production by the fetus. Corticoids, on the other hand, are low for the first three days after birth in both blood and urine, with maternal levels above umbilical cord ones; so these are virtually ruled out as the fetal cortex product. One theory is that the fetal cortex produces DHA, which is metabolized into estrogens in the placenta, this being the source of the very high levels of estrogen found in the pregnant woman. The evidence for this, in part, is that mothers carrying anencephalic fetuses (who lack most of their brain and have usually only small adrenal cortices) have low levels of estrogens. Apart from this, other substances may be produced by the fetal cortex, since newborns excrete a number of steroid metabolic products not seen in children or adults.

This subject has some importance in view of work during the last few years on the behavioral and endocrine effects of stimulating (originally "gentling") rats in the neonatal period. Rats who have been stimulated by handling or other means during the first few days after birth are said to show less "emotional" behavior in an open field test when adult than do unstimulated rats. They are also said to have a higher level of blood corticosterone (the chief corticoid in rats) during infancy. The idea behind this work is that a high level of corticosterone early in infancy may act to organize some area of the brain concerned with later emotional reactivity, in the same way as testosterone in the rat neonate organizes the hypothalamus in relation to later sexual activity (discussed later). But even in the rat the endocrine situation is confused at present, and transference of these results to the human has as yet no justification, particularly in view of the very considerable endocrinological and growth differences between the two species. The rat is born very much earlier in its progress to adulthood than the human, so that the first five or six days after birth in the rat correspond developmentally to somewhere in the fourth and fifth intrauterine months in the human. It would indeed be of great interest to know whether differences in stimuli reaching the human fetus affected its endorine function in a manner that might affect, in turn, its brain development. But our ignorance about this is at present complete.

Growth hormone is secreted by the pituitary gland from about the tenth postmenstrual week. The fetal blood level, as estimated by radio-immunoassay, increases to reach a peak at about 25 to 30 weeks and appears to become less again by the time of birth. The levels are much higher than those seen in children or adults, and this would correspond with the very high fetal growth rate between 20 and 34 weeks. The chorion secretes a growth-hormone-prolactin-like substance also, but this circulates only in the maternal blood and does not apparently cross to any great extent into the fetus (Kaplan and Grumbach, 1967).

Gonadal Hormones and Sexual Differentiation

The action of genes on the Y chromosome causes the previously undifferentiated gonad to become recognizably a testis at the ninth week of fetal age reckoned postmenstrually (or the seventh week postfertilization). Whether this is the result of hormonal action is at present uncertain. At about the eleventh postmenstrual week Leydig cells appear in the testis and increase rapidly in number until about the twenty-fourth week, after which time their absolute volume remains constant till birth, though the percentage of the whole testis they occupy declines considerably. The Leydig cells secrete testosterone or a closely related substance, and this causes the previously undifferentiated external genitalia progressively to form a penis and scrotum, beginning at the twelfth postmenstrual week (Jirasek, 1967; Niemi, Ikonen, and Hervonen, 1967). Very probably the initial growth and secretion of the Leydig cells is caused by the great increase in secretion of chorionic gonadotrophin early in pregnancy. The excretion of this substance in the mother's urine reaches its peak about the tenth to twelfth postmenstrual week (where its presence is used as the basis for pregnancy tests). Chorionic gonadotrophin drops to fairly low levels by 18 weeks and it is therefore conjectured that LH from the fetal pituitary may be responsible for sustaining the Leydig cells from this age on.

In the female, differentiation of the ovary and external genitalia proceeds, it seems, more passively. In the absence of the Y chromosome, nothing happens at the ninth week and at about the tenth postmenstrual week the gonad turns into an ovary. The external genitalia become female at around the fourteenth week, apparently without hormonal intervention.

There is another aspect of this sexual differentiation, so far studied only in animals, but of much importance in man in principle and perhaps in practice too. In the rat the Leydig cell secretion acts on the brain as well as on the external genitalia. In all mammals investigated endocrinological and to a large extent behavioral maleness is dependent on the structure of the hypothalamus. If a female pituitary is grafted into an adult male whose own pituitary has been removed, then, when vascular connections with the hypothalamus have been established, the pituitary will secrete gonadotrophic hormones in a male, not a female cycle. The converse is also true.

In the rat, differentiation of the hypothalamus is caused by testosterone secreted by the Leydig cells during the first two or three days after birth. This is a true critical or sensitive period. Testosterone given a few days before birth will not cause brain differentiation, nor will testosterone given from five days after birth on to a rat whose testes were removed at birth. The message has to reach the hypothalamus at exactly the right time. A single injection of female sex hormone on the fifth day after birth will stop the proper male differentiation, and a single injection of testosterone into a female on the fifth day will produce the "androgen-sterilized female," a rat without female reproductive cycles when it becomes adult. It is known that some areas of the brain selectively take up testosterone. These must include areas concerned in sexual behavior as well as in control of gonadotrophin releaser. Female rats given testosterone neonatally do not show any sexual female behavior when adult, even though ovariectomized and given estrogen-progesterone replacement therapy so that their sex-hormone state is that of a normal female. If ovariectomized and given testosterone, however, they behave as males. Neonatal administration of estrogen to male rats also causes disruption of adult male sexual behavior, even when testosterone replacement is given to the adult, but this is not as complete as in the case of the female (Harris and Levine, 1965). Thus, just as in the case of the external genitalia, the female central nervous system differentiates passively shortly after birth; the male is actively organized by the secretion of the testes.

It is already clear that the rat is not an exception among mammals in this respect. To what extent and with what timing an analogous situation holds in man is not yet known. Birth in the rat corresponds probably to about the twentieth to twenty-fifth week postmenstrual age in man, though since man seems to develop Leydig cells relatively earlier than other mammals investigated, perhaps we should think in terms of about the fifteenth to twentieth week. This would in fact correspond well with fetal testosterone secretion. Whether this work has significance for human sexual behavior patterns is not known, but it would be strange if it failed to do so. It may be that certain forms of homosexuality (assuredly not all forms) may be caused by a disturbance of intrauterine processes of this sort.

Birth to Adolescence

Differences between individuals in tempo of growth are probably mostly due to small differences in rates of secretion of hormones, themselves caused, perhaps, by differences in the setting of feedback mechanisms in the brain. Which hormones are concerned with which developmental clocks, we do not know. The smallness of the postulated hormonal differences between children is such that we could not estimate them reliably by our present chemical techniques. The general tempo may perhaps be related to differences in thyroid hormone secretion. Differences in adrenal androgen secretion may in whole or part cause the differences in skeletal maturation, but here also the levels with which such a hypothesis is concerned are below those accessible to our present methods.

The rate of secretion of *thyroid hormone* appears to drop gradually during the first two years and then remain practically constant till adolescence. So far as rate of growth is concerned, the action of the thyroid is permissive, not controlling. In hypothyroidism in childhood growth is delayed; skeletal maturity, dental maturity, and growth of the brain are all affected.

The mineralocorticoid secretion of the adrenal changes little during chidhood, and the cortisol secretion rate rises gradually in proportion to the increase in body size. The secretion of androgenic adrenal hormones remains at a very low level until puberty. The response of the adrenals to ACTH however, in terms of secretion of both cortisol (chiefly) and androgens, is much the same in the child as in the adult, when differences in body size are taken into account.

The Leydig cells disappear almost entirely after birth and can hardly be identified again until puberty. The secretion of testosterone ceases or is very low, and the secretion of estrogens is also at a very low level.

Growth hormone secretion continues, perhaps decreasing slightly from its level after birth, although this is not certain. Growth hormone is not secreted continuously, but only in response to a number of stimuli such as a rapid lowering of blood sugar, a rise in certain amino acids in the blood, physical exercise, or emotion. Thus special test situations have to be created for its estimation; and some of these preclude the use of healthy subjects. Our knowledge is thus fragmentary.

Endocrinology of Adolescence

At adolescence considerable changes in hormone secretion occur. The testes and ovaries, the adrenal and thyroid glands have an adolescent growth spurt in weight. The anterior pituitary also has a spurt, but more in girls than boys. Before puberty there is little if any sex difference in pituitary weight; after, girls have a distinctly larger pituitary, with a higher proportion of acidophil cells, probably secreting lactogenic hormone.

The first event in the sequence of puberty, immediately preceding the morphological changes, is an increased secretion of gonadotrophic hormones by the pituitary. The cells which secrete gonadotrophins cannot be seen in the pituitary before puberty in children, and bio-assay of glands also indicates that human and monkey pituitaries store very little follicle-stimulating or luteinizing hormone before puberty. This is in sharp contrast to the situation in rats, where gonadotrophin content reaches its maximum about 20 days after birth and subsequently falls until puberty, which occurs around 40 to 50 days after birth (Donovan and van der Werff ten Bosch, 1965). This is an important warning that in matters of growth and sexual development we must not be too ready to generalize from rodents to man; primates as a group differ considerably from other mammals in their patterns of growth (see Tanner, 1962, p. 233).

The rising level of FSH causes the follicles of the ovaries and the tubules of the testis to develop. Probably the rise in LH causes the Leydig cells of the testis to develop and to secrete testosterone, which in turn is responsible for many of the specifically male aspects of adolescence.

In both boys and girls there is a low and roughly constant excretion of estrogen from about 3 to 7 years, followed by a gradual rise in both sexes. As adolescence begins in girls, usually with the development of the breast bud, estrogen excretion rises very sharply and becomes cyclic (for literature see Tanner, 1969). The values reached during the cycle continue to increase until several years after menarche. In boys there is also a rise in estrogen excretion, occurring midway through puberty, at stages 3 or 4, (out of 5) of genitalia and pubic hair development. The levels reached are, naturally, much lower than in girls. Small amounts of estrogen continue to be excreted in adult men. They probably come chiefly from the adrenal cortex and from the metabolism of other steroid hormones.

In boys the secretion of testosterone greatly increases at puberty. In this instance we already know something of the mechanism concerned, thanks to Lindner's (1961) work on Leydig cell secretion in the bull. This mechanism has general importance, in that it probably characterizes many developmental sequences. In the spermatic vein of the prepuberal calf there is a considerable amount of androstenedione, a precursor of testosterone, but very little testosterone itself. Androstenedione has only a very weak androgenic action. At puberty the ratio of the two substances in spermatic vein blood is changed; in adult animals testosterone greatly predominates. The interesting thing is that injection of chorionic gonadotrophin (the nearest approach available to the natural stimulus, LH, at the time of the experiments) does not cause a conversion of androstenedione to testosterone, but merely an increase in androstenedione secretion. Only after puberty does gonadotrophin cause an increased testosterone secretion. Thus at puberty the Leydig cell acquires the capacity to convert androstenedione to testosterone; and this is by an increase in the amount of the enzyme 17β-hydroxysteroid dehydrogenase (as has been shown in the rat by Inano, Hori, and Tamaoki, 1967). Women evidently lack the mechanism for making this change, either because it can only happen in the Leydig cell, which they do not possess, or because the activator of the enzyme is missing, perhaps for chromosomal reasons.

Adrenocortical Hormones. Two out of the three major groups of adrenocortical hormones circulate in the blood at relatively unchanged levels from birth on: these are cortisol and aldosterone. The excretion of cortisol metabolites increases in keeping with the increase of body size, but it has no particular spurt beyond this at adolescence.

The secretion of adrenal androgenic hormones, on the other hand, increases greatly at puberty, in both boys and girls. Before puberty very little DHA or DHA sulphate can be demonstrated in blood or urine. The androgen metabolites in the urine, that is the 17-oxosteroids, increase sharply at about the time the height spurt begins. This occurs in both sexes, but in boys the 17-oxosteroids reach a level about one and a half times that in girls. The sex difference is probably entirely due to the fact that testosterone is also partly metabolized to 17-oxosteroids so that the boys' levels include both adrenal and testicular androgen metabolites. It seems likely that the adrenal contribution is fairly similar in both sexes. At least seven distinct substances are excreted, however, and it is not known whether men and women differ in the relative proportion of each that they excrete.

The cause of the increase in androgen secretion is far from clear. ACTH cannot be responsible, for it always causes a much greater increase in corticoid than in androgen secretion, yet the corticoids rise only slightly at puberty. Either some still unknown pituitary hormone is concerned ("adrenarche hormone") or else something modifies the response of the adrenal to ACTH at this time (see Tanner, 1962). This adrenal component of adolescence is sometimes referred to as "adrenarche." This should really read "androgen-adrenarche" since only the androgen function of the adrenal is concerned.

These adrenal androgens are clearly important in bringing about some of the changes of puberty, particularly in girls, in whom they cause growth of the pubic and axillary hair. Occasionally children are seen in whom pubic and sometimes axillary hair develops very early, before the occurrence of other signs of sexual maturity. The patients are mostly girls and a high proportion have brain damage. Bone maturation is advanced and the patients are large. The condition is known as "premature adrenarche" or "premature pubarche" and is associated with levels of 17-oxosteroid excretion characteristic of late adolescents. The disorder probably represents an isolated release of the hypothetical "adrenarche hormone."

The differential growth of hair at pubes, axilla, and face seems most easily explicable on the basis of locally different thresholds to stimulation, coupled perhaps with a predilection of hair at each site for either testicular or adrenal hormone. On this hypothesis, the skin of the pubes has the lowest threshold and responds to the small amount of adrenal androgen secreted by both girls and boys early in puberty. Axillary hair has a higher threshold, develops later and is somewhat more responsive to testosterone; the beard has a still higher threshold to adrenal androgens and a more pronounced preference for testosterone. This is probably an oversimplified view; a sequence of changes in hair follicle receptivity may also occur.

The cause of the adolescent growth spurt in body size is not yet known. The excess of the male over the female spurt is probably due to testosterone, as is the excess of male muscle and bone development. The rest of the spurt, common to both sexes, must be due to an increase in growth hormone secretion or to the adrenal androgens or to a combination of both. The part played by growth hormone at adolescence is not yet clear, but it should become so in the next few years, now that methods for its estimation are reliable.

Much is still uncertain about the endocrinology of adolescence. The synergies of hormone action are exceedingly complicated, the technical methods are complex and costly, and the absolutely essential longitudinal studies on hormonal production have not yet been attempted. Further details of what is known in this field can be found elsewhere (Tanner, 1969; Tanner and Gupta, 1968).

The Initiation of Puberty

The manner in which puberty is initiated has a general importance for the clarification of developmental mechanisms. Certain children develop all the changes of puberty, up to and including spermatogenesis and ovulation, at a very early age, either as the result of a brain lesion or as an isolated developmental, sometimes genetic, defect. The youngest mother on record was such a case, and gave birth to a full-term healthy infant by Caesarian section at the age of 5 years 8 months. The existence of precocious puberty and the results of accidental ingestion by small children of male or female sex hormones indicate that breasts, uterus and penis will respond to hormonal stimulation long before puberty. Evidently an increased end-organ sensitivity plays little or no part in pubertal events.

The signal to start the sequence of events is given by the brain, not the pituitary. Just as the brain holds the information on sex, so it holds information on maturity. The pituitary of a newborn rat successfully grafted in place of an adult pituitary begins at once to function in an adult fashion, and does not have to wait till its normal age of maturation has been reached (Harris and Jacobsohn, 1952). It is the hypothalamus, not the pituitary, which has to mature before puberty begins.

Maturation, however, does not come out of the blue and at least in rats a little more is known about this mechanism. In these animals small amounts of sex hormones circulate from the time of birth, and these appear to inhibit the prepubertal hypothalamus from producing gonadotrophin releasers. At puberty it is supposed that the hypothalamic cells become less sensitive to sex hormones. The small amount of sex hormones circulating then fails to inhibit the hypothalamus, gonadotrophins are released, and the level of sex hormones rises until the same feedback circuit is re-established, but now at a higher level of gonadotrophins and sex hormones. The sex hormones are now high enough to stimulate the growth of secondary sex characters and support mating behavior (Donovan and van der Werff ten Bosch, 1965).

The idea of a single feedback system operating at two different levels is very attractive, since it links with other developmental notions, and makes the evolution of the delay in primate puberty easier to comprehend. So far, however, it has been shown to be true only in rodents, although there are a few bits of supporting evidence from human pathology.

The basic change in hypothalamic receptivity at puberty remains unexplained. It may be itself a consequence of change in afferent input, though from where is not known.

VI. GROWTH AND DEVELOPMENT OF THE BRAIN

We know all too little about the growth of the brain and the development of its organization. Anatomical studies of brain structure are immensely laborious and few workers have had the courage, persistence, and technical support needed to carry out morphological analyses of the brains of children at different ages. Physiological studies are practically confined to the electroencephalogram and biochemical investigations have scarcely begun. In the last decade, however, interest has greatly increased, and mapping of the concentrations and activities of chemical substances at various stages of development has begun in animals.

Gross Morphological Development

From early fetal life the brain, in terms of its gross weight, is nearer to its adult value than any other organ of the body, except perhaps the eye. In this sense it develops earlier than the rest of the body (see Fig. 6). At birth it averages about 25% of its adult weight, at 6 months nearly 50%, at 2½ years about 75%, at 5 years 90%, and at 10 years 95%. This contrasts with the weight of the whole body, which at birth is about 5% of the young adult weight, and at 10 years about 50%.

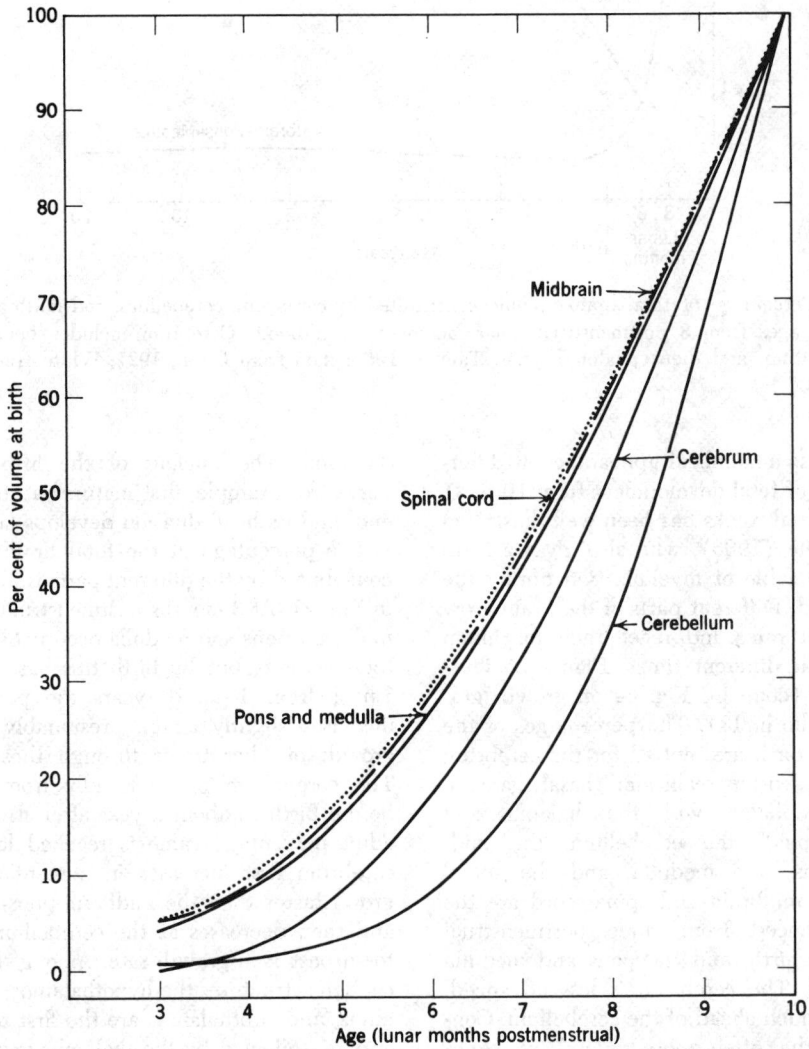

Fig. 26. Percentage of their volume at birth reached at earlier months by parts of the brain and spinal cord. Cerebrum includes hemispheres, corpus striatum, and diencephalon. (From Tanner, 1961, data from Dunn, 1921.)

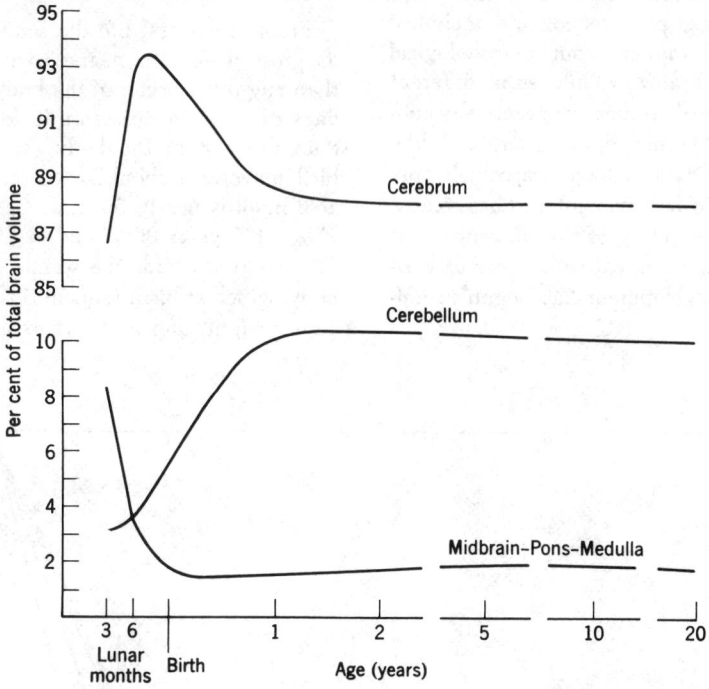

Fig. 27. Percentage of total brain volume contributed by cerebrum, cerebellum, and midbrain-pons-medulla at ages from 3 postmenstrual lunar months to adulthood. Cerebrum includes hemispheres, corpus striatum, and diencephalon. (From Tanner, 1961; data from Dunn, 1921, White House Conference, 1933.)

The gross anatomical appearance at different stages of fetal development from 10 to 41 postmenstrual weeks has been well illustrated by Larroche (1966), who also gives a comprehensive table of myelinization during the fetal period. Different parts of the brain grow at different rates and reach their maximum velocities at different times. Figure 26 illustrates this (compare Fig. 34 on growth gradients in the limbs). The percentages of the volume at birth are plotted for the cerebrum (including corpus callosum, basal ganglia, and diencephalon, with the thalamus and hypothalamus), the cerebellum, the midbrain, pons, and medulla, and the spinal cord. The midbrain and spinal cord are the most advanced from three postmenstrual months to birth, and the pons and medulla come next. The cerebrum is less advanced, although much ahead of the cerebellum. Contrary to the often-quoted "law" of cephalocaudad or head-to-tail development, the development of the central nervous system structures is more usually in a caudocranial

direction. The nucleus of the fifth cranial nerve, for example, first matures at its caudal end, and its head division develops later.

The percentage of the total brain volume contributed by the different parts is illustrated in Fig. 27. At 3 months postmenstrual age the midbrain pons and medulla occupy 8% of the total volume, but by birth this has fallen to 1.5%; from 1 to 10 years the percentage increases slightly again, presumably due to growth of fiber tracts through those areas. The cerebellum grows rapidly from shortly before birth to about a year after it; thus its adult percentage value is reached late. The cerebrum first increases in percentage as it grows faster than the midbrain-pons-medulla and then decreases as the cerebellum comes to surpass it in growth rate. Among the diencephalic structures the hypothalamus, epithalamus, and subthalamus are the first to differentiate, followed by the thalamus and corpus striatum. The thalamus and hypothalamus together constitute 10% of brain volume at 3 postmenstrual months and 3% at birth; the corpus striatum also constitutes 10% at 3 months and falls to about 5% at birth (Jenkins, 1921; Dekaban, 1954). These parts of the brain reach their maximum velocity of growth at about 2 months, the cerebral hemispheres at about 3 months, and the cerebellum at about 6 months.

Cerebral Cortex Development

Most of our knowledge about the development of the structure of the cerebral cortex is due to the enormously painstaking studies of Conel (1939, 1941, 1947, 1951, 1955, 1959, 1963), who published analyses of a small number of children at birth, 1 month, 3 months, 6 months, 15 months, 2 years, and 4 years. Rabinowicz (1967) has similarly described the 36-week premature. Further histological data for the prenatal period are given in Larroche (1966).

The cerebral cortex is identifiable at about 8 weeks; thereafter it gradually increases in width, at first uniformly, but by about 20 weeks it is increasing to different degrees in different parts (Klosovskii, 1963). By about 26 postmenstrual weeks most of the cortex shows the typical structure of six somewhat indeterminate layers of nerve-cells, with a layer of fibers on the inside. The layers do not advance in maturity simultaneously; the cells of the fifth layer are the most advanced up to birth and for a little time beyond, followed in order by those of the sixth, third, fourth, and second (Rabinowicz, 1967). All the nerve cells present in the adult are thought to be formed during the first 20 or 30 postmenstrual weeks. Thereafter, it is said, the cells differentiate, axons and dendrites grow, nucleoprotein appears in the cytoplasm, and the axons acquire varying amounts of myelin as sheaths; but no new cells are formed. This view has lately been challenged, although only to the extent of supposing that a small number of new nerve cells may appear. Neuroglia, the cells of the supporting tissue, may differentiate for somewhat longer. Neuroglia outnumber neurones after the early period of development, and they eventually constitute some 90% of the cells present in the brain.

From these cellular changes a series of criteria for maturation of parts of the cortex can be developed, in just the same way as the criteria for skeletal maturity are developed from a consideration of the appearances of the bones. Conel uses nine criteria, including the "density" of neurones (i.e., the number of neurones per unit volume of cortex), which decreases as axons and dendrites grow in between them; size of neurones, which increases; condition of Nissl substance and neurofibrils; length of axons and dendrites; and degree of myelination.

Two clear gradients of development occur during the first two years after birth. The first concerns the order in which general functional

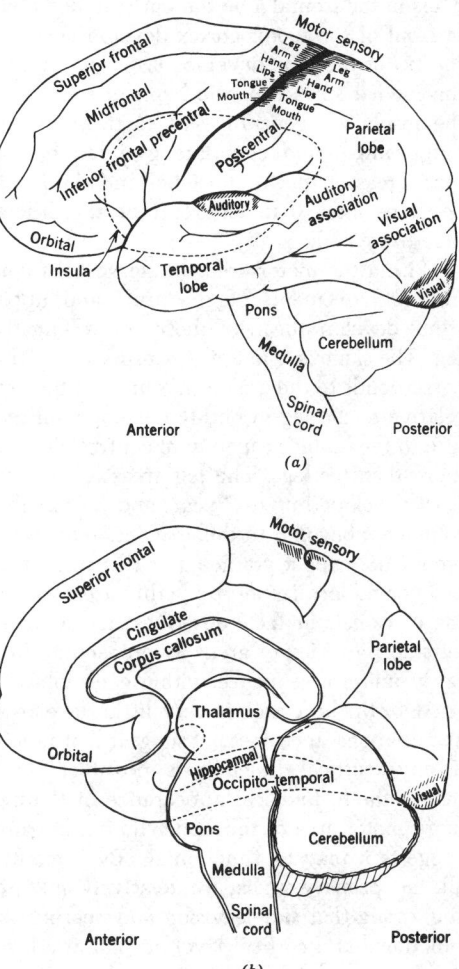

Fig. 28. Lateral and medial views of brain, to show divisions of cerebral cortex, areas of localization of function, and location of thalamus, cerebellum, pons, medulla, and spinal cord. (a) Lateral view of cortex. (b) Medial view of cortex and subcortical structures. (From Tanner, 1961, after various maps, including Penfield and Rasmussen, 1950.)

areas of the brain develop, the second the order in which bodily localizations advance within the areas. The most advanced part of the cortex is the primary motor area located in the precentral gyrus (see Fig. 28). Next comes the primary sensory area in the postcentral gyrus; then the primary visual area in the occipital lobe; then the primary auditory area in the temporal lobe. All the association areas lag behind the corresponding primary ones. Gradually the waves of development spread out, as it were, from the primary areas. Thus in the frontal lobe the parts immediately in front of the motor cortex develop next and the tip of the lobe develops last. The gyri on the medial surface of the hemisphere and in the insula are generally last to develop; the hippocampal and cingulate gyri lag behind most areas of the frontal lobe; and the insula develops later than any part of the frontal lobe examined.

Within the motor area the nerve cells controlling movements of the arms and upper trunk develop ahead of those controlling the leg. The same is true in the sensory area. This corresponds to the greater maturity of the arm relative to the leg in bodily development and also to the infant's capacity to control his arms more than his legs. The leg areas remain the least developed up to 2 years and presumably somewhat beyond. In the association areas we would not expect gradients of this sort, since little or no localization by bodily areas occurs there. Conel, in fact, describes development outside the primary areas as proceeding in a fairly uniform sequence within each lobe.

At birth the cortex is very little developed and its appearance does not suggest that much, if any, cortical function is possible. By 1 month the histological appearance of the primary motor area of the upper limb and trunk suggests it may be functioning. By 3 months all the primary areas are relatively mature, suggesting that simple vision and hearing are functional at a cortical level but not at a level involving any interpretive functions dependent upon the association areas. At this age the motor area is clearly the most advanced part of the cortex, and within it the hand, arm, and upper trunk are the most advanced parts.

By 6 months most areas have advanced further and many of the exogenous fibers coming to the cortex have become myelinated, although few association fibers within the cortex are yet mature. There has been a particularly rapid development in the part of the cortex controlling eye movement. Between 6 and 15 months the rate of development is greatest in the temporal lobe and in the cingulate and insula, next greatest in the occipital, and least in the parietal and frontal lobes, which have already passed through most of their course. The primary motor area is still slightly in advance of all the others but within it the leg still remains behind the rest. The child's behavior reflects this; he is beginning to control his hands and arms quite well, but he controls his legs less successfully. Many children are unable to walk at 15 months and few do so skillfully. The visual association area has matured somewhat and is ahead of the auditory. By 2 years the primary sensory area has caught up the primary motor, and the association areas have developed further. But some areas, most notably the hippocampal and cingulate gyri and particularly the insula, are still clearly immature.

During this period from birth to 4 years and presumably for some time after, there is a continuous increase in the number and size of dendrites in all layers of the cortex, and in the number and complexity both of exogenous fibers from lower in the brain, and in association fibers within and between cortical areas. The "connectivity" (i.e., the probability of one cell influencing others through its connections with them) increases, and this is clearly of paramount importance to the exercise of the more complicated brain functions.

It is clear from the studies on myelination by Yakovlev and Lecours (1967) that the brain goes on developing in the same sequential fashion at least till adolescence and perhaps into adult life. Myelination of nerve fibers is only one sign of maturity, and fibers can and perhaps sometimes do conduct impulses before they are myelinated. But the information from myelin studies agrees well with Conel's information on nerve cell appearances where the two overlap. As a rule the fibers carrying impulses to specific cortical areas myelinate at the same time as those carrying impulses away from these areas to the periphery: thus maturation occurs in arcs or functional units as we might expect rather than in geographical areas (Anokhin, 1964).

A number of tracts have not completed their

myelination even three or four years after birth. The fibers which link the cerebellum to the cerebral cortex and which are necessary to the fine control of voluntary movement only begin to myelinate after birth and do not have their full complement of myelin till about age 4. The reticular formation, a part of the brain especially developed in primates and man and concerned with the maintenance of attention and consciousness, continues to myelinate at least until puberty and perhaps beyond. Myelination is similarly prolonged in parts of the forebrain near the midline. Yakovlev suggests this is related to the protracted development of behavioral patterns concerned with metabolic, visceral, and hormonal activities during reproductive life.

Throughout brain growth from early fetal life the appearance of function is closely related to maturation in structure. It is of much interest that fibers of the sound-receiving system ("the acoustic analyzer") begin to myelinate as early as the sixth fetal month, but they complete the process very gradually, continuing until the fourth year. In contrast, the fibers of the light-receiving system or optic analyzer begin to myelinate only just before birth but then complete the process very rapidly. Yakovlev points out that in fetal life the sounds of the functioning of maternal viscera are the chief sensory stimuli, apart from anti-gravity sensation. They are evidently not perceived at a cortical level; but at a subcortical one the analyzer is working. After birth, however, visual stimuli rapidly come to predominate, for man is primarily a visual animal. These signals are very soon admitted to the cortex; the cortical end of the optic analyzer myelinates in the first few months after birth. The cortical end of the acoustic analyzer, on the other hand, myelinates slowly, in a tempo probably linked with the development of language.

There is clearly no reason to suppose that the link between maturation of structure and appearance of function suddenly ceases at age 6 or 10 or 13. On the contrary, there is every reason to believe that the higher intellectual abilities also appear only when maturation of certain structures or cell assemblies, widespread in location throughout the cortex, is complete. Dendrites, even millions of them, occupy little space, and very considerable increases in connectivity could occur within the limits of a total weight increase of a few per cent. The stages of mental functioning described by Piaget and others have many of the characteristics of developing brain or body structures and the emergence of one stage after another is very likely dependent on (i.e., limited by) progressive maturation and organization of the cortex.

Influences on Brain Development

To what extent environmental stimulation can influence brain maturation or organization is not clear. Cajal, the great pioneer of brain histology, believed simply that use of a cell caused axons and dendrites to grow or, in modern terms, increased its connectivity. Hebb thinks the same; but there is little experimental evidence yet to support their view. Many aspects of brain maturation seem quite unaffected by variations of environmental input within the range of what we consider normal environments. Thus prematurely born children in most respects develop quite in parallel with children of the same postfertilization age growing in the uterus (see Section II), at least till the normal time of birth. Premature babies (excluding those born prematurely by reason of some severe defect) become able to stand and to walk no sooner by being exposed to the stimuli of the outside environment longer. Calculated from birth, one series of prematures reached these milestones later than babies born at term, but calculated more correctly from fertilization, they reached them at just the same time (Douglas, 1956).

This is not to say by any means that maturation of the brain is unaffected by any outside conditions. Certain states, such as malnutrition or the presence of toxic substances, can certainly affect neural growth, if they are extreme. Conel remarks that at all ages some infants' brains were more myelinated than others, and that this was general over the whole cortex and not confined to any one area. He remarks also that several of the infants with the least myelin for their age had a malnourished appearance. To what extent malnutrition can in fact retard or abolish brain maturation in man is still a matter for research. It is certainly true that brain growth, both in man and experimental animals, is less affected than body growth by malnutrition at any postnatal period. This is largely because the brain completes such a relatively higher proportion of its growth *in utero*. But to say it is less affected is not to imply it is not affected at all. In rats malnutrition certainly causes delay in brain maturation, as does lack of thyroid hormone (Eayrs and Horn, 1955; Eayrs and Lishman, 1955).

More specific environmental factors may also be important at particular times. For the human, our ignorance in this regard is complete. In some animals, however, certain neural cells seem clearly to need an environmental stimulus for maturation to occur properly. The visual system of the kitten provides an example (Hubel and Wiesel, 1963; Wiessel and Hubel, 1963). Normally a kitten opens its eyes about 8 days after birth and at this time its visual system appears to be fully functional. But if its eyes are stitched closed from before the usual opening time until 3 months, then the cells of the lateral geniculate nucleus atrophy, or at least fail to develop normally. It seems that the experience of light (not form) is necessary to put the finishing touches to these cells, or to prevent their falling back into an atrophy of disuse. Once they have experienced light, however, they can thereafter go on without it, at least for a considerable time, for stitching the eyes of adult cats for several months leaves the cells intact.

Probably each species of animal differs in the amount and nature of input from the environment required for full development of its nervous system. The environment must be relied upon to provide the right stimulus at the right time. In this sense animals are born into "expected" environments—indeed, into "required" ones. What precisely are the requirements for the human neonate we do not know. There is no doubt that in the brain associations of nerve cells, diffuse in location but linked in function, are built up progressively during the course of growth. These cell assemblies must be presumed to have a high degree of stability, though the groupings of the particular cells constituting them may change. It seems probable, but at present wholly unproven, that optimal size and permanence of an assembly is secured by giving it particular stimulation at a particular time. It seems likely, too, that assemblies built early in childhood are under most circumstances more resistant to decay or change

than later-built ones. We have no answer to the all-important question of what happens to the cell assemblies if we attempt to teach something too soon, or, conversely, if we delay teaching something too long, so that a new neural organization is starved of exercise.

Motor Development: Wetting and Walking

The development of the brain is reflected no less in motor behavior than in increasing intellectual ability. In the early years the ability to carry out motor acts is the most important guide to the child's mental development.

The sequence of motor development during infancy has been dealt with elsewhere in this book. Detailed description of the development of late motor skills is beyond the scope of this book (see Ministry of Education, 1952, for aged 5 to 11; see also Clarke and Wickens, 1962; Glasgow and Kruse, 1960). Changes in muscle size and strength at adolescence have been described in Section III. There remain a few points to be made.

Sphincter Control. In the newborn baby micturition is a reflex act, which follows handling or other nonspecific stimuli or the taking of a meal. Babies may be conditioned very early to empty the bladder when placed on a pot, but voluntary control only appears at 15 to 18 months. The first stage is when the child is aware of the imminent passage of urine and tells the mother, but too late. A little later he tells her in sufficient time for the pot to be brought. It seems that sensory development at the cortical level is as important as motor control; indeed for a much longer period the child may forget to go to the toilet when occupied with a new toy or in some absorbing play.

Most children are dry by day by 18 months, but some, although perfectly normal, not until 3 years. At night about 50% of children are dry by age 2, and about 75% by age 3. By age 5 only 90% are dry, the remaining 10% wetting the bed occasionally or regularly throughout childhood. As in most motor developments girls on average mature earlier than boys, and in a large national survey in Britain it was found that bed-wetting after age 5 occurred in 12.1% of boys but only 9.7% of girls, a highly significant difference (Pringle, Butler, and Davie, 1966). The percentage of children who wet during the day after age 3 was the same, however, in boys (4.4%) and girls 4.3%), suggesting that the girls' advantage occurs under circumstances where conscious control is not operating.

Walking. The way in which the ability to walk develops has been described and illustrated in detail by McGraw (1943). At first the child develops inhibitory control over the reflex neonatal movements of the legs, then he makes stamping leg movements when supported, then deliberate forward steps when supported, then independent steps but with the arms widely extended, feet far apart, and knees flexed. Only when these developments are completed does the child walk with heel-toe progression, and still later with the arms swinging synchronously with the legs.

In the series of longitudinal studies in Brussels, London, Paris, Stockholm, and Zurich, coordinated by the International Children's Center, the mothers were asked at what age their child first walked a few steps without support. Since they were interrogated when the children were 9 months, 12 months, 18 months, 2 years, and 3 years, they were not called on to remember over a period of longer than 6 months. The age of walking, defined in this way, was distributed normally when age was expressed in logs, but not otherwise (Hindley et al., 1966). No social class differences were found, nor were any sex differences, in any of the five samples. But the means of the samples differed significantly; the Stockholm children walked at an average of 12.5 months and the Paris children at 13.8 months with the others intermediate. The range of normal variation of this event is about 10 months to about 19 months. At least this is so for Europeans, but East African children and probably Negro children in general have considerably accelerated motor development; in Uganda many children were able to walk alone by 9 months (Geber and Dean, 1964).

VII. THE ORGANIZATION OF THE GROWTH PROCESS

The growth of the child is a very regular and very organized process. The potential structure of the adult organism is, for the most part, contained in the highly condensed codescript of the genes. For this reason identical twins resemble each other very closely in appearance. They are not, however, absolutely the same. During the long and complex process which intervenes between the primary chemical action of the genes and the finished adult form there are many opportunities for slight deviations to occur.

When the single egg divides to give identical twins, it is unlikely that exactly equal amounts of cytoplasm go to each half. It is therefore unlikely that exactly the same concentration of chemical reactants will be formed in the two organisms. During subsequent development these differences could become progressively multiplied. Then, as growth continues, the two organisms are affected differently by the environment, for their positions in the uterus and their blood supplies are never quite the same. Finally, after birth, even under favorable circumstances of upbringing the two children are never identical in their total environment, for their food habits are never quite the same, their illness experiences never precisely similar. Yet uniovular twins do, in fact, greatly resemble each other. Their similarity, not their difference, requires an explanation.

Regulation of Growth; Canalization and Catch-Up

It is thought that the processes of growth are self-stabilizing, or, to take another analogy, "target-seeking." Children, no less than rockets, have their trajectories, governed by the control systems of their genetical constitution and powered by energy absorbed from the natural environment. Deflect the child from its growth trajectory by acute malnutrition or illness, and a restoring force develops so that as soon as the missing food is supplied or the illness terminated the child catches up toward its original curve. When it gets there, it slows down again to adjust its path onto the old trajectory once more.

It used to be thought that this self-correcting and goal-seeking capacity was a very special property of living things. We now realize that complex inanimate systems consisting of many interacting substances frequently show this capacity, especially if they are "open," that is, in continuous interaction with surrounding systems.

The property of returning to the original growth curve after being pushed off trajectory has been called *canalization* or *homeorhesis* by Waddington (1957). (Homeostasis is the maintenance of a static situation and homeorhesis the maintenance of a flowing or developing one.)

The growth in height of a healthy, well-nourished child was illustrated in Fig. 2. Figure 29 shows the effect on the growth of a young child of two periods in which food intake was much reduced for psychological reasons. The distance curve is shown in Fig. 29a; the velocity curve in part b. When food intake is restored to normal there is a period of what is called catch-up growth. The velocity during each period of catch-up reaches more than twice the average velocity for the chronological age. In this instance the catch-up is probably complete in that the child is

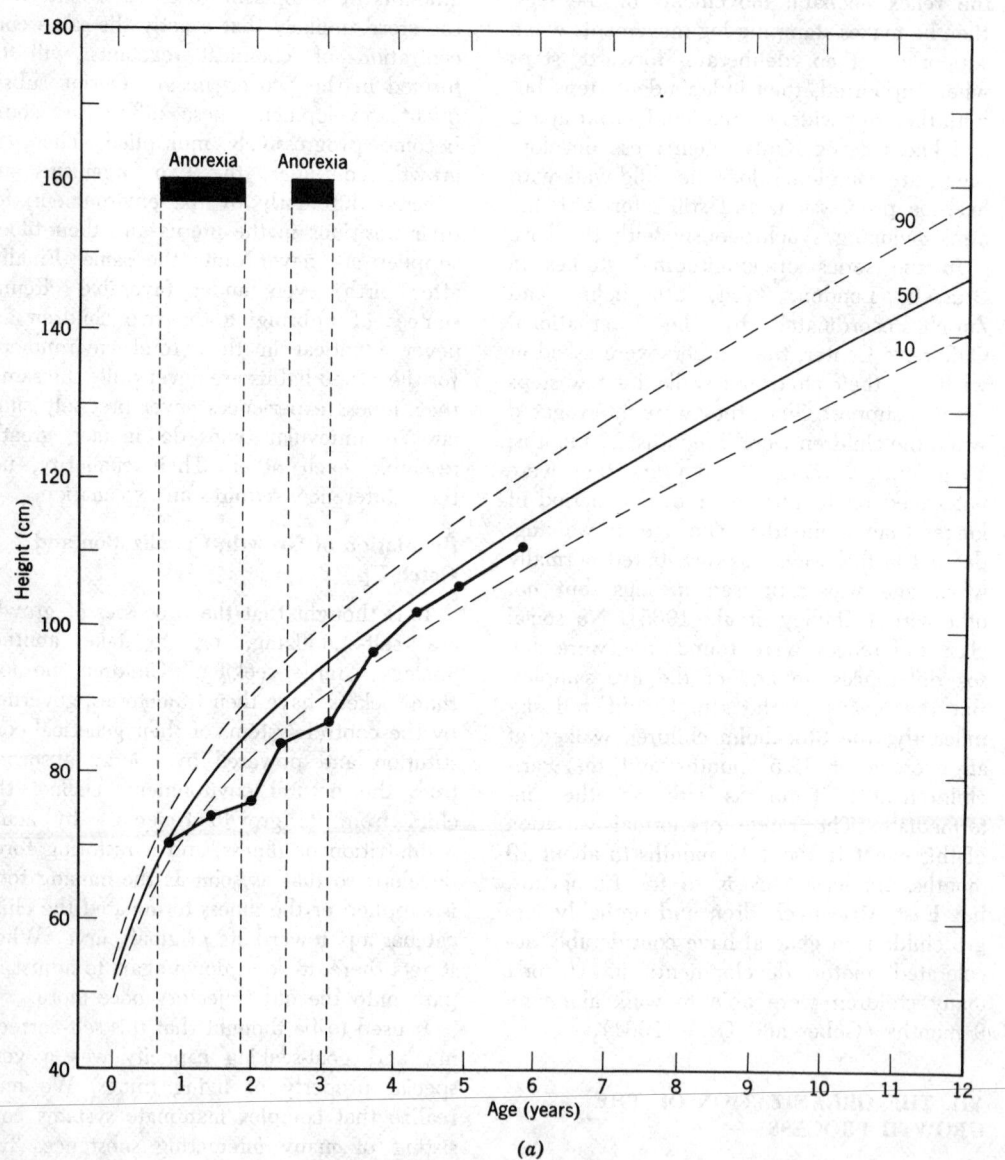

Fig. 29. Two periods of catch-up growth following episodes of anorexia nervosa in a young child. For explanation of charts, see text. (From Prader, Tanner, and von Harnack, 1963.)

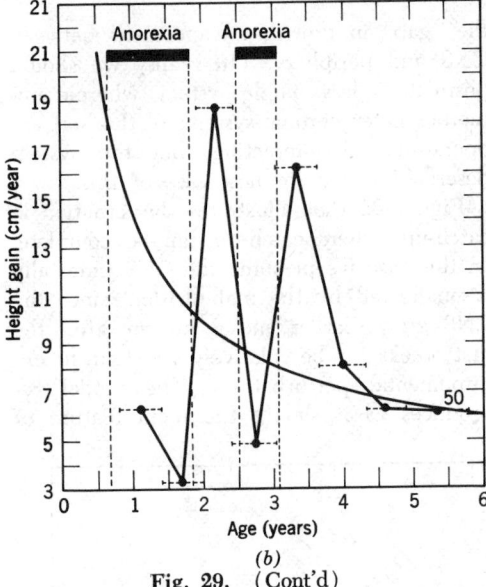

(b)

Fig. 29. (Cont'd)

quite normal in length and velocity of length by age 5. [The allied term "compensatory growth" is normally used to refer to growth of organs or parts rather than to the whole animal and describes a different phenomenon. Thus when one kidney is removed, the other undergoes compensatory growth or hypertrophy; when a limb of an amphibian is removed, it, or something similar, may grow again and this also may be called compensatory growth (see Goss, 1964).]

Figure 30 shows a second instance of catch-up, this time following removal of an adrenal tumor which had been secreting excessive quantities of cortisol (Cushing's syndrome). By age 4 the child was very small, but when the tumor was removed a remarkable catch-up ensued. At age 11, however, the child had only reached the twentieth percentile for height, so perhaps her regulatory forces had been insufficient to make good the effects of her long period of growth retardation.

The mechanism of canalization is at present very little understood. Females are better canalized than males, in respect of most characters, in man and all other mammals that have been investigated. Thus girls slow their growth less in response to malnutrition or disease than boys (see Tanner, 1962, p. 127). We have no direct evidence on the extent of canalization in brain growth or in the development of mental abilities. However,

there seems every reason to suppose the principle applies here also, particularly at the time when the brain is developing rapidly. The fact that girls trisomic for chromosome 21 have higher IQs than trisomic boys may be an example of better female canalization of brain development in a situation of chemical stress. Heterozygotes seem also to be better canalized in respect to a number of stresses than homozygotes, to judge by the evidence from inbred strains of animals.

The earlier and the more prolonged the stress, the more difficult it is for regulation to be fully effective in restoring the prestress situation. Rats may be malnourished from birth till 21 days by being placed in an overnumerous litter so that the mother's milk is insufficient. At weaning (21 days postbirth) they are smaller than well-fed rats. If after weaning they are allowed unlimited access to food, they do show a catch-up, but it is insufficient to bring them up to the size of the well-fed rats; they remain small throughout their lives (Widdowson and McCance, 1960). If, in contrast, rats are malnourished from 21 days to 77 days and then fed without restriction, a complete catch-up in weight occurs by 133 days in females and a very nearly complete one in males (Widdowson, Mavor, and McCance, 1964). Once again it must be remembered that the rat is born very early compared with the human, and the human equivalent to the rat suckling-period starvation is starvation *in utero*. It is indeed true that babies born at 40 weeks with an abnormally low birth weight and length fail to catch up after birth and remain small throughout their lives (see Section II).

The evidence leads us to suppose that it is both the duration of the malnutrition and the magnitude of the normal rate of growth at the time the malnutrition is applied that determine whether a full catch-up is possible. If true, this means that the critical factor is the *amount* of unsatisfied growth potential accumulated. Presumably this must be a real substance or state of the organism, and for this and other reasons, I have proposed a hypothetical mechanism for growth regulation (Tanner, 1963). The main points of the mechanism are illustrated in Figs. 31, 32, and 33.

The supposition is that in the normally

developing central nervous system a substance accumulates, or some cells mature, in a manner which traces out the brain's growth curve. This is called the "time tally" in Fig. 31, but in reality the tally will not signal clock time, of course, but the maturation tempo for each individual. Suppose further that body growth is also represented by some substance, called in Fig. 31 "inhibitor," at present wholly hypothetical both as to nature and provenance. The normal velocity of growth may then be thought to be proportional to the "mismatch" (M in Fig. 31) between these two signals; in other words, to

the "gap" in growth advancement between CNS and periphery. (In reality we should postulate a less simple system, wherein numerous heterochronic systems of this sort are operating, all interacting, but the system described is the simplest case of this.)

Figure 32 then illustrates the situation in catch-up, where catch-up can be complete. In this case we presume the CNS time tally is unaffected by the malnutrition, since the CNS grows earlier and is known, after the first weeks, to be relatively resistant to environmental perturbations. The model reproduces as it should the main feature of

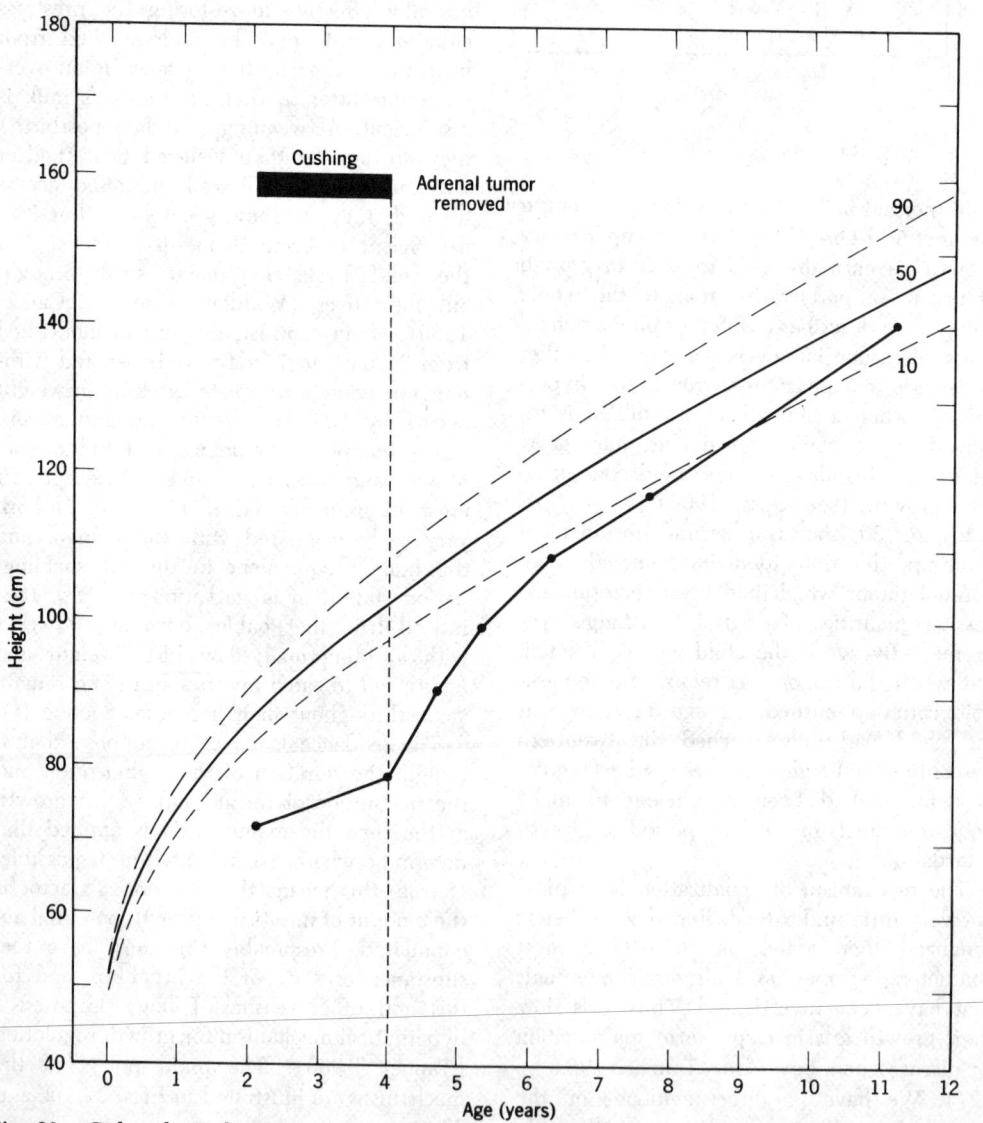

Fig. 30. Girl with Cushing's syndrome showing catch-up after removal of adrenal tumor at age 4. For explanation of charts, see text. (From Prader, Tanner, and von Harnack, 1963.)

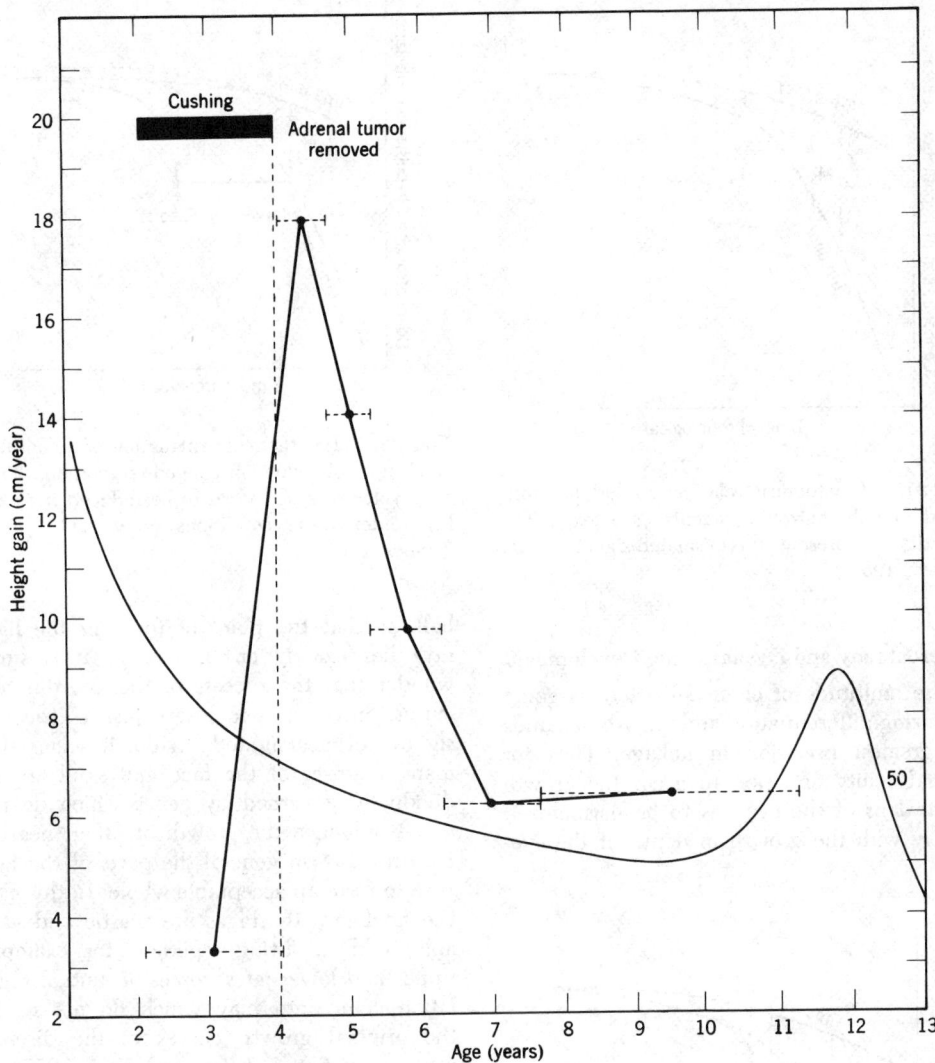

Fig. 30. (Cont'd)

catch-up, that is, the greater-than-normal growth velocity, since the mismatch (M_2) at refeeding is greater than the mismatch when starvation began.

If, however, starvation occurs at a time when the brain is still developing, the situation illustrated in Fig. 33 may result. Here the time tally itself is affected, though less than the general bodily growth. On refeeding a complete catch-up will not occur, since the "sizostat" has been reset. The model reproduces the threshold feature of complete catch-up described above; the faster the CNS

(or, more accurately, the area concerned with the time tally) is growing and the longer the starvation occurs, the more the sizostat gets "bent" and the less complete is the catch-up.

This is only a hypothetical model, and it may prove to be an erroneous one so far as size regulation goes. But it is a general model of the interaction of heterochronic processes and as such has a considerable importance for the understanding of dysharmonic growth processes and for the special case of sensitive or critical periods.

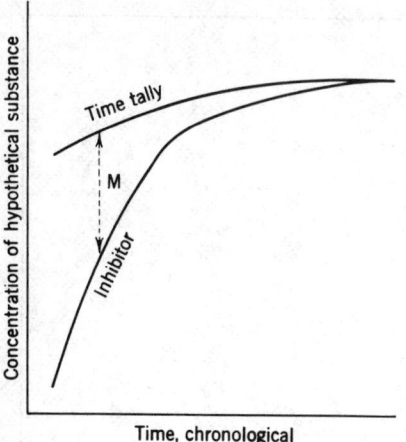

Fig. 31.   Hypothetical relations underlying supposed growth-controlling agents (see text). The quantity M represents the mismatch signal. (From Tanner, 1963.)

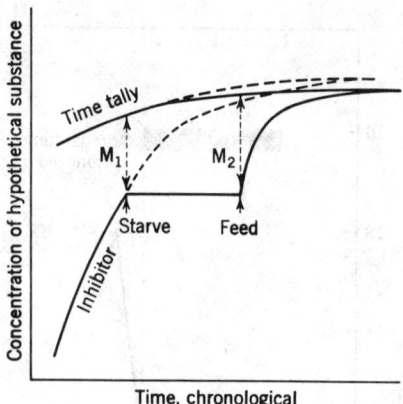

Fig. 33.   Hypothetical explanation of incomplete catch-up following prolonged starvation. Time tally velocity is supposed to be reduced irreversibly under these conditions (see text). (From Tanner, 1963.)

Heterochrony and Dysharmonic Development

The multitude of chemical reactions going on during differentiation and growth demands the greatest precision in linkage. Thus for normal acuity of vision to occur the growth of the lens of the eye has to be harmonized closely with the growth in depth of the eye-

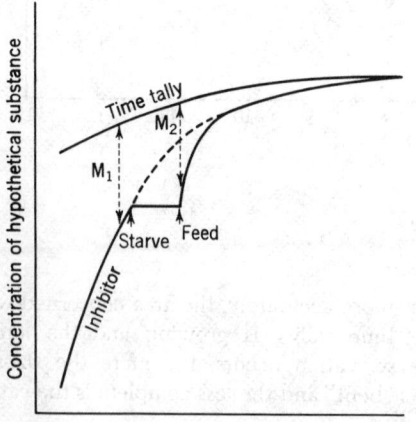

Fig. 32.   Velocity expected in catch-up growth, assuming control system of Fig. 31. Catch-up velocity is proportional to the mismatch M_2 which is greater than the mismatch when starvation began and equal to mismatch at an earlier age, as represented by $M_1 = M_2$. (From Tanner 1963.)

ball, so that the point of focus of the light rays lies exactly on the retina. It is small wonder that the success of this coordination varies, and most people are just a little far-sighted or nearsighted. Again, it seems that many features of the face and skull are individually governed by genes which do not much influence the growth of other, nearby, features. But in general the parts of the face fuse to form an acceptable whole. In this case the final growth stages are plastic and variable, and in fitting together, for example, upper and lower jaws, forces of mutual regulation come into play which do not reflect the original growth curves of the discrete parts (see Kraus, Wise, and Frei, 1959).

The regulative forces harmonizing the velocity of growth of one part with that of another do not always succeed, even in arriving within an acceptable area around the target. If the original genetic forces begin by being too unbalanced, as in trisomy, normal development cannot occur.

Variation in the speed of development of different structures and functions (heterochronisms) underlie many individual differences in bodily structure. Examples are the longer arms and legs relative to trunk in men as opposed to women, or in Negroes as opposed to whites. It is an open question to what extent similar heterochronisms may explain differences in personality structure. Some psychological abnormalities or culturally excessive deviations from the average (analogous with an inconvenient degree of nearsightedness) may arise from insufficient harmonization of the speeds at which different structures and functions develop. This could occur either for genetical reasons, the child carrying, by chance, a relatively dysharmonic set of genes, or for environmental reasons, the development of one area of the personality having been speeded up by external forces, perhaps early in childhood, while another was relatively retarded.

This general point of view, derived from experimental embryology, clearly has possibilities for behavioral research, even though it would be unwise to press the analogy too far. Not all human behavior is open to such delightfully simple explanations as that of *Oedipus anser* studied by Lorenz (1960). Domesticated strains of geese mature earlier than wild geese, and in the offspring of a wild gander and a domesticated goose dysharmonization occurs between sexual maturation and the earlier mother-following response. The mother-following response still remains operative when the sexual response appears, and the young male bird consequently insists on copulating with its mother. Since the wild father's sexual activity arises only later in the spring, it is unnecessary that he be killed first: he remains wholly indifferent to the drama.

The behavior of children with precocious puberty provides an instructive example of an extreme, pathological degree of heterochrony, in which a fully developed endocrine system acts upon a less developed brain. Psychosexual advancement by no means keeps pace with endocrine development. The hormones need a mature brain equipped with adolescent experience to work on if adult sex behavior is to occur. This is not to say that the hormones are without effect. In one of the best-described cases to date (Money and Hampson, 1955) the psychosexual development of a boy with simple precocious puberty was at a level characteristic of his chronological age, but more energized than normally. The boy was 6½ years old, with a skeletal age of 15. He had begun to have seminal emissions at 5 and to masturbate at 6. He experienced numerous dreams involving kissing women all over the body, which he would relate only to a male interviewer, with the

air of a "roué narrating his escapades in all-male company." He had no knowledge of copulation, and overt sexual behavior toward women had never been a problem. Several women on the hospital staff, however, said they felt uncomfortable under his gaze, which carried a considerable message of seduction.

Sensitive or Critical Periods

The much-discussed critical periods are extreme examples of the linking of differential growth events previously discussed. By "critical period" we mean a certain stage of limited duration during which a particular influence, from another area of the developing organism, or from the environment, evokes a particular response. The response may be beneficial, indeed perhaps essential to normal development, or it may be pathological. The term "sensitive period" is now displacing the term critical period. This describes the usual situation more accurately, since usually these periods consist of a number of hours, days, or weeks, during the beginning and end parts of which the organism is slightly sensitive to the specific influence, with a period of maximum sensitivity in the middle. It is not as a rule an all-or-none phenomenon.

Two examples of sensitive periods have already been given. One concerned the sexual differentiation of the hypothalamus in the rat, the other the differentiation of the external genitalia in the male mammal. Sensitive periods have long been part of the embryologists, conceptual apparatus. A tissue is said to show "competence" to a stimulus at a defined time, and to lose this competence as maturation progresses.

Sensitive periods may be times of particular vulnerability of the organism, though more in the specific than the general sense. If male sex hormone is not secreted by the testes of the neonatal rat, the hypothalamus is forever damaged. Thus the neonatal rat is especially vulnerable at this time to testicular disease or damage. But he may not be particularly vulnerable to the general stress of malnutrition, for malnutrition slows down the whole of development, so that the hypothalamus may wait, and the sensitive period, considered in clock time, may be lengthened. If the hypothalamus slows down less than the testicular development, after a time given by the difference between the development rates of the two systems, the sensitive period passes and the developmental disaster has occurred. We are seeing again an example of heterochronism.

The period of vulnerability has particularly been discussed in relation to brain development. Flexner (1952) and others have suggested that the period during which the brain is growing at its maximum speed and acquiring many enzyme systems is a specially vulnerable one. This is at about 41 to 45 days postfertilization in the guinea pig, and in the second week after birth in the earlier-born rat. However, the degree to which various stresses and deprivations can irreversibly affect brain structure at this time is not yet certainly known.

Sensitive periods in bodily development in general seem to be less in evidence during postnatal growth, although this may only reflect on our inability to detect them. If they continue to occur during the postnatal growth of the brain, they may well be of the greatest concern for educationists. Indeed, it is widely

believed, on educational grounds, that periods of sensitivity to various environmental sensory inputs do indeed exist, whether or not these are linked with or caused by underlying sensitive periods in brain maturation in structure. Certainly there is a formal analogy between "readiness" to read, for example, and competence in brain systems. It seems likely the connection will be shown to be more than formal when research on brain growth has advanced.

Growth Maturity Gradients

One way in which the organization of growth shows itself is through the presence of maturity gradients. One such is illustrated in Fig. 34. In Fig. 34b the percentage of the adult value at each age is plotted for foot length, calf length, and thigh length in boys. At all ages the foot is nearer its adult status than the calf, and the calf is nearer than the thigh. A maturity gradient is said to exist in the leg, running from advanced maturity at the far end of the limb to retarded maturity at the end nearest the trunk. The word gra-

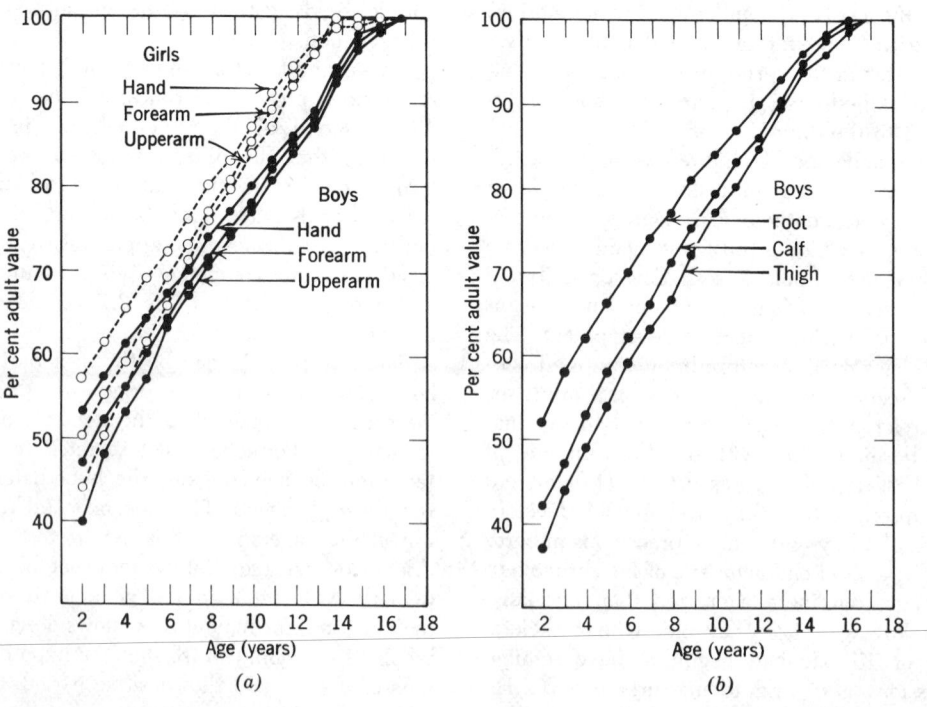

Fig. 34. Maturity gradients in upper and lower limbs. Length of segments of limbs plotted as percentage of adult value. Note hand is nearer adult value than forearm, and forearm nearer than upper arm at all ages, independent of sex difference in maturity. (From Tanner, 1962; data of Simmons, 1944.)

dient has arisen because of the supposed mechanism by which this occurs. It is thought that in the embryonic limb bud, before any differences between the three segments can be discerned, there must be differences in the concentration of some chemical substance. Thus a concentration gradient of the chemical substance leads eventually to a maturity gradient in developing physical structure.

Figure 34a illustrates the same gradient in the arm, together with the fact that girls are more advanced toward maturity than boys, without this affecting the gradient within the limb.

Many other growth maturity gradients are known, some covering small areas only and operating for short periods, others covering whole systems and operating throughout the whole of growth. The head is at all ages in advance of the trunk and the trunk in advance of the limbs. In the hand and foot the second digit is the most advanced, and the third, fourth, and fifth follow in that order.

Much of the growth of the brain is organized by means of such gradients, and several have already been described in Section VI.

Stages of Development: General and Singular

In child development there has been much argument as to whether development is continuous or whether it occurs in stages. Again, supposing stages do exist, there is argument as to whether any *general* ones occur, characterizing a simultaneous achievement of a number of anatomical, physiological, and psychological developments.

In physical growth, there is continuity and little evidence for discrete stages. Even in the development of motor skills such as crawling and walking development is more continuous than sudden. It is sometimes said that a child walks or does not walk, in a tone which implies that one day the child, previously unable to walk at all, suddenly finds the ability to walk unaided. Close observation of the development of such an ability, however, by no means supports this notion (McGraw, 1943); on the contrary, the ability to walk develops gradually.

In some creatures, such as insects at metamorphosis, general stages of development do occur. But in man only at adolescence do we have anything approaching a general stage;

here, it is true, developments in anatomy, physiology, and behavior tend to occur synchronously. But even here the degree of synchrony is only relative. Skeletal age and dental age are largely independent of each other; and the spurt in bodily development is not matched by any great rise in intellectual capacity.

Physical development is best envisaged as a series of many successive processes, overlapping one another in time and linked loosely or tightly as the case may be. Out of the complexity of the linkages, under equilibratory forces, emerges an overall order with visible changes in the varying sections following one another with the regularity of a continuously changing mosaic. The process is one of continuous unfolding and movement, with speeds varying from time to time in different parts of the mosaic; it is not a series of kaleidoscopic bumps. Only in certain restricted areas do rapid reassortments of the pieces occur, as they fall into new and increasingly precise patterns.

Spirals of Development

To conclude this general discussion we may revert to an example given earlier. At adolescence the great increase in sex hormone secretion is accomplished and controlled, it seems, by the use of a previously established feedback circuit, now elevated to greater levels at all points. The evolutionary and developmental usefulness of such a mechanism (compare "ritualization" in behavior) is obvious. We may call it developmental "spiralling." It is appropriate to call attention to its occurrence here, because it has theoretical relevance to psychological development. It seems likely that behavioral patterns also develop by reverberation and amplification of earlier-laid-down behaviors, perhaps with the objects changed and the emotions renamed. The analogy with physical development may be close; its pursuance may lead to increased knowledge of what is permanent and what changeable among the mechanisms of the brain.

VIII. INTERACTION OF HEREDITY AND ENVIRONMENT IN CONTROLLING GROWTH

Factors affecting the rate of growth must be considered separately from factors affecting the size, shape, and body composition of the child. The genetical control of rate seems to be independent of the genetical control of final size and, to a large extent, of shape (to be discussed later); and environmentally produced changes in rate do not necessarily produce any alteration in final physique. Size and shape are themselves to a large extent affected separately by genetical and environmental influences.

Rate of growth at any age is the outcome of the interaction of genetical and environmental factors. Some of the factors, like season of the year, are short-term ones reflecting the immediate environmental conditions; others, especially but not exclusively the genetical ones, are longer term and act by hastening or retarding physiological maturation from an early age. Others, such as socioeconomic class or the number of children in the household, reflect a complicated mixture of hereditary and environmental, physiological and behavioral influences.

Final size and shape also reflect the continuous interaction of hereditary and environmental forces. It is a long way from the possession of a certain set of genes to the acquisition of a height of 6 feet or the development of the menarche at age 12.5. Furthermore, as explained in Chapter 7, it is a truism in modern genetics that this interaction may be nonadditive. This means bettering the nutrition by a fixed amount will not in principle produce an increase of 10%, say, in the height of all persons but only in persons of certain "susceptible" genotypes. It is therefore impossible to specify in general the relative importance of heredity and environment in contributing to the variance of a particular trait. The nearer optimal the environment, the more the genes have a chance to show their hand, it is true; but this is a general statement only and undoubtedly many subtle and specific interactions occur, as explained in the previous section.

Hereditary factors are, however, clearly of immense importance in the control of growth. The fundamental plan is laid down very early. An immature limb-bud removed from a fetal or newborn mouse and implanted under the skin of an adult mouse of the same inbred strain will continue to develop until it closely resembles an adult bone. Furthermore, the cartilage scaffolding of the bone, removed at a stage preceding actual bone formation, will

do the same (Felts, 1959). The structure of the adult bone, in all its essentials, is implicit in the cartilage model of months before. The later action of the bone's environment, represented by the muscles pulling on it and the joints connecting it to other bones, seems limited to the making of finishing touches.

Genetics of Growth

The genetical control of rate of growth is manifested most simply in the inheritance of age at menarche. Identical twin sisters growing up together under average West European economic conditions reach menarche an average of 2 months apart (see Tanner, 1962), Nonidentical twin sisters, with the same proportion of identical genes as ordinary sisters, reach menarche on average about 10 months apart. The sister-sister and mother-daughter correlation coefficients for menarcheal age are both about .4, which is only slightly below the same correlations for height. Thus a high proportion of the variability of age at menarche in populations living under European conditions is due to genetical causes. The inheritance is probably transmitted as much by the father as the mother, and is due not to a single gene, but to many genes, each of small effect.

This genetical control evidently operates throughout the whole process of growth, for the conclusions regarding age at menarche apply also to skeletal maturity at all ages. Reynolds (1943) calculated the correlations for age of first appearance of 38 epiphyseal ossification centers in twins, sibs, and first cousins. In 6 pairs of identical twins the correlation was .71, in 22 pairs of sibs .28, and in 8 pairs of cousins .12. Garn and Rohmann (1962) were able to report from the unique Fels Research Institute data parent-offspring correlations in age of epiphyseal appearances in the first five years; they vary from .2 to .5. Some bones were more subject to hereditary influence than others. Hewitt (1957) found a sib-sib correlation of .45 in a composite measure of bone age in the hand and wrist over the whole period birth to age 5. Sibs also resembled each other in the shape of their velocity curve of skeletal maturation; that is, in whether they gained much in the first 3 years and little in the next 2, or vice versa.

The age of eruption of the teeth is to a large extent genetically controlled (Garn, Lewis, and Kerewsky, 1965). So also, and

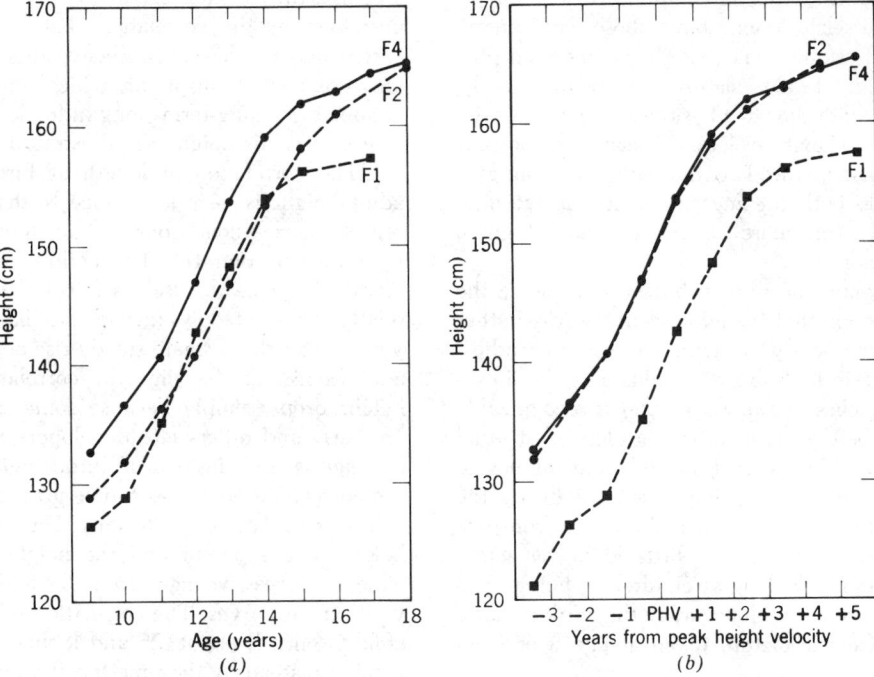

Fig. 35. Growth in height of three sisters. (*a*) Height plotted against chronological age. (*b*) Height plotted against years before or after year of peak height velocity. Note the coincidence of curves of F2 and F4 when equated for developmental age (part *b*). (From Tanner, 1962; data Ford, 1958.)

to an even greater extent, are the *sequences* in which the ossification centers and the teeth appear (Garn, 1962; Garn, Lewis, and Polachek, 1960). The manner in which this occurs implies the existence of genetically controlled factors acting locally on one or a few teeth only, an example of local growth maturity gradients, discussed in the previous section (see Tanner, 1960).

Sex-linked genes appear to be concerned in both time of eruption and final size of the teeth (Garn, Lewis, and Kerewsky, 1965a,b). The evidence for this is that for tooth size the sister-sister correlation is .64, brother-brother .38, and sister-brother .21 (see Chapter 7). The same may perhaps be true of some aspects of skeletal development, but it is very hard to disentangle in these data the relative importance of sex-linkage, sex-control, and the greater regulating power of the female.

Under reasonable environmental conditions the genetical control extends down to many of the details of velocity and acceleration curves of growth. This is demonstrated by the records of three sisters given in Fig. 35. In Fig.

35*a* the heights are plotted against chronological age, and in part *b* they are plotted against developmental age as given by years before or after peak height velocity at adolescence. Two of the sisters have curves which are practically superimposable except that they are on a different time base, one being almost a year in advance of the other. These two therefore differ radically in one parameter of their growth curve, but little in the other parameters. The third sister differs little from the others in velocity when plotted against developmental age, but markedly in actual height.

There is considerable evidence that in general genes controlling rate of growth are wholly or mostly independent of those controlling the final size attained. Body shape, however, as distinct from size, is somewhat related, under normal circumstances, to rate of growth. There are differences in physique between those who mature early and those who mature late, and these differences can be seen both before adolescence has started and after it is over (during adolescence they are obscured or magnified by the early maturers being larger and more muscular simply because of the spurt itself). Among boys, those with muscular physiques (i.e., high in mesomorphy; Sheldon, 1940) mature on average early; those with linear physiques (high in ectomorphy) mature late. Linear, ectomorphic girls also mature late, but early-maturing girls include both the muscular and the fat individuals (or, more accurately, those high in endomorphy).

It would be wrong, however, to leave the impression that the adolescent spurt, whether occurring early or late, causes any radical change in body build. It adds only the finishing touches to a physique that is recognizable years before. Anyone who has looked at serial pictures of children followed from infancy to adulthood must be impressed chiefly by the similarity of shape the child shows from one age to the next. There is little doubt that someone used to looking at children's photographs could predict with accuracy the adult somatotype from a picture taken at age 5 or even earlier.

Not all genes are active at birth. Some are not switched on till later and some can express themselves only in the physiological surroundings provided by the later years of growth. The effects of the latter are said to be "age-limited."

This is the probable explanation of the curve described by the correlations between measurements of a child at successive ages and his measurements as an adult, which have been obtained in long-term longitudinal studies. The curves for height are illustrated in Fig. 36. The correlation of length at birth with adult height is very low, since birth weight reflects uterine conditions and not fetal genotype (see Section II). The child's genes increasingly make themselves felt and the correlation rises steeply during the first three years. After this a small, steady rise occurs till adolescence; at this time the correlation for height drops, simply because some children are early and others late developers. If skeletal age is used instead of chronological age the correlation continues to rise gradually.

The correlation coefficients between the height of the parent and the height of the child at successive ages from birth describe very similar curves. The correlation when the child is born is about .25 and it then rises to reach a plateau by the time the child is about 3. The child's resemblance to his parents in size (relative, of course, as well as absolute) becomes increasingly marked as he grows older. The same types of curves are seen in the development of resemblance in IQ. Most data on height show mother-daughter correlations

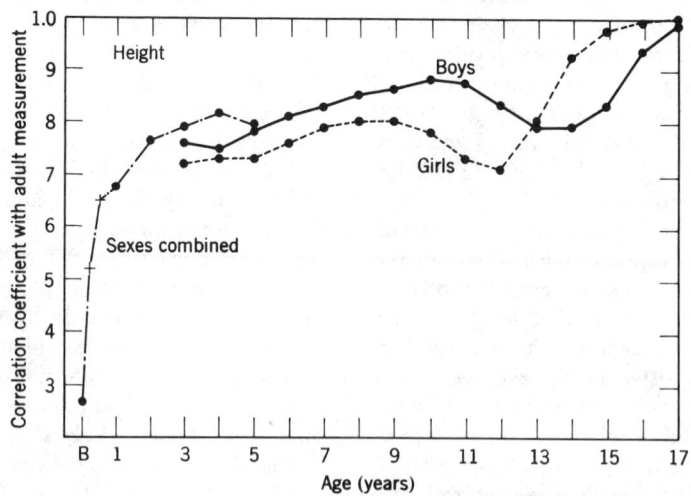

Fig. 36.   Correlations between adult height and heights of same individuals as children. Sexes combined lines (0–5) from 124 individuals of Aberdeen study (Tanner, Healy, Lockhart, MacKenzie, and Whitehouse, 1956) with + points from Bayley (1954). Boys' and girls' lines (3–17) from 66 boys and 70 girls of California Guidance Study (Tuddenham and Snyder, 1954). All data pure longitudinal. (From Tanner, 1962.)

to be above mother-son correlations at all ages up to puberty (Tanner and Israelsohn, 1963; Garn, 1966). The father correlations are less precisely estimated, since it is much harder to pursuade the fathers to attend for measurement, and relying on their own estimates of their height is hazardous. In general, however, it seems that the father-son correlations during childhood may be above the father-daughter ones.

Little is known about the genetics of the magnitude of the adolescent spurt. Since there is a considerable degree of independence between the amounts of growth before and during adolescence, it seems quite possible that newly acting genes may come into play at this time.

Race and Ecological Conditions

There are racial differences in rate and pattern of growth, leading to the racial differences seen in adult body build. Some of these are clearly genetically controlled, whereas others depend perhaps on climatic differences and certainly on nutritional ones (see Tanner, 1966a, for review).

We must suppose that in each of the major populations of the world the growth of its members was gradually adjusted, by means of selection, to the environmental conditions in which they evolved. We should be able to see the remnants of this process in modern populations—the remnants only, because relatively recent migrations have much altered the distributions of peoples, so that many no longer live in the areas in which they evolved. There is, in fact, a quite close positive relation between the linearity of peoples, as judged by their adult weight for height, and the average annual temperature of where they live (Roberts, 1953; Schreider, 1957).

Hiernaux' (1963; 1964) study of the growth of two East African groups living in Rwanda is especially interesting. The Tutsi are tall, linear people, with an average male height and weight of 176 cm and 57 kg; the Hutu are shorter and stockier, with averages of 167 cm and 58 kg. The Tutsi could be taller either because they go on growing for a longer period of time, or because they are longer at birth and grow at a slightly greater rate throughout childhood, ending their growth at the same time. The second possibility is in fact what occurs. Both Tutsi and Hutu grow slowly compared with Europeans, probably because their nutrition is suboptimal, but both have menarche at about 16.5 years and show the reversal of boys-taller to girls-taller at the same age of 14 years. When the study was made (1957-1958) both groups were growing up in the same environment, but the Tutsi were better nourished, being the ruling caste.

It is clearly established that Negroes are ahead of whites in skeletal ossification at birth. This probably reflects an inherited difference in hormone secretion during the late fetal period, for Negroes' permanent teeth also erupt earlier, and the basis of these is laid down *in utero*, though later than the primary teeth, whose eruption differs less between the races. The Negro child maintains his advancement (which is paralleled by advancement in motor development) for about two or three years if living in good economic circumstances. After this the African child comes to equal, or more usually to fall behind the European in maturity. This may be a natural occurrence, the mean velocity curves of the two races having different shapes, just as do the velocity curves of males and females in both races. Or it may reflect simply the better nutrition of the European.

The extent to which nutrition, climate, altitude, and other ecological conditions are the causes of the differences between populations is not known. We must presume that these ecological features originally governed the selection of growth-controlling genes and hence led to the emergence of the differences we see now. It seems improbable that many of the differences in growth pattern are directly due to the action of climate and altitude on the growing individual, except in such instances as emphysematous chests in very high altitude dwellers. A test of this is provided by people of one race who grow up in the area mostly inhabited by another. Europeans reared in the Sudan do not grow up with the Nilotic physique, nor do Africans reared in Liverpool grow thick, European-type calves. Englishmen who pass their youth in Japan are not, so far as we know, characteristically short-legged. But there are few actual studies on these lines. Eveleth (1965) found some differences in size and to a lesser extent in body shape between American children living in the subtropical climate of Rio de Janeiro (and conserving their American food habits) and chil-

dren of apparently comparable social groups
living in the United States. It is very hard to
be sure of true comparability, however. Indeed all studies of migrants are presented with
two great difficulties. First, migrant parents
seem never to be a random sample of the population they leave, being usually larger and
more intelligent than the stay-at-homes (even
if they only migrate from one English county
to another); and second, food habits and opportunities are seldom the same in migrants
and sedentes.

We have to distinguish between ecological
effects on differential body growth, leading to
adults with different shapes and body compositions, as described above, and ecological effects on overall rate of growth and maturation.
The two may interact but do not necessarily
do so. So far as growth rate is concerned, climate, contrary to popular belief, has probably
little effect. The average age of menarche of
well-off Buganda girls in East Africa is 13.4
years; that of Burmese and Assamese girls
living under good nutritional and medical circumstances but with a hot weather temperature of 112°F is 13.2 years (see Tanner,
1966b). These figures are entirely comparable
with averages for Europe (discussed later).

Eveleth's (1966) American children reared
for several years in Rio de Janeiro erupted
their permanent teeth a few months earlier
than their American-living controls, but they
reached menarche at a very similar age (12.6
years). In girls of the same race and population there is little real evidence that climate
is responsible for a significant amount of variation in menarcheal age. Altitude has been
considered to slow up growth, but in studies
to date it has been impossible to separate the
effects of altitude itself from those due to the
relative undernutrition which everywhere characterizes people living in mountainous areas
(Valsik, Stukovsky, and Bernátová, 1963;
Wurst, Wassertheurer, and Kimeswengen,
1961).

Season of the Year

In most European and American data a
well-marked seasonal effect on velocity of
growth can be seen. Growth in height is fastest in the spring and growth in weight fastest
in the fall. This effect is illustrated by the
growth curves of a pair of identical twins
reared together, seen in Fig. 37. The average
velocity of height in the March to May quarter
is almost twice that in the September to Oc-

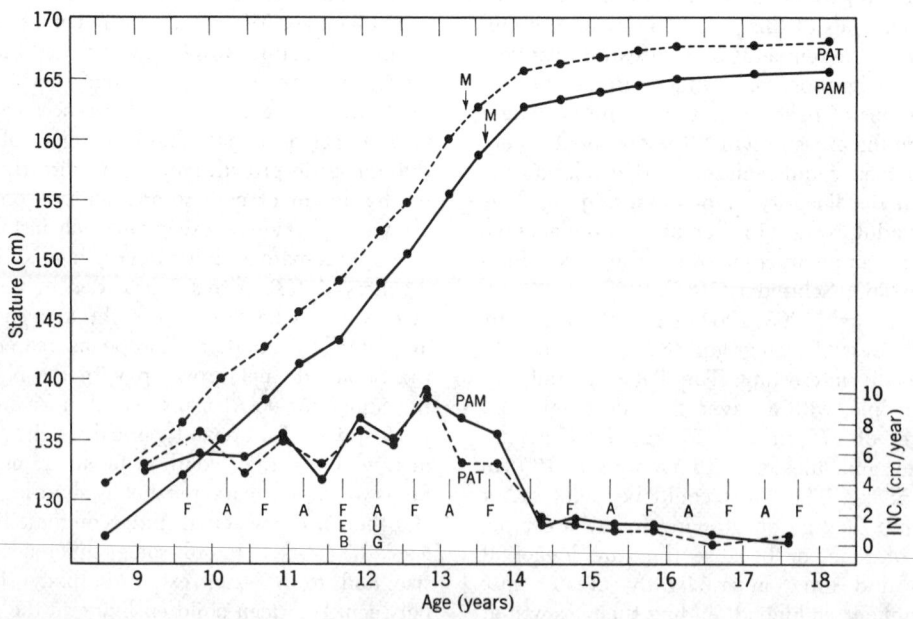

Fig. 37. Growth in height of identical twin girls, showing seasonal effect on rate of growth. (From
Tanner, 1962.)

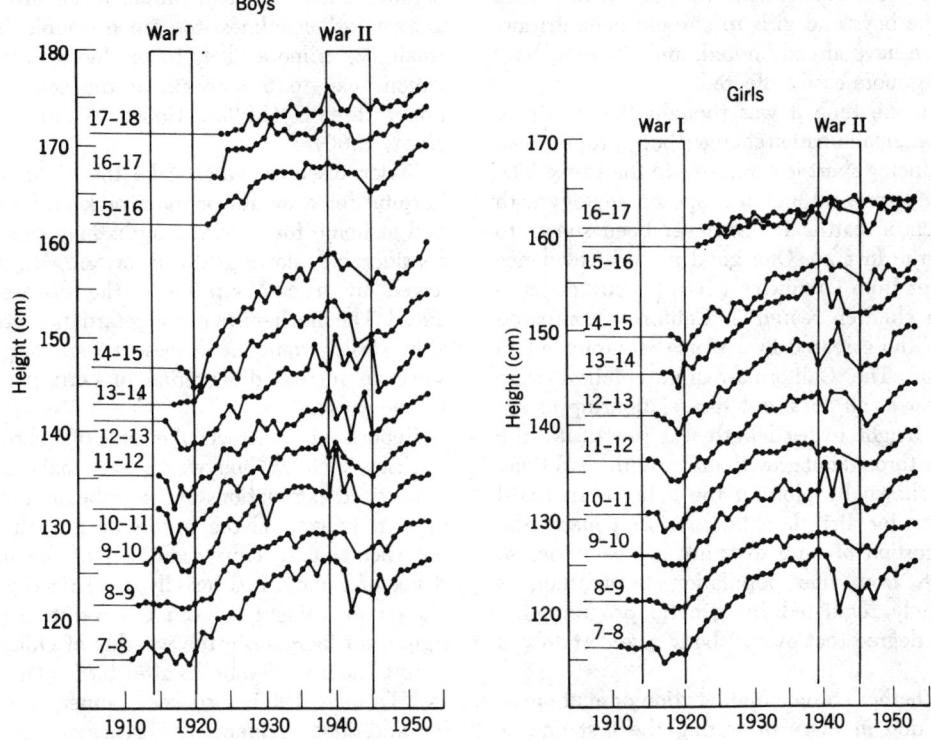

Fig. 38. Effect of malnutrition on growth in height. Heights of Stuttgart schoolchildren (7–8 to 14–15 Volkschule; 15–16 up, Oberschule) from 1911 to 1953. Lines connect points for children of same age and express secular trend and effect of war conditions. (From Tanner, 1962; data from Howe and Schiller, 1952, and personal communication.)

tober quarter in most of the older European data. Children differ surprisingly, however, both in the time of year at which they grow fastest, and in the degree to which they show the seasonal trend at all. The differences probably reflect individual variation in endocrine and hypothalamic reactivity. In countries where malnutrition is rife seasonal effects can occur, of course, for purely nutritional reasons (see Billewicz, 1967).

Nutrition

Malnutrition delays growth, as is shown from the effects of famine associated with war. In Fig. 38 the heights of children in Stuttgart, Germany, are plotted at each year of age, from 1911 to 1953. There is a uniform increase at all ages from 1920 to 1940 (see discussion of secular trend following), but in the later years of both world wars the height drops as the food intake of the children becomes restricted.

Children subjected to an episode of acute starvation recover more or less completely by virtue of their regulative powers (see Section VII), provided the adverse conditions are not too severe and do not last too long. Chronic malnutrition is another affair. Most members of some populations, and some members of all populations, grow to be smaller adults than they should, because of chronic undernourishment during all or most of their childhood.

We should distinguish nutritional effects on rate of growth, on final size, and on shape and tissue composition. Size and rate are much more easily affected than shape and tissue composition, so that in malnutrition shape changes seldom occur before size and rate changes are pronounced. Differences in gene complex between different populations seem most frequently to affect shape and tissue composition; thus we have some guide as to the likelihood of a given population difference being due mostly to genetic influences or mostly to starvation and disease. The responses of the boys and girls to chronic malnutrition, as we have already noted, are different, boys being more easily affected.

At one time it was thought that acute or chronic malnutrition changed body proportions, producing short legs relative to the trunk. The notion arose through a supposed analogy with effects in cattle. It has never been shown to be true in man. One good piece of evidence comes from Greulich's (1957) study of Japanese children reared in California compared with those reared in a worse environment in Japan. The California-reared children were bigger at all ages, but the relationship of sitting height to leg length was practically the same throughout growth under both conditions (as shown by plotting the data on standard charts for British children). In general the proportion of limb to trunk, which varies so much from one population to another, is strongly regulated by genetic programming to a degree that overall body size certainly is not.

Whether chronic malnutrition or acute malnutrition *in utero* or during the first one or two years after birth can affect brain growth and development permanently is a question of much importance. It is by no means yet settled.

The endocrine changes in malnutrition have recently been much clarified. Contrary to what was once thought, adrenal cortex secretion seems to be unaffected, and the secretion of growth hormone is increased, in a manner that agrees with the predictions of the model of growth regulation described above, on the presumption that growth-hormone secretion is proportional to the mismatch signal.

Disease

Minor and relatively short illnesses such as measles, influenza, antibiotic-treated middle ear infection, or even pneumonia cause no discernible retardation of growth rate in the great majority of well-nourished children (Tanner 1962; Meredith and Knott, 1962). In children with a less adequate diet they may cause some disturbance, though this has not been securely established. Often children with continuous colds, ear disease, sore throats, and skin infections are on average smaller than others, but inquiry reveals that they come from economically depressed and socially dis-

organized homes where proper meals are unknown and cleanliness too much trouble. The small size is more likely to be due to malnutrition than to the effects of the continued minor disease (Miller, Court, Walton, and Knox, 1960).

Major diseases which take the child to a hospital for a month or more or keep him in bed at home for several months may cause a considerable slowing down of growth, followed by a catch-up when the disease is cured. The mechanism of the retardation probably varies from one disease to another; in some an increased secretion of cortisol may be the cause.

Reports on the effects of eradicating chronic diseases such as hookworm and malaria in parasitized populations are now beginning to appear. In general the results on growth are not spectacular. Thus reduction of the incidence of malaria in a heavily parasitized population in Tanganyika did not result in any significant increase in the weights of children during the first 18 months after birth (Draper and Draper, 1960; also see Tanner, 1966a, for additional evidence). Disease which reduces the amount of hemoglobin in the blood reduces growth rate, as do some diseases of the kidneys. But much more of the slowing of growth in underdeveloped countries is due to malnutrition than to disease, probably.

Acheson (1966) thinks that even a relatively mild disease or subnutrition will cause the formation of new cartilage to slow down while permitting the turning of cartilage into bone to continue. Such an imbalance would result in a reduced final height. While this probably occurs in severe disorders, there is little evidence that it occurs in mild diseases or temporary undernutrition.

Psychological Disturbance

Really severe psychological stress seems capable of retarding growth. In a famous experiment, Widdowson (1951) studied (as she thought) the effects of increased rations on orphanage children living on the poor diet available in Germany in 1948. The design of the experiment (see Fig. 39) was to give orphanage B a food supplement after a six-months' control period and to compare the growth of the children there with those in orphanage A, which was not to be supplemented. As shown in Fig. 39, however, the

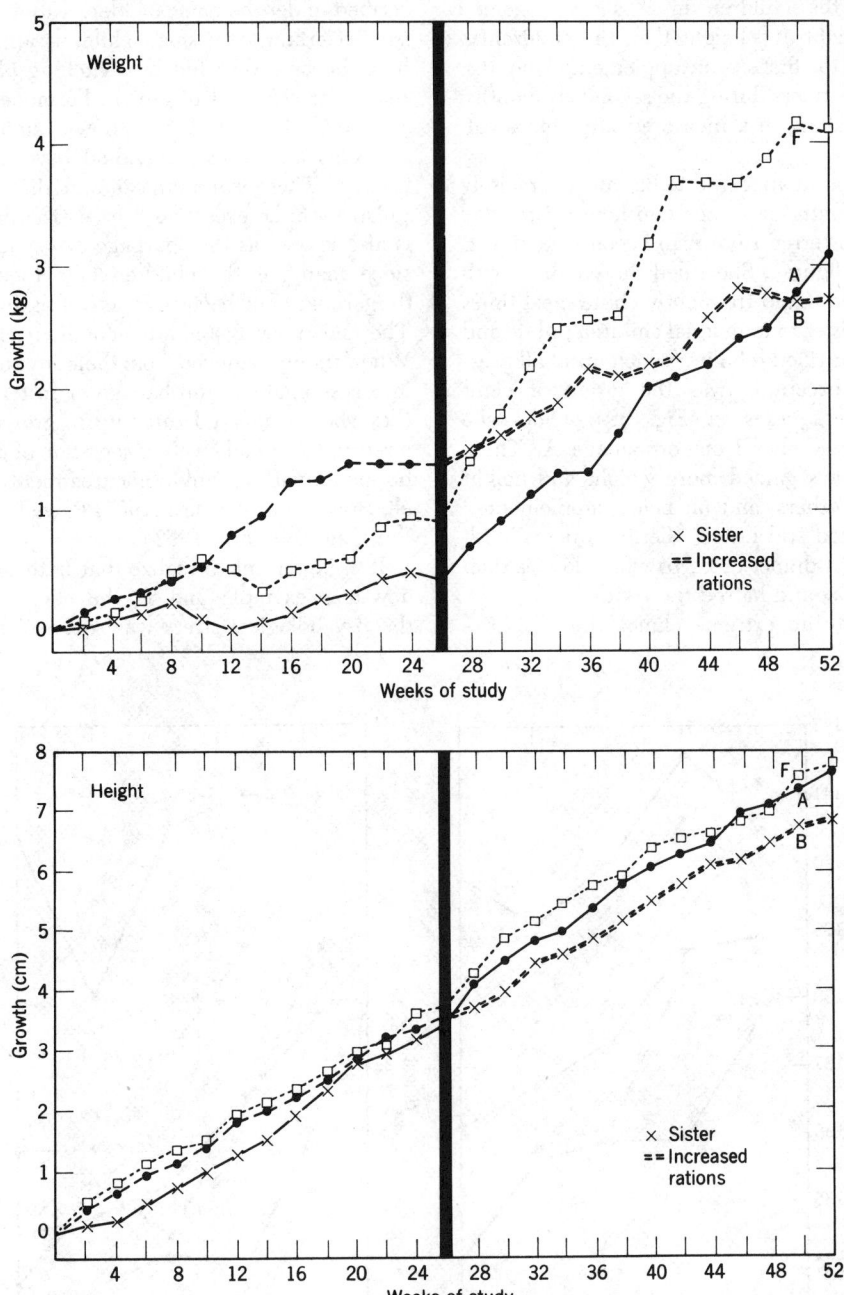

Fig. 39. Influence of sister-in-charge S on growth in weight and height of orphanage children. Presence of S marked by X plots, increased rations by $=$ $=$. Orphanage B diet supplemented at time indicated by vertical bar, but sister simultaneously transferred to B (- - -) from A (——). Note magnitude of growth follows presence or absence of sister, not amount of rations. The curves - - - are for eight favorites of sister, transferred with her to B from A. (From Tanner, 1962; redrawn from Widdowson, 1951.)

result was just the reverse of that expected. Though the children in B actually gained more weight and height than the children in A during the first six, unsupplemented months, they gained less during the second six months, despite taking in a measured 20% more calories.

The reason appeared to be that at precisely the six-month mark a certain house-sister had been transferred from A to become head of B (see the figure). She ruled the children with a rod of iron and frequently chose meal times to administer to individual children public and often unjustified rebukes, which upset all present. An exception was the group of eight favorites (squares in Fig. 39) whom she brought with her from orphanage A. These eight always gained more weight and height than the others, and on being supplemented in B gained still faster. "Better" quotes Widdowson, "a dinner of herbs where love is than a stalled ox and hatred therewith."

Recently an extreme clinical form of pre-

sumably the same phenomenon has been described under the name of "deprivation dwarfism." Certain very small children appear to have become dwarfed by switching off their release or synthesis of growth hormone under the stress of wholly broken-down family relationships and much individual psychological trauma. These children eat and drink compulsively to an excessive degree (the disorder is also known as the "garbage-can syndrome" since many of the children take food from the garbage) and become fat as well as dwarfed. They sleep poorly and are mentally backward. When simply removed from their environment into a sympathetic orphanage or foster home they show a marked catch-up in growth and a return to normal levels of secretion of growth hormone, without any other treatment (Powell, Brasel, and Blizzard, 1967; Powell, Brasel, Raiti, and Blizzard, 1967).

It is important to realize that both in Widdowson's example and in the clinical cases the psychological stress was severe. There is

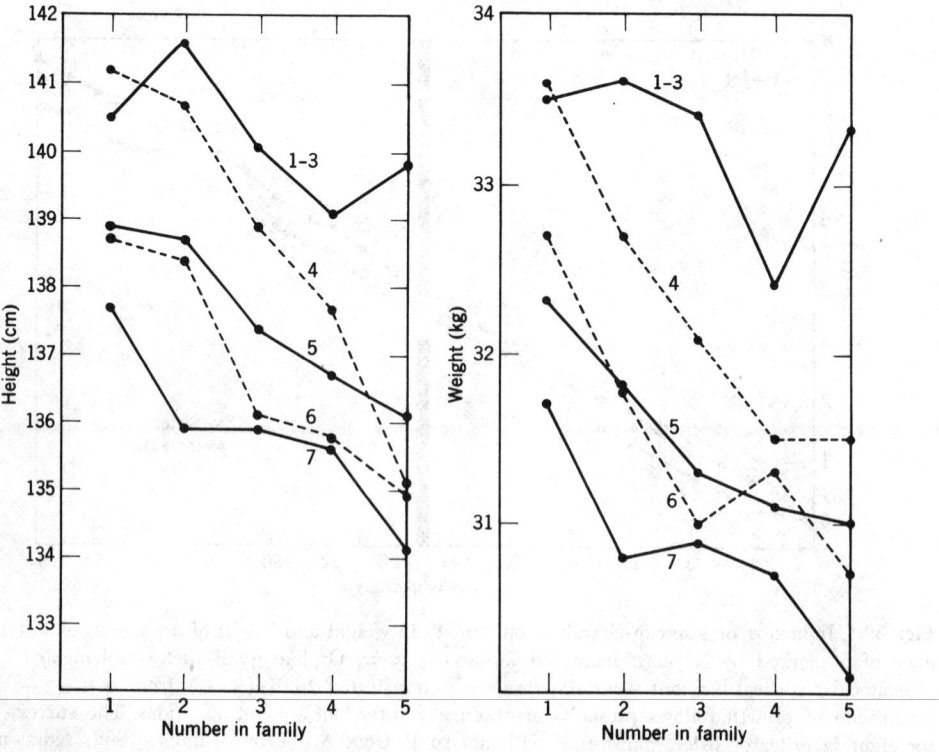

Fig. 40. Relation between height and weight of 11-year-old children and number of children in family in different socioeconomic classes in Scotland in 1947. Classes marked 1–3, 4, 5, 6, and 7. (From Tanner, 1962; data from Scottish Council for Research in Education, 1953.)

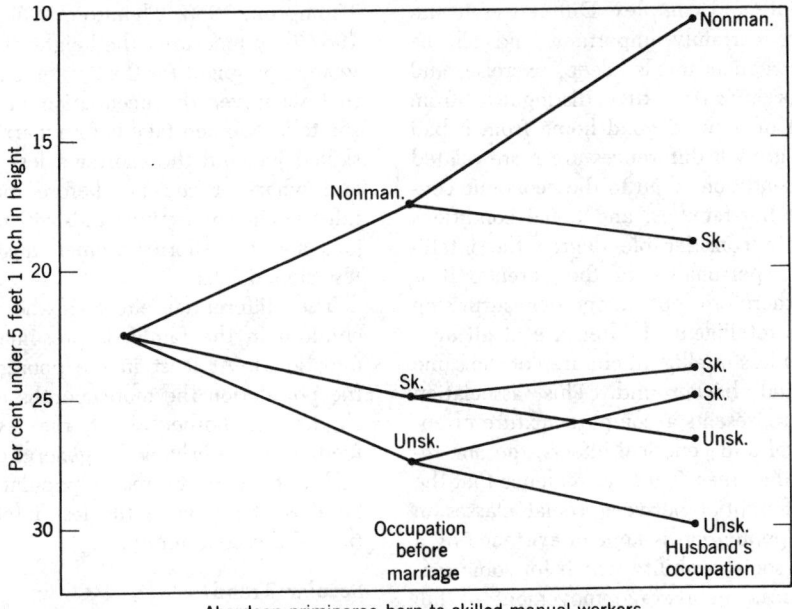

Fig. 41. Percentage of daughters of skilled manual workers under 5 feet 1 inch tall taking non-manual and manual jobs and marrying men in nonmanual, skilled manual, and unskilled manual occupations. (From Tanner, 1962; redrawn from Thomson, 1959.)

no evidence that the ordinary ups and downs of family and school life have any effect on a child's growth.

Socioeconomic Class: Number of Children in Family

Children from different socioeconomic levels differ in average body size at all ages, the upper groups being larger (Tanner, 1962; Graffar and Corbier, 1966). In most studies socioeconomic status has been defined according to father's occupation, though in recent years it is becoming clear that in many countries this does not distinguish people's living standards or style of living as well as formerly. An index reflecting housing conditions is a necessary adjunct, as is some measure of the child-centeredness of the family budget.

The difference in height between children of the professional and managerial classes and those of unskilled laborers in Britain is currently about 1 inch at 3 years rising to nearly 2 inches at adolescence (this is approximately equivalent to 20 years of secular trend). In weight the difference is less, since the lower socioeconomic class children have a greater

weight for height, due to greater relative breadth of bone and muscles. In Fig. 40 the heights and weights of a random sample of all 11-year-old Scottish children are plotted in relation to socioeconomic class and number of children in family. Classes 1 to 3 here represent professional persons, employers and salaried staff, class 4 nonmanual wage earners, and so on down to class 7, unskilled manual workers. The tendency for the better-off children to be larger is visible in families of all sizes.

Part of the socioeconomic height difference is due to earlier maturation of the well-off, though some is due to their being larger as adults. The difference associated with number of siblings probably is entirely due to rate of growth and disappears when adult size is reached (for full discussion see Tanner, 1966c). In most data there is a difference of age of menarche of around 2 to 4 months between girls in the best-off and worst-off classes in European countries, although the latest British data show no difference at all despite a persisting height difference (Douglas and Simpson, 1964).

The causes of the socioeconomic differential

are multiple and complex. Differences in nutrition are certainly important, and all the habits of regular meals, sleep, exercise, and general organization that distinguish, from this point of view, a good home from a bad one. The growth differences are more related to home conditions than to the economic conditions of the families, and home conditions reflect to a considerable degree the intelligence and personality of the parents. It is perhaps therefore not altogether surprising that more intelligent children are at all ages taller than less intelligent children of the same occupational background. This association probably represents a complex mixture of environmental and genetical effects, the one reinforcing the other. There is evidence that the height differential between social classes in the adult population is kept in existence by a system of social mobility which for some reason produces an average movement of tall persons upward and short persons downward (Schreider, 1964; Tanner, 1966c). The most striking demonstration of this is shown in Fig. 41, taken from the work of Baird and his associates in Aberdeen (Scott, Illsley, and

Thompson, 1956; Thomson, 1959). In 1950-1957 they measured the height of some 7500 women pregnant for the first time and showed that whatever the occupation of the father, the taller women take before marriage a more skilled job and the shorter a less skilled job; and whatever the job before marriage the taller women marry husbands with more skilled jobs and the shorter women husbands with less skilled jobs.

The differential effect of the number of children in the family is presumably mainly nutritional. At least in the poorer groups of the population the more mouths to feed and children to bother about, the less well the feeding, and perhaps the general care, is carried out. Also, in many populations larger families characterize the less intelligent section of the community.

Secular Trend

During the last hundred years there has been a striking tendency for children to become progressively larger at all ages (Tanner, 1966b). This is known as the "secular trend." The magnitude of the trend in Europe and

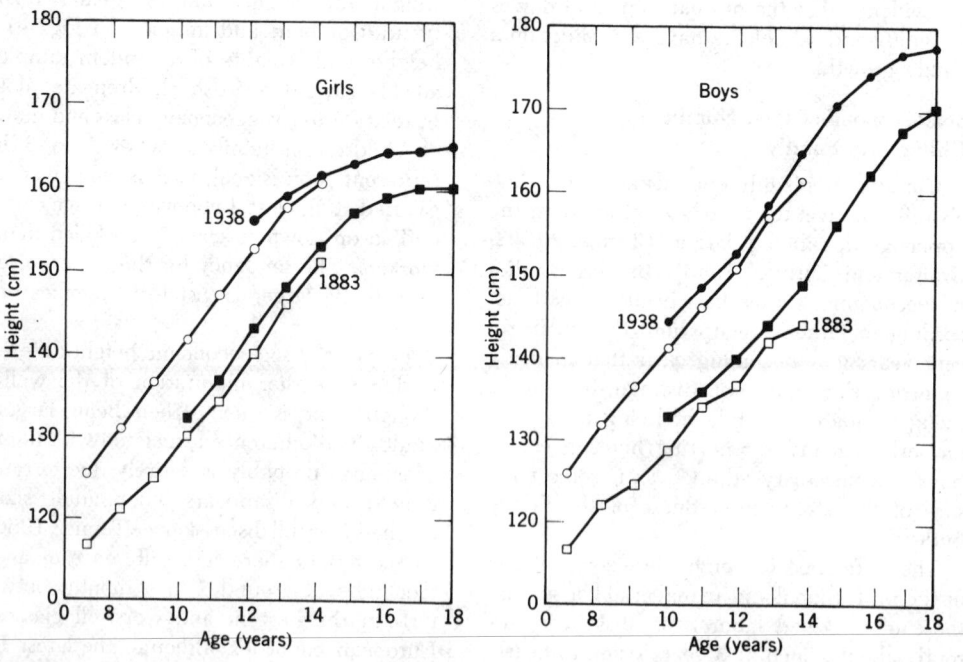

Fig. 42. Secular trend in growth of height. Height of Swedish girls and boys measured in 1883 (lower curve) and in 1938–1939. Elementary schools 7–14, secondary schools, 10–18. Distance curves; cross-sectional. (From Tanner, 1962; data from Broman, Dalberg, and Lichtenstein, 1942, Tables 11–14.)

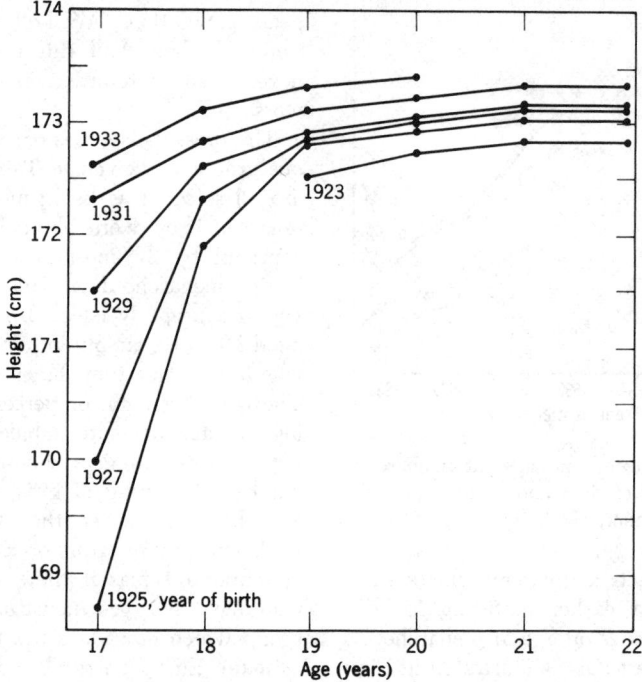

Fig. 43. Secular trend in height of French university students during 1940s. Average of all men students, mixed longitudinal data, according to year of birth. Note greater maximal height in more recently born, and earlier approach to maximum. (From Tanner, 1962; redrawn from Aubenque, 1957.)

America is such that it dwarfs the differences between socioeconomic classes. In Fig. 42 are plotted the heights of Swedish boys and girls measured in 1883 and 1938. The difference amounts to about 1½ years of growth. At the age when growth ceases, as shown by the 18-year-old girls in the figure, the secular trend is less than in childhood, but it still exists.

The data from Europe and America agree well: from about 1900, or a litle earlier, to the present, children in average economic circumstances have increased in height at age 5 to 7 by about 1 to 2 cm each decade, and at 10 to 14 by 2 to 3 cm each decade. Pre-school data show that the trend starts directly after birth and may, indeed, be relatively greater from age 2 to 5 than subsequently. The trend started, at least in Britain, a considerable time ago, because Roberts, a factory physician, writing in 1876 said that "a factory child of the present day at the age of nine years weighs as much as one of 10 years did in 1833 . . . each age has gained one year in forty years." The trend in Europe is still continuing at the time of writing (1967) but there

is some evidence to show that in the United States the best-off sections of the population are now growing up at something approaching the fastest possible speed.

During the same period there has been an upward trend in adult height, but to a considerably lower degree. One of the difficulties is that in earlier times final height was not reached till 25 years or later, whereas now it is reached at 18 or 19. Figure 43 shows this for French students. Those born in 1925 grew very considerably from 17 to 18, in contrast to those born in 1933. The difference between these two groups at age 17 is considerable, but at maximal adult height, aged 20, much less. Data do exist, however, which enable us to compare fully grown men at different periods. They lead to the conclusion that in Western Europe men increased in adult height little if at all from 1760 to 1830, about 0.3 cm per decade from 1830 to 1880, and about 0.6 cm per decade from 1880 to 1960. The trend is apparently still continuing in Europe.

Most of the trend toward greater size in children reflects a more rapid maturation; only

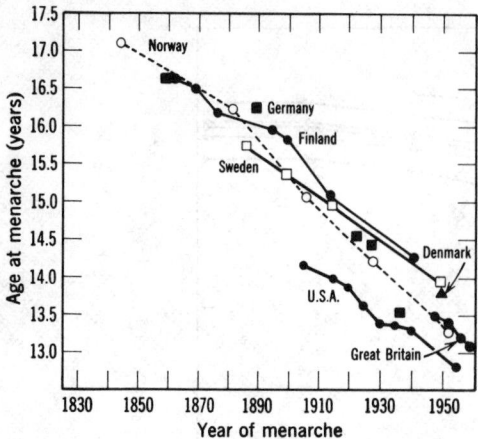

Fig. 44. Secular trend in age at menarche, 1830-1960. Sources of data and method of plotting detailed in Tanner, 1962.

a minor part reflects a greater ultimate size. The trend toward earlier maturing is best shown in the statistics on age at menarche. A selection of the best data is illustrated in Fig. 44 (the sources are detailed in Tanner, 1966b). The trend is about 4 months per decade since

1850 in average sections of Western European populations. Well-off persons show a trend of about half this magnitude, having never been so retarded in menarche as the worse-off.

The present-day ages of menarche for various groups are given in Table 1. These data are all selected as being modern and highly reliable. They were obtained, with few exceptions, by the most valid method for collecting menarche data. This is to make a survey of a properly-selected population of girls aged 10 to 16, simply inquiring their age and whether or not they have yet menstruated. The resulting data, of percentage menstruating at each age, are subjected to probit or logit analysis to give the mean age of menarche. (Inquiring of girls in a school what age they were when they first menstruated leads not only to errors of recollection, but to an important bias if there remain any girls who have not yet menstruated.) The only group which nowadays has menarche as late as many European rural and poorly off communities a hundred years ago is the Bundi of New Guinea.

Table 1. Age of Menarche in Recent Years (All estimates by probits or logits unless indicated)

Location		Year	Mean age and S.E.	Author[a]
Norway	Oslo	1952	13.4[b]	Kiil, 1953
Sweden	All	1951	13.9 approx.	Romanus, 1952
Denmark	Copenhagen	1950	13.8 ± 0.3	Bojlen et al., 1954
	Copenhagen	1963	13.1 ± 0.12	Andersen, unpubl.
Holland		1956	13.7 ± 0.06	Rusbach et al., 1961
Switzerland	Basle	1956	13.5 ± 0.10	Heimendinger, 1964
England	London	1959	13.1 ± 0.02	Scott, 1961
	Bristol	1956	13.2 ± 0.02	Wofinden et al., 1958
Scotland	Edinburgh	1952	13.4	Provis et al., 1955
Hungary	Budapest	1959	12.8 ± 0.08	Thoma, 1960
	Szeged	1961	13.0	Farkas, 1962, 1964
	All	1959	13.2 ± 0.02	Bottyan et al., 1963
Poland	Warsaw	1965	13.0 ± 0.04	Milicer and Szczotka, 1966
	Wroclaw	1961	12.6 ± 0.06	Zukowski et al., 1964
Rumania	3 towns	1963	13.5 ± 0.06	Cristescu et al., 1964
	3 village areas		14.6 ± 0.07	
U.S.S.R.[c]	Moscow	1965	13.0	Vlastowsky, 1966
	Tbilisi	1962	13.2	
	2 provincial towns	1960-1962	13.7	
	Rural area	1958	14.3	
	Buriat Rep. villages	1957	15.0	
Yugoslavia	Zemun	1963	14.3 ± 0.06	Zivanovic et al., 1964
France	All	1950	13.5 ± 0.01	Aubenque, 1964
Italy	Florence	1960	12.5 ± 0.11[d]	Young et al., 1963

Table 1.   (Continued)

Location		Year	Mean age and S.E.	Author[a]
U.S.A.	Denver (well-off)	1955	12.6[d]	Deming, 1958
	California	1950	12.8 ± 0.12[d]	Nicholson et al., 1953
Cuba	Negro	1963	12.3 ± 0.08	Laska-Mierzejewska, 1965
	White		12.4 ± 0.03	
	Mulatto		12.6 ± 0.06	
Chinese	Hong Kong	1962		Lee et al., 1963
	rich		12.5 ± 0.18	
	average		12.8 ± 0.20	
	poor		13.3 ± 0.19	
Burma and Assam	town, well-nourished	1957	13.2 ± 0.08	Foll, 1961
India	Madras, urban	1960	12.8 ± 0.14	Madhavan, 1965
	Madras, rural		14.2 ± 0.13	
	Kerala, urban		13.2 ± 0.17	
	Kerala, rural		14.4 ± 0.14	
Ceylon	Colombo	1950	12.8 ± 0.07	Wilson et al., 1950, 1953
	rural		14.4 ± 0.16	
Nigeria	Ibo(well-off)	1960	14.1 ± 0.16	Tanner et al., 1962
East Africa	Buganda			
	Kampala (well-off)	1960	13.4 ± 0.16	Burgess et al., 1964
South Africa	Bantu			
	Transkai Reserve	1958		Burrell et al., 1961
	not poor		15.0 ± 0.03	
	poor		15.4 ± 0.04	
East Africa	Rwanda, Tutsi	1957	16.5 ± 0.16	Hiernaux, 1965
	Rwanda, Hutu		17.1 ± 0.30	
New Guinea	Bundi (Highlands)	1964	18.8 ± 0.33	Malcolm, 1966, unpubl.
	Chimbu (Highlands)		17.5 ± 0.35	
	Megiar (Coast)		15.6 ± 0.22	

a References not in bibliography can be found in Tanner (1966b) from which most of this table is taken.
b Estimate only.
c The U.S.S.R. figures were obtained by graphical probits only.
d Longitudinal data (Demings figure may represent a biased selection of the Denver longitudinal sample, and be lower than is representative.)

There is at present little sign that the trend shown in Fig. 43 has stopped. It seems likely that the biological limit for European populations may be represented by an average of around 12¼ years. There is, of course, no reason a priori to suppose that rapid growing up is in itself biologically, psychologically, or sociologically either advantageous or disadvantageous.

The causes of the trend (or acceleration of growth as it is sometimes called) are probably multiple. Certainly better nutrition is a major one, and perhaps in particular more protein and calories in early infancy. A lessening of disease may also have contributed. Some authors have supposed that the increased psychosexual stimulation consequent on modern urban living has contributed, but there is no positive evidence for this. Girls in single-sex schools have menarche at exactly the same age as girls in coeducational schools, but whether this is a fair test of differences in psychosexual stimulation is hard to say.

The trend toward increased height in adults does not necessarily have the same causes. Probably better nutrition has contributed to it also, but there may in addition be a genetical explanation. If some degree of dominance occurs in genes increasing stature, then increased outbreeding, producing more heterozygotes, would increase the height of a population. There is increasing evidence that such dominance does in fact occur. As for outbreeding, that has been increasing steadily since the invention of the bicycle.

ACKNOWLEDGMENTS

I wish to thank Mr. R. H. Whitehouse, Dr. S. Hammar, Mr. H. Goldstein, and Mr. P. C. R. Hughes for making measurements and calculations on which a number of the figures are based, Dr. W. A. Marshall for a most helpful reading of the manuscript, and the Nuffield Foundation and the Medical Research Council for financial support.

References

This list consists of literature cited. It is naturally not comprehensive. Bibliographies suitable as sources for further reading will be found in the starred references.

*Acheson, R. M. Maturation of the skeleton. In F. Falkner (Ed.), *Human development*, Philadelphia, Pa.: Saunders, 1966.

Anokhin, P. K. Systemogenesis as a general regulator of brain development. *Prog. Brain Res.*, 1964, **9**, 54–86.

Aubenque, M. Note documentaire sur la statistique des tailles des étudiants au cours de ces dernieres années. *Biotypologie*, 1957, **18**, 202–214.

Bayley, N. Some increasing parent-child similarities during the growth of children. *J. educ. Psychol.*, 1954, **45**, 1–21.

Bayley, N., and Pinneau, S. R. Tables for predicting adult height from skeletal age: revised for use with the Greulich-Pyle hand standards. *J. Pediat.*, 1952, **40**, 423–441. (Erratum corrected in *J. Pediat.*, **41**, 371.)

Billewicz, W. J. A note on body weight measurements and seasonal variation. *Hum. Biol.*, 1967, **39**, 241–250.

Broman, B., Dahlberg, G., and Lichtenstein, A. Height and weight during growth. *Acta paediat.* (Uppsala), 1942, **30**, 1–66.

Büchi, E. C. Änderungen der Köperform beim erwachsenen Menschen. Eine Untersuchung nach der Individualmethode. *Anthrop. Forsch.*, 1950, **1**, 1–44.

Butler, L., and Metrakos, J. D. A study of size inheritance in the house mouse. I. The effect of milk source. *Canad. J. Res., Sec. D.*, 1950, **28**, 16–34.

Clarke, H. H., and Wickens, J. S. Maturity, structural, strength and motor ability growth curves of boys 9–15 years of age. *Res. Q., Am. Ass. Hlth. phys. Educ.*, 1962, **33**, 26–39.

Conel, J. L. *The postnatal development of the human cerebral cortex. Vol. I. The cortex of the newborn.* Cambridge, Mass.: Harvard University Press, 1939.

Conel, J. L. *The postnatal development of the human cerebral cortex. Vol. II. The cortex of the one-month infant.* Cambridge, Mass.: Harvard University Press, 1941.

Conel, J. L. *The postnatal development of the human cerebral cortex. Vol. III. The cortex of the three-month infant.* Cambridge, Mass.: Harvard University Press, 1947.

Conel, J. L. *The postnatal development of the human cerebral cortex. Vol. IV. The cortex of the six-month infant.* Cambridge, Mass.: Harvard University Press, 1951.

Conel, J. L. *The postnatal development of the human cerebral cortex. Vol. V. The cortex of the fifteen-month infant.* Cambridge, Mass.: Harvard University Press, 1955.

Conel, J. L. *The postnatal development of the human cerebral cortex. Vol. VI. The cortex of the twenty-four month infant.* Cambridge, Mass.: Harvard University Press, 1959.

Conel, J. L. *The postnatal development of the human cerebral cortex. Vol. VII. The cortex of the four-year child.* Cambridge, Mass.: Harvard University Press, 1963.

Dargassies, S. S-A. Neurological maturation of the premature infant of 28 to 41 weeks gestational age. In F. Falkner (Ed.), *Human development.* London: Saunders, 1966.

Dawkins, M. J. R. Changes in glucose-6 phosphatase activity in liver and kidney at birth. *Nature,* 1961, **91,** 72–73.

Dekaban, A. Human thalamus. An anatomical, developmental and pathological study. II. Development of the human thalamic nuclei. *J. comp. Neurol.,* 1954, **100,** 63–97.

Deming, J. Application of the Gompertz curve to the observed pattern of growth in length of 48 individual boys and girls during the adolescent cycle of growth. *Hum. Biol.,* 1957, **29,** 83–122.

Deming, J., and Washburn, A. H. Application of the Jenss curve to the observed pattern of growth during the first eight years of life in forty boys and forty girls. *Hum. Biol.,* 1963, **35,** 484–506.

Dickinson, A. G. Some genetic implications of maternal effects—a hypothesis of mammalian growth. *J. agric. Sci.,* 1960, **54,** 379–390.

*Donovan, B. T., and van der Werff ten Bosch, J. J. *Physiology of puberty.* London: Arnold, 1965.

Douglas, J. W. B. The age at which premature children walk. *Med. Off.,* 1956, **95,** 33–35.

Douglas, J. W. B., and Simpson, H. R. Height in relation to puberty, family size and social class. *Milbank meml. Fund Q. Bull.,* 1964, **42,** 20–35.

Draper, K. C., and Draper, C. C. Observations on the growth of African infants with special reference to the effects of malaria control. *J. trop. Med. Hyg.,* 1960, **63,** 167–171.

Dreyfus-Brisac, C. The bioelectrical development of the central nervous system during early life. In F. Falkner (Ed.), *Human development.* London: Saunders, 1966.

Drillien, C. M. *The growth and development of the prematurely born infant.* Edinburgh: Livingstone, 1964.

Dunn, H. L. The growth of the central nervous system in the human fetus as expressed by graphic analysis and empirical formulae. *J. comp. Neurol.,* 1921, **33,** 405–491.

Eayrs, J. T. Effects of thyroid hormones on brain differentiation. In M. P. Cameron and M. O'Connor (Eds.), *Brain-thyroid relationships.* London: Churchill, 1964.

Eayrs, J. T., and Horn, G. The development of cerebral cortex in hypothyroid and starved rats. *Anat. Rec.,* 1955, **121,** 53–61.

Eayrs, J. T., and Lishman, W. A. The maturation of behaviour in hypothyroidism and starvation. *Br. J. Anim. Behav.,* 1955, **3,** 17–24.

Engle, E. T., and Rosasco, J. The age of the albino mouse at normal sexual maturity. *Anat. Rec.,* 1927, **36,** 383–388.

Eveleth, P. B. The effects of climate on growth. *Ann. N. Y. Acad. Sci.,* 1965, **134,** 750–759.

Eveleth, P. B. Eruption of permanent dentition and menarche of American children living in the tropics. *Hum. Biol.,* 1966, **38,** 60–70.

Falkner, F. (Ed.) Child development: an international method of study. *Ann. Paediat. Suppl.,* 1960, **72,** 237 pp.

Felts, W. J. L. Transplantation studies of factors in skeletal organogenesis. I. The subcutaneously implanted immature long-bone of the rat and mouse. *Am. J. phys. Anthrop.*, N.S., 1959, **17**, 201–215.

Flexner, L. B. The development of the cerebral cortex: a cytological, functional and biochemical approach. *Harvey Lect.*, 1952, **47**, 156–179.

Flux, D. S. Growth of the mammary duct system in intact and ovariectomized mice of the CHI strain. *J. Endocr.*, 1954, **11**, 223–237.

Ford, E. H. R. Growth in height of ten siblings. *Hum. Biol.*, 1958, **30**, 107–119.

French, F. S., and Van Wyke, J. J. Fetal hypothyroidism. I. Effects of thyroxine on neural development. II. Fetal versus maternal contributions to fetal thyroxine requirements. III. Clinical implications. *J. Pediat.*, 1964, **64**, 589–600.

Garn, S. M. Changes in areolar size during the steroid growth phase. *Child Dev.*, 1952, **23**, 55–60.

*Garn, S. M. The genetics of normal human growth. In L. Gedda (Ed.), *De Genetica Medica.* Roma: Istituto Gregorio Mendel, 1962.

Garn, S. M. Body size and its implications. *Rev. Child Dev. Res.*, 1966, **2**, 529–561.

Garn, S. M., Helmrich, R. H., Flaherty, K. M., and Silverman, F. N. Skin dosages in radiation-sparing techniques for the laboratory and field. *Am. J. phys. Anthrop.*, 1967, **26**, 101–106.

Garn, S. M., Lewis, A. B., and Kerewsky, R. S. Genetic, nutritional and malnutritional correlates of dental development. *J. dent. Res.*, 1965, **44**, 228–242. (a)

Garn, S. M., Lewis, A. B., and Kerewsky, R. S. X-linked inheritance of tooth size. *J. dent. Res.*, 1965, **44**, 439–441. (b)

Garn, S. M., Lewis, A. B., and Polacheck, D. L. Sibling similarities in dental development. *J. dent. Res.*, 1960, **39**, 170–175.

Garn, S. M., and Rohmann, C. G. Parent-child similarities in hand-wrist ossification. *Am. J. Dis. Child.*, 1962, **103**, 603–607.

Garn, S. M., Rohmann, C. G., and Blumenthal, T. Ossification sequence polymorphism and sexual dimorphism in skeletal development. *Am. J. phys. Anthrop.*, 1966, **24**, 101–116.

Garn, S. M., Rohmann, C. G., Wagner, B., and Ascoli, W. Continuing bone growth throughout life: a general phenomenon. *Am. J. phys. Anthrop.*, 1967, **26**, 313–318.

Gavan, J. A. Growth and development of the chimpanzee; a longitudinal and comparative study. *Hum. Biol.*, 1953, **25**, 93–143.

Geber, M., and Dean, R. F. A. Le développement psychomoteur et somatique des jeunes enfants Africains en Ouganda. *Courrier*, 1964, **14**, 425.

Glasgow, R. B., and Kruse, P. Motor performance of girls age 6 to 14 years. *Res. Q. Am. Ass. Hlth. phys. Ed.*, 1960, **31**, 426–433.

Goss, R. J. *Adaptive growth.* London: Logos, 1964.

Graffar, M., and Corbier, J. Contribution à l'étude de l'influence socio-économique sur la croissance et le développement de l'énfant. *Courrier*, 1966, **16**, 1–25.

Grether, W. F., and Yerkes, R. M. Weight norms and relations for chimpanzee. *Am. J. phys. Anthrop.*, 1940, **28**, 181–197.

Greulich, W. W. A comparison of the physical growth and development of American-born and native Japanese children. *Am. J. phys. Anthrop.*, 1957, **15**, 489–515.

Greulich, W. W., and Pyle, S. I. *Radiographic atlas of skeletal development of the hand and wrist.* (2nd ed.) Stanford, Cal.: Stanford University Press, 1959.

Gruenwald, P. Growth of the human foetus. In A. McLaren (Ed.), *Advances in Reproductive Physiology.* Vol. II. London: Logos, 1967.

Harris, G. W., and Jacobsohn, D. Functional grafts of the anterior pituitary gland. *Proc. R. Soc. B.*, 1952, **139**, 263–276.

Harris, G. W., and Levine, S. Sexual differentiation of the brain and its experimental control. *J. Physiol.*, 1965, **181**, 379–400.

Hewitt, D. Some familial correlations in height, weight and skeletal maturity. *Ann. hum. Genet.*, 1957, **22**, 26–35.

Hiernaux, J. Heredity and environment: their influence on human morphology. A comparison of two independent lines of study. *Am. J. phys. Anthrop.*, 1963, **27**, 575–589.

Hiernaux, J. Weight/height relationship during growth in Africans and Europeans. *Hum. Biol.*, 1964, **36**, 273–293.

Hiernaux, J. Shape differentiation of ethnic groups and of sexes through growth. *Hum. Biol.*, 1968, **40**, 44–62.

Hindley, C. B., Filliozat, A. M., Klackenberg, G., Nicolet-Meister, D., and Sand, E. A. Differences in age of walking in five European longitudinal samples. *Hum. Biol.*, 1966, **38**, 364–379.

Howe, P. E., and Schiller, M. Growth responses of the school child to changes in diet and environmental factors. *J. appl. Physiol.*, 1952, **5**, 51–61.

Hubel, D. H., and Wiesel, T. N. Receptive fields of cells in striate cortex of very young, visually inexperienced kittens. *J. Neurophysiol.*, 1963, **26**, 996–1002.

Inano, H., Hori, Y., and Tamaoki, B. Effect of age on testicular enzymes related to steroid bioconversion. In G. E. W. Wolstenholme and M. O'Connor (Eds.), *Endocrinology of the testis*. London: Churchill, 1967.

Israelsohn, W. J. Description and modes of analysis of human growth. In J. M. Tanner, (Ed.), *Human Growth*. Oxford: Pergamon, 1960. (*Sym. Soc. Hum. Biol.*, **3**, 21–41.)

Jenkins, G. B. Relative weight and volume of the component parts of the brain of the human embryo at different stages of development. *Contr. Embryol.*, 1921, **13**, 41–60.

Jirasek, J. E. The relationship between the structure of the testis and differentiation of the external genitalia and phenotype in man. In G. E. W. Wolstenholme and M. O'Connor (Eds.), *Endocrinology of the testis*. London: Churchill, 1967.

Jones, H. E. *Motor performance and growth. A developmental study of static dynamometric strength*. Berkeley: University of California Press, 1949.

Jones, M. C. The later careers of boys who were early—or late—maturing. *Child Dev.*, 1957, **28**, 113–128.

Jonxis, J. H. P. The development of haemoglobin. *Pediat. Clins. N. Am.*, 1965, **12**, 535–550.

Jost, A. Anterior pituitary function in foetal life. In A. W. Harris and B. T. Donovan (Eds.), *The pituitary gland*. Vol. 2. London: Butterworth, 1966. Pp. 299–323.

Kaplan, S. L., and Grumbach, M. M. Growth hormone secretion in the human foetus and in anencephaly. *Excerpta med., Int. Congr.*, 1967. Series 142, Abstract 98.

Klosovskii, B. N. *The development of the brain and its disturbances by harmful factors*. London: Pergamon, 1963.

Knobloch, H., and Pasamanick, B. Mental subnormality. *New Engl. J. Med.*, 1962, **266**, 1045–1051; 1092–1097; 1155–1161.

Kraus, B. S., Wise, W. J., and Frei, R. H. Heredity and the craniofacial complex. *Amer. J. Orthod.*, 1959, **45**, 172–217.

Larroche, J. C. The development of the central nervous system during intrauterine life. In F. Falkner (Ed.), *Human Development*. London: Saunders, 1966.

Lauritzen, C., and Lehmann, W. D. Levels of chorionic gonadotrophin in the newborn infant and their relationship to adrenal dehydro-epiandrosterone. *J. Endocr.*, 1967, **39**, 173–182.

Lindner, H. R. Androgens and related compounds in the spermatic vein blood of domestic animals. II. Species-linked differences in the metabolism of androstenedione in blood. *J. Endocr.*, 1961, **23**, 139–159.

Lorenz, K. In J. M. Tanner and B. Inhelder (Eds.), *Discussions on child development*. London: Tavistock, 1960. Vol. 4, p. 128.

MacDowell, E. C., Allen, E., and MacDowell, C. G. The prenatal growth of the mouse. *J. gen. Physiol.*, 1927, **11**, 57–70.

McGraw, M. B. *The neuromuscular maturation of the human infant*. New York: Columbia University Press, 1943.

McKeown, T., and Record, R. G. Observations on foetal growth in multiple pregnancy in man. *J. Endocr.*, 1952, **8**, 386–401.

McKeown, T., and Record, R. G. The influence of placental size on foetal growth in man, with special reference to multiple pregnancy. *J. Endocr.*, 1953, **9**, 418–426.

McLaren, A. Genetic and environmental effects on foetal and placental growth in mice. *J. Reprod. Fert.*, 1965, **9**, 79–98.

McLaren, A., and Michie, D. Studies on the transfer of fertilised mouse eggs to uterine foster-mothers. I. Factors affecting the implantation and survival of native and transferred eggs. *J. exp. Biol.*, 1956, **33**, 394–416.

Meredith, H. V., and Knott, V. B. Illness history and physical growth. III. Comparative anatomic status and rate of change for school children in different long-term health categories. *Am. J. Dis. Child.*, 1962, **103**, 146–151.

Miller, F. J. W., Court, S. D. M., Walton, W. S., and Knox, E. G. *Growing up in Newcastle-upon-Tyne: a continuing study of health and illness in young children within their families*. London: Oxford University Press, 1960.

Ministry of Education. *Moving and growing*. London: His Majesty's Stationery Office, 1952.

Ministry of Health. Standards of normal weight in infancy. *Minist. Hlth. Rep. Publ. Hlth. No. 99.* London: His Majesty's Stationery Office, 1959.

Minkowski, A. Development of the nervous system in early life. In F. Falkner (Ed.), *Human development*. London: Saunders, 1966.

Money, J., and Hampson, J. G. Idiopathic sexual precocity in the male. *Psychosom. Med.*, 1955, **17**, 1–15.

Mussen, P. H., and Jones, M. C. Self-conceptions, motivations and impersonal attitudes of late- and early-maturing boys. *Child Dev.*, 1957, **28**, 243–256.

Mussen, P. H., and Jones, M. C. The behavior-inferred motivations of late– and early-maturing boys. *Child Dev.*, 1958, **29**, 61–67.

Naeye, R. L., Benirschke, K., Hagstrom, J. W. C., and Marcus, C. C. Intra-uterine growth of twins as estimated from live-born birth-weight data. *Pediatrics*, 1966, **37**, 409–416.

Nicholson A. B., and Hanley, C. Indices of physiological maturity, derivation and inter-relationships. *Child Dev.*, 1953, **24**, 3–38.

Niemi, M., Ikonen, M., and Hervonen, A. Histochemistry and fine structure of the interstitial tissue in the human foetal testis. In G. E. W. Wolstenholme and M. O'Connor (Eds.), *Endocrinology of the testis*. London: Churchill, 1967.

Papousek, H. A physiological view of early autogenesis of so-called voluntary movements. *Plzen. lék. Sb. Suppl.*, 1961, **3**, 195–198.

Penfield, W., and Rasmussen, T. *The cerebral cortex of man. A clinical study of localization of function*. New York: MacMillan, 1950.

Powell, G. F., Brasel, J. A., and Blizzard, R. M. Emotional deprivation and growth retardation simulating idiopathic hypopituitarism. I. Clinical evaluation of the syndrome. *New Engl. J. Med.*, 1967, **276**, 1271–1278.

Powell, G. F., Brasel, J. A., Raiti, S., and Blizzard, R. M. Emotional deprivation and growth retardation simulating idiopathic hypopituitarism. II. Endocrinologic evaluation of the syndrome. *New Engl. J. Med.*, 1967, **276**, 1279–1283.

Prader, A., Tanner, J. M., and Von Harnack, G. A. Catch-up growth following illness or starvation. *J. Pediat.*, 1963, **62**, 646–659.

Pringle, M. L. K., Butler, N. R., and Davie, R. *Eleven thousand seven-year olds.* London: Longmans, 1966.

Rabinowicz, T. Quantitative appraisal of the cerebral cortex of the premature infant of 8 months. In A. Minkowski (Ed.), *Regional development of the brain in early life.* Oxford: Blackwell, 1967.

Raiha, N., and Hjelt, L. The correlation between the development of the hypophysial portal system and the onset of neurosecretory activity in the human foetus and infant. *Acta paediat.*, 1957, **72**, 610–616.

Reynolds, E. L. Degree of kinship and pattern of ossification. *Am. J. phys. Anthrop.*, N. S., 1943, **1**, 405–416.

Reynolds, E. L., and Wines, J. V. Physical changes associated with adolescence in boys. *Am. J. Dis. Child.*, 1951, **82**, 529–547.

Roberts, D. F. Body weight, race and climate. *Am. J. phys. Anthrop.*, 1953, N.S., **11**, 533–558.

Scammon, R. E. The first seriatim study of human growth. *Am. J. phys. Anthrop.*, 1927, **10**, 329–336.

Scammon, R. E. The measurement of the body in childhood. In J. A. Harris, C. M. Jackson, D. G. Paterson, and R. E. Scammon. *The Measurement of man.* Minneapolis: University of Minnesota Press, 1930.

*Schreider, E. Gradients écologiques, régulation thermique et differenciation humaine. *Biotypologie*, 1957, **18**, 168–183.

Schreider, E. Recherches sur la stratification sociale des caracteres biologiques. *Biotypologie*, 1964, **25**, 105–135.

Scott, E. M., Illsley, R., and Thomson, A. M. A psychological investigation of primigravidae. II. Maternal social class, age, physique and intelligence. *J. Obstet. Gynaec. Br. Emp.*, 1956, **63**, 338–343.

Scott, J. A. *Report on the heights and weights (and other measurements) of school pupils in the county of London in 1959.* London: County Council, 1961.

Scott, J. A. Intelligence, physique and family size. *Br. J. prev. soc. Med.*, 1962, **16**, 165–173.

Scottish Council for Research in Education. *Social implications of the 1947 Scottish mental survey.* London: University Press, 1953.

Sereni, F., and Principi, N. The development of enzyme systems. *Pediat. Clins. N. Am.* 1965, **12**, 515–534.

Sheldon, W. H. *The varieties of human physique.* New York: Harper, 1940.

Shuttleworth, F. K. Sexual maturation and the physical growth of girls age six to nineteen. *Monogr. Soc. Res. Child Dev.*, 1937, **2**, No. 5.

Shuttleworth, F. K. The physical and mental growth of girls and boys age six to nineteen in relation to age at maximum growth. *Monogr. Soc. Res. Child Dev.*, 1939, **4**, No. 3.

Simmons, K. The Brush Foundation study of child growth and development. II. Physical growth and development. *Monogr. Soc. Res. Child Dev.*, 1944, **9**, No. 1.

Simmons, K., and Greulich, W. W. Menarcheal age and the height, weight and skeletal age of girls age 7 to 17 years. *J. Pediat.*, 1943, **22**, 518–548.

Stolz, H. R., and Stolz, L. M. *Somatic development of adolescent boys. A study of the growth of boys during the second decade of life.* New York: MacMillan, 1951.

Tanner, J. M. Current advances in the study of physique. Photogrammetric anthropometry and an androgyny scale. *Lancet*, 1951, **1**, 574–579.

*Tanner, J. M. Boas' contributions to knowledge of human growth and form. In W. Goldschmidt (Ed.), *The anthropology of Franz Boas: essays on the* *centennial of his birth.* Mem. Amer. Anthropol. Assoc., 1959, No. 89. (*Amer. Anthropol.*, **61**.)

Tanner, J. M. Genetics of human growth. In J. M. Tanner (Ed.), *Human Growth.* Oxford: Pergamon, 1960. (*Sym. Soc. Hum. Biol.*, **3**, 43–58.)

Tanner, J. M. *Education and physical growth. Implications of the study of children's growth for educational theory and practice.* London: University Press, 1961.

*Tanner, J. M. *Growth at adolescence.* (2nd ed.) Oxford: Blackwell Scientific Publications. Philadelphia: Davis, 1962.

Tanner, J. M. The regulation of human growth. *Child Dev.*, 1963, **34**, 817–848.

Tanner, J. M. *The physique of the olympic athlete.* London: Allen & Unwin, 1964.

Tanner, J. M. Radiographic studies of body composition. In J. Brozek (Ed.), *Body composition.* Oxford: Pergamon, 1965. (*Symp. Soc. Hum. Biol.*, **7**, 211–238.)

Tanner, J. M. Growth and physique in different populations of mankind. In P. T. Baker and J. S. Weiner (Eds.), *The biology of human adaptability.* Oxford: Clarendon, 1966. (a)

*Tanner, J. M. The secular trend towards earlier physical maturation. *T. Soc. Geneesk.*, 1966, **44**, 524–539. (b)

*Tanner, J. M. Galtonian eugenics and the study of growth. The relation of body size, intelligence test score, and social circumstances in children and adults. *Eugen. Rev.*, 1966, **58**, 122–135. (c)

Tanner, J. M. Puberty. In A. McClaren (Ed.), *Advances in reproductive physiology*, Vol. 2. London: Logos, 1967.

Tanner, J. M. Growth of bone, muscle and fat during childhood and adolescence. In G. A. Lodge (Ed.), *Growth and development of mammals.* London: Butterworth, 1968.

Tanner, J. M. Growth and endocrinology in the adolescent. In L. I. Gardner (Ed.), *Endocrine and genetic diseases of childhood.* Philadelphia: Saunders, 1969.

Tanner, J. M., and Gupta, D. A longitudinal study of the excretion of individual steroids in children from 8 to 12 years old. *J. Endocr.*, 1968, **41**, 139–156.

Tanner, J. M., Healy, M. J. R., Lockhart, R. D., MacKenzie, J. D., and Whitehouse, R. H. Aberdeen growth study. I. The prediction of adult body measurements from measurements taken each year from birth to 5 years. *Archs. Dis. Childh.*, 1956, **31**, 382–381.

Tanner, J. M., Hiernaux, J., and Jarman, S. Growth and physique studies. In J. S. Weiner (Ed.), *International biological programme: handbook of agreed methods, human adaptability section.* In press.

Tanner, J. M., and Israelsohn, W. J. Parent-child correlations for body measurements of children between the ages of one month and seven years. *Ann. hum. Genet.*, 1963, **26**, 245–259.

Tanner, J. M., Whitehouse, R. H., and Healy, M. J. R. *A new system for estimating skeletal maturity from the hand and wrist, with standards derived from a study of 2,600 healthy British children. Parts I and II.* Paris: Centre International de l'Enfance, 1962.

Tanner, J. M., Whitehouse, R. H., and Takaishi, M. Standards from birth to maturity for height, weight, height velocity and weight velocity: British children 1965. *Archs. Dis. Childh.*, 1966, **41**, 454–471; 613–635.

Thompson, D'A. W. *On growth and form.* Cambridge: University Press, 1942.

Thompson, A. M. Maternal stature and reproductive efficiency. *Eugen. Rev.*, 1959, **51**, 157–162.

Tuddenham, R. D., and Snyder, M. M. Physical growth of California boys and girls from birth to eighteen years. *Univ. Calif. Publs. Child Dev.*, 1954, **1**, 183–364.

Valsik, J. A., Stukovsky, R., and Bernatova, L. Quelques facteurs geographiques et sociaux ayant une influence sur l'âge de la puberté. *Biotypologie*, 1963, **24,** 109–123.

Vincent, M., and Hugon, J. L'insuffisance ponderale du prematuré Africain au point de vue de la santé publique. *Bull. Wld. Hlth. Org.*, 1962, **26,** 143–174.

Waddington, C. H. *The strategy of the genes. A discussion of some aspects of theoretical biology.* London: Allen & Unwin, 1957.

White House Conference on Child Health and Protection, Section I. *Growth and development of the child. Part II. Anatomy and physiology.* New York: Century, 1933.

Widdowson, E. M. Mental contentment and physical growth. *Lancet*, 1951, **1,** 1316–1318.

Widdowson, E. M., and McCance, R. A. Some effects of accelerating growth. I. General somatic development. *Proc. R. Soc. Brit.*, 1960, **152,** 188–206.

Widdowson, E. M., Mavor, W. O., and McCance, R. A. The effect of undernutrition and rehabilitation on the development of the reproductive organs: rats. *J. Endocr.*, 1964, **29,** 119–126.

Wiesel, T. N., and Hubel, D. H. Effects of visual deprivation on morphology and physiology of cells in the cats' lateral geniculate body. *J. Neurophysiol.*, 1963, **26,** 978–993.

Wurst, F., Wassertheurer, H., and Kimeswengen, K. *Entwicklung und Umwelt des Landkindes.* Wien: Ostenreichocher Bundesverlag, 1964.

Yakovlev, P. I., and Lecours, A. R. The myelogenetic cycles of regional maturation of the brain. In A. Minkowski (Ed.), *Regional Development of the Brain in Early Life.* Oxford: Blackwell, 1967.

Young, H. B. Ageing and adolescence. *Dev. Med. child Neurol.*, 1963, **5,** 451–460.

Young, W. C., and Yerkes, R. M. Factors influencing the reproductive cycle in the chimpanzee: the period of adolescent sterility and related problems. *Endocrinology*, 1943, **33,** 121–154.

Zeller, W. *Konstitution und Entwicklung.* Gottingen: Psychologisch Rundschau, 1952.

4 Physiological Development

DOROTHY H. EICHORN

Regardless of age, size, or complexity, all organisms perform the same basic physiological functions to remain alive. Each obtains from food the materials for repair or replacement of cells and energy for all its activities. Release of energy from nutrients requires oxidation. For the control of both oxidative and synthetic reactions secretions such as enzymes must be produced. Waste products accumulate from all metabolic reactions, and, as is known from chemical laws of mass action, will slow and eventually block these reactions, unless the organism has some means of excretion. If nutrients and oxygen are to reach all cells and their parts and wastes to be removed from them, circulation is needed. To respond to changes in the internal and external environments, the organism must be irritable. Not only the avoidance of danger and acquisition of food, but also the mechanics of digestion, respiration, and circulation involve movement.

Whether an organism is growing or not, it carries on all these activities. For growth to occur, some must be intensified, but the processes that fulfill the replacement function also underlie development. Only the creation of new individuals by organisms that reproduce sexually adds any function beyond those necessary for the existence and reproduction of single cells.

Viewed structurally, there is great diversity among species, and even within the same organism during the course of development, in the organs that support any given process, but the essential functions are the same in plant and animal, unicellular or multicellular, at all stages. If the student focuses on function, he will find the facts of human

physiological development easier to assimilate. The details that make for difficulty in understanding arise because (1) the human prenatal and postnatal environments are strikingly different, and each requires special adaptations, (2) complex organisms inherit many of their basic mechanisms from earlier, simpler forms, and have at least temporarily some structures characteristic of these simpler forms, and (3) the larger the organism becomes, the more remote are most of its cells from environmental supports, so specialized cells and organ systems, each with multiple controls, must be developed and integrated.

Many students of behavior think of its morphologic and physiologic bases in terms of only two or three systems—the neural, the muscular, and parts of the endocrine—and of these only in relation to the external environment—the processes of perceiving and responding to external stimuli. Yet most cells of the human body are carefully shielded from the general external environment. Those that are not completely insulated can exist only because they are also in a well-regulated internal environment, one that is essentially the same for all cells. Every functional system contributes to the compensatory mechanisms that keep the fluids surrounding each cell relatively constant in temperature, acid-base balance, concentration of nutrients and ions, osmotic pressure (pressure resulting in diffusion between solutions of different concentrations), and other characteristics. In the preceding chapter and several of the succeeding ones, the development of neuromuscular functions that mediate interactions with the external environment are described. Here

157

the emphasis will be on the processes that permit life to continue and development to proceed in the face of change in both the organism and its external environment.

As is true in the study of behavior, the development of functions can be dealt with in either of two ways. The level of development of all organic activities can be considered at a number of successive ages, or each different function can be traced individually throughout the course of its development. The first method has the advantage of calling attention to the fact that all systems are interrelated but the rate of development or decline is not the same for all. However, one tends to lose sight of the pattern of changes in particular functions. Further, as the organism becomes more complex, so do the interactions within a single system. To present a coherent picture of the intricacies of all activities simultaneously is virtually impossible except during the earliest stages of gestation when the organism is very small and relatively simple in structure. Therefore, after an overview of beginning phases, major functions will be approached separately.

EMBRYONIC DEVELOPMENT AND PLACENTATION

Nowhere are the principles outlined in the first two introductory paragraphs better illustrated than in the succession of means by which the human being secures food and oxygen and eliminates its wastes. Unlike the ova of lower vertebrates, those of most mammals have almost no yolk. Rather than drawing on a stored supply of food, the mammalian embryo quickly establishes a parasitic relationship with the mother. In the human this process is particularly elided, for the first phases of differentiation of the embryo itself are also relatively more rapid than in other mammals, imposing increased demands for food, oxygen, and elimination very early in gestation. Throughout most of the many months that the intricate digestive, respiratory, and excretory structures necessary for postnatal function are developing, the placenta acts as intestinal wall, lung, and kidney (and serves storage, endocrine, and barrier functions as well). About three weeks are required, however, for the human embryo to build up a placenta and vascular connec-

tions with it. Meanwhile, its cells carry on their essential metabolic activities through direct absorption from, and excretion into, the surrounding environment.

The first week or fortnight after conception is termed the ovular phase or period of the zygote, the second or third to the eighth week is called the embryonic period or period of organogenesis, and the remainder of gestation is the fetal period. Before it burrows into the lining of the uterus, the zygote spends about three or four days traversing the fallopian tube and another three or four free in the uterine cavity. During this time the ovum, which is the largest human cell, subdivides into a hollow ball of ordinary-sized cells, the blastocyst. It contains fluid rather than the yolk found in the blastocyst of lower vertebrates. At one end is the inner cell mass from which the embryo develops. Because very little growth occurs—the blastocyst is only a little larger than the original ovum—little food is needed, but the human zygote may utilize secretions from the fallopian tube.

While the fertilized ovum is still in the tube, the trophoblast, a layer of cells not part of the embryo proper, probably has begun to differentiate and cover the blastocyst. At least in human embryos recovered at seven or eight days after conception, trophoblast is already quite thick over the area that has started to invade the uterine wall. Trophoblast cells secrete fluid into the cavity of the blastocyst, phagocytize nutrient materials, and adhere to and destroy some of the endometrium (the mucous membrane lining the uterus). Once implantation has begun the embryo has available not only glycogen-containing secretions from uterine glands, but also cellular constituents and fluids from endometrial cells and blood vessels eroded by the trophoblast. Trophoblastic or histotrophic nutrition is characteristic of the second to fourth weeks, that is, from the initiation of implantation to the establishment of placental exchange, but may continue concomitantly with the latter for several more weeks.

A more effective method for securing food and oxygen than phagocytosis and direct absorption is urgently needed, for by the third week the embryo is growing rapidly. When the developing organism begins to enter the uterine lining between the seventh and ninth day it is already more than a simple blastocyst. The inner cell mass is now an embryonic disc with a definite layer of entoderm and a plate of potential ectodermal and mesodermal cells, the trophoblast consists of two layers—a thin generative layer of cytotrophoblast and a thick outer syncytium of cells that have lost their boundaries, and another extraembryonic membrane, the amnion, is separating from the embryo. The fluid-filled amnion helps to prevent adhesions and mechanical injury. Later in gestation the fetus may swallow amniotic fluid and excrete fluid into the amnion.

Differentiation, particularly of the extraembryonic structures and the embryonic cardiovascular system, is prodigious during the second and third weeks. Textbooks on developmental psychology usually stress the precocity of neural development but do not mention the accelerated rate of differentiation of the intraembryonic and placental circulatory systems. Near the end of the second week a third extraembryonic structure, the yolk sac, is distinguishable, and within a few days it has blood vessels. The yolk sac can be considered vestigial only in terms of its original function, for it is the site of the first blood formation in the human being and remains for some weeks a source of blood cells. The proliferating trophoblast acquires a core of mesoderm and is called trophoderm or serosa. Early in the third week both the body stalk, a narrow strip of mesoderm connecting the embryo and the trophoderm, and the allantois, an extraembryonic membrane which soon coalesces with the trophoderm to form the chorion, or fetal side of the placenta, can be seen. The clusters of trophoderm are organizing into bushy tufts or villi and developing lacunae that unite to become the intervillous space into which blood from eroded maternal vessels flow. As mesoderm and blood vessels differentiate from allantoic tissue, they penetrate the villous branches, transforming them, by the end of the third week, into true chorionic villi.

Simultaneous with these elaborations of the extraembryonic structures is the differentiation of the embryonic cardiovascular system. During the third week the paired strands of cells that constitute the primordia of the heart appear, one on each side of the gut. They are hollowed out, brought together,

and fused into a simple tubular heart. Meanwhile the primary blood vessels arise in much the same fashion. Cords of cells develop lumina (cavities), merge into small channels, and then enlarge. From the paired aortas thus formed branches are put out, among the largest of which are the arteries that extend from the dorsal aorta (running from the heart to the caudal end of the embryo) to the yolk sac and to the chorion. The intraembryonic portions of the former are the omphalomesenteric arteries and their continuations in the yolk sac are the vitellines, but for convenience both are often called vitelline arteries. The arteries to the chorion are known as the allantoics in recognition of their destination—the vascular plexus derived from the allantois and now investing the trophoderm—or as the umbilical arteries, because they run through the body stalk, the forerunner of the umbilical cord. Paired veins develop similarly but slightly later, and, again, those returning to the embryo from the yolk sac and from the chorion are very prominent.

The heart begins to beat about the end of the third week, but its early contractions are autonomous; innervation is not completed for several weeks. Fluid is present in the venous circuits to the heart, and immediately before circulation is initiated blood corpuscles from the yolk sac are added. When the contractions of the heart become sufficiently strong, these corpuscles move with each beat. As soon as networks of small channels differentiate to connect arteries and veins, the intraembryonic, yolk sac, and chorionic or placental circulations begin. This is probably early in the fourth week but may be late in the third. The course and dynamics of the fetal and postnatal circulations are described in the section on the cardiovascular system. Several important facts about the prenatal circulation and placental structure and physiology should be noted here, however.

First, all three vascular arcs undergo many further transformations. The straight tubular heart bends and twists and develops by the end of the second month into a four-chambered structure, differing in small but important respects from the adult heart. Metabolic need is the primary determinant of the course and size of blood vessels, but some temporary routes represent recapitulations of phylogeny. Moreover, vascular channels may be altered because other structures interfere, as illustrated by the interruption of the umbilical veins by the rapidly enlarging embryonic liver. Channels develop connecting these veins with the vascular network in the liver, so that eventually all blood returns from the placenta to the heart through the liver. Further, the umbilical veins coalesce in the umbilical cord, so that only the left umbilical vein carries blood from the placenta to the liver; the right simply drains the body wall and flows into the left. Because tissue needs to be well provided with blood only while metabolically active, some channels develop extensively and then regress. For example, the yolk sac and its vessels are of large size for several weeks, but shrink and become nonfunctional after the fifth or sixth week. Within the embryo, all new tissue must be vascularized, and, of course, the process continues postnatally in all growing tissue, but the more active organs always are the better supplied. Thus during gestation the placental circulation is much greater than that to the lungs. After birth, however, the reverse is true, the pulmonary circuit being large and the umbilical vein remaining only as ligaments and the umbilical arteries as minor vessels to tissue between their original branching point and the umbilicus and as fibroid cords.

Not only purely vascular changes occur in the placenta and accessory structures. Not until the fifth week does a true umbilical cord come into being. As mentioned previously, the body stalk originates from extraembryonic mesoderm. After the allantoic or umbilical arteries and veins appear they push out to the chorion through this rapidly growing stalk, and the allantois is also embodied within it. At the edge of the umbilicus the amnion and the body wall of the embryo are continuous, so the umbilical ring is the juncture of embryonic and extraembryonic tissue. Both the stalk of the yolk sac and the body stalk with its incorporated blood vessels and allantois pass through this open ring, which becomes progressively smaller. During the fifth week the amnion envelops these stalks and forces them together, forming the umbilical cord. Elongation of the cord continues to a final length somewhat greater than that of the fetus.

In contrast to the regression of the yolk sac, growth and modifications of both the maternal and fetal sides of the placenta persist throughout gestation. Although the size of the placenta relative to that of the uterus is greatest at the fifth month, growth is maintained thereafter. At least as important for the function of the placenta as its size are the alterations in its structure. While the early invasive action of the trophoblast is predominant, the villi have comparatively few short branches but cover the entire chorionic surface. Those not in the region of implantation later atrophy, whereas the villi in the discoid placental area elaborate. Not only do the branches increase in size and complexity, they also become more organized in external and internal structure. Instead of many hundreds of villous clumps covered with sprawling trophoblast, there are 15 or 16 treelike groupings called cotyledons separated by septa. Within the spaces bounded by these septa the ends of the majority of villi lie unattached and surrounded by the blood that oozes from eroded maternal blood vessels. The termini of some "anchoring villi," however, come into progressively closer contact with the endometrium. Their trophoblast is lost, as is the outer lining of the uterus below them, so the connective tissue core of the villi adheres to the connective tissue of the uterus. Less complete reduction of the trophoblastic covering of the free villi also occurs, the outer syncytial cells thinning markedly and almost all of the inner cytotrophoblast layer disappearing. This attenuation of the epithelial covering of the free villi begins once the chorion is well established, that is, at about the end of the second month, but is more extensive during the last three months of gestation.

To some extent these processes enhancing transfer of nutrients, gases, and wastes across the placenta are counteracted as gestation proceeds by the deposition of a fibrinoid substance which is probably an amalgamation of material from the maternal blood, the uterine lining, and the chorion (Arey, 1965; Patten, 1953). Certainly in abnormal circumstances interference with placental exchange has been observed (Nesbitt, 1966). In any event, the amount of tissue through which metabolic interchange must take place varies during prenatal existence although in principle three cellular layers of the villi separate the fetal from the maternal blood—the endothelial lining of the capillaries, stroma or supporting tissue, and the syncytial layer of the trophoblast. For more detail about the histology of the placenta and the development of the fetus and its accessory structures the student should consult specialized articles and volumes such as those of Amoroso (1961), Aherne and Dunnill (1966), Arey (1965), Patten (1953), and Villee (1960).

Because the normality and rate of prenatal development are highly dependent upon the nature and amount of substances passing the placenta, the subject of placental permeability is of great practical as well as theoretical significance (Benirschke, 1965; Dancis, 1965; Hepner and Bowen, 1960; Warkany, Monroe, and Southerland, 1961; Wigglesworth, 1966; Wilson, 1964). Summaries of early research are included in the classic works of Needham (1931) and Windle (1940). More recent reviews can be found in Adamsons (1965), Hagerman and Villee (1960), Page (1960), Villee (1960), and Widdas (1961).

Permeability is neither qualitatively nor quantitatively fixed from species to species, cell to cell, or moment to moment. Instead it fluctuates with substance, environmental conditions such as temperature and oxygen supply, level of metabolic activity, and characteristics of the membrane. The supply of nutrients in the maternal blood often exceeds current fetal need, particularly early in gestation. In the human and many other animals, nutrients are then stored, probably selectively, by the fetal placenta for later release. At a given point in time, therefore, the amount of a nutrient transferred may be modified by the reserve accumulated as well as by the concentration gradient between maternal and villous blood. Special mechanisms exist whereby molecules too large to diffuse through the pores of a membrane (e.g., glucose, amino acids, and vitamins) or small molecules indiffusible for other reasons (such as the ions of most electrolytes) can be transferred. If a membrane is damaged, leakage may also be a factor. As has been demonstrated in the rare instances in which red blood cells have passed the placenta (Page, 1960), even large particles can

leak through damaged membranes if the hydrostatic pressure is sufficiently great.

The surface area and thickness of a membrane are important factors in the regulation of transport across it. In general, placental size increases and the density of the placental barrier decreases throughout gestation. There are, however, differences among species and developmental variations within species in the size of the placenta relative to the fetus and in the number and thickness of the cellular layers separating fetal and maternal blood. Size has been estimated in terms of surface area, volume, and weight. These measures are intercorrelated, but none is an exact guide to functional capacity. Neither weight nor volume directly reflects the absorptive area, and not all the surface area is involved in metabolic interchange. Some of it, such as the septa, chorionic plate, and fibrinoid areas, lacks capillaries narrowly separated from maternal blood.

Early in gestation the weight of the placenta increases faster than that of the fetus, but later the reverse is true. For each species there is a time at which the placental: fetal weight ratio is maximal and one at which the weights become equal. Thereafter, fetal weight is progressively greater. In some species placental growth ceases before the end of gestation, but in monkey and man the weight of the placenta increases to the normal time of delivery.

At term the human placenta is about 14% of fetal weight. Its surface area has been estimated to range from about 7 square meters (Dodds, 1922) to 14.7 square meters, or about 160 square feet (Dees-Mattingly, 1936; Wilkin, 1958). Recently Aherne and Dunnill (1966), using improved methods, estimated the surface area of the intervillous space and villi (exclusive of microvilli) to be 11 square meters at term, and the villous area which contained capillaries close to the surface to increase from 0.4 square meters at 28 weeks to 1.8 at full term. That any of these figures is considerable is indicated by the fact that the surface area of the skin of a full-term newborn infant is about 0.22 square meters and that of the "standard 70 kilogram adult male" about 1.74.

In all likelihood the absorptive area of a normal placenta throughout most or all of the time the fetus is dependent upon it for metabolic interchange is not only adequate to meet fetal needs but also provides a margin of safety. This margin may narrow near the end of gestation. Fetal weight is significantly correlated with placental weight in many species, including man (Adair and Thelander, 1925; Calkins, 1937; McKeown and Record, 1953; Aherne, 1966; Winick, Coscia, and Noble, 1967), but variations in birth weights, independent of placental size and gestational age, have been observed to develop between single and multiple births very late in gestation in both man (McKeown and Record, 1953) and the guinea pig (Ibsen, 1928).

Grouping placentae by the number of layers of maternal and fetal tissue between the two bloods yields five classes:

1. Epitheliochorial (maternal endothelium, connective tissue, and epithelium, and fetal chorion, mesenchyme, and endothelium).
2. Syndesmochorial (lacking maternal epithelium).
3. Endotheliochorial (lacking both maternal epithelium and connective tissue).
4. Hemochorial (only fetal endothelium and chorion—trophoblast and stroma).
5. Hemoendothelial (only fetal endothelium).

Pigs and horses fall in the first classification, sheep and cattle in the second, the dog and cat in the third, monkeys and man in the fourth, and the rat, rabbit, and guinea pig in the fifth.

Across species and developmentally within species the width of the placental barrier is negatively correlated with permeability. Yet the correlation is far from perfect, and a specific substance may pass a dense placenta but not a simpler one. For example, in the rat, which has both a hemoendothelial placenta and a simultaneously functional thicker yolk sac placenta, the dye toluidin blue passes the latter more easily than the former (Windle, 1940). A striking illustration of developmental changes is found in the rabbit. During a gestation period of about 4½ weeks its placenta is reduced from syndesmochorial to hemoendothelial (Windle, 1940; Amoroso, 1952).

Morphological variations in placentae have

an important bearing upon the validity of our knowledge about human prenatal function. Still more frequently than is the case under postnatal circumstances, ethical and practical considerations contraindicate experimentation with human beings. Unfortunately, generalization of observations or experimental results from one species to another or of measurements taken at one point in time on a fetus to other periods is even more hazardous before birth than after. To all the usual factors restricting the comparability of species must be added not only structural variations of the placenta, but also length of gestation, degree of maturity at analogous stages (e.g., birth), physiological characteristics of the placenta (such as pressure and concentration gradients, oxygen supply, and storage, enzymatic and other metabolic activities), and the kind and extent of fetal and maternal adaptations to the conditions of gestation.

Selection of an appropriate species for studying a particular function is difficult because one that resembles man more closely in size or the manner in which the activity is carried out may differ markedly in gestation period or placental morphology and function. For several reasons the sheep and rabbit are subjects of choice for investigations of prenatal respiration, as are the rat and guinea pig for nutritional studies. However, the sheep's placenta is less advanced than man's and its gestation period is only about half as long. Some peculiarities of the placenta in the rabbit and rat have been detailed earlier; both have short gestations.

Normal prenatal development requires physiologic adjustments of the mother as well as of the fetus, and the human being is a prime example of a species in which modifications of the maternal physiology are extensive. Periodic changes in the secretion of gonadal hormones condition the uterus for implantation, increasing the size of uterine glands and the amount of fluid and glycogen they contain. If conception occurs, the production of many hormones by the pituitary, thyroid, and adrenocortical glands eventually rises. Probably in response to hormonal stimulation, blood and tissue fluid volumes become greater.

As gestation proceeds, more blood flows through the uterus (Assali, Douglass, Baird,

Nicholson. and Suyemoto, 1953; Huckabee, 1962; Metcalfe, Romney, Ramsey, Reid, and Burwell, 1955) and the total peripheral resistance of the maternal circulatory system drops, increasing the venous return to her heart and hence her cardiac output. Under normal circumstances the mother's cardiac output rises gradually during the first 7 months of pregnancy to 30 to 50% above the nongravid level and then drops somewhat during the last 8 weeks (Bader, Bader, Rose and Braunwald, 1955; Burwell and Metcalfe, 1958; Hamilton, 1949). Oxygen consumption rises approximately 30% as the time for delivery is approached. At the same time the expanding uterus pushes the abdomen against the diaphragm, reducing the respiratory excursion. To adjust to this handicap and to the increased demand for oxygen, the rate and depth of respiration increase.

The methods used in prenatal experiments also limit the conclusions that can be drawn from them. Prematurely delivered fetuses are obviously not functioning in a normal prenatal environment, and spontaneous prematurity is presumptive evidence of abnormality in mother, fetus, placenta, or some combination of the three. Even when the placenta is left attached and intact and sufficient time is allowed for recovery from anesthesia and possible surgical shock, any surgical intervention alters the normal physiologic condition of mother, fetus, and placenta. Anesthesia is essential for all but the most minor surgery, but anesthetic procedures vary in the degree to which they prevent shock as well as in the complications they may induce in fetus and mother. Windle's summary (1940, p. 10) of the dilemma posed by prenatal research still applies:

The problems involved in most investigations in physiology of the fetus are complicated because one is dealing with two organisms maintaining mutual although precarious relationship to one another. It is true that the fetus cannot be studied under physiologic conditions when the health of the mother is jeopardized, but on the other hand the best of conditions in the mother do not insure that behavior of the extracted fetuses will always be normal.

Although improved techniques devised since that statement was written help to minimize the physiologic disturbances created by experimental manipulations, the reservations outlined here should be kept in mind when evaluating any research on prenatal function.

HEMATOLOGY

Most cells of a complex multicellular organism are remote not only from the external environment but also from the organism's specialized tissues for nutrition, excretion, and internal secretion (e.g., of hormones). If the essential needs of each cell are to be met and its environment kept relatively constant, a link between all cells and the sources of food, oxygen, and internal secretions and the organs of elimination—kidneys, intestine, lungs, and skin—is necessary. This function is fulfilled by the body fluids—blood, interstitial fluid, and lymph.

As the primary vehicle of distribution, blood plays a role in almost every bodily activity. However, it remains in a system of closed vessels and is not in direct contact with cells (except those lining the walls of the blood vessels) so a means of interchange between blood and cells is needed. The medium of exchange is provided by interstitial fluid, which occupies the space around cells and is derived from the plasma of blood, largely through diffusion and filtration. Lymph is the fluid that drains from the intercellular spaces into the system of lymphatic vessels and thence back into the blood via lymphatic ducts emptying into the venous circulation.

Blood is composed of a complex fluid, plasma, which contains a large number of dissolved materials and in which are suspended the formed elements of blood—erythrocytes (red corpuscles), leukocytes (white cells), and thrombocytes (platelets). About 90% of plasma is water. Among the substances dissolved within it are the major blood proteins, digested forms of nutrients, wastes, gases, electrolytes, hormones, and enzymes. The proteins contribute to acid-base regulation, nutrition, coagulation, and immunological responses and to such functional characteristics of plasma as its viscosity, specific gravity, and osmotic pressure. In addition to transporting oxygen, erythrocytes are important in the maintenance of the acid-base balance, viscosity, and specific gravity of the blood, and their membranes contain a number of agglutinogens, the determiners of blood types.

Most white cells (leukocytes) are involved in defense against foreign matter such as bacteria and allergens. Platelets participate in several aspects of blood clotting.

Sites of Hematopoiesis. Hematopoiesis (hemopoiesis) is the general term for blood cell formation. Erythropoiesis, leukopoiesis, and thrombopoiesis refer to the formation of red cells, white cells, and platelets, respectively. Under normal circumstances all the formed elements of adult blood, except the majority of lymphocytes and monocytes (two types of white cells), are produced in the bone marrow. The source of monocytes is not definitely known, but lymphocytes and probably the monocytes are formed in lymphoid tissue in many parts of the body, for example, the lymph nodes, spleen, tonsils, thymus, liver, gastrointestinal tract, and bone marrow.

Despite the fact that bone marrow appears during the sixth prenatal week, blood cell formation does not begin there until almost mid-gestation. Instead, the final stage of hematopoiesis, known as the myeloid (bone marrow) period, is preceded by two successive and overlapping stages during which other tissues are the primary centers of blood formation.

In the embryo, blood cells and blood vessels arise from mesenchyme, the embryonic connective tissue. The earliest sites of hematopoiesis are the "blood islands" in the yolk sac (Bloom and Bartelmez, 1940; Wintrobe, 1961), and these islands probably also secrete plasma. Although neither the time limits of this first stage, the mesoblastic period, nor of the succeeding stages can be stated exactly, blood islands and primitive blood cells are known to be present early in the third week. Active hematopoiesis continues in the yolk sac to the sixth or seventh week and then declines rapidly. By the ninth week blood formation there is negligible.

The second or hepatic (liver) period begins about the fourth or fifth week, and within a few more weeks the liver has replaced the yolk sac as the prime site of hematopoiesis (Gilmour, 1941; Wintrobe, 1961). At about the third month hemopoie-

sis also starts in the spleen. It is always slight relative to that in the liver; it reaches a maximum about the fourth month and then subsides but may continue to a slight degree throughout the remainder of gestation. A brief phase of hematopoiesis also occurs in the thymus during the hepatic period.

Between the fourth and fifth months hematopoiesis is initiated in the bone marrow and lymph nodes. Blood cell formation is much greater in the bone marrow and accelerates, whereas production in the lymph nodes rises for only a brief time and then stays steady to term. Since hemopoiesis continues in the liver until two or three weeks after birth, although at a decelerating rate after the fifth month, there is considerable overlap between the hepatic and myeloid periods.

As noted earlier, the bone marrow becomes the exclusive normal site of erythropoiesis, thrombopoiesis, and the formation of most white cells within a few weeks after birth. However, the liver and spleen and perhaps other tissues retain their potential for hematopoiesis throughout infancy and early childhood and thus serve as emergency sources in times of crisis. Formation of blood cells in these sites is called extramedullary hematopoiesis.

Until a child is about 5 years old, the demand for blood cells is so great that red marrow fills all bones. Fat begins to appear in the marrow of long bones between the fifth and seventh year. With increasing age thereafter fat gradually replaces active marrow in the distal parts of the skeleton. By 18 or 20 years the centers of hematopoiesis are confined primarily to bones in the trunk —vertebrae, ribs, sternum, clavicles, and scapulae, and the innominate bones which make up the greater part of the pelvis—but some blood cell formation continues in the skull and the proximal epiphyses of the femur and humerus (Custer, 1949). The inactive, fatty areas of bone replace extramedullary centers as the reservoir for additional hematopoiesis during stress.

Erythrocytes. All the blood cells of the adult go through a series of transformations before they are released into the circulation, and some further developments may occur there. The normal stages of erythropoiesis are, in chronological order: pronormoblast (proerythroblast); basophilic, polychromatic, and orthochromatic normoblast (or early, intermediate, and late erythroblast); reticulocyte; erythrocyte. Sometimes the term erythroblast is used to mean all nucleated red cells, regardless of stage or normality. All the forms listed above are nucleated except reticulocytes and erythrocytes, the two types of red cell normally found in the circulating adult blood. The more immature forms in the series are rather large, but as maturation proceeds through successive cell divisions, the red cells become progressively smaller. Before a red cell enters the adult circulation, it normally extrudes its nucleus. A network of material with an affinity for basic dyes remains, so the cell at this stage is called a reticulocyte. After two to five days in the circulation the network is lost, and the cell is known as an erythrocyte.

The basic stimulus to erythropoiesis is a reduction in the oxygen level in bone marrow, whether this results from anemia (deficiency in the quality or quantity of red cells), hypoxia (low oxygen content of inspired air), or some other cause. However, the response is mediated by erythropoietin, a hormone secreted into the blood, probably by the kidneys.

Embedded in the colorless, spongy stroma, or framework, filling the interior of the erythrocyte is the red, oxygen-carrying pigment, hemoglobin. Every molecule of hemoglobin consists of four subunits, each of which has a heme portion containing iron, in conjugation with a polypeptide. Two of the subunits have one type of polypeptide; the other two have the second type. The polypeptides in the predominant form of adult hemoglobin are the alpha and beta chains. Both contain 19 different amino acids, but the alpha has 141 amino acid units and the beta has 146. Collectively, the polypeptides make up the globin fraction of the hemoglobin molecule. There is only a low to moderate correlation between the total amount of hemoglobin in the blood and the number of erythrocytes. When the components of hemoglobin are deficient, red cells mature without a normal complement of hemoglobin.

Red cells wear out after circulating for about 120 days. Deteriorated cells are broken down in the reticuloendothelial system, a special sort of connective tissue. Globin and heme are split off, with the former re-

turning to the amino acid pool of the body. Heme is transformed through several steps to insoluble bilirubin, a yellow pigment. Bilirubin is released into the circulation and carried to the liver, where it is converted into soluble forms and excreted in the bile. If this process fails, or excessive destruction of red cells occurs, the result is hyperbilirubinemia, or jaundice. There has been considerable controversy about the cause of icterus neonatorum, a form of jaundice common among neonates.

Much of the iron removed from the hemoglobin molecule when erythrocytes are destroyed is returned to the bone marrow to be reused in the formation of new hemoglobin. Unless the portion excreted is replaced by dietary intake, iron deficiency anemia ensues. Among other causes of insufficient or abnormal erythropoiesis are protein lack, vitamin deficiencies (particularly of the B vitamins), low levels of glucocorticoids (a class of adrenal hormones), or of thyroid or pituitary hormones, and genetic defects.

In general, the younger the individual, the more does the red blood cell picture present conditions that would be abnormal in the adult. This statement is qualified because some measures have curvilinear trends. The first characteristic to approximate adult levels—the proportion of immature cells in the circulation—shows only minor reversals. Release of nucleated cells into the circulation is indicative of pathology in adults; an elevated reticulocyte count is the normal sign of active red cell proliferation. Fetal blood, however, contains a large number of even less mature cells.

About the third week, when the first cells appear in the blood of the embryo, at least 99% are nucleated (Playfair, Wolfendale, and Kay, 1963). Further, they are large, primitive erythroblasts sometimes referred to as "first generation" or "provisional" erythroblasts. As these cells degenerate or are destroyed by phagocytes (cells that engulf and ingest other cells, microorganisms, and foreign matter), they are replaced by the second or "definitive" generation of smaller normoblasts (Bloom and Bartelmez, 1940). At 6 weeks most (92%) of the circulating red cells are still of the primitive type. The proportion drops to 53% by the end of the second fetal month, and at the end of the fourth all of the red cell precursors are of the second generation. Concurrently, the number of very immature forms (erythroblasts and normoblasts) reaching the circulation decreases, while the more mature forms, at first almost entirely reticulocytes, increase. Only 3% (Thomas and Yoffey, 1962) to 8% (Wintrobe, 1961) of circulating red cells are nucleated at 10 to 12 weeks. By midgestation the proportion is less than 1% and remains at this level until delivery (Anderson, 1941; Gilmour, 1941).

Reticulocytes rather than nucleated cells are the predominant form of red corpuscle in the third fetal month. In turn, they are replaced by erythrocytes. This process is somewhat slower, especially after the first half of gestation, than was the decline of erythroblasts and normoblasts. Between the third and sixth months reticulocytes decrease from 90% of circulating red cells to 15-30% (Windle, 1941). According to Seip (1955), the proportion declines almost linearly from about 16% at 22 weeks to 4-6% at term. These figures are consistent with those reported in most previous and subsequent studies and are significantly higher than the normal adult range of 0.2 to 2.0% (McDonald, Dodd, and Cruickshank, 1965) or 0.5 to 1.5% (Smith, 1966).

Many other characteristics of red cells, for example, their size and total number, have a similar age curve—that is, rapid development during the first half of gestation and a slower, steadier rate of change thereafter. Underlying this pattern is probably an interaction between the degree of maturity of blood-forming tissue and the demand for red cells. Some abatement of this demand is likely, because as gestation proceeds the increment in size during a given period of time becomes a progressively smaller fraction of the size at the beginning of the interval (Arey, 1965).

At birth and for several months thereafter many readjustments in the red cell picture take place. Unless one knows the meaning of the various indices used to assess the size and quantity of cells and the hemoglobin content of cells or whole blood, neither the prenatal trends nor the postnatal reversals can be adequately understood.

An absolute increase in the total numbers of formed elements would be expected throughout development, for the larger the organism, the greater is the volume of blood required to supply its organs. By the same token, the total amount of hemoglobin should also increase. To allow for differences in size, both among and within age and sex groups, cell counts and hemoglobin content are stated in relative terms.

Total counts of red cells (RBC), platelets, and white cells (WBC) or each category of the latter are given as the number of million cells per cubic millimeter (cu.mm. or mm.^{3}) of blood. A supplementary measure for red cells is the hematocrit (HCT), or packed cell volume (P.C.V.), which expresses the percentage of the volume of a given amount of blood that is occupied by red cells. The hematocrit is not a substitute for red cell count, because the same volume could be made up of a large number of small cells or a smaller number of larger cells. Among the measures of cell size are diameter, thickness, and volume. These may be measured directly, but estimates are sometimes used. For example, the mean corpuscular volume (M.C.V.) is calculated by dividing the volume of packed red cells per 1000 milliliters (ml.) of blood by the red cell count in millions per cubic millimeter, yielding a quotient in cubic microns (cu.μ).

In lieu of the older and less accurate color indices (the color of a blood sample is matched with one of a set of standards), ratios of the hemoglobin content of blood to the red cell count or the volume of packed red cells are now favored for the assessment of the hemoglobin content of red cells. The mean corpuscular hemoglobin (M.C.H.) is a measure of the weight, in micromicrograms ($\mu\mu$G. or $\mu\mu$Gm.), of the hemoglobin in the average red cell. It is derived by dividing the number of grams of hemoglobin per 1000 ml. of blood by the red cell count in millions per cubic millimeter. By contrast, the mean corpuscular hemoglobin concentration (M.C.H.C.) is an estimate of the concentration of hemoglobin in the average red cell, that is, the ratio of the weight of hemoglobin to the volume in which it is contained. This quotient is a percentage, obtained by multiplying the number of grams of hemoglobin per 100 ml. of blood by 100 and dividing the result by the volume of packed red cells in milliliters per

100 ml. of blood. If the mean corpuscular hemoglobin does not change in proportion to the mean corpuscular volume, the mean corpuscular hemoglobin concentration will deviate from normal, for it is the ratio of M.C.H. to M.C.V. This fact is particularly useful in the diagnosis of anemias. Cell volume and the weight of hemoglobin per cell change in parallel in most anemias, so the M.C.H.C. is constant. In certain anemias, however, the decrement in hemoglobin is greater than that in cell size, and the M.C.H.C. becomes subnormal. The so-called "physiological anemia" of infancy, to be discussed shortly, is of the former type.

The increment in number of red cells per unit volume of blood is rapid until mid-gestation when production slows (Singer, Chernoff, and Singer, 1951; Thomas and Yoffey, 1962; Walker and Turnbull, 1953; White and Beaven, 1959; Wintrobe and Shumacher, 1936). Thomas and Yoffey (1962) report a secondary rise in the third trimester. More regular and gradual increases in packed cell volume and amount of hemoglobin per 100 ml. of blood result from the relationships between curves for cell volume and cell count in the first case and mean corpuscular hemoglobin and cell count in the second (Wintrobe, 1961). Because mean corpuscular volume and mean corpuscular hemoglobin decrease at comparable rates, the mean corpuscular hemoglobin concentration stays at about the same level throughout gestation (Windle, 1941; Wintrobe and Shumacher, 1936).

Of great concern to hematologists, embryologists, and pediatricians are the qualitative differences between fetal and adult hemoglobin. The heme fraction and the pair of alpha chains are identical in both hemoglobins, but instead of the pair of beta chains of adult hemoglobin (Hb-A), fetal hemoglobin (Hb-F) has a pair of gamma chains (Schroeder, Shelton, Shelton, Cormick, and Jones, 1963; White and Beaven, 1959). Although beta and gamma chains contain the same number of amino acids, the composition differs. Fetal and adult hemoglobin differ in many physical and chemical properties, the most important of which physiologically is the greater oxygen affinity of Hb-F (see the section on Respiration). To date there is no conclusive evidence that the dif-

ference in oxygen affinity between fetal and adult blood actually arises from the beta and gamma chains rather than from other properties of the red cells or their environment.

The values reported for fetal hemoglobin at different ages vary considerably from study to study. In part the lack of consistency stems from the use of methods of assessment that differ in sensitivity and variability. Further, fetal red cells contain small amounts of adult hemoglobin and two other minor hemoglobins. The latter two constitute about 10% of the total hemoglobin and are included by some investigators in their figures, that is, they differentiate only between Hb-A and all other hemoglobin. Adult blood also has two minor components—Hb-A$_2$ and very small amounts (0.5–1%) of Hb-F.

During gestation very little shift in the proportions of fetal and adult hemoglobin is observed. About 95% of the hemoglobin at 8 to 20 weeks is Hb-F, although small amounts of adult hemoglobin can be detected (Fraser and Raper, 1962; Walker and Turnbull, 1955; Zipursky, 1966). Most investigators report fetal hemoglobin values of about 90% at 34-36 weeks (Beaven, Ellis, and White, 1960; Cook, Brodie, and Allen, 1957; Cottom, 1955; Schulman, Smith, and Stern, 1954). In fact, the 90-91% level seems to be a criterion of prematurity. Infants born before 34-36 weeks have more than 90% Hb-F, whereas those born after this age have less than 90%. A negative correlation between gestational age and proportion of Hb-F is established at this point, with a decline of 3-4% in Hb-F each week thereafter to term (Cook, Brodie, and Allen, 1957). The range of Hb-F content found at birth varies from 45-90%, with means of 70–85% (Abrahamov, Salzberger, and Bromberg, 1956; Armstrong, Schroeder, and Fenninger, 1963; Cook, Brodie, and Allen, 1957; Cottom, 1955; Schulman, Smith, and Stern, 1954; Singer, Chernoff, and Singer, 1951; Zipursky, 1966). However, the concentration varies from cell to cell, and over 90% of red cells in the blood of newborn infants contain some fetal hemoglobin (Zipursky, 1966).

Even less agreement exists on the rate of the postnatal decline in Hb-F. Beaven, Ellis, and White (1960) report that after the fourth month no more than 10% of hemoglobin is of this type. In the age range 6 months to 10 years less than 1% Hb-F was found in about two-thirds of their subjects. On the other hand, Chernoff and Singer (1952) found levels of 15% fetal hemoglobin at 1 year, 5% at 2, and less than 2% after 4 years.

The factors determining whether the hemoglobin manufactured will be predominantly of the fetal or adult type are not known. When fetal red cells are incubated under conditions of glucose deficiency or low oxygen, fetal hemoglobin is more likely to be formed (Allen and Jandl, 1960). Thus one hypothesis is that in the fetal environment, where glucose and oxygen are in relatively short supply, hemopoietic tissue somehow responds to such lack by producing fetal hemoglobin.

It is of some interest that the myoglobin (muscle hemoglobin) of fetuses and newborn infants is entirely of a fetal type, MbF. During the first six postnatal months MbF is completely replaced by adult myoglobin (Singer, Angelopoulos, and Ramot, 1955). As is true for fetal hemoglobin, the significance of this shift has not been determined.

Despite the slowing of erythropoiesis during the second half of gestation, the picture at delivery is one of hyperactive red cell formation. A temporary resurgence of nucleated red cells, both erythroblasts and normoblasts, occurs in many infants, particularly the premature (Smith, 1959). Within 24 hours an abrupt decline ensues, and by the end of the first week almost all the nucleated cells are gone. Some investigators (Findlay, 1946; Gairdner, Marks, and Roscoe, 1952; Wegelius, 1948) also report an increase in reticulocytes lasting from a few hours to 3 or 4 days. Seip (1955) found that the term level (4-6%) was maintained for 3 days, then dropped rapidly, reaching the adult range by the end of the seventh day. No sharp decrement is seen in Washburn's (1935) longitudinal data until the second to eighth week. However, those data show a brief increase between 6 and 10 weeks, followed by a second decline to adult values at about 4 months.

In addition, the erythrocytes of the newborn infant are larger and have a higher hemoglobin content than the adult's, and their numbers are as great or greater (Smith, 1959; Smith, 1966; Wintrobe, 1961; Wol-

man, 1957). Some investigations reveal a further rise in red cell count lasting from a few hours to several days (Findlay, 1946; Gairdner, Marks, and Roscoe, 1952; Guest, Brown, and Wing, 1938; Wegelius, 1948). During the first day hemoglobin levels of subjects in these studies increased even more sharply, but they too began to drop after about the fourth day.

The brief perinatal burst of erythropoiesis is most frequently interpreted to be the result of relative anoxia late in gestation and/or during delivery. Evidence for anoxia during labor is much better than that for an increase in oxygen deprivation as term approaches (James and Adamsons, 1964; Nesbitt, 1966; Smith, 1959; Walker and Turnbull, 1959). Moreover, the red cell and hemoglobin values available in the literature, particularly for neonates, should not be accepted uncritically, for a number of methodological, environmental, and genetic factors influence these measures.

One important variable is the source of the blood sample. Among adults hematocrits determined on venous blood are slightly higher than those done on arterial blood, while samples from peripheral or small vessels yield hematocrits as high as those from larger vessels only when the microhematocrit is used (McGovern, Jones, and Steinberg, 1955). For about the first postnatal week, however, simultaneous capillary and venous determinations show the former to be higher (DeMarsh, Alt, and Windle, 1948; Gatti, 1967; Mollison, Veall, and Cutbush, 1950; Mugrage and Andresen, 1936; Newman and Gross, 1967; Oettinger and Mills, 1949; Oh and Lind, 1966). The greater concentration of capillary blood probably comes about because the relatively inactive peripheral circulation allows more time for water to diffuse out of the capillaries. Smith (1959) collated red cell counts and hemoglobin levels from many studies on the basis of whether the blood was obtained from capillaries, veins, or the umbilical cord. In addition to reflecting the capillary-venous difference, his tables suggest that measures made on cord blood are lower than those taken on venous blood. Since simultaneous comparisons of cord and venous blood have not been made, one cannot be sure whether this difference represents an age trend or a concentration gradient.

Although the very high values for erythrocytes and hemoglobin frequently cited as characteristic of the newborn are based on capillary samples, dehydration from reduced water intake during the first few days of life may contribute to spuriously high values regardless of the source. Red cell and hemoglobin levels may actually begin to drop within the first day, with the decline being masked by a decrease in blood volume (Wolman, 1957). Water loss is the primary factor in the early neonatal weight decrement, and transfer of water from the blood is one line of defense against cellular dehydration.

A related factor of considerable significance is the time at which the umbilical cord is clamped. Delayed clamping can result in the transfusion of large quantities of blood from the placenta to the infant (see blood volume, below). Transfusion per se would not influence counts or concentrations, but it has this effect because fluid adjustments occur in which water leaves the plasma and enters the intercellular spaces or tissues. In a recent review of the effect of time of clamping of the cord on a variety of functions, Moss and Monset-Couchard (1967) list 20 studies that included hematological evaluations. Despite variations in the source of blood samples and in the definition of early or late clamping, almost all studies showed late clamping to produce higher red cell and hemoglobin values. The differences ranged from about 0.5 to 1.5 million for erythrocyte counts, 11 to 15 cc. per kilogram of body weight for red cell volume, 1 to 4 grams for hemoglobin levels, and 3 to 12% for hematocrit. On the other hand, infants whose cords are clamped early have higher reticulocyte counts (DeMarsh, Alt, and Windle, 1948).

With distressing frequency investigators attempting to establish age standards have failed to control not only for the time of clamping of the cord but also for gestational age, multiple births, and anemias. The more premature the infant, the lower his blood values are likely to be and the greater will be the effect of placental transfusion at delivery, for red cell, iron, and hemoglobin levels increase with gestational age, whereas the proportion of blood in the placenta decreases.

The fact that multiple births have an above average incidence of prematurity and iron-deficiency anemia is not the only reason why their exclusion is desirable. More and more cases of placental transfusions between monozygotic twins, either prenatally or during delivery, are being discovered (see reviews in Corney and Aherne, 1965; Falkner, 1966; Rausen, Seiki, and Strauss, 1965). In this syndrome one twin is plethoric (has an excess volume of blood) while the other is anemic. The effects vary from mild to severe (Benirschke, 1958; Corney and Aherne, 1965; Naeye, 1963) and include abnormalities in growth, cardiovascular and renal function, vision, and hearing. It has been suggested that the rather common occurrence of iron-deficiency anemia in one of a pair of twins when both have similar diets and growth rates may be instances in which the transfusion was not great and was not detected (Smith, 1966; Woodruff, 1958). The plethoric twin is usually but not always the larger (Falkner, Banik, and Westland, 1962; Kerr, 1959; Littlewood, 1963; Valaes and Doxiadis, 1960) and is equally susceptible to severe disorders and death (Minkowski, 1962). Not all the deleterious effects are apparent at birth (Corney and Aherne, 1965), and the abnormalities and differences between twins in size and other variables often persist for years (Becker and Glass, 1963; Falkner, 1966; Herlitz, 1942). The fact that prenatal environmental factors may make monozygotic twins more dissimilar than are dizygotic twins or even unrelated individuals obviously has implications for developmental research far exceeding the relatively minor confounding of hematological norms that results from including subjects whose blood values are not normal.

Although anemia is basically an abnormally low level of hemoglobin in the blood, it can arise because the hemoglobin content of all cells is reduced or because the number of red cells is insufficient. These states, in turn, stem from deficient or defective red cell formation, excessive destruction of red cells, or a combination thereof. Among the conditions that produce anemic newborns are bleeding from the fetus into the mother through a damaged placenta, blood loss from the placenta itself during delivery, a variety of genetic defects, and fetal-maternal blood group incompatibilities, of which the best known is the instance in which an Rh-negative mother carries an Rh-positive fetus. Descriptions of these and other disorders and a review of the literature on them can be found in Smith (1966). Dietary deficiencies and infections, which play a major role in anemias in older infants and children, are of comparatively little importance in neonates. Within a fairly wide range, maternal hemoglobin levels are not correlated with the production of hemoglobin by the fetus (Woodruff, 1956, 1958, 1961; Woodruff and Bridgeforth, 1953). However, if the mother's levels are very low, her offspring is much more likely to be anemic (Strauss, 1933; Woodruff and Bridgeforth, 1953). The incidence of neonatal anemia is also higher among premature and later-born infants and multiple births than in full-term and first-born infants and singletons, whose prenatal supply and storage of iron and other nutrients is better (Guest and Brown, 1957; Woodruff, 1958).

Whether or not a true increase in red cell and hemoglobin values takes place during the first few days after birth, there is no doubt that the normal infant enters postnatal life with every sign of active erythropoiesis and that within a week or so the rate of red cell formation is on the decline. As the high blood values at birth and possible increases during the first few days have been inferred to represent a response to decreasing oxygen tension, so the decreases which soon follow have been attributed to the removal of the stimulus to erythropoiesis by the more highly oxygenated postnatal environment. A time lag would be expected, because the primary response is by the erythropoietic tissue, and some days would be required for the change to be reflected in the circulation. Consonant with this interpretation is the fact that decreased or increased activity of the bone marrow, as appropriate, precedes the trends in blood values reported below (Smith, 1966).

The greatest variation in blood values "among infants or children apparently in states of good health and nutrition occur during the first three years of life" (Guest, Brown, and Lahey, 1957, p. 359). Other authorities agree on this point as well as to the contention that "optimal" standards, that is, those based on well-nourished children, are preferable to those derived from a more representative sample, because the latter will include many anemic children (Moe, 1965; Whipple, 1966).

Despite the wide range from study to study in absolute values at given ages and discrepancies as to the age at which minimum levels are found, the general age trends are quite consistent (Albritton, 1952; Berry, Cowin, and Magee, 1952; Gairdner, Marks, and Roscoe, 1952; Faxén, 1937; Guest and Brown, 1957; Guest, Brown, and Wing, 1938; Hawkins, Speck, and Leonard, 1954; Horan, 1950; Leichsenring, Norris, and Halbert, 1952; Leichsenring, Norris, Lamison, and Halbert, 1955; Merritt and Davidson, 1933; Moe, 1965; Mugrage and Andresen, 1936; Sjöstrand, 1949; Smith, 1959; Smith, 1966; Wintrobe, 1961; Wolman, 1957).

The decline in red cell count is gradual in onset, but after the second week becomes marked, reaching a low point at from 6 weeks to 5 months. Most investigators report minima approximately 1.5 million cells per cubic millimeter below birth means at about 2 months, with a slow increase thereafter, totaling about 0.7 million/cu.mm. by puberty. A brief secondary rise in reticulocytes is often observed as red cell proliferation is reactivated. During adolescence there is very little change in erythrocyte count among females—the average RBC from 10 years through middle age ranging from 4 to 5.5 million/cu.mm. Males, however, have a decided increment, amounting to about 0.3 million/cu.mm. from 10 to 14 and an equal increase between 14 and 17 years, for which rising testosterone secretion is probably the stimulus. The administration of testosterone to children with certain forms of anemia, to eunuchs, and to female or castrated male experimental animals produces a greater volume of red cells (McCullagh and Jones, 1942; Shahidi and Diamond, 1959; Van Dyke, Coutopoulos, Williams, Simpson, Lawrence, and Evans, 1954).

Across both species and age, erythrocyte count and size are negatively correlated (Wintrobe, 1961). Although average cell size decreases during gestation, it is still very large at birth (mean corpuscular volume of 106-125 μ and mean corpuscular diameter of 8-9 μ). The decline in size begins immediately, reaching a minimum MCV of 71-77 μ at 6 to 12 months and a minimum MCD of 5-7 + μ at from 3 to 12 months. Between 12 and 18 months the trend reverses, but cell size remains below the adult means of 85-90 μ for MCV and 7.2-7.9 μ for MCD at least until puberty.

Because red cell size and number decline simultaneously, the drops in hemoglobin per unit volume of blood and in volume of packed red cells (hematocrit) are even sharper and the subsequent rise slower than for erythrocyte count. Hemoglobin levels decrease by about 8-10 grams per milliliter of blood between birth and 3 to 6 months, then increase by 1.5 to 2 gr./ml. by 2 to 5 years. The levels remain fairly steady throughout the remainder of childhood. There is a further increase of about 0.5 gm/ml. for females between 14 and 17 years. Males have increments of 1 gm./ml. between 10 and 14 years, 1.5 gr. between 14 and 17, and 0.5 gr. from then to adulthood. The hematocrit curve, although somewhat more variable from study to study, takes a similar pattern, decreasing from a range of 52-66% in the first few days to a low of 34-37% at 6 weeks to 12 months. Very gradual increases beginning in the second or third year bring the means to 38-42% by 5 to 10 years. Averages for females increase by only about 1% between 10 and 14, 1% from 14 to 17, and 2% from then to adulthood. The increments for males during these periods are 3%, 4%, and 2%, respectively. Since there are no sex differences in cell size nor in the average hemoglobin content per cell, the greater hematocrit and total hemoglobin content of the blood in males is attributable to their higher erythrocyte count.

For the most part, the decline in mean corpuscular hemoglobin parallels that in mean corpuscular volume, so mean corpuscular hemoglobin concentration stays quite steady. However, during the first few weeks to 2 months when newer, smaller cells are beginning to appear the decrease in MCV is not matched by that in MCH, and the MCHC rises slightly. A slight decline thereafter to a minimum at about 2 years is also reported in several of the studies cited above. Considerable controversy has surrounded the question of whether the osmotic and mechanical fragility of infants' erythrocytes was greater than in older persons. There is little question that when tested in vitro or by injection into an adult, the life span of neonatal red cells is shorter than that of adult cells. The decreased rate of red cell proliferation rather than a difference in the quality of cells is now, however, believed to account for the faster rate of breakdown of the neonatal erythrocytes (Smith, 1959; Smith, 1966). With more old cells and fewer new ones in the blood of the young infant, a reduction in the mean life span would be predictable.

White Cells

The five major types of white cell (leukocyte) normally found in adult blood are neutrophils, eosinophils, basophils, lymphocytes, and monocytes. In contrast to red cells, all leukocytes are large and nucleated, but the various types and subgroups within them can be differentiated on the basis of the structure of the nucleus, whether or not the cytoplasm contains granules, and staining properties. Each category also has a characteristic size range. Collectively, neutrophils, eosinophils, and basophils are called granulocytes, in recognition of their granular cytoplasm, or polymorphonuclear leukocytes, because their nuclei are lobulated.

Granulocytes are considered to differentiate in the bone marrow from myeloblasts into promyelocytes, myelocytes, and metamyelocytes. During the myelocyte stage the granules in different cells acquire distinctive staining affinities, so from that point the precursors of neutrophils, eosinophils, and basophils can be discriminated. Before being released into the circulation, lypmphocytes pass through two stages, the lymphoblast and the prolymphocyte. The precursor of the monocyte is the monoblast.

Neither the functions of white cells nor the factors governing their formation are well understood. However, both the total number of circulating leukocytes and the proportions of the various types are known to fluctuate not only from day to day but within a single day in the presence of microorganisms and allergens and in response to physical exertion and pain or other mental stress. Except for lymphocytes, white cells apparently are drawn to the sites where they are needed primarily by chemical stimuli, such as the release of nucleic acid from destroyed tissue. When the demand for white cells increases, both the rate of production and the degree of mobilization of cells from storage areas rises. On the other hand, the white cells move quite rapidly from the blood into affected tissue. Further, a condition that stimulates an increase in one class of white cell may reduce the numbers of another. For example, glucocorticoids from the adrenal cortex, the secretion of which increases during stress, lower the lymphocyte count, both by destroying lymphocytes and by inhibiting their production. These hormones also decrease the numbers of eosinophils and basophils in the circulation and increase the neutrophil, platelet, and red cell counts. The concurrent existence of factors promoting and reducing the total number and proportions of white cells underlies the wide and frequent variations observed and makes for some discrepancies in the norms provided by different authorities and in estimates of the life span of leukocytes. Nevertheless, because the proportions of white cells do increase or decrease differentially under various conditions, a differential count, that is, separate counts of each major type, is often of more significance than a combined total count.

Under basal conditions the total white cell count in adults is 4000-7000, although it may rise to 10,000-11,000 with normal activities. Mature neutrophils with a segmented nucleus consisting of 2 to 5 lobes constitute 50-65% of all leukocytes, and nonsegmented forms, known as stab or staff cells, make up another 4-5%. In the advent of invasion of the body by bacteria that cause fever, the number of neutrophils increases markedly and promptly. These cells are very mobile and can pass through capillary walls, a process called diapedesis, to phagocytize bacteria. They also transport pathogenic organisms to lymph nodes, where other phagocytes assist in their destruction, and sometimes carry portions of disintegrated red cells back to the bone marrow.

The granules in both neutrophils and eosinophils seem to be lysomes that help to digest phagocytized matter, but eosinophils are apparently not as active or sturdy as

neutrophils. Eosinophils phagocytize antigen-antibody complexes, and their proportion, normally about 1-4% of white cells, is increased in persons with allergies and after anaphylactic reactions (extreme sensitivity to foreign matter). However, the action against allergens does not begin as rapidly as does the attack of neutrophils on bacteria. Elevated eosinophil counts also accompany parasitic infections, skin diseases, and blood disorders.

Very little is known about the functions of basophils, which number only 0.1-0.4% of white cells. Although they contain heparin, an acid that prevents clotting, their role in the total system controlling the coagulation of blood or its prevention has not been determined.

All granulocytes are short-lived, circulating for durations estimated at between 2 days and 2 weeks. Like erythrocytes, they are destroyed by the reticuloendothelial system.

Some 20–40% of leukocytes are lymphocytes. They exist in the blood in both small and large forms, the former being more numerous, and they are highly motile cells. Considerable evidence has accumulated to indicate that during gestation and early infancy a substance secreted by the thymus renders the lymphocytes capable of making the antibodies that produce delayed hypersensitivity reactions and rejection of tissue transplants from other organisms (Altemeier and Smith, 1965; Berman, 1963; Burnet, 1962; Dameshek, 1962, 1963; Fichtelius, 1958a, 1958b; Gitlin, 1964; Gorman and Chandler, 1964; Miller, 1964, 1966). There may be two populations of small lymphocytes, one arising in the thymus and "seeding" other lymphoid organs with immunologically competent cells and a second with some different function. Two subgroups of lymphocytes, not necessarily the same ones, have also been distinguished on the basis of life-span. Some survive for only several days, while others circulate for 100–200 days.

Monocytes constitute 5 to 10% of the circulating leukocytes. They, too, possess ameboid movement but are less active than neutrophils or lymphocytes. Because monocytes are larger than most of the other white cells, they can phagocytize whole red cells as well as fragments of nuclei and cytoplasm. In addition, they may have some function in antibody formation. The number of monocytes is increased in the acute phase of rheumatic fever, in active tuberculosis, and in the recovery phases of pneumonia and other acute infections.

Although the primitive blood cells are believed to have the potential to produce leukocytes as well as erythrocytes, very few white cells are found in the blood during the mesoblastic period (Bloom and Bartelmez, 1940; Matsuda, Schroeder, Jones, and Weliky, 1960; Smith, 1966; Thomas and Yoffey, 1962; Wintrobe, 1961). There is some disagreement as to the time of appearance of different classes of white cells and their relative proportions during the first half of gestation. According to some older studies (Doan, 1932; Knoll, 1949, cited in Smith, 1966, and in Wintrobe, 1961; Zanaty, 1934, cited in Wintrobe, 1961), the majority of white cells in the blood during the second month are myeloblasts and about 25% are more mature forms of granulocytes. The granulocyte count rises to fairly large numbers by the fourth month, at which time the first small lymphocytes, like those in adult blood, appear. More recently, however, Playfair, Wolfendale, and Kay (1963) and Thomas and Yoffey (1962) have reported that over half of the white cells found in the circulation in the second month are lymphocytes, and that their numbers increase rapidly from the tenth to the twenty-fifth week and more slowly thereafter. Playfair et al. (1963) detected mature granulocytes in fetuses about 10 weeks of age with a subsequent steady increase, whereas Thomas and Yoffey (1962) state that the small quantity of granulocytes did not begin to be augmented until the twenty-sixth week.

Granulocytes are found in the yolk sac and liver during the hepatic period, and the thymus produces not only lymphocytes but also a few myelocytes. Until the fifth month the spleen is primarily engaged in the proliferation of red cells, but then lymphocyte formation becomes predominant.

At birth the total white cell count and the absolute counts for each type of leukocyte are usually very high, but the relative proportions are more like those of the adult than is true later in infancy (Albritton, 1952; Kato, 1935; Smith, 1959; Smith, 1966; Washburn, 1935; Wintrobe, 1961; Wolman, 1957). An occasional newborn has a total count as low as 3600 or as high as 45,000, but the range in most samples is 7000–35,000, with a mean of about 18,000. Proportions of neutrophils, eosinophils, basophils, lymphocytes, and monocytes average approximately 60, 2–3, 0.5, 30, and 6%, respectively. There is some evidence that the leukocytes found in cord blood show poorer ameboid movement and phagocytic capability than those of adults (Matoth, 1952).

Almost all investigators have observed a prompt increase in the total count (to a mean of 20,000–22,000), most classes of white cells reaching a lifetime high sometime during the first 24 hours. Neutrophils rise to about 70%, whereas lymphocytes drop to about 20%. A peak for monocytes of 9–17% occurs between 3–4 days and 2–3 weeks. Eosinophils may be relatively low at birth and rise to a maximum of 5–6% between the first and fourth day (Kato, 1935; Mitchell, 1955), while the proportion of basophils seems to change very little. Some myelocytes may be present, and young neutrophils (nonsegmented and bilobed forms) may constitute as much as 20–40% of the neutrophils.

Between the second and fourth day a sharp decline in total count begins and continues for a few days to two weeks. Then a small increase ensues for several weeks or months, followed by a slow decline to adult levels at puberty or during early adolescence. Fluctuations in the neutrophil and lymphocyte counts are responsible for this curvilinear trend, for the numbers of other white cells decline gradually. The outstanding developmental trend is a reversal in the relative proportions of these cells. After the immediate postnatal increase, the total numbers of neutrophils decline for a week or two and then rise gradually to the adult value sometime between mid-childhood and puberty. The percentage of neutrophils, however, declines from its early peak of about 70% to a low of 30–32% between the second week and the sixth month, rising to the adult proportion by late childhood or early adolescence. At the same time the lymphocyte count follows the pattern of the total white cell curve, but the proportions are almost the inverse of those for neutrophils. From a minimum of about 20% at the end of the first day, the percentage of lymphocytes increases to approximately 60% by 2 weeks to 6 months, then decreases gradually to the adult level of about 30% between mid-childhood and puberty.

Changes in the availability of oxygen would not be expected to influence the neonatal white cell count, since variations in altitude have little effect on adult counts (Smith, 1959). In addition, white cells are known to require a good oxygen supply for their development (Smith, 1966), so a decline in white cells soon after birth cannot be explained in terms of an improved oxygen supply. Although dehydration might produce the brief postnatal increase in total white cell count, it does not account for the shifts in relative proportions of different types of white cells. The most reasonable hypothesis that has been offered for the latter phenomenon is the transition at birth from a relatively sterile environment to a germ-filled one (Allansmith, 1966; Kato, 1935). An increase in granulocytes is the typical reaction of older persons to infection.

Individual differences in white cell counts are greater than those among adults, at least until puberty. The range is so great during early infancy that an elevated white cell count is of little diagnostic utility. Other aspects of the white cell picture also lack the significance they have in adults (Smith, 1966). Before fat begins to infiltrate the bone marrow, a relatively mild infection may result in a disproportionate increase in white cell count, and in severe infections myelocytes and metamyelocytes may be released into the circulation. Immature lymphocytes appear in the circulation of infants and children more often than they do in adults, particularly in the presence of chronic upper respiratory infections and enlarged tonsils, and the blood of completely healthy young infants may contain some abnormal lymphocytes similar to those found in older persons with mononucleosis. Children with allergies but no other demonstrable illness may show eosinophil ratios as high as 25% for many years.

Platelets and Coagulation. Normal platelets are small, nonnucleated bodies of complex composition and, contrary to earlier opinion, high metabolic activity. They are formed from pseudopodia (protrusions) that break off from the cytoplasm of megakaryocytes. Originally, megakaryocytes are derived from the primitive blood cells of the embryo, as are erythrocytes and granulocytes. As blood formation shifts from one hemopoietic center to another, megakaryocytes appear successively in the yolk sac, liver, spleen, and bone marrow (Smith, 1966; Wintrobe, 1961). Once the hepatic period is well established the number of megakaryocytes increases. The production of platelets also begins very early, but it is slow until the myeloid period (Windle, 1940). In adults megakaryocytes are probably produced only in the bone marrow, although many are present in the lungs and some in the spleen. The megakaryocytes in these other organs are now assumed to have been carried there after developing in the bone marrow, but they retain the ability to form platelets.

To prevent blood loss from a damaged vessel two processes, hemostasis and thrombosis, occur, and platelets participate in each in several ways. Hemostasis (arrest or escape of blood) takes place through contraction of the vessel walls and adhesion of their surfaces. Platelets carry serotonin, a powerful vasoconstrictor, and release it at the site of injury. In addition, platelets possess properties of adhesiveness and aggregation. The formation of clumps of platelets along the injured vessel wall supplements contraction in arteries and arterioles and is even more important in helping to seal off veins, for they are not so well supplied with contractile muscle.

Thrombosis or clot formation can be regarded in a somewhat arbitrary fashion as consisting of three phases: (1) formation of plasma thromboplastin (intrinsic prothrombinase) and tissue thromboplastin (extrinsic prothrombinase); (2) conversion of prothrombin to thrombin, a step which requires both thromboplastin and calcium; and (3) combination of thrombin and fibrinogen to produce a fibrin clot. Plasma thromboplastin is elaborated more rapidly than is extrinsic prothrombinase. Once the latter has begun to form, however, the two mechanisms function simultaneously. Plasma contains all the elements needed to carry out the complete coagulation sequence, but tissue prothrombin cannot be converted to thrombin until it has been activated by certain other factors in the blood. At least twelve different "factors" or "principles," four of which are thromboplastin, prothrombin, calcium, and fibrinogen, have been implicated in the clotting process. It may be, however, that clots can be formed even if one is deficient. Platelets either contain or have absorbed on their surfaces (this alternative currently seems the more likely) a large portion of the factors required for coagulation. Some of the specific activities that have been attributed to platelets are participation in the elaboration of thromboplastin, acceleration of the conversion of prothrombin to thrombin and of fibrinogen to fibrin, and neutralization of the anticoagulant activity of heparin.

At birth the shape and size of the platelets are more variable than in older persons (Smith, 1966; Tocantins, 1938). Probably because of methodological difficulties—no method for counting platelets is completely satisfactory or entirely consistent from one user to another—platelet counts equal to, higher than, and lower than those of adults have been reported in newborns (Albritton, 1952; Guest, Brown, and Lahey, 1957; Smith, 1966). The weight of the evidence suggests average counts at the lower end of the adult range increasing gradually to adult means by 3 to 6 months (Albin, Kushner, Murphy, and Zippin, 1961; Grossman, Heyn, and Rozenfeld, 1952; Larrieu, Soulier, and Minkowski, 1952; Merritt and Davidson, 1933).

For some time it has been known that coagulation is delayed in newborn infants and becomes even slower on the second to fourth day. Neither a quantitative nor qualitative deficiency of the platelets per se seems to be responsible, however (Smith, 1959). Immaturity of the liver and a "physiologic" deficiency of vitamin K may well be major variables. Drawing on the data of McElfresh (1961) and of Aballi and deLamarens (1962), Smith (1966) has organized a developmental table for nine coagulation factors. Omitted are calcium, of which the normal newborn has adequate blood levels, thromboplastin (a product of the clotting sequence that participates in later phases), and the fibrin-stabilizing factor, which prevents clots from dissolving in certain solvents. The cord blood levels of seven of the nine

factors listed are lower than adult norms. Of these, six are produced in the liver, including all four of the vitamin K-dependent factors.

During the first few days after birth several factors, prothrombin in particular, are reduced below birth values. At 14 days four of the six liver-produced factors have attained low normal levels; one is 23–79% of the adult norm. However, prothrombin may not reach adult levels until the end of the first year (Plum, 1949), and the plasma thromboplastin component (Christmas factor) may remain somewhat low, as revealed in delayed thromboplastin formation, until 6 months (McElfresh, Sharpsteen, and Akabane, 1956). Plasma thromboplastin antecedent (Factor XI) rises almost to adult levels by 2 months (Hilgartner and Smith, 1965). Fibrinogen, one of the liver-made factors not dependent upon vitamin K, develops less rapidly than some other factors in young fetuses (Heikinheimo, 1964), but is only slightly low at birth and is normal by 3 days. The seventh factor deficient at birth, one of those involved in thromboplastin formation, rises to adult levels by 14 days.

Insufficient reserves, liver immaturity, and a bacteria-free intestinal tract all contribute to vitamin K deficiency in the newborn infant. With the ingestion of food, not only is Vitamin K absorbed, but intestinal flora that synthesize this vitamin also develop. Administration of vitamin K does more to improve coagulation in the full-term infant than in the premature (Aballi, Banus, deLamerens, and Rozenquaig, 1957), but not all coagulation factors are augmented (Hilgartner and Smith, 1965). Feeding cow's milk also helps to increase prothrombin levels, because breast milk has only about one-fourth as much vitamin K content (Smith, 1959).

Immunology. The human body has three systems for defending itself against pathogenic microorganisms (and the toxins that some produce), transplants of foreign tissue, and allergens (other foreign proteins and certain nonprotein substances that cause hypersensitivity reactions). First, barriers such as the skin and the mucosal linings of the respiratory, intestinal, and urogenital tracts and their chemical secretions, in some instances aided by ciliary action (vibration of hairlike processes), help to prevent the entry of invaders. Phagocytes, of which the granular leukocytes are one group, are another line of defense. Antibodies constitute the third system.

In the discussion of white cells the antibody activity of lymphocytes against allergens and transplants of foreign tissue has already been mentioned. Lymphoid tissues also manufacture immunoglobulins, a group of structurally related proteins, each member of which is an antibody complementary to a specific antigen (foreign substance that stimulates production of an antibody). In contrast to barriers and phagocytes, which are species-characteristic, antibody immunity is much more idiosyncratic, being acquired primarily in response to the particular antigens to which a person is exposed. Isohemagglutinins (antibodies for blood group agglutinogens found in the species but not in the individual himself) are partial exceptions. Some, mainly those for the A and B agglutinogens, appear spontaneously, rather than requiring the stimulus of a specific antigen. Additional ones may be formed in response to stimulation, however.

Antibodies are carried in the gamma globulin fraction of blood proteins. Five classes of gamma globulins differing in physical, chemical, and functional properties have been identified. Between 80 and 90% of the immunoglobulins in adult blood are of the class called gamma G in the recommended international nomenclature (*Bulletin of the World Health Organization*, 1964, Vol. 30). At least four subclasses of gamma G have been recognized, and they are found in interstitial fluid as well as in blood. Most of the antibodies to viruses, bacteria, and toxins belong to this group of immunoglobulins. Some specific examples are antibodies to measles, mumps, pertussis, poliomyelitis, diphtheria, tetanus, and influenza.

Gamma A class makes up 5–15% of adult circulating immunoglobulins. It includes antibodies involved in sensitivity reactions and the release of histamine, but may be like the gamma G class in being heterogeneous in both structure and function. The major class of immunoglobulins in external secretions—tears, saliva, secretions of the breast and of the respiratory and intestinal tracts—is gamma A.

About 5% of the immunoglobulin population of adult serum is of the gamma M class. Few gamma M antibodies are found in other body fluids. Some of the specific antibodies in the gamma M class are the isohemagglutinins, rheumatoid factors, cold agglutinins, Wasserman antibodies, and antibodies against some of the group of bacteria known as gram negative. However, protective, although very low titers (concentration) of antibodies against most antigens have been discovered in this class. One antigen may be opposed by several different antibodies, and in some instances in which there are antibodies of both gamma M and gamma G classes for the same antigen the former are several hundred times more potent (Robbins, Kenny, and Sutter, 1965).

Two minor groups of immunoglobulins, gamma D and gamma E, have also been identified, but virtually nothing is known about the functions or development of these two classes.

The duration of immunity to different types of infections varies with the "memory" of the immunological system for the antigen in question and with the specificity of the pathogen. The life span of circulating antibodies is quite short—gamma G, A, and M immunoglobulins have a half-life in serum of about 23, 6, and 5 days, respectively. However, antibodies for certain microorganisms and toxins circulate long after recovery from the original infection, perhaps because some antigen remains in the body. In other instances an antibody disappears from the blood, but if the antigen is later reintroduced the speed with which that antibody is produced is greater than in the first attack—the lymphoid tissue "remembers" how to make it. The measles virus is an example of an antigen that is both highly specific and to which resistance, once acquired, is high for very extensive periods of time. On the other hand, there are hosts of bacteria and viruses that cause upper respiratory infections with very similar symptoms. Young children frequently have such disorders, but after exposure to a sufficient variety of the antigens usually found in their environments, the incidence of upper respiratory infections decreases.

As techniques for the stimulation and detection of antibody formation have improved, three long-held beliefs about the immunological status of the human fetus and young infant have been refuted. They are: (1) the infant is immunologically incompetent until some months after birth, (2) antigens do not pass the placenta, (3) the neonate has not developed his blood group. Supporting these assertions were a number of observations. The immunoglobulins in the fetal and neonatal circulation seemed to be almost entirely of maternal origin, grafts of foreign tissue were rejected less rapidly by newborns than by older persons, the response of neonates to artificial immunization was very limited, the isoagglutinins in the serum of young infants were passively acquired from the mother *in utero,* and the A and B blood group agglutinogens were weaker at birth than at later ages (see reviews by Evans and Smith, 1963; Miller, 1966; Smith, 1959; Smith, 1966). None of this evidence has been completely contradicted, but additional facts have shown that the inferences drawn from them were not justified.

From about the twentieth fetal week, when lymphoid tissue is established in the spleen and lymph nodes—the thymus appears at 12 weeks (Kay, cited in R. T. Smith, 1966)—gamma G and M immunoglobulins can be detected in the spleen and in a small number of cells in the blood (van Furth, Schuit, and Hijmans, 1965). The latter, particularly those of the gamma G class, could be of maternal origin, because transfer of this type of immunoglobulin to the fetus begins very early in gestation, increases gradually until the eighth month, and then seems to rise quite abruptly (Pfau, 1954). Good evidence for fetal synthesis of gamma G immunoglobulins has been adduced, however (Fudenberg and Fudenberg, 1964; Martensson and Fudenberg, 1965), and it is now thought that very small amounts are produced throughout the latter two-thirds of gestation (Allansmith, 1966; R. T. Smith, 1966).

Contrary to the widely quoted results of Hitzig (1963), those of other investigators demonstrate the presence of gamma M immunoglobulins in the serum of almost all infants at birth, albeit at very low titers—5–14% of adult levels (Allansmith and Buell, 1964; Franklin and Kunkel, 1958; Fulginiti, Sieber, Claman, and Merrill, 1966; West, Hong, and Holland, 1962). Such gamma M

immunoglobulins as are present in the fetus are almost entirely self-produced rather than being passively acquired from the mother (Gitlin, Kumate, Urrusti, and Morales, 1964; Kochwa, Rosenfield, Tallal, and Wasserman, 1961).

Only rarely have gamma A immunoglobulins been found to cross the placenta or be produced by the fetus (Allansmith, Maloney, and Wymer, 1966; Fulginiti, Sieber, Claman, and Merrill, 1966). All statements about the absence of any class of immunoglobulins in any subject should, however, be qualified by the adjective detectable, because no assay technique is completely sensitive, and techniques vary in sensitivity. For example, the minimum levels per 100 ml. of serum detectable by the tests used by Fulginiti et al. (1966) were 20–40 mg. for gamma G, 4–14 mg. for gamma A, and 6–15 mg. for gamma M immunoglobulins.

At full-term delivery gamma G levels equal to, higher than, and lower than those in the maternal serum have been observed. All investigators agree that the titers in the infant's blood begin to decline almost immediately, but the lowest point has been reported at ages from 3 weeks to 6 months (Allansmith, 1966; Allansmith, Maloney, and Wymer, 1966; Barrett and Volwiler, 1957; Bridges, Condie, Zak, and Good, 1959; Hitzig, 1963; Oberman, Gregory, Burke, Ross, and Rice, 1956; Orlandini, Sass-Kortsak, and Ebbs, 1955; Stiehm and Fudenberg, 1965; West, Hong, and Holland, 1962). The decline occurs because maternal gamma G immunoglobulins disappear steadily, and replacement by immunoglobulins synthesized by the infant is not sufficiently rapid. Active production of gamma G immunoglobulins is established in most infants by 3 to 6 weeks (Allansmith, 1966; R. T. Smith, 1966), but several more months may be required before the supply is large enough to reverse the overall decline in blood levels.

In one large cross-sectional sample aged birth to 16 years (Allansmith, 1966), the mean gamma G titer was within the lower levels of the adult range by the end of the first year. Increases continued to 18 months, when there was a reversal to about the 12-month mean which lasted until 3 years. Thereafter the average titer began to climb again and had not reached a plateau at 16 years. Mean levels more than doubled between 24 and 52 weeks in infants observed by Fulginiti et al. (1966), and by the latter age were about three-fourths of the adult average. Several studies show adult means to be approximated between 1 and 7 years (Bridges, Condie, Zak, and Good, 1959; R. T. Smith, 1966).

Among adults the level of gamma A immunoglobulins usually considerably exceeds that for the gamma M class, but the reverse is true in infants. Relative levels shift between the third and sixth year. Probably because of insufficiently sensitive tests, some investigators have not detected gamma A immunoglobulins in the sera of infants until after the third month (Hitzig, 1963; West, Hong, and Holland, 1962). However, 23 of 27 infants tested by Fulginiti et al. (1966) at 6 weeks had this class of immunoglobulins, as did all 21 of the group assayed at 12 weeks. The mean was about 20% of the adult level at 1 year. In other studies gamma A production was found to be well established by the end of the first month (Allansmith, 1966; Allansmith, Maloney, and Wymer, 1966). Longitudinal observations showed the first appearance of this class to be between the fifth and twenty-eighth day. By the end of the first year, the group average was about one-fourth of the adult's. The curve of subsequent increases seems to parallel that for the gamma G immunoglobulins (Allansmith, 1966; Hitzig, 1963; West, Hong, and Holland, 1962), although Allansmith's (1966) data strongly suggest an adolescent spurt in the gamma A titers of girls.

That the greatest proportion of the postnatal increase in gamma M immunoglobulins occurs during the first year is a generalization supported by all the data available. A rapid rise during the second and third months, with levels above those of adults being reached by 6 to 12 months, characterizes some observations (Hitzig, 1963; R. T. Smith, 1966; West, Hong, and Holland, 1962). From cross-sectional sampling at birth and at 6, 12, 24, and 52 weeks (Fulginiti et al., 1966), a marked increment between birth and 6 weeks and a more gradual rise thereafter to somewhat over 50% of the adult mean by 52 weeks would be inferred. Frequent longitudinal sampling (Allansmith, Maloney, and Wymer, 1966) yielded a group

curve that was positively accelerated during the first week. Following much slower increases in the second week and little change in the next two, a decrease ensued at the end of the first month. Most individual curves, however, were steplike in pattern, plateaus alternating with steep rises. Allansmith's (1966) cross-sectional data also show a drop in gamma M immunoglobulins at about 30 days. The titers then rise to adult levels by 10–12 months and even higher by about 2 years. Another decline seems to take place sometime between 2 and 4 years. West, Hong, and Holland (1962) also report a decrease between the first and fourth year. From 4 to 16 years the means fluctuate irregularly with no real trend.

The immunoglobulin levels of infants are generally far less stable than those of adults (Allansmith, 1966). Even though the adult responds to antigens, synthesis of new antibodies seems to be balanced by the disappearance of old ones. At least in part the fluctuations in infants may result from competition for the antibody activity of an immature system, that is, synthesis of one class of immunoglobulins is curtailed when production of another rises.

In addition to assays of classes of immunoglobulins, there is also a considerable body of data on the specific antibodies to be found in the circulation at birth. Smith (1959) provides a good review of this literature. Given adequate concentrations in the maternal blood, the fetus acquires antibodies to diphtheria and tetanus toxins and to the viruses causing measles, mumps, poliomyelitis, and Cocksackie infection which continue to provide protection for as long as 6 to 12 months after delivery. Passive immunity of shorter duration has been demonstrated to streptococcal and staphylococcal infections, influenza and typhoid "H" bacilli, and to pneumococci. If the mother receives large injections of diphtheria toxoid or pertussis (whooping cough) vaccine during pregnancy, the fetus itself seems to produce antibodies as well as to receive larger quantities from the mother. Apparently neonates are fairly susceptible to pertussis because maternal antibodies usually are low rather than because this antibody cannot pass the placenta.

The relative resistance of the placenta to

the transfer of gamma M immunoglobulins is reflected in the low blood titers of the newborn for antibodies to typhoid "O" bacillus, epidemic diarrhea, and other intestinal infections caused by bacteria of the E. *coli* strain. On the other hand, the fact that this class of immunoglobulins does not easily pass the placenta serves to protect the fetus to a considerable extent from hemolytic disorders, because isoagglutinins for the A and B blood group antigens and the saline ("complete" or "agglutinating") type of Rh antibodies are carried by gamma M immunoglobulins. The "incomplete" or "blocking" Rh antibodies, which are transferred more readily, are of the gamma G class.

Unfortunately, the placenta is not completely impermeable to maternal isohemagglutinins, nor, contrary to assertions in even current reviews, is the human infant incapable of synthesizing "natural" A and B agglutinins until the third to sixth postnatal month. Low levels of anti-A or anti-B or both types of saline-active isohemagglutinins were detected in the cord sera of 148 of 250 newborns examined recently (Thomaidis, Fouskaris, and Matsaniotis, 1967). As should be the case, no isohemagglutinins were found in the cord sera of 50 infants with O blood type. Of those infants who did have A or B agglutinins, the source could not be determined in 130 cases. Ten had isohemagglutinins appropriate to the maternal blood type but not to their own. Such instances of ABO isoimmunization by placental passage of maternal agglutinins have been reported previously (Morville, 1929; Smith, 1928; Tovey, 1945). Heretofore it has been assumed that all cases of hemolytic disorder resulting from fetal-maternal blood group incompatibilities or from failure to match bloods before transfusing neonates arose in this way. Another eight infants, however, had A or B agglutinins that could not, because of fetal-maternal differences in blood type, have been of maternal origin.

The appearance of A and B isoagglutinogens early in the second fetal month with subsequent increases in levels was established some years ago (Levine, Burnham, Katzin, and Vogel, 1941; Smith, 1928). Rh, M, N, C, D, and E agglutinogens have also been identified late in the second prenatal month (Bornstein and Israel, 1942; Chown and

Lewis, 1948). The strength of the A antigen increases markedly during the first five postnatal months and more gradually thereafter, approximating adult levels by 2 to 4 years (Grundbacher, 1964). There are also definite variations in the strength of the A antigens and the A_1 and A_2 subtypes (Grundbacher, 1965). Other antigens have not been as well studied, but it has been asserted that the B antigen in fetal erythrocytes is also not as potent as at later ages (Grundbacher, 1964). Nevertheless, the newborn "has a blood type," and the Grundbacher study suggests that neonates are also able to produce isohemagglutinins.

Although both the fetus and the newborn have been shown to be immunologically competent, the neonate may not react as adequately as older children to antigens in terms of either the quantity of antibodies produced or the speed of proliferation. It has been reported that responses to smallpox vaccination and to immunization for pertussis and diphtheria are not as good during the early postnatal months as later. However, the problem of poor response is largely eliminated if a sufficiently potent smallpox vaccine is used (Espmark and Rabo, 1965). In diphtheria immunization there seems to be an age difference in the effectiveness of different types of antigens (Smith, 1959). Immaturity of the immunological mechanisms is one possible factor limiting the response of young infants to antigens. However, the premature infant may become immunologically competent at about the same rate as the full-term one (Uhr, Dancis, and Neumann, 1960), suggesting that environmental factors, that is, the extent of exposure to antigens, may be more influential (Miller, 1966). Complications are posed by the fact that upon leaving the uterine environment the infant is suddenly exposed to a flood of antigens competing for the antibody activity of an underdeveloped, or at least relatively unpracticed, system. Immunity acquired from the mother prenatally may also interfere with the infant's responsivity. However, breast milk offers no significant protection to the human infant (Smith, 1959) and hence may be inferred not to constitute another possible source of inhibition to antibody synthesis by the infant himself.

Although the fetus is considered to be

shielded from infectious agents, clinical data indicate the presence of fetal disease not only in cases of placental pathology but also when the placenta is apparently normal (Smith, 1959). The filterable viruses in particular seem to pass the intact placenta. Infants have been born with signs of measles, mumps, chickenpox, smallpox, and poliomyelitis or have developed the disease so soon after delivery that it must have been contracted prenatally when there was no sign of placental damage. The mother, however, had had the infection during pregnancy.

CIRCULATION

Course of Circulation

Between the beginning of the fourth week, when the embryonic circulation is established, and the end of the second month, when the state prevailing during the remainder of gestation is reached, many innovations and renovations take place in the cardiovascular system. Several were mentioned in the preceding section and a few more, necessary to the understanding of the fetal circulation, will be described here. There is also a brief neonatal transition period during which the course of the fetal circulation, diagrammed schematically in Fig. 1, is converted to the postnatal condition sketched in Fig. 2. General circulation in the adult will be outlined first to facilitate appreciation of the differences between it and the prenatal version and of the transitions that must be made after birth.

Deoxygenated venous blood returns from the systemic circulation (the greater part of the circulatory system, excluding the pulmonary circulation) through two large veins, the superior vena cava (serving the head and arms) and the inferior vena cava (serving the trunk and legs). It enters both the right atrium and the right ventricle, since the valve between the two chambers is open. Then the atrium contracts, forcing more blood through the open valve into the ventricle, which becomes distended as this extra blood is added to that already in the ventricle from passive filling. Next the ventricle contracts, and blood moves behind the cusps of the valve between atrium and ventricle, closing it, so blood is driven through the

valves opening into the pulmonary artery. The pulmonary artery divides into two branches, one to each lung. After giving up carbon dioxide and taking up oxygen in the capillaries surrounding the alveoli of the lungs, the blood returns through veins that unite to form larger veins and finally reaches the left atrium through one of the two pulmonary veins. The left atrium contracts, forcing blood through the open valve into the left ventricle. Blood then closes this valve in the same manner in which it closes the valve between the right atrium and ventricle, so that when the left ventricle contracts blood is forced through the open valve into the aorta, and on through the systemic circulation. Of course, these processes go on simultaneously, all parts of the heart and circulatory system being in almost constant action.

Figure 1 shows five structures that alter the course of the circulation in the fetus—the foramen ovale, ductus aterreriosus, ductus venosus, umbilical vein, and umbilical arteries. As noted in the preceding section, the original pair of umbilical veins coalesces into one. During most of gestation the circulatory system consists of two distinct arcs of afferent and efferent vessels—the intraembryonic or systemic and the extraembryonic; the vitelline arteries and veins running to and from the yolk sac have by this time been abandoned. All sets of channels have in common a receiving and pumping organ, the heart, and a primary distributing vessel, the aorta.

During fetal life most of the blood entering the right atrium comes from the superior vena cava. The major portion of blood coming up the inferior vena cava is detoured through the foramen ovale directly into the left atrium, which is closer to the inferior vena cava than it is in the adult. A projection of the anterior rim of the foramen ovale, the crista dividens, diverts some of the flow, but probably more important is the proximity of cava and atrium and the fact that the pressure on the caval side of the valve is greater than that in the left atrium. Although the location of the foramen ovale in the fetus was correctly pictured by Barclay, Franklin, and Prichard (1944) and by Barcroft (1946) several decades ago and, indeed, four centuries ago by Fabricius (translated by Adelmann, 1942), most descriptions

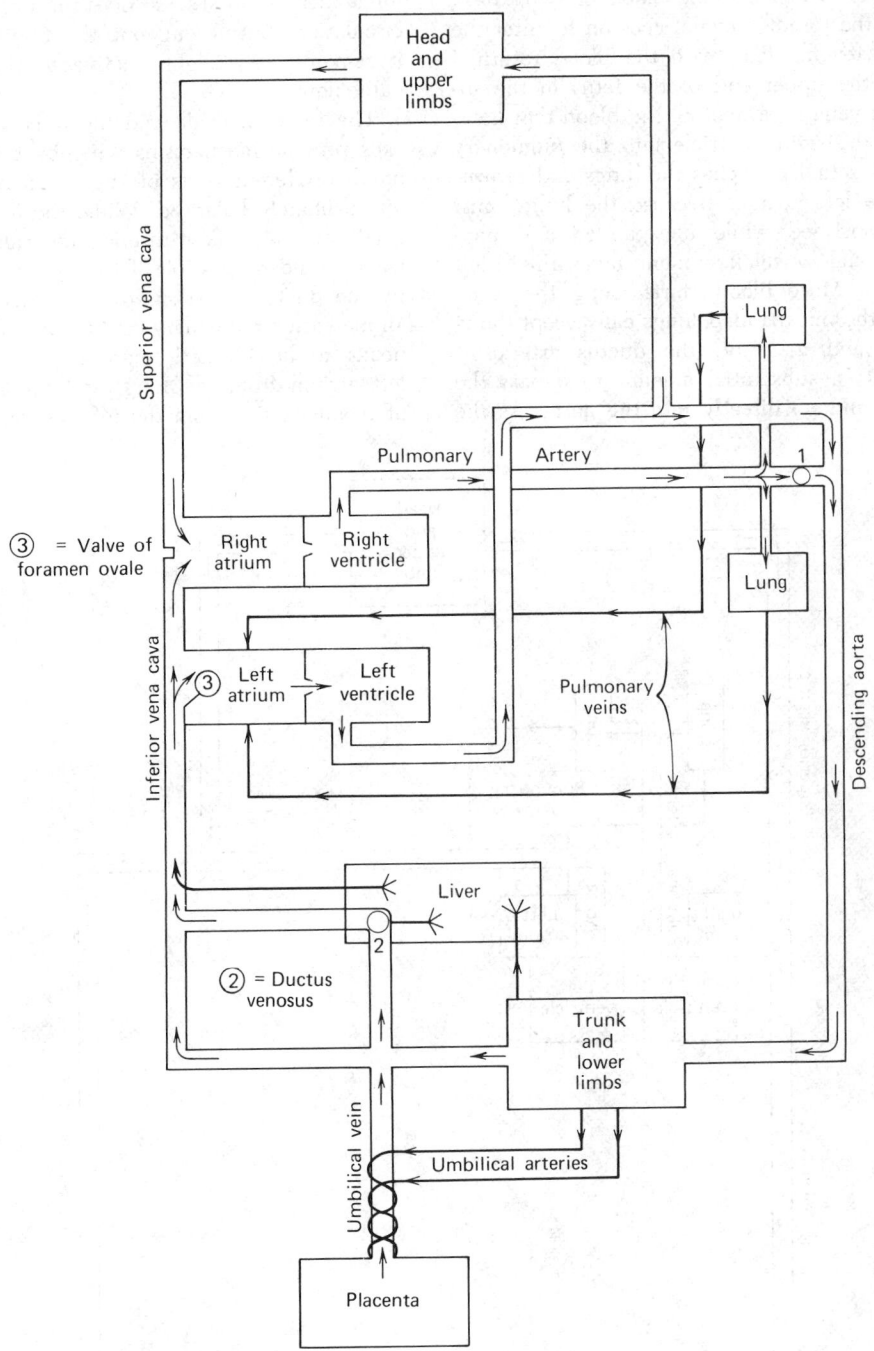

Fig. 1. Fetal circulation.

and diagrams place this valve in its eventual postnatal position between the right and left atria. The student should not be misled by the frequent repetition of this error. An excellent diagram by Born, Dawes, Mott, and Widdicombe (1954), reproduced in a number of articles in which the placement of the foramen is misstated, illustrates the true position clearly.

A smaller part of the inferior caval stream,

some of which may be blood eddying back from the foramen ovale, goes on to enter the right atrium along with the blood returned from the upper end of the fetus in the superior vena cava. Not all the blood that flows from the right ventricle into the pulmonary artery actually reaches the lungs and returns to the left atrium. Because the lungs must be nourished while unexpanded and non-functional, a small amount takes this adult course. More blood starts along the route than the unexpanded lungs can accept, however, and a shunt, the ductus arteriosus, permits a substantial amount to bypass the lungs and go directly into the aorta. As the

lungs increase in size, so does the pulmonary circulation, but throughout the fetal period it remains very slight relative to the postnatal flow.

The foramen ovale and the ductus arteriosus provide mechanisms whereby the loads on the different parts of the heart are kept approximately balanced. While the lungs are small very little flow through the right ventricle would be possible if the bypass offered by the ductus arteriosus did not exist. With an increasing pulmonary circulation less blood needs to be shunted, more returns to the left atrium from the lung, and the amount of blood passing from the inferior vena cava

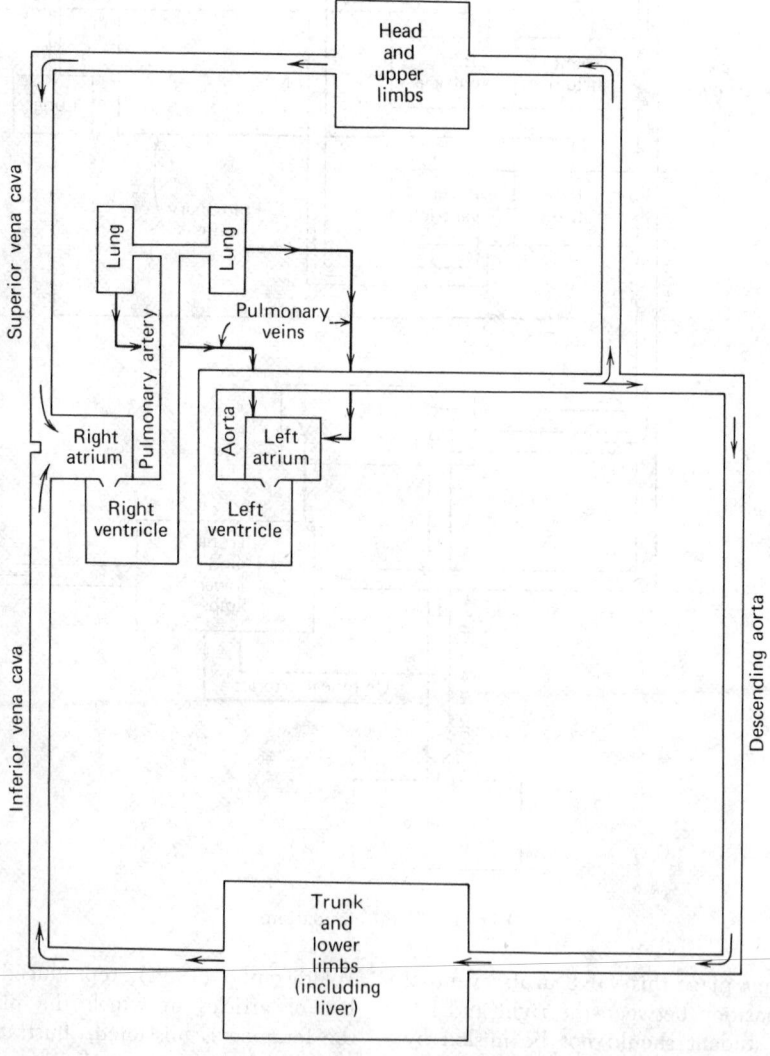

Fig. 2. Postnatal circulation.

to the left atrium by way of the foramen ovale declines. The approximate equalization of pumping load means that muscle on both sides of the heart is stimulated to develop. If there were no shunt such as that through the ductus arteriosus, the right ventricle would be less well prepared for the work it must perform as soon as breathing expands the lungs and the pulmonary circulation increases dramatically.

Blood coming into the left atrium from the lungs and through the foramen ovale is ejected into the left ventricle and then out into the aorta, as it is in the adult. From the aorta it also follows the adult course into the systemic circulation, some going to the head, neck, and arms via the ascending aorta and returning to the right atrium in the superior vena cava and part going to the trunk and legs in the descending aorta and returning to the left and right atria through the inferior vena cava. In the fetus, however, a large portion of the blood moving down the dorsal aorta passes out the umbilical arteries to the placenta to give up carbon dioxide and wastes and pick up oxygen and nutrients.

When well-oxygenated blood is brought back to the fetus through the umbilical vein it enters the left side of the liver. Here it takes one of two paths to the inferior vena cava. The first is indirect, via the network of sinusoids that began to develop when the liver first interrupted the course of the umbilical veins. The other is a direct shunt to the inferior vena cava, the ductus venosus, which formed slightly later as the volume of blood in the coalesced umbilical vein became larger. Whether or not blood takes this course has been thought to be determined by the opening and closing of a sphincter at the entrance of the ductus venosus (Barclay, Franklin, and Prichard, 1944; Nesbitt, 1966; Reynolds, 1953; Smith, 1959). How constricture would be controlled is not really understood, but innervation by a branch of the vagus nerve and responsiveness to shifts in blood pressure within the umbilical vein have been proposed (Reynolds, 1953). If a large volume of blood were driven in from the placenta, as it is when the uterus contracts, the sphincter could close, diverting the blood into the vascular network of the liver. Temporary storage in the liver would

prevent a sudden overloading of the heart. In addition, a decrease in umbilical vein pressure could stimulate constriction of the sphincter. The primary site of resistance to flow in the placental circuit by which pressure is maintained in the umbilical blood vessels is the liver sinusoids rather than the villous capillaries. Were all the blood to bypass the liver, the blood pressure might not be sufficient to keep the umbilical channels open. Contraction of the ductus venosus, forcing blood through the sinusoids, could promote an increase in pressure. However, the histological evidence for a true sphincter has recently been questioned (Lind, 1966).

Before other aspects of the fetal circulation are considered, let us digress to clarify the fact that in the fetus some veins, in particular the umbilical, contain more highly oxygenated blood than do the arteries. Those who think of arteries as carrying oxygenated blood and veins as bearing deoxygenated blood often find this point confusing. In fact, such a definition is not completely applicable even to the adult circulation, for the portal vein, which collects blood from capillaries in the digestive tract, takes blood to the liver rather than directly toward the heart. From the liver the blood is collected into another set of veins and delivered to the inferior vena cava. An accurate conception of arteries and veins that fits all situations is based on the direction of flow and the morphology of the vessel walls. Arteries carry blood away from the heart and are well-supported by smooth muscle and elastic tissue against the high and changing pressures to which they are subjected. Veins carry blood toward the heart under relatively constant conditions of lower pressure and hence have more nonelastic connective tissue in their walls and relatively little muscle or elastic fibers. This definition places the role of the umbilical vein in the proper context.

One of the questions that has intrigued investigators for many years is the extent to which the better oxygenated blood returning to the fetus via the umbilical vein and the liver becomes mixed in the inferior vena cava and the heart with much less oxygenated blood from the systemic circulation. The first definitive, as well as quantitative evidence came from a classic series of studies on the oxygen saturations of blood in the primary vascular channels of the fetal sheep (Kellogg, 1930; Barclay, Franklin, and Prichard, 1944; Barcroft, 1946). Later work (Dawes, Mott, and Widdicombe, 1954; Assali and Morris, 1964b; Romney, 1966) refined the gas analysis approach and added information from high-speed cineangiocardiograms of human and other fetuses (Lind and Wigelius, 1954; Reynolds, 1953; Cassels, 1966). The latter technique involves injecting contrast material into the blood so that its movement can be visualized in a cinematic X-ray. Although much of the research has been done under conditions that must be labeled "unphysiologic"—human data have been obtained largely from nonviable fetuses; lower animals have undergone anesthesia, removal from the uterus, and manipulation of the highly sensitive umbilical vessels and maternal and fetal tissue—the results from many sources are remarkably coherent. No quantitative data from direct measurements of oxygen saturation *in utero* are available for human beings, but the picture of blood flow pattern drawn from angiograms differs only in degree, for example, in the amount of flow through a particular region, from that in other species. In the following description figures in parentheses refer to average oxygen saturations in the fetal lamb (Born, Dawes, Mott, and Widdicombe, 1954).

The blood carried to the liver in the umbilical vein is the most highly oxygenated (80%) of any in the fetal body. Contrary to assertions in the older literature, a considerable amount of it is shunted directly into the inferior vena cava through the ductus venosus. Upon entry it is combined, to an extent still undetermined, with the smaller venous return of poorly oxygenated blood (26–27%) coming from the sinusoids of the liver in the hepatic portal vein and from other veins draining the trunk and legs. Most of this mixed but still relatively highly saturated (67%) inferior caval stream passes through the foramen ovale into the left atrium, as noted. A smaller stream moves on to the right atrium, there to join the blood of low oxygen saturation (31%) returning via the superior vena cava from the head, neck, and arms. It is this mixture of moderately oxygenated blood (52%) that flows from the right ventricle into the pulmonary artery. Some reaches the lungs and returns to the

left atrium, mixes with the more highly oxygenated blood that entered it via the foramen ovale, and passes on to the left ventricle and thence out the aorta to arteries feeding the cephalic end of the fetus. The oxygen saturation (62%) of the blood in the ascending aorta is only slightly lower than that of inferior caval blood entering the left atrium through the foramen ovale (67%).

At the point where the ductus arteriosus merges into the aorta, the remaining, larger portion of blood ejected from the right ventricle is also combined with more highly saturated blood following the course from left atrium to left ventricle to aorta. This mixture flowing down the descending aorta to the trunk, legs, and placenta is a little less oxygenated (58%) than that in the ascending aorta. Recently the concept of a differential in the oxygen pressures of the two systemic circuits has been challenged (Kaiser, 1966). But others maintain that vital organs such as the heart and brain are protected by a good oxygen supply at the expense of less essential tissue (Reynolds, 1953; Cassels, 1966). Given that physiological interactions are far more important in controlling the course of circulation than is the mere anatomical existence of shunts, it is not surprising that discrepancies exist both in data and in their interpretation. Relatively slight changes in heart rate, velocity of blood flow, and relative pressures (such as might occur either normally or in response to experimental manipulations) can modify the distribution of blood and hence its oxygen saturation in a particular channel at any point in time.

Physiological variables are also primary in the transformation of the fetal circulatory system to an adult one. Within moments after birth the normal infant becomes an air-breathing creature, his connection with the placenta is severed, and the transition to the adult type of circulation begins. Yet anatomical closure of most of the special fetal channels is quite slow. How soon these several channels close, anatomically and physiologically, and how closure is brought about are issues that have long concerned both basic scientists and clinicians. Persistent patency of the ductus arteriosus, for example, is one of the most frequently occurring congenital heart disorders and probably plays a part in the serious and baffling syndrome known as idiopathic respiratory distress. The complex of factors involved in expansion of the lungs requires detailed and separate consideration. Here we shall stress only the role of pulmonary changes in functional control of the transitional circulation.

Whether or not the infant breathes, support by the placenta is short-lived, for its pulsations soon cease even if no one cuts and ties the cord. The umbilical cord of man has no sphincter such as is found in some other species, but its vessels are supplied with smooth muscle—the arteries better than the vein. Constriction of human umbilical vessels has been observed in response to a variety of mechanical, thermal, and chemical stimuli. The portion of the cord within the uterus may be compressed. In addition, sponging or simply handling the cord initiates contractions in both directions from the site of irritation. Following an easy delivery, in which intrauterine compression may be assumed to have been minimal, and with little handling of the cord, blood may flow in the umbilical vessels for several minutes (Stembra, Hodr, and Janda, 1965). On the other hand, blood flow continuing for more than a few minutes is indicative of some abnormality in the transitional circulation (Desmond, Kay, and Megarity, 1959).

Cooling, which takes place when the infant leaves the maternal body and is augmented by evaporation in air, also stimulates constriction of the umbilical vessels. From experiments in which cord blood has been perfused with oxygen or with drugs such as adrenaline and noradrenaline, it has been inferred that both increase in oxygen saturation subsequent to breathing and secretion of catecholamines in response to the stress of birth produce vasoconstriction (Nyberg and Westin, 1957; Panigel, 1962; Smith, 1959).

Whatever the mechanism responsible for cessation of blood flow in the cord may be, elimination of the placental circuit has marked effects on the neonatal circulation. The vast vascular plexus of the placenta receives as much as half of the total cardiac output of the fetus. When this circulatory arc is removed, the venous return through the inferior vena cava to the heart is reduced, as is the pressure in this channel and the

force of blood against the foramen ovale. Breathing usually begins even before cord pulsations cease, and the expansion and ventilation of the large vascular bed of the lungs decrease pulmonary resistance. With an increase in blood flow to the lungs there is also, of course, a greater venous return to the left atrium. The changes in both the placental and pulmonary circulations alter pressure relationships between the right and left atria. Instead of the pressure being higher on the right side, as it was in the fetus, it becomes higher on the left. The hemodynamic balance which made for a right-to-left shunt through the foramen ovale shifts to a left-to-right pressure gradient serving to hold shut the valve of the foramen ovale.

During fetal life the two sides of the heart are at least equally well developed, and the right ventricle may be larger than the left (see below). In the early postnatal period, however, the weight of the right ventricle declines, while the muscle of the left increases markedly. The difference in the thickness and thus the elasticity of the walls of the two ventricles may also help to maintain greater pressure in the left atrium.

Although a high degree of functional closure is achieved within a few minutes after respiration is established, a small amount of right-to-left—that is, fetal—shunting, has been shown to continue for up to eight days in a large proportion of normal human neonates (Lind and Wegelius, 1954; Prec and Cassels, 1955; Condorelli and Ungari, 1960). Because functional closure depends upon pressure relationships, and these in turn depend in part upon pulmonary blood flow, the potential for reversion to the fetal condition exists. Both reversal of flow and failure of functional closure have been observed in asphyxiated newborns (Lind and Wegelius, 1954; James, Burnard, and Rowe, 1961), but such right-to-left shunts do not, in and of themselves, seem to have the detrimental effects in infancy that a patent ductus arteriosus does. However, closure *in utero* does give rise to enlargement of the heart and congestive heart failure (Naeye and Blanc, 1964). Normally, anatomical closure starts within a few days after birth, as the valve begins to adhere to the rim of the foramen ovale and clots form in the hole or holes in the valve, but very often never becomes complete. Scammon and Norris (1918) observed incomplete anatomical closure in 50% of children under the age of 5 years and 25% of persons over 15 or 20 years old. Postmortem data do not necessarily reflect accurately the normal course of closure, but they are our primary source of information.

Removal of the placental circulation obviously terminates the flow of blood through the ductus venosus from the umbilical vein. Nevertheless, if this channel remained open, liver function might be impaired because blood coming to the liver in the portal vein was diverted directly into the inferior vena cava. Because the ductus venosus is so inaccessible anatomically, relatively little is known about its closure or the consequences of its patency. Autopsy data (Scammon and Norris, 1918) indicate that anatomical closure takes place much earlier and more regularly than for the ductus arteriosus and foramen ovale—complete closure is reported in 40% of cases by 1 month, about 75% by 6 weeks, and approximately 100% by 2 to 3 months. Studies in which dyes or radio-opaque substances were injected suggest that functional closure is essentially accomplished within 1–3 hours after delivery (Jegier, Blankenship, and Lind, 1963) but may not be complete for 1 or 2 days (Peltonen and Hirvonen, 1965). Since the existence of a true sphincter at the entrance of the ductus venosus has been questioned (see earlier discussion), the mechanism of functional closure is a matter of conjecture.

Much more is known about the time and manner of closing of the ductus arteriosus. This is a very large vessel—almost equal in size to the aortic arch of the full-term fetus, and the results of its failure to close are serious. For these reasons, the ductus arteriosus has attracted attention at least since the time of Galen and has been the subject of a considerable proportion of the large body of research on the transitional circulation that has accumulated during the last decade. Most of the earlier studies were of anatomic closure (Gérard, 1900; Schaeffer, 1914; Noback and Rehman, 1941; Jager and Wollenman, 1942), but it was understood by the end of the last century that while this process ordinarily required some months, physiologic closure took place quite rapidly (Gérard, 1900).

The mechanism for functional closure is contraction of the smooth muscle in the wall of the ductus, and constricture is also the chief means by which the middle portion of the ductus closes anatomically, although thrombosis plays a part. At each end, occlusion takes place through thickening of the tissue. Eventually the ductus becomes a fibrous ligament. According to Scammon and Norris (1918), the incidence of complete anatomic closure is low during the first month, rises to about 50% by 2 months, and is about 90% by the end of the first year. Christie (1930) reported only 12% patency at 2 months and 1% at 1 year.

Work utilizing cineangiographic, indicator dilution, and oxygen analysis techniques (including improved polarography) and electromagnetic measures of blood flow has made it clear that although this vessel contracts very soon after breathing begins, blood may flow through it in either or both directions for as many as 8 days (Eldridge and Hultgren, 1955; Adams and Lind, 1957; Rowe and James, 1957; Burnard, 1958, 1959; Condorelli and Ungari, 1960; Saling, 1960; Moss, Emmanouilides, and Duffie, 1963; Assali and Morris, 1964a; Jegier, Blankenship, Lind and Kitchin, 1964; Gessner, Krovetz, Benson, Prystowsky, Stenger and Eitzman, 1965).

The direction and volume of blood shunted is influenced by so many variables that the course and timing of functional closure cannot be specified precisely. In general, the normal pattern is quite prompt but incomplete constricture, with some flow continuing in the fetal direction (right-to-left) for an hour or so, followed by bidirectional shunting for about another 6 hours, then left-to-right shunting for a half day or more, and finally complete physiological closure. Pressure changes like those underlying functional closure of the foramen ovale accompany the reversal in direction of flow through the ductus arteriosus. Before delivery, the pressure in the pulmonary arteries is greater than that in the descending aorta. Breathing lowers pulmonary vascular resistance, while removal of the placental vascular bed increases resistance in the systemic circuit. Hence the pressure in the pulmonary artery becomes somewhat lower than that in the aorta. At first flow through the ductus arteriosus may be bidirectional, for crying, coughing, and the like, can cause temporary pressure shifts that reverse the flow to the fetal direction. However, as constricture of the ductus becomes greater and pulmonary arterial pressure continues to drop, the flow becomes completely left-to-right before ceasing.

Results from both *in vivo* and *in vitro* experiments support the hypothesis that the primary stimulus for functional closure is an increase in oxygen tension (Born, Dawes, Mott, and Rennick, 1956; Assali, Morris, Smith, and Manson, 1963; Kovalčik, 1963; Adams, Moss, and Emmanouilides, 1966). There is also indirect evidence from observations on deliveries at high altitudes (Alzamora et al., 1953; Alzamora-Castro, Battilana, Abugattas, and Sialer, 1960; Peñaloza et al., 1964) and on premature (Powell, 1963; Moss, Emmanouilides, Rettori, Higashino, and Adams, 1965) and full-term neonates with respiratory distress syndrome (Record and McKeown, 1953; Rudolph, Auld, Golinko, and Paul, 1961). These conditions are associated with an above average incidence of low oxygen saturation, patent ductus arteriosus, and bidirectional shunting.

The ductus is also responsive to adrenaline and noradrenaline (Kennedy and Clark, 1941, 1942; Kovalčik, 1963). Apparently a direct response to chemical stimulation underlies the reactions to oxygen and these catecholamines, for the ductus arteriosus is not known to have autonomic innervation (Boyd, 1941). After several hours, the ductus loses its sensitivity to oxygen and fails to dilate if the oxygen saturation of the blood drops.

The effects of patent ductus arteriosus range from an almost complete lack of symptoms to labored breathing, congestive heart failure, and death, depending in large measure upon the extent to which the channel remains open and the presence of complications (Keith, Rowe, and Vlad, 1967). Susceptibility to fatigue is very common, particularly in younger children, and may in some instances help to prevent overexertion and more serious effects. Among the more severely impaired, growth failure, respiratory infections, and heart murmurs are the most frequent symptoms, and the incidence of heart enlargement is fairly high. When surgery is delayed beyond the age of three years, growth retardation often continues,

even in relatively mild cases. Slow growth, respiratory difficulties, and enlargement of the heart are not, of course, unique to patent ductus arteriosus. This syndrome is typical of any disorder that results in a poor supply of oxygen to the tissues.

Statistics on the incidence of disease cannot be accepted at face value, because of variations in the adequacy of diagnosis, reporting, and follow-up. Further, in mortality data, death is attributed to one cause, although the occurrence of multiple disorders is common. For example, figures on neonatal mortality show respiratory disease as the leading cause of death, while cardiac disease usually ranks about fifth, but the latter is often a complication of the former. Congenital heart disease is known to account for the largest proportion of cardiac disorders in children, and recent studies indicate a much higher incidence than was formerly believed to exist (Keith, Rowe, and Vlad, 1967). Current figures, which may still be too low, show over eight cases of congenital heart disease per thousand births. If stillbirths are excluded, the number drops to six or seven per thousand. However, many of these children succumb during the first year, particularly during the first month.

Given the intricacy of the circulatory system which is developed during gestation, the complexity of the circulatory adjustments to be made at birth, and the hazards imposed by delivery, it is perhaps surprising that most neonates make the transition from fetal to adult circulatory patterns so well. In a large majority, the system functions essentially as an adult one within about three hours after birth, despite the potential for some reversals during the first week or so and anatomical differences of longer duration.

Heart and Blood Vessels

Because modifications in work load are quite promptly reflected in the musculature of the region of the heart affected, the marked developmental changes which occur in the size and form of the heart are of particular interest. In all species that have been examined the walls of the ventricles are about equal in weight until fairly late in gestation, but soon after birth the left ventricle begins to grow more rapidly than the right and remains larger thereafter. Data on relative size during the interval between these two periods are much less consistent, particularly for the human being. Whether the discrepancies arise from true species differences, variations in method, or from abnormalities associated with the cause of death in man has not been determined.

Equal weights (Keen, 1955) and greater weight of the left ventricle (Brock, 1954) at term have been reported for human infants. However, more studies, especially recent ones, indicate a larger weight gain for the right ventricle from the sixth or seventh fetal month, with as much as a 33% difference in the full-term newborn (Patten, 1933; Emery and MacDonald, 1960; Hort, 1955, 1966). In addition, other kinds of data suggest greater development of the right ventricle in the perinatal period. The total size of the transverse sections of blood vessels leading to and from the right heart exceeds that for the left in the neonate (Patten, 1930/31), and Hort (1966) cites evidence for a greater capacity of the neonatal right ventricle when filled. Also, the most obvious feature of the late prenatal and early neonatal electrocardiogram is right ventricular preponderance (see discussion of Electrocardiogram).

According to some investigators (Brock, 1954; Emery and Mithal, 1961), there is no absolute loss in the weight of the right ventricle, only a slower rate of gain than is characteristic of the left ventricle. But the preponderance of evidence (Keen, 1955; Hort, 1955, 1966; Recavarren and Arias-Stella, 1964) supports Müller's (1883) early finding of real atrophy. Both Keen (1955) and Hort (1955) find a very considerable decrement in weight during the first month, followed by a smaller loss in the second month to a minimum of about 20% of birth weight. Shortly, a slow gain ensues, so that the right ventricle regains its birth weight sometime between 6 and 12 months.

Accepting the pattern of developmental changes in the human ventricles presented by recent studies, Hort (1966) marshalls rather convincing physiological hypotheses to explain the changes observed. He assumes that "the growth or atrophy of the heart muscle is regulated through the systolic force of tension that the muscle fibers develop by

their contraction" (1966, p. 210), and suggests factors that could modulate the force required of the two ventricles late in gestation and after delivery.

The amount of blood reaching the lungs from the right ventricle equals the amount delivered to the left atrium, and hence to the left ventricle, at all times. However, during the fetal period the volume of blood entering the ductus arteriosus from the right ventricle may not always be the same as that passing through the foramen ovale into the left heart. Hort (1966) argues for such a difference during the latter part of gestation. Because the growth rate of the foramen ovale decreases relative to that of the fetus as a whole, the amount of blood that can be shunted through the foramen ovale may not keep pace with the volume coming to the right heart in the superior and inferior vena cavae. More blood would then flow into the right ventricle. If the amount shunted through the ductus arteriosus now exceeds that reaching the left heart through the foramen ovale, the stroke volume of the right ventricle will be increased relative to the left.

The reversal in growth rates of the two ventricles after birth cannot be accounted for by some analogous change in stroke volume. Although the volume of blood returning from the placenta is eliminated, a greater amount reaches the right ventricle from the systemic circulation once the foramen ovale closes, and with constricture of the ductus arteriosus, the stroke volumes of the two ventricles become very similar. The lesser work load of the left ventricle probably stems instead from the lowering of resistance in the lungs and the consequent drop in pulmonary arterial pressure. The level of this pressure determines the tension that the right ventricle must develop to force blood into the pulmonary artery.

For a few days after birth the pressure in the pulmonary artery can vary widely, as mentioned earlier, but on the average it is about equal to the aortic pressure. Then it falls fairly dramatically and continuously until three months, when the mean ratio of aortic to pulmonary pressure approximates that of the adult. Hort (1966) aligned his age curves for the weight of the right ventricle with pressure curves (Rowe and James, 1957) and found them to parallel one another closely. As will be described later, the decline in pulmonary resistance and pressure is concomitant with a postnatal pattern of dilatation and thinning of the small arteries in the lungs.

In contrast to the postnatal course of the right ventricle, the left ventricle increases in weight at a rate greater than that of the body as a whole. The underlying variable may be the rise in pressure in the general circulation which takes place subsequent to a very brief drop in the first hour after birth. By about three months of age, the relative size and form of the various regions of the heart are comparable to those of the adult.

The total weight of the heart at birth constitutes a larger proportion of body weight than it does at most later ages. If placental weight is taken into consideration, however, the ratio of heart to body weight is like that of the adult. Elimination of the placenta reduces the weight of tissue to be served by about 15 to 20%, so the ratio increases slightly during the first month despite very little increment in total heart weight (Smith, 1959, pp. 126–128). During the remainder of the first year body weight triples while heart weight only doubles, presumably because of its initial advantage. Thereafter, the rate of growth of the heart almost parallels that of the body it must supply with blood. Between the end of the first year and adulthood, the ratio of heart to total weight declines by about 0.05% in males and 0.10% in females (Müller, 1883).

Although the embryonic and fetal development of vascular channels has been quite thoroughly researched (Arey, 1965; Patten, 1953), surprisingly few data are available on the postnatal growth of the major blood vessels. In the embryonic period the arteries are relatively large; during the remainder of gestation and during childhood, their diameter becomes progressively smaller in proportion to the size of the heart and the body as a whole (White House Conference, 1933). The decreasing heart:artery ratio may be a factor in the developmental increase of blood pressure (see below). Existing data indicate that the absolute growth rate of the arteries postnatally is associated with the weight or volume of the regions to which they carry blood.

Current concern about infant respiratory disorders is reflected in the considerable amount of research on the pulmonary vascular bed (Avery, 1964; Wagenvoort and Wagenvoort, 1966). The walls of the newborn's pulmonary arteries and arterioles, like those of the aorta, are very thick, and the pulmonary trunk and main arteries also have a great many elastic membranes. In the adult the walls of the pulmonary trunk are much thinner than those of the aorta and have little elastic membrane. Differences between the adult and the fetus and newborn in the thickness of the arterial walls are greater yet in the intrapulmonary arteries, particularly the muscular arteries and arterioles.

Soon after respiration is established, the media of the pulmonary vascular channels begins to thin rapidly and continues to do so until about the third week. The decrease is more gradual thereafter, and by 12 to 18 months, the relative thickness of the walls is comparable to that of the adult (Wagenvoort and Wagenvoort, 1966). Dilatation of the vessels rather than atrophy of their tissue is probably responsible for the widening of the lumina of the pulmonary vascular channels.

That developmental variations in the thickness of the smaller blood vessels bear importantly upon modifications in the vascular resistance of the lungs is suggested by other data (Wagenvoort and Wagenvoort, 1966). During gestation, when pulmonary resistance is high, the small arteries and arterioles have relatively thicker walls than do the larger muscular arteries. They apparently dilate more extensively after birth, however, for their walls are thinner in proportion to the diameter of the vessels than are those of the larger arteries until the end of the fourth or fifth week. At this time a slight but permanent reversal to a difference in the fetal direction takes place. Expansion of the small arteries and arterioles should contribute greatly to the reduction in vascular resistance and the resultant rise in blood flow observed in the lungs during the neonatal period.

There is a fairly sizable literature on the structural and functional development of the smallest blood vessels, the cappillaries, in various tissues of the human body. From post-mortem analyses on the liver, cerebral cortex, and cerebellum it is known that with advancing gestational age the distance between capillaries decreases, while the lengh of the capillary network and the number of capillaries per unit tissue increases rapidly (Mali and Räihä, 1935; Levine and Gordon, 1942; Niemineva, 1950; Niemineva and Tervillä, 1953; Diemer and Henn, 1964). Between full-term birth and adulthood, capillary density per unit tissue triples (Diemer and Henn, 1964), but the timing of the postnatal growth has not been traced. A large increment in the number of cerebral arterioles during the first six postnatal weeks with little systematic growth throughout the remainder of the first year has been reported (Rhodes and Hyde, 1965). However, the authors of that study believe that their failure to demonstrate an increase after six weeks may have a methodological basis.

As was pointed out very early in this chapter, the degree of vascularization of any organ is influenced by its metabolic activity. Diemer and Henn (1964) discuss their finding of a relatively low capillary density in the cortex of the newborn infant in these terms. Unfortunately, definitive development data on the oxygen consumption of the human brain are lacking; the only other evidence for a low cerebral metabolic rate in the neonate is also indirect (Kety, 1955; Kerpel-Fronius, Varga, and Mestyán, 1961). In lower animals (e.g., the rat) parallels exist between capillary density and oxygen consumption not only for adult and newborn, but also for different regions of the brain at a given age (Himwich, 1951; Flexner, 1955). With respect to the latter fact, it is of interest that the ratio of capillaries in white matter to the total number in the cortex is higher in the newborn (1:2) than in the adult (1:3) (Diemer and Henn, 1964). This observation suggests that the metabolic activity of subcortical tissue is relatively higher in proportion to that of the cortex in the newborn. Myelinated fibers make up the white matter, and little myelinization occurs in the cortex prenatally. Regional differences in capillarization within the brain have also been detected in human fetuses beginning quite early in gestation (Craigie, 1945). Analogously, early in the fetal period the oxygen consumption of the thalamus, caudate nucleus, and frontal cortex are low, whereas that of the medulla is relatively high (Himwich, Benardon, and Tucker, 1960) By term the metabolic activity of the other structures exceeds that of the medulla.

Investigations of capillary fragility have been prompted in part by concern about the susceptibility of the human infant to hemorrhage during labor. Most studies have used the technique of applying suction to induce pressure changes that produce petechiae (small purplish red spots caused by interadermal or submucous hemorrhage). Measured in this way, capillary permeability decreases during gestation and for at least the first postnatal week (see review in Smith, 1959, pp. 137–139). No attempt has been made to verify an early report indicating some decline in capillary resistance after the first few weeks (Abt, Farmer, and Epstein, 1936).

With a quite different approach evidence has also been obtained for a decrease in capillary permeability with age (Celander, 1966; Celander and Marild, 1962). The investigators regard their method as simply a means of assessing the extent of the capillary surface area to which blood is flowing. However, they offer no rationale for dismissing the likelihood that differences in permeability are responsible for their findings (Young, 1966). The calf and foot are placed in a water-filled venous occlusion plethysmograph (apparatus for recording volume changes) originally devised to study other aspects of the peripheral circulation in infants (Celander and Thunell, 1960, 1961; Celander and Marild, 1962). From the rate of outward filtration at different degrees of occlusion, a capillary filtration coefficient is calculated. This index represents the amount of fluid leaving the blood per unit time and tissue at various levels of capillary blood pressure. Although the capillary filtration coefficient varies with temperature and the volume of blood flow, it is on the average about twice as high in the full-term infant and five times as high in the premature infant as in the adult.

The response of the capillaries of the premature and full-term infant to other physiological stimuli also differ (Arajarvi, 1953; Eckstein, 1935). Neither dilatation after warming nor contraction in response to an injection of adrenalin is as adequate in the premature as in the full-term infant. Upon exposure to cold, however, the capillaries of the premature contract as promptly as those of the mature newborn.

Blood Volume

Plasma volume and red cell volume together make up blood volume. Normally plasma volume is almost constant and alterations in blood volume are caused by changes in red cell volume, which shifts considerably in a variety of circumstances (see discussion of Hematology). The total volume of blood in the body influences, and is influenced by, both fluid balance and cardiovascular function. In addition to the mechanisms controlling water intake and excretion, interchange of water among the fluid compartments (intracellular fluid, interstitial fluid, and plasma) helps to preserve the stability of each.

Intracellular fluid is protected from change at the expense of both other compartments, whereas water passes in and out of the interstitial compartment most readily. If interstitial adjustments are insufficient to sustain intracellular fluid at normal levels, plasma water is reduced or augmented. Diarrhea and vomiting, to which the infant is highly susceptible, are particularly likely to lead to dehydration in young children, because the younger the child, the greater is the relative water content of the body and the larger is the proportion in the extracellular compartments. Other conditions that result in a decrease of plasma volume are hypothyroidism, shock, burns, and hemorrhage.

When a large amount of blood is lost rapidly, pressure is reduced throughout the cardiovascular system. A decrease in venous pressure leads to a drop in cardiac output (volume of blood pumped by the heart each minute), further lowering the arterial pressure. The latter is a major factor in maintaining an adequate flow of blood to all tissues. To compensate for the decline in cardiac output, several reactions occur. A reflex triggers an increase in heart rate (cardiac output is a multiplicative function of stroke volume—the volume of blood ejected at each heart beat—and heart rate). Simultaneously, water is transferred from the interstitial compartment to plasma to restore blood volume to normal.

Blood volume and many of the variables to be considered in later sections are related to body size or some aspect of it. Neither the course of developmental changes nor some other comparisons such as those between the sexes, can be examined meaningfully unless these measures are expressed in terms of units per body size. Selection of an appropriate referent is, however, often difficult. One problem is that the effective variable may not be weight, height, or surface area, but rather the amount of a particular sort of tissue, such as lean body mass. Another is that different-sized units do not bear the same relationship to each other throughout development nor for all body builds at any one age. Illustrative of the former fact is Table 1 (adapted from Smith, 1959), which shows that the younger the child, the greater is his surface area relative to his weight.

Table 1.

Age	Proportion of Adult Weight	Proportion of Adult Surface Area
4 days, premature	0.024	0.090
15 days	0.048	0.150
6 months	0.080	0.210
1 year	0.145	0.340
6 years	0.250	0.525
12 years	0.340	0.630

As can be inferred from the table, if the underlying variable actually is surface area, weight will not provide a sufficient correction, and the measure per unit weight for an infant or child will be large relative to the adult.

According to the data of Morse, Cassels, and Schultz (1947), the correlation between total blood volume and weight is linear in children aged 1 to 17 years, but the correlations with age, height, and surface area are not. At greater heights or ages, for example, there is a larger increase in blood volume than would be predicted from a linear relationship. Russell (1949) found higher correlations of blood or plasma volume with weight than with height or surface area among children 3 months to 13 years of age. Nevertheless, he advocated height as a standard, because weight is less stable, changing considerably even during the course of one day with variations in hydration, food intake, and excretion. The standards of Brines, Gibson, and Kunkel (1941) are also based on height. Weight is still a widely used referent, however, particularly for infants and adults.

Probably because of differences in technique and the suitability of size referents, a rather wide range of values for blood volume have been reported at all ages. In principle, blood volume and either of its components can be measured, but in fact all methods have inherent sources of error. Among young infants another important factor is the extent of placental transfusion, and none of the normative data available comes from studies in which this factor has been carefully and systematically controlled.

Blood may be transferred from fetus to placenta, but transfer from placenta to fetus has received more attention. How much blood the infant will gain or lose is influenced by the strength and frequency of uterine contractions, pulsation of the cord, the length of time the cord is left attached, gravity (i.e., the position of the infant relative to the placenta), and whether or not the cord is deliberately "stripped" (see reviews in Moss and Monset-Couchard, 1967; Smith, 1959; Smith, 1966; and Watson and Lowrey, 1967). Increases in infant weight have been observed after each uterine contraction, but decreases occur if the cord pulsates strongly or if the fetus is held above the mother. Most of the effect on weight takes place within a few minutes of delivery, with almost no change after 10 to 20 minutes.

From serial measurements of blood volume in normal full-term infants Usher, Shephard, and Lind (1963) estimated that if the cord were not clamped for 5 minutes the total blood volume of an infant of average birth weight would rise about 60%. Their actual observations show a much smaller increase. One-fourth of the transfusion was accomplished within 15 seconds of birth and one-half to three-fourths by 60 seconds. Within 4 hours of birth the blood volume of infants with delayed clamping was reduced from 99 to 89 ml./kg., presumably because fluid had shifted from plasma to the interstitial compartment. Among infants whose cords had been clamped immediately there were no changes in blood volume during the same time period. At 3 days these infants had an average blood volume of 82 ml./kg. and red cell and plasma volumes of 31 ml./kg. and 51 ml./kg., respectively. Infants in the "late-clamping" group had a mean blood volume of 93 ml./kg., red cell volume of 49 ml./kg., and plasma volume of 44 ml./kg.

Most sources indicate that total blood volume is high in the premature infant, intermediate in the full-term infant, and lowest in the adult. The volume of red cells is almost equal for premature and full-term infants and higher in both than in the adult. Plasma volume is quite elevated among the premature, but only slightly so in the normal newborn when comparisons are based on body weight. Representative figures are a total blood volume of 108 ml./kg. for the premature, 85–90 ml./kg. for the full-term infant, and 75–80 ml./kg. for the adult. The adult average is probably approximated by about 2 months.

Among adults the male has a blood volume per unit weight about 16% greater than that of the female. The preponderance of evidence suggests that this difference does not appear until puberty, when red cell volume, total blood volume, and perhaps plasma volume increase more rapidly in the male (Brines, Gibson, and Kunkel, 1941; Sjöstrand, 1953; Tanner, 1962). Because blood volume seems to be higher in adults with relatively large amounts of muscle (Hicks, Hope, Turnbull, and Verel, 1956) and muscle mass increases more rapidly during adolescence in males, the sex difference in blood volume may arise from a difference in the relative proportions of tissue with high metabolic activity (Tanner, 1962).

Cardiac Output

The cardiac output of the human being is usually measured by some variant of either an indicator dilution or Fick method. For example, a known amount of dye is injected into the right atrium or a large vein, and a curve of the indicator concentration in successive samples of arterial blood is plotted against time. Dividing the amount of indicator injected by its average arterial concentration, with appropriate adjustments for the interval of time involved, yields an estimate of the flow of blood from the heart per minute.

According to the Fick principle, the amount of a substance taken up by an organ in a given amount of time is equal to the arteriovenous difference in the level of the substance multiplied by the blood flow. One way in which this principle can be applied to determine cardiac output is to divide the oxygen consumption of the lungs per unit time by the difference in oxygen content of venous and arterial blood across the lungs. In the direct Fick method oxygen saturation is actually measured; indirect methods utilizing estimates derived in other ways are not very reliable.

As ordinarily used, these procedures measure the output of only the left ventricle. By proper selection of sampling site, right ventricular output can also be measured, but the outputs of the two ventricles may be considered equal after the neonatal period. The existence of shunts so alters the pattern of oxygen or indicator concentrations and timing of indicator dilution curves basic to the calculation of cardiac output from either ventricle that estimates derived from the two ventricles may differ, and both may be inaccurate. Fortunately, techniques for detecting shunts can be incorporated in studies of blood flow.

No measures of cardiac output in the human fetus are available. However, several studies of newborn infants have been reported. An excellent example of problems and methods is a recent study (Gessner, Krovetz, Benson, Prystowsky, Stenger, and Eitzman, 1965), in which a dye dilution technique was used. One catheter with two separated side holes was positioned so that the two sideholes straddled the foramen ovale. Dye could then be injected into either one or both atria at the same time.

Only left atrial curves, that is, curves obtained after separate injection into the left atrium, proved to be suitable for estimating ventricular outputs and the amount of left-to-right shunting. Injection into the right atrium was useful for detecting right-to-left shunts, but shunted blood reappeared at the sampling site (the abdominal artery) before the peak concentration of the initial dye curve had been reached, invalidating the determination of cardiac outputs. Following left atrial injection, shunted blood returned dye to the abdominal artery shortly after the

first peak had been observed. Therefore left ventricular output had to be calculated from a formula in which only the first part of the dye curve is utilized instead of from the standard equation. By adjusting left ventricular output for the extent of left-to-right shunting, the right ventricular output was derived.

The generally rapid circulation time of infants (Blankenship, Lind, and Arcilla, 1965; Gessner et al., 1965; Lesser, Meyer, and Henderson, 1952; Slobody, Rook, Levbarg, and Morey, 1950; Yang, Slobody, Mendlowitz, and Tyree, 1955), particularly in combination with inaccuracies inherent in the customary flush technique for dye injection, also create difficulty in securing reliable dye curves. Circulation time is the interval required for blood to travel from one point in the circulation to another. It can be measured with injected dyes, radioactive isotopes, or a variety of substances that give rise to discriminable reactions, such as flushing or a bitter taste. Among adults the average arm-to-lips time is 14 to 15 seconds; for children aged 2 to 12 years and infants under 2 the means are about 11 and 7 seconds, respectively (Averbuck and Friedman, 1935; Brandfonbrener, Landowne, and Shock, 1955; Hubbard, Preston, and Ross, 1942; Oberst and LaRoche, 1954; Sutliff and Holt, 1925; Witzberger and Cohen, 1943). With the flush technique the instant at which dye begins to enter the circulation cannot be determined, and, unless timing is carefully controlled, the dye may be injected in two doses. A special syringe and injection technique designed to provide instantaneous dye ejection and recording were used in the study of Gessner et al. (1965) summarized above.

Circulation time is directly related to cardiac output, and both of these measures are positively correlated with metabolic rate. When oxygen consumption rises, as it does, for example, during exercise, excitement, eating, or hyperthyroidism, the cardiac output of normal subjects increases to keep the tissues adequately supplied with oxygen. Because cardiac output is associated with metabolism and the latter, in turn, with body size, cardiac output is often reported in terms of the cardiac index, the blood flow in liters per minute per square meter of surface area. The validity of this index is still being debated, and height has been claimed to be as good a referent (Krovetz, McLoughlin, Mitchell, and Schiebler, 1967). To date, however, the data available in a form to permit developmental comparisons are based either on surface area or weight.

Under basal conditions the cardiac output of adults averages 70–80 ml./kg./min., or a cardiac index of 3.0–3.2 L./min./sq.m. of surface area (Dittmer and Grebe, 1959; Hamilton, 1962). Prec and Cassels (1955), the first investigators to measure the cardiac output of the neonate, obtained a mean cardiac index of 2.5 for infants aged 2 to 26 hours. On a weight basis, this would be more than twice the adult output. Dye was injected into the umbilical vein (hence the dye curves are right atrial ones), an ear oximeter was used for sampling, and outputs were calculated from the standard Stewart-Hamilton equation. The oximeter is an inexact instrument for measuring dye concentrations; the problems associated with right atrial curves and timing of injection have been described. Although Adams and Lind (1957) arrived at an almost identical mean and range with the Fick method, they used assumed oxygen consumptions for all but three infants, and the oxygen content of their blood samples may have been affected by shunting. The means in these two studies are close to those estimated by Gessner et al. (1965) for right ventricular output, 2.6, but the higher individual values observed are in the range of their mean left ventricular cardiac index, 4.0.

The highest cardiac outputs reported for any age group—348 ml./kg./min. for the left ventricle and 348 for the right—are those from Burnard's (1966) work with infants 2 to 28 hours old. He measured right ventricular output by the Fick method and left ventricular output with a thermal dilution technique and injection directly into the left atrium. His simultaneous measures of oxygen consumption are about 50% greater than basal levels for age (see section on Basal Metabolism), indicating that the subjects were not in a basal condition. On the other hand, Gessner et al. (1965) made repeated measurements on the same infants during the first 2 hours of life and excluded from analysis any made while the baby was active. Average left ventricular output was about 250 ml./

kg./min. The derived estimate for right output was considerably lower. Their data are also consistent with mean pulmonary blood flows found in other recent studies of neonates (Cho, Clements, Cotton, Klaus, Sweet, Thomas, and Tooley, 1965; Klaus, Braun, and Tooley, 1961) and with data on the neonatal sheep (Cross, Dawes, and Mott, 1959) and rabbit (Dawes and Mestyan, 1963). However, their measures might be invalid if any significant degree of left-to-right shunting through the foramen ovale occurred. Their methods can be assumed to check only on shunting via the ductus arteriosus.

In none of the studies done to date has the effect of placental transfusion been controlled. However, nine of the newborns tested by Gessner et al. were delivered by elective caesarean section and had their cords clamped more promptly than the five infants who were delivered vaginally. At about one hour after birth the left and right ventricular outputs were 3.5 and 2.3 L./min./sq.m., respectively, for the former group and 5.0 and 3.1 for the latter. The absolute volume of left-to-right shunting was also greater in the babies delivered in the normal way.

Granting the reservations applicable to all the data available and taking account of the particular limitations of some, two inferences may be hazarded. The relatively large surface area of the neonate imposes a functional demand on his heart that is, in terms of his weight, several times that of the adult. Further, some factor, perhaps a higher metabolic rate, makes for a cardiac output larger than the adult's even per unit of surface area.

These conclusions are supported by the results of investigations on older infants and children. Unfortunately, in these studies a single cardiac index is reported for a wide range of ages. With only one exception (Jegier, Sekelj, Davenport, and McGregor, 1961), however, they agree in showing the cardiac index to be above the adult average. Means reported include 4.1 L./min./sq.m. in children aged 6 to 16 years (Sproul and Simpson, 1964), 4.3 in two groups, one with a mean age of 12 (Brotmacher and Fleming, 1957) and another with an average age of 8.7 years, but a range from less than 1 week to 19.9 years (Krovetz, McLoughlin, Mitchell, and Schiebler, 1967), and 4.6 in a sample aged 5 months to 14 years (Agustsson, Bicoff, and Arcilla, 1963).

Blood Pressure

The pressure exerted by blood against the walls of the vessels that contain it can be measured with varying degrees of difficulty and accuracy in all vascular channels and in the chambers of the heart. When unqualified, the term blood pressure is usually intended to mean the pressure in the aorta and large arteries, particularly the brachial ,artery in the upper left arm. Systolic pressure is the highest pressure reached in the large arteries during ventricular systole, and diastolic pressure is the minimum to which the pressure falls at the point in ventricular diastole immediately before the beginning of the next systole. If these two pressures are reported jointly, the systolic is, by convention, placed above the diagonal and the diastolic below it, for example, 120/60.

To assess intraarterial pressure directly, a needle which is attached to some measuring and recording device is inserted. Although direct measurements are the most accurate, they have disadvantages, especially when they are to be repeated over a period of time. The apparatus is expensive, and aseptic conditions must be maintained. Indirect methods require a cuff that can be inflated and gradually deflated and a manometer.

The oldest and still the most widely used techniques in routine clinical practice are palpation and auscultation. In palpation a finger is placed on the artery at the wrist or ankle (a leg is often the site of measurement in infants and young children) or just below the cuff. The pressure in the cuff is increased above the expected pressure or until the pulse disappears, and then is lowered in steps until the pulse is felt again. This approach gives an approximation of systolic pressure—about 2-5 mm. Hg lower than that obtained by auscultation and considerably below the direct pressure—but no estimate of diastolic pressure. It is particularly unsatisfactory with infants and children because the pulse in their arms and legs is often difficult to feel.

For auscultation a stethoscope is placed over the artery immediately below the cuff. The cuff is inflated and deflated as for palpation until the pressure in the artery just

exceeds that in the cuff. When this point, the systolic pressure, is reached a tapping sound can be heard. With continued deflation the sound at first grows louder, then becomes dull and muffled, and eventually disappears in most adults. Neither muffling nor cessation of sounds is a very reliable index of diastolic pressure in children. Among 120 children aged 3 to 19 years examined by Moss and Adams (1963) only 67% had both sounds. No muffling could be heard in 16%, and muffling was not followed by complete cessation of sound in 27%. The correlations with direct measures were low (.32–.36) for both points. In general, muffling yielded estimates that were too high and complete cessation readings that were too low, but the variability was somewhat less for muffling.

Because all heart sounds are less easily discriminated in children, and because auscultation involves more cooperation from the subject than can regularly be expected of infants, Goldring and Wohltmann (1952) devised a variation called the "flush" technique. Sufficient pressure is applied to the hand to blanch the area without causing crying. A pressure cuff is then attached and inflated. Pressure on the hand is removed and the cuff slowly deflated. As soon as normal color (flush) appears, the pressure, which is then about midway between the systolic and diastolic pressure, is read. If the foot is used instead of the hand, the pressure is 5–10 mm. Hg higher. In addition to yielding only a single value, the flush method may produce variable results, in part as a function of the speed of deflation and in part because of failure to recognize the first flush (Keith, Rowe, and Vlad, 1967; Moss and Adams, 1964).

Basically, the oscillometric method substitutes instrumental recording for palpation or listening for sounds, a definite asset in working with infants and children. The occluding cuff is placed on the arm or leg and manipulated as in auscultation. An oscillometer is applied at a lower point. While the pressure in the cuff is greater than the systolic pressure no blood flows, and hence no vibrations occur to be sensed by the oscillometer. In fact, there may be a few pulsations of small amplitude as the systolic pressure is approached, but when it is reached the amplitude of the oscillations suddenly rises to about 3 mm. in infants and 5–6 mm. in older children. The point at which the pulsations become reduced again is the diastolic pressure. Additional advantages of oscillometry are readings close to those from direct measures and the fact that the cuffs can be attached but not inflated until after the infant goes to sleep. If automatic recording is incorporated into the system, repeated observations can be made with less stress for either infant or observer, and with less expenditure of the observer's time (Currens, Brownell, and Aronov, 1957; Gupta and Scopes, 1965).

Similar advantages can be claimed for several other kinds of apparatus that have been introduced in research settings, such as a differential optical pulse indicator (Rice and Posener, 1959), a photocell oscillometer (Goodman, Cumming, and Raber, 1962), and plethysmographs (Celander and Thunnel, 1960; Karlberg, Moore, and Oliver, 1965; Levison, Kidd, Gemmell, and Swyer, 1966; Schaffer, 1955), all of which record vibrations passing beyond the site of pressure, and a microphone placed beneath the occluding cuff (Morse, Brownell, and Currens, 1960). On the other hand, it is fairly difficult to keep a plethysmographic system leakproof, and anything greater than minor movements will cause artifacts in almost any automatic recording.

At best, even reasonably reliable measures, particularly from infants and young children, demand much attention to procedural detail. Largely for this reason, assessments of blood pressure, although theoretically important, are rare in developmental psychophysiological studies. Basal measures in adults are taken 10 to 12 hours after the last meal and following a 30-minute rest. No young infant would be in normal condition if deprived of food for so long a time, and unless sleep occurs spontaneously or is induced, only the most ingenious experimenter will have a relaxed rather than an active subject at the end of an idle half hour. Standard, as contrasted with basal conditions are less stringent, measurements being made after an interval of rest and no sooner than two hours after eating.

Activity, emotional upset, and variations in respiration all influence blood pressure.

Even in newborns, for example, crying will increase the systolic pressure by 30 mm. Hg or more (Gupta and Scopes, 1965; Woodbury, Robinow, and Hamilton, 1938; Young and Holland, 1958). Raising a young infant's head or holding him in a sitting position elevates the arterial pressure (Gupta and Scopes, 1965). In infants less than 24 hours old, Gupta and Scopes (1965) also observed increments in directly recorded pressures of as much as 20 mm. Hg during sucking, whether or not food was ingested. After sucking ceased, pressures returned to resting levels, stayed constant for 30 to 60 minutes, and then declined markedly if the infant fell into a deep sleep. "As the child emerges from this deep phase of sleep the blood pressure again rises to approximately the resting level" (Gupta and Scopes, 1965, p. 639). Many investigators prefer postprandial conditions for infants, but the findings just cited indicate that the values recorded will vary with the state of the child.

Unlike some other physiological measures, blood pressure does not seem to be affected by moderate changes in environmental temperature in either premature or full-term infants (Contis and Lind, 1963; Gupta and Scopes, 1965; Levison, Kidd, Gemmell, and Swyer, 1966) or older children and adolescents (McKee and Eichorn, 1953). Gupta and Scopes also found no evidence of diurnal rhythms in young infants.

Especially in infants and young children, inappropriate cuff size is a major source of error. A cuff that is too narrow relative to the length of the limb yields measures that are too high, because greater inflation pressure is needed to compensate for the reduced compression of the artery. Conversely, too wide a cuff may give readings that are too low. When a longer portion of the artery is compressed, resistance increases, decreasing the blood flow. Hence the pulse may disappear before reaching the far end of the cuff. The most widely recommended criterion for cuff width is a size about two-thirds the length of the segment of the limb to which it is attached (Keith, Rowe, and Vlad, 1967; Watson and Lowrey, 1967).

From simultaneous comparisons of auscultatory and intraarterial pressures in 128 children 3 to 19 years old, Moss and Adams (1965) report that cuff widths of 5 cm.

at 3 to 5 years, 7 cm. from 5 to 8, 9.5 cm. from 8 to 14, and 12 cm. after 14 produce systolic pressures that do not differ by more than 8 mm. Hg from direct measures. These sizes are slightly smaller than those that Keith, Rowe, and Vlad (1967) have found to agree well with direct recordings: 3 cm. for prematures, 4.5 cm. for full-term to 2 years, 7 cm. for 2 to 4 years, 10 cm. for 5 to 9 years, and 13 cm. for 10 to 14 years. Except for the larger sizes suggested for children under 4 by these authors, their standards are similar to the widths recommended by the American Heart Association Committee on Blood Pressure (Bordley, Connor, Hamilton, Kerr, and Wiggers, 1951). However, the proper size to use with young infants groups is still a matter of controversy.

Since 1938, when Woodbury, Robinow, and Hamilton reported that only a 2.5 cm. cuff gave readings that closely paralleled direct ones, this size has been widely adopted. On the other hand, Schaffer's (1955) repeated assessments on infants during their first day with 2.5, 4, and 8 cm. cuffs and an impedance plethysmograph and electric manometer showed the narrow, short cuff (2.5 × 4 cm.) to yield unreliable results and probably spuriously high ones, at least with sensitive recording apparatus. Reinhold and Pym (1955) also considered measures made with a 2.5 cm. cuff to be more variable than those done with a 6 cm. cuff, but the mean systolic pressure of about 50 mm. Hg obtained with the latter in infants 1 to 3 days old is very low compared to most direct readings. Recording with a photocell oscillometer in a small group of infants aged 1 week to 30 months, Goodman, Cumming, and Raber (1962) got close agreement with intraarterial pressures and among each other for cuff widths varying from 2 to 3.7 cm. A sharp drop in levels was observed when a 6.5 cm. width was used.

On the basis of a study with children aged 1 day to 4 years, Moss and Adams (1964) concluded that cuff size was not so important with the flush method. Mean pressures were lower the larger the cuff, but the differences among cuffs of 5, 9, and 12 cm. were not statistically significant. Several other investigations do suggest that in newborns the most stable results with this method are achieved with a 4 cm. cuff (see review in Young, 1961).

How great the methodological differences in recorded arterial pressures are relative to age changes can be inferred from the data assembled in Tables 2, 3, and 4. Omitted from these tables are studies in which subjects were grouped over a wide time span for the particular ages concerned, for example, several days in the case of newborns, in which the recording technique was not constant, or in which age or cuff size was not specified. To provide illustrations of flush values through most of the first year an exception to the cuff width criterion, which does not seem to be a major one for this technique, was made for the data from Watson and Lowrey (1967). Research on older children was not included if pressures were reported for only one sex or for the sexes combined.

Regardless of technique, and despite the great variability among young subjects, most studies show the early weeks and months to be a period of comparatively rapid increase in pressure. Yet the values obtained vary so widely with method that were data collected with different methods (or with the same technique but a different cuff size) to be utilized for establishing age trends, the latter could be obliterated or even inverted. Of course, flush pressure is intermediate between the systolic and diastolic levels and so would be expected to differ from those values as assessed by any means. When measures are made by other indirect methods, cuff size is in general more influential than recording technique in determining the absolute values observed during infancy and early childhood. Pressures taken with a cuff of 4 or 5 cm. within the first few days of life range between the mid-forties and low sixties, with an average in the mid-fifties. Higher levels, closer to intraarterial pressures, are characteristic with narrower cuffs.

Additional sources of variation during the early days are time elapsed since delivery, time of clamping of the umbilical cord, mode of delivery, and degree of asphyxiation. Ashworth and Neligan (1959) found the mean systolic pressure to drop abruptly from a high of 92 mm. Hg during the first few minutes after birth to an average low of 60 four hours later in normal infants whose cords

Table 2. Blood Pressure During Early Infancy[a]

Study	Cuff Size	Birth	1	2	3	4-5	6-7	9-10	3-4	6	3	6
			Days						Weeks		Months	
Bowman, 1933, oscillometer	5 cm.		55/38	60/41	60/42	60/44						
Rucker and Connell, 1924, oscillometer	4 cm.		55/40	58/41	54/39	59/42	62/44	64/42				
Salmi, 1935 auscultation	4 cm.		46/26	64/38		75/47						
Levinson et al., 1966 strain-gauge	4 cm.		62	67	71	76	82					
Goodman et al, 1962 oscillometer	3 cm.	79	59-65[b]	69	73	82			89	95	100	100
Dexter and Weiss, 1941 oscillometer	2.5 cm.	74/38	78/40	84/42		92/50						
Contis and Lind, 1963, xylol bead pulse indicator	2.5 cm.		78-90[b]		82	90	97					
Holland and Young, 1956 palpation	2.5 cm.		67-70[b]		72			73	77	78	86	93
Woodbury et al., 1938, direct and palpation	— 2.5 cm.	80/46	85	85	92							
Gessnet et al., 1965, direct	—	70/39										
Moss and Adams, 1964, direct flush, leg	5, 9&12 cm.	53										
Forfar and Kibel, 1956, flush, arm	5 cm.		60	65		79	84	92				
flush, leg	5 cm.		65-68[b]	74		89	88	79				
Watson and Lowrey, 1967, flush	not stated		52					72	62		69	71

[a] Means for both systolic and diastolic pressures are listed where available. Some means were read from authors' graphs or computed from their data.

[b] Ranges on Day 1 indicate means obtained at different times during the first 24 hours.

were clamped early. If clamping was delayed, so also was the decrement, but it occurred within the first 24 hours. Regardless of time of clamping, a steady rise ensued throughout the remainder of the first week, but during the second day pressures never exceeded those recorded immediately after delivery. In another study (Goodman, Cumming, and Raber, 1962) the mean fall in pressure was marked but smaller, 20 mm. Hg, and the minimum was reached on the average at two hours instead of four. The following rise was very gradual during the rest of the first day and steeper thereafter, birth levels being regained by the fourth day. Infants delivered by caesarian section have lower systolic pressures than normal vaginal births (Holland and Young, 1956; Neligan, 1959), whereas respiratory distress may raise (Neligan, 1959) or lower (Gupta and Scopes, 1965; Holland and Young, 1956) the blood pressure.

Such information as has been secured on blood pressures during human gestation comes from measures made at or after delivery on premature infants. Therefore, interpretations must be tempered not only by the possibility of abnormalities in the subjects and differences between extrauterine and intrauterine environments, but also by a number of the methodological factors mentioned earlier, such as time since delivery and treatment of the cord. Probably the most definitive data are those reported several decades ago by Woodbury, Robinow, and Hamilton (1938). Recording directly from a cannula in the umbilical artery at delivery, they obtained pressures of 33–39/21, 55/25, 70/35, 85/45, and 80/46 at 5, 6.5, 7, 8, and 9 fetal months, respectively.

Most subsequent investigators have been concerned with methodological issues (Kafka,

1967), reflexes (Moss, Duffie, and Emmanouilides, 1963; Young and Holland, 1958), or the effect of birth weight (Bucci, Scalamandre, and Savignoni, 1963; Levison, Kidd, Gemmell, and Swyer, 1966) or various disorders (Gupta and Scopes, 1965; Neligan, 1959; Neligan and Smith, 1960), and only a few have categorized their subjects by gestational age. Rarely have infants that could be considered to be younger than 7 fetal months been included. Despite the limitations of individual studies and variations from study to study in the absolute levels recorded, most of the accumulated data support the conclusion that pressures are lower in prematures than in normal full-term infants and probably increase at least until the eighth prenatal month. In all other species that have

Table 3. Age and Sex Norms for Systolic Blood Pressure

Study:	Allen-Williams, 1945		Lincoln, 1928		Londe, 1966		Sundal, 1932		Richey, 1931		Shock, 1944	
Method:	Auscultation		Auscultation		Auscultation		Palpation		Auscultation		Auscultation	
Cuff size in cm.	4 (under 2 yrs), 6 (2-4 yrs.), 8 (4-5 yrs.)		9.5		9 (younger) 13.5 (older)		12		12		12.5	
Age in Years	M	F	M	F	M	F	M	F	M	F	M	F
0.75	89	93	—	—	—	—	—					
1.5	96	95										
2.5	99	92										
3.0			93	89			78	78				
3.5	100	100										
4.0			94	93	98	98	80	80				
4.5	99	99										
5.0			98	95	101	102	83	82	80	85		
6.0			98	97	105	105	85	84	85	85		
7.0			98	99	106	107	88	87	89	89		
8.0			100	100	108	108	90	88	92	93		
9.0			101	101	111	112	91	90	95	93		
10.0			105	104	114	114	93	95	95	96		
11.0			104	105	114	121	98	102	96	101		
11.5											103	107
12.0			102	104	116	117	104	106	98	102	104	104
12.5											105	106
13.0			105	105	120	121	108	108	101	103	106	105
13.5											108	108
14.0					120	119	110	109	106	104	111	108
14.5											111	106
15.0					125	115	113	109	110	106	110	105
15.5											111	104
16.0							113	108	112	107	112	107
16.5											111	105
17.0							114	108	112	103	115	107
17.5											114	105
18.0							114	109	113	101		
19.0							115	110	117	105		
20-30							114	113			112-114	108-110

been examined blood pressure rises during gestation, but there is considerable variability in pattern of increments (Dawes, 1961).

Whether age or weight is the more important factor cannot be stated conclusively, but the evidence for man tends to favor weight. Goodman et al. (1962) worked with infants of 23–36 weeks gestational age as well as with full-term babies. Systolic pressures in the premature were correlated with both weight and age, increasing to the thirty-second fetal week. Among infants born at 27 to 34 weeks, Levison and his associates (1966) found no systematic variation of systolic pressure with gestational age. Nor was there any difference in pressures between infants weighing 500–1000 grams and those

of 1000–1500 grams. However, pressures rose linearly with weight above the latter size. Similarly, Bowman's (1933) data reveal very little difference in either systolic or diastolic pressure on the fourth day of life between infants weighing 2–3 or 3–4 pounds, but systolic pressures were higher and equal in the 4–5 and 5–6 pound groups and slightly greater in infants of 6–7 pounds. In contrast, Gupta and Scopes (1965) observed no differences in pressures during the first 6 hours after delivery between a group weighing over 2500 grams at birth and one with birth weights of 1501 and 2500 grams; levels were somewhat lower in infants whose birth weights were less than 1500 grams. Their subjects had various disorders or were "nor-

Table 4. Age and Sex Norms for Diastolic Blood Pressure

Study:	Allen-Williams, 1945		Lincoln, 1928		Londe, 1966		Richey, 1931		Shock, 1944	
Method:	Auscultation		Auscultation		Auscultation		Auscultation		Auscultation	
Cuff size (cm.)	4 (under 2 yrs), 6 (2-4 yrs.), 8 (4-5 years)		9.5		9 (younger) 13.5 (older)		12		12.5	
Age (Yrs.)	M	F	M	F	M	F	M	F	M	F
0.75	60	62								
1.5	66	65								
2.5	64	60								
3.0			66	67						
3.5	67	64								
4.0			67	66	57	60				
4.5	65	66								
5.0			70	67	60	60	49	58		
6.0			70	69	60	64	53	56		
7.0			70	70	63	63	56	57		
8.0			73	71	61	65	57	59		
9.0			72	71	65	67	60	60		
10.0			75	74	66	64	61	61		
11.0			73	74	65	69	63	64		
11.5									69	73
12.0			73	75	67	65	62	65	71	71
12.5									70	72
13.0			75	74	65	69	62	66	70	70
13.5									69	68
14.0					68	67	64	67	68	68
14.5									68	67
15.0					67	67	66	67	69	68
15.5									70	68
16.0							66	69	71	69
16.5									70	68
17.0							67	67	72	69
17.5									71	69
18.0							69	66		
19.0							69	66		
20-30									75-80	72-76

mal" but small for gestational age and were examined under a variety of circumstances. No real trend with weight is discernible in the few premature (defined as a birth weight of less than 2.5 kg.) infants studied by Holland and Young (1956).

Circulatory and respiratory adjustment to extrauterine life only briefly reverse the rising trend of blood pressure which apparently begins early in gestation and continues at varying rates throughout the rest of the life span. Judging by the values derived by most investigators, the increase in systolic pressure is in the neighborhood of 20 mm. Hg between the first day and the fifth to tenth, and a major part of it may represent a return to birth levels. Some 3 to 9 more months are required to achieve another rise of about equal magnitude. The negatively accelerated rate of increase is even more clearly seen in the fact that 15 to 20 years pass before a comparable or somewhat smaller increment has taken place.

Because the development of diastolic pressure has been less thoroughly documented, particularly during infancy, generalizations must be somewhat more tentative and imprecise. By combining figures from different studies an increase of about 15–20 mm. Hg between the first few days and the third to fifth year may be inferred. A further rise of 10–15 mm. Hg, largely within the next decade, can be observed in data for the sexes separately (Lincoln, 1928; Londe, 1966; Richey, 1931; Shock, 1944; Stocks, Stocks, and Karn, 1927), girls only (Burlage, 1923; Nylin, 1935; Schwenk, Eggers-Hohmann, and Gensch, 1955), boys only (Hahn, 1952; Schwartz, Britten, and Thompson, 1928), and mixed sex groups (Faber and James, 1921; Graham, Hines, and Gage, 1945).

Except for the work of Sundal (1929), which is based on palpation, research on age changes after the first year or so has been done by auscultation. Pressure standards across age have yet to be established by direct recording, although some information may be gleaned from comparative plots of auscultatory and direct measures (Moss and Adams, 1963, 1965). Beyond late childhood normative data have almost always been obtained with a cuff 12 to 13 cm. in width—Lincoln's (1928) was 9.5 cm. Thus at older ages differences among studies in

pressure levels stem primarily from situational factors other than recording technique or cuff size. Shock (1944) secured the only truly basal measures. Practiced subjects do not account for the comparatively low norms from his longitudinal study, because equal levels characterized controls put through the same procedures at just one age.

Although the subjects in the studies of Lincoln (1928), Richey (1931), and Sundal (1929) were not in a basal state, the conditions were good, in that measurements were semilongitudinal, were made chiefly in the morning, and the children were in settings with which they were familiar. As already noted, Sundal also used palpation, a method which typically gives values 2–5 mm. lower than does auscultation. Blood pressures about as low as those in the four studies previously cited have been reported by Nylin (1935) from a study of various physiological functions in a small group of girls aged 10 to 15 years, for girls 3 to 16 years old (Downing, 1947), males aged 4 to 49 (Schwartz, Britten, and Thompson, 1928), and the sexes combined (Faber and James, 1921). Despite the care with which Londe (1966) made his determinations, they were taken in the course of routine physical examinations in a physician's office or a pediatric clinic and reflect the higher levels to be expected in such situations. Like pressures have been obtained under rather comparable circumstances by Burlage (1923) and Schwenk, Eggers-Hohmann, and Gensch (1955) in girls, Hahn (1952) in boys, for the sexes combined by Graham, Hines, and Gage (1945), and in each sex by Stocks, Stocks, and Karn (1927).

Again, were values derived in different situations to be combined to form age curves, the increase seen in separate studies during childhood and adolescence could be obliterated. Only in Shock's (1944) data is a small and temporary reversal of the upward trend in diastolic pressure between 12 and 14½ years evident. He suggests that so slight a decrease may be masked in cross-sectional observations, but his basal conditions may also have helped to reveal this digression. Further, the sex difference that develops in adolescence is not readily apparent, at least in its earlier phases, unless pressures are determined under carefully controlled conditions.

Of the two major factors governing blood pressure, peripheral resistance may reasonably be assumed to be more influential than cardiac output in producing developmental changes. Data indicative of a decline in cardiac output with age have already been summarized. A countercourse for peripheral resistance is evidenced by a rate of blood flow through the limbs of infants about twice that of adults (Celander, 1966; Celander and Thunell, 1961; Kidd, Levison, Gemmell, Aharon, and Swyer, 1966), for blood flow is inversely proportional to resistance. Noting these trends, Young (1961, 1966) proposes limited peripheral resistance as the primary cause of low arterial pressure among infants. She hypothesizes that resistance is restricted by inadequate vasoconstriction resulting from some deficiency in the tonic activity of neural and chemical mechanisms regulating blood flow through channels other than those to the skin. Within a few days after birth the vasomotor tone of skin vessels over the entire surface of the infant seems about equivalent to that in the adult (Bower, 1954; Brück, Brück, and Lemtis, 1957; Young, 1962; Young and Cottom, 1966). However, these vessels are thought not to be involved in the control of pressure through the redistribution of blood.

Also cited by Young (1961) as a partial explanation of the brief postnatal drop in pressure are observations suggesting that peripheral resistance declines because asphyxia renders the vasomotor centers and blood vessels even less responsive. Individual differences in the duration and degree of asphyxia and in the distribution of body fluids brought about by forces exerted on the fetus during labor are advanced as possible sources of the wide variation in blood pressure among newborns. According to several authorities, the brief decrement in pressure after delivery may be precipitated by expansion of the pulmonary and intestinal vascular beds and a decline in plasma volume (Contis and Lind, 1963; Lipton, Steinschneider, and Richmond, 1965).

In all likelihood, degenerative as well as maturational changes underlie increases in peripheral resistance with age. The rising trend in blood pressure among older persons has for many years been attributed to decreasing distensibility and hence greater resistance of the arterial walls consequent upon arteriosclerotic lesions. There is also good reason to believe that fatty streaks begin to infiltrate the vasculature during childhood, sometimes as early as the first year (see review in Giersten, 1964).

That increment in cardiac output may play a role in at least one aspect of developmental change in blood pressure is implicit in Tanner's (1962) rationale for the appearance of a sex difference during adolescence. He states that "establishment of a greater basal stroke volume at adolescence (Nylin, 1935), coincident with the greater increase in heart size" and perhaps supplemented by an increased blood volume, is probably responsible for the higher pressures of males. Cardiac output is a multiplicative function of stroke volume and heart rate; blood volume and heart size are two determinants of stroke volume.

Age, physiological maturity (as measured by skeletal age, menarcheal age, age at maximum growth in height, or age at reaching successive stages of secondary sexual characteristics), weight, height, and the levels of various physiological parameters are all to some degree intercorrelated (Nicholson and Hanley, 1953; Shock, 1943, 1944; Tanner, 1962). Which of the first four factors are most closely associated with blood pressure cannot yet be decided. When systolic pressure is examined in relation to menarcheal age, it is found to reach a peak before menarche and then to decline gradually for several years (Shock, 1943). Early maturing girls (Schwenk, Eggers-Hohmann, and Gensch, 1955; Shock, 1944) and boys (Shock, 1944) develop higher systolic and diastolic pressure sooner than do late maturers. At the same time, the early maturing are also heavier and taller. Hypertension is more common among obese adults than the underweight or those of appropriate weight for height. Among children the evidence is less conclusive.

In very young normal and premature infants positive associations of blood pressure with both weight and postnatal age have been reported, but their statistical significance was not tested (Forfar and Kibel, 1956; Levison, Kidd, Gemmell, and Swyer, 1966). Positive although insignificant correlations with weight exist in Allen-Williams' (1945) measures on boys and girls aged 6 months to 5 years. Londe (1966) found systolic pressure to be significantly correlated with weight in both sexes at most ages from 4 to 15 years. The coefficients for height were lower and insignificant. Generally low, positive associations obtained between diastolic pressure and weight and height, but only those with weight in girls approached significance. On the other hand, Richey's (1931) data show significant correlations from age 5 to 19 years between weight and diastolic as well as systolic pressure for each sex and between diastolic pressure and height for girls. Height also influenced systolic pressure in girls 11 to 15 years old and boys over 10. For his sample of boys aged 11 to 15 years Hahn (1952) states that blood pressure is more highly correlated with weight, surface area, and height than with age, and the correlation was stronger for the first two variables. However, the figures he presents do not seem to justify the latter claim. Stocks and Karn (1924) also demonstrated an association between systolic pressure and both weight and height and between diastolic pressure and height in boys aged 9 to 15 years.

A related question of concern is the predictability of hypertension. Prompted by evidence that elevated resting pressures were prognostic of later disease in young adults (Diehl and Hesdorffer, 1933; Levy, Hillman, and Stroud, 1944), Harris (1958) examined blood pressure records on subjects in a longitudinal study. Two groups of 24 boys each and two of 20 girls each were selected from the total sample on the basis of having the highest and lowest blood pressure for their sex at 15, 16, and 17 years. Plots of systolic and diastolic levels beginning at age 5 showed these subgroups already to be well separated by that age. Unfortunately, possible causal associations could not be ascertained because the "highs" of both sexes were early maturers as well as more mesomorphic or endomorphic, and no history of cardiovascular dysfunction in the "highs" at any age was presented.

If blood pressure responses to stress are more reproducible than resting levels, as some research indicates (Lacey and Lacey, 1958, 1962; Sontag, 1958; Tanner, 1958) then they may also be more effective in the prognosis of cardiovascular disease. A unique pair of studies utilizing the cold pressor test illustrates the potential of this approach. In the first study Hines (1937) examined 400 children 6 to 18 years old. Subjects plunged one hand up to the wrist in water of 4° C and held it there for one minute. The reflex rise in blood pressure was recorded from the opposite arm. After reevaluation of 207 members of the original sample 27 years later Barnett, Hines, Schirger, and Gage (1963) reported that both responsivity to the imposed stress and hypertension were predictable from the earlier measures.

Electrocardiogram

To differentiate the electrocardiogram from the electrocorticogram (a recording from the cerebral cortex) the original abbreviation, EKG, from the German spelling, is preferable to ECG. The EKG is a record of the electrical field effects generated by the action potentials of the nerve fibers of many cardiac muscle cells. From it may be determined the site of the pacemaker; conduction routes; and the rate, rhythmicity, patterns of excitability and refractoriness, and electrical axis of the heart. A large body of empirical data relating abnormalities in these characteristics to various cardiac disorders has been accumulated.

For the standard limb leads used in electrocardiography since the turn of the century surface electrodes are placed on each arm and on the left leg. Bipolar recordings (i.e., those obtained between two active electrodes) are made between the two arms (lead I), the right arm and left leg (lead II), and the left arm and leg (lead III). Illustrated in Fig. 3 are the typical pattern of deflections derived from lead II in a normal adult and the intervals of the cardiac cycle usually included in an analysis of the EKG. Other parameters regularly of interest are the duration, direction, amplitude, and shape of P, Q, R, S, and T waves.

The P wave arises from atrial depolarization initiated by the spread of excitation originating in the sinus node. After a brief isoelectric period throughout the heart, the ventricles become depolarized, producing the QRS complex. Included in the P-R interval is the time required for the excitation wave to depolarize some of the atrial muscles

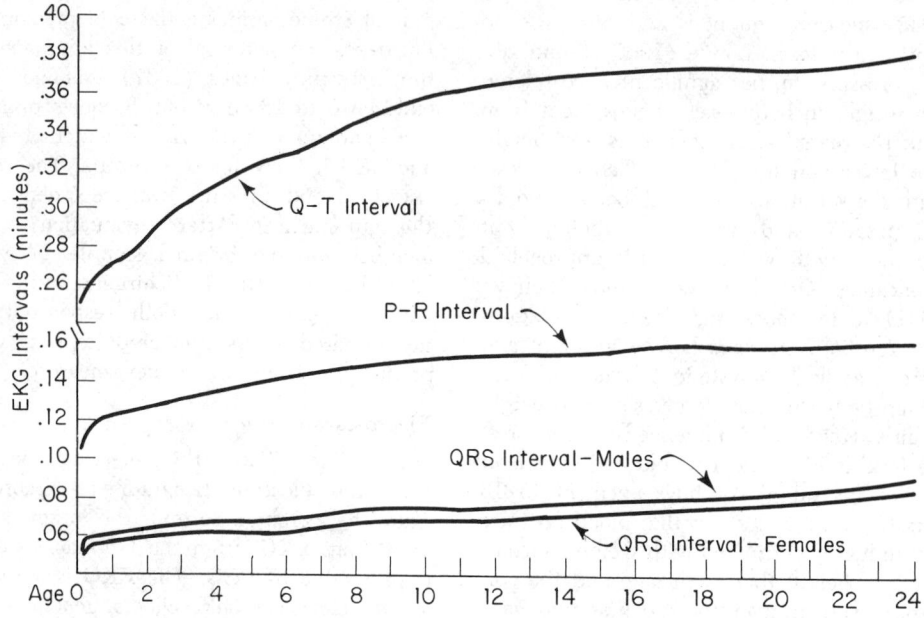

Fig. 3. Fiftieth percentiles for EKG intervals (in minutes). Redrawn from McCammon (1961).

and pass down through the atrioventricular node and the bundles of fibers which carry impulses to the ventricular muscle. The T wave reflects ventricular repolarization; atrial repolarization is generally masked by the QRS complex. Continuing ventricular depolarization and perhaps some slight beginning repolarization occurs during the S-T segment. Subsequent to the T wave, a U wave, thought to be produced by slow repolarization of the papillary muscles projecting from the walls of the ventricles, is sometimes observed. There is often some variation among the three leads in the amplitude and duration of waves and the length of intervals.

Current clinical routine also calls for at least nine other tracings, six from the chest (precordial leads) and three from the limbs. Although the different "views" provided by additional leads are very useful in the diagnosis of pathology, more normative material indicating something about the maturation of cardiac function and understandable by persons without extensive background in EKG analysis are derived from the standard limb leads. Further, the only developmental data on the EKG of the fetus *in utero* are based on records that closely resemble the configurations observed postnatally in these leads.

Quite by accident Cremer (1906) picked up the EKG of a fetus near term while recording that of the mother with standard limb leads and a string galvanometer. Using the electrodes attached to the surface of the maternal abdomen and a standard EKG machine, a number of subsequent investigators had good success in deliberate attempts to duplicate his feat (see summary bibliographic table in Bernstein and Borkowski, 1955). At least during the latter part of gestation such simple apparatus suffices in a large proportion of cases to demonstrate the existence of a living fetus and to provide tracings from which manual counts of fetal heart rate can be made. Southern (1954) was even able to measure amplitudes and durations. If EKGs of this caliber are to be secured with any degree of regularity, however, better instrumentation is required to overcome the impediments to *in utero* recording.

Amniotic fluid and maternal tissue attenuate the weak signal produced by the fetal heart. Further insulation against the transmission of impulses seems to be added, particularly in the seventh and eighth months, by the fetal coating of vernix caseosa, an oily secretion containing discarded skin cells (Goodyer, 1942; Wimmer, 1954). Except under a few special circumstances mentioned later, potential size per se does not now constitute a major restriction on the quality of intrauterine EKGs. Adequate amplification is supplied by electroencephalographs or high-sensitivity fetal electrocardiographs. Getting an input that is sufficiently free of artifacts is another matter. The "noise" from fetal or maternal muscles, the mother's heart beat, or alternating current in the environment may be great enough to obscure any fetal EKG. On the other hand, relatively little noise will interfere with a low level potential.

Unless a satisfactory signal to noise ratio can be achieved, automated heart rate counts (see following section, Heart Rate) and analyzable EKG configurations are precluded. Some means must be found to increase the fetal potential without simultaneously enhancing the artifacts, or to reduce the interference, or both. At times the signal reaching the surface is so small or the artifacts are so strong that closer electrode contact with the fetus than is possible with abdominal or limb leads is the only solution. Such small signals may arise, for example, in early gestation, polyhydramnios (excessive amniotic fluid), or maternal obesity; strong artifacts are characteristic of labor, when the potentials generated by uterine contractions are especially powerful. Establishing direct contact maximizes the fetal signal, essentially eliminates the maternal EKG, and materially decreases the noise from most other sources.

One approach is to insert fine electrodes through the abdominal wall and under the skin of the fetus (Caldeyro-Barcia, Poseiro, Pantle, Negreiros, Gomez-Rogers, Faundes, Henry, Zambrana, Arellano, Filler, and Cabot, 1961). After the cervix is dilated and the membranes ruptured, a flexible rod electrode, insulated except at the tip, can be introduced into the uterus via the cervix until it touches the fetus (Hon, 1959; Smyth, 1953; Sureau, 1956). Alternatively, an electrode may be attached to the presenting part of the fetus (Hon, 1967). For close but indirect contact during early pregnancy Bernstine (1961) recommends vaginal leads, a collar electrode fitted about the cervix, or an electrode clamped to the cervix.

Asepsis must be maintained while employing any of the electrodes described above. Because surface abdominal leads are easier to apply and involve no risk, they are still favored whenever recording conditions are, or can be made, suitable. By a combination of procedures an acceptable signal to noise ratio can be effected in most situations, and sometimes even during labor (Larks and Larks, 1965). Many of the basic precautions are those regularly observed in electroencephalography, where surface potentials are very small and artifacts from muscle, the EKG, and electrical noise also a problem.

As instrumentation and techniques have improved, the utility of fetal electrocardiography as an obstetric and research tool has become more extensive (Bernstine, 1961; Cameron, 1967; Kendall, Farell, and Kane, 1964; Larks and Larks, 1966). Not only can the presence of a fetus, multiple conceptions, and type of presentation (say, occipital or breech) be determined without the hazards of radiography, but evidence of viability can also be obtained. Monitoring high-risk pregnancies and deliveries by electrocardiography is feasible when other methods, such as listening for fetal heart sounds or biochemical assays of the oxygen, carbon dioxide, and acid content of the blood, are not. Blood samples cannot be taken until after the onset of labor, whereas detection of fetal heart sounds is rarely possible in the same circumstances that require special electrocardiographic procedures, for example, early gestation, polyhydramnios, and labor. Yet these are the conditions in which assessment of fetal status may be most needed. Only when the EKG is used to trigger a cardiotachometer (see Heart Rate section to follow) can the rapid changes in rate which occur in response to changes in intrauterine pressures, oxygen levels, and the like be fully appreciated.

In general, intrauterine EKGs give a more accurate picture of normal development than do those obtained from extirpated fetuses. The premature often are not healthy specimens, and their heart rates may be slowed by anoxia or cooling subsequent to delivery. However, abortuses have furnished the earliest records of the human EKG. The QRS complex and T wave were detectable in a tracing from the heart of a 6 mm. embryo

(Marcel and Exchaquet, 1938), a length that is reached just about at the age (30 days or slightly younger) when the primitive heart tubes fuse and the complete EKG should theoretically first be present. Other direct recordings made as early as the sixth to tenth week indicate that a fully differentiated EKG is already present by these ages (Borkowski and Bernstine, 1955; Goodyer, 1942; Heard, Burkley, and Schaefer, 1936; Lind, Stern, and Wegelius, 1964). By about 11 weeks *in utero* records can be reliably obtained, although auscultation of fetal heart sounds is not possible until about the eighteenth week (Mattingly and Larks, 1963).

When the subjects are in good physiological condition the heart rates observed early in gestation are as rapid as or somewhat higher than is typical of the neonate at rest or in a state of minimal metabolism. If the pulse is faster, one would expect the intervals of the cardiac cycle to be shorter, and they seem to be. Some of the best supporting data comes from studies done in Sweden on fetuses aged 10 or 12 to 25 weeks delivered by caesarian section at legal abortions (Lind, Stern, and Wegelius, 1964). Before the fetus was removed from the uterus and while the placenta was in place, the placental circulation intact, cord color and pulsations good, EKGs were obtained. The investigators concluded that the P-Q, QRS, and Q-T segments were probably somewhat shorter than in the full-term newborn, but, because the size of the heart was so small at these ages, the absolute speed at which excitation spread through the heart was considerably slower. Smaller heart size and less well developed muscle probably also account for the lower amplitudes of these EKGs, for attenuation obviously is not a factor in direct fetal recording.

Aside from these differences in amplitude and conduction times, fetal EKGs resemble neonatal ones in showing right ventricular preponderance and aberrations of the T wave. The amplitudes of QRS complex recorded from midline abdominal leads before delivery are correlated with those obtained in lead II after delivery in the same infants (Larks and Larks, 1966). Correlations for the R and S waves were significant and moderate (.6) and for the Q wave, which is more difficult to record and measure, signifi-

cant but low (.3). In addition, the calculated electrical axes had similar prenatal and postnatal means and were highly correlated (.79). A previous study (Larks and Larks, 1965) established a normal range for axis deviations and related abnormalities to complications of gestation and delivery. During normal labor changes in pressure in the umbilical artery resulting from cord compression by uterine contractions have sometimes been found to produce marked changes not only in the QRS complex but also in the P wave and the ST segment (Hon, 1966).

Methodological difficulties do not disappear once the infant becomes accessible. Overriding of the P wave of one cardiac cycle by the T wave of the preceding one is the most frequent problem, because while the heart rate is rapid there is almost no T–P interval (the period during which all chambers of the heart are in diastole). Movement artifacts are if anything more troublesome when the limb leads are on the infant himself. Chest leads are much less susceptible to interference from movement, but unless small electrodes are used and care is exercised in applying and removing electrode paste electrical phantoms will be recorded (McNamara, 1964; Ziegler, 1951). With telemeters or portable, battery-operated tape recorders long-term recording on a moving subject can be made quite successfully (Morgan, Deane, and Guntheroth, 1965). Fortunately, prior ingestion of food has no consistent effect in infants and children despite frequent reports of postprandial changes in adults (Gooch, Mintz, and Nova, 1967).

Associated with the hemodynamic, and probably also the respiratory, metabolic, and electrolytic transitions of the first week or so after birth are a succession of alterations in the EKG. The time at which the cord is clamped seems to have little influence (Buckels and Usher, 1965). However, rather precise knowledge of the time that has elapsed since delivery is essential for evaluation of the normality of the EKG of the newborn, for Walsh's (1963a, 1963b, 1963c, 1964, 1966) serial examinations of full-term and premature infants show that shifts occur with great rapidity during the first few hours following delivery. Within 30 to 60 minutes the P wave and all intervals are prolonged. The amplitude of the QRS complex is increased, particularly in chest leads representing right ventricular activation; Q waves are absent in left precordial leads, but good-sized, positive T waves appear in all chest leads. A few hours later the duration of the P wave, which was primarily responsible for the lengthened P–R interval, and of the P–R and QRS segments are considerably decreased, the voltage of the R and S waves is reduced in most chest leads, Q waves are found in one (V_6), and the T waves are positive in the right but negative or absent in the left chest leads. Further contrast among leads in the incidence and amplitude of the Q, R, S, and T waves, apparent on the second and third days, continue to develop through the end of the first week. By this time the Q–T interval has shortened significantly, the decrease being most notable between the third to the fifth or sixth days.

"Intervals which reflect atrial and atrioventricular conduction show relatively little change after the first hour of life, whereas those which involve ventricular conduction are not only influenced by events attending birth, but also by those affecting the first few months of life" (Walsh, 1964, p. 190). Lengthened P waves often characterize enlargement of the left atrium (Walsh, 1966). Left to right shunting through the ductus arteriosus in the course of the transition from the fetal to postnatal circulation increases the load on the left heart during diastole. Further, vagal activity may bring about the temporary postnatal slowing of the P–R and QRS segments and increased voltage of the QRS, and the responsivity of the heart to vagal control may be heightened because the oxygen content of the blood, reduced during delivery, stays low for about the first hour (Walsh, 1966).

Although Ziegler (1951) accounted for the decrement in the Q–T interval in terms of the concomitant increase in pulse rate (the duration of Q–T is negatively correlated with heart rate at all ages), Walsh (1964) points out that neither in his data nor in Ziegler's is the reduction in Q–T per unit change in heart rate anywhere nearly sufficient to produce the observed decrease in Q–T time. Nor did Ziegler find the length of QRS or Q–T to be effected by heart volume (1963a), as others have thought it to be (Wilson and Herrmann, 1930). The likelihood remains,

however, that the length of Q–R and the amplitude of the R wave are related to some degree to the *relative* thickness of the walls of the ventricles (Emery and Mithal, 1961; Keen, 1955; Sodi-Pallares, Portillo, Cisneros, De La Cruz, and Acosta, 1958; Walsh, 1963c). Compared to the T wave, the QRS complex is quite stable, especially after the early neonatal period. Ziegler (1966) attributes this greater stability to the fact that anatomic factors largely govern the QRS complex, whereas the T wave is much more dependent on functional variables. For example, abnormalities of the T wave or the Q–T interval tend to occur in disturbances of electrolyte (especially potassium and calcium) or acid-base balance (Keith, Rowe, and Vlad, 1967; McNamara, 1964).

All investigators have described peculiarities of the T wave and right ventricular preponderance as the most outstanding features of the neonatal EKG. Of particular interest is the fact that by such criteria as ventricular weight, thickness of the ventricle walls, or heart volume the left ventricle is better developed than the right at the end of the first month or sooner (Emery and Mithal, 1961; Keen, 1955; Kjellberg, Rudhe, and Zetterström, 1954; Lind, 1950; Lind and Wegelius, 1954; Patten, 1933; Scammon, 1923; Sodi-Pallares et al., 1958), yet electrical right ventricular dominance persists for several months. Before birth resistance to flow is high in the lungs, and the right ventricle pumps against this resistance and that of the systemic circulation (via the ductus arteriosus). As the pulmonary resistance begins to drop shortly after delivery and shunting declines, the work of the right ventricle decreases even though it pumps about as much blood as the left. On the other hand, with increasing age, resistance in the systemic circulation rises, so the work of the left ventricle becomes greater.

Walsh's (1964, 1966) comparisons of healthy premature and full-term infants reveal the role of postnatal experience with changed work loads in the gradual development of left ventricular dominance. Two groups of prematures differing in age (44 versus 90 days) and hence weight were matched by weight with two groups of full-term infants. To achieve a weight match the latter were, of course, younger (about 5½ days) in terms of postdelivery age. The EKGs of the premature, who, although younger on a gestational age basis, had circulatory systems that had operated longer in the postnatal fashion, showed more evidence of left ventricular preponderance. Differences between premature and full-term infants in most characteristics of the EKG were marked only in the first week or two. Nevertheless, some other factors, maturational and/or experiential, must influence the cardiac reactions represented in the EKG, because, despite equal heart rates in all groups, the Q–R, QRS, and Q–T intervals were significantly longer among the full-term infants, and the P–R duration and P amplitude tended to be greater.

Beyond early infancy the rate of change in parameters of the EKG becomes much slower. So slight are the shifts in amplitude that when mentioned at all in normative material the maximum for healthy individuals of a wide age range is usually all that is given. For example, the P wave is generally said not to exceed 2.5 mm. up to 1 year nor 3 mm. between 1 and 14 years (Keith, Rowe, and Vlad, 1967). By convention, 1 cm. of deflection equals 1 mv. Throughout life the T wave continues to be the most labile of the EKG configurations, and it is the most delayed in reaching the adult pattern. Not until 16 years can the T wave in the first chest lead be expected to be upright in most members of a normal population, although it may be so by 12 years in a sizable number (Keith, Rowe, and Vlad, 1967; Sodi-Pallares et al., 1958; Ziegler, 1951).

Standards for interval durations are sometimes also stated simply as normal maxima over a fairly wide age span (Epstein, 1948; Keith, Rowe, and Vlad, 1967; Kossman, 1953), but averages and/or ranges for more restricted age groups are available (Burnett and Taylor, 1936; Hafkesbring, Drawe, and Ashman, 1937; Seham and Moss, 1942; Sodi-Pallares et al., 1958; Ziegler, 1951). Unique among the latter both for their detail and for the nature of the sample from which they are drawn are the norms reported by McCammon (1961). The minima, maxima, and tenth, twenty-fifth, fiftieth, seventy-fifth, and ninetieth percentiles for the P–R, QRS, and Q–T intervals in each of the three

standard limb leads are tabulated by month from 1 through 6 months, at 3 months intervals from 9 months through 14 years, at 14½ years, and yearly from 15 through 24 years. Variations from the stated ages were not more than 1 week before 3 years, 2 weeks from 3 to 10 years, and 1 month after that age. Included in the analysis were 4993 records on 214 healthy upper-middle class subjects followed for periods varying from 6 months to over 24 years. Except for a few studies in early infancy, these are the only longitudinal data of this kind on normal subjects.

Figure 3 combines the medians for boys from Lead II for the three intervals measured by McCammon. Even such major segments of the cardiac cycle last only tenths or hundredths of a second, so the average increase from age to age across such short time spans are only thousandths of a second and are far exceeded by the range at any one age. Given the small size of the intervals and increments, irregularities in the curves would be expected. Nevertheless, the group trends rise steeply for all three intervals during the first six to nine months and much more gradually thereafter.

By 10 years the median for P–R is essentially at the adult level, with about half of the increment accomplished by 4 years. This interval also proved to be a very stable individual characteristic after the age of 2 years. Within any given year the values for a subject fluctuated very little, and his position in the group remained consistent across time. Exceptions were observed when a changing pacemaker was present, a phenomenon that occurred on several occasions in almost 25% of the children, primarily between the ages of 4 and 14 years. Contrary to the contention in almost all treatises on EKG development that the P–R interval varies directly with age and inversely with pulse rate, McCammon demonstrated that the association with heart rate is not linear.

Following a strategy previously used with adults (Schlamowitz, 1946), pulse rates and P–R durations were determined for a subsample before graded exercise on a bicycle ergometer and at 1-minute intervals for 5 minutes postexercise. As was true for adults, P–R duration did not vary systematically with pulse rate when age was thus held constant.

Graphs of the regular records also showed pulse rate to very labile, while the length of the P–R segment for an individual was, as noted above, highly stable. The linear correlation between pulse rate and P–R was -.01. However, the plot suggested a curvilinear association, which was confirmed by a chi-square test. That is, there was a tendency for P–R to be shorter when the pulse rate was either very fast or very slow. McCammon speculates that both the P–R interval and pulse rate are a function of some other factor or factors, rather than having the direct and bifactorial dependence inferred heretofore.

Chest X-rays on these subjects also failed to verify the supposition of some investigators (Hafkesbring, Drawe, and Ashman, 1937; Alimurung and Massell, 1956) that increasing heart size underlies the prolongation of the P–R segment with age. Individuals with heart sizes much above or below the mean for age had P–R durations across the entire range of normal values. A priori this hypothesis is suspect, for the developmental curve for heart size follows the general growth curve for weight (Maresh, 1948), whereas that for the P–R interval levels off by about 10 years and has no adolescent spurt.

Marked sex differences and indications of an adolescent spurt were found in the QRS norms. The age curves at the ninetieth percentile closely resemble those for physical growth, but this pattern is increasingly attenuated as one moves down the percentile ranks. Probably because the termination of the QRS complex is difficult to determine precisely, intraindividual variations in its duration were quite large.

Although the length of the Q–T interval approximated the adult median by 10 to 12 years, a very slow increase was observed to the oldest ages included. A number of formulas have been devised for correcting Q–T for heart rate, and most involve a different constant for women than for men and children. In this sample the correlation between pulse rate and the length of Q–T was substantial (-.59), but no sex differences were found until a correction was applied. After correction the Q–T duration was shorter in girls until they were about prepuberal. Then the sex difference reversed. McCammon com-

ments that the degree of separation of the sexes is surprising in view of the small differences in pulse rate. Correction for heart rate also eliminated age changes in the length of Q–T until adolescence, when a downward trend ensued. During this period the prolongation of the Q–T segment for some undetermined reason increasingly fails to keep pace with the decline in heart rate.

Not illustrated in the tables or graphs of any study is the dramatic increase in the T–P interval with increasing age and decreasing heart rate. Prolongation of the time during which all chambers of the heart are in diastole is greater on both an absolute and proportionate basis than for any other interval. At a heart rate of 150 beats per minute, which is typical of a 1-month-old infant while awake but not too active, the entire cardiac cycle takes 0.4 seconds. Only a little over 0.04 seconds is consumed by the T–P interval. The adult heart rate under similar conditions is about half as fast, and thus the cardiac cycle is twice as long. Yet the T–P segment is about 0.22 seconds, or over four times longer. Little hearts get little rest.

Heart Rate

Apart from their bearing on events occurring within the cardiac cycle, variations in heart rate among individuals or within the same individual during successive cycles are of inherent interest. Indeed, for both theoretical and pragmatic reasons, cardiac rate has been chosen more frequently than any other functional measure for psychophysiological research as well as for monitoring the condition of patients in clinical situations.

Heart rate is influenced by many aspects of mental and physical state, such as attention, emotion, pain, posture, exercise, digestion, respiration, oxygenation, metabolic rate, internal and external temperature, thyroxin, epinephrine, norepinephrine, and blood pressure. Such sensitivity to change in a wide variety of psychological, physiological, biochemical, and mechanical factors makes cardiac rate a useful response measure, but it also means that experimental conditions must be carefully controlled whether the effects of a particular variable are being explored or basal rates are sought. Despite the latter reservation, heart rate also offers practical advantages from the point of view of measurement. It can be determined intermittently or continuously with relative ease by at least one of several methods even under circumstances where a full EKG, blood pressure, metabolic rate, or like measures are difficult or impossible to obtain or simply not applicable (e.g., respiratory rate during gestation).

As for blood pressure, the oldest and still the most widely used techniques for obtaining heart rate are palpation and auscultation. Palpation is especially simple and convenient. If a finger is placed over a surface artery, pulsations are felt which arise from a sudden increase in the pressure and velocity of the blood generated by each contraction of the heart. In adults, pulse counts are usually taken at a radial (wrist) artery, but during infancy pulsations are often easier to feel over the carotid (side of the neck) or temporal (above and to the outer side of the eye) arteries. With certain exceptions already noted, auscultation of heart sounds through the maternal abdomen and hence rate counts can be accomplished by midgestation. After birth heart sounds can readily be heard through the chest wall, often without the aid of a stethoscope.

It is common in clinical practice to estimate heart rate per minute by counting the pulse for 15 seconds and multiplying the result by 4. Given the lability of cardiac rate, however, particularly in the young, more representative and reliable values can be obtained by making counts for a full minute and repeating them at least twice. In some experimental situations briefer intervals are deliberately examined to assess the degree of acceleration or deceleration occasioned by stimulation and the time required for recovery. For such work continuous, automatic recording is highly desirable, and instantaneous (beat-by-beat) rates cannot be secured in any other way.

Both instantaneous and average rates can be determined from any time-calibrated recording that contains a signal corresponding to a regularly recurring element of the cardiac cycle. Besides the action potentials from which the EKG is derived, mechanical displacements generated by the activity of the heart can be utilized as input. Over half a century ago Canestrini (1913) used a pneumograph placed over the anterior fontanel to pick up the vibrations of the pulse wave and a system of levers to transduce them for kymographic (smoked drum) recording. Heart sounds associated with different phases of the cardiac cycle are registered in a phonocardiogram as waves varying in amplitude and frequency. When the heart pushes blood into the aorta, an opposing force simultaneously accelerates the body in the opposite direction. The oscillations produced by these movements are detected by the ballistocardiograph, an instrument for measuring cardiac output, and heart rate can be measured from the resulting waveform. If only heart rate is to be assessed, the standard table model of the ballistocardiograph is unnecessarily complicated and expensive. An inexpensive version, consisting of a phono cartridge attached to the ankle, is entirely adequate for recording heart rate (Brown and Saucer, 1958).

Counting the number of waves per unit time to get average rates is tedious and time-consuming. Measuring the interval between analogous waves in successive cycles in order to compute instantaneous rate is even more so, and only a few devoted investigators have made the attempt (Sontag and Wallace, 1936). Alternatively, the intervals may be read manually and punched on cards for cardiotachometric plotting, that is, transformation to instantaneous rate at successive beats, by a computer (Welford, Sontag, Phillips, and Phillips, 1967). Less time is spent doing arithmetic, but the original reading is still laborious. By far the most convenient means for determining beat frequencies is an instantaneous rate meter. Usually the EKG is fed directly into a cardiotachometer, which is triggered by the R wave and electronically converts each R-R interval to an instantaneous rate. Recently Urbach and his associates (1965) incorporated a rate meter into a telemetered system.

If instantaneous or average rates in a given situation (e.g., age norms under basal conditions) are the only concern, the fact that the association between beat interval and rate is not linear poses no problems. When short-term changes in rate are to be analyzed, however, a decision must be made as to the more appropriate unit of measurement. Resolutions of this dilemma and related issues in the choice of a response measure for studying variations in rate and temporal aspects of a rate curve have been reviewed by Steinschneider (1967).

That simple techniques can yield reliable results when carefully applied is indicated by the similarity of the values reported in many older studies in which heart rate was determined by auscultation or palpation to those obtained instrumentally. In 1906 Vierordt gave 130–160 beats per minute as the normal range for cardiac rate during gestation and an average rate of 180 at birth, with a profound drop (mean of about 45 beats) within the next hour. Subsequent series of fetal EKGs, taken from the surface of the maternal abdomen or directly from intrauterine electrodes and totalling hundreds of cases, show average rates of 130–155 (see review in Bernstine, 1961; Brady and James, 1962; Welford, Sontag, Phillips, and Phillips, 1967). Little attention has been directed toward tracing changes in rate with fetal age, but in one study a decline between the fifth and ninth months (means of 156 and 142, respectively) and a slight increase in the tenth was observed (Sontag and Richards, 1938). On the other hand, the course of heart rate during and immediately after labor recently has been the subject of much detailed research.

The accounts of normal and abnormal labors provided by different investigators (Brady and James, 1962, 1963; Caldeyro-Barcia et al., 1963, 1966; Hon, 1959a, 1959b, 1962, 1963, 1966; Mendez-Bauer et al., 1963; Romney, 1966; Sanders, Lind, and Peltonen, 1961; Vallbona et al., 1963) are remarkably consistent. Continuous cardiotachometric records show the average heart rate of fetuses who undergo a normal labor and are in good condition at birth, as demonstrated by Apgar scores (Apgar, 1953) of 7 or above, to be somewhat above 140 before the onset of labor and between episodes of slowing and acceleration during labor. Among depressed infants (Apgar scores of 6 or less) born after abnormal labors this "basal" rate is at least 20 beats higher. Aside from minor rapid fluctuations, which are present throughout labor, the heart rate of normal fetuses remains at about the "basal" level

during much of the first stage. Near its end and in the second stage larger (10–25 beat) but brief (about ½- to ¾-minute) decrements or increments occur, decrements being more common. The second stage is also characterized by more frequent variations in cardiac rate. Beginning at the time of crowning and continuing until the first cry there is a period of marked bradycardia (very slow heart rate) when frequencies may normally be below 100.

Several types of bradycardia, apparently with different causes and diagnostic significance, have been described. As labor advances the incidence of bradycardia of short duration associated with uterine contractions, compression of the cord and head, manipulation of the fetus, and pelvic examinations increases in almost all cases. The profound drop at crowning is a reflex response to compression of the cranium on the maternal perineum. Unless slowing occurs in the absence of such factors or persists longer than 60 seconds beyond the end of a contraction the infant is not likely to be depressed at birth. Normal transient bradycardia is thought to result from vagal stimulation, because the conditions under which it occurs would produce hypoxia and because the response can be blocked by administering atropine (which counteracts vagal action) to either fetus or mother. More extreme and prolonged slowing, especially if it is present in early as well as late labor, is indicative of fetal distress. The perinatal mortality rate is tripled among infants in whom bradycardia continued for over half an hour. As might be expected, severe bradycardia is most often noted in circumstances that augment the normal, transient disturbance of the uteroplacental circulation, for example, maternal hypoxia and hypertension, toxemic pregnancies, intense uterine contractions, and looping of the cord about the fetal neck.

The same factors that appear to precipitate normal "dips" in heart rate may sometimes produce temporary tachycardia (excessively rapid heart rate). In other instances no probable cause of the acceleration can be discovered. Persistent tachycardia has been observed in connection with acidosis and respiratory depression and is prognostic of poor condition at birth. However, the likelihood of death, even among fetuses with tachycardia of several hours duration, is less than in those suffering much shorter periods of bradycardia. Tachycardia has been interpreted as a defensive response stemming from an increase in the activity of the sympathetic nervous system initiated by acidosis and hypoxia. With a faster heart rate, cardiac output rises, improving the metabolic interchange between fetus and mother. A rise in sympathetic tone also promotes vasoconstriction in nonessential tissues, so blood is diverted to the heart, brain, and placenta. Between uterine contractions or with the cessation of other sorts of interference with the uteroplacental circulation a drop in heart rate helps to conserve the energy resources (stored glycogen) of the heart. It is of interest here that when the mother is given injections of glucose, bradycardia during crowning is eliminated.

Although the overall postnatal trend in cardiac frequency is downward (see Tables 5 and 6), there is a reversal during the early days. In addition, vigorous and distressed infants continue to differ in their patterns of change in heart rate following delivery. After the first cry, beat frequency normally rises abruptly (in about 2 minutes) from the low level induced by crowning to a peak of 170–180. When the cord of healthy neonates is clamped before respiration is initiated, bradycardia intervenes briefly. Otherwise, the time of clamping has no particular effect on heart rate. Whether clamping is early or late, the heart rate next stabilizes temporarily at about 165–170. Between 15 and 60 minutes later the rate has dropped by 40 to 50 beats per minute. Asphyxiated babies who do not breathe promptly (Apgar scores are, of course, low) have continuing and increasing bradycardia until the lungs expand. Thereafter, their heart rates are generally higher than normal, with a mean over 180.

Normally heart rate declines further but more gradually during the first day and then begins to rise slowly (see data from Benedict and Talbot, 1915, in Table 5). Often the decrease begins while the baby is very active, but it is not interrupted when sleep ensues. A decrement during activity is in direct contrast to the situation at all later ages. As the means and ranges obtained by Eichorn (1951) and by Keating and Edwards (1888)

illustrate (see Table 5), even a quiet waking state is characterized by higher rates than is sleep. In the former study rates were read from EKGs, whereas in the latter palpation was used. Again, the agreement in values is notable. The data of Lipton et al. (1965) included in the table show the reduction in heart rate when very young infants are swaddled. While swaddled the subjects spent more time sleeping and almost never cried.

Exactly how long the accelerative phase of the rate curve lasts cannot be specified because the day-to-day change in rate has not been traced beyond the first week. Judging from the means found by Eichorn (1951) in cross-sectional groups and by McCammon (1961) in a longitudinal study, deceleration begins some time between 3 weeks and 2 months. Lipton, Steinschneider, and Richmond (1960) tested 14 infants at ages of 2 to 5 days and again at 2½ and 5 months and report significantly higher heart rates both before and after stimulation during the first week. Variability in rate was also significantly greater then. The lability of beat frequency in the young has often been remarked and can be seen in the ranges listed in Table 5. Irregularity of fetal heart rate has been regarded as evidence of vagal tone and the integrity of the autonomic system (Cameron, 1967). Sinus arrhythmia—acceleration of heart rate toward the end of inspiration and slowing toward the end of expiration—is so regular a phenomenon in infants, even the newborn, and children (Keith, Rowe, and Vlad, 1967; Lipton, Steinschneider, and Richmond, 1965; Urbach et al., 1965; Vallbona et al., 1963) that its absence is suggestive of abnormality in cardiac or autonomic function.

Once the long-term decline in heart rate begins it continues without further interruption except for a possible leveling-off or even slight reversal during the time the adolescent growth spurt is at its peak (see Table 6). As is true of most functional measures, the rate of change is steepest during infancy. The norms selected for Table 6 also show the influence of sex and conditions of measurement on the frequencies observed. Of particular interest is the contrast between the means reported by Iliff and Lee (1952) and by McCammon (1961). These data are from the same longitudinal sample examined in

Table 5. Heart Rate during Infancy

Benedict and Talbot, 1915

| | | Minimal Metabolism | |
		Mean	Range
Day	1	112	96–129
	2	114	88–138
	3	116	82–144
	4	116	98–132
	5	116	96–134
	6	122	108–138

Lipton, Steinschneider, and Richmond, 1960

| | | Median | |
		Free	Swaddled
Days	2–5	127	113

Eichorn, 1951

| | | Asleep | | Awake | | Activity |
		Mean	Range	Mean	Range	Range
Days	6–10	136	114–159	150	132–171	153–192
	11–20	136	114–156	149	129–171	147–192
	21–30	131	111–150	141	114–165	126–192
	31–60	131	105–150	138	114–162	132–210
	61–90	123	108–138	133	117–156	129–183

Keating and Edwards, 1888

		Asleep: Range	Awake: Range
Month	1	108–140	126–156
	2	100–132	110–150
	3–6	106–118	110–140
	6–12	114–120	114–142

McCammon, 1961

| | | EKG, supine | | | |
| | | 50th percentile | | Range | |
		M	F	M	F
Month	1	152	151	105–185	105–200
	2	146	151	120–185	110–215
	3	141	143	115–185	100–220
	4	138	142	110–175	110–205
	5	137	146	120–165	125–170
	6	138	138	110–185	110–190
	9	136	133	110–200	110–190
	12	132	127	90–190	100–170
	15	126	129	85–185	90–190
	18	122	120	95–180	90–200
	21	119	120	85–155	85–190
	24	116	116	80–155	85–190
	27	114	113	80–165	85–150
	30	110	107	80–160	75–160
	33	111	108	75–150	85–155
	36	103	106	70–135	85–150

different situations. McCammon's come from the EKGs described in an earlier section. The subjects were lying quietly but were neither sleeping nor in a basal state. For their study Iliff and Lee used pulse rates taken early in the morning immediately after tests of basal metabolism and while the children were fasting, quiet, and relaxed. Metabolic tests on infants were made after feeding at various times of day. They slept during the test, and pulse rates were determined as soon as they awoke. Pulse was counted for at least 30 seconds during palpation of the wrist in children and auscultation (with a stethoscope placed over the heart) or sometimes palpation of the ankle in infants. The lowest rate under these conditions was recorded.

Among the developmental changes that may underlie the overall decline in heart rate are decreasing metabolic rate and body temperature and increasing respiratory efficiency, vagal control, blood pressure, and

Table 6. Age and Sex Norms for Heart Rate

Study:	Allen-Williams, 1945		Lincoln, 1928				McCammon, 1961		Iliff and Lee, 1952		Shock, 1944	
Conditions:	Sleeping		Horizontal		Vertical		EKG, Supine		Basal		Basal	
Age (yrs.)	M	F	M	F	M	F	M	F	M	F	M	F
0.5							138	138	135	126	—	—
0.75	122	109	—	—	—	—	136	133	—	—	—	—
1.0							132	127	—	—	—	—
1.5	102	110	—	—	—	—	122	120	105	104	—	—
2.0			108	95	108	114	116	116			—	—
2.5	100	106					110	107	93	93	—	—
3.0			95	96	102	103	103	106			—	—
3.5	100	102					102	104	87	89	—	—
4.0			92	91	100	99	99	97			—	—
4.5	101	101					98	93	84	84	—	—
5.0			88	91	95	99	97	96			—	—
5.5							88	90	79	79	—	—
6.0			86	90	95	94	87	91			—	—
6.5							86	87	76	77	—	—
7.0			85	87	92	94	86	86			—	—
7.5							84	84	75	76	—	—
8.0			81	83	90	92	83	81			—	—
8.5							82	82	73	73	—	—
9.0			82	84	88	90	80	82			—	—
9.5							76	87	70	70	—	—
10.0			79	84	89	89	77	78			—	—
10.5							76	74	67	69	—	—
11.0			80	80	85	91	73	76			—	—
11.5							77	74	67	69	68	74
12.0			79	83	82	89	74	83			70	71
12.5							72	77	66	69	67	69
13.0			79	74		82	74	72			66	68
13.5			—	—	—	—	72	74	65	68	66	70
14.0			—	—	—	—	68	76			67	68
14.5			—	—	—	—	72	70	62	66	66	68
15.0			—	—	—	—	68	72			65	67
15.5			—	—	—	—			61	65	63	67
16.0			—	—	—	—	64	69			62	66
16.5			—	—	—	—			61	66	61	66
17.0			—	—	—	—	64	71			59	64
17.5			—	—	—	—			60	65	59	64
18.0			—	—	—	—	67	68				
19.0			—	—	—	—	64	71				
20-30			—	—	—	—	63-68	64-75			60-61	65-69

muscularity and volume of the heart. The basic function of the heart is to keep the tissues supplied with oxygen and nutrients and sufficiently free of wastes. As growth rate declines, so also does metabolic rate; hence relatively less blood flow is required. The major determinants of blood flow are resistance to flow (vasomotor tone), arterial pressure, and cardiac output, which is the product of stroke volume and heart rate. Under normal conditions, blood pressure and heart rate are negatively correlated. The role of increased heart volume and strength and vasomotor tone have already been cited as influences in the developmental increase in blood pressure. Heart rate is positively correlated with body temperature and changes approximately 11 beats per minute for each change of 1°F in oral temperature (Tanner, 1951). Body temperature tends to vary directly with metabolic rate.

Smith (1959) attributes the immediate postnatal deceleration in heart rate to alterations in vascular resistance, cardiac output, and other aspects of circulatory dynamics rather than to a reduction in metabolic rate, for the latter may actually be increasing. Another possible factor is body temperature, which drops several degrees within an hour after birth and remains low for several more. The extent and direction of the sex difference in temperature which appears during adolescence (see Table 6) and continues into adulthood is just about sufficient to account for the sex difference in heart rate which develops concurrently (Tanner, 1962).

As Lipton et al. (1965) note, an increase in cardiac rate during the first few weeks or months is contradictory to the change that would be predicted from the inverse associations of heart rate with blood pressure and heart weight and volume. They suggest that biochemical changes and increasing sympathetic tone may be responsible for increments in both heart rate and blood pressure. Physiological anemia (see Hematology) may play a role in the transient rise in heart rate. As blood levels of hemoglobin drop, an increase in cardiac output may be needed to offset the lower oxygen-carrying capacity of the blood. From Smith's view of the causes for the fall in heart rate on the first day, the succeeding temporary rise would simply represent a recovery period during which heart rate returns to levels approximating those before labor.

RESPIRATION

The drama of the first breath has touched the imaginations of physiologists and pediatricians as well as psychoanalysts and poets. In a few brief moments each newborn must abandon one respiratory system—the placenta and its circulation—and make functional another, which is not only untried but also solid and full of fluid. As one authority on the physiology of the newborn has put it, "The first breath of a newborn baby must give even the most experienced physician a small thrill of excitement. Until that sudden indrawing of air occurs the baby's life is in doubt, even though the heart is beating. . . . Other problems may be put off for hours, days or weeks, but if the baby is to live, it must begin moving air into and out of its lungs within minutes after emerging from the birth canal" (Smith, 1963, p. 27). He goes on to point out that the newborn is a "physiologically displaced person" thrust "into an entirely new medium with such novel physical properties it is astonishing that the infant is able to deal with it so promptly and effectively."

By comparison, the facts that must be known to understand the respiratory process —the anatomy of the respiratory tract, the mechanics of breathing, the physiology and biochemistry of gas transport, exchange, and utilization, and the chemical and neural control mechanisms—may seem prosaic, if intricate. The primary function of respiration is, of course, to supply the tissues with oxygen so that the energy in food can be released for work and heat and to remove the carbon dioxide produced during this combustion. As one of several interrelated and integrated functions, however, respiration also contributes to the control of body temperature and the maintenance of fluid and acid-base balance.

The metabolic processes through which oxygen passes from the blood into the cells and is utilized and by which carbon dioxide is produced and returned to the blood are called internal respiration, gaseous metabolism, or intermediary metabolism. In the last analysis the rate of combustion determines the amount of air that must be taken into the lungs in order to reduce the excess carbon dioxide and to replace the oxygen that has been removed from the blood. Nevertheless, this phase of respiration customarily is treated apart from external respiration. Subsumed under the latter term are the processes involved in the exchange of oxygen and carbon dioxide between body and environment, that is, the inspiration and expiration of air and the passage of oxygen from the alveoli (terminal air sacs of the lungs), to the blood and of carbon dioxide from the blood to the alveoli .

The circulation supplies the connecting link between external and internal respiration, and the circulatory and respiratory systems are closely integrated. If either is impaired, compensatory adjustments occur in the other. Indeed, the heart may quite properly be considered one of the most important organs of respiration. It and the gas transport mechanism of the blood are limiting factors in the efficiency of respiration, for the ability of the heart to pump blood and the oxygen-carrying capacity of the blood set the rate at which oxygen can be delivered to the cells.

Breathing is the mechanical aspect of the respiratory process. The amount of gas interchange with the atmosphere is determined by the mechanics of respiration, and these in turn depend upon the structural characteristics of the chest and respiratory tract (nasal passages, larynx, trachea, bronchi, and lungs), especially the lungs. Because the development of respiratory function is almost impossible to interpret without some knowledge of the essential apparatus, the more significant features of anatomical development will be reviewed first.

Anatomical Development

Almost coincidentally with the initiation of circulation to the fetal "lung," the placenta, in the fourth week, the bud of the primitive endodermal tube that constitutes the primordium of the lung appears. A day or two later two primary branches, the major bronchi, can be distinguished. Next, the right bronchus, which is larger, produces two side buds and the left only one. This unequal division presages the final plan of the lungs—three lobes on the right and two on the left. By successive generations of branchings these three new buds and the original two each gives rise to the bronchial tree of one of the five lobes of the mature lung. Cartilage begins to be deposited in the bronchi and larger bronchial tubes at approximately the tenth week, and by the twenty-fourth about as much has been laid down as is present at full term.

Once the bronchial trees are well established, the many lobules that comprise each lobe of the adult lung start to develop. From each of the many terminal bronchioles a number of irregular passageways, the alveolar ducts, are extended. Eventually every duct acquires bushy sacs of alveoli. Several alveolar sacs converge on a common chamber, the atrium, and the atria lead into the alveolar duct.

Very shortly after definitive alveoli begin to be elaborated, the cuboidal or columnar cells of their epithelial lining start to become flattened or platelike, and a network of capillaries proliferates close to the expanding airways. Within another four weeks there are two distinct classes of epithelial cells, one of which contains a substance called surfactant or its precursor. Whether these cells secrete or simply store this material is not known.

Until differentiation of the alveoli and adjacent capillaries, thinning of the alveolar lining, and production of the surfactant have progressed far enough to permit gas exchange commensurate with tissue needs, the fetus cannot survive independently. The alveoli and capillaries provide the surface for the interchange of oxygen and carbon dioxide, and a thin alveolar epithelium makes rapid diffusion of these gases possible. In the mature lung the alveoli remain open and diffusion continues throughout the respiratory cycle. Surfactant is thought to form a surface film on the alveolar lining that helps to keep the air spaces from collapsing each time air is exhaled. The properties and roles of this surface-active material are dealt with more fully in the discussion of the first breath which follows (see pp. 50–51).

Exactly when new bronchial tubes and bronchioles cease to be formed and when the alveoli first appear, change the structure and composition of their epithelial lining, and become invested with capillary loops are still matters of dispute. Recent work indicates that most of the bronchial branching takes place by the fourteenth fetal week (Bucher and

Reid, 1961; Cudmore, Emery, and Mithal, 1962).

Although some authorities set the time of appearance of alveoli and capillaries, flattening of the alveolar epithelium, and secretion of surfacant at 26 to 28 weeks (Avery, 1964; Avery and Mead, 1959; Potter, 1953), most studies place these events between the fourth and sixth months (Barnard and Day, 1937; Bucher and Reid, 1961; Campiche et al., 1963; Gruenwald, 1963, 1966; Loosli and Potter, 1959; Palmer, 1936; Reynolds et al., 1965; Short, 1950). Seven months is the typical "zone of viability," but the fact that some infants born at younger gestational ages survive also supports the contention that these processes basic to postnatal respiratory function have an earlier beginning. This argument is not conclusive, because even at full-term individual differences in the maturation of the lungs are considerably greater than they are at later ages (Cudmore, Emery, and Mithal, 1962; Kikuchi, 1962).

There is general agreement that the number of alveoli and terminal airways and the area of air-tissue interface increase markedly after birth (Barnard and Day, 1937; Bremer,

1935; Bucher and Reid, 1961; Dunnill, 1962; Emery and Mithal, 1960; Engel, 1947, 1962; Foman, 1961; Kikuchi, 1962; Wilson, 1928), although estimates of the timing of different types of growth vary. Discrepancies are to be expected, for measurements on the lungs are fraught with technical difficulties, the number of subjects is usually small, tissue must be obtained from autopsies, so some can be assumed to come from cases with respiratory disorders (and, probably, deficient development), and, as just noted, individual differences are considerable in the young.

In Table 7 the widely cited data of Dunnill (1962) are presented together with ratios that illustrate growth rates. The number of alveoli increases at a decelerating pace. By 4 years the child has almost 90% of the alveoli and half of the terminal airways of the adult. At about 8 years the adult levels are reached (the apparent small increment in alveoli thereafter may not be significant). However, the air-tissue interface (amount of alveolar surface area available for gas exchange) more than doubles between then and adulthood, its growth curve approximating that of body mass. Increase in lung size

Table 7. Age Trends in Terminal Respiratory Units

				Age			
	Birth	3 Months	7	13	4 Years	8	Adult
Number of alveoli[a] (x 10^6)	24	77	112	129	257	280	296
Ratio to birth value	—	3.2	4.7	5.4	10.7	11.7	12.3[b]
Number of airways[a] (x 10^6)	1.5	2.5	3.7	4.5	7.9	14.0	14.0
Ratio to birth value	—	1.7	2.5	3.0	5.3	9.3	9.3[b]
Air-tissue interface[a] (sq.m.)	2.8	7.2	8.4	12.2	22.2	32.0	75.0
Ratio to birth value	—	2.6	3.0	4.4	7.9	11.4	26.8[b]
Body surface area[c] (sq.m.), Ratio to birth value	—	1.4	1.8	2.1	3.2	4.4	9.0[b]
Air-tissue interface per unit body surface area	13.3	24.8	22.1	27.1	33.1	34.8	39.5
Body weight,[c] ratio to birth value	—	3.6	4.8	6.1	10.1	16.4	18.5

[a] Data from Dunnill, 1962. Ratios were calculated from these data.

[b] Dunnill estimates these ratios as 10, 10, 21, and 9, respectively.

[c] Data for these ratios were taken from pooled age norms from several sources.

after the formation of new units ceases comes, of course, from the growth of existing ones. Other investigators (Engel, 1962; Kikuchi, 1962) report that the transition to growth only by expansion of tissue already present occurs at around 3 to 5 years. As long as new units are being differentiated, the possibility of replacing destroyed tissue may remain. Thereafter, regeneration is unlikely.

Engel's (1966) distinction between immature and mature alveolation is of interest in its own right and also helps to explain inconsistencies among anatomists in the age at which alveoli are reported to appear and in the numbers estimated. During late prenatal and early postnatal development the alveoli are small (about one-fourth the adult diameter) and quite flat and undifferentiated. By the end of the first year they are larger, more elevated, and much better differentiated.

Whereas the number of alveoli, their surface area, and the total lung volume (about 1/20 to 1/40 of adult value; Engel, 1962, favors the latter estimate) of the newborn are small, the trachea, bronchi, and bronchioles are about one-third, one-half, and one-fourth, respectively, of adult size. Their postnatal growth curve also differs, being more like the "general" curve of growth, with a rapid increase during infancy, an adolescent spurt, and slow, steady increments during the interim. About 30% of the neonate's lung volume is made up of interstitial tissue, in contrast to 10-15% in the adult. Thus the anatomical "dead space" of the neonate's lungs (area not used in gas exchange) is proportionately greater. Helping to offset the resultant reduction in respiratory capacity is the fact that the surface area for gas interchange is greater per unit tissue while the alveoli are small than it is after they increase in size and change in shape.

The large width of the upper parts of the respiratory tract, their absolutely short length, and the deficiency of mucous glands in their linings render the infant more susceptible to infections. At the same time, the smaller absolute size of the passages means that they are more easily obstructed by foreign objects, inflamed tissue, or collapse of the supporting walls. For a number of reasons the lung of the young infant is less resistant to atelectasis (collapse) than is that of the adult. The bronchiolar muscle is thin, offering less sup-

port, there is less collateral ventilation among the terminal air spaces, and the alveoli are smaller in diameter and have a greater curvature. In premature infants and some full-term ones suffering from respiratory distress, the likelihood of atelectasis is enhanced by a deficiency in the amount or composition of surfactant. Because secretion of this substance is now believed to begin quite early in gestation, a deficiency is attributed to some factor, such as an inadequate pulmonary blood supply, that reduces the amount of surfactant or changes its nature.

Among the structural determinants of the resistance of the airways to the passage of air are the length of the tubes, the number in parallel, and their width. The last is the most important, resistance varying inversely with the fourth power of the radius of the tubes. Because the tracheobronchial tree is wide, the amount of pressure needed for the first inflation of the lungs and the degree of resistance to subsequent inflations in the infant are quite great.

The physical growth of the lungs and the temporary expansion of them with each inspiration are limited by the size of the chest. So small is the chest of the fetus that the lungs, although small in proportion to an adult's, are squeezed between the ribs and bear the marks of them. Early postnatal growth of both the chest and lungs are rapid but proportionate, so the depth of respiration continues to be restricted. Later the rate of growth in thoracic diameter begins to outstrip the rate of increase in lung volume.

Additional handicaps to deep respiration are the poor development of the thoracic muscles, the position of the ribs, and the large size of the heart, liver, and stomach. Like all of the infant's muscles, those of inspiration are weak. The tissue of infants has a high proportion of water and a low proportion of nitrogen, an essential component of protein for muscle. Even if the muscles were stronger, little or no elevation of the rib cage is possible because the ribs are still cartilaginous and positioned horizontally. Little change in position occurs during the first year. Throughout the second and third the descent is fairly rapid. By age 7 the angle of descent has become quite similar to that of the adult. The large heart occupies a disproportionate amount of the small thorax, and the large size of the abdominal organs such as the liver and stomach prevents adequate contraction of the diaphragm.

How this combination of anatomical limitations influences the character of respiration can be seen when one considers the two ways in which inspiration may take place in the adult. The diaphragm can contract, pushing out the abdomen and increasing the linear dimension of the thorax. Alternatively, the ribs can be raised, increasing the cross-sectional area of the chest. Actually, both sorts of expansion occur to some degree in both costal and diaphragmatic or abdominal breathing, but the sequence is different. In costal breathing, the upper ribs move first, followed by bulging of the abdomen. In diaphragmatic breathing the abdomen is extended first, followed by some movement of the thorax. Either type of inspiration is sufficient to fulfill the respiratory needs of a normal person even during mild exercise. Both usually occur in older children and adults.

At all ages diaphragmatic movements provide a greater amount of the total volume of air inspired under ordinary conditions. Among infants, breathing is primarily abdominal, despite the handicaps already mentioned. Costal respiration begins to play a larger role sometime between the fifth and seventh years.

The fluid filling the fetal lungs has been the source of two research questions: (1) Where does it come from?, and (2) How is it removed? For many years it was believed that this liquid was amniotic fluid, inspired during fetal respiratory movements. These movements were another issue of controversy, for some viewed them as "practice" for postnatal existence. Evidence for such movements, and particularly for the aspiration of amniotic fluid as the source of lung fluid, is tenuous (see reviews in Smith, 1959; Adams, 1966; Avery, 1964; James, 1966; James and Adamsons, 1964). Today respiratory movements are thought to occur during the latter part of gestation only under abnormal conditions, for example, when there is some interference with placental gas exchange. Although occasional respiratory-like movements may be normal earlier in gestation, they would be very unlikely to be effective in moving anything into the rather solid lungs. The hypotheses now favored are that lung fluid is either actively secreted by the lungs or is an ultrafiltrate of blood plasma from the pulmonary capillaries. Because lung fluid and blood differ in some respects, the second alternative requires the additional assumptions of selective reabsorption or secretion of some constituents. Elimination of lung fluid is one of the many events accompanying the onset of breathing.

Onset of Respiration

The establishment and continuation of respiration adequate to postnatal needs involves not only removal of fluid from the lungs but also development of sufficient pressure to overcome the initial strong resistance to inflation, retention of a volume of air between inspirations, even distribution of that volume throughout the lungs, a large increase in pulmonary blood flow over the fetal level (which is brought about by redistribution of the cardiac output), and a nice adjustment of the circulatory and respiratory systems so that the alveoli are perfused by a volume of blood appropriate to the required rate of gas exchange. To an astonishing extent these processes are accomplished by the end of the first respiratory cycle in healthy newborns.

In the course of a vaginal delivery pressure of the pelvic muscles and vaginal walls on the cartilaginous and therefore rather unresistant thorax squeezes a considerable amount of fluid from the lungs. It is expelled through the nose and mouth, and more fluid usually drains out under the force of gravity when the infant is suspended by its feet at delivery. The amount of fluid lost in this way is between one-fourth and one-third of the functional residual capacity (volume of air left in the lungs at the end of a normal expiration) of an infant several days old (Karlberg, 1960). That remaining must be cleared rapidly because by 15 minutes or so after delivery the functional residual capacity is very close to the typical neonatal level. Observations on lambs (Boston, Humphreys, Reynolds, and Strang, 1965) and rabbits (Aherne and Dawkins, 1964) suggest pulmonary lymphatics as one route of elimination. Other possibilities are evaporation and absorption into the blood (Avery, 1964; James and Adamsons, 1964).

Even after the respiratory passageways are open and some air remains in the lungs between inspirations, force must be generated to bring new air into the lungs. Air flow in and out of the lungs is governed by changes in the intrapulmonary (intra-alveolar) pressure. Between respiratory cycles no air moves because the pressure within the lungs is the same as that of the atmosphere. During inspiration the volume of the lungs is increased, and, because gases expand to fill the volume available to them, the air already in the lungs also expands, intra-alveolar pressure is reduced below atmospheric, and air flows into the lungs. When the inspiratory muscles stop contracting, the elastic fibers of the lungs retract to their original length, intrapulmonic pressure increases above that of the atmosphere, and air is forced out of the lungs. The inspiratory force must also be sufficient to offset the resistance to flow offered by the respiratory tract (discussed earlier) and by the viscosity and turbulence of air.

Additional pressure is required at birth to overcome the viscosity of the lung fluid and the resistance produced by surface tension at the air-liquid interface and force open the undistended lungs. Experimental work with mature fetal lambs (Strang, 1965) shows that a considerable opening pressure must be generated before any air enters the lungs. Beyond that point a small increment in pressure will bring about almost complete inflation. Water is several dozen times as viscous as air and a thousand times as dense. On the other hand, less pressure is required to inflate a lung that contains some fluid than one that is completely collapsed (Avery, Frank, and Gribetz, 1959). This advantageous effect of fluid may result from its effects on the curvature of the airways. Because the surface tension forcing the walls together is inversely proportional to the radius of curvature, spaces distended with fluid are less likely to collapse. Moreover, lungs containing fluid may not be so easily blocked by inspissated material (Avery, 1964).

Of the various sources of resistance to inflation, surface tension at the air-liquid interface is probably the greatest. Almost half the pressure needed for the initial inflation is used to counteract this tension (Nelson, 1966). The fact that surface tension is strongest in small air spaces means not only that the small alveoli are more subject to collapse, but also that in an interconnecting system, such as the air sacs, air from smaller units will tend to empty into larger ones. Unequal distribution of gases interferes with efficient respiration. Surfactant supplies two properties that alter the surface tension of lung fluid (see review in Mead, 1961). First, lung fluid containing surfactant is able to develop very low tension. Second, surfactant permits surface tension to vary directly with surface area rather than simply inversely with curvature. Thus as the surface area is extended surface tension increases. Conversely, if the alveoli are compressed (a normal occurrence during expiration), surface tension decreases markedly. It is this characteristic that maintains the stability of the air spaces. With pressures in air spaces about equal regardless of their size, air does not move from smaller sacs into larger ones.

Given lungs partially emptied of fluid through pressure on the thorax, the infant delivered vaginally is further aided in inflating his lungs by a reflex expansion of the chest. When the compressed thorax is freed from the confines of the birth canal, an elastic recoil of the chest walls sucks air into the respiratory tract (Karlberg, 1960). The amount of air taken in just about replaces the amount of fluid lost (7 to 42 ml.) and can be as much as 20-25% of the total lung capacity. Individual differences in fluid loss and the extent of the recoil may account in part for differences among healthy infants in the effort required for inflation. Some vigorous newborns seem to breathe almost without effort (James, 1966). Measurements made during the first breath (Karlberg, Cherry, Escardo, and Koch, 1962) show intrathoracic pressures to range from 20 to 70 cm. H_2O below atmospheric pressure and the intake of air to vary from 20 to 80 ml. Although the pressures applied and the work required to generate them are considerable, they are no greater than those typical during a good cry after respiration is established.

Why breathing begins is as intriguing a question as how the first breath is accomplished mechanically. The obvious answer— the baby needs to renew his supply of oxygen and rid himself of carbon dioxide—is not sufficient. First and most important, such a statement says nothing about the trigger mechanism(s). Second, newborns who are not asphyxiated, sedated, or otherwise impaired usually breathe almost immediately and before they are severed from the placental "lung." Speculation about, and investigation of, the way in which respiration is stimulated center around two general classes of stimuli—chemical and sensory.

Once established, spontaneous respiration is controlled by impulses from respiratory centers (inspiratory center and expiratory center) in the medulla oblongata in the lower brain stem. The activity of these centers is regulated primarily by the degree to which they are stimulated by chemoreceptors, receptor cells sensitive to variations in blood chemistry. An increase in the carbon dioxide pressure or hydrogen ion concentration or a decrease in the oxygen pressure of arterial blood activates the respiratory center, but this action is mediated by the chemoreceptors.

In the adult the central chemoreceptors, which probably lie on the ventral surface of the brain stem, are the major chemical regulatory mechanism. They seem to respond chiefly to the hydrogen ion concentration in the cerebrospinal fluid. Hydrogen ions and carbon dioxide pass from the blood into this fluid. The carbon dioxide is hydrated to form carbonic acid (H_2CO_3). Then much of the acid dissociates, increasing the hydrogen ion concentration. In this way the hydrogen ion concentration of the cerebrospinal fluid parallels the partial pressure of carbon dioxide in arterial blood, and hence an increase in carbon dioxide rather than a decrease in oxygen is the chief means by which respiration is adjusted to metabolic need.

The peripheral chemoreceptors, the aortic and carotid bodies (located below the aortic arch and in the bifurcation of each common carotid artery, respectively), normally play a more minor role, although they have an important emergency function. Unlike the central receptors, these bodies are sensitive to a reduction in the partial pressure of oxygen, as well as to increases in the partial pressure of carbon dioxide or in hydrogen ion concentration and have their maximum effect during asphyxia. Whereas the central chemoreceptors are readily depressed by anoxia, excess carbon dioxide, or anesthesia, the peripheral receptors react to oxygen lack. They continue to stimulate the respiratory center despite depression of the central receptors.

As the peripheral receptors are the stimulus for the last gasp, so it is thought they may be the deciding factor in the first. During labor and delivery gas exchange through the placenta is impaired, although to varying degrees depending upon the circumstances. At birth the oxygen tension of arterial blood is below normal and the carbon dioxide pressure and hydrogen ion content above normal even in the healthy products of uneventful labors. Considerable evidence has been amassed to indicate that both the central and peripheral chemoreceptors are well developed by term (see reviews in Brady and Tooley, 1966; Cross, 1961; Nelson, 1966; Purves and Biscoe, 1966). However, if the central receptors are depressed, activity of the peripheral ones may well become the major rather than the minor mediator of chemical stimulation to breathing.

Experimental results and clinical experience support the inference that sensory stimuli are somehow important in the initiation of respiration. The traditional spanking for nonbreathers is but one example. From a watery environment in which it is weightless, warm, and somewhat shielded from light, sound, and vibration, the fetus is propelled by vigorous pressures into a cold, bright, noisy one in which he has weight and is subjected to manipulations. A true experiment in which one possible determinant is systematically varied while others are held constant is difficult to accomplish even for the chemical variables. Especially with the human infant, real control of the sensory variables is impossible.

From work with lower animals (see reviews in James and Adamsons, 1964, and Purves and Biscoe, 1966) it appears that none of the chemical factors (oxygen, carbon dioxide, hydrogen ions) singly will bring about breathing. In combination they are effective. On the other hand, cooling, which is marked at birth (see Temperature), will stimulate regular respiration in the absence of changes in the gas tensions or hydrogen ion concentration of the blood (Dawes, 1965, 1966). Tactile stimuli alone, even when intense and repetitive, will not (Harned, Wolkoff, Pickrell, and MacKinney, 1961).

The failure of independent chemical changes to induce respiration is interpreted to mean either that the chemoreceptors of the newborn are not responsive to oxygen lack except in the presence of high carbon dioxide pressure and/or hydrogen ion concentration or that the threshold of the respiratory center is so high that stimulation from the peripheral chemoreceptors is not sufficient to induce increased activity. In the adult the responsivity of the respiratory center depends upon the activity of the reticular formation of the hindbrain, and its excitability is a function of the input from sensory receptors. After delivery the level of activity seems to rise, and the flood of sensory impulses may be the reason. Stimulation of baroreceptors by a rise in blood pressure subsequent to cutting of the cord and increased secretion of epinephrine in response to stress may also act as supplementary stimulants to breathing. To date, the evidence suggests that the initiation of respiration is typically multiply-determined. Certainly, if one were designing the ignition for so important a system, prudence would dictate alternative mechanisms.

Development of Pulmonary Function

Standard tests of pulmonary function include lung volume and its components, the distensibility of the lungs and chest, resistance of the airways, respiratory rate, and timed breathing capacities. Also of concern are the distribution of air among alveoli and between alveoli and dead space, the transfer of gases between alveoli and blood in the pulmonary capillaries, and alveolar-arterial differences in oxygen and carbon dioxide tensions. Most of these measures require voluntary effort and conformity to instructions. Among the other problems in testing infants and young children are keeping activity level similar from subject to subject and the apparatus properly adjusted to variations in size and position. Although means have been devised to estimate most aspects of pulmonary function even in newborn infants, of necessity they are often approximations of the conditions prescribed for adults.

When the various tests are used to chart the course of normal development additional difficulties arise. Not only must body size be taken into account, a step that involves a decision as to which measure, say, weight, height, or surface area, is most appropriate, but sometimes also total lung volume or oxygen requirement, that is, metabolic rate.

In view of these considerations it is not surprising that authorities sometimes differ in their interpretations of the adequacy of lung function in the young relative to the adult and that comparative statements typically must be made in general rather than exact terms.

The classic instrument for obtaining most measures of lung capacity is the spirometer. In essence this apparatus consists of a container of gas from which the subject breathes via a tube held in his mouth (his nose is occluded) and a recording device for continuous registration of changes in the volume of gas in the container. During the first few weeks of life infants do not normally breathe through their mouths, and children less than about 5 years old cannot be depended upon to retain a tube in their mouths. Therefore a nasal or facial mask is coupled to the tubing. Lung volumes can also be derived from airflow measurements made with a pneumotachygraph, which is a mesh screen of known resistance to air flow through which the subject breathes. It is attached to a mask, but no tubing is required.

One major disadvantage of masks and tubing is the increase in the dead space through which air must be moved. What would for an adult be a relatively small amount of instrumental dead space may be equal to or greater than the anatomic dead space in infants and cause alterations in the rate and pattern of breathing. Probably the most successful attempt to design a valved nasal mask with little dead space and resistance to air flow is that recently reported by Silverman, Sinclair, and Buck (1966).

The study of pulmonary function need not be entirely a saga of "through childhood with tube and mask." Alternative techniques for measuring lung capacities in which neither piece of equipment is required are standard and impedance plethysmography and barometry. For standard plethysmography the subject lies in an airtight box with only his head or face exposed. As the air around his body expands and contracts with movements of the thorax, the changes in volume can be recorded with a spirometer connected to the box or the changes in pressure with pressure transducers. A total body plethysmograph—one in which the subject is completely enclosed—is used for barometry and impedance plethysmography. The barometric method depends upon the fluctuations in pressure produced in the chamber when inspired air is warmed by the lungs, becomes saturated with water vapor, and expands. In impedance plethysmography changes in thoracic gas volume are detected by measuring increases and decreases in the conduction of a small alternating current passed between two electrodes attached to the chest. From simultaneous comparisons of volumes and respiratory rates determined by air-flow meter, barometry and impedance plethysmography, and pneumographic recording with a strain gauge like that used in measuring limb blood flow (see Blood Pressure), Polgar (1965) concluded that barometry is the most satisfactory method for infants.

Not all the subdivisions of total lung capacity (maximum volume of air that can be contained in the lungs without rupture) usually measured in adults have been studied in infants and children. Those most frequently assessed are: (1) tidal volume, the amount of air moved into or out of the lungs with each breath during normal, quiet respiration; (2) vital capacity, the largest volume of air that can be expired after a maximal inspiration, and (3) functional residual capacity, the amount of air left at the end of a passive expiration.

Lung volumes vary with height and surface area and to a lesser yet marked degree with chest dimensions and weight but are largely independent of age per se (Demuth, Howatt, and Hill, 1965; see also reviews in Shock, 1966, and Smith, 1959). For this reason, most data have been reported as a function of one or more physical measurements without reference to age. Only vital capacity, which is regarded as one of the most useful indicators of pulmonary function, has been related to age with sufficient frequency and at enough points to produce a relatively systematic picture of age trends and sex differences. Unfortunately, the failure of most investigators to adjust for size before plotting by age reduces the inferences that can be drawn about the effect of maturational variables other than gross size.

Although infants cannot be asked to perform a maximal inhalation and exhalation, they can easily be provoked into a highly reliable approximation of it—"crying vital capacity." Within 7 minutes after delivery this volume ranges from about 50 to 100% of that measured several days later (Sutherland and Ratcliff, 1961). From reviews of the literature Nelson (1966) concludes that the vital capacity (and total lung capacity) of the neonate per unit weight is considerably less than that of the adult, whereas Smith (1959) considers vital capacity per unit sur-

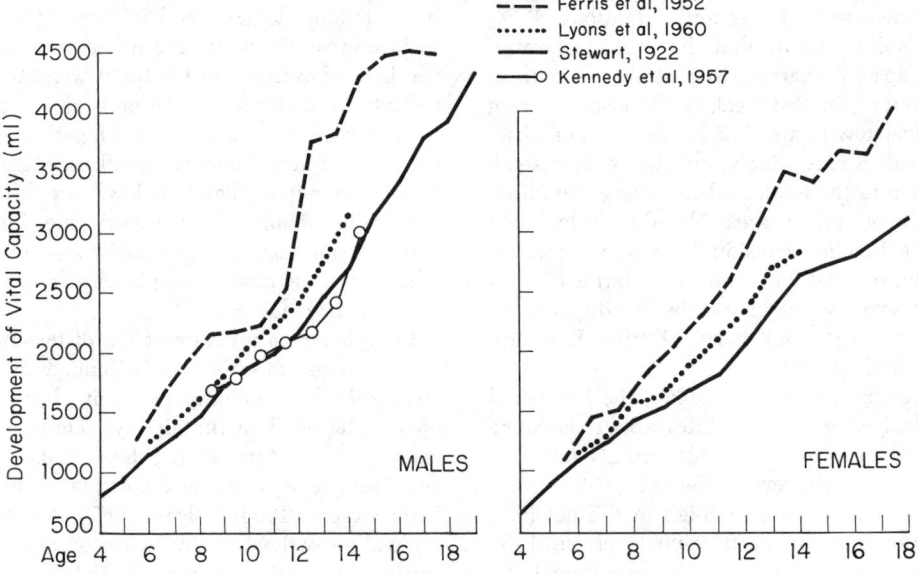

Fig. 4.   Development of vital capacity. (a) Males. (b) Females.

face area to be small, but per unit weight to be roughly equivalent to the adult's. Nelson (1966) also suggests that the vital and total lung capacities of the infant are low because the chest is too flimsy to provide the mechanical leverage needed for full inspiration.

As can be seen in Fig. 4 the curves of increase in vital capacity are similar to the "general" growth curve and show a progressive sex difference. The apparent variations from study to study in absolute values are not statistically significant, but they probably stem from differences in methodologies and subject size. When surface area is taken into account, vital capacity changes little between 10 and 18 years in girls yet increases gradually in boys (Moore, 1951; Shock, 1942). The fact that the increment in boys during adolescence is greater than would be predicted from total body size has been interpreted to mean that lung growth in this period is proportionately greater in males than females (Morse, Schultz, and Cassels, 1952; Tanner, 1962).

Evaluation of the functional residual capacity of the neonate has been of particular concern. This volume must be sufficient to prevent collapse of the lungs. Otherwise almost as much force would be required for each inspiration as for the first breath. Further, this air acts as a buffer during inspiration so that gas tensions in the alveoli are kept relatively stable. All investigators agree (see reviews in James and Adamsons, 1964, and Nelson, 1966) that the functional residual capacity characteristic of the neonate at the end of the first week is established during the first few minutes of breathing. The absolute values vary widely, but they too are small relative to the adult's when referred to either weight or surface area. Nor does calculation of the functional residual capacity, vital capacity, or total lung volume in terms of both body size and basal metabolic rate improve the picture (Cook, Cherry, O'Brien, Karlberg, and Smith, 1955).

According to Avery (1965), the functional residual capacity constitutes about the same proportion of the total lung capacity in infant and adult. However, Nelson (1966) concludes that this ratio is high in the newborn and does not decline to adult levels until the differentiation of new alveoli ceases and the rib cage is completely ossified. He attributes the higher ratio to a smaller retractive force of the lung consequent upon a smaller number of alveoli and a lower total alveolar surface tension. In support of this hypothesis he cites evidence for a decrease in functional residual capacity per unit body weight during early infancy. Over a wider age range (4 to 18 years), however, the association with weight is positive rather than negative (DeMuth, Howatt, and Hill, 1965).

Neonatal tidal volume is only slightly lower than the adult's on the basis of weight, but it is especially low when referred to surface area (Nelson, 1966; Smith, 1959). The ratio of tidal volume to functional residual capacity is identical in infant and adult, indicating that the alveolar gas tensions of the infant remain as stable from inspiration to inspiration. If this were not so, the protection against atelectasis offered by the functional residual capacity would be impaired.

About one-third to one-half of the small tidal volume of the neonate is distributed in the dead space (see reviews in Avery, 1964, 1965, and Nelson, 1966). A figure of 30% is average for adults, so infants with a comparable value are not wasting any larger fraction of their total ventilatory volume. The distribution of air among the alveoli is also equally good in neonate, child, and adult (Strang and McGrath, 1962; Orzalesi, Hart, and Cook, 1965). However, the amount of air required to ventilate the alveoli is dictated by metabolic demand and is proportional to surface area. Therefore the infant must overventilate in relation to his body weight, and the ratio of alveolar ventilation to dead space is very high. The latter ratio, together with the product of pulmonary compliance and resistance (see immediately below), are the primary determinants of respiratory rate. Singly and in combination these factors require a progressive increase in respiratory frequency as body size decreases.

Compliance, a measure of the distensibility of the lungs and thorax, is defined as the change in lung volume per unit change in pressure applied to the airways. Despite the many problems surrounding the determination and interpretation of lung compliance in infants (Avery, 1964; Polgar, 1967), the average values arrived at by many different investigators (see summaries in Nelson, 1966, and Polgar, 1967) are remarkably similar. At delivery lung compliance is comparatively poor. It improves rapidly between 3 and 8 hours later, probably because most of the fluid has been removed from the lungs. Relative to body weight, tidal volume, or functional residual capacity, lung compliance at tidal volumes is equivalent to adult ratios. Across a wider range of lung volumes the neonate is not in as good a position. However, compliance increases with age. The source of the apparent limitation in the young may not be a lesser elasticity of the lung but rather an artifact of having a lung with a larger amount of functional tissue per unit of potential air space.

In contrast to the lung, the thorax of the newborn is extremely compliant and becomes less so with age. The balance between the elastic recoil of the lung, which tends to produce collapse, and that of the chest, which makes for expansion, governs the resting volume at the end of expiration. Within the lung, as we have seen, collapse is counteracted by surfactant. Although the net balance of factors apparently leaves the lungs at the end of expiration rather near to the collapse volume, the normal full-term infant shows no real functional handicap. However, this set of conditions is one more reason that the premature infant, whose status is more marginal in all phases of respiratory function, is particularly susceptible to respiratory distress. After the growth of the thorax begins to outpace that of the lung, the balance of distending and compressing forces swings in the opposite direction, and the negative intrapleural pressure characteristic of the adult thorax at rest develops.

As would be anticipated from the anatomic data cited earlier, the absolute resistance of the airways to air flow is high in the newborn (Nelson, 1966; Polgar, 1967). Relative to the adult a much larger proportion of the resistance is attributable to lung tissue and a lesser proportion to the nasal passages (Polgar, 1967). When resistance is calculated in terms of the average air flow through the airways (ventilation per minute) or per unit of lung tissue, however, the infant is found not to be at a disadvantage. Indeed, as pulmonary resistance declines with the loss of fluid from the lungs, the infant comes to be in a more favorable position with respect to resistive forces.

The volume of air brought into the lung in a given interval of time is the product of the tidal volume times the respiratory rate. When inspiration begins, gas in the dead space is drawn back into the alveoli first, and the fresh air from the atmosphere follows. Thus the alveolar ventilation per unit time is the tidal volume minus the volume in the dead space multiplied by respiratory frequency. In rapid, shallow breathing energy is wasted in frequent ventilation of the dead space. On the other hand, the energy cost of a large increment in tidal volume is high because of the effort required to stretch the lungs. Some increase in both the depth and rate of respiration is the most efficient way for the adult to cope with an increased demand for gas exchange. If an impediment to air flow or some other pathological condition reduces tidal volume or alveolar ventilation, then breathing must be more frequent. For this reason respiratory rate, a seemingly gross measure, has diagnostic utility.

Although even the newborn infant can increase his tidal volume, the structural and mechanical characteristics of his respiratory apparatus make rapid, shallow respiration more economical in terms of energy cost (Polgar, 1967). The individual factors limiting the depth of respiration in the young have been mentioned at various points in the preceding discussion. In brief, these are: weak inspiratory muscles, lack of firm ribs positioned at a descending angle, large size of the organs in the thorax and abdomen relative to the space to accommodate them, rather stiff lungs, and considerable absolute resistance to air flow. Yet the demand for gas exchange in the young is high per unit of lung tissue, air-tissue interface, or body size. To compensate for the low tidal volume in the face of this need, respiration must be more rapid. Because the infant also typically meets any increased need for gas exchange or reduction in alveolar ventilation by raising his respiratory rate, this measure is useful not only clinically but also for psychophysiological studies.

Unfortunately, acquiring accurate records of respiratory rate, especially in young infants, is not easy. Rates counted by observers are likely to be low because respiratory movements are not always detectable, or cannot be distinguished from other movements and because the observer tires or is distracted. The traditional pneumograph, a flexible, accordianlike rubber tube, also may fail to detect shallow breaths. On the other hand, the weight or tactual stimulation of this or other equipment may alter the rate or pattern of respiration. In any event, erratic breathing such as occurs with sighing, crying, or aperiodic breathing (see review in Smith, 1959), for whatever cause, interferes with both observational and instrumental recording and necessitates making repeated counts over a stated interval.

With increasing age, respiration becomes deeper, gas exchange more efficient (see below), and the oxygen requirement per unit size decreases (see Metabolism), so respiratory rate declines. Illustrative data are presented in Table 8. Those of Dietel (reproduced in Peiper, 1963, p. 311) were secured by counting the moist spots on a sheet of cellulose loosely suspended in front of the infant's nose while he slept after feeding. Eichorn's (1951) subjects were also tested after feeding. Records were made not only during sleep but also during repetitive visual

and auditory stimulation and while the infant was awake but unstimulated. Rates during either visual or auditory stimulation (not shown) were intermediate between the sleeping and unstimulated waking rates. An infant's rubber pneumograph was fastened around the subject's abdomen, and the movements were recorded on a photopolygraph. Iliff and Lee (1952) made counts from visual observations of at least 30 seconds. Infants were asleep and older children rested quietly in a basal metabolism chamber. As described earlier (see Heart Rate), the infants had been fed, but the older children were fasting. The data of Shock and Soley (1939) are also from a longitudinal study. Respiratory rates were counted from the spirograms taken during three determinations of basal metabolism on each of two successive days. Two one-minute counts were made for each gas-sampling period.

Although rates obtained by different investigators on older children agree quite well, the variation among and within studies of infants is even greater than is reflected in Table 8. Deming and Hanner (1936) studied

Table 8. Age Trends in Respiratory Rate

Study: Dietel, 1954				Iliff and Lee, 1952				Shock and Soley, 1939		Eichorn, 1951				
Condition: Asleep				Asleep		Basal		Basal			Awake		Asleep	
Day	Mean	Range	Years	M	F	M	F	M	F	Days	Mean	Range	Mean	Range
1	46	28-78	0.5	31	30					6-10	77	54-108	53	27-69
2	46	32-72	1.5	26	27					11-20	75	33-114	51	27-84
3	44	32-68	2.5			25	25			21-30	68	57-102	53	27-84
4	42	28-66	3.5			24	24			31-60	64	45-90	43	21-81
5	40	28-64	4.5			23	22			61-90	59	42-81	39	30-66
6	39	26-62	5.5			22	21							
7	38	26-62	6.5			21	21							
			7.5			20	20							
			8.5			20	20							
			9.5			19	19							
			10.5			19	19							
			11.5			19	19							
			12.0					16.3	16.1					
			12.5			19	19							
			13.5			19	18							
			14.0					17.0	15.6					
			14.5											
			15.5											
			16.0					15.6	15.2					
			16.5											
			17.5											
			18-27					14.0	14.7					
			27-43					13.7	14.4					

18 infants for the first 11 days of life, using half-minute counts obtained in a plethysmograph. Mean resting rates ranged from 40 to 57 and showed no trend during this period. With more carefully controlled conditions and an improved plethysmograph, Cross (1949) found an average rate of 28.6 (range = 14-51) in 36 infants aged a few hours to 13 days. In another study the mean rate declined from about 53 in the first hour after birth to 43–44 by 12 hours and remained at that level during the rest of the first day (Malan, 1966). Rates were counted by observation when the babies were neither crying nor eating. Like heart rate, respiratory rate in most of the 2- to 5-day-old infants studied by Lipton, Steinschneider, and Richmond (1960) was lower ($M = 54.7$) when they were swaddled than when free ($M = 56.6$). Their measurements were made with a nasal thermistor.

All in all, the guess may be hazarded that the respiratory rate during the first week taken with a reasonably sensitive instrument under an age-appropriate approximation of "basal" conditions is somewhere around 50/minute and declines to a third or less of that figure by the end of adolescence.

After air has reached the alveoli, oxygen must diffuse through the alveolar wall, the interstitial space, the capillary lining, and the red cell membrane and combine with hemoglobin for transport to the cells. Carbon dioxide, which is more readily diffusible, takes an inverse course, except that it exists in the blood in several combined forms instead of attaching to hemoglobin. According to Nelson (1966), the ability of the newborn infant to transfer gases is less than that of the adult because "both the effective pulmonary capillary blood volume and membrane diffusing capacity are relatively low." The former deficiency arises because, although the distribution of air among alveoli is even, not all alveoli are equally well perfused with capillary blood (Ledbetter, Homma, and Farhi, 1967). As new generations of alveoli are formed and their walls become thinner, membrane diffusing capacity increases (Nelson, 1966). Between 4 and 18 years the pattern of increase in diffusing capacity is very like that in lung volume, height, weight, and surface area (DeMuth, Howatt, and Hill, 1965). Gas exchange becomes more efficient during adolescence, the percentage of oxygen in ex-

pired air decreasing and the percentage of carbon dioxide increasing between 12 and 16 years (Shock and Soley, 1939). Greater changes are observed in boys, but by 16 neither sex has achieved the levels characteristic of 20-year-olds.

Until fairly recently the fetus was generally believed to exist in a state of relative oxygen deprivation, hypercapnia (excess carbon dioxide in the blood), and acidosis. These inferences were drawn primarily from measurements made at delivery on blood from the umbilical cord or the arteries of the infant. The fact that the blood of many infants who are vigorous at birth has a low oxygen saturation and fairly high carbon dioxide tension and low pH (these two measures are particularly exaggerated in depressed neonates) suggests that this condition is not of long duration (James and Burnard, 1961). Now that fetal capillary blood (Saling, 1964) and the oxygen tension of fetal tissue (Caldeyro-Barcia et al., 1966) have been sampled during labor, it is known that the hypercapnia and acidosis and to a considerable extent the hypoxemia (low oxygenation of blood) arise during labor and delivery and do not accurately represent conditions *in utero* (see reviews in James and Adamsons, 1964; Romney, 1966; Stahlman, 1966; and Towell, 1966). Continuous gas-sampling from fetal animals (Adamsons, James, Towell, and Lacey, 1965; Meschia, Cotter, Breathnach, and Barron, 1965; Misrahy, Beran, Spradley, and Garwood, 1960) and observations on a few human fetuses during intrauterine exchange transfusion (Freda and Adamsons, 1964; James and Adamsons, 1964) also show that the normal fetus has well oxygenated tissues and is neither hypercapnic nor acidotic.

Other data from which fetal oxygen deprivation had been deduced have not been refuted but rather reinterpreted in the light of new information and consideration of additional factors. It is true, for example, that the maternal blood exposed to the chorionic villi has a lower oxygen tension than the alveolar air with which the blood in adult pulmonary capillaries equilibrates (Romney, 1966; Sjöstedt, Rooth, and Caligra, 1960), that the placenta itself consumes oxygen (Campbell, Dawes, Fishman, Hyman, and James, 1966; Tremblay, Sybulski, and Maughan, 1965), and that oxygen diffuses through the placenta more slowly than through the adult alveolar membranes (Eastman and Hellman, 1961). Relative to fetal metabolic needs, however, the placenta performs about as well as the adult lung in most aspects of oxygen transfer (James and Adamsons, 1964). The rate of blood flow rather than diffusion is the limiting factor in the degree of exchange of substances across the placenta. Both the fetal cardiac output and rate of placental blood flow are sufficiently high to offset the low oxygen tensions of placental and fetal blood (see reviews in Nesbitt, 1966; Romney, 1966; Stahlman, 1966; and Towell, 1966). Of course, interference with the placental or fetal circulations can reduce the amount of oxygen available to the fetal tissues.

Certain pecularities of fetal blood (see Erythrocytes), have long been recognized as a protection against oxygen lack. For several reasons the oxygen-carrying capacity of fetal blood is higher than that of adult blood. When enclosed in erythrocytes and in the blood stream, fetal hemoglobin has a greater affinity for oxygen at a given oxygen tension, although when separated from the red cells it does not (Allen, Wyman, and Smith, 1953; Nechtman and Huisman, 1964). Whatever the environmental source of the difference may be, the net result is that fetal blood takes up oxygen at tensions at which the maternal blood in the placenta releases it. The uptake at the placenta is further enhanced by simultaneous release of carbon dioxide (Bohr effect). At the oxygen tensions of fetal tissues and with the acidity there, however, the fetal oxyhemoglobin curve is such that an inverse and equally advantageous phenomenon is observed—oxygen is released more readily. These characteristics of the fetal oxygen dissociation curve, first demonstrated *in vitro* (in a test tube), have now been shown to hold *in vivo* across its entire range (Oh, Arcilla, and Lind, 1965). The reader will also recall that as gestation proceeds the number of erythrocytes and their hemoglobin concentration increases, becoming as high as or higher than in the adult.

Within minutes after the establishment of respiration a marked rise in arterial oxygen tension and drop in carbon dioxide tension occurs, and the alveolar oxygen tension and alveolar-arterial difference in carbon dioxide tension are like those of the adult (Nelson, 1966). However, the arterial oxygen tension (and hence the alveolar-arterial difference) does not reach adult levels for several days, even in normal full-term infants (Thibeault, Clutario, and Auld, 1966). Alveolar and arterial carbon dioxide tensions—the latter is considered to be the most reliable index of the adequacy of alveolar ventilation (Avery, 1964)—are somewhat low for several weeks (Stahlman, 1961) or months (Nelson, 1966). Although the acidosis present at delivery increases briefly, the acid-base balance is close to normal within 2 or 3 hours and like that of the mother near term by 1 to 3 days (Assali and Morris, 1964; James and Burnard, 1961; Weisbrot, James, Prince, Holaday, and Apgar, 1958). The latter state is one of compensated alkalosis, that is, the pH of the blood is normal, but the carbon dioxide tension is below 40.

The delay in achieving normal adult oxygen and carbon dioxide tensions is usually attributed to the continuation of shunting, which permits some blood to bypass the lungs, but imperfect adjustment between alveolar ventilation and perfusion of the pulmonary capillaries with blood probably is also a factor (Ledbetter, Homma, and Farhi, 1967). Probably the temporary rise in acidosis is a joint result of the loss of the placenta as a route for excreting hydrogen ions and the inability of the kidneys to handle the increased load (Assali and Morris, 1964). Respiratory adjustment to acidosis, that is, the exhalation of carbon dioxide, is rapid, but the metabolic response via the kidney is slower. A low plasma bicarbonate level is the primary characteristic of the compensated alkalosis that follows, and this, too, reflects the function of renal (kidney) and other ion transport mechanisms. Perhaps the rather slow-acting central chemoreceptors are as sensitive in the neonate as adult, but their homeostatic "set-point" for carbon dioxide is lower, like that of the pregnant female, because of depletion of the bicarbonate buffer system (Nelson, 1966). If the control mechanism were "set" differently, the ventilatory stimulus for exhalation of carbon dioxide would continue until the kidney and other ion transport mechanisms were able to conserve bicarbonate.

Because the blood loses its qualitative and quantitive fetal characteristics somewhat gradually, neonatal blood also has a higher oxygen saturation at a given tension than does adult blood. On the other hand, this aid to the oxygenation of tissues may in part be counteracted by the retention of another peculiarity of fetal blood—a low level of carbonic anhydrase (Smith, 1959). This enzyme catalyzes the conversion of carbonic acid to carbon dioxide and water, facilitating the transfer of carbon dioxide from tissue to blood and blood to lungs, and, indirectly the uptake of oxygen. However, the significance of the deficiency really is not known. Males have been reported to show a larger increase than females during adolescence in the blood levels of carbonic anhydrase (Lawrence, 1947). There is a rise in the alveolar and arterial carbon dioxide tensions of boys during adolescence (Shock, 1941), and the sex difference is maintained in adulthood (Shock and Hastings, 1935).

Sufficient cooperation and motivation can be secured from children beyond the preschool age to make timed and other special tests of pulmonary function. A number of investigators have tested maximal breathing capacity, the volume breathed during 15 seconds when the subject respires as deeply and rapidly as possible (Cassels and Morse, 1962; Ferris, Whittenberger, and Gallagher, 1952; Ferris and Smith, 1953; Kennedy, Thursby-Pelham, and Oldham, 1957; Moore, 1951), and flow rates, the rate of air flow adjusted to a standard respiratory rate (Chiang and Han, 1965; DeMuth, Howatt, and Hill, 1965; Heaf and Gillam, 1962; Kennedy et al., 1957; Lyons, Tanner, and Picco, 1960; Murray and Cook, 1963; Nairn, Bennet, Andrew, and MacArthur, 1961; Strang, 1959). In general it can be said that these measures follow the same developmental pattern as vital capacity, increasing steadily with age and size until puberty. Then a steeper increment occurs, particularly in boys, for whom the increases are greater than would be predicted from physical growth alone. Factor analyses by varimax rotation yield an axis that involves vital capacity, functional residual capacity, diffusing capacity, thoracic cage size, and to some degree peak expiratory flow rate (DeMuth et al., 1965). A second axis is highly related to various measures of flow rate.

Age trends after adjustment for size have been examined only for maximum breathing capacity. Allowing for surface area, there is still an increase from 10 to 20 years in both sexes. Many sex differences observed when measures are related to body size disappear when vital capacity is used as the referent (DeMuth, 1965). Longitudinal studies show the relative standing of individuals on various lung volumes and other measures to be consistent across time (DeMuth et al., 1965).

Neither timed vital capacity nor the flow rate at the point at which half the vital capacity has been expired follow the general growth pattern. The trend for the latter measure is like that for airway conductance, the reciprocal of airway resistance (DeMuth et al., 1965). In contrast to their performance on all other tests, children aged 6 to 14 deliver a higher proportion of their vital capacity in 1 second (timed vital capacity) than do adults (Lyons et al., 1960).

METABOLISM

In its most general sense metabolism (derived from a Greek word meaning alter, change, or turn about) encompasses all the physical and chemical processes by which food is converted into energy, new tissue, and wastes. Thus construed the term includes respiration, digestion, absorption, catabolism (the breakdown of ingested or stored substances into simpler compounds), anabolism (synthesis of more complex compounds from simpler ones), energy transformations, secretion, and excretion. Usually, however, metabolism is defined more specifically as the chemical transformations occurring between absorption (the uptake of nutrients from the digestive tract into the blood) and elimination. External respiration, digestion, and elimination involve physical as well as chemical action.

Metabolic reactions have two aspects that may be, and typically are, studied separately. Biochemists analyze the series of changes which newly absorbed or stored nutrients undergo as they are completely catabolized to wastes (largely carbon dioxide and water) or through which by-products of catabolism are recombined for storage or the repair or creation of cells (anabolism). Individually these intricate sequences are referred to as fat metabolism, protein metabolism, and carbohydrate metabolism. Collectively they are known as intermediary metabolism. As noted earlier, internal respiration is involved, for all but a few limited metabolic reactions require the presence of oxygen at some point and carbon dioxide is one of the end-products of most. The major "wastes" of intermediary metabolism are important factors in the regulation of fluid and acid-base balances, resspiration, and the maintenance of body temperature. However, developmental variations in metabolism are of a quantitative rather than a qualitative nature, hence there is no need to consider intermediary metabolism any further here.

Energy transformations, the other aspect of metabolism, are the source of power for all physiological processes. The form in which energy is expended in a particular process may be chemical, electrical, thermal, or mechanical, but it is originally derived from the chemical energy liberated when food is oxidized. At each step in the breakdown of food a small amount of chemical energy is released. Some of this energy is used immediately to fuel ongoing bodily functions. Any excess is dissipated as heat or stored in the fats, proteins, and carbohydrates or special energy-rich phosphate compounds synthesized by the body. If the intake of food is insufficient to supply the energy needed to perform work and maintain body temperature, stored energy is used.

Because energy can be neither created nor destroyed, only transformed, the energy released from ingested food = work energy + heat energy ± stored chemical energy (energy balance equation). In principle, the metabolic rate (amount of energy transformed per unit time) can be determined by measuring the terms on either side of this equation, but in practice problems arise. The heat produced when a given weight of a particular food is completely oxidized outside the body is calculated from the increase in temperature of a known volume of water caused by burning the sample in a metal chamber (bomb calorimeter) filled with oxygen and immersed in the water. Although fats and carbohydrates yield as much energy when catabolized as they do in the calorimeter, proteins are incompletely oxidized in the body and do not. Further, determining the quantities and qualities of food eaten is a time-consuming process for both subject and experimenter.

Among the variables that affect energy output and its distribution as work, heat, or chemical stores are size, age, sex, environmental and body temperatures, activity, secretion of thyroid hormone and epinephrine, and emotional stress (via muscular tension and increased production of epinephrine). To simplify the calculations of metabolic rate, energy production is measured under circumstances designed to eliminate some sources of variation. The subject should be reclining, physically and mentally relaxed, in the postabsorptive or fasting state (i.e., 12 to 14 hours after eating) in an environment of known and constant temperature following 30 to 60 minutes of horizontal rest. These so-called basal conditions, already mentioned in the sections on heart rate and blood pressure were originally defined for determining metabolic rate because it is so easily altered. Values obtained in this situation are not as low as they are during sleep, when, in addition to being in the postabsorptive state, the subject is more relaxed.

Under fasting conditions energy storage, which is difficult to assess, is eliminated or negative. All energy used for work is eventually converted to heat, thus with the storage component removed, all of the energy output of the body appears as heat. This heat production may be measured directly in a large calorimeter or indirectly by measuring oxygen consumption or the end products of metabolism (carbon dioxide, water, and protein residues such as urea).

Either direct calorimetry or measuring the end products of metabolism is tedious and requires equipment usually available only in specialized laboratories. By contrast, oxygen consumption can be determined fairly easily. Under basal conditions oxygen consumption is set by immediate need, for no oxygen debt is being repaid or incurred, and oxygen is never stored. Therefore the oxygen used in a given period of time directly reflects the amount of energy released.

Techniques for measuring oxygen consumption fall into two classes—open-circuit methods and closed-circuit or spirometric methods. In the former the subject breathes atmospheric air through one tube and exhales into another from which the expired air is collected for analysis of its composition. The spirometer has already been described (see Respiration). Adaptations, similar to those for studying lung volumes, are necessary for infants. These include low dead-space masks (Pribylová and Znamenáček, 1966), hoods (Karlberg, 1952; Mestyán, Jarái, Bata, and Fekete, 1964; Oliver and Karlberg, 1963), and small chambers (Adamsons, Gandy, and James, 1965; Hill and Rahimtulla, 1965; Levison and Swyer, 1964; Stern, Lees, and Leduc, 1965) much like a total body plethysmograph (see Respiration).

Basal metabolic rates obtained in these ways may be expressed simply as oxygen consumption per unit time. More frequently oxygen consumption is converted to an estimate of heat production by multiplying by a constant representing the caloric value of oxygen for an ordinary mixed diet. For very young infants the current trend is not to convert to Calories (see Table 9) because the assumptions made in doing so may not be fulfilled (James and Adamsons, 1964).

Despite a rather voluminous literature extending over more than a century (see reviews in Benedict and Talbot, 1921; Karlberg, 1952; Sargent, 1961; Shock, 1966; Tanner, 1962), considerable disagreement still exists on appropriate standards for basal metabolic rate, especially for infants and young children.

The controversy centers around referents, that is, whether values should be expressed in terms of surface area, weight, or height, muscle mass, etc., and whether age standards should also be used. Even when expressed in the same terms, however, the averages obtained by different investigators for a given age or size often vary more than those for adjacent age or size groups within a single study. The variations arise primarily from sample differences in body size and adequacy of nutrition and from methodological differences, not only in instrument but in many other variables such as time of day, number and length of tests, time since eating, preliminary rest and adaptation periods, and whether average values or lowest values were reported. Absolute differences notwithstanding, the trends observed in different studies are consistent in their major characteristics (see Table 9 and Fig. 5). On the basis of weight or surface area, basal metabolic rate begins to increase very soon after birth, reaches a peak sometime in the first year, and remains at this level until the second or third year when a decline begins which continues over the rest of the life span.

Table 9. Energy Metabolism in the Perinatal Period

Age	Pribylová and Znamenáček, 1966 O_2 Consumption (in ml./kg./min.) at Environmental Temperatures of:		Age	Brück, 1961 Heat Production (in kcal./kg./hr.) at Ambient Temperatures of:		
	33°C	23°C		32-34°C	28°C	23°C
5 mins.	3.79	5.10	0–6 hrs.	1.43	1.96	2.98
15	4.58	6.88	2–3 days	1.58	2.92	3.57
30	4.54	7.24	4–6 days	1.58	3.74	—
45	4.92	6.71	7–9 days	1.53	3.62	4.12
1 hr.	5.10	6.42				
2	4.94	6.14				
3	4.71	6.64				

Age	Hill and Rahimtulla, 1965, O_2 Consumption (ml./kg./min.)	Age	Levison and Swyer, 1964, O_2 Consumption (ml./kg./min.)
0–6 hrs.	4.76	0–12 hrs.	5.3
18–30 hrs.	6.59	2–3 days	5.3
2–4 days	6.70	4–5	5.5
6–10 days	7.02	6–8	5.7
		9–14	5.8

In the latest edition of Smith's *Physiology of the Newborn Infant* (1959) the averages reported by Benedict and Talbot in their classic monograph on the metabolism of the newborn infant (1915) are cited as similar to those obtained by subsequent investigators. Compared to the adult figure of 1.00 Cal./kg./hr., the heat production of the full-term newborn was found to be high, 1.75 Cal./kg./hr. (Benedict and Talbot, 1915) to 2.00 (Marsh and Murlin, 1925), or an oxygen consumption of 6.2 ml./kg./min. (Cross, Tizard and Trythall, 1957) to 6.6 (Benedict and Talbot, 1915). When referred to surface area it was lower—29.16 Cal./sq.m./hr. for the newborn and 35-50 for the adult (Marsh and Murlin, 1925)—as would be expected from the adult-infant contrast in amount of surface area per unit weight (see p. 28).

By an interesting coincidence, the most recent reference in Smith's (1959) review, a 1958 paper by Cross, Tizard, and Trythall, precipitated a series of studies which led to a revision of these estimates of neonatal metabolic rate and to a better understanding of the control of heat production and other aspects of temperature regulation (see Body Temperature). They reported that the oxygen consumption of newborns decreased when breathing an air mixture so mildly hypoxic as to have no effect on adult man or animals. Research with animals was first undertaken in an attempt to understand this unusual result (see reviews in Adamsons, 1966, and Oliver, 1965). A similar response was observed in newborn animals only in a cool environment. Later this finding was confirmed for the human infant (Oliver and Karlberg, 1963). After further exploration it was concluded that the neutral thermal environment (environment in which the basal metabolic rate is minimal) for the newborn of homeothermic (warm-blooded) species is warmer than for the adult and declines fairly rapidly with age (see review in Mount, 1966). First Brück (1961) and then others (Adamsons et al., 1965; Hill and Rahimtulla, 1965; Oliver and Karlberg, 1963) demonstrated a comparable phenomenon in man. Except for Day's (1943) work with premature infants, the influence of thermal variables had previously been overlooked.

As can be seen in Table 9, these recent studies place the minimal metabolic rate at birth at about 4.6 to 4.8 ml. oxygen/kg./hr., a value that is only about 33% rather than 200% greater than that of the adult. Also of interest is the fact that this level is in the range of the 4-5 ml./kg./hr. estimated for the fetus late in gestation (see reviews in Adamsons, 1966; Nesbitt, 1966; Romney, 1966). Like their predecessors, most contemporary investigators find not only an increase in rate during the first day but also further increments in the next few days or weeks, although the timing and extent of the gains are not the same from study to study.

Both in terms of their nature and the ways in which they are presented, the most definitive data on metabolic rate during infancy and early childhood are those from the longitudinal studies at the Child Research Council in Denver, Colorado (Lee and Iliff, 1956; Lewis, Duval, and Iliff, 1943). The population studied is the same as that from which the EKG, heart rate, and respiratory rate data summarized in previous sections were secured. One virtue of these data can be seen in Fig. 5—the overlapping of basal with sleeping, postprandial measures. Except for Karlberg (1952), who examined young infants 4 to 6 hours after a meal and older ones after 12 to 14 hours, most investigators have accepted the conclusion of Benedict and Talbot (1921) that restlessness accompanying hunger causes a greater increase in metabolism than does digestion and have not attempted to approximate basal conditions with children. Lee and Iliff provide systematic data on this point. In the age range at which both types of determinations were made—21 to 36 months—values obtained while the child was awake and fasting were 3 to 9% higher than in the sleeping, postprandial state. Further, measures taken on infants in the latter state were reliable and reproducible. Their variability compared favorably with that for basal determinations in older children and did not differ for tests made between ½ and 3½ hours after feeding.

Another strong point of the papers of Iliff and her associates is that results are referred to several different standards, permitting comparisons among referents within each study as well as with trends and absolute values from other laboratories. Only central line

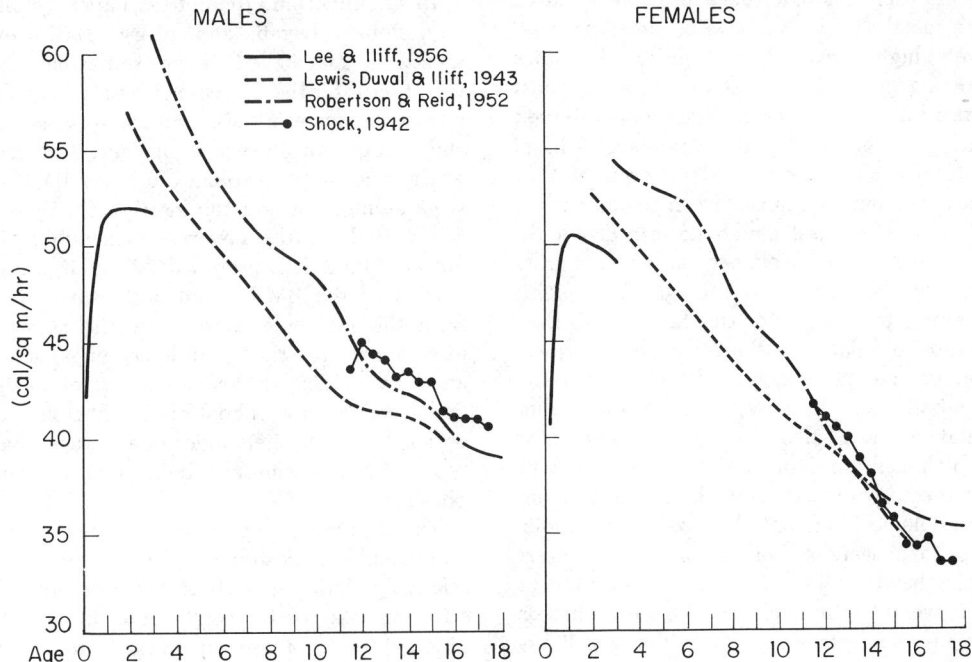

Fig. 5.   Age trends in energy metabolism (cal./sq.m./hr.). *(a)* Males. *(b)* Females.

values plotted from the means for Calories per unit surface area for age are incorporated in Fig. 5. However, the tables and graphs of Lee and Iliff (1956) show that on the basis of either Cal./sq.m./hr. or Cal./cm./hr., metabolic rate rises rapidly to 8 months, the surface area values then remaining constant until 24 months in girls and perhaps as late as 36 months in boys. Calories per unit height continue to increase gradually through age 3. Essentially no change is observed from 1 through 36 months in Cal./kg./hr. Discussion of hypotheses about the factors responsible for these patterns and the increment immediately after birth will be postponed until adolescent changes have been described.

The primary questions for the adolescent period are whether or not there is a reversal in the decline in basal metabolic rate that begins in early childhood, the issue of "physiologic instability," and sex differences. Detailed references bearing on the following conclusions can be found in Sargent (1961), Shock (1966), and Tanner (1962). All possible variations in both mean and individual curves at puberty have been reported, that is, increases, decreases, and no change. Of

course, no change or a slowing in the rate of decline is consistent with the notion of a "prepubertal reaction" first proposed by Du-Bois (1927). Taking the balance among studies and putting particular emphasis on those in which basal metabolism could be related to indicators of puberty, such as menarche or maximum growth in height (Eichorn, 1955; Shock, 1943), there does appear to be a prepubertal slowing of the deceleration in metabolic rate coincident with the growth spurt (see also Sargent, 1961), followed by a steeper decrement. Despite reports of fluctuations in individual curves during adolescence, the only systematic analysis of intraindividual variability during this period (Eichorn and McKee, 1958) offers no support for the advent of increased instability. Perhaps the fluctuations sometimes observed are artifacts resulting from variations in weight, which affect either weight or surface area standards, or from the fact that random errors are no longer masked by more sizable age changes.

When either surface area or height standards are used, sex differences exist across the entire age span beyond one month according to the Colorado data previously cited. The metabolic rate of boys becomes progressively higher than that of girls, all studies showing marked differences in adolescents and adults. Sex differences are not observed during infancy and early childhood if basal metabolic rate is computed in terms of Calories per unit weight. The increase in sex differences in basal metabolic rate at adolescence cannot be explained simply by gross size, that is, surface area, height, or weight. Attempts to account for this fact are, as they should be, related to the more general question of the basic factors determining basal metabolic rate. Because muscle has a higher metabolic rate than fat, lean body mass (which can be estimated in several ways) has been proposed as a better and more "physiologic" referent for basal metabolic rate than weight, height, or surface area. Males have a relatively higher proportion of their weight in muscle than females, whereas the inverse is true for fat. Although differences in muscle mass do account for part of the differences both between the sexes and within sex and size groups, they do not seem to be the complete explanation (Garn and Clark, 1953; Garn, Clark, and Portray, 1953; Tanner, 1962). Hormonal factors are another obvious possibility, particularly as adolescence is approached. There is some evidence that basal metabolic rate is correlated with ketosteroid production in boys but not in girls (Clark and Garn, 1953).

Several variables used to estimate lean body mass (fat-free body weight, body weight minus extracellular fluid, and body weight minus both extracellular fluid and fat) as well as more widely used standards such as surface area and body weight have recently been compared as referents for neonatal metabolic rate (Sinclair, Scopes, and Silverman, 1967). Only weight minus extracellular fluid met the mathematical criteria (Tanner, 1949) for a ratio standard. Many investigators have contrasted the relative merits of height, weight, and surface area as standards with varying results. For example, Lee and Iliff (1956) find the largest number of cases within ±15% of the mean using surface area as the referent. According to Sargent's (1961) analyses, however, surface area does not correct sufficiently for differences in physical size, and weight for height is the best standard.

In an important theoretical paper (Holliday, Potter, Jarrah, and Bearg, 1967) evidence is marshalled for a somewhat different basis for the decrease of basal metabolic rate with increasing size both across species and ontogenetically within species. Two factors are needed to explain the lower BMR of large animals, but for the most part, only one is required for the lower rate in adults. In both instances it is proposed that a large proportion of the BMR of an organism derives from the metabolic activity of the primary internal organs—the brain, liver, lungs, heart, and kidney. This approach is a variant on the tissue composition school of thought, in that organs of high metabolic rate rather than types of tissue (muscle, bone, fat) are emphasized.

The decrease in basal heat production per unit weight is postulated to stem from the relatively slower growth of these organs relative to total body weight. Put in slightly different terms, these vital organs must develop rapidly during gestation and early infancy to support life; they constitute a larger proportion of body weight at these times. With increasing age a progressively larger part of growth occurs in other organs and tissues, for example, fat and muscle. To account for species differences a decrease in organ metabolic rate with body size is also assumed. Within a species, however, no decrease during growth in the metabolic activity of the vital organs is posited after early infancy (say the first half year or so in man). Evidence for an increase during this period comes not only from the rise in total basal metabolic rate, but also from studies indicating increased activity of the kidney (Holliday et al., 1967) and brain (Kerpel-Fronius, Varga, and Mestyán, 1961). It should be noted in passing that a low rate of cerebral metabolism has been suggested as one reason that the fetus and newborn infant are more resistant to anoxia than older persons (Kerpel-Fronius et al., 1961).

Dawes lists other changes that would make for an increase in oxygen consumption during early infancy: adaptation to an environment cooler than the intrauterine one, the work required for respiration, increased gastrointestinal activity after feeding begins, improved muscular tonus, and the increased muscular work required to oppose gravity in a gaseous as contrasted to a fluid medium. Although muscular activity is responsible for only a small proportion of the BMR in either the basal or postprandial state (Holliday et al., 1967), this factor and perhaps others, such as hormonal levels, could account for the residual variance. That is, these variables may be the fine adjustments imposed upon the more major one of organ metabolism.

Of course, a person's food intake must include enough calories to cover the energy cost not only of this basal metabolic rate but also of the factors that are eliminated or minimized in the basal state—activity, growth (storage), specific dynamic action of food (S.D.A., the energy cost of digestion and assimilation), and loss in excreta. Like the BMR, these variables are influenced by age, size, and sex and other individual characteristics such as endocrine function. The absolute number of calories needed daily for each of these categories, particularly activity, increases from birth through the cessation of growth, then drops. After remaining relatively constant during young adulthood, caloric needs decline further in middle and old age.

In computing the allowance for activity, nutritionists take into account the increased energy demand that activity makes on vital activities, for example, respiration and circulation, as well as the cost of muscular movements. Even for adults, some allowance must be made for growth, because the need for repair and replacement of cells continues. The composition of the diet affects both S.D.A. and the caloric loss in excreta. For example, the S.D.A. of proteins is much higher than that of fats and carbohydrates.

None of the specific nutrients (vitamins, minerals, protein, etc.) that have been shown to be essential in the human diet are age, size, or sex specific in a qualitative sense. Instead, the variations in requirements are quantitative (National Academy of Sciences, 1958). Certain deficiencies are more common in particular age or sex groups either because of relatively higher requirements or the nature of the typical diet. Iron deficiency, probably the most common of nutritional deficiencies, is illustrative of both causes. Infants, children, adolescents, and adolescent and adult females have a relatively greater need for iron than do adult males. Milk, the primary constituent of the young infant's diet, is a poor source of iron.

BODY TEMPERATURE

The temperatures of different regions of the body and the extent of the range among them varies with environmental and physiological conditions. However, animals that are homeothermic ("warm-blooded") must keep their core temperature—the temperature of internal tissues and the central nervous system—within quite narrow limits if life is to be maintained. "Under normal conditions thermal constancy exceeds that of other variables defining the internal environment" (Adamsons, 1966, p. 599).

Tight controls are assumed to be necessary because the rate of all chemical reactions, especially those catalyzed by enzymes, is much influenced by temperature. Many vital processes are brought about by chemical reactions, but without enzymes most of these reactions would take place so slowly that they would be completely ineffective. For example, almost all the thousands of steps in intermediary metabolism are accelerated by enzymes. The optimal temperature range for the operation of enzymes is very small. Below this range reactions become progressively slower, and above it they occur with increasing rapidity until a point is reached at either extreme at which the enzyme in question is inactivated. Tissues with a high basal metabolic rate, such as the brain, are less tolerant of temperature change than are less active ones, such as the skin. In this connection, the convulsions and delirium accompanying high fever immediately come to mind.

Body temperature reflects the balance between heat production and the heat lost through radiation, convection, conduction, and evaporation. Radiation is the transfer of heat in the form of electromagnetic waves between objects that are not in contact. Because radiation takes place from and to the surface of the body, the variables involved in such loss or gain of heat are the effective radiating area exposed (which can be altered by changes in position and the amount and type of clothing), the average surface temperature of the body, the mean radiant temperature of objects in the environment, and the emissivities of the skin and object surfaces.

For convection—the exchange of heat through the movement of molecules in a fluid or gas—the important factors are the temperatures of the skin and of the air or fluid, the effective convective area of the body, and air flow. Within the body, heat moves from the core to the surface by convection through the blood stream and the upper respiratory tract. In the former case, of course, blood is warmed, and in the latter, air is. Comparatively little heat is lost from the surface of the body by convection unless air is moving. However, convection promotes conduction, the transfer of heat from an object to those it is touching in proportion to the temperature difference between them. Again, human beings usually lose little heat this way, but some is conducted through the tissues, and some is lost in warming ingested fluids and food. If the body is immersed in water, considerable conductive loss occurs.

Even when an organism is neither panting nor sweating, some heat is constantly lost through vaporization of water from the lungs and skin. The magnitude of the evaporative loss depends upon the rate of alveolar ventilation, the amount of sweating, skin temperature, and the humidity and movement of air. Water continuously diffuses through the skin (insensible perspiration) and is evaporated, removing heat from the body surface. At high temperatures sweating is prominent in man and panting in lower animals.

Automatic protection in a cold environment is offered by insulation (fat and hair), circulatory adjustments (cutaneous vasoconstriction and shifts in limb blood flow), and increased heat production. Although human beings have little hair and do not benefit much from its erection in cold, they can add to their insulation with clothing. In all homeotherms stability of the core temperature is accomplished at the expense of the periphery. Constriction of the blood vessels in the skin reduces the amount of heat carried to the surface. As a result, temperature at the periphery is lowered, the gradient between surface and environment decreases, and less heat is lost. Cooling is particularly noticeable in the limbs, which account for a large proportion of surface area. In the adult, for example, the hands and feet make up about 15% of the total surface area, yet the heat lost from

them can be reduced by vasoconstriction to 2% of the total loss.

Below a given temperature (25° C in the nude adult male), vasoconstriction is maximal, so cold must be counteracted by increasing heat production. Metabolic rate can be raised by shivering or through voluntary or semivoluntary movements. Shivering is the more effective mechanism, because no heat is wasted in doing work or by increased exposure of the skin. Nonshivering thermogenesis, brought about by increased secretion of certain hormones, is thought not to be an important source of heat production in the adult. As we shall see, peculiarities of the newborn may make this variable more effective. Whatever the cause of increased heat production, more fuel is required. If the intake is not increased, body stores are used.

When a homeotherm is in a warm environment very little adjustment can be achieved by lowering the metabolic rate, despite the common adult reaction "it's too hot to move or eat." Often infants become restless when too warm and thereby increase their heat production. The major facts, however, are that a minimal metabolic rate is needed to supply energy for vital functions and that above a critical temperature the rate of biochemical reactions, and hence heat production, increases progressively with environmental temperature. Again, circulatory adjustments are the first line of defense. Blood flow to the surface and through the extremities is increased. But in heat, too, there is a maximum temperature beyond which changes in circulation are inadequate (34° C in adult man). Sufficient heat cannot be dissipated because the temperature gradient between the skin and the surroundings is so far reduced or even negative. At this point evaporative loss via sweating must occur. If the organism is working, the temperature at which sweating begins is lower.

A neutral thermal environment is one in which core temperature remains within the normal range while oxygen consumption is minimal. From the preceding description of variables influencing heat loss, it is clear that this set of thermal conditions includes not only air temperature but also such variables as the temperature of objects in the environment, air flow, and relative humidity. The characteristic core temperature of homeotherms differs from species to species, with age within a species, and to a slight degree among adults within a species. So also do the level and range of the neutral thermal environment, a fact which came to be recognized in the course of recent research, particularly with the newborn, causing a change in the definition of homeothermy. No longer is maintenance of a constant body temperature over a wide range of environmental conditions the crux of the definition. Rather, the distinguishing characteristic of homeotherms is that in the event of heat loss exceeding heat production, responses occur that lead to the conservation of heat, and, when needed, an increase in metabolic rate.

Reflex reactions directed toward maintaining thermal stability are integrated by two perhaps not completely independent hypothalamic centers, one in the posterior hypothalamus controlling responses to cold and one in the anterior hypothalamus for reactions to heat. Input to these centers comes from central receptors within the anterior hypothalamus and from temperature receptors in the skin. Because the degree of hypothalamic cooling required to activate strong reactions is greater than that typical on exposure to cold, cutaneous receptors are thought to play the major role in stimulating the defense mechanisms against a decline in body temperature. In contrast, central receptors apparently provide the primary stimulus for response to heat. The latency of sweating is long, and sweating seems to be more highly correlated with brain temperature than with skin temperature. Efferent impulses activating reactions to heat and cold are mediated by the sympathetic nervous system. Within the hypothalamic centers catecholamines may serve as synaptic mediators, serotonin for the cold center and norepinephrine for the heat center.

According to the old definition of a homeotherm given earlier, the newborn human infant was considered poikilothermic (cold-blooded). By the new one, he is a homeotherm, albeit a less adequate one than his parents. Contrary to frequent assertions, his difficulties do not arise from immaturity of the neural regulatory mechanisms, for within 15 minutes of birth premature as well as full-term infants respond to cooling by vasoconstriction and a marked increase in heat production

(Adams, Fugiwara, Spears, and Hodgman, 1964; Adamsons, Gandy, and James, 1965; Brück, 1961; Přibylová and Znamenáček, 1966). There is speculation that the low arterial oxygen tension consequent upon labor and delivery would probably make it impossible for the newborn to increase his heat production immediately (Adamsons et al., 1965; Oliver, 1965).

At least by the age of 2 to 3 hours the metabolic response to cold is as good as that of the adult on the basis of body weight (Adamsons et al., 1965; Brück, 1961; Hill and Rahimtulla, 1965). The magnitude of this reaction is particularly surprising in view of the fact that human infants ordinarily receive little or no food during the first 1 or 2 days of postnatal existence.

On exposure to heat premature and full-term infants also show a vasomotor response, vasodilation (Adams, Fujiwara, Spears, and Hodgman, 1964; Brück, 1961; Young and Cottom, 1966), on the first day, although as noted earlier (see Circulation) it may not be as good as it is a few days later. Panting respiration has been noted in the premature (Adams et al., 1964). Unlike previous investigators (see review in Lipton, Steinschneider, and Richmond, 1965), Brück (1961) produced some sweating in full-term infants on their first day. He did not attempt to test the response of premature infants to high temperatures. Others (Adams et al., 1964; Day, Caliguiri, Kamenski, and Ehrlich, 1964) have since reported the sweating response to be poor, especially in the premature infant, but the problem seems to lie more in the glands themselves (Watson and Lowrey, 1967) than in their control.

In dealing with cold, the neonate is also handicapped primarily by physical characteristics, in this case, small size, a large surface area to mass ratio, and poor insulation (Adamsons, 1966; Hill, 1961; Mount, 1966; Oliver, 1965). Insulation, surface area, and the temperature gradient between the skin surface and the surroundings determine the rate of heat loss from the body. The lower limit of thermal conditions at which a homeotherm can maintain his core temperature is set by his maximal metabolic response to cold and his minimal effective thermal conductance. Thermal conductance is the difference between core and skin temperatures and varies with insulation, the surface area-mass ratio, and vasomotor control. Only with respect to the last factor is the newborn in as favorable a position as the adult.

Because the neonate's layer of subcutaneous fat is thinner, his thermal conductance is greater. Therefore his skin temperature is higher relative to the surroundings and he loses more heat. At resting levels his metabolic rate per unit surface area is lower than the adult's, and his metabolic reaction to cold, although comparable on a weight basis, is poorer relative to surface area. Thus the point at which heat production can no longer match heat loss is reached sooner. These physical factors combine to produce a heat loss about four times greater than that of the adult (Brück, 1961).

Given such limitations, the neonate would be expected to need a neutral thermal environment higher in temperature and narrower in range than does the adult. Other conditions (e.g., humidity, approximation of environmental temperature to that of radiant surfaces) being equal, the neutral thermal environment for the adult is 26 to 31° C (see review in Oliver, 1965), whereas that of full-term neonates is at least 32-34° C (Brück, 1961; Oliver and Karlberg, 1963; Scopes, 1966). Conditions in these studies may have reduced losses through radiation (Oliver,

1965). Hill and Rahimtulla (1965) report an even higher critical temperature—36°C—on the first day (below the critical temperature metabolic rate begins to rise). Critical temperature declined to 32° C at 7-9 days, but thermal conductance did not change. Scopes (1966) also found a decrease during the first 2 weeks, the critical temperature reaching 29-30° C at 14 days.

Almost all of the observations thus far cited were made on naked infants, and the generalizations from them must be so qualified. The ancient practice of wrapping the babe in swaddling clothes may hamper modern nursing care and experimental observations, but it materially reduces all possible heat losses. Whether swaddling per se makes any difference in the patterns observed may be questioned on the basis of comparable findings with respect to postnatal trends in rectal temperature from both older studies of swaddled infants (see summary in Smith, 1959) and more recent work with naked ones (see Table 10).

In only one study—one in which the infants were delivered into warm wrappings and placed in a preheated incubator (Přibylová and Znamenáček, 1966)—has the rather dramatic immediate postnatal drop in internal temperature been completely eliminated. Several variables confounded in this treatment

Table 10. Perinatal Body Temperatures

	Přibylová and Znamenáček (1966) Mean rectal temperature (°C) at environmental temperatures (°C) of:	
	33°	23°
Birth	37.44	37.40
15 mins.	37.16	36.33
30 mins.	37.13	35.95
45 mins.	37.19	35.40
1 hr.	37.24	35.20
2 hr.	37.35	35.10
3 hr.	37.33	35.13

		Fisher, Odie, and Makoski (1966) Temperature range (°C):		
		Ambient	Rectal	Skin
0–4 hours	Incubated	23.0–28.8	32.3–36.6	29.0–35.4
	Nonincubated	32.0–40.0	36.6–39.2	35.5–37.7
4–24 hours	Incubated	23.3–29.0	31.9–37.4	32.5–36.6
	Nonincubated	31.0–40.0	36.6–38.1	35.5–37.7

are at least partially disentangled in research conducted by Miller and Oliver and summarized by Oliver (1965). To appreciate the point of their comparisons, a brief digression into the natural history of life in the contemporary delivery room and newborn nursery is in order.

Both theoretical calculations and actual measurements show the core temperature of the fetus at term to be about 0.5° C higher than that of the mother, and the skin temperature to be about 2.5° greater than postnatally (see review in Adamsons, 1966). From his liquid environment of about 37° C the fetus is born wet into a gaseous one that is invariably colder—delivery room temperatures are sometimes as low as 15° C, and at least in Great Britain, rarely over 28° C (Scopes, 1966). Until he dries or is dried, considerable heat will be lost through evaporation as well as by other routes, these losses being increased by the steep gradient between the temperatures of the skin and the surroundings. Current routine subjects him to at least one further wetting—a bath in the newborn nursery —and this may be preceded by one in the delivery room. Under these circumstances the drop in core temperature is so steep and rapid, and the accompanying heat loss so great, that a heat production per unit weight twice as great as the adult's would not offset it (Adamsons, 1966).

To the compound of natural and environmental hazards already described other environmental ones may then be added. Despite warm rooms or incubators, typical nursery arrangements make for a radiant heat loss far in excess of that usual for adults (see review in Oliver, 1965). That the full-term newborn's internal temperature begins to climb within 2-3 hours is certainly a triumph of homeothermy.

The experiment described by Oliver (1965) indicates that bathing and subsequent management do affect the postnatal pattern of change in rectal temperature. A group of infants bathed in both delivery room and nursery and otherwise routinely managed had a mean drop in temperature of 2.5° C. One in which only the nursery bath was omitted showed a decline of about 2°. Both groups took 8 hours to achieve a normal core temperature. On the other hand, infants wrapped

and blanketed and placed in an incubator lost only 1° of temperature and returned to normal within 3 hours.

Oliver (1965) also summarizes evidence for the importance of a controlled thermal environment in reducing neonatal mortality and discusses the applications of recent research to the management of both healthy and "high-risk" infants. Several investigators have examined the effect of body and environmental temperature on hormone, carbohydrate, and water metabolism and acid-base balance (Adamsons, 1966; Fisher, Odie, and Makoski, 1966; Přibylová and Znamenáček, 1966).

In the course of his monumental studies Brück (1961) made several observations about the mechanisms underlying the newborn infant's responses to cold that were subsequently confirmed and expanded by other investigators. First, he noticed that when infants who had been exposed to subneutral environmental temperatures were placed in a neutral thermal environment, their metabolic rate dropped promptly although their rectal temperatures were still low. This phenomenon suggested that the metabolic response to cold was activated by a lowering of skin rather than core temperature. Second, he noted increases in heat production not only following increased activity but also when the infants appeared to be neither moving nor shivering.

As yet there is no consensus on the influence of internal temperature. A significant association between rectal temperature and oxygen consumption has been observed by some workers and not by others (see reviews in Adamsons, 1966; and Scopes, 1966). On the other hand, the role of skin and environmental temperature, or more particularly the gradient between them, has been verified. Oxygen consumption is most highly correlated with the gradient between surface and environmental temperatures (Adamsons et al., 1965). When the gradient was less than 1.5° C oxygen consumption was minimal. Every degree of increment in the gradient beyond this level produced an increase in oxygen consumption of about 0.6 ml. Lower but significant correlations existed between oxygen consumption and absolute skin or environmental temperature. Simply varying facial temperature by either heating or cooling the foreheads of infants is enough to stimulate changes in oxygen consumption (Mestyán, Jarái, Bata, and Fekete, 1964).

Not all observers agree that the newborn infant shivers (Adamsons, 1966; Scopes, 1966; Thompson, 1964). However, the existence of nonshivering thermogenesis suggested by observations on human infants (Brück, 1961; Oliver and Karlberg, 1963) has been verified in lower animals using electromyograms (muscle potentials), denervation, and paralysis of muscles with drugs (see reviews in Oliver, 1966; Thompson, 1964). The idea that norepinephrine mediated this response was also revolutionary, but its thermogenic effect is now supported by work with human infants (Karlberg, Moore, and Oliver, 1965; Stern, Lees, and Leduc, 1965) and experimental tests in animals via injections and blocking agents (Moore and Underwood, 1960a, 1960b; Scopes and Tizard, 1963). Human adults, long known to have a thermo-

genic response to epinephrine, may also have one to norepinephrine, but if so, it is much less than that of the newborn (Budd and Warhaft, 1966; Joy, 1963; Steinberg, Nestel, Buskirk, and Thompson, 1964).

Converging lines of evidence pointed to brown fat as the locale of nonshivering thermogenesis in neonatal animals (Dawkins and Hull, 1963; Heim and Hull, 1966) and probably human beings (Aherne and Hull, 1966; Dawkins and Scopes, 1965; Silverman, Zamelis, Sinclair, and Agate, 1964). A review by Hull (1966) should be consulted for details on the structure and function of brown adipose tissue. Suffice it to say here that it is distinctive from white fat, is found in considerable amounts in newborn animals but soon atrophies, has a rich supply of blood and of sympathetic nerves, and responds to cold or infusion of norepinephrine with an increase in oxygen consumption and blood flow. In the human infant brown fat is found around

Table 11. Longitudinal Trends in Body Temperature

Study:	Bayley and Stolz (1937)		Iliff and Lee (1952)			Bayley and Stolz (1937)		Iliff and Lee (1952)		Eichorn and McKee (1953)	
Conditions:	Developmental Examination		Post Feeding and Sleeping BMR			Developmental Examination		Basal		Basal	
Measure:	Mean Rectal (°F)		Mean Rectal (°F)			Mean Oral (°F)		Mean Oral (°F)		Mean Oral (°F)	
	M	F	M	F	yrs.	M	F	M	F	M	F
1 mo.	98.97	98.96			3.5			98.7	98.7		
2	99.16	99.09			4.5			98.6	98.5		
3	99.42	99.35			5.5			98.5	98.5		
4	99.36	99.37			6.0	99.2	99.2				
5	99.37	99.40			6.5			98.4	98.5		
6	99.38	99.27	99.1	99.1	7.0	98.8	98.8				
7	99.88	99.58			7.5			98.3	98.4		
8	99.78	99.73			8.5			98.3	98.3		
9	99.88	99.48			9.5			98.1	98.2		
10	99.66	99.53			10.5			98.0	98.1		
11	99.67	99.49			11.5			98.0	98.0	97.9	98.0
12	99.95	99.49			12.0					97.9	97.9
13	99.70	99.70			12.5			97.8	97.9	97.9	97.8
14	99.70	99.59			13.0					97.8	97.9
15	99.86	99.40			13.5			97.7	97.9	97.9	98.0
18	99.95	99.70	99.1	99.1	14.0					97.7	98.0
21	99.84	99.32			14.5			97.6	97.9	97.8	97.9
24	99.73	99.58			15.0					97.6	98.0
27	99.60	99.50			15.5			97.4	97.9	97.6	98.0
30	99.62	99.17	99.0	98.8	16.0					97.5	97.9
3.0 yrs.	99.22	98.72			16.5			97.3	97.8	97.4	97.8
3.5			98.9	98.8	17.0					97.4	97.8
4.0					17.5			97.2	97.9	97.4	97.8

the neck, adrenal, and kidneys, behind the sternum, and between the shoulder blades (Aherne and Hull, 1966). These stores are reduced or depleted in infants dying from cold exposure (Aherne and Hull, 1966).

How long nonshivering thermogenesis continues to be important in heat production and temperature regulation has not been determined; studies on children with congenital heart disease suggest at least the first six postnatal months (Oliver, 1965). The longitudinal data presented in Table 11 indicate that the "set point" for basal body temperature is high during infancy and declines with age. Unlike the studies included in Table 10, all of these were conducted before thermocouples were available for insertion in the rectum or thermistors for attachment to the skin. However, either rectal or oral temperatures taken with a clinical thermometer under carefully controlled conditions parallel core temperature. Core temperature is slightly higher than the rectal temperature. If the thermometer is in the mouth for a sufficient length of time and the influence of such factors as mouth-breathing and intake of food or fluid is excluded, oral temperature parallels rectal but is 0.5 to 0.75° F higher.

The curvilinear trend in the temperature measures of Bayley and Stolz (1937), which are not basal, is quite similar to that noted in basal measures by Benedict and Talbot (1921). The fact that there is no difference in Iliff and Lee's means at 6 and 18 months hints at a comparable trend. Of the variables that Bayley and Stolz (1937) examined—crying, season, time of day, illness, and obesity—only the last showed any evidence of an association with body temperature. The correlations between rectal temperature and an index of body build were low but positive and significant. Among adolescents, Eichorn and McKee (1953) found a positive association between oral temperature and subcutaneous fat in girls and oral temperature and basal metabolic rate in boys. In their data the decline in temperature was reversed at menarche in girls and rose for about two years thereafter before resuming the decline. At what would be corresponding chronological ages, Iliff and Lee report simply a cessation of the decline.

Despite the diurnal variations noted by many investigators, within-day and day-to-day variations, notable in young children (Bayley and Stolz, 1937; Ludwig and Stolz, 1931), also decrease with age (Bayley and Stolz, 1937; Eichorn and McKee, 1958). These findings suggest that thermal stability continues to improve well beyond infancy.

NEUROPHYSIOLOGY

Perhaps this section should be called "Electroencephalography," for that is, with minor exceptions, the subject matter with which it deals. The selective emphasis is dictated not by the relative worth of the various types of data bearing upon the functional development of the nervous system but rather by the nature of the information available and the topical coverage elsewhere in this book. If value judgments had to be made, strictly behavioral studies would readily be conceded to have provided a larger amount of more immediately useful data not only for the psychologist and neurologist but also for the neurophysiologist. "Higher nervous activity," as the Russian psychologists and physiologists term it, is characterized by flexibility, interaction, and integration, all of which are reflected in adaptive, coordinated, attentive behaviors, and by modifiability, as evidenced in learning and memory. These behaviors constitute the theme of most of the other chapters.

Many insights into the development of normal and abnormal neural function have also been gained from the study of neuromuscular reflexes, such as the grasp, startle, and various withdrawal responses (Dekaban, 1959; Peiper, 1963). Similarly, some investigations of visceral (e.g., circulatory, glandular and gastrointestinal) activity have as their aim the evaluation of the integrity of the autonomic nervous system (Lipton, Steinschneider, and Richmond, 1965). In large measure such vital homeostatic processes are regulated by this division of the nervous system, and about the only way of assessing its function in the intact human being is to examine the rate of reaction and recovery and the degree of stability of these activities. With few exceptions, research on reflexive behavior and autonomic function set in the context of neural maturation has been conducted with young infants and hence is included in Chapter 5 (Infancy by William Kessen). Developmental changes in some of the processes subject to autonomic control, that is, heart rate, blood pressure, and sweating, have been considered in preceding sections of this chapter from the point of view of the physiology of the effector system. Too often the fact that a deficiency in function may result from the state of the effector system rather than from its innervation is ignored when a visceral response is used to evaluate the reactivity of the autonomic nervous system. A case in point—the relatively poor sweating response of neonates —was noted in the discussion of temperature regulation.

Our understanding of function is also broadened by the contributions of neuroanatomy and neurochemistry. Important aspects of the anatomical development of the nervous system are summarized in Chapter 3 (Physical Growth by J.M. Tanner). Chemical reactions underlie the action potentials of nerves, and transmission at most synapses is chemically mediated. During the past decade developmental patterns in the composition (lipid, protein, water, etc.), enzymic concentrations, and metabolism of the brain have become foci of research. To date, however, most of the work has been with lower animals, and measures on the living human being are particularly scarce (McIlwain, 1966). Except for the research on the electroretinogram reviewed in the chapter on perception (Chapter 10), the only systematic body of developmental data on the electrical activity of the human nervous system comes from the electroencephalogram.

Basis of the Electroencephalogram

If sufficiently amplified, the variations in potential produced by the electrochemical activity of the brain can be recorded from electrodes on the scalp. This tracing is called an electroencephalogram (EEG). One obtained from the surface of the exposed brain or from electrodes inserted into the cortex is also sometimes referred to as an EEG, but the term electrocorticogram (ECG) distinguishes these recordings from those made at the scalp. Although the tracing from a single pair of electrodes—one on the scalp and one elsewhere on the body (monopolar recording) or two on the scalp (bipolar recording)— technically constitutes an EEG, localization of the region of origin of potentials, comparisons among regions, and economy of time make a number of simultaneous recordings essential.

For many years the most widely accepted hypothesis about the origin of brain waves was that they resulted from the summation of action potentials generated in cortical cells and passed along their axons in the form of the classic all-or-none spike. This concept was challenged by several pieces of evidence (Brazier, 1961). Microelectrode recordings from individual cortical cells show no particular correspondence with the EEG. Further, the impedance (resistance to current flow) of the cerebral cortex is high, and the direct current flow from the inner layers is not strong enough to be detected at the scalp.

Today the EEG is thought to originate from current flow in the thousands of dendrites in the outer layers of the cortex. The physical characteristics of these layers and the nature of dendritic transmission are such that they should produce a pattern like that of the EEG. However, as has been shown by research with lower animals in which pathways to the cortex were stimulated or interrupted at various points, the surface activity is influenced by impulses from the lower levels of the specific sensory systems and the reticular activating system in the brain stem which are relayed via the nonspecific nuclei in the hypothalamus. For example, if a circular incision is made around a cortical area, synchronized electrical activity is not interrupted as long as the blood supply is not affected. Rhythmicity is decreased when the connections to deeper levels are cut.

Methodology

The EEG is being used with increasing frequency in behavioral studies, for example, studies of learning, sensory acuity and adaptation (habituation), stress, individual differences, and response to therapy. As is the case with all research, both the producers and consumers must be aware of the methodological pitfalls, for the value of any study is limited by the care with which the data were collected, and the results must be interpreted in terms of the methods used. These truisms apply with particular force to the fluctuations in potential differences recorded at the scalp. The very characteristic that makes these fluctuations of interest, namely, that they are readily produced by a variety of chemical, physiological, and psychological variables, means that the experimental conditions must be very carefully controlled. Further, the potentials are of such small magnitude that they are easily masked by larger voltages arising from internal and external sources, and the basic parameters on which evaluations are based—frequency, amplitude, and time relationships—are subject to distortion by the apparatus used for amplification and recording. Artifacts can also be mistaken for true "brain waves."

Space does not permit a comprehensive treatment of the many sources of interference and artifacts nor of the techniques for recognizing and coping with them. For greater detail on the electrophysiological characteristics of living tissue, the design and inherent limitations of instruments, and the ways in which distortion and artifacts can be detected and corrected, textbooks on electroencephalography such as those by Hill and Parr (1963) and Kiloh and Osselton (1961) and instrument manuals should be thoroughly studied. Ellingson (1967a, 1967b) gives good discussions of methodological issues, particularly in dealing with infants.

In certain respects the standard conditions for obtaining an electroencephalogram are diametrically opposed to those for basal metabolic rate and other measures thus far considered. Neither fasting nor a preceding period of protracted sleep is desirable. Fasting is contraindicated because at a blood sugar level of about 70 mg./100 cc. (fasting levels are 60-70) the brain waves become slower than normal, and their frequency is progressively reduced as the level falls further.

Sleep records are of both research and clinical interest, and natural sleep is preferable to that induced by drugs, particularly if the effects of sensory stimulation are to be studied. Although there are sedatives that do not ordinarily affect the EEG, idiosyncratic drug reactions are legion. Physical and mental relaxation are prerequisites for a normal "basal" record, that is, one taken while the subject is awake but resting. Light "blocks" the primary rhythm of the resting EEG, so the subject is instructed to keep his eyes closed. Infants will sometimes do so spontaneously, and until the age of 3 months or so it makes little difference whether they do or not.

For older children and adults, the International 10-20 System (Jasper, 1958) of electrode placement has been gaining widespread adoption. Nineteen electrodes are applied at well-defined locations on the scalp, and a "reference" electrode is attached to each ear lobe. This is too many electrodes for a small skull even if the subject's and experimenter's patience were adequate to the task of applying them. When electrodes are too close together the interelectrode resistance is increased and the amplitude of the potential differences is decreased. A radiographically based 16-electrode adaptation of the 10-20 system and simpler arrays (topographical location of electrodes on the head) have been used with infants (Hellström, Karlsson, and Müssbichler, 1963; Ellingson, 1967b). Aside from maintaining sufficient distances between electrodes, the primary criteria are adequate sampling of different regions of the brain and exact placements, preferably ones that can be described in terms of measured distances. The relative positions of external landmarks and the location of regions of the brain in terms of these are not the same in infants and adults.

The long-continued debate over the relative merits of monopolar and bipolar recording has never been resolved. Ellingson (1967b) makes some constructive suggestions in terms of the age of the subject. Because reference electrodes on the ear are not really "indifferent" but pick up activity from adjacent portions of the temporal lobe whenever the rhythms in this region are strong, as they are, for example, in premature infants, the EEG will be deceptively diffuse. On the other hand, a vertex reference lead is poor for sleep recording, for the same reason. During sleep the most salient activity in premature infants and neonates is in this area, and monopolar recordings will be both more diffuse and more synchronous than the underlying activity actually is.

Distinctive features of the EEG used in the analysis of both spontaneous and induced activity include frequency, amplitude, waveform, a number of aspects of temporal and spatial distribution—rhythmicity, continuity, differentiation among cerebral regions, symmetry or synchrony of homologous areas in the right and left hemispheres of the brain—and responsiveness to stimulation. Berger

(1929) labeled the 10 cycle per second waves predominant over the occipital region in the resting record of adults the "alpha rhythm." On the basis of further empirical observations, subsequent investigators divided the frequency spectrum of the EEG into several "bands" designated by Greek letters. Not all workers accept this convention, and the definitions used by those that do vary somewhat. The groupings currently in general usage are: delta, under 4 cps (cycles per second); theta, 4–7 cps; alpha, 8–13 cps; and beta, over 13 cps. Sometimes the beta band is restricted to frequencies of 14–25 sec. and faster ones are classed as gamma (Gibbs, 1944; Walter, 1963). In some studies done before the theta division was made, waves up through this range were classified as delta (Henry, 1944).

Ontogeny of the Waking EEG

From either a rational or pragmatic standpoint, normative data on the EEG may be organized under three rubrics: activity while awake but at rest, sleep patterns, and evoked responses. The waking, resting state serves as the standard or reference condition for the sequence of stages of sleep and as the context for most experimental manipulations, although the effects of sensory stimulation and certain other variables are also often examined during sleep.

Tracings from fetuses in utero and premature infants are considered first. The terms waking and sleeping cannot properly be applied to those obtained before 8 fetal months, however, for one of the major characteristics of the EEG before this age is the absence of a sleep-wakefulness cycle.

In most respects the problems of in utero electroencephalography and the techniques for coping with them are like those for in utero electrocardiography. Achieving an adequate signal-to-noise ratio is more difficult because the EEG potentials are of even smaller magnitude than those generated by the fetal heart. Only electrodes over abdominal areas near to the place where the fetal head can be felt will pick up the EEG, but a number of leads should be attached elsewhere to allow for movements of the head and to control for artifacts. Unless the tracing is reasonably similar to that of the newborn infant and differs from simultaneously recorded tracings at other abdominal sites, it probably is being produced by contractions of the uterus or abdominal muscles, the fetal or maternal EKG, fetal movements, or some combination of these potential sources.

While recording fetal EKGs at the end of the seventh and eighth months of his wife's first pregnancy, Lindsley (1942) noticed patterns in certain abdominal leads that could reasonably be interpreted as an EEG. He verified his impression by the methods just described and by comparing the tracings with a neonatal EEG from the same infant. In the prenatal record most of the waves had a frequency of 6–7/sec., but brief periods of faster activity were frequent. The postnatal tracing from the precentral (motor) region was almost identical. Some years after Lindsley's findings were published reports of intrauterine EEGs (Bernstine and Borkowski 1955), and of direct recordings from abortuses (Okamoto and Kirikae, 1951) and premature infants (Hughes, Davis, and Brennan, 1951) began to appear.[1]

Even with the accumulation of additional observations on fetuses in utero (Bernstine, 1961; Bernstine and Borkowski, 1956; Gianelli, Pavoni, and Scopetta, 1963; Huhmar and Järvinen, 1963) and abortuses (Aresin, 1962; Bernstine, 1961; Borkowski and Bernstine, 1955; Schwartze and Aresin, 1964) the circumstances of recording are such that the data are neither plentiful nor very informative. Except for one study in which intracerebral electrodes were used (Bergstrom and Bergstrom, 1963), intrauterine tracings have not been obtained until fairly late in gestation, and no localization is possible. A few fetuses have been examined before they were removed from the amniotic sac (Bergstrom and Bergstrom, 1963; Okamoto and Kirikae,

---

[1] Abortuses may be the product of either spontaneous or induced deliveries; the criteria for inclusion in this group are a weight of less than 500 grams (which corresponds to a fetal age of about 5½ months) and failure to survive. If a fetus weighs more than 500 grams at birth it is classed as premature whether or not it is viable. Extensive bibliographies and reviews of the methods and results of work with fetuses in utero, abortuses, and premature infants can be found in the interpretive summaries of Bernstine (1961), Dreyfus-Brisac (1964, 1966), and Ellingson (1967b),

1951), but no abortus can be assumed to be in a normal physiological state. EEGs from both types of sample may be simply and similarly described as composed of discontinuous, irregular slow waves (0.5–2/sec.) of low to moderate amplitude upon which a considerable amount of low voltage faster activity (as high as 40/sec.) is superimposed. Thus, in very general features these tracings resemble those from older viable premature infants (see below). The significance of studies on abortuses lies mainly in the demonstration that the human cortex is generating electrical potentials by at least the second fetal month (Bernstine, 1961; Schwartze and Aresin, 1964).

In contrast, a detailed account of the evolution of the EEG from the fifth month through term has been derived from the much larger literature on premature infants (Bernstine, 1961; Dreyfus-Brisac and Blanc, 1956; Dreyfus-Brisac, 1962, 1964, 1966; Ellingson, 1964a, 1964b, 1967b; Mai and Schaper, 1953; Palesi and Vannucchi, 1958, 1959; Polikanina, 1963). With minor exceptions (Dreyfus-Brisac, 1966; Dreyfus-Brisac, Flescher, and Plassart, 1962), the EEGs of premature infants surviving to a given age are like those of infants born at that age, so earlier tracings from the more premature probably reflect maturation in utero quite accurately. This inference is not applicable to records made on fetuses delivered in the fifth month nor to most born during the sixth, for they are likely to be anoxic, and few infants born under 7 months of age live very long. Also, individual variations in rate of development are considerable (Ellingson, 1967b). Some infants of less than average maturity may in the course of a week become relatively advanced while others remain generally retarded or advanced. Further complications are introduced by the fact that there are a number of ways of estimating fetal age (e.g., from the first or last day of the last menstrual period or from 2 weeks after the first day) and a term for each (e.g., gestational age or menstrual age), but the usage of these terms by different authors is not consistent. In the present discussion ages are based on a 9-month schema, because the average gestation period is 270 days.

Granting the reservations about viability, individual differences, and specificity of ages, a number of generalizations about the prenatal development of the EEG can be drawn from the work with premature infants. The features common to the period from 5 through 7 months are: discontinuity, occasional paroxysmal outbursts (sudden appearance of a series of potentials differing in frequency and/or amplitude from the prevailing activity), failure to react to stimulation, and absence of interhemispheric (bilateral) synchrony and of a sleep-waking cycle (Dreyfus-Brisac, 1962, 1964, 1966). On the other hand, many rapid changes can also be discerned during this time (Dreyfus-Brisac, 1962, 1964, 1966; Ellingson, 1964a, 1967b). In the fifth-month record, polymorphic rhythms appear in bursts, chiefly over the occipital areas, between periods of electrical silence lasting from a few seconds to a few minutes. Superimposed faster activity is seen in the occipital, occipitotemporal, and central regions. The tracing lacks organization and intrahemispheric or interhemispheric synchrony. Notable in the sixth month are a diminution of disorganization and polymorphism and an increase in theta activity and intrahemispheric synchrony. Throughout the seventh month discontinuity decreases progressively, especially in the occipital or occipitotemporal areas. This degree of localization, although built up over the preceding months, is peculiar to the seven-month EEG. Slow waves, mixed with the theta prevalent in the preceding month, predominate.

Several major transitions take place at eight months (Dreyfus-Brisac, 1962, 1964, 1966; Ellingson, 1964a, 1967b). First, a sleep-waking cycle, barely distinguishable near the end of the seventh month, is established, and diffuse reactions to sensory stimuli occur during sleep. These phenomena are discussed in the appropriate sections that follow. Second, bilateral symmetry begins to emerge, initially in the central areas and thereafter in the frontals. Third, activity is now continuous in the waking state, but it is less rhythmic than at 7 months. Some delta and a small amount of alpha and beta activity are present. However, theta frequencies become prevalent again. Finally, the occipital predominance disappears from the waking record, so the topographical pattern is once more diffuse. During the ninth month the only modification is in the sleep sequence. Indeed, from 8 months through at least the first month after term the waking record remains essentially unchanged (Dreyfus-Brisac, 1966; Ellingson, 1967b).

Why regularity and localization give way to seemingly less mature patterns is not known. Perhaps the apparent regression reflects the emergence of cortical function. A subcortical origin has been hypothesized for EEG activity at earlier stages (Dreyfus-Brisac, 1962, 1966; Ellingson, 1964a, 1967b). More specifically, Ellingson (1964a, 1967b) speculates that the occipitotemporal predominance of activity may indicate origin in the limbic system (a complex system involving parts of the "old brain"). Because she observed potentials primarily in association with body movements, Samson-Dollfus (1955) made the further suggestion that the activity is evoked rather than spontaneous. In any event, the inception of, or an increment in, autonomous cortical activity could mask impulses coming from lower levels.

Observations on the development of the EEG after full-term birth dates from early papers of Berger (1932, 1933), the "father of electroencephalography." Other reports of age changes, some of which included repeated examinations of the same subjects and comparisons of sleeping and waking records, soon followed (Bernhard and Skoglund, 1939; Davis and Davis, 1936; Henry, 1944; Lindsley, 1936, 1938, 1939; Loomis, Harvey, and Hobart, 1936; Smith, 1937, 1938a, 1938b, 1938c, 1939, 1941). By and large, the waking EEG in the first few months of life is like that described above for the eight-month record, diffuseness being emphasized (Dreyfus-Brisac, 1966; Ellingson, 1967b).

A tendency toward concentration of theta activity over the central region in some neonates has been remarked (Ellingson, 1958, 1964a; Smith, 1938a, 1939, 1941), although Dreyfus-Brisac (1966) considers this localization a sign of drowsiness. Open eyes are known to be a fallible criterion of wakefulness in young infants (Ellingson, 1958). There does appear to be a little improvement in regularity, particularly over the central areas, during the early postnatal months. However, no remarkable transformations are seen in the waking record until the third to fourth month. Like the eighth fetal month, this age

marks a significant turning-point. The advent of an occipital "alpha rhythm" and its blocking by sensory stimuli, attention or stress are particularly striking. In addition, refinements in other forms of evoked responses are perceptible (see below).

Whereas alpha band refers simply to a range of frequencies, the designation of alpha rhythm is by tradition reserved for waves of these frequencies that are present in the occipital and parietal areas when the subject is relaxed with eyes closed but are "blocked" by arousal, particularly by visual stimuli (Storm van Leeuwen et al., 1966; Walter, 1963). Using all these criteria except frequency, Lindsley (1936, 1938, 1939) and Smith (1937, 1938a, 1938b, 1939, 1941) reported that the alpha rhythm first appeared over the occiput at about the third month postterm with a frequency of approximately 4/sec. and increased in frequency thereafter until late childhood or early adolescence (see Fig. 6). Parietal rhythms, originally faster, increased more gradually.

Some activity in the alpha frequency band is present even in newborn infants (Dreyfus-Brisac, 1966; Ellingson, 1964a; Gibbs and Knott, 1949; Smith, 1938a, 1938b, 1941), but it does not fulfill the other criteria for an alpha rhythm (Kellaway, 1964). For this reason, most electroencephalographers have accepted the view of the development of the alpha rhythm outlined by Lindsley and Smith. A few, however, take exception. Walter (1963) quarrels with a definition of alpha rhythm that excludes the frequency criterion, although the early-appearing alpha frequencies he isolates are not responsive to visual stimulation for several years and hence do not meet another criterion for alpha rhythm. Recently several other investigators have reported considerable fast activity, particularly in the alpha range, in the newborn with the suggestion that the adult form of the rhythm may be intrinsic rather than the product of evolution from slower activity (Churchill, Grisell, and Darnley, 1966; Liberson and Frazier, 1962; Shepovalnikov, 1962; Sidorenko, 1961). To date, however, adequate controls for artifacts from muscle tremor have not been instituted.

There are also indications that the alpha and beta frequencies present in the newborn may be associated with natal circumstances.

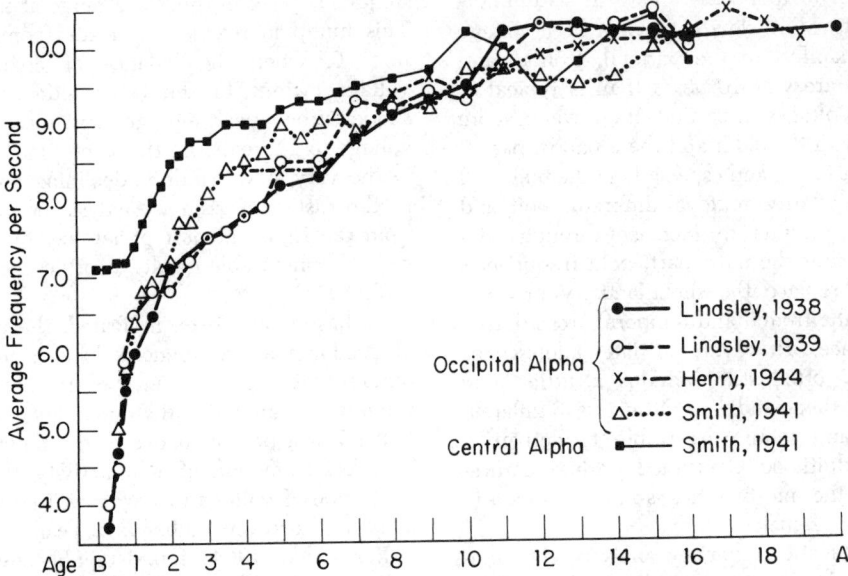

Fig. 6. Development of the alpha rhythm (average frequency per second).

Alpha activity was found to be greatest over the right hemisphere in infants among whom the presenting position of the head was right occiput anterior, transverse or posterior and greatest on the left among those with left occiput transverse or posterior presentation (Churchill et al., 1966). Only 35-45% of newborns have activity in the alpha frequency range (Churchill et al., 1966; Kellaway, 1964), and it disappears from all but the central leads during the neonatal period (Kellaway, 1964). Beta rhythms, found in about the same proportion of infants and especially prominent in the premature, are gone by about 4 weeks (Kellaway, 1964). They recur later in the year (Glaser, 1963).

In the early research on age changes the primary aim was to trace evolution of the dominant rhythms. Few electrodes were used and visual analysis and manual measurements had to be relied upon. Despite these limitations, several trends besides the initially rapid and then more gradual increase in the frequency of the occipital and parietal "alpha rhythm" were discovered. The amplitude of this rhythm increased in some subjects for periods varying from months to years and then declined, so that group averages showed a curvilinear pattern. Weinbach (1938) found frequency to be most highly correlated with brain weight, while amplitude was associated

first with estimated number of active neurons and later with skull thickness. Lindsley (1939) also pointed to the possible role of the closure of the fontanelles in the reduction of recorded voltage. Organization, regularity, and bilateral symmetry were reported to increase rapidly from the fourth month to the end of the first year and more gradually thereafter. The overall range of frequencies, relatively narrow in the first year, was observed to expand, becoming almost as wide as that of the adult by age 10.

These findings were augmented in succeeding studies by using more leads (Dreyfus-Brisac, Samson, Blanc, and Monod, 1958; Ellingson, 1964a; Gibbs and Gibbs, 1950; Novikova, 1961; see also reviews of Dreyfus-Brisac, 1966, and Ellingson, 1967b), and, at times, by automatic frequency analyzers (Bartoshuk, 1964; Corbin and Bickford, 1955; Fujimori, Yokota, Ishibashi, and Takei, 1958; Gibbs and Knott, 1949; Walter, 1963). Judged only by the occipital area, the EEG would be said to approximate adult levels of symmetry by about 1 year, frequency by 10 years, reactivity to stimulation by 12 years, and amplitude by mid-adolescence, although individual differences are admittedly great.

When all regions are explored simultaneously, however, a different developmental picture emerges. Even at 4 years a minor amount of temporal asymmetry is within normal limits. More slow activity of high voltage is still manifest in the parietal, frontal, and temporal areas at 10 years than is typical of adults. Voltages wax and then wane more gradually in the delta and theta bands, particularly the latter, and especially in the temporal lobes. Regularity, regional differentiation, and stability continue to increase through adolescence. For the most part, beta frequencies come to replace the theta activity predominant in the frontal and temporal areas during adolescence. However, in late adolescence the EEG often still contains a little more temporal theta and is a little less regular in pattern and more susceptible to activation than in adulthood. Continued gradual maturation into the mid-twenties is more common in males than females.

In automatic frequency analysis, the component voltage at each integral and half integral (cycle per second and half cycle per second) is measured and graphed. The integrated voltage from one or more regions or pairs of homologous regions may be assessed individually or pooled. Because analyzers cannot tell fact from fiction, artifact-free sections of record should be used. The operator is also the one who must separate sleeping, drowsy, and waking segments, but not all have done so. This may be one reason why a higher incidence of slow frequencies among infants and children is found with automatic than with manual analysis. On the other hand, the analyzer detects frequencies that are hidden from the eye by the masking of some smaller components by larger ones, so the underlying spectrum is more faithfully reproduced.

Although relatively few automatic analyses have been done on a normative developmental basis, the results are consistent. The range of frequencies observed is like that from manual measurement, and the overall trend is similar. To quote Gibbs and Knott (1949), whose pioneer work was based on summated activity from the left frontal, parietal, occipital, and temporal areas: "With each successive year the peaks of component voltage move further out toward the high-frequency end of the spectrum. Up to the end of the first year this acceleration only extends the shoulder of the low-frequency peak out to nine cycles." A "hump" appears on the shoulder of the low-

frequency peak in the 9 cps range at 2 years. This hump increases in size and complexity until 6, when the balance of component voltage swings to the faster side. Then a single, strong peak emerges and increases in voltage to 11 years. At the same time voltage in the very slow bands is declining and that in the fast ones rising. Analysis of voltages from the right and left parieto-occipital area yielded comparable results (Corbin and Bickford, 1955).

As has already been indicated, the pattern of predominant frequencies looks somewhat different at the lower end of the age continuum in automatic than manual analyses. Instead of a predominance of the theta band with lesser amounts of delta activity, the concentration of voltage in very slow frequencies is as high or even higher at 2 years.

Bartoshuk (1964) found reliably less slow activity and more fast activity in the waking than sleeping records from both the frontal-precentral and parietal-occipital areas of newborn infants. Both waking and sleeping samples showed more slow activity (1.4–6.0 cps) in the frontal-precentral region and more beta activity in the parietal-occipital.

Ontogeny of Sleep Patterns in the EEG

Except for Smith's (1938) "Preliminary Observations on the Pattern Sequence during Sleep" in infants and young children, the development of the electroencephalographic concomitants of the sleep-waking cycle received no systematic attention until almost 20 years after Berger's (1929) original paper on the EEG. Within the next decade, however, correlative studies of several sorts had coalesced to make research on sleep active, exciting, and productive.

Impetus for clinical studies of sleep, which proved to be the most valuable activator of abnormalities in children's EEGs (Fois, 1961; Paine and Oppé, 1966), came primarily from Gibbs and Gibbs' (1947, 1950) reports on the diagnostic value of sleep recordings. Concurrently, the normative data basic to clinical evaluation began to accumulate. The resurgence of interest in infancy that had become apparent by the early 1950s (Dreyfus-Brisac and Blanc, 1956; Dreyfus-Brisac and Monod, 1956; Kellaway, 1952; Kellaway and Fox, 1952; Schaper, 1953a, 1953b; Schroeder and Heckel, 1952) was signaled first by new data on full-term newborns while asleep, drowsy, and awake (Hughes, Eheman, and Brown, 1948; Hughes, Eheman, and Hill, 1949) and then by observations on premature infants under similar conditions (Hughes, Davis, and Brennan, 1951). Detailed analyses that still constitute the standard reference on normal sleep patterns from birth through 60 years were included in Volume I of the Gibbs' *Atlas of Electroencephalography* (1950). Although their terms for sleep stages are not consistently used by all investigators (see discussion in Lindsley, 1960), and later research, particularly with premature infants, has somewhat modified their conclusions, delineation of the notable features of the Gibbs' sequence will provide an overview of age changes and make fitting more recent data on young subjects into their niches easier.

According to the Gibbs, seven stages of sleep can be discriminated in the adult EEG: drowsiness, very light sleep, light sleep, moderately deep sleep, deep sleep, early morning sleep, and arousal. The patterns are topographically more differentiated than those of the waking record and more complex in their development, yet individual differences at any given age are less marked. Across the age span entry into and arousal from sleep show the greatest changes. In infants under 1 month, the Gibbs could distinguish mainly light and deep sleep. Subsequent workers agree that it is difficult to discriminate phases of sleep or sleep from waking. However, they have demonstrated an incipient differentiation of sleep from wakefulness during the seventh fetal month in the form of a slight increase in the amplitude of slow waves. This shift becomes more pronounced at 8 months, when superimposed low-voltage fast activity is common. Beginning in the second month steady, high amplitude waves are seen in drowsiness, their frequency increasing from 2–4/sec. to 4–6/sec. by 1 year. This activity has since been called "hypnagogic" (Kellaway and Fox, 1952) and "oscitant" (Ellingson, 1967b). During the second year the incidence of these waves begins to decline, and they appear in bursts rather than runs. At the same time fast activity (20–30/sec.), first present in the second half of the first year, increases in amount. Paroxysmal slowing remains common through 14 years, but fast activity decreases rapidly after 2 and is gone by 10, when the adult pattern of flattening with some slowing becomes typical.

The biparietal humps characteristic of very light sleep throughout the rest of the life span begin to appear in the last half of the first year and reach adult incidence in the second. By about 3 months the spindles of light sleep, present even in the first 2 months, also are as prominent as at later ages, although they are not as well formed until 3 years.

Whereas the Gibbs characterized deep sleep as a state in which almost all activity is very slow (0.5–2.0/sec.) with a little superimposed fast activity, others have since found a recurrent pattern in this stage, the *tracé alternant* (see reviews in Dreyfus-Brisac, 1966; Ellingson, 1967b). Bursts of irregular slow activity mixed with somewhat rhythmic 4–6/sec. waves with superimposed faster low-voltage activity alternate with periods of comparative electrical silence. This pattern is first seen during the last month of gestation.

Before 2 months it is difficult to differentiate any specific signs associated with spontaneous arousal from sleep (as distinguished from applied stimulation). Then continuous high amplitude slow waves are present in about half the subjects. The incidence of this pattern increases during the first year, remains constant through 6 years, and then declines to disappear by 20. While it is present, frequency increases and amplitude decreases somewhat with age. Normal adults never show this type of slowing, but return quickly to the waking pattern. An intermediate phase of paroxysmal slow activity on arousal, maximally present at 10-14 years but occasionally seen as early as 3 years, is found in a small proportion of adults.

The discovery of a new phase of sleep during the mid-1950s considerably altered the subsequent course of developmental work on sleep stages. Observations on young infants revealed alternations between quiet sleep and periods of body and eye movements (Aserinsky and Kleitman, 1955), and recurrent phases were found during deep sleep in adults in which a desynchronized EEG, much like that of the aroused, alert state, and accompanied by rapid eye movements (REM) replaced slow waves (Aserinsky and Kleitman, 1953, 1955; Dement and Kleitman, 1957). Both developmental and comparative studies with lower animals indicated that the REM state was a primitive form of sleep (Jouvet, 1961, 1963; see review of Snyder, 1965, for references on a wide variety of species). Meanwhile neurophysiologists had been exploring the role of the reticular system in sleep and waking (Lindsley, Schreiner, Knowles, and Magoun, 1950, Magoun, 1964; Moruzzi and Magoun, 1949), and a hierarchy of reticular centers for arousal, REM, and quiet sleep were outlined (Moruzzi, 1964). An important supplement to the electrophysiological researches on sleep was provided by investigators concerned with activity cycles, psychophysiological state, and control of the conditions under which stimulation is administered. They used observational and polygraphic measures of respiration, heart rate, body and eye movements to scale the sleep-waking continuum (see reviews in Crowell, 1967, and Steinschneider, 1967). To refine the definitions of phases of the sleep-waking cycle or to have independent measures, EEG and polygraph recording and observation were combined (Delange, Castan, Cadilhac, and Passouant, 1962; Goldie and Van Velzer, 1965; Parmelee, Wenner, Akiyama, Stern, and Flescher, 1967; Parmelee, Wenner, Akiyama, Schultz, and Stern, 1967; Petre-Quadens, 1966, 1967; Roffwarg, Dement, and Fisher, 1964; Roffwarg, Muzio, and Dement, 1966; see also reviews in Dreyfus-Brisac, 1964, and Ellingson, 1967b).

As work using several techniques of assessing waking and sleeping states progressed, it was demonstrated that REM sleep is characterized not only by fast, low-voltage, desynchronized EEG activity and rapid eye movements, but also by irregular heart rate and respiration, and a lack of both neck muscle tonus and phasic movements of the face and limbs. The *tracé alternant* is present during quiet sleep, respiration and heart rate are regular and slower, and, while tonus returns in the anterior neck muscles, other muscles are relaxed and few body movements occur. These two stages of sleep can be distinguished as early as the seventh fetal month, but the distinction is difficult. With increasing age, both the EEG and other patterns become clearer (Parmelee, Wenner, Akiyama, Stern, and Flescher, 1967). For example, muscle potentials are present during REM sleep in the 7-month fetus, whereas by term EMG (electromyograph) activity usually disappears in active sleep (Petre-Quadens, 1967).

The proportion of active sleep declines steadily from the seventh fetal month through 3 months post-term, while quiet sleep increases more gradually; the remainder of the time is accounted for either by transitional sleep or less time spent in sleep (Parmelee, Wenner, Akiyama, Schultz, and Stern, 1967; Petre-Quadens, 1967). However, computer coding of EEG and polygraph records reveals some increase in active sleep through the eighth fetal month, more transitional sleep, and a greater and more regular decline in the latter than in active sleep. The absolute and relative amount of REM sleep decreases throughout the life span (Roffwarg, Dement, and Fisher, 1964; Roffwarg, Muzio, and Dement, 1966). In contrast, the time spent in quiet sleep increases a little during the first 2 years and does not begin to decline to any extent until 10–13 years.

The progressive differentiation of sleep phases has been interpreted as a reflection of the maturation of the functional divisions of the reticular formation (Parmelee et al., 1967). The pontine reticular substance is the primary center for active sleep, the medullar for quiet sleep, and the mesencephalic portion for arousal (Moruzzi, 1964). A progressive shift from primarily pontine to medullar control with age is suggested by the decreasing predominance of active sleep and the increase in quiet sleep, while maturation within both regions is indicated by the fact that each phase becomes better defined. Improvement in the capacity to sustain wakefulness, a trend very noticeable even between term and the third postnatal month, suggests increasing activity not only in the mesencephalic segment but also at higher levels and greater interaction within the central nervous system.

Ontogeny of Evoked Responses

Although the waking and sleeping patterns thus far described must be influenced in some measure by a conglomerate of external as well as internal stimuli, they are referred to as spontaneous rhythms. Evoked responses are potential changes induced by discrete sensory stimuli, usually deliberately applied. They are superimposed on background activity, complex in wave form, and time-locked to stimulation, responses occurring at both the onset and termination of the stimulus. As yet "off" responses have received less systematic attention than "on" responses, especialy in developmental studies. Because ongoing activity often masks evoked potentials, they may not be detected without the aid of some kind of summating or averaging device. Electronic techniques in which variations in voltage over a period subsequent to stimulation are repeatedly stored, algebraically summed, and then averaged are now widely used. Brain waves that are not associated with the timing of the stimuli should be randomly distributed among positive and negative values and thus will cancel each other out to yield a sum of zero. On the other hand, responses that are temporally related to stimulation will be regularly positive or negative at given points in the succeeding time interval. Statistical as well as experimental controls are essential in work with evoked potentials. These and other aspects of methodology have recently been reviewed (Ellingson, 1967a, 1967b), and several current summaries of the developmental literature on evoked potentials are also available (Ellingson, 1964b, 1967b, Goldring, Sugaya, and O'Leary, 1964).

Some evoked responses, or segments of them, are nonspecific in that they are elicited by stimuli of more than one modality, for example, both audition and vision. There has been controversy about the existence of truly specific responses for a particular sensory modality. Whether or not the components of the induced wave forms are different for different senses is still unsettled, but there is good evidence for specificity of cerebral region for both visual and somatosensory stimuli. To date, specific auditory responses have not been demonstrated in the human being, probably because the primary projection areas are so deep that surface electrodes are inadequate for detecting them. In addition to being utilized in research on the cortical projection of sensory inputs, evoked responses have been useful in studying interaction between neural systems, the influence of stimulation on states of consciousness, and other aspects of neurophysiological function. They also offer another means of assessing the physiological development of the nervous system.

Nonspecific responses do not appear until about the last month of gestation. At this time auditory stimuli may flatten ongoing activity, intensify and then flatten sleep potentials, or produce topographically diffuse bursts irregular in wave form (Dreyfus-Brisac and Blanc, 1956; Ellingson, 1958, 1960; Engel, 1961). After the third postnatal month either somesthetic or auditory stimuli will *increase* the amplitude of sleep waves or evoke sharp, slow potentials of negative polarity. During deep sleep the latter may be followed by a series of potential changes called the K-complex, a typical response to auditory stimulation during sleep in the adult. By the end of the first year, several other responses to auditory stimuli are observed: diphasic high-amplitude potentials over the vertex, slow waves of moderate amplitude in frontal leads, and high-voltage slow waves over the occiput (Dreyfus-Brisac and Blanc, 1956; Ellingson, 1958, 1964a).

Because hearing cannot be tested in infants and young children by conventional audiometry, electroencephalographic reactions to auditory stimuli have also been the subject of considerable clinically motivated research (Appleby, 1965; Barnet and Lodge, 1966, 1967a, 1967b; Derbyshire, Fraser, McKermott, and Bridge, 1956; Ortiz-Estrada, Deutsch, and Hernandes-Orozco, 1963; Rapin, 1964; Wedenberg, 1956; Weitzman, Fishbein, and Graziani, 1965; Williams and Graham, 1963). Otherwise, developmental work has been concentrated on specific responses to visual stimuli, and nonspecific responses in general as well as specific responses to somesthetic stimuli have been neglected. This fact is somewhat surprising in view of anatomical data showing that the somesthetic area is better developed at birth than other sensory areas (Conel, 1939) and at least one report indicates that in newborn infants nonspecific responses are most likely to occur to somesthetic stimuli. At birth auditory stimulation is only moderately effective, and nonspecific visual responses are relatively rare, although specific ones are present long before term.

If even brief flashes are presented, specific visual responses can be detected in the occipital area. When these responses first appear is not known, but they have been observed in the youngest premature infants thus far tested, one of 24 weeks (Engel, 1964) and another of 28 weeks (Ellingson, 1960). In adults the specific visual response is polyphasic, consisting of both positive and negative components, but as first seen in the fetus (premature infant) it is a monophasic negative wave. An initial positive wave is added sometime during the last 2 fetal months. "All normal full-term human newborns display visual evoked responses" in electronically averaged recordings, and 98% show at least the diphasic pattern (Ellingson, 1967b, p. 83). A double positive phase or a positive-negative-positive pattern is seen in most (Ellingson, 1967b; Ferriss, Davis, Dorsen, and Hackett, 1967). One of the most outstanding features of the neonatal response is its "fatigability" (Ellingson, 1960). Perhaps this term is misleading in its implications, but it reflects well an observer's subjective feeling when he attempts to elicit responses in close succession (Eichorn, 1951). Unless approximately 1 second intervenes between stimuli, a response to the second stimulus is unlikely. Longer intervals are required for premature infants.

With increasing age the variability of the specific visual response in both amplitude and wave form decreases (Ellingson, 1960), and successive responses ("following" or "driving") can be elicited at progressively closer intervals (Eichorn, 1951; Ellingson, 1967b). Other changes include the appearance of additional negative waves—one before the two positive waves and several "late" ones that extend the temporal course of the response beyond 250 msec.—and alterations in regional distribution, latency, and voltage (Ellingson, 1960, 1966; Engel, 1964, 1965; Engel and Butler, 1963; Ferriss et al., 1967; Hrbek and Mares, 1964).

Until about 3 months all components of the visual evoked response are confined to the occipital region. After that age the later components can be detected as far forward as the central area, so these negative waves may be considered a nonspecific response. The average time elapsing between presentation of a stimulus and the greatest amplitude of the major positive wave is about 220 msec.

6 weeks before term. Latency decreases rapidly and almost linearly to about 190 msec. at full-term. The decrement is still rapid but decelerating through the third month, when the mean is about 100 msec. Thereafter a gradual decline continues to 14-18 weeks, when the adult latency of 80-90 msec. is approximated. The data just cited are Ellingson's (1960, 1964a, 1966); those of other investigators differ somewhat in absolute means and in postnatal trends (Engel, 1961; Engel and Butler, 1963), including a possible decrease in latency through 4 to 8 years. At birth voltages (amplitudes) may be as high as in older children and then decrease briefly (Ellingson, 1964a). From 1 month to 7 or 8 years, however, the amplitude of all components increases markedly (Dustman and Beck, 1966). The subsequent decline in voltage is temporarily reversed around age 13 to 14 and then resumes until amplitudes like those of young adults are reached at 17 to 19 years (Dustman and Beck, 1966).

Overview

Many intriguing parallels can be drawn between the development of spontaneous and evoked potentials, the anatomical and biochemical maturation of the brain, and behavioral development (Eichorn, 1963; Eichorn and Jones, 1958; Goldring, Sugaya, and O'Leary, 1964; Purpura, 1961a, 1961b; Scheibel and Scheibel, 1964). With a few exceptions (Purpura, 1961a, 1961b; Scheibel and Scheibel, 1959, 1961, 1962), however, these remain in the realm of speculation. One message does seem clear from all types of physiological data: the perinatal period is one of rapid, complex, and often temporary changes in most functions, and prediction to subsequent status is usually poor. Probably the developmental psychologist is expecting too much when he searches for significant associations between behavior at this time and at later stages.

References

Aballi, A. J., Banus, V. L., deLamerens, S., and Rozenquaig, S. Coagulation studies in the newborn period, alterations of thromboplastin generation and effects of vitamin K in full-term and premature infants. Am. J. Dis. Child., 1957, 94, 589–600.

Aballi, A. J., and deLamerens, S. Coagulation changes in the neonatal period and in early infancy. *Pediat. Clin. N. Amer.*, 1962, **9**, 785–817.

Abrahamov, A., Salzberger, M., and Bromberg, Y. M. Fetal hemoglobin in postmature newborn infants. *Am. J. clin. Pathol.*, 1956, **26**, 146–150.

Abt, A. F., Farmer, C. J., and Epstein, I. M. Normal ascorbic acid determinations in blood plasma and their relationship to capillary resistance. *J. Pediat.*, 1936, **8**, 1–19.

Adair, F. L., and Thelander, H. A. Study of the weight and dimensions of the human placenta in its relation to the weight of the newborn infant. *Am. J. Obstet. Gynec.*, 1925, **10**, 172–205.

Adams, F. H. Functional development of the fetal lung. *J. Pediat.*, 1966, **68**, 794–801.

Adams, F. H., Fujiwara, T., and Rowshan, G. The nature and origin of the fluid in the fetal lamb lung. *J. Pediat.*, 1963, **63**, 881–887.

Adams, F. H., Fujiwara, T., Spears, R., and Hodgman, J. Gaseous metabolism in premature infants at 32–34° C. ambient temperature. *Pediatrics*, 1964, **33**, 75–82.

Adams, F. H., and Lind, J. Physiologic studies on the cardiovascular status of normal newborn infants (with special reference to the ductus arteriosus). *Pediatrics*, 1957, **19**, 431–437.

Adams, F. H., Moss, A. J., and Emmanouilides, G. C. Closure of the ductus arteriosus and foramen ovale. In D. E. Cassels (Ed.), *The heart and circulation in the newborn and infant*. New York: Grune and Stratton, 1966. Pp. 80–87.

Adams, F. H., Moss, A. J., and Fagan, L. The tracheal fluid in the fetal lamb. *Biol. neonat.*, 1963, **5**, 151–158.

Adamsons, K., Jr. Transport of organic substances and oxygen across the placenta. In D. Bergsma, K. Abramson, K. Benirschke, and H. Hodes, (Eds.), *Symposium on the placenta*. New York: The National Foundation, 1965. Pp. 27–34.

Adamsons, K., Jr. The role of thermal factors in fetal and neonatal life. *Pediat. Clin. N. Am.*, 1966, **13**, 599–619.

Adamsons, K., Jr., Gandy, G. M., and James, L. S. The influence of thermal factors upon oxygen consumption of the newborn human infant. *J. Pediat.*, 1965, **66**, 495–508.

Adamsons, K., Jr., James, L. S., Towell, M. E., and Lacey, J. F. Physiologic observations during induced anemia in utero in the rhesus monkey. *J. Pediat.*, 1965, **67**, 1042.

Agustsson, M. H., Bicoff, J. P., and Arcilla, R. A. Hemodynamic studies in fifty-two normal infants and children. *Circulation*, 1963, **28**, 683.

Aherne, W. A weight relationship between the human foetus and placenta. *Biol. neonat.*, 1966, **10**, 113–118.

Aherne, W., and Dawkins, M. J. R. The removal of fluid from the pulmonary airways after birth in the rabbit, and the effect on this of prematurity and prenatal hypoxia. *Biol. neonat.*, 1964, **7**, 214–229.

Aherne, W., and Dunnill, M. S. Morphometry of the human placenta. *Brit. med. Bull.*, 1966, **22**, 5–8.

Aherne, W., and Hull, D. Brown adipose tissue and heat production in the newborn infant. *J. Path. Bact.*, 1966, **91**, 223–234.

Albin, A. R., Kushner, J. H., Murphy, A., and Zippin, C. Platelet enumeration in the neonatal period. *Pediatrics*, 1961, **28**, 822–824.

Albritton, E. C. (Ed.) *Standard values in blood*. Philadelphia: Saunders, 1952.

Alimurung, M. M., and Massell, B. F. The normal P-R interval in infants and children. *Circulation*, 1956, **13**, 257–262.

Allansmith, M. Development of immunity. In F. Falkner, (Ed.), *Human development*. Philadelphia: Saunders, 1966.

Allansmith, M., and Buell, D. N. The relationship of gamma-1A globulin and reagin in cord sera. *J. Allergy*, 1964, **35**, 339–345.

Allansmith, M., Maloney, J., and Wymer, B. Change in immunoglobulin levels in the same babies from birth to age 6 months. *Fed. Proc.*, 1966, **25**, 489. (Abstract.)

Allen, D. W., and Jandl, J. H. Factors influencing relative rates of synthesis of adult and fetal hemoglobin *in vitro*. *J. clin. Invest.*, 1960, **39**, 1107–1113.

Allen, D. W., Wyman, J., and Smith, C. A. The oxygen equilibrium of fetal and adult human hemoglobin. *J. biol. Chem.*, 1953, **203**, 81–87.

Allen-Williams, G. M. Pulse-rate and blood pressure in infancy and early childhood. *Archs. Dis. Child.*, 1945, **20**, 125–128.

Altemeier, W. A., and Smith, R. T. Immunologic aspects of resistance in early life. *Pediat. Clin. N. Am.*, 1965, **12**, 663–686.

Alzamora, V., Rotta, A., Battilana, G., Abugattas, R., Rubio, C., Bouroncle, J., Zapata, C., Santa-Maria, E., Binder, T., Subiria, R., Parades, D., Pando, B., and Graham, G. G. On the possible influence of great altitude on the determination of certain cardiovascular anomalies. *Pediatrics*, 1953, **12**, 259–262.

Alzamora-Castro, V., Battilana, G., Abugattas, R., and Sialer, S. Patent ductus arteriosus and high altitude. *Am. J. Cardiol.*, 1960, **5**, 761–763.

Amoroso, E. C. Histology of the placenta. Foetal and neonatal physiology. *Br. med. Bull.*, 1961, **17**, 81–90.

Amoroso, E. C. Placentation. In A. S. Parkes (Ed.), *Marshall's physiology of reproduction*. (3rd. ed.) London: Longmans, Green, 1952. Vol. 2, pp. 127–311.

Anderson, G. W. Studies on nucleated red count in the chorionic capillaries and the cord blood of various ages of pregnancy. *Am. J. Obstet. Gynec.*, 1941, **42**, 1–14.

Apgar, V. A proposal for a new method of evaluation of the newborn infant. *Anesth. Anal.*, 1953, **32**, 260–267.

Appleby, S. The slow vertex maximal sound evoked response in infants. *Acta otolaryng.*, 1965, Suppl. **206**, 146–152.

Arajarvi, T. Microscopic investigations into the capillaries of newborn, especially premature infants. *Études Neo-Natales (Studies)*, 1953, **2**, 139–162.

Aresin, L. Beitrag zur embryonalen Electroenzephalographie. *Confnia Neurol.*, 1962, **22**, 121–127.

Arey, L. B. *Developmental anatomy*. (7th ed.) Phildelphia: Saunders, 1965.

Armstrong, D. H., Schroeder, W. A., and Fenninger, W. D. A comparison of the percentage of fetal hemoglobin in human umbilical cord blood as determined by chromatography and by alkali denaturation. *Blood*, 1963, **22**, 554–565.

Aserinsky, E., and Kleitman, N. Regularly occurring periods of eye motility and concomitant phenomena during sleep. *Science*, 1953, **118**, 273–274.

Aserinsky, E., and Kleitman, N. A motility cycle in sleeping infants as manifested by ocular and gross bodily activity. *J. appl. Physiol.*, 1955, **8**, 11–18.

Ashworth, A. M., and Neligan, G. A. Changes in the systolic blood pressure of normal babies during the first twenty-four hours of life. *Lancet*, 1959, **1**, 804–807.

Assali, N. S., Douglass, R. A., Jr., Baird, W. W., Nicholson, D. B., and Suyemoto, R. Measurement of uterine blood flow and uterine metabolism, IV. Results in normal pregnancy. *Am. J. Obstet. Gynec.*, 1953, **66**, 248–253.

Assali, N. S., and Morris, J. A. Circulatory and metabolic adjustments of the fetus at birth. *Biol. neonat.*, 1964, **7**, 141–159. (a)

Assali, N. S., and Morris, J. A. Maternal and fetal circulations and their interrelationships. *Obstet. gynec. Surv.*, 1964, **19**, 923–948. (b)

Assali, N. S., Morris, J. A., Smith, R. W., and Manson, W. A. Studies on ductus arteriosus circulation. *Circulation Res.*, 1963, **13**, 478–489.

Averbuck, S. H., and Friedman, W. Circulation time in normal children. *Am. J. Dis. Child.*, 1935, **49**, 361–366.

Avery, M. E. *The lung and its disorders in the newborn infant.* Philadelphia: Saunders, 1964.

Avery, M. E. Physiologic considerations of the respiratory system. In G. M. Owen (Ed.), *Problems in neonatal surgery.* Rep. 49th Ross Conf. on Pediat. Res. Columbus, Ohio: Ross Laboratories, 1965. Pp. 75–81.

Avery, M. E., Frank, N. R., and Gribetz, I. The inflationary force produced by pulmonary vascular distension in excised lungs. The possible relation of this force to that needed to inflate the lungs at birth. *J. clin. Invest.*, 1959, **38**, 456–462.

Avery, M. E., and Mead, J. Surface properties in relation to atelectasis and hyaline membrane disease. *Am. J. Dis. Child.*, 1959, **97**, 517–523.

Bader, R. A., Bader, M. D., Rose, D. F., and Braunwald, E. Hemodynamics at rest and during exercise in normal pregnancy as studied by cardiac catheterization. *J. clin. Invest.*, 1955, **34**, 1524–1536.

Bakwin, H. M., and Bakwin, R. M. Body build in infants: VI. Growth of the cardiac silhouette and the thoraco-abdominal cavity. *Am. J. Dis. Child.*, 1935, **49**, 861–869.

Barclay, A. E., Franklin, K. J., and Prichard, M. M. L. *The foetal circulation and cardiovascular system and the changes that they undergo at birth.* Oxford: Blackwell, 1944.

Barcroft, J. *Researches on pre-natal life.* Oxford: Blackwell, 1946.

Barnard, W. G., and Day, T. D. The development of the terminal air passages of the human lung. *J. Pathol. Bacteriol.*, 1937, **45**, 67–73.

Barnet, A. B., and Lodge, A. Diagnosis of deafness in infants with the use of computer-averaged electroencephalographic responses to sound. *J. Pediat.*, 1966, **69**, 753–758.

Barnet, A. B., and Lodge, A. Click evoked EEG responses in normal and developmentally retarded infants. *Nature*, 1967, **214**, 252–255. (a)

Barnet, A. B., and Lodge, A. Diagnosis of hearing loss in infancy by means of electroencephalographic audiometry. *Clin. Proc. Children's Hospital, D. C.*, 1967, **22**, 1–18. (b)

Barnett, P. H., Hines, E. A., Schirger, A., and Gage, R. P. Blood pressure and vascular reactivity to cold pressor test: restudy of 207 subjects 27 years later. *J. Am. med. Ass.*, 1963, **183**, 845–848.

Barrett, B., and Volwiler, W. Agammaglobulinemia and hypogammaglobulinemia: the first five years. *J. Am. med. Ass.*, 1957, **164**, 866–870.

Bartoshuk, A. K. Human neonatal EEG: frequency analysis of awake and asleep samples from four areas. *Psychon. Sci.*, 1964, **1**, 281–282.

Bayley, N., and Stolz, H. R. Maturational changes in rectal temperatures of 61 infants from 1 to 36 months. *Child Dev.*, 1937, **8**, 195–206.

Beaven, G. H., Ellis, M. J., and White, J. C. Studies on human foetal haemoglobin. II. Foetal haemoglobin levels in healthy children and adults and in certain haematological disorders. *Br. J. Haematol.*, 1960, **6**, 201–222.

Becker, A. H., and Glass, H. Twin-to-twin transfusion syndrome. *Am. J. Dis. Child.*, 1963, **106**, 624–629.

Benedict, F. G., and Talbot, F. B. *The physiology of the newborn infant; character and amount of the katabolism.* Washington, D.C.: Carnegie Instit. Publ. No. 233, 1915.

Benedict, F. G., and Talbot, F. B. Metabolism and growth from birth to puberty. Washington, D.C.: Carnegie Instit. Washington, Publ. No. 302, 1921.

Benirschke, K. General discussion, some correlations of structure and functions in the placenta. In C. A. Villee (Ed.), *Gestation. Transactions of the fifth conference*. New York: Josiah Macy, Jr., Foundation, 1958. Pp. 163–247.

Benirschke, K. Major pathologic features of the placenta, cord, and membranes. In D. Bergsma, K. Abramson, K. Benirschke, and H. Hodes (Eds.), *Symposium on the placenta*. New York: The National Foundation, 1965. Pp. 52–63.

Berger, H. Über das Elektrenkephalogramm des Menschen: IV. *Arch. Psychiat. Nervenk.*, 1932, **97**, 6–26.

Berger, H. Über das Elektrenkephalogramm des Menschen: V. *Arch. Psychiat. Nervenk.*, 1933, **98**, 231–257.

Bergstrom, R. M., and Bergstrom, L. Prenatal development of stretch reflex functions and brain stem activity in the human. *Ann. Chirur. Gynaecol. Fenn.*, 1963, **52** (Suppl. 117), 1–21.

Berman, L. The immunologically competent cell ("immunocyte") system—an attempt at a delineation of cellular relationships. *Blood*, 1963, **21**, 246–249.

Bernhard, C. G., and Skoglund, C. R. Alpha frequency and age. *Skand. Arch. Physiol.* 1939, **82**, 178–184.

Bernstine, R. L. *Fetal electrocardiography and electroencephalography.* Springfield, Ill.: Thomas, 1961.

Bernstine, R. L., and Borkowski, W. J. Prenatal fetal electrocardiography. *Am. J. Obstet. Gynec.*, 1955, **70**, 631–638.

Bernstine, R. L., and Borkowski, W. J. Foetal electroencephalography. *J. Obstet. Gynaec. Br. Emp.*, 1956, **63**, 275–279.

Bernstine, R. L., Borkowski, W. J., and Price, A. Prenatal fetal electroencephalography. *Am. J. Obstet. Gynec.*, 1955, **70**, 623–630.

Berry, W. T. C., Cowin, P. J., and Magee, H. E. Haemoglobin levels in adults and children. *Br. med. J.*, 1952, **1**, 410–412.

Bordley, J., III, Connor, C. A. R., Hamilton, W. F., Kerr, W. J., and Wiggers, C. J. Recommendations for human blood pressure determinations by sphygmomanometers. *Circulation*, 1951, **4**, 503–509.

Borkowski, W. J., and Bernstine, R. L. Electroencephalography of the fetus. *Neurology*, 1955, **5**, 362–365.

Born, G. V. R., Dawes, G. S., Mott, J. C., and Widdicombe, J. G. Changes in the heart and lungs at birth. *Cold Spr. Harb. Symp. Quant. Biol.*, 1954, **19**, 102–108.

Bornstein, S., and Israel, M. Agglutinogens in fetal erythrocytes. *Proc. Soc. Exp. Biol. Med.*, 1942, **49**, 718–720.

Boston, R. W., Humphreys, P. W., Reynolds, E. O. R., and Strang, L. B. Lymphflow and clearance of liquid from the lungs of the foetal lamb. *Lancet*, 1965, **2**, 473–474.

Bower, B. D. Pink disease: autonomic disorder and its treatment with ganglion-blocking agents. *Q. J. Med.*, 1954, **23**, 215–230.

Bowman, J. E. The blood pressure in the newborn. *Am. J. Dis. Child.*, 1933, **46**, 949–953.

Boyd, J. D. The nerve supply of the mammalian ductus arteriosus. *J. Anat.*, 1941, **72**, 146–147.

Blankenship, W., Lind, J., and Arcilla, R. A. Atrial pressures and pulmonary circulation time in the newborn infant. *Acta paediat. Scand.*, 1965, **54**, 446–456.

Bloom, W., and Bartelmez, G. W. Hematopoiesis in young human embryos. *Am. J. Anat.*, 1940, **67**, 21–53.

Brady, J. P., and James, L. S. Heart rate changes in the fetus and newborn infant during labor, delivery, and the immediate neonatal period. *Am. J. Obstet. Gynec.*, 1962, **84**, 1–12.

Brady, J. P., and James, L. S. Fetal electrocardiographic studies; tachycardia as a sign of fetal distress. *Am. J. Obstet. Gynec.*, 1963, **86**, 785–790.

Brady, J. P., and Tooley, W. H., Cardiovascular and respiratory reflexes in the newborn. *Pediat. Clin. N. Am.*, 1966, **13**, 801–821.

Brandfonbrenner, M., Landowne, M., and Shock, N. W. Changes in cardiac output with age. *Circulation*, 1955, **12**, 557–566.

Brazier, M. A. B. *A history of the electrical activity of the brain. The first half century.* New York: Macmillan, 1961.

Bremer, J. L. Postnatal development of alveoli in mammalian lung in relation to the problem of alveolar phagocyte. Carnegie Institute, Washington. *Contributions to embryology*, 1935, **25**, 83–111.

Bridges, R. A., Condie, R. M., Zak, S. J., and Good, R. A. The morphologic basis of antibody formation development during the neonatal period. *J. Lab. clin. Med.*, 1959, **53**, 331–357.

Brines, J. K., Gibson, J. G., 2nd, and Kunkel, P. The blood volume in normal infants and children. *J. Pediat.*, 1941, **18**, 447–457.

Brock, J. *Biologische Daten fur den Kinderarzt.* (Erster Band.) Berlin: J. Springer, 1954.

Broman, I. Zur Kenntnis der Lungenentwicklung. *Anat. Anz.*, 1923, **57** (Ergänzungsheft), 83–96.

Brotmacher, L., and Fleming, P. Cardiac output and vascular pressures in ten normal children and adolescents. *Guy's Hosp. Rep.*, 1957, **106**, 268–272.

Brown, C. C., and Saucer, R. T. *Electronic instrumentation for the behavioral sciences.* Springfield, Ill.: Thomas, 1958.

Brück, K. Temperature regulation in the newborn infant. *Biol. neonat.*, 1961, **3**, 65–119.

Brück, K., Brück, M., and Lemtis, H. Hautdurchblutung und Thermoregulation bei neugeborenen Kindern. *Pflüger's Arch. ges. Physiol.*, 1957, **265**, 55–65.

Bucci, G., Scalamandrè, A., and Savignoni, P. La pression arterielle systolique chez le nouveau-né prématuré. *Cah. Coll. Med. Paris*, 1963, **4**, 742–746.

Bucher, H., and Reid, L. Development of the intrasegmental bronchial tree: the pattern of branching and development of cartilage at various stages of intrauterine life. *Thorax*, 1961, **16**, 207–218.

Buckels, L. J., and Usher, R. Cardio-pulmonary effects of placental transfusion. *J. Pediat.*, 1965, **67**, 239–247.

Budd, G. M., and Warhaft, N. Cardiovascular and metabolic responses to noradrenaline in man, before and after acclimatization to cold in Antarctica. *J. Physiol.*, 1966, **186**, 233–242.

Burlage, S. R. The blood pressure and heart rate in girls during adolescence. *Am. J. Physiol.*, 1923, **64**, 252–284.

Burnard, E. D. A murmur from the ductus arteriosus in the newborn baby. *Br. med. J.*, 1958, **1**, 806–810.

Burnard, E. D. The cardiac murmur in relation to symptoms in the newborn. *Br. med. J.*, 1959, **1**, 134–138.

Burnard, E. D. Discussion. In D. E. Cassels (Ed.), *The heart and circulation in the newborn and infant.* New York: Grune and Stratton, 1966. Pp. 135–137.

Burnet, M. Role of the thymus and related organs in immunity. *Br. J. Med.*, 1962, **5**, 807–811.

Burnett, C. T., and Taylor, E. L. Electrocardiograms on 167 average healthy infants and children. *Am. Heart J.*, 1936, **11**, 185–205.

Burwell, C. S., and Metcalfe, J. *Heart disease in pregnancy.* London: J. & A. Churchill, 1958.

Caldeyro-Barcia, R., Mendez-Bauer, C., Poseiro, J. J., Escareena, L. A., Pose, S. U., Bieniarz, J., Arnt, I., Gulin, L. and Althabe, O. Control of human fetal heart rate during labor. In D. E. Cassels (Ed.), *The heart and circulation in the newborn and infant*. New York: Grune and Stratton, 1966. Pp. 7–36.

Caldeyro-Barcia, R., Poseiro, J. J., Negreiros de Paiva, C., Gómez-Rogers, C., Faúndes-Latham, A., Zambrana, M. A., Arellano-Hernandez, G., Beauquis, A., Peña-Ortiz, P., Aguero-Lugones, F., and Filler, W. Effects of abnormal uterine contractions on a human fetus. *Mod. Probl. Pediat.*, 1963, **8**, 267–296.

Caldeyro-Barcia, R., Poseiro, J. J., Pantle, G., Negreiros, C., Gómez-Rogers, C., Faúndes, A., Henry, J. H., Jr., Zambrana, A., Arellano, G., Filler, W., Jr., and Cabot, H. M. Effects of uterine contractions on the heart rate of the human fetus. 4th. Intern. Conf. on Med. Electronics, N.Y., 1961.

Calkins, L. A. Placental variation. *Am. J. Obstet. Gynec.*, 1937, **33**, 280–290.

Cameron, M. D. Fetal electrocardiography: a survey of the literature. *Dev. Med. Child Neurol.*, 1967, **9**, 329–337.

Campbell, A. G. M., Dawes, G. S., Fishman, H. P., Hyman, A. I., and James, G. B. The oxygen consumption of the placenta and foetal membranes in the sheep. *J. Physiol.*, 1966, **182**, 439–464.

Campiche, M. A., Gautier, A., Hernandez, E. I., and Raymond, A. *Pediatrics*, 1963, **32**, 976–994.

Canestrini, S. Ueber das Sinnesleben des Neugeborenen. *Monogr. Gesamtgeb. Neurol. Psychiat.*, 1913, No. 5. Berlin: Springer. P. 104.

Cassels, D. E. (Ed.) *The heart and circulation in the newborn and infant*. New York: Grune and Stratton, 1966. Discussions, pp. 70–72; 130–131.

Cassels, D. E., and Morse, M. *Cardiopulmonary data for children and young adults*. Springfield, Ill.: Thomas, 1962.

Celander, O. Studies of the peripheral circulation. In D. E. Cassels (Ed.), *The heart and circulation in the newborn and infant*. New York: Grune and Stratton, 1966. Pp. 98–110.

Celander, O., and Mårild, K. Reactive hyperaemia in the foot and calf of the newborn infant. *Acta Paediat.*, 1962, **51**, 544–552.

Celander, O., and Thunell, G. A plethysmographic method for measuring the systolic and diastolic blood pressure in newborn infants. *Acta Paediat.* 1960, **49**, 497–502.

Celander, O., and Thunell, G. Mercury-in-rubber strain gauge for measurements of blood pressure and peripheral circulation in newborn infants. *Acta Paediat.*, 1961, **50**, 505–510.

Chernoff, A. I., and Singer, K. S. Studies on abnormal hemoglobins. IV. Persistence of fetal hemoglobin in the erythrocytes of normal children. *Pediatrics*, 1952, **9**, 469–474.

Chiang, S. T., and Han, T. S. Peak flow rate in relation to age, sex, and anthropometric measurements. *Acta Paediat. Scand.*, 1965, **54**, 439–445.

Cho, J., Clements, J. A., Cotton, E., Klaus, M. H., Sweet, A. T., Thomas, M. A., and Tooley, W. H. The pulmonary hypoperfusion syndrome: a preliminary report. *Pediatrics*, 1965, **35**, 733–742.

Chown, B., and Lewis, M. A-B-O and Rh blood antigen of fetuses of about 45 and 55 days. *Can. med. Ass. J.*, 1948, **58**, 504.

Christie, A. Normal closing time of the foramen ovale and the ductus arteriosus. *Am. J. Dis. Child.*, 1930, **40**, 323–326.

Churchill, J. A., Grisell, J., and Darnley, J. D. Rhythmic activity in the EEG of newborns. *Electroencephalog. clin. Neurophysiol.*, 1966, **21**, 131–139.

Clark, L. C., and Garn, S. M. Relationship between ketosteroid excretion and basal oxygen consumption in children. *J. appl. Physiol.*, 1954, **6**, 546–550.

Condorelli, S., and Ungari, C. The period of functional closure of the foramen ovale and the ductus Botalli in the human newborn. *Cardiologia*, 1960, **36**, 274–287.

Conel, J. L. *The postnatal development of the human cerebral cortex.* Vol. I. *Cortex of the newborn.* Cambridge, Mass.: Harvard University Press, 1939.

Contis, G., and Lind, J. Study of systolic blood pressure, heart rate, body temperature of normal newborn infants during the first week of life. *Acta Paediat.*, 1963 (suppl. 146), 41–47.

Cook, C. D., Brodie, H. R., and Allen, D. W. Measurement of the fetal hemoglobin in newborn infants. *Pediatrics*, 1957, **20**, 272–278.

Cook, C. D., Cherry, R. B., O'Brien, D., Karlberg, P., and Smith, C. A. Studies of respiratory physiology in the newborn infant. I. Observations on normal premature and full-term infants. *J. clin. Invest.*, 1955, **34**, 975–982.

Corbin, H. P., and Bickford, R. F. Studies of the electroencephalogram of normal children: comparison of visual and automatic frequency analysis. *Electroencephalog. clin. Neurophysiol.*, 1955, **7**, 15–28.

Corney, G., and Aherne, W. The placental transfusion syndrome in monozygous twins. *Archs. Dis. Child.*, 1965, **40**, 264–270.

Cottom, D. G. Foetal haemoglobin and postmaturity. *J. Obstet. Gynaec. Br. Emp.*, 1955, **62**, 945–948.

Craigie, E. H. The architecture of the cerebral capillary bed. *Biol. Rev.*, 1945, **20**, 133–146.

Cremer, M. Über die direkte Ableitung der Aktion ströme des menschlichen Herzens vom Ösophagus und über das Electrokardiogramm des Fötus. *Münch. med. Wschr.*, 1906, **53**, 811–813.

Cross, K. W. The respiratory rate and ventilation in the newborn baby. *J. appl. Physiol.*, 1949, **109**, 459–474.

Cross, K. W. Respiration in the newborn baby. *Br. med. Bull.*, 1961, **17**, 160–163.

Cross, K. W., Dawes, G. S., and Mott, J. C. Anoxia, oxygen consumption and cardiac output in newborn lambs and adult sheep. *J. Physiol.*, 1959, **146**, 316–343.

Cross, K. W., Tizard, J. P. M., and Trythall, D. A. H. The gaseous metabolism of the newborn infant. *Acta paediat.*, 1957, **46**, 265–285.

Cross, K. W., Tizard, J. P. M., and Trythall, D. A. H. The gaseous metabolism of the new-born infant breathing 15% oxygen. *Acta paediat.*, 1958, **47**, 217–237.

Cudmore, R. E., Emery, J. L., and Mithal, A. Postnatal growth of the bronchi and bronchioles. *Archs. Dis. Child.*, 1962, **37**, 481–484.

Currens, J. H., Brownell, G. L., and Aronow, S. An automatic blood-pressure-recording machine. *New Eng. J. Med.*, 1957, **256**, 780–784.

Custer, R. P. *An atlas of the blood and bone marrow.* Philadelphia: Saunders, 1949.

Dameshek, W. The thymus and lymphoid proliferation. *Blood*, 1962, **20**, 629–632.

Dameshek, W. "Immunoblasts" and "immunocytes"—an attempt at a functional nomenclature. *Blood*, 1963, **21**, 243–245.

Dancis, J. The role of the placenta in fetal survival. *Pediat. Clin. N. Am.*, 1965, **12**, 477–92.

Davis, H., and Davis, P. A. Action potentials of the brain of normal persons and in normal states of cerebral activity. *Archs. neurol. Psychiat.*, 1936, **36**, 1214–1224.

Dawes, G. S. Changes in the circulation at birth. *Br. med. Bull.*, 1961, **17**, 148–153.

Dawes, G. S. Oxygen supply and consumption in late fetal life and the onset of breathing at birth. In W. O. Fenn and H. Rahn (Eds.), *Handbook of physiology.* Section 2. *Respiration.* Washington, D. C.: American Physiological Society, 1965. Pp. 1313–1328.

Dawes, G. S. Initiation and continuation of respiration. In T. K. Oliver (Ed.), *Neonatal respiratory adaptation*. Washington, D. C.: Public Health Service Publication 1432, 1966.

Dawes, G. S., and Mestyán, G. Changes in oxygen consumption of newborn guinea pigs and rabbits on exposure to cold. *J. Physiol.*, 1963, **168**, 22–42.

Dawkins, M. J. R., and Hull, D. Brown fat and the response of the newborn rabbit to cold. *J. Physiol.*, 1963, **169**, 101.

Dawkins, M. J. R., and Scopes, J. W. Nonshivering thermogenesis and brown adipose tissue in the human newborn infant. *Nature*, 1965, **206**, 201–202.

Day, R. Respiratory metabolism in infancy and in childhood. XXVII. Regulation of body temperature of premature infants. *Am. J. Dis. Child.*, 1943, **65**, 376–398.

Day, R. L., Caliguiri, L., Kamenski, C., and Ehrlich, F. Body temperature and survival of premature infants. *Pediatrics*, 1964, **34**, 171–181.

Dees-Mattingly, M. Absorptive area and volume of chorionic villi in circumvallate placentas. *Am. J. Anat.*, 1936, **59**, 485–507.

Dekaban, A. *Neurology of infancy*. Baltimore, Md.: Williams and Wilkins, 1959.

Delange, M., Castan, P., Cadilhac, J., and Passouant, P. Les divers stades du sommeil chez le nouveau-né et le nourisson. *Rev. Neurol.*, 1962, **107**, 271–276.

DeMarsh, Q. B., Alt, H. L., and Windle, W. F. Factors influencing the blood picture of the newborn. *Am. J. Dis. Child.*, 1948, **75**, 860–871.

Dement, W., and Kleitman, N. Cyclic variations in EEG during sleep and their relation to eye movements, body motility, and dreaming. *Electroencephalog. clin. Neurophysiol.*, 1957, **9**, 673–690.

Deming, J., and Hanner, J. P. Respiration in infancy. II. A study of rate, volume, and character of respiration in healthy infants during the neonatal period. *Am. J. Dis. Child.*, 1936, **51**, 823–831.

DeMuth, G. R. Prediction of lung function values in children. *Am. J. Dis. Child.*, 1965, **109**, 443–446.

DeMuth, G. R., Howatt, W. F., and Hill, B. M. The growth of lung function. *Pediatrics*, 1965, **35**, 161–218.

Derbyshire, A. J., Fraser, A. A., McKermott, M., and Bridge, A. Audiometric measurements by electroencephalograph. *Electroencephalog. clin. Neurophysiol.*, 1956, **8**, 467–478.

Desmond, M., Kay, J., and Megarity, A. The phases of "transitional distress" occurring in neonates in association with prolonged postnatal umbilical cord pulsations. *J. Pediat.*, 1959, **55**, 131–151.

Diehl, H. S., and Hesdorffer, M. B. Changes in blood pressure of young men over a seven year period. *Archs. int. Med.*, 1933, **52**, 948–953.

Diemer, K., and Henn, R. The capillary density in the frontal lobe of mature and premature infants. *Biol. neonat.*, 1964, **7**, 270–279.

Dittmer, D. S., and Grebe, R. M. (Eds.) *Handbook of circulation*. Phildelphia: Saunders, 1959.

Doan, C. A. Current views on the origin and maturation of the cells of the blood. *J. Lab. clin. Med.*, 1932, **17**, 887–898.

Dodds, G. S. The area of the chorionic villi in the full-term placenta. *Anat. Rec.*, 1922, **24**, 287–294.

Downing, M. E. Blood pressure of normal girls from three to sixteen years of age. *Am. J. Dis. Child.*, 1947, **73**, 293–316.

Dreyfus-Brisac, C. The electroencephalogram of the premature infant. *World Neurol.*, 1962, **3**, 5–15.

Dreyfus-Brisac, C. The electroencephalogram of the premature infant and full-term newborn. Normal and abnormal development of waking and sleeping patterns. In P. Kellaway and I. Peterson (Eds.), *Neurological and electro-*

encephalographic correlative studies in infancy. New York: Grune and Stratton, 1964. Pp. 186–207.

Dreyfus-Brisac, C. The bioelectrical development of the central nervous system during early life. In F. Falkner (Ed.), *Human development.* Philadelphia: Saunders, 1966. Pp. 286–305.

Dreyfus-Brisac, C., and Blanc, C. Electroencéphalogramme et maturation cérébrale. *Encéphale,* 1956, **3,** 205–245.

Dreyfus-Brisac, C., Flescher, J., and Plassart, E. L'électroencéphalogramme, critère d'âge conceptionnel du nouveau-né à terme et prématuré. *Biol. neonat.,* 1962, **4,** 154–173.

Dreyfus-Brisac, C., and Monod, N. III. Veille, sommeil et réactivité chez le nouveau-né à terme. *Electroencephalog. clin. Neurophysiol.,* 1956, Suppl. 6, 425–431.

Dreyfus-Brisac, C., Samson, D., Blanc, C., and Monod, N. L'électroencéphalogramme de l'enfant normal de moins de 3 ans. *Études Neo-Natales,* 1958, **7,** 143–175.

Dubois, A. B., Botelho, S. Y., and Comroe, J. H., Jr. A new method for measuring airway resistance in man using a body plethysmograph: values in normal subjects and in patients with respiratory disease. *J. clin. Invest.,* 1956, **35,** 327–335.

DuBois, E. F. *Basal metabolism in health and disease.* Philadelphia: Lea and Febiger, 1927.

Dunnill, M. S. Postnatal growth of the lung. *Thorax,* 1962, **17,** 329–333.

Dustman, R. E., and Beck, E. C. Visually evoked potentials: Amplitude changes with age. *Science,* 1966, **151,** 1013–1015.

Eastman, J. J., and Hellman, L. M. *Williams obstetrics.* (12th ed.) New York: Appleton-Century-Crofts, 1961.

Eckstein, A. Untersuchungen über die Angioarchitektonik des Gehirns im frühen Kindesalter. *Z. Neurol.,* 1935, **154,** 298–313.

Eichorn, D. H. Electrocortical and autonomic response in infants to visual and auditory stimuli. Unpublished doctoral dissertation, Northwestern University, 1951.

Eichorn, D. H. A comparison of laboratory determinations and Wetzel Grid estimates of basal metabolism among adolescents. *J. Pediat.,* 1955, **46,** 146–154.

Eichorn, D. H. Biological correlates of behavior. In H. W. Stevenson (Ed.), *Child psychology, Part I, 63rd Yearbook Nat. Soc. Study Educ.* Chicago: University of Chicago Press, 1963. Pp. 4–61.

Eichorn, D. H., and Jones, H. E. Maturation and behavior. In G. H. Seward and J. P. Seward (Eds.), *Current psychological issues.* New York: Henry Holt, 1958. Pp. 211–248.

Eichorn, D. H., and McKee, J. P. Oral temperature and subcutaneous fat during adolescence. *Child. Dev.,* 1953, **24,** 235–247.

Eichorn, D. H., and McKee, J. P. Physiological instability during adolescence. *Child Dev.,* 1958, **29,** 255–268.

Eldridge, F. L., and Hultgren, H. N. The physiologic closure of the ductus arteriosus in the newborn infant. *J. clin. Invest.,* 1955, **34,** 987–996.

Ellingson, R. J. Electroencephalograms of normal, full-term newborns immediately after birth with observations on arousal and visual evoked responses. *Electroenceph. clin. Neurophysiol.,* 1958, **10,** 31–50.

Ellingson, R. J. Cortical electrical responses to visual stimulation in the human infant. *Electroencephalog. clin. Neurophysiol.,* 1960, **12,** 663–677.

Ellingson, R. J. Studies of the electrical activity of the developing human brain. In A. Himwich and H. E. Himwich (Eds.), *Progress in brain research.* Vol. 9. *Developing brain.* Amsterdam: Elsevier, 1964. Pp. 26–53. (a)

Ellingson, R. J. Cerebral electrical responses to auditory and visual stimuli in the infant (human and subhuman studies). In P. Kellaway and I. Petersen (Eds.), *Neurological and electroencephalographic correlative studies in infancy.* New York: Grune and Stratton, 1964. Pp. 78–116. (b)

Ellingson, R. J. Regional physiology of the central nervous system. In E. A. Spiegel (Ed.), *Progress in neurology and psychiatry.* New York: Grune and Stratton, 1965. Pp. 57–85.

Ellingson, R. J. Development of visual evoked responses in human infants recorded by a response averager. *Electroencephalog. clin. Neurophysiol.,* 1966, **21,** 403–404.

Ellingson, R. J. Methods of recording cortical evoked responses in the human infant. In A. Minkowski (Ed.), *Regional development of the brain in early life.* Oxford: Blackwell, 1967. Pp. 413–435. (a)

Ellingson, R. J. The study of brain electrical activity in infants. In L. P. Lipsitt and C. C. Spiker (Eds.), *Advances in child development and behavior.* Vol. 3. New York: Academic Press, 1967. Pp. 53–97. (b)

Emery, J. L., and MacDonald, S. The weight of the ventricles in the later weeks of intra-uterine life. *Br. Heart J.,* 1960, **22,** 563–570.

Emery, J. L., and Mithal, A. The number of alveoli in the terminal respiratory unit of man during late intrauterine life and childhood. *Archs. Dis. Childh.,* 1960, **35,** 544–547.

Emery, J. L., and Mithal, A. Weights of cardiac ventricles at and after birth. *Br. Heart J.,* 1961, **23,** 313–316.

Engel, R. Evaluation of electroencephalographic tracings in newborns. *Lancet,* 1961, **81,** 523–532.

Engel, R., and Butler, B. V. Appraisal of conceptual age of newborn infants by electroencephalographic methods. *J. Pediat.,* 1963, **63,** 386–393.

Engel, R. Electroencephalographic responses to photic stimulation, and their correlation with maturation. *Ann. N. Y. Acad. Sci.,* 1964, **117,** Art. 1, 407–412.

Engel, S. *The child's lung.* London: Arnold, 1947.

Engel, S. *Lung structure.* Springfield, Ill.: Thomas, 1962.

Engel, S. *The prenatal lung.* Oxford: Pergamon Press, 1966.

Epstein, N. The heart in normal infants and children. *J. Pediat.,* 1948, **32,** 39–45.

Espmark, J. A., and Rabo, E. The formation of neutralizing antibody following smallpox vaccination in young infants with maternal immunity. *Acta paediat. Scand.,* 1965, **54,** 341–347.

Evans, D. G., and Smith, J. W. Response of the young infant to active immunization. *Br. med. Bull.,* 1963, **19,** 225–229.

Faber, H. K., and James, C. A. The range and distribution of blood pressures in normal children. *Am. J. Dis. Child.,* 1921, **22,** 7–28.

Fabricius, H. *The embryological treatises.* (Trans. by H. B. Adelman.) Ithaca, N. Y.: Cornell University Press, 1942.

Falkner, F. General considerations in human development. In F. Falkner (Ed.), *Human development.* Phildelphia: Saunders, 1966. Pp. 10–39.

Falkner, F., Banik, N.D.D., and Westland, R. Intrauterine blood transfer between uni-ovular twins, *Biol. neonat.,* 1962, **4,** 52–60.

Faxén, N. Red blood picture in healthy infants. *Acta paediat.,* 1937, **19** (Suppl. 1), 1–142.

Ferris, B. G., and Smith, C. W. Maximum breathing capacity and vital capacity in female children and adolescents. *Pediatrics,* 1953, **12,** 341–352.

Ferris, B. G., Whittenberger, J. L., and Gallagher, J. R. Maximum breathing capacity and vital capacity of male children and adolescents. *Pediatrics,* 1952, **9,** 657–670.

Ferriss, G. S., Davis, G. D., Dorsen, M. McF., and Hackett, E. R. Changes in latency and form of the photically induced average response in human infants. *Electroencephal. clin. Neurophysiol.*, 1967, **22**, 305–312.

Fichtelius, K. E. A difference between lymph nodal and thymio lymphocytes shown by transfusion of labelled cells. *Acta Anat.*, 1958, **32**, 114–125. (a)

Fichtelius, K. E. Further studies on the difference between lymphocytes of lymph nodes and thymus. *Acta Haemat.*, 1958, **19**, 187–190. (b)

Fichtelius, K. E., and Diderholm, H. On the recirculation of lymphocytes from the lymph to the blood. *Acta Haemat.*, 1959, **22**, 322–328.

Findlay, L. The blood in infancy. *Archs. Dis. Childh.*, 1946, **21**, 195–208.

Fisher, D. A., Oddie, T. H., and Makoski, E. J. The influence of environmental temperature on thyroid, adrenal, and water metabolism in the newborn human infant. *Pediatrics*, 1966, **37**, 583–591.

Flexner, L. B. Enzymatic and functional patterns of the developing mammalian brain. In H. Waelsch, (Ed.), *Biochemistry of the developing nervous system.* New York: Academic Press, 1955. Pp. 281–295.

Fois, A. *The electroencephalogram of the normal child.* Springfield, Ill.: Thomas, 1961.

Fomon, S. J. (Ed.) Normal and abnormal respiration in children. *37th. Ross Conference on Pediatric Research.* Columbus, Ohio: Ross Laboratories, 1961.

Forfar, J. O., and Kibel, A. M. Blood pressure in the newborn estimated by the flush method. *Archs. Dis. Childh.*, 1956, **31**, 126–130.

Franklin, E. C., and Kunkel, H. G. Comparative levels of high molecular weight (19S) gamma-globulin in maternal and umbilical cord sera. *J. lab. clin. Med.*, 1958, **52**, 724–729.

Fraser, I. D., and Raper, A. B. Observations on the change from foetal to adult erythropoiesis. *Archs. Dis. Childh.*, 1962, **37**, 289–296.

Freda, V., and Adamsons, K., Jr. Exchange transfusion in utero: report of case. *Am. J. Obstet. Gynec.*, 1964, **89**, 817–821.

Fudenberg, H. H., and Fudenberg, B. R. Antibody to hereditary human gamma-globulin (Gm) factor resulting from maternal-fetal incompatibility. *Science*, 1964, **145**(1), 170–171.

Fujimori, B., Yokota, T., Ishibashi, Y., and Takei, T. Analysis of the electroencephalogram of children by histogram method. *Electroencephalog. clin. Neurophysiol.*, 1958, **10**, 241–252.

Fulginiti, V. A., Sieber, O. F., Jr., Claman, H. N., and Merrill, D. Serum immunoglobulin measurement during the first year of life and in immunoglobulin-deficiency states. *Pediatrics*, 1966, **68**, 723–730.

Gairdner, D., Marks, J., and Roscoe, J. D. Blood formation in infancy. Part II. Normal erythropoiesis. *Archs. Dis. Childh.*, 1952, **27**, 214–221.

Ganong, W. F. *Review of medical physiology.* Los Altos, Cal.: Lange Medical Publications, 1967.

Garn, S. M., and Clark, L. C. The sex difference in the basal metabolic rate. *Child Dev.*, 1953, **24**, 215–224.

Garn, S. M., Clark, L. C., Jr., and Portray, R. Relationship between body composition and basal metabolic rate in children. *J. appl. Physiol.*, 1953, **6**, 163–167.

Gatti, R. A. Hematocrit values of capillary blood in the newborn infant. *J. Pediat.*, 1967, **70**, 117–119.

Gerard, G. De l'obliteration du canal arterial, les theories et les faits. *J. Anat.* (Paris), 1900, **36**, 323–357.

Gessner, I., Krovetz, L. J., Benson, R. W., Prystowsky, H., Stenger, V., and Eitzmann, D. V. Hemodynamic adaptations in the newborn infant. *Pediatrics*, 1965, **36**, 752–762.

Gianelli, A., Pavoni, M., and Scopetta, V. Elettroencefalografia fetale. I. Nota preliminare. *Arch. Obstet. Ginec.*, 1963, **68**, 228–234.

Gibbs, E. L., and Gibbs, F. A. Diagnostic and localising value of electroencephalographic studies in sleep. *Res. Publ. Ass. nerv. ment. Dis.*, 1947, **26**, 366–376.

Gibbs, F. A., and Gibbs, E. L. *Atlas of electroencephalography.* Vol. I. Cambridge, Mass.: Addison-Wesley, 1950.

Gibbs, F. A., and Knott, J. R. Growth of the electrical activity of the cortex. *Electroencephalog. clin. Neurophysiol.*, 1949, **1**, 223–229.

Giersten, J. C. Atherosclerosis in an autopsy series. *Acta path. et Microbiol. Scandinav.*, 1964, **61**, 233–242.

Gilmour, J. R. Normal haemopoiesis in intrauterine and neonatal life. *J. Path. Bact.*, 1941, **52**, 25–55.

Gitlin, D. Protein metabolism, cell formation and immunity. *Pediatrics*, 1964, **34**, 198–210.

Gitlin, D., Kumate, J., Urrusti, J., and Morales, C. The selectivity of the human placenta in the transfer of plasma proteins from mother to fetus. *J. clin. Invest.*, 1964, **43**, 1938–1951.

Glaser, G. H. The normal electroencephalogram and its reactivity. In G. H. Glaser (Ed.), *EEG and Behavior.* New York: Basic Books, 1963. Pp. 3–23.

Goldie, L., and Van Velzer, C. Innate sleep rhythms. *Brain*, 1965, **88**, 1043–1056.

Goldring, D., and Wohltmann, H. Flush method for blood pressure determinations in newborn infants. *J. Pediat.*, 1952, **40**, 285–289.

Goldring, S., Sugaya, E., and O'Leary, J. L. Maturation of evoked cortical responses in animal and man. In P. Kellaway and I. Petersen (Eds.), *Neurological and electroencephalographic correlative studies in infancy.* New York: Grune and Stratton, 1964. Pp. 68–77.

Gooch, W. M., Mintz, A. A., and Nova, J. J. The lack of effect of glucose ingestion upon electrocardiograms in children. *J. Pediat.*, 1967, **71**, 410–413.

Goodman, H. G., Cumming, G. R., and Raber, M. B. Photocell oscillometer for measuring systolic pressure in newborn. *Am. J. Dis. Child.*, 1962, **103**, 152–159.

Goodyer, A. V. N. Clinical fetal electrocardiography. *Yale J. Biol. Med.*, 1942, **15**, 1–19.

Gorman, J. G., and Chandler, J. G. Is there an immunologically incompetent lymphocyte? *Blood*, 1964, **23**, 117–128.

Graham, A. W., Hines, E. A., Jr., and Gage, R. P. Blood pressure in children between the ages of five and sixteen years. *Am. J. Dis. Child.*, 1945, **69**, 203–207.

Grossman, B. J., Heyn, R. M., and Rosenfeld, I. H. Coagulation studies in the newborn infant. I. Normal infants. *Pediatrics*, 1952, **9**, 182–191.

Gruenwald, P. Normal and abnormal expansion of the lungs of newborn infants obtained at autopsy. II. Opening pressure, maximal volume, and stability of expansion. *Lab. Invest.*, 1963, **12**, 563–576.

Gruenwald, P. Pulmonary surfactant and stability of aeration in young human fetuses. *Pediatrics*, 1966, **38**, 4–6.

Grundbacher, F. J. Changes in human A antigen of erythrocytes with the individual's age. *Nature*, 1964, **204**, 192–194.

Grundbacher, F. J. Quantitative variation of the A antigen at birth: its significance in ABO hemolytic disease and in the infant's development. *Acta paediat. Scand.*, 1965, **54**, 550–556.

Guest, G. M., and Brown, E. W. Erythrocytes and hemoglobin of the blood in infancy and childhood. III. Factors in variability, statistical studies. *Am. J. Dis. Child.*, 1957, **93**, 486–509.

Guest, G. M., Brown, E. W., and Lahey, M. E. Normal blood values in infancy and childhood. *Pediat. clin. N. Am.*, 1957, **4**, 357–369.

Guest, G. M., Brown, E. W., and Wing, M. Erythrocytes and hemoglobin of the blood in infancy and childhood. II. Variability in number, size, and hemoglobin content of the erythrocytes during the first five years of life. *Am. J. Dis. Child.*, 1938, **56**, 529–549.

Gupta, J. M., and Scopes, J. W. Observations on blood pressure in newborn infants. *Archs. Dis. Childh.*, 1965, **40**, 637–644.

Hafkesbring, E. M., Drawe, C. E., and Ashman, R. Children's electrocardiograms —measurements for 100 normal children. *Am. J. Dis. Child.*, 1937, **53**, 1457–1469.

Hagerman, D. D., and Villee, C. A. Transport functions of the placenta. *Physiol. Rev.*, 1960, **40**, 313–330.

Hahn, L. The relationship of blood pressure to weight, height and body surface area in school boys aged 11 to 15 years. *Archs. Dis. Child.*, 1952, **27**, 43–53.

Hamilton, H. F. H. The cardiac output in normal pregnancy as determined by the Cournand right heart catheterization technique. *J. Obstet. Gynaec. Br. Emp.*, 1949, **56**, 548–552.

Hamilton, W. F. (Ed.) *Handbook of physiology.* Section 2 (*Circulation*), Vol. 1. Washington: American Physiological Society, 1962.

Harned, H. S., Jr., Wolkoff, A. S., Pickerell, J., and MacKinney, L. G. Hemodynamic observations during birth of the lamb. *Am. J. Dis. Child.*, 1961, **102**, 180–189.

Harris, R. E. Some observations on blood pressure in children. In J. P. Ambuel, (Ed.), *Physical and behavioral growth.* Rep. 26th Ross Pediat. Res. Conf. Columbus, Ohio: Ross Laboratories, 1958, 49–52.

Hawkins, W. W., Speck, E., and Leonard, V. G. Variation of the hemoglobin level with age and sex. *Blood*, 1954, **9**, 999–1007.

Heaf, P. J., and Gillam, P. M. Peak flow rates in normal and asthmatic children. *Br. med. J.*, 1962, **5292**, 1595–1596.

Heard, J. D., Burkley, G. G., and Schaeffer, C. R. Electrocardiograms derived from eleven fetuses through the medium of direct leads. *Am. Heart J.*, 1936, **11**, 41–48.

Heikinheimo, R. Coagulation studies with fetal blood. *Biol. neonat.*, 1964, **7**, 319–327.

Heim, T., and Hull, D. The blood flow and oxygen consumption of brown adipose tissue in the newborn rabbit. *J. Physiol.*, 1966, **186**, 42–55.

Hellstrom, B., Karlsson, B., and Mussbichler, H. Electrode placement in EEG of infants and its anatomical relationship studied radiographically. *Electroencephalog. clin. Neurophysiol.*, 1963, **15**, 115–117.

Henry, C. E. Electroencephalograms of normal children. *Monogr. Soc. Res. Child Dev.*, 1944, **9** (Serial 39, No. 3).

Hepner, R., and Bowen, M. The placenta and the fetus. *J. Am. med. Ass.*, 1960, **172**, 427–432.

Herlitz, G. Zur Kenntis der anämischen und polyzytämischen Zustande bei neugeborenen sowie des Icterus gravis neonatorum. *Acta paediat.*, 1942, **29**, 211–253.

Hicks, D. A., Hope, A., Turnbull, A. L., and Verel, D. The estimation and prediction of normal blood volume. *Clin. Sci.*, 1956, **15**, 557–565.

Hilgartner, M. W., and Smith, C. H. Plasma thromboplastin antecedent (factor XI) in the neonate. *J. Pediat.*, 1965, **66**, 747–752.

Hill, J. R. Reaction of the newborn animal to environmental temperature. *Br. med. Bull.*, 1961, **17**, 164–167.

Hill, J. R., and Rahimtulla, K. A. Heat balance and the metabolic rate of newborn babies in relation to environmental temperature; and the effect of age and of weight on basal metabolic rate. *J. Physiol.*, 1965, **180**, 239–265.

Himwich, H. *Brain metabolism and cerebral disorders.* Baltimore, Md.: Williams & Wilkins, 1951.

Himwich, W. A., Benardon, H. B. W., and Tucker, B. E. Metabolic studies on perinatal brain. In P. W. Bowman, and H. V. Mautner (Eds.), *Mental retardation.* New York: Grune and Stratton, 1960. Pp. 173–179.

Hines, E. A., Jr. Reaction of the blood pressure of 400 school children to a standard stimulus. *J. Am. med. Ass.*, 1937, **108**, 1249–1250.

Hitzig, W. H. *Die Plasmaproteine in der klinischen Medizin.* Berlin: Springerverlag, 1963.

Holland, W. W., and Young, I. M. Neonatal blood pressure in relation to maturity, mode of delivery, and condition at birth. *Br. med. J.*, 1956, **2**, 1331–1333.

Holliday, M. A., Potter, D., Jarrah, A., and Bearg, S. The relation of metabolic rate to body weight and organ size. *Pediat. Res.*, 1967, **1**, 185–195.

Hon, E. H. The fetal heart rate patterns preceding death in utero. *Am. J. Obstet. Gynec.*, 1959, **78**, 47–56. (a)

Hon, E. H. Observations on "pathologic" fetal bradycardia. *Am. J. Obstet. Gynec.*, 1959, **77**, 1084–1099. (b)

Hon, E. H. Electronic evaluation of fetal heart rate. VI. Fetal distress—working hypothesis. *Am. J. Obstet. Gynec.*, 1962, **83**, 333–353.

Hon, E. H. Classification of fetal heart rate. I. Working classification. *Obstet. Gynec.*, 1963, **22**, 137–146.

Hon, E. H. The human fetal circulation in normal labor. In D. E. Cassels (Ed.), *The heart and circulation in the newborn and infant.* New York: Grune and Stratton, 1966. Pp. 37–52.

Hon, E. H. Instrumentation of fetal heart rate and fetal electrocardiography. III. Fetal ECG electrodes: further observations. *Obstet. Gynec.*, 1967, **30**, 281–286.

Horan, M. Studies in anaemia of infancy and childhood. *Archs. Dis. Child.*, 1950, **25**, 110–128.

Hort, W. Morphologische Untersuchungen am Herzen vor, wahrend und nach der postnatalen Kreislaufumschaltung. *Virchow Arch. Pathol. Anat.*, 1955, **326**, 458–484.

Hort, W. The normal heart of the fetus and its metamorphosis in the transition period. In D. E. Cassels (Ed.), *The heart and circulation in the newborn and infant.* New York: Grune and Stratton, 1966. Pp. 210–224.

Hrbek, A., and Mares, P. Cortical evoked responses to visual stimulation in fullterm and premature newborns. *Electroencephalog. clin. Neurophysiol.*, 1964, **16**, 575–581.

Hubbard, J. P., Preston, W. N., and Ross, R. A. The velocity of blood flow in infants and young children determined by radioactive sodium. *J. clin. Invest.*, 1942, **21**, 613–617.

Huckabee, W. E. Uterine blood flow. *Am. J. Obstet. Gynec.*, 1962, **84**, 1623–1633.

Hughes, J. G., Davis, B. C., and Brennan, M. L. Electroencephalography of newborn infant; studies on premature infants. *Pediatrics*, 1951, **7**, 707–712.

Hughes, J. G., Ehemann, B., and Brown, U. A. Electroencephalography of newborn; studies on normal, full-term, sleeping infants. *Am. J. Dis. Child.*, 1948, **76**, 503–512.

Hughes, J. G., Ehemann, B., and Hill, F. S. Electroencephalography of newborn; studies on normal, full term infants while awake and while drowsy. *Am. J. Dis. Child.*, 1949, **77**, 310–314.

Huhmar, E., and Jarvinen, P. A. Observations on fetal electroencephalography. *Ann. Chir. Gynaec. Fenn.*, 1963, **52**, 372–375.

Hull, D. The structure and function of brown adipose tissue. *Br. med. Bull.*, 1966, **22**, 92–96.

Ibsen, H. L. Prenatal growth in guinea pigs with special reference to environmental factors affecting weight at birth. *J. exper. Zool.*, 1928, **51**, 51–91.

Iliff, A., and Lee, V. A. Pulse rate, respiratory rate, and body temperature of children between two months and 18 years of age. *Child Dev.*, 1952, **23**, 237–245.

Jager, B. V., and Wollenman, O. J., Jr. Anatomic study of closure of ductus arteriosus. *Am. J. Pathol.*, 1942, **18**, 595–613.

James, L. S. Onset of breathing and resuscitation. *Pediat. clin. N. Am.*, 1966, **13**, 621–634.

James, L. S., and Adamsons, K., Jr. Respiratory physiology of the fetus and newborn infant. *New Eng. J. Med.*, 1964, **271**, 1352–1360.

James, L. S., Burnard, E. D., and Rowe, R. D. Abnormal shunting through the foramen ovale after birth. *Am. J. Dis. Childh.*, 1961, **102**, 550.

James, S., and Burnard, E. Biochemical changes occurring during asphyxia at birth and some effects on the heart. *Ciba Foundation symposium on somatic stability of the newly born.* Boston: Little, Brown, 1961. Pp. 75–91.

Jasper, H. H. The ten twenty electrode system of the International Federation. *Electroencephalog. clin. Neurophysiol.*, 1958, **10**, 371–375.

Jegier, W., Blankenship, W., and Lind, J. Venous pressure in the first hour of life and its relationship to placental transfusion. *Acta paediat.*, 1963, **52**, 485–496.

Jegier, W., Blankenship, W., Lind, J., and Kitchin, A. The changing circulatory pattern of the newborn infant studied by the indicator dilution technique. *Acta paediat.*, 1964, **53**, 541–552.

Jegier, W., Sekelj, P., Davenport H. T., and McGregor, M. Cardiac output and related hemodynamic data in normal children and adults. *Can. J. biochem. Physiol.*, 1961, **39**, 1747–1753.

Jost, A., and Policard, A. Contribution experimentale à l'etude du développement prénatal du poumon chez le lapin. *Arch. Anat. Micr.*, 1948, **37**, 323–332.

Jouvet, M. Telencephalic and rhombencephalic sleep in the cat. In G. E. W. Westenholme and M. O'Connor (Eds.), *The nature of sleep.* Boston: Little, Brown, 1961. Pp. 188–208.

Jouvet, M. The rhombencephalic phase of sleep. In G. Moruzzi, A. Fessard, and H. Jasper (Eds.), *Progress in brain research.* Vol. 1. *Brain mechanisms.* New York: Elsevier, 1963. Pp. 406–424.

Joy, R. J. T. Responses of cold-acclimatized men to infused norepinephrine. *J. appl. Physiol.*, 1963, **18**, 1209–1212.

Kafka, H. A simple method for blood pressure measurements in the premature and newborn infant. *Pediatrics*, 1967, **40**, 106–108.

Kaiser, I. H. Correlation of circulatory changes before birth. In D. E. Cassels (Ed.), *The heart and circulation in the newborn and infant.* New York: Grune and Stratton, 1966. Pp. 65–69.

Karlberg, P. Determination of standard energy metabolism (basal metabolism) in normal infants. *Acta paediat.*, 1952, **41**, Suppl. 89.

Karlberg, P. The adaptive changes in the immediate postnatal period, with particular reference to respiration. *J. Pediat.*, 1960, **56**, 585–604.

Karlberg, P., Cherry, R. B., Escardo, F. E., and Koch, G. Respiratory studies in newborn infants. II. Pulmonary ventilation and mechanics of breathing in first few minutes of life including onset of respiration. *Acta paediat.*, 1962, **51**, 121–136.

Karlberg, P., Moore, R. E., and Oliver, T. K. Thermogenic and cardiovascular responses of the newborn baby to noradrenaline. *Acta paediat. Scand.*, 1965, **54**, 225–238.

Kato, K. Leucocytes in infancy and childhood; statistical analysis of 1,081 total and differential counts from birth to 15 years. *J. Pediat.*, 1935, **7**, 7–15.

Keating, J. M., and Edwards, W. A. Clinical studies on the pulse in childhood. *Archs. Pediat.*, 1888, 344–353.

Keen, E. N. The postnatal development of the human cardiac ventricles. *J. Anat.* (Lond.), 1955, **89**, 484–502.

Keith, J. D., Rowe, R. D., and Vlad, P. *Heart disease in infancy and childhood.* (2nd Ed.) New York: Macmillan, 1967.

Kellaway, P. The development of sleep spindles and of arousal patterns in infants and their characteristics in normal and certain abnormal states. *Electroencephalog. clin. Neurophysiol.*, 1952, **4**, 369.

Kellaway, P. Electroencephalographic characteristics of the newly born. In J. L. Kay (Ed.), *Physical diagnosis of the newly born. Rep. 46th Ross Conf. Pediat. Res.* Columbus, Ohio: Ross Laboratories, 1964. Pp. 86–96.

Kellaway, P. K., and Fox, B. J. Electroencephalographic diagnosis of cerebral pathology in infants during sleep. I. Rationale, technique, and the characteristics of normal sleep in infants. *J. Pediat.*, 1952, **41**, 262–287.

Kellogg, H. B. Studies on the fetal circulation of mammals. *Am. J. Physiol.*, 1930, **91**, 637–48.

Kendall, B., Farrell, D. M., and Kane, H. H. Uses of the fetal ECG. *Am. J. Nursing*, 1964, **64**, 75–78.

Kennedy, J. A., and Clark, S. L. Observations on the ductus arteriosus of the guinea-pig in relation to its method of closure. *Anat. Rec.*, 1941, **79**, 349–371.

Kennedy, J. A., and Clark, S. L. Observations on the physiological reactions of the ductus arteriosus. *Am. J. Physiol.*, 1942, **136**, 140–147.

Kennedy, M. C. S., Thursby-Pelham, D. C., and Oldham, P. D. Pulmonary function studies in normal boys. *Archs. Dis. Childh.*, 1957, **32**, 347–354.

Kerpel-Frönius, E., Varga, F., and Mestyán, G. Clinical aspects of stability. In G. E. W. Wolstenholme (Ed.), *Somatic stability of the newly born.* London: J. & A. Churchill, 1961. Pp. 326–328.

Kerr, M. M. Anaemia and polcythaemia in uniovular twins. *Br. med. J.*, 1959, **2**, 902–903.

Kety, S. S. Changes in cerebral circulation and oxygen consumption which accompany maturation and aging. In H. Waelsch (Ed.), *Biochemistry of the developing nervous system.* New York: Academic Press, 1955. Pp. 208–217.

Kidd, L., Levison, H., Gemmel, P., Aharon, A., and Swyer, P. R. Limb blood flow in the normal and sick newborn. *Am. J. Dis. Child.*, 1966, **112**, 402–407.

Kikuchi, N. Normal and retarded development of the lung and alveolar hypoplasia of neonatal infants. *Tohoku J. exper. Med.*, 1962, **77**, 99–119.

Kiloh, L. G., and Osselton, J. W. *Clinical electroencephalography.* London: Butterworths, 1961.

Kjellberg, S. R., Rudhe, U., and Zetterstrom, R. Heart volume variations in the neonatal period. *Acta Radiol.*, 1954, **42**, 173–180.

Klaus, M., Braun, J., and Tooley, W. H. Pulmonary capillary blood flow in the newborn infant. *Am. J. Dis. Child.*, 1961, **102**, 466–467.

Kochwa, S., Rosenfield, R. E., Tallal, L., and Wasserman, L. R. Isoagglutinins associated with ABO erythroblastosis. *J. clin. Invest.*, 1961, **40**, 874–880.

Kossmann, C. E. The normal electrocardiogram. *Circulation*, 1953, **8**, 920–936.

Kovalcik, V. The response of the isolated ductus arteriosus to oxygen and anoxia. *J. Physiol.*, 1963, **165**, 185–197.

Krovetz, L. J., McLoughlin, T. G., Mitchell, M. B., and Schiebler, G. L. Hemodynamic findings in normal children. *Pediat. Res.*, 1967, 1, 122–130.

Lacey, J. I., and Lacey, B. C. Verification and extension of the principle of autonomic response stereotypy. *Am. J. Psychol.*, 1958, 71, 50–73.

Lacey, J. I., and Lacey, B. C. The law of initial value in the longitudinal study of autonomic constitution: reproducibility of autonomic responses and response patterns over a four-year interval. *Ann. N.Y. Acad. Sci.*, 1962, 98, 1257–1290.

Larks, S. D. *Fetal electrocardiography.* Springfield, Ill.: Thomas, 1960.

Larks, S. D. Resemblance of the fetal ECG complex to the standard Lead II QRS of the newborn. *Obstet. Gynec.*, 1964, 24, 1–5.

Larks, S. D., and Larks, G. G. The electrical axis of the fetal heart: a new criterion for fetal well-being or distress. *Am. J. Obstet. Gynec.*, 1965, 93, 975–983.

Larks, S. D., and Larks, G. G. Components of the fetal electrocardiogram and intrauterine electrical axis: quantitative data. *Biol. neonat.*, 1966, 10, 140–152.

Larrieu, M. J., Soulier, J. P., and Minkowski, A. Le sang du cordon ombilical: étude compléte de sa coagulabilité, comparaison avec le sang maternel. *Étud. néonatal.*, 1952, 1, 39–60.

Lawrence, W. J. The carbonic anhydrase content of the blood of one hundred normal Australian subjects. *Med. J. Australia*, 1947, 1, 587–589.

Ledbetter, M. K., Homma, T., and Farhi, L. E. Readjustment in distribution of alveolar ventilation and lung perfusion in the newborn. *Pediatrics*, 1967, 40, 940–945.

Lee, V. A., and Iliff, A. The energy metabolism of infants and young children during postprandial sleep. *Pediatrics*, 1956, 18, 739–749.

Leichsenring, J. M., Norris, L. M., and Halbert, M. L. Hemoglobin, red cell count, and mean corpuscular hemoglobin of healthy infants. *Am. J. Dis. Child.*, 1952, 84, 27–34.

Leichsenring, J. M., Norris, L. M., Lamison, S. A., and Halbert, M. L. Blood cell values for healthy adolescents. *Am. J. Dis. Child.*, 1955, 90, 159–163.

Lesser, R. E., Meyer, R., and Henderson, A. T. Circulation times in newborn infants by the fluorescein method. *Am. J. Dis. Child.*, 1952, 83, 645–648.

Levine, P., Burnham, L., Katzin, E. M., and Vogel, P. The role of iso-immunization in the pathogenesis of erythroblastosis fetalis. *Am. J. Obstet. Gynec.*, 1941, 42, 925–937.

Levine, S. Z., and Gordon, H. H. Physiologic handicaps of the premature infant. I. Their pathogenesis. *Am. J. Dis. Child.*, 1942, 64, 274–296.

Levison, H., Kidd, B. S. L., Gemmell, P. A., and Swyer, P. R. Blood pressure in normal full-term and premature infants. *Am. J. Dis. Child*, 1966, 111, 374–379.

Levison, H., and Swyer, P. R. Oxygen consumption and the thermal environment in newly born infants. *Biol. neonat.*, 1964, 7, 305–312.

Levy, R. L., Hillman, C. C., and Stroud, W. D. Transient hypertension—its significance in terms of later development of sustained hypertension and cardiovascular disease. *J. Am. med. Ass.*, 1944, 126, 829–833.

Lewis, R. C., Duval, A. M., and Iliff, A. Standards for the basal metabolism of children from two to 15 years of age inclusive. *J. Pediat.*, 1943, 23, 1–18.

Liberson, W. T., and Frazier, W. H. Evaluation of EEG patterns of newborn babies. *Am. J. Psychiat.*, 1962, 118, 1125–1131.

Lincoln, E. M. The hearts of normal children. I. Clinical studies, including notes on effort syndrome. *Am. J. Dis. Child.*, 1928, 35, 398–410.

Lind, J. Heart volume in normal infants; roentgenological study, *Acta radiol.*, 1950, Suppl. 82, 3–127.

Lind, J. Discussion. In D. Cassels (Ed.), *The heart and circulation in the newborn and infant.* New York: Grune and Stratton, 1966. Pp. 130–132.

Lind, J., Stern, L., and Wegelius, C. *Human foetal and neonatal circulation.* Springfield, Ill.: Thomas, 1964.

Lind, J., and Wegelius, C. Human fetal circulation: changes in the cardiovascular system at birth and disturbances in the post-natal closure of the foramen ovale and ductus arteriosus. *Cold Spr. Harb. Symp. Quant. Biol.*, 1954, **19**, 109–125.

Lindsley, D. B. Brain potentials in children and adults. *Science*, 1936, **84**, 354.

Lindsley, D. B. Electrical potentials of the brain in children and adults. *J. gen. Psychol.*, 1938, **19**, 285–306.

Lindsley, D. B. A longitudinal study of the occipital alpha rhythm in normal children: frequency and amplitude standards. *J. genet. Psychol.*, 1939, **55**, 197–213.

Lindsley, D. B. Heart and brain potentials of human fetuses in utero. *Am. J. Psychol.*, 1942, **55**, 412–416.

Lindsley, D. B., Schreiner, L. H., Knowles, W. B., and Magoun, H. W. Behavioral and EEG changes following chronic brain lesions in the cat. *Electroencephalog. clin. Neurophysiol.*, 1950, **2**, 483–498.

Lindsley, D. B. Attention, consciousness, sleep, and wakefulness. In J. Field, H. W. Magoun, and V. E. Hall (Eds.), *Handbook of physiology.* Section 1, Vol. 3. Washington, D.C.: American Physiological Society, 1960. Pp. 1553–1593.

Lipton, E. L. Autonomic function in the neonate. VII: Maturational changes in cardiac control. *Child Dev.*, 1966, **37**, 1–16.

Lipton, E. L., Steinschneider, A., and Richmond, J. B. Autonomic function in the neonate. II: Physiologic effects of motor restraint. *Psychosom. Med.*, 1960, **22**, 57–65.

Lipton, E. L., Steinschneider, A., and Richmond, J. B. The autonomic nervous system in early life. *New Eng. J. Med.*, 1965, **273**, 147–154, 201–208.

Littlewood, J. M. Polycythaemia and anaemia in newborn monozygotic twin girls. *Br. med. J.*, 1963, **2**, 857–859.

Londe, S. Blood pressure in children as determined under office conditions. *Clin. Pediat.*, 1966, **5**, 71–78.

Loomis, A. L., Harvey, E. N., and Hobart, G. Electrical potentials of the human brain. *J. exp. Psychol.*, 1936, **19**, 249–279.

Loosli, C. G., and Potter, E. L. Pre- and postnatal development of the respiratory portion of the human lung. *Am. Rev. resp. Dis.*, 1959, **80** (1, part 2), 5–10.

Ludwig, G. N., and Stolz, H. R. Temperature variations in normal preschool children. *Child Dev.*, 1931, **2**, 225–228.

Lyons, H. A., Tanner, R. W., and Picco, T. Pulmonary function studies in children. *Am. J. Dis. Child.*, 1960, **100**, 196–207.

Magoun, H. W. The ascending reticular system and wakefulness. In J. F. Delafresnaye (Ed.), *Brain mechanisms and consciousness.* Oxford: Blackwell, 1964. p. 1–20.

Mai, H., and Schaper, G. Elektrencephalographische Untersuchungen an Frühgeborenen. *Ann. Paediat.*, 1953, **180**, 345–365.

Malan, A. F. Respiratory rates and patterns in normal newborn infants. *Clin. Pediat.*, 1966, **5**, 593–596.

Mali, A., and Räihä, C. E. Vergleich zwischen dem Kapillarnetz des frühegeborenen und des reifen Kindes und über die Bedeutung des unentwickelten Kapillartnetzes bei der Entstehung gewisser bei Frügeburten vorkommender Eigenschaften. *Acta paediat.*, 1935, **18**, 118–141.

Marcel, M. P., and Exchaquet, J. P. L'electrocardiogramme du foetus humaine avec un cas de double rythme auriculaire verifie. *Arch. Mal. Coeur.*, 1938, **31**, 504–512.

Maresh, M. M. Growth of the heart related to bodily growth during childhood and adolescence. *Pediatrics*, 1948, **2**, 382–404.

Marsh, M. E., and Murlin, J. R. Energy metabolism of premature and undersized infants. *Am. J. Dis. Child.*, 1925, **30**, 310–320.

Mårtennsson, L., and Fudenberg, H. H. Gm genes and γ-G-globulin synthesis in the human fetus. *J. Immunol.*, 1965, **94**, 514–520.

Matoth, Y. Phagocytic and ameboid activities of the leukocytes in the newborn infant. *Pediatrics*, 1952, **9**, 748–755.

Matsuda, G., Schroeder, W. H., Jones, R. T., and Weliky, W. Is there an "embryonic" or "primitive" human hemoglobin? *Blood*, 1960, **16**, 984–966.

Mattingly, R. F., and Larks, S. D. The fetal electrocardiogram. *J. Am. med. Ass.*, 1963, **183**, 245–248.

McCammon, R. W. A longitudinal study of electrocardiographic intervals in healthy children. *Acta paediat.*, 1961, **50**, Suppl. 126.

McCullagh, E. P., and Jones, R. Effect of androgens on the blood count of men. *J. clin. Endocrinol.*, 1942, **2**, 243–251.

McDonald, G. A., Dodds, T. C., and Cruickshank, B. *Atlas of hematology*. Baltimore, Md.: Williams and Wilkins, 1965.

McElfresh, A. E. Coagulation during the neonatal period. *Am. J. med. Sci.*, 1961, **242**, 771–779.

McElfresh, A. E., Sharpsteen, J. R., and Akabane, T. The generation of thromboplastin and levels of plasma thromboplastin component in the blood of infants. *Pediatrics*, 1956, **17**, 870–876.

McGovern, J. J., Jones, A. R., and Steinberg, A. G. The hematocrit of capillary blood. *New Eng. J. Med.*, 1955, **253**, 308–312.

McIlwain, H. *Biochemistry of the central nervous system*. London: J. A. Churchill, 1966.

McKee, J. P., and Eichorn, D. H. Seasonal variations in physiological functions during adolescence. *Child Dev.*, 1953, **24**, 225–234.

McKeown, T., and Record, R. G. The influence of placental size on foetal growth in man, with special reference to multiple pregnancy. *J. Endocrinal.*, 1953, **9**, 418–426.

McNamara, D. G. Electrocardiography of the neonate. In J. L. Kay (Ed.), *Physical diagnosis of the newly born, Rep. 46th Ross Conf. Pediat. Res.* Columbus, Ohio: Ross Laboratories, 1964. Pp. 56–64.

Mead, J. Mechanical properties of the lungs. *Physiol. Rev.*, 1961, **41**, 281–330.

Méndez-Bauer, C., Posiero, J. J., Arellano-Hernández, G. Zambrana, M. A., and Caldeyro-Barcia, R. Effects of atropine on the heart rate of the human fetus during labor. *Am. J. Obstet. Gynec.*, 1963, **85**, 1033–1053.

Merritt, K. K., and Davidson, L. T. The blood during the first year of life. 1. Normal values for erythrocytes, hemoglobin, reticulocytes and platelets, and their relationship to neonatal bleeding and coagulation time. *Am. J. Dis. Child.*, 1933, **46**, 990–1010.

Meschia, G., Cotter, J. R., Breathnach, C. S., and Barron, D. H. The hemoglobin, oxygen, carbon dioxide and hydrozen ion concentrations in the umbilical bloods of sheep and goats as sampled via indwelling plastic catheters. *Q. J. exp. Physiol.*, 1965, **50**, 185–195.

Mestyán, J., Járai, I., Bata, G., and Fekete, M. The significance of facial skin temperatures in the chemical heat regulation of premature infants. *Biol. neonat.*, 1964, **7**, 243–254.

Metcalfe, J., Romney, S. L., Ramsey, L., Reid, D. E., and Burwell, C. S. Estimation of uterine blood flow in normal human pregnancy at term. *J. clin. Invest.*, 1955, **34**, 1632–1638.

Miller, J. F. A. P. Immunity in the foetus and the newborn. *Br. med. Bull.*, 1966, **22**, 21–26.

Miller, J. F. A. P. The thymus and the development of immunologic responsiveness. *Science*, 1964, **144**, 1544–1551.

Minkowski, A. Le retentissment cardiaque de la polycythémic néo-natale (jumeaux) et post-natale (enfants uniques). *Biol. neonat.*, 1962, **4**, 61–74.

Misrahy, G. A., Beran, A. V., Spradley, J. F., and Garwood, V. P. Fetal brain oxygen. *Am. J. Physiol.*, 1960, **199**, 959–964.

Mitchell, R. G. Circulating basophilic leucocyte counts in the newborn. *Archs. Dis. Childh.*, 1955, **30**, 130–132.

Moe, P. J. Normal red blood picture during the first three years of life. *Acta paediat. Scandinav.*, 1965, **54**, 69–80.

Mollison, P. L., Veall, N., and Cutbush, M. Red cell and plasma volume in newborn infants. *Archs. Dis. Child.*, 1950, **25**, 242–253.

Moore, R. E. The vital capacity and maximal breathing capacity of adolescent boys. *Great Ormond St. J.*, 1951 (No. 2), 137–150.

Moore, R. E., and Underwood, M. C. Noradrenaline as a possible regulator of heat production in the newborn kitten. *J. Physiol.*, 1960, **150**, 13–14. (a)

Moore, R. E., and Underwood, M. C. Possible role of noradrenaline in control of heat production in the newborn mammal. *Lancet*, 1960, **278**, 1277–1278. (b)

Morgan, B. C., Deane, P. G., and Guntheroth, W. G. Long-term continuous electrocardiographic recording in pediatric patients. *Pediatrics*, 1965, **36**, 792–797.

Morse, M., Cassels, D. E., and Schultz, F. W. Available and interstitial fluid volumes of normal children. *Am. J. Physiol.*, 1947, **151**, 438–447.

Morse, M., Schultz, F. W., and Cassels, D. E. The lung volume and its subdivisions in boys 10–17 years of age. *J. clin. Invest.*, 1952, **31**, 380–391.

Morse, R. L., Brownell, G. L., and Currens, J. H. The blood pressure of newborn infants: indirect determination by an automatic blood pressure recorder in 20 infants. *Pediatrics*, 1960, **25**, 50–53.

Moruzzi, G. Reticular influences on the EEG. *Electroencephalog. clin. Neurophysiol.*, 1964, **16**, 2–17.

Moruzzi, G., and Magoun, H. W. Brain stem reticular formation and activation of the EEG. *Electroencephalog. clin. Neurophysiol.*, 1949, **1**, 455–473.

Morville, P. Investigation on isohemagglutination in mothers and newborn children. *Acta path. Microbiol. Scand.*, 1929, **6**, 39–44.

Moss, A. J., and Adams, F. H. Index of indirect estimation of diastolic blood pressure. *Am. J. Dis. Child.*, 1963, **106**, 364–367.

Moss, A. J., and Adams, F. H. Flush blood pressure and intra-arterial pressure. *Am. J. Dis. Child.*, 1964, **107**, 489–491.

Moss, A. J., and Adams, F. H. Auscultatory and intra-arterial pressure: a comparison in children with special reference to cuff width. *J. Pediat.*, 1965, **66**, 1094–1097.

Moss, A. J., Duffie, E. R., and Emmanouilides, G. Blood pressure and vasomotor reflexes in the newborn infant. *Pediatrics*, 1963, **32**, 175–179.

Moss, A. J., Emmanouilides, G., and Duffie, E. B. Closure of the ductus arteriosus in the newborn infant. *Pediatrics*, 1963, **32**, 25–30.

Moss, A. J., Emmanouilides, G. C., Rettori, O., Higashino, S. M., and Adams, F. H. Postnatal circulatory and metabolic adjustments in normal and distressed infants. *Biol. neonat.*, 1965, **8**, 177–197.

Moss, A. J., and Monset-Couchard, M. Placental transfusion: early versus late clamping of the umbilical cord. *Pediatrics*, 1967, **40**, 109–126.

Mount, L. E. Basis of heat regulation in homeotherms. *Br. med. Bull.*, 1966, **22**, 84–87.

Mugrage, E. R., and Andresen, M. I. Values for red blood cells of average infants and children. *Am. J. Dis. Child.*, 1936, **51**, 775–791.

Müller, W. *Die Massenuerhaltnisse des menschlichen Herzens.* Hamburg and Leipzig: Leopold Voss, 1883.

Murray, A. B., and Cook, C. D. Measurement of peak expiratory flow rates in 220 normal children from 4.5 to 18.5 years of age. *J. Pediat.*, 1963, **62**, 186–189.

Naeye, R. L. Human intrauterine parabiotic syndrome and its complications. *New Eng. J. Med.*, 1963, **268**, 804–809.

Naeye, R. L., and Blanc, W. A. Prenatal narrowing or closure of the foramen ovale. *Circulation*, 1964, **30**, 736–42.

Nairn, J. R., Bennet, A. J., Andrew, J. D., and MacArthur, P. A study of respiratory function in normal school children. The peak flow rate. *Archs. Dis. Child.*, 1961, **36**, 253–258.

Nechtman, C. M., and Huisman, T. H. J. Comparative studies of oxygen equilibria of human adult and cord blood red cell hemolysates and suspensions. *Clin. chim. Acta*, 1964, **10**, 165–174.

Needham, J. *Chemical embryology.* New York: Macmillan, 1931.

Neligan, G. The systolic blood pressure in neonatal asphyxia and respiratory distress syndrome. *Am. J. Dis. Child.*, 1959, **98**, 460–461.

Neligan, G. A., and Smith, C. A. The blood pressure of newborn infants in asphyxial states and in hyaline membrane disease. *Pediatrics*, 1960, **26**, 735–744.

Nelson, N. M. Neonatal pulmonary function. *Pediat. clin. N. Am.*, 1966, **13**, 769–799.

Nesbitt, R. E. L., Jr. Perinatal development. In F. Falkner (Ed.), *Human development.* Philadelphia: Saunders, 1966. Chap. 5, pp. 123–149.

Newman, A. J., and Gross, S. Capillary and venous hematocrits in the newborn. *Clin. Pediat.*, 1967, **6**, 6–8.

Nicolson, A. B., and Hanley, C. Indices of physiological maturity: derivation and inter-relationships. *Child Dev.*, 1953, **24**, 3–38.

Niemineva, K. On the capillary net of the human cerebral hemispheres during the early fetal period. *Ann. med. exper. biol. Fenn.*, 1950, **28** (Facs. 3), 262–269.

Niemineva, K., and Tervilla, L. On the capillary bed of the human fetal cerebellar hemispheres. *Acta Anat.*, 1953, **19**, 204–209.

Noback, G. J., and Rehman, I. The ductus arteriosus in the human fetus and newborn infant. *Anat. Rec.*, 1941, **81**, 505–527.

Novikova, L. A. Age features in the electrical activity of the brain as seen in children and juveniles. *Pavlov J. higher nerv. Activ.*, 1961, **11**, 61–71.

Nyberg, G., and Westin, B. The influence of oxygen tension and some drugs on human placental vessels. *Acta physiol. Scandinav.*, 1957, **39**, 216–227.

Nylin, G. The physiology of the circulation during puberty. *Acta med. Scandinav.*, 1935, Suppl. 69, 1–77.

Oberman, J. W., Gregory, K. O., Burke, F. G., Ross, S., and Rice, E. C. Electrophoretic analysis of serum proteins in infants and children. I. Normal values from birth to adolescence. *New Eng. J. Med.*, 1956, **255**, 743–750.

Oberst, B. B., and LaRoche, F. Circulation time in the newborn infant, using the fluorescein dye method. *J. Pediat.*, 1954, **45**, 580–582.

Oettinger, L., and Mills, W. B. Simultaneous capillary and venous hemoglobin determinations in the newborn infant. *J. Pediat.*, 1949, **35**, 362–365.

Oh, W., Arcilla, R. A., and Lind, J. *In vivo* blood oxygen dissociation curve of newborn infants. *Biol. neonat.*, 1965, **8**, 241–252.

Oh, W., and Lind, J. Venous and capillary hematocrit in newborn infants and placental transfusion. *Acta Paediat. Scand.*, 1966, **55**, 38–48.

Okamoto, Y., and Kirikae, T. Electroencephalographic studies on brain of foetus, of children of premature birth and new-born, together with a note on reactions of foetus brain upon drugs. *Folia Psychiat. Neurol. Japonica*, 1951, **5**, 135–146.

Oliver, T. K. Temperature regulation and heat production in the newborn. *Pediat. clin. N. Am.*, 1965, **12**, 765–779.

Oliver, T. K., Jr., and Karlberg, P. Gaseous metabolism in newly born human infants. *Am. J. Dis. Child.*, 1963, **105**, 427–435.

Orlandini, T. O., Sass-Kortsak, A., and Ebbs, J. H. Serum gamma globulin levels in normal infants. *Pediatrics*, 1955, **16**, 575–584.

Ortiz-Estrada, P., Deutsch, E., and Hernandes-Orozco, F. An electroencephalographic method for evaluation of hearing in children. *Ann. Otol.*, 1963, **72**, 135–148.

Orzalesi, M. M., Hart, M. C., and Cook, C. D. Distribution of ventilation in normal subjects from 7 to 45 years of age. *J. appl. Physiol.*, 1965, **20**(1), 77–78.

Page, E. W. Physiology of the human placenta at term. *Clin. Obstet. Gynec.*, 1960, **3**, 279–285.

Paine, R. S., and Oppé, T. E. *Neurological examination of children.* Clinics in Developmental Medicine 20/31. Medical Education and Information Unit. The Spastics Society in association with William Heineman Medical Books Ltd., 1966.

Palesi, S., and Vannucchi, C. Studio dell'elettroencefalogramma dello immaturo in prima giornata di vita. *Clin. Pediat.*, 1958, **40**, 904–918.

Palesi, S., and Vannucchi, C. Evoluzione dell'elettroencefalogramma dell'immaturo durante le prime tre settimane di vita. *Clin. Pediat.*, 1959, **41**, 601–611.

Palmer, D. M. The lung of a human fetus of 170 mm. C. R. length. *Am. J. Anat.*, 1936, **58**, 59–72.

Panigel, M. Placental transfusion experiments. *Am. J. Obstet. Gynec.*, 1962, **84**, 1664–1683.

Parmelee, A. H., Jr., Wenner, W. H., Akiyama, Y., Schultz, M., and Stern, E. Sleep states in premature infants. *Dev. Med. Child Neurol.*, 1967, **9**, 70–77.

Parmelee, A. H., Jr., Wenner, W. H., Akiyama, Y., Stern, E., and Flescher, J. Electroencephalography and brain maturation. In A. Minkowski (Ed.), *Regional development of the brain in early life.* London: Blackwell, 1967. Pp. 459–480.

Patten, B. M. The changes in the circulation following birth. *Am. Heart J.*, 1930/31, **6**, 192–205.

Patten, B. M. The circulatory system: embryological. In *Growth and development of the child.* Part 2: Anatomy and physiology, The White House Conference. New York: Century, 1933.

Patten, B. M. *Human embryology.* (2nd ed.). Philadelphia: Blakiston, 1953.

Peiper, A. *Cerebral function in infancy and childhood.* Translation of third revised German edition. New York: Consultants Bureau, 1963.

Peltonen, R., and Hirvonen, L. Experimental studies on fetal and neonatal circulation. *Acta paediat. Scand. Suppl.* 1965, **161**, 1–55.

Penaloza, D., Aria-Stella, J., Sime, F., Recavaren, S., and Marticornena, E. The heart and pulmonary circulation in children at high altitudes. *Pediatrics*, 1964, **34**, 568–582.

Petre-Quadens, O. On the different phases of the sleep of the newborn with special reference to the activated phase, or phase d. *J. neurol. Sci.*, 1966, **3**, 151–161.

Petre-Quadens, O. Ontogenesis of paradoxical sleep in the human newborn. *J. neurol. Sci.*, 1967, **4**, 153–157.

Pfau, P. Die Serumproteine von Feten, Neugeborenen und über tragenen Säuglingen. *Arch. Gynak.*, 1954, **185**, 208–220.

Playfair, J. H. L., Wolfendale, M. R., and Kay, H. E. M. The leucocytes of peripheral blood in the human foetus. *Br. J. Haemat.*, 1963, **9**, 336–344.

Plum, P. The prothrombin content of the blood during the first years of life. *Acta paediat.*, 1949, **38**, 526–537.

Polgar, G. Opposing forces to breathing in newborn infants. *Biol. neonat.*, 1967, **11**, 1–22.

Polgar, G. Comparison of methods for recording respiration in newborn infants. *Pediatrics*, 1965, **36**, 861–868.

Polikania, R. I. (Peculiarities of natural sleep in premature babies in early post-natal life). *Zh. vyssh. nerv. Deiat. Pavlova (Moskva)*, 1963, **13**, 62–72.

Potter, E. L. Pulmonary pathology in the newborn. *Adv. pediat.*, 1953, **6**, 157–189.

Potter, E. L., and Bohlender, G. P. Intrauterine respiration in relation to develop-ment of the fetal lung: with report of two unusual anomalies of the respira-tory system. *Am. J. Obstet. Gynec.*, 1941, **40**, 14–22.

Powell, M. L. Patent ductus arteriosus in premature infants. *Med. J. Aust.*, 1963, **2**, 58–60.

Prec, K. J., and Cassels, D. E. Dye dilution curves and cardiac output in newborn infants. *Circulation*, 1955, **11**, 789–798.

Přibylová, H., and Znamenáček, K. The effect of body temperature on the level of carbohydrate metabolites and oxygen consumption in the newborn. *Pedia-trics*, 1966, **37**, 743–749.

Purpura, D. P. Analysis of axodendritic synaptic organizations in immature cere-bral cortex. *Ann. N. Y. Acad. Sci.*, 1961, **94**, 604–654. (a)

Purpura, D. P. Ontogenetic analysis of some evoked synaptic activities in super-ficial neocortical neuropil. In E. Florey (Ed.), *International symposium on nervous inhibition*. New York: Pergamon Press, 1961. Pp. 424–446. (b)

Purves, M. J., and Biscoe, T. J. Development of chemoreceptor activity. *Br. med. Bull.*, 1966, **22**, 56–60.

Rapin, I. Evoked responses to clicks in a group of children with communication disorders. *Ann. N. Y. Acad. Sci.*, 1964, **112**, 182–203.

Rausen, A. R., Seki, M., and Strauss, L. Twin transfusion syndrome. *J. Pediat.*, 1965, **66**, 613–628.

Recavarren, S., and Areas-Stella, J. Growth and development of the ventricular myocardium from birth to adult life. *Br. Heart J.*, 1964, **26**, 187–192.

Record, R. G., and McKeown, T. Observations relating to the aetiology of patent ductus arteriosus. *Br. Heart J.*, 1953, **15**, 376–386.

Reinhold, J., and Pym, M. The determination of blood pressure in infants by the flush method. *Archs. Dis. Childh.*, 1955, **30**, 127–129.

Reynolds, E. O. R., Orzalesi, M. M., Motoyama, E. K., Craig, J. M., and Cook, C. D. Surface properties of saline extracts from lungs of newborn infants. *Acta Paediat. scand.*, 1965, **54**, 511–518.

Reynolds, S. R. M. Circulatory adaptations to birth. *Sci. Monthly*, Oct. 1953, 205–213.

Rhodes, A. J., and Hyde, J. B. Postnatal growth of arterioles in the human cerebral cortex. *Growth*, 1965, **29**, 173–182.

Rice, H. V., and Posener, L. J. A practical method for the measurement of systolic blood pressures of infants. *Pediatrics*, 1959, **23**, 854–860.

Richey, H. G. The blood pressure in boys and girls before and after puberty. *Am. J. Dis. Child.*, 1931, **42**, 1281–1330.

Robbins, J. B., Kenny, K., and Suter, E. Isolation and biological activities of rabbit γM-and γG-anti-Salmonella Typhimurium antibodies. *J. exp. Med.*, 1965, **122**, 385–402.

Roberts, L. N., Smiley, J. R., and Manning, G. W. A comparison of direct and in-direct blood-pressure determinations. *Circulation*, 1953, **8**, 232–242.

Robertson, J. D., and Reid, D. D. Standards for the basal metabolism of normal people in Britain. *Lancet*, 1952, **262**, 940–949.

Roffwarg, H. P., Dement, W. C., and Fisher, C. Preliminary observations of the sleep-dream pattern in neonates, infants, children and adults. In E. Harms (Ed.), *Problems of sleep and dreams in children*. International Monographs on Child Psychiatry, Vol. 2. New York: Macmillan, 1964. Pp. 60–72.

Roffwarg, H. P., Muzio, J. N., and Dement, W. C. Ontogenetic development of the human sleep-dream cycle. *Science*, 1966, **152**, 604–619.

Romney, S. L. Fetal hypoxic stress in the human. In D. E. Cassels (Ed.), *The heart and circulation in the newborn and infant*. New York: Grune and Stratton, 1966. Pp. 53–64.

Ross, R. B. Comparison of foetal pulmonary fluid with foetal plasma and amniotic fluid. *Nature*, 1963, **199**, 1100.

Rowe, R. D., and James, L. S. The normal pulmonary arterial pressure during the first year of life. *J. Pediat.*, 1957, **51**, 1–11.

Rudolph, A. M., Auld, P. A. M., Golinko, R. J., and Paul, M. H. Pulmonary vascular adjustments in the neonatal period. *Pediatrics*, 1961, **28**, 28–34.

Russell, S. J. M. Blood volume studies in healthy children. *Archs. Dis. Child.*, 1949, **24**, 88–98.

Saling, E. Neve Untersuchung-sergebnisse über den Kreislauf des Kindes unmittelbar nach der Geburt. *Arch. Gynäk.*, 1960, **194**, 287–306.

Saling, E. Technikder enduskopischen microblutentnahme am Feten. *Geburtsh. Frauenheilk.*, 1964, **24**, 464–469.

Samson-Dollfus, D. *L'électro-encéphalogramme du prematuré jusqu'à l'age de trois mois et du nouveau-né à terme*. Paris: Foulon, 1955.

Sanders, R., Lind, J., and Peltonen, T. Phonocardiograms before and after the first cry of the newborn infant. *Ann. paediat. Fenn.* 1961, **7**, 112–123.

Sargent, D. W. *An evaluation of basal metabolic data for children and youth in the United States*. Home Economics Res. Rep. No. 14, Human Nutrition Res. Div., Agricultural Res. Service, U. S. Dept. Agriculture. Washington, D. C.: U. S. Government Printing Office, 1961.

Scammon, R. E. A summary of the anatomy of the infant and child. In I. A. Abt (Ed.), *Pediatrics*, Vol. 1. Philadelphia: Saunders, 1923. Chap. 3. Pp. 257–444.

Scammon, R. E., and Norris, E. H. On the time of the post-natal obliteration of the fetal blood-passages (foramen ovale, ductus arteriosus, ductus venosus). *Anat. Rec.*, 1918, **15**, 165–180.

Schaeffer, J. P. The behavior of elastic tissue in the post-fetal occlusion and obliteration of the ductus arteriosus (Botalli) in sus scrota. *J. exp. Med.*, 1914, **19**, 129–143.

Schaffer, A. I. Neonatal blood pressure studies. *Am. J. Dis. Child.*, 1955, **89**, 204–209.

Schaper, G. Zum Hirnstrombild bei schlafenden Frühgebornen. *Mschr. Kinderheilk.*, 1953, **101**, 149–151. (a)

Schaper, G. Das Hirnstrombild des schlafenden Säuglings in 2. Trimenon. *Mschr. Kinderheilk.*, 1953, **101**, 258–262. (b)

Scheibel, M. E., and Scheibel, A. B. Development of reticulocortical control in the newborn. *Am. Acad. Neurol.*, 1959, p. 29. (Abstracts of 11th annual meeting.)

Scheibel, M. E., and Scheibel, A. B. Neural correlates of psychophysiological development in the young organism. *Anat. Rec.*, 1961, **139**, 319–320.

Scheibel, M. E., and Scheibel, A. B. Some structuro-functional correlates of maturation in young cats. *Electroencephalog. clin. Neurophysiol.*, 1962, **14**, 429.

Scheibel, M. E., and Scheibel, A. B. Some neural substrates of postnatal development. In M. Hoffman and L. Hoffman (Eds.), *Review of child development
research*. Vol. 1, New York: Russell Sage, 1964.

Schlamowitz, I. An analysis of the time relationships within the cardiac cycle in
electrocardiograms of normal men. III. The duration of the P-R interval and
its relationship to the cycle length (R-R interval). *Am. Heart J.*, 1946, **31**,
473–476.

Schroeder, C., and Heckel, H. Zur Frage der Hirtätigheit beim Neugeborenen.
Geburtsh. Frauenheilk., 1952, **12**, 992.

Schroeder, W. A., Shelton, J. R., Shelton, J. B., Cormick, J., and Jones, R. T. The
amino acid sequence of the gamma chain of human fetal hemoglobin. *Biochemistry*, 1963, **2**, 992–1008.

Schulman, I., Smith, C. H., and Stern, G. S. Studies on the anemia of prematurity:
I. Fetal and adult hemoglobin in premature infants. II. The blood volume in
premature infants. III. The mechanism of the anemia. *Am. J. Dis. Child.*,
1954, **88**, 567–595.

Schwartz, L., Britten, R. H., and Thompson, L. R. Studies in physical development and posture. 1. The effect of exercise on the physical condition and
development of adolescent boys. 2. Bodily growth with age. 3. Physical fitness
as reflected in tests of muscular strength. *Publ. Hlth. Bull.* (Wash.), 1928,
No. 179, 124 pp.

Schwartze, V. P., and Aresin, L. Die Wirkung von Transfusionen mit sauerstoffan-
gereicher Blut auf das EEG menschlicher Embryonen. *Biol. neonat.*, 1964, **7**,
76–82.

Schwenk, A., Eggers-Hohmann, G. and Gensch, F. Artevieller Blutdruck, Vaso-
motorismus und Menarchetermin bei Mädchen im 2. Lebensjahrzehnt.
Arch. Kinderheilk., 1955, **150**, 235–249.

Scopes, J. W. Metabloic rate and temperature control in the human baby. *Br. med.
Bull.*, 1966, **22**, 88–91.

Scopes, J. W., and Tizard, J. P. M. The effect of intravenous noradrenaline on
the oxygen consumption of newborn animals. *J. Physiol.*, 1963, **165**, 305–326.

Seham, M., and Moss, A. J. Electrocardiography in pediatrics. *Archs. Pediat.*,
1942, **59**, 419–445.

Seip, M. The reticulocyte level, and the erythrocyte production judged from
reticulocyte studies, in newborn infants during the first week of life. *Acta
Paediat.*, 1955, **44**, 355–369.

Setnikar, I., Agostoni, E., and Taglietti, A. The fetal lung, a source of amniotic
fluid. *Proc. Soc. exp. Biol. Med.*, 1959, **101**, 842–845.

Shahidi, N. T., and Diamond, L. K. Testosterone-induced remission in aplastic
anemia. *Am. J. Dis. Child.*, 1959, **98**, 293–302 .

Shepovalnikov, A. (Rhythmic components of the electroencephalogram of suckling children.) *Zh. vyssh. nerv. Deiat. Pavolva (Moska)*, 1962, **12**, 797–808.

Shock, N. W. Age changes and sex differences in alveolar CO_2 tension. *Am. J.
Physiol.*, 1941, **133**, 610–616.

Shock, N. W. Standard values for basal oxygen consumption in adolescents. *Am.
J. Dis. Child.*, 1942, **64**, 19–32.

Shock, N. W. The effect of menarche on basal physiological functions in girls. *Am.
J. Physiol.*, 1943, **139**, 288–292.

Shock, N. W. Basal blood pressure and pulse rate in adolescents. *Am. J. Dis.
Child.*, 1944, **68**, 16–22.

Shock, N. W. Physiological growth. In F. Falkner (Ed.), *Human development*.
Philadelphia: Saunders, 1966. Pp. 150–177.

Shock, N. W., and Hastings, A. B. Studies of the acid-base balance of the blood

III. Variations in the acid-base balance of the blood in normal individuals. *J. biol. Chem.*, 1935, **104**, 585–600.

Shock, N. W., and Soley, M. H. Average values for basal respiratory functions in adolescents and adults. *J. Nutrit.*, 1939, **18**, 143–153.

Short, R. H. D. Alveolar epithelium in relation to growth of the lung. *Phil. Trans. R. Soc. London,* 1950, **235**, 35–86 (Series B., Biol. Sc.).

Sidorenko, I. G. (Electroencephalogram of full-term neonate). *Vop. Ohr. Mater-inst. Detstva,* 1961, **6**, 43–48.

Silverman, W. A., Sinclair, J. C., and Buck, J. B. A valved mask for respiratory studies in the neonate. *J. Pediat.*, 1966, **68**, 468–470.

Silverman, W. A., Zamelis, A., Sinclair, J. C., and Agate, F. J. Warm nape of the newborn. *Pediatrics,* 1964, **33**, 984–987.

Sinclair, J. C., Scopes, J. W., and Silverman, W. A. Metabolic reference standards for the neonate. *Pediatrics,* 1967, **39**, 724–732.

Singer, K., Angelopoulos, B., and Ramot, B. Studies on human myoglobin. II. Fetal myoglobin: its identification and its replacement by adult myoglobin during infancy. *Blood,* 1955, **10**, 987–998.

Singer, K., Chernoff, A. I., and Singer, L. Studies on abnormal hemoglobins. I. Their demonstration in sickle cell anemia and other hematologic disorders by means of alkali denaturation. *Blood,* 1951, **6**, 413–435.

Sjöstedt, S., Rooth, G., and Caligara, F. The oxygen tension of the blood in the umbilical cord and the intervillous space. *Archs. Dis. Child.,* 1960, **35**, 529–533.

Sjöstrand, T. The total quantity of hemoglobin in men and its relation to age, sex, body weight and height. *Acta physiol. Scand.,* 1949, **18**, 324–336.

Sjöstrand, T. Volume and distribution of blood and their significance in regulating the circulation. *Physiol. Rev.,* 1953, **33**, 202–228.

Slobody, L. B., Rook, G. D., Levbarg, M., and Morey, M. Studies of the cardiovascular and renal systems in the newly born infant using flourescein. I. Circulation time immediately after birth. *Pediatrics,* 1950, **6**, 254–261.

Smith, C. A. *The physiology of the newborn infant.* (3rd ed.) Springfield, Ill.: Thomas, 1959.

Smith, C. A. The first breath. *Sci. Amer.*, 1963, **209**, 27–35.

Smith, C. H. Iso-agglutinins in the new-born, with special reference to their placental transmission. *Am. J. Dis. Child.,* 1928, **36**, 54–69.

Smith, C. H. *Blood diseases of infancy and childhood.* St. Louis, Mo.: Mosby, 1966.

Smith, J. R. Electroencephalogram during infancy and childhood. *Proc. Soc. exp. Biol. Med.,* 1937, **36**, 384–386.

Smith, J. R. The electroencephalogram during normal infancy and childhood: I. Rhythmic activities present in the neonate and their subsequent development. *J. genet. Psychol.,* 1938, **53**, 431–453. (a)

Smith, J. R. The electroencephalogram during normal infancy and childhood: II. The nature of the growth of the alpha waves. *J. genet. Psychol.,* 1938, **53**, 455–469. (b)

Smith, J. R. The electroencephalogram during normal infancy and childhood: III. Preliminary observations on the pattern sequence during sleep. *J. genet. Psychol.,* 1938, **53**, 471–482. (c)

Smith, J. R. The "occipital" and "precentral" alpha rhythms during the first two years. *J. Psychol.,* 1939, **7**, 223–226.

Smith, J. R. The frequency growth of the human alpha rhythms during normal infancy and childhood. *J. Psychol.,* 1941, **11**, 177–198.

Smith, R. T. Human immunoglobulins—a guide to nomenclature and clinical application. *Pediatrics,* 1966, **37**, 822–827.

Smyth, C. N. Experimental electrocardiography of the foetus. *Lancet,* 1953, **1,** 1124–1126.

Snyder, F. Progress in the new biology of dreaming. *Am. J. Psychiat.,* 1965, **122,** 377–391.

Sodi-Pallares, D., Portillo, B., Cisneros, F., DeLaCruz, M. V., Acosta, A. R. Electrocardiography of infants and children. *Pediat. clin. N. Am.,* 1958, **5,** 871–905.

Sontag, L. Discussion. In J. P. Ambuel (Ed.), *Physical and behavioral growth.* Rep. 26th Ross Pediat. Res. Conf. Columbus, Ohio: Ross Laboratories, 1958, 52–53.

Sontag, L. W., and Richards, T. W. Studies in fetal behavior. 1. Fetal heart rate as a behavioral indicator. *Monogr. Soc. Res. Child Dev.,* 1938, **3** (No. 4).

Sontag, L. W., and Wallace, R. F. Changes in the rate of the human fetal heart in response to vibratory stimuli. *Am. J. Dis. Child.,* 1936, **51,** 583–589.

Southern, E. M. Electrocardiography and phonocardiography of the foetal heart. *J. Obstet. Gynec. Br. Emp.,* 1954, **61,** 231–237.

Sproul, A., and Simpson, E. Stroke volume and related hemodynamic data in normal children. *Pediatrics,* 1964, **33,** 912–918.

Stahlman, M. Perinatal circulation. *Pediat. clin. N. Am.* 1966, **13,** 753–767.

Stahlman, M. Ventilation control in the newborn. *Am. J. Dis. Child.,* 1961, **101,** 216–227.

Steinberg, D., Nestel, P. J., Buskirk, E. R., and Thompson, R. H. Calorigenic effect of norepinephrine correlated with plasma free fatty acid turnover and oxidation. *J. clin. Invest.,* 1964, **43,** 167–176.

Steinschneider, A. Developmental psychophysiology. In Y. Brackbill (Ed.), *Infancy and early childhood.* New York: Free Press, 1967. Pp. 3–47.

Stembra, Z. K., Hodr, J., and Jandra, J. Umbilical blood flow in healthy newborn infants during the first minutes after birth. *Am. J. Obstet. Gynec.,* 1965, **91,** 586–594.

Stern, L., Lees, M. H., and Leduc, J. Environmental temperature, oxygen consumption and catecholamine excretion in newborn infants. *J. Pediat.,* 1965, **36,** 367–373.

Stewart, C. A. Vital capacity of the lungs of children in health and disease. *Am. J. Dis. Child.,* 1922, **24,** 451–496.

Stiehm, E. R. and Fundenberg, H. H. Antibodies to gamma-globulin in infants and children exposed to isologous gamma-globulin. *Pediatrics,* 1965, **35,** 229–235.

Stocks, P., and Karn, M. N. *Blood pressure in early life. a statistical study.* London: Cambridge University Press, 1924.

Stocks, P., Stocks, A. V., and Karn, M. N. Goitre in adolescence: anthropometric study of the relation between the size of the thyroid gland and physical and mental development. *Biometrika,* 1927, **19,** 292–353.

Storm van Leeuwen, W., Bickford, R., Brazier, M., Cobb, W. A., Dondey, M., Gastaut, H., Gloor, P., Henry, C. E., Hess, R., Knott, J. R., Kugler, J., Lairy, G. C., Loeb, C., Magnus, O., Oller Daurella, L., Petsche, H., Schwab, R., Walter, W. G., and Widen, L. Proposal for an EEG terminology by the terminology committee of the International Federation for Electroencephalography and Clinical Neurophysiology. *Electroencephalog. clin. Neurophysiol.,* 1966, **20,** 306–310.

Strang, L. B. The ventilatory capacity of normal children. *Thorax,* 1959, **14,** 305–310.

Strang, L. B. The lungs at birth. *Arch. Dis. Child.,* 1965, **40,** 575–582.

Strang, L. B., and McGrath, M. W. Alveolar ventilation in normal newborn infants studied by air wash-in after oxygen breathing. *Clin. Sci.*, 1962, **23**, 129–139.

Strauss, M. B. Anemia of infancy from maternal iron deficiency in pregnancy. *J. clin. Invest.*, 1933, **12**, 345–353.

Sundal, A. Der normale Blutdruck im Alter von 3-20 Jahren. Eine Untersuchung an 1932 Kindern und Jungendlichen in Oslo (Norwegen). *Z. Kinderheilk.*, 1929, **47**, 742–761.

Sureau, C. Recherches d'electrocardiographic foetale au cours de la gestation et du travail. *Gynec. Obstet.* (Paris), 1956, **55**, 21–33.

Sutherland, J. M., and Ratcliff, J. W. Crying vital capacity. *Am. J. Dis. Child.*, 1961, **101**, 67–74.

Sutliff, W. D., and Holt, E. The age curve of pulse rate under basal conditions. *Archs. intern. Med.*, 1925, **35**, 224–241.

Tanner J. M. The fallacy of per-weight and per-surface area standards and their relation to spurious correlation. *J. appl. Physiol.*, 1949, **2**, 1–15.

Tanner, J. M. The relationship between the frequency of the heart, oral temperature and rectal temperature in man at rest. *J. Physiol.*, 1951, **115**, 391–409.

Tanner, J. M. Discussion. In J. P. Ambuel (Ed.), *Physical and behavioral growth.* Rep. 26th Ross Pediat. Res. Conf. Columbus, Ohio: Ross Laboratories, 1958, 53.

Tanner, J. M. *Growth at adolescence.* (2nd ed.). Oxford: Blackwell, 1962.

Thibeault, D. W., Clutario, B., and Auld, P.A.M. Arterial oxygen tension in premature infants. *J. Pediat.*, 1966, **69**, 449–451.

Thomaidis, T., Fouskaris, G., and Matsaniotis, N. Isohemagglutinin activity in the first day of life. *Am. J. Dis. Child.*, 1967, **113**, 654–657.

Thomas, D. B., and Yoffey, J. M. Human foetal haemopoiesis. I. The cellular composition of foetal blood. *Br. J. Haemat.*, 1962, **8**, 290–295.

Thompson, S. G. (Ed.) Thermoregulation of the newly born. Suppl. #2, *Rep. Ross Pediatric Res. Conf.* Columbus, Ohio: Ross Laboratories, 1964.

Tocantins, L. M. Mammalian blood platelet in health and disease. *Medicine*, 1938, **17**, 155–260.

Tovey, G. H. A study of the protective factors in heterospecific group pregnancy and their role in the prevention of haemolytic disease of the newborn. *J. Path. Bact.*, 1945, **57**, 295–298.

Towell, M. E. The influence of labor on the fetus and newborn. *Pediat. clin. N. Am.*, 1966, **13**, 575–598.

Tremblay, P. C., Sybulski, S., ad Maughan, G. B. Role of the placenta in fetal malnutrition. *Am. J. Obstet. Gynec.*, 1965, **91**, 597–605.

Uhr, J. W., Dancis, J., and Neumann, C. G. Delayed-type hypersensitivity in premature neonatal humans. *Nature*, 1960, **187**, 1130–1131.

Urbach, J. R., Phuvichit, B., Zweizig, H., Millican, E., Carrington, E. R., Loveland, M., Williams, J. M., Lamberts, R. L., Duncan, A. M., Farrell, S. L., Simons, P. O., and Spurgeon, I. L. Instantaneous heart rate patterns in newborn infants. *Am. J. Obstet. Gynec.*, 1965, **93**, 965–974.

Usher, R., Shephard, M., and Lind, J. The blood volume of the newborn infant and placental transfusion. *Acta paediat.*, 1963, **52**, 497–512.

Valaes, T., and Doxiadis, S. A. Intrauterine blood transfer between uniovular twins. *Archs. Dis. Child.*, 1960, **35**, 503–505.

Vallbona, D., Desmond, M. M., Rudolph, A. J., Pap, L. F., Hill, R. M., Franklin, R. R., and Bush, J. B. Cardiodynamic studies in the newborn. II. Regulation of heart rate. *Biol. neonat.*, 1963, **5**, 155–199.

Van Dyke, D. C., Coutopoulos, A. N., Williams, B. S., Simpson, M. E., Lawrence, J. H., and Evans, H. M. Hormonal factors influencing erythropoiesis. *Acta haematol.*, 1954, **11**, 203–222.

Van Furth, R., Schuit, H. R. E., and Hijmans, W. The immunological development of the human fetus. *J. exp. Med.*, 1965, **122**, 1173–1188.

Vierordt, K. *Anatomische, physiologische und physikalische Daten und Tabellen.* Jena: Fischer, 1906.

Villee, C. A. (Ed.) *The placenta and fetal membranes.* Baltimore, Md.: Williams & Wilkins, 1960.

Wagenvoort, C. A., and Wagenvoort, N. The pulmonary vascular bed in the normal fetus and newborn. In D. E. Cassels (Ed.), *The heart and circulation in the newborn and infant.* New York: Grune and Stratton, 1966.

Walker, J., and Turnbull, A. C. (Eds.) *Oxygen supply to the human foetus.* Oxford: Blackwell, 1959.

Walker, J., and Turnbull, E. P. N. Haemoglobin and red cells in the human foetus. *Lancet*, 1953, **2**, 312–318.

Walker, J., and Turnbull, E. P. N. Haemoglobin and red cells in the human foetus. III.-Foetal and adult haemoglobin. *Archs. Dis. Childh.*, 1955, **30**, 111–116.

Walsh, S. Z. The ECG during the first week of life. *Br. Heart J.*, 1963, **25**, 784–794 (a).

Walsh, S. Z. Electrocardiographic intervals during the first week of life. *Am. Heart J.*, 1963, **66**, 36–41 (b).

Walsh, S. Z. Evolution of the electrocardiogram of healthy premature infants during the first year of life. *Acta paediat.*, 1963, Suppl. 145, 1–38 (c).

Walsh, S. Z. Comparative study of electrocardiograms of healthy premature and full-term infants of similar weight. *Am. Heart J.*, 1964, **68**, 183–192.

Walsh, S. Z. The electrocardiogram of the neonate and infant. In D. Cassels (Ed.), *The heart and circulation in the newborn and infant.* New York: Grune & Stratton, 1966. Pp. 263–273.

Warkany, J., Monroe, B. B., and Southerland, B. S. Intrauterine growth retardation. *Am. J. Dis. Child.*, 1961, **102**, 249–279.

Washburn, A. H. Blood cells in healthy young infants. III. A study of 608 differential leukocyte counts with a final report on 908 total leukocyte counts. *Am. J. Dis. Child.*, 1935, **50**, 413–430.

Watson, E. H., and Lowrey, G. H. *Growth and development of children.* Chicago: Yearbook Medical Publishers, 1967.

Wedenberg, E. Auditory tests on newborn infants. *Acta Otolaryng.*, 1956, **46**, 446–461.

Wegelius, R. On changes in the peripheral blood picture of the newborn infant immediately after birth. *Acta. paediat.*, (Suppl. 4), 1948, **35**, 1–107.

Weinbach, A. P. Some physiological phenomena fitted to growth equations: II. Brain potentials. *Hum. Biol.*, 1938, **10**, 145–150.

Weisbrot, I. M., James, L. S., Prince, C. E., Holaday, D. A., and Apgar, V. Acid-base homeostasis of the newborn infant during the first 24 hours of life. *J. Pediat.*, 1958, **52**, 395–403.

Weitzman, E. G., Fishbein, W., and Graziani, L. Auditory evoked responses obtained from the scalp electroencephalogram of the full term human neonate during sleep. *Pediatrics*, 1965, **35**, 458–462.

Welford, N. T., Sontag, L. W., Phillips, W., and Phillips, D. Individual differences in heart rate variability in the human fetus. *Am. J. Obstet. Gynec.*, 1967, **98**, 56–61.

West, C. D., Hong, R., and Holland, N. H. Immunoglobulin levels from the newborn period to adulthood and in immunoglobulin deficiency states. *J. clin. Invest.*, 1962, **41**, 2054–2064.

Whipple, D. V., *Dynamics of development: euthenic pediatrics.* New York: McGraw-Hill, 1966.

White, J. C., and Beaven, G. H. Foetal haemoglobin. *Br. med. Bull.*, 1959, **15**, 33–39.

White House Conference on Child Health and Protection. *Growth and development of the child.* Part II. *Anatomy and physiology.* New York: Century, 1933.

Widdas, W. F. Transport mechanisms in the foetus. Foetal and neonatal physiology. *Br. med. Bull.*, 1961 **17**, 107–111.

Wigglesworth, J. S. Foetal growth retardation. *Br. med. Bull.*, 1966, **22**, 13–25.

Wilkin, P. Morphogénèse. In J. Snoeck (Ed.), *Le Placenta Humain.* Paris: Masson, 1958. Pp. 23–70.

Williams, W. G., and Graham, J. T. EEG responses to auditory stimuli in waking children. *J. Speech Res.*, 1963, **6**, 57–63.

Wilson, H. G. Postnatal development of the lung. *Am. J. Anat.*, 1928, **41**, 97–122.

Wilson, F. N., and Herrmann, G. Relation of QRS-interval to ventricular weight. *Heart*, 1930, **15**, 135–140.

Wilson, M. G. Placental abnormalities and fetal disease. *Am. J. Dis. Child.*, 1964, **108**, 154–163.

Wimmer, P. Ergebnisse der Abdominal-Elektrokardiographie. *Geburtsh. Frauenheilk.*, 1954, **14**, 115–125.

Wimmer, P. Diagnostic possibilities of abdominal fetal electrocardiography in obstetrics. *Med. Wschr.*, 1955, **33–34**, 1131–1135.

Windle, W. F. *Physiology of the fetus.* Philadelphia: Saunders, 1940.

Windle, W. F. Development of the blood and changes in the blood picture at birth. *J. Pediat.*, 1941, **18**, 538–550.

Winick, M., Coscia, A., and Noble, A. Cellular growth in human placenta. I. Normal placental growth, *Pediatrics*, 1967, **39**, 248–251.

Wintrobe, M. M. *Clinical hematology.* (5th ed.) Philadelphia: Lea and Febiger, 1961.

Wintrobe, M. M., and Shumacker, H. B., Jr., Erythrocyte studies in the mammalian fetus and newborn. *Am. J. Anat.*, 1936, **58**, 313–328.

Witzberger, C. M., and Cohen, H. G. Circulation time in infants and young children determined by the fluorescein method. *J. Pediat.*, 1943, **22**, 726–730.

Woodbury, R. A., Robinow, M., and Hamilton, W. F. Blood pressure studies on infants. *Am. J. Physiol.*, 1938, **122**, 472–479.

Woodruff, C. W. Maternal factors in hypochromic anemia of infancy. *J. Am. med. Ass.*, 1956, **162**, 659.

Woodruff, C. W. Multiple causes of iron deficiency in infants. *J. Am. med. Ass.*, 1958, **167**, 715–720.

Woodruff, C. W. The utilization of iron administered orally. *Pediatrics*, 1961, **27**, 194–203.

Woodruff, C. W., and Bridgeforth, E. B. Relationship between the hemogram of the infant and that of the mother during pregnancy. *Pediatrics*, 1953, **12**, 681–685.

Yang, D. C. Y., Slobody, L. B., Mendlowitz, M., and Tyree, M. Digital blood flow in normal newborn infant measured calorimetrically. *Proc. Soc. exp. Biol. Med.*, 1955, **88**, 626–628.

Young, I. M. Vasomotor tone in the skin blood vessels of the newborn infant. *Clin. Sci.*, 1962, **22**, 325–332.

Young, I. M., and Holland, W. W. Some physiologic responses of neonatal arterial blood pressure and pulse rate. *Br. med. J.*, 1958, 2, 276–278.

Young, M. Blood pressure in the newborn baby. Foetal and neonatal physiology. *Br. med. Bull.*, 1961, **17**, 154–159.

Young, M. Responses of the systematic circulation of the newborn infant. *Br. med. Bull.*, 1966, **22**, 70–72.

Young, M., and Cottom, D. An investigation of baroreceptor responses in the newborn infant. In D. Cassels (Ed.), *The heart and circulation in the newborn and infant*. New York: Grune and Stratton, 1966. Pp. 111–120.

Ziegler, R. F. *Electrocardiographic studies in normal infants and children*. Springfield, Ill.: Thomas, 1951.

Ziegler, R. F. The T wave of the electrocardiogram: methods of measurement and interpretation. In D. Cassels (Ed.), *The heart and circulation in the newborn and infant*. New York: Grune and Stratton, 1966. Pp. 274–296.

Zipursky, A. Fetal hemoglobin levels in the fetus and newborn and the postnatal decline of fetal hemoglobin levels. *Fetal Hemoglobin*. Report of the fifty-second Ross Conference on Pediatric Research. Columbus, Ohio: Ross Laboratories, 1966, **52**, 14–18.

PART II

INFANCY AND
EARLY EXPERIENCE

5. *Human Infancy: A Bibliography And Guide*[1]

WILLIAM KESSEN   MARSHALL M. HAITH   PHILIP H. SALAPATEK

As men and as psychologists, we have long been concerned with beginnings. Tiedemann, whose words opened the modern study of children (". . . it is by experience and exercise that we learn to be served by our senses and to perceive correctly; observations made on men . . . found in the wild . . . have shown that the faculties of mind develop bit by bit and one after the other"), laid out many of the problems that direct the work of men who nowadays study human infants. What does the newborn infant bring, in body and behavior, to his first encounters with the world? How do "experience and exercise" modify the infant's behavior? To what degree does the baby's later behavior *emerge* from an innate potential? When we observe the young child, how much do we see the species—the child as representative of Man—and how much do we see a person, individual and perhaps unique? How does the world of the adult, physical and social, come to be represented in the mind of the child? How well can we predict the future course of a person's life from our knowledge of his infancy? Finally, the most durable of questions, what methods can we validly use to understand the infant; what are the windows on the baby's mind? To be sure, the rhetoric of the psychology of infancy has changed often but the organizing themes of study have remained remarkably stable. What is the *initial state* of the newborn's behavioral system? What events and processes determine the *transformation* of the initial state?

Certainly, the study of the infant cannot be confined to beginnings. We see the baby, in the first 18 months of life, undergoing continuous and rapid change. Whether one sees the newborn child as neurologically insufficient (Flechsig, 1920), cognitively confused (James, 1890), narcissistic (Freud, 1905), solipsistic (Piaget, 1927), or merely ugly (Hall, 1891), the distance between the new child and the walking, talking, socially discriminating, and perceptive person whom we see hardly 500 days later is awesome. Hall, for all of his interest in observing development, found distasteful the baby who arrives with its "monotonous and dismal cry, with its red, shriveled, parboiled skin, . . . squinting, cross-eyed, pot bellied, and bow legged . . ." (Hall, 1891). James, more sensitive to the psychological issues, speaks of "the baby, assailed by eyes, ears, nose, skin, and entrails at once, [who] feels that all is one great blooming, buzzing confusion . . ." (James, 1890, p. 488). Compare the description of a somewhat advanced 18-month-old:

. . . this little girl could walk up and down stairs without climbing but in an almost adult manner, and could be trusted on the stairs alone. She could climb up to stand on a chair,

[1] Many zealous searchers worked to construct the bibliographic basis of the present chapter—among them, John Dow, Anne-Marie Leutzendorff, Marion Kessen, Robert Milstein, and Linda More. Lyn Wickelgren's review of the literature on vision was essential. All the many versions of the chapter were typed by Jayne Rightmer and checked by Keith Nelson. Grants to Professor William Kessen from the United States Public Health Service (HD-0890) and the Carnegie Corporation of New York and to Professor Marshall M. Haith from the United States Public Health Service (HD-2680) supported the research represented here.

could seat herself at table, could jump off a step, kick a ball. . . . She helped to dress herself, taking off some of her garments unaided, including shoes and socks. She put away toys, with encouragement, and could be trusted with breakables. . . she was talking freely and clearly in short sentences. . . . She named ten pictures . . . and gave her first name but not her second name. . . she scribbled freely with a pencil, made strokes and attempted the circle . . . (Griffiths, 1954, p. 97).

Unhappily, we know far less of the middle and end of this period of startling change than we know of its beginning. The majority of studies of the human infant—if we take the upper bound of infancy to be that time in the middle of the second year when vocabulary explodes (Lenneberg, 1967)—is directed to an understanding of the first days and weeks of life. Technical knowledge of newborn behavior, although insufficient to our wish, greatly exceeds our knowledge of the 2-, 6-, 12-, and 15-month-old child. For reasons rooted as much in the easy accessibility of newborn children as in theoretical demand, the bibliography of studies on infancy is largely a bibliography on the study of the newborn infant.

Even so, the growth of research on infants over the past 60 years has been prodigious. Baldwin's (1901) listing had only a handful of papers on infancy despite his desire to reach back in time and across national boundaries. As late as 1933, Hurlock, in describing "experimental studies of the newborn," cited 76 references. Pratt (1954), in his chapter for the second edition of *Carmichael's Manual*, surveyed about 500 studies of the very young child. The bibliography of the present chapter lists upward of 2000 titles. Clearly, the literature of infancy is beyond summary in detail. Rather, the pages that follow represent an attempt to disentangle and differentiate the problems, methods, prejudices, and theories that have determined the course of research on the young infant in the twentieth century. The program of the chapter, then, contains the following elements: (1) a brief treatment of theoretically general issues; (2) a sketch of methods used in the study of the young child, (3) an illustrative guide to the several different ways in which investigators have at-

tempted to understand the infant, (4) a more narrowly defined treatment of three aspects of the infant's behavior that are of particular interest to us, and (5) a bibliography of early infancy comprehensive enough to carry the student as far as he wants to go in the research literature.

SEVERAL GENERAL THEORETICAL ISSUES

It has become a platitude to say that selection of problem for study, method of data collection and analysis, theoretical expectations, and even the researcher's friends are determined by the same variables. Similarly, somewhat loosely defined *schools* of the psychology of infancy exist, and the empirical literature can be organized to emphasize the distinctions that exist among various conceptions of the child. In our search for expository clarity, we have separated somewhat discussions of theory, method, and findings, but the divisions are at best artificial. The psychology of infancy does not represent a full matrix in which each available method has been applied to each available observational opportunity and the outcome evaluated in the light of each theory. To be sure, some attempts have been made to state encompassing positions (e.g., Preyer, 1880, 1882; Stern, 1914; Koffka, 1924; Gesell, 1928; Watson, 1928; Freud, 1940; Piaget, 1946) but, by and large, the study of infancy is a loose confederation of ideas about babies and about psychology. All theories of the infant have had something to say about environment and behavior but even conceptions as fundamental as *stimulus* and *response* do not have commonly shared definitions. Moreover, students of infancy have given vastly more attention to definition of the response—*measures of the infant*—than they have to definition of the stimulus—*the nature of the environment*.

The Nature of the Environment

Whatever their research concern, all psychologists must attend to the issue commonly known as the *definition of the stimulus*. The clarification of this problem may be more troublesome for students of the very young child than for their colleagues who observe adult forms. The infant is, in fundamental ways, incomplete and the use of adult categories of the environment to define the stimulus field of the child can be misleading (consider, for example, the problem of color perception discussed by Pratt, 1954). Moreover, limitations in the behavioral repertoire of infants—for example, the absence of language—make difficult the establishment of the converging operations that permit us to make confident definition of the environment of adults.

Wolf (1957) proposed that in trying to make sense of the infant's environment, useful rough distinctions could be made among *stimulation, reality,* and *world. Stimulation* represents the organization of the environment into the abstract, precise, and often quantified dimensions of physics and sensory physiology. The study of auditory threshhold in which careful control is maintained over the stimulus and the definition of visual stimuli in terms like *luminence* and *wave length* are cases in point. A large and increasing number of studies of infants attempt a definition of the infant's environment as stimulation. *Reality* encompasses the world of common objects. The environment is defined in the categories that most adults, whether psychologists or not, find comfortable. The infant is presented with a *ball,* a *dangling ring,* a *doll,* or a *staircase.* Clearly, such a definition of the environment blends out of *stimulation* and shares with physically defined stimuli the characteristic of remarkably high agreement among adults in the circumstances of appropriate application of the terms. But the environment defined by the usual adult is not the environment of the physicist-physiologist and, more consequentially, it need not be the environment of the infant. In writing of the infant's *world,* Wolf noted that the child must be considered to have his own theory of the environment and that we may make grossly unjustified inferences about the child's world if we speak of presenting him with a *mother's face,* a musical *phrase,* or a complicated *figure.* A future psychology of infancy will permit us to make statements about the child's ordering of his experience with more assurance than is now possible, and, in the meantime, empirical studies of the infant should be read with an eye on their definition of the environment. Kagan has pointed out the dangers of giving normal adult modes of thought a favored position in our attempts to comprehend the mind of the child:

It is threatening to abandon the security of the doctrine of absolutism of the stimulus event. Such a reorientation demands new measurement procedures, novel strategies of inquiry, and a greater tolerance for ambiguity. (1967, p. 141).

The difficulties of defining the environment of the infant will appear several times in the present chapter; in particular, the discussion of vision illustrates the vagaries of the issue.

Measures of the Infant

The definition of the response is hardly a less complicated issue than the definition of the stimulus, but the literature of infancy appears to show more regularity in the use of behavioral categories than it does in the definition of the environment. The imbalance partly reflects a recognition that precision in psychological analysis and comparison among different studies rest on the reliability of observations and partly reflects the fascination with method and measure that characterizes academic psychology. The recent history of infancy studies may, with only mild unkindness, be seen as largely representing an increase in the precision with which we measure the behavior that used to be measured less precisely. As will be seen in a later discussion of the several views of infants, there is substantial variation in the procedures and metrics of behavioral analysis; nonetheless, a brief listing of commonly used categories of measures of the infant may put the research literature into preliminary organization.

First, some old home truths. Measures of the infant serve several, sometimes mixed, functions, chief among them the *establishment of developmental norms,* the *assessment of individual variation,* and the *diagnosis of process or structure* (i.e., the measure of the interaction between infant and environment). Thus heart rate may be seen as a measure of cardiac function that changes systematically over the first months of life, or as an indicator of stable differences from one infant to another, or as a measure of sensory sensitivity and attention in the infant. Although the several functions of measure are by no means incompatible and a rare study will give them all proper due, there is usually a clear emphasis in particular studies on one function or another.

Physical Growth. After birth, infants continue the growth rates characteristic of the fetal period and then, near the end of infancy, enter the period of stable linear growth that will be characteristic until the spurt of adolescence. In the first 2 years, children go from about 20 inches in length (30% of AS [adult status]) to about 34 inches (50% of AS), and from a brain weight of ¾ pound (25% of AS) to a brain weight of almost 2½ pounds (75% of AS). Students of physical growth, struck by the regularity and possibility of quantification of physical growth in children, have devoted great energy to the study of anatomical change in the first years of life. Sophisticated procedures have been used to assess height, weight, relation of limb size, variations in patterns of tissue growth, ossification, among others (see, e.g., the discussion of growth in Falkner, 1966). The development of the brain has been of particular interest to students of growth (especially Conel, *passim*). The rate of growth in brain size is at a maximum near birth, and by age 6 children have achieved almost all of their adult brain size. No other anatomical

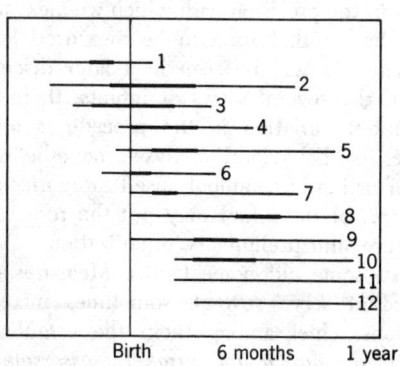

Birth   6 months   1 year

Fig. 1. The beginning and end of myelinization-gliosis in neural development. The process is at its maximum during the times shown by broadened lines. (1) Auditory nerve; (2) internal capsule; (3) pyramidal tract (mid-olivary level); (4) pyramidal tract (crus cerebri); (5) optic tract; (6) cerebellar subcortical: central; (7) cerebellar subcortical: peripheral; (8) cerebral subcortical: central; (9) striae of striatum; (10) corpus callosum; (11) cerebral subcortical: occipital; (12) cerebral subcortical: frontal. (From Dodgson, 1962, p. 207.)

system changes so quickly. Much of the change in brain weight can be ascribed to postnatal myelinization and gliosis. Although myelinization of all cranial nerves save the optic and olfactory is complete at birth, only a relatively small proportion of cerebral neurons (primarily in the afferent projection systems) has been myelinated. Moreover, changes in the nervous system are rapid enough to make the brain of the 2-year-old child hardly discriminable in histological characteristics from the adult brain (Dekaban, 1959; Gruner, 1962; Kennedy, 1961). Figure 1 records the changes that take place in myelinization and gliosis during the first 2 years of life.

Normative Measures. A large number of normative measurements have been made of physical growth in the fetal, newborn, and young infant (see, e.g., Bayley and Davis, 1935; Thomson, 1956). Merminod (1962) and Falkner (1966) present fairly comprehensive reviews of work on external measurements, bone age, water, fat, and protein composition of the body, as well as currently available data on variation in early physical growth that can be assigned to variations in nutrition, variations in social environment, and sex differences. A persistent and striking finding is the individual regularity of certain aspects of physical growth. Although the several measures of physical status in newborn babies are not highly intercorrelated (Bakwin and Bakwin, 1934; Carter and Krause, 1936) and no measure of newborn status correlates highly with terminal size, within a few weeks *length* at least has become a reliable indicator of adult stature. Bayley (1946) found correlations above .50 between length at 3 months and height at 18 years in her California sample and her data are congruent with British data (Merminod, 1962) in finding that the height of the 2-year-old child (who is almost exactly half his adult height) correlates at about .70 with his ultimate height. Regularity of this sort is not characteristic of any other physical growth measures, and it is, of course, not even approached by any measure of infantile *behavior*.

Effects of Nutrition. It has been known for some time that improved nutrition will increase rates of growth (e.g., Greulich, 1957) and may be critical to understanding the striking changes in the physical dimensions of human beings through the ages (Tanner,

1962). Correspondingly, undernourished babies (e.g., those born during wartime) are small and grow slowly (Dean, 1951). Recently, chiefly through large-scale investigations by agencies such as the *Centre Internationale de l'Enfance,* systematic studies have been made of the effects of generalized malnutrition, recovery from malnutrition, and the effects of malnutrition on intellectual as well as physical growth. Work with African children suffering from kwashiorkor (Dean, 1960) suggests that infants show sharp gains in weight and height when given calorically sufficient supplementary diets but that their physical measurements never come up to standard. Dean (1962) even suggests that there may be a falling away from expected development after age 4 even though the children continue an adequate diet.

Effects of malnutrition on cognitive growth cannot be readily documented. Large-scale studies of malnourished African children are only now under weigh, but the work of Cravioto (1969) in Latin America has suggested that prolonged malnutrition decreases intellectual competence in the school-age child. Available evidence does not suggest, however, that short-term and moderate malnutrition—again, in wartime babies—has significant effects on intellectual development. The effects of social environment on growth are hard to dissect from genetic variation. However, studies by Graffar (1962) and Acheson (1959), among others, indicate that the children of the higher social classes are taller and heavier than working-class children by the second or third year of life.

Racial Variation. Studies of racial difference are almost hopelessly confounded with issues of nutrition, early environment, and cultural variation. Earlier studies of indigent blacks (e.g., Bakwin and Patrick, 1934), showing that they were smaller and lighter than whites, have been corrected by studies of family children (e.g., Scott, Cardozo, Smith, and DeLilly, 1950; Crump, Horton, Masuoka, and Ryan, 1957) that show insignificant differences between blacks and whites on initial measures and early development. On the other hand, there is some evidence (Falkner, Pernot-Roy, Habich, Sénécal, and Massé, 1958) that African blacks are advanced in skeletal maturation at birth. Continuing studies of the *Centre Internationale de l'Enfance*

(cited by Falkner, 1966) suggest that there may also be racial differences in rates of growth and patterns of growth during the first four years of life.

Sex Differences. Differences between boys and girls in physical growth in the first years do not submit to easy generalization. Generally, boys are somewhat larger in external measures and show greater variability in development (e.g., Bakwin and Bakwin, 1934; Garn and Rohmann, 1960). Boys show higher mortality (Childs, 1965) and a greater susceptibility of their skeletal growth to variations in the environment (Acheson, 1966). The greater variability and vulnerability of boys, even in the first years, has been remarked by several authors (see Kagan and Kogan, Chapter 18 of this book). Douglas and Blomfield (1958), however, present evidence in support of a contrary conclusion. They show, for example, that girls in families of "nonmanual" workers grow relatively faster in the preschool years than their male peers and that girls from lower-class families are more likely to be admitted to the hospital. Bayley (1954) has shown that, in spite of the demonstrated more stable skeletal maturation of girls, terminal height can be much more reliably predicted from boys' length in the first years of life than can the terminal height of girls. It may be, as Bayley has suggested, that growth is under the control of different variables at different ages and that these variations interact with sex. Acheson Merminod(1962) has pointed to the probable important effect of timing of environmental variation on growth, particularly as the variation may be mediated by hormonal changes.

Physique and Behavior. Studies of interrelations among measures of physical status and behavior in young infants (e.g., Crowell, 1962) have found little or no significant relation between anatomical and behavioral measures, a finding congruent with recent careful work on the relation between physical measures and intelligence in older children (e.g., Lenz' note in Merminod, 1962, p. 156f.).

Physiological Measures. At least since Canestrini's (1913) ingenious use of cranial blood pulsation as an index of sensory functions in young infants, physiological measures have been used by students of infancy. Respiration and heart rate were often part of early investigations; developmental studies of the electroencephalogram began to appear shortly after the procedures had been developed for adults (e.g., Dreyfus-Brisac, Flescher, and Plassart, 1962; Engel, 1961; Smith, 1938); evoked potentials both auditory (Barnet and Goodwin, 1965) and visual (Ellingson, 1960; Dustman and Beck, 1966) have been assessed in infants; and, at one time or another, the behavior of babies has been related to stomach contractions (Carlson and Ginsburg, 1915), body temperature (Grossman and Greenberg, 1957), skin color change (Simons, 1925), vasodilation in the skin (Richmond and Lustman, 1955), basal skin conductance (Weller and Bell, 1965), skin potential (Wenger and Irwin, 1936; Stechler, Bradford, and Levy, 1966), and electroretinography (Barnet, Lodge, and Armington, 1965), among others. The use of physiological measures in the study of early development has been reviewed by Eichorn (1963, 1968) and by Steinschneider (1967).

The Uses of Heart Rate. Apart from their intrinsic interest to students of physiological development (Phillips, Agate, Silverman, and Steiner, 1964; Shock, 1966; Lipton, Steinschneider, and Richmond, 1966), physiological measures have served the study of developmental change, of individual variation, and of psychological process. In recent years, the analysis of cardiac response—typically heart rate—and its relation to stimulation, on one hand, and to other measures of the baby, on the other, has become the physiological measure of greatest interest to American investigators. Measures of cardiac activity can illustrate the remarkable range of use of physiological indicators in the study of infants.

Bridger and Reiser (1959) extended procedures used with adults in a study of the cardiac response of 40 children in the first week of life to air-stream stimulation of the skin. They found that the cardiac response to stimulation (acceleration of heart rate or deceleration) bore a strong relation to prestimulus heart rate. Moreover, it was possible to plot, for each baby, a regression line relating initial level of heart rate and response to stimulation. Certain characteristics of these regression lines—particularly that value of initial heart rate at which the stimulus produced neither acceleration nor deceleration—

were remarkably consistent in 15 babies who were tested on two different days. The operation of such a *law of initial value* in cardiac response to stimulation (a law that governs other measures of infants, both physiological and behavioral) requires that studies which use cardiac acceleration or deceleration as indicants of underlying psychological process be interpreted with care. Richmond and his colleagues have analyzed the parameters of cardiac response in 16 newborn females in some detail (Lipton, Steinschneider, and Richmond, 1961; Richmond, Lipton, and Steinschneider, 1962; Steinschneider, Lipton, and Richmond, 1964). The usual finding of a negative relation between prestimulus measures of the *magnitude* of the cardiac response and response to stimulation was obtained. Moreover, stable individual variation in slope of the regression line relating initial rate and response was demonstrated as well as individual variation in the newborn's capacity to return to prestimulus levels. Four temporal parameters (e.g., time to peak magnitude) were found to be generally independent of prestimulus characteristics and generally stable as a measure of individual variation. By and large, the several measures of cardiac functioning were not highly interrelated. In a follow-up study of 14 infants through the first 5 months of life Lipton, Steinschneider, and Richmond (1966) noted that, in addition to other maturational changes in cardiac response, infants at 10 weeks and 5 months of age showed higher intercorrelations of response measures than were typical for newborn infants. Again, as is commonly found with other measures of infants, there is a tendency for cardiac functioning to become stabilized during the first months of the infant's life.

Psychophysiological measures, including heart rate, have long been proposed as indicators of underlying psychological process (see Peiper, 1963, for a summary of early work). Perhaps the simplest of these is as a sign that the organism has detected an environmental change; for example, the infant's detection and discrimination of sounds has been assessed by variations in cardiac response (Bridger, 1961; Bartoshuk, 1964). Changes in heart rate have also been used as indicators of habituation (e.g., Keen, Chase, and Graham, 1965) and of learning (e.g.,

Polikanina, 1961). A variety of physiological measures has been used in studies of the infant's changes from asleep to waking—the heavily engaged problem of infantile *state*. Prechtl (1965), for example, described polygraphic procedures for recording simultaneously four channels of electroencephalography, six channels of electromyography, respiration, heart rate, and two channels carrying human judgment in the investigation of newborn state and the transition between different states of the young organism. Achievement and need in physiological measurement of the infant are revealed in Prechtl's assertion that "not less than 16" parameters of neurophysiological and other functions must be assessed in order to comprehend the problem of behavioral state.

Recently, interest has been shown in the use of physiological measures (again, particularly changes in heart rate) as measures of *attention* in young infants. Graham and Clifton (1966) have reviewed the literature linking heart rate changes to changes in attention. Lewis, Kagan, Campbell, and Kalafat (1966) concur that cardiac deceleration is a useful measure of the child's attention to visual and auditory information and that cardiac changes may reveal even more complicated psychological process. For example, ". . . work . . . with infants . . . suggests that, other things equal, a deceleration is most likely to occur in an infant when [he] confronts a moderate discrepancy from an existing schema, when the event surprises the infant" (Kagan, 1967). Kagan has also presented evidence for developmental changes in heart rate over the first two years of life (Kagan, personal communication). It should be noted that most psychophysiological studies of infants, even if aimed toward an analysis of developmental or environmental variables, also permit an examination of the stability of individual differences.

Physiological Measures and Behavior. The rapidly accelerating growth of interest in psychophysiological measures poses several problems for the psychology of infancy. The prosaic but nontrivial problem remains of establishing common or translatable procedures from one man's laboratory to another's. Assuming the accomplishment of that goal, there remains the major empirical problem of determining the nature of the interrelations among several physiological measures and among physiological and behavioral measures. A start has been made, for example, in Prechtl's (1965) work and in preliminary studies by Bridger, Birns, and Blank (1965). In measuring heart rate, judged movement, judged muscle tension, vocalization, and a combined behavioral measure ("excitation") under three conditions, Bridger et al. found that heart rate correlated highly with judged excitation ($p = .79$) and that both heart rate and judged excitation showed high individual stability ($W = .91$ for heart rate and .69 for excitation) across conditions of stimulation. Similar studies hold promise of providing an empirical matrix of interrelations among physiological and behavioral measures. Beyond the empirical matrix, however, lies the need for theoretical proposals about the relevance and significance of physiological measures in understanding the infant. We can say for physiological measures of the infant what will be said repeatedly and in different contexts through the present chapter—that we have only a rickety theoretical structure on which to display our growing sophistication of method and measure.

From one point of view, the literature on physiological measures as well as the literature on behavioral measures can be seen to demonstrate a paradox of precision. Most investigators start with interest in a process rather than a measure, in a problem rather than in a variable. Early studies, whether of activity or perception or thought, are typically imprecise in two ways: first, observations are not finely made and, second, several different *measures* may stand for the *process* studied (e.g., infantile distress may be indicated by vocalization, facial expression, and color change much as the beginnings of object permanence may be indicated by the child's response to hidden toys or peek-a-booing parents). The paradox lies in the fact that as precision of measurement increases there is a tendency for the relation between measure and process to become strained. Sometimes the measure is held to *become* the process (e.g., heart rate deceleration *as* attention); sometimes the honing of the measure takes on such interest of its own that the connection with process fades almost altogether (e.g., the persistence of studies of general activity in infants). In a sense, as we become more exact in our measures, we become less well connected with the problems that set us to search. The psychology of infancy has not been fully successful in refining its conceptual foundations to make optimal use of its refined measures of the response.

Behavioral Measures. The larger part of the psychology of infancy depends on measures of overt behavior, the gestures and movements of the baby described topographically or instrumentally. The variety is in fact so great and so defining of the several ways in which human infancy has been understood that a taxonomy of responses seen in infants would be of little value. Attempted catalogues have been neither uniform nor obviously cumulative (see, for example, Blanton, 1917; Dennis, 1934c; Peiper, 1963; Pratt, 1954; Richards and Irwin, 1934; Sherman and Sherman, 1925). Most behavioral measures have been of patterned activity—simple reflexes, movements of orientation toward aspects of the environment, avoidance responses, and emotional expression—but a good deal of continuing interest has been given over to the observation of *general activity* or *mass activity* in the young infant. A sketch of the history of general activity as a measure of the infant may serve to outline more general issues in the study of babies.

General Activity. General bodily activity of the infant puzzled and interested early observers of infants for a number of reasons. General activity was puzzling in that, unlike the reflexes, it showed no obvious relation to particular events in the environment; "spontaneous" movements (Preyer, 1880) seem neither adaptive nor instrumental. Preyer posed the question of the relation between early general activity and later adaptive behavior and proposed something like a reinforcement mechanism to account for the selection and preservation of parts of the baby's unpredictable activity. General activity was also of interest because, in spite of its unpredictability in detail, it showed obvious variation from time to time for a single child and substantial variation from one child to another. Early students of infants were especially interested in quieting; Moore (1896), for example, discussed the role of "inhibitory movements" in early intellectual and emotional development. However, as for most other observers (e.g., inventors of tests for infant development), general activity was not of inordinate importance to Preyer, Moore, and their contemporaries; relatively gross characterizations of activity seemed sufficient.

Just before 1930, however, general activity became prominent as a measure of the infant. In substantial part the enlarged interest in activity and its precise measurement grew from a desire to make the study of infancy truly a part of the new natural science of psychology. Weiss (1929) opened a long series of studies at Ohio State University with a hopeful paper on the measurement of behavior. Then, too, something of a theoretical controversy fed the interest in infantile activity. Students of fetal behavior, and of reflex activity more generally, were divided on the issue of whether early behavior was diffuse and general, becoming more specific and reflexive or, on the contrary, whether early behavior was largely reflexive with the discussion of "mass activity" representing a failure to recognize component particular reflexes. The argument was taken up among students of infancy, with Dennis (e.g., 1932) defending the position that the baby's behavior could most economically be represented as a collection of specific reflexes that became generalized through maturation and learning and with Irwin and Weiss maintaining that specific behaviors differentiated "from a primitive matrix of mass activity towards specialization" (Irwin and Weiss, 1930). On several occasions, Pratt (1934f, 1936, 1937) reviewed these positions and attempted to compromise them, although his theoretical preference for the differentiation point of view showed through, and he wrote contemptuously of "fictionalized part activity" (Pratt, 1936). He spoke for a careful separation of stimulus-specificity and response-specificity and he drew the controversy to a close in a familiar way by defining the issues as largely empirical. Pratt proposed a grand array of observations with stimuli along one dimension and responses along the other. He felt that, in this way, over the years, psychologists might come to a "quantitative expression" of the relation between stimuli and responses (Pratt, 1937). Pratt's position bypasses rather than solves most of the theoretical issues that turn on the definition of *stimulus, response,* and *process* but a sizable proportion of research in infancy—again, particularly on the newborn child—can be seen as candidate for Pratt's matrix. But by the 1940s mass activity had lost its status as an article of controversy and had become largely just another measure in the search for empirical regularity. And, certainly, in the intervening decades, infantile activity has been the behavioral measure most often subjected to apparatus and to attempts of quantification. Three families of procedures have been used to make precise descriptions of activity— *human judgment, stabilimeters,* and *film.*

Human judgments of activity have appeared most often and in the largest variety. Sherman and Sherman (1925) were content with recording "jerking"; Pratt, Nelson, and Sun (1930) attempted to describe the movement of body parts in the language of muscle mechanics and used "general activity" as a category only when the observer could not give a more precise description; categorical assessments of activity vary from a few rough divisions (e.g., Prechtl's [1965] *no movement, gross movement*) to many carefully described divisions (e.g., Birns' [1965] six-category system); Kestenberg (1965) used choreographic terms to describe "rhythms of movement." The variety is so great that the number of procedures for assessing activity by direct human observation is only slightly smaller than the number of studies in which activity is observed. Moreover, systems of description which are formally the same (e.g., categorical systems of four levels) have not been systematically compared. The deficiencies of direct human observation are well balanced, however, by the consideration that it does not require elaborate apparatus, that most systems can be easily taught, and that quite high reliability between observers can be obtained (Birns, 1965). But the major advantage of direct observation—and it is an advantage that permits serious metrical analysis—may lie in the possibility of making human judgment precise. After observing hundreds of infants of a particular age under a range of circumstances, the observer can build for himself a stable representation of the dimension of general activity. An experienced observer may then measure activity quite as sensitively as some instruments and, evaluated against the typical imprecision of stimulus control and theoretical analysis in

studies of infancy, his accuracy may be quite sufficient in many research applications.

Stabilimeter is a generic term for devices that more or less directly reduce the activity of the infant to a two-dimensional representation—time and position change. The instrument used by Weiss and his colleagues (Weiss, 1929) is typical; movements which the baby made as he lay on a pad were translated through tambours to a kymograph which displayed left-right and top-bottom movements. Instrumental variation is common. Wada (1922) rigged tambours to a crib at home to record diurnal variation in activity; Marquis (1931) used a platform with a fixed hinge at one end and a spring support at the other; Lipsitt and deLucia (1960) described a similar form that permitted, as well, the recording of some specific respones; Crowell, Yasaka, and Crowell, (1964) used photoelectric sensors and spring suspension to obtain both analogic and digital representations of activity. Variety of this sort makes stabilimetric recording liable to one of the limitations of direct observation—that comparison from one study to another is difficult. The instruments, however, provide a permanent record of observations made and permit fully objective scoring of the record. The latter advantage of stabilimetry is not always used. Although Irwin (*passim*) counted oscillations of recorded movement per unit time and Marquis (1931) counted half-minutes of recorded activity, some investigators (e.g., Lipsitt, 1963) have found that human observers, by inspection alone, can *judge* level of activity from stabilimetric records with sufficient accuracy.

Film, too, has a long history of use in recording the behavior of infants (e.g., Simons, 1925). Gesell and his colleagues were devoted to the use of filmed records (see, especially, *An Atlas of Infant Behavior,* 1934) and they developed objective procedures for scoring filmed records (Gesell, 1935a). Although more concerned with specific behavior patterns than with general activity, the Gesell group demonstrated the use of film in the study of individual differences in activity (Ames, 1942) and in the examination of phenomena such as laterality where a whole-body measure of activity will not serve (Ames, 1949a). Other procedures for the use of film in recording infantile activity have been reported by Bell (1960) and by Kessen, Hendry, and Leutzendorff (1961). Bell had human observers judge filmed records to assess level of activity (as well as three dozen other characteristics of the babies); Kessen et al. proposed a measure of limb movement which permitted the study of patterns of movement among limbs and which could be calibrated from one laboratory to another. The advantage of precision available from filmed records has been offset somewhat by two disadvantages—relatively long processing time and the lack of fast and accurate techniques for scoring film. The first difficulty will be reduced, if not eliminated, by the introduction of television monitoring and videotape recording to infancy studies (Engel and Hansel, 1961); the second has been mitigated by the description of efficient procedures for reducing filmed and videotaped data (Haith, 1966).

Despite its origin in controversy and its appeal to investigators caught up in a search for precise measures, infantile activity has survived as a prominent indicator of the baby's behavior because it is relatively sensitive to environmental variation and because it holds promise as a revealing mark of stable differences among babies. Activity has been reported to vary systematically with time since feeding (Irwin, 1932), level of ambient illumination (Irwin and Weiss, 1934a; Irwin, 1941), swaddling (Crowell et al., 1964), nonnutritive sucking (Kessen and Leutzendorff, 1963), procedures designed to produce temporal conditioning (Marquis, 1941), psychophysiological measures of arousal (Bridger, Birns, and Blank, 1965; Gordon and Bell, 1961), repeated presentation of stimulation (Bridger, 1961; Birns, 1965), the complexity contained in a visual dispaly (Haith, Kessen, and Collins, 1969), and the list can be extended.

Activity level of infants has been proposed as an important dimension of human variation by a number of investigators. Mittelman (1955) has connected variations in motor patterns to symptom formation. Stambak (1956; Lézine and Stambak, 1959) has reported that variations in motor tonicity can be linked to variations in locomotor development, feeding responses, and patterns of exploration. Kestenberg (1965) has proposed a longitudinal study of the correlates of con-

genital patterns of rhythm in movement. Fries (Fries and Lewi, 1938; Fries and Woolf, 1953) has long maintained the theoretical significance in understanding later personality of a "Congenital Activity Type." Recognizing that early variations in activity are not related in a simple fashion to adult personality, Fries has asserted that Congenital Activity Type influences the child's relation to others, patterns of psychological defense, and susceptibility to pathology. Thomas, Birch, Chess, Hertzig and Korn (1963) have described, among other measures, individual stability in activity level over the first two years of life. Schaffer (1966) presented evidence that infants of low activity level respond to social deprivation less well than their high-activity agemates. Even more provocative are reports of significant correlations between *fetal* activity reported by mothers and developmental test scores during the first eight months of life (Richards and Newbery, 1938; Walters, 1965).

In general, the weight of assertion about the importance of general activity in determining future development seems more than the available data can bear. Suggestive findings by several investigators of *short-term* regularities in activity level are hardly sufficient to justify the claims made for general activity as a central dimension of personality. Kagan (personal communication) has, in another connection, stated the general form of a question that must be put to proposals about the relation of early activity to later behavior. No one is seriously interested in variation in early activity as a predictive indicator of variation in activity among adults or even among older children. Rather, each theorist proposes a (different) set of transformations such that early differences in activity level show up in later differences in patterns of tension discharge, symptom formation, or strategies of problem-solving. The conceptual links between early behavior and its later manifestations are not always clearly shown and the demonstrated empirical support for the transformations that have been proposed is slight. Kagan lodged the issue in the contrast between genotypic and phenotypic characterizations of the infant's behavior; the phenotypical expression of general activity is seen to be of interest only as it indicates some psychological process or genotype.

Here, too, the study of infantile activity can stand as typical for other behavioral measures of the baby. Only short-term stable individual variation has been demonstrated; theoretical statements about the psychological process underlying variation in activity have been vague or careless; and demonstrations of continuity in process—genotype continuity —have been rare. indeed.

Activity as Representative of Behavioral Measures of Infants. General activity has been widely used in infancy research, it has attracted more apparatus than most behavioral measures, and it has been assigned great weight in attempts to understand early individual differences. For these reasons, general activity may serve to represent, *primus inter pares,* other behavioral measures. The following problems, which we have seen illustrated for activity, must be engaged in the use of other behavioral measures.

Measurement. There are three questions to ask about measurement. First, does the measure reliably indicate changes in the same baby across varying conditions? An affirmative answer can be given at several levels of precision, but, at a minimum, the question requires only that a *change* in the value of the observed variable be reliably detectable. Limited by the danger of regression effects and by slight generalizability, change measures that are reliable within subjects are common in infancy research. Second, does the measure reliably indicate differences between babies? Here at least an ordinal scaling must be possible for the measure under observation. Much of the attention given to the assessment of general activity—and, again, other behavioral measures follow the example—has been devoted to finding an affirmative answer. Finally, can the measure be applied uniformly from one observational setting or laboratory to another? A positive answer to this question would permit us, for example, to determine whether the most active baby observed in Akron was more active than the most active baby observed in Sacramento. Although filmed and videotaped records of infants offer some promise that fully generalizable measures will be found, it is a fair reading of the literature to say that few, *if any*, standard and precise metrics of infant behavior have ever been developed and applied widely. Of course, serious and informative studies of babies do

not require an affirmative answer to our third question, but the lack of a shared system of measurement limits the cumulative impact of infancy studies.

Observation in Context. It is often said of research that all empirical observations represent an interaction of many variables, and consideration of context—the setting for observation in all its complexity—is of prime importance in infancy studies. The paucity of standard measures, the absence of unifying conceptual schemes, and the fast rate of change of behavior in the first 18 months of life all impose a need to recognize and to describe, even if one cannot precisely measure, the instrumental and procedural characteristics that distinguish one study from another. Until a rough taxonomy of research procedures, settings, and apparatus is established, interpretations linking one study with another will be somewhat shaky. Bell (1963) has analyzed, for the limited case of the newborn infant, the disconcerting range of factors in the setting or in the baby that must be understood in order properly to interpret observations which are apparently straight-forward. Even for general activity, the behavior of newborn infants most often observed, general principles of great scope cannot be stated. At least part of the disability can be charged to the fact that psychologists of infancy, particularly the experimental psychologists of infancy, have developed neither standard procedures for observing the baby nor translation rules for relating the work of one laboratory to the work of another.

From Observation to Interpretation. An examination of the use of behavioral measures in infancy studies leads inescapably to the conclusion that *response*, like *stimulus*, is defined by hunch, prejudice, and theory as well as by replicable observation. However tough-minded and empirical an investigator aims to be, he shifts easily from a description of observed behavior to a discussion of assumed process. Explanation is, of course, both a normal part of any systematic study and the conceptual basis of response definition in the infant. It is worth noting here chiefly because of the strongly descriptive character of much research in infancy. Hall's program has been followed—". . . only the laborious comparison of many special and painstaking observations can yield results of value" (Hall, 1891)—but a psychology of infancy is far more than *look-see,* however sophisticated. Once again, the case of general activity serves in its illustrative role. Variation in activity has been explained in so many different ways (see Gordon and Bell, 1961, for a brief summary) that the weak connections between observation and interpretation are fully exposed.

Mental Structures of the Infant

In addition to Hall's empiricistic successors, who took variance wherever they found it, several general theoretical positions have influenced the conduct of research on babies. Though none was developed as a theory of early behavior in the first instance, propositions about babies can be drawn from them all. More or less coherent conceptual treatments of the infant are contained in or implied by the work of Freud and his followers (Freud, 1905; Rapaport, 1951; Spitz, 1965, to name a few), Koffka (1924), Gesell (especially 1925 and Gesell, Thompson, and Amatruda, 1934), Piaget, (1927, 1936, 1937, 1945), child psychologists and psychiatrists influenced by the ethological movement (e.g., Bowlby, 1958), and the investigators in several traditions who see the infant chiefly as a learner (Watson, 1928; Stevenson, 1962; Bijou and Baer, 1961). Several chapters of this book contain resumés of major theoretical positions in child psychology and the relevance of the theories for infancy can be seen there. Morover, some comparisons among theories have been made over the past decade (Baldwin, 1967; Kessen, 1965; Maier, 1965; Wolff, 1960). Therefore no review of psychological theories of infancy will be undertaken here.

However, unlike some areas of child psychology, infancy has attracted the attention of almost every theory of the child; thus several comments about theories of the child —the mental structures ascribed to infants— may be in order. It was suggested earlier that there is not a generally accepted body of *facts* which different theories can aim to encompass; rather, each conceptual point of view brings with it, explicitly or implicitly, rules for determining what constitutes a fact about the baby—that is, what constitutes a relevant arrangement of the environment and a relevant observation of the child for the particular theory under consideration. The

differences that separate theories of infancy are fundamental. They are not different ways of talking about the child; they are different ways of knowing what the child is. Decisions about the elemental nature of the baby interlock with the selection of problems for study; assumptions about process and the selection of typical problems, in turn, influence procedures for obtaining information and the ways the "facts" are finally reported. It is neither surprising nor inconsequential that theorists of the infant cluster with men of like mind; investigators separated in time and space are linked by their adherence to a particular way of seeing children.

Just as theories do not meet on the same domain of observations, neither do they maintain nonoverlapping, independent territories. Occasionally, varying conceptual attitudes are brought to bear on what seems to be roughly the same phenomenon. Perhaps the clearest example of this direct encounter is the diversity of treatment, theoretical and empirical, given social development in the first year of the child's life (see Maccoby, Chapter 21 of this book). Ainsworth(1963), Gewirtz (1961), and Spitz (1965) manage to make disconcertingly different statements about the baby and his first social attachments. A disagreement about the nature of the infant does not necessarily imply the existence of a contradiction, the incompatibility of varying explanations, or the existence of a "correct" alternative among the candidates. We are quite without systematic ways of making evaluative comparisons among theories of the baby. Rather, in the pages ahead, as we discuss procedures and problems, there will emerge several loosely connected sets of techniques, definitions, and conceptual propositions which represent the major points of view that exist in the field of infancy.

SOURCES OF INFORMATION ABOUT INFANTS

Observations of infants have been made because the researcher was fascinated by his own children, because the regularities of early development called almost aloud for precise and numerical description, because a problem of interest to the investigator in another domain (e.g., language, embryological differentiation, perception of space) seemed amenable to clarification by observation of infants and, less happily, because certain observations made on animals or adults had not yet been made on infants. The diversity of approaches to the study of infants and the remarkable relation between approach and outcome can be fairly represented if we consider *baby biographies, normative studies of development, longitudinal studies of early personality, laboratory studies,* and *other systematic procedures.* The categories are neither exhaustive nor exclusive but they permit the sorting of most observations on babies.

Baby Biographies

Many studies of the child depend on reports of parents but, because it is in the Western mode to keep the child at home during the first years of life, the study of infancy is unusually indebted to the relatively small number of parents who have watched and recorded the behavior of their children and then gone on to order and organize their observations in a way that permits sharing them with colleagues. Tiedemann (1787, translated by Murchison and Langer, 1927), who is often afforded the ritual honor of being the first baby biographer, apparently drew his inspiration from the self-revealing work of Rousseau and from the contemporary interest in developmental physiology. Almost 100 years later, again provoked by the more general biological problem of development posed by Darwin, the era of the baby biography began, grandly in the work of Preyer (1882), more modestly in notes about their children by eminent men like Taine (1877), Darwin (1877), and Champneys (1881). Dennis searched the literature for baby biographies in 1936 and found evidence of narrative accounts of infancy by 48 authors. When infancy studies became more rigidly scientific, enthusiasm for narrative parental accounts diminished; nonetheless, profoundly important examples of the form have appeared since in the work of Piaget (1936, 1937, 1945), in Valentine's (1930) study of fear, and in the observations of students of early language acquisition (e.g., Lewis, 1951; Leopold, 1939, 1947, 1949).

There is, of course, no agreed-on procedure for making a baby biography; they share the characteristic of being observational records on one or a few children made by parents of the observed child and continuing over several months (in some cases, over several years) of the child's life. Within so lightly defined a category there are studies of precise and limited intentions (e.g., Fairbanks, 1942, studied changes in the pitch of hunger wails over the first nine months of his son's life) as well as major attempts to understand the full scope of the baby's development. Biographical studies, of whatever dimension, suffer from the possibility of grossly contaminated observation by a loving parent who is typically also a professional psychologist with a point to make. The biographies also do not permit a systematic parametric analysis of variables influencing the child, a characteristic which may help to explain why no one has made the careful comparative study that the rich biographical literature demands. The limited summary of the biographies by Dennis and Dennis (1937) is encouraging, nonetheless, in demonstrating the regularity, across different accounts, of the timing of developmental changes.

Careful study of the biographies is justified because, even if one stipulates the bias of the parent-observer, he has a far better understanding of the baby's environment than is approached by the usual study of many children, whether normative or experimental. More than that, the biographer can organize his observation and speculations around the elemental fact that he is seeing a single coherent *person*; his descriptive task and his theory, if you like, are defined by the continuing and connected existence of another human being. More formal approaches to the psychology of infancy can offer neither conceptual coherence nor procedural elegance sufficient to match the biographer's *coherence of person.*

For all the technical arguments that can be made about the reliability and comparability of biographical data, the parental studies of early life have two remarkable properties that make them a major source of interest to observers of babies. First, biographies contain an enormous amount of information. Taken together, they comprise the most general and inclusive source of information about the child in the first two years of life that is available to us. The student of children who wishes to see the baby portrayed in broad and sometimes hesitant strokes, but fully human and fully persuasive, will wisely read Preyer (1882), Moore, (1896), Shinn (1900), and Piaget (especially 1936). Mrs. Moore wanted to describe all of her baby's mind, even though she recognized the necessity of abstraction and weakly supported generalization; Table 1, which shows some of her observations on recognition and inference, will illustrate the peculiarly important contribution of the baby biographer.

The empirical richness of the biographies is as remarkable as their selective character. To be sure, some accounts have been explicitly narrow in scope—most obviously those concerned with language—but all biographies, even those that aim for simple observational generality, represent their time and their authors. Darwin (1877) and Mrs.

Hall (1896–1897) concentrated on the development of emotion or, better, the development of sentiment. Tiedemann (1787) and Preyer (1882) wrote out of current psychology about sensation, volition, and the role of experience. Baldwin (1906), Mrs. Moore (1896), and Piaget (*passim*) saw the child as young philosopher and logician. The Kelloggs (1933), in their valuable study of early development in chimpanzee and baby, wanted to know how much a common environment could reduce species differences. The selectivity of attitude and the variety of conclusions shown in the biographies is not so much a measure of the inelegance of the method but rather of the fact that early human development is so many-sided that there exist many ways to make useful analytic reduction. Even so, there are communalities enough in the

Table 1. K. C. Moore's Summary (1896) of the Development and Relation of Recognition, Inference and Reconstruction in Her Son

Simple Recognition Based on Experience	Recognition Connected with Expectation	Inference, the Habit of Basing Conclusions upon Analogous Items of Experience	Reconstruction	
			Either a Simple Reorganization of Experience	Or a Reorganization involving an Inference
5th week: He recognized the human face.	21st week: He recognized hands extended to him and expected to be taken up.	24th week: He tried to take the hand of his own reflection in the mirror.	81st week: He threw his baby doll on the floor and ran into another room calling "Bye, bye, baby!" Then exclaiming, "Poor baby cry!" he ran back and picked it up.	66th: He found on the floor a bit of black wool about the size of a fly which he at once called a fly. He picked it up, carried it to the window and stuck it on the screen. Then pointed to it, exclaiming, "fly! fly!" a number of times.
7th week: The sounds of the voice.	22nd week: The spoon, and prepared to receive water	25th: Seeing a visitor wearing a hat he evinced delight; when she went out and did not take him he was distressed.		
9th week: He recognized the breast when he saw it; and the face of his mother.	23rd: His mother's hat, expecting to be taken out when she wore it.		He laid the doll on the bed springs and worked them up and down, giving the doll a ride as his grandmother rode him.	
12th week: His own hand.		59th: Seeing a cow for the first time the child called her a bird.		
16th: His thumb; the nipple.	27th: He recognized a tune, and expected it if he saw the movements which accompanied the song.	64th: A caterpillar he called a fly.	93d: Upon going into the bathroom he asked for a large empty bottle which was often given him to play with. Having received it he said, "Mamma, neck." His mother, who was busy, did not heed him. Then he	
17th: He recognized his ball at a distance of some feet.		83d week: In the afternoon the child walked in the station with his parents and rode in the street car. In the evening he and his mother went back to the station alone. When the		
18th: Footsteps on the stairs.	35th: Repeatedly threw his spoon on the floor and looked after it; sometimes he held out his hand as if to receive something, seeming to expect it to come to him.			
24th week: He recognized his grandfather, whom he had not seen for two weeks.				
34th: Changes in				

Table 1. K. C. Moore's Summary (1896) of the Development and Relation of Recognition, Inference and Reconstruction in Her Son

Simple Recognition Based on Experience	Recognition Connected with Expectation	Inference, the Habit of Basing Conclusions upon Analogous Items of Experience	Reconstruction	
			Either a Simple Reorganization of Experience	Or a Reorganization involving an Inference
the facial expression of people.	44th: His father was accustomed to take him from his chair every evening after dinner. When the child saw his father fold his napkin he was delighted, expecting to be taken up.	child found himself next to a man in the street car he called him papa, and insisted upon getting up on his lap, all without having looked in the man's face. In the station he ran after a man who walked a little in advance, calling him papa. When the man turned his face, the child at once saw that he was not his father.	said, "Mamma, hand!" and taking her hand he got her to sit down beside him. He then went through the performance of tipping the bottle as if pouring something out on his hand with which he afterwards rubbed his mother's neck as his had been rubbed with oil some three weeks before.	
43rd: He recognized and imitated a number of sounds.				
56th: The child liked to stand on a chair and look out of the window. If his mother moved the chair toward the window, calling him to come, he hastened toward the window; if she spoke the words without moving the chair, or adjusted the chair without addressing him, it meant nothing to him.	44th: When he saw his mother brush her hair (an operation usually performed before donning her hat) he expected to be taken out.			
	46th: His mother was accustomed to sit in a certain chair. One day the child saw his mother in the room, but while he was playing she took her seat in another chair. He soon looked at her chair, and not seeing her there began to worry as if alone, looking repeatedly at the chair. At last he chanced to perceive her, was satisfied and began to play again. Soon he looked up at her chair again, and, evidently having forgotten where she sat, behaved as at first. After having a second time discovered her he remembered where she was. Nor did he on the next or following days have	87th: He called a watch a clock.

95th: A picture was shown to the child. It represented a girl standing on a road in front of a fence. Her shadow lay on the ground behind her. He was asked to point out her shadow. He looked on the fence for it and could not find it, neither could he on the next day satisfy himself as to the shadow which he sought to find on the fence.

95th: He went with his mother to a strange house. He ran about the rooms examining everything. Of a large standing lamp he said: "See the big tree"; of the books behind glass | 101st: He put the scissors on a book and said they were riding on horseback.

103d: He lost a pin which fell down a crack. When he complained that it was gone his mother asked him where it was. He replied: "Gone to church; gone a sleigh ride." He saw "bizz" (his own moving shadow) on the floor and watched it. When asked what "bizz" was doing he replied that "bizz" was eating a big apple.

104th: The child gave his mother a pin; then offered one to his aunt (not present) and to many other persons whom he called by name, extending his hand now here, | 103d: One day while out, the child saw a man standing in the midst of a flock of chickens. He was too far away to see what the man and the chickens were doing; but was told that the man was feeding the chickens. The next day he described to his mother what he had seen, adding that the man fed the chickens with beef tea from a cup.

104th: His grandfather showed him the picture of a bunch of grapes, and promised that when the child visited him he should pick grapes. In a few weeks his grandfather went home. There- |
| 75th: A little playmate who had been away for four weeks was upon his return immediately recognized. He was seen for the first time in his wonted surroundings. | | | | |

Table 1. K. C. Moore's Summary (1896) of the Development and Relation of Recognition, Inference and Reconstruction in Her Son

Simple Recognition Based on Experience	Recognition Connected with Expectation	Inference, the Habit of Basing Conclusions upon Analogous Items of Experience	Reconstruction	
			Either a Simple Reorganization of Experience	Or a Reorganization involving an Inference
trouble in remembering where in any part of the room she sat.	doors: "See the books in the window!"		now there, as if giving the same pin to each in turn.	after the child in telling about his grandfather always represented him as picking grapes.
		98th: In the forenoon he saw a neighboor sweeping snow. In the afternoon when questioned as to her whereabouts he replied that she was sweeping the snow (he had not in the meantime seen her).		
		100th: Seeing his mother tacking down an oil cloth on the kitchen floor he exclaimed that the kitchen was broken (he had seen things mended with hammer and tacks.)		
		101st: The corner of his napkin bent up against his face, and this he attributed to the wind which blew under his cape and raised it in a similar manner.		
		103d: He broke the petiole from the blade of a leaf and asked his mother to mend it. She replied that she could not do so. He sat as if thinking for a few moments, then looked up and said, "Mamma mend(ed) the sofa; mamma mend(ed) the rabbit."		

records—for example, in records of emotional expression and of language—to justify more careful comparative study of them.

The biographies have the defects of their virtues: idiosyncratic selection makes comparison difficult, variation in observational procedure limits parametric analysis of variables, and the coherence of person that makes them convincing human documents often frustrates the student in search of an objective account. But, despite their weaknesses, the biographies are essential in our studies of language, emotional expression, problem solving, representation, and imitation in infants and they remain invaluable sources of observations and of leads toward better controlled observations on other matters of interest to the psychologist of infancy, particularly in the period between the newborn's hospital stay and the child's entrance into nursery school.

Normative Studies of Behavioral Development

The second major source of information about infants lies in large-scale studies of developmental regularities in behavior, the normative investigations that have produced, among their other achievements, the infant test. Bayley (in this book) deals with empirical and procedural issues in the measurement of development across the growth span; the account here will therefore review briefly only normative studies of mental development in infancy. Binet (Binet and Simon, 1905) included in his first intelligence scale a few items appropriate for the infant (e.g., visual following of a lighted match, prehension of an object seen, the execution of simple commands) but his later revision provided only for assessing the behavior of children at least 3 years old. Kuhlman (1912) began modifying the Binet scale for younger children and published items appropriate for children from 3 to 24 months of age in 1922. Simon (1916) proposed a detailed "questionnaire" to guide the observation of children between birth and 2 years and parts of his proposal were translated by Reymert in 1920. With the publication of Gesell's (1925) first scale of infant behavior, procedures for assessing early development came thick and fast. Developmental schedules, rarely altogether independent of one another and often leaning heavily on Gesell,

were described by Hallowell (1927), Linfert and Hierholzer (1928), Jones (1926), Stutsman (1931), Shirley (1931, 1933), Bühler and Hetzer (1932, 1935), and by Bayley (1933, 1936). Although the pace slowed after the mid-1930s, several new scales of infant development (as well as revisions of earlier procedures) have appeared; for example, the tests of Cattell (1940), Brunet and Lézine (1951), Griffiths (1954), and, in preliminary form, Uzgiris and Hunt (1964). For the narrower range of newborn behavior, early catalogues like Blanton's (1917) have been succeeded by standardized tests like Graham's (1956; Graham, Matarazzo, and Caldwell, 1956; Rosenblith, 1961; Rosenblith and Lipsitt, 1959).

Prodigious effort has been expended in the development, standardization, and application of normative schedules for infant behavior. Bühler and her colleagues made 'round-the-clock observations of children at intervals of 1 month in order to develop time-representative items. Boyd and Shirley made 1370 home visits and carried out 1944 behavioral examinations in the 2 years of their longitudinal study (Shirley, 1931). Bayley (1965) organized the testing of over 1400 infants under 15 months. Gesell, during the 25 years he studied infants systematically at the Yale Clinic of Child Development, applied his developmental schedule to thousands of normal and pathological babies, accumulating along the way miles of filmed records. The list could be extended to include scores of research applications of developmental scales for infants. From these studies has come the largest body of *descriptive* data available in the literature of infancy. However, in addition to variation among the tests themselves in content, standardization procedures have not been of uniform high quality (compare, for example, Gesell et al., 1934, with Griffiths', 1954, sophisticated standardization), and testing procedures, even for the same tests, have varied. Nonetheless, uniformities in the ways the tests were constructed (Hindley, 1962) have exerted regularizing force on most of the scales. Items assessing development of locomotion are often used as are measures of speech development—though here the differences among tests are substantial (McCarthy, 1954). Characteristically present also are items assessing sensory and percep-

Table 2. Items Drawn from Four Infant Tests Which Are Considered Appropriate for Six-Month-Old and One-Year-Old Infants

Gesell and Amatruda (1941)	Bayley (1933a)	Cattell (1940)	Griffiths (1954)
(Key age, 28 weeks)		(Key age, 6 months)	(Key age, 6 months)
Lifts head.	5.8 mo. Exploitive paper play. Present a piece of paper to child so he may grasp edge of it.	Secures cube on sight. When child is sitting in upright position before table a one-inch cube is placed within easy reach.	Plays with own toes.
Sits erect momentarily.			Sits with slight support.
Radial palmar grasp of cube.			Anticipatory movements when about to be lifted.
Whole hand rakes pellet.	5.8 mo. Accepts second cube. When child is holding one cube, place a second in easy reach.		Manipulates bell.
Holds two cubes more than momentarily.		Lifts cup. Place straight-sided aluminum cup upside down within easy reach of child as he is sitting at table.	Makes 4+ different sounds.
Retains bell.			Secures dangling ring.
Vocalizes m-m-m and polysyllabic vowel sounds.	5.9 mo. Vocalizes pleasure.		Hands explore table surface.
Takes solid food well.	5.9 mo. Vocalizes displeasure.	Fingers reflection in mirror. While child is in sitting position, a framed mirror is held before him in such a manner that he can see his reflection but not that of his mother or other persons.	Holds two cubes.
Brings feet to mouth.	6.0 mo. Reaches persistently. Place cube just far enough away from child so he cannot reach it. Credit if he reaches persistently.		
Pats mirror image.			
	6.1 mo. Turns head after spoon. Hold spoon so that it protrudes over edge of table by child's side and when he is interested, suddenly drop it to floor.	Reaches unilaterally. Child sits with shoulders square to front and both hands an equal distance from examiner. A two-to-three inch door key or peg is presented in perpendicular position.	
		Reaches persistently. One-inch cube is placed on table just out of child's reach. Credit if child reaches several times.	
	6.1 mo. Mirror image approach. Hold mirror before child, bringing it close enough so that he may reach it easily.		
	6.2 mo. Picks up cube deftly.	Approaches second cube. Child is presented with one cube and as soon as he has taken it a second is held before him in such a position as to favor his grasping,	
	6.3 mo. Says several syllables		

Table 2. Items Drawn from Four Infant Tests Which Are Considered Appropriate for Six-Month-Old and One-Year-Old Infants

Gesell and Amatruda (1941)	Bayley (1933a)	Cattell (1940)	Griffiths (1954)
		but is not actually placed in his hand.	
(Key age, 52 weeks)		(Key age, 12 months)	(Key age, 12 months)
Walks with one hand held.	11.5 mo. Inhibits on command. When child puts an object in mouth or on some other pretext, say "no, no." Credit if he inhibits.	Beats two spoons together. Two spoons are taken, one in each hand, and beaten gently together while child watches, then they are presented to child, one in each hand.	Side-steps around inside cot or play-pen holding rails.
Tries to build tower of cubes, fairly.			Obeys simple request, "Give me cup," etc.
Dangles ring by string.			Plays "pat-a-cake" (claps hands).
Tries to insert pellet in bottle.	11.6 mo. Repeats performance laughed at.		Reacts to music vocally.
Two words besides "mama" and "dada."		Places cube in cup. Aluminum cup and one-inch cube are placed before child and he is asked to put "block" in cup. If no response, placing cube in cup is demonstrated and request repeated.	Babbles monologue when alone.
Gives toy on request.			Says three clear words.
Cooperates in dressing.			Interested in motor-car.
Releases ball towards adult. (56 weeks).			Uses pencil on paper a little.
	11.6 mo. Strikes doll. Place small rubber whistle doll on table. Hit it smartly to produce whistle, encourage child to do the same. Credit if he imitates the hitting motion.	Marks with pencil. Piece of paper and pencil are placed before child with request, "——write." If no response writing is demonstrated and request repeated. Credit if child makes any marks on paper.	Manipulates box, lid, and cubes.
	11.7 mo. Imitates words. Say several words, as mama, dada, baby, etc., and credit attempts to imitate.		
	12.1 mo. Spoon imitation. Rattle spoon in cup with stirring motion. Credit if child succeeds in making a noise in cup by a similar motion with spoon.	Rattles spoon in cup. Aluminum cup is placed before child and spoon is moved back and forth in it, hitting edges; then spoon is placed beside cup with handle toward child.	
	12.2 mo. Holds cup to drink. Hand cup to child saying, "Take a drink." Credit if he takes it in his hands, and	Speaking vocabulary —two words. "Ma-ma" and "da-da" are not credited.	
		Hits doll. Rubber doll with whistle is put face up on table	

Table 2. Items Drawn from Four Infant Tests Which Are Considered Appropriate
for Six-Month-Old and One-Year-Old Infants

Gesell and Amatruda (1941)	Bayley (1933a)	Cattell (1940)	Griffiths (1954)
	holds it adaptively to drink. 12.6 mo. Adjusts round block. Three-hole (Gesell) form board is laid on table with round hole at child's right. Give round block to him with no directions. Credit if child puts block in round hole.	before child, and hit gently with open hand several times. Credit if child makes a definite attempt to hit doll.	

tual functioning, social responsiveness, and memory or learning. Table 2 illustrates the similarities and differences among infant tests by listing the items deemed appropriate for the 6-month-old and the 1-year-old from the work of Bayley, Cattell, Gesell, and Griffiths.

Normative studies of early development have had two aims: to describe the regular change in behavior with age for all children—the stability of the species—and to describe variations among babies that might permit reliable diagnosis and prediction—the stability of the person. With rare exception, the inventors of developmental schedules have been primarily concerned with the second, the *diagnostic* issue. Their search has been for ways to foresee the later development of babies for practical (e.g., in justification of adoptive placement) as well as for theoretical reasons. But the literature supports the conclusion that, however well we may know the timing and sequence of many responses in

the human infant as member of a species, we have not been able to devise procedures sufficient to the diagnostic and predictive task. Intratest and interobserver reliabilities are generally high (see, for example, Griffiths, 1954; Cattell, 1940; Werner and Bayley, 1966). Short-term test-retest reliabilities are also positive and sometimes high (Bayley, 1933b), although the summary of several studies in Table 3 shows that test-retest correlations rarely exceed .50 during the first three years of life. Several of the tests seem to be accounting for common variance. Pease, Rosauer, and Wolins (1961) in a comparative study of the Bayley, the Gesell, and the Cattell, and Caldwell and Drachman (1964) in a comparison of the Cattell, the Griffiths, and a modified Gesell have shown that, across a narrow age range, the several scales intercorrelate highly. But the capacity of infant development scales to forecast later measures of intelligence is slight. Bayley (1933, 1949),

Table 3. Intercorrelations of Averaged Test Scores within the First Three Years of Life

	4, 5, 6 Months	7, 8, 9 Months	10, 11, 12 Months	13, 14, 15 Months	18, 21, 24 Months	27, 30, 36 Months
1, 2, 3 m.	.57	.42	.28	.10	−.04	−.09
4, 5, 6 m.		.72	.52	.50	.23	.10
7, 8, 9 m.			.81	.67	.39	.22
10, 11, 12 m.				.81	.60	.45
13, 14, 15 m.					.70	.54
18, 21, 24 m.						.80

Hindley's (1962) casting of Bayley's (1933b) longitudinal data.

Anderson (1939), Cattell (1940), and Wittenborn (1957), among others, have demonstrated that the correlation between developmental measures in the first 18 months of life and tested intelligence scores between 5 and 18 years is effectively zero. Anderson's study may be taken as representative. Using three of the standard tests and some items of his own, he found that intelligence scores at 5 years correlated with 24-month scores at .45, with 18-month scores at .23, with 12-month scores at .06, with 9-month scores at .00, with 6-month scores at −.06, and with 3-month scores at .01. Whatever the reasons for the findings of low predictive value—general lack of stabilization in infantile functions, failure to sample "appropriate" behaviors, or the differentially greater impact of early experience on intelligence—Anderson's summary remains appropriate.

Infant tests, as at present constituted, measure very little, if at all, the function that is called "intelligence" at later ages. . . . It is unfortunate that workers in the pre-school period have used age-progression as virtually the only criterion for validating their tests (1940).

Not all investigators are convinced that accurate prediction of later intelligence cannot be made from early observations of babies. Illingworth (1961), Escalona and Moriarity (1961), Holden and Solomons (1962), Donofrio (1965), and Knobloch and Pasamanick (1959, 1962, 1963) have all argued for the clinical utility of early developmental testing. Each of these studies, however, involves either a sample biased toward low scores in a way that makes statistical interpretation difficult or it adds to developmental test scores another sort of observation such as "clinical appraisal based on test performance" (Escalona and Moriarity, 1961) or "a diagnosis of neurological status" (Knobloch and Pasamanick, 1959). The arguments presented suggest that characteristics of the test situation and aspects of the baby's behavior beyond his measurable performance on test items must be taken into account. Certainly it is the case that, over the years, pediatricians and neurologists have developed techniques for the assessment of the infant's neurological condition that may amplify and correct the findings of developmental tests. Although rarely cast in the strict psychometric form of infant tests, the behavioral observations of André-Thomas and his colleagues (e.g., Saint-Anne Dargassies, 1962) and of Peiper (1963) are essential to an understanding of the infant, particularly of the newborn. Parmalee (1962) has published a summary of current European neurological studies and Saint-Anne Dargassies (in Falkner, 1966) has summarized her observations on premature and term babies. Fiorentino (1963) has described a large number of reflex tests of central nervous system development in the 1½ years of life. A far simpler procedure for the evaluation of the newborn infant proposed by Apgar (1953; and James, 1962) has been used by students of infancy in assessing the sequelae of prematurity and perinatal anoxia.

On balance, the obvious contribution of the normative studies has been to describe in some detail the expected course of development in the first two years of white, Western, family-reared children. They also provide a procedure for assessing short-term developmental effects such as the relation of fetal activity to early development (Richards and Newberry, 1938; Bernard, 1964; Walters, 1965) and of the action of contemporaneous environmental change on behavior—for example, the effect of separation. Test performance has been used to measure cross-cultural and subcultural variation (e.g., Knobloch and Pasamanick, 1953; Geber and Dean, 1957; Vincent and Hugon, 1962), to measure the effect of institutionalization (Lipton and Provence, 1963), and to find the influence of sex, birth order, and characteristics of parents (Bayley and Schaefer, 1964; Bayley, 1965) as well as in extensive studies of prematurity and early pathology.

The search for normative measures with predictive power goes on. One tactic is represented by Uzgiris and Hunt, who have begun their search for test items on theoretical rather than empirical grounds, drawing largely from the work of Piaget (1936, 1937, 1945). Another, older procedure seeks items in present tests that are differentially sensitive to later performance. Anderson (1939) and Maurer (1946) made early use of the procedure; Werner and Bayley (1966) have recently shown that *reliabilities* are higher for test items that deal with independent movements of the baby's body and activity directed toward objects than they are for responses which involve a social partner. Cameron, Levson, and Bayley (1967) have recently followed up weak suggestions in the literature (e.g., Abt, Adler, and Bartelme, 1929; Catalano and McCarthy, 1954; Karelitz, Fisichelli, Costa, Karelitz, and Rosenfeld, 1964) that vocalization and early speech may be more intimately related to mature intelligence than other aspects of early infant behavior. Still, Stott and Ball (1965), after a close quantitative analysis of several currently used infant tests, conclude that there is "a great lack of consistency among and within the scales . . . in terms of factor content and meaning, thus pointing up the need for more consistent and adequate test scales."

Studies of Early Variation in Personality

When Mary Shirley reported her observations on personality development in the first two years of life, she commented: "there are no studies of personality at the infant level with which the results of this study can be checked and its theoretical interpretations compared" (Shirley, 1933). As she wrote, several studies that aimed to follow children from birth until maturity were being started and, over the years, several more have been initiated. But, for all the keen and apparently increasing interest in the longitudinal study of behavior (Bell, 1953; Anderson, 1954; Kessen, 1960; Schaie, 1965), the public literature on connections between baby's behavior in the first years of life and his personality during adolescence or adulthood is very small. Stone and Onqué (1959), in their survey of follow-up studies of personality, found only a scattering of reports that involved very young children. Among them were Washburn's study of laughing and smiling in the first year (1929) and of child-care procedures in the first two years (Washburn and Putnam, 1933), a report on MacFarlane's (1938) study of guidance, studies on a very small number of children by the Gesell group (Gesell and Ames, 1937; Ames, 1944) and their successors at Yale's Child Study Center (Coleman, Kris, and Provence, 1953; Wolf, 1953), a study of Shirley's babies after 15 years (Neilon, 1948), and some parts of Bayley's unique work. Reports on work completed or planned linking infant behavior to later personality have since

been presented by Meili (1957), Escalona and Heider (1959), Skard, Inhelder, Noelting, Murphy, and Thomas (summarized in David and Brengleman, 1960), Kagan and Moss (1962), Thomas, Birch, Chess, Hertzig and Korn (1963), and Schaefer and Bayley (1963).

The variability in instrument and procedure that characterizes longitudinal studies of motor and mental development is, not surprisingly, of a low order when compared with studies of early personality. We have some sense of what adult intelligence is and how to assess it; we have only a beginning notion of the dimensions of adult personality. Studies of infantile personality share an interest in some large categories (e.g., activity, impulsivity, and social response, particularly dependency and aggression) but there appear to be *no two studies* in the literature where the same instruments and the same procedure for personality assessment were used. Table 4 lists the categories for describing early behavior used by Gesell and Ames (1937), Bayley (Schaefer and Bayley, 1963), Kagan and Moss (1962), and Thomas et al. (1963). The rarity and value of data connecting infantile with adult characteristics make the diversity of technique insignificant, but there exists a clear need for integration and organization of information from the several studies. In general, short-term stability of observed characteristics has been established. Schaefer and Bayley compare four age groupings between 10 months and 36 months, Kagan and Moss compare years 1, 2, and 3 with years 4, 5, and 6, Thomas et al. present interview data drawn from six periods in the first two years —all concur in finding significant stability in observations of personality traits. But, in the few studies that report extensive data from infancy to adolescence or early adulthood, there is the familiar decay in the strength of relation from age period to age period. The work of Kagan and Moss and of Schaefer and Bayley can illustrate the conclusion. Kagan and Moss (1962) report some 174 correlations of characteristics of children in the first 3 years of life with characteristics of adults; of these, only 4 are statistically stable. Schaefer and Bayley (1963) report 784 correlations of characteristics observed between 10 months and 3 years with characteristics of adolescence; of these, 44 are statistically stable. In

Table 4. Examples of Categories Used to Describe Dimensions of Early Personality in Four Studies

Gesell and Ames (1937)	Kagan and Moss (1962)	Thomas et al. (1963)	Schaefer and Bayley 1963)
Energy output.	Passive and dependent behavior.	Activity level.	Responsive to persons.
Motor behavior.	Aggression.	Rhythmicity.	Rapid.
Self-dependence.	Achievement.	Approach-withdrawal.	Active.
Social responsiveness.	Interaction with oppo-	Adaptability.	Not shy.
Family attachment.	site sex.	Intensity of reaction.	Happy.
Communicativeness.	Physical-harm anxiety.	Threshold of respon-	Positive behavior.
Adaptivity.	Social interaction.	siveness.	Calm.
Exploration of	Compulsivity.	Quality of mood.	
environment.	Hyperkinesis.	Attention span and	
Humor sense.		persistence.	
Emotional maladjustment.			
Emotional expressiveness			
Reaction to success.			
Reaction to restriction.			
Readiness of smiling.			
Readiness of crying.			

the latter case, a disproportionate number of high correlations were reported for the girls in the sample and in the pattern that relates rapidity and activity in early life with adolescent characteristics of independence, boldness, irritability and defiance. The Schaefer and Bayley work also contains the provoking suggestion, in part confirmed by Kagan and Moss, that characteristics of mothers in the first three years of life, for boys at any rate, may be a better indicator of adolescent behavior than the child's own earlier behavior. It should be noted, however, as Bloom (1965) has noted for other human characteristics, that there is a tendency for personal stability to increase markedly during the second three years.

Strangely, some of the apparently most successful long-term predictions have been made in the *gross* categories of individuality used by Gesell and Ames (1937) and by Escalona and Heider (1959). Even more dramatic is Neilon's (1948) study in which she made a clinical assessment of 16 of Shirley's original 25 children when they became 17 years old. She gave clinical sketches of the children at 17 to some 15 judges together with clinical sketches of the children made at 2 years of age. The task of the judges was to match the two sets of data. Matches were made at statistically stable levels and the pattern of concurrence is strikingly close. As in the case of the baby biographies, we may be able to construct some sense of the

person but be unable to dissect and analyze our judgments into diagnostic and predictably effective categories. In spite of slight evidence of stability, our inability to make predictions of later personality from observations in the first three years of life is so much against good sense and common observation, to say nothing of the implication of *all* developmental theories, that the pursuit of predictively effective categories of early behavior will surely continue unabated.

Laboratory Studies

The line between sensitive observation in natural settings and systematic laboratory studies is not easy to draw. Defined loosely, laboratory studies are distinguished by attempts to control stimuli and to vary them systematically, by close attention to the reliablity of response measures, and by the use of comparable observations on a fair number of infants. The use of strict experimental procedures, with random assignment of subjects to differing treatments, has not been a distinguishing mark of laboratory studies. More often, and particularly in the older infancy work, the laboratory was a setting for carefully controlled and systematic observation rather than a place to carry out experiments of canonical design. For instance, the early German work represented so well in Canestrini's (1913) monograph was sensitive to consideration of the regularity of stimulus presentation and uniformity of response recording, but by and large each baby seen was offered as many stimuli as age and state of wakefulness would permit, in no regular order or design. Canestrini reports on 279 acoustical stimulations in which he used 13 different sound-producing sources ranging from 7 occasions of "a strange person's whisper" to 53 presentations of a ringing bell. The germinal work of Pratt, Nelson, and Sun (1930) represented a further refinement of procedures of careful observation of the infant in a controlled context. Procedures of observation in a laboratory setting have continued to be used effectively, particularly in attempts to establish norms for development (Gesell, 1934; Papoušek, 1967) and in observations of states of wakefulness and sleep (Dittrichová, and Lapácková, V., 1964; Prechtl, 1958; Wolff, 1966).

Systematic psychophysical studies in which several values of a stimulus dimension are presented in a controlled fashion are relatively rare in the infancy literature. Jensen's (1932) investigation of the infant's response to taste and temperature has long stood as a model. In his observations on response to salt, for example, Jensen used five levels of salinity and repeated his presentation to each infant a large number of times. The revival of interest in early visual functioning that has characterized the last decade has led psychologists of infancy to new attention to the use of the strict psychophysical procedures (Hershenson, Kessen, and Munsinger, 1967).

The great bulk of random-assignment experiments on infants, those in the manner so common to general psychology, have been studies of learning. A range of studies from Marquis' (1941) study of activity change under modification of feeding schedule to Siqueland and Lipsitt's (1966) study of conditioned head-turning represents the common characteristics of experiments with infants. The use of procedural paradigms tested with animals and adults, close attention to control of the stimulus conditions and the quantification of response, and generally a commitment to an associationistic view of the child are shared characteristics of experimental studies of the newborn, as they are of experimental studies of the older infant (Rheingold, 1956; Papoušek, 1967; Brackbill, Fitzgerald, and Lintz, 1967).

A powerful but rarely used application of experimental design is the co-twin study in which one member of a twin pair is given training or exposure to stimulation which is not available to his sibling (Gesell and Thompson, 1929; Strayer, 1930).

The carefully controlled experiment, with suitable comparison groups, remains one of the most precise instruments available to students of infancy. However, its precision and ultimate utility are constrained by the relevance and generality of the questions posed to the procedure and it is difficult to resist the conclusion that many experimental studies of infant behavior are regularizations of common sense, or, worse, laboriously magnified observations that have the scope of a single developmental test item. It should also be noted that even the most carefully managed experimental studies confound treatment with the effects of age, a general characteristic of child study which is amplified by the rapid development of the infant in the first 18 months of life.

Other Systematic Procedures

Observation in Natural Settings. The work of the European animal ethologists (Tinbergen, 1951; Lorenz, 1966) has led to the application of ethological attitudes and procedures to the study of infants. The work of Ambrose (1961) and of Spitz and Wolf (1946) on smiling, of Bowlby (1958), Robertson (1962), and Schaffer (Schaffer and Emerson, 1964) on early separation and the origins of anxiety, and the work of Ainsworth (1963) on mother-attachment define the evolving tradition. Clearly, studies of this order share many characteristics of procedures described earlier but the ethological dedication to the analysis of naturally occurring phenomena, resting as it does on a unique theory of the child, warrants separate mention.

Retrospective Studies. Freud's epochal theory of the nature of early infancy is a monument to the use of retrospective studies to draw conclusions about the first months of life. His methods of inquiry and procedures for inference continue, *mutatis mutandis*, in the work of contemporary psychoanalysts (clinical studies in *Psychoanalytic Study of the Child, passim.*) In addition to retrospective studies of infancy based on the recollections of patients in therapy, there is a substantial body of literature about infancy drawn from the recollection of parents. Sears, Maccoby, and Levin's *Patterns of Child Rearing* (1957) is a model for the strategy.

Cross-Cultural Studies. Anthropologists, particularly those influenced by psychoanalysis, have long been interested in variation among cultures in patterns of early development and of early mother-child interaction (Mead, 1954; Whiting, 1963; Whiting and Child, 1953). Interest in cross-cultural comparison continues to the present, with a particular interest on Africa (e.g., Ainsworth, 1963; Geber and Dean, 1959) and such study has been given important support by the establishment of cooperative groups such as the *Centre Internationalle de l'Enfance* (Falkner, 1966).

SEVERAL VIEWS OF THE INFANT

The diversity of methods used to study infancy is well matched by the diversity of conclusions drawn by investigators about the nature of the young child. Because of our limited access to the infant over so important a period of his development, because students of infancy come from several disciplinary homes and with widely varying theories, explicit and implicit, about the nature of man, and, centrally, because the human infant is so rapidly changing a phenomenon and so variable a source of data, a visitor from another planet who selected randomly from the enormous literature on infancy would be hard-pressed to recognize that a single species was under examination. Such diversity is not regrettable. Perhaps our best hope for understanding the infant depends on our approaching him from several sides and with several procedures. In order to comprehend the pluralism of infancy studies, we have divided an overall guide to the bibliography into the following sections— the infant as an *assembly of reflexes*, the infant as *emerging behavior*, the infant as *sensory surface*, the infant as *learner*, the infant as *perceiver and thinker*, and the infant as *social partner*. Necessarily somewhat arbitrary, and unhappily obscuring the overlap that exists among categories, the divisions can be defended, at least as a device for sorting studies and at best as collecting together closely related attitudes toward the nature of

the child and the proper procedures for understanding him.

The Infant as an Assembly of Reflexes

The remarkable density of studies of reflex activity in the newborn and the young infant may plausibly be understood on several grounds. First, scientific physiology in the nineteenth century—that is, the physiology of Helmholtz, Dubois-Reymond, and their students—depended heavily on the reflex as the fundamental unit in their conception of man (see Fearing, 1930). Many of the academic neurologists who played an important role in early studies of newborn behavior were clearly in the Helmholtzian mold. Neurologists saw the reflex as the clearest window on the diagnosis of brain function. Second, although Wundt and many of his American students did not consider reflexive behavior to be a proper part of psychology, the incorporation of Russian reflexology into American behaviorism made the study of reflexes an important part of developmental study. Finally, and perhaps of greatest relevance, the clarity and regularity of reflex behavior stood out from the otherwise chaotic and confusing activities of the newborn infant in a way that made the reflex appear to be the obvious and systematic way to understand the young infant.

Lists of Reflexes. The taxonomic task— the description of infantile reflexes—sometimes takes on the character of *list-making*. Cattaneo (1902) described six reflexes and their variation in a pathological sample over the first two years of life; Burr in 1921 and DeAngelis in 1923 listed "the" half-dozen reflexes of early infancy; among Blanton's (1917) several dozen responses of the first month were nearly a score that could be seen as reflexes; Dennis (1934c), the chief bibliographer of infancy in the 1930s, brought together a list of almost 100 responses of the newborn infant, many of which were reflexes. Descriptive aspects of the work of André-Thomas and Saint-Anne Dargassies (1960, 1962), the encyclopedia of Peiper (1963), and the standard texts of pediatric neurology (e.g., Dekaban, 1959) add richly to our collegation of reflexes. A few patterns appeared in almost everyone's list—patellar and abdominal and cremasteric reflexes, reflexes of the foot, reflexes of feeding (especially rooting, sucking, and swallowing) and crying and grasping, and reflexes of the whole body (startle and Moro). Yet, beyond these favorites, investigators have given concentrated attention to a staggering variety of reflexive patterns. To illustrate by sampling, Alexander (1911) described the nystagmatic response to active and passive turning of the baby's head, Hollis (1913) described the facial grimace of the child about to cry. Thornval (1921) treated of the nystagmic response to water of varying temperatures placed in the child's ear, Bauer (1926) described the newborn's primitive crawling, Wagner (1938) noted the temporal characteristics of hiccups, Stirnimann and Stirnimann (1940) assessed the grasping reflex of the foot in 1000 infants, Lønnum (1956) compared the abdominal skin reflex in newborn infants with its appearance in brain-damaged adults, Mitchell (1962) presented early developmental data on the Landau reflex (a regular response of infants to ventral suspension), Parmelee (1963) described Babkin's hand-mouth reflex in prematures, Zapella (1963) studied the appearance of foot-placing in children under 2 months of age, Prechtl, Grant, Lenard, and Hrbek (1967) made a polygraphic study of the lip-tap reflex, and Schmidt, Leurs, and Weidtman (1968) presented over 600 observations of children in the first 9 months of life on the reflexive response of the infant's head and back to the stimulus of being flicked on the nose.

Of course, almost all investigators of reflexive behavior in the young infant were sensitive to two limitations in the view of the child as an assembly of reflexes. First, not all behavior, even in the newborn baby, could be conceived as reflexive. The earlier discussion of general activity (see especially the work of Bryan, 1930; Gilmer, 1933; and Pratt, 1936) illustrates the troublesome problem of "spontaneous" activity. Moreover, a number of attempts to contrast *reflex* and *instinct* that appear in the literature from before Stern (1914) to after Bowlby (1958) illustrate the problem of mixed categories. Second, sensitive observers of behavior that can usefully be called reflexive recognized that wide variability exists, from occasion to occasion and from baby to baby, in the stability and reliability of the relation between stimulus and response. For example, observa-

tions made in several laboratories on movements of the head when the baby lies on his stomach indicate both the complexity of the response and the variety of variables that influence it (Prechtl, 1958; Turkewitz, Gordon, and Birch, 1965a, 1965b). To be sure, the alert infant stimulated on and near the mouth will move his head from side to side and will often open his mouth and grasp the stimulating object with his lips. However, it has been observed that the response not only changes with age (e.g., in the definition of the area near the mouth that will evoke the reflex) but also that the response varies widely during a single observation in amplitude and frequency, that the likelihood of eliciting the response depends on the sleep state of the baby and on time since last feeding, and that there is evidence for adaptation of the reflex under repeated stimulation. Prechtl (1958) has attempted to encompass part of the variability in head-turning by distinguishing a fixed-form response—side-to-side movement—from a variable form response—directed head-turning. It is a uniform finding in the literature that comparable complexity is found in other reflexive behavior when a close examination is made of response topography and conditions of elicitation.

Several groups of reflexes, at one time or another over the past 30 years, have received close attention from pediatricians, neurologists, and psychologists. The reflexes of feeding hold first place among these (see, in particular, Peiper's (1963) remarkable treatment of the relation among sucking, swallowing, and breathing) and a later section of the present chapter will treat sucking in detail.

The Babinski Reflex. As noted earlier, the reflexive movements of the foot—*plantar* and *Babinski*—have been favored objects of study. The Babinski remains an important index of abnormality in the functioning of the adult central nervous system (Nathan and Smith, 1955) but attempts to find clear-cut developmental patterns have been generally unsuccessful. Bendix (1931) had remarked on the relative variety of the Babinski in newborn infants and the work of Pratt (1934a, 1934b, 1934c) demonstrated in thousands of observations the variability of the response of newborn infants to plantar stimulation. Observing eight anatomical segments of leg and foot, Pratt found it necessary to list eight different patterns of response in order to account for just half of the obtained reactions. Pratt also demonstrated a variability in the response dependent on variation in stimulus and variation in state and his conclusions were generally confirmed in an exhaustive analysis of the literature made by Richards and Irwin (1934b).

The Moro Reflex as Representative Example. Close to the Babinski in level of interest aroused among students of the infant is the embracing reflex *(Umklammerungsreflex)* described in 1918 by Moro. Consideration of the Moro reflex will lend support to the conclusion that striking changes have been made over the intervening 50 years in technical procedures for studying infants. Moro described the response as comprising a symmetrical moving of the arms away from the body followed by a return of both arms to midline; he reported that the reflex was elicited by sharply hitting the surface on which the child lay and he speculated that the response represented a primitive tendency of the infant to clasp and cling to the mother. In support of his more general proposition that the first three months of life represented a time of utter helplessness and dependence, Moro noted the disappearance of the *Umklammerungsreflex* in the second quarter of the first year. Every aspect of Moro's somewhat offhand description of the response has been studied in substantial detail. Confusion of the Moro response with startle patterns similar to the startle response of adults continued in the literature (e.g., Irwin, 1932; Wagner, 1938a) until the careful photographic work of Hunt and his colleagues demonstrated that the Moro and the startle pattern were distinguishable characteristics of infant behavior (Hunt, Clarke, and Hunt, 1936; Clarke, Hunt, and Hunt, 1937). As Moro had suggested, the response he described is common in the newborn period and shortly thereafter but becomes less easily observable in the third month and, except in premature and damaged infants, has generally disappeared by the fifth month of life. The startle pattern, on the other hand, is rare during the first weeks of life (although it can occasionally occur as if superimposed on the Moro), increases in frequency and stability during the first years of life and becomes generally in-

distinguishable from the adult startle pattern. McGraw (1937) treated the disappearance of the Moro and the appearance of the startle as the development of a single process, but her findings are compatible with the interpretation made by Hunt.

Argument has persisted too on the adequate stimulus for eliciting the Moro response. Besides the original disturbance to equilibrium, it has been observed that loud sounds, changes of position, and changes of temperature will also provoke the reaction (see Mitchell, 1960, for a summary statement). Peiper has maintained that the vestibular apparatus was critical in stimulating the response while André-Thomas has supported the involvement of stretch receptors in the muscles of the neck. Apparently critical studies reported by Prechtl (1965) indicate that either stimulus will produce the Moro even in the absence of the other.

The functional significance of the Moro reflex remains in some doubt. Although some commentators have argued with Moro's interpretation of the response as related to primate clinging (Goldstein, Landis, Hunt, and Clarke, 1938), recent observations by Prechtl (1965) suggest that Moro was not far off the mark. Prechtl found that when head-drop stimulation is given an infant while his palmar grasp reflex is being stimulated, the "clinging" component of the response is strongly facilitated; Prechtl is of the opinion that the conditions under which the response is ordinarily elicited are not biologically adequate but that, were the baby clinging to a maternal surface, loss of support would properly elicit increased abduction and grasping. The 12- channel electromyographic record that Prechtl uses to support his conclusion is a long distance from Moro's brief verbal sketch and we surely know far more about the precise conditions of elicitation and the precise form of the response than was known 50 years ago. It is, however, not altogether obvious that our understanding of the Moro response in the context of the baby's other behavior has been significantly advanced.

The Grasp Reflex. Study of the infantile grasp reflex shows, perhaps even more strikingly than the Moro, the process of *making precise* what was a relatively casual but accurate observation. An English medical officer named Robinson reported an "infantile atavism" in 1891. He reported that newborn infants could support their own weight when suspended and he published a photograph of a child clinging to a leafy tree branch in expression of Robinson's conviction that the response was related to our having a "quadrumanous ancestor." The grasp response was noted by many investigators and Richter (1934) systematically observed that the newborn human being could hang by two hands for a minute or so, although there was the usual great variability from subject to subject and from occasion to occasion. Myrtle McGraw (1940d) observed nearly 100 children between the newborn period and 7 years of age to demonstrate the triphasic development of the reflex. She found for grasping, as she had found for the Moro-startle pattern, that the infant's ability to support his weight was relatively high during the first weeks of life, declined to a very low level after the first half year and then became steadily better in "voluntary or deliberate" suspension from age 1 to age 7. In her sample, children did not achieve again until age 5 the capacity to support themselves that was characteristic of a baby at age 40 days. The gains since Robinson's observations have been substantial and largely in refinement of early accounts.

Reflexes, the Brain, and Psychology. Moro's emphasis on the importance of the first three months of life for nervous system development reflected the general opinion among neurologists, best expressed by Flechsig (1920), that the newborn was unfinished and that birth marked only a midway point in the myelinization and functioning of cerebral pathways. The process that began in the fifth fetal month neared its completion only in the fourth postnatal month. Although a few radical behaviorists spoke of learning reflexes (Hollingworth, 1928; Kuo, 1924), many observers of the young infant believed that the changes in behavior observed during the first months of life could be largely ascribable to anatomical changes in the central nervous system (see, for example, Catel, 1932, who referred to the newborn as "an incomplete and helpless creature"). Much of the interest in the infant as an assembly of reflexes has derived from the concern of neurologists to chart normal development and, even more critically, to detect pathological development. The work of Peiper (1963), of André-

Thomas and Saint-Anne Dargassies (1960, 1962), and the continuing concern of neurologists in reflexive behavior (Dekaban, 1959; Fiorentino, 1963) are, in large measure, attempts to build a research basis for clinical neurology. The infant in the early weeks of life, in this view, has been seen as a structurally incomplete organism (Conel, *passim*) and the observation of reflexes has been in demonstration of cerebral insufficiency. Even André-Thomas, sensitive to the continual development that connects early infantile behavior with the complexity of the older child, wrote about the instability of the baby's "first impressions" (André-Thomas, 1954), and Peiper (1963) is unequivocating in his conclusion that the "mature newborn infant is a pallidum creature without functional cerebral hemispheres" although "the most important neurological differences between newborn infants and adults have already disappeared at the end of the first year of life."

What then is the place of the reflex in the psychology of early infancy? Is the enormous literature on reflexes to be seen as reflecting merely the life-keeping economy of the young child, a collection, in Prechtl's keen phrase, of "phylogenetic relicts"? Titchener long ago posed the issue sharply:

The human infant, in particular as the incomplete form of a very highly developed organism, embodies two courses of development, a phylogenetic and an ontogenetic, in their most complex modes. The newborn child hangs to your finger, supporting its full weight upon its arms; the boy, a few years later, will hang in like manner from the horizontal bar. . . . While both performances are conditioned on racial inheritance, the later is not the direct outgrowth of the earlier, and we should go widely astray if we argued from likeness of form to continuity in ontogenesis (1909).

At the very least, Titchener's implied request for an empirical demonstration of the connection between behavior in the first weeks of life and later characteristics of human beings has not been persuasively answered. Reflex behavior plays a role in the study of the child as emergent behavior, as a marker of sensory competence, as the first link in studies of learning, and as a theoretical idea of some power in the work of Piaget. Yet, sucking aside, the literature of infancy is strangely quiet about demonstrating the continuity, for the *normal* child, between early reflexive behavior and significant social and cognitive behavior of later life.

The Infant as Emergent Behavior

Emergent behavior is proposed as a category to contain responses which develop in a regular age-related fashion through the first 18 months of life. The development of prone locomotion is the prototypical example, perhaps, of emergent behavior; Arnold Gesell was certainly the chief architect and polemicist of the view of the child as a system of naturally emerging behavior. Gesell's interest, like that of the neurologist of early reflexive behavior, was to chart the course of changes in behavior uniformly characteristic of the human species and tightly tied to age.

All things considered, the inevitableness and surety of maturation are the most impressive characteristic of early development. It is the hereditary ballast which conserves and stabilizes the growth of each individual infant. . . . [Without it] the infant would be a victim of . . . flaccid malleability . . . (Gesell, 1928).

Certainly Gesell had reason to be enthusiastic about age-related behavior in infancy. Even a casual survey of the developmental tests mentioned earlier in this chapter provides a long list of responses that share two critical characteristics—very nearly universal appearance in human beings and a very sharp rise in probability of occurrence as a function of age. Among the countless possible examples, consider a typical observation by M. C. Jones (1926) (no radical maturationalist!) made on a group of several hundred American children. Of the babies studied, 25% blinked at the approach of an object by the end of the second month; 75% blinked at the end of the third month; the dates of the first and third quartiles in Jones' sample for sitting were 205 days and 250 days; and other examples can be supplied at length. Of course, the regularity of occurrence does not explain itself; students of infancy remain divided in the emphasis they give to autoch-

thonous physiological factors, on one hand, and to species-general uniformities in the environment of young children, on the other. Whatever the point of departure, however, the study of the infant as emerging behavior has been a major theme of psychology through the twentieth century. In addition to the normative studies described earlier—those largely aimed at the construction of test items—there are a large number of more highly focussed and detailed studies of emergent behavior in the literature. The following sketch of several areas of investigation will serve to illustrate the range of method and findings.

Prone Progression. Trettien (1900) analyzed about 200 responses to a syllabus (questionnaire) of G. Stanley Hall's on creeping and walking. Although his conclusions may seem somewhat overdrawn today—for example, he maintained that, in assuming the upright position, man expresses "the limit of organic evolution"—his observations on the sequence, timing, and variety of locomotor responses conform to later reports. Careful tracings of motion photography permitted Burnside (1927) to describe the topography of early locomotion in fine detail. The two classic studies of locomotion appeared in 1940. Gesell and Ames (1940) used motion photography to distinguish 23 stages of prone behavior organized into 4 cycles during the first 60 weeks of life. The first cycle ended with pivoting on the stomach at about 30 weeks, the second with creeping at 45 weeks, the third with "plantigrade progression" at 50 weeks, and the fourth with walking at 60 weeks. Gesell and Ames also attempted to give some interpretation to their observations by the use of the spiraling notion of *reciprocal interweaving*. McGraw (1940b) organized her 3000 observations of 82 infants in the first 5 years of life to demonstrate 7 "distinct phases" in the development of locomotion from reflex stepping in the newborn to the mature walking characteristic of children at the beginning of the third year. Like Gesell and Ames, she put the peak time of "deliberate stepping" at about 60 weeks of life. McGraw's study at once illustrates the regularity of behavioral sequences in young infants and the economy of description possible when scoring categories are carefully selected. The explanatory scheme imposed on her data by McGraw involved quasi-neurological considerations of cortical inhibition and integration. Studies of motor development that concentrate on the first months of life (e.g., Bergeron, 1938, 1948) have emphasized the stabilization of behavior at about three months that has been so commonly observed in reflexive behavior.

Although, as noted earlier, racial or cultural differences have been found in earlier motor behavior, sketchy available evidence suggests that age of walking is a remarkably stable *human* characteristic (Smith, Lecker, Dunlap, and Cureton, 1930) except under conditions of great deficit of environmental support (Dennis and Najarian, 1957).

Prehensile Skill. The work of Halverson (1931–1937) on grasping patterns in the first year of life is perhaps the most carefully documented account of emergent infantile behavior. Based largely on the analysis of photographic records using both longitudinal and cross-sectional procedures and presenting the child with varying stimulus materials, Halverson has presented verbally and pictorially a very nearly full description of early prehension. Other investigators have gone beyond Halverson's taxonomic account of sequence and topography. Stirnimann (1941), noting the differences between the newborn's grasp of a human finger and his grasp of similar artifical stimuli, concluded that early grasping must be understood as the first expression of a social drive. In a preliminary report of research, Bruner (1969) again has emphasized the important role that the interaction of grasping, vision, and sucking play in early development of mind (see also Piaget, 1936, 1937). Studies of bilaterality and early hand-preference have shown that early bilaterality observed in the tonic-neck reflex (Ames, 1949) is succeeded by a period of mixed preference with clear tendencies for a single hand to be more active emerging only after 6 months of age (Lippman, 1927; Ames, 1949; Flament, 1963; Haith, Kessen, and Collins, 1969). Some evidence suggests that handedness is related both to genetic and to intrauterine factors (Churchill, Igna, and Senf, 1962).

Crying and the Development of Affect. The study of early emotional development shows none of the clarity and stability that characterizes studies of locomotion and prehension. Newborn crying has been described

in some detail (Aldridge, Sung, and Knop, 1945a, 1945b, 1945c; Aldridge, Norval, Knop, and Venegas, 1946) with the data indicating the relevance of feeding cycle (babies cry most just before feeding), the sensitivity of crying to care-taking routines (crying can be halved by moderate increases in amount of nursing care), and the absence of contagion from the crying of one infant to that of others. Crying has been shown to be inhibited both by feeding (Marquis, 1943) and by nonnutritive sucking (Cohen, 1967). There is formal evidence in support of the common observation that crying can be reduced by holding the baby (Peiper, 1963) and by continuous auditory stimulation (Salk, 1961; Brackbill, Adams, Crowell, and Gray, 1966). Attempts to find evidence linking amount of crying to characteristics of delivery have been generally unsuccessful (Ruja, 1948).

The development of technically advanced devices for recording the sounds of crying (Fisichelli, Karelitz, Eichbauer, and Rosenfeld, 1961) promises more differentiating observations on early crying. The relation of crying and other early vocalizations to infant speech has been examined by Lewis (1951), Murai (1960), and Bullowa, Jones, and Bever (1964), among others.

The peculiar asynchrony between the infant's reflexive response to a painful stimulus and his later crying has been noted (Taylor-Jones, 1927; Peiper, 1963) and the proposal has been made that motor and autonomic components of the infant's response to pain may be initially somewhat independent (Levy, 1960; Kessen and Mandler, 1961). The most systematic treatment of the development of affect in the first months particularly in relation to pain has been given by André-Thomas (1954; André-Thomas and Autgaerden, 1959). He describes the change from early polar extremes of *affect* (simple approach and withdrawal) to later subtle and socialized *affectivity* (affection and sympathy on one side, defense and counterattack on the other). Other attempts to make some sense of early affective development have been made by Schmale (1964) and by Spitz (1965). Schmale (1964) emphasizes the primacy of anxiety as affect and charts a possible course for the development of the infant's sense of helplessness. Spitz proposes that three "organizers," comparable to the physiological organizers of embryological development, mark emotional change in the first year of life. The baby's first social smile, his anxiety at 8 months, and his head-shaking sign of negation are, in Spitz's view, benchmarks for early emotional differentiation.

With the exception of smiling and other signs of attachment, the empirical base for the early differentiation of emotional expression is shaky. Most secondary sources depend on the work of Bridges (1931–1937), who described a differentiating branching of emotional expression from initial excitement to later excitement and distress to still later excitement, distress, and delight, and finally to a wide range of emotional expression at 2 years of age (Bridges, 1932). She proposed an analogous ontogenesis in primary drives (Bridges, 1936). Acceptance of Bridges' simple scheme must be guarded by consideration that her samples were small, that the children observed were institutionalized foundlings, and that criteria for assignment to categories were ill-defined. Darwin's (1877) and Mrs. Hall's (1896, 1897) biographical accounts of emotional development are more persuasive than Bridges' apparently systematic assessment, a contrast which dramatizes the need for an adequate descriptive account of emotional development in infancy.

Sleep. With the care for detail characteristic of her time, Wagner (1937, 1938, 1939) studied newborn sleep. She used records of gross movement, eye movement, and mouth movement to establish seven levels of the sleep-waking dimension and she assessed the infant's responsiveness under each level of stage to stimuli in several sensory modalities. In spite of wide variability within and between subjects, she found that deep sleep (the condition of infants about 13% of the time) was relatively easy to judge, that "body jerks" were most frequent in light sleep, and that the baby was uniformly more responsive as motility increased. Reynard and Dockeray (1939), on evidence from stabilimetric records, concluded that "complete waking" and deep sleep were easily recognized and tended to persist over time but that no clear transition patterns could be established for their five intermediate stages. More recently, Brown (1964) and Wolff (1966) have proposed quite similar categorizations of sleep-waking with emphasis on patterns of respiration and

motility. Wolff's observations led him to conclude that the infant is likely to be responsive to external stimuli more during intermediate states than while deeply asleep or very active and that spontaneous motor patterns such as startles, mouthing, sobbing respirations, and erections occur rhythmically and most often under conditions of minimal external and visceral stimulation. Electroencephalographic markers of the development of sleep over the first 18 months of life have also been reported (Mirzoiants, 1961).

Studies of the development of sleep patterns in the first year of life reveal some congruent findings. Children in the first weeks of life sleep between 14 and 15 hours each day (Irwin, 1930; Kleitman and Englemann, 1953; Parmelee, Schulz, and Disbrow, 1961); within the major diurnal rhythm there appear a number of minor rhythms. Night sleep goes from about 60% of the total in the first weeks to about 80% or even higher at 18 months (Irwin, 1930; Kleitman and Englemann, 1953). The duration of the longest single period of sleep (on a criterion that included light and deep sleep) increases from about 4½ hours in the first days of life (Parmelee et al., 1961) to over 10 hours by the twenty-fifth week (Parmelee, 1961). Regular cycles of shorter duration also appear. Tcheng and Laroche (1965) found, in children up to 2 months of age, cycles of activity that lasted about 70 minutes. Periods of deep sleep approximately 21 minutes long were bounded on either side by periods of "half-sleep" of approximately equal duration. Their findings are congruent with those Aserinsky and Kleitman (1955) who, on criteria of gross motility and eye movements, described deep-sleep periods of about 24 minutes within a more variable motility cycle of about 1 hour, and with those of Weitzman, Fishbein, and Graziani (1965). Dittrichová and Lapácková (1964) observed 12 infants over the first 24 weeks of their lives. She reported dramatic and abrupt changes in the third month of life when babies begin to manipulate toys, begin to vocalize comfort sounds, and decrease their crying markedly. Hellbrügge, Lange, Rutenfranz, and Stehr (1964) have drawn together available evidence on sleep and other circadian rhythms and have concluded that, although the sleep-wake cycle begins to stabilize in the third week of life, the natural periodicity of the newborn infant (approximately 24.4 hours in duration) does not become adapted to a 24-hour cycle until well into the sixth month of life. Roffwarg, Muzio, and Dement (1966) have presented evidence that rapid-eye-movement (REM) sleep (so-called "dreaming" sleep) occupies almost half the sleep time of newborn infants and decreases rapidly to about one-quarter of the sleep time of children of 2 years. They propose, in explanation of so puzzling a finding, that endogenous neural activity underlying REM sleep prepares the higher centers of the late fetus and newborn "to handle the enormous rush of stimulations" encountered after birth.

Besides the empirically demonstrated patterns of emerging behavior in infants, only a small fraction of which are represented in the foregoing account, there are implicit or asserted propositions about age-related change (*maturation*) in all theories of psychological development. In the psychoanalytic theory of psychosexual development (Freud, 1905; Erikson, 1955), in Piaget's account of cognitive development (Piaget, 1936), and among the psychologists primarily interested in learning (e.g., Spiker, 1966) recognition has been shown, with greater or less precision, of the importance of species-general and age-related changes in early behavior that cannot be positively accounted for with available models for environmental impact. In the specialized studies of particular emerging behavioral patterns and in the more general catalogue of the developmental test, a detailed profile of early human development can be seen.

The Infant as Sensory Surface

Beyond the clinical concern with adequate functioning of sensory systems in the infant, there are two related intellectual sources of psychology's concern with the infant as a sensory surface. The antecedents of academic psychology in the sensory physiology of the nineteenth century joined well with the systematic associationism of American psychology that looked for all important behavioral control in the history of environmental impart. From Preyer's (1880) careful treatment of sensation to the present, there has been a connected tradition of research on the infant's sensory capacities.

The earlier discussions of reflexive and emergent behavior necessarily involved a recognition of sensory process. The vestibular change that elicits the Moro response, the bright light that causes pupillary contraction, the dangling ring or the pile of cubes that are presented in a developmental test, and the parental command all measure to some degree the infant's ability to detect and process sensory information. Early reflexive behavior, in particular, involves the infant's ability to respond to labyrinthine, deep-touch, and kinesthetic stimulation. A survey of the classical literature on the reflexes and on emergent behavior might, taken altogether, provide an index to the infant's receptive capacities. However, so attractive a solution is not feasible for at least three reasons. The literature represented in the preceding two sections does not commonly use standard stimuli, it only rarely involves comparable response measures, and it is generally insensitive to variations in the state of the infant and the context of stimulation. These limitations are shared with many investigations aimed directly at the study of sensory function. Moreover, as will be seen, many studies of infantile sensation give insufficient room to epistemological issues and to parametric variation. The first of these problems was alluded to earlier in a discussion of the contrasts among stimulation, world, and reality. Psychologists of infancy will probably miss some of the most fascinating problems of early development and, more, they may be led into error if they assume that the surround of the infant can be most economically organized in terms of physicalistic description of stimuli or in terms of common objects.

Although the epistemological difficulties seem esoteric and dispensible to empiricist psychologists, the rarity of parametric study of stimulus dimensions cannot be lightly ignored. After a century of research, it is no longer profound to assert that the young infant responds (or does not respond) to a particular configuration of the environment. A full account of infancy requires, rather, systematic variation of environmental variables; in the blessed case, the dimensions of variation are drawn from a conceptual analysis of the baby's nature.

Excellent summaries of the literature on sensory functioning in the newborn and young infant are available and no attempt will be made to duplicate them here. Preyer (1880) presents a good summary of nineteenth-century and earlier studies, Peiper (1963) brings together European studies up to 1950; and Pratt's (1954) chapter on the newborn in the second edition of *Carmichael's Manual* concentrated heavily on the sensory capabilities of the infant. Work since the mid-1950s has not been uniformly distributed across age or modality. The characteristic primacy of newborn studies continues and, even more strikingly, *vision* has received more attention than all other sensory channels. Because early visual development has been at a focus of recent research and because a detailed treatment of vision illustrates more general problems of method and inference, a later section of the present chapter will be given over to a consideration of research on early visual development. Here, audition and the other senses will be treated briefly.

Audition. From Preyer's (1880) first doubts about the newborn infant's ability to hear at all, there has been a connected series of studies by physicians and psychologists on auditory functioning in the infant. As usual, the range of interest is from clinical procedures for detecting deafness to issues of epistemological implications about the infant's first conceptions of space.

Clinical Tests of Hearing. All techniques used to study audition in the infant are, in a sense, available for clinical application, but some investigators have focused sharply on the problem of devising ways of diagnosing hearing loss early in infancy. Demetriades (1923) reviewed the available work on hearing and added his own observations that most children would blink to the sound of a tuning fork within the first 24 hours of life. Conditioning of foot-withdrawal was used by Aldrich (1928) to show auditory sensitivity in a 3-month-old child. Typical of screening procedures used are those described by Froeschels and Beebe (1946), who found a positive response of almost all their observed newborns to complex whistles, and by Hardy, Dougherty, and Hardy (1959), who studied the capacity of a large number of complex sound makers to distract children in the first weeks of life. Recently, Goodman, Appelby, Scott, and Ireland (1964) and Weitzman, et al. (1965) have used computer-analyzed EEG responses to repeated sounds as an index of auditory sensitivity. In both studies, all newborn infants observed showed a recognizable evoked response. Richmond, Grossman, and Lustman (1953) returned to blinking as a response to intense (113 db) sounds as evidence for infantile hearing.

Dimensions of the Stimulus. To what aspects of the auditory stimulus is the infant sensitive? A clear answer to so reasonable a question is difficult for several reasons. Often researchers have used complex natural sounds that do not submit readily to dimensional analysis—the squeak of a rubber rat (Miller, Schweinitz, and Goetzinger, 1963), the crinkling of paper (Eisenberg, Griffin, Coursin, and Hunter, 1964), and miscellaneous "soundmakers" (Ewing and Ewing, 1947). Even when some care is taken to specify the stimulus, however, variation in the conditions of observation make impossible the statement of parametric values (see Eisenberg, 1965, for a discussion of problems in controlling auditory signals). Consider the baby's response to variations in *frequency*. Marginal differential responses to frequency variation or none at all have been reported by Stubbs (1934), who observed breathing and activity changes, by Keen (1964), who observed sucking, by Goodman et al. (1964), who observed evoked cortical potentials, and by Leventhal and Lipsitt (1964), who observed changes in movement and breathing. On the other hand, Haller (1932) reported that infants were disturbed by high pitch, Bronshtein, Antonova, Kamenetskaya, Luppova, and Sytova (1958) reported rather fine tuning of sucking-inhibition to variations in freqeuncy, Eisenberg et al. (1964) reported that high-frequency sounds provoked unique behavior, Eisenberg (1965) suggested that the infant is differentially tuned to frequencies in the range of human speech (500–900 cycles per second), and Birns, Blank, Bridger, and Escalona (1965) reported that a low-frequency tone (perhaps 150 cycles per second) more effectively inhibited behavior than did a high-frequency tone (500 cycles per second) in infants under high arousal. Kasatkin and Levikova (1935b) used conditioning procedures in showing that 3-month-old infants could differentiate pure tones about an octave apart. The studies cannot be systematically compared with one another and no study—with the possible exception of Bronshtein et al. (1958)—is of sufficient scope to justify a summary statement about the infant's sensitivity to frequency.

Somewhat less ambiguous statements can be made about the infant's response to *intensity* of sound although here, too, interpretation is made difficult by the existence of unknown differences among laboratories, particularly in the level of ambient baseline noise. Early investigators (e.g., Froeschels and Beebe, 1946; Haller, 1932; Stubbs, 1934) agreed that a high-intensity tone was more likely to provoke a response by the baby than a low-intensity tone. More recent studies have moved toward the statement of more subtle functional relations. For example, several studies suggest that infants increase their likelihood of response quite sharply at about 60 decibels of intensity, again assuming a relatively low level of ambient noise (Bartoshuk, 1964a; Eisenberg, 1965; Steinschneider, Lipton, and Richmond, 1966). The relation between intensity and response for sounds above threshhold has also been studied. Steinschneider et al. (1966) found that general motor responsivity increased with increasing intensity between 55 and 100 decibels and that aspects of the cardiac response also showed systematic change. Respiratory behavior also changed systematically with intensity (Steinschneider, 1968). From his finding of a relation between heart rate and sound intensity between 48 and 78 decibels, Bartoshuk (1964a) fitted a power function to his results. Barnet and Goodwin (1965) found no systematic relation between cardiac change and intensity but they reported that the amplitude of a component of the cortical-evoked response changed linearly with stimulus intensity. The emerging simplicities become tangled again by suggestions that the baby's left and right ears differ in sensitivity and that he may show orientation *toward* relatively low-intensity tones and orientation *away from* high-intensity tones (Turkewitz, Birch, Moreau, Levy, and Cornwell, 1966).

A number of attempts have been made to assess the role of other stimulus dimensions—in particular duration (Keen, 1964; Stubbs, 1934) and complexity (Eisenberg et al., 1964)—but agreed-on summary statements have not developed. The great interest shown over the last decade in the habituation of the infant's response to repeated sounds is recounted later in this chapter.

Orientation toward Sound. The ability of children to turn their head and eyes appropriately toward a sound presented at their left or at their right seems to be well established by about 6 months of age (Chun, Pawsat, and Forster, 1960). The question arises, for a response so important to the organization of space, at what age and under what circumstances infants first show sound localization. Almost casual references to the newborn infant's orientation of head and eyes toward the source of the sound appear in the literature (e.g., Froeshels and Beebe, 1946) and interest in the issue was renewed by Wertheimer's (1961) observation of appropriate lateral eye-movement in a 10-minute-old child. Leventhal and Lipsitt (1964), in a study of adaptation and recovery of movement, found evidence of differentiation of location of sound. Following Schneirla's (1959) proposals about the relation of approach and intensity of stimulation, Turkewitz et al. (1966) showed a systematic relation between eye movement and location of auditory stimulation but had to call on differential sensitivity of the two ears in order to comprehend their findings. Turkewitz, Moreau, and Birch (1966) have further suggested that differential lateral responsiveness may be accounted for not so much by an innate connection between visual and auditory systems but by the asymmetrical position of the head (and assumed differential adaptation to ambient sounds) immediately before testing. With both electromyographic and photographic procedures available for the precise study of eye movements, further studies of early localization and its control are called for.

State, Arousal, and Quieting. Uniformly, investigators agree that the baby's state of arousal or wakefulness is important in determining his response to sound stimulation. Pratt (1934), for example, found that whether the baby was wet or dry, awake or asleep, was far more influential than variation in stimulus characteristics. The difficulty of interpreting an increase in activity for a quiet baby and a decrease in activity for an active baby (whether as regression toward the mean or a representing the "law of initial value") appeared in Haller's (1932) observation that her sounds caused more "comfort" responses in crying babies and more "discomfort" responses in sleeping babies and babies quietly awake. Stubbs (1934) found the greatest change in activity when the babies were awake and silent, less response when they were asleep or crying. With a very intense stimulus, Richmond, et al. (1953) found blinking almost invariably in light sleep, less often in deep sleep, and least of all when the baby was actively nursing. Barnet and Goodwin (1965) found larger evoked EEG responses during deep sleep than during light sleep. Birns et al. (1965) made their observations of auditory sensitivity only under conditions of high arousal. The complexities and confusions of the literature connecting auditory responsiveness to variations in state cannot be systematically clarified without further regularization of the indicators of variation in state.

The common observation that babies quiet to rhythmic stimulation has been subjected to more careful analysis in response to Salk's (1962) assertion that the infant was imprinted on the mother's heart beat. Salk observed that the presence of recorded heart beats during the first days of life resulted in increased weight gain and less crying. A failure to replicate Salk's findings by Tulloch, Brown, Jacobs, Prugh, and Greene (1964) used stimuli of such different intensity from his that a firm conclusion cannot be drawn. However, Brackbill et al. (1966) have made careful controlled observations of the effects of rhythmic sound and have concluded that, although sounds demonstrably reduce crying and heart rate, no special virtue attaches to heart beat over other rhythmic sounds.

Changes with Age. The response of fetuses to sound has been reported by Forbes and Forbes (1927) and by Sontag and Wallace (1935). Chun et al. (1960) reported the increasing ability of infants in the first year of life to localize sounds and they concluded, as noted earlier, that the ability was clearly demonstrable at 26 weeks of age. Children of 3, 4, and 5 months of age were studied by Miller et al. (1963) under stimulation with complex sounds. The procedure was held to be ineffective diagnostically for younger children but sensitive to developmetal change in the period studied.

Individual Differences. Stable individual variation in the responsiveness of young infants to sounds have been reported by, among others, Birns (1965), Bridger (1961), and Steinschneider et al. (1966).

Other Senses. The volume of research on vision and hearing in young infants may not properly represent their importance in the economy of the child. Stone and Bakwin (1948) emphasized the role of experience in the development of vision and audition and asserted that "the other senses . . . require no experience and appear to be highly meaningful to the young baby." The centrality of vision and hearing has also been denied by Baldenweck and Guy-Arnaud (1940), who made the even stronger assertion that "only the vestibular apparatus seems to be as adapted to its function at birth as it will ever be." Nonetheless, it is a fact of the literature that, although tactile sensitivity and kinesthetic sensitivity are implicitly under study in a large number of investigations, systematic assessment of the senses other than vision and hearing have been rare.

In studies of *olfaction,* Engen, Lipsitt, and Kaye (1963) and Lipsitt, Engen, and Kaye (1963) reported changes in threshhold to asafoetida over the first days of life and differentiating response to acetic acid, anise, asafoetida, and phenylethyl alcohol. Studies of olfaction, in infants as in adults, suffer from the difficulties of matching intensities of different chemical substances and from the unusually fast adaptation time of the receptor. Jensen's (1932) defining study of *taste* has already been described. Other studies of sensitivity to *temperature* change range from the effects of clothing on activity by Irwin and Weiss (1934b) to Usol'tsev and Terekhova's (1958) use of thermal conditioned stimuli. The Russian investigators found that both warm and cold stimuli showed broad generalization gradients and babies even up to 6 months of age had difficulty in differentiating among thermal stimuli. Crudden (1937) and Stirnimann (1939) demonstrated that newborn infants respond to both warm and cold stimulation; Stirnimann's conclusion that babies approach warm stimuli and withdraw from cold has not been replicated. Babies have also been shown to adjust the total number of calories taken in food with changes in ambient temperature (Cooke, 1952).

Tactile sensitivity is, of course, assessed

with every stimulation of the rooting reflex or the head-turning reflex and with stimulation to produce many other localized responses of the baby. Lustman (1956) and Bridger and Reiser (1959) have used air-stream stimulation to assess body-part and individual variation in tactile sensitivity. Several investigators have examined the baby's response to electrotactual stimulation. Lipsitt and Levy (1959) reported that electrotactual threshold decreases over the first days of life and a study of Kaye and Lipsitt (1964) showed that the early change in threshold could not be accounted for by changes in basal skin conductance. Evidence for habituation to electrotactual stimulation (i.e., increase in threshold with repeated stimulation over the first days of life) has been presented by Gullickson and Crowell (1964). The possibility of a negative relation between muscle strength and tactile sensitivity, particularly as it may underlie sex differences, has been debated by Rosenblith and DeLucia (1963) and Bell and Darling (1965). The expectable influence of state on the baby's response to tactile stimulation has been found by Lewis, Bartels, and Goldberg (1967).

The assortment of studies reported in the treatment of infant as sensory surface is at once exciting and distressing. It has been clearly and repeatedly established that the normal newborn infant responds to stimulation in all sensory modalities; he is, in every sense, competent. Yet, demonstrations *that* the baby responds cannot substitute for careful studies of *how* response changes with variations in the dimensions of stimuli employed. Such study will require more attention to standardization of the stimulus and comparability of response and procedure than has been typical in the past. It is a measure of the need for research that we do not have valid curves of spectral sensitivity or audiograms or tactile threshold for infants. Nor is it a novelty to report that there are few studies of changes in sensitivity between the first few days of life and the time of rich and demanding differentiation made by the child near the end of the first year of life.

The Infant as Learner

Many strands come together in the study of the baby as someone who learns. The progressive and ameliorative attitude of the gen-

eral culture, the finely worked procedures of learning studies in animals, and the claims of philosophic empiricism in both its English and its Russian forms come together in a view of the child as defined by his encounters with the teaching environment. In addition to Stevenson's chapter in this book, several summary statements of the literature on early learning have appeared in the 1960s. Brackbill (1962) and Kasatkin (1968) have written reviews of Russian studies on infant learning, continuing the earlier summary by Razran (1933). Work by American scholars of early learning has been ably summarized by Lipsitt (1963, 1966, 1967) and by Horowitz (1968).

There can be no doubt that the behavior of the child changes with his experience during the first months of life; in this broad sense, he learns. In addition to the common observations of parents and the evidence of normative studies, the work of many investigators on early adaptation to feeding patterns can be cited (Call, 1964; Davis, Sears, Miller, and Brodbeck, 1948; Gunther, 1961; Piaget, 1936). Most laboratory studies of early learning, however, have more narrowly focused on demonstrations of the traditional paradigms of learning. The impact of early experience on children has, essentially, been pressed into three paradigmatic molds—classical conditioning, operant or instrumental learning, and habituation. Such a limitation of scope has the advantage of permitting a focused consideration of a group of theoretical and empirical issues and of supporting the comparison of studies from different laboratories. Clearly, however, the general utility of a learning analysis of infancy depends not only on the precision and comparability of the observations made but also on the degree to which the formal paradigms properly reflect the nature of the child. As will be seen, there has been an uneven evolution from excessive enthusiasm for the relevance of simple conditioning models for understanding development (e.g., Watson, 1925) to a recognition that early learning, in the narrowly paradigmatic sense, can be comprehended only in the context of the child's developing conceptual and cognitive abilities (e.g., Papoušek, 1967a; Sameroff, 1969). Nonetheless, the traditional organization of the research on early learning will be maintained in this discussion. Studies of classical conditioning and of operant learning will be treated here; a more detailed discussion of the phenomena of habituation will be presented later in this chapter.

Classical Conditioning. The study of classical conditioning in young children falls naturally into three periods of time. Krasnogorski's (1909) opening observations in 1907 on a single 14-month-old child were followed over the next 25 years by a number of studies both in the Soviet Union and in the United States. His own work and observations of others led Krasnogorski to the conclusion that only simple conditioned responses can be formed in the first half-year of life and that differentiated responses began to appear early in the second half-year. Somewhat more extensive observations by Denisova and Figurin (1926) indicated that simple conditioned responses (depending on the context of observation and the stimuli used) could be observed as early as the beginning of the second month of life and they, too, observed differentiated responses in the sixth month. These early Russian studies, among others, have been summarized by Razran (1933); invariably only a small number of children was involved in the studies and observations on required control groups were not reported. In the United States, Mateer (1918), studying conditioned mouthing in children between 1 and 7 years of age, found rapid acquisition and extinction of the response on the average, and a substantial correlation ($r \sim .60$) between age and rate of conditioning. Watson's enthusiasms for a psychology based on reflex activity and especially his commitment to the conditioning of emotion (Watson, 1926) led to several observations on the relation of emotional development and conditioning procedures. Among these were Watson and Watson's (1921) fabled and incomplete observations on a child named Albert, Jones' (1926) toleration extinction of fear in a 3-year-old named Peter, Jones' (1930a) observation on 3 infants between 3 and 9 months of age that conditioned galvanic skin responses can be formed by shocking the babies, and Bregman's (1934) failure to establish conditioned emotions with a milder unconditioned stimulus. It was also during this period of initial enthusiams that Aldrich (1928) used conditioning procedures to diag-

nose hearing loss and that the radical behaviorists (e.g., Kuo, 1924, and Hollingworth, 1928) maintained that even the reflexes were learned.

A second period in the study of early conditioning opened with Marquis' (1931) question, "Can conditioned responses be established in the newborn infant?" The application of a learning interpretation to early behavioral change demanded the demonstration that even the youngest child could be conditioned. Marquis paired buzzer and feeding of eight infants during feeding periods over several days and found evidence of an increase in sucking and mouthing on presentation of buzzer alone. Wenger (1936) attempted to show conditioning in young infants but used too few subjects to obtain stable results. Wickens and Wickens (1940) observed responses to buzzer alone after paired buzzer and shock but found that a control group given shock alone showed the same pattern of response to buzzer that was shown by their "conditioned" group. Marquis (1941) presented evidence for temporal conditioning in the changed activity of babies when they were shifted from a three-hour feeding schedule to a four-hour schedule. During the 1930s, claims were also made for fetal conditioning in human beings by Ray (1932) and by Spelt (1948). The provocative observations made by students of perinatal conditioning were enough subject to alternative interpretation and to criticism on procedural grounds that Marquis' initial question could not be answered in the mid-1940s (Dennis, 1943). During this time, somewhat firmer evidence for conditioning was found for mouthing movements (Kantrow, 1937) and for defensive eye-blink (Morgan and Morgan, 1944) for children in the middle of the second month and older.

The third, most vigorous period of interest in early conditioning has been over the last 15 years. Researchers in the paradigm of classical conditioning have ranged widely and, among their studies of the newborn period alone, have touched on the change in leucocyte production with change in the temporal characteristics of feeding (Krachkovskaia, 1959), conditioned autonomic changes and facial expression to an unpleasant odor (Polikanina, 1961) sucking to the conditioned stimulus of a pure tone (Lipsitt and Kaye,

1964), and conditioning of the Babkin reflex to passive movement (Kaye, 1965). Conditioning in older infants has been reported for the orienting reflex (Kasatkin, Mirzoiants, and Khokhitva, 1953), for eye-blink to a visual stimulus (Rendle-Short, 1961), for eye-blink differentiated to tone (Janoš, 1965), for pupillary dilation and contraction to a temporal interval (Brackbill et al., 1967), for the eye-blink to sound (Lintz, Fitzgerald, and Brackbill, 1967), and for changes in visual preference (Lu, 1967). A study by Dashkovskaia (1953) can be taken as representative of the Soviet work during the period. A group of 10 infants in the first 10 days of life was given paired trials of a muffled electric bell and sugar solution, 10 infants had a red light paired with sugar solution, and 5 had bell paired with air-puff to eyes. For most children "distinct" but "unstable" conditioned responses appeared near the end of the period of observation after approximately 50 pairings of conditioned and unconditioned stimuli. Dashkovskaia pointed out individual variation among the infants, she noted the striking difference between normal infants and those with birth injuries, and she recounted the pattern of development of conditioned reflexes that Kasatkin (1968) has summarized in four stages. According to the Russian investigators, the course of early conditioning is seen in the change from (1) initial nonspecific responses to (2) a period of inhibition and orienting responses to (3) unstable conditioned responses and finally to (4) stable conditioned responses. Kasatkin summarizes a wide range of research (Brackbill, 1962) by asserting that "with a few exceptions, conditioned reflexes are weak and unstable up to the fourth to fifth weeks of life. . . . A firm and well-expressed conditioned reflex is sometimes formed in the fourth week and almost always in the second month." Part of the variation is assigned to the conditioned stimulus used; both simple conditioned responses and differentiated responses occurring earlier for vestibular and auditory stimuli than for taste and visual ones. In a review of the literature on early conditioning, Lipsitt (1963) concurs with the conclusion that it is difficult to demonstrate aversive or defensive conditioning in the first weeks but that a far better case can be made for the early conditioning of appetitional responses, especially sucking. An attempt to resolve the divergencies of the literature, recently made by Sameroff (1969), will be discussed later.

In any case, there is widespread agreement that conditioning becomes markedly easier as the child grows older. Kasatkin (1968) asserts that, whether pairing of auditory conditioned stimuli and either defensive or appetitional unconditioned stimuli is begun at age 10 days or age 30 days, stable conditioned responses will occur at the same time —at about 32 days of age. In a careful comparison of premature infants with full-term babies, Janoš (1958) found that stable conditioning occurred at the same *gestational age* in both groups with no advantage to the premature infants for their longer time in extrauterine life.

Operant Learning. The role of response-contingent reinforcement in early behavioral change lies implicit in early work (Myers, 1922a, 1924; Watson, 1926), but systematic study of infants in the instrumental paradigm started late and American studies of operant learning in newborn infants are a genuine novelty.

The possibility of controlling amount of smiling in 4-month-old infants was demonstrated by Brackbill (1958) and the influence of adult smiling and touching on vocalization of infants in the same age range has been shown by Rheingold, Gewirtz, and Ross (1959) and by Weisberg (1963). Smith and Smith (1962) showed that children of about 1 year of age would work to change the orientation of their playpen in order to bring visual displays into view. The ability of year-old infants to respond differentially to lights of different colors when reinforced for hand-tapping by the appearance of chimes was assessed by Simmons (1964). Siqueland (1964) has shown that head rotation to left or right in 4-month-old infants can be selectively reinforced with milk reinforcement, a procedure adapted from Papoušek (1959). Sensitive use of operant procedures has been made by Lipsitt, Pederson, and DeLucia (1966) in a study of year-old children whose rate of response controlled the brightness of a visual display and by Weisberg and Fink (1966) to assess the behavior of 18-month-old children to fixed-ratio schedules of reinforcement. Levison and Levison (1967) have used operant head-turning in studies of the effectiveness of visual displays in controlling the behavior of 3- month- old children. Increasing sophistication and precision in the use of tried-and-true operant procedures in the study of infants hold promise of permitting a more careful assessment of infantile sensory sensitivity, per- ceptual organization, memory, and motiva- tional variation than has been possible in the past.

The laboratories at Brown University have reported several applications of operant pro- cedures to infants in the first days of life. Lipsitt and Kaye (1965) showed changes over time in amount of sucking to the alter- nated presentation of a rubber nipple (on which sucking increased) and a straight rub- ber tube (on which sucking decreased). In- creased tube-sucking with reinforcement of dextrose solution has also been reported (Lipsitt, Kaye, and Bosack, 1966). Siqueland and Lippsitt (1966) showed an increase in directional head-turning with the contingent application of dextrose-solution reinforcement in children under 4 days of age. Observations by Kron (1967) suggest that changes in the patterns of sucking bursts may be determined by schedules of feeding reinforcement and Sameroff (1969) has shown that short-term changes can be induced in the patterns of sucking by delivering milk on a component- contingent basis.

The most extensive studies of infantile learning to be reported in English are those of Papoušek (1959, 1961, 1967a, 1967b). In a procedure which mixes somewhat the classical and operant paradigms, Papoušek reinforced with milk the infant's turning of his head toward right or left on the signal of a sound. Ten trials each day were given to a group of children under observation for several months; each of them went through a cycle of acquisition, extinction, reacquisition, discrimination of buzzer and bell as signals for left or right head-turn, and two reversals of the discrimination of sounds. With a strin- gent criterion of learning (five consecutive re- sponses to the auditory signal during a 10- trial session), he found that infants who were started in the procedure during the new- born period acquired the conditioned response after 177 trials (near the end of the first month of life). Papoušek (1967) calls atten- tion to the fact that only the extinction pro- cedure shows no systematic relation to age. He has found (Papoušek, personal communi- cation), as has his colleague Janoš (1965), that gestational age and ease of conditioning are highly correlated. Papoušek has also found remarkable individual variation in rate of conditioning.

The Context of Learning. Even with the spurt of studies of infantile learning that has occurred in the past decade, the number of studies is insufficient to the important ques- tions that can be posed. Nevertheless, a num- ber of tentative general principles and, per- haps of greater importance, a number of critical questions can be stated on the basis of data in hand. The least disputable principle is that age, with whatever process that age reflects or hides, is influential in determining the course of early learning. Procedures of marginal effectiveness in the first weeks of life give notable effects at 3 months. Here again the rate of developmental change puts de- mands on theories of infancy and on experi- mental procedures to guarantee that changes shown do not represent general maturational change in sensitivity or response effectiveness rather than learning.

A host of empirical and theoretical issues arise from the distinction that Lipsitt (1963) emphasizes between operant control and oper- ant learning. Many of the studies listed earlier can be seen as involving changes in the rate or occasions of occurrence of a well-estab- lished response rather than the acquisition of new responses. The distinction reflected in the classical literature of learning between *habit* and *performance* is relevant as well to inter- pretation of experimental effects as transient fatigue, adaptation, or habituation. It is sig- nificant that so little is known about the persistence of behavioral patterns established naturally or in laboratory settings. Almost no studies have examined infants over a long enough period of time to establish measures of persistence of behavior acquired early in life. Systematic studies of infantile memory over more than a few days are limited to a handful of studies (Burtt, 1932, 1937; Janoš, 1965; Levy, 1960; Papoušek, 1967).

Every aspect of the study of babies is re- lated to the issue of *state* or level of arousal, and learning is no exception. Gottlieb and Simner (1966) have noted the close and complex relation between measures of arousal such as heart rate change and measures commonly used as indicators of learning such as sucking. Koch (1968) related ease of conditionability to time since waking and time since feeding. The relevance of arousal to interpretations of early learning has been put forcefully by Kron (1968a), who suggested that many of the procedural operations used in studies of early learning may be as readily interpreted as changing the state of the baby and thereby changing the likelihood of the response under observation. Once more, the developmentally crucial difference between habit and performance must be noted.

A significant attempt to reconcile conflicting evidence on early, especially newborn, learning has been made by Sameroff (1969). Following Piaget (1936), Sameroff proposed that classical conditioning can take place only after the response systems relevant to the unconditioned and conditioned stimuli have been organized and differentiated. He pointed out also that studies of early learning can be more easily understood if the distinction is maintained between stimuli which provoke defensive or avoiding responses and those which provoke orienting or approach responses (see André-Thomas, 1954; Schneirla; 1958, and Sokolov, 1960). Sameroff proposed that conditioning is possible only after congenital defensive responses have been somewhat habituated.

Does the baby behave as he should according to the simple paradigms of learning? Papoušek (1967b) has given the question empirical import by observing the response of young infants to simple, predictable patterns of stimulation; for example, the signal for a left turn of the infant's head alternates regularly with a signal for a right turn. Apparently, in the first months of life, babies adopt what can be called "strategies" for anticipating sequential events. Papoušek outlines the theoretical problem and puts the psychology of infant learning on a new path when he says "sometimes, we even had the impression that successful solving of the problem itself elicited more pleasure in the subject than the reward." It is beyond doubt that babies are shaped by their early experience and the exciting task of the next generation of researchers will be to enlarge and complicate the paradigms of learning to make room for the complexity of the infant.

The Infant as Perceiver and Thinker

A notable discrepancy exists between the amount of interest currently invested in early cognitive development—the infant as perceiver and thinker—and the amount of research that has been carried out. Charlesworth (1968) has observed that the great bulk of research on infantile cognition has taken place since 1960; psychology is truly only at the edge of its study of perception, thinking, problem-solving, dreams, play, and language in the very young child (Kessen, 1966). There are one major and several minor exceptions to the principle of waywardness and lag in the study of early cognition. Minor exceptions can be seen in the interest of many investigators around the turn-of-the-century in early language and in the continuing *theoretical* interest of students of perception in the child's first view of his world. The major exception, and one that has transformed the study of infants irreversibly, is the work of Jean Piaget.

Perception. Theoretical controversy over the nature of human perception has long had implication for the psychology of infancy (Hochberg, 1963). The classical issue of whether perception was innately organized (Pastore, 1960) or derived from an increasing sensitivity to critical features of the environment (Gibson, 1969) or constructed from motor acts (Piaget, 1936) clearly calls for an answer from young children. Only recently, and in large part as a consequence of the observations of Robert Fantz, have these arguments been subjected to empirical observation of babies. The detailed treatment of infantile vision later in the chapter summarizes the evidence now available on early development of visual perception and its implication for the classic controversies about perception.

Language. Almost at the same time that interest in early perception was revived there appeared a new flurry of studies of early language. Although the procedures for gathering data about the child's early speech have been closely akin to those used by investigators of many years ago (Dewey, 1894; Strayer, 1930), recent observations on early language have been illuminated by their connections with linguistic theory and with general theory of cognitive development. In a chapter of this *Manual* McNeill presents a summary and an analysis of what is now known about the acquisition of language.

The Special Place of Piaget's Work. After his first observations on his eldest daughter, Piaget (1927) concluded that "the first year of the child is still, unhappily, a mysterious abyss for the psychologist." Piaget's willingness to enter the abyss and to begin to unravel some of the mysteries stands as the most important contribution yet made to an understanding of the human infant. The study of infancy has been a major and continuing theme in Piaget's work, but his primary observations and most important theoretical postulations about the nature of young children were contained in three books: *The Origins of Intelligence in Children* (1936), *The Construction of Reality in Children* (1937), and *Play, Dreams, and Imitation* (1945). His profound and complicated account of infancy, drawn largely from observations on his own three children, does not submit to easy abbreviation here. Fortunately, Flavell (1963) and Wolff (1960), among others, have prepared analytic and comparative accounts of Piaget's theory of the infant mind.

Piaget sees the infant as actively engaged with his environment. On the basis of congenitally organized reflexes—vision, prehension, sucking, and phonation—the child builds ever more complicated ways of dealing with environmental events. His adaptation is the result of a shifting balance between understanding the world in terms of his present structures *(assimilation)* and modifying those structures to fit the demands of the environment *(accommodation)*. The normal child in the usual environment of infants thereby develops, in a regular sequence, conceptions of space, time, and object which are increasingly like those of the adult. Piaget's observational techniques and the conceptual use to which he puts what he sees can be best understood with an example.

At 0;2 (4) [age two months and four days] Laurent by chance discovers his right index finger and looks at it briefly. At 0;2 (11) he inspects for a moment his open right hand, perceived by chance. At 0;2 (14), on the other hand, he looks three times in succession at his left hand and chiefly at his raised index finger. At 0;2 (17) he follows its spontaneous movement for a moment, then examines it several times while it searches for his nose or rubs his eye. Next day, same observation. At 0;2 (19) he smiles at the same hand after having contemplated it eleven times in succession. . . . The same day he looks very attentively at his two clasped hands. At 0;2 (21) he holds his two fists in the air and looks at the left one, after which he slowly brings it toward his face and rubs his nose with it, then his eye. A moment later the left hand again approaches his face; he looks at it and touches his nose. He recommences and laughs five or six times in succession while moving the left hand to his face. He seems to laugh before the hand moves, but looking has no influence on its movement. . . . At a given moment he turns his head to the left but looking has no effect on the direction. . . . At 0;2 (23) he looks at his right hand, then at his clasped hands (at length). . . .

It may thus be seen of what the coordinations between vision and the first circular reactions of the hand and fingers consist. We can say that the visual schemata tend to assimilate the manual schemata without the converse being yet true. In other words, the glance tries to follow what the hand does, but the hand does not tend in any way to realize what the glance sees; it does not even succeed in remaining in the visual field! Later, on the contrary, the hand will be regulated by vision, and vice versa; this will enable the child to grasp the objects seen. But, for the time being, the hand moves independently of the glance, the few vague circular reactions to which it gives rise being only directed by touch, kinesthetic sensations, or sucking. The relations between sight and hand movements are therefore different from those which exist between sucking and these movements; in the case of sucking, the schemata external to the hand movements control them and incorporate them (sucking entails circular reaction of the arms and hands) while in the case of vision hand movements are autonomous and the glance is limited to assimilating without controlling them. . . .

By means of such combinations of naturalistic observations and contrived intervention, Piaget developed a systematic account of intellectual change over the first months of life.

Along the way, he has addressed fundamental issues that have not had a place in American studies of babies—among them, the development of intention, the separation of means and goals, the growing use of instruments in the solving of problems, and the formation of categories of knowledge such as space and object. Piaget's theoretical apparatus is, of course, not universally accepted (Kessen and Kuhlman, 1962) and replication of his observations is essential, both in the mode he preferred and in the more usual style of experimental study. Nonetheless, White (1969) speaks for many students of children when he describes Piaget's *Origins of Intelligence* as "far and away the most outstanding body of work on human infancy."

The Return of Prehension. Piaget's emphasis on the development of independent motor systems—for example, looking and grasping—and their subsequent coordination has produced a revival of interest in the study of early patterns of prehension and their relation to looking, sucking, and the development of the notion of permanent objects. Brainard (1927) had noted the changes that take place in the coordination of eye and hand during the first half-year of life. The development of such coordination has been given a neurophysiological definition (Zagora, 1959) and the development of stable handedness in patterns of reaching and manipulation has been assessed longitudinally (Flament, 1965). In a series of studies of infants in an institution, White and his colleagues have carefully charted the normal course of visually directed reaching and have, further, demonstrated that the rate of development can be modified by experimentally introduced stimulation of the children (White, 1968, 1969; White, Castle, and Held, 1964). Bruner has taken the early development of grasping and its coordination with looking and sucking as a model for problem solving in the very young infant (Bruner, 1967; Bruner, Simenson, and Lyons, 1968; Bruner and Watkins, 1968).

Play, Interest, and Attention. Piaget's treatment of cognitive development brings into a sharp light the behavior of infants that seems closely related neither to the alleviation of primary drives nor to the actions of a social partner. The principle that children are active explorers of their environment and are pleased by cognitive achievements has been put in

several forms by Berlyne (1960), Hunt (1961), Rheingold, Stanley, and Cooley (1962), Stott (1961), and Wolff (1966). Although empirical work has not kept pace with speculations about the broader base of infantile motivation, several patterns of study have begun to emerge. In addition to Piaget's observations on *play* (1945), Friedlander and Kessler (1968) have described procedures for recording play patterns over long periods of time, and observations on patterns of free play at the Fels Research Institute (Goldberg and Lewis, 1969) and at Harvard (Kagan, personal communication) have begun to present evidence on the developmental stability of patterns of play and on the continuity of individual differences. Charlesworth (1969) has presented a detailed treatment of *surprise* as a factor in early motivation and cognitive development. A number of researchers have called attention to the importance of *complexity* as a variable governing the interest and attention of the young infant (Berlyne, 1960; Brennan, Ames, and Moore, 1966; Charlesworth, 1966; Munsinger and Weir, 1967; Thomas, 1965). *Discrepancy from a familiar pattern* as an influential determiner of attention, an idea elaborated by Sokolov (1960) and given application to early cognitive development by Jeffrey (1968), has been closely analyzed in Kagan's longitudinal study of early development (Kagan and Lewis, 1965; McCall and Kagan, 1967b). Evidence also has begun to accumulate on the importance of *arousal* or alertness in studies of attention (Korner and Grobstein, 1966; Stechler, Bradford, and Levy, 1966) and on the existence of puzzling variation in patterns of attention from one child to another (Kagan, personal communication; McCall and Kagan, 1967b).

Except for the work of Piaget, the study of the infant as thinker has just begun. Among the promising directions for development are a closer look at memory and time-sense in infants (Allen, 1931b; Watson, 1967), the establishment of links between early conditioning and problem-solving (as, for example, in Papoušek's infant strategists) and in the formal treatment of Piaget's theory of early cognitive change (Liu In-Mao, 1961).

The Infant as Social Partner

Psychologists have long been concerned with charting the course the child takes as he becomes a social being, effective in changing the behavior of others and responsive himself to social partners. From the early observations of Kaila (1932) and Spitz and Wolf (1946c), the focus of research on the infant as social partner has been concentrated on the study of smiling and attachment to the care-taking mother. The relevant research has been given close treatment by Maccoby elsewhere in this book, and her discussion will not be duplicated here.

The sixfold division of infancy research used in the foregoing discussion is necessarily abstract and necessarily artificial. There are serious connections among the areas of interest elliptically designated as reflex, emergent, sensory, learning, cognitive, and social. Nonetheless, the division roughly describes variation in research that characterizes the twentieth century and gives some sense of the change from dominant conceptions of the infant as creature of reflexes to conceptions of the infant as influential in determining the nature of his environment.

In the next section of the present report, a shift is made from a general and summary statement of available research to a more highly concentrated treatment of three collections of research—sucking, habituation, and vision—in illustration of the complex interaction of problem statement, method, and findings in the study of infants.

THE CASE OF SUCKING

Sucking as an Organized Biological Behavior

Rooting. The awake, hungry, newborn infant exhibits rapid pendular searching movements in response to tactile stimulation in the region around the mouth (Peiper, 1963; Prechtl, 1958). This pattern of searching movements, called the rooting reflex, is held to optimize the infant's chances of finding and grasping the nipple. Pepys is credited by Peiper with writing in 1667 the first description of rooting that occurred even before the first feeding. Several writers have corroborated the existence of the rooting response in the newborn (Blanton, 1917; Blauvelt, 1964; Gentry and Aldrich, 1948a; Peiper, 1963; Turkewitz, Gordon, and Birch, 1965b; Watson, 1919; Wolff, 1959), in the fetus (Hooker, 1952), and in the premature infant (Prechtl, 1958; Saint-Anne Dargassies, 1955).

Gentry and Aldrich (1948a) and Prechtl (1958) found rooting in about two-thirds of awake full-term babies tested before feeding. Blauvelt and McKenna (1961) have provided a detailed temporal analysis of rooting.

Several investigators have found that the rooting response is affected by state of arousal; the response increases in probability and in vigor as the baby becomes more alert (Peiper, 1963; Prechtl, 1958; Gentry and Aldrich, 1948a; Wolff, 1959). Wolff (1959) has argued that state of arousal is a more crucial variable than time since last feeding. Of 48 babies, 46 were reported by him to root when alert even immediately after a meal. The nervous organization of the rooting reflex is most assuredly quite low. It has been shown repeatedly that anencephalics and microcephalics root in patterns much like those of the normal baby (Blanton, 1917; Ingram, 1962; Peiper, 1963; Prechtl, 1958).

Mechanics and Components of Milk Extraction. The newborn infant has three sets of oral pads which are believed to facilitate and support the sucking act (Middlemore, 1941; Peiper, 1963). One set is on the outer and inner aspects of the lips and a second set on the gums; these two sets of pads form a closed-pressure seal around the nipple. A third set of pads on the inside of the cheeks is believed to support the cheeks so they are not sucked in by the negative intraoral pressure established during sucking.

According to Peiper (1963), Erasmus Darwin correctly noted in the eighteenth century that the infant does not sip milk at the breast but, instead, takes the nipple into his mouth and draws milk out by repeatedly pressing the nipple between his gums. Further analysis of the act has shown that sucking is made up of two major components—the establishment of *negative pressure* within the mouth and the lapping or *expressing* of the nipple.

It has been demonstrated that the sucking infant rhythmically establishes a condition of *negative pressure* in his mouth, but there is not a complete consensus as to how this pressure is established and exactly what role it plays in extracting milk from the nipple. Jensen (1932) summarized early work in support of the hypothesis that the infant, like the adult, sucked by establishing negative pressure through inspiration. In contrast, Auerbach (in Jensen, 1932) was the first of many investigators to maintain that infant and adult use markedly different techniques to establish negative pressure. The adult establishes negative pressure by thoraxic inspiration but the infant was said to use "mouth sucking"—a procedure whereby the oral cavity, closed off at the back and sealed by lips and gums at the front, is increased in volume by dropping the lower jaw (Kasahara, 1916). Although Auerbach's view is generally held to be correct (Peiper, 1963), it has not gone unchallenged. Halverson (1944), for example, found costal respiration to predominate over abdominal respiration during vigorous sucking, an observation suggesting thoracic involvement in the infant's sucking act.

The second mechanism used by the infant for extracting milk is called *expressing*. After the nipple is sucked into the mouth, the jaw and curved tongue are raised. The tongue presses the nipple against the hard palate and presses out milk by moving from the front to the back of the mouth. Cinemaradiographic evidence of this process has been provided by Ardran, Kemp, and Lind (1958a, 1958b) and by Lassrich (1959). Ardran, Kemp, and Lind found no evidence that milk was taken in during the phase of negative pressure when the tongue and jaw were dropped. Their evidence suggested that this phase chiefly provided time and negative pressure for refilling the teat. On the other hand, Colley and Creamer (1958) found insignificant pressure changes inside the nipple and argued against the position that the nipple was being pressed against the roof of the mouth. Variation in procedure, particularly in rigidity of nipples used, probably accounts for the discrepancy in observations; Sameroff (1968) obtained convincing evidence that both negative pressure and expressing can be used by newborn infants to extract milk.

Coordination of Sucking, Respiration, and Swallowing. A smooth feeding performance requires coordination of sucking, swallowing, and respiration. Swallowing apparently depends on the amount of milk in the mouth (Halverson, 1938); babies almost never swallow when sucking air (Jensen, 1932). The baby does not visibly interrupt his breathing when swallowing, but it does not follow that he can breathe and swallow simultaneously. Halverson (1944) and Lassrich (1959) found

swallowing to require less than 0.5 seconds for the infant as opposed to 1.5 seconds for the adult (Peiper, 1963). Inasmuch as swallowing occurs in the interval between inspiration and expiration the effect of swallowing on respiration has often gone undetected.

There is disagreement as to whether or not sucking and respiration are coordinated. Balint (1948) and Colley and Creamer (1958) found no relationship between sucking and breathing but Peiper (1963) and Halverson (1944) found definite relationships of 1:1 or 2:1 sucks to respirations, and several reports of deepened inspiration during sucking have been made (Ribble, 1939, 1944; Halverson, 1941, 1944). Halverson (1944) noted that the pattern of breathing changes during vigorous sucking; costal breathing predominates with sucking bursts often anticipated by abdominal tensing. He concluded that the best coordination of sucking, breathing, and swallowing occurs when a suck is made during an inspiration and a swallow is made between an inspiration and an exhalation. Peiper (1931) found that respiration rate slowed during sucking and that both sucking and breathing slowed when the infant was changed from nonnutritive to nutritive sucking. He argued that a hierarchical control of swallowing, sucking, and breathing exists with swallowing controlling sucking and sucking controlling breathing.

Effects of Age. Although most babies suck at birth or before, very little is known about how the mechanics of sucking change over age. Ribble (1939) reported that some premature babies have trouble grasping the nipple and do not suck strongly enough to draw milk from the breast. Halverson (1946) found the coordination of sucking, swallowing, and breathing to be highly variable from one premature baby to another. In his study of infants from birth to 18 weeks Halverson (1946) found good coordination of sucking, respiration, and swallowing in one baby at 8 hours, in 3 babies in the first 3 days, in 8 others at one time or another; in 2 babies, smooth coordination never appeared during the study. Prechtl (1956b) reported that the newborn infant tends to use negative pressure as his chief milk-getting technique, whereas after some weeks the child will tend to use expression. Auerbach wrote (Halverson, 1938) that the infant sucked by downward stroking of the jaw for the first 4 to 5 months and later used thoraxic inspiration. It is noteworthy that Ardran et al. (1958a), who studied 41 infants "from a few days to several months" did not report age changes in the form of the sucking response. Bruner (1967) has reported that sometimes at 2 months, but at least by 4 months, a baby presented with a novel stimulus may stop the phase of negative pressure but will continue expressing.

Sucking and Mode of Feeding. Ardran et al. (1958a,b) found no essential differences between the baby's technique for sucking breast and his technique for sucking bottle, but Peiper (1963) emphatically insisted that differences exist. Several studies have shown that infants can drink from a cup from birth (e.g., Sears and Wise, 1950); clearly, the specific sucking mechanics described earlier do not provide the only method a baby can use to feed.

Pathology. The absence of coordinated sucking, swallowing, and breathing may be indicative of brain trauma or retardation (Blanton, 1917; Kasahara, 1916; Ribble, 1939; Watson, 1919). However, sucking alone is usually intact even with relatively severe trauma (Blanton, 1917; Kasahara, 1916; Peiper, 1963; Ribble, 1939). Peiper (1963) discussed a variety of evidence from human monsters and lower animals that sucking is organized at a relatively primitive level of the nervous system.

Rhythms and Rates of Sucking. The infant generally sucks in a more or less regular pattern of bursts and pauses. During bursts of nonnutritive sucking, his rate varies around two sucks a second (Wolff, 1969). Although sucking rate has been reported by many investigators, several important variables are often not specified—age and health of the baby, time since last feeding, state of arousal, whether the baby is sucking for nutriment or on a pacifier, the nature of the nipple, and rate of milk flow. Moreover, several measures of the response can be calculated from the sucking record; for example, sucking rate during sucking, sucking frequency per unit time, duration of a sucking burst, duration of a rest between bursts, and number of sucks per burst. As Balint (1948a) and Kaye (1967) have pointed out, experimenters frequently do not make clear whether their rate-of-sucking calculation was obtained by calculating mean sucking rate during a burst of sucking or by assessing frequency of sucking over a fixed time period. Further, some experimenters have reported ranges for individual subjects and others have reported ranges of group means. Over a wide range of variables it appears that sucking rate during bursts is fairly uniform from 1 to 2.5 sucks per second, close to the value of 1.5 sucks per second reported by Ardran and Kemp (1959) using cinemaradiographic analysis. Sucking bursts seem to occur in packages of from about 5 to 24 sucks per burst.

Balint (1948b) reported two additional sucking frequencies found in a large portion of his subjects, which were later confirmed by Kaye (1966). A "restart" frequency of from 6 to 10 per second sometimes appeared at the beginning of a sucking burst and a quivering frequency, from 12 to 45 per second, appeared to be caused by tongue or jaw quivering. Neither frequency was related to the infant's age but the quivering appeared in 66% of the females and only 39% of the males, the only substantial sex difference reported for nutritive sucking.

Care has not always been taken to define the parameters separating one burst from another. Investigators attempting to quantify the burst variable have used either a 1-second or 2-second no-sucking interval to define the beginning or end of a burst (Halverson, 1944; Kaye, 1967; Sameroff, 1967). The pause between bursts has been considered to be either a rest period (Halverson, 1944), a play period (Halverson, 1944), or a period during which information is being processed (Bronshtein et al., 1958; Bruner, 1967; Haith, 1966; Haith et al., 1969; Keen, 1964; Piaget, 1952).

Variables Affecting Sucking Rate and Rhythm.

Hunger. Rather strong contradictions exist in the literature regarding the effect of hunger on the various parameters of sucking. Susswein (cited in Peiper, 1963) reported that the baby sucks continuously for the first several minutes of a feeding, then breaks into bursts and pauses as he becomes satiated, an observation confirmed by Norval (1946). Kaye (1966) experimentally confirmed an earlier correlational finding (Levin and Kaye, 1964) that sucking rate changed with amount of nutrient consumed. But Kron, Stein, and Goddard (1967) observed no change of sucking rate over 9 minutes of feeding. Similarly, Balint (1948b) found the rate of sucking to remain constant within ½ sucks per second in over 90% of his sample and the pause-burst pattern to remain essentially constant for 75%. Jensen (1932) reported that 10 of 17 of his subjects sucked air for as long as 15 minutes after a feeding.

Fatigue has been implicated in the depression of sucking rate over time during nonnutritive sucking; full recovery is held to occur after a rest of 60 seconds (Kaye, 1967). However, it is unclear whether or not recovery after a rest reflects the dissipation of fatigue or the response to a change of stimulus. Norval (1946) reported a recovery of sucking rate when the infant was moved from one breast to the other and the positive relationship between arousal and sucking rate has been well documented both observationally (Levin and Kaye, 1964) and experimentally (Bridger, 1962b; Jensen, 1932; Kaye, 1966). In fact it can be argued that arousal, not hunger, plays the major role in determining the rate of sucking (Bridger, 1962b; Kaye, 1966; Kessen, 1967).

Age. Bronshtein, Antonova, Kamenetskaya, Luppova, and Sytova (1958) reported that infants over 1 day of age have a higher maximum rate of sucking than infants under 24 hours of age but that pauses and the number of sucks per burst were independent of age. Bruner (1967), however, reported that younger infants pause irregularly; as they grow older, they change to a more regular pattern. Balint (1948b) found that babies held fairly closely to their basic sucking frequency over 2 to 2½ months of follow-up study while Kasahara (1916) reported that babies over a week of age do not pause while sucking nutritively, whereas newborns do.

Rate of Milk Flow. Colley and Creamer (1958) and Halverson (1944) found sucking rate and the presence of pauses to be affected by milk flow, possibly through the control that swallowing exerts over sucking. Some of the discrepancies found in the reports of sucking rates and burst patterns might be accounted for by variation in rate of milk flow.

Individual Stability. Infants show a fairly regular rate of responding both within an experimental session (Haith, 1966; Haith, Kessen, and Collins, 1969; Kron, Ipsen, and Goddard, 1968; Levin and Kaye, 1964; Sameroff, 1967; Wolff, 1969) and over longer periods of time (Balint, 1948b).

Natural Cycles of Feeding. A great deal has been written about whether the baby's cyclic demands for nourishment should be met (demand feeding) or whether the baby should be made to adapt to an imposed regular schedule of feeding (scheduled feeding). Frank (1966) noted that the changing advice to mothers from pediatricians and federal publications through the decades from 1900 is an instructive lesson in how the "truth" about infant rearing changes. In a personal communication to Frank, Anton Carlson reported that the 4-hour schedule of feeding apparently originated with a barium X-ray study of 3 newborns in 1900 which showed that the stomach emptied after about 4 hours. The generalization from 3 newborns fed a foreign substance to milk-drinking infants in general is, at best, dubious. The history of the demand-schedule issue has also been reviewed by Weinfeld (1950).

Only a few studies have been carried out on the plasticity of the newborn to an imposed schedule. Both Bystroletova (1954) and Marquis (1941) reported that babies adapted to their feeding schedule during the first 10 days of life. If fed on demand, the newborn baby may require from 10 to 14 feedings a day (Trainham and Montgomery, 1946; Simsarian and McLendon, 1942, 1945) in a more or less irregular pattern but, in a matter of several days or a few weeks, most infants will settle down to a fairly regular pattern of 5 to 6 feedings a day. Aldrich and Hewitt (1947) studied 100 demand-fed babies for over a year to discover their preferred feeding rhythm; their data are shown in Fig. 2. Self-regulating rhythms appear to approximate the commonly prescribed 4-hour interval for many infants.

Scheduled feeding has been justified as necessary to avoid the harmful effects of overeating, especially in the premature infant. However, it has been found that premature infants do well on a demand schedule (Horton, Lubchenco, and Gordon, 1952) and that demand feeding generally results in faster weight gain and earlier release from the

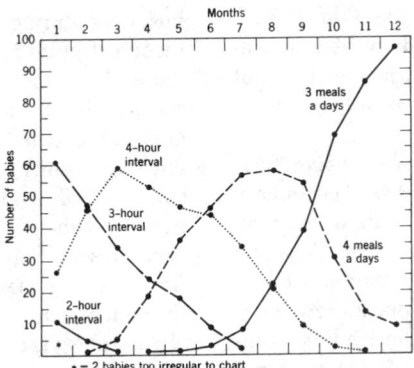

Fig. 2. Self-regulating schedule of feeding for 100 infants. (From Aldrich and Hewitt, 1947, p. 347).

hospital nursery.

Sucking as an Indicator of Underlying Process

The sucking response is one of the few organized responses present at birth and has the several advantages of being relatively easy to define, measure, elicit, and record. Perhaps for these reasons, sucking frequently has been used as an indicator of underlying process in the young infant. Over the years, some aspect of sucking has been called on to assess discrimination, learning, attention, habituation, arousal, and frustration.

Discrimination. A number of studies have used the sucking response to measure the sensitivity of the newborn (e.g., Dockeray, 1934; Jensen, 1932). Peiper (1963) reviewed classical evidence that sweet substances provoked sucking movements. Dockeray (1934) reported that some infants consistently responded negatively to acidic formulas. Nelson (Jensen, 1932) observed differential responding to sugar, salt, quinine water, and citric solutions by, respectively, 50, 40, 33, 32, and 23% of infants observed. Jensen (1932) obtained no differential response between sugar and milk and differential but irregular responses to varying concentrations of salt. Bronshtein et al. (1958) reported increased sucking to sugar solutions and decreased sucking to salt solutions. Dockeray (1934) reported no effect of odor on sucking but Bronshtein et al. (1958) found differential responding to three odors. Temperature sensitivity in infants has not been widely studied. Kasahara (1916) reported lower and upper limits of temperature that infants will tolerate to be approximately

30 and 40°C, whereas Jensen (1932) reported values of 19 and 52°C. Reported discrimination of sound intensity and frequency as measured by variation in sucking (Bronshtein et al., 1958) has not been replicated (Keen, 1964), nor have Bronshtein and his co-workers' reports of visual discrimination using similar procedures found support (Haith et al., 1969; Kaye, 1967; Sameroff, 1967).

Learning. The discrepancy between the amount and quality of research on newborns and the amount and quality of research on older infants is quite apparent in studies that use the sucking response as a conditioned response or as an indicator of learning. Unfortunately, without systematic observation of changes across age in the acquisition and extinction of learned responses, it is often difficult to interpret experimental findings. The presence of differences between treated and untreated samples of the same age invites many interpretations, particularly when only a small number of trials are presented, when all of the training takes place in a single session, or when appropriate control groups are absent. Long-term developmental studies of sucking as a learned response, comparable to the work of Papoušek (1967) on head-turning, are rare, and the results of many available studies can be understood as representing transient changes in adaptation or arousal.

Developmental Studies. Ripin (1930), studying the sucking responses anticipatory to feeding in babies during the first half-year of life, found occasional anticipatory responses as early as 1 month, but she concluded after examining changes in behavior over 6 months that true expectancies were not established until the third month of life. Kasatkin (1952a) and Dashkovskaia (1953) described "unstable" conditioning in the first days of life, but "stable" conditioning appeared only after the newborn period.

Naturalistic Observations of Learning. Several studies have deviated from customary learning paridigms to study infant learning in relatively natural circumstances. A single infant, reportedly a newborn traumatized at the breast by partial suffocation, subsequently "fought" the mother during the feeding situation (Gunther, 1961). Call (1964) reported film-documented cases of newborn infants who moved their heads from side to side and grasped the mother's breast when placed in the feeding position. The adjustment of activity patterns in newborn infants fed at different intervals has been observed (Marquis, 1943; Bystroletova, 1954). Thompson (1926) reported that an infant could learn to feed from a poorly shaped nipple by a "fading" procedure using a breast shield. When newborn infants repeatedly have a nipple inserted in their mouths and then withdrawn, they tend to quiet faster on insertion and cry sooner on withdrawal during late trials (Cohen, 1967).

Short-Term Laboratory Studies. Along more conventional lines, Marquis (1931) reported conditioning of mouth opening and the cessation of activity and crying after repeated pairings of buzzer and milk bottle. Dashkovskaia (1953), using sound stimulation as a conditioned stimulus, reported a confirmation of these findings with newborns, but she was not able to establish conditioning to a light conditioned stimulus. Sameroff (1968) observed the effects of differential milk reinforcement on the two major components of sucking. He found a lowered amplitude of the suctioning component when the expressing component was reinforced. In a second experiment he demonstrated that the magnitude of the expressing component, after brief practice by the baby, roughly matched the effort necessary to obtain milk.

Lipsitt and his colleagues at Brown University have carried out a number of studies of the conditioning of sucking in newborns. In one study (Lipsitt and Kaye, 1964) in which tone and nipple-induced sucking were paired, they found greater mouthing to the tone in experimental than in control babies

but only during the extinction phase. In a second study, Lipsitt and Kaye (1965) found more nipple-sucking in groups which received opportunity to suck nipple and tube, in an alternating schedule, than in a group receiving opportunity to suck only the nipple. In still a third study, sucking frequency on a tube by babies who received dextrose during tube presentation was compared with sucking frequency by babies who received dextrose through a syringe 20 seconds after withdrawal of the tube (Lipsitt et al., 1966). During test trials, tube-dextrose babies gave more mouthing responses than did tube-alone babies.

The results of these studies, taken together, have been considered to constitute evidence for learning in the suckling infant. However, even in the most carefully executed and adequately controlled experiments on learning in the literature of infantile sucking, the possibility remains that experimental manipulations may have systematically influenced arousal in favor of the experimental groups. There can be no doubt that sucking behavior changes in response to environmental change during the first days of life; what remains in doubt is a conclusion about the most productive explanation to put on the facts. Two recent proposals (Kron, 1968a; Sameroff, 1969) that go beyond the limited and limiting issue of whether or not the newborn infant can learn (Kessen, 1963; Lipsitt, 1966) were discussed earlier.

Attention, the Orienting Response, and Sucking. One of the best-known correlates of attention and of the orienting response is inhibition of ongoing activity (Berlyne, 1960; Sokolov, 1963). Observations on inhibition of sucking during visual exploration were, in fact, made by Piaget (1936) and by Fleischl (1957). Studying infants from birth to several months of age, Bronshtein et al. (1958) reported inhibition of sucking to visual and to auditory stimuli and, further, an attenuation of the tendency to inhibit sucking as stimuli were repeatedly presented. However, for the most part, the "Bronshtein effect" has been difficult to replicate. Some of the difficulties in replication probably derive from the vague description of procedures, stimuli, and age range in the original report. For example, most of the attempts at replication in the United States have been carried out with *newborns* on *nonnutritive* sucking. Brackbill (1962) reported after visiting Russian laboratories that full manifestation of inhibition, habituation, and subsequent dishabituation of *nutritive* sucking to a visual stimulus could be demonstrated in only one-third of the babies between a few hours and 17 days of age.

Kaye and Levin (1963) attempted to replicate the Bronshtein effect in two independent studies but could not find even initial inhibition of sucking. Additional studies by Kaye (1967) have produced similar requests. Keen (1964) found differential changes in sucking during presentation of tone for two durations, but the absence of no-tone observations makes it difficult to determine whether these differences reflected relative facilitation or relative inhibition of the response. Haith (1966) reported that suppression of newborn sucking was stronger to a light moving intermittently than to stationary light. In contrast to prior studies, Haith made the nipple available to infants only during discrete trials. Kaye (1967) reported studies of audition in which a similar procedure was used but he found no stable differences in performance attributable to tone. Under somewhat different procedures, Kaye (1967) was also unsuccessful in his attempt to replicate the Haith study with visual stimuli. Sameroff (1967) presented light, tone, and light and tone to newborns and found no effect on time spent sucking. However, he did find that the number of sucking bursts was fewer during all experimental presentations than during any control interval. Using 2- to 4-month-old infants, Haith, Kessen, and Collins (1969, and Collins, Kessen, and Haith, personal communication) found inhibition of sucking to both stimulus movement and to flashing lights but no stable relation was found between sucking inhibition and stimulus complexity. Moreover, there was no evidence of habituation of sucking inhibition with repeated stimulus presentation.

Sucking without Nutrient

In addition to its obvious contribution to efficient feeding, sucking is significant in other aspects of the infant's life. Commentators working from both observation and clever speculation have, moreover, assigned critical theoretical weight to sucking, especially sucking that does not produce nutrient. In fact, a great deal of research and speculation about sucking in infancy has hinged on the simple fact that infants suck on fingers, thumbs,

sleeves, toys, pacifiers, and other objects vigorously and for long periods of time without resulting nutritive intake.

In their attempts to account for such behavior, theorists have put forth a surprisingly varied set of arguments. According to some observers, nonnutritive sucking satisfies a "need" to suck, it serves to "pacify" the infant during moments of distress, it serves as one of a number of responses to dissipate a build-up of freely displaceable energy, it becomes positively reinforcing through its association with food, it acquires an erotogenic quality through its association with mother's breast and food, it is a prewired species-specific response to high arousal, it is a species-specific response which serves to attach the mother to her offspring, or, because the oral region is invested with a rich network of nerves and blood vessels, nonnutritive sucking occurs because it feels good.

A number of review papers and theoretical articles have dealt with available research and the theoretical issues involved in the study of nonnutritive sucking (Honzik and McKee, 1962; Kessen and Mandler, 1961; Orlansky, 1949; Palermo, 1956; Ross, Fisher, and King, 1957). The next paragraphs will deal first with the normative aspects of nonnutritive sucking, then with research relevant to the question of whether or not an inborn "need" to suck exists, and, finally, with evidence bearing on the power of sucking to pacify or calm the infant.

Normative Data. Ribble (1944) reported that 60% of 600 infants observed had to be "taught" to suck by moving the infant's jaw up and down over the mother's breast. Her assertion has not been confirmed and is clearly contradicted by a vast amount of literature. A number of investigators have reported finger sucking and hand-mouth contact shortly after birth and even before the first feeding (Blanton, 1917; Blauvelt, 1964; Kessen, Williams, and Williams, 1961; Ripin, 1930; Watson, 1919). Dramatic photographic documentation of the fetus' ability to suck its thumb was recently displayed in a national magazine (*Life*, April 1965).

The reported incidence of nonnutritive sucking among infants has ranged from 44% (Heering, 1932) to 100% (Kunst, 1948). Brazelton (1956) reported that 90% of the infants he observed engaged in nonnutritive

Table 5. Thumbsuckers

	n	Percentage of Thumb-suckers	Onset		Termination								
			3 mos.	6 mos.	9 mos.	12 mos.	1	2	3	4	5	6	7
Brazelton (1956)	70	87%	100%	100%	74%	93%	93%						
Davis (1940)	150	33			No report but some → 15 yrs.								
Heering (1932)	25	44	100		Observed to 17 wks.								
Traisman and Traisman (1958)	2,650	46	75	(?)		4	19		50%				
Klackenberg (1949)	259	50				50	53				79%		
Kunst (1948)	143	100	100	100									
Roberts (1944)	15		83	100	No Report								
Yarrow (1954)	66	64	63	90		28				50		75	86%
Lewis (1930)	30	18-41	67	77	3	13		20	30%	50	60%	70	

sucking. Kunst and Brazelton counted any kind of hand sucking—of finger, first, or thumb—in their estimates, whereas other investigators reporting an incidence of from 44 to 64% (Heering, 1932; Traisman and Traisman, 1958; Yarrow, 1954) apparently counted only sucking of the thumb. Table 5 presents a synopsis of data on onset and termination of nonnutritive sucking.

Investigators have not reported dates of termination of hand-sucking as thoroughly as onset. Brazelton (1956) reported that 74% of his subjects by 9 months and 93% by 12 months had discontinued the habit except when tired, hungry, or unhappy, but the dates of termination of all sucking were not reported. Most investigators have apparently concentrated on all hand-sucking regardless of state. Traisman and Traisman (1958) found that the mean age of termination was approximately 3.8 years. Yarrow (1954) found that half of his subjects had stopped sucking by 4 years. Lewis (1937) reported that 70% of his 30 cases stopped before 6 years. Although thumbsucking persists past 6 years in only a small percentage of subjects, Yarrow reported 14% of the babies he saw who thumb-sucked had not stopped by 7 years of age and several investigators have reported that a small percentage of children persist until adolescence (Davis, 1940; Honzik and McKee, 1962; Swinehart, 1938).

The specific correlates of thumb-sucking are not well known. As the infant grows older the incidence of thumb-sucking becomes associated with particular states. As common experience would suggest, Brazelton (1956)

found that although thumb-sucking disappeared as a common activity for the infant at approximately 12 months, the response continued to appear under conditions of distress. Kunst (1948) found a positive relationship between hunger and tendency to suck. Moreover, infants sucked primarily when they were awake until 17 to 19 weeks of age but then a reversal occurred, with infants sucking more during sleep until 1 year of age. Kunst also observed more sucking in bed than out, a finding she attributed to boredom but which might just as well be attributed to a drowsy state.

Honzik and McKee (1962) have summarized the literature regarding sex differences in thumbsucking. Gesell and Ilg (1937) reported that males sucked more than females but the basis for their statement is unclear. Honzik and McKee presented data from three studies to support their argument for a greater tendency of females to suck, a tendency which they attribute to greater tactile sensitivity. However, a number of studies have not confirmed this finding (Davis, 1940; Kunst, 1948; Traisman and Traisman, 1958) and there is some slight suggestion that Gesell and Ilg's original thesis is correct.

The Need to Suck. The occurrence of nonnutritive sucking has been variously held to reflect a primary drive or need to suck (Levy, 1937; Ribble, 1944), a derived or secondary drive to suck (Sears and Wise, 1950), the presence of an acquired secondary reinforcing property of stimulation produced by sucking (Palermo, 1956), the presence of autoerotic impulses within the child (Freud, 1905) or the presence of some unfulfilled need which the mother should attempt to rectify.

Palermo (1956) pointed out that three forces shaped modern thought to regard thumb-sucking as unhealthy and unnatural, a view which is, to some extent, now on the decline. First, the discovery of the germ and the accompanying hygienic revolution led to the reasonable belief that only clean objects should be permitted to enter the mouth; second, orthodontists (Lewis, 1930, 1937; Swinehart, 1938) reported evidence suggesting that thumb-sucking resulted in malocclusion and jaw deformation; finally, and by far most influentially, Freud's writings were interpreted to mean that a thumb-sucking child was manifesting his autoerotic needs and impulses, engaging in a primitive form of masturbation (Freud, 1905).

Levy is credited with the first attempt to make an empirical study of the etiologic factors involved in the development of persistent thumb-sucking (Levy, 1928). From interviews with over 60 mothers, he concluded that thumb-suckers had fewer feedings per day, were more likely to be on schedule as opposed to demand feeding, and were less likely to have pacifiers. In a later publication Levy (1937) commented that he could always relate the amount of thumb-sucking to the amount of sucking deprivation the child had experienced. Levy and many investigators have taken these findings as demonstration of an inborn primary *need* of the infant to suck, an important correlate of which is the intake of milk. Ribble (1944), for example, concluded that infants need 2 hours of sucking activity each day until they are 4 months of age. If they receive less opportunity they will suck their fingers.

The Levy-Ribble position on the fundamental need to suck was often taken to represent the view of psychoanalysis (McKee and Honzik, 1962) in spite of Freud's assertion "that the stimulus from the warm stream of milk was really the cause of the pleasurable sensation. To be sure, the gratification of the erogenous zone was at first united with the gratification of the need for nourishment." Whatever the logic of the argument the contrast between innate need and acquired-drive interpretations of nonnutritive sucking has served as a springboard for the confrontation of psychoanalytic and learning theories of behavior.

Roberts (1944), from interview data, concluded that thumb-suckers fed for substantially shorter periods than did nonthumb-suckers. Roberts also reported that the onset of thumb-sucking often followed shortly on a sharp decrease in feeding time. Many studies have not confirmed the Levy-Roberts findings. A number of retrospective studies have found more thumb-sucking in children who, because of late weaning or longer feedings, had greater access to sucking opportunity than those who had less opportunity (Bernstein, 1955; Sears and Wise, 1950; Yarrow, 1954). Yarrow, for example, found more severe and longer thumb-sucking in a late-weaned as opposed to an early-weaned group. In their large-scale study which involved repeated current interviews with mothers, Traisman and Traisman (1958) found an indefinite relationship between speed of feeding and percentage of babies who thumb-sucked. If nonnutritive sucking is an inverse function of degree of opportunity for nutritive sucking, one would suspect that demand-fed babies would not be thumb-suckers. This prediction has not been confirmed by the available reports (Simsarian, 1947; Trainham and Montgomery, 1946).

Blau and Blau (1955) observed one infant between 3 and 7 weeks of age for about 20 hours a day. The infant was given alternating fast and slow feedings (nipples with many or few holes). Contrary to a need-for-sucking hypothesis, fast feedings were followed by less crying, less nonnutritive sucking, and less activity in the 10-minute period following feeding. Brodbeck (1950) reported stronger sucking to a finger test by newborn babies fed from a small-hole nipple than by babies fed from a large-hole nipple before, after, and between regular 4-hour feedings.

It is possible to feed infants from a cup soon after birth with no detrimental effect on weight gain (Fredeen, 1948). One would suspect from a need-to-suck hypothesis that these infants would engage in more nonnutritive sucking than infants fed by bottle or breast. However, from a learning-theory position, from a strict interpretation of Freud, and from Piaget's statements about reflex extension, the prediction would be made that stronger and more nonnutritive sucking would occur in children who suck nutritively. Brodbeck (1950) fed one group of babies from a bottle for 4 days and then from a cup for 4 days and compared their sucking strength before, after, and between feedings with a group of babies fed routinely by bottle for 8 days. The first group showed a decrease in sucking strength after a switch to cup-feeding, whereas the bottle-fed group continued strong. Davis, Sears, Miller, and Brodbeck (1948) studied the response of three groups of infants for the first 10 days of life to a sucking test. The babies were bottle-, cup-, or breast-fed. There was a significant increasing trend in sucking responsiveness over days for the breast-fed group only; the trends for cup-fed and bottle-fed groups over days were flat. No differences were found between the groups in general body motility or in crying between feedings. These data were taken as evidence against the Levy-Ribble hypothesis.

Interest in the etiology of thumb-sucking has waned since the 1950s, perhaps as parental concern with thumb-sucking has changed. But the problem of comprehension has not gone away; the data do not allow a strong statement about the causes of nonnutritive sucking in the species or of variation among babies in amount and topography of sucking.

Pacification. The comforting effects of sucking, whether of thumb, fist, or nipple, are relatively well known. Pacifiers are frequently, if reluctantly, used by mothers for the purpose of quieting distressed babies. Although the sucking-quieting effect is well known, little experimental research has been addressed to the antecedents of this relationship or to the mechanism of its operation. The crying and thrashing infant will fairly abruptly cease crying and moving when a pacifier is placed into his mouth, only to begin again when the nipple is removed. The duration of the crying after the nipple is placed into the mouth and the latency to cry after it is removed depends on the degree of hunger and on the baby's familiarity with the nipple (Cohen, 1967; Marquis, 1943). Nurses often mollify newborns with sugar-soaked cotton pacifiers during circumcision. A similar procedure is used in the ritual circumcision of males by Jews where the baby sucks on wine-soaked cotton. Cohen (unpublished) recorded heart rate during circumcision and found little change in the rate or form of the heart record among infants who sucked on a pacifier. Infants who did not suck, however, showed violent tachycardia and dramatic changes in the form of the electrocardiogram. Wolowick (cited in Peiper, 1963) found an increase in the infant's threshold to shock during sucking and Birns, Blank, and Bridger (1966) found less response to cold-stress during sucking. The occurrence of sucking inhibits activity and reduces level of arousal.

Kessen and his colleagues have regarded limb movement as an indication of infant distress, although it has not been assumed that limb movement *only* reflects distress. Kessen and Leutzendorff (1963) found the quieting phenomenon not to be a general property of tactile stimulation alone. Limb activity was dramatically reduced in the stimulation period only during sucking opportunity and recovered rapidly when the nipple was withdrawn. It is possible that the soothing effect of a pacifier derives from the association of the sucking act with nutritive reinforcement, an hypothesis set forth by Palermo (1956). Kessen, Leutzendorff, and Stoutsenberger (1967) observed infants 1, 2, and 3 days of age. Of the 50 infants studied, 30 were seen on the first day of life both before and after the first feeding. The quieting-when-sucking phenomenon was observed in babies *before* the first feeding; that is, the pacifying effects of sucking do not depend on association with food.

Kessen and Mandler (1961) have argued, from a variety of evidence, that the running off of an organized behavioral act inhibits anxiety and resulting distress. They hypothesized that the congenitally organized response sequence of sucking relieves distress, quieting the infant, and that nutriment, whose physiological effects require relatively long periods of time, may become positively reinforcing through association with sucking and not the other way around. Bridger (1962b) also has argued that specific drives, for example, for food, are not present at birth, and that sucking is a species-specific response to high arousal level.

Rovee and Levin (1966) have challenged the universality of the sucking-quieting relationship. In the Kessen and Leutzendorff (1963) and Kessen et al. (1967) studies, infants were moderately aroused by diapering before observation but they were usually not crying. Rovee and Levin studied the relationship between initial arousal level and tendency to quiet when given an opportunity to suck. They found that very active babies decreased in activity when presented with the nipple, moderately active babies did not change activity level, and very quiet babies increased in activity when presented with the nipple. They replicated the Kessen et al. finding of an inverse relationship between sucking frequency and amount of activity decrement. There was also a high inverse correlation between time-to-accept nipple and baseline activity. Since an earlier study by Kaye and Levin (1964) had shown a strong inverse relationship between nipple-in time and arousal, apparently the very quiet babies were asleep and were awakened by the lip-stroking procedure used to facilitate nipple acceptance. Clearly, distress cannot be inhibited if it is not present.

There remain questions about the mechanisms involved in the sucking-quieting phenomenon. Halverson (1938) noted an increase in muscle tension during and sometimes before a sucking burst. Further, if sucking behavior pacifies the aroused infant one might expect to see infants sucking on their own thumbs and fists with a resulting decrement in activity. Wolff (1959, 1966) reported that spontaneous hand-mouth contacts in newborns tended to reduce crying but only before a meal. Hand-mouth contact also reduced the probability of spontaneous startles; Wolff used this evidence to argue that the sucking act discharges freely displaceable energy, which is constantly being generated in the infant. However, Williams and Kessen (1961) found no stable relation between hand-mouth activity and overall limb activity in newborns.

Virtually no experimental work has been carried out to study the relationships between activity and sucking in infants over a few days of age. Access to a pacifier has been suggested for restless infants (Ribble, 1944) and has been found to be helpful for treating "colicky" infants (Levine and Bell, 1950). Kunst (1948) noted that, until about 5 months of age, infants suck on their thumbs more while awake than asleep; after 5 months, a reversal in the pattern occurs. Infants sucked more when hungry and more in bed than out.

From what little evidence and casual observation is available, it appears that non-nutritive sucking may play different roles for the newborn and for the older infant. The newborn sucks most when highly aroused and is, in general, soothed through the sucking act. In the older infant thumbsucking seems, except for the hunger drive, to occur most frequently when the infant is in a low state of arousal.

The literature on sucking is vast and various; the iterated concern of child psychologists confirms the assertion of Piaget (1937) that the first changes in sucking are "the beginning of psychology."

THE CASE OF HABITUATION

The newborn infant enters the world with a number of built-in reactions to stimuli. Abrupt stimulation of the neck muscles elicits a Moro reflex; tactile stimulation at the side of the mouth of a hungry infant elicits a rooting reflex; a bright flash of light elicits eye-clamping; a sharp sound elicits tightening of the eyelids. It is obvious to the student of children that these responses change over age; responses are elaborated, modified, and, in the case of many newborn reflexes, often deleted from the child's behavioral repertoire. Much infant research in the past has concentrated on acquisition of new responses and on the refinement and recombination of old responses as the child grows. Only recently have child psychologists placed heavy emphasis on changes in the strength of unlearned responses with experience, particularly on the changing power of stimuli to alert or excite the child.

Current theoretical and empirical work on alerting characteristics of stimuli, for both children and adults, grows from a revived interest in *attention* and in *habituation of attention*. The behavior of dogs in Pavlov's laboratory when presented with a novel stimulus —stiffening of the ears, inhibition of ongoing behavior, and other signs of vigilance— led Pavlov (1927) to postulate an unconditioned orienting reflex, the "what is it?" response. The observed pattern of behavior appears to optimize further reception of the stimulus; the attention of the organism is fully directed toward the novel event and he is better able to evaluate its significance. However, taken by itself, the observation that a stimulus change regularly elicits attention and orientation carries with it rather disturbing implications. Although initial orientation and attention to a stimulus may be biologically useful, continued alerting to a stimulus that has no significance for the organism would make him a victim of irrelevant environmental variability. The problem becomes vivid when one considers the limitless variety of stimuli arriving at the infant's receptors.

Psychologists have generally considered selective *increasing* of attention (e.g., positive conditioning) to be the basic mechanism of selective attention. The mother's face is selected out of the myriad of visual stimuli and increased in salience because of its importance in the biological economy of the child. Recent research, however, has challenged the notion that nonsignificant stimuli which occur regularly are simply unattended; instead, it is argued that the organism actively ignores or filters stimuli which are of no use to him. Thus the emerging picture is one of an infant who gives high priority to novel events. If they are significant, he continues to attend; if not, he habituates.

An Example of Habituation and Some Definitions

Sharpless and Jasper (1956) carried out a fundamental study of habituation of the arousal reaction in the cat. Tones were repeatedly presented to sleeping cats while the investigators monitored brain activity by implanted electrodes. The response to the first presentation of a 500 Hz tone consisted of desynchronization of the brain-wave pattern (lower voltage and increased wave frequency) for as long as 3 minutes. The same tone was presented repeatedly and, with repetition of the stimulus, desynchronization lasted for shorter and shorter periods. However, when a new stimulus was presented (e.g., a 100 Hz or 1000 Hz tone) brain-wave desynchronization immediately reappeared. In this manner, Sharpless and Jasper demonstrated that habituation occurred specifically to the 500-cycle tone presented repeatedly and they eliminated, with appropriate controls, the possibility that the animal had gone into a deeper sleep or that the ear had in some way fatigued. Although Sharpless and Jasper did not find dishabituation to the familiar (i.e., repeated) stimulus after response to the novel stimulus (Pavlov's "disinhibition"), they did find some

recovery of desynchronization. However, if they permitted the activating effects of the novel stimulus to wear off completely, no response to the habituated stimulus was found. Apparently the effect of the novel stimulus was simply to activate the animal, essentially putting him in a different state during the presentation of the familiar stimulus. Habituation has, of course, been studied in other animals and in adult human beings (see, especially, Sokolov, 1963) but the Sharpless and Jasper study can be taken as representative in considering attempts to define habituation.

Conventional learning phenomena and habituation share a common characteristic in that the behavior of the animal changes with exposure to the stimulus. They differ in that learning typically consists of the acquisition of a new response or a change in the control of an old response, whereas habituation consists of the weakening of an unlearned response to stimulation. Whether or not habituation is a kind of learning can be argued; many investigators of infancy have considered it so (Bartoshuk, 1962; Engen and Lipsitt, 1965; Fantz, 1964). Thorpe (1956) has treated habituation as a kind of learning and he described both phenomena as examples of adaptation by the organism. In Thorpe's words, "habituation can . . . be defined as a relatively permanent waning of a response as the result of repeated stimulation which is not followed by any kind of reinforcement. . . . [It is] a simple learning not to respond to stimuli which tend to be without significance in the life of the animal."

Thompson and Spencer (1966) also regarded habituation as a kind of learning and emphasized that the response which is habituated is itself unlearned. They note that most investigators have considered habituation to be a response decrement which cannot be attributed either to simple response adaptation or to effector fatigue. Thompson and Spencer have proposed the most specific definition of habituation available, a definition which they presented as a list of nine essential characteristics of the phenomenon:

Given that a particular stimulus elicits a response, repeated applications of the stimulus result in a decreased response. . . . If the stimulus is withheld, the response tends to recover over time. . . . If repeated series of habituation training and spontaneous recovery are given, habituation becomes successively more rapid. . . . Other things being equal, the more rapid the frequency of stimulation, the more rapid is habituation. . . . The weaker the stimulus, the more rapid is habituation. Strong stimuli may yield no significant habituation. . . . The effects of habituation training may proceed beyond a zero asymptotic response level. . . . Habituation of response to a given stimulus exhibits stimulus generalization to other stimuli. . . . Presentation of another (usually strong) stimulus results in recovery of the habitated response. . . .

Significance of Habituation in Infants

Investigators have seen the study of habituation as significant for probing a variety of seemingly unrelated processes. Studies of attention, memory, model development, discrimination, and learning are cases in point.

Habituation promises to be a useful tool for the study of memory. Clearly, if an infant responds differently to stimulus X on trial 10 from the way he behaved on trial 1, state factors controlled, he has "remembered" stimulus X. Excitement about the phenomenon of habituation has been generated by an interest in knowing what the information storage capacities of the young infant are and how they develop (Fantz, 1964; Lewis, Bartels, Fadel, and Campbell, 1966; Pancratz and Cohen, 1968). Sokolov (1963), in a theory not unlike Hebb's (1949), has been most explicit about the form of memory implied by selective habituation. He proposed that a "neuronal model" preserves information about the *intensity, quality, duration,* and *order of presentation* of stimuli. This model or schema becomes more specific with each repetition of the stimulus. Each stimulus later in the series is then compared to the model. If the input coincides with the representation in memory, the stimulus is "recognized" and no orienting response is given. If, however, a mismatch between model and input occurs, the input disconfirms the organism's expectancy and an orienting response is elicited. A slight extension of Sokolov's proposal brings us close to studies of attention in infants (see, especially, Jeffrey, 1968). Several investigators (Berlyne, 1960; Dember and Earl, 1957; Finley, 1967; Haith et al., 1969; McCall and Kagan, 1967b) have suggested that discrepancy

or disconfirmation of an expectancy, rather than novelty strictly or complexity, is the most relevant consideration in infantile attention. In Sokolov's terms, it is the mismatch between the neuronal model—the schema or expectancy—and the input which is critical because of the baby's attempt to fit the input to the model. By this reasoning, an input too discrepant from any of the baby's models might not be attended because it cannot be related to any available expectancy. If one adds to this notion Berlyne's (1960) proposition that discrepancy produces arousal which the infant tries to reduce, it follows that an infant will be excited by slight discrepancies from expectancy, will examine the perturbing event, and will thereby reduce the effective uncertainty of the stimulus. In this way, the models or schemas of the baby become increasingly more complicated (Berlyne, 1960; Munsinger and Kessen, 1964; Piaget, 1936). There is a suggestion that moderate as opposed to large or small discrepancies from habituated stimuli elicit greater attention in the infant (Cohen, 1968; Finley, 1967; Kagan, personal communication; McCall and Kagan, 1967b). If discrepancy from a model has motivating effects, the habituation paradigm may serve as an important tool for studying the development of such models.

An additional significant implication of selective habituation is the evidence it provides that an infant is able to discriminate two stimuli (Kessen, 1963). Although any study which uses a so-called "novel" stimulus to demonstrate the selectivity of habituation to a familiar stimulus does, in effect, establish the discriminability of the two events, studies which have specifically used habituation as a tool for studying infantile discrimination have been carried out with variation in auditory stimuli (Bridger, 1961; Bronshtein et al., 1958) auditory localization (Leventhal and Lipsitt, 1964), visual stimuli (Bronshtein et al., 1958; Saayman, Ames, and Moffett, 1964), vibration, pressure, and olfactory stimuli (Bronshtein, et al., 1958).

Habituation has also been of significance because of its relation to learning. As noted earlier, the typical argument has been that habituation represents learning not to respond to certain stimuli. Since habituation may predate positive learning in that it does not require the occurrence of a new response, habituation may provide an index of early learning that avoids the troublesome problem that ease of response elicitation is often confounded with age.

Variables under Study in Habituation Research

A large number of studies document the decrease in infantile responding with repeated stimulation. The studies have differed widely in the modality studied, the parameter of stimulation varied, and the responses used. Response decrement has also been examined in its connections with nervous system functioning, age, sex, and state. After a brief survey of such studies, substantial questions of interpretation—in particular, the criteria which warrant the conclusion that response decrement in fact represents habituation—will be addressed.

Sensory Modality. Studies of habituation have been carried out in virtually every sensory modality; however, auditory stimuli have been by far the most popular. Investigations of the newborn have employed pure-tone stimuli (Bridger, 1961; Bronshtein et al., 1958; Keen, 1964), modulated pure tones (Eisenberg, Coursin, and Rupp, 1966), pulsed auditory stimuli (Barnet and Goodwin, 1965; Bartoshuk, 1962a, 1962b; Clifton, 1968; Keen, Chase, and Graham, 1965; Leventhal and Lipsitt, 1964), modulated pulsed stimuli (Bartoshuk, 1964) and complex sounds (Bronshtein et al., 1958; Eisenberg, Griffin, Coursin, and Hunter, 1964). But, on older infants, only two studies of habituation to auditory stimuli have been reported. Pure tones were used by Bronshtein et al., (1958) and Kagan and Lewis, (1965). Music and voices were used by Kagan and Lewis (1965). Habituation to the location of auditory stimulation has also been studied only in the newborn (Sokolov, 1960; Leventhal and Lipsitt, 1964).

Habituation studies using olfactory stimuli have been run almost exclusively with newborns (Bronshtein et al., 1958; Engen and Lipsitt, 1965; Engen et al., 1963; Kussmaul, 1896). Studies on the response to repeated presentations of an air jet, presumably a tactile stimulus, have been carried out by Bridger (1961) and by Stechler, Bradford, and Levy (1966) on newborns and by Bronshtein et al (1958) on both newborns and older infants. Habituation of response to temperature

stimuli has been reported by Bronshtein et al. (1958).

In the visual mode, the response to repeated presentations of light onset was studied by Bronshtein et al. (1958), Peiper (1926a), and Pratt (1934) on newborns and by Bronshtein et al. (1958), Cohen (1965), Kagan and Lewis 1965), and Lewis et al. (1966) in older infants. Repeated presentations of visual stimulus movement have been used in both studies of the newborn (Haith, 1966) and in studies of older infants (Cohen, 1965; Haith et al., 1969; Kagan and Lewis, 1965; Lewis, et al., 1966). No one has reported changes in responsiveness of newborns to repeated presentations of pictures or real objects. However, for older infants, the stimuli of choice for habituation studies have been stationary visual pictures. Investigators have used geometric forms (Kagan and Lewis, 1965; McCall and Kagan, 1967b; Pancratz and Cohen, 1968; Saayman et al., 1964), pictures of real objects, faces, or toys (Fantz, 1964; Kagan and Lewis, 1965; Meyers and Cantor, 1966, 1967) or real faces (Charlesworth, 1966).

Parameters of Stimulation. The habituation phenomenon has been used to study the rapidity with which a child reaches a stable low level of response as a function of a variety of stimulus parameters. The dimension of stimulus complexity has been studied with flashing or moving lights varying in predictability of shift in location (Cohen, 1965; Haith et al., 1969; Kagan and Lewis, 1965). Investigators have examined rate of habituation as a function of stimulus duration (Bridger, 1961; Clifton, 1968; Keen, 1964; Keen et al., 1965) interstimulus interval (Bartoshuk, 1962a, 1962b; Bridger, 1961; Keen, 1964; Pratt, 1934a, 1934b), and the interval between familiarization and test (Pancratz and Cohen, 1968). Oddly, with few exceptions (Barnet and Goodwin, 1965; Bronshtein et al., 1958; Engen et al., 1963) the effect of stimulus intensity on habituation rate has not been extensively studied. Finally, Charlesworth (1966) studied the effect of predictability of the spatial location in which a face would appear on persistence of a child in playing a game.

Responses. Although the primary measure used in habituation studies of animals and adults is desynchronization of the EEG pattern, no studies using this measure on infants have been reported. Barnet and Goodwin (1965) found no habituation of the evoked potential with repeated presentations of click stimuli. Heartrate change or latency to peak heartrate change has been used as the response in a number of studies (Barnet and Goodwin, 1965; Bartoshuk, 1962a,1962b; Bridger, 1961; Canestrini, 1913; Clifton, 1968; Eisenberg et al., 1966; Engen et al., 1963; Kagan and Lewis, 1965; Keen et al., 1965; McCall and Kagan, 1967b; Meyers and Cantor, 1966, 1967). Among the remaining physiological measures which have been used are respiration (Canestrini, 1913; Engen and Lipsitt, 1965; Engen et al., 1963; Keen et al., 1965; Leventhal and Lipsitt, 1964; Peiper, 1963), galvanic skin response (Jones, 1930a), and galvanic skin potential (Stechler, Bradford, and Levy, 1966).

The cochleopalpebral response was reportedly used by Moldenhauer in 1881 (Peiper, 1963) and more recently was used by Eisenberg et al. (1964). Behavioral startle or components of the startle response have been used in a number of studies of newborn habituation (Barnet and Goodwin, 1965; Bridger, 1961; Eisenberg et al., 1966; Eisenberg et al., 1964; Peiper, 1926a,1963). Total fixation time, number of looks, and duration of first fixation were measures in studies using single visual stimulus presentations (Cohen, 1968; Kagan and Lewis, 1965; Lewis et al., 1966; McCall and Kagan, 1967b; Meyers and Cantor, 1966, 1967; Pancratz and Cohen, 1968; Saayman et al., 1964), multiple-stimulus presentations (Cohen, 1968; Fantz, 1964; Saayman et al., 1964), and displays of moving lights (Cohen, 1968; Kagan and Lewis, 1965; Lewis et al., 1966).

Habituation of suppression of ongoing activity has been studied using the sucking response (Bronshtein et al., 1958; Haith, 1966; Haith et al., 1969; Kaye and Levin, 1963; Keen, 1964) and limb or body activity (Engen and Lipsitt, 1965; Engen et al., 1963; Haith et al., 1969; Kagan and Lewis, 1965; Leventhal and Lipsitt, 1964; Pratt, 1934a). Finally, the decrease in vocalization over trials to both auditory and visual stimuli has been studied by Kagan and Lewis (1965).

Central Factors in Habituation. If the process of habituation depends on central nervous system involvement in the form of model-building of prior input, one might suspect that the rate of habituation would reflect the relative integrity of certain brain structures. Bronshtein et al. (1958) reported that habituation of sucking suppression to auditory input did not occur in about half of the infants suffering trauma at birth whereas it occurred in almost three-quarters of the normals. Slower habituation was reported in the "suspect" babies even after the signs of the trauma had disappeared and they were considered clinically normal. Absence of habituation to sound stimuli was also reported in hydrancephalic infants. Eisenberg et al. (1966) reported that whereas normal infants required from 20 to 37 trials to habituate to a modulated tone falling from 5000 to 200 Hz in 4 seconds, 2 "suspect" babies required almost twice as long and 2 high-risk babies reportedly did not habituate at all.

Age Factors in Habituation. Although the role of maturation in affecting rate of habituation is an important issue theoretically, age variation is sorely underresearched. There seem to be no published studies which have explored habituation in the same infants over several months in the first two years of life, although such a study is now being carried out (Kagan, personal communication). A few cross-sectional age studies have been carried out but have usually covered only a small age range. Cohen (1965) found a somewhat faster falloff in fixation time to patterns of flashing lights over trials in 18- than in 13-week-old infants. Fantz (1964) found reduced attention to repeatedly presented pictures and increased attention to a novel picture in infants between 2 and 6 months of age but not in infants between 1 and 2 months. Lewis et al. (1966) found a fairly direct relationship between the decrement in fixation time to flashing lights and to faces as a function of age; infants generally habituated faster with increasing age over the first 18 months of life.

The literature is inconsistent with regard to rate or presence of habituation in very young infants. Fleischer (1953) and Peiper (1963) have both reported habituation of movement in the fetus to a strong auditory stimulus. Peiper (1963) also reported habituation of a respiratory response to auditory stimuli in premature babies, but Polikanina and Pobatova (1955) reported no habituation of the orienting response to sound in premature babies. They did find habituation in full-terms. Bronshtein et al. (1958) discussed the findings of other Russian investigators who reported a "delay in cessation" of responding in premature but healthy infants. Analysis of age differences in habituation over the first few days of life by American investigators have generally produced negative results (Bartoshuk, 1962b; Haith, 1966; Keen et al., 1965).

Sex Differences in Habituation. The role of sex in determining presence and rate of habituation is somewhat perplexing. Studies investigating sex differences in newborn habituation have had negative outcomes (Haith, 1966; Keen, 1964). Meyers and Cantor (1966) reported increasing heart rate responsiveness to pictures over trials by males and decreasing responsiveness by females (5 months of age), which would suggest faster habituation by females. This finding was supported in a study by McCall and Kagan (1967b) in which it was shown that discrepancy between old and new stimuli was an effective variable in the comparison of responsiveness for 4-month-old females but not for males. However, these findings to some extent are contradicted in other studies by the same investigators. Kagan and Lewis (1965) found a significant decrement in responsiveness for male, but not for female, 13-month-olds to blinking lights. Meyers and Cantor (1967) found a larger difference in heart rate responsiveness to novel stimuli in 6-month-old males than in females. Moreover, Pancratz and Cohen (1968) found habituation to pictures of geometric objects in 4-month-old males but not in females and also selective recovery of response to a new stimulus picture in males but not in females. Lewis et al. (1966), studying habituation of fixation time to pictures in 3-, 6-, 9-, 13-, and 18-month-old infants, found sex of the baby to be irrelevant to rate of habituation.

State and Habituation. Only Barnet and Goodwin (1965) have specifically studied habituation as a function of the baby's state. Further, such data are essential to a complete understanding of the mechanisms involved in habituation. There is the danger that many of the studies reporting age differences, the effects of birth trauma, and the effects of various parameters of stimulation have inadvertently studied the effects of state on rate of habituation.

Problems in the Interpretation of Habituation Studies

The baby's tendency to respond less and less to repeated stimulation cannot be interpreted uniformly as habituation. Appropriate control manipulations must be used to eliminate alternative interpretations of response decrement.

Studies of habituation in infants have typically been concerned with eliminating three determinants of response decrement: sensory accommodation, effector fatigue, and state of alertness or arousal. *Sensory accommodation* is generally not a problem in behavioral studies, especially when auditory or visual stimuli are used. For example, Barnet and Goodwin (1965) found no decrement in the evoked potential to sound in newborns even when 250 clicks were presented at a 1-per-second rate. However, experiments which use exceptionally long stimulus durations and brief interstimulus intervals (Bridger, 1961) may be vulnerable to the effects of sensory accommodation (Bartoshuk, 1964). Response decrement to olfactory stimuli is more difficult to interpret because the olfactory receptors adapt relatively rapidly and recover slowly (Engen and Lipsitt, 1965; Engen et al., 1964). The involvement of *effector fatigue* as an alternative to habituation can be eliminated by showing that a novel stimulus will still produce a response. Procedures used to rule out effector fatigue will be considered in greater detail later. A far more pervasive problem than sensory accommodation or effector fatigue in infant habituation studies is holding the infant's state of alertness or *arousal* constant throughout the experiment.

A number of studies reported earlier in the present chapter demonstrate the proposition that infantile responsiveness is affected by state. Moreover, level of arousal changes rapidly in infants and most rapidly in newborns. Therefore the possibility must be considered that, without suitable controls, findings of response decrement reflect progressive drowsiness or progressive irritation rather than habituation. A number of studies have, in fact, discussed "habituation" in a paradigm with no controls for state change (Barnet and Goodwin, 1965; Haith, 1966; Kagan and Lewis, 1965; Lewis et al., 1966; Peiper, 1963). A more subtle difficulty is that investigators attentive to the issue of alertness have often considered "state" to be affected only by the amount of time the baby is in the experiment. An important variable controlling state, however, is likely to be the stimulus which is presented to the baby as part of the experimental regimen. For example, some studies have used strong stimuli which initially elicit startle responses (Barnet and Goodwin, 1965; Bridger, 1961; Peiper, 1926a, 1963) or a concomitant of the defensive reaction such as heart rate acceleration (Bartoshuk, 1962a, 1962b; Bridger, 1961; Clifton, 1968). But a child who has been "frightened" by a strong stimulus cannot be assumed to be in the same state after its presentation as he was before. If awakened by a startle response, the infant may sink into an even deeper sleep afterward, with the consequence that he will be less responsive to additional stimulations. Wolff's (1966) observations on "freely displaceable energy," as well, suggest a continuing effect of a startling stimulus. It is also reasonable to expect that presentation of very rhythmic stimuli often used in habituation studies may produce drowsiness in babies. For example, consider the case in which infants are presented with a rhythmic stimulus for 24 trials (Cohen, 1965). As an apparent control for change in state, another group waits a period equivalent to the duration of 20 trials and then is presented with the rhythmic stimulus for 4 trials. A difference in response between the groups on the last 4 trials might reflect, not habituation, but drowsiness in the experimental group produced by the stimulus itself.

Test of Response Recovery and Dishabituation. Investigators have used a response-recovery strategy to eliminate state-change and effector-fatigue interpretations of response decrement. A second stimulus S_2 is presented after the infant's response to the first stimulus S_1 has waned. If the novel S_2 but not the familiar S_1 elicits a response, then neither variation-of-state nor effector-fatigue interpretations can be invoked to account for lack of responsiveness to S_1. Clearly, however, one must insure, either through counterbalancing S_1 and S_2 or by other procedures, that S_2 is not *always* more effective in eliciting the response than S_1.

Yet another method of demonstrating habituation to S_1 believed to eliminate the problem of equating responsiveness to S_1 and S_2 is the dishabituation paradigm—first S_1, then S_2, and then S_1 again, are each presented a number of times. If a response decrement to a repeated S_1 is obtained which recovers after S_2, the earlier diminution of responding is not easily attributable to effector fatigue or a consistent shift in state. However, the effect of S_2 in this paradigm may be on the state of the organism. A number of investigators have argued that S_2 does not in fact disrupt the process of habituation; rather, its presentation increases general excitability and potentiates the later response to S_1 (Sokolov, 1960; Thompson and Spencer, 1966). Only a few studies on infants have used precisely the dishabituation paradigm (Bartoshuk, 1964; Keen, 1964; Pancratz and Cohen, 1968).

Variants on the preceding two procedures have been used by a number of investigators. Pancratz and Cohen (1968) showed 4-month-old infants a geometric form (S_1) for 10 trials. The babies were then given 6 trials during which familiar stimulus trials alternated with trials on which novel stimuli were presented. A similar design was used by Meyers and Cantor (1967). In an ingenious design, Meyers and Cantor (1966) controlled familiarity on a continuum for several stimuli at the same time. Four different pictures were presented to babies in four phases. In phase 1, one stimulus (S_1) was shown 4 times; in phase 2, S_1 and a second stimulus (S_2) were each presented 4 times, in phase 3, S_1, S_2, and S_3 were each presented 4 times; in phase 4, S_1, S_2, S_3, and S_4 were each shown 4 times. Thus in phase 4 the ratio of familiarity of the stimuli was 4:3:2:1.

Fantz (1964) used a simultaneous-presentation method to explore the effects of stimulus familiarity on fixation time. A group of 28 infants 6 to 25 weeks of age were given 10 paired-comparison stimulus presentations, 1 minute in duration, with a particular stimulus shown on every trial (S_1) and the other changed on every trial (S_2). Infants 2 to 3 months of age and 4 to 6 months of age showed a decrement in relative amount of looking at the novel stimulus over trials but no reliable effects of novelty was demonstrated for children 1 to 2 months of age or 3 to 4 months of age.

An interesting modification of the test for specificity of response decrement was carried out by Engen and Lipsitt (1965) in what might be called a whole-part design. Two groups of newborns were first given familiarization trials in which they were presented a mixture of amyl acetate and heptanol and then tested on amyl acetate or heptanol separately. In a study using spatial shift as the dimension on which S_1 and S_2 differed, Leventhal and Lipsitt (1964) habituated newborns to a tone in one ear and then presented the tone in the other ear, and found response recovery. A still different way of testing specificity was used by Bartoshuk (1962a) and by Eisenberg et al. (1966). Following the earlier lead of Sharpless and Jasper (1956), these investigators first repeatedly presented a frequency-modulated tone and then reversed the order of frequency changes to test for specific habituation. Such a procedure nicely equates the amount of total energy in S_1 and S_2 but not necessarily the potency.

The problem of equal potency can easily be solved by counterbalancing assignment of the stimuli, but such a control is missing in studies of auditory habituation (Bartoshuk, 1962a; Eisenberg et al., 1966), olfactory habituation (Engen and Lipsitt, 1965), and studies of habituation to stimulus location (Leventhal and Lipsitt, 1964). Reports of procedure in some studies have not been complete enough to judge whether or not adequate counterbalancing was used (Bridger, 1961; Bronshtein et al., 1958). Still other studies, often cited as demonstrating habituation, have used reasonable counterbalancing precautions but have not found evidence of selective response decrements (Keen, 1964; Leventhal and Lipsitt, 1964).

The necessity for counterbalancing is often subtle. Eisenberg et al. (1966) repeatedly presented to newborns a 4-second tone falling from 5000 to 200 Hz, with resulting habituation. When the modulated tone was presented in reverse, increasing from 200 to 5000 Hz, the infants showed increased response. It is possible that the infants were responding only to the early portion of the signal and that lower frequencies elicited greater responsiveness. A similar argument can be made to Bartoshuk's (1962b) study of response to patterned stimuli. In a somewhat different manner, Leventhal and Lipsitt (1964) repeatedly presented a stimulus to newborns in one ear and then tested for location-specific

habituation by presenting the stimulus to the other ear. Significant recovery of responsiveness to the stimulus in the new location was found, but asymmetry of brain or ear may have been operative (Turkewitz et al., 1966). There have been only a few studies that have used a complete counterbalanced design or randomization of stimuli (Engen et al., 1963; Fantz, 1964; Meyers and Cantor, 1966, 1967; Pancratz and Cohen, 1968).

Taken as a whole, the habituation literature confirms the notion that with experience, even newborn infants modify their responses to a wide range of signals. Few behavioral phenomena rival habituation in usefulness as a measure of the infant's sensitivity and few have as many implications for theories of psychological development. Future research on the control of habituation by variation in stimulus, age, and personal characteristics will further clarify the role of habituation in the baby's early adaptation to the environment.

THE CASE OF EARLY VISION

Considerations of Anatomy and Physiology

Although anatomical and neurophysiological differences between the visual systems of newborn and adult do not necessarily imply qualitative functional differences, gross discrepancies often provide a lead toward assessing differences in visual capacity. The eye approximately doubles in size and weight from birth to maturity (Mann, 1964), but there is great variability in growth rate from one part of the eye to another. The greatest relative postnatal gain is in the iris, ciliary body, and choroid; the growth of the lens, retina, anterior chamber, cornea, and intrabulbar portion of the optic nerve is distinctly less than of the eyeball as a whole. The cornea is relatively large at birth and corneal refraction is high. The newborn lens is more spherical than the adult's, a fact that is probably relevant to newborn refractive processes, as is the differential development of the ciliary muscles. The retina is not fully differentiated at birth. The nuclei are closer together and more numerous in the various nuclear layers, the macula is not fully developed, and although the distance from the optic disc to the macula is the same as in the adult, a line passing through the center of the cornea and lens will at birth strike the retina at a point between the fovea and the disc. From the eighth month of intrauterine life to the fourth month after birth, the macula undergoes constant differentiation. During this period the nuclear and bipolar layers thin, the cone nuclei increase in number, the cones themselves become highly specialized, and the fovea externa develops.

At birth the fibers of the optic nerve are myelinated, but the nerve sheath is thinner than in the adult. Myelinization of the optic nerve is complete about the tenth week after birth. Although it appears fairly certain that the central nervous system (CNS) contains its entire allotment of neurons at birth, there is evidence to suggest that later cortical myelinization, differentiation, and rearrangement of these neurons occurs (Conel, 1939b, 1941). All in all, however, the anatomical evidence points to intact, if immature, visual structures at birth (Ellingson, 1960; Hershenson, 1967).

Physiological and neurophysiological evidence also tends to point toward relatively intact and well-developed visual structures. Contrary to the earlier findings of Zetterström (1951, 1952, 1955), Horsten and Winkelman (1962, 1964; Winkelman and Horsten, 1962) found cones as well as rods clearly distinguishable in the seventh month of gestation and were able to record electroretinograms (ERG) in the newborn not essentially different from those of the adult. Barnet, Lodge, and Armington (1965) also demonstrated a response to light of long wavelength in the newborn ERG. As Hershenson (1967) points out, although the maturation of the retina continues throughout childhood, there is little doubt that both the photopic and scotopic systems are differentiated and functional at birth.

It is more difficult to assess the developmental level of neurophysiological function in the CNS at birth. Bartoshuk (1964b; Bartoshuk and Tennant, 1964) has shown that substantial sleep-wake differences can be found in newborn EEG records, that there is a reasonable amount of bilateral covariation, and that sustained slow rhythmicity is present. Yet evoked responses in the visual system are immature in a number of ways; they vary in form and amplitude, they show a longer latency than adult responses (Elling-son and Lindsley, 1949; Smith, 1938a, 1938b, 1939), and their appearance is confined to the occiput, or, at best, they are found in other areas only infrequently and with variable shape and extreme sensitivity to changes in frequency (Ellingson, 1958, 1960). However, these features may only reflect quantitative immaturity—slower conduction, structural and metabolic properties of an immature brain, and a sluggish activation system (Hershenson, 1967; Hrbek and Mares, 1964a, 1964b). In sum, the neural pathways of vision are apparently functional at birth but neurophysiological indicators of functioning usually show differences in degree from the patterns of adults.

Oculomotor Facility and Reflexes of the Eye

Gross Postural Adjustments. Although the neck muscles are poorly developed at birth and the head will flop if the baby is held erect, there is evidence to indicate that the newborn, when lying on his back, can make certain immediate adjustments of the head in response to visual stimulation. Gutman (1924) reports turning away of the head from noxious stimulation in newborns. A number of researchers (Blanton, 1917; Genzmer, 1882; Moore, 1896; Peiper, 1928; Preyer, 1888; Shinn, 1893; Talbot, 1882) have observed slow, inaccurate, but nevertheless consistent, positive orientation of the head, as well as the eyes, to light stimuli of relatively low intensity. McGinnis (1930) reports slight newborn head movements in the direction of moving stripes. Ling (1942) observed adjustive head movements to bring a moving disc into view from the first days of life onward.

Oculomotor Responses. The most convincing overall evidence that infants under 5 days of age are capable of selective oculomotor response is to be found in studies of visual preference to be dealt with later. Briefly, both casual observation and controlled experimentation have indicated that the alert newborn, when presented with two visual stimuli, will sometimes orient the head and eyes more toward one than the other (Fantz, 1956, 1963, 1965; Hershenson, 1964; Hershenson, Munsinger, and Kessen, 1965, among others). The fact that some type of differential response is possible even in this early period of life implies the presence of a certain degree of visual sensitivity. The level of sensitivity can be assumed to depend on a number of factors contributing to selective oculomotor responding—the pupillary reflex, monocular adjustment and binocular coordination, accommodation of the lens, the area of the retina on which the image falls, and the physiological state of the receptors and receptor pathways. In addition to the general and indirect evidence in favor of early oculomotor capacity drawn from studies of preference, there exists well-controlled experimentation on specific aspects of selective oculomotor responding in the infant.

Pupillary Reflex. Early researchers generally agreed that the pupillary reflex is functional and lively at birth (the evidence is summarized by Pratt et al., 1930). Sherman, Sherman, and Flory (1936) and Beasley (1933b) found that the reflex, although somewhat sluggish at birth, rapidly perfects itself during the early part of the first week. Therefore it appears almost certain that there is early regulation of the light entering the eye when looking occurs under conditions of varying brightnesses. As a caution, however, it must be noted that Ling (1942) reported a positive correlation between level of illumination, duration of fixation, and number of eyeblinks in infants under four weeks of age. The finding indicated that while the pupillary reflex occurs, the newborn experiences some difficulty in adapting comfortably to increases in illumination, a difficulty that may be related to the lack of pigmentation in the iris and the incomplete development of the sphincter and dilator of the pupil at birth (Mann, 1964).

Monocular Adjustment and Binocular Coordination. Almost every type of eye movement can be recorded from the newborn (Ling, 1942) but there exists virtual unanimity that control of the eyes improves over the first few months (Dayton and Jones, 1964; Dayton, Jones, Steele, and Rose, 1964; Duke-Elder, 1949; Ling, 1942; McGinnis, 1930).

The one-eye response of the newborn to simple geometrical forms has been reported by Salapatek (1968). Binocular optokinetic nystagmus has been reliably elicited just after birth in a number of experiments (Dayton, Jones, Aui, Rawson, Steele, and Rose, 1964; Fantz, Ordy, and Udelf, 1962; Gorman, Cogan, and Gellis, 1959; McGinnis, 1930).

McGinnis (1930) recorded coordinate compensatory eye movements in a baby as young as 3 days of age, but such eye movements appeared rather late in the average infant (about 2 to 3 weeks of age). Ling (1942) found evidence of coordinate compensatory eye movements at 32 hours of age but also found that until the fourth or fifth week of age, the movements were effective only for head movements of very low velocity and very limited scope.

There exist widely divergent opinions as to the time of the first appearance of binocular fixation (Beasley, 1923b; Duke-Elder, 1949; Lucas, 1927; Feldman, 1920). Ling (1942) pointed out that differences in the literature are largely ascribable to differences in the definition of fixation and to the absence of a distinction between conjugate deviation and convergence coupled with the failure to record either accurately. Ling, using direct observation and photographic technique, found that, although the eyes moved coordinately in the same direction from the very first days following birth, binocular convergence first appeared as a series of small globus jerks only at a median of 4 weeks of age and did not become a smooth continuous process until about 8 weeks of age. It is somewhat unfortunate that Ling studied binocular fixation and convergence in response to a 2-inch circular disc slowly moving in and out radially through a distance ranging from 2 inches from the eyes to 36 inches from the eyes. Haynes, White, and Held (1965) have shown that the infant does not exhibit any great degree of variable accommodation until approximately 2 months of age but, rather, accommodation is fixed and appropriate only for objects about 8 inches from the eyes. In Ling's study, therefore, it is possible that early absence of convergence simply reflected a lack of the ability to maintain focus upon the disc as it moved. Wickelgren (1967), with precise photographic recording, found that divergence or ocular flare was uniformly present in the first days of life.

Research concerned with the newborn's and young infant's ability to follow moving stimuli with the eyes has tended, in more controlled situations, to find a series of jerky fixations and refixations coupled with relatively good conjugate deviations of the eyes (see McGinnis, 1930, for a summary of early work).

McGinnis found that during the first two weeks (even in the first hours after birth) movements of the visual field had a definite effect upon eye movements. However he also found that during the first two weeks, although the majority of the eye movements tended to be in the direction of the movements of the object, the pursuit movements were often broken by large movements in the opposite direction. He also found that first sustained pursuit at three to four weeks of age consisted of many jerky refixations, but that, by six weeks of age, ocular pursuit was smooth and involved effective head movements.

Dayton and his co-workers (Dayton and Jones, 1964; Dayton et al., 1964) have provided evidence that argues for the capacity of newborn infants to pursue moving objects visually. Electrooculographic recordings were taken from each eye separately while babies were presented with dots 14 inches above the eyes. An observer judged, and marked on the electrooculographic record, when pursuit was occurring. From birth there was a remarkable coincidence of horizontal movements from each eye when the dot was being followed. However, there was a substantial change over age; refixations in the newborn varied from 1 to 1.5 per second; in the adult, measurable refixation movements rarely occurred. In the infant the frequency of these movements decreased gradually up to 3 months of age. The amplitude or the excursion of the refixations in degrees was very large in the newborn, varying from 8 to 20°, but by 3 months of age decreased to from 4 to 8°. The velocity of the eye movements was found to vary directly with the velocity of the moving dot and conjugate movements were found when the target was moved randomly at a variable speed.

Accommodation of the Lens. The structure of the eye at birth would lead one to believe that the newborn eye would be farsighted (Mann, 1964). Evidence from experiments where the ciliary muscles were immobilized by atropine have almost without exception indicated the predominance of hyperopia in newborns (Cook and Glasscock, 1951; Duke-Elder, 1949; Pratt, 1954; Pratt, Nelson, and Sun, 1930; Slataper, 1950). However, as Duke-Elder (1949) points out, in the normal state the lens is not immo-

bilized and therefore can sometimes correct for extralens refractive errors by means of appropriate accommodation when these errors are not gross. Haynes, White, and Held (1965; White, 1963) tested accommodative responses under nondrugged conditions throughout the first four months after birth. The experimenters measured accommodation to a fixated red annulus with a retinoscope within four ranges of distance. Prior to one month of age the infant's accommodative response did not adjust to changes in target distance, but rather the system appeared to be locked in at one focal distance whose median value for the group was 19 centimeters. Flexibility of response began at about the middle of the second month of age, and performance comparable to that of the normal adult was attained by the fourth month.

Central and Peripheral Vision. There is known to be an increase in the density and a rearrangement of macular receptors in the early months and a correlated improvement in the baby's ability to fixate centrally. Ling (1942) ignored the problem of central fixation in newborns, stating that such a question was insolvable because no test could be devised that would ascertain whether or not the image actually fell on the macula. Fantz et al. (1962) sought to answer the question by comparing the number and direction of separate fixations on a striped figure and a plain surface figure presented simultaneously to infants ranging in age from 1 to 22 weeks. Both measures indicated preference for the striped pattern in all infants. However, as Fantz noted, the stimulus object, when centrally fixated, occupied peripheral as well as macular portions of the retina.

Visual Acuity. It is important in vision both to be able to get the eye to where it should be and also to be able to see clearly what is there when the eye arrives. Gorman, Cogan, and Gellis (1957), measuring optokinetic nystagmus to a field of moving stripes in infants under 5 days of age, found that 93 of 100 infants responded to stripes subtending a visual angle of only 33.5 minutes of arc.

Although Gorman and his co-workers' finding, in itself, is impressive evidence for the existence of a fair degree of visual acuity in the newborn infant, Fantz, Ordy, and Udelf (1962) have pointed out that the reflex response to a moving pattern occupying most of the visual field may be a very different type of visual performance from the "voluntary" attention to the pattern of localized stationary objects (see also Riesen, 1960). Fantz et al. presented infants 1 to 22 weeks of age with two stationary stimuli at varying distances, one of which had stripes of varying widths and the other of which was a plain grey surface. It was found that the infants under 2 months of age fixated most upon the striped stimulus if the stripes were as narrow as 40 minutes of a visual angle. Between 2 and 4 months the minimum width necessary in order to bring out this preference was only 20 minutes, and for infants older than 4 months only slightly more than 10 minutes of visual angle. In a more recent study, Fantz (1965) reported even finer acuity in young infants. Dayton and his associates (Dayton, Jones, Aiu, Rawson, Steele, and Rose, 1964) add further substantiation to the impressive acuity capabilities of the newborn. They found at least 20/150 vision in newborns by eliciting optokinetic nystagmus to moving stripes of different widths.

Dimensions of Effective Visual Stimulation

Brightness. Blanton (1917) reported that many of the newborn infants she observed fixated a light. She also reported that one infant, 34 days of age, when placed in bright sunlight first shut his eyes then opened them and stared straight at the sun with his pupils constricted. According to Champneys (1881), his son, when 1 week old, looked at a candle, and bright light always gave him much pleasure throughout the first 9 months of his life. Hall (1891) observed a baby blink and turn his head away from direct sunlight on the first day of life. The infant also exhibited "surprise and fear" when he encountered a sunny window. However, on the second day following birth the infant turned his eyes and then his head toward a lamp set at 90° from midline. Watson (1925c) found that newborns and infants moved their eyes toward a faint light in a dark room.

Hershenson (1964) presented 20 newborns, 2 to 4 days of age, with paired combinations of three uniform grey panels of differing brightness. He found that newborns oriented more toward the panel of intermediate than of dim or bright intensity and more toward the panel of bright than of dim intensity. Hershenson concluded that these significant

transitive preferences were indicative that brightness exists as a discriminable dimension of stimulation for the newborn. Salapatek (1968) reported interactions between brightness of figure and ground that are relevant to preference. Until preference is assessed in visual fields not containing sharp brightness transitions and in fields containing parametrically varied figure-ground brightness ratios, the exact nature of the relationship between brightness and fixation preferences will remain unclear.

Apart from the question of preference for varying brightness, a large body of experimental evidence indicates that the newborn and infant differentially respond to various brightness values in response systems other than visual orientation (Irwin and Weiss, 1934a, 1934b; Pratt, 1934b; Redfield, 1939; Smith, 1936; Weiss, 1934). Weiss (1934) reported decreased bodily activity with increases of light intensity. Other investigators (e.g., Pratt, 1934; Smith, 1936) have found variations in activity level as a function of brightness by infants whose eyes were closed and who were presumably asleep.

Doris, Felzen, and Poresky (1968) reasoned that, because the retina at birth may be functionally more of a rod retina than a mixed rod and cone retina, it was possible that the relationship between visual acuity and brightness would not be as marked in the newborn as in the older infant or adult. They tested the visual acuity of 20 newborns under 2 levels of brightness. Doris et al. argue that the pattern of their results is consistent with the hypothesis that visual acuity in the newborn period is not as sensitive to changes in brightness as it is in the case of 2- to 4-month-olds.

Color. Color, unlike brightness, has been studied in numerous observations and experiments since the late nineteenth century. However, the failure to control differences in brightness has caused grave difficulties in interpreting the results of research on infant color perception. Color discriminations by newborns and young infants may be on the basis of brightness alone; equating colored stimuli to be of equal intensity by adult standards may be an inadequate brightness control for research with newborns (Pratt, 1954; Mann, 1964).

Preyer (1888) gave his son identical forms

of different colors. The child could not discriminate the colors until 21 months of age, when he became able to discriminate red and yellow from the series. Baldwin (1906) remarked on a 9-month-old infant who preferred blue to other colors. Holden and Bosse (1900) studied 30 infants and found that none younger than 6 months of age responded to color; thereafter, red, orange, and yellow were the preferred colors. Marsden (1903a, 1903b) held up two colored cards before his son and moved them apart to see which was followed; later he used grasping and reaching as measures of discrimination. The infant first perceived and followed the yellow card at 4 months and soon afterward followed the red one as well. McDougall (1908) found that two infants first differentially grasped colored objects at 5 months; red was preferred to green and blue. Myers (1908) found that his single subject first preferred red and yellow at the age of 6 months by grasping those colors instead of others as did Wooley's (1909) baby. In observations of several infants from 1 to 14 days of age Canestrini (1913) found no distinct physiological reactions to different colors. After concluding that brightness and novelty influenced the babies' choices, Valentine (1914) showed that yellow and red were more readily followed and grasped.

A series of studies has used the Purkinje shift as an indication of infant color perception. Peiper (1963) in 1927 presented white and colored lights to four light- and dark-adapted premature infants. He measured their threshold with the eye-neck reflex to light flashes. Peiper found that for light-adapted subjects yellow had the greatest brightness value and, when the infant was dark-adapted, that blue had the greatest brightness value. Unfortunately, Peiper's results were not definitive; only one of his four subjects showed an unmistakable Purkinje shift of relative brightness values toward the short end of the spectrum as found in adults. Smith (1936) questioned Peiper's data and method. From a study of 20 infants in which change in activity was the measure of response, she concluded that newborn males are totally color blind and that females are partially color blind. Trincker and Trincker (in Peiper, 1963) in 1954 used Peiper's method with infants up to 10 weeks

of age and found the Purkinje shift uniformly. The degree of the shift increased with age. Pratt et al. (1930) equated colors for intensity by adult standards and measured infant's activity changes to stimuli. The results strongly supported the conclusion that responding was dependent on brightness rather than color.

Staples (1931, 1932) studied visual orientation and grasping in 262 infants from 10 weeks to 2 years of age. Colored stimuli were consistently looked at and grasped more than a grey comparison stimulus. Red was selected more than any other color paired with it. Staples concluded that color was perceived to some degree by 3 months of age. The most careful of the early studies on infant color perception was carried out by Chase (1937). She assumed that only if the infant could discriminate between colors equated for intensity would he be able to follow one color moving across a background of another color. The subjects were 24 infants from 15 to 70 days of age. Pursuit was observed in 90 to 100% of all presentations involving different colors. Control presentations (in which the stimulus was the same color as the field) elicited no pursuit at all.

Stirnimann (1944) measured the duration of gaze on colored cards varying in saturation, brightness, and position in 350 newborn infants. In the first two weeks of life, blue was preferred to red and green; looking time for red and blue increased during that time. Both saturation and brightness seemed to influence preferences so that the exact role of color as a stimulus was unclear.

Spears (1964, 1966) assessed discrimination of Munsell colored papers in 60 infants 4 months of age. The response measure was relative time spent looking at the various stimuli, which were presented in paired comparisons. Spears found a preference ordering of blue, red, yellow, grey with only the preference for blue over grey statistically stable. In tests of color and shape together, the only color trend was a preferene for red over grey. In an attempt to control for the brightness variable, Wickelgren (1967) presented 16 newborn infants with stimuli varying both in color and in brightness. The stimuli for the paired comparisons design were bright or dim red and grey slides. By presenting bright red and dim red slides in comparison with bright grey and dim grey slides, Wickelgren made it possible to find color preferences existing regardless of brightness level. No such preferences were found.

Recent studies of the electroretinogram (Barnet, Lodge, and Armington, 1965; Horsten and Winkelman, 1962, 1964) indicated that a light of strong intensity can evoke newborn ERG response to color like that of adults. Possibly stimuli bright enough to cause the newborn infant's cones to fire are too bright for the infant to look at them. If this is true, it may not be possible to use looking as a behavioral index of newborn color perception.

Despite the interest and effort that have produced studies of early color sensitivity, no positive report is free of the possibility that differences in brightness constituted the relevant stimulus dimension.

Movement. Little research has been done to determine specifically the necessary conditions for pursuit of moving objects. Jones (1926), Beasley (1933a, 1933b), Morgan and Morgan (1944), Wolff and White (1965) varied the direction of movement; they studied the baby's response to vertical, horizontal, and circular stimulus movement and obtained widely different results on the basic question of the age at which the infant follows movement in each direction. Dayton and Jones 1964a, 1964b) found good evidence that newborn infants can pursue a moving series of dots. The presence of optokinetic nystagmus in newborns and young infants also stands as evidence for visual tracking (Doris and Cooper, 1966; Gorman, Cogan, and Gellis, 1959; McGinnis, 1930; Tauber and Koffler, 1966). Beyond these studies only a beginning has been made toward determining infant preference for movement and there have not been any careful studies with techniques refined enough to determine response changes with variation in movement conditions.

One recent study of visual movement preferences in infants between 7 and 24 weeks of age was that of Silfen and Ames (1964). The stimuli were a moving and a stationary vertical belt of black and white checks. At 7 weeks there was no clear preference for movement at any speed; at 16 weeks there was a marked preference for speeds increasing up to the next-to-fastest speed used but dropping at the highest speed. At 24 weeks a pref-

erence was found for the faster speed over the entire range of speeds used. Recognizing that 7-week-old babies might discriminate movement but simply have no preference for it, Silfen and Ames (1964) ran a second experiment using several procedures to find whether infants at 7 weeks response to movement at all. Only an extension in the range of speeds produced a slight but insignificant trend toward greater response to faster movement.

Fantz and Nevis (1967b) also examined preference for movement in 20 infants tested weekly in the first 6 months of life. A rotating red spot on a yellow disc was paired with a complex stationary comparison object made of wire mesh over white wood with holes. The results of the comparison showed that from 2 to 6 weeks of age the 20 subjects preferred the moving stimulus; then preference for the stationary stimulus rose to a peak at about 14 weeks and then declined until there was no preference for either object at about 23 weeks. The finding of preference for movement under 2 months is contrary to the findings in a pilot study of Fantz and Nevis as well as that in the Silfen and Ames study. Variation of color and depth in the Fantz and Nevis study makes simple interpretations hard to come by.

A group of studies have used lights flashed sequentially as stimuli. The lights have been assumed to represent movement but it should be noted at the outset that responses might be to the on-off quality of the stimulus and not to the change in position as such. Kagan and Lewis (1965) and Lewis et al. (1966) studied infant attention with three patterns of blinking lights, along with other stimuli. A group of 32 infants was tested at 6 and 13 months. The patterns were a single blinking light in the center of the visual field, a blinking light moving horizontally across the field, and a blinking light that described a square helix. For all three light patterns the total looking time dramatically decreased over trials. There was no significant difference in looking time among the three light patterns for 6-month-olds, and 64 6-month-old infants run in a second experiment showed essentially the same results except that there was no decrease in looking at the helix over trials. At 13 months the original infants showed a clear preference for the single blinking light over the row and over the helix.

A study by Haith (1966) used suppression of sucking rate as a measure of responsiveness. Haith studied 41 infants from 3 to 5 days of age who were presented with lights that flashed sequentially in a retangular pattern. Suppression of sucking was reliably greater when the light moved than when it was stationary. Cohen (1965) studied newborn preferences and modification of preferences over trials. Lights blinking in 16 positions and in 4 positions were preferred to a single blinking light. It is not clear how Cohen's finding can be made congruent with the observation of Kagan and Lewis (1965a) that a single light blinking was preferred to horizontal or a square pattern in older infants.

A study of the ability of 3-month-old infants to anticipate regular patterns of blinking lights has been reported by Nelson (1968). After several exposures to a horizontal sequence of lights, the babies tended to move their eyes to the place where a light was about to appear.

Distance, depth, and size. As was noted earlier, there exists virtual agreement that one possible index of distance—appropriate convergence—is not available to the newborn (Beasley, 1923b; Feldman, 1920; Ling, 1942; Lucas, 1927; McGinnis, 1930). Indeed, Wickelgren (1967) found that divergence is uniformly present in the first days of life, and, further, that the extent of this divergence varies with the nature of the stimulus (e.g., patterned or plain). In view of such findings, it is difficult to suppose that either retinal disparity or convergence could function at birth as a valid cue for distance. Nor does it seem likely that accommodatory feedback from the ciliary muscles can serve the newborn as an index of distance. Haynes, White, and Held (1965) showed that the newborn does not exhibit variable refraction of the lens as a function of variations in the distance of a test object but, rather, he exhibits fixed refraction on a plane about 8 inches from the eye. Tendencies towards appropriate variable accommodation comparable to that of an adult first begin during the second month and approach perfect performance only in the fourth month. It is possible, however, that the newborn could make use of the retinal consequences of viewing stimuli through a refractively-fixed lens. In such a system, the degree of blurring of a constant, well-defined stimulus beyond the point of fixed refraction would be well correlated with its objective distance. Therefore, one might expect the commonly found preference for patterned stimuli in the newborn to depend on the distance of the stimuli. Fantz, Ordy and Udelf (1962) made observations relevant to such a possibility. They presented infants 1 to 22 weeks of age with a choice between a black and white vertically striped panel and a plain grey panel at each of three test differences—5, 10 and 20 in. from the infant's eyes. The "preferred distance" hypothesis was not supported by the finding that the striped pattern was preferred over the plain grey pattern at all ages and that the relative preferences for pattern was equal at all test distances.

Most reports have indicated that appropriate, stable binocular convergence for objects at different distances improves markedly during the second month (Beasley, 1923b; Feldman, 1920; Ling, 1942; Lucas, 1927; McGinnis, 1930), although the accuracy of measurement in these studies is not sufficient to indicate whether or not the infantile visual system manages binocular fusion to the same degree as does the adult. Advances in the oculomotor system are, however, accompanied by rather marked changes in the infant's response to objects changing distance. White (1963) reported that infants first exhibit partial, irregular eyeblinks to a fast approaching object at 3 weeks of age. From 3 weeks to 14 weeks the effective stimulus drop decreased and the reliability and vigor of the eyeblinks increased. Greenberg, Uzgiris, and Hunt (1968) provided evidence that placing an attractive pattern over the cribs of infants beginning at 5 weeks of age could reduce the age at which the blink-response becomes regular by approximately 3 weeks in comparison with infants not provided with overhead patterning.

Obviously, however, a true distance concept involves much more than mere transitive adjustments in reflex response systems as a function of variations in the distance of a stimulus. And, with the exception of Piaget's (see especially Piaget, 1936) extensive observations of spatial development during infancy, the empirical literature on the perceptual development of distance discrimination remains sparse. Bower (1964) trained infants,

70 to 85 days old at testing, to turn their heads in the presence of a 12-inch cube at a distance of 3 feet. Following training, size of cube and cube distance were varied to determine whether retinal size was the critical variable or whether the infant could respond to absolute size. The pattern of generalization responses led Bower to conclude that the babies had size constancy and could discriminate real distance. Bower (1965b) conducted a similar study with infants 40 to 60 days of age in which the babies saw real cubes or images of the cubes projected on a screen. Discrimination of real distance, independent of retinal size, appeared to occur in both binocular and monocular conditions; however, the discrimination broke down under the "projection" condition. Bower interpreted these results as indicating that motion parallax is the necessary cue for the perception of distance in infants, while pictorial or perspective cues are virtually useless. In still a further report (Bower, 1966c) provided data indicating that binocular parallax or disparity may also be a weak, but significant, cue for distance discrimination at the two-month age level. The Bower studies are unique in suggesting the presence of real size and distance discrimination in infants during the third month of life and merit replication.

The literature on preference for three-dimensional visual stimuli underlines the expansion of the infant's world that takes place during the third month. Fantz (1961a) presented infants between one and six months of age with a solid sphere and a flat circle. Under both monocular and binocular conditions, there was a preference for the sphere when both objects were textured and directly lit. However, under binocular viewing, this relationship was not found for the youngest infants. In further studies, Fantz reported an increasing preference with age for a three-dimensional over a two-dimensional head (Fantz, 1965; Fantz & Nevis, 1967a, 1967b).

Experimental data bearing directly upon visually judged distance and size constancy are rare for children between 3 and 24 months of age. Naturally occurring reaching and grasping, however, have received particular attention (e.g., Bruner, 1969, Halverson, passim; Piaget, 1936; White, 1969) as indicative of an increasing ability on the part of the infant to execute distance-appropriate move-

ments in space. However, the increasing ability of the infant with increasing age to reach or grasp an object reveals little in itself about his ability to discriminate distance because, on the one hand, depth discrimination may precede the requisite manual skill or, on the other, because the ability may reflect only the development of a tendency to move the hand toward an object until contact.

Cruikshank (1941) observed the reaching responses of infants 10- to 50-weeks of age, toward a small rattle at 25 cm. and at 75 cm. from their eyes, and a rattle three times as large as the small rattle at 75 cm. from the infant eyes. She found that between 10 and 14 weeks, 50% of the infants, and at 20 weeks 90% of the infants, reached for the small rattle at 25 cm. Responses to both the large and small rattle at 75 cm., however, were lower than the small rattle at 25 cm. in both age groups. Moreover, with age, responses to the far distance decreased relative to the near distance. Cruikshank concluded that reaching was based on distance rather than retinal size, and that size constancy was present.

Shirley (1933a) reported very similar results for a group of infants presented with a bell in and out of range; between 13 and 19 weeks less than 10% of the infants reached for the bell out of range. From 19 weeks on, there was an increase in reaching out of range which peaked at 22 weeks (70% of the babies) although reaching within range was still more common. The caution that the reaching response may not always provide a true index of the perception of distance is underscored by Shirley's comment that "babies under 6 months reached for a toy that was out of range even though they seemed to recognize that it was beyond their grasp."

Relevant to the older infant's perception of distance and depth are a series of studies indicating a tendency on the part of infants to avoid visually indicated depth when they become capable of crawling (Gibson & Walk, 1960; Walk, 1968; Walk & Dodge, 1962). Moreover, Walk and Dodge (1962; Walk, 1968) reported that a depth gradient will be avoided under monocular views although less powerfully in the early stages of crawling. Scarr and Salapatek (in press) provided additional evidence of the onset of cliff avoidance between 7 and 9 months of age, with an increase in the intensity of this tendency between 7 and 13 months. Fear of depths was rare in crawling infants below 7 months, and was never observed in infants below 7 months of age who did not crawl.

Orientation and slant. Watson (1966a) examined the smiling of infants under six months of age to stimuli varying in spatial orientation. Twenty infants from 12 to 20 weeks of age were each presented with the experimenter's fixed, smiling, and bobbing face in normal orientation and at rotations of 90°, 180°, and 270°. The maximum magnitude of smiling and speed of first smile were considerably greater for the zero orientation of the face than for all other orientations. In a second experiment, infants between 7 and 26 weeks of age were presented a multi-colored cloth mask, mother's face, and stranger's face in three orientations. For both the mother's and the stranger's face, there was more time spent smiling at a zero degree orientation, chiefly by children 14 weeks old, than at a 90-degree or 180-degree orientation. No differences among orientations were found for the mask. Bower (1966b), employing much simpler stimuli, provided data suggesting that both shape constancy and slant perception may be present in infants during the second and third month.

Complexity, form, and faces. A relatively large body of data has been accumulated on the issue of whether or not infants show selective visual attention to patterns of a particular level of complexity. In much of the research there has been the additional attempt to demonstrate a shift upwards, with increasing age, in the level of complexity preferred. For the most part, the literature has produced conflicting results; response measures used to assess visual preference vary, there is often a failure to equate for brightness and color of stimuli, and, in particular, confusion has centered around the definition of visual complexity. Some investigators have attempted to define complexity on the basis of varying *sensory* input provided by stimulation. Thus, patterns with more sides, or more angles, or more contour, or a greater number of distinct elements are generally assumed to be more complex. Other investigators have defined complexity in a more cognitive fashion. Visual complexity is seen as jointly determined by "sensory complexity" and the baby's prior knowledge of or association to the stimulus. Thus, the preference of an infant for a geometrically simple stimulus (e.g., two eye spots) over a rather complex geometric figure at a certain age may be interpreted as a response to greater cognitive complexity because the eye spots for the first time are recognized as defining features of a face.

The distinction between sensory and cognitive complexity is relevant as well to more general questions that can be posed for early perception. First, what is the baby's congenital organization of visual form? What are the givens of form perception? The answers in the literature have not always been unambiguously stated, but several clusters of proposals emerge. The baby initially may respond to some particular element (e.g., a corner or a contour) of the visual display. He may, alternatively, be sensitive to the overall complexity, however defined, of the presented stimulus. Or, and not necessarily in contradiction with the foregoing propositions, the infant may be sensitive to aspects of the environment that are of significance for him; the prime instance, of course, is the human face. Still another congenital strategy for handling visual stimulation may be a responsiveness to discrepancy, to the violation of an expectation.

Tied to the question of initial sensitivity is, of course, the question of the mechanisms for change. How does the child come to perceive the visual world in terms like those of the adult? Although the question is of central theoretical significance and has been treated at some length by theorists of perception (see Gibson, 1969, for a general review), there is little subtlety in the empirical studies addressed to the question of perceptual change. The bulk of the work has turned on the important but insufficient issue of whether or not complex visual functioning is available to the child without specific experience with environmental contingencies.

Not surprisingly, the variety of method that has marked other research with infants holds for the study of complexity and form. Stimuli have been presented singly or in pairs; measures have ranged from human judgment to precise photographic recording; the stimuli themselves are wildly assorted— dots, geometric forms, faces, and intricate constructions, among others. And, throughout the literature, not only of complexity but of perceptual studies with infants more generally, there arises the question of the distinction between preference and discrimination. A baby may have a fully adequate representation of a stimulus but still not provide evidence of his ability to detect it. As usual in the assessment of infantile capacity, there are likely to be many false negative results.

The studies that are reported in the next pages have all been designed to produce observations that will illuminate our understanding of the infant's early responses to visual complexity. Of course, in many of them, the definition of complexity can be stated in terms other than the terms used in reporting the research. To take one oft-noted example, a number of variations in complexity can also be seen as variations in number or length of contours.

Stirnimann (1944) measured differential fixation on a patterned surface as compared to a homogeneous surface and found that infants as young as one day of age looked longer at the patterned surfaces. Berlyne (1958b) presented infants between three and nine months of age with pairs of figures side by side, one of which was judged to be complex and the other simple. He found that the first fixation was significantly more often directed toward the more complex figures. Fantz (1958) found that infants between one week and six months old looked longer at a red checkerboard pattern when it was paired either with a solid red surface of equal area or a solid red surface with less area. However, this preference was consistently shown only after two months of age. Further evidence of preference for pattern was provided by Fantz' (1965) observation of infants between 2 days and 6 months of age who were presented with a number of different arrangements of paper squares. These studies provide evidence that, during the first year of life, there is some tendency for infants to prefer relatively complex, apparently meaningless, two-dimensional patterned visual stimuli over unpatterned stimuli. However, the studies do not permit the determination of preferred levels of complexity or of change in preference with age.

Only a few studies have varied stimulus complexity along a clearly quantifiable dimension. Typically these studies have defined complexity by number of different elements in a stimulus. Spears (1966) presented five regular polygons differing in number of turns and color to four-month old infants. He found no significant visual preferences along either the shape or color dimension alone; with dimensions combined, there was a suggestion of preference predominantly on the basis of color. Hershenson (1964) found that newborns preferred a simple 4-square checkerboard pattern over a 144-square checkerboard but he found no preference for a 16-square checkerboard over a 4-square of a 144-square checkerboard. Hershenson, Munsinger, and Kessen (1965) determined that newborns looked longer at flat outline 10-turn random shapes than at 5-turn shapes. No preference was found in comparisons of 20-turn random shapes with 5- and 10-turn random shapes.

Brennan, Ames, and Moore (1966) studied the visual preferences of infants of three ages for black and white checkerboards of varying numbers of squares. They found that three-week old infants looked at a 2 x 2 checkerboard (Low) longer than at an 8 x 8 checkerboard (Intermediate) and at an 8 x 8 checkerboard longer than at a 24 x 24 checkerboard (High). Eight-week old children showed significantly different preferences in the order Intermediate-High-Low and 14-week old children showed an ordered preference from High to Intermediate to Low. Congruent results were found in a second study in which the stimuli were presented in pairs. The data of Brennan et al. and the Hershenson (1964) findings provide some support for the proposition that infants tend to prefer patterns of a particular level of complexity, and that this preferred level of complexity increases with age. However, the proposition requires demonstration on a wider range of stimuli and for children of a wider range of age.

Additional data, although to some degree ambiguous, provide evidence that the infant organizes form from a very early age on a basis other than mere count of elements. Stirnimann (1944) found that newborns prefer a horizontal line over a circle. Fantz (1964) found clear change from a preference for a red horizontal striped pattern over a red bull's eye before eight weeks to a preference for the bull's eye over the striped pattern from about eight weeks to six months. In Fantz' (1965) study of varying arrangements of squares, patterns were significantly preferred over the plain grey square at all age levels but, somewhat surprisingly, the response to grey increased significantly with age. Occasional changes in preference for the five patterns across age are also difficult to interpret. A regular horizontal-vertical linear arrangement of black squares was looked at longest by infants under two weeks of age but stood fourth for infants of four to six months of age. However, a 6 x 6 checkerboard ranked lowest for infants under two weeks, third highest for infants three to four months old, and second highest for four- to six-month old infants. A comprehensive set of principles has not been adduced to account for these results.

Fantz and Nevis (1967a) presented forty-nine infants from approximately two weeks of age through 22 weeks of age with four patterns of black line segments—a circular bull's eye and the segments in random, radial, and horizontal arrangement. The horizontal pattern was preferred by babies under one month and showed an initial rise in fixation time (from two to six weeks); after two months, the radial and random patterns dropped in preference while the bull's eye remained high. A replication of the study with infants under five days of age showed no differentiation among the four patterns. The preferences of infants between one day and six months for four arrangements of 25 white squares on blue felt were also examined. The patterns were equally fixated by newborn infants, followed by increasing differentiation with age—a radial and a regular diagonal pattern became more preferred, a random pattern remained relatively constant in preference value, and there was a marked, consistent decline in preference for a regular linear arrangement of squares. Longitudinal data from ten university-faculty and ten foundling-home infants, presented with 18 pairs of stimuli of varied complexity once each week between 2 and 24 weeks of age, generally corroborated changing trends in preference noted earlier. Among the many observations reported for the babies was an increasing preference for a circular arrangement of circular stripes over a horizontal arrangement of linear stripes from approxi-

mately six to eight weeks on. The same was true for a checkerboard over a regular lattice arrangement of squares, for a polka dot pattern over a many-turn random shape pattern, and for a red checkerboard over a red square.

In a study of infants between 10 and 13 weeks of age, Graefe (1963) presented two stimuli in a central adjacent position and then moved them apart slowly, noting which stimulus the infant followed visually. Graefe's patterns and the infant's response to them are shown in Figure 3. Although some of the differences obtained are striking they do not lead to clear-cut interpretation.

The emotional reaction and visual orientation of 8-, 9-, and 10-week old infants toward punctate or continuous circular outlines, either regular or grossly distorted, were reported by Lang (1966). At eight weeks of age infants showed no differential perceptual behavior towards the stimuli but, by 10 weeks of age, the babies showed a more relaxed approach to the regular circular forms than to the distorted forms, whether punctate or continuous.

A number of studies have been concerned with the baby's response to visual figures with social significance, especially human faces. Generally, the data indicate that, at birth, patterns with social significance are no more preferred than meaningless geometric figures with approximately the same amount of patterning. However, beyond the first weeks of life, faces, human figures, and other social objects appear to become increasingly capable of attracting attention regardless of the amount of patterning. Stechler (1964) found that newborns preferred a schematic face to a diagonal of three dots and the diagonal to a blank stimulus; however, contour, as well as "faceness," varied in the stimuli. Fantz (1963) found that infants from 10 hours to 5 days of age looked longer at a schematic black and white face than at newsprint, more at newsprint than at a black and white bull's eye, and more at the bull's eye than at a red, white, or yellow plain surface. With another group of infants under one week of age (Fantz, 1966), patterned ovals were preferred to plain ones or ones with fewer features but no consistent differential fixation in favor of faces with features in the correct arrangement as opposed to scrambled faces

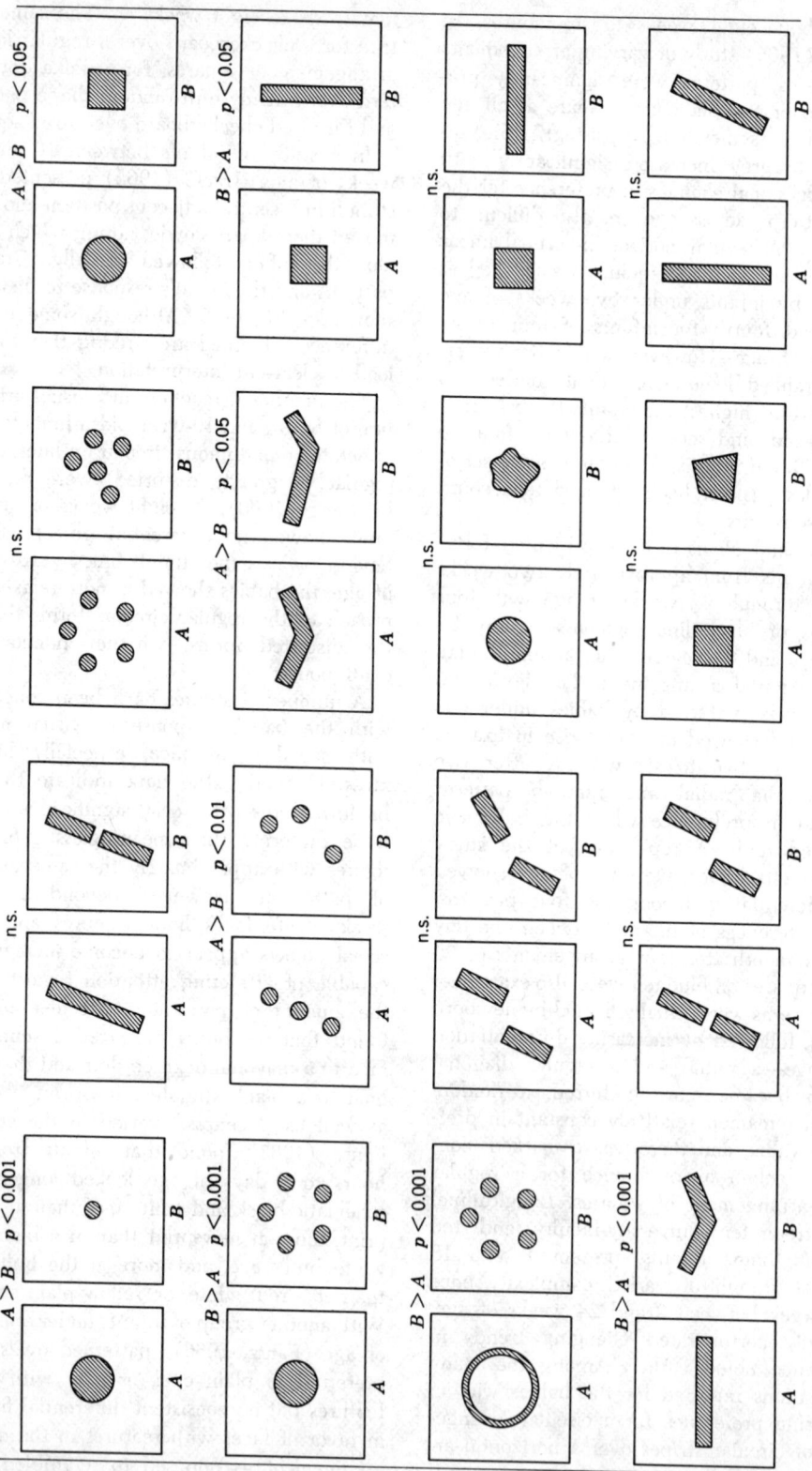

Fig. 3. Pairs of patterns used by Graefe (1963) to study differential following of infants' eyes. Directions of difference in preference and associated levels of significance are shown above each pair of patterns.

was shown. Hershenson (1964) has also reported indifference to faces in newborns.

Fantz and Nevis (1967a, 1967b) found that an oval with "eye spots" correctly located was slightly preferred by institution infants from the first month to the sixth, that a head model with painted features was not reliably preferred over a photograph of the model until 20 weeks of age, and that a correct arrangement of schematic facial features was not reliably preferred over the scrambled features until late in the first six months. Fantz (1961b) had shown earlier that infants from four to six months looked mostly at a diagram of a red and black "real" face, somewhat less often at the same face with its black features scrambled, and largely ignored an oval if its surface merely contained a solid area of black equal to the sum of the features on either of the former figures.

Thomas (1965) recorded length of fixation time of infants ranging in age from 2 through 25 weeks to four stimuli presented in permuted pairs. He found that for the 25 infants from 2 to 14 weeks of age, the order of increasing preference for the stimuli was two broad horizontal stripes, a stylized human face, a stylized clothed human female figure, and a checkerboard pattern. In contrast, the 24 infants between 15 and 26 weeks of age looked increasingly longer at stripes, checkerboard, figure and face. Lewis, Meyers, Kagan, and Grossberg (1963) presented 16 male and 16 female infants 24 weeks of age with six different pictures—a male face, a female face, a bull's eye, a checkerboard, a nursing bottle, and a panda bear. A slight difference was found among the six stimuli with male and female faces attracting somewhat longer fixations than other patterns.

The persisting problem of whether the baby's preference was determined by "faceness" or "complexity" was tackled by Haaf and Bell (1967) by presenting four-month old infants with four stimuli differing in an uncorrelated fashion along the dimensions of degree of "faceness" and amount of pattern detail or complexity. The order of preference, indicated by duration of fixation, perfectly paralleled the ordering of stimuli along the dimension of faceness but not along the dimension of complexity.

A final recent research concern in the realm of infant perception, preference, and discrimination has centered about the age-old question of part- and whole-from perception. In an attempt to discover the features to which newborn infants were attending, Salapatek and Kessen (1965) photographically recorded in some detail their visual scanning of a blank surface and of a plane triangle. The size of the infant's scan pattern was far smaller when a large triangle was in the field than when the field was blank. Moreover, for the large majority of new-borns, the eyes were directed toward an angle. Thus, the newborn can select and maintain a focused scan on a relatively circumscribed feature of a visual pattern. Salapatek (1968) presented newborns with black and white, solid and outline, plane geometric circles and triangles of each of three magnitudes, and with a plain homogeneous control field. In general, the results replicated the earlier study: (1) on the plain surface, infants scanned extensively, more broadly in the horizontal than in the vertical dimension; (2) with the introduction of any geometric figure, there was a significant decrease in the scope of the scan; and (3) many newborns examined only a very limited portion of the figure, even when it was of the smallest magnitude. Unlike the earlier study, however, angles were not necessarily the part of the triangle regularly selected for direct inspection. The infants' scan was more compressed on smaller than on larger figures and there was some tendency for infants to avoid directly inspecting figures whose centers were bright. The studies suggest a rather limited selection of features for inspection by the human newborn. Data recently collected by Bower, however, strongly suggest that by the second or third month of life, the infant may process visually rather extensive general properties of an object (Bower, 1965a, 1965b, 1966c).

Clearly, the child at three months still has a long way to go toward the organization of his visual surround. The foregoing pages have dealt with only the beginnings of the sophistication of vision and the critically important integration of vision with other activities of the infant.

CONCLUSION

This chapter does not provide a map of a well-charted terrain; rather it contains hints about ways through the forest. Much more is known about human infancy in 1969 than when Darwin wrote about his son in 1876 or when Piaget wrote about his daughter in 1927, but the distance gone is a small part of the distance yet to go. The bibliography which follows these pages is a strange mixture of false starts, wise guesses, tedious documentation, clever design, and a few insights that hold hope. Comforting and frustrating, the complexity of the infant continues to mock the simplicity of his students.

References

Abraham, K. Contributions to the theory of the oral character. In *Selected Papers.* London: Hogarth Press, 1949. Pp. 370–392.

Abramson, J. H., Singh, A. R., and Mbambo, V. Antenatal stress and the baby's development. *Archs. Dis. Childh.*, 1961, **36**, 42–49.

Abravanel, E. Developmental changes in the intersensory patterning of space. In *Proc. 75th Ann. Conv. Am. Psychol. Assoc.*, 1967, **2**, 161–162.

Abt, I. A. Breath-holding in infants. *Trans. Am. pediat. Soc.*, 1918, **30**, 25–30.

Abt, I. A., Adler, H. M., and Bartelme, P. The relationship between the onset of speech and intelligence. *J. Am. med. Assoc.*, 1929, **93**, 1351–1355.

Acheson, R. M. The environment and growth of children. *Ir. J. med. Sci.*, 1959, **11**, 11–19.

Acheson, R. M. Maturation of the skeleton. In F. Falkner (Ed.), *Human development*. Philadelphia, Pa.: Saunders, 1966. Pp. 465–502.

Ackerman, D. S. The critical evaluation of the Viennese tests as applied to 200 New York infants six to twelve months old. *Child Dev.*, 1942, **13**, 41–53.

Adams, A. B. Choice of infant feeding technique as a function of maternal personality. *J. consult. Psychol.*, 1959, **23**, 143–146.

Ahrens, R. Beitrag zur Entwicklung des Physiognomie- und Mimikerkennens. *Z. exp. angew. Psychol.*, 1954, **2**, 412–454.

Ahvenainen, E. K., and Veistola, T. Evaluation of the newborn. *Ann. paediat. Fenniae*, 1959, **5**, 27–32.

Ainsworth, M. D. *Deprivation of maternal care. A reassessment of its effects.* Geneva: World Health Organization, 1962.

Ainsworth, M. D. The development of infant-mother interaction among the Ganda. In B. M. Foss (Ed.), *Determinants of infant behavior*. Vol. II. New York: Wiley, 1963.

Ainsworth, M. D. Patterns of attachment behavior shown by the infant in interaction with his mother. *Merrill-Palmer Q.*, 1964, **10**, 51–58.

Albright, R. W., and Albright, J. B. The phonology of a two-year-old child. *Word*, 1956, **12**, 382–390.

Aldrich, C. A. The prevention of poor appetite in children. *Ment. Hyg.*, 1926, **10**, 701–711.

Aldrich, C. A. A new test for hearing in the new-born: the conditioned reflex. *Am. J. Dis. Child.*, 1928, **35**, 36–37.

Aldrich, C. A. Physiology of the cry of the newborn infant. *Proc. Mayo Clin.*, 1945, **20**, 60–62.

Aldrich, C. A., and Hewitt, E. S. A self-regulating feeding program for infants. *J. Am. med. Assoc.*, 1947, **135**, 340–342.

Aldrich, C. A., and Norval, M. A. A developmental graph for the first year of life. *J. Pediat.*, 1946, **29**, 304–308.

Aldrich, C. A., Norval, M. A., Knop, C., and Venegas, F. The crying of newly born babies. IV. A follow-up study after additional nursing care had been provided. *J. Pediat.*, 1946, **28**, 665–670.

Aldrich, C. A., Sung, C., and Knop, C. The crying of newly born babies: I. The community phase. *J. Pediat.*, 1945, **26**, 313–326. (a)

Aldrich, C. A., Sung, C., and Knop, C. The crying of newly born babies: II. The individual phase. *J. Pediat.*, 1945, **27**, 89–96. (b)

Aldrich, C. A., Sung, C., and Knop, C. The crying of newly born babies. III. The early period at home. *J. Pediat.*, 1945, **27**, 428–435. (c)

Aldrich, C. G., and Doll, E. A. Comparative intelligence of idiots and normal infants. *J. genet. Psychol.*, 1931, **39**, 227–257.

Alexander, G. Die Reflexerregbarkeit des Ohrlabyrinthes am menschlichen Neugeborenen. *Z. Sinnesphysiol.*, 1911, **45**, 153–196.

Allen, C. N. Bibliographies in child study and developmental psychology. *Psychol. Bull.*, 1931, **28**, 277–296. (a)

Allen, C. N. Individual differences in delayed reaction of infants. A study of sex differences in early retentiveness. *Archs. Psychol.*, 1931, **19**(127). (b)

Almy, M. *Child development.* New York: Henry Holt, 1955.

Alpert, A., Neubauer, P. B., and Weil, A. P. Unusual variations in drive endowment. *Psychoanal. Study Child.*, 1956, **11**, 125–163.

Ambrose, A. The age of onset of ambivalence in early infancy: indications from the study of laughing. *J. Child Psychol. Psychiat.*, 1963, **4**, 167–181.

Ambrose, J. A. The changing responsiveness of infants to the presence of an adult. *Bull. Br. Psychol. Soc.*, 1957, **32**.

Ambrose, J. A. The development of the smiling response in early infancy. In B. M. Foss, (Ed.), *Determinants of infant behavior.* New York: Wiley, 1961. Pp. 179–196.

Amen, E. W. Individual differences in apperceptive reaction: a study of the response of preschool children to pictures. *Genet. Psychol. Monogr.*, 1941, **23**, 319–385.

Ames, L. B. The sequential patterning of prone progression in the human infant. *Genet. Psychol. Monogr.*, 1937, **19**, 409–460.

Ames, L. B. Some relationships between stair climbing and prone progression. *J. genet. Psychol.*, 1939, **54**, 313–325. (a)

Ames, L. B. Precursor signs of plantigrade progression in the human infant. *J. genet. Psychol.*, 1939, **55**, 439–442. (b)

Ames, L. B. The constancy of psycho-motor tempo in individual infants. *J. genet. Psychol.*, 1940, **57**, 445–450.

Ames, L. B. Motor correlates of infant crying. *J. genet. Psychol.*, 1941, **59**, 239–247.

Ames, L. B. Supine leg and foot postures in the human infant in the first year of life. *J. genet. Psychol.*, 1942, **61**, 87–107.

Ames, L. B. Early individual differences in visual and motor behavior patterns: a comparative study of two normal infants by the method of cinemanalysis. *J. genet. Psychol.*, 1944, **65**, 219–226.

Ames, L. B. Free drawing and completion drawing: a comparative study of preschool children. *J. genet. Psychol.*, 1945, **66**, 161–165.

Ames, L. B. Bilaterality. *J. genet. Psychol.*, 1949, **75**, 45–50. (a)

Ames, L. B. Development of interpersonal smiling responses in the preschool years. *J. genet. Psychol.*, 1949, **74**, 273–291. (b)

Ames, L. B. The sense of self of nursery school children as manifested by their verbal behavior. *J. genet. Psychol.*, 1952, **81**, 193–232.

Ames, L. B. Longitudinal survey of child Rorschach responses: younger subjects two to ten years. *Genet. Psychol. Monogr.*, 1960, **61**, 229–289.

Ames, L. B., and Learned, J. Imaginary companions and related phenomena. *J. genet. Psychol.*, 1946, **69**, 147–167.

Ames, L. B., and Learned, J. The development of verbalized space in the young child. *J. genet. Psychol.*, 1948, **72**, 63–84.

Ames, L. B., and Learned, J. Developmental trends in child kaleidoblock responses. *J. genet. Psychol.*, 1954, **84**, 237–270.

Ames, L. B., Learned, J., Metraux, R. W., and Walker, R. N. *Child Rorschach responses: developmental trends from two to ten years.* New York: Hoeber, 1952.

Ames, L. B., Learned, J., Metraux, R. W., and Walker, R. N. Development of perception in the young child as observed in responses to the Rorschach Test blots. *J. genet. Psychol.*, 1953, **82**, 183–204.

Anderson, J. E. Methods of child psychology. In L. Carmichael (Ed.), *Manual of child psychology.* (2nd ed.) New York: Wiley, 1954.

Anderson, J. E. Child development: an historical perspective. *Child Dev.*, 1956, **27**, 181–196.

Anderson, L. D. The predictive value of infancy tests in relation to intelligence at five years. *Child Dev.*, 1939, **10**, 203–212.

Anderson, L. D. A longitudinal study of the effects of nursery-school training on successive intelligence-test ratings. *39th Yb. Natn. Soc. Stud. Educ.*, Part II, 1940. Pp. 3–10.

Anderson, R. B., and Rosenblith, J. F. Light sensitivity in the neonate: a preliminary report. *Biologia Neonat.*, 1964, **7**, 83–94.

André-Thomas. Ontogenèse de la vie psycho-affective et de la douleur. *L'Encéphale*, 1954, **43**(4), 289–311.

André-Thomas. L'équilibre et la fonction labyrinthique chez le nouveau-né et le nourrisson. *L'Encéphale*, 1955, **44**, 97–137.

André-Thomas. Integration in the infant. *Cerebral Palsy Bull.*, 1959, **1**(8), 3–12.

André-Thomas and Autgaerden, S. *Psycho-affectivité des premiers mois du nourrisson: Evolution des rapports de la motilité, de la connaissance, et de l'affectivité.* Paris: Masson, 1959.

André-Thomas, Chesni, Y., and Saint-Anne-Dargassies, S. *The neurological examination of the infant.* London: Medical Advisory Committee of the National Spastics Society, 1960.

Anson, B. J. Development of the auditory ossicles. *Laryngoscope, St. Louis*, 1946, **56**, 561–569.

Antonov, A. N. Physiology and pathology of the newborn: bibliography of the material for the period 1930–1940. *Monogr. Soc. Res. Child Dev.*, 1947, **10**, 1x + 217.

Apgar, V. Proposal for new method of evaluation of newborn infants. *Anesth. Analg.*, 1953, **32**, 260–267.

Apgar, V., Girdany, B. R., McIntosh, R., and Taylor, H. C., Jr. Neonatal anoxia: I. A study of the relation of oxygenation at birth to intellectual development. *Pediatrics*, 1955, **15**, 653–662.

Apgar, V., Holaday, D. A., James, L. S., Weisbrot, I. M., and Berrien, C. Evaluation of the newborn infant: second report. *J. Am. med. Assoc.*, 1958, **168**, 1985–1988.

Apgar, V., and James, L. S. Further observations on the newborn scoring system. *Am. J. Dis. Child.*, 1962, **104**(4), 419–428.

Ardran, G. M., and Kemp, F. H. A correlation between sucking pressures and the movement of the tongue. *Acta, Pediat.*, 1959, **48**, 261–272.

Ardran, G. M., Kemp, F. H., and Lind, J. A cineradiographic study of bottle feeding. *Br. J. Radiol.*, 1958, **31**, 11–22. (a)

Ardran, G. M., Kemp, F. H., and Lind, J. A cineradiographic study of breast feeding. *Br. J. Radiol.*, 1958, **31**, 156–162. (b)

Aronfreed, J. The origin of self-criticism. *Psychol. Rev.*, 1964, **71**(3), 193–218.

Aronovitch, G. On the nature of the cremasteric reflex. *J. nerv. ment. Dis.*, 1926, **64**, 235–240.

Arrington, R. E. *Interrelations in the behavior of young children*. New York: Teachers College, 1932.

Arvis, P. Contribution à l'étude de l'imitation chez l'enfant. *J. Psychol. norm. Pathol.*, 1959, **56**, 327–335.

Aserinsky, E., and Kleitman, N. A motility cycle in sleeping infants as manifested by ocular and gross bodily activity. *J. appl. Physiol.*, 1955, **8**, 11–18.

Ausubel, D. P. *Theory and problems of child development*. New York: Grune & Stratton, 1958.

Ausubel, D. P. A critique of Piaget's theory of the ontogenesis of motor behavior. *J. genet. Psychol.*, 1966, **109**, 119–122.

Avery, M. E. Some effects of altered environments: relationships between space medicine and adaptation at birth. *Pediatrics*, 1965, **35**, 345–354.

Avery, M. E., and O'Doherty, N. Effects of body tilting on the resting end—expiratory position of new born infants. *Pediatrics*, 1962, **29**, 255–260.

Babinski, J. Sur le réflexe cutané-plantaire dans certaines affections organiques du système nerveux central. *C. r. Séanc. Soc. Biol.*, 1896, **48**, 207–208.

Babinski, J. Du phénomène des orteils et de sa valeur sémiologique. *Sem. méd.*, 1898, **18**, 321–322.

Babinski, J. De l'abduction des orteils (signe de l'éventail). *Rev. neurol.*, 1903, **11**, 1205–1206.

Babinski, J. Réflexes de défense. *Rev. neurol.*, 1915, **27**, 145–155.

Babinski, J. Réflexes de défense. *Rev. neurol.*, 1922, **38**, 1049–1082.

Babkin, P. S. The establishment of reflex activity in early postnatal life. In *Central nervous system & behavior*, 3rd Conf. on CNS and Behav., Princeton, N. J., 1960. U.S. Dept. HEW, PHS. (OTS 62–13772.) Pp. 24–31.

Babska, Z. Formirovanie otozhdestvleniia vida predmitov u detei vtorogo i tretago goda zhizni. *Vop. Psikhol.*, 1959, **5**, 131–138.

Bakwin, H. Loneliness in infants. *Am. J. Dis. Child.*, 1942, **63**, 30–40.

Bakwin, H. Poor appetite in the newborn and young infant. *J. Pediat.*, 1953, **42**, 505–508.

Bakwin, H. Early infantile autism. *J. Pediat.*, 1954, **45**, 492–497.

Bakwin, H., and Bakwin, R. M. Body build in infants. I. The technique of measuring the external dimensions of the body in infants. *J. clin. Invest.*, 1931, **10**, 369–376. (a)

Bakwin, H., and Bakwin, R. M. Body build in infants. II. The proportions of the external dimensions of the healthy infant during the first year of life. *J. clin. Invest.* 1931, **10**, 377–403. (b)

Bakwin, H., and Bakwin, R. M. Body build in infants. V. Anthropometry in the new-born. *Hum. Biol.*, 1934, **6**, 612–626.

Bakwin, H., and Patrick, T. W. The weight of Negro infants. *J. Pediat.*, 1934, **24**, 405–407.

Bakwin, R. M. Similarities and differences in identical twins. *Ped. Sem.*, 1930, **38**, 373–397.

Baldenweck, L., and Guy-Arnaud. Valeur fonctionelle du labyrinthe vestibulaire chez le nouveau-né. *Presse Médicale, Jan.-Juin*, 1940, **48**, 47–49.

Baldwin, A. L. *Behavior and development in childhood*. New York: Dryden Press, 1955.

Baldwin, A. L. *Theories of child development*. New York: Wiley, 1967.

Baldwin, J. M. *Dictionary of philosophy and psychology.* London: MacMillan, 1901.

Baldwin, J. M. *Mental development in the child and the race.* London: MacMillan, 1906.

Baliassnikowa, N. J., and Model, M. M. Zur Neurologie des Saugens. Z. *Kinderforsch,* 1931–1932, **39,** 1–16.

Balikov, H. Functional impairment of the sensorium as a result of normal adaptive processes. *Psychoanal. Study Child,* 1960, **15,** 235–242.

Balint, E. On being empty of oneself. *Int. J. Psychoanal.,* 1963, **44,** 470–480.

Balint, M. Individual differences of behavior in early infancy, and an objective method for recording them: I. Approach and the method of recording. *J. genet. Psychol.,* 1948, **73,** 57–79. (a)

Balint, M. Individual differences of behavior in early infancy, and an objective method for recording them: II. Results and conclusions. *J. genet. Psychol.,* 1948, **73,** 81–117. (b)

Baltes, P. B. Longitudinal and cross-sectional sequences in the study of age and generation effects. *Hum. Dev.,* 1968, **11,** 145–171.

Banham, K. M. The development of affectionate behavior in infancy. *J. genet. Psychol.,* 1950, **76,** 283–289.

Barany, R. Über einige Augen- und Halsmuskelreflexe bei Neugeborenen. *Acta otofaryngol.,* 1918, **1,** 97–102.

Barany, R. Zur Klinik und Theorie des Eisenbahn-Nystagmus. *Arch. Augenheilk.,* 1921, **88,** 139–142.

Barnet, A. B. Maturation of electroencephalographic evoked potentials. AD-437 930. Office of Technical Services, U. S. Dept. of Commerce, 1964, 18.

Barnet, A. B., and Goodwin, R. Averaged evoked electroencephalographic responses to clicks in the human newborn. *Electroenceph. clin. Neurophysiol.,* 1965, **18,** 441–449.

Barnet, A. B., Lodge, A., and Armington, J. C. Electroretinogram in newborn human infants. *Science,* 1965, **148,** 651–654.

Barry, H., III, Bacon, M. K., and Child, I. L. A cross-cultural survey of some sex differences in socialization. *J. abnorm. soc. Psychol.,* 1957, **55,** 327–332.

Bartels, M. Pupillenverhältnisse bei Neugeborenen. Z. *Augenheilk.,* 1904, **12,** 638–644.

Bartels, M. Über die Regulierung der Augenstellung durch den Ohrenapparat. *Albrecht. v. Graefes Arch. Ophthal.,* 1910, **76,** 1–97.

Bartels, M. Über Augenbewegungen bei Neugeborenen. *Dt. med. Wschr.,* 1932, **58,** 1477–1478.

Barth, H. Untersuchungen zur Physiologie des Saugens bei normalen und pathologischen Brustkindern. Z. *Kinderheilk.,* 1914, **10,** 129.

Bartoshuk, A. K. Human neonatal cardiac acceleration to sound: habituation and dishabituation. *Percept. mot. Skills,* 1962, **15,** 15–27.(a)

Bartoshuk, A. K. Response decrement with repeated elicitation of human neonatal cardiac acceleration to sound. *J. comp. physiol. Psychol.,* 1962, **55,** 9–13. (b)

Bartoshuk, A. K. Human neonatal cardiac responses to sound: a power function. *Psychonom. Sci.,* 1964, **1,** 151–152. (a)

Bartoshuk, A. K. Human neonatal EEG: frequency analysis of awake and asleep samples from four areas. *Psychonom. Sci.,* 1964, **1,** 281–282. (b)

Bartoshuk, A. K., and Tennant, J. M. Human neonatal EEG correlates of sleep-wakefulness and neural maturation. *J. Psychiat. Res.,* 1964, **2,** 73–83.

Basan, L. I. A method for the examination of higher nervous activity in infants under natural conditions. *Pavlov. J. higher nerv. Activ.,* 1960, **10,** 853–857.

Bauer, J. Das Kriechphänomen des Neugeborenen. *Klin. Woch.,* 1926, **5,** 1468–1469.

Bayley, N. A study of the crying of infants during mental and physical tests. *J. genet. Psychol.*, 1932, **40**, 306–329.

Bayley, N. *The California first-year mental scale*. Berkeley: University of California Press, 1933. (a)

Bayley, N. Mental growth during the first three years: a developmental study of sixty-one children by repeated tests. *Genet. Psychol. Monogr.*, 1933, **14**, 1–92. (b)

Bayley, N. The development of motor abilities during the first three years. *Monogr. Soc. Res. Child Dev.*, 1935, No. 1. Pp. 1–26.

Bayley, N. *The California Infant Scale of Motor Development*. Berkeley: University of California Press, 1936.

Bayley, N. *Studies in the development of young children*. Berkeley: University of California Press, 1940. (a)

Bayley, N. Mental growth in young children. *39th Yb. Nat. Soc. Stud. Educ.*, Part II, 1940, 11–47. (b)

Bayley, N. Factors influencing the growth of intelligence in young children. *39th Yb. Nat. Soc. Stud. Educ.*, Part II, 1940, 49–79. (c)

Bayley, N. Tables for predicting adult height from skeletal age and present height. *J. Pediat.*, 1946, **28**, 49–64.

Bayley, N. Consistency and variability in the growth of intelligence from birth to eighteen years. *J. genet. Psychol.*, 1949, **75**, 165–196.

Bayley, N. Some increasing parent-child similarities during the growth of children. *J. educ. Psychol.*, 1954, **45**, 1–21.

Bayley, N. Individual patterns of development. *Child Dev.*, 1956, **27**, 45–74.

Bayley, N. Comparisons of mental and motor test scores for ages 1–15 months by sex, birth order, race, geographical location, and education of parents. *Child Dev.*, 1965, **36**, 379–411. (a)

Bayley, N. Research in child development: A longitudinal perspective. *Merrill-Palmer Q.*, 1965, **11**, 183–208. (b)

Bayley, N., and Davis, F. C. Growth changes in bodily size and proportions during the first three years: a developmental study of 61 children by repeated measurements. *Biometrika*, 1935, **27**, 26–87.

Bayley, N., and Jones, H. E. Environmental correlates of mental and motor development: a cumulative study from infancy to six years. *Child Dev.*, 1937, **8**, 329–341.

Bayley, N., and Schaefer, E. S. Correlations of maternal and child behavior with the development of mental abilities: data from the Berkeley Growth Study, *Monogr. Soc. Res. Child Dev.*, 1964, No. 97.

Bayley, N., and Stolz, H. R. Maturational changes in rectal temperatures of 61 infants from 1 to 36 months. *Child Dev.*, 1937, **8**, 195–206.

Beadle, K. R., and Crowell, D. H. Neonatal electrocardiographic responses to sound: methodology. *J. Speech Hear. Res.*, 1962, **5**, 112–123.

Bean, C. H. An unusual opportunity to investigate the psychology of language. *J. genet. Psychol.*, 1932, **40**, 181–202.

Beasley, W. C. Visual pursuit in 109 white and 142 Negro newborn infants. *Child Dev.*, 1933, **4**, 106–120. (a)

Beasley, W. C. An investigation of related problems in the vision of newborn infants. *Psychol. Bull.*, 1933, **30**, 626. (b)

Bechterew, W. Über die objective Untersuchung der kindlichen Psyche. *Russk. Wratch.*, 1908. (Abstr. in *Folia Neuro-biol.*, 1908, **2**, 362–366).

Becker, J. Über Haut und Schweissdrüsen bei Foeten und Neugeborenen. *Z. Kinderheilk.*, 1921, **30**, 3–20.

Becker, J. Über periphere Nervenendigungen in den äuzeren Genitalien von Neugeborenen. *Z. Kinderheilk.*, 1933, **55**, 264–268.

Beckey, R. E. A study of certain factors related to retardation of speech. *J. Speech Disord.*, 1942, **7**, 223–249.

Behrens, M. L. Child rearing and the character structure of the mother. *Child Dev.*, 1954, **25**, 225–238.

Beitel, L. Testergebnisse bei frühgeborenen Kindern. *Z. Kinderheilk.*, 1940, **61**, 533–547.

Bell, R. Q. Convergence: an accelerated longitudinal approach. *Child Dev.*, 1953, **24**, 145–152.

Bell, R. Q. Relations between behavior manifestations in the human neonate. *Child Dev.*, 1960, **31**, 463–477.

Bell, R. Q. Some factors to be controlled in studies of the behavior of newborns. *Biologia Neonat.*, 1963, **5**, 200–214.

Bell, R. Q. Level of arousal in breast-fed and bottle-fed human newborns. *Psychosom. Med.*, 1966, **28**, 177–180.

Bell, R .Q., and Costello, N. S. Three tests for sex differences in tactile sensitivity in the newborn. *Biologia Neonat.*, 1964, **7**, 335–347.

Bell, R. Q., and Darling, J. F. The prone head reaction in the human neonate: relation with sex and tactile sensitivity. *Child. Dev.*, 1965, **36**, 943–949.

Beller, E. K. Dependency and autonomous achievement striving related to orality and anality in early childhood. *Child Dev.*, 1957, **28**, 287–315.

Beltran, J. R. La psicología experimental en el estudio de los problemas del niño recién nacido. In E. Mouchet (Ed.), *Temas actuales de psicología normal y patológica*. Buenos Aires: Editorial Médico-Quirúrgica, 1945, 71–86.

Bendix, B. Der Babinski-Reflex bei Kindern der ersten Lebenszeit. *Z. Kinderheilk.*, 1931, **51**, 93–98.

Benedek, T. Adaptation to reality in early infancy. *Psychoanal. Q.*, 1938, **7**, 200–214.

Benedek, T. The psychosomatic implications of the primary unit: mother-child. *Am. J. Orthopsychiat.*, 1949, **19**, 642–654.

Benedict, F. G., and Talbot, F. B. *The gaseous metabolism of infants with special reference to its relation to pulse-rate and muscular activity*. Washington, D. C.: Carnegie Inst., 1914, No. 201.

Benedict, F. G., and Talbot, F. B. The physiology of the newborn infant. Character and amount of katabolism. Washington, D. C.: Carnegie Inst., 1915, No. 223.

Benedict, R. Child rearing in certain European countries. *Am. J. Orthopsychiat.*, 1949, **19**, 342–350.

Benjamin, E. The period of resistance in early childhood. *Am. J. Dis. Child.*, 1942, **63**, 1019–1079.

Bennett, I., and Hellman, I. Psychoanalytic material related to observations in early development. *Psychoanal. Study Child*, 1951, **6**, 307–324.

Beres, D., and Obers, S. J. The effects of extreme deprivation in infancy on psychic structure in adolescence: a study in ego development. *Psychoanal. Study Child*, 1950, **5**, 212–235.

Bergeron, M. Les manifestations motrices chez l'enfant de la naissance à trois mois. *Ann. Méd. Psychol.*, 1938, **96**, 367–372.

Bergeron, M. Esquisse du développement moteur chez l'enfant au cours des dix premiers mois. *Enfance*, 1948, **1**, 256–261.

Bergeron, M. *Psychologie du premier âge*. Paris: Presses Universitaires de France, 1951.

Bergman, P., and Escalona, S. K. Unusual sensitivities in very young children. *Psychoanal. Study Child*, 1949, **4**, 333–352.

Bergman, P., Malasky, C., and Zahn, T. Development changes in sucking strength and manual strength. *Percept. mot. Skills*, 1966, **23**, 595–606.

Berlyne, D. E. The influence of complexity and novelty in visual figures on orienting responses. *J. exp. Psychol.*, 1958, **55**, 289–296.

Berlyne, D. E. The influence of the albedo and complexity of stimuli on visual fixation in the human infant. *Br. J. Psychol.*, 1958, **49**, 315–318.

Berlyne, D. E. *Conflict, arousal, and curiosity.* New York: McGraw-Hill, 1960.

Berman, P. W., Graham, F. K., Eichman, P. L., and Waisman, H. A. Psychologic and neurologic status of diet-treated phenylketonuric children and their siblings. *Pediatrics*, 1961, **28**, 924–934.

Berman, P. W., Waisman, H. A., and Graham, F. K. Intelligence in treated phenylketonuric children: a developmental study. *Child Dev.*, 1966, **37**, 731–747.

Bernard, J. Prediction from human fetal measures. *Child Dev.*, 1964, **35**, 1243–1248.

Bernard, J., and Sontag, L. W. Fetal reactivity to tonal stimulation: a preliminary report. *J. genet. Psychol.*, 1947, **70**, 205–210.

Bernstein, A. Some relations between techniques of feeding and training during infancy and certain behavior in childhood. *Genet. Psychol. Monogr.*, 1955, **51**, 3–44.

Bersot, H. Variabilité et corrélations organiques. Nouvelle étude du réflexe plantaire. *Schweiz. Arch. Neurol. Psychiat.*, 1919, **4**, 277–323; **5**, 305–324.

Bersot, H. Développement réactionnel et réflexe plantaire du bébé né avant terme à celui de deux ans. *Schweiz. Arch. Neurol. Psychiat.*, 1920, 1921, **7**, 212–231; **8**, 47–74.

Bertoye, P., and Dumorand, C. Troubles de croissance du nourrisson par choc affectif. *Revue Hyg. Méd. soc.*, 1957, **5**, 187–189.

Bijou, S. W., and Baer, D. M. *Child development.* New York: Appleton-Century-Crofts, 1961.

Binet, A. Recherches sur les mouvements chez quelques jeunes enfants. *Rev. Philos.*, 1890, **29**, 297–309. (a)

Binet, A. Perceptions d'enfants. *Rev. Philos.*, 1890, **30**, 582–611. (b)

Binet, A. La peur chez les enfants. *L'Année Psychol.*, 1895, **2**, 223–254.

Binet, A., and Simon, T. Méthodes nouvelles pour un diagnostic du niveau intellectuel des anormaux. *L'Année Psychol.*, 1905, **11**, 191–244.

Birch, H. G., Thomas, A., Chess, S., and Hertzig, M. E. Individuality in the development of children. *Dev. Med. child Neurol.*, 1962, 4(4), 370–379.

Birdsong, McL., and Edmunds, J. E. Harlequin color change of the newborn. Report of a case. *Obstet. Gynec.*, 1956, **7**, 518–521.

Birns, B. Individual differences in human neonates' responses to stimulation. *Child Dev.*, 1965, **36**, 249–256.

Birns, B., Blank, M., and Bridger, W. H. The effectiveness of various soothing techniques on human neonates. *Psychosom. Med.*, 1966, **28**, 316–322.

Birns, B., Blank, M., Bridger, W. H., and Escalona, S. K. Behavioral inhibition in neonates produced by auditory stimuli. *Child Dev.*, 1965, **36**, 639–645.

Blanton, M. G. The behavior of the human infant during the first thirty days of life. *Psychol. Rev.*, 1917, **24**, 456–483.

Blatz, W. E., and Millichamp, D. A. The development of emotion in the infant. *Univ. Toronto Stud. Child Dev.*, 1935, No. 4.

Blau, T. H., and Blau, L. R. The sucking reflex: the effects of long feeding vs. short feeding on the behavior of a human infant. *J. abnorm. soc. Psychol.*, 1955, **51**, 123–125.

Blauvelt, H. Capacity of a human neonate reflex to signal future responses by present action. *Child Dev.*, 1962, **33**, 21–28.

Blauvelt, H. Differential latency of oral response on the first day of life. *J. genet. Psychol.*, 1964, **104**, 199–205.

Blauvelt, H., and McKenna, J. Capacity of the human newborn for mother-infant interaction. II. The temporal dimensions of a neonate response. *Psychiat. Res. Rep.*, 1960, **13**, 128–147.

Blauvelt, H., and McKenna, J. Mother-neonate interaction: capacity of the human newborn for orientation. In B. M. Foss (Ed.), *Determinants of infant behavior*. New York: Wiley, 1961.

Bliss, D. Thumb and finger sucking. *N. Z. dent. J.*, 1945, **41**, 103–104.

Bloch, O. Notes sur le langage d'un enfant. *Mém. Soc. Linguistique Paris*, 1913, **18**, 37–59.

Bloch, O. Les premiers stades du langage de l'enfant. *J. Psychol. norm. Path.*, 1921, **18**, 693–712.

Bloch, O. La phrase dans le langage de l'enfant. *J. Psychol. norm. Path.*, 1924, **21**, 18–43.

Block, J. Personality characteristics associated with fathers' attitudes toward child-rearing. *Child Dev.*, 1955, **26**, 41–48.

Bloom, B. S. *Stability and change in human characteristics*. New York: Wiley, 1965.

Bohn, W. E. First steps in verbal expression. *Ped. Sem.*, 1914, **21**, 578–595.

Bonaventura, E. Lo studio sperimentale del carattere nel bambino lattante. *Riv. psicol. norm. patol.*, 1936, **32**, 37–53.

Boon, A. A. Aspekte des Kinderspiels. *Prax. Kinderpsychol. Kinderpsychiat.*, 1952, **1**, 217–227.

Bordley, J. E., and Hardy, W. G. A study in objective audiometry with the use of a psychogalvanometric response. *Ann. Otol. Rhinol. Lar.*, 1949, **58**, 751–760.

Borkowski, W. J., and Bernstine, R. L. Electroencephalography of the fetus. *Neurology*, 1955, **5**, 362–365.

Bostock, J., and Shackleton, M. G. Enuresis and toilet training. *Med. J. Aust.*, 1951, **2**, 110–113.

Boulanger-Balleyguier, G. L'évolution de l'irritation pendant la première année. *Psychologie Française*, 1965, **10**, 369–375.

Bower, T. G. R. Discrimination of depth in premotor infants. *Psychon. Sci.*, 1964, **1**, 368.

Bower, T. G. R. The determinants of perceptual unity in infancy. *Psychon. Sci.*, 1965, **3**, 323–324. (a)

Bower, T. G. R. Stimulus variables determining space perception in infants. *Science*, 1965, **149**, 88–89. (b)

Bower, T. G. R. Heterogeneous summation in infants. *Anim. Behav.*, 1966, **14**, 395–398. (a)

Bower, T. G. R. Slant perception and shape constancy in infants. *Science*, 1966, **151**, 832–834. (b)

Bower, T. G. R. The visual world of infants. *Sci. Am.*, 1966, 80–92. (c)

Bower, T. G. R. The development of object-permanence: some studies of existence constancy. *Percept. Psychophys.*, 1967, **2**, 411–412.

Bowlby, J. The influence of early environment in the development of neurosis and neurotic character. *Int. J. Psychoanal.*, 1940, **21**, 154–178.

Bowlby, J. Some pathological processes set in train by early mother-child separation. *J. Ment. Sci.*, 1953, **99**, 265–272.

Bowlby, J. The nature of the child's tie to his mother. *Int. J. Psychoanal.*, 1958, **39**, 350–373.

Bowlby, J. Note on Dr. Lois Murphy's paper. *Int. J. Psychoanal.*, 1964, **45**, 44–46.

Bowlby, J. *Maternal care and mental health*. New York: Schocken, 1966.

Bowlby, J., Ainsworth, M., Boston, M., and Rosenbluth, D. The effects of mother-child separation: a follow-up study. *Br. J. med. Psychol.*, 1956, **29**, 211–247.

Bowles, M. E. Emotions of deaf compared with those of hearing children. *Ped. Sem.*, 1895, **3**, 330–.

Boyd, W. The beginnings of syntactical speech: a study in child linguistics. *Child Study*, 1913, **6**, 21–24; 47–51.

Boyd, W. The development of a child's vocabulary. *Ped. Sem.*, 1914, **21**, 95–124.

Boyd, W. The development of sentence structure in childhood. *Br. J. Psychol.*, 1927, **17**, 181–191.

Brackbill, Y. Extinction of the smiling response in infants as a function of reinforcement. *Child Dev.*, 1958, **29**, 115–124.

Brackbill, Y. Experimental research with children in the Soviet Union: report of a visit. *Am. Psychologist*, 1960, **15**, 226–233.

Brackbill, Y. Research and clinical work with children. In R. Bauer (Ed.), *Some views on Soviet psychology*. Washington. D. C.: American Psychological Association, 1962.

Brackbill, Y. (Ed.) *Research in infant behavior: a cross-indexed bibliography.* Baltimore, Md.: Williams and Wilkins, 1964.

Brackbill, Y. (Ed.) *Infancy and early childhood: a handbook and guide to human development*. New York: Free Press, 1967.

Brackbill, Y., Adams, G., Crowell, D. H., and Gray, M. L. Arousal level in neonates and preschool children under continuous auditory stimulation. *J. exp. child Psychol.*, 1966, **4**, 178–188.

Brackbill, Y., Fitzgerald, H. E., and Lintz, L. M. A developmental study of classical conditioning. *Monogr. Soc. Res. child Dev.*, 1967, **32,** Whole No. 116.

Brackbill, Y., and Thompson, G. G. *Behavior in infancy and early childhood: a book of readings*. New York: Free Press, 1967.

Braen, B. B. An evaluation of the Northwestern infant intelligence test: Test B. *J. consult. Psychol.*, 1961, **25**, 245–248.

Brain, W. R., and Curran, R. D. The grasp-reflex of the foot. *Brain*, 1932, **55**, 347–356.

Brainard, P. P. Some observations of infant learning and instincts. *Ped. Sem.*, 1927, **34**, 230–254.

Braunschwig, M., and Braunschwig, G. *Notre enfant: journal d'un père et d'une mère*. Paris: Hachette, 1913.

Brazelton, T. B. Sucking in infancy. *Pediatrics*, 1956, **17**, 400–404.

Brazelton, T. B. Psychophysiologic reactions in the neonate. II. Effect of maternal medication on the neonate and his behavior. *J. Pediat.*, 1961, **58**, 513–518.

Brazelton, T. B. A child-oriented approach to toilet training. *Pediatrics*, 1962, **29**, 121–128. (a)

Brazelton, T. B. Crying in infancy. *Pediatrics*, 1962, **29**, 579–588. (b)

Brazelton, T. B. Observations of the neonate. *J. Am. Acad. Child Psychiat.*, 1962, **1**, 38–58. (c)

Brazelton, T. B. The early mother-infant adjustment. *Pediatrics*, 1963, **32**, 931–937.

Brazelton, T. B., Scholl, M. L., and Robey, J. S. Visual responses in the newborn. *Pediatrics*, 1966, **37**, 284–290.

Breckenridge, M. E., and Murphy, M. *Growth and development of the young child*. Philadelphia, Pa.: Saunders, 1963.

Bregman, E. O. An attempt to modify the emotional attitudes of infants by the conditioned response technique. *J. genet. Psychol.*, 1934, **45**, 169–198.

Brennan, W., Ames, E. W., and Moore, R. W. Age differences in infants' attention to patterns of different complexities. *Science*, 1966, **151**, 354–356.

Brian, C. R., and Goodenough, F. L. The relative potency of color and form perception at various ages. *J. exp. Psychol.*, 1929, **12**, 197–213.

Bridger, W. H. Sensory habituation and discrimination in the human neonate. *Am. J. Psychiat.*, 1961, **117**, 991–996.

Bridger, W. H. Ethological concepts and human development. Chapter 12 in *Recent Advances in Biological Psychiatry*, **4**, 1962. Pp. 95–107. (a)

Bridger, W. H. Sensory discrimination and autonomic function in the newborn. *J. Am. Acad. Child Psychiat.*, 1962, **1**, 67–91. (b)

Bridger, W. H., Birns, B. M., and Blank, M. A comparison of behavioral ratings and heart rate measurements in human neonates. *Psychosom. Med.*, 1965, **27**, 123–134.

Bridger, W. H., and Reiser, M. F. Psychophysiologic studies of the neonate: an approach toward methodological and theoretical problems involved. *Psychosom. Med.*, 1959, **21**, 265–276.

Bridges, K. M. B. *The social and emotional development of the pre-school child.* London: Kegan Paul, 1931.

Bridges, K. M. B. Emotional development in early infancy. *Child Dev.*, 1932, **3**, 324–341.

Bridges, K. M. B. A study of social development in early infancy. *Child Dev.*, 1933, **4**, 36–49.

Bridges, K. M. B. The development of the primary drives in infancy. *Child Dev.*, 1936, **7**, 40–56.

Bridges, K. M. B. Measuring emotionality in infants: a tentative experiment. *Child Dev.*, 1937, **5**, 36–40.

Brigance, W. N. The language learning of a child. *J. appl. Psychol.*, 1934, **18**, 143–154.

Brodbeck, A. J. The effect of three feeding variables on the non-nutritive sucking of the newborn infants. *Am. Psychologist*, 1950, **5**, 292–293.

Brodbeck, A. J., and Irwin, O. C. The speech behavior of infants without families. *Child Dev.*, 1946, **17**, 145–156.

Brody, S. *Patterns of mothering: maternal influence during infancy.* New York: International Universities Press, 1956.

Brody, S. Self-rocking in infancy. *J. Am. Psychoanal. Assoc.*, 1960, **8**, 464–491.

Broesan, A. Erziehungsschwierigkeiten unter dem Aspekt der Künkel'schen Psychologie. *Prax. Kinderpsychol. Kinderpsychiat.*, 1953, **2**, 62–65.

Brohm, F., Šupáček, I., and Tichá, H. Metodika vyšetřování sluchu kojenců a malých dětí při depistáži sluchových vad. *Čslká. Pediat.*, 1961, **16**, 551–556.

Bronfenbrenner, U. Early deprivation in mammals and man. In G. Newton (Ed.), *Early experience and behavior.* Springfield, Ill.: Thomas, 1966.

Bronshtein, A. I., Antonova, T. G., Kamenetskaya, A. G., Luppova, N. N., and Sytova, V. A. On the development of the functions of analyzers in infants and some animals at the early stage of ontogenesis. In *Problems of evolution of physiological functions.* Moscow Acad. Sci., 1958. Israel Program for Scientific Translations, 1960. Pp. 106–116. (U.S. Dept. of Commerce OTS 60–51066.)

Bronshtein, A. I., and Petrova, E. P. Issledovanie zvukovogo analizatora novorazhdennykh i detei rannego grudonogo vozrasta. *Pavlov Zh. vyssh. nerv. Deyat.*, 1952, **2**, 333–343.

Bronson, W. C. Early antecedents of emotional expressiveness and reactivity control. *Child Dev.*, 1966, **37**, 793–810.

Brown, C. A. The development of visual capacity in the infant and young child. *Cerebral Palsy Bull.*, 1961, **3**, 364–372.

Brown, E. S. The baby's mind. *Babyhood*, 1890.

Brown, J. L. States in newborn infants. *Merrill-Palmer Q.*, 1964, **10**, 313–327.

Brown, J. L. The structure of the visual system. In C. H. Graham (Ed.), *Vision and visual perception.* New York: Wiley, 1965.

Brown, R., and Bellugi, U. Three processes in the child's acquisition of syntax. *Harvard Educ. Rev.*, 1964, **34**, 133–151.

Bruner, J. S. Origins of mind in infancy. Invited address before Div. 8 at the 75th anniversary of Amer. Psychol. Assoc., Washington, D. C., Sept. 1, 1967. (Mimeographed.)

Bruner, J. S. Eye, hand, and mind. In D. Elkind and J. H. Flavell (Eds.), *Studies in cognitive development*. New York: Oxford University Press, 1969. Pp. 223–235.

Bruner, J. S., Simenson, J., and Lyons, K. The growth of human manual intelligence. I. Taking possession of objects. 1968. (Mimeographed.)

Bruner, J. S., and Watkins, D. The growth of human manual intelligence: II. Acquisition of complementary two handedness. 1968. (Mimeographed.)

Brunet, O. Baby-tests. *Enfance*, 1948, **1**, 250–255, 361–366.

Brunet, O., and Lézine, I. *Le développement psychologique de la première enfance: Présentation d'une échelle française pour examen des tout petits*. Paris: Presses Universitaires de France, 1951.

Brunk, C. The effects of maternal over-protection on the early development and habits of children. *Smith Coll. Stud. Soc. Work.*, 1932, **2**, 261–273.

Brunswik, E., and Cruikshank, R. M. Perceptual size-constancy in early infancy. *Psychol. Bull.*, 1937, **34**, 713–714.

Bryan, E. S. Variations in the responses of infants during the first ten days of postnatal life. *Child Dev.*, 1930, **1**, 56–77.

Buchner, M. *Die Entwicklung der Gemütsbewegungen im ersten Lebensjahre*. Langensalza: Beyer, 1909.

Buck, F. From fundamental to accessory in the development of the nervous system and of movements. *Ped. Sem.*, 1898, **6**, 5–64.

Buckman, S. S. Babies and monkeys. *Nineteenth Cent.*, 1894, **36**, 727–743.

Buckman, S. S. The speech of children. *Nineteenth Cent.*, 1897, **41**, 793–807.

Bühler, C. Die ersten sozialen Verhaltungsweisen des Kindes. *Quell. Stud. Jugendk.*, 1927, **5**, 1–102.

Bühler, C. *The first year of life*. New York: John Day, 1930.

Bühler, C., and Hetzer, H. Das erste Verständnis für Ausdruck im ersten Lebensjahr. *Z. Psychol.*, 1928, **107**, 50–61.

Bühler, C., and Hetzer, H. Individual differences among children in the first two years of life. *Child Study*, 1929, **7**, 11–13.

Bühler, C., and Hetzer, H. *Kleinkinder tests*. Leipzig: Barth, 1932.

Bühler, C., and Hetzer, H. *Testing children's development from birth to school age*. New York: Farrar Rinehart, 1935.

Bühler, C., Hetzer, H., and Mabel, F. Die Affektwirksamkeit von Fremdheitseindrücken im ersten Lebensjahr. *Z. Psychol. Physiol. Sinnesorg.*, 1928, **108**, 30–49.

Bühler, C., and Spielmann, L. Die Entwicklung der Körperbeherrschung beim Kinde im ersten Lebensjahr. *Z. Psychol.*, 1928, **107**, 3–30.

Bullowa, M., Jones, L. G., and Bever, T. G. The development from vocal to verbal behavior in children. In U. Bellugi and R. Brown (Eds.), The acquisition of language. *Monogr. Soc. Res. Child Dev.*, 1964, **29**, No. 92.

Burling, R. Language development of a Garo and English speaking child. *Word*, 1959, **15**, 45–68.

Burlingham, D. T. The relationship of twins to each other. *Psychoanal. Study Child*, 1949, **3 & 4**, 57–72.

Burlingham, D. T. *Twins: a study of three pairs of identical twins*. New York: International Universities Press, 1952.

Burlingham, D. T. Some notes on the development of the blind. *Psychoanal. Study Child*, 1961, **16**, 121–145.

Burlingham, D. T., and Barron, A. T. A study of identical twins: their analytical material compared with existing observation data of their early childhood. *Psychoanal. Study Child*, 1963, 18, 367–423.

Burns, B. D. The central control of respiratory movements. *Br. med. Bull.*, 1963, 19, 7–9.

Burnside, L. H. Coordination in the locomotion of infants. *Genet. Psychol. Monogr.*, 1927, 2, 279–372.

Burr, C. W. The reflexes in early infancy. *Am. J. Dis. Child.*, 1921, 21, 529–533.

Burtt, H. E. An experimental study of early childhood memory. *J. genet. Psychol.*, 1932, 40, 287–295.

Burtt, H. E. A further study of early childhood memory. *J. genet. Psychol.*, 1937, 50, 187–192.

Burtt, H. E. An experimental study of early childhood memory: final report. *J. genet. Psychol.*, 1941, 58, 435–439.

Butler, N. M. The meaning of infancy and education. *Educ. Rev., New York*, 1897, 13, 58–75.

Bychowski, Z. Über das Verhalten einiger Haut– und Sehnen-Reflexe bei Kindern im Laufe des ersten Lebensjahres. *Dt. Z. Nervenheilk.*, 1907, 34, 116–127.

Byington, G. M. Incidence of breast feeding in Detroit. *Psychosom. Med.*, 1945, 7, 173.

Bystroletova, G. N. Obrazovanie u novorozhennykh detei uslovnogo refleksa na vremia v sviazi s sutochnym ritmom kormleniia. *Zh. vyss. nerv. Deyat.*, 1954, 4, 601–609.

Cahn, P. La carence affective telle qu'elle s'inscrit dans les Baby-Tests. *Psychologie Française*, 1963, 8, 133–137.

Caldwell, B. M. Assessment of infant personality. *Merrill-Palmer Q.*, 1962, 8, 71–88. (a)

Caldwell, B. M. The usefulness of the critical period hypothesis in the study of filiative behavior. *Merrill-Palmer Q.*, 1962, 8, 229–242. (b)

Caldwell, B. M., and Drachman, R. Comparability of 3 methods of assessing developmental level of young infants. *Pediatrics*, 1964, 34, 51–57.

Caldwell, B. M., Graham, F. K., Pennoyer, M. M., Ernhart, C. B., and Hartmann, A. F., Sr. The utility of blood oxygenation as an indicator of post-natal condition. *J. Pediat.*, 1957, 50, 434–445.

Caldwell, B. M., and Hersher, L. Mother-infant interaction during the first year of life. *Merrill-Palmer Q.*, 1964, 10, 119–128.

Caldwell, B. M., Hersher, L., Lipton, E. L., Richmond, J. B., Stern, G. A., Eddy, E., Drachman, R., and Rothman, A. Mother-infant interaction in monomatric and polymatric families. *Am. J. Orthopsychiat.* 1963, 33, 653–664.

Caldwell, B. M., and Richmond, J. B. Programmed day care for the very young child—A preliminary report. *J. marr. Fam.*, 1964, 26, 481–488.

Calkins, M. W. Wellesley College Psychological Studies: A. The emotional life of children. *Ped. Sem.*, 1894–1896, 3, 319–341.

Call, J. D. Newborn approach behaviour and early ego development. *Int. J. Psychoanal.*, 1964, 45, 286–294.

Callejas Davalos, R. Estudio de las percepciónes psico-neurofisiologicas del feto y del recién nacido. *Rev. med. Cubana*, 1942, 53, 201–209.

Cameron, J., Levson, N., and Bayley, N. Infant vocalizations and their relationship to mature intelligence. *Science*, 1967, 157, 331–333.

Campbell, R. V. D., and Weech, A. A. Measures which characterize the individual during the development of behavior in early life. *Child Dev.*, 1941, 12, 217–236.

Canestrini, S. Über das Sinnesleben des Neugeborenen (nach physiologischen Experimenten). *Gesamtgebiete Neurol. Psychiat.*, 1913, 5, 1–104.

Caplan, G. (Ed.) *Emotional problems of early childhood.* New York: Basic Books, 1955.

Caplan, H., Bibace, R., and Rabinovitch, M. S. Paranatal stress, cognitive organization and ego function: a controlled follow-up study of children born prematurely. *J. Child Psychiat.*, 1963, 2, 434–450.

Capper, A. The fate and development of the immature and of the premature child. Part I. *Am. J. Dis. Child.*, 1928, 35, 262–288. (a)

Capper, A. The fate and development of the immature and of the premature child. Part II. *Am. J. Dis. Child.*, 1928, 35, 443–491. (b)

Cardullo, H. M., and Holt, L. E., Jr. Ability of infants to taste PTC: its application in cases of doubtful paternity. *Proc. Soc. Exp. Biol. Med.*, 1951, 76, 589–592.

Carlson, A. J., and Ginsburg, H. The tonus and hunger contractions of the stomach of the newborn. *Am. J. Physiol.*, 1915, 38, 29–32.

Carmichael, L. Behavior during fetal life. In P. L. Harriman, *Encyclopedia of Psychology.* New York: Philosophical Library, 1946. Pp. 198–205.

Carmichael, L. The experimental embryology of mind. *Psychol. Bull.*, 1941, 38, 1–28.

Carmichael, L. (Ed.) *Manual of child psychology.* (2nd ed.) New York: Wiley, 1954.

Carmichael, L., and Lehner, G. F. J. The development of temperature sensitivity during the fetal period. *J. genet. Psychol.*, 1937, 50, 217–227.

Caron, R. F., and Caron, A. J. The effects of repeated exposure and stimulus complexity on visual fixation in infants. *Psychonom. Sci.*, 1968, 10, 207–208.

Carter, H. D., and Krause, R. H. Physical proportions of the human infant. *Child Dev.*, 1936, 7, 60–68.

Casler, L. The effects of extra tactile stimulation on a group of institutionalized infants. *Genet. Psychol. Monogr.*, 1965, 71, 137–175. (a)

Casler, L. The effects of supplementary verbal stimulation on a group of institutionalized infants. *J. Child Psychol. Psychiat.*, 1965, 6, 19–27. (b)

Castner, B. M. The development of fine prehension in infancy. *Genet. Psychol. Monogr.*, 1932, 12, 105–193.

Castro, F. Sécrétion lactée du nouveau-né prolongée jusqu'au onzième mois. *C. r. Soc. Biol., Paris,* 1930, 105, 485–486.

Catalano, F. L., and McCarthy, D. Infant speech as a possible predictor of later intelligence. *J. Psychol.*, 1954, 38, 203–209.

Catel, W. Über die Hirntätigkeit des Neugeborenen. *Dt. med. Woch.* 1932, 58, 997–1002. (a)

Catel, W. Zum Spontannystagmus des Neugeborenen. *Dt. med. Woch.*, 1932, 58, 1478–1479. (b)

Cattaneo, C. Über einige Reflexe im ersten Kindesalter. *Jb. Kinderheilk.*, 1902, 55, 458–463.

Cattaneo, C., and Marimo, F. Ricerche sul alcune sensibilità e sul senso stereognostico nella età infantile. *Pediatria-Naples,* 1902, 10, 593–608.

Cattell, P. The development of intelligence and motor control in infancy. *Rev. educ. Res.*, 1936, 6, 3–16.

Cattell, P. The development of motor functions and mental abilities in infancy. *Rev. educ. Res.*, 1939, 9, 5–17.

Cattell, P. *The measurement of intelligence of infants and young children.* New York: Psychological Corp., 1940.

Cavanaugh, M., Cohen, I., Dunphy, D., Ringwall, E., and Goldberg, I. Predictions from the Cattell Infant Intelligence Scale. *J. consult. Psychol.*, 1957, 21, 33–37.

Cemach, A. J. Beiträge zur Kenntnis der Kochlearen Reflexe. *Beitr. Anat., Physiol. Path. Ther. Ohr. Nase. Hals.,* 1920, **14,** 1–82.

Champneys, F. H. Notes on an infant. *Mind,* 1881, **6,** 104–107.

Chaney, B. L., and McGraw, M. B. Reflexes and other motor activities in new-born infants. *Bull. Neurol. Inst. New York,* 1932, **2,** 1–56.

Chapman, A. H. Early infantile autism. *Am. J. Dis. Child.,* 1960, **99,** 783–786.

Charlesworth, W. R. Persistence of orienting and attending behavior in infants as a function of stimulus-locus uncertainty. *Child Dev.,* 1966, **37,** 473–491.

Charlesworth, W. R. Cognition in infancy: where do we stand in the mid-sixties? *Merrill-Palmer Q.,* 1968, **14,** 25–46.

Charlesworth, W. R. The role of surprise in cognitive development. In D. Elkind and J. H. Flavell (Eds.), *Studies in cognitive development.* New York: Oxford University Press, 1969. Pp. 257–314.

Chase, W. P. Color vision in infants. *J. exp. Psychol.,* 1937, **20,** 203–222.

Chen, H. P., and Irwin, O. C. Development of speech during infancy: curve of differential percentage indices. *J. exp. Psychol.,* 1946, **36,** 522–525. (a)

Chen, H. P., and Irwin, O. C. Infant speech vowel and consonant types. *J. speech Disord.,* 1946, **11,** 27–29. (b)

Chen, H. P., and Irwin, O. C. The type-token ratio applied to infant speech sounds. *J. speech Disord.,* 1946, **11,** 126–130. (c)

Chess, S., Thomas, A., and Birch, H. Characteristics of the individual child's behavioral responses to the environment. *Am. J. Orthopsychiat.,* 1959, **29,** 791–802.

Child, I. L., and Adelsheim, E. The motivational value of barriers for young children. *J. genet. Psychol.,* 1944, **65,** 97–111.

Childs, B. Genetic origin of some sex differences among human beings. *Pediatrics,* 1965, **35,** 798–812.

Chrisman O. One year with a little girl. *Educ. Rev.,* 1895, **9,** 52–71.

Christoffel, H. Einige fötale und frühstkindliche Verhaltensweisen. *Int. Z. Psychoanal. Imago,* 1939, **24,** 447–460.

Chun, R. W. M., Pawsat, R., and Forster, F. M. Sound localization in infancy. *J. nerv. ment. Dis.,* 1960, **130,** 472–476.

Church, J. (Ed.) *Three babies: biographies of cognitive development.* New York: Random House, 1966.

Churchill, J. A. Current research in chronic neurologic diseases of children. *Merrill-Palmer Q.,* 1963, **9,** 95–100.

Churchill, J. A., Igna, E., and Senf, R. The association of position at birth and handedness. *Pediatrics,* 1962, **29,** 307–309.

Ciurlo, L. Sulla funzione olfattoria nel neonato. *Valsalva,* 1934, **10,** 22–34.

Clarke, F. M. A developmental study of the bodily reaction of infants to an auditory startle stimulus. *J. gen. Psychol.,* 1939, **55,** 415–427.

Clarke, F. M., Hunt, W. A., and Hunt, E. B. Incidental responses in infants following a startle stimulus. *J. genet. Psychol.,* 1937, **17,** 398–402. (a)

Clarke, F. M., Hunt, W. A., and Hunt, E. B. Plantar responses in infants following a startle stimulus. *J. genet. Psychol.,* 1937, **50,** 458–461. (b)

Clifton, R. K. Newborn heart-rate response and response habituation as a function of stimulus duration. *J. exp. child Psychol.,* 1968, **6,** 265–278.

Cobb, K., Goodwin, R., and Saelens, E. Spontaneous hand positions of newborn infants. *J. genet. Psychol.,* 1966, **108,** 225–237.

Cohen, A. I. Hand preference and developmental status of infants. *J. genet. Psychol.,* 1966, **108,** 337–345.

Cohen, D. J. The crying newborn's accommodation to the nipple. *Child Dev.,* 1967, **38,** 89–100.

Cohen, L. B. Observing responses, visual preferences, and habituation to visual stimuli in infants. Doctoral dissertation, Univer. of Cal. at Los Angeles, 1965.

Cohen, M. Sur les langages successifs de l'enfant. *Collection Linguistique*, 1925, **17**, 109–127.

Cohen, M. Observations sur les dernières persistances du langage enfantin. *J. Psychol. norm. Path.*, 1933, **30**, 390–399.

Cohen, M. Sur l'étude du langage enfantin. *Enfance*, 1952, **5**, 181–249.

Colby, M. G., Macy, I. G., Poole, M. W., Hamil, B. M., and Cooley, T. B. Relation of increased vitamin B (B_1) intake to mental and physical growth of infants. Preliminary report. *Am. J. Dis. Child.*, 1937, **54**, 750–756.

Coleman, R. W., Kris, E., and Provence, S. The study of variations of early parental attitudes. *Psychoanal. Study Child.*, 1953, **8**, 20–47.

Coleman, R. W., and Provence, S. Environmental retardation (hospitalism) in infants living in families. *Pediatrics*, 1957, **19**, 285–292.

Colley, J. R. T., and Creamer, B. Sucking and swallowing in infants. *Br. med. J.*, 1958, **2**, 422–424.

Combes, L. Quelques observations sur le langage des enfants. *Bull. Soc. libre étude Psychol. Enf.*, 1900–1905, **1–5**, 452–454, 571–577, 594–599.

Conel, J. L. The brain structure of the newborn infant and consideration of the senile brain. *Res. Publs. Assoc. Res. nerv. ment. Dis.*, 1939, **19**, 247–255. (a)

Conel, J. L. *The postnatal development of the human cerebral cortex.* Vol. 1. *The cortex of the newborn.* Cambridge, Mass.: Harvard University Press, 1939. (b)

Conel, J. L. *The postnatal development of the human cerebral cortex.* Vol. 2. *The cortex of the one-month infant.* Cambridge, Mass.: Harvard University Press, 1941.

Conel, J. L. *The postnatal development of the human cerebral cortex.* Vol. 3. *The cortex of the three-month infant.* Cambridge, Mass.: Harvard University Press, 1947.

Conel, J. L. *The postnatal development of the human cerebral cortex.* Vol. 4. *The cortex of the six-month infant.* Cambridge, Mass.: Harvard University Press, 1951.

Conel, J. L. *The postnatal development of the human cerebral cortex.* Vol. 5. *The cortex of the fifteen-month infant.* Cambridge, Mass.: Harvard University Press, 1955.

Conel, J. L. *The postnatal development of the human cerebral cortex.* Vol. 6. *The cortex of the twenty-four-month infant.* Cambridge, Mass.: Harvard University Press, 1959.

Cook, E., and Bevan-Brown, M. *The psychology of childbirth.* Christchurch, N. Z.: Christchurch Psychological Society, 1947.

Cook, E., and Bevan-Brown, M. *Psychological preparation for childbirth.* Christchurch, N. Z.: Christchurch Psychological Society, 1948.

Cook, R. C., and Glasscock, R. E. Refractive and ocular findings in the newborn. *Am. J. Ophthal.*, 1951, **34**, 1407–1413.

Cooke, R. E. The behavioral response of infants to heat stress. *Yale J. Biol. Med.*, 1952, **24**, 334–340.

Cooley, C. H. A study of the early use of self-words by a child. *Psychol. Rev.*, 1908, **15**, 339–357.

Cornieley, H. *Die sprachliche Entwicklung eines Kindes.* Bern: Lang, 1935.

Cort, R. L. Clinical observations in newborn premature infants. *Archs. Dis. Childh.*, 1962, **37**, 53–62.

Cotelessa, M. La motilita reflessa del neonato e del lattante. *Lattante*, 1931, 9–10, 707–737, 761–790.

Court, S. R. A. Numbers, time and space in the first five years of a child's life. *Ped. Sem.*, 1920, 27, 71–89.

Courtney, D. M., and Johnson, B. Skill in progressive movements of children. *Child Dev.*, 1930, 1, 345–347.

Cramaussel, E. *Le premier éveil intellectuel de l'enfant.* Paris: Alcan, 1909.

Cramaussel, E. Le sommeil d'un petit enfant. *Archs. Psychol.*, 1910, 10, 321–326. (a)

Cramaussel, E. Le sommeil d'un petit enfant. *Archs. Psychol.*, 1911, 11, 172–181 (b)

Cramaussel, E. Ce que voient des yeux d'enfant. *J. Psychol. norm. Path.*, 1924, 21, 161–169.

Cravioto, J., and De Licardie, E. R. Intersensory development of school-age children. In N. S. Scrimshaw and J. E. Gordon (Eds.), *Malnutrition, learning, and behavior.* Cambridge, Mass.: MIT Press, 1968.

Cronbach, L. J. Year-to-year correlations of mental tests: a review of the Hofstaetter analysis. *Child Dev.*, 1967, 38, 283–289.

Crowell, D. H. Associations among anatomical and behavioral variables of full-term neonates. *Child Dev.*, 1962, 33, 373–380.

Crowell, D. H. Patterns of psychophysiological functioning in early infancy: a preliminary analysis with autonomic lability scores. *Merrill-Palmer Q.*, 1967, 13, 37–53.

Crowell, D. H., Peterson, J., and Safely, M. A. An apparatus for infant conditioning research. *Child Dev.*, 1960, 31, 47–51.

Crowell, D. H., Yasaka, E. K., and Crowell, D. C. Infant stabilimeter. *Child Dev.*, 1964, 35, 525–532.

Cruchet, R. Évolution psycho-physiologique de l'enfant du jour de sa naissance à l'âge de deux ans. *Année psychol.*, 1911, 17, 48–63.

Cruchet, R. La mesure de l'intelligence chez l'enfant de la naissance à 2 et 3 ans. *J. de méd. de Bordeaux*, 1930, 107, 951–960.

Crudden, C. H. Reactions of newborn infants to thermal stimuli under constant tactual conditions. *J. exp. Psychol.*, 1937, 20, 350–370.

Cruikshank, R. M. The development of visual size constancy in early infancy. *J. genet. Psychol.*, 1941, 58, 327–351.

Crump, E. P., Gore, P. M. and Horton, C. P. The sucking behavior in premature infants. *Hum. Biol.*, 1958, 30, 128–141.

Crump, E. P., Horton, C. P., Masuoka, J., and Ryan, D. Growth and development. I. Relation of birthweight in Negro infants to sex, maternal age, parity, prenatal care, and socioeconomic status. *J. Pediat.*, 1957, 51, 678–697.

Cuignet, L. De la vision chez le tout jeune enfant. *Ann. Ocul.*, 1871, 66, 117–126.

Cunningham, B. V. An experiment in measuring gross motor development of infants and young children. *J. educ. Psychol.*, 1927, 18, 458–464.

Cunningham, B. V. Infant IQ ratings evaluated after an interval of seven years. *J. exp. Educ.*, 1934, 3, 84–87.

Cunningham, K. S. The measurement of early levels of intelligence. *Teachers Coll. Contr. Educ.*, 1927, No. 259.

Curti, M. W., Marshall, F. B., and Steggerda, M. The Gesell schedules applied to one-, two,- and three-year-old Negro children of Jamaica, B. W. I. *J. comp. Psychol.*, 1935, 20, 125–156.

Cutler, R., Heimer, C., Wortis, H., and Freedman, A. M. The effects of prenatal and neonatal complications on the development of premature children at two and one-half years of age. *J. genet. Psychol.*, 1965, 107, 261–276.

Czerny, A. Beobachtungen über den Schlaf im Kindesalter unter physiologischen Verhältnissen. *Jb. Kinderheilk.*, 1892, 33, 1–28.

Damborská, M., Blazkóvá, E., and Štěpánová, P. Rozvoj zraku u ústvních dětí. během prvnich mesicu života. Česk. Pediat., 1959, 14, 914–919.

Damborská, M., Filova, V., and Štěpánová, P. Rozvoj sluchu u ústavních dětí. Česk. Pediat., 1959, 14, 911–913.

Dambroská, M., and Neubauerová, H. Pérezúv reflex. Česk. Pediat., 1960, 15, 333–338.

Damborská, M., Neubauerová, H., and Štěpánová, P. Vývoj zraku u dítěte v druhém čtvrtleti. Česk. Pediat., 1961, 16, 496–501.

Daniels, E. E., and Maudry, M. Die Entwicklung der Abwehrreaktionen auf Störungsreize. Z. Psychol., 1935, 135, 259–287.

Dann, M., Levine, S. Z., and New, E. V. A long term follow-up study of small premature infants. Pediatrics, 1964, 33, 945–955.

Darwin, C. The expression of the emotions in man and animals. London: Murray, 1872.

Darwin, C. A biographical sketch of an infant. Mind, 1877, 2, 285–294.

Dashkovskaia, V. S. Pervye uslovnye reaktsii u novorzhdennykh deteĭ v norme i pri nekotorykh patologicheskikh sostoiàniiakh. Zh. vўssh. nerv. Deyat., 1953, 3, 247–259.

Davenport, C. B. Child development from the standpoint of genetics. Scient. Mon., 1934, 39, 97–116.

David, M., and Appell, G. A study of nursing care and nurse-infant interaction. In B. M. Foss (Ed.), Determinants of infant behavior. New York: Wiley, 1961. Pp. 121–136.

David, H. P., and Brengleman, J. C. (Eds.) Perspectives in personality research. New York: Springer, 1960.

Davids, A., Holden, R. H., and Gray, G. B. Maternal anxiety during pregnancy and adequacy of mother and child adjustment eight months following childbirth. Child Dev., 1963, 34, 993–1002.

Davidson, P. E. The recapitulation theory and human infancy. Teach. Coll. Contr. Educ., 1914, No. 65.

Davis, C. M. The self-selected diet of a newly weaned infant. J. Am. dent. Assoc., 1927, 14, 1119–1134.

Davis, C. M. Self selection of diet by newly weaned infants: an experimental study. Am. J. Dis. Child., 1928, 36, 651–679.

Davis, H. V., Sears, R. R., Miller, H. C., and Brodbeck, A. J. Effects of cup, bottle and breast feeding on oral activities of newborn infants. Pediatrics, 1948, 2, 549–558.

Davis, P. B. A study of thumbsucking: summary of a questionnaire answered by 250 parents. The trained nurse, 1940, 104, 422–425.

Davis, R. E., and Ruiz, R. A. Infant feeding method and adolescent personality. Am. J. Psychiat., 1965, 122, 673–678.

Day, E. J. The development of language in twins. I. A comparison of twins and single children. Child Dev., 1932, 3, 179–199. (a)

Day, E. J. The development of language in twins. II. The development of twins: their resemblances and differences. Child Dev., 1932, 3, 298–316. (b)

Dayton, G. O., Jr., and Jones, M. H. Analysis of characteristics of fixation reflexes in infants by use of direct current electrooculography. Neurology, 1964, 14, 1152–1156.

Dayton, G. O., Jr., Jones, M. H., Aiu, P., Rawson, R. A., Steele, B., and Rose, M. Developmental study of coordinated eye movements in the human infant. I. Visual acuity in the newborn human: a study based on induced optokinetic nystagmus recorded by electrooculography. Arch. Ophthal., 1964, 71, 865–870.

Dayton, G. O., Jr., Jones, M. H., Steele, B., and Rose, M. Developmental study of coordinated eye movements in the human infant. II. An electroocu-lographic study of the fixation reflex in the newborn. *Arch. Ophthal.*, 1964, **71**, 871–875.

Dean, R. F. A. The size of the baby at birth and the yield of breast milk. Studies of undernutrition, Wuppertal 1946–1949. *Spec. Rep. Ser. med. Res. Coun., London*, 1951, No. 275.

Dean, R. F. A. Treatment of kwashiorkor with moderate amounts of protein. *J. Pediat.*, 1960, **56**, 675–689.

Dean, R. F. A. Nutrition and growth. *Mod. Probl. Paediat.*, 1962, **7**, 191–198.

DeAngelis, F. Reflexes of the newborn. *Am. J. Dis. Child.*, 1923, **26**, 211–215.

Dearborn, G. V. N. *Moto-sensory development: observations on the first three years of a child.* Baltimore, Md.: Warwick and York, 1910.

Debesse; M. La créativité de l'enfant et la création artistique. *Gawein*, 1960, **8**, 194–200.

DeBruin, M. Over het verschijnsel van Babinski en soortgelijke reflexen bij zeer jonge kinderen. *Ned. Tijdsch. Geneesk.*, 1928, **72**, 3002–3027.

DeBruin, M. Respiration and basal metabolism in childhood during sleep. *Acta Paediat.*, 1936, **18**, 279–286.

Décarie, T. G. *Intelligence and affectivity in early childhood.* New York: International Universities Press, 1965.

de Crinis, M. Die Entwicklung der Grosshirnrinde nach der Geburt in ihren Beziehungen zur intellektuellen Ausreifung des Kindes. *Wein. klin. Wschr.*, 1932, **45**, 1161–1165.

Decroly, O. *Études de psychogénèse.* Brussells: Lambertin, 1932.

Degtyar, E. N. The elaboration of association in very young children. *Pavlov J. higher nerv. Activ.*, 1961, **11**, 83–88. (a)

Degtyar, E. N. Interaction between temporary connexions of different types in the elaboration of a stereotype in children. *Pavlov J. higher nerv. Activ.*, 1961, **11**, 663–668. (b)

Degtyar, E. N. Sravnitelnaia kharakteristika fiziologicheskikh uslovnii pri vyra-botke stereotipa v pervoi i vtoroi signalnoi sistemakh. *Zh. vÿssh. nerv. Deyat.*, 1962, **12**, 63–68.

Deisher, R. W., and Goers, S. S. A study of early and later introduction of solids into the infant diet. *J. Pediat.*, 1954, **45**, 191–199.

Dekaban, A. *Neurology of infancy.* Baltimore, Md.: Williams & Wilkins, 1959.

Delafresnaye, J. F. (Ed.) *Brain mechanisms and learning.* Oxford: Blackwell, 1961.

de Lissovoy, V. Head banging in early childhood. *Child Dev.*, 1962, **33**, 43–56.

Delman, L. The order of participation of limbs in responses to tactual stimulation of the newborn infant. *Child Dev.*, 1935, **6**, 98–109.

DeLucia, C. A. A system for response measurement and reinforcement delivery for infant sucking-behavior research. *J. exp. child Psychol.*, 1967, **5**, 518–521.

DeLucia, C. A. Apparatus for recording eyeblink. *J. exp. child Psychol.*, 1968, **6**, 427–430.

Dember, W. N. Birth order and need affiliation. *J. abn. soc. Psychol.*, 1964, **68**, 555–557.

Dember, W. N., and Earl, R. W. Analysis of exploratory, manipulatory, and curi-osity behaviors. *Psychol. Rev.*, 1957, **64**, 91–96.

Demetriades, T. The cochlea-palpebral reflex in infants. *Ann. Otol. Rhinol. Lar.*, 1923, **32**, 894–903.

Denisova, M. P., and Figurin, N. L. Periodicheskie iavleniia vo sne u detei. *Nov. refleks. fiziol. nerv. sist.*, 1926, **2**, 338–345.

Denisova, M. P., and Figurin, N. L. K voprosu o pervỹkh sochetatelnykh pishchevykh refleksakh u grudnykh detei. *Vop. genet. Refleks. Pedol.*, 1929, **1**, 81–88.

Dennis, W. Discussion: the role of mass activity in the development of infant behavior. *Psychol. Rev.*, 1932, **39**, 593–595. (a)

Dennis, W. Two new responses of infants. *Child Dev.*, 1932, **3**, 362–363. (b)

Dennis, W. The age at walking of children who run on all fours. *Child Dev.*, 1934, **5**, 92–93. (a)

Dennis, W. Congenital cataract and unlearned behavior. *J. genet. Psychol.*, 1934, **44**, 340–351. (b)

Dennis, W. A description and classification of the responses of the newborn infant. *Psychol. Bull.*, 1934, **31**, 5–22. (c)

Dennis, W. The effect of restricted practice upon the reaching, sitting, and standing of two infants. *J. genet. Psychol.*, 1935, **47**, 17–32. (a)

Dennis, W. An experimental test of two theories of social smiling in infants. *J. soc. Psychol.*, 1935, **6**, 214–223. (b)

Dennis, W. Laterality of function in early infancy under controlled developmental conditions. *Child Dev.*, 1935, **6**, 242–252. (c)

Dennis, W. A psychologic interpretation of the persistance of the so-called Moro reflex. *Am. J. Dis. Child.*, 1935, **50**, 888–893. (d)

Dennis, W. A bibliography of baby biographies. *Child Dev.*, 1936, **7**, 71–73.

Dennis, W. Infant development under conditions of restricted practice and of minimum social stimulation: a preliminary report. *J. genet. Psychol.*, 1938, **53**, 149–158.

Dennis, W. Does culture appreciably affect patterns of infant behavior? *J. soc. Psychol.*, 1940, **12**, 305–317. (a)

Dennis, W. Infant reaction to restraint: an evaluation of Watson's theory. *Trans. N. Y. Acad. Sci.*, 1940, **2**, 202–218. (b)

Dennis, W. Is the newborn infant's repertoire learned or instinctive? *Psychol. Rev.*, 1943, **50**, 330–337.

Dennis, W. Causes of retardation among institutional children: Iran. *J. genet. Psychol.*, 1960, **96**, 47–59.

Dennis, W., and Dennis, M. G. Behavioral development in the first year as shown by forty biographies. *Psychol. Rec.*, 1937, **1**, 349–361.

Dennis, W., and Dennis, M. G. The effect of cradling practices upon the onset of walking in Hopi children. *J. genet. Psychol.*, 1940, **56**, 77–86.

Dennis, W., and Najarian, P. Infant development under environmental handicap. *Psychol. Monogr.*, 1957, **71**, Whole No. 436.

Dennis, W., and Sayegh, Y. The effects of supplementary experiences upon the behavioral development of infants in institutions. *Child Dev.*, 1965, **36**, 81–90.

de Sa, A., and Soonawalla, R. A study of stress responses in children and neonates. *Ind. J. Child Hlth.*, 1959, **8**, 138–141.

Desmond, M. M., Franklin, R. R., Vallbona, C., Hill, R. M., Plumb, R., Arnold, H., and Watts, J. The clinical behavior of the newly born. I. The term baby. *J. Pediat.*, 1963, **62**, 307–325.

Despert, J. L. Anxiety, phobias, and fears in young children, with special reference to prenatal, natal, and neonatal factors. *Nerv. Child*, 1946, **5**, 8–24.

Devereux, G. The Mohave neonate and its cradle. *Primitive Man*, 1948, **21**, 1–18.

Dewey, E. *Behavior development in infants.* New York: Columbia University Press, 1935.

Dewey, J. The psychology of infant language. *Psychol. Rev.*, 1894, **1**, 63–66.

Dietrich, H. F. A longitudinal study of the Babinski and plantar grasp reflexes in infancy. *Am. J. Dis. Child.*, 1957, **94**, 265–271.

Disher, D. R. The reactions of newborn infants to chemical stimuli administered nasally. *Ohio Univ. Stud.*, 1934, No. 12, 1–52.

Dittrichová, J. Die geistige Entwicklung der Frühgeborenen im ersten Lebensjahr. *Prax. Kinderpsychol. Kinderpsychiat.*, 1961, **10**, 51–56.

Dittrichová, J., and Lapácková, V. Development of the waking state in young infants. *Child Dev.*, 1964, **35**, 365–370.

Dix, K. W. *Körperliche und geistige Entwicklung eines Kindes*. Band. I. *Instinkt-bewegung*. Leipzig: Wunderlich, 1911.

Dix, K. W. *Körperliche und geistige Entwicklung eines Kindes*. Band II. *Die Sinne*. Leipzig: Wunderlich, 1912.

Dix, K. W. *Körperliche und geistige Entwicklung eines Kindes*. Band III. *Vorstellen und Handeln*. Leipzig: Wunderlich, 1914.

Dixon, J. C. Development of self recognition. *J. genet. Psychol.*, 1957, **91**, 251–256.

Dockeray, F. C. Differential feeding reactions of newborn infants. *Psychol. Bull.*, 1934, **31**, 747.

Dockeray, F. C., and Rice, C. Responses of newborn infants to pain stimulation. *Ohio Univ. Stud.*, 1934, No. 12, 82–93.

Dockeray, F. C., and Valentine, W. L. A new isolation cabinet for infant research. *J. exp. Psychol.*, 1939, **24**, 211–214.

Dodgson, M. C. H. *The growing brain: An essay in development neurology*. Baltimore, Md.: Williams & Wilkins, 1962.

Doellerdt, M. *Die Fortentwicklung von 100 lebend aus der Klinik entlassenen Frühgeburten bei vorwiegender Beachtung ihrer geistigen Fähigkeiten*. Jena: Neuenhahn, 1939.

Donders, F. C. Die projection der Gesichtserscheinungen nach den Richtungslinien. *Abrecht v. Graefes Arch. Ophthal.*, 1871, **17**, 1–68.

Donders, F. C. Versuch einer genetischen Erklärung der Augen-Bewegungen. *Pflügers Arch. ges. Physiol.*, 1876, **13**, 373–421.

Donofrio, A. F. Clinical value of infant testing. *Percept. mot. Skills*, 1965, **21**, 571–574.

Dordi, A. M. Ricerche sperimentali sull' azione del riflesso psichico visivo e del succhiamento sulla secrezione gastrica del lattante. *Riv. clin. ped.*, 1931, No. 9, 791–802.

Doris, J., Casper, M., and Poresky, R. Differential brightness thresholds in infancy. *J. exp. child Psychol.*, 1967, **5**, 522–535.

Doris, J., and Cooper, L. Brightness discrimination in infancy. *J. exp. child Psychol.*, 1966, **3**, 31–39 .

Douglas, J. W. B. Subsequent development of premature babies. *Proc. Roy. Soc., Med.*, 1953, **46**, 884–885.

Douglas, J. W. B., and Blomfield, J. M. *Children under five*. London: Allan and Unwin, 1958.

Douglas, J. W. B., and Mogford, C. Health of premature children from birth to four years. *Br. Med. J.*, 1953, **1**, 748–754.

Dreger, R. M. Comparative psychological studies of Negroes and Whites in the United States: a reclarification. *Psychol. Bull.*, 1963, **60**, 35–39.

Dreyfus-Brisac, C. The bioelectrical development of the central nervous system during early life. In F. Falkner (Ed.), *Human development*. Philadelphia, Pa.: Saunders, 1966.

Dreyfus-Brisac, C., Flescher, J., and Plassart, E. L'électroencéphalogramme: critère d'âge conceptionnel du nouveau-né à terme et prématuré. *Biologia Neonat.*, 1962, **4**, 154–173.

Drillien, C. M. Studies in prematurity. Part 4. Development and progress of the prematurely born child in the pre-school period. *Archs. Dis. Childh.*, 1948, **23**, 69–83.

Drillien, C. M. Growth and development in a group of children of very low birth weight. *Archs. Dis. Childh.*, 1958, **33**, 10–18.

Drummond, M. D., and Gilliland, A. R. The validation of the Gilliland-Shotwell Infant Intelligence Scale. *Am. Psychologist*, 1946, **1**, 464.

Dubnoff, B. A comparative study of mental development in infancy. *J. genet. Psychol.*, 1938, **53**, 67–73.

Dudley, D., Duncan, D., and Sears, E. A study of the development of motor co-ordination in an infant between the ages of fifty-eight and sixty-seven weeks. *Child Dev.*, 1932, **3**, 82–86.

Duke-Elder, W. S. *Textbook of ophthalmology.* Vol. IV. London: Kimpton, 1949. (a)

Duke-Elder, W. S. *The practice of refraction.* (5th ed.) London: Churchill, 1949. (b)

Dumpert, V. Zur Kenntnis des Wesens und der physiologischen Bedeutung des Gähnens. *J. Psychol. Neur.*, 1921, **27**, 82–95.

Dunbar, F. Effects of the mother's emotional attitude on the infant. *Psychosom. Med.*, 1944, **6**, 156–159.

Dunham, E. C. The appraisal of the newborn infant. *U. S. Child. Bur. Publ.*, 1938, No. 242.

Du Pan, R. M., and Roth, S. The psychologic development of a group of children brought up in a hospital type residential nursery. *J. Pediat.*, 1955, **47**, 124–129.

Dupérié, R., and Bargues, R. À propos des réflexes inconditionnels du nourrisson: le réflexe de l'étreinte de Moro. *Gaz. hebd. des sci. méd. de Bordeaux*, 1932, **53**, No. 5, Jan. 31.

Dustman, R. E., and Beck, E. C. Visually evoked potentials: amplitude changes with age. *Science*, 1966, **151**, 1013–1015.

Eckstein, A. Zur Physiologie der Geschmacksempfindung und des Saugreflexes bei Säuglingen. *Z. Kinderheilk.*, 1928, **45**, 1–18.

Eckstein, A., and Paffrath, H. Bewegungsstudien bei frühgeborenen und jungen Säuglingen. *Z. Kinderheilk.*, 1928, **46**, 595–610.

Eckstein, A., and Rominger, E. Beiträge zur Physiologie und Pathologie der Atmung. Die Atmung des Säuglings. *Z. Kinderheilk.*, 1921, **28**, 1–37.

Edelson, H. Separation anxiety in young children: a study of hospital cases. *Genet. Psychol. Monogr.*, 1943, **28**, 1–95.

Edgerton, A. E. Ocular observations and studies of the newborn with a review of the literature. *Arch. Opth.*, 1934, **11**, 838–867.

Eichorn, D. H. Biological correlates of behavior. In H. W. Stevenson (Ed.), *Child psychology, 62nd yearbook, Nat. Soc. Study Educ.* Chicago: N.S.S.E., 1963, 4–61.

Eichorn, D. H. Biology of gestation and infancy: fatherland and frontier. *Merrill-Palmer Q.*, 1968, **14**, 47–81.

Eichorn, D. H., and Bayley, N. Growth in head circumference from birth through young adulthood. *Child Dev.*, 1962, **33**, 257–271.

Eisenberg, L., and Kanner, L. Early infantile autism, 1943–1955. *Am. J. Orthopsychiat.*, 1956, **26**, 556–566.

Eisenberg, R. B. Auditory behavior in the human neonate. I. Methodologic problems and the logical design of research procedures. *J. Audit. Res.*, 1965, **5**, 159–177.

Eisenberg, R. B., Coursin, D. B., and Rupp, N. R. Habituation to an acoustic pattern as an index of differences among human neonates. *J. Audit. Res.*, 1966, **6**, 239–248.

Eisenberg, R. B., Griffin, E. J., Coursin, D. B., and Hunter, M. A. Auditory behavior in the human neonate: a preliminary report. *J. Speech Hearing Res.*, 1964, **7**, 245–269.

Eissler, K. Zur genaueren Kenntnis des Geschehens an der Mundzone Neugeborener. *Z. Kinderpsychiat.*, 1938, **5**, 81–85.

Elkonin, D. B. The physiology of higher nervous activity and child psychology. In B. Simon (Ed.), *Psychology in the Soviet Union*. London: Routledge & Kegan Paul, 1957. Pp. 47–68.

Ellingson, R. J. Electroencephalograms of normal full-term newborns immediately after birth with observations on arousal and visual evoked responses. *Electroencephal. clin. Neurophysiol.*, 1958, **10**, 31–50.

Ellingson, R. J. Cortical electrical responses to visual stimulation in the human infant. *Electroenceph. clin. Neurophysiol.*, 1960, **12**, 663–677.

Ellingson, R. J., and Lindsley, D. B. Brain waves and cortical development in newborns and young infants. *Am. Psychologist*, 1949, **4**, 248–249.

Elze, C. Über das Nervensystem eines menschlichen Embryo von etwa 10 mm. Länge. *Wein. klin. Wschr.*, 1941, **54**, No. 6.

Engel, E. Das Elektrokardiogramm des gesunden Frühgeborenen, Neugeborenen, und Säuglings. *Z. Kinderheilk.*, 1937, **59**, 359–378.

Engel, C. E., and Hansell, P. Use and abuse of the film in recording the behavior and reactions of the newborn infant. *Cerebral Palsy Bull.*, 1961, **3**, 472–480.

Engel, G. L., Reichsman, F., and Segal, H. A study of an infant with a gastric fistula. I. Behavior and the rate of total hydrochloric acid secretion. *Psychosom. Med.*, 1956, **18**, 374–398.

Engel, R. Evaluation of electroencephalographic tracings of newborns. *Lancet*, 1961, **81**, 523–532.

Engel, R. Abnormal electroencephalograms in the newborn period and their significance. *Am. J. ment. Defic.*, 1964, **69**, 341–346.

Engel, R., and Butler, B. Appraisal of conceptual age of newborn infants by electroencephalographic methods. *J. Pediat.*, 1963, **63**, 386–393.

Engen, T., and Lipsitt, L. P. Decrement and recovery of responses to olfactory stimuli in the human neonate. *J. comp. physiol. Psychol.*, 1965, **59**, 312–316.

Engen, T., Lipsitt, L. P., and Kaye, H. Olfactory responses and adaptation in the human neonate. *J. comp. physiol. Psychol.*, 1963, **56**, 73–77.

Engstler, G. Über den Fussohlenreflex und das Babinski-Phänomen bei tausend Kindern der ersten Lebensjahre. *Wien. klin. Woch.*, 1905, **18**, 567–569.

Epstein, W. Experimental investigations of the genesis of visual space perception. *Psychol. Bull.*, 1964, **61**, 115–128.

Erickson, M. H. On the possible occurrence of a dream in an eight-month-old infant. *Psychoanal. Q.*, 1941, **10**, 382–384.

Erikson, E. The psychosocial development of children. In J. M. Tanner and B. Inhelder (Eds.), *Discussions on child development*. Vol. III. New York: International Universities Press, 1955. Pp. 169–216.

Ernhart, C. B., Graham, F. K., Eichman, P. L., Marshall, J. M., and Thurston, D. Brain injury in the preschool child: some developmental considerations. II. Comparison of brain injured and normal children. *Psychol. Monogr.*, 1963, **77**, No. 574.

Erwin, D. An analytical study of children's sleep. *J. genet. Psychol.*, 1934, **45**, 199–226.

Escalona, S. K. Feeding disturbances in very young children. *Am. J. Orthopsychiat.*, 1945, **15**, 76–80.

Escalona, S. K. An appraisal of some psychological factors in relation to rooming-in and self-demand schedules. In M. J. E. Senn (Ed.), *Problems of infancy and childhood, 1st Conference*. New York: Josiah Macy, Jr., Foundation, 1947. Pp. 58–62.

Escalona, S. K. The psychological situation of mother and child upon return from the hospital. In M. J. E. Senn (Ed.), *Problems of infancy and childhood, 3rd Conference*. New York: Josiah Macy, Jr., Foundation, 1949. Pp. 30–51.

Escalona, S. K. The use of infant tests for predictive purposes. *Bull. Menninger Clin.*, 1950, **14**, 117–128. (a)

Escalona, S. K. When mother and child return from the hospital. *Menninger Q.*, 1950, **4**, 8–16. (b)

Escalona, S. K. Emotional development in the first year of life. In M. J. E. Senn (Ed.), *Problems of infancy and childhood, 6th conference*. New York: Josiah Macy, Jr., Foundation, 1953. Pp. 11–47.

Escalona, S. K. Patterns of infantile experience and the developmental process. *Psychoanal. Study Child*, 1963, **18**, 197–244.

Escalona, S. K. *The roots of individuality*. Chicago, Aldine, 1968.

Escalona, S. K., and Heider, G. M. *Prediction and outcome: a study in child development*. New York: Basic Books, 1959.

Escalona, S. K., and Leitch, M. Early phases of personality development. A nonnormative study of infant behavior. *Monogr. Soc. Res. Child Dev.*, 1952, **17**, No. 1.

Escalona, S. K., and Moriarty, A. Prediction of school age intelligence from infant tests. *Child Dev.*, 1961, **32**, 597–605.

Escherich, T. Über die Säugbewegung beim Neugeborenen. *Münch. med. Woch.*, 1888, **35**, 687–689.

Eulenburg, A. Über einige Reflexe im Kindersalter. *Neurol. Centralbl.*, 1882, **1**, 169–172.

Evans, J. N. A visual test for infants. *Am. J. Ophthal.*, 1946, **29**, 73–75.

Evdokimov, S. A., and Zakliakova, V. N. Pribor dlia registratsii migatelnogo refleksa u detei. *Zh. vӳssh. nerv. Deyat.*, 1962, **12**, 354–357.

Ewing, I. R., and Ewing, A. W. G. *Opportunity and the deaf child*. London: University of London Press, 1947.

Fairbanks, G. An acoustical study of the pitch of infant hunger wails. *Child Dev.*, 1942, **13**, 227–232.

Fajans, S. Untersuchungen zur Handlungs- und Affektpsychologie. Herausgegeben von Kurt Lewin. XII. Die Bedeutung der Entfernung für die Stärke eines Aufforderungscharakters beim Säugling und Kleinkind. *Psychol. Forsch.*, 1933, **17**, 215–267. (a)

Fajans, S. Unterschungen zur Handlungs- und Affekpsychologie. Herausgegeben von Kurt Lewin. XIII. Erfolg, Ausdauer und Aktivität beim Säugling und Kleinkind. *Psychol. Forsch.*, 1933, **17**, 268–305. (b)

Falkner, F. (Ed.) *Human development*. Philadelphia, Pa.: Saunders, 1966.

Falkner, F. Pernot-Roy, M. P., Habich, H., Sénécal, J., and Massé, G. Some international comparisons of physical growth in the two first years of life. *Courrier*, 1958, **8**, 1–11.

Fantz, R. L. A method for studying early visual development. *Percept. mot. Skills*, 1956, **6**, 13–15.

Fantz, R. L. Pattern vision in young infants. *Psychol. Rec.*, 1958, **8**, 43–47.

Fantz, R. L. A method for studying depth perception in infants under six months of age. *Psychol. Rec.*, 1961, **11**, 27–32. (a)

Fantz, R. L. The origin of form perception. *Scient. Am.*, 1961, **204**, 66–72. (b)

Fantz, R. L. Pattern vision in newborn infants. *Science*, 1963, **140**, 296–297.

Fantz, R. L. Visual experience in infants: decreased attention to familiar patterns relative to novel ones. *Science*, 1964, **146**, 668–670.

Fantz, R. L. Visual perception from birth as shown by pattern selectivity. *Ann. N. Y. Acad. Sci.*, 1965, 118, 793–814.

Fantz, R. L. Pattern discrimination and selective attention as determinants of perceptual development from birth. In A. H. Kidd, and J. L. Rivoire (Eds.), *Perceptual development in children.* New York: International University Press, 1966.

Fantz, R. L., and Nevis, S. Pattern preferences and perceptual-cognitive development in early infancy. *Merrill-Palmer Q.*, 1967, 13, 77–108. (a)

Fantz, R. L., and Nevis, S. The predictive value of changes in visual preferences in early infancy. In J. Hellmuth (Ed.), *The exceptional infant.* Vol. I. Seattle: Special Child Publs., 1967. Pp. 349–414. (b)

Fantz, R. L., and Ordy, J. M. A visual acuity test for infants under six months of age. *Psychol. Rec.*, 1959, 9, 159–164.

Fantz, R. L., Ordy, J. M., and Udelf, M. S. Maturation of pattern vision in infants during the first six months. *J. comp. physiol. Psychol.*, 1962, 55, 907–917.

Farago, J. Über das Verhalten einiger Reflexe der neugeborenen Kinder. *Arch. f. Kinderheilk.*, 1887, 8, 385–389.

Fearing, F. *Reflex action: a study in the history of physiological psychology.* Baltimore, Md.: Williams and Wilkins, 1930.

Fedorov, V. K. O nekotorȳkh fiziologicheskikh mekhanizmakh nachol'nogo razvitiya psikhicheskoǐ zhizni rebenka. *Vop. Psikhol.*, 1961, 7, 101–107.

Feldman, W. M. *The principles of ante-natal and post-natal child physiology, pure and applied.* London: Longmans, Green, 1920.

Feldman, W. M. The nature of the plantar reflex in early life and the causes of its variations. *Am. J. Dis. Child.*, 1922, 23, 1–40.

Ferenczi, S. Stages in the development of the sense of reality. In J. S. Van Teslaar (Ed.), *An outline of psychoanalysis.* New York: Boni and Liveright, 1924.

Ferguson, A. D., Cutter, F. F., and Scott, R. B. Growth and development of Negro infants. VI. Relationship of certain environmental factors to neuromuscular development during the first year of life. *J. Pediat.*, 1956, 48, 308–313.

Field, H., Copack, P., Derbyshire, A. J., Driessen, G. J., and Marcus, R. E. Responses of newborns to auditory stimulation. *J. Audit. Res.*, 1967, 7, 271–285.

Figurin, N., and Denisova, M. Etapy rasvitia povedemia rebyonka ot rojdenia do goda. *Vop. genet. Reflex. Pedol. Mladench.*, 1929, 19–89.

Fillmore, E. A. Iowa tests for young children. *Univ. Iowa Stud. Child Welf.*, 1936, 11, No. 4.

Finley, G. E. Visual attention, play, and satiation in young children: a cross cultural study. Unpublished doctoral dissertation, Harvard University, 1967.

Fiorentino, M. R. *Reflex testing methods for evaluating C. N. S. development.* Springfield, Ill.: Thomas, 1963.

Fisch, R. O., Walker, W. A., and Anderson, J. A. Prenatal and postnatal developmental consequences of maternal phenylketonuria. *Pediatrics*, 1966, 37, 979–986.

Fischer, L. K. Hospitalism in six-month-old infants. *Am. J. Orthopsychiat.*, 1952, 22, 522–533.

Fischer, L. K. The significance of atypical postural and grasping behavior during the first year of life. *Am. J. Orthopsychiat.*, 1958, 28, 368–375.

Fish, B. The study of motor development in infancy and its relationship to psychological functioning. *Am. J. Psychiat.*, 1961, 117, 1113–1118.

Fishler, K., Graliker, B. V., and Koch, R. The predictability of intelligence with Gesell Developmental Scales in mentally retarded infants and young children. *Am. J. ment. Defic.*, 1965, 69, 515–525.

Fisichelli, V. R., and Karelitz, S. The cry latencies of normal infants and those with brain damage. *J. Pediat.*, 1963, **62**, 724–734.

Fisichelli, V. R., Karelitz, S., Eichbauer, J., and Rosenfeld, L. Volume-unit graphs: their production and applicability in studies of infants' cries. *J. Psychol.*, 1961, **52**, 423–427.

Fisk, B. The maturation of arousal and attention in the first months of life: a study of variations in ego development. *J. Child Psychiat.*, 1963, **2**, 253–270.

Fitchen, M. Speech and music development of a one year old child. *Child Dev.*, 1931, **2**, 324–326.

Fitzgerald, J. E., and Windle, W. F. Some observations on early human fetal movements. *J. comp. Neurol.*, 1942, **76**, 159–167.

Fitzgerald, W. J. The influences of propiomazine on maternal analgesia, length of labor and infant condition. *Clin. Med.*, 1965, **72**, 333–340.

Fitz-Simons, M. J. Some parent-child relationships as shown in clinical case studies. *J. exp. Educ.*, 1933, **2**, 170–196.

Flament, F. Développement de la préférence manuelle de la naissance à six mois. *Enfance*, 1963, No. 3, 241–262.

Flament, F. Analyses de quelques structures gestuelles dans l'activité manipulative du nourrisson. *Psychologie Française*, 1965, **10**, 265–276.

Flechsig, P. E. *Anatomie des menschlichen Gehirns und Rückenmarks auf myelogenetischer Grundlage.* Leipzig: G. Thieme, 1920.

Fleischl, M. F. The problem of sucking. *Am. J. Psychother.*, 1957, **11**, 86–97.

Flint, B. M. Babies who live in institutions. *Bull. Inst. Child Study, Toronto*, 1957, **19**, 1–5.

Flint, B. M. *The security of infants.* Toronto: University of Toronto Press, 1959.

Fonarev, A. M. Soglasovannost' v dvizheniyakh glaznykh yablok y novorozhdennykh detei i voprosy vospriyatiyva prostranstva. *Dokl. akad. Pedag. Nauk. RSFSR*, 1959, No. 4, 85–88.

Fonarev, A. M. Kabina s odnorodonoi opticheskoi srednoi dlya issledovaniya nervnoi deyatel'nosti detei. *Vop. Psikhol.*, 1962, **8**, 133–137.

Foote, E. *Six children.* Springfield, Ill.: Thomas, 1956.

Forbes, H. S., and Forbes, H. B. Fetal sense reaction: Hearing. *J. comp. Psychol.*, 1927, **7**, 353–355.

Foss, B. M. (Ed.) *Determinants of infant behavior.* New York: Wiley, 1961, 1963, 1965.

Foulke, K., and Stinchfield, S. M. The speech development of four infants under two years of age. *J. genet. Psychol.*, 1929, **36**, 140–171.

Fowler, M. B. The role of language in early child development. *Childh. Educ.*, 1941, **17**, 247–252.

Fowler, W. Cognitive learning in infancy and early childhood. *Psychol. Bull.*, 1962, **59**, 116–152.

Fradkin, H., and Krugman, D. A program of adoptive placement for infants under three months. *Am. J. Orthopsychiat.*, 1956, **26**, 577–593.

Fraiberg, S. On the sleep disturbances of early childhood. *Psychoanal. Study Child*, 1950, **5**, 285–309.

Fraiberg, S., Siegel, B. L., and Gibson, R. The role of sound in the search behavior of a blind infant. *Psychoanal. Study Child*, 1966, **21**, 327–357.

Frank, A. A study in infant development. *Child Dev.*, 1938, **9**, 9–26.

Frank, H. Untersuchung über Sehgrössenkonstanz bei Kindern. *Psychol. Forsch.*, 1925, **7**, 137–145.

Frank, L. K. The newborn as a young mammal with organic capacities, needs, and feelings, *Psychosom. Med.*, 1945, **7**, 169–171.

Frank, L. K. The beginnings of child development and family life education in the twentieth century. *Merrill-Palmer Q.*, 1962, **8**, 207–227.

Frank, L. K. *On the importance of infancy.* New York: Random House, 1966.

Franus, E. Reakcje strachu malych dzieci wywolane bodzcami dzialajacymi na analizator rownowagi. *Psychol. Wych.,* 1961, **4,** 281–294.

Franus, E. Jeszcze o reakcjach strachu niemowlat na widok i glos osoby nieznanej i zamaskowanej. *Psychol. Wych.,* 1962, **5,** 392–401.

Fredeen, R. C. Cup feeding of newborn infants. *Pediatrics,* 1948, **2,** 544–548.

Freedman, D. G. The infant's fear of strangers and the flight response. *J. child Psychol. Psychiat.,* 1961, **2,** 242–248.

Freedman, D. G. Smiling in blind infants and the issue of innate vs. acquired. *J. child Psychol. Psychiat.,* 1964, **5,** 171–184.

Freedman, D. G., and Keller, B. Inheritance of behavior in infants. *Science,* 1963, **140,** 196–198.

Freud, A. Observations on child development. *Psychoanal. Study Child,* 1951, **6,** 18–30.

Freud, A., and Burlingham, D. T. *Infants without families.* New York: International Universities Press, 1944.

Freud, A., and Dann, S. An experiment in group upbringing. *Psychoanal. Study Child,* 1951, **6,** 127–168.

Freud, S. Klinische Studie über die halbseitige Cerebrallähmung der Kinder. *Beiträge Kinderheilk.,* 1891, **3.**

Freud, S. Über familiäre Formen von Cerebralen Diplegien. *Neurolog. Centralbl.,* 1893, **12.** (a)

Freud, S. Zur Kenntnis der cerebralen Diplegien des Kindesalters (im Anschlusse an die Little'sche Krankheit). *Beiträge Kinderheilk.,* (Neue Folge,), 1893, **3.** (b)

Freud, S. Die infantile Cerebrallähmung. In C. W. H. Nothnagel, *Handbuch der speziellen Pathologie und Therapie.* Vienna, 1897. Vol. 9.

Freud, S. *Drei Abhandlungen zur sexual Theorie.* Leipzig: F. Deuticke, 1905.

Freud, W. E. Assessment of early infancy. *Psychoanal. Study Child,* 1967, **22,** 216–238.

Freudenberg, E. Der Morosche Umklammerungsreflex und das Brudzinski Nackenzeichen als Reflexe des Säuglingsalters. *Münch. med. Woch.,* 1921, **68,** 1646–1647.

Friedlander, B. Z., and Kessler, J. W. Long term recording of an infant's selective play for perceptual rewards. 1968. (Mimeographed.)

Friedrich, G. *Psychologische Beobachtungen an zwei Knaben.* Langensalza: Beyer & Söhne, 1906.

Fries, M. E. Behavior problems in children under three years of age: their recognition, treatment and prevention. *Archs. Pediat.,* 1928, **45,** 653–663.

Fries, M. E. Factors in character development, neurosis, psychosis and delinquency: a study of pregnancy, delivery, lying-in period and early childhood. *Am. J. Orthopsychiat.,* 1937, **7,** 142–181.

Fries, M. E. Diagnosing the child's adjustment through age-level tests. *Psychoanal. Rev.,* 1947, **34,** 1–31.

Fries, M. E., Brokaw, K., and Murray, V. F. The formation of character as observed in the well baby clinic. Preliminary report. *Am. J. Dis. Child.,* 1935, **49,** 28–42.

Fries, M. E., and Lewi, B. Interrelated factors in development: a study of pregnancy, labor, delivery, lying-in period and childhood. *Am. J. Orthopsychiat.,* 1938, **8,** 726–752.

Fries, M. E., and Woolf, P. J. Some hypotheses on the role of the congenital activity type in personality development. *Psychoanal. Study Child,* 1953, **8,** 48–62.

Froeschels, E., and Beebe, H. Testing the hearing of newborn infants. *Arch. Otolar.*, 1946, **44**, 710–714.

Fudel-Osipova, S. I., and Khokhol, E. N. Narushenie uslovnoreflektornoi deiatelnosti u detei, bolnykh zatiazhnoi dispepsiei. *Zh. vÿssh. nerv. Deyat.*, 1953, **3**, 260–266.

Furfey, P. H. The relation between socio-economic status and intelligence of young infants as measured by the Linfert-Hierholzer scale. *Ped. Sem.*, 1928, **35**, 478–480.

Furfey, P. H., Bonham, M. A., and Sargent, M. K. The mental organization of the newborn. *Child Dev.*, 1930, **1**, 48–51.

Furfey, P. H., and Muehlenbein, J. The validity of infant intelligence tests. *J. genet. Psychol.*, 1932, **40**, 219–223.

Fürnrohr, W. Studien über den Oppenheimschen "Fressreflex" und einige andere Reflexe. *Dt. Z. Nervheilk.*, 1904, **27**, 375–413.

Fuster, M. Observations sur le langage de deux petites filles de 4 mois à 3 ans. *Bull. Soc. libre Étude Psychol. Enf.*, 1900–1905, **1–5**, 253–255.

Gaddini, R. D., and Gaddini, E. Rumination in infancy. In L. Jessner and E. Pavenstedt (Eds.), *Dynamic psychopathology in childhood*. New York: Grune & Stratton, 1959. Pp. 166–185.

Galant, J. S. Über die rudimentären neuropsychischen Funktionen der Säuglinge. *Jb. Kinderheilk.*, 1931, **133**, 104–108.

Galant, S. *Der Rückgratreflex*. Basel, 1917.

Gale, M. C., and Gale, H. The vocabularies of three children of one family to two and half years of age. *Psychol. Stud., Univ. Minn.*, 1900, No. 1, 70–117.

Gallagher, J. J. Clinical judgment and the Cattell infant intelligence scale. *J. consult. Psychol.*, 1953, **17**, 303–305.

Gamper, E., and Untersteiner, E. Über eine komplex gebaute postencephalitische Hyperkinese und ihre möglichen Beziehungen zu dem oralen Einstellungsmechanismus des Säuglings. *Archs. Psychiat. Nervenkrankh.*, 1924, **71**, 282–303.

Gardner, D. B., Pease, D., and Hawkes, G. R. Response of two-year-old children to controlled-stress situations. *J. genet. Psychol.*, 1961, **98**, 29–35.

Gardner, D. B., and Swiger, M. K. Developmental status of two groups of infants released for adoption. *Child Dev.*, 1958, **29**, 521–530.

Gardner, E., Gray, D. J., and O'Rahilly, R. *Anatomy: a regional study of human structure.* Philadelphia, Pa.: Saunders, 1960.

Gardner, G. E. Problems of early infancy. *J. Am. Psychoanal. Assoc.*, 1955, **3**, 506–514.

Garn, S. M., and Rohmann, C. G. Variability in the order of ossification of the bony centers of the hand and wrist. *Am. J. phys. Anthrop.*, 1960, **18**, 219–229.

Garth, T. R., and Porter, E. P. The color preferences of 1032 young children. *Am. J. Psychol.*, 1934, **46**, 448–451.

Gatewood, M. C., and Weiss, A. P. Race and sex differences in newborn infants. *Ped. Sem.*, 1930, **38**, 31–49.

Geber, M. The observation of quality and quantity in the psychological testing of infants. In K. Soddy (Ed.), *Mental health and infant development*. New York: Basic Books, 1956. Pp. 273–282.

Geber, M. The psycho-motor development of African children in the first year, and the influence of maternal behavior. *J. Soc. Psychol.*, 1958, **47**, 185–195.

Geber, M. Tests de Gesell et de Terman-Merrill appliqués en Uganda. *Enfance*, 1958, **11**, 63–67.

Geber, M. Problèmes posés par le développement du jeune enfant Africain en fonction de son milieu social. *Travail hum.*, 1960, **23**, 97–111.

Geber, M., and Dean, R. F. A. Gesell tests on African children. *Pediatrics*, 1957, **20**, 1055–1065. (a)

Geber, M., and Dean, R. F. A. The state of development of newborn African children. *Lancet*, 1957, **272**, 1216–1219. (b)

Gellermann, L. W. Form discrimination in chimpanzees and two-year-old children. I. Form (Triangularity) *per se*. *J. genet. Psychol.*, 1933, **42**, 3–27. (a)

Gellermann, L. W. Form discrimination in chimpanzees and two-year-old children. II. Form versus background. *J. genet. Psychol.*, 1933, **42**, 28–50. (b)

Gentry, E. F., and Aldrich, C. A. Rooting reflex in the newborn infant: incidence and effect on it of sleep. *Am. J. Dis. Child.*, 1948, **75**, 528–539. (a)

Gentry, E. F., and Aldrich, C. A. Toe reflexes in infancy and the development of voluntary control. *Am. J. Dis. Child.*, 1948, **76**, 389–400. (b)

Genzmer, A. *Untersuchungen über die Sinneswahrnehmungen des neugeborenen Menschen*. Halle: Max Niemeyer, 1882.

Gesell, A. L. Mental and physical correspondence in twins. *Scient. Mon.*, 1922, **14**, 305–331.

Gesell, A. L. *The mental growth of the pre-school child: a psychological outline of normal development from birth to the sixth year, including a system of developmental diagnosis*. New York: Macmillan, 1925.

Gesell, A. L. *Infancy and human growth*. New York: Macmillan, 1928.

Gesell, A. L. The individual in infancy. In C. Murchison (Ed.), *The foundations of experimental psychology*. Worcester, Mass.: Clark University Press, 1929. Pp. 628–660. (a)

Gesell, A. L. Maturation and infant behavior pattern. *Psychol. Rev.*, 1929, **36**, 307–319. (b)

Gesell, A. L. *An atlas of infant behavior*. New Haven, Conn.: Yale University Press, 1934.

Gesell, A. L. Cinemanalysis: A method of behavior study. *J. genet. Psychol.*, 1935, **47**, 3–15. (a)

Gesell, A. L. Morphology of behavior in child development. *Jugendkunde*, 1935, **5**, 91–96. (b)

Gesell, A. L. The psychological hygiene of infant feeding. *Ment. Hyg.*, 1938, **22**, 216–220. (a)

Gesell, A. L. The tonic neck reflex in the human infant: its morphogenetic and clinical significance. *J. Pediat.*, 1938, **13**, 455–464. (b)

Gesell, A. L. Reciprocal interweaving in neuromotor development. A principle of spiral organization shown in the patterning of infant behavior. *J. comp. Neurol.*, 1939, **70**, 161–180.

Gesell, A. L. The genesis of behavior form in fetus and infant; the growth of the mind from the standpoint of developmental morphology. *Proc. Am. Phil. Soc.*, 1941, **84**, 471–488.

Gesell, A. L. Behavior aspects of the care of the premature infant. *J. Pediat.*, 1946, **29**, 210–212. (a)

Gesell, A. L. The ontogenesis of infant behavior. In L. Carmichael (Ed.), *Manual of child psychology*. New York: Wiley, 1946. Pp. 295–331. (b)

Gesell, A. L. Differential diagnosis of mental deficiency in infancy. *Neb. St. med. J.*, 1947, **32**, 304–307.

Gesell, A. L. Growth potentials of the human infant. *Sci. Mon.*, 1949, **68**, 252–256.

Gesell, A. L. Human infancy and the embryology of behavior. In A. Weider (Ed.), *Contributions toward medical psychology*. New York: Ronald Press, 1953. Pp. 51–74.

Gesell, A. L., and Amatruda, C. S. *The embryology of behavior; the beginnings of the human mind*. New York: Harper, 1945.

Gesell, A. L., and Amatruda, C. S. *Developmental diagnosis.* New York: Hoeber, 1941.

Gesell, A. L., Amatruda, C. S., Castner, B. M., and Thompson, H. *Biographies of child development: the mental growth of careers of eighty-four infants and children.* New York: Hoeber, 1939.

Gesell, A. L., and Ames. L. B. Early evidences of individuality in the human infant. *Scient. Mon.,* 1937, **45,** 217–225.

Gesell, A. L., and Ames, L. B. The ontogenetic organization of prone behavior in human infancy. *J. genet. Psychol.,* 1940, **56,** 247–263.

Gesell, A. L., and Ames, L. B. Ontogenetic correspondences in the supine and prone postures of the human infant. *Yale J. biol. Med.,* 1943, **15,** 565–573.

Gesell, A. L., and Ames, L. B. The development of handedness. *J. genet. Psychol.,* 1947, **70,** 155–175. (a)

Gesell, A. L., and Ames, L. B. The infant's reaction to his mirror image. *J. genet. Psychol.,* 1947, **70,** 141–154. (b)

Gesell, A. L., and Ames, L. B. Tonic-neck-reflex and symmetro-tonic behavior. *J. Pediat.,* 1950, **36,** 165–176.

Gesell, A. L., and Halverson, H. M. The development of thumb opposition in the human infant. *J. genet. Psychol.,* 1936, **48,** 339–361.

Gesell, A. L., and Halverson, H. M. The daily maturation of infant behavior: a cinema study of postures, movements, and laterality. *J. genet. Psychol.,* 1942, **61,** 3–32.

Gesell, A. L., and Ilg, F. L. *Feeding behavior of infants: a pediatric approach to the mental hygiene of early life.* Philadelphia, Pa.: Lippincott, 1937.

Gesell, A. L., and Ilg, F. L. *Infant and child in the culture of today: the guidance of development in home and nursery school.* New York: Harper, 1943.

Gesell, A. L., Ilg, F. L., and Bullis, G. E. *Vision. Its development in infant and child.* New York: Hoeber, 1949.

Gesell, A. L., and Thompson, H. Learning and growth in identical infant twins: an experimental study by the method of co-twin control. *Genet. Psychol. Monogr.,* 1929, **6,** 1–124.

Gesell, A. L., and Thompson, H. Twins T and C from infancy to adolescence: a biogenetic study of individual differences by the method of co-twin control. *Genet. Psychol. Monogr.,* 1941, **24,** 3–121.

Gesell, A. L., Thompson, H., and Amatruda, C. S. *Infant behavior: its genesis and growth.* New York: McGraw-Hill, 1934.

Gewirtz, J. L. A learning analysis of the effects of normal stimulation, privation and deprivation on the acquisition of social motivation and attachment. In B. M. Foss (Ed.), *Determinants of infant behavior.* New York: Wiley, 1961. Pp. 213–290.

Gewirtz, J. L. The course of infant smiling in four child-rearing environments in Israel. In B. M. Foss (Ed.), *Determinants of infant behavior.* Vol. III. New York: Wiley, 1965. Pp. 205–248.

Gewirtz, J. L. The course of smiling by groups of Israeli infants in the first eighteen months of life. *Scr. Hierosolymitana,* 1965, **14,** 9–58.

Gewirtz, J. L. On the choice of relevant variables and levels of conceptual analysis in environment-infant interaction research. Presented at the Merrill-Palmer Institute Conference on Research and Teaching of Infant Development. Feb. 15–17, 1968. *Merrill-Palmer Q.,* 1969, **15,** 7–47.

Gibson, E. J. *Principles of perceptual learning and development.* New York: Appleton-Century-Crofts, 1969.

Gibson, E. J., and Walk, R. D. The "visual cliff." *Scient. Am.,* 1960, **202,** 64–71.

Gibson, J. P. Reaction of infants to cold formulas. *J. Pediat.,* 1958, **52,** 404–406.

Gibson, R. M. Personality development. *Psychosom. Med.,* 1965, **27,** 229–237.

Gidoll, S. H. Quantitative determination of hearing to audiometric frequencies in the electroencephalogram. *Archs. Otolar.*, 1952, **55**, 597–601.

Giesecke, M. The genesis of hand preference. *Monogr. Soc. Res. Child Dev.*, 1936, **1**, No. 5.

Gilliland, A. R. The measurement of the mentality of infants. *Child Dev.*, 1948, **19**, 155–158.

Gilliland, A. R. Environmental influences on infant intelligence test scores. *Harvard educ. Rev.*, 1949, **19**, 142–146.

Gilliland, A. R. Socio-economic status and race as factors in infant intelligence test scores. *Child Dev.*, 1951, **22**, 271–273.

Gilmer, B. v. H. An analysis of the spontaneous responses of the newborn infant. *J. genet. Psychol.*, 1933, **42**, 392–405.

Glaser, K. Semi-self-demand feeding schedule for prematurely born infants. *Am. J. Dis. Child.*, 1948, **75**, 309–315.

Glaser, K., Parmelee, A. H., and Plattner, E. B. Growth pattern of prematurely born infants. *Pediatrics*, 1950, **5**, 130–144.

Glichlich, L. B. Developmental evaluation of the infant in the first four months of life. *Bull. Marquette Univ. Sch. Med.*, (Milwaukee, Wisc.), 1961.

Goldberg, S., and Lewis, M. Play behavior in the year old infant: early sex differences. *Child Dev.* 1969, **40**, 21–31.

Golden, M., and Birns, B. Social class and cognitive development in infancy. *Merrill-Palmer Q.*, 1968, **14**, 139–150.

Goldfarb, W. Infant rearing as a factor in foster home replacement. *Am. J. Orthopsychiat.*, 1944, **14**, 162–166.

Goldfarb, W. Effects of psychological deprivation in infancy and subsequent stimulation. *Am. J. Psychiat.*, 1945, **102**, 18–33.

Goldstein, K., Landis, C., Hunt, W. A., and Clarke, F. M. Moro reflex and the startle pattern. *Archs. Neurol. Psychiat.*, 1938, **40**, 322–327.

Gollin, E. S. Research trends in infant learning. In J. Hellmuth (Ed.), *Exceptional Infant.* Seattle, Wash.: Special Child Publications, 1967. Pp. 241–266.

Goodenough, F. L. The expression of the emotions in infancy. *Child Dev.*, 1931, **2**, 96–101.

Goodenough, F. L., Foster, J. C., and van Wagenen, M. J. *The Minnesota preschool test.* Minneapolis: University of Minnesota Press, 1932.

Goodman, W. S., Appelby, S. V., Scott, J. W., and Ireland, P. E. Audiometry in new-born children by electroencephalography. *Laryngoscope*, 1964, **74**, 1316–1328.

Gordon, K. A study of hand and eye preference. *Child Dev.*, 1931, **2**, 321–324.

Gordon, M. B. The Moro embrace reflex in infancy: its incidence and significance. *Am. J. Dis. Child.*, 1929, **38**, 26–34.

Gordon, N. S., and Bell, R. Q. Activity in the human newborn. *Psych. Rep.*, 1961, **9**, 103–116.

Gorman, J. J., Cogan, D. G., and Gellis, S. S. An apparatus for grading the visual acuity of infants on the basis of opticokinetic nystagmus. *Pediatrics*, 1957, **19**, 1088–1092.

Gorman, J. J., Cogan, D. G., and Gellis, S. S. A device for testing visual acuity in infants. *Sight-Saving Rev.*, 1959, **29**, 80–84.

Gottlieb, G., and Simner, M. L. Relationship between cardiac rate and non-nutritive sucking in human infants. *J. comp. Physiol. Psychol.*, 1966, **61**, 128–131.

Gottschadt, K. (Ed.) Internationales Symposion der Deutschen Akademie der Wissenschaften zu Berlin über "Probleme der Entwicklungs-Psychologie." *Z. Psychol.*, 1961, **165** (1–4).

Götz, G. Beiträge zum Frühgeburtenproblem. Mit Nachforschungen über Frühgeborene. *Mschr. Kinderheilk.*, 1940, **82**, 158–196.

Govallo, V. I. Kharakter dvigatel-noĭ aktivnosti vo vremia sna i bodrstvovaniia u deteĭ pervogo goda zhizni s razlichnymi tipologicheskikh osobennostiami nervnoĭ sistemi. *Dokl. Akad. Nauk. SSSR*, 1961, **136**, 989–992.

Graefe, O. Versuche über visuelle Formwahrnehmung im Säuglingsalter. *Psychol. Forsch.*, 1963, **27**, 177–224.

Graffar, M. Influence du milieu social sur la croissance. In A. Merminod (Ed.), *The growth of the normal child during the first three years of life.* Basel: Karger, 1962.

Graham, F. K. Behavioral differences between normal and traumatized newborns. I. The test procedures. *Psychol. Monogr.*, 1956, **70**, No. 427.

Graham, F. K., Caldwell, B. M., Ernhart, C. B., Pennoyer, M. M., and Hartmann, A. F., Sr. Anoxia as a significant perinatal experience: a critique. *J. Pediat.*, 1957, **50**, 556–569.

Graham, F. K., and Clifton, R. K. Heart-rate change as a component of the orienting response. *Psychol. Bull.*, 1966, **65**, 305–320.

Graham, F. K., Ernhart, C. B., Craft, M., and Berman, P. W. Brain injury in the preschool child: some developmental considerations. I. Performance of normal children. *Psychol. Monogr.*, 1963, **77**, No. 573.

Graham, F. K., Ernhart, C. B., Thurston, D., and Craft, M. Development three years after perinatal anoxia and other potentially damaging newborn experiences. *Psychol. Monogr.*, 1962, **76**, No. 522.

Graham, F. K., Matarazzo, R. G., and Caldwell, B. M. Behavioral differences between normal and traumatized newborns. II. Standardization, reliability, and validity. *Psychol. Monogr.*, 1956, **70**, No. 428.

Graham, F. K., Pennoyer, M. M., Caldwell, B. M., Greenman, M., and Hartmann, A. F., Sr. Relationship between clinical status and behavior test performances in a newborn group with histories suggesting anoxia. *J. Pediat.*, 1957, **50**, 177–189.

Granqvist, H. *Birth and childhood among the Arabs; studies in a Muhammadan village in Palestine.* Helsinki, Finland: Söderström, 1947.

Granqvist, H. *Child problems among the Arabs: studies in a Muhammadan village in Palestine.* Helsinki, Finland: Söderström, 1950.

Grant, E. I. The effect of certain factors in the home environment upon child behavior. *Univ. Iowa Stud. Child Welf.*, 1939, **17**, 61–94.

Grastyan, E. The significance of the earliest manifestations of conditioning in the mechanism of learning. In J. F. Delafresnaye (Ed.), *Brain mechanisms and learning.* Oxford: Blackwell, 1961. Pp. 243–263.

Gray, P. H. Theory and evidence of imprinting in human infants. *J. Psychol.*, 1958, **46**, 155–166.

Greenacre, P. Infant reactions to restraint: problems in the fate of infantile aggression. *Am. J. Orthopsychiat.*, 1944, **14**, 204–218.

Greenberg, D., Uzgiris, I., and Hunt, J. McV. Hastening the development of the blink-response with looking. *J. genet. Psychol.*, 1968, **113**, 167–176.

Greenberg, N. H. Studies in psychosomatic differentiation during infancy. I. A longitudinal anterospective approach for the study of development during infancy. *Arch. gen. Psychiat.*, 1962, **7**, 389–406.

Greenberg, N. H. Origins of head-rolling (spasmus nutans) during early infancy. *Psychosom. Med.*, 1964, **26**, 162–171.

Greenberg, N. H. Developmental effects of stimulation during early infancy: some conceptual and methodological considerations. *Ann. N. Y. Acad. Sci.*, 1965, **118**, 831–859.

Greene, W. A., Jr. Early object relations, somatic, affective, and personal. *J. nerv. ment. Dis.*, 1958, **126**, 225–253.

Greenwood, A. K. Das erste Halbjahr eines Säuglings. *Int. Z. indiv. Psychol.*, 1933, **11**, 464–467.

Grégoire, A. L'apprentissage de la parole pendant les deux premières années de l'enfance. *J. Psychol. norm. Path.*, 1933, **30**, 375–389.

Grégoire, A. *L'apprentissage du langage: Les deux premières années.* Paris: Alcan, 1937.

Grégoire, A. *L'apprentissage du langage. II. La troisieme année et les années suivantes.* Paris: Droz, 1947.

Greulich, W. W. A comparison of the physical growth and development of American-born and native Japanese children. *Am. J. phys. Anthrop.*, 1957, **15**, 489–516.

Griffiths, R. *The abilities of babies; a study in mental measurement.* New York: McGraw-Hill, 1954.

Grossman, H. J., and Greenberg, N. H. Psychosomatic differentiation in infancy. I. Autonomic activity in the newborn. *Psychosom. Med.*, 1957, **19**, 293–306.

Gruner, J. E. Histological study of the maturation of the nervous system. *Dev. Med. Child Neurol.*, 1962, **4**, 626–639.

Gryborski, J. D. The swallowing mechanism of the neonate. I. Esophageal and gastric motility. *Pediatrics*, 1965, **35**, 445–452.

Gudden, H. Das Verhalten der Pupillen beim Neugeborenen und im ersten Lebensjahr. *Münch. med. Woch.*, 1910, **57**, 405–406.

Guernsey, M. A quantitative study of the eye reflexes in infants. *Psychol. Bull.*, 1929, **26**, 160–161.

Guillaume, P. Le problème de la perception de l'espace et la psychologie de l'enfant. *J. Psychol. norm. Path.*, 1924, **21**, 112–134.

Gullickson, G. R., and Crowell, D. H. Neonatal habituation to electrotactual stimulation. *J. exp. child Psychol.*, 1964, **1**, 388–396.

Gundobin, N. Die Eigntümlichkeiten des Kindesalters. *Jb. Kinderheilk.*, 1907, **65**, 720–732.

Gunther, M. Instinct and the nursing couple. *Lancet*, 1955, **268**, 575–578.

Gunther, M. Infant behavior at the breast. In B. M. Foss (Ed.), *Determinants of infant behavior.* New York: Wiley, 1961. Pp. 37–44.

Gutmann, M. I. Über Augenbewegungen der Neugeborenen und ihre theoretische Bedeutung. *Archs. ges. Psychol.*, 1924, **47**, 108–121.

Gutteridge, M. V. *The duration of attention in young children.* Aust. Coun. Educ. Res.: Educ. Res. Series, 1935, No. 41.

Gutteridge, M. V. A study of motor achievements of young children. *Archs. Psychol.*, 1939, No. 244, 1–178.

Haaf, R. A., and Bell, R. Q. A facial dimension in visual discrimination by human infants. *Child Dev.*, 1967, **38**, 893–899.

Haas, M. B., and Harms, I. E. Social interaction between infants. *Child Dev.*, 1963, **34**, 79–97.

Hahn, C. *Des Prématurés.* Paris: G. Steinheil, 1901.

Haith, M. M. The response of the human newborn to visual movement. *J. exp. child Psychol.*, 1966, **3**, 235–243.

Haith, M. M., Kessen, W., and Collins, D. Response of the human infant to level of complexity of intermittent visual movement. *J. exp. child Psychol.*, 1969, **7**, 52–69.

Hakulinen, A., Hirvonen, L., and Peltonen, T. Response of blood pressure to sucking and tilting in the newborn infant. *Ann. Paediat. Fenniae*, 1962, **8**, 56–61.

Hall, A. J. Some observations on the acts of closing and opening the eyes. *Br. J. Ophthal.*, 1936, **20**, 257–295.

Hall, G. S. Notes on the study of infants. *Ped. Sem.*, 1891, **1**, 127–138.

Hall, G. S., and Smith, T. L. Curiosity and interest. *Ped. Sem.*, 1903, **10**, 315–358.

Hall, W. S. The first five-hundred days of a child's life. *Child Study Mon.*, 1896–97, **2**, 330–342; 394–407; 458–473; 522–537; 586–608.

Haller, M. W. The reactions of infants to changes in the intensity and pitch of pure tone. *J. genet. Psychol.*, 1932, **40**, 162–180.

Halverson, H. M. An experimental study of prehension in infants by means of systematic cinema records. *Genet. Psychol. Monogr.*, 1931, **10**, 107–286.

Halverson, H. M. A further study of grasping. *J. gen. Psychol.*, 1932, **7**, 34–64.

Halverson, H. M. The acquisition of skill in infancy. *J. genet. Psychol.*, 1933, **43**, 3–48.

Halverson, H. M. Complications of the early grasping reactions. *Psychol. Monogr.*, 1936, **47**, 47–63.

Halverson, H. M. Studies of the grasping responses of early infancy: I. *J. genet. Psychol.*, 1937, **51**, 371–392. (a)

Halverson, H. M. Studies of the grasping responses of early infancy: II. *J. genet. Psychol.*, 1937, **51**, 393–424. (b)

Halverson, H. M. Studies of the grasping responses of early infancy: III. *J. genet. Psychol.*, 1937, **51**, 425–449. (c)

Halverson, H. M. Infant sucking and tensional behavior. *J. genet. Psychol.*, 1938, **53**, 365–430.

Halverson, H. M. Genital and sphincter behavior of the male infant. *J. genet. Psychol.*, 1940, **56**, 95–136.

Halverson, H. M. Variations in pulse and respiration during different phases of infant behavior. *J. genet. Psychol.*, 1941, **59**, 259–330.

Halverson, H. M. The differential effects of nudity and clothing on muscular tonus in infancy. *J. genet. Psychol.*, 1942, **61**, 55–67.

Halverson, H. M. Mechanisms of early infant feeding. *J. genet. Psychol.*, 1944, **64**, 185–223.

Halverson, H. M. A study of feeding mechanisms in premature infants. *J. genet. Psychol.*, 1946, **68**, 205–217.

Hammond, W. H. The constancy of physical types as determined by factorial analysis. *Hum. Biol.*, 1957, **29**, 40–61.

Hardy, J. B., Dougherty, A., and Hardy, W. G. Hearing responses and audiologic screening in infants. *J. Pediat.*, 1959, **55**, 382–390.

Hardy, W. G., and Bordley, J. E. Evaluation of hearing in young children. *Acta oto-lar.*, 1951–1952, **40**, 346–360.

Hardy, W. G., and Bordley, J. E. Special techniques in testing the hearing of children. *J. speech hear. Disord.*, 1951, **16**, 122–131.

Harper, P. A., Fischer, L. K., and Rider, R. V. Neurological and intellectual status of prematures at three to five years of age. *J. Pediat.*, 1959, **55**, 679–690.

Harris, D. B. Early deprivation and enrichment, and later development: an introduction to a symposium. *Child Dev.*, 1965, **36**, 839–842.

Harris, D. B., and Harris, E. S. A study of fetal movements in relation to mother's activity. *Hum. Biol.*, 1946, **18**, 221–237.

Harris, J. A. On correlation between age of parents and length and weight of the newborn infant. *Proc. Soc. exp. Biol. Med.*, 1926, **23**, 801–805. (a)

Harris, J. A. Relationship between pregnancy order and birth order and length and weight of newborn infants. *Proc. Soc. exp. Biol. Med.*, 1926, **23**, 806–808. (b)

Harris, J. D. Habituation response decrement in the intact organism. *Psychol. Bull.*, 1943, **40**, 385–422.

Hartmann-Karplus, D. Untersuchungen über Juckempfindung, Kratzen und Pilomotorenreflex im Säuglingsalter. *Ann. Paediat.*, 1931, **132**, 140–158.

Hassin, G. B. Acute (epidemic?) encephalitis: report of a case in a newborn twin with histologic observations. *Archs. Neur. Psychiat.*, 1927, **18**, 44–55.

Haynes, H., White, B. L., and Held, R. Visual accommodation in human infants. *Science*, 1965, **148**, 528–530.

Hazard, C. The relation of reflex conduction rate in the patellar reflex to age in human beings. *Univ. Iowa Stud. Child Welf.*, 1936, **12**, 181–197.

Hazzard, F. W. Development of an infant in grasping, reaching and body movements. *Child Dev.*, 1931, **2**, 158–160.

Hazzard, F. W. A thumb sucking cure. *Child Dev.*, 1932, **3**, 80–81.

Heathers, G. The adjustment of two-year-olds in a novel social situation. *Child Dev.*, 1954, **25**, 147–158.

Heck, J., and Zetterström, B. Analyse des photopischen Flimmerelektroretinogramms bei Neugeborenen. *Ophthalmologica*, 1958, **135**, 205–210.

Heck, W. E. Vestibular responses in the newborn. *Arch. Otolar.*, 1952, **56**, 573.

Heering, G. A. A study of thumb sucking in infants from two to seventeen weeks of age. *Child Dev.*, 1932, **3**, 273–277.

Heider, G. M. Vulnerability in infants and young children: a pilot study. *Genet. Psychol. Monogr.*, 1966, **73**, 1–216.

Heinicke, C. M. Some effects of separating two-year-old children from their parents: a comparative study. *Hum. Relat.*, 1956, **9**, 105–176.

Heinstein, M. Behavioral correlates of breast-bottle regimes under varying parent-infant relationships. *Monogr. Soc. Res. Child Dev.*, 1963, **28**, Whole No. 88.

Hellbrügge, T., Lange, J. E., Rutenfrantz, J., and Stehr, K. Circadian periodicity of physiological functions in different stages of infancy and childhood. *Am. N. Y. Acad. Sci.*, 1964, **117**, 361–373.

Hendry, L. S., and Kessen, W. Oral behavior of newborn infants as a function of age and time since feeding. *Child Dev.*, 1964, **35**, 201–208.

Herbertson, Mrs. The beginning of childhood; notes on the first one-half of the third year. *Paidologist*, 1899, **1**, 83–93.

Herlitz, G. Studien über die konsensuelle Hautgefässreaktion Neugeborener bei Kälteeinwirkung. *Acta paediat., Stockholm*, 1942, **30**, 434–447.

Herring, A. An experimental study of the reliability of the Bühler baby tests. *J. exp. Educ.*, 1937, **6**, 147–160.

Herrmann, M. Beobachtungen über den Einfluss der Nahrungstemperatur auf das Verhalten des Säuglings. *Monatssch. Kinderheilk.*, 1931, **51**, 49–69.

Hershenson, M. Visual discrimination in the human newborn. *J. comp. physiol. Psychol.*, 1964, **58**, 270–276.

Hershenson, M. Development of the perception of form. *Psychol. Bull.*, 1967, **67**, 326–336.

Hershenson, M., Kessen, W., and Munsinger, H. Pattern perception in the human newborn: a close look at some positive and negative results. In W. Wathen-Dunn, (Ed.), *Symposium on models for the perception of speech and visual form*. Cambridge, Mass.: MIT Press, 1967. Pp. 282–290.

Hershenson, M., Munsinger, H., and Kessen, W. Preference for shapes of intermediate variability in the newborn human. *Science*, 1965, **147**, 630–631.

Herzfeld, B. Das neugeborene Kind und seine Eigentümlichkeiten. *Jb. Kinderheilk.*, 1922, **99**, 75–85.

Hess, J. H. Experiences gained in a thirty year study of prematurely born infants. *Pediatrics*, 1953, **11**, 425–434.

Hess, J. H., Mohr, G. J., and Bartelme, P. F. *The physical and mental growth of prematurely born children.* Chicago: University of Chicago Press, 1934.

Hetzer, H. *Kindheit und Armut: psychologische Methoden in Armutsforschung und Armutsbekämpfung.* Leipzig: S. Hirzel, 1929.

Hetzer, H. *Psychologische Untersuchung der Konstitution des Kindes.* Leipzig: J. A. Barth, 1937.

Hetzer, H., Beaumont, H., and Wiehemeyer, E. Das Schauen und Greifen des Kindes. Untersuchungen über spontanen Funktionswandel und Reizauslese in der Entwicklung. II. Optische Rezeption und Bilderfassen im zweiten Lebensjahr. *Z. Psychol. Physiol. Sinnesorg.,* 1929, **113,** 268–286.

Hetzer, H., and Jenschke, M. T. Nachprüfung von Testgutachten im zweiten Lebensjahr. *Z. Kinderforsch.,* 1930, **37,** 653–660.

Hetzer, H., and Koller, L. Vier Testreihen für das zweite Lebensjahr. *Z. Psychol.,* 1930, **117,** 257–306.

Hetzer, H., and Reindorf, B. Sprachentwicklung und soziales Milieu. *Z. angew. Psychol.,* 1928, **29,** 449–462.

Hetzer, H., and Tudor-Hart, B. H. Die fruhesten Reaktionen auf die menschliche Stimme. *Quell. Stud. Jugendk.,* 1927, **5,** 103–124.

Hetzer, H., and Wislitzky, S. Experimente über Erwartung und Erinnerung beim Kleinkind. *Z. Psychol.,* 1930, **118,** 128–141.

Hetzer, H., and Wolf, K. Babytests. *Z. Psychol.,* 1928, **107,** 62–104.

Hilden, A. H. A longitudinal study of intellectual development. *J. Psychol.,* 1949, **28,** 187–214.

Hill, J. Infant feeding and personality disorders. A study of early feeding in its relation to emotional and digestive disorders. *Psychiat. Q.,* 1937, **11,** 356–382.

Himelstein, P. Research with the Stanford-Binet, Form L-M: the first five years. *Psychol. Bull.,* 1966, **65,** 156–164.

Hindley, C. B. The Griffiths scale of infant development: scores and predictions from 3 to 18 months. *J. child Psychol. Psychiat.,* 1960, **1,** 99–112.

Hindley, C. B. Methods of studying psychological development. *Mod. Probl. Pediat.,* 1962, **7,** 112–128.

Hoch, P., and Zubin, J. (Eds.) *Psychopathology of childhood.* New York: Grune & Stratton, 1955.

Hochberg, J. E. Nativism and empiricism in perception. In L. Postman (Ed.), *Psychology in the making.* New York: Knopf, 1963. Pp. 255–330.

Hoefer, C., and Hardy, M. Later development of breast-fed and artificially fed infants. *J. Am. Med. Assoc.,* 1929, **92,** 615–619.

Hoeland, H. Über die Hexenmilch und die histologischen Veränderungen in den Brüsten des Neugeborenen. *Mschr. Geburtsh. Gynäk.,* 1927, **77,** 114–120.

Hoffer, W. Mouth, hand and ego integration. *Psychoanal. Study Child,* 1949, **3** & **4,** 49–56.

Hoffer, W. Development of the body ego. *Psychoanal. Study Child,* 1950, **5,** 18–23.

Hofstaetter, P. R. The changing composition of "intelligence": a study in T-technique *J. genet. Psychol.,* 1954, **85,** 159–164.

Hogan, L. E. *A study of a child.* New York: Harper, 1898.

Hogbin, H. I. A New Guinea infancy, from conception to weaning in Wogeo. *Oceania,* 1943, **13,** 285–309.

Hogg, I. D. Sensory nerves and associated structures in the skin of human fetuses of 8 to 14 weeks of menstrual age correlated with functional capability. *J. comp. Neurol.,* 1941, **75,** 371–410.

Holden, E. S. On the vocabularies of children under two years of age. *Trans. Am. Philol. Assoc.,* 1877, **8,** 58–68.

Holden, R. H., and Solomons, G. Relations between pediatric, psychological, and neurological examinations during the first year of life. *Child Dev.*, 1962, **33**, 719–727.

Holden, W. A., and Bosse, K. K. The order of development of color perception and of color preference in the child. *Arch. Ophthal.*, 1900, **29**, 261–277.

Hollingworth, H. L. How we learn our "reflexes." *Psychol. Rev.*, 1928, **35**, 439–442.

Hollis, W. A. Facial crinkles and emotional grimace. *Lancet*, 1913, **1**, 23–26.

Holmes, S. J. Recapitulation and its supposed causes. *Quart. Rev. Biol.*, 1944, **19**, 319–331.

Holmes, U. T. The phonology of an English-speaking child. *Am. Speech*, 1927, **2**, 219–225.

Holt, K. S. Early motor development: posturally induced variations. *J. Pediat.*, 1960, **57**, 571–575.

Holt, L. E., Jr., Davies, E. A., Hasselmeyer, E. G., and Adams, A. O. A study of premature infants fed cold formulas. *J. Pediat.*, 1962, **61**, 556–561.

Honzik, M. P. Developmental studies of parent-child resemblance in intelligence. *Child Dev.*, 1957, **28**, 215–228.

Honzik, M. P. Hutchings, J. J., and Burnip, S. R. Birth record assessments and test performance at eight months. *Am. J. Dis. Child.*, 1965, **109**, 416–426.

Honzik, M. P., and McKee, J. P. The sex-differences in thumb-sucking. *J. Pediat.*, 1962, **61**, 726–732.

Hooker, D. The origin of the grasping movement in man. *Proc. Am. Phil. Soc.*, 1938, **79**, 597–606.

Hooker, D. Fetal behavior. *Res. Publ. Assoc. nerv. ment. Dis.*, 1939, **19**, 237–243.

Hooker, D. Fetal reflexes and instinctual processes. *Psychosom. Med.*, 1942, **4**, 199–205.

Hooker, D. *The prenatal origin of behavior.* Lawrence: University of Kansas Press, 1952.

Hopkins, J. Bibliographie des recherches psychologiques conduites en Afrique. *Rev. Psychol. Appl.*, 1962, **12**, 201–213.

Hopper, H. E., and Pinneau, S. R. Frequency of regurgitation in infancy as related to the amount of stimulation received from the mother. *Child Dev.*, 1957, **28**, 229–235.

Horowitz, F. D. Infant learning and development: retrospect and prospect. *Merrill-Palmer Q.*, 1968, **14**, 101–120.

Horsten, G. P., and Winkelman, J. E. Electrical activity of the retina in relation to histological differentiation in infants born prematurely and at full term. *Vision Res.*, 1962, **2**, 269–276.

Horsten, G. P. M., and Winkelman, J. E. Electro-retinographic critical fusion frequency of the retina in relation to the histological development in man and animals. *Ophthalmologica.*, 1964, **18**, 515–521.

Horton, F. H., Lubchenco, L. O., and Gordon, H. H. Self-regulatory feeding in a premature nursery . *Yale J. Biol. Med.*, 1952, **24**, 263–272.

Howard, R. W. The language development of a group of triplets. *J. genet. Psychol.*, 1946, **69**, 181–188.

Hoyer, A., and Hoyer, G. Über die Lallsprache eines Kindes. *Z. angew. Psychol.*, 1924, **24**, 363–384.

Hrbek, A., and Mareš, P. Cortical evoked responses to visual stimulation in fullterm and premature newborns. *Electroenceph. clin. Neurophysiol.*, 1964, **16**, 575–581. (a)

Hrbek, A., and Mareš, P. The development of electrophysiological reactivity of CNS in children. *Activitas nerv. sup.*, 1964, **6**, 92–93. (b)

Hrbek, A., and Mareš, P. Development of the visual system in mature and premature infants. *Rev. Czech. Med.*, 1965, **11**, 81–90.

Hsu, E. H. On the application of Viennese infant scale to Peiping babies. *J. genet. Psychol.*, 1946, **69**, 217–220.

Hubbard, R. M. A study of the reliability and validity of the Bühler Infant Scale. *J. genet. Psychol.*, 1935, **47**, 361–384.

Hückstedt, B. Experimentelle Untersuchungen zum "Kindchenschema." *Z. exp. angew. Psychol.*, 1965, **12**, 421–450.

Hughes, J. G., Davis, B. C., and Brennan, M. L. Electroencephalography of the newborn infant. VI. Studies on premature infants. *Pediatrics*, 1951, **7**, 707–712.

Hughes, J. G., Ehemann, B., and Brown, U. A. Electroencephalography of the newborn: I. Studies on normal, full term, sleeping infants. *Am. J. Dis. Child.*, 1948, **76**, 503–512. (a)

Hughes, J. G., Ehemann, B., and Brown, U. A. Electroencephalography of the newborn: III. Brain potentials of babies born of mothers given "seconal sodium." *Am. J. Dis. Child.*, 1948, **76**, 626–633. (b)

Hughes, J. G., Ehemann, B., and Brown, U. A. Electroencephalography of the newborn: IV. Abnormal electroencephalograms of the neonate. *Am. J. Dis. Child.*, 1948, **76**, 634–647. (c)

Hughes, J. G., Ehemann, B., and Hill, F. S. Electroencephalography of the newborn: II. Studies on normal, full term infants while awake and while drowsy. *Am. J. Dis. Child.*, 1949, **77**, 310–314.

Hull, C. L., and Hull, B. I. Parallel learning curves of an infant in vocabulary and in voluntary control of the bladder. *Ped. Sem.*, 1919, **26**, 272–283.

Humphreys, M. W. A contribution to infantile linguistics. *Trans. Am. Philol. Assoc.*, 1880, **11**, 5–17.

Hunt, J. McV. *Intelligence and experience.* New York: Ronald Press, 1961.

Hunt, J. McV. Intrinsic motivation and its role in psychological development. In D. Levine (Ed.), *Nebraska symposium on motivation.* Lincoln: University of Nebraska Press, 1965. Pp. 189–282.

Hunt, W. A., Clarke, F. M., and Hunt, E. B. Studies of the startle pattern. IV. Infants. *J. Psychol.*, 1936, **2**, 339–352.

Hunt, W. A., Clarke, F. M., and Hunt, E. B. The startle pattern in infants in response to non-auditory stimuli. *J. genet. Psychol.*, 1938, **52**, 443–446.

Hunt, W. A., and Landis, C. Studies of the startle pattern: I. Introduction. *J. Psychol.*, 1936, **2**, 201–205.

Hunt, W. A., and Landis, C. A note on the difference between the Moro reflex and the startle pattern. *Psychol. Rev.*, 1938, **45**, 267–269.

Hurlock, E. B. Experimental studies of the newborn. *Child Dev.*, 1933, **4**, 148–163.

Illingworth, R. S. *The development of the infant and young child.* Edinburgh and London: Livingstone, 1960.

Illingworth, R. S. Delayed maturation in development. *J. Pediat.*, 1961, **58**, 761–770. (a)

Illingworth, R. S. The predictive value of developmental tests in the first year, with special reference to the diagnosis of mental subnormality. *J. child Psychol. Psychiat.*, 1961, **2**, 210–215. (b)

Illingworth, R. S. *An introduction to developmental assessment in the first year.* London: Heinemann, 1962.

Ingram, T. T. S. Clinical significance of the infantile feeding reflexes. *Dev. Med. Child Neurol.*, 1962, **4**, 159–169.

Irvine, E. E. Observations on the aims and methods of child rearing in communal settlements in Israel. *Hum. Relat.*, 1952, **5**, 247–275.

Irwin, O. C. The amount and nature of activities of newborn infants under constant external stimulating conditions during the first ten days of life. *Genet. Psychol. Monogr.*, 1930, **8**, 1–92.

Irwin, O. C. A cold light for photographing infant reactions with the high speed motion picture camera. *Child Dev.*, 1931, **2**, 153–155.

Irwin, O. C. The amount of motility of seventy-three newborn infants. *J. comp. Psychol.*, 1932, **14**, 415–428. (a)

Irwin, O. C. The distribution of the amount of motility in young infants between two nursing periods. *J. comp. Psychol.*, 1932, **14**, 429–445. (b)

Irwin, O. C. Infant responses to vertical movements. *Child Dev.*, 1932, **3**, 167–169. (c)

Irwin, O. C. The latent time of the body startle in infants. *Child Dev.*, 1932, **3**, 104–107. (d)

Irwin, O. C. Motility in newborn infants. *Proc. Iowa Acad. Sci.*, 1932, **39**, 243. (e)

Irwin, O. C. The relation of body motility in young infants to some physical traits. *J. exp. Educ.*, 1932, **1**, 140–143. (f)

Irwin, O. C. Dennis on mass activity: a reply. *Psychol. Rev.*, 1933, **40**, 215–219. (a)

Irwin, O. C. Motility in young infants: I. Relation to body temperature. *Am. J. Dis. Child.*, 1933, **45**, 531–533. (b)

Irwin, O. C. Motility in young infants: II. Relation to two indexes of nutritional status. *Am. J. Dis. Child.*, 1933, **45**, 534–537. (c)

Irwin, O. C. Qualitative changes in a vertebral reaction pattern during infancy: a motion picture study. *Univ. Iowa Stud. Child Welf.*, 1936, **12**, 199–207.

Irwin, O. C. Effect of strong light on the body activity of newborns. *J. comp. Psychol.*, 1941, **32**, 233–236. (a)

Irwin, O. C. The profile as a visual device for indicating central tendencies in speech data. *Child Dev.*, 1941, **12**, 111–120. (b)

Irwin, O. C. Reliability of infant speech sound data. *J. speech Disord.*, 1945, **10**, 227–235.

Irwin, O. C. Infant speech: equations for consonant-vowel ratios. *J. speech Disord.*, 1946, **11**, 177–180.

Irwin, O. C. Development of speech during infancy: curve of phonemic frequencies. *J. exp. Psychol.*, 1947, **37**, 187–193. (a)

Irwin, O. C. Infant speech: the problem of variability. *J. speech Disord.*, 1947, **12**, 173–176. (b)

Irwin, O. C. Infant speech: variability and the problem of diagnosis. *J. speech Disord.*, 1947, **12**, 287–289. (c)

Irwin, O. C. Infant speech: consonantal sounds according to place of articulation. *J. speech Disord.*, 1947, **12**, 397–401. (d)

Irwin, O. C. Infant speech: consonant sounds according to manner of articulation. *J. speech Disord.*, 1947, **12**, 402–404. (e)

Irwin, O. C. Infant speech: development of vowel sounds. *J. speech hear. Disord.*, 1948, **13**, 31–34. (a)

Irwin, O. C. Infant speech: the effect of family occupational status and of age on use of sound types. *J. speech hear. Disord.*, 1948, **13**, 224–226. (b)

Irwin, O. C. Infant speech: the effect of family occupational status and of age on sound frequency. *J. speech hear. Disord.*, 1948, **13**, 320–323. (c)

Irwin, O. C. Infant speech: speech sound development of siblings and only infants. *J. exp. Psychol.*, 1948, **38**, 600–602. (d)

Irwin, O. C. Infant speech: consonantal position. *J. speech hear. Disord.*, 1951, **16**, 159–161.

Irwin, O. C. Infant speech: effect of systematic reading of stories. *J. speech hear. Res.*, 1960, **3**, 187–190.

Irwin, O. C., and Chen, H. P. A reliability study of speech sounds observed in the crying of newborn infants. *Child Dev.*, 1941, **12**, 351–368.

Irwin, O. C., and Chen, H. P. Development of speech during infancy: curve of phonemic types. *J. exp. Psychol.*, 1946, **36**, 431–436. (a)

Irwin, O. C., and Chen, H. P. Infant speech: vowel and consonant frequency. *J. speech Disord.*, 1946, **11**, 123–125. (b)

Irwin, O. C., and Curry, T. Vowel elements in the crying vocalization of infants under ten days of age. *Child Dev.*, 1941, **12**, 99–109.

Irwin, O. C., and Weiss, A. P. A note on mass activity in newborn infants. *Ped. Sem.*, 1930, **38**, 20–30.

Irwin, O. C., and Weiss, L. A. Differential variations in the activity and crying of the newborn infant under different intensities of light: a comparison of observational with polygraph findings. *Univ. Iowa Stud. Child Welf.*, 1934, **9**, No. 4, 137–147. (a)

Irwin, O. C., and Weiss, L. A. The effect of clothing on the general and vocal activity of the newborn infant. *Univ. Iowa Stud. Child Welf.*, 1934, **9**, No. 4, 149–162. (b)

Irwin, O. C., and Weiss, L. A. The effect of darkness on the activity of newborn infants. *Univ. Iowa Stud. Child Welf.*, 1934, **9**, No. 4, 165–174. (c)

Irzhanskaia, K. N., and Felberbaum, R. A. Nekotorye dannye ob uslovnoreflektornoi deiatelnosti nedonoshennykh detei. *Fiziolog. Zh. SSSR*, 1954, **40**, 668–672.

Isaacs, S. *Social development in young children: a study of beginnings.* New York: Harcourt, Brace, 1933.

Ischikawa, T. Beobachtungen über die geistige Entwicklung eines Kindes in seinem ersten Lebensjahre. *Beitr. Kinderforsch. Heilerz.*, 1910, 7–53.

Jackson, E. B., and Klatskin, E. H. Rooming-in research project: development of methodology of parent-child relationship study in a clinical setting. *Psychoanal. Study Child*, 1950, **5**, 236–274.

Jackson, E. B., Klatskin, E. H., and Wilkin, L. C. Early child development in relation to degree of flexibility of maternal attitude. *Psychoanal. Study Child*, 1952, **7**, 393–428.

Jackson, I. M. The cry of the child in utero. *Br. med. J.*, 1943, **2**, 266–267.

Jackson, R. L., Westerfield, R., Flynn, M., Kimball, E. R., and Lewis, R. B. Growth of well born American infants fed human and cow's milk. *Pediatrics*, 1964, **33**, 642–652.

Jacobi, W., and Demuth, F. Die wahre Acidität der Mundflüssigkeit beim Säugling und Neugeborenen. *Z. Kinderheilk.*, 1923, **34**, 293–296.

James, W. *The principles of psychology.* New York: Henry Holt, 1890.

James, W. T. The effect of satiation on the sucking response in puppies. *J. comp. physiol. Psychol.*, 1957, **50**, 375–378.

Janoš, O. Vyšší nervová činnost nedonošených dětí v prvních měsících života. *Česk. Pediat.*, 1958, **8**, 951–955.

Janoš, O. Development of higher nervous activity in premature infants. *Pavlov. J. higher nerv. Activ.*, 1959, **9**, 760–767.

Janoš, O. *Věkové a individuální rozdíly ve vyšší nervové cinnosti kojencu.* Prague: Státní zdrovotnické nakladatelství, 1965.

Jaroschka, K. Ein Beitrag zur Kenntnis der Sekretionsvorgänge der Brustdrüse von Säuglingen. *Mschr. Kinderheilk.*, 1929, **42**, 523–527.

Jeffrey, W. E. The orienting reflex and attention in cognitive development. *Psychol. Rev.*, 1968, **75**, 323–334.

Jenkins, R. L. The prediction of the intelligence quotients of younger siblings. *J. genet. Psychol.*, 1933, **42**, 460–464.

Jensen, K. Differential reactions to taste and temperature stimuli in newborn infants. *Genet. Psychol. Monogr.*, 1932, **12**, 361–479.

Jersild, A. T. Emotional development. In L. Carmichael, (Ed.), *Manual of child psychology.* (2nd ed.) New York: Wiley, 1946. Pp. 752–790.

Jervis, J. L. Akustische Rezeption im zweiten Lebensjahr. *Z. Psychol.*, 1931, **123**, 259–290.

Jessner, L., and Pavenstedt, E. (Eds.), *Dynamic psychopathology in childhood.* New York: Grune and Stratton, 1959.

Johnson, B. J. *Mental growth of children in relation to rate of growth in bodily development.* New York: Dutton, 1925.

Jones, H. E. The galvanic skin reflex in infancy. *Child Dev.*, 1930, **1**, 106–110. (a)

Jones, H. E. The retention of conditioned emotional reactions in infancy. *J. genet. Psychol.*, 1930, **37**, 485–498. (b)

Jones, H. E. The conditioning of overt emotional responses. *J. educ. Psychol.*, 1931, **22**, 127–130. (a)

Jones, H. E. Dextrality as a function of age. *J. exp. Psychol.*, 1931, **14**, 125–143. (b)

Jones, H. E., and Hsaio, H. H. Pregnancy order and early development. *Child Dev.*, 1933, **4**, 140–147.

Jones, H. E., and Jones, M. C. Fear. *Childh. Educ.*, 1928, **5**, 136–143.

Jones, M. C. The elimination of children's fears. *J. exp. Psychol.*, 1924, **7**, 382–390. (a)

Jones, M. C. A laboratory study of fear: The case of Peter. *Ped. Sem.*, 1924, **31**, 308–315. (b)

Jones, M. C. The development of early behavior patterns in young children. *Ped. Sem.*, 1926, **33**, 537–585.

Joseph, S. Zur Biologie der Brustdrüse beim Neugeborenen. *Mschr. Geburtsch. Gynäk.*, 1929, **83**, 219–224.

Juarros, C. Aportación al conocimiento de algunos problemas planteados por el estudio del signo de Babinski. *Siglo Medico*, 1930, **85**, 689–694.

Jundell, I. On mixed diet during the first year of life. *Acta Paediat.*, 1921–22, **1**, 240–255.

Jundell, I. Mixed diet during the first year of life. *Acta Paediat.*, 1923–1924, **3**, 159–167.

Kagan, J. On the need for relativism. *Am. Psychologist*, 1967, **22**, 131–142.

Kagan, J., Henker, B. A., Hen-Tov, A., Levine, J., and Lewis, M. Infants' differential reactions to familiar and distorted faces. *Child Dev.*, 1966, **37**, 519–532.

Kagan, J., and Lewis, M. Studies of attention in the human infant. *Merrill-Palmer Q.*, 1965, **11**, 95–127.

Kagan, J., and Moss, H. A. *Birth to maturity.* New York: Wiley, 1962.

Kahn, W. Über die Dauer der Darmpassage im Säuglingsalter. *Z. Kinderheilk.*, 1921, **29**, 321–330.

Kaila, E. Reaktionen des Säuglings auf das menschliche Gesicht. *Ann. Univ. Aboensis.* 1932, **17**, 1–114.

Kantrow, R. W. An investigation of conditioned feeding responses and concomitant adaptive behavior in young infants. *Univ. Iowa Stud. Child Welf.*, 1937, **13**, No. 3.

Kaplan, S. A clinical contribution to the study of narcissism in infancy. *Psychoanal. Study Child*, 1964, **19**, 398–420.

Karelitz, S., Fisichelli, V. R. The cry thresholds of normal infants and those with brain damage. An aid in the early diagnosis of severe brain damage. *J. Pediat.*, 1962, **61**, 679–685.

Karelitz, S., Fisichelli, V. R., Costa, J., Karelitz, R., and Rosenfeld, L. Relation of crying activity in early infancy to speech and intellectual development at age three years. *Child Dev.*, 1964, **35**, 769–777.

Karelitz, S., Karelitz, R. F., and Rosenfeld, L. S. Infants' vocalizations and their significance. In P. W. Bowman and H. V. Mautner (Eds.), *International medical conference on mental retardation: Proceedings.* New York: Grune & Stratton, 1960. Pp. 439–446.

Karlberg, P. Determination of standard energy metabolism (basal metabolism) in normal infants. *Acta paediat., Stockholm*, 1952, **41**, Suppl. 89.

Karlova, A. N. Orienting reflexes in young children. *Pavlov J. higher nerv. Activ.*, 1959, **9**, 34–41.

Karn, M. N. Length of human gestation with special reference to prematurity. *Ann. Eugen., Camb.*, 1947, **14**, 44–59.

Kasahara, M. The curved lines of suction. *Am. J. Dis. Child.*, 1916, **12**, 73–87.

Kasatkin, N. I. Razvitie slukhovykh i zritelnykh uslovnykh refleksov i ikh differentsirovka u mladentsev. *Pediatriia*, 1935, No. 8, 127–137.

Kasatkin, N. I. *Rannie uslovyne refleksy v ontogeneze cheloveka.* Moscow: USSR Acad. Med. Sci., 1948.

Kasatkin, N. I. Rannie uslovnye refleksy rebenka. *Zh. vÿssh. nerv. Deyat.*, 1952, **2**, 572–581. (a)

Kasatkin, N. I. Uslovnye refleksy i khronaksiia kozhi detei. *Fiziolog., Zh. SSSR*, 1952, **38**, 434–443. (b)

Kasatkin, N. I. Ranii ontogenez reflektornoi deiatelnosti rebenka. *Zh. vÿss. nerv. Deyat.*, 1957, **7**, 805–818.

Kasatkin, N. I. The origin and development of conditioned reflexes in early childhood. In M. Cole and I. Maltzman (Eds.), *Handbook of contemporary Soviet psychology.* New York: Basic Books, 1969. Pp. 71–85.

Kasatkin, N. I., and Levikova, A. M. The formation of visual conditioned reflexes and their differentiation in infants. *J. gen. Psychol.*, 1935, **12**, 416–435. (a)

Kasatkin, N. I., and Levikova, A. M. On the development of early conditioned reflexes and differentiations of auditory stimuli in infants. *J. exp. Psychol.*, 1935, **18**, 1–19. (b)

Kasatkin, N. I., Mirzoiants, N. S., and Khokhitva, A. Ob orientirovochnykh uslovnykh refleksakh u detei pervogo goda zhizni. *Zh. vÿss. nerv. Deyat.*, 1953, **3**, 192–202.

Kaye, H. Skin conductance in the human neonate. *Child Dev.*, 1964, **35**, 1297–1305.

Kaye, H. The conditioned Babkin reflex in human newborns. *Psychonom. Sci.*, 1965, **2**, 287–288.

Kaye, H. The effects of feeding and tonal stimulation on non-nutritive sucking in the human newborn. *J. exp. Child Psychol.*, 1966, **3**, 131–145.

Kaye, H. Infant sucking behavior and its modification. In L. P. Lipsitt, and C. C. Spiker, (Eds.), *Advances in child development and behavior.* Vol. 3. New York: Academic Press, 1967. Pp. 1–52.

Kaye, H., and Levin, G. R. Two attempts to demonstrate tonal suppression of nonnutritive sucking in neonates. *Percept. mot. Skills*, 1963, **17**, 521–522.

Kaye, H., and Lipsitt, L. P. Relation of electrotactual threshold to basal skin conductance. *Child Dev.*, 1964, **35**, 1307–1312.

Keen, R. E. Effects of auditory stimuli on sucking behavior in the human neonate. *J. exp. Child Psychol.*, 1964, **1**, 348–354.

Keen, R. E., Chase, H. H., and Graham, F. K. Twenty-four hour retention by neonates of an habituated heart rate response. *Psychonom. Sci.*, 1965, **2**, 265–266.

Keitel, H. G., Cohn, R., and Harnish, D. Diaper rash, self-inflicted excoriations, and crying in full-term newborn infants kept in the prone or supine position. *J. Pediat.*, 1960, **57**, 884–886.

Kellogg, W. N. A method for recording the activity of the human fetus *in utero*, with specimen results. *J. genet. Psychol.*, 1941, **58**, 307–326.

Kellogg, W. N., and Kellogg, L. A. *The ape and the child: a study of environmental influence upon early behavior.* New York: McGraw-Hill, 1933.

Kelting, L. S. An investigation of the feeding, sleeping, crying, and social behavior of infants. *J. exp. Educ.*, 1934, **3**, 97–106.

Kennard, M. A. Relation of age to motor impairment in man and subhuman primates. *Archs. Neurol. Psychiat.*, 1940, **44**, 377–397.

Kennedy, C. Physiologic characteristics of growth of the human brain. *J. Pediat.*, 1961, **59**, 928–938.

Kennedy, H. E. Cover memories in formation. *Psychoanal. study Child*, 1950, **5**, 275–284.

Kennel, J. H., and Bergen, M. E. Early childhood separations. *Pediatrics*, 1966, **37**, 291–298.

Kenyeres, E. Les premiers mots de l'enfant et l'apparition des espèces de mots dans son langage. *Archs. Psychol.*, 1926–1927, **20**, 191–218.

Kepecs, J. G., Robin, M., and Munro, C. Tickle: the organization of a patterned response. *Archs. gen. Psychiat*, 1961, **5**, 237–245.

Kessen, W. Research design in the study of developmental problems. In P. H. Mussen (Ed.), *Handbook of research methods in child development.* New York: Wiley, 1960. Pp. 36–70.

Kessen, W. "Stage" and "structure" in the study of children. In W. Kessen and C. Kuhlman (Eds.), Thought in the young child, *Monogr. Soc. Res. Child Dev.*, 1962, Whole No. 83, 65–82.

Kessen, W. Research in the psychological development of infants: an overview. *Merrill-Palmer Q.*, 1963, **9**, 83–94.

Kessen, W. *The Child.* New York: Wiley, 1965.

Kessen, W. Questions for a theory of cognitive development. In H. W. Stevenson (Ed.), Concept of development. *Monogr. Soc. Res. Child Dev.*, 1966, **31**, Whole No. 107, 55–70.

Kessen, W. Sucking and looking: two organized congenital patterns of behavior in the human newborn. In H. W. Stevenson, E. H. Hess, and H. L. Rheingold (Eds.), *Early behavior: comparative and developmental approaches.* New York: Wiley, 1967. Pp. 147–179.

Kessen, W. The construction and selection of environments: a note. In D. C. Glass (Ed.), *Environmental Influences.* N. Y.: Rockefeller University Press, 1968. Pp. 197–201.

Kessen, W., Hendry, L. S., and Leutzendorff, A.-M. Measurement of movement in the human newborn: a new technique. *Child Dev.*, 1961, **32**, 95–105.

Kessen, W., and Kuhlman, C. (Eds.) Thought in the young child: report of a conference, with particular attention to the work of Jean Piaget. *Monogr. Soc. Res. Child Dev.*, 1962, Whole No. 83.

Kessen, W., and Leutzendorff, A.-M. The effect of non-nutritive sucking on movement in the human newborn. *J. comp. physiol. Psychol.*, 1963, **56**, 69–72.

Kessen, W., Leutzendorff, A.-M., and Stoutsenberger, K. Age, food deprivation, non-nutritive sucking, and movement in the human newborn. *J. comp. physiol. Psychol.*, 1967, **63**, 82–86.

Kessen, W., and Mandler, G. Anxiety, pain, and the inhibition of distress. *Psychol. Rev.*, 1961, **68**, 396–404.

Kessen, W., Williams, E. J., and Williams, J. P. Selection and test of response measures in the study of the human newborn. *Child Dev.*, 1961, **32**, 7–24.

Kestenberg, J. S. On the development of maternal feelings in early childhood: Observations and reflections. *Psychoanal. Study Child*, 1956, **11**, 257–291.

Kestenberg, J. S. The role of movement patterns in development: I. Rhythms of movement. *Psycholanal. Q.*, 1965, **34**, 1–36. (a)

Kestenberg, J. S. The role of movement patterns in development: II. Flow of tension and effort. *Psychoanal. Q.*, 1965, **34**, 517–563. (a)

Kimura, T. Studies on the electroencephalogram of the newborn. *Iryo*, 1951, **5**, 6–11.

Kiss, T. Az örömérzés elsö megnyilvánulásai a gyermeknél. *Pszichol. Tanulmanyok*, 1958, **1**, 85–93.

Kistyakovskaya, M. I. Ob ustoǐchivosti zritelnykh reakǐsti deteǐ pervykh mesiatsev zhizni. *Vop. Psikhol.*, 1959, **5**, 123–133.

Kistyakovskaya, M. I. Razvitie dvizheniǐ ruki u rebenka pervogo polugodyaǐ zhizni. *Vop. Psikhol.* 1962, No. 1, 89–100.

Kistyakovskaya, M. I. O stimulakh vyzyvayushchikh polozhiteľnye emotsii u rebenka pervykh mesyatsev zhizni. *Vop. Psikhol.*, 1965, No. 2, 129–140.

Klackenberg, G. Studies in maternal deprivation in infants' homes. *Acta Paediat.*, 1956, **45**, 1–12.

Klaften, E., and Wagner, R. Die galvanische Nervenerregbarkeit in der Neugeborenenperiode. *Z. Kinderheilk.*, 1934, **56**, 201–207.

Klatskin, E. H. Intelligence test performance at one year among infants raised with flexible methodology. *J. clin. Psychol.*, 1952, **8**, 230–237. (a)

Klatskin, E. H. Shifts in child care practises in three social classes under an infant care program of flexible methodology. *Am. J. Orthopsychiat.*, 1952, **22**, 52–61. (b)

Klatskin, E. H., and Jackson, E. B. Methodology of the Yale rooming-in project on parent-child relationship. *Am. J. Orthopsychiat.*, 1955, **25**, 81–108.

Klatskin, E. H., Jackson, E. B., and Wilkin, L. C. The influence of degree of flexibility in maternal child care practices on early child behavior. *Am. J. Orthopsychiat.*, 1956, **26**, 79–93.

Klatskin, E. H., McGarry, M. E., and Steward, M. S. Variability in developmental test patterns as a sequel of neonatal stress. *Child Dev.*, 1966, **37**, 818–826.

Kleeman, J. A. A boy discovers his penis. *Psychoanal. Study Child*, 1965, **20**, 239–266.

Kleeman, J. A. Genital self-discovery during a boy's second year: a follow up. *Psychoanal. Study Child*, 1966, **21**, 358–392.

Kleeman, J. A. The peek-o-boo game: Part I. Its origins, meanings, and related phenomena in the first year. *Psychoanal. Study Child*, 1967, **22**, 239–273.

Klein, M., Heimann, P., and Moneykyrle, R. E. (Eds.) *New directions in psychoanalysis: the significance of infant conflict in the pattern of adult behavior.* New York: Basic Books, 1957.

Klein, R., and Wander, E. Gruppenbildung im zweiten Lebensjahr. *Z. Psychol.*, 1933, **128**, 257–280.

Kleitman, N., and Engelmann, T. G. Sleep characteristics of infants. *J. appl. Physiol.*, 1953, **6**, 269–282.

Klingman, W. O. Life begins. *Proc. 7th Inst. except. Child, Child Res. Clin.*, 1940, 8–14.

Kluckhohn, C. Some aspects of Navaho infancy and early childhood. *Psychoanal. soc. Sci.*, 1947, **1**, 37–86.

Knapen, M. T. *L'enfant Mukongo.* Louvain, Belgium: Editions Nauwelaerts, 1962.

Knobloch, H., and Pasamanick, B. Further observations on the behavioral development of Negro children. *J. genet. Psychol.*, 1953, **83**, 137–157.

Knobloch, H., and Pasamanick, B. A developmental questionnaire for infants forty weeks of age: an evaluation. *Monogr. Soc. Res. Child Dev.*, 1955, **20**, No. 2.

Knobloch, H., and Pasamanick, B. The relationship of race and socio-economic status to the development of motor behavior patterns in infancy. *Psychiat. res. Reps.*, 1958, **10**, 123–133.

Knobloch, H., and Pasamanick, B. Syndrome of minimal cerebral damage in infancy. *J. Am. med. Assoc.*, 1959, **170**, 1384–1387.

Knobloch, H., and Pasamanick, B. An evaluation of the consistency and predictive value of the 40 week Gesell Developmental Schedule. *Psychiat. res. Reps.*, 1960, **13**, 10–31. (a)

Knobloch, H., and Pasamanick, B. Environmental factors affecting human development before and after birth. *Pediatrics*, 1960, **26**, 210–218. (b)

Knobloch, H., and Pasamanick, B. The developmental behavioral approach to the neurologic examination in infancy. *Child Dev.*, 1962, **33**, 181–198.

Knobloch, H., and Pasamanick, B. Predicting intellectual potential in infancy. *Am. J. Dis. Child.*, 1963, **106**, 43–51.

Knobloch, H., Rider, R., Harper, P., and Pasamanick, B. Neuropsychiatric sequelae of prematurity; a longitudinal study. *J. Am. med. Assoc.*, 1956, **161**, 581–585.

Knobloch, H., Rider, R., Pasamanick, B., and Harper, P. An evaluation of a questionnaire on infant development. *Am. J. Publ. Hlth.*, 1955, **45**, 1309–1320.

Knop, C. The dynamics of newly born babies. *J. Pediat.*, 1946, **29**, 721–728.

Koch, J. Orientacni podminenene motoricke reflexy u jednoletých deti. *Activ. nerv. super.*, 1960, **2**, 413–418.

Koch, J. The change of conditioned orienting reactions in five month old infants through phase shift of partial biorhythms. *Hum. Dev.*, 1968, **11**, 124–137.

Ködding, I. Der Lidschlag im Kindesalter. *Mschr. Kinderheilk.*, 1940, **84**, 212–223.

Koffka, K. *The growth of the mind; an introduction to child psychology.* New York: Harcourt, Brace, 1924.

Kohts, N. La conduite du petit du chimpanzé et de l'enfant de l'homme. *J. Psychol. norm. Path.*, 1937, **34**, 494–531.

Köllreutter, W. Die Schwerhörigkeit der Neugeborenen als reine Störung im schallzuleitenden Teile des Ohres. *Z. Ohrenheilk.*, 1906, **53**, 123–131.

Kollman, A. Über den Zeitpunkt des Abfalles des Nabelschnurrestes bei Frühgeburten. *Arch. Kinderheilk.*, 1938, **113**, 24–30.

Koltsova, M. M. O vozniknovenii i razvitii vtoroi signalnoi sistemy u rebenka. *Trudÿ-fiziol. Inst.*, 1949, **4**, 49–102.

Koltsova, M. M. Ob uslovnykh refleksakh na otnosheniia razdrazhitelei u detei rannego vozrasta. *Trudÿ-Inst. Fiziol., I. P. Pavlova*, 1952, **1**, 266–271. (a)

Koltsova, M. M. O razvitii vnutrennego tormozheniia u rebenka. *Fiziol. Zh. SSSR*, 1952, **38**, 27–32. (b)

Koltsova, M. M. O fiziologicheskikh mekhanizmakh razvitiia protsessa obobshcheniia u rebenka. *Zh. vÿss. nerv. Depat.*, 1956, **6**, 201–211.

Koltsova, M. M. *O formirovanii vysshei nervnoi deiatelnosti rebenka.* Leningrad: Medgiz, 1958.

Koltsova, M. M. The role of temporary connexions of associative type in the development of systematized activity. *Pavlov J. higher nerv. Activ.*, 1961, **11**, 56–60.

Korner, A., and Grobstein, R. Visual alertness as related to soothing in neonates: implications for maternal stimulation and early deprivation. *Child Dev.*, 1966, **37**, 867–876.

Korumaru, S., Okada, Y., Hanada, M., Uchida, S., and Oue, M. Fright reactions of newborn infants. *Jap. J. Child Psychiat.*, 1964, **5**, 220–233.

Krachkovskaia, M. V. Reflex changes in the leukocyte count of newborn infants in relation to food intake. *Pavlov J. higher nerv. Activ.*, 1959, **9**, 193–199.

Krasnogorski, N. I. Opyt polucheniia iskusstvennykh uslovnykh refleksov u detei rannego vozrasta. *Russkii Vrach,* 1907, **36,** 1245–1246.

Krasnogorski, N., I. Über die Bedingungsreflexe im Kindesalter. *Jb. Kinderheilk.,* 1909, **69,** 1–24.

Krasnogorski, N. I. Die letzten Fortschritte in der Methodik der Erforschung der bedingten Reflexe an Kindern. *Jb. Kinderheilk.,* 1926, **114,** 255–267.

Krause, P. *Die Entwicklung eines Kindes von der Geburt bis zum Eintritt in die Schule.* Leipzig: Wunderlich, 1914.

Kris, E. Some comments and observations on early autoerotic activities. *Psychoanal. Study Child,* 1951, **6,** 95–116.

Kris, E. Neutralization and sublimation. *Psychoanal. Study Child,* 1955, **10,** 30–46.

Kriuchkova, A. P., and Ostrovskaia, I. M. O vozrastnykh i individualnykh osobennostiiakh vysshei nervnoi deiatelnosti detei pervogo goda zhizni. *Zh. vÿss. nerv. Deyat.,* 1957, **7,** 63–74.

Kron, R. E. Instrumental conditioning of nutritive sucking behavior in the newborn. *Recent advances in Biological Psychiatry,* 1966, **9,** 295–300.

Kron, R. E. The effect of arousal and of learning upon sucking behavior in the newborn. In *Recent advances in biological psychiatry,* 1968, **10,** 302–313. (a)

Kron, R. E. The influence of interfeeding interval on newborn sucking behavior. 1968. (b) (Mimeographed.)

Kron, R. E., Ipsen, J., and Goddard, K. E. Consistent individual differences in the nutritive sucking behavior of the human newborn. *Psychosom. Med.,* 1968, **30,** 151–161.

Kron, R. E., Stein, M., and Goddard, K. E. A method of measuring sucking behavior of newborn infants. *Psychosom. Med.,* 1963, **25,** 181–191.

Kron, R. E., Stein, M., and Goddard, K. E. Newborn sucking behavior affected by obstetric sedation. *Pediatrics,* 1966, **37,** 1012–1016.

Kron, R. E., Stein, M., Goddard, K. E. and Phoenix, M. D. Effect of nutrient upon the sucking behavior of newborn infants. *Psychosom. Med.,* 1967, **29,** 24–32.

Kroner, T. Über die Sinnesempfindungen der Neugeborenen. *Breslauer aerzt. Zsch.,* 1882, **4,** 37–41.

Krüger, A. M. Über das Verhältnis des Kindes zum Tiere. *Z. angew. Psychol.,* 1934, **47,** 9–46.

Kuhlmann, F. A revision of the Binet-Simon system for measuring the intelligence of children. *J. Psycho-Asth.,* 1912, **16,** 113–139.

Kuhlmann, F. *A handbook of mental tests.* Baltimore: Warwick & York, 1922.

Kulka, A., Fry, C., and Goldstein, F. J. Kinesthetic needs in infancy. *Am. J. Orthopsychiat.,* 1960, **30,** 562–571.

Kunst, M. S. A study of thumb and finger sucking in infants. *Psychol. Monogr.,* 1948, **62,** Whole No. 290.

Kuo, Z. Y. A psychology without heredity. *Psychol. Rev.* 1924, **31,** 427–448.

Kussmaul, A. *Untersuchungen über das Seelenleben des neugeborenen Menschen.* Tübingen: Franz Pietzcker, 1896.

Kutvirt, O. Über das Gehör der Neugeborenen und Säuglinge. *Beitr. Anat. Physiol. Path., Ther. Ohr. Nase. Hals.,* 1912, **5,** 249–257.

Ladd, G. T. Development of attention in infancy. *Childhood,* 1893, **2,** 197.

Lakin, M. Personality factors in mothers of excessively crying (colicky) infants. *Monogr. Soc. Res. Child Dev.,* 1957, **22**(1) (Ser. 64).

Lambanzi, R., and Pianetta, C. Recherches sur le réflexe buccal. *Rev. Psychiat.,* 1906, **10,** 148–154.

Landauer, K. Die kindliche Bewegungsunruhe. *Int. Z. Psychoanal.,* 1926, **12,** 379–390.

Landis, C., and Hunt, W. A. *The startle pattern*. New York: Farrar and Rinehart, 1939.

Lang, A. Von der Störbarkeit zur Schüchternheit in der Entwicklung des Kindes: II. Konstanz vom ersten ins achte Jahr. *Schweiz. Z. Psychol. Anwend.*, 1962, **21**, 113–125.

Lang, A. Perceptual behavior of 8- to 10-week-old infants. *Psychonom. Sci.*, 1966, **4**, 203–204.

Lang, A. Über Wahrnehmungsverhalten beim 8 bis 10 wöchigen Säugling. *Psychol. Forsch.*, 1967, **30**, 357–399.

Langford, W. S. Disturbance in mother-infant relationship leading to apathy, extra-nutritional sucking, and hair-ball. In G. Caplan (Ed.), *Emotional problems of early childhood*. New York: Basic Books, 1955. Pp. 57–76.

Langmeier, J. Spánek malých dětí v rodinách a v nemocnici. *Česk. Pediat.*, 1959, **14**, 628–639.

Langworthy, O. R. Development of behavior patterns and myelinization of the nervous system in the human fetus and infant. Contribution to Embryology, No. 139. Reprinted from: Publ. No. 443, Carnegie Inst., Washington, Sept., 1933, 1–57.

Lantuéjoul, R., and Hartmann, E. Note sur le réflexe cutané-plantaire chez le jeune enfant, notamment au moment de la naissance. *Rev. Neurol.*, 1923, **39**, 387–398.

Laroche, J. L., and Tcheng, F. C. Y. *Le sourire du nourrisson*. Louvain: Publications Universitaires, 1963.

Lassrich, M. A. Zur Entwicklung der motorischen Funktion des oberen Verdauungstraktes. In F. Linneweh, (Ed.), *Die physiologische Entwicklung des Kindes*. Berlin; Göttingen, Heidelberg: Springer, 1959. Pp. 256–271.

Lawrence, M. M., and Feind, C. R. Vestibular responses to rotation in the newborn infant. *Pediatrics*, 1953, **12**, 300–306.

Lebedinskaia, Ye, I., and Polyakova, A. G. Certain age modifications of the interaction of the first and second signal systems in children two to seven years of age. In *The central nervous system and behavior*, 3rd Macy Conf., Princeton, N. J., Feb. 21–24, 1960. Pp. 488–499.

Lebovici, M. S. Notions nouvelles sur le développement du nourrisson dans ses répercussions psychologiques ultérieures. *Sem. Hôp. Paris*, 1950, **26**, 2256–2258.

Lederer, R. K. Studies in infant behavior. V. Part One: An exploratory investigation of handed status in the first two years of life. *Univ. Iowa Stud. Child Welf.*, 1939, **16**, 8–103.

Lehner, G. F. J. A study of the extinction of unconditioned reflexes. *J. exp. Psychol.*, 1941, **29**, 435–456.

Lehrman, D. S., Hinde, R. A., and Shaw, E. (Eds.) *Advances in the study of behavior*. Vol. I. New York: Academic Press, 1965.

Leitch, M. A commentary on the oral phase of psychosexual development. *Bull. Menninger Clin.*, 1948, **12**, 117–125.

Leitch, M., and Escalona, S. The reaction of infants to stress. *Psychoanal. Study Child*, 1949, **3**, 121–140.

Lenneberg, E. H. *Biological foundations of language*. New York: Wiley, 1967.

Lenneberg, E. H., Rebelsky, F. G., and Nichols, I. A. The vocalizations of infants born to deaf and hearing parents. *Hum. Dev.*, 1965, **8**, 23–27.

Leopold, W. F. *Speech development of a bilingual child*. Evanston, Ill.: Northwestern University Press, 1939, 1947, 1949.

Lesný, I., and Kuliš, Z. Results of neurological investigation of children carried out two years after abnormal delivery. *Prakt. Lék.*, 1962, **42**, 57–59.

Leuba, C. Children's reactions to elements of simple geometric patterns. *Am. J. Psychol.*, 1940, **53**, 575–578.

Leuba, C. Tickling and laughter: two genetic studies. *J. genet. Psychol.*, 1941, **58**, 201–209.

Leventhal, A. S., and Lipsitt, L. P. Adaptation, pitch discrimination, and sound localization in the neonate. *Child Dev.*, 1964, **35**, 759–767.

Levin, G. Kesher umaga shel hatinok im hazulat. *Ofakim.*, 1961, **15**, 82–85.

Levin, G. R., and Kaye, H. Nonnutritive sucking by human neonates. *Child Dev.*, 1964, **35**, 749–758.

Levin, G. R., and Kaye, H. Work decrement and rest recovery during nonnutritive sucking in the human neonate. *J. exp. child Psych.*, 1966, **3**, 146–154.

Levine, M. I. A modern concept of breast feeding. *J. Pediat.*, 1951, **38**, 472–475.

Levine, M. I., and Bell, A. I. The treatment of "colic" in infancy by use of the pacifier. *J. Pediat.*, 1950, **37**, 750–755.

Levine, S., and Alpert, M. Differential maturation of the central nervous system as a function of early experience. *Archs. gen. Psychiat.*, 1959, **1**, 403–405.

Levison, C. A., and Levison, P. K. Operant conditioning of head turning for visual reinforcement in three-month infants. *Psychonom. Sci.*, 1967, **8**, 529–530.

Levy, D. M. Resistant behavior of children. *Am. J. Psychiat.*, 1925, **4**, 503–507.

Levy, D. M. Finger sucking and accessory movements in early infancy: an etiologic study. *Am. J. Psychiat.*, 1928, **7**, 881–918.

Levy, D. M. Thumb or fingersucking from the psychiatric angle. *Child Dev.*, 1937, **8**, 99–101.

Levy, D. M. Psychic trauma of operations in children, and a note on combat neurosis. *Am. J. Dis. Child.*, 1945, **69**, 7–25.

Levy, D. M. *Behavioral analysis.* Springfield, Ill.: Thomas, 1958.

Levy, D. M. The infant's earliest memory of innoculation: a contribution to public health procedure. *J. genet. Psychol.*, 1960, **96**, 3–46.

Levy, D. M., and Patrick, H. T. Relation of infantile convulsions, head-banging and breath-holding to fainting and headaches (migraine?) in the parents. *Arch. neurol. Psychiat.*, 1928, **19**, 865–887.

Levy, D. M., and Tulchin, S. H. The resistance of infants and children during mental tests. *J. exp. Psychol.*, 1923, **6**, 304–322.

Levy, D. M., and Tulchin, S. H. The resistant behavior of infants and children: II. *J. exp. Psychol.*, 1925, **8**, 209–224.

Levy, R. J. Effects of institutional vs. boarding home care on a group of infants. *J. Personality*, 1947, **15**, 233–241.

Lewin, B. D. Sleep, the mouth, and the dream screen. *Psychoanal. Q.*, 1946, **15**, 419–434.

Lewis, J. M., and Haig, C. Vitamin A requirements in infancy as determined by dark adaptation. *J. Pediat.*, 1939, **15**, 812–823.

Lewis, M. M. *Infant speech.* (2nd ed.) New York: Humanities Press, 1951.

Lewis, M. M. *How children learn to speak.* New York: Basic Books, 1959.

Lewis, M. The meaning of a response, or why researchers in infant behavior should be oriental metaphysicians. *Merrill-Palmer Q.*, 1967, **13**, 7–18.

Lewis, M., Bartels, B., and Goldberg, S. State as a determinant of infants' heart rate response to stimulation. *Science*, 1967, **155**, 486–488.

Lewis, M. and Goldberg, S. Perceptual-cognitive development in infancy: a generalized expectancy model as a function of the mother-infant interaction. *Merrill-Palmer Q.*, (In press)

Lewis, M., Goldberg, S., and Rausch, M. Attention distribution as a function of novelty and familiarity. *Psychonom. Sci.* (In press.)

Lewis, M., Kagan, J., Campbell, H., and Kalafat, J. The cardiac response as a correlate of attention in infants. *Child Dev.*, 1966, **37**, 63–71.

Lewis, M., Kagan, J., and Kalafat, J. Patterns of fixation in the young infant. *Child Dev.*, 1966, **37**, 331–341.

Lewis, M., and Spaulding, S. J. Differential cardiac response to visual and auditory stimulation in the young child. *Psychophysiology*, 1967, **3**, 229–237.

Lewis, S. J. Thumb-sucking: a cause of malocclusion in the deciduous teeth. *J. Am. dent. Assoc.*, 1930, **17**, 1060–1073.

Lewis, S. J. The effect of thumb and finger-sucking on the primary teeth and dental arches. *Child Dev.*, 1937, **8**, 93–98.

Lewis, S. J., and Lehman, I. A. Observations in growth changes of the teeth and dental arches. *Dent. Cosmos*, 1929, **71**, 480–499.

Lézine, I. Essai d'exploration des possibilités d'adaptation visuelle des enfants de deux à douze mois. *Enfance*, 1965, **18**, 553–586.

Lézine, I., and Stambak, M. Quelques problèmes d'adaptation du jeune enfant en fonction de son type moteur et du régime éducatif. *Enfance*, 1959, **12**, 95–115.

Liamina, G. M. Mechanism by which children master pronunciation during the second and the third year. In *The central nervous system and behavior*, 3rd Macy Conf., Princeton, N. J., Feb. 21–24, 1960, 509–528.

Lindner, G. *Aus dem Naturgarten der Kindersprache. Ein Beitrag zur kindlichen Sprach- und Geistesentwicklung in den ersten vier Lebensjahren.* Leipzig: Grieben, 1898.

Lindsley, D. B. Heart and brain potentials of human fetuses in utero. *Am. J. Psychol.*, 1942, **55**, 412–416.

Line, W. The growth of visual perception in children. *Br. J. Psychol., Monogr. Suppl.* XV, 1931.

Linfert, H. E., and Hierholzer, H. M. A scale for measuring mental development of infants during the first year of life. *Stud. Psychol. Psychiat.*, 1928, **1**, No. 4.

Ling, B. C. Form discrimination as a learning cue in infants. *Comp. Psychol. Monogr.*, 1941, **17**, No. 2, 1–66.

Ling, B. C. A genetic study of sustained visual fixation and associated behavior in the human infant from birth to six months. *J. genet. Psychol.*, 1942, **61**, 227–277.

Linhart, J. *Vyšší nervová činnost dítěte. I díl. Obecné zákonitosti vyšší nervové činnosti dětí.* Praha: Státní pedagogické nakladatelství, 1953.

Lintz, L. M., Fitzgerald, H. E., and Brackbill, Y. Conditioning the eyeblink response to sound in infants. *Psychonom. Sci.*, 1967, **7**, 405–406.

Lippman, H. S. Certain behavior responses in early infancy. *J. genet. Psychol.*, 1927, **34**, 424–440.

Lipsitt, L. P. Learning in the first year of life. In *Advances in child development and behavior*. Vol. I. New York: Academic Press, 1963. Pp. 147–195.

Lipsitt, L. P. Learning in the human infant. In H. W. Stevenson, H. L. Rheingold, and E. Hess (Eds.), *Early behavior: comparative and developmental approaches*. New York: Wiley, 1967. Pp. 225–247.

Lipsitt, L. P. Learning processes of human newborns. *Merrill-Palmer Q.*, 1966, **12**, 45–71.

Lipsitt, L. P. The concepts of development and learning in child behavior. In D. B. Linsley and A. A. Lumsdaine (Eds.), *Brain function*. Vol. IV. Berkeley: University of California Press, 1967. Pp. 211–248.

Lipsitt, L. P., and DeLucia, C. An apparatus for the measurement of specific responses and general activity of the human neonate. *Am. J. Psychol.*, 1960, **73**, 630–632.

Lipsitt, L. P., Engen, T., and Kaye, H. Developmental changes in the olfactory threshold of the neonate. *Child Dev.*, 1963, **34**, 371–376.

Lipsitt, L. P., and Kaye, H. Conditioned sucking in the human newborn. *Psychonom. Sci.*, 1964, **1**, 29–30.

Lipsitt, L. P., and Kaye, H. Change in neonatal response to optimizing and non-optimizing sucking stimulation. *Psychonom. Sci.*, 1965, **2**, 221–222.

Lipsitt, L. P., Kaye, H., and Bosack, T. N. Enhancement of neonatal sucking through reinforcement. *J. exp. child Psychol.*, 1966, **4**, 163–168.

Lipsitt, L. P., and Levy, N. Electrotactual threshold in the neonate. *Child Dev.*, 1959, **30**, 547–554.

Lipsitt, L. P., Pederson, L. J., and DeLucia, C. A. Conjugate reinforcement of operant responding in infants. *Psychonom. Sci.*, 1966, **4**, 67–68.

Lipton, E. L., and Steinschneider, A. Studies on the psychophysiology of infancy. *Merrill-Palmer Q.*, 1964, **10**, 103–117.

Lipton, E. L., Steinschneider, A., and Richmond, J. B. Autonomic function in the neonate: II. Physiologic effects of motor restraint. *Psychosom. Med.*, 1960, **22**, 57–65.

Lipton, E. L., Steinschneider, A., and Richmond, J. B. Autonomic function in the neonates: III. Methodological considerations. *Psychosom. Med.*, 1961, **23**, 461–471. (a)

Lipton, E. L., Steinschneider, A., and Richmond, J. B. Autonomic function in the neonate: IV. Individual differences in cardiac reactivity. *Psychosom. Med.*, 1961, **23**, 472–484. (b)

Lipton, E. L., Steinschneider, A., and Richmond, J. B. Autonomic function in the neonate: VIII. Cardiopulmonary observations. *Pediatrics*, 1964, **33**, 212–215.

Lipton, E. L., Steinschneider, A., and Richmond, J. B. Swaddling, a child care practice: historical, cultural and experimental observations. *Pediatrics*, 1965, **35**, 521–567.

Lipton, E. L., Steinschneider, A., and Richmond, J. B. Autonomic function in the neonate: VII. Maturational changes in cardiac control. *Child Dev.*, 1966, **37**, 1, 1–16.

Lipton, R. C., and Provence, S. *Infants in institutions: a comparison of their development with family-reared infants during the first year of life.* New York: International Universities Press, 1963.

Liu In-Mao. An invariant function interpretation of developmental process. *Acta Psychol. Taiwan.*, 1961, No. 3, 90–93.

Locke, N. M. A comparative study of size constancy. *J. genet. Psychol.*, 1937, **51**, 255–265.

Loebenstein, F. *Formunterscheidung im ersten Lebensjahr.* Leipzig: Robert Noske, 1927.

Lohr, W. Verhalten und Spannungszustände bei Säuglingen im Alter von zehn bis achtzehn Wochen in einer Wahrnehmungssituation. *Z. exp. angew. Psychol.*, 1960, **7**, 493–531.

Lohr, W., Meili, R., and Pulver, U. Über den Ursprung von Persönlichkeitseigenschaften. *Schweiz, Z. Psychol. Anwend.*, 1964, **23**, 1–25.

Lombroso, C., and Grossi Bianchi, M. L. Variazioni dell'elettroencefalogramma nei primi cinque anni di vita. *Minerva pediat.*, 1951, **3**(2), 120–124.

Lombroso, P. La evoluzione delle idee nei bambini. *Riv. Sci. Biol., Torino*, 1899, **1**, 641–664.

Lønnum, A. The abdominal skin reflexes in man: an analysis of reflex findings in early infancy and in patients with cerebral disease. *Acta Psychiat., Kbh.*, 1956, Suppl. 108, 243–253.

Lorenz, E. Über des Brustdrüsensekret des Neugeborenen. *Jb. Kinderheilk.*, 1929, **124**, 268–274.

Lorenz, K. *On Aggression.* New York: Harcourt, Brace and World, 1966.

Loth, G. Neurologische Untersuchungen an Frühgeburten und jungen Säuglingen. *Z. Kinderforsch.*, 1952, **72**, 42–49.

Löwenfeld, B. Systematisches Studium der Reaktionen der Säuglinge auf Klänge und Geräusche. Z. Psychol., 1927, 104, 62–96.

Lu, E. G. Early conditioning of perceptual preference. Child Dev., 1967, 38, 415–424.

Lucas, W. P. The modern practice of pediatrics. New York: Macmillan, 1927.

Luria, A. R. Eksperimentalnaia psikholgiia i razvitie rebenka. Nauchnoe Slovo, 1929, 3, 77–97.

Luria, A. R. The directive function of speech in development and dissolution. Word, 1959 15, 341–352.

Lustman, S. L. Rudiments of the ego. Psychoanal. Study Child, 1956, 11, 89–98.

Lustman, S. L. Psychic energy and mechanisms of defense. Psychoanal. Study Child, 1957, 12, 151–165.

Lynip, A. W. The use of magnetic devices in the collection and analysis of the preverbal utterances of an infant. Genet. Psychol. Monogr., 1951, 44, 221–262.

Macfarlane, J. W. Studies in child guidance: I. Methodology of data collection and organization. Monogr. Soc. Res. Child Dev., 1938, 3, No. 6.

MacKinney, L. G., Ehrlich, F. E., and Chase, H. C. A study of factors affecting the neurological status of young children. I. Plan of study and some neonatal findings. Am. J. Publ. Hlth., 1955, 45, 653–661.

MacMahon, B., and Sowa, J. M. Physical damage to the fetus. In Milbank Memorial Fund, Causes of mental disorders: a review of epidemological knowledge, 1959. Pp. 51–110.

MacRae, J. M. Retests of children given mental tests as infants. J. genet. Psychol., 1955, 87, 111–119.

Magnus, R., and de Kleijn, A. Die Abhängigkeit des Tonus der Extremitätenmuskeln von der Kopfstellung. Pflügers Arch. ges. Physiol., 1912, 145, 455–548.

Mahler, M. S. Thoughts about development and individuation. Psychoanal. Study Child, 1963, 18, 307–324.

Mahon, R. A partir de quel âge le foetus peut-il présenter des mouvements actifs? Bull. Soc. Obstét. Gynéc. Paris, 1937, 26, 61.

Maier, H. W. Three theories of child development. New York: Harper & Row, 1965.

Major, D. R. First steps in mental growth. New York: Macmillan, 1906.

Malakhovskaia, D. B. Interaction between the conditioned and unconditioned plantar reflex in young children. Pavlov. J. higher nerv. Activ., 1959, 9, 38–44.

Malapert, P. Enquête sur le sentiment de la colère chez les enfants. L'Année Psychol., 1902, 9, 1–40.

Malrieu, P. La construction de l'objet et les attitudes sociales de l'enfant de la naissance à deux ans. J. Psychol. norm. Path., 1951, 44, 425–437.

Malrieu, P. Vie sociale et prélangage dans la première année. J. Psychol. norm. Path., 1962, 59, 139–165.

Mandell, S., and Sonneck, B. Phonographische Aufnahme und Analyse der ersten Sprachäusserungen von Kindern. Arch. ges. Psychol., 1935, 94, 478–500.

Mann, I. The development of the human eye. London: Brit. Med. Assoc., 1964.

Marden, P. M., Smith, D. W., and McDonald, M. J. Congenital anomalies in the newborn infant, including minor variations. J. Pediat., 1964, 64, 357–371.

Margoshes, A., and Collins, G. Right handedness as a function of maternal heartbeat. Percept. mot. Skills, 1965, 20, 443–444.

Marinesco, G., and Kreindler, A. Des reflexes conditionnels. J. Psychol. norm. Path., 1933, 30, 855–886.

Marinesco, G., and Kreindler, A. *Des réflexes conditionnels. Études de physiolgie normale et pathologique.* Paris: Felix Alcan, 1935.

Marquis, D. P. Can conditioned responses be established in the newborn infant? *J. genet. Psychol.,* 1931, **39,** 479–492.

Marquis, D. P. A study of activity and postures in infants' sleep. *J. genet. Psychol.,* 1933, **42,** 51–69.

Marquis, D. P. Learning in the neonate: the modification of behavior under three feeding schedules. *J. exp. Psychol.,* 1941, **29,** 263–282.

Marquis, D. P. A study of frustration in newborn infants. *J. exp. Psychol.,* 1943, **32,** 123–138.

Marsden, R. E. The early color sense—further experiments. *Psychol. Rev.,* 1903, **10,** 297–300. (a)

Marsden, R. E. A study of the early color sense. *Psychol. Rev.,* 1903, **10,** 37–47. (b)

Marston, L. R. The emotions of young children: an experimental study in introversion and extroversion. *Univ. Iowa Stud. Child Welf.,* 1925, **3,** No. 3.

Mason, M. F., Kennedy, J. A., and Barcroft, J. Direct determination of foetal oxygen consumption. *J. Physiol.,* 1938, **93,** 21–22.

Mast, E. T. Motivating factors in child learning. *Child Dev.,* 1937, **8,** 273–278.

Mateer, F. *Child behavior: a critical and experimental study of young children by the method of conditioned reflexes.* Boston: Badger, 1918.

Maudry, M., and Nekula, M. Social relations between children of the same age during the first two years of life. *J. genet. Psychol.,* 1939, **54,** 193–215.

Maurer, K. M. Intellectual status at maturity as a criterion for selecting items in preschool tests. *Univ. Minn. Inst. Child Welf. Monogr.,* 1946, No. 21.

Mautner, H. Drug action on underdeveloped and damaged brains. *Archs. Pediat.,* 1955, **72,** 265–274.

Mayerhofer, A. Schwimmbewegungen bei Säuglingen. *Arch. Kinderheilk.,* 1953, **146,** 137–142.

McCall, R. B., and Kagan, J. Attention in the infant: effects of complexity, contour, perimeter, and familiarity. *Child Dev.,* 1967, **38,** 939–952. (a)

McCall, R. B., and Kagan, J. Stimulus-schema discrepancy and attention in the infant. *J. exp. child Psychol.,* 1967, **5,** 381–390. (b)

McCarthy, D. A. The vocalizations of infants: Part I. Studies; Part II. Methods of recording. *Psychol. Bull.,* 1929, **26,** 625–651.

McCarthy, D. A. The language development of the preschool child. *Univ. Minn. Inst. Child Welf. Monogr.,* 1930, No. 4.

McCarthy, D. A. Language development in children. In L. Carmichael (Ed.), *Manual of child psychology.* (2nd ed.) New York: Wiley, 1954.

McCarthy, D. A. Language development. *Monogr. Soc. Res. Child Dev.,* 1960, **25,** whole No. 77.

McCurry, W. H., and Irwin, O. C. A study of word approximations in the spontaneous speech of infants. *J. speech hear. Disord.,* 1953, **18,** 133–139.

McDougall, W. An investigation of the colour sense of two infants. *Br. J. Psychol.,* 1908, **2,** 338–352.

McGinnis, J. M. Eye movements and optic nystagmus in early infancy. *Genet. Psychol. Monogr.,* 1930, **8,** 321–430.

McGrade, B. J., Kessen, W., and Leutzendorff, A.-M. Activity in the human newborn as related to delivery difficulty. *Child Dev.,* 1965, **36,** 73–79.

McGraw, M. B. A comparative study of a group of southern white and Negro infants. *Genet. Psychol. Monogr.,* 1931, **10,** 1–105.

McGraw, M. B. From reflex to muscular control in the assumption of an erect posture and ambulation in the human infant. *Child Dev.,* 1932, **3,** 291–297.

McGraw, M. B. Discussion: grasping in infants and the proximo-distal course of growth. *Psychol. Rev.*, 1933, **40**, 301–302.

McGraw, M. B. *Growth: a study of Johnny and Jimmy.* New York: Appleton-Century, 1935.

McGraw, M. B. The Moro reflex. *Am. J. Dis. Child.*, 1937, **54**, 240–251.

McGraw, M. B. Behavior of the newborn infant and early neuro-muscular development. *Res. Publ. Assoc., nerv. ment. Dis.*, 1939, **19**, 244–246. (a)

McGraw, M. B. Swimming behavior of the human infant. *J. Pediat.*, 1939, **15**, 485–490. (b)

McGraw, M. B. Neural maturation as exemplified in achievement of bladder control. *J. Pediat.*, 1940, **16**, 580–590. (a)

McGraw, M. B. Neuromuscular development of the human infant as exemplified in the achievement of erect locomotion. *J. Pediat.*, 1940, **17**, 747–771. (b)

McGraw, M. B. Neuromuscular mechanism of the infant: development reflected by postural adjustments to an inverted position. *Am. J. Dis. Child.*, 1940, **60**, 1031–1042. (c)

McGraw, M. B. Suspension grasp behavior of the human infant. *Am. J. Dis. Child.*, 1940, **60**, 799–811. (d)

McGraw, M. B. Development of neuro-muscular mechanisms as reflected in the crawling and creeping behavior of the human infant. *J. genet. Psychol.*, 1941, **58**, 83–111. (a)

McGraw, M. B. Development of the plantar response in healthy infants. *Am. J. Dis. Child.*, 1941, **61**, 1215–1221. (b)

McGraw, M. B. Development of rotary-vestibular reactions of the human infant. *Child Dev.*, 1941, **12**, 17–19. (c)

McGraw, M. B. Neural maturation as exemplified in the changing reactions of the infant to pin prick. *Child Dev.*, 1941, **12**, 31–42. (d)

McGraw, M. B. Neural maturation as exemplified in the reaching prehensile behavior of the human infant. *J. Psychol.*, 1941, **11**, 127–141. (e)

McGraw, M. B. Neural maturation of the infant as exemplified in the righting reflex, or rolling from a dorsal to a prone position. *J. Pediat.*, 1941, **18**, 385–394. (f)

McGraw, M. B. Neuro-motor maturation of anti-gravity functions as reflected in the development of a sitting posture. *J. genet. Psychol.*, 1941, **59**, 155–175. (g)

McGraw, M. B. Appraising test responses of infants and young children. *J. Psychol.*, 1942, **14**, 89–100.

McGraw, M. B. *The neuromuscular maturation of the human infant.* New York: Columbia University Press, 1943.

McGraw, M. B. Maturation of behavior. In L. Carmichael (Ed.), *Manual of child psychology.* New York: Wiley, 1946. Pp. 332–369.

McGraw, M. B., and Breeze, K. W. Quantitative studies in the development of erect locomotion. *Child Dev.*, 1941, **12**, 267–303.

McKee, J. P., and Honzik, M. P. The sucking behavior of mammals: an illustration of the nature-nurture question. In L. Postman (Ed.), *Psychology in the making.* New York: Knopf, 1962. Pp. 585–661.

McKinnon, K. M. *Consistency and change in behavior manifestations as observed in a group of sixteen children during a five-year period.* New York: Bureau of Publ., Teachers College, 1942.

McLeish, Mrs. Andrew. Observations on the development of a child during the first year. *Trans. Ill. Soc. Child Study*, 1898, **3**, 109–124.

McLellan, M. S., and Webb, C. H. Ear studies in the newborn infant. II. Age of spontaneous visibility of the auditory canal and tympanic membrane and the appearance of these structures in healthy newborn infants. *J. Pediat.*, 1961, **58**, 523–527.

Mead, C. D. The age of walking and talking in relation to general intelligence. *Ped. Sem.*, 1913, **20**, 460–484.

Mead, M. *Coming of age in Samoa*. New York: Morrow, 1932.

Mead, M. Some theoretical considerations on the problem of mother-child separation. *Am. J. Orthopsychiat.*, 1954, **24**, 471–483. (a)

Mead, M. The swaddling hypothesis: its reception. *Am. Anthrop.*, 1954, **56**, 395–409. (b)

Meerloo, J. A. M. Rhythm in babies and adults. *Archs. gen. Psychiat.*, 1961, **5**, 169–175.

Mehlman, J. The tonic neck reflex in newborn infants. *J. Pediat.*, 1940, **16**, 767–769.

Meierhofer, M. Fehlentwicklung der Persönlichkeit bei Kindern in Fremdpflege. *Schweiz. Med. Wschr.*, 1955, 862–866.

Meili, R. Observations of behavior in the third and fourth months relevant to character formation. *Schweiz. Z. Psychol. Anwend.*, 1953, **12**, 257–275.

Meili, R. Genesis of anxiety in infants. *Schweiz. Z. Psychol. Anwend.*, 1955, **14**, 195–212.

Meili, R. *Anfänge der Charakterentwicklung: Methoden und Ergebnisse einer Längsschnitt-Untersuchung*. Bern: Huber, 1957.

Meili, R. A longitudinal study of personality development. In L. Jessner and E. Pavenstedt (Eds.), *Dynamic psychopathology in childhood*. New York: Grune and Stratton, 1959. Pp. 106–123.

Meili-Dworetzki, G. Lust und Angst: Regulative Momente in der Persönlichkeitsentwicklung zweier Brüder. *Beitr. genet. Charakterologie*, 1959, No. 3, 7–112.

Melcher, R. T. Children's motor learning with and without vision. *Child Dev.*, 1934, **5**, 315–350.

Melcher, R. T. Development within the first two years of infants prematurely born. *Child Dev.*, 1937, **8**, 1–14.

Menaker, W. Neugier im 1. und 2. Lebensjahr. *Z. Psychol.*, 1936, **137**, 131–167.

Menninger, K. A. An anthropological note on the theory of pre-natal instinctual conflict. *Int. J. Psychoanal.*, 1939, **20**, 439–442.

Menzies, H. F. Children in day nurseries; with special reference to the child under two years old. *Lancet*, 1946, **251**, 499–501.

Mercurio, R. Le basi biopsichiche dell'assistenza al neonato e al lattante. *Pediatria*, 1935, No. 4.

Meredith, H. V. Physical growth from birth to two years: II. Head circumference. Part I. A review and synthesis of North American research on groups of infants. *Child Dev.*, 1946, **17**, 1–61.

Meredith, H. V. Body size in infancy and childhood: a comparative study of data from Okinawa, France, South Africa and North America. *Child Dev.*, 1948, **19**, 179–195.

Meredith, H. V. Birth order and body size: II. Neonatal and childhood materials. *Am. J. phys. Anthrop.*, 1950, **8**, 195–224.

Merminod, A. (Ed.) *The growth of the normal child during the first three years of life*. Basel: Karger, 1962.

Merry, F., and Merry, R. *The first two decades of life*. New York: Harper, 1958.

Mestyán, G., and Varga, F. Chemical thermoregulation of full-term and premature newborn infants. *J. Pediat.*, 1960, **56**, 623–629.

Metraux, R. W. Speech profiles of the preschool child 18 to 54 months. *J. speech hear. Disord.*, 1950, **15**, 37–53.

Meumann, E. *Die Entstehung der ertsten Wortbedeutungen beim Kinde.* Leipzig, 1802.

Meyer, A. A note on the postnatal development of the human cerebral cortex. *Cerebral Palsy Bull.,* 1961, **3**, 263–268.

Meyer, T. (Ed.) *Aus einer Kinderstube. Tagebuchblätter einer Mutter.* Leipzig: Teubner, 1914.

Meyers, C. E. The effect of conflicting authority on the child. *Univ. Iowa Stud. Child Welf.,* 1944, **20**, 31–98.

Meyers, W. J., and Cantor, G. N. Infants' observing and heart period responses as related to novelty of visual stimuli. *Psychonom. Sci.,* 1966, **5**, 239–240.

Meyers, W. J., and Cantor, G. N. Observing and cardiac responses of human infants to visual stimuli. *J. exp. child Psychol.,* 1967, **5**, 1–15.

Michalowicz, M. Zaburzenia psychiczne wieku niemowlecego. *Zdrowie psych.,* 1946, **1**, 24–44; 65–79.

Mickens, C. W. Practical results of child study. *Child Study Monogr.,* 1897–1898, **3**, 198–205.

Middlemore, M. P. *The nursing couple.* London: Hamish Hamilton, 1941.

Miller, G. F., Miller, M. D., and Nice, M. M. A boy's vocabulary at eighteen months. *Proc. Okla. Acad. Sci.,* 1923, **3**, 140–144.

Miller, H. C., Proud, G. O., and Behrle, F. C. Variations in the gag, cough, and swallow reflexes and tone of the vocal cords as determined by direct laryngoscopy in newborn infants. *Yale J. Biol. Med.,* 1952, **24**, 284–291.

Miller, J., de Schweinitz, L., and Goetzinger, C. P. How infants three, four, and five months of age respond to sound. *Except. Child.,* 1963, **30**, 149–154.

Minkovskii, M. A. O sheinikh i labirintnikh refleksakh u chelooe-cheskogo zarodisha. In *Problems of nervous physiology and of behavior.* Tiflis: Georgian Branch, Academy of Sci., USSR, 1936, 249–257.

Minkowski, M. Some reflections on the neurophysiology of the newborn and the infant and its relation with that of the foetus. *Rev. Neurol.* (Paris), 1955, **93**, 247–256.

Minkowski, M. A., and Sainte-Anne-Dargassies, S. Les convulsions du nouveau-né. *Évolut. psychiat.,* 1956, No. 1, 279–289.

Mintz, B. (Ed.) *Environmental influence on prenatal development.* Chicago: University of Chicago Press, 1958.

Mirzoiants, N. S. Uslovnyi orientirovochnyi refleks i ego differentsirovoka u rebenka. *Zh. vyssh. nerv. Deyat.,* 1954, **4**, 616–619.

Mirzoiants, N. S. The electrical activity in the cortex of young children when falling asleep and in the initial phases of natural sleep. *Pavlov J. higher nerv. Activ.,* 1961, **11**, 449–454. (a)

Mirzoiants, N. S. Electrical changes in the child brain in response to rhythmic photic stimulation. *Pavlov J. higher nerv. Activ.,* 1961, **11**, 1054–1060. (b)

Misumi, J. Experimental studies of the development of visual size constancy in early infancy. *Jap. J. Psychol.,* 1950, **20**, 16–26.

Mitchell, R. G. The Moro reflex. *Cerebral Palsy Bull.,* 1960, **2**, 135–141.

Mitchell, R. G. The Landau reaction (reflex). *Dev. Med. child Neurol.,* 1962, **4**, 65–70.

Mittelmann, B. Motility in infants, children and adults. *Psychoanal. Study Child,* 1954, **9**, 142–177.

Mittelmann, B. Motor patterns and genital behavior: fetishism. *Psychoanal. Study Child,* 1955, **10**, 241–263.

Mittelmann, B. Motility in the therapy of children and adults. *Psychoanal. Study Child,* 1957, **12**, 284–319.

Mittelmann, B. Intrauterine and early infantile motility. *Psychoanal. Study Child,* 1960, **15**, 104–127.

Mohr, G. J. Emotional factors in nutrition work with children. *Ment. Hyg.*, 1928, 12, 366–377.

Mohr, G. J., and Bartelme, P. Mental and physical development of children prematurely born. Preliminary report on mental development. *Am. J. Dis. Child,* 1930, 40, 1000–1015.

Moloney, J. C. The Cornelian Corner. *Psychiat. Q.*, 1946, 20, 603–609.

Monod, H. Les méthodes de mesure de la fréquence cardiaque. *Travail hum.*, 1960, 23, 341–360.

Montagu, M. F. A. *Prenatal influences.* Springfield, Ill.: Thomas, 1962.

Montgomery, J. C. Rooming-in of mother and baby in hospital. *Ill. med. J.*, 1952, 102, 191–196.

Moore, K. C. The mental development of a child. *Psychol. Rev. Monogr. Suppl.*, 1896, 1, No. 3.

Moore, K. C. Comparative observations on the development of movements. *Ped. Sem.*, 1901, 8, 231–238.

Moore, T. W. Studying the growth of personality. *Vita hum.*, 1959, 2, 65–87.

Moore, T., and Ucko, L. E. Night waking in early infancy: Part I. *Archs. Dis. Childh.*, 1957, 32, 333–342.

Morens, Z. Psychodrama in the crib. *Group Psychother.*, 1954, 7, 291–302.

Morgan, G. A., and Ricciuti, H. A. Infants' responses to strangers during the first year. In B. M. Foss (Ed.), *Determinants of infant behavior.* IV. New York: Wiley, 1968. Pp. 253–272.

Morgan, J. J. B., and Morgan, S. S. Infant learning as a developmental index. *J. genet. Psychol.*, 1944, 65, 281–289.

Morgan, S. S,., and Morgan, J. J. B. An examination of the development of certain adaptive behavior patterns in infants. *J. Pediat.*, 1944, 25, 168–177.

Moro, E. Über die Gesichtsreflexe bei Säuglingen. *Wien. klin. Wschr.*, 1906, 19, 637–639.

Moro, E. Das erste Trimenon. *Münch. med. Wschr.*, 1918, 65, 1147–1150.

Morrison, H. J. Breast feeding. *U. S. Armed Forces med. J.*, 1950, 1, 1473–1482.

Morse, J. L. A study of the plantar reflex in infancy. *Pediatrics*, 1901, 11, 13–17.

Moss, H. A. Methodological issues in studying mother-infant interaction. *Am. J. Orthopsychiat.*, 1965, 35, 482–486.

Moss, H. A. Sex-age and state as determinants of mother-infant interaction. *Merrill-Palmer Q.*, 1967, 13, 19–36.

Moss, H. A., and Kagan, J. Stability of achievement and recognition seeking behaviors from early childhood through adulthood. *J. abnorm. soc. Psychol.*, 1961, 62, 504–513.

Müller, E. *Über Reflexe beim Neugeborenen.* München: C. Wolf & Sohn, 1911.

Mumford, A. A. Survival movements of human infancy. *Brain*, 1897, 20, 290–307.

Munn, N. L., and Stiening, B. R. The relative efficacy of form and background in a child's discrimination of visual patterns. *J. genet. Psychol.*, 1931, 39, 73–90.

Munro, M. F. Three years in the life of a child. *Educ. Rev.*, 1896, 16, 367–377.

Munsinger, H., and Kessen, W. Uncertainty, structure, and preference. *Psychol. Monogr.*, 1964, 78, whole No. 586.

Munsinger, H., and Weir, M. W. Infant's and young children's preference for complexity. *J. exp. child. Psychol.*, 1967, 5, 69–73.

Murai, J. Speech development of infants: analysis of speech sounds by sona-graph. *Psychologia*, 1960, 3, 27–35.

Murchison, C., and Langer, S. Tiedemann's observations on the development of the mental faculties of children. *Ped. Sem.*, 1927, 34, 205–230.

Murlin, J. R., Conklin, R. E., and Marsh, M. E. Energy metabolism of normal newborn babies; with special reference to the influence of food and of crying.
Am. J. Dis. Child., 1925, **29,** 1–28.

Murphy, D., and Thorpe, E., Jr. Breathing measurements on normal newborn infants. *J. clin. Invest.,* 1931, **10,** 545–558.

Murphy, L. B. Comment on Dr. Bowlby's note. *Int. J. Psychoanal.,* 1964, **45,**
47–48. (a)

Murphy, L. B. Some aspects of the first relationship. *Int. J. Psychoanal.,* 1964,
45, 31–43. (b)

Muzio, O. Sulla audizione dei neonati. *Ann. lar.,* 1933, **33,** 105–110.

Myers, C. S. Some observations on the development of the colour sense. *Br. J.
Psychol.,* 1908, **2,** 353–362.

Myers, G. C. Grasping, reaching, and handling. *Am. J. Psychol.,* 1915, **26,** 525–
539.

Myers, G. C. Motor emotional expressions of an infant. *J. Phil., Psychol., scient.
Meth.,* 1915, **12,** 44–45.

Myers, G. C. When does the body begin to think. *J. Phil., Psychol., scient. Meth.,*
1918, **15,** 132–133.

Myers, G. C. Infant's inhibition: a genetic study. *Ped. Sem.,* 1922, **29,** 288–
294. (a)

Myers, G. C.: The evolution of an infant's walking. *Ped. Sem.,* 1922, **29,** 295–
301. (b)

Myers, G. C. Some whys of whims—a genetic study. *Ped. Sem.,* 1924, **31,** 78–83.

Nagera, H. Sleep and its disturbances approached developmentally. *Psychoanal.
Study Child,* 1966, **21,** 393–447.

Nassau, E. Die Kitzelreaktion beim Säugling. *Jb. Kinderheilk.,* 1938, **151,** 46–49.

Nathan, P. W., and Smith, M. C. The Babinski response: a review and new observations. *J. Neurol. Neurosurg. Psychiat.,* 1955, **18,** 250–259.

Nechaeva, I. P. K funktsionalnoi kharakteristike slukhogo analizatora rebenka rannego vozrasti. *Zh. vÿssh. nerv. Deyat.,* 1954, **4,** 610–615.

Neilon, P. Shirley's babies after fifteen years: a personality study. *J. genet. Psychol.,* 1948, **73,** 175–186.

Nelson, K. Organization of visual-tracking responses in human infants. *J. exp. child
Psychol.,* 1968, **6,** 194–201.

Nelson, V. L., and Richards, T. W. Studies in mental development: I. Performance
on Gesell items at six months and its predictive value for performance on
mental tests at two and three years. *J. genet. Psychol.,* 1938, **52,** 303–325.

Nelson, V. L., and Richards, T. W. Studies in mental development: III. Performance of twelve-month-old children on the Gesell schedule, and its predictive
value for mental status at two and three years. *J. genet. Psychol.,* 1939, **54,**
181–191.

Nelson, V. L., and Richards, T. W. Fels mental age values for Gesell schedules.
Child Dev., 1940, **11,** 153–157.

Nettl, B. Infant musical development and primitive music. *Sw. J. Anthrop.,* 1956,
12, 87–91.

Neugebauer, H. Aus der Sprachentwicklung meines Sohnes. *Z. angew. Psychol.,*
1915, **9,** 298–306.

Neugebauer, H. Das Gefühls-und Willensleben meines Sohnes in seiner frühen
Kindheit. *Z. angew. Psychol.,* 1929, **34,** 275–310. (a)

Neugebauer, H. Kind und Musik. *Z. päd. Psychol.,* 1929, **30,** 46–49. (b)

Neugebauer, H. Materialien zur Kinderpsychologie. *Z. angew. Psychol.,* 1929,
32, 294–320. (c)

Neugebauer, H. Das Denken und die Intelligenz meines Sohnes in seiner frühen
Kindheit. *Z. angew. Psychol.,* 1930, **36,** 393–437.

Neugebauer, H. Spiel und Phantasie in der frühen Kindheit meines Sohnes. *Z. angew. Psychol.*, 1932, **42**, 220–248.

Neugebauer-Kostenblut, H. Über die Entwicklung der Frage in der frühen Kindheit. *Z. angew. Psychol.*, 1913–1914, **8**, 145–153.

Newberry, H. Studies in fetal behavior: IV. The measurement of three types of fetal activity. *J. comp. Psychol.*, 1941, **32**, 521–530.

Newhall, S. M. Identification by young children of differentially oriented visual forms. *Child Dev.*, 1937, **8**, 105–111.

Newton, N. R. The relationship between infant feeding experience and later behavior. *J. Pediat.*, 1951, **38**, 28–40.

Niederland, W. G. The earliest dreams of a young child. *Psychoanal. Study Child*, 1957, **12**, 190–208.

Norman, E. Some psychological features of babble. In D. Jones, and D. B. Fry (Eds.), *Proc. 2nd Int. Congr. Phonetic Sci.* London: Cambridge Univ. Press, 1936.

Norman, H. N. Fetal hiccups. *J. comp. Psychol.*, 1942, **34**, 65–73.

Norris, A. S. Prenatal factors in intellectual and emotional development. *J. Am. med. Assoc.*, 1960, **172**, 413–416.

Norval, M. A. Sucking response of newly born babies at breast: a study of fifty cases. *Am. J. Dis. Child.*, 1946, **71**, 41–44.

Nothmann, H. Zur Frage der "psychischen" Magensaftsecretion beim Säugling. *Arch. Kinderhielk.*, 1909, **51**, 123–138.

Noyes, A. G. *How I kept my baby well.* Baltimore, Md.: Warwick & York, 1913.

Ohwaki, Y. Die ersten zwei Jahre der Sprachentwicklung des Japanischen Kindes. Ein Beitrag zur Psychologie der Kindersprache. *Tohoku psychol. Fol.*, 1933, **1**, 71–110.

Okamoto, N. Verbalization process in infancy: transpositive use of sounds in development of symbolic activity. *Psychologia, Kyoto*, 1962, **5**, 32–40.

Olson, W. *Child development.* Boston: Heath, 1959.

Oltuszewski, W. *Die geistige und sprachliche Entwicklung des Kindes.* Berlin: Fischer's Medic. Buchhandlung, H. Kornfield, 1897.

Orlansky, H. Infant care and personality. *Psychol. Bull.*, 1949, **46**, 1–48.

Orme, J. E. Intelligence, season of birth and climatic temperature. *Br. J. Psychol.*, 1963, **54**, 273–276.

Osborne, C. A. The sleep of infancy as related to physical and mental growth. *Ped. Sem.*, 1912, **19**, 1–47.

Ottinger, D. R., and Simmons, J. E. Behavior of human neonates and prenatal maternal anxiety. *Psychol. Rep.*, 1964, **14**, 391–394.

Ouroussov, M. P. *Education from the cradle.* London, 1890.

Ourth, L., and Brown, K. B. Inadequate mothering and disturbance in the neonatal period. *Child Dev.*, 1961, **32**, 287–295.

Overstreet, R. An investigation of prenatal position and handedness. *Psychol. Bull.*, 1938, **35**, 320.

Pacella, B. L., and Barrera, S. E. Postural reflexes and grasp phenomena in infants. *J. Neurophysiol.*, 1940, **3**, 213–218.

Palermo, D. S. Thumbsucking: a learned response. *Pediatrics*, 1956, **17**, 392–399.

Palmer, C. D. Principles of child growth and development. *J. educ. Res.*, 1960, **53**, 273–275.

Pancratz, C. N., and Cohen, L. B. Recovery of habituation in infants. 1968. (Mimeographed.)

Papoušek, H. A method of studying conditioned food reflexes in young children up to the age of six months. *Pavlov J. higher nerv. Activ.*, 1959, **9**, 136–140.

Papoušek, H. Podmíněné motorické potravové reflexy u kojenců: I. Experimentální podmíněné sací reflexy. *Česk. Pediat.*, 1960, **15**, 861–872. (a)

Papoušek, H. Podmíněné motorické potravové reflexy u kojenců: II. Nová experimentální vyšetrovací metoda. Česk. Pediat., 1960, 15, 981–988. (b)

Papoušek, H. Podmíněné motorické potravové reflexy u kojenců: III. Experimentální podmíněné rotační reflexy hlavy. Česk. Pediat., 1960, 15, 1057–1065. (c)

Papoušek, H. Conditioned head rotation reflexes in infants in the first months of life. Acta Pediat., 1961, 50, 565–576.

Papoušek, H. On the development of the so-called voluntary movements in the earliest stages of the child's development. Česk. Pediat., 1962, 17, 588–591.

Papoušek, H. Experimental studies of appetitional behavior in human newborns and infants. In H. W. Stevenson, E. H. Hess, and H. L. Rheingold (Eds.), Early behavior. New York: Wiley, 1967. Pp. 249–277. (a)

Papoušek, H., and Bernstein, P. The functions of conditioning stimulation in human neonates and infants. Paper read at conference on "The functions of stimulation in early postnatal development," London, 1967. (b)

Paramonova, N. P. O vozrastnykh osobennostiakh vzaimodeistviia dvukh signalnykh sistem. Zh. výssh. nerv. Deyat., 1957, 7, 651–658.

Parmelee, A. H., Jr. Infant speech development: a report of the study of one child by magnetic tape recordings. J. Pediat., 1955, 46, 447–450.

Parmelee, A. H., Jr. Sleep patterns in infancy: a study of one infant from birth to eight months of age. Acta Pediat., 1961, 50, 160–170.

Parmelee, A. H., Jr. European neurological studies of the newborn. Child Dev., 1962, 33, 169–180.

Parmelee, A. H., Jr. The hand-mouth reflex of Babkin in premature infants. Pediatrics, 1963, 31, 734–740. (a)

Parmelee, A. H., Jr. The palmomental reflex in premature infants. Dev. Med. Child Neurol., 1963, 5, 381–387. (b)

Parmelee, A. H., Jr. A critical evaluation of the Moro reflex. Pediatrics, 1964, 33, 773–788.

Parmelee, A. J., Jr., Brück, K., and Brück, M. Activity and inactivity cycles during the sleep of premature infants exposed to neutral temperatures. Biologia Neonat., 1962, 4, 317–339.

Parmelee, A. H., Jr., Schulz, H. R., and Disbrow, M. A. Sleep patterns of the newborn. J. Pediat., 1961, 58, 241–250.

Pasamanick, B. A comparative study of the behavioral development of Negro infants. J. genet. Psychol., 1946, 69, 3–44.

Pasamanick, B., and Knobloch, H. Early language behavior in Negro children and the testing of intelligence. J. abnorm. soc. Psychol., 1955, 50, 401–402.

Pastore, N. Perceiving as innately determined. J. genet. Psychol., 1960, 96, 93–99.

Patton, R. G., and Gardner, L. I. Influence of family environment on growth: The syndrome of "maternal deprivation." Pediatrics, 1962, 30, 957–962.

Pavlov, I. P. Conditioned reflexes. London: Oxford University Press, 1927.

Pease, D., Rosauer, J. K., and Wolins, L. Reliability of three infant developmental scales administered during the first year of life. J. genet. Psychol., 1961, 98, 295–298.

Peatman, J. G., and Higgons, R. A. Development of sitting, standing, and walking of children reared with optimal pediatric care. Am. J. Orthopsychiat., 1940, 10, 88–111.

Peatman, J. G., and Higgons, R. A. Relation of infants' weight and body build to locomotor development. Am. J. Orthopsychiat., 1942, 12, 234–240.

Peckham, G. Infancy in the city. Pop. Sci. Mon., 1886, 28, 683–689.

Peckham, R. H. Visual discrimination in pre-school children. Child Dev., 1933, 4, 292–297.

Peiper, A. Beiträge zur Sinnesphysiologie der Frühgeburt. Ann. Paediat., 1924, 104, 195–199. (a)

Peiper, A. Untersuchungen über den galvanischen Hautreflex. *Ann. Paediat.*, 1924, **107**, 139–150. (b)

Peiper, A. Die Hirntätigkeit des Neugeborenen. *Jb. Kinderheilk.*, 1926, **111**, 290–314. (a)

Peiper, A. Über einen Augenreflex auf den Hals im frühen Säuglingsalter. *Jb. Kinderheilk.*, 1926, **113**, 87–89. (b)

Peiper, A. Über die Helligkeits- und Farbenempfindungen der Frühgeburten. *Arch. Kinderheilk.*, 1926, **80**, 1–20. (c)

Peiper, A. Untersuchungen über die Reaktionszeit im Säuglingsalter: I. Reaktionszeit auf Schallreiz. *Mschr. Kinderheilk.*, 1926, **31**, 491–506. (d)

Peiper, A. Untersuchungen über die Reaktionszeit im Säuglingsalter: II. Reaktionszeit auf Schmerzreiz. *Mschr. Kinderheilk.*, 1926, **32**, 136–143. (e)

Peiper, A. Über das Unterscheidungsvermögen des Kleinkindes. *Ann. Paediat.*, 1927, **117**, 350–363.

Peiper, A. *Die Hirntätigkeit des Säuglings.* Berlin: Springer, 1928. (a)

Peiper, A. Die Hirntätigkeit des Säuglings. *Ergebn. inn. Med. Kinderheilk.*, 1928, **33**, 11–21. (b)

Peiper, A. Die Schreitbewegungen der Neugeborenen. *Mschr. Kinderheilk.*, 1929, **45**, 444–448.

Peiper, A. Sinnesreaktionen der Neugeborenen. *Z. Psychol.*, 1930, **114**, 363–370.

Peiper, A. Die Nahrungsaufnahme des Säuglings. *Mschr. Kinderheilk.*, 1931, **50**, 20–28.

Peiper, A. Diagnostisch wichtige Reflexe des Kindesalters. *Kinderärztl. Praxis*, 1933, **4**, 189–194. (a)

Peiper, A. Die Atmung des Neugeborenen. *Jahreskurse ärztl. Fortbild.*, 1933, **24**, 21–25. (b)

Peiper, A. Erregung und Hemmung. *Ann. Paediat.*, 1934, **143**, 143–152.

Peiper, A. Die Entwicklung des Mienenspiels. *Mschr. Kinderheilk.*, 1935, **63**, 39–91.

Peiper, A. Comments upon J. M. Smith's work "The relative brightness values of three hues for newborn infants." *Child Dev.*, 1937, **8**, 299–300. (a)

Peiper, A. Die Erscheinung der Dominanz und die Erregungsstufen des Saugzentrums. *Jb. Kinderheilk.*, 1937, **149**, 201–206. (b)

Peiper, A. Sinnesphysiologie und Hirntätigkeit. *Mschr. Kinderheilk.*, 1937, **69**, 327–335. (c)

Peiper, A. Die Erscheinung der Dominanz bei Reizlöschung. *Jb. Kinderheilk.*, 1938, **151**, 1–2.

Peiper, A. Die Führung des Saugzentrums durch das Schluckzentrum. *Pflüg. Arch. gesam. Physiol.*, 1939, **242**, 751–755. (a)

Peiper, A. Die Saugstörung. *Mschr. Kinderheilk.*, 1939, **79**, 241–255. (b)

Peiper, A. Das "Wegbleiben." *Mschr. Kinderheilk.*, 1939, **79**, 236–240. (c)

Peiper, A. Unreife des Frühgeborenen. *Mschr. Kinderheilk.*, 1940, **81**, 321–333.

Peiper, A. Die neurologischen Grundlagen der psychischen Entwicklung. *Mschr. Kinderheilk.*, 1941, **87**, 179–203.

Peiper, A. *Die Eigenart der Kindlichen Hirntätigkeit.* Leipzig: Thieme, 1949.

Peiper, A. *Cerebral function in infancy and childhood.* New York: Consultants Bureau, 1963.

Peiper, A., and Isbert, H. Über die Körperstellung des Säuglings. *Jb. Kinderheilk.*, 1927, **115**, 142–176.

Pendleton, W. R. Hiccups among infants. *Am. J. Dis. Child.*, 1927, **34**, 207–210.

Pennoyer, M. M., Graham, F. K., Hartmann, A. F. Sr., Jones, B., McCoy, E. L., Swarm, P. A., Meyer, R. J., and Endres, R. K. The relationship of paranatal experience to oxygen saturation in newborn infants. *J. Pediat.*, 1956, **49**, 685–698.

Perez, B. *La psychologie de l'enfant: les trois premières années.* Paris: 1878.

Perez, B. Les facultés de l'enfant à l'époque de la naissance. *Rév. Philosophique,* 1882,13, 133–145.

Perez, B. L'âme de l'embryon et l'âme de l'enfant. *Rév. Philosophique,* 1887, 23, 582–602.

Perez, B. *The first three years of childhood.* (Ed. and trans. by A. M. Christie.) London: Swan Sonnenschein, 1892.

Pernot-Roy, M. P. Étude longitudinale sur la croissance de l'enfant. Résultats de quelques mésures somatiques effectuées pendant les trois premières années de la vie. *Arch. franç. Pédiat.,* 1959, 16, 202–214.

Peterson, F., and Rainey, L. H. The beginnings of mind in the newborn. *Bull. Lying-In Hosp., New York,* 1909–1911, 7, 99–122.

Petö, E. Contribution to the development of smell feeling. *Br. J. Med. Psychol.,* 1936, 15, 314–320.

Petö, E. Säugling und Mutter. *Z. psychoanal. Pädag.,* 1937, 11, 244–252.

Pfister, H. Über das Verhalten der Pupille und einiger Reflexe am Auge im Säuglings- und frühen Kindesalter. *Arch. Kinderheilk.,* 1899, 26, 11–14.

Phillips, S., Agate, F., Silverman, W., and Steiner, P. Autonomic cardiac activity in premature infants. *Biologia Neonat.,* 1964, 6, 225–249.

Piaget, J. *La représentation du monde chez l'enfant.* Paris: Alcan, 1926. [*The child's conception of the world.* New York: Humanities Press, 1951.]

Piaget, J. La première année de l'enfant. *Br. J. Psychol.,* 1927, 18, 97–120.

Piaget, J. La causalité chez l'enfant. *Br. J. Psychol.,* 1928, 18, 276–301.

Piaget, J. Das Umdrehen des Gegenstandes beim Kind unter einem Jahr. *Psychol. Rundschau,* 1932, 4, 110–115.

Piaget, J. *La naissance de l'intelligence chez l'enfant.* Neuchâtel: Delachaux et Niestlé, 1936. [*The origins of intelligence in children.* New York: International Universities Press, 1952.]

Piaget, J. *La construction du réel chez l'enfant.* Neuchâtel: Delachaux et Niestlé, 1937. [*The construction of reality in the child.* New York: Basic Books, 1954.]

Piaget, J. *La formation du symbole chez l'enfant.* Neuchâtel: Delachaux et Niestlé, 1945. [*Play, dreams and imitation in childhood.* New York: Norton, 1951.]

Piaget, J. *La psychologie de l'intelligence.* Paris: Presses Universitaires de France, 1946. [*The psychology of intelligence*. London. Routledge, Kegan Paul, 1950. Trans. from 2nd French ed.]

Piaget, J. *Six études de psychologie.* Genève: Gonthier, 1964. [*Six psychological studies.* New York: Random House, 1967.]

Piaget, J., and Inhelder, B. *La représentation de l'espace chez l'enfant.* Paris: Presses Universitaires de France, 1948. [*The child's conception of space.* London: Routledge, Kegan Paul, 1956.]

Piaget, J., Inhelder, B., and Szeminska, A. *La géometrie spontanée chez l'enfant.* Paris: Presses Universitaires de France, 1948. [*The child's conception of geometry.* New York: Basic Books, 1960.]

Pick, H. L., Jr. Perception in Soviet psychology. *Psychol. Bull.,* 1964, 62, 21–35.

Pidgeon, D. A. Date of birth and scholastic performance. *Educ. Res.,* 1965, 8, 3–7.

Pieper, W. J., Lessing, E. E., and Greenberg, H. A. Personality traits in cesarean—normally delivered children. *Archs. gen. Psychiat.,* 1964, 11, 466–471.

Pietrusky, F. Das Verhalten des Auges im Schlaf. *Klin. Mbl. Augenheilk.,* 1922, 68, 355–360.

Pike, E. G. Controlled infant intonation. *Language Learning,* 1949, 2, 21–24.

Pinneau, S. R. A critique on the articles by Margaret Ribble. *Child Dev.,* 1950, 21, 203–228.

Pinneau, S. R. *Changes in Intelligence Quotient—infancy to maturity*. Boston: Houghton Mifflin, 1961.

Pinneau, S. R., and Hopper, H. E. The relationship between incidence of specific gastro-intestinal reactions of the infant and psychological characteristics of the mother. *J. genet. Psychol.*, 1958, **93**, 3–13.

Ploss, H. *Das kleine Kind vom Tragbett bis zum ersten Schritt*. Leipzig: 1881.

Poláček, E., and Polanská, M. Concentration test in infants. *Česk. Pediat.*, 1962, **17**, 1–10.

Polak, P. R., Emde, R. N., and Spitz, R. A. The smiling response to the human face: I. Methodology, quantification and natural history. *J. nerv. ment. Dis.*, 1964, **139**, 103–109. (a)

Polak, P. R., Emde, R. N., and Spitz, R. A. The smiling response to the human face. II: Visual discrimination and the onset of depth perception. *J. nerv. ment. Dis.*, 1964, **139**, 407–415. (b)

Polan, G. G., and Spencer, B. L. A check list of symptoms of autism of early life. *W. Va. med. J.*, 1959, **55**, 198–204.

Polgar, G. Comparison of methods for recording respiration in newborn infants. *Pediatrics*, 1965, **36**, 861–868.

Poli, C. L'udito dei neonati. *Arch. ital. di otol.*, 1894, **2**.

Polikanina, R. I. The relation between autonomic and somatic components in the development of the conditioned defense reflex in premature infants. *Pavlov J. higher nerv. Activ.*, 1961, **11**, 51–58.

Polikanina, R. I. Osobennosti estestvennogo sna nedonshennykh detei v rannii period postnatalnoi zhizni. *Zh. vўssh. nerv. Deyat.*, 1963, **13**, 62–72.

Polikanina, R. I., and Probatova, L. E. Razvitie orientirovochnoĭ reaktsii na zvukovoe razdrazhenie u nedonoshennykh deteĭ. *Zh. vўssh. nerv. Deyat.*, 1955, **5**, 226–236. (a)

Polikanina, R. I., and Probatova, L. E. Stanovlenie i razvitie pishchevogo dvigatel'nogo uslovnogo reflekso na zvuk u nedonoshennykh deteĭ. *Zh. vўssh. nerv. Deyat.*, 1955, **5**, 237–246. (b)

Polikanina, R. I., and Probatova, L. E. Razvitie orientirovochnoi reaktsii i dvigatel'nogo pishchevogo uslovnogo refleksa na svet u nedonoshennykh deteĭ. *Zh. vўssh. nerv. Deyat.*, 1957, **7**, 673–682.

Polikanina, R. I., and Probatova, L. E. On the problem of formation of the orienting reflex in prematurely born children. In L. G. Voronin, A. N. Leontiev, A. R. Luria, E. N. Sokolov, and O. S. Vinogradova (Eds.), *Orienting reflex and exploratory behavior*. Washington: American Institute of Biological Sciences, 1965. Pp. 330–340.

Popper, E. Studien über Saugphänomene. *Arch. Psychiat. Nervenkh.*, 1921, **63**, 231–246.

Portmann, A. Die biologische Bedeutung des ersten Lebensjahres beim Menschen. *Schweiz. med. Wschr.*, 1941, **71**, 921–924.

Portmann, A. Die biologische Bedeutung des ersten Lebensjahres beim Menschen. *Universitas*, 1949, **4**, 1081–1088.

Postman, L. (Ed.) *Psychology in the making*. New York: Knopf, 1962.

Poyntz, L. The efficacy of visual and auditory distractions for preschool children. *Child Dev.*, 1933, **4**, 55–72.

Pratt, K. C. Note on the relation of temperature and humidity to the activity of young infants. *Ped. Sem.*, 1930, **38**, 480–484.

Pratt, K. C. A note upon the relation of activity to sex and race in young infants. *J. soc. Psychol.*, 1932, **3**, 118–120.

Pratt, K. C. The effects of repeated auditory stimulation upon the general activity of newborn infants. *J. genet. Psychol.*, 1934, **44**, 96–116. (a)

Pratt, K. C. The effects of repeated visual stimulation upon the activity of new-born infants. *J. genet. Psychol.*, 1934, **44**, 117–126. (b)

Pratt, K. C. Generalization and specificity of the plantar response in newborn infants. The reflexogenous zone: I. Differential sensitivity and effector-segment participation according to the area of stimulation. *J. genet. Psychol.*, 1934, **44**, 265–300. (c)

Pratt, K. C. Generalization and specificity of the plantar response in newborn infants. The reflexogenous zone: II. Segmental patterning of responses. *J. genet. Psychol.*, 1934, **45**, 22–38. (d)

Pratt, K. C. Generalization and specificity of the plantar response in newborn infants. The reflexogenous zone: III. The effects of the physiological state upon sensitivity, segmental participation, and segmental patterning. *J. genet. Psychol.*, 1934, **45**, 371–389. (e)

Pratt, K. C. Specificity and generalization of behavior in newborn infants. A critique. *Psychol. Rev.*, 1934, **41**, 265–284. (f)

Pratt, K. C. Problems in the classification of neonate activities. *Q. Rev. Biol.*, 1936, **11**, 70–80.

Pratt, K. C. The organization of behavior in the newborn infant. *Psychol Rev.*, 1937, **44**, 470–490.

Pratt, K. C. The neonate. In L. Carmichael (Ed.), *Manual of child psychology.* (2nd ed.) New York: Wiley, 1954. Pp. 215–291.

Pratt, K. C., Nelson, A. K., and Sun, K. H. The behavior of the newborn infant. *Ohio State Univ. Stud., Contrib. Psychol.*, 1930, No. 10.

Prechtl, H. F. R. Angeborene Bewegungsweisen junger Katzen. *Experientia*, 1952, **8**, 220–221. (a)

Prechtl, H. F. R. Über die Adaptation des angeborenen Auslösemechanismus. *Naturwissenschaften*, 1952, **39**, 140–141. (b)

Prechtl, H. F. R. Zur Physiologie der angeborenen auslösenden Mechanismen. *Behaviour*, 1953, **5**, 32–50.

Prechtl, H. F. R. Die Eigenart und Entwicklung der frühkindlichen Motorik. *Klin. Wschr.*, 1956, **34**, 281–284. (a)

Prechtl, H. F. R. Neurophysiologische Mechanismen des formstarren Verhaltens. *Behaviour*, 1956, **9**, 243–319. (b)

Prechtl, H. F. R. The directed head turning response and allied movements of the human baby. *Behaviour*, 1958, **13**, 212–242.

Prechtl, H. F. R. Problems of behavioral studies in the newborn infant. In D. S. Lehrmann, R. A. Hinde, and E. Shaw (Eds.), *Advances in the study of behavior.* Vol. I. New York: Academic Press, 1965. Pp. 75–98.

Prechtl, H. F. R., Akiyama, Y., Zinkin, P., and Grant, D. K. Polygraphic studies of the full-term newborn infant. I. *Dev. Med. Child Neurol.* (In press.)

Prechtl, H. F. R., and Beintema, D. J. *The neurological examination of the full term newborn infant.* London: Heinmann, 1964.

Prechtl, H. F. R., and Dijkstra, J. Neurological diagnosis of cerebral injury in the newborn. In B. S. tenBerge (Ed.), *Prenatal care.* Groningen, The Netherlands: Noordhoff, 1960.

Prechtl, H. F. R., Grant, D. K., Lenard, H. G., and Hrbek, A. The lip-tap-reflex in the awake and sleeping newborn infant. *Exp. Brain Res.*, 1967, **3**, 184–194.

Prechtl, H. F. R., and Knol, A. R. Der Einfluss der Beckenendlage auf die Fussohlenreflexe beim neugeborenen Kind. *Arch. Psychiat. Z. ges. Neurol.*, 1958. **196**, 542–553.

Prechtl, H. F. R., and Schlidt, W. M. Auslösende und steuernde Mechanismen des Saugaktes. *I. Z. vergl. Physiol.*, 1950, **32**, 257–262.

Prechtl, H. F. R., and Schlidt, W. M. Auslösende und steuernde Mechanismen des Saugaktes. II. *Z. vergl. Physiol.*, 1951, **33**, 53–62.

Preyer, W. Psychogenesis. *Dt. Rundschau*, 1880, **23**, 198–221.

Preyer, W. *Die Seele des Kindes*. Leipzig: Grieben, 1882.

Preyer, W. *The mind of the child. Part I. The senses and the will*. New York: Appleton, 1888. (Translation of W. Preyer, *Die Seele des Kindes*.)

Preyer, W. *The mind of the child. Part II. The development of the intellect*. New York: Appleton, 1893. (Translation of W. Preyer, *Die Seele des Kindes*.)

Preyer, W. Embryonic motility and sensitivity. (Trans. by G. E. Coghill and W. K. Legner of selected sections of *Specielle Physiologie des Embryo*, 1885.) *Monogr. Soc. Res. Child Dev.*, 1937, **2**, No. 6.

Přibylová, H., and Znamenáček, K. Some aspects of thermoregulatory reactions in newborn infants during the first hours of life. *Biologia Neonat.*, 1964, **6**, 324–339.

Prior, M. D. Notes on the first three years of a child. *Ped. Sem.*, 1895, **3**, 339–341.

Provence, S., and Lipton, R. C. *Infants in institutions*. New York: International Universities Press, 1962.

Provence, S., and Ritvo, S. Effects of deprivation on institutionalized infants. *Psychoanal. Study Child*, 1961, **16**, 189–205.

Prugh, D. G. Childhood experience and colonic disorder. *Ann. N. Y. Acad. Sci.*, 1954, **58**, 355–376.

Przetacznikowa, M. Rozwoj psychiczny dzieci w pierwszym roku zycia w przekroju trzech srodowisk wychowawczych. *Psychol. Wych.*, 1960, **17**, 32–46.

Pulver, U. *Spannungen und Störungen im Verhalten des Säuglings*. Bern and Stuttgart: Hans Huber, 1959.

Putnam, M. C., Rank, B., and Kaplan, S. Notes on John I. *Psychoanal. Study Child*, 1951, **6**, 38–58.

Pyle, S. I. Effect of the difference in standards in interpreting skeletal age of infants. *Merrill-Palmer Q.*, 1958, **4**, 74–87.

Queck-Wilker, H. *Ein erstes Lebensjahr. Beobachtungen an einem Kinde nach Tagebuchaufzeichungen*. Langensalza: Beyer & Söhne, 1912.

Rabin, A. I. Behavior research in collective settlements in Israel. 6. Infants and children under conditions of "intermittent" mothering in the Kibbutz. *Am. J. Orthopsychiat.*, 1958, **28**, 577–584.

Rabin, A. I. The maternal deprivation hypothesis revisited. *Israel. Ann. Psychiat. rel. Disc.*, 1963, **1**, 189–200.

Rabinovitch, R., and Fischhoff, J. Feeding children to meet their emotional needs. *Am. diet. Assoc.*, 1952, **28**, 614–621.

Rademacher, J. T. Koude kinderen zuigen soms niet. *Ned. Tijdschr. Geneesk.*, 1938, **82**, 289–293.

Raehlmann, E., and Witkowski, L. Über atypische Augenbewegungen. *Arch. Anat. Physiol.*, 1877, 454–471.

Rapaport, D. *Organization and pathology of thought*. New York: Columbia University Press, 1951.

Rasmussen, V. *Child psychology*. Vol. I. *Development in the first four years*. London: Gyldendal, 1920.

Rasmussen, V. *Diary of a child's life from birth to the fifteenth year*. London: Gyldendal, 1931.

Rasmussen, V. *Ruth: Tagebuch über die Entwicklung eines Mädchens von der Geburt bis zum 18 Lebensjahr*. Berlin: Oldenbourgh, 1934.

Ray, W. S. A preliminary report on a study of fetal conditioning. *Child Dev.*, 1932, **3**, 175–177.

Razran, G. H. S. Conditioned responses in children: a behavioral and quantitative critical review of experimental studies. *Arch. Psychol.*, 1933, **23**, No. 148.

Recamier, P. C. Étude clinique des frustrations précoses. *Rev. franç. Psychoanal.*, 1953, **17**, 328–350.

Redfield, J. E. A preliminary report of dark adaptation in young infants. *Child Dev.*, 1937, **8**, 263–269.

Redfield, J. E. The light sense in newborn infants. *Univ. Iowa Stud. Child Welf.*, 1939, **16**, No. 2, 105–145.

Rendle-Short, J. The puff test. *Arch. Dis. Childh.*, 1961, **36**, 50–57.

Reymert, M. L. Questionnaire for the observation of a young child from birth to two years of age. *Ped. Sem.*, 1920, **27**, 200–204.

Reynard, M. C., and Dockeray, F. C. The comparison of temporal intervals in judging depth of sleep in newborn infants. *J. genet. Psychol.*, 1939, **55**, 103–120.

Rheingold, H. L. Mental and social development of infants in relation to the number of other infants in the boarding home. *Am. J. Orthopsychiat.*, 1943, **13**, 41–44.

Rheingold, H. L. The modification of social responsiveness in institutional babies. *Monogr. Soc. Res. Child Dev.*, 1956, **21**, No. 63.

Rheingold, H. L. The effect of environmental stimulation upon social and exploratory behavior in the human infant. In B. M. Foss (Ed.), *Determinants of infant behavior.* New York: Wiley, 1961. Pp. 143–171.

Rheingold, H. L. The measurement of maternal care. *Child Dev.*, 1960, **31**, 565–575.

Rheingold, H. L., and Bayley, N. The later effects of an experimental modification of mothering. *Child Dev.*, 1959, **30**, 363–372.

Rheingold, H. L., Gewirtz, J. L., and Ross, H. W. Social conditioning of vocalizations in the infant. *J. comp. physiol. Psychol.*, 1959, **52**, 68–73.

Rheingold, H. L., Stanley, W. C., and Cooley, J. A. Method for studying exploratory behavior in infants. *Science*, 1962, **136**, 1054–1055.

Rhodes, A. A comparative study of motor abilities of Negroes and whites. *Child Dev.*, 1937, **8**, 369–371.

Ribble, M. A .The significance of infantile sucking for the psychic development of the individual. *J. nerv. ment. Dis,.* 1939, **90**, 455–463.

Ribble, M. A. Disorganizing factors of infant personality. *Am. J. Psychiat.*, 1941, **98**, 459–463.

Ribble, M. A. Infantile experience in relation to personality development. In J. McV. Hunt (Ed.), *Personality and the behavior disorders.* New York: Ronald, 1944. Pp. 621–651.

Ribble, M. A. *The personality of the young child.* New York: Columbia University Press, 1955.

Ribble, M. A. *The rights of infants: early psychological needs and their satisfaction.* (2nd ed.) New York: Columbia University Press, 1965.

Ricciuti, H. Object groupings and selective ordering behavior in infants 12–24 months old. *Merrill-Palmer Q.*, 1965, **11**, 129–148.

Ricciuti, H. Social and emotional behavior in infancy: Some developmental issues and problems. *Merrill-Palmer Q.*, 1968, **14**, 82–100.

Richards, T. W. Gross metabolic changes characteristic of the activity of the neonate. *Child Dev.*, 1935, **6**, 231–241.

Richards, T. W. The importance of hunger in the bodily activity of the neonate. *Psychol. Bull.*, 1936, **33**, 817–835. (a)

Richards, T. W. The relationship between bodily and gastric activity of newborn infants: I. Correlation and influence of time since feeding. *Hum. Biol.*, 1936, **8**, 368–380. (b)

Richards, T. W. The relationship between bodily and gastric activity of newborn infants: II. Simultaneous variations in the bodily and gastric activity of newborn infants under long-continued light stimulation. *Hum. Biol.*, 1936, **8**, 381–386. (c)

Richards, T. W., and Irwin, O. C. Die Veränderung der Fussohlenreaktion bei Neugeborenen unter der Einwirkung von Reizung und anderen Einflüssen. Z. Kinderheilk., 1934, 57, 16–20. (a)

Richards, T. W., and Irwin, O. C. Experimental methods used in studies on infant reactions since 1900. Psychol. Bull., 1934, 31, 23–46. (b)

Richards, T. W., and Irwin, O. C. Plantar responses of infants and young children: an examination of the literature and reports of new experiments. Univ. Iowa Stud. Child Welf., 1934, 11, No. 1. (c)

Richards, T. W., and Nelson, V. L. Studies in mental development: II. Analysis of abilities tested at the age of six months by the Gesell schedule. J. genet. Psychol., 1938, 52, 327–331.

Richards, T. W., and Nelson, V. L. Abilities of infants during the first eighteen months. J. genet. Psychol., 1939, 55, 299–318.

Richards, T. W., and Newbery, H. Studies in fetal behavior: III. Can performance on test items at 6 months postnatally be predicted on the basis of fetal activity? Child Dev., 1938, 9, 79–86.

Richards, T. W., Newbery, H., and Fallgatter, R. Studies in fetal behavior. II. Activity of the human fetus in utero and its relation to other prenatal conditions, particularly the mother's basal metabolic rate. Child Dev., 1938, 9, 69–78.

Richards, T. W., and Simons, M. P. The Fels Child Behavior Scales. Genet. Psychol. Monogr., 1941, 24, 259–309.

Richardson, H. M. The growth of adaptive behavior in infants: an experimental study at seven age levels. Genet. Psychol. Monogr., 1932, 12, 195–359.

Richardson, H. M. The adaptive behavior of infants in the utilization of the lever as a tool: a developmental and experimental study. J. genet. Psychol., 1934, 44, 352–377.

Richmond, J. B. Observations of infant development: clinical and psychological aspects. Merrill-Palmer Q., 1964, 10, 95–101.

Richmond, J. B., Eddy, E., and Green, M. Rumination: a psychosomatic syndrome of infancy. Pediatrics, 1958, 22, 49–55.

Richmond, J. B., Grossman, H. J., and Lustman, S. L. A hearing test for newborn infants. Pediatrics, 1953, 11, 634–638.

Richmond, J. B., and Lipton, E. L. Some aspects of the neurophysiology of the newborn and their implications for child development. In L. Jessner, and E. Pavenstedt (Eds.), Dynamic psychopathology in childhood. New York: Grune & Stratton, 1959.

Richmond, J. B., Lipton, E. L., and Steinschneider, A. Autonomic function in the neonate: V. Individual homeostatic capacity in cardiac response. Psychosom. Med., 1962, 24, 66–74.

Richmond, J. B., and Lustman, S. L. Autonomic function in the neonate: I. Implications for psychosomatic theory. Psychosom. Med., 1955, 17, 269–275.

Richter, C. P. High electrical resistance of the skin of new-born infants and its significance. Am. J. Dis. Child., 1930, 40, 18–26.

Richter, C. P. The grasp reflex of the newborn infant. Am. J. Dis. Child., 1934, 48, 327–332.

Ricketts, A. F. A study of the behavior of young children in anger. Univ. Iowa Stud. Child Welf., 1934, 9, No. 5.

Riesen, A. H. Receptor functions. In P. H. Mussen (Ed.), Handbook of research methods in child development. New York: Wiley, 1960. Pp. 284–307.

Ripin, R. A study of the infant's feeding reactions during the first six months of life. Arch. Psychol., 1930, No. 116.

Ripin, R. A comparative study of the development of infants in an institution with those in homes of low socio-economic status. *Psychol. Bull.*, 1933, **30,** 680–681.

Ripin, R., and Hetzer, H. Frühestes Lernen des Säuglings in der Ernähfungssituation. *Z. Psychol.*, 1930, **118,** 82–127.

Ritala, A. M. Über die Vererbung der Konstitution der Eltern auf das neugeborenen Kind. *Acta Soc. Med. 'Duodecim,'* 1935, **23,** Ser. B. 20.

Ritter, C. Über das Verhältnis der Extremitätenbeuger zu Streckern beim Neugeborenen unter Berücksichtigung seiner Haltung. *Jb. Kinderheilk.*, 1924, **104,** 293–300.

Ritvo, S., and Solnit, A. J. Influences of early mother-child interaction on identification processes. *Psychoanal. Study Child*, 1958, **13,** 64–85.

Robertiello, R. C. The importance of trauma during the first year of life. *Psychoanal. Rev.*, 1956, **43,** 501–503.

Roberts, E. Thumb and finger sucking in relation to feeding in early infancy. *Am. J. Dis. Child.*, 1944, **68,** 7–8.

Robertson, J. Some responses of young children to the loss of maternal care. *Nursing Times*, 1953, **49,** 382–386.

Robertson, J. Mothering as an influence on early development. A study of well-baby clinic records. *Psychoanal. Study Child*, 1962, **17,** 245–264.

Robinson, L. Darwinism in the nursery. *Nineteenth. Cent.*, 1891, **30,** 831–842. (a)

Robinson, L. Infantile atavism: being some further notes on Darwinism in the nursery. *Br. Med. J.*, 1891, **5,** 1226–1227. (b)

Roffwarg, H. P., Muzio, J. N., and Dement, W. C. Ontogenetic development of the human sleep-dream cycle. *Science*, 1966, **152,** 604–619.

Rogers, M., Lilienfield, A., and Pasamanick, B. Prenatal and paranatal factors in the development of childhood behavior disorders. *Acta Psychiat. neurol. Scand.*, Suppl. 102, 1955, 11–157.

Rogerson, B. C. F., and Rogerson, C. H. Feeding in infancy and subsequent psychological difficulties. *J. ment. Sci.*, 1939, **85,** 1163–1182.

Rolando, F. I riflessi del neonato normale. *Pediatria*, 1931, **39,** 645–650.

Roos, J. Nieuwe vondsten betreffende het leven van den foetus. *Tijdschr. Diergeneesk.*, 1939, **66,** 1–13.

Rose, J. A., and Sonis, M. The use of separation as a diagnostic measure in the parent-child emotional crisis. *Am. J. Psychiat.*, 1959, **116,** 409–415.

Rosenblith, J. F. Neonatal assessment. *Psychol. Rep.*, 1959, **5,** 791.

Rosenblith, J. F. Manual for behavioral examination of the neonate. *Am. Psychol. Assoc.*, 1961. (a)

Rosenblith, J. F. The modified Graham behavior test for neonates: test re-test reliability, normative data, and hypotheses for future work. *Biologia Neonat.*, 1961, **3,** 174–192. (b)

Rosenblith, J. F. Prognostic value of neonatal assessment. *Child Dev.*, 1966, **37,** 623–631.

Rosenblith, J. F., and DeLucia, L. A. Tactile sensitivity and muscular strength in the neonate. *Biologia Neonat.*, 1963, **5,** 266–282.

Rosenblith, J. F., and Lipsitt, L. P. Interscorer agreement for the Graham behavior test for neonates. *J. Pediat.*, 1959, **54,** 200–205.

Rosenfeld, A. Drama of life before birth. *Life*, April, 1965.

Rosenthal, M. J. Psychosomatic study of infantile eczema: I. Mother-child relationship. *Pediatrics*, 1952, **10,** 581–592.

Ross, S., Fisher, A. E., and King, D. Sucking behavior: a review of the literature. *J. genet. Psychol.*, 1957, **91,** 63–81.

Roudinesco, J., and Appell, G. Les répercussions de la stabulation hôpitalière sur le développement psycho-moteur des jeunes enfants. *Sem. Hôp. Paris*, 1950, **26**, 2271–2273.

Roudinesco, J., David, M., and Nicolas, J. Responses of young children to separation from their mothers. *Courrier*, 1952, **2**, 66–78.

Roudinesco, J., and Geber, M. De l'utilisation du test de Gesell pour l'étude du comportement des jeunes enfants. *Enfance*, 1951, **4**, 309–322.

Rovee, C. K., and Levin, G. R. Oral "pacification" and arousal in the human newborn. *J. exp. child Psychol.*, 1966, **3**, 1–17.

Rowan-Legg, C. K. Self demand feeding of infants. *Can. Med. Assoc. J.*, 1949, **60**, 388–391.

Rubinfine, D. L. Maternal stimulation, psychic structure and early object relations. *Psychoanal. Study Child*, 1962, **17**, 265–282.

Rubinow, O., and Frankl, L. Die erste Dingauffassung beim Säugling. *Z. Psychol.*, 1934, **133**, 1–71.

Ruja, H. The relation between neonate crying and length of labor. *J. genet. Psychol.*, 1948, **73**, 53–55.

Runge, M. Der erste Schrei und der erste Athemzug. *Berl. klin. Wschr.*, 1895, **32**, 93–95.

Russel, A. Über Formauffassung zwei- bis fünfjähriger Kinder. *Neue Psychol. Stud.*, 1931, **7**, 1–108.

Rycroft, C. Two notes on idealization, illusion, and disillusion, as normal and abnormal psychological processes. *Int. J. Psychoanal.*, 1955, **36**, 81–87.

Saayman, G., Ames, E. W., and Moffett, A. Response to novelty as an indicator of visual discrimination in the human infant. *J. exp. child Psychol.*, 1964, **1**, 189–198.

Sachs, R. Beobachtungen über das physiologische Verhalten des Gehörorgans Neugeborener. *Arch. Ohrenheilk.*, 1893, **35**, 28–38.

Sadger, J. Preliminary study of the psychic life of the fetus and the primary germ. *Psychoanal. Rev.*, 1941, **28**, 327–358.

Saint-Anne Dargassies, S. La maturation neurologique des prématurés. *Etudes Neonat.*, 1955, **4**, 71–116.

Saint-Anne Dargassies, S. Neurologic development of the infant: the contributions of André-Thomas. *World Neurol.*, 1960, **1**, 71–77.

Saint-Anne Dargassies, S. Le nouveau-né à terme: Aspect neurologique. *Biologia Neonat.*, 1962, **4**, 174–200. (a)

Saint-Anne Dargassies, S. The first smile. *Dev. Med. child Neurol.*, 1962, **4**, 531–533. (b)

Salapatek, P. H., and Kessen, W. Visual scanning of triangles by the human newborn. *J. exp. child Psychol.*, 1966, **3**, 155–167.

Salber, E. J. Breast feeding in Boston. *Pediatrics*, 1965, **37**, 299–303.

Salk, L. The effects of the normal heartbeat sound on the behavior of the newborn infant: implications for mental health. *World ment. Hlth.*, 1960, **12**, 168–175.

Salk, L. The importance of the heartbeat rhythm to human nature: theoretical, clinical, and experimental observations. *Proc. 3rd World Congress Psychiatry*. Vol. 1. Montreal: McGill University Press, 1961. Pp. 740–746.

Salk, L. Mothers' heartbeat as an imprinting stimulus. *Trans. N. Y. Acad. Sci.*, 1962, **24**, 753–763.

Salzen, E. A. Visual stimuli eliciting the smiling response in the human infant. *J. genet. Psychol.*, 1963, **102**, 51–54.

Sameroff, A. J. An apparatus for recording sucking and controlling feeding in the first days of life. *Psychonom. Sci.*, 1965, **2**, 355–356. (a)

Sameroff, A. J. An experimental study of the response components of sucking in the human newborn. *Dissert. Abstr.*, 1965, **26**, 2341. (b)

Sameroff, A. J. Nonnutritive sucking in newborns under visual and auditory stimulation. *Child Dev.*, 1967, **38**, 443–452.

Sameroff, A. J. The components of sucking in the human newborn. *J. exp. child Psychol.*, 1968, **6**, 607–623.

Sameroff, A. J. Can conditioned responses be established in the newborn infant? 1969. (Mimeographed.)

Sancipriano, M. La formazione spirituale del bambino lattante. *Pediat. med. prat.*, 1938, **13**, 369–385.

Sander, L. W., and Julia, H. L. Continuous interactional monitoring in the neonate. *Psychosom. Med.*, 1966, **28**, 822–835.

Sanford, H. N. The Moro reflex in the newborn. *Am. J. Dis. Child.*, 1933, **46**, 337–340.

Sanger, M. Language learning in infancy: a review of the autistic hypothesis and an observational study of infants. *Harvard educ. Rev.*, 1955, **25**, 269–271.

Sayegh, Y., and Dennis, W. The effect of supplementary experiences upon the behavioral development of infants in institutions. *Child Dev.*, 1965, **36**, 81–90.

Scammon, R. E. The prenatal growth of the human pancreas. *Proc. Soc. Exp. Biol. Med.*, 1927, **24**, 391–394. (a)

Scammon, R. E. The prenatal growth of the human thymus. *Proc. Soc. Exp. Biol. Med.*, 1927, **24**, 906–909. (b)

Scammon, R. E., and Kittelson, J. A. The growth of the gastro-intestinal tract of the human fetus. *Proc. Soc. Exp. Biol. Med.*, 1927, **24**, 303–307.

Schachter, J., Bickman, L., Schachter, J. S., Jameson, J., Lituchy, S., and Williams, T. A. Behavioral and physiologic reactivity in human neonates. *Ment. Hyg.*, 1966, **50**, 516–521.

Schachter, M. Considérations sur l'activité cérébrale du nourrisson. *J. Neur. Psychiat.*, 1932, **32**, 405–416. (a)

Schachter, M. Le comportement neuropsychique du nourrisson. *Rev. méd. de l'Est*, 1932, **60**, 808–819. (b)

Schachter, M. Les cris des nourrissons et des petits enfants. *Bull. méd.*, 1932, **46**, 637–642. (c)

Schachter, M. Study of diurnal and nocturnal rhythms in the child: spasmus nutans, salaam tics, jactatio capitis nocturna. *Encéphale*, 1954, **43**, 173–192.

Schaefer, E. S. A circumplex model for maternal behavior. *J. abnorm. soc. Psychol.*, 1959, **59**, 226–235.

Schaefer, E. S., and Bayley, N. Maternal behavior, child behavior, and their intercorrelations from infancy through adolescence. *Monogr. Soc. Res. Child Dev.*, 1963, **28**, No. 3.

Schaefer, H. H. Vibration as reinforcer for infant children. *J. exp. anal. Behav.*, 1960, **3**, 160.

Schäfer, P. Beobachtungen und Versuche an einem Kinde in der Entwicklungsperiode des reinen Sprachverständnisses. *Z. paedag. Psychol. Jugendk.*, 1922, **23**, 269–289.

Schaffer, H. R. Objective observations of personality development in early infancy. *Br. J. med. Psychol.*, 1958, **31**, 174–183.

Schaffer, H. R. Changes in developmental quotient under two conditions of maternal separation. *Br. J. soc. clin. Psychol.*, 1965, **4**, 39–46.

Schaffer, H. R. Activity level as a constitutional determinant of infantile reaction to deprivation. *Child Dev.*, 1966, **37**, 595–602.

Schaffer, H. R., and Callender, W. M. Psychologic effects of hospitalization in infancy. *Pediatrics*, 1959, **24**, 528–539.

Schaffer, H. R., and Emerson, P. E. The development of social attachments in infancy. *Monogr. Soc. Res. Child Dev.*, 1964, **29**, No. 3.

Schaffner, B. Group processes. *Trans. 2nd Conf. Josiah Macy, Jr. Found.*, Princeton, N. J., Oct. 9–12, 1955.

Schaie, K. W. A general model for the study of developmental problems. *Psychol. Bull.*, 1965, **64**, 92–107.

Schaltenbrand, G. Normale Bewegungs- und Lagereaktionen bei Kindern. *Dt. Z. Nervenheilk.*, 1925, **87**, 23–59.

Scheidemann, N. V., and Robinette, G. E. Testing the ocular dominance of infants. *Psychol. Clin.*, 1932, **21**, 62–63.

Schmale, A. H. A genetic view of affects. *Psychoanal. Study Child*, 1964, **19**, 287–310.

Schmeidler, G. R. The relation of fetal activity to the activity of the mother. *Child Dev.*, 1941, **12**, 63–68.

Schmidt, E., Leurs, H. L., and Weidtman, V. Über einen nasolabial auslösbaren Reflex beim Neugeborenen. *Z. Kinderheilk.*, 1968, **102**, 109–119.

Schmidt, G. Reizreaktionsexperimente über das Lächeln bei Säuglingen. *Psychiat. Neurol. med. Psychol.*, 1965, **17**, 188–201.

Schmitz, H. A. Der Säugling: Ein soziales Wesen. *Acta paedopsychiat. Basel*, 1962, **29**, 172–178.

Schneeberger de Ataide, J. *Some aspects of motor activity in the first two years.* Lisboa, Portugal: Instituto Antonio Aurelio de Costa Terreira, 1957.

Schneersohn, F. Play and nervousness in infancy. *Z. Kinderpsychiat.*, 1955, **22**, 80–105.

Schneirla, T. C. An evolutionary and developmental theory of biphasic processes underlying approach and withdrawal. In M. R. Jones (Ed.), *Current theory and research in motivation.* Vol. 7. Lincoln: University of Nebraska Press., 1959. Pp. 1–45.

Schneirla, T. C. Aspects of stimulation and organization in approach/withdrawal processes underlying vertebrate behavioral development. In D. S. Lehrmann, R. A. Hinde, and E. Shaw (Eds.), *Advances in the study of behavior.* Vol. I. New York: Academic Press, 1965. Pp. 1–74.

Schoeler, H. Zur Identitäts-Frage. *Graefes Arch. Opthal.*, 1873, **19**, 1–15.

Schultze, K. W. Schicksal von 683 Frühgeburten. *Z. Geburtsh. Gynäk.*, 1939, **118**, 405–419.

Schunk, P. Der Wortschatz eines dreieivierteljährigen Kindes. *Z. allg. dt. Sprachvereins*, 1900, **15**, 167–168.

Schur, E. Studien über das statische Organ normaler Säuglinge und Kinder. *Z. Kinderheilk.*, 1922, **32**, 227–239.

Schwarting, B. H. Testing infants' vision. *Am. J. Ophthal.*, 1954, **38**, 714–715.

Scoe, H. F. Bladder control in infancy and early childhood. *Univ. Iowa Stud. Child Welf.*, 1933, **5**, No. 4.

Scott, R. B., Cardozo, W. W., Smith, A. de G., and DeLilly, M. R. Growth and development of Negro infants: III. Growth during the first year of life as observed in private pediatric practice. *J. Pediat.*, 1950, **37**, 885–893.

Scott, R. B., Ferguson, A. D., Jenkins, M. E., and Cutter, F. F. Growth and development of Negro infants: V. Neuromuscular patterns of behavior during the first year of life. *Pediatrics*, 1955, **16**, 24–30.

Scott, W. C. The demonstration of object relations and affect in a set situation in infants of 6 to 12 months. *Proc. 3rd World Congress of Psychiatry.* Vol. 1. Toronto: University of Toronto Press; Montreal: McGill University Press, 1961. Pp. 56–59.

Scupin, E., and Scupin, G. *Bubi im ersten bis dritten Lebensjahre.* Leipzig: Grieben, 1907.

Scupin, E., and Scupin, G. *Bubis erste Kindheit*. Leipzig: Dürr'sche Buchhandlung, 1933.

Sears, R. R. Effects of cup, bottle and breast feeding on oral drive of newborn
infants. *Am. Psychol.*, 1948, 3, 264.

Sears, R. R., Maccoby, E., and Levin, H. *Patterns of child rearing*. Evanston, Ill.:
Row Peterson, 1957.

Sears, R. R. and Sears, P. S. Minor studies of aggression: V. Strength of frustra-
tion-reaction as a function of strength of drive. *J. Psychol.*, 1940, 9, 297–300.

Sears, R. R., and Wise, G. W. Relation of cup feeding in infancy to thumb-sucking
and the oral drive. *Am. J. Orthopsychiat.*, 1950, 20, 123–138.

Seidman, J. *The child: a book of readings*. New York: Rinehart, 1958.

Seitz, P. F. D. Psychocutaneous conditioning during the first two weeks of life.
Psychosom. Med., 1950, 12, 187–188.

Semb, G., and Lipsitt, L. P. The effects of acoustic stimulation on cessation and
initiation of non-nutritive sucking in neonates. *J. exp. child Psychol.*, 1968,
6, 585–597.

Semmig, H. *Das Kind: Tagebuch eines Vaters*. Rudolfst, 1876.

Senn, M. J. E. *Problems of infancy and childhood: Seven conferences. 1947–1953*.
New York: Josiah Macy, Jr., Foundation, 1948–1954.

Senn, M. J. E. Editorial on finger sucking. *Pediatrics*, 1956, 17, 313.

Shapiro, H. The development of walking in a child. *J. genet. Psychol.*, 1962, 100,
221–226.

Share, J., Koch, R., Webb, A., and Graliker, B. The longitudinal development of
infants and young children with Down's Syndrome (mongolism). *Am. J.
ment. Defic.*, 1964, 68, 685–692.

Share, J., Webb, A., and Koch, R. A preliminary investigation of the early developmental status of mongoloid infants. *Am. J. ment. Defic.*, 1961, 66, 238–241.

Sharpless, S., and Jasper, H. Habituation of the arousal reaction. *Brain*, 1956, 79,
655–680.

Sheridan, M. D. The child's acquisition of speech. *Br. med. J.*, 1945, 1, 707–709.

Sherman, M. The differentiation of emotional responses in infants. I. Judgments
of emotional responses from motion picture views and from actual observation. *J. comp. Psychol.*, 1927, 7, 265–284. (a)

Sherman. M. The differentiation of emotional responses in infants. II. The ability
of observers to judge the emotional characteristics of the crying of infants,
and the voice of an adult. *J. comp. Psychol.*, 1927, 7, 335–351. (b)

Sherman, M., and Sherman, I. C. Sensori-motor responses in infants. *J. comp.
Psychol.*, 1925, 5, 53–68.

Sherman, M., Sherman, I., and Flory, C. D. Infant behavior. *Comp. Psychol.
Monogr.*, 1936, 12.

Shinn, M. W. Notes on the development of a child. *Univ. Calif. Stud.*, 1893–
1899, 1–4.

Shinn, M. W. *The biography of a baby*. New York: Houghton Mifflin, 1900.

Shinn, M. W. Notes on the development of a child. Part II. The development of
the senses in the first three years of childhood. *Univ. Calif. Publ. Educ.*,
1904, 4.

Shipley, T., and Anton, M. T. The human electroretinogram in the first day of life.
J. Pediat., 1964, 65, 733–739.

Shirley, M. M. *The first two years. A study of twenty-five babies. Vol. I. Postural
and locomotor development*. Minneapolis: University of Minnesota Press,
1931.

Shirley, M. M. *The first two years. A study of twenty-five babies. Vol. II. Intellectual development*. Minneapolis: University of Minnesota Press, 1933. (a)

Shirley, M. M. *The first two years. A study of twenty-five babies. Vol. III. Per-*

sonality manifestations. Minneapolis: University of Minnesota Press, 1933.(b)

Shirley, M. M. Development of immature babies during their first two years. *Child Dev.*, 1938, **9**, 347–360.

Shirley, M. M. A behavior syndrome characterizing prematurely-born children. *Child Dev.*, 1939, **10**, 115–128.

Shock, N. W. Physiological growth. In F. Falkner (Ed.), *Human development.* Philadelphia, Pa.: Saunders, 1966. Pp. 150–177.

Shotwell, A. M. Suitability of the Kuhlmann-Binet Infant Scale for assessing intelligence of mental retardates. *Am. J. ment. Defic.*, 1964, **68**, 757–765.

Shotwell, A. M., and Gilliland, A. R. A preliminary scale for the measurement of the mentality of infants. *Child Dev.*, 1943, **14**, 167–177.

Sicherer, O. V. Ophthalmoskopische Untersuchung Neugeborener. *Dt. med. Wschr.*, 1907, **33**, 1564.

Sigismund, N. M. *Kind und Welt. Vätern, Müttern und Kinderfreunden gewidmet: I. Die fünf ersten Perioden des Kindesalters.* Vieweg: Braunschweig, 1856.

Sikorsky, A. J. Du développement du langage chez les enfants. *Arch. Neurol.*, 1881, **6**, 319–336.

Silver, H. K., and Deamer, W. C. Graphs of the head circumference of the normal infant. *J. Pediat.*, 1948, **33**, 167–171.

Silverman, W. A., Zamelis, N., and Sinclair, N. M. Warm nape of the newborn. *Pediatrics*, 1964, **33**, 985–987.

Simmons, M. W. Operant discrimination learning in human infants. *Child Dev.*, 1964, **35**, 737–748.

Simmons, M. W., and Lipsitt, L. P. An operant-discrimination apparatus for infants. *J. exp. Anal. Behav.*, 1961, **4**, 233–235.

Simon, A. J., and Bass, L. G. Toward a validation of infant testing. *Am. J. Orthopsychiat.*, 1956, **26**, 340–350.

Simon, B. (Ed.) *Psychology in the Soviet Union.* London: Routledge & Kegan Paul, 1957.

Simon, T. Les deux premières années de l'enfant. *Bull Soc. libre Etude psychol. Enf.*, 1916, **108**, 1–64.

Simons, A. Kopfhaltung und Muskeltonus. *Zentbl. ges. Neur. Psychiat.*, 1925, **40**, 372–375.

Simonsen, K. M. *Examination of children from children's homes and day-nurseries by the Bühler-Hetzer developmental tests.* (Trans. by Poul Prom.) Copenhagen: Nyt Nordisk Forlag, 1947.

Simpson, Sir W. G. A chronicle of infant development and characteristics. *J. ment. Sci.*, 1893, **39**, 378–389, 498–505.

Simsarian, F. P. Case histories of five thumbsucking children breast fed on unscheduled regimes, without limitation of nursing time. *Child Dev.*, 1947, **18**, 180–184.

Simsarian, F. P., and McLendon, P. A. Feeding behavior of an infant during the first twelve weeks of life on a self-demand schedule. *J. Pediat.*, 1942, **20**, 93–103.

Simsarian, F. P., and McLendon, P. A. Further records of the self-demand schedule in infant feeding. *J. Pediat.*, 1945, **27**, 109–114.

Siqueland, E. R. Operant conditioning of head turning in four-month infants. *Psychonom. Sci.*, 1964, **1**, 223–224.

Siqueland, E. R. Reinforcement patterns and extinction in human newborns. *J. exp. Child Psychol.*, 1968, **6**, 431–442.

Siqueland, E. R., and Lipsitt, L. P. Conditioned head-turning in human newborns. *J. exp. Child Psychol.*, 1966, **3**, 356–376.

Skard, A., Inhelder, B., Noelting, G., Murphy, L., and Thomas, H. Longitudinal research in personality development. In H. P. David and J. C. Brengelmann

(Eds.), *Perspectives in personality research.* New York: Springer, 1960. Pp. 247–269.

Skawran, P. Furcht und Angst im frühen Kindesalter und ihre Abhängigkeit von "Grundeinstellungen." *Arch. ges. Psychol.*, 1930, **77**, 109–128.

Skerrett, H. S. Trainability and emotional reaction in the human infant. *Psychol. Clin.*, 1922, **14**, 106–110. (a)

Skerrett, H. S. The educability of a two-year old. *Psychol. Clin.*, 1922, **14**, 221–224. (b)

Skinner, E. F. The superficial abdominal reflexes. *J. ment. Sci.*, 1936, **82**, 394–410.

Slataper, F. J. Age norms of refraction and vision. *Arch. Ophthal.*, 1950, **43**, 466–481.

Slutskaia, M. M. Perevod oboronitelnykh refleksov v pishchevye u oligophrenic i u normalnykh detei. *Zh. Nevropatol.,* 1928, **21**, 195–205.

Smillie, D. The roots of personal existence. *J. humanist Psychol.*, 1961, **1**, 89–93.

Smillie, D. Familial resemblance in physique change in infancy. *Merrill-Palmer Q.*, 1962, **8**, 27–32.

Smith, C. A. The first breath. *Scient. Am.*, 1963, **209**, 27–35.

Smith, C. A. Human milk and breast feeding. *Pediatrics*, 1964, **34**, 873–874.

Smith, J. M. The relative brightness values of three hues for newborn infants. *Univ. Iowa Stud. Child Welf.*, 1936, **12**, No. 1, 91–140.

Smith, J. M. Reply to Peiper. *Child Dev.*, 1937, **8**, 301–304.

Smith, J. R. The electroencephalogram during normal infancy and childhood: I. Rhythmic activities present in the neonate and their subsequent development. *J. genet. Phychol.*, 1938, **53**, 431–453. (a)

Smith, J. R. The electroencephalogram during normal infancy and childhood: III. Preliminary observations on the pattern sequence during sleep. *J. genet. Psychol.,* 1938, **53**, 471–482. (b)

Smith, J. R. The "occipital" and "pre-central" alpha rhythms during the first two years. *J. Psychol.*, 1939, **7**, 223–226.

Smith, K. U., and Smith, W. M. *Perception and Motion.* Philadelphia, Pa.: Saunders, 1962.

Smith, K. U., Zwerg, C., and Smith, N. J. Sensory feedback analysis of infant control of the behavioral environment. *Percept. mot. Skills*, 1963, **16**, 725–732.

Smith, M. Wild children and the principle of reinforcement. *Child Dev.*, 1954, **25**, 115–123.

Smith, M. E., Lecker, G., Dunlap, J. W., and Cureton, E. E. The effects of race, sex, and environment on the age at which children walk. *Ped. Sem.*, 1930, **38**, 489–498.

Snyder, F. F., and Rosenfeld, M. Intra-uterine respiratory movements of the human fetus. *J. Am. med. Assoc.*, 1937, **108**, 1946–1948.

Soddy, K. (Ed.) *Mental health and infant development.* New York: Basic Books, 1956.

Söderling, B. The first smile. *Acta Paediat.*, 1959, **48**, Suppl. 117, 78–82.

Sokolov, E. N. *Perception and the conditioned reflex.* New York: Macmillan, 1963.

Solomons, G., and Solomons, H. C. Factors affecting motor performance in four-month-old infants. *Child Dev.*, 1964, **35**, 1283–1296.

Soltmann, O. Experimentelle Studien über die Funktionen des Grosshirns der Neugeborenen. *Jb. Kinderheilk.*, 1876, **9**, 106–148.

Soltmann, O. Über einige physiologische Eigentümlichkeiten der Muskeln und Nerven des Neugeborenen. *Jb. Kinderheilk.*, 1878, **12**, 1–20.

Sonahara, T. Über den Einfluss der Saccharinreizungen auf die Leersaugbewegungen bei den Neugeborenen: Eine systematische psychologische

Untersuchung von Neugeborenen. 1, 2. *Jap. J. exp. Psychol.*, 1934, 1, 1–18. (a)

Sonohara, T. Systematic studies on psychology of human neonates. Reactions to bitter stimuli. *Jap. J. exp. Psychol.*, 1934, 1, 127–141. (b)

Sonohara, T. Systematic observation on daily progress of five newborn infants in their first ten days. *Jap. J. exp. Psychol.*, 1936, 3, 187–218.

Sonohara, T. Psychological research on the newborn child. *Jap. J. exp. Psychol.* 1937, 4, 35–54. (a)

Sonohara, T. On sucking movements of nursing babies. *Jap. J. exp. Psychol.*, 1937, 4, 55–62. (b)

Sontag, L. W. War and the fetal-maternal relationship. *Marr. fam. Liv.*, 1944, 6, 3–4.

Sontag, L. W. The possible relationship of prenatal environment to schizophrenia. In D. D. Jackson (Ed.), *The Etiology of schizophrenia*. New York: Basic Books, 1960. Pp. 175–187.

Sontag, L. W., and Nelson, V. L. A study of identical triplets: Part I. Comparison of the physical and mental traits of a set of monozygotic dichorionic triplets. *J. Hered.*, 1933, 24, 473–480. (a)

Sontag, L. W., and Nelson, V. L. Monozygotic dischorionic triplets: Part II. Behavior of a set of identical triplets. *J. genet. Psychol.*, 1933, 42, 406–422. (b)

Sontag, L. W., and Richards, T. W. Studies in fetal behavior: I. Fetal heart rate as a behavioral indicator. *Monogr. Soc. Res. Child Dev.*, 1938, 3, No. 4.

Sontag, L. W., and Wallace, R. F. The movement response of the human fetus to sound stimuli. *Child Dev.*, 1935, 6, 253–258.

Sontag, L. W., and Wallace, R. F. Changes in the rate of the human fetal heart in response to vibratory stimuli. *Am. J. Dis. Child.*, 1936, 51, 583–589.

Spears, W. C. Assessment of visual preference and discrimination in the four-month-old infant. *J. comp. physiol. Psychol.*, 1964, 57, 381–386.

Spears, W. C. Visual preference in the four-month-old infant. *Psychonom. Sci.*, 1966, 4, 237–238.

Spelt, D. K. The conditioning of the human fetus in utero. *J. exp. Psychol.*, 1948, 38, 338–346.

Sperling, M. Animal phobias in a two-year old child. *Psychoanal. Study Child*, 1952, 7, 115–125.

Sperling, M. Etiology and treatment of sleep disturbances in children. *Psychoanal. Q.*, 1955, 24, 358–368.

Spiker, C. C. The concept of development: relevant and irrelevant issues. In H. W. Stevenson (Ed.), Concept of development. *Monogr. Soc. Res. Child Dev.*, 1966, 31, No. 107, 40–54.

Spiker, C. C., and Irwin, O. C. The relationship between IQ and indices of infant speech sound development. *J. speech hear. Disord.*, 1949, 14, 335–343.

Spitz, R. A. Hospitalism: an inquiry into the genesis of psychiatric conditions in early childhood. *Psychoanal. Study Child*, 1945, 1, 53–74.

Spitz, R. A. Hospitalism: a follow-up report on investigation described in volume 1, 1945. *Psychoanal. Study Child*, 1946, 2, 113–117.

Spitz, R. A. Autoeroticism: some empirical findings and hypotheses on three of its manifestations in the first year of life. *Psychoanal. Study Child*, 1949, 3–4, 85–120. (a)

Spitz, R. A. The role of ecological factors in emotional development in infancy. *Child Dev.*, 1949, 20, 145–155. (b)

Spitz, R. A. Relevancy of direct infant observation. *Psychoanal. Study Child*, 1950, 5, 66–73.

Spitz, R. A. The psychogenic diseases in infancy. *Psychoanal. Study Child*, 1951, **6**, 255–275.

Spitz, R. A. The primal cavity. *Psychoanal. Study Child*, 1955, **10**, 215–240.

Spitz, R. A. Some observations on psychiatric stress in infancy. In H. Selye (Ed.), *Fifth annual report on stress*. New York: MD Publs., 1956. Pp. 193–204.

Spitz, R. A. On the genesis of superego components. *Psychoanal. Study Child*, 1958, **13**, 375–404.

Spitz, R. A. Autoeroticism re-examined. *Psychoanal. Study Child*, 1962, **17**, 283–315.

Spitz, R. A. *The first year of life: a psychoanalytic study of normal and deviant development of object relations*. New York: International Universities Press, 1965.

Spitz, R. A., and Wolf, K. M. Analitic depression: an inquiry into the genesis of psychiatric conditions in early childhood. II. *Psychoanal. Study Child*, 1946, **2**, 313–343. (a)

Spitz, R. A., and Wolf, K. M. Environment vs. race—environment as an etiological factor in psychiatric disturbances in infancy. *J. nerv. ment. Dis.*, 1946, **103**, 520–521. (b)

Spitz, R. A., and Wolf, K. M. The smiling response: a contribution to the ontogenesis of social relations. *Genet. Psychol. Monogr.*, 1946, **34**, 57–125. (c)

Spitzer, R. L., Kramer, Y., and Rabkin, R. The neck-righting reflex in children. *J. Pediat.*, 1958, **52**, 149–151.

Spock, B. *The common sense book of baby and child care*. New York: Duell, Sloan & Pearce, 1946.

Spock, B. Innate inhibition of aggressiveness in infancy. *Psychoanal. Study Child*, 1965, **20**, 340–343.

Stambak, M. Contribution à l'étude du développement moteur chez le nourrisson. *Enfance*, 1956, **9**, 49–59.

Stambak, M. *Tonus et psychomotricité dans la première enfance*. Neuchâtel: Editions Delachaux et Niestlé, 1963.

Staples, R. Color vision and color preference in infancy and childhood. *Psychol. Bull.*, 1931, **28**, 297–308.

Staples, R. The responses of infants to color. *J. exp. Psychol.*, 1932, **15**, 119–141.

Statten, P., and Wishart, D. E. S. Pure-tone audiometry in young children: psychogalvanic-skin-resistance and peep-show. *Ann. Otol. Rhinol. Lar.*, 1956, **65**, 511–534.

Stechler, G. Newborn attention as affected by medication during labor. *Science*, 1964, **144**, 315–317.

Stechler, G., Bradford, S., and Levy, H. Attention in the newborn: effect on motility and skin potential. *Science*, 1966, **151**, 1246–1248.

Stechler, G., and Latz, E. Some observations on attention and arousal in the human infant. *J. Am. Acad. child Psychiat.*, 1966, **5**, 517–525.

Stedman, D. J., and Eichorn, D. H. A comparison of the growth and development of institutionalized and home-reared mongoloids during infancy and early childhood. *Am. J. ment. Defic.*, 1964, **69**, 391–401.

Steinschneider, A. Developmental psychophysiology. In Y. Brackbill (Ed.), *Infancy and early childhood: a handbook and guide to human development*. New York: Free Press, 1967. Pp. 1–47.

Steinschneider, A. Sound intensity and respiratory responses in the neonate. *Psychosom. Med.*, 1968, **30**, 534–541.

Steinschneider, A., Lipton, E. L., and Richmond, J. B. Autonomic function in the neonate: VI. Discriminability, consistency, and slope as measures of an individual's cardiac responsivity. *J. genet. Psychol.*, 1964, **105**, 295–310.

Steinschneider, A., Lipton, E. L., and Richmond, J. B. Auditory sensitivity in the infant: effect of intensity on cardiac and motor responsivity. *Child Dev.*, 1966, **37**, 233–252.

Sterba, E. Analysis of psychogenic constipation in a two-year-old child. *Psychoanal. Study Child*, 1949, **3–4**, 227–252.

Stern, C., and Stern, W. *Monographien über die seelische Entwicklung des Kindes: II. Erinnerung, Aussage und Lüge in der ersten Kindheit.* Leipzig: J. A. Barth, 1909. Pp. 111–160.

Stern, C., and Stern, W. Die Kindersprache. *Monogr. über die seelische Entwicklung des Kindes*, 1922, 1.

Stern, W. *Psychologie der frühen Kindheit bis zum sechsten Lebensjahr.* Leipzig: Quelle & Meyer, 1914.

Stern, W. *Psychology of early childhood.* New York: Henry Holt, 1924.

Stern, W. *Die Intelligenz der Kinder und Jugenlichen.* Leipzig: J. A. Barth, 1928.

Stevenson, H. W. Piaget, behavior theory, and intelligence. In W. Kessen and C. Kuhlman (Eds.), Thought in the young child. *Monogr. Soc. Res. Child Dev.*, 1962, **27**, No. 83.

Stevenson, S. S. Paranatal factors affecting adjustment in childhood. *Pediatrics*, 1948, **2**, 154–162.

Stewart, A. H. Excessive crying in infants: a family disease. In M. J. E. Senn (Ed.), *Problems of infancy and childhood.* New York: Josiah Macy, Jr. Foundation, 1952. Pp. 138–160.

Stewart, A. H., Weiland, J. H., Leider, A. R., Mangham, C. A., Holmes, T. H., and Ripley, H. S. Excessive infant crying (colic) in relation to parent behavior. *Am. J. Psychiat.*, 1954, **110**, 687–694.

Stirnimann, F. Versuche über Geschmack und Geruch am ersten Lebenstag. *J. Kinderheilk.*, 1936, **146**, 211–277. (a)

Stirnimann, F. Le goût et l'odorat du nouveau-né. *Rev. franç. Pédiat.*, 1936, **12**, 453–485. (b)

Stirnimann, F. Les réactions du nouveau-né contre l'enchaînement. *Rev. franç. Pédiat.*, 1937, **13**, 496–502.

Stirnimann, F. Versuche über die Reaktionen Neugeborener auf Wärme- und Kältereize. *Z. Kinderpsychiat.*, 1939, **5**, 143–151.

Stirnimann, F. *Psychologie des neugeborenen Kindes.* Zürich and Leipzig: Rascher, 1940.

Stirnimann, F. Greifversuche mit der Hand Neugeborener. *Ann. Paediat.*, 1941, **157**, 17–27.

Stirnimann, F. Über den Moroschen Umklammerungsreflex beim Neugeborenen. *Ann. Paediat.*, 1943, **160**, 1–10.

Stirnimann, F. Über das Farbempfinden Neugeborener. *Ann. Paediat.*, 1944, **163**, 1–25.

Stirnimann, F., and Stirnimann, W. Der Fussgreifreflex bei Neugeborenen und Säuglingen: Seine diagnostische Verwendbarkeit. *Ann. Paediat.*, 1940, **154**, 249–264.

Stoffels, M. J. La réaction dite de colère chez les nouveau-nés. *J. Psychol. norm. path.*, 1940/41, **37/38**, 92–148.

Stone, A. A. and Onqué, G. C. *Longitudinal studies of child personality.* Cambridge: Harvard University Press, 1959.

Stone, L. J. A critique of studies of infant isolation. *Child Dev.*, 1954, **25**, 9–20.

Stone, S., and Bakwin, H. Breast feeding. *J. Pediat.*, 1948, **33**, 660–667.

Stott, D. H. An empirical approach to motivation based on the behaviour of a young child. *J. child Psychol. Psychiat.*, 1961, **2**, 97–117.

Stott, L. H. The persisting effects of early family experiences upon personality development. *Merrill-Palmer Q.*, 1957, **3**, 145–159.

Stott, L. H., and Ball, R. S. Infant and preschool mental tests: review and evaluation. *Monogr. Soc. Res. Child Dev.*, 1965, **30**, No. 101.

Strang, R. *An introduction to child study.* New York: Macmillan, 1959.

Strauss, M. A. Anal and oral frustration in relation to Sinhalese personality. *Sociometry*, 1957, **20**, 21–31.

Strayer, L. C. Language and growth: the relative efficacy of early and deferred vocabulary training studied by the method of co-twin control. *Genet. Psychol. Monogr.*, 1930, **8**, 209–319.

Strümpell, L. Notizen über die geistige Entwicklung eines weiblichen Kindes während der ersten zwei Lebensjahre. In *Psychologische Pädagogik.* Leipzig: Georg Böhme, 1880.

Stubbs, E. M. The effect of the factors of duration, intensity, and pitch of sound stimuli on the responses of newborn infants. *Univ. Iowa Stud. Child Welf.*, 1934, **9**, No. 4, 75–135.

Stubbs, E. M., and Irwin, O. C. Laterality of limb movements of four newborn infants. *Child Dev.*, 1933, **4**, 358–359.

Stubbs, E. M., and Irwin, O. C. A note on reaction times in infants. *Child Dev.*, 1934, **5**, 291–292.

Stutsman, R. *Mental measurement of preschool children.* New York: World, 1931.

Sully, J. Babies and science. *Cornhill Mag.*, 1881, **43**, 539–554.

Sully, J. Infant psychology. *J. educ.*, 1894, **16**, 202–204.

Sully, J. *Studies of childhood.* New York: Appleton, 1903.

Sureau, M., Fischgold, H., and Capdevielle, B. L'EEG du nouveau-né: normal de 0 à 36 heures. *Electroenceph. clin. Neurophysiol.*, 1949, **1**, 376.

Sureau, M., Fischgold, H., and Capdevielle, B. L'EEG du nouveau-né normal et pathologique. *Electroenceph. clin. Neurophysiol.*, 1950, **2**, 113–114.

Sutton-Smith, B. Piaget on play: a critique. *Psychol. Rev.*, 1966, **73**, 104–110.

Swinehart, E. W. Structural and nervous effects of thumbsucking. *J. Am. dent. Assoc.*, 1938, **25**, 736–747.

Sylvester, E. Pathogenic influences of maternal attitudes in the neonatal period. In M. J. E. Senn (Ed.), *Problems of infancy and childhood.* New York: Josiah Macy, Jr. Foundation, 1948. Pp. 67–70.

Sylvester, E. Developmental truisms and their fate in child rearings: clinical observations. In M. J. E. Senn (Ed.), *Problems of infancy and childhood.* New York: Josiah Macy, Jr., Foundation, 1953. Pp. 9–37.

Szuman, S. Geneza przedmiotu o dynamicznej integracji sfer zmyslowych we wczesnem dziecinstwie. *Kwart. Psychol.*, 1932, **3**, 363–394.

Taine, H. Note sur l'acquisition du langage chez les enfants et dans l'espèce humaine. *Rév. Phil.*, 1876, **1**, 5–23.

Taine, H. M. Taine on the acquisition of language by children. *Mind*, 1877, **2**, 252–259.

Talbot, E. (Ed.) *Papers on infant development.* Boston: Educ. Dept., Am. Soc. Sci. Assoc., 1882.

Talbot, F. B. Physiology of the newborn infant. *Am. J. Dis. Child.*, 1917, **13**, 495–500. (a)

Talbot, F. B. Twenty-four hour matabolism of two normal infants with special reference to the total energy requirements of infants. *Am. J. Dis. Child.*, 1917, **14**, 25–33. (b)

Taniewski, J. Odczyny blednikowe u dzieci w pierwszym roku zycia. *Otolar. Polska*, 1950, **4**, 35–41.

Tanner, A. E. *The child: his thinking, feeling, and doing.* New York: 1904.

Tanner, A. E. The new-born child. *Ped. Sem.*, 1915, **22**, 487–501.

Tanner, J. M. *Education and physical growth.* London: University of London Press, 1961.

Tanner, J. M. *Growth at adolescence*. (2nd ed.) Oxford: Blackwell, 1962.

Tanner, J. M., Healy, M. J. R., Lockhart, R. D., Mackenzie, J. D., and Whitehouse, R. H. Aberdeen growth study. I. The prediction of adult body measurements from measurements taken each year from birth to 5 years. *Archs. Dis. Childh.*, 1956, **31**, 372–381.

Tauber, E. S., and Koffler, S. Optomotor response in human infants to apparent motion: evidence of innateness. *Science*, 1966, **152**, 382–383.

Tayler-Jones, L. A study of behavior of the newborn. *Am. J. Med. Sci.*, 1927, **174**, 357–362.

Taylor, J. H. Innate emotional responses in infants. *Ohio Univ. Stud.*, 1934, No. 12, 69–81.

Taylor, R. Hunger and appetite secretion of gastric juice in infants' stomachs. *Am. J. Dis. Child.*, 1917, **14**, 258–266. (a)

Taylor, R. Hunger in the infant. *Am. J. Dis. Child.*, 1917, **14**, 233–257. (b)

Tcheng, F. C. Y., and Laroche, J. L. Phases de sommeil et sourires spontanés. *Acta Psychol. Amsterdam*, 1965, **24**, 1–28.

Tennes, K. H., and Lampl, E. E. Stranger and separation anxiety in infancy. *J. nerv. ment. Dis.*, 1964, **139**, 247–254.

Teodorescu, I., Tanasescu, Gh., and Popa, S. Despre unil factori care influenteaza dezvoltarea fizica a copitutui in primul an de viata. *Pediatria*, 1958, **7**, 123–136.

Terman, L. M. An experiment in infant education. *J. appl. Psychol.*, 1918, **2**, 219–228.

Thelander, H. E. Childhood ecology: factors influencing maturation. *Calif. Med.*, 1954, **81**, 314–315.

Thelander, H. E., and Fitzhugh, M. L. Posture habits in infancy affecting foot and leg alignments. *J. Pediat.*, 1942, **21**, 306–314.

Thelander, H. E., Gratton, R., and Loring, C. A developmental study of triplets. *J. Am. med. Women's Assoc.*, 1961, **16**, 445–449.

Thiemich, M. Über die motorische Innervation beim Neugeborenen und jungen Säuglingen. *Jb. Kinderheilk.*, 1917, **85**, 395–399.

Thomas, A., Birch, H. G., Chess, S., Hertzig, M. E., and Korn, S. *Behavioral individuality in early childhood*. New York: New York University Press, 1963.

Thomas, A., Birch, H. G., Chess, S., and Robbins, L. Individuality in responses of children to similar environmental situations. *Am. J. Psychiat.*, 1961, **117**, 798–803.

Thomas, A., Chess, S., Birch, H. G., and Hertzig, M. E. A longitudinal study of primary reaction patterns in children. *Compreh. Psychiat.*, 1960, **1**, 103–112.

Thomas, H. Visual-fixation responses of infants to stimuli of varying complexity. *Child Dev.*, 1965, **36**, 629–638.

Thomas, J. E., and Lambert, E. H. Ulnar nerve conduction velocity and H-reflex in infants and children. *J. appl. Physiol.*, 1960, **15**, 1–9.

Thompson, H. The growth and significance of daily variations in infant behavior. *J. genet. Psychol.*, 1932, **40**, 16–36.

Thompson, H. Measurement of infant behavior. *J. exp. Educ.*, 1935, **3**, 230–232.

Thompson, H. Sleep requirements during infancy. *Psychol. Monogr.*, 1936, **47**, 64–73.

Thompson, H., and Bearg, P. A. The behavior examination of infants as an aid to early diagnosis of central nervous system disease. *J. Pediat.*, 1940, **16**, 570–579.

Thompson, J. On the lip reflex (mouth phenomenon) of new-born children. *Rev. Neurol. Psychiat.*, 1903, **1**, 145–148.

Thompson, J. Development of facial expressions of emotion in blind and seeing children. *Arch. Psychol.*, 1941, No. 264.

Thompson, J. M. Survey of the literature on psychological aspects of eating in infancy and early childhood. *Psychol. Serv. Center J.*, 1950, **3**, 203–226.

Thompson, R. F., and Spencer, W. A. Habituation: a model phenomenon for the study of neuronal substrates of behavior. *Psychol. Rev.*, 1966, **73**, 16–43.

Thompson, T. W. A baby's nursing difficulties. *Ped. Sem.*, 1926, **33**, 709–716.

Thompson, V. J. The effects of sudden weaning. *Proc. S. Afric. Psychol. Assoc.*, 1953, No. 4, 29–30.

Thomson, J. Infant growth. *Archs. Dis. Childh.*, 1956, **31**, 382–389.

Thornval, A. L'épreuve calorique chez les nouveau-nés. *Acta oto-laryng.*, 1921, **2**, 451–454.

Thurstone, L. L., and Jenkins, R. L. *Order of birth, parent-age, and intelligence.* Chicago: University of Chicago Press, 1931.

Tiedemann, D. Beobachtungen über die Seelenfähigkeiten bei Kindern. *Hess. Beitr. gelehrs. Kunst*, 1787, **2**, 313–333; **3**, 486–502.

Tilley, L. S. Record of development of two baby boys. *Publs. Assoc. Collegiate Alumnae*, 1910, Series 3, No. 22, 1–83.

Tilney, F., and Casamajor, L. Myelinogeny as applied to the study of behavior. *Arch. Neurol. Psychiat.*, 1924, **12**, 1–66.

Tinbergen, N. *The study of instinct.* Oxford: Clarendon Press, 1951.

Tischler, H. Schreien, Lallen und erstes Sprechen in der Entwicklung des Säuglings. *Z. Psychol.*, 1957, **160**, 210–263.

Titchener, E. B. *A textbook of psychology.* New York: Macmillan, 1909.

Togel, H. 16 Monate Kindersprache. *Beitr. Kinderforsc. Heilerz.*, 1905, **13**, 1–36.

Tonkova-Yampolskaia, R. V. K kharakteristike sosudistykh uslovnykh refleksov u detei mladshego vozrasta. *Zh. vÿssh. nerv. Deyat.*, 1956, **6**, 697–701.

Tonkova-Yampolskaia, R. V. The features of vascular conditioned reflexes in children in the third year of life. *Pavlov J. higher nerv. Activ.*, 1961, **11**, 89–93.

Tonkova-Yampolskaia, R. V. On the question of studying physiological mechanisms of speech. *Pavlov J. higher nerv. Activ.*, 1962, **12**, 82–87.

Tourney, A. L'asymétrie dans le développement sensitive-moteur de l'enfant. *J. Psychol. norm. Path.*, 1924, **21**, 135–144.

Tracy, F. *The psychology of childhood.* Boston: Heath, 1895.

Trainham, G., and Montgomery, J. C. Self-demand feeding for babies. *Am. J. Nurs.*, 1946, **46**, 767–770.

Trainham, G., Pilafian, G. J., and Kraft, R. M. A case history of twins fed on a self-demand regime. *J. Pediat.*, 1945, **27**, 97–108.

Traisman, A. S., and Traisman, H. S. Thumb- and finger-sucking: a study of 2,650 infants. and children. *J. Pediat.*, 1958, **52**, 566–572.

Tramer, M. Die Entwicklungslinie eines psychotischen Kindes. *Schweiz. Arch. Neur. Psychiat.*, 1931, **27**, 383–392.

Tramer, M. Tagebuch über ein geisteskrankes Kind. *Z. Kinderpsychiat.*, 1934, **1**, 91–97, 123–126, 154–161, 187–194; 1935, **2**, 17–28, 86–90, 115–124.

Trettien, A. W. Creeping and walking. *Am. J. Psychol.*, 1900, **12**, 1–57.

Trincker, D., and Trincker, I. Die ontogenetische Entwicklung des Helligkeits-und Farbensehens beim Menschen: I. Die Entwicklung des Helligkeitssehens. *Albrecht v. Graefes Arch. Ophthal.*, 1955, **156**, 519–534.

Tulloch, J. D., Brown, B. S., Jacobs, H. L., Prugh, D. G., and Greene, W. A. Normal heartbeat sound and the behavior of newborn infants: a replication study. *Psychosom. Med.*, 1964, **26**, 661–670.

Turkewitz, G., Birch, H. G., Moreau, T., Levy, L., and Cornwell, A. C. Effect of intensity of auditory stimulation on directional eye movements in the human neonate. *Anim. Behav.*, 1966, **14**, 93–101.

Turkewitz, G., Fleischer, S., Moreau, T., Birch, H. G., and Levy, L. Relationship between feeding condition and organization of flexor-extensor movements in the human neonate. *J. comp. physiol. Psychol.*, 1966, **61**, 461–463.

Turkewitz, G., Gordon, E. W., and Birch, H. G. Head turning in the human neonate: effect of prandial condition and lateral preference. *J. comp. physiol. Psychol.*, 1965, **59**, 189–192. (a)

Turkewitz, G., Gordon, E. W., and Birch, H. G. Head turning in the human neonate: spontaneous patterns. *J. genet. Psychol.*, 1965, **107**, 143–158. (b)

Turkewitz, G., Moreau, T., and Birch, H. G. Head position and receptor organization in the human newborn. *J. exp. child Psychol.*, 1966, **4**, 169–177.

Twitchell, T. E. The automatic grasping responses of infants. *Neuropsychologia*, 1965, **3**, 247–259. (a)

Twitchell, T. E. Normal motor development. *J. Am. Physi. Ther. Assoc.*, 1965, **45**, 5. (b)

Uklonskaya, R., Puri, B., Choudhuri, N., Dang, L., and Kumari, R. Development of static and psychomotor functions of infants in the first year of life in New Delhi. *Ind. J. Child Hlth.*, 1960, **9**, 596–601.

Updegraff, R. The determination of a reliable intelligence quotient for the young child. *J. genet. Psychol.*, 1932, **41**, 152–166. (a)

Updegraff, R. Ocular dominance in young children. *J. exp. Psychol.*, 1932, **15**, 758–766. (b)

Updegraff, R. Preferential handedness in young children. *J. exp. Educ.*, 1932, **1**, 134–139. (c)

Updegraff, R. The correspondence between handedness and eyedness in young children. *J. genet. Psychol.*, 1933, **42**, 490–492.

Usoltsev, A. N., and Terekhova, N. T. Functional peculiarities of the skin-temperature analyzer in children during the first six months of life. *Pavlov J. higher nerv. Activ.*, 1958, **8**, 174–184.

Uzgiris, I. C., and Hunt, J. McV. A scale of infant psychological development. 1964. (Mimeographed.)

Vajnorsky, J., Brachfeld, K., and Strakova, M. Prispevek k reflexum novorozeneckeho obdobi. *Česk. Pediat.*, 1958, **13**, 227–230.

Valcarce, M. La afectividad durante los dos primeros anos de la vida. *Rev. Psicol. Gen. Aplic.*, 1964, **19**, 985–993.

Valentine, C. W. The colour perception and colour preferences of an infant during its fourth and eighth months. *Br. J. Psychol.*, 1913–1914, **6**, 363–386.

Valentine, C. W. Reflexes in early childhood: their development, variabilty, evanescence, inhibition, and relation to instincts. *Br. J. med. Psychol.*, 1927, **7**, 1–35.

Valentine, C. W. The innate basis of fear. *J. genet. Psychol.*, 1930, **37**, 394–420.

Valentine, C. W. The psychology of imitation with special reference to early childhood. *Br. J. Psychol.*, 1930, **21**, 105–132.

Valentine, W. L., and Dockeray, F. C. The experimental study of the newborn, 1926–1936. *Educ. Res. Bull. Ohio St. Univ.*, 1936, **15**, 127–133.

Valentine, W. L., and Wagner, I. Relative arm motility in the newborn infant. *Ohio Univ. Stud.*, 1934, No. 12, 53–68.

Valbona, C., Desmond, M. M., Rudolph, A. J., Pap, L. F., Hill, R. M. Franklin, R. R., and Rush, J. B. Cardiodynamic studies in the newborn: II. Regulation of the heart rate. *Biologia Neonat.*, 1963, **5**, 159–199.

Van Wagenen, R. K., and Murdock, E. E. A transistorized signal-package for toilet training of infants. *J. exp. child Psychol.*, 1966, **3**, 312–314.

Variot, M. G. Sur les facteurs normaux et morbides qui peuvent avancer ou re-

440　W. KESSEN, M. M. HAITH AND P. H. SALAPATEK

tarder le début de la marche bipède chez les jeunes enfants. *Bull. mém. soc.*, 1927, **43**, 353–361. (a)

Variot, M. G. La prélocomotion chez le jeune enfant avant la marche bipède. *Rev. scient.*, 1927, **65**, 70–74. (b)

Variot, M. G. Présentation de deux frères dans lesquels le début de la marche bipède a coincidé avec une taille de 80 centimètres. *Bull. mém. soc. d'anthrop. Paris,* 1927, **8**, 13–15. (c)

Variot, M. G. Observations sur l'élevage et la croissance de trois jumelles agées de vingt-deux mois. *Soc. méd. Hôpi. Paris, Bull. mém.*, 1928, **52**, 512–527.

Variot, M. G., and Gotou. Le début de le marche bipède chez le jeune enfant, dans ses rapports avec l'âge et la taille. *Bull. mém. soc. d'anthrop. Paris,* 1927, **8**, 17–23. (a)

Variot, M. G., and Gotou. La marche bipède chez le jeune enfant dans ses rapports avec le poids de naissance, le poids actuel, le dentition, l'alimentation, et la sexe. *Bull. mém. soc. d'anthrop. Paris,* 1927, **8**, 23–30. (b)

Vassella, V., and Karlsson, B. Asymmetric tonic neck reflex. *Dev. Med. child Neurol.*, 1962, **4**, 363–369.

Vatsuro, E. G. Orientirovochnyĭ i issledovatel'skiĭ refleksy i razvitie ikh v ontogeneze i filogeneze. *Vop. Psikhol.*, 1962, No. 1, 113–120.

Veinger, R. A. K vozniknoveniiu kozhno-galvanicheskogo refleksa pri zritelnykh i zvukovykh razdrazheniiakh u detei v postnatalnom ontogeneze. *Fiziol. Zh. SSSR*, 1950, **36**, 653–659.

Velton, H. V. The growth of phonemic and lexical patterns in infant language. *Language*, 1943, **19**, 281–292.

Vereecken, R. *Spatial development.* Groningen: J. B. Wolters, 1961.

Vinay, C. La psychologie du nouveau-né. *Sem. Méd.*, 1897, **17**, 33–36.

Vincent, M., and Hugon, J. Relationships between various criteria of maturity at birth. *Biologia Neonat.*, 1962, **4**, 223–279.

Voegelin, C. P., and Adams, S. A phonetic study of young children's speech. *J. exp. Educ.*, 1934, **3**, 107–116.

Voelckel, E. Untersuchungen über die Rechtshändigkeit beim Säugling. *Z. Kinderheilk.*, 1913, **8**, 351–358.

Vormittag, S. Untersuchungen über die Atmung des Kindes: I. Atemzahl und Atemform des gesunden Kindes. *Mschr. Kinderheilk.*, 1933, **58**, 249–265.

Vulliamy, D. G. *The newborn child.* Boston: Little, Brown, 1961.

Wada, T. An experimental study of hunger and its relation to activity. *Arch. Psychol.*, 1922, **8**, 65–73.

Waggoner, R. W., and Ferguson, W. G. The development of the plantar reflex in children. *Arch. Neurol. Psychiat.*, 1930, **23**, 619–633.

Wagner, I. F. The establishment of a criterion of depth of sleep in the newborn infant. *J. genet. Psychol.*, 1937, **51**, 17–59.

Wagner, I. F. The body jerk of the neonate. *J. genet. Psychol.*, 1938, **52**, 65–77. (a)

Wagner, I. F. A note on the hiccough of the neonate. *J. genet. Psychol.*, 1938, **52**, 233–234. (b)

Wagner, I. F. The sleeping posture of the neonate. *J. genet. Psychol.*, 1938, **52**, 235–239. (c)

Wagner, I. F. Curves of sleep depth in newborn infants. *J. genet. Psychol.*, 1939, **55**, 121–135.

Wagoner, L. C. A note on the grasping reflex. *Ped. Sem.*, 1924, **31**, 333–335.

Waldrop, M. F., and Bell, R. Q. Effects of family size and density on newborn characteristics. *Am. J. Orthopsychiat.*, 1966, **36**, 544–550.

Walk, R. D., and Dodge, S. H. Visual depth preception of a 10-month-old monocular human infant. *Science*, 1962, **137**, 529–530.

Walk, R. D., and Gibson, E. J. A comparative and analytical study of visual depth perception. *Psychol. Monogr.*, 1961, **75**, Whole No. 519.

Walker, R. N. Body build and behavior in young children: 1. Body build and nursery school teachers' ratings. *Monogr. Soc. Res. Child Dev.*, 1962, **27**, Whole No. 84.

Walters, C. E. Prediction of postnatal development from fetal activity. *Child Dev.*, 1965, **36**, 801–808.

Warden, C. J. Notes on a male infant. *Ped.Sem.*, 1928, **35**, 328–330.

Warner, F. Muscular movements in man and their evolution in the infant. *J. ment. Sci.*, 1889, **35**, 23–44.

Washburn, A. H. All human beings start life as babies. *Pediatrics*, 1965, **37**, 828–832.

Washburn, R. W. A study of the smiling and laughing of infants in the first year of life. *Genet. Psychol. Monogr.*, 1929, **6**, 397–537.

Washburn, R. W., and Putnam, M. C. A study of child care in the first two years of life. *J. Pediat.*, 1933, **2**, 517–536.

Watkins, C. H. The growth of the arterial system in the human fetus. *Proc. Soc. exp. Biol. Med.*, 1927, **24**, 394–398.

Watson, J. B. *Psychology from the standpoint of a behaviorist*. Philadelphia, Pa.: Lippincott, 1919.

Watson, J. B. Experimental studies on the growth of the emotions. *Ped. Sem.*, 1925, **32**, 328–348. (a)

Watson, J. B. Recent experiments on how we lose and change our emotional equipment. *Ped. Sem.*, 1925, **32**, 349–371. (b)

Watson, J. B. What the nursery has to say about instincts. *Ped. Sem.*, 1925, **32**, 293–327. (c)

Watson, J. B. Behaviorism—a psychology based on reflexes. *Archs. Neurol. Psychiat.*, 1926, **15**, 185–204.

Watson, J. B. *Psychological care of infant and child*. New York: Norton, 1928.

Watson, J. B., and Morgan, J. J.B. Emotional reactions and psychological experimentation. *Am. J. Psychol.*, 1917, **28**, 163–174.

Watson, J. B., and Rayner, R. Conditioned emotional reactions. *J. exp. Psychol.*, 1920, **3**, 1–14.

Watson, J. B., and Watson, R. R. Studies in infant psychology. *Scient. Mon.*, 1921, **13**, 493–515.

Watson, J. S. Perception of object orientation in infants. *Merrill-Palmer Q.*, 1966, **12**, 73–94. (a)

Watson, J. S. The development of generalization of "contingency awareness" in early infants: some hypotheses. *Merrill-Palmer Q.*, 1966, **12**, 123–135. (b)

Watson, J. S. Memory and contingency analysis in infant learning. *Merrill-Palmer Q.*, 1967, **13**, 55–76.

Weech, A. A., and Campbell, R. V. D. The relation between the development of behavior and the pattern of physical growth. *Child Dev.*, 1941, **12**, 237–240.

Weinfeld, G. F. Self-demand feeding. *Med. Clin. N. Am.*, 1950, **34**, 33–40.

Weinfeld, G. F. Opinions of pediatricians on certain problems of infant care. *Arch. Pediat.*, 1949, **66**, 266–269.

Weisberg, P. Social and nonsocial conditioning of infant vocalizations. *Child Dev.*, 1963, **34**, 377–385.

Weisberg, P., and Fink, E. Fixed ratio and extinction performance of infants in the second year of life. *J. exp. Anal. Behav.*, 1966, **9**, 105–109.

Weiss, A. P. The measurement of infant behavior. *Psychol. Rev.*, 1929, **36**, 453–471.

Weiss, L. A. Differential reactions of newborn infants to different degrees of light intensity. *Proc. Iowa Acad. Sci.*, 1933, **40**, 198–199.

Weiss, L. A. Differential variations in the amount of activity of newborn infants under continuous light and sound stimulation. *Univ. Iowa Stud. Child Welf.*, 1934, **9**, No. 4, 9–74.

Weitzman, E. D., Fishbein, W., and Graziani, L. Auditory evoked responses obtained from the scalp electroencephalogram of the full-term human neonate during sleep. *Pediatrics*, 1965, **35**, 458–462.

Welch, L. The development of discrmination of form and area. *J. Psychol.*, 1939, **7**, 37–54. (a)

Welch, L. The development of size discrimination between the ages of 12 and 40 months. *J. genet. Psychol.*, 1939, **55**, 243–268. (b)

Welch, L. The span of generalization below the two-year age level. *J. genet. Psychol.*, 1939, **55**, 269–297. (c)

Welch, L. The genetic development of the associational structures of abstract thinking. *J. genet. Psychol.*, 1940, **56**, 175–206.

Weller, M. G., and Bell, R. Q. Basal skin conductance and neonatal state. *Child Dev.*, 1965, **36**, 647–657.

Wellman, B. L., Case, I. M., Mengert, I. G., and Bradbury, D. E. Speech sounds of young children. *Univ. Iowa Stud. Child Welf.*, 1931, **5**, No. 2.

Wenar, C. Competence at one. *Merrill-Palmer Q.*, 1964, **10**, 329–342.

Wendt, H. W. Risk-taking as a function of preverbal "imprinting." *Arch. ges. Psychol.*, 1961, **113**, 325–350.

Wenger, M. A. An investigation of conditioned responses in human infants. *Univ. Iowa Stud. Child Welf.*, 1936, **12**, No. 1, 7–90.

Wenger, M. A., and Irwin, O. C. Variations in electrical resistance of the skin in newborn infants. *Proc. Iowa Acad. Sci.*, 1935, **42**, 167–168.

Wenger, M. A., and Irwin, O. C. Fluctuations in skin resistance of infants and adults and their relation to muscular processes. *Univ. Iowa Stud. Child Welf.*, 1936, **12**, No. 1, 141–179.

Werboff, J. Research related to the origins of behavior. *Merrill-Palmer Q.*, 1963, **9**, 115–122.

Werner, E. E., and Bayley, N. The reliability of Bayley's revised scale of mental and motor development during the first year of life. *Child Dev.*, 1966, **37**, 39–50.

Wertheimer, M. Psychomotor coordination of auditory and visual space at birth. *Science*, 1961, **134**, 1692.

Weymouth, F. W., and Hirsch, M. J. Relative growth of the eye. *Am. J. Optom.*, 1950, **27**, 317–328.

White, B. L. An experimental approach to the effects of experience on early human behavior. In J. P. Hill (Ed.), *Minnesota Symposium of Child Psychology*. Vol. I. Minneapolis: University of Minnesota Press, 1967. Pp. 201–226.

White, B. L. Informal education during the first months of life. In R. D., Hess and R. M. Bear (Eds.), *Early education*. Chicago: Aldine, 1968. Pp. 143–169.

White, B. L. The initial coordination of sensorimotor schemas in human infants— Piaget's ideas and the role of experience. In D. Elkind and J. H. Flavell (Eds.), *Studies in Cognitive Development*. New York: Oxford University Press, 1969.

White, B. L. Child development research: an edifice without a foundation. *Merrill-Palmer Q.* (In press.)

White, B. L., and Castle, P. W. Visual exploratory behavior following postnatal handling of human infants. *Percept. mot. Skills*, 1964, **18**, 497–502.

White, B. L., Castle, P. W., and Held, R. Observations on the development of visually-directed reaching. *Child Dev.*, 1964, **35**, 349–364.

White, B. L., and Held, R. Plasticity of sensorimotor development in the human infant. In J. F. Rosenblith and W. Allinsmith (Eds.), *The causes of behavior: readings in child development and educational psychology*. Boston: Allyn & Bacon, 1966.

White, R. W. Motivation reconsidered: The concept of competence. *Psychol. Review*, 1959, **66**, 297–333.

Whiting, B. B. *Six cultures*. New York: Wiley, 1963.

Whiting, J. W. M., and Child, I. L. *Child training and personality: a cross cultural study*. New Haven, Conn.: Yale University Press, 1953.

Wickelgren, L. Convergence in the human newborn. *J. exp. child Psychol.*, 1967, **5**, 74–85.

Wickens, D. D., and Wickens, C. A study of conditioning in the neonate. *J. exp. Psychol.*, 1940, **26**, 94–102.

Wilcox, B. M., and Clayton, F. L. Infant visual fixation on motion pictures of the human face, *J. exp. child Psychol.*, 1968, **6**, 22–32.

Williams, C. T. Some facts about premature infants. *N. Orl. med. surg. J.*, 1940, **93**, 244–246

Williams, J. P., and Kessen, W. Effect of hand-mouth contacting on neonatal movement. *Child Dev.*, 1961, **33**, 243–248.

Williams, J. R., and Scott, R. B. Growth and development of Negro infants: IV. Motor development and its relationship to child rearing practices in two groups of Negro infants. *Child Dev.*, 1953, **24**, 103–121.

Williams, T. A., Schachter, J., and Tobin, M. Spontaneous variation in heart rate: relationship to the average evoked heart rate response to auditory stimuli in the neonate. *Psychophysiology*, 1967, **4**, 104–111.

Wilson, J., and Halverson, H. M. Development of a young blind child. *J. genet. Psychol.*, 1947, **71**, 155–175.

Windle, W. F. *Physiology of the fetus: origin and extent of function in prenatal life*. Philadelphia, Pa.: Saunders, 1940.

Windle, W. F. Developmental physiology. *Ann. Rev. Physiol.*, 1943, **5**, 63–78.

Winitz, H. Spectrographic investigation of infant vowels. *J. genet. Psychol.*, 1960, **96**, 171–181.

Winitz, H. Repetitions in the vocalizations and speech of children in the first two years of life. *J. speech hear. Disord., Monogr. Suppl.*, 1961, No. 7, 55–62.

Winitz, H., and Irwin, O. C. Infant speech: consistency with age. *J. speech hear. Res.*, 1958, **1**, 245–249. (a)

Winitz, H., and Irwin, O. C. Syllabic and phonetic structure of infant's early words. *J. speech hear. Res.*, 1958, **1**, 250–256. (b)

Winkelman, J. E., and Horsten, G. P. M. The ERG of premature and full-term infants during their first days of life. *Ophthalmolgica*, 1962, **143**, 92–101.

Winnicott, D. W. The observation of infants in a set situation. *Int. J. Psychoanal.*, 1941, **22**, 229–249.

Wittenborn, J. R. *The placement of adoptive children*. Springfield, Ill.: Thomas, 1957.

Wolf, K. M. Observations of individual tendencies in the first year of life. In M. J. E. Senn (Ed), *Problems of infancy and childhood*. New York: Josiah Macy, Jr., Foundation, 1952. Pp. 97–137.

Wolf, K. M. Observations of individual tendencies in the second year of life. In M. J. E. Senn (Ed.), *Problems of infancy and childhood*. New York: Josiah Macy, Jr., Foundation, 1953. Pp. 121–140.

Wolf, K. M. The origins of individuality. 1957. (Mimeographed.)

Wolff, L. V. The response to plantar stimulation in infancy. *Am. J. Dis. Child.*, 1930, **39**, 1176–1185.

Wolff, P. H. Observations on newborn infants. *Psychosom. Med.*, 1959, **21**, 110–118.

Wolff, P. H. The developmental psychologies of Jean Piaget and psychoanalysis. *Psychol. Iss.*, 1960, **2**, No. 1.

Wolff, P. H. Observations on the early development of smiling. In B. M. Foss (Ed.), *Determinants of infant behaviour.* II. New York: Wiley, 1963. Pp. 113–138.

Wolff, P. H. The development of attention in young infants. *Ann. N. Y. Acad. Sci.*, 1965, **118**, 815–830.

Wolff, P. H. The causes, controls, and organization of behavior in the neonate. *Psychol. Iss.*, 1966, **5**, No. 17.

Wolff, P. H. The serial organization of sucking in the young infant. 1969. (Mimeographed.)

Wolff, P. H., and White, B. L. Visual pursuit and attention in young infants. *J. Am. Acad. Child Psychiat.*, 1965, **4**, 473–484.

Wölfflin, E. Reduplikation in der Kindersprache. *Z. dt. Wschg.*, 1901, **1**, 263–264.

Wolstenholme, G. E. W., and O'Connor, C. M. (Eds.) *CIBA Foundation symposium on somatic stability in the newly born.* Boston: Little, Brown, 1958.

Woodward, O. M. *The earliest years. Growth and development of children under five.* New York: Pergamon Press, 1966.

Wooley, H. T. Some experiments on the color perception of an infant and their interpretation. *Psychol. Rev.*, 1909, **16**, 363–376.

Wooley, H. T. The development of right-handedness in a normal infant. *Psychol. Rev.*, 1910, **17**, 37–41.

Wooley, H. T. The validity of standards of mental measurement in young children. *Sch. & Soc.*, 1925, **21**, 476–482.

Woolley, P. V., Jr., and Valdecanas, L. Q. Growth of premature infants. *Am. J. Dis. Child.*, 1960, **99**, 642–647.

Yang, D. *The nervous system.* New York: Academic Press, 1960.

Yarrow, L. J. The relationship between nutritive sucking experiences in infancy and non-nutritive sucking in childhood. *J. genet. Psychol.*, 1954, **84**, 149–162.

Yarrow, L. J. Maternal deprivation: toward an empirical and conceptual re-evaluation. *Psychol. Bull.*, 1961, **58**, 459–490.

Yarrow, L. J. Research in dimensions of early maternal care. *Merrill-Palmer Q.*, 1963, **9**, 101–114.

Yarrow, L. J., and Goodwin, M. S. Some conceptual issues in the study of mother-infant interaction. *Am. J. Orthopsychiat.*, 1965, **35**, 473–481.

Ylppö, A., Hallman, N., Landtman, B. ,and Piipari, R. Effect of short time hospitalization on the behavior and on some somatic functions of children. *Ann. Paediat. Fenniae*, 1956, **2**, 3–24.

Youngstrom, K. A. Acetylcholine esterase concentration during the development of the human fetus. *J. Neurophysiol.*, 1941, **4**, 473–477.

Ypes, M. Some data on infants reared in incubators. *Maandschrift voor Kindergeneesk.*, 1936, **5**, 236.

Zador, J. Über die Beeinflussbarkeit und Pathogenese des Babinskischen Reflexes. *M. Psychiat. Neurol.*, 1927, **64**, 336–349.

Zagora, E. Observations on the evolution and neurophysiology of eye-limb coordination. *Ophthalmologica*, 1959, **138**, 241–254.

Zapella, M. The placing reaction in the newborn. *Dev. Med. Child Neurol.*, 1963, **5**, 497–503.

Zetterström, B. The clinical electroretinogram: IV. The electroretinogram in children during the first year of life. *Acta Ophthal.*, 1951, **29**, 295–304.

Zetterström, B. The electroretinogram in prematurely born children. *Acta Ophthal.* **30**, 1952, 405–408.

Zetterström, B. Flicker electroretinography in newborn infants. *Acta Ophthal.*, 1955, **33**, 157–166.

Zilahi, A. Zur Erziehung des Säuglings. *Int. Z. Indiv. Psychol.*, 1929, **4**, 287–296.

Zitran, A., Ferber, P., and Cohen, D. Pre- and paranatal factors in mental disorders of children. *J. nerv. ment. Dis.*, 1964, **139**, 357–361.

Zoepffel, H. Ein Versuch zur experimentellen Festellung der Persönlichkeit im Säuglingsalter. *Z. Psychol.*, 1926, **111**, 273–306.

6. *The Onset and Early Development of Behavior*

LEONARD CARMICHAEL

HUMAN FETAL BEHAVIOR BEST UNDERSTOOD BY COMPARING WITH EARLY BEHAVIOR OF OTHER ANIMALS

This chapter is primarily concerned with the development of behavior in the human infant before birth. At the outset, however, we must emphasize that the first responses of the human fetus and the gradual emergence of more and more complex patterns of behavior during prenatal and early postnatal life can best be understood when considered in a general biological setting. The comparison of the behavior of the human fetus before birth with other mammalian fetuses is much more illuminating in understanding what the young human organism can do than is a comparison of the behavior of the adult human being with the behavior of any other adult mammal. The mental life of the fully grown, effective, modern human being in so many ways depends on language and on almost incredibly complex cultural learning that a comparison with organisms that do not use real language or display behavior related to cognition, which is in large measure dependent on cultural learning, has limited significance. The difference as adults between man and even the highest of the other apes in the use of language and all that language involves for mental life has been emphasized by Chomsky (1968). The prelinguistic child, on the other hand, is in many respects a mammal among mammals for comparative purposes. Thus much that is vitally important about the behavior of the human fetus or the young child can be learned indirectly from comparative animal studies. This is because controlled experiments may be conducted on immature mammals, other than man, that would be impossible with human subjects. Nature, too, has organized what may be called a series of important experiments in this field. Different species of animals are born at very varying levels of functional maturity. Some, like the opossum and other marsupials, are at birth in certain respects comparable to early human fetuses. Others, like the ungulates (e.g., the typical African antelopes), are so far advanced at birth that their locomotor and perceptual abilities are almost as effective as they are in adults of the same species. In animals born in a "precocious" state it seems clear that the growth processes of fetal maturation rather than individual learning have produced the behavioral capacities that are uniformly seen in prenatal life and in the first hours after birth. In comparison, it becomes clear that the human baby at birth is not as immature as the marsupial nor nearly as far advanced as the ungulate. A proper understanding of the complementary roles of maturation and learning in the development of human prenatal and postnatal behavioral capacity can thus be illuminated by comparing early prenatal and neonatal human behavior changes with the fetal and early postnatal behavior of a variety of other mammals.

The word *altricial* is often used to describe species (sometimes including man) in which the neonate is largely helpless and requires much care and nursing by adults. This term has long been applied to birds such as doves and pigeons which are hatched naked or nearly naked and thus need the warmth of the nest and care by parents if they are to develop normally. This term is now used not

447

only in ornithology but to describe mammals born in a relatively immature state. The word *precocial* is used as applying to certain species of birds (called *Praecoces*). This term applies to hens, ducks, and other species that are so far advanced at hatching that they can follow the mothers and feed themselves. Such birds, in general, belong to nidifugous (i.e., species of birds that leave the nest soon after hatching) and are mainly ground nest builders. The term precocial is also now applied to mammals that are born with well developed sense organs and with a capacity for effective locomotion at birth.

In this chapter, after the concepts "behavior" and "development" as applied to early life have been discussed, a review is therefore given of some of the known facts of the development of behavior in nonhuman animals and especially fetal mammals. The history of man's interest in human prenatal life is briefly presented in connection with some of the topics that are treated. On the basis of these considerations, modern scientific studies of specifically human fetal behavior are described and evaluated.

THE DEFINITION OF THE WORD "BEHAVIOR" AS USED IN THE STUDY OF FETAL LIFE

When the word behavior is used in this chapter, it will be considered as applying in a very general way to what the organism is capable of doing at any developmental level. In the past some students have attempted to distinguish between behavior, at least as seen in adult life, as studied by psychologists, sociologists, and other "behavioral scientists" and behavior as studied by physiologists. This distinction may have validity in some studies of adult human beings but it does not apply in the description of prenatal or early neonatal behavior. It is convenient in the mature man or woman to differentiate between "psychological behavior," which is related to such matters as problem-solving, memory, "thought" and the use of language, as distinct from "physiological behavior," which involves human reflexes such as breathing and other patterns of response important, for example, in the ingestion of food and in reproduction. But this distinction cannot expediently be made in

describing behavior observable before birth or in early postnatal life. (See Lehrman, Hinde, and Shaw, 1965.)

Ethologists and other modern zoologically oriented students of animal behavior are probably justified in classifying some of the behavioral systems that they record and study in animals in terms of the ends or objectives that such behavior appears to the human observer to secure for the animal under study. One example is the list used in the study of dog behavior as given by Scott and Fuller (1965). These authors use the terms investigative behavior, shelter building, grooming, feeding, attention-getting, fighting, predation, escape, dominance seeking, sexual behavior, eliminative behavior, and comfort seeking in describing what dogs do. But terms such as these are seldom appropriate in a consideration of fetal responses. It is true that one who wishes a description of fetal behavior in terms of what it does *for the organism* at the time that the behavior act appears can assert that such responses often seem to prepare the organism for some specific later function. For example, many mammalian fetuses show rhythmic limb activities that can be called trotting movements long before birth. These patterned responses, like a great many others that regularly take place before birth, may be considered "trial runs" of behavior sequences serving no specific fetal function. Such behavior is nevertheless very important at developmental periods later in life. Fetal responses, like the "Ahlfeld movements"—the premature breathing movements of the fetal chest—may not only help prepare this important respiratory mechanism for later air breathing but also may have some purely prenatal function in facilitating fetal circulation.

The fact that behavior sequences can be commonly called out by experimental means at a time in development *prior* to that at which they ordinarily play an essential role in the life process of the organism has been proposed by the present author as a basic law of development. It has been named by the present author *the law of anticipatory function*. This law points to the fact that the maturation of behavior follows a predetermined course, which largely depends on the genetically determined structural growth that takes place in an environment that is "normal" or "characteristic" of the environments in which the species of organisms under study have evolved and in which they can maintain themselves. To put this another way, this law asserts that it is biologically essential to have the structures that make later adaptive responses ready at a period somewhat prior to the time when such reactions must work if the animal is to survive and lead a life that is characteristic of its species. This timing of developmental functional capacity as seen in all typical units of behavior is almost certainly determined by the genetic code.

In general, what has been said in the preceding paragraphs makes it clear that behavior as it is observed in fetal life and indeed to some extent in early neonatal life is best described in objective and measurable or at least potentially measurable terms. This measurement involves change in space of a total organism or in any part system of such an organism such as can be seen in neck or head bending or in limb movement.

THE MEANING OF THE WORD "DEVELOPMENT"

The second major word that is used in the title of this chapter is "development." The key to understanding the study of the growth of any organic structure or function in the *individual*, that is, in *ontogeny*, or in the *race*, that is, in *phylogeny*, is *emergence*.

Names such as the "doctrine of levels" and "creative synthesis" have been applied to the concept of emergence in organic development. The point that this term emphasizes is that as structures or processes grow or evolve, new totalities come into being not only by a simple adding together of what has been present and observable before but also by a creation of truly novel items which have genuinely new properties.

The failure to recognize the fact that novel characteristics must be described as aspects of new totalities and not as somehow hidden in the elements that make up these totalities has been called the error of potentiality (Lange, 1925). This classical mistake has been described by some logicians as the source of many of the world's worst metaphysical as well as scientific fallacies. To say this in other words, the error of potentiality

is a mistake leading to the assumption that because certain antecedent events or properties can be demonstrated to be always necessary in order to have a known subsequent event or property, therefore the full physical or other characteristics of the later-formed totality are somehow present in the simpler elements that are always present when the new totalities are formed. Oxygen and hydrogen are necessary if we are to have water, but "wetness" is not a characteristic of either of these gases before combination. C. Lloyd Morgan (1923), a distinguished classical student of animal behavior, has well pointed out that in the study of what animals do, it is best to assume that any organic capacity is not present until it can be observed (see also Lovejoy, 1926, 1936, 1957; Ralston, 1933).

Thus, in this chapter, in considering the novel emergence of specific acts of behavior as any individual grows, we do not intend to suggest that such a response at any stage is to be "explained" completely because of any previous reactions of that organism as a fetus or as a neonate. The point emphasized is, thus, that behavior typical of each species at every developmental stage is, as such, a fact of science. As King (1968) has said, "not only is there a constant interaction between endogenous developmental processes and the environment during ontogeny, but natural selection is also constantly molding ever more intricate interactions." But this does not mean that it is not important to know the history of each organism for anyone who wishes to understand the emergence of any act of adaptive or maladaptive behavior at any developmental period. The questions that must occupy us are concerned with the objective descriptive stages of behavior and with temporal stages of growth. To understand these growth processes, we must ask when does a particular behavior act first appear in ontogeny and how does it change as the animal matures?

WHEN DOES BEHAVIOR BEGIN?

Many of the early writers on child psychology, such as G. Compayre (1896), used to teach that the study of child psychology begins at birth. Throughout the history of biological sciences, however, the incompleteness of an assertion such as this has been obvious to many writers. Today it is safe to say that we must study the prenatal period if we are to determine what Gesell (1928, 1929a) has well called the "ontogenetic zero" of behavior or mind.

Ordinarily, in considering any mammal, ontogenetic development is taken as beginning at the time of individual fertilization. Under normal conditions in order that fertilization take place, there must be antecedent life in both the ovum and the sperm before true fertilization. Even though living material may some time in the future be synthesized from nonliving material, it is a safe working rule to accept the dictum: "All life comes from previous life." Each new mammalian individual, then, must be considered as beginning in processes initiated at fertilization but also as a continuation of life processes existing in the male and female germ cells before fertilization.

It is thus impossible to say that fertilization is, in all senses, the beginning of the new individual. Some specific characteristics of all reproductive cells can be traced back unchanged through countless generations. Logically, it is difficult to distinguish between the dynamic processes that are essential in structural development and the later observed processes of the organism, which we call behavior. This distinction, indeed, can be made only by the use of agreed-upon definitions. In this chapter, the beginning of true behavior, and hence the starting point of ontogenetic behavioral psychology, is to be placed at the point where neurally induced muscular activity begins. Such neuromuscular response can be shown to take place only after prior activities of a special sort have developed in the central nervous system (i.e., that lead to so-called "spontaneous behavior") or in external environments that initiate sense organ activity and determine coded inputs in sensory nerves that lead to central nervous activity and to the activation of motor neurons and then to response of muscles or glands. Much that is important in understanding the ontogenetic development of behavior patterns in man can be gained from a modern comparative study of identifiable behavior patterns as seen in phylogeny (Carmichael, 1936, 1954).

It is easy to deal with the emergent or novel creation of behavior in the abstract, but, when one turns to specific experimental studies of this emergence, the difficulty of the problem becomes clearer. This author has studied in some detail, as will be noted later, the very first responses of many organisms. For example, let us take the guinea pig fetus. Logically, it is clear that there must be a time in growth when stimulation of this organism's receptors will not be effective. Then, at an immediately subsequent time, say 1 second later, when such stimulation is given, behavior results. At time A this response is not possible, but after added growth—that is, at subsequent time B— it is possible. The possibility of this first response is considered as dependent upon elaborate changes which include growth and which are taking place in the organism under consideration. Let us trace these changes back in the history of the individual. Cell division, cell differentiation, cell migration, organ formation, and a whole series of other dynamic changes are essential before behavior begins.

As a result of all this growth, a structure capable of making this first behavioral reaction *emerges*. Without these countless antecedent cellular and subcellular processes, the first external response of an appendage or of the trunk of the living organism could not occur. These processes, moreover, must not be thought of as a simple unfolding of preformed organs. This old "preformism view," which is a typical biological expression of the error of potentiality discussed previously, is no longer held. Rather, at each stage the living organism is now considered to be maintaining itself in a dynamic relationship with the energies and the foodstuffs of its environment. This is not to say that the organism is being formed wholly by its environment, as the other old and now long-discarded view, that of "epigenesis," held. Indeed, today it is clear that inheritance and environment always cooperate in development. The old quarrel between preformism and epigenesis is now seen to have been sometimes a battle of words engaged in before relevant facts were known.

The discovery of the mammalian sperm in 1677 by Van Leeuwenhoek and of the mammalian and human ovum by Karl Ernst von

Baer (1827) are discussed in a full historical setting by G. W. Corner (1958). One who is interested in a modern summary of the growth of the anatomical processes on which behavior depends may consult A. E. Needham (1964). Details of this growth are now recognized as dependent on the genetic code or DNA (deoxyribonucleic acid) and on RNA (ribonucleic acid), which can be described as picking up and carrying the message of the code into the cytoplasm, where it supervises the formation of proteins.

A number of technical terms that are now commonly used by those who consider this development of the individual in relation to its genes and the environment in which it exists may be introduced here. The term *gamete* refers to a male or female reproductive cell with half the typical number of chromosomes of the species. When a gamete combines with another gamete, a diploid cell or *zygote* is produced. In other words, the zygote is a fertilized ovum, formed by the union of reduced male and female reproductive cells. The organism considered as a complete assemblage of its genes is called a *genotype*. The individual organism that develops from the genotype is called a *phenotype*. It is important to remember that organisms with the same phenotype may not have the same genetical constitution. An organism showing certain dominant factors may have inherited different recessive factors, as is explained in the modern science of genetics.

The chromosomes with which each fertilized ovum starts life contain information for a set of enzymes that are in the genes of each chromosome. This is the "blueprint" or "coded punch card" that is the DNA, which as a totality constitutes the genetic code. It is important to remember that in evolutionary terms, each organism's genetic code has evolved and survived because organisms with that code have been able to react in an adaptive way to their environments. Thus, as will be emphasized later in this chapter, the "information" in the code is, in one sense, environmental information.

This chapter is not the place to review the complex quantitative science of modern genetics. The reader who is interested may consult the following books and references given

in them: Burdette (1963) and Fuller and Thompson (1960).

It is, nevertheless, appropriate to note here that during the last few decades much information has been secured concerning what is now often called "genetic disease." Under this heading are included many characteristics of the behavior and in the broadest sense the psychology of the developing human infant. Evidence shows that there is a basis—a genetic basis—for many bodily malformations seen at birth, some forms of mental retardation, and certain neural and sensory defects. In fact, there is some evidence that there are now known more than 300 so-called "hereditary diseases" (Lock, 1962). All this evidence points to the importance of an understanding of genetics in a consideration of the early development of behavior. In this connection, note that there is increased assurance that embryos with chromosomal anomalies are frequently aborted. It has also been shown that in the human being the percentage of chromosomal abnormalities in early spontaneous abortions is higher than in abortions occurring after the twelfth week (Jacobson and Barter, 1967). There is some evidence that 2% of infants have congenital defects recognizable at birth (Lock, 1962).

The importance of chromosomal defects in relation to human mental life is nowhere better illustrated than in recent studies of mongolism. This subject and the research papers on which present knowledge is based are well reviewed in a paper by C. B. Jacobson (1967). The basic defect in Down's syndrome (mongolism) was uncertain until the development of modern cytogenetic techniques about a decade ago. An extra chromosome (trisomy) has been consistently found in over 95% of individuals who show Down's syndrome. This chromosomal characteristic is present in all tissues studied in individuals showing the syndrome.

Information of the sort just given shows how the student of the development of behavior must keep in view the findings of modern genetics as well as all the factors that determine embryological growth.

The processes basic to the reproduction of living animals are brought about in a number of different ways. In some animals the egg, after fertilization, continues to develop in protective coverings still within the maternal body. In other animals the egg leaves the body and continues development outside. In many animals the growth of all the fundamental organ systems is complete before hatching or birth. This condition may be considered as characteristic of many vertebrates, some worms, and certain arthropods. In the coelenterates, insects, and vertebrate amphibians, varying stages of growth after the new organism emerges from the egg are the rule. Common usage seems to have established the fact that the first stage of the development of any organism is to be described as *germinal*, the next stage as *embryonic*, and the latest stage preliminary to birth as *fetal*. The word *larval* is used to characterize independent, living, but organically immature organisms.

In describing larval development, two classes of such growth, direct and indirect, have been set up. In the first, development is linear—that is, each developmental stage produces an organism which is in most respects more like the adult than was the organism in its preceding stage. In the case of indirect larval development, however, organs often of a high order of complexity are produced which are later destroyed before maturity is reached. The term *metamorphosis* is applied to development of this latter sort. The terms *larval* and *pupal* are applied to describe stages in indirect development. Too little is known concerning the effect of environmental modification during the larval stage upon adult animals. This is a field in which more experimental investigation is almost certain to be done. For example, what influence will certain experimentally induced forms of activity in the wormlike larva have upon the fully developed *imago*, such as an adult butterfly? It is interesting in this connection to notice that among writers even on so-called inherited human instinct many examples are taken from types which pass through larval stages (cf. Bergson, 1911; McDougall, 1923; Thorpe, 1963).

The degree of maturity reached before the new organism begins an independent existence varies markedly from type to type. In so-called *oviparous* species, such as most fish and certain amphibians, eggs are laid as single cells and are subsequently fertilized after they have left the mother's body. In *viviparous* animals, such as certain fish and most mammals, on the other hand, all the early developmental stages are normally passed within the mother's body. Between these two extremes are the so-called *ovoviviparous* organisms, in which fertilization takes place before the egg is laid. Birds are good examples of this type. It is interesting to note that the so-called evolutionary level does not give a clear indication of the sort of reproduction which may be expected of an animal. The common dogfish bears its young inside the body until they are developed so that they may have an independent existence. On the other hand, the monotremes among the primitive mammals lay eggs. There are, moreover, certain forms in which favorable or unfavorable environmental conditions seem to determine the fact of the hatching of eggs inside or outside the mother's body (Hertwig, 1912).

Among the mammals, as already noted, it is also interesting to observe that there is a great diversity in the degree of development that has been reached at the time of normal birth. Thus the young of the opossum are born in many respects as relatively early embryos, as contrasted with the newborn guinea pig, in which almost full-grown characteristics are observed (Hartman, 1920; Avery, 1928). This fact should be kept in mind at all times as these pages are read. To put this in another way, it may be said that the behavioral age or even the "mental age" of different species of mammals is very different at the time of birth. Montague (1964) emphasizes the fact that in some species the newborn organisms are almost as dependent on the mother as they were before they were born. In fact, no one can fully understand fetal and neonatal behavior without studying in detail the maternal behavior of each species of mammal that is being considered. (Rheingold, 1963).

Corner (1944), in his admirable book, *Ourselves Unborn: An Embryologist's Essay on Man*, presents a clear description of the anatomical development of man, taking into account its aberrations. He says: ". . . we begin our lives in continuance of a long past and in progression toward an unseen goal; that life is precarious from the first day to the last. . . ."

Flanagan (1962, in a popular and very well illustrated book, gives a summary of human embryology and an excellent account for the nontechnical reader of some aspects of human development during the first nine months of life.

THE DEVELOPMENT OF BEHAVIOR IN THE LOWER VERTEBRATES

There are stages in the morphological development of the fish, amphibian, reptile, bird, infrahuman mammal, and man which are so similar that they make the study of one form important for a complete understanding of the development of other forms. This fact has long been recognized in anatomical embryology. By analogy, the same may be held to be true of behavior. Care must be taken, however, not to pretend to see homologies of behavior until by direct observation such homologies can be shown to exist. Figure 1 gives a somewhat too idealized picture of some of these relationships. For example, in certain forms nourishment during the entire fetal period is provided by the yolk of the egg, from which the organism develops. This means that behavior in connection with alimentation is less important in such types than in others in which at an early developmental stage the ingestion of food is necessary. In spite of this difficulty, the study of fish and amphibians has provided much information of importance to one who would understand the gradual development of behavior. Swen-

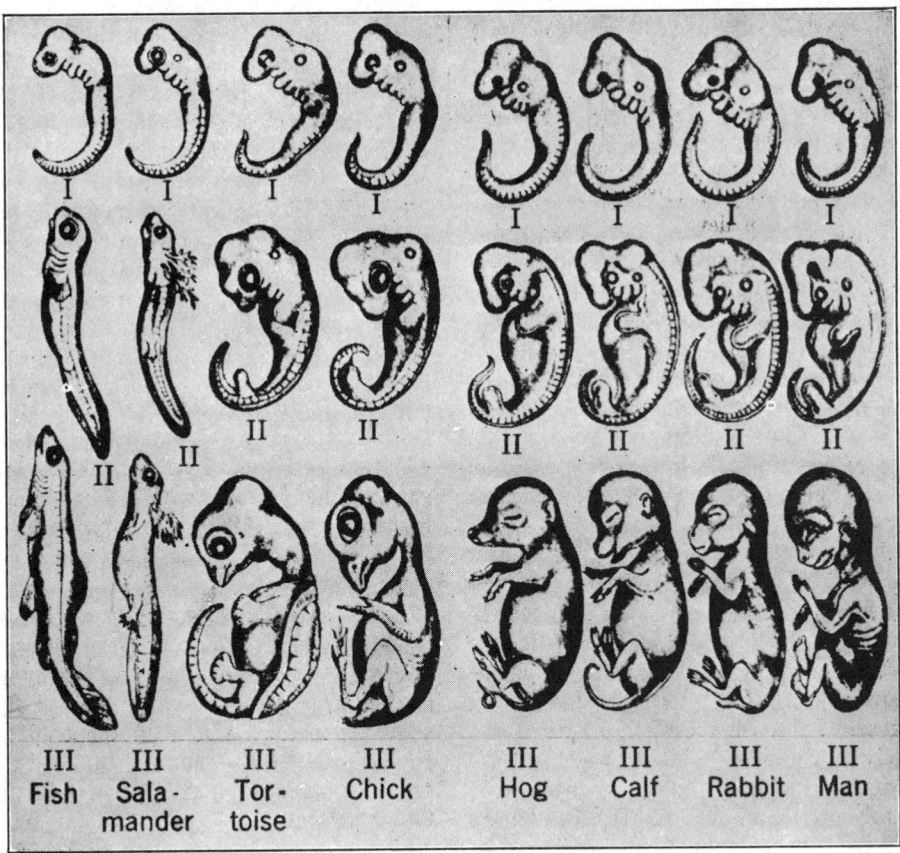

Fig. 1. A series of drawings constructed to emphasize similarities in structure in various embryos at three comparable and progressive stages of development (marked I, II, III). (From Romanes, 1896). This old diagram is presented here as a schematic device only. Research since it was drawn has made some alteration in the relationships demonstrated here. See for comparison diagrams in Ferris (1922).

son (1928a) has courageously attempted to set up seven fundamental acts of behavior as basic to the responses of lower vertebrates, mammals, and even man. These forms of behavior are progression, respiration, ingestion, expression, excretion, phonation, and reproduction. The fact that some of these processes can be studied in the amphibian larva as well as in the human infant makes the complete understanding of the simpler organism especially important. Coghill (1929c) and others (e.g., Windle and Griffin, 1931) have developed this point of view in various papers. A good history of the development of the study of vertebrate embryos is given by the scientist who did so much for the study of behavior that he may be considered the founder of the experimental study of early behavior. This man is William Preyer, for some years professor of physiology at Jena. His book, *Specielle Physiologie des Embryo. Untersuchungen über die Lebenserscheinungen vor der Geburt*, published in 1885, may be taken as a subsequent investigation in this field. Part of this fundamental work has been translated by Coghill and Legner (1937).

In this work Preyer summarizes and reviews a good many observations made on the early movements of fish embryos. Some of these studies were based on the observations of fish embryos growing after definitely dated periods of fertilization. Slow rotary movements characterize the early behavior of many fish embryos. Fillipi is quoted by Preyer as finding in *Alosa finta* such movements soon after fertilization. In a species of trout Preyer found movement of trunk at a definite number of days subsequent to fertilization. In general, on the day following the first trunk movement the first neck-head movement is noted. Then, in a few days, energetic movements of the whole tiny fish body may be observed. After the liberation of such organisms from their egg coverings, it is found that pressure stimulation on the body surface is followed by responses involving apparently the entire musculature of the trunk. Preyer points out that these movements involve fully developed reflexes. He makes this conclusion because the movements described consist in the total organism's drawing together of the head and tail. This same response occurs no matter what the locus may be of the point of pressure stimulation. As growth goes on, however, the strength of movement increases, and the movements become more and more regular and specific in relation to the exact locus of the area stimulated. Preyer gives quantitative tables of the increase in rapidity of the movements of the heart and the gills as development progresses. Myrberg (1965) has presented a full descriptive analysis of the behavior of the African cichled fish. Parental behavior, egg incubation, and the establishment of the free-swimming phase are discussed.

White (1915) describes the development of behavior in brook trout embryos. His observations cover the period from hatching until the yolk sac is absorbed. He notes that "the hatching is initiated by movements starting at the head and later extending through the whole length of the body. . . ." After hatching, the swimming reaction is gradually made more nearly perfect. Touch and mechanical jars are effective stimuli immediately after hatching, and, interestingly enough, at this time the head is found to be the region least sensitive to pressure stimuli. Rheotropism, or response to water flow in currents, negative phototaxis, or the avoidance of light, and photokinetic responses, or responses initiated but not necessarily directed by light, are also present at this time. Excess carbon dioxide in the water in which fish are studied is activating up to a point, and then depressing on bodily functions. The dependence of the fish upon the chemical make-up of its external water environment presents many analogies with the dependence of the higher animal upon the chemical make-up of the liquid internal environment of its own blood stream in which its own central nervous system maintains itself. Or, to put this another way, the internal environment of the fish embryo is seen to be most closely related to its external environment. Before the nourishment-supplying yolk sac disappears at about 2 months, the reaction of the fish to stimuli seems to be away from the point of contact. After this, some embryos studied become quite suddenly exploratory and aggressive and hence move toward the point stimulated (Preyer, 1885). This striking observation may remind the reader that an intimate relationship exists between the degree of maturation of an organism and the "drive" which the organism shows in relation to external stimulation.

From the general standpoint of the development of behavior, however, the work of Tracy (1926) is especially worthy of note. This investigator has studied fish embryos, especially those of the toadfish. He has carefully observed and recorded the growth of activity in this form from its first movement to a final free-swimming condition. The first activity of the embryo in this form as in so many others is what may be termed in Parker's sense the preneural and "independent effector" action of the heart (Parker, 1919). The first behavioral movement of the fish is the bending of the trunk in the anterior region. At times this movement is to the right, at times to the left. It is probable that the afferent proprioceptor or muscle-sense system is not functional at first. At an early point a spontaneous flutter movement develops. This movement probably is important in freeing the organism from the remaining egg membranes. In general, toadfish larvae when hatched lie at the bottom of the containing vessel in a quiescent state. Then suddenly they move. On the basis of careful study, Tracy concludes that this "spontaneous" behavior is related to cumulative changes in the blood of the organism such that at a certain point the central nervous system is directly stimulated or the threshold of the central nervous system is so altered that previously inoperative sensory impulses break over into motor outlets. Thus he concludes that spontaneous movements are the result of metabolites and oxygen deficiency in the blood stream. Soon after the onset of such responses, the organism becomes very sensitive to external stimuli. The mucous membrane area about the mouth is the first to be sensitized. In general, the spread of sensitivity is from this point toward the tail or possibly to the region that has just become most active. The "cephalocaudal progression" of sensory and motor development which some writers propose as a law is, however, far from regular in this organism.

Tracy draws some fundamental conclusions from these studies. He holds that if external conditions could be kept constant the activities of the organism would be determined by its own life processes or metabolism. This would mean that all behavior would be rhythmic, like that of an excised muscle in a balanced salt solution. At a later point we shall note that T. G. Brown (1915) holds that early mammalian reflexes may be of this nature. In conclusion, Tracy says: "From the beginning, and more or less continuously during its whole existence, the animal is driven through its environment as a result of stimuli which arise periodically in connection with its metabolic processes." The nature of later behavior may be thought of, he further suggests, as dependent upon neural development and the interference in the intrinsic rhythms of behavior brought about by the stimulation of the special exteroceptors of the organism by external energies. The basic relevance of this observation even for adult human behavior has been considered elsewhere (Carmichael, 1947).

Development of Behavior in Amphibians

We now turn to the study of the development of behavior in amphibians. Swammerdam, in his *Bibel der Natur* (1752), written before 1685, makes observations on the behavior of frog embryos five days after fertilization and at other periods (Preyer, 1885; Swammerdam, edited, 1907). Swammerdam has also recorded observations concerning the development of behavior in snails and other invertebrates. Leeuwenhoek (1967) made observations in this same field. Among other early students of behavior in invertebrates may be mentioned Stiebel (1815), Grant (1827), and Home (1827). Bischoff (1842) published a confirmation of the description of movements previously observed by Swammerdam in amphibians. He added a notation of the fact that the rate of these movements is a function of the temperature of the water in which the animals are maintaining themselves. Preyer (1885) reviews all this work as well as that of Perschir and Cramer on the amphibian embryo. Preyer himself made elaborate observations on the early movements of frog and salamander embryos. He noted that stimulating the embryo led first to a slight twitch in the anterior portion of the organism. Following this movement in time he noted that the body was bent so as to bring the head and tail nearer together. Reference to Preyer's original draw-

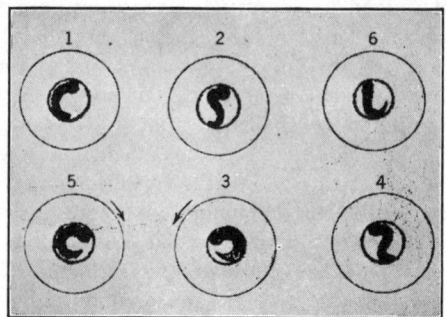

Fig. 2. Diagram of various positions of frog embryos (*Rana temporaria*) just before emergence from the egg. Note especially the C and S reactions. (From Preyer, 1885.)

ings, reproduced as Figure 2, as well as to the text of his book shows that he considered these C or reverse C movements very important. It is also clear from his drawings that he observed the fundamental S or sigmoid form of reaction. The importance of this S movement in freeing the organism from the egg is pointed out. That this movement is also related to the activity of swimming is an important consideration.

Other students have worked on the relationship between temperature and embryonic movements in larval amphibians (Preyer, 1885). Many others have used this convenient laboratory type in work in experimental embryology. Much of this experimental embryology has direct bearing on the problems of this chapter. (See Detwiler, 1920, 1921, 1922, 1923a, 1923b, and the bibliographies given by him.)

If Preyer may be called the father of the scientific study of the development of behavior, G. E. Coghill (see references in the bibliography) must be remembered as the investigator who first charted the relationship between the detailed growth of the nervous system and the consequent alterations which occur in behavior. This investigator is notable also because of the completeness of his work on the salamander *Amblystoma*, as well as on other types. The life of Coghill with his complete bibliography by C. J. Herrick (1949) ably discusses the fundamental contributions of this original scientist to the study of behavior. Coghill's first paper in this field was written in 1902, and from that time until his death in 1941 he published a most important

series of papers on the development of behavior in relation to the growth of the structures on which behavior depends. In the course of his many papers, Coghill reported detailed studies of the neural mechanism underlying the first movement and the later sequences of movements as they develop in *Amblystoma*. The first response results from the contraction of muscles just behind the head. As the embryo advances in age, this contraction becomes, after a period of gradual transition lasting for about 36 hours, one which involves the whole animal. The result of this reaction, is that the organism assumes a position which may be described as that of a tight coil. This C or exaggerated C coil is sometimes oriented to the right and sometimes to the left. It may reverse instantly. At this point in development, all behavioral activities are initiated in the head region and progress toward the tail.

In commenting upon this sequence, Coghill (1929a) notes that at this time: "Nothing really new has yet been introduced into the behaviour pattern of the animal since its first movement was performed, and the coil reaction gives the animal no locomotor power. Nevertheless the coil has in it the primary locomotor factor: cephalocaudal progression of muscular contraction." The transition from this behavioral level to the S reaction is amazingly simple. One C contraction begins, for example, on the left, but before it has reached the tail another contraction to the right begins.

The components of this movement may be made clearer by consulting Fig. 3. As this reaction gains speed, its performance exerts pressure upon the water and thus drives the organism forward. Thus the S reaction becomes the basis of swimming or aquatic locomotion. This fundamental pattern of behavior may well be a peculiarly significant stage in many other types of growing organisms. This same stage is seen clearly in the swimming of the lower vertebrates. It is somewhat obscured in the four-legged mammals and still more obscured in man, but that this S reaction plays its part in the growth of behavior in these higher organisms seems to be an established fact. Five stages in the development of this basic swimming activity have been made out by Coghill (1929a).

1. The nonmotile stage, in which direct muscle stimulation by mechanical or electrical

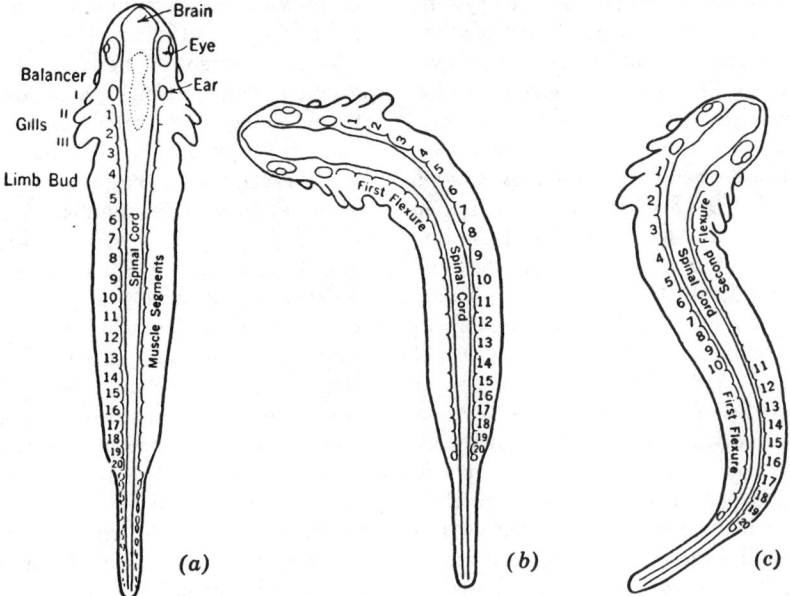

Fig. 3. Three diagrams of *Amblystoma*. (a) The organism in an early swimming stage but without indication of muscle contraction. (b) The beginning of a swimming movement as a first flexure by contraction of a number of anterior muscle segments. (c) The swimming movement in which the first flexure has passed tailward and the second flexure is beginning in the anterior region. (From Cogill, 1929a.)

means leads to muscular contraction and hence to externally observable response.

2. The early C flexure stage, in which light touch on the skin of any portion of the body leads to a response.

3. The tight-coil stage, in which the contractions noted in stage 2 become more pronounced and the extent of the contraction greater.

4. The S reaction, which is characterized by a reversal of flexure before the previous flexure has been completely executed as a coil, thus leading to the sinuous behavior of the total organism.

5. The speeding-up of the S reaction so as to produce the typical swimming movement of the amphibian larva.

Youngstrom (1937) in studies upon *Anura* (frogs, toads, etc.) concludes that the Coghillian sequence of developing behavior applies with only slight variations to the *Anura* studied. Wang and Lu (1940, 1941), too, have shown that the stages through which the frog passes are similar to those described by Coghill. These investigators have also shown that severance of the spinal cord arrests the

development of swimming at about Coghill's stage 4.

Coghill studied in great detail the neural structure characteristic of the salamander in each of the five stages noted above. On the basis of these investigations he shows how the known structure of the nervous system may make possible the behavior which has previously been described. It is important to recognize that for the most part Coghill (1929a) believed that in young organisms movement is typically away from the point of stimulation.

As already noted, the salamander has, besides aquatic locomotion, other significant behavior systems. Of these, walking or terrestrial locomotion and feeding require special consideration. The *Amblystoma* swims before its anatomical development has progressed to the point where it has true limbs. Structurally and functionally the forelimbs are in advance of the developing hindlimbs. In this organism, however, at first both sets of limbs, when they appear, move only in relation to the larger trunk movements previously described as those of swimming. Coghill shows why this must be so because of the developing nervous system. Gradually, however, independence of limb action or *individuation* of limb behavior over the dominance of the trunk movements begins (1930e). First the forelimbs gain a certain autonomy, and later the hindlimbs also. "It is obvious, therefore," observes Coghill (1929a), "that the first limb movement is an integral part of the total reaction of the animal, and that it is only later that the limb acquires an individuality of its own in behaviour." He then suggests that the forelimb itself may be considered to possess a pattern of development which is comparable to that of the total organism. At first, if movement occurs at all, the whole limb moves. Later, elbow flexion and wrist and digit movement in turn gain independence of the total member. It is important to recognize that during this developmental sequence the time relations of the swimming reaction may be considered as in a way superimposed upon limb activity. Thus one may, if he wishes to, think of the alternate movements of walking in a four-legged organism as a growth out of the basic trunk movements of swimming previously described. Coghill (1929a), indeed, says: "Movement of the trunk in walking is nothing more nor less than the swimming movement with greatly reduced speed." Gradually the sinuous movement of the trunk is reduced as walking becomes more independent, and eventually the characteristic land locomotion of the salamander appears.

There can be little doubt that this basic and important developmental sequence is determined in each organism by its own genetic code. As we compare lower vertebrates, mammals, and man, we can see that some especially "deeply organized" aspects of this code determine such anatomical facts as bilateral symmetry, the vertebral column, the spinal cord, the attachment of appendages, and what can be called the fundamental working plan of the vertebrate. But these "deeply established" aspects of the genetic code can also be seen in behavior. The sequence of trunk bending and of patterned limb movements just reviewed can be observed at least from fish to man.

It is interesting that the C posture and the S posture are seen in certain adult fish during courtship (Myrberg, 1965).

The development of the feeding reaction in this same organism has been similarly studied by Coghill (1929a). This response begins with a movement of the trunk; then comes a reaction which involves a sudden lunge of the whole organism; after this there is a gradual correlation between this lunge movement and the activity of the jaws and the muscles of the esophagus. In summarizing this whole development, Coghill (1929a) says: "Behaviour develops from the beginning through the progressive expansion of a perfectly integrated total pattern and the individuation within it of partial patterns which acquire various degrees of discreteness." It should also be noted that as this development continues new senses become important in relation to behavior. Coghill (1930a) believes that "the individual acts on its environment before it reacts to its environment." In considering these beautifully elaborated generalizations of Coghill's, it is important to remember that in some details a different sequence in the development of behavior may well characterize the growth of a mammal and a salamander. One should not forget also that even Coghill's own neurological studies point to specific relationships between the locus of stimulation and the muscles that are caused to respond (1929a). In comparing the salamander and the guinea pig, for example, it may be noted that the limbs are quite fully formed before the first behavioral response or reflex takes place in the guinea pig, but in the salamander behavior begins before there is any real morphological forelimb at all.

In a series of papers Carmichael has presented the results of his studies of the development of behavior in *Amblystoma* and the frog under conditions such that experimental groups of animals were raised under unusual environmental circumstances (Carmichael, 1926a, 1927, 1928, 1929). A technique devised by Randolph (1900) and developed by Harrison (1904) was employed. For a consideration of the effect of the anesthetic chloretone on the organism in question, a paper by Matthews and Detwiler (1926) should be consulted. At a period before motility had begun, numerous developing *Amblystoma* was divided into two groups. The first of these groups was used as a control. The second was used as an experimental group. The experimental group was placed in water containing the anesthetic. The control group was allowed to develop normally in water. Later, at a developmental point previously described by Herrick and Coghill (1915), vigorous responses began in the control group. At this time the experimental group showed morphological development but otherwise remained absolutely inert because of the action of the anesthetic. However, in a short time—often only a minute or two—after the drugged embryos were placed in fresh water, they began to swim well." In fact, a number of the eighteen *Amblystoma* embryos swam so well in less than one half hour after they had shown the first sign of movement that they could with difficulty, if at all, be distinguished from the members of the control group who had been free swimmers for five days" (Carmichael, 1926a). In evaluating this work, the publication of Fromme (1941) should be consulted as this investigator reports that in an experiment similar to that of Carmichael impaired behavior of short duration was observed.

In later experiments efforts were made to control stimulation in other ways (Carmichael, 1928). These investigations led to the conclusion that the development of the neural and other mechanisms upon which behavior depends does take place in these organisms whether or not they are as individuals responding to external stimulation. This seems to have a negative implication concerning an extreme interpretation of Child's (1921) environmentalist theory of the causation of growth in the nervous system. Nothing in these experiments is to be taken, however, as invalidating the idea that the growth of the nervous system itself involves activity. Studies such as those of Burr (1932) and P. Weiss (1926, 1939) on this same organism emphasize the dynamic character of such growth processes. For a general consideration of the relationship between neural growth and the development of behavior see Hooker (1950) and Hooker and Hare (1954).

In the reptile class comparatively little work has been done, although Preyer (1885) reported some occasional observations on snakes. Tuge (1931) also did some very interesting work upon the growth of behavior in the turtle. In this work the sequence of Coghill is seen as modified by the existence of the shell which especially characterizes this form. Smith and Daniel (1947) have also made some interesting observations on the early responses of the turtle.

In these relatively simple vertebrates, a principle can be seen most clearly that applies in all animals, including birds, mammals, and man. As morphological growth of an organism in its environment takes place, one can see the genetic code at work as developmental stage succeeds developmental stage. The neural mechanisms so developed can be thought of as information processing devices that have allowed organisms possessing such structures to adapt effectively to the environments in which they exist and survive. Later, each individual processes the "environmental information" acting on its own individual external sense organs in such a way that adaptive behavior results.

DEVELOPMENT OF BEHAVIOR IN THE EMBRYOS OF BIRDS

From an evolutionary point of view, the bird may be thought of as presenting an interesting comparison with the lower vertebrate and the mammal. The amphibian embryo provides unusually favorable material for morphological and behavioral developmental study. The growing salamander or frog embryo may be observed, without interference of any sort, through its translucent egg covering and in free life after leaving these coverings. Its egg yolk provides food during a long part of the early developmental period. On the other hand, the study of the development of behavior in the mammal involves relatively complex surgery and, at present at any rate, a certain disturbance of the normal environment of the growing organism. The bird embryo is harder to study than the amphibian but easier than the mammal. It may be studied in a relatively normal environment, but a special technique is necessary to render the development of the bird embryo continuously observable. Down through the years, however, the chicken's egg has been the subject of embryological study. Needham (1931) reviews the use that has been made of the hen's egg in embryology since earliest times. This writer describes the history of the artificial incubation of hens' eggs. He notes also the beginning of systematic observation of embryos taken from eggs in various periods of incubation at the time of Hippocrates (about 460 B.C.). From that time on, the hen's egg has been extensively used in morphological studies of development. Among those who have contributed to this development are Aristotle, Aelian, Pliny, Plutarch, Albertus Magnus, Leonardo da Vinci, Aldrovandus, Fabricius (who made beautiful illustrations of a series of chick embryos), Highmore, Sir Thomas Browne, Harvey, and Malpighi. Today the many admirable manuals on the embryology of the chick, such as those by Patten (1929) and F. R. Lillie (1919), present a large amount of evidence in regard to the structural development of the chick. Schneirla (1965) notes that altricial birds first respond in a general way to mechanical stimuli but adaptive discrimination develops as visual and auditory clues become effective.

Preyer (1885), reviewing certain of these facts many years ago, noted that, whereas the structural development of the chick is comparatively well known, its behavioral development is not. Although advances have been made since that time, this observation is still true. A few casual observations on this development, nevertheless, were made at an early time. Harvey as long ago as 1651 noted that the chick in the sixth day of development showed a bending and stretching of the head (Preyer, 1885). About a century later Béguelin noted the heartbeat of the small embryo on the third day, and on the sixth day the oscillation of the whole body, and from that point on he records elaborate changes in movement. He records the fact that he was able to observe the development for 15 days in the same living and developing embryo (Preyer, 1885). Home, in 1822, was probably the first to note the movement of the extremities on the sixth day (Preyer, 1885). Von Baer, in 1828, published rather extensive studies on the development of behavior in the chick, in which he noted the inception of the pendular movement of the whole embryo as a result of amnion contractions (Preyer, 1885). Amnion contractions, he noted, were most marked on the eighth day and were successively less on the succeeding days. This same investigator reported general activity of the embryo on the eleventh, twelfth, and thirteenth days. The amnion contractions of the bird's egg have no complete parallel in other forms. The growing chick seems, as it were, to be tossed in a blanket as it grows. Von Baer also saw

what he considered to be the beginning of breathing movements in the 14- to 16-day embryo. Several other investigators are quoted by Preyer as having also made observations upon the development of behavior in the chick. By far the most extensive study up to his time on the development of the bird embryo, however, was made by Preyer himself. The extent of his study may be indicated by the fact that he used some 500 eggs in his experiments.

In this work Preyer gave much attention to the movements of the amnion which have been referred to above. Preyer pointed out that the rhythmic movement of the amnion when at its maximum extent, between the seventh and ninth days, leads to such an agitation of the fetus that no study of fetal activity can be made without taking these contractions into account. The amnion contractions are generally described as independent muscle reactions. They are non-neural. Preyer also describes the gradual development of behavior of the chick embryo from its earliest head movement to the behavior necessary for hatching. Since the time of Preyer there have been a number of special studies on particular aspects of the fetal and hatching behavior of the birds, such as those by Breed (1911), W. Craig (1912), Clark and Clark (1914), and Patten and Kramer (1933). For the purposes of this chapter Kuo's work is especially important. This work is presented in a series of papers (Kuo, 1932a, 1932b, 1932c, 1932d, 1932e, 1938, 1939a; and Gottlieb and Kuo, 1965). The work of Orr and Windle (1934) and of Hamburger and Balaban (1963), Hamburger and Hamilton (1951), Koecke (1958) is also very important.

To collect material for the study of the morphological development of the egg, it is necessary only to open the shells at known periods of incubation. Opening of eggs without special precaution leads to the early death of the embryo, but this is not important if the organism to be studied is placed at once in a fixative to prepare it for the histologist. A number of techniques, however, have been devised to open the shell and still allow the continuous observation of the early development of behavior in the bird. One of these methods, devised by Kuo (1932a), has yielded excellent results. Kuo's method makes possible an uninterrupted study of the developing fetus without interfering in any essential way with the natural membranes of the egg, or, more important, with respiration of the embryo. Kuo's operation may be described as follows: The shell of the blunt end of the egg is cut off with a fine pair of scissors as far as the inner membrane. The whole inner membrane, however, is allowed to remain intact. A very small amount of melted petrolatum is immediately and rapidly applied to this membrane with a Chinese writing brush. At the temperature of the incubator the petrolatum remains liquid but, when applied by an expert does not spread. This treatment produces a transparent membranous window through which the embryo and the extraembryonic structures and functions can be observed. This technique renders the membrane so transparent that it is almost as satisfactory as removing the membrane. In the course of observations Kuo uses three incubators, one in which the eggs are kept before they are experimented upon, another in which the operation is performed, and the third a special observation incubator fitted with appropriate glass plates through which a microscope may be used. For a criticism of Kuo's technique, see Becker (1940, 1942).

Kuo has also devised a transparent dial graded in fractions of a millimeter which may be put over the cut end of the egg, thus making the quantitative measurement of fetal movements possible. The writer has collaborated with Kuo in making a moving-picture film of the typical stages of development of the chick embryo. For the most part these pictures were taken through the membrane treated as described above. This procedure has been described (Kuo and Carmichael, 1937). In connection with this technique a consideration of the air space of the hen's egg and its changes during incubation is interesting. (See Romijn and Roos, 1938.) S. H. Salter (1966) has developed a technique to record activity in eggs while the egg remains intact. A transducer is used that resembles a loudspeaker without a diaphragm. The egg to be studied rests on a cradle on top of the apparatus so that movements in the egg produce damped oscillations proportional to their amplitude. Sound signals produced in the egg can also be recorded. The eggs used in the experiment were those of the bobwhite quail.

Using his special technique, Kuo has studied many thousands of eggs, and on the basis of this study he has made definite statements in regard to the developmental sequence of behavior in the chick embryo. This work deserves special consideration in this chapter because it is the work of a scientist who is interested in the psychological significance of behavior and because it places emphasis on the part played by the environment in the determination of the course of behavioral development. The results are also presented in such a way that they are peculiarly applicable to psychological problems.

Kuo has traced the chronology and general nature of behavior in the chick embryo (1932a), the mechanical factors in the various stages leading to hatching (1932b), the influence of prenatal behavior upon postnatal life (1932d), and many other special topics such as the relationship between acetylcholine and the onset of behavior (1939a). In the last-named study Kuo shows that the first true neurally determined responses do not appear until after this substance may be detected. This suggests that there may be a chemical mediation of the first response of the chick. For a modern discussion of the physiology of neuromuscular transmission, see Field, Magoun, and Hall (1959). A reference to Fig. 1 will show that at one typical stage the embryo of the chick is very similar to the fetus of the reptile and, indeed, to the fetus of man. It must, however, be remembered that the arrangement of the embryo of the bird in relation to its extrafetal membranes is, as suggested above, in a number of ways peculiar. A description of this anatomical relationship may be found in Patten (1929).

Kuo's work on the chick may possibly best be summarized by indicating briefly something of the observed movement and the time at which the movement was *first* observed. It should be noticed that the writer, by using the time at which the movement was first observed, may do an injustice in certain cases to the facts as presented by Kuo, because that investigator shows that in many cases the movement does not, on the average, arise until some hours or even days after it was first observed in peculiarly favorable specimens. A summary of the commencement of the passive and active movements characterizing the developmental behavior of the chick may, however, give the best generalized picture of the development of the chick that is possible in the compass of this chapter. The following activities are among those noted: heartbeat, at 36 hours; head vibration, 66 hours; body vibration, 66 hours; head lifting, 68 hours; head bending, 70 hours; trunk movement, 84 hours; amnion contraction, 86 hours; yolk sac movement, 86 hours; swinging, 86 hours; head turning, 90 hours; movement of forelimbs, 90 hours; movement of hindlimbs, 90 hours; movement of tail, 92 hours; movement of toes, 5 days; response to electricity (in an embryo removed from the shell and placed in a physiological salt solution), 6 days; eyelid movement, 6 days; response to pressure, 6 days; movement of eyeball, 7 days; swallowing, 8 days; leg folding, 9 days; fixation of body position, 9 days; bill clapping, 9 days; response to touch (in physiological salt solution), 9 days; first wriggling, 11 days; turning of body, 12 days; protrusion of neck, 16 days; respiratory movement, 16 days; response to rotation, 17 days; tearing of membrane, 17 days; peeping, 17 days; response to light, 17 days; response to sound, 18 days; response to vibration, 18 days; hatching, 19 days. Final leaving of the shell does not typically occur, however, until the twentieth or the twenty-first day (Kuo, 1932a).

Alconero (1965) has shown that grafts from 3 day chick embryos show spontaneous motility only when the grafts contain sections of the spinal cord. This supports the view that spontaneous motility observed in vivo is neurogenic from the beginning.

Kuo has not been content with a mere passive description of the movements indicated above in their time sequences, but in every case he has attempted to give a description of the mechanical and environmental factors which are important in determining the special movements and the special modifications of movements that he notes. Thus, for example, he points out that the beating of the heart leads to a general rhythmic vibration of the inert fetal body which starts the head into passive mechanical movement. In connection with the heart beat of the chick, it may be noted that the structural and functional change of this organ during growth has been intensively studied by Patten and Kramer (1933). Almost from the first appearance of the cells which are to form the organ, beating may be noted. This passive mechanical movement continues until at length it gives place on the fourth or fifth day to a true active movement. Head movement in the chick begins as an up-and-down bowing. Gradually, as a result of the change of the weight of the head and of associated structures in the egg, this up-and-down movement is changed to a sidewise movement, which is eventually inhibited by the altered relationship between the fetus and the yolk sac.

Kuo makes similar observations in regard to the movement of the appendages and to other special behavioral functions. He notes that during the period of the most forceful amnion activity, from the seventh to the ninth day, the mechanical movement of the fetus so stimulates it that there is a large increase in the active movements of the embryo. These movements are considered significant in the development of further movement. It is also observed that an active movement originating in the embryo may incite further activity of contraction in the temporarily relatively quiescent amnion. Indeed, possibly as a result of this reciprocal activation during the period of vigorous amnion contractions, the movements of the developing chick in this period are almost ceaseless. It thus comes about that every part of the musculature of the embryo has been exercised before half its incubation period is over. This fact led Kuo (1932b) to point out that any correlation which it is desired to make between the development of behavior and the development of the nervous system in the chick must take into special consideration the changing conditions of response due to morphological growth and increase in weight of the body parts themselves and especially to the changing relationships between these growing body parts and the environment in which the growth is taking place.

It is interesting to note that the specialized movements of the eye and of the eyeball occur as early as the eighth or ninth day but that the first light response of the organism does not ordinarily appear until the seventeenth to the nineteenth day under experimental conditions. Thus the eye reflexes are present in the absence of effective visual stimuli. These early eye movements, indeed, have been found by Kuo to occur in conjunction with movement of the body in space instead of in response to visual stimuli. A similar temporal sequence in mammals and its probable mechanisms as worked out by the writer will be discussed below. Only in the later periods of development do the eyes begin to acquire a relative degree of independence from the rest of the organism. Kuo reports that in general the responses to touch, pressure, and electricity, which may be elicited from at least the tenth day onward, are similar to the normally excited responses which he has observed. In conclusion, Kuo asserts that practically every physiological effector mechanism is thus shown to be in a functional condition long before hatching. Thus the organs begin to function in many cases before they reach adult form; indeed, many function in rudimentary form. He feels that, as is true in the development of structure, too much stress cannot be laid on the fact that the development of behavior is gradual and continual. In Kuo's opinion, the early embryonic movements may be thought of as the elements out of which every later response of the adult bird is built. In this connection he points out that certain of the typical postural attitudes of the adult fowl are but returns to the tonus condition of the attitudes of pre-hatching life (1932d). This same observation, incidentally, although too infrequently presented, can be made in respect to mammals and man, and as such will do much to explain the maturation of many allegedly saltatory behavior patterns of postnatal life.

Gottlieb and Kuo (1965) have recently published an extensive study of the development of the embryo of the Peking duck (Anas platyrhynchos). In this study the techniques described previously for research on the development of behavior in the chick before hatching were used. In these experiments the air space was shifted from the blunt end of the egg to allow the opening of a window for the study of embryos of less than 12 days of development. The stages of development noted above for the chick were also found in general as characteristic of the duck. The cited paper gives precise details concerning amnion contractions, heartbeat, passive and active head movements,

eye movements, oral movements, neck movements, wing movements, hindlimb movements, tail movements, hatching movements, vocalization "combination movements," and responses to external stimulation. The authors stress the role of self-stimulation in the facilitation of motor patterns in the duck. They say, ". . . there is as yet no evidence to show that conventional learning theory is relevant to the prenatal development of behavior. . . ." They quote Thorpe (1956): "What is happening inside the egg when we detect movements of the embryo is, mainly if not entirely, a process of maturation of the innate behavior patterns." G. Gottlieb (1965) has also demonstrated that chickens and ducks have prenatal auditory sensitivity and chicks and ducks soon after hatching respond to the maternal call of their own species better than the maternal call of the other species.

In a recent book, Kuo (1967) stresses the complexity and variability of behavior at all developmental levels and introduces the concept of behavioral gradients and the concept of behavioral potentials.

In the carrier pigeon Tuge (1934) has shown that active movements as opposed to passive movements begin at about 105 hours after the beginning of incubation. The first movements observed are extensions and flexions of the head. In 10 additional hours muscles of the neck, trunk, rump, and tail are also involved. "Spontaneous" movements begin before response to chemical or tactile stimuli can be evoked. At about 125 hours in the incubation period the first flexion of the head and neck to tactile stimulation is called out. The reflexogenous zone spreads from the cephalic to the caudal region as development proceeds. Local reflexes of the wings and legs appear at about 155 hours.

Orr and Windle and their collaborators (Orr and Windle, 1934; Windle and Orr, 1934a; Windle and Barcroft, 1938; Windle and Nelson, 1938; Windle, Scharpenberg, and Steele, 1938) have studied in detail the development of the bird. In 1934 Orr and Windle reported that the first response to a blunt vegetable fiber needle takes place in the embryonic chick at 6½ to 7 days after the onset of incubation. This first response is a quick movement of the wing away from the trunk, a lateral flipperlike extension. This movement remains localized. The local reflexes of the embryo do not seem to develop from a generalized behavior pattern but rather arise independently. In another paper (Windle and Orr, 1934a) these two investigators show that the flexion of the chick fetus which takes place on the fifth day is of a sort which cannot be explained by the spinal cord structure at that time. Probably the mechanism that sets off this behavior is chemical in nature. The motor and sensory sides of the nervous system develop independently of each other, and the motor side is functional first. For a detailed report of the neural structure of the chick as its behavior develops, the reader should consult Windle and Orr's paper (1934a). Windle and his collaborators (Windle and Barcroft, 1938; Windle and Nelson, 1938; Windle, Scharpenberg, and Steele, 1938) have also published a series of papers upon the initiation of respiration and the development of respiration in the duck and the chick. Peters, Vonderahe, and Powers (1958) have studied by electric means the development of the eye and optic lobes in the chick embryo.

Kuo has also developed an elaborate theory of the growth of behavior in relation to environmental factors. He points out that the intensity of stimulation must be controlled if one is to make any statement concerning the generality or specificity of an organism's response. He has pointed out that the physiological *and* behavioral growth of the organism may be summarized in ten stages: (1) cardiac movement, (2) active head movement, (3) trunk movement and response to electric currents, (4) first limb and tail movements and first amnion contraction, (5) head turning and lateral flexion, (6) the hyperactive period from 6 to 9 days, (7) reduction of bodily activities, (8) period of relative quiet (15 to 18 days), (9) prehatching stage, (10) hatching behavior (Kuo, 1938). This is a descriptive procedure much preferred to any too easy generalization attempting to summarize the whole course of behavioral growth. Kuo (1939b, 1939c) has also given an interesting review of the whole question of which comes first, total patterns or local reflexes.

As previously suggested, the possible importance of chemical mediation in the determination of the onset of behavior requires study. Kuo (1939a) published a paper summarizing his investigations in this field.

Oppenheim (1966) has demonstrated that the removal of the amnion on days 9, 10, and 11 has no effect on the cyclic motility of the chick embryo. These observations lead us to question the importance of amnion activity in the initiation and maintenance of cyclic embryonic activity at the ages studied.

It has previously been noted that some birds are far advanced at hatching; these are the so-called precocial birds. Such birds, as soon as they are out of the shell, are ready to be acted upon by the new external environment in very specific ways. In recent years the term *imprinting* has been applied by ethologists and other students of animal behavior to a rapid acquisition of behavior that commonly occurs early in life (or at some *critical period*) and that is relatively immune to extinction or forgetting. Lorenz (1935) points out that imprinting can be seen very clearly in the following of the mother or some other moving object by newly hatched birds. This is said to be a condition where the motor responses are innate and ready soon after hatching but the "releaser" (effective specific environmental stimulus complex) is not innate. Lorenz says that this process of imprinting is basically different and cannot be identified with learning. But this question is an involved one and is clearly and exhaustively considered by W. Sluckin (1964). [See also Schiller (1957), Gray, (1963), and Moltz (1960 and 1968.)]

The idea of imprinting is not new. It was clearly described by D. A. Spalding (1873) in an epoch-making paper. The present writer made reference to this work in 1925 (Carmichael, 1925). Spalding's research was, indeed, discussed in some detail in James' *Principles of Psychology* (1890).

W. Craig (1914), one of the present writer's teachers, early pointed out another form of imprinting that has since been more completely studied. He notes that ring doves removed from their parents at a young age directed sexual responses at 1 year to the hand of the experimenters and at first ignored female doves as objects of courtship. The previously isolated doves still reacted positively to the human hand even after normal sex behavior had been established. (See also Craig, 1908.)

H. F. Harlow and his associates have made dramatic and important discoveries concerning the development of infant-mother affection, mother-infant affection, peer affection, heterosexual affection, and parental affection. These are put through an orderly series of maturational stages (Harlow and Harlow, 1965).

Other examples of the importance of maturation and of early experience or imprinting on courtship, aggression, and anxiety have been described. Much of this work is summarized by Beach and Jaynes (1954). Andrew (1964) has shown that "naive" day-old chicks can be caused to respond to objects in their environment when these chicks were injected with testosterone and kept in isolation until tested. Two of the chicks at once mounted the imprinting object and carried on copulation movements after their first approach to it. Other papers which describe the effect on the time of appearance of specific behavior patterns by the injection of testosterone in chicks can be reviewed in this connection.

Many experiments have been carried out, especially on nidifugous birds, to study the imprinting of a following response. Fabricius (1955) has studied this in detail. E. Hess has shown in excellent laboratory experiments that when ducklings are hatched, the first moving object they see is ordinarily the mother duck. Thus the young, immature animals will typically follow her, but if they see another moving object, they will follow it (Hess, 1958; 1962). Jaynes, in a series of papers, has studied the interaction of learned and innate behavior with special reference to imprinting and emergent discrimination (Jaynes, 1956, 1957, 1958a, 1958b). See also Moltz (1960, 1968).

The fact that birds can be imprinted by sound has been shown by Grier, Counter, and Shearer (1967). A batch of eggs was exposed to a patterned sound continuously from day 12 to day 18 of incubation while a control group was hatched in quiet. In a postnatal test, all chicks tended to creep toward a stationary sound source but the experimental group showed a preference for the sound heard during incubation. In a second test, the experimental chicks followed a moving model longer when it emitted the familiar sound than when it emitted a novel sound or no sound at all. These results indicate that imprinting follows the law of anticipatory function as defined previously.

THE DEVELOPMENT OF PRENATAL BEHAVIOR IN THE INFRAHUMAN MAMMAL

The development of behavior in the infrahuman mammal is in a number of respects more significant for one who would understand the growth of behavior and psychological functions in man than is the consideration of the amphibian or bird presented above. There are peculiar difficulties, however, in studying the development of fetal behavior in mammals. These difficulties can be made clear only by a brief review of the bodily structures and functions involved in the prenatal development of typical placental mammals, including man. In barest outline, disregarding many differences between various species of such mammals and many consequent qualifications, this process of development may be reviewed as follows:

The tiny fertilized mammalian egg is not at first attached but, probably as a result of ciliary action and the muscular contraction of the tubes, moves from the oviduct where it has been fertilized to the uterus. Parker (1931) has summarized the evidence in this field. During the process of movement, which occupies 4 to 10 days, depending on the type of mammal under consideration, the processes of development have begun which are to form the embryo and its membranes. Two embryonic folds are early formed which join to make up the then enclosing amniotic sac. This sac gradually enlarges. It is filled with a special liquid, the so-called amniotic fluid, which has a very definite chemical make-up and a specific gravity of 1006–1081 (Feldman, 1920). The specific gravity of this liquid is thus not far from that of the developing embryo, a fact of great importance in understanding the mechanics of certain forms of receptor–nervous-system–effector action in the fetus at a later period. That there is a change in the specific gravity of the fetus during development has been shown by Stephenson and Roberts (1962) in the sheep at 50 days it is 1.03 but at 140 days, about 1.06 (Stephenson and Roberts, 1962). As growth continues, the sac **more** and more completely surrounds the embryo.

It is quite appropriate, as numerous writers have pointed out, to compare the "weightless condition" of the mammalian fetus with the traveler in space. It will be emphasized later that because of this condition, the fetus shows many types of behavior that are not observed for some time after birth. Reynolds (see Avery, 1965) says, "It is a captivating thought that the uterus is the assigned space capsule of mankind and that all have been, so to speak, in weightless orbit—before they were born." Avery discusses this idea from a physical and psychological point of view in some detail.

The embryo thus immersed and supported is relatively independent of most direct mechanical surface contacts. Coincident with this development the other fetal sacs are formed. One of these, the vitelline sac, corresponds to the yolk sac of lower forms, although of course in the higher mammalian types it contains virtually no yolk. In later development of the fetus this sac is relatively much reduced in size, and at the time of birth is known as the umbilical vesicle. Snell and Stevens (1966) have given an admirable description of the early embryology of the mouse. Sections of embryos spaced at 6-hour intervals from 4 to 9 days were used in the study. The diagrams and reproduced sections make this treatment very clear and the authors also give full citation of relevant literature.

Now that so much attention is being given to organ transplants in adult human beings, it is interesting to think that the fetus is in a sense a foreign organism that has a different genetic code from the mother and yet is a successful graft. If the factors influencing this "graft" could be understood it might be more easy to improve the steps now used in heart or kidney grafts.

The allantois also makes its appearance as an outgrowth of the developing digestive tract of the embryo. This saclike structure comes in contact with the previously formed primitive chorion, with which it fuses to make up the true chorion. This doubly derived chorion now rapidly becomes a completely enclosing membranous wall outside the amniotic sac. The chorion continues to be attached to the embryo proper, however, by means of the allantoic stalk, which comes

to conduct as well the two allantoic arteries and the two allantoic veins.

As this development has progressed, therefore, the mammalian egg has become attached to the wall of the maternal uterus. As the very complex morphological changes, some of which have been suggested earlier, take place, the circulatory system of the fetus and its membranes continues to develop. This fetal circulatory system is mechanically completely separated from the maternal blood system, but the separation is, in certain areas, only that of a cell wall. By interchange through living membranes, therefore, oxygen and food materials pass from the maternal blood system into the independent embryonic blood system; similarly, carbon dioxide and other metabolites pass in the opposite direction into the maternal blood stream. Some antibodies, blood components, proteins, and other substances also pass the placental barrier. Typically, in the higher mammals only part of the chorion is directly attached to the maternal uterus. This area of attachment is called the placenta. As noted later in the chapter, the exchange of endocrines through the placenta is important. The placenta may best be thought of as involving two parts, one derived from the embryo and the other from the maternal uterus. The part derived from the maternal uterus becomes larger and larger, eventually encapsulating the developing embryo and its membranes, which have just been described. This true maternal membrane, as distinguished from the previously considered fetal membranes, is called the *decidua capsularis*.

In human development, as the fetus grows this decidua capsularis comes to be in contact with the mucous membrane lining of the rest of the uterine cavity, the so-called *decidua vera*. Thus as it grows the fetus is enveloped in an elaborate series of membranes. Figure 4 shows these relationships in very schematic form in the human organism. These developed membranes serve an important function. They provide within the mother's body a strong, many-layered sac in which is maintained a liquid environment of very constant temperature and remarkably constant physical and chemical constitution. Hsu (1948) has shown that in white rats increasing the temperatures somewhat above normal affects pregnancy. The results

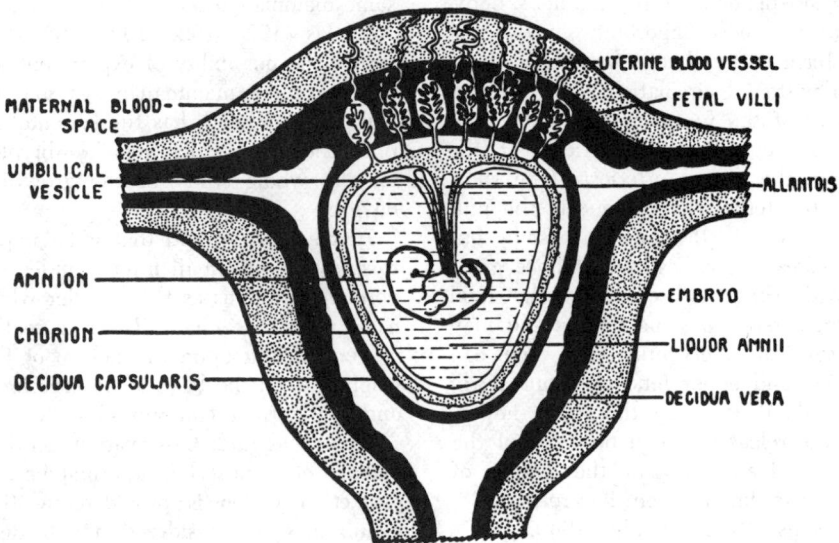

Fig. 4. Diagram representing the relationship between the uterus, the membranes, and the embryo during early pregnancy. (From Carmichael, 1933.)

suggest that with elevated temperatures the percentage of pregnancies affected is greater when the heat treatment is earlier. This result emphasizes the importance of constant and normal conditions of the uterus during pregnancy.

For an elaborate consideration of fetal development made clear by excellent diagrams, see Spee (1915). See also Barclay, Franklin, and Prichard (1946, 1947) for a consideration of changes in fetal circulation at birth. (See also Strang, 1964.)

By means of the association at the placenta, as just noted, the independently developing embryo is able, parasitically as it were, to receive food materials, oxygen, and other substances from the maternal blood supply and to send back into that system the waste products of its own organic life. The extremely important and technical topic of fetal respiration has been intensively studied by Barcroft and his associates and by many other workers. For a review of this literature see Barcroft (1938, 1946) and Windle (1940). The mechanism of the fetal membranes, therefore, makes possible fetal respiration, nutrition, and excretion. It is in a physical world of this sort that we must consider the fetal mammal as developing and in its later stages as actively responding. The nature of this very special environment must

not be forgotten in considering every evidence of sensory or behavioral life which the fetus shows. It must be emphasized, however, that there are great differences in detail in the relationship between fetus and maternal organism in different mammals. As Windle (1940) has pointed out, "Time and again in the study of prenatal physiology it will appear that species variations in the intimacy between maternal and fetal blood streams may explain differences in experimental results."

The relationship between blood flow in the umbilical cord and the rate of fetal growth in the sheep and guinea pig has been studied by Greenfield, Shepherd, and Whelan (1951).

The rupture of the fetal membranes during parturition is produced by the contractions of the muscular walls of the uterus. The physiology of this process is complex and important. (See Barron, 1940.)

Parturition and birth are important processes in the life of every mammal. The word *parturition* is derived from the Latin and means "in labor." It is a name for the actions and processes of the mother that lead to the giving of birth to offspring. The word *birth* is a name for the processes in the period during which a mammalian fetus becomes established as an individual that is physiologically independent of the mother's body.

One of the most important physiological facts of birth is the change from fetal circulation to postnatal circulation. This involves the closing of the foramen ovale (the fetal opening between the two auricles of the heart) and the ductus arteriosis (the short vessel in the fetus which connects the pulmonary artery with the aorta). In some human neonates known as blue babies (i.e., babies with congenital cyanosis) the fetal circulation persists to some degree and may require surgical intervention. No one can fully understand either fetal or neonatal responses without realizing the great importance in the release of such behavior of the adequacy or inadequacy of the supply of oxygen to the brain. (See Barcroft, 1938, 1946, etc.; also W. F. Windle, 1940.)

A new book, *Fetal and Neonatal Physiology*, by G. S. Dawes (1968) considers in detail the development in the fetus and in the newborn organism of the structure, functions, and responses that are necessary to maintain the normal internal environment and to allow growth and development. Here the modern literature on fetal circulation, birth changes, and the circulation of the blood in the newborn are fully considered. The comparative "critical periods of development" for the brain of man and other mammals is well considered in this volume.

A short time after the birth of the young mammal or the child there follows the expulsion of the now discarded enveloping membranes. This "afterbirth" consists largely of the remains of the decidua, the chorion, and the amnion. In infrahuman mammals this afterbirth is customarily eaten by the mother (Tinklepaugh and Hartman, 1930). This is an interesting response to be considered in relation to the problem of the special hungers and patterned "instincts" of the organism.

There are those who advocate in human birth draining the blood of the afterbirth into the newborn child.

From what has been said, it is obvious that the developing mammal is so well protected that it is difficult to study its growth at different periods, and nearly impossible—although the "impossible" has been accomplished, as will be pointed out later—to observe continuously the development of the

same mammalian fetus. A series of papers by Nicholas (1925, 1926, 1927, 1929a) demonstrates the possibility of experimental manipulation of the mammalian egg and growing embryo. This work has fundamental implications not only for the "new" embryology but for the whole study of the growth of behavior.

It may still be said that it is "impossible" to study the mammalian fetus under as nearly normal conditions as those under which Kuo has studied the chick. There is real danger in generalizing upon the nature of fetal development on the basis of observations made under abnormal conditions, as Kuo himself (1932c) has said. Observations on the mammalian fetus must be abnormal because the protection which is provided by the fetal membranes just considered must be destroyed if some forms of direct observation are to be possible.

It will, of course, be unnecessary here to give an account of the development of behavior in all classes and orders of mammals. Indeed, no special studies have been made of most mammalian forms. For example, so far as the writer is aware, no special study has been made of the development of behavior in the fetal monotremes. The study of the development of behavior in these primitive Australian egg-laying mammals would probably provide fundamentally significant facts that might be applied to higher, truly viviparous forms. In both the ornithorhynchus and the echidna, eggs with soft shells, rich in yolk, undergo segmentation in the uterus and are then laid and incubated. The incubation by the ornithorhynchus is in a nest; by the echidna, in a pouch. When hatched, the young of this subclass are nourished by the secretion of great glands possibly more like sweat glands than like the true mammary structures of higher mammals. But a detailed description of behavioral growth in these forms is not, so far as the writer can discover, available. (See Burrell, 1927.)

Study of the development of behavior in what is generally considered the next higher subclass above the monotremes— namely, the marsupials—has been carried on. Indeed, the marsupials are found to be very favorable material for developmental studies. The young of animals in this subclass are born in a condition which can be considered only that of a relatively immature fetus (Langworthy, 1928). In the marsupials, although early development occurs in the maternal uterus, and although the fetus is nourished by secretions from the uterine wall, no true placenta is formed. Possibly for this reason these true mammalian fetuses are born while still at an early period of development and are as yet open to easy continual external observation during most of the important growth stages in which behavior change may be noted. This fact has made this form a favorite one for studies of neurological development by such students as Weed and Langworthy (1925a, 1925b) and Langworthy (1928). After birth the young are cared for by the mother for many weeks in a pouch, the marsupium, into which the mammary nipples open (Hartman, 1920). In certain of the marsupials, indeed, the once independent fetus again becomes functionally but not structurally attached to the mother, as for a long period after the maternal nipple is taken into the mouth the nipple is never removed until the animal is ready to enter upon truly free life (Hartman, 1920).

From the standpoint of the student of the development of behavior, the most adequately studied form of this subclass is the Virginia opossum. In a series of complete and brilliant papers, Hartman (1916a, 1916b, 1919a, 1919b, 1920) has brought together the knowledge in regard to the development of the fetus in the opossum and related types. Until his own work was begun, Hartman points out that the birth of the opossum and the behaviorally significant journey of the newborn organisms to the pouch had been observed and described by but one man, Middleton Michel. Michel's observations, which are reprinted by Hartman (1920), led to a belief that the mother transferred the newborn animals to the pouch. Hartman's work, however, has shown that the newborn organisms travel directly from the vulva to the maternal pouch without the aid of the mother. He says:

Unerringly the embryo traveled by its own efforts; without any assistance on the mother's part, other than to free it of liquid on its first emergence into the world, this ten-day-old embryo, in appearance more like a worm than a mammal, is able, immediately upon release from its liquid medium, to crawl a full three inches over a difficult terrain. Indeed, it can do more: after it has arrived at the pouch it is able to find the nipple amid a forest of hair. This it must find—or perish.

Hartman has further shown that this essential journey is to be considered a negative geotropism, because under experimental conditions embryos can be made to travel away from the pouch if only the skin upon which they are moving is tilted upward. The locomotion of the embryo is described as a kind of overhand swimming stroke in which the head sways as far as possible to the side opposite the hand which is taking the propelling stroke. It is further noted that "With each turn of the head the snout is touched to the mother's skin . . . and if the teat is touched, the embryo stops and at once takes hold."

The conclusion may be suggested, therefore, that this young mammalian organism, less than 2 weeks removed from an unfertilized ovum, has already developed to a point of independent ability so far as air respiration, alimentary canal digestion, and the receptor-neuromuscular mechanism of geotropically oriented simple progression are concerned. McCrady (1938) has devoted a book to the description of the development of the opossum, a notable book in many respects but especially because of its beautiful drawings.

McCrady, Wever, and Bray (1937) have studied the electrical responses from the cochlea of the pouch-young opossum. These investigations have correlated reflex startle responses and the electrical output of the ear. The first responses of a startle type were found at 50 days. Nine days later the electrical output showed that the sensitivity of the ear was in about the midaudible range with 2000 cycles as the maximum. At 82 days the maximum had shifted to 7000 cycles. A linear relationship between intensity of stimulus and electrical response was found. This suggests that these young organisms have a very efficient electrical-acoustical apparatus. Hill and Watson (1958) have described the early development of the brain in a number of marsupials. The development of temperature regulation in the opossum has been described by Petajan and Morrison (1962).

Goerling, in an article also reprinted by Hartman (1920), gives an account of the birth of the kangaroo, an animal of the same subclass as the opossum. It has been observed that in the kangaroo the young animal moves through the fur from the opening of the urogenital canal to the pouch. The following observation is recorded in regard to the fetus: "It moved about slowly, very slowly, through the fur upwards, using the arms in its progress, and continually moving the head from side to side . . ." (Hartman, 1920). Thirty minutes were required for the passage, but during this time the mother gave no assistance whatsoever. Goerling further notes that the arms of the newborn kangaroo are strongly developed. The small hands open and close like a cat's paws. He says: "By these strong little arms and hands the young one is enabled to labour its way to the pouch, the place of safety and nourishment" (Hartman, 1920). It is further pointed out that, so far as the sucking reflex is concerned, once a young kangaroo is removed from the teat which it has taken in its mouth it is apparently unable to reatach itself. Figure 5 shows the early fetal appearance of the pouch-young kangaroo (Parker and Haswell, 1921).

In the series of papers referred to above, Hartman reports his studies of the early embryology of the opossum but without any detailed reference to the onset and development of behavior before the early motility stage in which it is found at birth. It is interesting to

Fig. 5. A so-called mammary fetus of the kangaroo attached to the maternal teat. (From Parker and Haswell, 1921.)

note, however, on the basis of the evidence given above, that in the marsupials young organisms which might even still be called embryos are born in what is in many respects a very early fetal condition. Their behavior, as indicated above, is significant at any rate in a number of ways for the general student of the development of response. Once in the pouch these organisms can be studied without the usual difficulties of disturbed respiration and digestion of higher mammalian fetuses of comparable developmental age which still depend upon the placental circulation. The reports just given suggest that in this organism there is a general conformity with the pattern of development of the amphibian larvae considered previously. As in the case of *Amblystoma*, the young opossum moves with a wriggling movement which from the description, "the head swaying as far as possible to the side opposite the hand which is taking the propelling stroke" (Hartman, 1920), suggests the double S movement elaborated by Coghill and others as a characteristic of the onset of aquatic locomotion in larval amphibians. It is also significant to note that it is the forelimbs, both in the opossum and even in that characteristically hindlimbed organism, the kangaroo, which are mentioned as the first effective agents of locomotion.

This again at least does not contradict the view that behavior typically develops from the anterior to the posterior segments of the organism. This generalization may be said to be essentially true of behavior growth in invertebrates, amphibians, and bird embryos. Moreover, there is nothing in the development of the feeding reaction which is presented that shows its essential sequence to be different from that already noted in lower types. Langworthy (1925, 1928) and Weed and Langworthy (1925a, 1925b) have studied the development of progression and body posture in pouch-young opossums. They find that decerebration of young opossums does not lead to decerebrate rigidity, but rather to an increase in progression movements. This suggests that at this period the cortex has as yet established little dominance over the other neural determinants of behavior. Similarly, they note, after giving a complete review of the work on the nervous system of the opossum, that electrical stimulation of the brains of pouch-young opossums gives contralateral leg responses but no other responses for over 50 developmental days (Weed and Langworthy, 1925b). These observations are important in regard to the part played by myelinization of the nervous system in behavior and, incidentally, seem to confirm the priority of forelimb progression in the early behavioral repertory of this form. Larsell, McCrady, and Zimmerman (1935) have studied the morphological and functional development of the membranous labyrinth of the inner ear of the opossum. Nerve endings are present around the receptor "hair cells" before the ear is functional. Vestibular reflexes appear at about 43 days after insemination; acoustic reflexes appear at 50 days. Myelin appears on the vestibular nerve fibers at the time reflexes first appear. It increases as the reflexes become more pronounced. The evolution of marsupial reproduction is clearly treated by Kean (1961).

Of all orders of infrahuman mammals, the rodents have probably been most completely studied, so far as the development of behavior is concerned. It is difficult to say when the study of behavioral growth in rodent fetuses began. They are convenient animals to work with, and it is highly probable that some member of this order was used by the classic embryologists, whose work will be reviewed historically in the course of a discussion of the specific development of behavior in man is given. It is known, at any rate, that the dead embryos of typical rodents—namely, the rabbit, guinea pig, and mouse—besides many other animal forms, were discussed by Hieronymus Fabricius in his monumental work De Formato Foetu in 1604 (Needham, 1931). It is highly probable that this writer or some of the other great embryologists of the Renaissance observed the behavior of fetal rodents, because at this time embryology was still much concerned with the Aristotelian problem of the development of the vegetable, sensible, and rational souls in all the forms which were studied.

It was not until Preyer began his series of experiments on fetal guinea pigs and other animals that the modern period of the study of the behavioral growth of the rodent began. In his summarizing work of 1885, Preyer gives an elaborate history of the study of the development of behavior in each form which he considers. Significantly enough, however, in this treatise, when he deals with the development of mammalian behavior, he begins almost without historical references.

Preyer (1885), in his own experiments, however, used a number of different types of mammals and a number of different techniques in his study of the development of behavior. His most significant work was done on the guinea pig. In studying this rodent he used at least six methods:

1. The animal was placed on its back, and the movements of the external abdominal wall of the pregnant mother were observed without interference. He also made such observations on pregnant females on which so-called animal hypnosis or tonic immobility had been induced by an appropriate posture and pressure manipulation. As a result of these types of direct observation he concluded that there are periods of quiescence, lasting sometimes for more than an hour, interspersed with periods of great activity in fetal behavior, at least during the latter part of the pregnancy.

2. In another experiment he placed a long, thin needle directly through the abdominal wall and the fetal sacs of the pregnant female and pressed it into the fetus. This needle was inserted so that, when the fetus moved, the needle, forming a sort of lever, could be observed to change its position. As a result of these investigations, the frequency of fetal activity was noted. It is all too clear to the modern investigator accustomed to the use of anesthetics in animal experiments that the fetus and the mother could hardly be considered "normal" during these studies.

3. He listened to the fetal movements through a stethoscope and recorded that in the later stages of pregnancy they made a peculiar Knistern and Knacken.

4. By operation he found it possible to allow a single limb to extrude from the sac in such a way that its movement could be observed.

5. By experimental surgery it proved possible to observe the movements of the fetus still in the mother's body. In this situation he was able to note the effect of changing the blood supply upon fetal behavior and to come to the conclusion that, although deprivation of oxygen did at times lead to general fetal movements, such deprivation was not an essential cause of such movements.

6. He also removed guinea pig fetuses in the air-breathing stage and studied them when supported by blood-warm physiological salt solution and in a warm chamber. In observing the movements of such fetuses he characterized their responses as "*schr manigfaltig, ungeregelt, asymmetrisch, arhythmisch.*"

It is interesting to note that these are virtually the same words used by Minkowski and many others later in describing early human fetal movements. Preyer also observed certain movements of stretching and of reflex contraction and extension which would be difficult for the fetus while confined in the sac. This phenomenon has been seen many times by the writer, who knows of no evidence that Preyer used any anesthetics in employing any of the methods noted above. The criticism of the more painless work of later investigators, that possibly the fetal material was anesthetized, cannot therefore be urged against this pioneer work of Preyer, which may, however, be criticized on humane grounds.

In one case Preyer (1882) notes that, when his observations were made on a guinea pig in the still intact sac, touching the skin of the face led to a localized brushing movement on the part of the forelimb of the fetus as if to wipe away the offending stimulus which was touching the pad of the vibrissae. We shall see that the study of the development of this ability in the fetus may throw light upon certain aspects of the old question as to whether or not the perception of space is natively or empirically determined.

Preyer gives a rather general description of development in the fetal guinea pig. In a fetus 20 to 21 mm in length no movement was seen, but he adds that this may not be interpreted as assurance that no movement had previously occurred while the organism was in the uterus. In one of 81 to 83 mm, however, opened under blood-warm salt solution, the heart was seen to beat strongly and chest movements were noted. In much larger fetuses, 105 to 111 mm long, a complete repertory of action almost like that seen in the adult animal was recorded. Many other observations are given on fetuses whose lengths are not recorded. On the basis of these observations on fetuses, often approximately dated by statements in regard to the hair and teeth condition of the organism, it is possible to say that Preyer noted in the development of behavior in the guinea pig a gradual change in response with growth The very early movements changed by gradual development until elaborate adaptive responses appeared. Concerning a series of carefully weighed litters in later stages he gives a detailed account of definite responses. These activities include the pinna reflex to sound, now often called *Preyer's reflex*, the pupillary reflex to light, and even the cerebral inhibition of reflexes as a result of antagonistic stimuli (1885). He points out that in a 173-gm guinea pig the teeth of the organism were so well developed that they bit his fingernail sharply. On the basis of all this observational and experimental work, Preyer turns to his consideration of the development of behavior in the human fetus, to which reference is made below.

The first systematic study of the development of fetal behavior in guinea pigs, from the point of view of behavioral psychology, is Avery's (1928), carried out in the Psychological Laboratory of Stanford University. As a background for the study of prenatal development, Avery carefully investigated the responses to stimulation shown by newborn guinea pigs. (See also Draper, 1920.) As contrasted with the naked and almost helpless neonatal marsupials described previously, the guinea pig is at birth in many respects structurally and functionally a mature animal. It is born with a sleek coat of fur. Its teeth are well erupted. Its eyes and ears are open. Its heart pulsations and breathing may be quite continuous and regular. It is able to roll from back to side, side to back, and side to haunches. It can crawl, stand, and walk.

To the pinch stimulus applied to the foot it responds by kick or withdrawal of foot. The electrical stimulus elicits a muscular twitch, respiratory gasp, and jump. It can execute the scratch reflex spontaneously or when stimulated in the facial region. Although muscular weakness is evident the patterns of response show good coordination. (Avery, 1928.)

The sensory control of behavior, this investigator points out, has also progressed to a remarkable degree. Lid and pupillary reflexes are present. The newborn animal avoids objects without touching them as it moves about.

The ears are functional, and total bodily movements and pinna twitches are elicited by appropriate auditory stimulation. Needle pricks and heated objects lead to quick response. Olfactory stimuli evoke movement of the head. The complex movements of swallowing are well developed. So far as more integrated behavior is concerned, Avery reports that the young run together when separated from each other and run to the mother when separated from her. Somewhat similar observations were also made by Preyer (1882). The young lick themselves, swim when placed in deep water, chew shavings, and attempt to disengage a foot held by an observer. No retreat responses were noticed when young guinea pigs were placed with an adult white rat. The prenatal development of behavior of this Minerva-like organism is therefore peculiarly interesting because it is such a complete story.

Avery's work on prenatal development must be strictly evaluated, however, in terms of the rather special conditions which he employed in his experimental study. Abandoning the techniques used by some of the earlier investigators in mammalian behavioral development, Avery removed from the mother each fetus that he studied. He thus, of course, intercepted placental circulation and therefore brought about all the changes which have been found to result from oxygen deprivation and an increasing concentration of metabolites in the fetal blood stream. He often worked with dying fetuses. Thus his work is strictly comparable to most of the work on human fetuses reviewed below. Observations were most often made on a large metal tray placed on a well-lighted observation table. "An electric heater, reflector type, was placed nearby. It served to dry the young and to keep them warm. A temperature of 98° F. was maintained on the observation table" (Avery, 1928). This technique provided that, so far as early embryos were concerned, they were studied not only without normal respiration but in what was apparently a continually drying condition.

Avery also considered the question of whether or not there is a distinction between the responses of fetuses taken from young and old mothers. He came to the conclusion that there is no significant difference in the maturity of response elicited from the fetuses of young and fully adult mothers. This conclu-

sion is unlike that of King (1915) and of Angulo y González (1932b) in regard to the white rat, in which various parental conditions were found to influence fetal development.

By the use of X-rays Avery also ingeniously studied the orientation of the fetuses in the uterus of the guinea pig. This study convinced him that gravitation is apparently not very significant in determining rapid changes in the orientation of the fetus in the uterus. He concludes: "The shifts of the foetuses in utero are inadequate to explain their activity after experimental delivery." As a final conclusion to his study Avery says: "These results substantiate the belief that certain congenital response mechanisms exist in foetal and newborn guinea pigs. Some of these are subject to early modification through experience." For an interesting early study in this field, see Virey (1833).

Carmichael (1934a) studied a large number of fetal guinea pigs in a series of experiments in which as many factors as possible were controlled. This study involved more than 2 years of work and the typing of more than 2000 pages of protocols dictated at the time of the experiments. In most cases motion-picture records of behavior were also made. The apparatus used is shown in Fig. 6. A summary of results follows:

1. Heartbeat was the only activity observable in the youngest fetuses studied in this investigation.

2. Before any behavior was observed the skeletal muscles of the still immobile fetus could be made to respond by direct electrical stimulation.

3. In a 28-day fetus behavior involving skeletal muscles response without electrical stimulation was observed.

4. The first "spontaneous" movement observed was a lateral flexion of the neck and a synchronous and possibly independent movement of the forelimbs.

5. The first sensory area from which behavior was released in the present study was . . . the concha of the ear.

6. In general, responses at every stage are a function of what were called . . . (a) modes of stimulation and (b) variable conditions of the organism.

7. The first stimulus-released response noted

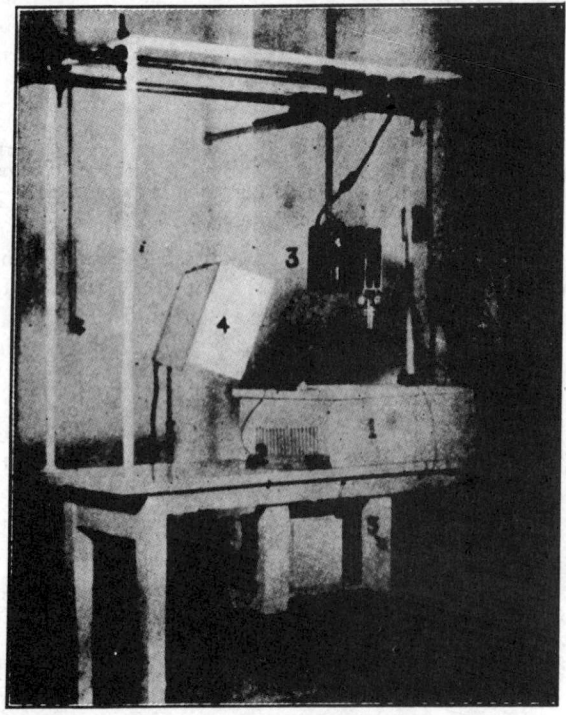

Fig. 6. Photograph of apparatus. (1) Constant-temperature tank in which is inserted a tray filled with physiological saline solution. Maternal animal is held in this bath by suitable supports and fetal organisms are then exposed for study. (2) Holder and graded series of esthesiometers. (3) Electrically driven motion-picture camera for recording. (4) Reflectors for two 1000-watt lamps used to illuminate the field. (5) Foot-operated switch to start and stop the recording motion-picture camera. (From Carmichael and Smith, 1939).

in the study may be characterized, at its first appearance, as a pattern of behavior, which involves a relationship between neck flexion and forelimb movement.

8. Many of the points indicated . . . when stimulated, release behavior from the first which in spite of very great variability could always be considered as a special "pattern of behavior."

9. Each behavior pattern released by the stimulation of a particular area may be said to undergo a series of changes during fetal life.

10. Photic stimulation of the eye may lead to motor responses of the limbs, etc., before the eyes are normally open in the fetus, when such stimulation is made possible by an operative exposure of the eye.

11. Auditory stimuli released behavior in a 63-day fetus after the liquid had been removed from the external meatus.

12. Needle stimulation ("pain stimuli") in general released responses which were quite comparable to responses released by pressure stimuli rather than to the vigorous responses characteristic of the adult animal when subjected to pain stimulation.

13. Temperature stimuli well above and well below the temperature of the fetus, when applied to the skin, release behavior.

14. In late fetuses compensatory movements during rotation and in the immediate postrotational period were demonstrated.

15. There is evidence that in late fetal life higher brain centers influence responses which are characteristically called "spinal reflexes."

16. As development progresses, the amount of "motor diffusion resulting from specific receptor stimulation" decreases, at least in certain areas and under certain stimulus conditions.

17. The study does not confirm in detail

the specific laws of development, alleging that development is in all respects cephalo-caudal, proximo-distal, or from "fundamental" to "accessory" muscles.

18. It is possible to view most of the typical patterns of behavior released by the stimulation of given areas as capable of securing some end or ends, which during fetal life itself or during subsequent independent life may serve adaptive needs of the organism.

19. The present study does not give unqualified support to any of the more general theories of the development of behavior, such as those summarized by the words "individuation" or "integration."

After this general study it became apparent that a more detailed study of certain aspects of fetal behavior in the guinea pig was important. Bridgman and Carmichael (1935) studied 47 fetal litters *at just about the time that behavior first begins.* As a result of this study the following conclusions were drawn:

1. Prior to the onset of behavior in the fetal guinea-pig, myogenic contractions can be elicited from certain muscles. That these early responses are truly myogenic, and not sensory-motor responses, there is little doubt, because of their character, particularly as compared to later movements.

2. Active behavior in the fetal guinea pig begins in the last hours of the twenty-fifth day. Previous observers had placed the onset at least 1 day later than this.

3. True behavior, that is, response that results from stimulation, and which is secondarily induced by nervous discharge, can be elicited 10 to 14 hours before "spontaneous" behavior appears. These stimulated responses are of a sufficiently different character from the earlier myogenic contractions to be classified as active; i.e., involving neural activity.

4. The first active responses of the fetal guinea pig are definite in character, and involve movements of the head, brought about by contraction of the neck muscles, and of the fore leg. The evidence is as yet inconclusive concerning which of these components arises first.

5. It is seen that, from the earliest period, the neck and limb responses occur sometimes together, and sometimes independently, and that throughout the developmental period

studied, independent elements of behavior are present at all times. That is, no gradual progressive "individuation" of the specific responses out of a total pattern is seen.

6. Because of the simple and specific nature of much of the earliest behavior of the fetal guinea pig, it is thought that these responses may advantageously be described as reflexes. Moreover, no need to use such words as "generalized," "totally integrated," or "nonspecific" in the description of this behavior has arisen.

The development of temperature sensitivity in the fetal guinea pig has been studied by Carmichael and Lehner (1937). The results of this study are summarized in Fig. 7. This figure shows that in fetuses of all ages there is an increase in released behavior as stimuli (drops of water) are used which are either warmer or cooler than the physiological zero (about 37.5° C.) of the organism. The conclusions of this study may be summarized in the following statements:

1. Temperature stimuli . . . are effective in releasing responses during most of the motile fetal period of the guinea pig.

2. At each of three fetal development periods, as these periods were established for the purposes of this study—young, mid, and old—the greater the difference between the temperature of the stimulus and the physiological zero of the organism, the greater the relative number of responses released by that stimulus.

3. At the youngest ages studied, there appears to be a slight tendency for cold stimuli

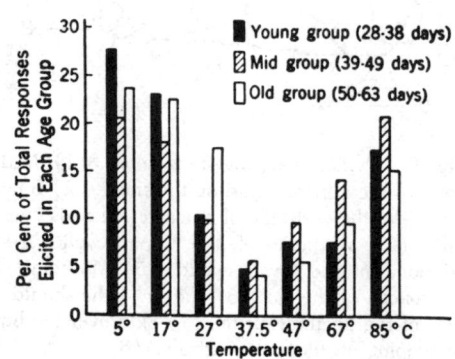

Fig. 7.   Response of guinea pig fetuses to thermal stimuli. (From Carmichael and Lehner, 1937.)

to be relatively more effective than warm stimuli if certain assumptions of equality are made concerning units of measurement.

4. During the "young" period of fetal life, as defined above, there appears to be development of temperature sensitivity. Sensitivity is greater, that is, in the mid period studied than in the initial period. There is no corresponding increase during the other periods studied. In the last period, the growth of the insulating hair coat unquestionably modifies the effectiveness of the stimuli as applied in this investigation.

5. There is no great change in the percentage of specific and general responses released by the stimuli used at any of the three periods studied, nor does the effective intensity of stimulation (as measured by the greater degree of difference from physiological zero) change in a definite manner as development progresses in its efficacy in releasing either general or specific responses. There is a slight preponderance of specific over general responses, as these two words are defined in this paper in each period, but this finding can hardly be considered as statistically significant.

6. There is some shift in the relative sensitivity of the six areas stimulated during fetal development. These data may be considered as supporting the generalization made by previous investigators that the development of sensitivity spreads from the cephalic to the caudal regions of the body and from the prox-

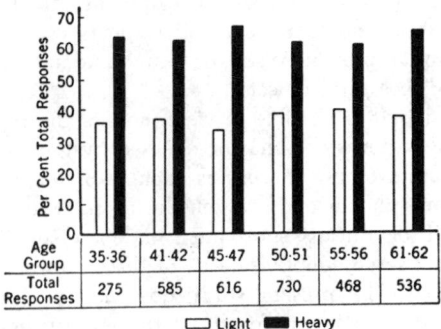

Fig. 9. Percentage of responses at each fetal age group studied. (Normal gestation period is 68 days.) (From Carmichael and Smith, 1939.)

Group 35-36 days
Total responses 275 Light 36.5% Heavy 63.5%

Group 41-42 days
Total responses 585 Light 37.5% Heavy 62.5%

Group 45-47 days
Total responses 616 Light 33.6% Heavy 66.4%

Group 50-51 days
Total responses 730 Light 38.4% Heavy 61.6%

Group 55-56 days
Total responses 468 Light 39.7% Heavy 60.3%

Group 61-62 days
Total responses 536 Light 35.4% Heavy 64.6%

imal to the distal region of limbs.

Bonardi (1946) has also made observations on the stimulation of the nose with cold and hot water at various fetal ages. At the temperatures used cold water was more effective than hot water in releasing behavior.

Hooker (1944) and other investigators have emphasized the importance of the use of quantified pressure stimuli in working upon fetal material. Carmichael and Smith (1939) attempted to study this question in detail. (See also Carmichael, 1937.) First they decided to use certain well-established reflexogenous zones as shown in Fig. 8. They then prepared a series of calibrated von Frey esthesiometers. In each case the lightest esthesiometer that would elicit a response was used, as well as one 7 to 9 points higher in the scale of esthesiometers. The quantitative conclusions of this study are shown in Fig. 9. An example of the difference in response to the light and heavy stimuli is shown in Fig. 10. In summary of this study it may be said that pressure stimuli are like temperature stimuli in the importance of intensity upon resulting response.

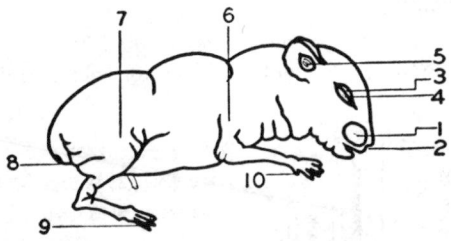

Fig. 8. Typical reflexogenous zones. (1) Midpoint of the vibrissae pad on the snout. (2) Inner surface of the vestibule of one external naris (nostril). (3) Midpoint of the upper eyelid. (4) Midpoint of the lower eyelid. (5) Midpoint of the concha of the ear. (6) Skin over the shoulder joint of the pectoral girdle. (7) Skin over the hip bone joint of the pelvic girdle. (8) Anus. (9) Point in medial plantar surface of one hindpaw. (10) Point in medial palmar surface of one forepaw. (From Carmichael and Smith, 1939.)

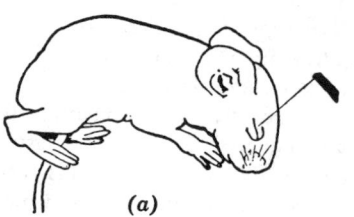 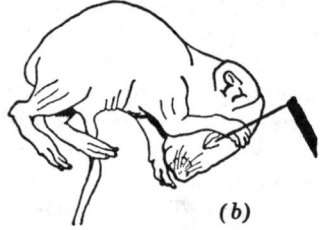

Fig. 10. Outline tracings from motion-picture film of two postures of 51-day guinea pig fetus. (a) Resting posture of the fetus as stimulated with light esthesiometer. Only response in this case was an eye wink. (b) One phase of movement elicited by a heavier esthesiometer. In this case, the entire trunk and all limbs are involved in the reaction. Note the precise localization of the stimulated spot by the forepaw. (From Carmichael and Smith, 1939.)

Moreover, the present results show that the same relative proportion of general and specific responses seems to be released at all of the typical fetal ages studied. This finding adds further confirmation to the view that specific responses are early developed in fetal life. Thus it becomes more than ever clear that the widely accepted formula that all specific behavior develops from the individuation of previously more general patterns of behavior needs revision. Such revision can come only from continued study of fetal behavior as released by stimuli of quantitatively known character (Carmichael and Smith, 1939).

Jasper, Bridgman, and Carmichael (1937) have studied the electrical brain potentials of the fetal guinea pig. The conclusions are:

1. The brain potentials of the guinea pig first appear when the age of 48-56 days of gestation has been attained.

2. No quantitative ontogenetic trend in the characteristic frequency of potential variation, nor in the total range of frequencies, has been discovered. The appearance of secondary groupings of characteristic frequencies is found more often as age increases.

3. The average amplitude of the characteristic frequencies at any age shows an irregular yet definite increase with age.

4. Definite though not invariable effects of stimulation on the character of the cortical electrogram have been noted, occurring as early as the 60th day of gestation.

5. The guinea pig brain first exhibits electrical activity at a time when behavioral indications also point to maturation of higher nervous centers.

In connection with this study it was noted that tying off the umbilical cord abolished most cortical activity but did not for some time abolish the lower reflexes of the fetus.

In another study using high-gain electrical amplification of bioelectric phenomena in the fetal guinea pig, Rawdon-Smith, Carmichael, and Wellman (1938) have demonstrated that the cochlear electrical response (the so-called Weaver-Bray effect) is present in a guinea pig fetus of 52 postinsemination days. The electrical response secured at 52 days had a peak voltage of 1 to 2 microvolts to a stimulus of 600 cycles per second at an intensity of 100 decibels above human threshold. Declining responses were noted to tones below this and above 2000 cycles per second. The rise in electrical output was rapid as development progressed, for by 62 days 100 microvolts was recorded. It is interesting to note that the time of onset of the electrical response of the fetal ear—52 days—is exactly the same time at which the first overt behavior released by auditory stimuli can be observed in the fetal guinea pig.

Of all rodents, however, not the guinea pig but the white rat seems to be the most generally studied laboratory mammal. It is not surprising, therefore, that in recent years an increasing amount of attention has been given to the prenatal development of behavior in this convenient organism. One of the most elaborate studies of this sort is reported in an unpublished thesis by Swenson (1926) and in several other papers by Swenson (1925, 1928b, 1929).

Swenson's observation began with fetuses showing absolutely no movement save heartbeat and continued at convenient stages to birth. It is difficult to generalize about any such developmental sequence because the omission of any of the details of the onset of behavior is likely to give a prejudiced picture of the total process. It is possible in review here, however, to give a few of the salient points of the growth of behavior in the rat as found by Swenson. The first movement noticed was a slight lateral bending of the head. This same movement, differently interpreted, may be characterized as a slight cephalic trunk-bending movement. From this early action to the precise adaptive movements of tongue and paws in late fetuses, there is found a continuous quantitative and qualitative change in the movements as observed in litters of increasing gestation age.

Angulo y González (see references in bibliography), also associated with Coghill, has published some very important studies of the development of behavior in the fetal albino rat. He used much the same technique as Swenson in operating on the mother rat and in preparing the fetal material for observation. He selected his material with unusual care. Of the 643 fetuses used in one study, all came from healthy female rats of known stock 110 to 190 days of age, his previous work having indicated that these precautions were necessary in order to obtain scientifically comparable results at various gestation ages. In his work moving-picture records were taken to supplement the written protocols. Angulo y González in his experimental report gives the percentages of fetuses showing each movement at each age. For these detailed conclusions the reader is advised to consult the original papers (1929a, 1930b, 1932a, 1939). This same author, after using the drug *curare*, which alters the physiological relationship of motor nerves and muscles, was able to stimulate muscles directly in young fetuses. This indicates that the first responses of the rat fetus may be purely myogenic.

It is interesting to note that both Swenson and Angulo y González independently first observed movement in the rat fetus in the three hundred and seventy-eighth hour after insemination. Angulo y González' general description of the developmental process, particularly so far as the process of "individuation" of behavior is concerned, may best be given in his own words:

During the early stages of development the appendages move only with the trunk. Thus, upon stimulation of the snout the reaction more frequently obtained is a total mass reaction which involves the trunk and appendages. This total mass reaction we called a total pattern. This total-pattern reaction consists of a primary or basic movement, lateral flexion of the trunk, and a series of secondary movements. Similarly, there develops later a total pattern consisting of a basic movement of head extension and a series of secondary movements. The basic movements, during the early period of behavioral development, assert their sovereignty upon the secondary movements. During the later period of the development of fetal behavior, we find a number of specific reflexes showing what at first seems to be a breaking up of the total patterns into individual and specific reflexes. But close study has convinced me that the process by means of which the individuation and specificity of certain reflexes is attained is not a disintegration or breaking up of the established pattern, but, rather, is due to an inhibitory action by means of which the primary or basic movements are in a large measure arrested. In other words, the total-pattern reaction is never abolished completely, nor is the dominance of the primary over the secondary movements lost (1932a).

This same investigator (1933a) has suggested that there are three phases in the development of somatic activity in albino rat fetuses: (1) a myogenic phase in which behavior can be elicited only by direct muscle stimulation; (2) a neuromotor stage in which internal stimuli acting upon the nervous system initiate behavior; (3) a sensory-motor phase in which true reflex action begins.

Angulo y González (1934a) has also shown that the dissolution of the behavioral systems of the fetal rat is in inverse order to its evolution, which is in general cephalocaudal and proximodistal. The relationship of this observation to Hughlings Jackson's generalizations (1884) should be noted. Angulo y González (1934b, 1939, 1940) has studied in detail the change in neural mechanisms which are correlated with behavioral development.

Besides these studies of the whole developmental sequence in the rat there have been a number of investigations devoted to certain aspects of the growth of the activity of the response mechanism in the rat. Lane (1917) has studied the development of the correlation between structure and function of the special senses in the white rat. His method of preparing fetal material consisted of killing the pregnant mother and studying the excised fetuses in a warm chamber. This method is open to the limitations pointed out in the evaluation of Avery's work given above. During the observation period the fetus was bathed in a warm physiological salt solution.

Lane's (1917) observations on the development of the senses in the white rat may be summarized as follows.

Touch. He found no evidence of this sense in 7½-mm embryos, which are generally agreed to be immobile. Neurologically, at this stage he found both sensory and motor fibers developed. The sensory fibers, however, had not as yet reached the periphery. In 16-mm embryos, that is, in organisms approximately 17 gestation days old, the tactual sense is reported as present on the flanks and snout, as evidenced by motor response to needle pricks. Lane reports no response to stimulation with a sable brush at this time. This is contrary to the findings of all subsequent investigators and is probably a function of the special condition of the embryos used. In 23- to 28-mm embryos, that is, embryos approximately 19 to 20 gestation days old, he reports response to stimulation with a fine sable brush as well as with a needle prick. The snout region is most sensitive, although stimulation about the shoulder, upper arm, hip, rump, and thighs also evokes motor responses. He reports that there is a noticeable increase in the number of vibrissae as well as a greater complexity in the neural fiber basket of the vibrissae follicle. In very late fetuses and newborn rats a still better development of the tactual sense is found, responses being elicited by stimulation of any point on the entire body, including the tail. Pain as the result of needle stimulation is at this period shown by squeaks. The fibrillae baskets in the vibrissae follicles are now elongated cylinders, from the base of which neural fibrils in comparatively large bundles are seen to emerge, distad to the base of the

follicle itself. In later stages there is no particular advance noted in tactual sensitivity, although the snout region continues to be superior to the rest of the surface in sensitivity.

Equilibrium. In regard to this sense, this investigator found in 7½-mm embryos that stimulation leads to no behavioral trace whatsoever. Histologically, he reports the semicircular canals to be as yet undeveloped. In the 16-mm embryo Lane again found no experimental evidence of the sense of equilibrium, although the semicircular canals are now well developed. In 23- to 28-mm embryos, Lane still finds no experimental evidence of a sense of equilibrium. Histologically, the differentiation of the cells of the cristae is at this time further advanced than in the previous stage, although the sensory and supporting elements are not yet distinguishable. Slight indications of central connection with the cerebrum are noted. In a 35-mm fetus the sense of equilibrium was first observed, as seen in the righting responses of the organism when in contact with a surface. Structurally, the semicircular canals are now virtually complete. On the first day after birth, however, the righting responses were better developed, as were the histological and neural connections seen in the semicircular canals. In later stages there was manifested a greater perfection of the sense of equilibrium accompanying an increasing power of coordinated movement. Lane makes no reference to the part possibly played by neck proprioceptors or by other receptor fields in determining these righting responses, nor is any reference made to the analysis of postural reactions suggested by the school of Magnus, which will be referred to later.

Smell. Lane reports no satisfactory method of smell stimulation in rat embryos from 7½ to 28 mm in length. Histologically, he says: "During these stages the olfactory apparatus is being gradually laid down, both as regards its sensory and peripheral portions. The histological differentiation of the olfactory epithelium has not advanced sufficiently far to enable the sensory cells proper to be identified." Using a brush placed in an odoriferous substance, Lane obtained no certain response to olfactory stimuli in 35-mm fetuses. Histological development, however, is noted as continuing. Small's work (1899) on smell in the newborn rat is quoted, and the statement is made by Lane that "there is on the whole a gradual perfecting of the olfactory sense from day to day." No experimental proof is given of this statement, and it is hard to understand its basis in view of the difficulty reported by Liggett (1928) in dealing with this sense in the white rat.

Taste. In this sense, Lane reports that the 35-mm fetuses were able to swallow, but neither in these nor in those of any preceding stage were any true evidences of a sense of taste discovered. At no time previous to birth could taste buds or other fully differentiated organs of taste be demonstrated. On the first day after birth, however, he notes that sugar solutions were received with less objection than salt or acid solutions. Lane again makes a generalized statement that in postnatal life this sense is gradually perfected, although no experimental evidence is given to support the view.

Hearing. Here Lane reports that "absolutely no response to sound was noted before the twelfth day after birth," and that "from that day to the sixteenth or seventeenth day there is a gradual increase in the ability to perceive sound." No evidence is given for this conclusion in the monograph, however, save that change is inferred from structure. In his conclusions he says:

Previous to the twelfth day the portions of the ear concerned with the perception of sound have been undergoing a gradual development, but have not yet reached that degree of differentiation of the organ of Corti necessary for the perception of sound. By the twelfth or thirteenth day the organ of Corti is apparently differentiated for at least part of its extent, though the lumen of the external auditory meatus is not fully opened. The next few days witness the completion of the differentiation of the apparatus of hearing.

For a study of the early growth of the inner ear of the rat, see Wada (1923).

No better example of cross-species comparison can be given than a consideration of the late development of hearing in the rat and fetal hearing in the guinea pig as described above. The prenatal development of this sense in the guinea pig and the very similar postnatal development in the rat illustrate how important timing is in developmental processes which are almost certainly in a basic way genetically determined.

Vision. As far as this sense is concerned, the report of Lane is: "Absolutely no response to light was obtained before the opening of the eyes on the sixteenth or seventeenth postnatal day." This was determined by the use of an electric flashlight. The objection may be raised, on the basis of a good deal of other experimental work, that this stimulus was possibly not strong enough to bring about response. No record is given of the pupillary response which might have been obtained had the eyelids been opened by operation. Histological evidence, however, is given to suggest that there is a neural and receptor development paralleling the reported functional development.

From the report just given of Lane's work, as well as from the incidental observations in the work of Swenson and Angulo y González, it becomes obvious that, of all the sensory fields in the white rat, that of skin sensitivity is apparently earliest and most completely developed during prenatal life. The development of this sense in the fetal rat was quite extensively investigated by Raney, working with the writer (Raney and Carmichael, 1934). In this work the pregnant female was deeply anesthetized and the spinal cord completely transected between the sixth and seventh cervical vertebrae. The result of this operation was to provide an effectively immobilized and, so far as the field of the operation is concerned, a completely desensitized adult organism in which, however, circulation and respiration continue in a virtually normal condition. After a period of 1½ to 2 hours, the fetuses were shelled out, with placental circulation maintained, into physiological salt solution held at 37.5° C. by thermostatic control. Raney and Carmichael's work was conducted not only in an effort to study the effect of change of skin sensitivity at various fetal developmental ages, but also to consider the origin of what may be called "local sign," at least insofar as such local sign may be demonstrated in the progress of localizing movements of the limbs of the fetus resulting from punctiform stimulation.

Klemm (1914), in his history of space perception, referred to the development of the view that space is perceived in relation to body movement. James (1890, Vol. II) also considered the factors leading to this view, and Peterson's experimental work (1926) on local signs as orientation tendencies again emphasized this conception. Raney and Carmichael's work shows that with increasing gestation age the fetus first becomes sensitive to areal stimulation, as, for example, to stimulation with a camel's-hair brush approximately 5 mm in diameter. Response to punctiform stimulation by a single light hair is observed to begin some time later. The first appearance of sensitivity is in the head region and is observed to pass gradually caudad (that is, toward the tail). The first responses to stimulation are slight movements of the trunk occurring during the sixteenth day, as noted by previous investigators. As development continues, stimulation at any sensitive point may elicit much more complicated behavior, often involving neck, trunk, forelimb, hindlimb, and other muscle movements. The peculiar sensitivity to tactual stimulation of the region from which the vibrissae issue is noted throughout this developmental sequence. The early function of this tactual organ, as it may be called, is particularly interesting in reference to the full innervation of this area as shown by Lane and in the behavioral observations on the function of the vibrissae in young rats by Small (1899), and especially in the special study of this receptor field by Vincent (1912).

Raney and Carmichael (1934) have found, however, where the mechanical possibility of movement is present, that is, where the limb may touch the surface, that the responses may gradually become more and more precisely related to the point of stimulation. Thus at an early gestation age stimulation of the region of the vibrissae may lead to slight trunk movements. Later such stimulation may lead to the movement of many muscle groups of the fetus, including the limbs. At a still later time, the principal response may be merely the forepaw moved ever so slightly toward the point stimulated. If the point touched is on the body wall, the movement may be toward that point. If it is on the nose, it may be toward that point. It

must be noted, however, that, even at the best time for such differentiated response in late gestation periods, the stimulation of any point may also bring out very general activity. It is possible that such generalized response is due to interruption of some "spontaneous" movement, or that it is related to the strength of stimulation. The frequency of stimulation or the immediate past activity of the organism may also be important in inducing such activity. The significance of intensity of stimulation in this connection in the guinea pig fetus has been explained. This is not the place for a full consideration of the theoretical implications of Raney and Carmichael's study as it bears on space perception, but the results suggest a certain reformulation of one form of a modified genetic theory of the perception of extension as considered by Boring (1929).

To return now to experimental fetal studies, Lincoln (1932), also working in collaboration with Carmichael, was able to show in the rat fetus something of the elaborate sensory and behavioral sequences which are antecedent to the sucking reflex as that reflex is seen at birth. The report of this investigation is recorded in library copies of a thesis. (See also Carmichael, 1934a.) This work is especially interesting in relation to Lane's work on the correlation between structure and function in the nursing reflex of the young rat and guinea pig. In Lane's work (1924) special attention is given to the development of the tongue both as a locus of taste receptors and as a prehensile organ. Further references to the sucking reflex are given below.

Angulo y González (1937) has shown that the sensory system follows the motor system in development. The earliest functional sensory endings develop in the region of the snout as tactile receptors. The receptors in the forelimbs, for example, are later in development than those in the snout. The total arc connections seem to be formed by the growth of collateral fibers which establish functional connections after the sensory and motor systems are complete. The study of fetal behavior and of the functions of the fetal sense organs is important in an understanding of perception, as indicated later.

Windle (1934b) has demonstrated that

all the spinal reflex arcs are present at 11 mm but they are incomplete because sensory collaterals are just beginning to enter the mantle layer of the spinal cord. The main difference between the nervous system of motile and nonmotile fetuses lies in the number and length of these elements. This same investigator (1944) in an excellent synthesizing article has emphasized that a close correlation can be demonstrated between the time of appearance of reflexes and the anatomical completion of the neural mechanism on which these responses depend.

Besides the special studies noted above, there have been a number of other investigations dealing with particular muscle groups or special behavioral characteristics of the white rat fetus. Corey (1931) has studied the causative factors of the initial inspiration of mammalian fetuses, using the white rat as material. In this study it is concluded that the initial respiration of the fetus is normally brought about by a change in the relationship between carbon dioxide and oxygen in the blood in cooperation with the stimulating effect of the drying of the skin. Blincoe (1928a, 1928b) has worked on the development of behavior in the motor system of the forelimb of the rat. He has elaborately studied the anatomy of the limb before the fifteenth day, that is, just before the onset of motility. An effort has also been made to present a correlation between this stage of development in the rat and in man. In the later study he points out that it seems that the arm of the rat shows "the static assembling of many bodily components which await some complementary addition to render them a dynamic whole" (1928b). It is suggested that this addition is to be found in functional innervation. In this connection see also a paper by Barron (1934) on the results of his experiments on the peripheral anastomoses between the forelimb and hindlimb nerves of albino rats.

Also working with the rat fetus, Windle, Minear, Austin, and Orr (1935) have shown that physiological muscular development may be summarized in the course which it takes. In general this development proceeds from the head to the tail region and distad and ventrad from the dorsal part of the trunk. (See also Windle and Baxter, 1935, 1936.)

Bors (1925), Nicholas (1925, 1926, 1929c), Hooker and Nicholas (1927, 1930), Nicholas and Hooker (1928), and others have performed experimental operations on rat fetuses. Following a very elaborate technique, these students have been able to operate on mammalian fetuses without interrupting pregnancy. In the course of this work they have made a number of incidental observations on the development of motility, and Hooker and Nicholas (1930) particularly have pointed out the fact that during intrauterine existence "movements are restricted to a large degree and there is also a greater degree of independence of the individual cord segments than is found in later postnatal stages." These observations are significant, for they were made under conditions more nearly approaching those of normal development than any other studies of the development of mammals.

Straus and Weddell (1940) have shown that the earliest visible contractions of the forelimb muscles of the rat appear during the latter half of the fifteenth or the first half of the sixteenth postinsemination day. The extensor muscles are more readily stimulated than the flexor muscles, and if a nerve trunk can be stimulated the response is greater than if the muscle must be directly stimulated. (See also Straus, 1939.)

Corey (1934) has shown that in the fetal rat the cortex is not extensively involved in the production of fetal movements. Becker, King, Marsh, and Vierck (1964) have studied the respiratorylike movements of the fetus of the rat and guinea pig. They question whether or not such movements are normal or seen only in fetuses experimentally deprived of oxygen. (See also Vierck, King, and Ferm, 1966.)

A number of studies of special aspects of the development of behavior have been made on the rabbit; a few of these have been referred to earlier. Preyer (1885) made some observations on fetal organisms of this type. Langworthy (1926) has worked on progression in very young rabbits. He points out that in such animals decerebration does not lead to extensor rigidity but to prolonged progression movements. In the more mature newborn guinea pig, however, rigidity follows decerebration. This difference is attributed to the degree of myelinization in the central nervous system. The importance of myelinization, or the formation of the myelin sheaths, on neurons is discussed below. Zuntz (1877) also used the rabbit fetus in his work on respiration. Richter (1925) has observed sucking movements in rabbit fetuses about 20 days old. Pankratz (1930, 1931b) has adapted Swenson's technique to the study of the rabbit. Mechanical stimulation of nose, head, and neck led to response of simple lateral flexion of neck and trunk in 15- to 16-day rabbit fetuses. In a 17-day fetus there was a marked ventrolateral flexion of head and upper trunk, with some movement of the forelimbs. In 20-day-old fetuses, opening and closing of the mouth, active movements of the forelimbs, flexion of the hindlimbs, and lateral flexion of the whole trunk were observed. As the gestation period advanced the movements became more complex.

Thyroid may be necessary for normal development of the mammalian brain *in utero*. In a study using 160 rabbits, the clearest effects on the weight of the body and brain were seen after birth but thyroid treatment had some influence during fetal life (Cuaron, Gamble, Myant, and Osorio, 1963).

The cat has proved itself to be an eminently suitable animal for the laboratory study of the development of fetal behavior. Its neuromuscular system is quite highly organized. Its gestation age of over 60 days allows for the development of an organism at birth that is relatively mature. Much is also known as a result of past research concerning its structural development (Hill and Tribe, 1924; Latimer, 1931; Latimer and Aikman, 1931), anatomy, and certain of its adult behavioral characteristics, such as the righting response (Camis, 1930). These factors combine to make the animal peculiarly satisfactory for research upon the development of fetal behavior. The general purposes of this chapter, therefore, demand a rather complete summary of the investigations of fetal behavior in the cat.

Windle and Griffin (1931) reported a study in which a large number of cat fetuses of precisely known or accurately estimated gestation age were experimentally studied. The technique employed by these investigators involved an operation on the brain of the mother cat such that later, without anesthesia, it was possible to study the fetal organisms under warm physiological salt solution with fully maintained placental circulation. The methods of studying the fetuses varied more or less according to age. In all, 34 pregnant cats were used, giving 125 living embryos and fetuses for study. Of the litters of the 34 cats thus employed, 19 were of known age since copulation. The ages of the other fetuses were calculated from their body measurements, a procedure that is not in all respects satisfactory.

These investigators reported that no movement was seen in the 23-day stage or on any day previous to that. In later studies, however, it was established that movement does take place on the twenty-third day (Windle and Becker, 1940a). In the 24- and 25-day stage, what the reader may now begin to consider as the characteristic response of young fetuses, namely, the very slightest slow ventral lateral head flexion, was observed in a number of embryos. This was also independently confirmed by Windle (1930a). The earliest limb reflexes are well-localized movements occurring on the side of stimulation at the twenty-fourth day (Windle, 1934a). In the 26- to 27-day stage, movements were in general more complex and of greater amplitude or duration and strength than those noted previously. Generalized trunk undulations, however, still formed the permanent background of activity, but forelimb flexion had also begun. The investigators have pointed out that, at this stage, rotation of head and trunk appears to be coordinated with older components, but that this activity results in movements which strikingly resemble the righting reflexes seen in later fetal life. At this stage the fetuses seem unresponsive to brush or probe. At 28 days slight flexion of the hindlegs was noticed, and at this time also the first responses to touch, particularly in the head region, were observed. Stimulation of this sort was followed by typical apparently "random" head-trunk-limb undulations. At 30 days the activity recorded was still more complex. Active flexion of the hindlimbs was noted, and at the same time definite, although sluggish, mouth movements appeared. From this time until birth, continued and progressive increase in the specificity of behavior was noted by these observers.

So far as the development of sensory capacity in these animals is concerned, it has already been noted that no external response to stimulation is found in fetuses of less than 26 mm, that is, of approximately 28 gestation days. These investigators hold that there is evidence, however, of exteroceptive and proprioceptive function even in the first animals that show spontaneous movements. "The fact that the unilateral trunk or neck flexions seemed always to be executed toward the observer and away from the surface on which they rested may indicate that the earliest sensation is one of deep pressure" (Windle and Griffin, 1931). So far as behavior at the 26-mm stage is concerned, it is held that the activity noted may be the result of a "primitive type of proprioception." This would explain the spread of motor response, although there is some possibility that the wavelike progression of muscular contraction noted is due to the function of long association pathways in the central nervous system.

The first so-called cutaneous reflexogenous zone, that is, cutaneous area, in which stimulation can be shown to lead to response included the nose areas and in general most of the head. Pronounced response in the fetuses at 28 days followed stimulation of the nose. Gradually, as fetuses of later ages were considered, the area spread caudally to the neck, pectoral region, forelimbs, trunk, hindlimbs, and finally to the tail. Windle and

Griffin point out: "It is interesting to note that spontaneous motor activity always involved a part of the body before responses could be elicited either locally or at a distance from the point stimulated." The strength of stimulation was also reported as significant in determining the nature of response. Usually the light touch of a brush was found to be ineffective in specimens less than 60 mm long. In a few fetuses a little longer than this a response was secured when the brush was applied to the nose. It was noticed that a light stimulus which caused no response if once applied was sometimes adequate if repeated several times. This effect of summation of stimuli is noted in many fetal forms under a variety of conditions. Very little difference could be observed between strong innocuous stimulation and stimulation producing observable protoplasmic damage. The authors believe that the primitive type of pressure-touch sensitivity, which they postulate as the characteristic state of the receptor surface or early fetuses, was not replaced by definite touch and pain until relatively late in fetal life. In fetuses of 75 to 80 mm marked differences between the responses to light and to strong stimuli were observed, and pain responses were thought to be definitely present.

In the cat, vestibular function probably appears in prenatal life. No absolute evidence of its presence is found until very shortly before birth. It should be borne in mind in

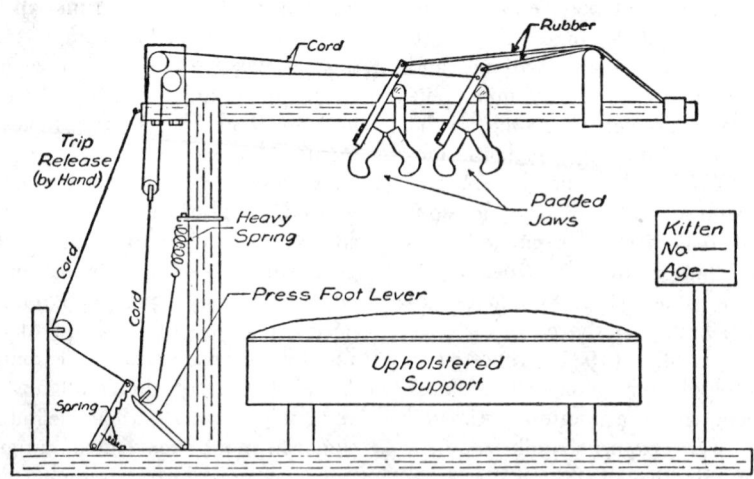

Fig. 11. Apparatus used in the study of the development of the air-righting reflex in small mammals. (From Warkentin and Carmichael, 1939.)

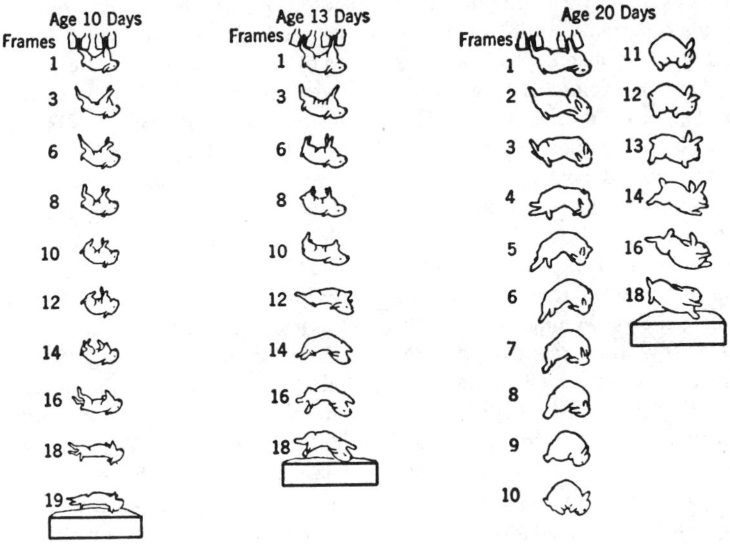

Fig. 12. Diagrams of movement sequences during falling in a young rabbit at three different ages —10 days, 13 days, 20 days. Not every frame is shown. The frames represented are numbered at the left of each diagram, the numbering for each falling sequence beginning with "Frame 1" as the last frame before the jaws opened. Since the film was photographed at the rate of 64 frames per second, and the exposure per frame was about 2 sigma, the time interval from one frame to the next was roughly 15 sigma. All diagrams are drawn to the same scale; hence the animal is larger at the later ages because of normal gain and size and weight during the days represented. (From Warkentin and Carmichael, 1939.)

all considerations of this sense in fetal life that there are great difficulties in testing it accurately in a squirming fetus. In a later study, however, Windle and Fish (1932) demonstrated by the use of several techniques, including the operative interference with the vestibular apparatus, that the true vestibular righting reflex elicited in animals in contact with a surface probably appears in fetal kittens of 100- to 115-mm crown-rump length, that is, on about the fifty-fourth day of gestation. These same investigators (Fish and Windle, 1932) considered the onset of rotary and postrotary nystagmus in the eyes of newborn cats.

For an important early study of the developing of the "falling reflex," see Muller and Weed (1916). Carmichael (1934b) and later Warkentin and Carmichael (1939) studied the genetic development of the kitten's capacity to right itself when falling through the air. Rabbits were also used in the second study. The apparatus used to release the animals is shown in Fig. 11, and a typical sequence as drawn from high-speed moving-picture films is shown in Fig. 12. These

studies were correlated with studies on the development of vision in kittens (Warkentin, 1938). They show that there is a genetic relationship between the time sequence of the partial responses making up air righting and the performance of the act. Thus an animal may be able to perform all the behavioral acts needed in air righting before the total pattern in time can be accomplished in the short period allowed by a free fall.

From study of the vestibular sense, Windle and Griffin (1931) turn to a consideration of the development of posture and progression in general. In this study they follow in part the analysis of Hinsey, Ranson, and McNattin (1930). Walking can be shown to require the coordination of several behavioral patterns, including the ability to maintain an erect posture. In this connection the analysis of Magnus (1924), which shows that posture may depend on impulses from the various receptor groups of the nonauditory labyrinth, from the proprioceptors of the muscles and associated structures, and from the exteroceptors including touch and the distance receptors, is distinctly relevant. In view of the facts it becomes obvious that the maintenance of erect posture may demand quite elaborate stimulation and the establishment of postural tonus by the proper neurological balance between flexor and extensor muscle groups. This complex mechanism makes possible successful opposition to gravity and behavioral acts dependent upon such opposition. For an illuminating evaluation of the effect of gravity on the development of behavior in mammals, the reader should consult a treatment of this subject by Holt (1931). Windle and Griffin (1931) further show that the essential receptor and effector mechanisms necessary for progression involve an added condition, by means of which alternate and rhythmic changes in the limbs are brought about. This last component is necesary if balance is to be changed in such a way that stepping movements may be accomplished.

Windle and Griffin report that these mechanisms, which are essential to locomotion, develop at different times during fetal growth. The onset of the righting reflex has just been reviewed. The first positive evidence of rhythmic movement of the forelimbs involving flexion and extension movements, was seen in a 58- to 60-mm fetus. At this time the hind-leg movements were less rhythmical. Occasionally in a 100-mm fetus complete stepping movements were observed. In this connection the study of Laughton (1924) on the nervous mechanism of progression in mammals should also be consulted. It is further suggested by Windle and his associates that the unilateral rhythmic flexion-extension of the limb as seen in the scratching reflex may have a relationship to the occurrence of the alternate rhythms of locomotion. The first indication of the scratch phenomenon was thought to have been observed at the 75- to 80-mm stage, following ear stimulation. These observations show that the walking movement even as seen in prenatal life involves a complex series of factors which are concerned with virtually the entire receptive field and the entire muscular system of the organism.

Besides this characteristic behavior pattern, these same investigators have also studied the development of the sucking reaction, a response which, like that of locomotion, is characteristic of early mammalian behavior and to which reference has been made. The first head raising and lowering of the jaw were noted in 27- to 28-mm fetuses. This early prefeeding response was followed in the 45- to 50-mm organisms by tongue reflexes which were so amplified in the 70- to 80-mm organisms as possibly to be characterized as sucking. In the 95- to 103-mm organisms, this response had developed so much farther that it was present in virtually its adult form (Windle and Griffin, 1931; Windle and Minear, 1934). Windle and Minear have also shown that the response to faradic shock given to the snout changes with age. At first the reaction is dominantly away from the stimulus (that is, on the opposite side); later, homolateral responses appear. Windle (1937) and his collaborators (Windle, O'Donnell, and Glasshagle, 1933) have also studied the detailed neurology related to the first forelimb responses. At 14 mm, or about 23 days, true reflexes are elicited. At this time the sensory collaterals of the cord are just complete. Windle emphasizes the fact that these responses are not part of a total mass reaction pattern when they first appear. He had previously (1935) shown that the simplest forms of reflex pathways are laid down in the central nervous system before higher integration systems are functional. (See also Windle, Orr, and Minear, 1934.) This same investigator (Windle, 1939) suggests that calcium and potassium deficiencies may account for certain delays observed in the onset of fetal movements.

Another elaborate study of the development of behavior in the fetal cat was undertaken in 1928 by Coronios, working in collaboration with Carmichael and other investigators (Coronios, 1930, 1931, 1933; Coronios, Schlosberg, and Carmichael, 1932). Unlike Windle and Griffin, Coronios used only fetuses from litters whose insemination age he knew accurately. In Coronios' work the pregnant female was prepared for observation under deep ether anesthesia. While the animal was anesthetized the carotid arteries were ligated, a cannula inserted in the trachea, and a complete midbrain section carefully performed. After this section, the anesthetic was immediately discontinued. The decerebrate adult cat was then allowed to remain quiet for 1½ or 2 hours before the fetuses were exposed for observation by an operative technique. Before the observations began, the cat was placed in a specially devised bath apparatus in which physiological salt solution was maintained thermostatically at 37.5° ± 0.5° C. Into this blood-warm liquid the fetuses were shelled out one by one. A summary of the behavior observed at various copulation ages may be found in Fig. 13. In a supplement to this chart Coronios (1933) offers the following conclusions:

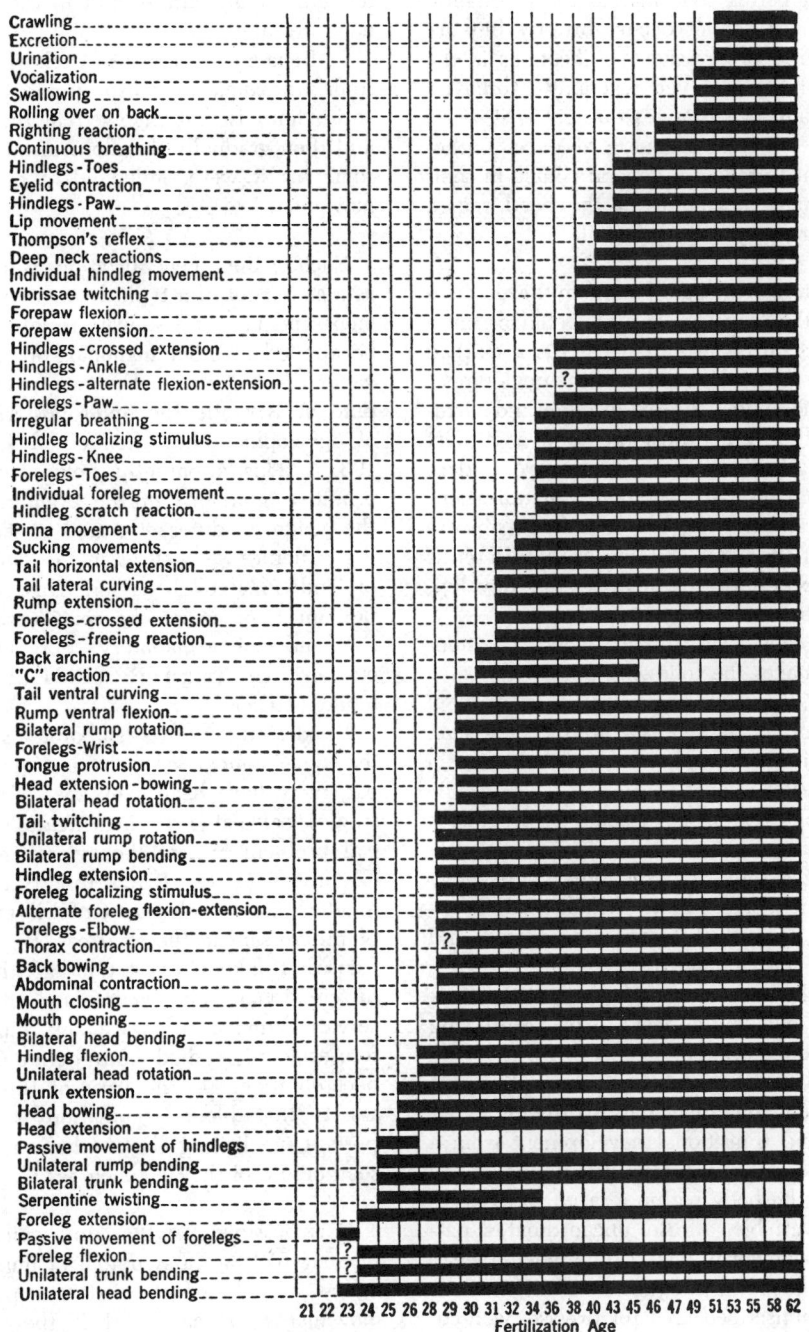

Fig. 13. A chart constructed to show the development of behavior in cat fetuses of various gestation ages. (From Coronios, 1933.)

In the early stages the behavior is diffuse, variable, relatively uncoordinated, and weak. With the increase in gestation age, the reactions become more vigorous, more regular in their appearance, less variable, individualized, and better coordinated. These qualitative changes do not occur abruptly but are continuously progressive modifications in the quality of the observed reactions. Moreover, these qualitative changes do not, as it were, "invade" the total organism at once. Rather they seem to follow a general course in their development, beginning at the head region and progressing toward the tail.

It is interesting again to note in this description of the development of behavior in a highly organized mammalian fetus a marked similarity to the description of the devlopment of behavior noted in *Amblystoma* and virtually all other forms considered above. It must be emphasized, however, that there is danger in making too sweeping generalizations about fetal behavior, but it is impossible to deny that there are certain descriptive terms which accurately characterize the development of behavior in many forms.

As a conclusion to his work, Coronios (1933) makes the following points:

1. Before birth there is a rapid, progressive, and continuous development of behavior in the fetuses of the cat.

2. The development of behavior progresses from a diffuse, massive, variable, relatively unorganized state to a condition where many of the reactions are more regular in their appearance, less variable, better organized, and relatively individualized.

3. In the early stages of prenatal development the behavior appears to be progressing along a cephalocaudal course.

4. The development of the sensitivity of the reflexogenous zones passes through a continuous and transitional development from a time when rather vigorous stimulation of any "spot" of the body within a large area serves to elicit variable, diffuse, uncoordinated patterns of behavior to a later time when a weak stimulus becomes adequate, within a much more circumscribed area for precise, well-coordinated, uniform, and less variable patterns of behavior. The direction of such development is cephalocaudal.

5. The "primitive" reactions of breathing, righting, locomotion, and feeding are the products of a long and continuously progressive course of prenatal development.

6. Behavior development appears first in the gross musculature, and in the fine musculature later.

7. Behavior develops in each of the limbs from a proximal to a distal point; that is, the entire limb is first involved in the response and then gradually the more distal joints become, as it were, independent of the total movement.

Each of these generalizations is to be taken as a statement of a typical course of development and not as a specific formula that can be applied to other mammals or man in advance of observation. For example, from the time of Aristotle the anteroposterior course of development has been noted (Needham, 1931). This apparently holds true in the primitive gradients of the organism and in the weight of different organs of its developing structure, as well as in the development of "individuated" behavior. This generalization must, of course, be considered descriptive and not explanatory. For further discussion, see Kingsbury (1924, 1926) and Child (1925).

Besides these two elaborate studies of the development of behavior in the fetal cat, there have been a number of incidental studies calculated to investigate some special problem in fetal behavioral growth. T. G. Brown (1914, 1915) reports an experiment on the development of the mechanism of progression in the fetal cat. He used four fetuses of unknown gestation age, the placental circulation being maintained and the observations made in a warm salt solution. The fetuses were studied both before and after decerebration. On the basis of this work he asserts that blood stimulation is very important in eliciting the rhythmic movements seen before birth. He concludes:

It is possible that the "quickening" movements which are a symptom of human pregnancy may be due to similar progression movements in man; and if they are thus evoked by some such accidental asphyxia as that conditioned by pressure upon the umbilical cord they may tend, in an indiscriminate manner it is true, to relieve that pressure (1915).

He also suggests on the basis of other observations a phylogenetic theory of the development of locomotion based on Sherrington's view of motor half-centers in the central nervous system.

Langworthy (1929) has also studied the development of behavior in the fetus of the cat. He reported a study on six fetuses near term and a number of kittens of varying ages after natural birth. In these fetuses after decerebration he found behavior that is characteristic of the late cat fetus, although less well-defined hindleg movements were observed than those reported by Brown. The behavior of the fetal and young organisms was then correlated with structural studies of the nervous system. He reported in summary of this work:

Bilateral movements of the extremities begin to coordinate when the ventral commissural fibers of the cord receive their myelin sheath. The animals turn the body at a time when myelinated vestibular fibers reach the spinal cord. The hindleg movements become better coordinated when myelinization becomes marked in the lumbar portion of the cord.

Krnjevic and Silver (1966) have carried out a histochemical study of the developing forebrain of the cat embryo. They believe that acetylcholinesterase-containing elements have a purely telencephalic origin.

Tilney has prepared a chart showing the stream of behavior reaction in the cat similar to the chart concerning the development of behavior in the guinea pig cited above (Woodworth, 1929). In this chart many behavioral acts are shown as appearing in postnatal life which the studies given above show in prenatal life. This is true of "primitive escape," "snatching," and, indeed, virtually all the reactions shown in the chart. The "sudden emergence" of some of these behavior patterns noted below the chart, as in most "saltatory maturation," may seem therefore to involve the reactivation under different environmental conditions of behavior which has had a prenatal developmental history. Similar facts of human fetal development are significant in interpreting the conclusions of Gesell (1929b) and Shirley (1931a, 1931b) concerning human behavioral maturation. Windle and Orr (1934b) have shown that when the fetus is dying there is likely to be a vermiform contraction. These general reactions may appear after the heart has ceased to beat.

A number of special studies have been made on other mammals. Erasmus Darwin (1796) quotes an account from Galen of the fetal development of the goat. The fetus, after removal, got to its feet and walked, shook itself, scratched, smelled of objects, and then drank milk. Huggett (1927, 1930) has used this same ungulate in elaborate studies of the onset of breathing reflexes in the fetus, which will be considered below. He used animals 1 or 2 months before full term. The size of the animal made it convenient for operative purposes, but some difficulties which experimenters with small animals are spared may be noted, since a "domestic bath" had to be used to hold the saline solution into which the fetus was delivered (1927).

Scharpenberg and Windle (1938) have now shown that, in the sheep, myogenic responses precede neurogenic ones. Some sensory collateral fibers have grown out from the dorsal funiculus and have reached the internuncial neurones of the cord at the time the first true reflex arcs are established. The most elaborate studies of the fetus of the sheep, however, have been made by Barcroft and Barron (1939). These investigators outline the results of an elaborate series of studies upon this large fetus. In this animal the first spontaneous movements appear on the thirty-fifth day after insemination. These responses involve forelimb, neck, and trunk movements. By the thirty-eighth day the observed movements are more "definite" and the movements are larger and more numerous. Such spontaneous movements are quite transient. Even in a 40-day fetus they may last only 5 minutes after delivery. Maintained posture following movement is seen by the forty-second day. In their study of responses these investigators stimulated by various means the fields related to some of the important peripheral nerves of the body. As a conclusion of the study of the maxillary nerve, for example, they state that the motor response to specific stimulation is at first confined to a few muscles, then more muscles become involved, but at length only those are activated which respond in the adult sheep. Again, in regard to the sensory nerves distributed to the trunk and limbs they conclude that local muscular reactions are first evoked, but with increasing development more and more muscles may be brought into play.

Barcroft and Barron (1936) have also studied the genesis of respiratory movements in the fetus of the sheep. Barcroft, Barron, and Windle (1936) have shown in the same large embryo localized responses to mechanical and electrical stimulation. These writers conclude that behavior may be considered to have its genesis in localized patterns of response. This conclusion is qualified, however, in a later paper by Barcroft and Barron (1937a), in which a neurological distinction is drawn between reflexes and local contractions, for example, of the neck. These same investigators in another paper (1937b) give an excellent description of the movements of the fetal sheep in midfetal life. Barcroft himself gives a more general description of this work in a paper entitled "The Mammal before and after Birth" (1935; see also 1946).

Barcroft's summary of much of this work appears in his excellent volume of Terry Lectures entitled The Brain and Its Environment (1938). In this volume brain activity in relation to its internal environment in fetal and neonatal life is brilliantly described. In all of Barcroft's work the importance of the changing internal environment of the fetus subjected to experimental study is emphasized. For a comprehensive evaluation of these problems see Barron (1950) and Windle (1950).

Comline, Silver, and Silver (1965) have studied the factors responsible for the stimulation of the adrenal medulla during asphyxia in lambs at 115 and 140 gestational days. Eidelberg, Kolmodin, and Myerson (1965) in experiments on 50 unanesthetized fetal sheep from 30 to 150 gestation days of age have shown that the electrical steady potential in the fetal sheep brain can be recorded at 30 days and that there is a slight increase in steady potential values during all of the rest of pregnancy.

The dynamics of circulation in the fetal lamb and its changes in the lamb after birth have been studied by Assali et al. (1965).

Bolk (1926) has made a comparative morphological study of fetuses of the gorilla, chimpanzee, and man in relation to a theory of development. Tinklepaugh, Hartman, and Squier (1930) have studied fetal heart rate in the monkey. Hines and Straus (1934) have studied the motor cortex of fetal and infant rhesus monkeys. The gestation period of the macaques used was taken as 168 days. Fetuses 85 days old showed good contralateral responses of shoulder and head on cortical stimulation. The fingers gained cortical representation during the first week after birth, as did also the facial areas and lower extremities. It seems that the muscles innervated by the dorsal strata of the limb plexus (extensor system) are the first muscles of the extremeties to gain representation in the motor cortex.

Incidental observations on other animal fetuses are given by J. F. Craig (1930) in his revision of Fleming's Veterinary Obstetrics. Needham (1931) gives tables of the gestation times of scores of animals which are valuable for comparative purposes. For an even more complete table, see Altman and Dittmer (1962).

THE EFFECT OF DRUGS ON FETAL DEVELOPMENT

Preyer (1882, 1885, 1893), as already noted at several points, was a true pioneer in the scientific study of the behavior of the fetus. In his 1885 book he pointed out that the drug curare could inhibit behavior by paralyzing the newborn animals but that immature fetuses were resistant to doses that were large enough to paralyze an adult. In conducting these experiments, he made the important discovery that transmission of this drug through the placenta to the mother from the fetus could take place as maternal paralysis was observed to follow fetal injections.

Ruckert (1930) much later showed that acetylcholine acted on certain guinea pig fetuses and caused them to contract. This pattern of response persisted for a time in neonatal life.

In general, as already noted, it can be said that recent work has shown that the placenta is not as much of a barrier to drugs as had once been thought. Drugs with molecular weights of less than 1000 can apparently cross the barrier (Eastman, 1956).

Factors that lead to the development of malformation in fetal life are called *terato-genic*. The fact that malformation could be caused by drugs was not widely understood until the tragedy of the malformations that resulted from the administration of thalidomide. Thalidomide was first synthesized in 1953. When pharmacologically tested, for example, by Somers (1962), it appeared to be nontoxic. It was considered to be a good so-called hypnotic drug with favorable sedative effects. It was described as a new nonbarbiturate, sleep-inducing drug (Lasagna, 1960).

In December, 1959, a report of malformation (*Phocomelia*) related to thalidomide was published (Weidenbach, 1959). Soon other similar reports were made (Collins, 1964). In 1962 Lenz reported on 52 malformed infants whose mothers had taken thalidomide during the early stages of pregnancy. Many later reports confirmed this finding. The major defect produced in the fetus by the drug is a malformation of the limbs. The long bones such as the radius, femur, and tibia do not develop in a normal way when the drug acts on a fetus. Fingers are often absent or fused. There are internal organic abnormalities as well (Lenz, 1962).

From an embryological point of view, it seems that the damage results mostly between the third and eighth postinsemination weeks. This has been attributed by Pliess (1962) to interference in development in the critical or determinant time for the active growth of mesodermal structures.

Experimental work has demonstrated that thalidomide apparently does not affect all mammals equally but some species are vigorously affected by it. When thalidomide was given to pregnant mice, many litters were found to contain embryos with congenital abnormalities (DiPaolo, 1963). In an experiment in which control animals were studied as well as those receiving thalidomide, results show that no malformations were found in the control animals but 6.9% of the fetuses of animals receiving the drug showed malformations (King and Kendrick, 1962). In rhesus monkeys, thalidomide sometimes seems to kill the embryo, probably prior to implantation. Thalidomide produces abnormalities in rabbits similar in some respects to those in human beings and hence rabbits have been much used in studies of the effect of this drug on fetuses (Taussig, 1962a, 1962b).

Comprehensive bibliographies listing hundreds of papers on the effect of thalidomide have been brought together (Food and Drug Administration, 1963). The whole problem of drug dangers to the fetus from maternal medication has been well summarized by Arena (1964). Baker (1960) has prepared an admirable bibliography of 354 references and summaries of the effects of drugs on the fetus. He concludes by pointing out that at the present time more children die from congenital malformations than from certain contageous diseases which were dangerous before the modern era of chemotherapy. His paper discusses the effects of powerful analgesics, mild analgesics, sedatives, tranquilizers, anesthetics, carbon monoxide, curare and related drugs, anticoagulants, antibiotics, antithyroid drugs, carcinogenic drugs, lead, and nicotine. The effect of cigarette smoking on premature birth has been studied by Simpson (1957). One of the first or pioneer studies on chromosomal damage in human leukocytes induced by LSD has been investigated by Cohen, Marinello, and Back (1967).

Radiation damage to the fetus has also been extensively studied (Yamazaki, Wright, and Wright, 1954; Yamazaki, 1966; Miller, 1956; Furchtgott, 1964; Rugh, 1958). The effect of high altitude on pregnancy has been studied. Some striking effects are found but much further work is needed (see Montague, 1964).

The very large body of literature on morphological effects of drugs on mammalian fetuses cannot be fully reported here. It is important, however, to note that marked changes in the structure of the fetus produce marked changes in behavior. It is clear, therefore, that any generalization about the fact that embryonic development is a result of the working of the genetic code alone must be qualified by a full consideration of the effect of drugs and other agents on the embryological development of the fetus after conception. Woollam (1962) has indeed pointed out that the thalidomide disaster may be considered as an experiment in mammalian teratology and, it may be added, in the development of mammalian behavior. Physical growth and the growth of behavior involves a long series of what are called in this chapter emergent developmental changes. It is hard or impossible in considering this complex development, as seen in some obvious organic defect or in some atypical form of behavior, to determine a single explanation of how the defect arose. Every "normal" development is subject to unpredictable variations. Distinctions between genetic and environmental effects in fetal development are thus very hard to establish. There is evidence that prenatal and premating stress may affect adult behavior (Joffe, 1965). As Weiss (1955a) has noted, selective damage to a particular organ by an environmental factor can be referred to differential susceptibilities of different parts of the body. Thus environmental damage, in one respect, may be said to go back to the genes of the organism.

It is, of course, well known that malformed fetuses are often aborted before reaching full term, but the birth of many malformed fetuses (or "monsters," as they are sometimes called) shows that this is not an invariable rule.

In recent years a large literature has developed concerning the effect of rubella (German measles) and many other maternal diseases on the fetus (Mintz, 1958). Maternal influenza has been studied by Coffey and Jessop (1959). In almost all such cases, the structural malformation and especially the atypical brain development that is observed can be seen to lead to the growth of behavior patterns that are not the normal ones of the species. Dagg (1966) has prepared an admirable summary of the whole subject. He gives emphasis to abnormalities found in the mouse fetus but his work has implications for other mammals and especially for the importance of the critical periods in fetal life when teratogenic agents are most apt to produce abnormalities.

It is important in considering abnormal fetal development to differentiate anomalies caused by teratogenic factors from those resulting from mutant genes and linkages. The latter topic has been fully reviewed by M. C. Green (1966; see also bibliography of this topic in E. L. Green, 1966). M. C. Green has also well summarized present knowledge of how the genes act in normal as well as abnormal development. She points out that in seeking answers to the general questions of how genes (or the genetic code) control development, it is important to remember that in multicellular organisms many kinds of cells are formed. It is clear that although each cell type contains the full pattern of genes that are present in the zygote, only *certain genes are active* in each different kind of cell and then only at specific times. In other words, multicellular development depends on the fact that some genes are called into action at particular times and promote changes that may then call other genes into action or repress the activity of other genes that have been previously active. This involved mechanism is of the greatest significance for the student of behavior. As the relationships of these involved factors become better known, it will almost certainly become clear that some specific changes of behavior that are seen in individuals, even in adult life, may have a basis in genes. For example, some of the changes of senescence almost certainly have their basis in mechanisms such as those just described.

GENERAL ASPECTS OF HUMAN FETAL DEVELOPMENT

Prescientific Study

From one point of view at any rate, all that has gone before in this chapter has been intended to prepare the reader for the consideration of the prenatal development of behavior in human beings. Behavioral development before birth has long been a subject of notice in the human race, but only comparatively recently has it been studied in a systematic and scientific manner.

That the fetus moves before birth is knowledge as old as mankind. Certainly there are references to this phenomenon in the folklore of primitive peoples (Ploss and Bartels, 1927). It is interesting to notice also, so far as the anthropomorphic theory of primitive deities is concerned, that the process of making gods in the image of man even included speculations about god embryos. For a consideration of this topic, see Briffault's work *The Mothers* (1927) and Witkowski (1887). There are references to prenatal development of behavior in Biblical literature and in ancient Indian and Chinese writings. The Egyptians early began to consider this matter, as is shown in a hymn to the sun god attributed to Amenophis IV (about 1400 B.C.):

Creator of the germ in woman,
Maker of seed in man,
Giving life to the son in the body of his
    mother,
Soothing him that he may not weep,
Nurse (even) in the womb.
Giver of breath to animate everyone that he
    maketh
When he cometh forth from the womb on
    the day of his birth.

(Needham, 1931[1])

Aristotle taught that the vegetative or nutritive soul existed in the unfertilized material of the embryo (Needham, 1931).[2]

One of the problems that grow out of the view that the fetus early comes to have an independent existence is the value placed upon human fetal life. This problem of evaluation is essentially ethical rather than scientific. As such, it continues even at the present time to be significant. It is not, however, a topic within the scope of this chapter. Among the numerous treatments of this topic, the monograph by Goeckel (1911) dealing with the changes that have taken place in the evaluation of the life of the unborn human fetus is important. In this monograph the author reviews primitive opinion and the statements of Roman and old Germanic law in regard to the fetus. He presents an excellent bibliography of Roman Catholic theological pronouncements and of civil legal opinions on the value of the life of the fetus. The legal aspect of prenatal life is also given special consideration in a paper by Morache (1904). As already noticed, the earlier history of the evaluation of fetal life is fully considered in Witkowski's detailed *Histoire des accouchements chez tous les peuples* (1887). Much of this work, however, seems to be based upon Cangiamila's *Embryologia Sacra* of 1775, which the writer has not seen.

Modern thinking about the value of the fetus is reviewed in such papers as those of Hughes (1905), Arendt (1910), and Glenn (1911), which treat various aspects of the ethics of dealing with the life of the unborn child. Present civil and religious discussions of birth control and so-called legal abortions show how current are ethical and legal problems in this field.

From early times people have believed that the mother's thoughts and experiences directly influence the fetus. For many years, however, this view of prenatal influence has existed in the popular rather than in the scientific tradition. That "thought transference" or some mysterious nervous relationship exists between mother and fetus is not generally held today by scientific investigators. Save in the chemical interchange between the two blood streams or in mechanical or infectious transmissions, biology and psychology offer no basis for this view. Compayré (1896) gives a brief history of this superstition. He describes the now amusing assertions of Malebranche in regard to the complete intercerebral sharing of all mental processes between fetus and mother and then carries the subject on to the speculations current in nonscientific writings at the end of the nineteenth century. Compayré does not, however, refer to the remarkable assertions of the philosopher Hegel (1894) concerning psychological embryology, in which mother and fetus are said to be in undivided "psychic unity." This magic relationship is held to be of the nature of animal magnetism, by which the character and talent of the mother are communicated to the child.

That superstitious views of prenatal influence are still discussed may be discovered by reading articles by Coughlin (1905), Walton (1910), Christenbery (1910–1911), Tompkins (1911–1912), Barham (1915–1916), and R. L. Brown (1918). An example of such an observation is the following case described by Morrison (1920). A mother of five healthy children had two teeth removed during pregnancy. She feared that the child

---

[1] For much of the historical material given in various parts of this chapter, the writer is indebted for actual references and for many interpretations to Needham's illuminating history of embryology (1931). For a study of the ideas of primitive peoples concerning generation as they have evolved into modern scientific understanding, the reader is urged to consult Meyer's *The Rise of Embryology* (1939).

[2] A more detailed history of prescientific studies of fetal behavior is given in the previous edition of this chapter. See second edition (1954) of *Carmichaels Manual of Child Psychology.*

would have a harelip. She became obsessed with the idea. The child was born with a harelip. It proved difficult to convince the mother that maternal impressions were not an accepted scientific cause. In this case just given, one is apparently dealing with an unusual coincidence which seems very like a causal connection to those who participate in it emotionally. To the parent such a conclusion may thus be psychologically if not scientifically pardoned. Until new evidence is presented, however, such cases cannot be considered as having scientific significance. We may still say with some assurance that "prenatal influence" in the sense discussed is a superstition.

Sontag (1966) has summarized the literature showing that pregnant rats and other mammals produce offspring that are affected by adult environmental conditions. Pregnant rats that are fondled produce less "neurotic" offspring. It is also asserted that severe maternal emotions cause a change in the activity level of the human fetus. In eight cases in which maternal emotion caused increases in fetal activity level the offspring later showed no congenital defects but some were hyperactive, irritable, or had frequent stools.

Scientific Study

We must now turn back in our consideration to the scientific study of the fetus in order to consider what is known about the actual behavioral development of the unborn child. For the purpose of understanding this prenatal development of human behavior, some general idea of morphological development provides a useful baseline upon which

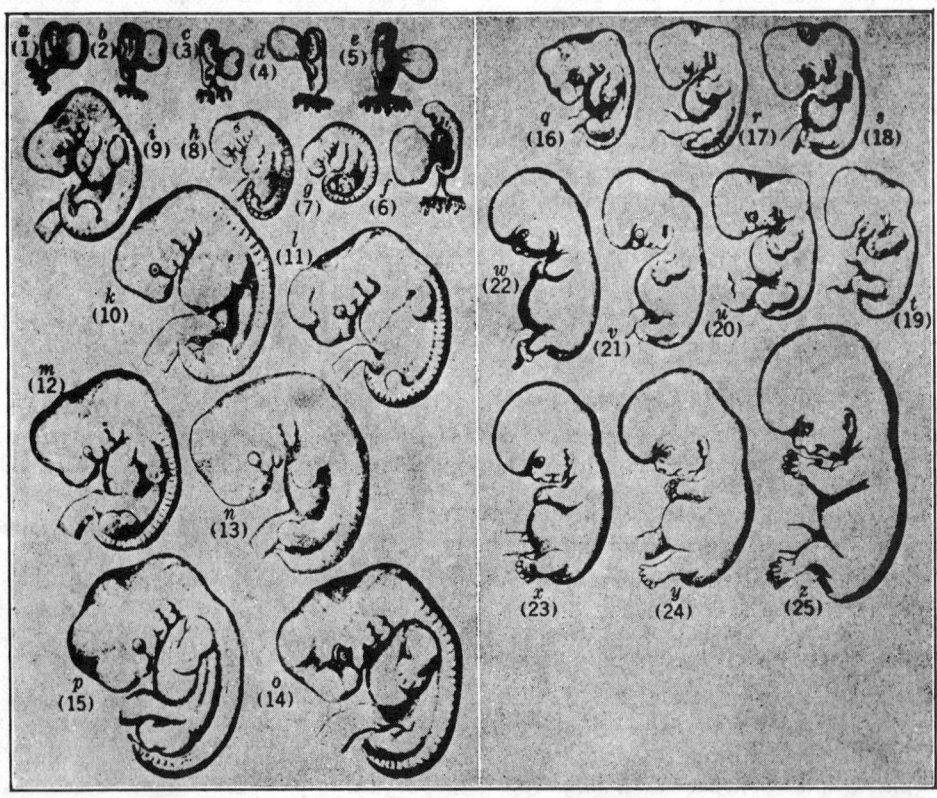

Fig. 14. The human embryo of His[1]*Normentafel* as given by Keibel and Elze. The letters designating each fetus, its size in millimeters, and its estimated age in days are: *a*, 2.1, 12–15; *b*, 2.12, 12–15; *c*, 2.15, 12–15; *d*, 2.2, 12–15; *e*, 2.6, 18–21; *f*, 4.2, 18–21; *g*, 4.0, 23; *h*, 5.5, 24–25; *i*, 7.5, 27–30; *k*, 10.0, 27–30; *l*, 9.1, 27–30; *m*, 9.1, 27–30; *n*, 10.5, 31–34; *o*, 11.0, 31–34; *p*, 11.5, 31–34; *q*, 12.5, 31–34; *r*, 13.7, 31–34; *s*, 13.8, about 35; *t*, 13.6, about 35; *u*, 14.5, about 37–38; *v*, 15.5, about 39–40; *m*, 16.0, about 42–45; *x*, 17.5, 47–51; *y*, 18.5, 52–54; *z*, 23.00, 60. (From Keibel and Elze, 1908.)

to represent the changing continuum of behavior. (See Goldstein, 1904, for an important early approach to this subject.) Figure 14, taken from Keibel and Elze (1908), shows a selected series of human embryos and fetuses 2.1 to 23 mm in length. The length of each specimen is given in the legend below the figure.

Many efforts have been made to compile a table from which the ages of fetal human organisms can be estimated on the basis of known physical measurements. Scammon (1927), indeed, estimated that there were 7500 titles on the growth and physical development of the fetus, infant, and child. The construction of satisfactory norms of growth in prenatal life has proved to be a very hard scientific task because of the difficulties that must be overcome in evaluating the material to be measured. In the first place, even if organisms of truly known age were plentifully available, each age norm would necessarily be stated in terms of some statistical average, because of the many factors such as genetic stock, nourishment, and specific pathology which influence fetal size. For a consideration of some of these factors in infrahuman mammals, see the work of Bluhm (1929).

A greater stumbling block than this variability of size at any true age, however, is found in the fact that it is peculiarly difficult in the human individual to place correctly the starting point of development, even though, in the light of the discussion given at the beginning of this chapter, such point be taken as the moment of fusion of the nuclei of the two parent cells. As a matter of fact, this moment can never be absolutely accurately determined, and therefore many different ways of approximating the zero point of development have been used in the history of human embryology. Even now no complete agreement has been reached as to the most desirable procedure in arriving at this calculation. Of these methods the following are probably most important:

1. *Menstruation age.* In this scale the age of the fetus is calculated from the first day of the last period of menstruation prior to the onset of pregnancy (Mall, 1918).

2. *Mean menstruation age.* This age is similar to the above, except that it is based on the average calculated from many cases. Thus if 51 days is taken as a mean, there is a possible deviation from 40 to 62 days, so far as the relationship to morphological measurement is concerned (Mall, 1918).

3. *Conception age.* The age of the fetus is calculated from the last day of the last menstrual period prior to pregnancy. This is the age used by His and adopted by Minot (1892).

4. *Copulation, or insemination, age.* This age, based upon calculation and upon trustworthy cases of known copulation time, is found to be approximately 10 days shorter than the mean menstrual age defined above (Mall, 1918).

5. *Ovulation age.* This age is calculated from the time of ovulation. It is at present extremely difficult to determine directly the time of ovulation. Determinations are complicated by many factors, such as the observation that it is difficult to know how long spermatozoa may live after entering the female genital tract, and by many other considerations. A complete and critical study of the time of ovulation and the fertile period of the menstrual cycle is given by Hartman (1936) in a book devoted to a consideration of recent data and theories in this field.

6. *Fertilization, or true, age.* This age cannot at present be directly determined, but must be calculated from 1, 2, or 4 above. In general it may be said that the present evidence points to the fact that fertilization occurs in less than 48 hours after copulation (Mall, 1918).

A standard table of age-length equivalents during the prenatal period of development is still further complicated by the fact that the linear measurements of the specimens have been obtained by different methods. The measurements commonly used include the crown-rump length and crown-heel length or standing height. The second of these is really related to the first, that is, it is crown-rump length added to the rump-heel length (Minot, 1903). Besides these two usual measurements, there is the *Näckenlange* of His, that is, the length measured from a particular point in the caudal bend to a particular point in the neck band of the specimen (His, 1880, 1882, 1885).

Of these measurements the crown-rump

measurement is possibly best for embryological purposes (Minot, 1903), but in most of the work on the development of behavior the crown-heel length has been employed (Minkowski, 1923, 1928a; cf. also Scammon and Calkins, 1929).

In a subject so full of possible divergences of opinion, therefore, it is little wonder that many apparently conflicting tables of age-length relationships have been produced. Among the tables frequently referred to are those of C. M. Jackson (1909), Preyer (and the other embryologists summarized by him) given in Minot (1892), and the summarizing table from Keith (1913). Instead of giving all these tables and many others to which reference might be made, or of attempting any averaging of the results, it has seemed wise to present Mall's (1910) table, which seems to the writer to be based on excellent evidence. This table, based on Mall's own work and upon the collection of material by Issmer, is given as Table 1. Mall (1918) has reviewed his work subsequent to the publication of this table and finds the table still accurate. It should be noted, however, that particularly so far as the younger stages are concerned there is a possibility of great variability in judging age from such a table as that given. Weight is probably a better index but is seldom given (Minot, 1892). Therefore, in all age determinations given in this chapter, it should be borne in mind that the word "approximate" should really be placed in front of almost any statement of fetal age. Streeter (1920) has prepared a series of growth curves of the human fetus based upon most carefully computed data. In his tables and graphs the relationships of weight, sitting height, head size, foot length, and menstrual age of the human embryo are presented. Hooker (1944) has suggested that length and weight provide a more useful index of behavioral development than does age (Gesell, 1928).

Estimation of gestational age from weight of a fetus is subject to uncertainty. Sex, race, genetic background, nutrition and other factors are important in determining weight. Recent work suggests deriving equations which contain a parameter for estimating the weight of the fetuses at various gestational ages. This equation may be fruitful in comparing weight of fetuses from different popu-

Table 1. Abbreviated Data from Mall to Show Relationship between Various Age Determinations of the Fetus and *CH* (Crown-Heel) and *CR* (Crown-Rump) Measurements of Height in Millimeters

Prob-able Age in Weeks	Prob-able Age in Days	Mean Men-strual Age	Mean Length of Embryo (*CH*)	Mean Length of Embryo (*CR*)
1	7			
2	14			
3	21	31	.5	.5
4	28	37	2.5	2.5
5	35	43	5.5	5.5
6	42	51	11	11
7	49	59	19	17
8	56	65	30	25
9	63	72	41	32
10	70	79	57	43
11	77	86	76	53
12	84	94	98	68
13	91	100	117	81
14	98	108	145	100
15	105	114	161	111
16	112	121	180	121
17	119	128	198	134
18	126	136	215	145
19	133	143	233	157
20	140	150	250	167
21	147	157	268	180
22	154	165	286	192
23	161	171	302	202
24	168	177	315	210
25	175	185	331	220
26	182	192	345	230
27	189	199	358	237
28	196	205	371	245
29	203	212	384	252
30	210	219	400	265
31	217	228	415	276
32	224	234	425	284
33	231	241	436	293
34	238	248	448	301
35	245	256	460	310
36	252	262	470	316
37	259	271	484	325
38	266	276	494	332
38½	270	280	500	336

From Keibel and Mall (1910).

lations (Spencer and Coulombe, 1964).

The study of the embryology of the brain both in terms of its gross structure and its histology is important in understanding the physical basis of behavior growth. The present state of this subject is well reviewed by Robinson and Tizard (1966). They point

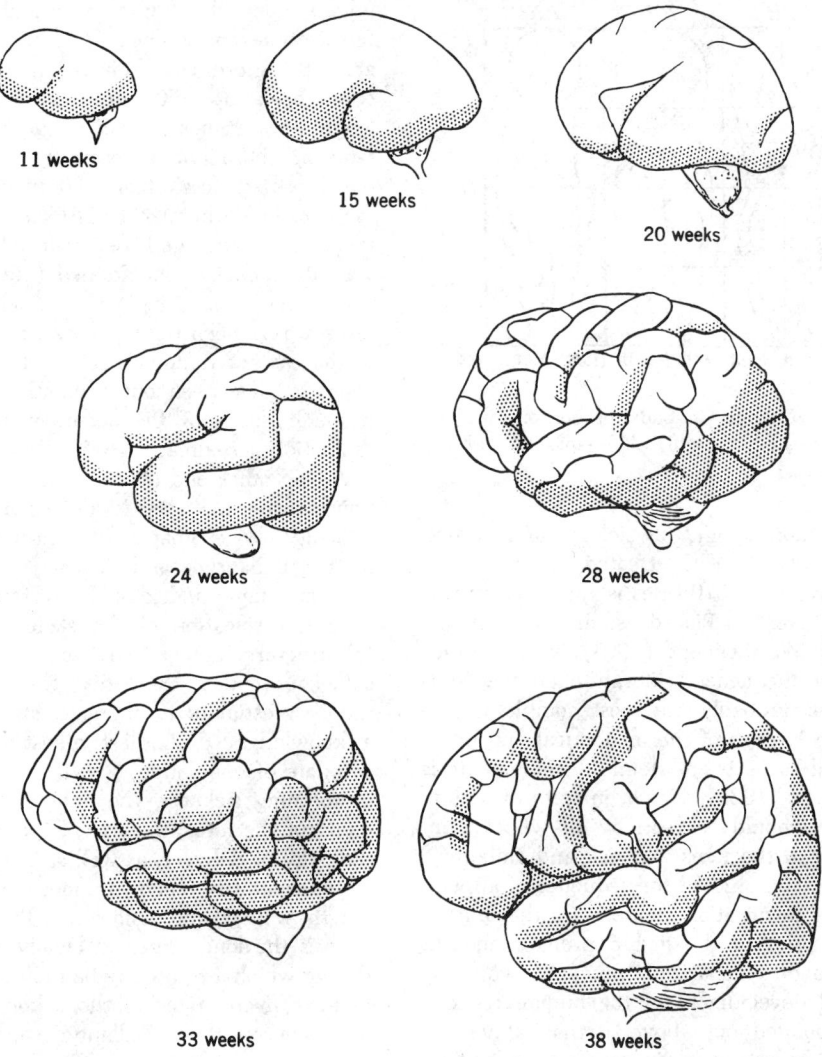

11 weeks

15 weeks

20 weeks

24 weeks

28 weeks

33 weeks

38 weeks

Fig. 15. The external appearance of the brain of babies born at different gestational ages. After Larroche, 1962.)

out that the brain of a full-term infant is ¼ the weight of the adult human brain. This can be compared with a proportion of about ⅟₂₀ for other organs. It is also important to note that all neurons are present at 7½ months from conception. The later fourfold growth of the brain is mainly due to the deposit of myelin and the elaboration of dendritic processes and vascular tissue. Figure 15 shows the external appearance of the human brain at various fetal ages. The difficulty of predicting behavior from a study of the brain alone has been emphasized by many writers (Carmichael, 1940a). See also

Borkowski and Bernstine (1955) for the electroencephalogy of the fetus.

Arising immediately out of the relationship between growth and age of the fetus is a whole series of studies on the morphological development of the fetus, which of course cannot be reviewed in this chapter. Figure 16 shows graphically the significance of such knowledge for one who thinks of the fetus as a "smaller infant." The literature on general fetal development has several times been summarized, the early work having been brought together in an excellent summary by Pinard (1877). In this summary the work

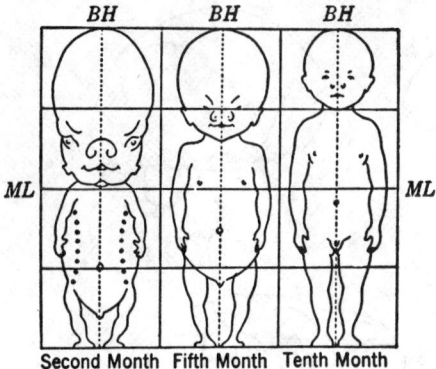

Fig. 16.   Changes in body proportions in fetal
life. *BH*—body height; *ML*—midline. (From
Hess, 1922.)

on the morphology, physiology, and pathology of the fetus is treated separately. A bibliography of 870 titles is appended to this treatise. Next to Pinard's summary in importance is Wertheimer's (1904), which brings together the general literature on the fetus to 1904. Probably the most complete summary in English of the anatomical and physiological aspects of fetal development is Feldman's (1920), which, in spite of certain lacunae, should be read by all who are interested in the fetus. Noback and Robertson (1951) have studied the sequence of appearance of ossification centers in the human skeleton during the first 5 prenatal months and have summarized previous work on skeletal development of the human fetus.

As pointed out above, it may almost be said to be necessary, in order to understand the development of behavior, to have some reference line in terms of measurements of anatomical development. It has become a convention by following such a temporal line to divide the prenatal life of the human being into three periods (Feldman, 1920; Williams, 1931). The first period of 1 or sometimes 2 weeks is spoken of as the *germinal* period. From the third to fifth or sixth week is the *embryonic* period. From the sixth week to birth is the *fetal* period. The normal term of pregnancy is usually placed at 280 days (Williams, 1931), although estimates varying between 270 and 284 days have been given by various investigators and summarized by Needham (1931). It must be obvious, however, that such figures are mean-

ingless unless the method of calculating true fertilization time is given. The normal length at birth is ordinarily given as 500 mm in crown-heel, or 320 mm in crown-rump, length. Sometimes, however, premature infants are born and successfully reared who have passed less than 180 days in the mother's body; but 180 or 181 days is usually taken as the average lower limit below which viability cannot be maintained (Hess, 1922). Claims have been made that much younger fetuses have been raised, but as, for example, in the case of Rodman's fetus which was alleged to have been but 4 months old, there is much doubt of the accuracy of the age estimation (Rodman, 1815; Baker, 1825).

At the other end of the scale the terminal point of postmaturity is also open to great difficulty of estimate. In considering this matter, Ballantyne and Browne (1922) hold that no single index such as fetal length, weight, ossification of the skeleton, placental structure, or cord structural condition is sufficient to date the fetus. They state that the best estimate is obtained by combining a knowledge of the last menstrual period, the date of copulation, the date of the onset of morning sickness, the date of the quickening of the fetus, the size of the uterus, the difficulty of delivery, as well as the evidences of postmaturity such as measurements of length, weight, and ossification. Probably 334 days is the longest period legally considered during which a fetus may be thought possibly to have lived in the mother's body and still be delivered alive (Ballantyne and Browne, 1922). Thus, from one point of view at any rate, the human fetal life span that will be dealt with in this chapter must be taken as lasting from fertilization until birth, a time which in the extremest possible cases may vary by as much as 154 days!

That mere age or anatomical development is not enough to determine developmental level is suggested by Arshavsky (1968), who says, "The physiologically immature neonate differs from the physiologically mature by neither length of the gestation period nor birth weight, but by physiological peculiarities suggested by retarded development."

In this chapter most of the references to fetal behavior are made to unborn fetuses. It should be kept in mind, however, that the study of correctly dated premature infants may throw light upon the later fetal period. In interpreting the sensory ability or response activity of a prematurely born infant, it is not safe to attribute the same abilities to the unborn fetus of the same age. As suggested in the first part of this chapter, the greatest errors in genetic science are made by suggesting that because environmental conditions of one sort produce behavior of a particular kind in one individual, therefore these same abilities must be "implicit" in an organism living under wholly dissimilar conditions. A normal fetus of the same age as a successfully air-breathing premature infant may act in a very different way from the comparison organism. This is true not only because of mechanical differences of bodily make-up, such as the presence or absence of liquid in the ear, but because of the gross differences brought about by the change from placental respiration to pulmonary respiration and from placental nourishment to alimentary canal nourishment. The sheer mechanical change from life in a liquid with the specific gravity of the amniotic fluid to life in air is most important. Similarly, the effectiveness of external stimulation is vastly changed in the transition from a relatively constant stimulus world before birth to a continually changing and varied set of physical energies after birth. An excellent brief summary of the development of the fetus week by week is given by Williams (1931). In the present chapter, save for the tables of fetal length and age, and save for the reproduction of the famous Keibel and Elze series of embryos and fetuses given above, no detailed consideration can be given to gross structural change which occurs during prenatal growth.

An interesting graphic representation of prenatal physical development is that in Fig. 17, reproduced from Scammon and Calkins and redrawn by Needham (1931), in which the age, height, or weight can, to the limits of accuracy of the original data, be read off

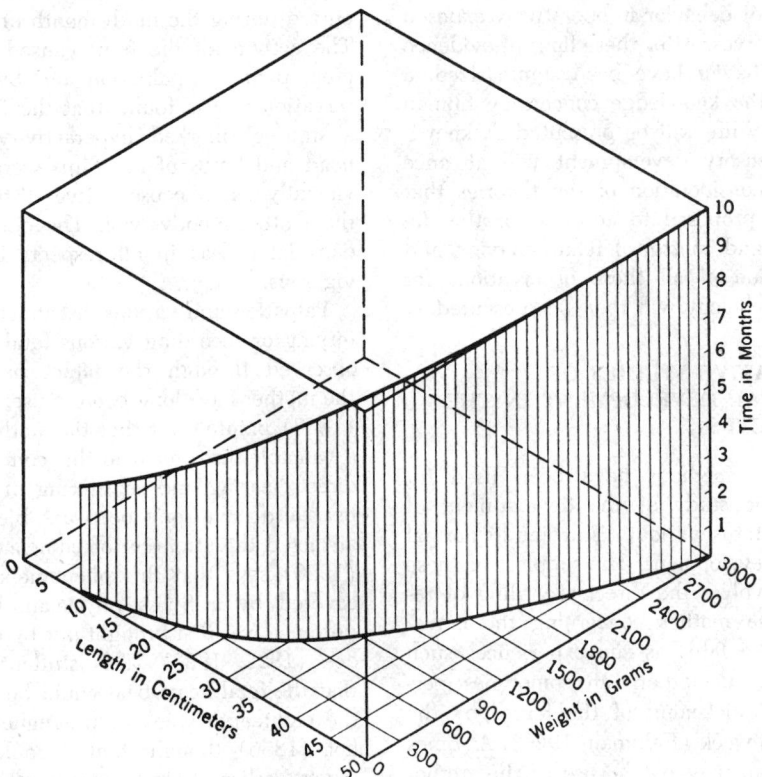

Fig. 17. Three-dimensional isometric projection from which height, weight, and age of human embryos may be read off if one is known. (From Scammon and Calkins, 1924.)

if any one of these measurements is known. (See also Streeter, 1920.)

In a paper entitled "Physical Fitness in Terms of Physique, Development and Basal Metabolism" Wetzel (1941) presents a critique of a new method of evaluating individual progress from birth to maturity which suggests that there are types of physique which influence all growth tables. A similar observation could undoubtedly be made of fetal life as well. In this connection a study of body build by Sheldon and his collaborators (Sheldon, Stevens, and Tucker, 1940) should be consulted. For a convenient graphic age conversion scale, see McCarthy (1936).

In the paragraphs below a review of the development of behavior in human fetal life without detailed reference to morphology is presented. In this presentation brief consideration will be given to clinical observations made on fetal movements without operation on the mother or the interruption of pregnancy. After this discussion, as accurate and complete a summary as possible will be given of the experimental studies on the development of behavior in operatively exposed human embryos. After these lines of evidence of fetal behavior have been summarized, a review of the knowledge concerning human fetal sensory life will be presented. A knowledge of sensory development will at once lead to a consideration of the theories that have been proposed to account for the development and control of fetal behavior, and an evaluation of all these observations for human psychology will then be presented.

NONOPERATIVE STUDIES OF BEHAVIORAL DEVELOPMENT IN THE HUMAN FETUS

Numerous methods have been used for the scientific study of the development of the human fetus without disturbing its normal course of development. The simplest of these methods involves the direct recording of reports of the mother concerning the movements of the fetus as she experiences such movements. A mother can sometimes perceive the "quickening of the fetus" by the seventeenth week (Feldman, 1920). At times the physician may by the use of the stethoscope hear fetal movements as early as the fourteenth week (Mailliot, 1856; Neu, 1915).

It is customary, however, to say that the first time at which such movements can be detected by the physician is in the fifteenth or sixteenth week (Feldman). Feldman points out that in fetuses of 8 weeks the umbilical cord shows regular spiral twists. Since such twists are not characteristic of animals that carry many young and therefore have little room for the fetus to turn in, it is assumed that the movements of the fetus even at such an early age determine the twisting of the cord. The writer, however, can see no reason why such twisting might not result from passive as well as from active movements.

In later periods of pregnancy, mothers give reports of movement involving part of the body. Sometimes the movements of the extremities or of the trunk alone are noted. Mermann (1887), for example, reports a case of rhythmic movement of the fetal back palpated through the mother's abdominal wall in a fetus of 7 months. Whitehead (1867) gives an extended report of a case of violent convulsion of the fetus while still in the uterus. This convulsive condition occurred during the ninth month of pregnancy. The activity of the fetus caused the mother great pain. By palpation and by direct observation it was found that the fetus was in a state of marked hyperactivity. Both the head and limbs of the fetus were moved so violently as to cause active disturbances of the mother's body wall. The child, born 21 days later, was in all respects healthy and vigorous.

Palpation and various instruments for magnifying or recording various fetal movements observed through the intact body wall of the mother have long been in use. MacKeever (1833) pointed out that the stethoscope was a valuable instrument in this connection. The direct hearing and registering of fetal heart beat also have long been a subject that has attracted the attention of clinicians. Feldman (1920) says that this phenomenon was discovered by a Swiss physician, but its importance was first brought out by de Kergaradee (1822, 1823). This student concluded that the fetal heart beat could be heard from the eighteenth week of pregnancy on. Mailliot (1856) thought that it could be heard much earlier. Later, among others, DeLee (1927, 1928) and Hyman (1930) made special studies of the fetal heartbeat, including such phenomena as irregularities in its rhythm.

In 1891 Pestalozza succeeded in taking a cardiograph of the second twin after the first twin had been born (Feldman, 1920). In this he was more successful than Hicks (1880), who by the use of an instrument like a cardiograph obtained certain records which were, however, so badly obscured by the rhythmic activities of the mother that they could scarcely be identified. Krumbhaar and Jenks are reported by Feldman (1920) as having obtained typical electrocardiographic tracings of the fetal heart. (See also Sachs, 1922.) Maekawa and Toyoshima (1930) have, by the use of amplifiers and a string galvanometer with electrodes placed on the front abdominal wall of the mother, secured excellent electrographic tracings of the fetal heart. After birth the beat of the same heart is also recorded for purposes of comparison.

Stimulated by this work, Carmichael in 1935 attempted, with equivocal results, to record normal fetal heart activity by high-gain amplification. More recently, Mann and Bernstein (1941) and Geiger, Monroe, and Goodyer (1941) have published in this field, and the physiological psychologist D. B. Lindsley (1942) has published a most interesting paper on the heart and brain potentials of human fetuses *in utero*. In this paper a reliable method of recording maternal and fetal electrocardiograms is given. What is even more interesting, however, is the fact that this investigator has also been able to record fetal electroencephalograms. In the latter case, during the seventh and eighth months of human pregnancy electrodes were at times placed on the maternal abdominal wall over the palpated head of the fetus. By suitable amplification and recording, fetal electroencephalograms were secured by this means. The records were typical of those from the precentral region of the brain in the newborn. In all work upon fetal or neonatal heart rate the effect of asphyxia must be considered (Barcroft, 1938). A fall in heart rate that is nonvagal has been demonstrated in fetal rabbits by tying off the umbilical cord (Bauer, 1938).

A number of recent studies have been made of the electroencephalograms of the fetus showing irregular slow waves with superimposed fast waves (Borkowski and Bernstine, 1955). Anoxia leads to high-amplitude–low-frequency activity which may end in complete absence of electrical activity (Huhmar and Jarvinen, 1963). The electroencephalograms of the fetus during birth is similar to that of the alert neonate (Rosen and Satran, 1965).

Recently, ultrasonic pulse echo techniques have been used in estimating fetal development. Studies show that it is possible within known limits of accuracy to estimate the weight of the fetus by this technique. Animal studies show that there are no toxic effects by the use of this method (Thompson, Holmes, Gottesfeld, and Taylor, 1965).

Among the other early movements of the fetus which are often directly recorded are the so-called *Ahfeld breathing movements,* or the rhythmic contractions of the fetal thorax felt through the mother's body. These movements should not be confused with uterine contractions occurring after the third month, sometimes called *Ahlfeld's sign,* which incidentally may have something to do with the onset of behavior, if an analogy with the amnion contraction of the chick noted above may be suggested (Kuo, 1932c). In spite of the difficulty of the ancients concerning fetal respiration that involves the intake of no air into the lungs, it has of course long been understood, as Leonardo da Vinci knew, that the fetus does not breathe water (Needham, 1931). The gaseous interchange of the mammalian fetus occurs in the placenta between the bloodstream of the mother and that of the fetus. The general significance of this process and its detailed consideration have been studied by many physiologists. The history of the early advance of knowledge on this matter is summarized by Starling (1900), and the generally accepted facts about the fetus are brought together by Sarwey (1915) and more recently by Barcroft and Mason (1938). (See also Bylicki, 1921.)

The liquid environment, of course, completely precludes true lung breathing, but at least since 1798 movements of the chest and thorax of the fetus similar to breathing movements have been occasionally noticed. Béclard (1815) observed such movements in various mammalian embryos without removing the amniotic sac through which they were observed. Ahlfeld (1890) has developed a view on the nature and significance of certain irregular but vaguely rhythmic movements of the fetus which seem to be caused by the contraction of the same muscles which will make respiration possible in postnatal life. (See also Kouwer, 1919, and Kellogg, 1930.) Ahlfeld has made graphic records of these movements, which in typical cases vary from 38 to 76 per minute. C. A. Smith (1946) has presented an admirable summary of the fetal aspects of respiration. He discusses the experimental literature in this field. The point is made that respiratory movements of the fetus of animals studied cannot be considered as automatic, constant, and progressive. His view is rather that here again, as in so many other aspects of fetal behavior, we see the setting off of a response pattern under certain conditions which otherwise, although acquired early, is normally held in abeyance for later use.

If these speculations are in any sense correct, therefore, the so-called first breath of the child may be considered to be just a change in the way in which the same neuromuscular mechanism determines the oxygenation of the blood (Walz, 1922). For an excellent popular statement concerning the onset of breathing, see Henderson (1937).

Barcroft and Karvonen (1948) have studied the effects of carbon dioxide and of cyanide on fetal respiratory movements. They conclude that cutaneous sensory stimulation rather than asphyxia is responsible for the commencement of air breathing.

A number of investigators have severely criticized the Ahlfeld concept of prenatal breathing movements. Walz (1922) attributed these objections to the fact that the initial statement of Ahlfeld's view was unfavorably received by the two leading obstetricians of Germany at the time, and that the weight of authority long kept this phenomenon from being correctly evaluated. It should be noted, however, that Huggett (1930), in an experimental study of fetal respiratory reflexes previously referred to, says: "The exact mechanism suggested by Ahlfeld is not in every sense confirmed."

A good many speculations have been made as to the causes involved in the first intake of air breath. As noted above, many students have held that the increase of metabolites, and especially of carbon dioxide tension in the blood, is one of the essential causes of the first gasp (Corey, 1931). Cohnstein and Zuntz (1884) observed that in a fetal lamb clamping of the umbilical cord led to the first intake of air. Carmichael has noticed this same result in fetal cats, rats, and guinea pigs. Indeed, the procedure of clamping the umbilical cord to study the effect of the blood stimulus on general bodily movements has been part of the experimental technique of several investigators and notably so of Swenson (1926) in his study of the fetal rat. Angulo y González (1933b) reports that in fetuses of 19 postinsemination days in which tactile stimulation of the hindleg aroused no response there was immediate response after ligation of the umbilical cord. The general result of this procedure seems to be an increase in amount and vividness of activity for a time. Pflüger (1877), however, held that some external stimulus, such as cold air, was necessary besides blood change to bring about the first breathing act (cf. Huggett, 1930). Preyer (1885) also suggested a relationship between cutaneous stimulation of some sort and the onset of breathing. Corey (1931) holds that an increase in the metabolites of the blood stream and some external stimulus, such as drying of the skin, seem usually to be antecedent to the initial respiratory gasp. It is suggested by Fender, Neff, and Binger (1946) that *asphyxia neonatorum* may play some part in the development of certain cases of epilepsy in human beings. For a general consideration of this problem see Windle (1950).

Goodlin (1965) has studied the factors associated with breathing in fetal rabbits in an incubator. These studies seem to indicate that external stimuli are not alone responsible for the first breath. It is interesting that these studies show that the smaller fetuses of the litter have the best breathing record.

Snyder and Rosenfeld (1937) have made direct studies of the onest of respiratory movements. They have studied the fetuses of the cat, rabbit, guinea pig, and man. Rhythmic respiratory movements are initiated in all these types in the uterus. Oxygen and carbon dioxide affect fetal breathing movements; a certain level of carbon dioxide, for example, is essential to the maintenance of fetal respiration.

Windle, Monnier, and Steele (1938) and

Abel and Windle (1939) show that there are no respiratory movements in cat fetuses less than 13 mm in length. But in the middle third of the gestation period delicate and rapid rhythms of respiration may begin. Under certain conditions carbon dioxide breathed in by the mother starts such movements. There is no significant increase in blood volume at birth in the pulmonary system. There is a circulation in the lungs during the last part of pregnancy capable of caring for oxygenation when air breathing is established. For a more detailed consideration of the blood gases of the cat fetus, see Steele and Windle (1939), and for a consideration of the physiology and anatomy of the respiratory system in the fetus and newborn infant, see Windle (1941b). See also Potter and Bohlander (1941), Whitehead, Windle, and Becker (1942), and Zettleman (1946).

Besides "breathing movements" there are other movements of the fetus which are indirectly significant in behavior. The movements of the organs of the digestive tract as seen in fetal organisms have been studied by a number of investigators. Yanase (1907a, 1907b) has studied peristaltic intestinal movements in fetal guinea pigs, cats, rabbits, and men. As a result of these studies, he concludes that peristaltic movements may begin long before birth. The status of gastrointestinal activity *in utero* has also been studied, especially in the cat and guinea pig, by Becker, Windle, Barth, and Schulz (1940); Becker (1941); and Becker and Windle (1941). In man such movements are possible in the seventh week. So far as hunger contractions are concerned, Patterson (1914) has shown that hunger contractions are practically continuous in young dogs. As age advances these contractions decrease in magnitude. Carlson and Ginsburg (1915), working on fetal dogs and newborn children, have written: "The empty stomach at birth and in the prematurely born exhibits the typical periods of tonus and hunger contractions of the adult, the only difference between infant and adult being the greater frequency and relatively greater vigor of these periods in the young." For other aspects of the function of the stomach before birth, see Sutherland (1921).

Certainly, in view of the large amount of work on the "hunger drive" as a determiner

of activity, part of which is summarized by Warden (1931), the possibility that these stomach and intestinal contractions are stimuli to "random" and "spontaneous" skeletal muscle movement, and indeed to much of the behavior of the premature or full-term infant, cannot be neglected by one who would understand fetal behavior. Such behavior initiated by internal stimulation may well be considered merely the setting into action of inborn neural mechanisms. In this connection, see De Snoo (1937) and Sontag, (1941).

Excretion of urine by the human fetus is well established. Fetal urine is the source of part of the amnionic fluid (Potter, 1961).

The question has often been raised as to whether gross external fetal movements of the various sorts considered above have any part in the rearrangement of the fetus in the uterus in the normal position for delivery at birth. As so often happens when a phenomenon is difficult to explain, it has been alleged that the position of the fetus is governed by instinct (Dubois, 1833). Mechanical and physical explanations have been advanced by Paramore (1909), Barnum (1915), Griffith (1915), McIlroy and Leverkus (1924), and others. Possibly it may be said that no absolutely positive proof has been advanced to show that active fetal movements are essential in determining the normal position of the fetus at the time of delivery. Langreder (1949a; 1949b) has considered the posture of the fetus in relation to fetal reflexes and position at birth.

It seems increasingly clear that fetal attitude or posture, however, is a result of fetal movements in the late fetal period. The normal attitude of moderate flexion of the spine with limbs well flexed and close to the body may be changed by vigorous kicks of the legs or by the umbilical cord becoming wound around the neck and other anomalies (Barnett and Nairn, 1965).

In the study of the changes of fetal position before birth, much has been learned by the use of the X-ray. Avery (1928) attempted to study the changes in position of guinea pigs by the use of roentgenograms. This work of Avery's was directly adapted from human clinical procedures used in the study of the fetus. The use of the X-ray in the study of the fetus has given a new clue to the determination of the fetal age by the study of the ossification of the fetal skeleton, although it is by no means an absolute clue. Hess (1918) has brought together much of the literature on this subject and suggests approximate norms of ossification at certain periods. (See also Mall, 1906, and Adair, 1918.) The study by Rudolph and Ivy (1933) on the rotation of the fetal head shows that uterine contractions and the movement of the fetus both contribute to this change in posture. Danforth and Ivy (1938) have shown that uterine activity is in part at any rate a function of calcium. Augmentation of uterine activity is brought about by increasing the calcium present; by decreasing the calcium the action is depressed. In this connection it is interesting to note that Good (1924) has shown that a patient may have the spinal cord completely severed and still give birth to a baby normally and painlessly.

A phenomenon of prenatal and immediately postnatal behavior which has long attracted attention is the first cry of the human organism. Kant (1799) found significance in the first sound uttered by the human infant. Preyer (1893), indeed, qoutes Kant as saying:

The outcry that is heard from a child scarcely born has not the tone of lamentation, but of indignation and of aroused wrath; not because anything gives him pain, but because something frets him; presumably because he wants to move, and feels his inability to do it as a fetter that deprives him of his freedom.

Both Preyer (1893) and Compayré (1896) have pointed out the futility of such verbal fancies. Such speculation, however, is not as yet entirely dead. An analytical psychiatrist who is quoted by Blanton (1917) has written of the cry of the human infant at birth: "It is an expression of its overwhelming sense of inferiority on thus suddenly being confronted by reality, without ever having had to deal with its problems." By operative technique Minkowski (1922) has found that crying occurs as early as the sixth month in the prematurely delivered fetus. In clinical practice many cases of *vagitus uterinus*, or fetal crying, have been reported. A typical case is that reported by M. Graham (1919), in which in a difficult delivery, the fetal sac having been ruptured by operative means to assist delivery, the crying of the still unborn fetus could be distinctly heard. Many such cases are reported, but they need not be reviewed here. (See also Feldman, 1920.)

All cases of fetal crying reported above seem to be the result of appropriately activated muscles, which bring about the expulsion of air in such a way as to cause it to vibrate. There seems to be no reason to assume that this phonation has any greater mechanistic significance than many of the other random acts of the child. It catches the notice of the observer, however, because from such behavior language develops in later life. This function is, of course, one of the most important aspects of adult human behavior, and an aspect which will in itself come to be, at least in the subvocal stage of "verbal thought," peculiarly important even in strictly introspective psychology.

Fetal hiccup has also been reported by a number of observers. These cases are summarized by DeLee (1928). See also a study by Norman (1942).

Recently an effort has been made to predict postnatal development from fetal activity. Thirty-five women recorded felt movements during the last three months of pregnancy. These babies after birth were tested on the Gessell Developmental Schedule at 12, 24, and 36 weeks. Total fetal activity correlated significantly with some Gessell scores. At 36 weeks, for example, all correlations between fetal activity and motor, language, and "total Gessell scores" were significant (Walters, 1965).

Two types of fetal crying have been reported. One is a soft whimper early in labor and the second is loud and gasping and related to fetal asphyxia (Blair, 1965).

This concludes the consideration of human fetal behavior of the sort that can for the most part be studied during the normal course of development. In the next pages the study of the development of human fetal behavior in fetuses removed from the uterus before the end of the normal term of gestation will be considered. The relationship of criteria of maturity at birth has been considered. (See Vincent and Hugon, (1962; and papers in Wynn, 1965.)

THE STUDY OF BEHAVIOR IN OPERATIVELY REMOVED HUMAN FETUSES

Most of the living human fetuses to which reference will be made in the next paragraphs were removed while still alive from the mother's body because some disease of the mother rendered the artificial termination of pregnancy medically necessary. Minkowski's technique (1928a) is typical. This investigator and a collaborator removed each fetus that was to be studied by a Caesarean section, usually performing the operation under a local anesthetic. The fetus, placenta, and amnion were removed. The fetus was then placed in a bath of physiological salt solution at normal blood temperature. This meant that such fetuses were cut off from their oxygen supply, and the movements which resulted must be thought of as the movements of increasingly asphyxiated organisms. This is important in the evaluation of the behavior reported, for, as we have pointed out, increased metabolites in the blood at first lead to hyperactivity and then to hypoactivity.

The behavioral development of the human fetus as determined in operatively removed cases will be considered here in one series. This has its disadvantages because in certain reports estimated age is given; in others only measurements are presented; but certainly for an understanding of development it is most important to give estimated age. The writer has attempted to make a summarizing table of human fetal development, but he does not feel that such a table gives a correct impression. One who wishes to see this material expressed as well as possible in tabular form should consult Coghill (1929c).

The development, then, of human fetal behavior as observed by various investigators in relation to estimated postinsemination age or menstrual age may be given as follows.

Fetuses Less than 9 Weeks Old

In very young human fetuses operatively removed from the mother, the first movement observed is of the beating heart. For several centuries there has been a scientific controversy as to whether the heartbeat is to be thought of as primarily determined by direct muscle or by neural stimulation. It now seems that the early embryonic heartbeat must be thought of as essentially an independent muscle contraction (Parker, 1919). Therefore, in most of the work on the development of behavior the beating of the heart is not considered to mark the onset of "true behavioral life." Pflüger (1877) has demonstrated the beginning of heartbeat in the fetus as being in the third week, that is, in a fetus of approximately 4 mm. (See also Strassmann, 1903.)

For a consideration of the mechanism of the initiation of contraction in different parts of the heart of a typical vertebrate, see Goss (1937, 1938, 1940) and Copenhaver (1939).

Williams (1931) gives an excellent summary of development in this early period. The germinal stage of the human being may be considered to be the first week or two of life. The third week is thought of as the onset of the true embryonic period. At this period the medullary groove begins to be formed. A little later cell structures which make up the primitive heart are laid down and, as just noted, these cells begin the lifelong beat of the heart. At about this time, also, cerebral and optic vesicles begin to be differentiated and limb buds first appear. The muscles also develop rapidly in fine structure during this period.

In the second month there is continued morphological growth both in total height and weight and in the fine structure of the organs of the growing individual. Windle and Fitzgerald (1937) in a paper on the development of the spinal reflex show that all the elements needed for a reflex arc in the central nervous system are laid down during the sixth week but no spinal arcs are complete before the eighth week. Bolaffio and Artom (1924) note in this period that isolated limbs torn during delivery can be stimulated directly.

Minkowski (1920b) reports that at the end of the second month cutaneous stimulation elicits response. This finding is not confirmed by Bolaffio and Artom (1924), for they point out that at this time the skin is very thin and may involve in its stimulation the activation of receptors in underlying tissues.

Much is known of the structural and minute functional development of the receptors, nervous system, and effectors in this as in all later embryonic and fetal stages. It is not, however, until the fetus reaches the length of 15 mm, or is about 4 weeks old, so far as the writer can discover, that any direct statement can be made in regard to the activity of any part of the response mechanism, and this is a negative statement. In a fetus of this length, Minkowski (1928b) reports that is was impossible to bring about muscular response even to an electric current of 40 milliamperes. He made observations on two fetuses of this length with the same conclusion.

This finding is not entirely unexpected, since Hewer (1927) has shown that histologically the musculature of the fetus develops at uneven rates, the unstriped musculature, which is the first to develop, being clearly formed in an embryo 1 mm in length. Striped musculature could not be detected in a fetus smaller than 2.5 mm long, and it did not take on its definitive characteristics in fetuses less than 22 weeks old. Special changes of structure are also noted by this same investigator in regard to heart musculature.

Possibly the youngest human fetus to be observed to move is one reported by Yanase (1907b) in his studies of the development of intestinal movement noted above. In a fetus 20 mm long and of an estimated age of 6 weeks, one movement involving the right arm is rather casually noted. The next youngest human fetus to be reported moving is a fetus 22 mm long and probably about 6 weeks old described by Strassmann (1903) in a case of extrauterine pregnancy. He observed through a rupture in the tube wall slow movements, backward and forward, of the arms and legs of the fetus. In evaluating this observation it should be noted that Strassmann's report is given in such a manner as possibly to lead to a questioning of his observations, since apparently the fetus was observed in such a way that rhythmic mechanical movement of the adult body was possible. Certainly all observers of fetal behavior have had difficulty in deciding whether or not they were seeing something which was not the result of passive external mechanical movement. It should be borne in mind, therefore, that possibly these two earliest observations should be substantiated before they are finally accepted. In a fetus of 30 mm, or an estimated age of 8 weeks, Minkowski (1923) observed a wormlike movement of the arms, legs, and trunk.

In Hooker's (1939b) description of his carefully controlled work the statement is made that no response to tactile stimulation has been observed before the eighth week of menstrual age. In a 25-mm fetus of a menstrual age of 8 to 8½ weeks, however, response to tactile stimulation has been recorded. This same investigator has repeated this observation on two other fetuses of approximately the same age. At this stage tactile stimulation is effective only in the area over the mouth and immediately adjacent to that supplied by the mandibular and maxillary divisions of the fifth nerve. Hogg (1941) points out that the cutaneous nerves and nerve endings are very immature when responses are first elicited. No encapsulated endings are seen. Excitation is probably dependent upon deformation of the growing tips of the fibers by displacement of the surrounding tissue at this time, according to this author. Stimulation in this area in a fetus of this age led to contraction of the long muscles of the body and neck to produce body flexion. Limb girdle muscles related to both upper extremities were also activated. Rotation of the rump, caused by activation of the pelvic girdle muscles, was observed in very slight degree. Hooker notes that at this period a hair capable of exerting a pressure greater than 25 mg may cause direct mechanical stimulation. Faradic stimulation at this time is also effective. No spontaneous movements were noted by Hooker at or before this age.

Fitzgerald and Windle (1942) report that in a study of 15 fetuses 7 weeks to a little over 8 weeks old, fetal movement was seen in only three organisms. These responses were individual reflexes of trunk, arms, or legs when oxygenated blood was still supplied to them. For an excellent summary of the early development of human behavior, see Hooker (1943).

Fetuses 9 Through 12 Weeks Old

In a fetus of 35 mm (estimated age 8 or 9 weeks) Minkowski (1928b) reports muscle contraction to galvanic current. Minkowski's work shows that fetuses of 40 to 50 mm (9 to 10 weeks) sometimes still show this characteristic muscle response, possibly without neural activation. The observation coincides with the observations noted above on the fetuses of lower mammals, in which the musculature comes to respond to direct stimulation before true neuromuscular action begins. The most elaborate studies of this sort of muscular response have been made by

Wintrebert (1904). (See also Minkowski, 1924.)

Among the many significant observations that may be made at this period, it is interesting to note that the vestibular apparatus seems to be anatomically developed to its full (Minkowski, 1922).

A fetus of 42 mm was removed under operation by Woyciechowski (1928) to interrupt a pathological pregnancy. At the operation a mass was removed from the uterus. As soon as the mass was taken out, a fetus of 42 mm dropped from the excised sphere of tissue. This fetus, estimated by the operator to be of approximately 2 months' gestation age, was seen to move both arms and legs spontaneously. When it was touched by a finger an energetic "protective movement" began which involved a much stronger moving of the arms and hands and the opening of the mouth. The observations made upon the movement of this fetus were checked by another observer. In spite of cooling, the movements of the fetus lasted in an active form for more than 5 minutes.

In fetuses of the 9- to 10-week age period, Minkowski (1921b, 1922) noticed slow, asymmetrical, arrhythmic, noncoordinated movements. He also noted (1922) that at this time neurologically the elements of the spinal reflex arc are developed anatomically.

Bolaffio and Artom (1924) studied a fetus of about this same age. They report that dropping the fetus from a height of a few centimeters to a table led to active contractions of the flexor muscles of the limbs. Further, they noted that tapping the table lightly with the fingers elicited responses of energetic movements involving the elevation of the scapulas, movement of the arms, and flexion of the thighs and legs. These movements were elicited for about 3 minutes, after which they rapidly diminished in intensity and ceased. During the active period, stimulation by a blunt metal rod of the skin of the breast and of the abdomen led to no response. After the cessation of activity, direct brain stimulation led to no muscle response.

In a fetus less than 8 weeks old, Minkowski (1922) reports that percussion of the patellar tendon resulted in contraction of the quadriceps muscle. After this contraction had taken place, irradiation followed to other muscles. In this fetus the heartbeat was rela-

tively constant at 80 beats per minute, but covering the fetus with normal salt solution at 40° C. led to an increase in the beat of the heart from a basal beat of 80 to 100 beats per minute. Extirpation of the cerebral hemispheres in this fetus did not change the reflexes described. Sectioning the medulla just above the cord region, however, abolished the reflexes due to change in the position of the body. In a fetus about 9½ weeks old Hooker (1944) notes that stretch of limb muscles is effective in stimulating proprioceptive organs and initiating response.

In a fetus about 2 months old, Bolaffio and Artom report that stroking and tapping elicited slow local contractions of all the muscles of the limbs. For example, if these stimuli were applied to the palm of the hand, adduction and internal rotation of the corresponding arm were noted; if to the leg, flexion of the corresponding thigh. These investigators state, moreover, that mechanical stimulation of the cortex in this fetus gave a constant movement of elevation of the left shoulder, but no contraction of either of the lower limbs or of the right shoulder. After this same fetus was decerebrated they note a greater vividness (*vivacitá*) of the local contractions referred to above and the reappearance of diffusion of movement at a distance from the stimuli which had ceased. In this experiment mechanical stimulation of the medulla led to respiratory movements. They further suggest that even in a fetus of this age removal of the cerebral cortex does remove some inhibition from the lower reflexes. It is interesting to note that during this period the neural and muscular mechanisms basic to sucking are developed so that they may function. A study of the evolution of this mechanism throughout the rest of the fetal period is instructive. For suggestions, see Feldman (1920) and, for the later period, Irwin (1930).

Bolaffio and Artom report in regard to another fetus about 2 months of age that gentle stimulation of the skin of the whole body was followed by no response, but percussion led to definite responses. Definite percussion blows on the forearm sometimes led to flexion, adduction, and slight internal rotation of the arm. Percussion on any part of the lower limb led to flexion and adduction of the thighs with slight flexion of the legs. If the percussion is rather light, the contractions are limited to the homolateral limbs; if somewhat more energetic, contractions also of the heterolateral limbs are reported. Percussion on the breast and abdomen gave homolateral responses about the pectoral muscles and bilateral responses about the abdominal muscles. Hooker (1944) reports that in fetuses of about 8 weeks the reflexogenous zone of the cutaneous surface of the infant spreads from a very localized area, including part of the upper lip and the skin about the nostrils, to the whole upper lip, chin, and part of the neck. The responses made at this time are stereotyped and mechanical in nature. That the fetuses are ready for such responses is shown by Windle and Fitzgerald (1937). These workers demonstrate that the elements of the reflex arc are laid down by the sixth week. Spinal cord arcs do not seem to be complete before the eighth week. It should be emphasized that Hooker (1944) says in commenting on this stage that "each stimulation in the reflexogenous area evokes a response which, within the limits of ordinary biological variation, is identical with every other one secured."

It is generally thought that even during the third month the cerebral cortex has as yet assumed no functions in relation to the general bodily activity. Bolaffio and Artom, however, report that removal of the cortex in a fetus of this age seems to remove inhibition from the reflexes of the lower limbs. This result is difficult for the writer to interpret. During this period sucking is theoretically possible; that is, the neuromuscular mechanisms necessary to bring about this response have probably already been determined. The reader who wishes a complete consideration of this earliest feeding reaction of the human individual should read the specific references given above to this reaction and then should refer to the summary of the knowledge of the reaction given by Feldman (1920). (See also Irwin, 1930.)

Arshavsky (1959) has pointed out that the function of the digestive system at various developmental stages are appropriate to the nutritive medium typically available at each age. He notes that the amnionic fluid enters the mouth and stomach in the fetal period. This fetal feeding reaction is considered as a necessary precursor to the taking of milk in early postnatal life.

After superficial and deep stimulation of numerous points on the body of a decerebrate fetus of 90 mm, Bolaffio and Artom at first recorded very vivid contractions of apparently all muscles. After about 3 minutes, however, the contractions were still bilateral, but limited now to segments and homologous regions of the body. As time passed, the contractions became more and more circumscribed, and after about 3 minutes they were limited to the muscles corresponding to the stimulated point. After 15 minutes every reaction had ceased.

During the third month Minkowski (1922; 1928a) reports labyrinthine reflexes, but Bolaffio and Artom (1924), obtaining the same responses that Minkowski reports, interpret them rather as responses elicited as the result of the stimulation of proprioceptors in the neck. Minkowski (1922) reports tendon reflexes at this age, but Bolaffio and Artom do not find them until the sixth month. Here once more the decision must be a very difficult one to make, if the writer may judge from his own observations on infrahuman fetuses. Stimulation at the locus of a tendon may lead to a response, but this may be due to several possible forms of stimuli, such as (1) cutaneous stimulation, (2) direct muscle stimulation, or (3) a true tendon-stretch muscle stimulation. Mere observation of the response makes very difficult the decision as to which of these forms of stimulation has been effective. Bolaffio and Artom's careful work, however, seems to indicate that at first muscle sensitivity dominates when the tendons are stimulated, but in later fetuses true tendon reflexes begin gradually to arise.

Golubeva, Shuleikina, and Vainshtein (1959) have studied the neural basis of the development of motor activity from 16½ to 29 weeks of gestation. Every reaction studied such as grasping, sucking, sneezing show two phases in development. The first is a response directly related to the maturation of local and specific morphological structures. The second phase is that of an adaptive action and is due to the maturation of appropriate brain centers.

Hooker (1939a), in summarizing development during this period, says that by 9½ weeks of menstrual age responses include rotation of rump and body flexion. The neck-trunk reactions are usually contralateral. At this period "spontaneous" human responses were first observed. This same investigator notes that from 9½ to 12 weeks a "total pattern" of response is dominant. At 11 weeks palmar stimulation causes a quick but incomplete finger closure, which marks the onset of the grasping reflex. Hooker (1938) studied the development of this reflex in great detail. He (1939a) further noted the onset of the plantar reflex during this period. Hooker (1944) also noted that by 11 weeks stimulable cutaneous reflexogenous zones have spread over the whole upper extremity, and the sole of the foot has also become stimulable. Patterned eye movements seem to begin at this time.

Fetuses 13 through 16 Weeks Old

By 13 weeks the top and back of the head alone remain insensitive (Hooker, 1944). Minkowski (1922), studying a fetus in the early part of this period (110 mm), recorded the fact that touching the lower lip or tongue with a blunt probe led to a closing of the mouth, brought about through the lowering and lifting of the jaw. He also noticed in the same fetus that reflexes of the trunk and extremities were seen prominently, but after the transection of the cord in the dorsal region the lower reflexes were discontinued at once. This seemed to prove that conduction of activation in this case, at any rate, was through the cord. After this operation, moreover, he noticed that the short reflexes remained unchanged but were themselves abolished after total extirpation of the cord. Destruction of the lumbar and sacral cord abolished the hindlimb reflexes, whereas similar destruction of the cervical cord abolished those of the forelimbs.

The so-called spontaneous movements observed by Hooker at 14 weeks include the activity of most body parts as well as of the "organism as a whole." For the first time these movements, like those at about the same period elicited by tactual stimulation, may be characterized as "graceful" and delicate." Hooker (1944) points out that by this period, except for movements of respiration and vocalization and the true grasping reflex, the fetus already shows most of the responses that can be elicited in the neonate.

In a fetus of 135 mm Minkowski (1922) notes that a touch on the skin, using a blunt stimulus, led to reactions of diverse parts of the body. Characteristic of such stimulation were the flexion of both arms, the repeated opening and closing of the mouth, and simultaneous retraction of the head. He notes that at this stage of fetal development every part of the skin can act as a reflexogenous zone for various reactions. These reactions, however, tend to spread more or less over the entire fetal organism. Direct muscle excitability still remained at this stage 1 hour after the cord had been extirpated. Total removal of the cerebral cortex did not change the observable responses noted above. Transection at the midbrain, however, seemed to weaken the responses, although they still continued.

In a fetus 160 mm long Minkowski (1922) reports spontaneous dorsal flexion of the great toe, although he could secure no direct response to the touch of the sole of the foot. Distinct contractions of the abdominal walls were evoked in this fetus by brushing. Touching the closed eyelid in this fetus evoked a contraction of the orbicularis muscle.

Erbkam (1837) reports a study of a fetus, accidentally delivered, approximately 170 mm long. He noted the contraction of both arms and legs and the movement of the head from side to side, "as if to breathe." In this fetus the heart beat for 10 minutes. After that time the water in which the fetus was lying became cool and the heartbeat became slower. When more warm water was poured in, however, the heartbeat became lively. The eyes of this fetus were closed. The great physiologist Johnnes Müller saw the fetus and agreed with the author that it was of approximately 4 months' fetal age.

In a fetus of 180 mm Minkowski (1923) noted spontaneous movements of all the extremities and the head. These were noted before the umbilical cord was ligated. In this fetus, touching the sole just at the time of delivery led to the dorsal extension of the big toe, the Babinski reflex. Later the plantar flexion followed (1923; 1928a).

In a fetus 190 mm long Minkowski (1924) obtained definite indication of reciprocal muscle innervation. He also reports at this stage that diagonal reflexes were established; that is, stimulating one foot of the fetus would lead to the movement of the arm on the opposite side. In certain instances the stimulation of the sole of the foot on one side even led to the movement of one finger, the little finger, on the hand of the opposite side of the body. These diagonal reflexes are considered by Minkowski (1922) as significant in relation to the trotting reflex.

This elaborately patterned series of movements, as has been noted, is an especially basic constellation of inborn responses in mammalian and also in submammalian vertebrates.

During this period the sole of the foot reflexes are thought by Minkowski (1928a) to have their connection in the spinal cord and the tegmentum. In terms of response this involves the domination of the response of extension over flexion. (See also Dewey, 1935.) For a photographic sequence of the foot reflexes of a 14-week fetus, see Fig. 18, from Hooker (1939b). Liesch (1946) has described the stimulation of mucous membrane areas and other cutaneous areas in a fetus 200 mm in length and of an estimated age of 4 months.

Fetuses from 17 Weeks to Normal Birth Time

In experiments previously referred to, Barcroft (1938) has shown that after about one-third of the normal fetal period has passed in the sheep a remarkable change takes place. At this point the organism, which has already developed most of the basic patterns of behavior, becomes more quiescent. Spontaneous movements decrease. This is due to the fact that at this time a less adequate supply of oxygen is provided for the fetal central nervous system. At about the sixteenth week Hooker (1944) notes that a similar sluggishness begins in the human fetus. This again gives emphasis to the fact that in the study of the fetus positive evidence that such and such a response can be elicited is much more important than a negative finding when one is seeking for the neurological correlates of behavior.

In several fetuses approximately 200 mm long, that is, about 17 weeks old, Minkowski found that brushing the sole of the foot led to plantar flexion of the toes, except the big toe, which did not move. This was directly related to Minkowski's elaborate study of the reflexes of the sole of the foot. (See 1922;

1923; 1928a.) Direct mechanical stimulation of the motor roots of the spinal nerve at this stage showed that intersegmental spinal conduction is well established (1922). Mechanical stimulation of the cranial nerves at the level of the medulla led to the opening and closing of the mouth. It is presumed by Minkowski that this reaction resulted from the direct stimulation of the facial nerve. At this period direct stimulation of the cortex does not lead to response (Bolaffio and Artom, 1924), but breathing changes do result from stimulation of the medulla.

In a fetus of 210 mm Minkowski (1922) observed opening and closing of the mouth accompanied by arm movements. The duration of such movements at this period was limited. Maximum responsiveness seldom lasted more than 1 minute at the most. In a fetus of 230 mm Minkowski noted for the first time continued rhythmic contractions of the sort often described as Ahlfeld's breathing movements.

In a fetus of this same length Bolaffio and Artom (1924) noted that by employing superficial stimulation they were able to elicit localized muscular contractions in the limbs and other specialized muscle groups. By using strong and deep stimulation on a single segment of one limb, it is possible to elicit flexion of the whole contralateral limb. They also noted that stroking the ridge of the tibia gave vivid adduction of the homolateral thigh. In regard to the development of cortical dominance at this time it is interesting to note that mechanical stimulation of the Rolandic zone of the brain, either through the cranial cap or after its removal, did not call forth any reaction. Nevertheless, removal of the hemispheres did lead to more vivid local responses than in preceding excitations when the brain was intact. Stroking the pectoral muscles called forth adduction of the contralateral limb. In this case also these investigators reported that, if the intensity of the stimuli was increased somewhat, they got contraction of the whole corresponding limb. By stimulating the medulla they were able to call forth violent respiratory movements with active participation of the cervical, thoracic, and abdominal muscles, and those of the diaphragm. These movements were so violent they also led to elevation of the shoulder and adduction of

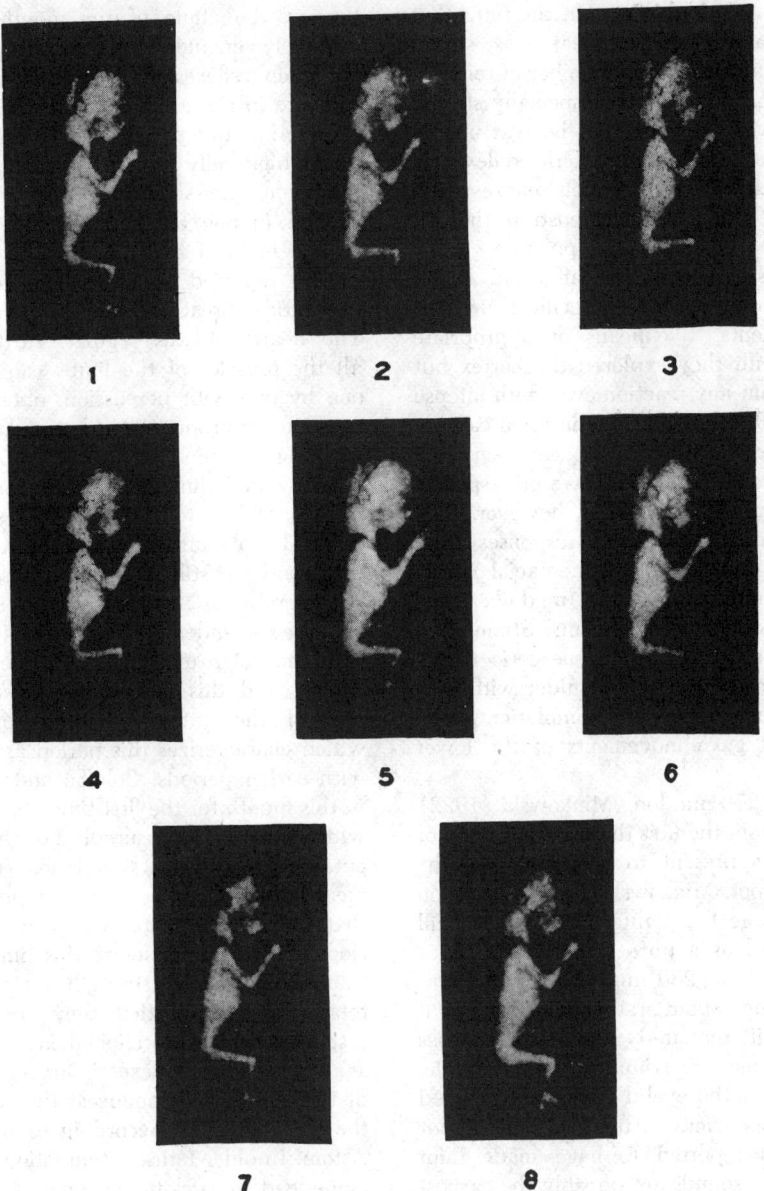

Fig. 18. Response to tactile stimulation of the sole. Probable menstrual age 14 weeks. Stimulation was applied by stroking the sole of the right foot with a 2-gram hair (1). The response consisted of the following elements; (a) Extreme dorsiflexion of the hallux (2 to 4) and "fanning" of the other toes (3 to 6). The toes, other than the hallux, ultimately show slight plantar flexion (6 and 7). (b) Flexion at the hip (2 to 4), slight flexion at the knee (3 to 5), and slight dorsiflexion of the foot (2 to 4). (c) Return to normal posture (5 to 8). (From Hooker, 1939.)

the arms. It is further significant to realize that these investigators found, after repeated successive experiments and as the vitality of the fetus became less, that the muscular contractions disappeared first in the lower limbs and then later in the upper limbs.

In a fetus of 240 mm Krabbe (1912) reported slow movement of the limbs and contraction of the muscles as the result of percussion. He also obtained strong abdominal reflexes as the result of light blows. The plantar reflex occurred without involving the participation of the big toe. In the fetus that he investigated the heartbeat was strong and he was able to elicit a number of reflexes, the abdominal reflex being especially strong. The fetus was a female, but he was unable to elicit the female cremasteric reflex. He felt that both bone and tendon reflexes were present and was able to demonstrate that direct muscle stimulation was possible.

In a fetus of 260 mm Bolaffio and Artom (1924) attempted certain specific neurological experiments. By means of appropriate electric stimuli they explored the cortex but did not obtain any reaction even with intense stimulation. By operation the internal capsule and peduncles of the brain were exposed, but still electric stimulation gave no response. When they reached the pons, however, they got ready and synchronous responses from the muscles innervated by the facial nerve. Finally, stimulation of the medulla gave energetic respiratory movements. Stimulation of the cervical cord led to energetic movements of elevation of the shoulder with flexion of the upper limbs, and stimulation of the lumbar cord gave movements of the lower limbs.

In a fetus 270 mm long Minkowski (1922) noted that from the first the plantar flexion of the toes was present to stimulation of the sole of the foot. Minkowski is of the opinion that at this age the plantar flexion must still be considered as a pure spinal reflex.

In a fetus of 280 mm Minkowski was able to bring about rather elaborate but quite well-differentiated muscular responses to a single electric stimulus. For example, the muscles of the eyelid could be activated with great specificity. After exposure in air this fetus is reported to have made faint sounds. These sounds are possibly the earliest observed in a human organism. They may be taken by those who are interested in zero points as the onset of functional activity in the great mechanism which makes human speech possible.

In a fetus of the same length Bolaffio and Artom (1924) observed that every muscle reacted even to quite energetic stimulation, such as percussion, by local contraction. This specificity is more marked in the head region than in the leg region of the fetus. Percussion in front of the ear led to a movement of closing of the eye with eleva-

tion of the angle of the mouth and chin. Strangely enough, however, it seems that the deep reflexes are not easily obtained at this age in the arms. Stimulation of the legs shows that the patellar reflex can be called forth bilaterally and the Achilles tendon reflex on one side. No plantar reflex was elicited in one fetus at this age.

In a fetus of 310 mm Bolaffio and Artom further reported the observation of periodic respiration. Breathing was "by fits and starts." The heartbeat was regular. At this period all the muscles of the limbs can be excited one by one with percussion, obtaining vivid reaction. Appropriate local stimulation serves to bring out most of the typical percussion reflexes, including minor responses of the fingers, of the toes, and of the sole of the foot. The plantar reflex, however, and some of the others, still seem to be absent.

Generally in the sixth month there is an increased tendency of various receptor-neuromuscular mechanisms to act independently, and this independent contraction is part of the greater vividness of response which characterizes this period as contrasted with earlier periods. Bolaffio and Artom find in this month for the first time tendon reflexes which seem to be assuredly not the result of cutaneous or muscle stimulation. Their judgment on this matter is based on the facts that the specific responses given at this period are not found before this time but continue to increase in strength during the later fetal periods, and that they are the same responses which are elicited in early infancy as true tendon reflexes. Direct stimulation of the mouth and tongue at this age elicited the sucking reflex, according to Bolaffio and Artom. In older fetuses stimulation of the lips alone leads to sucking movements which may or may not be accompanied by the protrusion of the tongue. As noted, Minkowski found this reflex at an earlier period.

These same investigators, using a slightly larger fetus (330 mm), again reported superficial respiratory movements. These breathing reactions ceased after a minute or two. They reappeared when pressure and percussion of the thorax were used. In this fetus they noted also that with percussion the muscles gave powerful and localized contractions. The tendon reflexes which could be elicited included those of the biceps and triceps and the Achilles reflex. Direct stimulation of the cortex still brought no response. In this fetus it seems that no true cutaneous reflexes could be called forth either before or after the removal of the brain. In another fetus of exactly the same size these same investigators report that the fetus cried weakly and moved about spontaneously but with less strong movements than those characteristic of a fetus at term. When death seemed imminent in this fetus the top of the skull was removed and the cortex directly stimulated electrically. All the various zones of the cerebral cortex were stimulated with negative results. Stimulation of lower brain centers, however, led to specific results such as increased breathing rate, shoulder, arm, and finger movements.

Bolaffio and Artom also reported the behavior of a fetus of 340 mm which appeared to be slightly undernourished. This fetus made weak crying sounds and breathed weakly. After about 2 hours it stopped breathing. During the period before breathing stopped they elicited contractions by tapping one by one the muscles and groups of muscles of the body. In this specimen by stroking the sole of the foot the plantar flexion of the toes was brought out. All these reactions became more vivid just before the death of the fetus. This suggests a change in the higher brain centers as a result of a lack of oxygen.

Certain responses noted in the seventh month, although definite, nevertheless are seen to involve synergic muscle groups (Bolaffio and Artom, 1924). This finding must be taken into consideration in evaluating statements given in regard to the randomness of activity in the newborn child. It may well be that much of the apparent "mass activity" of the newborn child (Irwin and Weiss, 1930) is not truly diffuse response of the sort found in the early fetus, but rather the activation of groups of synergic muscles in the sense of the term as used by Sherrington and his associates (Creed, Denny-Brown, Eccles, Liddell, and Sherrington, 1932). Krabbe, Minkowski, and Bolaffio and Artom all report abdominal reflexes at this period. A number of other specific reflexes are also clearly brought out at this time. The knee jerk is definitely elicited. The plantar reflex, according to Minkowski, now probably involves not only the centers concerned during previous months but also part of the lenticular nucleus and the red nucleus. Bolaffio and Artom feel that at this period the plantar reflex in its typical form is much like that of adult life but that it is still much more variable than it will be at a later period. This leads them to be critical of statistical work on reflexes, such as that of De Angelis (1922). (Cf. also Cesana, 1911.) The corneal reflexes are seen in the seventh month. Direct stimulation of the cornea of the eye leads from this time on to an increasingly strong response. Decerebration in this month was found to lead to increased vividness of most reflexes, but also to a tendency to reflex spread.

In a still larger fetus Bolaffio and Artom reported that with slight percussion of all the muscles of the limbs they observed vivid responses not limited to single muscles. Such responses spread to synergic muscle groups. With percussion of the pectoral muscles they obtained adduction and internal rotation of the arm and flexion of the forearm. They obtained bilaterally the patellar reflex and an extension of the leg, sometimes associated with flexion of the thigh. Associated with this pattern of response was the dorsal flexion of the foot. The Achilles tendon reflexes, however, were not always obtained even in a fetus as old as this one. These investigators also failed to get abdominal reflexes in fetuses of this age. However, the slight excitation of the sole called forth a definite unified toe phenomenon, and then a more energetic stimulation called forth flexion of the toes. The sucking reflex was secured only by stimulating the tongue. They reported that the movement of grasping which they got by applying pressure to the palms of the hand was energetic. These same investigators reported that from the seventh month to birth they investigated 13 fetuses of 7 months, 3 of 8 months, and a large number of mature fetuses. In this study they have not considered protocols of any fetuses which, because of condition of nutrition or on account of the presence of disease, did not present normal situations. They assert that from the end of the sixth month the movements of the fetus became so powerful and complex as to render very difficult and sometimes impossible detailed and specific report of behavior.

During the last two months of pregnancy the muscular reflexes decreasingly tend to prevail over the tendon reflexes, according to Bolaffio and Artom. By the end of the ninth month the tendon reflexes are so well established that they prevail over special muscular reflexes. All the tendon reflexes are found to be present during this period of fetal life, with the exception of those of certain of the upper limbs which are elicited with difficulty because of the small size of the member. Contralateral adductor reflexes are sometimes called out in this period. Even in the fetuses nearest term, the cremasteric reflex was difficult to elicit (Bolaffio and Artom, 1924).

At any prenatal age, including this last period, however, it is noticed that very light stimulation of the hand gives variable and inconstant movements, whereas strong stimulation, possibly involving the muscle or other underlying tissue, leads uniformly to grasping (Bolaffio and Artom, 1924). Bolaffio and Artom, therefore, believe that the grasping reflex is not to be thought of as a purely cutaneous reflex in prenatal life. Minkowski (1928a) finds this reflex at an earlier period. Iris reflexes are present during the prenatal period (Bolaffio and Artom, 1924). The reaction of the iris, however, is slow, and very strong light is needed to call out the response. (See also Minkowski, 1928a.) It is difficult to say when the response would begin if stimuli as strong as direct sunlight could always be used. Bolaffio and Artom do not note the fact, but it seems obvious that, with such strong stimulation as they recommend, the danger of independent muscle effector action of the sort described by Parker (1919) must be guarded against.

There is some evidence that the cerebral cortex is directly stimulable at this period, although as yet the evidence is not conclusive (Bolaffio and Artom, 1924), as will be pointed out later in considering the possibility of fetal learning.

General Characteristics of Fetal Behavior

It is possible to add to this consideration of month-by-month fetal development some general statements that have been made by those who have been most directly concerned

in these investigations. Thus Minkowski holds that one may say that every part of the skin can, as its receptivity is progressively established, serve as a reflexogenous zone for quite variable reactions which tend to spread more or less over the whole fetal organism. In the whole developmental process the gradual acquisition of postural responses and muscle tone is peculiarly important. The development of these responses will be considered in the section in which the origin and development of the proprioceptive and static senses are discussed. Minkowski offers in part explanation of the spread of reflexes during the early periods the fact that the spinal cord tracts as well as the nerve trunks have no medullary sheaths before the fourth month of fetal life. Illustrations of Minkowski's anatomical work on the nervous system are given in several places (1921a; 1928a). There is a suggestion that from this time on there is an anatomical increase in specificity correlated with the differentiation of the nervous elements in ways possibly ivolving the nature of protoplasm, neurofibrils, medullary sheaths, synapses, long conduction paths, and other cell changes (Minkowski, 1922). These gradual alterations in the nervous system, it is suggested, lead progressively to the possibility of more and more circumscribed and definite response. Compared with the diffuse character of early fetal response, therefore, in the late fetus, Minkowski (1920a) feels that all the well-known special reflexes have more or less been established. The preceding discussion, however, has shown that the process of development of these reflexes is a complex one and that later in adult life injury to the nervous system may bring about reactions which were characteristic of a previous period, even of a fetal period (Minkowski, 1922). For the historical breaking of ground in this connection, see H. Jackson's essay (1884) on the evolution and dissolution of the nervous system. For a consideration of the psychological development of the fetus see Minkowski (1947–1948; 1962).

It must be impossible to read what has gone before in this chapter without realizing that there is a general relationship in sequence of development of behavioral capacities from fish to man. It must be noted, however, that there are peculiar dangers in generalizing from, for example, the amphibian development of behavior, or even the rodent or cat development of behavior, to the growth of adaptive actions in man. For example, it has been shown clearly that in fish, amphibians, and lower mammals the first responses involve a unilateral bending of the trunk. This stage may or may not exist in the human individual, but at any rate no observations have so far been made in which trunk movements unaccompanied by arm movements are observed in early fetuses.

The basic pattern for the development of locomotion and other "individuated" responses, as suggested by Coghill and his students, may be seen in a less typical form in human development than might be supposed, although Coghill (1929c) himself has called attention to the attractive possibilities of the analogy. Little evidence of rhythm in the limbs of the human fetus has been determined. It may well be, therefore, that locomotorlike movements of the limbs do not appear until very late in the human fetal period. Windle and Griffin (1931) have summarized this comparative evidence, and they suggest that the movements observed in the kitten fetuses with which they have worked possibly should not be compared directly to human fetal movements because of the differences between the two in the type of adult locomotion. In a similar way the locomotor mechanisms in fish and amphibians which require a high degree of trunk-muscle integration may be difficult to compare with the conditions obtaining in a mammal that stands erect.

Too much emphasis cannot be placed upon the fact that easy generalizations, such as the assertion that all behavioral development occurs from a generalized total pattern of the organism to the specific responses of adult life, must be taken with great caution. While this description may be true in many respects, particularly if the word "pattern" is given an unambiguous meaning, it seems certain on the basis of the specific responses considered above that it cannot be indiscriminately applied. Before generalizations can be made with assurance, there must be a large amount of accurate measurement and the determination of a series of statistical norms in regard to the development of each of the specific developmental stages in each form considered. Typical cross sections in

development in every form and in all responses from significant receptor surfaces must be considered before such a generalization can be made. Certainly the late fetus has an elaborately organized and in some respects quite specific response mechanism. To some stimuli the relatively early fetus makes quite definite responses.

It seems hard to believe that anyone who knows anything of the structure and function of the tracts and centers of the central nervous system can read the report of fetal activity at various developmental levels given above and still feel that there is much to be gained by saying that before birth the organism reacts as a whole, as certain psychologists, possibly under the influence of one form of the *Gestalttheorie*, have suggested. Much of the nervous system may, in some sense, be involved in any partial activity of the system, but this does not mean that the system is not in many respects sharply differentiated. Certain essential relationships between diffuseness and specificity and between individuation and integration of behavior will become clearer after the parts played by the specific senses in fetal life have been considered.

The account presented above from the reports of several investigators gives a picture of the development of behavior in human fetal organisms of estimated ages. No effort has been made to include all known published accounts of fetuses but only those in which behavior significant for the general problem of this chapter was noted. Minkowski (1923) refers to at least 11 fetuses not considered here in which primarily the only reflexes studied were those released by stimulation of the sole of the foot. In the study of this response Bersot (1918; 1919; 1920; 1921) has also considered fetal activity in detail in relation to a study of the development of the clinically significant plantar reflex. This same response has been considered from a scientific and theoretical point of view by Feldman (1922) and by Minkowski (1926) in work that has been referred to above. For an account of a fetus investigated by Winterstein, see Minkowski (1928a).

Hooker has given permission to refer to his *Preliminary Atlas of Early Human Fetal Activity* (1939b), which was issued for restricted use only. Reference previously has been made to this work, but the author wishes to call special attention to it because it contains very beautiful reproductions of photographs of human fetal material 8½ to 14 weeks of menstrual age. A careful study of this atlas may give a more adequate picture of early human fetal behavior than any other single reference known to the present author. Milner (1967) has presented an outline of pattern of prenatal neural and behavioral development that should be consulted in this connection.

THE SPECIAL SENSES IN HUMAN PRENATAL LIFE

Historically there has been much speculation in regard to the role of the senses before birth. In earlier psychology these speculations centered largely about the question of whether or not some sort of dim conscious awareness exists in the infant before birth. More recently this essentially nonexperimental question has given place to one that may be studied. The question now asked is: How and when does the stimulus control of fetal behavior determined by the activation of the various receptor systems begin before birth, and how do behavior capacities develop? Objective techniques for study of the senses in the premature or newborn infant have been devised, of which those of Canestrini (1913) and A. P. Weiss (1929) are significant examples. These techniques have not only made quantitative study of the senses possible in a new way, but they have also added to the general knowledge of the part that stimulation plays in the subtle alterations of bodily activity. In this chapter, therefore, the various specific senses will be considered in turn in relation to fetal behavioral or mental life when such behavioral or mental life is considered as including not only experience but also specific receptor-controlled behavior.

After each of the senses has been treated, some generalizations will be made by the author on the significance for psychology of receptor-aroused activity in the fetus. The reader should be reminded that the material presented above on the development of the senses in lower animals and especially the elaborate work on the guinea pig has much relevance in a consideration of the growth of the human senses. In this section, however, the whole emphasis is placed upon human development except where specific reference to infrahuman forms is considered necessary for strictly comparative purposes. Of all the traditional topics of scientific psychology, it seems that perception may have most to learn from a proper comparative study of fetal and neonatal senses.

Perception

In the study of perception there has been a long debate between those who believe in nativism (the idea that ability to perceive space, movement, time, objects, and related aspects of the "external world" is inborn and not dependent on individual experience) and empiricism (the idea that such perceptions originate in individual experience or learning). Modern study of receptor mechanisms shows in detail how external environmental energies activate sense organs. This activation leads to the release of coded impulses in the sensory nerves associated with such receptors. Coded messages then pass into the central nervous system and initiate other coded processes which ultimately, in typical cases, lead to adaptive adjustment on the part of the total organism by activating its appropriate effector organs. The point to emphasize here is that the effect of the environment on the organism is transformed into coded information in the receptors and in sensory or afferent neurons. Broadbent and others (1961) present a good case for preferring the language of information flow to that of stimulus and response in his consideration of human perception and animal learning. As mentioned elsewhere in this chapter, adaptive or even maladaptive relationships to its environment may thus be thought of as a result of muscular or glandular response to coded information about the external world. Perception thus can be viewed as a result of neural (including neurochemical) activity which was started by coded inputs. The central neural processes (molar or molecular) which are involved in this activity are a result of the evolutionary processes that have led to the origin of the species in question and thus make the adaptation of that species to its environment possible. Present behavior of the sort involved in perception thus partly depends on molar or molecular mechanisms that are genetically determined. Specific responses of each individual at certain ontogenetic stages lead, as a result of learning, to specific perceptual responses that are empirically acquired.

The old arguments between supporters of nativism and empiricism were largely discussed before some of these modern facts about the physiology of the sense organs and the nervous system were known. It is not by accident that the man who is sometimes called the first modern physiologist, Johannes Müller, is generally considered as having "given formal status to the nativistic theory in 1826" (Boring, 1942). Müller and Sir Charles Bell (Carmichael, 1926a) are properly considered as the scientists first to explain the phenomena basic to the idea of the so-called "specific energies of nerves." This view of neural action is the precursor of our modern knowledge about coded sensory inputs. As Barlow (1961) well says, "There are two encouraging results of considering the operation of the sensory side of the nervous system as a reversible coder for removing redundancy. One is that this is a subdivisible operation and so could be brought about by the large number of semi-independent units which appear to make up the central nervous system; the other is that mental acts, when broken down in this way, may be reduced to a level of simplicity which can be understood and investigated by the physiologist."

Arguments about nativism and empiricism in perception, however, are by no means all history. Some of the modern work in this field shows the great importance of a study of fetal and newborn organisms in understanding the psychology of the newborn and indeed the adult human individual. Bishop Berkeley, in his famous *An Essay Towards A New Theory of Vision* (1709), is generally credited with establishing the view that perception (such as that of visual space) is dependent not only on the eyes but also on touch. Berkeley's view is well summarized by Pastore (1965). Berkeley, as noted by Pastore, asserted, "Consider, for example, a globe as the first object within reach of an infant. The visual sensation is a certain gradation of colors in the same plane . . . in conjunction with that sensation, the infant extends his arms and feels the rotundity of the globe. After many trials, the visual

sensation serves as a sign (or suggests) the tactual idea of palpation of the globe. . . . The infant will thus have the perception of solidity even when touch . . . is prevented."

This empiricistic or "learning theory" of the visual perception of space has had many proponents down to the present day. But as Pastore has clearly shown, it was essentially disproved more than a century ago by Samuel Bailey (1842, 1855). Bailey pointed out that the behavior of newborn mammals offers a better test of Berkeley's theory than does a study of the newborn human infant. Bailey (as paraphrased by Pastore) says, "The infant, in being born 'helpless' does not have the necessary 'organic maturity' of senses and limbs their development is one of 'gradual growth.'" Bailey then goes on to discuss the fact that animals born or hatched in a relatively mature state (in the terminology of this chapter, "precocious" animals) have essentially identical optical structures with those of man. Bailey then further points out that immediately after birth, such precocious animals can run about, snatch at objects and leap from one spot to another with the greatest precision and without learning.

The present author has made many similar observations on newborn mammals. A newborn giraffe, for example, a few minutes after birth, can, without any trial and error, visually localize a sound at a distance and show other types of immediate adaptive visual perception (Carmichael, 1957). The admirable experimental work of Eleanor J. Gibson and her associates (1960) on the visual cliff contributes very important evidence on the matter. She says, "From our first few years of work with the visual cliff we are ready to venture the rather broad conclusion that a seeing animal will be able to discriminate depth when its locomotion is adequate even when locomotion begins at birth. (See also J. Gibson, 1958.)

The present author's work on the development of "local sign" in the tactual perception of space in fetal animals similarly points to the correctness of a nativistic view of perception (Carmichael, 1961).

Before leaving the early work of Bailey and his refutation of Berkeley and the other older empiricists, it is interesting to note that John Stuart Mill went out of his way to attack Bailey for an odd but possibly significant reason. Mill was a social reformer as well as a great psychologist and economist. He wrote in relation to Bailey's work and that of another nativist, Sir William Hamilton, ". . . the prevailing tendency to regard all marked distinctions of human character as innate, and in the main indelible . . . is one of the chief hindrances to the rational treatment of great social questions and one of the greatest stumbling blocks to human improvement" (quoted by Pastore from Mill's autobiography).

In the present author's opinion the last word on this socially important question has not been written but the work of Bailey each year seems more surely correct. A rational consideration of what is really innate in human nature, with all its implications for "the rational treatment of great social questions," still needs active study.

The Cutaneous Receptors

In a consideration of the senses of touch, an effort is made to suggest such differences as have been noted in fetal life between light and deep pressure, temperature, and cutaneous pain. The development of skin in the human fetus has been anatomically described by a number of writers. This work is summarized by Feldman (1920). In appearance the skin of the late fetus or early premature infant is very red, owing to the visibility of the vascular system just beneath it. At 2 or 3 months before birth the skin is still quite thin and is covered with *lanugo hairs,* which apppear at about the fifth month of pregnancy. The skin of the fetus during midpregnancy is typically much wrinkled, because of the comparative absence of subcutaneous fat. The hair on the scalp at this period is short and poorly pigmented. The nails grow gradually during late fetal life (Hess, 1922).

There has been much speculation on the skin as a sensory surface during the uterine life of the fetus. Cabanis is quoted by Genzmer (1882) as holding the skin to be a peculiarly important receptor field at this period. Bichat (1827) and Magendie, as noted above, discussed the skin sensibility of the fetus. Some casual observations are also reported in relation to the material summarized previously in this chapter concerning the possibility of stimulating the fetus by pressing on the abdominal wall of the mother. Of course, stimulation of this sort may well activate the deep-lying proprioceptors as well as the true tactile receptors. In the review of the literature in the experimental study of the development of fetal behavior in infrahuman organisms, many references have already been made to tactual stimulation. In the human field alone, Minkowski, Bolaffio and Artom, Krabbe, Hooker, and others have considered fetal responses that are released by cutaneous stimulation as indicated above. Hooker has been especially careful to use quantified stimuli. The part played by the sense of touch in animals and man in discrimination and even in responses of equilibration is considered by Kidd (1907).

A. Pressure. In summarizing the work that has been done on human and infrahuman fetuses, the following factors may possibly be isolated as important in a consideration of the pressure sense before birth.

1. *Place Stimulated.* In general, cutaneous sensitivity seems to begin in the oral-nasal region, that is, the region involving the mucous membrane of the nostrils and the red of the lips (Genzmer, 1882; Windle and Griffin, 1931; Hooker, 1944). In rodents the pads of the vibrissae also very early become sensitive (Lane, 1917; Raney and Carmichael, 1934; Carmichael, 1934a), and in many animals the regions about the eyes and the openings of the ears are also very early sensitive, as is the anal region (Coronios, 1931). In the human infant Kussmaul (1859) found the eyelashes very sensitive, but this was not confirmed by Genzmer (1882). Most studies seem to suggest that, with individual variations, skin sensitivity develops by spreading out over the face region and then progressively over the surface of the body. In this development in certain organisms, such as the toadfish, the salamander, the rat, and the cat, a fairly well-worked-out course of temporal difference in the arrival of sensitivity in increasingly caudal segments of the body may be observed. In animals with tails this even goes on out to the end of the tail.

In this general course of development, however, certain exceptions have been seen, as noted above by the writer in a study of the development of the receptive zones of the fetal guinea pig. Sensory development in general has been treated by Minkowski and other investigators as the spreading of what they have termed reflexogenous zones. This term has much to recommend it because at present almost the only method used in the study of fetal sensory capacity on the skin is the recognition of behavior correlated with the experimental stimulation. Windle and Griffin (1931) suggest in general that motility precedes the ability of a part to be stimulated. In his consideration of the "reflex circle," Holt (1931) has suggested the large part that self-stimulation may possibly play in the development of specific forms of behavior as organisms develop. Certainly no one who has watched an active mammalian fetus can help being struck by the fact that in its movements it stimulates almost its entire body surface by its own moving paws and head. It is peculiarly striking to watch a 48-day guinea pig fetus, for example, stimulate its head and face by appropriately cupped "hands." These scrubbing movements, performed not once but over and over again, are such that the surface must certainly be irritated by the friction.

2. *Areal versus Punctiform Stimuli.* Minkowski (1922), Coronios (1931), Windle and Griffin (1931), Carmichael (1934a), Raney and Carmichael (1934), and Hooker (1936) have all apparently noticed that stroking produces stimulation when single punctate stimulation does not bring about response. Following this suggestion, Raney has been able to show that stimulation of a point on the skin by a single hair may not bring about response, but stimulating the same area immediately around such a point with a brush made up of comparable hairs will sometimes do so. (In this connection, see also Kuo, (1932e.)

3. *Summation of Stimuli.* Carmichael (1934a) and others have noted that a single touch with a light hair may fail to bring out response, but several touches apparently of the same intensity at the same point may be effective in eliciting response.

4. *Weak and Strong Stimulation.* Genzmer (1882) long ago noted that in a premature infant entirely different responses might be elicited to weak and strong cutaneous stimulation. The distinction in terms of the strength of cutaneous pressure is one that has too infrequently been made in studies of fetal development. Thus, as previously noted, Bolaffio and Artom disagree with Minkowski as to the point at which cutaneous reflexes begin in the developing fetus. This disagreement may be based on the fact that Bolaffio and Artom

(1924) indicate the possibility that Minkowski was unwittingly stimulating the underlying musculature and thus that the massive responses which he reports in young fetuses are not cutaneous but are due to the stmulation of deep receptors. The possibility of direct muscle stimulation in such cases must also be remembered. Holt (1931) considers that the distinction between strong and weak stimulation is a peculiarly important one in the development of the functional activity of the growing organism. He believes that light stimulation will usually lead to response moving toward the stimulus, or *adiently,* whereas only secondarily does strong stimulation of the same receptor field lead to *abient,* or withdrawal and avoidance, responses. Richter (1925) and others have confirmed this observation. Indeed, Coronios, Schlosberg, and Carmichael (1932) have been able to take moving pictures showing exactly this response as the result of stimulating the paw of a fetal kitten.

Under other circumstances, however, observations have not been such as to confirm this generalization. Thus Coghill (1929a) asserts that the first responses of *Amblystoma* are all away from the region stimulated. Windle and Griffin (1931) point out that the unilateral trunk or neck flexions of the earliest fetuses seem to be executed toward the observer and away from the surface on which the animal is resting. Kuo (1932e) also uses the strength of the stimulus as a peculiarly important part of the theory of development which he has proposed. It seems possible that in responses in which apparently the same receptor field is stimulated first lightly and then more strongly two distinct neural mechanisms may sometimes be brought into play. It might be suggested speculatively that the facts behind the differentiation between the allegedly developmental epicritic and protopathic sensitivity, as proposed by Head and Rivers and especially as explained by Boring (1916) and later by Sharpey-Schäfer (1928), will ultimately provide some clue in the explanation of this diversity of response to different stimulus intensity.

Windle and Griffin (1931) also discuss a developmental system of cutaneous receptor mechanisms. The difference in responses to light and heavy tactile stimulation makes peculiarly uncertain the interpretation of results of investigators who do not indicate that they have considered the strength of the stimulus as important in describing the fetal responses which they have elicited in experimental work. It is all the more peculiar that this distinction should not have been continuously made, because of the statement in regard to the difference in responses to weak and strong stimuli made, as noted above, many years ago by Genzmer. As previously reported, Smith and the writer (Carmichael and Smith, 1939) have demonstrated a quantitative relationship between the extent and spread of response and the intensity of punctiform stimulation when calibrated esthesiometers were used.

5. Localization. Preyer (1882) believes that the first localization response to tactile stimuli is the seeking of the nipple by means of the cutaneous stimulation of the lips. Many specific references have been given above to the motor responses of various fetuses set off by tactual stimulation. It has been suggested in connection with the work of Raney and Carmichael (1934) that such responses possibly develop greater accuracy in localization as age progresses.

6. Cutaneous Reflexes. As suggested in the preceding paragraphs, the skin may be thought of as a mosaic of points, each spot of which is the locus of stimulation for a more or less specific behavioral response. Many writers have discussed the significance of cutaneous reflexes in adult life. Givler (1921) has suggested the wide significance of the development of one such reflex, that of grasping. Hooker's (1938) careful observations on the grasping reflex show that it develops during fetal life in two phases: finger closing, and gripping. Finger closing appears as a quick flexion of the digits except the thumb at about 11 weeks of menstrual age. Gripping is first observed in the eighteenth week. It is still weak in the twenty-fifth week of menstrual age. In the first 25 weeks of fetal life the thumb seems to play no role in fetal grasping.

Minkowski, as noted, considers in detail the variations in the pattern of the reflexes elicited by the stimulation of the skin of the sole of the foot. Sucking, in its later stages, is possibly conditioned by a number of exteroceptive and interoceptive stimuli, such as the stomach contraction of hunger, but it is in essentials always a cutaneous and mucous membrane reflex. The cremasteric reflex and certain of the abdominal reflexes also result from stimulation of the cutaneous field. In a paper on reflex sweating in the fetus, it is pointed out that human sweat glands can be seen in the palm and sole of the foot by the sixteenth fetal week and in the axilla by the nineteenth week. The secretory activity is established late in fetal life (Higasihara, Hurusawa, Simada, and Tanaka, 1965).

In general, then, it may be pointed out that many of the specific acts of the fetus are induced by stimulation of cutaneous pressure receptors. Mucous membrane reflexes (Minkowski, 1928a) are also probably best thought of as involving receptor mechanisms, so far as pressure is concerned, that are similar to cutaneous reflexes. Peiper (1928) has tabulated the cutaneous responses seen in newborn children. The writer must here again emphasize his belief that, given a stimulus just above the lower threshold and a quiescent fetus in a standard posture, there is typically *one behavior act or reflex* set off by the stimulation of each cutaneous area. These cutaneous "push buttons" are remarkably specific in their behavioral relations when the complexity of the central nervous system is considered.

B. Temperature. Warmth is one of the skin senses attributed by the philosopher John Locke (1849 edition) to the fetus. In spite of this early sanction it is difficult to understand how marked differences in temperature can normally be present in prenatal life. In the study of the temperature sense in the prematurely delivered infant the matter is further complicated by the great variability of body temperature which characterizes the premature infant (Hess, 1922; Evensen, 1931). Currently accepted views in regard to the mechanism of temperature stimulation start with the assumption that the temperature to which the skin is adapted must be taken as the physiological zero point. From this zero other stimuli are to be considered as above or below; therefore quantified work in regard to temperature in the premature infant is rendered difficult when only absolute temperatures of stimuli are recorded.

Some indications, however, of responses to both warm and cool stimuli in premature infants are given by both Kussmaul (1859) and Genzmer (1882). For the most part these observations agree with those of the following investigators of the temperature sense of newborn children: Preyer (1882), Canestrini (1913), Blanton (1917), and Peiper (1928). These opinions are criticized by Pratt, Nelson, and Sun (1930), who also add their own controlled experimental observations. These three collaborators report that newborn infants react much less strongly to stimuli warmer than the body than to stimuli that are cooler. The writer has described above a study of fetal temperature sensitivity (Carmichael and Lehner, 1937) in which some observations on the temperature responses of guinea pigs were made. In this study unmistakable reactions to temperature both of warm and cool stimuli were obtained under controlled conditions. Drops of blood-warm water call out no response save as they arouse tactile receptors, but cold- or hot-water drops do call out such activities. This sensitivity has appeared by approximately the middle of the gestation period. Here again the "more intense" stimulus (warm *or* cold) calls out more active responses than the "less intense" stimulus. Thermal homeostasis in the fetus and the newborn does not seem to have been thoroughly studied (Adamsons and Towell, 1965). It has been known for years that body temperatures regulation in the newborn fluctuates more than in the older infant. Premature infants show greater thermal instability than normal-term babies (Miller, Miller, and Westin, 1964; Daniel, Dawes, James, Ross, and Windle, 1966).

C. Pain. Locke (1849 edition) also attributed the experience of pain to the fetus. Since his speculation there has been little direct experimentation upon the fetal pain sense. A number of casual observations show, however, that the application of stimuli that must have caused gross destruction of skin and protoplasm has not called out very pronounced movements on the part of the fetus. Genzmer (1882), on the basis of such observations, holds that the pain sense is very poorly developed in the fetus. On the first day of a premature infant's neonatal life he stimulated it until blood came and got no response. It is certainly true that increase in pressure over that necessary to bring out the typical responses to deep pressure does not always seem in the guinea pig fetus, at any rate, to increase the extent or intensity of re-

sponse. Thus in certain cases the light pressure of a fine hair may lead to extension and stronger pressure of a heavier hair to retraction, but very strong and even obviously destructive stimulation of the same point may or may not make any observable difference in the elicited response over that noted to strong pressure stimulation. Similar observations have been made on the cat fetus (Windle and Griffin, 1931). There can be no doubt that protoplasm-destroying stimuli sometimes bring about violent responses in late fetuses, but even this reaction does not always occur. Speculations on the part played by pain in relation to unpleasantness and discomfort will be referred to in the consideration of the organic senses.

The foregoing paragraphs may be summarized by the statement that there is much evidence that the specialized skin senses have developed to an active functional state long before birth and are able when appropriately stimulated to initiate the release of behavior that is typically very precisely related to the point stimulated.

The Proprioceptive Senses

The neuromuscular spindles may be taken as typical of the many classes of proprioceptors. They are found in the fourth month of fetal life in practically all muscles, including the extrinsic muscles of the tongue and the external eye muscles (Elwyn, 1929). Historically it was not until quite recently that the kinesthetic senses came to be distinguished at all from touch. Carmichael (1926b) has described the history of knowledge concerning the "muscle sense." Much that Bichat (1819) wrote about the active touch of the fetus probably referred to the proprioceptive rather than to the cutaneous sense. Kussmaul (1859) and Genzmer (1882) both refer to responses which must have involved muscle-sense stimulation. Preyer (1885) makes similar references. Peterson and Rainey (1910) also hold that not only touch but also the activity of the muscles of the fetus must lay the foundation "under the threshold of consciousness for a sense of equilibrium and vague spatial relationships." In his study of the relationship between local reflexes and posture, Coghill (1929a) comes to the conclusion that ". . . the limb is able to respond very precisely to stimuli arising within the body (proprioceptive) as the result of a particular posture before it can respond to stimuli that arise exclusively from the outside world (exteroceptive). . . ."

In experimental work on operatively exposed human and infrahuman fetal material during the active period, the proprioceptive senses are always much in evidence. Indeed, in the responses in fetal rats both Swenson (1926) and Angulo y González (1932a) find evidence of this sense in a 16-day fetus. Coronios (1933) and Windle and Griffin (1931) deal with this sense in detail. (See also Windle, 1940.) As noted in the consideration of the cutaneous senses, these investigators report activities that show that the posture of the cat fetus at the time of stimulation seems in certain cases to determine the response that will be elicited. This point is substantiated by many protocols of the experimental studies of fetal behavior that the present writer has recorded. It is possible that this fact alone may be taken as indicating an early onset of proprioceptive control of behavior.

In this connection one must remember as pointed out above the differential gravitational action on the limb and body in air and in the liquid of the amniotic sac. In one of the studies of a very young human fetus—by Strassmann (1903), noted above—it is recorded that the observer pressed against, in a manner which apparently means moved, the limb of the fetus. As a result of this stimulation the experimenter could feel the foot press down on his hand. The writer has noticed this same response in young guinea pig fetuses. Even when very gentle or even relatively strong tactual stimulation would not release a response in the forelimb of the fetus, it not infrequently has happened that a forcible movement of the limb itself by the experimenter gave a specific and direct response. As the skin was not anesthetized in the cases reported, this may not of course be thought of as a wholly proprioceptive stimulus, but, as cutaneous stimulation was ineffective in producing the same response, the facts seem to favor the view that the responses noted were proprioceptively aroused. This conclusion must be taken with reservations because the bending and stretching of the skin which result from the bending of a limb are a very strong pressure stimulus.

There is still other evidence that the proprioceptors are effective very early in fetal development. Hooker and Nicholas (1930) have reported experiments on fetal rats in which the spinal cords were completely sectioned at various levels. After some of these experiments it was found that stimulation above or below the sectioned point of the cord might lead to responses in parts of the body innervated by segments of the cord above or below the cut. The question at once arose as to how these impulses were transmitted. As one of the possible explanations of this transmission, these investigators have suggested the following course of events. An exteroceptive stimulus leads to afferent conduction over peripheral nerves to the cord above the region of the section. From this still intact segment of the cord impulses pass out over efferent peripheral nerves to trunk muscles leading to this response. This response mechanically moves the adjoining musculature and thus directly stimulates the proprioceptors in it. These newly activated proprioceptors then initiate afferent impulses which pass into the cord below or above the region of the cut, as the case may be, and thus in turn activate arcs in the intact region of the cord above or below the section, which in turn lead to responses obviously innervated by connections in the cord beyond the section. (See also Hooker, 1911.)

Recent studies of Mavrinskaya (1960, 1962) on the correlation of development of skeletal muscle nerve endings with the appearance of motor activity in the human fetus show that primitive sensory and motor nerve endings are present at the 7 to 8 week stage. This is two to three weeks earlier than has previously been reported. Sensory and motor endings arise simultaneously in the muscles studied. Indirect evidence leads Mavrinskaya to the conclusion that by the eleventh developmental week these endings are functional. This mechanism, he concludes, is basic in the primary movements of the developing fetus. Such movements are, he believes, reflex in nature. In another area, Larroche (1962) has studied some anatomical aspects of brain development that are important in the growth of behavior.

Windle and Griffin (1931) report many evidences of movement that may be considered on the basis of the analysis of Sherrington and his school of reflex physiologists as at least in part proprioceptively innervated. These investigators report that a quiescent embryo held in the cramped condition of the sac will, on the cutting of the sac, sometimes at once assume an exaggeratedly stretched position. It seems as though it were attempting to exercise itself after the close confinement of its entire previous existence. It may be remarked that the writer has seen and photographed similar responses. These maintained "extensor thrusts" are in many respects similar to the tonus of decerebrate rigidity as seen in the adult animal and may possibly involve proprioceptive stimulation. The experiments of Weed (1917) Weed and Langworthy (1926), and Langworthy (1928, 1929) give very clear evidence of other reactions involving this receptor system. The writer has sometimes noted when dealing with a late guinea pig fetus that, if the fetus, still wholly immersed in the bath, is held by its own forepaws on a submerged projection, the animal will seem to try to crawl up onto the projection. Correlated movements are here used which seem, to superficial observation, similar to those employed by a swimmer lifting himself out of the water onto a diving raft. This well-integrated and apparently purposeful activity seems to involve complex proprioceptively directed responses.

Most students of the development of fetal behavior agree that locomotion, as, for example, in the first crawling movements of the fetal opossum considered above, sucking, and breathing are three of the earliest essential behavior systems of the newborn animal. It is interesting to note that each of these in its developed form may involve marked proprioceptive stimulation. The geotropic responses of the opossum fetus considered above, occurring less than 2 weeks after copulation, seem, in the light of Crozier's work (1929) on geotropism in the rodent, to represent a response in which proprioceptive stimulation plays a part. Hunter (1931) has pointed out in a similar study that the vestibular apparatus and other stimulus factors are probably also important in determining such responses.

As noted above, Minkowski (1922; 1928a) reports that there are true tendon reflexes in the early fetus. This is questioned, however,

by Bolaffio and Artom (1924). These latter observers suggest that the responses seen by Minkowski in very early fetuses may have been the result of other forms of stimulation. The mechanism of deep stimulation which they suggest and true tendon-stretch stimulation both involve proprioceptive activity. Indeed, it may be said that the whole study of prenatal behavior in man and in the lower mammals indicates that the proprioceptors in muscles and tendons, and possibly joints, are functional well before birth. By the time of birth these mechanisms have undergone such development that they are among the best-organized receptor fields so far as the initiation and control of behavior are concerned.

The Receptors in the Nonauditory Labyrinth

Adult posture, righting responses, and other reactions to gravity, tonus changes due to rotation, and other alterations of the body in space are often held to result from stimulation of receptors in the nonauditory labyrinth and associated receptor fields (Camis, 1930). As suggested above in a consideration of the development of behavior in the fetal cat, the change of body posture in space has been shown sometimes to involve various combinations of nonauditory labyrinthine, kinesthetic, and exteroceptive stimuli. In the fetus it is peculiarly difficult to isolate the part played by the body exteroceptors and muscle proprioceptors from the part played by the receptors in the nonauditory labyrinth. It should be noted that there is some evidence also that in certain types there is an auditory function subsumed by receptors in this *non*auditory receptor complex.

Historically, comparatively little reference has been made to the static senses in connection with fetal mental life as this life was considered in the older speculative child psychology. Some reference, however, has been made to the part played by these receptors in determining the position of the fetus in relation to gravity. Lane (1917) has noted in his study of the development of the senses in the fetal rat considered above that there is an apparent correlation between the histological development of the semicircular canals and the acquisition of postural righting responses on the part of the fetus. In Lane's work, however, no effort to differentiate between proprioceptive and static stimuli is reported.

The development of the labyrinth has been considered by many writers, including Streeter (1906) and Larsell (1929). (Cf. also Bowen, 1932, and McCrady, Wever, and Bray, 1937.) Minkowski (1922), as noted previously, has demonstrated from neurological studies that the labyrinth is fully differentiated in a human fetus of 40 mm. As noted above also, Windle and Griffin (1931) report that in very early cat embryos of 26 or 27 days ". . . rotation of head and trunk appeared to be indefinitely coordinated with the older components, namely, lateral and ventral head and trunk flexion. This activity resulted in motions that strikingly resembled the righting reflexes seen in late fetal life." Windle and Fish (1932) show that in cat fetuses several days before normal birth true labyrinthine reflexes do appear. These reactions make possible what has been called the first "purposeful" movement of the cat, that is, successful locomotion (Windle and Griffin, 1931). This complex behavior act, as already suggested, is held to be a combination of equilibration, body-righting responses, general postural tonus, and rhythmic movement of the limbs.

Coronios and Carmichael have both noticed that, in late cat and guinea pig fetuses, turning the animal over while it is completely immersed in the warm bath does not always lead to righting movements. If the cord is ligated and the same fetus is placed on its side on the experimental table, righting may begin at once. This is possibly to be interpreted as indicating that at this period righting still, at any rate, involves exteroceptive and proprioceptive as well as vestibular functions.

Similarly, Coronios and Carmichael have both been able to elicit typical Magnus reflexes of limb extension as the fetal mammal's neck is turned to the right or the left. These responses are strikingly similar to those of decerebrate mammals and tend to confirm the observation agreed upon by all other investigators that for the most part the young fetus is not under the active control of the cerebral hemispheres. Minkowski (1922) reports labyrinthine reflexes in early human fetuses. He suggests that it is not only possible to elicit responses from general labyrinthine stimulation but also possible to distinguish between the reflexes attributed by Magnus and his colleagues to the utriculus-sacculus complex of receptors as contrasted with those attributed to the complex of semicircular-canal receptors. His analysis leads him to believe that most of the fetal responses to nonauditory labyrinthine stimulation are the result of semicircular-canal receptor action.

Minkowski (1922) states further that in his opinion the early anatomical development and functional use of the vestibular apparatus in the fetus are probably related to the fact that the fetus is living in a fluid medium the specific gravity of which is almost equal to its own specific gravity. Therefore it is almost "weightless," a condition in which he believes the labyrinthine reflexes may be seen to operate to excellent advantage. Minkowski (1928a) is careful, however, not to disregard the possibility that the phenomena noted as the basis for attributing labyrinthine function to the fetus may be the result of the stimulation of proprioceptors in the neck and related receptors. Magnus (1924), in reviewing this work, seems to emphasize the part of the tonic neck reflexes in such activities.

There is some reason to believe that the first eye movements of the fetus are in response to changes of the bodily position of the fetus in space; that is, the first eye movements are occasioned not by retinal stimulation but as part of the general tonus changes of the body brought about by gross movements in space. This fact is brought out very clearly in Kuo's work (1932a). Early eye muscle movements, indeed, may be thought of as specific. These movements take place, however, at the same time that other responses are active and hence may be called part of the "generalized" pattern of responses. Later specific responses are observed which can then be said to differentiate themselves out of the more complex pattern (Minkowski, 1924; 1928a; Tracy, 1926).

There is no reason to believe, however, that these early "postural" responses of the eye muscles are as definitely related to specific aspects of semicircular-canal stimulation as they are in the adult condition so well summarized by Maxwell (1923), Favill (1929), and Holsopple (1929).

Eye movements in adult life that are determined by vestibular function may be modified in various ways (Dodge, 1923). Wellman and Carmichael have made preliminary and as yet unpublished studies of the origin and development of eye movements in the fetal guinea pig. Although these results are still tentative, the following statements may be made, based upon the electrical recording of eye movements in living fetuses:

1. Vestibular stimulation brings about responses before light stimulation is effective in causing eye movements.

2. Optokinetic (that is, light-induced) responses can be called out in the fetal guinea pig which have some of the same characteristics as such responses in older animals.

In these experiments a moving field of bars of light and shade gradients is passed near the eyes of the fetus. The resulting reactions show the slow and fast photic responses typical of such stimuli in adult animals.

It is thus difficult to say with assurance the exact part which the labyrinthine senses play in determining behavior before birth, but it is certain that the tonus adjustments of the body muscles in postural responses, including precise adjustments of eye muscles, are among significant prenatal activities. An understanding of these responses in fetal and adult life is important (Magnus, 1925). One of the points, however, at which a knowledge of the development of proprioceptive responses in the fetus is most important is the evaluation of the studies of postnatal life in which the alleged saltatory character of certain responses there noted is observed in the light of the knowledge of prenatal postural responses. Popularly speaking, the postural actions of the fetus may be considered a fundamental preparation for a diversity of actions in postnatal life. Walking and localizing responses of arms, trunk, and legs can take place only in an organism in which postural mechanisms are developed. It is almost as if these senses provide the essential "gyro-control" necessary before a reaction can be made, just as gyro-apparatus on a warship is necessary if the guns are to be pointed effectively in a heavy sea. In considering the part played by incoming nerve impulses, which themselves result from motor reactions, one should consider the whole nature of "feedback" systems in biology as related to similar electronic systems (Wiener, 1948).

The Organic Senses

Historically there has been some speculation in regard to the organic senses in the fetus. Some have held that the fetus lives in a perfect world in which hunger, thirst, and all other needs are cared for before they arise (Bichat, 1827). Locke (1849 edition), on the contrary, held at an early period in the total story of speculation about fetal life that the unborn child has "perhaps some faint ideas of hunger and thirst." Kussmaul (1859) agrees with this view. As noted above, Yanase (1907a; 1907b) has studied the movement of the fetal intestines. In the rhythmic nature of these movements is found a basis for possible organic experience and, indeed, for the indirect activation of the skeletal musculature.

The work of Patterson (1914) and Carlson and Ginsburg (1915) on newborn infants and on dogs delivered before normal time indicates something of the nature of the tonus changes of the stomach which may occur in late fetal life. These changes in these organisms are found under appropriate conditions to be rapid and active. This coincides with the observations of Preyer (1893) and of Peterson and Rainey (1910) on the hunger of newborn full-term or even premature infants. Some suggestion of the developmental course of hunger activities and stimulation may be obtained from an observation of Hess (1922) that very early premature fetuses are much less able than later premature infants to show the usual signs of needing to be fed. Jensen (1932) notes the dependence in the infant of the reflex of sucking, a reflex incidentally too often considered merely tactual, on the concomitance of hunger stimuli and tactual stimuli. Preyer (1893) notes the whole sequence of bodily changes, even including those of the eye muscles, which come to be related to the hunger activities of the newborn child.

The theory of "drive" or motivation held by some modern comparative psychologists, which correlates such activities to some extent with organic stimulation, finds support in the observations of the "random" activity of the fetus which is shown by Irwin (1930) and others to accompany hunger stimuli. As noted above, this activity may not be "random" in the ordinary sense of the word but rather the consecutive or concomitant release of a series already described patterns of behavior. (See Carmichael, 1941.)

This concept of "drive" is closely related to phenomena considered by certain of the older descriptive psychologists as characterizing the motivating power of the affective processes. That is, "drive" is related to the bodily basis of pleasantness and unpleasantness. Thus Preyer (1882; 1885) and others have discussed reaction related to pleasantness and unpleasantness as apparent before birth or immediately after birth. These conclusions are inferences based on unaided observation of facial expression and on instrumentally recorded bodily changes, such as breathing and directly measured cerebral volume (Canestrini, 1913). Facial expression is reported by Minkowski as beginning in the relatively early weeks of active fetal life, and so it seems that this expressive pattern of so much significance in pleasant and unpleasant situations of later life has had ample opportunity for exercise during the prenatal period.

It may be noted in passing that the rate of fetal heartbeat can be modified by external stimulation, thus possibly leading to vascular stimuli of the sort often considered to fall under the heading of "organic experience." The possibility of respiratory experiences, or "feelings of suffocation," is certainly present, so far as may be judged from a knowledge of stimulation and response. But there is, of course, no evidence that any introspective state actually follows such stimulation.

In conclusion, it may be said that there are possibly certain organic changes in the stomach, intestines, heart, and vascular and respiratory systems that occur before birth which may be important in receptor stimulation. See Cannon and Rosenblueth, 1937.) It is possible that the stimulation of these receptor systems may lead to fetal activity which does not, of course, have any specific external end in view until, as a result of external stimulation and learning, such stimula-

tion in postnatal life comes to initiate adaptive responses which some wish to characterize as "end-seeking." It may also be noted that no one who has worked with fetal material has failed to see that, after repeated responses, "fatigue" sets in, and for a time stimulation is difficult or impossible (Peiper, 1925).

The question whether fetal quiescence is to be considered as fetal sleep has also been debated (Preyer, 1885). A suggestion has recently been made that there is a "sleep-wake" cycle that is similar in mother and fetus and that this rhythm is carried over into the postnatal period (Payne and Bach, 1965).

This 24-hour clock has been demonstrated to play an important role in the lives of adult animals and men. This mechanism is inborn and is in complete independence of homeostasis as demonstrated by Richter (1967).

Taste. The histological work on the development of the taste mechanism in the embryo is summarized by Keibel and Mall (1910). Taste buds are said by Parker (1922) to begin to appear in man during the third fetal month. The taste receptors are also found to be much more widely distributed in fetal life than in adult life. Parker thus points out that there is evidence of a real retraction of the sensory field in man from the late fetal period to the adult state. At first, taste buds are found on the tonsils, hard palate, and parts of the esophagus. Later, functional taste cells are almost always limited to the tongue (1922). Here is a striking example of a "reflexogenous" or receptor zone which changes as a function of developmental time.

Historically, there have been several different speculative opinions concerning this sense in prenatal life. The early opinions are summarized by Bichat (1827). It is undoubtedly true that the amniotic fluid might serve as a taste stimulus. Since change is ordinarily thought of as essential to real external stimulation, however, the question may be debated as to whether or not the change in the amniotic fluid as pregnancy progresses is enough to make it at any point a taste stimulus (Feldman, 1920). To the writer this seems unlikely. A safe conclusion seems to be that, although the mechanism for taste is present before birth, there is no adequate stimulation of this sense until after birth. Here again we have an illustration of what the present writer has called the law of *anticipatory morphological maturation.*

Experiments on the sense of taste in newborn children have been carried out by Kussmaul (1859), Genzmer (1882), and Peterson and Rainey (1910) using the method of general observation of facial expression after stimulation. The conclusion of these writers is that sweet is distinguished, even by premature infants, from salt, sour, and bitter. It is difficult to be sure, however, that salt, sour, and bitter are stimuli for behavior that is specific. Canestrini (1913) and Jensen (1932) have worked out a method of experimentally recording bodily changes which result from taste. Pratt, Nelson, and Sun (1930) find that under the conditions of their experiment, involving very dilute concentrations, there is not as strong evidence in regard to taste differentiation at birth as had previously been supposed. These later experimenters conclude that the stimulating efficiency of various sapid substances in early life is not only quantitatively but also qualitatively different from the condition in adult life. (See Pfaffman, 1936, in this connection.)

It may thus be said that the receptors for taste are probably never normally activated before birth. The receptor-neuromuscular mechanism, however, has been shown, by work on premature infants, to be ready to function in late fetal life whenever appropriate stimulating conditions are brought to bear upon it. Most experimenters seem to conclude that sweet stands in a class by itself so far as the infant is concerned. Salt, sour, and bitter are apparently distinguishable with greater difficulty. References to the sense of taste in infrahuman fetuses have been given above.

Smell. Bedford and Disse and others quoted by Parker (1922) have considered the embryonic development of the receptor cells of the nervous fibers of the olfactory epithelium. Lane (1917), as already noted, has studied the development of the olfactory structures in the rat. Feldman (1920) points out that the olfactory and tactual parts of the brain were found by Flechsig to be the earliest to be myelinated in the fetus. Historically, save where taste and smell have

been grouped together, there seems to have been general agreement, in the early period at least, that while the nasal cavity is filled with the amniotic liquid there can be no *adequate* olfactory stimulation. Preyer (1885) specifically defends this conclusion, basing his statement on Weber's assertion (1847) that substances that could be smelled when vaporized were quite unable to arouse the sense of smell when introduced into the nose as liquids.

A great deal of relevant work in this field has been critically summarized by Parker (1922). This work shows that there is excellent reason to believe "that the olfactory organs of an air-inhabiting vertebrate can be stimulated by ordinary solutions, though this form of stimulation cannot be looked upon as normal." Even though this is true, however, the same difficulty as that met with in the sense of taste must be remembered to exist. Even though the amniotic fluid may be an effective inadequate stimulus for the olfactory receptors, there is little reason to suppose that there would be sufficient change in the liquid to effect significant stimulation during prenatal life.

In this sense field, therefore, the study of smell reactions of prematurely delivered infants will again be very significant in any determination of how the functional development of the olfactory mechanism progresses during late fetal life. Kussmaul (1859) found that asafetida and certain other odors, but not irritating substances, led to responses in a 1-month premature infant. He is not sure that he was able to secure responses in earlier premature infants. Peterson and Rainey (1910) also found smell reactions in premature infants.

Historically, there has long been a belief that the newborn child could distinguish odors effectively. Feldman (1920) asserts that the Jewish sages in the time of the Talmud believed that a blind baby could tell his mother's milk by smell and taste. Rousseau also commented on the sense of smell in newborn infants (Feldman, 1920). Preyer (1882) reports that an 18-day infant refused a breast nipple on which kerosene had been placed but eagerly took the other odorless breast immediately after the refusal. Preyer (1882) also demonstrated that newborn guinea pigs apparently select their food by the sense of smell. He asserted, moreover, that in young animals, including man, the sense of smell in general is most important in determining behavior. Indeed, in infrahuman animals it is suggested that this significant aspect of behavior determination by smell does not come to be neglected to the extent that it is by civilized man.

Experimental work on the sense of smell in newborn infants, which is probably also generally applicable to late premature infants, has been summarized by Canestrini (1913), Peiper (1928), and Pratt, Nelson, and Sun (1930). Canestrini concludes that there has been some exaggeration in regard to the effectiveness of the sense of smell in young animals. He feels that most of the work on smell has been concerned with stimuli which act on the receptors related to the trigeminal cranial nerve components of the nasal receptor surfaces. These trigeminal components are probably best considered as the "common chemical sense" (Parker, 1922) and not in the usual sense of the term "tactual" as suggested by Pratt, Nelson, and Sun (1930). Certainly the trigeminal endings are not "olfactory" in the ordinary sense. Stimulation of the common chemical sense receptors typically sets off violent reactions, such as sneezing. A characteristic irritant of this sort is ammonia. It is significant in this connection to notice that Pratt, Nelson, and Sun found ammonia to be a peculiarly effective "smell" stimulus. Probably the responses of a newborn infant to ammonia should be considered as responses to the common chemical sense rather than to true olfactory stimulation.

In summary: The neural mechanism for olfaction—that is, the mechanism related to the so-called first cranial nerve—is developed before birth, and the possibility of inadequate stimulation exists before birth. It is probably true, however, that olfaction does not generally occur in its normal form until the nasal cavity comes to be filled with air. Premature infants, at least in the last month, are able to smell substances when air enters the olfactory cavity. Much work on smell, however, has probably been vitiated by the fact that the free nerve endings of the trigeminal nerve (the fifth cranial nerve), the receptors for the common chemical sense, have been stimulated rather than the true olfactory spindles.

Hearing. Anatomically the development of the ear in the individual has been extensively studied. This work is summarized by Keibel and Mall (1910). Hess (1922) shows an original drawing of a section through the ear of a late fetus. Stevens and Davis (1938) have summarized much of the experimental work upon the adult auditory mechanism.

Historical opinion on the sense of hearing in the human fetus is probably best summarized in the words of Kussmaul (1859): "Von allen Sinnen schlummert das Gehör am tiefsten." The history of experiment on the sound response of full-term and prematurely born infants is excellently summarized by Pratt, Nelson, and Sun (1930). The general conclusion of these authors is in harmony with that of the later investigators, that hearing becomes effective only in the very early part of postnatal life.

Most of the early investigators of the development of audition concluded that the auditory mechanism was developed to a point at which it could be functional before birth but that the infant remained deaf until by breathing, crying, and possibly yawning the Eustachian tube was opened. Only in this way, they suggested, could the somewhat gelatinous liquid of the fetal middle ear be drained out (Preyer, 1882). Peterson and Rainey (1910) specifically secured evidence of auditory response in a prematurely delivered infant as soon as there had been an opportunity for the draining of the middle ear. More modern work seems to have offered no reason to differ with this conclusion so far as stimuli of normal intensity are concerned. Preyer (1882) also reports that newborn guinea pigs are deaf for ½ hour after birth and are then sensitive to tonal stimuli of a great variety of frequencies (C of third octave to E of eighth). Avery (1928) has secured comparable results on late guinea pig fetuses prematurely delivered, as noted above. The experiment of Rawdon-Smith, Carmichael, and Wellman (1938), which shows by electrical methods of recording the onset of functional activity in the cochlea, has already been referred to. This experiment shows that the guinea pig fetus can hear before birth, judging by both electrical and behavioral criteria.

Although there has been some speculation

on the fact that the sounds inside the mother's body might act as sound stimuli to the fetus, little evidence has been brought forward to make this seem certain (Preyer, 1885). There are experimental findings which suggest that loud auditory stimuli may activate the human fetus. Peiper (1925) was led to this study because he noted that in six neonates, very soon after birth, changes in the breathing curve were found in response to a special sound stimulus. The change in the breathing curve is reported as marked. He therefore decided to try to find out whether or not any indication of hearing before birth could be secured. It had been discovered that auditory and other sudden stimuli give two sorts of responses in the newborn—one, a change in breathing rhythm, and the second, a change in the level of general movements. Peiper felt that there was no sure reason to believe that the unborn child would respond differently if it could be stimulated in its auditory receptors. The breathing center in the brain is open to stimulation before birth. He therefore thought of the possibility of using the prenatal "breathing movements" of Ahlfeld as an indicator of sound response. The disadvantage was found, however, that these movements were not always present, and so the number of subjects was limited. But with proper recording apparatus he was able to take records of the general movement of the fetus through the body wall of the mother.

It was obvious that sounds would be much muffled on their way to the fetus. Therefore a very loud sound was chosen as a stimulus, an automobile horn being used. The experimenter waited until the fetus was absolutely quiet and the mother had been prepared so that she would not herself respond to the stimulus. Incidentally, it proved impossible to train all mothers in this way. The stimulus was given in a quiescent interval. In more than a third of the subjects studied, definite fetal reactions were secured to stimulation of this sort. There were, however, individual differences in responsiveness. Sometimes the response was given on one day and not on the next. The movements which the fetus made in response to the stimuli also showed individual differences. Most often, however, the fetus seemed to draw its whole body together. Peiper (1925) comments that it

might seem to one who had not been present at the experiments that the movement was a response of the mother and not of the fetus. He is certain, however, that one who had actually observed the experiment would be convinced that the response was fetal and not maternal. As an additional safeguard, a pneumograph was placed on the mother's chest and her breathing curve taken during the experiment. After a good deal of practice it was possible to train some mothers so that they made practically no response, and thus the fetal response could be recorded. Continued stimulation led to a diminution of the effect. This corresponds to a frequently observed phenomenon of fetuses and neonates: their responses are easily fatigued or exhausted. Peiper even goes so far as to suggest that this change in response may be thought of as a simple kind of attention. He also states that one mother remarked that she had noticed definite movements of the fetus while attending a concert.

Forbes and Forbes (1927) have reported a case of apparent fetal hearing. Thirty-one days before her baby was born a pregnant woman was lying in a metal bathtub full of warm water. A 2-year-old child was playing on the floor beside the tub. Accidentally the child struck the side of the tub with a small glass jar, and at once a sudden jump of the fetus was felt by the mother, which gave a sensation quite unlike the usual kicks or limb movements. A few days later an observer struck the side of the tub below the water line a quick rap with a small metallic object, meanwhile watching the mother's abdomen. A fraction of a second after the rap, a single quick rise of the anterior abdominal wall was clearly visible. The mother at this moment felt the same jump inside her abdomen as previously reported. Her own muscles were entirely relaxed, and she was not at all startled by the noise, nor was she conscious of perceiving any vibration through the skin. The mother's tactual sense later tested showed that the same intensity of vibration could be perceived only by those portions of the skin coming in contact with the tub. In the infant in question, 8 days after birth, it is interesting to note that while the baby was nursing an auditory stimulus occurred which resulted in the flattening of the baby's ear against the side of the head for a few seconds, after which the ear relaxed again. These same investigators also report another case in which concerts attended toward the end of pregnancy resulted in troublesome activity on the part of the fetus. The conclusion of these writers (1927) is:

Good evidence exists that the human fetus 4 or 5 weeks before birth can respond with sudden movements to a loud sound originating outside the body of the mother. It seems probable that this is a true auditory-muscular reflex but the possibility of reception through tactile organs in the skin cannot be excluded.

Recently the fetal heart rhythms of 32 pregnant women in the latter part of pregnancy were studied. Tones of 1000 and 2000 cycles per second of an intensity of 100 decibels were given for 5 seconds. Acceleration of fetal heart to the 1000 cycles per second tone averaged 7 beats a minute. To the 2000 cycles per second tone the increase was 11 beats a minute. The mother's heart did not show any acceleration. The hearing of premature infants has been studied by a similar technique (Johansson, Wedenberg, and Westin, 1964).

The response of the fetus to auditory stimulation has been made the basis of several studies of fetal learning, to which reference is made below.

In summary: It may be said that the auditory mechanism seems to be well developed structurally during later fetal life, but in general, possibly because of the closure of the external ear or because of the gelatinous liquid which fills the middle ear, the fetus is probably deaf to sounds of normal intensity before birth and during a short period immediately after birth. Strong sounds, however, especially those which can directly pass through the mechanical blocks noted, seem to be able to bring about auditory stimulation before birth, although it is still possible that such responses are tactual rather than truly auditory.

Vision. The specific morphological cellular changes which are the essential antecedents to the development of the function of the human eye begin in the second or third week of development of the embryonic period, and from that time on an elaborate series of events occurs until, in the normal human individual, binocular convergence and the diverse activities associated with visual space perception and stereoperception develop in the young child. The anatomical aspects of this growth have been summarized by Keibel and Mall (1910) and by Mann (1928). Hess (1922) has described in some detail the eye of an early premature infant.

So far as the function of sight in normal prenatal life is concerned, there has been general agreement that the absence of radiation of the sort that typically activates the retina makes true sight all but impossible in prenatal life (Preyer, 1885). The possibility does exist that under very strong light stimulation, if the head were in just the right place, radiation falling on the mother's abdomen might stimulate the fetal retina, but this seems most unlikely. There is evidence, however, given by Kussmaul (1859), that pronounced differences between light and dark bring about specific reactions in an infant born 2 months before term. Peterson and Rainey (1910) also found light reactions in premature infants. Genzmer (1882) does not confirm this observation. Preyer (1885) agrees that adequate stimuli are impossible during fetal life, but he considers the possibility that inadequate stimuli of pressure similar to the stimuli which bring about phosphenes might be effective in prenatal life.

There is evidence that even at normal birth the optic nerve and related structures have not fully developed anatomically (Pratt, Nelson, and Sun, 1930). This knowledge has led to speculation in regard to the neural basis of the development of eye muscle function in neonatal life. This whole question has been considered by Preyer (1882) in relation to the nativistic and empiristic theories of the visual spatial world, with the conclusion that the evidence is conflicting.

The writer has taken a few records of the eye movements of human babies, using the electrical recording method. These movements were induced by placing the baby's head in a large rotating drum on which there were striations. The results of these experiments showed that it was possible to elicit optokinetic nystagmus in early infants. This technique may also be used as an objective means of determining lower brightness and color vision thresholds in normal or premature newborn infants. For a description of this technique especially as applied to recording of eye wink and eyeball movements see Carmichael and Dearborn (1947).

One of the best indices of the sensitivity of the fetus to light, although possibly not to the full neural mechanism involved in true visual responses, is thought to be the onset of the light-stimulated pupillary reflex. Portal (1818) alleged that responses of the iris diaphragm did not appear during fetal life. Hess (1922) and others, however, have shown that in premature infants strong light stimulus leads to contraction of the pupil, followed in 2 or 3 seconds by dilation again. Bolaffio and Artom (1924) and Minkowski (1928a), as noted above, have been unable to make unequivocal statements about light reflexes in late fetuses. As pointed out in another part of this chapter, care must be exercised, especially when strong light is used, not to confuse the independent, non-neurally determined muscular response of the iris to light with the true iris reflex. The development of the pupillary response in postnatal life has been summarized by Peiper (1928).

Much of the evidence in regard to the general muscular movements of the eyes in the first days of life has been summarized by Pratt, Nelson, and Sun (1930). Early eye movements have been carefully studied in the newborn child by Sherman and Sherman (1925). As already noted above, however, there is excellent evidence to show that during fetal life eye movements occur as part of the general tonus change of the body musculature resulting from the spatial reorientation of the entire fetal body. (See Carmichael, 1940b.) Preyer (1882) and many students since his time have discussed the development of function in the auxiliary musculature of the eye, including the mechanism of winking. In general, great differences are noted in the tonus and general behavior of the lids in the newborn child as contrasted with those of the older child. Some hints of the beginning of this development are to be found in the reports on fetal development given by Minkowski. In a fetus of only 160 mm he found that touching the closed eyelid led to a contraction of the orbicularis muscle (1922).

So far as infrahuman organisms are concerned, there is the greatest divergence from type to type in respect to the time of the opening of the eyes. The subject was early investigated, Emmert, one of the first students of fetal mammals, having studied this phenomenon in the mouse (Emmert and Burgätzy, 1818). Certainly no generalizations can be made from form to form in regard to eyelid activities at the time of birth. The guinea pig is born with eyes open and apparently in an adult functional condition, whereas the lids of the rat do not gain their adult condition until the sixteenth or seventeenth postnatal day (Lane, 1917). Warkentin and Smith (1937) and Warkentin (1938) have studied the development of a number of visual functions by various techniques in developing animals. (See also Mowrer, 1936, for a general consideration of learning versus maturation in this field.)

In summary: Concerning vision in the fetus it can be said that the specific morphological changes that lie behind the development of the visual mechanism occur from possibly the second week after fertilization until well after birth. Light stimuli at intense levels ordinarily do not affect the retina before birth, but in premature infants it can be shown that the eye is probably sufficiently structurally developed before birth to make possible the light or iris reflex and the differentiation between light and dark. The functional development of the neuromuscular apparatus of the eye is also gradual. Indications have been obtained in regard to the relationship between vestibular stimulation and eye movements before birth which suggest that vestibular control is more primitive than visual control. Eyelid reactions are also found to undergo a progressive series of changes before normal birth.

THE SENSES IN GENERAL RELATIONSHIP TO THE ONSET OF MENTAL LIFE IN THE PRENATAL PERIOD

For the psychologist there are at least two major problems connected with the study of the senses. The first of these is the classic problem of the relationship between the senses and what the philosophers have long called conscious experience. The second is the relationship between receptor activity and the initiation, modification, and control of behavior. As noted above, this control must be considered in certain cases to include a continuous "feedback" relationship with existing continuous or periodic activity (Wiener, 1948). Many psychologists, on the basis of some excellent reasons, hold that ultimately these two problems reduce to one, as Langfeld (1931) and others have urged in the interpretation of consciousness in terms of response. Historically, however, and indeed at the present time, the two problems are ordinarily treated as separate, or at any rate as separable. Some prefer to say that consciousness and behavior are aspects of the total functional description of the relationship between the adult (or immature) human organism and its environment. Here, although no attempt will be made to find an ultimate answer to the question whether these problems are really one or two, they will be treated as independent.

A study of the fetal senses contributes little to our knowledge of the so-called introspective psychology of consciousness. There has been some speculation concerning sensory experience before birth, but little of scientific validity has been written. As incidentally noted above, several of the empiristic philosophers concerned themselves with prenatal life. John Locke (1849 edition) did not neglect the possibility that some dim ideas were present before birth. Cabanis (Genzmer, 1882) held that quite elaborate sensory experiences were present in the fetus, even to the consciousness of self. (Cf. Compayré, 1896.) Kussmaul (1859) held that the child came into the world with a dim perception of an outer world. Preyer (1882) also attributed experience of a sort to the fetus. Peterson and Rainey (1910) say: "The newborn comes into the world with a small store of experience and associated feelings and a shadowy consciousness."

Such observations could be added to by other excerpts from early psychologists, but on the whole they seem profitless. Compayré (1896), more than 70 years ago, summarized the scientific arguments against such speculations as well as against the fancies of the Neo-Platonists that "our birth is but a sleep and a forgetting." The gist of his argument is that there can be no evidence on the matter. With this point of view the writer is in accord.

James (1890) and, more recently, Koffka (1924) and his associates made much of the fact that in early postnatal life specific experiences, like specific acts of behavior, become individuated out of totalities rather than at first synthesized out of discrete elements. Thus James (1890, Vol. I) says: "The baby, assailed by eyes, ears, nose, skin, and entrails at once, feels it all as one great blooming, buzzing confusion." And again: "Our original sensible totals are, on the one hand, subdivided by discriminative attention, and, on the other, united with other totals." Koffka (1924) similarly asserts: "From an unlimited and ill-defined background there has arisen a limited and somewhat definite phenomenon, a quality." Certainly if these descriptions are adequate to the experiential life of the neonate, there is no reason to suppose that they may not also be adequate, although possibly in a still vaguer form, to conscious fetal life. If the writer were asked to make a guess in regard to the matter, he would say that he feels that the description given above by Koffka is probably relatively adequate as a description of the development of fetal conscious experience. It may be pointed out that such experience may parallel reactions to many different and quite specific types of receptor stimuli.

So far as the present writer is concerned, there is no objection to applying to ontogeny, that is, growth in the individual, a point of view similar to that now generally accepted in regard to the growth of consciousness in the development of the animal series. Such judgments must be treated as complex inferences, however, and not as facts of observation. The writer further points out that a scientific definition of the word "consciousness" as commonly used has not yet been presented in a form to win general acceptance. The problem of the nature of consciousness and its relation to the brain is still viewed as a scientific and not merely as a philosophical question. A recent book, *Brain and Conscious Experience*, edited by J. C. Eccles (1966), is devoted largely to a consideration of the concept of consciousness from the point of view of neurophysiology.

The second large problem which concerns the psychologist in relation to receptor activity has grown out of the approach to the study of mental life which deals explicitly with the processes of behavior. The problem of the receptor or, possibly better, of stimulus control of behavior is, however, much older than the so-called school of behaviorism. Kussmaul (1859) explicitly defended this view in undertaking his study of premature and normal newborn infants. It is related to a much more general position, as is the view expressed by Forel and quoted by Canestrini (1913): "Das wahre Baumateriel der Organismen liefern die Reize der Aussenwelt." One who takes a type of "communication theory" approach to behavior can consider that all behavior is a result of genetically determined responses that result from mutations that led to survival in the ancestors of each organism or to encoded environmentally determined learning in the individual under consideration.

It seems more and more certain that, whatever else scientific psychology may do, it must thus concern itself increasingly with the relationship between the environment external to the receptors, be they extroceptors, interoceptors, or proprioceptors, and to the responses of the organism to such stimulation. In any consideration of fetal psychology, therefore, special attention should be given to the facts of the stimulus control of behavior. In order to understand this relationship, it will be necessary to review the current status of fact and theory in regard to the causes underlying the beginning and differentiation of activity in the fetal organism. This consideration may well serve as a conclusion to this chapter, because any such discussion will necessarily involve a review of many of those processes of fetal life which are even inferentially significant for general psychology. For an excellent consideration of this general field see Hooker (1942; 1952; etc.).

In the beginning of this chapter, something was said of the early processes of morphogenesis in the developing organism. It was suggested that the point should be kept continually in view by one who is interested in behavioral development, that the general growth of structure and function always occurs in an organism that is in an environment. Organisms do not live or grow in a physical or biological vacuum. From the first cell division in the developing individual, each process of structural and functional modification is, moreover, to be considered as a complex resultant of activities. Some of these determinants are intrinsic in the cell and are, indeed, in the correst sense of the term hereditary, but such intrinsic determinants always act in a dynamic system which is also subjected to extrinsic influences. Development is apparently always a resultant of these two sets of forces working *interdependently*. For some of the evidence on this matter, see earlier papers by Carmichael (1925, 1938). Sharp (1926) summarizes this point of view when he says in his consideration of general cytology:

The cell should not be thought of as a static . . . structure. It is rather a dynamic system in a constantly changing state of molecular flux, its constitution at any given moment being dependent upon antecedent states and upon environmental conditions.

To put this in another way, the problem is not whether a given type of behavior is a result of heredity or environment. This is true because the environment is essential in the development of all inherited mechanisms that determine behavior. The real question is to determine whether a behavior act under study is a result of the work of the genetic code or of the individually determined engram.

If space permitted a review of the present status of that part of scientific embryology which is devoted to developmental mechanics, it would become apparent that the process of growth in the organism involves a most complex series of energy relationships, some of which, it seems probable, have as yet only begun to be unraveled. (See Arshavsky, 1967).

Joseph Altman (1966), in his consideration of the organic foundations of animal behavior, well considers the relationship just discussed in terms of different modes of neural and behavioral programming. He emphasizes three phases:

1. Fixed morphogenetic programming, which occurs without individual experience and is not generally altered by experience.
2. Modifiable epigenetic programming,

which consists of essential inborn components but requires individual exxperience for its realization. Acquired transactional programming, in which new schemata of behavior are formed on the basis of individual experience.

There seems, therefore, to be excellent evidence for the view elsewhere discussed by the writer (1925) at greater length that, from the movement that growth has begun in the fertilized ovum until senescence or death, development consists of the alteration of existing structures and functions in an organism living in a continually changing environment. It cannot be overemphasized that there is both an external and an internal environment. As noted elsewhere in this chapter, the alterations that take place in the chemistry of the blood stream, which supplies the central nervous system, are fundamental in altering the way in which this system responds to the afferent neural impulses which come in from its receptors.

Above all, it must be remembered that the genetic code continues to influence growth and behavior as long as the organism lives.

Conel (1939–1963) has studied in detail the postnatal development of the human cerebral cortex. This elaborate series of investigations discusses the cytoarchitectonic pattern of the cerebral cortex at various early postnatal ages. This investigator points out, for example, that the behavior of the human infant during the first month of life may be mediated by subcortical centers. He concludes, "The gradual development of the structural components of the cortical mechanism suggests that function also develops gradually." Noback (1959) has also worked in this area.

In the area of human neonatal sleep, Bartoshuk (1964) has investigated four areas of awake and sleep samples using the electroencephalographic techniques.

Hamburger and his associates (1957; 1963; 1964; 1965; 1966; 1967) in a general consideration of the ontogeny of behavior and its structural basis presents strong evidence for his previously expressed view that the early development of behavior is genetically determined. He says, "The architecture of the nervous system and the concomitant behavior patterns result from self-generating growth and maturation processes that are determined entirely by inherited intrinsic factors, to the exclusion of functional adjustment, exercise or anything else akin to learning."

The fact that learning is possible in fetal life has been noted previously in this chapter. This question can thus be raised: To what degree are the normal behavior changes that are observed in the early ontogenetic development of any typical mammal or in man a result of specific individual environmental stimulation (i.e., to some type of learning or conditioning) or the result of the working out of the genetic code?

Ray (1932) has attempted to condition fetal responses. Spelt (1938), using the auditory responses of the fetus described above, has reported the conditioning of the human fetus. These and other studies of early postnatal learning may be taken as demonstrating that the neural mechanism of the late fetus has matured to a level at which environmentally determined learning is possible. This, of course, should not be taken as indicating that *all* behavior changes after learning has begun is a result of further learning.

The present author will try, in the following paragraphs, to suggest one answer to this old and crucially important question on the basis of his years of observation of fetal behavior and his study of the publications of others in this field. No claim is made for originality in what is presented here, and it will not always be possible to cite specific references for the ideas that are given. This is a field in which much active research and theoretical writing is in progress and anything asserted about it at one time must always be considered subject to change as additional scientific evidence is secured.

As has been pointed out before, it is a truism that all behavior depends on structure. Behavior, indeed, is structure in action. Behavior is anything a human being or other animal does. Structure in the sense used here may be at the molecular as well as at the molar level. As has been said more than once in this chapter, the developing organism always exists in an environment. The genetic code of each species has indeed evolved in organisms that exist in what may be called "normal" prenatal and postnatal environments for the species. Fuller and Thompson (1960) well express this fact: "The development of any trait always involves genetic and environmental determinants" and "a trait is called hereditary if most of the variation within a population is associated with genetic endowment."

Today there seems little doubt that it can be asserted with assurance that in all mammals including man, early behavior is a result of the activation of structures that are as they are largely as a result of genetic endowment. Typical of such behavior is the elaborate repertory of specific responses that the present author has described above, to take but one example, as characterizing the developing prenatal guinea pig. This is true "species-specific behavior." It is possible to quibble about the words used, but there can be no doubt that these standard prenatal reactions are as surely hereditary as in hair color, tooth pattern, or species-specific skeletal makeup.

As any mammal passes through ontogenetic development, it comes to a stage or period at which some type of learning or conditioning can be demonstrated as important in determining the adjustments that the individual mammal makes to the environment in which it is adaptively existing. This does not mean that the genetic code has ceased to operate in the altering of some of the structures on which some observable behavior change depends. In other words, even after an animal can learn, some of its behavior changes are a result of maturation rather than learning. There is, therefore, in postnatal life, a close and interlocking interrelationship between "maturation" and "learning" in determining the multitudinous specific structural changes on which new adaptive acts depend. In this connection, a point should be emphasized again that is clearly made by Margaret Green (1966). She says, "In multicellular organisms many kinds of cells are formed and it is clear that although each kind contains the whole array of genes present in the zygote, only certain genes are active in each different kind of cell. In some way, genes are called into action at particular times and promote changes which may then call certain other genes into action or repress activity of others already active."

It may be helpful here to consider this mechanism of embryologic growth and of behavior change in different words. No one doubts that if any population of organisms is to survive and reproduce its kind and escape extinction, enough of its members must adapt successfully to what is ordinarily its own geographically isolated niche so as to allow the essential reproductive activity that alone makes it possible for the gene pool of the population of organisms in question to remain at a viable level. This means that each species of organism and its environment must communicate at all times and they must communicate in an adaptive way. The genetic code may thus be thought of as a record or, to use a standard analogy, as a "punch card" by means of which adaptive communication between the ancestors of the living members of a species and their environments have taken place and allowed the origin and the viable life of the ancestors of present representatives of any species. Each phylogenetic code has developed by mutation and the organisms possessing such codes are those that survive as a result of all the processes called "natural selection."

Because of its inborn genetic code, therefore, each new organism is able to communicate adaptively with its environment on a basis that is similar in some respects to that which previously allowed the survival of its ancestors.

As Hirsch (1962) well says, "We cannot understand the behavior of an organism without understanding the organism not only as an integrated and coordinated system responsive to its environment but also as a member of a population with a unique evolutionary history adapting it to the niche it presently occupies."

In the ontogeny of the human beings and all other mammals, as just pointed out, the genetic code produces a stage or stages at which adaptive changes are not only made on the basis of ancestral information concerning what is adaptive, in communication between the organism and its environment, but also in the production of a new, vitally important characteristic by means of which new environmental information can produce structural changes basic to individual habits or other individually determined acts of adaptive behavior. That is, the genetic code determines a level or a series of levels of development at which learning or specific types of learning are possible. Barlow (1961), in considering the physiology of sensory inputs, emphasizes that such messages are compressed by removing redundancy and thus suggests the idea that the code which compresses messages may also constitute the basis of memory. (See paragraphs on perception above.)

This view that the changes of behavior that result from both maturation and learning are to be considered as dependent on mechanisms by means of which an organism "communicates" with its environment needs much further study and amplification. It may be that the key to both these processes will be found in a new understanding of the engram. In this sense the term engram is used to describe the physical basis of habit, that is, a hypothetical more or less permanently altered state of living tissue resulting from previous excitation. If this view is adopted, it may be said that just as a record of the successful communications between a species of organisms and their environments (which have led to survival) are stored in the DNA-RNA mechanisms, so also it may be that individual adaptive changes in behavior which are based on learning are dependent on individually acquired coded molecular changes.

It is clear that the changes established by individual experience do not directly alter the phylogenetic code. This code is carried in the germ cells of each succeeding generation until changed by mutation. Biology has clearly demonstrated that the so-called Lamarkian theory of evolution—that acquired characteristics somehow become hereditary characters—is not true. In other words, except as mutations change the code of the germ cells of populations of organisms the adaptive acts of the adults of any population do not alter the basic genetic code of that population.

The two codes mentioned above do, however, play complex roles in the determination of the structures, whether molecular or molar—on which the adaptive responses of organisms to the information secured from the environment at any time depend. The full ontogeny of individual behavior can thus be thought of as dependent in an intricate way on both of these coded systems. An example may make this more clear. The terrestrial locomotion of mammals, including men, can, as indicated above, be shown to depend in a basic way on the genetic code and also upon the particular engram system of the individual, which has been determined by the organism's specific learned habits of locomotion in the particular environment in which it exists and has developed. The complexity of this problem is well analyzed by Hyden (1967; 1967a) in his paper on behavior, neural function, and RNA.

As already suggested, there is much that is still speculative in the consideration of the role of phylogenetic and ontogenetic codes, as just presented, but this view is given here as a means of stimulating further study and research. For a consideration of some of the problems involved in thinking of a chemical basis of learning of the sort suggested here, the reader should consult a paper and references given by Agranoff (1967) in a consideration of memory and protein synthesis. In a consideration of the chemical basis of memory, see Flexner, Flexner, and Stellar (1963; 1967) and the references given by them.

The immediately preceding paragraphs contain statements that must be viewed today as speculative. What has been written is intended to suggest that scientific work of great importance is now in progress that may soon give a firm scientific basis for an understanding of the growth of normal and abnormal behavior and of applied procedures to modify behavior whether the molecular basis of such behavior is seen to be "inborn" or "acquired." This will then indeed show how important it is for the psychologist to understand the onset and early development of behavior.

The student who wishes further study in this field should consult, besides the detailed references given, papers by Hooker (1936, 1939a, 1942, 1943; and especially 1952), which summarize much of the work in this field; the summary of the early work on the development of behavior by Dewey (1935); and the important book *Physiology of the Fetus: Origin and Extent of Function in Prenatal Life* by Windle (1940). Chapter 17, "The embryology of behavior" in Marler and Hamilton (1966) is an especially valuable short introduction to this field.

The late Sir Joseph Barcroft's important work, to which many references are given in this chapter, is also summarized in a book, *Researches on Pre-Natal Life* (1946). Early development in general is summarized in a chapter, "Ontogenetic Development," by Carmichael in the *Handbook of Experimental Psychology*, edited by S. S. Stevens, 1951.

This chapter may well end by two quotations from poets. The first is from Oliver Wendell Holmes (noted by Irving in his foreward to Smith's excellent *The Physiology of the Newborn Infant*, 1946):

So the stout fetus, kicking and alive,
Leaps from the fundus for his final dive.
Tired of the prison where his legs were
    curled
He pants, like Rasselas, for a wider world.

No more to him their wanted joys afford
The fringed placenta and the knotted cord.

The second is prose, written by a poet—Coleridge (1885):

Yes—the history of a man for the nine months preceding his birth would probably be far more interesting and contain events of greater moment, than all the three score and ten years that follow it!

Poets have a way of understanding what psychologists sometimes miss!

References

Abel, S., and Windle, W. F. Relation of the volume of pulmonary circulation to respiration at birth. *Anat. Rec.*, 1939, **75**, 451–464.

Adair, F. L. The ossification centers of the fetal pelvis. *Am. J. Obstet.*, 1918, **78**, 175–199.

Adamsons, K., and Towell, M. E. Thermal homeostasis in the fetus and newborn. *Anesthesiology*, 1965, **26**, 531–48.

Agranoff, B. W. Memory and protein synthesis. *Scient. Am.* 1967, **216**, 115–122.

Ahlfeld, J. F. Beiträge zur Lehre vom Uebergange der intrauterinen Athmung zur extrauterinen. In *Beiträge zur Physiologie, Festschrift zu Carl Ludwig, zu seinem 70. Geburtstage gewidmet von seinen Schülern*. Leipzig: Vogel, 1890. Pp. 1–32.

Alconero, B. The nature of the earliest spontaneous activity of the chick embryo. *J. Embryol. exp. Morph.*, 1965, **13**, 255–256.

Altman, J. *Organic foundations of animal behavior*. New York: Holt, Rinehart and Winston, 1966.

Altman, P. L., and Dittmer, D. S. *Growth, including reproduction and morphological development*. Washington, D. C.: Federation of American Societies for Experimental Biology, 1962.

Andrew, R. J. The development of adult responses from responses given during imprinting by the domestic chick. *Anim. Behav.*, 1964, **12**, 542–8.

Angulo y González, A. W. The motor nuclei in the cervical cord of the albino rat at birth. *J. comp. Neurol.*, 1927, **43**, 115–142.

Angulo y González. A. W. Priliminary report on the motor-cell columns in the cervical region of the albino rat before birth. *Anat. Rec.*, 1928, **38**, 46–47.

Angulo y González, A. W. Is myelinogeny an absolute index of behavioral capability? *J. comp. Neurol.*, 1929, **48**, 459–464. (a)

Angulo y González, A. W. Neurological interpretation of fetal behavior: the motor-cell columns of the albino rat before birth. (Abs.) *Anat. Rec.*, 1929, **42**, 17. (b)

Angulo y González, A. W. Endogenous stimulation of albino rat fetuses. *Proc. Soc. exp. Biol. Med.*, 1930, **27**, 579. (a)

Angulo y González, A. W. Motion-picture records showing the typical stages in the development of muscular activity in albino-rat fetuses which are used in connection with the corresponding changes in the nervous system. *Anat. Rec.*, 1930, **45**, 284. (b)

Angulo y González, A. W. Neurological interpretation of fetal behavior: The progressive increase of muscular activity in albino-rat fetuses. (Abs.) *Anat. Rec.,* 1930, **45,** 254. (c)

Angulo y González, A. W. The prenatal development of behavior in the albino rat. *J. comp. Neurol.,* 1932, **55,** 395–442. (a)

Angulo y González, A. W. The prenatal growth of the albino rat. *Anat. Rec.,* 1932, **52,** 117–138. (b)

Angulo y González, A. W. Development of somatic activity in the albino rat fetuses. *Proc. Soc. exp. Biol. Med.,* 1933, **31,** 111–112. (a)

Angulo y González, A. W. Endogenous stimulation of albino rat fetuses. *Anat. Rec.,* Suppl., 1933, **55,** 3. (b)

Angulo y González, A. W. Functional dissolution of the nervous system in albino rat fetuses induced by means of asphyxia. *Anat. Rec.,* Suppl., 1934, **58,** 45. (a)

Angulo y González, A. W. Neurological interpretation of fetal behavior: structural changes in the nervous system of the albino rat and their relation to behavioral development, *Anat. Rec.,* Suppl., 1934, **58,** 2. (b)

Angulo y González, A. W. Further studies upon development of somatic activity in albino rat fetuses. *Proc. Soc. exp. Biol. Med.,* 1935, **32,** 621–622.

Angulo y González, A. W. Neurological interpretation of fetal behavior: the development of the sensory system in albino rat. *Anat. Rec.,* Suppl., 1937, **67,** 4.

Angulo y González, A. W. Histogenesis of the monopolar neuroblast and the ventral longitudinal path in the albino rat. *J. comp. Neurol.,* 1939, **71,** 325–359.

Angulo y González, A. W. The differentiation of the motor-cell columns in the cervical cord of albino rat fetuses. *J. comp. Neurol.,* 1940, **73,** 469–488.

Anokhin, P. K. Systemogenesis as a general regulator of brain development. In W. Himwich and H. Himwich (Eds.), *The developing brain. Progress in brain research,* Vol. 9, New York: Elsevier, 1964. Pp. 54–86.

Arena, J. M. Drug dangers to the fetus from maternal medications. *Clin. Pediat.,* 1964, **3,** 450, 465, 471.

Arendt. Wann ist die Perforation des lebenden Kindes notwendig? *Dtsch. med. Presse,* 1910, **14,** 167–168.

Arshavsky, I. A. Mechanisms of the development of nutritional functions during the intrauterine period and following birth. *Zh. obshch. Biol.,* 1959, **20,** 104–114.

Arshavsky, I. A. Essays on physiological growth, Moscow: Academy of Medical Science of the U.S.S.R., 1967.

Arshavsky, I. A. Adaptive and homeostatic mechanisms in the development of physiologically mature and immature organisms. In G. Newton and S. Levine, *Early experience and behavior,* Springfield, Ill.: Thomas, 1968.

Assali, N. S., Kirschbaum, T., Lucas, W., and Beck, R. Dynamics of the fetal lamb circulation before and after birth. *Physiologist,* 1965, **8,** 339–340.

Avery, G. T. Responses of fetal guinea pigs prematurely delivered. *Genet. Psychol. Monogr.,* 1928, **3,** 245–331.

Avery, M. E. Some effects of altered environments; relationships between space medicine and adaptations at birth. *Pediatrics,* 1965, **35,** 345–354.

Bailey, S. *A review of Berkeley's theory of vision designed to show the unsoundness of that celebrated speculation.* London: James Ridgeway, 1842.

Bailey, S. (Ed), *Letters on the philosophy of the human mind.* London: Longmans, Green, 1855.

Baitsell, G. A. (Ed.) *The evolution of man.* New Haven, Conn.: Yale University Press, 1922.

Baker, J. B. E. The effects of drugs on the fetus. *Pharmac. Rev.,* 1960, **12,** 37–90.

Baker, T. E. Description of a singularly small child. *Trans. med. phys. Soc. Calcutta,* 1825, **1,** 364–365.

Baker, T. E. Nachricht von einem ausserordentlich kleines Kind. *Z. organ. Physik,* 1827, **1**, 260–261.

Ballantyne, J. W., and Browne, F. J. The problem of foetal post-maturity and prolongation of pregnancy. *J. obstet. gynaec. Brit. Emp.,* 1922, **29** (New Ser.), 177–238.

Barclay, A. E., Franklin, K. J., and Prichard, M. M. L. *The foetal circulation and cardiovascular system and the changes that they undergo at birth.* Springfield, Ill.: Thomas, 1946.

Barclay, A. E., Franklin, K. J., and Prichard, M. M. L. *The circulation in the foetus.* Springfield, Ill.: Thomas, 1947.

Barcroft, J. The mammal before and after birth. *Irish J. Med. Sci.,* 1935, **1**, 289–301.

Barcroft, J. Fetal circulation and respiration. *Physiol. Rev.,* 1936, **16**, 103–128.

Barcroft, J. *The brain and its environment.* New Haven, Conn.: Yale University Press, 1938.

Barcroft, J. *Researches on pre-natal life.* Springfield, Ill.: Thomas, 1946.

Barcroft, J., and Barron, D. H. The genesis of respiratory movements in the foetus of the sheep. *J. Physiol. (London),* 1936, **88**, 56–61.

Barcroft, J., and Barron, D. H. The establishment of certain reflex arcs in foetal sheep. *Proc. Soc. exp. Biol. Med.,* 1937, **36**, 86–87. (a)

Barcroft, J., and Barron, D. H. Movements in midfoetal life in the sheep embryo. *J. Physiol. (London),* 1937, **91**, 329–351. (b)

Barcroft, J., and Barron, D. H. The development of behavior in foetal sheep. *J. comp. Neurol.,* 1939, **70**, 477–502.

Barcroft, J., Barron, D. H., and Windle, W. F. Some observations on genesis of somatic movements in sheep embryos. *J. Physiol. (London),* 1936, **87**, 73–78.

Barcroft, J., and Karvonen, M. J. Action of carbon dioxide and cyanide on fetal respiratory movements; development of chemo-reflex function in sheep. *J. Physiol. (London),* 1948, **107**, 153–161.

Barcroft, J., and Mason, M. F. The atmosphere in which the foetus lives. *J. Physiol. (London),* 1938, **93**, 22.

Barham, W. B. Maternal impressions. *Va. Med. Semi-mo.,* 1915–1916, **20**, 454–459.

Barlow, H. B. The coding of sensory messages. In W. H. Thorpe and O. L. Zangwill (Eds.), *Current problems in animal behavior.* Cambridge: Cambridge University Press, 1961. Pp. 331–360.

Barnett, E., and Narin, A. A study of foetal attitude. *Br. J. Radiol.,* 1965, **38**, 338–349.

Barnum, C. G. The effect of gravitation on the presentation and position of the fetus. *J. Amer. Med. Ass.,* 1915, **64**, 498–502.

Barron, D. H. The results of peripheral anastomoses between the fore and hind limb nerves of albino rats. *J. comp. Neurol.,* 1934, **59**, 301–323.

Barron, D. H. The functional development of some mammalian neuromuscular mechanisms. *Biol. Rev.,* 1941, **16**, 1–33.

Barron, D. H. Genetic neurology and the behavior problem. In P. Weiss (Ed.), *Genetic neurology.* Chicago: University of Chicago Press, 1950. Pp. 223–231.

Bartoshuk, A. Human neonatal EEG frequency analysis of awake and sleep samples from four areas. *Psychonom. Sci.,* 1964, **1**, 281–282.

Bauer, D. J. The effect of asphyxia upon the heart rate of rabbits at different ages. *J. Physiol. (London),* 1938, **93**, 90–103.

Beach, F. A., and Jaynes, J. Effects of early experience upon the behavior of animals. *Psych. Bull.,* 1954, **51**, 239–63.

Becker, R. F. Experimental analysis of Kuo Vaseline technique for studying behavior development in chick embryos. *Proc. Soc. exp. Biol. Med.*, 1940, **45**, 689–691.

Becker, R. F. The status of gastro-intestinal activity in utero. *Quart. Bull. Northwestern Univ. Med. School*, 1941, **15**, 85 ff.

Becker, R. F. Experimental analysis of the Vaseline technique of Kuo for studying behavioral development in chick embryos. *J. genet. Psychol.*, 1942, **60**, 153–165.

Becker, R. F., King, J. E., Marsh, R. H., and Vierck, A. B. Intrauterine respiration in the rat fetus. I. Direct observations with the guinea pig. *Am. J. obstet. Gynec.*, 1964, **90**, 236–246.

Becker, R. F., and Windle. W. F. Origin and extent of gastro-intestinal motility in the cat and guinea pig. *Am. J. Physiol.*, 1941, **132**, 297–304.

Becker, R. F., Windle, W. F., Barth, E. E., and Schultz, M. D. Fetal swallowing, gastro-intestinal activity and defecation in amnio. *Surgery Gynec. Obstet.*, 1940, **70**, 603–614.

Béclard, P. A. Untersuchungen, welche zu beweisen scheinen, das der Fötus das Schafwasser athmet. *Dtsch. Arch. Physiol.*, 1815, **2**, 154–155.

Bergson, H. *Creative evolution.* (Trans. by A. Mitchell.) New York: Holt, 1911.

Berkeley, G. An essay towards a new theory of vision (1709). In A. C. Fraser (Ed.), *The works of George Berkeley, Vols. I, II.* Oxford: Clarendon Press, 1901. Pp. 93–210.

Bersot, H. Variabilité et corrélations organiques. Nouvelle étude de réflexe plantaire. *Schweiz. Arch. Neurol. Psychiat.*, 1918, 1919, **4**, 177–323; **5**, 305–324.

Bersot, H. Développement réactionnel et réflexe plantaire du bébé né avant terme à celui de deux ans. *Schweiz. Arch. Neurol Psychiat.*, 1920, 1921, **7**, 212–239, **8**, 47–74.

Bichat, M. F. X. *Anatomie générale précédée des récherches physiologiques.* Paris: Brosson, Gabon, 1819. *General anatomy applied to physiology and medicine.* (Trans. by G. Hayward.) Boston: Richardson and Lord, 1822.

Bichat, M. F. X. *Physiological researches upon life and death.* (2d Amer. ed., including notes by F. Magendie. Trans. by F. Gold.) Boston: Richardson and Lord, 1827. *Récherches physiologiques sur la vie et le mort.* (5th ed.) Paris: Gabon, 1829.

Bischoff, T. L. W. *Entwicklungsgeschichte des Kaninchen-Eies.* Brunswick: Vieweg, 1842.

Blair, R. G. Vagitus uterinus: crying in utero. *Lancet*, 1965, II, 1164–1165.

Blanton, M. G. The behavior of the human infant during the first thirty days of life. *Psychol. Rev.*, 1917, **24**, 456–483.

Blincoe, H. Anatomy of the fore limb of the albino rat at approximately the time in fetal life when muscular movements bigin. *Anat., Rec.*, 1928, **38**, 40. (a)

Blincoe, H. The anatomy of the fore limb of the albino rat at approximately the time in fetal life when somatic movement begins. *Anat. Rec.*, 1928, **40**, 277–295. (b)

Bluhm, A. Über einige das Geburtsgewicht der Säugetiere beeinflussende Faktoren. *Arch. Entwicklungsmech. Organ.*, 1929, **116**, 348–381.

Bolaffio, M., and Artom, G. Ricerche sulla fisiologia del sistema nervosa del feto umano. *Arch. sci. biol.*, 1924, **5**, 457–487.

Bolk, L. Vergleichende Untersuchungen an einem Fetus eines Gorillas und eines Schimpansen. *Z. Anat. Entwicklungsgeschichte.*, 1926, **81**, 1–89.

Bonardi, G. Rapporti fra lo sviluppo del riflesso di flessione dorsale del capo e lo sviluppo della respirazione nel feto di cavia. *Bollet. del Soc. Italiana di Biol. Speriment.*, 1946, **21**, 833–834.

Boring, E. *Sensation and perception in the history of experimental psychology.* New York: Appleton-Century, 1942.

Borkowski, W. J., and Bernstine, R. L. Electroencephalography of the fetus. *Neurology*, 1955, **5**, 362–365.

Bors, E. Die Methodik der intrauterinen Operation am überlebenden Säugetier-foetus. *Arch. Entwicklungsmech. Organ.*, 1925, **105**, 655–666.

Bowen, R. E. The ampullar organs of the ear. *J. comp. Neurol.*, 1932, **55**, 273–313.

Breed, F. S. The development of certain instincts and habits in chicks. *Behav. Monogr.*, 1911, **1**(1), vi; 178.

Bridgman, C. S., and Carmichael, L. An experimental study of the onset of behavior in the fetal guinea-pig. *J. genet. Psychol.*, 1935, **47**, 247–267.

Briffault, R. *The Mothers*. Vol. 1. New York: Macmillan, 1927.

Broadbent, D. E. Human perception and animal learning. In W. H. Thorpe and O. L. Zangwill (Eds.), *Current problems in animal behavior*. Cambridge: Cambridge University Press, 1961. Pp. 248–272.

Brown, R. L. Maternal impressions. *W. Va. Med. J.*, 1918, **13**, 86.

Brown, T. G. On the nature of the fundamental activity of the nervous centers; together with an analysis of the conditioning of rhythmic activity in progression, and a theory of the evolution of function in the nervous system. *J. Physiol. (London)*, 1914, **48**, 18–46.

Brown, T. G. On the activities of the central nervous system of the unborn foetus of the cat; with a discussion of the question whether progression (walking, etc.) is a "learnt" complex. *J. Physiol. (London)*, 1915, **49**, 208–215.

Burdette, W. J. *Methodology in basic genetics*. San Francisco, Cal.: Holden-Day, 1963.

Burr, H. S. An electro-dynamic theory of development suggested by studies of proliferation rates in the brain of *Amblystoma*. *J. comp. Neurol.*, 1932, **56**, 347–371.

Burrell, H. *The platypus*. Australia: Angus and Robertson, Ltd., 1927.

Bylicki, L. À la biologie du foetus. *Gynéc. obstet.*, 1921, **4**, 541–543.

Camis, M. *The physiology of the vestibular apparatus*. (Trans. by R. S. Creed.) Oxford: Clarendon Press, 1930.

Canestrini, S. Über das Sinnesleben des Neugeborenen. (*Monogr. Gesamtgeb. Neurol. Psychiat.*, No. 5.) Berlin: Springer, 1913. P. 104.

Cannon, W. B., and Rosenblueth, A. *Autonomic neuro-effector systems*. New York: Macmillan, 1937.

Carlson, A. J., and Ginsburg, H. Contributions to the physiology of the stomach: XXIV. The tonus and hunger contractions of the stomach of the new-born. *Am. J. Physiol.*, 1915, **38**, 29–32.

Carmichael, L. Heredity and environment: Are they antithetical? *J. abnorm. soc. Psychol.*, 1925, **20**, 245–260.

Carmichael, L. The development of behavior in vertebrates experimentally removed from the influence of external stimulation. *Psychol. Rev.*, 1926, **33**, 51–58. (a)

Carmichael, L. Sir Charles Bell: A contribution to the history of physiological psychology. *Psychol. Rev.*, 1926, **33**, 188–217. (b)

Carmichael, L. A further study of the development of behavior in vertebrates experimentally removed from the influence of external stimulation. *Psychol. Rev.*, 1927, **34**, 34–47.

Carmichael, L. A further experimental study of the development of behavior. *Psychol. Rev.*, 1928, **35**, 253–260.

Carmichael, L. The experimental study of the development of behavior in vertebrates. *Proc. Papers 9th Int. Congr. Psychol.*, New Haven, 1929, 114–115.

Carmichael, L. Origin and prenatal growth of behavior. In C. Murchison (Ed.), *A handbook of child psychology*. (2d ed., rev.). Worcester: Clark University Press, 1933. Pp. 31–159.

Carmichael, L. An experimental study in the prenatal guinea-pig of the origin and development of reflexes and patterns of behavior in relation to the stimulation of specific receptor areas during the period of active fetal life. *Genet. Psychol. Monogr.*, 1934, **16**, 337–491. (a)

Carmichael, L. The genetic development of the kitten's capacity to right itself in the air when falling. *J. genet. Psychol.*, 1934, **44**, 453–458. (b)

Carmichael, L. A re-evaluation of the concepts of maturation and learning as applied to the early development of behavior. *Psychol. Rev.*, 1936, **43**, 450–470.

Carmichael, L. Stimulus intensity as a determiner of the characteristics of behavior in the fetal guinea pig. (Abs.) *Science*, 1937, **86**, 409.

Carmichael, L. Fetal behavior and developmental psychology. *Rapp. et C. R. onzième congr. int. psychol.*, Paris, 1938, 108–123.

Carmichael, L. The physiological correlates of intelligence. *Yearb. Nat. Soc. Stud. Educ.*, 1940, **39** (I), 93–155. (a)

Carmichael, L. A technique for the electrical recording of eye movements in adult and fetal guinea pigs. (By title.) *Psychol. Bull.*, 1940, **37**, 563. (b)

Carmichael, L. The experimental embryology of mind. *Psychol. Bull.*, 1941, **38**, 1–28.

Carmichael, L. 1946. *Manual of child psychology.* New York: Wiley (2nd ed.: 1954).

Carmichael, L. The growth of the sensory control of behavior before birth. *Psychol. Rev.*, 1947, **54**, 316–324.

Carmichael, L. Ontogenetic development. In S. S. Stevens, *Handbook of experimental psychology,* New York: Wiley, 1951. Pp. 281–303.

Carmichael, L. The phylogenetic development of behavior patterns. In D. Hooker, and C. C. Hare (Eds.), *Genetics and the inheritance of integrated neurological and psychiatric patterns.* Baltimore, Md.: Williams and Wilkins, 1954.

Carmichael, L. *Basic psychology.* New York: Random House, 1957.

Carmichael, L. Evidence from the prenatal and early postnatal behavior of organisms concerning the concepts of local sign. *Acta psychol.*, 1961, XIX, 166–170.

Carmichael, L. The early growth of language capacity in the individual. In E. H. Lenneberg (Ed.), *New directions in the study of language,* Cambridge: M. I. T. Press, 1964. Pp. 1–22.

Carmichael, L., and Dearborn, W. F. *Reading and visual fatigue.* Boston: Houghton Mifflin, 1947.

Carmichael, L., and Lehner, G. F. J. The development of temperature sensitivity during the fetal period. *J. genet. Psychol.*, 1937, **50**, 217–227.

Carmichael, L., and Smith, M. F. Quantified pressure stimulation and the specificity and generality of response in fetal life. *J. genet. Psychol.*, 1939, **54**, 425–434.

Cesana, G. Lo sviluppo ontogenico degli atti riflessi. *Arch. Fisiol.*, 1911, **9**, 1–120.

Child, C. M. *The origin and development of the nervous system from a physiological viewpoint.* Chicago: University of Chicago Press, 1921.

Child, C. M. *Physiological foundations of behavior.* New York: Holt, 1924.

Child, C. M. The physiological significance of the cephalocaudal differential in vertebrate development. *Anat. Rec.*, 1925, **31**, 369–383.

Chomsky, N. *Language and mind.* New York: Harcourt, Brace and World, 1968.

Christenbery, H. E. Maternal impressions. *J. Tenn. Med. Ass.*, 1910–1911, **3**, 274–277.

Clark, E. L., and Clark, E. R. On the early pulsations of the posterior lymph hearts in chick embryos: Their relation to the body movements. *J. Exp. Zoöl.*, 1914, **17**, 373–394.

Coffey, V. P., and Jessop, W. J. E. Maternal influenza and congenital deformities. *Lancet*, 1959, **2**, 935–938.

Coghill, G. E. The cranial nerves of *Amblystoma tigrinum*. *J. comp. Neurol.*, 1902, **12**, 205–289.

Coghill, G. E. The cranial nerves of *Triton taeniatus*. *J. comp. Neurol.*, 1906, **16**, 247–264.

Coghill, G. E. The development of the swimming movement in amphibian embryos. (Abs.) *Anat. Rec.*, 1908, **2**, 148.

Coghill, G. E. The reaction to tactile stimuli and the development of the swimming movement in embryos of *Diemyetylus torosus*, Eschscholts. *J. comp. Neurol.*, 1909, **19**, 83–105.

Coghill, G. E. The correlation of structural development and function in the growth of the vertebrate nervous system. *Science*, 1912, **37**, 722–723. (a)

Coghill, G. E. The primary ventral roots and somatic motor column of *Amblystoma*. *J. comp. Neurol.*, 1913, **23**, 121–143. (b)

Coghill, G. E. Correlated anatomical and physiological studies of the growth of the nervous system of Amphibia: I. The afferent system of the trunk of *Amblystoma*. *J. comp. Neurol.*, 1914, **24**, 161–233.

Coghill, G. E. Correlated anatomical and physiological studies of the growth of the nervous system of Amphibia: II. The afferent system of the head of *Amblystoma*. *J. comp. Neurol.*, 1916, **26**, 247–340.

Coghill, G. E. Correlated anatomical and physiological studies of the growth of the nervous system in Amphibia: III. The floor plate of *Amblystoma*. *J. comp. Neurol.*, 1924, **37**, 37–69. (a)

Coghill, G. E. Correlated anatomical and physiological studies of the growth of the nervous system of Amphibia: IV. Rates of proliferation and differentiation in the central nervous system of *Amblystoma*. *J. comp. Neurol.*, 1924, **37**, 71–120. (b)

Coghill, G. E. Correlated anatomical and physiological studies of the growth of the nervous system of Amphibia: V. The growth of the pattern of the motor mechanism of *Amblystoma punctatum*. *J. comp. Neurol.*, 1926, **40**, 47–94. (a)

Coghill, G. E. Correlated anatomical and physiological studies of the growth of the nervous system in Amphibia: VI. The mechanism of integration in *Amblystoma punctatum*. *J. comp. Neurol.*, 1926, **41**, 95–152. (b)

Coghill, G. E. Correlated anatomical and physiological studies of the growth of the nervous system of Amphibia: VII. The growth of the pattern of the association mechanism of the rhombencephalon and spinal cord of *Amblystoma punctatum*. *J. comp. Neurol.*, 1926, **42**, 1–16. (c)

Coghill, G. E. The growth of functional neurones and its relation to the development of behavior. *Proc. Amer. Phil. Soc.*, 1926, **65**, 51–55. (d)

Coghill, G. E. Correlated anatomical and physiological studies of the growth of the nervous system of Amphibia: VIII. The development of the pattern of differentiation in the cerebrum of *Amblystoma punctatum*. *J. comp. Neurol.*, 1928, **45**, 227–247.

Coghill, G. E. *Anatomy and the problem of behavior*. Cambridge: University Press. New York: Macmillan, 1929. (a)

Coghill, G. E. The development of movement of the hind leg of *Amblystoma*. *Proc. Soc. exp. Biol. Med.*, 1929, **27**, 74–75. (b)

Coghill, G. E. The early development of behavior in *Amblystoma* and in man. *Archs. Neurol. Psychiat.*, 1929, **21**, 989–1009. (c)

Coghill, G. E. Correlated anatomical and physiological studies of the growth of the nervous system of Amphibia: IX. The mechanism of association of *Amblustoma punctatum*. *J. comp. Neurol.*, 1930, **51**, 311–375. (a)

Coghill, G. E. The development of half centers in relation to the question of antagonism in reflexes. *J. Gen. Psychol.*, 1930, **4**, 335–337. (b)

Coghill, G. E. The genetic interrelation of instinctive behavior and reflexes. *Psychol. Rev.*, 1930, **37**, 264–266. (c)

Coghill, G. E. Individuation versus integration in the development of behavior. *J. Gen. Psychol.*, 1930, **3**, 431–435. (d)

Coghill, G. E. The structural basis of the integration of behavior. *Proc. Nat. Acad. Sci.*, 1930, **16**, 637–643. (d)

Coghill, G. E. Correlated anatomical and physiological studies of the growth of the nervous system of Amphibia: X. Corollaries of the anatomical and physiological study of *Amblystoma* from the age of the earliest movement to swimming. *J. comp. Neurol.*, 1931, **53**, 147–168.

Coghill, G. E. Integration and motivation of behavior as problems of growth. *J. genet. Psychol.*, 1936, **48**, 3–19.

Coghill, G. E., and Legner, W. K. Embryonic motility and sensitivity. (Trans. of W. Preyer. *Specielle physiologie des embryos.*) *Monogr. Soc. Res. Child Develpm.*, 1937, **2**, 1–115.

Cohen, M., Marinello, M., and Back, N. Chromosomal damage in human leukocytes induced by lysergic acid diethylamide. *Science*, 1967, **155**, 1417–1419.

Cohnstein, J., and Zuntz, N. Untersuchungen über das Blut, den Kreislauf und die Athmung beim Säugetierfötus. *Pflüg. Arch. ges. Physiol.*, 1884, **34**, 173–233.

Collins, I. S. Hazards of drug therapy. *Med. J. Australia*, 1964, **1**, 222–230.

Comline, R. S., Silver, I. A., and Silver, M. Factors responsible for the stimulation of the adrenal medulla during asphyxia in the fetal lamb. *J. Physiol.*, 1965, **178**, 211–238.

Compayré, G. *The intellectual and moral development of the child:* Pt. 1. (Trans. by M. E. Wilson.) New York: Appleton, 1896.

Conel, J. L. *The postnatal development of the human cerebral cortex.* Vols. 1–7. Cambridge: Harvard University Press, 1939–1963. [Ref. in these chapters are to Vol. I. (1939) and Vol. II (1941).]

Copenhaver, W. M. Initiation of beat and intrinsic contraction rates in the different parts of the *Amblystoma* heart. *J. exp. Zoöl.*, 1939, **80**, 193–224.

Corey, E. L. Causative factors of the initial inspiration of the mammalian fetus. (Abs.) *Anat. Rec.*, Suppl., 1931, **48**, 41.

Corey, E. L. Effects of brain cautery on fetal development in the rat. *Proc. Soc. exp. Biol. Med.*, 1934, **31**, 951–953.

Corner, G. W. *Ourselves unborn: an embryologist's essay on man.* New Haven, Conn.: Yale University Press, 1944.

Corner, G. W. *Anatomist at large.* New York: Basic Books, 1958.

Coronios, J. D. Preliminary note: technique for observing and motion-picture recording of fetal behavior (cat). *J. genet. Psychol.*, 1930, **37**, 544–545.

Coronios, J. D. The development of behavior in the fetal cat. (Abs.) *Psychol. Bull.*, 1931, **28**, 696–697.

Coronios, J. D. Development of behavior in the fetal cat. *Genet. Psychol. Monogr.*, 1933, **14**, 283–386.

Coronios, J. D., Schlosberg, H., and Carmichael, L. Moving-picture film showing the development of fetal behavior in the cat. (With accompanying booklet.) Chicago: Steolting, 1932.

Coughlin, R. E. Report of two cases of maternal impression. *Brooklyn Med. J.*, 1905, **19**, 199–200.

Craig, J. F. *Fleming's veterinary obstetrics.* (4th ed.) London: Baillière, 1930.

Craig, W. The voices of pigeons regarded as a means of social control. *Am. J. Sociol.*, 1908, **14**, 86–100.

Craig, W. Behavior of the young bird in breaking out of the egg. *J. Anim. Behav.*, 1912, **2**, 296–298.

Craig, W. Male doves reared in isolation. *J. Anim. Behav.*, 1914, **4**, 121–133.

Creed, R. S., Denny-Brown, D., Eccles, J. C., Liddell, E. G. T., and Sherrington, C. S. *Reflex activity of the spinal cord.* Oxford: Clarendon Press, 1932.

Crozier, W. J. The study of living organisms. In C. Murchison (Ed.), *The foundations of experimental psychology.* Worcester: Clark University Press; London: Oxford University Press, 1929, Pp. 45–127.

Cuaron, A., Gamble, J., Myant, N. B., and Osorio, C. The effect of thyroid deficiency on the growth of the brain and on the deposition of brain phospholipids in fetal and newborn rabbits. *J. Physiol.*, 1963, **168**, 613–630.

Dagg, C. P. Teratogenesis. In E. L. Green (Ed.), *Biology of the laboratory mouse.* New York: McGraw-Hill, 1966, Pp. 309–328.

Daniel, S. S., Dawes, G. S., James, L. S., Ross, B. B., and Windle, W. F. Hypothermia and the resuscitati noof asyhyxiated fetal rhesus monkeys. *J. Pediat.*, 1966, **68**, 45–53.

Danforth, D. N., and Ivy, A. C. Effect of calcium upon uterine activity and reactivity. *Proc. Soc. exp. Biol. Med.*, 1938, **38**, 550–551.

Darwin, E. *Zoonomia; or the laws of organic life.* New York: T. and J. Swords, 1796.

Dawes, G. S. *Fetal and neonatal physiology: a comparative study of changes at birth.* Chicago: Yearbook Medical Publishers, 1968.

DeAngelis, F. I riflessi nel neonato. *Pediatria*, 1922, **30**, 1107–1113.

Decker, J. D. Motility of the turtle embryo, *Chelydra serpentina* (*Linne*). *Science*, 1967, **157**, 952–954.

Decker, J. D., and Hamburger, V. The influence of different brain regions on periodic motility of the chick embryo. *J. exp. Zool.*, 1967, **165**, 371–384.

Dekaban, A. *Neurology of infancy.* Baltimore, Md.: Williams and Wilkins, 1959.

De Kergaradec, L. Ueber die Ausculation, angewandt auf das Studium der Schwangerschaft. *Notizen Geb. Natur Heik.*, 1822, 1823, **2**, 191, 202–207; **3**, 159.

DeLee, J. B. Counting fetal heart beat. *J. Amer. Med. Ass.*, 1927, **88**, 1000.

DeLee, J. B. *The principles and practice of obstetrics.* (5th ed.) Philadelphia: Sanders, 1928.

De Snoo, K. Das trinkende Kind im Uterus. *Mschr. Geburtsh. Gynäk.*, 1937, **105**, 88–97.

Detwiler, S. R. Functional regulations in animals with composite spinal cords. *Proc. Nat. Acad. Sci.*, 1920, **6**, 695–700.

Detwiler, S. R. Experiments on the hyperplasia of nerve centers. *China Med. J.*, 1921, **35**, 95–107.

Detwiler, S. R. Experiments on the transplantation of limbs in *Amblystoma*: further observations on peripheral nerve connections. *J. Exp. Zoöl.*, 1922, **35**, 115–161.

Detwiler, S. R. Experiments on the reversal of the spinal cord in *Amblystoma* embryos at the level of the anterior limb. *J. exp. Zoöl.*, 1923, **38**, 293–321. (a)

Detwiler, S. R. Experiments on the transplantation of the spinal cord in *Amblystoma*, and their bearing upon the stimuli involved in the differentiation of nerve cells. *J. exp. Zoöl.*, 1923, **37**, 339–393. (b)

Dewey, E. *Behavior development in infants: a survey of the literature on prenatal and postnatal activity, 1920–1934.* New York: Columbia University Press, 1935.

Dipaolo, J. A. Congenital malformation in Strain A mice: its experimental production by thalidomide. *J. Am. Med. Ass.*, 1963, **183**, 139.

Dodge, R. Habituation to rotation. *J. exp. Psychol.*, 1923, **6**, 1–35.

Draper, R. L. The prenatal growth of the guinea-pig. *Anat. Rec.*, 1920, **18**, 369–392.

Dubois, P. Causes de la présentation de la tête, dans l'accouchement. *Arch. gén. méd.*, 1933, **1** (2d ser.), 292–295.

Eastman, N. J. *Williams obstetrics.* (11th ed.) New York: Appleton-Century-Crofts, 1956.

Eccles, J. C. (Ed.) *Brain and conscious experience.* New York: Springer-verlag, 1966.

Eidelberg, E., Kolmodin, G. M., and Myerson, B. A. Ontogenesis of steady potential and direct cortical response in fetal sheep brain. *Exper. Neurol.*, 1965, **12**, 198–214.

Elwyn, A. The structure and development of the proprioceptors. In F. Tilney *et al.* (Eds.), *The cerebellum: an investigation of recent advances.* (Proc. Ass. Res. Nerv. Ment. Dis., 1926.) Baltimore: Williams and Wilkins, 1929. Pp. 244–280.

Emmert, A. G. F., and Burgätzy, J. J. Beobachtungen über einige schwangere Fledermäuse und ihre Eihüllen. *Dtsch. Arch. Physiol.*, 1818, **4**, 1–33.

Erbkam: Lebhafte Bewegung eines viermonatlichen Fötus. *Neue Z. Geburtsk.*, 1837, **5**, 324–326.

Evensen, H. *Entwicklung und Schicksal der zu früh geborenen Kinder.* (Dissertation.) Berlin: Friedrich-Wilhelms-Universität, 1931.

Fabricius, E. Experiments on the following response of mallard ducklings. *Br. J. Anim. Behav.*, 1955, **3**, 122.

Favill, J. The relationship of eye muscles to semicircular canal currents in rotationally induced nystagmus. In F. Tilney *et al.* (Eds.), *The cerebellum: an investigation of recent advances.* (Proc. Ass. Res. Nerv. Ment. Dis., 1926.) Baltimore: Williams and Wilkins, 1929. Pp. 530–546.

Feldman, W. M. *Principles of antenatal and post-natal child physiology, pure and applied.* London and New York: Longmans, Green, 1920.

Feldman, W. M. The nature of the plantar reflex in early life and the causes of its variations. *Amer. J. Dis. Child.*, 1922, **23**, 1–40.

Fender, F. A., Neff, W. B., and Binger, G. Convulsions produced by fetal anoxia; experimental study. *Anesthesiol.*, 1940, **7**, 10–13.

Ferris, H. B. The natural history of man. In G. A. Baitsell (Ed.), *The evolution of man.* New Haven, Conn.: Yale University Press, 1922. Pp. 39–79.

Field, J. H. W., Magoun, H. W., and Hall, V. E. (Eds.), *Neurophysiology. Handbook of physiology, Vol. I.* Washington, D.C.: American Physiological Association, 1959.

Fish, M. W., and Windle, W. F. The effect of rotatory stimulation on the movements of the head and eyes in newborn and young kittens. *J. comp. Neurol.*, 1932, **54**, 103–107.

Fitzgerald, J. E., and Windle, W. F. Some observations on early human fetal movements. *J. comp. Neurol.*, 1942, **76**, 159–167.

Flanagan, G. L. *The first nine months of life.* New York: Simon and Schuster, 1962.

Flexner, J. B., Flexner, L. B., and Stellar, E. Memory in mice as affected by intracerebral puromycin. *Science*, 1963, **141**, 57–59.

Flexner, L. B. Dissection of memory in mice with antibiotics. *Proc. Am. Phil. Soc.*, 1967, **111**, 343–346.

Flexner, L. B., Flexner, J. B., and Roberts, R. B. Memory in mice analyzed with antibiotics. *Science*, 1967, **155**, 1377–1383.

Fromme, A. An experimental study of the factors of maturation and practice in the behavioral development of the embryo of the frog. *Rana pipiens. Genet. Psychol. Monogr.*, 1941, **24**, 219–256.

Forbes, H. S., and Forbes, H. B. Fetal sense reaction: Hearing. *J. comp. Psychol.*, 1927, **7**, 353–355.

Fuller, J. L., and Thompson, W. R. *Behavior genetics.* New York: Wiley, 1960.

Furchtgott, E., Lore, R., and Morgan, W. Depth perception in prenatally x-irradiated rats. *Perceptual and motor skills*, 1964, **19**, 703–710.

Geiger, A. J., Monroe, W. M., and Goodyer, A. V. N. Clinical fetal electrocardiography: its practical accomplishment. *Proc. Soc. exp. Biol. Med.*, 1941, **48**, 646–648.

Genzmer, A. *Untersuchungen über die Sinneswahrnehmungen des neugeborenen Menchen.* (Dissertation, 1873.) Halle: Niemeyer, 1882.

Gesell, A. *Infancy and human growth.* New York: Macmillan, 1928.

Gesell, A. The individual in infancy. In C. Murchison (Ed.), *The foundations of experimental psychology.* Worcester: Clark University Press; London: Oxford University Press, 1929. Pp. 628–660. (a)

Gesell, A. Maturation and infant behavior pattern. *Psychol. Rev.*, 1929, **36**, 307–319. (b)

Gibson, E., and Walk, R. The "visual cliff." *Scient. Am.*, 1960, **202**, 64–71.

Gibson, J. Visually controlled locomotion and visual orientation in animals. *Br. J. Psychol.*, 1958, **49**, 182–194.

Givler, R. C. The intellectual significance of the grasping reflex. *J. Phil.*, 1921, **18**, 617–628.

Glenn, W. F. Is a foetus a person? *South. Pract.*, 1911, **33**, 117–120.

Goeckel, H. *Die Wandlungen in der Bewertung des ungeborenen Kindes.* (Dissertation.) Heidelberg, 1911.

Goldstein, K. Kritische und experimentelle Beiträge zur Frage nach dem Einfluss des Zentralnervensystems auf die embryonale Entwicklung und die Regeneration *Arch. Entwicklungsmech. Organ.*, 1904, **18**, 57–110.

Golubeva, E. L., Shuleikina, K. V., and Vainshtein, I. The development of reflex and spontaneous activity of human fetus in the process of embryogenesis. *Obstet. Gynecol.* (USSR), 1959, **3**, 59–62.

Good, F. L. Pregnancy and labor complicated by diseases and injuries of the spinal cord. *J. Am. Med. Ass.*, 1924, **83**, 416–418.

Goodlin, R. C. Fetal incubator studies: factors associated with breathing in fetal rabbits. *Biol. Neonat.*, 1965, **8**, 274–280.

Goss, C. M. Early development of the rat heart in vitro. *Anat. Rec.*, Suppl., 1937, **67**, 20.

Goss, C. M. The first contractions of the heart in rat embryos. *Anat. Rec.*, 1938, **70**, 505–524.

Goss, C. M. First contractions of the heart without cytological differentiation. *Anat. Rec.*, 1940, **76**, 19–27.

Gottleib, G. Prenatal auditory sensitivity in chickens and ducks. *Science*, 1965, **147**, 1596–1598.

Gottleib, G., and Kuo, Z. Development of behavior in the duck embryo. *J. comp. physiol. Psych.*, 1965, **59**, 183–188.

Graham, M. Intrauterine crying. *Brit. Med. J.*, 1919, **1**, 675.

Grant, R. E. Beobachtungen über den Bau und das Wesen der *Flustrae. Z. organ. Physik*, 1827, **1**, 401–418.

Gray, P. H. A checklist of papers since 1951 dealing with imprinting in birds. *Psychol., Rec.*, **13**, 445–454.

Green, E. L. *Biology of the laboratory mouse.* New York: McGraw-Hill, 1966.

Green, M. C. Genes and development. In E. Green (Ed.), *Biology of the laboratory mouse.* New York: McGraw-Hill, 1966. Pp. 329–336.

Greenfield, A. D. M., Shepherd, T. J., and Whelan, R. F. The relationship between the blood flow in the umbilical cord and the rate of foetal growth in sheep and guinea pig. *J. Physiol.* London, 1951, **115**, 158–162.

Grier, J. B., Counter, S. A., and Shearer, W. M. Prenatal auditory imprinting in chickens. *Science*, 1967, **155**, 1692–1693.

Griffith, W. S. A. An investigation of the causes which determine the lie of the foetus in utero. *Lancet*, 1915, **2**, 319–325.

Hamburger, V. The concept of "development" in biology. In D. H. Harris (Ed.), *The concept of development*. Minneapolis: University of Minnesota Press, 1957. Pp. 49–58.

Hamburger, V. Some aspects of the embryology of behavior. *Quart. Rev. Biol.*, 1963, **38**, 342–365.

Hamburger, V. Ontogeny of behavior and its structural basis. In D. Richter (Ed.), *Comparative neurochemistry*. Oxford: Pergamon Press, 1964.

Hamburger, V., and Balaban, M. Observations and experiments on spontaneous rhythmical behavior in the chick embryo. *Develop. Biol.*, 1963, **7**, 533–545.

Hamburger, V., Balaban, M., Oppenheim, R., and Wenger, E. Periodic motility of normal and spinal chick embryos between 8 and 17 days of incubation. *J. exp. Zool.*, 1965, **159**, 1–13.

Hamburger, V., and Hamilton, H. L. A series of normal stages in the development of the chick embryo. *J. Morphol.*, 1951, **88**, 49–92.

Hamburger, V., and Oppenheim, R. Prehatching motility and hatching behavior in the chick. *J. exp. Zool.*, 1967, **166**, 171–204.

Hamburger, V., Wenger, E., and Oppenheim, R. Motility in the chick embryo in the absence of sensory input. *J. exp. Zool.*, 1966, **162**, 133–160.

Harlow, H. F., and Harlow, M. K. The affectional systems. In A. M. Schrier, H. F. Harlow, and F. Stollnitz (Eds.), *Behavior of non-human primates*, Vol. II. New York: Academic Press, 1965. Pp. 287–334.

Harrison, R. G. An experimental study of the relation of the nervous system to the developing musculature in the embryo of the frog. *Am. J. Anat.*, 1904, **3**, 197–220.

Hartman, C. G. Studies in the development of the opossum *Didelphys virginiana* L.: I. History of the early cleavage. *J. Morphol.*, 1916, **27**, 1–41. (a)

Hartman, C. G. Studies in the development of the opossum *Didelphys virginiana* L.: II. Formation of the blastocyst. *J. Morphol.*, 1916, **27**, 42–83. (b)

Hartman, C. G. Studies in the development of the opossum *Didelphys virginiana* L.: III. Description of new material on maturation, cleavage and entoderm formation. *J. Morphol.*, 1919, **32**, 1–73. (a)

Hartman, C. G. Studies in the development of the opossum *Didelphys virginiana* L.: IV. The bilaminar blastocyst. *J. Morphol.*, 1919, **32**, 73–142. (b)

Hartman, C. G. Studies in the development of the opossum *Didelphys virginiana* L.: V. The phenomena of parturition. *Anat. Rec.*, 1920, **19**, 251–261.

Hegel, G. W. F. *Philosophy of mind.* (Trans. by W. Wallace.) Oxford: Clarendon Press, 1894.

Henderson, Y. How breathing begins at birth. *Science*, 1937, **85**, 80–91.

Herrick, C. J. *George Ellett Coghill: Naturalist and philosopher.* Chicago: University of Chicago Press, 1949.

Hertwig, R. *A manual of zoology.* (Trans. by J. S. Kingsley.) New York: Holt, 1912.

Hess, E. Imprinting in animals. *Scient. Am.*, 1958, **198**, 81–90.

Hess, E. Imprinting and the "critical period" concept. In E. Bliss (Ed.), *Roots of behavior*. New York: Harper, 1962. Pp. 254–263.

Hess, J. H. The diagnosis of the age of the fetus by the use of roentgenograms. *Ill. Med. J.*, 1918, **33**, 73–88.

Hess, J. H. *Premature and congenitally diseased infants*. Philadelphia: Lea and Febiger, 1922.

Hewer, E. E. The development of muscle in the human foetus. *J. Anat.*, 1927, **62**, 72–78.

Hicks, J. B. On recording the fetal movements by means of a gastrograph. *Trans. Obstet. Soc. London*, 1880, **22**, 134.

Higasihara, Y., Hurusawa, S., Simada, Y., and Tanaka, I. Observations on the axon reflex sweating in the fetus. *Kumamoto Med. J.*, 1965, **18**, 43.

Hill, J. P., and Watson, K. M. The early development of the brain in marsupials. *J. Anat.*, 1958, **92**, 493–497.

Hill, J. P., and Tribe, M. The early development of the cat (*Felis domestica*). *Quart. J. Micro. Sci.*, 1924, **68**, 513–602.

Himwich, W., and Himwich, H. (Eds.) *Progress in brain research*, Vol. 9. New York: Elsevier, 1964.

Hines, M., and Straus, W. L. The motor cortex of fetal and infant rhesus monkeys (*Macaca mulatta*). *Anat. Rec.*, Suppl., 1934, **58**, 18.

Hinsey, J. C., Ranson, S. W., and McNattin, R. F. The role of the hypothalamus and mesencephalon in locomotion. *Arch. Neurol. Psychiat.*, 1930, **23**, 1–42.

Hirsch, J. The contributions of behavior genetics to the study of behavior. In F. J. Kallmann (Ed.), *Expanding goals of genetics in psychiatry*. New York: Grune and Stratton, 1962. Pp. 25–31.

His, W. *Anatomie menschlicher Embryonen*. (3 vols.) Leipzig: Vogel, 1880, 1882, 1885.

Hogg, I. D. Sensory nerves and associated structures in the skin of human fetuses of 8 to 14 weeks of menstrual age correlated with functional capability. *J. comp. Neurol.*, 1941, **75**, 371–410.

Holsopple, J. Q. Space and the nonauditory labyrinth. In C. Murchison (Ed.), *The foundations of experimental psychology*. Worcester: Clark University Press; London: Oxford University Press, 1929. Pp. 414–433.

Holt, E. B. *Animal drive and the learning process*, Vol. I. New York: Holt, 1931.

Home, E. Über die Fortpflanzung der Auster und der Flussmuschel. (Croonian Lecture, 1826.) *Z. organ. Physik*, 1827, **1**, 391–396. (See also *Phil. Trans. Roy. Soc. London*, Pt. 1, 1827, 39.)

Hooker, D. The development and function of voluntary and cardiac muscle in embryos without nerves. *J. exp. Zool.*, 1911, **11**, 159–186.

Hooker, D. Early fetal activity in mammals. *Yale J. Biol. Med.*, 1936, **8**, 579–602.

Hooker, D. The development of reflexes in the mammalian fetus. *Anat. Rec.*, Suppl., 1937, **70**, 55.

Hooker, D. The origin of the grasping movement in man. *Proc. Amer. Phil. Soc.*, 1938, **79**, 597–606.

Hooker, D. Fetal behavior. *Res. Publ. Ass. Nerv. Ment. Dis.*, 1939, **19**, 237–243. (a)

Hooker, D. *A preliminary atlas of early human fetal activity*. Privately published: 1939. (b)

Hooker, D. Fetal reflexes and instinctual processes. *Psychosom. Med.*, 1942, **4**, 199–205.

Hooker, D. Reflex activities in the human fetus. In R. G. Barker, J. S. Kounin, and H. F. Wright (Eds.), *Child behavior and development*. New York: McGraw-Hill, 1943. Pp. 17–28.

Hooker, D. *The origin of overt behavior*. Ann Arbor: University of Michigan Press, 1944.

Hooker, D. Neural growth and the development of behavior. In P. Weiss (Ed.), *Genetic neurology*. Chicago: University of Chicago Press, 1950. Pp. 212–213.

Hooker, D. *The prenatal origin of behavior*. University of Kansas Press, 1952.

Hooker, D., and Hare, C. C. (Eds.) *Genetics and the inheritance of integrated neurological and psychiatric patterns.* Baltimore: Williams and Wilkins, 1954.

Hooker, D., and J. S. Nicholas. The effect of injury to the spinal cord of rats in prenatal stages. (Abs.) *Anat. Rec.,* 1927, **35**, 14–15.

Hooker, D., and J. S. Nicholas. Spinal cord section in rat fetuses. *J. comp. Neurol.,* 1930, **50**, 413–467.

Hsu, C. Y. Influence of temperature on development of rat embryos. *Anat. Res.,* 1948, **100**, 79–90.

Huggett, A. St. G. Foetal blood-gas tensions and gas transfusions through the placenta of the goat. *J. Physiol.,* 1927, **62**, 373–384.

Huggett, A. St. G. Foetal respiratory reflexes. *J. Physiol.,* 1930, **69**, 144–152.

Hughes, H. Status of the foetus in utero. *N. Y. Med. J.,* 1905, **82**, 963.

Huhmar, E., and Jarvinen, P. Observations on fetal EEG. *Ann. Chir. et Gynaec. Fenn.,* 1963, **52**, 372–375.

Humphrey, T. The development of mouth opening and related reflexes, involving the oral area of human fetuses. *Alabama J. Med. Sci.,* 1968, **5**, 126–157.

Hunter, W. S. The mechanisms involved in the behavior of white rats on the inclined plane. *J. Gen. Psychol.,* 1931, **5**, 295–310.

Hyden, H. Biochemical and molecular aspects of learning and memory. *Proc. Am. phil. Soc.,* 1967, **111**, 326–342. (a)

Hyden, H. Behavior, neural function and RNA. In J. N. Davidson and W. E. Cohn (Eds.), *Progress in nucleic acid research and molecular biology,* Vol. VI. New York: Academic Press, 1967. (a)

Hyman, A. S. Irregularities: phonocardiographic study of the fetal heart sounds from fifth to eighth months of pregnancy. *Am. J. obstet. Gynec.,* 1930, **20**, 332–347.

Irwin, O. C. The amount and nature of activities of new-born infants under constant external stimulating conditions during the first ten days of life. *Genet. Psychol. Monogr.,* 1930, **8**, 1–92.

Irwin, O. C., and A. P. Weiss. A note on mass activity in newborn infants. *J. genet. Psychol.,* 1930, **38**, 20–30.

Jackson, C. M. On the prenatal growth of the human body and the relative growth of the various organs and parts. *Am. J. Anat.,* 1909, **9**, 119–165.

Jackson, H. Evolution and dissolution of the nervous system. *Lancet,* 1884, **1**, 555–558; 649–652; 739–744.

Jacobson, C. B. The nature of the chromosomal defect in mongolism. *Proc. Child. Hosp. Wash., D. C.,* 1967, **23**, 43–48.

Jacobson, C. B., and Barter, R. H. Some cytogenetic aspects of habitual abortion. *Am. J. obstet. Gynec.,* 1967, **97**, 666–680.

James, W. *The principles of psychology.* (2 vols.) New York: Holt, 1890.

Jasper, H. H., Bridgman, C. S., and Carmichael, L. An ontogenetic study of cerebral electrical potentials in the guinea pig. *J. exp. Psychol.,* 1937, **21**, 63–71.

Jaynes, J. Imprinting: the interaction of learned and innate behavior. I. Development and generalization. *J. comp. physiol. Psychol.,* 1956, **49**, 201–206.

Jaynes, J. Imprinting: the interaction of learned and innate behavior. II. The critical period. *J. comp. physiol. Psychol.,* 1957, **50**, 6–10.

Jaynes, J. Imprinting: the interaction of learned and innate behavior. III. Practice effects on performance, retention and fear. *J. comp. physiol. Psychol.,* 1958, **51**, 234–237. (a)

Jaynes, J. Imprinting: the interaction of learned and innate behavior IV. Generalization and emergent discrimination. *J. comp. physiol. Psychol.,* 1958, **51**, 238–242. (b)

Jensen, K. Differential reactions to taste and temperature stimuli in newborn infants. *Genet. Psychol. Monogr.,* 1932, **12**, 363–479.

Joffe, J. M. Genotype and prenatal and premating stress interact to affect adult behavior in rats. *Science*, 1965, **150**, 1844–1845.

Johansson, B., Wedenberg, E., and Westin, B. Measurement of tone response by the human fetus. *Acta Otolaryng.*, 1964, **57**, 188–192.

Kant, I. *Anthropologie*. Leipzig, 1799.

Kean, R. I. *The evolution of marsupial reproduction*. Wellington: New Zealand Forest Service, 1961.

Keibel, F., and Elze, C. *Normentafel zur Entwicklungsgeschichte des Menschen*. Jena: Fischer, 1908.

Keibel, F., and Mall, F. P. *Manual of human embryology*. Philadelphia: Lippincott, 1910.

Keith, A. *Human embryology and morphology*. London: Arnold, 1913.

Kellogg, H. B. Studies on fetal circulation of mammals. *Am. J. Physiol.*, 1930, **91**, 637–648.

Kidd, W. *The sense of touch in mammals and birds, with special reference to the papillary ridges*. London: Adam and Charles Black, 1907.

King, C. T. G., and Kendrick, F. J. Teratogenic effects of thalidomide in the Sprague Dawley rat. *Lancet*, 1962, **2**, 1116.

King, D. H. On the weight of the albino rat at birth and the factors that influence it. *Anat. Rec.*, 1915, **9**, 213–231.

King, J. A. Species specificity and early experience. In G. Newton and S. Levine (Eds.), *Early Experiences and Behavior*. Springfield, Ill.: Thomas, 1968.

Kingsbury, B. F. The significance of the so-called law of cephalocaudal differential growth. *Anat. Rec.*, 1924, **27**, 305–321.

Kingsbury, B. F. On the so-called law of antero-posterior development. *Anat. Rec.*, 1926, **33**, 73–87.

Klemm, G. O. *A history of psychology*. (Trans. by E. C. Wilm and R. Pintner.) New York: Scribner's, 1914.

Koecke, H. V. Normalstadien der Embryonalentwicklung bei der Hausente (*Anas boschas domestica*). *Embryologia*, 1958, **4**, 55–78.

Koffka, K. *The growth of the mind: An introduction to child psychology*. (Trans. by R. M. Ogden.) New York: Harcourt, Brace; London: Kegan Paul, 1924.

Kouwer, B. J. Adembewegingen van de vrucht voor en na de geboorte. *Ned. Tijdschr. Geneesk.*, 1919, **11**, 815–822.

Krabbe, K. Les réflexes chez le foetus. *Rev. neurol.*, 1912, **24**, 434–435.

Krnjevic, K., and Silver, A. Acetylcholinesterase in the developing forebrain. *J. Anat. (London)*, 1966, **100**, 63–89.

Kuo, Z. Y. Ontogeny of embryonic behavior in Aves: I. The chronology and general nature of the behavior of the chick embryo. *J. exp. Zool.*, 1932, **61**, 395–430. (a)

Kuo, Z. Y. Ontogeny of embryonic behavior in Aves: II. The mechanical factors in the various stages leading to hatching. *J. exp. Zool.*, 1932, **62**, 453–487. (b)

Kuo, Z. Y. Ontogeny of embryonic behavior in Aves: III. The structure and environmental factors in embryonic behavior. *J. comp. Psychol.*, 1932, **13**, 245–272. (c)

Kuo, Z. Y. Ontogeny of embryonic behavior in Aves: IV. The influence of embryonic movements upon the behavior after hatching. *J. comp. Psychol.*, 1932, **14**, 109–122. (d)

Kuo, Z. Y. Ontogeny of embryonic behavior in Aves: V. The reflex concept in the light of embryonic behavior in birds. *Psychol. Rev.*, 1932, **39**, 499–515. (e)

Kuo, Z. Y. Ontogeny of embryonic behavior in Aves: XII. Stages in the development of physiological activities in the chick embryo. *Am. J. Psychol.*, 1938, **51**, 361–378.

Kuo, Z. Y. Development of acetylcholine in the chick embryo *J. Neurophysiol.*, 1939, **2**, 488–493. (a)

Kuo, Z. Y. Studies in the physiology of the embryonic nervous system. *J. comp. Neurol.*, 1939, **70**, 437–459. (b)

Kuo, Z. Y. Total pattern or local reflexes? *Psychol. Rev.*, 1939, **46**, 93–122. (c)

Kuo, Z. Y. *The dynamics of behavior development: an epigenetic view.* New York: Random House, 1967.

Kuo, Z. Y. and Carmichael, L. A. technique for the motion-picture recording of the development of behavior in the chick embryo. *J. Psychol.*, 1937, **4**, 343–348.

Kussmaul, A. *Untersuchungen über das Seclenleben des neugeborenen Menschen.* Leipzig: Winter, 1859.

Lane, H. H. The correlation between structure and function in the development of the special senses of the white rat. *Univ. Okla. Bull.* (New ser. No. 140) (*Univ. Stud.*, No. 8), 1917, 1–88.

Lane, H. H. A mechanism showing a remarkable correlation between structure and function in connection with the nursing reflex in the young mammal. *Kan. Univ. Sci. Bull.*, 1924, **15** (Whole ser. 26), 247–253.

Lange, F. A. *History of materialism* (1873.) (Trans. by E. C. Thomas.) New York: Harcourt, Brace; London: Kegan Paul, 1925.

Langfeld, H. S. A response interpretation of consciousness. *Psychol. Rev.*, 1931, **38**, 87–108.

Langreder, W. Ueber Fötalreflexe und deren intrauterine Bedeutung. *Z. Geburtsh. Gynakol.*, 1949, **131**, 236–251. (a)

Langreder, W. Welche Fötalreflexe haben line intrauterine Aufgabe. *Dtsch. Med. Wschr.*, 1949, **74**, 661–667. (b)

Langworthy, O. R. The development of progression and posture in young opossums. *Am. J. Physiol.*, 1925, **74**, 1–13.

Langworthy, O. R. Relation of onset of decerebrate rigidity to the time of myelinization of tracts in the brainstem and spinal cord of young animals. *Contr. Embryol., Carnegie Inst. Wash.*, 1926, **17**, No. 89, 125–140.

Langworthy, O. R. The behavior of pouch-young opossums correlated with the myelinization of tracts in the nervous system. *J. comp. Neurol.*, 1928, **46**, 201–247.

Langworthy, O. R. A correlated study of the development of reflex activity in fetal and young kittens and the myelinization of tracts in the nervous system. *Contr. Embryol., Carnegie Inst. Wash.*, 1929, **20**, No. 114, 127–171.

Larroche, J. C. Some anatomical aspects of the brain development. *Biologia neonat.*, 1962, **4**, 126–153.

Larsell, O. The comparative morphology of the membranous labyrinth and the lateral line organs in their relation to the development of the cerebellum. In F. Tilney *et al.* (Eds.), *The cerebellum: an investigation of recent advances.* (*Proc. Ass. Res. Nerv. Ment. Dis.*, 1926.) Baltimore, Md.: Williams and Wilkins, 1929.

Larsell, O., McCrady, E., and Zimmerman, A. Morphological and functional development of the membranous labyrinth in the opossum. *J. comp. Neurol.*, 1935, **63**, 95–118.

Lasagna, L. Thalidomide—a new nonbarbiturate sleep-inducing drug. *J. chron. Dis.*, 1960, **11**, 627–631.

Lashley, K. S. The problem of serial order in behavior. In L. A. Jeffrees (Ed.), *Cerebral mechanisms in behavior—the Hixon Symposium.* New York: Wiley, 1951.

Latimer, H. B. The prenatal growth of the cat: II. The growth of the dimensions of the head and trunk. *Anat. Rec.*, 1931, **50**, 311–332.

Latimer, H. B., and J. M. Aikman. The prenatal growth of the cat: I. The growth in weight of the head, trunk, forelimbs, and hindlimbs. *Anat. Rec.*, 1931, **48**, 1–26.

Laughton, N. B. Studies on the nervous regulation of progression in mammals. *Amer. J. Physiol.*, 1924, **70**, 358–384.

Leeuwenhoeck, A. Part of a letter dated Delft, September 10, 1697, concerning the eggs of snails, the roots of vegetables, teeth, and young oysters. *Phil Trans.*, 1697, **19**, 790–799.

Lehrman, D., Hinde, R., and Shaw, E. (Eds.) *Advances in the study of behavior*, Vol. I. New York: Acadamic Press, 1965.

Lenz, H. How can the physician prevent dangers for the offspring? (Ger.) *Med. Welt*, 1962, **48**, (1), 2554–2558.

Liesch, E. La motilità riflessa durante lo sviluppo fetale nell'uomo. *Bollet. del Soc. Italiana di Biol. Speriment.*, 1946, **21**, 831–833.

Liggett, J. R. An experimental study of the olfactory sensitivity of the white rat. *Genet. Psychol. Monogr.*, 1928, **3**, 1–64.

Lillie, F. R. *The development of the chick.* New York: Holt, 1919.

Lincoln, A. W. *The behavioral development of the feeding reaction in the white rat.* Unpublished master's thesis, Brown University, 1932.

Lindsley, D. B. Heart and brain potentials of human fetuses in utero. *Am. J. Psychol.*, 1942, **55**, 412–416.

Lock, F. R. Human congenital anomalies—some current concepts. *Obstet. Gynec.*, 1962, **20**, 867–873.

Locke, J. *Essay concerning human understanding.* (1690.) Philadelphia: Kay and Troutman, 1849.

Lorenz, K. Der Kumpan in der Umwelt des Vogels: die Artgenosse als auslosendes Moment sozialer Verhaltungsweisen. *J. Orn.*, 1935, **83**, 137–213; 289–413.

Lovejoy, A. E. *The great chain of being.* Boston: Harvard University Press, 1936 (2nd ed., 1957).

Lovejoy, A. O. The meanings of "emergence" and its modes. *Proc. 6th Int. Congr. Philosophy, Cambridge, Mass.*, 1926, 20–33.

MacKeever, T. On the information afforded by the stethoscope in detecting the presence of foetal life. *Lancet*, 1833, **24**, 715.

Maekawa, M., and Toyoshima, J. The fetal electro-cardiogram of the human subject. *Acta Scholae Med. Univ. Imp.*, *Kioto*, 1930, **12**, 519–520.

Magendie, F. *See* Bichat, 1827.

Magnus, R. *Körperstellung.* Berlin: Springer, 1924.

Magnus, R. Animal posture. (Croonian Lecture.) *Proc. Roy. Soc. London*, 1925, **98B**, 339–353.

Mailliot, L. *L'asucultation appliquée à l'étude de la grossesse.* Paris: Baillière, 1856, (German summary by Sickel in *Schmidt's Jb. ges. Med.*, 1857, **93**, 258–260).

Mall, F. P. On ossification centers in human embryos less than one hundred days old. *Am. J. Anat.*, 1906, **5**, 433–458.

Mall, F. P. Determination of the ages of human embryos and fetuses .In F. Keibel, and F. P. Mall. *Manual of human embryology*, Vol. I. Philadelphia: Lippincott, 1910, Pp. 180–201.

Mall, F. P. On the age of human embryos. *Am. J. Anat.*, 1918, **23**, 397–422.

Mann, H., and Bernstein, P. Fetal electro-cardiography. *Am. Heart. J.*, 1941, **22**, 390–400.

Mann, I. C. *The development of the human eye.* Cambridge: University Press, 1928.

Marler, P. R., and Hamilton, W. J. *Mechanisms o fanimal behavior.* New York: Wiley, 1966.

Matthews, S. A., and Detwiler, S. R. The reactions of *Amblystoma* embryos following prolonged treatment with chloretone. *J. exp. Zool.*, 1926, **45**, 279–292.

Mavrinskaya, L. F. On correlations of development of skeletal muscle nerve endings with appearance of motor activity in human embryo. *Arkh. Anat.*, 1960, **38**(2), 61–68.

Mavrinskaya, L. F. Histological changes of cholinesterase in developing somatic musculature of human embryos. *Arkh. Anat.*, 1962, **42**, 30–43.

Maxwell, S. S. *Labyrinth and equilibrium*. Philadelphia: Lippincott, 1923.

McCarthy, D. A graphic age conversion scale. *Child Develpm.*, 1936, **7**, 74.

McCrady, E. *The embryology of the opossum*. Philadelphia: Wistar Institute of Anatomy and Biology, 1938.

McCrady, E., Wever, E. G., and Bray, C. W. The development of hearing in the opossum. *J. exp. Zool.*, 1937, **75**, 503–517.

McDougall, W. *Outline of psychology*. New York: Scribner's, 1923.

McIlroy, A. L., and Leverkus, D. Changes in polarity of the foetus during the later weeks of pregnancy. *Lancet*, 1924, **2**, 267–271. Also in *Proc. Roy. Soc. Med. (Sect. Obstet. Gynec.)*, 1924, **17**, 89–99.

Mermann. Ueber eigenthümliche rhythmische Fötalbewegungen. *Cbl. Gynäk.*, 1887, **11**, 622–624.

Medical Reference Staff, Division of Research and Reference, Bureau of Medicine, Department of Health, Education and Welfare, Food and Drug Administration. *Thalidomide: reports collected from the literature*. Washington, D. C.: 1956–1963.

Meyer, A. W. *The rise of embryology*. Palo Alto, Calif.: Stanford University Press, 1939.

Mill, J. S. *Autobiography of John Stuart Mill*. (Published after his death: 1873) New York: Columbia University Press, 1960.

Miller, J. A., Miller, F. S., and Westin, B. Hypothermia in the treatment of asphyxia neonatorum. *Biol. neonat.*, 1964, **6**, 148–163.

Miller, R. W. Delayed effects occuring within the first decade after exposure of young individuals to the Hiroshima atomic bomb. *Pediatrics*, 1956, **18**, 1–18.

Milner, E. *Human neural and behavioral development*. Springfield, Ill.: Thomas, 1967.

Minkowski, M. Movimientos y reflejos del feto humano durante la primera mitad del embarazo. *Trabojos del Laboratorio de Investigaciones Biologicas, Univ. Madrid*, 1920, **18**, 269–273. (a)

Minkowski, M. Réflexes et mouvements de la tête, du tronc et des extrémités du foetus humain pendant la première moitié de la grossesse. *C. R. Soc. Biol., Paris*, 1920, **83**, 1202–1204. (b)

Minkowski, M. Sur les mouvements, les réflexes, et les réactions musculaires du foetus humain de 2 à 5 mois et leur rélations avec le système nerveux foetal. *Rev. neurol.*, 1921, **37**, 1105–1118, 1235–1250. (a)

Minkowski, M. Ueber Bewegungen und Reflexe des menschlichen Foetus während der ersten Hälfte seiner Entwicklung. *Schweiz. Arch. Neurol. Psychiat.*, 1921, **8**, 148–151. (b)

Minkowski, M. Ueber frühzeitige Bewegungen. Reflexe und muskuläre Reaktionen beim menschlichen Fötus und ihre Beiziehungen zum fötalen Nerven- und Muskelsystem. *Schweiz. med. Wschr.*, 1922, **52**, 721–724, 751–755.

Minkowski, M. Zur Entwicklungsgeschichte, Lokalisation und Klinik des Fussohlenreflexes. *Schweiz. Arch. Neurol. Psychiat.*, 1923, **13**, 475–514.

Minkowski, M. Zum gegenwärtigen Stand der Lehre von den Reflexen in entwicklungsgeschichtlicher und der anatomisch-physiologischer Beziehung. *Schweiz. Arch. Neurol. Psychiat.*, 1924, **15**, 239–259; 1925, **16**, 133–152, 266–284.

Minkowski, M. Sur les modalités et la localisation du réflexe plantaire au cours de son évolution du foetus à l'adulte. C. R. *Congr. Médecins, Aliénistes et Neurologistes de France,* Geneva, 1926, **30,** 301–308.

Minkowski, M. Neurobiologische Studien am menschlichen Foetus. *Handb. Biol. ArbMeth.,* 1928, Pt. V, **5B,** 511–618. (a)

Minkowski, M. Ueber die elektrische Erregbarkeit der fötalen Muskulatur. *Schweiz. Arch. Neurol. Psychiat.,* 1928, **22,** 64–71. (b)

Minkowski, M. Zum Problem der ersten Anfänge einer seelischen Entwicklung beim Fötus. *Z. Kinderpsychiat.,* 1947–1948, **14,** 87–94.

Minkowski, A. The early developing nervous system in the frame of body growth. *Biologia neonat.,* 1962, **4,** 121–125.

Minot, C. S. *Human embryology.* New York: William Wood, 1892.

Minot, C. S. *A laboratory text-book of embryology.* Philadelphia, Pa.: Blakiston, 1903.

Mintz, B. *Environmental influences on prenatal development.* Chicago: University of Chicago Press, 1958.

Moltz, H. Imprinting: empirical and theoretical significance. *Psychol. Bull.,* 1960, **57,** 291–314.

Moltz, H. An epigenetic interpretation of the imprinting phenomenon. In G. Newton and S. Levine (Eds.), *Early experiences and behavior.* Springfield, Ill.: Thomas, 1968.

Montague, A. *Life before birth.* New York: New American Library, 1964.

Morache, G. La vie intra-utrine et sa durée. *J. méd. Paris,* 1904, **2,** 14–16.

Morgan, C. L. *Emergent evolution.* London: Williams and Norgate, 1923.

Morrison, F. J. Maternal impressions. *Va. Med. Mo.,* 1920, **47,** 127.

Mowrer, O. H. "Maturation" vs. "learning" in the development of vestibular and optokinetic nystagmus. *J. genet. Psychol.,* 1936, **48,** 383–404.

Muller, H. R., and Weed, L. H. Notes on the falling reflex in cats. *Am. J. Physiol.,* 1916, **40,** 373–379 .

Murchison, C. *A handbook of child psychology.* (2nd ed.) Worcester, Mass.: Clark University Press, 1933.

Myrberg, A. A. A descriptive analysis of the behavior of the African cichlid fish *Pelmatochromis Guentheri (Sauvage). Anim. behav.,* 1965, **13,** 312–329.

Needham, A. E. *The growth process in animals.* London: Pitman, 1964.

Needham, J. *Chemical embryology.* (3 vols.) Cambridge: University Press, 1931.

Neu, M. Die Diagnose der Schwangerschaft. In A. Döderlein (Ed.), *Handbuch der Geburtshilfe.* Wiesbaden: Bergmann, 1915, Pp. 246–328.

Nicholas, J. S. Notes on the application of experimental methods upon mammalian embryos. *Anat. Rec.,* 1925, **31,** 385–394.

Nicholas, J. S. Extirpation experiments upon the embryonic forelimb of the rat. *Proc. Soc. exp. Biol. Med.,* 1926, **23,** 436–439.

Nicholas, J. S. The application of experimental methods to the study of developing *Fundulus* embryos. *Proc. Nat. Acad. Sci.,* 1927, **13,** 695–698.

Nicholas, J. S. An analysis of the responses of isolated portions of the Amphibian nervous system. *Roux' Arch. Entwicklungsmech. Organ.,* 1929, **118,** 78–120. (a)

Nicholas, J. S. Transplantations of tissues in fetal rats. *Proc. Soc. exp. Biol. Med.,* 1929, **26,** 731–732. (b)

Nicholas, J. S., and Hooker, D. Progressive cord degeneration and collateral transmission of spinal impulses following section of the spinal cord in albino rat fetuses. *Anat. Rec.,* 1928, **38,** 24.

Noback, C. R. *The heritage of the human brain.* New York: American Museum of Natural History, 1959.

Noback, C. R., and Robertson, C. G. Sequences of appearance of ossification centers in the human skeleton during the first five prenatal months. *Am. J. Anat.*, 1951, **89**, 1, 1–28.

Norman, H. N. Fetal hiccups. *J. comp. Psychol.*, 1942, **34**, 65–73.

Oppenheim, R. Amniotic contraction and embryonic motility in the chick embryo. *Science*, 1966, **152**, 528–529.

Orr, D. W., and Windle, W. F. The development of behavior in chick embryos: The appearance of somatic movements. *J. comp. Neurol.*, 1934, **60**, 271–283.

Pankratz, D. S. The possible relations of the development of the suprarenal gland to the origin of foetal movements in the albino rat. *Anat. Rec.*, 1930, **45**, 235.

Pankratz, D. S. A preliminary report on the fetal movements in the rabbit. (Abs.) *Anat. Rec.*, Suppl., 1931, **48**, 58–59.

Paramore, R. H. A critical inquiry into the causes of the internal rotation of the foetal head. *J. Obstet. Gynec., London*, 1909, **16**, 213–232.

Parker, G. H. *The elementary nervous system*. Philadelphia: Lippincott, 1919.

Parker, G. H. *Smell, taste, and allied senses in the vertebrates*. Philadelphia: Lippincott, 1922.

Parker, G. H. The passage of sperms and of eggs thorugh the oviducts in terrestrial vertebrates. *Phil. Trans. Roy. Soc., London*, 1931, **219**, 381–419.

Parker, T. J., and Haswell, W. A. *A textbook of zoology*. Vol. II. London: Macmillan, 1921.

Pastore, N. Samuel Bailey's critique of Berkeley's theory of vision. *J. Hist. Behav. Sci.*, 1965, **1**, 321–337.

Patten, B. M. *The early embryology of the chick*. (3d ed.) Philadelphia: Blakiston, 1929.

Patten, B. M., and Kramer, T. C. The initiation of contraction in the embryonic chick heart. *Am. J. Anat.*, 1933, **53**, 349–375.

Patterson, T. L. Contributions to the physiology of the stomach: XIII. The variations in the hunger contractions of the empty stomach with age. *Am. J. Physiol.*, 1914, **33**, 423–429.

Payne, G. S., and Bach, L. M. N. Perinatal sleep-wake cycles. *Etudes Neo-nateles*, 1965, **8**, 308–320.

Peiper, A. Sinnesempfindungen des Kindes vor seiner Geburt. *Mschr. Kinderheilk.*, 1925, **29**, 236–241.

Peiper, A. *Die Hirntätigkeit des Säuglings*. Berlin: Springer, 1928.

Petajan, J. H., and Morrison, P. Physical and physiological factors modifying the development of temperature regulation in the opossum. *J. exp. Zool.*, 1962, **149**, 45–57.

Peters, J. J., Vonderahe, A. R., and Powers, T. H. Electrical studies of functional development of the eye and optic lobes in the chick embryo. *J. exp. Zool.*, 1958, **139**, 459–468.

Peterson, F., and Rainey, L. H. The beginnings of mind in the newborn. *Bull. Lying-In Hosp. City of N. Y.*, 1910, **7**, 99–122.

Pfaffman, C. Differential responses of the new-born cat to gustatory stimuli. *J. genet. Psychol.*, 1936, **49**, 61–67.

Pflüger, E. Die Lebensfähigkeit des menschlichen Foetus. *Pflüg. Arch. ges. Physiol.*, 1914, **33**, 423–429.

Pinard. Fétus, anatomie et physiologie. Fétus, pathologie. *Dictionnaire encyclopedique des sciences médicales*. (Ser. 4.) Vol. II. Paris: Masson, 1877. Pp. 472–556.

Pliess, G. Contribution to the teratological analysis of the new Wiedemann dysmelia syndrome (Thalidomide abnormalities). Beitrag zur teratologischen Analyse des Neuen Wiedemann Dysmelie-Syndroms (Thalidomid-Mibbildungen?) *Med. Klin.*, 1962, **57**, 1567–1573.

Ploss, H., and Bartels, M. *Das Weib in der Natur- und Völkerkunde.* (3 vols.) (11th ed.) Berlin: Neufeld, 1927.

Portal, Ueber die Pupillarmembran. *Dtsch. Arch. Physiol.*, 1918, **4**, 640–641.

Potter, E. L. *Pathology of the fetus and the infant.* (2nd ed.) Chicago: Yearbook Medical Publishers, 1961.

Potter, E. L., and Bohlander, G. P. Intrauterine respiration in relation to development of fetal lung, with report of two unusual anomalies of respiratory system. *Am. J. obstet. Gynec.*, 1941, **42**, 14–22.

Pratt, K. C., Nelson, A. K., and Sun, K. H. The behavior of the newborn infant. *Ohio State Univ. Stud., Contr. Psychol.*, 1930, No. 10.

Prechtl, H. F. R. Problems of behavioral studies in the newborn infant. In D. Lehrman, R. Hinde, and E. Shaw (Eds.), *Advances in the study of behavior*, Vol. I. New York: Academic Press, 1965. Pp. 75–98.

Preyer, W. *Die Seele des Kindes.* Leipzig: Fernau, 1882. (5th ed., 1900.) *The mind of the child:* Pt. 1. *The senses and the will;* Pt. 2. *The development of the intellect.* (Trans. by H. W. Brown.) New York: Appleton, 1888, 1889.

Preyer, W. *Specielle Physiologie des Embryo. Untersuchungen über die Lebenserscheinungen vor der Geburt.* Leipzig: Grieben, 1885.

Preyer, W. *Die geistige Entwicklung in der ersten Kindheit.* Stuttgart: Union, 1893. *Mental development in the child.* (Trans. by H. W. Brown.) New York: Appleton, 1893.

Ralston, H. J. *Emergent evolution and purpose.* Boston: Badger, 1933.

Randolph, H. Chloretone (acelonchloroform): An anesthetic and mascerating agent for lower animals. *Zool. Anz.*, 1900, **23**, 436–439.

Raney, E. T., and Carmichael, L. Localizing responses to tactual stimuli in the fetal rat in relation to the psychological problem of space perception. *J. genet. Psychol.*, 1934, **45**, 3–21.

Rawdon-Smith, A. F., Carmichael, L., and Wellman, B. Electrical responses from the cochlea of the fetal guinea pig. *J. Exp. Psychol.*, 1938, **23**, 531–535.

Ray, W. S. A preliminary report on a study of fetal conditioning. *Child Develpm.*, 1932, **3**, 175–177.

Rheingold, H. E. (Ed.) *Maternal behavior in mammals.* New York: Wiley, 1963.

Richter, C. P. Some observations on the self-stimulation habits of young wild animals. *Arch. Neurol. Psychiat.*, 1925, **13**, 724–728.

Richter, C. P. Sleep and activity: their relation to the 24-hour clock. In Association for Research in Nervous and Mental Disease, *Sleep and altered states of consciousness.* Baltimore, Md.: Williams and Wilkins, 1967. Vol. XLV, pp. 8–29.

Robinson, R. J., and Tizard, J. P. M. The central nervous system in the new born. *Br. Med. Bull.*, 1966, **22**, 49–55.

Rodman, J. Case of a child born between the fourth and fifth month and brought up. *Edinburgh Med. Surg. J.*, 1815, **11**, 455–458.

Romanes, G. J. *Darwin, and after Darwin:* Vol. I. *The Darwinian theory.* Chicago: Open Court, 1896.

Romijn, C., and Roos, J. The air space of the hen's egg and its changes during the period of incubation. *J. Physiol.*, 1938, **94**, 365–379.

Rosen, M., and Satran, R. Fetal electro-encephalography during birth. *Obstet. Gynec.*, 1965, **26**, 740–745.

Ruckert, W. Über die tonischen Eigenschaften fötaler Muskeln. *Arch. exp. Path. Pharmak.*, 1930, **150**, 221–235.

Rudolph, L., and Ivy, A. C. Internal rotation of the fetal head. *Am. J. obstet. Gynec.*, 1933, **25**, 74–94.

Rugh, R. X-irradiation effects in the human fetus. *J. Pediat.*, 1958, **52**, 531–538.

Sachs, H. Elektrokardiogrammstudien am Foetus in utero. *Arch. ges. Physiol.*, 1922, **197**, 536–542.

Salter, S. H. A note on the recording of egg activity. *Anim. Behav.*, 1966, **14**, 41–43.

Sarwey, O. Anatomie und Phpsiologie der Schwangerschaft. Pt. 2. In A. Döderlein (Ed.), *Handbuch der Geburtshilft.* Wiesbaden: Bergmann, 1915. Pp. 153–245.

Scammon, R. E. The literature on the growth and physical development of the fetus, infant, and child: a quantitative summary. *Anat. Rec.*, 1927, **35**, 241–267.

Scammon, R. E., and Calkins, L. A. The relation between the body-weight and age of the human fetus. *Proc. Soc. exp. Biol. Med.*, 1924, **22**, 157–161.

Scammon, R. E., and Calkins, L. A. *The development and growth of the external dimensions of the human body in the fetal period.* Minneapolis: University of Minnesota Press, 1929.

Scharpenberg, L. G., and Windle, W. F. A study of spinal cord development in silver-stained sheep embryos correlated with early somatic movements. *J. Anat.*, 1938, **72**, 344–351.

Schiller, C. H. (Ed.) *Instinctive behavior.* New York: International University Press, 1957.

Schneirla, T. C. Aspects of stimulation and organization in approach-withdrawal processes underlying vertebrate behavioral development. In D. S. Lehrman, R. A. Hinde, and E. Shaw (Eds.), *Advances in the study of behavior*, Vol. I. New York: Academic Press. Pp. 1–74.

Scott, J. P., and Fuller, J. L. *Genetics and the social behavior of the dog.* Chicago: University of Chicago Press, 1965.

Sharp, L. W. *An introduction to cytology.* New York: McGraw-Hill, 1926.

Sharpey-Schäfer, E. The effects of denervation of a cutaneous area. *Quart. J. exp. Physiol.*, 1928, **19**, 85–107.

Sheldon, W. H., Stevens, S. S., and Tucker, W. B. *The varieties of human physique.* New York: Harper, 1940.

Sherman, M., and Sherman, I. C. Sensorimotor responses in infants. *J. comp. Psychol.*, 1925, **5**, 53–68.

Shirley, M. M. A motor sequence favors the maturation theory. *Psychol. Bull.*, 1931, **28**, 204–205. (a)

Shirley, M. M. Is development saltatory as well as continuous? *Psychol. Bull.*, 1931, **28**, 664–665. (b)

Simpson, W. J. A preliminary report on cigarette smoking and the incidence of prematurity. *Am. J. obstet. Gynec.*, 1957, **73**, 808–815.

Sluckin, W. *Imprinting and early learning.* London: Methuen, 1964.

Small, W. S. Notes on the psychic development of the young white rat. *Am. J. Psychol.*, 1899, **11**, 80–100.

Smith C. A. *The physiology of the newborn infant.* Springfield, Ill.: Thomas, 1946.

Smith, K. U., and Daniel, R. S. Maturational development and integration of response in the sea turtle. (Abstract.) *Am. Psychol.*, 1947, **2**, 266.

Snell, G. D., and Stevens, L. C. Early embryology. In E. L. Green (Ed.), *Biology of the laboratory mouse.* (2nd ed.) New York: McGraw-Hill, 1966. Pp. 205–245.

Snyder, F. F., and Rosenfeld, M. Direct observation of intrauterine respiratory movements of the fetus and the role of carbon dioxide and oxygen in their regulation. *Am. J. Physiol.*, 1937, **119**, 153–166.

Somers, G. F. Thalidomide and congenital abnormalities. *Lancet*, 1962, **1**, 912–913.

Sontag, L. W. The significance of fetal environmental differences. *Am. J. obstet. Gynec.*, 1941, **42**, 996–1003.

Sontag, L. W. Implications of fetal behavior and environment for adult personalities. *Ann. N. Y. Acad. Sci.*, 1966, **134**, 782–786.

Spalding, D. A. Instinct, with original observations on young animals. *Macmillan's Magazine*, 1873, **27**, 282–293. Reprinted in *Brit. J. animal Behav.*, 1954, **2**, 2–11.

Spee, F. Anatomie und Physiologie der Schwangerschaft. Pt. 1. In A. Döderlein (Ed.), *Handbuch der Geburtshilfe*. Wiesbaden: Bergmann, 1915. Pp. 1–152.

Spelt, D. K. Conditioned responses in the human fetus in utero. *Psychol. Bull.*, 1938, **35**, 712–713.

Spencer, R. P., and Coulombe, M. J. Observations on fetal weight and gestational age. *Growth*, 1964, **28**, 243–247.

Starling, E. H. The muscular and nervous mechanisms of the respiratory movements. In E. Sharpey-Schäfer (Ed.), *Text-book of physiology*. Vol. 2. Edinburgh: Pentland, 1900. Pp. 274–312.

Steele, A. G., and Windle, W. F. Some correlations between respiratory movements and blood gases in cat foetuses. *J. Physiol.*, 1939, **94**, 531–538.

Stephenson, S. K., and Roberts, J. Specific gravity changes during the development of the sheep foetus. *Nature*, 1962, **196**, 788–789.

Stevens, S. S., and Davis, H. *Hearing: its psychology and physiology*. New York: Wiley, 1938.

Stiebel, F. Ueber die Entwicklung der Teichhornschnecken *(Limneus slagnalis)*. *Dtsch. Arch. Physiol.*, 1815, **1**, 423–426.

Strang, L. B. Changes in the pulmonary circulation in the foetus and newly born. *Maandschrift voor kindergeneeskunde*, 1964, **32**, 549–556.

Strassmann, P. Das Leben vor der Geburt. *Samml. klin. Vortr., N. F., Gynäk.*, 1903, No. 353, 947–968.

Straus, W. L. Changes in the structure of skeletal muscle at the time of its first visible contraction in living rat embryos. *Anat. Rec.*, 1939, Suppl., **73**, 50.

Straus, W. L., and Weddell, G. Nature of the first visible contractions of the forelimb musculature in rat fetuses. *J. Neurophysiol.*, 1940, **3**, 358–369.

Streeter, G. L. On the development of the membranous labyrinth and the acoustic and facial nerves in the human embryo. *Am. J. Anat.*, 1906, **6**, 139–165.

Streeter, G. L. Weight, sitting height, head size, foot length, and menstrual age of the human embryo. *Contr. Embryol., Carnegie Inst. Wash.*, 1920, **11**, No. 55, 143–170.

Sutherland, G. F. Contributions to the physiology of the stomach: LVII. The response of the stomach glands to gastrin before and shortly after birth. *Am. J. Physiol.*, 1921, **55**, 398–403.

Swammerdam, J. *Bibel der Natur*. Leipzig: J. F. Gleditschens, 1752.

Swammerdam, J. (Edited.) Versuche, die besondere Bewegung der Fleischstränge am Frosche betreffend. In *Opuscula selecta neerlandecorrim de arte medica*, Fasc. 1, 82–135. Amsterdam: F. van Rossen, 1907.

Swenson, E. A. The use of cerebral anemia in experimental embryological studies upon mammals. *Anat. Rec.*, 1925, **30**, 147–151.

Swenson, E. A. *The development of movement of the albino rat before birth*. Unpublished doctor's thesis, University of Kansas, 1926.

Swenson, E. A. Motion pictures of activities of living albino-rat fetuses. (Abs.) *Anat. Rec.*, 1928, **38**, 63. (a)

Swenson, E. A. The simple movements of the trunk of the albino-rat fetus. *Anat. Rec.*, 1928, **38**, 31. (b)

Swenson, E. A. The active simple movements of the albino-rat fetus: The order of their appearance, their qualities, and their significance. (Abs.) *Anat. Rec.*, 1929, **42**, 40.

Taussig, H. B. The thalidomide syndrome. *Scient. Am.*, 1962, **207**, 29–35. (a)

Taussig, H. B. Thalidomide and phocomelia. *Pediatrics*, 1962, **30**, 654–659. (b)

Thompson, H. E., Holmes, J. H., Gottesfeld, K., and Taylor, E. S. Fetal development as determined by ultrasonic pulse echo techniques. *Am. J. obstet. Gynec.*, 1965, **92**, 44–52.

Thorpe, W. H. *Learning and instinct in animals.* (1st ed.) Cambridge: Harvard University Press, 1956. (2nd ed.) London: Methuen Press, 1963.

Tinklepaugh, O. L., and Hartman, C. G. Behaviorial aspects of parturition in the monkey (*Macacus rhesus*). *J. comp. Psychol.*, 1930, **11**, 63–98.

Tinklepaugh, O. L., Hartman, C. G., and Squier, R. R. The fetal heart rate in the monkey (*Macacus rhesus*). *Proc. Soc. exp. Biol. Med.*, 1930, **28**, 285–288.

Tompkins, J. McC. Influences during pregnancy upon the unborn child. *Old Dominion J. Med. Surg., Richmond*, 1911-1912, **13**, 219–224.

Tracy, H. C. The development of motility and behavior reactions in the toadfish (*Opsanus tau*). *J. comp. Neurol.*, 1926, **40**, 253–369.

Tuge, H. Early behavior of embryos of the turtle, *Terrapene carolina* (L). *Proc. Soc. exp. Biol. Med.*, 1931, **29**, 52–53.

Tuge, H. Early behavior of the embryos of carrier-pigeons. *Proc. Soc. exp. Biol. Med.*, 1934, **31**, 462–463.

VanLeeuwenhoeck, A. For full bibliography, see A. W. Meyer, *The rise of embryology.* Palo Alto, Calif.: Stanford University Press, 1939.

Vierck, C. J., King, F. A., and Ferm, V. H. Effects of prenatal hypoxia upon activity and emotionality of the rat. *Psychon. Sci.*, 1966, **4**, 87–88.

Vincent, M., and Hugon, J. Relationships between various criteria of maturity at birth. *Biologia neonat.*, 1962, **4**, 223–279.

Vincent, S. B. The function of the vibrissae in the behavior of the white rat. *Behav. Mongr.*, 1912, **1**, No. 5. Pp. 81.

Virey. Rémarques sur la position du foetus dans l'utérus dans les diverses séries des animaux. *Arch. gén. méd.*, 1833 (2nd ser.), **1**, 295–298.

von Baer, K. E. For full biblography, see A. W. Meyer, *The rise of embryology.* Palo Alto, Calif.: Stanford University Press, 1939.

Wada, T. Anatomical and physiological studies on the growth of the inner ear of the albino rat. *Amer. Anat. Memoirs, Wistar Inst. Anat. Biol.*, 1923, **10**, 174.

Walters, C. E. Prediction of postnatal development from fetal activity. *Child Devel.*, 1965, **36**, 801–808.

Walton, C. E. Maternal impressions. *J. Surg. Gynec. Obstet., N. Y.* 1910, **32**, 27–29.

Walz, W. Ueber die Bedeutung der intrauterinen Atembewegungen. *Mschr. Geburtsh. Gynäk.*, 1922, **60**, 331–341.

Wang, G. H., and Lu, T. W. Spontaneous activity of the spinal tadpoles of the frog and the toad. *Science*, 1940, **92**, 148.

Wang, G. H., and Lu, T. W. Development of swimming and righting reflexes in frog (*Rana guetheri*): Effects thereon of transection of central nervous system before hatching. *J. Neurophysiol.*, 1941, **4**, 137–146.

Warden, C. J., et al. *Animal motivation: Experimental studies on the albino rat.* New York: Columbia University Press, 1931.

Warkentin, J. *A genetic study of vision in animals.* Unpublished doctor's thesis, University of Rochester, 1938.

Warkentin, J., and Carmichael, L. A study of the development of the air-righting reflex in cats and rabbits. *J. genet. Psychol.*, 1939, **55**, 67–80.

Warkentin, J., and Smith, K. U. The development of visual acuity in the cat. *J. genet. Psychol.*, 1937, **50**, 371–399.

Weber, E. H. Ueber den Einfluss der Erwärmung and Erkältung der Nerven auf ihr Leitungsvermögen. *Arch. Anat. Physiol.*, 1847, 342–356.

Weed, L. H. The reactions of kittens after decerebration. *Am. J. Physiol.*, 1917, **43**, 131–157.

Weed, L. H., and Langworthy, O. R. Decerebrate rigidity in the opossum. *Am. J. Physiol.*, 1925, **72**, 25–38. (a)

Weed, L. H., and Langworthy, O. R. Developmental study of excitatory areas in the cerebral cortex of the opossum. *Am. J. Physiol.*, 1925, **72**, 8–24. (b)

Weed, L. H., and Langworthy, O. R. Physiological study of cortical motor areas in young kittens and in adult cats. *Contr. Embryol., Carnegie Inst. Wash.*, 1926, **17**, No. 87, 89–106.

Weidenback, A. Totale phokomelie. *Zbl. Gynak.*, 1959, **81**, 2048–2052.

Weiss, A. P. The measurement of infant behavior. *Psychol. Rev.*, 1929, **36**, 453–471.

Weiss, P. The relations between central and peripheral coordination. *J. comp. Neurol.*, 1926, **40**, 241–252.

Weiss, P. *Principles of development.* New York: Holt, 1939 .

Weiss, P. Nervous system neurogenesis. In B. B. Willier, P. Weiss, and V. Hamburger, (Eds.), *Analysis of development.* Philadelphia: Saunders, 1955. Pp. 346–401.

Weiss, P. Specificity in growth control. In E. G. Butler, (Ed.), *Biological specificity and growth.* Princeton, N. J.: Princeton University Press, 1955. Pp. 195–206. (b)

Wertheimer, E. Foetus. In C. Richet, (Ed.), *Dictionnaire de physiologie*, Vol. VI, Paris: Alcan, 1904. Pp. 499–634.

Wetzel, N. C. Physical fitness in terms of physique, development and basal metabolism. *J. Am. Med. Assn.*, 1941, **116**, 1187–1195.

White, G. M. The behavior of brook trout embryos from the time of hatching to the absorption of the yolk sac. *J. Anim. Behav.*, 1915, **5**, 44–60.

Whitehead, J. Convulsions in utero. *Br. Med. J.*, 1867, 59–60.

Whitehead, W. H., Windle, W. F., and Becker, R. F. Changes in lung structure during aspiration of amniotic fluid and during air-breathing at birth. *Anat. Rec.*, 1942, **83**, 255–265.

Wiener, N. *Cybernetics, or control and communication in the animal and the machine.* New York: Wiley, 1948.

Williams, J. W. *Obstetrics.* New York: Appleton, 1931.

Windle, W. F. The earliest fetal movements in the cat correlated with the neurofibrillar development of the spinal cord. (Abs.) *Anat. Rec.*, 1930, **45**, 249.

Windle, W. F. Correlation between the development of local reflexes and reflex arcs in the spinal cord of cat embryos. *J. comp. Neurol.*, 1934, **59**, 487–505. (a)

Windle, W. F. Correlation between the development of spinal reflexes and reflex arcs in albino-rat embryos. (Abs.) *Anat. Rec.*, Suppl., 1934, **58**, 42 (b).

Windle, W. F. Neurofibrillar development of cat embryos: Extent of development in the telencephalon and diencephalon up to 15 mm. *J. comp. Neurol.*, 1935, **63**, 139–172.

Windle, W. F. On the nature of the first forelimb movements of mammalian embryos. *Proc. Soc. exp. Biol. Med.*, 1937, **36**, 640–642.

Windle, W. F. Calcium and potassium deficiency as possible causes of certain delayed fetal movements. *Physiol. Zool.*, 1939, **12**, 39–41.

Windle, W. F. *Physiology of the fetus: origin and extent of function in prenatal life.* Philadelphia: Saunders, 1940.

Windle, W. F. Physiology and anatomy of the respiratory system in the fetus and newborn infant. *J. Pediat.*, 1941, **19**, 437–444.

Windle, W. F. Genesis of somatic motor function in mammalian embryos: a synthesizing article. *Physiol. Zool.*, 1944, **17**, 247–260.

Windle, W. F. Asphxia neonatorum. Its relation to the fetal blood, circulation and respiration and its effects upon the brain. *Amer. Lecture Ser. Publ.*, **52**. Springfield, Ill.: Thomas, 1950. Pp. 70.

Windle, W. F., and Barcroft, J. Some factors governing the initiation of respiration in the chick. *Am. J. Physiol.*, 1938, **121**, 684–691.

Windle, W. F., and Baxter, R. E. Development of reflex mechanisms in the spinal cord of albino rat embryos. Correlations between structure and function and comparisons with the cat and the chick. *J. comp. Neurol.*, 1935, **63**, 189–200.

Windle, W. F., and Baxter, J. The first neurofibrillar development in albino rat embryos. *J. comp. Neurol.*, 1936, **63**, 173–185.

Windle, W. F., and Becker, R. F. The course of the blood through the fetal heart. An experimental study in the cat and guinea pig. *Anat. Rec.*, 1940, **77**, 417–426.

Windle, W. F., and Fish, M. W. The development of the vestibular righting reflex in the cat. *J. comp. Neurol.*, 1932, **54**, 85–96.

Windle, W. F., and Fitgerald, J. E. Development of the spinal reflex mechanism in human embryos. *J. comp. Neurol.*, 1937, **67**, 493–509.

Windle, W. F., and Griffin, A. M. Observations on embryonic and fetal movements of the cat. *J. comp. Neurol.*, 1931, **52**, 149–188.

Windle, W. F., and Minear, W. L. Reversal of reaction pattern in the course of development of the snout reflex of the cat embryo. (Abs.) *Anat. Rec.*, 1934, Suppl., **58**, 92.

Windle, W. F., Minear, W. L., Austin, M. F., and Orr, D. W. The origin and early development of somatic behavior in the albino rat. *Physiol. Zool.*, 1935, **8**, 156–175.

Windle, W. F., Monnier, M., and Steele, A. G. Fetal respiratory movements in the cat. *Physiol. Zool.*, 1938, **11**, 425–433.

Windle, W. F., and Nelson, D. Development of respiration in the duck. *Am. J. Physiol.*, 1938, **121**, 700–707.

Windle, W. F., O'Donnell, J. E., and Glasshagle, E. E. The early development of spontaneous and reflex behavior in cat embryos and fetuses. *Physiol. Zool.*, 1933, **6**, 521–541.

Windle, W. F., and Orr, D. W. The development of behavior in chick embryos: Spinal cord structure correlated with early somatic motility. *J. comp. Neurol.*, 1934, **60**, 287–308. (a)

Windle, W. F., and Orr, D. W. Vermiform contractions of the musculature of cat embryos at death. *Anat. Rec.*, 1934, Suppl., **58**, 92. (b)

Windle, W. F., Orr, D. W., and Minear, W. L. The origin and development of reflexes in the cat during the third fetal week. *Physiol. Zool.*, 1964, **7**, 600–617.

Windle, W. F., Scharpenberg, L. G., and Steele, A. G. Influence of carbon dioxide and anoxemia upon respiration in the chick at hatching. *Am. J. Physiol.*, 1938, **121**, 692–699.

Wintrebert, M. P. Sur l'existence d'une irritabilité excito-motrice primitive, indépendante des voies nerveuses chez les embryons ciliés de Batraciens. *C. R. Soc. Biol., Paris*, 1904, **57**, 645.

Wintrebert, M. P. La contraction rhythmée anecurale des myotomes chez les embryons de selaciens: I. Observation de *Scylliorhinus canicula* L. Gill. *Arch. zool. expér.*, 1930, **60**, 221.

Witkowski, G. J. *Histoire des accouchements chez tous les peuples.* Paris: Steinheil, 1887.

Woodworth, R. S. *Psychology.* (Rev. ed.) New York: Holt, 1929.

Woollam, D. H. Thalidomide disaster considered as an experiment in mammalian teratology. *Br. Med. J.*, 1962, **2**, 236–237.

Woyciechowski, B. Ruchy zarodka ludzkiego 42 mm. *Polsk. Gazeta Lekarska*, 1928, **7**, 409–411.

Wynn, R. W. (Ed.) *Fetal homeostatis*, 2 vols. New York: Academy of Science, 1965.

Yamazaki, J. N. A review of the literature on radiation dosage required to cause manifest central nervous system disturbances in utero and postnatal exposure. *Pediatrics*, 1966, **37**, 877–903.

Yamazaki, J. N., Wright, S. W., and Wright P. M. Outcome of pregnanacy in women exposed to atomic bomb in Nagasaki. *Am. J. Dis. Child.*, 1954, **87**, 448–463.

Yanase, J. Beiträge zur Physiologie der peristaltischen Bewegungen des embryonalen Darmes: I. Mitteilung. *Pflüg. Arch. ges. Physiol.*, 1907, **117**, 345–383. (a)

Yanase, J. Beiträge zur Physiologie der peristaltischen Bewegungen des embryonalen Darmes: II. Mitteilung. *Pflüg. Arch. ges. Physiol.*, 1907, **119**, 451–464. (b)

Youngstrom, K. A. Studies on the developing behavior of *Anura. J. comp. Neurol.*, 1937, **68**, 351–379.

Zettleman, H. J. Initial fetal atelectasis. *Am. J. obstet. Gynec.*, 1946, **51**, 241–245.

Zuntz, N. Ueber die Respiration des Säugethier-Foetus. *Pflüg. Arch. ges. Physiol.*, 1877, **14**, 605–637.

7. Studies of Early Experience[1]

WILLIAM R. THOMPSON AND JOAN E. GRUSEC

Developmental psychology, with which this book is concerned, has tended to employ two major methodological orientations to its subject-matter. The first—and certainly the more usual—is the *normative-descriptive*. This has been the approach traditionally taken by most workers in child psychology. The kinds of datum gathered by Gesell and his colleagues at Yale are prototypic of this approach in that they are basically descriptions of the behavior of children at each chronological age level. The work of Piaget and others at Geneva has been similar, although the use of simple age as the major anchoring variable has been rather less emphasized. That is to say, Piaget has attempted to derive stages based on *developmental* sequences, although these are not necessarily perfectly correlated with chronological age. Ultimately, however, such so-called stages are based on description supplemented by a good deal of guesswork and without much reference to any basic theoretical conceptualizations of whether there are changes taking place in the developing organism that demand such psychological transitions.

The second orientation is the *experimental-predictive*. Here the focus is less on empirical assays of what the organism is like at certain periods of its development than on the later outcomes of certain treatments that are imposed either by nature or by deliberate experimental manipulation early in life. The

[1] This chapter was prepared with the aid of grants from the National Research Council, the Arts Research Committee of Queen's University, and the Ontario Alcohol and Drug Addiction Research Foundation.

retrospective clinical investigations of Freud —though he himself did virtually no work with children—belong to this orientation, as does most of the work done on development in animals, that is, the so-called studies of early experience.

It is of some importance to note that the two approaches have seldom been combined, for a variety of historical reasons. Thus we find very little attention paid, in most of the work on early experience, to descriptions of the behavioral characteristics of a young animal, which might permit the isolation of those characteristics responsible for determining the later residua of whatever treatment the experimenter has imposed. On the other hand, most child psychologists have been content to deal with their subjects descriptively at some particular age level as if they all occupied a kind of neutral and uniform environment and had no past and no future.

One result of this disparity between the two orientations has been an almost complete lack of fruitful theorizing pertaining uniquely to the area of developmental psychology. There are certainly broad schemas such as those of Gesell (1946) and Werner (1957), but these have not readily been translatable into sets of specific questions that can be asked and answered in a precise experimental manner. The same can be said of at least many of the conceptions of Piaget. On the animal side, we again find a lack of theorizing and, instead, an endless proliferation of studies dealing with more and more exotic independent and dependent variables. These experiments leave no doubt that early experience is extremely important. But they do not explore the nature of the residual effects nor

565

the manner in which they are stored by organisms at a young age. Yet these are the basic issues we wish to understand.

THE ESSENTIAL PROBLEM

It is easy to demonstrate that a rat or mouse that has been handled, shocked, vibrated, cooled, or heated as an infant behaves differently from an animal that has not undergone such treatments As we just stated, early experince is important. This is a simple enough postulate, yet its terms are rich in possible meanings. "Early experience" covers presumably all age levels from conception to maturity—a lengthy period during which the experiences of animals with respect to some imposed treatment cannot be uniform. The response of a human fetus to anxiety in its mother surely cannot be the same as that of the four-year-old child and hence the residual effects of these experiences, if any, are bound to be different. The question we must ask is how the early period of life can be broken up in a manner that takes account, not so much of the changes in chronological age that are occurring, but rather of the changes in developmental characteristics that are also going on. For although these latter changes must vary with age, the relationships they may have with age are not necessarily one to one. Age proceeds, by definition, in terms of uniform increments. Such developmental variables as differentiation and growth, however, are usually considered to be sigmoid or logistic in form. When we attempt to make predictions about the effects some early experience may have later in life, it is such basic dimensions as these to which we should turn our attention.

What we are suggesting, in short, is that more information be obtained about the properties—physiological and psychological—of young organisms and that these be used to formulate theoretical models that will put more predictive potency into the rationale that lies behind the study of early experience.

The same kind of examination must be made of the term "important." It is very seldom that any careful definition of this key word is attempted. Schaefer and one of the writers (Thompson and Scheafer, 1961) suggested it must involve the following dimensions:

1. Extent of change in a particular function; for example, the size of increment or decrement in open-field activity as shown by a treated group of animals as compared with controls.

2. The potential reversibility of the change; that is, how easy or difficult it is, by using special procedures, to produce a reversion to the control level.

3. The permanence or duration of the change; that is, the lack of any tendency for treated animals spontaneously to drift back to a normal level.

4. The generality of the change—meaning simply the number of discrete functions or structures affected by the treatment.

Together, these constitute the operational meaning of "important" when we use this term in connection with the effects of early experience.

One further point must be made most emphatically. The meanings specified above can have usefulness only when the experimental comparisons made are of a four-way type: that is, between young treated and nontreated and adult treated and nontreated groups. The use of such a 2×2 design is usually impracticable with human subjects for obvious reasons, but with animals it should be (though it seldom is) regarded as mandatory. Obviously, we can say little about the unique characteristics of young systems unless we can compare them with adult organisms.

Besides a formal explication of the phrase "early experience is important," we may arrive at some understanding of the theoretical problems that are latent in the phrase by sketching the historical background out of which empirical work arose. Let us now examine this.

HISTORY OF WORK ON EARLY EXPERIENCE

The history of the general problem as it has been commonly understood is far broader in scope than the history of the problem as we have more precisely defined it. That is to say, there has been a great deal of work done on topics like the nature of growth, the problem of maturation versus learning, the modifiability of child intelligence by special procedures such as orphanage rearing, nursery school experience, and the like. However, in only a few of these areas has there been any real theoretical interest in or experimental provision for educing from the data critical information about properties that may distinguish the young from the mature organism. To take an example, during the late 1930s and early 1940s, a series of studies was carried out by Wellman, Skeels, Skodak and others at Iowa purporting to show that the IQs of mentally defective children could be significantly raised by exposure to special schooling. Institution rearing, on the other hand, was supposed to have the opposite effect. These results were subsequently challenged by a number of critics, including especially Goodenough (1939) and McNemar (1940), on the grounds of inadequate control and statistical procedure. Consequently, their validity must be considered doubtful; but whatever the case, certainly no conclusion can be drawn from such data regarding the importance of the *youth* of the subjects as a major factor influencing the outcome. The interest of the Iowa group was more broadly in the problem of modifiability of intelligence in general rather than merely in young systems. Thus such studies stand a little apart from the category we wish mainly to consider in this chapter.

The commitment that must define this category—and it may be held implicitly and explicitly—is to the notion that an experience imposed on an organism will have diffferent effects according to whether it is mature or immature since the immature organism has certain special properties. Using this notion as a guideline we may trace four theoretical traditions that together include most of the work on early experience: (1) the tradition of developmental biology; (2) the psychiatric and psychoanalytic tradition; (3) the tradition of physiological psychology; and (4) the ethological tradition.

The Tradition of Developmental Biology

Major ideas about the process of biological development have been well reviewed by Hunt (1961) and Kuo (1967). One of the major issues on which most theorists have taken a position has concerned the plasticity or modifiability of the developing organism and the extent to which its phonotype may deviate from its expected genetic pathway or

"creode" as Waddington (1957) has called it. The logic of Darwinian evolutionary theory coupled with classical Mendelian genetics works better if it can be assumed that the phenotype on which selection acts bears a relatively fixed relation to genotype, so that the "right" individuals—that is, those with the greatest probability of survival—are the ones selected. Certainly, the kinds of characters with which both Darwin and Mendel were concerned, such as flower color, or avian plumage, were stable enough. And even behavioral traits could be viewed in the same way. In his book *Expression of Emotions in Man and Animal* (1872) Darwin attempted to show how the apparently fluid behaviors involved in animal communication were made up of fairly fixed components and that the residuals of these could also be found in human beings. A further step was taken by a number of developmental biologists who attempted to define more precisely the essential building blocks of behavior. Their work, for the most part, was done on lower organisms such as paramecia, stentor, hydra, and planaria. Thus Jacques Loeb (1890) formulated his famous tropism theory, according to which the directed behaviors of many species—for example, the medusa, *Tiaropsis indicans*—could be explained in terms of mechanical contraction or extension of musculature in the region of the stimulated surface area. The result of this was an orientation directly toward or away from the source of stimulation, thus rectifying, as it were, the animal's relation with the external world.

In a similar vein, von Uexküll, from his work on the sea urchin, proposed the concept of *reflex*, by which he meant the relatively invariant relation between certain afferent nerves and certain muscles. At least in its broader sense, it was intended to include the behavior of animals without as well as animals with nervous systems—though for the former, von Uexküll preferred to use the term *antitype* rather than reflex (see Jennings, 1915).

Although a radically mechanistic approach to behavior may have been highly compatible with Darwinian theory and was certainly fashionable around the turn of the century, it was not one that fitted all the facts. One of the first to demonstrate this was H. S. Jennings with his extensive studies on a variety of protozoa, especially amebas, and some of the lower metazoa. He introduced his work by stating:

The modifiability of the characteristics of organisms has always been a subject of the greatest importance in biological science. . . . In the processes of behavior we have characteristics that are modifiable with absolute ease. . . . (The general problem) is: what lasting changes are producible in organisms by the environment or otherwise, and what are the principles governing such modifications? Perhaps in no other field do we have so favorable an opportunity for the study of this problem, fundamental for all biology, as in behavior (1915, p. VI).

The data obtained by Jennings clearly showed that the lower organisms he studied were not, at least in the usual sense, machines. Their behavior showed variety and spontaneity to an extent not readily encompassed by such notions as tropism and reflex. Thus the behavior of an ameba was clearly adaptive and the rules that governed such adaptiveness "apparently form the fundamental basis of intelligent action. This fundamental basis then clearly exists even in the Protozoa; it is apparently coextensive with life. It is difficult if not impossible to draw a line separating the regulatory behavior of lower organisms from the so-called intelligent behavior of higher ones; the one grades insensibly into the other. From the lowest organism up to man behavior is essentially regulatory in character and what we call intelligence in higher animals is a direct outgrowth of the same laws that give behavior its regulatory character in the Protozoa" (Jennings, 1915, p. 335).

Out of this interest in the modifiability of behavior and the general search for units out of which behavior is built has emerged a great deal of basic empirical work. Some of this has focused primarily on the plasticity problem; some of it primarily on the building-blocks problem. Thus we have a line of research starting mainly with Coghill on amblystoma, Kuo on the chick, Barcroft on sheep, and Windle on the cat which has attempted to show just how maturation proceeds (see Carmichael, 1954; Kuo, 1967). Coghill (1929), on the basis of his research findings, put for-

ward the view that specific forms of action come to be individuated out of an initial matrix of total, massive responding. Kuo, on the other hand, working with avian embryos and using more precise techniques, as well as Windle (1940) and others, came to an opposite conclusion: specific movements or reflexes appear first and these form the elements out of which later complex behaviors are constituted (see Carmichael, 1954; Kuo, 1967). Such a disagreement is very difficult to settle empirically since the exact spatial limits of any response are hard to define and, in any case, depend greatly on the intensity and coarseness of the stimulus used to evoke it. However, such descriptive work on developmental sequences is not essentially relevant to our present discussion. The interested reader may consult Carmichael (1954), Kuo (1967), and Aaronson et al. (1966) for reviews of it. Our concern here is rather with the extent to which such early behaviors are modifiable before they assume their stable and crystallized adult forms. The two basic viewpoints about this problem have nicely been summarized by Gottlieb:

One viewpoint holds that behavioral epigenesis is predetermined by invariant organic factors of growth and differentiation (particularly neural maturation), and the other main viewpoint holds that the sequence and outcome of prenatal behavior is probabilistically determined by the critical operation of various endogenous and exogenous stimulative events (Gottlieb, 1966a).

The first position is currently held by Hamburger and his colleagues at Washington University, the second by Kuo, Gottlieb, Schneirla, and others. Whatever the final conclusion may be, there is no doubt that the disagreement has generated a most useful and active line of research. There seem to be strong indications that many embryo motor systems show rhythms or discharges that are called out by spontaneous activity of spinal motor neurons (Hamburger, 1962; Alconero, 1965). On the other hand, it is equally true that, under at least some circumstances, exogenous or endogenous stimulation is an important contributing factor to developmental changes. Thus it appears that cardiac beat and amnion contractions produce motility in avian embryos and that there is, in fact, a high correlation between heart rate and frequency of bodily movements (Kuo, 1967). Furthermore, Gottlieb (1966b) has put forward the interesting idea—which he is able to back with some data—that the responsiveness of chicks and ducks to their species call is produced, at least in part, by self-stimulation arising from their own vocalizations at hatch.

It is obvious that this kind of research, even from our very brief account of it, has bearing on the early experience problem, since it deals directly with the plasticity of young systems and the degree to which the developmental course their behavior follows can be altered by environmental influences.

The Psychiatric Tradition

Sigmund Freud was perhaps the first to emphasize the importance of childhood events in determining later behavior. Certainly, other psychologists were engaged in studying children, but not with a view to specifying long-term outcomes resulting from some kind of early treatment. Freud himself, aside from his brief contact with "Little Hans," did not work with children and his construction of the stages of psychosexual development was made on the basis of inference from the reported experiences of his adult patients. Nonetheless, he set the stage for the emergence of a strong tradition of child psychiatry. Prominent in this movement were such workers as Anna Freud, Melanie Klein, and Susan Isaacs, all of whom attempted to validate and extend the formulations of Freud through actual observations of children. Much of this early work, set as it was in the rather cabalistic framework of psychoanalytic theory, tended to receive scant attention from orthodox academic psychology. It was not until the later 1930s and early 1940s that a link between theory and experiment was made by Margaret Ribble (1939, 1944). Her observations carried out on 600 infants seemed to show that adequate "mothering" was a prerequisite to normal development. Deprived of continued, uninterrupted contact with a mother or substitute caretaker, the newborn would often commence to manifest a variety of undesirable and often fatal symptoms collectively described by Ribble as *maramus*. Both her data

and her theoretical treatment of them were open to many criticisms, which were later forthcoming (Orlansky, 1949; Pinneau, 1950, 1955). Nonetheless, there is no doubt that her basic findings caught the attention both of the public and of professional psychologists and laid the groundwork for several important lines of research. Since we discuss these in more detail in the main body of the chapter, we need only mention them here very briefly.

One basic line of research is simply an attempt to replicate and extend in various directions Ribble's basic data. Studies such as those of Goldfarb (1945a) and Provence and Lipton (1962) on orphanage rearing and those of Spitz (1945) and Bowlby (1952) on separation and lack of mothering are examples. They have, in the main, confirmed the original findings of Ribble. A rather more unexpected line of work, however, was that started with the experiments of Bernstein (1952) and of Weininger (1953) on the effects of "mothering" or "gentling" on the later behavior of young rats. The number of studies devoted to examining this problem has been very great and it is still being examined. Generally, the data have given at least indirect support to the conclusions initially drawn by Ribble. Young rats and mice that are given additional stimulation in moderate amount turn out to be healthier, less emotional, better motivated, and faster learners than those left alone with their mothers. It is curious that the natural mother should turn out to be apparently less than adequate in this respect; but perhaps from the standpoint of survival and adaptation to a lab situation, the kind of "personality" the mother rat or mouse puts into her young is optimal.

For the most part, such experimentation on early stimulation has been of a highly empirical character. Every conceivable aspect of the problem has been examined: the type and intensity of stimulation; the age at which it is administered; the type of behavioral and physiological and biochemical effects that it has; and the characteristics of the animal on which it is imposed. Such studies have certainly resulted in the accumulation of a great deal of information. But it has become very clear that what is needed is some kind of theoretical ordering of such data—conceptualizations that point up the most fruitful directions that future research should follow. As we shall show later, there are now signs that theorizing is indeed on the increase.

The Tradition of Physiological Psychology

A critical problem for physiological psychologists working between the 1920s and 1940s was just how the residuals of learning are laid down in the brain. Karl Lashley, who initially hypothesized a connectionistic view, after many years of experimentation moved to a field-theoretical approach. The greater feasibility of the field-theoretical approach was suggested to him by two sets of data in particular: first, the high positive relation between loss of learning and retention capacity, on the one hand, and amount of loss of brain tissue *independent of locus;* and, second, the *generalizations* that animals were able to make between figures or patterns on which they had been trained to ones they had never seen before. Such facts raised a dilemma and, as Hebb has so clearly pointed out, different theorists took different positions with respect to it. Speaking of two of these, Hebb says:

Köhler (1940), for example, starts out with the facts of perceptional generalization, in his theory of cortical fields of force, and then cannot deal with learning. He has no apparent way of avoiding a fatal difficulty about the nature of the trace, its locus and structure.

. . . The theory elaborated by Hull (1943), on the other hand, is to be regarded as providing first of all for the stability of learning. It has persistent difficulties with perception (1949, p. 15).

In his work *The Organization of Behavior* from which we have drawn this quote, Hebb attempted a solution to the problem. Perhaps its two most central propositions were as follows:

1. The functions of perception and of learning depend on the establishment in the cortex of complex neuronal networks of neurons—or cell assemblies—whose integrity as units is maintained by structural changes occurring at the synapses between them. Such networks may be spread over widely dispersed cortical areas and may involve many alternative pathways.

2. Learning during adulthood depends on the kind of learning that has gone on early in life. The two types of learning have quite different properties, varying with phylogenetic level. Such a skill as learning to perceive, which mainly constitutes primary learning, for example, occurs relatively slowly in higher primates, but rather quickly in lower species; whereas the kind of conceptual learning that goes on at maturity tends to be much more efficient in higher than in lower animals.

Hebb's analysis of the mechanisms of the development of learning in animals is one of the most subtle and incisive that has been made. It has been explored experimentally, however, only with respect to its broad emphasis on the importance of early experience for later ability and intelligence. One of the first such studies was done by Hebb himself. He (and his daughters) reared seven rats at home as pets. These were later compared with cage-reared controls on Hebb-Williams maze performance. The free-environment animals were markedly superior, thus demonstrating the importance of early learning in determining adult intellectual ability. This key experiment has served as a paradigm for many subsequent studies, for example, those of Hymovitch (1952), Forgays and Forgays (1952), Forgus (1954; 1955a; 1955b) on rats and the series on dogs mainly by Thompson, Heron, Melzack, and others (cf. Thompson and Melzack, 1956). Work on the problem still continues (e.g., Schweikert and Collins, 1966; Fuller and Clark, 1966a, 1966b). The results of all this work support, in the main, Hebb's emphasis on the importance of perceptual learning early in life. It is of some interest to note at this point that such experience produces not only clear behavioral but also clear anatomical and biochemical effects in the central nervous system, as shown by the extensive series of Krech, Rosenzweig, and others at Berkeley (cf. Rosenzweig, 1966). Much of the tradition we have outlined has been well reviewed by Hunt (1961) and by Newton and Levine (1967).

The Ethological Tradition

Ethology a movement mainly among European naturalists, has also produced significant contributions to the study of early experience. Interest in the social structure of animal populations has led naturally to the question of how social attachments between animals—whether these have to do with reproduction, maternal care, or general communication—arise in the first place. Konrad Lorenz (1935), one of the initiators of work in the area, put forward the view that, in the case of birds—particularly such precocial species as domestic chickens, ducks, and geese—the hatchling learns in one brief exposure a relatively permanent attachment to an object presented to it at this time, normally the mother. Lorenz (1935) called this rather unique form of learning *imprinting*. A large volume of work on this topic has since appeared, concerned with such problems as the characteristics of the mother or surrogate that maximize imprinting, the age at which it optimally occurs, the species in which it can be found, its reversibility, ways of measuring it, and its relation to adult behavior, in particular, mate choice. Although imprinting may be thought originally to have represented a rather recondite phenomenon of interest only to naturalists, it has clearly come to offer a kind of paradigm for considering all aspects of early socialization and hence to have importance to all psychologists studying learning and development. Even these workers dealing directly with children have been influenced by the imprinting studies; for example, Bowlby, who has proposed a theory of infant maternal attachment with a strong ethological bias (Bowlby, 1957), 1958). The concept of imprinting has also been extended in a number of directions to take in territorial and food preferences (see Hess, 1959). The general problem with which these deal, however, is the same—the effects of early experience on later behavior.

The preceding overview of the history of work in the area indicates that it is of a very basic nature, drawing together many divergent methodologies and theoretical points of view. For this reason, perhaps, it is a difficult task to find a "best way" of reviewing relevant literature. We have chosen to order the empirical work mainly according to age level. Prior to this we present a short discussion of what properties characterize young living systems and the major methods used in the early experience work. We shall end the chapter by presenting some of the theoretical models

that have been put forward to handle the early experience problem.

THE NATURE OF YOUNG ORGANISMS

The most obvious characteristic that distinguishes young from adult organisms is age. However, by itself, the simple passage of time is an empty variable and has no special implications. We must focus instead on those dimensions which change as a function of age and which carry implications for the input, output, and storage characteristics of young organisms. For it is these functions that are of major relevance to any real understanding of how early experiential effects operate.

A good many such basic developmental variables have been specified by different writers. Let us now look at some of these.

Differentiation

Differentiation refers, generally, to the transition from a relatively unitary system to one with independent parts. At the physiological and morphological levels, we find occurring with age such processes as histogenesis, regionalization, and morphogenesis, whereby qualitative differences in form, structure, and function start to become apparent. Thus a zygote becomes a blastula and gradually, through gastrulation, the distinctive ectoderm and endoderm cell layers form, followed eventually by the mesoderm. Each of these structures is potentially directed to certain functions such as neural conduction and sensory reception, digestion and metabolism, and body support.

At the behavioral level the dimension is somewhat more difficult to define. On the input side, we may think of it as having to do with the improvement in discriminative ability that occurs with increasing age up to and perhaps beyond maturity. Hebb (1949) has suggested that initially the newborn perceives only unities but not identities. The speed of learning this second type of task may vary according to the species, lower ones accomplishing it in a much shorter time than higher species, due possibly, according to Hebb (1949, p. 124), to a larger association cortex to sensory cortex ratio in the higher. This kind of perceptual differentiation is similar to that described by Gibson and Gibson (1955), namely, the progressive increase in correspondence between the input systems and environmental stimulation. It may be contrasted with the so-called "enrichment" theories, which attempt to account for improvement in perceptual discrimination by postulating that cues became "distinctive" by gradually acquiring associations with other stimuli or responses. There are undoubtedly such acquisitions, but it seems likely that they pertain to later rather than early learning in Hebb's terms, and are dependent, in the first instance, on an initial refinement of the perceptual system simply through its exposure to the environment.

In the case of some sensory modes, the motor side must also be implicated. Eye movements and accommodation certainly play a part in the building up of differentiation in the visual system. Haynes, White, and Held (1965), for example, have used the techniques of dynamic retinoscopy to demonstrate that accommodation in the human infant is initially poor. Until around the fourth month, proper focus occurs only for objects at a distance of around 19 cm. Likewise, the work of Kessen (1967) and his associates at Yale suggests that visual scanning plays a critical role in the building up of percepts of shapes such as triangles.

On the motor side as such, differentiation must also occur. It seems convenient, as Thompson (1966, 1968) has attempted to show, to consider this separately from the input side, since this division allows us to think of development in terms of an S-R framework. In any case, common observation suggests that as an organism matures, there is an increasing independence of muscles or muscle groups. Thus the prehension of objects initially involves the whole limb, which is used in a kind of "raking" movement. This gross movement gradually becomes refined into the delicate and economical finger-thumb opposition normally used by an adult, to pick up some object (Halverson, 1931). As with input systems, it is likely that differentiation on the output side may follow a two-stage development, the first being concerned with the laying down of basic skills, the second with the learning of the more refined and complex coordinations often demanded of adults. Thus by the time a child is 10, he usually will have a repertoire of movements sufficient to meet most of the demands his culture may place on

him—for example, crawling, walking, running, climbing, and writing. On these basic skills will be built—with a great deal more rapidity—various special sets of responses such as riding a bicycle, driving a car, ballet, swimming, piano playing, and so forth.

It is probable that differentiation proceeds at different rates in different systems. For example, tactual differentiation may well be considerably ahead of visual or auditory differentiation. Comparing the average rate for input with the average rate for output, it is also likely that the auditory differentiation lags considerably behind the tactual. Thus the young infant's perceptual capacities are considerably closer to the level they will eventually reach than are his motor abilities. By 8 months of age he can discriminate through most of his sensory systems a considerable range of fine differences. But his locomotor, manual, or vocal skills at the same age are very far from the level of refinement they will show at maturity. We shall examine, later in this chapter, some possible consequences of these kinds of postulated differences in respect to rate of differentiation.

Growth

This developmental parameter refers basically to the increments in size or in number of elements that occur in living systems as they change with age (Shock, 1951). Thus most organisms get bigger as they get older. Some level off as they approach sexual maturity, but others, for example, many plant forms and some fish, continue the process until they die. We also find increments in subsystems of the whole, for example, number of fibers in spinal nerves in human beings (cf. Zubek and Solberg, 1954), total brain weight, density of neural and glial cells, cell mitochondria, and quantity of chemical compounds such as ACh, ChE, and GABA per unit mass of tissue (cf. Himwich, 1962). Kascer has suggested (cf. Waddington, 1957), in accordance with the above, that growth produces an increase in the redundancy of a system and that a consequence of this will be a difference between young and mature systems with respect to "buffering" characteristics. Thus it seems reasonable to suppose that the mature organism, because it has more replicated parts serving the same function, will be better able to withstand the impact of some disturbing environmental event, in the sense that the deviations from the normal level that are allowed will be smaller and the speed of return to normal will be more rapid. It is these kinds of parameters that are at least implicitly referred to when we speak of young systems as being more unstable or more plastic. For example, the response of the newborn rat to water overload is a great deal slower than that of the older animal and it may remain overhydrated for a much longer time after treatment (McCance, 1961; Vesterdal, 1961). The problem of equating the stimulus between age groups is, of course, a formidable one. As Vesterdal (1961) points out, 30 ml of water per kilogram given to an infant weighing 3 kg will be more or less equivalent to an ordinary feeding; but the same ratio administered to an adult weighing 75 kg would amount to 2250 ml—a quantity much above normal intake.

It is rather difficult to think in terms of psychological functions as showing size increments in the same manner as do various physiological systems. But, on the other hand, it is quite sensible to ask about their buffering characteristics as a function of age. It would be very useful to know the extent to which performance in various tasks is disturbed in organisms of different ages. It seems likely, for example, that the same IQ level might be differently susceptible to mild stress in young as against mature organisms. Such a problem—as well as many others like it—is readily testable both in human beings and in lower animals. The work of Campbell and his associates at Princeton (Campbell, 1967; Campbell and Riccio, 1966; Riccio and Campbell, 1966) represents a very good start on this line of research. They have been systematically exploring the response of young as compared with mature animals of different species to a variety of treatments such as cold stress, food deprivation, and electric shock. An example of some of their data is shown in Fig. 1. The major point emerging from the work is clear. Young rats do not behave like adults when subjected to cold stress and consequently it is of great importance to define a treatment imposed not only in physical terms—for example, so many milliamperes of shock stress—but also in terms of the immediate effects they have. It will also be evident that there is some ambiguity in specifying the

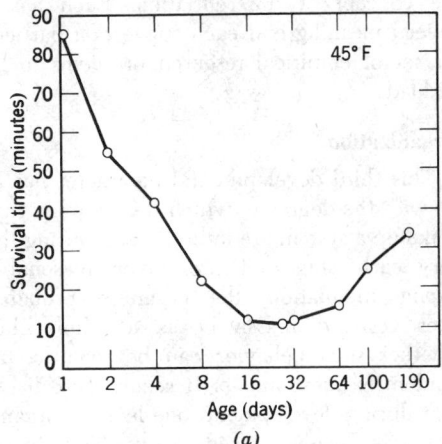

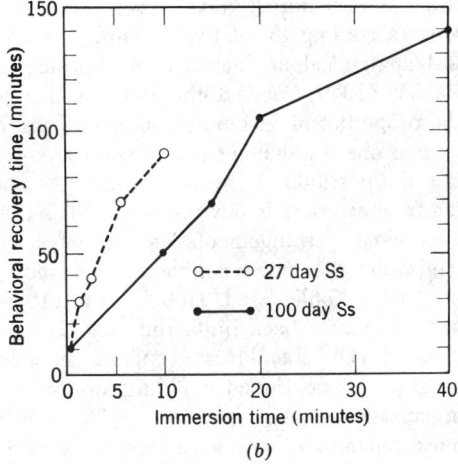

Fig. 1. The effects of cold stress. (a) Survival time in rats of different ages following immersion in 45°F water. (b) Behavioral recovery time as a function of age and duration of immersion.

behavior of immature systems in terms of such broad categories as "stability" or "plasticity." They furnish a good theoretical starting point but require close empirical explication. In general, however, we certainly have grounds for believing that, with a physically equivalent stress or environmental event, young systems will be more seriously disturbed than more mature ones; and it is therefore possible that any residual effects will be more important in the sense we have defined this term.

The dimension of growth is one which has heuristic value for the experimental study of development over and above that afforded by the concept of differentiation. Each has a special meaning and each suggests a particular set of empirical research problems to be tackled.

Organization

This third developmental parameter has to do with the degree to which the subparts that make up a system are interrelated. During the very early stages of life, given reasonably strong stimulation, the organism probably does respond massively as a whole, but whether such behavior can be regarded as random is questionable. It seems more likely that during development, one level of organization replaces a preceding one. Thus in respect to brain function, firing in response to a stimulus may initially occur over widespread areas according to relatively simple mechanical, anatomical, or electrochemical principles. Köhler (1940) viewed the brain as having the properties of a volume conductor; and as long as one is unwilling (as he was) to entertain the possibility of structural changes arising from exposure to environment, which then impose new arrangements on the extant organization, then one is confined to the kinds of parameter Köhler used. Hebb's view (1949) has, of course, been quite different. His notions of cell assembly and phase sequence suggest the continued building up of new organizations which, in their specific aspects, must depend on the unique experience of the individual during his lifetime. Whatever their idiosyncratic features, however, these organizations must effect an increasing coherence in the interactions of the living system with the environment and a shift from stimulus control to control by autonomous central processes.

Although the concept of organization has a certain theoretical appeal, it is not one that so far has lent itself very well to direct empirical study. For one thing, the extent to which organizational changes occur in a system must depend a great deal on the degree of differentiation and the extent of growth in that system. Thus differentiation must continually operate to break up extant organizations, whereas the buffering given by increments in growth may work to preserve them. Even were these somehow constant, organization would still be hard to define in a precise operational way. That this is so is indicated

by the famous so-called Leeper-Young controversy. This centered around the problem of whether emotion had an organizing or disorganizing effect on behavior. Though generating a good deal of lively theorizing, the debate led to very little actual empirical work—a minor study by the senior author being one exception (Thompson and Higgins, 1958).

Whatever the difficulties may be, however, organization does seem to represent a parameter that should be included in any consideration of development; and it is always possible that some ingenious person—particularly if he is experimentally minded—will come up with some way of making the concept empirically useful.

Other Developmental Parameters

The three dimensions we have so far discussed perhaps underlie all others that various workers have attempted to specify. Thus Gesell's (1946) principles of developmental direction, functional asymmetry, reciprocal interweaving, individuating maturation, and self-regulatory fluctuation are descriptive and perhaps derivable form those we have dealt with. At the same time, since they are less abstract, they may offer to the student of development more immediate empirical possibilities. Certainly, they have proven useful in normative studies of the behavior of developing organisms. Our main concern here is whether they have in the past, or may in the future, contribute in any way to research and theorizing on problems of early experience. The answer to the first part of this question must be in the negative. One does not commonly find them discussed as relevant dimensions by workers in this area. The same applies in the case of differentiation, growth, and organization. On the other hand, the latter three notions, in the opinion of the writers, may well have direct value—a point we will attempt to make later on.

We now turn to a consideration of some empirical work on the nature of young organisms and aspects of early life that appear to be critical. This is not intended by any means to be an exhaustive review of all the literature on this topic. Such information can be obtained from several other chapters in this book. All we wish to do is to present a few examples of work which may throw light on the main problem before us—why early experience is important

CRITICAL ASPECTS OF EARLY EXPERIENCE

Our discussion of the major dimensions of development and the various empirical studies that pertain to them suggests that generally organisms get bigger and better as they mature. They are able to discriminate increasingly finer differences, are able to perform more and different kinds of acts, and become perhaps more strongly buffered against the exigencies of environment. Much the same applies to the subsystems that make up the whole organisms, and each is likely to manifest its own particular rate and pattern of change.

An excellent summary of the kind of changes that have been demonstrated for various physiological, neural, and biochemical functions has been made by Himwich (1962). This is partly reproduced in Table 1. Although such detailed data as these may not immediately aid our understanding of the exact nature of early experience, they do show clearly that the young organism is strikingly different from the adult in very many aspects. They further supply us with useful developmental norms for specific variables against which the

effects of experimental treatments may be compared.

Our major concern here, of course, is with behavior, and how storage that occurs in early life affects various kinds of measurable responses in the adult. Thus the features of early experience that are of most critical concern to us must be the nature of storage at any particular age and the permanence of such storage. It is undeniably difficult to unconfound these two questions, since a clue to the type of storage or learning that predominates at any particular age level is given mainly by some measure taken later that also reflects permanence. However, if we consider that different types of learning—for example, habituation, classical conditioning, and instrumental or operant learning—are distinguishable, then it should be possible not only to assess the overall amount of change that can be produced in organisms of different ages but also to parcel out the relative contributions made to this total change by each type of storage separately. Thus we might find that effects due to habituation are dominant in a very young animal and that these effects are much more marked than any that can be induced through the same type of learning at a later age. A design like this would allow us to ex-

Table 1. Development of Various Physiological and Behavioral Functions in the Brains of Guinea Pigs.

	Age from Conception							
	34	39	44	49	54	59	64 Birth	69
Anatomy			5 cortical layers etc.					
Biochemistry			Adult level RNA			H^2O falls		
			Adult level DNA			Na, Ca fall		
	GAG high, falls etc.		GAG low, + increases Protein					
			Respiratory enzymes increases				Adult level	
Neurophysiology			Adult EEG				Cortical polarization Spreading depression	
			Strychine spike			Response to afferent stimuli		
Behavior			Eyes open				Adult reactions	

From Himwich (1962) (modified).

amine separately the two major problems: What is early experience like? And how lasting are its effects? At present, however, almost none of the empirical work done on the topic has been sufficiently precise to yield the relevant data. Thus most of the work of Campbell and his associates (see Campbell, 1967) has used—as a critical index for drawing conclusions about early memory—a conditioned avoidance response. Data based on this rather complex indicator have suggested that memory is poorer in young than in adult subjects. But it might well be that a more careful dissection the of response into components would yield a different conclusion.

One important line of work should be mentioned in this connection. Lynn (1966) has ably reviewed a large body of Russian literature dealing more specifically with the ontogeny of the so-called orientation reaction in both human young and in the young of various lower species. Several workers have agreed in formulating a three-stage sequence: (1) a stage of autonomic reactions with no behavioral orientation of defensive reaction; (2) a stage involving "passive" defensive reactions and avoidance of stimulation; (3) a stage of normal orientation to stimuli of moderate intensity and defensive reactions to very strong stimulation. In general, most of the studies discussed by Lynn tend to show that habituation in very young animals is slower than in adults. Conditioning, on the other hand, improves with age only up to a point after which it declines again, presumably due to the increasing dominance of the "second signalling system." Some current research by the senior author and his colleagues is aimed precisely at elucidation of this problem. This point will be discussed later in the chapter in the context of theoretical models about early experience.

The notion of *critical* or *sensitive period*, which is often used to explain the lasting effects of certain early experience, also tends to confound problems of storage-mechanism with problems of storage-duration. In its usual meaning, it has involved a particular age level presumably set by maturational factors during which certain responses are more or less irreversibly learned. The most classic example is, of course, imprinting. Thus as a result of exposure to a parent or parent-surrogate at around 12 to 14 hours to posthatch, a young

chick tends later to follow this object or those similar to it, this attachment being less marked if the exposure occurs later or earlier than the critical age. Although it is recognized now that the limits of a critical period are probably not as narrow as originally thought (see Bateson, 1966), it is held by many workers that there are stages during development when certain kinds of experience are most likely to be stored. Such a notion seems, at first sight, to contradict the postulate we suggested earlier: susceptibility to environmental influence decreases linearly as a direct function of age. That it need not do so, however, is indicated by inspection of one model put forward by Hess (1959) to explain the occurrence of a critical period for imprinting. A slightly modified summary of it is presented in Fig. 2a. Note that the existence of a critical period is based on the two separate curves, each of which show a simple relation with age, namely, fear and locomotor ability. These are shown in Figs. 2b and 2c. Fear itself is actually educed from a further relation—that between age and the ability of the animal to discriminate familiar from unfamilar aspects of the environment. The intersect of the fear and locomotor curves is taken to be the critical period for imprinting of the following response. Were imprinting measured by other indicators, however, it is likely that the critical period would cover a different age range. Many other variables will be implicated in this also (Bateson, 1966).

The major point we wish to make is that the idea of critical period involves assumptions about the relation of buffering or memory storage to age and also assumptions about what kinds of input and output systems can be regarded as the best indicators of the event under study—for example, in the case of imprinting, the following of some discriminable object by a young chick. It should be noted that the time at which some function emerges and becomes available for involvement in the residual effects of early experience may be difficult to pin down. Thus it is doubtful whether following can be implicated in imprinting if critical exposure occurs before a chick is mobile. On the other hand, many complex adult responses may have precursors in early behavior. A good example of this is the precocial sexual behavior that may be elicited under certain conditions in very

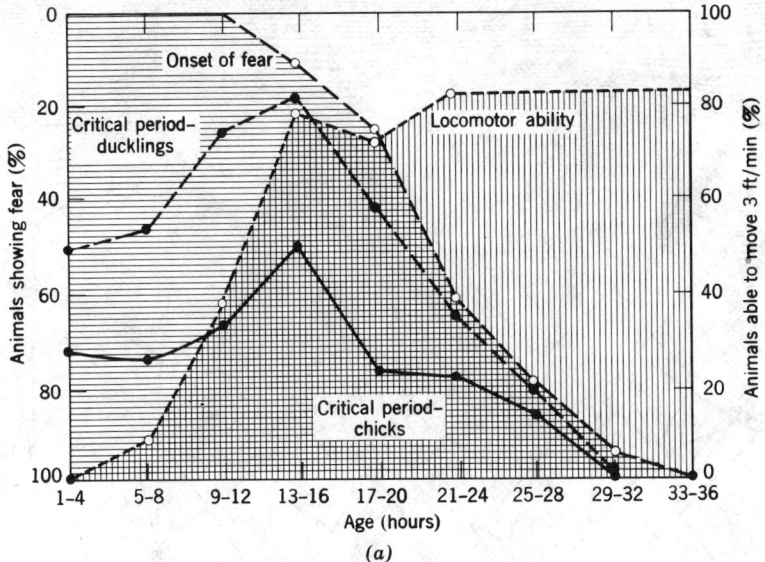

(a)

young birds (Andrew, 1963). It is difficult to say when a particular behavior pattern has its onset and how mature it must be before it can be altered in a relatively permanent way by environmental stimulation. At the human level, this has represented a problem of some magnitude. Freud's designation of the ages at which the various stages of psychosexual development occurred has been considerably altered by later workers. The formulations of Melanie Klein (1950), for example, which presuppose, in very young children, attitudes and social perceptions of a most complex kind, certainly seem to strain our credulity. Yet it is quite possible that some precursors of adult social behavior do make their appearance as early as the age of 1 or 2 years and are available for manipulation at this time.

There is one additional consideration concerning the critical aspects of early experience. Whatever treatments are imposed on a young organism, these can have effects only within certain limits set by genotype. This genotype may be permissive or nonpermissive to environmental influences, in the sense that it may allow very small or very large deviations from a projected developmental pathway. As we noted earlier, this notion has been put forward most explicitly by Waddington (1957). His schematic representation of the situation —the epigenetic landscape—is reproduced in Fig. 3. It can be seen here that genes determine the magnitudes and kinds of phenotypic

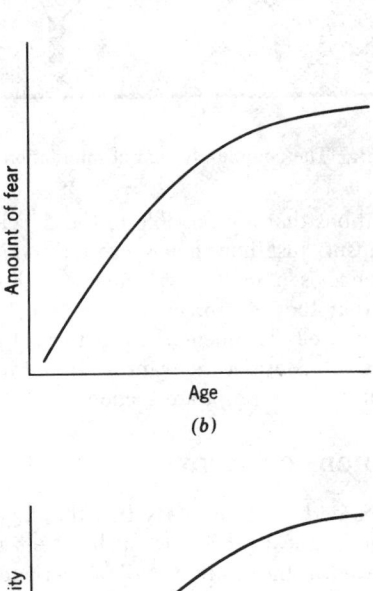

Fig. 2. Hess' model of the critical period in avian species. (a) The general model. (b) Fear as a function of age. (c) Locomotor capacity as a function of age.

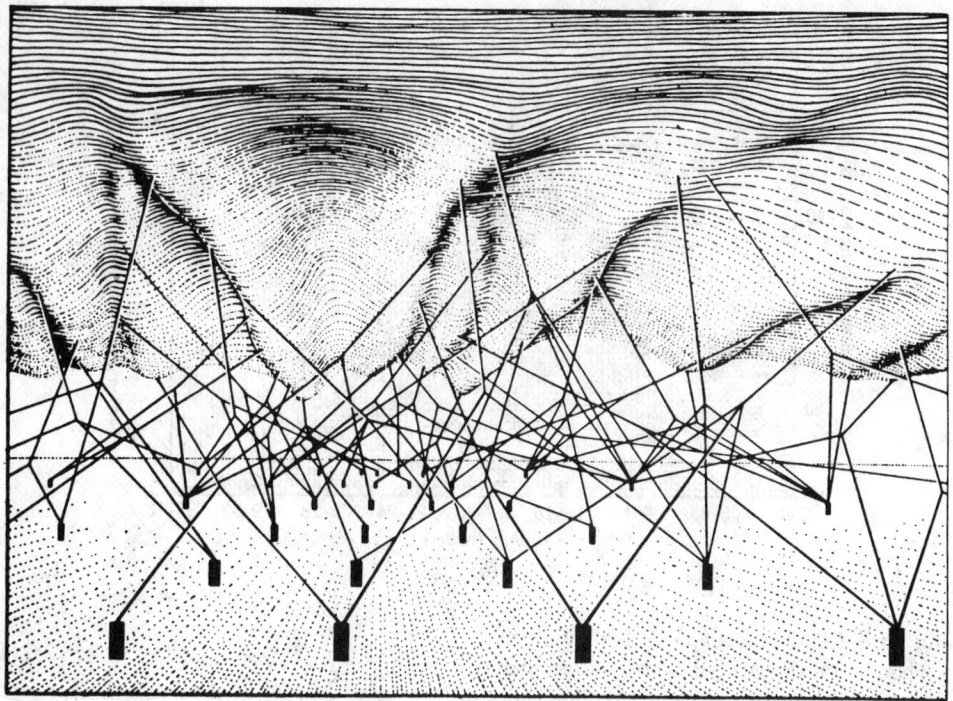

Fig. 3.   The complex system of interactions underlying the epigenetic landscape.

deviations that are possible to the developing organism. Just how genes exert this kind of influence is a matter of conjecture, but the fact that they do so, in respect to behavior, is now well documented by empirical work. We shall consider relevant studies in more detail in the appropriate section.

METHODS OF STUDY

It is perhaps true to say that the degree of methodological precision that has been so far achieved in the study of early experience has not been up to handling properly the kinds of dimensions we have articulated. The usual treatments by which the effects of early experience are tested involve either adding or taking away certain kinds of exogenous stimulation. Thus a rat may be given special handling in addition to that normally given to it by its mother (Denenberg, 1966), or it may be reared in a so-called enriched environment or rat "nursery" of the kind first used by Hymovitch (1952), Forgays and Forgays (1952), and others. Conversely, restriction may be imposed, as in the case of the dog experiments carried out at McGill University

by Thompson and others (Thompson and Melzack, 1956). There has also been a strong interest in the effects of various agents, the exact nature and direction of whose action may be uncertain, for example, drugs or noxious stimulation and stress. A large amount of work has studied the effects in offspring of treatments applied to the mother during pregnancy, for example, experimentally produced anxiety, anoxia, X-irradiation, and a variety of chemical compounds.

The restriction technique has often been applied to the motor side. Spaldings classic experiments (1873) on flying in birds involved the use of this method, as did those of Carmichael (1926) on swimming in amblystoma. In Spalding's experiments restriction involved mechanical immobilization of wings; in Carmichael's immobilization of all movement by treating the water with chloretone. Recently, Held and his colleagues (Held et al., 1959, 1961, 1963) have used a modification of it by means of an experimental condition that permitted only passive—not self-produced—movements. Thus kittens were held in a restraining apparatus which moved them through an experimental environment, simulating the manner in which they would explore it under normal conditions. Presumably, what Held has called reafferent stimulation is different in the two cases, and the difference shows up in terms of tests of visual-motor coordination given later. The actual procedure involved, it must be pointed out, is somewhat crude inasmuch as it is extremely difficult to specify exactly all the effects that ensue when an experimenter directs the movements of a subject. Restraint may produce emotional behavior, for example, as well as interfere with practice of sensory-motor skills. But conceptually, such a method represents a step forward, since it involved an attempt to unconfound the effects of restricting input from the effects of limiting kinesthetic feedback arising from voluntary movement. We will return to Held's work later in the chapter.

At the human level, it is very rare to find use made of the type of experimental manipulation that can so readily be carried out with animals. Investigators must look at natural situations which appear to be relevant, for example, nursery schools or other enriching environments, orphanages, lower-class homes, maternal-child separations, and others considered to be restricting or traumatic. The difficulties of control are, of course, formidable and we must therefore be very cautious about the inferences drawn from data based on such methods. Furthermore, because these are naturally occurring situations, they do not lend themselves to precise conceptual or experimental analysis. Thus institutionalization may have effects in respect to the sheer amount of general stimulation it involves, the perceptual richness or complexity it supplies, and finally the kinds of social structure it entails. These factors, which can be fairly well separated in a rat or dog study, are not easily untangled. Nevertheless, in our discussion of the work on early experience in children, we shall attempt as far as possible to achieve such a separation in line with the animal studies, even though it may appear somewhat artificial.

What will be needed in the future is a far greater refinement in the specification of independent and dependent variables. This applies both to animal and human studies. One especially important aspect of this is the careful evaluation of the immediate effects of whatever treatment is imposed on a young animal. Certainly, it seems reasonable to suppose that the residual effects of some early experiences are more likely to be interpretable in terms of the initial reactions of the subject to the experience rather than in terms of the physical attributes of this variable. The work of Campbell (1967), as mentioned earlier, hits exactly at this problem and will undoubtedly supply much essential baseline information. Likewise much of the current research on human neonates (see Campbell and Thompson, 1968) will be of great value to understanding the problem of early experience and its effects on later behavior.

REVIEW OF STUDIES OF EARLY EXPERIENCE

We now turn to a review of the literature on the problem we are discussing. Though it might have been more desirable to mesh together more closely the animal and human work, this is not easily accomplished. Their traditions, methods, and theoretical frameworks are, for the most part, different. Consequently, we shall consider the two categories separately and attempt at the end of the chapter to indicate possible lines of convergence.

Prenatal Influences

Before the advent of embryology, it used to be thought that almost any event influencing a mother during pregnancy could also influence the unborn fetus. Thus a mother frightened by, say, a dog, could supposedly pass on to her child a phobia of dogs. Such a view was presumably based, at least implicitly, on the assumption that neural connections of some kind existed between the maternal and fetal systems. When embryology was able to establish that no such connections did in fact exist, the idea of maternal impression fell into disrepute. Indeed, there occurred a tendency for medical opinion to swing almost to the diametrically opposed position—that the fetus was almost independent of the mother and would maintain its integrity no matter what environmental contingencies might be imposed on the mother during gestation. It soon became evident, however, that placental exchange between maternal and fetal circulatory systems was not limited to the transmission of nutritive materials or excretory products but could also carry a great variety of powerful chemical compounds (Page, 1957). These could be either endogenous substances—such as the hormonal products of stress—or exogenous agents taken in by the mother, either accidentally or sometimes for medical reasons.

The embryological evidence suggests, in fact, that the placental system is a highly fluid one. A great range of substances can pass through the intercellular barrier between mother and fetus, its extent depending on the genotype of the animal, the time of gestation, and the quantity and character of the agent involved (Windle, 1940; Flexner and Gellhorn, 1942; Hooker, 1952; Nalbandov, 1958; Page, 1957). In addition, the placenta itself appears to show hormonal activity, secreting ACTH, adrenocorticoids and glucocorticoid substances (Assali and Hammermesz, 1954; Johnson and Haines, 1952; Wiele and Jailer, 1959). Alterations of maternal physiology are known to produce striking changes in the fetus. For example, adrenalectomy of pregnant rats produces fetal adrenal hypertrophy (Ingle and Fisher, 1938; Josimovitch, Hadman, and Deane, 1954; Knobil and Briggs, 1953); cold and ACTH applied to the mother produce a rise in fetal cholesterol level and a large amount of ACTH results in a depletion of adrenal ascorbic acid in the fetus (Jones, Lloyd, and Wyatt, 1953).

The exact mechanisms by which maternal physiological changes are transmitted to and exert an influence on the fetus must be exceedingly complex. However, that these changes can have some influence is certainly clear enough. Since the early work of Gregg (1941) linking abnormalities in the newborn infant, especially blindness, with german measles (rubella virus) in the mother, a great volume of studies has appeared demonstrating teratological effects ensuing from numerous different agents. Poisons, atmospheric changes (hypoxia or anoxia), ionizing radiations, numerous hormones and chemical substances, antibiotics, infectious agents, vitamins in excessive dosages or vitamin deficiencies, and many others have been implicated in such birth defects as cleft lip and cleft palate, absence of limbs, eyes, or tail, hernias, cranial malformations, and many other such gross abnormalities (Kalter and Warkany, 1959;

Montagu, 1961; Fraser, 1958, 1962; Fraser et al., 1953).

Such studies as these are of less importance to us here, however, than those aimed at establishing *behavioral* effects produced by some prenatal treatment—particularly treatments of a psychological nature, for example, emotional stress. The literature covering these kinds of problems does not go back much more than 10 years but has now become fairly extensive. We shall review the highlights of it for human and animal subjects separately.

ANIMAL STUDIES ON BEHAVIORAL EFFECTS OF PRENATAL EXPERIENCE

Chemical Manipulations

An early series of studies was carried out by Hamilton, Harned, and others on the effects on rat offspring of sodium bromide fed to their pregnant mothers in various dosages through a stomach tube. Testing indicated a retardation in learning ability on several learning tasks (Harned, Hamilton, and Borrus, 1940; Hamilton and Harned, 1944). Dosage level apparently was not a variable of major importance. Experimentals tended to be more seizure-prone but showed less emotional elimination in several different situations. The outstanding characteristics of the treated offspring were high aggressiveness and lack of control (Hamilton, 1945). Armitage (1952), using sodium barbitol and pentobarbitol, also found deficits in learning in experimental offspring as compared with controls. However, an improvement in intelligence was claimed by Dispensa and Hornbeck (1941) using prenatal administration of dessicated thyroid hormone. The same workers were able to find no effects from administration of anterior pituitary extract.

Since this early line of work, numerous agents have been screened for their effects on behavioral functions of offspring. Some of these yielding positive results have been alcohol (Vincent, 1958), epinephrine (Thompson and Olian, 1961; Thompson and Goldenberg, 1962; Thompson, Goldenberg, Watson, and Watson, 1963; Thompson, Watson, and Charlesworth, 1962; Young, 1963; Young, 1964; Lieberman, 1963), drugs affecting serotonin activity such as iproniazid, reserpine, 5 HTP, and BAS (Werboff, Gottlieb, Havlena, and Word, 1961), and isocarboxazid (Werboff, Gottlieb, Dembicki, and Havlena, 1961). Chlorpromazine and meprobamate (Werboff and Havlena, 1962; Werboff and Kesner, 1963), and labeled chlorpromazine (S^{35} CP^z) (Ordy, Samorajski, Collins, and Rolstein, 1966), a deficiency in such essential substances as phenylalanine (Thompson and Kano, 1965) and protein (Caldwell and Churchill, 1966, 1967) have also been shown to produce alterations in offspring behavior. Profound central nervous system changes can also occur. Thus Zamenhof et al. (1966) injected purified bovine pituitary growth hormones into female rats between the seventh and twentieth day of pregnancy. The offspring showed unchanged body weights but significant increases in brain weight, brain DNA content, cortical cell density, and neuron to glial cell ratios. Descriptions of some of the drug studies have been included in the review by Karnofsky (1965).

It is difficult to draw any very precise conclusions about specific drug effects from such work. Almost any compound put into a pregnant animal by any route seems to have effects on a variety of behaviors provided the dosage is sufficient. It is worth pointing out in this connection that very few studies have in fact aimed at demonstrating effects specific to a certain compound. Neither control procedures nor techniques of measurement of the independent variables have been set up in a manner appropriate to this end. Thus the otherwise interesting study by Vincent (1958) showing that alcohol ingested by pregnant mother rats alters emotionality, motivation, and learning of offspring (in both directions depending on dosage level) failed completely to demonstrate that alcohol per se was implicated to the exclusion of other components of the situation—particularly nutritional deficit—that may have been involved. Nor was it made clear that any other chemical substance differing in only a few respects from alcohol in its molecular structure would have different effects; nor was any attempt made to dissect more exactly the components of behavior affected. A study of Thompson and Kano's (1965) aimed at exploring some of these problems. It attempted specifically to examine the effects of phenylalanine overload in pregnant rats both on the relevant metabolic system in offspring—that is, the phenylalan-

ine hydroxylaze system—and also on emotional as distinct from intellectual behavior. It is significant that the changes found were not specific to this biochemical system and were mainly emotional rather than intellectual in character. Such results seem to indicate that we can hope for very little precision in this field, and it may well be that it is the stress components of drug administration rather than their chemical characteristics that produce an effect. We will return to this point shortly.

X-Irradiation

Literature on some of the neural and behavioral effects of ionizing radiation have been reviewed by Furchtgott (1963), Werboff (1964), and Garcia, Kimeldorf and Hunt (1961). Levinson (1952), one of the first experimenters in this field, irradiated pregnant rats with 300 to 600 r at days 11, 13, 15, 17, or 19 of gestation. The learning of offspring on a Lashley III maze was significantly decreased. Since numbers in the subgroups were very small, no analysis could be made of dosage or drugs effects. Furchtgott and his colleagues (1958a, 1958b, 1958c) later attempted to replicate and extend Levinson's findings. They found a suggestion that the earlier the age, the lower the dosage necessary to produce learning deficits. Thus at days 14 and 15 of gestation, 100 r was effective, but at 18 days neonatally, only subjects receiving 300 r showed changes. Locomotor coordination, on the other hand, was more easily altered with low dosage levels at later stages of gestation. Fetal irradiation was shown to result in increased general activity, longer cage-emergence latencies (time taken to leave home cage and emerge into a strange environment), and increased emotional defecation. The authors interpreted this to mean that irradiation during early development affects fearfulness primarily.

Work in other laboratories has to some extent borne out these general conclusions with some modifications. Werboff, Broeder, Havlena, and Sikov (1961) have demonstrated that radiation at any level between 25 and 100 r could alter threshold in offspring to seizures (bell plus metrazol). Radiation during early gestation produced an *increase* in threshold, later in gestation a *decrease* in threshold. In another experiment, Werboff, Havlena, and Sikov (1962) were able to show that changes in emotionality and also in maze-learning ability ensued on administration of low dosages of radiation well below those used by Furchtgott et al. on their animals. They expressed disagreement with the general proposition that emotionality was always increased and learning ability decreased as a result of fetal radiation. In fact, some of their animals showed exactly opposite effects. A later study by Werboff, Havlena, and Sikov (1963) showed that the threshold for behavioral effects was probably between 15 and 25 r, at least after the fifth day of gestation. It was recognized by Werboff et al. that before this time even smaller dosages might have effects. This notion was also put forward experimentally by Luchsinger (1963) and by Kaplan, Rugh, and White (1963). Thus there appears to be an interaction between dosage level and age of organism on which it is imposed.

The extent of exposure to radiation is an additional factor. Some Russian investigators, Piontkovsky and Semagin (1963), found that only 1 r administered between days 1 and 20 of gestation led to a slower rate of formation and stabilization of simple stereotyped conditioned responses. Interestingly enough, this treatment also produced a significant reduction of thickness of frontal cortex. A rather thorough study by Fowler et al. (1962) using 150 r of X-irradiation administered on day 13 to 14 of gestation demonstrated that treated fetuses subsequently showed decreased ability on the more difficult problems of the Hebb-Williams maze test and decreased open-field adaptiveness. Various neurological abnormalities in neocortex and in various subcortical structures were also reported (Fowler et al., 1962; Hicks et al., 1959). Quite a large volume of work has been done on the problem in the Soviet Union. Some of this has been reviewed in a conference proceedings edited by Werboff (1963).

Atmospheric Changes

Little has been done on the behavioral effects in offspring of maternal exposure to this variable. Becker and Donnell (1952) showed deficits in the learning by guinea pigs of a complex task as a result of severe asphyxia at birth. Experimental animals were markedly less active and gave the appearance of being less inquisitive and more apathetic and lethargic than controls.

One of the more extensive studies on the topic was carried out by Meier, Bunch, Nolan, and Scheidler (1960) at Washington University. They examined the effects of natal anoxia on young rats and kittens and of prenatal anoxia at various gestation ages on rats. They found that 60 min oxygen deprivation at birth (2.91% equivalent oxygen) produced deficits in learning ability in rats and 30 min deprivation decreased responsiveness of kittens in a puzzle-box situation and more "stereotyped" modes of solution in a discrimination task. Finally, a 2-hour exposure of pregnant female rats to 6.21% equivalent oxygen had significant effects on learning ability of offspring. Treatment early in gestation *facilitated* maze performance, treatment late in gestation *hindered* it. The authors speculated that two factors might be involved as target functions at different stages of development. One of these was presumably vulnerable early in gestation and the impact of a treatment on it would improve performance. The other would be vulnerable at a later stage and its response to treatment would reduce learning ability. In view of Furchtgott's rather similar data, which we discussed above, this seems like a reasonable idea.

Just how anoxia (and X-irradiation) have their effects has been the subject of a controversy. Some investigators have felt that they are the result of a direct insult to the fetus, others that they come about indirectly through maternal influence. This problem has been reviewed by Meier (1962).

General Stress

We have already noted that almost any kind of treatment imposed on the developing fetus can have effects, and any differences appearing between specific agents probably relate to the general stress or effects these agents have rather than to their intrinsic characteristics. It is significant that, in fact, different injection procedures (subcutaneous versus intraperitoneal) or different placebos (saline versus distilled water) can also produce behavioral changes of an order as great as that produced by various chemical compounds (Havlena and Werboff, 1963a). Consequently, there is every reason to believe that any treatment that can produce a stress response in a pregnant female and in the fetus is likely to leave residua that will later become manifest in various forms of behavior. A fairly extensive line of work has been concerned with exactly this problem.

The first attempt to study the effects of maternal stress during pregnancy on emotional behavior of offspring was initiated by Thompson (1957). Female rats were just trained to avoid shock at the sound of a buzzer by opening a door and running to the safe side of a two-compartment box. It was assumed that the habit was maintained by an acquired anxiety drive. After reaching a criterion level of responding they were mated together with control females to a common sample of males. As soon as they were pregnant, the experimental females were given three daily exposures to the conditioned anxiety-evoking signal but were denied the opportunity to perform the instrumental response that had up to then brought about anxiety reduction. At parturition, some of the offspring were left with their natural mothers, and others were fostered either to different mothers of the same or of a different treatment group. Testing was carried out on two ages using two measures of emotionality. Main results are shown in Fig. 4. It is clear that anxiety during pregnancy does indeed alter offspring behavior, in this case the change being in the direction of increased emotionality or fearfulness.

These results have since been replicated in the main by a number of investigators (Doyle and Yule, 1959; Hockman, 1961; Ader and Belfer, 1962; Thompson, Charlesworth, and

Watson, 1962; Thompson and Quinby, 1964). It is noteworthy that direction of effects is not always toward increased emotionality but sometimes the opposite (Thompson and Quinby, 1964). Furthermore, fostering may interact with prenatal experience in complex ways (Hockman, 1961; Thompson, Watson, and Charlesworth, 1962) either to facilitate or inhibit the effects of the latter. Morra (1965) used fear conditioning prior to pregnancy but with radiant heat rather than shock as a UCS. He found that behavior decrements (open-field and water T-maze) were produced in many by stress in the second half of pregnancy. A higher level of prenatal stress produced greater behavioral deficit. Fertility and viability were also affected.

If conditioned anxiety can alter offspring behavior it might be expected that any kind of stress will do the same. This indeed seems to be the case. Various forms of physical stress have been examined. Offspring from mother rats subjected to audiogenic seizures during pregnancy show changes in behavior, as demonstrated by Thompson and Sontag (1956). Weir and DeFries (1964) and DeFries (1964 used swimming in water 25°C for 3 min, 3 min exposure to a "tilt box," and 2 min in a brightly lit open field. These conditions were imposed on two strains of mice daily during gestation. The usual kinds of change in emotionality were found, although their extent and direction varied with genotype and postnatal treatment. Crowding of pregnant mice produces lowered activity, slowness of responding, and reduced defecation in their young tested at 30 and 100 days of age (Keeley, 1962). Extra handling given to mother rats during gestation reduces emotionality in experimental offspring (Ader and Conklin, 1963). A greater susceptibility to gastric erosion follows immobilization stress, especially in female offspring (Ader and Plaut, 1967). The imposed stress does not necessarily have to occur during pregnancy. Thus Denenberg and Whimbey (1963a) have demonstrated that the offspring of female rats handled in infancy show significant decreases in emotional behavior (open-field activity and defecation) as compared with controls from females not manipulated in infancy. Ressler's studies (1966a, 1966b) demonstrate essentially the same conclusion.

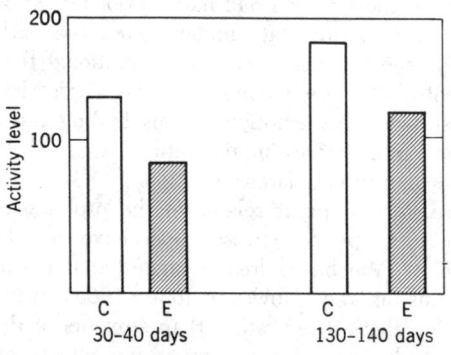

Fig. 4. Open-field activity levels in rat offspring from mothers made anxious during pregnancy (Es) and normal mothers (Cs). Low activity is taken to mean high emotionality. (Thompson, 1957.)

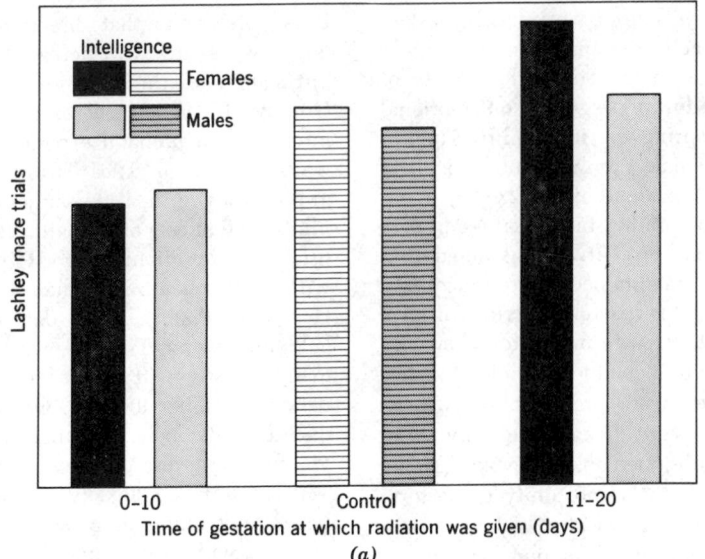

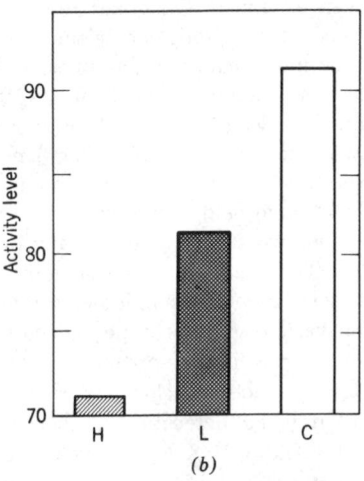

Fig. 5. Effects on behavior of rat offspring of (a) X-irradiation adminstered to their mothers early or late in gestation. (b)Two levels of anxiety-stress administered to their mothers during the whole of gestation. H = high anxiety; L = low anxiety; C = control. (Thompson and Quinby, 1964.)

General Conclusions

Three points of special interest should be noted here. First, changes that ensue from some prenatal stress may vary in extent and direction depending on amount of stress and the age at which stress is imposed. These two points are illustrated in Fig. 5 based on Werboff et al. (1962) and Thompson and Quinby (1964). In the former, intelligence is increased over controls by radiation given early in pregnancy, reduced if given late in pregnancy. In the second study, emotionality as measured by activity level tends to be increased as a direct function of pregnancy anxiety.

Such bidirectionality is possibly a function of the sequencing of test procedure and how often tests are given. Thus DeFries and Weir (1964) showed that the initial test (open-field activity) given to treated and untreated offspring may bias the results of a later testing. Groups that were tested at 120 days of age showed only characteristics exactly opposite those which had had a prior test at 40 days. Experimental animals given the early plus the late test were more emotional than controls. Those having only the single, late test were less emotional. This finding raises some most interesting theoretical issues, which we shall discuss later on.

A second point relates to the problem of whether specific stressors can have specific effects. We have already suggested that this seems unlikely. However, Joffe (1965), using a "conflict" stress rather than stressors of the kind described above, found no effects on emotionality but a reduction in Hebb-Williams maze performance. Whether the effects of conflict on the mother have to do only with intelligence in the offspring seems, however, very doubtful. Most maze tests involve emotional and temperamental components and it is possible that these influenced error scores in learning without showing up in the other tests.

A third important point has been made by Webster (1967), who suggested that the effects of prenatal stress may often result from the alteration of the nutritional status of the animal on which the stress is imposed. He was, in fact, able to demonstrate that deficits in maze learning of offspring were strongly correlated with weight loss of mothers during treatment. This is not an unexpected finding, since food deprivation has clear and dramatic teratogenic effects in some breeds of mice (Runner and Miller, 1956), and hence it might certainly be expected to exert effects on behavior. But since it is a factor that is very seldom controlled in behavior studies, the emphasis given to it by Webster is very worthwhile.

HUMAN DATA

Work on the problem of prenatal influences involving human beings has been less convincing than that done with animals. In fact, it is only the positive findings coming out of the animal studies that give credibility to the conclusions drawn concerning human beings. Generally the work has been epidemiological and retrospective in nature. That is to say, large samples of children having some kind of abnormality are located and the pregnancy records of their mothers are assessed. The positive relationships that are often established, however, are correlational, and casual by inference only. Since proper control procedures, especially for genetic and postnatal variables, are seldom carried out, this inferential step has usually been a very large one.

Sontag (1941) was one of the first to examine the problem. He suggested that the chemical substances which appear in a mother's blood during emotional stress and which are transmitted to her child may have adverse effects on that child. He reports that fetal bodily movements are markedly increased when mothers undergo stress. The effects of brief maternal stress on fetal movement endure for several hours, while prolonged maternal stress produces concomitant increased activity in the fetus throughout the whole stress period. In addition, infants born to dis-

turbed mothers continue to have high activity levels after birth. They are irritable and may often have feeding, sleeping, and gastrointestinal disturbances. Early and prolonged stress seems to have more damaging effects than stress occurring later in pregnancy (Gebhard et al., 1958; Wallin and Riley, 1950).

According to Sontag, then, mothers who are emotionally upset during their pregnancies may give birth to neurotic offspring because of the unsatisfactory fetal environment they have provided them. Any conclusions about "blood-borne anxieties," however, must be modified by the knowledge that mothers who are under stress when they are pregnant may also continue to be anxious and emotionally upset after they have given birth. Thus some, much, or all of their infants' distress may be due to tense mother-child relations following birth. Colic, characterized by excessive crying and symptoms of acute distress in the digestive tract, has also been attributed to maternal tenseness and anxiety during pregnancy. Mothers of colicky babies seem to be less accepting of their roles as mothers, more concerned about their ability to care for their child, and less secure and in harmony with other people than mothers of noncolicky babies (Stewart et al., 1954; Lakin, 1957). Again, however, we have no reason to assume that anxiety during pregnancy is the causal factor in the production of colic. It may be that the tenseness a mother displays in caring for her child after birth is the important thing in its development. Again, it is not unlikely that a mother would become anxious and have doubts about her ability as a mother *because* her child was acutely upset no matter what she did to try and comfort him.

Other variables, besides maternal emotional stress, affect the welfare of a developing fetus. The use by the mother of certain drugs may cause various kinds of damage to the fetus. Thalidomide, for example, is responsible for malformation of the limbs when used early in pregnancy. It interferes with growth of the long bones of the arm, with the result that the fetus' hands extend almost directly from its shoulders. The legs are less affected, but do show a similar distortion in growth (Taussig, 1962). Large doses of quinine, used in the treatment of malaria, often cause deafness because of their effect on the fetal inner ear. Maternal use of narcotics may produce temporary dysfunctioning in the fetus. Montagu (1950) suggests that heavy use of painkilling drugs prior to delivery may affect the oxygen supply to the fetal brain and even lead to permanent brain damage with resulting intellectual impairment. Although there is no evidence that maternal smoking has enduring effects on fetal development, Sontag and Wallace (1935) do report that the fetal heart rate often accelerates following the mother's smoking. There is little evidence pertaining to the effect on the fetus of a mother's use of alcohol.

Fetal infection from maternal disease is infrequent, although in some rare cases infants have been born with mumps, measles, chickenpox, or smallpox transmitted from the mother (Goodpasture, 1942). Maternal syphilis, however, can have a damaging effect on the fetus. The child of a syphilitic mother, if it avoids abortion, miscarriage, or stillbirth, may be born weak, deformed, or mentally deficient (Montagu, 1959). It can also manifest the symptoms of syphilis, although these may not appear until many years after birth. Rubella (German measles), contracted by a mother in her first two or three months of pregnancy, is highly likely to produce a variety of congenital abnormalities including deaf mutism, cardiac lesions, and microcephaly (Swan and Tostevin, 1946). This diversity of abnormalities is explained by the fact that during early stages of development several organs are in the process of differentiation and hence susceptible to injury. Pronounced thyroid deficiency results in cretinism, characterized by impaired intellectual functioning, failure of bones and cartilage to develop, a protruding abdomen, and rough, coarse skin.

Small amounts of X-irradiation in the maternal pelvic region do not appear to damage the fetus. Murphy (1929), however, reports that large doses of therapeutic X-irradiation given to mothers during pregnancy do result in physical and mental abnormalities in offspring, including intellectual retardation, physical deformation, and blindness. In a study of the effects of exposure to atomic attack, Neel (1953) reports a great increase in stillbirths, abortions, and malformations among infants born to mothers who had been in Nagasaki and Hiroshima during atomic attack.

Because the unborn child's nourishment comes from the maternal bloodstream through the placenta, nutritional deficiencies in the mother, especially severe ones, will be reflected in fetal development. Hepner (1958) and Knoblock and Pasamanick (1958) report a greater incidence of mental deficiency and physical abnormality (e.g., general physical weakness, epilepsy, rickets, cerebral palsy) in children whose mothers have experienced serious malnutrition during pregnancy. Similarly, Pasamanick, Lilienfeld, and their colleagues (Pasamanick and Knoblock, 1961; Lilienfeld et al., 1955) have claimed a relationship between incidence of complications during the mother's pregnancy and various behavioral changes in the offspring, including tics, speech defects, and behavior disorders. Stott (1957, 1958), on the basis of data obtained mostly from retarded or mongoloid children, has attempted to relate causally pregnancy stress, early illness, malformation, and "unforthcomingness," a trait assessed by the Bristol social adjustment guides and defined in terms of a lack of assertiveness, "will and effectiveness." In these studies, it must be pointed out that control of other variables was loose and the samples atypical. Furthermore, it is now known that mongolism or Down's syndrome is due to a chromosomal anomaly. Consequently, we must view the conclusions with some skepticism.

Prolonged malnutrition of the mother is one of the most common causes of fetal and neonatal death and of incurable damage to infants (Antonov, 1947; Smith, 1947; Stearns, 1958). In an experimental study of maternal diet, Ebbs, Tisdall, and Scott (1942) supplemented the diet of a group of mothers who had been receiving a nutritionally inadequate diet for the first four or five months of their pregnancies. The diet supplement continued until five weeks after their babies were born. Mothers in a control group continued to eat nutritionally inadequate food for their whole pregnancy. There was a much smaller incidence of miscarriages, premature births, and stillbirths in the experimental than in the control group. In addition, babies born to mothers in the experimental group were healthier during their first six months.

Postnatal Influences

The largest volume of work on the early experience problem has been directed to demonstrating the effects on later behavior of different kinds of treatment administered to a young organism during the critical phases of its postnatal development. Like the studies on prenatal influences described above, work here has also been strongly empirical in character. Various sectors of research in the area have been reviewed Beach and Jaynes (1954), King (1958), Thompson (1960, 1966, 1968), Denenberg (1962a, 1966), Hunt (1961), Sluckin (1964), Casler (1961), and by the various contributors to Stevenson, Hess, and Rheingold (1967) and to Newton and Levine (1967). Since the number of studies done over the last 20 years probably amounts to close to 1000, we shall not attempt to provide a complete review of them. In view of their largely parametric style, this would, in any case, be an almost unmanageable task. Instead, we present some of the major conclusions that seem to have emerged regarding the types of variables that are involved in early experience and the kinds of effects they produce.

ANIMAL STUDIES

General Massive Stimulation

As we indicated earlier, an interesting line of work on animals grew directly out of Ribble's observation that "mothering" had an important role in promoting the healthy development of human neonates. Initial experiments carried out on rats by Bernstein (1952) and Weininger (1953, 1956) involved a so-called "gentling" procedure—that is, the handling of young rats for certain durations of time—and the later behavioral assessment of these animals together with "nongentled" controls. Results were quite clear-cut and dramatic. They showed, in essence, that such early manipulation produced large decreases in emotionality and an increase in exploratory activity and also alterations of a physiological nature, for example, a smaller enlargement of adrenals in response to a severe adulthood stress such as immobilization coupled with complete food and water deprivation (Weininger, 1953). Handled animals were more stress resistant than nonhandled rats.

From the early 1950s, studies have proliferated at an exponential rate. All conceivable variations of the problem have been examined; but it still seems true that really fruitful theoretical directions and solid empirical generalizations which are not so broad as to be trivial have failed to emerge in any clear fashion. We shall summarize material under two main headings: treatments and effects, and essential parameters.

Treatments and Effects. It was supposed in the initial phases of work on the effects of early manipulation that being "gentle" to a young animal was a critical aspect of the treatment (Bernstein, 1952; Weininger, 1953). This assumption was based at least in part on the work of Ribble (1944) cited earlier, in which the notion "love object" had been explicitly stressed. What subsequent studies clearly showed, however, was that not only the "gentleness" with which handling was carried out irrelevant to the effects produced (see, e.g., Eells, 1961), but also that handling itself—in the sense of experimenter-contact—was also not a necessary condition. Thus a noxious stimulation such as electric shock (Levine, 1956; Salama and Hunt, 1964) or shaking or moving the living cages of the animals (Levine, 1959) produces behavioral changes indistinguishable from those produced by handling. The same applies to the many other types of treatment that have been used, including level of ambient stimulation (Denenberg et al., 1966; McMichael, 1966), husbandry conditions, for example, procedures for cage maintenance and mode of feeding (Denenberg and Whimbey, 1963; Ader, 1965), consistency or roughness of handling (Eells, 1961), temperature alterations including cooling (Schaefer, 1963; Schaefer et al., 1962; Hutchings, 1963) or heating (Kline and Denenberg, unpublished; cf. Denenberg, 1966; Werboff and Havlena, 1963), and auditory or vibratory stimulation (Lindzey et al., 1960, 1963; Winston, 1963).

Bovard (1958) attempted to distinguish two stimulation procedures: Type I, involving actual stroking of an animal as in the Weininger and Bernstein studies; Type II, in which the animal is simply removed from its home cage to a different environment and then replaced after a period of time. However, since these procedures have much the same effects, as Bovard points out, the distinction really is of questionable value.

Social conditions of rearing also appear to be important. Ottinger et al. (1963) have shown that multiple mothering—rotation of a litter from a real to a foster mother—produces increases in offspring emotionality, as does also the level of maternal emotionality. Some workers have suggested that litter size can be an important variable. Seitz, in two studies (1954, 1958), showed that animals reared in large litters tended to be more emotional than those raised in small litters, apparently due to the greater amount of individual attention accorded to a pup by the mother when it does not have to contend with many others as well. These general findings were confirmed by Carlson (1961) but not by Broadhurst and Levine (1963). The discrepancy may well have been due, as suggested by Denenberg (1966), to the genetic difference between the strains involved in their studies. Certainly, some genotypes are better "buffered" than others and less readily show effects as a consequence of minor environmental manipulations.

Mixing of genotypes in a litter apparently has effects on later behavior. Ressler (1962) showed that BALB/C mice reared by foster mothers of the same or of a different strain (C57BL/10) elicit more maternal handling than if reared by their own mothers. The same does not apply in the case of C57BL pups, however. Reading (1966) has further shown that the later behavior of these same two strains is affected, compared to controls, by alien maternal rearing, it being apparently pulled away from that predicted by their genotype in the direction of that of the alien strain. Work on the effects of interspecies rather than interstrain rearing has been carried out by Denenberg and his colleagues (Denenberg et al., 1964, 1966; Hudgens et al., 1967). They have shown that mouse pups can be quite satisfactorily reared by rat mothers. Mice so reared turned out to be different from mouse-reared mice, the former showing greater weights at weaning and at 48 days and also less aggressiveness. It was also true in the Hudgens study, however, that mortality rate through weaning was approximately 75% for the animals fostered to rat mothers as compared with about 25% for mice reared by mothers of their own species. Hudgens and his colleagues argue that this selective bias is not serious. But in the opinion of the writers they do not make a convincing case for ignoring it, though it is admittedly difficult to assess properly the co-

gency of their arguments on the basis of their report.

The general conclusion that may be derived from all these studies is that treatment effects are nonspecific and that any differences in kind or magnitude are due not to any special features of a treatment but rather to variation in such fundamental parameters as its intensity and the age at which it is administered. An important qualification to this notion should also be made: the specificity of the linkage between effects (however general they may be) and some treatment probably increases with age. In other words, shocking a neonatal rat is likely to result in an animal which shows, in adulthood, a change in level of emotional responsiveness to any kind of stimulus situation. Shocking a postweanling rat, on the other hand, may produce changes that are similar in kind and extent but linked to the context in which the original experience occurred. Gauron (1964) has emphasized the idea of trauma-specificity and has presented relevant evidence. He found that rats exposed early in life to a water stress (immersion) performed poorly in a water-escape maze later in life, but behaved similarly to controls in an avoidance learning situation. It is quite possible, of course, that the difference was due not to the "trauma-relevance" of the tests but rather to the relative amount of stress each entailed. Consequently, Gauron's thesis cannot be regarded as proved. The senior author has put forward a similar view (to be discussed later), but one that postulates a dependence of degree of trauma-specificity on age and the accompanying differentiation of input systems. Brookshire, Littman, and Stewart (1961), in their distinction between three residua of early trauma—"pure shock effect," "acquired fear," and "instrumental habit"— seem to be making a similar point. They refer to the possibility that a trauma may have three kinds of effect: one mediated purely by its action as a stressor; a second mediated by the generalization to other cues of the fear response it produces; and a third mediated by the "shaping" it can exert on different operants.

An important study by Lindholm (1962) bears on these distinctions. He was able to show that with a certain age group of rats (20 to 30 days), noxious stimulation could have the paradoxical effect of establishing a conditioned fear to a specific but of reducing fear in general. It is clear from this result that the category of "emotionality" may be too broad to be always useful. Finally, Henderson (1965) has suggested that the mechanism responsible for later effects on emotionality— especially as measured by activity scores— may relate to shaping of operant movement responses by the reinforcement involved in any stress rather than to the stimulation effects it has. A study designed by this worker to test this possibility yielded negative results (Henderson, 1966b). Thus shaping does not seem to be an important factor at a very young age at least. Again, however, it is still possible that such learning is involved, though to such a small extent that its effects are not readily discernible by the tests conventionally used.

As the preceding discussion has indicated, the major target systems for early stimulation appear to be those connected with emotional behavior. Changes show up on such variables as open-field activity level of defecation, avoidance learning, shock escape learning, various "time of emergence" tests, responsiveness to stress including survival time, different measures of exploratory behavior, social behavior, dominance, and water-maze learning (see Denenberg, 1966; Thompson, 1966, 1968). On the physiological side, effects have been demonstrated with respect to general growth rate (Levine, 1961), adrenal size (Weininger, 1956), adrenal ascorbic acid activity (Levine et al., 1958, 1959), formation of gastric erosions (Ader, 1965), leukocyte changes in response to stress (Levine, 1961), plasma corticosterone level (Denenberg et al., 1967; Haltmeyer et al., 1967), subcortical cholinesterase activity (Tapp and Markowitz, 1963), and survival time in response to carcinoma implantation (Newton et al., 1962). Such results as these have led some if not most workers to the conclusion that early manipulations of most kinds do not *directly* affect intellectual functions. Denenberg and Morton (1962b) have put forward this view on the basis of their data showing no effects of early preweaning handling on Hebb-Williams maze performance. Their conclusion is supported by Schaefer (1963) and by Winston (1963). It is still true, of course, that most

tests of intelligence in animals involve components of emotionality and motivation. Consequently, unless these are parcelled out by some procedure (e.g., extensive pretraining) they will inevitably show up in tests of exploration and maze learning. Meyers (1962), for example, has reported effects on the tendency of animals to "explore" an alley, but it is very doubtful if his measures reflect anything beyond what is commonly thought of as emotionality or responsiveness to stress. DeNelsky and Denenberg (1967), on the other hand, have claimed to have been able to pull apart experimentally factors of emotionality from factors of exploration and curiosity. They found that handling produced rats that were less emotional (as measured by defecation and general activity level) but more exploratory in the sense that their activity increased in proportion to the amount of "complexity" (tactual variation) offered by the environment. Nonhandled controls showed decreasing activity with increasing environmental variation. A similar finding was reported earlier by Halliday (1966).

Relevant Parameters. If it is granted that the behavior most affected by massive stimulation early in life have to do with emotion or arousal level, three important questions may still be asked. (1) Is it possible to articulate more precisely this rather broad category? (2) What can be said about the direction of changes produced? (3) To what extent is the "earliness" of the stimulation a necessary condition for producing lasting changes?

In response to the first problem, not a great deal can be said. The only real attempt at dimensional analysis of emotionality has been made by Whimbey and Denenberg (1966), who factor analyzed results obtained on 23 tests of early stimulation effects. Three of the six obtained factors were reported as being clearly identifiable: "emotional reactivity," "consumption-elimination," and "field exploration." Although the rationale of the study was a good one, such results are not very informative. In the opinion of the writers, experimental rather than statistical dissection of the behaviors involved in early experience effects will be more likely to yield fruitful conclusions. The studies of DeNelsky and Halliday cited above appear to be oriented in this direction.

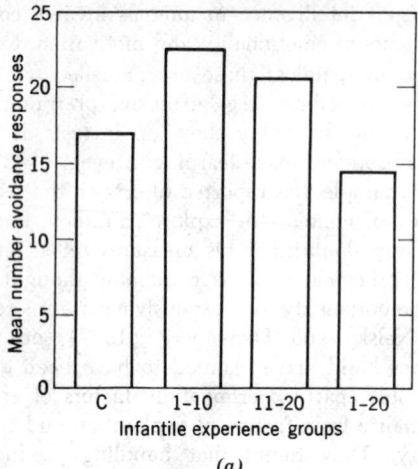

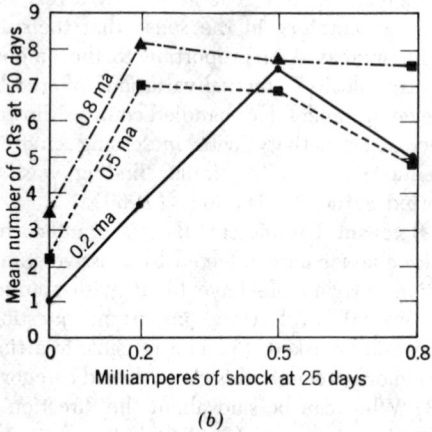

Fig. 6. (a) Number of avoidance responses in adult mice as a function of amount and age of infantile handling. (b) Number of avoidance responses in adult mice as a function of shock level used during training and amount of shock stimulation received at 25 days of age.

Data in regard to the second question are more definitive. Denenberg (1959) and Denenberg and Karas (1960) were among the first to demonstrate emotional reactivity may be either increased or decreased depending on intensity of stimulation. Their main results for avoidance learning in mice are shown in Fig. 6. Additional data bearing on this point have been provided by Denenberg (1962b) using rats, his measures being weight, avoidance learning, and survival time following complete deprivation. Again, the relation between these variables and number of days of handling was generally curvilinear in form.

Numerous other investigators, notably Levine, Chevalier, and Korchin (1956), Meyers (1965), and Henderson (1964), have reported similar results. The data of Meyers' (1965) are summarized in Fig. 7.

Besides duration and physical level of stimulation, frequency and the extent of massing or spacing of stress (Karas and Denenberg, 1961; Henderson, 1966c) are also important variables, presumably because these relate directly to intensity.

It should be obvious, of course, that effects will be unidirectional if only a limited intensity range is studied. Thus Denenberg and Haltmeyer (1967) showed that plasma corticosterone level assayed in rats following shock in adulthood at either of two levels decreased as a function of number of days of handling. These data are presented in Fig. 8. Whether the curves would in fact inflect if more or less stimulation were imposed is unknown. The authors take the position that they would not and that this physiological variable bears a *monotonic* relation to level of infantile stimulation. Although such a point of view appears to be at odds with the behavioral data cited above, it need not be, provided one assumes that a certain score on a test (e.g., avoidance learning) can occur for quite different reasons; thus an animal can perform poorly because it

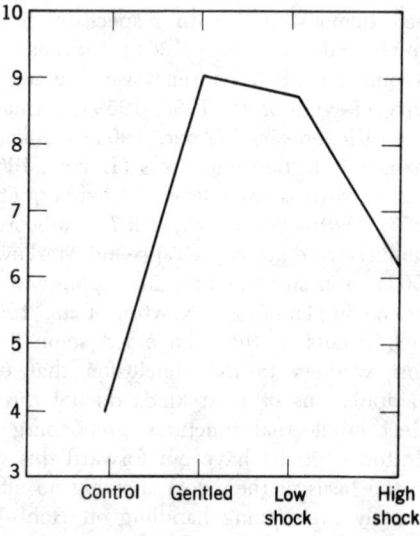

Fig. 7. A U-shaped function relating exploratory activity and degrees of intensity of stimulation. (Meyers, 1965.)

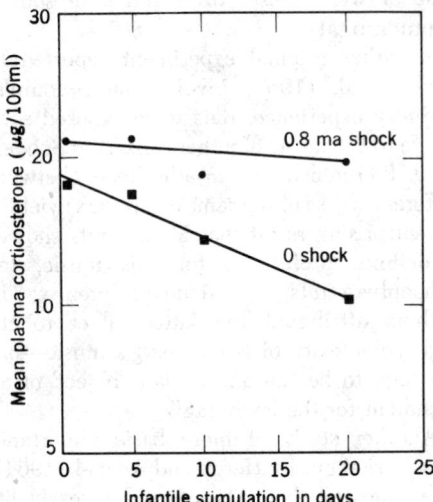

Fig. 8. Mean plasma corticosterone response as a function of preassay shock level and amount of prior stimulation (handling). (Denenberg and Haltmeyer, 1967.)

is very *emotional* or, conversely, because it is very *unemotional*. A fuller statement of this notion has been made by Denenberg (1964) and will be discussed later in more detail.

Age is another parameter showing somewhat the same relation to direction of effects. This point has been demonstrated by Bell et al. (1962, 1963) and by Henderson (1964). Figure 9 summarizes the results of the second of these investigators relating the effects of shock or handling at each of seven ages to defecation and avoidance-learning scores measured at 60 and 85 days of age, respectively. The age effect is very clear empirically speaking, though the theoretical reason for it is less obvious. Furthermore, it is not certain to what extent such a sensitive period is liable to shift according to the level of stimulation used. When both age and manipulation intensity are varied at the same time, results of manipulation intensity tends to overwhelm those of age (Denenberg and Kline, 1964). For this reason, Denenberg (1962) has argued that a search for critical periods in relation to early stimulation effects may be a fruitless task.

The final question concerns the extent to which the kinds of change discussed are dependent on stimulation early in life and whether they can as readily be produced in adult animals. It is usually assumed that the immaturity of the animal is an important if not a necessary condition for producing drastic alterations, but few studies have explicitly shown this to be so. In fact, some of those investigators who have utilized adult control groups, for example, Dolittle and Meade (1957), Ader (1959), and Brookshire, Littman, and Stewart (1961), have shown that prior experience is certainly important, but not exclusively early experience. Doty and Doty (1967) used five age groups—3-, 15-, 250-, 400-, and 600-day-old animals—to study the effects of handling on behavior. Their results indicated that all age levels were affected and only temporarily. Age was a major variable determining activity level, regardless of extrastimulation treatment.

On the other hand, other investigators have obtained positive results. Levine (1956), for

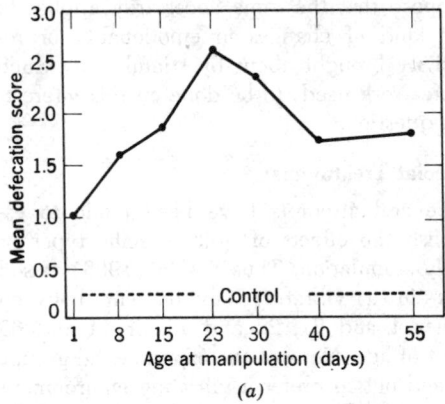

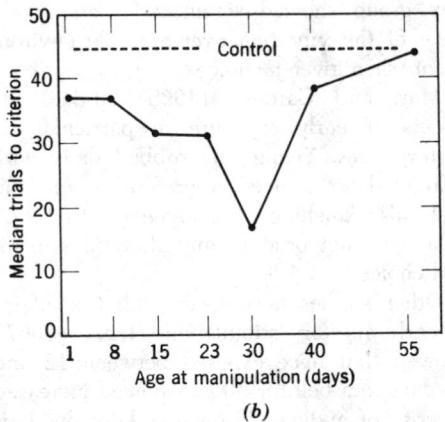

Fig. 9. (*a*) Open-field defecation as a function of age of stimulation (shock). (Henderson, 1964.) (*b*) Trials to criterion in avoidance responding in adult mice as a function of age of stimulation (shock).

example, used a group of rats handled in infancy, one not handled, and an adult-handled group. He found that the early treated animals were the least emotional, the controls the most emotional, and the adult-handled rats in between. These conclusions are in general agreement with data reported earlier by Hunt (1941) and Wolf (1943). As matters stand, then, the problem can still be considered to be not completely settled. Before it can be, it will certainly be necessary to dissect more closely the experience that is being put in; since it is quite likely that some types of storage occur more readily in young and other types more readily in older animals. Campbell (1967) has argued, on the basis of a good deal of data, that adults do, in fact, retain conditioned avoidance responses better than young rats. But it would be a mistake to suppose that the same necessarily applies to the kind of changes in emotionality or reactivity brought about by stimulation. Much more work needs to be done on this interesting question.

Special Treatments

Several attempts have been made to establish the effects of quite specific types of early stimulation. Thus Soskin (1963) raised rats in a vibrating environment between either 1 and 21, 22 and 43, or 44 and 65 days of age. None of the experimental groups turned out to prefer a vibrating environment when tested in adulthood, but the 1 to 21 day group showed significantly less avoidance of the vibration over a stable environment when given a choice.

Marr and Gardner (1965) studied the effects of early exposure to particular olfactory cues. Young rats rubbed daily with cologne later showed a preference for animals also smelling of cologne. Methyl salicylate did not produce any alterations in social choice.

Other studies have dealt with the effects of early auditory stimulation. Henry (1967) showed that mice exposed between 12 and 20 days to a bell for 30 sec showed increased severity of audiogenic seizures later on. It is of interest that the strain used (C57BL/6) is considered to have normally a high threshold to sound-induced seizures. It is also worth noting that such a "priming" had effects whether the animals were awake at the time or were anesthetized (ether or sodium pentobarbital).

A rather original experiment reported by Cross et al. (1967) involves more complex auditory experience. Rats were exposed early in life to the music of either Mozart or Schoenberg. Preference tests in adulthood (between different works of the same composers) yielded the surprising result that Mozart rats showed a definite preference for this music, but Schoenberg rats showed no preference. The authors attributed the latter effect to the high complexity of Schoenberg's music—one too high to be "an appropriate 'object' of attachment for the lowly rat."

Another study of more basic importance was carried out by Heron and Anchel (1964). They showed that rats exposed in early life to synchronous sensory bombardment manifested in adulthood EEG patterns that were altered toward being phased to this synchrony.

Procedures that involve manipulation of food intake have been used by a number of investigators. As early as 1941, Hunt (1941) found that feeding frustrations imposed on infant rats produced an increment in hoarding behavior later on. Likewise, Amsel and Penick (1962) using a similar manipulation involving degree of accessibility of food also found effects on later behavior. Rosen and Wejtko (1962) found that delaying weaning of rats until 42 days had no effects on emotional or eating behavior but did lower dominance in a competitive feeding situation. Novakova (1966) studied the relation between weaning age and acquisition rate and stability of a conditioned reflex (drinking on a signal). He found that rate of learning was inversely proportional to earliness of weaning, those weaned at 15 days showing the slowest acquisition rate, those weaned at 30 days the fastest rate. Similarly, stability of the trace was least in the early group and greatest in the late group.

As might be expected, neonatal X-irradiation affects later behavior (Meier et al., 1960; Agrawal et al., 1967) as does hyperoxia (Greenbaum and Gunberg, 1962). Meier and Garcia-Rodriguez (1966) have implicated, in the case of rhesus monkeys, mode of delivery (caesarian versus normal) as a factor that can alter emotional and avoidance learning ability.

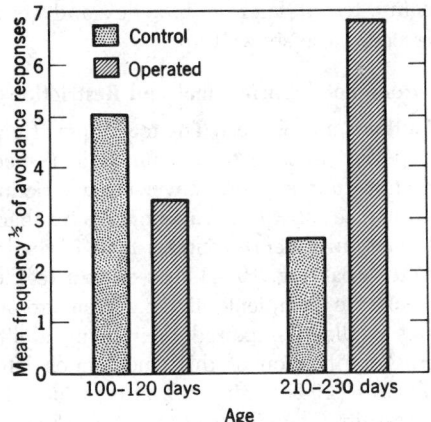

Fig. 10. Avoidance responding as affected by occipital cortex ablation at two age levels. (Isaac and Baker, 1963.)

Brain insult occurring early in life might be predicted to have severe effects, and Hebb (1942, 1949) has argued persuasively for this point of view. Indeed, it does seem to be true that clean surgical removal of large amounts of brain in the adult often exerts only small effects on psychometric intelligence. Support is given to these data by some of the animal work. Thus Isaac and Baker (1963) showed that bilateral and occipital cortex ablation produced large defects in conditioned avoidance learning in relatively young animals (around 100 days) compared to older subjects (210 days). Surprisingly enough, the older subjects showed a facilitation of learning ability compared with controls. These data are shown in Fig. 10. The reason for this is not clear. On the other hand, other work on animals, for example, the early studies of Kennard (1936) on monkeys and of Tsang (1937) on rats, have yielded opposite results. These investigators found that early operated subjects showed smaller deficits and any losses in function that were initially produced were recovered faster in these.

It is not entirely clear to what variables this apparent contradiction is due. It is possible, however, that rearing conditions have an important influence on the effects of brain injury and that the relatively rich environmental conditions to which most human adults have been exposed throughout their lives may serve to buffer biological intelligence against trauma. Most laboratory animals, on the other hand, do not have such an advantage, spending most of their lives in semirestriction. The validity of this notion is supported by the work of Schwartz (1964), who found that early brain lesions in rats (18 to 24 hours after birth) produced significant changes in Hebb-Williams maze performance only if the animals were reared in a restricted environment. Free-environmental rearing minimized the effects of ablation. These interesting results are presented in Fig. 11. It should be noted, however, that the data of Isaac and Baker showing a *facilitating* effect of late lesions on performance can hardly be explained by reference to environmental variables. Possibly changes in arousal level were involved, these, in turn, affecting responsivity to the CS and UCS involved in the learning task.

A great deal of work has been carried out on the effects of early chemical manipulations. Deprivation of an essential dietary component such as protein will produce changes in learning ability at later testing (Penner, 1966). Likewise, adrenalin given preweaning can increase emotionality (Henderson and Eisner, 1966) and such substances as reserpine and deanol also produce changes in various behavioral dimensions including emotionality and discrimination learning (Meier and Huff, 1962). Meier and Huff argue, on the basis of their results, for a nonassocia-

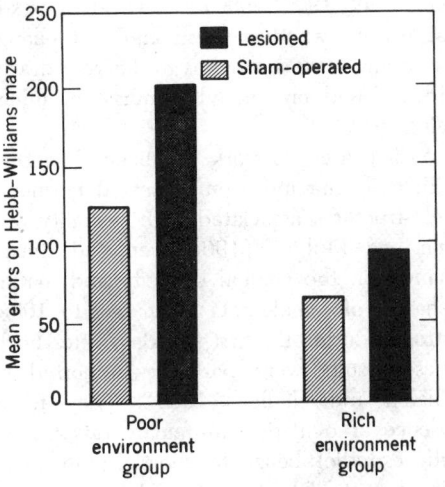

Fig. 11. Hebb-Williams maze performance as a function of neonatal cortical lesions and subsequent mode of rearing. (Schwartz, 1964.)

tionistic learning mechanism as the means by which the residua of early drug treatment are stored. In this connection, it is of interest to note that the magnitude of effects of early stimulation depends heavily on the chemical state of the animal. Young (1964) has shown that these were mitigated in rats if, prior to treatment, at 2 to 4 days, the animals were injected with either norepinephrine or chloropromazine.

One of the more interesting lines of work in the present context, since it may bear on the well-known syndrome in human beings, has been on experimental phenylketonuria. Excessive overloading of phenylalanine plus tyrosine was imposed by Woolley and Van Der Hoeven (1964) on newborn mice. They reported maze deficits in adulthood as a result of this treatment and argued that a serotonic deficiency was directly implicated. On the other hand, as we noted earlier, Thompson and Kano (1965) did not find changes in intelligence as a result of maternal phenylalanine overload prenatally, though large changes in emotionality did appear. It is possible that the maze test of Woolley and Van Der Hoeven assessed emotional as much as intellectual differences and were the former taken out the latter might well not have appeared. Postweaning administration of the compound under discussion does appear to affect intelligence in rats (Louttit, 1962; Polidora et al., 1966), and monkeys (Waisman et al., 1959, 1960). However, it is still not certain whether these kinds of change are in any sense analogous to the very drastic effects found on phenylketonuria in human beings.

A final area of work has been concerned with early manipulation of sexual hormones and structures associated with sexuality. Levine and Mullins (1964) reported drastic changes in the vaginal cyclicity and mating behavior of female rats given 5μg to 100μg estrogen during the first few days after birth. These results were partially supported by Whalen and Nadler (1965). They found absence of ovulation in female rats treated with estradiol benzoate shortly after birth, and absence of lordosis, though some passive receptivity to males. Gray et al. (1965) reported that early injection in rats of either male or female sex hormone decreased emo-

tionality tested later in life. Sex and strain differences also showed up.

Environmental Enrichment and Restriction

Methods and Effects. The technique of giving special practice to an animal in respect to certain functions or, conversely, restricting performance of those functions dates back to the late nineteenth century. In 1873 Spalding (see Spalding, 1954) showed that restriction of the incipient flight movements of young swallows impaired their flying ability later. A replication of this study much later by Dennis (1941) using buzzards yielded the same results. The effects of retriction of swimming in amblystoma was studied in a series of investigations started by Carmichael (1926). He found that paralysis of movement induced by immersion in chloretone produced no effects. Matthews and Detwiler (1926), however, were able to demonstrate that prolonged immersion in the solution beyond a certain period resulted in definite impairment. Restriction on the sensory side was used by Metfessel (1940) to explore the mode of song acquisition in roller canaries. Young birds which had never been allowed to hear the species song were still able to reproduce it properly. On the other hand, certain aspects of the song—vibration frequencies—could be altered by enforced exposure to an electronic oscillator. These observations have recently been extended by a number of workers (see Marler and Hamilton, 1966) to song acquisition in the white-throated sparrow of the Bay area in northern California.

Work on the effects of *general* restriction and *general* enrichment was given its initial impetus by the theoretical stress laid by Hebb (1949) on the importance of early learning. We have already referred to his own study on the intelligence of home-reared compared with laboratory-reared rats. Several of his students and colleagues at McGill followed up these initial observations, notably Hymovitch (1952), Forgays and Forgays (1952), and Forgus (1954). They all were able to show quite clearly that the problem-solving ability of rats, as indicated chiefly on the Hebb-Williams maze test, was markedly raised by rearing in a so-called "rich" environment. This environment usually was defined loosely in terms of increased physical space and greater sensory complexity.

Another series of similar experiments was also started at McGill around 1950 on a higher species—the dog (Clarke et al., 1951). The general method was roughly similar to that used in the rat studies. Thus comparisons were made on a variety of tests between Scottish terriers that had been reared in relatively restricted laboratory cage situations with dogs raised as pets either in the lab or in homes in Montreal. The initial finding of Clarke et al. showed that such manipulations produced dramatic differences in intelligence, emotionality, motivation, and social behavior. Follow-up studies were carried out over the next few years by Thompson, Heron, Melzack, and others (see Thompson and Melzack, 1956). Procedure was the same as that of Clarke et al. with some additional control over degree of restriction. In a series of papers it was demonstrated that restriction produced greatly heightened diffuse activity level (Thompson and Heron, 1954a), marked deficiency in tests of problem solving, maze ability, and delayed responding (Thompson and Heron, 1954b), a tendency to epileptiform seizures (Thompson, Melzack, and Scott, 1956), and diminished social capacity (Melzack and Thompson, 1956). In addition, the restricted animals showed a curious apparent insensitivity to pain (Melzack and Scott, 1957). One experimental dog, for example, would continually approach and contact a lighted cigar or match without showing any obvious signs of distress but only general excitement. This qualitative finding was confirmed in a more controlled manner using an electrified, remote-controlled toy car. Some of the findings are shown in Table 2. The results were summarized by one of the experimenters as follows (Thompson, 1955, pp. 130–131):

. . . . the restricted dogs present a picture of retarded psychologic development. In almost every way, their behaviour is more like that of puppies than of mature dogs.

The "puppylike" behavior that ensues on restriction is indeed striking and contrasts sharply with the more serious demeanor of normally raised animals. It fact it was quite characteristic for most visitors to the laboratory to mistake the normal dogs for the deprived ones on account of the general ebul-lience and alertness of the latter. It should be remarked, however, that a very severe restriction imposed on a few animals did produce an initial traumatic reaction at the time the subjects were first exposed to the world. This factor has been emphasized, as we shall see shortly, by other workers.

These findings have, in the main, been confirmed and extended by later investigators using other dog breeds (Melzack, 1962; Melzack and Burns, 1965; Fuller and Clark, 1966a, 1966b; Fuller, 1966). However, interpretations of how the effects of restriction operate to produce the results they do have varied somewhat. This point we shall take up later.

The effects of restriction and enrichment on higher species were studied initially in more specific contexts. Thus the work of Riesen and his students (Riesen, 1958, 1961) has focused mainly on the specific perceptual handicaps that result from various types of visual deprivation. This work has shown clearly that exposure to light during early development is necessary for normal visual function later on. Chimpanzees reared in complete darkness show gross deficits, for example, lack of ability to fixate objects, impaired blink reflexes, poor depth perception, and poor size discrimination (Riesen, 1947).

Table 2. Effects of Early Restriction on Various Adult Behaviors in Dogs

Activity Levels (minimum activity in 4½-hour tests)	
Normal	14.11
Restricted	21.32

Intelligence	
Delayed response (median delay reached in second)	Maze errors for 18 problems
Normal	240	237
Restricted	0	344

Social Behavior	
Dominance (number of wins)	Social contact with another dog (seconds)
Normal	57	97.7
Restricted	7	64.5

From Thompson and Heron (1954a, 1954b); Melzack and Thompson (1956).

However, it was pointed out by Riesen (1951) that dark-rearing also produced physiological changes in the visual system—in particular, a marked pallor of the optic disk. This finding was confirmed by Brättgard (1952) using rabbits. Such a defect can be partly mitigated by rearing animals in such a way that they receive diffuse but not patterned light stimulation. Under these conditions perceptual losses are again obtained though of considerably less severity. A daily ration of patterned light stimulation (1½ hours) was sufficient to allow almost normal development of visual function (Riesen et al., 1951). Later work has borne out and extended these general conclusions (see, e.g., Riesen et al., 1964).

The effects of specific restrictions have also been studied in lower species. Thus Spigelman and Bryden (1967) used rats to examine the effects of deprivation of one modality on performance that depended on the use of a different one. They found that animals peripherally blinded by enucleation shortly after birth did poorly compared to late-blinded animals on an auditory localization task. Curiously enough, the late-blinded performed better than sighted animals, although it is likely this difference was due to chance. Finally, early-blinded did better than late-blinded or sighted on a nonspatial auditory learning task.

Besides such specific deficits that ensue on restriction, other changes are produced. Especially since the work of Harlow (1958) on the development of affectional systems in primates, much attention has been given to the effects of different rearing procedures on social behavior. Starting in the late 1950s and 1960s, there has been a rapidly growing body of literature dealing with the general effects on primate behavior of partial or complete isolation. Three of the major centers for this work have been the University of Wisconsin, Cambridge University, and Yerkes Lab at Orange Park. At the first of these institutions, studies have been reported by Mason and Fitz-Gerald (1962), Rowland (1964), Mason and Sponholz (1963), and Griffin and Harlow (1966) among others. For the most part, early isolation produces striking deficits in social behavior and temperament. Animals so reared are socially inept and often very emotional as compared to normals. Learning

generally does not appear to be so greatly affected, though Griffin and Harlow (1966) have suggested that more complete testing procedures might well uncover deficits. The Cambridge studies have focused more on early social behaviors—particularly those occurring between adults and young and the effects of manipulation of these (e.g., by mother-infant separation) on behavior (e.g., Spencer-Booth et al., 1965; Hinde et al., 1966; Hinde and Spencer-Booth, 1967).

At Yerkes Lab, Menzel and colleagues (1963, 1964) compared normally laboratory-reared, restricted, and wild-born chimpanzees. He found that restriction produced timidity and lack of willingness to approach novel objects in their environments. Such differences in "responsiveness" appeared to be mainly a function of differences between rearing and testing environments. They tended to decline with age. These findings appear to be in essential agreement with those of the dog and monkey studies described previously.

Melzack (1965) has argued, somewhat in the same vein, that restricted dogs do not really have behavioral deficits and are on a continuum with normals in respect to psychological functioning. Restriction has the effect simply of increasing the novelty of cues in any testing situation confronted. Thus prior experience fails to make the positive contribution to performance that it does in the case of normals. In other words, restricted rearing produces a *different kind* of background but not necessarily abilities that are defective in any usual sense of this term. Melzack's point of view is backed up by data indicating that the EEGs of restricted dogs shift from predominantly low to high frequencies when they are permitted to look through their cage doors at a novel environment. Changes of comparable magnitude do not occur with normal animals (Melzack and Burns, 1965).

If early experiences of the kinds we are discussing affect behavior, they also must produce physiological effects. We noted earlier Schwartz' finding (1964) that the deleterious effects of very early brain damage in rats on later problem-solving ability can be attenuated by free-environmental rearing. In this study, cortical removal was carried out prior to environmental treatment. Thus it is reasonable to ask what would happen if the two treatments were reversed. Such a question was posed in an experiment by Smith (1959), who compared the effects of extrastriate posterior or anterior cortical lesions in cage-reared as against free-environment reared rats. The results turned out to be rather complex. In the cage-reared animals, there appeared to be a positive relation between lesion size and loss in maze performance. This finding was considered to be in accord with Lashley's principle of mass action. In the "free" group, however, no such relationship appeared; for these subjects, locus appeared to be of importance—those with small *posterior* lesions performing worse than those with large *anterior* lesions. Such data are difficult to interpret, more especially since a later study (Wittrig, 1966) has reached the almost opposite conclusion that enriched early environmental experience may enhance cortical equipotentiality. The discrepancy between these two sets of results undoubtedly lies in the procedural differences involved and more exact specifications of which of these are the most critical should provide some interesting research possibilities.

Besides the possible influences early rearing experience may have on brain functioning, it has become very clear, in the last decade, that its effects can also extend to brain anatomy, physiology, and biochemistry. This has now been demonstrated quite decisively by the Berkeley studies of Krech, Rosenzweig, and their colleagues. These investigators have shown using rats that: (1) brain cholinesterase activity correlates positively with genetically based maze ability; (2) enriched environmental rearing results in significant increases in brain acetylcholinesterase activity in both the cortex and the rest of the brain; (3) enriched environmental rearing results in increased brain weight, mostly attributable to cortical thickness, and glia to neuron ratio increases. There is also a suggestion that those specific cortical areas that are subjected to greater input show greater anatomical change; (4) such effects can be obtained by manipulation of adult as well as of young animals; (5) an impoverished condition of rearing (i.e., confinement in a highly uniform and monotonous environment) will produce results opposite to those described above. This effect is due specifically to lack of stimulation rather than to any stressful aspects of the situation (Rosenzweig, 1966; Krech et al., 1966).

This carefully done series of studies thus demonstrates clearly that early experiential variables can have profound influences on brain physiology and biochemistry. Which changes are the most crucial with respect to behavior still constitutes a problem. It is quite likely that the increase in acetylcholinesterase activity may indicate an increased number of functional synaptic connections and that this may be the dimension critical to improved intellectual functioning. However, this is a problem that still remains to be solved.

RNA (ribonucleic acid) has received a great deal of attention in connection with learning and memory functions. It is apparently also susceptible to early environmental manipulation, as shown in a study by DeBold et al. (1967). These investigators demonstrated with rats that rearing in dark from weaning for various periods of time and then being transferred to light produced alterations in the highest molecular weight fraction of RNA from occipital cortex. The Berkeley Laboratories have also implicated RNA in the effects of differential rearing procedures (Rosenzweig, 1966).

The apparent fact that the adult brain—at least in the case of the rat—is as responsive to environmental manipulation as the young brain is also worth noting, since it contradicts the common presumption concerning the greater plasticity of youth. Whether the same will also turn out to be true for higher species, however, remains to be seen.

The Essential Parameters. The major question arising from the studies we have discussed concerns the specification of the variables mainly responsible for mediating the effects of restriction or enrichment—as well as the exact nature of the behavior changes they produce. One would expect at least that age would be implicated and this does in fact seem to be the case. Thus Hymovitch (1952), one of the few to employ an adult control group, found that late manipulation of environment produced no appreciable changes in the learning ability of rats. On the other hand, the same was not found by Woods (1959). His adult group did, in fact, show marked improvement in maze performance as a result of exposure to a free environment. Consequently, we must be a little cautious about drawing definite conclusions concerning the importance of age.

It should be noted also that age is a variable with two aspects. Thus some environmental experience may or may not have an effect, not only because of the particular developmental status an animal has but also because of the experience the animal has had up to that point. These are two separate problems, but they are hard to disentangle.

It is clear also that the independent variables are very complex. The categories "enriched" and "restricted" are global ones involving many factors. The former usually is defined operationally in terms of larger amounts of space, more complex sensory (especially visual) stimulation, and the provision for more complex modes of motor response. The latter category, of course, involves presumably the opposite features. What is not yet fully understood is which of such dimensions is mainly operative in producing changes in behavior, and also whether the same variable is involved in effects of both enrichment and restriction.

Hymovitch (1952) was one of the first workers to focus on this problem. In his free-environment situation, he had some subjects which were allowed to roam freely about the full extent of the cage, while others were confined in small wire-mesh cages in the enclosure. The confined subjects had extra visual stimulation but no opportunity to respond very much to it. Results showed that the two experiences had equivalent effects on problem-solving ability. Consequently, Hymovitch concluded that perceptual experience was the critical factor in early emotional experience. On the other hand, two experimenters from the McGill laboratory, Forgays and Forgays (1952), made a similar comparison and found the very opposite to hold true. Thus rats allowed motor activity in addition to broad perceptual experience showed better performance than subjects provided only with the latter. What probably is critical is the similarity between the so-called rearing environment and the later testing situation. This point was demonstrated by the Forgays, who reasoned that the free-environment situation involved continued opportunity to fixate on distant visual cues, whereas restriction necessarily forced animals to attend to proximal stimuli. If this were true, then changing the position of the maze in reference to the room after a certain level of performance had been achieved should produce a greater disturbance for free-environment than for restricted animals. This, in fact, turned out to be the case.

The series of studies carried out by Forgus (1954, 1955a, 1955b, 1958) has made essentially the same point. That is to say, the findings seem to indicate that the effects of rich or impoverished rearing are "good" or "bad" relative to the demands of a criterion task. Theoretically, this means that provided the appropriate test could be supplied, restriction might turn out to have good effects and free-environment rearing to produce deficits in performance. Perhaps the most sensible position to take is to define as a rich environment one that will facilitate performance on a maximum number of task dimensions. This has been generally the position taken by Meier and McGee (1959), who suggested that an enriched early environment furnishes opportunity for progressive stimulus differentiation in all modalities including the kinesthetic. The more modalities that are involved, the richer the experience can be considered to be and the more performance in a variety of tasks should be facilitated.

We may still ask, however, whether such a passive exposure to a complex environment and the perceptual differentiation this produces is the only variable at work. It can be argued that active exploration of the world and the setting up of certain sensorimotor coordinations will also be of great importance. This notion has been put forward especially by Held and his colleagues, who have stressed the importance of the motor side in sensorimotor development—particularly the place of reafferent stimulation that ensues on muscle action. In a series of experiments using human and animal subjects, these workers have manipulated this variable by comparing the results of discrimination training under conditions of self-produced or active movement with those under conditions of passive or experiment-produced movement (Held and Hein, 1963; Held and Schlank, 1959; Held and Bossom, 1961). In one of these experiments, for example, an ingenious carousel arrangement was used. This allowed one member of a pair of subjects to explore actively the surrounding environment but the other, yoked to the first and restrained in a box, had only passive exposure to the same environment. Subsequent testing indicated that the "passive" kittens compared to the "active" animals were deficient on tests of visually guided paw placement, discrimination on a visual cliff, and development of a blink response (Held and Heim, 1963). The general conclusion is that both for the normal development and maintenance of visual spatial performance, the patterns of reafferent stimulation arising from active or self-induced movement are essential. Although their experimental procedures involve difficulties that make precise control over the relevant variable rather imprecise, these do not greatly detract from the validity of this idea.

If the advantages of enriched environmental rearing lie in the maximizing of compatibility between general living circumstances and test conditions, we might expect that the noncompatibility that ensues on severe restriction will have at least two effects. The one we have emphasized so far has been of a cognitive sort in that it relates to the adequacy of intellectual preparation that a subject, because of prior rearing conditions, can bring to some criterion task. However, there is an affective factor also involved. A sharp disparity between what an animal has become used to over a long period of time and what is suddenly imposed on him is likely to produce serious emotional disturbance, and this in turn may cause a deficit in performance. The importance of such a factor has been particularly stressed by Fuller and Clark (1966a, 1966b), who have referred to it as the "postisolation" syndrome. In one experiment they were able to show that the trauma of emergence could be reduced by means of a tranquilizer—chloropromazine—and this resulted in a smaller deficit in performance. Similarly, in a second study they found that approach and contactual behavior to objects and other dogs following a period of isolation could be aided by supplying some pretest familiarization with the testing space.

In the opinion of the writers, it is quite likely that postisolation depression is of importance. But it perhaps should not be regarded as an exclusive alternative to the factor of perceptual-motor experience, nor, indeed, is it probably as critical as the latter.

In the McGill studies both with dogs and rats, pretraining procedures prior to many of the tests used guaranteed that emotionality was a very minor factor in determining scores. And it seems improbable that the emotional trauma of being taken out of isolation could be long enough or intense enough to produce by itself large and inevitable losses in intelligence and other functions. Nonetheless, Fuller and Clark have done a useful service in drawing the attention of researchers to the postisolation syndrome. It is certainly an effect that must be reckoned with in any early isolation study.

Early Social Influences

One of the most important types of early environmental influence relates to the social interactions that occur between a young organism and its parents, peers, or others close to it physically. In psychology, Freud was one of the first to suggest that the patterns that were set up in early childhood could become prototypic of all later social behavior and attitudes. His specific formulations were couched in rather overdramatic and literary terms but there is no gainsaying the validity of the general point. In biology, Charles Darwin came to regard emotional expression and its role in animal communication as having a prominent role in determining the course of evolutionary change. Subsequently, a great many workers in the biological area, particularly those concerned with ecology, have concerned themselves with trying to specify the dimensions of social behavior that contribute to population parameters and the dependence of these on genotype and environment.

In the present context, however, this orientation is of less relevance. What we wish to discuss here relates not so much to group characteristics, but rather to the nature of social interactions between individuals and how these are influenced by the encounters one animal has with another early in life. Since the volume of work done is enormous, we shall consider only three particular lines of work as reasonably representative of this focus: (1) the work on imprinting, especially in avian species; (2) socialization processes in the dog; and (3) affectional systems in primates. We shall review briefly each of these areas and also discuss some selected studies that seem to be of importance.

Imprinting. The extensive work in this area has been reviewed by Sluckin (1964) and by Bateson (1966). It has been known since the nineteenth century and probably well before that very shortly after hatch, young birds will respond positively to different objects in the environment and as a result may show to these strong and relatively permanent attachment behavior. The person most responsible for putting into a formal theoretical context what had previously been simply an interesting bit of natural history was Konrad Lorenz (1935). He emphasized the following aspects of imprinting: (1) the critical period during which it can occur; (2) its irreversibility; (3) its species characteristics in respect to the kinds of stimuli and response patterns it involves. Much of the work done on the subject has been directed toward exploring one or other of these problems. What has become more and more clear is that the phenomenon is a general one that probably takes in a great diversity of apparently distinct types of early learnings, including, for example, attachment to territories and food objects (Hess, 1964; Bateson, 1966). In addition, it seems likely that taken broadly it also occurs in species other than precocial birds, for example, some mammals such as goats and sheep (Scott, 1945; Smith et al., 1966; Cairns and Johnson, 1966; Cairns, 1966a), perhaps some of the canidae (Scott and Fuller, 1965), and possibly primates (Sackett et al., 1965).

From the standpoint of the early experience framework, the important feature of the phenomenon of imprinting lies in the fact that it represents a case of long-term social attachment set up during a short (and perhaps critical) period during development. In lower animals at least, such an attachment is usually defined in terms of a stronger following response to the surrogate as against weaker following of a neutral object, or a simple preference of the former over the latter (Bateson, 1966).

Besides these, other measures can be used to indicate attachment. For example, avoidance of unfamiliar objects is stronger in birds imprinted on a particular surrogate (Jaynes, 1956; Guiton, 1959); likewise, distress calling often occurs in the temporary absence of the imprinted object and the general resistance of the animal to stress seems to be greater (Thompson and O'Kieffe, 1962). It has been shown that the surrogate can quite readily function as a reinforcing stimulus in a maze-learning (Campbell and Pickleman, 1961) or bar-pressing situations (Peterson, 1960; Hoffman et al., 1966a, 1966b). Finally, there is limited evidence that imprinting influences mate-choice in the direction of choosing animals like the imprinted object, as well as promoting flocking and general social behavior later in life, although the conditions under which this occurs may be rather particularized (Bateson, 1966). When such a relationship does obtain, it is possible that it may have important evolutionary consequences, and some workers (e.g., Mainardi et al., 1965) have constructed models relating polymorphism and eventual speciation to mate-preferences arising from early imprinting. Data relevant to this hypothetical relation have been gathered by Cooke (unpublished manuscript, 1968) on the blue goose and the snow goose.

As indicated previously, the precocity and rapid development of the species usually involved in imprinting studies have tended to give to the phenomenon a quality of special mystery and drama that may make it seem to have a narrower application than it really does. For whatever reasons, most young animals probably become attached to and prefer those social objects to which they are first exposed; and indeed it does not strain credibility to suppose, as both Gray (1958) and Bowlby (1958) have suggested, that this applies as much in the case of children as in birds and lower species. Certainly, the consequences of making and breaking of early social attachments have been explicitly the concern of much of classical psychoanalytic theory and its more modern offshoots. This point will be taken up again in the section dealing with studies on children.

We may next ask what happens when social attachment or imprinting does not have the opportunity to occur early in life? Some of the more important work in this problem has been carried out with dogs and monkeys. Let us now consider a sample of these researches.

Social Isolation in Dogs. During the late 1940s, a program of work was set up at the Jackson Laboratory, Bar Harbor, Maine, to study the genetics and social behavior of the dog. A book of this title summarizing almost

20 years of work has been published (Scott and Fuller, 1965). One of the most interesting lines of research carried out was concerned with the socialization process. Several studies may be cited here as representative.

The first (Elliot and Scott, 1961) concerned itself with the immediate effects on puppies of isolation from the mother. Dependent variables measured were activity level and amount of vocalization. Besides isolation itself, a major independent variable was age. Results are summarized in Fig. 12. They show quite clearly that, in terms of the behavioral indices used, emotional upset is maximal around 6 to 8 weeks of age. This presumably indicates that social attachment to the mother is strongest around this age in the puppy. Hence Scott (1962) and Scott and Fuller (1965) have referred to the time between about 4 to 14 weeks as the *socialization period*. It is also true, however, that it seems to be a time when affective relations with any part of the environment—animate or inanimate—may be formed and when a puppy is likely to show the greatest emotional response to any unusual or disturbing stimulus (Fox and Stelzner, 1966). Consequently, we should perhaps be careful not to categorize it in too narrow terms.

If it is true that the formation of social attachments is one of the more important processes going on in the 4 to 14-week-old puppy, we might then guess that isolation during this time would have drastic effects on later social behavior. This indeed seems to be true. Pfaffenberger and Scott (1959) studied the reasons for failure in animals being trained as guide-dogs for the blind. One of the most critical factors turned out to be a protracted period during early life involving minimal human contact. For accidental reasons, some dogs were kept in the school for some weeks beyond the end of the socialization period (i.e., around 12 to 14 weeks) before being farmed out to homes. These animals tended to perform poorly in the criterion tests. Similarly, Freedman, King, and Elliot (1961) found that the extent to which a dog would make social contact with another dog or with a human being was directly proportional to the amount of social contact it had been permitted with them between 4 and 14 weeks. According to the authors, animals isolated between these ages were never able to

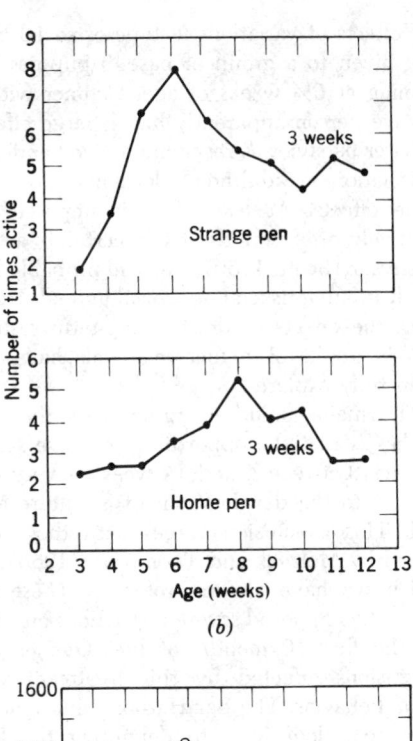

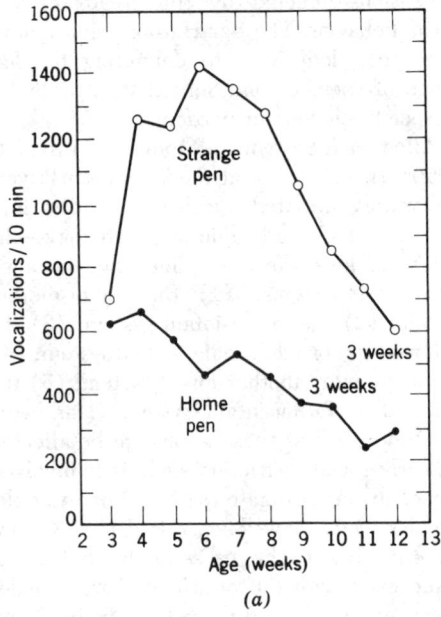

Fig. 12. (*a*) Vocalization in puppies as a function of familiarity or nonfamiliarity of environment and age. (*b*) Activity scores at different ages as a function of the same two variables. In both cases, note peaking at 6 to 10 weeks. (Modified from Elliot and Scott, 1961.)

develop the ability to socialize normally. The dimensions of contact have also been examined. Stanley and Elliot (1962) explored the effects of variations in type of social contact given to a group of basenji puppies beginning at 6½ weeks of age. Contact with a passive person apparently has as large effects on later behavior as receiving active handling.

Isolation in adulthood does not have the same effects. At least if it is imposed for relatively brief periods, it will certainly act as a stressor (Scott, 1950), but will probably not result in an antisocial or asocial animal. However, the effects of drastic long-term restriction in adults of higher mammals have not been fully explored.

The major point emerging from the dog studies is that the opportunity to have social contacts between 4 and 14 weeks is very important to the development of a mature animal. This conclusion agrees with those obtained by Melzack and Thompson (1956), to which we have already referred. These investigators imposed severe restrictions on dogs for the first 10 months of life. One of the dimensions affected by this treatment was social behavior. The Bar Harbor studies, however go a long way to delimiting the age range of specific conditions that are relevant to social behavior in particular.

Affectional Systems in Monkeys. In the late 1950s, H. F. Harlow at the Wisconsin Private Laboratory initiated a series of studies in a curiously neglected topic in psychology—the nature of love. He has defined five so-called affectional systems: (1) the infant-mother system; (2) the infant-infant system; (3) the heterosexual or adult male-female system; (4) the maternal or mother-infant system; (5) the paternal or father-infant system (Harlow et al., 1963). All of these appear to be affected by early social restriction such as is involved especially in surrogate-rearing. For example, females which have been raised in this manner turn out to be exceedingly difficult to breed even with the most experienced males (Harlow, 1965), and those that are bred and produce young make exceptionally poor mothers. Harlow et al. (1963, pp. 275–276) write of the behavior of unmothered mothers as follows:

All five females were totally hopeless mothers, and none of the infants would have survived without artificial feeding in the first days or weeks of life. Two mothers were essentially indifferent to their infants; three were violently abusive. Indeed, the last infant was separated when it became apparent that otherwise it would not live. The maternal inadequacies of these animals cannot be attributed to faulty responding by the babies. Early in life the babies repeatedly offered visual and auditory cues normally appropriate for creating maternal responses, and as far as the first four infants were physically able to initiate approach and body-contact responses, they made repeated attempts to attach to the mothers, only to be repulsed and rejected. So strong were these contact-seeking responses in two infants that they withstood brutal and continuous abuse by the mothers until they attained the breast for reasonable periods of time.

Temporary separations of short duration can also have effects on behavior and these appear to be similar to those found in human children. Jensen and Tolman (1962), Seay et al. (1962), and Seay and Harlow (1965) used various lengths and degrees of separation. They demonstrated increases, on the part of the infants, in "crying," self-directed mouthing, depression, and general lethargy. Hinde et al. (1966) and Kaufman and Rosenblum (1968) have verified and supplemented these main results. The latter two authors have usefully summarized the primate work on the problem and pointed up the similarities between such observations with monkeys and those with children. It is of interest to note, in this connection, that rearing monkeys with humans produces animals that prefer the company of human beings to other monkeys when given a choice at 2 to 3 years of age. Animals reared in isolation or with both humans and monkeys turn out to prefer monkeys (Sackett et al., 1965).

It is still uncertain how long or how severe social isolation must be to produce effects. Three months of social deprivation produces initially "severe depression" and heightened "self-directed" activities but apparently does not greatly affect social responses (Griffin and Harlow, 1966). On the other hand, social potentialities are effectively destroyed if isolation lasts as long as 6 to 12 months after birth (Harlow, 1965). As a result of such a prolonged period of social restriction, a monkey appears to become almost totally autistic and incapable of orienting appropriately to another animal whatever its sex or age. It is difficult to know exactly what are the most critical aspects of the isolation experience that produce such results. At least in the case of monkeys, physical contact between animals must be an important dimension. It does appear to be true that social and sensory deprivation tends to reduce the extent to which contacting behavior is initiated. That is to say, isolation produces monkeys that dislike touching another monkey. Since social behavior in this species involves a very heavy component of physical contact, it is therefore markedly distorted (Sackett, 1967).

The manner in which such a variable operates in other species is not known. It seems likely it is most important in the case of human beings. However, as with general environmental restriction, more work will be needed to locate the variables most critically implicated. For the time being, however, we must be content with the well-documented empirical evidence that social behavior in all its various forms, and in a variety of species, depends on the social attachments that are set up early in life.

HUMAN STUDIES

We have broken down our review of postnatal early experience studies in human beings according to a division similar to that used in our discussion of the animal work. However, as we have already indicated in our brief review of methods, the relevant experiential variables in humans tend to be rather broad ones that do not easily lend themselves to neat categorization. Thus "institutionalization" or "nursery school attendance" must incorporate many of the kinds of influence that we have been able to consider separately when dealing with the animal work. As a result, the recurrence of these variables across sections may give the appearance of redundancy. This is unfortunate but seems to be preferable to collapsing distinctions which the work done with animals suggests are of great importance.

General Massive Stimulation

Institutionalization and Stimulation. Children living in institutions have had an unbelievably high mortality rate, which has decreased only recently. Of 10,272 children admitted to the Dublin foundling home between 1775 and 1800, 45 survived (Kessen, 1965). At the beginning of this century one of the major foundling homes in Germany had a mortality rate of 71.5% in infants during their first year of life (Spitz, 1945). By the 1930s the situation had improved sufficiently that the death rate among institutionalized children compared favorably with that of noninstitutionalized children. At this time, however, a new problem came into focus. Investigators began to report that among children reared in an institutional setting the incidence of psychological disturbance was alarmingly high (Durfee and Wolf, 1933; Lowrey, 1940; Bender and Yarnell, 1941; Bakwin, 1949). Two factors were generally deemed responsible for the observed psychological abnormalities—lack of stimulation and absence of the mother.

The first large-scale study of institution infants less than 1 year old was undertaken by Spitz (1945). He compared the development in the first year of life of infants raised in two different kinds of institutions. The one, *Nursery*, was for the children of delinquent girls who were in a penal institution; the other, *Foundling Home*, was for children whose mothers could not support them. In Nursery the occupants were provided with toys, could see all that was going on around them from their cribs, and were fed, nursed, and cared for by their own mothers or by full-time mother substitutes. Children in Foundling Home, on the other hand, had few toys and could see little of the world around them because sheets were regularly hung over the foot and side railings of their cots. They interacted with other people only at feeding time, when busy nurses came to look after their needs. They lay supine in their cots for so many months that hollows were worn into their mattresses and, by the time they were physically able to turn themselves in their cots (about 7 months of age), these hollows prevented them from doing so. Thus, at the age of 10 or 12 months, they were observed lying only on their backs and playing with the only toys they had—their hands and feet.

When he compared the Developmental Quotient scores (Hetzer and Wolf, 1928) of the two sets of infants, Spitz found a large difference. There was a dramatic reduction in score between the first and last third of the first year of life for Foundling Home infants. On the other hand, the comparable scores of Nursery infants and of two control groups of noninstitutionalized infants remained approximately the same. Foundling Home children also showed a marked reduction over the year in "Body Mastery" scores as compared to scores of Nursery children. Apart from severe developmental retardation, Spitz also noted unusual reactions to strangers by Foundling Home children in the last third of their first year of life, ranging from extreme friendliness to blood-curdling screams. In addition, they were extremely susceptible to infection and illness of any kind, despite what Spitz reports as impeccable hygiene and precautions against infection in the home. During Spitz' stay an epidemic of measles struck the institution, leaving a staggering number of the children dead.

A follow-up two years later (Spitz, 1946) revealed continuing large developmental differences between Foundling Home and Nursery children. Although conditions in Foundling home had been greatly improved—the children had been moved into a large, sunny room where they interacted with each other and with nurses who were constantly in attendance—the 21 whom Spitz was able to study were retarded in physical development, toilet training, speech, and ability to feed and dress themselves. Thus the unfortunate conditions under which they had lived for their first year of life seemed to have had irreversible effects on their subsequent development. The children in Nursery generally left the institution when they were 1 year old, but Spitz was able to observe a few who were there between 13 and 18 months of age. Their development was quite adequate and, in fact, in most cases the Developmental Quotient surpassed the normal age level. During the 3½ years in which Spitz had contact with Nursery not a single child died.

The effects of institutionalization which Spitz found in Foundling Home children could well be attributed to a lack of general environmental stimulation. Spitz chose, however, to maintain that the children suffered because their perceptual world was lacking in human contact—that of either a mother or a mother-substitute. He argued that "perception is a function of libidinal cathexis and therefore the result of the intervention of an emo-

tion of one kind or another" (1945, p. 67); and it is only through the intervention of a mother that emotions are provided for a child. The children in the Nursery experienced an adequate mother-child relationship. It was, in fact, an exaggerated one. Since many of the opportunities these mothers might have had for social contact were obviously denied them in the penal setting, they focused even more of their emotional attachments on their babies. They were in constant competition with other Nursery mothers as to who had the best baby and were intensely jealous of any attention others gave to their infant. It may be that this intensified care given to Nursery children produced the accelerated development which Spitz noted in his follow-up.

Spitz was not alone in attributing the detrimental effects of institutionalization to maternal deprivation. As we have indicated earlier, Ribble (1944) maintained that the newborn child urgently needs a long and constant period of psychological mothering, by its own mother or a single mother substitute, to counteract biological anxiety and maintain body integration while the nervous system is maturing. Babies deprived of mothering, she reported, develop marasmus, a condition of physical debilitation. Marasmic children also display a form of either negativistic excitement or regressive quiescence. When given care and massage by a "foster mother" these children show a remarkable recovery, with restored appetite, alertness, and reflex excitability.

The severe retardation of infants in institutions is still being documented (Provence and Lipton, 1962). In studying the occupants of a nursery where there was minimal contact between caretakers and children and lack of individualized care these investigators noted substantial impairment in social responsiveness, language development, body awareness, and pain avoidance. They found a large discrepancy between maturation of the motor apparatus and its use by the infant, a difficulty in modulating motor impulses to produce smooth movements, and a diminished impulse to reach out toward people and objects. Again, they attribute much of this retardation to lack of continuous care by a mother figure.

Goldfarb (1945a, 1945b, 1947, 1949) compared the development of children who had lived in an institution up to the age of 3, at which time they had been placed in a foster home, with that of children who had been placed in a foster home before age 1. All the children had been separated from their mothers before they were 9 months old. The 30 children whom Goldfarb studied most intensively ranged in age from 10 to 14 years, and all were living with foster parents at the time of his investigation. The institution in which half of these children had lived for the first 3 years of their lives was very similar to Spitz' Foundling Home. Although it was immaculate in physical hygiene, it involved for the children almost complete social and sensory isolation during the first year of their lives. They were cared for by a number of staff members with frequent personnel changes both during the course of a day and over a period of months. Thus they lacked any opportunity for intense and continuous contact with a specific adult. Conditions in the institution during the next 2 years of these children's lives were only slightly better. These children, as compared with the 15 who had had immediate placement in a foster home after separation from their mothers, were deficient in intelligence, ability to conceptualize, and speech development. They were also restless, less able to concentrate, and poorer in school achievement. They were unpopular, socially immature, aggressive, and insatiable for affection, although unable to form any genuine attachment. An inability to adhere to rules or to display any sign of guilt after deviation completed a picture remarkably like that painted by Bender (1947) in her description of the so-called "psychopathic behavior disorder in childhood." These emotional and intellectual consequences were blamed by Goldfarb on the lack of mothering during the first three years of life. In spite of the fact that the foster homes to which both groups of children had been assigned were equivalent in the environments they provided, the differences existed. Goldfarb thus concluded that the early effects of institutionalization were irreversible.

Retrospective studies of adopted children continue to suggest that maternal separation early in life may have lasting negative effects. It appears that a greater proportion of adopted children are being treated for emotional disturbance than one would expect

from their incidence in the general population (Bostock, 1961). Those with emotional problems display impulsivity, hostility, delinquency, and other aggressive symptoms. Menlove (1965) found the incidence of hyperactivity, hostility, and negativism to be greater among a group of adopted than nonadopted children.

In a report prepared on behalf of the World Health Organization, Bowlby (1952), citing an extensive list of studies including his own (Bowlby, 1940, 1944), concluded that when a child is deprived of maternal care his physical, intellectual, and social development is almost always retarded. In addition, Bowlby indicated that the effects of early deprivation are permanent. "This is a sombre conclusion which must now be regarded as established" (p. 15). It appeared to Bowlby that maternal deprivation before the age of 6 months was less detrimental than that occurring later. But lack of opportunity during the first 3 years of life for the formation of attachment to a mother-figure, deprivation of a mother-figure for a limited period of time, or changes from one mother-figure to another during the same period of time were all experiences, he felt, which would produce the affectionless and psychopathic character so many investigators had described. Beyond the age of 3, Bowlby suggested, a child becomes more able to tolerate maternal absence for a few days or weeks at a time, and, by age 7 or 8, of a year or more.

Criticism of the Early Studies. In spite of the large volume of work pointing to the negative consequences of a lack of early mothering, the findings and conclusions have not gone unchallenged. The methodological adequacy of many of the studies has been questioned, studies which suggest that not all children are adversely affected by institutionalization have been reported, and reinterpretations of the data have been made. We shall deal with each of these in turn.

Methodological Criticisms. The work of Ribble and Spitz has come under extensive fire by Pinneau (1950, 1955). In a 1950 *Child Development* article Pinneau criticized Ribble for her assumptions that in infancy there is a tendency to functional disorganization and that psychological mothering is needed for normal development. The evidence shows, Pinneau claimed, that the normal infant circulatory system is fully adequate to meet the demands placed on it, that handling is not necessary for the majority of babies to help them breathe properly, and that the sensitivity of the infant's digestive system is not due to a lack of mothering. In concluding that marasmus is not due to lack of mothering Pinneau regretted, along with others (e.g., Orlansky, 1949), that Ribble had not drawn a line between her empirical findings and her personal opinions. At the same time, though it may be true that data on the physiological make-up of infant systems does not completely favor Ribble's position, it does not favor Pinneau's either (see Wolstenholme and O'Connor, 1961).

Pinneau's criticism of Spitz (Pinneau, 1955) included criticism of Spitz' failure to state whether or not there were congenital abnormalities in Foundling Home children which might have accounted for their developmental retardation. Spitz also failed to pay attention to possible differences between the mothers of the two groups of children which might, at least partially, have caused the differences in the children. These included factors such as the mothers' intellectual and socioeconomic backgrounds and conditions of health. In addition, Pinneau pointed to the questionable validity of the Hetzer-Wolf baby tests which Spitz had employed and to their lack of predictive ability for later performance.

Spitz lost many of the children in his sample through outplacement. It seems evident that these would be the more desirable ones, and that hence only the less well-developed children would be left behind for him to study. Again, one wonders if the high mortality rate among foundling home children was due to maternal deprivation or, rather, if it was because these infants were more susceptible, because of their inactivity, to such problems as respiratory infection.

Children who are committed to institutions do not constitute a random sample from the general population. For that reason the results of institutionalization studies cannot be generalized to the general population. It seems possible that a high proportion of mothers who give up their children to institutions are likely to be from a lower socioeconomic class, unwed or deserted by their husbands. We might then expect their offspring to have a poorer genetic gackground than that of children reared in a home. If a mother gives up her child the chances seem great that her pregnancy was unwanted and that she was anxious and tense during it. It is also likely that she may have received less adequate medical attention during pregnancy than do mothers of wanted children and that she may have had a more difficult birth with resultant damage to her child. All these factors, as we have noted in a previous section, may produce serious—although undiagnosed—psychological and physical disturbances in the child before he is ever placed in an institution. Brain-damaged children suffer more from isolation than do normal children (Bender, 1950). Hence we would expect a quite different reaction to the social and sensory isolation of an institution from damaged children, who may constitute a large percentage of its population, than from normal children.

Goldfarb's studies have also come under critical attack (e.g., O'Connor, 1956; Casler, 1961). Perhaps the most important criticism is that his two groups of children may well not have been matched for every variable except the incidence of institutionalization. Goldfarb is careful to show that the foster homes in which his children had spent the greater part of their lives were identical and that, in fact, the true mothers of the *institution* children were superior to those of the noninstitution ones. Unanswered, however, is the question of why 15 of the children had spent the first 3 years of their lives in an institution. Was there something wrong with them that they had not been placed in foster homes soon after separation from their mothers? How did they differ from the children who did go almost immediately into foster homes, and what made them less desirable for this kind of placement?

Contradictory Data. Not every observer found the overwhelmingly negative effects of institutionalization described by Bowlby in his WHO report. Nor were others so pessimistic about the eventual fate of children who were raised in foundling homes. In a follow-up study of 60 children who had been admitted to a tuberculosis sanitarium before they were 4 years old, Bowlby, Ainsworth, Boston, and Rosenbluth (1956) were forced to conclude that the case against maternal deprivation had been overstated. These children, aged 6 to 14 years at the time of the study, had spent varying amounts of time in the sanitarium, ranging from a few months to over 2 years. Compared to a matched control group of school classmates they did not show any reduction in intellectual functioning. It was true that, according to the examiner's judgment, fewer of the institutionalized than the control children could respond well in the test situation and, according to teachers, they displayed more withdrawal and apathy, rough behavior and temper. On the other hand, few of the sanitarium children were delinquent and over half of them were capable of establishing good social relationships with their peers. Thus Bowlby et al. stated that the belief which they had had to that point, that institutionalization and privation commonly lead to the development of psychopathy and affectionless characters, was incorrect.

In a study of six orphaned children who had spent most of their lives in a concentration camp, Freud and Dann (1951) found that, at the age of 3, these children were not delinquent, deficient, nor psychotic, nor was their ability to form emotional relationships and attachments, at least for each other, impaired. Similarly, Freud and Burlingham (1944) noted that children in their nursery often developed better than in the average household. Rheingold (1956) found that the average intellectual level of institution infants she studied was within normal limits on the Cattell scale, a report in striking contrast to those noting a severe reduction in intellectual functioning among orphanage children. In a later study Rheingold and Bailey (1959) report that these same children were friendly, intelligent, and in no way emotionally or mentally retarded. And, finally, in a study of another group of "deprived" infants, Rheingold (1961) states that they were as interested and competent as home-reared control infants and even more positively responsive to the examiner than the control children.

In a study of children raised in a foundling home ("the Creche") in Beirut, Dennis and Najarian (1957) did find these children exhibited some intellectual retardation but found no evidence that this retardation was irreversible. A ratio of one attendant to ten children meant that children in the Creche received little more than the essentials of physical care. They were not held while they were

being fed, but, instead, were given a bottle propped on a small pillow from which they drank as they lay on their backs. The infants were swaddled—a Near Eastern practice— until they were 4 months old so that their opportunity for activity in arms and legs was severely restricted. The cribs in which they lived were covered around the sides, as in Spitz' Foundling Home. Compared to children raised in homes in Beirut these babies, after 3 months of age, were significantly lower in intelligence as measured by a modified Cattell infant scale. However, children in the same institution who were between 4½ and 6 years of age were not retarded in their performance on the Goodenough draw-a-man test, the Knox cube test, or the Porteus mazes when compared to American norms. Since the older children had received the same kind of care as the infants Dennis and Najarian measured, and the home's admission requirements had not changed, we can only assume that whatever experiences the infants had missed in infancy were made up at a later date. Hence, at least the effects of institutionalization on intellectual development appear reversible. Moreover, since Creche infants had never had their mothers with them, the retardation which Dennis and Najarian observed could not have been due to a break with the mother. Spitz' suggestion that this was the reason his Foundling Home infants were retarded is therefore questionable.

The fact that a number of investigators have not discovered negative effects in *all* children raised in institutions, *in spite of the fact that they had all suffered maternal deprivation*, means that other explanations for these effects, where they occur, must be sought. A likely explanation lies in the suggestion that children in institutions suffer from perceptual deprivation and restriction of learning opportunities.

Alternative Explanations. Dennis and Najarian suggest that Creche infants performed as poorly as they did on the Cattell infant scale because they had been deprived of normal opportunities for learning, which most children reared in family homes have had. Items measuring intellectual development between the ages of 3 and 12 months require an infant to sit on an adult lap, and this was a luxury to which Creche infants were unaccustomed. They were unable to hold their heads erect and steady and had had no opportunity to practice manual skills directed by vision, which are necessary for performance on the Cattell test. Once given the opportunities for learning which they had missed, these children should have performed as well as any noninstitutionalized infants and, indeed, by the age of 5 or so they appeared to do just this.

Clearly, an environment lacking variety in material surroundings, and in which there is minimal opportunity for interaction with caretakers, is going to be deficient in learning opportunities. We would expect its inhabitants to be retarded intellectually, in motor and language development, and in many social skills. These deficits we shall discuss later when we deal with the effect of qualitative alterations in an organism's environment. The data previously presented, however, on the effects of general, massive stimulation on animal development do suggest that much retardation in orphanage children is due to a lack of general stimulation. The variables of handling, shocking, stress, and so forth which have been discussed sound very much like the "stimulus feeding" Ribble suggests mothers provide when they stroke, hold, rock, and move in front of their infants. Mothers, in the course of daily care of their children, provide a great deal of stimulus feeding. But much of the kinesthetic and tactile stimulation to which home-reared children are exposed continuously may be denied to institution children, who spend so much time unhandled and lying in their cribs. Home-reared children are not generally left alone in cribs draped with sheets. They are given extensive auditory and visual stimulation in the course of being exposed to the activity going on around them. That the opportunities for this stimulation are generally mediated by a mother figure, however, does not mean that her absence will be detrimental to all forms of development. Provided that a child receives this perceptual stimulation, be it from a number of different caretakers or through inanimate means, he should suffer less than a child totally deprived.

The function of perceptual stimulation and the mechanisms through which it influences development have already been noted. Clearly, all that has been suggested in reference to the animal studies is relevant to the human data as well. In brief, one of the important functions of general stimulation may be to produce habituation in the young organism, that is, a tendency to be less aroused or more easily aroused by stimulus change. A child deprived of adequate amounts of stimulation may never show normal general reactivity to his environment. His general responsiveness to any alteration in stimulus conditions may be no different from what it would have been had there been no exposure to early stimulation. Thus he might be characterized by the adjectives nervous, phlegmatic, jumpy, emotional, docile—adjectives which might easily be applied to children in institutions. In addition, if children are not habituated to stimuli which elicit startle, defense, and emotional behavior, it is quite probable that their early learning experiences will be interfered with by these competing unlearned emotional behaviors.

It has been suggested (e.g., Thompson, 1958, 1960; Casler, 1961) that the ill effects that have been attributed to maternal deprivation during the first 6 months of life are, in fact, due to perceptual deprivation while those occurring after 6 months are due to perceptual deprivation and the affective compontents that accompany the breaking of an established emotional bond between mother and child. (We should also add to this the ill effects of never having formed an emotional attachment to a mother figure). The cutoff age of 6 months is by no means an arbitrary one. Bowlby (1958) notes that children who are separated from their mothers after this age fret, but those that are separated before do not. Spitz (1946) has suggested that it is not until the age of 6 months that the average infant is able to discriminate between his mother and other human beings. Thus we would not expect him to be upset before that time at any attempt to replace her. In a study of 76 babies admitted to hospital, and thereby separated from their mothers, Schaffer and Callender (1959) found that those 6 months of age or less did not protest and readily accepted mother substitutes. Those 7 months or older, however, were disturbed at the separation.

Schaffer (1958) further reports the existence of two posthospitalization syndromes in these infants—a "global" and an "overdependent" syndrome. The global pattern of behavior occurred mainly in infants who were under 7 months of age, whereas the overdependent was commonly found in those over 7 months. When these children returned home from the hospital, mothers of the younger infants reported that they exhibited an extreme preoccupation with the environment. For a lengthy period of time the child would engage in an unfocused inspection of his surroundings, rarely engaging in any other behavior such as vocalization or playing with toys. During this time the child was quite unresponsive to any person around him. Schaffer reports that some of the children also experienced somatic upset, in the form of feeding and sleep disturbances. Children who displayed the overdependent syndrome presented quite a different picture of behavior, with excessive clinging to their mothers and crying when left alone. This overdependence on the maternal figure was further revealed in a fear of strangers and the fact that familiar figures were sometimes regarded with suspicion. Thus we have support for the idea that early maternal-child separation has its effects not on the relationship between mother and child, but on behaviors which result from perceptual deprivation.

It is interesting that Schaffer describes the appearance of *both* syndromes in some children over 7 months of age, again indicating that maternal separation may have produced in them both perceptual deprivation and emotional upset as a function of the disruption of an established emotional bond. Schaffer explains the existence of the global syndrome in the following way. Piaget (1950) describes a level of cognitive development in infancy in which self and environment are merged. Schaffer suggests that under a condition of perceptual monotony such as exists in a hospital this natural tendency to merge with the environment is emphasized. When the monotony is reduced on the infant's return home the static perceptual field is disrupted. Such disruption is stressful and may cause somatic upset. Formation of a new perceptual field is necessitated and evidence of this is seen in the intensity with which the infant inspects his surroundings.

Increased Stimulation. So far we have been concerned with the absence or, rather, severe reduction of general stimulation. But what if infants are subjected to stimulation in excess of what they normally receive in the normal process of child-rearing? Some cross-cultural research is suggestive here (Geber, 1958; Geber and Dean, 1957; Whiting and Landauer, 1963). In assessing the development of a large number of African children, mainly from Uganda, Geber (1958) notes their extreme precociousness in the psychomotor area. From the first day after birth the African infant can keep his head from falling back when he is drawn into a sitting position and he can hold his back straight. In the first days of life he can focus his eyes (European infants are unable to do this until they are 8 weeks old), and by 6 weeks he can control his head, regardless of the position in which he is placed. At 4 months he can sit alone, at 8 months stand without support, at 10 months walk, and at 11 months use his thumb and forefinger accurately to pick up small objects. At each level he is 2 or 3 months ahead of the average development of a European child of the same age. In addition, Geber notes that these children display a lively interest in test materials, "talk" to the examiner, and smile in excess of what one would expect from their European counterparts.

This accelerated development Geber attributes to the massive stimulation which all infants receive from the time of birth. A Ugandan infant is never left alone by his mother but carried on her back, often with skin-to-skin contact, wherever she goes. In addition, he sleeps with her and is fed on demand by her. He is stimulated by her at her various occupations, hears all her conversations, is the subject of her warm and loving affection, and is often offered to others to hold. Geber suggests that the precocity she observed is not attributable solely to the advanced state of development of these children at birth. For children raised in the European way did not show a similar acceleration in development after the first month of life. Moreover, while most children were suddenly and dramatically weaned and often separated geographically from their mothers, with an accompanying reduction in social responsivity and liveliness, those who were weaned less suddenly maintained their lively behavior.

Landauer and Whiting (1963), having noted the effects of stress on physical development shown by studies with animals, located a number of societies in the Human

Relations Area Files in which various stressful procedures were involved in customary infant-rearing practices. These procedures included: (1) pain; (2) shaping, usually for cosmetic reasons; (3) extreme heat; (4) extreme cold; (5) administration of emetics or irritants; (6) abrasion, for example, scraping with shell; (7) intense stimulation such as subjecting to loud noises; (8) binding, for example, painful swaddling. Adult males were, on the average, 2 inches taller in these societies than in societies where early stress was not imposed. The correlation between intensity and frequency of stress and male adult height was $+.33$ $(p < .01)$. In addition, the effects on adult stature seemed to be produced maximally during the first 2 years of life.

Gunders (cited by Whiting, 1965) noted that in the animal studies on stress, whenever animals were stressed or stimulated, they were taken away from their mothers for a variable period of time. Thus she hypothesized that a crucial factor might be an event associated with separation from the mother. Assessing separation in the first 2 weeks of life, based on amount of physical contact with the mother, handling by others, and use of a wet nurse, she found a correlation of .53 $(p < .01)$ between separation and adult male height.

Landauer and Whiting did attempt to control for genetic, climatic, and nutritional variables in their study. However, we cannot discount the possibility that there is no causal relationship between early stress and adult height. It may be that stressful infant-rearing practices tend to occur in societies where hardship and stress are generally common. Thus, although early stress might not increase mortality rate, the general hardships of life might result in a strong selection against small size and physical weakness. Perhaps, too, early maternal separation, as defined by Gunders, might occur in societies where life is generally more difficult.

We do not yet know whether extremely massive stimulation is harmful. The animal data suggest it ought to be. But, so far, no researcher has reported the existence of child-rearing practices which subject a child to stimulation that is too great for optimal development.

Experimental Manipulation of General

Stimulation. A few attempts have been made to test experimentally the notion that early perceptual stimulation, in the form of handling, rocking, and stroking, is important for human development. Hopper and Pinneau (1957) investigated the effects of additional stimulation on regurgitation. If Ribble was correct in suggesting that stimulus feeding decreases the incidence of gastrointestinal disturbance, they reasoned, these effects should be revealed in a decrease in regurgitation. Twenty-one mothers were asked to spend at least 10 minutes more than usual before each feeding handling, rocking, swinging, rolling on the bed, fondling, tickling, and bouncing their infants. The diversionary explanation given to these mothers was that some experts feel such stimulation should be associated with an advance in speech development. At the end of 2 weeks the amount of regurgitation in the experimental babies was compared to that of the 21 controls who had not received the additional handling. According to the mothers' reports, although regurgitation was significantly reduced for both groups, there was no statistically significant difference as a function of the extra stimulation. Although the mothers supplied Hopper and Pinneau with data on incidence of vocalization, these are not reported.

More promising results have been obtained by Ourth and Brown (1961), White and Castle (1964), and Casler (1965). Ourth and Brown conducted their study in a hospital nursery with newborn infants. The 20 neonates in the experimental group were provided with extra handling at feeding time by either their mothers, the experimenter, or a nurse. This consisted of 60 minutes of firm support, fetal positioning, and mild, rhythmic stimulation, and was carried out, on the average, for 4½ days. The experimental group, compared to a control group receiving routine care stripped of all unessential attention, cried less both immediately before and during feeding sessions. A somewhat inelegant feature of the design, however, was that all the experimental infants were breast fed while all the controls were bottle fed. Thus we might conclude not that extra handling reduces upset but that infants who are breast fed cry less than those who are bottle fed. Ourth and Brown suggest the infants in their control group were disturbed because of a sudden reduction in stimulation to which they had become accustomed as fetuses. For experimental babies the additional stimulation was more nearly like the kind and amount provided in the fetal environment by the walking, breathing, and changing position of the mother.

To assess the effect of handling on visual exploratory behavior, White and Castle (1964) gave infants in a state hospital 20 minutes of extra rocking daily for between 6 and 36 days. During rocking the infants' eyes were covered with a blindfold to control for a possible increase in visual experience. When they were tested at the age of 37 days infants who had been rocked spent a greater proportion of their waking time attending to and exploring their visible environment than did those who had not received the additional experience. There was no difference between the two groups in the development of prehension, rate of weight gain, or general health. The difference in visual attention gradually declined with time, probably because of the monotony of the visual surround, but both groups exhibited a sharp increase in visual attention at a time when they were relocated in a more complex environment.

Casler (1965) provided eight institutionalized babies with additional tactile stimulation beyond the amount ordinarily provided by the institution. The importance of this particular sensory mode was suggested to him, among other things, by Harlow's work on contact comfort. Children who were under 1 year of age at the beginning of the experiment, and who had given no indication that they were brain-damaged, received 20 minutes of stimulation, 5 days a week, for 10 weeks. The experimenter looked at the child's midsection, said "Hello, baby" every 60 seconds, and stroked any part of his skin not covered by clothing except the hands and mouth region. A control group was treated in the same manner except that the tactile stimulation was omitted. (The experimenter's verbalization was employed to keep the attention of children in the control group.) At the end of the experimental treatment all children were tested on the Gesell Developmental Schedule as they had been just before the beginning of the experiment. Both groups had declined, perhaps because of the deprivation of other kinds of stimulation in the institution. The decline of the experimental

group, however, except for the motor subtest, was one half that of the control. Thus the tactile stimulation seemed to have improved functioning in the areas of sensorimotor adjustment, eye-hand coordination, capacity to start new adjustments in problem situations, language development, feeding ability, self-dependence in play, and cooperativeness. It is unfortunate that interpretation of the results of this study are made difficult by the fact that the tactile stimulation was administered by a social agent. For it is possible that, if stroking is reinforcing, the experimenter who did it became secondarily reinforcing. The experimental subjects may then have been made more socially responsive, through stimulus generalization, to other adults around them. And this increased responsiveness might have been revealed in faster learning and better performance on a developmental test. The results of a study in which tactile stimulation is provided by a machine would, as Casler notes, be most interesting.

The Existence of a Critical Period for General Stimulation. The existence of a critical period in animals for general stimulation has been previously documented. We have little evidence that such a critical period either exists or does not exist for humans. The only study which suggests that it might, at least for some functions, is that of Whiting and Landauer (1963). For additional evidence we must wait for more research.

Chemical and Nutritional Manipulations

Attempts to improve intellectual functioning by chemical means have been frequent and have generally been aimed at individuals functioning at the lower end of the intellectual continuum. But, except for mental deficiencies such as phenylketonuria, which result from known biochemical lesions, the results have not been promising.

Glutamic acid is the compound that has received the greatest attention as a possible agent for improving intellectual functioning. During the late 1940s and early 1950s innumerable studies appeared with the majority supporting the hypothesis that glutamic acid therapy has a beneficial effect on intellectual performance among the retarded. (These studies have been reviewed by Astin and Ross, 1960.) Most of the supporting studies, however, suffered from methodological inadequacies, whereas those that were better designed were, almost without exception, negative in their results. Thus it is evident that a specific effect of glutamic acid on intellectual functioning has yet to be demonstrated.

Vitamins, particularly B_1 and E, have also received considerable attention in the treatment of mentally deficient children (e.g., Rudolf, 1950; Giudice, 1961). None of the reported studies, however, have included suitable control groups. Studies on the effects of tranquilizers such as chlorpromazine and reserpine, and of stimulants, have not suggested that these drugs facilitate intellectual functioning (see review by Louttit, 1965). Albert-Gasorek and Argrett (1961) administered chorionic gonadotrophin to sexually immature mentally retarded boys and found a small but statistically significant increase in intellectual functioning as compared with a group of placebo controls. They attributed the increase in IQ at least in part to an increased basic metabolic rate.

By far the most gratifying results in the chemical and nutritional treatment of mental deficiency have come from the investigation of phenylketonuria. Phenylketonuria is transmitted as a recessive characteristic from a single autosomal gene, and is associated with the excretion of phenylpyruvic acid in the urine and marked elevation in phenylalanine blood levels. These large amounts of phenylalanine reflect an inability to metabolize this amino acid, and are due to a block in the major route of phenylalanine metabolism, hydroxylation to tyrosine. Evidence suggests that the lesion is a marked deficiency in a liver enzyme, so that phenylketonuria may be considered primarily a hepatic disorder with the accompanying mental retardation a secondary effect (Udenfriend, 1961). The mechanisms underlying this secondary effect are unclear. Treatment consists of putting the phenylketonuric on a diet low in phenylalanine to reduce and maintain serum phenylalanine at a low level. If the diet is introduced during the early months of life the chances are good that the individual will develop normally. The longer the delay in instituting treatment, however, the less effective it will be (Lyman, 1963).

Enrichment and Restriction

Institutions do not provide a great deal in the way of general, massive stimulation. Institutions are deficient, too, in the kinds of *specific* learning opportunities they provide for their occupants. Clearly, much of the developmental and intellectual retardation described by Spitz, Goldfarb, and others is due to the restricted and unstimulating environments in which the children they studied lived.

Nor are unstimulating environments confined to orphanage and hospital settings. Retardation in home-reared children who are provided with inadequate learning opportunities in their own families has also been reported. Coleman and Provence (1957), for example, describe two children raised in deprived family settings who were retarded in growth, gross motor development, language, social functioning, and in the ways they reacted to people and toys. Clarke and Clarke (1954) indicate that mentally retarded children who come from poor and unstimulating homes show an increase in IQ once they are institutionalized. Children who come from good homes, on the other hand, do not show this change. It is evident that dogmatic statements about the ill effects of maternal deprivation often disregard the hazards a child may suffer from having a bad mother or an indifferent mother substitute.

In addition to looking at enrichment and restriction in institutional settings we shall also discuss the extensive literature on the effects of nursery school on child development. The preschool, with its emphasis on creativity and on the development of motor, language, physical, and intellectual skills, is a device favored by many to provide a child with a stimulating environment. The hope is that he will benefit from the experience with accelerated development and that this acceleration will have enduring effects. Some have cautioned that the good effects of nursery school may be offset by the harmful effects of maternal separation which preschool attendance necessitates. Glass (1949), however, found no support for the notion that nursery care for the child around 2 is harmful. She reports only slight differences in eating, sleeping, elimination habits, and behavior problems between children of working mothers who attended a day nursery for 6½ to 10 hours daily and a control group who were cared for at home by their own mothers. The slightly greater proportion of problem behavior in the nursery school children, she suggests, was due to the existence of problems in the home which probably caused the child's need for day care in the first place.

Heinicke (1956) compared two groups of 2-year-olds who were experiencing their first maternal separation. One group was composed of children in a residential nursery school and the other of children in a day nursery school. Children in the residential nursery tended to show greater and more prolonged upset at separation from their mothers. Some of them also refused to recognize their parents when they visited after an absence of 3 weeks. The children in the day nursery, on the other hand, reacted in a normal fashion to their parents when they came to take them home at the end of the day. Loss of sphincter control, hostility, active affection-seeking, and an increase in auto-erotic behavior were observed in residential children. These behaviors were not seen in the day nursery children. On the basis of the two studies, then, we must conclude that the effects of short-term maternal separation which nursery school entails are nothing like those which longer-term maternal separation produces.

Institutionalization and Restriction of Experience. The deprived environment of many institutions and the restricted opportunities they allow for learning have been discussed previously. Provence and Lipton (1962) describe at length the shortness of time spent in actual care of an individual infant and the lack of personalized care. Infants in the institution they studied were fed, changed, and bathed on schedule, regardless of any particular need state they might or might not be experiencing at the time. In her observation of institutional and home-reared infants, Rheingold (1961) reports that 44% of her observations were made while home children were being cared for. Only 15% of observations of orphanage children were made where they were receiving care. Home children received much more of certain kinds of stimulation such as being talked to, fed, and played

with. Orphanage children received the same kind of stimulation, but less of it. The two sets of infants spent equal amounts of time in play but had different kinds of toys. Home children were provided with a wide assortment of stimulating toys, whereas institution children were forced to resort to their own hands, clothing, and bars of their cribs.

The severe reduction in social stimulation which an institution provides has been emphasized by Zigler and his associates (Zigler, 1966) as a nonintellective factor affecting intellectual performance of institutionalized children. They suggest that a child who desires social interaction because he is deprived of it may modify his performance on intellectual tasks as a result. If being correct means a child's interaction with an adult will be terminated, he may continue to be wrong. The perseveration noted in institutionalized children (Green and Zigler, 1962) may also reflect this increased motivation for social interaction. Thus the conditions of social impoverishment in an institution may tend to make a child look dull. On the other hand, we would also expect that social deprivation could lead to faster learning where social reinforcement was made contingent on good and efficient performance.

Modification of the Usual Institutional Environment. In a study of three Iranian orphanages Dennis (1960) notes the advantages of the better care which was given in one of them. In the deprived orphanages, conditions were similar to those we have described as typical. The children in these were retarded in sitting alone and in the onset of locomotion. Most of them, prior to walking, locomoted by scooting rather than creeping. In the third institution, however, the children were frequently handled, held in an attendant's arms while they were fed, propped in a sitting position, and frequently placed in a prone position. In spite of the fact that these children were probably initially more retarded than those observed in the first two institutions, their motor development resembled that of most home-reared infants.

Earlier, Dennis and Najarian (1957) had suggested that the poorer performance of orphanage children on the Cattell infant scale was due to their lack of opportunity for learning motor skills which the test demands. Dennis and Sayegh (1965) reasoned that if orphanage children were accustomed to sitting in an upright position, if their interest in objects were encouraged, and if·their skill in object manipulation were developed, their performance on the test should be much improved. Five days a week for 15 days they gave 1 hour's ·practice to institutionalized children in sitting and in watching and manipulating objects. This extra stimulation resulted in greater gains in developmental test scores by these children than by children who had not had the extra practice. Thus Dennis and Najarian's hypothesis was supported.

Rheingold (1956) divided 16 6-month-old infants, who had been institutionalized for at least 3 months, into two groups. Children in the experimental group received all their care from the experimenter herself. For 7½ hours a day, 5 days a week for 8 weeks she fed, diapered, soothed, held, talked to, and played with them. The eight control children were looked after according to the routine of the institution, receiving their care from 17 different persons. They were also alone more, being cared for on only 7% of the time sample observations as opposed to 23% for the experimental group. On the Cattell and on tests of postural development and cube manipulation the experimental infants had slightly, but not significantly higher scores than the controls. They were, however, more socially responsive to the experimenter almost at once, and, with time, they became more responsive to other persons as well.

One year later the children, all but one of whom had left the institution, were tested for social responsiveness and developmental progress (Rheingold and Bayley, 1959). The only statistically significant difference between them was that more of the experimental subjects vocalized during the social test. Thus, of the tested behaviors, only language development continued to be affected by the experimental manipulation. This fact suggests that verbal behavior may be more sensitive to the impoverishment of an institution environment than are many other classes of behavior. Rheingold, Gewirtz, and Ross (1959) have demonstrated that the vocal behavior of 3-month-old children can be increased by reinforcement in the form of smiling, auditory, and kinesthetic-tactile stimulation. Presumably attendants in orphanages, unlike mothers caring for their own children, are much too busy to respond to the vocalizations of their charges with smiles and vocalizations of their own. In addition, they offer few stimuli that might evoke vocalization. It is surely this lack of care and encouragement—a reduction in learning opportunities—that accounts for so much of the language retardation of orphanage children.

An early study on the effects of increased stimulation in an institutional setting was done by Skeels and Dye (1939). They shifted infants and very young children from an orphanage to an institution for mentally retarded girls. Here these infants received considerable stimulation and attention from the mildly retarded older girls. These mother-substitutes became very fond of their charges and would even spend part of their very small allowances on them. They trained them in eating and toilet habits and taught them to walk, talk, and play with toys. At the end of 2 years the children had shown, on the average, a 27 point increase in IQ. A control group of children who had been left in the institution showed a decrease in IQ of 26 points.

Positive Effects of Institutional Care. Often institutionalization may provide some benefits home-rearing does not. The Hampstead Nursery (Burlingham and Freud, 1944) is a case in point. It provided wartime homes for children whose family life had been broken up temporarily or permanently because of the war. Although a residential nursey, it was not run in the usual institutional way. Rather, it tried to establish for its residents what they had lost, that is, the security of a stable home and opportunities for individual development. Burlingham and Freud report that infants between birth and the age of 5 months, when not breast fed under either condition, developed better in their nursery than in the average household. This, they suggest, was due to better food and air and the skilled and regular handling of the nursery staff. The nursery children between the ages of 5 and 12 months were more active in watching people and more responsive to their coming and going.[2] They showed greater develop-

[2] This increased responsiveness no doubt reflects the fact that the children were exposed less to adults than are children raised in family homes.

ment in muscular control in the second year of life than home-reared children because they were allowed greater freedom of movement and had more space to play in than home children. Finally, they were better eaters, probably because less stress was placed on eating in the nursery than is usually the case in a home. Parents are very concerned that their children eat properly and this concern produces problems. Among other things, it is possible for children to use eating, or noneating, as a way of effectively manipulating their mothers. Such avenues of manipulation are not open to a child in an institution, where no one really appears to care whether or not he eats.

Even with the enriched environment the Hampstead Nursery offered, however, its residents showed retardation in some areas of development. Children in the second half of their first year were less advanced in reaching out for objects and in active play. Their habit training was slow, probably because staff had less time to spend in intensive training, and many of them lost bladder and sphincter control when they were placed in the nursery. They were also retarded in speech development. Obviously, a child who is in a residential nursery is living in a community of nontalking playmates, where speech is of no immediate help to him in making known his needs and wants.

Between 1947 and 1950 a number of children from Kent were taken into the Mersham Reception Centre. Some were placed there after being removed from their own homes by court order. Others went because they were orphaned or, for some other reason,

---

Thus the appearance of an adult would have greater novelty value for them than for home-reared children. And this novelty would produce more orienting, attending, and investigatory behavior whenever an adult was in the vicinity. It is interesting that observers seem to categorize increased attending to people as either good or bad, depending on whether they are discussing the good or bad characteristics of institutionalization. According to their frame of reference, they may describe the observed behavior positively as "an increase in social responsiveness" or negatively as "an insatiable craving for affection," and "socially immature." That this increased responsiveness can be both facilitating and detrimental is evident from, among other things, our discussion of Zigler's work.

could no longer live at home. Rather than make decisions about placement immediately the authorities felt it better that the children be detained for a while in the center. There they could be given the beneficial experience of a healthier environment, and they could be observed for a period of time so that their needs could be assessed and more appropriate recommendations for placement could be made. Although it is obviously desirable to move a child as few times as possible, it was felt that the drawbacks of a stay in a residential nursery might be offset, in this case, by the benefits of more careful final placement. Unfortunately, since no control group of children who were not admitted to a temporary residential setting was assessed, the study can be considered only a demonstration and the reported results only suggestive. Lewis (1954), who studied the children 2 to 3½ years after final placement, suggests an improvement in the behavior of almost ⅔ of the children. The children who had fared best were those placed in accord with the center's recommendation, either in a foster home, an approved school, or back in their own homes.

Institutionalization of Retardates. There has been some controversy about whether children who display severe mental retardation should be institutionalized (see Centerwall and Centerwall, 1960; Birch and Belmont, 1961). Again, it seems clear that when the institution provides an enriched environment geared to the needs of its residents, including a stable relation to competent adult attendants, and when this environment is better than that provided for the child in his home, significant improvements in aggressive and pathological behavior and in intellectual development will occur (Tizard, 1960).

Nursery School as Enrichment. Numerous attempts have been made to assess the effects, if any, of nursery school attendance on intellectual development. In addition, many investigators have been concerned with the effects of nursery attendance on social and physical development, emotional adjustment, and the learning of motor skills. Not all the studies have been methodologically adequate, for many of them have simply assessed the changes which have taken place over a period of time in children attending nursery school. The better designed studies have included a control group of children who have not attended nursery school and also measured changes in their behavior over the same period of time.

Much of the work on changes in intelligence has been carried out by investigators (e.g., Wellman, 1932; Skodak, 1939) from the Iowa Child Welfare Research Station, as part of a large-scale study of the effect of a number of different environmental conditions on intellectual development. In one study (Skeels, Updegraf, Wellman, and Williams, 1938) a nursery school was set up in an orphanage. Some of the children, who were retarded intellectually, socially, and in language development, were assigned to an experimental group which attended nursery school 6 hours a day. A matched control group was also selected from the orphanage population. The experimental group displayed a dramatic increase in IQ, whereas the control group did not. McNemar (1940) has criticized this study on statistical grounds, but a reanalysis of the data (Wellman and Pegram, 1944) has produced essentially the same results. Generally, consistent improvement in scores on intelligence tests by children attending nursery school has been reported by the Iowa investigators (Wellman, 1945). Moreover, this improvement seems to have been maintained over time. Woolley (1925) and Starkweather and Roberts (1940) have also reported gains in IQ by children attending nursery school at the Merrill-Palmer School in Detroit.

Other studies (e.g., Anderson, 1940; Jones and Jorgensen, 1940; Goodenough and Maurer, 1940), however, have not shown these beneficial effects of nursery attendance. Accordingly, the Iowa studies have been criticized. It has been suggested that the children had been coached by parents or nursery school teachers, that they had been tested so often that they had become practiced at taking IQ tests, and that the testers had been biased by their knowledge that the child was attending nursery school. These criticisms cannot be applied to all the studies, however. For example, in many of the studies the controls had been tested as often as the children who had attended nursery school. Truax (cited by McCandless, 1967) has shown that children without siblings are the ones who gain in IQ in nursery school. It seems that children who have little opportunity to play with other children lack the intellectual and

social stimulation provided by a preschool experience. And it is unlikely that examiner bias would operate differentially between only children and those with siblings.

It is a rather time-wasting exercise, as Truax' study reveals, simply to compare children who have gone to nursery school with those who have not. Any observer is aware of the very large differences that exist between nursery schools. Some offer genuinely enriched and stimulating environments to children who attend. Others are little better than glorified baby-sitting establishments. In most cases there are differences in attitudes and child-rearing practices between parents who want their children to go to nursery school and those who do not. These differences almost certainly mean that children who are tested in a nursery school and children in a control group are not from the same general population. This is not an appropriate criticism, of course, where children are randomly assigned to a preschool and a control group, but this is a condition which can only be met when children are living in institutions. If a child is not doing well in nursery school he may be withdrawn. Thus only those who are improving in performance are left to be tested by the psychologist. Even the most enriched preschool experience may have no effect on a child if he already comes from a very stimulating home environment. Again, the experiences which have proved beneficial for a middle-class child may not be those which will benefit a lower-class child. The deprived child may lack the experience that would enable him to benefit from the conventional nursery experience.

The preschool experience's influence on social development has also been assessed by many (e.g., Jersild and Fite, 1939; Hattwick, 1936; Brown and Hunt, 1961). Again the results are discrepant. These differences may be partly due to the diverse measures of "social adjustment" used by investigators.

It is clear that a more fruitful approach to assessing the effects of preschool attendance will come from research which relates these results to a specific aspect of the nursery experience. These aspects include the physical setting, the program, teacher-child relations, peer-group interaction, and personality characteristics of the individual child. Studies which do this have recently been reviewed by

Swift (1964). In essence, the studies suggest that a program's effectiveness depends on its appropriateness to the child's developmental level and the provision of experiences which supplement instead of duplicate those he is receiving elsewhere. The teacher's qualities are extremely important. She must actively engage in teaching the child new intellectual and social skills. The child's ability to utilize the peer-group aspect of the nursery experience depends on his age, temperament, and the experiences he has at home.

Education of Culturally Disadvantaged Children. Recent concern with the education of culturally disadvantaged children has produced attempts at detailed analysis of what an enriched or deprived environment may involve for a given child. Thus people have begun to try to understand the mechanisms whereby cultural deprivation impairs cognitive capacities and academic achievement. Hess and Shipman (1965), for example, argue that the control which mothers in deprived families employ restricts the number and type of alternatives for action and thought that are open to their children. These mothers use "restricted" rather than "elaborated" styles of verbal behavior (Bernstein, 1961). They say "Shut up" rather than "Would you keep quiet a minute? I want to talk on the phone." Thus the child does not have the opportunity to reflect, consider, and choose among alternatives for speech and action. He develops modes of behavior that are impulsive rather than reflective, present- rather than future-oriented, and disconnected rather than sequential.

In an analysis of the differences in cognitive functioning, linguistic functioning, and mother-child relationships among four different social status groups, Hess and Shipman conclude that deprivation means an environment in which behavior is controlled by rules rather than attention to individual characteristics of a given situation and where no attempt is made to teach a child about the relationships between two events. "This environment produces a child who relates to authority rather than to rationale, who, although often compliant, is not reflective in his behavior, and for whom the consequences of an act are largely considered in terms of immediate punishment or reward rather than future effects and long-range goals" (1965, p.

885). Presumably, a preschool program should be designed to develop in a child those behaviors which this kind of child-rearing makes difficult.

More precise analysis of deprived environments has led to the creation of a number of research projects concerned with the effects of preschool environment on culturally disadvantaged children. Gray and Klaus (1965) describe the culturally disadvantaged child in the following terms. They suggest that he receives less reinforcement for his behavior, especially from adults, that the reinforcement he does receive is probably not verbal, that he is urged "to stay out of trouble," and that the reinforcement he does get is diffuse rather than focused precisely on the adequacy of his performance. This last contention is supported by the findings of Zigler and Kanzer (1962). As a result, only a small part of the behavior of these children is under the control of adult verbal direction, their exploratory tendencies are inhibited, and, in general, they are not responsive to verbal reinforcement. Zigler and de Labry (1962) have also found that lower-class children are not motivated simply by being correct. They learn as rapidly as middle-class children, however, if they are given material reward. On the basis of their analysis Gray and Klaus have concentrated in their program on studying the development of attitudes to and aptitude for school achievement, the development of delay of gratification, some aspects of perceptual development and cognition, and language.

Both Gray and Klaus (1965) and Deutsch (1962) have worked with parents, as well as with children, in a "total push" program. Hodges, McCandless, and Spiker (1966), on the other hand, have developed a program to which only children are exposed. So far, the results of these experimental programs have been encouraging, with at least early gains in IQ reported. McCandless (1967), however, reports his impression that children given enriched training continue to improve only if they stay in demonstration programs or are placed in schools that enroll children from all socioeconomic levels. If they are returned to a school where the students come from an equally impoverished background, they lose their initial momentum. Teachers in this situation, appalled by the lack of essential skills possessed by the majority of their students, apparently tend to concentrate on this majority and to ignore those from the demonstration school projects. Hence students from such projects coast and rapidly lose their initial advantage.

Manipulation of the Social Environment: Social Development in Humans

The Development of Social Attachments: A Learning Analysis. In order to understand the effects of maternal separation per se we should first understand the development of social attachments under normal conditions. For some time the popular method of accounting for this development involved an emphasis on the mother-child feeding relationship (e.g. Sears, Maccoby, and Levin, 1957). Because the mother's presence was always associated with the reduction of primary drives, particularly hunger, she supposedly acquired secondary reinforcing properties. Thus the child found her reinforcing, that is, he became attached to her. The emphasis on the feeding situation, almost to the exclusion of other situations in which mother and child interact, was dictated primarily by psychoanalytic theory and its concern with the oral drive.

Sucking as the *basic* response underlying social attachment has recently been questioned. Human infants during the first $1\frac{1}{2}$ years of life frequently form specific attachments to individuals who never participate in routine caretaking activities (Ainsworth, 1963; Schaffer and Emerson, 1964b). Harlow's work, discussed elsewhere in this chapter, has demonstrated that contact comfort is a more important antecedent of attachment, at least in rhesus monkeys, than is feeding. The question of the importance of contact comfort or clinging in the development of human social responsiveness, however, remains unanswered. It is certainly clear that human mothers present a surface to their infants that is less supportive of clinging than do mother rhesus monkeys. Clinging does not generally appear in infants until *after* specific social attachments have been formed. It seems to become more important when the child becomes mobile, at which time he frequently clings to his mother's hand or skirts. Rheingold and Keene (1963) have observed that the human infant contributes much less to his own transport than do many other mammalian young; that

is, he hangs on less. Schaffer and Emerson (1964b) also report that infants whose mothers employ much physical contact in interacting with their children are no more attached than infants whose mothers rely primarily on other means. These include stimulation by their voice and facial expressions or diversion of attention from themselves through the provision of toys, food, and other objects whenever the infant demands attention.

Rheingold (1961) indicates that a basic and primary activity of the human infant is his visual exploration of the environment. Certain objects attract and hold his attention and the more interesting of these evoke facial, vocal, and bodily responses of delight. The reinforcing effectiveness of complex and changing stimulation has frequently been documented (e.g., Berlyne, 1958). One of the most interesting objects in the infant's environment, from the standpoint of complexity, is the human face, with its shiny and nonshiny surfaces, its bumps and contours. Hence we would expect that a face would be even more likely than other objects to elicit vocalization, smiling, and reaching out—all behaviors which are considered indicants of social responsiveness. Furthermore, unlike stuffed teddy bears and rattles, human faces generally respond to a child's evident delight by changing expression and vocalizing. Thus the child's social behaviors may be further increased in frequency by reinforcement through this stimulus change. In addition, the infant quickly discovers that it is the humans in his environment who are capable of providing him with stimulation and stimulus change from inanimate objects. They are the ones who move his carriage, who carry him around, who turn on the television, and who dangle various toys in front of him. Evidence supporting this hypothesis that distance receptors may play a more important role than feeding or clinging in the development of social responsiveness in human children has recently been summarized by Walters and Parke (1965).

Schaffer and Emerson (1964b) suggest that there are three stages in the development of social responsiveness. In the first the infant finds that he can receive stimulation from all parts of his environment. In the second he discovers that humans are the best providers of stimulation. This is a phase of indiscriminate attachment where the presence of *any* human will alleviate his distress at social isolation. The third phase, that of specific attachments, begins at the age of 7 months. It is only at this age—Piaget's sensorimotor stage IV— that we see the beginning of object conservation. Before this a specific social object has no meaning for the infant apart from its presence, and so it is not missed in its absence. Upset at separation from the mother, Schaffer hypothesizes, begins only at an age when the infant begins to search for objects that have been removed from his perceptual field. That 7 months is the point where specific attachments are formed is evident from data provided by Schaffer and Callender (1959). Children hospitalized after 7 months bitterly protest separation from their mothers and cling to them during visits. They display negativism toward hospital staff and are frightened of them. This behavior is interspersed with intervals of withdrawal and subdued behavior. Infants hospitalized before 7 months of age do not protest separation. They accept strangers as mother-substitutes without a change in their usual level of responsiveness (except for a noticeable absence of vocalization), and they adjust to radically different feeding routines with no apparent difficulty.

Schaffer (1963) provides evidence indicating that a phase of indiscriminate attachment is necessary before specific attachments can be formed. He compared two groups of hospitalized infants. Members of one group received very little stimulation, although they were visited by their mothers. The second group's members had been exposed to tuberculosis and were institutionalized for vaccination. This group received a great deal of stimulation from the many nurses who cared for them, although they were not visited by their own mothers. All the children were at least 30 weeks of age when they were reunited with their mothers. Those in the first group who had received little social stimulation took much longer to form a specific attachment to their mothers than did those who had received a great deal, even though this stimulation was not from their own mothers. Thus it would appear that general social stimulation must be provided before specific attachments can be formed. Prolonged exposure to the individual with whom the specific attachment is eventually formed is not necessary. Only the total amount of stimulation appears to be important.

Differences in social responsiveness between home- and institution-reared infants are especially understandable in terms of deprivation of social stimulation. Rheingold (1961) found 3- and 4-month-old infants in institutions were more socially responsive to a strange experimenter than were home-reared children. The institutionalized children gave the observer more consistent attention, smiled more readily at her, smiled, vocalized, and reached out toward her more often, and gave her fewer negative responses. Over the period of observation they vocalized with increasing frequency, whereas home children decreased their frequency of vocalization. The institutional children were certainly more deprived of social stimulation than are home-reared children. The high frequency and intensity of their social responding would seem to reflect this deprivation. They may also have been learning that strong responding was necessary in order to keep an adult near them. In addition, home-reared children probably were able to discriminate between their own mothers and a strange observer. Since many of the positive cues generally associated with the mother would be missing, the strength of their accustomed responses would be diminished. A child raised in an institution by a number of different caretakers could not so easily discriminate a stranger from a non-stranger. The increased social responsiveness in institutional children in the form of prompt attention when anyone entered their nursery and the poor discrimination between a regular attendant and a stranger's face have also been noted by Provence and Lipton (1962).

Smiling at a stationary, unsmiling human face does not occur in institutional infants until they are around 14 weeks old, and it reaches its maximum at 17 to 20 weeks of age. Home-reared children smile much earlier (6 to 10 weeks), with modal smiling occurring between 11 and 14 weeks (Ambrose, 1961). Smiling is probably more frequently elicited and reinforced among home-reared than institutional children; hence its earlier appearance. Again, home-reared children may learn to discriminate sooner between a familiar and a strange face. Thus they would sooner cease smiling at a face that had not been associated with reinforcement in the past.

Imprinting and the Development of Social Attachments. As indicated earlier, the similarity between imprinting and the development of social attachment in human infants has led a number of investigators to treat them as identical processes. Gray (1958) suggests that smiling in human infants is the motor equivalent of following responses in animals below the higher primates, whereas Caldwell (1962) proposes that the motor equivalent is the visual following response. Scott (1963b) maintains that any response which leads to prolonged contact with the maternal figure at the proper time will be important in the development of social attachment. He also indicates that an intense emotional experience, whether rewarding or punishing, will increase the formation of attachment. Thus Fisher (1955) found that puppies displayed attachment to a human with whom they had had only painful physical interaction if no other social contact was made available to them. We are reminded here of the observation (Lewis, 1954) that some children who have been severely neglected by their parents still display concern for those parents. It is also true, however, that, although the material needs and social training of these children have been neglected, they have generally received affection from their parents. Similarly, although Fisher punished his dogs, he may also have provided some gratification for them in the form of perceptual stimulation.

Bowlby's (1958) analysis of the attachment process is also greatly influenced by the work of ethologists. He suggests that sucking, clinging, and following are instinctual responses which keep an infant in close contact with his mother. These unlearned behaviors mature at different times during the first year of life and thus are centrally important at different times. In addition, crying and smiling on the infant's part serve to elicit maternal behavior from the mother, toward whom they are directed, and thus keep her in her infant's presence. Bowlby, however, does not present the conditions for attachment in a way that suggests that learning is not involved. Using certain assumptions from associative learning theory, Cairns (1966b) has proposed that mammalian attachment behavior is determined solely by the length of association with

an object in a given context and the relative cue weight of the object. Certainly this is an alternative conceptualization to a secondary reinforcement theory which must be considered.

If there exists a critical period for imprinting it seems too that there could well be a critical period for the development of social attachment in humans. Gray places it between 6 weeks and 6 months, beginning with what he suggests is the onset of learning ability, continuing with the smiling response, and ending with the development of fear of strangers. A similar position is taken by Scott (1963b). Although the period of 6 weeks to 6 months—the "period of primary socialization"—is critical for the formation of social relationships, Scott suggests that later ages are also critical with regard to psychological damage resulting from breaking off these relationships. The word "critical" now begins to lose much of the meaning with which it has been generally endowed.

Imprinting is a phenomenon whereby an organism learns to make social responses to objects to which it has been continually exposed. In nature this is usually to its own species, and it does not refer to attachment to a particular member of that species. Hence we are left somewhat in the dark as to whether there is a critical period for a generalized, nonspecific attachment to the human species, or whether it is for *specific* attachment to a given individual or individuals. Again, the idea that a devloping fear of strangers marks the end of the socialization period is made rather less satisfactory by the finding that stranger anxiety is *not* in a one-to-one relationship with either attachment or separation anxiety (Ainsworth and Wittig, in press; Ainsworth, 1963; Benjamin, 1963; Schaffer and Emerson, 1964b, Tennes and Lampl, 1964). Children who are attached may display no fear of strangers. Again, a fear of strangers may occur in a child before he actually develops a specific attachment. The intensities of the two phenomena—attachment and fear of strangers—do not coincide. Clearly, at the moment, the critical period hypothesis needs further clarification, as do the developmental mechanisms which might be involved in it.

Situations in which the Formation of Specific attachments Is Impeded. Infants in institutions are obviously deprived of the opportunity to form a specific attachment to a single caretaker. If, for present purposes, we adopt a secondary reinforcement theory, we may also say they have less chance to learn that people in general are reinforcing because they receive less caretaking. If the responses they make to social stimuli are not reinforced, these responses may, through habituation, soon disappear. Under normal rearing conditions most children must also learn to make certain operant responses like crying or reaching out in order to receive certain gratifications. If caretaking in an institution is given so that the child has no control over what happens to him—if reinforcement is not contingent on anything he does—he may soon appear quite socially unresponsive. All these conditions are encompassed in a description by Ainsworth and Wittig (in press) of the variables in mother-infant interaction which seem to foster both the growth of healthy attachment and of competence. These include (1) frequent and sustained physical contact, especially during the first year of life, together with the mother's ability to soothe her infant's discomfort through physical contact, (2) the mother's sensitivity to her baby's signals and her ability to time her interventions with his rhythms, (3) an environment where the infant feels he has some control over what happens to him, (4) the mutual delight which mother and baby take in their transactions with each other.

Institutions vary in the extent to which they support social responsiveness and competence. Even where attempts are made to provide intensive and personal care, however, the quality of emotional interchange may be limited. Nurses are reluctant to become too involved with children from whom they know they will be separated (David and Appell, 1961). The institution Rheingold (1961) studied was supportive to the extent that its occupants were socially responsive to a stranger. Others may provide less optimal conditions for learning. Provence and Lipton (1962) describe an institution in which the children showed little cooing or crying in response to people, where they showed a decreasing tendency over time to reach out for or move toward people and toys, and where they displayed no playful activity with others. The children were generally bland in affective expression and unafraid of strangers. When they were in distress they failed to turn to an adult—they gave no sign that they anticipated or expected that a need would be met. If something unpleasant was being done to them they only cried miserably, but made no attempt to push away from the noxious event. In this institution, whose environment is described in extensive detail in the report, there was an absence of specific maternal care, very little time was spent in actual care, and none of it was personalized. Children were fed and changed, not when they wanted it, but according to routine. Many of their distress signals went unanswered so that opportunities for learning the source of comfort were few. Feeding, diapering, changing of position, and being given a toy were done on schedule. Only occasionally were these related to the child's wishes. Clearly any behavior which the child might use to gain attention was extinguished, since care was independent of anything he did. And any secondarily reinforcing qualities adhering to caretakers must have been quite minimal in light of the restricted caretaking that was provided.

Provence and Lipton also report that the children were atypical in their approach to toys. They showed no preference for one over another, were not displeased at the loss of a toy, and made no attempt to recover it. They suggest that a normal infant invests toys with some of the feeling he has developed for his mother. Presumably, feelings of attachment to a mother might generalize to an inanimate object. It is also possible, however, that the impoverished environment offered by the institution produced retardation in the development of the concept of object constancy. These children may have been behaving like younger ones who, when a toy disappears from their surroundings, act as if it no longer exists. The children also rarely displayed any self-stimulating activities, except for rocking. Thumb-sucking and the mouthing of toys and other objects were rarely observed. Perhaps a mother must first make a child aware of the gratification of tactile stimulation before the child himself will reproduce it.

Provence and Lipton suggest the effects of institutionalization on social behavior are irreversible. Although the children improved dramatically after foster home placement, they were still impaired in utilization of the mother as a source of comfort, relief from tension, and help in problem-solving. They were indiscriminately friendly, and had problems in impulse control and ability to delay gratification. It may well be that the critical period for the establishment of emotional ties to a single individual had passed. Without a specific emotional attachment the internalization of parental standards is difficult, both because the process of identification with parental prohibitions is weakened and because the child has no need to maintain parental approval by performing the behaviors they want him to. On the other hand, it may be that there still had not been sufficient learning opportunities for impulse control and seeing the mother as a source of gratification by the time of the follow-up. These would be opportunities the children had been almost totally denied in the institution. Then, too, adults may find it difficult to tolerate a social behavior in an older child which they would accept and try to modify in a younger one. Thus foster parents may not provide the same learning conditions for older children from an institution that they would younger children. Again, the explanation may be a genetic one. As we have suggested earlier, children in an institution probably do not constitute a random sample from the general population. The genetic constitution of the children Provence and Lipton observed may have predisposed them to display aggressive, uncontrolled behavior.

One of the features of institutional care is that it provides interaction with many caretakers. Even if an institution's conditions were such as to provide excellent conditions for the learning of social behavior, it might be that the diffusion of attachment over a number of individuals could be detrimental to optimal behavioral development. If a young organism does not learn the components of an emotional attachment to a single mother-figure, he may have difficulty in forming anything but superficial attachments to others. Hence the indiscriminate friendliness which Goldfarb, Provence and Lipton, and others have noted.

Studies of children raised in Israeli kibbutzim are relevant here. From early infancy these children are placed in a nursery where they are cared for, along with a number of other children, by a substitute mother-figure, the *metapelet*. The *metapelet* is responsible for the everyday care and training, including impulse control, of the children. Their own mothers, who visit regularly and may even breast-feed their children for several months, seem primarily responsible for affectional gratification. Rabin (1958) found some evidence for developmental retardation among infants in the kibbutzim, which he attributes to a lesser total amount of stimulation than is ordinarily provided in family homes. Studies at later ages, however, suggest that these children are in no way retarded intellectually nor do they display any personality distortions. Rabin suggests they display better emotional control and greater maturity and ego-strength than children raised with their own families. There has been some suggestion that children who have lived all their lives on a kibbutz tend to lack emotional depth. Although they are capable of maintaining satisfactory relationships with their peers, there is a tendency for all relationships to be on the same level. It may be true, then, that one must learn how to form an intense emotional relationship with a single mother-figure before intense relationships with others can be formed in later life.

Other data on multiple mothering have been provided through the study of children in home-management houses—training centers for students of home economics. Typically, many students provide care, in turn, for these infants before they are placed in foster or adoptive homes, usually within 5 or 6 months. There is always a house mother available who provides some continuity in mothering. Follow-up studies of these children, at least in the preschool years, suggest no damage to them as reflected in their response to frustration or brief maternal separation (Gardner, Pease, and Hawkes, 1961) or in personality development (Gardner, Hawkes, and Burchinal, 1961).

In a study comparing children raised in "monomatric" families (where the mother was the exclusive caretaker of her infant) with those reared in "polymatric" families (where the infant was cared for by more than one person), Caldwell et al. (1963) found no difference between the two groups of children at 6 months of age. At 1 year, however, the infants from the monomatric families were more active, more emotionally dependent on their mothers, and more emotional in their interactions with their mothers. Mothers in monomatric families, however, had earlier been found to be more affectionate, active, sensuous, playful, and vocal with their infants, and more concerned with their well-being than mothers in polymatric families. Thus the observed differences in the behavior of the two groups of children might well have been due to their mothers' personality differences, rather than to the number of caretakers with which they were provided.

An unusual study of six German Jewish orphans (Freud and Dann, 1951) provides evidence that lack of a consistent mother-figure is not necessarily detrimental to the formation of social attachments. After their parents had been killed, these children had arrived at the same concentration camp when they were a few months old. After that, they were always together as a group. Because they were in a deportation camp their caretakers changed very often. When they were taken to England they were observed to have a most unusual emotional dependence on each other. All their positive feelings centered exclusively on their own group, where there was almost complete absence of jealousy, rivalry, and competition. Since they had experienced most of their satisfactions in each other's presence, they appeared to have developed the kind of attachment for each other that children raised in more normal environments have for their own mothers. Moreover, they soon came to make positive approaches to the adults who continuously looked after them in England. These responses were very similar to the approaches they made to each other.

Maternal Separation after a Specific Attachment Has Been Formed. The reaction of a child over 6 months of age to separation from his mother has been described by a number of observers (Bowlby, 1958; Robertson and Bowlby, 1952; Roudinesco, David and Nicolas, 1952; Spitz and Wolf, 1946). Typically, there are three stages. The first involves active protest and entails much crying and physical agitation. The second stage is one of despair with withdrawal and monotonous crying. The final stage is one of detachment. Here all adults are treated socially but casually and on the same level. The child appears preoccupied with material things and no longer seems to care for anyone. It is notable that the first two phases do not appear where the relationship with the mother has previously been severely impaired.

Gewirtz (1961) offers an explanation of this behavior in keeping with a learning analysis of the development of social attachment. He points out that maternal separation involves an abrupt and continuing change in what was earlier a satisfactory pattern of availability of cue and reinforcing stimuli to the child, after these have been conditioned as such for him. The initial response to this change is frustration—an increasing rate of responding and the emergence of emotional responses which are incompatible with the development of new and desirable responses. If the new caretaker is not able to respond to and provide reinforcement for what socially adequate responses the child may produce, these will soon extinguish. We might also suggest that the younger the child, the more restricted his behavioral repertoire and hence the greater his difficulty in producing new and acceptable responses. A period of depression at the loss of a valued object may be followed by apparent recovery from grief. The social detachment the child displays during this phase may well result from the repeated experience of becoming attached to a nurse who eventually leaves. After this happens a number of times, the child no longer becomes upset at separation from a caretaker.

What damage, if any, does a child experience from maternal separation after a specific attachment has been formed? Freud and Burlingham (1944) report that children who were separated from their families and placed in residential nurseries during World War II showed a great deal of initial disturbance, but they also point to the possibility of minimizing personality damage by providing substitute individualized relationships. In a follow-up study of 20 adults who had been placed in residential nurseries as children during the war, Maas (1963a, 1963b) found no severe cases of personality pathology. Most of these adults were functioning very well. There was a trend in the data, however, suggesting that separation was more damaging to children less than 1 year old than to those who were more than 1 year old. The former showed a greater incidence of disturbance in the personality-social area as adults. Bowlby, Ainsworth, Boston, and Rosenbluth (1956) report that children who had spent some time in a tuberculosis sanitarium before 4 years of age did show tendencies toward withdrawal, apathy, and aggression. They did not, however, show a disturbance in their capacity to establish relationships with their peers. In summary, then, the data do not suggest that every child who is separated from a figure to whom he has become attached will suffer irreversible damage. That some damage may occur, if the separation is not handled well and a suitable new environment is not provided, cannot be ruled out.

GENOTYPE AND EARLY EXPERIENCE

As we have suggested, any change in an organism's behavior produced by some environmental manipulation must also be conditioned by its genotype. Depending on how the genotype is constituted, an early experience may have a large effect or no effect at all, one that is permanent or one that is transient. Behavior, like any other chaacter—morphological or physiological—has hereditary determination at least in respect to many of its formal, measurable aspects.

It is obvious enough, of course, that many of the *content* aspects of behavior depend completely on environment, for example, the fact that one person speaks German and another Russian. However, the ease with which one individual, as compared to another, learns to speak a language (either as a native language or a foreign one) may be heavily influenced by genotype. Learning ability, in other words, is probably inherited. Evidence for this conclusion comes mostly from animal studies using both the method of selection and the method of strain differences (see Fuller and Thompson, 1960; Hirsch, 1967).

Since early environmental experiences must be retained by some learning or storage mechanisms, we may expect to find that the susceptibility of an organism to change as a result of environmental manipulation should vary according to genetic constitution. That is, some individuals may be expected to be strongly buffered, others weakly buffered.

Empirical evidence bearing directly on this point has been put forward by a number of workers. Hughes and Zubek (1956), using the McGill "bright" and "dull" rat strains selected by Thompson (1954), were able to show that dulls much more than brights showed improvement in maze performance as a result of glumatic acid treatment during infancy. A subsequent study by the same au-

thors (Hughes and Zubek, 1957) further demonstrated that the effect produced was fairly long and lasting, extending over a period of several months. Hughes and Zubek (1956) suggested that possibly dullness was due to a selected metabolic error relating to neural functioning and ACh activity for which exogenous glutamic acid provided some compensation.

Genetically selected maze ability is also differentially responsive to early environmental—as against chemical—manipulation. Cooper and Zubek (1958) were able to show that dulls gain much more than brights in Hebb-Williams maze ability as a result of exposure to enriched early experience. In a restricted environment, however, brights lose much more than dulls. These data are summarized in Table 3. They show that both strains are

Table 3. *The Effects of Enriched and Restricted Environmental Rearing on Maze Performance in "Bright" and "Dull" Rats (McGill Strains). Hebb-Williams Maze Error Scores Are Shown*

	Rearing Conditions		
	Normal Cage	Enriched	Restricted
Bright	117.0	111.2	169.7
Dull	164.0	119.7	169.5

equally susceptible to phenotypic changes but only in one direction. This presumably means that selection produced animals representing, respectively, the upper and lower limits of rat intelligence.

A study bearing more directly on this point was carried out by Thompson and Olian (1961). This has been referred to previously. Briefly, the data showed that the effects of administration of adrenalin to pregnant mice of three strains had effects on offspring activity level that varied with genotype. Offspring from the normally high-active strain—C57-BL/6s—showed reduced activity; those from the usually low-active A/Jax mothers showed increased activity over controls; and those from BALB/Ci mothers were not altered. These results suggested that the BALB genotype is rather strongly buffered as compared to the C57 and A/Jax genotypes. The general finding that an early treatment tends to increase the activity of the less genetically active strain and lower that of the genetically more active strain has been confirmed by DeFries (1964) and DeFries and Weir (1964). It is of some interest to note, however, that in the DeFries study C57s were the more active, but in the DeFries and Weir study BALBs were the more active strain under control conditions. This was ascribed to differences in the testing situation used in the two experiments. Whichever strain was the lower-active showed the increase as a result of treatment and whichever was the higher-active showed the decrease. Finally, DeFries (1964) showed that hybrids, which were normally more active than either of the pure strain animals, responded differentially to prenatal stress depending on the genotype of the mother. This involvement of maternal as well as fetal genotype was further demonstrated by DeFries, Weir, and Hegmann (1967). They studied effects on offspring activity of exposure of pregnant mothers to cold, shaking, noise, or adrenalin chloride. Differences in activity-level were found between the effects of physical and those of chemical stress. The two types of stress also interacted differently with genetic factors. The results of the studies outlined above as well as those of other investigators (King and Eleftherion, 1959; Lindzey, Lykken, and Winston, 1960; Levine and Wetzel, 1963; Levine and Broadhurst, 1963; Lindzey and Winston, 1962; Henderson, 1966a) indicate clearly that genetic differences exist with respect to buffering.

At the human level, fewer data are available. It was suggested by Kallman (1953) that schizophrenia—a syndrome he considered to be dependent on a single recessive gene—could be expressed or not depending on what he called a nonspecific constitutional defense mechanism having itself a polygenic basis. Thus a homozygous recessive individual might manifest schizophrenia in response to severe stress or not, depending on the strength of the defense system. A similar notion has recently been put forward—albeit in somewhat different terms—by Meehl (1962). This writer hypothesized that the various symptoms of schizophrenia will always appear in what he designated as the schizotaxic person, who carries the genes for the basic neural-integrative defect underlying the disease, provided there is also exposure to an unfavorable environment, and provided also that there is a low inherited capacity for resistance to stress. If these conditions are not all fulfilled, according to Meehl, schizophrenia will not appear, although the basic personality organization underlying it may be manifested in a well-compensated form. These ideas have received a good deal of support from Gottesman and Shields' (1966) analysis of their own and other workers' data. They conclude that a large proportion of cases of schizophrenia may be polygenically determined, the expression of the disease depending on the number of genes present and also on the amount of environmental stress. It would be useful to have further data implicating early experience variables.

These are interesting notions and intuitively make sense. It does indeed seem likely that many individuals who have a basic inherited disposition to some abnormality and who are exposed to environmental stress favoring its expression may still be protected by some secondary defense system which is itself also genetic. Unfortunately, however, no conclusive data directly bearing on such an assertion are available. One set of observations made by Bentley Glass a number of years ago (1954) is perhaps suggestive of the kind of work that badly needs to be done. His interest was in what he called "adaptability," the process by which living organisms make appropriate adjustments to changing environmental conditions. It is a concept similar to "buffering" but of a more evaluative character. To study it empirically, Glass observed the responses made by members of identical twin pairs in a visual-motor task—hitting a target with a needle—under normal conditions and under conditions of mild stress. The mild stress consisted simply of the ingestion of five cups of hot or cold coffee. Some of Glass' data are summarized in Fig. 13. The plots indicate a striking qualitative and quantitative similarity between twins under both the normal and stress conditions. This suggests that "adaptability" or responsiveness to some environmental treatment is indeed genetically conditioned. Obviously, as Glass himself has pointed out, these results are very preliminary and more data will be needed before any firm conclusions can be drawn. Nonetheless, the method seems to

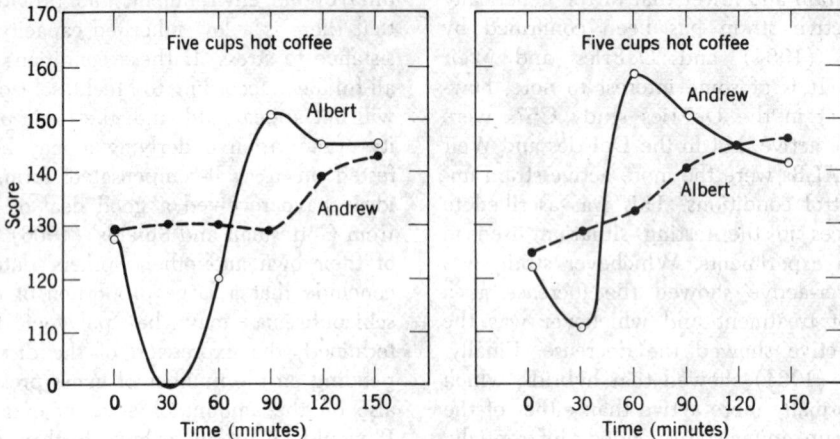

Fig. 13. The similarity of effects of a mild stress on visual-motor performance in a pair of identical twins. In the left graph, Albert drank the coffee; in the right one, Andrew drank it. (Glass, 1954.)

be capable of shedding considerable light on the problem we are discussing.

Granting that buffering and adaptability are genetically based, we may still inquire as to the exact nature of the genetic mechanisms involved. Lerner (1954), in a discussion of this problem, has suggested two main possibilities. First, it may be a property of degree of homozygosity—either in general or at specific loci. That is to say, it may have to do with heterosis or hybrid vigor. Data gathered by Winston (1964) give quite direct support to this alternative. This investigator compared the amount of behavioral change induced by early sound trauma in inbred mouse strains with the amount produced in hybrids between them. The hybrids turned out to be less readily influenced than the parental strains—a result which the author ascribed to heterosis.

On the other hand, there is the second possibility: buffering may be caused by particular genes at specific loci. The cogency of this notion is suggested first by the fact that differences may readily be found between inbred strains which are not known to differ in degree of heterozygosity. Indeed, if such differences do exist, it is unlikely they could be large enough to exert very much influence. Furthermore, it has been shown that buffering may be a character susceptible to selection. Sines (1959, 1961) was able to select a strain of rats that showed higher susceptibility to stomach ulcers following stress. The

females of the susceptible line showed, over the three generations of selection (up to F_2), a more rapid response, the percentage of individuals manifesting ulcers rising from 68% in the base population to 96% in the F_2 generation. It is not certain, however, whether this result was due to fixation of specific genes or to loss of heterozygesity. In the absence of either control or nonvulnerable lines, no firm conclusion can be drawn concerning the genetic mechanisms involved in the specific case of buffering. A long-term project has been undertaken by the senior author of this chapter to specify more exactly the genetic basis of susceptibility to early environmental manipulations. Preliminary results indicate that it is indeed possible to select lines strongly or weakly buffered against the effects of stimulation in infancy.

This brief sketch hardly does justice to the large body of literature relevant to the problem under discussion. For more detailed exposition the reader is referred to Chapter 2 of this book. All we wish to establish here is that genetic factors play a most important part in determining the magnitude and direction of the effects of early experience.

THEORETICAL MODELS OF EARLY EXPERIENCE EFFECTS

As we have already emphasized, there has been a marked poverty of theoretical treatment of early experience effects. Attempts that have been made have either been too broad to have real predictive power, or else they have been pitched to a level dealing with only particular sectors of the problem. We have suggested that two critical problems are involved: (1) the specification of those mechanisms by which the residua of an early experience may be stored, that is, mode of acquisition as a function of age; and (2) the specification of those properties of young systems that may affect long-term retention of any changes that are induced, that is, long-term memory as a function of age. We may deal with these questions in terms of physiological or behavioral categories.

Many of the theoretical positions attempting to deal with the first question have been descriptive in the sense that they have specified periods critical for certain types of storage on the basis of direct (or indirect) data rather than on the basis of any postulated developmental properties. Most psychoanalytic theories on early experience effects belong to this category in that they hypothesize the seriatim appearance of different "stages" during which environmental events imposed on the organism may be expected to have certain specific outcomes. Thus during the oral stage, matters pertaining to the mouth, the ingestion of food, or biting, have a special importance for determining certain aspects of personality. The ages at which these stages are located can only be loosely specified and, indeed, their occurrence and nature are based only on casual kinds of empirical data. Nevertheless, they accord generally with common sense and have apparently proved useful within the framework of practical psychoanalytic treatment. Within the framework of science, they must be regarded as having uncertain status; but the general underlying idea behind them—the proposition that the organism is constituted differently at different ages and therefore susceptible to certain kinds of influence and not others—is an entirely credible one.

This notion has, of course, had wide favor in the literature dealing with development in animals. Its most popular application has been in connection with the age at which social attachments are just made—in particular, in the matter of imprinting in avian species. As we have indicated, Lorenz (1935) conceived of a very brief period—perhaps a few hours duration in ducks, geese, and chicks—during which a very rapid, one-trial learning occurred, this having irreversible consequences. However, neither Lorenz nor other workers of similar persuasion have stated why this type of learning is most salient at this time as opposed to other ages, or why it should have such permanent effects. The implication has been that (1) before this time neither the motor nor sensory system is mature enough to allow retention of such information, and (2) events occurring first will exert a much greater influence than events occurring later—a primacy hypothesis. The first of these ideas has been stated formally by Hess (1959) in a model which we have already discussed. Whatever its empirical validity—and it does appear to have some—his model has considerable merit in that it makes an explicit attempt to go beyond a simple descriptive definition of the sensitive period and, instead, to specify those developmental variables that should make a certain age critical for certain types of storage.

Another worker who has attempted to search for mechanisms underlying so-called initial periods has been Margaret Vince (1959, 1960). From her studies of learning in juveniles of several species, she has obtained data suggesting that young birds are more highly motivated in the sense that they respond with more vigor both to familiar and slightly unfamiliar objects. However, they show less ability to inhibit responses which are not rewarded. Vince interpreted this to mean that "internal inhibition," in the Pavlovian use of the term, becomes more "stable" with age up to a point, beyond which it starts to decline again. A summary of her results is presented in Fig. 14. Admittedly, these data are difficult to interpret; but they do suggest that a research focus on inhibitory processes may contribute much to our understanding of critical periods in development.

Extensive use of the critical period concept has been made by Scott and his coworkers at Jackson Laboratory, Bar Harbor. The stages of development as he has outlined them for dogs are summarized in Table 4 (Scott, 1962) together with those educed by Nice (1943) for the song sparrow. It should be emphasized that both these schemes are based not on any theoretical notions about the nature of development, but rather on em-

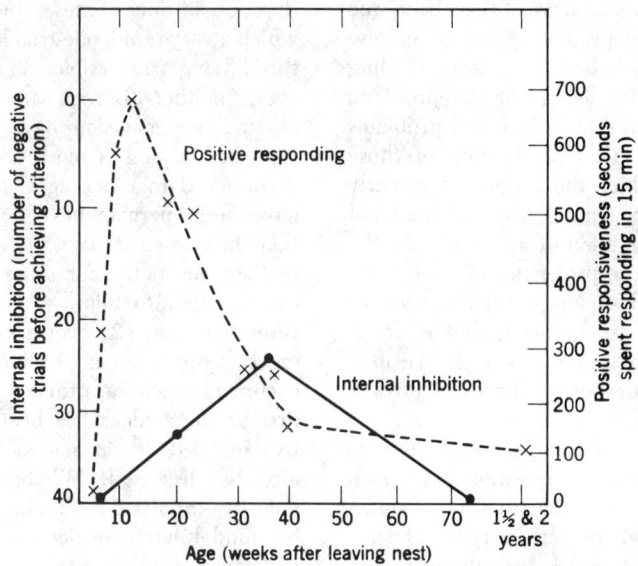

Fig. 14. Positive responsiveness and internal inhibition in some avian species as a function of age. (Vince, 1960.)

pirical data, particularly those relating to socialization. We have already discussed a sample of the extensive work done on this problem by Scott and his colleagues.

We should note, at this point, that not all workers have found the critical period concept to be useful in dealing with early experience effects. Schneirla and Rosenblatt (1963), in particular, have felt that its acceptance implies a nativism not in line with the facts about development. Their work on kitten behavior has suggested that the emergence of various patterns of behavior at certain ages depends not only on maturational factors but also strongly on factors of learning and experience that have gone on before—particularly those occurring as a result of highly standardized situations, for example, the female litter situation. Thus the apparent fixity of developmental sequences is derivable from

Table 4. Periods of Development for the Dog and the Song Sparrow.

Name of Period	Puppy Length of Period (weeks)	Initial Event	Name of Period	Song Sparrow Length of Period (days)	Initial Event
I. Neonatal	0-2	Birth, nursing	Stage 1 (nestling)	0-4	Hatching, gaping
II. Transition	2-3	Eyes open	Stage 2	5-6	Eyes open
III. Socialization	3-10	Startle to sound	Stage 3	7-9	Cowering—first fear reactions
			Stage 4 (fledgling)	10-16	Leaving nest— first flight
			Stage 5	17-28	Full flight
IV. Juvenile	10-	Final weaning	Stage 6 (juvenile)	29-	Independent feeding

both environmental and genetic factors working together rather than from genetic factors alone. This point of view, as Scott (1963) has pointed out, is not by any means completely antithetical to the critical period notion. Nonetheless, its emphasis on the importance of learning is certainly a useful one.

Another theory we have previously mentioned dealing with formation of early social attachments but not involving the idea of critical periods has been presented by Cairns (1966b). This is directed mainly to explaining the data on lower mammals but presumably has applicability to human infants as well. Starting from an Estes-type of position, the theory proposes that any object or class of objects that appears frequently in combination with other environmental or organismal events comes to have importance in maintaining a variety of maintenance behaviors such as ingesting and sleeping. The presence of the object then comes to be necessary for the stability of such response systems; its absence produces disruption of such responses. The greater probability of animate rather than inanimate objects figuring in such "attachments" is attributed to their greater salience and attention-getting characteristics. As Cairns suggests, the methodology implied by the model involves detailed analysis of the reciprocal behaviors involved in social attachments and focusing on approach and withdrawal responses rather than on general state variables such as emotionality and temperament. Cairns has initiated a program of work along these lines and deals in two papers (Cairns and Johnson, 1965; Cairns, 1966a) with the consequences of social attachment formation within and between species (lambs and dogs).

Two other models dealing with the effects of early experience have slightly different orientations. Brookshire, Littman, and Stewart (1961), on the basis of a study on the effects of early trauma in rats, have put forward a three-factor theory according to which an early experience may have three kinds of residual: a "pure-shock effect," acquired fear," and "instrumental-habit." Presumably the salience of each of these in determining of the type outcome of a trauma will depend on the age at which the trauma occurs. However, the authors did not concern themselves directly with any relevant dimensions of development,

and hence were not able to relate their three types of residua to any particular critical ages. In spite of this lack, the model is an interesting one and has considerable heuristic value.

Denenberg (1964) has formulated a model specifically to deal with the quantitative relation between amount of early stimulation and ensuing changes in emotionality. He has postulated, first, a monotonic relation between the two variables such that the greater the degree of stimulation, the *less* emotional the animal. Such a proposition initially appears to contradict the large amount of data showing bidirectional changes in treated animals. Denenberg has explained these by reference to the Yerkes-Dodson effect, suggesting that performance on a task will be a function of level of motivation (or emotionality) and degree of task complexity. The situation is diagramed in Fig. 15. What it means, essentially, is that depending on the nature of the task, a certain range of early stimulation can produce increasing or decreasing linear or bidirectional effects. Such a conclusion certainly makes a good deal of sense. However, the logic of the initial postulate seems questionable. It makes little sense to suppose that severe traumatic shock imposed on a very young animal is going to result in extreme docility. In fact, almost the opposite point of view has been considered quite plausible by Salama and Hunt (1964). The matter probably will only be settled when those theorizing about the relation in question can agree on adequate operational definition of the variables involved.

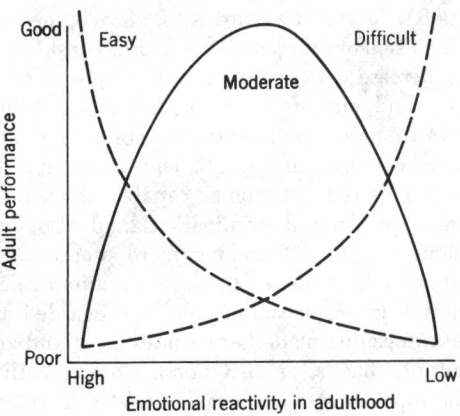

Fig. 15. Theoretical relationship between adult performance and level of emotionality for tasks of varying degrees of difficulty. (Denenberg, 1964.)

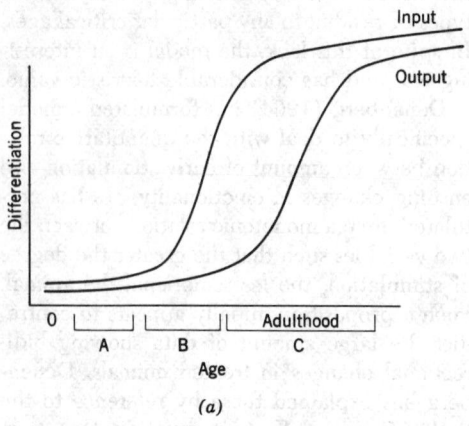

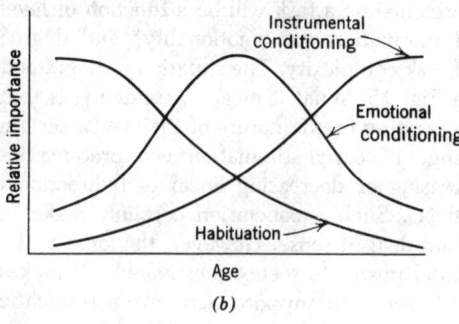

Fig. 16. (a) Input and output differentiation as a function of age. (b) Storage mechanisms salient at different ages, as predicted from a. (Thompson, 1966.)

The next schema to be considered is one that has been proposed by Thompson (1966, 1968). Its starting point is the developmental dimension of differentiation. This is considered to increase with age both on the input or sensory and output or motor sides, but it increases more rapidly in the case of the former, as schematized in Fig. 16. Thus an organism, as it gets older, becomes capable of making finer and finer discriminations and also becomes capable of making more precise and articulated responses to these discriminanda. Now learning or storage may be regarded as an association made between an input and an output, that is, an S-R bond. Consequently, the model states that some kinds of learning will be more probable at certain ages than at others. At a very young age, it will be undifferentiated input-undifferentiated output; at a somewhat later age, differentiated input-

undifferentiated output; and still later, differentiated input-differentiated output. These three types of storage are considered to correspond, respectively, to habituation-sensitization; classical or emotional conditioning; and instrumental or operant learning. It will be noted also that these categories are very similar to those suggested by Brookshire et al. (1961) referred to previously. However, they are derived directly from an application of a developmental dimension rather than a priori or empirically and could have been specified without the aid of any of the nomenclature of learning theory.

The author has further suggested that there must then exist three major developmental periods of age-zones, during each of which any given experience will have certain special outcomes according to the learning involved. These age-zones are described as follows:

1. The "temperament adaptation zone." During this time the organism, through the processes of habituation and sensitization, learns a characteristic level and range of responsiveness—not to any particular cues, but to the environment in general. Hence the category "temperament" seems most able to encompass the kinds of behavioral effects produced.

2. The "affective-meaning zone." Since input is relatively differentiated at this time (by definition), the organism can learn to respond to cues—but only in an undifferentiated manner. Storage that occurs under these conditions would seem to relate most closely to classical or emotional conditioning—that is, the attachment of emotional responses, positive or negative, to specific cues or cue categories. This period should be characterized by the formation of social attachments, of likes, dislikes, and so forth.

3. The "instrumental-meaning zone." During the third age zone, response differentiation becomes relatively high, thus resulting in the domination of storage by means of instrumental learning. The young organism no longer merely reacts to the world passively but can now commence to cope with it by means of specific, well coordinated acts.

These three stages or age zones may relate to age in a somewhat variable manner, depending on environmental factors and also on the genotype of the species involved. However, if the postulates concerning differentiation and its relation and development are correct, their order of occurrence should be invariant. The approach is thus epigenetic in the sense that the influences of both environment and motivational factors are recognized.

This model and the others we have considered, however, provide little information concerning the importance of early environmental events. It seems commonsensible, as we have already suggested, to suppose that young organisms are in some sense more plastic and therefore register the contingencies of environment with more permanence than do older animals. However, it must also be recognized that notions like plasticity, liability and the like are not only vague in character but also double-edged in the sense that they imply not only ease of entry of information but also perhaps the equal ease of loss of it. The senior author has hypothesized that, whatever the empirical data may finally show, the developmental dimension of growth is probably relevant to the problem under consideration. Growth was defined earlier in terms of increments in the quantity of the system or of the subsystems that make it up that occur directly as a function of age. Such increments may be taken to represent an increasing redundancy, which might be expected to affect the buffering characteristics of an organism. We might expect that a less redundant (and hence less well buffered) system would be more sensitive to the impact of some environmental event than one more strongly buffered; that is to say, it would be more strongly and permanently changed by any given early experience. However, whether any differences should imply more permanence of effects on the part of the less buffered cannot easily be decided by logical analysis. The important collection of essays edited by Wolstenholme and O'Connor (1961) deals directly with this problem; but the data cited by the various authors of those essays fail to yield any very clear-cut solution.

Granting, however, that such concepts as plasticity, lability, and buffering may have some value in formulating broad hypotheses concerning the importance of early experiences, we must recognize that it is also possible to deal with the same problem in a more economical manner without involving any special properties that may accrue to young

as opposed to more mature systems. Development is probably stochastic in the broad sense that the effect of any event occurring at a certain moment is influenced by whatever preceded it in time, either immediately or remotely. This should mean that any changes exerted on an organism very early in its life, provided they are retained for at least a short time, should have a disproportionately larger influence than events occurring at an older age. To give a simple example, a parent may designate his child who accidentally knocks over a glass of milk as "clumsy." This may set up in the child's mind an initial acceptance of the attribution of the trait to himself, which makes more likely the acceptance of it whenever a comparable situation again arises.

The most explicit statement of this kind of hypothesis has been made by Campbell and Jaynes (1966) in their "reinstatement" theory. The model starts from the findings of Campbell and others showing that the long-term retention of conditioned avoidance responses is, if anything, less stable in weanling as compared with adult rats (see Campbell, 1967). If we accept this conclusion that the isolated memory trace is so impermanent in young organisms, then we must account in some other way for the commonsense-based "fact" that early experience is important. The reinstatement notion attempts to do this by appealing essentially to the stochastic nature of development to which we have already referred. Thus it postulates that any given experience in early life will be retained provided only that it is reinstated in a minimal way at intervals. In this manner, it can be maintained at full strength for an indefinite time. Campbell and Jaynes (1966) present data purporting to show this. They compared memory of a conditioned avoidance response in three groups of animals. One group received at 25 days of age an initial trauma consisting of a number of shocks in a black box, plus three further reinstatement exposures to the situation; a second received the original trauma only; and a third received only the reinstatement trials. All groups were tested for avoidance of the black side in a black-white choice box. The first group showed, over a 30-min trial, significantly greater avoidance of the relevant cue. This rather neat experiment nevertheless has a number of flaws: (1) it did not involve any adult control groups; (2) the response involved was a relatively complex one, possibly involving a number of components perhaps differentially susceptible to early manipulation; (3) the first group received more training trials than the other two groups, regardless of how these were spread out in time. In view of these difficulties the paradigm study cannot be regarded as having supplied a very firm basis for the reinstatement model. At the same time, both the general ideas put forward by Campbell and Jaynes and their mode of empirical attack are exceedingly interesting and certainly deserve to be followed up.

Very few attempts have been made to formulate precise physiological theories about the effects of early experience. Bovard (1958) suggested that early stimulation acts as a stressor, having the effect of reducing pituitary-adrenal and sympathetico-adrenal medulla responsiveness to later stress. More centrally, the amygdaloid complex and the hypothalamus would also be involved. Such a notion has received support especially from the work of Levine (1961) and makes a good deal of intuitive sense. At the same time, it is very programmatic in scope and hardly suggests specific hypotheses that can be precisely tested.

The theories we have just discussed are broad enough to encompass both human and animal data, although we have focused mainly on the latter. Points of view geared specifically to human young, apart from those emerging from the psychoanalytic framework, are few and far between. Several have been mentioned in the sections on studies of children. Bowlby (1957, 1958) presented a theory to account specifically for mother-child attachments and the effects of disturbing these by separation. His model combines a psychoanalytic and an ethological approach. Specifically, he suggested that the close relation between mother and child emerges out of a number of unlearned behaviors—sucking, clinging, and following—each of which matures at different times during development. Some acts such as crying and smiling on the part of the baby activate or release various maternal behaviors. Such a point of view has considerable value in its emphasis on biologically based variables important to social relationships in human beings.

A second suggestion we consider to be useful was that made by Casler (1961) in his review of the literature on early experience. He pointed out that almost all studies done on this problem have confounded two kinds of variables. These are perceptual or sensory deprivation and maternal deprivation. The first relates to insufficient amounts or variety of inputs; the second, on the other hand, covers the breaking of an already formed attachment between a mother and a child with all the affective consequences that this implies. Thompson (1958, 1960) and Schaffer (1958) have also made this kind of distinction, as noted by Casler (1961). Further, Schaffer has suggested that perceptual deprivation probably has effects up to about 7 months of age, whereas maternal deprivation comes to be important some time after this age. He and Callender (1959), on the basis of data gathered on 76 infants hospitalized between 3 and 51 weeks, were able to educe two major types of syndromes. One of these was "global" in nature and was characterized by an "unfocused inspection of surroundings." The other, which they called "overdependent," involved strong tendencies to demand maternal attention. The first was associated with hospitalization during the first half-year; the second with hospitalization occurring after this age. The refinement of these notions suggested by Schaffer and Emerson (1964) has already been discussed and need not be reviewed here in detail. It should be noted that these authors use the "stage" concept, their formulation being based essentially on the increasing capacity of an infant to discriminate objects—animate and inanimate—in his environment. They do not deal very clearly, however, as Cairns has tried to do, with the reasons why actual social attachments come about, as distinct from specifying with what objects—animate and inanimate—in his endeal explicitly with the importance of early social relations as possibly providing "rules" for later behavior.

The preceding survey of theoretical developments concerning the early experience problem indicates fairly clearly that work in this area has been heavily oriented toward the amassing of empirical data. Even those models that are available are very programmatic in style and provide only broad guidelines for researchers. There are signs, however, that theorizing is on the increase, and before long the major issues will come to be more sharply defined than they have been up to now.

Conclusions

This chapter has attempted to review the salient lines of empirical and theoretical work done on the problem of early experience. It is clear that the area involves a number of quite diverse convergent traditions out of which have come a large volume of studies but little in the way of primary models that can effectively order the data available or supply to the field the kind of unity and theoretical integrity it needs. The chief reason for this appears to be that too little attention has been paid to analysis and definition of the nature of the basic dimension involved—development. We have pointed out, in agreement with Zigler (1963) and Wohlwill (1964), that age is not an experimentally manipulable variable and, in itself, is empty of any real psychological meaning. It is, however, a variable that is correlated with many other changes which do directly affect behavior. These include both genetics and environmental factors working in conjunction. Together they constitute what we ordinarily mean by the term development; and the passage of time, represented by age, gives them a chance to operate in psychologically significant ways. Thus the expression of certain genes may be so timed that certain types of behavior and certain capacities for discrimination and for articulated response will emerge at particular times. Similarly, between one age and a subsequent one, various environmental events may produce either regularities or irregularities in behavior. Thus a rat at the age of, say, 90 days, may be expected to respond in certain ways to an open-field situation not only because of the maturational processes that have gone on up to that age but also because it has been reared in a cage, exposed to a certain light-dark cycle, fed certain food, and so forth.

It is true that these two sets of variables are very difficult to unconfound and also very difficult to manipulate in the first instance. Certainly, we can vary environmental treatment given to some subjects but we can not do this without altering the rate of various developmental processes. Nor can we vary duration of a treatment independently of the maturational processes that have also been going on.

As a consequence, the study of development involves special problems that need not trouble much of the rest of experimental psychology, dealing as it does with short-term effects of different manipulable variables on adult behavior. As Wohlwill (1964) has pointed out in an incisive review of the problem, many psychologists have felt that the study of development cannot really be regarded as a *primary* field in the same sense that such areas as learning or perception can be. Admittedly, it will be difficult if not impossible to disentangle maturational from environmental variables. Yet this does not mean that regularities in development cannot be found; and we do not have to be committed to a preformist position to suppose that they can (Wohlwill, 1964). Indeed, the work of Schneirla and his colleagues on cats and kittens (Schneirla et al., 1963), focusing as it does on uniformities produced both by genetic and environmental factors in interaction, represents a good case in point.

At the same time, it is clearly necessary that the concept of development be explicated considerably further. We have suggested the kinds of dimension that it must involve; for example, differentiation, growth, and organization. These have so far not had great heuristic value, but this is not to say they might not have were they analyzed in a careful operational maner. It will be particularly desirable to find for them meanings that are more than merely descriptive but are compatible with a genuine experimental framework. The attempt made by the senior author (Thompson, 1966) to distinguish input from output differentiation represents perhaps a step in this direction, since it does give to the term an S-R orientation. How empirically useful this will turn out to be remains to be seen.

Our review of the work done on early experience, both on the level of humans and on lower animals, indicates clearly that the problem is a very viable one; but equally it shows the strong need for more theorizing and a closer liaison between what we have designated as the normative-descriptive and experimental-predictive orientations. Thus while it may be obvious from the large number of studies carried out that early experience is important, it is less obvious how or why this should be so. To comprehend this broad statement in more precise and articulated terms, we will have to understand more thoroughly just what early experience is and what we imply by the term important. This task will, in turn, require theorizing of the kind already suggested.

On the whole, the animal and human data fit well together. Indeed, we might say that their compatibility is greater than it is in most fields, perhaps because the divergence between man and lower species is least during the earliest stages of development. The constructs needed to describe processes of verbal learning and memory storage are very different from those used to describe classical conditioning in a dog. But those needed to descibe those psychological functions appearing in a human infant may also prove to be useful for dealing with the behavior of a newborn kitten or even a rat.

The various theoritical models we have reviewed, though they can hardly match in sophistication and power those elaborated in some other areas of psychology, do suggest that this may be so. Consequently, we may well have, in the area of early experience work, a unique opportunity to provide some very basic principles that will exert a unifying effect on many disparate sectors of the whole field of psychology: between the normative and experimental orientation, between human and animal studies, between a hereditarian as against environmental orientation, and between clinically oriented and general psychology. The fact of development is a fundamental feature of all *living* forms of life. From the simplest plant form to man, all of them have a starting point, grow up, and, in some sense, die. Attention to this basic commonality can be expected to provide rich dividends for the progress of psychology as a whole.

References

Aaronson, L. R., Lehrman, D. S., Rosenblatt, J. S., and Tobach, E. (Eds.) *Development and evolution of behavior.* San Francisco: Freeman, 1966.

Ader, R. The effects of early experience on subsequent emotionality and resistance to stress. *Psychol. Monogr.*, 1959, **73** (2, Whole No. 472).

Ader, R. Effects of early experience and differential housing on behavior and susceptibility to gastric erosions in the rat. *J. comp. physiol. Psychol.*, 1965, **60,** 233–238.

Ader, R., and Belfer, M. L. Prenatal maternal anxiety and offspring emotionality in the rat. *Psychol. Rep.*, 1962, **10,** 711–718.

Ader, R., and Conklin, P. M. Handling of pregnant rats: effects on emotionality of their offspring. *Science,* 1963, **142,** 411–412.

Ader, R., Plant, S. M. Effects of prenatal maternal handling and differential housing on offspring emotionality, plasma corticosterone level and susceptibility to gastric erosions. Paper read at annual meeting, American Psychosomatic Society, New Orleans, La., April, 1967.

Agrawal, H. C., Fox, M. W., and Himwich, W. Neurochemical and behavioral effects of isolation-rearing in the dog. *Life Sciences,* 1967, **6,** 71–78.

Ainsworth, M. D. The development of infant-mother interaction among the Ganda. In B. M. Foss (Ed.), *Determinants of infant behavior.* New York: Wiley, 1963. Vol. 2, pp. 67–112.

Ainsworth, M. D., and Wittig, B. A. Attachment and exploratory behavior of one-year-olds in a strange situation. In B. M. Foss (Ed.), *Determinants of infant behavior.* Vol. 4, New York: Wiley, to be published.

Albert-Gasorek, K., and Argrett, J. M. Fluctuations in intellectual functioning associated with changing sexual maturity. *J. Neuropsychiat.*, 1961, **3,** 85–90.

Alconero, B. B. The nature of the earliest spontaneous activity of the chick embryo. *J. Embryol. exp. Morphol.*, 1965, **13,** 255–266.

Ambrose, J. A. The development of the smiling response in early infancy. In B. M. Foss (Ed.), *Determinants of infant behavior.* New York: Wiley, 1961. Vol. 1, pp. 179–196.

Amsel, A., and Penick, E. C. The influence of early experience on the frustration effect. *J. exp. Psychol.*, 1962, **63**, 167–176.

Anderson, L. D. A longitudinal study of the effects of nursery school training on successive intelligence test ratings. *Yearbook of the National Society for Studies in Education*, 1940. Vol. 39, Part 2, pp. 3–10.

Andrew, R. J. Effect of testosterone on the behavior of the domestic chick. *J. comp. physiol. Psychol.*, 1963, **56**, 933–940.

Antonov, A. N. Children born during the siege of Leningrad in 1942. *J. Pediat.*, 1947, **30**, 250–259.

Armitage, S. G. The effects of barbiturates on the behavior of rat offspring as measured in learning and reasoning situations. *J. comp. physiol. Psychol.*, 1952, **45**, 146–152.

Assali, N. S., and Hammermesz, J. Adrenocorticotropic substances from human placenta. *Endocrinology*, 1954, **55**, 561–567.

Astin, A. W., and Ross, S. Gluamic acid and human intelligence. *Psychol. Bull.*, 1960, **57**, 429–434.

Bakwin, H. Emotional deprivation in infants. *J. Pediat.*, 1949, **35**, 512–521.

Bateson, P. P. G. The characteristics and context of imprinting. *Biol. Rev.*, 1966, **41**, 177–220.

Beach, F. A., and Jaynes, J. Effects of early experience upon the behavior of animals. *Psychol. Bull.*, 1954, **51**, 239–263.

Becker, R. F., and Donnell, W. Learning behavior in guinea pigs subject to asphyxia at birth. *J. comp. physiol. Psychol.*, 1952, **45**, 153–162.

Bell, R. W., and Adams, D. A. Emotionality following handling within the first five days of life in the rat. *Can. J. Psychol.*, 1962, **16**, 234–238.

Bell, R. W., and Denenberg, V. H. The interrelationships of shock and critical periods in infancy as they affect adult learning and activity. *Anim. Behav.*, 1963, **11**, 21–27.

Bender, L. Psychopathic behavior disorders in children. In R. M. Lindner and R. V. Seliger (Eds.), *Handbook of correctional psychology.* New York: Philosophical Library, 1947.

Bender, L. Anxiety in disturbed children. In P. H. Hoch and J. Zubin (Eds.), *Anxiety.* New York: Grune and Stratton, 1950. Pp. 119–139.

Bender, L., and Yarnell, H. An observation nursery: a study of 250 children in the psychiatric division of Bellevue Hospital. *Am. J. Psychiat.*, 1941, **97**, 1158–1174.

Benjamin, J. D. Further comments on some developmental aspects of anxiety. In H. S. Gaskill (Ed.), *Counterpoint.* New York: International Universities Press, 1963. Pp. 121–153.

Berylne, D. E. The influence of the albedo and complexity of stimuli on visual fixation in the human infant. *Br. J. Psychol.*, 1958, **49**, 315–318.

Bernstein, B. Social class and linguistic development: a theory of social learning. In A. H. Halsey, J. Floud, and C. A. Anderson (Eds.), *Education, economy and society.* Glencoe, Ill.: Free Press, 1961.

Bernstein, L. A note on Christie's "Experimental naivete and experiential naivete." *Psychol. Bull.*, 1952, **49**, 38–40.

Birch, H. G., and Belmont, L. The problem of comparing home rearing versus foster-home rearing in defective children. *Pediatrics*, 1961, **28**, 956–961.

Bostock, J. Thieving in childhood. *Med. J. Aust.*, 1961, **1**, 813–815.

Bovard, E. W. The effects of early handling in viability of the albino rat. *Psychol. Rev.*, 1958, **65**, 257–271.

Bowlby, J. The influence of early environment. *Int. J. Psycho-Analysis*, 1940, **21**, 154–178.

Bowlby, J. Forty-four juvenile thieves. *Int. J. Psychol-Analysis*, 1944, **25**, 1–57.

Bowlby, J. Maternal care and mental health. *WHO Monogr.*, 1952, No. 2.

Bowlby, J. An ethological approach to research in child development. *Br. J. med. Psychol.*, 1957, **30**, 230–240.

Bowlby, J. The nature of the child's tie to his mother. *Int. J. Psycho-Analysis*, 1958, **39**, 350–373.

Bowlby, J., Ainsworth, M., Boston, M., and Rosenbluth, D. The effects of mother-child separation: a follow-up study. *Br. J. med. Psychol.*, 1956, **29**, 211–247.

Brattgard, S. O. The importance of adequate stimulation for the chemical composition of retinal ganglion cells during early postnatal development. *Acta. Radiol.*, 1952, Suppl. 96.

Broadhurst, P. L., and Levine, S. Behavioral consistency in strains of rats selectively bred for emotional elimination. *Br. J. Psychol.*, 1963, **54**, 121–125.

Brookshire, K. H., Littman, R. A., and Stewart, C. N. Residue of shock-trauma in the white rat: a three-factor thesis. *Psychol. Monogr.*, 1961, **75** (10, Whole No. 514).

Brown, A. W., and Hunt, R. Relations between nursery attendance and teachers' ratings of some aspects of children's adjustment in kindergarten. *Child Dev.*, 1961, **32**, 585–596.

Burlingham, D., and Freud, A. *Infants without families*. London: Allen and Unwin, 1944.

Cairns, R. B. Development, maintenance, and extinction of social attachment behavior in sheep. *J. comp. physiol. Psychol.*, 1966, **62**, 298–306. (a)

Cairns, R. B. Attachment behavior of mammals. *Psychol. Rev.*, 1966, **73**, 409–426. (b)

Cairns, R. B., and Johnson, D. L. The development of interspecies attachment. *Psychon. Sci.*, 1965, **2**, 337–338.

Caldwell, B. M. The usefulness of the critical period hypothesis in the study of filiative behavior. *Merrill-Palmer Q. behav. Devel.*, 1962, **8**, 229–242.

Caldwell, B. M., Hersher, L., Lipton, E. L., Richmond, J. B., Stern, G. A., Eddy E., Drachman, R. and Rothman A. Mother-infant interaction in monomatric and polymatric families. *Am. J. Orthopsychiat.*, 1963, **33**, 653–664.

Caldwell, D. F., and Churchill, J. A. Learning impairment in rats administered a lipid-free diet during pregnancy. *Psychol. Rep.*, 1966, **19**, 99–100.

Caldwell, D. F., and Churchill, J. A. Learning ability in the progeny of rats administered a protein-deficient diet during the second half of gestation. *Neurology*, 1967, **17**, 95–99.

Campbell, B. A. Development studies of learning and motivation in infraprimate mammals. In H. W. Stevenson, E. H. Hess, and H. L. Rheingold (Eds.), *Early behavior*. New York: Wiley, 1967.

Campbell, B. A., and Jaynes, J. Reinstatement. *Psychol. Rev.*, 1966, **73**, 478–480.

Campbell, B. A., and Pickleman, J. R. The imprinting object as a reinforcing stimulus. *J. comp. physiol. Psychol.*, 1961, **54**, 592–596.

Campbell, B. A., and Riccio, D. C. Cold induced stress in rats as a function of age. *J. comp. physiol. Psychol.*, 1966, **61**, 234–239.

Campbell, D., and Thompson, W. R. Development. *Ann. Rev. Psychol.*, 1968, **19**, 251–292.

Carlson, P. V. The development of emotional behavior as a function of diadic mother-young relationships. Unpublished doctoral dissertation, Purdue University, 1961.

Carmichael, L. The development of behavior in vertebrates experimentally removed from the influences of external stimulation. *Psychol. Rev.*, 1926: **33**, 51–58.

Carmichael, L. The onset and early development of behavior. In L. Carmichael, (Ed.), *Manual of child psychology.* (2nd ed.) New York: Wiley, 1954.

Casler, L. Maternal deprivation: a critical review of the literature. *Monogr. Soc. Res. Child Dev.*, 1961, **26**, No. 2.

Casler, L. The effects of extra tactile stimulation on a group of institutionalized infants. *Genet. psychol. Monogr.*, 1965, **71**, 137–175.

Centerwall, S. A., and Centerwall, W. R. A study of children with mongolism reared in the home compared to those reared away from the home. *Pediatrics,* 1960, **25**, 678–685.

Clarke, A. D. B., and Clarke, A. M. Cognitive changes in the feebleminded. *Br. J. Psychol.*, 1954, **45**, 197–199.

Clarke, R. S., Heron, W., Fetherstonaugh, M. L., Forgays, D. G., and Hebb, D. O. Individual differences in dogs: preliminary report on the effects of early experience. *Can. J. Psychol.*, 1951, **5**, 150–156.

Coghill, G. E. *Anatomy and the problem of behavior.* Cambridge: Cambridge University Press, 1929.

Coleman, R. W., and Provence, S. Environmental retardation (hospitalism) in infants living in families. *Pediatrics*, 1957, **19**, 285–292.

Cooper, R. M., and Zubek, J. P. Effects of enriched and restricted environments on the learning ability of bright and dull rats. *Can. J. Psychol.*, 1958, **12**, 159–164.

Cross, H. A., Halcomb, C. G., and Malter, W. W. Imprinting or exposure learning in rats given early auditory stimulation. *Psychon. Sci.*, 1967, **7**, 233–234.

Darwin, C. *The expression of emotions in man and animals.* New York: Appleton-Century-Crofts, 1872.

David, M., and Appell, G. A study of nursing care and nurse-infant interaction. In B. M. Foss (Ed.), *Determinants of infant behavior,* New York: Wiley, 1961. Vol. 1, Pp. 121–141.

DeBold, R. C., Firschein, W., Carrier, S. C., III, and Leaf, R. C. Changes in RNA in the occipital cortex of rats as a function of light and dark rearing. *Psychon. Sci.*, 1967, **7**, 379–380.

DeFries, J. C. Prenatal maternal stress in mice. *J. Hered.*, 1964, **55**, 289–295.

DeFries, J. C., and Weir, M. W. Open field behavior of C57BL/6J mice as a function of age, experience, and prenatal maternal stress. *Psychon. Sci.* 1964, **1**, 389–390.

DeFries, J. C., Weir, M. W., and Hegmann, J. P. Differential effects of prenatal maternal stress on offspring behavior in mice as a function of genotype and stress. *J. comp. physiol. Psychol.*, 1967, **63**, 332–334.

DeNelsky, Garland Y., and Denenberg, V. H. Infantile stimulation and adult exploratory behavior: effects of handling upon tactual variation seeking. *J. comp. physiol. Psychol.*, 1967, **63**, 309–312.

Denenberg, V. H. Interactive effects of infantile and adult shock levels upon learning. *Psychol. Rep.*, 1959, **5**, 357–364.

Denenberg, V. H. The effects of early experience. In E. S. E. Hafez (Ed.), *The behavior of domestic animals.* Baltimore, Md.: Williams and Wilkins, 1962. (a)

Denenberg, V. H. An attempt to isolate critical periods of development in the rat. *J. comp. physiol. Psychol.*, 1962, **55**, 813–815. (b)

Denenberg, V. H. Critical periods, stimulus input, and emotional reactivity. *Psychol. Rev.*, 1964, **71**, 335–351.

Denenberg, V. H. Animal studies on developmental determinants of behavioral adaptability. In O. J. Harvey (Ed.), *Experience structure and adaptability*. New York: Springer, 1966.

Denenberg, V. H., and Haltmeyer, G. C. Test of the monotonicity hypothesis concerning infantile stimulation and emotional reactivity. *J. comp. physiol. Psychol.*, 1967, **63**, 394–396.

Denenberg, V. H., Hudgens, G. A., and Zarrow, M. X. Mice reared with rats: modification of behavior by early experience with another species. *Science*, 1964, **243**, 380–381.

Denenberg, V. H., Hudgens, G. A., and Zarrow, M. X. Mice reared with rats: effects of mother on adult behavior patterns. *Psychol. Rep.*, 1966, **18**, 451–456.

Denenberg, V. H., and Karas, G. G. Interactive effects of age and duration of infantile experience on adult learning. *Psychol. Rep.*, 1960, **7**, 313–322.

Denenberg, V. H., and Kline, N. J. Stimulus intensity vs. critical periods: a test of two hypotheses concerning infantile stimulation. *Can. J. Psychol.*, 1964, **18**, 1–5.

Denenberg, V. H., and Morton, J. R. C. Effects of environmental complexity and social groupings upon modification of emotional behavior. *J. comp. physiol. Psychol.*, 1962, **55**, 242–246. (a)

Denenberg, V. H., and Morton, J. R. C. Effects of preweaning and postweaning manipulations upon problem-solving behavior. *J. comp. physiol. Psychol.*, 1962, **55**, 1096–1098. (b)

Denenberg, V. H., Ottinger, D. R., and Stephens, M. W. Effects of maternal factors upon growth and behavior in rats. *Child Dev.*, 1962, **33**, 65–71.

Denenberg, V. H., Schell, S. F., Karos, G. G., and Haltmeyer, G. C. Comparison of background stimulation and handling as forms of infantile stimulation. *Psychol. Rep.*, 1966, **19**, 943–948.

Denenberg, V. H., and Whimbey, A. E. Behavior of adult rats is modified by the experience their mothers had as infants. *Science*, 1963, **142**, 1192–1193. (a)

Denenberg, V. H., and Whimbey, A. E. Infantile stimulation and animal husbandry: a methodological study. *J. comp. physiol. Psychol.*, 1963, **56**, 877–878. (b)

Dennis, W. Spalding's experiment on the flight of birds repeated with another species. *J. comp. Psychol.*, 1941, **31**, 117–120.

Dennis, W. Causes of retardation among institutional children: Iran. *J. genet. Psychol.*, 1960, **96**, 47–59.

Dennis, W., and Najarian, P. Infant development under environmental handicap. *Psychol. Monogr.*, 1957, **71**, No. 7.

Dennis, W., and Sayegh, Y. The effect of supplementary experiences upon the behavioral development of infants in institutions. *Child Dev.*, 1965, **36**, 81–90.

Deutsch, M. The disadvantaged child and the learning process: some social, psychological and developmental considerations. Columbia University, New York: Paper prepared for the Ford Foundation "Work Conference on Curriculum and Teaching in Depressed Urban Areas," 1962.

Dispensa, J., and Hornbeck, R. T. Can intelligence be improved by prenatal endocrine therapy. *J. Psychol.*, 1941, **12**, 209–224.

Dolittle, R. F., and Meade, R. The effect of gentling on some psychological and physiological phenomena. Paper read at the meetings of the Eastern Psychological Association, New York, April, 1957.

Doty, B. A., and Doty, L. A. Effects of handling at various ages on later open-field behavior. *Can. J. Psychol.*, 1967, **21**, 463–470.

Doyle, G. A., and Yule, E. P. Early experience and emotionality: the effects of prenatal maternal anxiety on the emotionality of albino rats. *J. soc. Res. Pretoria*, 1959, **10**, 57–66.

Durfee, H., and Wolf, K. Anstalspflege und Entwicklung im 1. Lebensjahr. Z. *Kinderforsch.*, 1933, **42**, 273–320.

Ebbs, J. H., Tisdall, F. F., and Scott, W. A. The influence of prenatal diet on the mother and child. *Milbank mem. Fund Q. Bull.*, 1942, **20**, 35–36.

Eells, J. F. Inconsistency of early handling and its effect upon emotionality in the rat. *J. comp. physiol. Psychol.*, 1961, **54**, 690–693.

Elliot, O., and Scott, J. P. The development of emotional distress reactions to separation in puppies. *J. genet. Psychol.*, 1961, **99**, 3–22.

Fisher, A. E. The effects of differential early treatment on the social and exploratory behavior of puppies. Unpublished doctoral dissertation, Pennsylvania State University, 1955.

Flexner, L. B., and Gellhorn, A. The comparative anatomy of placental transfer. *Am. J. obstet. Gynecol.*, 1942, **43**, 985.

Forgays, D. G., and Forgays, J. W. The nature of the effect of free environmental experience in the rat. *J comp. physiol. Psychol.*, 1952, **45**, 322–328.

Forgus, R. H. The effects of early perceptual learning on the behavioral organization of adult rats. *J. comp. physiol. Psychol.*, 1954, **47**, 331–336.

Forgus, R. H. Influence of early experience on maze-learning with and without visual cues. *Can. J. Psychol.*, 1955, **9**, 207–214. (a)

Forgus, R. H. Early visual and motor experience as determinants of complex maze-learning under rich and reduced stimulation. *J. comp. physiol. Psychol.*, 1955, **48**, 215–220. (b)

Forgus, R. H. The interaction between form pre-exposure and test requirements in determining form discrimination. *J. comp. physiol. Psychol.*, 1958, **51**, 588–591.

Fowler, H., Hicks, S. P., D'Aneto, J., and Beach, F. A. Effects of fetal irradiation on behavior in the albino rat. *J. comp. physiol. Psychol.*, 1962, **55**, 309–314.

Fox, M. W., and Stelzner, D. Approach/withdrawal variables in the development of social behaviour in the dog. *Anim. Behav.*, 1966, **14**, 362–366.

Fraser, F. C. Recent advances in genetics in relation to pediatrics. *J. Pediat.*, 1958, **52**, 734–757.

Fraser, F. C. Methodology of experimental mammalian teratology. In W. J. Burdette (Ed.) *Methodology in mammalian genetics.* San Francisco: Holden-Day, 1962.

Fraser, F. C., Fainstat, T. A., and Kalter, H. The experimental production of congenital defects with special reference to cleft palate. *Neonatal Stud.*, 1953, **2**, 43–57.

Freedman, D. G., King, J. A., and Elliot, O. Critical period in the social development of dogs. *Science*, 1961, **133**, 1016–1017.

Freud, A., and Burlingham, D. T. *Infants without families.* New York: International Universities Press, 1944.

Freud, A., and Dann, S. An experiment in group upbringing. *Psychoanal. Study Child*, 1951, **6**, 127–168.

Fuller, J. L. Transitory effects of experiential deprivation upon reversal learning in dogs. *Psychon. Sci.*, 1966, **4**, 273–274.

Fuller, J. L., and Clark, L. D. Genetic and treatment factors modifying the post isolation syndrome in dogs. *J. comp. physiol. Psychol.*, 1966, **61**, 251–257. (a)

Fuller, J. L., and Clark, L. D. Effects of rearing with specific stimuli upon post isolation behaviour in dogs. *J. comp. physiol. Psychol.*, 1966, **61**, 258–263. (b)

Fuller, J. L., and Thompson, W. R. *Behavior genetics.* New York: Wiley, 1960.

Furchtgott, E. Behavioral effects of ionizing radiations: 1955–61. *Psychol. Bull.*, 1963, **60**, 157–199.

Furchtgott, E., and Echols, M. Locomotor coordination following pre- and neonatal X-irradiation. *J. comp. physiol. Psychol.*, 1958, **51**, 292–294. (a)

Furchtgott, E., and Echols, M. Activity and emotionality in pre- and neonatally X-irradiated rats. *J. comp. physiol. Psychol.*, 1958, **51**, 541–545. (b)

Furchtgott, E., Echols, M., and Openshaw, J. W. Maze learning in pre- and neo-natally X-irradiated rats. *J. comp. physiol. Psychol.*, 1958, **51**, 178–180.

Garcia, J., Kimeldorf, D. J., and Hunt, E. L. The use of ionizing radiation as a motivating stimulus. *Psychol. Rev.*, 1961, **68**, 383–395.

Gardner, D. B., Hawkes, G. R., and Burchinal, L. G. Noncontinuous mothering in infancy and development in later childhood. *Child Dev.*, 1961, **32**, 225–234.

Gardner, D. B., Pease, D., and Hawkes, G. R. Responses of two-year-old children to controlled stress situations. *J. genet. Psychol.*, 1961, **98**, 29–35.

Gauron, E. Infantile shock traumatization and subsequent adaptability to stress. *J. genet. Psychol.*, 1964, **104**, 167–178.

Geber, M. The psychomotor development of African children in the first year and the influence of maternal behavior. *J. soc. Psychol.*, 1958, **47**, 185–195.

Geber, M., and Dean, R. F. A. Gesell tests on African children. *Pediatrics*, 1957, **20**, 1055–1065.

Gebhard, P. H., Pomeroy, W. B., Martin, C. E., and Christenson, C. V. *Pregnancy, birth, and abortion.* New York: Harper and Row, 1958.

Gesell, A. The ontogenesis of infant behavior. In L. Carmichael (Ed.), *Manual of child psychology.* New York: Wiley, 1946.

Gewirtz, J. L. A learning analysis of the effects of normal stimulation, privation and deprivation on the acquisition of social motivation and attachment. In B. M. Foss (Ed.), *Determinants of infant behavior*, New York: Wiley, 1961. Vol. 1, pp. 213–290.

Gibson, J. J., and Gibson, E. J. Perceptual learning: differentiation or enrichment. *Psychol. Rev.*, 1955, **62**, 32–41.

Giudice, A. del. Vitamin E for mental defect. *The Summary*, Shute Foundation for Medical Research, London, Ontario, Canada, 1961, **13**, 1–4.

Glass, H. B. The genetic aspects of adaptability. *Proc. Ass. Res. nerv. ment. Dis.*, 1954, **23**, 367–377.

Glass, N. Eating, sleeping, and elimination habits in children attending day nurseries and children cared for at home by mothers. *Am. J. Orthopsychiat.*, 1949, **19**, 697–711.

Goldfarb, W. Effects of psychological deprivation in infancy and subsequent stimulation. *Am. J. Psychiat.*, 1945, **102**, 18–33. (a)

Goldfarb, W. Psychological privation in infancy and subsequent adjustment. *Am. J. Orthopsychiat.*, 1945, **15**, 247–255. (b)

Goldfarb, W. Variations in adolescent adjustment of institutionally reared children. *Am. J. Orthopsychiat.*, 1947, **17**, 449–457.

Goldfarb, W. Rorschach test differences between family-reared, institution-reared, and schizophrenic children. *Am. J. Orthopsychiat.*, 1949, **19**, 625–633.

Goodenough, F. L. A critique of experiments on raising the I.Q. *Educ. Meth.*, 1939, **19**, 73–79.

Goodenough, F. L., and Mauer, K. M. The mental development of nursery school children compared with that of non-nursery school children. *Yearbook of the National Society for Studies in Education*, 1940. Vol. 39, Part II, pp. 161–178.

Goodpasture, E. W. Virus infection of the mammalian fetus. *Science*, 1942, **95**, 391–396.

Gottesman, I. I., and Shields, J. Contributions of twin studies to perspectives on schizophrenia. In B. A. Maher (Ed.), *Progress in experimental personality research.* New York: Academic Press, 1966. Vol. 3.

Gottlieb, G. Conceptions of prenatal behavior. In L. R. Aaronson, D. S. Lehrman, J. S. Rosenblatt, and E. Tobach (Eds.), *Development and evolution of behavior.* San Francisco: Freeman, 1966. Vol. 1. (a)

Gottlieb, G. Species indentification by avian neonates: contributory effect of pre-natal auditory stimulation. *Anim. Behav.*, 1966, **14**, 282–290. (b)

Gray, J. A., Levine, S., and Broadhurst, P. L. Gonadal hormone injections in infancy and adult emotional behavior. *Anim. Behav.*, 1965, **13**, 33–45.

Gray, P. H. Theory and evidence of imprinting in human infants. *J. Psychol.*, 1958, **46**, 155–166.

Gray, S. W., and Klaus, R. A. An experimental preschool program for culturally deprived children. *Child Dev.*, 1965, **36**, 887–898.

Green, C., and Zigler, E. Social deprivation and the performance of feeble-minded and normal children on a satiation type task. *Child Dev.*, 1962, **33**, 499–508.

Greenbaum, M., and Gunberg, D. L. The effect of neonatal hyperoxia on sexual arousal and emotionality in the male rat. *Anim. Behav.*, 1962, **10**, 28–33.

Gregg, N. McA. Congenital cataract following German measles in the mother. *Trans. opth. Soc. Aust.*, 1941, **3**, 35–46.

Griffin, G. A., and Harlow, H. F. Effects of three months of total social deprivation on social adjustment and learning in the Rhesus monkey. *Child Dev.*, 1966, **37**, 533–548.

Guiton, P. Socialization and imprinting in Brown Leghorn chicks. *Anim. Behav.*, 1959, **7**, 26–34.

Halliday, M. S. Some effects of early experience on exploratory behavior in the rat. *Anim. Behav.*, 1966, **14**, 583.

Haltmeyer, G. C., Denenberg, V. H., and Zarrow, M. X. Modification of the plasma corticosterone response as a function of infantile stimulation and electric shock parameters. *Physiol. Behav.*, 1967, **2**, 61–63.

Halverson, H. M. An experimental study of prehension in infants by means of systematic cinema records. *Genet. psychol. Monogr.*, 1931, **10**, 107–286.

Hamburger, V. Ontogeny of behaviour and its structural basis. *Compar. Neurochem. Proc. Int. Neurochem. Sympos.*, 1962.

Hamilton, H. C. The effect of the administration of sodium bromide on the behavior of the offspring: IV. Emotionality (heredity) and experimentally induced seizures. *J. Psychol.*, 1945, **19**, 17–30.

Hamilton, H. C., and Harned, B. K., The effect of the administration of sodium bromide to pregnant rats on the learning ability of the offspring: III. Three-table-test. *J. Psychol.*, 1944, **18**, 183–195.

Harlow, H. F. The nature of love. *Am. Psychol.*, 1958, **13**, 673–685.

Harlow, H. F. Total social isolation: effects on Macaque monkey behavior. *Science*, 1965, **148** (Whole No. 3670), 666.

Harlow, H. F., Harlow, M. K., and Hansen, E. W. The maternal affectional system of Rhesus monkeys. In H. Rheingold (Ed.), *Maternal behavior in mammals*. New York: Wiley, 1963.

Harned, B. K., Hamilton, H. C., and Borrus, J. C. The effect of bromide administration to pregnant rats on the learning ability of offspring. *Am. J. med. Sci.*, 1940, **200**, 846.

Hattwick, B. W. The influence of nursery school attendance upon the behavior and personality of the preschool child. *J. exp. Educ.*, 1936, **5**, 180–190.

Havlena, J., and Werboff, J. Postnatal effects of control fluids administered to gravid rats. *Psychol. Rep.*, 1963, **12**, 127–131.

Haynes, H., White, B. L., and Held, R. Visual accommodation in human infants. *Science*, 1965, **148**, 528–530.

Hebb, D. O. The effect of early and late brain injury upon test scores, and the nature of normal adult intelligence. *Proc. Am. Phil. Soc.*, 1942, **85**, 275–292.

Hebb, D. O. *Organization of behavior*. New York: Wiley, 1949.

Heinicke, C. M. Some effects of separating two-year-old children from their parents: a comparative study. *Hum. Relat.*, 1956, **9**, 105–176.

Held, R., and Bossom, J. Neonatal deprivation and adult rearrangement: complementary techniques for analyzing plastic sensory-motor coordinations. *J. comp. physiol. Psychol.*, 1961, **54**, 33–37.

Held, R., and Hein, A. Movement-produced stimulation in the development of visually guided behavior. *J. comp. physiol. Psychol.*, 1963, **56**, 872–876.

Held, R., and Schlank, M. Adaptation to disarranged eye-hand coordination in the distance-dimension. *Am. J. Psychol.*, 1959, **72**, 603–605.

Henderson, N. D. Behavioral effects of manipulation during different stages in the development of mice. *J. comp. physiol. Psychol.*, 1964, **57**, 284–289.

Henderson, N. D. Acquisition and retention of conditioned fear during different stages in the development of mice. *J. comp. physiol. Psychol.*, 1965, **59**, 439–442.

Henderson, N. D. Inheritance of reactivity to experimental manipulation in mice. *Science*, 1966, **153**, 650–652. (a)

Henderson, N. D. Behavior shaping in studies of preweaning stress. *Psychon. Sci.*, 1966, **5**, 125–126. (b)

Henderson, N. D. Effects of intensity and spacing of prior stimulation on later emotional behavior. *J. comp. physiol. Psychol.*, 1966, **62**, 441–448. (c)

Henderson, N. D., Eisner, H. C. Effects of preweaning injections of adrenalin on later open-field behavior of rats. *Psychon. Sci.*, 1966, **5**, 91–92.

Henry, K. R. Audiopnic seizure susceptibility induced in C57/BL/6J mice by prior auditory exposure. *Science*, 1967, **158**, 938–940.

Hopner, R. Maternal nutrition and the fetus. *J. Am. Med. Ass.*, 1958, **168**, 1774–1777.

Heron, W., and Anchel, H. Synchronous sensory bombardment of young rats: effects on the electroencephalogram. *Science*, 1964, **145**, 946–947.

Hess, E. H. The conditions limiting critical age for imprinting. *J. comp. physiol. Psychol.*, 1959, **52**, 515–518.

Hess, E. H. Imprinting in birds. *Science*, 1964, **146**, 1128–1139.

Hess, R. D., and Shipman, V. C. Early experience and the socialization of cognitive modes in children. *Child Dev.*, 1965, **36**, 869–886.

Hetzer, H., and Wolf, K. Baby tests. *Z. Psychol.*, 1928, **107**, 62–104.

Hicks, S. P., D'Amato, C, J., and Lowe, M. J. The development of the mammalian nervous system: I. Malformations of the brain, especially the cerebral cortex, induced in rats by radiation: II. Some mechanisms of the malformations of the cortex. *J. comp. Neurol.*, 1959, **113**, 435–470.

Himwich, W. A. Biochemical and neurophysiological development of the brain in the neonatal period. In C. C. Pfeiffer and J. R. Smythies, *International Review of Neurobiology*, 1962. Vol. 4, pp. 117–159.

Hinde, R. A., and Spencer-Booth, Y. The behavior of socially living Rhesus monkeys in their first two and a half years. *Anim. Behav.*, 1967, **15**, 169–196.

Hinde, R. A., Spencer-Booth, Y., and Bruce, M. Effects of 6-day maternal deprivation on Rhesus monkey infants. *Nature*, 1966, **210**, 1021–1023.

Hirsch, J. *Behavior-genetic analysis.* New York: McGraw-Hill, 1967.

Hockman, C. H. Prenatal maternal stress in the rat: its effects on emotional behavior in the offspring. *J. comp. physiol. Psychol.*, 1961, **54**, 679–684.

Hodges, W. L., McCandless, B. R., and Spicker, H. H. The development and application of a diagnostically-based curriculum for culturally deprived preschool children. Washington, D.C., *U.S. Office of Education Research Proposals*, 1964–1966.

Hoffman, H. S., Schiff, D., Adams, J., and Searle, J. L. Enhanced distress realization through selective reinforcement. *Science*, 1966, **151**, 352–354. (a)

Hoffman, H. S., Schiff, D., Adams, J., and Searle, J. L. Behavioral control by an imprinted stimulus. *J. exp. Analysis Behav.*, 1966, **9**, 177–189. (b)

Hopper, H. E., and Pinneau, S. R. Frequency of regurgitation in infancy as related to the amount of stimulation received from the mother. *Child Dev.*, 1957, **28**, 229–235.

Hooker, D. *The prenatal origins of behavior*. Lawrence: University of Kansas Press, 1952.

Hudgens, G. A., Denenberg, V. H., and Zarrow, M. X. Mice reared with rats: relations between mothers' activity level and offsprings' behavior. *J. comp. physiol. Psychol.*, 1967, **63**, 304–308.

Hughes, K. R., and Zubek, J. P. Effect of glutamic acid on the learning ability of bright and dull rats. *Can. J. Psychol.*, 1956, **10**, 132–138.

Hughes, K. R., and Zubek, J. P. Effect of glutamic acid on the learning ability of bright and dull rats: II. Duration of the effect. *Can. J. Psychol.*, 1957, **11**, 182–184.

Hull, C. L. Principles of behavior. New York: Appleton-Century-Crofts, 1943.

Hunt, J. McV. The effects of infant feeding frustration upon adult hoarding in the albino rat. *J. abnorm. soc. Psychol.*, 1941, **36**, 338–360.

Hunt, J. McV. Intelligence and experience. New York: Ronald Press, 1961.

Hutchings, D. E. Early "experience" and its effects on later behavioral processes in rats: III. Effects of infantile handling and body temperature reduction on later emotionality. *Trans. N.Y. Acad. Sci.*, 1963, **25**, 890–901.

Hymovitch, B. The effects of experimental variations in early experience in problem-solving in the rat. *J. comp. physiol. Psychol.*, 1952, **45**, 313–321.

Ingle, D. J., and Fisher, G. T. Effects of adrenalectomy during gestation on size of adrenals in new-born rats. *Proc. Soc. exp. Biol. Med.*, 1938, **39**, 149–150.

Isaac, W., and Baker, E. J. A changing effect of cortical ablation with age. *J. comp. physiol. Psychol.*, 1963, **56**, 167–168.

Jaynes, J. Imprinting: the interaction of learned and innate behavior. I. Development and generalization. *J. comp. physiol. Psychol.*, 1956, **49**, 201–206.

Jennings, H. S. *Behavior of the lower organisms*. New York: Columbia University Press, 1915.

Jensen, G. D., and Tolman, C. W. Mother-infant relationship in the monkey *Macaca nemestrina*: the effect of brief separation and mother-infant specificity. *J. comp. physiol. Psychol.*, 1962, **55**, 131–136.

Jersild, A. T., and Fite, M. D. The influence of nursery school experience on children's social adjustments. *Monogr. Soc. Res. Child Develop.*, 1939, No. 2.

Joffe, J. M. Emotionality and intelligence of offspring in relation to prenatal maternal conflict in albino rats. *J. genet. Psychol.*, 1965, **73**, 1-11.

Johnson, R. H., and Haines, W. J. Extraction of adrenal cortex hormonal activity from placental tissue. *Science*, 1952, **116**, 456–457.

Jones, H. E., and Jorgensen, A. P. Mental growth as related to nursery school attendance. *Yearbook of the National Society for Studies in Education*, 1940. Vol. 39, Part II, pp. 207–222.

Jones, J. M., Lloyd, C. W., and Wyatt, T. C. A study of the interrelationships of maternal and fetal adrenal glands of rats. *Endocrinology*, 1953, **53**, 182–191.

Josimovich, J. B., Hadman, A. J., and Deane, H. W. A histophysiological study of the developing adrenal cortex of the rat during fetal and early postnatal stages. *Endocrinology*, 1954, **54**, 627–639.

Kallman, F. J. *Heredity in health and mental disorder*. New York: Norton, 1953.

Kalter, H., and Warkany, J. Experimental production of congenital malformations in mammals by metabolic procedure. *Physiol. Rev.*, 1959, **39**, 69–115.

Kaplan, S. J., Rugh, R., and White, R. K. The behavior of 100 day old male rats resulting from fetal X-irradiation. *Atompraxis*, 1963, **9**, 11–16.

Karas, G. G., and Denenberg, V. H. The effects of duration and distribution of infantile experience on adult learning. *J. comp. physiol. Psychol.*, 1961, **54**, 170–174.

Karnofsky, D. A. Drugs as teratogens in animals and man. *Ann. Rev. Pharmacol.*, 1965, **5**, 447–472.

Kaufman, I. C., and Rosenblum, L. A. The reaction to separation in infant monkeys: anaclitic depression and conservation-withdrawal. *Psychosomat. Med.*, 1968 (in press).

Keeley, K. Prenatal influence on behavior of offspring of crowded mice. *Science*, 1962, **135**, 44–45.

Kennard, M. A. Age and other factors in motor recovery from precentral lesions in monkeys. *Am. J. Physiol.*, 1936, **115**, 138–146.

Kessen, W. *The child.* New York: Wiley, 1965.

Kessen, W. Sucking and looking: two organized congenital patterns of behavior in the human newborn. In H. W. Stevenson, E. H. Hess, and H. L. Rheingold (Eds.), *Early behavior.* New York: Wiley, 1967.

King, J. A. Parameters relevant to determining the effect of early experience upon the adult behavior of animals. *Psychol. Bull.*, 1958, **55**, 46–58.

King, J. A., and Eleftherion, B. E. Effects of early handling upon adult behavior in two subspecies of deermice. Peromyscus Maniculates. *J. comp. physiol. Psychol.*, 1959, **52**, 82–88.

Klein, M. *Contributing to psycho-analysis.* London: Hogarth Press, 1950.

Knobil, E., and Briggs, F. N. Fetal-maternal endocrine interrelations: the hypophyseal-adrenal system. *Endocrinology*, 1955, **57**, 147–152.

Knoblock, H., and Pasamanick, B. Seasonal variations in the births of the mentally deficient. *Am. J. publ. Hlth.*, 1958, **48**, 1201–1208.

Köhler, W. *Dynamics in psychology.* New York: Liverwright, 1940.

Krech, D., Rosenzweig, M. R., and Bennett, E. L. Environmental impoverishment, social isolation and changes in brain chemistry and anatomy. *Physiol. Behav.*, 1966, **1**, 99–109.

Kuo, Z. Y. *The dynamics of behavior development.* New York: Random House, 1967.

Lakin, M. Personality factors in mothers of excessively crying (colicky) infants. *Monogr. Soc. Res. Child Develop.*, 1957, **22**, No. 64.

Landauer, T. K., and Whiting, J. N. M. Infantile stimulation and adult stature of human males. *Am. Anthrop.*, 1963, **66**, 1007–1028.

Lerner, I. M. *Genetic homeostasis.* New York: Wiley, 1954.

Levine, S. A further study of infantile handling and adult avoidance learning. *J. Personality*, 1956, **25**, 70–80.

Levine, S. The effects of differential infantile stimulation on emotionality at weaning. *Can. J. Psychol.*, 1959, **13**, 243–247.

Levine, S. Psychophysiological effects of early stimulation. In E. L. Bliss (Ed.), *Roots of behavior.* New York: Hoeber, 1961.

Levine, S., Alpert, M., and Lewis, G. W. Differential maturation of an adrenal response to cold stress in rats manipulated in infancy. *J. comp. physiol. Psychol.*, 1958, **51**, 774–777.

Levine, S., and Broadhurst, P. L. Genetic and autogenetic determinants of adult behavior in the rat. *J. comp. physiol. Psychol.*, 1963, **56**, 423–428.

Levine, S., Chevalier, J. A., and Korchin, S. J. The effects of early shock and handling on later avoidance learning. *J. Personality*, 1956, **24**, 475–493.

Levine, S., and Lewis, G. W. The relative importance of experimenter contact in an effect produced by extra-stimulation in infancy. *J. comp. physiol. Psychol.*, 1959, **52**, 368–369.

Levine, S., and Mullins, R. F., Jr. Hormonal influences on brain organization in infant rats. *Science*, 1966, **152**, 1585–1591.

Levine, S., and Wetzel, A. Infantile experiences, strain differences, and avoidance learning. *J. comp. physiol. Psychol.*, 1963, **56**, 879–881.

Levinson, B. Effects of fetal irradiation on learning. *J. comp. physiol. Psychol.*, 1952, **45**, 140–145.

Lewis, H. *Deprived children*. New York: Oxford University Press, 1954.

Lieberman, M. W. Early developmental stress and later behavior. *Science*, 1963, **141**, 824–825.

Lilienfeld, A. M., Pasamanick, B., and Rogers, M. E. The relationship between pregnancy experience and the development of certain neuropsychiatric disorders in childhood. *Am. J. publ. Hlth.*, 1955, **45**, 637.

Lindholm, B. W. Critical periods and the effects of early shock on later emotional behavior in the white rat. *J. comp. physiol. Psychol.*, 1962, **55**, 597–599.

Lindzey, G., Lykken, D. T., and Winston, H. D. Infantile trauma, genetic factors and adult temperament. *J. abnorm. Soc. Psychol.*, 1960, **61**, 7–14.

Lindzey, G., and Winston, H. Maze learning and effect of pretraining in inbred strains of mice. *J. comp. physiol. Psychol.*, 1962, **55**, 748–752.

Lindzey, G., Winston, H. D., and Manosevitz, M. Early experience, genotype and temperament in Mus musculus. *J. comp. physiol. Psychol.*, 1963, **56**, 622–629.

Loeb, J. *Der Heliotropis mus der threre und seine Liberstimmung mit dem Heliotropismus der Pflanzen*. Wurzburg: Hertz, 1890.

Lorenz, K. Der Kumpan in der Umwelt des Vogels. *J. Ornithol.*, 1935, **83**, 137–213.

Louttit, R. T. Effect of phenylalanine and isocarboxazid feeding on brain serotonin and learning behavior in the rat. *J. comp. physiol. Psychol.*, 1962, **55**, 425–428.

Louttit, R. T. Chemical facilitation of intelligence among the mentally retarded. *Am. J. ment. Defic.*, 1965, **69**, 495–501.

Lowrey, L. G. Personality distortion and early institutional care. *Am. J. Orthopsychiat.*, 1940, **10**, 576–586.

Luchsinger, V. P. Effects of fetal X-irradiation on maze performances of two generations of albino rats. *Diss. Abstr.*, 1963, 2592.

Lyman, F. L. *Phenylketonuria*. Springfield, Ill.: Thomas, 1963.

Lynn, R. *Attention, arousal and the orientation reaction*. Oxford: Pergamon Press, 1966.

Maas, H. Long-term effects of early childhood separation and group care. *Vita hum.*, 1963, **6**, 34–56. (a)

Maas, H. The young adult adjustment of twenty wartime residential nursery children. *Child Welfare*, 1963, **42**, 57–62. (b)

Mainardi, D., Scudo, F. M., and Barbieri, D. Assortative mating based on early learning. *Acta Biomed.*, 1965, **36**, 583–605.

Marler, P. R., and Hamilton, W. J. *Mechanisms of animal behavior*. New York: Wiley, 1966.

Marr, J. H., and Gradner, L. E., Jr. Early olfactory experience and later social behavior in the rat: preference, sexual responsiveness, and care-of-young. *J. genet. Psychol.*, 1965, **107**, 167–174.

Mason, W. A., and Fitz-Gerald, F. L. Intellectual performance of an isolation reared monkey. *Percept. Mot. Skills*, 1962, **15**, 594.

Mason, W. A., and Sponholz, R. R. Behavior of Rhesus monkeys raised in isolation. *Psychiat. Res.*, 1963, **1**, 1–8.

Matthews, S. A., and Detwiler, S. R. The reactions of Amblystoma embryos following prolonged treatment with chlorotone. *J. exp. Zool.*, 1926, **45**, 279–292.

McCance, R. A. Characteristics of the newly born. In G. E. W. Wolstenholme and M. O'Connor (Eds.), *Somatic stability in the newborn.* Boston: Little, Brown, 1961.

McCandless, B. R. *Children: behavior and development.* New York: Holt, Rinehart, and Winston, 1967.

McMichael, R. E. Early experience effects as a function of infant treatment and other experimental conditions. *J. comp. physiol. Psychol.,* 1966, **62,** 433–436.

McNemar, Q. A critical examination of the University of Iowa studies of environmental influences upon the I.Q. *Psychol. Bull.,* 1940, **37,** 63–92.

Meehl, P. E. Shizotaxia, schizotypy and schizophrenia. *Am. Psychol.,* 1962, **17,** 827–838.

Meier, G. W. In defense of "Prenatal Anoxia and Irradiation: Maternal-Fetal Relations." *Psychol. Rep.,* 1962, **11,** 27–31.

Meier, G. W., Bunch, M. E., Nolan, C. T., and Scheidler, C. H. Anoxia, behavioral development and learning ability: a comparative experimental approach. *Psychol. Monogr.,* 1960, **1** (Whole No. 488), 74.

Meier, G. W., and Garcia-Rodriguez, C. Continuing behavioral differences in infant monkeys as related to mode of delivery. *Psychol. Rep.,* 1966, **19,** 1219–1225.

Meier, G. W., and Huff, F. W. Altered adult behavior following chronic drug administration during infancy and prepuberty. *J. comp. physiol. Psychol.,* 1962, **55,** 469–471.

Meier, G. W., and McGee, R. K. A re-evaluation of the effect of early perceptual experience on discrimination performance during adulthood. *J. comp. physiol. Psychol.,* 1959, **52,** 390–395.

Melzack, R. Effects of early perceptual restriction on simple visual discrimination. *Science,* 1962, **137,** 978–979.

Melzack, R. Effects of early experience on behavior: experimental and conceptual considerations. In P. H. Hoch and J. Zubin (Eds.), *Psychopathology of perception.* New York: Grune and Stratton, 1965.

Melzack, R., and Burns, S. K. Neurophysiological effects of early sensory restriction. *Exper. Neurol.,* 1965, **13,** 163–175.

Melzack, R., and Scott, T. H. The effects of early experience on the response to pain. *J. comp. physiol. Psychol.,* 1957, **50,** 155–161.

Melzack, R., and Thompson, W. R. Effects of early experience on social behavior. *Can. J. Psychol.,* 1956, **10,** 82–90.

Menlove, F. L. Aggressive symptoms in emotionally disturbed adopted children. *Child Dev.,* 1965, **36,** 519–532.

Menzel, E. W., Jr. Patterns of responsiveness in chimpanzees reared through infancy under conditions of environmental restrictions. *Psychol. Forsch.,* 1964, **27,** 337–365.

Menzel, E. W., Jr., Davenport, R. K., Jr., and Rogers, C. M. The effects of environmental restriction upon the chimpanzee's responsiveness to objects. *J. comp. physiol. Psychol.,* 1963, **56,** 78–85.

Metfessel, M. Relationships in heredity and environment in behavior. *J. Psychol.,* 1940, **10,** 177–198.

Meyers, W. J. Critical period for the facilitation of exploratory behavior by infantile experience. *J. comp. physiol. Psychol.,* 1962, **55,** 1099–1101.

Meyers, W. J. Effects of different intensities of postweaning shock and handling on the albino rat. *J. genet. Psychol.,* 1965, **106,** 51–58.

Montagu, A. *Human heredity.* New York: Harcourt, Brace, and World, 1959.

Montague, M. F. A. Constitutional and prenatal factors in infant and child health. In M. J. E. Senn (Ed.), *Symposium on the healthy personality.* New York: Josiah Macy, Jr., Foundation, 1950. Pp. 148–175.

Montague, M. F. A. *Prenatal influences.* Urbana, Ill.: Thomas, 1962.

Morra, M. Level of maternal stress during pregnancy periods on rat offspring behavior. *Psychon. Sci.,* 1965, **3,** 7–8.

Murphy, D. P. The outcome of 625 pregnancies in women subjected to pelvic roentgen irradiation. *Am. J. Obstet. Gynec.,* 1929, **18,** 179–187.

Nalbandov, A. V. *Reproductive physiology.* San Francisco: Freeman, 1958.

Neel, J. V. The effect of exposure to the atomic bombs on pregnancy termination in Hiroshima and Nagasaki: preliminary report. *Science,* 1953, **118,** 537–541.

Newton, G., Bly, C. G., and McCrary, C. Effects of early experience on the response to transplanted tumor. *J. nerv. ment. Dis.,* 1962, **134,** 522–527.

Newton, G., and Levine, S. *Early experience and behavior: psychological and physiological effects of early environmental variation.* Urbana, Ill.: Thomas, 1968.

Nice, M. M. Studies in the life-history of the song sparrow. II. The behavior of the song sparrow and other passerines. *Trans. Linn. Soc. N.Y.,* 1943, **6,** 1–329.

Novakova, V. Weaning of young rats: effect of time on behaviour. *Science,* 1966, **151,** 475–476.

O'Connor, N. The evidence for the permanently disturbing effects of mother-child separation. *Acta psychol.,* 1956, **12,** 174–191.

Ordy, J. M., Samorajski, T., Collins, R. L., and Rolsten, C. Prenatal chlorpromazine effects on liver, survival and behavior of mice offspring. *J. Pharmacol. exp. Ther.,* 1966, **151,** 110–125.

Orlansky, H. Infant care and personality. *Psych. Bull.,* 1949, **46,** 1–48.

Ottinger, D. R., Denenberg, V. H., and Stephens, M. W. Maternal emotionality, multiple mothering and emotionality at maturity. *J. comp. physiol. Psychol.,* 1963, **56,** 313–317.

Ourth, L., and Brown, K. B. Inadequate mothering and disturbance in the neonatal period. *Child Dev.,* 1961, **32,** 287–295.

Page, E. W. Transfer of materials across the human placenta. *Am. J. Obstet. Gynec.,* 1957, **74,** 705–718.

Pasamanick, B., and Knoblock, H. Epidemiologic studies on the complications of pregnancy and the birth process. In G. Caplan (Ed.), *Prevention of mental disorders in children.* New York: Basic Books, 1961.

Penner, L. R., Jr. The effect of pre- and early postnatal protein deficiency on maturation and intelligence of the albino rat. *Diss. Abstr.,* 1966, **27,** 988.

Peterson, N. Control of behavior by presentation of an imprinted stimulus. *Science,* 1960, **132,** 1395–1396.

Pfaffenberger, C. J., and Scott, J. P. The relationship between delayed socialization and trainability in guide dogs. *J. genet. Psychol.,* 1959, **95,** 145–155.

Piaget, J. *The psychology of intelligence.* London: Routledge and Kegan Paul, 1950.

Pinneau, S. A critique on the articles by Margaret Ribble. *Child Dev.,* 1950, **21,** 203–228.

Pinneau, S. The infantile disorders of hospitalism and anaclitic depression. *Psychol. Bull.,* 1955, **52,** 429–452.

Piontkovsky, I. A., and Semagin, U. W. Higher nervous activity of adult rats prenatally irradiated with small doses of X-rays. *J. comp. physiol. Psychol.,* 1963, **56,** 748–751.

Polidora, V. J., Cunningham, R. F., and Waisman, H. A. Dosage parameters of a behavioral deficit associated with phenylketonuria in rats. *J. comp. physiol. Psychol.,* 1966, **61,** 436–441.

Provence, S., and Lipton, R. C. *Infants in institutions.* New York: International Universities Press, 1962.

Rabin, A. I. Some psychosexual differences between kibbutz and non-kibbutz Israeli boys. *J. Project. Tech.*, 1958, **22**, 328–332.

Reading, A. J. Effect of maternal environment on the behavior of inbred mice. *J. comp. physiol. Psychol.*, 1966, **62**, 437–440.

Ressler, R. H. Parental handling in two strains of mice reared by foster parents. *Science*, 1962, **137**, 129–130.

Ressler, R. H. Inherited environmental influences on the operant behavior of mice. *J. comp. physiol. Psychol.*, 1966, **61**, 26–267. (a)

Ressler, R. H. Avoidance conditioning in mice: prenatal influence of mother's treatment before mating. *Am. Zool.*, 1966, **6**, 7. (b)

Rheingold, H. L. The modification of social responsiveness in institutional babies. *Monogr. Soc. Res. Child Develop.*, 1956, **21**, No. 2.

Rheingold, H. L. The effect of environmental stimulation upon social and exploratory behavior in the human infant. In B. M. Foss (Ed.), *Determinants of infant behavior*, New York: Wiley, 1961. Vol. 1, pp. 143–177.

Rheingold, H. L., and Bayley, N. The later effects of an experimental modification of mothering. *Child Dev.*, 1959, **30**, 363–372.

Rheingold, H. L., Gewirtz, J., and Ross, H. Social conditioning of vocalizations in the infant. *J. comp. physiol. Psychol.*, 1959, **52**, 58–73.

Rheingold, H. L., and Keene, G. C. Transport of the human young. In B. M. Foss (Ed.), *Determinants of infant behavior*, New York: Wiley, 1963. Vol. 3, pp. 87–110.

Ribble, M. Significance of infantile sucking for psychic development. *J. nerv. ment. Dis.*, 1939, **90**, 455–463.

Ribble, M. A. Infantile experience in relation to personality development. In J. McV. Hunt (Ed.), *Personality and the behavior disorders*. New York: Ronald Press, 1944. Pp. 621–651.

Riccio, D. C., and Campbell, B. A. Adaptation and persistence of adaptation to a cold stressor in weanling and adult rats. *J. comp. physiol. Psychol.*, 1966, **61**, 408–410.

Riesen, A. H. The development of visual perception in man and chimpanzee. *Science*, 1947, **106**, 107–108.

Riesen, A. H. Post-partum development of behavior. *Chicago med. Sch. Q.*, 1951, **13**, 17–24.

Riesen, A. H. Plasticity of behavior: psychological aspects. In H. F. Harlow and C. N. Wolsey (Eds.), *Biological and biochemical bases of behavior*. Madison: University of Wisconsin Press, 1958.

Riesen, A. H. Stimulation as a requirement for growth and function in behavioral development. In D. W. Fiske and S. R. Maddi (Eds.), *Functions of varied experience*. Homewood, Ill.: Dorsey Press, 1961.

Riesen, A. H., Chow, K. L., Senomes, J., and Nissen, H. W. Chimpanzee vision after four conditions of light deprivation. *Am. Psychol.*, 1951, 282. (Abstract)

Riesen, A. H., Ramsey, R. L., and Wilson, P. D. Development of visual acuity in Rhesus monkeys deprived of patterned light during early infancy. *Psychon. Sci.*, 1964, **1**, 33–34.

Robertson, J., and Bowlby, J. Responses of young children to separation from their mothers. *Courr. Cent. int. Enf.*, 1952, **2**, 131–142.

Rosen, J., and Wejtko, J. Effects of delayed weaning on rat emotionality: related to dominance behavior in the rat. *Arch. genet. Psychiat.*, 1962, **7**, 77–81.

Rosenzweig, M. R. Environmental complexity, cerebral change, and behavior. *Am. Psychol.*, 1966, **21**, 321–332.

Roudinesco, J., David, M., and Nicolas, J. Responses of young children to separation from their mothers. I. Observation of children ages 12 to 17 months recently separated from their families and living in an institution. *Courr. Cent. int. Enf.*, 1952, **2**, 66–78.

Rowlands, G. L. The effects of total social isolation upon learning and social behavior in Rhesus monkeys. Unpublished doctoral dissertation, University of Wisconsin, 1964.

Rudolf, G. de M. The treatment of mental defectives with aneuria for one year. *J. Ment. Sci.*, 1950, **96**, 265–271.

Runner, M. N., and Miller, J. R. Congenital deformity in the mouse as a result of fasting. *Anat. Rec.*, 1956, **124**, 437–438.

Sackett, G. F. Some persistent effects of different rearing conditions on preadult social behavior of monkeys. *J. comp. physiol. Psychol.*, 1967, **64**, 363–365.

Sackett, G. P., Porter, M., and Holmes, H. Choice behavior in Rhesus monkeys: effect of stimulation during the first month of life. *Science*, 1965, **147**, 304–306.

Salama, A. A., and Hunt, J. "Fixation" in the rat as a function of infantile shocking, handling, and gentling. *J. genet. Psychol.*, 1964, **105**, 131–162.

Schaefer, T. Early "experience" and its effects on later behavioral processes in rats: II. A critical factor in the early handling phenomena. *Trans. N. Y. Acad. Sci.*, 1963, **25**, 871–889.

Schaefer, T., Weingarten, F. S., and Towne, J. C. Temperature change: the basic variable in the early handling phenomenon. *Science*, 1962, **135**, 41–42.

Schaffer, H. R. Objective observations of personality development in early infancy. *Br. J. med. Psychol.*, 1958, **31**, 174–183.

Schaffer, H. R. Some issues for research in the study of attachment behavior. In B. M. Foss (Ed.), *Determinants of infant behavior*, New York: Wiley, 1963. Vol. 2, pp. 179–199.

Schaffer, H. R., and Callender, W. M. Psychologic effects of hospitalization in infancy. *Pediatrics*, 1959, **24**, 528–539.

Schaffer, H. R., and Emerson, P. E. Patterns of response to physical contact in early human development. *J. Child Psychol. Psychiat.*, 1964, **5**, 1–13. (a)

Schaffer, H. R., and Emerson, P. E. The development of social attachments in infancy. *Monogr. Soc. Res. Child Develop.*, 1964, **29**, No. 1. (b)

Schneirla, T. C., and Rosenblatt, J. "Critical periods" in the development of behavior. *Science*, 1963, **139**, 1110–1115.

Schwartz, S. Effect of neonatal cortical lesions and early environmental factors on adult rat behavior. *J. comp. physiol. Psychol.*, 1964, **57**, 72–77.

Schweikert, G. E., and Collins, G. The effects of differential postweaning environments on later behavior in the rat. *J. genet. Psychol.*, 1966, **109**, 255–263.

Scott, J. P. Social behavior, organization, and leadership in a small flock of domestic sheep. *Comp. Psychol. Monogr.*, 1945, **18**, 1–29.

Scott, J. P. The relative importance of social and hereditary factors in producing disturbances in life adjustment during periods of stress in laboratory animals. *Proc. Ass. Res. Nerv. Ment. Dis.*, 1950, **29**, 61–71.

Scott, J. P. Critical periods in behavioral development. *Science*, 1962, **138**, 949–958.

Scott, J. P. Reply to Schneirla and Rosenblatt. *Science*, 1963, **139**, 1115–1116. (a)

Scott, J. P. The process of primary socialization in canine and human infants. *Monogr. Soc. Res. Child Develop.*, 1963, **28**, No. 1. (b)

Scott, J. P., and Fuller, J. L. *Genetics and the social behavior of the dog.* Chicago: University of Chicago Press, 1965.

Sears, R. R., Maccoby, E. E., and Levin, H. *Patterns of child rearing.* Evanston, Ill.: Row, Peterson, 1957.

Seay, B., Hansen, E., and Harlow, H. F. Mother-infant separation in monkeys. *J. Child Psychol. Psychiat.*, 1962, **3**, 123–132.

Seay, B., and Harlow, H. F. Maternal separation in the Rhesus monkey. *J. nerv. ment. Dis.*, 1965, **140**, 434–441.

Seitz, P. F. D. The effects of infantile experience upon adult behavior in animal subjects. I. Effects of litter size during infancy upon adult behavior in the rat. *Am. J. Psychiat.*, 1954, **110**, 916–927.

Seitz, P. F. D. The maternal instinct in animal subjects. *Psychosomat. Med.*, 1958, **20**, 215–226.

Shock, N. W. Growth curves. In S. S. Stevens (Ed.), *Handbook of experimental psychology.* New York: Wiley, 1951. Pp. 330–346.

Sines, J. D. Selective breeding for development of stomach lesions following stress in the rat. *J. comp. physiol. Psychol.*, 1959, **52**, 615–617.

Sines, J. D. Behavioral correlates of genetically enhanced susceptibility to stomach lesion development. *J. psychonom. Res.*, 1961, **5**, 120–126.

Skeels, H. M., and Dye, H. A. A study of the effects of differential stimulation in mentally retarded children. *Proc. Am. Ass. Ment. Def.*, 1939, **44**, 114–136.

Skeels, H. M., Updegraff, R., Wellman, B. L., and Williams, H. M. A study of environmental stimulation: an orphanage preschool project. *University of Iowa Studies in Child Welfare*, 1938, **15**, 7–191.

Skodak, M. Children in foster homes: a study of mental development. *University of Iowa Studies in Child Welfare*, 1939, **16**, No. 1.

Sluckin, W. *Imprinting and early learning.* London: Methuen, 1964.

Smith, C. A. Effects of maternal undernutrition upon the newborn infant in Holland (1944–1945). *J. Pediat.*, 1947, **30**, 229–243.

Smith, C. J. Mass action and early environment in the rat. *J. comp. physiol. Psychol.*, 1959, **52**, 154–156.

Smith, F. V., Von-Toller, C., and Boyes, T. The critical period in the attachment of lambs and ewes. *Anim. Behav.*, 1966, **14**, 120–125.

Sontag, L. W. The significance of fetal environmental differences. *Am. J. Obstet. Gynec.*, 1941, **42**, 996–1003.

Sontag, L. W., and Wallace, R. F. The effect of cigarette smoking during pregnancy upon the fetal heart rate. *Am. J. Obstet. Gynec.*, 1935, **29**, 3–8.

Soskin, R. A. The effect of early experience upon the formation of environmental preferences in rats. *J. comp. physiol. Psychol.*, 1963, **56**, 303–306.

Spalding, D. A. Instinct: with original observations on young animals. Reprinted *Br. J. Anim. Behav.*, 1954, **2**, 2–11.

Spencer-Booth, Y., Hinde, R. A., and Bruce, M. Social companions and the mother-infant relationship in Rhesus monkeys. *Nature*, 1965, 208–301.

Spigelman, M. N., and Bryden, M. P. Effects of early and late blindness on auditory spatial learning in the rat. *Neuropsychologia*, 1967, **5**, 267–274.

Spitz, R. A. Hospitalism: an inquiry into the genesis of psychiatric conditions in early childhood. *Psychoanal. study Child*, 1945, **1**, 53–74.

Spitz, R. A. Hospitalism: an inquiry into the genesis of psychiatric conditions in early childhood: a follow-up report. *Psychoanal. study Child*, 1946, **2**, 113–117.

Spitz, R. A., and Wolf, K. Anaclitic depression. *Psychoanal. study Child*, 1946, **2**, 313–342.

Stanley, W. C., and Elliot, O. Differential human handling as reinforcing events and as treatments influencing later social behavior in Basenji puppies. *Psychol. Rep.*, 1962, **10**, 775–788.

Starkweather, E. K., and Roberts, K. E. I.Q. changes occurring during nursery school attendance at the Merrill-Palmer School. *Yearbook of the National Society for Studies in Education*, 1940. Vol. 39, Part II, pp. 315–335.

Stearns, G. Nutritional state of the mother prior to conception. *J. Am. med. Ass.*, 1958, **168**, 1655–1659.

Stevenson, H. W., Hess, E. H., and Rheingold, H. L. *Early behavior: comparative and developmental approaches.* New York: Wiley, 1967.

Stewart, A. H., Weiland, I. H., Leider, A. R., Mangham, C. A., Holmes, T. H., and Ripley H. S. Excessive infant crying (colic) in relation to parent behavior. *Am. J. Psychiat.*, 1954, **110**, 687–694.

Stott, D. H. Physical and mental handicaps following a disturbed pregnancy. *Lancet,* 1957, 1006–1012.

Stott, D. H. Some psychosomatic aspects of casualty in reproduction *J. psychosomat. Res.*, 1958, **3**, 42–55.

Swan, C., and Tostevin, H. Congenital abnormalities in infants following infectious diseases during pregnancy, with special reference to rubella. A third series of cases. *Med. J. Aus.*, 1946, **1**, 645–659.

Swift, J. W. Effects of early group experience: the nursery school and day nursery. In M. L. Hoffman and L. W. Hoffman (Eds.), *Review of Child Development Research.* New York: Russell Sage, 1964. Vol. 1, pp. 249–288.

Tapp, J. T., and Markowitz, H. Infant handling: effects on avoidance learning, brain weight, and cholinesterase activity. *Science*, 1957, **125**, 698–699.

Taussig, H. B. The thalidomide syndrome. *Scient. Am.*, 1962, **207**, 29–35.

Tennes, K. H., and Lampl, E. E. Stranger and separation anxiety in infancy. *J. nerv. ment. Dis.*, 1964, **139**, 247–254.

Thompson, W. D., and Sontag, L. W. Behavioral effects in the offspring of rats subjected to audiogenic seizures during the gestation period. *J. comp. physiol. Psychol.*, 1956, **49**, 454–456.

Thompson, W. R. The inheritance and development of intelligence. *Proc. Res. Assoc. nerv. ment. Dis.*, 1954, **33**, 209–231.

Thompson, W. R. Early environment—its importance for later behavior. In P. H. Hoch and J. Zubin (Eds.), *Psychopathology of childhood*, New York: Grune and Stratton, 1955.

Thompson, W. R. Influence of prenatal maternal anxiety on emotionality in young rats. *Science*, 1957, **125**, 698–699.

Thompson, W. R. Motivational factors in development. *Aust. J. Psychol.*, 1958, **10**, 127–143.

Thompson, W. R. Early environmental influences on behavioral development. *Am. J. Orthopsychiat.*, 1960, **30**, 306–314.

Thompson, W. R. Early experiential and genetic influences on flexibility. In O. J. Harvey (Ed.), *Experience structure and adaptability.* New York: Springer, 1966.

Thompson, W. R. Development and the biophysical bases of personality. In E. Borgatta and W. Lambert (Eds.), *Handbook of personality.* Chicago: Rand McNally, 1968.

Thompson, W. R., and Goldenberg, L. Some physiological effects of maternal adrenalin injections during pregnancy on rat offspring. *Psychol. Rep.*, 1962, **10**, 759–774.

Thompson, W. R., Goldenberg, L., Watson, J., and Watson, M. Behavioral effects of maternal adrenalin injection during pregnancy in rat offspring. *Psychol. Rep.*, 1963, **12**, 279–284.

Thompson, W. R., and Heron, W. The effects of early restriction on activity in dogs. *J. comp. physiol. Psychol.*, 1954, **47**, 77–82. (a)

Thompson, W. R., and Heron, W. The effects of restricting early experience on the problem-solving capacity of dogs. *Can. J. Psychol.*, 1954, **8**, 17–31. (b)

Thompson, W. R., and Higgins, W. H. Emotion and organized behavior: some experimental data bearing on the Leeper-Young controversy. *Can. J. Psychol.*, 1958, **12**, 61–68.

Thompson, W. R., and Kano, K. Effects on rat offspring of maternal phenylalanine diet during pregnancy. *J. Psychiat. Res.*, 1965, **3**, 91–98.

Thompson, W. R., and Melzack, R. Early environment. *Scient. Am.*, 1956, **114**, 38–42.

Thompson, W. R., Melzack, R., and Scott, T. H. "Whirling" behavior in dogs as related to early experience. *Science*, 1956, **123**, 939.

Thompson, W. R., and O'Kieffe, M. The effects of imprinting on stress-response in chicks. *Science*, 1962, **135**, 918–919.

Thompson, W. R., and Olian, S. Some effects on offspring behavior of maternal adrenalin injection during pregnancy in three inbred mouse strains. *Psychol. Rep.*, 1961, **8**, 87–90.

Thompson, W. R., and Quinby, S. Prenatal maternal anxiety and offspring behavior: parental activity and level of anxiety. *J. genet. Psychol.*, 1964, **105**, 359–371.

Thompson, W. R., and Schaefer, T. Early environmental stimulation. In D. W. Fiske and S. Maddi (Eds.), *Function of varied experience*, Chicago: Dorsey Press, 1961.

Thompson, W. R., Watson, J., and Charlesworth, W. R. The effects of prenatal maternal stress on offspring behavior in rats. *Psychol. Monogr.*, 1962, **76** (Whole No. 557)

Tizard, J. Residential care of mentally handicapped children. *Br. med. J.*, 1960, **1**, 1041–1046.

Tsang, Y. C. Visual sensitivity of rats deprived of visual cortex in infancy. *J. comp. Psychol.*, 1937, **24**, 255–262.

Udenfriend, S. Phenylketonuria. *Am. J. Clin. Nutr.*, 1961, **9**, 691–694.

Vesterdal, J. Kidney function and the excretion of water and solutes. In G. E. W. Wolstenholme and M. O'Connor (Eds.), *Somatic stability in the newborn*. Boston: Little, Brown, 1961.

Vince, M. A. Effects of age and experience on the establishment of internal inhibition in finches. *Br. J. Psychol.*, 1959, **50**, 136–144.

Vince, M. A. Developmental changes in responsiveness to the great Tit (Paras major). *Behaviour*, 1960, **15**, 219–243.

Vincent, N. M. The effects of prenatal alcoholism upon motivation, emotionality and learning in the rat. *Amer. Psychol.*, 1958, **13**, 401. (Abstract)

Waddington, C. H. *The strategy of the genes.* London: Allen and Unwin, 1957.

Waisman, H. A., Wang, H. L., Harlow, H. F., and Sponholz, R. B. Experimental phenylketonuria in the monkey. *Proc. Soc. exp. Biol. Med.*, 1959, **101**, 864–865.

Waisman, H. A., Wang, H. L., Palmer, G., and Harlow, H. F. Phenylketonuria in infant monkeys. *Nature, London*, 1960, **188**, 1124–1125.

Wallin, R., and Riley, R. Reactions of mothers to pregnancy and adjustment of offspring in infancy. *Am. J. Orthopsychiat.*, 1950, **20**, 616–622.

Walters, R. H., and Parke, R. D. The role of the distance receptors in the development of social responsiveness. In L. P. Lipsitt and C. C. Spiker (Eds.), *Advances in child development and behavior.* New York: Academic Press, 1956. Vol. 2.

Webster, R. L. Postnatal weight and behavior changes as a function of components of prenatal material injection procedures. *Psychon. Sci.*, 1967, **7**, 191–192.

Weininger, O. Mortality of albino rats under stress as a function of early handling. *Can. J. Psychol.*, 1953, **7**, 111–114.

Weininger, O. The effects of early experience on behavior and growth characteristics. *J. comp. physiol. Psychol.*, 1956, **49**, 1–6.

Weir, M. W., and DeFries, J. C. Prenatal influence on behavior in mice: evidence of a genetic basis. *J. comp. physiol. Psychol.*, 1964, **58**, 412–417.

Wellman, B. L. The effect of preschool attendance upon the I.Q. *J. exp. Educ.*, 1932, **1**, 48–69.

Wellman, B. L. I.Q. changes of preschool and nonpreschool groups during the preschool years: a summary of the literature. *J. Psychol.*, 1945, **20**, 347–368.

Wellman, B. L., and Pegram, E. L. Binet I.Q. changes of orphanage preschool children: a reanalysis. *J. genet. Psychol.*, 1944, **65**, 239–263.

Werboff, J. (Ed.) *Prenatal irradiation effects on CNS development and postnatal behavior. Conf. Proc.*, Washington, D.C., 1963.

Werboff, J. Prenatal irradiation: effects on the development of the central nervous system and postnatal behavior. *Science*, 1964, **144**, 84–86.

Werboff, J., Broeder, J. D., Havlena, J., and Sikov., M. R. Effects of prenatal X-ray irradiation on audiogenic seizures in the rat. *Exper. Neurol.*, 1961, **4**, 189–196.

Werboff, J., Gottlieb, J. S., Dembicki, E. L., and Havlena, J. Postnatal effects of antidepressant drugs administered during gestation. *Exper. Neurol.*, 1961, **3**, 542–555.

Werboff, J., Gottlieb, J. S., Havlena, J., and Word, T. J. Behavioral effects of prenatal drug administration in the white rat. *Pediatrics*, 1961, **27**, 318–323.

Werboff, J., and Havlena, J. Postnatal behavioral effects of tranquilizers administered to the gravid rat. *Exper. Neurol.*, 1962, **6**, 263–269.

Werboff, J., and Havlena, J. Febrile convulsions in infant rats and later behavior. *Science*, 1963, **142**, 684–685.

Werboff, J., Havlena, J., and Sikov, M. R. Effects of prenatal X-irradiation on activity, emotionality and maze-learning ability in the rat. *Rad. Res.*, 1962, **16**, 441–452.

Werboff, J., Havlena, J., and Sikov, M. R. Behavioral effects of small doses of acute X-irradiation administered prenatally. *Atompraxis*, 1963, **9**, 103–105.

Werboff, J., and Kesner, R. Learning deficits of offspring after administration of tranquilizing drugs to the mothers. *Nature*, 1963, **197**, 106–107.

Werner, H. The concept of development from a comparative and organismic point of view. In D. Harris (Ed.), *The concept of development*. Minneapolis: University of Minnesota Press, 1957.

Whalen, R. E., and Nadler, R. D. Modification of spontaneous and hormone-induced sexual behavior by estrogen administered to neonatal female rats. *J. comp. physiol. Psychol.*, 1965, **60**, 150–152.

Whimbey, A. E., and Denenberg, V. H. Programming life histories: creating individual differences by the experimental control of early experiences. *Multiv. Behav. Res.*, 1966, **1**, 279–286.

White, B. L., and Castle, P. W. Visual exploratory behavior following postnatal handling of human infants. *Percept. Mot. Skills*, 1964, **18**, 497–502.

Whiting, J. W. M. Menarcheal age and infant stress in humans. In F. A. Beach (Ed.), *Sex and behavior*. New York: Wiley, 1965.

Whiting, J. W. M., and Landauer, T. K. Some effects of infant stress upon human stature. Unpublished manuscript, Harvard University, 1963.

Wiele, R. L. V., and Jarler, J. W. Placental steroids. *Ann. N. Y. Acad. Sci.*, 1959, **75**, 889–894.

Windle, W. F. *Physiology of the fetus*. Philadelphia: Saunders, 1940.

Winston, H. D. Influence of genotype and infantile trauma on adult learning in the mouse. *J. comp. physiol. Psychol.*, 1963, **56**, 630–635.

Winston, H. D. Heterosis and learning in the mouse. *J. comp. physiol. Psychol.*, 1964, **57**, 279–283.

Wittrig, J. J. Extravisual placitivity of posterior cortex in rats as a function of variation in proximal and distal input during development. *Percept. Mot. Skills*, 1966, **23**, 211–219.

Wolf, A. The dynamics of the selective inhibition of specific functions in neurosis: a preliminary report. *Psychosom. Med.*, 1943, **5**, 27–38.

Wolstenholme, G. E. W., and O'Connor, M. *Somatic stability in the newly born.* Boston: Little, Brown, 1961.

Woods, P. J. The effects of free and restricted environmental experience on problem solving behavior in the rat. *J. comp. physiol. Psychol.*, 1959, **52**, 399–402.

Woolley, D. W., and Van Der Hoeven, T. Serotonin deficiency in infancy as one cause of a mental defect in phenylketonuria. *Science*, 1964, **144**, 883–884.

Woolley, H. T. The validity of standards of mental measurement in young children. *School and Society*, 1925, **21**, 476–482.

Young, R. D. Effect of prenatal maternal injection of epinephrine on postnatal offspring behavior. *J. comp. physiol. Psychol.*, 1963, **56**, 929–932.

Young, R. D. Drug administration to neonatal rats: effects on later emotionality and learning. *Science*, 1964, **143**, 1055–1057.

Zamenhof, D., Mosley, J., and Schiller, E. Stimulation of the proliferation of cortical neurons by prenatal treatment with growth hormone. *Science*, 1966, **152**, 1396–1397.

Zigler, E. Metatheoretical issues in developmental psychology. In M. Marx (Ed.), *Psychological theory.* New York: Macmillan, 1963.

Zigler, E. Mental retardation: current issues and approaches. In L. W. Hoffman and M. L. Hoffman (Eds.), *Review of child development research.* New York: Russell Sage, 1966. Vol. 2, pp. 107–168.

Zigler, E., and de Labry, J. Concept-switching in middle-class, lower-class, and retarded children. *J. Abnorm. Soc. Psychol.*, 1962, **65**, 267–273.

Zigler, E., and Kanzer, P. The effectiveness of two classes of verbal reinforcers on the performance of middle and lower class children. *J. Personality*, 1962, **30**, 157–163.

Zubek, J. P., and Solberg, P. A. *Human development.* New York: McGraw-Hill, 1954.

PART III

COGNITIVE DEVELOPMENT

8. The Learning Theory Tradition and Child Psychology

SHELDON H. WHITE

> ". . . So, when on one side you hoist in Locke's head, you go over that way;
> but now, on the other side, hoist in Kant's and you come back again, but
> in very poor plight. Thus, some minds for ever keep trimming boat. Oh,
> ye foolish! Throw all these thunderheads overboard, and then you will float
> light and right."
>
> *Moby Dick*, HERMAN MELVILLE

> "Every psychological explanation comes sooner or later to lean either on
> biology or on logic (or on sociology, but this in turn leads to the same
> alternatives)."
>
> *The Psychology of Intelligence*, JEAN PIAGET

The most significant programmatic approach of American psychology, the stimulus-response tradition, still remains an identifiable approach among psychologists who study children. Among child psychologists, as among psychologists in general, it is a waning tradition; we are in the midst of what Hebb (1960) has described as the second American revolution. The first American revolution overthrew introspection, the Psychology of Consciousness, and Titchenerian structuralism; it established stimulus-response analysis, the Psychology of Behavior, and the learning theories. It took a long time to happen. We sometimes describe Watson's 1913 paper, "Psychology as the Behaviorist Views It," as both the opening gun and the decisive ideological stroke of the revolution, but it seems more reasonable to view the changeover as something that took an academic generation to complete itself.

For American psychologists, the case for behaviorism must have been an argument-in-being as early as Dewey's attack on the reflex arc in 1896; the case for Structuralism must have been an argument-in-being as late as 1933, when Boring published his *Physical Dimensions of Consciousness*. Perhaps the slow entry of behaviorism required a period during which young blood gradually supplanted an older generation. Perhaps there was a little more to the slowness than that. At this distance, it seems clear that the turn to a stimulus-response psychology was not as revolutionary as it seemed and that it basically was a reissuing of Psychology's traditional interest in central processes on a new scientific platform. A new platform seemed necessary at the turn of the century because the then-traditional program of Psychology had been built to accept introspective analyses of consciousness, and this platform could not accommodate data not cast in the form of decompositions of conscious material: Thorndike and Pavlov on comparative psychology, Freud on abnormal psychology, Hall on child study, Binet on psychometrics.

It took time for the right compromise to be worked out. It took time to try to consider the possibility of a psychology of animal consciousness (Washburn, 1908; Judd, 1910), for Thorndike (1913) to reject the hypothesis of ideomotor action, and, finally, for Tolman (1922a, 1922b, 1923, 1925, 1926, 1927, 1932) to develop a series of translations and, ultimately, "operational definitions" to persuade many that the interests of a mentalistic psychology could be located, and worked with, in the behavior of a laboratory rat.

If one may judge by the course of the first revolution, the second will take time. We seem right now to be working toward a kind of cognitive functionalism based on a progressive alignment of the guesswork of psychology and neurophysiology. Function words— "short-term memory," "arousal," "concrete operations," "pleasure centers," "analysis-by-synthesis," "feature detectors," "mediation," "orienting-exploratory behavior"—are proposed on the one side from behavior analysis and on the other from neurophysiological analysis, with each side trying to come to terms with the function that the other proposes. These functions are then arranged into schemes which are speculative models of central processing mechanisms. There is a frank interest in hypothetical constructs, in the conceptual nervous system, and in thinking. (The issue and reissue of books about thinking shows such an increase in operant rate as to suggest that someone, somewhere, is reinforcing the word—*Thinking* by Bartlett [1962] and *Thinking* by Humphrey [1963], *The Psychology of Thinking* by Vinacke [1952], *Thought and Language* by Vygotsky [1962], *A Study of Thinking* by Bruner, Goodnow, and Austin [1962], *Thinking: From Association to Gestalt* by Mandler and Mandler [1964], *Modes of Thinking in Young Children* by Wallach and Kogan [1965].)

The learning theory tradition brings into child psychology emphases which are not constant but which show some of the effects of this evolutionary process. After all, a good part of the revolution was generated out of the tradition itself. As Hunt noted a few years ago:

It can be said that stimulus-response methodology has been undoing stimulus-response theory. Or, at any rate, stimulus-response method has produced evidence that has demanded so much revision in stimulus-response theory that the new theory has few resemblances to the one which originally went by that name . . . (Hunt, 1961, p. 8).

Although the learning theory tradition is still a viable intellectual force among psychologists, still discussed and taught to students, there has been a significant alteration in the pattern of research activities built upon it. Papers devoted to basic research, or to development or analysis of the learning theories, have shown a marked decline—a comparison of the journals of today with those of a decade ago will show this. At the same time, the stimulus-response tradition shows an intensification of effort in what were once its fringe areas—analysis of social and clinical psychological phenomena, behavior therapy, and behavior engineering. It is this changing pattern of stimulus-response studies, a body of research activity floating free of its theoretical core, which has in recent years come to impinge upon child psychology.

Other approaches to child psychology, with which the tradition is necessarily in interaction, are themselves changed from what they were. Under the sway of one of the strongest of the revolutionary forces, Piaget, they have become significantly more ideological—receptive not only to Piaget, but to Werner, to the psycholinguistics-cum-nativism inspired by Chomsky, to ethology, and to the Russian scheme. It is not true today, as it once seemed to be, that the S-R psychologists alone offered an organized theoretical program to a body of child psychologists largely interested in norms rather than theory, largely interested in the issues of social adjustment rather than the issues of psychological analysis. Within child psychology, the confrontation is now with alternative and seemingly worthwhile conceptions of theory, of usable data, and of the learning and problem-solving processes themselves.

We are not concerned here to discuss the learning theories themselves. Most psychologists know something about them; they have been summarized well elsewhere (Hilgard and Bower, 1966; Koch, 1959); they are not germane to child psychology, strictly speaking. The learning theories were not designed to accommodate the data of children's learning, and it is only by making some assumptions that one can connect them to such data in a general sort of way. What has been brought to child psychology is a surrounding pattern of analyses, an understructure and a superstructure. The understructure, or pretheory, seems most clearly visible in historical examination. The superstructure is made up of a set of speculative analyses, or interventive programs, which carries the S-R approach to topics in cognition, social and clinical psychology, education, psychotherapy, or applied psychology. To encompass these, our discussion will sample the range of such activities being undertaken with children today.

Prominent among the sources of the American S-R tradition was the work of Ivan Pavlov. From the early decades of this century until quite recently, the American behavioristic tradition and Russian reflexology coexisted apart from one another—both descendants of Pavlov, but each working through the issues posed by Pavlov in diverging ways. About a decade ago, American psychologists reestablished contact with the Russian work, at first through some significant secondary sources (Razran, 1961; Berlyne, 1960) and then through translations and more extended reviews (e.g., Luria, 1960, 1961, 1966a, 1966b, 1968; Sokolov, 1963; Vygotsky, 1962; Zeigarnik, 1965; Uznadze, 1966; Pevzner, 1961; Konorski, 1967; Bernstein, 1967; O'Connor, 1961; Lynn, 1966).

While Soviet psychology has not developed the range of activities characteristic of American psychology—because, for one thing, the Russians subdivide psychological research differently among the specialties of physiology, psychology, and pedagogy (Brackbill, 1960)—it has developed an interestingly divergent set of analyses of the problems of learning and adaptation toward which both Russians and Americans were pointed by Pavlov. More neurological than the American S-R approach, Russian reflexology has kept alive an interplay between neurophysiology and psychology. Where the Americans have placed intervening variables between the stimulus and the response, the Russians have placed hypothetical constructs. This does make a difference in practice, in spite of in-principle arguments to the contrary. The Americans begin things with stimuli, hypothetical start buttons which defy exact empirical definition. The Russians, aware that there is as much efference as afference to the intake of experience, have been concerned to analyze out mechanisms—the orienting reflex, orienting-investigatory behavior—which are likely to be important factors in the definition

of the stimulus. The Americans have populated the innards of the organism with logicisms, if-then wiring which sometimes proliferates into complex skeins of logical or mathematical central hypotheses (e.g., Berlyne, 1965). The Russian conceptions of central processing have employed more complex physicalistic metaphors, which often are fragmentary and vague. These divergences in the Russian and American S-R traditions have led to significantly different approaches to learning and cognitive development. Today, certain contrasts between Russian work and American work seem to suggest some of the less obvious assumptions and goals built into the learning theory tradition. We will later be concerned with such contrasts.

BEHAVIORISM AND GENETIC PSYCHOLOGY: THE FIRST CONFRONTATION

It seems worthwhile to begin by asking why the stimulus-response tradition came so late to child psychology. S-R analyses of children's behavior did not become really prominent or widespread in American psychology until the middle 1950s. Yet, for several decades before this, the learning theories had been overwhelmingly in the center of theoretical efforts in psychology, coexisting with a sizable establishment of child psychologists who took no substantial guidance from them.

The anomaly is a little more surprising because John B. Watson had specifically made child psychology the intended center of his behavioristic reform. In 1917, Watson was awarded $100 by the Committee on Grants for Research of the American Association for the Advancement of Science to allow him to study the development of reflexes and instincts in infants. This was eight years after the first American description of Pavlov's work (Yerkes and Morgulis, 1909), four years after the declaration of Behaviorism (Watson, 1913), four years after Hunter's important comparisons of animals and infants (Hunter, 1913), and coincident with the first American research on conditioning—significantly, research employing children as subjects (Mateer, 1918). Watson did establish an infant laboratory and it bore fruit in some of the well-remembered documents of the Behaviorist era: Watson's analysis of the emotions

(Watson, 1919), his conditioning of Albert (Watson and Rayner, 1920), and his sponsorship of an environmentalism based on conditioned reflexes (Watson, 1926). But the infant work helped to promote a revolution in psychology at large while having curiously little lasting influence upon those psychologists who studied children.

In a recent volume, Kuo (1967), one of the earliest and most active behaviorists, regards this as a historical misfire:

In reviewing the history of the behavioristic movement one most important aspect has long been overlooked: the ontogenetic implications. These were clear to me in the basic tenets of behaviorism, in Watson's own later interest in the behavior of human neonates, in the vigorous anti-instinct campaign in the 1920's, and in Watson's effort . . . to catch up with the anti-instinct trend. An objective and unbiased historian of science should have been able in the late 1920's to forecast the future trend of development of the original Watsonian behaviorism, namely, the ontogenetic approach to the study of animal behavior. . . . The studies of various aspects of the ontogeny of postnatal behavior after World War II must be regarded as a continuation of the 1930's trend and partly as a silent (in most cases) protest against the rat-learning psychologists from Tolman to Hull, Skinner, and their followers, who seem to have deviated from the original tenets of Watsonian behaviorism (Kuo, 1967, p. 10).

In this quotation, Kuo seems to underestimate the persistent drive of Watson (and Tolman and Hull and Skinner) to use animal studies as a vehicle for the indirect study of human behavior. Watson's own motives for the study of infant behavior were clear; he saw in such studies a vehicle for the reform of society:

The behaviorist has an axe to grind, you say, by being so emphatic? Yes, he has—he would like to see the presuppositions and assumptions that are blocking us in our efforts to spend millions of dollars and years of patient research on infant psychology removed because then, and only then, can we build up a real psychology of mankind (Watson, 1926, p. 11).

Behaviorism ought to be a science that prepares men and women for understanding the principles of their own behavior. It ought to make men and women eager to rearrange their own lives, and especially eager to prepare themselves to bring up their own children in a healthy way. I wish I could picture for you what a rich and wonderful individual we should make of every healthy child if only we could let it shape itself properly and then provide for it a universe in which it could exercise that organization—a universe unshackled by legendary folk-lore of happenings thousands of years ago; unhampered by disgraceful political history; free of foolish customs and conventions which have no significance in themselves, yet which hem the individual in like taut steel bands. I am not asking for revolution; I am not asking people to go out to some God-forsaken place, form a colony, go naked and live a communal life, nor am I asking for a change to a diet of roots and herbs. I am not asking for "free love." I am trying to dangle a stimulus in front of you, a verbal stimulus which, if acted upon, will gradually change this universe. For the universe will change if you bring up your children, not in the freedom of the libertine, but in behavioristic freedom—a freedom which we cannot even picture in words, so little do we know of it. Will not these children, in turn, with their better ways of living and thinking, replace us as society and in turn bring up their children in a still more scientific way, until the world becomes a place fit for human habitation? (Watson, 1930, pp. 303-304).

One wishes that Watson's faith in Behaviorism might have worked out. Watson's utopian behaviorism finds echoes in Skinner's writings in our own day, but it was not the promise of social reform that initially won psychologists to the behavioristic cause. Most psychologists seem to have bought a methodological behaviorism stripped of the extremes of peripheralism, environmentalism, and utopianism espoused by Watson. Probably they bought it because it was crystallized into workable programs of scientific research and development by the various learning theorists, principally Tolman, Hull, and Skinner.

The Impact of the Learning Theories

The learning-theory movement was a complex and many-faceted social movement within Psychology. As is the case with any social movement, different individuals probably went along with it with a variety of understandings, purposes, and configurations of consent. What was the broadest basis of consent, the least disputed understanding and agreement among the users of the learning theories? It seems likely that most people went along with the learning theories because, first, they offered a peremptory though plausible solution to certain epistemological, metatheoretical issues that were a plague and a puzzle to psychologists at the turn of the century and, second, because they presented a well-reasoned plan for cooperative research to psychologists concerned to establish for their field a mutual, cumulative, scientific effort.

Epistemology and Methatheory. At the turn of the century, psychological writing was almost buried in discussion. Anyone disheartened by the routine "stamp collecting" research often found in current psychological journals should read the *Psychological Reviews* of the opening decades of this century to get a sense of a different boredom. There is a tortuous obscurity to much of the writing, a ponderousness, as various authorities are compared and reconciled, as tiny psychological issues are sifted for hemidemisemiquavers of implication, as author after author weighs in with his own elaborate statement of position on the mind-body problem. In the midst of this sea of dialogue, the modern reader can almost feel the relief as a modern piece of stamp collecting comes along—a close, careful naturalistic observation of animals (Watson, 1908), or an empirical investigation of handwriting analysis (Hull, 1919).

Much of the obsessing was about a circle of interconnected issues having to do with epistemology, the mind-body problem, and the relationship between physics and psychology. There was, on the one hand, a concern that these questions be settled adequately because they were fundamental for Psychology's initiation of empirical inquiry and, on the other hand, an exasperation with all the disputing and a frequently voiced desire, expressed by Titchener no less than Watson, that the problems of psychology be separated from the problems of philosophy. Behaviorism and, subsequently, the learning theories offered a preemptive way out, and it was taken.

We are generally aware of certain ideological elements which were put together in the construction of the learning theories: Darwinism, Behaviorism, the connectionism of Thorndike, the reflexology of Pavlov, and the logical positivism of the Vienna Circle. These contributed semifinished ingredients to the system builders. One important ingredient, a physicalistic epistemology of "naive realism," from which standpoint the mind-body issue could be dismissed as a pseudo problem, was a solution to the problems so prominent at that time. Today, living in a different ideological environment, we tend to underestimate the significance of that solution.

Cooperative Program. Once it was settled that the psychologist might look easily at a world of objects and movements, there remained questions of how, and for what the examination should be directed. The ingredients of the learning theories, woven into elaborated programs by the system builders, provided a justified agenda. There was a vision of reinforcement as a natural selection process in the environment which could select out adaptive animal behaviors—hence the justification for an intensive examination of learning as a reinforcement process. There were techniques for the study of learning on which the field could to some extent standardize because of the belief that such techniques got close to the basic and universal forms of learning. Finally, there was an understanding of science as a process where empirical laws are collected to be organized into deductive theories, and there was a miscellany of papers designed to show that the S-R scheme under development could, in principle, be brought to a point where it might assimilate subtle or complex forms of human behavior (e.g., Hull, 1930, 1938)—these offered a vision of future significance for series of small-scale studies.

So much controversy of so many sorts has swirled about what learning theories could or could not do, their rightness or wrongness, that it is easy to miss one's way as one tries to discuss their purposes. What seems clear and evidential, above all, is that the learning theories provided a basis for the creation of a great volume of American research work. Filtering out the enthusiasms, the inadvertences, and the stubbornnesses which carry opponents and proponents of a system to extremes, the learning theory movement has probably not been widely accepted because its adherents have believed that: (1) all human beings are "nothing but" simple mechanical contrivances; (2) all human behavior is learned behavior; (3) the stimulus is cause and the response is effect. The theories have had a thrust which leads in those directions, but for every adherent who takes his theory "that far" there are others who do not. However, though individuals have not bought such arguments in principle, the theories have had a *de facto* influence channelling research in selected directions as though such principles were held. A fairly clear case for this can be made with respect to the heredity-environment issue (White, 1968a).

In the view being advanced here, behaviorism and the learning theories won the adherence of many because they found for Psychology a reasonable species of psychological reality, and because they then laid down a paradigm of cooperative research procedure which might search that reality with a hope of significant findings. If one paid the price of the assumptions (thoughtful, intelligent assumptions, articulated by some of the best minds of the field), one could stop the hair-splitting and the throat-clearing and one could move into intensive scientific development. It was not necessary, and it is unlikely, that all who adopted this paradigm were intuitively persuaded by the model of organismic behavior implied within it. There is a statement by David Hume which goes, roughly, "If I had to live by my philosophy I would die within a week." However, the collective wisdom of psychologists in this tradition was inexorably formed by the model; journal articles traded information about S-R regularities, but the myriad of odd phenomena regularly turned up as by-products of S-R analyses—"set" effects, sensitization, habituation, sensory preconditioning, expectancy effects, etc.—were either set aside or else attempts were made to digest them into the S-R scheme.

The Genetic Tradition

We have this strong force in the theoretical psychology of the early decades, specifically aimed toward child study by Watson, and it is difficult to find any clear influence in the child psychology of the era—some enhancement of the study of learning, occasional papers expressing antipathy for the S-R model of man, and sympathy for opposing Gestalt arguments. Others beside Watson brought animal procedures to child psychology without conspicuously attaching theoretical strings (e.g., Weinbridge and Gabel, 1919). The study of children's learning moved off at a modest pace, using techniques borrowed from the Ebbinghaus tradition and from comparative psychology, the learning construed in the less drastic and less committing stimulus-response psychology of Thorndike's *Educational Psychology* (1913-1914), the research material organized—clustered would be a better word—only somewhat around issues of possible educational interest, such as massed versus distributed practice, or whole-part learning. The learning processes were a minor interest in the child psychology of the 1930s and 1940s. The first few volumes of *Child Development* from 1929 on place very little emphasis on learning work; parallel volumes of the *Journal of Genetic Psychology* contain a great deal of animal work but also show a steady, small, miscellaneous stream of papers on children's learning.

Part of this disengagement of child psychologists from the learning theory movement might be attributed to a generally pragmatic and undoctrinal style of this group, somewhat isolated from the main body of psychologists and committed more to interdisciplinary explorations. Not only learning theory but also psychoanalysis was not caught up. Systematists more indigenous to child psychology— Hall, Baldwin, Werner, the early Piaget— did not have a strong following. It is common to hear descriptions of the child psychology of the 1930s and 1940s as an enterprise devoted to atheoretical fact-gathering, and there seems to be some truth to that. Probably, the general torpor and dilapidation of research in child psychology so frequently commented upon in the early 1950s—see the *Annual Review* entry on "Developmental Psychology" by Barker (1951), and then successive years—reflects a kind of entropy of purpose due to this disinclination to articulate theory and program.

However, one has the definite feeling that learning theory did not cross over to child psychology in the 1930s and 1940s because of factors more active than the disinclination to theorize. However pragmatic and atheoretical the child psychological literature might have appeared in contrast with other areas of psychology burgeoning with learning theories and personality theories, one did have a group of researchers who were vigorous in generating and trading research information. This implies a shared theory in some sense of the term. Furthermore, the active period of the Child Development Movement in the 1930s coincided with the period when the learning theories were most actively under development in American psychology, when they were most exciting, and when it was most possible to be optimistic about possibilities. This vigorous thrust might, perhaps, have been walled off by theoretical passivity, but it seems more likely that it was checked by the existence of another point of view which was antipathetic to it. There are signs that a belief system with some integrity was maintained among child psychologists without much overt rehearsal. One might have called this belief system the "genetic point of view" at the turn of the century, and today one would be inclined to call it the "comparative-developmental point of view"—giving to Werner, rather than Piaget, the broadest contemporary statement of the position if not the most penetrating use of it.

There is an intricate and interesting history to be traced here, which we shall discuss in outline form. We are interested in why the learning theory tradition did not take root in child psychology in the 1920s and why it did in the 1950s. The argument, so far, is that there existed a not-well-articulated genetic tradition which was vigorous enough to successfully oppose its assumptions in the first half of this century. It is thus possible to look over that half century and argue, looking at the learning theory tradition, that Psychology has been too environmentalistic in its assumptions about human adaptation, or else, looking at the genetic tradition, that Psychology has

been too hereditarian in its assumptions (Hunt, 1961).

The genetic tradition arose from the speculations about human development formulated by the Evolutionists such as Spencer, Darwin, and Galton, and it has had a continuous influence upon American psychologists. For various reasons, the spokesmen who might have been prominent exemplifications of the position were not perfectly reputable in an era when American psychologists were concerned with the clarity and researchability of a theory. There was Hall, who was entirely too poetic and whose Recapitulationism, taken literally, could be disproved by empirical test (Grinder, 1967). There was Freud, who embedded his system in Wagnerian scenarios which almost disguised the fact that his theory of child development was another rendition of the genetic point of view. And, a little later, there was Werner's *Comparative Psychology of Mental Development*, whose influence is now growing but whose system for a long time seemed too loose and too philosophical for wide acceptance.

The transcription of the genetic point of view into a rigorous and tough-minded program for maintaining and containing research, always a central issue for American experimental psychologists, never took place, and has not yet taken place. The dynamics of the position—its view of what forms the child—did dictate that one should be concerned to understand the detailed flow of normative ontogenesis of behavior, and that within that framework one should be concerned about the potential for adjustment.

Certain interesting views of inquiry were opened up by the anthropometry of Galton, the norm-gathering of Binet and Henri in the 1890s, and the questionnaires of G. Stanley Hall. Hall fostered these in the Child Study Movement, and for a time promulgated a covering evolutionary ideology (Hall, 1908), but his system shriveled after his death into a few catch-phrases remembered only in textbooks about childhood and adolescence (Grinder, 1967). The approach, if not the words of Hall must have been sustained to some extent in the Child Development Movement, where there are so many similarities. There was the eclecticism, cross-disciplinary but centering in Psychology; there was the devotion to broad norm-gathering; there was the orientation to Education; there was a commitment to a geneticism which, faintly but firmly, kept alive the ideas of an innate hierarchy of talent, and the view of human development as a progression through maturational schedules. Terman and Gesell, Hall's students at Clark, were bellwethers in the developmental psychology of the 1930s and 1940s. Terman's interest in genius and stupidity was sustained from his earliest work as a student' in Hall's laboratory (Terman, 1906). His work continued a scientific extension of the intermixture of psychometry, anthropometry, and eugenic utopianism which motivated Sir Francis Galton. Gesell maintained interest in psychological embryology, acknowledging Hall's influence and developing what would appear to be the sensible empirical core of his system.

Huxley was right when he insisted that the study of embryology subtends the entire life cycle. The higher as well as lower orders of behavior were built by evolutionary processes, and they survive only through embryological (ontogenetic) processes however much they bear the final impress of acculturation. Learning is essentially growth; and even creative behavior is dependent upon the same kind of neuronic growth which fashions the capacities of the archaic motor system, *in utero* and *ex utero*. The performances of genius belong to a hierarchical continuum because there is only one physiology of development. There is but one embryology of behavior (Gesell, 1952, p. 153).

In brief, the learning theory tradition growing out from Watsonian behaviorism did not win a strong following among child psychologists because of their concern to develop a quite different set of assumptions about children, a genetic tradition, with an integrity of its own and research concerns of its own. In our own day, that genetic tradition has been rearoused as a force in American child psychology primarily because of the new vigor and incisiveness manifest in Piaget's work and the work of the Russian developmental theorists. Piaget's work is either child psychology or it is an empirical analysis of historic epistemological issues using children. The Russian work is child psy-

chology incidental to, and integrated with, the pursuit of a psychobiology of behavior. One sees that the new geneticism is something more than the reassertion of a maturational, stagelike, recapitulationistic process of growth and one must move outside child psychology to fully understand what it represents.

One cannot fully understand the point of view of genetic psychologists toward children unless one understands something about a great deal of other information not having to do with children which forms the point of view. Indeed, lengthy and detailed observations of children began some years after the point of view was formed at around the time of Darwin. The same might be said of the learning theory point of view: it states what *should* be true of children in consistency with a body of assumptions and data outside child psychology. In this writer's judgment, the conflict between the learning theory tradition and the tradition of genetic psychology was and is another chapter of the ancient and honorable conflict between empiricist and rationalist views of man.

Psychologists have a sense of the historical continuities which has led to a continuous reassertion of an associationistic scheme for psychological affairs, because good histories (Warren, 1921; Boring, 1951) have traced the lineage clearly. We do not have nearly as good a sense of the continuous reassertion of psychological schemes descending from Cartesian rationalism. One suspects a good history of this kind could be written. There is a tradition which has elaborated exactly those elements of Descartes' epistemology which the British empiricists were concerned to expunge: the acceptance of acts of reflection in the psyche, and the attempt to classify them; the acceptance of a priori intuitions in the mind; the concern to align brain and mind; and, finally, the assertion of discontinuities between lower-order and higher-order mental processes, the argument that they differ qualitatively rather than quantitatively. This is a characterization of Descartes' psychology, but it is also a description of the psychology of Piaget.

Evolutionism, and the various theories of human mental functioning which flowed from it, added a genetic wing to the rationalist scheme of things. That new genetic psychology seems to have begun with Herbert

Spencer, whose philosophical influence was extended toward Piaget via Bergson, toward neurology and psychiatry via Hughlings Jackson, and toward the American genetic tradition via G. Stanley Hall. The great principle of development which Spencer applied to everything, that all systems progress from "an indefinite, incoherent homogeneity to a definite, coherent heterogeneity," survives today in child psychology as Werner's orthogenetic law.

In the terms just sketched, one would argue that Watson's behaviorism, and the subsequent elaboration of the learning theories, did not have a significant influence on child psychology in the early decades of this century because child psychologists had a rival theoretical scheme, more or less implicit and unrehearsed, in the genetic-rationalist tradition. Not really well suited to development through research, not persuasively reasserted, this tradition failed to keep things going and the child development movement lost vigor. That which organized and rationalized its research ventures was not rehearsed and adjusted and expanded. Ultimately, the learning theory tradition did infuse a programmatic sector into child psychology—because there was a vacuum?—because of change in the learning theory tradition? What did come into child psychology was a tradition in evolution, the evolution intended to accommodate the S-R analysis to the rationalist and developmental issues.

THE LEARNING THEORY TRADITION TODAY: HOMOGENEITY AND HETEROGENEITY

A significant movement toward stimulus-response analysis did emerge among child psychologists in the mid-1950s, unified in some senses and conglomerate in others. The unity was somewhat submerged in that there was not much theoretical or programmatic writing designed to explain or justify these kinds of efforts. In the mid-1950s, the learning theories, their assumptions, and their various extensions, were so widely understood in the professional culture of American psychologists that such efforts seemed more or less natural. The diversity resulted from the fact that the S-R tradition moved into child psychology embedded in several programmatic

packages. These packages—at least two distinct approaches to the strategy of basic research, at least a half-dozen more S-R approaches to issues other than learning—had, generally speaking, been developed outside child psychology and then diffused into it. Though all of these programs flew the flag of behavior theory or behavior analysis, they were discrete in the sense that a faith in one did not, logically or in fact, imply a faith in the others. Proponents of behavior analysis were divided about whether basic research should proceed by an atheoretical functional analysis or a learning theory approach, and they showed varied patterns of interest in extensions of the S-R scheme to cognitive, social, and clinical phenomena, or to the development of interventive techniques for behavior therapy, behavior engineering, or programmed learning.

This differentiation of approaches has been hardening, and today it would be careless to view all of the proponents of a stimulus-response psychology as interested in learning theory, S-R analysis of human behavior, behavior therapy, etc. There are commonalities, but they are subtle and one must pick and choose one's way carefully to find them; there is probably no completely uncontroversial way to do so.

One thing which unites stimulus-response psychologists is, of course, their commitment to a psychology of Ss and Rs, and to transactions with observable behavior change. What is often called the "learning theory point of view" would seem to amount to these assumptions:

1. The environment may be unambiguously characterized in terms of stimuli.

2. Behavior may be unambiguously characterized in terms of responses.

3. A class of stimuli exist which, applied contingently and immediately following a response, increase it or decrease it in some measurable fashion. These stimuli may be treated as reinforcers.

4. Learning may be completely characterized in terms of various possible couplings among stimuli, responses, and reinforcers.

5. Unless there is definite evidence to the contrary, classes of behavior may be assumed to be learned, manipulable by the environ-

ment, extinguishable, and trainable (White, 1969).

The first two assumptions have to do with the reality of the psychologist as scientist. Though to many psychologists these seem to be easy and convenient, our glance at history shows that they imply significant commitments. The last three represent a Darwinistic conception of behavior adaptation—the survival of the fittest response through reinforcement—which can be traced back to Thorndike (1913-1914, 1931) and which, with variations, runs through the learning theories.

The learning-theory tradition has characteristically been a rigorous movement, paying great attention to observational proof and parsimony of interpretation. There has been an emphasis on small-scale experiments with tight control of conditions, usually experiments on learning where specifiable changes in conditions produce countable changes in behavior (White, 1963). There has been an emphasis on bringing terminology "close to behavior." Operational definitions are sought for key terms (Spiker and McCandless, 1954); other systematic positions are examined for the possibility of an S-R translation, and in applied work the thrust of the tradition is toward the maximum reduction of problems and goals to observable, countable patterns of behavior (Krasner and Ullman, 1965). In keeping with this urge to avoid vagueness, this tradition more than any other has brought instrumentation into child psychology to regularize the administration of experimental procedures.

There is, then, a unifying commitment to a scientific universe of Ss and Rs, an understanding of behavioral adaptation as a process of response selection by reinforcement, and a methodological drive toward precision of observation and parsimony of interpretation. With this in mind, we can look at the diversity of expression of the learning theory tradition within child psychology. The literature has encompassed the following:

1. A small literature of operant analysis, with methodology carefully articulated but not oriented to theory, based on the program of B. F. Skinner (1938, 1953). This is largely concerned with the functional analysis of the behavior of the child, with both normal and disturbed patterns of behavior analyzed as under the control of reinforcement contingencies in the environment (e.g., Bijou and Baer, 1960, 1963; Ferster, 1961).

2. A small body of studies directed at assumptions or variables of concern to the theoretical position of Hull (1943) and Spence (1936, 1956), and in some general sense oriented toward the understanding of construct, law, and theory on which that position rests (e.g., Spiker, 1963; Castaneda and Palermo, 1955; Zeaman and House, 1963).

3. An eclectic group of studies, not identified with any program, yet analyzing procedures of classical conditioning, instrumental learning, verbal learning, and so forth, to look for the sorts of regularities that might usually be caught up in such programs (e.g., Stevenson and Weir, 1959; Weir, 1964; Lipsitt, 1963, 1967; Palermo, 1961, 1962; Brackbill, Fitzgerald, and Lintz, 1967).

4. A ramified set of attempts to translate issues of socialization and social interaction into stimulus-response terms, and to explore such issues experimentally. This includes studies of social reinforcement (Gewirtz and Baer, 1958a, 1958b; Stevenson, 1965; Gewirtz, 1967; Landau and Gewirtz, 1967), studies of imitation and "vicarious reinforcement" (Bandura and Walters, 1963; Bandura, 1965b; Baer and Sherman, 1964) and the analysis of conscience (Aronfreed, 1964).

5. Attempts to enlarge the framework of stimulus-response analysis to encompass verbal behavior (Skinner, 1957), curiosity and exploration (Berlyne, 1960), attention (Zeaman and House, 1963), symbolization (Kendler and Kendler, 1962; Reese, 1962), inference (Kendler and Kendler, 1967), and reasoning and planning (Maltzman, 1955; Staats, 1961; Berlyne, 1965).

6. Finally, a series of practical attempts at education, behavior engineering, and behavior modification, which have in common the attempt to train humans using manipulations of contingent reinforcement schedules. These efforts are manifold and widely directed. One major sector works toward the teaching of the normal child (Lumsdaine and Glaser, 1960; Skinner, 1968) and the other toward special education or behavior therapy (Krasner and Ullman, 1965; Ullman and Krasner, 1965; Bijou and Baer, 1967).

It might be said that this list of topics

underestimates the diversity of these efforts. It implies that the S-R tradition has been carried in all these directions without any "bending." It does not convey a proper impression of the huge volume of work fitting under these categories.

In the 15 to 20 years since the learning theory tradition entered child psychology, there has been a continuous acceleration of the volume of published efforts, but at the same time there has been a diminution in the first two categories of effort given above—less laboratory studies of schedules of reinforcement, and less basic research devoted to the development of the Hull-Spence theory. The two significant nuclei, the Hull-Spence learning theory and Skinner's program, still have some direct influence in the way their collaterals are evolving. Those coming from the Hull-Spence tradition have been devoted to continuing theoretical analysis, trying to open up new veins of S-R analysis which might provide theory to account for children's behavior. Those coming from Skinner's orientation have, like him, disregarded theoretical analysis for its own sake and have moved out of the laboratory toward behavioral engineering. Substantially different issues arise in the course of the theoretical thrust and the practical thrust.

THEORY-DIRECTED ANALYSIS

The traditional purpose of the learning theories was to serve as a framework for a cumulative development and integration of research information about learning. To provide the basic research, a family of procedures has been used, descendants of the verbal learning studies of Ebbinghaus and G. E. Müller, the salivary conditioning of Pavlov, and the trial-and-error problems of Thorndike. All these form a family because they have special characteristics in common, differentiating them from other procedures through which one might conceivably make observations or inferences about learning processes. In most of the special procedures, the subject's time to observe or act is parcelled out in trials. The time and place of learning is fixed and the environment is isolated, uninterrupted, and asocial. Discrete cues are made prominent. Criteria, set up by observer or instrument, are enforced so that countable,

timeable, scorable responses are fished from the stream of behavior. The typical research procedures for the study of learning have regularized it, made the learning situation more repeatable across individuals and laboratories. They have emphasized the maximum quantification of antecedents, consequents, and the time course of the process. The theories of learning were based upon the possibilities of controlled variation and experimentation possible when learning had been so regularized. One influence of the learning theory tradition upon child psychology has been, simply, to provide support for the dissemination of such regularized techniques as instruments for basic research into children's learning (Spiker, 1960; White, 1963).

The significance of the fact that such techniques have become conventional should not be underestimated; their almost exclusive use is in itself tantamount to what some might call the adoption of a theory of learning. Using these techniques as a window, one often does not "see" learning when the stimulus conditions are out of the view of the experimenter, when the change in behavior occasioned by learning does not occur fairly promptly, or when the effects of something learned may manifest themselves with equal probability in any of a dozen response indices. One tends to underestimate how much the problem of everyday learning may depend on the noisiness of the unpurified environment (White, 1966a). And, in child psychology, one tends to confuse the learning registered by the instrument with another, unregistered, learning process through which the child is trying to adapt to the instrument (Levin and Hamermesh, 1967). Of course, all this is not to say that experimenters cannot and do not make the effort to see beyond their formal data, or that this tradition alone runs the risk of instrumental nearsightedness. The point being emphasized is that a significant part of the learning theory tradition has been carried into child psychology by the sheer adoption of the specialized observational procedures adapted to that tradition.

If one looks for the programmatic impact of the learning theories upon the study of children's learning one must proceed a little carefully. No learning theory has ever been constructed from studies of children or been specifically directed toward them. Strictly speaking, there is no learning theory in child psychology. Setting aside direct applicability, there is a way in which the Hull-Spence theory and its collaterals have been construed as a potential basis for the understanding of children's learning:

1. One assumes, as Hull and Spence did, that there is an elementary bonding process through which bits of the environment become attached to bits of behavior. One assumes that the universal and elementary basis of all learning is the formation of an S-R bond. This is a behavioristic form of an old neurological suggestion that all organismic adaptation rests on more or less complicated forms of the reflex arc. Hull's systematic contribution (Hull, 1943, 1951) was primarily an attempt at an intensive analysis of the S-R bonding process. His theory provides an intensive analysis of one encounter during which a set of stimulus conditions are an occasion for a response. In this analysis, the stimulus conditions are described as quantified variables and their influence traced schematically to intervening variables, whose influence in turn is traced to response characteristics. The system provides that some of the flow through these lines of influence will influence performance momentarily, while others will make for the lasting influence that we call learning.

2. One assumes that all the more complex kinds of problem-solving are potentially decomposable into sets of interacting S-R bonds. Spence (1936, 1937, 1956) and Hull (1952) attempted a rigorous decomposition of one order of complexity—the situation, in two-choice discrimination learning, where the subject's behavior may be viewed as the resultant of the interaction of two competing S-R links. This analysis has been quite controversial, as well it should be, since it offers a test for the most significant promissory note of this type of theory—that a rigorous way can be found to multiply the one-S–one-R analysis through "composition laws" into a predictive schematic for complicated kinds of learning, conceived as many-S–many-R situations. Other examples of the attempt to provide such composition laws rigorously are Miller's (1959) analysis of conflict and displacement, Spiker's (1963) stimulus interaction hypothesis, and Zeaman and House's

(1963) attentional theory of discrimination learning.

3. All of the worked-out decompositions have been for experimental situations that are limited in complexity, but a large number of other analyses have been offered in which various interesting domains of behavior have been interpreted as S-R systems without much specification of the form of the composition laws which might be predictive for them. This is the speculative superstructure of S-R analysis extending from the learning theory base to the significant targets of psychological analysis. It contains a large literature, of mixed value. The best of this literature consists of carefully worked out treatments of imitation (Miller and Dollard, 1941; Bandura and Walters, 1963), psychopathology and therapy (Dollard and Miller, 1950), frustration-aggression (Dollard et al., 1939), symbolic processes (Mowrer, 1960), and thinking (Berlyne, 1965). In these treatments there is manifestly some effort, not always successful, to keep novel S-R constructions within the epistemological and metatheoretical boundaries within which the terminology was framed. In less useful speculative treatments, the S-R terminology seems to degenerate into a catch-all scientistic jargon. On the more careful side we have the laborious and intricate literature which tries to capture a little bit of the activity of representation in an S-R mediation scheme (Kendler and Kendler, 1962; Reese, 1962); on the less careful side we have the practice, common now, of using the term "mediation" as an acceptable way to say "thinking." Today, too, there are the offerings in educational psychology in which various generalizations are wrenched from their origins in experimental situations and unhesitatingly offered up as laws of classroom learning. Disregarding these latter misconstructions of the learning theory analysis (the price of popularity, which psychoanalysis has paid and which genetic epistemology is beginning to pay) one must accept the body of careful speculative extensions as an effort to display and justify the ultimate promise of the learning theories.

Keeping in mind these three levels of development of the Hull-Spence theory, one may suggest the linkages of that theory to basic research on learning in child psychology. Since Hull's formal system, laid out on animal data and the data of human classical conditioning, was intended to portray universal processes of S-R bond formation in all species, it is at least conceivable that the system could have been superimposed on the results of suitable data-gathering efforts using children. This possibility has aroused little interest among child psychologists. In the formal sense, Hull's theory is a first approximation to what we today call mathematical models of learning (Spence, 1952, 1953). The later, tighter body of mathematical models has not drawn forth much research and development among child psychologists, only sporadic and casual occasional papers on children's probability learning (e.g., Messick and Solley, 1957; Ross and Levy, 1958; Stevenson and Zigler, 1958; Atkinson, Sommer, and Sterman, 1960; McCullers and Stevenson, 1960; Kessen and Kessen, 1961; Siegel and Andrews, 1962; Brackbill, Kappy, and Starr, 1962; Craig and Meyers, 1963; Bogartz, 1965). If anything, the trend in child psychology is away from theorizing construed as mathematical modelling to predict behavioral probabilities.

The countervailing tendency among child psychologists has been to accept the exact analysis of the S-R bond as a given or as something to be worked out elsewhere and to concentrate efforts on the analysis of the more complex levels of behavior. At the second level of development of the Hull-Spence scheme, there is the discrimination analysis. Discrimination problems can be given to preschool children in formats quite analogous to those used with animals. Here, in the children's literature, one finds what little formal theorizing there is (Spiker, 1963; Zeaman and House, 1963) and here one finds a small reconsideration of the continuity-noncontinuity controversy resolved by the postulation of central stimulus-selection mechanisms. The newer analyses of the child in the discrimination situation run together with the newer analyses of the animal in that situation (Fellows, 1968; Riley, 1968). But here, as everywhere, the child psychologist's adoptions of the instruments and the formal theoretical apparatus of the tradition are mostly not being used for the development of a formal theory; effort is concentrated on those aspects of the discrimination situation which offer a jumping-off place for the exploration of factors of attention and symbolization. Examining the spectrum of S-R efforts in the time of the new American revolution, this seems predominantly to be the case. Most of the work in child psychology is at the third level of development of the Hull-Spence analysis, the attempt to "open up" the theoretical scheme to make it a vehicle for the understanding of significant issues in human behavior. There are a series of such programs, which can be seen as attempts to modify and enlarge the analysis to accommodate it to the human factors and the developmental factors with which the child psychologist must deal.

Analysis of the Stimulus

The problem of the exact definition of the stimulus arises before one attempts to bring the S-R analysis to human behavior; it is a fundamental issue for that analysis, never really resolved. In an early paper, Skinner recognized the problem:

In the description of behavior it is usually assumed that both behavior and environment may be broken into parts, which may be referred to by name, and that these parts will retain their identity from experiment to experiment. If this assumption were not in some sense justified, a science of behavior would be impossible . . . (Skinner, 1935, p. 40).

Despite the truce with the problem worked out by Skinner in that paper, the problem of the stimulus, the "environment broken into parts," has persisted for behavior theory. The problem is that one cannot seem to find a part of the environment which in and of itself, disregarding the subject, is always a stimulus for behavior. In recent years, S-R psychologists within and without child psychology have tried to grapple with the issue of the definition of the stimulus and, in so doing, have reintroduced the term "attention" to behavior analysis.

Stimulus Saliency. In all behavior analysis, it has been recognized that some parts of the environment are more likely to be stimuli than others because of intrinsic properties of intensity, change, size, etc. In a recent, influential book, Berlyne (1960) attempted an examination of the issue of attention, orienting, and stimulus selection. With the publication of that book, an interest in what he has termed "collative variables" of novelty, change, complexity, conflict, surprisingness, and structure has developed in the subsequent experimental literature. Cantor (1963) has provided a review of research directed at substantiating the special saliency of complex and novel stimuli for children's behavior.

Berlyne's analysis is less concerned with the intrinsic properties of environmental events which cause them to draw attention, and more with attention as it is determined by a strategic interplay between what the environment offers and the central structures within the subject. Several researchers have been concerned to show that the efficacy of a stimulus may be altered by the subject's history with it. Cantor and his associates have explored what seems to be a stimulus satiation effect upon reaction time (Cantor and Cantor, 1964, 1965, 1966; Witte and Cantor, 1967; Bogartz and Witte, 1966; Witte, 1967). Another set of studies has shown that stimuli which are associated with rewards acquire salience for the subject (Nunnally, Stevens, and Hall, 1965; Nunnally, Duchnowski, and Parker, 1965; Parker and Nunnally, 1966; Nunnally, Duchnowski, and Knott, 1967; Nunnally and Faw, 1968). Such experiments begin to introduce conditionality into the effectiveness of a stimulus. Despite their obvious relevance, experiments which attempt to monitor at least the overt accompaniments of the stimulus selection process, scanning behavior, are still few (White and Plum, 1964; Wright and Smothergill, 1967). Such experiments would obviously be useful in providing a bridge between the kinds of stimulus-enhancing and stimulus-diminution factors suggested in the Cantor and Nunnally series and the dimension-selecting mechanisms which are proposed to exist in the Zeaman and House theory.

The S-R tradition has thus made an acknowledgment of attentional factors when they are determined by the intrinsic saliency of the stimulus, by the overt scanning of the subject, or by the relatively recent history of the subject with the stimulus. Berlyne's theoretical analysis goes further, of course, but it seems significant that subsequent experimental work has been so heavily directed toward the novelty and complexity of stimuli, the most "out there" of his collative variables. Other collative variables depend upon the postulation of central mechanisms which effectively select those parts of the environment that will be stimuli, central structures which have as yet been given no detailed and incisive representation in the S-R schematization. We turn now to an examination of some of the recent attempts to approach such central terms.

Attempts to Model Conceptualization, Inference, and Planning

As has been suggested earlier, the original basis on which the learning theories were established in psychology was once to provide a step-by-step empirical route toward the analysis of complex human adaptive mechanisms. A good number of the early theoretical writings of Tolman and Hull were directed to offering behavioristic or S-R accounts of higher mental processes, and continuous with the history of the S-R tradition there have been numerous attempts to provide accounts of expectancies, sets, concepts, inferences, and strategies within the scope of the system. Within child psychology, one finds representations of some of these efforts. It seems significant that despite the long history of S-R attempts in these directions, so much of the present work seems at its beginning, tentative and prefatory. Where a large literature has developed, as is the case with the mediation hypothesis, it has eventuated in very little systematic development.

Discrimination Learning Set. Stemming from Harlow's work with animals, there has been some exploration of the phenomenon of learning set with children and the work with children has largely substantiated what has been concluded from the animal studies. Experiments have demonstrated cumulative nonspecific transfer—learning to learn—from one discrimination problem to the next, and they have suggested that such transfer is associated with the progressive suppression of position-guided strategies and, possibly, some change in the visual search patterns of the child as he moves from one problem to the next (Reese, 1963).

The present-day efforts, with animals and children, represent a more or less rigorous realization of the view of the discrimination learning process suggested by Lashley and Krechevsky some decades ago. Partly as a result of this realization, there are newer models of discrimination learning which blend together noncontinuous factors (stimulus analyzer selectors or dimension selectors) with continuous learning processes (Sutherland, 1959; Mackintosh, 1965; Zeaman and House, 1963). These provide that the organism can switch attention from one type of cue to another in the course of learning and provide a partial accommodation to the data at hand. The error factors appear to involve something more than inappropriate stimulus control over the subject's behavior, and this residual has not yet been incorporated into the theorizing. There are different strategies, or stereotypes, which can follow when subjects are position-guided and the systematic treatments do not offer a differentiation among the strategies. Furthermore, there are age changes in proneness to selection of a strategy (Weir, 1964; Levinson and Reese, 1967) which need explanation. The learning set analyses seem to have forced the establishment of enough central processing to account for central switching from one stimulus dimension to another and sudden learning; they have opened issues of strategy selection and age change, but no extensive analysis has been given to those issues in this line of work. There are other avenues which do lead to formulations concerning temporally organized response sequences and age change with respect to their use.

Mediation Theory. By far, the most extensively explored issues in the S-R literature of child psychology have to do with a pair of age shifts in learning occurring in children between 5 and 7 years of age. There have been hundreds of investigations of a change in the child's reaction to the transposition experiment in this age range (Kuenne, 1946) and a parallel change in reversal-nonreversal shift problems (Kendler and Kendler, 1962). This literature has mostly been concerned with whether such phenomena can be accounted for by central mediational processes (Kendler and Kendler, 1962; Reese, 1962), by age changes in attentional processes (Zeaman and House, 1963), or the development of stimulus differentiation (Tighe, 1965; Youniss and Furth, 1965). However, as one examines the voluminous literature on these problems

one is more impressed by the number and complexity of the side issues they have engendered than by their tendency to converge on some decisive clarification of the source of the original experimental effects (White, 1963; Zeiler, 1967; Weiss, 1967). White (1965, 1966a, 1966b, 1968b) has suggested that these age-shifts in learning experiments are part of a large spectrum of change in the 5-7 age range, involving not only many other behavior changes but also changes in physical growth and in susceptibility to pathology. One implication of such an analysis might be that these experimental situations and their variants offer too narrow a window through which to explore the underlying developmental process. Certainly, however, some facets of development could and should be better revealed by an examination of the changes in learning.

It is quite common for experiments in the learning theory tradition to uncover phenomena reflecting developmental changes or cognitive phenomena, and it is always an intriguing issue to try to handle them in some sort of systematic way. The issue, always, is whether such special phenomena, now located and demonstrable within an experimental S-R format, can be shown to have some explanation which is intrinsic to the S-R scheme. In terminology with which we have all become familiar, the issue is whether the S-R schema can be adapted to an observed novelty through assimilation or accommodation. To assimilate is essentially to account for the phenomenon in the terms of the theory; thus a broad set of phenomena in classical conditioning and associative transfer has been linked to some quantitative assumptions about drive-habit interaction in Hullian theory (Spence and Taylor, 1951; Spence, 1956; Castaneda, 1965). To accommodate, on the other hand, is to make some alteration in the theory which remains within certain ground rules basic to the construction of the theory; the ground rules are, essentially, the assumptions that form the "learning theory point of view," discussed earlier. Spiker's stimulus interaction hypothesis (1963) and Zeaman and House's attentional theory (1963) are examples of permissible alterations. Failure to adapt, to either assimilate or accommodate, would be represented by a concession to maturational or central causation not portrayable in S-R terms and not moved by the dynamics envisaged by the system.

Bearing in mind that the ultimate thrust into higher mental processes was the long-range goal of the Hullian system, the transposition and reversal-nonreversal shift phenomena have a special significance.

First, given a system which is largely built upon animal problem-solving, it is significant that these age changes between 5 and 7 seem to represent shifts from the approaches to these problems characteristic of animals toward the approach characteristic of human adults. If one could identify what is new in the older child's approach, one would probably have located a significant human factor.

Second, there is a relationship of these age shifts to language which strikes peculiarly closely to a long-suggested human factor. Children to show the older pattern of performance often give, or can be made to give, labels for stimuli that might lead them to the older behavior. These labels can be conceived of as the "pure stimulus acts," or response-produced cues, which behavior theorists have consistently postulated, in animal experiments as well as human, as a rigorous systematic basis for phenomena of anticipation, expectancy, or symbolization (Hull, 1930; Osgood, 1953).

Thus children in this age range make a move toward adultlike performance, and they do so in a way that suggests that response-produced cues might be fairly employed as a theoretical accommodation to the phenomena. The issues now reside in the fine grain of the data and, as well, in the fine grain of the hypothesis. There are ways in which verbalization might lead to the age shifts which would fit tightly neither into the theoretical framework nor, perhaps, within the ground rules (Vygotsky, 1962). One must elaborate the mediational hypothesis so that it describes not only the "before" and "after" learning processes, but also the mechanism of age change. Reese (1962), staying within the system of discourse, suggests overtraining as an explanation, but Kendler and Kendler (1962) suggest that it must be due to development, maturation and experience, conceding to factors outside the system. If labeling does not always accompany the older pattern of performance, and if teaching of labeling does not always produce it, it is

possible to hold that verbalization is not a cause but a correlate of the age-shifts, and to suggest as an alternative that changes in the attention of the child might account for them. Complicating the problem of decision among the overlapping theoretical alternatives is the fact that the experiments in this area regularly turn up odd experimental effects, which now form a good-sized family of unsolved side issues.

The voluminous and tortuous literature which all this has generated has not yet brought off the proof that the S-R scheme explains the older child's pattern. That explanation, even if successful, would really give the system little thinking power. What would be installed in the center would be a mediating word or act, cued as a response by the external stimulus, giving to the subject the ability to make a response not determined by his reinforcement history with the external stimulus.

Part of this limitedness is unnecessary in learning theory terms. It arises from a deceptiveness in the diagrammatic form in the S-R scheme, recognized in other contexts but not often brought up in discussions of children's mediation. The prototypical episode in Hullian theory begins with an S, or groups of Ss, moves through the intervening variables, and ends with an R. However, behavior theorists have had to recognize that, even in the simplest learning situations, the sequence S-R is an abbreviation for a sequence of behavioral episodes which must properly be diagrammed in some form like $S - R_1 - S_1 - R_2 - \ldots - R$ (Spence, 1956, p. 44). Diagrammed at full length, what behavior theorists have called an S-R connection becomes an organized assembly of adaptive behavior virtually identical to what Piaget has called a sensorimotor schema, and the mediational properties of a "response-produced cue" become—what? Perhaps something like the plan of Miller, Galanter, and Pribram (1960), perhaps something like the orienting-investigatory schemata of conceptualization of the Russians (Zaporozhets, 1961), perhaps something like the operation of Piaget (1960).

There is no explicit theoretical treatment which develops the possibility of a mediational use of a nonabbreviated S-R connection, but one can imagine a number of interesting possibilities. Any one of them would make the issue of mediation more complicated, richer, probably even less able to be settled by empirical test, than the question whether the child does or does not depend upon cue words like "larger" and "smaller" in his vocabulary. But it would instantly move behavior theory closer to comprehending findings like those of McKee and Riley (McKee and Riley, 1962; Riley and McKee, 1963; Riley, McKee, and Hadley, 1964), who have shown that transposition implies more general ordering ability than would be implied by the possession of locally appropriate ordering labels.

Inference and Reasoning. There has been some effort to examine the ways in which S-R links might be strung together in sequences, to form a basis for what are usually called reasoning and planning.

One line of work has produced a sequence of studies directed at children's inference. The sequence of studies has been reviewed in Kendler and Kendler (1967) in a close-knit analysis which is, in itself, a model of the process of experimental inference; the paper offers a superb example of the programmatic development of an idea through a succession of procedures and experiments. The searching serial quality of the set of studies reported in this paper is worth some emphasis. A problem which plagues the learning theory tradition because of its closeness to procedures and emphasis on testable hypothesis is the very readiness with which any issue draws swarms of "one-shot" literature entries—studies which must be accommodated because they do, after all, present data but which are so raw and chancy in inception, execution, and interpretation that it is difficult to know what weight to place upon them. A collection of such studies addressed to an issue—e.g., transposition, the controversies about latent learning, place versus response learning, etc., can bring in so much noise that they hinder as much as help. Many one-shot studies are valuable, of course, and one could not draw a line which excluded the bad from the good. Nevertheless, one can safely argue that there has been, and is, too little of the thoughtful programmatic experimentalism manifest in the Kendlers' efforts, in Osler's analyses of concept attainment (Osler and Fivel, 1961; Osler and Trautman, 1961; Osler and Weiss, 1962; Osler and Shapiro, 1964; Osler and Kofsky,

1965, 1966) and in Lipsitt's explorations of infant learning (Lipsitt, 1963, 1967).

The Kendlers' analysis of inference directs itself to Hull's analysis of reasoning, defined as "the joining of two-behavior chain segments previously learned on separate occasions so that together they solve a problem faced by the organism." In the course of their efforts, they come to the conclusion that Hull's formulation does not yield derivations valid for their data; they find that their test of reasoning shows a sharp increase in children between 8 and 12 years of age; they find interactions of inference with assigned verbal labels which lead them to conclude that verbal mediation has an important bridging function for the inference process. Again, their experimental analysis is quite precisely delimited; their theoretical analysis places in the center the simple labeling response or a response term like it:

. . . . we should again make explicit that representational responses are not synonymous with verbal labels. As far as we know, any response with adequate feedback could serve the purpose. We used linguistic labels for reasons already enumerated. It also seems likely that, among articulate humans, verbal labels are among the most common responses used for representation simply because they are so well suited to this function. They are so available, discriminable, easily fractionated, can occur without interference with any other ongoing activity, can so easily move forward in the behavior sequence (Kendler and Kendler, 1967, pp. 188-189).

The Kendlers, here as in their reversal-nonreversal analyses, stop short of the proliferative possibilities introduced by their vicarious cue-producing response. Presumably, a response-produced cue could produce another vicarious response-produced cue which in turn could lead to others and one could then conjecture branching sequences of invisible S-R links to serve as a basis for quite complex central mediating processes. The Kendlers and other behavior theorists have probably stopped short of this kind of expansion because it is obvious that one is instantly deploying the scheme into conjectural and untestable areas. But there is a neobehavioristic group spearheaded by Osgood and Berlyne which has developed these kinds of constructions.

Berlyne's recent volume *Structure and Direction in Thinking* must be considered a landmark in the S-R analyses of higher mental processes, with particular interest for child psychologists. Unlike other behavior theorists, who often set forth theoretical schemes on carefully delimited domains as though the only facts that needed adjusting to were the incontrovertibly proven facts and the only real issues were the precisely formulated issues, Berlyne is unusually catholic and wide-ranging in his acknowledgment of diverse facts, issues, and formulations. Although other behavior theorists have been timorous about venturing more than a pseudopod of S-Rism into the unobservable areas of human mentalism, Berlyne has been quite bold in doing so. The two big problems in the center are, probably, what we generally call attention and reasoning and in separate books Berlyne has made a significant effort to encompass each (Berlyne, 1960, 1965).

The directed thinking book hearkens back to the second most venturesome of the S-R systematists, Hull himself, and the ideas which Berlyne develops have their germs in early theoretical papers in which Hull was trying to foresee the ultimate possibilities of an S-R analysis (Hull, 1930, 1931, 1934, 1935, 1938). The theoretical structures which are used are familiar in the learning theory lexicon: habit, the fractional anticipatory goal response, stimulus generalization, the habit family hierarchy, and so forth. These are worked up to model sequential thought processes in a way which has been tried before, by Hull in the previously cited papers and by others (Maltzman, 1955; Staats, 1961). Berlyne, however, offers certain new interpretations of these speculative habit structures which enables them to be subject to operations, transformations, groupings, etc. At the heart of the effort is the union between the speculative scheme of reasoning of S-R and Piaget, but there is more to the synthesis than that. The system also gives a place to such factors as imagery, multiple sensory representation, and certain of the transformational devices of the psycholinguists.

The complete treatment needs to be read, if only because there is not much writing anywhere which is so broadly in tune with what the issues are for an analyst of reasoning. There is, of course, something slightly outrageous about the casting of all this in the S-R terminology. One has obviously moved things a good distance away from the "learning theory point of view," empiricism, behaviorism, and the traditional view of parsimony. That the treatment is possible at all is due to a quality in the treatment of the terms "stimulus" and "response," which should really be more explicitly acknowledged in the learning theorists' use of them. On the one hand the terms have been used to denote empirical units, the "behavior and environment broken into parts," which Skinner (1935) was at pains to justify, and on the other hand they have had a logical status. The terms "stimulus" and "response" have come to stand for "if" and "then" in a calculus of sequential psychological contingency. On many occasions, the empirical and logical uses of the S-R terminology can be confused and confusing, but Berlyne's use of it makes a fairly clean break with the empirical side. Essentially, the innards of Berlyne's reasoning organism are wired with if-then statements, or systems of them.

Berlyne (1954) has freely admitted the difficulties with this speculative S-Rism, but he has argued that the rigor of the S-R terminology makes the effort worth a try. One cannot speak of empirical rigor in this kind of effort, but one can speak of a rigor of delineation of antecedent and consequence in hypothesized processing sequences. This is not the "right" rigor in the classical S-R sense, but there are plenty of cases in the history of psychology where right things have been done in the wrong way and wrong things have been done in the right way. This kind of effort is almost *sui generis*. It floats free of its origin and it needs to be judged on its own terms. Right now, it has some intrinsic interest for child psychologists because it has accomplished some important junctures among what might have seemed to have been incommensurable sets of independent analyses. It will not be testable and provable or disprovable in the usual sense in which we understand those terms. But it rests on facts and on reasonable interpretations of those facts; its linkages are quite reasonable; it has a form of truth value because of that. In time, we may know enough to rewrite it, make it closer to a larger network of facts, locate it better in neural processes, perhaps give it more exact predictive and explanatory power. We have no alternative to a treatment like this, really, because we have not yet found any better way to build a behavior theory.

Attempts to Examine Social and Personality Processes

We turn, now, to a set of theoretical efforts in which the S-R scheme is brought away from its originating thrust toward human problem-solving, and we consider a set of efforts in which the S-R terminology has been brought toward the other great concern of psychologists in the first half of this century: a personality theory, an interwoven consideration of individual differences, social influences, and psychopathology. The originating development of the S-R scheme toward a theoretical account of personality issues was, again, out of Yale: Miller and Dollard's (1941) analysis of imitation, Dollard and Miller's (1950) account of personality and psychopathology, and Mowrer's (1950) treatment of personality. These larger efforts were accompanied by a large number of research efforts, using animals and humans, in which experimental techniques were developed to attempt to bring fear, anxiety, conflict, regression, displacement, fixation, etc., into the laboratory. There are obvious difficulties in establishing an experimental tradition around such topics with human subjects, but certain kinds of studies—of imitation, of social interaction effects—can be conducted in an experimental manner using children. Other topics are approachable through observations of co-incidence, correlational methods. In recent years, still another empirical approach is at hand, in which a theoretical analysis is interwoven with an applied effort at behavioral or social engineering. Now we cannot speak of a laboratory tradition; we begin with speculative analyses which by their nature must touch empirical ground when and as they can.

The S-R analysis of learning and cognitive processes worked its way into child psychology through a number of spin-offs in which procedures and issues elaborated in the general experimental literature migrated into use with children. The learning theory approach to personality processes came in less adventi-

tiously and it came in earlier. Robert Sears, concerned at first with the experimental testing of psychoanalytic hypotheses (Sears, 1943), became the first to organize a learning-theory-based analysis into child psychology and one can trace most of the efforts to provide an S-R analysis of personality development to his influence. His move into child psychology was a logical one. The conditions for learning are at hand to be studied wherever one can produce some learning, but the conditions for the development of personality would seem to be either in childhood or in genetics. Thus personality theories of the S-R stripe or any other variety must inherently be concerned about developmental issues.

Antecedent-Consequent Analysis of Child-Rearing Consequences. The development of an antecedent-consequent analysis of the growth of the child's personality would seem to have been built around three consecutive programs of research organized by Sears and his associates and described in three major reports (Sears et al., 1953; Sears, Maccoby, and Levin, 1957; Sears, Rau, and Alpert, 1965) and numerous collateral papers. Though these programs originated in an attempt to apply something much like the Hull scheme to socialization, a number. of important modifications of the scheme had to be made to confront the problem, and it is questionable whether the final form of the efforts was in any vital way formally dependent upon, or a serious test of, the originating learning theory.

That Sears was initially concerned to develop a Hull-like theory seems clear in his presidential address to the American Psychological Association in 1951:

. . . the data of social psychology have been meager and those of personality limited mainly to clinical observations.

Yet it is clear that further development in these fields will require an adequate theory. By a theory I mean a set of variables and the propositions that relate them to one another as antecedents and consequents. This involves such logical impedimenta as definites, postulates, and theorems. And it requires the following of certain rules, such as that the definitions of variables must be mutually exclusive; that intervening variables must ultimately be reducible to operations; that the reference events specified as the consequents in theorems must be measured independently of the antecedents from which they are derived and so on. The general procedure of theory construction is sufficiently standard that it needs no explication here (Sears, 1951, p. 476).

Sears' efforts have been most consistently concerned with the analysis of dependency and aggressiveness in children, dependency construed in the S-R scheme as a secondary reinforcement process arising because the parent is instrumental for and contiguous to the reduction of primary drives in the child, aggression analyzed in the terms of the frustration-aggression hypothesis, of which Sears was a co-developer (Dollard et al., 1939). In the analyses of child-rearing practices which were undertaken, characteristics of parents and homes were treated as independent variables and dispositions of the child, often far removed in time, were treated as dependent variables. In those analyses, consequently, Hull's analysis of the force field surrounding a single S-R episode would not be applicable and, instead, we deal with the causal connections between antecedents and consequents. The antecedents and consequents are not one event, but rather a string of events having a similar force as, for example, when a mother consistently punishes overt aggression and the child is regularly quite aggressive in doll play. In several significant ways, the approach of Sears and his group vacated the observational base of the learning theorists, slicing the stream of behavior quite differently, while retaining their concern for the dynamics and terminology of S-R analysis.

Sears (1951) has projected an even more radical departure of antecedent-consequent analysis from conventional behavior theory. He points out that personality and social psychology, concerned with interpersonal transactions, have need of *dyadic* theorizing which acknowledges the two-person interaction. This seems to be an argument that antecedent behaviors on the part of one person and consequent behaviors on the part of another cannot be fully comprehended without taking into account the fact that the individuals are in an established interdependency upon one another and, consequently, react to one another's behaviors in terms of expectancies. The expectancies of the actors participate in the defining of what is to be an antecedent or a consequent.

The various translations of the Sears group, done or projected, move the grounds for discussion of their organizing framework a distance away from the originating learning theory tradition. In fact, the theory once hoped for by Sears has not yet come into being. His originating efforts had success in one sense; they did create a good-sized body of research on children's socialization. Probably, the development of theory has not taken place because deductive psychological theories do not seem as accessible a goal as they once did, and because studies of the effects of child-rearing practices and interrelationships of personality variables have not yet made it easy to see regularities across studies (Kohlberg, 1963; Caldwell, 1964). There are still-unsolved technical problems in observing such regularities.

Imitation and Social Reinforcement. Through the work of some of Sear's students, there have developed some other veins of research into social processes in childhood. These efforts are not directly derivative from Sears' antecedent-consequent approach. They are often characterized as social learning theory. They involve small-scale laboratory studies using children and in the ideas which guide them they make a fresh connection with the learning theory tradition.

Bandura and Walters (1963) have set forth an important new treatment of the imitative process in children. They, like Sears, emphasize consideration of the dyadic nature of human transactions and they point out convincing experimental evidence of the significance of imitation as a basic mechanism of learning. They suggest that some modification of the learning theories is necessary to account for this. Accommodation of the learning theory to imitation has existed for some time in treatments by Miller and Dollard (1941) and Mowrer (1950), but those treatments are essentially accounts of the establishment of the eliciting powers of the model through reinforcement. Experiments exist which support them. One can increase imitation by increasing the rewarding powers of the model (Bandura and Huston, 1961; Bandura, Ross, and

Ross, 1963) and one can, through reinforcement, increase the child's generalized tendency to imitate (Baer and Sherman, 1964). However, Bandura and Walters point out that individuals without any status in the reinforcement history of the child—strangers—can serve as models for imitation and that therefore imitation can serve as a generalized basis for the transmission of behavior patterns outside a context of reinforcement and nonreinforcement.

In the history of the development of learning theories, there somehow developed a consensus that there are two fundamental types of learning, in the Hull-Spence terminology called *classical* and *instrumental* conditioning and in Skinner's terminology *respondent* and *operant* conditioning. The assumption that there are only these two types has not been probed very extensively, probably because it is difficult to conceive of a direct test of the far-reaching assumption thot one or two learning processes are the prototypes of all adaptation. One can ask if at least one of the two types is detectable in all species which give some evidence of learning; one can ask if at least one of the two mechanisms is detectable in infancy coexisting with the first clear signs of environmental adaptation; one can ask if all forms of adaptation which do not look like these two types are somehow reducible as special cases of them. The first two kinds of tests have been sporadically attempted (e.g., Hilgard and Marquis, 1940, p. 30–32; Lipsitt, 1963) without any strong contradiction of the existence of the basic dichtomy. With respect to the third test, things are more ambiguous, because it is always debatable whether or not an analysis of an observed adaptation does or does not successfully reduce it to the proposed basis. Thus, there now exist a set of observed forms of adaptation whose relationship to classical and instrumental conditioning has at best been conjectural: sensory preconditioning, habituation, stimulus predifferentiation, learning sets, sensitization, imprinting, and imitation. Several of these are of considerable interest to the child psychologist, because they imply accounts of the development of the child through experience not conceived as reinforcement history. Imitation, in one sense firmly linked to behavior theory, is a good case in point.

Bandura (1965b) has offered an incisive and scholarly analysis of the mechanism of imitation and its influence, and his review sets the imitative tendency within the learning theory framework, with one or two amendments. Observational learning does require the assumption that imaginal and verbal representation of a model's behavior can be developed in the observer through contiguity, and that such representations can then serve as directions ("discriminative stimuli," "templates") for the organization of the observer's subsequent behavior. The tendency to imitate gives to the child a mechanism of "no-trial learning," Bandura's phrase, which would enable him through observation of others' behavior to develop new response patterns (Bandura, Ross, and Ross, 1961; Bandura, Grusec, and Menlove, 1966), modify his behavior according to the permissions and prohibitions in his environment, (Walters and Parke, 1964), and interpret his own emotional reaction to it (Schachter and Singer, 1962). Evidence that observation will accomplish these things has been provided in a great number of experiments (Bandura, 1965b). Imitation thus provides a basis for a broad spectrum of adaptation, and it could account for an enormous amount of the child's learning in life. Bandura argues that, in fact, it must be quite pervasive in its influence because of its efficiency, because there are so many kinds of adaptation to physical and social risks where trial-and-error learning would be inconceivable, and because the child learns so much for which it is difficult to imagine a reinforcement shaping history.

Whether or not the imitative tendency derives from the mechanisms of learning theory, the wide practical importance of imitation envisaged by Bandura would seem to necessitate a radical reorientation of experiment and theory having to do with children's learning. Most of our studies of children's learning are not intentionally conceived as dyadic. If imitative learning is a central factor, this experimental emphasis needs to change.

Most of the experimentation on imitation to date has attempted to demonstrate the range of effects it can have and it has been incidentally directed at establishing its precise linkages to processes of classical and instrumental conditioning. The delayed reproduction of the model's behavior requires that there exist within the subject imaginal and verbal representations of the model's series of stimuli, which, in turn, serve as discriminative stimuli guiding the observer's reproduction. These, it is argued, are cue-producing symbolic responses developed according to the usual associative learning principles. Again, here, there is an appeal to central representational elements which, by the very nature of the imitative phenomenon, must be something more than the single cue-producing response conditioned to the single stimulus. This is a substantial admission of a central operator, though not all concede its necessity (Gewirtz and Stingle, 1968).

The radical theoretical reorientation provided by imitation comes where one tries to project outward from mechanisms and functions toward some kind of account of the child's development through experience. One does not have to search the child's history for hypothetical reinforcement sequences which could shape him toward adulthood; one imagines, in addition to this, an extensive influence of unreinforced observation of others. In so doing, the learning theory view veers abruptly toward the reconstructions of the cognitive development of the child offered by Piaget (1962) and of his psychosocial development by Kohlberg (Kohlberg, 1966), ostensibly treatments offered from a point of view quite different from the learning theory tradition. These offer free play to central operations, whereas the representational scheme offered by Bandura is used judiciously simply as a carrier of the model's earlier performance to the observer's later copy. If one assumes the possibility of central operations upon such a carrier, and it seems more likely than not that evidence for this could be developed, one forms an alliance with the constructions of Berlyne's neobehaviorism. All in all, the introduction of a mechanism of imitation would require a rather drastic revision of all previous projections from the learning theory framework.

Another large vein of research activity has been developed from studies of a special dyadic situation, conceived as a paradigm for the study of social reinforcement. In this situation, the rate at which a child performs a simple repetitive response, his baseline, may be increased or decreased by supportive comments delivered by others. This measurement of the effectiveness of a social stimulus

through its ability to deflect ongoing steady behavior is analogous to a technique widely used for the study of fear in animals, where the effects of a fear-evoking stimulus are measured by its ability to elicit cessations in a stream of positively rewarded responses (Estes and Skinner, 1941). Here, the development of a considerable body of data reflecting manifold and complex social influences upon the child's behavior has been, so far, an inductive process without much accompanying theoretical development (Stevenson, 1965). The experimental paradigm is treated curiously like a behavioristic projective test for uncovering the effects of social motivation. Not all are agreed that a social motive, per se, is involved. One issue, an effect of isolation on social reinforcement first described by Gewirtz and Baer (Gewirtz and Baer, 1958a, 1958b; Gewirtz, Baer, and Roth, 1958) has led to extended replication and the development of several possible lines of explanation of social influences in this situation (Walters and Ray, 1950; Erickson, 1962; Stevenson and Odom, 1962; Hill and Stevenson, 1964; Lewis, 1965; Rosenhan, 1967; Landau and Gewirtz, 1967; Gewirtz, 1967). These offer, in microcosm, a spectrum of S-R treatments of social influence in the contemporary literature.

THE EXPERIMENTAL ANALYSIS OF BEHAVIOR

In our discussion of the learning theory tradition in child psychology, we have been using an organization which simplifies discussion but is slightly inaccurate. We have discussed basic research and theory building largely as derivative from the Hull-Spence tradition, and we will now proceed to discuss the experimental analysis of behavior ("descriptive behaviorism," "functional analysis," "operant analysis") largely as a platform for applied efforts. Within child psychology, the pattern of contemporary work is mostly arranged this way—though one must note the existence of behavior therapies built from the Hull-Spence analysis or extensions of it (e.g., Wolpe, 1958; Bandura, 1961, 1965a), and theoretical arguments using the viewpoint of functional analysis (e.g., Gewirtz, 1961; Gewirtz and Stingle, 1968). The divergence between the two treatments of stimulus-response analysis is substantial and there is a sense in which it almost subsumes the applied-basic distinction. Functional analysis searches for those environmental conditions which control the animal's behavior; the behavior theorists are always concerned with the adequacy of a network of postulated relationships among variables. One tries to manage the subject and the other tries to explain him; these differences in approach are there whether the view is toward basic or applied problems, and whether the topic is learning or social behavior.

Again, here, we deal with an S-R program that was first well developed outside child psychology and which then exported component efforts into it. The general systematic stance of the program is familiar to most psychologists (Skinner, 1938, 1953, 1959b; Keller and Schoenfeld, 1950; Holland and Skinner, 1961; Hilgard and Bower, 1966; Reynolds, 1968). Despite the popularity of the approach of experimental analysis, there are not many ideological fissures within the group subscribing to the program. On the surface, at least, this is a movement which deliberately travels light theoretically and perhaps because of this it has not generated the proliferation of idiosyncratic analyses and speculative theorizing which now has acted to partition off subgroups of individuals who have become specialized in their commitment to behavior theory. To a rather remarkable extent, the individuals committed to functional analysis have held to those thrusts set up by Skinner.

A good deal of the uniqueness of functional analysis seems to have been laid down in a special treatment of animal research, first fully described in 1938 in Skinner's *The Behavior of Organisms*. An animal is brought to repeated delivery of an index response by a shaping procedure in which successive approximations to the response are rewarded. When the animal regularly delivers the response, his rate of delivery—the basic datum of this method—is subject to manipulation by various schedules of reinforcement, fixed programs of reward contingency and time interval which govern whether and when the running responses of the animal will bring a reinforcement. When an animal adopts a stable and characteristic pattern of response to the schedule, the schedule is said to control his behavior. Similarly, when a stimulus, signalling the enforcement of a particular schedule, influences the animal's behavior, there is said to be stimulus control. There may, also, be compoundings of stimuli and schedules offering too much intricacy for straightforward adaptation by the animal; then a second-order shaping process is devised in which one begins with a simple schedule and moves to successive approximations until the animal is adapted to the multiple schedule. This constant emphasis on control "sets" the system in the direction of the behavior engineering efforts toward which it has tended. Where the traditional motto of hard-nosed psychology has been "Predict and Control," a different kind of scientific determinism is called into play here, a determinism in which one controls and therefore predicts.

Method, this method of working with subjects, is one important unifier of those interested in the experimental analysis of behavior. There has been sustained laboratory exploration of schedule effects accompanied by the innovation of new schedules. Some of the schedule information has been codified in a large handbook (Ferster and Skinner, 1957) and, since 1958, more has appeared regularly in the *Journal of the Experimental Analysis of Behavior* devoted almost exclusively to the development of the method. Some have argued that the widespread influence of Skinner's systematic writings has been brought about by the utility and versatility of his experimental procedures. Such an argument has a little evidence going for it. Skinner's experimental chamber is an unusually convenient way of gathering behavioral data from animals: simple, automatable, sensitive, and flexible, it has been given extensive technical development, and it is now one of the bread and butter items of the psychological equipment industry.

Despite all the obvious usefulness of the operant paradigm, it would be a serious underestimation of the intellectual force of the program built around it to see that program only as sophisticated gadgetry with an ideological penumbra. The program, by choice, does not espouse a theory of behavior (Skinner, 1950). However, a unique approach to the study of behavior has been gradually developed in association with the instrumentation which, if it is not a theory, at least stands in serious competition to other approaches which include theoretical proposals.

Operant Conditioning: Paradigm and Approach

Skinner (1959), in a classic piece of scientific autobiography, has been kind enough to the future psychologist to give a straightforward chronological account of the development of his paradigm. The paper has a wry quality characteristic of much of Skinner's writings; it tells a candid story of the bumbling, chancy process of scientific discovery in the laboratory, and that story takes on satiric overtones because it is given in response to a rather solemn and formalized survey of the methodological status of psychology. This mixture of seriousness and sardonic irreverence extends beyond Skinner; it is a part of the style of the experimental analysis movement, which we will have occasion to refer to again. We know from the paper, at any rate, that the development of the paradigm was not a calculated innovation in psychological outlook. That innovations flowed from the method would confirm a point which Skinner might like: new behavior by the experimenter is tantamount to new thinking by the experimenter.

Used as a basic research instrument, the operant conditioning paradigm has some unique features which may set the stage for some of the uniquenesses in the generalized approach of the experimental analysis group. **Subject-Experimenter Relation.** The operant conditioning technique has a peculiar immediacy which is a little difficult to describe; one must see the technique in operation for a while in order to appreciate it. A frequent objection to the paradigm is that, figuratively and often literally, it obscures the animal. The animal, shut inside an experimental chamber, becomes a featureless thing to which one pumps in cues and pellets and from which one gets the movements of counters and pens. The charge is that the experimenter has avoided the opportunity to be enlightened by naturalistic observation of the animal, as to a certain extent he has, but a peculiar reverse compensation emerges. In no other experimental format are the hard data so much on line with the experimenter's ac-

tivity. In most experimental formats, the experimenter will not fully see the force of his data until some time after he has seen his subjects; he must group, average, compute, plot, to know exactly what the subjects did. In the operant conditioning paradigm, the experimenter facing his buttons and switches and cumulative recorders is virtually in dyadic relationship with his subject. The subject's behavior shows a certain rate of response; the experimenter changes something; the animal very soon begins to visibly change his behavior pattern. One suspects that in the experience of this immediacy may be the origin of the word "control" so widely used in experimental analysis.

Procedural Flexibility. Most psychological research formats are what one might call testing formats, in that a fixed procedure is applied to a group of subjects who do more or less adequately in response to its demands. In the operant conditioning procedure, perhaps because of the immediacy which we have just discussed, procedure is often not fixed but rather there is an informal feedback from the subject's behavior to the procedure. The experimenter is flexible and opportunistic in his initial shaping of the animal's index response and, similarly, he proceeds by reasonable-seeming steps in his attempts to make various schedules assume control over the subject's behavior. Here, too, we arrive at an estimate of the subject's capacity but we make that estimate in a training format and the estimate has somewhat different implications. On the negative side, one must accept the fact that the training format is not only an estimate of the capacity of the subject as adapter but also, to some extent, of the capacity of the experimenter as trainer. On the positive side, the experimenter is given the flexibility to probe freely, to find out just what environment it takes to get the adaptation, and to get a more rounded picture of the exact circumstances upon which the adaptation depends. In principle, the sequential probing necessary for this could be done using judicious sequences of fixed-procedure experiments but this is time consuming and, in practice, such follow-through experiments are rarely executed.

Single Case Work. Operant conditioning typically generates relatively great quantities of recorded responses from a single subject, and this stream of responses graphed on a cumulative recorder is, in effect, "smoothed" so that stable patterns of responding are seen in the single case record. In the more usual experimental formats, one cannot have objective, visible pictures of trend unless the records of a number of individual cases are averaged together. Moment-to-moment aberrations of the individual's response are in either case washed out—in the case of operant conditioning washed together with the individual's later responses, in the more usual formats averaged with the responses of other individuals. The latter device, grouping across individual differences, presents some known problems because group trends may be mischievously fictitious representations of behavioral regularities (Sidman, 1952). The classic case in psychology is where one way of grouping data leads one to talk about a gradual learning process, and another way to consider sudden learning (House and Zeaman, 1960; White and Plum, 1964). It is true that experimental analysts have been prone in the past to accept the results of one or two wellworked case studies to be generalizable to all individuals (or, occasionally, to all species), but this is not an intrinsic flaw of the method.

Behavior, Dispositions, and Time. The ability of the operant conditioning format to picture stable trends in the individual subject is of some importance because this, in turn, brings about a subtle but important reorientation to psychological terminology. Much more than any other psychological paradigm, the operant conditioning paradigm develops information about the subject in real time. It deals with rate of reaction, behavior-and-time, rather than behavior frozen, sectioned, and stained. Temporal and frequency characteristics are "in" the descriptive terminology. Most other psychological work envisages a typical situation, a test or a trial, conceived as something administered to the subject to probe his dispositions to behave. One has repetition of the "same thing" over time. The Hullian theory, as we have seen, poses its entire theoretical analysis as an analysis of the vectors that impinge on the subject's behavior in a prototypical trial. To abstract behavior from the flow of time in this way leads one, seemingly inevitably, to reified nominalizations. Some characteristic of the subject leads one to conclude that the subject *is* something—intelligent, anxious, creative, fearful, rigid, retarded, mature, immoral, etc., etc. It then takes repeated sophisticated dialectic to keep the term in proper bounds, to keep reiterating that most statements of psychological disposition in the subject are not measurements of some part of him or truth about him, that a dispositional statement in psychology usually states some probabilistic consistency in a subject that depends upon a situation for its manifestation and that it usually alludes to some characteristic which he shows relatively more frequently than others. Operant analysis, which looks at adaptation as an increase or decrease of rate from baseline, which does not deal with the typical but the recurrent, somehow has a natural way of keeping psychological nominalizations on what would seem to be a more realistic plane of discourse.

Descriptive Behaviorism. We turn finally, to the last special characteristic of experimental analysis, one that seems linked to the special set toward terminology given in this approach. All stimulus-response psychology emphasizes parsimony and edges toward nothing-butism, but the experimental analysis tradition is easily the most radical in its insistence on purely behavioral terminology. Not only the soft words which give all psychologists trouble, but also the ordinary little English words ("need," "try," "see," "want"), or the terminology of behavior theory ("habit," "drive," "motive," "fear") are frequently given semantic quotes in the writings of the experimental analysts. Terminology which asserts or implies central states of the subject is thus consistently handed to the reader between thumb and forefinger, as something which it is necessary to use but which one really cannot fully accept. At the same time one is given redefinitions in those writings, again and again and again, like a litany.

When a man controls himself, chooses a course of action, thinks out the solution to a problem, or strives towards an increase in self-knowledge, he is *behaving* (Skinner, 1953, p. 228).

To the question *What is drive?*, we must now answer that drive as the *name* for a fact—the fact that certain operations can be performed on an organism (for example, depriving it of food) that have an effect upon behavior which is different from that of other operations. Drive is not a *thing* . . . (Keller and Schoenfeld, 1950, p. 265).

The debunking quality of these repeated disclaimers from time to time joins with the wry style of the group to produce what seem to be calculatedly barbaric allusions.

Most operants occur with a high frequency only under certain conditions. One rarely, if ever, recites the Gettysburg address unless faced with an audience of listeners . . . (Reynolds, 1968, p. 9).

The reinforcers portrayed in Heaven and Hell are far more powerful than those which support the "good" and "bad" of the ethical group or the "legal" and "illegal" of government control, but this advantage is offset to some extent by the fact that they do not actually operate in the lifetime of the individual. . . . In actual practice a threat to bar from Heaven or to consign to Hell is made contingent upon sinful behavior, while virtuous behavior brings a promise of Heaven or a release from the threat of Hell (Skinner, 1953, p. 353).

To most psychologists not soaked in this style of discourse such statements have a startling quality. The classification of the Gettysburg Address as an "operant" instantly brings to mind all of the qualities of the Gettysburg Address which the author of this quotation is not taken into account. The portrayal of Heaven and Hell as cosmic techniques for religious control seems like jargonistic imperialism carried off into infinity. But, by and large, this is a group which when writing outside its own technical journals is rather sensitive to words and jargon. One concludes, eventually, that there is a certain base rate of leg-pulling, a certain generalized willingness to put grandiosity and pomposity in its place wherever the occasion occurs, in such writings. But it all has a serious edge. Directly and indirectly, seriously or half-humorously, the experimental analysis group maintains a steady attack on the psychological discourse of everyday language and of everyday psychology, which it conceives of as a flawed lexicon

where descriptions of behavioral events are mixed with gratuitous and often unrecognized assumptions.

In the preceding discussion, we have tried to deal with certain specializations of outlook which have become associated with the experimental analysis of behavior. These are seen as capitalizations upon the new outlook offered by the method of operant analysis which, in the aggregate, amount to a new way of doing business with psychological data (Sidman, 1960). As experimental analysis has moved into child psychology, its proponents have developed a pattern of effort quite different from the work built out of behavior theory.

Functional Analysis of the Child's Behavior

In the dozen years or so since the experimental analysis of behavior has been brought in volume to the study of children's behavior, it has undergone a rather rapid evolution. Beginning in the middle 1950s, Bijou (1955, 1957, 1958a, 1958b, 1961; Bijou and Sturges, 1959; Bijou and Baer, 1960; Bijou and Orlando, 1961) published a series of laboratory reports which described the beginnings of a laboratory exploration of schedule effects with children, but the development of such a laboratory effort quickly abated in the child psychology literature and laboratory work is not, at this writing, prominent in the emerging literature. In its place, there has come a second wave of development of applied efforts toward behavior modification.

The deployment of techniques of behavior modification is at this moment proceeding with great rapidity. An increasing body of reports now exist which demonstrate some effectiveness of behavior modification across a good sample of problems and subject characteristics. In work with diagnostically normal children, there have been reports of obtained improvement in cases of regressed crawling (Harris et al., 1964), vomiting (Wolf et al., 1965), mutism (Kerr, Meyerson, and Michael, 1965), prolonged crying (Hart et al., 1964), isolation or timidity in play (Allen et al., 1964; Johnston et al., 1966), tantrums (Williams, 1959; Wolf, Risley, and Mees, 1964), and stuttering (Goldiamond, 1965). At the same time, behavior modification techniques have been brought into use with various diagnostic groups and there has been some demonstrated improvement of behavior problems of handicapped children (Meyerson, Kerr, and Michael, 1967), brain-injured (Hall and Broden, 1967), retarded (Birnbrauer et al., 1965; Wiesen et al., 1967), autistic (Wolf, Risley, and Mees, 1964; Metz, 1965), and schizophrenic patients (Lovaas et al., 1965; Hingtgen, Sanders, and DeMyer, 1965). Behavior modification techniques have been brought to educational issues and used for remediation of reading problems (Staats et al., 1964; Staats, 1965) and for the betterment of the classroom group's functioning (Zimmerman and Zimmerman, 1962; Brown and Elliott, 1965; Mithaug and Burgess, 1967; Quay et al., 1967). Here the movement toward behavior modification joins another great applied offshoot of experimental analysis, the movement toward programmed instruction. We come almost full circle when we find fine-tooled programming efforts which have a searching quality and an analytic edge usually thought to be characteristic of the best "basic" research (e.g., Sidman and Stoddard, 1966, 1967; Stoddard and Sidman, 1967; Stoddard, 1968; Touchette, 1968.

The conveying of experimental analysis out of the laboratory and into a series of applied efforts raises several interesting questions. There is nothing unique to child psychology about this trend to practical intervention. The applied efforts in child psychology are part and parcel of a movement toward interventive efforts led by Skinner and characteristic of the group interested in experimental analysis. For most psychologists, this leap from the laboratory into application violates the expected. The traditional wisdom says that scientific development proceeds by a crystallization of basic research information into systematic theory and then by an extension of theory to the design of solutions for practical problems. There is a rhetoric in the behavior modification and programmed learning which goes toward this model. The applied efforts are sometimes said to be applications of "laboratory principles of learning." Such claims are usually dropped into discussion without elaboration and, in truth, one familiar with the psychological learning literature has a hard time finding backing for it. The centerpiece of psychology's conception of learning, the law of effect, is hardly a discovery of the twentieth century or a novelty in human engineering. The lore of the research literature—the regularities and laws and curves—does not seem to have manifest value for application nor is its presence easily detected as an influence on behavior modification efforts. Without the backing of laboratory proofs, the traditional wisdom would tend to question the legitimacy of the scientific validity of such work.

However, one feels distinctly uneasy about the dismissal of such efforts as scientistic adventurism. The traditional wisdom presupposes basic research as an enterprise cumulating hard, systematic data, which gradually give an explanation or an understanding of the critical issues of a discipline; the point of the learning theory movement seems to have been to set up exactly that kind of cumulative enterprise, and one point of the second American revolution seems to be that learning theory failed to be convincing in its efforts. One can, more generally, ask whether the basic research of psychology has yet shown the trend towards utility. One can ask whether the applied versus basic distinction in psychology can be given full credence. Do we really get more incisive information about human behavior from within than from outside the laboratory? Have psychoanalysis and psychometrics taken more from the laboratory than they have given to it? In view of such reservations, it is conceivable that here, as elsewhere, one finds Skinner finessing the traditional conceptions of scientific development of the discipline to work from an intuitive, and perhaps truer, conception of what moves it is possible for psychologists to make.

What has come from the laboratory into behavior modification? Not a theory. Not laws of learning, as they are usually conceived. What has come from the laboratory is an analytic posture, the tendency to construe behavioral affairs as a history of recurrent responses moderated by contingent reinforcement influences, and some methods of manipulating such responses. In two small books, Bijou and Baer (1961, 1965) have given a rough sketch of the child in his environment, giving full allowance to biological and maturational factors, but essentially arguing that the impingement of the environment upon the child's behavior and his adaptation to it can be envisaged in terms of his reinforcement history—that is, in terms of respondent and operant conditioning and certain elaborations of those mechanisms which lead to discrimination, differentiation, and chaining. A sweeping regularization of the child as a behaving system is involved: "The developing child may be adequately regarded, in conceptual terms, as a cluster of interrelated responses interacting with stimuli" (Bijou and Baer, 1961, p. 14).

This is the analytic posture of experimental analysis toward the child. It is a less simple posture than it would appear to be on the surface. The stimulus and response are observable events, parts of behavior and environment, but which parts are germane to the psychologist are selected empirically in terms of observed functional relationships. A stimulus or a response enters into the psychological analysis only when it has been shown to enter a functional equation. In a peculiar way, without relinquishing a positivistic stance, the analysis embraces a phenomenological point. The subject participates in the definition of what is a stimulus for him. Stimuli and responses are grouped into equivalence classes in a similar way, by empirically observed functional equivalence. This device, in turn, allows the system to collect disparate observables into types or syndromes without tying them together through a central mechanism or state. Some would argue that these definitional devices go a long way around to avoid what seems obvious: that there is a center, which accomplishes these special selections of stimulus and response. It may be said, however, that the analysis simply asserts in a principled way what most psychologists actually do in their development of nomenclature for environment and behavior.

With the developing child so pictured, his response patterns, seen as a set of operants, become manipulable in much the same way as the index response of the laboratory. Hypothetically, at least, they should be subject to shaping, extinction, and the effects of various schedules, just as the pigeon's window pecking or the rat's bar pressing operants. Unlike the laboratory case, of course, one does not have one's subject on a deprivation schedule; the child subject is not working for food or water or shock avoidance. The experimental analysts working with children have therefore had to be concerned with the critical question of reinforcement controlled by the experimenter. Money, food, and tokens have been used in some cases. In most, the behavior modification efforts have relied upon the most natural and ubiquitous source of contingent reinforcement in the human environment, the approvals and disapprovals registered by teachers, parents, peers, or experimenter. The approach that weaves all this together into an applied program builds from the unique emphases of the laboratory approach; the set toward control, the procedural flexibility, the willingness to work with single cases, and the stress on behavioristic exemplification of nominalisms.

The positivism in which this work is conceived makes it difficult, at this stage, to discern how the behavior modification efforts can or will contribute to some betterment of our understanding of the child. The understanding of learning, or of the development of the child, upon which the movement now proceeds is, from the perspective of most psychologists, relatively rudimentary; the movement sets aside most of the enormous mass of information and speculation about learning and development whose significance now bedevils the understanding of the mass of psychologists. It seems to get along without it. In some writings, there is an edge of hostility toward traditional psychological terminology, which is seen as mystifying or obscuring matters that are straightforward when they are examined in behavioral terms. Meyerson, Kerr, and Michael (1967) quote an imaginary dialogue about mental retardation in this spirit:

"Why doesn't Mary walk?"
"Well, she's severely mentally retarded, and it is not uncommon among the severely mentally retarded that they don't walk."
"I see, but what is the reason for it?"
"She's slow in development."
"I see. And what is it that is responsible for her slow development?"
"It is the fact that she is mentally retarded."
"I see. And how do you know that she is mentally retarded?"
"Why you can see for yourself. She doesn't walk, she doesn't talk, she isn't toilet trained and doesn't do many other things like a mentally normal child" (Meyerson, Kerr, and Michael, 1967, pp. 224–225).

This quotation alludes to the tendency of diagnosticians to label behavior disorders as manifestations of a central pathology which often cannot be independently substantiated. Without some neurological or biochemical evidence to the contrary, the behavioral modifier prefers to deal with psychotherapy as a cluster of deviant behaviors, capable of removal by training efforts which shape the behaviors toward the normal range. That an abnormal behavior pattern can be deflected by reinforcement procedures is sometimes taken as *prima facie* evidence that that the abnormality was originally learned. In the case of childhood autism, an origin in reinforcement history has been speculatively traced out (Ferster, 1961).

Most psychologists see the processes of adaptation, psychotherapy, and child development in more complicated ways than they are envisaged in much of the rhetoric surrounding behavior modification. The early successes of the behavior modification efforts are quite provocative, but there are not yet the definitive successes which might serve as a kind of shield for the line of reasoning that lies behind them. The problems they seem to have definitely cleared up are minor, and one suspects a technology of behavior modification would not be needed to solve them. Patients with significant diagnostic entities have been benefited but not yet to a practical extent. Skepticism is still possible. Earlier applied efforts growing out of the experimental analysis movement have not yet had unequivocal success. Behavior shaping developed as a commercial animal training venture ultimately did not prove fully adequate to its proponents (Breland and Breland, 1961). Teaching machines and programmed learning have as yet only a tiny and uncertain place in the American educational system. Behavior modification must survive the period of early enthusiasm before its practical and theoretical weight can be felt.

That the movement may develop considerable theoretical significance seems likely. American inquiry into children's learning and cognitive processes has probably been a little too well-designed and well-controlled; the inquiry could use a clinical edge. The behavior modifiers and programmed learners have thrown open a window to the child in his natural confrontation with the issues of adaptation and education. Already, reading in the case protocols, one can find significant and provocative accounts of side effects of intervention, side effects more interesting than the reinforcement effect itself. In some of the intervention procedures themselves, one suspects that there are more agents than reinforcement schedules at work upon the subject; the focusing of his attention, the organization of his behavior over time, the reduction of stress—which might require more than the law of effect for their conceptualization. Behavior modification techniques right now represent new behavior for the experimental psychologist, behavior which is currently being reinforced, and one might reasonably expect that behavior in the terms of that discourse to eventuate in what others might call new thinking.

SOME SUMMARY COMMENTS

In this section, before turning to a consideration of the Russian form of stimulus-response analysis, it seems well to try to give some general perspective on the contemporary influence of the learning theory tradition. It must be said, again, that the problem of obtaining such a perspective is considerable. Within child psychology, one finds a series of outcroppings of the learning theory tradition, heterogeneous with respect to the amount and depth of the issues they address in the literature of child psychology, relatively more homogeneous in their conception of procedure, method, strategy, significant variables, terminology, and the nature of scientific development. The homogeneities lie in the diverse connections of the various efforts with the programs of Hull, Spence, and Skinner and, behind them historically, we find what seems to be the least common denominator of the group as a whole, the learning theory point of view, formed before the learning theories in the Behaviorism of the 1910s and 1920s.

For child psychologists at least, the tradition offers no articulated learning theory or even a theory of child development. It nevertheless has a "position" that is generally understood and, in the sloganizing way in which various theoretical positions are often seen to be in contention, it stands as a force against the geneticism of Piaget and Werner in that it is usually seen as a debater which is insistent on environment, learning, reinforcement, and peripheralism, against others who contend for maturation, stages, development, and central structures as causative agents. The debating position is not imaginary; the characteristic arguments regularly flicker in the writings of the S-R proponents. But there is no one drawn-together statement of the position acceptable to all proponents. The only approximation to it is the pair of short books by Bijou and Baer (1961, 1965), but those two volumes would probably seriously misrepresent the S-Rism of Berlyne, of Bandura, and of the Kendlers.

Looked at more closely, the literature of the learning theory tradition reveals its diversity and within that diversity another, less recognized, pattern. The theoretical wing of the literature, largely descended from the Hull-Spence tradition, has less and less been preoccupied with the characteristic variables and system-building of that tradition, but has more and more drawn toward the edge of the behavioristic grounds. The basic research and systematization is building around issues of novelty, familiarization, attention, inference, strategy, and imitative learning. Those concerned with the experimental analysis of behavior have more and more moved toward interventive and applied efforts where, holding to the behavioristic view of affairs, they have nevertheless moved into ground which most psychologists would consider out of the reach of a purely behavioristic conception. The stimulus-response analysis holds the methodological ground it has generally always held in psychology, that of a conservative, behavioristically parsimonious physicalism though that ground become more difficult to hold as proponents are pulled with the general trend of psychology toward a new cognitivism, an interest in biological variables, and maturation.

The cause of this difficulty is of some interest. The general tendency and the natural tendency is to view the learning theory tradition as a general conception of human nature, and to consider its adequacy in that regard. Seeing the learning theory tradition in this way, one can recognize the force of certain devastating criticisms of the position which have regularly appeared recently, and one can anticipate the early demise of this peculiarly shortsighted construction of the last generation of psychologists. Or, taking the longer view, one may recognize in the learning theories their descent from traditional Associationism, and one may see in their waning the cure of a much older obsession:

Associationism has been our only really general theory since we began to think about human behavior. It may be that in this complicated field we have stumbled upon the right answer at our first attempt, that somehow or another we already find ourselves in the alley leading to the food-box with only minor obstacles to surmount. The likelihood seems small, for the maze must be large. Alternatively we have been scrabbling for a century or two at the rather ill-defined end of of a *cul-de-sac* whose entrance was rendered attractive in the eighteenth century by the rapid growth of classical physics and, above all, chemistry. History would support the latter alternative" (Drever, 1968, p. 27).

The learning theory tradition is waning, and the arguments against it have considerable point, but one misses one point of discussion in the current round of post-mortems. Behaviorism and the learning theory tradition were descendants of associationism, but this was only an incidental fact of the thrust which lay behind their development. They were, or shortly became, general conceptions of human nature, but they did so in the face of exactly the same arguments at the turn of the century as those raised at the middle of the century. The ideological shortcomings of the learning theory tradition have been constant, and constantly recognized, and the rise and fall of the tradition may have to do with other issues—programmatic issues. There are two key questions that the learning theory tradition seems addressed to. (1) Can psychology become a self-contained science? (Can one find a way to build a behavior theory?) (2) Can psychology develop a cooperative and cumulative research tradition? In this view, the learning theory tradition failed to catch hold because the behavior theories did not manage to become self-propagating and self-organizing. The vast mass of learning literature lies, impossible to read and remember, beside the vast mass of other research findings which accumulates, largely unsynthesized, in the back journals. If this view is correct, the originating questions that motivated the learning theory effort lie once more on the table.

There is no great urge to take the issues up. We have all become a little tired of methodology, of scientific prospecti, of those seductive analogies between psychology and physics-seen-at-a-distance. To a greater extent than before, psychologists within and without the tradition are following their noses, less and less able or concerned to keep their ideological lines clear. The result is more scattershot and more interesting. The syntheses appear, but they are less planned, less predictable, more intuitive. Perhaps, aided and abetted by the learning theories, we have reached a more adequate plane of scientific discourse which is not, as expected, a level of all-embracing empiricism. Rather, that plane may be one where the intuition of the psychologist-at-large has been sophisticated, where method and modelling have their place, but where the interchange among diverse psychologists may take place usefully without a perfectly adequate intersubjective language, uniform body of methods, or spelled out program. One needs to take account of the psychology of science as well as the philosophy of science. When scientists communicate, they are not always exchanging facts and they do not always need a purified thing-language. They are often intercalibrating schemata and they may need a discourse replete with analogies, metaphors, and models to bring this about.

The preceding quotation from Drever may be modified slightly. There has always been a general theory opposed to Associationism which has been waiting in the wings of American psychology. It has been peculiarly at home in American developmental psychology; we speak here of the genetic-rationalist tradition outlined earlier. It is, one suspects, the viable alternative to the associationist tradition. To work meaningfully within the tradition, it has at least usually been the case that one must treat behavioral manifestations as an expression of sources not discernible within the observable realm, that one must move to a parsimony of comprehensive consistency rather than a parsimony of simplicity or seeableness. One must relinquish reliance on the-single cause–single-effect conception of explanation. In short, one must relinquish a

great many of the guidelines to which American research practices have traditionally hewed closely.

RUSSIAN REFLEXOLOGY AND CHILD PSYCHOLOGY

The Russian treatment of stimulus-response psychology and the extension of that treatment to child psychology, offers a contrast to the American development of the tradition.

Americans are inclined to feel an amused kind of skepticism about Russian claims to have invented things first, but in the case of behaviorism there is some evidence suggesting that the Russians did, indeed, see the point first. The following quote is taken from I. M. Sechenov's *Reflexes of the Brain,* published in 1863, and represents an unmistakable assertion of the behavioristic thesis:

All the endless diversity of the external manifestations of the activity of the brain can be finally regarded as one phenomenon,—that of muscular movement. Be it a child laughing at the sight of toys, or Garibaldi smiling when he is persecuted for his excessive love for his fatherland; a girl trembling at the first thought of love, or Newton enunciating universal laws and writing them on paper,—everywhere the final manifestation is muscular movement. In order to help the reader to reconcile himself with this thought more readily, I will remind him of the frame-work created by the mind of humanity to include all manifestations of brain activity; this frame-work is *"word and deed."* Under *deed,* the popular mind conceives, without question, every external mechanical activity of man based exclusively on the use of muscles. And under *word,* as the educated reader will realize, is understood a certain combination of sounds produced in the larynx and the cavity of the mouth, again by means of muscular movements (Sechenov, 1863, p. 390).

Sechenov's anticipation of the behavioristic thesis seems something more than the chancy anticipations of all psychological points which one repeatedly finds in the literature and philosophy of earlier times. The thesis that one knows another man only by his behavior is, after all, not very far from common sense and it would be a distinct surprise if it took mankind until the twentieth century to first see it and speak about it. Behaviorism was a "discovery" for psychologists only when and as it became a strong principle of organization of the inquiry process of the field; the point of the Sechenov "discovery" was that there seems every reason to believe that it was definitive and generative for the evolution of a line of Russian psychological endeavor. Sechenov's scheme for brain and mind was not very influential upon European psychological analysis—something very much like his scheme, promulgated by the British neurologist Hughlings Jackson did have influence—but his treatment was immensely popular in Russia, and it had direct and important influence on Ivan Pavlov (Babkin, 1949).

The behavioristic point was only incidental to Sechenov's psychophysiology, which sketched a grand design for the understanding of the interplay between mind and body (Yaroshevski, 1968). Pavlov, after him, seems to have accepted the design and begun its substantiation, to have placed it on an experimental format, and to have begun the process of working out the system in detail. The behavioristic thesis was a part of that design, and there is some evidence that it took Pavlov a little trouble to accept it; when he did, he did so vehemently (Pavlov, 1928). Pavlov's writings were the major point of contact between American Soviet psychology for a good many years, and it is only recently that the two national groups have again begun comparing notes. The evolution of conditioning in the Soviet Union has been quite different from its history here and consequently the impingement of the conditioning tradition upon child psychology has been quite different. A number of circumstances make this so.

Some recent surveys (Bauer, 1952; Mintz, 1958; O'Connor, 1961) enable us to get a perspective on the Russian discipline of psychology as a whole. These surveys, and the good number of direct translations of Russian work, give us some sense of a spectrum of psychological efforts organized quite differently from our own. One must envisage first a disciplinary line which comes between the conditioning tradition and psychology. Conditioning work has been considered to be a part of physiology, and is typically published in a different journal (*The Journal of Higher Nervous Activity*) than work considered psychological (*Questions of Psychology*). This is not to imply that conditioning, and Pavlov, are not important sources for the Russian psychological work. They are not the only sources and, apparently, they have not been the centers of so strongly formed a programmatic movement as has developed in American psychology.

The status of psychology as a discipline has been politically touchy in the past decades. There were no psychological journals from 1935 to 1954. Sources disagree somewhat about just how contaminating political pressures have been upon Russian psychological efforts, but it seems that, at least superficially, Russian psychologists have had to be concerned about the compatibility of their work with dialectical materialism and their writings have showed some care to be politically progressive. Intelligence testing was officially forbidden by the Communist party in 1936. Dialectical materialism has been seen as incompatible with notions of the active unconscious, with materialism (the physicalistic positivism which has been influential in American psychology), and with extreme idealism, a pure phenomenology. Not necessarily for political reasons, the spectrum of Russian psychology as a discipline has failed to include good-sized components of our own: psychoanalysis, social psychology, and industrial psychology.

There are thus differences in the political and professional matrix of forces in Soviet and American psychology and because of these differences comparisons need to be made with caution. Nevertheless, it is at least interesting to try to imagine the Russian development of S-R psychology as a kind of control for the American experience. Pavlovian conditioning was enormously influential upon Russian psychology, but it was never made the centerpiece of an effort at scientific and methodological reform of the discipline. There was no equivalent of the behavioristic revolution and consequently there seems now to be no equivalent of the cognitivist counterrevolution. Rather, elements of the prebehavioristic psychology have survived to the present day in Russia, coexisting with the development of conditioning methodology.

Textbooks of psychology typically define it as the science of mind or psyche. The interests of researchers are directed toward consciousness and the analysis of the reflective processes by which it forms a judgment of experience and a guidance of voluntary behavior. Research on conditioning is not seen as incompatible with this:

The stress on consciousness and cognitive factors in behavior is not contradicted by the acceptance of the conditioned reflex as a basis of adaptive behavior. The conditional reflex is apt to be viewed not as a blindly functioning habit based on stimulus-response connections but as a flexible form of adjustment which enables the organism to respond to signals (Mintz, 1958, p. 497).

The more relaxed view of conditioning provokes a quite different treatment of it. Where in American psychology the stimulus has been made an undefined term in a calculus of learning and the S-R connection an undefined term in a calculus of higher-order behavior, the Russians have not logicized these terms. The stimulus is seen as the outcome of a process that requires explaining through conjoint behavioral and neuropsychological analysis:

The understanding of sensory (especially auditory) processes underwent a radical change as a result of the introduction of Pavlov's *reflex theory of sensation* and concept of *analyzers . . . sensation incorporates the process of analysis and synthesis of signals while they are still in the first stages of arrival* (Luria, 1966a, p. 97).

Because the treatment of behaviorism and conditioning has not been seen as methodologically preemptive, those working with conditioning phenomena can coexist with other veins of research which are continuations of German introspectionism. The work of the Georgian group, a major sector of Russian activity, seems to be essentially an elaboration of the analysis of sets first begun by the Würtzburg group (Uznadze, 1966; Natadze, 1961).

There are also, it might be said, some procedural effects of the fact that the Russians did not develop a methodological revolution. Russian papers do not as sharply separate philosophical and psychological issues, and research reports are not so scrupulous in separating findings from interpretation. Procedures are not always so completely reported. Statistics are not a *sine qua non* in research work, and statistical regularities are accepted only when their implications can be shown to have some satisfactory bearing on an otherwise tenable line of explanation of the individual's behavior.

Given this kind of setting for the Russian treatment of the conditioning, the impingement of stimulus-response analysis upon child psychology is of an entirely different character in Russian work. It does not convey an insistence on parsimony or a resistance to explanations which appeal to central factors or hypothetical constructs. It is intrinsically more speculative since it is not so associated with the canons of testability and rigorous and comprehensive experimental proof. Carrying a much lighter methodological load, the analysis has traveled a useful distance into the issues which are now so central to the American behavior theory group—attention and reasoning.

At several levels, the Russians have been concerned with the subject's work with the stimulus as a precursor to his formation of an adaptation to it. At the level of conditioning, the Russians have identified an orienting reflex, a set of postural and autonomic reactions most typically identified by vasomotor components in finger and forehead, which is an important precursor and participant to the establishment of classical conditioning. The orienting reflex is presumed to be a formant of what one would usually call attention to the stimulus, and an elaborate experimental analysis of the reflex has led to the suggestion that it is reflective of the processes of neuronal modelling of the stimulus (Sokolov, 1963).

At a more molar level, orienting-investigatory behavior of the child has been envisaged as separate from and a precursor to the learning of voluntary motor patterns:

One could assume that preliminary orientation leads to formation of the habit itself and the formation of that system of connections which forms its basis. Our data, however, do not confirm this notion. What occurs is that, following the preliminary orientation, the motor system in the process of development appears not to have been assimilated yet and a number of additional motor exercises is needed before the habit is finally established.

Although getting somewhat ahead, we could say that, in the process of orientation, not the system of the performed motor reactions is formed but *the image,* under control of which the subsequent functioning of this system is made possible (Zaporozhets, 1965, p. 436).

A staged sequence of interaction between the orienting activity and the establishment of the motor pattern is found.

1. There is a "chaotic" orientation pattern, widely distributed, as the child establishes initial familiarity with the task.

2. The orienting reactions begin to be channelled toward those aspects of the situation which are relevant to the task, and there seem to be strategic connections or anticipation involving one and another. A system of orientation is formed.

3. With the establishment of the motor learning, the motor and external verbal reactions associated with the orienting system diminish, are inhibited, and they form an image which, in effect, exists as a schema of the voluntary behavior.

4. If, finally, the now correctly executed adaptive reaction is repeated again and again, it becomes stereotyped and automatized, and there is an extinction of most orienting reactions. The extinction is not complete and, for example, agents offering reinforcement continue to elicit orienting (Zaporozhets, 1961, 1965).

At the level of the conditioned reflex, and at the level of voluntary behavior, an orienting process is seen as a precursor to adaptation and as an index to the formation of an adequate central representation of the relevant environment—in the case of voluntary behavior, part and parcel of the forming of the representation. In addition, several interesting development trends have been acknowledged. The habituation of initial orientation is more rapid as children grow older and, in several ways, seems indicative of "higher" or more intact functioning (Lynn, 1966). During the preschool era, the orienting-investigatory activity of the child is seen to show a developmental move from motor-tactile to visual exploration (Zaporozhets, 1961).

A connected vein of Russian investigation has examined the directing or regulating functions which language exerts upon behavior. The relevant research by Luria (1961) and Vygotsky (1962) is the best-known Russian work to American child psychologists. Just as the line of research previously discussed traces the internalization of movement and visualization patterns to become cognitive representations of the situation and directors of adaptive activity, so here the directive functions of language are traced ontogenetically. Luria traces the initial influence of language, in the younger years, first as an excitatory influence, later as both excitatory and inhibitory, finally as regulative and directive. Vygotsky traces this regulatory language as it is used by the young child to explicitly direct himself and then, subsequently, as it internalizes to become an organ of planning and reasoning.

All this has some similarity to the American conception of mediation as the basis for abstract thought processes. Indeed, the Russian conception is a somewhat looser and broader version of the behavior theory conception of meditation. They are different elaborations, perhaps, of Pavlov's initial suggestion that human higher mental processes should be conceived of as a "second signal system."

On the whole, this parallelism between the Russian child psychology and the American learning theory tradition is misleading if it is taken as a sign that these two traditions differ in degree rather than in kind. The Russian tradition is quite willing to work with judicious mentalizing and neurologizing—in fact, sees the ultimate understanding of psychological data to lie in the understanding of consciousness through the synthesis of behavioral and neurological information. There is not acceptance of the learning theory point of view. Nevertheless, the Russian work can be seen as supporting and extending the present cognitivist trends within the behavior theory group. Their work has already been interjected in significant ways because of its considerable influence on Berlyne's neobehavioristic formulations (Berlyne, 1960, 1965). It is exactly with respect to the issues addressed in those volumes, attention and reasoning, that the Russians have established an experimental foothold while the grasp of behavior theory is still not secure.

References

Allen, K. E., Hart, B. M., Buell, J. S., Harris, F. R., and Wolf, M. M. Effects of social reinforcement on isolate behavior of a nursery school child. *Child Dev.*, 1964, **35**, 511–518.

Aronfreed, J. The origin of self-criticism. *Psychol. Rev.*, 1964, **71**, 193–218.

Atkinson, R. C., Sommer, G., and Sterman, M. B. Decision making by children as a function of amount of reinforcement. *Psychol. Rep.*, 1960, **6**, 299–306.

Babkin, B. P. *Pavlov: a biography.* Chicago: University of Chicago Press, 1949.

Baer, D. M., and Sherman, J. A. Reinforcement control of generalized imitation in young children. *J. exp. Child Psychol.*, 1964, **1**, 37–49.

Bandura, A. Psychotherapy as a learning process. *Psychol. Bull.*, 1961, **58**, 143–159.

Bandura, A. Behavioral modification through modelling procedures. In L. Krasner and L. P. Ullmann (Eds.), *Research in behavior modification.* New York: Holt, Rinehart, and Winston, 1965. (a)

Bandura, A. Vicarious processes: a case of no-trial learning. In L. Berkowitz (Ed.), *Advances in experimental social psychology.* Vol. II. New York: Academic Press, 1965. (b)

Bandura, A., Grusec, A. E., and Menlove, F. L. Observational learning as a function of symbolization and incentive set. *Child Dev.*, 1966, **37**, 499–506.

Bandura, A., and Huston, A. C. Identification as a process of incidental learning. *J. abnorm. soc. Psychol.*, 1961, **63**, 311–318.

Bandura, A., Ross, D., and Ross, S. A. Transmission of aggression through imitation of aggressive models. *J. abnorm. soc. Psychol.*, 1961, **63**, 575–582.

Bandura, A., Ross, D., and Ross, S. A. A comparative test of the status envy, social power, and secondary reinforcement theories of identificatory learning. *J. abnorm. soc. Psychol.*, 1963, **67**, 527–534.

Bandura, A., and Walters, R. H. *Social learning and personality development.* New York: Holt, Rinehart, and Winston, 1963.

Barker, R. G. Child psychology. *Ann. Rev. Psychol.*, 1951, **2**, 1–22.

Bartlett, F. *Thinking.* New York: Basic Books, 1962.

Bauer, R. A. *The new man in Soviet psychology.* Cambridge, Mass.: Harvard University Press, 1952.

Berlyne, D. E. Knowledge and stimulus-response psychology. *Psychol. Rev.*, 1954, **61**, 245–254.

Berlyne, D. E. *Conflict, arousal, and curiosity.* New York: McGraw-Hill, 1960.

Berlyne, D. E. *Structure and direction in thinking.* New York: Wiley, 1965.

Bernstein, N. *The co-ordination and regulation of movements.* London: Pergamon Press, 1967.

Bijou, S. W. A systematic approach to an experimental analysis of young children. *Child Dev.*, 1955, **26**, 161–168.

Bijou, S. W. Methodology for an experimental analysis of child behavior. *Psychol. Rep.*, 1957, **3**, 243–250.

Bijou, S. W. Operant extinction after fixed interval schedules with young children. *J. exp. Analysis Behav.*, 1958, **1**, 25–29. (a)

Bijou, S. W. A child study laboratory on wheels. *Child Dev.*, 1958, **29**, 425–427.

Bijou, S. W. Discrimination performance as a base line for individual analysis of young children. *Child Dev.*, 1961, **32**, 163–170.

Bijou, S. W., and Baer, D. M. The laboratory-experimental study of child behavior. In P. H. Mussen (Ed.), *Handbook of research methods in child development.* New York: Wiley, 1960.

Bijou, S. W., and Baer, D. M. *Child development*. Vol. 1. *A systematic and empirical theory*. New York: Appleton-Century-Crofts, 1961.

Bijou, S. W., and Baer, D. M. Some methodological contributions from a functional analysis of child development. In L. P. Lipsitt, and C. C. Spiker (Eds.), *Advances in child development and behavior*. Vol. 1. New York: Academic Press, 1963.

Bijou, S. W., and Baer, D. M. *Child development*. Vol. 2. *Universal stage of infancy*. New York: Appleton-Century-Crofts, 1965.

Bijou, S. W., and Baer, D. M. *Child development: readings in experimental analysis*. New York: Appleton-Century-Crofts, 1967.

Bijou, D. W., and Orlando, R. Rapid development of multiple-schedule performances with retarded children. *J. exp. Analysis Behav.*, 1961, **4**, 7–16.

Bijou, S. W., and Sturges, P. T. Positive reinforcers for experimental studies with children—consumables and manipulatables. *Child Dev.*, 1959, **30**, 151–170.

Birnbrauer, J. S., Wolf, M. M., Kidder, J. D., and Taque, C. E., Classroom behavior of retarded pupils with token reinforcement. *J. exp. Child Psychol.*, 1965, **2**, 219–235.

Bogartz, R. S. Sequential dependencies in children's probability learning. *J. exp. Psychol.*, 1965, **70**, 365–370.

Bogartz, R. S., and Witte, K. L. On the locus of the stimulus familiarization effect in young children. *J. exp. Child Psychol.*, 1966, **4**, 317–331.

Boring, E. G. *The physical dimensions of consciousness*. New York: Dover, 1963. (First edition, 1933.)

Boring, E. G. *A history of experimental psychology*. (2nd ed.) New York: Appleton-Century-Crofts, 1951.

Brackbill, Y. Experimental research with children in the Soviet Union: report of a visit. *Am. Psychol.*, 1960, **15**, 226–233.

Brackbill, Y., Fitzgerald, H. E., and Lintz, L. M. A developmental study of classical conditioning. *Monogr. Soc. Res. Child Dev.*, 1967, **32**, Serial No. 116.

Brackbill, Y., Kappy, M. S., and Starr, R. H. Magnitude of reward and probability learning *J. exp. Psychol.*, 1962, **63**, 32–35.

Breland, K., and Breland, M. The misbehavior of organisms. *Am. Psychol.*, 1961, **16**, 681–684.

Brown, R., and Elliott, R. Control of aggression in a nursery school class. *J. exp. Child Psychol.*, 1965, **2**, 103–107.

Bruner, J. S., Goodnow, J. J., and Austin, G. A. *A study of thinking*. New York: Science Editions, 1962.

Caldwell, B. M. The effects of infant care. In M. L. Hoffman and L. W. Hoffman, *Review of child development research*. Vol. 1. New York: Russell Sage, 1964.

Cantor, G. N. Responses of infants and children to complex and novel stimulation. In L. P. Lipsitt and C. C. Spiker (Eds.), *Advances in child development and behavior*. Vol. 1. New York: Academic Press, 1963.

Cantor, G. N., and Cantor, J. H. Effects of conditioned-stimulus familiarization on instrumental learning in children. *J. exp. Child Psychol.*, 1964, **1**, 71–78.

Cantor, G. N., and Cantor, J. H. Discriminative reaction time performance in preschool children as related to stimulus familiarization. *J. exp. Child Psychol.*, 1965, **2**, 1–9.

Cantor, G. N., and Cantor, J. H. Discriminative reaction time in children as related to amount of stimulus familiarization. *J. exp. Child Psychol.*, 1966, **4**, 150–157.

Castaneda, A. The paired-associates method in the study of conflict. In L. P. Lipsitt and C. C. Spiker (Eds.), *Advances in child behavior and development*. Vol. 2. New York: Academic Press, 1965.

Castaneda, A., and Palermo, D. S. Psychomotor performance as a function of amount of training and stress. *J. exp. Psychol.*, 1955, **50**, 175–159.

Craig, G. J., and Meyers, J. L. A developmental study of sequential two-choice decision making. *Child Dev.*, 1963, **34**, 483–493.

Dewey, J. The reflex arc concept in psychology. *Psychol. Rev.*, 1896, **3**, 357–370.

Dollard, J., Doob, L. W., Miller, N. E., Mowrer, O. H., Sears, R. R., Ford, C. S., Hovland, C. I., and Sollenberger, R. T. *Frustration and aggression.* New Haven, Conn.: Yale University Press, 1939.

Dollard, J., and Miller, N. E. *Personality and psychotherapy.* New York: McGraw-Hill, 1950.

Drever, J. Some early Associationists. In B. B. Wolman (Ed.), *Historical roots of contemporary psychology.* New York: Harper and Row, 1968.

Erickson, M. T. Effects of social deprivation and satiation on verbal conditioning in children. *J. comp. physiol. Psychol.*, 1962, **55**, 953–957.

Estes, W. K., and Skinner, B. F. Some quantitative properties of anxiety. *J. exp. Psychol.*, 1941, **29**, 390–400.

Fellows, B. J. *The discrimination process and development.* London: Pergamon Press, 1968.

Ferster, C. B. Positive reinforcement and behavioral deficits of autistic children. *Child Dev.*, 1961, **32**, 437–456.

Ferster, C. B., and Skinner, B. F. *Schedules of reinforcement.* New York: Appleton-Century-Crofts, 1957.

Gesell, A. In C. Murchison (Ed.), *A history of psychology in autobiography.* Worcester, Mass.: Clark University Press, 1952.

Gewirtz, J. L. A learning analysis of the effects of normal stimulation, privation and deprivation on the acquisition of social motivation and attachment. In B. M. Foss (Ed.), *Determinants of infant behavior.* New York: Wiley, 1961.

Gewirtz, J. L. Deprivation and satiation of social stimuli as determinants of their reinforcing efficacy. In J. P. Hill (Ed.), *Minnesota symposium on child psychology.* Vol. 1. Minneapolis: University of Minnesota Press, 1967.

Gewirtz, J. L., and Baer, D. M. The effect of brief social deprivation on behaviors for a social reinforcer. *J. abnorm. soc. Psychol.*, 1958, **56**, 49–56. (a)

Gewirtz, J. L., and Baer, D. M. Deprivation and satiation of social reinforcers as drive conditions. *J. abnorm. soc. Psychol.*, 1958, **57**, 165–172. (b)

Gewirtz, J. L., Baer, D. M., and Roth, C. M. A note on the similar effects of low social availability of an adult and brief social deprivation on young children's behavior. *Child Dev.*, 1958, **29**, 149–152.

Gewirtz, J. L., and Stingle, K. G. Learning of generalized imitation as the basis for identification. *Psychol. Rev.*, 1968, **75**, 374–397.

Goldiamond, I. Stuttering and fluency as manipulatable operant response classes. In L. Krasner, and L. P. Ullmann (Eds.), *Research in behavior modification.* New York: Holt, Rinehart, and Winston, 1965.

Grinder, R. E. *A history of genetic psychology.* New York: Wiley, 1967.

Hall, G. S. *Adolescence.* New York: Appleton, 1908.

Hall, R. V., and Broden, M. Behavior changes in brain-injured children through social reinforcement. *J. exp. Child Psychol.*, 1967, **5**, 463–479.

Harris, F. R., Johnston, M. K., Kelley, C. S., and Wolf, M. M. Effects of positive social reinforcement on regressed crawling of a nursery school child. *J. educ. Psychol.*, 1964, **55**, 35–41.

Hart, B. M., Allen, K. E., Buell, J. S., Harris, F. R., and Wolf, M.M. Effects of social reinforcement on operant crying. *J. exp. Child Psychol.*, 1964, **1**, 145–153.

Hebb, D. O. The American revolution. *Am. Psychol.*, 1960, **15**, 735–745.

Hilgard, E. R., and Bower, G. H. *Theories of learning.* (3rd ed.) New York: Appleton-Century-Crofts, 1966.

Hilgard, E. R., and Marquis, D. G. *Conditioning and learning.* New York: Appleton-Century-Crofts, 1940.

Hill, K. T., and Stevenson, H. W. The effectiveness of social reinforcement following social and sensory deprivation. *J. abnorm. soc. Psychol.*, 1964, **68**, 579–584.

Hingtgen, J. N., Sanders, B. J., and DeMyer, M. K. Shaping cooperative responses in early childhood schizophrenics. In L. P. Ullmann and L. Krasner (Eds.), *Case studies in behavior modification.* New York: Holt, Rinehart, and Winston, 1965.

Holland, J. G., and Skinner, B. F. *The analysis of behavior: a program for self-instruction.* New York: McGraw-Hill, 1961.

House, B. J., and Zeaman, D. A. Visual discrimination learning and intelligence in defectives of low mental age. *Am. J. ment. Defic.*, 1960, **65**, 51–58.

Humphrey, G. *Thinking.* New York: Science Editions, 1963.

Hull, C. L. An experimental investigation of certain alleged relations between character and handwriting. *Psychol. Rev.*, 1919, **26**, 63–74.

Hull, C. L. Knowledge and purpose as habit mechanisms. *Psychol. Rev.*, 1930, **37**, 511–525.

Hull, C. L. Goal attraction and directing ideas conceived as habit phenomena. *Psychol. Rev.*, 1931, **38**, 487–506.

Hull, C. L. The concept of the habit-family hierarchy and maze learning. *Psychol. Rev.*, 1934, **41**, 33–52.

Hull, C. L. The mechanism of the assembly of behavior segments in novel combinations suitable for problem solutions. *Psychol. Rev.*, 1935, **42**, 219–245.

Hull, C. L. The goal-gradient hypothesis applied to some "field-force" problems in the behavior of young children. *Psychol. Rev.*, 1938, **45**, 271–299.

Hull, C. L. *Principles of behavior.* New York: Appleton-Century-Crofts, 1943.

Hull, C. L. *Essentials of behavior.* New Haven, Conn.: Yale University Press, 1951.

Hull, C. L. *A behavior system.* New Haven, Conn.: Yale University Press, 1952.

Hunt, J. McV. *Intelligence and experience.* New York: Ronald, 1961.

Hunter, W. S. The delayed reaction in animals and children. *Anim. Behav. Monogr.*, 1913, **2**, 1–86.

Johnston, M. K., Kelley, S. C., Harris, F. R., and Wolf, M. M. An application of reinforcement principles to development of motor skills in a young child. *Child Dev.*, 1966, **37**, 379–387.

Judd, C. H. Evolution and consciousness. *Psychol. Rev.*, 1910, **17**, 77–97.

Keller, F. S., and Schoenfeld, W. N. *Principles of psychology.* New York: Appleton-Century-Crofts, 1950.

Kendler, H. H., and Kendler, T. S. Vertical and horizontal processes in problem solving. *Psychol. Rev.*, 1962, **69**, 1–16.

Kendler, T. S., and Kendler, H. H. Experimental analysis of inferential behavior in children. In L. P. Lipsitt and C. C. Spiker (Eds.), *Advances in child development and behavior.* Vol. 3. New York: Academic Press, 1967.

Kerr, N., Meyerson, L., and Michael, J. A procedure for shaping vocalizations in a mute child. In L. P. Ullmann and L. Krasner (Eds.), *Case studies in behavior modification.* New York: Holt, Rinehart, and Winston, 1965.

Kessen, W., and Kessen, M. L. Behavior of young children in a two-choice guessing problem. *Child Dev.*, 1961, **32**, 779–788.

Koch, S. (Ed.) *Psychology: a study of a science.* Vol. 2. *General systematic formulations, learning and special processes.* New York: McGraw-Hill, 1959.

Kohlberg, L. Moral development and identification. In H. Stevenson (Ed.), *Child psychology: sixty-second yearbook of the National Society for the Study of Education.* Part 1. Chicago: University of Chicago Press, 1963.

Kohlberg, L. A cognitive-developmental analysis of children's sex-role concepts and attitudes. In E. Maccoby (Ed.), *The development of sex differences.* Stanford, Cal.: Stanford University Press, 1966.

Konorski, J. *Integrative activity of the brain.* Chicago: University of Chicago Press, 1967.

Krasner, L., and Ullmann, L. P. *Research in behavior modification.* New York: Holt, Rinehart, and Winston, 1965.

Kuenne, M. R. Experimental investigation of the relation of language to transposition behavior in young children. *J. exp. Psychol.,* 1946, **36,** 471–490.

Kuo, Z-Y. *The dynamics of behavior development: an epigenetic view.* New York: Random House, 1967.

Landau, R., and Gewirtz, J. L. Differential satiation for a social reinforcing stimulus as a determinant of its efficacy in conditioning. *J. exp. Child Psychol.,* 1967, **5,** 391–405.

Levin, G. R., and Hamermesh, D. R. Procedure and instructions in children's matching-to-sample. *Psychonom. Sci.,* 1967, **8,** 429–430.

Levinson, B., and Reese, H. W. Patterns of discrimination learning set in preschool children, fifth-graders, college freshmen, and the aged. *Monogr. Soc. Res. Child Dev.,* 1967, **32,** Serial. No. 115.

Lewis, M. Social isolation: a parametric study of its effect on social reinforcement. *J. exp. Child Psychol.,* 1965, **2,** 32–40.

Lipsitt, L. P. Learning in the first year of life. In L. P. Lipsitt and C. C. Spiker (Eds.), *Advances in child development and behavior.* Vol. 1. New York: Academic Press, 1963.

Lipsitt, L. P. Learning in the human infant. In H. W. Stevenson, E. H. Hess, and H. L. Rheingold (Eds.), *Early behavior: comparative and developmental approaches.* New York: Wiley, 1967.

Lovaas, O. I., Freitag, G., Gold, V. J., and Kassorla, I. C. Experimental studies in childhood schizophrenia: Analysis of self-destructive behavior. *J. exp. Child Psychol.,* 1965, **2,** 67–84.

Lumsdaine, A. A., and Glaser, R. *Teaching machines and programmed learning: a source book.* Washington, D. C.: National Education Association, 1960.

Luria, A. R. *The nature of human conflicts: an objective study of disorganization and control of human behavior.* New York: Grove Press, 1960.

Luria, A. R. *The role of speech in the regulation of normal and abnormal behavior.* New York: Liveright, 1961.

Luria, A. R. *Higher cortical functions in man.* New York: Basic Books, 1966. (a)

Luria, A. R. *Human brain and psychological processes.* New York: Harper and Row, 1966. (b)

Luria, A. R. *The mind of a mnemonist.* New York: Basic Books, 1968.

Lynn, R. *Attention, arousal and the orientation reaction.* London: Pergamon, 1966.

MacKintosh, N. J. Selective attention in animal discrimination learning. *Psychol. Bull.,* 1965, **64,** 124–150.

Maltzman, I. Thinking: from a behavioristic point of view. *Psychol. Rev.,* 1955, **62,** 275–286.

Mandler, J. M., and Mandler, G. *Thinking: from association to gestalt.* New York: Wiley, 1964.

Mateer, F. *Child behavior: a critical and experimental study of young children by the method of conditioned reflexes.* Boston: Badger, 1918.

McCullers, J. C., and Stevenson, H. W. Effects of verbal reinforcement in a probability learning situation. *Psychol. Rep.,* 1960, **7,** 439–445.

McKee, J. P., and Riley, D. A. Auditory transposition in six-year-old children. *Child Dev.*, 1962, 33, 469–476.

Melville, H. *Moby Dick*. New York: Dutton, 1907. Pp. 285.

Messick, S. J., and Solley, C. M. Probability learning in children: some exploratory studies. *J. genet. Psychol.*, 1957, 90, 23–32.

Metz, J. R. Conditioning generalized imitation in autistic children. *J. exp. Child Psychol.*, 1965, 2, 389–399.

Meyerson, L., Kerr, N., and Michael, J. L. Behavior modification in rehabilitation. In S. W. Bijou and D. M. Baer (Eds.), *Child development: readings in experimental analysis*. New York: Appleton-Century-Crofts, 1967.

Miller, G. A., Galanter, E., and Pribram, K. H. *Plans and the structure of behavior*. New York: Holt, Rinehart, and Winston, 1960.

Miller, N. E. Liberalization of basic S-R concepts: extensions to conflict behavior, motivation and social learning. In S. Koch (Ed.), *Psychology: a study of a science*. Vol. 2. New York: McGraw-Hill, 1959.

Miller, N. E., and Dollard, J. *Social learning and imitation*. New Haven, Conn.: Yale University Press, 1941.

Mintz, A. Recent developments in psychology in the U.S.S.R. *Ann. Rev. Psychol.*, 1958, 9, 453–504.

Mithaug, D. E., and Burgess, R. L. Effects of different reinforcement procedures in the establishment of a group response. *J. exp. Child Psychol.*, 1967, 5, 441–454.

Mowrer, O. H. *Learning theory and personality dynamics*. New York: Ronald, 1950.

Mowrer, O. H. *Learning theory and the symbolic processes*. New York: Wiley, 1960.

Natadze, R. G. Studies on thought and speech problems by psychologists of the Georgian S.S.R. In N. O'Connor (Ed.), *Recent Soviet psychology*. New York: Liveright, 1961.

Nunnally, J. C., Duchnowski, A. J., and Knott, P. D. Association of neutral objects with rewards: effects of massed versus distributed practice, delay of testing, age and sex. *J. exp. Child Psychol.*, 1967, 5, 152–163.

Nunnally, J. C., Duchnowski, A. J., and Parker, R. K. Association of neutral objects with rewards: effects on verbal evaluation, reward expectancy, and selective attention. *J. Pers. soc. Psychol.*, 1965, 1, 270–274.

Nunnally, J. C., and Faw, T. T. The acquisition of conditioned reward value in discrimination learning. *Child Dev.*, 1968, 39, 159–166.

Nunnally, J. C., Stevens, D. A., and Hall, G. F. Association of neutral objects with rewards: effects on verbal evaluation and eye movements. *J. exp. Child Psychol.*, 1965, 2, 44–57.

O'Connor, N. (Ed.) *Recent Soviet psychology*. New York: Liveright, 1961.

Osgood, C. E. *Method and theory in experimental psychology*. New York: Oxford, 1953.

Osler, S. F., and Fivel, M. W. Concept attainment: I. The role of age and intelligence in concept attainment by induction. *J. exp. Psychol.*, 1961, 62, 1–8.

Osler, S. F., and Kofsky, E. Stimulus uncertainty as a variable in the development of conceptual ability. *J. exp. Child Psychol.*, 1965, 2, 264–279.

Osler, S. F., and Kofsky, E. Structure and strategy in concept attainment. *J. exp. Child Psychol.*, 1966, 4, 198–209.

Osler, S. F., and Shapiro, S. L. Studies in concept attainment: IV. The role of partial reinforcement as a function of age and intelligence. *Child Dev.*, 1964, 35, 623–633.

Osler, S. F., and Trautman, G. E. Concept Attainment: II. Effect of stimulus complexity upon concept attainment at two levels of intelligence. *J. exp. Psychol.*, 1961, **62**, 14–23.

Osler, S. F., and Weiss, S. R. Studies in concept attainment: III. Effects of instructions at two levels of intelligence. *J. exp. Psychol.*, 1962, **63**, 528–533.

Palermo, D. S. Backward associations in the paired-associate learning of fourth and sixth grade children. *Psychol. Rep.*, 1961, **9**, 227–233.

Palermo, D. S. Mediated association in a paired-associate transfer task. *J. exp. Psychol.*, 1962, **64**, 234–238.

Parker, R. K., and Nunnally, J. C. Association of neutral objects with rewards: effects of reward schedules on reward expectancy, verbal evaluation, and selective attention. *J. exp. Child Psychol.*, 1966, **3**, 324–332.

Pavlov, I. P. *Lectures on conditioned reflexes.* New York: Liveright, 1928.

Pevzner, M. S. *Oligophrenia: mental deficiency in children.* New York: Consultants Bureau, 1961.

Piaget, J. *The psychology of intelligence.* Paterson, N.J.: Littlefield, Adams, 1960. P. 3.

Piaget, J. *Play, dreams and imitation in childhood.* New York: Norton, 1962.

Quay, H. C., Sprague, R. L., Werry, J. S., and McQueen, M. M. Conditioning visual orientation of conduct problem children in the classroom. *J. exp. Child Psychol.*, 1967, **5**, 512–517.

Razran, G. The observable unconscious and the inferable conscious in current Soviet psychophysiology: interoceptive conditioning, semantic conditioning, and the orienting reflex. *Psychol. Rev.*, 1961, **68**, 81–147.

Reese, H. W. Verbal mediation as a function of age level. *Psychol. Bull.*, 1962, **59**, 502–509.

Reese, H. W. Discrimination learning set in children. In L. P. Lipsitt and C. C. Spiker (Eds.), *Advances in child development and behavior.* New York: Academic Press, 1963.

Reynolds, G. S. *A primer of operant conditioning.* Glenview, Ill.: Scott, Foresman, 1968.

Riley, D. A. *Discrimination learning.* Boston: Allyn and Bacon, 1968.

Riley, D. A., and McKee, J. P. Pitch and loudness transposition in children and adults. *Child Dev.*, 1963, **34**, 471–482.

Riley, D. A., McKee, J. P., and Hadley, R. W. Prediction of auditory discrimination learning and transposition from children's auditory ordering ability. *J. exp. Psychol.*, 1964, **67**, 324–329.

Rosenhan, D. Aloneness and togetherness as drive conditions in children. *J. exp. Res. Pers.*, 1967, **2**, 32–40.

Ross, B. M., and Levy, N. Patterned prediction of chance events by children and adults. *Psychol. Rep.*, 1958, **4**, 87–124.

Schachter, S., and Singer, J. E. Cognitive, social, and physiological determinants of emotional state. *Psychol. Rev.*, 1962, **69**, 379–399.

Sears, R. R. *Survey of objective studies of psychoanalytic concepts.* New York: Social Science Research Council, 1943.

Sears, R. R. A theoretical framework for personality and social behavior. *Am. Psychol.*, 1951, **6**, 476–483.

Sears, R. R., Whiting, J. W. M., Nowlis, V., and Sears, P. Some child-rearing antecedents of aggression and dependency in young children. *Genet. Psychol. Monogr.*, 1953, **47**, 135–234.

Sears, R. R., Maccoby, E. E., and Levin, H. *Patterns of child rearing.* Evanston, Ill.: Row, Peterson, 1957.

Sears, R. R., Rau, L., and Alpert, R. *Identification and child rearing.* Stanford, Cal.: Stanford University Press, 1965.

Sechenov, I. M. Reflexes of the brain. In R. J. Herrnstein and E. G. Boring (Eds.), *A source book in the history of psychology*. Cambridge, Mass.: Harvard University Press, 1966. (Original ed., 1863.)

Sidman, M. A. note on functional relations obtained from group data. *Psychol. Bull.*, 1952, **49**, 263–269.

Sidman, M. *Tactics of scientific research*. New York: Basic Books, 1960.

Sidman, M., and Stoddard, L. Programming perception and learning for retarded children. In N. Ellis (Ed.), *International review of research in mental retardation*. Vol. 2. New York: Academic Press, 1966.

Sidman, M., and Stoddard, L. The effectiveness of fading in programming a simultaneous form discrimination for retarded children. *J. exp. analysis Behav.*, 1967, **10**, 3–15.

Siegel, S., and Andrews, J. M. Magnitude of reinforcing and choice behavior in children. *J. exp. Psychol.*, 1962, **63**, 337–341.

Skinner, B. F. The generic nature of the concepts of stimulus and response. *J. gen. Psychol.*, 1935, **12**, 40–65.

Skinner, B. F. *The behavior of organisms: an experimental analysis*. New York: Appleton-Century-Crofts, 1938.

Skinner, B. F. Are theories of learning necessary? *Psychol. Rev.*, 1950, **57**, 193–216.

Skinner, B. F. *Science and human behavior*. New York: Macmillan, 1953.

Skinner, B. F. *Verbal behavior*. New York: Appleton-Century-Crofts, 1957.

Skinner, B. F. A case history in scientific method. In S. Koch (Ed.), *Psychology: a study of a science*. Vol. 2. New York: McGraw-Hill, 1959. (a)

Skinner, B. F. *Cumulative record*. New York: Appleton-Century-Crofts, 1959. (b)

Skinner, B. F. *The technology of teaching*. New York: Appleton-Century-Crofts, 1968.

Sokolov, Ye. N. *Perception and the conditioned reflex*. New York: Macmillan, 1963.

Spence, K. W. The nature of discrimination learning in animals. *Psychol. Rev.*, 1936, **43**, 427–449.

Spence, K. W. The differential response in animals to stimuli varying within a single dimension. *Psychol. Rev.*, 1937, **44**, 430–444.

Spence, K. W. Mathematical formulations of learning phenomena. *Psychol. Rev.*, 1952, **59**, 152–160.

Spence, K. W. Mathematical theories of learning. *J. gen. Psychol.*, 1953, **49**, 283–291.

Spence, K. W. *Behavior theory and conditioning*. New Haven, Conn.: Yale University Press, 1956.

Spence, K. W., and Taylor, J. Anxiety and strength of the UCS as determiners of the amount of eyelid conditioning. *J. exp. Psychol.*, 1951, **42**, 183–188.

Spiker, C. C. Research methods in children's learning. In P. H. Mussen (Ed.), *Handbook of research methods in child development*. New York: Wiley, 1960.

Spiker, C. C. The hypothesis of stimulus interaction and an explanation of stimulus compounding. In L. P. Lipsitt and C. C. Spiker (Eds.), *Advances in child development and behavior*. Vol. 1. New York: Academic Press, 1963.

Spiker, C. C., and McCandless, B. R. The concept of intelligence and the philosophy of science. *Psychol. Rev.*, 1954, **61**, 255–266.

Staats, A. W. Verbal habit-families, concepts, and the operant conditioning of word classes. *Psychol. Rev.*, 1961, **68**, 190–204.

Staats, A. W., and Butterfield, W. H. Treatment of nonreading in a culturally deprived juvenile delinquent: an application of reinforcement principles. *Child Dev.*, 1965, **36**, 925–942.

Staats, A. W., Finley, J. R., Minke, K. A., and Wolf, M. M. Reinforcement variables in the control of unit reading responses. *J. exp. analysis Behav.*, 1964, **7**, 139–149.

Stevenson, H. W. Social reinforcement of children's behavior. In L. P. Lipsitt and C. C. Spiker (Eds.), *Advances in child development and behavior*. Vol. 2. New York: Academic Press, 1965.

Stevenson, H. W., and Odom, R. D. The effectiveness of social reinforcement following two conditions of social deprivation. *J. abnorm. soc. Psychol.*, 1962, **65**, 429–431.

Stevenson, H. W., and Weir, M. W. Variables affecting children's performance in a probability learning task. *J. exp. Psychol.*, 1959, **57**, 403–413.

Stevenson, H. W., and Zigler, E. Probability learning in children. *J. exp. Psychol.*, 1958, **56**, 185–192.

Stoddard, L. T. An observation on stimulus control in a tilt discrimination by children. *J. exp. Analysis Behav.*, 1968, **11**, 321–324.

Stoddard, L. T., and Sidman, M. The effects of errors on children's performance on a circle-ellipse discrimination. *J. exp. Analysis Behav.*, 1967, **10**, 261–270.

Sutherland, N. S. Stimulus analysing mechanisms. *In Proceedings of a symposium on the mechanisation of thought processes*. London: Her Majesty's Stationery Office, 1959.

Terman, L. M. Genius and stupidity: a study of the intellectual processes of seven "bright" and seven "stupid" boys. *Pedag. Sem.*, 1906, **13**, 307–373.

Thorndike, E. L. Ideo-motor action. *Psychol. Rev.*, 1913, **20**, 91–106.

Thorndike, E. L. *Educational psychology: Vol. I, The original nature of man; Vol. II, The psychology of learning; Vol. III, Mental work and fatigue and individual differences and their causes*. New York: Teachers College, 1913–1914.

Thorndike, E. L. *Human Learning*. New York: Century, 1931.

Tighe, L. S. Effect of perceptual training on reversal and nonreversal shifts. *J. exp. Psychol.*, 1965, **70**, 379–385.

Tolman, E. C. A new formula for behaviorism. *Psychol. Rev.*, 1922, **29**, 44–53. (a)

Tolman, E. C. Concerning the sensation quality: a behavioristic account. *Psychol. Rev.*, 1922, **29**, 140–145. (b)

Tolman, E. C. A behavioristic account of the emotions. *Psychol. Rev.*, 1923, **30**, 217–227.

Tolman, E. C. Purpose and cognition: the determiners of animal learning. *Psychol. Rev.*, 1925, **32**, 285–297.

Tolman, E. C. A behavioristic theory of ideas. *Psychol. Rev.*, 1926, **33**, 352–369.

Tolman, E. C. A behaviorist's definition of consciousness. *Psychol. Rev.*, 1927, **34**, 433–439.

Tolman, E. C. *Purposive behavior in animals and men*. New York: Century, 1932.

Touchette, P. E. The effects of graduated stimulus change on the acquisition of a simple discrimination in severely retarded boys. *J. exp. Analysis Behav.*, 1968, **11**, 39–48.

Ullmann, L. P., and Krasner, L. (Eds.) *Case studies in behavior modification*. New York: Holt, Rinehart, and Winston, 1965.

Uznadze, D. N. *The psychology of set*. New York: Consultants Bureau, 1966.

Vinacke, W. E. *The psychology of thinking*. New York: McGraw-Hill, 1952.

Vygotsky, L. S. *Thought and language*. Cambridge, Mass.: M.I.T. Press, 1962.

Wallach, M. A., and Kogan, N. *Modes of thinking in young children*. New York: Holt, Rinehart, and Winston, 1965.

Walters, R. H., and Parke, R. D. Influence of response consequences to a social model on resistance to deviation. *J. exp. Child Psychol.*, 1964, **1**, 269–280.

Walters, R. H., and Ray, E. Anxiety, social isolation, and reinforcer effectiveness. *J. Personality*, 1960, **28**, 358–367.

Warren, H. C. *A history of the association psychology.* New York: Scribner, 1921.

Washburn, M. F. *The animal mind.* New York: Macmillan, 1908.

Watson, J. B. Imitation in monkeys. *Psychol. Bull.*, 1908, **6**, 169–178.

Watson, J. B. Psychology as the behaviorist views it. *Psychol. Rev.*, 1913, **20**, 158–177.

Watson, J. B. A schematic outline of the emotions. *Psychol. Rev.*, 1919, **26**, 165–196.

Watson, J. B. What the nursery has to say about instincts. Experimental studies on the growth of emotions. Recent experiments on how we lose and change our emotional equipment. In C. Murchison (Ed.), *Psychologies of 1925.* Worcester, Mass.: Clark University Press, 1926.

Watson, J. B. *Behaviorism.* (1st ed.) Chicago: University of Chicago Press, 1930.

Watson, J. B., and Raynor, R. A. Conditioned emotional reactions. *J. exp. Psychol.*, 1920, **3**, 1–4.

Weinbridge, E. R., and Gabel, P. Multiple choice experiment applied to school children. *Psychol. Rev.*, 1919, **26**, 294–299.

Weir, M. W. Developmental changes in problem solving strategies. *Psychol. Rev.*, 1964, **71**, 473–490.

Werner, H. *Comparative psychology of mental development.* New York: Science Editions, 1961.

White, S. H. Learning. In H. W. Stevenson (Ed.), *Child psychology: sixty-second Yearbook of the National Society for the Study of Education.* Part 1. Chicago: University of Chicago Press, 1963.

White, S. H. Evidence for a hierarchical arrangement of learning processes. In L. P. Lipsitt, and C. C. Spiker (Eds.), *Advances in child behavior and development.* Vol. 2. New York: Academic Press, 1965.

White, S. H. Age differences in reaction to stimulus variation. In O. J. Harvey (Ed.), *Flexibility and creativity: nature and determinants.* New York: Springer, 1966. (a)

White, S. H. The hierarchical organization of intellectual structures. Paper presented at symposium, ("The role of experience in intellectual development," American Association for the Advancement of Science convention, Washington, D. C., December, 1966. (b)

White, S. H. The learning-maturation controversy: Hall to Hull. *Merrill-Palmer Q.*, 1968, **14**, 187–196. (a)

White, S. H. Changes in learning processes in the late preschool years. Paper presented at symposium, "Early learning," American Educational Research Association convention, Chicago, 1968. (b)

White, S. H. A contemporary perspective on learning theory and its relation to education. In J. I. Goodlad (Ed.), *Human behavior and childhood education.* Waltham, Mass.: Blaisdell, 1969.

White, S. H., and Plum, G. E. Eye movement photography during children's discrimination learning. *J. exp. Child Psychol.*, 1964, **1**, 327–338.

Wiesen, A. E., Hartley, G., Richardson, C., and Roske, A. The retarded child as a reinforcing agent. *J. exp. Child Psychol.*, 1967, **5**, 109–113.

Williams, C. D. The elimination of tantrum behavior by extinction procedures. *J. abnorm. soc. Psychol.*, 1959, **59**, 269.

Witte, K. L. Children's response speeds to familiarized stimuli. *Psychonom. Sci.*, 1967, **7**, 153–154.

Witte, K. L., and Cantor, G. N. Children's response speeds to the offset of novel and familiar stimuli. *J. exp. Child Psychol.*, 1967, **5**, 372–380.

Wolf, M. M., Birnbrauer, J. S., Williams, T., and Lawler, J. A note on apparent extinction of the vomiting behavior of a retarded child. In L. P. Ullman and L. Krasner (Ed.), *Case studies in behavior modification.* New York: Holt, Rinehart, and Winston, 1965.

Wolf, M. M., Risley, T. R., and Mees, H. I. Application of operant conditioning procedures to the behavior problems of an autistic child. *Behav. Res. Ther.,* 1964, **1**, 305–312.

Wolff, J. L. Concept-shift and discrimination-reversal learning in humans. *Psychol. Bull.,* 1967, **67**, 369–408.

Wolpe, J. *Psychotherapy by reciprocal inhibition.* Stanford, Cal.: Stanford University Press, 1958.

Wright, J. C., and Smothergill, D. Observing behavior and children's discrimination learning under delayed reinforcement. *J. exp. Child Psychol.,* 1967, **5**, 430–440.

Yaroshevski, M. G., I. M. Sechenov—The founder of objective psychology. In B. B. Wolman (Ed.), *Historical roots of contemporary psychology.* New York: Harper and Row, 1968.

Yerkes, R. M., and Morgulis, S. The method of Pawlow in animal psychology. *Psychol. Bull.,* 1909, **6**, 257–273.

Youniss, J., and Furth, H. G. Discrimination shifts as a function of degree of training in children. *J. exp. Psychol.,* 1965, **70**, 424–427.

Zaporozhets, A. V. The origin and development of the conscious control of movements in man. In N. O'Connor (Ed.), *Recent Soviet psychology.* New York: Liveright, 1961.

Zaporozhets, A. V. The role of the orienting activity and of the image in the formation and performance of voluntary movements. In L. G. Voronin, A. N. Leontiev, A. R. Luria, E. N. Sokolov, and O. S. Vinogradova (Eds.), *Orienting reflex and exploratory behavior.* Washington: American Institute of Biological Sciences, 1965.

Zeaman, D., and House, B. J. The role of attention in retardate discrimination learning. In N. R. Ellis (Ed.), *Handbook of mental deficiency.* New York: McGraw-Hill, 1963.

Zeigarnik, B. V. *The pathology of thinking.* New York: Consultants Bureau, 1965.

Zeiler, M. D. Stimulus definition and choice. In L. P. Lipsitt and C. C. Spiker (Eds.), *Advances in child development and behavior.* Vol. 3. New York: Academic Press, 1967.

Zimmerman, E. H., and Zimmerman, J. The alteration of behavior in a special classroom situation. *J. exp. Analysis Behav.,* 1962, **5**, 59–60.

9. Piaget's Theory[1]

JEAN PIAGET[2]

The following theory of development, which is particularly concerned with the development of cognitive functions, is impossible to understand if one does not begin by analyzing in detail the biological presuppositions from which it stems and the epistemological consequences in which it ends. Indeed, the fundamental postulate that is the basis of the ideas summarized here is that the same problems and the same types of explanations can be found in the three following processes:

a. The adaptation of an organism to its environment during its growth, together with the interactions and autoregulations which characterize the development of the "epigenetic system." (Epigenesis in its embryological sense is always determined both internally and externally.)

b. The adaptation of intelligence in the course of the construction of its own structures, which depends as much on progressive internal coordinations as on information acquired through experience.

c. The establishment of cognitive or, more generally, epistemological relations, which consist neither of a simple copy of external objects nor of a mere unfolding of structures preformed inside the subject, but rather involve a set of structures progressively constructed by continuous interaction between the subject and the external world.

We begin with the last point, on which our theory is furthest removed both from the ideas of the majority of psychologists and from "common sense."

I. THE RELATION BETWEEN SUBJECT AND OBJECT

1. In the common view, the external world is entirely separate from the subject, although it encloses the subject's own body. Any objective knowledge, then, appears to be simply the result of a set of perceptive recordings, motor associations, verbal descriptions, and the like, which all participate in producing a sort of figurative copy or "functional copy" (in Hull's terminology) of objects and the connections between them. The only function of intelligence is systematically to file, correct, etc., these various sets of information; in this process, the more faithful the critical copies, the more consistent the final system will be. In such an empiricist prospect, the content of intelligence comes from outside, and the coordinations that organize it are only the consequences of language and symbolic instruments.

[1] This chapter was written in French and translated by Dr. Guy Gellerier of the University of Geneva and Professor Jonas Langer of the University of California at Berkeley. We are also grateful to Professors Bärbel Inhelder and Hermione Sinclair for their assistance in the translation.

[2] The present chapter is, in part, the expansion of an article on my conceptions of development published in *Journal International de Psychologie,* a summary of previous publications, but it also takes into account recent or still unpublished work by the author or his collaborators and colleagues. As a matter of fact, "Piaget's theory" is not completed at this date and the author of these pages has always considered himself one of the chief "revisionists of Piaget." (Author's note)

But this passive interpretation of the act of knowledge is in fact contradicted at all levels of development and, particularly, at the sensorimotor and prelinguistic levels of cognitive adaptation and intelligence. Actually, in order to know objects, the subject must act upon them, and therefore transform them: he must displace, connect, combine, take apart, and reassemble them.

From the most elementary sensorimotor actions (such as pushing and pulling) to the most sophisticated intellectual operations, which are interiorized actions, carried out mentally (e.g., joining together, putting in order, putting into one-to-one correspondence), knowledge is constantly linked with actions or operations, that is, with *transformations*.

Hence the limit between subject and objects is in no way determined beforehand, and, what is more important, it is not stable. Indeed, in every action the subject and the objects are fused. The subject needs objective information to become aware of his own actions, of course, but he also needs many subjective components. Without long practice or the construction of refined instruments of analysis and coordination, it will be impossible for him to know what belongs to the object, what belongs to himself as an active subject, and what belongs to the action itself taken as the transformation of an initial state into a final one. Knowledge, then, at its origin, neither arises from objects nor from the subject, but from interactions—at first inextricable—between the subject and those objects.

Even these primitive interactions are so close-knit and inextricable that, as J. M. Baldwin noted, the mental attitudes of the infant are probably "adualistical." This means they lack any differentiation between an external world, which would be composed of objects independent of the subject, and an internal or subjective world.

Therefore the problem of knowledge, the so-called epistemological problem, cannot be considered separately from the problem of the development of intelligence. It reduces to analyzing how the subject becomes progressively able to know objects adequately, that is, how he becomes capable of objectivity. Indeed, objectivity is in no way an initial property, as the empiricists would have it,

and its conquest involves a series of successive constructs which approximates it more and more closely.

2. This leads us to a second idea central to the theory, that of *construction*, which is the natural consequence of the interactions we have just mentioned. Since objective knowledge is not acquired by a mere recording of external information but has its origin in interactions between the subject and objects, it necessarily implies two types of activity—on the one hand, the coordination of actions themselves, and on the other, the introduction of interrelations between the objects. These two activities are interdependent because it is only through action that these relations originate. It follows that objective knowledge is always subordinate to certain structures of action. But those structures are the result of a *construction* and are not given in the objects, since they are dependent on action, nor in the subject, since the subject must learn how to coordinate his actions (which are not generally hereditarily programmed except in the case of reflexes or instincts).

An early example of these constructions (which begin as early as the first year) is the one that enables the 9- to 12-month-old child to discover the permanence of objects, initially relying on their position in his perceptual field, and later independent of any actual perception. During the first months of existence, there are no permanent objects, but only percepual pictures which appear, dissolve, and sometimes reappear. The "permanence" of an object begins with the action of looking for it when it has disappeared at a certain point A of the visual field (for instance, if a part of the object remains visible, or if it makes a bump under a cloth). But, when the object later disappears at B, it often happens that the child will look for it again at A. This very instructive behavior supplies evidence for the existence of the primitive interactions between the subject and the object which we mentioned (¶ 1). At this stage, the child still believes that objects depend on this action and that, where an action has succeeded a first time, it must succeed again. One real example is an 11-month-old child who was playing with a ball. He had previously retrieved it from under an armchair when it had rolled there before. A moment later, the ball went under a low sofa. He could not find it under this sofa, so he came back to the other part of the room and looked for it under the armchair, where this course of action had already been successful.

For the scheme[3] of a permanent object that does not depend on the subject's own actions to become established, a new structure has to be constructed. This is the structure of the "group of translations" in the geometrical sense: (a) the translation $AB + BC = AC$; (b) the translations $AB + BA = O$; (c) $AB + O = AB$; (d) $AC + CD = AB + BD$. The psychological equivalent of this group is the possibility of behaviors that involve returning to an initial position, or detouring around an obstacle (a and d). As soon as this organization is achieved—and it is not at all given at the beginning of development, but must be constructed by a succession of new coordinations—an objective structuration of the movements of the object and of those of the subject's own body becomes possible. The object becomes an independent entity, whose position can be traced as a function of its translations and successive positions. At this juncture the subject's body, instead of being considered the center of the world, becomes an object like any other, the translations and positions of which are correlative to those of the objects themselves.

The group of translations is an instance of the construction of a structure, attributable simultaneously to progressive coordination of the subject's actions and to information provided by physical experience, which finally constitutes a fundamental instrument for the organization of the external world. It is also a cognitive instrument so important that it

[3] Throughout this paper the term *scheme* (plural, *schemes*) is used to refer to *operational* activities, whereas *schema* (plural, *schemata*) refers to the figurative aspects of thought—attempts to represent reality without attempting to transform it (imagery, perception and memory). Later in this paper the author says, ". . . images . . . , however schematic, are not schemes. We shall therefore use the term schemata to designate them. A schema is a simplified image (e.g., the map of a town), whereas a scheme represents what can be repeated and generalized in an action (for example, the scheme is what is common in the actions of 'pushing' an object with a stick or any other instrument)."

contributes to the veritable "Copernican revolution" babies accomplish in 12 to 18 months. Whereas before he had evolved this new structure the child would consider himself (unconsciously) the motionless center of the universe, he becomes, because of this organization of permanent objects and space (which entails moreover a parallel organization of temporal sequences and causality), only one particular member of the set of the other mobile objects which compose his universe.

3. We can now see that even in the study of the infant at sensorimotor levels it is not possible to follow a psychogenetic line of research without evolving an implicit epistemology, which is also genetic, but which raises all the main issues in the theory of knowledge. Thus the construction of the group of translations obviously involves physical experience and empirical information. But it also involves more, since it also depends on the coordinations of the subject's action. These coordinations are not a product of experience only, but are also controlled by factors such as maturation and voluntary exercise, and, what is more important, by continuous and active autoregulation. The main point in a theory of development is not to neglect the activities of the subject, in the epistemological sense of the term. This is even more essential in this latter sense because the epistemological sense has a deep biological significance. The living organism itself is not a mere mirror image of the properties of its environment. It evolves a *structure* which is constructed step by step in the course of epigenesis, and which is not entirely preformed.

What is already true for the sensorimotor stage appears again in all stages of development and in scientific thought itself but at levels in which the primitive actions have been transformed into *operations*. These operations are interiorized actions (e.g., addition, which can be performed either physically or mentally) that are reversible (addition acquires an inverse in subtraction) and constitute set-theoretical structures (such as the logical additive "grouping" or algebraic groups).

A striking instance of these operational structurations dependent on the subject's activity, which often occurs even before an experimental method has been evolved, is *atomism*, invented by the Greeks long before it could be justified experimentally. The same process can be observed in the child between 4 to 5 and 11 to 12 years of age in a situation where it is obvious that experience is not sufficient to explain the emergence of the structure and that its construction implies an additive composition dependent on the activities of the subject. The experiment involves the dissolution of lumps of sugar in a glass of water. The child can be questioned about the conservation of the matter dissolved and about the conservation of its weight and volume. Before age 7 to 8 the dissolved sugar is presumed destroyed and its taste vanished. Around this age sugar is considered as preserving its substance in the form of very small and invisible grains, but it has neither weight nor volume. At age 9 to 10 each grain keeps its weight and the sum of all these elementary weights is equivalent to the weight of the sugar itself before dissolution. At age 11 to 12 this applies to volume (the child predicts that after the sugar has melted, the level of the water in the container will remain at its same initial height).

We can now see that this spontaneous atomism, although it is suggested by the visible grains becoming gradually smaller during their dissolution, goes far beyond what can be seen by the subject and involves a step-by-step construction correlative to that of additive operations. We thus have a new instance of the origin of knowledge lying neither in the object alone nor in the subject, but rather in an inextricable interaction between both of them, such that what is given physically is integrated in a logicomathematical structure involving the coordination of the subject's actions. The decomposition of a whole into its parts (invisible here) and the recomposition of these parts into a whole are in fact the result of logical or logicomathematical constructions and not only of physical experiments. The whole considered here is not a perceptual "Gestalt" (whose character is precisely that of *non*additive composition, as Kohler rightly insisted) but a sum (additive), and as such it is produced by operations and not by observations.

4. There can be no theoretical discontinuity between thought as it appears in children and adult scientific thinking; this is the reason

for our extension of developmental psychology to genetic epistemology. This is particularly clear in the field of logicomathematical structures considered in themselves and not (as in ¶ 2 and ¶3) as instruments for the structuration of physical data. These structures essentially involve relations of inclusion, order, and correspondence. Such relations are certainly of biological origin, for they already exist in the genetic (DNA) programming of embryological development as well as in the physiological organization of the mature organism before they appear and are reconstructed at the different levels of behavior itself. They then become fundamental structures of behavior and of intelligence in its very early development before they appear in the field of spontaneous thought and later of reflection. They provide the foundations of these progressively more abstract axiomatizations we call logic and mathematics. Indeed, if logic and mathematics are so-called "abstract" sciences, the psychologist must ask: Abstracted from what? We have seen their origin is not in objects alone. It lies, in small part only, in language, but language itself is a construct of intelligence. Chomsky even ascribes it to innate intellectual structures. Therefore the origin of these logicomathematical structures should be sought in the activities of the subject, that is, in the most general forms of coordinations of his actions, and, finally, in his organic structures themselves. This is the reason why there are fundamental relations among the biological theory of adaptation by self-regulation, developmental psychology, and genetic epistemology. This relation is so fundamental that if it is overlooked, no general theory of the development of intelligence can be established.

II. ASSIMILATION AND ACCOMMODATION

5. The psychological meaning of our previous points (¶ 1 to 4) is that the fundamental psychogenetic connections generated in the course of development cannot be considered as reducible to empirical "associations"; rather, they consist of *assimilations*, both in the biological and intellectual sense.

From a biological point of view, assimilation is the integration of external elements into evolving or completed structures of an organism. In its usual connotation, the assimilation of food consists of a chemical transformation that incorporates it into the substance of the organism. Chlorophyllian assimilation consists of the integration of radiation energy in the metabolic cycle of a plant. Waddington's "genetic assimilation" consists of a hereditary fixation by selection on phenotypes (phenotypic variations being regarded, in this case, as the genetic system's "answer" to stresses produced by the environment). Thus all the organism's reactions involve an assimilation process which can be represented in symbolic form as follows:

$$(T + I) \rightarrow AT + E \qquad (1)$$

where T is a structure, I the integrated substances or energies, E the eliminated substances or energies, and A a coefficient > 1 expressing the strengthening of this structure in the form of an increase of material or of efficiency in operation.[4] Put in this form it becomes obvious that the general concept of assimilation also applies to behavior and not only to organic life. Indeed, no behavior, even if it is new to the individual, constitutes an absolute beginning. It is always grafted onto previous schemes and therefore amounts to assimilating new elements to already constructed structures (innate, as reflexes are, or previously acquired). Even Harlow's "stimulus hunger" cannot be reduced simply to subordination to the environment but must rather be interpreted as a search for "functional input" ("éléments fonctionnels") that can be assimilated to the schemes or structures actually providing the responses.

At this point it is appropriate to note how

[4] For example, take T to be an already established classification on a set of objects, O, which divides it into two distinct subclasses. I is a set of new objects that are added to the original ones and to which the classification T must be extended. When this is done (I has been assimilated to T), it turns out that there are say two new subclasses (the whole structure is now AT) and some properties of the new objects I (e.g., the number of elements in I, or their shape, size or color) have been neglected in the process. We now have $T + I \rightarrow AT + E$, where $T =$ the two original subclasses, $I =$ the new elements, $AT =$ the four subclasses, and $E =$ the irrelevant properties of the new elements, that is, the properties which are not used as criteria for classifying in this specific instance.

inadequate the well known "stimulus-response" theory appears in this context, as a general formulation of behavior. It is obvious that a stimulus can elicit a response only if the organism is first sensitized to this stimulus (or possesses the necessary reactive "competence" as Waddington characterizes genetic sensitization to specific inducers).

When we say an organism or a subject is sensitized to a stimulus and able to make a response to it, we imply it already possesses a scheme or a structure to which this stimulus is assimiliated (in the sense of incorporated or integrated, as defined previously). This scheme consists precisely of a capacity to respond. Hence the original stimulus-response scheme should not have been written in the unilateral S → R form, but in the form:

$$S \rightleftarrows R \qquad \text{or} \qquad S \rightarrow (AT) \rightarrow R \qquad (2)$$

where AT is the assimilation of the stimulus S to the structure T.

We thus return to the equation $T + I \rightarrow AT + E$ where, in this case, T is the structure, I the stimulus, AT the result of the assimilation of I to T, that is the response to the stimulus, and E is whatever in the stimulus situation is excluded in the structure.

6. If assimilation alone were involved in development, there would be no variations in the child's structures. Therefore he would not acquire new content and would not develop further. Assimilation is necessary in that it assures the continuity of structures and the integration of new elements to these structures. Without it an organism would be in a similar situation to that of chemical compounds, A, B, which, in interaction, give rise to new compounds C and D. (The equation would then be $A + B \rightarrow C + D$ and not $T \rightarrow AT$).

Biological assimilation itself, however, is never present without its counterpart, accommodation. During its embryological development, for instance, a phenotype assimilates the substances necessary to the conservation of its structures as specified by its genotype. But, depending on whether these substances are plentiful or rare or whether the usual substances are replaced by other slightly different ones, nonhereditary variations (often called "accommodates") such as changes in shape or height may occur. These variations are specific to some external conditions. Similarly, in the field of behavior we shall call accommodation any modification of an assimilatory scheme or structure by the elements it assimilates. For example, the infant who assimilates his thumb to the sucking schema will, when sucking his thumb make different movements from those he uses in suckling his mother's breast. Similarly, an 8-year-old who is assimilating the dissolution of sugar in water to the notion that substance is conserved must make accommodations to invisible particles different from those he would make if they were still visible.

Hence cognitive adaptation, like its biological counterpart, consists of an equilibrium between assimilation and accommodation. As has just been shown, there is no assimilation without accommodation. But we must strongly emphasize the fact that accommodation does not exist without simultaneous assimilation either. From a biological point of view, this fact is verified by the existence of what modern geneticists call "reaction norms" —a genotype may offer a more or less broad range of possible accommodations, but all of them are within a certain statistically defined "norm." In the same way, cognitively speaking, the subject is capable of various accommodations, but only within certain limits imposed by the necessity of preserving the corresponding assimilatory structure. In Eq. 1 the term A in AT specifies precisely this limitation on accommodations.

The concept of "association," which the various forms of associationism from Hume to Pavlov and Hull have used and abused, has thus only been obtained by artificially isolating one part of the general process defined by the equilibrium between assimilation and accommodation. Pavlov's dog is said to associate a sound to food, which elicits its salivation reflex. If, however, the sound is never again followed by food, the conditioned response, or temporary link, will disappear; it has no intrinsic stability. The conditioning persists as a function of the need for food, that is, it persists only if it is part of an assimilatory scheme and its satisfaction, hence of a certain accommodation to the situation. In fact, an "association" is always accompanied by an assimilation to previous structures, and this is a first factor that must not be overlooked. On the other hand, insofar as the "association" incorporates some new in-

formation, this represents an active accommodation and not a mere passive recording. This accommodatory activity, which is dependent on the assimilation scheme is a second necessary factor that must not be neglected.

7. If accommodation and assimilation are present in all activity, their ratio may vary, and only the more or less stable equilibrium which may exist between them (though it is always mobile) characterizes a complete act of intelligence.

When assimilation *outweighs* accommodation (i.e., when the characteristics of the object are not taken into account except insofar as they are consistent with the subject's momentary interests) thought evolves in an egocentric or even autistic direction. The most common form of this situation in the play of the child is the "symbolic games" or fiction games, in which objects at his command are used only to represent what is imagined.[5] This form of game which is most

[5] The categories of play defined by Piaget (in *Play, Dreams and Imitation,* 1951, for example) are the following:

a. Exercise Games. These consist of any behavior without new structuration but with a new functional finality. For example, the repetition of an action such as swinging an object, if its aim is to understand or to practice the movement, is *not* a game. But the same behavior, if its aim is functional pleasure, pleasure in the activity in itself, or the pleasure of "causing" some phenomenon, becomes a game. Examples of this are the vocalizations of infants and the games of adults with a new car, radio, etc.

b. Symbolic games. These consist of behaviors with a new structuration, that of representing realities that are out of the present perceptual field. Examples are the fiction games where the child enacts a meal with pebbles standing for bread, grass for vegetables, etc. The symbols used here are individual and specific to each child.

c. Rule Games. These are behaviors with a new structuration involving the intervention of more than one person. The rules of this new structure are defined by social interaction. This type of game ranges over the whole scale of activities, starting with simple sensorimotor games with set rules (the many varieties of marble games, for instance) and ending with abstract games like chess. The symbols here are stabilized by convention and can become purely arbitrary in the more abstract games. That is, they bear no more relation (analogy) with what they represent. (Translator's note) frequent at the beginning of representation (between 1½ and 3 years of age), then evolves toward constructive games in which accommodation to objects becomes more and more precise until there is no longer any difference between play and spontaneous cognitive or instrumental activities.

Conversely, when accommodation prevails over assimilation to the point where it faithfully reproduces the forms and movements of the objects or persons which are its models at that time, representation (and the sensorimotor behaviors which are its precursors and which also give rise to exercise games that develop much earlier than symbolic games) evolves in the direction of imitation. Imitation through action, an accommodation to models that are present, gradually extends to deferred imitation and finally to interiorized imitation. In this last form it constitutes the origin of mental imagery and of the figurative as opposed to the operative aspects of thought.

But as long as assimilation and accommodation are in equilibrium (i.e., insofar as assimilation is still subordinate to the properties of the objects, or, in other words, subordinate to the situation with the accommodations it entails; and accommodation itself is subordinate to the already existing structures to which the situation must be assimilated) we can speak of cognitive behavior as opposed to play, imitation, or mental imagery, and we are back in the proper domain of intelligence. But this fundamental equilibrium between assimilation and accommodation is more or less difficult to attain and to maintain depending on the level of intellectual development and the new problems encountered. However, such an equilibrium exists at all levels, in the early development of intelligence in the child as well as in scientific thought.

It is obvious that any physical or biological theory assimilates objective phenomena to a restricted number of models which are not drawn exclusively from these phenomena. These models involve in addition a certain number of logicomathematical coordinations that are the operational activities of the subject himself. It would be very superficial to reduce these coordinations to a mere "language" (though this is the position of logical positivism) because, properly speaking, they

are an instrument for structuration. For example, Poincaré narrowly missed discovering relativity because he thought there was no difference between expressing (or translating) phenomena in the "language" of Euclidian or of Riemanian geometry. Einstein was able to construct his theory by using Riemanian space as an instrument of *structuration*, to "understand" the relations between space, speed, and time. If physics proceeds by assimilating reality to logicomathematical models, then it must unceasingly accommodate them to new experimental results. It cannot dispense with accommodation because its models would then remain subjective and arbitrary. However, every new accommodation is conditioned by existing assimilations. The significance of an experiment does not derive from a mere perceptive recording (the "*Protokollsätze*" of the first "logical empiricists"); it cannot be dissociated from an *interpretation*.

8. In the development of intelligence in the child, there are many types of equilibrium between assimilation and accommodation that vary with the levels of development and the problems to be solved. At sensorimotor levels (before 1½ to 2 years of age) these are only practical problems involving immediate space, and as early as the second year, sensorimotor intelligence reaches a remarkable state of equilibrium (e.g., instrumental behaviors, group of displacements; see ¶ 2.) But this equilibrium is difficult to attain, because during the first months, the infant's universe is centered on his own body and actions, and because of distortions due to assimilation not yet balanced by adequate accommodations.

The beginning of thought creates multiple problems of representation (which must extend to distant space and can no longer be restricted to near space) as well as the problem of adaptation no longer measured by practical success alone; thus intelligence goes through a new phase of assimilatory distortion. This is because objects and events are assimilated to the subject's own action and viewpoint and possible accommodations still consist only of fixations on figural aspects of reality (hence on states as opposed to transformations). For these two reasons—egocentric assimilation and incomplete accommodation—equilibrium is not reached. On the other hand, from the age of 7 to 8 the emergence of reversible operations ensures a stable harmony between assimilation and accommodation since both can now act on transformations as well as on states.

Generally speaking, this progressive equilibrium between assimilation and accommodation is an instance of a fundamental process in cognitive development which can be expressed in terms of centration and decentration. The systematically distorting assimilations of sensorimotor or initial representative stages, which distort because they are not accompanied by adequate accommodations, mean that the subject remains centered on his own actions and his own viewpoint. On the other hand, the gradually emerging equilibrium between assimilation and accommodation is the result of successive decentrations, which make it possible for the subject to take the points of view of other subjects or objects themselves. We formerly described this process merely in terms of egocentrism and socialization. But it is far more general and more fundamental to knowledge in all its forms. For cognitive progress is not only assimilation of information; it entails a systematic decentration process which is a necessary condition of objectivity itself.

III. THE THEORY OF STAGES

9. We have seen that there exist structures which belong only to the subject (¶ 1), that they are built (¶ 2), and that this is a step-by-step process (¶ 7). We must therefore conclude there exist stages of development. Even authors who agree with this idea may use different criteria and interpretations of stage development. It therefore becomes a problem that requires discussion in its own right. The Freudian stages, for instance, are only distinct from each other in that they differ in one dominant character (oral, anal, etc.) but this character is also present in the previous—or following—stages, so that its "dominance" may well remain arbitrary. Gesell's stages are based on the hypothesis of the quasi-exclusive role of maturation, so that they guarantee a constant order of succession but may neglect the factor of progressive construction. To characterize the stages of cognitive development we therefore need to integrate two necessary conditions without introducing any contradictions. These conditions for stages are (a) that they must be defined to guarantee a constant order of succession, and (b) that the definition allow for progressive construction without entailing total preformation. These two conditions are necessary because knowledge obviously involves learning by experience, which means an external contribution in addition to that involving internal structures, and the structures seem to evolve in a way that is not entirely predetermined.

The problem of stages in developmental psychology is analogous to that of stages in embryogenesis. The question that arises in this field is also that of making allowance for both genetic preformation and an eventual "epigenesis" in the sense of construction by interactions between the genome and the environment. It is for this reason that Waddington introduces the concept of "epigenetic system" and also a distinction between the genotype and the "epigenotype." The main characteristics of such an epigenetic development are not only the well-known and obvious ones of succession in sequential order and of progressive integration (segmentation followed by determination controlled by specific "competence" and finally "reintegration") but also some less obvious ones pointed out by Waddington. These are the existence of "creodes," or necessary developmental sequences, each with its own "time tally," or schedule, and the intervention of a sort of evolutionary regulation, or "homeorhesis." Homeorhesis acts in such a way that if an external influence causes the developing organism to deviate from one of its creodes, there ensues a homeorhetical reaction, which tends to channel it back to the normal sequence or, if this fails, switches it to a new creode as similar as possible to the original one.

Each of the preceding characteristics can be observed in cognitive development if we carefully differentiate the construction of the structures themselves and the acquisition of specific procedures through learning (e.g., learning to read at one age rather than another). The question will naturally be whether development can be reduced to an addition of procedures learned one by one or whether learning itself depends on developmental laws which are autonomous.

This question can only be answered experimentally, but we shall discuss it further in Section IV. Whatever the answer is, it remains possible to distinguish between major structures, such as the operational "grouping," and particular acquisitions. It then becomes proper to inquire whether the construction of these major structures can be defined in terms of stages. If this were so, it would then become possible to determine their relations to developmental laws of learning.

10. If we restrict ourselves to major structures, it is strikingly obvious that cognitive stages have a sequential property, that is, they appear in a fixed order of succession because each one of them is necessary for the formation of the following one.

If we now consider only the principal periods of development, one can enumerate three of them:

a. A sensorimotor period lasts until approximately 1½ years of age with a first subperiod of centration on the subject's own body (lasting about 7 to 9 months) followed by a second one of objectivization and spatialization of the schemes of practical intelligence.

b. A period of representative intelligence leads to concrete operations (classes, relations, and numbers bound to objects) with a first preoperational subperiod (there is no reversibility or conservation, but the beginnings of directional functions and qualitative identities), which begins around 1½ to 2 years of age with the formation of semiotic processes such as language and mental imagery. This is followed by a second subperiod (at about 7 to 8 years) characterized by the beginnings of operational groupings in their various concrete forms and with their various types of conservation.

c. Finally, there is the period of propositional or formal operations. This also begins with a subperiod of organization (11 to 13 years old) and is followed by a subperiod of achievement of the general combinatory and the group INRC of the two kinds of reversibilities. (See ¶ 28 and fn 9.)

If we now consider the preceding sequence, it is easy to observe that each one of these periods or subperiods is necessary to the constitution of its successor. As a first example, why do language and the semiotic function emerge only at the end of a long sensorimotor period where the only significates are indexes and signals, and where there are no symbols or signs? (If the acquisition of language were only dependent on an accumulation of associations, as is sometimes claimed, then it could occur much earlier.[6]) It has been shown that the acquisition of language requires that at least two conditions be satisfied. First, there must exist a general context of imitation allowing for interpersonal exchange, and second, the diverse structural characters which constitute the one basic unit of Chomsky's (1957) transformational grammars must be present. For the first of these conditions to be met means that in addition to the motor techniques of imitation (and this is by no means an easy task) the object, spatiotemporal, and causal decentrations of the second sensorimotor subperiod must have been mastered. For the second requirement, our collaborator H. Sinclair, who specializes in psycholinguistics, has shown (in her recent work which will shortly be published) that Chomsky's transformational structures are facilitated by the previous operation of the sensorimotor schemes, and thus that their origin is neither in an innate neurophysiological program (as Chomsky himself would have it) nor in an operant or other conditioning "learning" process [as Chomsky (1959) has shown conclusively].

A second example of the sequential character of our periods and subperiods is the subperiod of ages 2 to 7, which itself results from the sensorimotor schemes elaborated in

---

[6] The contention is that there already exists symbol manipulation, that is, storage and computation, on indexes and signals during the sensorimotor stage. Therefore the absence of language cannot be attributed to the lack of such functions, and conditioning (classical or operant) should be possible at least on the input side. At this stage the child can discriminate between sounds and he should be able to respond selectively, verbally or otherwise, to phonetic inputs on a purely associative basis. It is claimed that this is impossible for more than a finite (and very limited) set of inputs because of the absence of the most essential linguistic structure (monoid) which would permit the generation and storage of rules allowing for the analysis and recognition of an unlimited set of organized sequences of sounds. (Translator's note)

the ninth and tenth months and which prepares the concrete operations of ages 7 to 10. This subperiod is characterized by some negative aspects (lack of reversibility and absence of the concept of conservation), but it also evolves some positive achievements such as the directional functions. [*fonctions orientées*—mappings where $y = f(x)$ with unity of the value $f(x)$ for any (x) and the qualitative identity $a = a$]. In fact, these functions already play an extensive role in preoperational thought. Their one-way orientation explains the general primacy of the concept of order at this level, with its adequate aspects, but this also is the source of systematic distortions (e.g., "longer" understood as "going farther"; estimation of a quantity of water by taking only its level into account). The elementary functions are nothing other than the connections inherent in the schemes of action (which, before they become operational, are always oriented toward a goal) and therefore originate in the sensorimotor schemes themselves. Qualitative identity (the type of identity expressed by the child when he says: "It is the same water," even if the quantity of water changes) has its origin in the concept of permanent object, and in the notion that the subject's own body (as well as those of other subjects) maintains its identity both in time and in space; and these are three achievements of the sensorimotor stage. On the other hand, the one-way, directional functions and the identities they involve constitute the necessary condition for future operations. Thus we can see that the stages between 2 and 7 years are simultaneously an extension of the sensorimotor stages and the basis of the future concrete operations.

The propositional operations that appear between ages 11 and 15 with the INRC group and general combinatorial structures, all consist of applying operations to operations and transformations to transformations. It is therefore obvious that the existence of this last stage necessarily involves the acquisitions of the previous one (concrete operations, or operations to the first power).

11. Thus defined, the stages always appear in the same order of succession. This might lead us to assume that some biological factor such as maturation is at work. But it is certainly not comparable to the hereditary neurophysiological programming of instincts. Biological maturation does nothing more than open the way to possible constructions (or explain transient impossibilities). It remains for the subject to actualize them. This actualization, when it is regular, obeys the law of creodes, that is, of constant and necessary progress such that the endogenous reactions find support in the environment and in experience. It would therefore be a mistake to consider the succession of these stages as the result of an innate predetermination, because there is a continual construction of novelty during the whole sequence.

The two best proofs of this last point are the possibilities of deviations from the norm (with regulation by homeorhesis) and of variations in the time tally with the possibility of accelerations or delays. Deviations may be brought about by unforeseen experiences encountered by the activity of the child himself as well as by adult pedagogical interventions. Some pedagogical interventions can, of course, accelerate and complete spontaneous development; but they cannot change the order of the constructions. For example, educational programs rightly introduce the concept of metric proportions a long time after the elementary arithmetical operations, although a proportion seems to consist only of an equivalence between two divisions, as in $4:2 = 6:3$. But there also exist untimely pedagogical interventions, such as those of parents who teach their children to count up to 20 or 50 before they can have any concept of number. In many cases, such premature acquisitions in no way affect the creode specific to the construction of integers. For instance, when two lines of m and n elements $(m = n)$, respectively, are first put into visual one-to-one correspondence and their lengths changed by changing the spacing of the elements, the fact that the child of a certain age can count will not prevent him from saying that the longer line has more elements. On the other hand, when a pedagogical intervention has been successful or when the child obtains by himself a partial conquest in a specific operatory domain, the problem of the interactions between the various creodes remains still unsolved. In the case of classes or relations, for example, are the additive and multiplicative operations always synchronic—as they often seem to be—or can one follow the other, and in that event does the final synthesis remain unchanged (as is probably the case)?

12. In considering the problem of duration or rate of succession of the stages, we can readily observe that accelerations or delays in the average chronological age of performance, depend on specific environments (e.g., abundance or scarcity of possible activities and spontaneous experiences, educational or cultural environment), but the order of succession will remain constant. Some authors even believe unbounded acceleration would be possible and desirable. Bruner (1960) went so far as to assert that if one tackles it the right way, one can teach anything to children of any age, but he does not seem to believe this any longer. On this point, however, we can quote two situations investigated by Gruber. The first is that of developing kittens. It has been shown that they go through the same stages as infants in acquiring the "concept" of permanent object, and further that they achieve in 3 months what the infant does in 9. However, they do not progress any further and one may wonder whether the child's slower rate of development does not, in this case, make for greater progress ultimately. The second study by Gruber concerns the remarkable tardiness with which some of Darwin's main concepts appeared to him, although they were logical consequences of his previous ideas. Is this remarkably slow speed of invention one of the conditions of fruitfulness or only a deplorable accident? These are major problems in cognitive psychology that are not yet solved. Nevertheless, we would like to put forward a plausible hypothesis. For a specific subject the speed of transition from one stage to the following one has an *optimal rate*. That is, the stability and even the fruitfulness of a new organization (or structurization) depends on connections which cannot be instantaneous but cannot be indefinitely postponed either since they would then lose their power of internal combination.

I.V. THE RELATIONS BETWEEN DEVELOPMENT AND LEARNING

13. If we give the name *learning* to every form of cognitive acquisition, it is obvious that development only consists of a sum or a succession of learning situations. Generally, though, the term is restricted to denote essentially exogenous acquisitions, where either the subject repeats responses, parallel to the repetition of external sequences (as in conditioning), or the subject discovers a repeatable response by using the regular sequences generated by some device, without having to structure or reorganize them himself through a constructive step-by-step activity (instrumental learning). If we accept this definition of learning, the question arises whether development is merely a succession of learned acquisitions (which would imply a systematic dependency of the subject on the objects), or whether learning and development constitute two distinct and separate sources of knowledge. Finally, there is, of course, the possibility that every acquisition through learning in fact represents only a sector or a phase of development itself, arbitrarily provided by the environment (which entails the possibility of a local deviation from the "normal" creodes) but remaining subject to the general constraints of the current developmental stage.

Before we examine the experimental facts, we would like to mention a talented behaviorist's attempt to reduce our theory to Hull's theory of learning. To effect this reduction, however, Berlyne (1960) was obliged to introduce two new concepts into Hull's theory. The first is stimulus-response generalization, which Hull foresaw but did not use. The second and more fundamental is the concept of "transformational responses," which are not restricted to repetitions but are amenable to reversible transformations in the same way as "operations." In discussing equilibration and regulation, Berlyne extends the concept of external reinforcements, introducing the possibility of "internal reinforcements" such as feelings of surprise, incoherence or coherence. Though these modifications of Hull's theory change its structure fundamentally, it is not certain that they are sufficient. The main question remains, indeed, whether the "transformational responses" are simple copies of observable external transformations of the objects or whether the subject himself transforms the objects by acting on them. The main point of our theory is that knowledge results from *interactions* between the subject and the object, which are *richer* than what the objects can provide by themselves. Learning theories like Hull's, on the other hand, reduce knowledge to direct "functional copies" which do not enrich reality. The problem we must solve, in order to explain cognitive development, is that of *invention* and not of mere copying. And neither stimulus-response generalization nor the introduction of transformational responses can explain novelty or invention. By contrast, the concepts of assimilation and accommodation and of operational structures (which are created, not merely discovered, as a result of the subject's activities), are oriented toward this inventive construction which characterizes all living thought.

To close this theoretical introduction to the problem of learning and development we would like to point out how peculiar it is that so many American and Soviet psychologists, citizens of great nations, which intend to change the world, have produced learning theories that reduce knowledge to a passive copy of external reality (Hull, Pavlov, etc.), whereas human thought always transforms and transcends reality. Outstanding sectors of mathematics (e.g., those that involve the continuum hypothesis) have no counterpart in physical reality, and all mathematical techniques result in new combinations which enrich reality. To present an adequate notion of learning one first must explain how the subject manages to construct and invent, not merely how he repeats and copies.

14. A few years ago the International Center of Genetic Epistemology investigated two problems:

a. Under what conditions can logical structures be learned, and are these conditions identical to those for learning empirical sequences?

b. And, even in this last case (probabilistic or even arbitrary sequences), does learning imply a logic analogous, for example, to the logic of the coordinators of action, the existence of which can be observed as early as during the organization of sensorimotor schemes?

On the first point, studies such as those of Greco, Morf, and Smedslund (1959) have shown that in order to learn how to construct and master a logical structure, the subject must start from another, more elementary logical structure which he will differentiate and complete. In other words, learning is no more than a sector of cognitive development which is facilitated or accelerated by experience. By contrast, learning under external reinforcement (e.g., permitting the subject to observe the results of the deduction he should have made or informing him verbally) produces either very little change in logical thinking or a striking momentary change with no real comprehension.

For example, Smedslund found that it was easy to make children learn the conservation of weight with pieces of clay whose shape was modified and whose constant weight could be read by the child on a pair of scales, because in this case, mere repetition of these observations facilitates generalization. The same processes of reinforcement by observation are not at all sufficient to induce the acquisition of transitivity in the weight equivalences: $A = C$ if $A = B$ and $B = C$. In other words, the logical structure of conservation (and Smedslund has checked the correlation between transitivity and operational conservation) is not acquired in the same way as the physical contents of this conservation.

Morf observed the same phenomenon in the learning of the quantification of inclusion: $A < B$ if $B = A + A'$. The spontaneous tendency of the child is to compare part A to the complementary part A' whenever his attention is called to the parts of the whole B and B ceases to be preserved as a whole.

By contrast, previous training on the intersection of classes facilitates learning of inclusion. It is true that the Dutch psychologist Kohnstamm (1956) has tried to show that it is possible to teach young subjects the quantitative dominance of the whole over the part ($B > A$) by purely didactic and verbal methods. Hence educational psychologists who believe that educational methods make it possible to teach anything at any age are considered optimistic and the psychologists of the Geneva school who assert that only an adequate spontaneous development makes understanding possible under any circumstances are considered pessimistic. However, the checks on Kohnstamm's experiment now being made in Montreal by Laurendeau and Pinard show that things are not as simple as they appear (verbally trained children make a great many mistakes on the relations between A and A'). One can easily understand that teachers of the traditional school will call anyone who believes in their methods an optimist, but, in our opinion, genuine optimism would consist of believing in the child's capacities for invention. Remember also that each time one prematurely teaches a child something he could have discovered for himself, that child is kept from inventing it and consequently from understanding it completely. This obviously does not mean the teacher should not devise experimental situations to facilitate the pupil's invention.

To turn to the second problem we mentioned, Matalon and Apostel have shown that all learning, even empiricist learning, involves logic. This is true in the sense of an organization of the subject's action as opposed to immediate perception of the external data; moreover, Apostel has started to analyze the algebra of the learning process and its necessary basic operations.

15. Following these investigations at the International Center of Genetic Epistemology, Inhelder in Geneva, with her colleagues Bovet and Sinclair (1967), and later Laurendeau (1966) in Montreal, with her colleagues Fournier-Choninard and Carbonneau, have carried out more detailed experiments. The aim of their inquiries was to isolate the various factors which may facilitate an operational acquisition, and to establish the possible relations with the factors involved in the "natural" constructions of the same concepts (e.g., conservation in the course of spontaneous development).

As an example, one of Inhelder, Bovet, and Sinclair's experiments (with Fot) is performed by showing the child transparent jars filled with the same quantities of liquid. Instead of pouring in the usual manner, these jars empty through taps in their bases into glass jars of various shapes, which in turn empty into more jars on other levels. The heights and widths of successive jars vary at each level, but at the bottom of the sequence are jars identical to the ones at the top. This arrangement should lead the child to perform both dimensional and quantitative comparisons and eventually to understand the reason for the equality of the quantities at the starting point and at the end point.

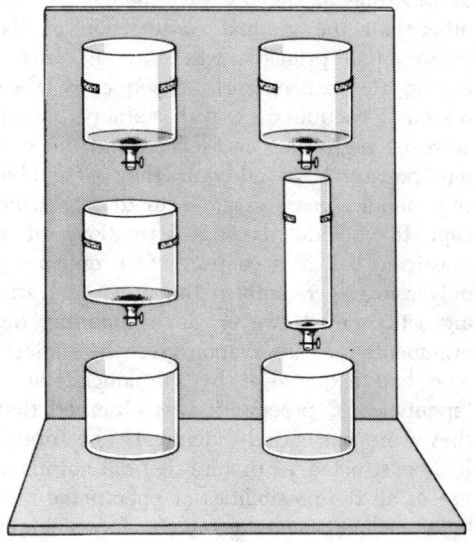

Fig. 1. Experimental apparatus for learning the concept of conservation of quantity.

It was discovered in this experiment that the results vary very significantly as a function of the initial cognitive levels of the children, which were classified according to the available schemes of assimilation. No child starting at a preoperational level succeeded in learning the logical operations underlying the elementary concepts of the conservation of physical quantities. The great majority (87.5%) did not even show any real progress, while a minority (12.5%) moved up to an intermediate level characterized by frequent oscillations where conservation would be alternatively asserted or denied. This uncertainty is ascribable to the fact that the coordination of the centrations or successive isolated states or their variations were still partial and transient. Clearly, it is one thing to observe that in a closed system of physical transformations nothing is created and nothing destroyed, and quite another to infer from this a principle of conservation. The situation is different with children who initially were already at this intermediate level. In this case only 23% did not achieve conservation, while 77% benefited in various degrees from the exercise and achieved a conservation based on a genuinely operatory structure. It is true that for about half of them (38.5%), this result involved only an extension of a structuration already started at the time of the pretest, whereas for the other half the gradual construction of the conservation principle was easy to observe during the experiment. Subsequently their reasoning acquired a real stability (there were no regressions in the first and the second posttests). In addition, they were able to generalize conservation, extending the concept to include the transformations of a plasticine ball in a context which outwardly only remotely resembled the previous learning situation. However, in comparing the arguments for conservation given by subjects who had acquired it by the much slower "spontaneous" process, it was observed that they were not entirely identical. The former had constructed a structure that did not make use of all the possibilities of operational mobility, which in its complete form entails general reversibility. In fact, they gave a majority of arguments by identity and compensation, which had been evolved in the experimental situation, and very few arguments by reversibility based on cancellation.

On the other hand, progress in the experimental situation was more general and complete in the cases of children who were initially at an elementary operational level (characterized by the acquisition of conservation of quantity during the experiment) but who had not yet acquired the more complex concept of conservation of weight, which, during spontaneous development, generally appears 2 or 3 years later. In this case progress is genuine when the experimental situation does not restrict the child to passive observation but involves a series of operational exercises (e.g., establishing equality of weight for objects of different sizes, and regardless of position on the scales, and, more essentially, comparing the weights of collections of different objects and establishing their equivalence or nonequivalence). After being subjected to this type of training sequence, 86% of the subjects achieved conservation (in three sessions). Among them, 64% were able to use the transitive properties of order or equality in weight and, using arguments based on total reversibility, showed that they felt these properties were logically evident. These kinds of acquisition are therefore clearly distinct from the pragmatic solution given by children who at a preopera-

tional level were subjected (as in Smedslund's experiment) only to empirical evidence.

Essentially what this experiment shows is that learning is subordinate to the subjects' levels of development. If they are close to the operational level, that is, if they are able to understand quantitative relations, the comparisons they make during the experiment are enough to lead them to compensation and conservation. But the farther they are from the possibility of operational quantification, the less they are likely to use the learning sequence to arrive at a concept of conservation.

An experiment carried out by Laurendeau consists of trying to induce progressive decentration and equilibration, and comparing the results thus obtained to those obtained by Skinner-type operant learning with external reinforcement. One group of subjects is asked to predict the level a liquid will reach when it is poured from one container to another of a different shape. The subjects are then shown the level reached when the liquid is actually poured so that they may see whether their prediction was correct. The subjects are then questioned about conservation, and when they deny it they are asked to add the quantity necessary to make the levels equal. This is repeated with containers whose shape is more and more different, until one is very wide and low and the other very high and thin, and it becomes obvious that equal levels do not produce equal quantities of liquid. In this third part of the experiment 12 gradually higher and thinner containers are used, the median ones (6 and 7) being equal; these are filled by the subject with quantities of liquid he judges to be equal. They are then poured into containers 5 and 8, respectively; the operation is then repeated and 6 and 7 are poured into 4 and 9, etc. With children between 5 and 6 a definite improvement in performance can be observed, and this is corroborated by the posttests given 1 week and 3 months later.

Subjects in a second group are asked to make the same prediction, but then they are asked only questions (some 20 in all) about conservation; correct answers are suitably rewarded. In fact, the child is very quickly able to give only correct answers and can still do this 2 or 3 days later, but posttests show that his learning is much more limited and less stable.

To summarize, learning appears to depend on the mechanisms of development and to become stable only insofar as it utilizes certain aspects of these mechanisms, the instruments of quantification themselves, which would have evolved in the course of spontaneous development.

V. THE OPERATIVE AND FIGURATIVE ASPECTS OF COGNITIVE FUNCTIONS

16. The stages described in Section III are only those concerning the development of intelligence, and the aspects of learning considered in Section IV are only relevant to these stages.

If we wish to obtain a complete picture of mental development, we must not only consider the operative aspect of the cognitive functions, but also their figurative aspect. We will call *operative* the activities of the subject that attempt to transform reality: (*a*) the set of all actions (except those which, like imitation or drawing, are purely accommodatory in intent) and (*b*) the operations themselves. "Operative" is thus a broader term than "operational," which is only related to the operators. In contrast, we shall call *figurative* the activities which attempt only to represent reality as it appears, without seeking to transform it: (*a*) perception, (*b*) imitation, in a broad sense (including graphic imitation or drawing), and (*c*) pictorial representations in mental imagery.

Before discussing these figurative aspects and their relations with the operative aspects of knowledge, we must briefly analyze their relations with the semiotic function (generally called symbolic function). In considering semiotic functions, Pierce introduced a distinction between "indexes" (perceptions), "icons" (images), and symbols, in which he included language. We prefer de Saussure's terminology, which is more widely used in linguistics, and which is characterized psychologically in the following way:

a. *Indexes* are signifiers that are not differentiated from their significants since they are part of them or a causal result for example

for an infant, hearing a voice is an index of someone's presence.

b. *Symbols* are signifiers that are differentiated from their significants, but they retain a measure of similarity with them, for example in a symbolic game representing bread by a white stone and vegetables by grass.

c. *Signs* are signifiers that are also differentiated from their signifiers but are conventional and thus more or less "arbitrary": the sign is always social, whereas the symbol can have a purely individual origin as in symbolic games or in dreams.

We shall thus call the semiotic function (or symbolic function, but semiotic has a broader meaning) the ability, acquired by the child in the course of his second year, to represent an object which is absent or an event which is not perceived, by means of symbols or signs, that is, of signifiers differentiated from their significants. Thus the semiotic function includes in addition to language, symbolic games, mental and graphic images (drawings), and deferred imitation (beginning in the absence of its model), which appears nearly at the same time (except for drawing, which appears slightly later), whereas indexes (including the "signals" involved in conditioning already play a role during the first weeks. The transition from indexes to symbols and signs—in other words, the beginning of the differentiation which characterizes the semiotic function—is definitely related to the progress of imitation, which at the sensorimotor level, is a sort of representation through actual actions. As imitation becomes differentiated and interiorized in images, it also becomes the source of symbols and the instrument of communicative exchange which makes possible the acquisition of language.

Thus defined, the semiotic function partially includes the figurative activities of knowledge, which in their turn partially include the semiotic function. There thus exists an intersection between their respective domains but not equivalence or inclusion. In effect, perception is a figurative activity, but it does not belong to the semiotic function since it uses only indexes and no representative signifiers. Language belongs to the semiotic function, but it is only partly figurative (mainly when the child is young, or less so with increased age, especially with the onset of formal operations). In contrast, imitation, mental imagery, and drawing are both figurative and semiotic.

17. The discussion of perception here is very brief; Seagrim's excellent translation of the author's *Perceptual Mechanisms* (1961) will be published in the near future. However, it is relevant to note here that, during our study of the development of perception in the child, we have been led to distinguish between "field effects" (field being understood here as field of visual motor centration, *not* as field in the sense of Gestalt theory) and the perceptual activities of exploration such as visual transports, relating, and visually placing in reference (as far as position or direction are concerned).

Field effects quantitatively decrease with age (this is the case for the primary opticogeometrical illustrations such as Müller Lyer's), but they retain their qualitative characteristics. Consequently, their evolution with age does not yield a succession of stages. For instance, based on the concept of visual centrations (studied with Vinh-Bang in ocular movements) we have been able to construct a probabilistic model of "encounters" and "couplings" (through successive centrations) which gives a general law for the plane primary illusions and can be used to compute for each one its theoretical positive and negative maximum point. These points have been checked experimentally and remain the same at every age, though the quantitative amount of the illusion decreases.

In contrast, perceptual activities are modified with age and roughly approximate stages can be distinguished. For example, if one exposes the same subject to 20 or 30 presentations of the Müller-Lyer or lozenge illusion (underestimation of the main diagonal), one observes an effect of learning which increases with age after 7 years. Noelting and Gonheim were able to show that it did not appear before 7. This perceptual learning (which is dependent on autoregulations or spontaneous equilibrations) is not reinforced, since the subject does not know the error in his estimate, it is the result of perceptual activities which become more efficient with age.

Moreover, while studying the way in which children perceptually estimate the horizontality of a line (e.g., in a tilted triangle), we

found (with Dadsetan) a real improvement toward 9 to 10 years, which is in direct correlation with the corresponding spatial operations. Here, as in all the cases in which we could study the relations between perception and intelligence, it is intelligence which directs the movements—naturally not by experimenting with the perceptual mechanisms but by indicating what must be looked at and which indexes are useful in making a good perceptual estimate.

18. We have studied mental images extensively with Inhelder (1966) and many other colleagues, especially considering their relations to intelligence (e.g., by asking subjects to imagine the result of pouring a liquid into a different container in a conservation experiment, before they have actually seen the result). Our first conclusion is that the image does not come from perception (it only appears at approximately 1½ years together with the semiotic function) and that it obeys completely different laws. It is probably the result of an interiorization of imitation. This hypothesis seems corroborated in the domain of symbolic games in their initial stages (fiction or imagination games, which show all the transitions between imitative symbols by gestures and actions and interiorized imitation or images).

Further, if one distinguishes "reproductive" images (to imagine an object or an event which is known but is not actually perceived at the time) and "anticipatory" images (to imagine the result of a new combination), our results have shown the following:

a. Before 7 years, one can find only reproductive images, and all of them are quite static. For example, the subjects experience systematic difficulty in imagining the intermediate positions between the initial vertical and final horizontal position of a falling stick.

b. After 7 to 8 years, anticipatory images appear, but they are not only applied to new combinations. They also seem to be necessary for the representation of any transformation even if it is known, as if such representations always entailed a new anticipation.

But this research has shown above all the strict interdependency between the evolution of mental images and the evolution of operations. Anticipatory images are possible only when the corresponding operations exist. In our experiments concerning conservation of liquids the younger subjects go through a stage of "pseudo-conservation" where they imagine that in a narrow container the level of the liquid would be the same as in a wide one (and it is only when they see that it is not the same level that they deny conservation). About 23% of the subjects know the level will rise, but this knowledge is contained in a reproductive image (founded on experience) and they conclude that there will be no conservation (when asked to pour the "same quantity" in the two containers, they pour liquid up to the same levels).

In short, while mental images can sometimes facilitate operations, they do not constitute their origin. On the contrary, mental imagery is generally controlled by the operations gradually as they appear (and one can follow their construction stage by stage).

19. The study of mental imagery led us to investigate the development of memory. Memory has two very different aspects. On the one hand, it is cognitive (entailing knowledge of the past), and in this respect it uses the schemes of intelligence, as we shall show shortly in an example. On the other hand, imagery is not abstract knowledge and bears a particular and concrete relation to objects or events. In this respect such symbols as mental images and, more specifically, "memory images" are necessary to its operation. Images themselves can be schematized, but in an entirely different sense, for images in themselves, however schematic, are not schemes. We shall therefore use the term schemata to designate them. A schema is a simplified image (for example, the map of a town), whereas a scheme represents what can be repeated and generalized in an action (e.g., the scheme is what is common in the actions of "pushing" an object with a stick or any other instrument).

The main result of our research has been, in this context, to show not the generality but the possibility that progress in memory is influenced by improvements in the operational schemes of intelligence. For example, we showed (with Sinclair and others) 3- to 8-year-old children an array of 10 wooden bars varying in length between 9 and 16 cm arranged according to their length, and we merely asked the subjects to look at the array. A week, and then a month later they were asked to draw the array from memory.

The first interesting result is that, after 1 week, the younger children do not remember the sequence of well-ordered elements, but reconstruct it by assimilating it to the schemes corresponding to their operational level: (a) a few equal elements, (b) short ones and long ones, (c) groups of short, medium, and long ones, (d) a correct sequence, but too short, (e) a complete seriation. The second remarkable result is that after 6 months (without any new presentation, memory was improved in 75% of the cases. Those who were at level *a* moved up to *b*. Many at level *b* moved up to *c* or even *d*. The *c*'s moved up to *d* or *e*, etc. The results, naturally, are not as spectacular in other experiments, and there is less progress as the model is less schematizable (in the sense of being made schematic, and not being assimilated to a scheme). The existence of such facts shows that the structure of memory appears to be partly dependent on the structure of the operations.

VI. THE CLASSICAL FACTORS OF DEVELOPMENT

20. We have seen that there exist laws of development and that development follows a sequential order such that each of its stages is necessary to the construction of the next. But this fundamental fact remains to be explained. The three classical factors of development are maturation, experience of the physical environment, and the action of the social environment. The two last cannot account for the sequential character of development, and the first one is not sufficient by itself because the development of intelligence does not include a hereditary programming factor like the ones underlying instincts. We shall therefore have to add a fourth factor (which is in fact necessary to the coordination of the three others—equilibration, or self-regulation (*auto régulation*).

It is clear that maturation must have a part in the development of intelligence, although we know very little about the relations between the intellectual operations and the brain. In particular, the sequential character of the stages is an important clue to their partly biological nature and thus argues in favor of the constant role of the genotype and epigenesis. But this does not mean we can assume there exists a hereditary program underlying the development of human intelligence: there are no "innate ideas" (in spite of what Lorenz maintained about the a priori nature of human thought). Even logic is not innate and only gives rise to a progressive epigenetic construction. Thus the effects of maturation consist essentially of opening new possibilities for development, that is, giving access to structures which could not be evolved before these possibilities were offered. But between possibility and actualization, there must intervene a set of other factors such as exercise, experience, and social interaction.

A good example of the gap that exists between the hereditary possibilities and their actualization in an intellectual structure can be provided by an inspection of the Boolean and logical structures discovered by McCulloch and Pitts (1947) in the neural connections. In this context the neurons appear as operators which process information according to rules analogous to those of the logic of propositions. But the logic of propositions only appears on the level of thought at around 12 to 15 years of age. Thus there is no direct relation between the "logic of the neurons" and that of thought. In this particular case, as in many others, the process must be conceived of not as progressive maturation, but as a sequence of constructions, each of which partly repeats its immediate predecessor but at a very different level and on a scope that goes far beyond it. What makes possible the logic of neurons is initially exclusively a nervous activity. But this activity makes possible in its turn a sensorimotor organization at the level of behavior. However, this organization, while retaining certain structures of the nervous activity, and consequently being partially isomorphic to it, results at first in a set of connections between behaviors which is much simpler than that of the nervous activity itself because these behaviors have to correlate actions and objects and are no longer limited to exclusively internal transmissions. Further, the sensorimotor organization makes possible the constitution of thought and its symbolic instruments, which imply the construction of a new logic, partially isomorphic to the previous ones, but which is confronted with new problems, and the cycle repeats. The propositional logic which is constructed between 12 and 15 years is thus by no means the immediate consequence of the logic of neurons, but

it is the result of a sequence of successive constructions that are not preformed in the hereditary nervous structure but are made possible by this initial structure. So we are now very far from a model of continuous maturation which would explain everything by preformed mechanisms. For this purely endogenous model, there must be substituted a series of actual constructions, the sequential order of which does not imply a simple predetermination but involves much more than this.

21. A second factor traditionally invoked to explain cognitive development is *experience* acquired through contact with the external physical environment. This factor is essentially heterogeneous, and there are at least three categories and meanings of experience, among which we shall distinguish two opposite poles.

a. The first is simple *exercise,* which naturally involves the presence of objects on which action is exerted but does not necessarily imply that any knowledge will be extracted from these objects. In fact, it has been observed that exercise has a positive effect in the consolidation of a reflex or of a group of complex reflexes such as sucking, which noticeably improves with repetition during the first days of life. This is also true of the exercise of intellectual operations which can be applied to objects, although these operations are not derived from the objects. In contrast, the exercise of an exploratory perceptual activity or of an experiment can provide new exogenous information while consolidating the subject's activity. We can thus distinguish two opposite poles of activity in exercise itself: a pole of accommodation to the object, which is then the only source of the acquisitions based on the object's properties; and a pole of functional assimilation, that is, of consolidation by active repetition. In this second perspective, exercise is predominantly a factor of equilibration or autoregulation, that is, it has to do with structurations dependent on the subject's activity more than with an increase in the knowledge of the external environment.

As regards experience proper in the sense of acquisition of new knowledge through manipulations of objects (and no longer through simple exercise), we must again distinguish two opposite poles, which will correspond to categories (*b*) and (*c*).

b. There is what we call *physical experience,* which consists of extracting information from the objects themselves through a simple process of abstraction. This abstraction reduces to dissociating one newly discovered property from the others and disregarding the latter. Thus it is physical experience that allows the child to discover weight while disregarding an object's color, etc., or to discover that with objects of the same nature, their weight is greater as their volume increases, etc.

c. In addition to physical experience (*b*) and to simple exercise (*a*), there is a third fundamental category, which strangely practically never has been mentioned in this context. This is what we call *logicomathematical experience.* It plays an important part at all levels of cognitive development where logical deduction or computation are still impossible, and it also appears whenever the subject is confronted with problems in which he has to discover new deductive instruments. This type of experience also involves acting upon objects, for there can be no experience without action at its source, whether real or imagined, because its absence would mean there would be no contact with the external world. However, the knowledge derived from it is not based on the physical properties of these objects but on properties of the actions that are exerted on them, which is not at all the same thing. This knowledge seems to be derived from the objects because it consists of discovering by manipulating objects, properties introduced by action which did not belong to the objects before these actions. For example, if a child, when he is counting pebbles, happens to put them in a row and to make the astonishing discovery that when he counts them from the right to the left he finds the same number as when he counts from the left to the right, and again the same when he puts them in a circle, etc., he has thus discovered experimentally that the sum is independent of order. But this is a logicomathematical experiment and not a physical one, because neither the order nor even the sum was in the pebbles before he arranged them in a certain manner (i.e., ordered them) and joined them together in a whole. What he has discovered is a relation, new to him, between the action of putting in order and the action of joining together (hence, between

the two future operations), and not, or *not only,* a property belonging to pebbles.

Thus we see that the factor of acquired experience is, in fact, complex and always involves two poles: acquisitions derived from the objects and constructive activities of the subject. Even physical experience (*b*) is never pure, since it always implies a logicomathematical setting, however elementary (as in the geometrical Gestalts of perception). This amounts to saying that any particular action such as "weighing" that results in physical knowledge is never independent of more general coordinations of action (such as ordering, joining together, etc.) which are a source of logicomathematical knowledge.

22. The third classical factor of development is the influence of the social environment. Its importance is immediately verified if we consider the fact that the stages we mentioned in Section III are accelerated or retarded in their average chronological ages according to the child's cultural and educational environment. But the very fact that the stages follow the same sequential order in *any* environment is enough to show that the social environment cannot account for everything. This constant order of succession cannot be ascribed to the environment.

In fact, both social or educational influences and physical experience are on the same footing in this respect, they can have some effect on the subject only if he is capable of assimilating them, and he can do this only if he already possesses the adequate instruments or structures (or their primitive forms). In fact, what is taught, for instance, is effectively assimilated only when it gives rise to an active reconstruction or even reinvention by the child.

An excellent example of this complex situation is provided by the difficult problem of the relations between language and thought. Many authors have maintained that language is not only the essential factor in the constitution of representation or thought, which raises a first question, but also that language is the origin of the logical operations themselves (e.g., classification, order, propositional operations), which raises a second question.

With respect to the first question, it is doubtless true that language plays a major part in the interiorization of action into representation and thought. But this linguistic factor is not the only one at work. We must refer to the symbolic or semiotic function as a whole—and language is only a part of this. The other instruments of representation are deferred imitation, mental imagery (which is an interiorized imitation and not a mere extension of perception), symbolic games (or games of imagination), drawing (or graphical imitation), etc.; and it is certainly imitation in the general sense which constitutes the transition between the sensorimotor and semiotic functions. Thus it is in the general context of the semiotic function that language must be considered, however important its part may be. The study of deaf-mutes, for example, shows how far the other symbolic instruments can reach when the development of articulate language is disturbed.

Turning to the question of the relations between language and logical operations, we have always maintained that the origin of logical operations is both deeper than and genetically prior to language; that is, it lies in the laws of the general coordinations of action, which control all activities including language itself.

An elementary logic already exists in the coordination of the sensorimotor schemes (cf. Section I: the group of translations, the conservation of the objects, etc.) It exists in a form of intelligence which is yet neither verbal nor symbolic. But there still remains to establish more precisely the relations between language and the logical operations on the level of interiorized thought.

This has recently been done by Sinclair in a set of experiments at the psychological and linguistic level, which are most instructive. She studied two groups of 5- to 7-year-old children, one clearly at a preoperational stage and unable to attain the concept of conservation, whereas the other possessed all the instruments that lead to conservation. She was then able to show that their language is on the average noticeably different when one examines them on subjects other than conservation, for instance, when one asks them to compare two or more objects such as a long, thin pencil and a short, thick one. The preoperational group uses mainly the nonrelational terms of a scale: "this one is long, this one is short, this one is thick, and this one is thin." The operational group, in contrast, uses mainly "vectors": "this one is smaller and thicker," etc. There is thus a clear relation between linguistic and operational level (and this is also true in other situations). But in which direction? To establish this, Sinclair then taught a group of younger subjects to use the verbal forms used by the older ones. Once this was done she again investigated their operational level and discovered that only approximately 10% had improved; this very small proportion could even represent intermediate cases, or cases who were already very near the operational threshold. We can thus observe that language does not seem to be the motor of operational evolution but rather an instrument in the service of intelligence itself (See Sinclair and Zwart, 1967).

To conclude ¶ 20, 21, and 22, it appears that the traditional factors (maturation, experience, social environment) are not sufficient to explain development. We must therefore appeal to a fourth factor, *equilibration*, and we must do this for two reasons. The first is that these three heterogeneous factors cannot explain a sequential development if they are not in some relation of mutual equilibrium, and that there must therefore exist a fourth organizing factor to coordinate them in a consistent, noncontradictory totality. The second reason is that any biological development is, as we now know, self-regulatory, and that self-regulating processes are even more common at the level of behavior and the constitution of the cognitive functions. We must thus consider this factor separately.

VII. EQUILIBRATION AND COGNITIVE STRUCTURES

23. The main aim of a theory of development is to explain the constitution *of the operational* structures of the integrated whole or totality (*structure opératoire d'ensemble*) and we believe only the hypothesis of progressive equilibration can account for it. To understand this we must first briefly consider the operational structures themselves.

The concept of structure became classical in psychology when it was introduced by Gestalt theory to combat association and its atomistic habits of thought. But the Gestaltists conceived of only one type of structure as applicable to the whole of psychology, from perception to intelligence. They did not distinguish two characters, which in reality are quite different. The first is common to all structures; they all possess holistic laws derived from the fact that they form a system, and these laws are distinct from the properties of the elements in the totality. The second character is nonadditive composition, that is, the whole is quantitatively different from the sum of the parts (as in Oppel's perceptual illusion). But in the field of intelligence, there exist structures which verify the first characteristic and not the second; the set of integers, for instance, has holistic properties as such ("group," "ring," etc.), but composition in it is strictly additive— $2 + 2 = 4$, no more, no less.

We have therefore attempted to define and analyze the structures specific to intelligence, and they are structures involving operations, that is, involving interiorized and reversible actions such as addition, set-theoretic union, logical multiplication, or, in other words, composition of a multiplicity of classes or relations "considered simultaneously." These structures have a very natural and spontaneous development in the child's thought: to seriate, for instance (i.e., to order objects accordiing to their increasing size), to classify, to put into one-to-one or one-to-many correspondence, to establish the multiplicative matrix, are all structures that appear between ages 7 and 11, at the level of what we call "concrete operations" which deal directly with objects. After 11 to 12 other structures appear, such as the four-group and combinatorial processes, which we shall describe later.

To investigate the properties of these concrete operational structures, and to establish their laws, we need to use the language of the logic of classes and relations, but this does not mean we are leaving the field of psychology. When a psychologist computes the variance of a sample or uses the formulas of factor analysis, it does not mean his field has become statistics and not psychology. To analyze structures we must do the same, but, since we are not dealing with quantities, we must simply resort to more general mathematical instruments such as abstract algebra or logic. But they are only instruments which will allow us to reach genuinely psychological entities such as operations, considered as interiorized actions or general coordinations of actions.

A totality structure such as a classification has the following properties, which characterize, simply, the operations that are actually present in the subject's action.

a. He can combine one class A with another A', to obtain class B, denoted $A + A' = B$ (he can then go on to perform $B + B' = C$, etc.).

b. He can dissociate A or A' from B, denoted $B - A' = A$, which constitutes the inverse operation. Notice this reversibility is necessary to the understanding of the relation $A < B$, and we know that until 7 or 8, the child does not grasp easily the idea that if he is given 10 primroses A, and 10 other flowers A', then there are more flowers B than primroses A, because to be able to compare the whole B to the part A, one must be able to combine the two operations $A + A' = B$ and $A = B - A'$, otherwise the whole B is not preserved, and A is then only compared to A'.

c. He will understand that $A - A = 0$, and $A + 0 = A$.

d. Finally, he will be able to associate $(A + A') + B' = A + (A' + B') = C$, while $(A + A) - A = 0$ is not equal to $A + (A - A) = A$.

We have called *groupements* these elementary groupings[7] (*structures de groupoïdes*),

---

[7] A grouping can be considered as a lattice that has been made reversible. In a lattice, if $A + A' = B$, where B is an upper bound of A and A', A can be recovered by operating on B: $B - A' = A$. But the more general case is where C is an upper bound of A and C', for example, and $A \pm D - C'$. In other words, the operation $A + A'$ can only be "reversed" between contiguous elements such as A and A', in the sense that in the 3-tuple A, A', B any two elements uniquely determine the third (Fig. F7a).

This is not the case for A, C', D, where $A + C' = D - D' - B' - A'$. Here we consider a grouping as a group where composition is restricted to contiguous elements only ($A + C'$, for example, is not defined without special conditions) and by the special identities $A + A = A$, $A + B = B$. A grouping is therefore only defined as a sequence of nested elements, such as a classification (Fig. F7b). It consists of (a) a direct operation: (b) an inverse operation: (c) an identity operation O: and (d) special identities:

$$A + A' = B$$
$$B - A' = A$$
$$A + O = A; \qquad A - A = O$$
$$A + A = A; \qquad -A - A = -A;$$
$$A + B = B$$

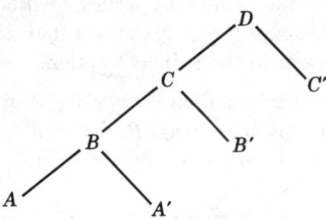

Fig. F7a.

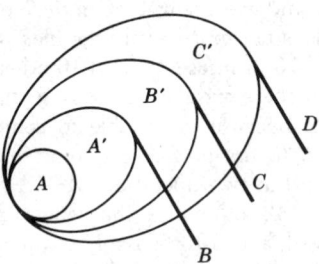

Fig. F7b.

which are more primitive than mathematical groups, but which are also much more limited structures and less elegant ones, in that composition is defined only between neighboring elements without general combinatorial properties and shows restricted associativity.[8] We have often been criticized for having thus only constructed structures that have no psychological reality. But such structures actually exist, primarily because they describe simply what happens in a classification, a seriation, etc., all

[8] Associativity is limited by the fact that the grouping only combines contiguous elements. $A + C'$ can only be constructed by operating step-by-step on the nearest contiguous classes A, A', B', up to D, the first class containing both A and C', then $A + C' = D - B' - A'$. Similarly, $A - C'$ only gives rise to the tautology $A - C' = (D \cdot - C' - B' - A') - C'$ where $(D - C' - B' - A') = A$. The consequence of these restrictions is that associativity is not verified before the elements in brackets have first been "reduced": $(A + A') + B' = B + B' = C$, but $A + (A' + B')$ has no meaning since $(A' + B')$ and is not defined as such. (For further details of the reduction rules, cf. Piaget, 1959.) In contrast, on the group of the integers under addition, any number can be immediately added to or subtracted from any other because an integer can be completely freed from its successors that "contain" it. (Translator's note)

of which are quite contemporaneous behaviors. Moreover, they can be recognized on the psychological level by the more general characters that reveal the existence of a totality structure, such as transitivity (for instance, in a seriation $A < C$ if $A < B$ and $B < C$) and the constitution of conservation concepts (conservation of a whole B when the arrangement of its parts A and A' is modified, conservation of length, quantity, etc.).

24. The problem then becomes that of understanding how the fundamental structures of intelligence can appear and evolve with all those that later derive from them. Since they are not innate, they cannot be explained by maturation alone. Logical structures are not a simple product of physical experience; in seriation, classification, one-to-one correspondence, the subject's activities add new relations such as order and totality to the objects. Logicomathematical experience derives its information from the subject's own actions (as we saw in ¶ 21), which implies an autoregulation of these actions. It could be alleged that these structures are the result of social or educational transmission. But as we saw (¶22), the child must still understand what is transmitted, and to do this the structures are necessary. Moreover, the social explanation only displaces the problem: how did the members of the social group acquire the structures in the first place?

But on all levels of development actions are coordinated in ways that already involve some properties of order, inclusion, and correspondence, and also foreshadow such structures (e.g., seriation for order, classification for inclusion, multiplicative structures for correspondence). What is more important, though, is that coordination of actions involves correction and self-regulation; in fact, we know regulatory mechanisms characterize all levels of organic life (this is true for the genetic pool as well as for behavior). But regulation is a process of retroaction (negative feedback), which implies a beginning of reversibility; and the relationship between regulation (which is correction of error with semireversibility in the retroaction) and operation, whose full reversibility allows for precorrection of errors (i.e., for "perfect" regulation in the cybernetic sense) becomes apparent.

Thus it seems highly probable that the

construction of structures is mainly the work of equilibration, defined not by balance between opposite forces but by self-regulation; that is, equilibration is a set of active reactions of the subject to external disturbances, which can be effective, or anticipated, to varying degrees. Equilibrium thus becomes identical with reversibility, but when one objects (as Bruner does, for example) that equilibrium therefore becomes superfluous, because reversibility is sufficient in itself, one forgets that it is not only the final state of equilibrium that must be considered, but that *equilibration* is essential as the self-regulating process leading to this final state and thus to the reversibility that characterizes the structures that must be explained.

25. Equilibration has explanatory value because it is founded on a process with increasing sequential probabilities. We can understand this better through an example. How can we explain the fact that when a spherical lump of clay is changed into the shape of a sausage in front of him, a child will begin by denying that the quantity of clay is preserved under this transformation, and end by asserting the logical necessity of this conservation? To do this we must define four stages, each of which *becomes more probable*, not a priori, but as a function of the present situation or of the one immediately preceding it.

a. Initially the child considers only one dimension, for instance, length (say 8 times out of 10). He then says the sausage contains more matter because it is longer. Sometimes (say 2 times out of 10) he says it is thinner, but forgetting its greater length, he concludes the quantity of matter has decreased. Why does he reason thus? Simply because the probability of considering one dimension only is greater. If the probability for length is .8 and that for width is .2, that for length *and* width is .16, because they are independent occurrences as long as compensation is not understood.

b. If the sausage is made longer and longer, or if the child becomes weary of repeating the same argument, the probability of his noticing the other dimension *becomes* greater (though it was not initially) and he will fluctuate between the two.

c. If there is oscillation, the probability

of the subject's noticing some correlation between the two variations (when the sausage becomes longer it becomes thinner) *becomes* greater (third stage). But as soon as this feeling of the solidarity existing between variables appears, his reasoning has acquired a new property: it does not rest solely on *configurations* any more but begins to be concerned with *transformations*: the sausage is not simply "long"; it can "lengthen," etc.

d. As soon as the subject's thought takes transformations into account, the next stage *becomes* more probable in which he understands (alternately or simultaneously) that a transformation can be reversed, or that the two simultaneous transformations of length and width compensate, because of the solidarity he has glimpsed [see stage (*c*)].

We can thus see that progressive equilibration has effective explanatory value. Stage (*a*) (which all those who checked our research have found) is not an equilibrium point because the child has noticed only one dimension: in this case the algebraic sum of the virtual components of work (to quote d'Alembert's principle on physical systems) is not zero since one of them, which consists of noticing the other dimension, has not been completed yet and will be sooner or later. The transition from one stage to another is therefore an equilibration in the most classical sense of the word. But since these displacements of the system are activities of the subject, and since each of these activities consist of correcting the one immediately preceding it, equilibration becomes a sequence of self-regulations whose retroactive processes finally result in operational reversibility. The latter then goes beyond simple probability to attain logical necessity.

What we have just said about an instance of operational conservation could be repeated about the construction of every operational structure. Seriation $A < B < C$, for example, when it becomes operational, is the result of coordinating the relations $<$ and $>$ (each new element in E in the ordered sequence having the property of being both $> D, C, B, A$, and $< F, G, H, \ldots$ and this coordination is again the result of an equilibration process of increasing sequential probabilities of the kind we have described. Similarly for inclusion of classes, $A < B$ if $B = A + A'$ and

$A' > O$ is obtained by an equilibration of the same type.

It is not therefore an exaggeration to say that equilibration is the fundamental factor of development, and that it is even necessary for the coordination of the three other factors.

VIII. THE LOGICOMATHEMATICAL ASPECTS OF STRUCTURES

26. The "concrete" operational structures we have just mentioned all presuppose the construction of certain quantities: extension of classes for classification (which explains the difficulty of quantifying the inclusion of classes), size of the differences for seriation, quantitative conservations, etc. But even before these quantitative structures are constructed, some partial and qualitative structures may be observed at the preoperational levels which are of great interest, because they constitute the first half, so to speak, of the logic of reversible operations. These are the directional functions (one-way functions that do not have inverses, which would imply reversibility) and the qualitative identities (see ¶ 10).

The functions, we remember are "mappings" in the mathematical sense, which have no inverses because, as we saw, they are psychologically related to the schemes of action, which are goal-directed. Suppose, for instance, we have a piece of string b, part a of which is at right angles to the rest (a') and can slide on a nail when a weight is connected with a' and a is held back by a spring. All children between 4 and 7 understand that if one pulls b, a grows shorter as a' grows longer. But they do not yet have conservation of the length of the whole b $(b = a + a')$, and what they perform is not a quantified operation but simply a qualitative or ordinal equation (longer = farther).

Similarly for identity, all children (or nearly all) agree, as we saw, that when a ball of clay is changed into a sausage, it is the "same" lump of clay even if quantity is not preserved. These identities are acquired early and the scheme of permanent objects we mentioned in ¶ 2 is one of them. In a recent book, Bruner considers them the origin of quanitative conservations. This is true in a sense (they are a necessary condition, but not a sufficient one), but a central difference remains: qualities (on which qualitative identity is founded) can be established perceptually, whereas quantity involves a lengthy structural elaboration whose complexity we have just seen (¶ 23 to 26).

In fact, functions and qualitative identity constitute only that half of a logic which is both preoperational and qualitative and leads to the logic of reversible and quantitative operations but is not powerful enough to account for it.

27. This quantification of concrete operations, as opposed to the qualitative nature of preoperational functions and identities, is revealed in particular by the construction, around 7 or 8, of the operations related to number and measure, which are partly isomorphic to one another but have very different content. The construction of cardinal numbers cannot be explained, as was believed by Russell and Whitehead, simply by one-to-one correspondence between equivalent classes, because the correspondence they used, by abstraction of qualities (in contrast with qualified correspondence between individual objects with the same properties) implicitly introduced unity and therefore number, which made their reasoning circular. In fact, when we deal with finite sets cardinal numbers cannot be dissociated from ordinal numbers and are subject to the three following conditions:

a. Abstraction from qualities, which makes all singular objects equivalent and therefore $1 = 1 = 1$.

b. The intervention of order: $1 \to 1 \to 1$ . . . , which is necessary to distinguish the objects from one another—otherwise $1 + 1 = 1$ would be true.

c. An inclusion of (1) in $(1 + 1)$, then of $(1 + 1)$ in $(1 + 1 + 1)$, etc.

The integers thus result from synthesis of order (seriation) and inclusion or nested sets (classification), which is made necessary by the abstraction from qualities. Hence the integers are built up from purely logical elements (seriation and classification), but they are rearranged in a new synthesis which allows for their quantification by an iterative process: $1 + 1 = 2$, etc.

Similarly, measurement in a continuum (e.g., a line, a surface) implies (*a*) its partition into segments one of which is then chosen as unity and made equivalent to others by congruence $a = a = a \ldots$, *(b)* its translation in a certain order, $a \rightarrow a \rightarrow a$, etc., to make it congruent to others, and *(c)* the units settling into its additive compositions, thus a into $(a + a)$ and $(a + a)$ into $(a + a + a)$. This synthesis of partition with nested segments and order in the translations of unity is thus isomorphic to the synthesis of order and inclusion which characterizes number, and this makes it possible to apply number to measurement.

It is thus clear that without having recourse to anything other than the synthesis of elementary "groupings" of inclusion or order relations, the subject attains a numerical or metrical quantification whose power by far surpasses the elementary quantification (relations from part to whole) of the extension of classes or of seriation based on differences evaluated simply by "more" or "less."

28. After the concrete operational structures mentioned in ¶23, two other new structures are constructed between ages 11

and 15 which make possible the manipulation of such propositional operations as implications $(p > q)$, incompatibilities $(p \mid q)$, and disjunctions $(p \vee q)$, etc. These two new structures are the four-group and combinatorial operations. Combinatorial activity at this stage consists of classifying all possible classifications (just as permutations are a seriation of seriations) aa, ab, ac, bc, bb, cc, etc., and this does not therefore constitute an entirely new operation but an operation on other operations. Similarly, the four-group $INCR$[9] results from connecting in a whole the inversions N and reciprocities R (thus the inverse of the reciprocal $NR = C$ appears, as well as the identity operation $I = NCR$). But inversion already exists in the groupements of classes, under the form $A - A = 0$, and reciprocity exists under the form $A = B$ therefore $B = A$ in the groupements of relations. The $INRC$ group is thus again an operational structure bearing on prior operations. As for the propositional operations, $p > q$, etc., which involve both combina-

---

[9] The $INRC$ group is a set of operations that act on the operations or elements of some other algebraic structure which has an involutive operation (an operation which is its own inverse: $N^2 = I$). An example of an involutive operation is the duality (de Morgan) law of Boolean algebra: $\overline{p \cup q} = \bar{p} \wedge \bar{q}$, which we can write $N(p \vee q) = \bar{p} \wedge \bar{q}$ (N for negative). If we define C (correlative) to be the rule that acts on the connectives, changing $\wedge$ into $\vee$ and conversely, and R (reciprocal) to be the rule that acts on the sign of the variables, changing p into $\bar{p}$ and conversely, then by using C and R in succession [on, say $(p \cup q)$], we get the same result as by using N. The following "state diagram" shows the relations between N, R, and C acting on $(p \vee q)$

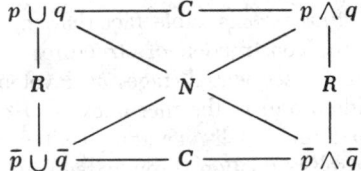

Identity I can now be defined as the rule that changes any formula into itself, and the following properties can easily be verified by "chasing around the diagram."

a. $RC = N$, $RN = C$, $CN = R$, and all couples are commutative—$RC = CR$, etc.

b. $C^2 = N^2 = R^2 = I$ (all transformations are involutive, i.e., each element has an inverse).

c. $RNC = I$.

From this we can show the set $[I, N, R, C]$ together with the operation of composition (in the usual sense of applying one transformation on the result of another) forms a noncyclic group of four elements (known as the Klien four-group).

The $INRC$ group can also be defined on physical systems that have the proper structure (i.e., an involutive transformation that can be "decomposed" into two other involutive transformations). In one of his experiments on double reference-systems Piaget uses a snail, which can move from left to right and conversely on a small board, which can itself be moved both ways on a table. We can define C to be the rule that reverses the movement of the snail: $C\ (L, L) = (R, L)$, for example [where (R, L) means the snail (first coordinate) is moving right, and the board moving left]. Then we can define R to be the rule that reverses the second coordinate, for example, $R\ (L, L) = (L, R)$ (this reverses the movement of the board). The "state diagram" has the same structure as before, and N (N reverses both movements) is the product of R and C.

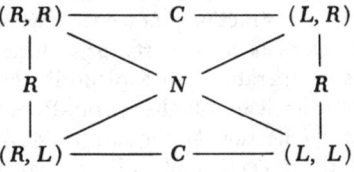

(**Translator's note**)

torial activity and the *INRC* group, they are new in their form, but in their content they deal with connections between classes, relations, or numbers, etc., and are therefore again operations on operations.

In general, the operations belonging to the third period of development (see ¶ 10, period *c* for ages 11 to 12) have their roots in concrete operations (subperiod *b II*, between 7 and 11) and enrich them, just as the source of concrete operations is in the sensorimotor schemes (period *a*, until about 2) which they also considerably modify and enrich. The sequential character of the stages (which we sufficiently stressed in ¶ 10) thus corresponds from the point of view of the construction of structures to a mechanism which we must now analyze, because it is too important for us to merely call it a sequential or progressive equilibration process. We must still understand how the constructions that bring about novelty occur, and this is a well-known problem in the development of mathematical structures.

29. We saw (¶ 21*c*) that before the level at which logicomathematical operations are constructed and thus become a deductive system we can speak of logicomathematical experiments, which extract information from the properties of actions applied to objects, and not from the objects themselves, which is quite another matter. We thus have, in contrast with abstraction proper, a new type of abstraction which we shall call *reflective abstraction* and which is the key to our problem. To abstract a property from an action or an operation, it is not enough to dissociate it from those that will be disregarded (e.g., a dissociation between the "form" to be retained and the "content" to be disregarded); the property or form thus retained must in addition be transferred somewhere, that is, on a different plane of action or operation. In the case of abstraction proper this question does not appear since we are dealing with a property of an object, which is assimilated by the subject. In the case of reflective abstraction, however, when the subject extracts a property or a form from actions or operations on a plane P_1, he must then transfer it to a higher plane P_2, and this is thus a reflection in a quasi-physical sense (as in the reflection of a light beam). But for this form or property to be assimilated on

this new plane P_2, it must be reconstructed on this new plane and therefore subjected to a new thought process which will this time mean "reflection" in a cognitive sense. Thus it is in both senses of the word that we must understand "reflective abstraction."

But if a new cognitive processing is necessary on plane P_2 to assimilate the properties or forms abstracted from plane P_1, this means new operations or actions on plane P_2 will be added to those of plane P_1 from which the required information was abstracted. Consequently, reflective abstraction is necessarily *constructive* and *enriches* with new elements the structures drawn from plane P_1, which amounts to saying it constructs new structures. This explains why the concrete operations based on sensorimotor schemes are richer than they were and why the same is true of propositional or formal operations, which are themselves based on concrete operations. As operations *on* operations, they add new modes of composition (combinatorial ones, etc.).

But reflective abstraction is the general constructive process of mathematics: it has served, for example, to evolve algebra out of arithmetic, as a set of operations on operations. Cantor constructed transfinite arithmetic in the same manner; he put into one-to-one correspondence the sequence 1, 2, 3, 4, . . . , with the sequence 2, 4, 6, 8. . . . This generates a new number ($\aleph_0$) which expresses the "power (a number) of the denumrable," but is an element of neither sequence. Present function theory constructs "morphisms" and "categories," etc., in the same manner, and this is also true for the Bourbaki with the "mother structures" and their derivatives.

It is thus a remarkable fact that the process of the construction of structures we observe in the sequential stages of development in children and in the mechanisms of equilibration through self-regulation (which result in this self-regulation through feedback of a higher order, which is a reversible operation) coincides with the constant constructive process used by mathematics in their indefinitely fruitful development. This is a solution to the problem of development which reduces to neither an empirical process of discovery of a "ready-made" external reality nor to a process of preformation or predetermination (a priori), which would also mean believing that everything is ready-made from the beginning. We believe truth lies between these two extremes, that is, in a constructivism which expresses the manner in which new structures are constantly being elaborated.

VIII. CONCLUSION: FROM PSYCHOLOGY TO GENETIC EPISTEMOLOGY

30. The theory we have outlined is necessarily interdisciplinary, and it involves, in addition to psychological elements, components belonging to biology, sociology, linguistics, logic, and epistemology. The relations with biology are obvious since the development of cognitive functions is a part of the epigenesis that leads from the first embryological stages to the adult state. From biology we essentially retain the three following points:

a. There can be no transformation of the organism or of behavior without endogeneous organizational factors, because the phenotype, although it is constructed in interaction with the environment, is the genome's "response" (or a response of the entire population's genetic pool, the individual genome being a cross section of the gene pool) to environmental "stresses."

b. Conversely, there is no epigenetic or phenotypic transformation independent of interaction with environmental influences.

c. These interactions involve continuous processes of equilibration or self-regulation, of which the equilibrium between assimilation and accommodation is an early instance. This also appears in sensorimotor, representative, and preoperational self-regulations, and even in operations themselves since they are anticipatory self-regulations and corrections of error which do not rely any more on the feedback from an error which has already happened.

The relations with sociology are also self-evident, because even if the origin of cognitive structures is in the general coordinations of action, they are also interpersonal or social as well as individual, since the coordination of the actions of individuals obeys the same laws as intra-individual coordination. This is not true of social processes involving constraint or authority, which lead to a socio-centrism closely akin to egocentrism, but it is true in situations of cooperation, which are in reality "co-operations." One of the fundamental processes of cognition is that of decentration relative to subjective illusion (see ¶ 8) and this process has dimensions that are social or interpersonal as well as rational.

The relations with linguistics would have very little meaning if linguistics were still defending positions like Bloomfield's, with its naive antimentalism. But we can adopt, in G. A. Miller's words, a position of "subjective behaviorism," and in linguistics proper, the contemporary work of Chomsky and his group on transformational grammars is not very far from our own operational perspectives and psychogenetic constructivism. But Chomsky believes in the hereditary basis of his linguistic structures, whereas it will probably be possible to show that the necessary and sufficient conditions for the construction of the basic units on which are founded the linguistic structures are satisfied by the development of sensorimotor schemes, and this is what Sinclair is working on at the present time.

The relations with logic are more complex. Modern symbolic logic is a "logic without a subject," whereas psychologically there exists no "subject without a logic." The subject's logic is undeniably poor and the groupement structures in particular are of little algebraic interest, except for the fact that related elementary structures do seem to arouse the mathematician's interest. But we must note that in studying the subject's logic we were able to formulate the laws of the four-group of propositional transformations *INRC* in 1949, that is even before logicians themselves began to look into it. On the other hand, present work on the limits of formalization, initiated with Gödel's proof, will, more or less necessarily, orient logic toward a kind of constructivism, and in this light the parallel with psychogenetic construction has some interest. Generally speaking, logic is an axiomatic system, and in our context we must ask: An axiomatization of what? It is certainly not an axiomatization of the subject's conscious thought processes, because they are inconsistent and incomplete. But behind conscious thought are the "natural" operatory structures, and it is obvious that, even though it can indefinitely surpass them (because the productivity of axiomatics has no formal limit), they became the basis of logical axiomatization through a process of "reflective abstraction."

31. Finally, there remains the great problem of the relations between the theory of the development of cognitive functions and epistemology. When one adopts a static rather than a psychogenetic point of view and when one studies, for example, the intelligence of an adult or of subjects considered at a single level, it is easy to distinguish psychological problems (how intelligence functions or what are its performances) from epistemological problems (what are the relations between the subject and the objects, and whether or not knowledge of the former adequately attains the latter). But when one adopts a psychogenetic point of view, the situation is completely different because one is then concerned with the formation or the development of knowledge, and it is essential to consider the roles of objects or of the activities of the subject, those issues which necessarily raise all the epistemological problems. In fact, those who attribute the formation of knowledge exclusively to experience, in the sense of physical experience, and those who introduce the activities of the subject in the sense of necessary organization will orient toward different epistemologies. To distinguish, as we have done (¶ 21), between two types of experience—one physical with abstraction beginning from objects and the other logicomathematical with reflective abstraction—is to make a psychological analysis, but one whose epistemological consequences are clear.

There are authors who fail to appreciate the interconnections between genetic psychology and epistemology, but this only indicates that they are choosing one epistemology among other possible ones, and that they believe their own epistemology is evident. For example, when Bruner tries to explain conservations by means of identities and symbolization based upon language and imagery, believing himself able to avoid operations and all epistemology, he is actually taking the point of view of empirical epistemology. At the same time he invokes an operation of identity without noticing that it implies others. In giving conservations a more operational explanation, and in supposing

that quantities call for a complex construction and not simply a perceptual activity, we *de facto* remove ourselves from empiricism in the direction of a constructivism, which is another epistemology; moreover, it is much closer to present biological trends, which underscore the necessity of constructive autoregulations.

If we turn now to the epistemological side, we discover that *its* trends also differ noticeably, according to whether it adopts a static or a historical and genetical point of view as is its natural internal tendency. When epistemology simply asks itself what knowledge is in general, it believes itself able to make abstractions without recourse to psychology, because, in fact, when knowledge is achieved, the subject retires from the scene. But, in reality, this is a great illusion, for all epistemology, even when it tries to bring down to *a minimum* the activities of the subject, makes implicit appeal to psychological interpretations. For example, logical empiricism attempts to reduce physical knowledge to perceptual states and logicomathematical knowledge to laws of an ideal language (with its syntax, its semantics, and its pragmatics, but without reference to transformational actions). Now, these are two highly conflicting hypotheses, first, because physical experience rests on actions and not only on perceptions and always supposes a logicomathematical framework drawn from the general coordination of actions (of such kind that the operationalism of Bridgman must be completed by that of Piaget!). Second, logicomathematical knowledge is not tautological but constitutes a structural organization drawn from reflective abstraction of the general coordination between our actions and our operations.

But, most importantly, it is impossible that epistemology is static in point of view, because all scientific knowledge is in perpetual evolution, including mathematics and logic itself [of which the constructivist aspect has become evident since the theorems of Gödel have shown the impossibility of a theory to be self-sufficient (complete)—therefore, the necessity of always constructing "stronger" ones; from whence finally the inevitable limits of formalization!] As Natorp said in 1910: ". . . science evolves continually. The progression, the method is everything . . .

a consequence, the *fact* of science can only be understood as *fieri*. Only the fieri is the fact. All being (or object) that science attempts to fix must again dissolve in the current of becoming. It is in the furthest removes of this becoming, and there only, that one has the right to say, It is (fact). Therefore, that which can and must be sought is 'the law of this process'" (p. 15).

32. These uncontestable declarations are tantamount to stating the principle of our "genetic epistemology," that in order to resolve the problem of what is knowledge (or its diversity of forms) it is necessary to formulate it in the following terms: How does knowledge grow? by what process does one pass from knowledge judged to be ultimately insufficient to knowledge judged to be better (considered from the point of view of science)? It is this that the proponents of the historicocritical method have well understood (see among others the works of Koyré and Kuhn). These critics, to understand the epistemological nature of a notion or a structure, look to see first how they were formed themselves.

If one takes a dynamic rather than a static point of view, it is impossible to maintain the traditional barriers between epistemology and the psychogenesis of cognitive functions. If epistemology is defined as the study of the formation of valid knowledge, it presupposes questions of validity, which are dependent on logic and on particular sciences, but also questions of fact, for the problem is not only formal but equally real: How, in *reality*, is science possible? In fact, all epistemology is therefore obliged to invoke psychological presuppositions, and this is true of logical positivism (perception and language) as well as of Plato (reminiscence) or of Husserl (intuition, intentions, significations, etc.). The only question is to know if it is better to content oneself with a speculative psychology or whether it is more useful to have recourse to a verifiable psychology!

This is why, as all our efforts lead to epistemological conclusions (this was moreover their initial goal), we have founded an International Center for Genetic Epistemology, so that psychologists, logicians, cyberneticists, epistemologists, linguists, mathematicians, physicists, etc., may collaborate there, depending on the problems being considered.

This center, which has already published 22 volumes (and several others are in press), has therefore had as its goal, from the beginning, to study a certain number of epistemological problems seeking to analyze experimentally the psychological data necessary for the other aspects of the problem.

We have thus studied the interrelations of logical structures from the double point of view of their psychological genesis and their formal genealogy (with Grize, Papert, Apostel, etc.), which has permitted us to find a certain covergence between the two methods. We have examined the problem with what the great logician Quine ironically called the "dogma" of logical empiricism, that is to say, the absolute distinction between the analytic and the synthetic: after having declared that all these authors, being occupied with that question, have had recourse to *factual* data, we have put them under experimental control and have declared that numerous intermediaries exist between these two sorts of relationships incorrectly judged as irreducible.

We have also studied the problems of the development of the notions of number, space, time, speed, function, identity, etc., and have been able to bring to all these questions new psychogenetic data, while completely removing from their regard epistemological conclusions, which are as far removed from the a priori as from the empirical, and suggesting a systematic constructivism. With regard to empiricism, we have above all analyzed the conditions for an adequate interpretation of experience, and have added to this result what a mathematician-philosopher has summed up in these terms: "Empirical study of experience refutes empiricism!" We have seen previously (¶ 14) several of our studies on the role of learning.

In a word, the psychological theory of the development of cognitive functions seems to us to establish a direct, and even quite intimate, relationship between the biological notions of interactions between endogenous factors and the environment, and epistemological notions of necessary interaction between the subject and the objects. The synthesis of the notions of structure and of genesis that determines psychogenetic study finds its justification in the biological ideas of autoregulation and organization, and touches on an epistemological constructivism which seems to be in line with all contemporary scientific work; in particular, with that which concerns the agreement between logicomathematical constructions and physical experience.

References

Apostel, L. *Etudes d'Epistémologie Génétique II:* Logique et équilibre. Presses Universitaires de France, 1957.

Berlyne, D., and Piaget, J. *Etudes d'Epistémologie Génétique XII: Théorie du comportement et opérations.* Paris: Presses Universitaires de France, 1960.

Bruner, J. *The process of education.* Cambridge, Mass.: Harvard University Press, 1960.

Chomsky, N. Review of B.F. Skinner, *Verbal Behavior in Language,* 1959, **35**, (1), 26–58.

Chomsky, N. *Syntactic structures.* The Hague: Mouton, 1957.

Greco: *Etudes d'Epistémologie Génétique VII: Apprentissage et connaissance, Ier et II parties.* Paris: Presses Universitaires de France, 1959.

Inhelder, B., Bovet, M., Sinclair, H., in *Revue suisse de psychologie,* 1967.

Kohnstamm, G. A. La méthode génétique en psychologie. *Psychologie française,* No. 10, 1956.

Laurendeau, M., and Pinard, A. in *Psychologie et épistémologie génétique.* Dunod, 1966.

Morf, A., Smedslund, J., Vinh Bang, Wohlwill, J.: *Etudes d'Epistémologie Génétique IX: L'Apprentissage des structures logiques.* Paris: Presses Universitaires de France, 1959.

Natorp, P. *Die logischen Grundlagen des exacten Wissenschaften.* Berlin, 1910.

Piaget, J. *Traité de logique.* Colin, 1959.

Piaget, J. *Les mécanismes perceptifs.* Paris: Presses Universitaires de France, 1961. (Contains contributions of Vinh Bang, Gonheim, Noelting, Dadsetan.)

Piaget, J., and Inhelder, B. *L'image mental chez l'enfant.* Paris: Presses Univer-

Pitts, W., and McCulloch, W. S. How we know universals: the perception of sitaires de France. 1966.

Sinclair, H., and Zwart, *Acquisition du langage et développement de la pensée.* auditory and visual forms. *Bull. Math. Biophys.,* 1947, **9**, 127–147.

Waddington, C. H. *The Strategy of the Genes.* Dunod, 1967.

10. Werner's Comparative Organismic Theory[1]

JONAS LANGER

The central theoretical issue is dialectical: how does a developing organism change qualitatively and at the same time preserve its integrity? It is important to keep this dialectical formulation[2] well in mind because

[1] As a student of Werner, I naturally find it almost impossible to differentiate precisely between Werner's views and those I have come to hold. Moreover, it is impossible to mark off where Werner's contributions end and those of his colleagues and students at Clark University begin, particularly the contributions of Bernard Kaplan and Seymour Wapner.

Since the theory is a comprehensive one and the theoretical issues involved in this discussion are complex, the reader may find it helpful to have an outline of the sequence of topics:

[2] Dialectical is being used in the Hegelian sense that development is the synthesis of antitheses, here, transformation and conservation.

the term "development" itself has tended to focus theoretical and empirical attention upon one pole of the dialectical process—the nature of adaptive change—at the expense of considering the other—the nature of organizational stability. A theoretical synthesis of both is necessary to the comprehensive developmental understanding of the integrity that marks a whole organism while it is altering through an ordered sequence of change.

Any narrowing of the developmental conception to the investigation of change alone must be distorting. It may lead to the misconception that development is the kind of anarchism where totally unrelated and radically discontinuous stages follow each other in sequence; or it may lead to the kind of historicism where new or modified behaviors are merely added on in continuous temporal order as the organism grows. The anarchic perspective misses the functional and structural integrity of organismic development. It may mistakenly imply organizational dissociation between different periods of life. Historicism assumes a continuous, ongoing organism. Consequently, it does not adequately examine how the current organization influences the development of subsequent new behavior patterns or the modification of old behavior patterns. As such, historicism fails to inquire into whether and how the ongoing organization is altered as a consequence of such acquisition or modification.

The dialectical nature of development also has implications for the persistent question of why does an organism that is well adapted at one stage ever progress to the next stage. Insofar as development is a dialectical process and the question of motive is legitimate in this context it should apply to organizational stability as well as change. Motivational questions about progress seem to have two related sources. The first is a generalization from empirical work on the motivation for the local or short-term acquisition and modification of a delimited performance or behavior pattern. Many investigators believe it to be legitimate to ask questions of motive, like what is the drive, instinct, reward, and/or reason for a given behavior (cf. Peters, 1958). The second source of motivational questions seems more theoretical. It is the view that development is nothing but the continuous, gradual, quantitative acquisition and slight modification of small bits of behavior over time (e.g., Bijou and Baer, 1961; Staats, 1968). Taken together these two ideas suggest that each bit of behavior acquisition and modification must be motivated and therefore the accumulation of bits over time, called behavioral growth, must be motivated. However, functional questions of motivation are misdirected when the process under consideration is long-term psychological development. Then motivational questions as to why a new stage develops when the organism is already adapted at one level are no more appropriate here than to the rest of evolutionary biology. It makes as little scientific sense to ask what motivates the development of a new stage of cognitive organization as, for example, to ask what motivates the evolution of a new species or what motivates the evolution of mature respiratory structures in humans.

The dialectical formulation of long-term change suggests that development is composed of a sequence of universal stages of organization, that is, structures and functions. Each stage of organization is simultaneously directed toward maintaining continuity or stability and generating discontinuity or transformation. The fundamental thesis is that evolution is a synthetic process that interweaves two antithetical organismic tendencies: to maintain continuity in order to conserve one's integrity (survival and organizational coherence) and to elaborate discontinuity in order to develop (Langer, 1969, p. 89).

There is, on one hand, the tendency of organisms to *conserve* their integrity, whether biological or psychological: in the face of variable and often adverse, external or internal conditions, the organism tends to maintain its existence as an integrated entity. There is, on the other hand, the tendency of organisms to *develop* towards a relatively mature state: under the widest range of conditions, organisms undergo transformation from the status of relatively little differentiated entities to relatively differentiated and integrated adult forms. (Werner and Kaplan, 1963, p. 5).

ORTHOGENESIS

In order to characterize these two dialectical but concurrent tendencies within the growing organism, Werner (1948) adapted the embryogenetic prinicple of orthogenesis and applied it to mental development.[3] The orthogenetic principle asserts that development is a process of increasing differentiation and specification of the organism's relatively global organization, coupled with a process of progressive centralization and hierarchic integration of the more individuated systems so that progressive equilibrium is achieved.

Progressive *differentiation* and specification of the organization of rudimentary action systems, such as sensory and motor systems, is one major side to development. Functionally, primitive systems may be fused with each others so that they have no flexible operative relationship to each other but rather operate in a rigidly fixed or fluctuating fashion. Differentiation leads to progressively discrete yet internally integrated means of action and intended ends that function in a flexible and

[3] In a recent work (Langer, 1969, Chap. 4) I have attempted to show that Werner's and Piaget's conceptions have common major theoretical and empirical features that make up much of the contemporary organismic approach to development. The present chapter will not, however, refer to Piaget's relevant work because it is presented by Piaget himself in this book. Rather, this chapter will refer extensively to Cassirer's philosophy of symbolic forms because his contributions to the study of genetic epistemology have made a major and direct impact upon comparative organismic theory.

stable fashion in relationship to each other. Structurally, primitive systems have no definite boundaries but are diffuse in both internal character and external relationship to each other. Differentiation leads to progressive individuation into definite and well articulated part systems that are coherently related to each other.

Progressive *hierarchic integration* is the reciprocal of progressive differentiation and the other major side to development. The most advanced (differentiated, specialized, and internally integrated) systems functionally regulate and structurally subordinate less developed systems. The long-range, developmental result of concomitant differentiation and hierarchic integration is the progressive construction of a holistic organization where the most central and advanced action systems regulate the more primitive systems.

The dialectical tension between the tendencies to change and to preserve stability is expressed in three theoretical ideas that are central to the orthogenetic conception of development (Werner, 1957).

1. *Discontinuity.* Differentiation is a process of altering a relatively global organization into a more individuated whole.

2. *Continuity.* Hierarchic integration serves to maintain the organism's integrity in the face of change over time. As a consequence, some forms of the organism's structures and functions are preserved by being subsumed by the more individuated systems that have developed; not all primitive systems are lost or altered in the course of developing competence.

3. *Synthesis* of these two antithetical tendencies. The organization of a new stage is a reorganization of the previous stage that combines both continuity and discontinuity. The total pattern is altered but still continuous with the previous pattern: (a) new structures and functions are dominant and hierarchically integrate or control others; (b) differentiation leads to specialization and newly individuated systems; and (c) primitive systems that are preserved operate differently due to increased centralization and their regulation by more differentiated and integrated systems (cf., Langer, 1969, pp. 172–177).

Several strategic ideas about research flow from the orthogenetic principle. To begin to study development requires an initial conception, however tentative, of the ideal end state or most mature organization that the organism may achieve in the course of its life. The reason for this is that developmental change is not an unlawful flux but rather directed alteration. To study and understand processes of mental development requires inquiry into its epistemological goal (cf., Cassirer, 1957). A comprehensive explanation of developmental processes will therefore require a coherent view of *final determination*, that is, a well established conception of the mental end state toward which development is directed and which lends significance to the processes of change. A complementary strategy is to inquire into the organization that constitutes the original mental state of the organism and the source or *material cause* of all further development (cf. Werner, 1948). This means determining the self-regulatory rules of coherence and the self-generative rules of adaptation that are inherent to the organism's original functional structures since these are the inherent rules of developmental transformation and construction. Furthermore, determining the nature of development (conservation and change) requires comparison of the transformed psychological state with its foundation. Finally, determining the form of organization that constitutes the original and most advanced mental stages of development provides the basis for both determining the form of the transitional stages and determining the organism-environment interactions that *logically imply* the transformative construction from stage to stage (cf. Langer, 1969).

Two major types of theoretical analysis flow from the orthogenetic formulation of the dialectical process of development. First, the orthogenetic conception of functional and structural development leads to an organismic analysis. In addition, the generality of the orthogenetic conception leads to a comparative analysis of psychological phenomena in the diverse contexts in which development may take place (Kaplan, 1966). It is to a consideration of these two types of analysis that the next two sections are addressed.

ORGANISMIC ANALYSIS

We may now return to the functional question of what causes an organism that is well-adapted at one stage of organization to change. Insofar as a functionally equilibrated state of adaptation has been achieved it provides the basis for coherent stability even at a stage of primitive organization (cf. Goldstein, 1939). When the organism's primitive instruments or means determine and satisfy the problems or ends dealt with, the organism is in a balanced, albeit primitive state of adaptation. In complementary fashion, when the organism's primitive adaptive ends determine the instruments or means that are required, then the organism's rudimentary systems of action are adequate and the organism is also in a balanced state. Both means-ends relationships imply coherent organizational stability and do not provide the functional conditions that would generate directed change.

The probability is exceedingly small that a living organism is in perfect and total functional equilibrium. Indeed,

. . . when one examines the developmental changes in means-ends relationships . . . one observes the effects that newly emerging goals or ends have on the formation and restructurization of biopsychological equipment and the effects which in turn such newly formed equipment has in the determination of biopsychological ends (Werner and Kaplan, 1963, p. 7).

In particular, it is to be expected that the organism's primitive means and ends, such as its sensorimotor means and ends, are rarely equilibrated perfectly:

. . . stability of behavior requires a flexibility of response in order to preserve the functional equilibrium of the organism in the face of mutable situations (Werner, 1948, p. 55).

But flexibility is not a characteristic of primitive systems of action. This suggests that primitive means and ends are never completely sufficient (adequate) or satisfying (adaptive). This is the functional disequilibrium that is necessary for means-ends reorganization:

. . . wherever functional shifts occur during development, the novel function is first executed through old, available forms; sooner or later, of course, there is a pressure towards the development of new forms which are of a more function-specific character; i.e., that will serve the new function better than the older forms (Werner and Kaplan, 1963, p. 60).

Or a previously subordinate functional system acquires regulative control:

a reorganization of processes conditioned either by the introduction of a new function, or by a change of dominance of function in a given process-pattern (Werner, 1937, p. 353).

When the organism develops, the more primitive systems are not necessarily lost but become relatively less important and salient in the more advanced functioning of the organism. They are used less and their efficiency may deteriorate as more sophisticated systems become more dominant in the organism's life:

. . . lower levels of functioning (both in terms of means and of ends) are subordinated to more advanced levels of functioning; they may come to the fore again under special internal or external conditions, for example, in dream states, in pathological states, under intoxication by certain drugs, or under various experimental conditions. They also, and characteristically, may come to the fore when the organism is confronted with especially difficult and novel tasks: in such cases one often finds a partial return to more primitive modes of functioning before progressing towards full-fledged higher operations; we may refer to this tendency as a manifestation of the *genetic principle of spirality* . . . (Werner and Kaplan, 1963, p. 8).

Spiral development means that

The organism at times seems to retreat from a locus of maturity which it has already attained. Temporarily such a retreat may look like an abandonment. It would be abandonment if it continued on one tangent. The course of development, however, being spiral, turns back toward the point of departure;

and it does not return precisely to this point. It returns to the same region but at a higher level. The neurological result is an interwoven texture which expresses itself in progressive patterns of behavior. The unity of the ground plan of the organism is preserved. It is a process of reincorporation and consolidation (Gesell, 1946, p. 317).

The genetic principle of spirality assumes that *analogous functioning* is one of the most general laws of development. Functional analogy between stages and systems of action implies that more primitive stages and systems are the primary sources or precursors of more advanced stages. It is clear that Werner's conception of functionally analogous processes is that of a fundamental law of development which informs the theoretical and empirical search for stages. This has been worked out in the greatest detail by Werner (1948) for the processes of relating, grouping, abstracting, generalizing, and representing, which make up concept formation.

There are, for example, three genetically parallel levels of establishing relations that involve analogous processes. Primitive, concrete "relating" is sensorimotor in form. Brightness transposition in chickens is a good example of the ability to establish sensorimotor relations:

When two areas of grey are united in a brightness configuration and acquire different functional values (+ and −)with respect to the food-seeking activity, we may safely assume that the animal has constructed a relationship on a sensori-motor level (Werner, 1948, p. 217).

According to Werner, one of Koehler's experiments with apes is a particularly apt demonstration of the concrete relations that can be constructed by sensorimotor activity. In order to rake in a distant object, a chimpanzee was provided with two bamboo rods, neither of which was long enough to get the desired object. The diameter of one rod A is smaller than that of B and can be fitted into B to make a long enough rod. If rod A must be pushed into B and B must be held steady so that A will fit in, then A is the active and B the passive rod. After having solved this problem through sensorimotor manipulations,

rod A was taken away and replaced with a third rod C whose diameter is larger than B. This requires that the chimpanzee act on the basis of (1) the relationship between (and not the absolute) sizes and (2) the relationship between (and not the absolute) active and passive elements. Upon sensorimotor inspection of the rods the chimpanzee solves the problem immediately.

"Relating" as a predominantly perceptual activity may proceed from simple to more complex levels. In one experiment (Werner, 1948, p. 220) children were presented with a card on which is presented four lines of a given size proportion. The task is to select other cards that show four lines with the same size proportion. Children can perform the task at a younger age if the lines are presented as a definite figure (see A) rather than as separate parts (see B).

(A)

(B)

Constructing relations at the most advanced level involves the formation of explicit abstract rules. Most often these rules are expressed linguistically, although they may involve even more abstract logical and mathematical forms. This would be the case if the preceding problem of relating lines were expressed and solved on the basis of a rule articulating the metric relations. It is Werner's central genetic hypothesis that even the construction of such abstract relations develops out of—and is a transformation of—concrete perceptual relations:

. . . two separate phases are often observable in the thought processes of comparison. The first is the formation of a perceptual relationship—the relation between two parts is grasped in a certain configuration. The second is the derivative abstract form of the relationship as expressed in a verbally constituted judgment (Werner, 1948, pp. 221–222).

The dialectical thesis serves to remind us of the organism's stable organization and therefore the central importance of structural considerations in the understanding of development. The assumption is that even in their initial infantile states, all organisms are organized and have some degree of competence. This organization provides the basis for acting. Its functional structures determine the range of conduct available to the organism and consequently the types of interaction with its environment that are open to it. It is obvious, for example, that a verbal environment cannot stimulate a verbal response from a newborn baby. The range of conduct and interactions therefore progress as the organization develops.

Now the organism's organization is composed of many parts or systems, such as those for locomotion, vision, and thinking, which have different characteristics. When these parts are in structural equilibrium, both within and between parts, they form a coherent whole and change will not occur (cf. von Bertalanffy, 1933). But the probability of total structural (part-whole) equilibrium may be assumed to be just as small as the probability of perfect functional (means-ends) equilibrium. Consequently, structural change is always expected:

Wherever there is life there is growth and development, that is, formation in terms of systematic, orderly sequence (Werner, 1948, p. 55).

In particular, it is to be expected that the organism's primitive structures are rarely equilibrated perfectly. For example, the young infant cannot reach for objects he is looking at and desires to grasp. More integrated structures are required for this coordination. This is the type of adaptive disequilibrium that is necessary for part-whole reorganization (cf. Langer, 1969a). Eventually, more integrated structures develop, such as those requisite for efficient hand-eye coordination.

COMPARATIVE ANALYSIS

Much of the richness of the orthogenetic approach is provided by the comparative analysis of evolutionary change, whether found within a line or direction of development or between lines of development. That is, comparison may be within species evolution (phylogenesis), long-term individual development (ontogenesis), short-term individual development (microgenesis), societal development (ethnogenesis), and psychopathological development (pathogenesis). Comparison may also be made between domains:

. . . the psychology of the individual and of the human race, animal and child psychology, psychopathology and the psychology of special states of consciousness—all these can be approached from the genetic standpoint. The final procedure of a comparative developmental psychology is to compare the results gained from work done in the specialized fields, and from the comparison to derive developmental laws generally applicable to mental life as a whole (Werner, 1948, p. 5).

Two early developmental conceptions, those of Hobhouse and J. M. Baldwin, were especially significant in the formulation of the comparative approach. Hobhouse's (1901) comparative focus was upon the phylogeny and ontogeny of mental activity. He delineated six means of acting that become progressively available within phylogenesis. The first and most primitive is the *reflex* or blind, mechanical reaction of a preformed structure to a sensory stimulus. The next three means of acting that evolve beyond reflexes become increasingly dependent upon interactive experience. The second means of action is *trial and error*. It permits the organism to call upon a variety of reactions when an obstacle is met, until the situation is changed or the organism is unable to master it. As a consequence, for example, a paramecium may learn habitual modes of response. The third means, that of *assimilation*, is the adjustment of the organism's action to suit its needs such that modification of behavior is possible in the future. Here Hobhouse refers to Lloyd Morgan's experiment in which chicks learned to discriminate between bitter and agreeable food so that they no longer pecked at the bitter food. The highest means of acting that is directly dependent upon experience is *practical judgment*. Different objects may be related in concrete experience or judgment, such as a chimpanzee's use of a stick as a tool with which to obtain a banana that is out of reach. The fifth means is *conceptual thought;* this means of acting is not dependent directly upon experience. It is a means of expressing explicit relations which is free from perception. It is the way in which knowledge, tradition, and culture are learned and used. The most advanced means of mental activity that evolves in phylogenesis is *analysis* by logical operations, which involves rational, logicomathematical systems.

These six means of activity characterize the direction of mental development within both phylogenesis and human ontogenesis. Hobhouse made it clear, however, that there were differences between phylogeny and ontogeny. The development of these six means of acting is obviously not a characteristic of the ontogeny of all species. The two most advanced means, conceptual thought and logical analysis, only evolve in human ontogenesis.

Baldwin's (1915) comparative focus was upon the relationship between the evolution of mental life in human ontogenesis and ethnogenesis rather than phylogenesis. This led him to establish the discipline he called *genetic epistemology* or how "thought or experience makes to render reality" by comparing the progressive "stages of thought" that evolve in ontogenesis and ethnogenesis so as to construct "a natural history of interpretation itself." Although Baldwin argued that there is parallel "movement in the internal organization of thought and values" between human ontogeny and ethnogenesis, he maintained that it is ontogenesis that gives ethnogenesis "its vital impulse and its progressive 'uplift.' "

Baldwin divides human ontogenesis into three progressive stages of interpretation. The first is the *prelogical* stage where the child's mode of action is "intuitive" and "quasi-discursive" or quasi-linguistic. The child makes no distinction between the subjective and objective factors in his experience. He accepts "the reality of the datum" of experience. Thus knowledge in the prelogical period is pragmatic and presentational: "a meaning of immediate presence and intuition." The interpretative mode of action at the next, the *logical*, stage is "discursive" or linguistic. Imaginative, esthetic schemes are used to unite thought (mediated interpretation of reality) with "the singular and the immediate." The person's imagination projects "its schematic and tentative readings" upon the environment. These imaginative projections have "the character of assumption, proposal. hypothesis." Therefore all imaginative interpretations "have the force of possibility and probability" such that "reality is embodied in all sorts of 'as if' construction." But the person now begins to use verification procedures in order to assess the validity of his imaginative assumptions. This leads to the logical processes of judgment, reasoning, and implication that determine "what is to be accepted as real." At the highest, *hyperlogical* stage of ontogenesis "Consciousness achieves a freeing from logic as before she worked to secure the freeing of logic." Now the interpretative mode of action becomes esthetic contemplation which "erects into postulates its ends, values, and goods."

Baldwin hypothesized that the ontogeny of subjective (individual) interpretationism is paralleled by the progressive construction in ethnogenesis of objective (societal) embodiments of interpretation "in laws, rites, customs, sanctions." He therefore proposed three stages of cultural evolution that parallel the ontogenetic stages of interpretation. At the prelogical stage, the group's interpretative mode of action is mystical and takes mythical and religious forms. At the logical stage the mode of action is speculative, taking scientific and critical forms. The interpretative mode of action is transformed into "aesthetic contemplation" at the hyperlogical stage and takes the form of advanced philosophical theory.

Although important in their own right, Hobhouse's and Baldwin's comparative formulations do not fully meet the criteria for a formal theory of development, namely, that the assessment of change should not be bound temporally or in content, output, and value (see the section on The Direction of Mental Development). Werner's formulation of formal coordinates provides the kind of theoretical dimensions that are required in order to make a purely formal comparative analysis within and between directions of evolution. Also, Werner extended the comparative analysis to include pathogenesis and microgenesis as well as phylogenesis, ontogenesis, and ethnogenesis.

Consider first an aspect of perceptual development. The comparative coordinates permit a purely formal analysis of the genetic level of perception and its change within and between ontogenesis, pathogenesis, and microgenesis. To this end a number of studies, summarized by Werner (1957), have investigated form perception on the Rorschach test. If we rate undifferentiated, diffuse, and amorphous percepts as developmentally low while we rate differentiated, articulated, and well-integrated percepts as developmentally high, then the findings may be outlined as follows:

1. Ontogenesis. There is a significant and continuous shift from low to relatively advanced responses from the age of 3 to 10 years.

2. Pathogenesis. Four groups were tested. Their status was ordered in terms of pathology from the most severe regressives (hebephrenic and catatonic schizophrenics) to paranoid schizophrenics to psychoneurotics to normal adults. Again there is a clear progression from low to high responses; with the percepts of the hebephrenic and catatonic schizophrenics paralleling those of the 3- to 5-year-olds and the percepts of the psychoneurotics being intermediate between the 10-year-olds and normal adults.

3. Microgenesis. (a) Rorschach cards were presented for 0.01 second, 0.1 second, 1 second, and 10 seconds to four independent groups of normal adult subjects, respectively. There is a clear progression from low to high percepts. (b) The same exposure times were used with four independent groups of hebephrenic and catatonic schizophrenics. Their responses were not very different from the normal adults at the 0.01 second exposure time. But unlike the normals their responses evidenced no microgenetic progress.

Now consider an aspect of the comparative development of concepts, specifically that of time concepts. One general hypothesis is that all primitive time cognition is egocentrically tied to the concrete, affective, and pragmatic aspects of the subject's conduct—it has the "concrete and affective character-of-action." One of the examples that Werner (1968) presents from ethnogenesis is that of the system of dividing up the day constructed by Uganda tribesmen who raise cattle. Their temporal scheme is based upon, and consists of, the order of the day's work events, such as milking time, watering time, and home coming time for the cattle. Primitive ontogenetic and pathogenetic cognition of time is also based upon a fusion of concrete acts and affective desire. One of the ontogenetic examples cited by Werner is that of a 6-year-old boy who pointed to different parts of the sky, saying "That's where the day comes out, and there, farther along, is the night, and right up at the top is Christmas day." Some of the pathogenetic examples that Werner analyzed follow:

Time, says one schizophrenic, falls together like a pack of cards. Another schizophrenic's experience of time during his quiet phase differed from his temporal experience during the phase of terrible anxiety. In the calm phase time moved on with great rapidity; ten months were as one. In the anxious phase, on the contrary, events hung motionless in a temporal vacuum (Werner, 1948, p. 190).

Head describes aphasiacs who, following a loss of the abstract schema, employed a concrete time-of-action . . . For instance, one patient had a concrete qualitative time scale made up of dominant movements in the succession of daily events: "Then, when you eat." "Then, when we arrive there," etc. (Werner, 1948, p. 190).

So far this comparative analysis of perceptual and conceptual development, as well as Hobhouse's and Baldwin's comparative analyses, focused upon the parallels within and between evolutionary domains. A thorough comparative analysis cannot afford to neglect the crucial differences, however:

For all practical purposes one may speak of a principle of parallelism: development in mental life follows certain general and formal rules whether it concerns the individual or the species. Such a principle implies that, apart from general and formed similarities, there do exist specific material differences in the comparable phenomena (Werner, 1948, p. 26).

These parallels must be taken as such, as merely indicating a similar mental structure in a general and purely *formal* sense. In a particular and *material* sense, there will be irreconcilable differences (Werner, 1948, p. 26).

While it is obvious that there are particular content differences in comparable mental achievements, it seems equally clear that there must also be general formal differences in the social and psychological processes that underlie such achievements. Indeed, Werner (1948), for example, details three basic differences between comparable primitive stages of ontogenesis and ethnogenesis. First, the young child is growing and his whole mental life is in the process of change. Adults in preliterate societies are fully developed and their mental life is relatively "fixed in tradition." Second, the child develops "out of his child's world into an alien world of adults." What he becomes is therefore greatly "the result of an interaction between these two worlds." By contrast the psychological world and status of an adult in a preliterate society is fairly permanent. Third, the child's "social pattern" of functioning is not well organized and formed while the social pattern of the adult in a preliterate society is well established. These fundamental differences do not negate the possibility of formal similarities and genetic parallels. But they also do not merely reflect trivial variations in the particular content of formally similar mental phenomena. Rather, there are also general formal differences in the organization of mental life at comparable primitive stages of ontogenesis and ethnogenesis.

INTERACTION

The organismic and comparative analyses suggest that all organisms are born with a minimal set of species-specific functional structures which permit them to interact with the environment in order to incorporate experience and stimulation; otherwise they would not develop. This is the basis for the root organismic metaphor of interaction (Pepper, 1942). The organism actively takes in and digests environmental properties. The consequences are physiological and/or psychological development. It is obvious that physiological structures can only assimilate those environmental properties for which it has appropriate physiological organs. Similarly, psychological structures can only assimilate that experience and information for which it has appropriate mental systems. Thus it is the organism's organization that selectively determines the character of its interaction and the significance of its experiences. These experiences, in turn, feed back upon the functional structures which were the orginal source of the interaction. In ways that are still little understood, such feedback eventually leads to the qualitative alteration of the organization of one stage into the next more advanced stage.

This is the *material cause* of development: the organization of preceding stages logically implies but does not contain the organization of subsequent stages. Since the organization at each stage is different from that of other stages, the organism's interactions with its environment change in the course of life. When these interactions are not disruptive, the conditions are propitious for the organism to remain in equilibrium and its organization will remain stable. When the feedback from these interactions perturb the organism, then the disequilibrating conditions necessary for change are present and the probability of functional and structural reorganization increases (Langer, 1969a).

The key to the process of development (stability and change) is interaction. The environment is the scene or object of the organism's actions and development while the organism is the actor or the subject in this scene. Consequently, the organism is not merely a reactor to the environment, but an operator upon its *Umwelt* or scene (von Uexküll, 1934). The analysis of development therefore requires investigating the lawful changes in actor-scene ratios (cf. Burke, 1945) or subject-object relations (Werner, 1948) that occur in progressive or regressive evolution.

At this point we need to introduce a further distinction. This is the difference between the form and the content of acts and their products—mental experiences, achievements, and development. The interaction that results in the person's acts and their products is, of course, a composition of organismic and environmental factors. The role of the organism's functional structures is mediated by its schemes of interacting (cf. Langer, 1969). These functional structures determine the *form* of schematizing activity and consequently the form of interaction with the environment. Schematizing progressively constructs the forms of the organism's products including its own development. The *content* of the organism's interaction is more directly the result of the physical and social environment. The role of the environment's functional structures is mediated by patterns of stimulation. Stimulation provides much of the content upon which the organism acts and, consequently, greatly determines the content of the organism's achievements and development.

Schemes and Schematizing Activity

The concept of the scheme or schema[4] and schematizing activity has become such a central idea in current theories of cognitive development that it would do well for us to dwell briefly upon its meaning. In his *Dictionary of Philosophy and Psychology*, J. M. Baldwin notes that a schema is a product according to Kant. It is a product of the transcendental imagination which through its exercise gives generality to sense experience and particularity to thought conceptions. A schema is also a mode of constructing or a formula for synthesizing. As a mode or a formula, it is a general rule that guides mental activity. As embodied in a characteristic form, a scheme is the particular mental product of this rule of action. For example, the schema of quantity is number and the schema of substance is permanence in time.

The more contemporary usage of schema was introduced by Head (1926). Head points out that Pick accepted Hughling Jackson's

[4] We cannot deal here, with the useful distinction introduced by Piaget between an operative scheme (e.g., conceptual conservation) and a figurative schema (e.g., perceptual constancy). Rather, we are using the terms synonymously and in a fashion that corresponds more closely to Piaget's use of scheme than schema.

hypothesis that, intellectually, speech disorders are failures to produce propositional statements. Pick made an analytic distinction between the construction of thought (the preliminary to any symbolic expression) and the formulation of speech (which underlies the executive process of verbal production). Thus he distinguished between the psychological schemata that make up thought from the grammatical schemata or rules for its formation in words.

Head extended this usage of schema to the hypothesis of a general bodily "postural appreciation" or "dispositional system" of standards "against which all subsequent changes in posture are measured before they appear in consciousness." This schema or model is a constantly changing standard and record of the body's movements in space:

By means of perpetual alterations in position we are always building up unwittingly a model of ourselves, which is constantly changing. Every new posture or movement is registered on this plastic schema and the activity of the cortex brings into relation with it each fresh group of afferent impulses, evoked by a change in the position of the body (p. 488).

Thus Head's concept of schema included both the process of "schema building"—of schematizing activity—and the product of this activity—the "schema built."

The main point is that schemes have both functional and structural aspects. Functionally, schemes are self-constructive; these self-constructive powers serve to organize one's experience into percepts and concepts. Thus schemes are rules for the cognitive organization and satisfaction of interests, attitudes, and needs. Structurally, schemes are the products or representational forms of knowledge, attitudes, and needs, which are constructed by their own active schematizing operations. They are the "stuff" of cognition. (For further theoretical implications of the concept of schemes and schematizing activity see Langer, 1969, pp. 169–172.)

Progressive Constructivism

Werner and Kaplan (1963) maintain that the course of development is marked by a ratio shift in interactive dominance from the

Table 1. Diagram of Developmental Transformations

Organism-*Umwelt* Relationships			Means-Ends Relationships
I Tropistic-re- flex actions	*to*	Stimuli	Biophysical and biochemical transmission culminating in stereotyped reaction patterns of parts of, or whole, organism
II. Goal-directed sensorimotor action	*upon*	Signaled things	Species-specific behaviors and individually learned patterns of response ("habits"); formation of signals (mammals); "natural" tool usage (apes); all predominantly in the service of biological ends
III. Contempla-tive knowledge	*about*	Objects	Construction of tools and formation of symbols in the service of knowing about and manipulating the environment

scene to the actor as they have outlined it in Table 1. At primitive stages of development the scene or psychological environment is the prime initiator of interaction. Although the organism's functional structures determine the form of its conduct, it is still a relatively passive reaction to environmental stimulation. Progressively, at more advanced stages of development, organisms become the prime initiators of interaction as well as the determiners of the forms of their own conduct in the interaction. In this sense, the actor's behavior has become relatively spontaneous, self-generated action upon the environment. The organism becomes increasingly sovereign in initiating and determining the character of its own actions; and it increasingly molds or constructs even the content of the scenes to suit its own needs and goals.

An interesting symptom of the developmental shift in dominance in the actor-scene ratio is reflected in the ontogenesis from naive acceptance to critical appraisal of events. The stages of this development were first worked out by Brind (and are reported by Brunswick, 1933). They have been essentially replicated (Schwartz and Langer, 1967; Langer, 1969a) with respect to the evaluation and handling of an impossible task. The observed ontongenetic shift is from (1) an initial naive credulity and acceptance to (2) criticalness and rejection to (3) a final criticalness coupled with either an attempt to rectify the situation or with amusement.

Egocentrism to Perspectivism

The developmental shift in dominance from the biophysical press of the scene to the constructive activity of the subject is marked by progressive differentiation of primitive egocentric interactions. Egocentric interactions are globally fused, that is, the organism does not discriminate between himself (his status as a subject, his acts, his experiences and his feelings) and the environment (its status as an object, its behavior, and its stimulation):

. . . the young child's acceptance of dreams as external to himself, the lack of differentiation between what one dreams and what one sees, as is found in psychosis, or in some nonliterate societies, the breakdown of boundaries of the self in mescaline intoxication and in states of depersonalization—all of these betoken a relative condition of genetic primordiality. . . (Werner, 1957, p. 127).

Werner (1948) cites the case of a paranoid schizophrenic who is fearfully observing doors swinging back and forth. This leads him to exclaim, "The door is devouring me!" Werner analyzes this behavior:

Affect . . . has once more become a factor in the configuration of the surrounding world . . . this occurs not in the sense that the world of things become invested with an especially strong overtone of emotion, but rather in the sense that affect actually forms the world itself. . . . The properties of things cease to be entirely objective, geometric, and "out there." Actually they acquire and express a much greater "depth" and inner significance (1948, p. 81).

Differentiation of primitive interactions in progressive development is accompanied by increasing integration of the actor with his scene:

Higher types of action are formally characterized by an interaction of personality with an outer discrete world, both polar elements being relatively self-subsistent (Werner, 1948, p. 191).

This means that the subject has relatively greater understanding of his environment and its influences on him and his effects on it. It also means increasing perspective on the part of the subject. He can increasingly sympathize with, empathize with, and adopt the perspectives of others as well as his own; and he can increasingly integrate all these to form a coherent basis for his own conduct:

. . . increasing subject-object differentiation involves the corollary that the organism becomes increasingly less dominated by the immediate concrete situation; the person is less stimulus bound and less impelled by his own affective states. A consequence of this freedom is the clearer understanding of goals, the possibility of employing substitutive means and alternative ends. There is, hence, a greater capacity for delay and planned action. The person is better able to exercise choice and willfully rearrange a situation. In short, he can manipulate the environment rather than passively respond to the environment. . . . At developmentally higher levels, therefore, there is less of a tendency for the world to be interpreted solely in terms of one's own needs and an increasing appreciation of the needs of others and of group goals (Werner, 1957, p. 127).

The findings of three sets of perceptual studies document the shift in actor-scene ratio from egocentrism to differentiated perspectivism. The first set deals with the perception of self-object relations, the second with the perception of the self, and the third with the perception of the scene.

The paradigm for experimental inquiry into self-object relations involves investigating the developing relation between perception of body and object positions (Wapner and Werner, 1965; Wapner, 1969). Subjects were placed in a tilted position in a dark room. Then they were required to indicate where a luminescent rod must be placed in order to locate their own position (self) vis-à-vis that of the true vertical (object). The angular separation between apparent body and apparent object position is used as an index of their perceptual relation for the subjects. There is a shift from perceiving body and vertical positions as relatively next to each other (from age 6 to 13) to seeing them as increasingly separate (from age 13 to 18). These data may be interpreted as measuring aspects of the ontongenetic shift from global syncresis to analytic discreteness in self-object relations.

The paradigmatic comparative analysis of progressive, arrested, and regressive shifts in self-perception involves experiments on apparent body size (Wapner, 1964; Wapner and Werner, 1965). In one series of studies the focus was on apparent head size as indicated by subjects placing their index fingers on a rod in front of them while keeping their eyes closed. The comparative findings may be summarized as follows:

1. There is an ontogenetic shift from great overestimation at 5 years to a relatively minor degree of overestimation by 18 years.

2. The natural ontogenetic articulation of the boundary between the self and the world may be simulated experimentally. For example, if one side of the child's head is touched, then his size estimate of the articulated but not the untouched side diminishes.

3. Retarded children overestimate their head size more than normal children.

4. Schizophrenics overestimate their head size more than normal individual's of the same age.

5. Adults given LSD-25, a drug assumed to induce regression, overestimate more than adults given a placebo.

6. Increasing overestimation accompanies old age.

Together these particular data are consistent with the more general comparative hypothesis that there is a shift from diffuse self-perception at primitive stages to an articulate self-perspective at advanced stages of development.

Experimental inquiry into the developmental shifts in the status attributed to objects in self-object interactions takes the following kind of form (Wapner, 1969).

Subjects are presented with a luminous ×
(two lines at right angles to each other) in
a dark room. They are seated in a chair that
is tilted 45° to the right. Consequently, when
asked what algebraic sign the object is they
can either respond that it is a plus or a multiplication sign. The hypothesis is that egocentric perception will lead to the judgment
that it is a plus sign because that is consonant
with the subject's own position of viewing the
object. On the other hand, a more perspectivistic outlook will tend to assess the object
in terms of its context in the total field and
relatively play down one's own subjective
orientation. The ontogenetic findings from
third-, fourth-, fifth-, and sixth-grade children
confirm the hypothesis. Third graders give the
highest frequency of "plus" responses and
sixth graders the highest frequency of "multiplication" sign responses.

In sum, these three findings indicate the
progress in perceptual judgments of the self,
the scene, and their relation in self-object interactions. Primitive stages are dominated by
egocentric constructions of the actor-scene
ratio, whereas more advanced stages are
marked by the construction of perspectivistic
ratios that seek to take into account and integrate multiple viewpoints.

THE DIRECTION OF MENTAL DEVELOPMENT

Werner made many deep changes in his
theory of mental development over the 40-
year span of his writings. The most profound
trend was a progressive movement away from
a temporal formulation that would only fit the
growth trends of individual life cycles, and a
movement toward an ever more logical and
abstract formal characterization of progressive, arrested, and regressive development
that could account for evolutionary mental
change wherever it occurs, whether in the
field of phylogenesis, ethnogenesis, ontogenesis, microgenesis, or pathogenesis. The aim
was to avoid being forced into the assumption
that development had taken place just because the organism under consideration (animal, man, patient, society) had passed through
a long period of time (Kaplan, 1966a).

This required conceptualizing primitive
and advanced stages of development in formal
terms that adequately cover the comparative

field of mental evolution. The aim was to establish dimensions of assessment that are: (1)
not temporally bound because chronological
growth alone does not insure either progressive or regressive alteration; (2) not content
bound because it is the form of the organism's
actions and products that mark his mental
development; (3) not output or achievement bound because a number of processes
having different developmental status may
lead to the same observed output by the organism (Werner, 1937); and (4) not value
bound because the theoretical requirement is
for objective rather than evaluative means of
assessing change and stability.

Formal Dimensional Coordinates

Werner's (1948) orthogenetic formulation
of development as the "increasing differentiation and centralization or hierarchic integration, within the genetic totality" was an
initial step in this direction, providing a purely
formal principle. On this basis, Werner further specified four formal sets of coordinates
for the analysis of the genetic level of mental
phenomena.

The central set of formal coordinates for
the functional analysis of development is that
of *syncretic* to *discrete*. Functional undifferentiatedness is especially marked by syncretic
fusion of systems of action. Synceresis may
obtain between subsystems within a system,
such a emotional undifferentiatedness during
infancy and early childhood (Bridges, 1931)
and such as the perceptual fusion of sensory
modalities in synesthesia (Werner, 1948).
Syncresis may also obtain between systems,
such as the affective and imaginal fusion implied in the confabulations of dream and
hypnogogic imagery (Silberer, 1951). Syncresis is also a mark of functionally undifferentiated mental forms (e.g., the several
meanings that may be fused in a dream
image but not necessarily in a conscious
thought) and functionally undifferentiated
subject- object relations (e.g., egocentrism).
Orthogenesis is marked by increasing functional discreteness or individuation of systems
of action. Again, this is true for the functional
relationship between subsystems within a system (e.g., the differentiation of various emotions and perceptual modalities during ontogenesis) and between systems (such as the
differentiation of the affective and the imag-

inal). The same holds for mental forms (such as the relatively discrete significance of different conscious thoughts) and subject-object relations (e.g., the differentiation aspect of perspectivism).

The central set of formal coordinates for the structural analysis of development is that of *diffuse* to *articulate*. Lack of structural differentiation and centralization is especially marked by the diffuse organization of parts (individual systems of action) and their lack of integration with the whole (the totality of systems). Structural diffuseness may be between: (1) parts or systems of action such as the "mass activity" of much of the newborn infant's behavior; (2) subsystems within a part or system such as the neonate's general use of his facial muscles, including those controlling the lips, when sucking; (3) parts of mental forms, such as the lack of articulation of the symbols and their referents in word realism (Vygotsky, 1934); and (4) characteristics of the actor-scene ratio; for example, as noted previously, the young child does not articulate well the boundaries between himself and the environment, resulting in relative overestimation of some of his body parts. Progressive structural "transformation of the diffuse into the articulated occurs as a dividing up, a progressive disjunction, of the whole into related parts" (Werner, 1948, p. 54). In particular, structural articulation takes place between: (1) parts or systems of action, such as the differentiated but integrated way in which different parts of the body are used in well executed sports play; (2) subsystems within a system, such as the muscles used in sucking efficiently; (3) parts of mental forms, such as the relative detachment of a symbol from what it refers to in conventional linguistic behavior; and (4) characteristics of the actor-scene relationship, such as the above noted progressive definition of body boundaries in development.

Two other sets of formal coordinates are relevant to the assessment of both structural and functional orthogenesis. These are the dimensions of *rigid* to *flexible* and *labile* to *stable*. At undifferentiated stages of development, mental organization is relatively rigid and yet unstable (Werner, 1948). Differentiation, centralization, and hierarchic integration lead to increased plasticity while insuring new stability of mental organization.

Primitive conduct is rigidly bound to the organism's attitudes. Progressive development is marked by differentiation and hierarchic integration of attitudes so that the organism flexibly (1) attributes differential status—either objectivity or subjectivity—to its various acts and (2) shifts the dominance from one to the other attitude depending upon factors such as organismic needs and environmental demands.

Primitive conduct that is labile is characterized by fluctuation in the self-concept. For example, the young child may think that he and others are transformed in essence by wearing different clothes or by saying they are different animals (e.g., De Vries, 1969). Often his lability is expressed in playful creation of imaginary friends and in playful "splitting" of his own character into a good and a bad self (Werner, 1948). The "good" self may scold the "bad" self, the "bad" self may transform itself into a "good" child, and so on. Development involves progressive stabilization of the self-concept so that the organism no longer acts as if it were being radically transformed or "split" in character but is a differentiated and hierarchically integrated whole. In human ontogenesis this means that the child's self-constructive activity is directed toward (1) differentiating himself as a stable, subjective entity that is discrete from others so that he feels and acts like a distinct individual and at the same time (2) integrating himself as a participant in, and member of his social order, thereby acquiring the same objective status as others. The most advanced forms of individuation involve the conception of oneself as a consciously active operator attributing the status of a relatively subjective character to the self, such as having internal, covert, and psychological character. At the same time it involves the conception of oneself as attributing a relatively objective character to other things, such as having external, overt, and physical character.

Mental Level

Consider for a moment what the utilization of these formal coordinates means for the comparative assessment of whether an organism is operating at a relatively primitive or advanced level. Such an assessment must include a consideration of at least three factors. The first consists of determining which *dimen-*

sional coordinates are relevant. The second is determining the *system of action* that produced the phenomenon to be analyzed. The third is the analysis of the *form* of the particular mental operation involved in the production of the phenomenon.

In order to make the point, it is necessary to recall some exceptional phenomena first, such as John Stuart Mill's writing philosophical treatises at 6 years of age and Mozart's composing music at 4 years. The systems of action that produced these phenomena are something like logical thinking and musical composition. And it could hardly be argued that the developmental level of the systems of action involved was primitive on any of the dimensional coordinates formulated by Werner. In terms of these systems of action, J. S. Mill and Mozart were obviously at advanced stages of development during their childhood, even though they were still at comparatively primitive levels of functioning in terms of their physiological and other aspects of their psychosocial development. This means that a given organism may be operating at many levels of development during the same chronological period of life. There need not be parallel rates of development of all the organism's systems of action.

Now let us recall some more typical phenomena. We are all used to observing rather primitive phenomena in adults in our society. For example, this author recently had to deal with an experienced paint salesman who could only mix paints absolutely by following a given formula and not proportionately by experimenting with the parts. In terms of Werner's formal coordinates, his paint-mixing behavior was rigid and diffuse even though he had spent much of his adult life at it. This is but one anecdote of primitive mental activity in literate adults in a Western culture.

Now consider some documented findings. Kohlberg (1968) reports that about two-thirds of adults in our culture reason at a relatively primitive level of moral judgment, that is, at stages 3 and 4 in Kohlberg's 6-stage scheme. Furthermore, Kramer (1968) presents longitudinal data which show that in some cases level of moral reasoning seems to temporarily slip back during late adolescence. The interpretation of such data is complex and subject to debate. Perhaps the system of moral reasoning actually regresses during late

adolescence to a more primitive stage. On the other hand, the data may mean that (1) the adolescent is more hierarchically integrated and can operate at many moral levels, or (2) these more primitive moral judgments are serving the purposes of another system of action, such as that of conventional mores, which is hierarchically subordinating the moral system, or (3) there is a conceptual syncresis between moral judgments and conventional mores that reflect initial attempts to differentiate and integrate these two forms of reasoning. Resolution of this question requires much additional data on subjects' abilities to appreciate, comprehend, and produce moral reasoning. But the major point is clear: the *potential* (rather than the *actual*) functional stage of an organism's system of action cannot be determined simply from observations of particular phenomenal manifestation of the range of the organism's capacities and of the cognitive structure of the systems involved. (For further discussion along these lines, see Kohlberg, 1968 and Turiel, 1969).

Finally, we should note Kohlberg's (1968) report that Taiwanese Atayals show the following development in their conception of dreams. Like children in our culture, they progress from the notion that dreams are concrete and external to the idea that they are imaginal and internal. However, Atayal adolescents, unlike adolescents in our culture, revert to an idea that dreams are concrete and external. Now it is clear that the Atayals develop advanced notions of dreams during late childhood. Then they seem to regress, perhaps like adolescents in our culture when they are reasoning morally. This would raise the same questions of further diagnosis we have just alluded to.

Before drawing this section to a close it is especially important to reinforce two points. First, in order to inquire into the processes underlying an organism's conduct and achievements it is necessary initially to diagnose adequately the level at which it is functioning. For example, if we presume that the normal human adult always operates contemplatively or logically, then we will misinterpret much of his conduct and profoundly misunderstand its etiology. We will fall into the same type of error if we presume that the behavior patterns of all animals are reactions to stimuli which are shaped by conditioning mechanisms regardless of the phylogenetic and ontogenetic status of the animals.

The second point is that the ascription of a mental phenomenon to one of the stages is without prejudice to its value, whether moral, esthetic, or any other value. Ideally, any psychological phenomenon under scientific consideration should be classifiable by this taxonomic scheme. Its location at a given level is obviously only the result of the comparative organismic perspective underlying this scheme. Its location is therefore meaningful and scientifically useful only in light of this particular comparative organismic perspective, which seems so far to comprehend and tie together a wide range of phenomena; that is, its location has explanatory and heuristic value only within the present theoretical system. However, its location is by no means immutable; if there were a different developmental perspective that constructed a radically different taxonomic scheme, then that same mental phenomenon might be ascribed to a very different developmental location. Which location would be most adequate might then be crucially tested. Unfortunately, from the scientific point of view, radically divergent taxonomic schemes of mental development are not yet available.

The general idea to be drawn from all these considerations is that childhood, nonliterate, and schizophrenic activities are not assumed to be synonymous with primitive stages of development. Nor are adult, literate, and normal activities synonymous theoretically with advanced stages of development.

COMPARATIVE MENTAL DEVELOPMENT

As previously noted, Werner and Kaplan delineate three fundamental evolutionary transformations in the organization of mental activity and their constructed products (see Table 1). These three transformations in mental representation may be taken to reflect the three major stages in the progressive constructivism of biopsychological evolution. These stages form a hierarchy where the most advanced forms of mental activity that arise during the final, most mature stage integrate the more primitive forms that are their precursors.

Neither the theoretical boundaries between the three stages nor the formal criteria for establishing stage boundaries were explicitly spelled out by Werner. Yet there is implicit order from the precursory stages of mental development to their final culmination in the stage of contemplative operations.

Three basic assumptions are made about the genesis of all mental activity. The first is that it is futile to seek the historical origins of mental operations in the absolute sense. A more appropriate theoretical and empirical strategy is to determine the analogous processes that underlie mental activity at different stages of evolution. This is the task of *genetic morphology* (Gesell, 1946.) It requires formal descriptive analyses of the patterns of functioning underlying psychological activity at different stages of evolution so that they may be related developmentally and epistemologically. The second assumption is that analogous but lower-order patterns of functioning are prerequisite to the emergence of higher-order patterns of functioning. The third assumption is that lower-order functional patterns do not ordinarily drop out when higher-order patterns emerge (e.g., Halpern, 1965). Very often they are hierarchically integrated into the emergent, more complex organization with the higher-order functions dominating, centralizing, and regulating the lower-order functional patterns. In his epistemological analysis, Cassirer (1957) comes to much the same conclusion about the history of physics:

. . . physical thinking has risen step by step to ever higher areas. . . . Each higher stage of objectivization sets a limit to the preceding stage; but in this limitation it does not destroy the earlier phase; rather it embraces it in its own perspective (p. 477).

This means that primitive systems may continue to develop and that they are integrated in the form they attain during a given stage of development rather than the form they took in the stage in which they originated.

As far as human ontogenesis is concerned it is clear that man primarily passes through the two most advanced stages outlined in Table 1. Werner's developmental characterization of man therefore focused upon the extremes of these two stages in order to clarify the most primitive and most mature forms of functioning:

In advanced forms of mental activity we observe thought processes which are quite detached from the concrete sensorimotor, perceptual and affective type. In the primitive mentality, however, thought processes always appear as more or less perfectly fused with functions of a sensori-motor and affective type. It is this absence of a strict separation of thought proper from perception, emotion and motor action which determines the significance of so-called concrete and affective thinking. Concrete and affective thinking are therefore characteristic examples of syncretic activity (1948, p. 213).

Much less attention was given to formulating a consistent set of intermediate, transitional stages that comprehensively take into account the variety of mental developments. Instead the transitional stages were loosely united into a larger stage of intuitive or perceptual representation. This is not to imply that Werner completely neglected the taxonomic task of working out the transitional stages. However, his efforts along these lines were restricted to establishing transitional stages of specific mental activities, such as the intuitive construction of spatial concepts. Werner did not attempt to formulate precisely general transitional stages that, for example, simultaneously encompass the construction of the fundamental cognitive concepts such as space, time, number, and causality.

The orthogenetic relationship of the three major stages of mental construction is such that the most advanced contemplative systems hierarchically integrate the more primitive sensorimotor and intuitive systems, when all three systems have developed in an organism. It is highly unlikely, for example, that adult humans ever construct a pristine percept that is untinged by any contemplative operation. This means, however, that perceptual or intuitive representation is not only a stage of development but one of three parallel systems of action that may develop into the most mature (differentiated and hierarchically integrated) organization possible. Consequently, development may be schematized, according to Werner, as a three-branched tree like that in Fig. 1.

The parallel branch model is consistent with the idea of spiral development. This principle suggests parallel development be-

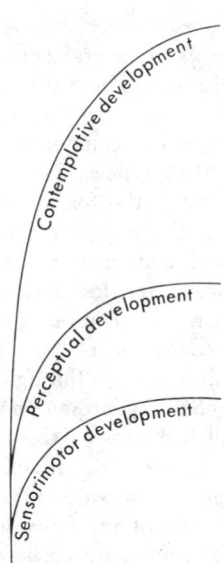

tween stages and systems of action from an initial state of egocentrism to a final state of perspectivism within each stage. The general theoretical hypothesis may be summed up as follows: Not only is there development *between* stages and systems of action (that may be measured along formal dimensions such as egocentrism to perspectivism) but parallel progress *within* any one stage and system of action (that should be measurable on the same dimensions). A major theoretical task that Werner began, then, is to work out the comparative development of each psychological stage and system of action from its most primitive manifestations to its most sophisticated forms. For example, with respect to perceptual representation, Werner hypothesized that:

In both microgenesis and ontogenesis the formation of percepts seems, in general, to go through an orderly sequence of stages. Perception is first global; whole qualities are dominant. The next stage might be called analytic; perception is selectively directed towards parts. The final stage might be called synthetic; parts become integrated with respect to the whole (1957, pp. 127–128).

The theme that runs through this developmental analysis is that the human psychological world in particular is not a reflected reality that merely mirrors the physical and social environment. Rather, it is a representational reality or product that is constructed by man's means of mental action that serve to achieve his ends. These constructed products or representations are the core of human mental life. They are composed of two reciprocal schematizing aspects (Werner and Kaplan, 1963). One is the formation of symbols (ranging from the imaginal and gestural to the verbal and mathematical) that conceptualize, depict, refer to, and communicate cognized experience. The other is the formation of cognized experience, including feelings, percepts, and concepts, through representation. Throughout the presentation that is to come we will first present the general schematizing or representational activity central to each stage. Then we will consider the symbolic and objectifying functions that mark each stage. The strategic basis for this theoretical analysis is summed up by Cassirer:

With the dissection of phenomenal reality into presentative and representative factors, into the representing and the represented, a new motif is acquired which operates with increasing force and henceforth determines the entire movement of theoretical consciousness (Cassirer, 1957, p. 142).

Precursory Acts

Werner (1948, p. 59) contends that the classification of development on the basis of a content analysis "is quite inadequate for the analysis of primitive psychic events" because "primitive mental life . . . reveals a relatively limited differentiation of object and subject, of perception and pure feeling, of idea and action, etc." The products of primitive mental constructions are basically global phenomena in which vital physiological, motoric, affective, and sensory processes are fused. In support of this contention, Werner summarizes the evidence from many studies on form discrimination in dogs. These studies show that their usual facility for form discrimination, such as between a circle and a triangle, is debilitated when the dogs' physical movements are restricted. The facilitative effect of physical movements in lowering visual recognition thresholds in adult humans (Miller, 1963; Dowling, 1965) provides reciprocal evidence.

Werner was particularly impressed by the dynamic character of primitive mental life:

The high degree of unity between subject and object mediated by the motor-affective reactivity of the organism results in a dynamic, rather than static, apprehension of things (1948, p. 67).

He cites phylogenetic evidence, such as the frog ignoring prey that does not move, and ontogenetic evidence, such as the neonate's greater responsiveness to suckable objects if they are moved suddenly. Werner (1948, p. 69) hypothesizes that it is the "dynamization of things based on the fact that the objects are predominantly understood through the motor and affective attitude of the subject" that underlies the lack of differentiating animate from nonanimate events. This is why some inanimate objects will be perceived immediately as animate or expressing "some inner form of life." It is this immediate dynamic mode of mental activity that he called *physiognomic* in order to distinguish it from the more matter-of-fact, *geometric-technical* mode of cognition. The physiognomic mode of mental activity lies at the heart of subjective constructions, that is, the individual's mythical, magical, and esthetic cognitions; whereas the geometric-technical mode represents the direction that the individual's objective constructions take, that is, his physical, social, and logical cognitions. Syncresis of these two modes is characteristic of primitive mental acts and their products. Their differentiation and synthesis in contemplative operations mark the potential richness and creativity of mature mental acts and their products.

Werner extends his contention that primitive mental life is the global product of fused functions to the hypothesis that even the different sensory modalities are relatively undifferentiated at primitive stages of development. Consequently, a given stimulus, such as a sound, is more likely to evoke other impressions, such as color and warmth, rather than its corresponding auditory sensation. An example of such undifferentiated, *synesthetic* experiences, cited by Werner, is that of 3-year-old Bubi Scupins saying that "The leaf smells green" and "That [a lilac] smells awfully nice and yellow." It is Werner's hypothesis that such expressions are not the result of the young child's linguistic inadequacy but an "actual undifferentiated experience of sensation." It should be noted that an adequate ontogenetic test of this hypothesis has still not been devised. Werner further hypotheizes that:

. . . synaesthesia as a primordial form of sensory experience may reappear as a consequence of a pathologically conditioned primitivation (1948, p. 92).

Primitive concrete action is characterized by *"immediacy, limited motivation, and lack of planning"* (Werner, 1948, p. 191). Personal motives do not play a role in primitive action. Primitive action is "set in motion by vital drives on the one hand, and the concrete signals of the milieu on the other" (Werner, 1948, p. 194). This is true for much of animal and infant behavior. For example, animals learn mazes more rapidly when hungry and infants learn how to find objects more easily if it is rewarding.

Primitive mental activity lacks the specificity and direction that is the mark of abstract intentional planning. Werner cites C. Buhler's finding that infants are even unable to master a situation such as that requiring brushing away a cloth which has been laid on their faces. Only about 25% of infants at the age of 1½ months show any purposeful movements directed toward getting rid of the cloth; only about 50% of the movements are purposeful even at 4½ months; and the majority of purposeful manipulations become successful at the age of 7 months.

The uncoordinated, global character of primitive mental activity means that representation does not yet articulate ". . . partial goals, the one following the other in succession. . . . There is a single goal which can be realized only in the totality of the course of the action" (Werner, 1948, p. 201). Eventually this diffuseness gives way to the individuation of the global activity, with parts of the body acquiring specific functions. The same is true of global goals. As they become increasingly volitional and representational they involve a routine with subparts. Each subpart has relative independence from its predecessor so that the whole does not necessarily have to be run through in an unbroken, rigid, and stereotyped fashion. Central control is achieved so that parts no longer have equal value and nonessential acts are subordinated

to essential acts. As an example, Werner cites Zeigarnik's findings that the disruption of an activity is a much more vivid experience for children than adults and leaves a stronger memory impression.

Uncoordinated acts are marked by the lack of integration between different movements that will eventually become coordinated parts of a larger whole, for example, hand-eye coordination. Lack of well established "syntactic relation" between parts accounts for the greater difficulty that children have with classical problem solving tasks that require coordination between partial instruments and acts. Progressively, this rigidity of action gives way to a plasticity of the external character of action and the inner motivations and goals of the actor. Thus the child can increasingly modify his behavior flexibly to accord with his representational assessment of the situation in which he finds himself.

The immediate, presentational character of primitive action is most evident in the global, helpless, and noninstrumental movements of the neonate. The immediate, presentational character of primitive action is also apparent in the difficulty young children and chimpanzees have in dealing with problem situations that require circuitous behavior, such as extending a rake through bars beyond a desired object in order to haul it in. Such observations are important because perhaps the most striking indication that cognition is becoming representational and conceptual is the evolution of circuitous behavior since a "mark of the release of the subject from the domination of the concrete field is the extension of the action beyond the visibly given field" (Werner, 1948, p. 194). Werner cites the following evidence: Chickens (Révész, 1921) and sea gulls do not seek food that they have seen hidden while crows and jackdaws (Hertz, 1926, 1928) are more like higher vertebrates such as apes (Tinkelpaugh, 1928), who will search for and recognize food that they have perceived being hidden. The human infant only begins to search for and recognize an object hidden in front of him at about 9 months of age (Buhler, 1931) and shows some freedom of action to retrieve hidden objects at 13 months (Stern, 1930). Cassirer states the case for the immense epistemological significance of this developmental phenomenon for the construction of organized mental life—for representation and conception—most elegantly:

This act of recognition is necessarily bound up with the function of representation and presupposes it. Only where we succeed, as it were, in compressing a total phenomenon into one of its factors, in concentrating it symbolically, in "having" it in a state of "pregnance" in the particular factor—only then do we raise it out of the stream of temporal change; only then does its existence, which had hitherto seemed confined to a single moment in time, gain a kind of permanence: for only then does it become possible to find again in the simple, as it were, punctual "here" and "now" of present experience a "not-here" and a "not-now." Everything that we call the identity of concepts and significations, or the constancy of things and attributes, is rooted in this fundamental act of finding-again. . . . But here there is a demand that consciousness —contrary to its fundamental character, contrary to the Heraclitean flux in which alone it seems to subsist—shall step twice, in fact many times, into the same river. Transcending objective time and experienced time, it must seize upon a permanent and stable content and posit it as identical with its self. Identifications of this kind—even if they do no more than establish and postulate purely sensuous qualities—contain the germ and beginning of every form of concept formation. For the identity or similarity which we apprehend in two different and temporally separate impressions is itself no mere impression that is added to the others and simply embeds itself in the same plane with them. If something that is given here and now is taken and recognized as a "this,"—if for example it is recognized as a certain shade of red or as a tone of a certain pitch—we already have to do with a genuinely "reflective" factor (1957, pp. 114–115).

Presentational Symbols. Even as they originate in the mental activity of the operating subject, symbols are not merely substitute signs that are originally learned as arbitrary and conventional labels for things. Rather, at first symbols inhere in and express or signal the thing-of-action construction of the objects they serve to determine, refer to, and represent:

For the analysis of sensory appearance showed that its very *appearing,* its presentation is impossible without an ordered and articulated system of purely representative functions. . . . Without the relations of unity and otherness, of similarity and dissimilarity, of identity and difference, the world of intuition can acquire no fixed form; but these relations themselves belong to the makeup of this world only to the extent that they are *conditions* for it, and not parts of it (Cassirer, 1957, p. 300).

Werner and Kaplan (1963) hypothesize that the original ontogenetic situation out of which the representational function develops is what they call the *primordial sharing situation.* In this situation the human infant is "sharing" rather than "communicating" an experience (the object of reference) with another person, usually the mother. That is, the primordial sharing situation is a sensorimotor affective "pre-symbolic situation in which there is little differentiation in the child's experience between himself, the other (typically the mother), and the referential object" (p. 42). The precursory components for symbolization, however, are present. Together, the mother and child are sharing the same thing. What is still necessary is that the child must differentiate and integrate the primordial sharing situation—himself, from objects of reference, from his means of symbolic communication, from his communicants (others) —so that his symbols represent his objects of reference in a communicative fashion to both others and himself.

Werner and Kaplan (1963) present the following sequence in the ontogenesis of reference. The first sign that the child is referring himself to a thing and/or indicating it to another is *reaching* (not grasping) outward. This is a concrete action (and possibly affective) indicator that there is a thing which is distant from the child's body toward which he is reaching. At the same time, the child begins to use *call-sounds* that accompany straining movements of his body toward things beyond his reach. These call sounds are the first manifestations of vocal demonstratives. The next step takes place when the child begins *touching* things at a distance from himself in order to indicate it to himself or others. The third step, that of *turning for looking* or turning toward things in order to refer to or indicate them, leads quickly into *pointing*. This becomes the human's specialized motor-gestural symbolic form of reference. During this same period the child begins to use specific forms of *vocal denotation* such as "da." These vocal denotatives are used both independently and in concert with pointing. Finally, the child begins to use truly *verbal demonstratives* such as "this" and "that." Again, verbal demonstratives are used together with and separately from pointing.

Two theoretical points are made about the developmental sequence of motor pragmatic or practical means of reference. First, the sequence follows the orthogenetic principle of progressive differentiation and articulation of global action patterns. The gross bodily movements used in reaching become progressively refined and articulate in form from a gross bodily movement to one in which the outstretched forefinger assumes the configuration of a pointer. Second, the sequence follows the organismic principle governing means-ends or form-function relations. At first the function of reference is tied syncretically to forms like reaching and touching, that primarily serve other functions. Eventually a specialized form (means), that of pointing, is shaped out of the percursory forms as if it were a tool designed specifically to serve the reference function (end).

Primitive symbolic forms of depicting referents are first constructed in the bodily and vocal medium and are presentational cognitions. Even a presentational symbol

. . . has a kind of transparency; an inner life shines through its very existence and facticity. The formation effected in language, art, and myth starts from this original phenomenon of expression; indeed, both art and myth remain so close to it that one might be tempted to restrict them wholly to this sphere. High as myth and art may rise, they remain on the soil of primary, "primitive" expressive experiences. Language, it is true, discloses the new turn, the transition to a new dimension, more clearly than the other two; we cannot doubt its connection with the world of expression. There is always a certain expressive value, a certain "physiognomic" character in words, even in those of highly developed language (Cassirer, 1957, p. 449).

The ontogenetic foundations of the representational function are those motor-gestural expressions that are marked by material similarity and spatiotemporal proximity between the symbolic and referential forms. These presentational symbols are the precursors of the linguistic and mathematical symbols that eventually develop. Material similarity and spatiotemporal proximity are first clearly apparent in the baby's motoric and vocal reactions or *co-actions*. For example, 5-month-old babies who get pleasure out of seeing a person in front of them rocking are capable of doing the same in order to make the interesting spectacle last. Co-action is a transitory expressive form toward true *imitative depiction* which

. . . comes into play only when the expression and the presented content are to some extent differentiated—on two different dimensions as it were. In the early movements of the child, there is an affective-sensory-motor unity: expressive movement does not "refer" to or represent the affective content but rather includes this content in the reactive pattern (Werner and Kaplan, 1963, p. 85).

At root, true imitative gestures are still presentational symbols even when some material difference is introduced. For example, a child may imitate the flickering of a light by fluttering his eyelids. Or he may imitate vocally the heard characteristics of objects or his own action. An example of depiction by such naturalistic onomatopoetic expressions used by a child 17 months old is *f-f-f* to designate a match stick because that is the sound of blowing when putting it out (Werner and Kaplan, 1963). This still involves a realistic pattern that presents the content the child is referring to. This is even true of anticipatory gestures such as making sucking and biting movements or sounds such as *num-num* in order to indicate the desire for liquid or food. Now there is a distinct increase in material differentiation and spatiotemporal distancing between the symbols and their referents. Yet they are still primarily pragmatic, presentational symbols.

The transition between presentational and truly representational vocal gestures takes place when the vocal patterns *analogically depict* referents that do not have any sound properties. Here there is greater material differentiation between the symbols and their referents than in onomatopoesis. Werner and Kaplan (1963) cite many examples, including an 18-month-old boy who called all round, rolling objects such as balls, coins, and rings *golloh*. Werner and Kaplan call these symbolic forms physiognomic and suggest that they are the genetic basis for sound or phonetic symbolism. Werner and Kaplan analyze four transitional forms between the natural depictive forms (onomatopoetic and physiognomic) and conventional forms of designation:

1. Assimilation of an onomatopoetic expression to the conventional linguistic code; for example, one French child went from using *bum* as an onomatopoetic expression for the noise of things dropped to the verb *bumer* to designate "to fall."
2. Composite forms in which a part is an infantile idiomatic expression and a part is conventional; for example, an 18-month-old boy called hammering *poch* which he transformed into *pochmaker* in order to designate workman.
3. Combinatory forms composed of both an idiomatic and a conventional name, such as *bah-sheep* and *shu-shu train*.
4. The child responds with his own idiomatic expression when asked to repeat a conventional word, such as *tah* for spoon and *peep-peep* for chicken.

Things-of-Action. The objects of cognition constructed by primitive mental activity do not have contemplative or abstract quality. For this reason they are not considered to be intuitive or conceptual constructs of mental operations but things-of-action. Thus Werner argues that the mental life of the very young child "can be understood only through the assumption that the motor-emotional and sensory factors are blended into one another." His mental constructs are things-of-action:

If it is admitted that the things of the child world are created as much by his motor-affective activity as by objective stimuli, it becomes intelligible, for instance, why a child can seriously consider a few wisps of straw to be a doll or a bit of wood to be a horse. (Werner, 1948, p. 65).

This hypothesis also fits some of the primitive behavior of brain-damaged patients. Werner notes, for example, that such patients cannot recognize a key in the abstract but may immediately recognize and name it when it is inserted and turned in a lock, that is, when it becomes a thing-of-action.

It is possible, following Werner, to distinguish for analytic purposes the products (constructs) of undifferentiated mental acts into "things-of-action" when referring to their object character and into "signal-things" when referring to their expressive and communicative character. Thus, boxes and chairs are different kinds of "signal-things" for dogs. Sarris (cited in Werner, 1948) performed the following experiment. A dog was trained to jump on a chair and sit on it at the command "Chair!" and to go and lie down in a basket at the command "Basket!" When the dog was presented with a box that was open at the top, he lay down in it when commanded "Basket." Anything that he could get into and lie down in had the "signal-quality" of basket. He did not respond to the command "Basket" when that same box was covered with a lid. At that point he only responded to the command "Chair" by jumping up and sitting on it. The signal-qualities for the dog were obviously guided by the actions he could perform on it.

Things-of-action are diffusely organized; they are not well articulated as discrete parts of the total environment; and they are rigidly dependent upon the whole constellation of the concrete, sensorimotor, and affective field. Werner cites, for example, the behavior of the spider (*Tegeneria domestica*) waiting for prey. Its behavior is rigid—it will only attack a fly caught in the outer meshes of the web—and diffuse—it will attack any object that vibrates, such as a tuning fork, even if it is not food, and not attack appropriate prey like a fly if it is stationary. This diffuse and inflexible character of sensorimotor products means that they are not articulated as objects that have essential and variable characteristics. They lack the permanence which is prerequisite for a stable, conceptual construction of the field:

A necessary prerequisite for the constant object is an articulation of the concrete field to the end that constant elements making up the object will be experienced in sharp contradistinction to the variable elements (Werner, 1948, p. 108).

The frog may starve to death if his prey is in front of him but static, when he has been conditioned to react to a particular motion. Such rigidity of behavior could not happen beyond the earliest period of the child's development. The reason for this is that in human ontogenesis things begin to be flexibly articulated at around 9 months of age. Consequently, they acquire a permanent "objective" form which is preserved across transformations of nonessential characteristics.

Permanence is only possible where things are abstracted out of their momentary, concrete action context and embedded in a minimal representational network. This network must include some construction of a stable spatial sense:

The "permanence" of the thing is bound up with the stability of . . . spatial unities. We judge that a thing is precisely this one and continues to be so, chiefly by designating its place in intuitive space as a whole (Cassirer, 1957, p. 142).

According to Werner, the most primitive sense of space is "syncretically bound" to the practical activity of the subject. It is therefore a subjective construction that is "physiognomic-dynamic" and "rooted in the concrete and substantial"—it is a "space-of-action." In human ontogenesis space is first known through bodily action, particularly the mouth's sucking on the things with which it comes into contact. It is therefore a transient space of immediate action. Growing out of this, in a few weeks, is "a space-of-nearness, of propinquity, in which the space surrounding the body becomes differentiated from the body proper" (Werner, 1948, p. 173). The infant's space becomes bounded by that which he can reach, touch, and see. The limits expand in distance as the infant's visual capacities increase but space still remains a space-of-relative nearness as long as he cannot locomote on his own power. In this sense, the knowledge of space remains a strictly presentational cognition. And his knowledge

or objectification of things in general remains that of a strictly presentational and pragmatic permanence.

Transitional Acts

The mental acts and products that are transitional between precursory and advanced mental life involve many of the features that are characteristic of both. They stand midway between, and are functionally analogous to and partially isomorphic with both concrete presentational and abstract representational phenomena. First of all, they have vestigial presentational characteristics, transitional mental activity being diffusely organized. In ontogenesis this is especially evident when we examine the child's drawing and melodic activities, whether they are spontaneous or copies. Their parallel diffuse organization is summarized in Table 2, as outlined by Werner (1948, pp. 122; 127–128).

Diffuse perceptual intuitions are characterized by three central features (Werner, 1948, pp. 128–135). The first is a sensitivity to transformations in the external environment and a corresponding lack of identity and conservation judgments. For example, the child may not recognize his parents if they are wearing new clothes. Corroborating evidence on intuitive identity judgments comes from a study calling for verbal judgments (Sigel, Saltz, and Roskind, 1967). Only 42% of 5- and 6-year-olds' responses are positive to questions such as "This father studied and became a doctor. Is he still a father?" Even at the ages of 7 and 8 not all the responses (only 71%) are positive. The second characteristic is lability. Often, for example, the young child changes the meaning of what he is drawing, what he is building with blocks, and even what the words he is using mean as his activity proceeds (Werner and Kaplan, 1952). Indeed, he does not intentionally begin to plan his activity is advance until he is about 4 or 5 years old. The third feature of perceptual intuitions is rigid conservatism or traditionalism. The young child, for example, is likely to insist that the parts of a game be repetitively repeated in a strict order.

Physiognomization is still at the heart of much of perceptual intuition, such as when one young child said "Poor, tired cup" upon observing a cup lying on its side (Werner,

Table 2. Parallels in Primitive Perceptual-Motor Activity

Graphic Activity	Tonal Activity
A tendency toward homogeneity and greater diffuseness may be revealed:	We may enumerate parallel trends in the tonal and graphic patterns:

Graphic Activity

1. In the strong emphasis on qualities-of-the-whole:
   a. Making a figure more uniform, indivisible: □ → O
   b. Closing an open figure: ⊃ → ⊙

2. In the homogeneization of directions and parts by:
   a. Making parts alike: ⊣ → ⊣⊢

   b. Simplifying directions: ✳ → ⟋

   c. Using Symmetry: S → C

Tonal Activity

1. Expression of the "quality-of-the-whole":
   a. Continuity: The "glissando" characteristic in the singing of very young infants tends to disappear with older children, but a marked inclination to increase the continuity of the original pattern remains in the event of large tonal intervals ("leveling tendency").
   b. Tonal closure: The tendency to a closure of the "open figures" in the drawings is translated here into a tendency to finish with a low note, as the note *par excellence*, rather than with the actual middle note.

2. Homogeneity of direction and parts:
   a. Parts are made more alike (see as examples above the two copies of Motif II).
   b. Simplification of direction: If the melodic movement is strongly articulated like this (♩♪♩♩) it will tend toward simplification into this:(♪♩♪♩)
   c. "Symmetrization" of ascending and descending parts frequently occurs whenever the model is asymmetrical:

      (♩♪♩♩) becomes (♩♪♪♩)

   (Aside from these deviations on a purely melodic basis obvious changes occur which follow a tendency to simplify the harmonic relationship.)

1948). Such physiognomization retains the relatively immediate, direct quality of presentational experience when compared with mediated, as-if constructions, such as in acts of personification:

Nature when known physiognomically is alive throughout, not because the soul, the vitality, is invested in the inanimate object, but rather because everything is understood to behave dynamically, quite apart from and prior to the differentiation between object and subject (Werner, 1948, p. 80).

Just as perceptual intuition is infused with affect during this transitional phase, so emotional experience is still relatively fused syncretically with somatic and perceptual-motor activity. Werner cites, as an example, the exclamation of a 4-year-old girl when given new clothes: "The beautiful clothes. I'm happy right in the bottom of my stomach!" And at a later age: "Oh, you're so wide when

you're happy!" Another important feature of the syncresis of the perceptual and the affective aspects of transitional mental activity is the fusion of ethical with esthetic judgments. Werner notes that it is not unusual for young children to identify "ugly" with "unjust" and "beautiful" with "good." Even adults often engage in the kind of borderline mental activity where they syncretically fuse "white" with "good" qualities and "black" with "bad" qualities.

The other side to perceptual intuitions is that they begin to exhibit precursory aspects of the abstract, representational features of the contemplative acts that fully develop during the next stage. For example:

In the construction of every spatial intuition, of every apprehension of spatial forms, of every judgment as to the position, magnitude, distance of objects, the individual experiences "weave themselves into the whole." In order to be spatially determined in relation to the whole, every spatial content must be referred to and interpreted according to certain typical spatial configurations. These interpretations, as effected in the sign language of sense perception, may be regarded as primary achievements of the concept (Cassirer, 1957, p. 286).

The general hypothesis is that intuitive interpretations and representations begin to

. . . articulate the individual and particular into a determinate totality, and in the particular they see a representation of this totality itself. As intuitive knowledge progresses along this path, each of its particular contents gains greater power to represent the totality of the others and to make it indirectly "visible." If we take this representation as a characteristic determinant of the function of the concept as such, there can be no doubt that the worlds of perception and spatio-temporal intuition can nowhere dispense with this function (Cassirer, 1957, p. 286).

The appearance of even rudimentary abstract features is dependent upon increasing subject-object differentiation and the initial development of perspectivism. The child begins to recognize that people may perceive the same event in different ways. He also begins to be able to look at the same event from different perspectives and adopt the point of view of others. However, he will not be able to integrate fully these different perspectives into a coherent world view or ideology until he reaches the truly abstract representational stage.

Progressive subject-object differentiation leads to intuition becoming more circuitous; less immediate mediational means (instruments and devices) are developed for achieving ends. At first this is seen in ontogenesis when children use parts of their body as instruments to deal with and master situations. Lewin's film of a 3-year-old child climbing on a stone and only then turning around in order to sit down demonstrates that even a simple, circuitous perceptual-motor act does not develop until well into childhood. The "increasing specificity of the subjective factor," as compared to objective factors in the determination of conduct, marks the "emergence of a specifically personal motivation"

that is "revealed in the growing intention and complexity of purely personal motives" (Werner, 1948, pp. 191; 194). Werner cites the following kind of evidence. A 2½-year-old child will have no difficulty performing a task (removing every second object in a series) if it has valence for him (each second object is a piece of candy). He will have difficulty with the same task if it has no valence for him (pasteboard coins). As the child begins to recognize that objectivity is dependent upon his own conduct he develops planful behavior. Illustrative of the child's growing capacity to anticipate the end effect of his action is his naming of what he is drawing (see Table 3, from Werner, 1948, p. 198).

Protosymbols. Human mentality reaches the level of abstract concepts through representation—through language and the naming process. However, abstract conceptual representation has its basis in the more primitive symbolic forms of stages "where language itself is identified with concrete action and where names are fused with objects they denote" (Werner, 1948, p. 254). In primitive symbolization names are material parts of the things they represent (e.g., word magic) and are sometimes conceived of as things themselves (Cassirer, 1953). Werner (1948) suggests the following developmental basis of symbolization:

In the physiognomic world the name is not a mere instrument of sound behind which there is meaning. The word, by virtue of its concrete physiognomy, is directly related to the object itself. Or it may even go beyond this because the word, in so far as it shares the physiognomy of the objects, is an integral part of this subject (p. 263).

Table 3. Early Age Levels at Which Objects Are Named in Drawing (After Hetzer)

Age (Years)	Not Named	Named Afterward	Named While Being Drawn	Named Prior to Being Drawn
3	90	10	0	0
4	18	9	37	36
5	0	0	20	80
6	0	0	0	100

Figures refer to percentage of cases.

Expressive physiognomic qualities that are intersensory in character may exist in the sounds articulated in the human voice . . . language itself has a physiognomic quality . . . language is the most flexible and refined instrument for expressing the dynamic-motor aspect of the objective world (p. 257).

[Eventually] names are no longer thought of as concrete and physiognomic in nature, as constituent parts of objects proper; they gradually achieve the status of symbols substituting for the objects themselves. At the same time the physiognomic quality of words may still remain as the sensuous ground from which the abstract meaning draws its vitality (p. 264).

Werner (1948) makes three points about the developmental relations of general concepts and symbols. The first is that primitive symbolization is characterized by a multiplicity of particular terms and a scarcity of general terms. The second is that it remains an open question whether or not preliterate people possess general ideas even when they are not explicitly expressed in their language. Generalization may be implicitly expressed in their language when there is no explicit expression. The third is that we may find a multiplicity of particulars and a scarcity of generalities even at advanced levels of mentality:

The difference between lower and more advanced societies does not consist of the fact that primitive forms of behavior are absent in the latter, but rather that the more primitive the society the greater the homogeneity and the consequent dominance of primitive behavior. As the society advances the stratifications of mental form stand out with increasing clarity (p. 271).

The underlying tenet about the emergence and development of mental processes is the principle of spiral development: all novel psychological functions are first actualized through the use of forms serving genetically prior functions. As applied specifically to the ontogeny of symbolization, this general tenet leads to the specific assumption that the function of linguistic representation emerges from and is rooted in prelinguistic, gestural, and intonational forms of symbolization. On the basis of this assumption, it is possible to order genetically analogous manifestations of the symbolic function in terms of the transformations in the form to function relations which these manifestations undergo during the transitional stage from (1) the initial prelinguistic state of syncretic symbolization where the expressive forms of gesture and intonation serve both the functions of representing some referent and the attitude (orientation, feeling, and conation) toward the referent, toward (2) the linguistic state of discrete symbolization where the representative function achieves the autonomy necessary to the development of a form—a medium of representation such as language—that uniquely serves its ends, such as reference, designation, and predication.

As the child begins to construct extended verbal expressions to communicate about events during this intermediate stage, these

. . . messages become increasingly differentiated and articulated, so that distinct aspects of an expression come specifically to represent distinct aspects of a complex state of affairs, such as the intent of the speaker, the different components of the situation, and so on (Werner and Kaplan, 1963, p. 31).

There are two major aspects to messages, according to Werner and Kaplan (1963). The first is the "attitudinal mode" of the message, that is, whether the intent is to command, declare, question, and so on. The other aspect is what the message signifies, that it, whether the reference is to oneself, another object, a concept, and so on. The prelinguistic, gestural, and intonational means of symbolization employed during the initial mental stage permit only some diffuse expression of attitude, such as the desire for contact or demand. They do not usually permit differentiated and integrated representation of the "three major components of a situation (self-other-object)."

The child's bodily or vocal symbols that no longer simply express an attitude but also refer to situations are said to be *monoremes*. At first, monoremes represent syncretically a fusion of attitude and reference. They are more like prelinguistic expressions, such as call-sounds that point to desiderata. Monoremic expression should be easiest to determine when the child's symbolic orientation is declarative; for example, when a child points at something and says *da* (there). Even then, however, the declarative aspect of the symbol is at best hypothetical and implicit.

The duration of the monoremic stage lasts from about six months to a year. According to Werner and Kaplan (1963, pp. 136–137), it is marked by two notable developments, an "increase in the *variety* of vocal forms" produced by the child in order to articulate the communicative, referential, and depictive moments of the speech situation, and a progressive differentiation of the nature of monoremes. The intonational variations in the child's monoremic symbols express "some degree of differentiation among attitudes but . . . not . . . differentiation between important elements of the situation, such as direction towards addressee and object of discourse." Toward the end of the monoremic stage,

the child produces monoremes in which such aspects of the situation as orientation toward an addressee and reference to an object of discourse are differentiated respectively by intonation and gesture, on one hand, and by the form of the vocable, on the other exact citation.

This movement reflects one of the major laws of development, the genetic principle of *shift of function*. The child is using his well-established expressive forms of "intonation and gesture for novel functions" such as indicating his attitude; and his vocal forms progressively become speech units or "names" that represent objects of reference.

It is not until the child reaches the two-vocable or *duoremic* stage that we may be sure that the child's intent is explicitly declarative. Now, the function of his verbal forms shifts from "names" to "words":

A name becomes a word only insofar as it fulfills a grammatical and syntactic function in an utterance, a function beyond its role as designator of something (Werner and Kaplan, 1963, p. 138).

Words, unlike names, are always parts of sentences. Words and sentences co-emerge in development. When vocables become words, then their referents become increasingly delimited. Werner and Kaplan cite an example from one of Gregoire's children. When the child was at the monoremic stage he used *bum* to refer to all events in which a loud, abrupt sound played a significant part. Later the child used *bum* or *popot* (porte, door) as holophrastic names to refer to door-closing or door-being-closed. When the child advanced to the two vocable stage he produced *bum-popot,* such that he delimited banging sound as the distinctive referent of *bum* and door as the referent of *popot*. These distinctively delimited representational relationships "become fixed and stabilized as the child uses them as pivot forms, as in *bum-sonnette* and *ouvrez-porte*."

A second, related aspect of the progressive differentiation of reference at the two-vocable stage is specification or "the ontogenetic change from vocables having a vague, over-inclusive referent to vocables having a definite more clearly specified referent" (Werner and Kaplan, 1963, p. 142). The most significant function of specification "for linguistic articulation of noun-verb relationships" is categorization of represented events, particularly into things and actions. Werner and Kaplan cite an example from Leopold. At 17 months a child used *auto* to represent the object in motion. At 19 months she began to use action terms (such as *choo-choo* to refer to motion) in combination with thing terms (such as *train* and *auto*) to produce two-vocable phrases (such as *choo-choo-train* and *choo-choo-auto*).

The categorical function of specification is "correlative with the integrative trend toward the structuring of sentences." At the beginning of the two-vocable or duoremic stage "*integration* is very concretely assured through the referential *overlap* of the two vocables." Werner and Kaplan cite the example of a child who says *da-digda*, where *da* refers to "there" and *digda* to "clock" and both refer to the totality of the sounding clock. The first form of integration then reflects overlapping or holophrastic reference.

Integration is also assured by the external, vehicular aspect of symbols. Werner and Kaplan hypothesize that one major means that the child uses to achieve sentence integration is intonation. During the monoremic stage intonation serves to designate the child's attitude, orientation, and emotion. During the duoremic stage its function changes to ensuring initial integration of words. Werner and Kaplan suggest two developmental steps in intonational integration. The first is even or monotonous stress where the child produces both vocables with the same intonation. The second step occurs when the child uses uneven stress so that the intensity, pitch, or duration of the intonation is different for the two words. The use of intonation as a means of representation reflects two major developmental principles: (1) the genetic principle of shift of function, here, the shift in the function of intonation from designation to sentence integration; and (2) the genetic principle of spiral development, here, "the temporary return to more primitive means of representation, such as intonation . . . when realizing more complex acts of mentation" (Werner and Kaplan, 1963, p. 132).

A major function of speech, particularly in its sentence form, is the construction and expression of predicative judgments or assertions. The earliest ontogenetic predications are judgments of identification:

In explicit verbal manifestation, these judgments take the form "this (pointing) is a B" or "A is a B." The earliest forms of identifying predications occur in situations in which the child "names" a presented content (Werner and Kaplan, 1963, p. 160).

Eventually, in later stages of development when the child has well developed his capacities for conventional sentential designation "identifying predications subserve class inclusion and exclusion: one asserts that 'A is a B' or 'A is not a B'" (Werner and Kaplan, 1963, p. 162). Before the child can produce judgments and predications of actions (by an agent) and of attribution (of a quality to a thing) he must be able "to distinguish between thing and some state of thing within a global, concrete happening." Then he must distinguish between states of action ("doing") and attribution ("belonging to").

Werner and Kaplan outline four sequential steps in the formation of predication or symbolic judgment:

(1) The earliest pre-predicative . . . utterances are, both referentially and linguistically, of an undifferentiated character, that is, they are monoremic. (2) Next come two-vocable utterances which are initially a junction of monoremes, in which each denotes the same event, while connoting somewhat different aspects of it . . . —a loose joining of relatively separate vocables. (3) At a later stage of the two-vocable utterances, the units become relatively distinct in reference and are eventually linked together in an intonational hypotaxis (uneven stress)—indicating that one referent is in some way dependent upon the other. (4) Finally, specific morphological means, such as form-words, come into play to establish integration of the vocables entirely within the linguistic medium per se; at this point "sentences" are fully established and, correlatively, so are "words" (1963, pp. 168–169).

The final major function that speech begins to serve in this intermediate stage is the formation and expression of "relations between thoughts." Werner and Kaplan hypothesize two ontogenetic phases:

. . . whereas the structures of the earlier utterances, depictive of the order of pragmatic-perceptual happenings, are closely tied to, and interwoven with, concrete contexts, later utterances are increasingly freed from contextual embeddedness; this decontextualization of speech goes hand in hand with a stress on conceptual-logical rather than pragmatic-perceptual relationships among experiences (thought) (1963, p. 182).

The authors document this hypothesis with many examples of the developing expression of coordinate, sequential, simultaneous, antithetical, subordinative and causal relations in child language. The idea is that at first the child's utterance closely reflects his observation so that he may say something like "The toy is broken—it doesn't move." Then the child begins to conceive of concrete causal relations; he observes an effect which leads him to anticipate and look for the cause so that the child may say something like "It doesn't move because it's broken." Eventually, at the next stage the child abstracts the logic of this class of events and may say something like "Because it is broken, it doesn't move" where the particularity of the figural event is expressed in relation to a logical ground about the class of causal events.

Perceptual Intuitions. During this stage, percepts retain four major characteristics of primitive mental activity The first is physiognomization. In a series of experiments with children ages 6 to 19, Wapner and Werner (1957) examined the effects of "directional dynamics" in pictured objects and visually presented words upon preception. One experiment, for example, compared the perceived speed of motion of (1) objects that have a static quality (e.g., a "sitting mouse") or objects that are pointed in the direction opposite of the movement (e.g., a series of triangles like ◁ moving left to right) with (2) objects that have a dynamic quality (e.g., a "running mouse") or objects that are pointed in the direction of the movement (e.g., the same series of triangles but whose apexes now faced in the same direction as the motion). The effects of the directional dynamics was greatest for the youngest subjects and decreased with age. Their studies lead the authors to conclude:

. . . these developmental trends have been related by us to the developmental principle of increasing object-subject differentiatedness. Developmental theory assumes that dynamic perception entails relative unity (undifferentiatedness) between object and organism. Since this undifferentiatedness decreases with age the potency of the dynamics inherent in objects decreases with increase in age (Wapner and Werner, 1957, p. 36).

The second characteristic is psychophysical undifferentiatedness. For example, a child who perceives a few pieces of straw as a doll may have no awareness that he is attributing these doll-like qualities to the straw. Rather, his percept may be the result of a lack of differentiation in his total psychological organization between his subjective (motor-affective-perceptual) state and the objective matter-of-fact attributes of things (e.g., Werner and Wapner, 1955; Langer, Wapner, and Werner, 1961; Langer, Werner, and Wapner, 1965).

The third primitive characteristic of intuitions is syncresis of percepts and images, for example, in eidetic imagery, which was first described in detail by Jaensch (1930). These images have much of the force, the "sensuous vivacity," and detail possessed by percepts.

Consequently, some children feel that their images are "real projections on some surface in outer space involving no effort of will" (Werner, 1948, p. 143). In this sense, eidetic imagery is tied to sensory phenomena. On the other hand, it also partakes of qualities characteristic of imaginal phenomena. Unlike sensory after-images, eidetic imagery can be influenced and intentionally altered by the creative will of the child. Eidetic imagery, like children's drawings is particularly susceptible to what Werner calls the "emotional perspective." Jaensch reports, for example, the case of a boy who was so impressed by a play that the actors grew to enormous proportions before his eyes.

The fourth primitive characteristic of intuitive perception is its lack of stability. In their sensoritonic theory, Wapner and Werner (1957) posit that the underlying mechanism of perception is an equilibration process between sensoritonic forces within the organism. The theory makes the holistic assumption that sensory and tonic (postural-muscular) forces "must be essentially of the same nature," even though they may appear to be different sources of perception, because they have parallel effects and they influence each other. The organism is in a relatively stable state when his interactions with the environment result in sensory and tonic states that are in equilibrium with each other. Unstable states are the result of interactions that result in sensory forces that perturb the tonic forces, or vice versa. Such an unstable state may be examined experimentally by tilting an individual in a dark room and testing its effect upon his perception of major spatial coordinates, such as the vertical represented by a luminescent rod. The hypothesis is that at primitive stages in the development of perceptual intuition the organism does not have stabilizing forces to counteract the perturbing forces in the direction of the tilt (cf. Goldstein, 1939). Consequently, the rod will appear to be vertical when it is actually tilted in the same direction as the organism. At advanced stages of perceptual intuition, on the other hand, the organism develops stabilizing counterforces in the direction opposite to those induced by the tilt in order to reestablish equilibrium. This often involves counteractive forces that overcompensate for the perturbation. Consequently, the resultant perception may not be "veridical." For example, the rod may be perceived as vertical when it is actually tilted in the direction opposite the tilt of the organism. The comparative data conform to this sensoritonic hypothesis:

1. Children 6 to 16 and older people 65 to 80 locate the apparent vertical to the same side as their own tilt (Comalli, Wapner, and Werner, 1959).
2. Catatonic-hebephrenic schizophrenic adults locate the apparent vertical to the side of their own tilt (Carini, 1955).
3. Normals, 16 to 50 years old, locate the apparent vertical opposite the side of their own tilt (Comalli, Wapner, and Werner, 1959).

The intuitive perceptual sense that develops also becomes progressively detached from the subject and objectified as a separate but still concretely understood external world. As a paradigmatic example of the progress achieved let us consider the intuition of space that develops beyond the immediately perceptible. Its most primitive manifestation is usually supported by the physiological maturation of locomotory powers that permit wider exploration and memory that permits the temporal extension of space into familiar but not presently experienced places. In this sense, spatial cognition begins to be representational. But, for these very same reasons, spatial knowledge is still very much tied to the particular activity of the subject; it is, in Werner's terms, a "personal space-of-action" and not a general concept. An example from human ontogenesis is that 3-year-olds are likely to be disoriented if they are taken into a familiar place by an entrance that they have previously used only as an exit.

The most advanced manifestation of the concrete intuition of space is one in which regions are differentiated and systematized into a whole organization. But it is still a personalized organization that is intrinsically interwoven with the idiosyncratic and physiognomic activity of the acting subject. This stage is central to ethnogenetic comparisons because much of the mythical organization of space seems to involve reasoning that does not go beyond the concrete intuitive level. This seems to be as true of the astrological, cosmic spatial concepts that are becoming increasingly prevalent in contemporary cul-

ture in the United States as it is, for example, in the religious partitioning of space in Zuni or early Babylonian ideologies (Cassirer, 1955).

[Highly organized mythical space] retains some of the salient properties of primitive space, particularly its concreteness and dynamism. This qualitative dynamism may come to view in such physiognomic or expressive terms as "holy" or "unholy," qualities on which a mythical space may be based (Werner, 1948, p. 171).

Myth arrives at spatial determinations and differentiations only by lending a peculiar mythical accent to each "region" in space, to the "here" and "there," the rising and setting of the sun, the "above" and "below." Space is now divided into definitive zones and directions; but each of these has not only a purely intuitive meaning but also an expressive character of its own. Space is not yet a homogeneous whole, within which the particular determinations are equivalent and interchangeable. The near and far, the high and low, the right and left—all have their uniqueness, their special mode of magical significance. Not only is the basic opposition of sacred and profane interwoven with all these spatial oppositions; it actually constitutes and produces them. One must immerse oneself in the artistic representations of the gods and demons of the directions—as we find them for example in the ancient Mexican culture—in order wholly to feel this expressive meaning, this physiognomic character which all spatial determinations possess for the mythical consciousness. Even the systematic order of space (for this is by no means lacking in mythical thinking) does not go beyond this sphere. The augur who marks off a templum, a sacred precinct in which he differentiates various zones, thus creates the basic precondition, the first beginning and impulse toward "contemplation." He divides the universe according to a definite point of view—he sets up a spiritual frame of reference, toward which all being and all change are oriented. This orientation is designed to insure a vision of the world as a whole, and with it a prevision of the future. But of course this vision does not move within a free, ideal, linear structure, as in the realm of pure "theory";

WERNER'S COMPARATIVE ORGANISMIC THEORY   763

the zones of space are inhabited by real, fateful powers, powers of blessing or of doom. The magical circle that embraces the whole existence of nature and of man is not burst asunder but only reinforced; the distances conquered by mythical intuition do not break its power but serve only to confirm it anew (Cassirer, 1957, pp. 150–151).

As for ontogenesis we find that although the child is beginning to differentiate locations, the way in which he relates them into a spatial organizations is still egocentrically bound to his own action at the beginning of this stage rather than in a perspective fashion. For example, by the age of 6 or 7 years, children know what right and left is on their own body. But they cannot tell right from left on other bodies; and they mirror image the movements of another person when required to imitate. Toward the end of this stage, the construction of spatial coordinates begin to be detached from the actions of the subject. Children begin to discriminate right from left on other bodies as well as their own. But even at 8 years they can still hardly imitate correctly someone facing them who moves his right and left hands (Wapner and Cirillo, 1968).

Werner cites further comparative evidence from pathogenesis. For example, Head (1926) reports that aphasiac patients place their right hand to their right eye when imitating Head's placement of his left hand to his left eye. The imitation, then, is mirror-like. Another aphasiac patient was only able to distinguish right from left in terms of his own activity—right is the side with which he writes. These kinds of observations led Werner (1948) to the hypothesis that mental disturbances are often marked by conceptual regression to relatively primitive notions of space: spatial cognition becomes egocentric, affectively laden, physiognomic, or dynamic —a concrete "space-of-action."

Werner's (1948) central hypothesis is that the perceptual intuition of space is rooted in "the property of a temporal succession, that is, irreversibility." As an example he cites the Scupins's report of their son Bubi's behavior when he was 7 years old:

Today Bubi was taken through the woods by the forester. Without following any path,

over brooks, mounds and through clearings he went to the tree-nursery where the men were digging. On the way back, at a spot some five-minutes' walk from the forester's lodge, the man showed the boy a strawberry patch. In the afternoon the child's mother, armed with a pail, thought she would let him lead her to the strawberries. Unable to reconstruct the return route in a reversed direction, the boy led her all the way through the woods, over the brooks and through cleared spots to the place where the men were at work at the nursery, and thus found his circuitous way to the strawberry patch. To her amused astonishment, Bubi's mother found that it had taken her three-quarters of an hour of trail-making to arrive at a place not five minutes' distance from the forester's house where they had started. A whole chain of associations and memories had guided him. He spoke in a long monologue, saying: "Here at the threshold the forester said, Watch out! Here's a step up! Here the forester said, Sit down and slide. Here—wait a minute—how do you go from here? Oh, yes . . .the grass is trampled . . . we're right. There's Gold Brook already! The forester jumped across first and reached over his stick to us. . . . Look! there are the men working!" (pp. 176–177).

Contemplative Acts

Abstact conceptual activity requires that from the totality of experience "a factor is not only detached by abstraction but at the same time taken as a representative of the whole" (Cassirer, 1957, p. 114). This means that symbols are created that not only stand for and are integrated with—but are fully detached and differentiated from—what they represent. This permits the articulation (differentiation and integration) of experience from many perspectives, not only one's immediate involvement. Symbolic representation is therefore necessary to the construction of ideological consciousness or theoretical cognition in which subjective perspectives are finally related in a logical fashion with objective perspectives.

Abstract contemplation, then, is based upon schematization that is intentional and planned (Werner, 1948; Werner and Kaplan, 1963). The detachment from immediate and pragmatic involvement permits contemplative schematization to go beyond presentational construction of here and now experience to an interpretative representation of past experience and future possibilities as well as of present activities. Observed transformations over time are no longer accepted in their presentational guise but are represented in relation to reversible mental interpretations. This means mental coordination of the observed present actual transformation with the nonpresent possible reversibility of that deformation. Intentional schematizing is also stable and flexible. Intentional schemes are constructs in which interpretations become principled in their meaning so that they do not simply fluctuate due to context. Yet they are plastic enough to permit for modification where the conditions indicate qualification. They have, then, the character of principles that have universal definition and particular qualification.

Thus schematization reaches its highest form during this stage when two criteria are met. The first is the development of the categorial and hypothetical "attitude toward the possible" (Goldstein, 1939). The most advanced manifestation of the *categorial attitude* is the ability to deal with possibilities as well as with actualities in a principled fashion:

Previously we mentioned a certain detachment from experienced situations as prerequisite to the adoption of the "categorial" attitude. Such detachment permits the normal person not merely to experience the actual situation and to undergo the effectiveness of operating factors, but also to explicate the given situation, to apprehend and thematize effective factors, and, eventually, to orient his actions with respect to factors thus rendered explicit (Gurwitsch, 1949, p. 183).

The second criterion is the development of the *transcendent capacity* to act mentally upon one's own psychological actions, thereby permitting the organism to contemplate its own thoughts and be conscious of its consciousness. Both these developments are prerequisite to the formation of theoretical, perspectivistic, and ideological cognition of physical, social, and psychological experience.

In theoretical cognition the "schematism of images has given way to the symbolism of principles" (Cassirer, 1957, p. 467). This permits the formation of logical systems of action

that create abstract or formal ordering relations. Thus the final character of mentation as representation emerges: abstract symbolism that permits the construction of principled concepts which are logically necessary, and have general meaning yet maintain their particular intuitive reference:

The meaning of a principle must ultimately be fulfilled empirically, hence intuitively; but this fulfillment is never possible directly; it can only occur when other propositions are derived by a hypothetical deduction from the assumption of the principle's validity. None of these propositions, none of these particular stages in a logical process, need be susceptible of direct intuitive interpretation. Only as a logical totality can the series of inferences be related to intuition, and confirmed and justified by intuition.

It is the construction of a network of logical principles, such as the principle of invariant relations in the concept of the conservation of energy, rather than the positing of the existence of particular things which characterizes the most advanced form of objective schemata:

Here the substantial is completely transposed into the functional: true and definitive permanence is no longer imputed to an existence propagated in space and time but rather to those magnitudes and relations between magnitudes which provide the universal constants for all description of physical process (Cassirer, 1957, p. 473).

The mental representatives of these functions are symbolic relational schemes, such as the operation of reversibility, that have the objective force of logical necessity.

Symbols. The progressive development of autonomous symbolization is marked by the construction—the appreciation and understanding, as well as the production—of symbolic forms that are progressively differentiated from the referents they represent. With respect to the linguistic medium this.

. . . increasing *distance* and independence of language from the domain of concrete, perceptual-motor experiences reflects itself in several ways: increasing reference to phenomena remote from concrete perception, formation of names to refer to class concepts rather than to individual concepts, formation of designators of abstract rather than context-bound relations, etc. (Werner and Kaplan, 1963, p. 184).

The concept of distancing leads to the derivative idea that "the use of purely linguistic operations for constructing referents and relations among referents" is a major of function of symbolization. This takes many forms in the course of ontogenesis. One form is "*composition,* the joining of two names to form a new unitary name." Many of the composites formed by children, such as "birthday-tree," are tied to specific spatiotemporal contexts and are of short-term duration; others endure a long time. A related form is "*derivation,* the adding of form-elements to a name in order to derive new names (and concepts)." This occurs when the child already discriminates between "nouns as thing-words and verbs as action-words" but for the purpose of a novel function, constructing new words, he returns to the use of a more primitive form in which things and actions are not differentiated, e.g., a 5-year-old boy called a towel a "wipe-it-dry."

A more advanced symbolic form of constructing relations between linguistic concepts is that of defining the meaning of words by other words (Lewis, 1929). At first the child's *lexical constructions* are "global, diffuse, and concretely contextualized." When 5- and 6-year-old children are asked what "bottle" means they give answers such as "There's lemonade in it" and "When a little boy drinks milk out of it." Eventually the child's lexical units become "relatively context-free" and general; for example, one child defined a bottle as "A container into which all kinds of liquids go."

When words acquire general, decontextualized meanings, then they truly attain the level of *autonomous lexical units.* Werner and Kaplan (1963) hypothesize six steps in the formation of autonomous symbols. This hypothesis is based upon a study (Werner and Kaplan, 1952) of 8½- to 13½-year-old children. These children were presented with twelve series of six sentences each. The same artificial word appeared in each series of six sentences. For example, the artificial word in

one series was "hudray" (its adequate translation was grow, increase, or expand) and one of the sentences was "If you eat well and sleep well you will *hudray.*" The child's task was to find the meaning of "hudray" that would fit all six sentences.

Young subjects tend to ascribe a "global connotative sphere" to the artificial word that reflects what the context means to them. This "word-sentence undifferentiatedness" means that they do not treat the word as an autonomous lexical concept. Not only do these children fuse the meaning of the word with that of its sentence context but they also fuse or intermingle the different structure of the various sentence contexts. For example, even a 10-year-old said that "hudray" means "feel good" in the above sentence; he then translated the second sentence "Mrs. Smith wanted to *hudray* her family" into "Mrs. Smith wanted her family to *feel good*"; after which he translated the third sentence "Jane had to *hudray* the cloth so that the dress would fit Mary" into "Jane makes the dress good to fit Mary so that Mary *feels good*"; and so on for the rest of the series. Thus the child's syncretic construction leads to a global and diffuse concept in which words and sentences are relatively undifferentiated.

A step beyond this "word-sentence fusion" is partial detachment and partial fusion of the word meaning with the sentence contexts. For example, one 10-year-old assigned the meaning "collect" to the artificial word "lidber" in the sentence "Jimmy *lidbered* stamps from all countries"; but then he went on to incorporate "stamps" into the meaning of "lidber" as in "The police did not allow the people to *lidber* on the street," which he translated as "The police did not allow the people to *collect stamps* on the street." Thus both word-sentence and sentence-sentence meanings overlapped.

A third level is achieved when children no longer have trouble assigning meaning to the word in each sentence, but the meaning is context specific. Each time the word appears they give it a new specific significance that fits the particular context rather than arriving at a general meaning that fits all the sentences in the series. The task demand of arriving at a general meaning is often dealt with at this stage by assigning "a meaning comprised of an *aggregation* of the context-specific meanings. For example, a 10-year-old first translated "contavish" as "cardboard" in the sentence "You can't fill anything with a *contavish*"; then as "room" in "The more you take out of a *contavish* the larger it gets"; and finally as "cardboard and room" when asked for a general meaning so that he then translated the second sentence into "The more *cardboard* you take out of a *room*, the larger the *room* gets."

At the next stage children assign both a different specific meaning to the artificial words in each context and a general meaning. Then they globally integrate "the specific meanings to the over-all meaning in a vague, subsumption-like relationship." That is, each specific referent is diffusely subsumed under a general class. This pluralization means that the sentence contexts are discretely articulated from each other. For example, one child interpreted the word "prignatus" as meaning "hit back" in "Boys sometimes *prignatus* their parents"; then as "lie" in "Mary did not know that Jane used to *prignatus*"; then as "holler at" in "Mother said, 'Jimmy you should never *prignatus* your own mother'"; and so on. The overall meaning that the child assigned to "prignatus" was "not respect your elders."

The development of the related operation of transposition follows pluralization as a means of trying actively to arrive at an overall meaning while retaining the word's context-specific significance that is also syntactically adequate:

This demand is . . . met by expanding the meaning of one context-specific solution— equating all the other context-specific meanings with that one solution. This "equating" is done by means of such expressions of assimilation as "like-a," "sort-of," "kind-of" (Werner and Kaplan, 1963, p. 196).

For example, an 11-year-old translated "corplum" as "bar" in "*Corplums* may be used to close off an open place" and then translated "A *corplum* may be used for support" as "A *leg of table* may be used for support; *bar* fits—a *leg of table* is a *sort-a* bar." Transposition permits the structuring of a discrete sentence context "but the meaning of the circumscribed vocable is not yet of a truly general character." For this reason it does not

yet have the most advanced character of a symbolic concept.

The final development of symbolic concepts described by Werner and Kaplan (1963) involves the formation of general meanings that transcend the specific contexts yet fit each particular manifestation in terms of both its semantic reference and its syntactic requirements. They cite the following response as an example of this principled form of symbolization:

For *prignatus,* one child gave *lie to* as its meaning in the first sentence: Boys sometimes *lie* to their parents; for the second sentence, the solution was cheat: Mary did not know that Jane used to *cheat; deceive* was the solution for the fourth sentence: You may *deceive* someone but you will not get away with it often. Deceive was then used to subsume both *lie to* and *cheat*; it was a word-meaning that could be fitted into all the sentence-contexts without entailing either vague reference or syntactic distortion (Werner and Kaplan, 1963, p. 197).

Concepts. Now the full organizational and functional nature of conceptual schematization becomes manifest. Concepts are the products of mental acts. All conceptual acts evaluate. This evaluation is *logical*: it seeks to come to a principled understanding of empirical actualities and hypothetical possibilities. This evaluation is *intentional*: it is directed toward transcending immediate practical involvement in order to achieve some understanding for the sake of understanding. This evaluation is *esthetic*: it demands continuing rotation of the problems and the solutions until a feeling of equilibrium—fittingness and elegance—is achieved. The resultant conception is not a static achievement but a dynamic process that points to certain judgments. Conceptual judgments are, of course, evaluative acts, which is what initiated the entire process: thus cognition comes full circle. At the same time, they are acts that evaluate in a new light thereby suggesting new considerations, problems, and ideas for consideration: thus cognition develops. Conception

. . . is no ready-made path but a function of pathfinding itself. Intuition follows set paths of combination, and herein consists its pure form and schematisms. The concept, however, reaches out beyond these paths in the sense that it not only knows them but also points them out; it not only travels a road that is opened and known in advance but also helps to open it (Cassirer, 1957, p. 289).

. . . each newly asquired concept is an attempt, a beginning, a problem; its value lies not in its copying of definite objects, but in its opening up of new logical perspectives, so permitting a new penetration and survey of an entire problem complex . . . one of its essential tasks is not to let the problems of knowledge come prematurely to rest, but to keep them in a steady flux, by guiding them toward new goals which it must first anticipate hypothetically. Here again we find that the concept is far less abstractive than prospective; it not only fixes what is already known, establishing its general outlines, but also maintains a persistent outlook for new and unknown connections (Cassirer, 1957, p. 306).

We are only now beginning to reveal some of the fundamental characteristics of the most mature forms of conceptual schematization, particularly as it manifests itself in scientific thinking (e.g., Snell, 1953; Kuhn, 1962). The study of sophisticated forms of thinking not only gives us some understanding of advanced conceptual activity but it indicates to us, and reinforces Werners hypotheses, about the intuitive sensorimotor precursors of full-fledged concepts.

The ability to take into account more than one's own subjective perspective seems to be one fundamental characteristic of sophisticated thought. The product of *perspectivism* is the formation of concepts that are relative to the perspectives they must take into account. This is apparent in the development of spatial ideas that become progressively based upon integration of other perspectives with that of the constructing subject. An ontogenetic illustration is the ability of older children to transpose rather than mirror the movements of others when imitating them. Transposition in imitation indicates "the internalization of the left-right distinction occurring in action and the representational

coordination of perspectives" (Wapner and Cirillo, 1968, p. 887). Thus spatial ideas become progressively detached from the subject's intuitive action and from concrete phenomenal relations. First, they become objectified as separate, concrete external containers with contained objects. Eventually, they become objectified as complex configurations for empirical examination and logical conceptualization.

A second major characteristic of advanced conceptual schematism is its progressive *transparency*. Conceptual transparency means that the mental operations involved are increasingly those of formulating and manipulating sets of hypothetical principles. These principles have their developmental foundation in concrete acts. But they become progressively detached from pragmatic, empirical intuitions. Increasingly they become based upon a hypothetical attitude that is directed toward the intention to know and understand. Principles therefore become progressively founded upon the construction of a logical network of theoretical possibilities. This is clearest in scientific thinking, which constructs hypothetical principles—theoretical fictions or mathematical functions—that are themselves not observable yet are said to represent the essential and universal properties of reality:

What we define as the ultimate physical reality has cast off all appearance of thingness: there is no longer any meaning in speaking of one and the same matter at different times. And yet . . . the abandonment of thingness does not impair the objectivity of physics but grounds it in a new and deeper sense. What we call the object is no longer a schematizable, intuitively realizable "something" . . . in accordance with the definition which Kant worked out clearly in principle, it is a mere X "in relation to which representations have synthetic unity" (Cassirer, 1957, p. 473).

Progressive transparency also means that the symbolic forms involved are increasingly those of constructing and manipulating *stipulated conventions*. These conventions have their developmental foundations in expressive acts and models. But they become progressively distanced from motivated, presentational signifiers and become transparent vehicular media for defining logical relations (Werner and Kaplan, 1963). Cassirer (1957) describes the epistemological development in the physical sciences from concrete concepts to principles:

> . . . a scientific principle, regardless of its particular character, belongs, if only because of its universal logical dimension, to a different sphere of validity . . . it is fully expressed only in a universal proposition. And every such proposition comprises a specific mode of postulation. Its relation to the world of intuitive phenomena is mediated throughout— that is, it passes through the medium of signification (p. 461).

A final, related characteristic of advanced conceptual schematism is its progressive *heuristic potency*. The categorical concern with the construction of hypothetical possibilities means that conceptualization is now intentionally directed toward the creation of new forms that transcend empirical experience. The intention is to create a psychological reality that has political, ethical, and esthetic as well as physical and logical form. This psychological reality marks the final hierarchic integration of objective and subjective systems in the creation of conceptual forms. Its manifestation in scientific thinking is the formulation of theoretical principles that are logically coherent and esthetically elegant. Its manifestation in personal thinking is the development of ideological cognition that not only makes rational sense but is emotionally satisfying.

CONCLUDING REMARKS

A chapter of length at least equal to the present would have to be written in order to seriously evaluate the success of the comparative organismic perspective. Also, it is obviously too soon to pass any definitive judgment upon the theory as a whole. Yet it seems clear that the approach has already borne fruit in a number of domains. It has been most successful in the study of cognitive phenomena, particularly phenomena of concept and symbol formation. It also has rich potential for the investigation of personality and social development from a genetic epistemological stance; but, to date, this potential remains relatively dormant except for some rudimentary stirrings (e.g., Werner, 1948, Chaps. XII and XIII; Kaplan, 1966a; Witkin, 1962; Langer, 1969, pp. 174–177, 1970; Kohlberg, 1969).

Ultimately, the genetic epistemological aim of comparative organismic theory is to comprehend the totality of mental life and its development. This requires a holistic conception of mental acts since they are the stuff of—construct and generate the development of—mental life. A holistic conception implies that mental acts are feelings as well as judgments. This means that they are both conceptual and motivated acts: the stuff of mental life and development is evaluative conduct.

It should be abundantly apparent by now that Werner's overall aim was to fashion a theoretical perspective that would be applicable to the study of all mental development, whether the primary purpose of the study is empirical, analytical, explanatory, descriptive, etc. This theoretical strategy rests upon the fundamental methodological assumption that all psychological investigations involve (1) a comparison of the invariant and changing features of the same mental phenomenon when it is in two states or (2) a determination of the similarities and differences in comparable mental phenomena. This means that the lawful investigation of psychological phenomena is at root developmental in nature. And it means that a comprehensive account is possible by creating a comparative psychology of mental development.

References

Baldwin, J. M. *Genetic theory of reality.* New York: Putnam, 1915.

Bertalanfly, L. von *Modern theories of development.* London: Oxford University Press, 1933.

Bijou, S. W., and Baer, D. M. *Child Development*. Vol. 1. *A systematic and empirical theory*. New York: Appleton-Century-Crofts, 1961.

Bridges, K. M. B. *Social and emotional development of the preschool child*. London: Kegan Paul, 1931.

Bühler, C. *Kindheit und Jugend*. 1931.

Burke, K. *A grammar of motives*. Englewood Cliffs, N.J.: Prentice-Hall, 1945.

Carini, I. P. An experimental investigation of perceptual behavior in schizophrenics. Microfilmed Ph.D. thesis, Clark University, 1955.

Cassirer, E. *Philosophy of symbolic forms*. Vol. 1. *Language*. (1923) New Haven, Conn.: Yale University Press, 1953.

Cassirer, E. *Philosophy of symbolic forms*. Vol. 2. *Mythical thought*. (1925) New Haven, Conn.: Yale University Press, 1955.

Cassirer, E. *Philosophy of symbolic forms*. Vol. 3. *Phenomenology of knowledge*. (1929) New Haven, Conn.: Yale University Press, 1957.

Comalli, P. E., Wapner, S., and Werner, H. Perception of verticality in middle and old age. *J. Psychol.*, 1959, **47**, 259–266.

De Vries, R. Constancy of genetic identity in the years three to six. *Monogr. soc. res. Child Dev.*, 1969, 34 (3, Whole No. 127).

Dowling, R. M. Visual recognition threshold and concurrent motor activity. *Percept. Mot. Skills*, 1965, **20**, 1141–1146.

Gesell, A. The ontogenesis of infant behavior. In L. Carmichael (Ed.), *Manual of child psychology*. 2nd edition. New York: Wiley, 1946.

Goldstein, K. *The organism*. New York: American Book Co., 1939.

Gurwitsch, A. Gelb-Goldstein's concept of "concrete" and "categorial" attitude and the phenomenology of ideation. *Philos. Phenomenol. Res.*, 1949, **10**, 172–196.

Halpern, E. The effects of incompatibility between perception and logic in Piaget's stage of concrete operations. *Child Dev.*, 1965, **36**, 491–497.

Head, H. *Aphasia and kindred disorders of speech*. New York: Macmillan, 1926.

Hertz, M. Beobachtungen an gefangenen Rabenvögeln. *Psychol. Forsch.*, 1926, **8**.

Hertz, M. Weitere Versuche an der Rabenkrähe. *Psychol. Forsch.*, 1928, **10**.

Hobhouse, L. T. *Mind in evolution*. New York: Macmillan, 1901.

Jaensch, E. R. *Eidetic imagery and typological methods of investigation*. New York: Harcourt, 1930.

Kaplan, B. The study of language in psychiatry: the comparative developmental approach and its application to symbolization and language in psychopathology. In S. Arieti (Ed.), *American handbook of psychiatry*. Vol. 3. New York: Basic Books, 1966a.

Kaplan, B. The "latent content" of Heinz Werner's comparative-developmental approach. In S. Wapner and B. Kaplan (Eds.), *Heinz Werner 1890–1964*. Worcester, Mass.: Clark University Press, 1966.

Kohlberg, L. Early education: a cognitive-developmental view. *Child Dev.*, 1968, **39**, 1013–1062.

Kohlberg, L. Stage and sequence: the developmental approach to socialization. In D. Goslin (Ed.), *Handbook of socialization*. Chicago: Rand McNally, 1969.

Kramer, R. B. Changes in moral judgment response pattern during late adolescence and young adulthood: retrogression in a developmental sequence. Unpublished doctoral dissertation, University of Chicago, 1968.

Kuhn, T. S. *The structure of scientific revolutions*. Chicago: University of Chicago Press, 1962.

Langer, J. Disequilibrium as a source of development. In P. H. Mussen, J. Langer, and M. Covington (Eds.), *Trends and issues in developmental psychology*. New York: Holt, Rinehart & Winston, 1969.

Langer, J. *Theories of development.* New York: Holt, Rinehart & Winston, 1969.

Langer, J. The development of the individual. Chapter 10 in *Psychology today: an introduction.* Del Mar: CRM, 1970.

Langer, J., Wapner, S., and Werner, H. The effect of danger upon the experience of time. *Am. J. Psychol.,* 1961, **74,** 94–97.

Langer, J., Werner, H., and Wapner, S. Apparent speed of walking under conditions of danger. *J. gener. Psychol.,* 1965, **73,** 291–298.

Lewis, C. I. *Mind and the world order.* New York: Dover, 1956.

Miller, A. Verbal satiation and the role of concurrent activity. *J. abnorm. soc. Psychol.,* 1963, **66,** 206–212.

Pepper, S. C. *World hypotheses.* Berkeley: University of California Press, 1942.

Peters, R. S. *The concept of motivation.* London: Routledge & Kegan Paul, 1958.

Révész, G. Tierpsychologische Untersuchungen (Vers. an Hühnern). *Z. Psychol.,* 1921, **88.**

Schwartz, C., and Langer, J. Aspects of classificatory conceptualization. Unpublished manuscript, University of California, 1967.

Sigel, I. E., Saltz, E., and Roskind, W. Variables determining concept conservation in children. *J. exp. Psychol.,* 1967, **74,** 471–475.

Silberer, H. Report on a method of eliciting and observing certain symbolic hallucination-phenomena. In D. Rapaport (Ed.), *Organization and pathology of thought.* New York: Columbia University Press, 1951.

Snell, B. *The discovery of the mind.* Cambridge: Harvard University Press, 1953.

Staats, A. *Learning, language, and cognition.* New York: Holt, Rinehart & Winston, 1968.

Stern, W. *Psychology of early childhood.* New York: Holt, 1930.

Tinkelpaugh, O. F. Representative factors in monkeys. *J. comp. Psychol.,* 1928, **8.**

Turiel, E. Developmental processes in the child's moral thinking. In P. H. Mussen, J. Langer, and M. Covington (Eds.), *Trends and issues in developmental psychology.* New York: Holt, Rinehart, & Winston, 1969.

Uexküll, J. von. A stroll through the world of animals and men. (1934) In C. H. Schiller (Ed.), *Instinctive behavior.* New York: International Universities Press, 1957.

Vygotsky, L. S. *Thought and language.* (1934) Cambridge: M.I.T. Press, 1962.

Wapner, S. An organismic-developmental approach to the study of perceptual and other cognitive operations. In C. Scheerer (Ed.), *Cognition.* New York: Harper and Row, 1964.

Wapner, S. Organismic-developmental theory: some applications to cognition. In P. H. Mussen, J. Langer, and M. Covington (Eds.), *Trends and issues in developmental psychology.* New York: Holt, Rinehart, & Winston, 1969.

Wapner, S., and Cirillo, L. Imitation of a model's hand movements: age changes in transposition of left-right relations. *Child Dev.,* 1968, **39,** 887–894.

Wapner, S., and Werner, H. *Perceptual development.* Worcester, Mass.: Clark University Press, 1957.

Wapner, S., and Werner, H. An experimental approach to body perception from the organismic-developmental point of view. In S. Wapner and H. Werner (Eds.), *The body percept.* New York: Random House, 1965.

Werner, H. Process and achievement. *Harvard Educ. Rev.,* 1937, **7,** 353–368.

Werner, H. The concept of rigidity. *Psychol. Rev.,* 1946, **53,** 43–52.

Werner, H. *Comparative psychology of mental development.* New York: International Universities Press, 1948.

Werner, H. The concept of development from a comparative and organismic point of view. In D. B. Harris (Ed.), *The concept of development.* Minneapolis: University of Minnesota Press, 1957.

Werner, H. and Kaplan, B. *Symbol formation.* New York: Wiley, 1963.

Werner, H., and Kaplan, E. The acquisition of word meanings: a developmental study. *Monogr. soc. res. Child Dev.*, 1952, **15** (1, Whole No. 51).

Werner, H., and Wapner, S. Changes in psychological distance under conditions of danger. *J. Personality*, 1955, **24**, 153–167.

Witkin, H. A., Dyk, R. B., Faterson, H. B., Goodenough, D. R., and Karps, S. A. *Psychological differentiation*. New York: Wiley, 1962.

11. Sensory and Perceptual Development[1]

HERBERT L. PICK JR., AND ANNE D. PICK

I. NATIVISM-EMPIRICISM IN RELATION TO THE DEVELOPMENT OF SPACE PERCEPTION

Perceptual development, at the intersection of the fields of perception and developmental psychology, has been included in the recent resurge of interest in both these fields. The revitalization of interest in perception no doubt stems partly from the failure of classical learning theory to handle adequately the stimulus input or even to define the effective stimulus. In any case general experimental psychology has achieved a new balance, with perception again sharing a position of prominence. In developmental psychology the disenchantment with the normative-descriptive

[1] This chapter was prepared while the first author held an NIH Career Development Award 5 KO3 HO 12396 and the second author held an NIH Postdoctoral Fellowship FD HD-32,895. The work was also supported by NIH grant MH 07631 to the University of Minnesota and by the Center for the Study of Human Learning at the University of Minnesota. The reader is also referred to other general review articles on perceptual learning and development by Eleanor Gibson (Gibson and Olum, 1960; Gibson, 1963a, 1963b) and by Wohlwill (1960, 1966). These sources have been especially helpful to the present authors. The authors are especially grateful to Professor Eleanor J. Gibson for allowing us to read the manuscript of her forthcoming book, *Principles of Perceptual Learning and Development* (1969). Our long association with her and with Professor Richard D. Walk, our former teachers has greatly influenced our ideas and approach to the problems of perceptual development, and we are pleased to acknowledge our indebtedness to them.

approach to the study of children has evolved into a more analytic investigation of the determiners of children's behavior.

A particularly important impetus to the study of perceptual development from the realm ' of developmental psychology is the work of Piaget. Piaget's view that an early sensorimotor stage is a precursor of intellectual development and his observations of the spatial conceptions of children have inspired interest in children's perception. At the same time, better techniques for measuring sensitivity in young children have been developed. These include use of unconditioned orienting responses (Bartoshuk, 1962a, 1964; Keen, 1964; Engen, Lipsitt, and Kaye, 1963), conditioning procedures (Papousek, 1967), studies of stimulus preference (Fantz, 1966; Ames and Selfan, 1965; Hershenson, 1964), and physiological techniques (Eichorn, 1963).

Another general impetus to the study of perceptual development is the importance attributed to early experience and sensory stimulation by Hebb and by the ethologists. Indeed, Hebb's ideas were developed in the context of perceptual problems and the perceptual aspects of discrimination learning. The ethologists' observations on the stimulus specificity in imprinting and the specificity of releaser stimuli called the attention of psychologists to the importance of stimulus determinants of behavior and of the possibility of changes of such determinants with development.

These trends all fell upon the background of a persistent concern of psychologists with the nature-nurture problem of perception— nativism versus empiricism. Hochberg (1962) recently reviewed the history of the controversy, pointing out changes in the specific questions, methods of study, and interpretation of results. It is clear from his review that neither the *strong* empiricist nor the *strong* nativist position has been held for a long time. These positions were, respectively, that *all* perception is based on prior experience which fell on an initially blank tablet of a mind, and that all perception is independent of prior experience and reflects the operation of an innate mind. The more typical and weaker positions have tended to emphasize just the role of prior experience, on the one hand, or the role of innate processing mechanisms, on the other. It is also clear from the Hochberg review that until recently few directly studied the development of perception; rather, inferences were made about perceptual development on the basis of introspection or experiments with adults.

Empirical and experimental work on the development of perception began fitfully in the 1930s and gained great momentum in the 1950s and 1960s. As data directly relevant to perceptual development were accumulated, the nature of the nativism-empiricism question changed. In general, investigators no longer were concerned with proving the innate or the acquired character of a specific type of behavior. Rather, they accepted a view of the interaction of heredity and environment in the development of perception and felt that the researchers' task was to define the nature of this relation. This change was perhaps instigated by some of the work on instincts by animal behaviorists (see Lehrman, 1953) and by some of the work on the nature of intelligence (see Anastasi, 1958).

Still, some of the problems of perceptual development were set by the long-standing nativism-empiricism controversy and are best understood in relation to these differing theoretical viewpoints. Both views focused on the paradox that our perception is better than it ought to be on the basis of a superficial analysis of the proximal stimulus. This paradox was most vividly exemplified by the the phenomenon of depth perception, wherein we see three dimensions although the retinal image is a two-dimensional stimulus. Both the nativists and the empiricists resolved this paradox by enriching the impoverished retinal image. The empiricists invoked the effects of past experience, adding them to the present stimulation

to produce a final resultant percept. The nativists invoked a physiological or pseudophysiological mechanism to modify the effects of the present stimulation. Although both groups addressed themselves to many aspects of perception, in recent years the investigation of depth perception seems to have been most closely associated with empiricists, whereas investigation of form perception has been more closely associated with nativists.

A. Development of Depth Perception

Brunswik has developed the most explicitly empiricist point of view currently concerned with depth perception (Brunswik, 1956; Postman and Tolman, 1959). In this view most of the classical cues of depth perception such as size of retinal image, degree of convergence of eyes, and linear perspective form the basis of depth perception. These cues are utilized according to an individual's past experience with them. The novel aspect of Brunswik's position is his suggestion that the cues are probabilistically weighted by the perceiver in terms of their validity, and this validity is an ecological variable which one can measure. Indeed one of Brunswik's students did measure the ecological validity for depth of such cues as brightness and vertical position in the visual field. A typical example of his data was that the height of objects in the visual field had a correlation of .6 with their distance from the S (Postman and Tolman, 1959, p. 552). Since in this theory accurate depth perception is based on prior experience with differentially valid cues, Brunswik would predict that depth perception should improve with age. Some of his work on the development of the perceptual constancies supports this prediction. Of course, all variations of the empiricist point of view predict improvement of perception with age. In the perception of depth there are obvious ways in which the effects of past experience could function. It is understandable then that empiricist psychologists have addressed themselves to this problem. Before 1960 the studies were confined exclusively to children of preschool age and above, and these will be reviewed presently.

Since 1960 techniques for investigation of sensitivity in neonates and young infants have been developed to the point where it is quite feasible to investigate perception of depth at this early age. The reader is referred to Chapter □ (by Kessen) for details of these techniques. It suffices to say here that so far procedures involving stimulus preference and operant conditioning have been used to assess infants' ability to perceive depth.

Fantz (1961a) observed durations of eye fixations when infants of 1 to 6 months of age were presented with a disc and sphere of equal diameters. Infants spent significantly more time fixating the sphere. Fixation preferences were tested using binocular and monocular viewing, rough and smooth test stimuli, and direct lighting. The most reliable preference for the sphere was manifest when textured objects were illuminated by direct light. The same preferences were manifest when viewing monocularly or binocularly. If it is assumed that infants fixate the sphere longer because they detect its solidity, this result is surprising; it implies that the pictorial cues of shading and texture operate earlier than the "primary" cue of retinal disparity.

The other stimulus preference method used to investigate infant depth perception employs the visual cliff developed by Walk and Gibson (1961). In this technique the infant is placed on a centerboard between two glass surfaces onto which he can crawl. The typical depth test consists of placing a surface directly under the glass on one side and a surface at some distance below the glass on the other side. A careful systematic program of research using this technique has been reported by Walk (1966). The visual cliff technique, of course, is applicable only to infants who can locomote and this usually occurs after 6 months of age. Using the most sensitive of a number of variations of the visual cliff procedure, Walk found that better than 90% of infants at all ages (6½ to 15 months) who respond in the cliff situation do avoid the deep side of the cliff. However, under certain conditions a number of babies who initially choose the shallow side can be coaxed across the deep side. Some of these conditions are: fewer older infants can be coaxed than younger infants; when the pattern under the deep side is more definitive (checks as opposed to homogeneous surface) fewer children can be coaxed across; when the pattern is deeper on the deep side fewer children will cross; depth and definition of pattern are more important for the older infants than the

younger. It would seem therefore that although young infants can make the discrimination between the deep and shallow side, the increased motivation of coaxing can override their normal avoidance of depth. One further point of interest is that older children who can be coaxed across the deep side have had significantly less crawling experience as defined by mothers' ratings of the time at which they started to crawl. Thus although the infants can discriminate, an experiential factor is playing a role in their performance in a depth situation.

Little work has been done directly with infants to ascertain the effective depth cues on the visual cliff. One demonstration (Walk and Dodge, 1962) with a monocular infant indicated that retinal disparity was not a necessary condition for appropriate responding. This result is congruent with the previously discussed results of Fantz.

Bower (1964, 1965a) used the generalization of an operant response to assess the effectiveness of certain depth cues for infants. In the first study (Bower, 1964) 70- to 85-day-old infants were conditioned to turn their heads when a 12-inch cube was presented at a distance of 3 feet. Bower then assessed generalization of this response to a 12-inch cube at a distance of 9 feet, to a 36-inch cube at distances of 3 and 9 feet, and to the original conditioning stimulus. There was most but not complete generalization to the 12-inch cube at 9 feet, next most to the 36-inch cube at 3 feet, and least to the 36-inch cube at 9 feet. This pattern of results is most easily interpretable in terms of amount of change in physical size and physical distance of the stimulus. A change in either size or distance produces a decrement in responding and a change in both (36-inch cube at 9 feet) produces the largest decrement. As Bower points out, these results suggest that such young infants are sensitive to variables specifying distance and size-at-a-distance. In particular, size of retinal image does not seem to be an important determiner of response since when that was invariant (36-inch cube at 9 feet) the least generalization of response occurred. In the second study (Bower, 1965a) these results were replicated with slightly younger infants (40 to 60 days) under monocular viewing conditions. Also in the second study another group was trained and tested on two-dimensional pictures of the displays used for conditioning and testing of the other groups. In this latter case there was most generalization in responding in the test condition in which the size and distance of the stimulus was changed, that is, the condition in which the retinal size of the stimulus was invariant. Bower interprets the different pattern of results obtained for this two-dimensional group to imply that motion parallax (a cue available for all the other groups) is necessary to discriminate between the sizes of objects at different distances which project the same size retinal image.

In Bower's situation the change in response with a change in distance of the cube of course implies discrimination of depth. That this is not just due to a change in size of retinal image may be deduced from the fact that a change in size of the stimulus elicits more generalization than a change in size and distance which still leaves the retinal image size the same. In essence, Bower's results imply a degree of size constancy in infants as well as discrimination of depth. Many investigators use size constancy as an indirect way of assessing depth perception, under the assumption that it requires that an organism register distance. This assumption may not be true and when possible should be directly verified as in Bower's experiments (see discussion below on relation of size and distance judgments in older children).

In summary, then, infants as young as 1 month appear to discriminate some of the cues which specify depth. Texture and shading appear to be effective cues in eliciting fixation. Binocular parallax is not a necessary cue, but nothing is known as to whether it would be sufficient for infants. Retinal image size by itself does not appear to be a necessary or sufficient cue.

There are two distinctions that can be made in relation to infants' responses to depth. The first is the distinction between preference and discrimination. In any of the preference measures of depth discrimination, failure to respond differentially does not imply lack of discrimination since there are obviously many reasons why a preference might not be manifest even though an organism is capable of discrimination. It is clear that in this case positive results are meaningful but negative results are not.

The second distinction is not as easily stated. It involves the question of whether it can be asserted that infants or animals perceive depth or whether they are simply reacting to cues that are normally correlated with depth. Here the term perceive is used to imply a sense of meaning. This might be considered a purely philisophical question (and indeed one of the authors, A. P., so considers it). However, there may be a sense in which it is psychologically meaningful. As an example consider a nonverbal organism trained to respond differentially to one depth cue in isolation from others. If this discrimination generalized to all other depth cues in isolation, it could reasonably be argued that the response is made on the basis of the meaning of the cue, that is, depth. This interpretation rests on the assumption that the physical similarity of one depth cue to another is not likely to give rise to so-called primary stimulus generalization. No such experiment has yet been done, but in principle it could be.

Assuming that young infants do respond to depth, this ability may nevertheless improve with age after infancy. Two kinds of studies yield normative data on this question. In one children are directly asked to make distance judgments or matches. In the other children are asked to make size judgments about objects at different distances with the implication that size constancy involves registering of distance—a questionable assumption, as previously noted.

As part of a more general study of the development of space perception, Smith and Smith (1966) asked children ranging in age from 5 to 12 and adults to perform a variety of tasks involving distance estimation. These investigators found that reproduction of distances by children in a free or unreduced viewing condition are as accurate as those of adults. However, under reduced viewing conditions there is improvement with age. This pattern of results may suggest that ability to utilize specific but not necessarily all depth cues improves with age. Alternatively, it may suggest that the redundant depth information provided by ordinary viewing situations is sufficient for even the youngest children to make precise depth judgments.

Studies investigating size constancy usually have shown improvement with age. Typical of these studies is one done by Zeigler and

Leibowitz (1957), who asked Ss to match an adjustable comparison rod 5 feet away to a standard rod whose distance was varied from 10 to 100 feet. The children tested (7 to 9 years of age) showed less constancy than a group of young adults. A somewhat different constancy experiment was conducted by Harway (1963), who asked Ss to generate successive intervals along the ground away from themselves in 1-foot units. A standard foot ruler was placed at their feet as a reference unit. All Ss showed a progressively increasing overestimation of the 1-foot units as the distance away from themselves increased. The younger Ss (5 to 10 years of age) showed considerably more overestimation than did the older Ss (12-year-olds and adults). There was a rather sharp break in performance between the 10- and 12-year-olds. Other normative studies, for the most part showing such improvement in constancy with age, are described in Wohlwill's (1960) excellent review.

One step beyond simply establishing an improvement in size constancy as a function of age is determining which, if any, depth cues change in effectiveness as a function of age. The evidence with respect to retinal disparity as studied by stereoscopic vision is also reviewed by Wohlwill (1960). The data are equivocal: some studies show increased depth responses as a function of age and others do not. Furthermore, the interpretation of some of the studies that do show a change with age is suspect because of the possibility that Ss could not focus on the stereoscopic images (Munn, 1965). One systematic study described by Wohlwill showing an age change is that of Leyer (1939), who presented stereograms tachistoscopically to children 8 to 19 years of age. Here the age trend may have been due to difficulty by younger Ss in focusing or accommodating during a short exposure. Johnson and Beck (1941) found stereoscopic vision present in 2-year-olds. They controlled the light stimulation entering the two eyes by using light differently polarized for each eye and appropriate filters over each eye. The stereoscopic stimulus was that of a doll. The images were projected on a screen an arm's length away from the child. When viewing the stereoscopic images S localized the doll as an adult would, about midway between the screen and himself. When one of the stereo images was turned off S localized

the image on the screen. A best guess at this point would be that stereoscopic vision does not improve with age, at least after infancy. Furthermore, in nonstereoscopic binocular viewing Smith and Smith (1966) found no improvement in depth judgments with age in a relatively rich viewing stiuation nor in judgments of curvature of a surface in depth under relatively restricted viewing conditions. Thus use of binocular cues in general may not change significantly with age.

There seems to be no information about the use of motion parallax by children. This is surprising in view of a recent interest in self-produced movement as a factor in perceptual development, which will be discussed in connection with the effects of early experience (Section IC). There also seems to be no specific information about the use of convergence as a depth cue as a function of age, in spite of the fact that this cue formed the basis of Berkeley's original empiricist theory. Wickelgren (1967) found a rather variable degree of convergence in neonates presented with pattern stimuli, so it is unlikely that this could be an effective depth cue at birth. Ability to accommodate or focus the lens of the eye does change with age but appears to be at adult level by 6 months (Haynes, White, and Held, 1965). However, no studies have been done on the development of the use of accommodation as a cue to depth.

There is some information about the use of pictorial cues for depth perception. Wohlwill (1962) studied linear perspective. He asked Ss of different ages to bisect a stimulus card presented in a frontal plane. The stimulus outline was the shape of a trapezoid with the narrow end up as would be projected to the eye by a horizontal plane rectangle below eye level. Various stimulus cards were used which had different amounts and regularity of texture. In all cases the texture gradient increased from bottom to top again, which would be the case for a horizontal textured field projected to the eye. All Ss made their bisection judgments too high on the card which would be predicted if they were responding to the linear perspective. In general, their bias was greater the denser the texture and the more regular the texture; both of these variables presumably provided more perspective information. The adults showed less bias than the children (first, fourth, and eighth grades). It should be kept in mind that the task was objective bisection of the stimulus card and not bisection of phenomenal depth. Thus children not only are able to respond to the depth information of linear perspective but apparently are less able than adults to ignore it.

Wohlwill has also directly studied the effects on depth perception of texture uninfluenced by perspective. In one study (Wohlwill, 1963a) he asked Ss to bisect fields extending away from themselves under instructions which set them toward making objective judgments. In another study (Wohlwill, 1965) he had Ss bisect photographic representations of the same fields presented in a frontal plane. In the first study there was increasing overconstancy as a function of age. That is, the adults and older children made their bisections further beyond a true bisection than the younger children. In the second study with photographs Ss of all ages showed underconstancy, but the adults and older children again made their bisections further up than the younger children so at least the direction of age differences was consistent in the two studies. In a very careful review of this general area Wohlwill (1963b) summarizes much evidence for trends toward constancy and overconstancy with age in both size constancy and distance judgments. He further adduces a great deal of evidence to the effect that overconstancy is due to a judgmental or cognitive process. This evidence is compelling but not without exception, and it must be reconciled with the fact that there is little correlation between intelligence and contancy (see Section IVA).

Familiar size as a cue to distance was investigated in a monograph by Smith and Smith (1966). They asked Ss ranging in age from 5 to 12 and adults to judge the distance of a baseball under both reduced and normal viewing conditions. Under the reduced conditions familiar size is presumably the effective depth cue. All Ss overestimated the distance under both viewing conditions, but the adults were more accurate than the children. When the mean values of the judgments under reduced viewing were corrected for the constant error existing under normal viewing conditions (perhaps assuming that it was produced by an artifact in the procedure) the age differences were less consistent but still

seemed to be present. Of course correcting the judgments in this way introduces a conservative bias since the familiar size cue may also be operating under the normal viewing conditions. Thus applying a correction factor from normal viewing could take the effect of the familiar size cue out of the results of the restricted viewing situation.

Smith and Smith also asked their Ss to make size judgments of the baseball. Under reduced viewing conditions about 23% of the children (but no adults) made judgments closer to visual angle matches than to size constancy matches. Under normal viewing conditions only about 7% of the children did this. An important point in this respect noted by the Smiths is that size judgments tended to be bimodally distributed around visual angle judgments and around size constancy judgments. One implication of this is that the grouped data of many constancy experiments lying between size constancy and visual angle matching may be masking two separate distributions conforming rather closely to each kind of judgment.

One final point about such size and distance judgment raised by the Smiths and by Wohlwill (1960) concerns the relation between size and distance perception. The classical size-distance invariance hypothesis is one possible relation. It can be derived from the general empiricist point of view and one way of stating it is that for a given size of retinal image, size and distance judgments should be positively correlated. An empiricist interpretation would be that we know from past experience that a given size of retinal image can be caused by large objects far away or small objects close by. Wohlwill reviews evidence of Denis-Prinzhorn (1961) to the effect that size and distance judgments are positively correlated for children but not for adults. This result is consistent with other studies of adults (e.g., Gruber, 1954). On the other hand, Smith and Smith, correlating size and distance judgments for children and adults in four different tasks, find similar patterns of negative or no relationships for both age groups. Thus the size-distance invariance hypothesis does not seem to hold for adults and the evidence is conflicting for children.

A general view of the work on depth perception suggests that distance perception improves after infancy and there is a trend toward overconstancy in size judgments. However, there are a number of exceptions to these generalizations which suggest situation-specific determiners of depth perception. There is a lack of systematic work on specific depth cues other than texture gradients. In this case the results are congruent with the preceding generalizations.

The classical empiricist interpretation of certain geometrical illusions is that susceptibility to the illusions depends upon incorrectly perceiving two-dimensional figures as perspective representations of three-dimensional stimuli. The Ponzo illusion (see Table 1), for example, can be attributed to the interpretation by Ss of converging lines as indicating depth through linear perspective. This illusion was shown by Leibowitz and Heisel (1958) and Leibowitz and Judisch (1967) to increase with age from 4 to 20 years. Such a developmental increase is predicted by the empiricist position since people are presumed to learn to use perspective cues as a function of experience.

The most recent and systematic exploration of the empiricist hypothesis about illusions is a cross-cultural investigation by Segall, Campbell, and Herskovitz (1963, 1966). Following Sanford (1908), they suggested that illusions such as the Müller-Lyer and Sander parallelogram (see Table 1) depend upon S interpreting oblique angles as right angles seen in perspective. To present this hypothesis more concretely, consider the possibility that the Müller-Lyer figures are viewed as representations of sawhorses. The portion of the illusion figure consisting of arrowheads and a line segment would be a sawhorse with the top near S and the legs extending away; the portion formed by the arrow tails would be a sawhorse with the top away from S and the legs extending toward him. The illusion then is attributed to the possibility that S interprets the two equal line segments on his retina as coming from unequal distances. In such a case S infers that the one which is further away (formed by the arrow tails) is larger.

In general, such inappropriate interpretations of two-dimensional cues are thought to depend on the degree to which the environment provides stimuli having properties similar to the cues. In particular, the degree to which an S interprets right angles as oblique angles seen in perspective (as in the Müller-Lyer and Sander parallelogram) depends on the degree to which the environment is "carpentered," that is, contains right-angled objects which would project oblique angles to the retina when viewed from most vantage points. Similarly, it was suggested that the horizontal-vertical illusion is a function of the degree to which S interprets a vertical line as the foreshortened projection of a line on a horizontal plane extending away from S. This in turn was thought to depend on the degree of open horizontal surfaces in the environment. Such an experience-based explanation of these illusions, of course, implies their development as a function of age.

To check this hypothesis, the susceptibility to the Müller-Lyer–Sander parallelogram and horizontal-vertical illusions was assessed in Ss from 15 cultures which varied widely in the degree of "carpentering" of environment and in the local geography. These cultures ranged from rural African to urban Western. The data seemed to support to a considerable extent the hypothesis with respect to the Müller-Lyer and Sander parallelogram illusions and to a lesser extent the horizontal-vertical illusion. However, developmental data on the Müller-Lyer illusion from this study and a number of other studies generally concur in finding a decrease in magnitude of illusion with age. Segall, Campbell, and Herskovitz argue that this result is not completely damaging to their thesis since most of the developmental data are from school-age children and by this time the carpentering of the environment may have had its effect.

Pollack (1969) has argued against the empiricist interpretation of the cross-cultural differences in susceptibility to the Müller-Lyer and Sander parallelogram illusions. His suggestion is that anatomical or physiological characteristics such as retinal pigmentation provide a more likely explanation. He supported this suggestion with evidence that Ss with higher foveal pigmentation manifest less susceptibility to the Müller-Lyer illusion (Pollack and Silvar, 1967). It may be that differences in foveal pigmentation are a function of environmental factors. Pollack has found an inverse correlation between magnitude of Müller-Lyer illusion reported for the various cultures and a combination measure of the environmental variables: nearness to equator, amount of sunshine, and density of forest cover. The implication is that these variables are related to density of retinal pigmentation. In short, the argument is that the cross-cultural differences found by Segall, Campbell, and Herskovitz are not a function of the degree of environmental "carpentering" but of differences in retinal pigmentation.

Before leaving the topic of depth perception it is well to consider some evidence that depth information can play an important role in other psychological processes. Several investigators have noted the ease with which children can learn a discrimination between stereometric objects as compared with two-dimensional projections of these objects. Stevenson and McBee (1958), for example, found that children can learn to discriminate among cubes faster than among painted squares or square cutouts. A recent study (Dornbush and Winnick, 1966) investigated whether such differences might not be due to the greater amount of stimulus information provided by three-dimensional stimuli such as perspective information. In one experiment they taught one group of Ss (5- and 7-year-old children) to discriminate between a cube and a parallelepiped of the same depth. A second group of Ss was trained to discriminate between a square and rectangle. The 5-year-olds learned the stereometric discrimination faster than the two-dimensional discrimination. There was no difference for the 7-year-olds. In a second experiment one group of children was taught to discriminate between two-dimensional perspective representations of the stereometric stimuli of the first experiment and a second group of children was again taught to discriminate between the square and rectangle. The 5-year-olds learned to discriminate between the perspective drawings more quickly than between the square and rectangle. Moreover, the absolute numbers of trials to learn the stereometric discrimination and the perspective discrimination were similar, as were the number of trials to learn the pattern discrimination in the two experiments. (Again, no difference was found for the 7-year-olds.) Thus for younger children the perspective information of stereometric stimuli may be an important factor in the ease with which such stimuli are discriminated.

However, there are others differences between planometric and stereometric stimuli

that might also be contributing factors and that should be investigated. These include the motion parallax resulting from S's movement in relation to a stereometric stimulus which is absent when moving in relation to a painted pattern stimulus. It is certainly the case that differences between stereometric and pattern stimuli are easily detected, that is, teaching a child to discriminate between a stereometric stimulus and a painted projection of the stimulus is very easy. It has been shown that this discrimination is easier than the discrimination between horizontal and vertical stripes for rats, infant monkeys, and children (Tighe, 1964; Tighe and Tighe, 1966). Such a stimulus difference can be considered to define a stimulus dimension of three-dimensionality. This dimension appears to be a very prepotent one and deserves more study.

B. Development of Shape Perception

It is appropriate to begin a consideration of the development of shape perception in the context of Gestalt psychology with its nativistic emphasis. It is not that empiricists have nothing to say about perception of shape—indeed the same kind of analysis that they make of size constancy can be made with shape constancy. (That is, it could be argued that Ss independently register shape of retinal image and stimulus slant and combine these to yield a veridically perceived shape.) Rather, the Gestalt psychologists contributed some of their most striking ideas to the study of shape perception. In this context the Gestalt laws of organization—proximity, good continuation, symmetry, etc.—were formulated and in this context figural after-effects formed the basis of Gestalt physiology. The Gestalt observation that figure-ground discrimination is a primitive organization of perception has often been applied to shape. For example, a contour is seen as belonging to the figure and not to the ground and the ground is seen as continuing behind the figure. The position holds that we see things the way we do because our brain functions in a certain way. The Gestalt laws of organization, for example, are thought to reflect the biases of brain processes as they interact with particular patterns of stimulation. Thus a "good form" such as a circle will be seen under more rapid tachistoscopic exposure or will be remembered for a longer time than would an irregular polygon. In any case, shape perception, except in a very restricted way (e.g., figural after-effects), should not depend on prior experience.

Shape perception in infants has only recently been directly studied. Fantz (1963, 1966) employed his preference technique first to show that infants, even neonates, could discriminate between complex forms. He, as well as a number of other investigators, varied the stimuli presented to the infant to determine the stimulus dimensions to which they were attending. The reader is again referred to the chapter by Kessen for a thorough discussion of this work and to the section on attention (VI) of the present chapter for additional consideration of these studies.

Bower has employed measures of response generalization to assess directly the function of certain Gestalt laws in infancy. In one study (Bower, 1965b) he used inhibition of an unconditioned sucking response to a "surprising" stimulus as an index of an infant's sensitivity to perceptual unity. For example, infants were shown a pair of vertical rods moving together from side to side. After they had been habituated to this and no longer ceased sucking upon presentation of the display it was changed. Now the rods moved toward and away from each other. For one change the height-separation ratio of the rods was kept constant so they projected the image of a rigid pair of rods approaching or receding from S. For the second change the rods had constant height so they project an image of two objects moving together and apart. This latter image of a previously rigid configuration of two rods might be surprising as a disruption of "common fate." The sucking rate of 10-week-old infants was in fact significantly suppressed when they were shown the second display change as compared with the first. Two other displays constructed on analogous principles to exemplify the Gestalt properties of proximity and continuation did not result in differential responding until 40 weeks of age. In a second study Bower (1967) again used the generalization of an operant response and was able to show that good continuation may be an effective shape variable for 5-week-old infants, although simple proximity still was not. These imaginative

experiments of Bower are excellent demonstrations of techniques for investigation of complex perceptual problems in infants. However, the particular choice of stimuli permit alternative explanations and the small number of stimuli limit the generality of the results, thus restricting the theoretical implications.

Bower (1966) has reported a somewhat more systematic exploration of shape constancy in infants. This study again employed generalization of an operant response, in this case head turning. The experiments involved conditioning an infant to respond to a particular shape at a particular slant, then testing for generalization to stimuli which (1) were physically the same shape, but were at different slants and projected different retinal images, (2) were physically different shapes but were at the same slant and projected different retinal images, and (3) were physically different shapes and were at different slants but projected the same retinal image. In all the experiments the first condition elicited the most generalization, that is, there was shape constancy. On the basis of these data Bower argues quite convincingly that the empiricist position of independent registry and subsequent combination of shape of projected images and slant must be incorrect. He concludes that infants are set to respond to higher-order invariants specifying shape-at-a-slant and that they ignore the lower-order invariants of simple slant or image shape.

It is clear, in summary, that infants, even as neonates, can discriminate among some aspects of shape. Just what the stimulus determinants are is not always clear. The work of Bower certainly suggests that infants respond to some very complex parameters of shape, but much more systematic work is needed before the nature of these parameters is understood. Some other possibilities will be considered in connection with the discussion of attention.

Considerable work has been done on various Gestalt factors in shape perception with older children. There have been several studies of figure-ground relations in children. Werner and Strauss (1941) and Dolphin and Cruikshank (1951), for example, examined the possibility that figure-ground differentiation was poorer in retarded children than in normals. Their results suggested that brain-damaged children (but not all retardates) are more oriented to ground than normal children, who are figure oriented. Spivack (1963) has suggested that these results may be due in part to the use of a different response criterion by the brain damaged. He himself (Spivack and Levine, 1959) provides some evidence that brain-damaged children show less reversal than normal children in stimuli with ambiguous figure-ground relations such as the Necker cube and the Shroeder staircase.

Elkind and Scott (1962), using a greater variety of ambiguous figures with children in nursery school and first, second, and third grades, found an increasing ability as a function of age to name alternative figures of the stimuli. They also found a correlation of .43 between IQ and number of figures named. Botha (1963), studying nursery school children, looked at the effect of pre-exposure on the reversal of an ambiguous figure. The stimulus could be seen either as a black figure on white ground or a white figure on black ground. The children were pre-exposed predominantly to one or the other of the two alternative ways of organizing the stimulus. Then they were shown the ambiguous stimulus. They reported seeing the alternative presented less often in the pre-exposure. This was also true of semiliterate natives but not of educated adults. The latter always reported seeing the black-on-white alternative, which the author attributes to long experience reading black print. Elkind, Koegler, and Go (1962) also conducted a pre-exposure experiment with ambiguous figures. This study was in fact a training experiment with 6-, 7-, and 8-year-olds. They were shown one set of ambiguous figures as a pretest, then a second set as a training set of figures, and finally the original set of figures as a posttest. The children were asked in the tests to report what they saw while looking at the ambiguous figures. Training consisted of giving successively more complete clues as to what the alternative organization of the figure might be. The children of all three ages improved from pretest to posttest in the number of figures named and they retained this improvement over a 1-month interval. In addition, there were significant age differences in both the pretests and posttests, with the older children reporting more figures than the younger. However, this experiment was weak insofar

as there was no control group to assess the effect of repeated presentation of the stimuli on pretest and posttest without the intervening training.

Other investigations of children conducted in the Gestalt tradition include studies of embedded figures, part-whole identifications, and identifications of incomplete figures. Ghent (1956) conducted an investigation of the ability of children 4 to 8 years old to identify overlapping and embedded figures. When overlapping figures represented real objects the children named the objects, when they were overlapping geometric figures the children identified the objects from an array, and when embedded figures were used the children had to trace out the hidden figure which matched the sample given them. Reliable age differences were found, with the older children being able to make more identifications than the younger. In addition, the children found the embedded figures more difficult than the overlapping realistic figures, which in turn were more difficult than the overlapping geometric figures. This result must be accepted with caution because of the differences in procedure among the three tasks and lack of control for order effects.

Part-whole identification in children has been studied by Elkind, Koegler, and Go (1964). They showed children figures which consisted of objects arranged to form larger objects. For example, candy canes were arranged in the shape of a scooter. The child was asked to describe each figure and was scored on whether he mentioned the parts only, the whole figure only, or both parts and whole. "part" responses dropped from 71% at 4 years of age to 21% at 9 years of age. Over this age range "whole" responses vary from 17 to 0%, while "part and whole" responses increase from 11 to 79%. On the surface these data do not seem to support the Gestalt view that perceptual development proceeds from global to analytic or that stimuli become more articulated. However, in such studies it is very difficult to control for the specific properties of the stimuli comprising the parts and the whole—their meaningfulness, their discriminability, etc. Thus it is difficult to make unequivocal interpretations of the results.

The perception of incomplete figures has been compared in children and adults in a series of studies by Gollin (1960b, 1962, 1965). In various experiments he showed Ss ranging from preschoolers (2½ years) to third graders and adults incomplete pictures which were made by eliminating large portions of the contour of line drawings of objects such as a shoe. Their task was simply to identify the picture. In one experiment successively more complete pictures were presented until S was able to identify the picture correctly. In other experiments only the most incomplete picture was ever shown. In general, as would be expected, the older Ss performed better than the younger Ss. For example, in one study the correlation between recognition ability and CA was .66. In many of the experiments Gollin was interested in training Ss to improve their recognition scores. Typically the training involved pre-exposure (naming or serial learning) to the complete outline figures or moderately incomplete figures and then testing for effect of training with very incomplete outlines of the same figures. The adults benefited more than the children when the training was on the complete outline figures, but there was no age difference when the training was on the moderately incomplete figures. This interaction between the variables of figure completeness and age might be due to the fact that there is a greater difference between the training stimuli and test stimuli when the complete figures are used for training than when the moderately incomplete figures are used. Older Ss with higher MA may be able to make this transfer better than younger Ss.

Some support for this hypothesis is found in another experiment in which Gollin found that Ss with higher IQ or higher CA were able to recognize the incomplete figures better after training on the complete figures. Potter (1966) has studied the recognition of figures impoverished by blurring rather than deletion although not from a Gestalt-theoretical point of view. The emphasis in this study was on cognitive factors in recognition. In general, adults recognized figures with more blurring than did children. However, older children and adults, perhaps because of more integrated responding, were more hindered by forming early hypotheses about the nature of a blurred figure than were younger children. The older Ss required relatively more focus-

ing of the figure than did younger Ss after an incorrect hypothesis had been made.

One additional study of Gestalt properties should be mentioned. This is a study by Graham, Berman, and Ernhart (1960) of the ability of preschool children to copy forms. Children 2½ to 5 years were asked to copy various forms including a straight line, a diamond, and other curved and straight line figures. Each reproduction was judged on whether it was more or less "primitive" than the original in terms of Werner's (1957) criteria of simplification, increased closure, and increased symmetry. As Werner would predict, simplification and increased closure were more common in younger children than in older; but so were their opposites, complication and decreased closure (or opening) of the figures. There was more increase of symmetry in the younger children than in the older, which is also in accord with Gestalt expectation. The reproductions were also judged for accuracy on several characteristics: form, curvature or linearity, openness or closedness, orientation, size relationship of parts, and accuracy of intersections. There was improvement in accuracy for all these characteristics as a function of age. The authors conclude that such a simple quantitative change of accuracy is a better description of improvement than a change in the Gestalt properties. Although there have been numerous studies of children's ability to copy forms using the Bender Gestalt test, by and large these studies have not broken down the results by type of error (e.g., Koppitz, 1960). Where the results have been so classified (e.g., Quast, 1961), the scoring categories have not for the most part been relevant to Gestalt properties. However, these scoring categories may have intrinsic merit and the reader is referred to Quast (1957, 1961) for such an analysis.

It is clear from a consideration of the various studies in the Gestalt tradition that there are developmental changes: better identification of the alternative organization of reversible figures, better identification of embedded figures, more identification of the parts and the whole of stimulus configurations, and better recognition of incomplete figures. Although many of these studies are intrinsically interesting, the general implications of the results are not really clear since the relevant stimulus dimensions are not clearly specified. This has been the traditional problem with the Gestalt properties and it has not been solved in these studies with children. There have been some provocative attempts at such specification with adults. For example, Hochberg and McAlister (1953) and Attneave (1954) independently suggested an information theory metric that may define the property of good organization. Hochberg and Brooks (1960) used a variation of this measure to predict whether ambiguous figures would be seen as two- or three-dimensional. Using children as Ss, Hochberg and Brooks (1964) also showed that this measure predicted which of several two-dimensional representations of a geometric solid would be chosen as most like the real solid. However, no direct age comparisons of the predictive value of this measure have been made. Such comparisons would be quite interesting.

Not all investigation of the development of shape perception has been done in the Gestalt tradition. There have been at least two other types of investigation. One, conducted most systematically by Soviet psychologists, is an examination of the perceptual activity of S while he is identifying or discriminating shapes. In a series of studies conducted in Zaporozhets' laboratory, Zinchenko and other colleagues (Lavrent'eva and Ruzskaya, 1960; Tarakanov and Zinchenko, 1960; Zinchenko, 1957, 1960; Zinchenko, Chzhitsin, and Tarakanov, 1962; Zinchenko, Lomov, and Ruzskaya, 1959; Zinchenko and Ruzskaya, 1960a, 1960b) investigated the eye movements involved in visual discrimination of shape and the hand movements involved in haptic discrimination of shape. These studies of children from 3 to 7 years have been reviewed elsewhere (Pick, 1964). It should be noted here, however, that at very young ages, when shape identification was poor, children tended to concentrate their eye or hand movements around the interior of objects and the movements had little relation to the shape. At intermediate ages the movements of the receptor organs conformed rather closely to the contour of the shape. With older children the movements became very abbreviated; they included points on the contour but jumped quickly around and did not at all trace the contour. It also is interesting

to note that these investigators started with the Berkleyian idea that touch teaches vision but were forced by their data (precise identifications earlier by vision than by touch) to reject this hypothesis.

A second type of study of the perceptual development of shape not in the Gestalt tradition is one exemplified by Gibson, Gibson, Pick, and Osser (1962). In such studies the stimuli are constructed so that inferences can be made about the perceptual process from an analysis of the discrimination errors. This study by Gibson et al. was conducted as part of a project investigating basic processes involved in reading, and its immediate goal was to trace the development of children's ability to discriminate letterlike forms. An analysis of printed capital letters was made and a set of standard nonsense line drawings was constructed following various constraints found in the real alphabet. For each standard form four classes of transformation were generated: rotations and reversals, changes of straight lines to curves and vice versa, topological transformations (adding or subtracting a piece to the standard), and perspective transformations (tilting the standard and reproducing the projected view). The children were shown a standard form and an array containing the transformations and some exact copies of the standard. They were asked to pick out all forms identical to the standard. Children at all ages (4 to 8) tended to confuse the perspective transformations with the standard and few children at any age tended to confuse topological transformations with the standard. Rotations and reversals and line-to-curve changes were confused with the standards by the young children but not by the older children. The greatest improvement in these latter discriminations came around 5 to 6 years when the children were presumably learning to read in school. The authors suggest that the kinds of discrimination the child was making in his everyday life transferred to form discrimination. This hypothesis, admittedly post hoc, accounts for the results quite well, although it should be recognized that the particular values of the specific transformations of the standard (e.g., perspective transformations were projected views of standards tilted 45°) might have affected the results. The hypothesis is particularly interesting in two respects. It suggests that children transfer perception of *critical features* from one situation in their environment to another and in fact to a completely novel situation (see also Section VIC). It also suggests that transfer occurs easily from three-dimensional to two-dimensional stimuli.

Another experiment in which inferences about the perceptual process are made from errors in discrimination is one reported by Kerpelman and Pollack (1964). In this study 4-, 5-, and 6-year-old children had to select from a circular array of shapes one that was identical to a standard shape in the center. One hypothesis investigated was that children of different ages might respond on the basis of different parts of shapes. The shapes were either irregular pentagons or only the tops, bottoms, or centers of these pentagons. In all conditions performance improved with age and for all ages bottoms were easiest to identify and centers most difficult. The easy identifiability of the bottoms may have implications for certain hypotheses about scanning behavior in shape perception. For example, Ghent (1961a) has argued that children tend to scan shapes from top to bottom (see Section IIIB) and the present results might seem inconsistent with that hypothesis. However, it is difficult to generalize confidently from these data without a careful analysis of the differences between specific shapes; perhaps the bottoms are more different from each other than the tops.

Research on the development of shape perception (as well as on shape perception in adults) is hampered by a lack of a good metric for shape. This is especially important for inferences about shape perception from error analysis since such analysis depends on the relation between shape differences and errors. If the stimulus differences are not quantifiable or if they are not psychologically meaningful, they are not likely to advance our understanding. The shape differences in the study by Gibson, Gibson, Pick, and Osser seemed to be psychologically meaningful. Other recent studies of shape perception have used stimuli generated on the basis of concepts from information theory. These shapes have certain mathematical properties but the differences between them may not be relevant to the differences between shapes in the real world. Finally the obvious comment should be made that the two approaches—the focus

on receptor organ activity and error analysis in the study of shape perception—should be combined. Not only could the results of one procedure verify the conclusions of the other, but by showing points of inconsistency further insight into the process of perception would be gained. [For a general theoretical analysis of the problems of shape perception the reader is referred to Uhr's (1963) discussion of the problems encountered in computer recognition of shape.]

How does shape perception interact with perception of other stimulus attributes? Recently there has been considerable interest in the relation between color and form perception. The problem has focused on the old observation of Brian and Goodenough (1929) that younger children match stimuli on the basis of color rather than form and older children do the opposite. The methodology of older studies of this phenomenon has been improved and the effects of such stimulus dimension preferences on learning have been explored.

The two currently most active researchers in this area are Corah (1964, 1966) and Suchman (Gaines, 1964; Suchman, 1966; Suchman and Trabasso, 1966a, 1966b). Corah has been interested in the possibility that the color preferences typically found for young children may be based on a difference in attention between younger and older children. It may be more difficult for a young child to attend to the contour of a figure than to the whole colored configuration. In one study (Corah, 1966) this hypothesis was investigated by varying the amount of color and complexity of contour. It was reasoned that if the amount of color was reduced, the preference would be reduced and if the complexity of the contour was increased, the preference for color would be increased since the complex contour would be more difficult to apprehend. A group of young children (4½ years) and a group of older children (8¾ years) were given a matching-to-sample task. The sample form was presented above two comparison forms. One matched the sample in shape and the other in color. The child's task was to pick the comparison stimulus most like the sample. Three types of problems were presented: (1) the shapes were very simple and very different (e.g., square and circle), (2) the shapes were simple but the comparison shapes were similar to the sample (e.g., a square and rectangle), and (3) the shapes were complex (pentagons) and the comparison shapes were similar to the sample shapes. In all three problems the colors were red, blue, and green but for half the problems the shapes were solidly colored and for half the problems just the outlines of the shapes were colored. As hypothesized for the younger children, there were more color responses with the solid colored and more complex shapes. However, overall these children made more form than color responses. For the older children there were no color responses under any of the conditions.

Suchman has been interested in the relation between color-form preference and ability to discriminate. In one of her studies Suchman (1966) compared 7- to 12-year-old hearing and deaf children. One of the two preference tests involved comparisons of three stimuli that varied in color, shape, and size. The stimuli were so selected that any pair had the same value on one of these dimensions but differed on the other two. The S's task was to choose the stimulus of the three he considered to be different.[2] In both this test and a sorting test of the Weigl or Goldstein-Scheerer type the hearing children displayed a preference for form and the deaf children for color. Furthermore, in discrimination tests of color and of form the hearing Ss discriminated form more accurately than the deaf Ss and the deaf Ss discriminated color more accurately than the hearing Ss. Although this seems to support a hypothesis of relation between preference and discrimination accuracy, the results of a direct comparison between children (both deaf and hearing) who preferred form and those who preferred color did not show a statistically significant relation between their preferences

[2] It should be pointed out that this procedure involves asking Ss to attend to differences between stimuli, whereas the more traditional matching-to-sample procedure involves Ss attending to similarities. Although these procedures may be logically equivalent, they may not be psychologically equivalent. It is possible that an S will attend to different stimulus dimensions when asked to look for similarities than when he is asked to look for differences. This possibility should be kept in mind when interpreting dimensional "preferences."

and accuracy of discrimination. Also, no relation was found in this study between color or form preference and performance in a discrimination learning problem in which the relevant cues were color or form. However, in another study (Suchman and Trabasso, 1966b) with 2- to 6-year-old hearing Ss such a relation was found. That is, color or form preference facilitated learning when the preferred dimension was the relevant one.

The difference in preference between deaf and hearing Ss is quite interesting since it suggests a very unexpected influence of early sensory deprivation on saliency of stimulus dimensions. This is a reliable result replicating an earlier study (Gaines, 1964), and it is not based on intellectual differences since the hearing and deaf children were matched for IQ and age. The underlying explanation for this difference in preference is not clear.

In spite of the interest in the relation between stimulus dimension preference and discrimination ability no one investigating such preferences has equated the discriminability of the stimulus differences on the basis of psychophysical experiments. If the young child's color preferences and the older child's form preferences merely reflect greater discriminability of the preferred dimension, the results are somewhat less interesting than if a preference is manifest independently of discriminability. It is also the case that most of the preference studies have utilized only a few colors and shapes. These dimensions should be sampled widely in order to generalize the results to color and form as stimulus dimensions. However, there are large numbers of studies using slightly different procedures, forms, and colors which typically find a greater degree of form preference in older children. Such consistency argues that this preference is a real one and not an artifact of the particular stimuli used. Quite interesting but not so consistently reported is the observation of a shift from form to color preference at a very early age (Brian and Goodenough, 1929).

Another stimulus dimension preference has been observed by Klein (1963). He noted that in tactual matching young children tend to match stimuli on the basis of texture, whereas older children tend to match on the basis of shape. Again the texture differences and the shape differences were not equated for discriminability and the results are limited to the shapes and textures used in this one study since no other work has been reported.

Tactual perception of shape is a problem that has recently elicited considerable interest. One type of tactual problem is analogous to the overlapping and embedded figures studied in the context of visual shape perception. Gollin (1960a, 1961) asked children and adults to discriminate tactually a figure made up of tacks placed in plywood. Their task was to indicate whether two figures were the same or different. In half of the pairs the figures were masked by having tacks of a different size placed at random around the basic figures. The remaining pairs were unmasked figures, that is, just the tacks defining each figure were present. Adults were better than first- through third-grade children at discriminating both types of figures. Masking the figures resulted in a decrement in the children's performance but not in the adults' performance. Also, adults and older children showed facilitation in discriminating the masked figures after tactual experience with the unmasked. The greater ability of older Ss in this task is similar to that found by Ghent (1956) for visually embedded figures, as has previously been discussed.

Other developmental studies of tactual shape perception have investigated stimulus properties in relation to shape discrimination. Hermelin and O'Connor (1961) used unfamiliar Greek and Russian letters in tactual and visual matching tasks. They found that retarded children were more accurate tactually than visually. Medinnus and Johnson (1966) failed to replicate this result, however, so the status of this finding is unclear. Soviet investigators (Lavrent'eva and Ruzskaya, 1960; Tarakanov and Zinchenko, 1960; Zinchenko, 1957, 1960; Zinchenko, Chzhitsin, and Tarakanov, 1962; Zinchenko, Lomov, and Ruzskaya, 1959; Zinchenko and Ruzskaya, 1960a, 1960b) have examined tactual discrimination tasks again in relation to response processes. Their conclusions for the development of tactual perception of planometric stimuli are similar to those for visual shape perception. Younger children are quite inaccurate and their exploratory movements do not conform to the contour of objects. As their exploration becomes more systematic the number of errors decreases. This improvement

occurs at a slightly older preschool age than with visual perception of the same shapes. However, the improvement in tactual perception never reaches the same level as visual perception during the preschool years.

The later development of tactual shape perception was the subject of a study by the present authors (Pick and Pick, 1966). This was a tactual replication of the study of Gibson et al. with letterlike forms. The forms were raised line drawings on a metal background. The children were blindfolded and explored the shapes simultaneously in pairs, each consisting of a standard form and a transformation. The Ss were children from 6 to 13 years of age and adults. The tactual perception of these forms was much more difficult than the visual perception of the forms. Even adults made an appreciable though smaller number of errors than the children. At all ages the perspective transformations were confused with the standards most often and the topological transformations least often. The line-to-curve transformations were of intermediate difficulty. These results are similar to those for visual perception of the forms. The main differenece between the visual and tactual results was with the rotations and reversals. These were as easy to discriminate tactually from the standards as were the topological transformations. This is reasonable if one considers how the child is exploring the stimuli. He typically moves his two hands over the two forms synchronously. A rotation or reversal of a form would be equivalent to a topological transformation in that the child is likely to find parts added or missing in corresponding places explored by the hands.

In general, very little work has been done in studying the development of tactual shape perception. Furthermore, the stimulus dimensions varied have been derived from visual studies and so a good metric for shape is lacking in tactual perception. In addition, it is not clear that the same shape dimensions are psychologically meaningful for both sensory modalities. An imaginative analysis of the shape dimensions psychologically important in tactual perception is needed. No work has been done with tactual shape perception of infants. One might speculate that infants would be particularly sensitive, for example, to the shapes of nipples, although tactual sensitivity of the mouth and tongue is not often studied.

The studies of the development of shape perception concur in finding that tactual perception develops more slowly and is less accurate than comparable visual performance. These findings place an additional burden of proof on empiricist theoretical statements that visual perception is dependent on prior tactual perception.

C. Effects of Early Experience on Perception

The nativist-empiricist controversy receives most precise definition in studies manipulating early experience. With such direct study the interactive relation between heredity and environment also becomes most clear. Of course manipulation of early experience is a procedure most generally applicable to animals. (See Chapter 12 for a more general discussion of this area.) However, in some cases mild or enriching manipulations can be undertaken with children, or advantage can be taken of pathologies such as congenital blindness or deafness to study the effects of early experience in humans. Generally speaking studies manipulating early experience can be divided into deprivation or enrichment studies. In addition, some investigators have suggested that perceptual rearrangements (distortion studies) provide information analogous to that from early experience studies. Studies of experimental manipulation in the environments of animals and their effects on perceptual development will be considered first and then the effects of early experience on human perceptual development.

Studies of the effects of early experience on shape perception have often used an enrichment design. Animals raised in a "normal" environment have been compared with animals raised in an "enriched" environment in subsequent ability to discriminate shapes. The basic question, of course, is whether any such enrichment is effective at all. Other important problems include the question of the existence of a critical period for the effects and the question of specificity between the early stimulation and the subsequent effects.

In one series of studies Gibson and Walk and their students (Gibson and Walk, 1956; Walk, Gibson, Pick and Tighe, 1958; Gibson, Walk, and Tighe, 1959; Walk, Gibson, Pick, and Tighe, 1959) conducted a total of nine different experiments. All of these were variations of a design which involved early exposure of rats to triangles and circles. In the first study of the series (Gibson and Walk, 1956) triangles and circles cut out of sheet metal were hung on the sides of the cages during rearing. This exposure markedly facilitated subsequent discrimination learning between triangles and circles. (These were painted on the doors of a Grice discrimination apparatus, which presented on each trial two alternatives at the end of an alley.) With this strong effect as a basis the investigators began a series of studies focusing on other variables such as the role of reinforcement, the timing of exposure, and the specificity of the exposed stimuli to the subsequently learned discrimination. In conducting these studies replications of the original study which were included in the designs frequently did not produce the original results. Examination of all the studies revealed that whenever the original results were replicated the pre-exposure forms were cutouts on the sides of the animals' cages. All failures to replicate occurred when the pre-exposure forms had been modified so that they were painted on a background. The authors suggest that the essential difference between the cutouts and painted forms was the presence of motion parallax when animals moved with respect to the former but not the latter. Possibly this parallax attracted the animal's attention to the edge of the form.

Because of the only intermittent success in replicating the original phenomenon during the series of studies, many of the follow-up experiments investigating other questions did not produce informative results. Those experiments investigating specificity of the early experience suggest that the facilitating effect generalizes over a wide range of stimuli. It was also determined that facilitation of triangle-circle discrimination would occur with only one of these as the pre-exposure form and it made little difference whether it was the subsequently positive or negative stimulus in the discrimination learning. Recently Kerpelman (1965) investigated the role of reinforcement using a design which also included a replication of the original Gibson and Walk experiment. His results indicated that reinforcement, eating in the presence of the stimuli, did play a role, even though differential reinforcement of the positive and negative stimuli did not occur.

In two experiments Forgus (1958a, 1958b) adduced additional evidence that early exposure of rats to outlines of forms facilitates later discrimination between them. The results of his experiments suggested that facilitation in the discrimination did not occur for forms identical to those pre-exposed but rather to variations of the original forms. For example, pre-exposure to the sides of a triangle without the angles markedly facilitated later discrimination of a complete triangle from a circle. This was not true when pre-exposure was to the complete figures. These results show the effect of early experience by capitalizing on the animal's response to a novel aspect of stimuli. It seems to be important that the novel aspect be of high information value such as angles.

In a broad sense studies of imprinting might be considered to demonstrate the effect of early enriching experience on later perception. These will not be reviewed here; the reader is referred to Chapters 6 and 12 for discussion of this phenomenon.

The deprivation technique for the study of effects of early experience is typified in a study by Riesen and Aarons (1959) which demonstrates the effect of visual deprivation on a subsequent visual discrimination. These investigators raised kittens in darkness for the first 6 weeks of life. Then they were subdivided into groups which were given (1) 1 hour per day of diffuse light stimulation without head movement or (2) 1 hour per day of pattern stimulation without head movement or (3) 1 hour per day of pattern vision with freedom of movement, or (4) normal rearing in the laboratory environment. All animals were trained between 14 and 18 weeks on a discrimination between a stationary and moving form and a brightness discrimination. The animals in all four groups were able to learn the brightness discrimination, but the animals who had pattern stimulation with free movement, groups (3) and (4), were vastly superior in learning the discrimination between stationary and moving form. Examination of the eyes of all the animals suggested that the peripheral parts of the visual system were unaffected by the differential rearing, as did the

fact that they all could learn the brightness discrimination. The critical factor appeared to be the possibility of movement in the presence of patterned visual stimulation and the deficit caused by the absence of this experience seemed to be central in nature.

The importance of movement, particularly *self-produced* movement in the presence of visual stimulation, has also been implicated in the development of depth perception. Held and Hein (1963) raised kittens in the dark until the age of 8 to 12 weeks. At this time they were exposed to visual stimulation for 3 hours per day in the following manner. An experimental and a control kitten were linked together at opposite ends of a pivoted bar. The bar was set inside a vertically striped cylinder and the kittens were harnessed in such a way that every movement that the experimental animal made pushed the control animal through an equal distance. The control animal was raised off the floor so it could not move itself. However, it was exposed to exactly the same changes in pattern of visual stimulation as was the experimental animal. The difference was that the changes were correlated with the movements the experimental animal was making. (This design epitomizes the yoked control.) Kittens were tested daily for visually guided paw placement (i.e., reaching out toward an approaching surface), and as soon as the experimental kitten made a paw placement both kittens of the pair were tested on a visual cliff. All experimental animals developed a paw placement to an approaching surface and a blink response to an approaching hand before the corresponding control animals. At the time of visual cliff testing all experimental animals made appropriate depth responses, that is, they chose the shallow side on all trials, but the control animals responded at an approximately random level. The initial inability of the control animals to make a paw placement is congruent with observations made by Riesen and Aarons on the kittens which were raised without the opportunity to move in the presence of patterned stimulation.

Held and Hein's study and nearly all the other studies of the effect of early experience on depth perception have used the method of deprivation rather than enrichment. Many of these studies have utilized the visual cliff.

The first of these studies of performance on the visual cliff compared dark-reared and light-reared rats on their preference for the shallow side of the cliff. In these studies (Walk, Gibson, and Tighe; 1957; Walk and Gibson, 1961) in which rats were raised in the dark for 90 days and then tested in a simple cliff situation no differences in preference were found between the normally reared animals and the dark-reared animals. However, subsequent studies (Nealy and Riley, 1963; Walk, Trychin, and Karmel, 1965) extending the dark-rearing period of rats to 140 or more days found a failure of depth discrimination on the cliff. The effect was not irreversible; after 2 weeks of exposure to light the animals began to discriminate depth.

Walk and Gibson (1961) also raised kittens in the dark until the age of 26 days. In contrast to the rats reared 90 days in the dark, these animals seemed functionally blind when they were placed on the visual cliff. They stumbled around, falling off the centerboard of the cliff indiscriminately to either side. They made no placing responses or tracking response of moving objects. Their only visual response was a pupillary reflex to changes in illumination. During several days of living in light their visual cliff behavior and paw placement gradually indicated depth discrimination. In contrast, control light-reared kittens showed good depth responses on the cliff and accurate paw placement. Thus the visual development of a kitten seems much more sensitive to early manipulation than that of the rat.

That early experience can affect the rat's visual development is demonstrated in more analytic experiments of Walk and Gibson (1961). In these experiments they investigated the effective depth cues on the visual cliff for light- and dark-reared rats. The typical cliff situation was modified in two ways. First, real differences in depth were eliminated by placing both visual surfaces directly underneath the glass. Differences in texture density of the retinal image were preserved by making one surface pattern so fine that it projected to the eye approximately the same sized pattern elements as the surface usually at the deep side of the cliff. In the second modification real differences in depth were preserved. Differences in texture density

were eliminated by making the elements of the pattern of the deep side of the cliff so large that they projected the same sized elements to the eye as the elements on the shallow side. Normal light- and dark-reared rats were tested in both these conditions. The light-reared rats made appropriate depth responses under both conditions: they chose the coarser textured pattern when depths on both sides were equal or they avoided the actual deep side when texture density differences had been eliminated. The dark-reared rats, however, responded to the real depth differences but not to the texture density differences with equated depth. The authors suggest that the effective cue for the dark-reared rats is the differential motion parallax present with real depth differences between the two sides of the cliff. For the light-reared rats both texture size and motion parallax are effective cues. The authors speculate that texture size may be a learned depth cue by virtue of its association with motion parallax. They do show that the preference for the larger texture size does develop gradually in dark-reared rats after they have been brought out into the light.

It has been found possible to modify the typical preference for the shallow side of the visual cliff. In two studies animals were raised on the deep side of a visual cliff and this experience tempered their visual preferences for the shallow side. Tallicaro and Farrell (1964) found that 35 hours of rearing chicks on the deep side of a visual cliff eliminated the usual preference for the shallow side. In fact, there was a slight but not statistically significant preference for the deep side. Kaess and Wilson (1964) found that 2 weeks of rearing rats on the deep side of a visual cliff reversed the typically found preference for the shallow side. Although the possibility of thus modifying a preference is very exciting, it says little about whether the animal innately discriminates depth. It certainly does not, as Tallicaro and Farrell suggest, cast doubt on whether animals innately avoid a cliff.

For obvious reasons, deprivation of early perceptual experience is not often undertaken with humans. However, studies have been conducted of naturally occurring deprivation, for example, of congenitally blind Ss whose sight has been restored. Senden (1960) reviewed a large number of cases derived from a variety of sources extending from medical reports to newspaper articles. Hebb (1949) interpreted these cases to show that such patients have considerable difficulty in perceiving or learning to perceive shape. However, Wertheimer (1951) has criticized his interpretation and indeed Hebb himself acknowledged the difficulty in making such use of nonscientific sources. More recently Gregory and Wallace (1963) carefully examined a 53-year-old man whose sight had been restored. This patient, who had been blind from the age of 10 months, was able to identify visually certain shapes soon after the operation. These were shapes he had been familiar with tactually, for example, upper-case printed letters. He was not able to identify complex shapes such as the expression in people's faces, and his susceptibility to geometric illusions was very low. No mention was made of any difficulty in identifying visual direction. If a capacity for identifying visual direction by pointing is present in persons with restored sight, a means is provided for intermodal transfer of shape perception from touch (or kinesthesis and proprioception) to vision. The shape of objects seen visually could be traced out and the response could be made to the tracing movement. It might also be possible to perceive the shape without actually making the movement since the information for the movement is present.

Gregory and Wallace's patient saw objects in depth, although his distance scale was somewhat distorted. On the other hand, he saw no depth in two-dimensional line drawings representing three-dimensional objects such as the Necker cube and the Schroeder staircase. This might suggest that visual experience is necessary for seeing depth in such stimuli. However, Hudson (1960) provided evidence that South African natives who had not attended school were also deficient in seeing depth in line drawings.

Is the ability to recognize (as distinguished from seeing depth in) two-dimensional representations of objects, in general, dependent on experience with such representations in our highly pictured world? Hochberg and Brooks (1962) performed the herculean task of raising their son to the age of 19 months

in the absence of two-dimensional representations of objects. At this age his recognition of photographs and other two-dimensional representations of objects was tested and proved to be excellent. Zimmerman and Hochberg (1963) reported a similar experiment with monkeys. Infant monkeys were taught an object discrimination and displayed considerable transfer to photographs of the objects. As the photographs were impoverished in various ways the amount of transfer decreased.

The role of early visual experience on tactual perception can be investigated by comparing the tactual perception of blind and sighted Ss. The relevant data from such experiments has been summarized by Pick, Pick, and Klein (1967) and will not be reviewed here. Most of that work has addressed the problem of shape perception and this may bias the results toward showing a considerable effect of early visual experience. Early visual experience might not effect the tactual perception of texture, for example. There is a commonly held view that visual experience markedly influences one's imagery even with nonvisual perception. Although this may well be true, there is little experimental evidence on the question.

The enrichment technique for investigation of perceptual effects of early experience has not been widely employed with human Ss. White (1968) has enriched the environment of institutionalized infants in particular ways such as increasing the amount of handling by 20 minutes per day in one case and introducing into cribs specific attention attracting objects in another case. He found specific perceptual effects, for example, on the amount of looking behavior and the age at which their hands are noticed. His manipulations, carried out against the background of very careful normative observations, show the power of this combination of techniques. The various educational intervention programs being conducted widely in this country also involve enrichment procedures but, by necessity, the nature of the intervention and analysis of effects are not very specific. If such massive enrichment can be demonstrated to have substantial effects, it is hoped that analytic investigations will be undertaken to determine the specific causes and effects.

II. BASIC SENSITIVITY IN CHILDREN AND PSYCHOPHYSIOLOGY OF PERCEPTUAL DEVELOPMENT

A. Visual Sensitivity

Infant perception has been one of the most exciting topics in perceptual development during recent years. This work has employed a variety of behavioral and physiological responses to index the fact that a stimulus has been registered by an S. The work has been reviewed in detail in Chapter 9 and it will be discussed here only insofar as it relates to developmental trends occurring after infancy.

The initial work in this area documented the fact that infants could make visual discriminations previously thought impossible. Fantz' pioneering work (Fantz, 1961b) is an example of this. He showed that infants preferred to look at complex patterned stimuli rather than homogeneous stimuli. Using this fact, he obtained a measure of the acuity of infants by pairing a homogeneous stimulus with a series of striped stimuli in which the width of stripe varied. It was reasoned that whenever a reliable preference was shown for the striped stimulus, then acuity must be at least high enough to resolve that width of stimulus. The results obtained were in good accord with measures using optokinetic nystagmus as an index of sensitivity (Fantz, Ordy, and Udelf, 1962; Gorman, Cogan, and Gellis, 1957; Dayton, Jones, Aiu, Rawson, Steel, and Rose, 1964). Such studies placed the acuity of infants of 0 to 1 month of age between 20/150 and 20/400 Snellen. In addition, acuity typically has been found to increase with age over the first few months of life.

The investigations of infant visual perception have been concerned with more than basic sensitivity and have tried to look at. stimulus dimensions comprising the infants' visual world. The work on depth and shape has already been briefly described. Responsiveness to stimulus dimensions of complexity, amount of contour, and brightness have also been investigated. The interesting literature describing these results has made clear the necessity of obtaining coherent series of responses so as to be able to infer the stimulus dimension determining the response [see Brennen, Ames, and Moore (1966) on complexity,

Hershenson (1964) for brightness, and Karmel (1966) for contour].

Acuity continues to rise very rapidly through infancy and early childhood, and maximum acuity is usually attained by the age of 10. (Weymouth, 1963). This maximum is typically 20/20 to 20/15 Snellen and it refers to acuity of eyes corrected for focusing difficulties, that is, acuity based on the resolution capability of the retina.

However, one of the primary causes of poor vision in real-life is the inability of the viewer to focus the image properly. Recent work of Haynes, White, and Held (1965) suggests that neonates do not accommodate (change their lens focus) to the changing distance of stimuli. Their eyes have a fixed focus set for targets at approximately 8 inches. During the first several months of life infants improve in ability to accommodate to targets of different distances, and by the age of 4 months they adjust their accommodation quite precisely to the distance of the target.

It is common ophthalmological practice to regard the relaxed, unaccommodated eye as the standard from which to judge the refraction condition of the visual system. The relaxed or unaccommodated eye should focus on the retina parallel rays of light (i.e., rays of light coming from a distant target). This means the refraction of the light at the cornea and at the lens should result in the image being focused on the retina. For infants and young children the image is often focused behind the retina and they are termed hypermetropic. As the child grows older his eye becomes bigger and the distance from lens to retina increases more than is necessary for focusing the image on the retina. The image would now be focused in front of the retina (myopia) except that the lens and cornea become less refractive with age, helping to balance the change of focus due to increased size of the eye. The balance is not quite correct and there is a tendency for children to be hypermetropic and for adults to be myopic.

There is very little information on absolute thresholds for detection of light in children. The probable reason for this is the tedious procedure for obtaining such thresholds, involving long periods of dark adaptation followed by exacting judgments. There are a few data on contrast sensitivity. Doris and Cooper (1966) varied the brightness of white stripes on a black background. They found that older infants (up to 69 days of age) showed optokinetic nystagmus with less bright stripes than did younger infants (down to 4 days of age). Unfortunately, the brightness of the background also varied and one cannot be certain whether the age change was a function of absolute or relative brightness. Pollack (1963) obtained an increase of contrast threshold as a function of age in children between 8 and 14 years. This is the only report of a decrease in sensitivity with children so young (see Eichorn, 1963). However, Pollack cites other evidence that sensitivity decreases as a function of age with older Ss. (This result is important for his theoretical position, which will be described subsequently.)

It is generally agreed that contrast sensitivity is closely related to contour formation. Hence it would be reasonable to expect developmental changes in other contour processes such as the type of masking described by Werner (1935): if a disc is presented briefly to an S, followed by a circumscribed ring, the disc may not be seen; the S reports that he has seen only a ring. On the other hand, if the disc alone is presented for the same amount of time, S has no trouble reporting it. Apprently the ring masks the perception of the disc. Parametric research has shown that the temporal duration of the disc and the interval between disc and ring are important determiners of degree of masking. Pollack (1965b) has investigated age changes in this phenomenon. He found that masking occurs with longer intervals between disc and ring in younger children (7 years) than in older children (10 years). Since masking has also been found to depend on figure-ground contrast, it was suggested that the effective age variable is the decrease in contrast sensitivity, which Pollack also observed.

Sensitivity to hue differences is also difficult to measure in young children because of the laborious psychophysical techniques necessary for precision. There were a number of early attempts to measure hue perception in infants, and these are reviewed in Munn (1965). The problem is an especially interesting one because languages divide the wavelength continuum differently. That is, some languages divide a given range of the visual wavelength continuum with many color names, whereas other languages use only a few names. It would be a very interesting example of perceptual learning if preverbal children discriminate along the wavelength continuum differently from verbal children, and it might suggest an effect of language on perception. Before this question is asked it will be necessary to determine how preverbal children perceive hue. As Munn pointed out, it is necessary to rule out discrimination between hues on the basis of differential brightness. Investigators of hue perception in infants have mostly used preference measures, but they have also used the tendency for infants to track spots of one hue when moved against backgrounds of another hue. The brightness of the hues was equated in many of these studies by using values obtained from adults. As Munn points out this is a questionable procedure because the relative brightness of different colors may not be the same for infants and adults.

There has been relatively little work on hue discrimination with older children. Navrat (1965), using children from 3 to 10 years, observed increasing precision with age in matching pigmented tints. On the other hand, Pollack (1966), using more precise measurement techniques, found no age changes in hue discrimination with children between the ages of 7 and 12 years.

B. Auditory Sensitivity

The work on infant perception has included some interesting documentation of infant's auditory perception. For example, Steinschneider, Lipton, and Richmond (1966) found that the auditory threshold to sounds for 2- to 5-day-old infants was less than 70 db (relative to 0.0002 dyn/cm²). These investigators used changes in heart rate as a measure of infant sensitivity. It is important to note that the sensitivity of the infant is at least as good as observed here. It is quite possible that sounds are detected at lower intensities but not reflected in changes of heart rate. Bartoshuk (1964) was able to scale auditory stimuli using the same physiological response. He presented a series of sounds from 48 to 78 db (relative 0.0002 dyn/cm²) to neonates 1 to 4 days old and measured their change in heart rate. He obtained a power function relating physiological response to physical intensity of the stimulus ($\triangle HR = I^n$ where

$\triangle HR =$ change in heart rate, $I =$ intensity, and n is the exponent). The value of the exponent was found to be 0.53. Stevens (1961), using adults, had found n to be 0.6 for a power function relating judged magnitude of sound to intensity. The close agreement raises the interesting possibility that sound intensity is perceived similarly over a very wide age range.

Evidence for frequency discrimination, like evidence for hue discrimination, is difficult to obtain in pure form in infants. However, Leventhal and Lipsitt (1964) obtained data suggestive of a frequency discrimination when the frequency change was 200 to 1000 cps but not when the change was from 200 to 500 cps. They used such measures as changes in activity level and heart rate as indices of sensitivity. In addition, using cardiac rate measures, Bartoshuk (1962a) and Bridger (1961) provide some evidence for frequency discrimination in neonates between 100 and 1000 cps and 400 and 1000 cps respectively.

Auditory acuity in older children also has not been intensively studied. There is, however, at least one precise normative study. Eagles, Wishik, Doerfler, Melnick, and Levine (1963) used a large sample of school children between the ages of 5 and 14. Their data show an increasing absolute sensitivity to sound until 12 to 13 years. At the age of 14 there was a slight decrease in sensitivity. The maximum age difference, which was between 5 and 13 year olds at 250 cps, is only 6 or 7 db (relative to 0.0002 db). However, such large numbers of Ss were used that this difference was easily significant. The age differences are greatest at the lower frequencies; they decrease but are still present at the highest frequency tested, 8000 cps. The age differences are quite consistent; they occur independently in boys, girls, Negroes, and whites.

Recently McKee and Riley have investigated relational learning using auditory parameters (McKee and Riley, 1962; Riley and McKee, 1963; Riley, McKee, and Hadley, 1964). They utilized a transposition design to assess the degree to which children respond relationally to frequency and intensity of sound. The basic result is that more children (first to third graders) respond relationally after learning an intensity discrimination than after learning a frequency discrimination.

In transfer tests after frequency discrimination training neither children nor adults as groups respond consistently (absolutely or relationally). The amount of relational responding to frequency was increased for all ages if the interval between the training sounds was made smaller (Riley and McKee, 1963). However, a check with magnitude estimation scaling techniques indicated that the small size of the intervals between the training stimuli did not account for the greater amount of relational transposition for the intensity dimension. The investigators suggest the intriguing hypothesis that Stevens' (1961) distinction between prothetic and metathetic stimulus dimensions might apply to type of transposition. He has noted that psychophysical scales with different properties are obtained for stimulus dimensions such as intensity, which seem to depend primarily on amount of stimulation, and for dimensions like frequency, which appear to depend upon locus of stimulation. Intensity is a prothetic dimension and frequency metathetic. If such dimensions are typically mediated by different physiological mechanisms, our perception of them might also lead to relational or absolute discrimination learning.

C. Sensitivity in the Lower Senses

Studies of tactual sensitivity in neonates have indicated that females are more sensitive to mild electric shock than males (Lipsitt and Levy, 1959). Stimulation of the neonates' feet with an aesthesiometer does not yield consistent sex differences, but stimulation of the abdomen with an air jet again produces greater sensitivity in females (Bell, 1964). Some previous observations had shown female adults to have higher tactual sensitivity than males. Ghent (1961b), in a study of children ages 5 to 11, found greater sensitivity in girls to stimulation of the center part of the upper arm. However, she found no higher sensitivity in girls to stimulation of the thumb, and over the age range studied there was a slight increase of sensitivity for boys but no consistent change for girls.

The response of children to simultaneous tactual stimulation has been studied by Fink and Bender (1953). When a child is stimulated simultaneously in two places on his body, for example, his cheek and hand, he may not detect one of the sources of stimulation (extinction) or he may misperceive the locus of one of the sources (displacement). Fink and Bender found that the incidence of such errors decreases from 3 to 15 years. There is a marked practice effect, and even the older children make many errors in the early trials. Stimulation of the face seems to dominate other parts of the body; stimulation of the face rarely results in extinction, and stimulation of another part of the body often is displaced toward the face. The mechanism for this phenomenon is not clear. The authors try to relate it to Gestalt principles such as good closure, but their explanation is not very convincing. In their procedure the stimuli were applied by E simply touching S. The synchrony and intensity of stimulation cannot be very carefully controlled using such a method. This tactual extinction and displacement need to be studied with a better technology because they may be related to work on the ability to process more than one channel of information at a time (see Broadbent, 1958). Bekesy (1967) has summarized a large number of technically elegant experiments with adults which appear to be related to these phenomena.

There has been some work with infants, for example, see Engen, Lipsitt, and Kaye (1963) on olfaction, but no other developmental investigations of basic sensitivity in other lower sense modalities. This is unfortunate since both theoretical and practical problems might well be illuminated with research, for example, on taste sensitivity. Taste buds are more widely distributed in the mouth of children than in adults, but there have been no systematic investigations to see if this wider distribution is correlated with greater sensitivity. Since gustatory stimuli are easy to mix, taste might be a convenient modality in which to do masking and detection experiments with children. In a practical vein, basic knowledge of children's taste sensitivity could be applied to preparation of food for children.

D.   Laterality and Sensitivity

Differential sensitivity as a function of side of stimulation has been reported for vision, audition, and touch. The development of such sensory asymmetry has important implications for brain function and for perceptual learning.

A large amount of research has been conducted on detection of stimuli presented to the right or left of a visual fixation point. A careful review of much of this work with adults can be found in Howard and Templeton (1966). If letters or words are flashed either on the right or the left but not both, those on the right are detected more easily. If letters or words are flashed simultaneously on the left and the right, those on the left are detected more easily. Two hypotheses have been advanced to account for these results; one has to do with differential localization of function in the brain and the other has to do with learned scanning tendencies. Mishkin and Forgays (1952), for example, concluded that training in reading establishes a more efficient neural organization in one visual hemisphere than in the other. Harcum (1964), on the other hand, posits the existence of a perceptual scan factor as well as a sensitivity factor. Only two developmental studies of this phenomenon have been conducted (Forgays, 1953; Dyer and Harcum, 1961). Forgays studied children from grades 1 through 12. He presented words either in the right or left visual field and found a gradually increasing advantage for words presented on the right. That this advantage is a function of experience or training is supported by other studies, which showed that for Hebrew readers words are recognized in the left visual field more easily (Mishkin and Forgays, 1952; Orbach, 1952). Dyer and Harcum also found a superiority of the right visual field for recognition of binary patterns. They attributed the result to a recency effect resulting from scanning left to right. The last element to be scanned is reported most accurately. If this interpretation is correct, Harcum's scan factor may be in reality a short-term memory phenomenon.

Greater auditory sensitivity on one side of the body than the other has been reported only under conditions in which the two ears are in competition. When different inputs are presented simultaneously to the two ears, the right ear has a higher accuracy for recognition of speech and the left ear for nonspeech sounds such as melodies (Kimura, 1963, 1964). In the only developmental study of this phenomenon (Kimura, 1963) the right ear advantage was greatest at the youngest age, 4 years. The lack of large differences at the older ages may have been attributable to a ceiling effect since absolute performance levels were high. In any event there was not the expected developmental increase of lateral differentiation. The right ear advantage has been thought to be related to cortical lateralization of speech. There is considerable evidence (Penfield and Roberts, 1959; Zangwill, 1960; Lenneberg, 1967) that such lateralization, usually with the left hemisphere dominant, develops during childhood. Children who have lesions of the left hemisphere at early ages regain language facility·completely, but adults with similar lesions remain permanently impaired. It may be that the perceptual advantage of the right ear is related to cortical dominance, but the relation must be a complex one. A possible mechanism for a lateral ear advantage (Shankweiler, 1966) would be stronger representation of the contralateral ear than the ipsilateral ear in the dominant hemisphere. Ongoing activity in the brain from this contralateral ear would block processing of input from the ipsilateral ear. Thus if the left hemisphere is responsible for processing speech, the right ear would have a competitive advantage from stronger cortical representation. Shankweiler summarizes some of the evidence for this hypothesis.

Observations of passive tactual thresholds by Weinstein and Sereson (1961) have revealed that sensitivity is greater in the nondominant hand than in the dominant. Ghent (1961b), in a previously mentioned study, investigated whether this differential sensitivity developed with age between 5 and 11 years. In boys the differential sensitivity had developed by 11 years but in the girls it had not. For the 9- and 11-year-olds and a few of the children of other ages thresholds were determined for a section of the upper arm. The sensitivity of the nondominant arm was higher than that of the dominant arm at all ages, but the differences were not statistically significant.

There is a large literature concerned with the relation between lateral dominance and reading disability. In this case lateral dominance has referred to motor dominance, usually handedness. Although motor dominance is not the concern of the present chapter its relation to the perceptual aspects of reading makes consideration relevant. An early hypothesis was that left-handedness or ambidexterity reflected abnormal cortical lateralization

of function. This abnormal lateralization was thought somehow to affect adversely reading ability. Belmont and Birch (1965) adduce evidence to the effect that differences in lateral dominance between normal and retarded readers are found when the retarded readers are sampled from a clinical setting but not when they are obtained from a normal population. It is not clear what kinds of bias the selection from clinical populations introduces. At least clinical samples are not pure cases of reading difficulty.

One problem with studies relating lateral dominance to other functions is the rather arbitrary definition of dominance. Most investigators fail to distinguish between sensory and motor dominance. Furthermore, most of the motor dominance studies have used limb preference as the definition of dominance, but limb skillfulness might be a more meaningful way of defining such dominance. Finally, while dominance is often operationally defined by the hand used in some overt behavior such as ball throwing, a cortical lateral dominance is often inferred. Recently a technique has been developed (Wada and Rasmussen, 1960) which defines the cortical lateralization of speech production in a much more functional way. This involves infusion of sodium amytal into the arteries supplying one side or the other of the brain. A temporary aphasia results from infusing into the "speech dominant" side. The time appears ripe for a careful extensive study of dominance and laterality. This might include determination of laterality for a large number of functions in the same Ss to see whether functions are lateralized in clusters. Replicating such studies at different ages would further define related functions and would suggest fruitful hypotheses about brain function.

III.   SENSORY INTERACTION[3]

A.   Development of Body Image

To what extent is a person aware of the parts of his own body? Does he perceive their position, size, and state accurately? There is an extensive literature on this topic (see Schilder, 1950), but much of the evidence consists of clinical observations. These are

[3] For a more extended treatment of some of these problems see Pick, Pick, and Klein (1967).

provocative, but they have not been investigated in normal populations. There is even very little clinical literature on the development of body image in children.

It is possible to distinguish two general types of questions about one's perception of his body. One has to do with being able to perceive parts of the body in relation to each other. The second has to do with perception of the body in relation to an external reference system. These capacities do not necessarily depend on a single mechanism. Schilder (1950), for example, describes the case of a patient who could indicate by appropriate marking of a diagram a position on a limb of the body that had been tactually stimulated, but the patient had no idea where the stimulated limb was when it was out of sight.

In investigations of body perception Ss are asked to make a response with respect to a stimulated part of the body. Often this means that S has to indicate a target part of his body with another bodily response. Any difficulty could be attributed to either perception of the target or the response indicator or both. Furthermore, Ss are often asked to *identify* stimulated parts of their body. This ability involves more than just discrimination of two parts of the body as different.

The simplest kind of appraisal of one's body perception is the determination of two-point thresholds at various places on the body surface. Dunford (1930) cites a study by Freedman which found a decrease in the two-point sensitivity (as measured by variability) for children up to the age of 12, then an increase. However, a study by Wundt is cited to the effect that children have a smaller space threshold than adults. This question is still unresolved.

At a somewhat more complex level of body perception, Ss can be asked to indicate a point on their body which E had stimulated. Dunford (1930) and Renshaw (1930) both reported developmental studies in which Ss were asked to localize points on their hand or arm that had been tactually stimulated by E. Localization was accomplished by pointing with a stylus held in the other hand. The two studies were consistent in finding that precision was greater in younger children than adults. Renshaw suggested that the decrease in precision with age might be due to a shift from tactual-kinesthetic orientation to visual

orientation. If this were the case, older children and adults might be better at localizing with a visual response while they were becoming worse at localizing with a tactual-kinesthetic response. A visual localizing procedure might involve touching S and having him open his eyes and report graphical coordinates of the point stimulated. Renshaw found preliminary support for this prediction in the same study and subsequently verified it (Renshaw and Wherry, 1931). Visual localization becomes more accurate with age, especially between 13 and 14 years, while tactual-kinesthetic localization as defined in this task becomes worse.

This interesting, unusual result of decreasing accuracy in performance with age should be replicated since the age trends found by both Dunford and Renshaw are rather irregular and are based on relatively few Ss. Another study (Renshaw, Wherry, and Newlin, 1930) provides evidence that the performance of well practiced Ss does not decay with age. The performance of congenitally blind Ss improved with age. That precision may generally be a function of amount of use is suggested by the fact that both Dunford and Renshaw found marked practice effects at all ages.

Clinical observations have indicated that there may be difficulties in discriminating between structurally similar body parts such as the same member on opposite sides of the body or adjacent fingers. Some of these observations have been the subject of developmental investigation. Kinsbourne and Warington (1963) report a study of children between the ages of 4½ and 7½ involving a number of finger differentiation tests. In one test blindfolded children were stimulated simultaneoulsy on two parts of their fingers. They had to report whether the points were on the same finger or on two different ones. In a second test E touched two different fingers and S was required to report how many fingers there were between the two. Performance in the tests improved from below 40% correct at age 4½ to close to 100% correct by age 7½. Unfortunately, the results are presented only in terms of percent correct and are not broken down into different types of errors.

Finger identification has been studied in a series of investigations by Benton, many of which are summarized in one source (Benton, 1959). Using a 50-item test battery Benton conducted a normative study of 150 school children between the ages of 6 and 9. The test items were of the nature of pointing to or naming individual fingers on oral command with eyes open or closed, or indicating which finger had been touched by E. Results indicate a marked improvement as a function of age. Since it is an identification experiment, it is not clear how much of the change represents perceptual improvement. The pattern of errors, however, is interesting. The order of number of errors from most to least is third finger, second finger, pointer finger, little finger, and thumb. The differential pattern of errors may well be a failure of discrimination rather than identification. The correlation between errors of the right and left hand was relatively high (.54). In a study of adults Elithorn, Piercy, and Crossky (1953) found that the second finger, rather than the third finger, was least accurately identified. Whether the difference between their and Benton's study represents a real developmental change or whether it is due to a somewhat more complicated procedure in their study is not clear. Benton (1955) found poorer performance on the same test battery in a group of retardates matched with normals on MA. This confirmed a similar finding of Werner and Garrison (1942).

So far the developmental studies of body image have dealt with precision of perception, but there are two studies relevant to the qualitative nature of the body image. Mc-Kinney (1964), in an imaginative study, asked children ranging in age from 4 to 8 to indicate which finger he touched. The interesting experimental condition was one in which the child had to turn his hand over before responding. The younger children made a great many errors in which they responded to the original spatial position rather than to the correct finger. This was not due to motor interference or distraction since the young children performed quite well in a condition in which they turned their hand over and back again before responding. McKinney suggests that the younger children are responding in terms of a visual image of the hand. He supported this hypothesis by showing that congenitally blind children did not make such errors.

The second study (Simmel, 1966) of qualitative aspects of the body image investigates the relation between age of amputation of a limb and occurrence of a phantom limb. It was found that if the amputation occurs very early a phantom limb is less likely to be experienced. For example, only 20 to 25% of Ss whose amputations occurred before the age of 4 reported phantoms, whereas 61 to 100% of Ss whose amputations occurred after the age of 4 reported phantoms. There was some confounding between age of amputation and time elapsed since amputation but probably not enough to account for the marked relationship.

The clinically observed difficulty in discriminating the right from left side of the body is not found in normative studies even in young children. However, the identification of the right and left parts of the body is an entirely different matter. There are a number of studies that show this ability is poorer in young children and improves steadily with age (Swanson and Benton, 1955; Benton, 1959; Belmont and Birch, 1963 and 1965). These studies evaluate right-left awareness by using such items as *raise your right hand,* and *point to your left ear with your right hand.* In Benton's (1959) study the test battery is most elaborate and involves performing the right-left identification tasks with eyes open and closed, with active movement and passive movement, and on pictures of other persons. Again there may be a perceptual and an identification component to the child's difficulty. The perceptual component is probably related to children's difficulty in discriminating right and left mirror images from each other (see Section IIIB on orientation). In addition, learning proper identification of right and left may be hampered by the fact that right and left do not have consistent meaning relative to the child. These terms are also used to label other people's position and are often reversed with respect to the child's orientation.

One could perhaps use a reaction time procedure for assessing the perceptual discriminative aspects of right-left perception. For example, the reaction times for same-different judgments could be compared for simultaneous stimulation of different parts on the same and opposite side of the body.

There appear to be no systematic studies

of the accuracy with which children perceive their own body dimensions. However, one study does touch on this problem. Smith and Smith's (1966) factor analytic study found two tasks involving estimation of arm length which yielded a perceptual factor. Unfortunately, the actual values of the estimates were not reported and two other tests of arm length estimation were not included in this factor.

One final aspect of body perception concerns the locus from which S perceives his own body. Natsoulas and Dubanoski (1964) investigated this problem with adults by tracing ambiguous (reversible) letters on the forehead, sides, and back of head. They asked S to report the letter they experienced. Thus if E traced a "b" on the forehead, S might perceive this as a "b" or a "d," depending on where his locus of perception was. They found that S tends to report as if he were standing behind the head and looking forward. Thus a "b" on the forehead from E's point of view is perceived as a "d," whereas a "b" on the back of the head is perceived as a "b." Recently Dubanoski (1965) and Podell (1966) have replicated this procedure with children. In general they both found the same pattern of results for children from 6 to 16 (Dubanoski) and from 3½ to 11 (Podell). In some conditions both these investigators found greater proportions of children than adults responding as if they were standing in front of the head and looking back. Dubanoski further showed that older children could, if required, make judgments as if viewing from E's point of view, whereas younger children could not. He related this to Piaget's observations that older children are better able to imagine relative orientations from different points of view.

B. Orientation

The perception of orientation of stimuli will be considered as a problem of sensory interaction since in some cases more than one modality is involved. For example, judgments of orientation often refer the visual orientation of a stimulus to the direction of gravity. Sometimes, of course, only one modality is involved, for example, when one visual stimulus is compared with another.

Howard and Templeton (1966) have made a comprehensive analysis of the meaning of various questions about orientation. Here the concern will be with the developmental aspects of such questions only. It has long been known that young children tend to confuse a visual shape with rotations and mirror images of itself. Recent documentation of this fact can be found in Gibson, Gibson, Pick, and Osser (1962), who reported that 4-year-olds made such confusions in approximately 45% of the relevant cases. In that study a standard shape was paired with 45, 90, and 180° rotations and right-left and up-down mirror images. Confusion errors between all of these transformations and the standard shapes decreased with age. However, the mirror images continued to produce more errors than the other rotations.

Paradoxical results have been reported by Ghent (1961a), who asked children between the ages of 4 and 8 to indicate which of two shapes (up-down mirror images of each other) was upside down. Four-year-old children showed remarkable intersubject consistency in their selections. The difference in results between Gibson et al. and Ghent might be due to the difference in the particular forms used or it might be due to the different question asked. In the study by Gibson et al. the Ss were asked in essence to make same-different judgments, whereas Ghent asked her Ss directly to identify an orientation. The questions asked might have produced the divergent results by directing the children's attention to different aspects of the stimuli. Ghent has also shown that the orientation of figures makes a difference in recognition tasks (Ghent, 1960; Ghent and Bernstein, 1961). Children were asked to identify forms shown tachistoscopically. Forms which were right-side up were identified more accurately than those which were upside down. This difference occurred both with forms representing real objects and with nonsense forms which previously had been found to have orientations that were reliably judged as right side up and upside down. The difference in accuracy between the two orientations decreased with age from 3 to 7 in the case of realistic forms. It seems quite clear that the observation often made that children look at pictures upside down does not mean that they are insensitive to differences in orientation.

Ghent has proposed a scanning mechanism

to account for these results (Ghent, 1961a). She hypothesizes that children tend to scan from top to bottom of a form. She further noted that many of the forms that were reliably identified as upside down had "focal points" at the bottom. Her suggestion is that the focal point attracts the initial attention of the child. When this is at the top, it is congruent with the normal scanning tendency and the form is judged as right side up. When the focal point is at the bottom, the child's attention is attracted to it and he has to scan from bottom to top. This is counter to his normal scanning tendency and the shape is judged as upside down. The scanning may well be implicit since Ghent herself has demonstrated the preceding results with tachistoscopic presentation at speeds too great for actual eye movements to occur.

Ghent's scanning hypothesis has been investigated in two studies. Wohlwill and Wiener (1964) reasoned that if Ghent's scanning hypothesis were correct, then orientation would be better discriminated in stimuli that had high directionality, internal detail, or were open in comparison with stimuli that had low directionality, no internal detail, or were closed. It was thought that the presence of these properties would facilitate scanning from a focal point. Ability to discriminate orientation was tested in 4-year-old children using a matching-to-sample technique. Only the variable of directionality made a significant difference. Although this variable lacks precise definition it is obviously most relevant to the scanning hypothesis. Ghent herself (Braine, 1965) did a study in which she asked 3- to 5-year-old children to identify a tachistoscopically exposed stimulus from an array of similar stimuli. The stimuli were designed so they had focal points at one end and distinguishing features at the other end. The hypothesis of the study was that young children would recognize the forms more rapidly when they had the focal point at the top and the distinguishing features at the bottom since this arrangement would be congruent with their natural scanning tendency. The younger children recognized the right side up figures more accurately than the upside down, but the results were reversed for the older children. There is some other evidence (Ghent, 1963) that older children and adults scan from top to bottom independently

of the specific stimulus. Thus the general interpretation of the results is that stimulus factors and scanning tendencies both operate for younger children, but only the scanning tendency is important for older children. They start at the top of the figure and if that is where the distinguishing feature is they can use it immediately.

One difficulty with the Ghent hypothesis is that there are apparent exceptions. In some cases stimuli with obvious focal points do not obey the rules. However, in many of these cases the form has a representative function and the judgment of orientation is made in terms of the object that is represented. In other cases there is no reasonable focal point; nevertheless, consistent judgments of orientation are made. This leads to a second difficulty for the Ghent hypothesis, which is the lack of a precise definition of focal point. In many cases observers would agree that a focal point is present. In some cases, however, observer agreement could not be obtained. In summary, it is quite likely that several factors influence judgments of orientation but Ghent has no doubt identified an important one.

There has been some investigation of the generality of the orientation phenomenon. Antonovsky and Ghent (1964) found similar identifications of orientation in Iranian children. Pick, Klein, and Pick (1967) found similar identifications on another set of nonsense forms, but the consistent identification disappeared when the task was performed tactually without vision. Neither were there consistent identifications by totally blind Ss. However, partially sighted Ss did show consistent tactual identifications which were similar to the visual identifications. Goldstein has investigated the effect of change of vertical orientation on recognition and learning of photographs of faces. Brooks and Goldstein (1963), studying children between 3 and 14 years, found that older children are relatively better at recognizing inverted photographs of their peers than are younger children. On the other hand, when the task was learning to associate a letter with a facial photograph, children performed relatively better than adults with inverted photographs (Goldstein, 1965). The paradox of these two sets of results has not yet been resolved.

As previously noted, confusions of right and left mirror images with each other are also quite common among children. In the study of Gibson, Gibson, Pick, and Osser (1962) the level of errors for up-down mirror images was approximately the same as that for right-left mirror images. It has more often been found, however, that right-left mirror images are more difficult. For example, Davidson (1935) found quite consistently with the letters *b, d, p,* and *q* that the right-left mirror images were confused more than the up-down. Further, Rudel and Teuber (1963) found that it is more difficult to learn to discriminate between right-left mirror images than between up-down mirror images. One possibility suggested for the difference in difficulty between these transformations is an interaction between the type of transformation and the direction of their alignment. Both transformations are usually presented in a horizontal alignment and this may make comparison of the left-right mirror images more difficult. Sekuler and Rosenblith (1964) and Huttenlocher (1967) have tested such a hypothesis. Sekuler and Rosenblith found a marked interaction, as predicted, in a situation involving same-different judgments. There were very few confusions of up-down mirror images when they were horizontally aligned, but a large number when they were vertically aligned. On the other hand, there were very few confusions of right-left mirror images when they were vertically aligned and a large number when they were horizontally aligned. Huttenlocher found similar results in a discrimination learning situation. Learning to discriminate between right-left mirror images was relatively more difficult when they were horizontally aligned than when they were vertically aligned. The converse was true with the up-down mirror images, although the magnitude of the difference was rather small.

Why should there be an interaction of this type? A scanning hypothesis might be invoked. Suppose S scanned repeatedly across a pair of stimuli in the direction of their alignment, as in a TV scanner, registering only the number of elements present on each scan. Then left-right mirror images would register identically in horizontal alignment, and up-down mirror images would register identically in vertical alignment. Discrimination based on such registration would seem to handle most of the existing results as far

as the difference between left-right and up-down mirror images are concerned. For example, in the Gibson, Gibson, Pick, and Osser study where the usual difference was not found, the situation did not involve consistent horizontal or vertical alignments of the stimuli. The model is, in essence, an extension of one suggested by Sutherland (1961) to account for shape discrimination performance in the octopus.

C. Intermodal Relations

The theoretical point of view most directly concerned with intermodal interaction is the sensory-tonic field theory developed by Heinz Werner and Seymour Wapner (Werner and Wapner, 1949). This point of view has been integrated with Werner's developmental theory (Wapner and Werner, 1957). The basic assertion is that perceptual experience is a function of the relation between stimulation and the organismic state. In this theory stimulation and body tonus or state can be considered to be distributed symmetrically or asymmetrically with respect to body axes. When stimulation and body tonus are congruent, as when they are both symmetrical, their relation is considered to be stable. When they are noncongruent, as when body tonus is asymmetric and stimulation symmetric, their relation is considered to be unstable. When unstable, there is a change in the state of the organism which is reflected in a change in perception. The paradigmatic problem is perception of verticality. The Ss are asked to judge whether a rod is aligned vertically or not. If the task is presented when S's body is upright and tonus is symmetrically distributed, the judgment is made accurately. If the body is tilted and tonus is asymetrically distributed, there is an unstable relation leading in some cases to incorrect judgment of the verticality of the rod. Asymmetric stimulation may be applied by such means as an extraneous sound to one side of the head, or by a nonsymmetric starting position of the rod to be judged. It is Werner's view that development proceeds by increasing differentiation and hierarchic integration. One implication of this view is that there is increasing differentiation of self from object as a function of age. It is then predicted that the effects of extraneous stimulation will decrease as a function of age.

Wapner and Werner (1957) report an interesting factorial experiment in which they examined the effect of body tilt and starting position of a rod on judgments of verticality. Using children ranging in age from 6 to 19 they found that the youngest Ss tended to report the rod as vertical when it was tilted slightly (0 to 4°) in the direction of the body tilt. The oldest Ss reported it as vertical when it was tilted in the direction opposite to the body. Starting position biases the Ss toward judging the rod as vertical when it is tilted in the same direction as its initial position. This effect is present at all ages but its magnitude decreases with age. The decrease is consonant with the hypothesized differentiation of self from object. The change in the effect of body tilt with age eventually leads to overcompensation in adults; they judge the rod as tilted away from the direction of their body tilt. Similar results of decreasing effect with age were shown by these investigators in two other situations. In one, the task was localizing the median plane when a figure in the visual field was asymmetrically placed. In the other, the task was maintaining head strain when illumination of the visual field was asymmetric.

The development of adaptation to visual distortion has been studied within the framework of sensory-tonic theory. Giannitrapani (1958) reasoned that if organism and environment are less differentiated in children, these children would feel greater impact of sensory distortion. This in turn would result in greater adaptation or adjustment to the visual distortion. Giannitrapani studied adaptation to visual magnification and tilt and to kinesthetic tilt, and he found the predicted trends. There were also some sex differences in the visual and kinesthetic tilt situations. Giannitrapani's analysis implies that the initial reaction of the children to the distortion would be greater than that of adults. An investigation by Klein (1966) measured the initial response to three situations in which visual and proprioceptive information were put into conflict by means of visual distortion. The task was to respond to the proprioceptive information, not the visual. The response of Ss at all ages was biased by the visual information, but there was a trend toward decreasing visual bias as a function of age.

The sensory-tonic field theory has instigated a great deal of interesting work on the problem of sensory interaction. It has been criticized (see Howard and Templeton, 1966) and probably fairly for making an artificial distinction between organism and stimulation. The distinction apparently intended is often that between exteroceptive and interoceptive stimulation. Furthermore, it is not always clear how the stimulation and tonus are asymmetric. For example, Howard and Templeton argue in one case that the tonus in body tilt is distributed on the side opposite that indicated by Wapner and Werner. The hypothesis of greater differentiation with increasing age is applied in this framework mainly to the concepts of self and environment, but this seems unnecessarily restrictive.

IV. PERCEPTION AND INDIVIDUAL DIFFERENCES

A. Perception and Intelligence

The classical empiricist position emphasizing the effects of experience on perception implies a relationship between perception and intelligence. Consider perceptual constancy as a model: it might be expected that degree of constancy would improve with increasing intelligence since constancy may involve integrating a number of different cues in order to make an accurate judgment. For size constancy, for example, the size of the retinal image is thought to be registered in relation to the distance of the object to yield an accurate perception. The evidence does not support this line of reasoning. There are a number of studies which show that degree of size constancy increases with chronological age but not with intelligence. Zeigler and Leibowitz (1957), for example, asked 13-year-old boys and men to estimate the size of rods placed at distances ranging from 10 to 100 feet. The task required that they select a comparison rod of the same size from a group of stimuli 5 feet away. The children and adults showed a similar high degree of constancy for near stimuli. As the distance increased the adults continued to show a high level of constancy, whereas the children showed progressively less constancy. On the other hand, Leibowitz (1961), in a very similar situation using adult college students and adult retardates with an MA of 8.7 years, found equal and high constancy at all distances for both groups.

One of the most instructive studies is that of Jenkin and Feallock (1960). These investigators used approximately matched CA and MA controls in a size constancy study similar in principle to the studies of Leibowitz. A group of retarded children with mean CA of 15 years, 10 months and mean MA of 8 years, 2 months was compared with normal children with mean CA 8 years, 3 months and with normal children of mean CA 13 years, 7 months. An additional group of normal adults, mean CA 26 years, 6 months, was also tested. Again constancy increased as a function of chronological age but not of mental age. The retardates showed approximately the same degree of constancy as the 13-year-old normals, more than the 8-year-old normal Ss, and less than the adults.

The Gestalt position is another theoretical orientation from which relatively explicit predictions have been made for retarded Ss. With some roots in Lewin's concept of rigidity (Lewin, 1935) but based primarily on Köhler's theory of brain physiology (Köhler and Wallach, 1944), predictions have been made that figural aftereffects should be more difficult to establish in retardates than in normals. It is reasoned that the hypothesized satiation which is considered responsible for figural aftereffects occurs more slowly in retardates. This prediction has been confirmed in a number of studies (e.g., Spitz and Blackham, 1959, and Spivack and Levine, 1959). Spivack and Levine found a correlation of about .50 between susceptibility to figural aftereffects and intelligence in retarded children, but a zero correlation in normal children. Gestalt physiology notwithstanding, the same predictions might have been made on the basis of the task requirements. The induction of figural aftereffects requires prolonged visual fixation, a task that may be more difficult for retardates than for normals. The satiation model has also been used to predict a lower reversal rate for reversible figures by retardates. Such a prediction has not been consistently confirmed (see Spivack and Levine, 1959). Comprehensive general reviews by Kodman, by Spitz, and by Spivack of research on sensory and perceptual processes in retarded Ss are available in Ellis (1963).

Pollack has pursued a promising approach to the relation between intelligence and perception (Jenkin and Pollack, 19-66; Pollack, 1969). He has observed, following Piaget, that there are two types of illusion. One type decreases in magnitude with increasing age, and a second type increases as a function of age. For Piaget the basis for changes in both these types of illusion are changes in the way a child scans. Pollack suggests that two different mechanisms are implicated. He refers the decrease in the first type of illusion to physiological processes independent of intelligence. For example, the Müller-Lyer illusion decreases with age and with increasing foveal pigmentation (see Section IA on depth perception). It also decreases with decreasing figure-ground contrast of the elements of the illusion (Pollack, 1963). Pollack found that contrast threshold increases in age from 8 through 12 and suggests that this might account for the decrease in the Müller-Lyer illusion. As predicted, the magnitude of the illusion was significantly correlated with contrast threshold but not with intelligence.

On the other hand, Pollack suggests that some of the illusions which increase in magnitude with age, such as the Usnadze illusion, are related to intelligence. The Usnadze effect is similar to a figural aftereffect except that the exposure times are shorter. If two concentric circles are presented successively, the inner after the outer circle, the inner circle appears to be smaller than it really is. This illusion increases with age, as do figural aftereffects (Piaget and Lambercier, 1944; Pollack, 1964). In the Delboeuf illusion, which is elicited by two concentric circles presented simultaneously, the inner one appears larger than it really is. The magnitude of this illusion decreases with age (Piaget, Lambercier, Boesch, and Albertini, 1942). Thus changing the presentation of an illusion from successive to simultaneous changes its direction and its relation with age. Pollack (1964) has been able to demonstrate an analogous result with the Müller-Lyer illusion. He used a modified form of the illusion and presented the elements successively. The direction of the illusion was reversed: the arrow-tail portion was judged shorter, and the magnitude of this reversed illusion increased with age. Furthermore, in this successive form of the illusion the magnitude of illusion is highly correlated with IQ. Within each age group from 8 to 11 years these correlations varied from .73 to .93.

The hypothesis proposed by Pollack (1966)

Table 1. Development of Susceptibility to Illusions

Illusion[b]	Reference	Age Groups Included	Age Trend Observed
Delboeuf	Giering (1905)[a]	6 and 14	Decrease
	Piaget, Lambercier, et al. (1942)	5–12 and adults	Decrease
	Piaget, Matalon, and Bang (1961)[a]	5–7 and adults	Decrease
	Rüssel (1934)[a]	4–6½	Small, irregular changes
	Santostefano (1963)	6, 9, and 12	No significant age trends
Parallel lines	Giering (1905)[a]	6 and 14	No age change
	Piaget and von Albertini (1950)[a]	5–9 and adults	Decrease
Titchener circles	Rüssel (1934)[a]	4–6½ and adults	Small decrease 4–6½
	Wapner and Werner (1957)[a]	6–adults	Irregular increase
	Wapner, Werner, and Comalli (1960)	6–80	Increase 6–44, then decrease
Size-weight[b]	Ciampi (see Rey, 1930[a])	3–15, adults, aments, and dements	Increase in frequency
	Ohwaki (1953)[a]	3–5 and aments	Increase in frequency
	Oostlander (1967)	3–18	No clear age trends
	Pick and Pick (1967)	4–adults	Increase in magnitude in haptic presentations; no change in visual and visual-haptic
	Rey (1930)[a]	5–adults and aments	Increase 5–9, then decrease
	Robinson (1964)	2–10	Decrease in magnitude
Müller-Lyer	Binet (1895)[a]	7–12 and 10–14	Less in older group
	Gaudreau, Lavoie, and Delorme (1963)	7–13 normals and 10–13 retardates	Decrease in normals, no change in retardates
	Murray (1967)	Kindergarten–2nd grade	No change
	Noelting (1960)[a]	5–10 and adults	Decrease
	Piaget and von Albertini (1950)[a]	5–9 and adults	Less for adults
	Piaget, Maire, and Privat (1954)[a]	4–10 and adults	Decrease
	Pintner and Anderson (1916)[a]	6–adults and aments	Decrease
	Pollack (1964)	8–12	Decrease
	Pollack (1966)	8–11	Increase in successive presentation, decrease in simultaneous (see text)
	Segall, Campbell, and Herskovitz (1966)	5–11 and adults	Children generally more susceptible
	Sun (1964) (Abstract only)	6–16	Decrease
	Van Biervliet (1896)[a]	12–16 and adults	Less for adults
	Walters (1942)[a]	6–19	Decrease 6–10, increase 15–19

Table 1. Development of Susceptibility to Illusions (Continued)

Illusion[b]	Reference	Age Groups Included	Age Trend Observed
	Wapner and Werner (1957)[a]	6–19	Decrease 6–12, increase 15–19
	Wapner, Werner, and Comalli (1960)	6–80	Least illusion 20–39
Horizontal-vertical	Doyle (1967)	7–11	Decrease
	Fraisse and Vautrey (1956)[a]	6, 9, and adults	Varies with type of figure
	Piaget, Matalon, and Bang (1961)	5–7 and adults	Decrease
	Rivers (1905)[a]	Children and adults	Less for adults
	Segall, Campbell, and Herskovitz (1966)	5–11 and adults	No clear age trends
	Walters (1942)[a]	6–19	Decrease
	Winch (1907)[a]	8–15 and adults	Slight decrease
	Würsten (1947)[a]	5–13 and adults	Increase 5–10, then decrease
Oppel-Kundt	Gaudreau, Lavoie, and Delorme (1963)	7–13 normals, 10–13 retardates	Normals decrease
	Piaget and Osterreith (1953)[a]	Children and adults	Decrease
	Piaget and Bang (1961)	5–7 and adults	Increase
Perspective	Wohlwill (1962)	7, 9, 14, and 20	Less effect of background on adults
Ponzo	Leibowitz and Heisel (1958)[a]	4–20	Increase 4–7
	Leibowitz and Judisch (1967)	3½–18½ and older children	Increase to adulthood, decrease in old age
Poggendorf	Vurpillot (1957)[a]	5, 7, 9, 12, and adults	Decrease
	Leibowitz and Gwozdecki (1967)	5–80 normal and 16–20 retardates	Decrease 5–10
Sander Parallelogram	Heiss (1930)[a]	Children of all ages	Decrease
	Segall, Campbell, and Herskovitz (1966)	5–11 and adults	Less in adults

Table adapted from Wohlwill (1960). We are indebted to Dr. Cynthia Gliner for bringing it up to date.

[a] Illusion cited by Wohlwill (1960) and study taken from his references.

[b] In each illustration of illusion comparison is to be made between segments marked *a* and *b*. For the size-weight illusion the larger of two equal weights is perceived as lighter. For the Poggendorf illusion the two segments of the diagonal are typically seen as nonlinear.

is that phenomena involving temporal integration are related to intellectual ability. This, of course, must be investigated empirically and Pollack is doing so. It leads one to speculate whether intermodal transfer or integration might also be related to intellectual capacity. Such an extension must be complex, and it leads to a paradox. For example, the size-weight illusion must depend on confusing weight and size information, that is, the senses interact, but inappropriately. It is the case that the magnitude of size-weight illusion is less in retardates than in normals (Spivack, 1963) and this illusion does not increase with age. Table 1, adapted from Wohlwill (1960), lists a number of perceptual illusions that have been studied developmentally and indicates the age trends if any were found.

B.   Perception in Cognition and Personality

A problem which has received considerable attention during the last few years is that of consistency and generality of cognitive and personality characteristics in perception and perceptual development. Witkin (Witkin, 1949; Witkin, Lewis, Hertzman, Machover, Meissner, and Wapner, 1954; Witkin, Dyk, Faterson, Goodenough, and Karp, 1962) and more recently Kagan (1965a and 1965b, 1966; Kagan, Moss, and Sigel, 1963; Kagan and Rosman, 1964; Kagan, Rosman, Day, Albert, and Phillips, 1964) and Gardner (Gardner, Holzman, Klein, Linton, and Spence, 1959; Gardner, Jackson, and Messick, 1960; Gardner and Schoen, 1962) have conducted extensive investigations of individual preferences or predispositions in perceptual functioning. These are presumed to account for qualitative differences in perceptual functioning when stimulus conditions and subject ability are held constant.

Kagan's procedures yield correlation data from many measures on early and middle elementary school children. Among these measures are (1) response times in perception tasks in which alternative solutions are available, (2) indices of the tendency to analyze visual stimuli into components, (3) errors in perceptual discrimination tasks, and (4) preferences for analytic groupings in a concept sorting task. Kagan concludes that his investigations reveal "two basic cognitive dispositions that appear to have generality and stability: the tendency to analyze visual arrays and the tendency to reflect upon alternative-solution hypotheses. . ." (Kagan et al., 1964, p. 36). These dispositions are postulated to be independent of each other and of verbal ability and "each of these dispositions contributes considerable variance to the production of the more complex cognitive products of analytic concepts . . . and recognition errors on tasks requiring complex perceptual discriminations. . ." (Kagan et al., 1964, p. 36). Thus measures (1) and (2) above are predictor variables, and measures (3) and (4) above are criterion variables.

The evidence with respect to Kagan's hypotheses is somewhat equivocal (see Kagan, 1966, Tables pp. 511–512). The measures of these dispositions tward visual analysis and reflection do appear to be independent of each other and are also unrelated to WISC verbal skill measures. However, the intrasubject consistency of these measures varies (see Kagan et al., 1964, Tables p. 24). The test-retest correlations for the visual analysis measure are − .05, + .49, + .20, and + .05 for different subject groups; those for one of the response time measures are higher: + .54, + .74, + .71 and + .51. The intra-individual consistency of the criterion variables is also reasonably high: rs of + .56, + .60, + .84, + .44, for perceptual recognition errors and + .70, + .43, and + .47 for the measure of analytic sorting.

The various measures of the reflection tendency response times are not highly related to each other; slightly less than half of the 24 correlations between response times on different tasks are + .40 or greater (see Kagan, 1966, Tables pp. 511–512). Thus it is not clear that these response time measures are tapping a general dimension of reflection-impulsivity.

Given the moderate degree of stability and generality of the measures of reflection- impulsivity and visual analysis, it would be surprising if these variables accounted for most of the variance in the criterion tasks. Indeed, this is the case (Kagan, 1966, Tables pp. 511–512): correlations between reflection measures (response times) and errors on the same perceptual recognition task range from − .11 to − .67 with a median r of about −.50; correlations between reflection measures in one perceptual task and perceptual recognition errors in a second task range from + .31 to

− .58 with a median *r* of about − .33. Correlations between reflection measures and analytic sorting, the other criterion variable, range from − .05 to + .47 with a median *r* of about + .15. Visual analysis, the second predictor variable, has correlations with perceptual recognition errors ranging from + .03 to − .41 with a median *r* of about − .22; visual analysis is related to analytic sorting as evidenced by *r*s of − .13, + .44, + .45, and + .10. Thus the independent predictor variables, reflection and visual analysis, account for only small amounts of the variance of the criterion variables of recognition errors and analytic sorting.

In summary, the evidence does not clearly support the hypothesis that the two dispositions toward visual analysis and reflection contribute substantially to production of analytic concepts and perceptual recognition errors. Particularly the measure of visual analysis shows less than desirable reliability. Furthermore, the several reflection measures show only moderate relationship to one another. Finally, these measures are not highly related to the criterion measures of analytic concepts and perceptual recognition errors.

The hypothesis that individual tendencies or "styles" of analyzing and responding to stimuli should have a broad effect on perceptual functioning is an appealing one and it may be that a different research strategy might provide stronger support for it. For example, Lee, Kagan, and Rabson (1963) conducted an experiment using as Ss boys who represented the extreme ends of a distribution of scores for production of analytic concepts in the sorting task. These two groups differed in the ease with which they acquired concepts based on similar elements of complex stimuli in a learning task. In other words, Ss who spontaneously grouped stimuli on the basis of certain characteristics also found it easy to learn concepts based on the same type of characteristics. Perhaps this strategy of utilizing Ss manifesting clear differences on some behavior dimension and then observing their performance in tasks whose requirements are carefully analyzed may reveal stable and general individual differences in perceptual functioning. A step-by-step analysis of subject characteristics, task requirements, and relationships between tasks may prove more fruitful than large correlational studies involving performance on widely differing and often unrelated tasks.

Witkin's program of research has been extremely ambitious and prolific. His goal has been to relate personality characteristics to perceptual functioning. Degree of dependence on the visual field has been studied using a variety of perceptual measures. Two of the measures used to define this dimension require S to establish the upright in the presence of a distorting visual frame of reference. One, a rod-and-frame task, requires S, while in the dark, to adjust a luminous rod to the true upright when both it and a surrounding luminous frame are tilted. Another task requires S to adjust a chair in which he is seated to upright when both the chair and the room in which it is located are tilted. The extent to which the S ignores the visual field (either the frame or the room) as a frame of reference and is able to set the rod or his own chair close to the true upright is a measure of his field dependence or independence. If he is dependent on the field, he would tend to set the rod or chair in alignment with the field. However, the measure recorded is the deviation from true upright in degrees (Witkin et al., 1954, p. 33). This measure does not take into account direction of deviation. One investigator (Gruen, 1955, 1957) observed many Ss who overcompensated in these tasks. Although overcompensation and undercompensation may both reflect an influence of the visual field, their underlying mechanisms may be quite different. Perhaps direction of deviation should be taken into account in these tasks.

A third task used as an index of relative degree of field dependence or independence is an embedded figures task in which subjects are asked to locate a simple figure in a more complex pattern. For this task the measure recorded is the amount of time elapsed before a correct solution is reached.

The developmental trends in all three tasks are quite consistent and similar. Between the ages of 8 and about 17 years there is a decrease in relative field dependency. That is, older Ss take less time to locate the embedded figures and they adjust the rod or chair closer to the true upright than do younger Ss. Thus field independence is considered a more advanced level of development than field dependence. There are also consistent sex differences with boys and men showing a greater degree of field independence than girls and women. It is interesting to note that Witkin has identified a response dimension which varies with age, and he uses it to interpret individual differences even in adults as reflecting different degrees of psychological development. However, he has stopped short of interpreting the lesser field independence of women as reflecting a lower level of psychological development!

The relationship among the measures for the various tasks is moderate. The median correlation coefficients between the rod-and-frame and embedded figures tasks of different groups are .32 for women and .44 for men. Those between the chair adjustment and rod-and-frame task are .37 for women and .42 for men. The median coefficients between the chair adjustment and embedded figure tasks are about .36 for women and about .33 for men (Witkin et al., 1954, Tables p. 144).

The personality variables hypothesized to be related to mode of perceptual functioning have been measured in a variety of tasks, for example, Rorschach, TAT, figure-drawing tests, and clinical interviews. An evaluation of the validity of these measures is beyond the scope of this chapter, but Postman (1955) and Zigler (1963) in reviewing Witkin's work have argued that this problem has not been adequately dealt with. It would seem to be an important problem since the underlying thesis of Witkin's work is that the personality variables determine the individual differences in perception. In the present context, then, it is relevant to review the degree of relationship between the perceptual and personality measures.

For adult groups of Ss, median correlations between perceptual measures and interview variables (e.g., ratings of degree of self-awareness, repression of hostility, self-esteem) range from .33 to .54. Median correlations between the perceptual measures and Rorschach measures (e.g., scores for Whole, Popular, Color, for m responses) range from .22 to .41. Median correlations between perceptual measures and figure drawing scores (e.g., lack of body confidence, lack of drive) range from .45 to .63; and the median correlations with TAT scores (e.g., lack of self-assertiveness, unfavorable outcome) range from about 0 to .45 (Witkin et al., 1954,

Tables pp. 191–192, 218, 246, 274). Thus the relationships between perceptual measures and personality measures can be described as low to moderate. It has been argued (see Postman, 1955; Zigler, 1963; Gruen, 1957) that there are some methodological problems with these procedures some of which would inflate the correlation coefficients, for example: the specific manipulations employed in obtaining the personality scores, familiarity by E with the hypothesis being tested in situations where scoring is quite subjective, and unreliability of scoring the personality measures.

It is difficult to assess the strength of the suggested personality-perception relationships in children since most of the studies do not present correlation coefficients. However, reference is made in one report (Witkin et al., 1964, p. 190) to correlations obtained with children between perceptual measures and figure drawing. These correlations range from .44 to .76. Zigler (1963) has suggested that such relationships may be accounted for by factors common to these measures and standard intelligence measures. This possibility has not been explored fully but did receive some support from Gruen (1957). He found lower intercorrelations than Witkin and different patterns of intercorrelation among the perceptual and personality measures separately, but he found personality-perception correlations of the same magnitude as Witkin. Furthermore, a factor analytic study (Goodenough and Karp, 1961) found significant relationships between the perception measures and performance on several subtests of the WISC.

In summary, it can be said that much research has been stimulated by Witkin's ideas. Many of the studies support the relationships hypothesized by him (Dyk and Witkin, 1965; Witkin, 1950, 1964; Witkin et al., 1966; Witkin and Wapner, 1950), but there are many that do not (Dana and Goocher, 1959, 1960; Vaught and Ellinger, 1966; Vaught and Auguston, 1967; Gruen, 1957). The lack of consensus among the studies may be due to the vagueness of the basic concepts and consequent difficulty in investigation or it may be that the relationships are not as decisive as Witkin suggests. A more general hypothesis is that Ss respond to these tasks differently and neither the perception nor the personality measures reflect unitary dimensions. In other words, the individual differences may reside not in the ways Ss perceive the world, but in terms of their interpretations of the task presented.

A third extensive program of investigation concerned with individual differences is that of Gardner (Gardner et al., 1959, 1960; Gardner and Schoen, 1962; Gardner and Long, 1962; Holzman and Klein, 1954). The particular individual tendencies which these investigators have explored are termed cognitive controls. These controls are viewed as structures or organizational tendencies that mediate an individual's perceptual cognitive and personality functioning. Examples of some controls are tendencies toward constriction or flexibility and toward leveling or sharpening. Each of several controls has been defined in terms of specific tasks, and factor analytic techniques have been employed to investigate the nature and generality of the hypothesized controls. The controls are assumed to be dimensions rather than dichotomies for categorization of behavioral tendencies.

The bulk of this careful and systematic investigation has been conducted with adult samples. The stability of the measures of cognitive controls appears fairly high: 3-year test-retest data on one sample yielded correlations ranging from .36 to .75 with a median r of about .60 (Gardner and Long, 1960). Unfortunately, little work with children has apparently been reported. However, Gardner suggests that studies with children of the development of stable cognitive control patterns are important parts of the general investigation (Gardner et al., 1959, 1960) and has indicated that an extensive investigation of this type is underway (Gardner, 1964). One study with children by the Gardner group is a cross-cultural study in which Mexican and U. S. children of the same age were compared in performance on an object sorting task (Mercado, Guerrero, and Gardner, 1963). The two groups differed somewhat in the types of categories formed with the objects; for example, the Mexican children made fewer categories than the U. S. children, but if single objects were not scored as categories, then the Mexican children made more categories with the objects. The general implications of these differences are not clear.

Gardner sees a close relation between the studies of cognitive control and Witkin's investigations of field dependence-independence and their development. In fact, one of Gardner's cognitive controls, "field articulation," seems to subsume the dimension of field dependence-independence, and two of its several measures are Witkin's rod-and-frame task and his embedded figures task.

Selective attention emerges as an important concept in Gardner's theoretical framework. This refers to a dimension of degree of attention to relevant though subtle aspects of stimulation rather than to irrelevant though compelling aspects in perceptual and cognitive tasks. Selective attention is viewed by Gardner as a crucial process in both Witkin's and his own studies.

A final note relevant to all of these investigations of individual differences concerns the problem of typologies. All three primary investigators—Kagan, Witkin, and especially Gardner—assert that the variables with which they are concerned are dimensions and not dichotomies. Nevertheless, in Kagan's and Witkin's work, and to a lesser extent in Gardner's, one finds these variables discussed at length as though they were categories of behavior. Kagan discusses reflective and impulsive types of individuals, and Witkin often discusses field-dependent and field-independent types of individuals. Furthermore, the nature of the studies conducted do not reveal whether the variables are dimensional or categorical. It would seem important to establish their nature early in the research programs. In short, it seems that studies of individual differences in perceptual development have not yet revealed any variables, either dimensional or categorical, which account for much of the subject variability in perceptual performance. It seems important to avoid the suggestion of dichotomies in this area until their presence is clearly established.

V. DEVELOPMENT OF PERCEPTION OF COMPLEX EVENTS

Processing of complex information undoubtedly involves at least perception, learning, and cognition. It would be fruitless to try to draw a sharp distinction between the end of one process and the beginning of another.

In this section only the perceptual aspects will be emphasized.

A. Perception of Moving Stimuli

There has been very little study of children's perception of real movement. As pointed out in Section II on sensitivity, the optokinetic response to a moving series of stripes has been used to measure acuity. The fact that even neonates exhibit such a response and the fact that they will track in the direction of a moving stimulus indicates an early gross sensitivity to motion. However, in these studies measurement of degree of sensitivity was not undertaken. Carpenter and Carpenter (1958) showed that two older children, 81 and 108 months, could discriminate between a stationary and moving stimulus. In this case speed of movement was varied and thresholds for detection of motion were determined. Edgren (1953) investigated the perception of motion in Ss from 8 years to old age. In many respects he replicated the classic work on this topic by Brown (1931). Brown had demonstrated that the phenomenal velocity of a moving stimulus varied as a function of distance, size of stimulus, and direction of movement, among other factors. Edgren presented the moving stimuli by means of motion pictures. Although this is not real movement, his results replicated the effects obtained by Brown with real movement for the variables of distance, size, and direction. The direction variable was the only one for which an age trend was obtained. Vertical movement was seen as faster than horizontal movement and this difference decreased slightly though significantly with age. Edgren suggests that the overestimation of vertical speed may be related to the fact that vertical distances are overestimated relative to horizontal as in the horizontal-vertical illusion. It might be pointed out as further support for Edgren's explanation that the horizontal-vertical illusion decreases with age (see Wohlwill, 1960).

There has been more direct concern with responsivity to apparent movement. Rock, Tauber, and Heller (1965) presented evidence that naive guppies and praying mantises respond with an optokinetic response to a sequence of illuminated stripes which are seen as moving by human adults, and Tauber and Koffler (1966) showed the same result

for human neonates. Haith (1966) also found that neonates respond to a sequence of lights which adults perceive as moving. His response measure was inhibition of sucking, which did not occur to a stationary light. Of course studying the perception of motion in nonverbal Ss poses a problem similar to that in studying the perception of depth: deciding whether differential response implies perception of the stimulus as *movement*. The optokinetic response as an index has some face validity for inferring that movement is perceived since the slow tracking component of nystagmus probably cannot occur (in humans) to discrete stimuli in different positions.

Older children, of course, can report when they see movement. Brenner (1957) presented to Ss ranging from $2\frac{1}{2}$ to 19 years a pair of stimuli designed to elicit apparent movement. Each stimulus was presented for 25 ms and the interstimulus interval was varied. The presentation of the stimuli was repeated continuously to give the Ss an opportunity to make a judgment. In such studies, as the interstimulus interval varies from short to long, Ss' reports vary from seeing two *simultaneous* stimuli to seeing one stimulus *moving* between two positions, to seeing two stimuli in *succession*. The data can be analyzed in terms of the range of interstimulus intervals in which Ss report movement. In Brenner's study the midpoint of this range was a shorter interval for the younger children than for the older. In addition, the range was less wide for the younger than for the older.

Pollack (1966) also studied apparent movement with children from 6 to 11 years of age. His stimuli were presented for 50 ms and again the interstimulus interval was varied. He found a curvilinear relation between the midpoint of the range of intervals eliciting reports of movement and age; the midpoints were longer for the youngest and oldest children, decreasing to a minimum for the 9-year-olds. This age trend was due almost entirely to variation in the transition from reporting movement to reporting succession. The transition occurred at longer intervals for the youngest and oldest children and at shorter intervals for the 9-year-olds. The transition from reporting simultaneity to reporting movement occurred at a constant interval at all ages. Pollack suggests that the difference between his and Brenner's results might be due to the very different stimuli used. For example, Brenner's stimuli were much larger, subtending a visual angle of 35° while Pollack's subtended only 2°. Such a difference might be reasonable from Pollack's point of view. He attributed the early downward trend in range midpoint to physiological age changes. If the crucial changes are changes in neural interaction in the peripheral visual system, they might well be manifest only over short distances on the retina, and so not be reflected in the perception of larger stimuli such as Brenner used.

Schiff (1965) examined the responses of a large number of species to an expanding visual stimulus. Animals from fiddler crabs to humans responded to an expanding shadow as if it were an approaching object. One S, a 5-year-old girl, consistently reported movement (as did the other human Ss) and in fact blinked and withdrew her head on several presentations.

In summary, it would seem that even young children are sensitive to movement and to stimuli eliciting apparent movement. The change in sensitivity with age needs more study. There are many other questions about perception of motion that have not been systematically explored. For example, investigation of children's sensitivity to trajectory of movement, their ability to extrapolate and predict time and point of impact might lead to interesting qualitative age differences in perception. A good review of the existing literature on these and related topics can be found in Gibson and Olum (1960).

B. Development of Language Perception

Little direct evidence is available about the early development of phoneme discrimination. Most of the ideas are based on inferences from such sources as the biographical studies of speech production (e.g., Velton, 1943; Leopold, 1939). Ervin and Miller (1963, pp. 111–114) have summarized the data from many of these studies and suggest some generalizations about the order in which phonemes are produced; for example, a vowel-consonant distinction is acquired first. These regularities in the development of phoneme production lend support to Jakobson's (Jakobson and Halle, 1956) hypotheses about the relation between distinctive or contrasting features of phonemes and the order in which phonemes are acquired. For example, vowels and consonants differ by many contrasting features, and this distinction appears early in language development.

One Soviet study of phoneme discrimination is summarized by Slobin (1966, pp. 381–382). Shvachkin trained Ss to associate words differing by one phoneme with different objects. The results, for Ss between 11 and 23 months of age, implied that vowels generally are discriminated before consonants. The trends are similar to those for speech production. The available stimulus information, as well as the number of distinctive features, may be relevant for the development of phoneme discrimination. In one study with adults (Woodward and Barber, 1960) it was found that phoneme differences were most discriminable when both auditory and visual information was available (a sound movie); next most discriminable when only auditory information was presented (sound without film); and very poorly discriminated when only visual information was presented (film without sound). Perhaps the number of phoneme contrasts and their redundancy in terms of the perceptual modalities are factors in determining the developmental order in which they are perceived.

There is evidence, from the Haskins Laboratory, that adult acuity for detection of some phoneme differences is a matter of improved discrimination at phoneme boundaries rather than degradation of acuity within phoneme categories (Liberman, 1957). Considerable evidence has been amassed by this research group to the effect that phoneme identification is more closely related to units of speech production than to simple units of acoustical analysis. For a thorough review of this research program and a discussion of the theory of speech perception which underlies it, see Liberman, Cooper, Shankweiler, and Studdert-Kennedy (1967).

Finally, it is not surprising to find a relation between children's ability to discriminate speech sounds and their early reading achievement. Deutsch (1964) found that discrimination of speech sounds was better for good readers than for poor readers in the early grades. Since reading involves decoding written language into the spoken language, it is to be expected that individuals poor at discriminating some of the speech sounds might also have difficulty learning to read.

At the syntactic and semantic level of language development the evidence, again, is primarily from studies of language production and hence is, by necessity, inferential with respect to language perception. Yet one of the important questions to be investigated is just that relationship between perception and production of language. Another question concerns the units in which spoken language is processed and stored.

Spoken language appears to be salient auditory stimulation fairly early in development. Slobin (1966, p. 367) summarized a Soviet study of Fradkina which found that in infants of 10 to 11 months of age it was very much easier to condition a response to a word than to other auditory stimuli. Information about the auditory units in which spoken language is processed comes from several types of studies. Conditioning experiments show fairly consistent developmental changes in the type of word to which a conditioned response will generalize. Riess (1946) found maximum generalization to homonyms of stimulus words in 8-year-old Ss, to antonyms in somewhat older children, and to synonyms in children 14 years and older. Razran (1961) described some Soviet experiments providing more evidence that with increasing development, generalization of a conditioned response occurs more on a semantic and less on a phonetic basis. In one of these experiments Luria observed generalization in normal and mentally retarded children of the same age. Extremely retarded Ss generalized a CR only on a phonetic basis, normal Ss generalized only on a semantic basis, and moderately retarded Ss generalized to words both phonetically and semantically related to the conditioned stimulus word.

Slobin (1966, pp. 365–366) summarized an experiment by El'kin in which the conditioned stimulus was an entire sentence. He then observed the strength of generalization to parts of the sentence in children of different ages. For his youngest Ss, 10 to 12 years, generalization was greater to words at the beginning or end of the sentence; for Ss 12 to 14 years, generalization was greatest to the subject and predicate; and in the oldest Ss, 14 to 16 years, semantically important parts of the sentences elicited maximum generalization.

The basis for the developmental changes found in these studies is not clear and one variable that might be involved is reading skill. Brown and Berko (1960a), in an experiment that involved free associations and use of new words, found that words were increasingly associated with each other on the basis of a syntactic relationship as children became older. From first to third grade there was a marked increase in associations that were the same part of speech as the stimulus word as compared with associations that were a different part of speech.

These developmental changes in generalization of conditioned responses and in free word associations may reflect changes in the aspect of the stimulus complex on which attention is focused. With increasing development, it may be semantic and syntactic variables rather than phonetic variables which are attended to and are perhaps the units in which speech is processed and stored.

Other information about the units of auditory perception of speech comes from experiments using tasks which require Ss to attempt some type of analysis of words or groups of words. Zhurova, as summarized by Slobin (1966, pp. 385–386), required children to isolate and pronounce only the first or last sounds of individual words. In general, it was more difficult to isolate the final sound than the first sound. Three- to five-year-old children first had to pronounce the entire word before they could pronounce only the requested sound. Six- to seven-year-old children could produce the requested sound alone. Thus the older children could better analyze the sounds of the word, or at least focus attention on one sound segment of the word.

A task which, in some sense, is the converse of Zhurova's was used by Bruce (1964). He asked 5- and 9-year-old children to respond with the word remaining after a particular sound was deleted from a larger word. As in the previous task, performance was best when the sound was removed from the beginning of the word and next best when it was removed from the end of the word. The 5-year-old Ss apparently could not perform this task at all, but the 9-year-olds could. Although it is difficult to compare age groups directly in these two studies, one might cautiously suggest that the task of producing the word remaining after a deletion is more difficult than producing the sound to be deleted from a particular location in the word. Perhaps the second task requires the capacity to analyze and focus attention on the sounds of the word separately; the first task requires, in addition, the capacity subsequently to, change the focus of attention from the isolated sound to the remaining sounds.

Huttenlocher (1964) asked children to perform an analysis of word sequences rather than single words. Children of 4 and 5 years were asked to reverse two-word utterances, of various types. Pairs of words which comprised a common grammatical sequence were difficult for the children to reverse, whereas pairs of letters or numbers, words of the same part of speech, and words forming an anomalous grammatical sequence were relatively easier. It seemed that the ability to separate the members of a pair was a significant factor in determining whether the sequence could be reversed. Thus the capacity to focus attention on the separate elements was a necessary condition for performing another operation, reversal, on the sequences.

These three studies provide us with some information about the units of speech which can be attended to by children of different ages since the different tasks may require that attention be focused on part of the speech stimulus in order to successfully perform the task. The data considered thus far present a paradox: on the one hand, older children seem to process speech in more complex units than younger; on the other hand, older children are also better able than younger children to analyze speech into smaller units and separate sounds. It may be that this paradox is related to the development of attention (see Section VI). Perhaps older children are simply better able to focus attention on whatever aspect of the speech stimulus is relevant. Normally, this will be a larger rather than a smaller unit, but if the task requires, this will be as small a unit as a single speech sound. The importance of the task requirements is illustrated in a study by Anisfeld (1966) in which he examined children's knowledge of pluralization using three slightly different production tasks and three different recognition tasks. The production tasks required Ss to produce various plural forms, whereas the recognition tasks required Ss to recognize the pictures to which various plural forms were appropriate. There were differences in difficulty among the two types of task; generally the recognition tasks were easier than the production tasks, but one of the recognition tasks was as difficult as two of the production tasks.

Two techniques used with adults might be adapted for use with children in order to tap more directly the perceptual processing of speech. Ladefoged and Broadbent (1960) and Fodor and Bever (1965) had Ss listen to spoken sentences and report the place in the sentences where an extraneous sound occurred. Sounds were frequently displaced to a syntactic boundary. In addition, if sounds were, in fact, located at a boundary, they were more often correctly perceived than when their actual location was in the middle of a linguistic segment. Mehler and Carey (1967) presented sentences against a background of white noise and asked Ss to write what they heard. Sentences differing in surface structure from those previously presented were inaccurately perceived. These studies demonstrated the effect on perception of linguistically defined units of speech. Whether the linguistic rules that affect perception will be the same for developing speakers and accomplished speakers should be investigated.

The precise nature of the relation between perception and production in language development is difficult to assess. Developmentally, there may be a lag between speech perception and production since the presence of such a delay between comprehension and production is quite well documented (e.g., Fraser, Bellugi, and Brown, 1963). The reasons for such a delay, such as S's interpretation of a task presented, are beginning to be investigated (Kaplan and Yonas, 1967).

The descriptive records of individual children's language development contain information about correlated changes in speech perception and production (Brown and Bellugi, 1964; Ervin, 1964; Brown and Fraser, 1964; Miller and Ervin, 1964). All such studies seem to agree that children's imitations of adult speech are shorter than the original, and that the reductions are systematic. The parts retained in imitations seem to be the most informative parts. Whether the reduction is based on analysis of information, or whether the more informative parts are in certain locations in sentences and the locations are perceived, or whether the more informative parts are more discriminable because of a factor such as greater stress is not clear at present.

There has been a great increase recently in investigations focusing on reading and learning to read. This may reflect the increased national interest in remedial reading programs. Psychologically, it reflects the the recognition of reading as a complex activity suitable for analysis in terms of basic perceptual and perceptual learning processes. Kolers, for example, described three levels of activity of a reader as including letter recognition, response to grammatical context, and perception of word meanings (Kolers, in press). His experiments with adult Ss have included studies of item recognition and of readability of text under a variety of geometric transformations (Kolers, 1968). He finds similarity for reading Hebrew and English in the order of difficulty of different transformations. He concludes that the transformation and not the orientation of single letters is related to the difficulty of reading transformed text.

Eleanor Gibson has conducted extensive theoretical and experimental analyses of the stages of reading and learning to read (Gibson, 1965; Gibson, 1969). In her view, the first phase of learning to read is acquiring the spoken language. Learning to read then involves learning to decode the written language to speech. This mastery of the written language proceeds through three generally sequential stages. The first is learning to discriminate among the written elements—the letters of the alphabet. Second, the child must learn to decode the letters to the sounds of speech. Finally, as he becomes a skilled reader he learns to use all the "rules" in the language such as spelling structure and grammatical structure. In short, he learns to process larger and more complicated units of the written language. Gibson and some other investigators have conducted experiments bearing on the perceptual learning processes of each of these levels and they will be discussed in that order.

The developmental course of letter discrimination was investigated in the study by Gibson, Gibson, Pick, and Osser (1962) discussed previously. Improvement in such discriminations occurred between the ages of 4 and 8 years. The rates of improvement depended on the type of discrimination involved, that is, whether or not the difference was critical for distinguishing among real letters (see Section IB).

The question of whether this improvement in letter discrimination with age might reflect some type of learning was asked in a study by Pick (1965). She trained kindergartners to make discriminations among standard letter-like forms and various transformations of the standard forms. Then, in a transfer task, the Ss made discriminations among forms which were either (1) the same standard forms as in the training stage, but new transformations (prototype group); or (2) different standard forms from those in the training stage but the same types of transformation (distinctive feature group); or (3) different standards and transformations from those in the training stage. The performance of the second group, whose members discriminated among forms they had never seen before but which varied among each other on the same dimensions as their training stage forms, was superior to that of the other two groups. Thus improvement in discrimination of forms like letters might primarily involve learning to attend to and respond on the basis of dimensional differences among the forms.

In another study Gibson (1965) found that for 4-year-olds, difficulty of matching real letters was highly related to the difficulty predicted on the basis of an analysis of the number of differences or distinctive features distinguishing one letter from another. Three studies investigated the utilization of such distinctive features in tasks of searching for a visual target letter (Gibson and Yonas, 1966a, 1966b; Yonas and Gibson, 1967). These are described in detail in Section VIC. These studies generally imply that distinctive features of letter forms rather than letter names or Gestalt shape variables are the basis for improved discrimination of the forms as a function of age and experience.

Once the letter forms are perceptually distinguished, the beginning reader is faced with the problem of decoding the graphemes into speech sounds. Bishop (1964), in an experiment with adults, compared the effect of letter-sound training with word training on performance in learning a new list of nonsense words. In a paired associate task, Ss either learned to associate single sounds such as *fa* with Arabic graphemes (phonics method) or they learned to associate two-syllable nonsense words such as *faru* with written words composed of two Arabic graphemes (whole-word method). Following training to a criterion, Ss in both groups were presented with a second paired associate task in which the items were two-syllable words to be associated with two-grapheme written words. The two-syllable words, both in the whole-word training list and in the transfer list for both groups, were composed of the letters and sounds used in the single-letter training. Ss trained with the single letter-sounds learned the second word list faster than Ss trained with a first list of words. Furthermore, the basis for transfer appeared to be the letter-sound relationships regardless of whether Ss had been trained with them or whether they had abstracted them from the list of words. Jeffrey and Samuels (1967) recently replicated this finding with kindergartners. They found a significant effect of letter training on correct responses on the first transfer trial as well as in number of trials to learn the new list. On this latter measure, Ss receiving word training were no faster at learning the second list than a control group of Ss who had received no training.

The units of processing at a more complex and skilled level of reading are surely not single letters. Adults find it extremely difficult to read material which is presented one letter at a time sequentially (Kohlers and Katzman, 1966; Newman, 1966). There is no particular reason to suppose that children who have attained some skill in reading find it any easier to process written text letter by letter.

The question of what the higher-order perceptual units of skilled reading are has been investigated in a number of experiments. Gibson, Pick, Osser, and Hammond (1962) found that for adults pseudo-words constructed according to the rules for English spelling were more easily perceived than pseudo-words which were not. The hypothesis entertained in this experiment was that the complex spelling-sound relationships define perceptual units in written material. The results of this experi-

ment have been replicated with children (Gibson, Osser, and Pick, 1963), with Braille readers (Pick, Thomas, and Pick, 1966), and with deaf readers (Gibson, Shurcliff, and Yonas, 1966). A variety of control procedures ruled out the possibility that some type of frequency of occurrence variable accounted for the ease with which the one group of words was perceived as compared with the other (see also Gibson, 1964). Since the deaf readers performed like the other Ss, and since they could not utilize the sound correspondence, it may not be the spelling-sound correspondences which operate as perceptual grouping principles but instead the spelling patterns themselves. Most of these Ss did not speak either though, and they may have learned to read in a manner quite different from normal readers. The question of the usual function of the sound relationship in forming larger perceptual units of written material is not settled by testing the deaf Ss. Bever and Bower (1966) are investigating the possibility that some readers may directly perceive written material ("visual readers"), whereas others perceive it in terms of the sound relationship.

The way in which the spelling patterns are learned is a problem only recently studied. Wallach (1963) found a significant positive relationship between fifth graders' spelling achievement scores and their accuracy in tachistoscopic recognition of letter sequences approaching real English words (e.g., mossia, everal) as compared to random sequences of letters. He interpreted this relationship as suggesting that spelling skill consists of learning the sequential probability arrangements of letters. Of course, the relationship could also be a function of learning spelling-sound regularities. Perhaps if Wallach had used nonsense letter sequences consisting solely of English spelling-sound regularities (instead of approximations) as compared with random letter sequences, the relationship between spelling skill and recognition accuracy would have been even greater.

Gibson, Farber, and Shepela (1967) studied directly the way in which spelling patterns might be learned. They used a learning set procedure and asked whether regularities in spelling patterns could provide a basis for improvement in performance across problems. The Ss were in kindergarten and first grade, and each problem was a pair of four-letter words or pseudo-words. The correct members of the pairs contained a common two-letter pattern in a given location. The incorrect members of the pairs differed from the correct members by only one letter. The results from the kindergartners were difficult to interpret since they could not pay attention to the task, but the first graders did form learning sets with the material. That is, they showed the improvement over problems that one would expect if they were basing their responses directly on the structural regularities and looking for such regularities in new problems.

The function of grammatical structure in processing written material has been the subject of some recent investigations. Levin and Mearini (1964) proposed the hypothesis that attention tends to be focused on those parts of a word that are more important or informative. Specifically, they hypothesized that Italian readers would attend more to the ends of words than English readers because there are more inflectional suffixes in Italian than in English. They presented children who were either English or Italian readers with a sorting task consisting of a number of nonsense words in which the location of the criterial attribute varied. The two groups performed equally well when the criterial attribute occurred at the beginning of the words, but when it occurred at the end of the word the Italian children performed better than the American children. Here the grammatical structure of the language seems to function to direct attention to one or another part of a word.

The technique of measuring the eye-voice span (EVS) has been used by Levin to investigate the function of grammatical structure in perceptual processing of written text with children and adults. This technique measures the "distance" that the eye is ahead of the voice in oral reading. The distance is determined simply by removing the text from an S while he is reading aloud and then counting the number of words he is able to report correctly. With unstructured lists of words the number of words in the EVS remains quite constant for a given S, but with sentences the size of the EVS varies with structural characteristics of the sentences (Levin and Turner, 1966; Levin and Kaplan, 1966). For example, these studies found that the EVS tends to reach to the end of a phrase rather than stopping before the phrase boundary. The EVS is shorter in active sentences than in comparable passive sentences, which are more constrained or predictable. Generally, the EVS increases with age and it is greater for fast readers than for slow ones.

The question can be raised as to whether these various grammatical constraints affect what the S can report by guessing on the basis of probabilities or whether they really affect what the S sees. That the effect is on the perceptual process and not just on facility of guessing is implied strongly by additional measures used in the Levin and Kaplan study. Ss were given a recognition test in which some of the words were from the experimental material and others had visual and semantic similarity to the experimental words. On this measure, the ratio of correct to incorrect recognitions was extraordinarily great. If the Ss are merely guessing when the EVS measures are taken, one might expect many of the guesses to be words visually and semantically similar to the correct words. On the other hand, it is possible that the correct words would have been highly probable guesses.

Sensitivity to grammatical context in oral reading was demonstrated in very young children by Weber (1967). She had first-grade children read aloud and she noted the errors they made. When an error was not compatible grammatically with the text, the children usually corrected it. On the other hand, if an error was not corrected, it usually proved to be grammatically compatible with the context. The better readers demonstrated these effects even more strongly than below-average readers.

The units of perceptual processing of written material again are obviously not single letters. Spelling structure (whether because of its relationship to speech patterns or independently of this relationship) and even more complex grammatical structure seem to operate in the formation of perceptual units in reading. Presumably, the skilled reader comes to be able to utilize more and more of these regularities of structure in the written language.

Just exactly how a reader progresses toward processing higher order and more complex units of material is not clear. Hochberg

(1966) has suggested that this perceptual learning involves changes in the way in which the material is coded and stored rather than changes in what is perceived. He had Ss make same-different judgments between pairs of written words presented either simultaneously or successively. In simultaneously presented words, if the shapes of the members of a pair differed (e.g., one in upper case, the other in lower case), response latency increased. When the words were presented successively, however. shape variables were irrelevant, but response latency increased if the words were unpronounceable or if they were presented in a geometric transformation. Presumably, shape differences affected the judgments in simultaneous presentation conditions by requiring S to read the words before making his judgment. Under successive presentations, when memory became involved and S had to read the words anyway it was not form variables but the variables affecting codability or readability which affected response times. Hochberg, in effect, suggests that changes in selection and attention and in coding are involved in the progression toward perceptual processing of increasingly complex structural regularities. Posner (1967) has utilized this type of technique in investigating the type of processing involved in perceptual matching, identification, and classification tasks in adults. This would also be a technique useful for such work with children.

Some studies have investigated the relationship between reading performance and other perceptual tasks. Birch and Belmont (1965) presented a task of auditory-visual matching of dot patterns to children from 5 to 12 years. Performance improved with age and most of the improvement occurred during the first couple of years. At these early age levels, but not later, task performance was also related to reading achievement. This result probably reflects the fact that the tasks required in reading change as the reader becomes more skilled. In a similar study, Muehl and Kremenak (1966) also found a high relationship between first graders' reading achievement and auditory-visual matching of dot patterns. To the extent that reading involves two modalities, it seems reasonable that other tasks involving the same two modalities show some relationship with reading. However, it might be observed that the pro-

cesses involved in recognition of dot patterns may not be similar enough to reading to elucidate the specific tasks involved in learning to read.

One final problem of perception and reading deserves some consideration. This is the relationship between tachistoscopic training and speed of reading. Most of the mechanical devices used in the "speed-reading" training programs—pacers, tachistoscopes, etc.—are assumed to be training eye movements and thereby increasing the speed of reading. Tinker (1958), in reviewing studies attempting to evaluate the effectiveness of these methods, concludes that systematic practice in reading results in as much improvement in reading speed as any programs involving mechanical devices. He also points out that changes in eye movements reflect but do not cause improvement in reading skill. Most of the relevant studies (e.g., Glock, 1949; Manolakes, 1952) used adult Ss and found no difference between the effect of specific training programs using tachistoscopic devices and systematic practice. One study (Manolakes, 1952) found a greater increase in words read per minute for Ss who practiced than for Ss who underwent the training program! It is doubtful whether the results of such studies would be different if children were used as Ss since Tinker's analysis of the eye movements as symptoms seems quite reasonable.

C. Eidetic Imagery

An eidetic image has traditionally been defined as ". . . a visual image of a figure, usually long in duration, localized in space in front of the S's eyes, positive in color, and usually in the plane where the original figure was shown" (Leask, Haber, and Haber, 1968, p. 1). The study of this phenomenon was once an extremely popular topic, but it received very little attention after 1932 (Kluever, 1932) until recently when Haber and Haber (1964) made the initial report of an extensive research program.

The Habers and their colleagues, in contrast to many of the early investigators, have done a very careful job of operationalizing criteria for the definition and identification of eidetic imagery. In the initial study (Haber and Haber, 1964) 12 of 155 school children reported a degree of imagery which was far superior on a number of measures than 72 others who had reported some imagery. For example, in these 12 children all images of the pictures displayed lasted longer than 40 seconds, their accuracy scores were higher, a much greater percentage of the images were positively colored, and all of them could be scanned with their eyes (as opposed to the image moving with the eyes). These results proved reliable on retesting after 8 months. A subsequent screening of 380 school children yielded 23 who seemed to have a reliable, qualitatively different kind of imagery (Leask, Haber, and Haber, 1968).

On the basis of subsequent work and overall examination of the data these investigators have suggested even more stringent criteria for identification of eidetic imagery. One possibility they have developed is to show an S a sequence of two meaningful pictures which can be superimposed to make a quite different picture. If an S has an eidetic image of the first picture and superimposes it on the second, he should be able to report the composite picture. When the 23 Ss who were thought to be eidetic were shown the sequence of two pictures, only 4 responded appropriately. In addition, 2 Ss with high eidetic imagery were matched with two control Ss in school grade and academic ability and were tested on their ability to report from the image or recall details of pictures that they were shown. The accuracy of all 4 Ss was approximately the same, suggesting that a criterion of exceptional memory may not turn out to be as important a distinguishing characteristic as was once thought. The investigators feel overall that there is a reliable phenomenon of eidetic imagery that occurs with a lower frequency than was thought on the basis of the early literature. This phenomenon deserves to be studied, especially in light of the current interest in various types of memory processes.

On the basis of the Habers' work there seems to be little evidence for a decrease in eidetic imagery with age, although this was a very common report in the early literature. It should be pointed out that the Habers have both cross-sectional and longitudinal data relevant to this question. Relevant to individual differences is a report by Sipola and Hayden (1965) of a very high incidence of eidetic imagery in a brain-damaged retarded sample of Ss. Doob (1966) has reviewed a number of studies of eidetic imagery in different cultures. The incidence varied from 0 to 20% in the various cultures.

The study of imagery, eidetic or other, is complex. To conduct such research with retardates or cross-culturally must multiply the difficulties. Nevertheless, the careful methodology of the Haber group provides a model for how to proceed.

VI. DEVELOPMENT OF ATTENTION[4]

Attention concerns the motivation of perception, its selectivity and maintenance. The study of attention has had an erratic history in general psychology, assuming central importance in the days of the structuralists (see Boring, 1950) and being virtually ignored from the 1930s to the 1950s. The study of attention revived from the impetus given during the war to studies of vigilance of watch standers. The study of the development of attention must be marked as part of the general interest in perceptual development.

A. Stimulus Determiners of Attention

Fantz (1958), in one of his early studies, observed infants' fixation preferences when they were shown a pair of figures; he noted that infants tended to show a preference for a more "complex" figure over a "simpler" figure. However, he also noted that the preference shown for a horizontally striped figure compared with a checkerboard figure showed a reversal at about 2 months of age. Fantz' definition of complexity was an intuitive one and a great deal of research with infants has been conducted using variations of his technique to ascertain the precise stimulus variables that are implied by this term. Complexity as measured by information content, novelty, amount of contour, and brightness has been investigated as a possible determiner of attention in infants. The reader is referred to Chapter 10 for details of many of these studies. One carefully controlled study (Bren-

[4] A promising and exciting approach based on concepts of information processing related to this section and Section IVA on perception and intelligence is exemplified by Neisser's (1968) book, *Cognitive Psychology*. Unfortunately, to date little developmental work has been done relevant to Neisser's ideas.

nen, Ames, and Moore, 1966) indicated a curvilinear relationship between fixation preference and complexity. The maximum duration of fixation occurred for stimuli of medium complexity. Stimuli of greater and lesser complexity elicited fixations of shorter duration. The point of maximum duration moves toward more complexity as a function of age between birth and 6 months. In this case complexity was defined as number of squares in a checkerboard pattern. A similar shifting curvilinear relationship was found by Sackett (1966) with infant monkeys. In his case complexity was defined as amount of contour change per unit area. This definition of complexity is congruent with that Brennen et al. (1966) applied to their stimuli.

There have been a number of developmental studies of older children which have varied such dimensions as stimulus complexity and have measured reported stimulus preference rather than fixation preference (Cantor, Cantor, and Ditrichs, 1963; Clapp and Eichorn, 1965). In one study (Munsinger, Kessen, and Kessen, 1964) a paired comparison design was used to evaluate the preference for pairs of random forms which varied in number of corners. The pairs of stimuli were presented to children in the first to eighth grades. In each case they were asked to indicate which of the two forms they preferred. The older children showed maximum preference for 10-cornered stimuli and decreasing preference for stimuli with more or fewer corners. This replicated a previous result with adults (Munsinger and Kessen, 1964). On the other hand, the younger children showed increasing preference with increasing number of corners. However, they did show a secondary preference peak for 10-cornered stimuli. These investigators hypothesized that stimulus preference is determined by an optimal complexity level which matches an information processing level of the organism. Since this would be expected to increase with age, the results of the younger children do not support the hypothesis. However, in the second part of the study the same procedure was used with letter sequences which varied from complete redundancy (repetition of the same letters) to maximally informative (random letters). Here maximum preference was shown by all ages for intermediate levels of redundancy with older Ss showing somewhat

higher preference for the less redundant material. These results support the initial hypothesis.

Thomas (1966) reported a similar study including two experiments that cover an age range from 6 to 19. His stimuli were generated by the same method used by Munsinger, Kessen, and Kessen. He measured preference for a stimulus initially by noting whether S fixated it longer than the stimulus with which it was paired, and 2 weeks later by a direct judgment of preference. These two measures were in very close agreement. The results indicated that, for younger children up to about 12, preference was an increasing function of complexity, defined as number of turns of the stimulus. Above this age the relationship between preference and complexity was curvilinear, with the maximum preference occurring at decreasing complexity values as age increased. Thus Thomas' results agree with those of Munsinger, Kessen, and Kessen with similar shapes, except for the particular age at which complexity values for maximum preference start to decrease. A completely satisfying explanation for these results is yet to be found. Thomas does make an interesting observation that older Ss show more inconsistency in their judgment, as indicated by lack of preference transitivity. (Stimulus A being preferred to stimulus B, and B to C, does not necessarily imply that A is preferred to C.) He suggests that different aspects of the stimuli may determine the preferences at different times. The results for complexity may not be generalizable to other kinds of stimuli. Clapp and Eichorn (1965) found no relationship between looking time of nursery school children and complexity (stimulus redundancy) when the stimuli were geometric forms varying in regularity. However, their study also differed from the ones just discussed in that stimuli were presented successively rather than in pairs. They did find that colored stimuli elicited longer viewing than black and white and that incongruous stimuli (e.g., a picture of a bird with two bodies and two heads but one pair of legs) elicited longer viewing time than normal stimuli.

Selectivity of perception can also be determined by other aspects of the situation than the stimulus itself. Reese, for example, presented a series of human or of animal pictures prior to exposure of an ambiguous figure (which could be seen either as a man or a rat). He found a preponderance of responses consistent with the forms previously shown (Reese, 1963a, 1963b; Reese and Ford, 1962). The Ss ranged in age from preschool to second grade and the result was stronger in the older children. Reese attributed the results to a mediation process by which an expectancy for the class of stimuli previously exposed causes a bias in coding the incoming stimulus. However, the mediation process may be simpler than the one implied. Exposure to a class of stimuli may cause S to attend to different parts of the stimulus than he would with another class of stimuli. This would put the selectivity in the perceptual rather than the response aspect of the identification.

Reese's suggestion of a mediating process for perceptual responses is related to the acquired distinctiveness hypothesis formulated succinctly by Miller (1948). This hypothesis suggests that if different responses are associated with two stimuli, the stimuli will become perceptually more different. This occurs because there are different response produced stimuli accruing to the initial stimuli. Conversely, stimuli which have similar responses associated with them become perceptually more similar. This phenomenon is called acquired equivalence. One way of studying this hypothesis has been to have Ss learn distinctive or common verbal labels for two or more stimuli and to observe whether this affects their discriminability. There have been numerous studies with this general paradigm, but they have failed to be crucial for the hypothesis since they have (1) used as a measure of discriminability a learning task that involved association as well as discrimination, or (2) used stimuli that were initially very discriminable, or (3) not determined the discriminability of the initial stimuli. Recently, Katz (1963) reported a study not subject to these deficiencies, which provides positive evidence for the hypothesis. She taught 7- and 9-year-old Ss verbal labels for a set of four nonsense forms and then tested their discriminability using same-different judgments. One group of Ss learned a common label for each pair of forms. One group learned different labels for all four forms. A third group simply observed the forms and

did not learn labels. The discriminability of the forms was then tested by showing Ss pairs of forms tachistoscopically and asking them to make same-different judgments. The *common label* group made more errors in identifying two shapes as the same when they were really different; the *different label* group made fewer such errors; and the *nonlabel* group gave intermediate results. These results are the best evidence obtained to date for a change in perception as a function of such association. As Katz points out, the results do not agree with other studies which have properly measured changes in perception, but these were done with adults. Perhaps the design with children is a more sensitive test of the hypothesis.

B. Maintenance of Perception

One of the traditional questions of attention is the extent to which a person is able to perform one task in the face of irrelevant stimulation, that is, distraction. The study of vigilance represents one extreme of this question: How well is a person able to perform one task over a long period of time in the absence of any extraneous stimulation?

There is a common hypothesis that mental retardates are more distractable than normal children. In this context Ellis, Hawkins, Preyer, and Jones (1963) investigated the effect of distraction on oddity problem learning (learning to pick the one of three objects which is different from the other two) in normal and retarded children between 6 and 8 years. The distracting condition was a mirror mounted on the apparatus and facing S. This distraction facilitated performance for the normals and had no effect for the retardates. On the other hand, Turnure and Zigler (1964) found that under certain conditions performance of retardates is facilitated by distraction. They used an object assembly task with 6-year-old retardates and found that a distraction was beneficial if it provided information which was subsequently useful, for example, when the distraction consisted of E working on a problem that was subsequently given to the child. Turnure (1966) used an oddity problem task and found that normal children 5½ years old were adversely affected by a mirror distraction, whereas the performance of older children was facilitated. He suggested that the distraction serves to mobilize the energy of the older children toward the task. The mirror mounted on the apparatus would also serve to keep the child oriented to the task, but this should be true for younger children as well as older children. In the same study a distracting noise was also introduced for some Ss, but this had no effect on the performance.

The second type of distraction problem of current interest in general perception is the study of perception under simultaneous input of information from two sources. Such experiments most often have taken the form of simultaneous input of two auditory messages and are referred to as selective listening experiments. They derive most directly from Broadbent (1958), who suggests that when the information load becomes too great for immediate transmission through man's perceptual channels he has a short-term storage available to hold the excess momentarily. If the delay in transmission exceeds a rather short time, the information in this short-term storage is lost. He conceives of a filterlike model which permits a person to transmit some of the information directly through the perceptual channels and to shunt some of it into storage. One implication of this is that if two messages are given to a person at the same time, he could choose to listen to one and ignore the other. Many interesting experiments have been done to try to ascertain on what stimulus characteristics the filter would work. It has been found that adults can selectively listen with ease to one of two messages which differ in spatial location or in voice quality but not when they differ in semantic content (Triesman, 1964a, 1964b).

Maccoby and Konrad (1966, 1967) have conducted a series of selective listening experiments with children. In these studies children, ranging in age from kindergarten through sixth grade, were asked to repeat one of two simultaneously presented messages. The messages, one in a man's voice, the other in a woman's voice, consisted of one or two words. In the first study (Maccoby and Konrad, 1966) the messages were presented through earphones, and the effects of age, practice, type of presentation, and number of syllables in the stimuli were investigated. The children were told before each pair of messages to report either the man or the woman's voice. The results showed significant improve-

ment with age and significant practice effects through two series of trials. The type of presentation was varied by presenting the messages both through the two earphones and one through each earphone. In the second procedure, the messages differed in spatial location as well as voice quality, and it is this condition that produces better selectivity. The performance with messages differing in spatial location alone was not determined. Multisyllable words were recognized better at all ages, but had relatively more advantage for the older children. The authors suggest older children may be better able to use the redundancy in language.

In a second study (Maccoby and Konrad, 1967) a condition of preknowledge about the voice to be selected was compared with a condition in which the voice to be reported was indicated after the messages were transmitted. It was hoped that this comparison would reveal whether the selectivity mechanism functioned before or after the stimulus. In this study, the messages were presented over two loud speakers rather than through earphones. Again performance improved with age. Preknowledge appeared to aid performance for the younger children and not for the older. However, only a main effect of preknowledge was statistically significant. In various conditions the effect of the familiarity of target words and sequential probabilities of pairs of words in the target messages were also studied. Both of these factors influenced the accuracy of performance, and sequential probability interacted with age. The high sequential probability phrases were more effective for the older Ss than the younger Ss. The authors interpret this result to mean that the older Ss are better able to fill in poorly heard phrases. The two studies together yielded overall age differences in performance but, for the most part, not the interaction that would have indicated qualitative developmental changes in the selective process itself.

In another study using the selective listening technique Neufeldt (1966) presented two digits simultaneously, one to each ear. The S's task was to report all he heard on each presentation. A group of 13-year-olds reported significantly more digits correctly than a group of 9-year-olds. This was true for both the first half of their report and the second, thus suggesting better perception and short-term memory for the older children. This interpretation is based on an assumption that if S is required to report all he has heard, performance on the initial half of the report (the first digit reported) reflects perception, whereas that on the last half (the second digit reported) reflects short-term memory. A group of organically brain damaged and a group of cultural-familial retardates, matched in MA to the 9-year-olds and in CA to the 13-year-olds, performed at approximately the same level as the 9-year-olds, suggesting that the differences found between the 9- and 13-year-olds is an MA difference rather than a CA difference. The 9-year-olds did significantly better than the organic retardates in the second half of their report, but not as well as the 13-year-olds. To the extent that the second half of the report does represent short-term memory, it suggests an IQ or developmental rate deficit.

In another experiment in this study, four stimuli were presented, one to each ear simultaneously, followed by a second to each ear. The Ss were directed to report the message either ear by ear, pair by pair (i.e., in temporal order), or by type (e.g., digit or letter, since in this case the messages were mixed digits and letters). In general, the 13-year-olds did better than the 9-year-olds. All Ss did relatively poorly reporting by pair. The normal 9- and 13-year-olds did equally well reporting by type or by ear, but both groups of retardates did better reporting by type than by ear. The author interprets this difference in performance as reflecting recall strategies. The normal Ss are relatively better able to shift recall strategies than the retarded Ss.

The possibilities of using the selective listening technique to explore developmental changes in perception and short-term memory have just begun to be exploited (see also Inglis and Caird, 1963; Broadbent and Gregory, 1965). However, developmental differences in selective listening may not be unequivocally interpretable since the process of selective listening is not completely understood for adults. Developmental studies will contribute to an understanding of the general process and vice versa.

The phenomenon of retinal rivalry has been thought to be a useful measure of attention in the sense of maintenance of perception. This is the alternation between seeing one and another of two stimuli, presented simultaneously one to each eye (see Woodworth and Schlosberg, 1954). One developmental study of this phenomenon with Ss from kindergarten to college age has been reported. Goldstein and Cofoid (1965) presented a vertical line to one eye and a horizontal line to the other eye, and Ss were asked to report what they saw. They noted how many times during a 3-minute observation period the S's report changed. There was a significant increase in alternation or change as a function of age and a somewhat greater frequency of alternation for girls than for boys. Control experiments and careful instruction of the younger Ss ruled out the possibility that the differences were due to experimental artifacts. It seems surprising that a measure of attention would show a decrement with age. However, the task in this experiment did not ask Ss to maintain attention. Thus results obtained with this method, in fact, may not be relevant to that aspect of attention.

C. Visual Search in Children

Woodworth and Schlosberg (1954) have reviewed the early literature on attention as measured by the number of objects that could be apprehended at a single glance (span of attention) and on changes of attention as indicated by number and loci of eye fixation. The final aspect of attention which will be considered here is visual search. There has been relatively little work investigating how children approach a perceptual search task. As in the case of investigation of shape perception (see Section IB), there are at least two possible strategies for studying search behavior in children. The exploratory behavior itself can be observed, for example, by recording and analysis of eye movements, or features of the search process can be inferred from measures of the results of search. Both methods have been used with children.

White and Plum (1964) photographed preschool children's eye movements while they performed a series of discrimination learning problems in a learning set design. The photographic records only permitted reliable judgments as to whether an S was looking right or left. Frequency of movements, defined as a change from looking right to looking left, was correlated with performance in the learning task. The total number of eye movements in a relatively easy, interesting problem series was greater than in more difficult series. There was some suggestion of an increase in number of eye movements until S reached a successful solution and a decrease thereafter. This seemed to be true for both intraproblem and interproblem performance.

Mackworth and Thomas (1962) devised an apparatus to photograph and measure eye fixation position to within 1° of visual angle (± ½ inch at a distance of 28 inches). Such precision permits detailed analysis of where Ss look in a visual display. Mackworth and Bruner (1966) used this device for an intensive study of the eye movements of 6-year-old children and adults. The Ss viewed a series of photographs of a picture which was either progressively blurred or was initially blurred and progressively brought into focus. Each successive exposure of a picture in the progression lasted 10 seconds, during which time eye position was recorded. The Ss commented on the picture after each exposure. Overall results showed that average fixation duration is slightly longer for children than for adults (373 versus 360 ms).

The authors point out that these durations are longer than those typically found for reading and they do not decrease so markedly with age. They suggest that pictorial viewing is not so developed a skill as reading. All the Ss tended to focus their fixations on fewer points as the stimulus became more blurred. Intersubject variability was extremely high so that there was no group trend toward concentration on particular points of the target. Children also scanned less effectively by failing to attend to the most informative aspects of the picture. Furthermore, they were more variable in exploration of repeated presentations of the same picture. Finally, children made many more very short eye movements, relative to the number of larger saccades. This last fact is interpreted to mean that they restrict their intake of information when faced with tasks that put a burden on their capacity for information processing—in other words, children develop a kind of tunnel vision. These results are admittedly preliminary since they are based on a restricted collection of stimulus materials and a narrowly prescribed task. However, the feasibility of the technique has been demonstrated and the type of analysis is both precise and imaginative.

Vurpillot (1966) used Mackworth's recording technique to observe the eye movements of children from 5 to 9 years old as they made same-different judgments about pairs of stimuli. The stimuli were outline drawings of houses, each with six windows. Corresponding windows in the pair of stimuli could contain the same or different designs and the children's task was to decide whether the two houses were exactly the same. The eye movement recording was precise enough to be able to follow Ss' scanning as they looked from window to window. Vurpillot was able to infer the strategies that the children of different ages were using. She found that the younger children spend less time scanning than the older children before making their judgment. This is apparently due to reaching a decision upon incomplete sampling of the stimulus. The children of intermediate age scan for as long or longer than the older children. They are not as sensitive to the demands of the task, and even after they find a difference they will go on to scan the whole array before making a judgment. Some of the different behaviors of children apparently reflect differences in short-term memory capacity. For example, more older children will scan several windows in one house before scanning the corresponding windows in another house.

There has been some work on search patterns in tactual exploratory behavior and this has been described previously (Section IB) in connection with shape discrimination. In addition, Gliner (1965) has shown that it is possible to reinforce the exploratory movement of the hands in tactual exploration so that children will explore texture cues or shape cues. As might be expected, such training can have a facilitating or inhibitory effect on discrimination learning, depending on relevance of the trained cues for the learning task.

Gibson and Yonas (1966a, 1966b) have conducted studies which are good examples of the way in which aspects of the search process can be inferred from the results. These investigators used a task originally devised by Neisser (1964) to study differences in search between children and adults. The task is to search through a list of rows of letters for a target letter. The farther through the list an S has to search, the longer is his search time. It is possible to calculate the average time for processing each letter and to study the effect on this time of such parameters as age, number of targets, confusability of the contextual letters.

In the first study (Gibson and Yonas, 1966a) Ss searched for one or two targets against a low confusion background, that is, a background of letters that are rarely confused with the target letter. In another condition the Ss searched for one target, which was embedded in a highly confusable background. Children from the second, fourth, and sixth grades and college sophomores served as Ss. Response time decreased significantly with age, and the low-confusion background produced shorter response times than the high-confusion background. However, there was no effect of number of targets nor was there an interaction of age with confusability or number of targets.

In a second study (Gibson and Yonas, 1966b) third-grade and college students searched for targets, again in the context of high- and low-confusion visual backgrounds. In addition, however, high- and low-confusion auditory backgrounds were introduced by presentation of spoken letters through earphones. In this experiment only the visual backgrounds affected search time; as in the first study, the high-confusion background resulted in longer response times. Interestingly, in the second study there was an interaction between the age and confusability of visual background. The children's response time was more severely affected by the high-confusion background than was the adults'. As the authors point out, this result may not have been found in the first study because of uncontrolled order effects. The investigators suggest application of this technique to a microanalysis of the strategies involved in the search process. By varying the number of distinctive features shared by the target and background letters, they hope to be able to infer the strategies utilized by children and adults in such tasks. Preliminary results by the same authors (Yonas and Gibson, 1967) from disjunctive reaction time procedures support the hypothesis that number of shared features between target and nontarget stimuli

is an important determiner of information processing time.

D. Perceptual Learning and Attention

Many different problems have been discussed in this section on attention. There is no general theory that attempts to encompass all of them. Indeed it is quite likely that at least the *maintenance* aspects of perception involve quite different processes than the *selective* aspects. The theoretical position of Eleanor Gibson, however, is one that focuses on the selective aspects of perceptual learning and development. One basic tenet of this position is that perceptual development consists of a progressive increase in sensitivity. This increase in sensitivity refers to both an increase of resolving power with respect to single stimulus dimensions and an increase in the number of stimulus dimension to which a person is sensitive. An example of the type of improvement predicted from this point of view is the results of the normative study by Gibson et al. (1962) of shape perception previously described (see Section IB). In that study, it will be recalled, children were asked to discriminate between standard forms and various transformations of them. Improvement with age occurred for discrimination of all the transformations reflecting an increasing sensitivity within specific stimulus dimensions. The different levels and rates of improvement for the different types of transformation were attributed to differential sensitivity to the various stimulus dimensions. For example, topological differences between stimuli ordinarily specify different objects in the world, and children early exhibit sensitivity to this type of difference since it is necessary for their real-life perception. On the other hand, perspective differences are typically found in the real world when the same object is seen from different viewpoints. Thus there is little reason for children to have an early sensitivity to this type of difference. The crux of this interpretation is that children are and become sensitive to specific stimulus dimensions and this sensitivity generalizes under appropriate conditions.

This interpretation was investigated in the previously cited study (see Section VB) by Pick (1965). It will be recalled that when kindergartners were trained to discriminate visually between standard forms and transformations of them, their learning appeared to be based on detection of distinctive features to a greater degree than on construction of prototypes or templates. The generality of these results to tactual perception was explored in the same study. Pick used essentially the same design in replicating the experiment under conditions of simultaneous as well as successive tactual comparison of the forms. When the comparison was simultaneous only distinctive feature learning occurred; when the comparison was successive both distinctive feature and prototype learning occurred. The author suggested that distinctive feature learning, which always occurred, was basic to such improvement in sensitivity. Prototype learning occurred only to the extent that memory was involved in order to compare one form with another. The importance of distinctive feature learning was also demonstrated in cross-modal replications of these experiments (Pick, Pick, and Thomas, 1966). The learning and generalization of distinctive features may be a very important way in which improvement in sensitivity occurs.

From Gibson's point of view sensitivity or changes of sensitivity could be built into the organism or could develop as a function of experience. It is essentially neutral with respect to the nativism-empiricism controversy. However, to the degree that experience is necessary for improvement in sensitivity, it does not function by association. That is, we do not perceive better or differently because we add meaning or implicit responses to the stimulus input. We perceive better because we have become sensitive to more or different properties of the stimulus. The kind of experience that will lead to improvement in perception is any experience that provides the opportunity for detection of more of the stimulus properties. This may, but does not have to be an identification learning task such as is used in traditional discrimination learning studies. Scanning the stimulus, for example, is at least as conducive to an improvement in perception. An experiment illustrating the expected results is one reported by Robinson (1955). He presented adult Ss with 10 fingerprints as stimuli in a study of the transfer of different kinds of training to a subsequent discrimination task. One group learned a different gang-

ster name for each print, another group learned to respond with "cops" to five of the prints and with "robbers" to the other five. A third group made same-different judgments among the fingerprints. In a transfer task requiring same-different judgments between fingerprints, all three of these groups made significantly fewer errors in a transfer task than a control group, which had received no training. The differences between the training groups were not significant. These results suggest that same-different training is as effective for improvement in discrimination as is training to associate distinctive labels. They are not congruent with the previously described results of Katz (1963), who, it will be recalled (see Section VIA), found that association training resulted in differential effects as compared with nonassociation training. The reasons for this incongruity are not known. Gibson would interpret the improvement in discrimination such as found by Katz also to be a function of learning to attend to the relevant properties of the stimuli rather than a direct function of association training.

Description of the mechanism for the detection of stimulus properties has been a problem in the theoretical position proposed by Gibson. However, recently (Gibson, 1969) she has attempted to specify the form of such a mechanism in more detail. She suggests that, peripherally, overt orienting or exploratory movements may mediate attention to the various features of the stimulus. (It cannot be emphasized too strongly that in Gibson's point of view these overt responses do not operate by changing the stimulus input after it comes in, but by causing a different stimulus to come in.) At the level of the central nervous system, Gibson suggests the existence of an abstracting process and of a filtering process similar to that suggested by Broadbent (1958). The nature of the abstracting process still lacks satisfying specificity. However, the filter model, by virtue of the work of such investigators as Broadbent (1958) and Triesman (1964a, 1964b), is quite meaningful. That is, the properties of one kind of filter model have been well investigated, but there is no equally well formulated model for the abstraction process. In referring to such processes Gibson points out that although the direct evidence for them is scant, there are many converging lines of evidence, which make their existence extremely likely. The reader is referred to Gibson's (1969) book for a development of this theoretical orientation including a careful review of the evidence and a consideration of the implications for a variety of interesting problems.

VII. THEORIES OF PERCEPTUAL DEVELOPMENT

Several theoretical points of view have been described in discussing specific topics in perceptual development: those of Brunswick, Gibson, and Pollack; the sensory tonic concepts of Werner and Wapner; Gestalt theory; the Soviet motor-copy view; and the individual difference approaches of Gardner, Kagan, and Witkin. It was thought that the research problems might be better integrated in the context of a theoretical perspective. However, it is apparent that the theories are not formal hypothetic-deductive systems but are more or less specific frames of reference for examining problems of perceptual development. This generalization is also true of a few additional points of view to be described.

All these theories may be compared on a number of dimensions. Several positions have already been characterized as being nativist or empiricist, or as involving mechanisms of enrichment or differentiation. They may also be characterized along an active-passive dimension. That is, many theories consider S's gross activity to be involved in perception, whereas others would consider S's to be relatively passive receivers of sensory information. Finally, and in many ways most importantly, the various theories differ greatly in the problems toward which they have been directed and the research which they have stimulated. The ideas of Piaget, Hebb, and a neurophysiological approach to perceptual development will be examined with these distinctions in mind.

A. Piaget

Flavell (1963) quotes the following definition of perception by Piaget: "We will call perception the most direct or immediate possible knowledge of a present object in the sensorial field (without affirming, however, that there exists a knowledge which is completely direct or immediate)" (p. 232). This definition has two important implications for the present purpose. First, it focuses attention on knowledge by perception and on knowledge by means other than perception. Illusions lend themselves very nicely to such a distinction. Illusory perception can be corrected by cognitive operations. Second, the implication in the definition that perception is not an immediate process raises the question of the perceptual process as it develops over time. It is with respect to this question that Piaget's mechanism of perception becomes apparent. The longer the duration of fixation of a stimulus, the larger it will appear. Such a relationship obtains because subjective size is conceived to depend on the number of interactions or encounters between elements of the stimulus and Ss' receptors, and the number of such encounters presumably increases with fixation time. When two stimuli are presented, the degree to which one is overestimated relative to the other depends on how the encounters of each stimulus are combined or coupled. The more such coupling is complete and balanced, the more veridical will be perception of relative size. Thus the effect of coupling is opposite to that of fixation. Errors involving the original encountering due to fixation are called Type I and, as indicated, often are in the direction of overestimation. These errors decrease with age. However, Ss' perceptual activity such as eye movements and scanning strategies control the completeness and balance of coupling.

The perceptual activity can also lead in some cases to nonveridical perception. Piaget speaks of such cases as Type II errors. These often increase as a function of age with an increase in Ss' perceptual activity. Examples of such errors include size constancy studies, which often produce results in the direction of overconstancy with increasing age, and figural aftereffects, the magnitude of which also appears to increase with age. Piaget's model, which he has developed in mathematical form (described in detail by Vurpillot, 1959), has been mostly applied to illusions. However, he has also applied it to psychophysical thresholds and it is possible to derive the Weber-Fechner law from it.

A study of an illusion which illustrates Piaget's interest in comparing perceptual and cognitive modes of knowing was reported by Piaget and Taponier (1956). If two equal parallel horizontal lines are presented so that they are laterally offset, the upper line is overestimated relative to the lower. Piaget and Taponier found that the degree of this overestimation increases as a function of age. However, when the lines are presented initially directly under each other so that no illusory effect occurs and are then displaced while S is watching, the task becomes one of conservation of length. In this case with increasing age, decreasing number of Ss make illusion-type judgments, which would be expected since there is increasing length conservation as a function of age. The procedure of comparing increasing *magnitude* of illusion with decreasing *numbers* of Ss exhibiting the illusion may be questionable. Nevertheless, it is an interesting demonstration of perceptual and cognitive development showing opposite age trends.

Piaget's interest in perceptual activity is illustrated by one of the most methodologically precise studies coming from his laboratory (Piaget and Vinh-Bang, 1961). This study was an investigation of temporal parameters of eye movements and fixations during a number of perceptual tasks. Such information presumably could provide precise empirical support for the effects of fixation and coupling. For example, when the perceptual task was to compare the lengths of two vertical line segments, one above the other, there was a tendency to overestimate the upper segment. Eye movement analysis indicated the upper segment was fixated more often. However, in general the lack of details about reliability of the measures makes interpretation of this study difficult.

Piaget's explanation of perception then is based on perceptual activity in the sense that Type I errors occur because of fixation duration and Type II errors because of changes of fixation or scanning. Pollack, as will be recalled, has also focused on developmental changes in illusions and, like Piaget, distinguishes between those that decrease and those that increase with age. However, in Pollack's view the mechanisms are quite different, being basic physiological aging factors for the second type.

B. Hebb

Hebb (1949, 1958), like Piaget, tends to emphasize activity in his analysis of percep-

tual development, although, like the Gestalt theorists, he considers the discrimination of figure and ground as a primitive basis for perception. He conceives of perception as a mediating process between sensation and response and his views of perceptual development concern the role of early experience in producing this mediating process. Perceptual activity is brought into the theory by invoking the hypothetical physiological entities of cell assembly and phase sequence. These concepts refer to integrated neural networks formed by the close association in time between stimulus configurations and receptor organ (e.g., eye) movement. In Hebb's view the formation of such neural networks is a prerequisite for any pattern perception. Thus even very primitive aspects of perception depend on prior experience and movements or scanning. It is not surprising then to find that much research conducted or stimulated by Hebb has investigated the effects of early perceptual experience. In the absence of prior visual experience, pattern perception should be very difficult. Hebb discusses studies of dark-reared animals and congenitally blind humans who have had their sight restored (Senden, 1960) and adduces evidence that under these conditions pattern perception is indeed defective (see Section IC). However, the human evidence is often very ambiguous (Wertheimer, 1951) and Gregory and Wallace (1963) have recently described a relatively clear counterexample—a case of a patient with restored sight who was able to make good shape identifications very soon after recovery of sight.

Another direction of work stimulated by Hebb has been examination of the perceptual effects of scanning tendencies. Highly practiced scanning movements in one direction may facilitate information reception in the direction of scan. Thus when single letters are flashed tachistoscopically to the left or right of a fixation point they are detected more accurately on the right. Furthermore, this selectivity increases with age (Forgays, 1953). It is as if the left-to-right scanning of reading habits makes one more sensitive to stimulus input from the side toward which the eyes are moving. It will be recalled that in her studies of perception of orientation, Ghent similarly suggested that Ss tried to scan from top to bottom of stimuli. When this scanning tendency is not congruent with where the eye is attracted by a point of high information content (focal point), S's judge the stimulus as upside down. Some critics have attacked Hebb's physiology for being too speculative. Nevertheless, he has had an extremely stimulating effect on the study of perceptual development, especially by means of manipulation of early experience.

C. Neurophysiological Approach

Hebb's ideas are also relevant to the neurophysiological approach to perceptual development. Teuber and Rudel (1962) have summarized considerable evidence concerning the perceptual effects of brain damage at various ages. These data are based on such tests as location of embedded figures and on tests of localization under conditions of body tilt. The study documents quite forcefully the thesis that the perceptual effects of brain damage depend on the age of S at testing and on the type of perceptual activity being tested. For example, the constant error in setting a luminous line to vertical when the body is tilted increases with age, but it increases more for normal than for brain-damaged children. On the other hand, setting body position to vertical from an initially tilted position results in higher constant error (further toward tilt and away from true vertical) in brain-damaged children than in normal controls, but this differences decreases with age.

Birch and Lefford (1963, 1967) have presented an integrated theoretical view of perceptual-motor development based on evidence from brain damage and the evolution of behavior. From both neurophysiological and comparative evidence they suggest three hypotheses about the development of perceptual-motor behavior.

1. There is a developmental shift from control of movement by proximal stimulus input (e.g., proprioception) to teloreceptive systems (e.g., vision). This hypothesis seems to suggest that young infants initially are more responsive to touch, proprioception, and vestibular stimulation and that with age, behavior comes to be controlled by such systems as vision and audition. Teloreceptive control is well instituted by 5 years of age (Birch and Lefford, 1967, p. 8).

2. There is a development of integration of the various sense modalities and activity is mediated by stimulation patterned from the several modalities. An example of this in infancy presented by Birch and Lefford is the fact that a rooting response can be elicited in the neonate by squeezing the ball of the thumb. However, within a few months this stimulus is no longer effective unless the arm is adducted at the shoulder and bent at the elbow; this means a patterning of tactual and proprioceptive stimulation is now necessary to elicit the response.

3. There is increased intrasensory differentiation as well as sensory integration. That is, there are changes in the aspects of stimulation within a single modality to which organisms respond. Such increased intrasensory differentiation was thought to be reflected in improvement in visual recognition of shapes, a task used in an investigation designed to evaluate the general position.

In this study ability to copy designs was correlated with performance in intersensory and intrasensory tasks. There was a strong association between intersensory performance and the perceptual-motor coordination required by the copying task. However, a positive association between intrasensory functioning and the copying task was found only with a variation of the copying task that involved ability to utilize supplementary visual cues. The age range of the children, 5 to 11 years, was already beyond the stage where there could be a test of the first hypothesis. However, it will be recalled that the related hypothesis that visual perception matures later than tactual has been called into question earlier in this chapter and elsewhere by the present authors (Pick, Pick, and Klein, 1967).

D. Conclusions

Birch and Lefford's third hypothesis of intrasensory differentiation is reminiscent of the theoretical points of view of Gibson and of Werner and Wapner. Is it possible to distinguish these various differentiation theories? Both Birch and Lefford and Werner and Wapner provide for increasing hierarchic integration along with increasing differentiation. This accounts for the obvious increase with age in ability to cope with complex aspects of the environment and in particular to respond in a similar way to stimuli which are functionally similar but physically very different. Gibson, on the other hand, accounts for this ability with the same mechanism as before, differentiation. Complex or higher-order variables of stimulation are distinguished and response is made to these. It is in this sense that the properties of the stimulus are emphasized and changes in attention to them are important rather than changes in processing of the same stimulus properties. Gibson would accept the importance of categorization and other mediation processes in cognitive tasks rather than in tasks involving perceptual change.

The clearest distinction in the concept of differentiation as employed by Gibson and the others is in the range of problems addressed and in the specificity with which it is applied. Both Birch and Lefford and Werner and Wapner have applied the concept mainly to intrasensory problems, whereas Gibson has used it in the study of intersensory problems (grapheme-phoneme units) as well as in the study of depth and shape perception. She has also been more precise in specifying the stimulus dimensions that are differentiated.

The study of the development of shape perception has been undertaken from more of the theoretical points of view considered in this chapter than has any other single problem. The Gestalt, Gibson, Hebb, and Soviet motor-copy views have all been centrally concerned with this problem and some of the other views have been concerned with it insofar as they have studied illusions and embedded figures. The Gestalt influence has been noted in problem areas other than the direct study of shape perception. The investigation of individual difference variables of field dependence and field articulation, the widespread use of various embedded figure tests, and the importance placed on figure-ground relations in the study of brain-damaged children reflect the pervasiveness of some of the Gestalt concepts.

The development of depth perception has not been a focal problem for many of the theoretical positions. Gibson has investigated the problem and Brunswik has inferred the effect of early experience. Perception as a cognitive process has been emphasized in Piaget's and Pollack's investigations as well as in Brunswik's analysis of size and shape constancy. None of the theoretical positions is seen as dealing completely and carefully

with all of the problems of perceptual development. In fact only the Gestalt theorists, and Hebb, and Gibson even address themselves to more than one or two aspects of perceptual development. A comprehensive theory probably awaits the interrelating of many of the problems previously described, which heretofore have been investigated only in isolation.

A concluding question about perceptual development is whether there are any such dramatic qualitative age changes in perception as the development of the conservations in cognition. At this point there is certainly no solid evidence for such changes, with the possible exception of imprinting. As far as basic sensitivity is concerned, it appears that the age changes that occur are very gradual. If qualitative changes are to be found, they will probably occur in changes of attention with age or in changes in perceptual integration across sense modalities or across time delays, although even in these areas the evidence to date suggests gradual change.

The problems of attention and perceptual integration have been rediscovered and are arousing great interest. The mechanisms of attention and education of attention, however, are not even clearly defined concepts, much less well understood, and it seems likely that they will be crucial in any general theory of perceptual development. Furthermore, even very basic questions such as span of attention have not been investigated from a developmental point of view. Perceptual integration, which must comprise a large part of real-life perception, has received relatively little emphasis in research. Yet there are a number of remedial (reading problem, retardation, etc.) procedures based on the supposed importance of sensory-motor coordination (Kephart, 1960; Delacatto, 1963). Such procedures both emphasize the need for basic research on perceptual integration and hold out promise of great reward.

The study of perceptual development has usually drawn its problems from the traditional study of perception, as witness the amount of literature in this chapter on perception of size, distance, shape, illusions, etc. The field may well be beginning to draw its problems from the real world. The recent research on reading is an example of this. The social problems of cultural and environmental deprivation may set additional problems. For example, practitioners in special education are becoming increasingly aware of "perceptual" deficits, not only of the blind and deaf but also of the physically handicapped and of those with learning disabilities. Problems derived from the real world can have theoretical as well as practical significance. A more analytic approach to the problem of deprivation and enrichment, for example, might be suggested. Such as analysis could then be integrated with the more analytic experimental approaches to the problem of deprivation recently undertaken by Hein and Held (1967). The results of such manipulations of early experience contrasted with the discovery of complex stimulus detectors (Hubel and Wiesel, 1962) and the suggestion of innate linguistic categories (e.g., McNeil, 1966) raise once again the initial question of this chapter, nativism versus empiricism, but it is at a new level of complexity.

References

Ames, E. W., and Selfan, C. K. Methodological issues in the study of age differences in infant's attention to stimuli varying in movement and complexity. Paper presented at the meetings of the Society for Research in Child Development, Minneapolis, 1965.

Anastasi, A. Heredity, environment and the question "How?" *Psychol. Rev.*, 1958, **65**, 197–208.

Anisfeld, M. The child's knowledge of English pluralization rules. *Project Literacy Reports* (Cornell University), 1966, No. 7, 45–51.

Antonovsky, H. F., and Ghent, L. Cross-cultural consistency of children's preference for the orientation of figures. *Am. J. Psychol.*, 1964, **77**, 295–297.

Attneave, F. Some informational aspects of visual perception. *Psychol. Rev.*, 1954, **61**, 183–193.

Bartoshuk, A. K. Human neonatal cardiac acceleration to sound: habituation and dishabituation. *Percept. Mot. Skills,* 1962, **15**, 15–27 (a).

Bartoshuk, A. K. Response decrement with repeated elicitation of human neonatal cardiac acceleration to sound. *J. comp. physiol. Psychol.*, 1962, **55**, 9–13. (b)

Bartoshuk, A. K. Human neonatal cardiac responses to sound: a power function. *Psychon Sci.*, 1964, **1**, 151–152.

Bekesy, G. V. *Sensory inhibition*: Princeton, N.J.: Princeton University Press, 1967.

Bell, R. Q., and Costello, N. S. Three tests for sex differences in tactile sensitivity in the newborn. *Biologia Neonat.*, 1964, **7**, 335–347.

Belmont, L., and Birch, H. G. Lateral dominance and right-left awareness in normal children. *Child Dev.*, 1963, **34**, 257–270.

Belmont, L., and Birch, H. G. Lateral dominance, lateral awareness and reading disability. *Child Dev.*, 1965, **36**, 57–71.

Benton, A. L. Right-left discrimination and finger localization in defective children. *A.M.A. Archs. Neurol. Psychiat.*, 1955, **74**, 583–589.

Benton, A. L. *Right-left discrimination and finger localization: development and pathology.* New York: Hoebar-Harper, 1959.

Bever, T. G., and Bower, T. G. How to read without listening. *Project Literacy Reports,* (Cornell University), 1966, No. 6, 13–25.

Bever, T. G., Fodor, J. A., and Weksel, W. On the acquisition of syntax: a critique of "contextual generalization." *Psychol. Rev.*, 1965, **72**, 467–482.

Binet, A. La measure des illusions visuelles chez les enfants. *Revue Philosoph.*, 1895, **40**, 11–25.

Birch, H. G., and Belmont, L. Auditory-visual integration, intelligence and reading ability in school children. *Percept. Mot. Skills*, 1965, **20**, 295–305.

Birch, H. G., and Lefford A. Intersensory development in children. *Monographs of the Society for Research in Child Development*, 1963, **28** (5, Serial No. 89).

Birch, H. G., and Lefford, A. Visual differentiation, intersensory integration, and voluntary motor control. *Monogr. Soc. Res. Child Dev.*, 1967, **32** (2, Serial No. 110).

Bishop, C. H. Transfer effects of word and letter training in reading. *J. Verb. Learn. Verb. Behav.*, 1964, **3**, 215–221.

Boring, E. G. *A history of experimental psychology*. (2nd ed.) New York: Appleton-Century-Crofts, 1950.

Botha, C. Practice without reward and figure-ground perception of adults and children. *Percept. Mot. Skills*, 1963, **16**, 271–273.

Bower, T. G. R. Discrimination of depth in premotor infants. *Psychon. Sci.*, 1964, **1**, 368.

Bower, T. G. R. Stimulus variables determining space perception in infants. *Science*, 1965, **149**, 88–89. (a)

Bower, T. G. R. The determinants of perceptual unity in infancy. *Psychon. Sci.*, 1965, **3**, 323–324. (b)

Bower, T. G. R. Slant perception and shape constancy in infants. *Science*, 1966, **151**, 832–834.

Bower, T. G. R. Phenomenal identity and form perception in an infant. *Percept. Psychophys.*, 1967, **2**, 74–76.

Braine, L. G. Age changes in mode of perceiving geometric forms. *Psychon. Sci.*, 1965, **2**, 155–156.

Braine, M. D. S. On learning the grammatical order of words. *Psychol. Rev.*, 1963, **70**, 323–348.

Brennen, W. S., Ames, E. W., and Moore, R. W. Age differences in infants' attention to patterns of different complexities. *Science*, 1966, **151**, 354–356.

Brenner, M. W. The developmental study of apparent movement. *Q. J. exp. Psychol.*, 1957, **9**, 169–174.

Brian, C. R., and Goodenough, F. L. The relative potency of color and form perception at various ages. *J. exp. Psychol.*, 1929, **12**, 197–213.

Bridger, W. H. Sensory habituation and discrimination in the human neonate. *Am. J. Psychiat.*, 1961, **117**, 991–996.

Broadbent, D. E. *Perception and communication*. New York: Pergamon Press, 1958.

Broadbent, D. E., and Gregory, M. Some confirmatory results on age differences in memory for simultaneous stimulation. *Br. J. Psychol.*, 1965, **56**, 77–80.

Brooks, R. M., and Goldstein, A. G. Recognition by children of inverted photographs of faces. *Child Dev.*, 1963, **34**, 1033–1040.

Brown, J. F. The visual perception of velocity. *Psychol. Forsch.*, 1931, **14**, 199–232.

Brown, R. Linguistic determinism and the part of speech. *J. abnorm. Soc. Psychol.*, 1957, **55**, 1–5.

Brown, R., and Bellugi, U. Three processes in the child's acquisition of syntax. In E. H. Lenneberg (Ed.), *New directions in the study of language*, Cambridge: MIT Press, 1964. Pp. 131–161.

Brown, R., and Berko, J. Word association and the acquisition of grammar. *Child Dev.*, 1960, **31**, 1–14. (a)

Brown, R., and Berko, J. Psycholinguistic research methods. In P. Mussen, (Ed.), *Handbook of research methods in child development*. New York: Wiley, 1960. Pp. 517–557. (b)

Brown, R., and Fraser, C. The acquisition of syntax. In U. Bellugi and R. Brown (Eds.), The acquisition of language. *Monogr. Soc. Res. Child Dev.*, 1964, **29**, (92), 43–79.

Bruce, D. J. The analysis of word sounds by young children. *Br. J. educ. Psychol.*, 1964, **34**, 158–170.

Brunswik, E. *Perception and the representative design of psychological experiments.* Berkeley: University of California Press, 1956.

Cantor, G. N., Cantor, J. H., and Ditrichs, R. Observing behavior in preschool children as a function of stimulus complexity. *Child Dev.*, 1963, **34**, 683–689.

Carpenter, B., and Carpenter, J. T. Perception of movement by young chimpanzees and human children. *J. comp. physiol. Psychol.*, 1958, **51**, 782–784.

Carroll, J. B., and Casagrande, J. B. The function of language classifications in behavior. In E. E. Maccoby, T. M. Newcomb and E. L. Hartley (Eds.), *Readings in social psychology.* New York: Holt, Rinehart & Winston, 1958. Pp. 18–31.

Clapp, W. F., and Eichorn, D. H. Some determinants of perceptual investigatory responses in children. *J. exp. Child Psychol.*, 1965, **2**, 371–388.

Corah, N. L. Color and form in children's perceptual behavior. *Percept. Mot. Skills*, 1964, **18**, 313–316.

Corah, N. L. The influence of some stimulus characteristics on color and form perception in nursery-school children. *Child Dev.*, 1966, **37**, 205–211.

Dana, R. H., and Goocher, B. Embedded-figures and personality. *Percept. Mot. Skills*, 1959, **9**, 99–102.

Dana, R. H., and Goocher, B. Pessimism reaffirmed: a reply to Witkin. *Percept. Mot. Skills*, 1960, **11**, 243–244.

Davidson, H. P. A study of the confusing letters B, D, P, Q. *J. genet. Psychol.*, 1935, **47**, 458–468.

Dayton, G. O., Jr., Jones, M. H., Aiu, P., Rawson, R. H., Steele, B., and Rose, M. Developmental study of coordinated eye movements in the human infant I: Visual acuity in the newborn human: a study based on induced optokinetic nystagmus recorded by electro-oculography. *Archs. Opthal.* 1964, **71**, 865–870.

Delacato, C. H. *The diagnosis and treatment of speech and reading problems.* Springfield, Ill.: Thomas, 1963.

Denis-Prinzhorn, M. Perception des distances et constance des grandeurs (etude genetique). *Archs. Psychol.*, Genève, 1961, **37**, 181–309.

Deutsch, C. Auditory discrimination and learning: social factors. *Merrill-Palmer Q.*, 1964, **10**, 277–296.

Dolphin, J. E., and Cruickshank, W. M. The figure-background relationship in children with cerebral palsy. *J. clin. Psychol.*, 1951, **7**, 228–231.

Doob, L. W. Eidetic imagery: a cross cultural will-o'-the-wisp? *J. Psychol.*, 1966, **63**, 13–34.

Doris, J., and Cooper L. Brightness discrimination in infancy. *J. exp. Child Psychol.*, 1966, **3**, 31–40.

Dornbush, R. L., and Winnick, W. A. The relative effectiveness of stereometric and pattern stimuli in discrimination learning in children. *Psychon. Sci.*, 1966, **5**, 301–302.

Doyle, M. Perceptual skill development: a possible resource for the intellectually handicapped. *Am. J. ment. Defic.*, 1967, **71**, 776–782.

Dubanoski, R. A. Inferring the phenomenal locus of the perceiver from responses to tactile stimulation. Unpublished masters thesis, University of Minnesota, 1965.

Dunford, R. E. The genetic development of cutaneous localization. *J. genet. Psychol.*, 1930, **37**, 499–513.

Dyer, D. W., and Harcum, E. R. Visual perception of binary patterns by preschool children and by school children. *J. educ. Psychol.*, 1961, **52**, 161–165.

Dyk, R. B., and Witkin, H. A. Family experiences related to the development of differentiation in children. *Child Dev.*, 1965, **36**, 21–55.

Eagles, E. L., Wishik, S. M., Doerfler, L. G., Melnick, W., and Levine, H. S. *Hearing sensitivity and related factors in children*. Published by Laryngoscope. 650 S. Kingshighway, St. Louis, Mo., 63110. 1963, Vol. XI, p. 220.

Edgren, R. D. A developmental study of motion perception, size constancy, recognition speed, and judgment of verticality. Unpublished doctoral thesis, Stanford University, 1953.

Eichorn, D. Biological correlates of behavior. In H. W. Stevenson (Ed.), *Child psychology, sixty-second yearbook of the National Society for the Study of Education*. Chicago: University of Chicago Press, 1963. Pp. 4–61.

Elithorn, A., Piercy, M. F., and Crosskey, M. A. Tactile localization. *Q. J. exp. Psychol.*, 1953, **5**, 171–182.

Elkind, D., Koegler, R. R., and Go, E. Effects of perceptual training at three age levels. *Science*, 1962, **137**, 755–756.

Elkind, D., Koegler, R. R., and Go., E. Studies in perceptual development: II. Part-whole perception. *Child Dev.*, 1964, **35**, 81–90.

Elkind, D., and Scott, L. Studies in perceptual development: I. The decentering of perception. *Child Dev.*, 1962, **33**, 619–630.

Ellis, N. R. (Ed.) *Handbook of mental deficiency*. New York: McGraw-Hill, 1963.

Ellis, N. R., Hawkins, W. F., Pryer, M. W., and Jones, R. W. Distraction effects in oddity learning by normal and mentally defective humans. *Am. J. ment. Defic.*, 1963, **67**, 576–583.

Engen, T., Lipsitt, L. P., and Kaye, H. Olfactory responses and adaptation in the human neonate. *J. comp. physiol. Psychol.*, 1963, **56**, 73–77.

Ervin, S. M. Imitation and structural change in children's language. In E. H. Lenneberg (Ed.), *New directions in the study of language*. Cambridge: MIT Press, 1964, Pp. 163–189.

Ervin, S. M., and Miller, W. R. Language development. In H. W. Stevenson (Ed.), *Child psychology: the sixty-second yearbook of the National Society for the Study of Education*. Chicago: University of Chicago Press, 1963. Pp. 108–143.

Fantz, R. L. Pattern vision in young infants. *Psychol. Rec.*, 1958, **8**, 43–47.

Fantz, R. L. A method for studying depth perception in infants under six months of age. *Psychol. Rec.*, 1961, **11**, 27–32. (a)

Fantz, R. L. The origin of form perception. *Scient. Am.*, 1961, **204**, 66–72. (b)

Fantz, R. L. Pattern vision in newborn infants. *Science*, 1963, **140**, 296–297.

Fantz, R. L. Pattern discrimination and selective attention as determinants of perceptual development from birth. In A. H. Kidd and J. L. Rivoire (Eds.), *Perceptual development in children*. New York: International Universities Press, 1966.

Fantz, R. L., Ordy, J. M., and Udelf, M. S. Maturation of pattern vision in infants during the first six months. *J. comp. physiol. Psychol.*, 1962, **55**, 907–917.

Fink, M., and Bender, M. B. Perception of simultaneous tactile stimuli in normal children. *Neurology*, 1953, **3**, 27–34.

Flavell, J. H. *The developmental psychology of Jean Piaget*. Princeton, N. J.: Van Nostrand, 1963.

Fodor, J. A. How to learn to talk: some simple ways. In F. Smith and G. Miller (Eds.), *The genesis of language*. Cambridge: MIT Press, 1966, Pp. 105–122; 288–294.

Fodor, J. A., and Bever, T. G. The psychological reality of linguistic segments. *J. verb. Learn. verb. Behav.*, 1965, **4**, 414–420.

Forgays, D. G. The development of differential word recognition. *J. exp. Psychol.*, 1953, **45**, 165–168.

Forgus, R. H. The effect of different kinds of form pre-exposure on form discrimination learning. *J. comp. physiol. Psychol.*, 1958, **51**, 75–78. (a)

Forgus, R. H. The interaction between form pre-exposure and test-requirements in determining form discrimination. *J. comp. physiol. Psychol.*, 1958, **51**, 588–591. (b)

Fraser, C., Bellugi, U., and Brown, R. Control of grammar in imitation, comprehension, and production. *J. verb. Learn. verb. Behav.*, 1963, **2**, 121–135.

Gaines, R. Color-form preferences and color-form discriminative ability of deaf and hearing children. *Percept. Mot. Skills*, 1964, **18**, 70.

Gardner, R. W. The development of cognitive structures. In C. Scheerer (Ed.), *Cognition theory, research, promise*. New York: Harper and Row, 1964. Pp. 147–171.

Gardner, R. W., Holzman, P. S., Klein, G. S., Linton, H. B., and Spence, D. P. Cognitive control. A study of individual consistencies in cognitive behavior. *Psychol. Issues*, 1959, **1** (4, Whole No. 4).

Gardner, R. W., Jackson, D. N., and Messick, S. J. Personality organization in cognitive controls and intellectual abilities. *Psychol. Issues*, 1960, **2**, (4, Whole No. 8).

Gardner, R. W., and Long, R. I. The stability of cognitive controls. *J. abnorm. soc. Psychol.*, 1960, **61**, 485–487.

Gardner, R. W., and Long, R. I. Control, defence, and centration effect: a study of scanning behavior. *Br. J. Psychol.*, 1962, **53**, 129–140.

Gardner, R. W., and Schoen, R. A. Differentiation and abstraction in concept formation. *Psychol. Monogr.*, 1962, **76** (41, Whole No. 560).

Gaudreau, J., Lavoie, G., and Delorme, A. La perception des illusions de Muller-Lyer et d'Oppel-Kundt chez les deficients mentaux. (Perception of Muller-Lyer and Oppel-Kundt illusions among mental deficients.) *Can. J. Psychol.*, 1963, **17**, 259–263.

Ghent, L. Perception of overlapping and embedded figures by children of different ages. *Am. J. Psychol.*, 1956, **69**, 575–587.

Ghent, L. Recognition by children of realistic figures presented in various orientations. *Can. J. Psychol.*, 1960, **14**, 249–256.

Ghent, L. Form and its orientation: a child's eye view. *Am. J. Psychol.*, 1961, **74**, 177–190. (a)

Ghent, L. Developmental changes in tactual thresholds on dominant and nondominant sides. *J. comp. physiol. Psychol.*, 1961, **54**, 670–673. (b)

Ghent, L. Stimulus orientation as a factor in the recognition of geometric forms by school-age children. Paper presented at the meetings of the Eastern Psychological Association, April, 1963.

Ghent, L., and Bernstein, L. Influence of the orientation of geometric forms on their recognition by children. *Percept. Mot. Skills*, 1961, **12**, 95–101.

Giannitrapani, D. Changes in adaptation to prolonged perceptual distortion: A developmental study. Unpublished doctoral dissertation, Clark University, 1958.

Gibson, E. J. Perceptual Development. In H. W. Stevenson (Ed.), *Child psychology, sixty-second yearbook of the National Society for the Study of Education*. Chicago: University of Chicago Press, 1963, Pp. 144–195. (a)

Gibson, E. Perceptual learning. *Ann. Rev. Psychol.*, 1963, **14**, 29–56. (b)

Gibson, E. J. On the perception of words. *Am. J. Psychol.*, 1964, **77**, 667–669.

Gibson, E. J. Learning to read. *Science*, 1965, **148**, 1066–1072.

Gibson, E. J. *Principles of perceptual learning and development*. New York: Appleton-Century-Crofts, 1969.

Gibson, E. J., Farber, J., and Shepela, S. Test of a learning set procedure for the abstraction of spelling patterns. *Project Literacy Reports* (Cornell University), 1967, No. 8, 21–30.

Gibson, E. J., Gibson, J. J., Pick, A. D., and Osser, H. A developmental study of the discrimination of letter-like forms. *J. comp. physiol. Psychol.*, 1962, **55**, 897–906.

Gibson, E. J., and Olum, V. Experimental methods of studying perception in children. In P. Mussen (Ed.), *Handbook of research methods in child development.* New York: Wiley, 1960, Pp. 311–373.

Gibson, E. J., Osser, H., and Pick, A. D. A study of the development of grapheme-phoneme correspondences. *J. verb. Learn. verb. Behav.*, 1963, **2**, 142–146.

Gibson, E. J., Pick, A. D., Osser, H., and Hammond, M. The role of grapheme-phoneme correspondence in the perception of words. *Am. J. Psychol.*, 1962, **75**, 554–570.

Gibson, E. J., Shurcliff, A., and Yonas, A. The role of pronounceability in perception of pseudo-words by hearing and deaf subjects. *Project Literacy Reports* (Cornell University), 1966, No. 7, 62–72.

Gibson, E. J., and Walk, R. D. Effect of prolonged exposure to visually presented patterns on learning to discriminate them. *J. comp. physiol. Psychol.*, 1956, **49**, 239–242.

Gibson, E. J., Walk, R. D., Pick, H. L., Jr., and Tighe, T. J. The effects of prolonged exposure to visual patterns on learning to discriminate similar and different patterns. *J. comp. physiol. Psychol.*, 1958, **51**, 584–587.

Gibson, E. J., Walk, R. D., and Tighe, T. J. Enhancement and deprivation of visual stimulation during rearing as factors in visual discrimination learning. *J. comp. physiol. Psychol.*, 1959, **52**, 519–521.

Gibson, E. J., and Yonas, A. A developmental study of visual search behavior. *Percept. Psychophys.*, 1966 **1**, 169–171. (a)

Gibson, E. J., and Yonas, A. A developmental study of the effects of visual and auditory interference on a visual scanning task. *Psychon. Sci.*, 1966, **5**, 163–164. (b)

Giering. H. Das Augenmass bei Schulkindern. *Z. Psychol.*, 1965, **39**, 42–87.

Gliner, C. R. M. Saliency and relevance of stimuli and observing responses in haptic discrimination. Unpublished masters thesis, University of Minnesota, 1965.

Glock, M. D. The effect upon eye-movements and reading rate at the college level of three methods of training. *J. educ. Psychol.*, 1949, **40**, 93–106.

Goldstein, A. G. Learning of inverted and normally oriented faces in children and adults. *Psychon. Sci.*, 1965, **3**, 447–448.

Goldstein, A. G., and Cofoid, D. A developmental study of retinal rivalry. *Percept. Mot. Skills*, 1965, **20**, 235–238.

Gollin, E. S. Tactual form discrimination: a developmental comparison under conditions of spatial interference. *J. exp. Psychol.*, 1960, **60**, 126–129. (b)

Gollin, E. S. Developmental studies of visual recognition of incomplete objects. *Percept. Mot. Skills*, 1960, **11**, 289–298. (b)

Gollin, E. S. Tactual form discrimination: developmental differences in the effects of training under conditions of spatial interference. *J. Psychol.*, 1961, **51**, 131–140.

Gollin, E. S. Factors affecting the visual recognition of incomplete objects: a comparative investigation of children and adults. *Percept. Mot. Skills*, 1962, **15**, 583–590.

Gollin, E. S. Perceptual learning of incomplete pictures. *Percept. Mot. Skills*, 1965, **21**, 439–445.

Goodenough, D. R., and Karp, S. A. Field dependence and intellectual functioning. *J. abnorm. soc. Psychol.*, 1961, **63**, 241–246.

Gorman, J. J., Cogan, D. G., and Gillis, S. S. An apparatus for grading the visual acuity of infants on the basis of opticokinetic nystagmus. *Pediatrics*, 1957, **19**, 1088–1092.

Graham, F. K., Berman, P. W., and Ernhart, C. B. Development in preschool children of the ability to copy forms. *Child Dev.*, 1960, **31**, 339–359.

Gregory, R. L., and Wallace, J. G. Recovery from early blindness: a case study *Exp. Psychol. Soc. Monogr.*, (Cambridge), 1963, No. 2.

Gruber, H. E. The relation of perceived size to perceived distance. *Am. J. Psychol.*, 1954, **67**, 411–426.

Gruen, A. The relation of dancing experience and personality to perception. *Psychol. Monogr.*, 1955, **69**, (14, Whole No. 399).

Gruen, A. A critique and re-evaluation of Witkin's perception and perception-personality work. *J. gen. Psychol.*, 1957, **56**, 73–93.

Haber, R. N., and Haber, R. B. Eidetic imagery: I. Frequency. *Percept. Mot. Skills*, 1964, **19**, 131–138.

Haith, M. M. The response of the human newborn to visual movement. *J. exp. Child Psychol.*, 1966, **3**, 235–243.

Harcum, E. R. Reproduction of linear visual patterns tachistoscopically exposed in various orientations. *College of William and Mary Monogr.*, 1964, 134 pp.

Harway, N. I. Judgment of distance in children and adults. *J. exp. Psychol.*, 1963, **65**, 385–390.

Haynes, H., White, B. L., and Held, R. Visual accommodation in human infants. *Science*, 1965, **148**, 528–530.

Hebb, D. O. *The organization of behavior.* New York: Wiley, 1949.

Hebb, D. O. *A textbook of psychology.* Philadelphia: Saunders, 1958.

Heiss, A. Zum Problem der isolierenden Abstraktion. *Neue Psychol. Stud.*, 1930, **4**, 285–318.

Hein, A., and Held, R. Dissociation of the visual placing response into elicited and guided components. *Science*, 1967, **158**, 390–391.

Held, R., and Hein, A. Movement-produced stimulation in the development of visually guided behavior. *J. comp. physiol. Psychol.*, 1963, **56**, 872–876.

Hermelin, B., and O'Connor, N. Recognition of shape by normal and subnormal children. *Br. J. Psychol.*, 1961, **52**, 281–284.

Hershenson, M. Visual discrimination in the human newborn. *J. comp. physiol. Psychol.*, 1964, **58**, 270–276.

Hochberg, J. Nativism and empiricism in perception. In L. Postman (Ed.), *Psychology in the making.* New York: Knopf, 1962. Pp. 255–330.

Hochberg, J. Perceptual "chunking" and storage in reading words. *Project Literacy Reports* (Cornell University), 1966, No. 7, 73–78.

Hochberg, J., and Brooks, V. The psychophysics of form: reversible-perspective drawings of spatial objects. *Am. J. Psychol.*, 1960, **73**, 337–354.

Hochberg, J., and Brooks, V. Pictorial recognition as an unlearned ability: a study of one child's performance. *Am. J. Psychol.*, 1962, **75**, 624–628.

Hochberg, J., and Brooks, V. Recognition by preliterate children of reversible-perspective figures. *Percept. Mot. Skills*, 1964, **19**, 802.

Hochberg, J., and McAlister, E. A quantitative approach to figural "goodness." *J. exp. Psychol.*, 1953, **46**, 361–364.

Holzman, P. S., and Klein, G. S. Cognitive system-principles of leveling and sharpening: individual differences in assimilation effects in visual time-error. *J. Psychol.*, 1954, **37**, 105–122.

Howard, I. P., and Templeton, W. B. *Human spatial orientation.* New York: Wiley, 1966.

Hubel, D. H., and Wiesel, T. N. Receptive fields, binocular interaction and functional architecture in the cat's visual cortex. *J. Physiol.*, 1962, **160**, 106–154.

Hudson, W. Pictorial depth perception in sub-cultural groups in Africa. *J. soc. Psychol.*, 1960, **52**, 183–208.

Huttenlocher, J. Children's language: word-phrase relationship. *Science,* 1964, **143,** 264–265.

Huttenlocher, J. Discrimination of figure orientation: effects of relative position. *J. comp. physiol. Psychol.,* 1967, **63,** 359–361.

Inglis, J., and Caird, W. K. Age differences in successive responses to simultaneous stimulation. *Can. J. Psychol.,* 1963, **17,** 98–105.

Jakobson, R., and Halle, M. *Fundamentals of language.* The Hague: Mouton, 1956.

Jeffrey, W., and Samuels, S. J. Effect of method of reading training on initial learning and transfer. *J. Verb. Learn. Verb. Behav.,* 1967, **6,** 354–358.

Jenkin, N., and Feallock, S. M. Developmental and intellectual processes in size-distance judgment. *Am. J. Psychol.,* 1960, **73,** 268–273.

Jenkin, N., and Pollack, R. H. Perceptual development: its relation to theories of intelligence and cognition. Proceedings of a conference sponsored by Institute for Juvenile Research, Illinois State Department of Mental Health, and National Institute of Child Health and Human Development, National Institute of Health, 1966.

Johnson, B., and Beck, L. F. The development of space perception: stereoscopic vision in preschool children. *J. genet. Psychol.,* 1941, **58,** 247–254.

Kaess, D. W., and Wilson, J. P. Modification of the rat's avoidance of visual depth. *J. comp. physiol. Psychol.,* 1964, **58,** 151–152.

Kagan, J. Reflection-impulsivity and reading ability in primary grade children. *Child Dev.,* 1965, **36,** 609–628. (a)

Kagan, J. Individual differences in the resolution of response uncertainty. *J. Personality soc. Psychol.,* 1965, **2,** 154–160. (b)

Kagan, J. Developmental studies in reflection and analysis. In A. H. Kidd and J. H. Rivoire (Eds.), *Perceptual development in children.* New York: International Universities Press, 1966. Pp. 487–522.

Kagan, J., Moss, H., and Sigel. I. The psychological significance of styles of perceptualization. In J. C. Wright and J. Kagan (Eds.), Basic cognitive processes in children. *Monogr. Soc. Res. Child Dev.,* 1963, **28** (2, Serial No. 86).

Kagan, J., and Rosman, B. Cardiac and respiratory correlates of attention and an analytic attitude. *J. exp. Child Psychol.,* 1964, **1,** 50–63.

Kagan, J., Rosman, B., Day, D., Albert J., and Phillips, W. Information processing in the child: significance of analytic and reflective attitudes. *Psychol. Monogr.* 1964, **78** (1, Whole No. 578).

Kaplan, E., and Yonas, P. Communication requirements and children's production of relational words. *J. exp. Child Psychol.,* 1967, **5,** 142–151.

Karmel, B. Z. The effect of complexity, amount of contour, element size, and element arrangement on visual preference behavior in the hooded rat, domestic chick, and human infant. Unpublished doctoral dissertation, George Washington University, 1966.

Katz, P. A. Effects of labels on children's perception and discrimination learning. *J. exp. Psychol.,* 1963, **66,** 423–428.

Keen, R. Effects of auditory stimuli on sucking behavior in the human neonate. *J. exp. Child Psychol.,* 1964, **1,** 348–354.

Kephart, N. C. *The slow learner in the classroom.* Columbus, Ohio: Charles Merrill, 1960.

Kerpelman, L. C. Preexposure to visually presented forms and nondifferential reinforcement in perceptual learning. *J. exp. Psychol.,* 1965, **69,** 257–262.

Kerpelman, L. C., and Pollack, R. H. Developmental changes in the location of form discrimination cues. *Percept. Mot. Skills,* 1964, **19,** 375–382.

Kimura, D. Speech lateralization in young children as determined by an auditory test. *J. comp. physiol. Psychol.,* 1963, **56,** 899–902.

Kimura, D. Left-right differences in the perception of melodies. *Q. J. exp. Psychol.*, 1964, **16**, 355–358.

Kinsbourne, M., and Warington, E. K. The development of finger differentiation. *Q. J. exp. Psychol.*, 1963, **15**, 132–137.

Klein, R. E. A developmental study of perception under conditions of conflicting sensory cues. Unpublished doctoral dissertation, University of Minnesota, 1966.

Klein, S. D. A developmental study of tactual perception. Unpublished doctoral dissertation, Clark University, 1963.

Kluever, H. Eidetic phenomena. *Psychol. Bull.*, 1932, **29**, 181–203.

Kodman, F., Jr. Sensory processes and mental deficiency. In N. R. Ellis, (Ed.), *Handbook of mental deficiency.* New York: McGraw-Hill, 1963, pp. 463–479.

Köhler, W., and Wallach, H. Figural after-effects: An investigation of visual processes. *Proc. Am. Phil. Soc.*, 1944, **88**, 269–357.

Kolers, P. A., and Katzman, M. T. Naming sequentially presented letters and words. *Language and Speech*, 1966, **9**, 84–95.

Kolers, P. A. The recognition of geometrically transformed text. *Percept. Psychophys.*, 1968, **3**, 57–64.

Kolers, P. A. Three stages of reading. In H. Levin and J. Williams (Eds.), *Basic studies on reading.* (in press).

Koppitz, E. M. The Bender Gestalt test for children: a normative study. *J. clin. Psychol.*, 1960, **16**, 432–435.

Ladefoged, P., and Broadbent, D. Perception of sequence in auditory events. *Q. J. exp. Psychol.*, 1960, **12**, 162–170.

Lavrent'eva, T. V., and Ruzskaya, A. G. Sravnitel'nyi analiz osyazaniya i zreniya: Soobschenie, V. Odnovremennoe intersensornoe sopostavlenie formy v doshkol'nom vozraste. (Comparative analysis of touch and vision: Communication V. Simultaneous intersensory comparison of form at a preschool age.) *Dokl. Akad. Pedagog. NAUK RSFSR*, 1960, **44**, 73–76.

Leask, J., Haber, R. N., and Haber, R. B. Eidetic imagery in children: II. Longitudinal and experimental results. Unpublished manuscript, University of Rochester, 1968.

Lee, L., Kagan, J., and Rabson, A. Influence of a preference for analytic categorization upon concept acquisition. *Child Dev.*, 1963, **34**, 433–442.

Lehrman, D. S. Problems raised by instinct theories. *Q. Rev. Biol.*, 1953, **28**, 337–365.

Leibowitz, H. W. Apparent visual size as a function of distance for mentally deficient subjects. *Am. J. Psychol.*, 1961, **74**, 98–100.

Leibowitz, H. W., and Gwozdecki, J. The magnitude of the Poggendorff illusion as a function of age. *Child Dev.*, 1967, **38**, 573–580.

Leibowitz, H. W., and Heisel, M. A. L'evolution de l'illusion de Ponzo en fonction de l'age. (The development of the Ponzo illusion as a function of age.) *Archs. Psychol., Genève*, 1958, **36**, 328–331.

Leibowitz, H. W., and Judisch, J. M. The relation between age and the magnitude of the Ponzo illusion. *Am. J. Psychol.*, 1967, **80**, 105–110.

Lenneberg, E. H. Color naming, color recognition, color discrimination: a reappraisal. *Percept. Mot. Skills*, 1961, **12**, 375–382.

Lenneberg, E. H. Understanding language without ability to speak: a case report. *J. abnorm. soc. Psychol.*, 1962, **65**, 419–425.

Lenneberg, E. H. *Biological foundations of language.* New York: Wiley, 1967.

Leopold, W. F. *Speech development of a bilingual child: a linguist's record.* (4 vols.) Evanston, Ill.: Northwestern University Press, 1939–1949.

Leventhal, A. S., and Lipsitt, L. P. Adaptation, pitch discrimination, and sound localization in the neonate. *Child Dev.*, 1964, **35**, 759–767.

Levin, H., and Kaplan, E. Studies of oral reading. X. The eye-voice span for active and passive sentences. Unpublished manuscript, Cornell University, 1967.

Levin, H., and Mearini, M. C. The incidence of inflectional suffixes and the classification of word forms. *J. Verb. Learn. Verb. Behav.*, 1964, **3**, 176–181.

Levin, H., and Turner, E. Sentence structure and the eye-voice span. *Project Literacy Reports* (Cornell University), 1966, No. 7, 79–87.

Lewin, K. A. *A dynamic theory of personality.* New York: McGraw-Hill, 1935.

Leyer, K. *Tiefenwahrnehmung in den Entwicklungsphasen. Z. Psychol.*, 1939, **146**, 229–279.

Liberman, A. M. Some results of research on speech perception. *J. acoust. Soc. Am.*, 1957, **29**, 117–123.

Liberman, A. M., Cooper, F. S., Shankweiler, D. P., and Studdert-Kennedy, M. Perception of the speech code. *Psychol. Rev.*, 1967, **74**, 431–461.

Lipsitt, L. P., and Levy, N. Electrotactual threshold in the neonate. *Child Dev.*, 1959, **30**, 547–554.

Maccoby, E. E., and Konrad, K. W. The effect of preparatory set on selective listening: developmental trends. *Monogr. Soc Res. Child Dev.*, 1967, **32** (4, Serial No. 112).

Maccoby, E E., and Konrad, K. W. Age trends in selective listening. *J. exp. Child Psychol.*, 1966, **3**, 113–122. (In press.)

Mackworth, N. H., and Bruner, J. S. Selecting visual information during recognition by adults and children. Unpublished manuscript, Harvard Center for Cognitive Studies, 1966.

Mackworth, N. H., and Thomas, E. L. Head-mounted and eye-marker camera. *J. opt. Soc. Am.*, 1962, **52**, 613–716.

Manolakes, G. The effects of tachistoscopic training in an adult reading program. *J. appl. Psychol.*, 1952, **36**, 410–412.

McKee, J. P., and Riley, D. A. Auditory transposition in 6-year-old children. *Child Dev.*, 1962, **33**, 469–476.

McKinney, J. P. Hand schema in children. *Psychon. Sci.*, 1964, **1**, 99–100.

McNeill, D. Developmental psycholinguistics. In F. Smith and G. A. Miller (Eds.), *The genesis of language.* Cambridge: MIT Press, 1966. Pp. 15–84.

Medinnus, G. R., and Johnson, D. Tactual recognition of shapes by normal and retarded children. *Percept. Mot. Skills*, 1966, **22**, 406.

Mehler, J., and Carey, P. Role of surface and base structure in the perception of sentences. *J. verb. Learn. verb. Behav.*, 1967, **6**, 335–338.

Mercado, S. J., Guerrero, R. D., and Gardner, R. W. Cognitive control in children of Mexico and the United States. *J. soc. Psychol.*, 1963, **59**, 199–208.

Miller, G. A., and Isard, S. Some perceptual consequences of linguistic rules. *J. verb. Learn. verb. Behav.*, 1963, **2**, 217–228.

Miller, N. E. Theory and experiment relating psychoanalytic displacement to stimulus-response generalization. *J. abnorm. soc. Psychol.*, 1948, **73**, 155–178.

Miller, W., and Ervin, S. The development of grammar in child language. In U. Bellugi and R. Brown (Eds.), The acquisition of language. *Monogr. Soc. Res. Child Dev.*, 1964, **29** (1, Whole No. 92), 9–34.

Mishkin, M., and Forgays, D. G. Word recognition as a function of retinal locus. *J. exp. Psychol.*, 1952, **43**, 43–48.

Muehl, S., and Kremenak, S. Ability to match information within and between auditory and visual sense modalities and subsequent reading achievement. *J. educ. Psychol.*, 1966, **57**, 230–238.

Munn, N. L. *The evolution and growth of human behavior.* Boston: Houghton Mifflin, 1955.

Munsinger, H., and Kessen, W. Uncertainty, structure, and preference. *Psychol. Monogr.*, 1964, **78** (9, Whole No. 586).

Munsinger, H., Kessen, W., and Kessen, M. L. Age and uncertainty: developmental variation in preference for variability. *J. exp. Child Psychol.*, 1964, **1**, 1–15.

Murray, F. B. Conservation of illusion-distorted length and illusion strength. *Psychon. Sci.*, 1967, **7**, 65–66.

Natsoulas, T., and Dubanoski, R. A. Inferring the locus and orientation of the perceiver from responses to stimulation of the skin. *Am. J. Psychol.*, 1964, **77**, 281–285.

Navrat, M. L. Color tint matching by children. *Percept. Mot. Skills*, 1965, **21**, 215–222.

Nealy, S. M., and Riley, D. A. Loss and recovery of discrimination of visual depth in dark-reared rats. *Am. J. Psychol.*, 1963, **76**, 329–332.

Neisser, U. Visual search. *Scient. Am.*, 1964, **210**(6), 94–101.

Neisser, U. *Cognitive psychology.* New York: Appleton-Century-Crofts, 1967.

Neufeldt, A. H. Short-term memory in the mentally retarded: an application of the dichotic listening technique. *Psychol. Monogr.*, 1966, **80** (12, Whole No. 620).

Newman, E. B. Speed of reading when the span of letter is restricted. *Am. J. Psychol.*, 1966, **79**, 272–278.

Ohwaki, S. On weight perception, especially the formation of Charpentier's illusion in children. *Jap. J. Psychol.*, 1953, **24**, 257. (English abstract)

Oostlander, A. M. The development of the weight-volume illusion. *J. exp. Child Psychol.*, 1967, **5**, 237–248.

Orbach, J. Retinal locus as a factor in recognition of visually perceived words. *Am. J. Psychol.*, 1952, **65**, 555–562.

Papoušek, H. Experimental studies of appetitional behavior in human newborns and infants. In H. W. Stevenson, E. H. Hess, and H. L. Rheingold (Eds.), *Early behavior.* New York: Wiley, 1967, Pp. 249–277.

Penfield, W., and Roberts L. *Speech and brain mechanisms.* Princeton, N.J.: Princeton University Press, 1959.

Piaget, J., and Lambercier, M. Recherches sur le developpement des perceptions: V. Essai sur un effet d' "Einstellung" survenant au cours de perceptions visuelles successives (effet Usnadze) *Archs. Psychol., Genève*, 1944, **30**, 139–196.

Piaget, J., Lambercier, M., Boesch, E., and von Albertini, B. Recherches sur le developpement des perceptions: I. Introduction a l'etude des perceptions chez l'enfant et analyse d'une illusion relative a la perception visuelle de cercles concentrigues (Delboeuf). *Archs. Psychol., Genève*, 1942, **29**, 1–107.

Piaget, J., Maire, F., and Privat, F. Recherches sur le developpement des perceptions: XVIII. La resistance des bonnes formes a l'illusion de Müller-Lyer. *Archs. Psychol., Genève*, 1954, **34**, 155–202.

Piaget, J., Matalon, B., and Vinh-Bang. Recherches sur le developpement des perceptions: XLII. L'evolution d'illusion dite "verticale-horizontale" de ses composantes (rectangle et equerre) et de l'illusion de Delboeuf en presentation tachistoscopique. (Research on the development of perceptions: XLII. The evolution of the horizontal-vertical illusion from its constituent elements and the Delboeuf illusion in tachistoscopic presentation) *Archs. Psychol., Genève*, 1961, **38**, 23–68.

Piaget, J., and Osterrieth, P. A. Recherches sur le developpement des perceptions: XVII. L'evolution de l'illusion d'Oppel-Kundt en fonction de l'âge. *Archs. Psychol., Genève*, 1953, **34**, 1–38.

Piaget, J., and Von Albertini, B. Recherches sur le developpement des perceptions: XI. L'illusion de Müller-Lyer. *Archs. Psychol., Genève*, 1950, **33**, 1–48.

Piaget, J., and Taponier, S. Recherches sur le developpement des perceptions XXXII. L'estimation des longeurs de deux droites horizontales et parralleles a extremites decalees. *Archs. Psychol., Genève,* 1956, **35,** 369–400.

Piaget, J., and Vinh-Bang. Recherches sur le developpement des perceptions: XLI. L'evolution de l'illusion des espaces divises (Oppel-Kundt) en presentation tachistoscopique. *Archs. Psychol., Genève,* 1961, **38,** 1–21. (a)

Piaget, J., and Vinh-Bang. Comparison des mouvements oculaires et des centrations du regard chez l'enfant et chez l'adults. (Comparison of the eye movements and fixations of children and adults.) *Archs. Psychol., Genève,* 1961, **38,** 167–200. (b)

Pick, A. D. Improvement of visual and tactual form discrimination. *J. exp. Psychol.,* 1965, **69,** 331–339.

Pick, A. D., and Pick, H. L., Jr. A developmental study of tactual discrimination in blind and sighted children and adults. *Psychon. Sci.,* 1966, **6,** 367–368.

Pick, A. D., Pick, H. L., Jr., and Thomas, M. L. Cross-modal transfer and improvement of form discrimination. *J. exp. Child Psychol.,* 1966, **3,** 279–288.

Pick, A. D., Thomas, M. L., and Pick, H. L., Jr. The role of graphemephoneme correspondences in the perception of Braille. *J. Verb. Learn. Verb. Behav.,* 1966, **5,** 298–300.

Pick, H. L., Jr. Perception in Soviet psychology. *Psychol. Bull.,* 1964, **62,** 21–35.

Pick, H. L., Jr., Klein, R. E., and Pick, A. D. Visual and tactual identification of form orientation. *J. exp. Child Psychol.,* 1966, **4,** 391–397.

Pick, H. L., Jr., Pick, A. D., and Klein, R. E. Perceptual integration in children. In L. P. Lipsitt and C. C. Spiker (Eds.), *Advances in child development and behavior.* New York: Academic Press, 1967. Vol. 3, pp. 192–220.

Pintner, R., and Anderson, M. M. The Müller-Lyer illusion with children and adults. *J. exp. Psychol.,* 1916, **1,** 200–210.

Podell, J. E. Ontogeny of the locus and orientation of the perceiver. *Child Dev.,* 1966, **37,** 993–997.

Pollack, R. H. Figural after-effects as a function of age. *Acta psychol.,* 1960, **17,** 417–423.

Pollack, R. H. Contour detectability threshold as a function of chronological age. *Percept. Mot. Skills,* 1963, **17,** 411–417.

Pollack, R. H. Simultaneous and successive presentation of elements of the Mueller-Lyer figure and chronological age. *Percept. Mot. Skills,* 1964, **19,** 303–310.

Pollack, R. H. Effects of figure-ground contrast and contour orientation on figural masking. *Psychon. Sci.,* 1965, **2,** 369–370. (a)

Pollack, R. H. Backward figural masking as a function of chronological age and intelligence. *Psychon. Sci.,* 1965, **3,** 65–66. (b)

Pollack, R. H. Hue detectability as a function of chronological age. *Psychon. Sci.* 1965, **3,** 351–352. (c)

Pollack, R. H. Temporal range of apparent movement as a function of age and intelligence. *Psychon. Sci.,* 1966, **5,** 243–244.

Pollack, R. H. Some implications of ontogenetic changes in perception. In J. Flavell and D. Elkind (Eds.), *Studies in cognitive development: essays in honor of Jean Piaget.* New York: Oxford University Press (1969).

Pollack, R. H., and Silvar, S. D. Magnitude of the Mueller-Lver illusion in children as a function of pigmentation of the Fundus oculi. *Psychon. Sci.,* 1967, **8,** 83–84.

Posner, M. I., and Mitchell, R. F. Chronometric analysis of classification. *Psychol. Rev.,* 1967, **74,** 392–410.

Postman, L. Association theory and perceptual learning. *Psychol. Rev.,* 1955, **62,** 438–446.

Postman, L., and Tolman, E. C. Brunswik's probabilistic functionalism. In S. Koch (Ed.), *Psychology: the study of a science.* Vol. I. New York: McGraw-Hill, 1959, 502–564.

Postman, L. Witkin, H. A., Lewis, H. B., Hertzman, M., Machover, K., Meissner, P. B., and Wapner, S. Personality through perception. *Psychol. Bull.,* 1955, **52,** 79–83.

Potter, M. C. On perceptual recognition. In J. S. Bruner, R. R. Olver and P. M. Greenfield (Eds.), *Studies in cognitive growth.* New York: Wiley, 1966.

Quast, W. Visual-motor performance in the reproduction of geometric figures as a developmental phenomenon in children. Unpublished doctoral dissertation, University of Minnesota, 1957.

Quast, W. The Bender Gestalt: a clinical study of children's records. *J. consult. Psychol.,* 1961, **25,** 405–408.

Razran, G. The observable unconscious and the inferable conscious in current Soviet psychophysiology. *Psychol. Rev.,* 1961, **68,** 81–147.

Reese, H. W. "Perceptual set" in young children. *Child Dev.,* 1963, **34,** 151–159. (a)

Reese, H. W. "Perceptual set" in young children: II. *Child Dev.,* 1963, **34,** 451–454. (b)

Reese, H. W., and Ford, L. H., Jr. Expectancy and perception of an ambiguous figure in preschool children. *J. Verb. Learn. Verb. Behav.,* 1962, **1,** 188–191.

Renshaw, S. The errors of cutaneous localization and the effect of practice on the localizing movement in children and adults. *J. genet. Psychol.,* 1930, **38,** 223–238.

Renshaw, S., and Wherry, R. J. Studies on cutaneous localization: III. The age of onset of ocular dominance. *J. genet. Psychol.,* 1931, **39,** 493–496.

Renshaw, S., Wherry, R. J., and Newlin, J. C. Cutaneous localization in congenitally blind vs. seeing children and adults. *J. genet. Psychol.,* 1930, **38,** 239–248.

Rey, A. Contribution a l'etude de poids chez les anormaux. *Archs. Psychol. Genève,* 1930, **22,** 285–297.

Riesen, A. H., and Aarons, L. Visual movement and intensity discrimination in cats after early deprivation of pattern vision. *J. comp. physiol. Psychol.,* 1959, **52,** 142–149.

Riess, B. F. Genetic changes in semantic conditioning. *J. exp. Psychol.,* 1946, **36,** 143–152.

Riley, D. A., and McKee, J. P. Pitch and loudness transposition in children and adults. *Child Dev.,* 1963, **34,** 471–482.

Riley, D. A., McKee, J. P., and Hadley, R. W. Prediction of auditory discrimination learning and transposition from children's auditory ordering ability. *J. exp. Psychol.,* 1964, **67,** 324–329.

Robinson, J. S. The effect of learning verbal labels for stimuli on their later discrimination. *J. exp. Psychol.,* 1955, **49,** 112–114.

Rock, I., Tauber, E. S., and Heller, D. P. Perception of stroboscopic movement: evidence for its innate basis. *Science,* 1965, **147,** 1050–1052.

Rudel, R. G., and Teuber, H. L. Discrimination of direction of line in children. *J. comp. physiol. Psychol.,* 1963, **56,** 892–898.

Russel, A. Ein entwicklungspsychologischer Beitrag zur Theorie der geometrischoptischen Täuschungen. *Archiv. ges. Psychol.,* 1934, **91,** 289–304.

Sackett, G. P. Development of preference for differentially complex patterns by infant monkeys. *Psychon. Sci.,* 1966, **6,** 441–442.

Sanford, E. C. *A course in experimental psychology. Part I: Sensation and perception.* Boston: Heath, 1908.

Santastefano, S. A developmental study of the Delboeuf illusion. *Percept. Mot. Skills*, 1963, **17**, 23–29.

Schiff, W. Perception of impending collision: a study of visually directed avoidant behavior. *Psychol. Monogr.*, 1965, **79** (6, Whole No. 604).

Schilder, P. *The image of appearance of the human body.* New York: International Universities Press, 1950.

Segall, M. H., Campbell, D. T., and Herskovits, M. J. Cultural differences in the perception of geometric illusions. *Science*, 1963, **139**, 769–771.

Segall, M. H., Campbell, D. T., and Herskovits, M. J. *The influence of culture on visual perception.* Indianapolis: Bobbs-Merrill, 1966.

Sekuler, R. W., and Rosenblith, J. F. Discrimination of direction of line and the effect of stimulus alignment. *Psychon. Sci.*, 1964, **1**, 143–144. (translated by P. Heath)

Senden, M. von. (Tr. P. Heath) *Space and sight.* New York: Free Press, 1960.

Shankweiler, D. Effects of temporal-lobe damage on perception of dichotically presented melodies. *J. comp. physiol. Psychol.*, 1966, **62**, 115–119.

Simmel, M. L. Developmental aspects of the body scheme. *Child Dev.*, 1966, **37**, 83–95.

Siipola, E. M., and Hayden, S. D. Exploring eidetic imagery among the retarded. *Percept. Mot. Skills*, 1965, **21**, 275–286.

Slobin, D. I. Abstracts of Soviet studies of child language. In F. Smith and G. Miller (Eds.), *The genesis of language.* Cambridge: MIT Press, 1966, Pp. 363–386.

Smith, O. W., and Smith, P. C. An illusion of parallelism. *Percept. Mot. Skills*, 1962, **15**, 455–461.

Smith, O. W., and Smith, P. C. A developmental study of the illusion of parallelism. *Percept. and Mot. Skills*, 1963, **16**, 871–878.

Smith, O. W., and Smith, P. C. Developmental studies of spatial judgments by children and adults. *Percept. Mot. Skills*, 1966, **22**, 3–73.

Smith, O. W., and Smith, P. C. Some comments on Wohlwill's critique. *Percept. Mot. Skills*, 1966, **23**, 221–222.

Spitz, H. H. Field theory in mental deficiency. In N. R. Ellis (Ed.), *Handbook of mental deficiency.* New York: McGraw-Hill, 1963. Pp. 11–40.

Spitz, H. H., and Blackman, L. A comparison of mental retardates and normals on visual figural after effects and reversible figures. *J. abnorm. soc. Psychol.*, 1959, **58**, 105–110.

Spivack, G. Perceptual processes. In N. R. Ellis (Ed.), *Handbook of mental deficiency.* New York: McGraw-Hill, 1963. Pp. 480–511.

Spivack, G., and Levine, M. Special after effects and measures of satiation in brain-injured and normal Ss. *J. Personality*, 1959, **27**, 211–227.

Steinschneider, A., Lipton, E. L., and Richmond, J. B. Auditory sensitivity in the infant: effect of intensity on cardiac and motor responsivity. *Child Dev.*, 1966, **37**, 233–252.

Stevens, S. S. Toward a resolution of the Fechner-Thurstone legacy. *Psychometrika*, 1961, **26**, 35–47.

Stevenson, H. W., and McBee, G. The learning of object and pattern discriminations by children. *J. comp. physiol. Psychol.*, 1958, **51**, 752–754.

Suchman, R. G. Color-form preference, discriminative accuracy and learning of deaf and hearing children. *Child Dev.*, 1966, **37**, 439–451.

Suchman, R. G., and Trabasso, T. Color and form preference in young children. *J. exp. Child Psychol.*, 1966, **3**, 177–187. (a)

Suchman, R. G., and Trabasso, T. Stimulus preference and cue function in young children's concept attainment. *J. exp. Child Psychol.*, 1966, **3**, 188–198. (b)

Sun, Shih-luh. (Age differences in the Müller-Lyer illusion) *Acta psycholog. Sinica*, 1964, No. 3, 223–228. (Abstract only seen by authors)

Sutherland, N. S. Methods and findings of experiments on the visual discrimination of shape by animals. *Exp. Psychol. Soc. Monogr.*, 1961, No. 1.

Swanson, R., and Benton, A. L. Some aspects of the genetic development of right-left discrimination. *Child Dev.*, 1955, **26**, 123–133.

Tallarico, R. B., and Farrell, W. M. Studies of visual depth perception: an effect of early experience on chicks on a visual cliff. *J. comp. physiol. Psychol.*, 1964, **57**, 94–96.

Tarakanov, V. B., and Zinchenko, V. P. Sravnitelnyi analiz osyazaniya i zreniyi: Coobschenie VI. Proizvol'noe i neproizvol'noe zapomenanie formy v doshkol' noĭ vozrasti. (Comparative analysis of touch and vision: Communication VI. Voluntary memory of form in preschool children.). *Dokl. Akad. Pedagog. NAUK RSFSR*, 1960, **4**, 49–52.

Tauber, E. S., and Koffler, S. Optomotor response in human infants to apparent motion: evidence of innateness. *Science*, 1966, **152**, 382–383.

Templin, M. C. *Certain language skills in children.* Minneapolis: University of Minnesota Press, 1957.

Templin, M. C. The study of articulation and language development during the early school years. In F. Smith and G. Miller (Eds.), *The genesis of language.* Cambridge: MIT Press, 1966. Pp. 173–186.

Teuber, H. L., and Rudel, R. G. Behavior after cerebral lesions in children and adults. *Devl. Med. Child Neurol.*, 1962, **4**, 3–20.

Thomas, H. Preferences for random shapes: ages six through nineteen years. *Child Dev.*, 1966, **37**, 843–859.

Tighe, T. J. Reversal and nonreversal shifts in monkeys. *J. comp. physiol. Psychol.*, 1964, **58**, 324–326.

Tighe, T. J., and Tighe, L. S. Overtraining and optional shift behavior in rats and children. *J. comp. physiol. Psychol.*, 1966, **62**, 49–54.

Tinker, M. Recent studies of eye movements in reading. *Psychol. Bull.*, 1958, **55**, 215–231.

Triesman, A. M. Verbal cues, language, and meaning in selective attention. *Am. J. Psychol.*, 1964, **77**, 206–219. (a)

Triesman, A. M. The effect of irrelevant material on the efficiency of selective listening. *Am. J. Psychol.*, 1964, **77**, 533–546. (b)

Turnure, J. E. Children's reactions to distractions: a developmental approach. Unpublished doctoral dissertation, Yale University, 1966.

Turnure, J. E., and Zigler, E. Outer-directedness in the problem solving of normal and retarded children. *J. abnorm. soc. Psychol.*, 1964, **69**, 427–436.

Uhr, L. "Pattern recognition" computers as models for form perception. *Psychol. Bull.*, 1963, **60**, 40–73.

Van Biervliet, J. J. Nouvelles mesures des illusions visuelles chez les adultes et les enfants. *Revue Philosoph.*, 1896, **41**, 169–181.

Vaught, G. M., and Auguston, B. Field-dependence and form discrimination in females. *Psychon. Sci.*, 1967, **7**, 333–334.

Vaught, G. M., and Ellinger, J. Field-dependence and form discrimination. *Psychon. Sci.*, 1966, **6**, 357–358.

Velton, H. V. The growth of phonemic and texical patterns in infant language. *Language*, 1943, **19**, 281–292.

Vurpillot, E. Piaget's law of relative centrations. *Acta Psychol.*, 1959, **16**, 403–430.

Vurpillot, E. The development of scanning strategies and their relation to visual differentiation. *J. exper. child Psychol.* (in press)

Wada, J., and Rasmussen, T. R. Intracortid injection of sodium amytal for the lateralization of cerebral speech dominance, experimental and clinical observations. *J. Neurosurg.*, 1960, **17**, 266–282.

Walk, R. D. The development of depth perception in animals and human infants. In H. W. Stevenson (Ed.), *Concept of development. Monogr. Soc. Res. Child Dev.*, 1966, **31**, (5, Serial No. 107), Pp. 82–108.

Walk, R. D., and Dodge, S. H. Visual depth perception of a 10 month old monocular human infant. *Science*, 1962, **137**, 529–530.

Walk, R. D., and Gibson, E. J. A comparative and analytic study of visual depth perception. *Psychol. Monogr.*, 1961, **75** (15, Whole No. 519).

Walk, R. D., Gibson, E. J., Pick, H. L., Jr., and Tighe, T. J. The effectiveness of prolonged exposure to cutouts vs. painted patterns for facilitation of discrimination. *J. comp. physiol. Psychol.*, 1959, **52**, 519–521.

Walk, R. D., Gibson, E. J., Pick, H. L., Jr., and Tighe, T. J. Further experiments on prolonged exposure to visual form: the effect of single stimuli and prior reinforcement. *J. comp. physiol. Psychol.*, 1958, **51**, 483–487.

Walk, R. D., Gibson, E. J., and Tighe, T. J. Behavior of light and dark-reared rats on a visual cliff. *Science*, 1957, **126**, 80–81.

Walk, R. D., Trychin, S. J., and Karmel, B. Z. Depth perception in the dark-reared rats as a function of time in the dark. *Psychon. Sci.*, 1965, **3**, 9–10.

Wallach, M. Perceptual recognition of approximations to English in relation to spelling achievement. *J. educ. Psychol.*, 1963, **54**, 57–62.

Walters, Sister A. A genetic study of geometrical-optical illusions. *Gene. Psychol. Monogr.*, 1942, **25**, 101–155.

Wapner, S., and Werner, H. *Perceptual development.* Worcester, Mass.: Clark University Press, 1957.

Weber, R. M. Grammaticality and the self-correction of reading errors. *Project Literacy Reports* (Cornell University), 1967, No. 8, 53–59.

Weinstein, S., and Sersen, E. A. Tactual sensitivity as a function of handedness and laterality. *J. comp. physiol. Psychol.*, 1961, **54**, 665–669.

Weir, R. *Language in the crib.* The Hague: Mouton, 1962.

Werner, H. Studies on contour: I. Qualitative analyses. *Am. J. Psychol.*, 1935, **47**, 40–64.

Werner, H. *Comparative psychology of mental development.* (Rev. ed.) New York: International Universities Press, 1957.

Werner, H., and Corrison, D. Measurement and development of the finger scheme in mentally retarded children: relation of arithmetic achievement to performance on the finger schema test. *J. educ. Psychol.*, 1942, **33**, 252–264.

Werner, H., and Strauss, A. A. Pathology of figure-background relation in the child. *J. abnorm. soc. Psychol.*, 1941, **36**, 236–248.

Werner, H., and Wapner, S. Sensory-tonic field theory of perception. *J. Personality*, 1949, **18**, 88–107.

Wertheimer, M. Hebb and Senden on the role of learning in perception. *Am. J. Psychol.*, 1951, **64**, 133–137.

Weymouth, F. W. Visual acuity of children. In M. J. Hirsch and R. E. Wick (Eds.), *Vision of children.* Philadelphia, Pa.: Chilton, 1963.

White, B. L. An experimental approach to the effects of experience on early human behavior. In J. Hill (Ed.), *Minnesota Symposium on Child Psychology*, Vol. 1. Minneapolis: University of Minnesota Press, 1968.

White, S. H., and Plum, G. E. Eye movement photography during children's discrimination learning. *J. exp. Child Psychol.*, 1964, **1**, 327–338.

Wickelgren, L. W. Convergence in the human newborn. *J. exp. Child Psychol.*, 1967, **5**, 74–85.

Winch, W. H. The vertical-horizontal illusion in school children. *Br. J. Psychol.*, 1907, **2**, 220–225.

Witkin, H. A. Perception of body position and of the position of the visual field. *Psychol. Monogr.*, 1949, **63** (7, Whole No. 302).

Witkin, H. A. Individual differences in ease of perception of embedded figures. *J. Personality*, 1950, **19**, 1–15.

Witkin, H. A. Origins of cognitive style. In C. Scheerer (Ed.), *Cognition. Theory, research, promise.* New York: Harper and Row, 1964. Pp. 172–205.

Witkin, H. A., Dyk, R. B., Faterson, H. F., Goodenough, D. R., and Karp, S. A. *Psychological differentiation.* New York: Wiley, 1962.

Witkin, H. A., Faterson, H. F., Goodenough, D. R., and Birnbaum, J. Cognitive patterning in mildly retarded boys. *Child Dev.*, 1966, **37**, 301–316.

Witkin, H. A., Lewis, H. B., Hertzman, M., Machover, K., Meissner, P. B., and Wapner S. *Personality through perception.* New York: Harper, 1954.

Witkin, H. A., and Wapner, S. Visual factors in the maintenance of upright posture. *Am. J. Psychol.*, 1950, **63**, 31–50.

Wohlwill, J. F. Developmental studies of perception. *Psychol. Bull.*, 1960, **57**, 249–288.

Wohlwill, J. F. The perspective illusion: perceived size and distance in fields varying in suggested depth, in children and adults. *J. exp. Psychol.*, 1962, **64**, 300–310.

Wohlwill, J. F. Overconstancy in distance perception as a function of the texture of the stimulus field and other variables. *Percept. Mot. Skills*, 1963, **17**, 831–846. (a)

Wohlwill, J. F. The development of "overconstancy" in space perception. In L. P. Lipsitt and C. C. Spiker (Ed.), *Advances in child development and behavior.* New York: Academic Press, 1963. Vol. I, pp. 265–312. (b)

Wohlwill, J. F. Texture of the stimulus field and age as variables in the perception of relative distance in photographic slides. *J. exp. Child Psychol.*, 1965, **2**, 163–177.

Wohlwill, J. F. Perceptual learning. *Ann. Rev. Psychol.*, 1966, **17**, 201–232.

Wohlwill, J. F. Smith and Smith's developmental studies of spatial judgments: a note. *Percept. mot. Skills*, 1966, **23**, 137–138.

Wohlwill, J. F., and Wiener, M. Discrimination of form orientation in young children. *Child Dev.*, 1964, **35**, 1113–1125.

Woodward, M. F., and Barber, C. G. Phoneme perception in lip reading. *J. Speech Hear. Res.*, 1960, **3**, 212–222.

Woodworth, R. S., and Schlosberg, H. *Experimental psychology.* New York: Holt, 1954.

Würsten, H. Recherches sur le developpement des perceptions: IX. L'evolution des comparaisons de longueurs de l'enfant a l'adulte avec variation d'angle entre la verticale et l'horizontale. *Archs. Psychol., Genève*, 1947, **32**, 1–444.

Yonas, A., and Gibson, E. J. A developmental study of feature-processing strategies in letter-discrimination. *Project Literacy Reports* (Cornell University), 1967, No. 8, 11–20.

Zangwell, O. L. *Cerebral dominance and its relation to psychological function.* Edinburgh, Scotland: Oliver & Boyd, 1960.

Zeigler, H. P., and Leibowitz, H. Apparent visual size as a function of distance for children and adults. *Am. J. Psychol.*, 1957, **70**, 106–109.

Zigler, E. A measure in search of a theory? *Contemp. Psychol.*, 1963, **8**, 133–135.

Zimmermann, R., and Hochberg, J. Pictorial recognition in the infant monkey. *Proceedings of the meeting of the Psychonomic Society*, 1963, p. 46. (Abstract)

Zinchenko, V. P. Nekotorye osobennosti orientirovochnykh dvizhenii ruki i glaza i ikh rol'v formirovanii dvigatel'nykh navykov. (Some properties of orienting movements of the hands and eyes and their role in the formation of motor habits.) (Authorized summary of candidate's dissertation.) Moscow: Institute of Psychology, 1957.

Zinchenko, V. P. Sravnitel'nyi analiz osyazaniya i zrenya: Soobschenie II. Osobenesti orientirovochno-issledovatel'skikh dvzhenii glaza u deteĭ doshkol'nogo vozrasta. (Comparative analysis of touch and vision: Communication II. Properties of orienting-investigatory eye movements in preschool children.) *Dokl. Akad. Pedag. Nauk RSFSR*, 1960, **4**(2), 53–60.

Zinchenko, V. P., Chzhi-tsin, V., and Tarakanov, V. V. Stanovlenie i razvitie pertstivnykh deistvii. (Formation and development of perceptive behavior.) *Vop. Psikhol.*, 1962, **8**(3), 1–14.

Zinchenko, V. P., Lomov, B. F., and Ruzskaya, A. G. Sravnitel'nyi analiz osyazaniya i zreniya: Soobschenie I. O tak nazivaem "Simultanoe" vospriyatie. (Comparative analysis of touch and vision: Communication I. On so called simultaneous perception.) *Dokl. Akad. Pedag. Nauk RSFSR*, 1959, **3**(5), 71–74.

Zinchenko, V. P., and Ruzskaya, A. G. Sravnitel'nyi analiz osyazaniya i zreniya: Soobschenie III. Zritel' no-gapitcheskii perenos v doshkol' nom vozraste. (Comparative analysis of touch and vision: Communication III. Visual-haptic transfer in preschool age.) *Dokl. Akad. Pedag. Nauk RSFSR*, 1960, **4**(3), 95–98. (a)

Zinchenko, V. P., and Ruzskaya, A. G. Sravnitel'nyi analiz osyazaniya i zreniya: Soobschenie VII. Nalichnye uroveni vospriyatiya formy u detei doshkolnoga vozrasta. (Comparative analysis of touch and vision: Communication VII. The observale level of perception of form in children of preschool age.) *Dokl. Akad. Pedag. Nauk RSFSR*, 1960, **4**(6), 85–88. (b)

12. Learning in Children

HAROLD W. STEVENSON[*]

Research on children's learning is for the most part a derivative of psychological studies of learning in animals and human adults. Although the impetus for studying children's learning is related to practical concerns in the educating and rearing of children, the field characteristically has been dominated by the methods and problems of the experimental psychologist. The studies typically have been laboratory investigations, and until very recently few studies had been conducted in naturalistic or classroom settings. Child psychologists have not rejected other methods as being unsuitable or inappropriate, but they have tended to use the experimental method because of the ease with which problems originating in the experimental study of learning in animals and human adults could be adapted to the study of children. The close alliance with experimental psychology has been productive. The number and quality of studies on children's learning published each year have continued to increase. In many ways, however, the consequence of such an approach has been to provide more information about the general phenomenon of learning than about the distinctive characteristics of learning in the immature organism.

The first studies of children's learning were straightforward adaptations of studies that had been conducted with animals. Among the earliest was Krasnogorski's (1909) study of the

development of conditioned responses in children. Krasnogorski, and somewhat later Mateer (1918), assessed the degree to which children's behavior, in this case salivation and chewing movements, could be modified by pairing conditioned and unconditioned stimuli. The success of these studies, and the seemingly general power of the conditioned response paradigm as a means of understanding behavioral change, led to the early promulgation by Watson (1928) of the conditioned response as the key to effective child training. Watson's defense of his position was not limited to discussions of the work of others, for some of the best known studies of children's learning were conducted in his laboratory (Jones, 1924a, 1924b; Watson and Raynor, 1920; Watson and Watson, 1921) on the instigation and elimination of children's fears by means of conditioning and extinction. As might be expected, Watson's espousal of learning as the primary source of behavioral change met with vigorous opposition, and arguments about the role of learning and maturation rocked the field for many years. In the end, Watson's major influence proved to be methodological rather than substantive. The strong behavioristic orientation of American studies of children's learning can be traced to Watson's emphasis on the objective study of behavior.

Partially as a response to the proponents of conditioning such as Watson, and partially as a result of the inherent importance of the topic, many early investigators were concerned with the acquisition of sensorimotor skills. A large proportion of the studies of sensorimotor learning were designed to answer the general question of whether a given amount of practice is equally effective, independent of the

[*] This paper was written while the author was in residence as a Fellow at the Center for Advanced Study in the Behavioral Sciences, supported in part by Special Fellowship (HD–35961) from the National Institute of Child Health and Human Development, U. S. Public Health Service.

child's level of maturation. Of these studies, perhaps the best known are those of Gesell and Thompson (1929), Hilgard (1932), and McGraw (1935). In these studies there typically were two groups of children: an experimental group, which received intensive training on a particular skill over a period of time, and a control group, which was given infrequent or no practice for the same period, followed by intensive training. The importance of the interaction of learning and maturation was clearly demonstrated, for when young children were given relatively simple tasks, such as learning to climb stairs, to cut, or to button, increasing maturation resulted in increasingly greater effectiveness of a given amount of training. By the late 1930s, however, interest in sensorimotor learning had waned, and only minimal attention has been given to the topic for the past several decades.

The early research also included an array of studies on diverse topics whose only common feature was an interest in contrasting the performance of children with that of lower animals or human adults. Examples of such comparative studies are those on delayed reactions by Hunter (1913, 1917), on maze learning by Hicks and Carr (1912), and on the solution of puzzles by Lindley (1897). These studies, and indeed most of the early studies of children's learning, were characteristically problem oriented. They were concerned with such questions as whether children performed more effectively than lower animals, whether differences in CA, IQ, or sex resulted in differences in performance, and how the performance of children differed from that of adults. The empirical orientation of such studies is not surprising, for theoretical positions of some complexity did not begin to be formulated in discussions of the psychology of learning until the 1930s.

Many early studies were also concerned with the pragmatic questions of whether performance in learning tasks could be improved by the introduction of incentives and whether training was task-specific or transferred to other types of tasks. The demonstration by Thorndike (1932) of the facilitative effects of introducing rewards on the performance of animals and human adults led directly to investigations of whether similar effects would be found with children. Although there were differences in the relative effectiveness of dif-

ferent incentives when, for example, the performance of children was compared with that of adults, the results generally indicated a higher level of performance when the child was presented an incentive for correct response than when he was not (Abel, 1936; Hurlock, 1931). Thorndike (1924) also stimulated an interest in transfer of training, but his work was preceded by that of such persons as Judd (1908) on the general effects of practice on rote memory. A typical study was that of McGinnis (1929), who investigated transfer in the stylus-maze learning of preschool children. A more exhaustive delineation of early studies of children's learning would include work on retention (e.g., Meek, 1925), forgetting (e.g., Ballard, 1913), and the effects of guidance on learning (e.g., Gates and Taylor, 1923; Goodenough and Brian, 1929). There were also many studies of problem solving, but this is the topic of another chapter in this book and the research will not be discussed here.

This early research accomplished little other than replicating the findings of earlier studies. Munn (1954, p. 449), in concluding his review of children's learning for the preceding edition of this *Manual,* summarized his impressions in the following way:

So far as discovering anything fundamentally new concerning the learning process, the investigations on learning in children have failed. One possible reason for this is that such investigations have from the first been patterned too much after the lines of earlier research with animals and adults in the laboratory. A more likely reason, however, is that the phenomenon of learning is fundamentally the same whether studied in the animal, child, or adult.

Although we may wish to qualify the second interpretation, Munn's general conclusion seems appropriate. Educational and child-rearing practices and other research in learning were not strongly influenced by the work that had been done with children. This does not mean, however, that teachers and parents were not influenced by psychological research in learning. Such research consistently has been a focus of attention in educational psychology and, especially in the heyday of conditioning, was an important source of advice about how parents should rear their children. The overall similarity in the results of studies with children and those with other subjects was interpreted by many as indicating that the results of studies on animals and adults could be applied directly to the child, and because of this child psychologists often found it convenient to discuss children's behavior in terms of learning principles. This, in addition to the efficient and replicable procedures of laboratory studies, gave child psychology a learning and experimental orientation that still persists.

It would be unfortunate if the more recent research on children's learning had produced only a proliferation of adaptations and translations of research with animals and human adults, but this has not been the case. Although the studies still are intimately related to the general body of research in learning, investigators have begun to capitalize on the characteristics of children that make them especially suitable subjects for yielding new information about the learning process. Two of the most important characteristics are the developmental changes in the role of language in the control of behavior and the degree to which the child's behavior is influenced by that of other persons. It seems logical, and the studies have offered support for such an argument, that the learning process would undergo changes as the child gains linguistic competence and undergoes socialization experiences. Research became more productive and the study of children's learning was vitalized when psychologists began to select children as subjects because of their distinctive characteristics and not merely because of curiosity about how children would perform in standard laboratory tasks or because they were readily available and cooperative.

A second factor that transformed research with children from a replicative to an innovative field of investigation was the development of increasingly sophisticated theoretical models and systems in general psychology. None of these has been concerned explicitly with developmental processes, but they have been a valuable source of ideas and, importantly, have elucidated the possible importance of particular variables in determining how children learn. Because of these theoretical advances, current research with children is typically variable-oriented, in contrast to the problem orientation of earlier studies. It would be an overstatement to say that all learning studies with children now seek to assess the significance of particular variables. Most commonly, however, questions are asked about how experimental variables influence learning either singly or in interaction, rather than questions such as how long it takes children to learn a certain task, whether performance differs according to age, sex, and intelligence, and how the performance of children differs from that of lower animals.

By now there have been so many studies of children's learning that it is impossible to review them adequately in one chapter. Fortunately, comprehensive reviews have appeared in the two previous editions of this book (Munn, 1946, 1954) and in the two editions of A Handbook of Child Psychology (Peterson, 1931, 1933). In addition, the recent rapid development of the field has led to the publication of numerous reviews of research on particular topics (Bijou and Baer, 1963, 1966; Cantor, 1965; Castaneda, 1965; Denny, 1964; Fowler, 1962; Gollin, 1965; House and Zeaman, 1963; Kendler, 1963; Lipman, 1963; Lipsitt, 1963, 1967; Long, 1959b; McPherson, 1948, 1958; O'Connor, 1958; Reese, 1963; Ross, 1963; Shepp and Turrisi, 1967; Spiker, 1963; Stevenson, 1963; Terrell, 1965; White, 1963; Zeaman and House, 1967). It seems desirable therefore to concentrate in this review on the topics that currently are receiving the greatest amount of attention. References to earlier research are made only when such information is necessary to place a topic in its historical context. Some topics included in earlier chapters such as sensorimotor learning, memory, and problem solving are omitted, either because they have been inactive areas of research or because they are discussed in detail elsewhere in this book. Thus this chapter generally supplements, rather than reiterates, what has been discussed in previous general reviews.

This chapter begins with a consideration of the most simple form of learning, the conditioned response, and proceeds through a discussion of more complex forms. Although it would have been desirable to organize the chapter around variables that influence learning or around basic processes in learning, the most convenient and economical mode of organization appeared to be by type of task.

Because so many different tasks have been used, and because the tendency has been to investigate particular topics with a limited number of tasks, a large amount of repetition would have been necessary if another mode of organization had been used. Basic studies that have used normal children as the subjects receive primary attention, and studies dealing with special populations, such as the retarded, the deaf, and the disturbed, have not been discussed. Because of the vast number of publications no attempt is made to include all possibly relevant studies. The review is selective and discusses critical studies as intensively as possible. An attempt is made, however, to refer to reviews or other bibliographic sources for the use of persons who are interested in pursuing particular areas of research.

CONDITIONING WITH INFANTS AND YOUNG CHILDREN

Everyone who has had a course in introductory psychology is familiar with the basic facts about conditioning. Classical and operant conditioning, experimental extinction, spontaneous recovery, and the like have been demonstrated repeatedly with mature organisms from a wide variety of species. The initial interest in research with children was to ascertain whether these processes could be established in the human infant and child, and when an affirmative answer was reached, attention was directed to the questions of when the infant could be conditioned, what kinds of conditioned stimuli were effective, and the kinds of responses that could be conditioned. The effectiveness and simplicity of the conditioning methodology have led to many attempts at training and therapy, and a sizable proportion of the work with children has dealt with these problems.

Neonatal Conditioning

Psychoanalytic theory proposed that the early experiences of the infant have a profound importance for later personality development. One test of the validity of this proposition, as well as Watson's (1928) proposition concerning the universal applicability of conditioning procedures, is to determine whether the neonate can be conditioned. Unless the neonate can be conditioned, it is doubtful that other types of experiences could have enduring

psychological effects. It would seem the question could be answered readily, but at one point the problems seemed to be nearly insurmountable. The report by Wickens and Wickens (1940) placed the results of earlier studies in question because of the lack of appropriate controls. As if it were not difficult enough to obtain subjects who meet the requirements of a stringent experimental design, neonates are troublesome subjects with which to work, for they are often asleep, irritable, or hungry.

Even more distressing than the inadequacies of the earlier studies were the actual results of the Wickens' investigation. During a series of training trials, neonates in an experimental group were presented with the sound of a buzzer as the conditioned stimulus and a shock to the foot as the unconditioned stimulus; in one control group the neonates were presented only the buzzer and in another only the shock. Clear evidence of conditioning was found for the experimental group, but similar results also were found for the group that had been presented only the shock during the training trials. One of the interpretations of these results was that the effective conditioned stimulus for both of these groups was a change in the stimulus complex and that as the shock had constituted such a change in the training period for the control group, the buzzer constituted such a change in the test trials and therefore was capable of eliciting the conditioned response of leg retraction. If this were the case, and neonates were so sensitive that any change in the environment might operate as a conditioned stimulus, it seemed unlikely that a study could be designed to assess the critical features of the conditioned response.

Following the Wickens' study, interest in the problem was dormant until new techniques were introduced in the mid-fifties. The Wickens' somewhat incongruous results turned out to be partly attributable to their use of electric shock as the unconditioned stimulus. Shock and other aversive stimuli, except, perhaps, so mild a stimulus as a puff of air to the eye (Lintz, Fitzgerald, and Brackbill, 1967), have the undesirable effect of heightening the organism's level of arousal and thereby altering threshold values for response. Such effects seem to occur with less frequency when the stimuli are non-noxious, and studies of appetitional conditioning have given much more clear-cut demonstrations of neonatal conditioning than had previously been available. The most notable work has been that of Papoušek at the Institute for the Care of Mother and Child in Prague.

Papoušek was fortunate in having infants available at the Institute from birth through the first six months of life. Thus he could begin his studies with infants of different ages and proceed through a series of conditioning, extinction, reconditioning, discrimination, and reversal procedures. Summaries of his work have appeared in several recent publications (Papoušek, 1965, 1967a, 1967b). Following is the basic procedure used in these studies.

The UCS (milk) was presented by the assistant, who sat screened behind S's head. If S responded to the bell and turned to the left, milk was offered to him immediately. The bell continued to ring until S started sucking the milk. If S did not respond to the presentation of the CS within 10 seconds, the assistant (nurse) tried eliciting the head turn by tactile stimulation, touching the left corner of his mouth with the nipple. If this stimulation was ineffective, she turned his head to the left and placed the nipple in his mouth. At the end of reinforcement the nurse turned his head back to the middle, leading it with the nipple, and then took the nipple from his mouth (Papoušek, 1967b, p. 255).

Ten such trials were given each day until five consecutive positive responses were made in a daily session. In the basic study, conditioning was begun with groups of infants with mean ages of 3, 86, and 142 days.

In the youngest group an average of 32.2 trials was necessary before the first conditioned head-turn appeared, and the average number of trials required to reach criterion was 177. Thus conditioning was demonstrated during the neonatal period and in some cases was quite rapid. Criterion was reached within 7 days by some infants, but others required more than a month of training. Generally, the rate of conditioning of newborns was slow in comparison to that of the two older groups of infants, who required an average of only 42.3 and 27.8 trials, respectively, to reach criterion.

Papoušek (1967b) discerned several stages through which the infants passed prior to the formation of stable conditioned responses. During the first phase, the CS elicited non-specific orientational behavior, then partial responses, and finally the first conditioned responses. This phase was relatively long in neonates and included signs of distress. The next phase was unstable conditioning, which in neonates sometimes included generalized movement of the whole body. Ultimately a phase of stable conditioning was reached in which the responses were stronger, faster, and made with signs of pleasure rather than distress.

A closely related study has been reported by Siqueland and Lipsitt (1966). Two groups of infants between 1 and 2 days of age were presented 30 trials in which a buzzer preceded tactile stimulation of the cheek by 2 seconds. One group was reinforced with a dextrose solution immediately following rotation of the head to the side of stimulation, whereas in the other group reinforcement occurred 8 to 10 seconds after termination of the tactile stimulus. After training, the Ss received 12 extinction trials. The results reflected significant effects of the reinforcement and extinction procedures in the experimental group and a relatively stable level of response across trials in the control group. Two aspects of the study yielded negative findings. Amount of deprivation did not influence the rate of conditioning, for there were no significant differences in performance of the Ss, with half of each group tested 1 hour after feeding and the others tested 2½ hours after feeding. Further, there was no reliable indication of conditioning with the measure used by Papoušek, for the Ss showed no significant tendency to anticipate the presentation of the UCS by rotating their heads following the onset of the buzzer.

Siqueland and Lipsitt (1966) applied the same basic procedure in studying learned differentiation of stimuli by neonates and the reversal of responses to positive and negative stimuli. In the first study, 1- to 5-day-old infants were presented 48 trials in which tactile stimuli, preceded by distinctive sounds, were presented alternately to the left and right cheeks. Response to one of the stimuli was reinforced and response to the other was not. The frequency of head-turns to the reinforced side increased significantly over trials, whereas there was no increase in the frequency of response to the nonreinforced side. A habituation effect was demonstrated in the control Ss for whom reinforcement was not contingent upon head-turning. With another group of 2- to 5-day-old infants head-turns preceded by one auditory stimulus were reinforced and those by another were not. After 60 acquisition trials the pattern of reinforcement was reversed for a second series of 60 trials. Clear evidence of the infants' ability to discriminate auditory stimuli was found; not only did the frequency of responses to the positive stimulus increase during training, but by the end of the reversal trials the frequency of response to the previously negative stimulus exceeded that to the previously positive (now negative) stimulus. The results of a study by Lipsitt, Kaye, and Bosack (1966) indicated that the effects found in the latter studies were not limited to the head-turning response. When the insertion of a rubber tube in the mouths of 1- to 4-day-old infants was followed by reinforcement with a dextrose solution the rate of sucking increased significantly, and when the reinforcement was omitted the rate dropped to a baseline level. Rate of sucking therefore was significantly altered by the reinforcement contingencies.

Further evidence of the modifiability of neonatal behavior has been reported by Kaye (1965) in a study of the Babkin reflex. In this study reflex pressure to the palms of a supine infant results in the infant's opening its mouth. The arms of 2- to 4-day-old infants were moved from the extended to the flexed position and pressure was applied to the palms when the arms were in the flexed position. In tests following 35 training trials, the frequency of mouth opening to arm movement alone was significantly higher than that which had been found in a baseline period and was consistently above that of control Ss for whom arm movement had not preceded pressure to the palm during the training trials.

Other recent studies of neonatal conditioning have been discussed by Brackbill and Koltsova (1968), Lipsitt (1963), and Papoušek (1967a). Among the most notable of the studies offering evidence of conditioning are those by Dashkovskaia (1953) on conditioning of the eye-blink reflex in 8-day-old infants and by Krachkovskaia (1967). In the second study an increase in leukocyte count, which typically occurs in infants following feeding, was found in 8-day-old infants at the time they usually were fed when the feeding was omitted to allow testing without food. A simi-

lar form of temporal conditioning had been reported earlier by Marquis (1941), who found an increase in bodily activity after the third hour in 9-day-old infants whose feeding was altered from a 3- to a 4-hour schedule. Considering all these studies, there seems to be little question that neonatal conditioning is possible.

The next obvious question is whether conditioning is possible prior to birth and in infants who are born prematurely. The best known study of prenatal conditioning is that of Spelt (1948), who reported what appeared to be conditioning of the fetus *in utero* during the last two months of gestation. Unfortunately, this study has not been followed by further research, and in the face of the inadequacies of the controls, especially of the mothers' perception of the UCS and the CS, it is difficult to conclude that successful conditioning was demonstrated. Premature infants apparently can be conditioned, but this problem, too, will require additional research before satisfactory conclusions can be drawn. Other than the disrupting effects that might occur from the greater incidence of physical anomalies in the premature, there would be no reason to expect that premature infants would be less susceptible to conditioning than would full-term babies, if both are tested at comparable gestational ages. When groups of prematures were matched with full-term infants on the basis of time since delivery, Janoš (1965) found slower conditioning in the prematures, but they were nevertheless able to reach a criterion of five consecutive eye-blinks to a tone. The argument has been made that the greater opportunities premature infants have for stimulation may result in faster conditioning, but at present there is no evidence that prematurity is especially advantageous to learning.

Habituation

The status of habituation is still being debated; some regard it as an example of learning, whereas others view it as the result of more basic neural processes (see Bartoshuk, 1962). At any rate, the diminution of response to repetitive stimulation illustrates a change in behavior as a function of repeated experience with a particular stimulus, a definition that often is used for learning. The process has been demonstrated in lower animals, neonates, and older infants. Recent interest in the study of habituation with neonates is attributable to a study reported by Bronshtein, Antonova, Kamenetskaya, Luppova, and Sytova (1958), in which a tone or odor followed the insertion of a pacifier in an infant's mouth. Initially, the infant ceased sucking when the odor or tone was presented, but with repeated presentations the stimulus became ineffective in suppressing sucking. A repetition of the study by Keen (1964) produced less striking results than those reported by Bronshtein et al.; when the duration of the tone and intertrial interval were carefully controlled there was less cessation of sucking to the tone than had been found in the earlier study. Also, habituation occurred much more slowly, and there was no evidence that the neonates discriminated between the two tones (400 versus 4000 cps) that were used. The inexplicitness of the Russian report makes it impossible to assess the basis for these discrepancies in results. Keen did find, as had Bridger (1961) in a study of cardiac acceleration to tones, that the duration of the stimulus played a more important role in producing habituation in neonates than did the interval between presentations. Other efforts (Kaye and Lavin, 1963; Solomons, Hardy, and Melrose, 1965) have been unable to produce habituation of the sucking response.

Two other studies using olfactory stimuli and body movement as the response have found evidence of habituation (Engen and Lipsitt, 1965; Engen, Kaye, and Lipsitt, 1963). The percentage of neonatal responses to the stimulus (anise or asafoetida) decreased with repetitive stimulation and the effect of previous experience generalized, for more rapid habituation was found to each odor when it was presented after habituation had occurred to the other. When two odors (amyl acetate and heptanal) were combined habituation to the mixture occurred, and when the odors were presented singly there was recovery of the habituated response.

Conditioning in Older Infants

In contrast to the small number of studies that have been conducted with neonates, there have been many studies of conditioning with older infants and children. Soviet psychologists and physiologists, trained in the Pavlovian school, have been responsible for a large proportion of this work. Reviews of the most sig-

nificant of these studies have been presented by Brackbill (1962) and Brackbill and Koltsova (1968). Despite the extensive work that has been done, a great deal of parametric work still is needed. Little is known, for example, about the effects of length of presentation of the CS and UCS, the interval between presentation of CS and UCS, the intensity of the CS, and reinforcement mechanisms in conditioning the young human being.

The Soviet work has been multifaceted, but two consistent lines of investigation have been studies of the effects of the CS on conditioning and of the development of higher-order and complex forms of conditioning. According to Brackbill (1962, p. 110), "Soviet physiologists maintain that in conditioning—at least in classical conditioning—there is only one really influential member of the triad, CS-UCS-CR, and that is the first member." Accordingly, much time has been spent in ascertaining developmental trends in conditioning as a function of the type of CS used. All types of stimuli have not been found to be equally effective at all ages, for maturational changes in the sensory apparatus appear to result in a developmental sequence in the relative effectiveness of a particular CS. This sequence, according to Kasatkin (Brackbill and Koltsova, 1968), is such that vestibular stimuli are effective earliest, followed by auditory, tactile, olfactory, taste, and visual stimuli, in that order. There are problems, of course, in equating the intensity of stimuli differing on qualitative dimensions, but for the present there is little evidence that this sequence is not correct.

Soviet investigators distinguish three categories of stimuli as being effective in eliciting responses in the human being. Unconditioned stimuli elicit reflexive responses, conditioned stimuli become capable of eliciting such responses through their association with unconditioned stimuli, and, at a later developmental level, words develop meanings that, if associated with the CS, become capable of eliciting the conditioned response. Conditioned stimuli constitute what are called the first signal system and words constitute the second signal system. A great deal of emphasis has been placed on the role of the second signal system in the development and control of human behavior. A study by Degtiar (1962; cited by Brackbill and Koltsova, 1968) illustrates the type of research that has been done on the emergence of the second signal system. Children from 1½ to 3 years of age readily developed conditioned responses to visual and auditory stimuli which generalized to the verbal cues "lamp" and "bell." The youngest Ss were incapable of generalizing the response to abstract designations of these stimuli and did not respond to the words "light" and "sound," even though they had been taught the meaning of these words before participating in the experiment.

A second example of studies of the second signal system is that of Koltsova (1967) on the role of excitation and inhibition in the development of generalization. In an initial experiment there were two groups of 2-year-old Ss. In the first group the presentation of geometrical figures was accompanied by a puff of air to the eye and the utterance "thing," whereas the presentation of objects such as a key or drumstick was never accompanied by the puff or the word. In the second group the presentation of small skeins of yarn was always followed by an air puff, but only those in which yellow predominated were accompanied by the word "thing." Stable discrimination between the positive and negative stimuli was found in the first group as successive stimuli were presented, but in the second group successive presentations of the same or different skeins resulted in increasingly weak and unstable responses and, eventually, extinction. When the children were asked to pick out a "thing" from sets of objects, clear differentiation was found in the first group, for the Ss always chose geometrical forms; but in the second group the Ss chose only the brightest and largest of the objects. The results of this and subsequent similar studies were interpreted as evidence of the necessity for developing inhibitory as well as excitatory processes before successful generalization from earlier conditioning can occur.

Many other examples of Soviet research could be cited, such as studies of auditory discrimination, color vision, and the conditioning of physiological responses, but most of these studies deal with capacity rather than process. Perhaps the major impact of these studies has been the demonstration of the ubiquity of the conditioning process. Conditioning has been shown to be an important tool for assessing the abilities of the preverbal child,

the functions of language, the operation of physiological processes, and the possibilities for remediation of defects or deficits in behavior.

The most noteworthy non-Soviet study of conditioning of older infants and young children is that by Papoušek (1967b). As indicated earlier, Papoušek found developmental changes in the rate with which head-turning could be conditioned. In rate of extinction, however, the three groups of Ss, now 32, 94, and 149 days of age, all met the criterion of five consecutive negative responses in approximately the same number of trials (25 to 27). The latency of the CR was longer for the youngest group, and for these Ss there was a significant correlation between trials to condition and trials to extinguish, but otherwise there was no basis for interpreting the remarkable similarity in rate of extinction among the three groups of Ss. Reconditioning occurred no more rapidly than original learning for the two oldest groups of Ss, but it was faster for the youngest group. Age differences also were found for speed of discrimination involving reinforcement of responses to a bell on the left and to a buzzer on the right, and for reversal of this discrimination. This same negative relation betwen age and number of trials to criterion has been reported in at least 13 other studies of conditioning (Brackbill and Koltsova, 1968).

The studies reviewed thus far have not been separated into those using classical conditioning procedures and those using instrumental or operant procedures. The distinction between those in which behavior is elicited (classical) and those in which behavior is emitted (operant) is of importance, however, in introducing the next group of studies, which are all the operant type. The operant method has been popularized by Skinner and his students, but the initial systematic studies of operant conditioning with children were conducted by Ivanov-Smolensky (1927). In Ivanov-Smolensky's studies, which have been reviewed by Razran (1933), the child was able to release a piece of food from a container by pressing a rubber bulb. The CS (bell or light) was presented just before the food was visible. Such a technique was effective in establishing stable conditioning, higher-order conditioning, and conditioning to chains of stimuli with young children.

Rheingold, Gewirtz, and Ross (1959) capitalized on the usefulness of operant techniques in their study of the conditioning of vocalization in the 3-month-old infant. Vocalizations were reinforced by a complex of social acts, including smiling, making "tssk" sounds, and touching the baby's abdomen. Such acts were effective in increasing the frequency of vocalization over that found in a baseline period and, when omitted, in reducing the frequency of vocalization to approximately the baseline level. The experiment was conducted in 9 daily 3-minute sessions over 6 days. The results appear to offer clear evidence of conditioning, but an alternative interpretation of the increase and subsequent decrease in vocalization is possible. The social stimuli may have had an arousing rather than a reinforcing function. The validity of such an interpretation was investigated by Weisberg (1963), who replicated the experimental conditions of the Rheingold et al. study adding groups for whom vocalization was reinforced by a nonsocial stimulus (door chime), groups in which either the social or nonsocial stimuli were not contingent upon S's vocalizing, and nonreinforced groups in which the adult was present and in which the adult was absent. Successful conditioning and extinction were found in the first group only, thereby supporting the conclusion that conditioning had been demonstrated in the earlier study.

Two other studies offer evidence of operant control of infants' social behavior. The frequency of smiling in 4-month-old infants increased significantly when an adult reinforced smiling by picking up the baby, smiling, and talking to him (Brackbill, 1958). Evidence of extinction, accompanied by an increase in protest responses, was found when reinforcement was discontinued. (The presence of such emotional responses during extinction was also noted by Rheingold et al.) Etzel and Gewirtz (1967) also used social stimuli to reinforce smiling in 6- and 20-week-old infants while simultaneously attempting to reduce the incidence of crying by nonreinforcement. These studies demonstrate with infants what will be abundantly clear in later discussions of research with older children: The adult may exert powerful control over behavior by following desired responses with reinforcement and by withholding reinforcement following undesired responses.

CONDITIONING STUDIES WITH OLDER CHILDREN

Studies of conditioning with older children have relied nearly solely on operant methods. The degree to which operant conditioning has captured attention is exemplified in the recent books on child development by Bijou and Baer (1961, 1965), where the principles of operant conditioning provide the guiding theme in their analysis of behavior. The basic tenets of such an approach have been summarized by these writers:

The positivistic approach is usually functional: an area of behavior is defined and then procedures are established to discover those variables which control it. As discoveries are made, responses are described as functions of certain experimental manipulations, usually of stimulus events in the past and present environments, and a set of empirical laws evolves. Concepts arise not because of their imaginative, logical, or global characteristics, but only as they serve to describe and summarize the experimental stimulus operations which control behavior. Hence, such concepts are functional in that they pertain only to those procedures demonstrated to influence the behaviors in question (Bijou and Baer, 1966, p. 719).

The basic principles of operant conditioning are simple, explicit, and applicable to a wide variety of behavior. Initially research was concerned with problems such as the kinds of response that could be modified, the classes of stimuli that were effective reinforcers, and the types of schedule of reinforcement that were optimally effective (e.g., Baer, 1960, 1961; Bijou, 1957, 1958; Bijou and Sturges, 1959, Long, 1959a). The cataloguist function has not dominated such research, however, and the principles have been investigated in a number of novel and interesting ways.

Verbal Conditioning

The verbal behavior of children, at least within the restricted settings that have been used, can be effectively controlled by making reinforcement contingent upon the emission of a particular verbal response. Of special interest has been the analysis of the relation of situational and antecedent conditions to children's conditionability. A good example is the developmental study by Baer and Goldfarb (1962) in which Ss in grades 3, 6, and 10 were asked to select a pronoun from a list and use it as the first word in a sentence. The experimenter (a male adult) made a supportive comment after each sentence that began with "I." Developmental changes in rate of conditioning differed for boys and girls. The greatest increment in "I" responses occurred for grade 3 boys and grade 10 girls, and the smallest increments for grade 3 girls and grade 10 boys. Sex differences were small at grade 6. The tendency, then, was for the conditioning procedure to be increasingly effective with girls and decreasingly effective with boys as age increased.

Rowley and Keller (1962) employed the same procedure with 9- to 12-year-olds, but they added a control group that received no reinforcement and a second experimental group whose reinforcement consisted of a nod of the head and a smile from the experimenter. Performance did not change across trials for the control Ss, but there was a moderate increase in the number of reinforced pronouns with physical reinforcement and a marked increase with verbal reinforcement. Boys and girls performed at approximately the same level and there were no differences in performance between groups scoring high and low on a test of manifest anxiety.

The degree to which preschool boys could be conditioned to answer "Mother" or "Father" to a series of simple questions about a family of four dolls was found to differ by Epstein and Liverant (1963), depending upon boys' sex-role identification. The Ss were obtained by selecting the highest and lowest scorers from a large sample of boys given a test of sex-role preferences. Conditioning occurred in all groups, but boys who were classified as high-masculine identifiers were more effectively conditioned by a male than by a female experimenter. The male experimenter was a more effective agent of reinforcement for the high- than for the low-masculine identifiers, and the only group in which "Father" was not more effectively conditioned than "Mother" was the low-masculine group tested by a male.

Reinforcement in the preceding studies involved a social response from the experimenter. Would verbal conditioning also occur if a nonsocial reinforcement were used? A study by Erickson (1962) indicated that it

would not. Sixth graders were reinforced with the automatic delivery of a marble or with the statement "Good" each time they verbalized the name of the animate object in pairs of animate and inanimate objects. Prior to this task the Ss spent 15 minutes working on a game in which they were praised by the experimenter or performed alone. Conditioning occurred with verbal reinforcement when there had been no social interaction in pretraining, but even this form of reinforcement was ineffective when the Ss had been praised in their pre-experimental sessions.

These studies illustrate how radically the experimental situation changes when the experimenter enters the scene. The sex of the subject, sex of the experimenter, sex-role preferences, and previous opportunities for social interaction, all seemingly strange variables to consider in studies of conditioning, became important determinants of how rapidly learning will occur. Much more will be said about such variables in later sections.

Drive Level

There has been a great deal of interest in the effects of high levels of drive on the conditioning of instrumental motor responses. Total drive level has been varied by increasing frustration, by using incentives of different value, and by selecting Ss differing in level of anxiety.

The impetus for using frustration comes from the hypothesis that nonreward in the context of reinforced trials leads to frustration, which increases drive, which, in turn, increases level of performance in situations employing simple, noncompetitive responses. One of the first investigations of this hypothesis with children was reported by Holton (1961). Preschool Ss were divided into three groups on the basis of pretraining experiences. Two groups received a large number of reinforcements (marbles) prior to receiving nonreward. In one of these groups, only a few more marbles were needed to reach the goal of filling a marble board that could be traded for a prize: a larger number of marbles was needed in the other group. A third group received a smaller number of reinforcements prior to nonreinforcement and needed only a small number of marbles to fill the marble board. The response measure was force exerted on a panel whose depression resulted in the delivery of a reward. The amount of force increased in all groups between the early reinforced period and the period following the introduction of nonreinforcement. The increase was greater when nonreinforcement occurred near the goal and followed a large number of reinforcements or when nonreinforcement occurred further from the goal. The effects of nonreinforcement therefore depended on both the prior number of reinforced trials and how close S was to reaching the defined goal.

Endsley (1966) tested 7- and 8-year-olds in a related study. The Ss' efforts in an initial task met with either success or failure. To have another try at the first task, the Ss were required to push a button on a second piece of apparatus. The first task was rigged so that the Ss could be made to fail either near or far from the defined goal. In contrast to Holton's findings, both near- and far-failure Ss responded faster after success than after failure. The total situation, however, was much more complex, and it is likely that failure elicited avoidance responses, such as looking back at the apparatus of the first task, which interfered with the Ss' subsequent response on the second task.

Frustration effects may also be operative under conditions of partial reinforcement, where the same response may, depending upon the schedule, terminate either in reinforcement or nonreinforcement. Several studies have used a lever-pulling task to investigate this problem. At the onset of a signal S is required to pull a lever through its full excursion to terminate the signal or to receive a marble reward. Two measures of response, starting and movement speeds, are commonly used, but since starting speed has proved to be less productive in most studies, only results obtained with movement speed will be discussed.

Bruning (1964) and Ryan and Moffitt (1966) have found that movement speeds were faster with 50% than with 100% reinforcement. Incentive level was also varied in these studies, but only in the Ryan and Moffitt study were significant incentive effects obtained—and these were in the direction opposite from that predicted. Groups working for incentives of low value increased their speeds, and the high-incentive groups showed

little change after an early, low asymptotic level of response. This inversion may be readily explained by the fact that all Ss were aware of the two incentives, a piece of string and a toy. It is not unlikely that working for a piece of string became increasingly frustrating when the Ss knew that other children were being rewarded with a toy.

A more elaborate study by Ryan (1966) included six schedules of reinforcement. Preschool children had faster movement speeds with partial than with consistent reinforcement. There was an orderly increase in the speeds as the percentage of reinforcement decreased between 100, 83, 66, and 50%, but the speeds decreased somewhat as the percentage of reinforcement decreased from 50 to 33 and 17%. These findings suggest an inverted U-shaped relation between asymptotic response speed and reward schedule. A subsequent study by Ryan and Voorhoeve (1966) replicated this effect. Response speeds of 5-year-olds increased as the percentage of reinforcement for lever-pulling decreased from 100 to 70 and 50%, but decreased again as the percentage of reinforcement dropped to 30 and 10%. The facilitation of response with partial reinforcement thus begins to be lessened as the likelihood of nonreinforcement exceeds that of reinforcement.

Two-lever tasks have also been used. Here, variation in percentage of reinforcement followed movement of the first lever, with movement of the second lever resulting in consistent reinforcement. Penney (1960) found that the movement speeds on a second lever were faster following nonreinforcement than following reinforcement on the first lever. Ryan (1965) replicated this effect in between-group comparisons where one group received 50% reinforcement on the first lever and the second group received 100%. The Ss worked either for a preferred or a nonpreferred incentive, but incentive level had no significant effect on movement speeds.

All of the preceding studies used tangible reinforcers. Ryan and Watson (1966) asked whether the same effects would be found with verbal reinforcement. When lever-pulling terminated in a supportive statement from the experimenter 33% of the time, movement speed increased as training progressed, but the speed changed only slightly when Ss were given 100% reinforcement. The effects, then, were not limited to the use of tangible reinforcement.

The conclusions from these studies are consistent: partial reinforcement results in faster responding than does continuous reinforcement, but incentive is not an effective variable in itself in influencing rate of response. The studies provide supportive evidence for a frustration or drive theory, but, as several of the investigators pointed out, the results may also be predicted from an associational framework if it is assumed that the Ss may have learned from everyday experience that they should try harder in the face of low success. When there is only partial success in the lever-pulling task, the Ss may apply this dictum and increase their efforts in the only available way by pulling the lever faster.

Finally, there are the studies on anxiety. Anxiety is assumed by some theorists to act as an irrelevant drive, energizing all existing habits. In the lever-pulling task, which involves a well-learned response, highly anxious children should have faster response speeds than children with lower levels of anxiety. Penney and McCann (1962) tested groups of third and fourth graders who received high and low scores on an anxiety questionnaire. An escape conditioning procedure was used, where movement of the lever terminated a loud, unpleasant tone. The high anxious Ss had faster response speeds than low anxious Ss. If anxiety is an enduring characteristic of the individual, prior adaptation to a noxious stimulus should have less effect in altering the total drive level of high anxious than of low anxious Ss. To test this possibility, Penney and Kirwin (1965) exposed half of their high and low anxious fourth and fifth graders to a series of trials with an intense tone. The Ss then were tested in the lever-pulling task, where response terminated the previously experienced tone. There was no significant difference in the response times of adapted and nonadapted high anxious Ss, but adapted low anxious Ss had significantly slower response times than their nonadapted counterparts. Thus adaptation appeared to have reduced the total motivational level of the low anxious but not of the high anxious Ss.

The general conclusion from these studies is straightforward. When response involves a well-learned habit such as lever-pulling, an increase in drive results in more efficient response. The effects appear to be similar whether drive level is increased by introducing frustration, by using a high level of incentive, or by selecting anxious children as Ss. As will be seen in later sections, these variables have a disruptive rather than a facilitative effect on performance when the correct response is initially weak in strength or when it is subject to interference from incorrect responses of higher strength.

Delay of Reward

A delay in the delivery of a reward in the conditioning of an instrumental response should, according to an associational interpretation, result in slower rates of response. According to this position, a delay increases the possibility that competing responses that are incompatible with the instrumental response will be conditioned. Further, the degree of interference should be a function of the similarity between the cues present during the delay period and those that elicit the instrumental response. Maximal similarity would occur if the stimulus situation did not change between the time of the onset of the cue and the delivery of the reward.

Rieber (1961a) tested these predictions with kindergarten children in a lever-pulling task. The excursion of the lever terminated in either immediate or a 12-second delay in reinforcement. In the delayed reinforcement groups the initiating signal (a light) remained visible during the delay period for half of the Ss and terminated with Ss' response for the other half. In line with the predictions, starting speed (i.e., the time between onset of signal and beginning of response) was fastest with immediate reinforcement and slowest when the signal remained on during the delay interval. Movement speeds revealed no difference between immediate and delayed reinforcement with immediate offset of the signal, but the speeds were slower when the signal remained on during the delay interval. It therefore appears that competing responses, presumably conditioned to the signal, had a greater differential effect on starting than on movement speeds. A more elaborate study by Rabinowitz (1966) confirmed Rieber's findings and added the information that the immediate delivery of tangible reinforcement increased movement speeds over those found when such reinforcement was absent, that delay of signal offset affected movement speeds, and that delay of delivery of the reinforcer affected starting speeds.

An additional study (Rieber, 1961b) included four groups of 6-year-olds who received either immediate or delayed reinforcement through 30 trials or were switched at trial 16 from one to the other condition. Starting speed proved to be the more sensitive measure. Immediate reinforcement resulted in faster speeds than delayed reinforcement when the conditions remained the same for all trials. Persisting effects of delayed reinforcement were evident in the second half of the trials, for among Ss who were switched to immediate reinforcement, starting speeds were slower than they were for Ss who received immediate reinforcement on all trials. Correspondingly, Ss who were switched from immediate to delayed reinforcement showed a marked decrease in their speeds during the second half of the trials.

A study by Rieber and Johnson (1964) attempted to determine whether children could learn to anticipate reward conditions and vary their responses accordingly. The task involved alternating trials of immediate and delayed reinforcement. Additional cues (lights) were provided to signal the type of trial that would occur. In contrast to the previous results, response speeds were faster on the trials with delayed reinforcement than they were on the immediately reinforced trials, and the effect appeared with delays of 4, 8, and 16 seconds Response speeds of all three groups were slower, however, than they were for a group of Ss that received consistent immediate reinforcement. Although the writers postulated that anticipation would be reflected in faster responding on immediately reinforced trials, the reverse argument can be made. The Ss may have learned to anticipate delayed reinforcement, and since anticipation of delay was frustrating, the speed of response increased. In this type of design, however, it is impossible to determine whether the differences are due to the residual effects of what occurred on the preceding trial or to the conditions prevailing on a particular trial.

Two other studies of the effects of delay on instrumental conditioning have been reported. Penney (1967) found response speeds in lever-pulling to escape a loud tone were faster with immediate than with delayed reinforcement. Groups receiving alternating and random delayed and immediate reinforcement were included in the study. The insertion of immediately reinforced trials on an alternating schedule with delayed reinforcement did not change performance from that which occurred when all trials involved a delay of reinforcement, but somewhat faster speeds of response were found when the delay occurred randomly across trials. Harris (1967) found no difference in speeds of response when the delay of reinforcement was constant and when it varied between two values. Of greater importance, however, was the finding that an enriched surround (the presence of a large variety of interesting toys) did not produce significantly lower response times than did a stimulus-poor surround, even though the opportunities for developing competing responses would seemingly be greater in the enriched surround.

The results are consistent in indicating a disrupting effect of delayed reinforcement on speed of response in the instrumental conditioning of a motor response such as lever-pulling. Support for an associational interpretation of the effect would appear to be somewhat weakened by Harris' findings, but there is no indication that motivational or other interpretations offer a more powerful means of explaining the results.

Stimulus Familiarization

It has been suggested in the literature that the effectiveness of a conditioned stimulus decreases as the S becomes increasingly familiar with it. A series of studies has explored this problem in the instrumental conditioning of young children by exposing the Ss to the CS for a series of trials prior to commencing the conditioning procedure. Cantor and Cantor (1964) presented a buzzer or a light to kindergarten Ss for 40 2-second exposures before introducing the Ss to a lever-pulling task in which both light and buzzer served as conditioned stimuli. Starting speeds were markedly faster for the novel than for the familiar stimulus when the familiar stimulus was a buzzer, but only slight differences were found when the familiar stimulus was a light. In this, and in the subsequent studies, speed of response decreased across trials for both types of stimuli.

In a second study (Cantor and Cantor,

1965) Ss were given 40 3-second exposures to a red or green light. The experimental task was modified so that Ss were required to press a button of a color corresponding to that of the light. Response speeds were faster for the novel than for the familiar stimulus. A trial-by-trial analysis indicated that the fastest speeds occurred when a novel stimulus followed a familiar stimulus and the slowest speeds when a familiar stimulus followed itself. The magnitude of the effect thus appeared to depend on whether or not the preceding trial involved a familiar stimulus.

The same apparatus and procedure were used in a third study (Cantor and Cantor, 1966), but the number of familiarization trials was varied. Kindergarten Ss were given either 5 or 35 exposures to one of the two lights; the total number of preliminary trials was held constant by using a third, irrelevant light. Although response times were faster to the novel than to the familiar stimuli, 5 exposures were as effective as 35 in reducing speed of response —a somewhat incongruous finding. Another effect of novelty appeared in an analysis of individual trials: response times were faster when there was a change in the stimulus than when the same stimulus was repeated.

The stimulus familiarization effect obviously is replicable, but what is the underlying mechanism? Several alternative interpretations have been offered, including (1) a prolonged attention response is conditioned during the familiarization trials that interferes with rapid responding in the motor task, (2) familiarization trials induce habituation that reduces the subsequent effectiveness of the stimulus in eliciting attending responses, and (3) novelty is surprising and may produce an increased level of drive or heightened orientation that facilitates the execution of the motor response. Studies exploring these hypotheses have not been exhaustive, but at this time habituation seems to be the most satisfactory explanatory mechanism.

In a study by Witte (1967) the stimulus was presented 20 times during the familiarization trials, but the length of exposure was 4.5 seconds for half of the Ss and 1.5 seconds for the other half. Starting speeds of preschool Ss in a lever-pulling task were faster to the stimulus that had been presented with the shorter exposure times, thus giving some support to the habituation hypothesis. A method-ological innovation was introduced by Bogartz and Witte (1966) which was relevant to the evaluation of the various hypotheses. The Ss were required to remove their finger from the button with stimulus onset during both the familiarization and conditioning trials. This procedure was adopted to decrease the possibility that competing responses could be conditioned during the familiarization trials. Again, however, kindergarten Ss showed faster response speeds to the novel than to the familiarized stimulus, a result that is hard to incorporate into a competing-response interpretation of the familiarization effect. Evidence against a surprise interpretation also was obtained. The authors noted that in prior studies the sequence of trials had been constructed, inadvertently, so that on 75% of the trials the stimulus was opposite to that presented on the previous trial. Such a sequence would be likely to produce an alternation pattern of responding, with faster responding on alternation than on repetitive response. Schedules therefore were constructed that involved 75% alternation-25% repetition or 75% repetition-25% alternation of response. The Ss in the first group responded faster on changed than on unchanged trials, whereas Ss in the latter groups responded faster on unchanged than on changed trials. The change effect therefore seems to be due to the structure of the schedules rather than to novelty. Thus only the habituation hypothesis appears not to have been discredited. A habituation hypothesis has considerable strength, for it not only accounts for an overall drop in response time across trials, but it also predicts that the drop will be faster for stimuli to which S has been exposed in pre-experimental trials.

Satiation and Deprivation

Satiation is another process whereby the effectiveness of a stimulus may be reduced, but in this case it is the role of the stimulus as a reinforcing agent, rather than as a conditioned stimulus, that is of special interest. A number of studies have demonstrated that the utility of a stimulus in reinforcing an instrumental response may be decreased by satiation and enhanced by deprivation operations. Two studies by Gewirtz and Baer (1958a, 1958b) illustrate this process with social reinforcers. The experimental task involved dropping marbles into two holes of a container.

After establishing a baseline of response, social reinforcement (praise) was given on a fixed-ratio schedule every fifth time S dropped a marble into the hole that had been preferred least during the last minute of the baseline period. Before introducing the experimental task, the preschool Ss were subjected to 20 minutes of social isolation by being left alone in an empty room, to 20 minutes of periodic praise as they performed a simple task, or, in the control condition, received no preliminary experience. The increase in the number of responses to the nonpreferred hole between baseline and experimental periods was greatest following isolation and least following satiation, indicating that the operations had been successful in altering the effectiveness of supportive statements as social reinforcers.

Similar effects have been reported for visual and auditory stimuli. Stevenson and Odom (1961) found that rate of lever-pressing for visual reinforcement increased rapidly following visual deprivation but showed little change after visual satiation. The two conditions were established by leaving 5- to 7-year-old Ss alone in an experimental room for 15 minutes. In the deprivation condition the room was empty and dimly lit and in the satiation condition the room was full of many interesting, colorful toys with which Ss could play.

Odom (1964) controlled Ss' stimulus input more adequately by fitting 8- to 10-year-olds with a space helmet equipped with earphones and a visual tunnel attached to the visor of the helmet. For a 10-minute period the Ss either viewed a uniformly dull visual field or saw a sequence of colors and heard either nothing or a series of varying tones. The experimental task involved turning a small wheel in one direction for presentation of colors and the other for presentation of tones. The number of responses made during 7 experimental minutes differed markedly, depending upon Ss' earlier experiences. The Ss who had been satiated for visual stimuli (and deprived of auditory stimuli) showed an increase in the number of responses that produced auditory stimuli, and the Ss who had been satiated for auditory stimuli (and deprived of visual stimuli) showed an increase in the number of responses that produced visual stimuli. The Ss who had been satiated or deprived of both types of stimuli showed equivalent frequencies of response in each direction.

Although the effects are not as simple as may appear in these sets of studies, there is little question that deprivation and satiation operations alter the effectiveness of relevant stimuli as reinforcers. The use of social reinforcement has proved to be especially complicated, for such factors as sex of S, sex of the experimenter, age of S, and characteristics of the experimenter have been found to be important variables in determining the effectiveness of supportive statements in modifying rate and type of instrumental response (see Stevenson, 1965).

Stimulus Generalization

Stimulus generalization occurs when novel stimuli, similar to the training stimulus and presented for the first time on test trials, elicit the conditioned response. Some degree of stimulus generalization has utility for the organism, but if generalization is too extensive, responses will be made to stimuli that are so dissimilar from the originally effective stimulus that the responses may turn out to be inappropriate. From a developmental point of view, it might be expected that mature Ss will show more restricted gradients of stimulus generalization than will younger Ss. Several studies have found that this is the case. Mednick and Lehtinen (1957) investigated age differences by training Ss to lift their finger from a button when a central light appeared. At the completion of the training trials peripheral lights, arranged on an arc in front of S, were intermixed with reappearances of the central light. The stimulus generalization gradient, as assessed by frequency of response to the peripheral lights, was flatter with 7- to 9-year-old Ss than with 10- to 12-year-olds. Tempone (1965) found a similar effect when MA rather than CA was varied. The Ss were all 8-year-olds, but had mean MAs of 6.6, 8.8, and 10.9 years. Decreasing amounts of stimulus generalization were found with increasing MA.

Why younger Ss show broader generalization gradients is not clear, but one possible basis is suggested in a study by Jeffrey and Skager (1962), who assumed that the greater generalization by the younger Ss may reflect a lack of interest in the task. In the previous two studies, the only reinforcement for correct response during training was verbal encouragement, an incentive that may be less effective with younger than with older Ss. Therefore, to heighten motivation a training condition was introduced in which Ss received a poker chip for correct response, lost a chip for incorrect response, and were told they later could cash in the chips to see a movie. The procedure was identical for control Ss, except that chips were not given and were not required for the movie. The proportion of 6- to 7-year-olds showing generalization to peripheral lights was significantly smaller with the added incentive than without it, but performance did not differ between the two conditions for 9- to 12-year-olds. Importantly, the performance of the younger Ss in the experimental group did not differ significantly from that of the older Ss. Developmental changes in stimulus generalization may therefore be minimized when younger Ss are highly motivated to respond correctly.

Numerous variables have been found to influence stimulus generalization in a series of studies with preschool Ss by Spiker and his colleagues. All of the studies used lever-pressing as the response and lights varying in hue or brightness as the stimuli. If the strength of the generalized tendency to respond to other stimuli is dependent upon the strength of the conditioned response, increasing the number of training trials should result in a greater degree of stimulus generalization. A study by Spiker (1956a) supported this hypothesis, for the amount of generalization was greater following 24 than following 12 training trials. The effect was replicated in a study of the effect of stimulus intensity on stimulus generalization (Spiker, 1956b). The Ss again were given 12 to 24 training trials, but half were trained with a dim light (2.5 foot-candles) and half with a bright light (250 foot-candles). This study tested the hypothesis that stimulus intensity influences motivational level of S. More intense stimuli are assumed to increase motivation, which, in a multiplicative relation with strength of response, increases the strength of the generalized habit. The results were supportive of the hypothesis, for a steeper gradient of stimulus generalization was obtained for Ss who had been trained with the bright light.

In a relevant study, Tempone (1966) varied the number of training trials with Ss at two levels of CA. In line with Spiker's reasoning, it was assumed that generalization would be increased for younger Ss as the number of training trials increased. With older Ss, however, the opposite effect was predicted. These Ss presumably respond on the basis of some form of mediation. As training increases, the cues defining the effective stimulus should become increasingly redundant, thus increasing the likelihood that a specific, relevant mediating response would be developed which would restrict the degree of stimulus generalization. Two groups of Ss, 6½ to 7½ and 10½ to 12 years old, were presented 15, 30, or 45 training trials in the spatial generalization task. The mean number of responses to the generalization lights decreased for older Ss and increased for the younger Ss with increasing amounts of training, thus supporting the predicted interaction between age and number of training trials.

The effects of providing a verbal mediator on stimulus generalization by preschool Ss was studied by Shepard (1956). After original training and a test for stimulus generalization, the Ss were provided with a common verbal response for the training stimulus and each of the test stimuli. With this type of training, the amount of generalization increased on the second test. Interestingly, however, the increase occurred for only half of the Ss; the other half showed no greater generalization after they had learned a common mediating response than they had in the first test. Even for the former Ss, the mediator was ineffective in raising the level of response for the test stimuli to that found for the training stimulus.

Generalization also may be increased if Ss are trained on multiple rather than single stimuli. White and Spiker (1960), assuming that training with variable stimuli would encourage Ss to generalize, trained an experimental group with three stimuli differing in hue and brightness and a control group with only one of the stimuli. Significantly more generalized responses were made by the experimental group, and younger Ss (42 to 54 months) showed more generalization than did older Ss (52 to 61 months). A final study (White, 1958) investigated the hypothesis that a novel stimulus differing from the training stimulus on only one dimension will elicit more generalized responses than will a novel stimulus differing on two dimensions. The test stimuli differed from the training stimuli in brightness, hue, or brightness and hue. As predicted, the test stimuli with the more variable attributes elicited fewer generalized responses than did the stimuli differing on only one dimension.

These studies leave the status of developmental changes in stimulus generalization unclear. They set forth the possibility that the broader generalization gradients found with younger and duller Ss may be due to motivational processes, but the validity of this argument cannot be assessed until more data are available. Studies with young children indicate that generalization may be increased by using intense training stimuli, extending the number of training trials, using multiple stimuli for training, and by providing a common verbal label for the training and test stimuli. The study by Tempone (1966) is a good example, however, of the desirability of testing children at different ages before concluding that a variable will influence generalization in a specific manner, for depending on the age of S, the variable may produce quite different results.

Extinction

There is only a small number of studies with children on the extinction of instrumental responses, in spite of the importance of this topic in behavior theory. Generally, the experimental variables have been selected from among those used in studies with lower animals. For example, greater resistance to extinction has been found with partial than with continuous reinforcement (e.g., Bijou, 1957; Lewis, 1952; Myers, 1960), with increasing amounts of training (Siegel and Foshee, 1953), and with greater numbers of incentives (Pumroy and Pumroy, 1961). The results are not in uniform agreement, however, for neither a partial reinforcement effect nor an incentive effect was found by Bruning (1964) when speed of response rather than number of responses was used to measure extinction, and Pumroy and Pumroy (1961) reported faster extinction with partial than with continuous reinforcement. The results of several large parametric studies may serve to resolve some of these discrepancies.

Kass (1962) used six percentages of reinforcement (0, 16⅔, 33⅓, 60, 80, and 100%) and Ss at four age levels (4, 6, 8, and 10 years) in a study with a simulated slot machine. The Ss were shown how to use the

machine, given 30 trials in which they could win pennies to purchase a prize, and then placed on extinction. The extinction trials continued until the Ss wanted to stop or until they had made 370 responses. Four-year-olds made a significantly smaller number of responses during the extinction trials than the three older groups, and, for all groups, the number of responses decreased significantly as the percentage of reinforcement received during training increased. Nearly as many responses were made by the 0% reinforcement group as by the group that had received 16⅔% reinforcement; thus the inverted U-shaped function between number of responses and percentage of reinforcement reported by Lewis (1952) was not found. The percentage of reinforcement received during training had equivalent effects at the four age levels.

A second study (Kass and Wilson, 1966) used the same general procedure, but the central variable was the number of training trials. Six- and 7-year-old Ss were given 3, 9, 21, 45, or 60 training trials with 33⅓ or 100% reinforcement. Responses made during extinction decreased significantly as the number of training trials increased and were uniformly higher following partial than following continuous reinforcement. An indication of the degree to which children persisted in this task is seen in the fact that after only three trials with partial reinforcement, an average of nearly 240 responses were made during extinction. The results were interpreted as providing support for a discrimination hypothesis of extinction, which states that extinction will be facilitated by the introduction of variables that increase the distinction between acquisition and extinction periods. Accordingly, it should be more difficult for Ss to discern that there has been a change in the schedule of reinforcement with partial than with continuous reinforcement and when only a restricted number of training trials has been presented.

Secondary Reinforcement

A closely related topic—its effects typically are assessed during extinction trials—is secondary reinforcement. Secondary reinforcement is assumed to occur when a stimulus, through its association with a reinforcer, acquires the capacity to influence behavior in a manner similar to that of the original reinforcer. The concept is used to explain the apparent strengthening of responses by what seem to be neutral stimuli, but a review of the experimental findings leaves the impression that it is an elusive process that is not readily demonstrated with human Ss. In fact, Longstreth (1966, p. 26), after reviewing the literature, concluded that "it becomes reasonable to argue that the phenomenon has not yet been clearly demonstrated with human Ss" and cites methodological and interpretive problems in many of the studies that seem to have yielded evidence for its occurrence. Longstreth's main criticisms are (1) there is a lack of evidence that groups receiving primary reinforcement behaved differently from those that did not, thus calling into question the basis for the conditioning of secondary reinforcers, and (2) the task may be constructed so that the sequence of responses leading to primary reinforcement serves to elicit the response on the subsequent trial rather than strengthen the preceding response. In view of the confused status of the concept, perhaps the most expeditious approach to reviewing the studies is to indicate the studies in which the effect has and has not been found.

A study by Sidowski, Kass, and Wilson (1965) illustrates some of the complexities. Their goal was to separate the potential cue and reinforcing functions of the neutral stimulus. The stimulus, a light, appeared (1) before and during response, (2) with the delivery of the primary reinforcer, a penny, or (3) during both the time of response and the delivery of the penny. The greatest number of responses occurred during extinction when the light was directly associated with primary reinforcement and the fewest, when the light served as a cue for response. The presentation of the light during both response and delivery of reinforcement resulted in an intermediate number of responses. The overall analysis of the data did not reveal a significant difference in the number of responses made when the light was present and when it was absent during the extinction trials, although a median split on number of responses indicated a greater number of Ss above the median when the light was present during the extinction trials.

The Myers (Myers and Myers, 1965) have published a large number of studies on secondary reinforcement and have been particularly interested in testing a discrimination hypothesis of secondary reinforcement. This hypothesis predicts that the strength of a response when primary reinforcement is absent is a function of the degree of similarity between the patterns of stimulation occurring in conditioning and in the test trials. From their studies, many of which are extremely elaborate, they have concluded that "the discrimination hypothesis accounts for data resulting from a choice between two responses, only one of which produces a secondary reinforcer. Under other test conditions, the method of conditioning is not relevant and secondary reinforcement is strongest when its percentage of occurrence is greatest" (p. 101). These studies received the brunt of Longstreth's (1966) criticisms.

The elusive nature of the secondary reinforcement effect is evident in a study by Kass, Beardshall, and Wilson (1966) where the apparatus and general procedure of the Sidowski, Kass, and Wilson (1965) study were used. A secondary reinforcement effect was not obtained. Seven- and eight-year-olds were tested with the simulated slot machine and either half or all of their responses were reinforced with a penny for 24 trials. A light was paired with the delivery of the penny for half of the Ss in each condition, and for the other half the light was absent. During the extinction trials a light appeared for half of the Ss and for the other half it did not. Only the percentage of reinforcement received during training exerted a significant effect on the number of responses made during extinction; the number was higher following 50% than following 100% reinforcement. Kass and Wilson (1966) reported a second nonconfirmatory study. Although number of training trials and percentage of reinforcement, the major variables investigated, significantly influenced performance, there was no indication that pairing a light with the delivery of the primary reinforcer had any significant effect on performance.

Longstreth (1966) has argued that what may appear at times to be a secondary reinforcement effect is actually the result of frustration that occurs when a cue is no longer followed by reinforcement, and he has presented several studies to support such an interpretation. For example, children were tested in a situation in which either a bright or a dim light led to reward and the other did not. Three stimulus conditions were operative during extinction: (1) the positive cue and the sound that accompanied the delivery of the reward; (2) the positive cue alone; and (3) the negative cue alone. Resistance to extinction was fastest in the first condition, a result opposite from that predicted from a secondary reinforcement hypothesis, but in line with predictions from a frustration position.

The final group of studies related to secondary reinforcement includes those of Nunnally and his associates, who have isolated some of the behavioral consequences of pairing a neutral stimulus with primary reinforcement. The apparatus used in most of these studies was a spin-wheel in which a pointer stopped on one of two or three nonsense syllables. When the pointer stopped on one, a penny was delivered; when it stopped on the others, the Ss had to give back a penny or nothing happened. In two studies (Nunnally, Duchnowski, and Parker, 1965; Nunnally, Stevens, and Hall, 1965) the nonsense syllable leading to reward was later described in more favorable terms than were the other nonsense syllables; it was more often expected to be associated with reward in another game; and it was looked at longer in a "looking box" than were the other nonsense syllables.

A study by Parker and Nunnally (1966) replicated these effects and found, in addition, that varying the percentage of reward in training affected the Ss' expectancies of receiving a reward from an object bearing the name of the nonsense syllable but did not influence other measures of response significantly. A final study (Nunnally, Knott, and Duchnowski, 1967) varied the amount of practice on the original task (5, 15, or 30 trials) and compared the effects of actually obtaining or relinquishing rewards versus defining the reward conditions as those that would prevail when the Ss played the game at a later time. Neither variable had a significant effect on performance. In this study, however, the nonsense syllable that led to reward or that was defined as the one that would lead to reward was evaluated more favorably and was more frequently expected to lead to reward in another game than were the other nonsense syllables, but perceptual responses, such as time spent viewing the syllable, eye movements, and pupillary responses, were not significantly different for the three types of nonsense syllable.

Research on secondary reinforcement is more disjointed than is the research in many other areas. The most dismaying aspect of the studies is that, with the same apparatus and procedure, the results are sometimes positive and more often negative. Because of the critical importance of the temporal relations among the various events involved in a study of secondary reinforcement, great care and control will be necessary before satisfactory statements about the utility of the concept can be made.

Behavior Modification

The discussion thus far has consisted of a review of laboratory studies, but the techniques of instrumental or operant conditioning also have been applied successfully to the treatment of a wide variety of behavior problems in children. The success appears to be attributable not only to the systematic control of the outcomes of behavior, but also to astute analyses of the effective conditions of reinforcement and to the confidence necessary to attack some of the most intractable types of behavior.

A study by Baer (1962) illustrates how a common form of undesired behavior, thumb-sucking, is influenced by the systematic withdrawal of positive reinforcement. Two Ss with a high incidence of thumb-sucking were shown animated cartoons. Whenever one of the Ss sucked his thumb the projector was turned off; the film continued only when S removed his thumb from his mouth. Thumb-sucking decreased in this S, but not in the second S, run in a yoked fashion with the first S but for whom the withdrawal and presentation of reinforcement were not contingent upon the thumb-sucking response. Lovaas, Freitag, Gold, and Kassorla (1965) have shown that withdrawal of reinforcement may also be effective in modifying a much more severe form of behavior, self-mutilation. Adults typically are astonished by such behavior and attempt to intercede by responding to the child when he commits such acts. The Lovaas et al. study clearly indicates the frequency of self-mutilation can be effectively decreased if the adult ignores rather than responds to such acts.

Noxious stimuli have also been used with

success. Lovaas, Schaeffer, and Simmons (1965) associated the presence of an adult with the cessation of electric shock. Autistic children, who previously had displayed minimal awareness of adults, learned to approach and embrace adults through this procedure. Shock has been used as a last resort and only with the most severely disturbed children; reliance usually is placed on application of positive forms of reinforcement. In a typical study, Patterson, Jones, Whittier, and Wright (1965) attempted to increase a hyperactive child's attention to what was going on in school. The child was equipped with a small earphone and a buzz in the earphone was established as a secondary reinforcer by being paired with candy during preliminary training. The child and the class were told that if the child sat still all would receive candy. A decrease in the frequency of the child's non-attentive responses was noted when a buzz was presented following each 10-second interval in which the child was attentive.

Many other studies of behavior modification with children could be discussed, such as those directed at increasing sociability (Allen, Hart, Buell, Harris, and Wolf, 1964), reducing aggression (Brown and Elliott, 1965), treating enuresis (Ellis, 1963), eliminating phobias (Lazarus, 1960), teaching autistic children to speak (Lovaas, Berberich, Perloff, and Schaeffer, 1966), and improving reading skills (Staats and Butterfield, 1965). Such a discussion would serve primarily to illustrate how extensively the techniques have been applied. The effects of the studies of behavior modification on child psychology have been healthful, for they offer vivid, and sometimes dramatic examples of how principles derived from laboratory experimentation may be applied successfully to the solution of practical problems.

DISCRIMINATION LEARNING

In contrast to studies of conditioning, where the approach is often highly empirical, interest in the study of children's discrimination learning began when child psychologists attempted to find out how well Spence's (1936, 1956) treatment of discrimination learning could predict the performance of children. It did not take long to see that the child was too complex for the model that had

been developed to account for the behavior of nonverbal organisms. This is not surprising, for the manifest simplicity of a discrimination learning task conceals a bewildering array of psychological processes. In a typical study, all that is asked of the child is that he select the correct stimulus from an array of two or more stimuli. Each time he chooses the stimulus deemed to be correct by the experimenter he discovers some prize or other indication that he has been correct. Eventually, if the problem is of an appropriate level of difficulty, he begins to choose the correct stimulus consistently. However, in presenting the problem to the child, a number of implicit assumptions are made. It is assumed that he is capable of attending to the relevant stimuli, of inhibiting attention to irrelevant cues, of discriminating the differences among the stimuli, of remembering the stimulus chosen, of being appropriately influenced by the consequence of his response, of being motivated to persist in trying to be correct, and of not elaborating the problem so that it becomes more difficult than it actually is. Thus what is often assumed to be one of the simplest forms of learning turns out to have many complex aspects.

Characteristics of the Stimuli

It is obvious that gross differences among stimuli will influence the rate of discrimination learning. But subtle differences among stimuli and their physical and temporal relation to response and reward also have been found to have significant effects. Since most of the studies have used visual materials, the discussion will center on visual stimuli.

The dimensionality of stimuli may vary; that is they may be two-dimensional patterns, planometric (depth is minimized), or stereometric (all three dimensions are fully represented). The influence of this attribute is clearly demonstrated in three studies, all with 3-year-old Ss, which found large differences in the average number of trials required by the children to learn a two-choice size discrimination: 335.8 (Kuenne, 1946), 54.8 (Alberts and Ehrenfreund, 1951), and 13.6 (Stevenson and Langford, 1957). Although the experimental procedures differed in several ways, a critical difference appears to be the way in which the stimuli were presented. In the first study the stimuli were patterns mounted on the doors of the boxes containing the incentives; in the second the incentive boxes were equipped with square doors of different sizes; and in the third the stimuli were blocks which S lifted to reveal the incentive. The use of blocks or doors as stimuli may have aided in divorcing the stimuli from a common background and in increasing the number of cues available to the Ss by requiring them to manipulate the stimuli. Stevenson and McBee's (1958) later finding that a three-choice size-discrimination was learned more readily when the stimuli were stereometric than when they were planometric or patterns affirms the importance of stimulus dimensionality on learning, as does the finding of Dornbush and Winnick (1966) that a square and rectangle are discriminated more easily when they are represented by stereometric as contrasted to planometric objects. The only contradictory evidence is found in a study by Kerpelman (1967) in which children learned to discriminate among irregular pentagons more rapidly when they were planometric than when they were stereometric. In such a complex discrimination the addition of a third dimension may have provided additional cues that confused rather than aided the Ss.

Spatial relations between stimulus, response, and reward may exert a significant effect on rate of learning. Murphy and Miller (1959) found that fewer trials were required by 10-year-olds to learn a two-choice discrimination if the cue and the locus of response and reward were contiguous than if they were separated. Similar findings were obtained in a more elaborate study with preschool Ss by Jeffrey and Cohen (1964). Learning was most rapid in a condition where the stimulus, response, and reinforcement were contiguous (S lifted a block to find the reward), and little change in performance occurred when all three components were separated spatially, or when there was contiguity of stimulus and reward or response and reward with separation of the other component. Since a high level of learning occurred in a group for which the stimulus and response were contiguous but the locus of reward was separated, it was concluded that the most important combination was the contiguity of stimulus and response. The results support the notion that Ss often restrict their attention to the locus of response; thus if the stimulus is near this area, differences among the stimuli are more likely to be observed.

Another important influence on rate of learning is the procedure by which the stimuli are presented. Two common procedures have been used in studies of discrimination learning: the simultaneous discrimination, as previously discussed, and the successive discrimination. Two or more different stimuli are presented on each trial in the simultaneous problem, whereas in the successive problem only one of the stimuli is presented on each trial. In the first, S's task is to learn to choose the stimulus that leads to reinforcement (e.g., the black stimulus); in the second, S must learn to make different responses to the various stimuli (e.g., choose "right" when the stimuli are black, "left" when they are white). The simultaneous problem has been found to be easier for children in a number of studies (Erickson and Lipsitt, 1960; Horowitz and Armentrout, 1965; Jeffrey, 1961; Rieber, 1964; Spiker and Lubker, 1965), but this is not always the case. Although the simultaneous problem may be easier than the successive problem when response is made directly to the stimuli, the opposite effect has been found when the stimulus and response are spatially separated (Lipsitt, 1961).

It appears that any procedure which increases the likelihood that Ss will compare and contrast the stimuli and thereby isolate their distinctive and relevant characteristics will result in faster learning. Evidence to support such a conclusion has been reported by Rieber (1966b), who forced Ss to delay their response following the simultaneous or successive presentation of stimuli (colored lights). When there was stimulus feedback, that is, when the stimulus reappeared as S responded to it or when all stimuli reappeared as S responded, the simultaneous problem was easier than the successive problem. When there was no feedback, the successive problem was easier. It was assumed that the reappearance of the stimuli emphasized their relevant characteristics, but without feedback the importance of the relevant dimension—color—was obscured by the simultaneous presentation of stimuli whose position also differed on different trials.

A direct test of the possibility that the presence of irrelevant dimensions may retard learning has been reported by Lubker (1967). Three groups of 8- to 10-year-olds were presented a two-choice simultaneous discrimination problem in which the relevant dimension was form. Blocks varying in form, brightness, and size were used for all groups of Ss, and the blocks were combined in different fashions to constitute three series of pairs of blocks which differed in the number of irrelevant dimensions presented. For one group, each pair of stimuli differed only in form; in a second, they also differed in brightness; and in a third, they differed in form, brightness, and size. Significantly slower learning occurred when either one or two irrelevant dimensions were present. The same result was found in a very similar study by Osler and Kofsky (1965) with 4-, 6-, and 8-year-olds in a discrimination task involving stimuli that varied in form, size, and color. Developmental changes were found in the children's tendencies to respond to the irrelevant cues. When the sequences of Ss' responses were analyzed, it was found that the two youngest groups responded more frequently to the irrelevant dimensions and to position cues than did the 8-year-olds.

The degree to which learning is retarded by the presence of irrelevant information is one index of how information may be used by children in guiding their response. Another index is the degree to which learning is facilitated when the superfluous information is redundant rather than irrelevant. Eimas (1965) gave kindergarten children a series of two-trial problems in which the cues varied in a systematic manner between the first and second trials. Performance improved in an orderly manner on trial 2 as the number of redundant cues increased. Even though the second problem could be responded to correctly on the basis of differences in one of the components, learning was more efficient when compound cues were available.

The remarkable degree to which children scan stimuli in their efforts to solve problems is seen in a study by White (1965) in which the cues were ever-changing. For example, if on a particular trial one of the two stimuli included a small square superimposed on a large square, only the small square along with

two vertical lines functioned as this stimulus on the subsequent trial. When the child responded correctly on this trial, the stimulus was transformed into one vertical line with a second line attached to a circle on the next trial, and so on through multiple changes, with each new stimulus retaining only a portion of the attributes of its immediate predecessor. Ten- and eleven-year-olds were capable of tracking such variations when they occurred for the positive stimulus, and although the Ss seemingly paid little attention to such changes in the negative stimulus, three-fourths of the Ss subsequently were capable of learning a problem in which changes were made in both the positive and negative stimuli. A less complex, related design was used by Walk and Saltz (1965), in which the number of positive and negative cues differed. Eight- and 9-year-olds performed better when there was a single positive than when there was a single negative cue, again indicating a greater tendency for children to be influenced by variations in the positive cue.

From this discussion we might deduce that children utilize all aspects of the stimulus situation with equal effectiveness in learning a discrimination problem. That they do not is illustrated in a series of studies in which the relevant cue coincides with or is discordant with the child's preferences. For example, after the fourth year children generally prefer form over color, even though below that age they tend to prefer color over form as a means of classifying stimuli (Suchman and Trabasso, 1966a). Suchman and Trabasso (1966b) have demonstrated with 10-year-olds that children who, in pretesting, showed a preference for form over color later learned to sort cards faster by form than by color, with the opposite effect occurring for children who preferred color over form. Smiley and Weir (1966) and Mumbauer and Odom (1967) have demonstrated similar effects in studies of color and form discrimination with kindergarten and preschool Ss. In a related experiment, Wolff (1966) found that some 7-year-old children preferred height and some preferred brightness as a means of classifying stimuli. When the children later were presented a two-choice discrimination utilizing stimuli that differed both in height and brightness, those who had preferred brightness learned a brightness discrimination more rapidly than a form discrimination and those who had preferred form learned the form discrimination more rapidly. Shepp (1963) found another example of how the choice of stimuli may affect learning in a study where pieces of candy were used both as discriminative stimuli and as reinforcers. More rapid learning occurred when the reward was candy of the same form and color as the positive cue than when it was dissimilar to both the positive and negative cues, or when it was identical to the negative cue. Thus the tendency to select a stimulus was greater when it was identical to the one functioning as the reinforcer.

These studies of stimulus factors indicate that children's performance cannot be subsumed under a theory such as Spence's, which conceptualizes discrimination learning as the result of incremental changes in the strength of approach and avoidance tendencies occurring as a consequence of reinforcement and nonreinforcement. Stimuli appear to function as sources of information for children, rather than as cues that elicit differential tendencies to respond. Seemingly small changes in the stimuli and the manner in which they are presented may produce striking differences in the rate of learning, and, on the other hand, radical changes in the stimuli do not necessarily mean that the child will fail to find relevant characteristics in the stimuli that provide a basis for correct response. Furthermore, the results of studies in which data from individual children are considered or in which the course of learning is plotted "backwards" from the point at which criterion is met indicate that discrimination learning may not be a gradual process. In either of these cases, evidence has been found for an initial plateau in which little improvement in performance takes place, followed by a period of rapid acceleration in the frequency of correct response (Rieber, 1966a; White and Plum, 1964; Zeaman and House, 1963). Such curves have been interpreted as indicating that two stages are involved in discrimination learning: an early phase in which S learns to attend to and discriminate among the stimuli, and a second, rapid phase in which the correct response is attached to the positive stimulus.

An important question that is not con-sidered by such two-stage models is how S discriminates among the stimuli. Is it a result of learning the distinctive features of the objects that are to be discriminated, or is it a result of matching sensory data to schema of objects that have been built up and refined through experience?

Pick (1965), studying reactions of Ss to six letterlike forms and their transformations, found that the detection of distinctive features may be the necessary and sufficient condition for improvement in discrimination when simultaneous comparison of objects is required. Pick, Pick, and Thomas (1966), employing essentially the same design and similar stimuli in a study of cross-modal transfer, obtained results supporting Pick's earlier observations. These studies are discussed in detail in Chapter 13 of this book.

What appears to emerge is a three- rather than two-process model of discrimination learning: the child must learn to attend to the stimuli, isolate the distinctive features that differentiate the stimuli, and attach the appropriate response to the stimulus leading to reward. The studies reviewed have been concerned primarily with the first two processes and indicate that the characteristics of the stimuli may facilitate such learning when the situation involves few irrelevant cues, the cues are redundant, the stimuli are presented near the locus of response, the mode of presentation provides an opportunity for contrasting the stimuli, and when the reinforced cue is in accord with the child's preferences.

Stimulus Pretraining

Other explorations of the influence of stimulus factors on discrimination learning have been concerned with the degree to which stimulus pretraining influences subsequent discrimination learning. These studies have been directed at assessing the utility of various theoretical analyses of discrimination learning. The two interpretations of the effects of stimulus pretraining on later learning that have received the greatest attention are those dealing with the development of observing responses and with the acquired distinctiveness of cues. The first postulates that learning may be facilitated if S learns to make observing responses "which, when made to one or the other of a given pair of stimulus complexes which are different, consistently results in distinctive stimulation from those two complexes" (Kurtz, 1955, p. 290). According to this view, pretraining may aid later learning by directing S's attention to the properties or dimensions of the stimuli that subsequently provide the cue for differential response.

The hypothesis of acquired distinctiveness of cues has been offered as a mechanism for accounting for the more rapid learning that occurs when Ss, in pretraining, have attached distinctive verbal or motor responses to the discriminative stimuli. It is assumed that the distinctive responses reduce stimulus generalization by making the total stimulus complex associated with each cue more distinctive. The stimulus complex is viewed as consisting of the external stimulus and the stimuli produced by the distinctive verbal or motor responses. A complementary hypothesis dealing with the acquired equivalence of cues is applied when a common verbal or motor response is attached to the discriminative stimuli during pretraining. In this case, stimulus generalization is assumed to be increased and the efficiency of learning impaired by the presence of an element common to all of the discriminative stimuli.

A third hypothesis was proposed by Spiker (1956a), who suggested that verbal responses attached to the discriminative stimuli during pretraining may facilitate later learning by making it easier for the S to rehearse the correct associations during the intertrial intervals. Although various forms of preliminary experience with the discriminative stimuli have been found to aid later learning, it has not been possible to design studies that offer exclusive support for a particular hypothesis. (For a detailed review of these studies, see Cantor, 1965.)

A typical experiment is that of Norcross and Spiker (1957) in which preschool children were pretrained with pictures of faces. One group learned distinctive names for pictures of two female faces; a second group learned distinctive names for pictures of two male faces; and the third had to respond to the female faces by saying "same" or "different," depending upon whether or not the faces were identical. Following pretraining the Ss were presented a two-choice discrimination task in which the female faces

were the discriminative stimuli. The first group performed significantly better on the discrimination task than the second or third groups, but the latter groups did not differ significantly in incidence of correct response. The possession of verbal labels thus enhanced performance on the discrimination task, but learning to orient to the distinctive features of the discriminative stimuli did not result in more efficient performance than did pretraining with a different set of stimuli.

Several of the difficulties that arise in research on stimulus pretraining are evident in this study. The Ss had more difficulty in learning to associate names with the female faces than in determining whether or not the pair was identical, thus the amount of pretraining experience with the stimuli differed for the first and third group. Second, it is questionable whether learning names for the pair of male faces constituted irrelevant pretraining, for the discovery of the bases of the differences between these faces involved comparison of the same facial features as was required later in the discrimination learning task. It is therefore impossible to determine whether or not a particular theoretical position was supported by the results of this study. In addition, the lack of a control group receiving no pretraining makes it impossible to ascertain whether the results reflected facilitation in the performance of the first group or interference in the performance of the last two groups.

Two additional problems encountered in studies of stimulus pretraining were avoided in a design used by Norcross (1958) to study the effects of similarity of previously acquired stimulus names on discrimination learning. A within-Ss design controlled for nonspecific transfer resulting from the effects of warm-up and learning-to-learn. If some Ss are required to learn names of the stimuli during pretraining and others are not, later differences in discrimination learning may be a result of the Ss' prior learning experience in the experimental setting. In Norcross' study, each S learned distinctive names to one pair of stimuli and similar names to a second pair during pretraining. As would be predicted from the hypothesis of acquired distinctiveness of cues, a higher level of performance was found for the pair of stimuli with distinctive names in the subsequent discrimination learning task involving both pairs of stimuli.

Reese (1960) extended Norcross' study to include different amounts of pretraining. In a carefully counterbalanced design, Ss were given no pretraining on one pair of stimuli, moderate pretraining on a second, and extended pretraining on a third. Although level of pretraining had no generally significant effects on discrimination learning, the pair of stimuli with distinctive names elicited better performance than did the pair not presented during the pretraining trials. For names of intermediate similarity, a high level of pretraining produced better performance than no pretraining. No facilitation was found with either level of pretraining when the names were extremely similar. Thus whether or not distinctive names facilitated learning depended on how well the names had been learned. A second study by Reese (1961a) also revealed no significant differences in ease of learning following different degrees of pretraining. Only in the early phases of test performance did the presence or absence of prior experience with the test stimuli influence the children's choices.

A somewhat different approach to evaluating the effects of stimulus pretraining was taken by White (1961), who assumed that pretraining with varied stimuli, each consistently yielding reward, would induce Ss to minimize or overlook stimulus differences in a later discrimination learning task. Preschool children were given 24 trials with (1) one of the discriminative stimuli, (2) a stimulus that was not used in the discrimination task, or (3) three different stimuli, one of which was included in the discrimination task. Other Ss were given eight trials with one of the discriminative stimuli or were given no pretraining. (The discriminative stimulus used in pretraining was always the stimulus that led to reinforcement in the discrimination learning task.) The facilitating effects of warm-up were reflected in the fact that any form of pretraining resulted in more efficient learning than did no pretraining. Earlier experience with varied stimuli led to poorer performance than did experience with the discriminative stimulus, but the number of the pretraining trials was not a significant variable in influencing performance. The conclusion that pretraining with varied stimuli had a detrimental effect on later performance is marred, how-ever, by the fact that the performance of Ss pretrained with the irrelevant stimulus differed significantly only from that of the Ss given no pretraining.

A final set of three studies indicates that stimulus pretraining may or may not be helpful, depending upon the consequences of the responses made during the pretraining period. Spiker (1959) presented preschool Ss with a two-part discrimination learning task. One group was given 24 preliminary trials in which a bright light was the positive cue and a dim light was the negative cue, followed by 24 trials in which a medium-bright light was substituted for the dim light. The study was undertaken to test the hypothesis that the use of highly similar stimuli during the preliminary phase would retard the development of appropriate orienting responses. The fact that the first group performed at a higher level during the terminal 24 trials than did the second group supports such a hypothesis, but another plausible explanation of the results is that the difficult task was frustrating and that frustration-produced responses disrupted subsequent performance.

Possible frustrating effects of pretraining also were found by Stevenson and Pirojnikoff (1958), who gave preschool Ss pretraining trials with all three of the forms that were later used in a discrimination learning task. One group of Ss received 100% reinforcement; that is, all choices made during pretraining were reinforced. Another group received 50% nondifferential reinforcement, and a third group received 0% reinforcement. A fourth group received no pretraining. The results differ from those found by White (1961) where pretraining was given with only one of the discriminative stimuli, for the 100% group and the control group showed equivalent rates of learning. Both groups learned more effectively, however, than did the 50% and 0% groups. The effects of frustration were evident in the performance of the last two groups, thus either inconsistent or no reinforcement during stimulus pretraining may produce effects that interfere with later learning. Such a possibility was supported in a study by Steigman and Stevenson (1960), where the pretraining was given with stimuli different from those used in the discrimination learning task. A low level of reinforcement during pretraining resulted in significantly poorer performance on a discrimination learning task than did high levels of reinforcement during pretraining.

The conclusions that can be derived from these studies are of relatively low order. It has been extraordinarily difficult to establish control groups that make it possible to interpret the results as providing definitive support for a particular hypothesis. Whatever the mechanism, there seems to be little disagreement that later discrimination learning is facilitated if the S learns distinctive names for the stimuli during pretraining and that such variables as the relative distinctiveness of the names and the amount of pretraining significantly affect the degree of facilitation that will occur. Further, any pretraining that increases the likelihood that the Ss will discover the distinctive features of the stimuli appears to facilitate later learning. Prior familiarization with the discriminative stimuli is not in itself sufficient to produce facilitation, for the effects of such familiarization depend upon such conditions as the reinforcement provided during pretraining and the other types of stimuli that are presented.

Reinforcement and Incentive Effects

Implicit in the design of any study of discrimination learning is the fact that response to only one member of the set of stimuli will be designated as correct. The experimenter must then decide how the child will be informed of the appropriateness of his response. A review by Bijou and Sturges (1959) of the types of stimulus and event that have been used as positive reinforcers indicates that information about the correctness of response has been imparted in a variety of ways, and in many studies the incentive conditions selected by the experimenter have been found to play a significant role in determining the course of children's performance.

Children in many ways are uncharitable Ss, for they often fail to behave in the manner predicted by learning theories or, in some cases, even by common sense. The vagaries of their behavior are strikingly evident in some of the studies of reinforcement effects on discrimination learning. A good example is the study by Miller and Estes (1961) in which 9-year-old boys received either a signal light, 1 cent, or 50 cents for each correct response in a two-choice discrimination task. The last two groups also had to forfeit the same amounts for each error. Not only did the Ss given a monetary reward perform significantly more poorly than the control group, but the group receiving 50 cents for correct response performed no better than the group receiving only 1 cent. How can such a finding be interpreted? First, elementary school children enter most experimental situations with a high level of motivation to perform well. Although they may have some trepidation about the strange situation, and indeed older children often appear to be very anxious about how well they will perform, such concerns usually are dispelled by the benign characteristics of most learning tasks. Thus, in contrast to what occurs when lower animals are used as Ss, the experimenter is faced with an eager and expectant S whose behavior is not easily controlled by physical sources of reinforcement. It is sometimes the case, and this appears to have occurred in the Miller and Estes study, that physical reinforcement is distracting and results in the S's dividing his attention between the accumulated rewards and the discriminative stimuli.

The Miller and Estes results have been substantiated in other studies, such as one by Terrell, Durkin, and Wiesley (1959), in which middle-class Ss learned a two-choice size discrimination more rapidly when a correct response was followed by a light than when it was followed by the light and a piece of candy. However, the performance of lower-class Ss included in the study places an important restriction on the results obtained with middle-class Ss, for the lower-class Ss performed more effectively when they were reinforced with candy than when they merely received a signal for correct response. It was assumed in designing this study that middle- and lower-class children differ in the degree to which they have learned to value nonmaterial incentives, and the significant interaction between social class and incentive effects supports such an assumption.

Subtle differences in incentive conditions may change the outcome of a study. Terrell (1958), for example, found no significant difference in performance among Ss whose correct responses were reinforced by a signal light, a piece of candy, or by allowing Ss to transfer a bean from one jar to another with the expectation that they could trade the beans for a bag of candy when they had enough of them. The signal light also followed correct response for the last two groups. A fourth group of Ss, who simply were promised a bag of candy after they had made the light go on enough times, performed more poorly than any of the other groups. Evidently, the vagueness of a promise with no accompanying evidence of progress or indication of what constituted attainment resulted in a deterioration of performance. Or was it that the children in the "promise" group were prohibited from making meaningful manipulative responses that, in themselves, may constitute a source of reinforcement? This possibility was studied by Terrell (1959), who told the Ss to imagine they received a piece of candy after each correct response and to put the imaginary candy in a make-believe bag that later could be exchanged for a real bag of candy. The Ss who had engaged in manipulation of the imagined objects learned a two-choice discrimination in significantly fewer trials than Ss who simply were promised a bag of candy when they made the light go on enough times.

These results do not mean that children are insensitive to the presence of material incentives in a discrimination learning task, since the studies typically involved a single testing session and arbitrary assignment of the child to a particular incentive group. Conditions can be arranged to reveal significant differences in performance as a function of the incentives used. Brackbill and Jack (1958) made the reasonable assumption that the effectiveness of different objects as incentives or reinforcers may differ, depending upon individual preferences. In their study, kindergarten boys either were allowed to select the incentive they wished to work for from among a group of three, or they arbitrarily were assigned one incentive. As predicted, the variability in the average number of trials required to meet criterion for learning a three-choice discrimination problem was greater for the group whose incentive was assigned.

Another effort to assess differential effects of incentives is a study with 10-year-olds by Witryol, Tyrrel, and Snowden (1964), who used a five- choice discrimination task. Each of the five stimuli was consistently paired with one of five incentives: a piece of bubble gum, a penny, a toy charm, verbal reinforcement, or nothing. Two indices of possible differences in the effects of the incentives were the rank-order of frequency of choices of each stimulus and changes in the frequency of choices across trials. The stimulus yielding a penny was chosen most frequently and the stimulus yielding nothing was, reasonably, chosen least frequently. The Ss selected the other three stimuli with roughly equal frequency. However, for boys, only choices of the stimulus that yielded a penny increased significantly across trials, and for girls, only the stimulus associated with supportive comments from a young male experimenter.

Two other studies found that a higher level of performance may occur if there is a possibility that the incentive will be retrieved by the experimenter when S makes an incorrect response. Brackbill and O'Hara (1958) gave kindergarten boys 15 pieces of candy and told some of the Ss that each time they made a correct choice they would find another piece of candy, but that each time they made an incorrect choice they would have to return a piece to the experimenter. Another group was not required to return the candy when they made incorrect choices. Learning was significantly faster for the first group, perhaps because the value of an incentive is increased when there is a possibility of losing it. But it is also possible that the introduction of a mild form of punishment results in S's paying closer attention to the discriminative stimuli.

Similar results were found by Stevenson, Weir, and Zigler (1959). In an effort to vary the amount of pre-experimental satiation for the incentive objects, the Ss were given either 5, 10, 20, or 40 colored stickers in the pre-experimental period. The Ss received a sticker for each correct response and half of the Ss were required to return a sticker after each incorrect response. Only those groups given the two smaller numbers of stickers and required to relinquish a sticker following incorrect response tended to learn the three-choice successive discrimination problem.

Over 80% of these Ss reached the criterion for learning, but 30% or fewer of the Ss in the other groups did so. The effects of introducing a penalty for incorrect response were dependent upon the number of incentive objects the Ss had available.

Facilitating effects of mild forms of punishment also have been found in studies where the punishment involved more than the penalty of returning prizes for incorrect responses. Penney and Lupton (1961), in line with the preceding results, found a higher level of performance in a two-choice pattern discrimination when children received candy for correct response and an unpleasant tone for incorrect response than when they received only candy for correct response. In fact, the second group continued to perform at a chance level throughout the task. A third group, which received only the tone for incorrect responses, showed the highest level of performance.

In a related experiment, Spence and Segner (1967) found that children presented candy for correct response and a buzzer for incorrect response learned a series of object discriminations more effectively than did a group receiving only reward for correct response. No significant difference was found between the performance of the group given both candy and the buzzer and a third group given only the buzzer. The study included complementary groups for whom the words "right" and "wrong" constituted the reinforcers. There were no significant differences in performance among the verbal reinforcement groups. Of additional interest is the finding that there was no significant difference in the effectiveness of material and nonmaterial rewards for middle- and lower-class children, a result different from that found by Terrell, Durkin, and Wiesley (1959). Spence and Segner were careful to point out the informational value of the presence or absence of reinforcement for a particular response; thus the Ss' set was presumably quite different in this study from that of the Ss in the other studies discussed. The interpretation favored by the authors for the poor performance of the candy-only group was that the delivery and accumulation of rewards may distract attention from the task and thereby interfere with performance.

Silence as used in studies such as the preceding one may play a different role, depending upon whether it is paired with the experimenter's saying "right" or "wrong." Offenbach (1966) has shown that silence acquires reinforcement value in a direction opposite to the verbal statement with which it is combined. That is, silence may acquire a positive value when the word "wrong" follows incorrect responses and a negative value when "right" follows correct responses. Silence therefore may impart different information, depending upon the S's expectations or prior experience.

Finally we consider what would happen if an intense form of punishment were used. Strong electric shock has been found to have strong effects on learning in lower animals; Nelson, Reid, and Travers (1965) attempted to determine whether such a strong aversive stimulus would result in similar effects with children. In a study that probably will not be repeated because of its ethical problems, children received either a tone, the words "right" or "wrong," or strong electric shock as feedback for correct and incorrect responses in tasks where one of two responses had to be associated with a series of words, or of combinations of letters or numbers. Despite the fact that the shock was so strong that it produced tears in some children, no significant differences in rate of learning were found among the various conditions. In contrast to animals, children appeared to respond to the informational value of the shock, rather than to its aversive qualities, in directing their response.

These studies, and others to be discussed in later sections, indicate the inappropriateness of mechanistic interpretations of the role of reinforcers and incentives in children's discrimination learning. Reward does not necessarily facilitate the acquisition of the correct response, nor does punishment necessarily decrease the tendency to make incorrect responses. Because children are social organisms who are highly dependent upon the manner in which the adult structures the task and who enter the experimental situation with preferences and great varieties of prior experiences, their interpretation of what is defined as a reward or a punishment and the way their performance is influenced by them may be very complex. As Spence and Segner (1967, p. 37) have pointed out, "it is becoming increasingly apparent that reinforcers do not have a simple set of properties that affect performance in a uniform manner but may play a number of complex roles, depending on such variables as the characteristics of the subjects, the task, the nature of the reinforcers themselves, and the precise manner in which they are introduced into the situation."

Delay of Reinforcement

There is a great deal of evidence that a delay in the time of reinforcement retards animal learning, but the findings with children are inconsistent. The majority of the studies of children's discrimination learning have found negligible effects of delaying reinforcement, but differences in the performance of groups receiving immediate and delayed reinforcement have been found in some studies. Several examples reveal the disparities among these sets of results. In a study by Ross, Hetherington, and Wray (1965) delays as long as 18 seconds did not significantly influence performance when the stimuli were not visible during the delay period; when the stimuli were visible, learning was retarded by a 12- but not by an 18-second delay. Hetherington, Ross, and Pick (1964) found significantly slower learning when the delay was 12 seconds, but not when it was 1.5 or 6 seconds. No effects of delays of 3 or 6 seconds were found by Erickson and Lipsitt (1960) in a three-choice discrimination problem. In a summary of seven studies by Brackbill and her associates involving 14 comparisons, immediate reinforcement resulted in faster acquisition in only one case (Brackbill, Wagner, and Wilson, 1964). On the other hand, two studies of form and size discrimination have found significantly slower learning for groups receiving a 7-second delay than for those receiving immediate reinforcement (Terrell and Ware, 1961; Ware and Terrell, 1961).

The last two studies offered a clue as to why, in some cases, delay may result in less efficient learning. In these two studies, 5- and 6-year-olds were presented simultaneous form and size discriminations; one problem was coupled with immediate reinforcement and the other with delayed reinforcement. The children seemed to lose interest in the problem involving delayed reinforcement. The

possibility that the detrimental effects of delayed reinforcement may be attributable to inattention resulting from boredom or frustration has been investigated in several subsequent studies. Fagan and Witryol (1966) found that such effects could be eliminated if the Ss were instructed to look at the source of reinforcement during the period of delay. Maintaining attention to the source of reinforcement presumably made it less likely that interfering responses would be learned during the delay period. Other Ss receiving delayed reward but no instructions about what to do during the delay period performed more poorly than a group receiving immediate reinforcement. Further support for the importance of the delay period as a time when interfering—or facilitating—responses can be made was found by Wright and Smothergill (1967). Immediate reinforcement was less effective than delayed reinforcement if active observing behavior occurred during the delay period.

The frequent failure to find significant effects of delay of reward with children thus may be a result of children's ability to maintain appropriate orienting responses during the period of delay—an incomparably more difficult feat for animals. Another related factor may be children's ability to bridge the period of delay with forms of self-instruction or mediating responses. A tendency for younger children to be more strongly affected in a negative manner by delay than older children has been noted by Terrell (1965), which may indicate that younger, less verbally facile children are less likely to make such responses spontaneously than are older children.

Brackbill and her associates have demonstrated a secondary gain from delay of reinforcement. In a series of studies they found no significant effects of delay of reinforcement on acquisition but consistent facilitating effects on retention of a discrimination. For example, Brackbill (1964) attempted to determine whether the introduction of a distracting task during the delay period would diminish the effects of delay on retention. The Ss were required to copy numbers during the 10-second delay between response and reinforcement. The immediately reinforced Ss were also required to copy numbers, but after the reinforcement had been delivered.

A 20-second intertrial interval was used for all groups. In contrast to previous findings, the Ss learned a series of 18 two-choice discriminations more slowly with immediate than with delayed reinforcement. Surprisingly, the delay group performed at the same level during acquisition trials as another delay group, which did not perform an intervening task. As was found in the previous studies, significantly greater numbers of trials were required to relearn the discrimination 1 or 8 days after acquisition by the Ss who received immediate reinforcement during training than by those for whom reinforcement had been delayed. Despite the consistency of this finding across a number of studies, its explication awaits additional research.

Response Biases

The discrimination learning situation may elicit response biases in children which are important considerations in evaluating performance. In a two-choice task with undiscriminable stimuli and nondifferential reward, Jeffrey and Cohen (1965) reported that 3-year-olds tend to persevere in making position responses, whereas 4-year-olds tend to alternate their choices between the stimuli. Schusterman (1963) has reported similar effects for 3- and 5-year-olds, but 10-year-olds were found to demonstrate neither response pattern. Rieber (1966a) repeated the Jeffrey and Cohen study with 7- and 9-year-old Ss. Nearly three-fourths of the Ss showed alternating behavior when either response was consistently reinforced, but the number of alternations dropped significantly under schedules of nondifferential partial reinforcement. Considering the three studies, it appears that a preference for alternation is present at age 4, persists through age 8, and drops out by age 10.

Stevenson and Weir (1961) investigated the effect of initial reinforcement or nonreinforcement of response in a three-choice spatial discrimination task on the tendency to repeat the response on the subsequent trial. At age 3 over 80% of the Ss repeated the response that had led to reinforcement on the previous trial, but by age 9 fewer than 30% did so. When the initial response was not reinforced, fewer than 50% of the 3-year-olds and practically none of the 5-, 7-, and 9-year-olds included in the study repeated the response.

Greene (1964) reported similar results in a study of preschool and kindergarten children. The Ss were presented varying numbers of trials in a two-choice color discrimination problem before a third, novel stimulus was introduced. On trial 2 nearly 70% of the Ss shifted their response to the stimulus that was not chosen on trial 1. A similar percentage of Ss chose the novel stimulus when it was introduced, and the tendency to shift to this stimulus was not influenced significantly by the number of prior trials with the two discriminative stimuli. In another study using the same problem, Greene and Terrell (1964) found that over 70% of the Ss in grades 1, 3, and 5 shifted their response on trial 2 to the stimulus that had not been chosen on the previous trial. In contrast to the Stevenson and Weir study, however, no differences in this tendency were found across grades, and a greater tendency was found to shift response after reinforcement than after nonreinforcement. The bases for the discrepancies are not clear.

These are paradoxical results for a reinforcement theorist. Reinforcement does not increase the tendency of older children to repeat a response; it has the opposite effect of increasing the likelihood that an alternative response will be made. Three-year-olds, however, are a different matter; they do behave as they should according to traditional concepts of reinforcement. This, it will be seen, is the first of many instances where the behavior of preschool children, but not of older Ss, conforms to reinforcement theory. The interpretation of the performance of the older Ss appears to require the introduction of new concepts and several alternatives have been offered. Children may switch their response to the new stimulus out of curiosity to discover what would happen if it were chosen; children may have learned to expect that adults are unlikely to reinforce a particular choice consistently; or children may wish to be "fair" and give each alternative an equal chance of being selected. At present, it is impossible to decide whether one of these alternative explanations is more relevant than the others.

Developmental Studies

Other than in the studies reviewed, there has been little interest in studying discrimination learning at different ages. At first, such studies would seem to be unproductive ventures, for there is little obvious basis for predicting anything other than an improvement in performance with increasing age. But several developmental studies have reported quite unexpected results.

Stevenson, Iscoe, and McConnell (1955) presented a two-choice size discrimination to Ss at six age levels between the preschool and college years. As expected, performance improved consistently between ages 4 and 11, with the 11-year-olds learning the problem in a very small number of trials. After this, however, performance became increasingly inefficient; the frequency of correct response decreased consistently across the next three age levels, ending with the college Ss performing at approximately the same level as the 4-year-olds. A curvilinear relation between age and rate of learning also was found in a study by Weir and Stevenson (1959), where Ss between the ages of 3 and 9 were presented a serial discrimination task involving drawings of five pairs of common objects. Learning was more rapid for 5- than for 3-year-olds, but both 7- and 9-year-olds performed less adequately than the 5-year-olds.

How can such odd results be interpreted? The older Ss in these studies appeared to be unable to accept the fact that the problems were as simple as they actually were. Consequently, they developed complex hypotheses about their solution that hindered the development of the more simple, correct response. The expectations that children have about the level of difficulty of the problem may lead to poor performance unless the expectations are roughly in concordance with the actual level of difficulty.

A second set of developmental studies explored changes in the ease of learning a relation between two members of a pair of stimuli. The discrimination of relations between sets of stimuli should be more difficult than the discrimination of common elements, if it is assumed that the former requires some type of higher order abstracting ability. Graham, Ernhart, Craft, and Berman (1964) found the opposite to occur. Children between the ages of 2 and 4½ years were presented pairs of stimuli, each pair consisting of a common stimulus and a second stimulus larger or smaller than the first. For some Ss, response to the relation between the stimuli

was reinforced (*i.e.*, the larger stimulus in each pair was reinforced) and for other Ss the stimulus that was common across the pairs was reinforced. Learning the absolute discrimination was harder at all ages, but the difficulty decreased with increasing age. Performance on the relational problem was maximal by the age of 3.

Further evidence of young children's ability to respond to relations between stimuli before the age at which they normally demonstrate relational concepts in other ways was found by Berman and Graham (1964). Preschool children were presented two squares, both of which were reinforced on a single trial. On the second trial, one of the first-trial stimuli and a new stimulus were presented. On trial 2 the children chose the stimulus of the same relative size more often than they chose the alternative stimulus. Hence the ability to respond to relations between stimuli is a primitive form of behavior that does not require verbal control.

Similar effects have been found for auditory discrimination (Riley, McKee, Bell, and Schwartz, 1967). First and third graders were instructed to make absolute or relative judgments concerning tones differing in loudness and pitch. The Ss followed instructions for amplitude better than for frequency, and Ss followed relative instructions better than absolute instructions. Children of these ages appeared to discriminate between amplitudes almost exclusively on a relational basis. Third graders performed better than first graders only when the discrimination trials were not preceded by pretraining with other stimuli and when the Ss were required to make either absolute or relative judgments, but not both. As the authors point out, however, a relational discrimination does not require Ss to remember relations among particular stimuli, but an absolute discrimination is dependent upon the retention of information about a specific stimulus. The relational discrimination may be a more primitive mode of response since it requires less differentiation of the specific attributes of the stimuli and is less dependent on memory.

LEARNING SET

There are many indications that experience with learning problems results in more efficient learning of new problems. Some factors contributing to this improvement are the elimination of biases and other incorrect response tendencies, development of appropriate observing responses and increased attention to relevant cues, modification of expectancies concerning the difficulty of the problem, and acquisition of strategies for maximizing the information from each response. When the problems are all of the same type, positive transfer across learning tasks should be maximal. This is the case, for when Ss, both human and nonhuman, are given a series of two-choice discrimination problems, a point is reached where the correct response is learned in no more than one trial. The S has learned how to learn, or has developed what is called a learning set.

The first studies of learning set with children as Ss were aimed at determining whether children could form learning sets (they could) and whether brighter children formed learning sets more rapidly than duller children (they did). Learning sets are developed by children with great rapidity; for example, Reese (1965) found that only 17% of trial-2 responses were incorrect when 3- to 5-year-olds were required to learn a series of two-choice object discrimination problems. In another study (Ellis, Girardeau, and Pryor, 1962), only one problem was necessary for children to develop a learning set if this problem was learned to criterion. The correlation between MA and number of problems necessary to reach criterion of learning set has been found to vary between −.50 and −.60 for younger Ss (e.g., Koch and Meyer, 1959). Although there has been no rigorous investigation of the effects of type of stimulus on rate of acquiring learning set, it appears that the type of stimulus plays a less important role in the development of learning set in children than in lower animals.

Two of the most definitive studies of the role of MA and IQ on the development of learning sets have been reported by Harter (1965; 1967). In the first study, children at three levels of MA (5, 7, and 9) and three levels of IQ (70, 100, 130) were presented 10 four-trial problems a day until they reached a criterion of over 90% correct response on five successive problems. Significant differences in performance were associated with MA, IQ, and the interaction

between MA and IQ. Thus both level of intellectual functioning and rate of intellectual growth were significantly related to the ease of developing learning sets. The interaction reflects the greater differences in performance among the MA groups at IQ 70 than at the higher IQ levels and the greater differences between IQ groups at MA 5 than at MAs 7 and 9. The interaction of MA and IQ and the low relationship of MA with performance for the children over 8 years old probably is due partly to a ceiling effect resulting from the simplicity of the problems.

In the second study, Harter included two MA levels, 5½ and 8½, and three IQ levels, 65, 100, and 130. The findings were similar to those of the first study, indicating more rapid development of learning set at the higher levels of MA and IQ. In their precriterion performance, younger Ss employed response-set hypotheses, evident in position preferences and position alternations, whereas older Ss employed hypotheses contingent on the outcome of the prior response, such as win-stay, lose-shift. The latter types of hypothesis are, of course, more useful in solving the problems. Level of IQ was not clearly associated with different types of hypothesis. In addition, half of the Ss were tested under a standard, neutral condition and half were praised for correct response. The two conditions did not influence the performance of the higher MA Ss significantly, but performance of the lower MA Ss was higher in the praise condition. Motivational differences associated with intellectual level may play an important role in determining the rate at which a learning set will be formed.

The effects of varying the difficulty of successive problems on the acquisition and retention of a learning set has been studied by Katz (1967). The Ss, preschool children from a culturally deprived population, were separated into average and low IQ groups (mean IQs of 102 and 84, respectively). The difficulty of the problems was increased by reducing the number of dimensions (shape, size, color) represented in geometric figures; in the easiest problems the stimuli differed on all three dimensions and in the most difficult problems they differed on only one dimension. In line with other results, groups given prior experience with object discrimination problems did better on three criterion problems than did a group with no prior experience. Within the pretrained groups the sequence of relative difficulty of the training problems did not influence performance on the criterion problems. When the two IQ groups were considered separately, however, a significant effect was found for the low IQ Ss: a transition from easy to moderately difficult or from easy to difficult problems produced decrements in performance. A portion of the Ss were retested after 6 months. The Ss who had received prior training showed greater improvement across the test problems than did the control Ss, indicating that the improved performance was due to enhanced speed of learning rather than to better immediate memory.

ODDITY LEARNING

Discrimination learning problems can be made more difficult if S is required to choose the odd object from among a set, rather than one particular object. In studies of oddity learning, three or more objects are presented on each trial; one of the objects is dissimilar from the others. Since different sets of objects are used on successive trials, S must abstract the quality of "oddity" as the relevant basis for response. An even more difficult problem, a conditional oddity problem, can be constructed if additional cues are provided to indicate the dimension of oddity relevant on a particular trial. For example, the discriminative stimuli may differ in color and form. If they are presented in the presence of one cue, oddity in color is the relevant dimension, whereas in the presence of a second cue, oddity in form is the relevant dimension.

Several developmental studies of oddity learning have been reported. Gollin and Shirk (1966) presented children between the ages of 4 and 7 an oddity problem involving color. The percentage of Ss capable of reaching criterion within 54 trials increased from 42% for the 4-year-olds to 88% for the 6-year-olds. These levels of performance were somewhat higher than those found in an earlier, similar study by Lipsitt and Serunian (1963), but the pattern of changes across age was highly similar.

Hill (1965a) also found developmental changes in oddity learning between the ages of 4 and 12. All of the 12-year-olds, over 50% of the 6-year-olds, but only 10% of the 4-year-olds were capable of reaching criterion within 200 trials in a task involving objects that differed in shape and color. Hill also compared performance on the oddity problem with that found in a two-choice discrimination and in a conditional oddity problem. The object discrimination problem was easier than the oddity problem, and the conditional oddity problem was quite difficult. Since the Ss were presented at least two of the problems, transfer effects could be assessed. Negative transfer was found for 4-year-olds when they were given the discrimination task after the oddity problem, and positive transfer was found for 12-year-olds when they were given the conditional oddity problem after the other two problems.

In a direct investigation of possible sources of transfer, Hill (1965b) pretrained 4- and 6-year-olds with a two-choice object discrimination task or with pairs of stimuli identical or different in form and color. Following pretraining, the Ss were presented an oddity problem with a new set of objects that differed in form and color. No differential effects of the two types of pretraining were found for 4-year-olds, but the 6-year-olds benefited more from pretraining that emphasized the attributes of similarity and difference between pairs of objects than they did when they simply were given a discrimination task during pretraining.

The effects of the presence of irrelevant stimulus dimensions on oddity learning was investigated with 8- to 10-year-olds by Lubker and Spiker (1966). The stimuli were squares, triangles, and circles that were either white or black and large or small. When only one within-trial irrelevant cue (brightness) and one irrelevant between-trial cue (size) were present, learning to discriminate oddity of form did not differ from the case where there were no irrelevant within-trial cues but different between trial cues. When, however, two irrelevant within-trial cues were present (i.e., the stimuli differed in form, size, and brightness) learning was less efficient than when there were no irrelevant within-trial cues.

Two other variables that influence oddity learning are stress and the similarity of the stimuli (Lipsitt and Lolordo, 1963). Nine-year-olds were tested with three colors that were either distinctive or similar; half were instructed there was a time pressure on their performance and half were given neutral instructions. Slower learning was found when the stimuli were similar than when they were distinctive, presumably because the similar stimuli aroused competing responses, which interfered with learning. The interaction between stress and task difficulty was also significant: learning was facilitated under stress when the stimuli were distinctive, but when the stimuli were similar stress had a deleterious effect on performance. In fact, the performance of the group given stress instructions and similar stimuli did not improve across 54 trials.

TRANSPOSITION

In the initial phase of the transposition problem, Ss are trained to respond, for example, to the larger of two stimuli. In the second, test phase the smaller of the original pair is replaced by a third, still larger stimulus. Will S now choose the originally positive stimulus or will he choose the larger stimulus of the pair? The general finding that animals of different species and humans of different ages tend to choose the larger stimulus on the first test trial was used by the Gestalt psychologists to support the view that learning is a result of developing an understanding of the relations that exist among stimuli, rather than acquiring specific stimulus-response connections. How, otherwise, could one account for the fact that Ss select the stimulus in the test set that they had not encountered previously in preference to a stimulus that had been reinforced consistently? Spence (1937) proposed a model to handle this question. Spence assumed that the habit strength developed to the positive stimulus during training generalized to other stimuli along the same dimension, as did the inhibitory strength developed to the negative stimulus. By summing the excitatory and inhibitory tendencies algebraically at different points along the stimulus continuum, it is possible to predict that transposition will occur for "near" stimuli (stimuli near the training set) but not for "far" stimuli (stimuli further removed on the stimulus dimension). The second prediction is not in accord with a relational theory, and evidence of a decrease

in the incidence of transposition as the test stimuli become more remote from the training stimuli (the "distance effect") was interpreted as an indication of the greater power of a stimulus-response, or absolute theory.

Many studies of transposition have used children as Ss, but current interest in the problem can be traced to the publication of a study by Kuenne (1946). Kuenne assumed that different frequencies of transposition would be obtained, depending upon the Ss' linguistic competence. The performance of young children who cannot verbalize relations among stimuli should conform to the predictions of Spence and be similar to that of nonverbal organisms. Older children, however, who can verbalize a relation such as "larger than," should depend upon the verbal cues to guide their response and their performance should be less dependent upon the absolute characteristics of the test stimuli. Accordingly, it was predicted that younger Ss would show a distance effect, but that transposition would be maintained at a high level by older Ss even for remote stimuli.

In a study of the performance of Ss varying in mental age from 3 to 6 years, Kuenne found support for these predictions. Transposition remained at a high level across all MA levels for a "near" set of stimuli, but decreased consistently for a "far" set as MA decreased. Post-test questioning of the Ss indicated that the younger Ss were less capable of verbalizing the size relation that existed within the pairs of stimuli; none of the Ss at the 3-year level and nearly all at the 5- and 6-year levels were able to verbalize the principle either spontaneously or upon questioning. Kuenne's results were replicated shortly afterward by Alberts and Ehrenfreund (1951).

Subsequent studies have not consistently supported Kuenne's two-stage model. For example, Stevenson, Iscoe, and McConnell (1955) found no marked changes in the incidence of transposition between the preschool and college years, and a distance effect was not obtained by Stevenson and Iscoe (1955) for the first-trial performance of retarded Ss, who presumably were preverbal in the sense that only 3 of the 44 Ss could verbalize the basis for solving the problem. Totally discrepant findings have been reported by Rudel (1958). The Ss, 21 to 45 months of age, were divided into preverbal and verbal groups according to their ability to pick out the "bigger" or "smaller" of a pair of squares at the completion of the testing session. The Ss were trained on a size discrimination in which the larger stimulus was correct for half of the Ss and the smaller stimulus was correct for the other half. Five sets of increasingly large stimuli were used in the test trials for different groups of Ss. A U-shaped curve was obtained: transposition decreased across the first three pairs of test stimuli but then increased for pairs 4 and 5. In addition, a significantly higher incidence of transposition was found when the smaller stimulus, rather than the larger stimulus, in the training pair had been correct and there was no overall difference in the performance of the preverbal and verbal Ss. Only the decrease in transposition found for pairs 1 to 3 by the preverbal Ss is in accord with Kuenne's model.

One of the most difficult sets of results for the model to explain is that reported by Johnson and Zara (1960). The behavior of half of the Ss in this study conformed to the model, but that of the other half did not. Two groups of Ss between the ages of 3 and 5 years were trained on a size-discrimination problem. When only one pair of stimuli was presented on the training trials, as had been the case in the previous studies, a distance effect was found. When, however, two pairs of training stimuli were used, the Ss transposed at a high level regardless of the distance between the training and test sets. The gradients posited by Spence cannot account for such an effect, although the effect can be understood if it is assumed that (1) when the same relation exists in multiple sets of training stimuli Ss are more likely to discover the relevance of the relation between the stimuli for solution of the problem and (2) Ss are able to utilize such information on the test trials. The results have been replicated by Sherman and Strunk (1964).

Additional discordant results have been reported by Hunter (1952) for 5-year-olds. As in the preceding two studies, Ss were trained with more than one set of stimuli, but in this study the different sets were presented successively rather than simultaneously. The procedure was rather complicated.

Different combinations of stimuli were used with different groups, but all embodied the following type of training. After Ss had learned to select the larger of two circles consistently, a new set of stimuli whose members were larger than the first set was presented. When the larger of these two stimuli was selected consistently, trials were given with a third set whose positive member was the stimulus that had not been reinforced during the second phase and whose negative member was a blank card. The last set was used to offset the inhibitory tendencies that would be predicted to develop during the second phase of training. On the test trials a pair of stimuli was used whose members consisted of a stimulus larger than any of those used during training and a stimulus whose size was intermediate between the stimuli reinforced during the first two phases of training. According to an absolute theory, the last stimulus should be chosen on the test trials, for its excitatory strength is postulated to be the sum of the generalized excitatory strengths derived from the training stimuli. Any generalized inhibitory strength to this stimulus should have been eliminated by the third phase of training. Thus the Ss should have chosen the smaller stimulus in the test set rather than the more distant, larger stimulus. Nevertheless, over 80% of the Ss made a relational response. Furthermore, when a similar procedure was followed in a second study with Ss whose mean age was 23 months, 80% of the Ss made a relational response on the test trials.

The results of the preceding three studies indicate that training with multiple sets of stimuli is conducive to making a relative response, even when the training is devised so that it supposedly yields gradients that, according to Spence's model, should result in absolute responding.

Another implication of the model was tested by Cole, Dent, Eguchi, Fujii, and Johnson (1964). Three-year-olds were trained with a "fading in" technique whereby the negative stimulus was represented initially by a thin line, which gradually evolved across the 30 training trials into a small square. The positive stimulus, a larger square, was complete on all trials. This technique made it very unlikely that the Ss would make errors and, consequently, that inhibitory tendencies would be developed for the negative stimulus. In such a situation, the Ss did transpose to ·a significant degree.

Spence's model obviously is inadequate for predicting the behavior of young children in transposition tasks. Does the second aspect of Kuenne's developmental model fare any better? The results of a study by Marsh and Sherman (1966) indicate that it does not. The purpose of this study was to determine whether the frequency of transposition could be increased by instructing Ss about the relevant dimension and eliciting relevant verbalizations prior to each response. Two groups of Ss with mean ages of 3.2 and 4.6 years were trained with a pair of squares differing in both size and brightness. The two dimensions were relevant and redundant in that, for example, the large black square was positive and the small white square was negative. The Ss were tested with the previously positive stimulus and a new stimulus that differed in both size and brightness from the other member of the pair. No age differences in performance were found, and the youngest Ss for whom size was verbalized did not transpose above chance on the test trials. Those for whom brightness was verbalized tended to choose the previously positive stimulus. When the study was repeated with 2-year-olds, now including a group receiving no instructions, the incidence of transposition again was not significant; the Ss in all groups tended to choose the previously positive stimulus. Thus activation of a verbal response through instructions is not sufficient to insure that performance of the young child will be influenced significantly by such verbalization. McKee and Riley (1962) reported similar results for auditory transposition. Labeling of tones as "high" or "low" did not facilitate transposition along a pitch dimension.

A different approach was taken by Zeiler (1966) with 4- and 5-year-olds, all of whom could verbalize size relations. The area-ratios of the stimuli used in this study were either 1.96:1 or 1.4:1. A gradient similar to those found by Kuenne and by Alberts and Ehrenfreund for preverbal Ss appeared for the stimuli with the lower area-ratio, but a uniformly high level of transposition was found for the stimuli with the high area-ratio. It is possible therefore that the difficulty of the original discrimination, rather than the presence or absence of verbal mediation, may determine whether or not a distance effect will be found. Stimuli with a low area-ratio are more difficult to discriminate, and, as indicated earlier, the younger Ss in the two earlier studies required far greater numbers of trials to solve the original discrimination than did the older Ss. If the original problem is as difficult, Ss may be more likely to develop a relational response than if the absolute characteristics of the training stimuli differ greatly.

The evidence appears to indicate, then, that such variables as stimulus conditions, characteristics of the Ss, and types of training will determine whether or not transposition occurs. Some studies support a relational interpretation, whereas some support an absolute interpretation. However, it may be inappropriate to attempt to categorize learning as either relational or absolute. Johnson and Bailey (1966) reported results from a very extensive study involving five training conditions, different numbers of training problems, and three age levels (kindergarten, fourth grade, and college Ss). Although the overall proportion of relational responses on the test trials was high (.73), the proportion varied widely, and systematically, across the various subgroups, depending upon the training conditions and the age of the Ss. For example, when kindergarten Ss were presented the stimuli successively and without opportunity for comparison, the proportion of relational responses was .29, but when the stimuli were presented successively and they could be compared, the proportion increased to .92. The results of this study are complex, but they indicate clearly it is possible to manipulate the incidence of absolute and relational responding by modifying the stimulus situation within a relatively restricted range.

The Intermediate-Size Problem

In addition to research on the two-stimulus problem, there has been a great deal of interest in the transposition of intermediate size. Researchers initially became interested in this problem because of the opposing predictions of the relational and absolute theories. According to relational theory, transposition of intermediate size should occur; according to absolute theory it should not. The basic assumptions of the absolute theory are the same as those previously discussed, but now there are two gradients of inhibitory tendencies and one of excitatory tendencies. By summing the strengths of these tendencies along the relevant stimulus dimension, the net excitatory strength is found to be greatest for the stimulus nearest in size to the initially positive stimulus. Thus in tests of transposition one step removed (a set of stimuli consisting, for example, of the two larger members of the original set and a new, still larger stimulus), pre-verbal Ss are predicted to choose the previously positive stimulus, thereby making an absolute response.

One of the first investigations of the transposition of intermediate size was reported by Stevenson and Bitterman (1955), whose Ss were 4- to 6-year-olds, none of whom could relate the significance of middle-size to the solution of the problem. Test trials were conducted with sets of stimuli one and five steps removed from the training set. Transposition was found for stimuli one step removed, and a distance effect was obtained. There was a much lower incidence of transposition for stimuli five steps removed than for stimuli two steps removed. These results were interpreted as indicating that during training Ss had learned something about both the relations that existed among the stimuli and the region occupied by the training stimuli on the stimulus continuum. Hence transposition would be predicted to occur when the test set is near the training set but to decrease as test sets become increasingly dissimilar to the training set. A similar view had been suggested by Hunter (1954).

One implication of this position is that the probability Ss will transpose depends on the discriminability of the test set from the training set. If the training stimuli are highly similar, transposition is more likely to occur than if the stimuli are dissimilar, since discriminating between-set differences should be more difficult when within-set differences among the stimuli are small. Reese (1962) tested this hypothesis by using two sets of stimuli, with area-ratios 1.3:1 and 2:1. Transposition was found for all groups on a near test, but on a far test the preschool Ss transposed only when the area-ratio of the stimuli was small.

Another implication of the "discriminability" hypothesis is that transposition on far tests should occur if it is made clear to the Ss that the relation learned during training is applicable to a broad range of stimuli. Gonzales and Ross (1958) trained 4-year-olds with two sets of stimuli selected from opposite ends of a size continuum and tested the Ss on a set intermediate between the two training sets. Far transposition was found for the 4-year-old Ss with this procedure. Subsequent studies by Caron (1966) and by Beatty and Weir (1966) with 3- and 4-year-olds confirmed this finding and showed that the effect was dependent upon training with extreme sets of stimuli rather than upon multiple-set training, as might be suggested by the Johnson and Zara (1960) results cited earlier. Two training problems were used in these studies, each involving two sets of stimuli. In one problem the sets were selected from one extreme on the size dimension, and in the other, one set was selected from each extreme. Only far tests of transposition were used. Of the 90 Ss in each of Caron's conditions, 25 transposed on the first test trial in the first condition and 55 in the second condition. In the Beatty and Weir study, 3 of 20 transposed in the first condition, but in the second condition 16 of 20 transposed on the far test. None of the Ss in a third condition, which involved training on only one set of stimuli, transposed. The likelihood that Ss will transpose on far tests thus is increased if training encompasses extreme instances in the range of stimuli, but, in contrast to the results of two-stimulus problems, the incidence of transposition is not increased greatly by multiple-set training.

There is other evidence that the intermediate-size problem involves processes different from the two-stimulus problem. The S's ability to verbalize relative size was an important variable in the two-stimulus problem, but stimulus conditions appear to play a more important role in determining performance on the intermediate-size problem. Studies by Caron (1966), Reese (1961b, 1962a), Reese and Fiero (1964), Rudel (1957), and Zeiler (1963a) found no relation between performance of Ss on test trials and their ability to verbalize the concept of middle-size. In another study (Reese, 1966) the experimenter named the correct or the incorrect stimuli for 3- to 5-year-old Ss during training, and a distance effect was found, even though this effect would not be expected when verbal mediation is possible. The incidence of transposition was higher, however, among Ss for whom the experimenter labeled the correct or incorrect stimuli than among Ss who received no directive instructions. The only other study in which differences were found among Ss who possessed the concept of middle-size and those who did not was reported by Caron (1967). First-trial choices on tests of transposition were equally high for both groups on near tests, but on a test six steps removed from the training stimuli, a greater number of the Ss who possessed the concept transposed. None of the studies offers any basis for determining why possessing labels for the stimuli exerts a significant effect on transposition in the two-stimulus problem but is only infrequently an important variable in the intermediate-size problem.

Zeiler (1963b) has presented a ratio theory of transposition that ignores the variable of level of conceptualization regarding intermediate size and derives its predictions solely on the basis of the characteristics of the stimuli present in the training and test situations. In many ways it is an attractive theory, for it offers a quantitative approach to the transposition problem, but experimental evidence has not given strong support to the predictions made. Basically, it is an application of Helson's (1964) theory of adaptation level. It is assumed that an adaptation level is established for the training trials which is a sum of the geometric mean of the values of the stimuli present and of a residual adaptation level derived from prior experience. The S learns to select a stimulus that has a particular ratio to the adaptation level. During the test trials, the S is predicted to choose the stimulus whose ratio to the adaptation level established upon the perception of the test stimuli is most similar to the ratio of the original positive stimulus to the training adaptation level. Zeiler (1963a, 1963b) presents a series of studies with children that seem to be in line with these predictions.

A critical response to Zeiler's work has been made by Riley, Sherman, and McKee (1966), who found it impossible to replicate certain of Zeiler's findings. One of Zeiler's (1963b) central experiments was repeated. A series of stimuli, 1 through 8, vary in size from small to large. During training, stimuli 1, 2, and 8 are presented to all Ss, with 2 being the positive stimulus. During testing, stimuli 1 and 2 are retained, but the third

member of the set may be stimulus 3, 4, 5, or 6. As the largest test stimulus decreased in size, Zeiler found an increasing tendency for the Ss to choose stimulus 1. The most striking departure from what would be predicted from any other position was performance with test stimuli 1, 2, and 3. Riley, Sherman, and McKee repeated the study, using only this test set. Whereas Zeiler had found the largest number of Ss chose stimulus 1 on the test trial, in the replication study the largest number chose the stimulus of intermediate size. A second group of 4-year-olds was instructed to look carefully at all of the stimuli, on the assumption that the Zeiler effect might depend upon S's attending to all of the stimuli. Again, the largest number of Ss chose the stimulus of intermediate size. Additional groups either were instructed to find the middle-sized stimulus, were told that the reward would always be under a particular square, or were told to find the one that fitted the board. The third instruction was meaningful, for strips had been pasted on the stimulus tray of the same width as the stimulus of intermediate size. Relative choices on the test trial were more frequent for Ss given the first set of instructions, but when the instructions emphasized the absolute characteristics of the stimuli, a preponderance of absolute choices was made. The issues are not settled, for Zeiler (1966) has responded by pointing out other studies in which the results were in line with adaptation level theory, but, nevertheless, concluded that "because of the growing catalog of situational variables that cause absolute learning, the ratio theory is also unconvincing" (p. 260).

What is left from the studies of transposition, then, is a large amount of data in search of a theory. Transposition has been discussed in some detail because it is one of the most thoroughly explored problems in experimental studies of children's learning and because the data demonstrate with awesome vividness the complexity of the learning process in even very young children. There is little question that theoretical analyses capable of handling data derived from lower animals are incomplete and inadequate for predicting results from studies with children. Relational theories, absolute theories, discriminability theories, and even mediation and ratio theories may provide satisfactory accounts for portions of the data, but new approaches, especially those emphasizing perceptual and verbal processes and their interaction with developmental level, will be necessary for a more comprehensive and satisfactory analysis of children's performance.

REVERSAL AND NONREVERSAL SHIFTS

One case of transfer of training is transposition, in which transfer is assessed with sets of stimuli differing on a single stimulus dimension and bearing the same within-set relationship. Two other types of transfer problems that have captured a great deal of interest are reversal and nonreversal shifts, where Ss are trained with a set or sets of stimuli which differ in at least one dimension and are tested with sets that require Ss to shift their responses either to a second value of the previously relevant dimension or to a previously irrelevant dimension. As in the studies of transposition, the research has tended to be developmental and the role of language has received special attention. Much of the research on shift behavior with children was stimulated by a series of studies published by T. and H. Kendler and their associates. The basic paradigm used in the studies and the predictions made from the stimulus-response and mediation theory espoused by the Kendlers have been as follows.

For example, if a subject is initially trained on stimuli that differ simultaneously in brightness (black vs. white) and size (large vs. small) by being rewarded to responses to black regardless of size, a reversal shift would consist of learning to respond to white, and a nonreversal shift would consist of learning to respond to small. Comparisons between these two types of shifts are of particular interest because theories based on single-unit versus mediated S-R connections yield opposed predictions about their relative efficiency. A single-unit theory assumes a direct association between the external stimulus and the overt response and would predict a reversal shift to be more difficult than a nonreversal shift. This is because reversal shift requires the replacement of a response that has previously been consistently reinforced with a response that has previously been consistently extinguished. In a nonreversal

shift previous training has reinforced responses to the newly positive and negative stimuli equally often. Strengthening one of these associations does not require as much extinction of its competitor as in a reversal shift and should, therefore, be acquired more easily.

A theory that includes a mediating link (or links) between the external stimulus and the overt response leads to a different prediction. The mediating link is conceived of as a perceptual or verbal response, often covert, to the relevant dimension, which produces cues that elicit the overt response. In a reversal shift, the initial dimension maintains its relevance, hence, so does the mediated response. Only the overt response needs to be changed, and since the experimental situation provides only one alternative overt response, the problem presents no great difficulty. In a nonreversal shift the previously acquired mediation is no longer relevant, consequently both the mediating and overt response must be replaced, making the task more difficult than a reversal shift. It is therefore to be expected that for subjects who mediate, a reversal shift will be acquired more easily than a nonreversal shift (Kendler, 1963, pp. 35-36).

Earlier research had demonstrated that reversal shifts are more difficult for lower animals but nonreversal shifts are more difficult for human adults. Research with children was undertaken to determine whether a transition period might be found during childhood, before which children's performance would be similar to that of lower animals and after which children would perform in the fashion of adults. In an initial study (Kendler and Kendler, 1959), 5- and 6-year-olds were used as Ss. Overall, the children did not perform more poorly on one type of shift than the other, apparently contradicting the predictions made from both the single-unit and mediational positions. However, when the Ss were separated according to the ease with which they had learned the initial discrimination (above and below the median number of training trials), slow learners were found to learn the reversal shift more slowly than the nonreversal shift, whereas fast learners learned the reversal shift more rapidly than the nonreversal shift. The deduction was made that the fast learners had approached the task with verbal labels, which facilitated both original learning and reversal performance, whereas the slow learners had not.

Shifting the age level downward should provide some clarification of the first study, for with 3- to 5-year-olds, who presumably are less likely to utilize verbal mediators, reversal learning should be more difficult than nonreversal learning. This was found to be true (Kendler, Kendler, and Wells, 1960). There was negative transfer from the training trials for a reversal shift but positive transfer for a nonreversal shift. The impact of the results is weakened, however, by the fact that Ss who were required to verbalize the basis of response during the terminal phase of the training trials performed no differently from those who were not required to verbalize, even though the use of verbal labels had been assumed to be helpful in reversal learning. The authors were forced to conclude that at this stage "verbal responses, though available, do not readily mediate between external stimuli and overt responses, but rather form parallel connections with little or no interaction" (p. 87).

Relevant verbalization also failed to produce faster reversal learning with 4- and 7-year-old Ss in a subsequent study (Kendler and Kendler, 1961). Verbalization exerted a significant influence on performance only when Ss were required to use irrelevant verbalizations during training (by labeling the irrelevant cue), and even then interference was found only in the performance of the older Ss. An unsystematic relation between verbalization and performance was evident in the performance of kindergarten Ss in a later study (Kendler, 1964), where Ss were told the basis for correct response and required to verbalize this prior to making each choice during the training trials. When the reinforcement contingencies were reversed, many Ss continued to verbalize the previously appropriate statement—while making the opposite choice from that embodied in their verbalizations!

The "optional shift" technique has been used to provide an indication of S's tendency to use reversal or nonreversal modes of response (Kendler, Kendler, and Learnard, 1962). Optional shift studies are conducted

in three phases. During initial training Ss are presented two pairs of stimuli whose members differ in size and brightness. One attribute of one dimension is reinforced; for example, black. One pair of the original stimuli is retained in a second phase, but white is now reinforced. Since in this example the white stimulus may also be the small stimulus, Ss could be learning to respond in the second phase on the basis of brightness (reversal shift) or size (nonreversal shift). A test then is conducted with the pair of stimuli used in the second phase and an additional pair of stimuli including, say, a large white stimulus and a small black stimulus. Choices of either of the latter stimuli are reinforced. If S chooses the white stimulus of the second pair on 8 of the 10 test trials he is classified as having shown a reversal shift, and if he chooses the black (small) stimulus he is classified as having shown a nonreversal shift. Five age levels were sampled: the mean ages were 3, 4, 6, 8, and 10 years. The percentage of Ss demonstrating reversal shifts increased with increasing age, as was predicted, but contrary to the predictions, the percentage of Ss demonstrating nonreversal shifts did not change. Rather, a decrease was found in the percentage of Ss responding in an inconsistent fashion.

The technique was used by Kendler (1964) with kindergarten children in a study of the effects of verbalization on performance. The proportion of Ss demonstrating reversal shifts was higher among Ss who were required to verbalize the basis of their response than among those who were not required to verbalize. As indicated previously, some of the Ss in the second phase continued to verbalize the response that was appropriate to the first phase but was now inappropriate. When the study was repeated and only relevant verbalization was permitted in the second phase, the incidence of reversal shifts was higher in the verbalizing than in the nonverbalizing groups—but only when brightness was the initially relevant dimension. When it was shape, there was no significant difference between the verbalizers and the nonverbalizers. (In this, as in all of the studies, the training conditions were counterbalanced so that each attribute of each dimension was relevant for one-fourth of the Ss.)

Since rate of learning was correlated with

the frequency of reversal shifts, it is possible that the results may be attributable to the number of training trials, rather than to the operation of verbal mediation. To determine whether larger amounts of training would produce a lower incidence of reversal learning, Kendler and Kendler (1966) gave half of their Ss 16 and half 36 training trials on the original discrimination. Within this range, there was no significant effect of increasing the number of training trials. Nine-year-old Ss did, however, make more optional reversals than did 4-year-olds.

The work of the Kendlers is central, but it comprises only a small portion of the research on reversal-nonreversal shifts. Scores of studies have been published; researchers have been stimulated both by the Kendlers' work and by the work of others on the role of attention in discrimination learning (Mackintosh, 1965; Sutherland, 1964; Zeaman and House, 1963). As more and more data have come in, theoretical notions about reversal-nonreversal problems have met the same fate as the early ideas about transposition: the problems have proved to be so complex that none of the theories is capable of handling the essential results. Each can incorporate part, but conditions can be rearranged easily so that quite different results are obtained. There were enough hints in the equivocal findings in much of the Kendlers' own research to indicate that later studies would topple some of the central units in the structure they had built. It appears that theories about children's learning must be judged effective if they produce sufficient data to insure their own demise! This would be a depressing fate if it were not also evident that there has been progress, if progress is viewed as the ability to ask increasingly sophisticated questions.

The research on the effects of overtraining on reversal learning is a good example of the transformations that occur when the studies start by asking a seemingly simple question. The effects of overtraining have been investigated extensively with animals, and generally overtraining has been found to facilitate reversal learning (Sperling, 1965). The results from a number of studies of object discriminations with children reached the same conclusion (Cross and Tyler, 1966; Eimas, 1966b; Furth and Youniss, 1964;

Marsh, 1964; Tighe and Tighe, 1966; Youniss and Furth, 1964a, 1964b, 1965). In spatial discriminations, however, overtraining had no effect or a detrimental effect on reversal learning (Eimas, 1966b; Stevenson and Weir, 1959a; Youniss and Furth, 1964b); but, as was found in the last study, the addition of irrelevant, nonspatial cues may result in a facilitative effect of overtraining in spatial discriminations. Overtraining also facilitates the learning of intradimensional shifts, where new stimuli from the same relevant dimension are substituted for the training stimuli (Eimas, 1966a; Furth and Youniss, 1964; Heal, 1966). On the other hand, overtraining has been found to have variable effects on the rate of learning extradimensional shifts, where the second set of stimuli is from a new stimulus dimension. In general, then, overtraining increases the ease of learning a reversal or intradimensional shift, thereby producing the same effect found with the introduction of verbal mediation. Such a conclusion, however, is subject to several qualifications.

Gollin (1964) found that although overtraining facilitated reversal performance of 4½- to 5½-year-olds, it had a detrimental effect on the performance of 3½- to 4½-year-olds. The facilitative effect of overtraining also was restricted to the older Ss in a study of 3- and 4-year-olds by Tighe and Tighe (1966). In addition, the effects in the last study were dependent upon the stimulus dimension relevant during original learning. Practically all Ss for whom the relevant dimension was height reversed without overtraining, but when diagonal and vertical stripes were the relevant dimension, practically none of the Ss reversed without overtraining. After overtraining, the 4-year-olds in the latter group showed significantly more reversals, but there was no change in the performance of the 3-year-olds. The frequency of reversal shifts by 8- and 10-year-olds also has been found to differ, depending upon the dimension that was relevant during the training trials (Eimas, 1967). The frequency of reversal shifts was greater when the relevant dimension was size than when it was brightness. Thus the frequency of reversal shifts may depend upon the saliency of the stimuli and overtraining may interact with saliency of stimuli and age in its effects on reversal learning.

Jeffrey (1965) has reported a study that shows how a modest change in the testing procedure can produce results that have a destructive effect on any theory that postulates changes with age in the ease of reversal learning. The study included 4-, 6-, and 8-year-olds and college students. The Ss were trained on a color discrimination and after reaching criterion the previously nonreinforced stimulus was now reinforced. In addition to changing the reinforcement contingencies, the form of the stimuli was changed from circles to squares. With this procedure, there were no developmental changes in ease of reversal learning. Such results may be interpreted as indicating that young children's difficulty in reversal learning may be due to a difficulty in abstracting a single common dimension among the stimuli rather than to a lack of verbal mediation. Changing one aspect of the cues between the training and test trials apparently emphasized a commonality between the two sets of trials that otherwise would have been difficult for the younger Ss to recognize.

An additional feature of Eimas' (1967) study should be discussed, since it introduced another variable that interacts with overtraining in influencing reversal performance. The Ss were trained in the "optional shift" technique, half with a constant irrelevant dimension, and half with a variable irrelevant dimension. More reversal shifts were made by the latter than by the former Ss. Further, overtraining increased the frequency of reversal shifts following variable irrelevant training but decreased the frequency following constant irrelevant training. The results are interpreted according to the two-stage attention theory of Zeaman and House (1963), summarized by Eimas as follows:

According to this model, discrimination learning requires the acquisition of a chain of two responses, the first a mediating attention response to the relevant stimulus dimension, and the second, an instrumental choice response to one of the outputs of the attention response—the positive discriminandum. Furthermore, during original learning, overtraining is assumed to increase the probability of attending to the relevant dimension

without differentially affecting instrumental habits, at least to any considerable degree. A major assumption of the model, related to transfer-of-discrimination learning, is that both members of the response chain transfer across problems, provided that other stimulus arrangements or dimensions that function to divert the locus of attention from the previously relevant dimension are not introduced (Eimas, 1967, p. 338).

The introduction of the novel stimuli on the shift trials is assumed to constitute a source of diversion of attention, with maximal effects occurring following overtraining on a constant irrelevant dimension. The incidence of reversal shifts is assumed to be decreased after overtraining with constant irrelevant stimuli because of S's heightened tendency to respond to the new cues introduced on the shift trials. The high incidence of reversals without overtraining with variable irrelevant stimuli is interpreted as indicating that attention was maintained toward the originally relevant dimension, despite the fact that only one of the original pairs of cues was retained in the shift trials.

These and other studies provide information about the Kendlers' notions about the effects of verbal mediation on reversal. According to the Kendlers, following the attainment of criterion on the first task, preschool Ss should learn a nonreversal shift more rapidly than a reversal shift, but older Ss should learn the reversal shift more rapidly. Evidence in support of the first prediction was found in studies by Marsh (1966) and Saravo (1967). There was no difference between the two types of shifts by the preschool Ss tested by Cobb and Price (1966). The second prediction also has received some support. Reversal shifts were learned more easily than nonreversal shifts by elementary school Ss in a study by Saravo (1967) when there were two or more dimensions varying simultaneously, and in a study by Sanders, Ross, and Heal (1965). No shift differences were found by Youniss and Furth (1965) for Ss of these ages.

Similar predictions would be made for intradimensional shifts. An intradimensional shift should be learned more rapidly by older Ss than an extradimensional shift, for the Ss should find it more difficult to adopt a new mediator, as would be necessary in the extradimensional shift, than to continue to apply the old mediator with new specific designations, as would be necessary in the intradimensional shift. The studies by Eimas (1966a), Furth and Youniss (1964), and Heal (1966) support such a deduction. Similar results were found for kindergarten Ss in a study by Trabasso, Deutsch, and Gelman (1966) when the stimuli were objects differing in color and shape, but the two types of shifts were of equivalent difficulty when the stimuli were patterns. More rapid learning of intradimensional shifts was found by Dickerson (1966) for preschool Ss, who, according to the predictions, should learn the extradimensional shift more easily. The methodology of this study has been criticized by Tighe and Tighe (1967), who found that if 4-year-olds are trained in a fashion comparable to that used in the other studies, extradimensional shifts were learned more rapidly than intradimensional shifts.

The majority of the results tend to be in line with the predictions that age—and presumably level of verbal facility—interacts with type of shift. When verbalization is directly manipulated, however, the results turn out to be more elusive. The results of Silverman (1966) offer clear support for the facilitative effects of verbalization, for 3- and 4-, as well as 7- and 8-year-olds, learned a reversal shift more rapidly when they were required to verbalize the relevant dimension during training than when they were not. No overall facilitating effects were reported by Morse and Shepp (1967) when kindergarten and first-grade Ss were required to verbalize during the training trials. Among the intradimensional shift Ss, however, those who spontaneously continued to verbalize during the shift problem learned more rapidly than did those who abandoned verbalization after the training trials. For the older Ss, verbalization impeded the learning of extradimensional shift problems. Unexpectedly, the kindergarten Ss who verbalized during the training period learned both types of problems more slowly than did those who did not verbalize.

Blank (1966), who informed half of her preschool Ss of the solution to the training problem, found that such information did not help Ss significantly on a reversal problem,

for their performance was similar to that of groups for whom the correct responses were not labeled. Similarly, Cobb and Price (1966) found no differences in the performances of preschool Ss who were given pretraining in learning relevant or irrelevant labels for the discriminative stimuli. Whatever the ultimate resolution of the sources of discrepancies among these studies, it is obvious that verbalization does not necessarily result in more effective learning of reversal and intradimensional shift problems.

One of the incidental results of a number of studies is the finding that the ease of making a reversal shift differs, depending upon the characteristics of the stimulus dimension that was relevant during training. Smiley and Weir (1966) investigated this problem directly by selecting color and form, dimensions for which Ss were known to have different preferences. The optional shift technique was used with kindergarten children. Prior to being presented the training problem, the Ss were given two series of trials on the basis of which they could be classified as being color or form dominant. During the training trials, either the dominant or nondominant dimension was reinforced. In the test series, a reversal shift was shown by 25 of the 32 Ss for whom the dominant dimension had been correct but only 8 of the 32 Ss for whom the nondominant dimension had been correct. In contrast to earlier findings, learning speed was not related to the incidence of reversal shifts but was significantly faster for Ss whose preferred dimension had been reinforced. There is a strong suggestion in these results that both rate of learning and frequency of reversal shifts may be a function of dimensional dominance rather than the operation of mediators, such that both speed of learning and frequency of reversals are increased if there is a fortuitous assignment of Ss to the condition in which their preferred dimension is reinforced.

Prior experience in differentiating the critical differences among the training stimuli has been found to decrease the number of trials required to learn a reversal shift (Tighe, 1965). The Ss who were given pretraining in making same-different judgments with the training stimuli learned a reversal shift more rapidly than did Ss who were given irrelevant pretraining in a control group or who were presented a nonreversal shift. Another important and related variable has been isolated by Johnson and White (1967) in a study of 6- and 7-year-olds. Some of the Ss were pretrained with problems involving the ordering of stimuli on a dimension. Those above the median in performance on these tests made significantly fewer errors in the reversal problem than did those below the median. Thus reversal shifts are more likely to occur when the Ss had a more highly developed concept of dimensionality. A final study of pretraining by Vaughter and Cross (1965) found that prior experience with both stimuli used in a reversal task produced superior performance to that found when the experience was limited to one of the stimuli or when no preliminary experience was given.

A complex but elucidating study by Mumbauer and Odom (1967) assessed the roles of verbalization, overtraining, and dimensional preference on reversal, intradimensional, and extradimensional shift problems. Preschool Ss were tested with stimuli that differed in form and color. Initial learning was faster when the Ss were required to verbalize prior to responding and when Ss were tested with form as the relevant dimension. A significant interaction between verbalization and dimension indicated that verbalizing had no influence on the performance of Ss for whom form was the relevant dimension, but it facilitated performance when color was relevant.

In the shift trials, the main effects of verbalization, dimension, and type of shift were significant. Learning was faster for Ss who verbalized, for whom form was correct, and extradimensional shifts were harder to learn than the other two types of shift. Several significant interactions were obtained, and the general pattern in these interactions was for the performance of one of the groups to diverge from that of the other groups, which did not differ significantly. In the verbalization by overtraining interaction, Ss who had not verbalized and who were not overtrained required approximately twice as many trials to learn the discriminations as did the Ss in the other three groups. The divergent group in the significant verbalization-by-dimension interaction was the nonverbalizing-color Ss; in the overtraining-by-dimension interaction it was the nonovertrained-color Ss; and in

the shift-by-dimension interaction it was the extradimensional shift-color Ss. Possibly the most critical is the shift-by-dimension interaction, which indicated that only extradimensional shift Ss shifted to color differed significantly from the other groups. Differences in shift performance therefore appear to be a result of dimensional preferences rather than the operation of a mediation process. The interaction between verbalization and overtraining, indicate that these variables produce similar but noncumulative effects on shift performance.

These, then, are some of the more important studies on reversal shifts. The Kendlers' position has been emphasized, for their arguments and the research done to evaluate their predictions have had the greatest impact on research in this area. For obvious reasons, summary statements are difficult to make. Judging by the deluge of recent publications, the investigation of shift behavior has been considered to be important, primarily as a means of investigating the relation between the learning and the development of language. The hypothesis that performance between the preschool and elementary school years is increasingly influenced by verbal mediation at first appeared to be attractive in its simplicity and clarity. The studies do not necessarily invalidate the hypothesis, but performance that was assumed to be dependent upon mediation can occur without it, and stimulus variables and training procedures appear to exert at least as strong an influence on children's performance.

VERBAL MEDIATION

Several other studies have been concerned with developmental changes in verbal mediation. For example, changes in the use of verbal mediation have been posited to be the basis for developmental changes in double-alternation behavior (Pufall and Furth, 1966). Developmental changes found in this problem closely correspond to those found for the other types of problem discussed. Four-year-olds had great difficulty in learning a LLRR pattern, but by age 6 the number of children acquiring the rule reached an asymptote not exceeded by children as old as 9.

Two periods in development are clearly defined: very early childhood, where relevant language has not been acquired and hence the child is incapable of using verbal mediators; and adulthood, where behavior is largely under the control of verbal mediators. As has been pointed out by Reese (1962b), there is a period in early childhood where verbal responses do not seem to serve as mediators, even though the child is capable of using words. This "mediational deficiency" has been noted by Kuenne (1946), Kendler, Kendler, and Wells (1960), and Luria (1957). A recent article by Flavell, Beach, and Chinsky (1966) contrasts this view, which asserts that the child's verbalizations fail to influence his behavior, with a "production deficiency hypothesis," which proposes that "the younger child tends not to produce the relevant words in the first place, and this suffices to explain the apparent nonmediated characteristics of his overt task behavior. It is stipulated that he knows the relevant words and that he can and does produce them in some situations; his deficiency here consists solely in the fact that this particular task (or perhaps task-like situations in general) fails to elicit them" (p. 284).

In a test of this hypothesis, 5-, 8-, and 10-year-old Ss were presented a recall task, during which the experimenter lip-read by observing the child as he performed. Eighteen of the 20 youngest Ss, but only 3 of the 20 oldest Ss, showed no perceptible evidence of verbal rehearsal. Only 1 of the youngest Ss, but 13 of the oldest Ss, showed three or more instances of perceptible verbalization. No definitive interpretation of the mechanism underlying these changes was possible, but the results support a view that words may play a less important role in the behavior of young children, not because they are elicited and fail to be effective in directing behavior, but simply because they are not used. The relation of learning and language is bound to continue to be an important topic for further research.

PROBABILITY LEARNING

The structure of a probability learning task is similar to that of a discrimination learning task, except that the probability that response will lead to reinforcement is less than 1.00. The problem would be of little interest if children simply learned to make the response that led to the greatest frequency of rein-

forcement more slowly than they would if the response were reinforced consistently. But they do not. Further, research with children would add little to the body of information about probability learning if the proportion of times with which children ultimately selected the more frequently reinforcing stimulus reached an asymptotic level equal to the probability with which the response was reinforced, a result that is commonly found with adults. But, again, they do not. Children's performance changes with age and other variables interact with age in their influence on the choices children make.

The apparent simplicity of the probability learning task is deceptive. As shall be seen, the alteration of the schedule of reinforcement transforms a discrimination learning task into one that lies along the hazy boundary separating learning and problem solving. Since no solution yields consistent reinforcement, Ss are required to function as prediction-makers to a greater degree than in other learning problems. Because of this, the task has been used to delineate the role of more complex processes, such as sets and strategies, in children's performance at different ages. Although in many cases the studies have produced different and unreconciled results, the topics will be discussed in some detail because of the potential importance of many of the variables in the description of developmental changes in children's learning.

Most of the research has been conducted with two types of problems. In the two-choice problem, choices of one stimulus are reinforced, say, 75% of the time and choices of the other stimulus are reinforced 25% of the time. The schedule of reinforcement may be contingent upon response, as indicated in this example, or may be noncontingent on response in that reinforcement is potentially available but not necessarily obtained, for 75% of the choices of one stimulus and 25% of the choice of the other. A three-choice spatial problem also has been used in which choices of one position are reinforced, for example, 66 or 33% of the time, and choices of the other two positions are never reinforced.

Developmental Changes

Among the first questions asked in studies with children was whether their performance changed with age, and, if so, what trend these changes might follow. An answer was obtained by Weir (1964a) who consolidated the data from a number of studies to produce a picture of changes among 3 to 18 years. The intermediate ages included 5-, 7-, 9-, 11-, and 15-year-olds. All had been tested with the three-choice problem under the same experimental conditions. Terminal levels of response, as indicated by the average numbers of responses made to the reinforced stimulus during the last 20 of the 80 trials presented, plotted according to age, produced a U-shaped function. With both 33 and 66% reinforcement, performance of the youngest and the oldest Ss exceeded that of Ss in the middle years of childhood. The rate at which these levels were approached was more rapid for the youngest than for the oldest Ss, whereas the performance of the middle groups tended to change very slowly or not at all. The general relations described by Weir have been found in the two-choice problem by Derks and Paclisanu (1967) for eight groups of Ss varying in age from 4 to 21 years, and portions of the curve have been replicated in other studies with both three-choice (Odom, 1967) and two-choice problems (Jones and Liverant, 1960).

Such age differences are interesting in themselves, but unless efforts are made to understand the underlying processes, the data constitute little more than another descriptive statement about normative changes in behavior. One bit of evidence that might indicate something about Ss' expectancies about the task may be obtained by determining the proportion of Ss at each age level who show maximizing behavior by the end of training, that is, the proportion of Ss who consistently choose the more frequently reinforcing stimulus. If Ss believe a solution yielding consistent reinforcement is possible, they should continue to vary their behavior in an effort to find such a solution. If, on the other hand, they do not have such expectancies, or if such expectancies have been extinguished, they should settle on a response that yields the greatest payoff. Weir (1964a) found that the proportion of Ss at each age level who show maximizing behavior in the three-choice problem followed a U-shaped function, indicating that the youngest Ss seemingly did not tend to have such expectancies and the oldest Ss apparently gave up such expectancies when they

found they were incapable of obtaining consistent reinforcement.

Another indication of the strategies employed by the Ss is the proportion of Ss who follow a simple LMR or RML spatial pattern of responses. Now, an inverted U-shaped function was obtained. Children between ages 7 and 10 employed these patterns with a high frequency, whereas both the youngest and oldest Ss used them less often. When Weir plotted the number of alternation patterns obtained in studies using a two-choice problem, an inverted U-shaped function again was found. It was suggested, in accounting for the frequent use of simple stereotyped patterns by the middle-aged child, that "the 7- to 10-year-old is at a point in development where his ability to generate complex hypotheses and employ complex search strategies is growing at a faster pace than his information-processing ability" (Weir, 1964a, p. 481). A more detailed discussion of this point will be made later.

A final analysis examined the effects of reinforcement and nonreinforcement on the Ss' tendencies to repeat a response. The youngest Ss were more likely to repeat a response, regardless of whether it was correct or incorrect, and the older Ss tended to show a win-shift, lose-shift strategy. Again, the relation between incidence of response repetition and age was curvilinear, with the Ss between 7 and 15 years more likely to adopt the win-stay, lose-shift strategy. In summarizing these analyses, Weir concluded that the developmental changes in probability learning are a consequence of "differential growth of the ability to generate hypotheses and employ strategies and the ability to process information Ss gain from their own responding" (Weir, 1964a, p. 473).

The possibility that level of performance in a probability learning task may depend upon Ss' expectancies for reinforcement was tested in a study by Stevenson and Zigler (1958). The finding of an initial study that the asymptotic level of response was higher for institutionalized retarded children than for noninstitutionalized normal children led to the hypothesis that the first group had learned from their everyday experience to expect lower degrees of success than had the latter Ss, thus making it easier for them to accept a solution that yielded only partial reinforcement. In a second study, normal preschool Ss were given pretraining games in which they experienced either uniformly high or low degrees of success. Following this, the Ss were presented the three-choice task with a 66-0-0% schedule of reinforcement. The prediction that Ss who had experienced low degrees of success in the pretraining games would perform at a higher level than those who had experienced a high degree of success was supported.

A subsequent study by Gruen and Zigler (1968) contrasted the performance of middle- and lower-class 6-year-olds. It was assumed that lower-class children have a background of more frequent failure than middle-class children; thus, following the reasoning just outlined, lower-class Ss should show a higher frequency of response to the reinforcing stimulus than middle-class Ss. The results supported this assumption. Success and failure experiences also were provided in a pretraining period, but they had no overall effect on performance. When, however, separate analyses were made according to social class, it was found that for the middle-class Ss, pretraining with low degrees of success increased the frequency of choices of the reinforcing stimulus over that found following pretraining with high degrees of success. The performance of the lower-class Ss was not influenced by pretraining. The short-term manipulation of success appeared to be insufficient to overcome the expectancies of the lower-class Ss regarding their potential for success.

Similar results were obtained by Odom (1967) in a study of 5-, 6-, and 10-year-old middle- and lower-class children. Lower-class Ss made a significantly higher frequency of response to the reinforced stimulus than did middle-class Ss. Lower-class Ss tended to make fewer pattern responses than middle-class Ss in both this and the previous study, which may indicate that the middle-class Ss demonstrated a higher level of cognitive development. In neither study, however, was there a significant within-group relation between IQ and frequency of correct response.

One of the arguments made by Weir (1964-a) was that, unlike younger Ss, Ss between the ages of 9 and 12 are able to develop patterned response strategies in the probability learning task, but, unlike still older Ss, they are unable to reject these simple strategies if they do not pay off consistently. Weir suggested that inadequate memory of past events and their outcome is responsible for such behavior. This possibility was investigated (Weir, 1967) by providing children with a memory-aid. The Ss were 6- and 9-year-olds and adults, half tested with a memory-aid and half without. In the memory condition the Ss were given a board in which pegs could be inserted to mark the response (LMR) just made and its outcome. There was a significant interaction between condition and age: the performance of the adult Ss was not influenced by the memory-aid; the performance of the 9-year-olds, as predicted, was higher with the memory-aid than without it; and the performance of the 6-year-olds was lower with the memory aid, apparently because they failed to understand its use and it consequently became an irrelevant task that disrupted performance. The results of a second study with 5- and 9-year-olds and adults revealed that the memory-aid had other functions than merely indicating the locus of reinforcement. When three containers, each located below the response button, were used, performance did not differ from that found with only one central container. This result was not unexpected, for in previous studies, all of which used only one central container, Ss usually were able to identify the locus of reinforcement, despite the fact that they failed to select it consistently.

The results of several additional developmental studies can be noted briefly. The only exception to the previously discussed developmental changes in performance was found by Craig and Myers (1963). Kindergarten Ss performed at a lower level than fourth and eighth graders in a two-choice problem. The use of a noncontingent schedule may account for the different results, but why this should be so is not clear. Kessen and Kessen (1961) contrasted the behavior of younger and older Ss, with median ages of 3 ½ and 4 ½ years, in a two-choice problem where the probabilities of reinforcement changed in the middle of the experiment. The younger Ss showed a greater reluctance to give up a rule that had previously been established and continued to respond in the second period on the basis of the schedule that had been in effect during the first period. The older Ss, however, were able to modify their performance as a function of the changed probabilities. A related effect was found by Odom and Coon (1966). The LMR pattern of responses were reinforced in the three-choice problem for 90 trials, after which 20 extinction trials were presented. Six-year-olds were unable to give up the pattern response when it was no longer reinforced, but 11- and 19-year-olds showed clear evidence of extinction.

A variant of the probability learning task was used in a hide-and-seek game presented to Ss at ages 3 to 5, 7 to 8, and 10 to 12 years by Stevenson and Odom (1964). The E hid objects in three boxes so that the percentage of reinforcement for choices of the various boxes was 75, 25, or 0%. On alternate trials S hid objects, and E looked in S's boxes according to a random schedule or a fixed schedule of 75–25–0% responses to the three boxes. Had the Ss adopted the optimal strategy for seeking by looking in the experimenter's 75% box and for hiding by placing their objects in the 0% box, a correlation between these two behaviors should have been obtained. There was no significant relation, however, between Ss' frequency of seeking in E's 75% box and of hiding in the 0% box at any age level, indicating that the strategy for response differed according to S's role as seeker or hider. As was found in the other tasks, however, Ss tended, with increasing age, to be more variable in their seeking behavior, to vary their responses more frequently after both reinforcement and nonreinforcement, to adopt patterned responses more frequently, and to utilize positional responses less frequently. In their hiding behavior Ss in the fixed condition did not relinquish the use of the 75% box, but they did show less variable behavior in this than in the random condition. The difference in performance between the two conditions was greater for the two oldest than for the youngest groups of Ss.

The study was repeated by Odom (1966a), but sex of E in relation to sex of S was varied. The Es hid trinkets in only one of the three boxes 66% of the time, and their seeking responses followed a random schedule. A significant sex of E by sex of S interaction was found with the 6-year-old Ss: boys made more correct responses than girls when E was a female, and girls made more correct responses than boys when E was a male. Thus the social setting, as well as the other variables that

have been discussed, may influence children's behavior in a probability learning task.

No sex differences in probability learning have been found, but the results of a study by Kass (1964) indicate that boys may be more likely to select situations that yield high or intermediate levels of reinforcement than are girls, who are more likely to select a situation that yields a low but consistent level of reinforcement. These results were derived from a study of children's choices of slot machines that were programmed so that each had an equal expected monetary return but a different probability of payoff.

Finally, Gratch (1964) studied possible differences in children's dependency upon adult approval of their performance in a probabilistic task at ages 6, 9, and 11 years. Two decks of cards differed in their construction so that one of two cards was more likely to appear in one deck than in the other. Teachers' ratings were obtained of the degree to which the children were dependent upon adult approval. The Ss were given practice on the two decks and then were asked whether or not they wished, in subsequent trials, to wager candy they had been given. The more dependent children showed a greater unwillingness to make such wagers than the less dependent children, but no differences in their actual guessing behavior were found. The older children evidenced more understanding of the structure of the task than the 6-year-olds, whose guesses were approximately the same for the two decks.

Incentive Effects

Incentive effects in probability learning generally have been studied on the assumption that effects found with no manifest incentives or with incentives of low value would be magnified when incentives were introduced. Brackbill, Kappy, and Starr (1962), for example, assumed that "Ss will maximize gain to the extent that there is something tangible to be gained by so doing" (p. 32). For each correct guess in a two-choice problem Ss were given 0, 1, 3, or 5 marbles which later could be turned in for a prize. The greatest difference in level of responding was attributable to the presence or absence of reward, but a decreasing hierarchy of "correct" responses (i.e., responses to the more frequently recurring stimulus) was found as the magnitude of reward decreased. Several other studies obtained similar findings. Lower levels of asymptotic response were found by Siegel and Andrews (1962) with preschool Ss when the rewards were of low value than when they were of high value. Lewis, Wall, and Aronfreed (1963) found with 7-, but not 11-year-olds that the addition of supportive comments from the experimenter resulted in a significantly higher level of correct responding than occurred when Ss were given only information about the outcome of their previous guesses. The 6- and 7-year-olds in a study by Walters and Foote (1962) were more likely to make the correct response when they were given tokens that could be exchanged for prizes than when they were rewarded only with tokens. Finally, Offenbach (1964) found a higher level of performance when kindergarten and fourth grade Ss were reinforced with 1 or 3 marbles that later could be exchanged for a toy than when no marbles were given for correct response. The Ss were penalized for incorrect response by being required to return an equivalent number of marbles.

An interaction between incentive effects and social class was reported by Rosenhan (1966). Six-year-olds were praised for response to the more frequently reinforcing stimulus in a 70:30 two-choice problem or were given statements of disapproval following responses to the less frequently reinforced side. It was assumed that lower-class Ss are more sensitive to the responses of an adult than are middle-class children. The prediction that performance would be more strongly facilitated by praise in the lower than in the middle-class children was supported, as was the prediction that the performance of the lower-class children would be more disrupted by disapproval. The performance of middle-class children fell between the two extremes formed by the lower-class children and showed a tendency to be higher in the disapproval condition.

The results of a study by Stevenson and Weir (1959b) were in the opposite direction from those found in the preceding studies. When 5-year-olds were tested with the three-choice problem, higher levels of response were obtained with incentives of low value than with incentives of high value, when the reinforced choice yielded both 66 and 33% reinforcement. Although the results differ from those of the other studies, they are in line

with the assumption that incentives affect performance by determining the degree to which Ss will attempt to find a solution to the problem. If Ss persist in attempting to find a solution, they must continue to vary their behavior, thereby reducing the frequency with which they select the reinforcing stimulus. Paradoxically, then, the desire to obtain more incentives of high value should result in Ss' actually obtaining fewer reinforcements. Results similar to those found in this study were obtained by Das and Panda (1963).

Several studies have attempted to clarify the basis of these differences in incentive effects. Stevenson and Hoving (1964) noted that in addition to many procedural differences among the studies, the ages of the Ss also differed. Therefore a study was undertaken with 4-, 9-, 14-, and 20-year-olds with the three-choice problem and two levels of incentive. A curvilinear relation between frequency of correct response and age was obtained, and the interaction between age and level of incentive was significant. The results of the Stevenson and Weir (1959b) study were replicated for the 4-year-olds. For the two intermediate ages, the level of response of the high incentive group was below that of the low incentive group. Level of incentive did not differentiate the performance of the oldest Ss. It thus appeared that the youngest Ss were performing in line with an expectancy theory, but that the performance of the older Ss could be predicted more satisfactorily from a utility theory.

The effects of age and incentive value also were studied by Bisett and Rieber (1966). Prior to introducing the experimental task, the 6- to 7- and 10- to 11-year-old Ss were presented a variety of incentives in paired comparisons to establish what, for each child, was an incentive of high and low value. This procedure had not been followed in the preceding studies, where differences in incentive value were established on the basis of the experimenter's judgment or from preferences children demonstrated in pretests. When the Ss were tested in a two-choice task with only one alternative yielding reinforcement, a higher level of performance was found at both age levels for Ss who were given incentives of high value.

Obviously, factors other than age must play an important role in determining the effects of incentives on probability learning. Weir and Gruen (1965) investigated two other sources of differences, the number of choices and the type of problem. The prototypes for the problems were the two-choice problem of Siegel and Andrews (1962) and the three-choice problem. The conditions of the Siegel and Andrews study were replicated and extended to include three choices. The three-choice problem was presented as it had been in previous studies and modified so that only two choices were available. The ratio of reinforcement was 75:25 when there were two choices and 75:12.5:12.5 when there were three choices. In all cases the Ss were preschool children. The results were consistent but perplexing. The Ss given a high level of incentive with the Siegel and Andrews two-choice problem performed at a higher level than the Ss given a low level of incentive (prizes versus knowledge of results), thus replicating the earlier results. When the Siegel and Andrews task was extended to include three choices, no differences in performance according to level of incentive were found. Furthermore, with the standard three-choice problem, Ss performed at a lower level with high incentives than with low incentives, thereby replicating earlier findings with this problem. When one of the alternative choices in the standard three-choice problem was eliminated, thus reducing it to a two-choice problem, the differences in performance between the two incentive conditions were minimal.

The results of these studies are tantalizing, for although the effects are replicable, the bases of the differences in results remain unknown. In general, the study of the effects of incentives on children's learning is a troublesome topic. In discrimination learning, differences in performance as a function of level of incentive were difficult to obtain; in probability learning differences were easy to find but hard to understand.

Effects of Instructions

It has been suggested in earlier studies and found in the direct verbalizations obtained by Stevenson and Weir (1963) during the course of Ss' performance that children enter the probability learning task with a strong expectation that consistent reinforcement is possible. Instructions that there is or is not a method whereby such a frequency can be obtained therefore should have strong differential effects on performance. Weir (1962) investigated this possibility by instructing Ss that there was a way of obtaining a reward on every trial, that there was not a way, or by giving no instructions. The Ss were 5- to 7- and 9-year-olds. The three-choice problem was used with 50% reinforcement of one response. The younger Ss performed at a higher level than the older Ss, but there was no main effect of instructions or an interaction between instructions and age.

A subsequent study by Gruen and Weir (1964) included a broader sampling of ages. The Ss were 7- to 8- and 12- to 14-year-olds and college students. The instructional conditions were the same as those of the previous study, but a penalty condition was added in which Ss were required to return a reinforcer following incorrect response. Again, instructions had no overall effect on performance. There was an instructions-by-age interaction, where only the college Ss performed in the manner predicted by showing a higher level of response when they were told that no solution was possible. The direction of the results was opposite from that predicted for the youngest Ss. Overall, level of performance varied directly with age and Ss penalized for incorrect response selected the reinforcing stimulus more frequently than did those who were not penalized. Apparently it is very difficult to disengage younger Ss from the sets with which they approach the task by means of verbal instructions.

Binary Prediction

Several studies of binary prediction offer additional information about variables that influence trial-to-trial changes in the performance of preschool children. A study by Bogartz and Pederson (1966) demonstrates the sensitivity of this type of task. Preschool Ss were told they would play a guessing game with lights and the sequence would always be blue-green-blue-green; they were shown how the lights alternated in color. In one phase of the study the lights appeared consistently in one window and in the other they alternated between an upper and lower aperture. There were more errors and latency of response was greater when the colors remained in the same position than when they alternated, and more errors generally were made when the intertrial interval was 10 seconds than when it was 3 seconds. The remarkable thing about these results is that differences appeared even after the Ss had been instructed about what would happen.

A second report by Bogartz (1966) presents the results of two other studies with preschool children. In the first, the Ss were given experience, in different orders, with three sequences of events in which the two components appeared as ABAB, ABBABB, or ABBBABBB. When the alternation sequence was presented first, performance improved rapidly, but when it was preceded by experience with either of the other sequences, there was little change in performance. The nonalternating sequences were very difficult for the preschool Ss to learn. In a second study, Ss were given preliminary experience with two events whose probability of recurrence varied so that it was low, at a chance level, or high. When the Ss later were tested with an alternation pattern, Ss who had experienced longer runs of single events showed the least tendency to predict an event opposite to the event that occurred on the preceding trial.

Mathematical Models

Persons interested in mathematical models will be dismayed by the lack of concern in this review with the relation between children's performance and the levels of response predicted from such models. The generation of mathematical models of behavior in situations with uncertain outcomes has occupied a great deal of attention in research with animals and human adults, but with the exception of such studies as those Atkinson, Sommer, and Sterman (1960), Atkinson, Calfee, Sommer, Jeffrey, and Shoemaker (1964), and Bogartz (1965, 1966), few studies have tested such models with children. Since appropriate tests require extended series of trials, and since it is difficult to retain children in testing situations for long periods of time, children may be ineffective Ss for such research. In addition, it is difficult to define a "pure" situation in which a model can be tested and at the same time maintain children's interest in the task. At any rate, it appears likely that the parameters for the equations used in contemporary models will have

to be modified and perhaps extended if they are to encompass developmental changes in performance and the effects of other variables that have been found to influence the behavior of children in probability learning.

CONCEPT LEARNING

Although studies of concept learning have been included in the past several sections, two groups of studies remain to be discussed. Early studies (see Munn, 1954) demonstrated the important roles that age and intelligence play in concept learning. Interest in these variables has persisted, but recent research has been more concerned with investigating the bases for such differences than with uncovering tasks that are sensitive to the effects of these variables.

Developmental Studies

Odom (1966b) has distinguished three levels of learning that may occur in a concept learning task. The most primitive is learning simple S-R relations for the various instances of a concept; an intermediate level involves learning to label the specific instances; and the most advanced level involves learning to label by categories rather than by instances. A situation similar to a reversal shift was devised with pictures of the heads and bodies of animals. During training, the heads of four animals and the bodies of four others were presented in pairs, with reinforcement following choices of heads. (Each category was reinforced for half of the Ss, but for simplicity only one of the sequences will be described.) The portion of the animal not presented during training was used in the transfer trials. The category relevant during training continued to be relevant for half of the Ss, and the other category became relevant for the remaining Ss. Thus in the first case "heads" remained relevant but was represented by new instances, and in the second case "bodies" became relevant—but, importantly, the bodies were those of the animals whose heads had been correct in the training period. The Ss were 5-, 11-, and 14-year-olds.

During original learning, the youngest Ss required four times as many trials to reach criterion as the oldest Ss. When the transfer trials required reversal of the original discrimination, the youngest Ss learned as rapidly as the oldest Ss. For example, they had little difficulty in learning that the body of the tiger was now correct after having learned that the head of the tiger was correct. The ease with which the youngest Ss learned the reversal apparently indicated that they were not responding at a primitive S-R level but had labeled the stimuli during the training trials and were using the labels to direct their performance in the transfer trials. When, however, the transfer trials required the Ss to continue to respond by category rather than by instance, the 5-year-olds made many more errors than the older Ss, who again learned very rapidly. It was concluded that even though the 5-year-olds had responded mediationally, they did not use mediational abilities to organize the stimuli by conceptual categories.

Osler and Kofsky have attempted to determine the effects of adding irrelevant information in a concept learning task at different ages. Their first study (Osler and Kofsky, 1965) established that the difficulty of a concept learning task could be increased by adding one or two irrelevant dimensions to the discriminative stimuli in a two-choice task. However, the performance of 4-, 6-, and 8-year-olds did not produce a significant interaction between age and number of irrelevant dimensions. A second study (Osler and Kofsky, 1966) explored the hypothesis that the structure of the task, as well as the presence of irrelevant information, may be an important variable in rate of learning concepts, and that its effects differ, depending upon the age of S. They assumed that younger Ss employ rote learning in a concept learning task, whereas older Ss respond on the basis of categories. The younger Ss therefore should be more strongly influenced by the number of S-R relations present in the task, and older Ss should be more strongly influenced by the number of categories or dimensions on which the stimuli vary. Five-, 8-, and 11-year-olds were tested with one of three sets of stimuli. In one set there were one relevant and three irrelevant dimensions, each represented by two values; in the second set, one relevant dimension represented by two values and one irrelevant dimension represented by eight values; and in the third set, one relevant and one irrelevant dimension, each represented by two values. Thus there were 16 different stimuli in the first two sets and four in the third. The dimensions of the stimuli differed according to form, color, size, and number. If the preceding reasoning is correct, the younger Ss should perform similarly with the first two sets, but older Ss should find the second set as easy as the third. The results supported these considerations. Five-year-olds made large and equivalent numbers of errors on the first two sets, but with the third set they learned nearly as rapidly as the older Ss. The older Ss learned the second and third sets with equal ease, but the 8-year-olds, and to some degree the 11-year-olds, found the first set quite difficult. Thus the crucial factor for the youngest Ss was size of set, and for older Ss, number of independent dimensions represented in the set.

In a subsequent study, Kofsky and Osler (1967) found the presence of irrelevant information may thwart successful performance by 5-year-olds because of their difficulty in shifting criteria for categorizing stimuli. Children at ages 5, 8, and 11 years showed preferences in the order with which they categorized stimuli such as those used in the previous study, but their preferences had a restrictive effect only on the ability of the youngest Ss to make additional sortings. In concept learning, then, young Ss may perform well if the initial basis for classifying the stimuli is in accord with their preferences, but if it is not they may make many errors before they discern other bases by which they can categorize the stimuli.

Another important process in concept learning is integration of information. The Kendlers have asked when children are able to integrate segments of behavior that previously have been learned but were not contiguously associated. A task was developed for studying this question. In a series of training trials Ss learned that X leads to Y, A leads to B, and B leads to G, the goal. Concretely, the Ss learned to press a lever or push a button to obtain Y and B (e.g., a marble and a steel ball, respectively), and to drop B in a hole to obtain a prize. Training consisted of two steps: first, learning which responses led to Y and B; and second, learning that B led to G. Kendler and Kendler (1962) found that very few 5-year-olds were capable of giving a direct, inferential solution in this problem. By the third grade, however, 73% of the Ss initially selected the A-B segment in a test trial and of these, 67% followed directly with the B-G segment.

In a second study (Kendler, Kendler, and Carrick, 1966) an effort was made to see whether performance of the younger Ss could be improved if verbal labels were given to Y and B. It was assumed that the label would provide a common stimulus element for the A-B and B-G segments, which would facilitate solution. Kindergarten Ss who labeled the stimuli performed only slightly more poorly than third-grade Ss. As predicted, kindergarten Ss performed more poorly when they did not use labels, but, unexpectedly, labels interfered with the performance of the older Ss. The last finding is interpretable if it is assumed that the labels arbitrarily given to the stimuli by the experimenter may produce interference if they differ from those the Ss spontaneously apply to the stimuli.

Performance in concept learning tasks does not always improve with increasing age. For example, in a study by Friedman (1965) with children between the ages of 6 and 10, performance dropped at ages 8 to 9 in learning a series of sequential-pattern problems. This decline was attributed to the ineffective operation of mediation at these ages. Presumably, younger Ss could learn a pattern of responses (opening doors of boxes in varying orders) by trial and error and the oldest Ss could apply rules leading to efficient performance. The 8- to 9-year-old was assumed to have progressed beyond the trial-and-error to a mediation stage, but "he has not yet learned to use his new tool efficiently. He is so rigid in the application of this newly developing ability that his predictions (i.e., hypotheses) mask the actual regularity of events, thus he is unable to modify his hypotheses so as to include new information" (p. 4). This interpretation is similar to that offered earlier for the poor performance of Ss at these ages in probability learning.

TeVault, Bailey, Cagan, Dionis, and Figelman (1966) attempted to determine whether the hypothesized changes between 8 and 9 year olds in ability to mediate could be demonstrated with a different task. Half of the Ss were assigned single responses to classes of stimuli (forms) and for the other half the assignment of responses to stimuli was random. Learning was more efficient in the first condition. There was no significant effect associated with age or the interaction of age with condition. The results were interpreted as not supporting the hypothesis offered by Friedman in the preceding study. Perhaps the most noteworthy aspect of this study, however, was the significant experimenter effect. The results differed, depending upon which of the five experimenters the Ss had been assigned to. Although experimenter effects have been found in studies in other areas of child psychology and in studies with adults, its operation in a study of this type indicates a potentially important source of variance that is often not considered in studies of children's learning. The possibility of significant experimenter effects complicates the design of research. At the same time, a failure to replicate prior results may be due to differences between or among the experimenters rather than to other, seemingly more basic differences in experimental effects.

A common theme runs through all these studies. The young child is viewed as a relatively rigid rote learner whose performance is determined by the number of relations to be learned and whose spontaneous use of verbal labels is restricted to nominal statements about the stimuli. The older Ss, on the other hand, are seen to be flexible and verbally facile and to use these characteristics in successive attempts to isolate the attributes of the stimuli that are relevant for correct response.

Role of Intelligence

Osler and her associates have investigated the relation between intelligence and concept learning in a series of studies. In the initial study (Osler and Fivel, 1961) the correct response in a two-choice discrimination depended upon S's isolating the concept of bird, animal, or living thing. These classes of stimuli were assumed to represent increasingly more difficult concepts. The Ss were 6-, 10-, and 14-year-old children, half above average (mean IQ of 121) and half of average IQ (mean IQ of 101). The older Ss and the brighter Ss at each age learned the concepts more rapidly, and there were no differences in the rate with which the three concepts were learned. To determine whether the concepts were learned rapidly or gradually, performance on the 10 trials preceding criterion were analyzed for each S. Those whose percentage of correct response fell below the median were classed as sudden learners, and above the median, as gradual learners. The incidence of sudden learners was a function of IQ, but not of age or concept, leading the writers to infer that the brighter Ss were better able to develop hypotheses than were the average Ss.

If bright children develop hypotheses more readily, stimuli that are likely to elicit a wide variety of irrelevant hypotheses should result in bright Ss' performing more poorly than would be the case if the stimuli permitted a more restricted number of hypotheses. The concept "two" was studied by Osler and Trautman (1961) with samples of Ss of the age and IQ levels used in the first study. The concept was represented either by dots or by pictures of common objects. It was assumed that the large number of irrelevant cues contained in the pictures would facilitate the formation of hypotheses. Correct response required that S select the member in each of a large number of pairs that contained two elements and reject the member that contained one or more than two elements. The main effect of age was significant, and IQ interacted significantly with method of representation. The bright Ss had more difficulty in learning the discrimination when the stimuli were objects than when they were dots, but the average Ss learned each with equal ease.

It should be noted that Wolff (1967) in a replication study found no significant interaction between IQ and method of presentation. Both the bright and average Ss performed more poorly when the stimuli were pictures of common objects. Wolff noted that the number of times "one" had been used as the negative instance by Osler and Trautman differed for the two types of stimuli and argued that this contributed to the differences in results. Additional research will be necessary to clarify this.

It is possible that the superiority of bright children lies in their greater capabilities in defining problems, rather than in their being more effective learners. Under the nonspecific instructions used by Osler and Fivel (1961), bright Ss performed at a higher level than average Ss. But could their greater effectiveness be traced to their discerning more readily the problem that was to be solved? To investigate this question, Osler and Weiss

(1962) repeated the earlier study with groups of the same ages and IQs, but added a condition in which the Ss were given the explicit instruction: "If you look at the pictures carefully you will see that there is something in the pictures like an idea that will tell you which one to choose to get a marble every time." The earlier results were replicated with nonspecific instructions but differences in the performance of the bright and average Ss disappeared when the instructions explicitly defined what the Ss were to do. As expected, type of instructions facilitated the performance of the average Ss and had no differential effect on the performance of the bright Ss.

In a final study of the series, Osler and Shapiro (1964) tested bright and average Ss with continuous and partial reinforcement. The task involved discriminating between two and three circles appearing in different spatial arrangements. The bright Ss were significantly superior to the average Ss when continuous reinforcement was available. With partial reinforcement, performance did not differ according to the level of IQ. Support thus was obtained for the hypothesis that the performance of bright Ss would be disrupted to a greater degree than would that of the average Ss when their efforts at generating rules met with only partial success.

These studies point to several factors that distinguish the concept learning of bright Ss. Bright Ss appear to be able to define problems more readily and to produce more hypotheses than average children. When the formulation of many hypotheses is of assistance in the development of the correct response and when there is consistent affirmation of the utility of a particular hypothesis, bright Ss perform at a higher level than average Ss. When the stimuli elicit few hypotheses and when the problem is clearly defined, IQ, at the levels tested, is not a critical variable in concept learning.

PAIRED-ASSOCIATE LEARNING

The learning of paired-associate lists is among the most venerable of psychological problems. There has been a long history of intensive research with human adults as Ss, but relatively few studies with children were published until recently. Why child psychologists shied away from this problem for so many years is not clear, especially since learning to associate names and places, dates and events, occupies so much of the child's time in school and, consequently, becomes a problem with practical significance. At any rate, once research with children began to be published, it rapidly became apparent that paired-associate learning was a sensitive means of investigating the effect of many variables that have important implications for a wide variety of learning tasks.

Associative Strength

The effects of the associative strength of the S and R elements have been studied by selecting response elements that differ in their associative strength to the stimulus elements in the child's natural language. Castaneda, Fahel, and Odom (1961) established the free-association value of a list of words for fifth and sixth graders and then constructed paired-associate lists by using strong or weak associates of the stimulus items. Learning was significantly faster when the associative strength was high, a result that would be expected except for the fact that it is difficult to demonstrate this effect with adult Ss. This finding has been replicated by McCullers (1961) and extended by Wicklund, Palermo, and Jenkins (1964). The availability of more extensive word association norms enabled the latter authors to make a more sensitive test of the effect of associative strength on learning. Lists of 10 items were constructed so that the responses were primary associations to the stimulus words or were of medium or very low strength. In addition, half of the primary responses were high-frequency responses and half were of low frequency. The ease with which fourth-grade Ss learned the lists varied directly with the strength of the associations and the primary responses were learned more rapidly when they were of high frequency.

Klinger and Palermo (1967) found the same general results when the lists were presented aurally to first and fourth graders. The effects differed at the two age levels. Performance was similar at the two ages on a control list in which the S-R relations had no associative strength. But when the lists contained items of either high or low associative strength, the older Ss learned with great rapidity, whereas the performance of the younger Ss began at a low level and never reached that of the older Ss. The greater linguistic experience of the older Ss apparently enabled them to benefit from lists that contained items with some natural associative S-R relation.

In a study by Shapiro (1965), items with high and low association value were arranged to form a noncompetitive list (the R was paired with the S that elicited it in free association) or a competitive list (the list was rearranged so that the R was paired with an S different from that which elicited it in free association). It was predicted that strongly associated elements arranged in a competitive list would generate a high degree of interference but that when arranged in a noncompetitive list they would produce facilitation. The Ss, fifth graders, were selected from the sample used in establishing the word association norms and their responses had either high or low degrees of commonality with the responses most frequently made by the Ss in the normative group. This variable was introduced to determine whether group norms would be a more effective basis for prediction when the responses of the individual S were in close concordance with these norms than when they were not. Learning was more rapid with high-association pairs, noncompetitive pairings, and for Ss with high commonality scores. Better performance for high-association pairs was found on the noncompetitive lists, but there was no difference in the competitive lists according to strength of S-R association.

A study of Palermo, Flamer, and Jenkins (1964) found similar effects when the association value of the response elements was varied by using consonant-vowel-consonant nonsense syllables with association values of 20, 50, and 80%. Adjectives served as the stimulus elements. The difference in rate of learning the extreme lists was significant for the fifth-grade Ss. Further, when the response elements were numbers that were presumably highly meaningful, the Ss learned the associations more rapidly than when they were nonsense syllables with low association values.

The facilitating effect of using items with high associative strength extends to studies where the response element is omitted on a portion of the trials (Carroll and Penney,

1966). The learning of items with low associative strength was more strongly disturbed
by the partial omission of the response element than was the learning of items with
high associative strength.

A different approach has been used by
Ramiriz and Castaneda (1967). They selected names of children who had received
either high or low sociometric ranks for use
as the stimulus elements. More behaviors
were assumed to be associated with the names
of children with high sociometric rank, thus
making their names more meaningful. The
rate of learning to associate consonants with
names was faster when the names were of
children with high sociometric ranks. That
the effect was not due to some other factor,
such as general association value of the names
or pronouncability, was seen in the fact that
children unfamiliar with the names learned
the two lists in equal numbers of trials.

Another related study is that of Paivio and
Yuille (1966), who found more efficient
learning when the materials were high-frequency, concrete nouns than when they were
high-frequency, abstract nouns. The effect
was more pronounced when the nouns functioned as stimulus elements than when they
were the response elements. The basis of the
effect is not clear, but concrete nouns may
elicit a greater number of facilitating associations than do abstract nouns.

Mode of Presentation

Since much of the formal learning of the
young child occurs through the auditory
mode, learning of paired associates might
be more rapid if the items were presented
by the aural than by the traditional visual
mode. Shapiro (1966) tested this possibility
with 10- and 11-, and 13- and 14-year-olds.
Lists contained items with high or low in-
terresponse competition and high or low associative strengths. Learning was faster with
the noncompetitive lists, and items of high
associative strength in noncompetitive lists
were learned more rapidly than were items
of low associative strength. The main effects
of age and mode of presentation were not
significant, nor were the interactions of these
variables with either of the other variables.
However, when the analyses were made
separately at each age, it was found that the
younger Ss but not the older Ss learned faster

with aural than with visual presentation. More
rapid learning with aural than visual presentation also was obtained by Budoff and Quinlan (1964) in a study with 7- and 8-year-
olds. When, however, the visual stimuli are
pictures rather than words, no differences
were found between modes in the rate of
learning by 7- and 8-year-olds (Hill and
Hecker, 1966).

These results suggest that young children
may have difficulty with visually presented
material because of their lack of experience
with written words. Levin, Watson, and Feldman (1964) therefore assumed that pretraining young children on the construction of
words might facilitate later learning. Since
an earlier study had indicated that the number of confusions in verbal learning was
greatest when two or more words shared an
initial grapheme and was least when they
shared medial graphemes, first-grade Ss were
trained on initial, medial, or terminal graphemes of an artificial orthography devised for
use in an eight-item paired-associate task.
The Ss were required to trace the graphemes
occupying one of the positions in each of the
artificial words three times. Overall, none of
the groups performed differently from a control group, which did not have the tracing
experience, but the number of correct responses in the paired-associate task was in
the predicted order, and the number of correct responses of the group tracing the initial
graphemes was significantly higher than that
of the group tracing the medial graphemes.

The most extensive investigation of this
topic has been reported by Otto (1961), who
selected Ss at grades 2, 4, and 6, who were
good, average, and poor readers, and who
had IQs between 95 and 110. The task involved learning to associate low association
value nonsense syllables with geometric
forms. Three modes of presentation were
used: (1) visual; (2) visual presentation of
the form, reading of the nonsense syllable
by the experimenter; and (3) a combination
of the first two, plus the requirement that S
trace the nonsense syllable with his finger.
The poor readers in grade 2 required approximately twice as long to learn the list as
the good readers, but by grade 6 the difference had decreased. There was no interaction
between reading level and mode of presentation, as might be expected, but mode of

presentation did interact significantly with grade. The combined mode of presentation (3) was most effective for the grade-2 Ss, the visual mode was most effective at grade 4, and at grade 6 the two modes were of approximately equal effectiveness. Verbalization of the response element produced the slowest learning at the two higher grades but was somewhat better than the visual mode at grade 2.

Several other studies deal with quite different questions related to the effects of different modes of presenting paired-associate materials. The learning of paired-associate lists often is discussed as involving two steps: first, delimiting the alternative responses, and second, attaching the responses to the stimulus elements. If this description is correct, learning should be faster if all response elements are presented to Ss on each trial than if, as is the usual case, they become known only during the course of successive trials. Carroll (1966) found the 10- and 11-year-olds did learn more rapidly in the former than in the latter case. It also is possible that learning would be faster if the lists were presented in a constant rather than a varied order. Samuels and Jeffrey (1966) found that the number of correct responses was higher with a constant order when the response items were of high similarity, but order was not a significant variable when the responses were of low similarity. Finally, learning of individual items may be more rapid if only a small number of items are presented. In a large parametric investigation, including lists of 4, 8, 12, and 20 items, Carroll and Burke (1965) found with tenth graders, however, that "items appear to be acquired one by one and at a rate that is relatively independent of the total number of items presented in a given trial or session. For example, it has been shown in this study that it takes about the same amount of exposure and response time for an S to acquire 4 items regardless of whether they stand alone or are embedded in a list of 20 items" (p. 552).

Affective Factors

The role of affective factors, such as anxiety, stress, and conflict, has been studied extensively in the paired-associate learning of adults. There are fewer studies with children,

but the results obtained with children and adults are similar. Most of these studies have sought to evaluate the hypotheses that (1) strength of response is a function of the product of level of drive and habit strength and (2) general level of drive is increased by the presence of affective factors such as those previously listed. According to these hypotheses, high drive should result in improved performance when habit strength of the correct response is high. When, however, the habit strength of the correct response is lower than that of alternative, competing responses, high drive should disrupt performance.

A study by Lipsitt and Spears (1965) illustrates how these predictions have been tested in paired-associate learning. Triads of stimuli were constructed so that one response was strongly associated with all three stimulus elements, but for two of the pairs, the correct response was a weak associate. For example, if the triad was fork-eat, knife-hat, spoon-door, the tendency to respond "eat" to each of the stimuli, should be strong for all Ss, but of greatest strength for the Ss with high drive. Two studies with sixth-grade Ss were reported. In one, drive level was manipulated by selecting Ss from extreme scores on a paper-and-pencil test of manifest anxiety, and in the second, an effort was made to increase drive for half of the Ss by giving instructions that emphasized the importance of responding correctly and doing as well as other children. The results partially confirmed the hypothesis. Performance on the low-association items was impaired for high-anxious and stress-instructed Ss, but no differences occurred for the high-association items, partly because they were learned with great ease. The mechanism assumed to account for differences in performance was not relevant, for the errors were mostly extralist errors and neither anxiety nor stress increased the tendency of Ss to make the high-association response, as was predicted.

More generally supportive evidence for the hypothesized mechanism was found by Castaneda (1961) in a motor paired-associate task with fifth graders as Ss. Five lights appeared in a horizontal array, and below each light was a response button. The Ss were assumed to have a strong tendency to press the button directly below each light. For some light-button combinations these tendencies resulted in correct response, but for other combinations correct response required the Ss to make a nondominant response. High levels of anxiety were predicted to result in better performance when the dominant response was correct (i.e., habit strength was high) but poorer performance when the dominant response was incorrect. In the second case, the heightened tendency to make the dominant, incorrect response would result in more errors. The results revealed a significant interaction between level of anxiety and type of button correct, with each of the differences being in the predicted direction. There were more dominant response errors for the high- than for the low-anxious Ss and the number of random errors made by the two groups did not differ. Similar results were found in the same type of task by Castaneda and Lipsitt (1959) when drive level was manipulated by introducing stress in the form of a time pressure for response. Impaired paired-associate learning with high levels of anxiety has been reported in several other studies. Stevenson and Odom (1965) obtained significant negative correlations between rate of learning and anxiety scores for boys at grades 4 and 6. The correlations for girls were negative but were not significant. Castaneda, Palermo, and McCandless (1956) presented high- and low-anxious Ss with a five-light–five-button motor paired-associate task. Performance of the two groups was compared for the two easiest and two most difficult combinations. Compared to the low-anxious Ss, high-anxious Ss performed better on the easy combinations and more poorly on the difficult combinations. These results are in line with the assumption that level of difficulty of the combinations was determined by the number of competing responses, all of which would be of higher strength for the high-anxious Ss. Poorer performance of high-anxious Ss also was found in a four-light–two-button task (Palermo, Castaneda, and McCandless, 1956). Here it was assumed that only two alternatives for response would increase the likelihood that competing responses would be present, thereby making this a relatively difficult task.

A within-Ss design has been used in several studies of this general problem. The proposition tested in these studies was that "conditions which produce associative interference,

that is, competition between incompatible response tendencies, may serve to engender motivational states in the S" (Castaneda, 1965, p. 2). To test this proposition, paired-associate lists were constructed in sets of two so that the presence of competing associations was maximized for some of the sets but minimized for others. Test pairs were interspersed among these two types of set, always following a set of items with high or low competing associations. Half of the test pairs were strong associates and half were weak, but neither had a strong associative relation with the other items. The measure of central interest was the number of trials to reach a criterion of one errorless trial on the test pairs. It was assumed that the competing associations would generate states of conflict that would result in an increased drive level, which, in turn, would facilitate performance for test pairs where the associative connections were strong and interfere with performance for test pairs where the associative connections were weak. A significant interaction was obtained between type of training pair and type of test pair. The predicted facilitating effect of conflict on the learning of the test pairs with strong associative connections was obtained, but the difference for the weakly associated test pairs was not reliable. A variant of this procedure was employed by McCullers (1967), and again performance for strongly associated test pairs improved as interference within a training pair increased but no effect was found for the weakly associated test pairs.

Mediation

The paired-associate task is a convenient, frequently used method for investigating the effects of verbal mediation on learning. Some studies with children have used the classical mediation paradigms developed in research with adults. In these paradigms, potential mediators are developed during the course of the experiment or are derived from associations occurring in natural language. For example, potential mediators may be developed during the course of a study by requiring Ss to learn three lists of pairs of words: first, they learn to associate A with B, then B with C, and, finally, A with C. Word B is assumed to function as a potential mediator which, if effective, would facilitate the learning of the association A-C. By appropriate arrangements, the mediator may be used as a potential source of interference in learning the A-C association. It is possible to eliminate the first of the three stages by selecting words for the A-B associations from high-frequency associates in word-association norms. Other techniques for providing potential mediators between the stimulus and response elements have involved linking the two elements by verbal and pictorial means, and by varying the syntactical relations embodied in the mediating words and pictures.

Norcross and Spiker (1958) were able to demonstrate both facilitation and interference in the paired-associate learning of 5- and 6-year-olds with the three-stage paradigm. Facilitation was produced by pairings such as those described in the preceding example; interference was produced by arranging the pairings in the third list so that the potential mediator would elicit incorrect responses and thereby interfere with learning. Wismer and Lipsitt (1964) obtained similar effects with fifth graders, although the interference effects were much more pronounced than were the facilitation effects.

The same types of effects have been found when conditions are arranged so that the presumed mediation occurs during the learning of the A-C list (Palermo, 1962). In this design, only A-B and A-C lists were presented and in each list there were six stimulus elements and three response elements. After the A-B list was learned, new responses were paired with the old stimuli in a manner that would be expected to produce facilitation, interference, or no effect. Using the facilitation arrangement as an example, the response "scissors" was paired with both "stool" and "shoe" in the first list. In the second list, both stimulus words were associated with the response "house." Since both stimulus elements were associated with the same response element in each stage, the strengthening of each association in the second stage should facilitate the learning of the other because of the tendency for each to elicit the common mediator "scissors."

Nikkel and Palermo (1965) used both A-B, B-C, A-C, and A-B, C-A, C-B paradigms in a study with sixth graders, where the words entering the A-B association were selected because of their high association value. Here, as in all of the studies, a control group, in

which the associations developed in the second stage were irrelevant for learning in the third stage, provided the basis for determining the presence of facilitation or interference. The results were similar for the two paradigms; the fastest learning of the A-C and C-B lists occurred in the facilitation conditions, and the slowest in the interference conditions. Thus existing language habits significantly influenced the acquisition of new verbal habits, apparently by implementing the mediation process. Palermo (1966) extended the findings with sixth graders to lists of the forms C-B, B-A, A-C and B-C, B-A, A-C. The relative differences among the facilitation, control, and interference conditions were as great in this study, where one or two backward associations were necessary for mediation to occur, as they were in the other studies, where only forward associations were involved.

A different approach was used by Reese (1965) in an investigation of the roles of verbal and visual content of the response items in paired-associate learning. The Ss were preschool children at three age levels (average ages 44, 58, and 77 months). The stimuli were pictures of animals and the responses were either pictures of objects or drawings of the animals engaged in activities with the objects (e.g., cat carrying an umbrella). On the first trial, the experimenter either verbalized the response or described the interaction between the animals and the objects. The group that saw and heard only the response was inferior in learning to the other groups, whose scores were approximately equal. The main effect of age was significant, but age did not interact with content of the response. Thus learning to associate two words was facilitated when the experimental conditions supplied a connective link, either verbal or visual, between the stimulus and response elements.

Numerous other studies have found that paired-associate learning is facilitated if the stimulus and response elements are connected by verbal or pictorial means. Davidson (1964) divided sixth graders into five groups, each trained under a different mediation condition. The stimuli were pictures of common objects. The conditions included (1) presentation of the pictures, (2) the experimenter named the pictures, (3) the experimenter named the pictures and provided a connecting preposition,

(4) the experimenter used the objects in the context of a descriptive sentence, and (5) the sentence of the preceding condition was read and a picture was presented that depicted the relation described in the sentence. The different treatments were applied only on trial 1. Learning was significantly slower in the first two than in the last three conditions, indicating that when a connective relation between the stimulus and response elements was present, even in the form of a preposition, learning was facilitated.

Syntactical mediation as a function of age has been studied by Jensen and Rohwer (1965) with children at six age levels between 5 and 17 years. On the initial trial, half of the Ss were asked to construct a sentence relating the stimulus and response elements (common objects) and half were not. A dramatic effect was obtained when Ss were asked to construct sentences: There were no age differences in rate of learning after age 7. When Ss were not required to construct sentences, age differences continued to be found. Even the performance of the oldest Ss was influenced by being asked to construct a sentence, apparently because this induced them to mediate earlier than otherwise would have been the case.

Providing verbal links between the stimulus and response elements obviously facilitates learning, but would similar facilitation occur if the links were presented pictorially? Rohwer, Lynch, Suzuki, and Levin (1967) extended Reese's (1965) study to include three verbal connectives—conjunctions, prepositions, and verbs—and three parallel pictorial connectives—coincidental, locational, and actional. Among the verbal connectives, only a connective verb produced more rapid learning than occurred in a control group where the objects merely were named. Among the pictorial connectives, more rapid learning occurred with actional (all materials were presented by means of movies) than with locational and with locational than with coincidental pictorialization. The order of the facilitative effects obtained with the verbal and pictorial connectives was approximately the same and equivalent effects were found for Ss at grades 1, 3, and 6.

A companion study (Rohwer, Lynch, Levin, and Suzuki, 1967) contrasted the rate of learning when the objects were presented pictorially and when printed names of the objects were used. Learning was more rapid at both grades 3 and 6 with pictorial than with printed materials, and, confirming the earlier results, learning was more efficient when the experimenter related the stimulus and response elements by a verb than when they were related by a preposition or a conjunction. Other studies (Rohwer, 1966; Rohwer and Lynch, 1967) add further evidence of the greater facilitating effects of verbs than of conjunctions or prepositions as connective links, but the basis of the facilitation by verbs remains unclear. It does not seem to be due solely to the fact that verbs exercise greater constraints on the number of possible words that can follow them than do prepositions or conjunctions, but alternative explanatory mechanisms have not been established.

Although the study by Martin and Jones (1965) of grammatical units in paired-associate learning does not deal with mediational processes, it is of relevance in the present discussion. Fifth and sixth graders were presented single-word nouns or noun phrases as stimulus elements and single-word verbs or verb phrases as response elements. The two words within each phrase either conformed to common grammatical order or the order was reversed (e.g., an apple versus apple an; woke up versus up woke). As measured by rate of learning, single-word nouns and noun phrases were functionally equivalent, except when the two words of the noun phrase were in the reverse grammatical order, but the Ss learned pairs involving single-word verbs more rapidly than verb phrases and these, in turn, more rapidly than pairs involving verb phrases in reversed grammatical order. Hence there was a significant influence of daily language habits on the ease of paired-associate learning.

The findings of these studies are remarkably consistent. Learning to associate words occurs more rapidly when a third word is available as a mediator or when a connective link between the words is established by verbal or pictorial means. Within the ages studied, the effects were of similar magnitude and age consistently failed to interact with experimental conditions. It appears that by the time children enter school the mediational processes occur in the same manner, although more slowly than they do at later ages.

Transfer

If a response is associated with a particular stimulus in an initial task and in a subsequent task a new response must be associated with the stimulus, the amount of training received on the first task should result in increasing interference in learning the new association. Spiker (1960) reported three studies aimed at determining (1) the relation between amount of initial practice and degree of interference and (2) whether similar results would be obtained if the effects of initial training were heightened by instructing Ss to rehearse or to use mnemonic devices (e.g., imagine a boat made of cake). Sixth graders received either 6 or 15 trials in learning four paired-associates. They were then presented a new list of eight items in which the stimuli of four of the original pairs were coupled with new responses, along with four new S-R pairs. The difference in rate of learning the two types of item was greater for the group that received the greater number of trials, apparently reflecting greater interference for these Ss in learning new responses to the old stimuli. At the same time, the extended training resulted in superior performance in learning the new S-R pairs, demonstrating a nonassociative form of facilitation. The same effects were produced by rehearsal and use of mnemonics.

Spiker and Holton (1958) found similar results when groups were given 5, 10, or 20 trials on the initial task: the more training given on task 1, the greater the interference on learning in task 2. The interference effect appeared to be attributable in part to the fact that Ss failed to respond within the time limit allowed (2 seconds). It seemed likely therefore that extending the amount of time for response would reduce the interference effect. This suggestion was tested by White, Spiker, and Holton (1960), who repeated the earlier study with a 4-second interval for response. Degree of training on task 1 now failed to produce differences in associative interference as measured by frequency of correct response. When speed of response was considered, some evidence of greater interference for a 20-trial group than for a 5-trial group was found. Extending the time interval for response also produced improved performance by preschool Ss (Price, 1963). These Ss performed more poorly with a 2-second than with a 6-second anticipation interval, but when, during the later stages of training, the interval was 6 seconds for all Ss, roughly equivalent levels of performance were attained. Since the level of performance of the 2-second group improved rapidly with the longer interval, shorter time intervals appeared to affect performance rather than learning.

A transfer design was used by Rice and DiVesta (1965) to test semantic and phonetic generalization in paired-associate learning. Third, fifth, and seventh graders initially learned nonsense syllable responses to a set of three training words. A second list of 12 items was constructed by substituting as stimulus elements a homonym, antonym, synonym, or a control word for each training word. No differential transfer was found for third graders in learning the second list; rate of learning to associate the nonsense syllables did not differ for the four categories of test stimuli. At grades 5 and 7, however, more correct responses were found for homonyms, antonyms, and synonyms than for the control words.

INCIDENTAL LEARNING

Until now, the problems have involved intentional learning where Ss were given explicit instructions about what they were to do and the cues provided a relevant basis for correct response. But does learning also occur when the Ss are not instructed to learn or when the cues contain information that is irrelevant for correct response? Casual observation indicates that learning does occur under such conditions, and the results of experimental studies have substantiated such observations. Depending upon such factors as the age of the child and the experimental conditions, however, the degree of incidental learning does differ.

Developmental Differences

One of the first developmental studies was reported by Stevenson (1954), who tested children between the ages of 3 and 7 years. At each end of a life-sized Y-maze were two boxes, one locked with a padlock. The S was told to go to the open box, find a key, and open the locked box to find a prize. In each open box was an assortment of objects, including on one side a small white purse, and on the other side a matchbox. Depending on the experimental condition, the key was on, under, or in the purse and matchbox. After an equal number of experiences with each side of the maze, the S was asked to find the purse or the matchbox. Since neither object had been mentioned by the experimenter and since there had been no necessity for Ss to learn their location, the ability of Ss to locate the object was assumed to be the result of incidental learning. The frequency of correct response increased significantly with increasing age and differed significantly among the experimental conditions. The greatest frequency of incidental learning occurred when the incidental object had to be manipulated (key in the object) and the least when no manipulation was necessary (key on the object).

Would the tendency to acquire irrelevant information continue to increase if still older Ss were tested? It can be argued that it would not. If the mature organism were responsive to the vast array of incidental stimuli that is continually available, he would be so flooded with momentarily useless information that appropriate response would be disturbed. To maintain behavior in an efficient and effective manner, the organism eventually must become selective in his attention, responding to relevant stimuli that have no immediate utility.

Maccoby and Hagen (1965) provided data relevant to this discussion in a developmental study of incidental recall in first, third, fifth, and seventh graders. It was assumed that the young child is handicapped in focusing his attention selectively because of his inexperience in discriminating between task-relevant and task-irrelevant aspects of a stimulus complex. As the child learns to categorize, code, and label objects, incidental learning may increase, but at a later stage selective attention becomes possible. Consequently, it was predicted that the relation between age and incidental learning would be curvilinear. A set of cards bearing different colors and different pictures was shown to the child. The cards were then turned over and the child was asked to point to the card bearing a particular color. Incidental recall was tested by asking the child to find cards bearing particular pictures. There was a very modest increase in number of correct responses between grades 1 and 5, and a significant decrease between grades 5

and 7. The correlations between performance on the intentional and incidental tasks were nonsignificant, indicating that the acquisitions of the central and incidental information were not reciprocal processes.

A curvilinear relation between incidental learning and chronological age also was found by Siegel and Stevenson (1966) with a different type of task. The Ss were between the ages of 7 and 14 years, roughly the ages of the Ss in the previous study. A standard three-choice successive discrimination problem was followed by the presentation of each of the discriminative stimuli imbedded in a stimulus complex. In this second phase, which constituted an overlearning period for the original discrimination, each stimulus complex was presented 12 times. To test incidental learning, the incidental objects then were presented separately. The question was whether the Ss would make the response to the incidental object that had been correct for the discriminative stimulus with which it had been associated. The frequency of correct response increased significantly between ages 7 to 8 and 11 to 12 and decreased significantly between ages 11 to 12 and 13 to 14. Again, there was no significant correlation between the measures of incidental and intentional learning.

A closely related study by Crane and Ross (1967) assessed the ability of 8- and 11-year-olds to profit by the presentation of information that was irrelevant to their performance at one stage, but later became relevant. A two-choice discrimination problem with either form or color as the relevant dimension was presented during an original learning period. The irrelevant cues appeared on every trial but in a varied manner, so that each cue was associated with reward on only half of the trials. If form was the relevant dimension, color was irrelevant, and vice versa. When Ss reached criterion on this problem, the irrelevant cues were made 100% redundant for the experimental groups. The original procedure was continued for the control groups. In the third stage, the irrelevant cues became relevant; the cue that had been associated consistently with reward was correct for half of the experimental Ss and the cue that had been paired with the nonreward was correct for the other half. The different conditions of the third stage resulted in different rates of learning by the younger, but not by the older Ss. The younger Ss learned the problem when the previously "positive" irrelevant cue was correct more rapidly than when the previously "negative" irrelevant cue was correct or than in the control condition. Thus the redundant cues of the overtraining phase had acquired functional significance for the younger Ss, but the older Ss appeared to have concentrated their attention more completely on the relevant aspects of the stimuli.

Other Studies

A study by Hetherington and Banta (1962) provides additional information about the relation between incidental and intentional learning. Six-year-olds were given a color-naming test in which cards of different colors also contained different pictures of common objects. After a delay of 2 days the Ss were asked to recall the names of the objects. The procedure was repeated, but now the Ss named the objects and were instructed to try to remember their names. As found in the previous studies, there was no significant relation between the intentional and incidental learning scores. What causes an S to demonstrate a high degree of incidental learning is not clear, but whatever the bases, they apparently are not the same as those producing a high degree of intentional learning.

Some studies with adults have found that increased motivation results in poorer incidental learning. The effect has been attributed to the restriction of perceptual range with heightened motivation. Kausler, Laughlin, and Trapp (1963) tested seventh and eighth graders to determine whether a similar effect would be found with children. A 14-item serial learning test involving seven forms was presented to the Ss. Each form appeared with two of seven colors. Incidental learning was measured by the number of correct form-color pairings the Ss could recognize when all combinations were presented on a printed sheet. Half of the Ss were told at the beginning of the study that they could win money as a prize, and half simply were asked for their cooperation. Incidental learning was greater when Ss were offered money, both for Ss who later stated they had tried to learn the color-form combinations and for Ss who stated they did not. Perhaps the type of drive as well as the strength of drive is important in determining the incidence of incidental learning. In this study a nonaversive drive was used, whereas the studies with adults involved aversive drive states such as hunger or anxiety.

INTERRELATIONS IN LEARNING

In the preceding section it was seen that incidental and intentional learning apparently involve different psychological processes, for scores obtained on tests of the two types of learning were not significantly correlated. This opens an interesting topic, that of ascertaining the interrelations among various tasks that are used to measure children's learning. Thus far, there has been no discussion of the correlations among scores obtained in different types of learning tasks. There is a very simple reason for this. The common practice has been for an investigator to use a particular type of problem to assess the influence of certain experimental variables, and rarely have the same Ss been presented more than one type of problem. Data are available, however, concerning the intercorrelations among scores obtained on a variety of learning tasks. These studies have tended to be undertaken by persons interested in the analysis of the psychometric structure of learning ability and have been concerned with the question of whether learning is a unitary function or whether it is necessary to posit different types of learning abilities.

One of the earliest studies with children was Husband's (1941) investigation of the effects of the range of intelligence on the interrelations among tasks. It had been suggested that the low correlations typically found among learning tasks with adults resulted from the restricted ranges of intelligence sampled in the studies. Husband presented a series of tasks to Ss in grades 7 and 8 with IQs ranging between 81 and 162. The median correlation among tasks was .10 and the range of correlation was similar to that found in the earlier studies. Although the median intertask correlation was low, high correlations sometimes were found between similar tasks, such as rate of learning a finger maze and a mental maze ($r = .37$).

A more extensive study was reported by Stake (1961), who presented 12 learning tasks to 240 Ss in grade 7. The tasks differed on three dimensions, content (verbal-nonverbal), type (rote, relational), and mode of presentation (group versus gamelike individual tests). Each S's performance on each task was fitted to a theoretical learning curve with three parameters. The highest intercorrelations were obtained with the parameter of asymptotic level as measured by total errors. The medians of the correlations between asymptotic level for each task and all other tasks varied between .10 and .30. The highest correlations were those between two forms of the same learning or memory task or between various memory and learning tasks. Stake concluded that his results provided no evidence for a general learning factor, for the separation of rote and relational learning, or for verbal tasks to load on a verbal learning factor. Further, mode of presenting the material had no differential effect on the correlations; individual differences in performance were comparable for Ss tested in groups and individually.

A study by Duncanson (1964) included three types of task: rote memory, paired associates, and concept formation. Three types of material were used in each task: verbal, numerical, and figural. The tasks were given to 102 Ss in grade 6. Duncanson obtained a set of coefficients for each S on the basis of the number of components necessary to describe his performance. The intertask correlation matrix yielded correlations of approximately the same magnitude as those found in previous studies. A number of significant correlations were found between the various rote memory and paired-associate tasks, but there were few instances of significant relations between either concept formation and rote memory or concept formation and paired associates. A factor analysis of the data yielded more distinct separations of the tasks than had been found by Stake. Tasks involving words had high loadings on verbal factors and tasks involving numbers and figures had high loadings on nonverbal factors. The most unexpected result was the specificity of the concept-formation factor, which was defined solely by the three concept-formation tasks.

Stevenson and Odom (1965) reported the interrelations among performance in five tasks: paired associates, two discrimination learning tasks, a concept-formation task, and anagrams. The Ss were 354 children enrolled in grades 4 and 6. The median correlation among the tasks was .17. There were no significant correlations between the two most complex tasks, concept formation and anagrams, but the correlations between what had been presumed to be the most simple and the most complex tasks, paired associates and anagrams, were consistently significant across both grade and sex. Consistently significant correlations also were found between the two forms of discrimination learning.

The previous study was extended by Stevenson, Hale, Klein, and Miller (1968) to include 12 different tasks, consisting of paired associates, discrimination learning, probability learning, incidental learning, and tasks involving verbal memory, concept of probability, concept of conservation, and anagrams. The Ss were over 600 children in grades 3 to 7. In analyses of the data obtained over a broad range of intelligence at grade 7, the median intercorrelation among tasks was .30; when the analyses included samples of Ss of average ranges of IQs across all grades, the median intercorrelation was .20. The correlations were somewhat higher than those found in the previous studies, but even here fewer than 10% of the correlations were above .50. Tasks that were highly similar in structure, such as the two paired-associate, the two memory, or the two concept of probability tasks, tended to be significantly related in all analyses. The presence of verbal material in a task appeared to be the single most important determinant of the frequency and magnitude of the correlations found in the study. The greatest number of significant correlations was produced by paired associates, verbal memory, and anagrams, all of which were highly dependent upon verbal processes. The frequency of significant correlations among the learning tasks was no greater than that among the remaining tasks, which were assumed to be examples of problem-solving tasks.

The number of studies is small, but the results are consistent. Low positive intercorrelations tend to be found among different learning tasks, except when the tasks are similar in structure, or, in some cases, similar in content. These results are comparable to those found in studies with human adults and animals, even though the studies with children have tended to include larger and more heterogenous samples of Ss. Thus far, at least, there appears to be little basis for assuming that learning represents a unitary function that operates in a similar manner across different learning tasks. Information is too limited to draw more than this negative conclusion, which, in itself, is absorbing information for anyone who is tempted to construct a theory of learning based on children's performance in a restricted sample of problems.

LEARNING AND INTELLIGENCE

Intelligence often is assumed to be closely related to the child's ability to learn and results of intelligence tests frequently are used to make predictions about future academic success. In fact, Binet's original work on the construction of intelligence tests was instigated by the request of city authorities to develop an instrument to identify slow learners before they entered the Paris public school system. Although there have been many studies of the relation of IQ to performance in school, there have been remarkably few studies of the relation of IQ to performance in standard learning tasks.

The early studies of sensorimotor learning reviewed by Munn (1954) generally revealed little, if any, correlation between children's rate of learning and IQ, and low correlations were reported for more complex serial learning tasks by Garrett (1928) and Garrison (1928). These studies were criticized, however, because of the restricted range of ability represented in the groups from which the Ss had been drawn. Husband (1941) attempted to counter this criticism by sampling from a broader range of intelligence, but the magnitudes of the correlations were similar to those that had been found in other studies. Some correlations, however, were moderately high; for example, the correlation between rate of learning a finger maze and IQ was .38 and between rate of learning a mental maze and IQ was .34. Similar results were found by Simrall (1947), who used gain scores of seventh graders derived from the repeated administration of the Thurstone Memory, Spatial Relations, and Perceptual tests. The gain scores were not highly correlated with IQ or with each other. On the basis of her study and previous studies, Simrall concluded that

intelligence could not be defined as the ability to learn.

The results of four recent studies do not lead to quite so negative a view. In the studies by Stake (1961), Duncanson (1964), Stevenson and Odom (1965), and Stevenson, Hale, Klein, and Miller (1968), high frequencies of significant correlations between performance on learning tasks and IQ were found. The median correlation between Otis IQ and error scores was .36 in the study by Stake. The tasks for which the correlations were above the median included various forms of paired-associate learning, memory for patterns of numbers, and verbal memory. Duncanson found a median correlation of .24 between Kuhlmann-Anderson IQ and the coefficient for the first component in his analysis of the learning curves obtained from three forms of paired-associate learning, concept formation, and rote learning. The highest correlations ($r = .43$ to .44) were between IQ and verbal paired-associate learning, verbal rote memory, and figural rote memory. In the study by Stevenson and Odom, correlations for paired-associate learning and anagrams with Lorge-Thorndike IQ ranged between .28 and .57. The concept-formation tasks used in all three studies yielded a median correlation of .11, with no correlations with IQ above .29. In the study by Stevenson, Hale, Klein, and Miller a median correlation of .34 was found between Lorge-Thorndike IQ and performance on 12 learning and problem-solving tasks when the analyses included seventh-grade Ss representing a broad range of intelligence, and a median correlation of .37 when the analyses included children in grades 3 to 7 with an average range of intelligence. Particularly high frequencies of significant correlations were found for tasks with verbal content: paired associates, verbal memory, and anagrams.

Another group of studies relating IQ and performance in learning tasks has been reviewed by Zeaman and House (1967). Although these were not correlational studies, level of intelligence was related to learning by comparing the performance of groups of Ss differing in IQ or MA. Comparisons of groups differing in IQ yielded fewer differences in performance than comparisons of groups differing in MA. Differences specifically associated with IQ appeared only when the groups differed greatly in intellectual level or when the tasks were very complex.

The results of these studies lead to the conclusion that although level of intelligence may be a significant determinant of performance in learning tasks, intelligence and learning ability are not identical functions. Those instances in which moderately high correlations have been found tended to use verbal material, tests of the ability to acquire associations, and material similar to that found in intelligence tests.

OBSERVATIONAL LEARNING

Nearly all of the previous studies have involved learning in one-person situations. A vast amount of learning occurs, however, in social situations where the child himself remains inactive but is able to view the efforts and effects of adults and peers as they engage in activities with objects and with each other. Such learning is described by such terms as observational learning or imitation. Problems of analysing performance in learning tasks become much more complex when all the variables that operate in a social context must be considered, and, as Bandura and Walters (1963) have pointed out, the principles derived from studies of animal and human learning in nonsocial contexts must be extended and modified, and new principles must be added, if learning in social situations is to be understood. Despite the apparent complexities, progress has been made in the past decade in clarifying many of the basic processes in observational learning. It would be impossible to present within this one chapter an adequate picture of all the ramifications of this research, but since many of the issues are discussed extensively in other chapters, the discussion here will be limited to a review of studies that have examined the conditions under which observational learning occurs and the variables that play an important role in determining its manifestation in performance.

In Discrimination Learning

Wilson (1958) was interested in determining whether preschool children are able not only to learn to imitate the responses made by an adult model but also to make the appropriate response in the absence of a model.

After an initial stage in which the child learned to imitate the model's choice of one of two identical containers, two containers differing in shape and color were introduced. The model consistently chose one of the containers for eight trials and then left the room, after which the game was resumed without the model. The experimental Ss learned the discrimination much more rapidly than a control group given standard discrimination learning trials throughout the study. Thus, even though they had not been instructed to do so, the children had learned the nature of the critical cues while imitating the model's choices.

McDavid (1959) found somewhat less positive results when Ss were rewarded consistently for imitating a model's choices of one of two objects. On trial 1, only 28% of the preschool Ss made an imitative response, and after 24 trials, 44% had not learned an imitative solution to the problem. The task differed from that used by Wilson in two important ways: the child never saw whether the model received a reward for his choice, and the color and position cues of the objects were irrelevant for solution. Thus learning to imitate was more difficult when the model's responses were not differentially associated with an external cue and when the results of the model's choice were unknown to the Ss. The number of imitative responses did increase across trials, and there was a significant interaction between sex of S and age of S. Imitation scores for older preschool boys were lower than those for younger preschool boys, but the scores for the girls increased with age. It was assumed that this interaction was related to the fact that boys more than girls progressively are taught to become more independent as they become older.

The implication that imitation would be less frequent when the model's responses were not associated differentially with environmental cues was investigated directly by McDavid (1962). Four-year-olds were tested in a three-choice discrimination learning task in which an imitative response was rewarded, but the consistency of the model's behavior varied. The model consistently chose one of the three stimuli for one group of Ss, chose one stimulus two-thirds of the time for another group, and one-third of the time for a third group. The frequency of imitative behavior increased as the model's behavior became increasingly consistent. The proportions of Ss meeting a criterion of six successive imitative responses were .90, .50, and .10 in three groups, respectively. An increasingly strong tendency to ignore the model's behavior was apparent as the conditions required greater degrees of attention to the discriminative cues.

A much more extensive series of responses were made by the model in a study by Bandura and Huston (1961). During the course of responding in a two-choice discrimination problem, the model exhibited verbal, motor, and aggressive responses that were irrelevant to the learning task. There was a high frequency of imitation of the incidental behavior; for example, 90% of the Ss imitated the model's aggressive response (knocking a doll off one of the discriminative stimuli) and 45% marched toward the stimuli in the manner performed by the model. Prior to the experimental session, half of the Ss had been exposed to the model for two 15-minute sessions in which the model behaved in a very nurturant manner, and half had been treated in a non-nurturant fashion. The frequency of imitation of the incidental responses was greater following the nurturant than non-nurturant interactions, but these conditions did not significantly influence the frequency with which the Ss imitated the model's choice of the discriminative stimuli. Partial support was obtained for a positive relation between the child's dependency as rated from observations of social interactions in the nursery school and frequency of imitative behavior; the correlation was significant for imitative verbal behavior, but not for the other categories.

The same task was used by Bandura, Ross, and Ross (1963b) to study the effects on imitative learning of the role adopted by the model. Two adults served as models, and before the discrimination learning task was introduced, an attempt was made to establish a different role for each adult. One adult was the controller and dispenser of resources; for example, he "owned" the toys and dispensed cookies and juice. The second adult assumed the role of consumer and was the recipient of the controller's favors. In a second situation, the Ss were the recipients and the other adult was ignored by the controller. During the discrimination learning task each adult exhibited a different set of novel, irrelevant verbal and motor responses while making his choices.

There was a greater tendency for the Ss to imitate the model who had been the controller of the resources, regardless of whether the other adult or the Ss themselves had been the recipient of the rewards, than to imitate the adult who was the child's rival as the consumer of the resources.

In a final study of the type, Fletcher and Orr (1967) found that observation of the correct choice in two-choice discrimination problems was relatively ineffective unless the Ss were required to point to the stimulus that was correct. No model was used in this study and the information about the response that was correct was provided by a signal light in front of each object.

Variables Influencing Observational Learning

Verbalization is another active form of response that may aid observational learning (Bandura, Grusec, and Menlove, 1966). Observational learning was more effective when the Ss verbalized the content of the observed behavior than when the Ss observed passively or were engaged in competing symbolization. The Ss watched a short film in which an adult displayed a series of novel patterns of behavior and used play materials in unusual ways. The Ss were instructed to verbalize the model's actions as they occurred, to count as they watched the film, or merely to pay close attention. When the Ss later were asked to demonstrate all the model's responses they could recall, the highest scores were obtained by the Ss who had verbalized while the model performed. The Ss who had been instructed to count obtained significantly lower scores than the passive observers, apparently reflecting an interfering effect of the competing verbalization. Half of the Ss had been tested under an incentive set in that they were told they would receive candy for each correct description, but these Ss did no better than did Ss who had not been given such a promise.

The results of another study (Rosenbaum, 1962) indicated that verbalization does not necessarily have to be made by S for recall to be improved. Recall of the names of objects was better when a peer or an adult verbalized the names of the objects in the presence of an attentive but silent S than when there was no verbalization.

The effects on children's imitation of the sex of the model and attentiveness of the model were studied by Rosenblith (1959, 1961). Before the study, kindergarten Ss were given the Porteus Maze test. In the experimental sessions, models of each sex were assigned to children of each sex, and for the first 10 minutes the model either maintained an attentive interaction with S or terminated it after 5 minutes and spent the rest of the time reading a book. At the end of this period, a maze the child previously had failed was presented to the model, who traced it slowly and correctly. The child, who had observed the model, then was given the maze. This procedure was followed for several different mazes. Observing a model was more effective than having additional trials with mazes in improving maze performance, and prior attention from the model resulted in greater improvement than did withdrawal of attention. Improvement was greater in boys than in girls, and the male was more effective than the female model. But these general statements must be qualified by the presence of significant interactions among the variables. Moreover, the second report made clear that the type of imitative response was also an important variable. A different constellation of results appeared when the measure was choices of a pencil of the same color the model used in completing his maze than when the measure was improvement in tracing mazes.

As part of a larger study, Hetherington (1965) investigated children's imitation of parental choices of objects. The parents, and then the child, was asked to point to pictures in a set of 20 pairs that he thought were the prettier. The Ss were 4- to 5-, 6- to 8-, and 9- to 11-year-olds. The interesting feature of the results was that the incidence of imitation was greater for the parent who had been evaluated as being the dominant member of the family rather than for the parent of the same sex as the child, as might ordinarily be expected.

Fifth graders who were rated as being above and below the median in self-esteem as measured by a paper-and-pencil test of self-evaluation were used by Gelfand (1962) in a study of imitation of preferences. Before introducing the experimental task, the Ss were subjected to failure or success experiences by receiving higher or lower scores than a companion in four learning and performance tasks. The second child then unwittingly

acted as a confederate in a matching test by following a cue provided earlier by the experimenter as the basis for making his choices. Self-esteem was not a significant variable in determining the number of imitative responses made by the Ss, but the frequency of imitation was significantly higher for Ss who had experienced failure than it was for the control Ss or those who had been successful in the first phase of the study.

To test whether the likelihood that behavior will be imitated is influenced by the consequences that follow the model's choices, Barnwell and Sechrest (1965) tested pairs of Ss in grades 1 and 3 under different conditions of reinforcement. One child was designated the model and was seated at a table with toys. He was asked to choose a toy to play with and after a period of time was praised or criticized for his efforts. The S, who had observed this sequence of events, then was asked which toy he wished to play with. When S was busy with his choice, the model was asked again which toy he wanted to play with. For first graders, the tendency was equally great in the observer and in the model to choose the same toy when the model was praised and to choose a different toy when the model was criticized. At the third grade, both Ss chose the same toy with equal frequency when the model had been praised, but the observer tended to choose the toy that had been chosen by the model, even though the model's play had been criticized; and, in fact, the models themselves chose the original toy as frequently as a novel toy. Thus the effects of success on imitative choices were roughly equivalent in all cases, but differences were found in the effects of direct and vicarious punishment at the two grade levels.

Another approach to this problem was taken by Kobasigawa (1965), who used a lever-pulling task and either allowed an adult performer to succeed in completing the defined goal or blocked his performance one-fifth or nine-tenths of the distance from attaining the goal. The Ss, first-grade boys, were asked to push a button that turned off a buzzer signaling the onset of each trial. The results were very similar to those found when the performances of Ss themselves were blocked in these manners. The amplitude and speed of Ss' button-pushing responses were greater when the performer was blocked near the goal than when he was far from success or was allowed to succeed. The strength of this effect was not influenced by the relation between the performer and the child established before the task by means of supportive or nonresponsive reaction to Ss as he played games with the experimenter.

Direct and vicarious effects of a shift in magnitude of reward on performance of kindergarten Ss in a lever-pulling task were investigated by Bruning (1965). For 30 acquisition trials Ss received either one or five pieces of candy and on 30 subsequent trials the level of incentive was either maintained at the original level or shifted to the alternative level. The Ss performed the task alone, or they observed during the first 30 trials and performed during the last 30 trials. Response speeds were faster with the lower level of incentive and a shift from a high to a low level of incentive produced increased speeds of response. The results were the same whether the S was an observer or a performer during the initial set of trials. Reward to one child affected not only his performance but also the subsequent performance of an observer who was present in the situation.

Baer and Sherman (1964) have shown that social reinforcement of imitative responses may result in the generalization of imitation to a response that was never reinforced. A highly novel procedure was used in this study. Preschool Ss were introduced to a talking puppet, which engaged them in conversation and induced them to imitate such behaviors as head-nodding, mouthing, and making strange verbalizations. The puppet praised the Ss for their performance and in the course of subsequent interactions began pressing a bar. Nearly two-thirds of the Ss demonstrated imitative bar-pressing and later, when reinforcement no longer followed the other imitative responses, extinction of imitative bar-pressing occurred.

Aggression

The study of imitative learning was extended by Bandura, Ross, and Ross (1963a) to a consideration of the learning of aggression through exposure to aggressive behavior in real-life models and as depicted in films by adult models or a cartoon character. In each case the models exhibited a wide range of verbal and physical aggression. After this exposure, the Ss (preschool children) were mildly frustrated by having some toys they were playing with taken away, and then they were led to an experimental room, which contained many of the objects that had been used by the model in displaying aggression. Exposure to filmed aggression, as well as to real-life aggression, increased the Ss' aggressive responses. All three experimental groups displayed more imitative aggression than did the control Ss who had not seen the film, and the effect was equally strong with Ss who had been exposed to aggressive models in person and in film. There was more imitative aggression by boys than by girls, and by Ss exposed to a male than to a female model. Hicks (1965) repeated the study, using films depicting male and female adults and male and female peer models. The male peer had the greatest immediate influence as a model for imitative aggression, but the adult male had the most lasting effect, as reflected in aggression scores obtained by the Ss after a 6- month interval.

Bandura, Ross, and Ross (1963c) found that preschool children displayed more imitative aggression after they had seen an aggressive model rewarded for his aggression than when the model was punished or no specific consequence followed the aggression. The potential power of observation as a means of acquiring complex forms of social behavior is clearly demonstrated in this series of studies.

Comments

Young children obviously are capable of learning to imitate the behavior of others and, in the course of doing so, of acquiring relevant information about the characteristics of the environment in which the imitative responses were made. Observing the consequences of a model's responses appears to influence the behavior of the child in a manner similar to that which occurs when the child has like experiences in the course of his own performance. Once another person is introduced into the learning situation as a significant participant, a host of variables that have received little attention in other studies of learning take on critical importance. The relation between the model and the child, the role adopted by the model, and the personality characteristics of the child are examples of the types of variable that seem to influence the degree to which observational learning occurs. It is likely that learning in what may appear superficially to be one-person situations also is subject to the effects of these variables.

CONCLUDING REMARKS

Although an attempt was made in this review to include topics currently receiving primary attention from developmental psychologists interested in children's learning, several potentially important topics have been omitted. Research on learning in school settings is perhaps the most glaring omission. There are two reasons why these studies have not been discussed. First, the studies usually have been undertaken in the context of projects on curriculum development or the use of mechanical and electronic aids in teaching and appear at present to have greater implications for education than for developmental psychology. Second, although many studies of school learning are under way, so few have been published that their importance for the psychological analysis of children's learning is difficult to ascertain. Another omission is the study of learning disabilities in children. These, and studies of learning in the mentally retarded, constitute a large body of research, and the only justification for their omission is that there was neither time nor space.

It has been difficult to decide which articles to include within each topic. Biases and preferences undoubtedly play a part in determining choices, but the goal was to include the most relevant and soundly executed studies that could be found. In some cases isolated but important studies have been omitted because there was no context in which they could be discussed.

What impressions remain after reviewing the literature? First, a strong impression is that a great deal has been done in a very short time. If the energetic pace of the past decade is maintained or accelerated, we soon should have a good grasp of how numerous variables influence children's learning. Studies completed more than 15 years ago seem to have done little more than set the stage for the recent work. The earlier studies provided interesting and useful normative and descriptive data and illustrated many of the ways in which children's performance might differ from that

of animals and human adults. As more and more of these differences have been uncovered, the influence of theories based on research with animals and adults has tended to decline in importance as directive influences on research with children.

Munn (1954, p. 449) concluded in his earlier review that, apparently, "the phenomenon of learning is fundamentally the same whether studied in the animal, child, or adult." It is probably impossible to devise situations that would critically test this conclusion. Even if it were correct in the broadest sense, many variables have been found to have differential effects on children's and animals' or adults' performance. In fact, variables often have different effects with children at different developmental levels. Such findings greatly add to the difficulty of the task of theory construction. It seems fair to say that no theory has survived the onslaught of the accumulated data. Different theoretical positions are capable of handling small amounts of the data, but none is effective in handling a significant portion of the results. Frequently, the behavior of very young children can be predicted from S-R models, but it is often easy to modify the task so that their performance violates the predictions that have been made. There was hope that the addition of mediation mechanisms would make it possible to predict the behavior of older children in S-R terms, but the results have offered only partial support for the utility of such constructs. Obviously, new approaches to theory construction are needed; and hopefully these will depart from the framework of traditional learning theories and incorporate a consideration of the role of developmental processes in learning.

After reading these studies, one is not impressed by statements implying nearly total malleability of the child. It is always possible to criticize studies by saying that the tasks were artificial or were inappropriately presented; however, there are too many instances in which learning did not occur or in which variables were ineffective to permit the assumption that other techniques would have permitted any child to discover and perform the correct response. For example, verbal instructions, incentives, models, and degree of training may be important factors in producing correct response at some ages or in some children, but such factors as the developmental status of the child, his past experiences, and his motivational state may place important restrictions on the degree to which the experimental variables can influence the child's performance.

What are the most salient features of children's learning? A brief statement cannot be adequate, but a number of points can be made. Learning occurs from the time of earliest infancy and at all ages there are large individual differences in the rate of attaining the correct response. The individual differences cannot be attributed to any single characteristic. Intelligence, which would seem to be a likely basis for such differences, especially among older children, proves to be a significant variable but is capable of accounting for only a moderate portion of the variability found. Children's motivation to learn appears to be very high, at least with these children, usually from middle-class families, who typically constitute the samples of Ss included in the studies. The high motivation does not appear to be strongly dependent upon a desire to obtain material rewards, for it is difficult to produce differences in performance by manipulating incentive conditions, except when the responses are already well learned or the Ss have been subjected to conditions of deprivation. This is not to say that the consequences of response do not have important effects on learning. Rather, the most important consequence appears to be knowledge of the correctness of response. After infancy, pleasing the experimenter and, later, pleasing themselves seem to be the most important incentives for children's acquiring the correct response biases and stimulus preferences, which, has been used, its influence in producing correct response appears to be due to its increasing the child's attention to the task.

Verbal instructions, the most common means by which adults attempt to impart information, do not appear to be a highly effective means for controlling the behavior of young children, especially when the effects of instructions are contrasted with those resulting from actual performance or observation of the performance of others. Even young children enter the experimental situation with strong response biases and stimulus preferences, which, if in accord with correct response, lead to rapid learning and otherwise interfere with performance. Young children seem to be more dependent upon the characteristics of the external situation than are older children. Older Ss are more likely to respond in terms of their own hypotheses and expectations. Such implicit response tendencies may facilitate learning unless they result in the child's overcomplicating or responding inappropriately to the experimental task. Two common obstacles to rapid learning are the child's failure to attend to the stimuli and to determine the critical features by which the stimuli differ. Once appropriate attentional and discriminative habits have been developed, the child can transfer prior learning to a new situation with great ease.

The role of language in learning is less simple than had been assumed. The child appears to go through at least three stages; first, he may not have the words that are necessary to direct behavior; then, he may acquire the words but not use them; and, finally, he may have the words and use them appropriately. The time at which words can function efficiently as mediators of response is probably later than had been assumed, for the performance of 6- and 7-year-olds does not consistently indicate that mediation has occurred. Labeling objects may improve learning by providing a verbal mediator or by focusing the child's attention on the stimuli and emphasizing the differences among stimuli.

Social variables, such as the child's relation with the experimenter, the social milieu in which he has been raised, and his opportunities to use the behavior of others as models for his own behavior, significantly influence the rate at which he will learn. It is doubtful that any task presented by an adult is totally uninfluenced by the operation of social variables. Personality characteristics of the child, most notably his level of anxiety and motivation to achieve, also have a significant effect on performance in learning tasks.

Only a few instances were noted where the experimental studies of children's learning have been utilized in practical situations. Nevertheless, the studies have many important implications for teaching and rearing children. It would be inappropriate to deduce from these studies that the variables necessarily would have the same effects on learning in everyday situations that they have in controlled laboratory settings. To answer such questions it will be necessary to undertake translational studies in which the effects of the variables are investigated in the context of the practical setting. The attempt in the 1930s to apply the results obtained with mature animals and human adults to the young child led to important lessons in the futility of incautious applications of laboratory research to everyday life. These settings are similar enough, however, so that experimental studies may be useful sources of information about how to construct tasks and situations that will result in better learning. The extension of interest to practical problems and the continuation of research in the laboratory should produce exciting advances during the next few decades in our knowledge about children's learning.

References

Abel, L. B. The effects of shift in motivation upon the learning of a sensori-motor task. *Arch. Psychol.*, 1936, **29**, (205).

Alberts, E., and Ehrenfreund, D. Transposition in children as a function of age. *J. exp. Psychol.*, 1951, **51**, 30–38.

Allen, E. K., Hart, B., Buell, J. S., Harris, F., and Wolf, M. Effects of social reinforcement on isolate behavior of a nursery school child. *Child Dev.*, 1964, **35**, 511–518.

Atkinson, R. C., Calfee, R. C., Sommer, G. R., Jeffrey, W. E., and Shoemaker, R. A test of three models for stimulus compounding with children. *J. exp. Psychol.*, 1964, **67**, 52–58.

Atkinson, R. C., Sommer, G. R., and Sterman, M. B. Decision making by children as a function of amount of reinforcement. *Psychol. Rep.*, 1960, **2**, 299–306.

Baer, D. M. Escape and avoidance response of pre-school children to two schedules of reinforcement withdrawal. *J. exp. Analysis Behav.*, 1960, **3**, 155–159.

Baer, D. M. Effect of withdrawal of positive reinforcement on an extinguishing response in young children. *Child Dev.*, 1961, **32**, 67–74.

Baer, D. M. Laboratory control of thumbsucking by withdrawal and re-presentation of reinforcement. *J. exp. Analysis Behav.*, 1962, **5**, 525–528.

Baer, D. M., and Sherman, J. A. Reinforcement control of generalized imitation in children. *J. exp. Child Psychol.*, 1964, **1**, 37–49.

Baer, P. E., and Goldfarb, G. E. A developmental study of verbal conditioning in children. *Psychol. Rep.*, 1962, **10**, 175–181.

Ballard, P. B. Obliviscence and reminiscence. *Br. J. Psychol. Monogr. Suppl.*, 1913, **1**, 82.

Bandura, A. Influence of models' reinforcement contingencies on the acquisition of imitative responses. *J. Personality soc. Psychol.*, 1965, 1, 589–595.

Bandura, A., Grusec, J. E., and Menlove, F. L. Observational learning as a function of symbolization and incentive set. *Child Dev.* 1966, **37**, 499–506.

Bandura, A., and Huston, A. C. Identification as a process of incidental learning. *J. Abnorm. soc. Psychol.*, 1961, **63**, 311–318.

Bandura, A,. Ross, D., and Ross, S. A. Imitation of film-mediated aggressive models. *J. Abnorm. soc. Psychol.*, 1963, **66**, 3–11. (a)

Bandura, A., Ross, D., and Ross, S. A. A comparative test of status envy, social power, and secondary reinforcement theories of identificatory learning. *J. Abnorm. soc. Psychol.*, 1963, **67**, 527–534. (b)

Bandura, A., Ross, D., and Ross, S. A. Vicarious reinforcement and imitative learning. *J. Abnorm. soc. Psychol.*, 1963, **67**, 601–607. (c)

Bandura, A., and Walters, R. H. *Social learning and personality development.* New York: Holt, Rinehart, and Winston, 1963.

Barnwell, A., and Sechrest, L. Vicarious reinforcement in children at two age levels. *J. educ. Psychol.*, 1965, **56**, 100–106.

Bartoshuk, A. K. Human neonatal cardiac acceleration to sound: habituation and dishabituation. *Percept. Mot. Skills*, 1962, **15**, 15–27.

Beatty, W. E., and Weir, M. W. Children's performance on the intermediate-size transposition problem as a function of two different training procedures. *J. exp. Child Psychol.*, 1966, **4**, 332–340.

Berman, P. W., and Graham, F. K. Children's response to relative, absolute, and position cues in a two-trial size discrimination. *J. comp. physiol. Psychol.*, 1964, **57**, 393–397.

Bijou, S. W. Patterns of reinforcement and resistance to extinction in young children. *Child Dev.*, 1957, **28**, 47–54.

Bijou, S. W. Operant extinction after fixed interval schedules with young children. *J. exp. Analysis Behav.*, 1958, **1**, 25–29.

Bijou, S. W., and Baer, D. M. *Child development*, Vol. 1. New York: Appleton-Century-Crofts, 1961.

Bijou, S. W., and Baer, D. M. Some methodological contributions from a functional analysis of child development. In L. P., Lipsitt and C. C. Spiker, *Advances in child development and behavior*. Vol. 1. New York: Academic Press, 1963. Pp. 197–232.

Bijou, S. W., and Baer, D. M. *Child development, Vol. II. Universal stage of infancy.* New York: Appleton-Century-Crofts, 1965.

Bijou, S. W., and Baer, D. M. Operant methods in child behavior and development. In W. Honig, (Ed.), *Operant behavior: areas of research and application.* New York: Appleton-Century-Crofts, 1966. Pp 718–789.

Bijou, S. W., and Sturges, P. T. Positive reinforcers for experimental studies with children—consumables and manipulatables. *Child Dev.*, 1959, **30**, 151–170.

Bisett, B. M., and Rieber, M. The effects of age and incentive value on discrimination learning. *J. exp. Child Psychol.* 1966, **3**, 199–206.

Blank, M. The effects of training and verbalization on reversal and extra-dimensional learning. *J. exp. Child Psychol.* 1966, **4**, 50–57.

Bogartz, R. S. Sequential dependencies in children's probability learning *J. exp. Psychol.*, 1965, **70**, 365–370.

Bogartz, R. S. Variables influencing alternation prediction by preschool children. *J. exp. Child Psychol.*, 1966, **3**, 40–56.

Bogartz, R. S., and Pederson, D. R. Variables influencing alternation prediction by preschool children: II. Redundant cue value and intertrial interval duration. *J. exp. Child Psychol.*, 1966, **4**, 211–216.

Bogartz, R. S., and Witte, K. L. On the locus of the stimulus familiarization effect in young children. *J. exp. Child Psychol.*, 1966, **4**, 317–331.

Brackbill, Y. Extinction of the smiling response in infants as a function of reinforcement schedule. *Child Dev.*, 1958, **29**, 115–124.

Brackbill, Y. Research and clinical work with children. In R. Bauer, (Ed.), *Some views on Soviet psychology.* Washington, D. C.: American Psychological Association, 1962.

Brackbill, Y. The impairment of learning under immediate reinforcement. *J. exp. Child Psychol.*, 1964, **1**, 199–207.

Brackbill, Y., and Jack, D. Discrimination learning in children as a function of reinforcement value. *Child Dev.*, 1958, **29**, 185–190.

Brackbill, Y., Kappy, M. S., and Starr, R. H. Magnitude of reward and probability learning. *J. exp. Psychol.*, 1962, **63**, 32–35.

Brackbill, Y., and Koltsova, M. M. Conditioning and learning. In Y. Brackbill, (Ed.), *Infancy and early childhood.* New York: Free Press, 1968.

Brackbill, Y., and O'Hara, J. The relative effectiveness of reward and punishment for discrimination learning in children. *J. comp. physiol. Psychol.*, 1958, **51**, 747–751.

Brackbill, Y., Wagner, J., and Wilson, D. Feedback delay and the teaching machine. *Psychology in the Schools*, 1964, **1**, 148–156.

Bridger, W. H. Sensory habituation and discrimination in the human neonate. *Am. J. Psychiat.*, 1961, **117**, 991–996.

Bronshtein, A. I., Antonova, T. G., Kamenetskaya, N. H., Luppova, V. A., and Sytova, V. A. On the development of the functions of analyzers in infants and some animals at the early stage of ontogenesis. *Problems of evolution of physiological functions.* Moscow: U.S.S.R. Academy of Science, 1958.

Brown, P., and Elliott, R. Control of aggression in a nursery school class. *J. exp. Child Psychol.*, 1965, **2**, 103–107.

Bruning, J. L. Effects of magnitude of reward and percentage of reinforcement on a lever movement response. *Child. Dev.*, 1964, **35**, 281–285.

Bruning, J. L. Direct and vicarious effects of a shift in magnitude of reward on performance. *J. Personality soc. Psychol.*, 1965, **2**, 278–282.

Budoff, M., and Quinlan, D. Auditory and visual learning in primary grade children. *Child. Dev.*, 1964, **35**, 583–586.

Cantor, G. N., and Cantor, J. H. Effects of conditioned-stimulus familiarization on instrumental learning in children. *J. exp. Child Psychol.*, 1964, **1**, 71–78.

Cantor, G. N., and Cantor, J. H. Discriminative reaction time performance in preschool children as related to stimulus familiarization. *J. exp. Child Psychol.*, 1965, **2**, 1–9.

Cantor, G. N. and Cantor, J. H. Discriminative reaction time in children as related to amount of stimulus familiarization. *J. exp. Child Psychol.*, 1966, **4**, 150–157.

Cantor, J. H. Transfer of stimulus pretraining in motor paired-associate and discrimination learning tasks. In L. P. Lippsitt and C. C. Spiker, (Eds.), *Advances in child development and behavior*, Vol. II, New York: Academic Press, 1965, Pp. 19–58.

Caron, A. J. Far transposition of intermediate-size in preverbal children. *J. exp. Child Psychol.*, 1966, **3**, 296–311.

Caron, A. J. Intermediate size transposition at an extreme distance in preverbal children. *J. exp. Child Psychol.*, 1967, **5**, 186–207.

Carroll, J., and Burke, M. Parameters of paired-associate verbal learning: length of list, meaningfulness, rate of presentation and ability. *J. exp. Psychol.*, 1965, **69**, 543–553.

Carroll, W. R. Response availability and percentage occurrence of response members, associative strength, and competition in paired-associate learning in children. *J. exp. Child Psychol.*, 1966, **3**, 258–266.

Carroll, W. R., and Penney, R. K. Percentage of occurrence of response members, associative strength, and competition in paired-associate learning in children. *J. exp. Child Psychol.*, 1966, **3**, 258–266.

Castaneda, A. Supplementary report: differential position habits and anxiety in children as determinants of performance in learning. *J. exp. Psychol.*, 1961, **61**, 257–258.

Castaneda, A. The paired-associates method in the study of conflict. In L. P. Lipsitt and C. C. Spiker, (Eds.), *Advances in child development and behavior*, Vol. 2. New York: Academic Press, 1965, Pp. 1–18.

Castaneda, A., Fahel, L. S., and Odom, R. Associative characteristics of sixty-three adjectives and their relation to verbal paired associate learning in children. *Child Dev.*, 1961, **32**, 297–304.

Castaneda, A., and Lipsitt, L. P. Relation of stress and differential position habits to performance in motor learning. *J. exp. Psychol.*, 1959, **57**, 25–30.

Castaneda, A., Palermo, D. S., and McCandless, B. R. Complex learning and performance as a function of anxiety in children. *Child Dev.*, 1956, **27**, 327–332.

Cobb, N. J., and Price, L. E. Reversal and nonreversal shift learning in children as a function of two types of pretraining. *Psychol. Rep.*, 1966, **19**, 1003–1010.

Cole, R. E., Dent, H. E., Eguchi, P. E., Fujii, K. K., and Johnson, R. C. Transposition with minimal errors during training trials. *J. exp. Child Psychol.*, 1964, **1**, 355–359.

Craig, G. J., and Myers, J. L. A developmental study of sequential two-choice decision making. *Child Dev.*, 1963, **34**, 483–493.

Crane, N. L., and Ross, L. E. A developmental study of attention to cue redundancy introduced following discrimination learning. *J. exp. Child Psychol.*, 1967, **5**, 1–15.

Cross, H. A., and Tyler, Z. E. The overlearning reversal shift effect in preschool children as a function of age. *Psychon. Sci.*, 1966, **6**, 175–176.

Das, J. P., and Panda, K. C. Two-choice learning in children and adolescents under rewarded and nonrewarded conditions. *J. genet. Psychol.*, 1963, **68**, 203–211.

Dashkovskaia, V. S. The first conditioned reactions in newborn infants under normal and in certain pathological conditions. *Zh. vyssh. nerv. Deiatel.*, 1953, **3**, 247–259.

Davidson, R. E. Mediation and ability in paired-associate learning. *J. educ. Psychol.*, 1964, **55**, 352–356.

Degtiar, E. N. Comparative characteristics of physiological conditions for the elaboration of a stereotype in the first and second signal systems. *Zh. vyssh. nerv. Deiatel.*, 1962, **12**, 63–68.

Denny, M. R. Research in learning and performance. In H. A. Stevens and R. Heber, (Eds.), *Mental retardation*, Chicago: University of Chicago Press, 1964, Pp. 100-142.

Derks, P. L., and Paclisanu, M. Simple strategies and binary prediction by children and adults. *J. exp. Psychol.*, 1967, **73**, 278–285.

Dickerson, D. J. Performance of preschool children on three discrimination shifts. *Psychon. Sci.*, 1966, **4**, 417–418.

Dornbush, R. L., and Winnick, W. A. The relative effectiveness of stereometric and pattern stimuli in discrimination learning in children. *Psychon. Sci.*, 1966, **5**, 301–302.

Duncanson, J. P. *Intelligence and the ability to learn.* Princeton, N. J.: Educational Testing Service, 1964.

Eimas, P. D. Stimulus compounding in the discrimination learning of kindergarten children. *J. exp. Child Psychol.*, 1965, **2**, 178–185.

Eimas, P. D. Effects of overtraining and age on intradimensional and extradimensional shifts in children. *J. exp. Child Psychol.*, 1966, **3**, 348–355. (a)

Eimas, P. D. Effects of overtraining, irrelevant stimuli, and training task on reversal discrimination learning in children. *J. exp. Child Psychol.*, 1966, **3**, 315–323. (b)

Eimas, P. D. Optional shift behavior as a function of overtraining, irrelevant stimuli, and age. *J. exp. Child Psychol.*, 1967, **5**, 332–340.

Ellis, N. R. Toilet training the severely defective patient: an S-R reinforcement analysis. *Am. J. ment. Defic.*, 1963, **68**, 98–103.

Ellis, N. R. Girardeau, F. L., Pryor, M. W. Analysis of learning sets in normal and severely defective humans. *J. comp. physiol. Psychol.*, 1962, **55**, 860–865.

Endsley, R. C. Effortfulness and blocking at different distances from the goal as determinants of speed and amplitude. *J. exp. Child Psychol.*, 1966, **3**, 18–30.

Engen, T., and Lipsitt, L. P. Decrement and recovery of responses to olfactory stimuli in the human neonate. *J. comp. physiol. Psychol.*, 1965, **59**, 312–316.

Engen, T., Lipsitt, L. P., and Kaye, H. Olfactory responses and adaptation in the human neonate. *J. comp. physiol. Psychol.*, 1963, **56**, 73–77.

Epstein, R., and Liverant, S. Verbal conditioning and sex-role identification in children. *Child Dev.*, 1963, **34**, 99–106.

Erickson, M. T. Effects of social deprivation and satiation on verbal conditioning in children. *J. comp. physiol. Psychol.*, 1962, **55**, 953–957.

Erickson, M. T., and Lipsitt, L. P. Effects of delayed reward on simultaneous and successive discrimination learning in children. *J. comp. physiol. Psychol.*, 1960, **53**, 256–260.

Etzel, B. D., and Gewirtz, J. L. Experimental modification of caretaker-maintained high-rate operant crying in a 6- and a 20-week-old infant (Infans tyrannotearus): extinction of crying with reinforcement of eye contact and smiling. *J. exp. Child Psychol.*, 1967, **5**, 303–317.

Fagan, J. F., and Witryol, S. L. The effects of instructional set and delay of reward on children's learning in a simultaneous discrimination task. *Child Dev.*, 1966, **37**, 433–438.

Flavell, J. H., Beach, D. R., and Chinsky, J. M. Spontaneous verbal rehearsal in a memory task as a function of age. *Child Dev.*, 1966, **37**, 283–299.

Fletcher, H. J., and Orr, B. M. Instructions and observational learning in preschool children. *Psychon. Sci.*, 1967, **7**, 83–84.

Fowler, W. Cognitive learning in infancy and early childhood. *Psychol. Bull.*, 1962, **59**, 116–153.

Friedman, S. R. Developmental level and concept learning: confirmation of an inverse relationship. *Psychon. Sci.*, 1965, **2**, 3–4.

Furth, H. G., and Youniss, J. Effect of overtraining on three discrimination shifts in children. *J. comp. physiol. psychol.*, 1964, **57**, 290–293.

Garrett, H. E. The relation of tests of memory and learning to each other and to general intelligence in a highly selected adult group. *J. educ. Psychol.*, 1928, **19**, 601–613.

Garrison, K. C. The correlation between intelligence test scores and success in certain rational organization problems. *J. appl. Psychol.*, 1928, **12**, 621–630.

Gates, A. I., and Taylor, G. A. The acquisition of motor control in writing by preschool children. *Teachers College Record*, 1923, **24**, 459–468.

Gelfand, D. M. The influence of self-esteem on rate of verbal conditioning and social matching behavior. *J. abnorm. soc. Psychol.*, 1962, **65**, 259–265.

Gesell, A., and Thompson, H. Learning and growth in identical infant twins. *Genet. Psychol. Monogr.*, 1929, **6**, 1–123.

Gewirtz, J. L., and Baer, D. M. Deprivation and satiation of social reinforcers as drive conditions. *J. Abnorm. soc. Psychol.*, 1958, **57**, 165–172. (a)

Gewirtz, J. L., and Baer, D. M. The effect of brief social deprivation on behaviors for a social reinforcer. *J. Abnorm. soc. Psychol.*, 1958, **56**, 49–56. (b)

Gollin, E. S. Reversal learning and conditional discrimination in children. *J. comp. physiol. Psychol.*, 1964, **58**, 441–445.

Gollin, E. S. A developmental approach to learning and cognition. In L. P. Lipsitt and C. C. Spiker, (Eds.), *Advances in child development and behavior, Vol. II.* New York: Academic Press, 1965, Pp. 159–186.

Gollin, E. S., and Shirk, E. J. A developmental study of oddity-problem learning in young children. *Child Dev.*, 1966, **37**, 214–217.

Gonzales, R. C., and Ross, S. The basis of solution by preverbal children of the intermediate size problem. *Am. J. Psychol.*, 1958, **71**, 742–746.

Goodenough, F. L., and Brian, C. R. Certain factors underlying the acquisition of motor skill by preschool children. *J. exp. Psychol.*, 1929, **12**, 127–155.

Graham, F. K., Ernhart, C. B., Craft, M., and Berman, P. W. Learning of relative and absolute size concepts in preschool children. *J. exp. Child Psychol.*, 1964, **1**, 26–36.

Gratch, G. An exploratory study of the relation of dependence upon adult, anxiety and age to children's risk taking. *Child Dev.*, 1964, **35**, 1155–1167.

Greene, F. M. Effect of novelty on choices made by preschool children in a simple discrimination task. *Child Dev.*, 1964, **35**, 1257–1264.

Greene, F. M., and Terrell, C. Response shifts in discrimination learning of children at three grade levels. *Child Dev.*, 1964, **37**, 661–668.

Gruen, G. E., and Weir, M. W. The effect of instruction, penalty, and age of probability learning. *Child Dev.*, 1964, **35**, 265–273.

Gruen, G., and Zigler, E. Expectancy of success and the probability learning of middle-class, lower-class, and retarded children. *J. abn. Psychol.*, 1968, **73**, 343–352.

Harris, L. The effects of stimulus setting and of variability of delayed reinforcement in children's visual orientation and speed of lever movement. *J. exp. Child Psychol.*, 1967, **5**, 350–361.

Harter, S. Discrimination learning set in children as a function of IQ and MA. *J. exp. Child Psychol.*, 1965, **2**, 31–43.

Harter, S. Mental age, IQ, and motivational factors in the discrimination learning set performance of normal and retarded children. *J. exp. Child Psychol.*, 1967, **5**, 123–141.

Heal, L. W. The role of cue value, cue novelty, and overtraining in a discrimination shift performance of retardates and normal children of comparable discrimination ability. *J. exp. Child Psychol.*, 1966, **4**, 126–142.

Helson, H. *Adaptation-level theory.* New York: Harper and Row, 1964.

Hetherington, E. M. A developmental study of the effects of sex of the dominant parent on sex-role preference, identification, and imitation in children. *J. Personality soc. Psychol.*, 1965, **2**, 188–194.

Hetherington, E. M., and Banta, T. J. Incidental and intentional learning in normal and mentally retarded children. *J. comp. physiol. Psychol.*, 1962, **55**, 402–404.

Hetherington, E. M., Ross, L. E., and Pick, H. L. Delay of reward and learning in mentally retarded and normal children. *Child Dev.*, 1964, **35**, 653–659.

Hicks, D. J. Imitation and retention of film-mediated aggressive peer and adult models. *J. Personality soc. Psychol.*, 1965, **2**, 97–100.

Hicks, V. C., and Carr, H. A. Human reactions in a maze. *J. anim. Psychol.*, 1912, **2**, 98–125.

Hilgard, J. R. Learning and maturation in preschool children. *J. genet. Psychol.*, 1932, **41**, 31–56.

Hill, S. D. The performance of young children on three discrimination-learning tasks. *Child Dev.*, 1965, **36**, 425–435. (a)

Hill, S. D. Transfer in discrimination learning. *Child Dev.*, 1965, **36**, 749–760. (b)

Hill, S. D. and Hecker, E. E. Auditory and visual learning of a paired-associate task by second grade children. *Percept. Mot. Skills*, 1966, **23**, 814.

Holton, R. B. Amplitude of instrumental response following cessation of reward. *Child Dev.*, 1961, **32**, 107–116.

Horowitz, F. D., and Armentrout, J. Discrimination-learning, manifest anxiety, and effects of reinforcement. *Child Dev.*, 1965, **36**, 731–748.

House, B. J., and Zeaman, D. Miniature experiments in the discrimination learning of retardates. In L. P. Lipsitt and C. C. Spiker, (Eds.), *Advances in child development and behavior*, Vol. 1. New York: Academic Press, 1963. Pp. 313–374.

Hunter, I. M. L. An experimental investigation of the absolute and relative theories of transposition behavior in children. *Br. J. Psychol.*, 1952, **43**, 113–128.

Hunter, I. M. L. Children's reactions to bivariant stimuli. *Br. J. Psychol.*, 1954, **45,** 288–293.

Hunter, W. S. Delayed reactions in animals and children. *Behav. Monogr.*, 1913, **2,** (6).

Hunter, W. S. Delayed reaction in a child. *Psychol. Rev.*, 1917, **24,** 75–87.

Hurlock, E. B. The psychology of incentives. *J. Soc. Psychol.*, 1931, **2,** 261–290.

Husband, R. W. Intercorrelations among learning abilities: III. The effects of age and spread of intelligence upon relationships. *J. genet. Psychol.*, 1941, **58,** 431–434.

Ivanov-Smolensky, A. G. On the methods of examining the conditioned food reflexes in children and mental defectives. *Brain*, 1927, **50,** 138–141.

Janoš, O. *Age and individual differences in higher nervous activity in infants.* Prague: SzdN., 1965.

Jeffrey, W. E. Variables in early discrimination learning: III. Simultaneous versus successive stimulus presentation. *Child Dev.*, 1961, **32,** 305–310.

Jeffrey, W. E. Variables affecting reversal-shifts in young children. *Am. J. Psychol.*, 1965, **78,** 589–595.

Jeffrey, W. E., and Cohen, L. B. Effect of spatial separation of stimulus, response, and reinforcement in selective learning in children. *J. exp. Psychol.*, 1964, **67,** 577–580.

Jeffrey, W. E., and Cohen, L. B. Response tendencies of children in a two-choice situation. *J. exp. Child Psychol.*, 1965, **2,** 248–254.

Jeffrey, W. E., and Skager, R. W. Effect of incentive conditions on stimulus generalization in children. *Child Dev.*, 1962, **33,** 865–870.

Jensen, A. R., and Rohwer, W. D., Jr. Syntactical mediation of serial and paired-associate learning as a function of age. *Child Dev.*, 1965, **36,** 601–608.

Johnson, P., and Bailey, D. E. Some determinants of the use of relationships in discrimination learning. *J. exp. Psychol.*, 1966, **71,** 365–372.

Johnson, P. J., and White, R. M., Jr. Concept of dimensionality and reversal shift performance in children. *J. exp. Child Psychol.*, 1967, **5,** 223–227.

Johnson, R. C., and Zara, R. C. Relational learning in young children. *J. comp. physiol. Psychol.*, 1960, **53,** 594–597.

Jones, M. C. The elimination of children's fears. *J. exp. Psychol.*, 1924, **7,** 382–390. (a)

Jones, M. C. A laboratory study of fear: the case of Peter. *Pedag. Semin.*, 1924, **31,** 308–315. (b)

Jones, M. H., and Liverant, S. Effects of age differences on choice behavior. *Child Dev.*, 1960, **31,** 673–680.

Judd, C. H. The relation of special training to general intelligence. *Educ. Rev.*, 1908, **36,** 28–42.

Kass, N. Resistance to extinction as a function of age and schedules of reinforcement. *J. exp. Psychol.*, 1962, **64,** 249–252.

Kass, N. Risk in decision making as a function of age, sex, and probability preference. *Child Dev.*, 1964, **35,** 577–582.

Kass, N., Beardshall, A., and Wilson, H. The effects of schedules of training upon the development of a conditioned reinforcer. *Psychon. Sci.*, 1966, **6,** 183–184.

Kass, N., and Wilson, H. Resistance to extinction as a function of percentage of reinforcement, number of training trials, and conditioned reinforcement. *J. exp. Psychol.*, 1966, **71,** 355–357.

Katz, P. Acquisition and retention of discrimination learning sets in lower-class preschool children. *J. educ. Psychol.*, 1967, **58,** 253–258.

Kausler, D. H., Laughlin, P. R., and Trapp, E. P. Effects of incentive-set on relevant and irrelevant (incidental) learning in children *Child Dev.*, 1963, **34,** 195–199.

Kaye, H. The conditioned Babkin response in human newborns. *Psychon. Sci.*, 1965, **2**, 287–288.

Kaye, H., and Levin, G. R. Two attempts to demonstrate tonal suppression of non-nutritive sucking in neonates. *Percept. Mot. Skills*, 1963, **17**, 521–522.

Keen, R. Effects of auditory stimuli on sucking behavior in the human neonate. *J. exp. Child Psychol.*, 1964, **1**, 348–354.

Kendler, H. H., and Kendler, T. S. Effect of verbalization on discrimination reversal shifts in children. *Science*, 1961, **134**, 1619–1620.

Kendler, T. S. Development of mediating responses in children. In J. C. Wright and J. Kagan (Eds.), *Basic cognitive processes in children. Monographs of the Society for Research in Child Development*, 1963, Vol. 28, No. 2. Pp. 33–51.

Kendler, T. S. Verbalization and optional reversal shifts among kindergarten children. *J. Verb. Learn. verb. Behav.*, 1964, **3**, 428–436.

Kendler, T. S., and Kendler, H. H. Reversal and nonreversal shifts in kindergarten children. *J. exp. Psychol.*, 1959, **58**, 56–60.

Kendler, T. S., and Kendler, H. H. Inferential behavior in children as a function of age and subgoal constancy. *J. exp. Psychol.* 1962, **64**, 460–466.

Kendler, T. S., and Kendler, H. H. Optional shifts of children as a function of number of training trials on the initial discrimination. *J. exp. Child Psychol.*, 1966, **3**, 216–224.

Kendler, T. S., Kendler, H. H., and Carrick, M. Verbal labels and inferential problem solution of children. *Child Dev.*, 1966, **37**, 749–764.

Kendler, T. S., Kendler, H. H., and Learnard, B. Mediated responses to size and brightness as a function of age. *Am. J. Psychol.*, 1962, **75**, 571–586.

Kendler, T. S., Kendler, H. H., and Wells, D. Reversal and nonreversal shifts in nursery school children. *J. comp. physiol. Psychol.*, 1960, **53**, 83–88.

Kerpelman, L. C. Stimulus dimensionality and manipulability in visual perceptual learning. *Child Dev.*, 1967, **38**, 563–572.

Kessen, W., and Kessen, M. L. Behavior of young children in a two-choice guessing problem. *Child Dev.*, 1961, **32**, 779–788.

Klinger, N. N., and Palermo, D. S. Aural paired-associate learning in children as a function of free-associative strength. *Child Dev.*, 1967, **38**, 1143–1152.

Kobasigawa, A. Observation of failure in another person as a determinant of amplitude and speed of a simple motor response. *J. Personality soc. Psychol.*, 1965, **1**, 626–630.

Koch, M. B., and Meyer, D. R. A relationship of mental age to learning set formation in the preschool child. *J. comp. physiol. Psychol.*, 1959, **52**, 387–389.

Kofsky, E., and Osler, S. F. Free classification in children. *Child Dev.*, 1967, **38**, 927–937.

Koltsova, M. M. The physiological mechanisms underlying the development of generalization in the child. In Y. Brackbill and G. G. Thompson, (Eds.), *Behavior in infancy and early childhood.* New York: Free Press, 1967. Pp. 250–258.

Krachkovskaia, M. V. Conditioned leukocytosis in newborn infants. In Y. Brackbill and G. G. Thompson, (Eds.), *Behavior in infancy and early childhood.* New York: Free Press, 1967. Pp. 240–245.

Krasnogorski, N. I. Ueber die Bedingungsreflexe im Kindesalter. *Jb. Kinderheilk. phys. Erzieh.*, 1909, **19**, 1–24.

Kuenne, M. R. Experimental investigation of the relation of language to transposition behavior in young children. *J. exp. Psychol.*, 1946, **36**, 471–490.

Kurtz, H. H. Discrimination of complex stimuli: the relationship of training and test stimuli in transfer of discrimination. *J. exp. Psychol.*, 1955, **50**, 283–292.

Lazarus, A. A. The elimination of children's phobias by deconditioning. In H. J. Eysenck (Ed.), *Behavior therapy and the neuroses.* New York: Macmillan, 1960, Pp. 114–122.

Levin, H., Watson, J. S., and Feldman, M. Writing as pretraining for association learning. *J. educ. Psychol.*, 1964, **55**, 181–184.

Lewis, D. J. Partial reinforcement in a gambling situation. *J. exp. Psychol.*, 1952, **43**, 447–450.

Lindley, E. H. A study of puzzles with special reference to the psychology of mental adaptation. *Am. J. Psychol.*, 1897, **8**, 431–493.

Lintz, L. M., Fitzgerald, H. E., and Brackbill, Y. Conditioning the eyeblink response to sound in infants. *Psychon. Sci.*, 1967, **7**, 405–406.

Lipman, R. S. Learning: verbal, perceptual-motor, and classical conditioning. In N. R. Ellis, (Ed.), *Handbook of mental deficiency.* New York: McGraw-Hill, 1963, Pp. 391–423.

Lipsitt, L. P. Simultaneous and successive discrimination learning in children. *Child Dev.*, 1961, **32**, 337–348.

Lipsitt, L. P. Learning in the first year of life. In L. P. Lipsitt, and C. C. Spiker, (Eds.), *Advances in child development and behavior,* Vol. 1. New York: Academic Press, 1963. Pp. 147–196.

Lipsitt, L. P. Learning in the human infant. In H. W. Stevenson, E. Hess, and H. L. Rheingold, (Eds.), *Early behavior: comparative and developmental approaches.* New York: Wiley, 1967. Pp. 225–248.

Lipsitt, L. P., Kaye, H., and Bosack, T. N. Enhancement of neonatal sucking through reinforcement. *J. exp. Child Psychol.*, 1966, **4**, 163–168.

Lipsitt, L. P., and Lolordo, V. M. Interactive effect of stress and stimulus generalization on children's oddity learning. *J. exp. Psychol.*, 1963, **66**, 210–214.

Lipsitt, L. P., and Serunian, S. A. Oddity problem learning in young children. *Child Dev.*, 1963, **34**, 201–206.

Lipsitt, L. P., and Spears, W. C. Effects of anxiety and stress on children's paired-associate learning. *Psychon. Sci.*, 1965, **3**, 553–554.

Long, E. R. Multiple scheduling in children. *J. exp. Analysis Behav.*, 1959, **2**, 268. (a)

Long, E. R. The use of operant conditioning techniques in children. In S. Fisher, (Ed.), *Child research in psychopharmacology.* Springfield, Ill.: Thomas, 1959. (b)

Longstreth, L. E. Frustration and secondary reinforcement concepts as applied to human conditioning and extinction. *Psychol. Monogr.*, 1966, **80** (Whole No. 619).

Lovaas, O. I., Berberich, J. P., Perloff, B. F., and Schaeffer, B. Acquisition of imitative speech in schizophrenic children, *Science*, 1966, **151**, 705–707.

Lovaas, O. I., Freitag, G., Gold, V. J., and Kassorla, I. C. Experimental studies in childhood schizophrenia: analysis of self-destructive behavior. *J. exp. Child Psychol.*, 1965, **2**, 67–84.

Lovaas, O. I., Schaeffer, B., and Simmons, J. Q. Building social behavior in autistic children by use of electric shock. *J. exp. Res. Personality*, 1965, **1**, 99–109.

Lubker, B. J. Irrelevant stimulus dimensions and children's performance on simultaneous discrimination problems. *Child Dev.*, 1967, **38**, 119–125.

Lubker, B. J., and Spiker, C. C. The effects of irrelevant stimulus dimensions on children's oddity-problem learning. *J. exp. Child Psychol.*, 1966, **3**, 207–215.

Luria, A. R. The role of language in the formation of temporary connections. In E. Simon, (Ed.), *Psychology in the Soviet Union.* Stanford, Cal.: Stanford University Press, 1957.

Maccoby, E. E., and Hagen, J. W. Effect of distraction upon central versus incidental recall: developmental trends. *J. exp. Child Psychol.*, 1965, **2**, 280–289.

McCullers, J. C. Effects of associative strength, grade level, and interpair interval in verbal paired-associate learning. *Child Dev.*, 1961, **32**, 773–778.

McCullers, J. C. Associative strength and degree of interference in children's verbal paired-associate learning. *J. exp. Child Psychol.*, 1967, **5**, 58–68.

McDavid, J. W. Imitative behavior in preschool children. *Psychol. Monogr.*, 1959, **73** (16).

McDavid, J. W. Effects of ambiguity of enviromental cues upon learning to imitate. *J. Abnorm. soc. Psychol.*, 1962, **65**, 381–386.

McGinnis, E. The acquisition and interference of motor habits in young children. *Genet. Psychol. Monogr.*, 1929, **6**, 203–311.

McGraw, M. B. *Growth: a study of Johnny and Jimmy.* New York: Appleton-Century, 1935.

Mackintosh, N. J. Selective attention in animal discrimination learning. *Psychol. Bull.*, 1965, **64**, 124–150.

McKee, J. P., and Riley, D. A. Auditory transposition in six-year-old children. *Child Dev.*, 1962, **33**, 469–476.

McPherson, M. W. A survey of experimental studies of learning in individuals who achieve subnormal ratings on standardized psychometric measures. *Am. J. ment. Defic.*, 1948, **52**, 232–254.

McPherson, M. W. Learning and mental deficiency. *Am. J. ment. Defic.*, 1958, **62**, 870–877.

Marquis, D. P. Learning in the neonate: the modification of behavior under three feeding conditions. *J. exp. Psychol.*, 1941, **29**, 263–282.

Marsh, G. Effect of overtraining on reversal and nonreversal shifts in nursery school children. *Child Dev.*, 1964, **35**, 1367–1372.

Marsh, G., and Sherman, M. Verbal mediation of transposition as a function of age level. *J. exp. Child Psychol.*, 1966, **4**, 90–98.

Martin, J. G., and Jones, R. L. Size and structure of grammatical units in paired-associate learning at two age levels. *J. exp. Psychol.*, 1965, **70**, 407–411.

Mateer, F. *Child behavior.* Boston: Badger, 1918.

Mednick, S. A., and Lehtinen, L. C. Stimulus generalization as a function of age in children. *J. exp. Psychol.*, 1957, **53**, 180–183.

Meek, L. H. A study of learning and retention in young children. *Teachers College Contributions to Education*, 1925, No. 164.

Miller, L. B., and Estes, B. W. Monetary reward and motivation in discrimination learning. *J. exp. Psychol.*, 1961, **61**, 501–504.

Morse, P. A., and Shepp, B. E. The effects of overt verbalization and overtraining on dimensional shifts. In B. E. Shepp, *Studies of discriminative learning and transfer in normal and retarded children.* Progress report, Brown University, 1967.

Mumbauer, C. C., and Odom, R. D. Variables affecting the performance of preschool children in intradimensional, reversal, and extradimensional shifts. *J. exp. Psychol.*, 1967, **75**, 180–187.

Munn, N. L. Learning in children. In L. Carmichael (Ed.), *Manual of child psychology.* New York: Wiley, 1946. (2nd ed., 1954).

Murphy, J. V., and Miller, R. E. Spatial contiguity of cue, reward, and response in discrimination learning by children. *J. exp. Psychol.*, 1959, **58**, 485–489.

Myers, N. A. Extinction following partial and continuous primary and secondary reinforcement. *J. exp. Psychol.*, 1960, **60**, 172–179.

Myers, N. A., and Myers, J. L. A test of a discrimination hypothesis of secondary reinforcement. *J. exp. Psychol.*, 1965, **70**, 98–101.

Nelson, R. B., Reid, I. E., and Travers, R. M. W. Effect of electric shock as a reinforcer of the behavior of children. *Psychol. Reps.*, 1965, **16**, 123–126.

Nikkel, N., and Palermo, D. S. Effects of mediated associations in paired-associate learning of children. *J. exp. Child Psychol.*, 1965, **2**, 92–101.

Norcross, K. J. Effects on discrimination performance of similarity of previously acquired stimulus names. *J. exp. Psychol.*, 1958, **56**, 305–309.

Norcross, K. J., and Spiker, C. C. The effects of type of stimulus pretraining on discrimination performance in preschool children. *Child Dev.*, 1957, **28**, 79–84.

Norcross, K. J., and Spiker, C. C. Effects of mediated association on transfer in paired-associate learning. *J. exp. Psychol.*, 1958, **55**, 129–134.

Nunnally, J. C., Duchnowski, A. J., and Parker, R. K. Association of neutral objects with rewards: effect of verbal evaluation, reward expectancy, and selective attention. *J. Personality soc. Psychol.*, 1965, **1**, 270–274.

Nunnally, J. C., Knott, P. D., and Duchnowski, A. J. Association of neutral objects with rewards: effects of different numbers of conditioning trials and of anticipated reward versus actual reward. *J. exp. Child Psychol.*, 1967, **5**, 249–262.

Nunnally, J. C., Stevens, D. A., and Hall, G. H. Association of neutral objects with rewards: Effect on verbal evaluation and eye movements. *J. exp. Child Psychol.*, 1965, **2**, 44–57.

O'Connor, N. Learning and mental defect. In A. M. Clarke and A. D. B. Clarke, (Eds.), *Mental deficiency: the changing outlook.* London: Methuen, 1958.

Odom, R. D. Effects of auditory and visual stimulus deprivation and satiation on children's performance in an operant task. *J. exp. Child Psychol.*, 1964, **1**, 16–25.

Odom, R. D. Children's probability learning as a function of the cross-sex effect. *Psychon. Sci.*, 1966, **4**, 305–306. (a)

Odom, R. D. Concept identification and utilization among children of different ages. *J. exp. Child Psychol.*, 1966, **4**, 309–316. (b)

Odom, R. D. Problem-solving strategies as a function of age and socioeconomic level. *Child Dev.*, 1967, **38**, 747–752.

Odom, R. D., and Coon, R. C. The development of hypothesis testing. *J. exp. Child Psychol.*, 1966, **4**, 285–291.

Offenbach, S. I. Studies of children's probability learning behavior: I. Effect of reward and punishment at two age levels. *Child Dev.*, 1964, **35**, 709–715.

Offenbach, S. I. Reinforcer acquisition during discrimination learning. *Psychol. Rep.*, 1966, **19**, 843–849.

Osler, S. F., and Fivel, M. W. Concept attainment: I. The role of age and intelligence in concept attainment by induction. *J. exp. Psychol.*, 1961, **62**, 1–8.

Osler, S. F., and Kofsky, E. Stimulus uncertainty as a variable in the development of conceptual ability. *J. exp. Child Psychol.*, 1965, **2**, 264–279.

Osler, S. F., and Kofsky, E. Structure and strategy in concept learning. *J. exp. Child Psychol.*, 1966, **4**, 198–209.

Osler, S. F., and Shapiro, S. L. Studies in concept attainment. IV. The role of partial reinforcement as a function of age and intelligence. *Child Dev.*, 1964, **35**, 623–633.

Osler, S. F., and Trautman, G. E. Concept attainment. II. Effect of stimulus complexity upon concept attainment at two levels of intelligence. *J. exp. Psychol.*, 1961, **62**, 9–13.

Osler, S. F., and Weiss, S. R. Studies in concept attainment. III. Effect of instructions at two levels of intelligence. *J. exp. Psychol.*, 1962, **63**, 528–533.

Otto, W. The acquisition and retention of paired-associates by good, average, and poor readers. *J. educ. Psychol.*, 1961, **52**, 241–248.

Paivio, A., and Yuille, J. C. Word abstractness and meaningfulness, and paired-associate learning in children. *J. exp. Child Psychol.*, 1966, **4**, 81–89.

Palermo, D. S. Mediated association in a paired-associate transfer task. *J. exp. Psychol.*, 1962, **64**, 234–238.

Palermo, D. S. Mediated association in the paired-associate learning of children using heterogeneous and homogeneous lists. *J. exp. Psychol.*, 1966, **71**, 711–717.

Palermo, D. S., Castaneda, A., and McCandless, B. R. The relationship of anxiety in children to performance in a complex learning task. *Child Dev.*, 1956, **27**, 333–337.

Palermo, D. S., Flamer, G. B., and Jenkins, J. J. Association value in the paired-associate learning of children and adults. *J. Verb. Learn. verb. Behav.*, 1964, **3**, 171–175.

Papoušek, H. The development of higher nervous activity in children in the first half-year of life. In P. H. Mussen, (Ed.), *European research in cognitive development. Monographs of the Society for Research in Child Development*, 1965, **30**, No. 2. Pp. 102–111.

Papoušek, H. Conditioning during early postnatal development. In Y. Brackbill, and G. G. Thompson, (Eds.), *Behavior in infancy and early childhood.* New York: Free Press, 1967, Pp. 259–274. (a)

Papoušek, H. Experimental studies of appetitional behavior in human newborns and infants. In H. W. Stevenson, E. Hess, and H. L. Rheingold, (Eds.), *Early behavior: comparative and developmental approaches.* New York: Wiley, 1967. Pp. 249–278. (b)

Parker, R. K., and Nunnally, J. C. Association of neutral objects with rewards: effects of reward schedules on reward expectancy, verbal evaluation, and selective attention. *J. exp. Child Psychol.*, 1966, **3**, 324–332.

Patterson, G. R., Jones, J. W., Whittier, J., and Wright, M. A. A behavior modification technique for the hyperactive child. *Behav. Res. Ther.*, 1965, **2**, 217–226.

Penney, R. K. The effects of nonreinforcement on response strength as a function of number of previous reinforcements. *Can. J. Psychol.*, 1960, **14**, 206–215.

Penney, R. K. Children's escape performance as a function of schedules of delay of reinforcement. *J. exp. Psychol.*, 1967, **73**, 109–112.

Penney, R. K., and Kirwin, P. M. Differential adaptation of anxious and non-anxious children in instrumental escape conditioning. *J. exp. Psychol.*, 1965, **70**, 539–541.

Penney, R. K., and Lupton, A. A. Children's discrimination on learning as a function of reward and punishment. *J. comp. physiol. Psychol.*, 1961, **54**, 449–451.

Penney, R. K., and McCann, B. The instrumental escape conditioning of anxious and nonanxious children. *J. Abnorm. soc. Psychol.*, 1962, **65**, 351–354.

Peterson, J. Learning in children. In C. Murchison, (Ed.), *A handbook of child psychology.* Worcester, Mass.: Clark University Press, 1931. (2nd ed., rev., 1933.)

Pick, A. D. Improvement of visual and tactual form discrimination. *J. exp. Psychol.*, 1965, **69**, 331–339.

Pick, A. D., Pick, H. L., Jr., and Thomas, M. L. Cross-modal transfer and improvement of form discrimination. *J. exp. Child Psychol.*, 1966, **3**, 279–288.

Price, L. E. Learning and performance in a verbal paired-associate task with preschool children. *Psychol. Rep.*, 1963, **12**, 847–850.

Pufall, P. B., and Furth, H. G. Double alternation as a function of age and language. *Child Dev.*, 1966, **37**, 653–661.

Pumroy, D. K., and Pumroy, S. S. Effect of amount and percentage of reinforcement on resistance to extinction in preschool children. *J. genet. Psychol.*, 1961, **98**, 55–62.

Rabinowitz, F. M. Conditioned stimulus duration and delay of reward as variables in a lever pulling situation. *J. exp. Child Psychol.*, 1966, **3**, 225–234.

Ramiriz, M., III, and Castaneda, A. Paired-associate learning of sociometrically ranked children's names. *Child Dev.*, 1967, **38**, 171–180.

Razran, G. H. S. Conditioned responses in children. *Archs. Psychol., N. Y.*, 1933, **148**, 720.

Reese, H. W. Motor paired associate learning and stimulus pretraining. *Child Dev.*, 1960, **31**, 505–514.

Reese, H. W. Level of stimulus pretraining and paired-associate learning. *Child Dev.*, 1961, **32**, 89–94. (a)

Reese, H. W. Transposition in the intermediate-size problem by preschool children. *Child Dev.*, 1961, **32**, 311–314. (b)

Reese, H. W. The distance effect of transposition in the intermediate-size problem. *J. comp. physiol. Psychol.*, 1962, **55**, 528–531. (a)

Reese, H. W. Verbal mediation as a function of age level. *Psychol. Bull.*, 1962, **59**, 502–509. (b)

Reese, H. W. Discrimination learning set in children. In L. P. Lipsitt and C. C. Spiker, (Eds.), *Advances in child development and behavior*. Vol. 1. New York: Academic Press, 1963. Pp. 115–146.

Reese, H. W. Discrimination learning set and perceptual set in young children. *Child Dev.*, 1965, **36**, 153–161. (a)

Reese, H. W. Imagery in paired-associate learning. *J. exp. Child Psychol.*, 1965, **2**, 290–296. (b)

Reese, H. W. Verbal effects in the intermediate-size transposition problem. *J. exp. Child Psychol.*, 1966, **3**, 123–130.

Reese, H. W., and Fiero, P. G. Overlearning and transposition. *Child Dev.*, 1964, **35**, 1361–1365.

Rheingold, H. L., Gewirtz, J. L., and Ross, H. W. Social conditioning of vocalizations in the infant. *J. comp. physiol. Psychol.*, 1959, **52**, 68–73.

Rice, U. M., and DiVesta, F. J. A developmental study of semantic and phonetic generalization in paired-associate learning. *Child Dev.*, 1965, **36**, 721–730.

Rieber, M. The effect of CS presence during delay of reward on the speed of an instrumental response. *J. exp. Psychol.*, 1961, **61**, 290–294. (a)

Rieber, M. Shifts in response-reward interval and its effect upon response speed. *Psychol. Rep.*, 1961, **60**, 393–398. (b)

Rieber, M. Delay of reward and discrimination learning in children. *Child Dev.*, 1964, **35**, 559–568.

Rieber, M. Response alternation in children under different reinforcement schedules. *Psychol. Sci.*, 1966, **4**, 145–150. (a)

Rieber, M. Role of stimulus comparison in children's discrimination learning. *J. exp. Psychol.*, 1966, **72**, 263–270. (b)

Rieber, M., and Johnson, B. M. The relative effects of alternating delayed reinforcement and alternating nonreinforcement on response speeds of children. *J. exp. Child Psychol.*, 1964, **1**, 174–181.

Riley, D. A., McKee, J. P., Bell, D. D., and Schwartz, C. R. Auditory discrimination in children: the effect of relative and absolute instructions on retention and transfer. *J. exp. Psychol.*, 1967, **73**, 581–588.

Riley, D. A., Sherman, M., and McKee, J. P. A. Comment on intermediate size discrimination and adaptation level theory. *Psychol. Rev.*, 1966, **73**, 252–256.

Rohwer, W. D., Jr. Constraint, syntax and meaning in paired-associate learning. *J. Verb. Learn. verb. Behav.*, 1966, **5**, 541–547.

Rohwer, W. D., Jr., and Lynch, S. Semantic constraint in paired-associate learning. *J. educ. Psychol.*, 1967, **57**, 271–278.

Rohwer, W. D., Jr., Lynch, S., Levin, J. R., and Suzuki, N. Pictorial and verbal factors in the efficient learning of paired associates. *J. educ. Psychol.*, 1967, **58**, 278–284.

Rohwer, W. D., Jr., Lynch, S., Suzuki, N., and Levin, J. R. Verbal and pictorial facilitation of paired-associate learning. *J. exp. Child Psychol.*, 1967, **5**, 294–302.

Rosenbaum, M. E. Effect of direct and vicarious verbalization on retention. *Child Dev.*, 1962, **33**, 103–110.

Rosenblith, J. F. Learning by imitation in kindergarten children. *Child Dev.*, 1959, **30**, 69–80.

Rosenblith, J. F. Imitative color choices in kindergarten children. *Child Dev.*, 1961, **32**, 211–223.

Rosenhan, D. L. Effects of social class and race on responsiveness to approval and disapproval. *J. Personality soc. Psychol.*, 1966, **4**, 253–259.

Ross, L. E. Classical conditioning and discrimination research with the mentally retarded. In N. R. Ellis, (Ed.), *International review of research in mental retardation*, Vol. 2. New York: Academic Press, 1967.

Ross, L. E., Hetherington, M., and Wray, N. P. Delay of reward and the learning of a size problem by normal and retarded children. *Child Dev.*, 1965, **36**, 509–518.

Rowley, V., and Keller, E. D. Changes in children's verbal behavior as a function of social approval and manifest anxiety. *J. abnorm. soc. Psychol.*, 1962, **65**, 53–57.

Rudel, R. G. Transposition of response by children trained in intermediate-size problems. *J. comp. physiol. Psychol.*, 1957, **50**, 292–295.

Rudel, R. G. Transposition of response for size in children. *J. comp. physiol. Psychol.*, 1958, **51**, 386–390.

Ryan, T. J. The effects of nonreinforcement and incentive value on response speed. *Child Dev.*, 1965, **36**, 1067–1081.

Ryan, T. J. Instrumental performance as related to several reward schedules and age. *J. exp. Child Psychol.*, 1966, **3**, 398–404.

Ryan, T. J., and Moffitt, A. R. Response speed as a function of age, incentive value, and reinforcement schedule. *Child Dev.*, 1966, **37**, 103–113.

Ryan, T. J., and Voorhoeve, A. C. A parametric investigation of reinforcement schedule and sex of S as related to acquisition and extinction of an instrumental response. *J. exp. Child Psychol.*, 1966, **4**, 189–197.

Ryan, T. J., and Watson. P. Children's response speeds as a function of sex and verbal reinforcement schedule. *Psychon. Sci.*, 1966, **6**, 271–272.

Samuels, S. J., and Jeffrey, W. E. Intralist similarity and facilitation of paired-associate learning by fixed order presentation. *Psychon. Sci.*, 1966, **5**, 141–142.

Sanders, B., Ross, L. E., and Heal, L. W. Reversal and nonreversal shift learning in normal children and retardates of comparable mental age. *J. exp. Psychol.*, 1965, **69**, 84–88.

Saravo, A. Effect of number of variable dimensions on reversal and nonreversal shifts. *J. comp. physiol. Psychol.*, 1967, **64**, 93–97.

Schusterman, R. J. The use of strategies in two-choice behavior of children and chimpanzees. *J. comp. physiol. Psychol.*, 1963, **56**, 96–100.

Shapiro, S. S. Paired-associate learning in children. *J. Verb. Learn. verb. Behav.*, 1965, **4**, 170–174.

Shapiro, S. S. Aural paired associates learning in grade-school children. *Child Dev.*, 1966, **37**, 417–424.

Shepard, W. O. The effect of verbal training on initial generalization tendencies. *Child Dev.*, 1956, **27**, 311–316.

Shepp, B. E. Some cue properties of incentives: discrimination of distinct rewards by retardates. *J. comp. physiol. Psychol.*, 1963, **56**, 1078–1080.

Shepp, B. E., and Turrisi, F. D. Learning and transfer of mediating responses in discriminative learning. In N. R. Ellis, (Ed.), *International review of research in mental retardation*. Vol. 2. New York: Academic Press, 1967.

Sherman, M., and Strunk, J. Transposition as a function of single versus double discrimination training. *J. comp. physiol. Psychol.*, 1964, **58**, 449–450.

Sidowski, J. B., Kass, N., and Wilson, H. Cue and secondary reinforcement effects with children. *J. exp. Psychol.*, 1965, **69**, 340–342.

Siegel, A. W., and Stevenson, H. W. Incidental learning: a developmental study. *Child Dev.*, 1966, **37**, 811–818.

Siegel, P. S., and Foshee, J. G. The law of primary reinforcement in children. *J. exp. Psychol.*, 1953, **45**, 12–14.

Siegel, S., and Andrews, J. M. Magnitude of reinforcement and choice behavior in children. *J. exp. Psychol.*, 1962, **63**, 337–341.

Silverman, I. W. Effect of verbalization on reversal shifts in children. *J. exp. Child Psychol.*, 1966, **4**, 1–8.

Simrall, D. Intelligence and the ability to learn. *J. Psychol.*, 1947, **23**, 27–43.

Siqueland, E. R. Operant conditioning of head turning in four-month infants. *Psychon. Sci.*, 1964, **1**, 223–224.

Siqueland, E. R., and Lipsitt, L. P. Conditioned head-turning in human newborns. *J. exp. Child Psychol.*, 1966, **3**, 356–376.

Smiley, S. S., and Weir, M. W. Role of dimensional dominance in reversal and nonreversal shift behavior. *J. exp. Child Psychol.*, 1966, **4**, 296–307.

Solomons, G., Hardy, J. C., and Melrose, J. Auditory reactions of the neonate. *The Journal-Lancet*, 1965, **85**, 17–21.

Spelt, D. K. The conditioning of the human fetus *in utero. J. exp. Psychol.*, 1948, **38**, 338–346.

Spence, K. W. The nature of discrimination learning in animals. *Psychol. Rev.*, 1936, **43**, 427–449.

Spence, K. W. The differential response in animals to stimuli varying within a single dimension. *Psychol. Rev.*, 1937, **44**, 430–444.

Spence, K. W. *Behavior theory and conditioning*. New Haven, Conn.: Yale University Press, 1956.

Spence, J. T., and Segner, L. L. Verbal versus nonverbal reinforcement combinations in the discrimination learning of middle- and lower-class children. *Child Dev.*, 1967, **38**, 29–38.

Sperling, S. E. Reversal learning and resistance to extinction: a review of the rat literature. *Psychol. Bull.*, 1965, **63**, 281–297.

Spiker, C. C. Effects of stimulus similarity on discrimination learning. *J. exp. Psychol.*, 1956, **51**, 393–395. (a)

Spiker, C. C. The stimulus generalization gradient as a function of the intensity of stimulus lights. *Child Dev.*, 1956, **27**, 85–98. (b)

Spiker, C. C. Performance on a difficult discrimination following pretraining with distinctive stimuli. *Child Dev.*, 1959, **33**, 859–864.

Spiker, C. C. Associative transfer in verbal paired-associate learning. *Child Dev.*, 1960, **31**, 73–88.

Spiker, C. C. Verbal factors in the discrimination learning of children. In J. C. Wright, and J. Kagan, (Eds.), *Basic cognitive processes in children. Monographs of the Society for Research in Child Development*, 1963, **21**, Whole No. 2. Pp. 53–68.

Spiker, C. C., and Holton, R. B. Associative transfer in motor paired-associate learning as a function of amount of first task practice. *J. exp. Psychol.*, 1958, **56**, 123–132.

Spiker, C. C., and Lubker, B. J. The relative difficulty of the successive and simultaneous discrimination problems. *Child Dev.*, 1965, **36**, 1091–1101.

Staats, A. W., and Butterfield, W. H. Treatment of nonreading in a culturally deprived juvenile delinquent: an application of reinforcement principles. *Child Dev.*, 1965, **36**, 925–942.

Stake, R. E. Learning parameters, aptitudes, and achievements. *Psychomet. Monogr.*, 1961, No. 9.

Steigman, M. J., and Stevenson, H. W. The effect of pretraining reinforcement schedules on children's learning. *Child Dev.*, 1960, **31**, 53–58.

Stevenson, H. W. Latent learning in children. *J. exp. Psychol.*, 1954, **47**, 17–21.

Stevenson, H. W. Discrimination learning. In N. R. Ellis, (Ed.), *Handbook of mental deficiency.* New York: McGraw-Hill, 1963, Pp. 424–438.

Stevenson, H. W. Scoial reinforcement of children's behavior. In L. P. Lipsitt, and C. C. Spiker, (Eds.), *Advances in child development*, Vol. II. New York Academic Press, 1965. Pp. 97–126.

Stevenson, H. W., and Bitterman, M. E. The distance-effect in the transposition of intermediate size by children. *Am. J. Psychol.*, 1955, **68**, 274–279.

Stevenson, H. W., Hale, G. A., Klein, R. E. .and Miller, L. K. Interrelations and correlates in children's learning and problem solving. *Monogr. Soc. Res. Child Dev.*, 1968, **33**, Whole No. 7.

Stevenson, H. W., and Hoving, K. L. Probability learning as a function of age and incentive. *J. exp. Child Psychol.*, 1964, **1**, 64–70.

Stevenson, H. W., and Iscoe, I. Transposition in the feebleminded. *J. exp. Psychol.*, 1955, **49**, 11–15.

Stevenson, H. W., Iscoe, I., and McConnell, C. A developmental study of transposition. *J. exp. Psychol.*, 1955, **49**, 278–280.

Stevenson, H. W., and Langford, T. Time as a variable in transposition by children. *Child Dev.*, 1957, **28**, 365–370.

Stevenson, H. W., and McBee, G. The learning of object and pattern discriminations by children. *J. comp. physiol. Psychol.*, 1958, **51**, 752–754.

Stevenson, H. W., and Odom, R. D. Effects of pretraining on the reinforcing value of visual stimuli. *Child Dev.*, 1961, **32**, 739–744.

Stevenson, H. W., and Odom, R. D. Children's behavior in a probabilistic situation. *J. exp. Psychol.*, 1964, **68**, 260–268.

Stevenson, H. W., and Odom, R. D. Interrelationships in children's learning. *Child Dev.*, 1965, **36**, 7–19.

Stevenson, H. W., and Pirojnikof, L. H. Discrimination learning as a function of pretraining reinforcement schedules. *J. exp. Psychol.*, 1958, **56**, 41–44.

Stevenson, H. W., and Weir, M. W. Developmental changes in the effects of reinforcement and non-reinforcement of a single response. *Child Dev.*, 1961, **32**, 1–6.

Stevenson, H. W., and Weir, M. W. Response shift as a function of overtraining and delay. *J. comp. physiol. Psychol.*, 1959, **52**, 327–329. (a)

Stevenson, H. W., and Weir, M. W. Variables affecting children's performance in a probability learning task. *J. exp. Psychol.* 1959, **57**, 403–412. (b)

Stevenson, H. W., and Weir, M. W. The role of age and verbalization in probability learning. *Am. J. Psychol.*, 1963, **76**, 299–305.

Stevenson, H. W., Weir, M. W., and Zigler, E. F. Discrimination learning in children as a function of motive-incentive conditions, *Psychol. Rep.*, 1959, **5**, 95–98.

Stevenson, H. W., and Zigler, E. F. Probability learning in children. *J. exp. Psychol.*, 1958, **56**, 185–192.

Suchman, R. G., and Trabasso, R. Color and form preference in young children. *J. exp. Child Psychol.*, 1966, **3**, 177–187. (a)

Suchman, R. G., and Trabasso, R. Stimulus preference and cue function in young children's concept attainment. *J. exp. Child Psychol.*, 1966, **3**, 188–198. (b)

Sutherland, N. S. The learning of discrimination by animals. *Endeavour*, 1964, **23**, 140–152.

Tempone, V. J. Stimulus generalization as a function of mental age. *Child Dev.*, 1965, **36**, 229–236.

Tempone, V. J. Mediational processes in primary stimulus generalization. *Child Dev.*, 1966, **37**, 687–696.

Terrell, G. The role of incentive in discrimination learning in children. *Child Dev.*, 1958, **29**, 231–236.

Terrell, G. Manipulatory motivation in children. *J. comp. physiol. Psychol.*, 1959, **52**, 705–709.

Terrell, G. Delayed reinforcement effects. In L. P. Lipsitt and C. C. Spiker, (Eds.), *Advances in child development and behavior*, Vol. II. New York: Academic Press, 1965. Pp. 127–158.

Terrell, G., Durkin, K., and Wiesley, M. Social class and the nature of the incentive in discrimination learning. *J. Abnorm. soc. Psychol.*, 1959, **59**, 270–272.

Terrell, G., and Ware, R. Role of delay of reward in speed and size of form discrimination learning in childhood. *Child Dev.*, 1961, **32**, 409–415.

TeVault, R. K., Bailey, M., Cagan, E., Dionis, J., and Figelman, E. Developmental level and concept learning: a possible artifact. *Psychon. Sci.*, 1966, **5**, 167–168.

Thorndike, E. L. Mental discipline in high school studies. *J. educ. Psychol.*, 1924, **15**, 83–98.
    1932.

Thorndike, E. L. *The fundamentals of learning.* New York: Teachers College,

Tighe, L. S. Effect of perceptual pretraining on reversal and nonreversal shifts. *J. exp. Psychol.*, 1965, **70**, 379–385.

Tighe, T. J., and Tighe, L. S. Overtraining and optional shift behavior in rats and children. *J. comp. physiol. Psychol.*, 1966, **62**, 49–55.

Tighe, T. J., and Tighe, L. S. Discrimination shift performance as function of age and shift procedure. *J. exp. Psychol.*, 1967, **4**, 466–470.

Trabasso, T., Deutsch, J. A., and Gelman, R. Attention in discrimination learning of young children. *J. exp. Child Psychol.*, 1966, **4**, 9–19.

Vaughter, R. M., and Cross, H. A. Discrimination reversal performance of children as a function of prereversal experience and overlearning. *Psychon. Sci.*, 1965, **2**, 363–364.

Walk, R. D., and Saltz, E. J. Discrimination learning with varying members of positive and negative stimuli by children of different ages. *Psychon. Sci.*, 1965, **2**, 95–96.

Walters, R. H., and Foote, A. A study of reinforcer effectiveness with children. *Merrill-Palmer Quarterly*, 1962, **8**, 149–157.

Ware, R., and Terrell, G. Effects of delayed reinforcement on associative and incentive factors. *Child Dev.*, 1961, **32**, 789–793.

Watson, J. B. *Psychological care of infant and child.* New York: Norton, 1928.

Watson, J. B., and Rayner, R. Conditioned emotional reactions. *J. exp. Psychol.*, 1920, **3**, 1–14.

Watson, J. B., and Watson, R. R. Studies in infant psychology. *Scient. Mon.*, 1921, **13**, 493–515.

Weir, M. W. Effects of age and instruction on children's probability learning. *Child Dev.*, 1962, **33**, 729–735.

Weir, M. W. Developmental changes in problem solving strategies. *Psychol. Rev.*, 1964, **71**, 473–490. (a)

Weir, M. W. Effect of patterned partial reinforcement on children's performance in a two-choice task. *Child Dev.*, 1964, **35**, 257–264. (b)

Weir, M. W. Age and memory as factors in problem solving. *J. exp. Psychol.*, 1967, **73**, 78–84.

Weir, M. W., and Gruen, G. E. Role of incentive level, number of choices, and type of task in children's probability learning. *J. exp. Child Psychol.*, 1965, **2**, 121–134.

Weir, M. W., and Stevenson, H. W. The effect of verbalization in children's learning as a function of chronological age. *Child Dev.*, 1959, **30**, 143–149.

Weisberg, P. Social and nonsocial conditioning of infant vocalizations. *Child Dev.*, 1963, **34**, 377–388.

White, S. H. Generalization of an instrumental response with variation in two attributes of the CS. *J. exp. Psychol.*, 1958, **56**, 339–343.

White, S. H. Effects of pretraining with varied stimuli on children's discrimination learning. *Child Dev.*, 1961, **32**, 745–753.

White, S. H. Learning. In H. W. Stevenson, (Ed.), *Child psychology. 62d Yearbook of the National Society for the Study of Education*, Part 1. Chicago: University of Chicago Press, 1963. Pp. 196–235.

White, S. H. Discrimination learning with ever-changing positive and negative cues. *J. exp. Child. Psychol.*, 1965, **2**, 154–162.

White, S. H., and Plum, G. E. Eye movement photography during children's discrimination learning. *J. exp. Child Psychol.*, 1964, **1**, 327–338.

White, S. H., and Spiker, C. C. The effect of a variable conditioned stimulus upon the generalization of an instrumental response. *Child Dev.*, 1960, **31**, 313–319.

White, S. H., Spiker, C. C., and Holton, R. B. Associative transfer as shown by response speeds in motor paired associate learning. *Child Dev.*, 1960, **31**, 609–616.

Wickens, D. D., and Wickens, C. A study of conditioning in the neonate. *J. exp. Psychol.*, 1940, **26**, 94–102.

Wicklund, D. A., Palermo, D. S., and Jenkins, J. J. The effects of associative strength and response hierarchy on paired-associate learning. *J. Verb. Learn. verb. Behav.*, 1964, **3**, 413–420.

Wilson, W. C. Imitation and the learning of incidental cues by preschool children. *Child Dev.*, 1958, **29**, 393–397.

Wismer, B., and Lipsitt, L. P. Verbal mediation in paired-associate learning. *J. exp. Psychol.*, 1964, **68**, 441–448.

Witryol, S. L., Tyrrel, D. J., and Snowden, L. M. Five-choice discrimination learning by children under simultaneous incentive conditions. *Child Dev.*, 1964, **35**, 233–243.

Witte, K. L. Children's response speeds to familiarized stimuli. *Psychon. Sci.*, 1967, **7**, 153–154.

Wolff, J. L. The role of dimensional preferences in discrimination learning. *Psychon. Sci.*, 1966, **5**, 455–456.

Wolff, J. L. Concept attainment, intelligence, and stimulus complexity: an attempt to replicate Osler and Trautman (1961). *J. exp. Psychol.*, 1967, **73**, 488–490.

Wright, J. C., and Smothergill, D. Observing behavior and children's discrimination learning under delayed reinforcement. *J. exp. Child Psychol.*, 1967, **5**, 430–440.

Youniss, J., and Furth, H. G. Reversal learning in children as a function of overtraining and delayed transfer. *J. comp. physiol. Psychol.*, 1964, **97**, 155–157. (a)

Youniss, J., and Furth, H. G. Reversal performance in children as a function of overtraining and response conditions. *J. exp. Child Psychol.,* 1964, **1,** 182–188. (b)

Youniss, J., and Furth, H. G. Discrimination shifts as a function of degree of training in children. *J. exp. Psychol.,* 1965, **70,** 424–427.

Zeaman, D., and House, B. J. An attention theory of retardate discrimination learning. In N. R. Ellis, (Ed.), *Handbook of mental deficiency.* New York: McGraw-Hill, 1963, Pp. 159–223.

Zeaman, D., and House, B. J. The relation of IQ and learning. In R. M. Gagne, (Ed.), *Learning and individual differences.* Columbus, O.: Merrill, 1967. Pp. 192–212.

Zeiler, M. D. New dimensions of the intermediate-size problem: neither absolute nor relational response. *J. exp. Psychol.,* 1963, **66,** 588–595. (a)

Zeiler, M. D. The ratio theory of intermediate-size discrimination. *Psychol. Rev.,* 1963, **70,** 516–533. (b)

Zeiler, M. D. Solution of the two-stimulus transposition problem by four- and five-year-old children. *J. exp. Psychol.,* 1966, **71,** 576–579.

13. Children's Reasoning and Thinking[1]

D. E. BERLYNE

The problem of defining reasoning and thinking, and thus specifying the boundaries of this chapter, is a formidable one. When definitions of thinking have been offered, they have almost invariably been lacking in precision, and, more often than not, they have borne the stamp of commitment to particular theoretical interpretations. Thought has sometimes been conceived so broadly that it encompasses virtually all conscious or internal phychological processes, as the word so often does in everyday speech ("Penny for your thoughts!"). An even more extreme view has maintained that "thought is simply behavior—verbal or nonverbal, covert or overt" (Skinner, 1957, p. 449).

In the history of psychology, there have been two traditions with contrasting views of the role of thinking. The rationalist-spiritualist tradition flourished in continental Europe during the seventeenth to nineteenth centuries. It had a strong inclination, traceable at least as far back as the works of Plato and Aristotle, to emphasize the uniqueness of human thought, its intimate connections with volition, and the determination of behavior by cogitation, understanding, and judgment. The rival empiricist-sensationist-associationist-materialist current, which was particularly strong in Great Britain during the same period and gradually spread over a wider area, tended to regard thought as a derivative of sensation and, to a lesser extent, of action. In the present century a similar division exists, although the two traditions have undergone radical transformations. Members of the Gestalt-cognitivist current see behavior as governed largely by "representations," "models," or "images" of external reality—in other words, by factors akin to thinking. They are, however, less inclined than their rationalist predecessors to treat thought as a prototype of psychological functioning. In its earlier phase, this current tended to characterize thought as a derivative of perception. More recently, its representatives have been greatly influenced by computer analogies and tend rather to analyze thought in terms of storing and processing information. On the other hand, the reflexologists and behaviorists of the early twentieth century and the later neobehaviorists of the S-R or neoassociationist current have been hesitant in assuming that representational processes intervene between stimulus and response. They have done so only when there seemed to be no alternative, and they have treated thoughts as covert or internal responses, derived from overt motor responses.

In this chapter we shall adopt a set of definitions that have been outlined elsewhere (Berlyne, 1965a) and are meant to represent the highest common factor of several approaches that have been proposed. The word *thinking* is applied when behavior can be assumed to depend on a chain of two or more representational or symbolic intraorganismic events. Neoassociationists would classify these events as both "symbolic responses" and "symbolic response-produced stimuli," having a prediliction for hypothesizing, as a working assumption, that central events are governed by some of the same principles that govern overt responses and

[1] The preparation of this chapter was facilitated by a grant from the Ontario Institute for Studies in Education.

external stimuli. Others (notably those partial to cognitivist theories) prefer not to adopt such a strategy.

Following suggestions made by such diverse writers as Maier (1929), Hull (1935), and Boiko (1955), we can regard *reasoning* as a process whereby several pieces of prior learning combine to produce a solution to a newly encountered problem. In other words, a new stimulus-response association (using this term in a purely statistical sense) can be assumed to result from the previous acquisition of two or more learned associations that differ from the new association and from one another in their stimulus terms, their response terms, or both.

Not all thinking is reasoning; autistic thinking (e.g., daydreaming) is not. Not all reasoning is thinking; there are several cases of reasoning (e.g., in lower animals) that can be explained by the intervention of a single covert symbolic response rather than a chain of symbolic responses. Any process that satisfies simultaneously the criteria for thinking and for reasoning can be called *directed thinking*.

According to a conceptualization that has been developed on the basis of these definitions (Berlyne, 1965a), directed thinking is essentially a process of arriving at beliefs, evaluations, and decisions through symbolization of sequences of transformations and their outcomes. This means that the salient attributes and problems of thinking emerge most clearly when a dynamic situation, involving a succession of changes in the stimulus field, is given representation within the organism. Directed thinking helps us out whenever we cannot tell how to react to a given event without identifying the chain of past changes that has led up to the event or the chain of future changes that the event heralds. Even a static situation can be handled in the same way, as we focus on various aspects or properties in turn and keep track of the relations that connect one with another by means of a sequence of thoughts representing transformations. The most unequivocal examples of directed thinking, fulfilling the criteria for both thinking and reasoning, are cases of deductive inference, in which two or more thoughts are pieced together to yield a conclusion that could not be reached if any of them were missing.

Other Categorizations

In accordance with the foregoing discussion, this chapter will not deal with many of the topics that developmental psychologists are wont to place under such headings as "thinking," "intellectual development," and "cognitive development" (see Berlyne, 1965, 1966a). For one thing, most of the investigations that have been subsumed under these headings have been studies of "concept formation," "concept attainment," or "concept learning." These, and the somewhat different investigations devoted by Piaget to the development of "concepts" or "notions," are dealt with in another chapter. The usual concept-formation experiment, in which the subject has to distinguish those stimulus objects to which a certain response, verbal or nonverbal, must be attached, involves discrimination learning. Most, but probably not all, of the experimental situations in question have required mediated or secondary generalization and discrimination, that is, the intervention of at least one symbolic response or label. In many cases, the task cannot be completed without recourse to inferential processes involving complicated chains of symbolic responses. So thinking can contribute to concept formation, and concept formation in its turn can indubitably affect the course, and especially the content, of directed thinking. But this does not mean that concept formation and thinking are the same thing (see Berlyne, 1966a).

Similarly, numerous phenomena that will not be treated here have been classified as "problem solving." Often this term means exactly the same as concept formation. At other times the term seems simply to cover any kind of learning in which stimuli have to be discriminated from one another or a correct response has to be selected from a set of competing responses. In the absence of an agreed-on definition of what constitutes a "problem," problem-solving does not seem to be a useful category of behavior, and it is especially hazardous to identify it with thinking.

Plan of the Chapter

Since reasoning and thinking are highly specialized and intricate ways of manipulating and responding to symbols, we cannot properly examine them and research devoted to them without first considering some questions relating to symbolic functions in general. We shall therefore first take up problems, ideas, and findings that concern the origins and development of symbolic functions. Then we shall turn to the development of ideational (that is, symbolic) control over behavior, of which rational control (control through reasoning) is a particular form. After these preliminaries we shall be in a position to look at work concerned directly with reasoning and thinking in the child and, finally, to glance at some of the much neglected motivational aspects of these functions.

ORIGIN AND DEVELOPMENT OF SYMBOLIC FUNCTIONS

Communicative and Representational Functions

Symbolic responses (in the form of speech, gestures, facial expressions, writing, and actions that create symbolic artifacts) often have a primarily *communicative* function. They are, in other words, used to influence the behavior of other human beings or animals. On the other hand, the symbolic responses with which we are concerned are used *representationally*. The organism that produces them uses them to influence its own behavior. Overt symbolic responses, which give rise to publicly available stimuli, can work in both of these ways at once. However, except in very early childhood, the representational function in human beings is performed mostly by internal symbolic responses, which can affect only the originator's nervous system. Covert representational responses come to predominate, presumably because of the advantages they offer in privacy, lack of repercussions from disturbance of other persons, and relatively low effort.

Various views have been expressed on the relations between the communicative and representational roles of symbols.

Mead (1934), in an account that has had a profound direct or indirect influence on neobehaviorist analyses of intellectual processes, traced the origin of symbolization back to the "gesture," which calls for an "adjustive response" in another organism. The gesture becomes a "significant symbol" when "the individual responds to his own stimulus in the same way as other people respond." This

capacity for "putting ourselves in the place of others" is the source of thought, "for in order that thought may exist there must be symbols, vocal gestures generally, which arouse in the individual himself the response which he is calling out in the other, and such that from the point of view of that response he is able to direct his later conduct."

Much of contemporary Russian developmental psychology bears the imprint of Vygotski's (1934) view, which, although it has a distinct Marxist tinge, has much in common with Mead's. The "use and . . . creation of implements of labor although present in embryonic form in some species of animals, are a specific characteristic of the human process of labor" (p. 48). This capacity gives rise eventually to the elaborate economic activities that characterize human societies, and these, in their turn, require collaboration and therefore efficient communication, which is ensured by language. The child has to learn to speak to others and to respond appropriately to what he hears others say to him. Gradually language, which originates as a means of social control, turns into a means of self-control. The child masters the use of his own verbal responses, particularly in the form of "inner speech," to regulate his own behavior. The influence of this view in the Soviet Union has been reinforced by Pavlov's emphasis on the "second signal system" or system of learned "connections" involving words (Pavlov, 1932). Human beings learn to respond to words as signals of signals belonging to the "first signal system," that is, as substitutes for nonverbal conditioned stimuli. Subsequently, kinesthetic stimulation from organs of speech is conveyed to the cerebral cortex, and its central correlates play their part in determining action.

Piaget (1947) agrees that the "system of collective signs" that constitutes language "conveys to the individual an already prepared system of ideas, classifications, relations—in short, an inexhaustible stock of concepts which are reconstructed in each individual after the age-old pattern which previously molded earlier generations."

Nevertheless, both Vygotski and Piaget deny that acquisition of verbal communication is the sole source of the internal representations on which thought depends. Vygotski (1934) uses both phylogenetic and ontogenetic arguments. He points out that chimpanzees possess rudimentary equivalents of human thought and speech. They are capable of elementary reasoning, exemplified by Köhler's (1921) famous experiments on "insight," and they vocalize to express affective states and to achieve "psychological contact with others of their kind." These two functions are, however, quite independent in the chimpanzee. Similarly, Vygotski refers to experiments by C. Bühler (1927) demonstrating insightful problem-solving in 10 to 12-month-old human infants, which are "exactly like those of the chimpanzees." The origins of speech also appear before the first birthday in the form of babbling and utterance of the first words. The first signs of coalescence and interdependence of intellectual and verbal capacities, as a result of which "thought becomes verbal and speech rational," do not appear until considerably later. So Vygotski is led to insist that thought and language originate independently and later come to merge in the kind of internal speech that constitutes much mature thinking.

Vygotski's successors have discerned some corroboration for his statements in an experiment by Bozhovich (cited by Zaporozhets and El'konin, 1964). Children between 3 and 5 years of age had to gain access to a picture, which was attached to one end of a lever, by using a rod to bring the lever nearer. The solution to the problem necessitated first moving the picture away from oneself, which was a source of difficulty. An earlier investigation by Levina had shown how children can at first solve such problems only by motor trial and error. When they are a little older, they can look at the stimulus objects and plan a course of action, which they then implement. Finally, they can plan a solution in the absence of the objects, using words to represent them. Bozhovich instructed his subjects to describe verbally in advance how they would carry out the task. The hope was that this prior verbalization might accelerate the appearance of a capacity for prior planning. Some children were unable to give any verbal description and sought a solution solely through motor activity. Some gave verbalizations that reflected the same mistakes as their actions. Some expressed verbally a solution that they had already dis-

covered. All in all, there was no evidence that the verbalization helped in the discovery of a solution. As Zaporozhets puts it, "Speech did not direct the intellectual process but was itself determined by it." The independence of reasoning and language in development is thus illustrated.

Piaget and Inhelder (1959) cite three arguments in denying that the acquisition of language is solely responsible for the classificatory and ordering "operations" on which logical thinking depends. They refer to studies of deaf-mute children, apparently revealing no serious abnormality in the development of ordering or of elementary classification. Second, Piaget's earlier investigations indicate that, when the child first takes over the language current in his environment, he assimilates it to his own intellectual structures and does not immediately take over the forms of classification implicit in adult speech. Finally, these authors' own developmental studies of logical operations show children to possess the linguistic tools that are necessary for adult logic (e.g., the ability to use quantifiers like "all" and "some") before they can use them reliably to frame correct statements or to arrive at valid inferences.

Piaget maintains strongly that the structures basic to logical thinking originate not in the grammatical training through which a child learns to piece together syntactically correct sentences but in his experience of "coordinating motor acts in sequences for the attainment of practical ends."

Analysis of the Symbolic Function and of Meaning

Many writers have referred to "representations," "symbols," and the like with little or no attempt at definition, evidently assuming that their connotations are self-evident. Others, in contrast, have endeavored to specify with some semblance of precision what constitutes a "sign" or "symbol" and to analyze the relation between a sign or symbol and the object for which it stands (its "significate" or "referent").

These attempts have been extremely varied, but they fall into a few categories. First, an object or stimulus has sometimes been held to evoke imagery or other mental content corresponding to the significate. According to Titchener (1909), "meaning" can be identified with "context": the meaning of a stimulus or an idea resides in the kinesthetic sensations or images that it evokes and that correspond to stimuli with which it has been accompanied in the past. Ogden and Richards (1923) are responsible for another mentalistic account that at one time enjoyed some vogue. A symbol, they maintained, evokes a conscious experience resembling what would have resulted from the "referent" if it had been present. Tolman's (1932) "sign-gestalt theory" constitutes a neobehaviorist equivalent of the same approach, and variants of it reappear continually. If a stimulus, S_1, has regularly been followed by another stimulus, S_2, then S_1 becomes a "sign" and evokes an expectation of the significate, S_2. But since Tolman believed that all learning, however elementary, consists in the acquisition of expectations or "cognitions" of this sort, such a definition can scarcely serve to mark off a domain of intellectual or ideational activity that can be contrasted with simpler psychological processes.

In contrast, the reflexologists and early behaviorists identified "meaning" with responses. Pavlov (1932) pointed out that innumerable conditioned stimuli can act as "signals" of the relatively few unconditioned stimuli of outstanding biological importance; they acquire their signalling function by frequently preceding or accompanying an unconditioned stimulus and manifest it by evoking responses associated with the unconditioned stimulus in anticipation of its appearance. Words, in their turn, act as signals (belonging to the second signal system) of nonverbal conditioned stimuli. Similarly, Watson (1924) equated meaning with the sumtotal of responses associated with a stimulus object: ". . . 'meaning' is just a way of saying that out of all the ways the individual has of reacting to this object, at any one time he reacts in only one of these ways . . ." (p. 250).

This approach has two serious shortcomings. Like the early introspective treatments, it regards "meaning" as an attribute of virtually all stimuli and therefore fails to capture the peculiarities of thinking and other ideational activity. Further, it fails to recognize that a subject's reaction to a verbal or other pattern of symbols is, more often than not, quite different from the reaction that the sig-

nificate would have evoked if it had been present. This is one fact that makes symbols so valuable. Morris (1946) gives the example of a motorist who is told that a landslide has blocked the road some distance in front of him. The communication makes him drive on a little further, until he finds a side road into which he can turn. This is not what he would have done if he had seen an obstruction in front of him.

Neobehaviorists, especially those of the S-R or neoassociationist current, have adopted more complicated definitions, although they still single out responses as the links between sign and significate. Morris (1946) offered an informal paraphrase of his formal definition of a sign as follows: "If something, A, controls behavior toward the goal in a way similar to (but not necessarily identical with) the way something else, B, would control behavior with respect to that goal in a situation in which it were observed, then A is a sign." A sign is defined as a "symbol" if it is produced by its interpreter (i.e., an organism for which it is a sign) and acts as a substitute for some other sign with which it is synonymous.

This analysis has undergone further development at the hands of Osgood (1952), whose definition has been accepted as the best available to date by several writers, apparently including Morris himself (1964). He states that "A pattern of stimulation which is not the object is a sign of the object if it evokes in an organism a mediating reaction, this (a) being some fractional part of the total behavior elicited by the object and (b) producing distinctive self-stimulation that mediate responses which would not occur without previous association of nonobject and object patterns of stimulation." Osgood clarifies this definition with the help of the diagram shown in Fig. 1, which also embodies a theory to explain how stimuli bocome signs. In this diagram R_T is the overt response pattern associated with S, the significate. s is the sign

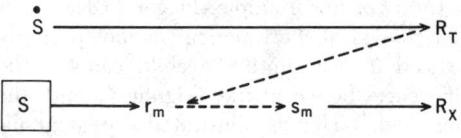

Fig. 1. Osgood's analysis of the sign-significate relation.

which, through conditioning, comes to evoke r_m, a "detachable" portion of R_T (i.e., elements of R_T that can occur in the absence of S). This r_m is the "mediator" (with which the "meaning" of the sign is identified). Then s_m, the stimulus aspect of r_m, evokes R_x, an overt response pattern which may be different from R_T.

Finally, the rather different and more radical proposals of Skinner (1957) must be mentioned, especially in view of the profound influence that this writer has had on recent developmental psychology. He prefers not to speak of signs, symbols, or meaning. Instead, he reduces thinking and intellectual activity generally to "verbal responses," overt and covert. Verbal responses are responses reinforced "through the mediation of a person." There are two ways in which they become connected with the external objects or events that, according to other terminologies, they "represent." A "mand" (e.g., a verbal request or command) is regularly reinforced by the appearance of a particular object or event. A "tact" (e.g., a sentence in the indicative mood or a name) has been regularly reinforced only in the presence of a particular object or event. Skinner's definition encompasses many forms of behavior that would not be considered verbal or symbolic in the usual senses. He is explicitly concerned to minimize the differences between thinking and other forms of behavior, so that his analysis is hardly capable of throwing light on the peculiarities of behavior that are controlled by thought processes.

The essence of the Morris-Osgood approach is the assertion that signs evoke some of the same behavior as the corresponding significates but generally not the same behavior in all respects. Other writers have singled out the ability to distinguish a sign or symbol from what it stands for as an indispensable attribute of the sign-significate relation. In other words, there must be some circumstance in which the subject would react differently to the two. For example, Piaget (1945) says that the "symbolic function" cannot properly be said to exist until the child can tell the difference between the "signifier" and the "signified." This is illustrated by symbolic play. A child may treat a doll as if it were a baby, but in other conditions he makes it clear that he can differentiate between the two.

Similarly, according to Werner and Kaplan (1963), "representation . . . implies some awareness, however vague, that vehicle and referential object are not identical but are, in substance and form, two totally different entities."

Origins of Internal Symbolic processes

There are two major views on the origins of internal symbolic events that can represent external events in their absence. The nineteenth-century associationists, like their empiricist predecessors, thought of "ideas" as faint copies of the sensations produced by stimuli impinging on sense organs. Plato's analogy of the impression left on a piece of wax after a seal has been withdrawn was widely accepted. The Gestalt school protested against this kind of psychology, but the view they favored was nevertheless similar. They spoke of the elements of memory and thought as "traces" of previous perceptions (Koffka, 1935). They contended, however, that a trace corresponds to a perceived pattern or configuration rather than a unitary sensation, which meant that structure and organization were important. Furthermore, they held that a trace undergoes endogenous changes, in accordance with the law of "*Prägnanz*," after it has been freed from the influence of its parent stimulus pattern. These changes generally turn it into a distorted representation, rather than a copy, of the parent pattern.

Other theorists, representing a surprising variety of traditions, have contended, on the other hand, that internal symbols derive from motor responses. The relatively late appearance, both phylogenetically and ontogenetically, of symbolic functions seems to them to argue against simple impressionability of the nervous system as a basis for these functions. Since particular thoughts are usually evoked by external stimuli and prior thoughts, it seems defensible to refer to them as "internal" or "implicit" responses. Whether thoughts are separable from activities of muscles and glands has been debated since the days of early behaviorism (see Humphrey, 1951). But even if they do not conform to the older and narrower definition of a response, they seem to qualify clearly enough as responses in the broad sense, that is, as events that can become associated with stimuli through learning (Miller and Dollard, 1941; Berlyne, 1965).

A hypothesis that has suggested itself to several writers is that internal symbolic responses are derivatives of motor responses that have become associated, through learning, with their significates. This hypothesis has, in fact, appeared in three distinguishable variants.

1. According to one view, thought elements can be identified with minute contractions, or perhaps only action currents, in muscles. These are insufficient to produce visible bodily movement but can supply kinesthetic stimuli to evoke subsequent responses (Watson, 1924; Washburn, 1926). Naturally, subvocal reactions of the speech organs have received most attention. But Watson, the outstanding spokesman of this view, recognized that attenuated reactions of the muscles subserving manual responses and of the muscles and glands of the viscera may also participate in thinking. This approach has, from time to time, encouraged statements to the effect that we think with the whole body rather than with the brain alone.

2. According to a different view, thought elements consist of neural processes that, if allowed to complete themselves, would lead to innervation of muscles but are cut short before motor pathways are reached. For example, Sechenov (1878) depicted a thought as a truncated reflex: inhibition prevents the final or motor segment of the reflex arc from coming into play. The sensory and central phases of the reflex occur alone, or, when a thought is evoked by another thought, the sensory as well as the motor phase may be lacking.

Piaget's (1949) scheme takes account of the reciprocal action between the organism and the environment. Originally, the organism does something to produce an environmental change, and this in its turn generates stimuli that act on the organism. Thought uses "internalized" versions of this process, whereby the motor act and the external environment are eliminated from the circuit. The neural process that used to produce the motor act leads directly to the neural process that would have resulted from the external stimulus.

3. A view developed by Hull (e.g., 1931) and made more explicit by Osgood (1953) holds an internal symbolic event (Hull's "fractional anticipatory goal response," (Osgood's "mediator") to consist of some components (which may or may not be reduced in amplitude), but not others, of a complex motor pattern evoked by the significate. But which components will occur in anticipation of, or in the absence of, the significate and thus serve to represent it? Osgood, following Hull, suggests that they will be the "detachable" components—those that are capable of occurring without the significate. This writer (Berlyne, 1965) has argued against such a view, suggesting that they will be component responses that do not delay or jeopardize subsequent reinforcement by occuring before the significate has been reached and that are thus relatively insusceptible to inhibition of delay.

These three variants are, of course, not mutually exclusive, so that there may be some truth in all of them.

Whatever form it takes, the reduction, attenuation, or internalization of a response has often been ascribed to the "law of least effort," "principle of reactive inhibition," and the like. There seems to be a deeply rooted tendency, which makes obvious biological sense, for an organism to perform a response with the least degree of vigor that is compatible with fulfillment of its function. Rats trained to press a bar in a Skinner box will gradually reduce the force that they exert until they reach the point beyond which reward will not be forthcoming (Skinner, 1938). Sequences of motor acts will sooner or later degenerate into brief gestures if these will do just as well, the most familiar example being the threatening gesture. The relevance of this phenomenon to communicative symbolization has been pointed out by Mead (1934) and by Mowrer (1954). The same kind of process can go much further when symbols are used representationally, since they then need to have sufficient intensity to preserve their stimulus value but need not be strong enough to affect the external environment.

Hull (1930) referred to "acts whose sole function is to serve as stimuli for other acts" as "pure stimulus acts." These became the "cue-producing responses" of Miller and Dollard (1941) and the "mediators" of Osgood (1952). In a strikingly similar vein, Vygotski (1960) made much of situations in which "the stimulus created by man himself determines his reaction." As illustrations, he cites tying a knot to remember something and casting lots to resolve a conflict. This is the root of "mastery of one's own process of behavior." The transition to mediating activity radically reorganizes the entire mental operation, as the use of a tool modifies the natural activity of organs and endlessly extends the system of activity of the mental functions. The former and latter together we designate by the term of *higher mental function* or *higher behavior*."

Some important aspects of the sign-significate relation can also be clarified by use of information-theoretic language (Berlyne, 1965, Chap. 1). There must be some degree of correlation or contingency or correspondence (not necessarily of similarity) between properties of the sign or symbol and properties of the significate. This implies that the sign or symbol contains information transmitted from the significate. It does not, however, mean that the properties of the significate must be causally determining the properties of the sign. The correlation between the two can be brought about indirectly through other factors, including some belonging to the distant past. Then, since a symbol plays some part in determining the response, information contained in the symbol (including some that comes from the significate) is transmitted further to the motor organs In this way, the symbol acts as an intermediary to ensure the transmission of information between the significate and the response, even though the significate may be outside the stimulus field.

Images, Words and Other Symbols

The kinds of internal symbols discussed most often are imagery and silent speech. Properties of images and covert verbal responses must, of course, be treated as intervening variables and be inferred from overt behavior (see Berlyne, 1965a).

The old-fashioned belief that the image is simply a trace left by an external stimulus has not survived closer inspection, so that the genesis of the image is now generally regarded as a gradual and complicated process. Piaget (1945) has characterized the image as "internalized imitation." He traces the development of imitation in the child up to the point where "deferred imitation" (i.e., imitation of a remembered model that is no longer present) appears in the course of the second year. He finds the first indications of imagery at

about this time and concludes that the two functions are intimately related. Imitation is, however, strongly biased toward "accommodation" (i.e., toward letting behavior be governed by properties of external objects). Another fountainhead of imagery, and of representational thought generally, is "symbolic" play or "role-playing." This, being essentially "assimilative" (i.e., determined by processes within the organism that are independent of the present external environment), compensates for the stimulus-bound nature of imitation. It provides an element of emancipation from the external environment and thus helps to establish the necessary equilibrium between accommodation and assimilation.

Piaget's (Piaget and Inhelder, 1967) more recent investigations of imagery contrast images of static situations with images representing the transformations that lead from one of these to another. The latter are mastered later than the former, since they must await the formation of the "operational" structures through which systems of transformations are handled in thought.

Other investigations (see Berlyne, 1965a) likewise draw attention to the complex, dynamic nature of imagery and its dependence on imitative and receptor-adjusting responses. Zaporozhets (1958), in particular, has dwelt, both theoretically and experimentally, on the way in which patterns of eye movements and manual exploratory responses correspond to spatial properties of external stimuli. Since they reproduce shapes and geometrical relations characterizing external objects and events, they can represent them in their absence.

The acquisition of linguistic symbols is a vast domain of developmental psychology in itself and is dealt with elsewhere in this *Manual*. However, we may note here Piaget's observation that both words and images begin to control behavior, and are mastered, at about the same time—toward the end of the second year—because the ability to speak, like the ability to imagine, depends on deferred imitation.

Several writers would, however, protest against any suggestion that thinking is confined to, or even dominated by, verbal and imaginal symbols. Both Sechenov's and Piaget's work bring out the dependence of directed thinking on organized sequences of internal symbolic events that correspond to, and thus represent, sequences of transformations. Trains of thought could not preserve their correspondence with reality and their internal consistency if all they did were to represent one stimulus situation after another. They also have to represent the transformations, whether they be physicochemical processes, logico-mathematical steps, or legal moves, that could lead from one represented stimulus situation to the next.

The motor acts that lead in a regular, predictable manner from one stimulus situation to another fall into two main classes. These are *executive* responses, which produce physical changes in external objects, and *receptor-adjusting* responses, which cause sense-organs to leave one combination of stimuli and focus on another. It is interesting that Piaget (e.g., 1949) singled out executive responses and Sechenov (1878) singled out receptor-adjusting responses as the raw material out of which the internalized elements of directed thinking are fashioned (Berlyne, 1965).

Stages in the Development of Symbolic Functions

Various aspects of the development of representational functions have been brought into focus by writers belonging to different traditions. This is an area on inquiry in which everybody is likely to show a particularly strong attachment to his own classificatory schemes and terminological creations, so that a consensual synthesis is still some way off.

Piaget (1947, etc.) has provided the most thoroughgoing account. During the *sensorimotor* stage, which occupies roughly the first two years of life, the child gradually masters those forms of adaptive interaction with external objects that are possible without symbolic mediation. Nevertheless, the primitive rudiments of symbolization—the first signs of an ability to take account of the properties of an object that is outside the stimulus field—appear during this period. For example (Piaget, 1937), by about the tenth month the child has attained the notion of an external object that does not go out of existence when it goes out of sight and does not change its characteristics when it changes its appearance. He looks for objects after they have disappeared from view and knows where he is likely to find them. Even earlier than this, he

shows expectation of events that have not yet occurred, when signals that have regularly preceded them are perceived. During the sensorimotor stage, perceptual "anticipations" and "perseverations" emerge, enabling the child to make comparisons between objects that are perceived successively rather than simultaneously. By the end of this stage, forms of "insightful" problem-solving, comparable to those achieved by Köhler's apes, are possible and constitute the highest levels of adaptation that behavior can reach without drawing on the resources of uniquely human symbolic capacities.

Like other writers, Piaget places roughly toward the end of the second year the great turning point when behavior comes under the control of words, images, and other symbolic processes. This is when thought becomes a major determinant of activity. During a *preconceptual* stage (roughly 2 to 4 years), the child possess only preconcepts. The notions of class-membership and class-inclusion are lacking, so that, to cite one of Piaget's examples, the child regards every snail he sees as an instance of "snail," that is, of the combination of properties constituting "snailishness." Whether the same snail keeps on reappearing or there are several distinct, but similar, snails is hardly a meaningful question. The child does not understand that every snail is a member of a class of snails, having some characteristics in common with all other snails as well as unique characteristics that confer on it its individuality. These limitations diminish during the *intuitive* stage (4 to 7 years). Class-membershp and class-inclusion now exist, as evidenced by the ability to form sentences containing quantifiers like "some" and "all." But these words are often used to state incorrect conclusions.

At about age 7, the stage of *concrete operations* begins. Thinking now makes use of "operations," defined (Piaget, 1953) as "actions which are internalizable, reversible, and coordinated in systems characterized by laws which apply to the system as a whole." The laws in question define organized systems of operations such as the "grouping" (*groupement*) invented by Piaget himself, and others familiar to mathematicians like the "group," the "semilattice," and the "lattice." With the help of these structures, the child is able to handle classification, ordering, and number.

This means that elementary forms of logical and mathematical reasoning are available.

Finally comes the stage of *formal operations* (beginning at about age 11 and complete by about 15), during which additional structures, necessary for advanced logical, mathematical, and scientific thinking, are completed. Formal operations are "operations on operations." Through them, relations between abstract entitles can be manipulated.

Ivanov-Smolenski (1956, 1963) was an outstanding pioneer among Pavlov's students in extending classical conditioning techniques to human children and particularly in investigating the relations between the first and second signal systems. He suggested a fourfold sequence. First comes the formation of "direct-direct" connections, that is, conditioned associations in which both stimulus and response are nonverbal. Then "verbal-direct connections" attach nonverbal responses to verbal stimuli. "Direct-verbal connections" (between verbal responses and nonverbal stimuli) come later, reflecting the well-known fact that the ability to respond to words is generally in advance of the ability to utter them appropriately. "Verbal-verbal connections" are the last to appear, and these constitute the interverbal associations on which thinking depends.

Gal'perin's (1954) description of four stages characterizing the learning of "every mental action" has had an enormous influence on recent Soviet psychology and has, in fact, inspired several innovations in teaching practice. The child has initially to master an action by interacting with concrete objects. This includes the learning of the necessary discriminations and the perfection of skilled movements. Next, the action must be transferred to the plane of "audible speech." The child learns to use words appropriately while in contact with the relevant external objects. "When a full reflection of a material action has been achieved on the plane of audible speech, the stage of transference to the mental plane begins." He then uses language and images "in his head." As a final stage, the action "in the head" is "abbreviated or compressed" and otherwise "consolidated" as a "mental action."

Werner and Kaplan (1963) describe the "primordial" symbol-situation as an intimate "sharing" relation bringing together four components, the addressor (or originator of the symbol), the addressee, the referent, and the symbolic vehicle. Ontogenesis is marked by progressively increasing "distancing" or "polarization." The person, whether addressor or addressee, becomes more and more distinct from the referent, as does the person from the symbolic vehicle, the symbolic vehicle from the referent, and the addressor from the addressee.

According to Bruner (1964, 1966a), the child first masters "enactive" representation (representing events through appropriate motor responses). He then becomes capable of "ikonic" representation, which "summarizes events by the selective organization of percepts and of images, by the spatial, temporal and qualitative structures of the perceptual field and their transformed images." Finally comes "symbolic" representation, which "represents things by design features that include remoteness, arbitrariness," the prime example being linguistic coding. An illustrative experiment was performed by Bruner and Kenney (1966), who confronted children ranging between 3 and 7 years of age with 9 beakers arranged in a matrix, arranged in order of increasing height from front to back and in order of increasing width from left to right. Over half of the children could replace beakers that were removed from the display and reproduce the whole arrangement when all had been removed. These tasks are held to require ikonic representation, since the children have to "'copy' something they have in mind." A transposition task in which a beaker that used to be in one corner is placed in another corner, so that the whole matrix has to be rotated, was not accomplished by 50% until they reached 7 years. This task appears to require verbalization of the relations governing the arrangement.

Since the words "ikonic" and "symbolic" have been used in connection with quite different classifications of sign processes, notably by Morris (1946), this writer (Berlyne, 1965) has suggested that the words "schematic" and "onomastic" be substituted for them. He has suggested further that the differences between Bruner's three forms of representation can best be specified in terms of "informational correspondence." As noted previously, there must be some degree of correspondence or information transformation between the nature of a sign or symbol as a whole and the nature of the significate as a whole. Informational correspondence [the opposite of Garner and McGill's (1956) "interaction uncertainty"] can be said to exist if there is some degree of correspondence or information transmission between particular parts or properties of the sign or symbol and particular parts of properties of the significate. From this point of view, enactive symbols possess informational correspondence with motor patterns, schematic (Bruner's "ikonic") symbols possess informational correspondence with external stimulus patterns, and onomastic (Bruner's "symbolic") symbols possess informational correspondence with neither.

DEVELOPMENT OF IDEATIONAL CONTROL OVER BEHAVIOR

Ever since Plato and Aristotle, reason and volition have been closely linked by philosophers. And at least since Descartes, an intimate connection, frequently amounting to identification, has been seen between thinking and consciousness. Abstruse and acrimonious debates have, of course, raged around these concepts for centuries. Awareness of what one is doing and why one is doing it was long regarded as a distinguishing mark of "rational" or "intelligent" behavior, through which it could be contrasted with behavior governed by "instinct" or "reflexes."

Even those who are primarily interested in publicly observable behavior and wish to steer clear of metaphysical arguments must recognize important and outwardly manifest differences between the kinds of behavior that are and are not amenable to control by ideational processes, that are and are not voluntary, that are and are not said to be accompanied by awareness. If the first of these characteristics is present, the other two seem generally to be present too. It is possible to base such distinctions on objective criteria—on attributes or accompaniments of the behavior that are fully accessible to an external observer—regardless of whether the philosophical connotations of "reason" or "will" (particularly "free will") are applicable or whether what we are calling "awareness" corresponds to consciousness in the sense of subjective experience.

We must therefore consider, with special attention to their developmental aspects, the distinctive characteristics of behavior that is "rational" (in the sense of subject to the influence of thinking and reasoning), accompanied by "awareness" (the use of which term might avoid the special connotations of "consciousness"), and "voluntary."

Awareness

Dollard and Miller (1950) have suggested that, from a behavioral point of view, the unconscious is the "unverbalized." In this they were echoing Freud's (1915) statement that repression prevents ideas from becoming conscious by denying them "translation. . . into words."

Eriksen (1960) has objected to this view. He points out that "one's verbal description of the facial appearance of another individual may be wholly inadequate in enabling another to recognize this person among a crowd. However, if the person giving the description possesses a mediocre artistic talent, it will be possible for him to draw a sketch of the person described which would greatly increase the chances of the individual's being recognized." If we "adhered strictly to a definition of awareness in terms of verbalization," he says, "we should have to conclude that somebody capable of a portrait but not of an adequate verbal description was not aware of the appearance of the person in question." It is noteworthy, however, that sketching is a form of symbolic behavior, so that Eriksen's criticism might be overcome if we recognized the hallmark of awareness to be symbolic representation, usually in verbal form, but occasionally in the form of nonverbal symbolic responses such as drawing, imitation, gestures. Since directed thinking (Berlyne, 1965) controls behavior through symbolic responses, it is easy to see why stimuli and motor activities that are deprived of symbolic representation cannot come within its purview.

East European writers have likewise attached great importance to whether or not stimuli and motor responses are, as they put it, "reflected in the second signal system." Ivanov-Smolenski (1949, 1951, 1956) has reviewed relevant experiments carried out in his own laboratory.

For work with children, Ivanov-Smolenski's group has made much use of motor conditioning with verbal reinforcement. In this technique the response consists of pressing a rubber bulb with the hand, and the unconditioned stimulus is the word "Press!" uttered by the experimenter. If the unconditioned stimulus is preceded by a light, a sound, or some other conditioned stimulus, this conditioned stimulus will normally come to evoke a conditioned anticipatory press. After the first conditioned response has appeared, reinforcement is usually maintained by saying "Right!" or "Wrong!" Differentiation can be set up by having two conditioned stimuli and saying "Don't press" after presenting the one that is to become inhibitory.

In some of the experiments, child subjects have been questioned after training. It is reported that the youngest children can describe the stimuli and the response correctly but cannot report the connection between them. Then comes a stage when positive or excitatory connections are correctly reported but the significance of a negative or inhibitory stimulus is not. Verbal reports then either fail to reflect the fact that the subject reacted differently to the two stimuli or assert that he refrained from making the motor response to the negative stimulus when he did not. It is interesting that, even when differentiation is fully reflected in the second signal system, the presence of the conditioned stimulus is generally not reported when an extraneous stimulus, productive of external inhibition, accompanies it.

Other experiments show that a stimulus may be sufficiently intense for the first signal system but not for the second. Kotliarevski used a slight increase in illumination as a conditioned stimulus for bulb-pressing. It proved effective, but the subject did not know why he responded. He said, "I just pressed" or "For some reason I felt like pressing." Faddeeva used a compound conditioned stimulus consisting of a bright red light coupled with a faint hooter sound. Subsequently, when the light was presented alone, the subjects (8- to 10-year-old children) always responded to it and reported its presence correctly. When the sound was presented alone, the subjects generally performed the motor response, but some reported having heard it, some did not, and some reported its presence but showed no awareness of the connection between it and their motor response.

In general, according to Ivanov-Smolenski's summary, the occurrence of the stimulus, the occurrence of the response, or the connection between the two may or may not be reported. Verbalization is likely to be deficient when the stimuli are weak or when the subjects are young children or adults suffering from various neurophychiatric disorders.

The development of verbal mediation with increasing age is further illuminated by Paramanova (1956), who, although not an associate of Ivanov-Smolenski, used his motor-conditioning technique. When differential training was given, some subjects learned not to respond to the negative stimulus very rapidly, but others were slow. The quick learners were found at all ages, but most of them were found among the older subjects, aged 5 to 6 years. They invariably answered questions about the procedure correctly. When the experimenters ceased to say "Don't press!" after the appearance of the negative stimulus, one or two subjects asked "Should I press?" The implication is that the response was under the control of verbal mediators and, in some subjects, was held in check until a verbal sanction had been given. The slow subjects were mostly younger subjects, aged about 3. The amplitude of their response to the negative stimulus gradually waned, and the latency gradually increased, until the response dropped out altogether. Verbal report was defective. When the positive stimulus was made negative and vice versa, older (5- to 6-year-old) subjects changed their manner of responding immediately, but the reversal took some time with the younger subjects. When reinforcement (i.e., telling the children whether they were right or wrong) ceased, 3-year-olds lost the differentiation, pressing the bulb in response to both positive and negative stimuli for some time. After that, they remained inactive until the instructions of the adult experimenter were renewed. Four-year-olds had some success at maintaining a differential performance, but there was considerable instability. Some used verbal instead of motor responses, remarking on the presence of the stimulus that had usually been paired with the experimenter's utterance. Some responded correctly but gave themselves audible instructions. By the fifth or sixth year, response to the positive stimulus and nonresponse to the negative stimulus persisted, although there was some tendency to error.

These experiments, Paramanova concludes, illustrate the tendency for direct control of behavior by external stimuli to give way gradually to the mediating influence of verbal stimuli. At first, the child is susceptible to control by verbal responses of adults, but he gradually becomes capable of self-control through his own verbal behavior.

Voluntary Behavior

There has been a strong tendency among psychologists interested in learning to identify voluntary behavior with instrumental conditioned responses. Skinner (1938, p. 112) says that "The operant field corresponds closely with what has traditionally been called 'voluntary' behavior." Similarly, Ivanov-Smolenski (1956) identifies "voluntary movements" with "conditioned-conditioned-reactions," his term for instrumental conditioned responses.

Instrumental conditioned responses have three characteristics, each of which has been singled out at one time or another as the distinguishing mark of voluntary activity. First, they are generally responses involving the motor division of the somatic nervous system and the skeletal (or, as they have sometimes been called, "voluntary") muscles. However, Skinner (1938, p. 112) pointed out quite early that "the 'voluntary' control of some autonomic activities is well established." Recent experiments by Miller (1966), in which visceral responses performed by curarized animals were followed by reward, seem to have conclusively and affirmatively settled the formerly disputed question of whether such responses can be subjected to instrumental conditioning. Second, instrumental responses are strengthened by rewarding consequences and apparently (although there has been some debate over this) weakened by punishing consequences. Third, instrumental conditioned responses frequently occur "spontaneously," that is, without being evoked by a specific external stimulus. As Kupalov (1964, p. 116), a leading Russian investigator of learned locomotor behavior in freely moving dogs, has put it, "those reactions are called voluntary that

are actively performed by animals and do not represent a response to a definite, special stimulus."

Some writers, mindful of the age-old inclusion of volition among the "higher mental functions," have felt that, to qualify as "voluntary," an action should not only be relatively independent of external stimulation but prompted by internal symbolic processes. James (1890) connected will with "ideomotor action," the process by which the idea of a movement leads to its realization, although he recognized that this would happen "unhesitatingly and immediately" only in "the absence of any conflicting notion in the mind." When there is "an antagonistic representation present simultaneously in the mind," he says, a "voluntary fiat" is needed to overcome it. Ach (1905, 1910) related will to the "determining tendencies" that, according to the introspective experiments of the Würzburg school, could be set up by an experimenter's instructions. Analogous determining tendencies could be set up by an intention or decision of the subject himself.

The approach, and even the aims, of these early psychologists were, of course, very different from those of contemporary behavior theorists. Nevertheless, a behaviorist equivalent of their emphasis on the control of behavior by ideational acts and self-instructions was the view that a voluntary response is one that a subject can bring on at any time with the help of subvocal speech. In a celebrated experiment by Hudgins (1933), human subjects were first taught by a classical-conditioning technique to constrict their pupils to a light-bell combination. The response was then conditioned to the word "Contract!" uttered by the experimenter while the subject produced the light-bell combination by squeezing a dynamometer, then to the verbal command alone, then to the subject's own pronunciation of the word "Contract!", and finally to the thought of the word. Other words, and even nonsense syllables, were used successfully in the same manner. Several later experimenters have brought other normally involuntary responses under the control of self-administered verbal stimuli by analogous techniques. Professional actors often bring on tears and other forms of emotional expression with the help of thoughts or postural adjustments that supply the necessary conditioned stimuli. Skinner (1938, pp. 112–114) lists, in fact, four ways in which a human being can induce specific autonomic reactions in himself "at will": he can use unconditioned exteroceptive stimuli, unconditioned proprioceptive stimuli, conditioned exteroceptive stimuli, and conditioned proprioceptive stimuli.

Nevertheless, although these procedures enable the subject to produce the responses in question "at any time" and are clearly a step toward voluntary control, it is possible to feel that voluntary control means more than the possibility of producing a response through internal verbal stimuli. Hilgard and Marquis (1940) refer to the products of Hudgins's technique as "semi-voluntary conditioned responses." Naturally occurring human voluntary responses have additional characteristics. They can be withheld when judged undesirable and they can be modified or interrupted while in process, if changes in the external stimulus situation warrant it.

Such a restricted, but still objective, conception of voluntary activity appears in Zaporozhets's (1958; 1960) account. He contrasts animals with plants, which have to rely on passive adaptation. Animals "carry out an active search for the sources of satisfaction of their vital needs." In higher animals, the search depends on the skeletal musculature, but its use introduces many possibilities of error, because of the large number of degrees of freedom open to muscular responses, because of variations in the effects of bodily movements in accordance with the initial states of the muscles, and because of the many random factors to which muscles are subject. For this reason, "sensory correction" is indispensable. The organism has to be sensitive to signals indicating ways in which an action must be modified.

Primitive animals can make use only of feedback that follows the completion of an action and tells whether or not the consequences are satisfactory. This information about consequences can lead to a repetition of the action with modifications or to trial-and-error learning. Human beings, however, are able to monitor the external situation and their own actions through feedback signals received while these actions are in progress. Consequently, the actions can be corrected between their initiation and their conclusion,

which will maximize the probability that the consequences will be satisfactory. To accomplish this, the subject needs to be guided by images of the external situation, of the consequences that an action is likely to have, and of the form a behavior chain should take. As we have already seen, Zaporozhets sees a vital role for orienting (exploratory, attentional) responses, leading from one crucial stimulus to another, in the formation of the appropriate images. He also acknowledges the importance of verbal habits belonging to the "second signal system."

Zaporozhets, assimilating ideas from several Russian authors, traces a course of development from excitomotor reactions (which depend on "irritability" and are evoked by simple stimuli) through sensorimotor reactions (which depend on "sensitivity' 'and are guided by orienting responses and thus by images), to voluntary reactions (which result from sensitivity to interoceptive and proprioceptive stimuli). Russian physiologists and psychologists have, since Pavlov (1932), always seen a close connection between "motor conditioned reflexes" (the term by which they usually refer to instrumental conditioned responses) and kinesthetic stimuli. Zaporozhets relates this course of development to the appearance of vertebrate animals, which surpass invertebrates in complicated motor and neural equipment, and with the movement of higher vertebrates from aquatic to terrestrial environments, where vital objects are commonly surrounded by other objects that can serve as either means or impediments to their attainment.

Zaporozhets's view, with its emphasis on feedback signals and orienting responses, receives support from an experiment conducted by one of his associates, Lisina (1958). She established voluntary control over a normally involuntary reaction in a very different manner from Hudgins and apparently more completely. The response in question was vasodilatation in the hand in response to electric shock (running counter to the normal vasoconstrictive response), and her techniques worked by enabling subjects to recognize the extent and direction of their own vasomotor responses. Some success was achieved when an auditory signal (a tone varying in pitch) or a visual signal (fluctuations of a recording pen) corresponded to vasodilation and vasoconstriction. But the most successful procedure consisted of training subjects to recognize the faint and normally undetected proprioceptive sensations that result from vasomotor responses.

Luria's Experiments

Luria has traced the development of voluntary behavior by studying effects of verbal instructions. He distinguishes various functions that words uttered by an experimenter can have. The presumption is that subvocal responses of the subject himself, by which he influences his own actions, can perform these functions also. They comprise an *orienting* function, an *inhibitory* function, an *impelling* (or *initiating*) function, and a genuine *regulatory* (including *preselecting*) function. These functions are established in turn.

The beginnings can be discerned (Luria, 1959; Luria and Poliakova, 1959) when an infant surrounded by toys is given some instruction such as "Give me the fish!" Shortly after the first six months of life, the child will simply look up at the experimenter. At 10 to 12 months, he will look at the fish. Even up to 1⅓ years, the instruction is unlikely to interrupt activities in which the child is immersed. If not otherwise occupied, he may well respond, early in his second year, to "Give me the fish!" by handing the experimenter the fish. This, however, will occur only if the fish happens to be prominent in the visual field. That a true regulatory function of language has not yet been achieved can be seen from the fact that, if the fish is some distance away and there is a brightly colored toy cat close by, the child will look at the fish but give the experimenter the cat. The instruction is not reliably carried out until about the middle of the second year. One especially noteworthy characteristic of behavior during the second year is its perseveration. If a child between 1 and 1⅙ years is asked to hand over the fish three or four times in a row, he will still hand over the fish when the instruction is changed to "Give me the horse!" If a 1⅙- or 1⅓-year-old child has just been putting rings on a stick and is told "Take off a ring!" while he is holding a ring in his hand, he is likely to respond by putting the ring on.

Another technique (Luria and Rozanova, 1959) consists of placing a coin under either a cup or a tumbler out of the child's sight and then telling him "Now the coin is beneath the cup. Find the coin!" From 1½ to 1⁵⁄₁₂, the child looks fleetingly at the object that has been mentioned. On hearing the word "Now," he may seize both objects or turn to one of them, remaining unaffected by the name of the correct object when it is given. By the middle of the third year, the instruction will be followed correctly, unless a delay of 10 seconds is imposed before the objects can be touched. The delayed reaction is fully mastered by the end of the third year.

Here we have the beginnings of the delayed effects of verbal instruction. Their later development has been traced by Luria's group (Luria, 1956, 1958, 1961) with the help of a simple technique. The child is presented with a rubber bulb and receives some instruction such as "When the light comes, on, press the bulb!" Between about 1⅔ and 2½, the child looks at the light on hearing the word "light" and starts pressing as soon as he hears the word "Press." There is no synthesis between the two clauses of the instruction and no storage of set or motivational condition such that the response is inhibited until the appropriate external stimulus appears. At this age, the child is, in fact, likely to continue to press until the light appears and then to stop in consequence of external inhibitions.

If, while he is pressing, he is told "That's enough!", this is unlikely to stop him but may, on the contrary, intensify the activity. If the admonition "Don't press!" is repeated, the result may be "complete irradiated inhibition and the discontinuance of all motor reactions." So we can see that the impelling function of verbal stimuli is uppermost at this stage. The inhibitory function is weak and nonselective.

By age 3½, the child will react appropriately to the instruction, pressing the bulb only when the light comes on. But inadequacies will become manifest when the task is made a little more complicated. If he is told "Press when a red light comes on but not when a green light comes on!", he will press in response to either light or to neither. If he is told "Press twice when the light comes on!", he is apt to press three or more times. All these deficiencies are overcome completely only at the age of 5 to 6 years.

Further insight into the factors at work has come from various training procedures with which Luria and his associates (Iakovleva, 1958; Tikhomirov, 1958) have tried to remedy the shortcomings that appear at various ages. For example, the child is taught to say "Go!" to himself when the signal light appears. Up to 2½, this does not work; the child either soon gives up saying "Go!" or finds himself unable to say the word and press simultaneously because of inhibition by negative induction. The device works much better in the third year and helps to reduce the intersignal responses to which children of this age are prone. Between 4 and 4½, the child can improve his powers of differentiation (pressing in response to one color but not another) if taught to say "I must!" or "I must not!" appropriately when the signal appears. Even at 2 to 3 years, performance is improved by providing "sanctioning afferentation," that is, an external stimulus (e.g., the sound of a bell or the sight of the light going off), when the motor response is performed correctly. Two-year-old children can become capable of withholding the pressing response between appearances of the light if they are taught to move the hand away from the bulb as soon as each movement has been completed and not to return it until the next signal is seen.

A 3- or 4-year-old child can be induced to press twice, and twice only, when the light is turned on, by training him to say "Go! Go!" on seeing the light. The true nature of this phenomenon is, however, revealed when he is told to say "I shall press twice!" instead. He then produces a single protracted movement instead of the two presses that are required. It can thus be seen that the two syllables "Go! Go!" produce two presses through their impelling function. The genuine regulatory function, involving response to the meaning of a verbal utterance, has not yet been perfected.

Zaporozhets's Experiments

The copious experimental material gathered by Zaporozhets (1960) and his group takes over where Luria's investigations leave off. They have carried the inquiry to the end of the preschool period (which in the Soviet Union lasts until the age of 7) and have concentrated on complex tasks in which sequences of motor responses have to be made to sequences of external stimuli and in which there is room for planning.

Great importance is attached to preparatory and orienting responses, which precede the executive responses that act on the external environment. Orienting responses bring behavior under the control of essential cues and enable images to be formed of simultaneous or successive patterns of external stimuli before they are encountered. Considerable emphasis is also placed on the development of the ability to imagine required bodily movements. For example, when a child of 3 to 4 years is asked to show how he would use a comb or a pair of scissors, he drags his fingers through his hair or performs movements with his forefinger and middle finger. From about 4 years on, he will place his hand in the posture it would have if he were actually manipulating a comb or a pair of scissors.

The tasks employed in experiments by Zaporozhets and his associates include learning to discriminate visual figures, to trace a path through a maze, to perform gymnastic exercises, and to press buttons in coordination with visual signals. The results show how spontaneous movements become more prominent, more efficient, and thus more capable of facilitating completion of the task, as the child grows older. Various procedures for inducing orienting responses and making them more effective have had notable success.

Other training procedures compare the efficacy of passive movement, demonstration of the correct behavior by the experimenter, and verbal instructions. Passive movement is generally more helpful with younger children, and imitation with older children. The relative merits of demonstration and verbal instruction depend on the complexity of the task and the nature of the cues on which its performance depends. Verbal instruction is more effective when the required bodily movements are relatively simple and when external stimuli are of particular importance (e.g., in button-pressing tasks). Demonstration and imitation work better when proprioceptive stimuli are more important and when the required movements are complex (e.g., in gymnastic exercises). One of the chief functions of verbal instructions is to draw attention to relevant cues in the external world. Relevant kinesthetic cues are brought to a child's attention most readily when he executes a pattern of movements that he has just witnessed.

The culmination of the development of voluntary movements and the link with thought processes become evident when internalization takes place. Inner speech comes to take the place of the audible speech through which verbal instructions are conveyed by adults. Conditioned orienting responses come to represent external stimuli in their absence. For example, a verbal instruction referring to a signal that is not yet present causes a child to look in the direction from which it can be expected. Ultimately, the progressive reduction of the orienting response with increasing age and with increasing mastery of a particular task leads to the formation of internalized equivalents of orienting responses, constituting imagery. As mastery proceeds, the executive response requires fewer and fewer preliminaries.

A particularly suggestive idea offered by Zaporozhets (see Berlyne, 1965a, Chap. 6) is that the processes through which we search for an idea or a solution when we think are internalized versions of the exploratory responses through which we search for concrete objects in the real world.

A recent addition to this series of investigations (Nepomniashchaia, 1965) considers the motivational side of volitional development. It starts out from Leont'ev's (1959) emphasis on a proper coordination between "motive" (the ultimate aim) and "goal" (a subsidiary goal that is a means to the ultimate aim). It shows how children below the age of 4½ will generally take up a task only if it is presented to them as a game to be carried out for its own sake (i.e., motive and goal coincide). They gradually develop the capacity to recognize actions as prerequisites for the later fulfillment of motives (e.g., making a toy, making a present to give to Mother). Anticipation of the ultimate consequences and recognition of the relation between the means and the end will then ensure enough motivation for the task to be taken up. We can thus see a progressive unfolding of the functions on which preparation and planning depend. Symbolic representation of events

that have not yet taken place and of the relations between components of the unified sequence is, of course, an essential ingredient.

CHILDREN'S REASONING

Although much human reasoning does not lead immediately, or at all, to overt action, reasoning is biologically important as a means of arriving at an adaptive response pattern, which generally means a response pattern that will be rewarded. Once the rewarding consequences have occurred, the response pattern will become more likely to be performed in the presence of pertinent stimulus conditions. So reasoning can be regarded as an adjunct to instrumental conditioning, an aid to the acquisition of learned behavior. In order to view reasoning in perspective, we must therefore compare it with other ways in which the first occurrence of an adaptive response pattern can come about.

Trial and Error. In accordance with Thorndike's (1898) description of "trial and error and accidental success," an organism can sample its behavior repertoire (with replacement) until a successful act turns up. The distribution on which the sampling is based will generally vary with the stimulus situation, since experienced members of higher animal species will be most likely, in the course of trial and error, to do things resembling what has worked in similar situations in the past. An experimenter relying on this process is compelled simply to wait until the selected response occurs spontaneously. If the response is a simple one, with a relatively high operant level, such as bar-pressing or panel-pecking in a Skinner box, he will not have to wait long. But if it is a complex combination or succession of acts, or a response with a low initial probability, trial and error alone cannot be expected to produce it at all.

Successive Approximation. An experimenter can speed up the emergence of a relatively improbable response pattern by requiring successively closer and closer approximations to it before delivering reward (*shaping*). Either an experimenter or nature alone can gradually steer an organism toward a behavior pattern by rewarding remote semblances of the optimal behavior to a slight degree and rewarding closer and closer approximation more and more intensely (*cybernetic search*).

Evocation. A stimulus can be administered that is known to evoke the adaptive response pattern. For example, Brogden (1939) used a tone that had been paired with electric shock to evoke leg retraction in the dog, and Konorski (1967) induced ear-scratching in the cat by placing cotton in the ear. In both experiments the response, once it had occurred, was reinforced with food. There are three special cases of this kind of technique that warrant particular notice. In *passive movement* a specific bodily movement is brought about by mechanical force. This technique was used in the original instrumental-conditioning experiments of Miller and Konorski (1928), who used a cable-and-pulley arrangement to make dogs flex their paws. Similarly, trainers of circus and domestic animals commonly push their pupils into the desired postures, and human beings may be taught skilled movements by having their limbs held and guided. The second special case is *imitation*, also known as *modelling* (Zaporozhets, 1960; Bandura and Walters, 1963). Here the stimuli that evoke the desired responses are the visual or auditory cues that come from another individual who is deliberately or inadvertently demonstrating the response. Finally, a response pattern can be evoked in human subjects by *verbal instruction*.

Deferred imitation. A human being can witness a response without at the time performing it himself and become in consequence likely to do the same on some future occasion. When this deferred imitation (Piaget, 1945) leads to a learned strengthening of the response, *observational learning* is said to occur. When learning depends on witnessing not only the act but also the consequences of the act for the individual performing it, the term *vicarious learning* is used (Bandura and Walters, 1963; Bandura, 1965).

Deferred Response to Verbal Instruction. A human subject may hear or read a verbal description of a course of action and, although he does not put the instruction into practice immediately, it may cause him to perform the described behavior in appropriate circumstances at a later time.

We can thus comprehend the problems raised by reasoning if we review the similarities and differences that relate it to these other processes. Reasoning clearly contrasts with trial and error by making it possible for adaptive behavior to emerge much more quickly and, more often than not, by bringing about forms of adaptive behavior that trial and error could never have generated at all. Like response to verbal instruction, reasoning depends on ability to respond appropriately to verbal stimulus patterns. But as with deferred imitation and deferred response to instruction, there must be response to internal representational structures that have been deposited during earlier learning experiences and are now revived after what may well be a considerable delay. However, the internal symbolic patterns that underlie deferred imitation and response to instruction need to be relatively faithful copies (imaginal or verbal) of those induced by the demonstration or the verbal description at the time of the original learning. The symbolic patterns that result from reasoning are, in contrast, unlike any that the subject has had at his disposal before; they have to be constructed out of elements belonging to several previous learning experiences. Lastly, we must note that imitation and verbal instruction (whether or not response to them is deferred), as well as passive movement and shaping, require the intervention of another organism. According to the definition offered by Mowrer (1950, p. 675), following a suggestion made by one of his students, they are all examples of *teaching*. Reasoning, on the other hand, is something to which an individual can resort on his own. The learning experiences on which a specific piece or reasoning builds may or may not have been induced by teaching. The presence of a teacher, who is eager to provide hints and feedback, may well assist reasoning while it is going on. But reasoning can proceed without external supports and is alone in this respect among the various short-cuts to adaptive behavior that make use of symbolic capacities.

Piaget

The development of inferential thinking has received its most ambitious theoretical analysis from Piaget. His is also the most thoroughgoing attempt that has been made so far to chart its course empirically.

Piaget traces the roots of logic back to the sensorimotor stage, which embraces the first two years of life when external stimuli evoke responses with little or no intervention of symbolic mediators. During this stage, the child learns to "coordinate schemata." This means both piecing together stimulus-response associations into sequences through which goals can be attained and recognizing two or more sequences as alternative, and therefore equivalent, ways of arriving at the same terminus from the same starting point. It is significant that these correspond to the two properties defining Hull's "habit-family hierarchies" (Berlyne, 1965), namely, the formation of "behavior chains" and the recognition of equivalence between behavior chains that lead to the same goal-situation from a common initial stimulus situation.

The ability to make use of systems of "coordinated" elements is later transferred from the level of motor actions to the level of internalized actions, which include symbols. In manipulating symbols, the child takes some time to relearn some of the lessons that he has already mastered while manipulating sensorimotor schemata. By the end of the sensorimotor stage, the child becomes capable of the simple forms of adaptive behavior that do not require human symbolic capacities. He becomes capable, for example, of the kinds of reasoning or "insightful" problem solving that Köhler (1921) and later experimenters observed in apes. He will use a stick to obtain an object that is otherwise out of reach. He will also perform actions that are prerequisites for later actions, for example, rotating a stick so that it can pass between the bars of a playpen, walking to the far end of a doll carriage in order to push it away from a wall. All of these solutions are discovered without overt trial and error.

Directed thinking appears once behavior has come under the influence of language, images, and other internal symbols, but thought processes are for some years subject to serious limitations. During the *preconceptual stage* (2 to 4 years), the child depends heavily on "transduction." This term, which Piaget has taken over from Stern (1914), denotes reasoning from the particular to the particular; it infers that, because one object or event has

a certain characteristic, a similar object or event will also have it. General statements, which are essential to induction and deduction, become important during the *intuitive stage* (4 to 7 years), but conclusions are likely to be erroneous. This is due an imperfect understanding of class-membership and class-inclusion (Piaget and Inhelder, 1959). Reasoning is also impeded at this stage by an undue dependence on perceptual data, coupled with a tendency to attend to one aspect of a stimulus situation while overlooking other, equally significant aspects (Piaget, 1945).

The stage of *concrete operations* (7 to 11 years) introduces the use of operations. Operations are organized in groupings (*groupements*). These approach the properties defining algebraic groups without quite fulfilling them (Piaget, 1941, 1947). With their help, the child is able to make correct inferences belonging to the algebra of classes, the algebra of relations, and elementary arithmetic.

Finally, the stage of *formal operations* (Inhelder and Piaget, 1955) coincides with early adolescence (11 to 15 years). Deductions identifiable with the propositional calculus are mastered. Implications can be derived from the relations between propositions, regardless of concrete content. Consequently, hypothetico-deductive reasoning, that is, the ability to state what *would* follow *if* something were the case (when it is not), becomes possible. So does reasoning that requires understanding of ratios and probabilities.

Inhelder and Piaget have analyzed this stage with the help of ingenous experiments in which the adolescent subject is confronted with phenomena illustrating simple physical and chemical principles and asked to work out the laws governing these phenomena. During the stage of formal operations, he first becomes capable of devising conclusive experiments by conceiving of, and then examining, all the possible combinations of events that could occur. In attempting to explain the kinds of reasoning that first appear during this stage, Inhelder and Piaget refer copiously to the "four group," a group of four transformations, each of which has two opposites, an "inverse" and a "reciprocal." They also make much of a system of relations between logical connectives, analogous to proportional relations between numbers, that Piaget has discovered. Commentators (e.g., Parsons 1960; Berlyne, 1965), while acknowledging the crucial role of algebraic groups in logical, mathematical, and scientific thinking, have questioned the suggestion that the adolescent actually makes use of these logical "proportions" or that the four group has the unique role that Piaget attributes to it.

Experiments Inspired by Piaget

The experiments that have been inspired by Piaget's writings but carried out in other laboratories have some way to go before they outstrip in number those carried out in Geneva, but they are catching up. Much of this work has been aimed at verifying Piaget's statements about the development of concepts or "notions" and is thus not directly relevant to our present discussion. Lately, however, there has been a growing body of work on quantitative invariants like quantity, number, and weight, which begin to be understood at about the age of 7. As argued elsewhere (Berlyne, 1965), the recognition that, say, quantity remains constant when a shape or spatial distribution changes must depend on deduction from stored information. This makes it a better paradigm for directed thinking, especially directed thinking about dynamic processes, than that old standby, the concept-formation experiment. Nevertheless, work on the origins of such judgments and on ways of accelerating their appearance is treated elsewhere in this *Manual* and has, in any case, been lucidly reviewed by Wallach (in press).

Braine (1959) has investigated inference from transitive relations $(A > B, B > C, \therefore A > C)$, using a nonverbal length-discrimination task. This is a step toward bridging the gap between Piaget's use of verbal responses to study reasoning and the experimental techniques of behavior theory. It was concluded that such inferences, which according to Piaget should not generally occur before the age of 7, actually ocur two years earlier.

The publication of Braine's monograph touched off a controversy with Smedslund (1963). He has criticized Braine's technique, asserting on a number of grounds that he failed to demonstrate that correct responses must have resulted from inference. He also claims, with support from experiments of his own, that transitivity of length is not generally recognized before the age of 8. Smedslund (1961, 1963) also attaches importance to the explanations that children give of their judgments. He maintains that, say, conservation of a property like weight or length can be said to have been "acquired" only when subjects defend their conclusions deductively, mentioning both of the premises from which the conclusion must be inferred. Nonverbal discrimination alone does not demonstrate that this stage has been attained.

Halpern (1965) has shown that a child's verbal explanations can be indicative of the progress he has made in moving from the reliance on perceptual cues that characterizes the intuitive stage to the predominance of thought processes that comes with the stage of concrete operations. She took children who, when confronted with three objects of equal size, acknowledged that, if A weights more than B and B more than C, A must weigh more than C, and who could also recognize that weight must remain unchanged when the shape of a ball of plasticine is altered. She then divided these children into two groups, according to whether their explanations of conservation of weight had been "empirical" (i.e., they directly or indirectly referred to observable features of the stimulus situation now confronting them) or "deductive" (i.e., they directly or indirectly referred to previous events, such as having seen objects weighed in the same test item). The empirically oriented children made more errors when tested for transitivity of weight with objects of differing sizes, especially when size was negatively correlated with weight. When these children were asked to compare A and C for weight, the influence of a demonstration on a balance that A weighs more than B and B more than C was unable to outweigh the influence of perceiving C to be larger than B.

More and more experimenters have been examining the changeover between concrete and formal operations. Lovell (1961) has repeated many of Inhelder and Piaget's experimental procedures and, with the exception of a few specific points, has come to the same general conclusions as they. Lunzer (1965) obtained relatively few successful solutions for children below the age of 10 or 11, when he set verbal problems depending on structures of a form A is to B as C is to D. This finding, he contends, is compatible with the argument that such problems, even if concrete in content, require formal operations, since the subject must recognize relations between relations. Nassefat (1963) gave 9- to 13-year-old subjects about 50 problems, which he divided into "concrete," "intermediate," and "formal," according to the kinds of thinking that they required. As expected, when performance was related to age, the concrete problems were the first, and the formal problems the last, to evoke a predominance of correct solutions. Likewise, there tended to be a progression with increasing age from answers showing "absence of correct perception of the data of the problem," to "insufficient perception of the data" then to "insufficient combination of the data," and finally to "correct perception and combination of data."

Case and Collinson (1962) questioned 11- to 18-year-old subjects about texts that they had read and gave 1, 2, or 3 points to each answer according to whether it manifested intuitive thinking, concrete operations, or formal operations, respectively. The score obtained by a summing of these points was positively correlated with chronological and mental age. But the mean was found to move by "blocks of ages" rather than increasing gradually with age. There was a significant difference between 15- to 17-year-old and 11- to 12-year-old subjects. Cowan (1963) gave 8- to 13-year-old subjects "concrete" problems (requiring them to compare A and C for weight after being told A weighs more than B and B weighs more than C) and "formal" problems (resembling the "concrete" problems except that relations between objects were denoted by nonsense syllables). There was a moderate positive correlation between overall performance and mental age, and there was some evidence that concrete reasoning is mastered earlier than formal reasoning. There was, however, no support for the assumption that "concrete or formal operations emerge suddenly at any given age level."

Other experimenters have looked for signs at much earlier ages of the kinds of reasoning associated with the stage of formal operations. Mogar (1960) gave demonstrations to children from kindergarten and second and fourth grade classes of phenomena having to do with floating and nonfloating bodies and with the projection of shadows. Adequate explanations of this phenomenon became commoner with increasing age within this range. Ervin (1960) took another of the problems used by Inhelder

and Piaget (1953). Second- and third-grade children were set the task of discovering the principles that govern the flexibility of a rod. A few children in each age group discovered all four operative variables (length, material, thickness, and form of cross section). Failures resulted from tendencies to repeat unsuccessful predictions, to focus on an unduly narrow range of hypotheses, to be confused over terminology, and especially to overlook uncontrolled variables.

McLaughlin (1963) has offered an alternative to Inhelder and Piaget's interpretation of the obstacles that have to be overcome before immature forms of thinking can be replaced. He holds that limitations of immediate memory or of attention can account for the belated appearance of more advanced thought processes, arguing that pre-operational, concrete-operational, and formal-operational thinking require, respectively, two, four, and eight concepts to be handled simutaneously.

The Influence of Köhler: Insight versus Trial and Error

Phenomena demonstrated in animals have served as reference points for investigators of reasoning in children. Köhler's (1921) experiments on "insightful" problem-solving in the chimpanzee have been a particularly fruitful source of experimental techniques and theoretical issues. The foremost question raised by Köhler was the relative importance of, on the one hand, the discovery of successful responses by trial and error and, on the other hand, sudden perceptual restructuring and understanding of relations between the elements of the problem situation. It has, however, become more and more evident that this is not a sharp dichotomy (see Berlyne, 1965). This "blindest" so-called "random" trial-and-error behavior is never a random sample of the responses of which the organism is capable but rather a selection of acts that have proved useful in somewhat similar situations in the past. And both American and Russian experiments (the latter carried out under Pavlov's supervision toward the end of his life) have shown how "insight" depends on prior acquisition through learning of the essential ingredients of the solution.

Piaget's reports of behavior in infants resembling that of Köhler's apes have already been mentioned. Historically, the first such observations seem to have been made by Bühler (1930). One infant whom he studied was able by the end of the tenth month to pull on a string and thus obtain a cookie that was attached to it. The ability to remove a ring from a post by lifting it rather than trying to pull it sideways did not, however, appear until the middle of the second year.

Two American experimenters, Alpert (1928) and Matheson (1931), have exposed preschool children to situations resembling those that confronted Köhler's chimpanzees. They were required to obtain otherwise inaccesible objects by means of sticks or strings, to move a block to a position where they could stand on it to reach something hanging form the ceiling, and so on. The commonest reaction observed by Alpert was "exploration and elimination," that is "a deliberate trying out . . . of one possibility after another or an investigation of the constituent parts of the situation." It was sometimes "guided by a partial understanding of or insight into the situation." The next most frequent was the "preparatory response," that is, reaching out with the hand. This usually occurred when the child was first placed in the situation, but it was apt to recur after failing to solve the problem. The "random response," comparable to the trial-and-error behavior of Thorndike's cats in the puzzle box, appeared generally as part of an emotional reaction to being thwarted. The "immediate solution," possibly preceded briefly by a preparatory response, occurred relatively rarely. Nevertheless, it appears that any type of response will lead to a solution "only if the subject has gained insight into the problem-situation." According to Matheson's records, "manipulation" and "pointing and reaching" (identifiable with trial-and-error) were most frequent, followed by "feelings of incapacity" and "asking the experimenter to help him." Like Alpert, Matheson states that "solutions which occurred without preliminary manipulation" were relatively rare. She equates them with Köhler's insight, which seems to be an example of a surprisingly widespread misconception. Reference to Köhler's protocols will make it clear that what he calls "insight" does not preclude prior trial and error. The general conclusion that "understanding may occur in differing degrees" seems well taken and agrees with comments made by other investigators of reasoning. Both Alpert and

Matheson found positive and moderate correlations between success at these tasks and chronological and mental age.

Richardson (1932, 1934) tested infants monthly between the ages of 6 months and 1 year for ability to obtain lures by pulling strings or turning levers. With increasing age, there was more and more of a tendency to pay attention to the strings or levers. The author concludes that "perceptive attitudes" and motor capacities develop hand in hand and that both of them contribute to the development of proficiency at tasks of this kind.

Some more original tasks were devised by Harter (1930). They all required the subject to find a way of removing or circumventing obstacles, so that an object could be transferred from one location to another. The salient observation was of "considerable overt trial and error." There was also evidence for some learning, since subjects made fewer random moves when faced with a specific task for the second time, but one-trial learning often taken as another criterion of insight, was not in evidence.

Russian Work: Transfer from Previous Learning

Beginning with Pavlov, Russian representatives of psychology and "physiology of higher nervous activity" have been unable to ignore Köhler's chimpanzee experiments. However, like many of their Western colleagues and for strikingly similar reasons, they have taken exception to Köhler's theoretical interpretation with its emphasis on "insight" as something that cannot be reduced to learning. They have felt challenged to show that the same phenomena can be explained by a suitable extension of Pavlovian conditioned-reflex principles.

Some pertinent experiments with children, paralleling the experiments with chimpanzees that were going on at about the same time under Pavlov's direction, were carried out in Ivanov-Smolenski's laboratory and reported in a book edited by him (Ivanov-Smolenski, 1934). As in the experiments by the same group that were mentioned earlier, the favorite response of pressing the rubber ball with the hand was generally used. No verbal instructions were generally given, except for utterances like "Press!" and "Don't press!" when these were selected as unconditioned stimuli. Furthermore, the subject was alone in an experimental chamber. In these conditions it is easier than it is in most human experiments to compare the behavior that emerges with animal behavior and with simple forms of conditioning' even though this behavior must be influenced by thought processes and by attempts to figure out what one is supposed to do.

Naroditskaia studied "The formation in childhood of new conditioned connections without previous elaboration." In an initial phase, children were taught, with a verbal unconditioned stimulus, to press a rubber bulb in response to either a red square or the sound of a bell. The response was followed by either the receipt of a piece of candy or the appearance of a picture. In a second phase, the conditioned stimulus was changed: the red square was replaced by a yellow rectangle or the bell by a tone. In a third phase, the original conditioned stimulus was used, but the response was changed by introducing either a bulb of a different shape or the same bulb in a different location. In a fourth phase, both stimulus and response were changed. These last three situations can be recognized as calling for Hull's (1943) "stimulus generalization," "response generalization," and "stimulus-response generalization," respectively. The crucial role of the last of these in reasoning has been elaborated on elsewhere (Berlyn, 1965a, Chap. 7). Naroditskaia found the percentage of subjects acting appropriately in all three transfer tasks to be 28 at preschool ages, 40 in 7-to 8-year olds, and 80 in 10-to 12-year-olds.

In Khozak's experiment, entitled "The formation of conditioned connections in the child by means of a cross-over on the basis of past experience," children were first confronted with a grey, pear-shaped bulb and the sound of a bell. They did not press the bulb. They were then taught to press a flat brown bulb in response to a flashing green light and to press a button in response to a rattling sound. Candy was given as a reward in both cases. After these two training experiences, they were presented with the initial situation. The majority of the children then pressed the pear-shaped bulb. Once again, we see an instance of stimulus-response generalization, although the factors at work are not altogether clear. Some children did not press the

bulb in the final stage but, when asked what they should be doing, they nevertheless answered "Press!" This might mean that the required association could be generated by a verbal mediator, elicited by the question, but would not appear without it. But it might mean instead that these children recognized the action that was appropriate but were prevented by some kind of timidity or scruple from performing it.

In an experiment on "The neurodynamics of suddenly arising conditioned closures in complex situations," Kotliarevski introduced an additional feature of Köhler's ape experiment, the necessity of a preparatory tool-using response before the directly reinforced response can occur. Children were taught to press the bulb, as a means of obtaining candy, on seeing a flashing yellow square. The response was, however, not reinforced when the square was accompanied by the sound of a bell. Later, they could reach the bulb only after loosening the tube to which it was attached and unwinding it from a hook or else by fitting two sticks together to form an instrument by which it could be pulled toward them. These supplementary actions were frequently evoked by the positive conditioned stimulus, the flashing yellow square. But inhibition generalized to the new situation when the square and bell were presented together. Both trial and error and sudden insight were observed. Like Naroditskaia, Kotliarevski found the frequency of success to increase with age between 5 and 12 years.

An active team headed by Rubinsthein (1958, 1959, 1960) has focused on another aspect of transfer from previous learning. They view thinking as an interplay of "analysis" and "synthesis." Pavlov used these terms to denote, respectively, the processes by which properties of stimuli are distinguished and registered (the work of the "analyzers," i.e., the sensory nerves and sensory areas of the brain) and the evocation of responses through "conditioned connections" or (in the case of verbal events) "associations." Rubinshtein extends these notions considerably. Under analysis, he includes taking cognizance of the data of a problem, picking out essential components, considering its different aspects. Analysis of sensory images is distinguished from analysis of verbal "images," which is essential to human thinking. There is "analogous filtering," which means simply focusing on one facet of a problem after another. But special importance is attributed to "analysis through synthesis." This occurs when elements of the problem are related to one another and especially when the requirements of the solution and the conditions within which the solution must be reached are considered jointly. In its turn, a new analysis or "formulation" of the problem leads to new "synthesis" by bringing new thoughts into play. This happens, for example, when relations emerge between the present problem and other problems to which solutions have been found in the past.

Some of the experiments illustrating these points have been done with children. For example, in an experiment by Zhukova (1960), children between 3 and 6 years of age had to select an instrument with which to extract a piece of candy from a container. One group was presented with hooks of different shapes and colors, while a second group had hooks of different shapes but of the same color. At first, no subject could solve the problem without trying out different hooks in turn, but, after a while, they could pick out a hook of the right shape without trial and error. This transition to "the plane of cognition" required about half as many trials in the second group as in the first group. It is suggested that the conditions used for the first group are representative of the conditions in which most everyday thinking goes on. The stimulus properties that could guide one to a solution are mixed up with other, irrelevant stimulus properties. The processes of structuring and generalization on which a "proper analysis" of the problem or discovery of its "functional meaning" depend are therefore impeded. The subjects of the second group were, in contrast, able to concentrate on the property that mattered, namely shape. In another experiment, Slavskaia (1960) presented children of 13 and over with geometrical problems, seeking the conditions in which supplementary questions, containing hints, could be useful. Subjects could, it turned out, take advantage of a supplementary problem only when analysis of the main problem had gone far enough for the relation between the two to be recognized.

Reasoning in preschool children has been one of the concerns of the Moscow school, which carries on the tradition of Vygotski. Several experimenters have taken it up under the direction of Leont'ev and Zaporozhets (El'konin, 1960; Zaporozhets and El'konin, 1964). Once again, subjects have to gain access to objects with the help of intermediary instruments (which sometimes have first to be constructed or modified). And again, the findings are deemed to refute Köhler's view. Transfer from previous learning, especially learning that has resulted from social interaction, is seen as the key to what Köhler called "insight." To quote Zaporozhets (1960, p. 212), "At first, the child carries out a transfer solely on the basis of an external similarity between situations, but subsequently —even in preschool years—he begins to grasp internal mechanical connections in the relations between objects and, after solving a series of similar but simpler mechanical tasks, he grasps the principles that unite them and forms the corresponding generalizations."

Under the joint influence of Pavlov's emphasis on the central role of the second signal system in human behavior and Vygotski's emphasis on words as transmitters of social influence, these Russian investigators dwell on the importance of speech as a vehicle of generalization that ensures appropriate transfer from relevant previous experiences to the present problem. There are some close parallels between their views on this matter and the views of American psychologists (e.g., Miller and Dollard, 1941; Staats and Staats, 1963) on the functions of verbal mediators. Furthermore, the importance attached to exploratory ("orienting") activity and the links established between this activity and imagery have drawn attention to the way in which images, like words, make it possible to plan a solution to a practical task beforehand and thus obviate the need for overt trial and error.

However, the ability to use these symbolic aids takes time to develop. Minskaia (1954) set children various tasks requiring manipulation of levers. Three different conditions were compared. One group had to discover the solution while handling actual levers ("the visuo-operative level"). A second group had to describe how they would solve the problem, using a drawing of the equipment ("the visuo-imaginal level"). The third group had to describe in words how the problem could be solved ("the verbal level"). More than 50% of the children in the first group succeeded, even at 3 to 4 years. This percentage was not reached until 4 to 5 years in the second group. In the third group, there was only 22% success even at 6 to 7 years, the oldest age group tested. Minskaia also examined the role of exploration ("orientation"), distinguishing four levels: "primitive-chaotic," looking round the room; paying attention to the lure but not particularly to the lever through which the lure was to be secured; concentrating on the lever and manipulating it; conceiving of the solution after simply examining the components of the lever visually. There were no successes at all with the first kind of exploration, but the percentage of success rose from the second to the fourth. The fourth kind became commoner with increasing age.

The importance of transfer from previous learning even for logical deduction is illustrated in an experiment by Ul'enkova (1954). The ability to make correct deductions from premises was almost absent at 3 to 4 years and gradually increased to 80% success at 7 years. The probability of success varied both with the form of the underlying syllogism and with the content of the premises, depending on how close they were to the child's experience. A training procedure, designed to "actualize" past experience and induce the formation of appropriate universal statements, had no effect on 3-year-olds, but improved ability to handle syllogisms in older children. Its efficacy increased with age. Four stages in the formation of deductive thinking were distinguished. First, the child does not form any universal statements or generalizations; he does not give grounds for his assertions or, if he justifies them, he does so haphazardly. Subsequently, the child operates with universal statements, but they are often invalid and they are, in any case, introduced inappropriately and haphazardly. In a third stage, the child uses appropriate and valid universal statements but does not consider all possible cases. Finally, the child overcomes all these deficiencies and can draw valid conclusions. This investigation clearly deals with some of the same processes as Piaget's developmental studies of logical thinking. It is a little hard to compare their

findings, since Ul'enkova's tests were based on the syllogisms of Aristotelian logic, whereas Inhelder and Piaget patterned their procedures after the inferential forms of modern symbolic logic. Ul'enkova's data seem, however, to suggest that processes associated by Inhelder and Piaget with early adolescence can actually appear earlier.

Maier and Hull: Synthesis of Learned Associations

Maier (1936) reported an experiment on reasoning in children in which he pursued a conceptualization arising out of his earlier experiments with rats and with human adults. He contrasted "reasoning" (the "ability to combine two isolated experiences") with "learning" (the "ability to combine two contiguous experiences"). His rat experiments had led him to conclude that these two abilities are distinct, since (1) brain injuries that impair reasoning do not affect learning, (2) reasoning is better in older rats and learning in younger rats, and (3) tests of reasoning ability are highly correlated with one another but not with tests of learning.

In the title of an article reinterpreting Maier's and Köhler's reasoning experiments, Hull (1935) spoke in the same vein of "The mechanism of the assembly of behavior segments in novel combinations suitable for problem solution." Related views have been expressed in the Soviet Union. Vatsuro (1948), who studied tool-using behavior in chimpanzees under Pavlov's direction, concluded that qualitatively new "dynamic patterns of temporary connections" can result from the interaction of distinct previously acquired conditioned reflexes. Boiko (1955, 1957) has described how new "temporary connections" can be formed "without preliminary elaboration" through the simultaneous evocation and interaction of two or more conditioned reflexes whose fields of cortical excitation overlap. This kind of process, he maintained, underlies the "higher mental processes," including deductive and inductive thinking.

In his experiment with children, Maier used an arrangement of enclosed alleys, shaped like a swastika, with a booth at the end of each arm. The booth could be entered from inside or from outside the apparatus. Following the procedure Maier had already introduced in his rat experiments, the child was initially given two distinct learning experiences. First he was allowed to explore the interior of the apparatus, and, second, he was led into one of the booths from outside and shown a toy windmill whose arms would rotate to the accompaniment of a tune if a coin were dropped into a slot. In the test phase, the child was taken out of the apparatus and into another booth, from which he was to find his way to the booth containing the toy. Above-chance success, regarded as an index of reasoning, was "rarely developed to a marked extent in children below 6 years of age." Since children are able to learn much earlier than that, Maier felt confirmed in his belief that learning and reasoning correspond to distinct abilities. Success at his reasoning task was correlated with mental and chronological age.

In a series of experiments inspired by Hull's (1935, 1952) analyses of reasoning, the Kendlers and various collaborators have used the kind of apparatus depicted in Fig. 2. The child is first trained to perform three responses: response A leading him to subgoal B, response X leading him to subgoal Y, and manipulating subgoal B leading him to the major goal, G. He is then presented with A and X simultaneously to see whether he will choose to perform A, the response by which he could attain the main goal. For example, in the first experiment, response A was pulling a ribbon, which caused subgoal B, a toy ladybug, to appear. Response X was pulling a chain, which caused subgoal Y, a toy chicken, to appear. The major goal, G,

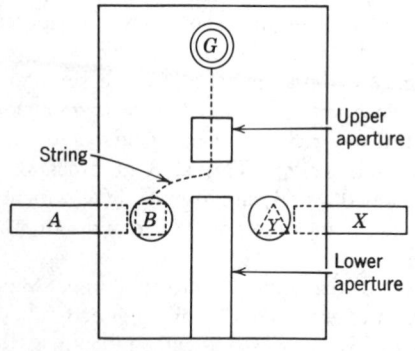

Fig. 2. Basic plan of apparatuses used in experiments on inference by Kendlers and associates. (From Kendler, Pliskoff, and D'Amato, 1958.)

was a toy car. In later experiments, different manipulanda and responses were used, but the general scheme was the same.

In the first experiment (Kendler and Kendler, 1956) there were eight groups of 3- and 4-year-old children. Four experimental groups had two trials with the A-B response, the X-Y response, and the B-G response, but the order differed from group to group. Four corresponding control groups underwent the same treatments except that the B-G response was not introduced; they were simply shown the main goal instead. In the subsequent test phase, the experimental groups performed the correct response (pulling A) significantly more often than the control groups. This contradicted Maier's conclusion that reasoning is not generally present before age 6. As far as the orders were concerned, there was evidence of inference when the A-B response was learned before the B-G response but not when the B-G response was learned first.

The details were modified in the second experiment (Kendler, Kendler, Pliskoff, and D'Amato, 1958). All subjects acquired the A-B response, the X-Y response, and the B-G response, in that order. The two independent variables of interest were "reinforcement during training" and "motivation during the test trial." Half of the subjects found a gold charm in the major-goal container and the other half did not. Furthermore, half of the subjects could see the major-goal container through a window during the test trial, and the other half could not. Subjects who received a charm during the training trials and also could see the major goal during the test trial performed better than subjects for whom one or both of these conditions were absent. "It was concluded that inferential behavior, like the simple bar-pressing habit in animals, is influenced by independent variations of reinforcement and motivational variables."

The third experiment (Kendler and Kendler, 1961) reverted to the question of whether the order of acquiring the components of the solution chain makes a difference. A third version of the apparatus was used. In the training phase, all six possible orders of acquiring the A-B, X-Y, and B-G responses were used for different experimental groups. The groups did not, however, differ significantly in incidence of inference. This finding failed to support explanations of inference derived from writings of Hull (1935, 1952), Skinner (1938), and Underwood (1952). How reasoning may be explained without assuming that the contributing associations must be acquired in a particular order has been discussed elsewhere (Berlyne, 1965a, Chap. 12).

A fourth experiment (Kendler and Kendler, 1962) introduced various complications into the procedure. The training phase was more elaborate, and the subgoals were interchanged for some subjects in the test phase, so that response A produced subgoal Y and response X produced subgoal B. Children of 8 to 10 years were tested as well as kindergarten children. A significant tendency to choose the correct response in the test phase was shown by the older children but not by the younger children. The discrepancy between this finding and the success that had been obtained with younger children in the earlier experiments was attributed to the higher socioeconomic status of the earlier subjects and the additional complexity of the present task. The behavior of the children for whom the correct response in the test phase produced the incorrect subgoal and vice versa showed that the formation of a solution chain is not determined solely by the presence of external stimulation from the appropriate subgoal but depends also on choice of the correct initial response.

The most recent experiment in the series (Kendler, Kendler, and Carrick, 1966) concentrated on the influence of verbal labels. Some subjects were taught to apply identical names to the subgoal object, B, that figured in the A-B association and to the B that figured in the B-G association. Some were taught to apply different names to them. Some were not led to apply any verbal labels to them at all during training. The dissimilar labels had no consistent influence on the incidence of correct solutions. The use of identical labels made correct solutions more frequent at the kindergarten level but either made no appreciable difference or had a detrimental effect in grade-3 children. To account for these findings, the authors suggest that older children supply their own verbal labels and that the induced labels either coincide with these, thus adding nothing, or conflict with them, impairing performance.

Investigations Arising Out of Educational Problems

Tests of reasoning ability have, of course, long been of interest to educational psychologists. A considerable body of theoretical writing has grown up along with the testing movement, much of it relating to classification of intellectual abilities with the help of factor analysis and other taxonomic techniques (e.g., Spearman, 1927; Thurstone, 1938; Guilford, 1967). For a long time, there was a wide and highly regrettable chasm between those who were measuring intellectual capacities and those who were doing experiments to discover the laws that govern intellectual processes. Fortunately, the educational reform movement of the 1960s has begun to bridge this gulf between applied and basic research.

An interesting example of a synthesis between the two approaches is Donaldson's (1963) book. She set children various problems such as are widely used in intelligence tests. They included matching problems, three-term-series problems, series-extrapolation problems, related-series problems, and problems requiring formal deductive reasoning. Her aim was to find out how errors arose, and her findings led her to place them in three major categories. There were "structural" errors (due to "failure to appreciate the relationships involved in the problem or grasp some principle essential to the solution"), "arbitrary" errors (due to "a lack of loyalty to the given"), and "executive" errors (due to "some failure in the actual carrying out of the manipulations required"). With reference to the last category, the author says that "some defect of concentration, of attention, or of immediate memory seems usually to lie at their origin."

The growing appreciation of creativity and independence of thought by contemporary society has encouraged educational psychologists to seek ways of promoting intellectual capacities rather than simply diagnosing them. By delving further into the operative mechanisms than was customary until recently, an investigation like Donaldson's can contribute to this change. Two studies supervised by Suppes (Suppes and Hill 1961; Suppes, 1966) were similarly prompted by hopes of advancing pedagogical technique. Children ranging between 6 and 8 years of age were set problems, each of which presented them with two or three premises and required them to state whether or not a particular proposition would follow.

The percentage of correct answers increased from 71.18 at 6 years to 85.58 at 8 years. A control group, for whom the first premise of each item was omitted, answered correctly 52.02% of the time. The inclusion of negative propositions among the premises raised the probability of error.

The second study was concerned with the ability of first-grade children to construct proofs in a simple mathematical system. One training procedure used discrimination learning with correction. After arriving at each line of the proof, the subject had to choose from four alternatives the kind of step that needed to be taken next. He was then shown the correct choice. Children trained with this procedure made fewer errors than others who were trained with a discovery method and not corrected until the whole proof had been completed.

Other experimenters have sought more directly to devise instructional methods that can improve the efficiency of reasoning. In the U.S.S.R., Landa (1959, 1961, 1962) has devised "algorithms" for training pupils in "rational methods of think." Algorithms resemble computer flow charts, except that "they take into account the experience in thinking operations possessed by the child." The pupil is taught to go through a prescribed sequence of steps, each of which involves asking himself a specific question about the problem material and performing one of a set of alternative operations in accordance with the answer to the question. Landa has applied this method, which draws on mathematical logic, cybernetics, and information theory, to geometry and to grammatical analysis and claims that it could enable problems to be solved more speedily, easily, and effectively.

In the United States, Crutchfield (Covington and Crutchfield, 1965; Crutchfield, 1966) and his associates have produced written and pictorial material, resembling comic strips, that is designed to "promote generalized problem-solving skills" in fifth- and sixth-grade children. A child is taught "the value, necessity, and techniques of identifying and defining a problem properly, of asking questions and taking time for reflection rather than leaping to conclusions, of looking carefully at details and searching for discrepancies, of generating many ideas and not fearing to come up with what may seem 'silly' ideas, of looking everywhere when stymied for possible clues and sources of ideas, etc." He is given opportunities to generate his own ideas and receives "immediate and frequent feedback" in the form of "good examples of fruitful questions and hypotheses." Preliminary studies have indicated "substantial increments in the performance of the trained children on a variety of criteria and tests of problem-solving and creative thinking."

MOTIVATIONAL FACTORS

During the last 100 years, there has been a great accumulation of data on how both adults and children think when a psychologist has just instructed them to do so. Remarkably little is known about the conditions that govern spontaneous thinking in early or later life. It is, of course, obvious that effects resembling those that result from verbal instructions to think can be induced by other factors in everyday life outside the laboratory, for example by a subject's self-instructions or their equivalents. But all too little attention has been paid to the problem of exactly how words uttered by an experimenter can set thought processes in motion so powerfully and exactly what other conditions can and cannot have the same kind of influence.

In other words, the investigation of the motivational factors that underlie thinking have been woefully neglected both by specialists in adult thinking and by specialists in children's thinking (see Berlyne 1960a, 1965a). The factors that need to be identified if the so-called motivational aspects of thinking are to be illuminated include those that determine when a piece of directed thinking will begin, why it is aimed at one problem rather than at others, how long a thought process will persist, and when it will be terminated either through discouragement at lack of success or through recognition that a solution has been attained.

There are nevertheless some directions in which we may seek hints concerning these matters.

Exploratory Behavior

There has been a great deal of experimental work on the determinants of exploratory responses in children (Berlyne, 1960a, 1966b; Cantor, 1963). Exploratory responses—which may include eye movements, head turning, locomotion, and manipulation—have in common the function of introducing, intensifying, or prolonging "indifferent" stimulation, that is, stimulation that is not detectably accompanied by biologically important effects on the organism apart from the sense organs and the nervous system. It is clear, however, that such stimulus-seeking behavior can perform several sharply different biological functions and that indifferent stimuli may be sought for various reasons.

One distinction (Berlyne, 1960a) that has appeared more and more important as research has proceeded is that between "specific" and "diversive" exploration. Specific exploration is likely to occur when the organism is disturbed by a specific lack of information (uncertainty), and it is directed toward portions of the external environment that may supply the information through which the uncertainty-induced discomfort (perceptual curiosity) can be relieved. Diversive exploration, which includes several, if not most, of the activities that we classify as "play" (Berlyne, 1969), is aimed at stimulation, regardless of source, that possesses characteristics such as novelty, surprisingness, and complexity to the right degree.

Other writers have been led by their observations to suggest essentially the same dichotomy. Lewis, Kagan, and Kalifat (1966), discussing eye movements in infants, state that "there appear to be two causes of long fixations: (1) a preference created by the pleasure derived from looking at the stimulus and (2) a desire to categorize a stimulus or comprehend its meaning." These clearly correspond to diversive and specific exploration, respectively. Likewise, Hutt (1966), who studied the behavior of 3- to 5-year-old children confronted with a rectangular box bearing a lever and four counters, distinguished two successive phases. First, there was "investigation" (i.e., specific exploration), during which "all receptors were oriented towards the object, the general expression being one of 'concentration.'" The goal of this behavior was "getting to know the properties." When the child "feels he knows the properties of the object in that environment," specific exploration gives way to "play": "vision and manipulation were no longer simultaneously directed toward the object" and "the behavior towards the object might almost be described as 'nonchalant.'" There was a "gradual relaxation of movement" and, in this phase of evidently diversive exploration, "the emphasis changes from the question of 'what does this *object* do?' to 'what can *I* do with this object?'"

Of these two forms of exploratory behavior, the diversive form may have more affinities with autistic or free-associative thinking, but directed thinking and reasoning must be more closely related to specific exploration. Thus specific exploration and directed thinking are aimed at access to information that can relieve specific subjective uncertainties. Both can be regarded as means of relieving an aversive condition due to lack of information. Both seem to arise from the kinds of motivational condition that, in everyday parlance, we call "curiosity."

There are, however, important differences between specific exploration and directed thinking. Whereas specific exploration leads to approriate external stimulus patterns, directed thinking is a form of "epistemic behavior" (Berlyne, 1954, 1960a), which means that its function is to supply "knowledge" or information stored in verbal or other symbolic stimulus patterns. Some epistemic activities, notably consultation (which includes directing spoken or written questions at another person or looking up reference books), bring the subject into contact with external symbolic formulas. Directed thinking, on the other hand, constructs patterns of symbolic responses inside the subject, whose stimulus aspects are then capable of guiding overt behavior in conjunction with external stimulus situations.

Specific exploratory responses are usually evoked by stimuli that are novel, surprising, complex, or ambiguous (Berlyne, 1960). These and other "collative" stimulus properties (properties dependent on comparison of two or more stimulus patterns) generally entail subjective uncertainty about inaccessible properties of the stimulus object or event. There have been several competing analyses of the essence of the collative stimulus properties, accounting for their motivational effects (Berlyne, 1963, 1965). Whichever precise formulation is favored, it is recognizable that they work by setting up discrepant processes in the central nervous system. They can be argued to motivate through *conflict,* which means, in the most general sense of the term, a condition in which mutually interfering processes occur simultaneously and in which selection of a motor response from a set of competing alternatives is therefore hampered.

In the case of the "problems" that give rise to directed thinking, and to epistemic (knowledge-seeking) behavior generally, not only is the "solution," the pattern that resolves the uncertainty, symbolic in form. The motivating conflict, whether it rises from contact with a puzzling external object, exposure to a puzzling verbal message, or immersion in a puzzling train of thought, is usually "conceptual conflict" or conflict between incompatible symbolic response tendencies. In other words, although extraneous sources of motivation may play an important part when thinking is aimed at the solution of a "practical" problem, directed thinking, it would seem from this line of argument, is initiated and kept going by factors stirring up mutually discrepant beliefs, attitudes, and trains of thought.

Piaget's Equilibration

Piaget (1957, etc.) has asserted that the major advances that mark the child's progress from less mature to more mature ways of perceiving and thinking are brought about chiefly by a process he calls "equilibration." This is a tendency for systems of conceptual and intellectual activities to form structures of progressively more complete equilibrium. Although he concedes that learning and maturation have their contributions to make, equilibration is deemed distinct from either of them. Piaget discusses equilibration in relation to the major transitions of intellectual development, such as the transition from unorganized, haphazard perception to the "perceptual activities" that mitigate "primary" illusions and the transition from "intuitive" to "operational" thinking. It seems reasonable, however, to suppose that similar factors will account for the initiation of a specific piece of thinking as well as the adoption of new overall strategies of thinking and the construction of the comprehensive systems of thought elements on which every specific thought process depends.

Piaget (e.g., 1967) dissociates equilibration from maturation on the grounds that the "dynamic structures" that underlie thinking are not innate but form very gradually. The stages that mark their construction do not correspond to a particular age but occur in a constant order of succession. Maturation simply fixes the limits beyond which development spurred by other factors cannot go. These points seem, however, to be equally applicable to aspects of behavior, like grasping and locomotion, that are generally cited as products of maturation. As for learning, Piaget and his associates (Gréco and Piaget, 1959; Goustard et al., 1959) have gathered evidence that the phenomena attributed to equilibration are not produced simply by exposure to external events illustrating logical and mathematical principles. This is the main basis for his distinction between equilibration and learning. But the view that learning results simply from experiencing external stimuli in particular sequences was characteristic of the eighteenth-century empiricists and the nineteenth-century associationists. It is not typical of the contemporary learning theorist, although Tolman (1932) admittedly put forward a rather similar conception in modern times.

We may conclude, rather, that what Piaget calls "equilibration" is a form of learning, limited by maturational factors, that is motivated by conflict and reinforced by conflict reduction (Berlyne, 1960b, 1965; Ranzi and Tampieri, 1966). This can be seen from some of the rather meager hints that Piaget has thrown out regarding the essence of equilibration. He says (1957), for example, that progressive equilibration makes for increasing ability to predict and *sécurité* (assurance, security, safety). It therefore seems to be a matter of relieving subjective uncertainty. Equilibration also means a balance between "assimilation" (determination of behavior by factors inside the organism) and "accommodation" (determination of behavior by properties of external objects). It therefore evidently minimizes conflict due to discrepancies between external stimuli and expectations, beliefs, or habits derived from previous learning. Equilibration is said to result from recognition of the inconsistency of judgement to which less mature forms of perception and thinking lead. The importance of conflict has received some confirmation from Smedslund's work (1961a, b) showing how conservation of quantitative invariants can be speeded up by a technique that forces a child to face the latent inconsistencies among his thought structures. Several new educational techniques (particularly the so-called "discovery" methods—see Berlyne, 1965b) seem similarly to improve retention and understanding by confronting a child with experience that reveals the gaps and discordances in his present knowledge.

Questions

Still further evidence on the development of motivational factors with relevance to thinking comes from studies of children's questions.

A question addressed to someone likely to know the answer is an epistemic response that often forms an alternative to directed thinking. We must thus suppose that these two epistemic activities have common sources of motivation. A question, whether put by somebody else or put to oneself, frequently starts off and directs a thought process. Furthermore, just as the existence of information (whether in the technical mathematical sense or in the everyday sense) necessitates prior uncertainty and just as curiosity is a product of previous knowledge supplying alternative hypotheses and competing response tendencies, a question is likely itself to be a product of previous thinking, from which subsequent thinking issues.

Studies of Spontaneous Questions

As Piaget (1923, Chap. 5) says, "There is no better introduction to child logic than the study of spontaneous questions." One might add that these questions must also have a great deal to tell us about the conditions that motivate recourse to logic. Fahey (1942) has supplied a useful review of empirical work and theoretical views on children's questions up to the end of the 1930s.

In the early days of child psychology, when day-by-day observation of individual children, usually the investigator's own offspring, was the standard source of information, plentiful collections of questions uttered by children in the course of their normal activities were accumulated and analyzed. Several works belonging to this period (e.g., Stern, 1914; Piaget, 1923) differentiate two phases. The first phase begins at about the age of 1½, when the child has discovered that everything has a name. It is characterized by an abundance of requests for names of objects and also of questions about place. Around 2⅔ begins the second phase, in which why-questions and when-questions predominate.

Piaget's (1923, Chap. 5) penetrating analysis of 750 why-questions asked by one boy between the ages of 6¼ and 7½ led him to distinguish a number of categories. There were requests for *explanations* (in terms of either *cause* or *end*) with reference to physical objects, requests for *motivation* with reference to psychological actions, and requests for *justifications* with reference to customs and rules or (logical justification) with reference to classification and connection of ideas. Piaget agrees with Stern that the earliest why-questions are not expressions of curiosity but rather simply expressions of "wonder at what is unusual" (Stern, 1914), of an affective reaction to "disappointment produced by the absence of a desired object or the nonarrival of an expected event, i.e., surprise and frustration." This tallies with the fact that these earliest why-questions do not seem to call for answers; the child will, in fact, sometimes answer them himself. A little later, however, the child is evidently directing why-questions at adults in the hope of having something explained to him, but both his questions and his reactions to the answers that he receives manifest "precausal" thought, in which physical causality, human intentions, and logical deduction are not clearly separated. It is interesting that, when conversations between two boys of about the same age were recorded (Piaget, 1923, Chap. 1), a very small percentage of the questions that passed between them were "whys." Causality, as Piaget points out, "remains the subject of conversation between children and adults or the child's own solitary reflection." Consultation of adults and directed thinking are evidently the only epistemic activities that are regularly rewarded by receipt of curiosity-reducing explanations.

To return to the first boy, questions that

did not begin with "why" consisted of questions relating to *causal explanation, reality and history, human actions and intentions, rules and usage, arithmetical relations,* and *classification and evaluation.*

A somewhat similar study, with concentration on why-questions, was carried out by Isaacs (1930). He disputes many of Piaget's points, particularly those that emphasize differences between the causal thinking of children and adults. He also goes further in analyzing the conditions that motivate why-questions, seeing the crucial factor as "a certain clash, gap or disparity between our past experience and any present event." When this occurs, "immediate experience turns into a sense of something wrong with knowledge, some unsuspected error, insufficiency, or confusion—or of something wrong with the perception of a supposed fact." So the role of conceptual conflict, which was recognized by Stern and Piaget, is brought out even more clearly.

Statistical analysis was applied to large samples of children's questions by McCarthy (1930) and by Davis (1932). Questions were found to appear at a faster rate in boys and in children of higher socioeconomic status. The rate increased with age up to about 30 months and then remained fairly steady for some years after. The incidence of different types of questions also varied with the same variables. Both authors found questions to occur much more frequently when a child is talking to an adult than when he is talking to another child.

Studies of Induced Questions

In children of school age, questioning has generally been studied by procedures that induce or invite questions. The early literature of this kind is also covered in Fahey's (1942) review.

Yamamoto (1962) has analyzed questions produced by 850 subjects (grade-1 to grade-12 children, as well as adult counsellors) who underwent an "Ask and Guess Test." The subject is shown a picture illustrating a familiar nursery rhyme. In the first part of the test, which is the only part of interest here, the child is instructed to ask as many questions as possible about what he sees in the picture. The number of questions asked tended to increase with age. Questions beginning with "why" were commonest; they comprised 70% of the questions asked by grade-1 to grade-3 subjects, but their incidence dropped at grade 4 and higher, while questions beginning with "what" became more frequent. "Be?" questions (i.e., questions inquiring whether or not something is the case) become more frequent with age throughout the range. To sum up, children appear to advance from "global" questions (why?) to "specific" questions (what?, when?, where?, who?, and which?) and finally to "definitive" questions (how?, and be?).

Aikawa and Horiuchi (1962) solicited why-questions from 1028 children between grades 2 and 9. The number of questions supplied reached a peak at grade 6 and then declined. Why-questions about "human life" increased with age, while why-questions about "things" and about "animals and plants" became gradually less frequent. Why-questions regarding "natural phenomena" rose from grades 2 to 4 and then became less numerous. Boys asked more why-questions about "heavenly bodies" and "instruments" than girls but fewer about "animals and plants." The authors conclude that a phase of "materially cognizing reality" corresponds to late infancy and early childhood, whereas, after a transitional level occupying middle and late childhood, there is a phase of "socially cognizing reality" coinciding with pre-adolescence.

In an experiment by Stirling (1937), questions were elicited while children were exposed singly to a variety of pictures and stories. Questions were more numerous, and bore on a large number of items, the older the child was. Older children also asked more questions about purposes, times, and places, and fewer about names and attributes of objects. The number of questions also increased with IQ and socioeconomic status.

This technique was extended by Berlyne and Frommer (1966), who used pairs of items—pictures, orally related stories, orally related stories accompanied by pictures, and a magic trick—representing different values of "collative" variables (Berlyne, 1960), such as novelty, surprisingness, incongruity, uncertainty, and amount of information. The subjects ranged in age from kindergarten to grade 6. Over all age groups there was evidence that novelty, uncertainty, incongruity, and surprisingness increased the incidence of questions. Number of questions increased with age in two of the schools from which subjects were taken but reached a peak in grade 3 at the remaining schools. This is likely to have been because the older children at this school turned out to be familiar with some of the stories that were used. Provision of answers to the questions increased the incidence of questions in grade-3 children but not in younger or older children. The authors suggested that "in the youngest children, the potential reinforcement value of answers may not have been operative and . . . , in the older children, some other factor may have made up for the lack of answers when they were not forthcoming."

At all ages, specific interrogations (questions beginning with an interrogative adverb) were commoner than yes-no questions (questions asking whether a particular proposition is true or false). Explanatory questions were more numerous than factual questions when children were faced with a surprising magic trick, but factual questions were commoner in situations where facts were conspicuously lacking, that is, with exposures to a picture of a boy or a girl not accompanied by oral information and with exposure to stories of uncertain outcome. Explanatory yes-no questions, which require formation of an explanatory hypothesis, were found to an appreciable extent only among older (grade 5) children exposed to surprising magic tricks. When confronted with a story of uncertain outcome, the proportion of children asking which of the alternative possibilities was realized went up with age, but most children below grade 3 did not ask such questions.

Questions in the Course of Problem-Solving

The vital role of questions, and especially of well chosen questions, in directed thinking is illustrated by two experimental studies. Liublinskaia (1948, cited by El'konin, 1960, p. 262, and Zaporozhets, 1964, pp. 210–211) observed preschool children faced with practical tasks and distinguished two kinds of verbal reaction: "play speech," reflecting emotional reactions to the situation, and "questioning speech," which is "directed to the establishment of new connections and relations as yet unknown to the child" (Za-porozhets, 1964). Questions about causes were likely to occur when the child was faced with some difficulty, such as the failure of a toy to work as expected. To quote from Zaporozhets's interpretation, "The appearance of such questions is extremely important, since it attests the occurrence within the child of the first representations of the presence of causal relations. Furthermore, these questions exert an essential influence on the very process by which the child solves a practical task, imparting to his actions a striving for a correct solution, and imparting to the thought process a definite direction." In the youngest children, attempts to remedy an impediment have a chotic character, but a question put by an adult can induce them to look for causes and to endeavor to put things right in a goal-directed and organized way. After experience of such interaction with adults, the child learns to put appropriate questions to himself spontaneously, and the formulation of a question, even in such a general form as "What's in the way?" or "What's gone wrong?", can make his search for an appropriate course of action more effective. The ability to do this in the face of practical problems comes, as one might expect, rather earlier than the ability to do it in the face of more abstract problems requiring logical inference.

Two variants of the "Twenty Questions" game were used by Mosher and Hornsby (1966) with children between 6 and 11 years. It is well known that the most rational strategy for games of this kind is what these authors call "constraint seeking," which means asking questions that narrow down the range of possibilities progressively and have equal chances of being answered affirmatively and negatively. The opposite of this strategy is what they call "hypothesis scanning." "A child simply asks a series of questions, each of which tests a self-sufficient, specific hypothesis that bears no necessary relation to what has gone before." In a first experiment, the children were confronted with 42 pictures of common objects and had to find out which one the experimenter had selected. Almost all the questions asked by 6-year-old subjects were of the "hypothesis-scanning" type. "Constraint-seeking" questions were somewhat more numerous than these at age 8 and comprised almost 80% of questions asked at age 11. When 8-year-old children asked a constraining question, it was usually followed by a series of specific-hypothesis questions rather than by further constraint seeking. On the other hand, 11-year-olds generally avoided voicing specific hypotheses until they felt ready to terminate the inquiry.

A second experiment used verbally described situations. For example, subjects were told, "A man is driving down the road in his car. The car goes off the road and hits a tree," and they had to find out what caused the accident. Here, in contrast with the first experiment, where the alternatives were restricted to a set of pictures in front of the subject, the possible solutions came from an unrestricted universe. As before, 11-year-olds used constraint seeking more often than hypothesis scanning. But at the ages of 6 and 8, there was more partiality for hypothesis scanning than in the previous experiment. Furthermore, the percentage of children who asked connected series of questions, "basing later questions upon answers obtained earlier," rose from 40 at the age of 6 to 80 at the age of 11. Interestingly enough, when children were offered a choice at the beginning of the game between a general and a specific question, one-third of the 6-year-olds and most of the 8-year-olds actually chose the general constraint-seeking question. As the authors put it, "They appeared able to *recognize* a better strategy in the verbal game, but they seemed less able to mount the strategy on their own initiative."

A related investigation has been conducted by Olson (1966). Children were presented with a board bearing a number of light bulbs arranged in a matrix pattern. They were told that some of the bulbs, but not others, would light up when pressed, and two diagrams representing alternative partitions of the matrix into active and inactive bulbs were shown. The subject had to find out which of the two diagrams represented the true state of affairs, and this entailed pressing bulbs on the board in order to see whether each of them would light up or not. These bulb-pressing responses were thus equivalents of questions. Three-year-old children pressed bulbs in a "somewhat orderly" manner but independently of the diagrams representing the alternative combinations. At 5 years of age this behavior was generally replaced by a "circuit-pattern-matching strategy": the child tried out each of the alternative solutions in turn, confining himself to bulbs that, according to the diagram, should light up. Finally, at about age 7, the "information-selection strategy" appeared. The child concentrated on "informative" bulbs—bulbs that would light up according to one solution but not according to the other and could thus offer a way of deciding between the alternatives rapidly. The author points out that the transition from the kind of search characteristic of the 3-year-old to the pattern-matching of the 5-year-old requires "not only the achievement of recognition of correspondence between a model and its referent, but also an achievement of the ability to reproduce." There must be "some interplay between the image and the action that it must guide. . . ." The information-selection strategy necessitates "being able to deal not with one image at a time, but rather with the properties or features of several images simultaneously." "Such a step," Olson writes, "corresponds to the development in the Twenty Questions game when children are able to ask 'indirect' questions about constraints, rather than testing hypotheses directly."

Procedures for Training in Questioning

As Mackworth (1965) has emphasized in a lecture on "Originality," "problem finding is more important than problem solving." Guilford (1956, 1967) has identified a dimension of "sensitivity to problems" as an important component of ability to think creatively. It is thus far from surprising to find questions assigned a prominent role in some of the newer pedagogical techniques, with their stress on training for creative problem-solving.

Some of the "discovery" methods confront children with questions and require them to find the answers to them through their own efforts. Others make the child formulate his own questions as an incentive and guide to fruitful discovery. There has therefore been considerable interest in the possibilities of training children to formulate questions more effectively and readily.

One notable example is the "Inquiry Training" project (Suchman, 1959, 1962, 1963). A procedure developed under its auspices begins with a short film demonstrating a surprising physical phenomenon (e.g., a brass ball that is small enough to pass through a ring case can no longer do so after it has been heated). This is followed by "episode analysis" (Stage I) or a verification that the content of the film has been correctly noted. The children are then invited to discover the principles governing the phenomenon they have witnessed. They do so by putting questions to the teacher. The questions must be ones that can be answered "yes" or "no" and correspond to possible experiments that could be performed.

This constitutes Stage II, aimed at "isolation of the relevant variables and necessary conditions" and "identification of conditions that are necessary for the outcome of the film demonstration." Then, Stage III is devoted to "induction or relational constructs." Hypotheses regarding physical principles and relationships must be formed, and ways in which they can be tested must be conceived. A validation study, comparing children exposed to the inquiry-training procedure with others who were simply exposed to the film and then to more conventional teaching, indicated that "The inquiry skills of fifth-grade children can be improved over a 15-week period." The total fluency of questioning was significantly greater in the experimental group, and, in particular, fruitful kinds of questions were more frequent.

Another, somewhat similar program has been tried out by Blank and Covington (1966). Their subjects, predominantly boys in grade 6, were divided into three groups. All were exposed to verbal descriptions of situations in which somebody had to make a choice between alternative courses of action. Group I went through an auto-instructional program, aimed at training them to tell when a question cannot be completely answered without additional items of information and to seek the additional items by formulating suitable questions. Group II had an "emasculated" form of the program, in which they were simply told that certain kinds of information were needed. Group III had no programmed material. The results of the auto-instructional program were tested in several different ways. There was a pretest and a posttest with oral and written problems. Then, performance on a science-achievement test requiring problem solving was measured.

Finally, teachers were asked to rate the children for participation in class discussions on scientific subject-matter. Between the pretest and posttest problems, there was a significant rise in the number of questions asked in Group I but not in the other two groups. Group I also exceeded the other two groups in their scores on the science-achievement test and in rated participation in class discussion.

Asking questions, like other forms of epistemic and exploratory behavior, has always to contend with competition from locomotor withdrawal or from withdrawal of attention as a means of reducing disturbance from novel or puzzling stimulus patterns. The educational system must presumably incline children toward approach and information-seeking, although this must not go too far. Excessive scrutiny of external objects and pondering before coming to a decision is characteristic of obsessive-compulsive neurosis. Children must presumably be taught to judge when persistent exploratory and epistemic efforts are worthwhile and when they are not worth embarking on or should be abandoned. If relatively brief training programs, such as those just described, can incline the child to seek information and to construct questions that will enable him to do so efficiently, much must depend on the environment to which he has been exposed in his early years. The degree to which parents and teachers encourage a child's questions and answer them patiently and fully will, we must suppose, have lasting effects. Whether a child has been led into epistemic efforts that lie within his capacities and extend them progressively or whether he has been frustrated by unsuccessful attacks on problems that exceed his capacities will, no doubt, also have an important influence.

Profound differences between social classes and ethnic groups in aptitude and taste for schoolwork have often been noted. These differences could be due in part to motivational differences dependent on factors like these. In experiments on exploratory behavior, Lore (1965) found that lower-class "culturally deprived" children, at 6 or 7 years of age, spent less time looking at visual patterns than middle-class "culturally enriched" children of comparable age. The difference in mean inspection time was particularly marked with irregular or incongruous (i.e., problem-raising or conflict-inducing) patterns. It seems likely that a similar difference would have emerged if epistemic behavior, including questioning and directed thinking, had been investigated instead.

Of late, considerable effort has been expended on working out teaching methods that could improve the efficiency of children's reasoning. Future research must pay at least as much attention to the motivational factors that govern readiness to embark on thinking, skillful choice between thinking and alternative epistemic activities (consultation, observation), and the ability to judge when epistemic efforts are worthwhile and how long they should continue.

References

Ach, N. *Über die Willenshätiqkeit und das Denken.* Göttingen: Vandenhoeck & Ruprecht, 1905.

Ach, N. *Über den Willensakt und das Temperament.* Leipzig: Quelle & Meyer, 1910.

Aikawa, T., and Horiuchi, S. A study in the development of whys: I. Investigations in the areas of whys which arise as a process of cognizing reality. *Jap. J. educ. Psychol.,* 1962, **10**, 139–149.

Alpert, A. The solving of problem-situations by preschool children: an analysis. *Teach. Coll. Contrib. Educ.,* 1928, No. 323.

Bandura, A. Vicarious processes: a cause of no-trial learning. In L. Berkowitz (Ed.), *Advances in experimental social psychology.* Vol. 2. New York: Academic Press, 1965.

Bandura, A., and Walters, R. H. *Social learning and personality development.* New York: Holt, Rinehart, and Winston, 1963.

Berlyne, D. E. A theory of human curiosity. *Br. J. Psychol.,* 1954, **45**, 180–191.

Berlyne, D. E. *Conflict, arousal, and curiosity.* New York: McGraw-Hill, 1960. (a).

Berlyne, D. E. Les équivalences psychologiques et les notions quantitatives. In D. E. Berlyne and J. Piaget, *Théorie du comportement et opérations.* (*Etudes d' Epistém. Génét.,* XII). Paris Press Universitaires de France, 1960. (b)

Berlyne, D. E. Motivational problems rainsed by exploratory and epistemic behavior. In S. Koch (Ed.), *Psychology: a study of a science.* Vol. 5. New York: McGraw-Hill, 1963.

Berlyne, D. E. *Structure and direction in thinking.* New York: Wiley, 1965. (a)

Berlyne, D. E. Curiosity and education. In J. D. Krumboltz (Ed.), *Learning and the educational process.* Chicago: Rand-McNally, 1965. (b)

Berlyne, D. E. The delimitation of cognitive development. *Monogr. Soc. Res. Child Dev.,* 1966, **107**, 71–81. (a)

Berlyne, D. E. Curiosity and exploration. *Science,* 1966, **153**, 25–33. (b)

Berlyne, D. E. Laughter, humor and play. In G. Lindzey and E. Aronson (Eds.), *Handbook of social psychology.* (2nd ed.) Cambridge, Mass.: Addison Wesley, 1969.

Berlyne, D. E., and Frommer, F. D. Some determinants of the incidence and content of children's questions. *Child Dev.,* 1966, **37**, 177–189.

Blank, S. S., and Covington, M. Inducing children to ask questions in solving problems *J. educ. Res.,* 1966, **59**, 21–27.

Boiko, E. I. [On the mechanisms of intellectual processes.] *Vop. Psikhol.,* 1955, No. 6, 39–71.

Boiko, E. I. [The interaction of conditioned-reflex processes in complex systematic reactions.] In *Voprosy izucheniia vysshei neirodinamiki v sviazi s problemami psikhologii.* Moscow: Acad. Pedag. Sci., 1957. [*Studies in higher neurody-*

namics as related to problems of psychology. Washington: OTS 60–21168, U. S. Dept. of Commerce, 1961]

Boiko, E. I. *Pogranichnye problemy psikhologii i fiziologii* [*Borderline problems of psychology and physiology*]. Moscow Acad. Pedag. Sci., 1961.

Braine, M. D. S. The ontogeny of certain logical operations: Piaget's formulation examined by non-verbal methods. *Psychol. Monogr.*, 1959, **73**, 43pp.

Brogden, W. J. Unconditioned stimulus substitutions in the conditioning process. *Am. J. Psychol.*, 1939, **52**, 46–55.

Bruner, J. S. The course of cognitive growth. *Am. Psychol.*, 1964, **19**, 1–15.

Bruner, J. S. On cognitive growth: I. In J. S. Bruner et al., *Studies in cognitive growth*. New York: Wiley, 1966.

Bruner, J. S. *Toward a theory of instruction*. Boston, Mass.: Belknap Press, 1966.

Bruner, J. S., and Kenney, H. J. On multiple ordering. In J. S. Bruner et al., *Studies in cognitive growth*. New York: Wiley, 1966.

Bühler, C. *Soziologische und psychologische Studien über das erste Lebensjahr.* Jena: Fischer, 1927.

Buhler, K. *Die geistige Entwicklung des Kindes.* (6th ed.) Jena: Fischer, 1930.

Cantor, G. N. Responses of infants and children to complex and novel stimulation. In L. P. Lipsitt and C. C. Spiker (Eds.), *Advances in child development and behavior.* Vol. 1. New York: Academic Press, 1963.

Case, D., and Collinson, J. M. The development of formal thinking in verbal comprehension. *Br. J. educ. Psychol.*, 1962, **32**, 103–111.

Covington, M. V., and Crutchfield, R. J. Experiments in the use of programed instruction for the facilitation of creative problem solving. *Programed Instruction*, 1965, **4**, (4), 3–5; 10.

Cowan, P. A. A developmental study of logical transformations. Unpublished doctoral thesis, University of Toronto, 1963.

Crutchfield, R. S. Sensitization and activation of cognitive skills. In J. S. Bruner (Ed.), *Learning about learning: a conference report.* Washington: U. S. Office of Education (Co-operative Research Monograph 16), 1966.

Davis, E. A. The form and function of children's questions. *Child Dev.*, 1932, **3**, 57–74.

Dollard, J., and Miller, N. E. *Personality and psychotherapy.* New York: McGraw-Hill, 1950.

Donaldson, M. *A study of children's thinking.* London: Tavistock, 1963.

El'konin, D. B. *Detskaia psikhologiia.* [*Child psychology*] Moscow: Uchpedgiz, 1960.

Eriksen, C. W. A study of awareness and its effects on learning and generalization. *J. Personality*, 1960, **28**, 503–517.

Ervin, Susan M. Experimental procedures of children. *Child Dev.*, 1960, **31**, 703–719.

Fahey, G. L. The questioning activity of children. *J. gen. Psychol.*, 1942, **60–61**, 337–357.

Freud, S. Triebe und Triebsschicksale. *Int. Z. ärztl. Psychoanal.*, 1951, 3, 84–100. [Instincts and their vicissitudes. In S. Freud, *Collected Papers*, Vol. 4. London: Hogarth, 1925.]

Gal'perin, P. I. [An experimental study in the formation of mental actions.] In *Doklady na soveshchanii po voprosam psikhologii* [*Reports of conference on psychological questions*]. Moscow: Acad. Pedag. Sci., 1954. [Translation in B. Simon (Ed.), *Psychology in the Soviet Union.* Stanford, Calif.: Stanford University Press, 1957.]

Garner, W. R., and McGill, W. J. The relation between information and variance analyses. *Psychometrika*, 1956, **21**, 219–228.

Goustard, M., Gréco, P., Matalon, B., and Piaget, J. *La logique des apprentissages* (*Etudes d'Epistém. Génét.*, X). Paris: Presses Universitaires de France, 1959.

Gréco, P., and Piaget, J. *Apprentissage et connaissance* (*Etudes d'Epistém, Génét.*, VII). Paris: Press Universitaires de France, 1959.

Guilford, J. P. The structure of intellect. *Psychol. Bull.*, 1956, **57**, 267–293.

Guilford, J. P. *The nature of human intelligence.* New York: McGraw-Hill, 1967.

Halpern, E. The effects of incompatibility between perception and logic in Piaget's stage of concrete operations. *Child Dev.*, 1965, **36**, 491–497.

Harter, G. L. Overt trial and error in the problem solving of preschool children. *J. genet. Psychol.*, 1930, **38**, 361–372.

Hilgard, E. R., and Marquis, D. G. *Conditioning and learning.* New York: Appleton-Century, 1940.

Hudgins, C. V. Conditioning and the voluntary control of the pupillary light reflex. *J. genet. Psychol.*, 1933, **8**, 3–51.

Hull, C. L. Knowledge and purpose as habit mechanisms. *Psychol. Rev.*, 1930, **37**, 511–525.

Hull, C. L. Goal attraction and directing ideas conceived as habit phenomena. *Psychol. Rev.*, 1931, **38**, 487–506.

Hull, C. L. The mechanism of the assembly of behavior segments in novel combinations suitable for problem solution. *Psychol. Rev.*, 1935, **42**, 219–245.

Hull, C. L. *Principles of behavior: an introduction to behavior theory.* New York: Appleton-Century, 1943.

Hull, C. L. *A behavior system; an introduction to behavior theory concerning the individual organism.* New Haven, Conn.: Yale University Press, 1952.

Humphrey, G. *Thinking.* London Methuen: New York: Wiley, 1951.

Hutt, C. Exploration and play in children. *Symp. zool. Soc. Lon.*, 1966, **18**, 61–81.

Iakobleva, S. V. [Conditions of formation of the simplest forms of voluntary action in children of preschool age.] In A. R. Luriia (Ed.), *Problemy vysshei nervnoi deiatel'nosti normal'nogo i anomal' nogo rebenka* [*Problems of higher nervous activity in the normal and abnormal child*]. Moscow: Acad. Pedag. Sci., 1958.

Inhelder, B., and Piaget, J. *De la logique de l'enfant à la logique de l'adolescent.* Paris: Press Universitaires de France, 1955. [*The growth of logical thinking from childhood to adolescence.* New York: Basic Books, 1958.]

Isaacs, N. Children's "why" questions. In S. Isaacs, *Intellectual growth in young children.* London: Routledge, 1930.

Ivanov-Smolenski, A. G. (Ed.) *Na puti k izucheniiu vysshikh form neirodinamiki rebenka* [*Towards the study of higher forms of neurodynamics in the child*]. Moscow: Medgiz, 1934.

Ivanov-Smolenski, A. G. [On the interaction of the first and second signal systems in some physiological and pathological conditions.] *Fiziol. Zh. SSSR*, 1949, **35**, 271–281.

Ivanov-Smolenski, A. G. [On the study of the joint operation of the first and second signal systems of the brain.] *Zh. vys. nerv. deiat.* 1951, **1** (1), 55–66.

Ivanov-Smolenski, A. G. *Opyt ob'ektivnogo izucheniia raboty i vzaimodeistviia signal'nykh sistem golovnogo mozga (v norme i patologii)* [*An attempt at objective study of the operation and interaction of the signal systems of the brain (in normality and pathology)*]. Moscow: State publishing House for Medical Literature, 1963.

James, W. *Principles of psychology.* New York: Holt, 1890.

Kendler, H. H., and Kendler, T. S. Inferential behavior in preschool children. *J. exp. Psychol.*, 1956, **51**, 311–314.

Kendler, H. H., Kendler, T. S., Pliskoff, S. S., and D'Amato, M.F. Inferential behavior in children: I. The influence of reinforcement and incentive motivation. *J. exp. Psychol.*, 1958, **55**, 207–212.

Kendler, T. S., and Kendler, H. H. Inferential behavior in children: II. The influence of order of presentation. *J. exp. Psychol.*, 1961, **61**, 442–448.

Kendler, T. S., and Kendler, H. H. Inferential behavior in children as a function of age and subgoal constancy. *J. exp. Psychol.*, 1962, **64**, 460–466.

Kendler, T. S., Kendler, M. M., and Carrick, M. Verbal labels and inferential problem solution of children. *Child Dev.*, 1966, **37**, 749–763.

Koffka, K. *Principles of Gestalt psychology.* New York: Harcourt, Brace, 1935.

Köhler, W. *Intelligenzprüfungen an Menschenaffen.* Berlin: Springer, 1921. [*The mentality of apes.* New York: Harcourt, Brace, 1925.]

Konorski, J. *The integrative activity of the brain.* Chicago: University of Chicago Press, 1967.

Kupalov, P. S. *Situatsionnye uslovnye refleksy u sobak v norme i patologii* [Situational conditioned reflexes in normality and pathology]. Moscow: Meditsina, 1964.

Landa, L. N. [Formation of a general method of thinking activity for solving problems in pupils.] *Vop. Psikhol.*, 1959, **5**(3), 14–27.

Landa, L. N. [Training pupils in the methods of rational thinking and problem of algorithms.] *Vop. Psikhol.*, 1961, **7**(1), 103–118.

Landa, N. L. [An experiment on the application of mathematical logic and information theory to several problems of teaching]. *Vop. Psikhol.*, 1962, **8**,(2), 19–40.

Leont'ev, A. N. *Problemy razvitiia psikhiki* [*Problems of the development of the mind*]. Moscow: Mysl', 1959.

Lewis, M., Kagan, J., and Kalafat, J. Patterns of fixation in the young infant. *Child Dev.*, 1966, **37**, 331–341.

Lisina, M. L. [The role of orientation in the conversion of involuntary into voluntary reactions.] In L. G. Voronin et al., (Eds.), *Orientirovochny refleksi i orientirovochno-issledovatel'skaia deiatelnost'. [The orienting reflex and exploratory behavior]*. Moscow: Acad. Pedag. Sci., 1958.

Liublinskaia, A. N. [Causal thinking in the acting child.] *Izvestiia Akad. Pedag. Nauk. RSFSR*, 1948, No. 17.

Lore, R. K. Some factors influencing the child's exploration of visual stimuli. Unpublished doctoral thesis, University of Tennessee, 1965.

Lovell, K. A follow-up study of Inhelder and Piaget's "The growth of logical thinking." *Br. J. Psychol.*, 1961, **52**, 143–153.

Lunzer, E. A. Problems of formal reasoning in test situation. *Monogr. Soc. Res. Child Dev.*, 1965, **30**, 19–43.

Luria, A. R. [On the regulatory role of speech in the formation of voluntary movements.] *Zh. vys. nerv. deiat.*, 1956, **6**, 641–662.

Luria, A. R. [The role of speech in the regulation of normal and abnormal behavior.] In A. R. Luria (Ed.), *Problemy vysshei nervnykh deiatel'nosti normal'nogo i anomal'nogo rebenka [Problems of higher nervous activity in the normal and abnormal child]*. Vol. II. Moscow: Acad. Pedag. Sci., 1958.

Luria, A. R. The directive function of speech in development and dissolution. *Word*, 1959, **15**, 341–352; 453–464.

Luria, A. R. *The role of speech in the regulation of normal and abnormal behavior.* New York: Liveright, 1961.

Luria, A. R., and Poliakova, A. G. [Observations on the development of voluntary action in early childhood. I. The execution of oral instructions in the early stages of the development of the child.] *Doklady Akad. Pedag. Nauk. RSFSR.* 1959, **3**, 75–80.

Luria, A. R., and Rozanova, V. A. [Observations on the development of voluntary action in early childhood. III. On the formation of the orienting role of speech in children of preschool age.] *Doklady Akad. Pedag. Nauk. RSFSR.* 1959, **6**, 59–62.

Mackworth, N. H. Originality. *Am. Psychol.*, 1965, **20**, 51–66.

Maier, N. R. F. Reasoning in children. *J. comp. Psychol.*, 1936, **21**, 357–366.

Maier, N. R. F. Reasoning in white rats. *Comp. Psychol. Monogr.*, 1929. **6**, No. 93.

Maier, N. R. F., and Schneirla, T. C. *Principles of animal psychology.* New York: McGraw-Hill, 1935.

Matheson, E. A study of problem solving behavior in pre-school children. *Child Dev.*, 1931, **2**, 242–262.

McCarthy, D. *Language development of the pre-school child.* Minneapolis: Univ. Minn. Inst. Child Welfare (Monogr. Ser. No. 4), 1930.

McLaughlin, G. H. Psychologic: A possible alternative to Piaget's formulation. *Br. J. educ. Psychol.*, 1963, **33**, 61–67.

Mead, G. H. *Mind self and society.* Chicago: University of Chicago Press, 1934.

Miller, N. E. Experiments relevant to learning theory and psychopathology. Lecture to XVIII International Congress of Psychology. Moscow, 1966.

Miller, N. E. Some reflections on the law of effect produce a new alternative to drive reduction. In D. Levine (Ed.), *Nebraska symposium on motivation, 1963.* Lincoln.: University of Nebraska Press, 1963.

Miller, N. E., and Dollard, J. *Social learning and imitation.* New Haven, Conn.: Yale University Press, 1941.

Miller, S., and Konorski, J. Sur une forme particulière des réflexes conditionnels *C.R. Soc. Biol., Paris,* 1928, **99**, 1155–1157.

Minskaia, G. I. [The transition from visuo-active to rational thought.] Unpublished candidate's thesis, Moscow State University, 1954.

Mogar, M. Children's causal reasoning about natural phenomena. *Child Dev.*, 1960, **31**, 59–65.

Morris, C. R. *Signs, language and behavior.* Englewood Cliffs,: N. J. Prentice-Hall, 1946.

Morris, C. R. *Signification and sgnificance.* Cambridge, Mass.: MIT Press, 1964.

Mosher, F. A., and Hornsby, J. R. On asking questions. In J. S. Bruner et al., *Studies in cognitive growth.* New York: Wiley, 1966.

Mowrer, O. H. *Learning theory and personality dynamics.* New York: Ronald Press, 1950.

Mowrer, O. H. The psychologist looks at language. *Am. Psychol.*, 1954, **9**, 660–694.

Nassefat, M. *Étude quantitative sur l'évolution des opérations intellectuelles.* Neuchâtel: Delachaux & Niestlé, 1963.

Nepomniashchaia, N. I. [The structure of voluntary activity in children of preschool age.] In A. V. Zaporozhets and I. Z. Neverovich (Eds.), *Razvitie poznavatel'nykh i volevykh protsessov u doshkol'nikov [The development of cognitive and volitional processes in preschool children].* Moscow: Prosveshchenie, 1965.

Ogden, C. K., and Richards, I. A. *The meaning of meaning.* New York: Harcourt, Brace, 1923.

Olson, D. R. On conceptual strategies. In J. S. Bruner et al., *Studies in cognitive growth.* New York: Wiley, 1966.

Osgood, C. E. The nature and measurement of meaning. *Psychol. Bull.*, 1952, **49**, 197–237.

Osgood, C. E. *Method and theory in experimental psychology.* New York: Oxford University Press, 1953.

Paramanova, N. P. [On the formation of the interaction of the two signal systems in the normal child.] In A. R. Luria (Ed.), *Problemy vysshei nervnoi dei-atel'nosti normal'nogo i anomal'nogo rebenka* [*Problems of higher nervous activity in the normal and abnormal child*]. Vol. I. Moscow: Acad. Pedag. Sci., 1956.

Parsons, C. Inhelder and Piaget's, "The growth of logical thinking." II. A logician's viewpoint. *Br. J. Psychol.*, 1960, 51, 75–84.

Pavlov, I. P. The reply of a physiologist to psychologists. *Psychol. Rev.*, 1932, 39, 81–127.

Piaget, J. *Le language et la pensée chez l'enfant.* Neuchâtel Delachaux & Niestlé, 1923. [*The language and thought of the child.* New York: Harcourt, Brace, 1928.]

Piaget, J. *La construction du réel chez l'enfant.* Neuchâtel: Delachaux & Niestlé, 1937. [*The construction of reality in the child.* New York: Basic Books, 1954.]

Piaget, J. Le mécanisme du développement mental et les lois du groupement des opérations. *Arch. Psychol., Genève.* 1941, 28, 215–285.

Piaget, J. La formation du symbole chez l'enfant. Neuchâtel. Delachaux & Niestlé, 1945. [*Play, dreams and imitation in childhood.* New York: Norton, 1951.]

Piaget, J. *La psychologie de l'intelligence.* Paris: Colin, 1947. [*The psychology of intelligence.* London: Routledge & Kegan Paul, 1950.]

Piaget, J. Le problème neurologique de l'intériorisation des actions en opérations réversibles. *Arch. Psychol., Genève*, 1949, 32, 241–258.

Piaget, J. *Logic and psychology.* Manchester: Manchester University Press, 1953.

Piaget, J. Logique et équilibre dans les comportements du sujet. In L. Apostel, B. Mandelbrot, and J. Piaget, *Logique et équilibre.* (*Etudes d'Epistém. Génét., II*). Paris: Presses Universitaires de France, 1957.

Piaget, J. *Six psychological studies.* New York: Random House, 1967.

Piaget, J. and Inhelder, B. *La genèse des structures logiques élémentaires: classifications et sériations.* Neuchâtel: Delachaux & Niestlé, 1959. [*The early growth of logic in the child.* New York. Harper and Row, 1944.]

Piaget, J., and Inhelder, B. *L'image mentale chez l'enfant.* Paris: Press Universitaires de France, 1967.

Ranzi, A., and Tampieri, P. I fattori dello sviluppo del pensiero: "equilibrazione" e apprendimento. *Riv. Psicol. Soc.*, 1966, 13, 399–430.

Richardson, H. M. The growth of adaptive behavior in infants: an experimental study at seven age levels. *Genet. Psychol. Monogr.*, 1932, 12, 195–359.

Richardson, H. M. The adaptive behavior of infants in the utilization of the lever as a tool: a developmental and experimental study. *J. genet. Psychol.*, 1934, 44, 352–377.

Rubinshtein, S. L. *O myshlenii i putiakh ego issledovanii* [*On thinking and ways of investigating it*]. Moscow: Acad. Sci. USSR, 1958.

Rubinshtein, S. L. [The principle of determinism and the psychological theory of thinking.] In B. G. Ananev et al. (Eds.), *Psiklogicheskaia Nauka v SSSR.*, Vol. I. Moscow: Acad. Pedag. Sci., 1959. [Translation in *Psychological Science in the USSR.* Washington: U. S. Joint Publications Research Service. OTS: 62–11,083), 1961.]

Rubinshtein, S. L., (Ed.) *Protsess myshleniia i zakonomernosti analiza, sinteza i obobshcheniia* [*The thought process and the laws governing analysis, synthesis and generalization*]. Moscow: Acad. Sci. USSR, 1950.

Sechenov, I. M. [Elements of thought.] *Vestnik Evropy.*, 1878, 3, 39–107. [English translation in I. M. Sechenov, *Collected works.* Moscow and Leningrad: Medgiz, 1935.]

Skinner, B. F. *The behavior of organisms.* New York: Appleton-Century-Crofts, 1938.

Skinner, B. F. *Verbal behavior.* New York: Appleton-Century-Crofts, 1957.

Slavskaia, K. A. [The thought process and the utilization of knowledge.] In S. L. Rubinshtein (Ed.), *Protsess myshleniia i zakonomernosti analiza, sinteza i obobshcheniia* [*The thought process and the laws governing analysis, synthesis and generalization*]. Moscow: Acad. Sci. USSR, 1960.

Smedslund, J. The acquistion of conservation of substance and weight in children. I. Introduction. *Scand. J. Psychol.,* 1961, **2**, 11–20.

Smedslund, J. The acquisition of conservation of substance and weight in children. V. Practice in conflict situations without external reinforcement. *Scand. J. Psychol.,* 1961, **2**, 156–160.

Smedslund, J. The acquisition of conservation of substance and weight in children. VI. Practice on continuous versus discontinuous material in conflict situations without external reinforcement. *Scand. J. Psychol.,* 1961, **2**, 203–210.

Smedslund, J. The development of concrete transitivity of length in children. *Child Dev.,* 1963, **34**, 389–405.

Spearman, C. *The abilities of man.* New York: MacMillan, 1967.

Staats, A. W., and Staats, C. K. *Complex human behavior.* New York: Holt, Rinehart, and Winston, 1963.

Stern, W. *Psychogie der frühen Kindheit bis zum sechsten Lebensjahre.* Leipzig: Quelle & Meyer, 1914. [*Psychology of early childhood up to the sixth year of age.* London: Allen & Unwin, 1924.]

Stirling, M. E. An analysis of questions asked by a group of preschool children in a controlled setting. Unpublished M. A. thesis, University of Toronto, 1937.

Suchman, J. R. Training children in scientific inquiry. Paper read at Soc. Res. Child Dev., Bethesda, Md., 1959.

Suchman, J. R. Inquiry training: building skills for autonomous discovery. *Merrill-Palmer Quart.,* 1961, 147–169.

Suchman, J. R. The inquiry process and the elementary school child. Paper read to Amer. Educ. Res. Assoc., Atlantic City, N. J., 1962.

Suppes, P. On the behavioral foundations of mathematical concepts. In L. D. Morrisett and S. Vinsonhaler. *Monogr. Soc. Res. Child Dev.,* 1965, No. 99.

Suppes, P. Mathematical concept formation in children. *Am. Psychol.,* 1966, **21**, 139–150.

Thorndike, E. L. *Animal intelligence.* New York: Macmillan, 1898.

Thurstone, L. L. Primary mental abilities. *Psychometr. Monogr.,* 1938, No. 1.

Tikhomirov, O. K. [On the formation of voluntary movements in children of preschool age.] In A. R. Luria (Ed.), *Problemy vysshei nervnoi deiatel'nosti normal'nogo i anomal'nogo rebenka* [*Problems of higher nervous activity in the normal and abnormal child*]. Vol II. Moscow: Acad. Pedag. Sci., 1958.

Titchener, E. B. *Lectures on the experimental psychology of the thought processes.* New York: Macmillan, 1909.

Tolman, E. C. *Purposive behavior in animals and men.* New York: Appleton-Century, 1932.

Ul'enkova, U. B. [The psychology of deductive syllogisms in preschool children.] Unpublished candidate's dissertation, State University of Moscow, 1954.

Underwood, B. J. An orientation for research on thinking. *Psychol. Rev.,* 1952, **59**, 209–220.

Vatsuro, E. G. [An investigation of higher nervous activity in an ape (chimpanzee).] Moscow: Acad. Med. Sci., USSR., 1948.

Vygotski, L. S. *Mishlenie i rech* [Thought and speech]. Moscow: Giz, 1934. [*Thought and language*: Cambridge, Mass.: MIT Press; New York: Wiley, 1962].

Vygotski, L. S. *Razvitie vysshikh psikhicheskikh funktsii* [*The development of higher mental functions*]. Moscow: Acad. Pedag. Sci., 1960.

Wallach, L. On the basis of conservation. In J. H. Flavell and D. Elkind (Eds.), *Piaget Festschrift*. Oxford University Press (in press).

Washburn, M. F. *The animal mind*. New York: Macmillan, 1926.

Watson, S. B. *Behaviorism*. Chicago: University of Chicago Press, 1924.

Werner, H., and Kaplan, B. *Symbol formation: an organismic developmental approach*. New York: Wiley, 1963.

Yamamoto, K. Development of ability to ask questions under specific testing conditions. *J. genet. Psychol.*, 1962, **101**, 83–90.

Zaporozhets, A. V. [The role of orienting activity and the image in the formation and persistence of voluntary movements.] In L. G. Voronin et al. (Eds.), *Orientirovochny reflex i orientirovochno-issledovatel'skaiá deiatel'nost' [The orienting reflex and exploratory behavior]*. Moscow: Acad. Pedag. Sci., 1958.

Zaporozhets, A. V. *Razvitié proizvol'nykh dvizhenii [The development of voluntary movements]*. Moscow: Acad. Pedag. Sci., 1960.

Zaporozhets, A. V. [The development of thinking.] In A. V. Zaporozhets and D. B. El'konin (Eds.), *Psikhologiia detei doshkol'nogo vozrasta [The psychology of preschool children]*. Moscow: Proveschenie, 1964.

Zhukova, I. M. [The role of analysis and generalization in cognitive activity.] In S. L. Rubinshtein (Ed.), *Protsess myshleniia i zakonomernosti analiza, sinteza i obobshcheniia [The thought process and the laws governing analysis, synthesis and generalization]*. Moscow: Acad. Sci. USSR, 1960.

14. Concept Development

JOHN H. FLAVELL[*]

CONCEPTS

The search for a satisfactory definition of the term "concept" is a lexicographer's nightmare. Like its complex and elusive instances —"art," "life," "religion," etc.—this concept seems to defy all attempts at adequate epitomization. There have been many such attempts, of course; nearly all writers who treat the topic begin with some sort of definition (e.g., Bruner, Goodnow, and Austin, 1956; Carroll, 1964; Harvey, Hunt, and Schroder, 1961; Hunt, 1962; Kendler, 1961; Klausmeier et al., 1965; Langer, 1948; Russell, 1956; Sigel, 1964; Vinacke, 1952). The various characterizations are far from identical, needless to say, and after pondering on them for a while the reader is tempted to think that their most important similarity is their common inadequacy. Each one leaves the reader with a sense that something has been omitted, distorted, or oversimplified—that something he intuitively feels to be true of at least some concepts has simply not been captured.

After further pondering he begins to suspect where the trouble lies. First, the array of entities that have been or could be included under the rubric "concept" is truly extraordinary. Second, a search for attributes common to this array gives meager returns: the

number of attributes is small; their applicability to the entire array is often dubious; the insight they give into the essential nature of concepts is frequently uncertain. Third, and in contrast, these entities differ from one another in an astonishing number of ways; the dissimilarities are, in fact, far more striking, clear-cut, and important-looking than the similarities.

Given this preponderance of differences over similarities, it is little wonder that the definitional enterprise has been so difficult, and its outcome so universally unsatisfactory. But if The Concept cannot be tightly defined, the concepts can certainly be described and discussed with profit. It is very instructive to look at putative similarities among concepts and see what problems emerge; it is probably even more instructive to examine some of the important differences, because the richer story lies there. Concepts are usually regarded as the fabric of mental life. It is not surprising, after all, to learn that the former is as complex and baffling a notion as the latter, and just as resistant to easy characterization.

Similarities among Concepts

Concepts as Equivalence Responses. One of the most serious contenders for the status of common attribute here is the notion of equivalence response. The argument is that all concepts imply similar or identical reactions to different environmental inputs. Kendler actually goes so far as to define concepts entirely in terms of "a common response to dissimilar stimuli" (1961, p. 447). This view of the nature of concepts leads to further assertions of considerable importance. For one thing, it explicitly locates concepts in orga-

[*] The author wishes to express his deepest appreciation to Samuel R. Cannizzo, Marvin W. Daehler, Terry G. Halwes, Barbara E. Moely, and Frances Wynns Knudtson for their bibliographic assistance in the preparation of this chapter. He is also much indebted to Joachim F. Wohlwill for his invaluable contributions to the ideas (at least the better ones!) presented in the final section on general issues.

nisms rather than in their external milieus. Carroll (1964) has observed that there could be no concepts in a totally inorganic world because they are "properties of organismic experience" (p. 180). In addition, this view indicates a semantic connection between "concept" and such terms as "class," "category," and "set," inasmuch as the latter also imply, psychologically speaking, an act of colligation or drawing-together of disparate elements for response purposes. Furthermore, it is always assumed that the organism has an organized network of such equivalence responses, and this implies discrimination as well as generalization. That is, the individual makes one response to one set of inputs, a different response to a second set, and so on.

The concept repertoire serves in this way to carve up or "chunk" the organism's entire world into functional units, yielding a complete mapping of responses into stimulus sets for the length and breadth of the psychological environment. Harvey, Hunt, and Schroder well describe, in the case of human organisms, this structuring-of-the-world function of concepts:

We assume that an individual interacts with his environment by breaking it down and organizing it into meaningful patterns congruent with his own needs and psychological make-up. As a result of this interchange, perceptual and behavioral constancies develop, which stem from the individual's standardized evaluative predilections toward differentiated aspects of his external world. We will refer to such evaluation tendencies as *concepts*. . . . A concept is a system of ordering that serves as the mediating linkage between the input side (stimuli) and the output side (response). In operating as a system of ordering, a concept may be viewed as a categorical schema, an intervening medium, or program through which impinging stimuli are coded, passed, or evaluated on their way to response evocation (1961, p. 1).

And further:

Once a concept develops, it serves as an experiential filter through which impinging events are screened, gauged, and evaluated, a process that determines in large part what responses can and will occur (pp. 2–3).

Difficulties in identifying concepts with equivalence responses. There appear to be two problems in defining concepts as equivalence responses. First, it is uncertain whether all concepts literally entail equivalence responses and, more generally, whether a description in terms of "equivalence" and "response" always gets to the heart of what is really involved in concept making and concept using. Second, it is similarly questionable whether all reactions which are indisputably equivalence responses are equally indisputably concepts.

For the first, the following statements seem to be true of at least some prima facie concepts: (1) the concept need not be acquired at all; (2) if acquired, it need not be acquired through a process of successive common responding to the different relevant objects; (3) there may in fact be only one such object to which the concept can apply, and hence the "equivalence" part of the characterization is not literally applicable.

1. A given organism may be genetically programmed to respond in a certain way to a specific set of inputs. There would be some discomfort, however, in asserting that it does not possess this "concept" prior to actually making the response across the stimulus set in question, that is, the assertion that the concept *is* the equivalence response seems forced.

2. I may acquire a given concept without constructing it from successive contacts with the relevant instances. I may, for example, attain an impeccable concept of "centaur" without ever "responding" to a set of pictures of centaurs, and would certainly have to do so without contact with instances of the real article. Again, an identification of concept and actual responses to concept instances seems unwarranted.

3. When the first wheel (or automobile, or digital computer, . . .) was built, there was by definition only one concept instance; there was and always will be but one exemplar of constructs like "Minoan Civilization." Some will recoil before the prospect of saying that the inventor of the wheel could not have a concept of one until a second was built, or that "Minoan Civilization" simply can never be a concept because it has no plural.

It is not argued that the notion of equivalence response cannot be made to apply in such cases, especially if it is liberalized to include response "dispositions" and "potential" equivalences. The animal, of course, could and certainly would make its innate response to the relevant stimulus set, given the opportunity; my concept of "centaur" would presumably allow me to "respond appropriately," should I chance to encounter such a creature; and the specialist could doubtless identify new instances of that ancient civilization as such, were these instances somehow to be created for him. The point is rather an uncertainty of how far the notion brings us in understanding how people, in particular, develop and utilize concepts. That they can and do use them to order and collectivize real sensory input is undeniable. The question is to what extent they do other, perhaps more important, things with and to their store of concepts, especially in the *absence* of any sensory input regarding concept instances.

The second difficulty with the criterion of equivalence response is that it buys us some "concepts" we may not want to pay for. I respond to all members of one diverse class of stimuli by sneezing; any member of another group of inputs makes me drowsy. Certain fish react by fighting all and only those intruders into its territory who bear certain markings. Indeed, even plants make what are essentially invariant responses to variant inputs. These and many other humble reactions appear to fit the definition of equivalence response, but most people would be loathe to apply the designation "concept" to them. Actually, it is difficult to avoid the conclusion that equivalence responses are intimately involved in adaptational patterns at all biological levels, and that identifying concepts with such responses virtually makes them synonymous with biological adaptation itself. To paraphrase Carroll, perhaps there could be no organic life without equivalence responses, as well as no concepts without organisms.

The only escape from this difficulty would be to restrict further the definition of a concept by adding new criterial attributes. Concepts would then be construed as but one species of equivalence response, a species whose special properties sharply distinguish it from other, nonconceptual equivalence responses. But what might these special properties be? The writer, for one, has been unable to find any satisfactory conjunction or disjunction of additional attributes that would delimit the class in an intuitively satisfying way.

One can, of course, always impose *arbitrary* criteria for one purpose or another—simply to constrain the behavioral domain one wants to investigate, for instance. Thus Hunt (1962) excludes all infrahuman equivalence responses from his definition of a concept for just this reason. What seems to be lacking so far is a *principled* distinction, one that suggests fundamental differences in process and mechanism between those equivalence responses we wish to call "conceptual" and all other kinds. While such a distinction may emerge when we learn more about these processes and mechanisms, none seems available at present.

Functional Similarities among Concepts. It is plain, then, that all problems in the conceptualization of concepts are not resolved by appeals to the notion of equivalence response. At the same time, there is obviously something of value in looking at concepts from this point of view. Concepts *do* serve to partition the subject's world into functional units, as nearly everyone has suggested. Moreover, interpreting concepts as equivalence responses leads to some plausible guesses about their adaptational values, about what they accomplish for the organism. That is, the selection of equivalence response as a formal similarity facilitates the identification of some likely functional similarities as well.

Bruner, Goodnow, and Austin (1956) have described several properties of this kind. First and foremost, concepts have the absolutely essential function of reducing the complexity of sensory input to manageable proportions. As they put it, "categorization serves to cut down the diversity of objects and events that must be dealt with uniquely by an organism of limited capacities" (p. 245). This simplification function has important consequences. For one thing, it allows the organism a viable economy of time and effort in dealing with the world. Old and new inputs alike usually can be quickly identified and appropriately reacted to by virtue of being assimilable to existing concepts. For another, it leads to the possibility of a highly adaptive anticipation of future events from present events. To know that a perceived object is an instance of a particular class is to know a great deal else that is not immediately perceptible: it is to know virtually all that it could do to you or you to it, because this information is implied in its class membership:

It is this future-oriented aspect of categorizing behavior in all organisms that impresses us most. It is not simply that organisms code the events of their environment into equivalence classes, but that they utilize cues for doing so that allow an opportunity for prior adjustment to the event identified (Bruner, Goodnow, and Austin, 1956, p. 14).

We . . . regard a concept as a network of sign-significate inferences by which one goes beyond a set of observed criterial properties exhibited by an object or event to the class identity of the object or event in question, and then to additional inferences about other *unobserved* properties of the object or event (*ibid.*, p. 244).

In sum, concepts perform a dual service: (1) they identify and classify input information; (2) they make it possible for the organism to "go beyond the information given" in all manner of adaptive ways. As Klausmeier et al. (1965) state:

Concepts serve two main functions in human behavior: as responses to objects and events by which they are classified and categorized, and as mediators between stimulating events and subsequent behavior (p. 5).

Conceptual Systems. There is one further property which surely characterizes all "higher-order" equivalence responses—at least, that is, all responses everyone would be comfortable in calling "concepts": the contents of the individual's conceptual repertoire are complexly interrelated to form conceptual systems. The defining attributes of one concept will themselves consist of other concepts, and that concept will in turn assist in the definition of still others. The easiest way to gain a sense of the extreme interconnectedness of concepts is to thumb through a dictionary. Most dictionary entries refer to concepts, and these concepts are of course always defined in terms of other concepts. Moreover, concepts make important mental liaisons with others which do not form their definitional

base, as every student of word association processes knows. In general, about the most certain prediction one can make regarding the psychological activation of any concept is that numerous others will be immediately activated in consequence. It is the fact that concepts are functionally interlocked to form complex systems, which gives the temporal flow of most thinking its smooth, continuous, and effortless quality.

The argument was made earlier that an equivalence-response characterization of concepts fails to convey all that we sense to be important about them. One thing it fails to convey is this extraordinary interdependence among concepts. Not only does the subject map sensory inputs into concepts, he also goes on to relate these concepts to numerous others. All things considered, it is not surprising that Harvey, Hunt, and Schroder (1961) could write an entire book about conceptual systems.

Differences among Concepts

The diversity found in the realm of concepts is of two, roughly distinguishable sorts. First, there is variation associated with concepts taken in their public, consensually valid aspect. Although concepts are fundamentally private, cognitive phenomena, they of course can be and are externalized as social objects, and agreement can often be reached as to what their exact, "correct" meaning should be. Susanne Langer had this public and external face of the concept in mind when she defined it as "that which all adequate *conceptions* [i.e., private and internal conceptual acts] of an object have in common" (1948, p. 58, our italics and insertion). In other words, it is possible to look upon concepts as detached, ideal entities, unrelated to any individual's living cognitive experiences, and to discern a number of dimensions on which these entities vary.

In addition to this variation in the nature of concepts taken per se, there are also differences in their relation to the individuals who use them. Knowing that a given concept, as a public entity, has certain attributes does not tell me what it means to you, how you represent it to yourself, how and under what conditions you can access and utilize it—in short, its role and status in your cognitive life. Just as concepts differ among themselves, so also do individuals differ in the way they apprehend, use, and otherwise "relate to" any given concept. Since this chapter is concerned with concept *development,* variations in the subject-concept relation among different individuals (younger versus older children) is of considerable interest.

Variation in Concepts. One of the best available treatments of how concepts differ is given in Klausmeier et al. (1965); the classification given below is derived in part from their analysis. It will become apparent that the dimensions proposed are not the only ones possible, nor are they entirely independent from one another; they do, however, collectively give a fair image of the heterogeneity of concepts.

1. Attributes. An object of perception or thought constitutes an instance of a well-defined concept if and only if it possesses the set of attributes given in the definition of that concept. Instances of the concept will invariably possess other, nondefining attributes as well. Some of these will characterize all the instances, just as the defining attributes do; others will characterize a greater or lesser portion, that is, they will be correlated at some level with the presence of an instance. For example, all mammals have hair and bones, and most are terrestrial, yet only the first of these three attributes is "criterial" for that class of animal. Noncriterial as well as criterial properties serve as cues for categorizing objects, however. I may be too far away from an animal to see whether it has hair or not, but I can still make an educated guess that it is a mammal from other, noncriterial cues (such as the region I am in, the animal's general shape and size, and the fact that I see it moving along the ground).

The attributes, criterial and noncriterial, associated with instance identification and concept use are a most heterogeneous lot. Literally anything that human beings are able to perceive or intellectually construct can serve as a conceptual attribute (recall the earlier remark that concepts have other concepts as their defining properties). An attribute may, for example, be some perceptible or measurable physical property of the instance, such as its color, texture, and composition. These are properties that generally come to mind in thinking about the criterial attributes of concept instances. But there are other attributes, increasingly less concrete, immediate, palpable, and "intrinsic" (Klausmeier et al., 1965, p. 4) than these familiar prototypes. A large and ill-bounded group of attributes refers to function and activity rather than structure, to potentiality rather than actuality. Objects are not only "red," "smooth," "tall," etc., but also "edible," "combustible," "soluble," and the like. We categorize objects not only in terms of their immediate, static properties but also in terms of nonimmediate, "transformational" ones: what the object could do or become under certain circumstances; what we could do to or with it under certain circumstances.

There are other concept-defining attributes which "inhere" still less in the concept's instances. Careful examination of an object in isolation will permit the conclusion that it is "round," and even that it is "combustible," but no such analysis could serve to establish that it is a "nephew," a "logical conclusion," or a "best seller." The defining properties of many interesting concepts are less "attributes" in the literal sense than they are assertions regarding the role and status of their instances within some system of interrelated objects. One may have to know a whole complex of historical and current information about the object and its conceptual environment in order to determine that it is a member of certain types of class. As Jenkins has put it, certain concepts are best described as "constructs in general systems of relationships" (1966, p. 68).

2. Structure. The meaning of a concept includes not only its set of criterial attributes but also an assertion about how these attributes must be interrelated or combined in the concept definition. Bruner, Goodnow, and Austin (1956) have distinguished three types of combination—*conjunctive, disjunctive,* and *relational.* If two properties must both be present for the object to constitute an instance of the concept, the definitional structure is conjunctive (e.g., a "bachelor" must be *both* male *and* unmarried). If the presence of either attribute suffices, it is disjunctive (e.g., *either* extreme social withdrawal *or* delusional thinking may win you the diagnosis of "schizophrenic"). If the relationship between the attributes must be of a certain kind, the structure is relational (e.g., "equilateral triangle" refers only to those triangles whose sides are equal). Any one or combination of these three types of attribute pattern may obtain for a given concept.

The nature and complexity of concept structure varies a great deal from concept to concept. The conjunction of but two attributes suffices to define "bachelor." In contrast, the definitional structure of the legal concept "tort" is something like this (Carroll, 1964): $(A + B + C + D + E + F + G + H)$ $(I + J)(K)(-L)(-M)(-N)(-O)$, where the letters refer to attributes (each one itself a structurally complex concept, be it noted), the plus sign to disjunction, the parentheses to conjunction, and the minus sign to absence of. In the same notation, "bachelor" would be described as $(A)(B)$.

Notice that disjunction, in contrast to conjunction and relation, serves to unite what may be very different objects under the same conceptual roof. A batter can fail to get on base (be categorized as "out") in quite a variety of ways. We all are accustomed to thinking of concept instances as possessing "common attributes." It became evident in the preceding section, however, that the elements of a concept's definition are often "attributes" only in the loosest sense. And in the case of disjunction concepts, the modifier "common" is equally inexact and misleading.

3. Abstractness. A concept is said to be "concrete" to the extent that its instances are tangible objects, and "abstract" to the extent that they are not. Thus "dog" and "telephone" would be categorized as concrete concepts, whereas "eternity" and "democracy" are abstract ones. The view that concepts are made up of other concepts is nowhere more evident than in the case of such abstract entities: their components are entirely conceptual—attributes, instances, and all.

4. Inclusiveness. Concepts vary in the number of instances they include. A concept may have no instances ("Sumerian jet pilots"), a small number ("North American countries"), a large number ("grains of sand"), or an infinite number ("integers").

5. Generality. Concepts also vary in their position in the classification hierarchy to which they belong; the higher they are in the taxonomic tree, the more general they are. By this definition, "mountain gorilla" would constitute a very specific concept,

"mammal" a more general one, and "organism" a very general one.

6. Precision. A concept is "precise" to the extent that our present knowledge would allow us to agree upon an explicit and workable set of rules for distinguishing instances from noninstances. Some concepts are extremely precise by this standard, for example, "bachelor" and "equilateral triangle." Others, like "masterpiece," "schizophrenic," and "grammatical English sentence," are, by the same token, quite imprecise. Most workaday concepts fall somewhere in between, and are often less precise than one would have thought (try writing an effective set of identification rules for "tree" contrasted with "bush").

The fact that one cannot formulate an explicit set of identification rules for a given concept does not necessarily mean that the users of the concept cannot identify instances with fair precision and consistency; that is, our inability to explicate these rules does not mean that they are not somehow represented, in an inarticulate and implicit form, in the subject's psychological structure. A native speaker of English can quickly and effortlessly sort most strings of words into the two classes of grammatical/acceptable versus ungrammatical/unacceptable English sentences, but linguistic science cannot yet adequately formulate the rule system he is implicitly using when he does so (e.g., Chomsky, 1965). As a matter of fact, many of the most engaging research problems in the life sciences have to do with explicating some organism's "concepts"—with understanding the implicit rules that govern its invariant reactions to variant inputs.

7. Power. A concept is "powerful" if it satisfies two conditions: (a) most people would agree that the concept is, for some reason, an important and central one; (b) its attainment makes possible or facilitates the attainment of a number of other important concepts. Metaphors like "key," "cornerstone," and "building block" come to mind in connection with concepts of this sort, because of their special location and role within systems of interconnected concepts. This dimension is of particular interest to developmental psychologists and educators, since it has to do with concept acquisition. The child acquires a multitude of concepts as he grows, but not all of them point beyond themselves to important further acquisitions. While the attainment of a concept like "cat" may not be wholly without significance for the child's overall intellectual growth, it scarcely has the formative, development-impelling power of "permanent object" or "measurement unit." It is such powerful concepts whose attainment the developmentalist wants to understand and the educator to foster.

Variation in the Subject-Concept Relation.

1. Validity. Although a given concept may have a relatively constant and fixed public meaning, it is obvious that individuals may differ widely in their private conceptions of it. There are two major variations here. First, the subject's operating interpretation of the concept may deviate from the accepted interpretation on any of a number of dimensions. His category may be narrower than the standard, or broader, or some distortion of it (for instance, what might be termed a "partial concept" or a "pre-concept"). The concept has one more or less definite meaning and individuals have various different approximations of that meaning. On the other hand, the individual's concept may deviate from the standard in that its meaning is less definite and fixed than that of the standard. Thus not only may it differ in meaning from the standard, it may also differ in meaning for the individual himself from occasion to occasion.

Both types of departure from validity can be noted in the ontogenetic acquisition of concepts (and also, of course, in the "microgenesis" of much adult new learning). For instance, Piaget's studies indicate that the young child's concept of, say, quantity tends at once to be different from and more unstable than the adult prototype. Quantity is likely to have a unidimensional rather than tridimensional meaning for the child ("more" means "taller" only, or "wider" only), and it may also refer to one dimension (e.g., height) in certain situations and another dimension (e.g., width) in other situations. An understanding of how certain powerful concepts stabilize and converge on their public prototypes during childhood is a major objective in the study of concept development.

2. Status. It is ambiguous simply to say that someone "has" a certain concept, because concepts can be "had" in rather different ways. In particular, the concept may have only the status of a vehicle or instrument of adaptation, or it may also have in varying measure the status of a well-articulated and fully coded object of thought. An individual could not be said to have a concept if he could not in some sense think *with* it; he might well be said to have it, however, even though he could not in the slightest degree think *about* it. Thus the concept-user might have no name for or awareness of a given concept; or he might know its name without being able to characterize it further; or he might be a highly articulate authority on its full and exact meaning, its implications for all manner of things, and its place in whole systems of related concepts. Concept as cognitive object and concept as cognitive instrument are imperfectly correlated within individuals: if one has the former one is rather likely to have the latter, but the converse is hardly true—remember the earlier example, "grammatical English sentence." Children especially are very likely to "have"—that is, indisputably operate in terms of—concepts which they cannot name, let alone define and discuss.

3. Accessibility. The old distinction between learning and performance applies to concept usage: an individual may have acquired a concept (of whatever validity and status) and yet, for any of a variety of reasons, be unable to gain access to and use it on some given appropriate occasion. The distinction is between what one knows—timelessly, as it were—and what one can do in this or that immediate situation. The hiatus between learning and performance can vary across individuals for the same concept and also within an individual across concepts.

In summary, the subject-concept relation may vary in at least the following three ways: (*a*) the nature and degree of resemblance between the subject's private conception and the public, "standard" concept (validity); (*b*) the extent to which the concept can function as intellectual object as well as intellectual instrument (status); (*c*) the extent to which the concept is available for use on appropriate occasions (accessibility). Ontogenetic changes in validity have traditionally received the greatest research emphasis, but a full account of conceptual development ought to encompass changes in status and accessibility as well. In addition to being of intrinsic interest, the fact of these latter changes has implications for the assessment of validity. In trying to establish that a child has just recently acquired a certain concept (in final, adult form or in any more primitive form—the point is the same), the investigator may have to negotiate, as obstacles to his assessment attempts, the fact that the child may be utterly inarticulate about his concept and that he may also have trouble bringing it into active service in all but the most obvious and compelling situations. It is important to find out when the child first has a given concept "in some sense." But when a concept is newly minted and freshly attained, it is likely to be unformulated, precariously utilizable, and therefore difficult to diagnose (Flavell and Wohlwill, 1969).

CONCEPT DEVELOPMENT

The research literature on concept development has grown so large that no chapter-length survey can cover it fully. We therefore set priorities for which studies to highlight, which to cite briefly, and which to exclude altogether. It will become apparent that some studies have been excluded from this chapter because, although relevant to concept development, they are better treated elsewhere in this book. For the remainder, the writer's biases have led him to emphasize investigations of the following kinds:

1. The investigation attempts to track some substantial and enduring developmental modification in the child's conceptual program. Not all studies involving concepts and using children as subjects do this. Many concept-formation or concept-learning experiments, for example, seem to measure the child's ability to utilize some concept he has already attained rather than assess his level of conceptual development. Although such experiments can certainly illuminate the learning and problem-solving abilities of children at various ages, their contribution to our understanding of concept development itself is often less apparent.

2. The concept under study has some prima facie importance as a cognitive acquisition. It may have considerable "power" as an adaptational tool or as a developmental formative (see previous section). Or it may appear to be a cognitive-developmental "universal," that is, a concept that is probably acquired by all normal children in all societies.

3. The research gives evidence regarding some unexpected or surprising acquisition. It may never have occurred to us, perhaps, that the concept studied exists as an active, if implicit, component of the adult cognitive system. Or perhaps, knowing this, we are surprised to learn that the concept *needs* acquiring at all, that is, that young children typically do not possess it. Piaget's studies of the attainment of conservation concepts are examples of what is meant here.

4. The study sheds some light on the all-important problem of how the child makes cognitive progress, that is, concerning the mechanisms or processes underlying developmental movement. We know very little about the mechanisms of development at present, and any investigation that even touches on the problem has an immediate claim on our attention.

5. The study contributes something to a unified and integrated picture of conceptual development, in which various acquisitions are seen as functionally and temporally interconnected. The study may show, for example, how some concept slowly evolves through a succession of preliminary versions or preconcepts. Or it may illustrate how certain attainments pave the way for later ones, which then play the same developmental role for still others. Or it may show how a certain concept, once achieved, enters into the construction of a whole array of disparate-looking attainments. In all such cases, the evidence presented reduces our sense of the heterogeneity of development by relating one acquisition to another, within and across time periods.

6. Implicit in most of the preceding points, the investigation was cast within or can be related after the fact to some existing developmental theory or pretheory. The study can thereby find its place within a larger body of research evidence dealing with the same theory and its data can be given a fuller

and more coherent interpretation. Nowhere do facts without theory stand in lonelier isolation than in the area of concept development.

If the reader interprets this discussion as meaning that he is in for a chapter featuring research in the Piagetian mode, he is of course right. Other recent reviews of conceptual development (Sigel, 1964; Wallach, 1963) have done the same thing, doubtlessly for the same reason. The reason is simply that, in this decade, there is really no other choice. Piaget-related studies comprise a large proportion of the existing publications on concept development, and a still larger proportion of the interesting ones (by the criteria just given—or by any other reasonable criteria). Furthermore, his is the only comprehensive and detailed theoretical system presently available in this area. This system has generated all manner of empirical findings to replicate and extend, specific hypotheses to test, and general issues concerning the nature of development to ponder and to translate into researchable problems. A contemporary survey of conceptual development research without a Piagetian emphasis would reflect not merely coolness and disinterest but an outright and peevish animus against his approach. Whatever may have been true in the past, few psychologists bear any such animus today.

For those who wish to pursue the subject of concept development more deeply than we do here, there are several useful sources. Piaget has recently written good summaries of his own work, in this book and elsewhere (Piaget and Inhelder, 1963, 1966). Other surveys and evaluations of Piagetian theory, research, or both include those by Baldwin (1967), Elkind and Flavell (1969), Flavell (1963a, 1963b), Hunt (1961, 1963), Inhelder (1962), Lovell (1962), Lunzer (1959, 1960a), Sigel (1964), Sigel and Hooper (1968), Wallace (1965), Wallach (1963), and Wohlwill (1962, 1963, 1966a). Wallace's book in particular—probably not well known in the United States—provides excellent coverage of non-Genevan research on Piaget's theory up to 1963 or so. There have also been two published conferences devoted to his approach (Kessen and Kuhlman, 1962; Ripple and Rockcastle, 1964).

Sigel's review (1964) also describes non-Piagetian research on concept development, as do earlier surveys by Russell (1956), Vinacke (1952), and Werner (1948).

NORMATIVE-DESCRIPTIVE STUDIES OF CONCEPT DEVELOPMENT

THE LOGICAL AND MATHEMATICAL WORLD

Classes

In the first section of this chapter, it was asserted that the relationship between an individual and a concept may vary along the three dimensions of *validity*, *status*, and *accessibility*, and that this variation is partly a function of the individual's developmental level. Since "concept" and "class" are so closely related in meaning, these dimensions are especially pertinent to the present topic. We shall begin, then, by rephrasing aspects of these earlier remarks as they apply to a developmental analysis of classification behavior.

The entities called "classes" have a dual status in human cognition. One the one hand, they are usually regarded as essential ingredients of the thinking process itself. Particular classes are constantly being retrieved or constructed by the individual and pressed into service as conceptual vehicles or instruments. On the other hand, classes can also constitute abstract objects of thought. The individual may, in addition to utilizing particular classes in his everyday thinking, have explicit or implicit knowledge of the logical properties of classes and classification systems in general. The distinction here is between classes considered as cognitive tools and classes taken as the elements of a subject matter or body of knowledge—between the classes the subject knows and what he knows about classes.

Moreover, the classes available to the subject and the manner in which he can utilize them in thinking must depend, among other things, upon his grasp of the basic nature of classes and their interrelations. For instance, his ability really to understand and reason about the assertion that the object before him is at one and the same time a beagle, a dog, a mammal, and a living organism must depend in part upon his tacit understanding of how logical classes—these or any others—may interrelate in hierarchical systems. Of course, what the individual knows about classes-in-general—his "metaconceptual" knowledge, as it were—will not be the only determinant of the categories he favors or his favored use of them. A disposition toward concrete, loosely organized categories in a young child is not explainable solely on the basis of an inadequate grasp of classificatory logic. On the other hand, advances in his understanding of the abstract properties of class systems will surely be one of the necessary conditions for the later formation and skillful utilization of higher-level categories.

If one turns to the developmental literature, it immediately becomes apparent that there is virtually no study in any area of conceptual growth that could not be construed as relevant to the development of classes-qua-intellectual-instrument (Wallace, 1965, p. 178). The child obviously classifies and categorizes phenomena within each of the conceptual domains treated in this chapter—number, space, causality, etc.—and the nature and manner of utilization of these categories change with age. For instance, the assertion that animistic thinking decreases with age can be paraphrased as the assertion that the child's implicit definitions of the classes "living" and "not living" undergo developmental alteration. There are some things to be learned about the development of the class-as-instrument aspect of the subject-class relation from the literature conventionally associated with this topic, for example, dealing with children's behavior on sorting tasks, but the intimate relation between "class" and "concept" should warn the reader to look beyond this literature (and this chapter section) for the fuller picture. As for the classes-qua-intellectual-object aspect, the pertinent studies are somewhat easier to demarcate. This area has been the particular province of the Genevan group, although there is also a good deal of non-Genevan research which bears on it directly or indirectly. For other treatments of the classification-development literature, see Vinacke (1952), Wallace (1965), and particularly Kofsky (1963).

The Beginnings of Classificatory Activity.

When does the child begin to classify objects and events? Our earlier difficulties in defining "concept" versus "equivalence response" suggest that there can be no unambiguous answer to the question. If classification behavior is taken to include similar behavioral reactions to nonidentical inputs, then it is apparent that the very young infant is continually engaging in it. As Inhelder and Piaget (1964, p. 13) have noted, much of the infant's everyday activity looks analogous to what in the older child would unequivocally be called classifying (e.g., assimilation of diverse objects to a common sensory-motor schema). There is also evidence that the very young child tends to group related or associated items in his recall. Although most developmental studies of associative clustering indicate that it increases with age (Austin, Gekoski, and Zivian, 1965; Bousfield, Esterson, and Whitmarsh, 1958; Rossi, 1964; Rossi and Rossi, 1965), even 2-year-olds show a significant amount of it (Rossi and Rossi, 1965).

One might prefer instead to set as the beginnings of classificatory activity the age at which the child starts manually to group together similar or related objects. Although this criterion is no less arbitrary than any other, it has the advantage of referring to overt, observable behavior, and behavior closely resembling what has traditionally been accepted as an expression of classification skills, namely, what an individual does in an object-sorting task. Stott (1961) reports a spontaneous instance of such grouping in his 15-month-old son. He observed the boy systematically gathering together all the red bricks from a multicolored assortment, despite the fact that they were scattered randomly among the other bricks and therefore not always the easiest to reach. One would think that evidence on infant sorting behavior could emerge only from chance observations of spontaneous behavior, such as Stott's. However, Ricciuti (1965; Ricciuti and Johnson, 1965) has devised an ingenious procedure for eliciting it under laboratory conditions. Eight objects are spread randomly before the child, four of one class (e.g., stringing beads) and four of another (e.g., clay balls). The instructions are simply: "See these?—You play with them—You fix them all up." Ricciuti (1965) has tested infants as young as 12 months of age with this procedure, and finds that some of them respond with such classificationlike behavior as serially touching, manipulating, or putting to one side all the members of one of the object classes (and, more rarely, both of the object classes). It is clear, then, that classificatory activity, whether broadly or narrowly defined, is in evidence during the period of infancy. As such, one must agree with Inhelder and Piaget (1964) and Ricciuti (1965) that its origins, at least, are not dependent upon the linguistic abilities so often associated with the notion of classification.

Classes in Isolation. As would be expected, the great majority of studies in this area deal with postinfancy development. Following Kofsky (1963), we shall review the evidence under two headings. This section discusses the child's behavior vis-à-vis any given class taken in isolation; for instance, the structure of the class he forms as a result of grouping certain objects together. The next section will deal with developmental changes in his grasp of the interactions and interrelations among classes; for example, his understanding of the rules governing class inclusion within a class hierarchy.

Ricciuti's data (1965) provide a good point of departure for the evidence regarding isolated classes. From the standpoint of logical classification, the behavior of his young Ss was impeccable: there were two readily discriminable classes of objects, each with its own set of common perceptual attributes, and some of these children moved all (and only) the members of the one class away from the members of the other. If you gave the average adult the same objects and asked him to sort them, he would certainly have made the same division. Ricciuti subsequently retested some of his 20-month-old Ss when they were 40 months of age (Ricciuti and Johnson, 1965). Not surprisingly, the frequency of this logical-looking behavior had increased. What was surprising, however, was that these children also showed a grouping activity which had been largely absent 20 months earlier and which was distinctly illogical, from a strictly classificatory point of view. They would, for instance, form two aggregates, each containing two objects from *each* class; moreover, the objects within each aggregate were brought close together to form what looked suspiciously like a 3-year-old's

version of an interesting design or pattern. Ricciuti and Johnson argue quite plausibly that these patterns reflect intellectual progress. The 40-month-old can group objects together on the basis of both common attributes and their joint contributions to pleasing spatial configuration; the 20-month-old can only group by common attribute, a more purely classificatory activity. The fact remains that these 3-year-olds do show a form of behavior in a classification setting which adults rarely show. An examination of the literature further suggests that this particular form is but one of a number of dispositions or tendencies at the level of the isolated class which exhibit developmental modification. The existence of these various developmental changes is easy to document, as will be shown. Their interpretation remains somewhat obscure, however.

Olver and Hornsby (Bruner, Olver, and Greenfield, 1966, Chap. 3) argue that an individual's classification of a set of objects exhibits both "semantic" and "syntactic" features, and that both undergo developmental change. The semantics of classification refers to the features of objects and events which form the basis for linking them together in a common group, for example, their perceptual or functional properties. The syntax of classification refers to the formal structure of the class thus constructed, for example, whether or not all of the class members share a common attribute. Developmental changes in the syntactic aspects—the "rules for grouping" as Kofsky (1963, p. 6) has called them—are the more interesting ones and will be described first.

The chapter by Olver and Hornsby just cited reports two studies of classification development. Since most of the major features of children's classificatory syntax reported elsewhere in the literature were also observed by these experimenters, their studies will be taken as the framework within which we discuss these features. Olver's procedure (see also Bruner and Olver, 1963) was to present a pair of words and ask how their referents were alike, then to present a third word and ask how all three were alike, then a fourth, and so on, through a list of eight. One of her lists included the words *banana, peach, potato, meat, milk, water, air,* and *germs,* for example. Her Ss were 6 to 18 years of age. Hornsby's procedure was closer to that of the traditional sorting test. Children of 6 to 11 years were presented with an array of 42 water-color pictures of familiar objects (apple, clock, umbrella, etc.). S was first asked to select from the array a group of pictures that were alike in some way, "any way at all in which a group of things is the same." After the child had completed his grouping, he was asked to tell how the pictures selected were alike, the pictures were returned to the array, and the child was then asked to form another group, and so on, through 10 sorting trials.

The classificatory behavior of the Ss in both studies was categorized under three main rubrics in terms of class structure or syntax:

1. *Superordinate groupings.* This is the familiar logical-classification grouping: all the objects in the class share one or more common attribute (e.g., banana, peach, and potato are "all food" or "all have skins"). As would be expected, there was a convergence with age toward the exclusive use of this grouping strategy in both studies.

2. *Complexive groupings.* These structures are not so easily characterized, as their name implies. There also appear to be a number of semidistinguishable subvarieties, but we shall not describe each one individually here (Bruner, Olver, and Greenfield, 1966, Chap. 3; Bruner and Olver, 1963). In general, complexive groupings appear to be the result of a conventional find-the-common-attributes strategy which the child fails, for any of a number of reasons, to carry off for the whole set of objects to be grouped. The child might, for instance, find a perfectly acceptable similarity between two of five objects in his group, but then find no similarity, a nonsimilarity (a contrast), or a different similarity for the remaining three. Or, alternatively, he might select one of the objects and treat it as a common property shared by all the rest. Bruner and his colleagues refer to this kind of complex as a "key ring"; for instance, *germs* function as the "ring" in the rationale, "Germs are in banana, peach, potato, meat, milk, water, and air." Whatever the particular form of the complex, it represents an *inconsistent* class (Kofsky, 1963) in the sense that not all the objects are taken as belonging to the class on the same basis, for the same reason (i.e.,

common attributes). Hornsby's data also give evidence of something like the complement of inconsistency; Kofsky refers to it as *nonexhaustiveness.* As in the complexive grouping, the child attempts to use equivalence or similarity relations to form his class, but he fails to include in his group all the objects that possess the property he has chosen as his criterion for class membership:

The young child will form a group consisting of *house* and *barn* "because they have red on them," and yet ignore the red *apple* and red *balloon.* Or he will select just two animals or two foods and fail to include the other animals or foods (Bruner, Olver, and Greenfield, 1966, p. 82).

In contrast to superordinate groupings, complexive groupings and allied phenomena show a definite decrease with age in both studies.

3. *Thematic groupings.* The less ambitious of Olver and Hornsby's complexive groupings come perilously close to ignoring the similarity or common-attribute constraints of the classification task altogether (e.g., "Bell is black, horn is brown, telephone is blue, radio is red"). Their thematic groupings systematically ignore them. The elements of the group are interrelated, but the relations are not those of equivalence or similarity. Rather, they are linked together, with greater or lesser ingenuity and logic, in some sort of story or thema; for example, "The little boy was eating a banana on the way to the store to buy some peaches and potatoes." Unlike both superordinate and complexive groupings, the link between items is not of the common-attribute variety; and unlike superordinate but like complexive groupings, the same link does not hold between all pairs of items. They could therefore be thought of not only as nonclasses but also as inconsistent nonclasses. Thematic groupings were virtually absent in Olver's protocols but were rather commonly seen in Hornsby's; like complexive groupings, they showed a clear decline with age.

As indicated, much of the developmental story on classificatory syntax can be derived from these two studies alone; the numerous other investigations in the literature mostly reinforce their conclusions and, in some instances, provide the basis for further conceptual elaboration of them. Let us begin with the thematic groupings. Formally speaking, they bear a striking resemblance to the configurations or patterns created by Ricciuti's 40-month-olds (Ricciuti and Johnson, 1965). In both cases, common properties are eschewed in favor of common participation in some totality. If the items to be grouped are meaningful ones, as in Hornsby's task, the totality is likely to be a thema or story. If they are relatively nonmeaningful, as in Ricciuti's and Inhelder and Piaget's (1964) tasks, it will tend to be a design, pattern, or constructed object of the jigsaw puzzle type. In either case, the result is not a class, as the complexive grouping strives to be and the superordinate grouping succeeds in being, but simply a structured whole. Correspondingly, the relation between item and totality is one of part to whole rather than class member to class (Inhelder and Piaget, 1964).

Inhelder and Piaget have done the most extensive work on preclasses of the Ricciuti variety, which they refer to as *graphic* (or *figural*) *collections*. These collections were frequently found in their 2½- to 5-year-old Ss. Recall that Ricciuti's 3-year-olds did both classlike and configurationlike sorting (Ricciuti and Johnson, 1965). Inhelder and Piaget's graphic collections often showed evidence of both sorting tendencies. In a typical graphic collection, the child might begin by putting similar objects together and then adjoin dissimilar ones to them, perhaps ending up with a meaningful structured whole (e.g., a jigsaw puzzle-like "house"). Some of Hornsby's examples of thematic groupings also look like admixtures of classes and nonclass wholes; in general, one would expect to find numerous transition structures between the thematic grouping or graphic collection and the complexive grouping. For an interesting analysis and interpretation of young children's graphic collections, see Inhelder and Piaget (1964; Flavell, 1963a, pp. 304–306). Many other studies, utilizing a variety of procedures, confirm the young child's predilection for graphic collections and thematic groupings (Annett, 1959; Goldman and Levine, 1963; Lovell, Mitchell, and Everett, 1962; Reichard, Schneider, and Rapaport, 1944; Sigel, 1953; Szeminska, 1965; Thompson, 1941; Vygotsky, 1962; Weigl, 1941).

There is also considerable supporting evidence for Olver and Hornsby's observations regarding complexive and related classificatory behavior. It was Vygotsky (1962, Chap. 5) who originally used the term "complex" in the early thirties, and the varieties he described are very similar to those reported by these authors. As indicated earlier, children's classification efforts at the level of the complexive grouping characteristically fail to satisfy the dual requirements of *consistency* (all members of the group share the same common property or properties) and *exhaustiveness* (all objects sharing the property or properties are included in the group). The frequent failure of young children to observe the consistency constraint has been noted by Annett (1958), Goldman and Levine (1963), Lovell, Mitchell, and Everett (1962), Thompson (1941), Vygotsky (1962), and Werner and Kaplan (1950). The child's failure to establish exhaustive classes in free-sorting tasks seems in part to be the consequence of a tendency to form two- and three-object groups (recall the preceding quotation from Bruner, Olver, and Greenfield, 1966). This tendency, nonexhaustive sorting, or the two in combination have also been reported in several studies (Annett, 1959; Goldman and Levine, 1963; Kofsky, 1966; Reichard, Schneider, and Rapaport, 1944; Szeminska, 1965).

There are other observations about children's classification below the level of the superordinate grouping that should be mentioned. Not surprisingly, the developmental level of the child's groupings is usually higher than that of his verbal definitions or explanations regarding them (Reichard, Schneider, and Rapaport, 1944; Saarinen, 1964; Vygotsky, 1962). Szeminska (1965) and Inhelder and Piaget (1964) have stressed the lack of planning and self-monitoring in the young child's classificatory activity: "If we try to analyse the course of behaviour and thinking at stage I [the stage of graphic connections], we are inevitably struck by the fact that the child is taking each step as he comes to it, forgetting what went before, and not foreseeing what must follow" (Inhelder and Piaget, 1964, p. 285). It is apparent that a systematic absence of foresight and hindsight would alone be sufficient to produce a nonsuperordinate end result. The young child's categories have also been characterized as fluid and unstable, subject to abolition or redefinition from moment to moment as conditions change (Kofsky, 1963; Vygotsky, 1962; Werner and Kaplan, 1950). Kofsky (1963, 1966) has devised an ingenious procedure for tapping one aspect of class stability. Her "conservation of class" task (analogous to the Piagetian tests for conservation of number, length, etc.) probes the child's understanding that members of a given class continue to retain their class-membership status even when separated from each other spatially. And, finally, Bruner and Olver (1963) epitomize much of what is known about children's classificatory syntax in suggesting that development here consists largely of:

. . . the growth of strategies of grouping that encode information in a manner (a) that chunks information in *simpler* form, (b) that gains *connectedness* with rules of grouping already formed, and (c) that is designed to *maximize the possibility of combinatorial operations* such that groupings already formed can be combined and detached from other forms of grouping. In a word then, what distinguishes the young child from the older child is the fact that the younger one is more complicated than the older one, not the reverse (p. 134).

Developmental changes in the semantic aspects of classificatory behavior are less clear cut, both factually and in terms of their probable significance for an understanding of cognitive growth. Generally speaking, there appears to be an ontogenetic shift—clearly evident in one study, less so in another— from equivalences based on the more concrete and immediately given perceptual, situational, and functional attributes of objects to equivalences of a more abstract, verbal-conceptual sort, in particular the use of class names ("animals," "fruit," etc.) as the basis for grouping. The relevant evidence is to be found in both the sorting and classification literature (Annett, 1959; Bruner and Olver, 1963; Bruner, Olver, and Greenfield, 1966; Goldman and Levine, 1963; Natadze, 1961; Reichard, Schneider, and Rapaport, 1944; Ricciuti, 1966a, 1966b; Sigel, 1953, 1954; Szeminska, 1965; Thompson, 1941) and in studies of children's vocabulary-definition preferences (Feifel and Lorge, 1950; Kruglov, 1953; Russell and Saadeh, 1962; Wolman

and Barker, 1965). Moreover, in tasks where all the available equivalence options are perceptual, there is a subsidiary research corpus of ancient lineage which reports developmental changes in the saliency of such attributes as the gradual dominance of form over color cues with increasing age. For good recent studies of this genre, see Corah (1966), Lee (1965), and Suchman and Trabasso (1966a, 1966b).

The evidence also strongly suggests that the property an individual will single out as the basis for linking objects together will depend upon factors in addition to his developmental status. It will depend upon the possibilities afforded by the available objects (the Olver and Hornsby studies, for instance, show this to be an extremely powerful determinant), upon the individual's style of conceptualization (e.g., Kagan, Moss, and Sigel, 1963), possibly upon the wording of the sorting instructions (the use of "belong together" versus "are alike in some way"), and other variables.

Classes in Interaction. Piaget and Inhelder have been the chief contributors to our developmental knowledge in this area (Piaget, 1952; Inhelder and Piaget, 1964; see also Flavell, 1963a, pp. 190–193, 306–309). The ontogenetic target here is an individual who understands and can think in terms of certain basic facts and rules concerning the interactions among classes. These include the recognition that a set of objects may be members of a number of classes simultaneously and a grasp of the exact quantitative relations holding among the extensions (i.e., the set of objects comprising the class members) of these classes. If the extensions of two classes overlap (i.e., there exist objects which are members of both), an understanding of this overlap can be described as a tacit understanding of class multiplication. For instance, the (logical) multiplication of the classes "Republicans" and "New Yorkers" yields the product class "Republican New Yorkers"—precisely those individuals who belong to both of these classes at once. The intersection of two classes may leave a nonintersecting remainder in both classes, as in the example just given (New Yorkers who are not Republican, and Republicans who are not New Yorkers). On the other hand, one of the classes may be wholly included within the other, with only the latter possessing a nonintersecting remainder. For example, all terriers are dogs but there are also dogs that are not terriers. An individual who grasps the structure of this or similar classification paradigms understands something of class addition as well as class multiplication. He not only can multiply the classes "dog" and "terrier" and get the class product "terrier," but he also can add (logically) "terrier" and "nonterrier dog" to get the sum or superordinate class "dog" ("Republicans" and "New Yorkers" can also be added in the same way, of course, but that fact is not germane to the present discussion).

The research of the Genevan group has been largely directed at studying the child's growing skill and knowledge regarding these and related properties of class systems. Inhelder and Piaget (1964) report a variety of experiments which suggest that young children have great difficulty with problems demanding an understanding of multiple class membership and class multiplication. Once they have imposed a classificatory division on a set of objects, for example, they find it difficult to reclassify these same objects on some other basis. In another of their studies, S is presented with a horizontal row of pictures of different colored *leaves*, which forms an L with a vertical row of pictures of diverse *green* objects. S's problem is to decide which picture should go in a blank space that lies at the juncture of the two series. The older Ss (about 9 to 10 years) quickly sense the class-intersect character of the problem and insert a picture of a *green leaf* in the blank space, whereas the younger ones characteristically choose a depicted object which belongs to only one of the two classes (e.g., another leaf of any color).

The young child's problems with class addition and related operations are illustrated by a more celebrated series of studies (Piaget, 1952; Inhelder and Piaget, 1964). These studies show that, whereas the young child has no difficulty in recognizing that a set of, say, ducks and nonduck birds together comprise a collection of birds, he is systematically incapable of correctly answering E's query as to whether there are more ducks or more birds in the set. The child's problem here is said to involve an inability simultaneously to hold in mind superordinate and subordinate classes, in order to compare their extensions.

Inhelder and Piaget (1964) also describe a number of other experimental probes into the child's understanding of superordinate-subordinate class relationship, for example, investigations of his growing ability to manipulate the quantifiers "some" and "all" with reference to the extensions of classes thus related. According to Piaget, the child gradually masters the basic rules and operations governing the interaction among classes during the early to middle elementary school years, and this mastery is interpreted in terms of the acquisition of concrete-operational structures.

There have been a number of attempts to replicate or extend Inhelder and Piaget's findings (Dodwell, 1962; Elkind, 1961c; Hood, 1962; Hyde, 1959; Kofsky, 1966; Lovell, Mitchell, and Everett, 1962; Morf, 1959; Sigel, Saltz, and Roskind, 1967; Wohlwill and Katz, 1967). In general, these investigators find roughly the same developmental phenomena that Inhelder and Piaget found, with perhaps a difference in detail here and there. The young child's difficulty with the class-inclusion problem (more ducks or more birds?), for example, has been repeatedly reconfirmed. There are other, nonreplication studies which also give corroborative information. For instance, the young child's relative inability to shift criteria and reclassify the same set of items in different ways is well documented (Heald and Marzolf, 1954; Reichard, Schneider, and Rapaport, 1944; Saarinen, 1964; Thompson, 1941). The classic papers by Welch and Long on the learning of class hierarchies should perhaps also be cited here (Welch, 1940; Welch and Long, 1940a, 1940b), although the writer has found it very difficult to interpret and evaluate these particular studies. Finally, there is an interesting study by Mosher which illustrates how the child's growing expertise with class hierarchies gets expressed in the information-seeking strategies he uses when playing the game of Twenty Questions (Bruner, Olver, and Greenfield, 1966, Chap. 4).

Conclusions. This discussion began with a distinction between classes as intellectual instrument and classes as intellectual object. What is to be learned from the literature just reviewed about the development of each of these? For classes as intellectual instrument, the answer is uncertain. There is still no convincing reason to suppose that an individual's behavior on a sorting task is a really faithful reflection of the spontaneous categorizations he makes in everyday situations. In particular, we suspect with Brown (1965, p. 328) that the typical adult utilizes categories of a wider genetic range in everyday life than you would be led to believe from the neat superordinate groupings he gives you on your sorting test. The problem is partly that we really are not sure what stimulus properties such tests have for Ss of various ages—just what implicit self-instructions the materials and formal instructions arouse in S.

For classes as intellectual object, the answer is a bit clearer, although some of the same interpretative problems apply here as well. The literature suggests that the child in our culture gradually acquires a functional command of the rules and regularities which obtain in the isolated class and in systems of interrelated classes. One can only assume that this growing understanding has important effects upon the categories the individual habitually uses, and especially upon the way he uses them in everyday reasoning and problem-solving situations.

Relations

The conceptual link between relations and classes is obviously a very close one. For instance, equivalence, difference, conjunction, disjunction, and other relations continually figure in our assignment of objects to classes. It is no surprise, then, to discover numerous parallels between the development of relational and classificatory thinking. First, the distinction betwen intellectual-instrument and intellectual-object aspects applies here as it did to classes. The child can be said to acquire a repertory of particular kinds of relations which he imposes on data, and he can also be said to acquire an understanding of the properties of relations in general. Second, relational thinking, like classificatory thinking, appears to have its origins in the sensorimotor period of infancy (Inhelder and Piaget, 1964, p. 13), although the relational equivalent of Ricciuti's (1965) study on early classification behavior has apparently not been done yet. Third, it is again possible to divide the developmental evidence according to its bearing on relations taken in isolation or in interaction with one another: the child learns what *a* relation is, and he also learns about *systems*

of relations. Moreover, Piaget's theoretical analysis has shown that systems of relations, like those of classes, are susceptible to the operations of logical addition and multiplication. In fact, of the eight concrete-operational groupings he uses as models for middle-childhood cognitive attainments, the most important are said to be the four dealing with the addition and multiplication of classes and relations (Inhelder and Piaget, 1964, p. 278). And finally, implied in what has just been said, the developmental mastery of the fundamental properties of relations and of classes appears to be roughly synchronous, that is, both are attained during the elementary school years.

Relations in Isolation. One way to approach this topic would be to chronicle the developmental acquisition of particular individual relations, taken in their intellectual-instrument aspect. For instance, Kreezer and Dallenbach (1929) and Robinowitz (1956) have shown that it is not until age 6 to 7 years or so that the child seems to have acquired the relation "opposite of." Similarly, there are many studies in the literature on children's learning concerning the age at which relational concepts such as "middle-sized" enter the child's functional repertoire. It might, however, be more illuminating (and would certainly be less space-consuming) to restrict our attention to the intellectual-object side of the problem, that is, to the child's progressive understanding of what a relation—any relation—is and implies. This also involves looking at the child's reactions to specific relational concepts, but with an eye to drawing more general conclusions.

The pertinent observations appear to have been made first by Piaget some years ago (Piaget, 1928, Chap. 2–3; Flavell, 1963a, pp. 276–278). His principal finding was that young children tend to misconstrue relations as absolute classes; this is true for both symmetrical relations (e.g., "brother of") and asymmetrical relations (e.g., "left of," "darker"). Such expressions are taken simply as class names for sets of objects sharing some common property rather than as relations holding between objects. Thus the relative, "darker," is interpreted as the absolute, "dark," and "brother" is at first simply "a boy." Furthermore, because the child is insensitive to the relational connotations of terms like "brother," he fails to realize that he himself is also a brother of his brother, that is, the reciprocal nature of such symmetrical relations escapes him. Piaget summarizes the young child's conception of relations as follows:

The conclusion to which we are finally led is this. The child does not realize that certain ideas, even such as are obviously relative for an adult are relations between at least two terms. Thus he does not realize that a brother must necessarily be the brother of somebody, that an object must necessarily be to the right or left of somebody, or that a part must necessarily be part of a whole, but thinks of all these notions as existing in themselves, absolutely (1928, p. 131).

Piaget attributes the young child's difficulty in grasping the relativity of relations to his cognitive egocentrism, defined as a generalized inability to envisage multiple perspectives or points of view, that is, to see things relatively rather than absolutistically. It is worth noting that something like this confounding of relations with classes was also detectable in the child's early classificatory activity, where objects are frequently grouped together on the basis of various (nonequivalence) relations holding between one object and another, thus giving rise to thematic groupings and graphic collections. Piaget's findings regarding the developmental aspects of relations in isolation have been substantially confirmed by other researchers (Danziger, 1957; Elkind, 1961e, 1962a).

Relations in Interaction. We have already said that the operations by which sets of classes can be interconnected have their analogues in the domain of relations. As in the section on classes, our description of these operations will be incomplete and nonrigorous, intended only to illustrate some basic points (Flavell, 1963a, Chap. 5). First, roughly parallel to the imposition of a class hierarchy on an object domain is the operation of seriating a set of objects, for instance, lining up a set of sticks in regular order from shortest to longest. The relations betwen the objects so seriated are then susceptible to a kind of logical addition, analogous to the addition of classes. For example, if the ordered series is represented as $A < B < C < D \ldots$ (A shorter than

B, B shorter than C, etc.), then the relation $(A < B)$ "plus" the relation $(B < C)$ "equals" the relation $(A < C)$; the addition of relations thus expresses the transitivity of these relations. The same would be true for certain symmetrical relations, such as "equals" or "is brother to": $A = B$ "plus" $B = C$ "equals" $A = C$; if A and B are brothers, and B and C are brothers, then so also must A and C be brothers. Furthermore, relations can be multiplied as well as added. Given a square matrix embodying two seriations in which, say, the objects become increasingly darker in color as one moves along the rows from left to right, and increasingly larger as one proceeds down the columns, some object X in the matrix can be conjunctively characterized as at once darker *and* larger than some Y, lighter *and* equal in size to some Z, etc. A product relation like "darker and larger" is thus the counterpart of a product class like "New York (and) Republican."

We can now define some developmental objectives regarding a basic understanding of relations in interaction. The child will need to acquire the ability to seriate correctly a potentially orderable but unordered collection of objects, and to understand clearly that the nth object in his constructed series occupies that position because it is at once larger, say, than object $n - 1$ and smaller than object $n + 1$. Given this ability and understanding, the interpolation of new and additional objects into the series will pose no problem, since the $[(n - 1) < n < (n + 1)]$ "rule" will guarantee the correct placement of each object. The child will also need to grasp the transitivity principle implied in the serial addition operation. He should eventually be able to regard the conclusion $A < C$ (or $A = C$) as logically necessary, given only the information $A < B$ and $B < C$ (or $A = B$ and $B = C$), regardless of countervailing suggestion from E or from the perceptual properties of A, B, and C themselves. Finally, he should acquire the same sensitivity to the multiplicative possibilities of sets of different relations that he does for sets of different classes (recall Inhelder and Piaget's experiment on the intersection of green objects and leaves), and he should also be able to reason in terms of product relations on problems where such reasoning might be helpful.

Piaget has analyzed the developmental

problem of relational systems in roughly the manner just described, and he has conducted his research accordingly. First, he has shown that young children have real difficulties in arranging unordered objects into an ordered series and, when first able to do this, cannot continue to insert new items into it correctly (Piaget, 1952, Chap. 6; Inhelder and Piaget, 1964, Chap. 9).

Similarly, the empirical establishment of a relation between A and B and between B and C does not initially suffice for definite conclusions regarding the relation between A and C. This absence of transitive inference has been found to characterize the young child's reasoning with respect to both asymmetrical (Piaget and Inhelder, 1941, Chap. 10) and symmetrical (*ibid.*, Chap. 11) relations. For instance, given three objects of varying sizes and colors of identical or different weights, the child will not reliably and with subjective certainty conclude that $A = C$ on the basis of $A = B$ and $B = C$, or that $A < C$ on the basis of $A < B$ and $B < C$.

Moreover, the multiplication of relations also appears to be an operation foreign to the young mind. In one of their studies, Inhelder and Piaget (1964, Chap. 10) gave children of different ages 49 cut-out pictures of leaves orderable both by size (7 sizes) and by shade of color (7 shades) and probed in various ways for their ability to construct the 7×7 matrix. The youngest Ss failed to seriate at all. Older ones could construct one of the series or sometimes both in succession, but without being able to effect a multiplicative synthesis of the two. After the age of 7 or so, partial or complete matrix-building became quite common. One gets the impression from reading Inhelder and Piaget's behavior records here (1964, p. 275) that these oldest Ss "knew what the game was" in a way that the younger ones did not. It should also be mentioned that Piaget assigns a very important and general mediative role to the child's growing ability to multiply relations: it is said to be a developmental bridge to the attainment of the various conservation concepts (e.g., Piaget, 1952, Chap. 1).

There have been a number of independent confirmations of Piaget's assertions regarding early difficulties in constructing series and in interpolating new elements into already-constructed ones (e.g., Chittenden, 1964; Elkind,

1964a; Lovell, Mitchell, and Everett, 1962). In addition, there are many studies on number development which support these assertions in a less direct manner (see the next section).

There can also be no doubt that a grasp of the transitivity rule develops with age (Chittenden, 1964; Hood, 1962; Hyde, 1959; Lovell and Ogilvie, 1961b; Youniss and Furth, 1965, 1966; and numerous other studies to be cited in later sections). The two experiments by Youniss and Furth are particularly interesting. In the earlier one (1965), children of grades K, 1, and 3 were required to learn arbitrary causal sequences, namely, which of three balls (identical in size but different colors) would push one another off an inclined plane. They found that the older groups, but not the younger one, learned a given sequence significantly faster if it embodied the transitivity principle (A pushes B off the plane, B pushes C, and A pushes C) than if it did not (A pushes B, B pushes C, but C pushes A). In the second study (1966) they found that kindergarten children learned transitive sequences more easily than intransitive ones only when the perceptual cues were congruent with the sequence (i.e., bigger balls pushing smaller ones); first- and third-graders, on the other hand, learned transitive sequences more easily regardless of the congruency-incongruency of these cues.

There is less evidence regarding the development of relational multiplication, but what there is confirms the Genevan findings (Bruner, Olver, and Greenfield, 1966, Chap. 7; Lovell, Mitchell, and Everett, 1962). Lovell, Mitchell, and Everett essentially repeated Inhelder and Piaget's original procedure and obtained similar developmental trends. Bruner and Kenney (Bruner, Olver, and Greenfield, 1966, Chap. 7) were more innovative. They presented children with a square matrix of nine beakers, the beakers increasing in height along one axis and in width along the other. The Ss were tested both for their ability to reproduce the original matrix from memory and for their ability to complete a transposed matrix which E began for them by moving the shortest and thinnest glass from its original position in the southwest corner of the matrix to the southeast corner. The results were dramatic. Whereas ⅗ of the 5-year-olds could reproduce the original matrix, not one could complete the transposed version. In contrast, ⅘ of the 7-year-olds succeeded on both tasks. It would be a fair interpretation of their data to say that the older child understands the multiplication-of-relations principle implicit in the arrangement of the glasses and therefore can transpose as easily as he can reproduce; this principle eludes the younger child, and hence he sees only a specific and immutable spatial configuration.

Number

We now consider normative-descriptive research dealing principally with the child's developing grasp of certain very basic and important properties of number and the number system. Developmental investigations of other mathematical concepts such as the concept of probability will be taken up in the next section.

Virtually everything of interest that we know about the early growth of number concepts grows out of Piaget's pioneer work in the area (Piaget, 1952; Churchill, 1961; Flavell, 1963a, pp. 309–316). Piaget saw early that revealing studies here must focus on tacit mathematical assumptions and beliefs which may be considerably removed from the child's overt behavior with respect to the number system, that is, they must deal with the genotypes rather than the phenotypes of mathematical behavior. He argued that what the child really understands about the nature of number cannot be reliably inferred from the conventional numerical operations (counting, adding, etc.) he is called upon to learn and perform in the traditional classroom; instead, new and radically different methods must be devised to probe for this understanding—for the child's number *concepts* in the true sense of the word. Although such an approach would probably elicit a condescending "of course" from today's educator or developmental psychologist, it is important to realize that it did not always seem self-evident. Consider the following excerpt from a 1942 book, *The Early Development of Number Concepts*. A test was given to some 1290 children just entering elementary school in order to find out what they already knew about arithmetic. The nature and rationale of this test are apparent from the author's conclusions:

It is obvious that whereas almost all pupils entering school can perform rote counting by units, only about 20 per cent can accomplish rote counting by tens, and the number who succeed in counting backwards is negligible. Practically all children entering school are competent to some degree in rational counting, and more than half succeed in actual counting up to 10 or 15. . . . Over 90 per cent of school entrants can give 2 objects, over 50 per cent can give 5 objects, and over 20 per cent can give 10 objects when they are required to do so by the teacher. . . . The addition combination $1 + 2$ is known to almost half the pupils, and $3 + 1$ by a third; $2 + 3$ and $5 + 1$ are known to about 20 per cent. The subtraction combination $3 - 1$ is known to three-quarters of the pupils, whereas the corresponding addition combination $3 + 1$ is only known to a third; $5 - 2$ is as well known as $1 + 2$, and $7 - 3$ is known to a quarter of the pupils (Scottish Council for Research in Education, 1942, p. 27).

Piagetian research on number development can be divided for convenience of presentation into two parts: Piaget's original studies, carried out in the 1930s and first published in English in 1952 (Piaget, 1952); subsequent research on the problem, done primarily by Piaget's collaborators during the last 10 years. The original studies have become very well known to the psychological and educational public and have often been repeated by others. The recent work, as yet unreplicated (by non-Genevans) and untranslated, will undoubtedly be less familiar to most readers.

The Original Studies. Piaget conceived the basic developmental problems in roughly the following way. What, exactly, are the essential cognitive components of an adequate elementary concept of number? That is, what must the child implicitly know about the properties of numbers in order to be credited with such a concept? Piaget believes that these cognitive components principally include a concrete-operational mastery of classification and seriation (the middle-childhood-level understanding of classes and relations described in the preceding two sections of this chapter). Number itself is actually conceptualized as a fusion or synthesis of classes and (asymmetrical) relations, according to a logical and epistemological analysis which will not be detailed here (see Flavell, 1963a, pp.

310–311 and the page references to Piaget, 1952, cited here). Because of the putative intimate relation among these three cognitive domains, several of Piaget's number-concept problems require for their solution the ability to classify and, especially, to seriate.

In one of his tasks, for example (Piaget, 1952, Chap. 5), the child is presented with two unordered but potentially orderable sets of 10 objects each: dolls of different heights and miniature walking sticks of different lengths. The child is told to arrange the dolls and sticks in such a way that each doll can easily find the stick that belongs to it. The solution is to seriate the objects in each set and bring the appropriate doll-stick pairs together, in optical correspondence, for instance, the fourth-largest doll must be placed opposite the fourth-largest stick. Once this is accomplished, E closes up one of the series so that each stick is no longer directly opposite its owner, and S is asked to find the stick that belongs to some particular doll selected by E. The most interesting finding was that there were a number of children who could readily solve the initial, double-seriation part of the problem but could not find the correct stick for a given doll when the optical correspondence between the two series—each doll opposite its stick—was destroyed. In particular, the child at this stage was prone to confuse the *ordinal* number of the correct stick (nth) with the *cardinal* number ($n-1$) of those smaller than it, thus often selecting the ($n-1$)th stick when the nth was called for. Several other of Piaget's studies (*ibid.,* Chap. 6) also pointed up the pre-operational child's difficulties in differentiating and coordinating the ordinal and cardinal aspects of number—in terms of Piaget's initial conceptualization, its relational and classificatory components, respectively.

By all odds the most famous of Piaget's investigations in this area deal with the conservation of number. The tasks he used to elicit conservation or nonconservation responses in children varied from study to study, but one basic paradigm is used in all cases. Two sets of objects are established as numerically equivalent, usually by one-one correspondence rather than enumeration; for example, E's row of objects and S's row of objects are set in direct, one-one optical correspondence, as with the sticks and dolls, or

E puts a marble in one container every time S puts a marble in another container. The objects in the one set may have some natural connection with those in the other (e.g., dolls in the one set, their beds in the other), or they may not (e.g., a set of white beads versus a set of red beads); Piaget refers to the former as "provoked" and the latter as "spontaneous" correspondence (Piaget, 1952).

Whatever the specific form of the task, at some point conditions are so arranged that there is a lack of optical correspondence between the members of the two sets, with the result that the young child may experience what amounts to a perceptual illusion as regards the relative numerosity of the two sets. If the two sets had been placed initially in optical correspondence, say, two rows of equally spaced and opposing objects, E may destroy the correspondence by lengthening one of the rows, by transforming one row into a heap or a tower, or by effecting spatial subgroups within one of the sets (Piaget in this instance would speak of the "additive composition of numbers," i.e., the recognition that the sum of the subsets equals the total set). If the numerical equivalence had instead been initially constituted by one-for-one insertion of marbles into each of two identical transparent containers, E will have insured an eventual optical noncorrespondence by pouring the contents of one into a third, differently shaped container. The child is then asked whether the two sets now contain identical numbers or amounts of objects. The prototypical conserver steadfastly affirms their continued equivalence; the nonconserver denies it.

There is considerable controversy regarding just what characteristics of the child's structure account for conservation versus nonconservation responses, in the area of number and elsewhere, and especially regarding the mechanisms by which the former replaces the latter in the course of development. We shall touch on such questions later. There is no controversy at all, however, about the reality of certain gross differences between the two types of responders. The nonconserver is distinguished from the conserver both by what he does and by what he fails to do. What he does is treat the problem as a perceptual rather than a cognitive one, and in so doing he is likely to make a judgment of nonequivalence on the basis of certain number-irrelevant cues such as length, width, and density. Thus the spread-out row is often said to contain more objects because "it is longer," the thin container because "it is higher" (i.e., the column of marbles is higher), etc. What he fails to do is draw logical conclusions from the fact that the two sets were initially established as equivalent by one-one correspondence (or by counting), and from the fact that the transformations which have been performed are not of the kinds that affect the numerosity of the sets. And what he does not have, quite obviously, is a coherent and differentiated—an "operational," as Piaget would put it—concept of number.

The claim that young children are systematically prone to nonconservation responses, in this and other areas, seems most improbable at first hearing, and it could have been predicted that subsequent researchers would leave no children untested in trying to support or falsify it. In the case of number conservation specifically, there is overwhelming evidence that the claim is indeed a valid one. We shall cite here only the replication-oriented studies of Piaget's conservation and other number-concept tasks; we defer to later sections consideration of investigations which verify the claim incidentally, while in the course of pursuing some other objective (attempts at training nonconservers to conserve, cross-cultural comparisons of the age at which conservation is attained, etc.).

Replications of one or more of Piaget's number-concept studies have been carried out by Almy, Chittenden, and Miller (1966), Beard (1963a), Dodwell (1960, 1961), Elkind (1964a), and Hood (1962). These investigators report essentially the same gamut of pre-operational and concrete-operational behaviors on the various tasks that Piaget found. The Almy, Chittenden, and Miller study provides especially strong confirmation in that it demonstrated progressive shifts from nonconservation to conservation responding in individual children, retested at 6-month intervals over a 2-year period (5 to 7 years of age).

It is unclear (at least to the writer) whether Piaget's theoretical analysis of the number concept as a synthesis of classificatory and relational operations actually ought to imply that the standard Piagetian tests for these operations (e.g., seriation and class-inclusion tasks) should be negotiated earlier than, or in strict synchrony with, more direct tests of the number concept itself (e.g., tests of cardinal-ordinal correspondence or of number conservation). Whatever the logical status of this implication, its factual status is certainly very doubtful. Neither Piaget nor anyone else (e.g., Beard, 1963a; Dodwell, 1961a; Hood, 1962) has shown any convincing empirical evidence that seriation and classification tasks are regularly mastered prior to number tasks. Although there is some agreement across studies as to the order of difficulty among the various tasks, those assessing classificatory and relational operations are not uniformly easier than those assessing numerical ones.

Finally, there is a study by Gunderson (1955), which, although not conceived within a Piagetian framework, lends some support to his view that the elementary numerical operations become interconnected within a more general cognitive structure during early middle childhood. She found that second-grade children, already skilled in simple addition and subtraction operations, were surprisingly adept at solving simple multiplication and division problems, even though they had not yet received any formal instruction in these latter operations.

Recent Genevan Research. Inhelder and Piaget (1963) have done further studies of the child's developing ability to infer conservation of number from the repeated or recursive application of the operation of one-one correspondence. A variety of new tasks were employed (the Genevans seem to have an inexhaustible supply of techniques for assessing conservation concepts!), of which the following is prototypical. The child repeatedly performs the action of simultaneously adding a bead to each of two glasses, one wide and one narrow. At various points, E: asks the child if the two sets of beads continue to be equal; covers the glasses with a cardboard box, has the child continue to drop marbles into the glasses through holes in the box, and then repeats the conservation question; asks if the sets would always continue to be equal if the child kept up the one-for-one process "all afternoon," or "for a long time." The child was further queried about each answer, as is usual in Piagetian research, and asked to justify his conclusions.

Two findings of this study are of particular interest. First, a number of the younger Ss were able to infer at any given point that the two sets continued to be equal, despite all appearances (the higher column of beads in the thinner glass), on the basis of their construction through the one-for-one operation. However, they were hesitant and uncertain about the equality after the cardboard boxes were added or when asked to extrapolate into the future. In contrast, one of the older Ss spoke for all concrete-operational thinkers in saying, "Oh yes, once you know, you know forever!" (*ibid.*, p. 66). Second, operational-looking judgments and justifications seem to emerge earlier on this type of task than on the traditional number-conservation tasks, for example, where one of two identical glasses of beads is abruptly poured into another, different-shaped one. Inhelder and Piaget apparently construe these precocious successes as involving a primitive form of recursive reasoning, which will subsequently play a role in the formation of a concrete-operational conception of the number series.

An earlier study reported in Apostel, Mays, Morf, and Piaget (1957, Chap. 4) was concerned with the distinction between logically based and empirically based conservation judgments, a distinction implicitly present in the findings just described. Their task was the following. Two rows of buttons are set in one-one optical correspondence, and the child agrees that the rows are numerically equal. E then divides one of the rows into two or more clusters of buttons; for example, a row of eight may be rearranged into groups of 3, 3, and 2. A screen is placed between S and this row so that the child can see E create the subsets (and E also describes everything he is doing) but cannot actually count the buttons. The child then is asked if the two sets are still equal, and E tries to determine whether the child feels it necessary to remove the screen and count the buttons to be sure. As usual, it is the intermediary reactions that are of greatest interest. There appears to be a stage when the child is unwilling to either assert or deny conservation before counting; conservation has for him the status of an empirical hypothesis that has to be tested. Moreover, the less advanced children of this stage have to keep reconfirming the equality, always by counting, for each new division of the same set of buttons. In addition, empirical verification through counting only leads to sure conservation judgments during this stage if the sets are relatively small (less than 15 or 20).

From this and other evidence, Piaget has elsewhere concluded that there is a *progressive arithmetization* of the number series in the course of development: numerical operations are at first constituted only for the domain of small, "familiar" sets, and they are then slowly extended over the entire series (Piaget, 1960, p. 65). On the other hand, the oldest Ss in the Apostel et al. sample (8 to 9 years) clearly regarded conservation as a logical necessity, given the nature of the transformation performed, and therefore disdained to count. As one of them said, "There's no need to count; it's just the same as it was before" (Apostel et al., 1957, p. 118).

The Genevans have explored still other variations of the conservation problem. Apostel et al. (1957, Chap. 5) describe a second task, also utilizing the screening procedure, in which symmetrical divisions are made in both rows of buttons. The top row may consist of 8 buttons subsequently partitioned into groups of 3 (left side) and 5 (right side), and the bottom row may consist of 8 buttons subsequently partitioned into groups of 5 (left side) and 3 (right side). The child's task is to judge whether a bar placed horizontally and vertically within the four-subset configuration will in each instance result in an equal number on either side of the bar. It does, of course:

$$\frac{3 \quad 5}{5 \quad 3} \quad \text{with the bar horizontal}$$

$$\begin{array}{c|c} 3 & 3 \\ 5 & 5 \end{array} \quad \text{with the bar vertical.}$$

As in the preceding study it was found that with increasing age the child feels increasingly less need to count in order to be sure of the equivalences. The most peculiar result, however, was that a number of the intermediate-stage Ss remained unconvinced that vertical bisection (which creates two *new* sets of two subsets each) resulted in numerical equality, even after counting!

Gréco (1962a) has also used a variation of the conservation procedure in an attempt to test the child's understanding of the commutativity law of addition: $x + y = y + x$. Two rows of 8 equally spaced counters are placed in optical correspondence, one row directly above the other; the leftmost 5 in each row are white and the rightmost (remaining) 3 are red. The 3 red counters in the bottom row are slowly displaced, one by one, to the left of the white counters in that same row (thus effecting a spatial permutation of the whites and the reds), and the conservation question is posed. The developmental succession of responses to this task closely resembles that which is generally found in traditional conservation studies; on this and other grounds one is led to wonder whether the task really tapped anything more specific than conservation-nonconservation.

There is another, more interesting study by Gréco (1962b). He has shown that at least some children pass through a curious transitional stage before acquiring a clear-cut, adult grasp of number conservation. During this stage, the child clearly recognizes that the numerical labels of two sets remain invariant under number-irrelevant transformations (e.g., spreading out the objects in one of the rows), but he seems not to grasp the quantitative implications of this fact. That is, he will defend (often with operational-like arguments) the position that "there are still seven here and seven there"; nevertheless, he will conclude that "there are more" in the longer row! Such a child is said to have acquired the conservation of *quotité*—of the numerical "names" which describe each set—but not yet the conservation of numerical *quantité* proper. Dodwell (1960) and Wohlwill and Lowe (1962) have noted a similar lack of integration between the absolute-numerical and relative-quantitative aspects of number in some of their young Ss.

Not all of the recent Genevan research in this area has dealt with number conservation. Morf (1962), for example, has tried to study the child's growing understanding of the fact that numbers form a connected, unbroken series, for example, that in counting one by one from 2 to 10, you must necessarily "pass through," say, 7. He used several variations of the following technique. The child is initially presented with two sets of cubes: a set of 30, aligned on a wooden ruler; a set of 9 (set A) grouped together on the table. E tips the ruler so that one or two of the 30 slide off onto the table, thus forming the beginning

of a second group of cubes on the table (set B). E then asks: "If I continue to make these blocks fall one by one, am I sure to end up having as many cubes on the left as on the right?" (i.e., must $B = A$ at some point as B continues to increase in size?) It is clear from Morf's behavior records that some of the children were unsure of what would happen for largely artifactual reasons (e.g., they wondered if the sliding-off process could in practice be arrested at precisely the $A = B$ point). On the other hand, his records suggest that some of the younger children really were unsure that B would have to equal A in going from $B < A$ to $B > A$. He reports such responses as, "You're not sure—there could be one not enough and then one too many," and, "There could be more and afterwards less and never the same thing" (Morf, 1962, p. 96).

The expression, "Given any number . . . ," is commonplace in mathematical arguments. Matalon (1963a, 1963b) and Gréco (1963a) have attempted to study the developmental acquisition of this concept of "any number" (*nombre quelconque*). Various techniques were used, all designed to probe for the insight that certain mathematical operations produce invariant results regardless of what numbers they are performed upon, and hence that the number in question need not be known or specified ("let n represent any given number . . ."). It is intuitively obvious that this kind of mathematical understanding is more subtle and abstract than any so far dealt with in this section, and it is no surprise to find that most of Matalon's and Gréco's *quelconque* problems appear to require formal rather than concrete operations for their systematic solution.

In one of Matalon's (1963a) studies, the child was asked, in effect, whether $2n + 1$ will be divisible by 2 (i.e., will be an even or an odd number), whatever value of n is selected. The developmental trends found were not very pronounced, but there was at least some indication that the older Ss (near-adolescents) tended to be more sensitive to the generality of the answer—to the "no-matter-what-number-you-choose" character of the problem. In another study, two rows of white and red counters were set before the child in optical correspondence, each white opposite a red. E then mixed the two sets together and asked S if the successive removal of randomly chosen pairs of counters from the pile would or would not leave a remainder. Some of the younger children were confident that pairwise depletion would leave no remainder, providing that each pair consisted of a red and a white counter, but were unsure for *paires quelconques*. The older ones recognized that any and all pairs were equivalent in this context.

Gréco's (1963a) tasks were too complex to be described here. In general, they also highlight the elementary school child's difficulties in seeing that all numbers can be regarded as equivalent for certain purposes of mathematical reasoning. In discussing these studies, Piaget speaks of a progressive *quelconquification* of numbers in the course of development, and he suggests that the child's increasing fluency with combinatorial operations plays a role in this process (Gréco, Inhelder, Matalon, and Piaget, 1963, pp. 13, 16). For other recent Genevan work on number concepts, see Vols. 11, 13, and 17 of Piaget's *Etudes d'épistémologie génétiques* monograph series (published by Presses Universitaires de France).

Other Concepts

This brief section deals with a residual cluster of interrelated concepts of a logical-mathematical sort concerning which we have at least some developmental information. The principal one is the concept of chance or probability. Piaget and Inhelder (1951) have made an extensive theoretical and experimental analysis of its evolution, and there is also a small follow-up literature by non-Genevan researchers. Piaget and Inhelder have cogently argued that the full development of elementary probabilistic reasoning must await certain formal-operational acquisitions, namely, the concept of proportion and the ability to engage in combinatorial thinking. Some interesting developmental research has been done on proportions and combinations, however, and an initial examination of this research will serve as an introduction to the probability studies.

Combinations and Proportions. In Piaget's theoretical system, combinatorial operations and an understanding of proportionality are characterized as *formal-operational schemas:* conceptual instruments or skills which are the developmental by-products of adolescent-level thought organization in general (Piaget's group-lattice structure), and which can mediate the solution of a wide range of superficially dissimilar problems (Inhelder and Piaget, 1958, pp. 307–329; Flavell, 1963a, p. 222). Thus Piaget frequently appeals to the adolescent's underlying grasp of combinations and/or proportions to account for his ability to master many of the scientific-reasoning tasks he and Inhelder have given to this age group, such as problems involving the determination of the chemical properties of an array of identical-looking liquids, the discovery of the metrical regularities involved in the projection of shadows, and also—as we shall see—certain probability problems (Inhelder and Piaget, 1958; Piaget and Inhelder, 1951).

In the specific case of combinations, Piaget has made a more direct probe for the child's understanding (Piaget and Inhelder, 1951, Chap. 7). The child is presented with several sets of colored tokens, each set of a different color. His task is to form as many distinct, unlike-color pairs of tokens as he can. Given three sets of red, blue, and yellow tokens, for instance, the only possible unlike-color pairs would be red-blue, red-yellow, and blue-yellow. Piaget found that a sure and systematic procedure for identifying all the possible combinations was seldom in evidence before the age of 11 to 12 years, the beginning of the formal-operational period. Other studies (*ibid.,* Chap. 8, 9) showed that a similar management of permutation and arrangement problems is also largely an adolescent rather than middle-childhood achievement.

As for proportions, Lunzer (1965b) reports a sharp increase in the ability to master verbal and numerical analogies problems across the age period 9 to 11 years. These problems clearly have a relations-between-relations, proportional structure (e.g., "oval-*sphere*-round-ring-diameter is to *circle* as *cube* is to *square*"), and Lunzer argues that this fact explains the concrete-operational child's difficulty in coping with them.

Bruner and Kenney (Bruner, Olver, and Greenfield, 1966, Chap. 8) have done a particularly ingenious developmental study of this concept. Children of 5, 6, 7, 9, and 11 years were presented with pairs of glasses containing water, and asked to judge which glass is fuller and which glass emptier. The glasses in each pair varied systematically on a number of dimensions: their absolute height and diameter, the absolute height of their liquid column, the degree (proportion) to which they are full and empty. They found that younger children tend to judge solely on the basis of an undifferentiated estimate of the amount of water in the two glasses: "fuller" or "full" means more or much water; "emptier" or "empty" means less or little water (the "much" or "little" often being indexed by the height of the liquid column without regard to its diameter). The 7- and 9-year-olds also tend to have an absolutistic conception of fullness and emptiness, but a more articulated one: "fuller" means the glass with the most filled space and "emptier" the one with the most unfilled space. However, since the same glass may show *both* of these properties (e.g., the larger of two glasses, both half full), these children are susceptible to inconsistent and contradictory judgments, which the younger ones escape. And, finally, consistent with Piaget's and Lunzer's findings, there is a decided increase from 9 to 11 years of age in the number of judgments reflecting a proportional conception of these terms. Lovell (1961) has replicated a number of Inhelder and Piaget's probability and scientific-reasoning tasks, and his data also attest to the formal-operational status of combinatorial and proportional thinking.

Probability. Piaget has proposed a theory concerning the ontogeny of probabilistic thinking (Piaget and Inhelder, 1951, pp. 226–250; Flavell, 1963a, pp. 341–347). It begins with an argument which the writer has summarized as follows:

In order to identify a set of phenomena as "chance events," one has first to identify a set of phenomena which are not chance events, a nonchance ground against which chance can emerge as figure. Only if cognitive processes are developed enough to order and organize the intrinsically certain, lawful, and predictable by means of rational operations, can things which are intrinsically uncertain, unlawful, and unpredictable be apprehended as such. Put most simply, a mind which knows no law can also know no lawlessness (Flavell, 1963a, pp. 341–342).

The pre-operational child lacks such operations and hence is generally unable to differ-

entiate clearly between the two realms; *a fortiori*, he cannot engage in genuine probabilistic thinking. The advent of concrete operations first makes such a differentiation possible, and during the latter part of this developmental period the child begins to train these operations on chance as well as nonchance events, in an attempt to extract whatever lawfulness and predictability he can. However, concrete-operational structures are essentially inadequate for most probability problems, and it is not until adolescence that his newly attained combinatorial and proportional schemas make possible any really systematic and effective treatment. Once given a systematic method for isolating all the possible combinations of a set of items, the child is in a position to understand the nature of random processes and to think about the chances of obtaining certain combinations from the total set of possible ones. Similarly, once endowed with a concept of proportionality, a genuine quantitative comparison of probabilities becomes possible. For example, only if such a concept is available can the child be sure that a collection of 2 red and 3 white marbles affords better odds for drawing a red than does a collection of 1 red and 2 whites, that is, that the proportion $\frac{2}{5}$ is greater than the proportion $\frac{1}{3}$.

Piaget and Inhelder (1951) used a number of different tasks to study ontogenetic changes in the child's understanding of probability (Flavell, 1963a, pp. 343–347). In one, an initially ordered arrangement of objects is progressively randomized, and E tries to assess S's grasp of the randomization process. Other studies dealt with the child's ability to predict the kind of distribution (normal, rectangular) which would result from random movements of objects under various physical constraints, and with the child's reaction to the progressively more nonrandom-looking behavior of a crooked roulette wheel. The last series consisted of lot-drawing tasks, of which that discussed next is perhaps the most interesting (Piaget and Inhelder, 1951, Chap. 6).

Two logically equivalent variations on a set of probability-comparison problems were given to children of different ages. The stimuli were in all instances white tokens, some blank on both faces and some with a cross on one face. In the one variation, the child is shown two small collections of these tokens;

although those with the crosses are turned face down, E makes sure that S is fully informed of the composition of each collection (e.g., 1 cross and 3 plain in one, 2 crosses and 3 plain in the other). The child's task is to judge, in effect, which collection would more likely yield a cross on a random draw. In the other variation, only a single collection is used, and S must decide which *kind* of token (cross or plain) a random draw is more likely to produce. The composition of the two collections in this procedure was varied in ways designed to reveal the cognitive level of the Ss; for example, simple ratios of 1/2 and 2/2 (for the two collections) versus more difficult ratios of 1/3 and 2/6, or of 1/2 and 2/3.

An analysis of Ss' responses to the various subtasks suggested the following developmental sequence (ages approximate, of course). The youngest children (4 to 7 years) either entirely fail to respond in terms of the quantitative relations involved, or can occasionally do so on an intuitive basis when the perceptual disproportions are particularly striking. Beginning at about 7 years of age, regular and systematic solutions to certain classes of tasks become manifest. In the case of the single-collection problem, the child now invariably selects the kind of token that is numerically superior; in the case of the two-collection problem, he analogously chooses the collection which has the most crosses in it. What he is still unable to do, as would be predictable from the proportion-concept studies reviewed previously, is to judge on the basis of the *proportion* of crosses-to-total, as opposed to the *absolute number* of crosses, in each of the two collections. For instance, he is inclined to think that 2/4 presents better odds than 1/2 simply because there are more crosses in the first collection. Toward age 11 (i.e., the end of Piaget's concrete-operational period) the child begins to reason in terms of the proportions in play, and he does so systematically in the years following. Here is an example of the kind of transitional thinking Piaget encountered in some of his Ss. The problem is the one just mentioned and the child is 9 years of age.

Here (2/4). No, it's there (1/2), because there is only one without a cross. (Why did you say the other one?) Because there are two crosses. (Well, which counts the most, two crosses or one without a cross?) One without a cross, two crosses . . . it's the same, because there are two crosses and two without crosses (in 2/4). (Then one of the two is easier?) No, it's the same, but it's surer here (2/4) because there are two crosses (very perplexed) (Piaget and Inhelder, 1951, p. 166).

In a related study (*ibid.*, Chap. 5), the child's task is to predict the likeliest draw (of either one or a pair of tokens) from a bag containing different numbers of tokens of several colors (e.g., 15 yellows, 10 reds, 7 greens, and 3 blues). Where the draw of only a single token is to be predicted, this task of course becomes a simple variate of the one-collection problem just described. Once again, the authors argue from their data that pre-operational children are largely incapable of assessing comparative probabilities.

There are three experiments by American psychologists which take the Piagetian lot-drawing procedures as their point of departure (Yost, Siegel, and Andrews, 1962; Davies, 1965; and Goldberg, 1966). Although the procedures and results of these three experiments of course differ from one another on a number of points, there are enough similarities to permit the following single statement of their collective message.

Probabilistic thinking undoubtedly undergoes developmental changes, as Piaget and Inhelder had claimed (the Davies study was in fact partly normative-developmental in design). However, at least the beginnings of this development occur earlier than Piaget and Inhelder would have us believe. There are a number of "noisy" variables in the Piaget and Inhelder procedures, features which may impede the behavioral actualization of what the child really knows about probability. If one uses a testing method designed to eliminate or neutralize such variables (e.g., a method that relies less heavily on the child's verbal skills, controls for his initial stimulus preferences, and provides better memory aids for the composition of the collections), it can be demonstrated that more young children will behave in accordance with the event probabilities than will be the case with Piaget and Inhelder's original methods.

All three of these experiments appear to have been carefully designed and executed, and the writer is not inclined to doubt their findings as such. The interpretation of these findings is quite another matter, however. As will be seen, there are now numerous studies in the Piagetian literature attempting to show that some given operation enters the child's repertoire earlier than Piaget had claimed. The problem which such studies bring forcibly to our attention is the very difficult and involved one of defining, both conceptually and operationally, precisely what is meant by "having" an item in one's cognitive system. If there could be agreement on just what it means to have "attained" any item, and on the exact test behavior that distinguishes attainment from nonattainment, the dating of cognitive acquisitions would be an easy matter. But there is no such agreement in the field at the present time; in fact, the problem itself has not yet attracted the serious attention it deserves. As in the case of the term "concept" itself, the difficulty is of course not in finding *some* definition (and *some* associated test criterion) but in finding a *principled, theoretically based* one—in effect, a revealing and heuristic way of conceptualizing the question. A later section of this chapter is devoted to this and related matters (Developmental Diagnosis of Conceptual Acquisitions). In the present case, it can at least be said that there is little in the data of the aforementioned three investigations that would lead one to conclude that the pre-operational child really "has"—to invoke that vague word again—very much in the way of probabilistic-thinking skills (Goldberg, 1966, Conclusions).

As already indicated, these three studies suggest that the growth period for probabilistic reasoning should be extended further toward the birth end of the ontogenetic span than Piaget would have it. To balance matters, there are three other studies which suggest that the typical level of functioning at the other end of this period may be lower than he supposed. Teachers of statistics will not be surprised to learn, for example, that untutored adults have been found to show rather poor intuitions about the concept of correlation (Smedslund, 1963d). Similarly, Ross has demonstrated that the reasoning of adolescents and adults in chance situations is likely to show nonprobabilistic as well as probabilistic features (Ross, 1966; Ross and Levy, 1958). He found, for instance, that the "gambler's fallacy" (exemplified in the belief that

a head becomes ever more probable, in a coin-tossing situation, as a run of tails grows longer) actually *increases* in frequency with age during the adolescent period. Piaget is probably right in believing that, as the child develops, he becomes increasingly able and disposed to train intellectual operations on probabilistic problems. Not all of these operations need conform to the tenets of probability theory, however, and a good number of them —for example, those that underlie gambler's-fallacy predictions—probably will not. As the Bruner and Kenney study so neatly illustrates (Bruner, Olver, and Greenfield, 1966, Chap. 8), intellectual development makes possible not only new truth, but also new and more exotic forms of error.

THE NATURAL WORLD

Objects

Some 40 years ago Piaget made an intensive and careful study of the sensorimotor development of his own three children. Most of what he discovered in this work is of significance for a treatment of concept development; but his findings regarding the infant's changing conception of objects (the so-called "object concept") deserve particular attention (Piaget, 1954; see also Flavell, 1963a, pp. 129–135, and Gouin-Décarie, 1965, Chap. 2). According to Piaget, during the period of infancy the child gradually and step by step makes an ontological discovery of enormous significance for his subsequent development: the objects that populate his world maintain a permanent existence and physical integrity independent of his own intermittent sensory and motor contacts with them. The child "has" such a concept, in other words, to the extent that he tacitly assumes that objects are no less in continued existence for being temporarily out of receptor contact, for example, for having disappeared from sight behind a screen. It is next to impossible to conceive of an intellectual genesis that would not presuppose either the innate or early acquired possession of this fundamental concept. Consequently, any demonstration that it is in fact a gradual acquisition rather than an initial given would qualify as a most important scientific discovery. Let us begin, then, by briefly summarizing Piaget's account of this acquisition.

Piaget's Analysis of the Growth of the Object Concept. Piaget traces this growth within the 6-stage framework utilized in all of his descriptions of sensorimotor development. The age range associated with each stage is intended to be approximate only.

Stages 1 and 2 (0 to 4 months). When an object disappears from view, the infant will at most fixate for a time on the position where it was last seen. This is in itself very weak evidence for the lack of an object concept, of course, but it has significance in combination with what is seen in later stages.

Stage 3 (4 to 8 months). There are a number of relevant achievements during this stage, of which two are perhaps the most interesting. First, the child makes a primitive beginning at regaining contact with absent objects by extrapolating the accommodatory movements made to them during their presence; thus he may lean over to look for an object that fell to the floor rather than simply stare at the point where it disappeared from view, as would have been the case in Stages 1 and 2. Second, he acquires the ability to anticipate a whole object on the basis of seeing only a part of it. However, his behavior in this situation also testifies to the immaturity of his object concept: if a sufficient fraction of the object shows from behind the screen, he reaches for it; if this fraction is then made to decrease, the reaching hand abruptly drops. More generally, it is characteristic of this stage that the child makes no attempt to retrieve an object manually once it has disappeared from view (e.g., by being covered with a cloth), in spite of the fact that such activity would by this age be well within his physical capabilities.

Stage 4 (8 to 12 months). The child now regularly searches for objects which he has just seen move behind screens, at first only if already in the act of reaching for them at the moment of disappearance, and then without this restriction. However, this behavior pattern—surely a milestone in the genesis of the object concept—remains subject to an important limitation. Having had repeated success at retrieving an object hidden in one place, the child continues to search in that place when the object is then hidden elsewhere, despite the fact that its disappearance at the new location had clearly been attended to.

Stage 5 (12 to 18 months). The child overcomes the previously mentioned limitation, now searching only where the object was last seen to disappear irrespective of what happened on previous trials. But this advance also contains the seeds of one further limitation: the child cannot yet infer invisible displacements, that is, further movements of the object after it has disappeared from view. Thus, if *E* carries a small object in his closed hand to a given hiding place and leaves it there, the Stage 5 child will search only where the object was last seen—in *E*'s hand.

Stage 6 (beginning at 18 months). At the end of the sensorimotor period the child becomes capable of representing whole sequences of invisible but inferable displacements, for example, if object-in-closed-hand is transported in succession to hiding places *A*, *B*, *C*, and *D*, the child will systematically search in all of them (and in the hand), as if he knew exactly what the possibilities were. At this point in development, Piaget is ready to credit him with a full-fledged concept of the independent and enduring object.

Replications and Extensions of Piaget's Work. For reasons we need not mention here, all of Piaget's studies tend to constitute very powerful stimuli for replication behavior on the part of his reader. A lack of independent confirmation of his infancy work, however, ought to make a reader exceptionally uncomfortable, in view of the not overlarge sample of Ss (three), their relationship to the investigator, and the casual-looking tenor of his observations-interventions. One might have thought that there would have been a veritable stampede of would-be confirmers (or disconfirmers) for this segment of his work. However, for reasons that can only be guessed at (the difficulty of infant research and its relative unpopularity until recently), replication attempts are just now appearing on the scene, and some of the best are still in progress at this writing. The most important questions for follow-up work on object-concept development would seem to be these two. (1) Are the various behaviors vis-à-vis objects which Piaget observed in his three infants found in all normal infants? (2) Do these behaviors always emerge in the particular ontogenetic sequence he described?

There are three major replication studies, one completed (Gouin-Décarie, 1965) and two still in progress (Uzgiris and Hunt, 1966a,

1966b; Escalona, 1966). The two projects in progress have as their eventual aim the construction of standardized developmental scales for testing sensorimotor intelligence. Both are large-scale and extremely well-designed investigations, and they have already yielded what looks like very clear and trustworthy evidence concerning the genesis of the object concept. In particular, their data strongly support three conclusions. First, large samples of infants regularly show the very same behavioral reactions in this area that Piaget's three children did. Second, standardized testing procedures for eliciting these reactions can be devised and the reactions elicited show very high interobserver and (short-term) test-retest reliability. And, finally, the scalability of the test items turns out to be essentially perfect, that is, virtually no children ever show reactions characteristic of a later Piagetian stage while failing to have achieved those characteristic of an earlier one. These studies also show promise of providing a wealth of additional detail about this evolution which Piaget, with his limited sample, could hardly have obtained. For instance, Uzgiris and Hunt (1966b) report what may be new intermediate or transitional reactions within Stages 5 and 6, and Escalona (1966) presents evidence suggesting a qualitative difference between Stage 6 performance and that of earlier stages.

The purpose of Gouin-Décarie's (1965) investigation was quite different: she tried to show chronological parallels between the development of the object concept and the development of interpersonal-affective "object relations" (in the psychoanalytic sense of the term). Like Escalona and Uzgiris and Hunt, Gouin-Décarie's data on the former development unequivocally supported Piaget's conclusions, in terms of both content and content sequence (the scalability of her items also turned out to be perfect). The data on the genesis of object relations and their alleged parallelism with object-concept development were also suggestive, but much less unambiguous. That some such parallelism must exist seems undeniable, since the significant people in the infant's life are, at minimum, also "objects." It is interesting in this connection that Schaffer and Emerson (1964) have recently shown that differentiated affective attachments to specific human objects occur at about the same time the infant begins to search in earnest for absent objects (i.e., early in Stage 4). Finally, Woodward (1959) can claim credit for the earliest replication study in this area, if one is willing to accredit retardates as surrogate infants! She found that the order of difficulty of object-concept items for severely retarded older children closely corresponded to their ontogenetic order as described by Piaget.

We shall close this section by describing two recent studies of a more innovative sort, methodologically innovative in the case of Charlesworth (1966) and substantively so in the case of Babska (1965). Charlesworth's investigation focused only on the acquisition of Stage 4 behavior, which he regards as the most important developmental step in the sequence. His design was a combination longitudinal and cross-sectional one, 12 of his 58 infant Ss being retested monthly across the period of transition. His procedure was as follows. S is seated in a high chair and his attention is drawn to a small preferred object on the high chair tray. E thereupon cups his hand over the object for 2 to 4 seconds and then removes his hand. On some trials (Real Condition), the object is again visible after the hand is lifted, and on some (Trick Condition) it has miraculously disappeared, thanks to a small, foot-operated "trap door" in the tray. The child's behavior throughout the procedure is filmed with a motion picture camera. Charlesworth's Real and Trick Condition trials provide him with a rich and varied set of responses for developmental diagnosis. The older infants could variously certify their Stage 4 status with behaviors such as these: active search for the object while it is under E's hand; an immediate reaching response toward the object after the hand is lifted (Real Condition); surprise, puzzlement, change in affect, and active visual or manual search for the unaccountably missing object (Trick Condition). Charlesworth's data suggest that of the two, the Trick Condition is in general the more sensitive measure of the child's cognitive progress. A global assessment of S's developmental status based upon such behaviors indicated that the transition to Stage 4 occurs at roughly 7 to 8 months, which accords fairly closely with Piaget's original findings. Charlesworth is currently exploring the feasibility of measuring the infant's autonomic responses in these conditions, as a more sensitive indicator of the infant's cognitive expectancies and his reaction to their violation (personal communication).

It might be supposed that the cognitive accomplishments of Stage 5, and especially of Stage 6, entail something more than just a tacit belief that the out-of-sight object continues to exist (the literal definition of the object concept). Also involved perhaps is a growing sensitivity to the cues that reliably indicate just where in space this existence is or could be manifested: at the place where the object last was seen (Stage 5) or at the places its conveyor "touched down" during its itinerary (Stage 6). Babska (1965) has studied what may be still higher developmental forms of this sensitivity. Her test materials were sets of four grey, identical boxes with white cardboard covers, each cover exhibiting a different picture (e.g., a hen, a horse, a woman's face, and a cat). The child is presented with one of the boxes and is shown that it contains a toy. The box is then taken away for 15 seconds, after which it is shown again in company with the other three boxes of the set. E now asks S to find the toy and give it to her. The critical box (or the whole set of boxes) is changed from trial to trial, and the only reliable algorithm by which the child can always succeed in immediately finding the toy is to choose the one identical in appearance to that which was previously shown to contain the toy. Successful responding thus involves selective attention to the particular visual characteristics of the hiding place on each given trial; neither attending to spatial-position cues nor repeating the previous trial's correct response is an appropriate strategy here. Babska found that the transition to a consistent management of this type of problem occurs much later than sensorimotor Stage 6; it occurs at around 3 years of age. Her work appears to open up a number of research possibilities regarding the cognitive skills underlying the retrieval of absent objects under different circumstances —a research area that might be titled "Beyond the Object Concept."[2]

[2] An ingenious series of experiments by Bower (1967) has come to the author's attention since the completion of this chapter. Bower appears to have demonstrated that infants as young as 2 to

Quantity

A great many concepts are "quantitative" in the sense of being susceptible to precise enumeration or measurement—number, length, area, time, velocity, etc. However, this section deals only with the three that Piaget has usually subsumed under the name *quantité*: substance (alternate designations: mass, matter, global quantity), weight, and volume. The development of these three concepts, and especially of their conservation, has been described in detail in one of Piaget's books (Piaget and Inhelder, 1941); there is elsewhere reported some additional evidence regarding conservation of substance (Piaget, 1952) and of volume (Piaget, Inhelder, and Szeminska, 1960).

Conservation of Substance, Weight, and Volume. We begin by briefly describing in turn the testing procedures used to assess nonconservation-conservation of each of these three concepts. In the case of substance, the procedure is as follows. Two quantities of a given material or substance X are initially established as equal, by virtue of having identical perceptual appearance or configuration. One of the two is then altered in some quantity-irrelevant way—for instance, changed in shape or divided into parts—and the child is asked if there is still "as much

3 months have what could be described as a perceptual version of the concept of object permanence. If an object disappears in an abrupt, discontinuous way (e.g., appears to "implode"), for example, the infant indeed acts as if it no longer existed for him, just as Piaget had suggested. However, if it disappears slowly and continuously (e.g., gradually moves behind a screen), he behaves for a time as though it were still present or would shortly reappear. Bower suggests that these primitive, perception-based discriminations regarding permanence and impermanence are later subordinated to conceptual rules—to the *concept* of object permanence. Unlike the 3-month-old, the 12-month-old has come to believe in the continued existence of certain objects (e.g., his mother) regardless of the psychophysical properties of their disappearance—even when his lower-order, perceptual operations have given him a verdict of out-of-existence rather than out-of-sight. If Bower's findings prove valid (his studies certainly should be replicated), they will substantially augment and elaborate our understanding of this highly important sector of human epistemological growth.

X" (or some equivalent expression) in the one as in the other. Several different materials have been used. The child may be presented with two identical balls of clay or plasticine, one of which is then elongated, flattened, cut into pieces, etc., prior to the conservation question. Or he may be given two identical glasses containing equal quantities of liquid, one of which is then poured into a narrower or wider glass, or into several little glasses. Or, as we have already seen, the contents of the glasses may be marbles or beads, the test thereby amounting to a variation on the standard conservation of number problem (conservation of "discontinuous" as opposed—in the case of clay and water—to "continuous" quantity).

Whichever procedure is used, the physical transformation which *E* has wrought in one of the quantities presents *S* with the temptation to index the relative amounts perceptually—by noting the differential heights of the liquid column in the standard and comparison glasses, the greater length of the elongated clay ball, etc.—rather than conceptually—by invoking the knowledge that nothing has been added or taken away during the transformation, etc. As in the number conservation test, the younger, nonconserving *S* succumbs to the temptation, assesses the quantities in terms of some one, striking perceptual feature, and wrongly concludes that there is "more *X*" here than there, for example "more water" in the narrower glass because of its higher liquid column.

As in the area of number, we still have much to learn about the cognitive structure and content of children who do and do not conserve global quantity or substance. It can at least be said that "amount" for the nonconserver is not yet a multidimensional affair, unreliably estimable by consideration of only a single dimension; everything points to the fact that the young child is quite content to estimate quantity (and, as subsequent sections will show, many other physical variables) by means of a single cue such as height. In the case of substance conservation particularly, however, an exact intellectual characterization of the conserver is equally difficult. For the present, it will suffice to point out two components his quantity concept need *not* have and, indeed, regularly does not have when the conservation we are

discussing is first attained. (1) There is no recognition that the weight and the volume of the transformed object—the very attributes by which its quantity or "amount" could be precisely measured—also remain invariant under the transformation. (2) The concept of "amount" that the child first attains, and to which he correctly ascribes quantitative invariance in the face of all manner of irrelevant physical changes, appears to be a global, nonmeasurable affair, not yet anchored to the more precise concepts of weight and volume.

In the case of weight, the materials regularly used are the clay or plasticine balls. After initially establishing that the two balls keep the arms of a scale balance horizontal when placed on opposite pans (and/or are judged equally heavy when held in the child's two hands), one of them is transformed (change of shape or division into pieces) and the child is asked if they still weigh the same, or would continue to balance on the scale. Two procedures have been used to assess conservation of volume. In the one devised earlier (Piaget and Inhelder, 1941, Chap. 3), the child is shown that a clay ball placed in a vessel of water causes the water level to rise to a certain point (which *E* carefully marks). After the child agrees that a second, identical ball would make the water rise to the same height, this ball is transformed in any one of the usual ways and the child is asked if it will now take up the same amount of space in the water, if it will make the water rise to the same point. In the later procedure (Piaget, Inhelder, and Szeminska, 1960, Chap. 14), 36 small metal cubes are arranged and rearranged to make different "houses" and the child is asked if all these houses have the same amount of "room" in them. The same materials have also been used in the older procedure for comparative purposes: the little cubes are put in a vessel of water and the child is asked to predict the height of the water level when the same cubes are rearranged in different configurations.

According to Piaget, the child attains conservation of these three concepts in an invariant developmental sequence: first substance (early middle childhood), then weight (late middle childhood), and finally volume (early adolescence). However, a number of studies by Piaget (Piaget, Inhelder, and Szeminska, 1960) and others (Elkind, 1961b, 1961f,

1962c; Lovell and Ogilvie, 1961a; Lunzer, 1960b; Uzgiris, 1964) have shown that the mean age of volume-conservation attainment is very much a function of the method used to test for it. For example, there is the finding by Piaget, Inhelder, and Szeminska (1960, Chap. 14), subsequently confirmed by Lovell and Ogilvie (1961a), that the recognition that the different "houses" constructed from a common set of cubes all have the same amount of room inside is normally acquired several years earlier (i.e., roughly concurrent with weight conservation) than the recognition that they will all cause the surrounding water to rise to the same level; Piaget, Inhelder, and Szeminska refer to the former as the conservation of "interior volume" and to the latter as that of "occupied volume."

On the other hand, studies by Elkind (1961b, 1961f, 1962c) and Uzgiris (1964) have shown that there are some perfectly reasonable-looking versions of the volume-conservation task which most early adolescents fail and which only an unimpressive majority of college students pass (Elkind, 1962c). The present writer has so far been unable to find a wholly satisfactory explanation for the extremely wide variation in difficulty level across these various tasks. He suspects, however, that the easiest ones may really be tapping a slightly refined form of substance conservation and that it is the more difficult ones which, despite their undoubted psychometric impurities, come closer to assessing what the individual really understands about volume per se and about the conditions under which it remains invariant.

Assuming for the moment that conservation of substance, weight, and volume are achieved in that ontogenetic order, how might this particular order be explained? The following is a highly oversimplified account of Piaget's attempt at explanation (Piaget and Inhelder, 1941; Piaget, Inhelder, and Szeminska, 1960; see also Flavell, 1963a, pp. 300-303). The ability to conserve substance or global quantity emerges from two schemas or skills developed early in the concrete-operational period. On the one hand, the child becomes capable of multiplying relations, for example, imagining that the elongated ball's added length may be compensated by its decreased thickness. On the other hand, he attains a kind of part-whole or "atomistic" conception

of substances: an intuition that a given amount of substance is composed of a fixed number of small parts or unit-amounts, which merely change their position in space under the standard transformations (in effect, a kind of number-conservation schema applied to continuous rather than discontinuous material). However, for various reasons having to do with his initial, egocentrically tainted conception of weight, the child is not at first ready to assume that the weight of these unit-amounts remains the same regardless of their locus within the whole, and hence there remain further obstacles to overcome before conservation can be generalized to this property. And, finally, there are still more advanced schemas and skills which must get into the repertoire before conservation of volume becomes a possibility: a clear differentiation between weight and volume and some grasp of their relationship within an atomistic conception (objects which are heavy for their volume are composed of dense, closely compacted units); an understanding of certain properties of lines and planes, which makes possible a metric, three-dimensional conception of volume.

Subsequent Research on the Quantity Conservations. As was true in the area of number, Piaget's work on substance, weight, and volume conservation has received a considerable amount of research attention by other investigators. Some of the relevant studies on volume conservation have already been cited. Additional evidence will now be presented by means of the stratagem used in the section on class concepts: describe a well-executed, prototypical study, and ring the findings of other investigators around its results. The best study for this purpose (and perhaps the best study in the area on most counts) is that by Uzgiris (1964). Tests of conservation of substance, weight, and (occupied) volume were individually administered to 120 first- through sixth-grade children. Four different types of material were used in testing for each of the three conservation concepts: plasticine balls, metal nuts, wire coils, and straight pieces of insulated wire. There were two principal findings.

Conservation of substance, weight, and volume are almost invariably achieved in that order for each of the four types of material. Out of 120 Ss, only 8 showed a deviation from this sequence on some one of the four materials. There are at least eight other studies that give evidence on this alleged substance-weight-volume sequence (in addition, of course, to Piaget's original positive findings; see Piaget and Inhelder, 1941, p. 12). Of the eight, the data of six either explicitly demonstrate (Chittenden, 1964; Kooistra, 1965; Sigel and Mermelstein, 1966; Smedslund, 1961b) or imply (Elkind, 1961b; King, 1963) a near-exceptionless sequence of acquisition for these concepts, whereas two (Beard, 1963b; Hyde, 1959) apparently find numerous deviations from the modal order. The combined evidence for the developmental gap (or, in Piaget's lexicon, developmental *décalage*) between weight and volume appears to this writer to be somewhat more compelling than that for the substance-weight *décalage* (e.g., Kooistra, 1965), and it may turn out that a small minority of children somehow achieve conservation of weight before or in rough synchrony with conservation of substance. (Lovell and Ogilvie, 1960, found that a few children actually appeal to weight invariance in justifying their substance conservation responses.) On the other hand, the data from some of the more carefully designed studies in this area (e.g., Chittenden, 1964; Uzgiris, 1964) are very convincing, and the research consensus may someday be that there is in fact a universal sequential invariance here, an invariance at the level of cognitive-structural genotype as contrasted with verbal-behavioral phenotype.

Uzgiris' second major finding was that there is a fair amount of individual inconsistency in level of conceptual response across task materials, especially at certain ages. Uzgiris offers the highly reasonable suggestion that it is the child in a transitional phase with respect to some conservation concept who is most subject to variation in performance concerning that concept as a function of specific features of the task situation; once the concept is well-consolidated, this situational variability would be expected to diminish. As will be shown later in the chapter, this interaction, possibly age-dependent, between performance level and task features is scarcely limited to the area of quantity concepts. Within this area, however, Beard (1963b), Lovell and Ogilvie (1960, 1961b), and Pratoomraj and Johnson (1966) have likewise noted that conservation judgments are partly dependent on the specifics of the task. Lovell and Ogilvie (1961b), for example, have shown that weight conservation judgments may be importantly influenced by the kind of transformation performed upon the materials: many children who recognized that the weight of an object is not altered when its shape changes still believed that making it harder or softer (water cooled until it turned to ice, hard butter allowed to soften, etc.) would change the weight.

It must be obvious that the research questions posed by Uzgiris and these other investigators are not the only ones, nor the only important ones, that might be asked about the ontogenesis of quantity concepts. There is, for instance, the vital problem of identifying the cognitive antecedents or "ingredients" of these various conservation concepts and, once identified, of determining their necessary- versus sufficient-condition status as "causes" of these concepts. However, this and other important problems are also better deferred to later chapter sections, so that they may be given a more general treatment. Suffice it to say here that Piaget's account of the cognitive acquisitions underlying these particular conservations has already come under fire (e.g., Bruner, Olver, and Greenfield, 1966; Lunzer, 1960b), and that there are a number of vexing methodological and theoretical problems involved in trying to decide what constitutes adequate research evidence on this sort of developmental question. One final investigation is worth citing if only because it can scarcely be well known as yet. In an unpublished doctoral study (1965), Anderson has found an increase from grades 3 through 6 in children's disposition to utilize atomistic conceptual models to explain the attributes and behavior of various natural phenomena such as water.

Space

This section reviews studies of the development of such spatial concepts as the conservation and measurement of length, distance, and area. As with previous topics, Piagetian or Piaget-inspired studies come close to exhausting the significant research literature in this area.

Piaget's Theory and Research on the Development of Spatial Concepts. Piaget makes a rather sharp distinction between the perception and representation of space (Piaget and Inhelder, 1956). The theory and research under discussion concerns representation rather than perception: the evolution of the child's intellectual representations and operations with regard to the spatial world—developmental changes in "how the child thinks about space" (*ibid.*, p. xii). His theory makes several claims about this evolution, of which the following two are held to be particularly important. First, an adult's cognitive representation of space derives from an ontogenetic history of actions performed upon objects, rather than from a history of direct perceptual "readings" of their properties; the way we eventually come to apprehend our spatial surroundings is thus primarily a function of past doings rather than past seeings. Second, not all the various spatial-geometric properties are acquired at the same time. In particular, topological properties (proximity, order, etc.) are said to be attained first, and then to provide a developmental foundation for later-acquired projective (perspectives, etc.) and Euclidean (rectilinear coordinates, etc.) properties.

Special theoretical and research attention has been given to the mastery of Euclidean concepts (Piaget and Inhelder, 1956, Part 3; Piaget, Inhelder, and Szeminska, 1960). The following passage describes what Piaget believes to be one of the major intellectual components of this mastery:

What the child needs eventually to establish—and does not at first possess—is a picture of space as a kind of all-enveloping container made up of a network of sites or subspaces. Within the container are objects, the things contained, which move from site to site, now occupying or filling a given site, now leaving it unoccupied and empty. Measurements of various kinds can be made within the container without regard for whether the sites along which the measurements occur are occupied or not. For example, the straight-line distance from me to you is the same whether or not the space between us is occupied by objects, whether or not the intervening spatial sites are filled or empty. Similarly, if I slide a block of wood along the table, the metric value of the space it occupied before the movement (its length, its surface area, its

volume) is precisely equivalent to that of the space it presently occupies, even though the former is now empty and the latter is now filled. In short, the child has finally to conceive of space as a medium which is homogeneous throughout from the point of view of measurement, in spite of its heterogeneity as regards filled versus empty subspaces or sites (Flavell, 1963a, p. 335).

The two Piaget volumes cited above report some three dozen developmental studies, and it is obviously impossible to summarize them all here. Several deal with the acquisition of various topological concepts (Piaget and Inhelder, 1956, Part 1). In one, Piaget and Inhelder claim to show that the child can distinguish, in both tactual discrimination and graphic reproduction task settings, topological features (e.g., a closed versus an open ring) earlier than he can discriminate Euclidean features (e.g., a square versus a triangle). Several other studies point up the child's initial difficulties with the topological property of order or sequence; for example, his inability to invert an order and to transform a circular order into a simple linear one. These experiments on spatial order have a better-known ancestor, reported in an earlier book (Piaget, 1946b): E slides three different-colored wooden balls into, say, the left-hand opening of a tunnel in a particular order (A, then B, then C), and then asks S a series of questions. In what order will the three balls exit at the right hand end of the tunnel (ABC)? In what order would they reemerge on the left side (CBA)? What will be the order of appearance on the right side when the whole tunnel is rotated 180° (CBA), or 360° (ABC), etc.? Pre-operational children tend to have problems with all but the first question, and occasionally even predict that the middle ball (B) will emerge first under one or another of the experimental conditions. Above all, they seem to lack any sense of a rule system governing the occurrence of direct versus inverse orders under the various rotations and directions of exit.

Another group of studies dealt with the acquisition of projective-geometric properties, especially with the child's growing awareness that a given object or array of objects has a different visual appearance when looked at from different viewpoints, and that its appearance from any given perspective may be "computed" from the cues presented (Piaget and Inhelder, 1956, Part 2). Consideration of this research will be deferred to the section titled Psychological Concepts, however, since the behavior in question can equally be construed as an instance of social-psychological (i.e., role-taking) cognitive activity.

The list of investigations centering on Euclidean-geometric acquisitions is much longer. The concept of an iterable (i.e., capable of repeated application) measurement unit is seen as one of the crucial mediators of operational progress in this area (Piaget, Inhelder, and Szeminska, 1960, Chap. 15). Reminiscent of the atomistic view of substance described in the previous section, it refers to the view that a given length (distance, area, volume) is potentially divisible into equal, unit part-lengths of arbitrary size, the total length thus being precisely measurable by repeatedly (iteratively) displacing one of these units along its entire extent. The following experiment nicely illustrates the developmental growth of this concept (*ibid.*, Chap. 2). The child is shown a block tower and asked to build another one of the same height. Conditions are so arranged that measurement is necessary for exact replication (e.g., the child cannot see the model while actually constructing the duplicate and the blocks available for the duplicate are of a different size than those used in the model), and various-sized sticks and paper strips are put at the child's disposal. The behavior of Piaget's Ss on this task yielded a rich sequence of developmental stages and substages, among which the following are particularly revealing. The basic transitivity property inherent in all metric comparisons eludes the youngest children, that is, that the establishment of A (the model tower) $= B$ (a stick of the same length), and $B = C$ (the duplicate tower), permits the certain inference $A = C$. This failure to utilize spontaneously a common measure recalls the developmental evidence on transitivity of symmetrical relations presented in an earlier section of this chapter (Relations). Also, only toward the middle of the concrete-operational years do children have a conception of length that allows them to utilize a stick or strip *shorter* than the model as an iterable unit measure—"the

tower I must build is exactly three-sticks-plus-this-much-leftover high."

Possession or nonpossession of this unit-parts schema almost certainly influences the child's response to some of the conservation of length problems Piaget has invented (*ibid.*, Chap. 5). He has shown, for example, that young children fail to maintain an initial judgment of length equivalence when one of two originally identical strips of paper is cut into pieces and the pieces are set end to end to form a jagged line; the reason is that they attend only to the endpoints of the line, rather than to its constituent part-lengths (the sequence of pieces).

The schema of empty and filled subspaces described in the preceding quotation is also thought to mediate conservation of length (*ibid.*, Chap. 4) and, especially, conservation of distance(*ibid.*, Chap. 3). As to conservation of length, Piaget has shown that two identical sticks of wood initially judged to be of equal length when placed side by side so that their ends coincide are, incredibly, no longer so judged by the young child when E slides one ahead of the other. The child appears to focus his attention solely on the leading edge of the stick that was moved, failing to note that the space which this front edge fills is equal to the space which its hind edge vacates. Conservation of distance is assessed by placing two objects at a certain distance from each other, having the child globally code this distance (e.g., "they are far apart"), and then asking him if they are "still just as far apart" after a cardboard screen is interposed between them. There is a stage in development when the child thinks the distance is now less than it was because he does not "count," as part of the total distance, the space occupied by the screen. If a small window is put in the screen, for instance, the distance between the objects is actually thought to increase when the window is open and diminish when it is closed!

Other studies deal with the apprehension of two-dimensional rather than one-dimensional Euclidean space. In one of these investigations, an assessment was made of the extent to which the young child "sees" objects as embedded in a two-dimensional spatial framework—the Euclidean "grid" of horizontal and vertical coordinates (Piaget and Inhelder, 1956, Chap. 13). In the case of horizontal coordinates, for example, the child is shown a glass jar with colored water in it and asked to predict (e.g., gesturally) the spatial orientation of the water level when the jar is tilted in various ways. At one stage, the child systematically predicts that the water line will remain perpendicular to the sides of the jar, regardless of how the jar is tilted—he appears to represent the water level with reference to a local and immediate rather than generalized spatial framework. A recent study by Smedslund (1963b) clearly shows that laboratory experience in actually observing the invariance of water level under tilt has little effect on the predictions of children who showed no signs of recognizing this invariance before training; like other cognitive immaturities Piaget has described, this one appears to be less corrigible than common sense would suggest. A related study by Piaget, Inhelder, and Szeminska (1960, Chap. 7) showed that younger children are also insensitive to the need for taking into account both vertical and horizontal axes when trying to measure an object's position in two-dimensional space (given a piece of paper with a dot on it, reproduce the exact position of the dot on a second piece of paper without recourse to superposition).

Conservation and measurement of area have been assessed by a variety of techniques. In one version (*ibid.*, Chap. 11) the child was presented with two identical cardboard rectangles, each made up of six detachable squares, and was shown that the same number of tiny wooden cubes exactly covered each rectangle. After a square had been detached from one of the rectangles and reattached elsewhere on the same rectangle, the child was asked if the set of cubes would still exactly and completely cover it, if there was still the "same amount of room" on the two rectangles, or similar questions designed to tune S in to area comparisons. It is abundantly clear from this and related investigations that young children fail to conserve area in the face of area-irrelevant transformations, again perhaps due to the absence of an atomistic, unit-parts view of surfaces, wherein whole areas are seen as composed of little part areas. As indicated in the previous section, Piaget has also done extensive research on three-dimensional conservation and measurement (i.e., conservation of volume).

Other Studies of Children's Spatial Concepts. There are a number of subsequent investigations that have made use of Piaget's testing procedures (or variations thereof) in this developmental area. Three are "omnibus" replication studies, employing a whole battery of Piaget's tasks for the express purpose of checking his results (Dodwell, 1963; Lovell, 1959; Lovell, Healey, and Rowland, 1962). More focus on one or a few of his procedures, for replication or other purposes (e.g., Beilin and Franklin, 1962; Braine, 1959; Charlesworth, 1962; Peel, 1959; Pratoomraj and Johnson, 1966; Rivoire, 1962; and a number of training studies, such as that by Smedslund, 1963b, cited above).

As always, it is very difficult to summarize in a few sentences the results of such a heterogeneous body of research. Generally, these investigators seem to find roughly the same varieties of age-related immature, transitional, and mature cognitive responses that Piaget found. Quite often, however, they report differences in major and minor detail: in mean ages of acquisition, ease of response classification, observed frequency of response types, intertask and intrachild inconsistencies which Piaget would not have led us to expect, and the like. As an example of this last, Beilin and Franklin (1962) found that conservation and measurement of length is definitely achieved earlier than the corresponding operations in the case of area, whereas Piaget, Inhelder, and Szeminska (1960, pp. 285–300) had believed them to be developmentally synchronous. Several studies lend at least qualified support to Piaget's hypothesis that topological properties are mastered earlier than projective and Euclidean ones (Dodwell, 1963; Lovell, 1959; Peel, 1959; Rivoire, 1962). However, the present writer believes that much more careful, parametric experimentation will be needed before the validity —and certainly the generality—of this particular developmental sequence is firmly established.

Several studies extend, supplement, or modify Piaget's research and theory in the domain of spatial representation. Vinh Bang (1965a, 1965b) and Lunzer (1965a) have both tested children's conservation-nonconservation judgments regarding bounded surfaces that are made to vary in shape: in some conditions, the perimeter is kept constant under the shape transformation with the area changing; in others, the perimeter varies while the area is kept the same. True to type, younger children tend to conserve neither area nor perimeter in the face of these perceived changes. The interesting finding, however, was that many older (concrete-operational) children systematically asserted the continued invariance of *both* perimeter and area (wrongly so for one or the other, of course, depending upon the experimental condition)— a kind of overgeneralization of the conservation strategy. Vinh Bang's interpretation of this finding seems a reasonable one: "Once the concept of conservation is acquired, the child of 8–9 years thinks that invariance in one domain implies invariance in another, especially when the domains are related, as in the case of a perimeter and the area it generates" (1965b, p. 58). The aforementioned paper by Lunzer (1965) also makes the intriguing suggestion that the child may develop an earlier and a later operational conception of length, closely kin to the previously made distinction between "interior" and "occupied" volume (Piaget, Inhelder, and Szeminska, 1960, pp. 374–376). For a commentary on these and other recent Genevan studies on spatial concepts, see Piaget (1964b).

Middle childhood seems to be the favored epoch for the attainment not only of "conservation" (and occasionally "overconservation," so it now appears) but also of something which Beilin (1964; 1969) describes as "quasiconservation." Imagine that the child is shown the two identical cardboard rectangles used in the area conservation task described earlier, but *after*, rather than *before*, one of the six detachable squares has been removed from its original locus and reattached in a different place on the same rectangle. We then ask him if the two pieces of cardboard have the same area (not if they *still* have the same area, as in the ordinary conservation procedure, because he of course had *not* seen them in their initial, perceptually identical state). Although the two cardboards may not appear equal in area under these circumstances, it is possible to infer that they are, either by mentally relocating the itinerant square at its original position to reconstitute an intact rectangle (a "translocative" solution), or by simply counting the squares in each figure (an "iterative" solution). Such is

the essence of Beilin's area quasiconservation task. His data suggest that it tends to be mastered at a later age than is the corresponding conservation task. Beilin's (1969) explanation for this age difference is that quasiconservation inferences require more cognitive initiative on S's part, since there has been no perceived transformation from initial identity that might suggest to the child the nature of the problem and of its solution (e.g., the inverse operation of translocation).

Recent work by Braine and Shanks (1965a, 1965b) on children's reactions to illusory size and shape changes has led to an important hypothesis regarding the nature and origin of conservation. Their data indicate that it is not until about age 5 that children become capable of distinguishing between real and phenomenal properties of objects; for example, the recognition that one object may *look* (phenomenal) bigger than another and yet not *really be* (real) bigger. Braine and Shanks propose that the acquisition of the real-phenomenal distinction is a necessary precondition for conservation and may, for certain conservations tested for under certain task conditions, also prove to be a sufficient one. Given the structure of the conservation task, it is hard to imagine how at least the initial, necessary-condition part of this proposal could be wrong. Other relevant investigations in the area of spatial concept development are those by Drake (cited in Bruner, Olver, and Greenfield, 1966), Huttenlocher (1967), Lord (1941), Meyer (1940), and Piaget (1963, pp. 9–10, 40–41).

Time, Movement, and Velocity

One might assume that developmental progress in these three conceptual domains would show numerous interactions and synchronisms, given their definitional interdependencies, and Genevan theory and research here has in fact proceeded from just this assumption. Thus it is that Piaget's volume on movement and velocity (1946b) is regarded as the direct continuation of his book on temporal concepts (1946a), the two together comprising an extensive research report of about 20 developmental studies (see also Flavell, 1963a, pp. 316–326; Fraisse, 1963). This section will begin with a sketch of his views concerning the developmental construction of these concepts.

Piaget's Developmental Analysis of Time, Movement, and Velocity Concepts. According to this analysis, the young child's intellectual representations of time begin by being thoroughly confounded with his representations of space. He tends to confuse successions of events in time and the resulting temporal intervals between these events with their spatial counterparts, that is, with the sequence of spatial points traversed in a movement and the spatial intervals or distances between these points. One way to demonstrate this confusion experimentally is to elicit comparative temporal judgments regarding two movements which are simultaneous and spatially parallel, but proceed at different velocities and hence cover different distances. The young child is very likely under these circumstances to deny the simultaneity of their starting and stopping, as well as the equality of the intervening temporal durations, because he mistakenly relies on purely spatial cues: the fact that the starting or stopping *spatial* positions of the two movements do not coincide, and that the *spatial* intervals traversed by each are not equal. As Piaget interprets such evidence, the young child implicitly regards each individual movement as having its own "local time" (1946a, p. 273), unrelatable to those inherent in other movements. One of the child's major developmental tasks therefore is to construct something analogous to the general Euclidian framework described in the preceding sections: an all-encompassing, "homogeneous time" (*ibid.*, p. 273) within which all movements proceed in common, and thus within which all movements can be ordered and compared on a common temporal basis.

The child's early conceptions of movement and velocity are equally discrepant from those he will eventually attain. Initially, both phenomena are indexed solely in terms of the perceived endpoints of spatial motions. In the case of movement, such indexing sheds further light on how the young child conceptualizes distance (see the previous section): one object is said to have moved further than another if it ends up ahead of the latter, regardless of the actual distances traversed. Similarly, accurate velocity comparisons are made only if the child can actually see one object pass, or end up ahead of another. If the passing occurs out of the child's sight, he is wholly unable to utilize the available time and distance information to judge their relative speeds.

The forgoing analysis of the pre-operational child's capabilities in the areas of time, movement and velocity implies that there is much developmental work for him to do in succeeding years. The following is a paraphrase of the experimental topics treated in the two books, giving a fair idea of what Piaget thinks this work includes:

In the case of time, there is first of all a conceptual grasp of temporal order of succession and of the temporal intervals between succeeding temporal points—analogous to the ordinal and cardinal aspects of number, respectively. Other achievements include an understanding of temporal simultaneity, additivity and associativity of temporal intervals, the measurement of time through the construction of the temporal unit, and finally, what Piaget calls "lived" time . . . , including the concepts of age and of internal, subjective time. In the case of movement, there are the concepts of spatial order, composition of displacements in space (distances), and relative movements. And for velocity, there is the notion of the time-distance relation and its ultimate measurement in a variety of situations: in successive versus simultaneous movements, for uniform versus accelerated motion, and in the case of relative velocities [the velocity of one object relative to that of another, simultaneously-moving object] (Flavell, 1963a, p. 318).

Piaget's Research on the Genesis of Time, Movement, and Velocity Concepts. One of Piaget's experiments well illustrates the young child's difficulty in keeping temporal estimates uncontaminated by spatial ones (Piaget, 1946a, Chap. 3). The child is shown two parallel "race tracks" on which two little "men" run. Starting even, one of the men runs a certain distance (call it a distance of 4 units) while the other one simultaneously runs a shorter distance (1 unit). Immediately thereafter, the second man runs again (1 more unit, say), while the first remains in place. Thus the facts are that the second man ran for a longer period of time and stopped running later than the first, whereas the first man ran the greater distance and ended up ahead of the second. Here is a 5½-year-old who interprets the situation differently:

"What did you see?—The yellow one (I) stopped and the other one (II) walked again. —Then which one stopped first?—The blue one (II).—Which first [E used "en premier" rather than "d'abord" in repeating the question]?—The blue one (II).—Which one walked for the longest time?—The yellow one (I).—Let's say that this one (I) stopped at noon. Now look, did this one (II) stop at noon too, or before, or after?—Before—at noon." As a control procedure, we make the two movements go in opposite directions. Both I and II leave from point A, but I goes to D_1 on the right while II simultaneously goes to B_2 on the left; II then continues on to C_2. All questions are now correctly answered: I "stops first" and II "walked the longest" (*ibid.*, p. 91).

Spatiotemporal undifferentiation also plagues the pre-operational child's judgments about "lived" (versus "physical") time (*ibid.*, Part 3), as the following study illustrates. The child is shown two series of pictures representing the year-by-year growth of two fruit trees. One of the trees is planted a year after the other but, growing at a faster rate, eventually outstrips the first in size, quantity of fruit, etc. Young children tend to judge this tree to be the older of the two, disregarding their knowledge that it was planted later.

Other investigations have dealt with the child's growing understanding of the metric properties of time, for example, that temporal intervals can be divided into subintervals which exhibit the properties of additivity and associativity. For instance, the child only gradually comes to realize that two durations must be equal if their component subdurations are equal (additivity), and the same is true for the equivalence $(A + B) + C = A + (B + C)$, where A, B, and C are temporal intervals which occur in sequence (associativity).

The best known study in the movement category was described in the previous section (inversion of spatial order under 180°, 360°, etc., rotations). The others largely concerned the concept of distance, with the usual emphasis on the development of a metric, sum-of-units view of this property (Piaget, 1946b, Part 2). Tasks requiring an understanding of relative movements prove to be particularly difficult for children: a snail moves along a board at the same time that the board moves along a table, in the same or opposite direction from the snail's movement; determine the net distance that the snail moves in relation to the table. Correct solutions to this problem do not occur in force until around 11 to 12 years of age, and there are reasons to suppose that the requisite mental operations are formal rather than concrete (*ibid.*, Chap. 5).

As for velocity, the writer has previously described one set of Piaget's investigations in the following way:

The first several experiments all bear on a single point: that children initially reduce velocity to an intuition of order and changes of order, i.e., that object traveled faster which, initially behind another, caught up to it and ended up ahead. We shall summarize these experiments by describing the typical reaction of the younger subjects to the velocity problem each experiment presented. When two parallel and simultaneous movements of unequal speed and distance take place inside tunnels, so that the child cannot see the faster one gaining on the slower one, the child thinks they traveled at equal speeds. When two simultaneous movements of unequal velocity and distance begin at a common point and end at a common point (the longer and faster one taking an angled or sinuous itinerary and the shorter and slower one following a straight-line path), the child believes the velocities were equal. When simultaneous movements proceed along concentric circles (the movement along the larger circle being of course faster), the child asserts equality of speed. When one object starts its movement at the same instant as a second but from a position considerably behind it, the young child will say it traveled faster if it ends up in front of the second when they both stop, but not if it ends up parallel to or just behind the second (in all three cases its actual speed was considerably greater than the second's). If two objects make parallel movements of equal distance, one starting before the other in time but both terminating simultaneously (termination points superimposed), the child either thinks the speeds were equal or else that the one which started first went faster, since it initially "passed" the (stationary) second one in the beginning of its movement (Flavell, 1963a, p. 324).

Children solve such problems with dispatch— but only once in possession of the necessary inferential machinery:

Ner (8; 11): "The big one goes faster [the object travelling along the larger circle in the above-mentioned concentric circle problem]. —Why?—Because it makes more of a trip in the same time" (Piaget, 1946b, p. 141).

Other experiments dealt with the child's understanding of relative velocity, acceleration, quantification of speed, and the like. Similar to the experiment on relative movements, most of the tasks used here seem to require something more than concrete-operational thinking for their solution.

Other Studies. There appear to exist only two broad-scale replications of Piaget's research in these areas, both by the indefatigable Lovell. One systematically repeated about a half dozen of Piaget's studies on time concepts (Lovell and Slater, 1960); the other did the same for virtually all of his velocity experiments (Lovell, Kellett, and Moorhouse, 1962). Predictably, these investigators observed roughly the same kinds of age-dependent immature and mature responses to these various tasks that Piaget found, and also the usual intertask variability in difficulty level. The congruence with Piaget's developmental findings appears to be particularly marked in the Lovell, Kellett, and Moorhouse study. With the exception of the one on spatial order (see Charlesworth, 1962), the small group of Piagetian experiments on the concept of movement appear not to have been systematically replicated yet.

Although only Piaget and his followers seem to have studied the growth of movement and velocity concepts, there exists a considerable extra-Piagetian literature on the development of temporal thinking (e.g., Ames, 1946; Bradley, 1947; Friedman, 1944a, 1944b; Oakden and Sturt, 1922; Springer, 1952; for reviews of this literature, see Fraisse, 1963; Jahoda, 1963a). It would be difficult to review most of this work with any enthusiasm, however. Largely atheoretical in orientation, these studies tend to focus on certain obvious and highly

phenotypical expressions of the child's grasp of time: his growing ability to cope with clock, calendar, and historical sequences, his evolving comprehension and utilization of time words ("yesterday," "next year," etc.), and the like. The results of these various studies do accord reasonably well with one another, and hence developmental generalizations about such behaviors can be made (see Jahoda, 1963a, for examples). The problem rather lies in trying to give these generalizations any theoretically interesting and meaningful interpretation. On the other hand, Fraisse's book (1963) provides an excellent survey and analysis of developmental changes —Piagetian and non-Piagetian, perceptual and conceptual—in this area. Although his views on the developmental psychology of time do not coincide with Piaget's on all points, their differences do not appear to be substantial enough to warrant review here.

Causality and Related Concepts

Previous chapter sections have reviewed studies of the child's developing conceptualization of certain measurable properties of the natural world's objects and events, properties like weight, length, area, time, and velocity. One might equally inquire into his evolving views about these objects and events themselves, as particular phenomena in that world. For example, how do children of different ages interpret the nature, origin, and activity of specific natural entities like shadows, night, sun, clouds, birth, life, death, and so on? There is a potential danger in posing such questions, however, since the number of investigatable entities here is practically inexhaustible. A determined but unreflective empiricist could readily find himself enmeshed in a multilifetime effort to trace the developmental course of this, that, and a hundred other specific concepts. A research program of this kind would be as poorly conceived as it is unfeasible, since its scientific yield would likely be very meager. A far better strategy would be to assess children's conceptual reactions to some carefully selected subset of the possible entities for the express purpose of diagnosing the nonspecific (i.e., to any particular entity) cognitive traits that underlie these reactions. This kind of strategy is a sensible one for any research enterprise, of course, but it is especially important where—

as in the present case—the risk of scientific nit-picking is particularly great.

Piaget's Theory and Research on Children's Causal Explanations. Early in his career, Piaget did a number of studies in which he elicited children's verbalized interpretations of diverse natural phenomena (1929, 1930). His scientific strategy was essentially the one just outlined: treat the child's particular interpretations of particular phenomena as symptomatic expressions of deeper-lying and more general cognitive tendencies—expressions of his "spontaneous attitude of mind" (Piaget, 1929, p. 123). The underlying tendencies or "attitudes" were conceived as existing at two levels. At the upper level are the child's tacit causal (initially "precausal") notions; it is these notions which at least partly determine how he answers Piaget's questions about various physical-biological phenomena (shadows, life, etc.). At the lower level, and in turn mediating his concept of causality, is the child's position on the developmental continuum from egocentric to socialized thought. Thus the child's ideas about causality are seen as a crucial intermediary between his implicit view of the natural world and the fundamental orientation of his mind. It is for this reason that there is much on children's world views in Piaget's *The Child's Conception of Physical Causality* (1930) and much on their causal thinking in his *The Child's Conception of the World* (1929).

The gist of Piaget's developmental theory here can be summarized as follows (Piaget, 1929, 1930; see also Flavell, 1963a, pp. 279–290; Laurendeau and Pinard, 1962, Chap. 1). An important manifestation of the young child's cognitive egocentrism is a relative undifferentiation between self and world, subjective and objective, psychological and physical. When his mind is directed toward genuinely psychological phenomena, this undifferentiation leads him to substantiate or "physicalize" these phenomena (a cognitive disposition which Piaget refers to as *realism*). Thus, for instance, dreams are initially conceived as external, palpable realities, potentially visible to others. When the child's mind turns to the realm of the genuinely physical, this same lack of differentiation leads him to the opposite kind of contamination, with psychological properties intruding into his conceptions of physical-natural phenomena. It is

this tendency to "humanize" the inorganic world that gets expressed in the variety of precausal "-isms" familiar to Piaget readers. Examples are: *animism*—the attribution of life and consciousness to inanimate objects; *dynamism*—the attribution of humanlike energy, strength, and capacity for spontaneous movement to such objects; *finalism*—explanations couched in terms of anthropocentric functional purpose (boats float so that people can ride on them); and *artificialism*—the positing of a human or (humanlike) divine architect to account for the origin of natural objects and events (if lakes are thought to be dug *by* men, the belief is artificialistic; if they are thought to exist *for* man's use and convenience, the belief is finalistic: both beliefs may, of course, coexist in the same child).

The data base for these categories of precausal explanations was a series of interview, question-and-answer studies with children of various ages. These studies are probably familiar to most readers, and we shall simply allude to a few of the more salient findings. Young children may attribute life and consciousness to a number of inanimate objects, especially if they regularly show movement (e.g., wind and bicycles). Subsequently, these traits are restricted to entities whose motion is self-engendered (wind, but not bicycles). Artificialistic and finalistic answers are given to questions about the origins of natural phenomena like lakes, mountains, night, etc. For instance, night comes "so we may sleep." The movement of clouds is first conceived as the result of human activity, with the clouds themselves playing an acquiescent and cooperative role in the causal process (a combination of artificialism and animism).

Replications of Piaget's Research on Precausal Thinking. This aspect of Piaget's research has had a much more troubled and uncertain career in the history of developmental psychology than have his other studies. Although there is much that we still do not understand about nonconservation of weight, say, there was not for long much dispute about its existence, as a readily elicitable response in young children, and about its decline with age. In contrast, both the existential and developmental statuses of precausal thinking have been subject to considerable controversy over the past four decades. As Laurendeau and Pinard's excellent survey of this literature shows (1962, Chaps. 2 to 4), some studies have failed to find any substantial amount of animistic, artificialistic, etc., reasoning in young children, whereas others report its presence in children and adults alike. Laurendeau and Pinard believe that both sets of discordant findings may be explained away on methodological and other grounds, and their own study was designed to settle the issue. Since this study appears to be the most thoroughgoing and careful normative-descriptive investigation of the subject ever done (or ever likely to be done), we shall summarize its procedures and findings. For a sample of other recent reviews and studies in this area, see Almy, Chittenden, and Miller (1966), Danziger and Sharp (1958), Jahoda (1958a, 1958b), Muuss (1961), Nass (1964), and Smith (1963).

Elaborate questionnaires were prepared on five topics previously investigated by Piaget: the concept of dream, the concept of life, the origin of night, the movement of clouds, and the floating and sinking of objects. The Ss were 500 French-Canadian children (Montreal area), 50 at each of ages 4, 4½, 5, 6, 7, 8, 9, 10, 11, and 12. The age groups were almost perfectly matched on a number of potentially relevant variables (such as sex and parents' occupational level), and the children at each age level comprised a representative sample of the local population. All Ss were tested individually by experimental examiners, either at school or at home (in the case of the youngest children). The children's answers to each of the five questionnaires were classified in terms of a Piagetian-type scale of developmental stages and substages. Three judges scored each response protocol, and interjudge agreement was very high.

The results of this study clearly support the conclusion that, when carefully questioned, young children do in fact give an abundance of the sorts of precausal explanation and interpretation reported in Piaget's early books, and also that these responses do in fact evolve and change with age in much the same way that he had originally described. Although Laurendeau and Pinard's data differed from Piaget's in certain details, the overall picture is decidedly one of consensus:

Not all the scales described by Piaget are found in the present classification. The differ-ences noted are of two main types: either Piaget reserves a stage to answers too scarce or too ambiguous to characterize a real level of development (e.g., substantial formation of the night by dark clouds, explanation of life by the usefulness of objects, etc.), or else he does not provide a particular place for certain answers which are in fact truly typical and numerous enough to correspond to a normal level in evolution of a concept (e.g., anthropomorphism related to the concept of life, artificialism in the explanation of the movement of clouds, etc.). These divergences, however, do not prevent a recognizable and fundamental resemblance between our scales and those of Piaget. In both investigations, the child's conception of the world develops from a level of pure precausality to a level of objective causality through intermediate steps in which the opposite conceptions are intermingled (Laurendeau and Pinard, 1962, pp. 247–248).

The writer suspects that there may have been at least two factors responsible for the prolonged distrust of Piaget's findings in this and related areas. First, the *Zeitgeist* of the pre-1960s made for considerable resistance to the very idea that young minds might be qualitatively as well as quantitatively different from older minds, in the domain of causal reasoning or anywhere else. It is simply far easier for us today to imagine that the young child's causal thinking *might* have just the characteristics Piaget attributed to it, given everything else we now know about pre-operational thinking in general and childish egocentrism in particular (see the next section); one might even go so far as to say that an absence of qualitative differences here would be incongruous with our contemporary image of the developing child.

The second factor was probably a marked sense of discomfort in trying to diagnose tacit and subtle cognitive orientations on the basis of purely verbal interchanges with young children—organisms whose language-to-cognition circuits are still quite poorly engineered. It must be admitted that such discomfort seems as justified now as it did in the past, Laurendeau and Pinard's results notwithstanding, and Piaget himself has joined the rest of us in sharing it. In the preface to the Laurendeau and Pinard book, he states:

In this respect, I must confess that had I been consulted, I would perhaps have attempted to dissuade my friends from such a return to precausality, not because I no longer believe in it, but because today verbal thinking seems to me marginal to real thinking which, even though verbalized, remains until about eleven or twelve years of age centered upon action (p. xii) . . . exclusively verbal thinking therefore no longer seems to be sufficient for the investigation of the child's thinking: it provides a series of instructive indications, which must, however, be related to other findings derived from operational tests proper (p. xiii).

How could one investigate the child's causal orientation without asking questions about perceptually absent and, to the child, undoubtedly recondite phenomena like night and shadows? An ingenious study by Ausubel and Schiff (1954) suggests one possible approach. Kindergarten, third-, and sixth-grade children were presented with a teeter-totter bearing a red wooden block on one arm and an identical green block on the other. The task was to predict which arm would fall when released. Each child had two series of trials, given in counterbalanced order. In the "relevant" series, the longer arm (the one extending farthest from the fulcrum) always fell, just as the laws of physics say it should. In the "irrelevant" series, the arm which bears the red block regularly fell, for no explicable reason. The kindergarten Ss learned to make correct predictions in about the same number of trials in each of the two series, whereas difficulty of the irrelevant series becomes progressively more pronounced in the two older groups. Similarly, the learning of the irrelevant cause-effect relation is harder when preceded by the relevant series than when given first, but again only for the older children. The logic of this study is similar to that of the Youniss and Furth (1965, 1966) experiments described earlier: make inferences about the child's cognitive skills and dispositions by seeing what he finds easier and harder to learn. This approach has much to recommend it when investigating the developmental growth of relatively nebulous and hard-to-articulate concepts such as causality.

Related Concepts. There is a handful of studies, some developmental and some nonde-velopmental, dealing with children's understanding of various biological phenomena: sexual anatomy (Kreitler and Kreitler, 1966), conception and birth (Kreitler and Kreitler, 1966; Nagy, 1953b), life (Safier, 1964; Steiner, 1965), various bodily processes (Nagy, 1953a), germs (Nagy, 1953c), and death (Anthony, 1939; Nagy, 1948; Safier, 1964; Steiner, 1965). Most of these studies rather smack of the overspecificity and low-altitude empiricism that was cautioned against at the beginning of this section. The most significant contribution to the field of cognitive development is probably Safier's (1964) study (the Kreitler and Kreitler, 1966, paper has import for psychoanalytic theory). Safier's research suggests that there are some interesting parallels in the child's evolving concepts of life and death: both are initially pervaded by the child's animistic orientation, etc. Death itself is at first conceived as reversible, subsequently irreversible or permanent but escapable, and ultimately both irreversible and inevitable.

THE SOCIAL WORLD

After surveying the research literature on cognitive growth a few years ago, Wallach had this to say about intellectual development with respect to the social world:

In our examination of current research on the development of children's thinking, we obviously have concentrated on the child's knowledge of the physical world—i.e., on the traditional definition of thinking as reasoning, problem solving, and understanding, concerning the non-social environment. . . . The extent to which thinking about the social environment follows similar or different ontogenetic patterns must remain an open question at this point (1963, p. 270).

The literature in this area is somewhat more substantial now than it was when Wallach's review was written, and the question he raises is correspondingly less open. There are in fact some indications that the "ontogenetic patterns" which are going to emerge here will turn out to be rather similar to those found in other conceptual areas. It is reasonable that this should be so. The mind of the child at any given level of its development would hardly be expected to change its basic design features when turning from logical-mathematical or physical to social content. We shall try to convey a sense of this cross-content homogeneity in the sections below.

Psychological Concepts

The following passage from one of Piaget's books (1954) is a good point of departure for this section:

Intelligence thus begins neither with knowledge of the self nor of things as such but with knowledge of their interaction, and it is by orienting itself simultaneously toward the two poles of that interaction that intelligence organizes the world by organizing itself (pp. 354-355). . . . In other words, the first knowledge of the universe or of himself that the subject can acquire is knowledge relating to the most immediate appearance of things or to the most external and material aspect of his being (p. 355).

Much of the research work already reviewed in this chapter supports the generalization that young children do not go beyond this "most immediate appearance of things" when reasoning about logical-mathematical and natural phenomena. It is only by penetrating the phenomenal surface, for instance, that the child can secure a conservation judgment in the face of countervailing appearances. What of Piaget's claim that the same is true for the self? Developmental research on the self-concept and related topics will be surveyed elsewhere in this book (see also Dubin and Dubin, 1965), but there are two pieces of evidence from Piaget's early work which we shall cite here. First, the young child's interpretations of his own psychological processes (notably, his daytime thoughts and nighttime dreams) tend to be "realistic" in the technical Piagetian sense, that is, these processes are construed as external-objective rather than internal-subjective in nature (Piaget, 1929; also recall the corroborative findings of Laurendeau and Pinard, 1962, in the case of dreams). Second, Piaget has also shown (1928, Chap. 4) that the young child is unable to gain access to his own cognitive processes, unable to treat his own thinking as an object of introspective thought.

Other human beings have features in common with both the self and with physical objects. Like the self, other individuals are sentient organisms endowed with distinctive, subjective-psychological properties. Like nonsocial objects, they are "out there," external to the self. And like both, according to the research evidence of Piaget and numerous others, the child's interpretations of them begin with surface manifestations and only gradually move into the psychological interior. That is, he initially represents and reasons about those aspects of other people that are most accessible to direct perception, thereby neglecting the crucial but covert processes of thought, perception, attitudes, feelings, etc. Let us briefly survey Piaget's evidence first.

Piaget's Research on the Development of Psychological Thinking. Several of Piaget's investigations have dealt with the child's ability to represent the perceptual experience of another individual when that experience differs from his own (Piaget and Inhelder, 1956, Chaps. 6, 8, 9). In the best known of these studies (*ibid.*, Chap. 8), the child sits facing a scale model of three mountains and is tested for his ability to predict their appearance from various other perspectives (from the right of where he is seated, from the opposite side, etc.). The most interesting finding was that a number of the younger children kept confusing their own perspective with the others: asked to find the photograph which represents how the mountains look from a given position, for example. the child tends to select the one that reproduces his own view. We have already described (Relations) how the pre-operational child's absolutistic and uniperspective egocentrism permeates his conceptual treatment of relational concepts such as "left" and "right," "brother," etc. (Piaget, 1928).

The cognitive experiences of other people are similarly underrepresented in the young child's thinking. For instance, he characteristically fails to pay attention to his listener's receptive capacities and informational needs when verbally communicating with him (Piaget, 1926). Because he does not monitor the listener's probable reactions to what he is saying and frame his messages accordingly, these messages tend to have an unedited, private-speech quality about them.

Finally, Piaget's data on moral development (1932) emphasize the young child's insensitivity to the inner motives and intentions of others. The individual who steals a more costly object to give to a needy friend is judged more culpable by young Ss than one who steals a less expensive item for purely selfish reasons. Analogously, the "whopper" innocently perpetrated by a young storyteller is initially estimated to be a more heinous offence than a plausible untruth, which was, however, clearly intended to deceive its hearer. Thus, although the young child is able and ready to consider the overt and objective aspects of interpersonal situations, the covert motivational processes of the participants escape him.

As he grows older, the child becomes increasingly sensitive to the existence of covert perceptual, cognitive, and motivational processes in other people (as well as in himself) and also increasingly accurate in his indentification and interpretation of these processes. Piaget (1928) believes that the major vehicle for the developmental decline of this and all other manifestations of cognitive egocentrism is social interaction, especially with peers. Conflicts, arguments, and other dissonant interpersonal experiences gradually compel the child to pay attention to perspective differences, and thereby eventually to generate some conceptions and information-gathering skills regarding human psychological processes.

Other Research. Although one would be ill-advised to write a textbook called *Social-Cognitive Development* on the basis of presently existing research data, there are at least the beginnings of a real literature in this area. Much of it has been stimulated by Piaget's pioneering studies, but the theoretical writings of Mead (e.g., 1947), Heider (1958), and others have also played a role. The writer and his associates (Flavell 1961, 1966a, 1966b; Flavell et al., 1968; Fry, 1966) have carried out what is probably the broadest-scale investigation in the area so far, and hence their work can serve as a convenient framework for reviewing the rest of the literature.

Flavell et al. have used the expression "role-taking activity" to refer to the processes under discussion, but "person perception," "interpersonal inference," "social cognition," or even the barbaric but apt "people-reading" might do as well. As we view it, role-taking activity may entail any of a number of per-

ceptual-cognitive processes in the role-taker, may take as its object any of a number of psychological processes in the other person, and may be carried out for any of a number of concrete purposes. Let us briefly amplify the latter two of these three features. The description of Piaget's work has already suggested that the object toward which this activity is directed can vary: the other's perceptual experiences; his cognitive experiences, predispositions, and capacities; his emotional states; his motives and intentions—in short, anything that people might construe to be a potentially "readable" or inferable psychological entity. Likewise, role-taking activity may be initiated for any of a variety of purposes: in order more effectively to cooperate with the other person, to understand and be understood in communicative interactions with him, to compete with him, simply to satisfy one's curiosity about him—the list could obviously be extended to include any motive which this particular kind of information-gathering might help to satisfy. Our research was concerned with developmental changes in role-taking activity or skill across a sampling of objects and purposes.

One of our tasks was closely patterned after the Piagetian model-mountain problem, and thus was intended to assess the child's ability to predict visual-perceptual experiences different from his own momentary one. The data showed very consistent and regular increases with age in this ability across middle childhood and adolescence. Subsequent research with maximally simple perspective-taking tasks led us to think that the very notion of perceptual perspective or point of view is probably absent in most 3-year-olds, gradually emerging in rudimentary form during the preschool period. Developmental findings consistent with these and Piaget and Inhelder's data have also been reported by Davol and Hastings (1966), Dodwell (1963), Gellert (1966), Laubengayer (1965), and Lovell (1959). Karplus (1964) has devised an ingenious teaching technique involving perceptual role-taking to convey to elementary school children the relativity of position and motion, and Laubengayer (1965) has had some success in furthering the perspective-taking ability of preschool children through systematic training. Moore (1958) has also demonstrated that the development of perceptual role-taking skill is not confined to the visual sphere: older children are more sensitive than younger ones to what others may be hearing as well as to what they may be seeing.

A different sort of task is needed to tap role-taking processes directed at the non-perceptual (e.g., cognitive or affective) experiences of the other person. In one of our investigations, middle-childhood and adolescent Ss are shown an ordered series of seven pictures which, comic-strip fashion, illustrate a story. After the child has narrated the story, three of the pictures are removed. The remaining four pictures were so constructed as to suggest a story also, but this story is quite different from the original, seven-picture one. A second E, supposedly unacquainted with any of the pictures, now enters the room. S's task is then to predict the story that this E would derive from the four-picture series. There is of course no *perceptual* role-taking problem here; both S and E see the same four pictures, and in the same orientation. The problem is instead to predict E's *cognitive* response to what he sees, that is, his interpretation of what the visual stimuli, in their ensemble, suggest or signify. We found that many second- and third-grade children (the youngest Ss in this study) could not accurately predict what story the four pictures would suggest to a naive other—one not "contaminated," as is the child, by having previously seen them in full, seven-picture context. A characteristic reaction is to predict cognitive responses to the four pictures which they themselves have come to make on the basis of previous experience (i.e., a seven-picture-story interpretation) but which the inexperienced other would be very unlikely to make, much as the young S in a perceptual role-taking task keeps misattributing his own perspective to the other observer. Another of our studies showed clear developmental trends in the ability to impute complex chains of reasoning to other people, particularly those that include a representation, by the other, of one's *own* cognitions—"I think that he thinks *that I think* such-and-so."

The data from these and other studies in the literature suggest that inferential activity regarding the cognitions, feelings, etc., of others changes with development in at least two ways. First, the child constructs an increasingly rich interpretation of the other's covert processes; more—and more complex—internal psychological events are attributed to him as the child matures. Second, what gets attributed to the other also becomes more accurate and objective, less tainted by the child's own, egocentric perspective. Dymond, Hughes, and Raabe (1952), Flapan (1965), and Rothenberg (1967) have found a substantial increase across middle childhood in the child's disposition and ability to explain surface behavior in terms of subsurface cognitions, feelings, motives, etc. Feffer (1959) and Gollin (1954) have devised formal test procedures for assessing such dispositions and abilities, and have also reported developmental changes across middle childhood (Feffer and Gourevitch, 1960) and adolescence (Gollin, 1958). Milgram and Goodglass (1961) found a decided increase from second through eighth grade in S's ability to make accurate guesses about the normative word associations of young children and adults. The Baldwins and their students have recently begun to investigate the development of various interpersonal concepts, using as their frame of reference the average adult's implicit "theory" of human behavior as described by Heider (1958). Thus far reported are interesting age changes in the child's interpretation and assessment of malevolent-benevolent intentions (Baldwin, 1965), kindness (Baldwin and Baldwin, 1967), and fairness (Shure, 1967), the latter reminiscent of Piaget's work (1932) on moral judgment. Whiteman (1967) has done an interesting developmental study of children's conceptions of psychological causality (i.e., human motivation), using kindergarten and third-grade S's. Although not quite resembling miniature psychoanalysts, Whiteman's older S's did show a surprisingly good ability to sense the motivational workings of classic defense mechanisms (displacement, projection, denial, etc.) behind the overt behavior of a story character; for example, to understand why a child who does not like to share her toys might anticipate nonsharing motives on the part of other children whom she had never even met before (projection).

As Piaget's early research (1926) has shown, one of the most important functions or purposes of role-taking activity is the monitoring and guiding of communication behavior. A message constructed without any attention to the informational needs and in-formation-processing capabilities of the in-tended audience would only be accidentally effective. A number of our studies inves-tigated developmental changes in the child's ability to tailor and adapt his verbal messages to particular listeners and circumstances. In one of these studies, Ss are given the task of explaining how to play a game to two adult listeners, one of whom can see the game materials and one of whom cannot (he is blindfolded). Older children construct much longer and more informative messages to the blindfolded listener, whereas younger children tend to say the same things to both. A few of the younger Ss went so far in their disre-gard of audience characteristics as to refer without further explanation to "this," "there," etc., when talking to the blindfolded listener. Similar age differences obtained in a study where the two listeners differed in cognitive (adult versus child) instead of perceptual (sighted versus blindfolded) receptive abil-ities. Other investigations showed develop-mental changes across middle childhood and early adolescence in the ability to: (1) modify a message on the basis of postmessage feedback regarding its communicative inad-equacy; (2) give a single, "lowest-common-denominator" message to several listeners who differ in initial informational level regarding the content to be communicated; (3) evaluate the adequacy of someone else's message; (4) communicate nonredundantly; and (5) con-struct an effective persuasive as opposed to informative message.

Recent studies by Glucksberg and Krauss (1967), Glucksberg, Krauss, and Weisberg (1966), and Krauss and Glucksberg (1965) have yielded very similar developmental find-ings. They too interpret the young child's communicative performance as reflecting an absence of editing and modification due to a failure to take note of the communication-relevant attributes of the listener. If this in-terpretation is correct, one would expect that role-taking and communication skills, inde-pendently assessed by means of two separate tasks, would covary within the individual. Such covariation has in fact recently been demonstrated, both in children (Cowan, 1966) and in adults (Feffer and Suchotliff, 1966; Phillips and Feffer, 1966). Role-taking ability has also been shown to correlate with other

variables. Swinson (1966) found significant correlations between Feffer's role-taking test and several of Piaget's concrete-operational tasks (e.g., conservation of quantity), with age, grade, and IQ partialled out. Rothenberg (1967) found small but statistically reliable correlations between social sensitivity and several measures of interpersonal adjustment and intelligence. Wolfe (1963) has further demonstrated significant interrelationships among several indices of role-taking ability. Other relevant studies in the area of inter-personal inference include Elkind (1967b), Kohlberg (1963), Muuss (1961), and Niel-sen (1951).

As already suggested, we have much yet to learn about the ontogenesis of role-taking and related "people-reading" abilities. There is, however, enough evidence available to risk an educated guess about its major features:

We ought now to be able to make some speculations — likewise preliminary — about what this development consists of, and when in childhood its various constituents tend to appear. The nature of these constituents can be epitomized by considering what one needs to know, or know how to do, in order to engage in behavior which is mediated by role-taking activity. There are five such con-stituents:

1) The understanding that there is such a thing as "perspective," that is, what you perceive, think, or feel in any given context need not coincide with what I perceive, think, or feel. (*Existence*)

2) The realization that an analysis of the other person's perpective is warranted in this particular situation, that is, such an analysis would be a useful means to whatever one's goal is here. (*Relevance*)

3) How actually to carry out this analysis, that is, possession of the ability to predict with accuracy the relevant attributes of the other. (*Ability*)

4) How to maintain in awareness the fruits of this analysis, in competiticn with the un-remitting press of one's own point of view, long enough for it to be able to fulfill its function as means or instrumentality for sub-sequent behavior. (*Performance*)

5) How then to employ the fruits of this analysis as a means to some behavioral end,

for example, as an effective monitor of verbal communication. (*Application*)

The evidence suggests that the development of *existence* is at least partly accomplished by the beginning school years. Young preschoolers often behave as if the very existence of perspective variation were foreign to them, whereas many older preschoolers clearly demonstrate an awareness of its existence, at least in task situations where the experimenter's instructions and the elemental nature of the role attributes in question conspire to facilitate such awareness. Correspondingly, there is some *ability* to predict with accuracy those perspectives whose existence the child is mature enough to recognize, but this ability appears to be extremely limited—limited primarily to the discrimination of the more obvious components of the other person's perceptual perspective.

On the other hand, really substantial prowess in *ability*, and in *relevance, performance,* and *application* as well, is probably not attained much before late middle childhood or early adolescence. We have been impressed with how rudimentary is the capacity, during the early school years, to tune in on the hidden role-taking requirements of ostensibly non-role-taking (e.g., communication) tasks (*relevance*); to predict complex perceptual inputs and subtle or intricate intellectual processes in the other person (*ability*); to keep one's image of the other person's role attributes unsullied by one's own ongoing perspective (*performance*); and to translate what one knows or can guess about the other person into effective social behavior regarding him (*application*). In contrast, the child 12 to 14 years old in our studies and in other studies shows himself to be a surprisingly adept role taker across a wide range of tasks and problems. Although the data are really not yet ample enough to justify it, one is tempted to predict that middle childhood will turn out to be *the* developmental epoch so far as basic role taking and allied skills are concerned, with the preschool period contributing the prologue and adolescence the epilogue (Flavell, 1966a, pp. 175–176).

Other Concepts

A survey of developmental research dealing with logical-mathematical, physical-biological, and psychological notions does not quite exhaust the existing concept-development literature. There is a small remainder, most of it concerned with the acquisition of political, economic, and religious concepts. The general tenor of this residual literature is suggested by Geis' remark in a recent book review: "The book will *certainly* be read by psychologists interested in political development, and *possibly* by *some* interested in cognitive and affective development" (Geis, 1966, p. 586, italics ours). That is to say, these studies do provide information of greater or lesser interest regarding the specific content area in question, but they typically contribute little to our overall understanding of cognitive development.

Politics. The handful of studies in this area can be sorted into two rough categories. One deals with the evolution of children's knowledge, attitudes, and interests regarding political figures and institutions. The other focuses on their developing sense of national identity, changing conceptions of their own and other geographical-political units (native city and country, foreign countries, etc.), and related topics.

The investigations of Greenstein (1961, 1965), Hess and Easton (1960; Easton and Hess, 1962), and O'Neill (1965) make up the first group. Greenstein and Hess and Easton administered survey questionnaires to large groups of middle-childhood and early-adolescent Ss, with very similar results (Greenstein, 1961). A general finding was that children develop strong feelings and opinions about political entities well before they achieve any clear understanding of them. They like and identify with a specific political party before learning how the parties differ; they think the President is extremely important and rate his performance in the job as superlative without any clear idea of what he actually does, let alone how competently he is doing it, etc. Images of the father and of the President are initially very similar, and Hess and Easton (1960) hypothesize that the President first emerges as a generalization from the father. The President appears to be the American child's earliest point of contact with the political system, with other offices and institutions initially apprehended in relation to him: the alderman, courts, legislature, and the like are perceived simply as the President's "helpers" (Greenstein, 1961). Gradually, the roles and functions of political offices become better understood and differentiated from their human incumbents. Greenfield's (1965) data show that by eighth grade, rate of approval of the President's performance has declined to a level similar to that found in a national survey of adults. O'Neill's (1965) interview study with an adolescent sample revealed some interesting developmental changes in political-philosophical concepts, such as the notion of a community, the nature and functions of government, and the idea of individual rights.

The second group is chiefly represented by a fairly elaborate study of Jahoda's, done in response to an earlier investigation by Piaget and Weil (1951). The empirical aspects of Jahoda's work are presented in three articles (1962, 1963b, 1963c), with an overview and theoretical analysis given in a subsequent paper (1964). We shall eschew Jahoda's (1964) detailed (and generally well-founded) critique of the Piaget and Weil study in favor of suggesting some developmental conclusions derived from both sets of findings. Young children are initially extremely vague about the denotation of their native city, state, and country and correspondingly confused about the partitive or inclusion relations among them. Thus Glasgow and Scotland (Jahoda), or Geneva and Switzerland (Piaget and Weil), may be represented by the young child as discrete, nonoverlapping physical domains. Similarly, the child may be unable to grasp the fact that he is at once Scottish and British (or Genevan and Swiss). Part of the problem could be a basic difficulty in handling the logical-inclusion operation (Piaget and Weil). However, a more powerful determinant after the child has reached early middle childhood could well be the abstractness and ill-defined character, for the child, of these geopolitical units (Jahoda). It goes without saying that coherent ideas and attitudes regarding foreign countries are not in evidence during this early period (Jahoda, 1962). Weinstein (1957) did a scalogram analysis of 5- to 12-year-old children's answers to a series of questions concerning national identity and the notion of flag. He found a fairly well-defined developmental sequence of 10 steps or levels in the cognitive mastery of these political concepts.

Economics. Schuessler and Strauss (1950; Strauss and Schuessler, 1951) tested for developmental changes in the child's abilty to identify coins, compare their values, and establish monetary-value equivalences among them. Although clear age trends were revealed, this study deserves to be remembered more for its methodology than for its substantive findings: so far as the writer knows, Schuessler and Strauss were the first to use scalogram-analysis techniques for assessing the sequential invariance of developmental stages. A second study (Strauss, 1952) had a broader focus, dealing with the meaning and uses of money within the economic system. The child only gradually sees, for example, that paying money and receiving change for goods bought from the storekeeper is more than a mere ritual; that there is a "maker" who sells goods to the storekeeper; that the "maker" and the storekeeper spend money received on a variety of things (more goods, their employees, items for personal needs, etc.); and that business is essentially an impersonal affair governed by the profit motive (a customer and a storekeeper need not like each other; a storekeeper sells goods for more than he pays for them—both these propositions often denied by young children).

The results of a later study (Danziger, 1958) roughly confirm Strauss' findings. In addition, Danziger emphasizes that what the child initially lacks and only gradually attains is a conception of the economic world as a system of reciprocal relationships—of balanced exchanges of money, goods, and services between boss and worker, seller and buyer.

Religion. The few existing studies on children's thinking in the area of religion well illustrate one leitmotif of this chapter: the overall level of the child's intellectual development operates like a "g" factor in specific content areas to determine in part his conceptual structuring of these areas. Goldman (1965), for example, had no great difficulty classifying children's interpretations of Biblical events (e.g., the temptations of Jesus) as reflecting Piaget's pre-operational, concrete-operational, and formal-operational modes of thinking, each class of interpretation predominating during its appropriate age span. He therefore concludes: "Religious thinking appears to take place, within the context of belief in the supernatural, according to the same processes and methods of thinking as applied to other fields of experience" (p. 167). Elkind's developmental studies of Jewish (1961d), Catholic (1962b), and Protestant (1963) children's conceptions of their respective religious denominations makes the point even more strongly (see Elkind, 1964b, for a resumé and discussion of his findings).

In general, it was found that the *form* of the child's thinking at a given age/stage was remarkably consistent across the three groups, with the *content* showing the expected inter-denominational variation. Moreover, the major formal changes are reminiscent of generalizations made in the previous section. For instance, the essential ingredients of one's religious identity are at first external (e.g., going to a certain church) and only later internal (e.g., possessing certain beliefs). The child's concept of prayer likewise exhibits this familiar developmental movement from outer to inner aspects (Elkind, Spilka, and Long, 1966). In the writer's judgment, Elkind's interesting studies have important implications for the field of religious education. Miscellaneous other investigations of children's conceptualizations of the social world include Case and Collinson (1962), Jahoda (1959), Meltzer (1925), Ordan (1945), Pflederer (1964), and Spiegel (1950).

GENERAL ISSUES IN THE FIELD OF CONCEPT DEVELOPMENT

The major purpose of this chapter has been to review the basic, normative-descriptive literature on conceptual growth, concept area by concept area. Such a review fails to highlight certain issues, questions, and problems common to all of these areas, which are repeatedly encountered whenever a deeper analysis of any of them is attempted. The remainder of the chapter will do little more than simply introduce some of these problems and call the reader's attention to pertinent bibliography. In this instance, brevity is dictated by more than the everpresent space limitations. There is reason to doubt whether our knowledge and understanding regarding these issues is sufficiently advanced as yet to make possible any really extended and authoritative review.

Developmental Diagnosis of Conceptual Acquisitions

All research on concept development, whatever its ultimate purpose, involves developmental diagnosis at some point. The experimenter must always, by one testing procedure or another, try to assess the child's status vis-à-vis predefined conceptual item (skill, notion, structure, operation). Evidence is rapidly accumulating, however, that precise estimation of children's cognitive-developmental status is a much more complicated and nettlesome problem than we had once thought. One might until recently have believed, for example, that nothing could be more straightforward than to find out whether a young child is capable of transitive inference. The notion of transitive inference is clearly definable, and the Genevans have long since provided us with simple but elegant procedures for its diagnosis. However, a recent controversy between Braine and Smedslund (Braine, 1959, 1964; Smedslund, 1963a, 1965, 1966b; see also Gruen, 1966; Wortman, 1964) has shown that the assessment of this inferential skill is a veritable mare's-nest of conceptual and methodological problems. We are now led to wonder what testing procedures, if any, will protect us here against diagnostic errors of both the false-positive and false-negative variety. Moreover, it must now be asked whether transitive inference is a monolithic, all-or-none entity or whether, instead, there may be several earlier and later, less and more mature forms of it. Similar questions are currently being raised concerning the nature and measurement of other Piagetian acquisitions (e.g., Bruner, 1964; Bruner, Olver, and Greenfield, 1966; Gruen, 1966; Inhelder, Bovet, Sinclair, and Smock, 1966; Kohnstamm, 1967; Pascual-Leone and Bovet, 1966).

The classification and resolution of diagnosis-and-assessment problems in this field are crucial for a number of reasons. We shall cite only two of the more important ones. First, exact developmental dating is obviously a prerequisite for describing the temporal relations among conceptual acquisitions, in particular, which ones emerge in a regular ontogenetic order, one always before another, and which ones emerge more or less concurrently. Information about temporal relations is in turn a necessary (but not sufficient) first step in determining the functional and structural relations among acquisitions. For instance, only if we could be sure that cognitive item A regularly precedes cognitive item B could we entertain the possibility that A might somehow help to mediate the attainment of B, might be an earlier and more immature form of B, etc. Similarly, only if we were certain that items X and Y developed in synchrony could we make hypotheses about the emergence of some superordinate structure upon which both depend. It is apparent that the functional and structural connections between, for instance, transitivity and other acquisitions cannot be even guessed at until we can decide whether it first appears at 4 to 5 years (Braine) or at 7 to 8 years (Smedslund and the Genevans).

Precise evaluation of the child's developmental status is also indispensable whenever we wish to assess the effects of experience on cognitive growth (for instance, the rapidly burgeoning ensemble of Piagetian "training studies"). The nature and magnitude, and hence the theoretical significance of training effects can be inferred only from information about cognitive status before and after the training experience. Much of the recent controversy concerning the influence of short-term experimental interventions on intellectual growth has hinged precisely on disagreements about the trainees' pretraining and posttraining intellectual structure (e.g., Kohnstamm, 1967, versus Pascual-Leone and Bovet, 1966).

Concern about diagnostic problems has resulted in the creation of a number of new testing procedures in recent years. Largely in reaction to reputed deficiencies in Piaget's "clinical method," many of these procedures require a minimum of verbal judgment and explanation on the part of the child. Braine (1959, 1962) has been an early and assiduous proponent of nonverbal methods here and has tried to devise procedures that will be sensitive to the first manifestations of a given acquisition. We have in previous sections mentioned the diagnostic innovations of Davies (1965), Goldberg (1966), and Yost, Sigel, and Andrews (1962) in the area of probability concepts, of Youniss and Furth (1965, 1966) with transitive inference, and of Ricciuti (1965) with early classificatory abilities. Charlesworth (1964, 1966; Charlesworth and

Zahn, 1966) has successfully employed surprise reactions as indicators of cognitive level in both infants and schoolchildren, and DeVries (1967) has done much the same with fear responses.

Also worth mentioning is an extinction procedure for evaluating the depth and solidity of conservation concepts, in which the child is presented with fabricated empirical evidence that appears to contradict his (correct) conservation judgment. The Genevans generally favor the use of such techniques, and have for years used verbal countersuggestion ("But another little boy told me . . .") for the same purpose. Invented by Smedslund (1961c), the extinction method has subsequently been used in studies by Brison (1965), Hall and Kingsley (1967), and Raven (1965). It has recently been criticized by Kohnstamm (1967)—probably rightly—as susceptible to assessment error of the false-negative variety (i.e., genuine conservers mistakenly diagnosed as nonconservers). In the writer's opinion, the current proliferation of new testing methods has done more to highlight the complexity of the developmental diagnosis problem than to clarify and resolve it. The road from observed test responses to conclusions about underlying structure remains a sinuous and treacherous one.

The fundamental difficulty appears to be one of conceptualizing, and subsequently finding ways to diagnose accurately, the different ways or senses in which a child may be said to "have" a cognitive item in his repertoire. Flavell and Wohlwill (1969) have recently suggested that Chomsky's (1965) competence-performance analysis of language behavior and development may also be useful in thinking about this and related problems in the area of intellectual development. Briefly stated, the argument is that any given conceptual item, for example, the notion of transitivity, may first emerge as a part of the child's intellectual "competence" considerably earlier than normal testing procedures would indicate. At this point in development, the item—while now genuinely "there," "in the system"—is conceived as being exceedingly fragile and difficult to elicit, highly vulnerable to blockage by innumerable "performance" factors (memory and attentional problems, interfering perceptual and conceptual sets, and the like). In the ensuing years (and it is normally a matter of years rather than months) the item slowly frees itself from performance limitations, gradually becomes consolidated, stabilized, and generalized, and eventually emerges as a reliably elicitable cognitive tool in most appropriate situations and under most internal and external conditions of testing. It might therefore be, for example, that Braine's 5-year-old, Smedlund's 8-year-old, and an adult mathematician could all be said to "have" a transitivity rule—in contrast, say, to a 2-year-old—but they would be said to "have" it in quite different ways. If this general view of how conceptual development typically proceeds is even approximately correct, a great deal of painstaking research awaits us, because we know almost nothing as yet about the details of the process. For related ideas regarding the nature of cognitive development and for some possible examples of temporary performance limitations on competence during its course, see Aebli (1963), Beilin (1966), Braine and Shanks (1965a, 1965b), Davies (1965), DeVries (1967), Dodwell (1963), Donaldson (1964), Elkind (1966, 1967a), Feigenbaum (1963), Fleischman, Gilmore, and Ginsberg (1966), Goldberg (1966), Goodnow (1962), Halpern (1965), Huttenlocher (1964), Inhelder, Bovet, Sinclair, and Smock (1966), Lunzer (1965b), Maccoby and Bee (1965), Mermelstein and Shulman (1967), Murray (1965, 1966, 1967a, 1967b), Pascual-Leone and Bovet (1966), Pinard and Laurendeau (1969), Pratoomraj and Johnson (1966), Santa Barbara and Paré (1965), Siget, Saltz, and Roskind (1967), Smedslund (1960, 1964a, 1966c, 1966d, 1966e), Szeminska (1965), Vygotsky (1962, Chaps. 5 and 6), Wallach and Sprott (1964), Wallach, Wall, and Anderson (1967), Wohlwill (1964b), Wohlwill and Katz (1967), and Zimiles (1963, 1966).

Developmental Sequences and Concurrences

As implied in the previous section, one of the major aims of cognitive-developmental study is to identify and interpret the temporal relations that may hold among conceptual acquisitions. For any pair of acquisitions A and B, the most interesting of such relations are invariant concurrence (A and B develop synchronously in all children) and invariant sequence (e.g., A develops earlier than B in all

children). There appear to be methodological problems in the initial empirical identification of invariant concurrences and sequences, conceptual problems in formulating reasonable hypotheses to explain them, and further methodological problems in the subsequent testing of these hypotheses. Much of what will be said about these problems derives from previous writings by Joachim Wohlwill and the present author (Flavell, 1966c; Flavell and Wohlwill, 1969; Wohlwill, 1963, 1966a; see also Pinard and Laurendeau, 1969).

Sequences. How can we ascertain whether one intellectual acquisition (A) invariably occurs earlier in childhood than another (B)? The crudest and least certain method is to show that the mean age at which a test for A is passed is lower than the mean age at which a test for B is passed, each test given to a different but roughly comparable sample of Ss. Many of Piaget's initial claims about developmental sequence (and concurrence) were based on such data. An obvious improvement on this method is to compare mean ages (or equivalent indices of difficulty level) when both tests are administered to the same sample (e.g., Beard, 1963a, 1963b; Beilin and Franklin, 1962; Elkind, 1961a, 1961b, 1961f). However, even within-sample comparisons of mean ages are insufficient in themselves to demonstrate *invariant* (i.e., exceptionless) sequences, because such comparisons would fail to detect a possible minority of out-of-sequence Ss, namely, children who pass test B but fail test A.

A more powerful measure of sequential invariance therefore would be one that scrutinizes the test response patterns of individual Ss for sequence reversals. Whereas a few reversals might be written off as measurement error, more than a few would suggest that the sequence under study is not truly invariant. There are now quite a number of studies in the literature that have analyzed pairs of cognitive acquisitions (e.g., conservation and transitivity of length) in essentially this fashion (e.g., Chittenden, 1964; Dodwell, 1960; Hyde, 1959; Keats, 1955; Kooistra, 1965; Lovell and Olgilvie, 1961a, 1961b, Lunzer, 1965a; Piaget and Inhelder, 1941; Raven, 1965; Shantz and Smock, 1966; Sigel and Mermelstein, 1966; Smedslund, 1961b, 1961f, 1962, 1964a; and Wortman, 1964). When sequences of three or more acquisitions (e.g., conservation of mass, weight, and volume) are tested for invariant order of emergence, one or another version of scalogram analysis is generally used, but the basic logic remains the same (e.g., Davol, Chittenden, Plante, and Tuzik, 1967; Dodwell, 1961; Escalona, 1966; Goldman, 1965; Gouin-Décarie, 1965; Kofsky, 1966; Lunzer, 1960b; Nassefat, 1963; Peel, 1959; Raven, 1965; Schuessler and Strauss, 1950; Smedslund, 1961f, 1962; Uzgiris, 1964; Uzgiris and Hunt, 1966a, 1966b; Wallace, 1966; Weinstein, 1957; Wohlwill, 1960). It would be expected that unambiguous-looking instances of sequential invariance thus identified in cross-sectional data would also be confirmed by longitudinal study, where an S's progress from A to B can be assessed directly. Escalona (1966) has in fact obtained this kind of confirmation in the case of the sequential growth of prehension skills in infancy (see also Almy, Chittenden, and Miller, 1966).

If our views on the problems and pitfalls of developmental diagnosis are as realistic as they are pessimistic, however, not even the most sophisticated of available testing and data analysis methods can assure an accurate identification of invariant sequences, particularly where the developmental onsets of the A's and B's in question are closely adjacent in ontogenetic time. Suppose, for example, that it is really (i.e., genotypically) the case that some A invariably begins its development shortly before some B does. Suppose further that our test for the presence of A in children's repertoire is, quite unknown to us, systematically less sensitive than our test for the presence of B, that is, it yields a higher percentage of false negatives. If these two tests were administered to a sample of children in the appropriate age range, the probable result is a substantial percentage of sequence reversals—children in whom both A and B are in fact evolving, but who pass the "easier" test for B and fail the "harder" test for A. Conversely, if the test for B were the less sensitive, an investigator might be led to infer an invariant A-B sequence when the genotypic facts were quite different (even including the possibility of an underlying B-A invariant sequence). It should be noted that longitudinal studies provide no inherent safeguard against such interpretation errors, as long as the two tests retain these properties.

If A were a much earlier acquisition than B, to be sure, differential sensitivities are likely to cause no difficulty; on the other hand, a finding of sequential invariance here would probably be of less theoretical interest. What we need, obviously, is some means of equating the "hit rates" of the tests we wish to compare. This may be possible when dealing with certain kinds of acquisitions, as Smedslund's (1964a) excellent study has tried to demonstrate in the case of conservation (A) and transitivity (B) of weight. Whether this kind of essential control can be enacted in all cases is uncertain at present (Flavell, 1966c). Where it cannot, the confidence level of an invariant-sequence assertion might be increased somewhat by utilizing a variety of different tests for each of the acquisitions being compared.

The empirical demonstration that some A reliably precedes some B in ontogenesis ought to be regarded as only the beginning of the developmentalist's task. The next step would obviously be trying to hypothecate an other-than-temporal connection between A and B, which could account for, or at least make plausible, the observed temporal one. There has been surprisingly little attention given in the literature to this aspect of the problem (Flavell and Wohlwill, 1969). For a formulation somewhat different from the one very tentatively proposed below, see Piaget (1957).

The A's and B's whose temporal relations have been or could be investigated are a most heterogeneous lot, comprising any and all conceptual milestones that our current pre-theories have defined for us. Correspondingly, the possible developmental liaisons among them that could be envisaged are also quite varied.

In many cases, there appears to be some kind of recognizable structural similarity between earlier A and later B. For instance, B may constitute a more perfected version of A—more stable, more generalizable, and more readily available to the child when the problem setting calls for it. Some of the adjacent pairs of stages in the evolution of the object concept and the conservation concepts might be cases in point. Alternatively, B might be a richer structure which has incorporated its predecessor as a subpart. Formal operations are related to concrete operations in this way.

In general, the developmental processes of differentiation and integration postulated by Werner (1948) and others are likely to result in sequences of cognitive items linked by one or another form of similarity or partial-identity relation.

There are other ordered acquisitions which exhibit no such similarity. The most important subcategory here includes sequences in which B effectively comes to replace or substitute for a quite different-looking A as the dominant mode of response to a certain class of stimulus situations. For instance, more mature forms of moral judgment gradually preempt less mature ones, with the only essential similarity between the two being the content area to which they apply (i.e., moral problems). More extreme cases of this general category are largely without interest: those pairs whose members are so dissimilar in structure, function, and age of acquisition that their invariant order of appearance invites no effort at explanation, say, the object concept (A) and the concept of proportionality (B).

There is a third and extremely interesting category of A-B liaison, which, although sometimes difficult to distinguish from the first, has more of a functional than structural quality about it. In this instance, the relation of A to B is essentially that of means to end or mediator to mediated: A evolves first, and sooner of later thereafter plays a key role (together with other mediators, perhaps) in the formation of B. Piaget's theory provides a number of alleged examples: a grasp of seriation is said to be one of the developmental bridges to an operational concept of number, the ability to multiply relations (e.g., coordinate height and width) is thought to help mediate conservation of liquid quantity, etc.

This third category poses more of a problem for the developmentalist than do the other two. Once we have established empirically that mastery of visible displacements invariably precedes that of invisible displacements (stages 5 and 6 of the object concept, respectively), for instance, few psychologists would doubt that the developmental relation between the two is essentially one of what we have termed similarity or partial identity, with the later formation constituting an elaboration-generalization of the earlier one. Likewise, once we have evidence that, say, the child's first moral judgments are always absolutistic and that they become progressively more relativistic with age, some sort of substitution-replacement characterization appears to be mandated. In neither case, of course, have we thereby told the whole developmental story. In particular, we have not described the mechanisms within the child or the forces within his milieu which help account for the transition from stage 5 to stage 6 and from absolution to relativism. Nonetheless, we do appear to have specified the other-than-temporal, formal nature of the observed temporal relation in a largely incontrovertible fashion.

The situation is quite different where an invariant sequence looks as though it might reflect a mediational linkage. Even if careful research could convince us that, for example, the ability to coordinate height-width relations is invariably present before the child attains conservation of liquid quantity (there is no such convincing evidence at present, by the way), we still could not be at all sure that the one plays any developmental role in the formation of the other. The fact that the former ability might be a logically plausible mediator of the latter is obviously not good enough. The ability to coordinate relations is only one of a number of plausible candidates that have recently been put forward in the case of substance conservation, and we simply have no way of knowing at present which of them, if any, actually assists in the real-life genesis of that concept (Wallach, 1969). Moreover, what may be plausible or even logically compelling for one psychologist need not be for another. For instance, Smedslund thinks that the empirically identified sequence, conservation of length prior to transitivity of length, "also makes good sense logically" (1964a, p. 28), but the present writer finds his argument unconvincing.

It is apparent, then, that if empirical research is initially required just to identify A as a possible universal mediator of B (quite obviously, any substantial number of observed B-A sequence children would rule out even the possibility), additional research must be carried out to show that it is so in actuality. The most convincing research demonstration here would probably take the general form of showing that the experimentally induced and thereby accelerated acquisition of A is regularly followed by an accelerated acquisition of B. Such research is beset with numerous methodological problems in practice, and unambiguous data on mediation are hard to come by (as only one of many cases in point, see Wallach, Wall, and Anderson, 1967). These problems are primarily the familiar ones of diagnostic assessment discussed previously, and they include those of ensuring that developmental movement really occurred with respect to both A and B subsequent to one's experimental intervention, and occurred *only* with respect to these (i.e., ensuring that the intervention did not as an unwanted by-product engender the development of some X, which might have done the real mediative work vis-à-vis B). If reasonably unambiguous positive findings could be obtained by such an experiment, however, the truth status of the hypothesized mediational linkage approaches that which can be bought more cheaply for other linkages. The aforementioned study shows that A *can* help to mediate B. Add to this the initial research finding that A invariably precedes B in normal development, and one is probably as close as one will ever get to proving that A routinely *does* help mediate B in the developmental histories of live children.

This is all that we shall say here about the sequence issue, but it is clearly not all that should be said. For instance, the exact definitions of and distinctions among the three types of relation just described remain extremely vague and uncertain and so, consequently, does the assignment of instances to each. We have also said nothing directly about the (likely) possibility of multiple mediators of a given B and of multiple "mediatees" of a given A. And, last, there is the question of the existence of noninvariant mediators (A helps to mediate B for some children but not for others) or, more generally, that of alternative developmental "routes" to any cognitive attainment (Flavell, 1966c), whether the milestones along these routes be linked by similarity/partial-identity, substitution, or mediation. Assuming that such questions have real referents, the study of concept development is assured a long if trying future.

Concurrences. The identification and interpretation of developmental concurrences has had a theoretical motivation quite different from that which underlies the search for developmental sequences, although the overall theoretical context is again Piagetian. Accord-

ing to Piaget, each of his three major developmental periods has two particularly significant features. Let us use the period of concrete operations as an example, since the concurrence issue has most often been raised in connection with that epoch. First, there emerge within this period a number of new intellectual operations of enormous power and generality, in the sense that each one can serve as a solution procedure for a large and extremely varied assortment of superficially unrelated tasks or problems. The number of different problems that might implicitly call for the operation of class multiplication for instance, would be vast indeed. Thus each operation is conceived as being profoundly genotypical, a veritable "cardinal trait" of cognition. The second important feature is that these operations are definitely not seen as leading separate and independent lives in the child's repertoire. Rather, they are said to be intimately connected, one with another, to form operational structures or systems. Sets of concrete operations are interlinked to form tight structures called "groupings," for instance, and these groupings are in turn conceived as variously interrelated. Piaget's term for the whole network of interrelated structures characteristic of a given developmental period, *structure d'ensemble* (e.g., 1955), conveys this sense of unity and interdependence.

The existence of developmental concurrences becomes an important theoretical issue given the validity of a certain line of reasoning with respect to what has just been said. We shall present this argument in its extreme form, although various weaker versions of it have been proposed or debated (useful sources here include Braine, 1959; Flavell and Wohlwill, 1969; Lunzer, 1960; Pinard and Laurendeau, 1969; Wohlwill, 1963, 1966a). If, in the first place, any given operation has the profundity and generality which Piaget's theory ascribes to it, then its acquisition should be manifested by the child's sudden ability to solve any and all cognitive tasks to which it is applicable. In other words, the picture ought to be one of pronounced developmental concurrence across this ensemble of tasks—either consistent success or consistent failure, depending upon whether the child has or has not yet acquired the underlying operation. If, in the second place, these highly general operations are also bound together into structures (with these structures in turn tightly interlinked), then one would likewise expect developmental synchronisms across operations. As soon as a child can master any task requiring one operation, therefore, he should be able to master any other task requiring any other operation, whether it belongs to the same grouping or not. To the extent that developmental reality fails to accord with this ideal picture, that is, it presents numerous asynchronisms within and between operations, to that extent would such key Piagetian expressions as "stage," "operation," and "structure" become imprecise and even misleading.

The research methods typically used to probe for concurrences are closely related to those employed in the identification of sequences. The investigator looks for high correlations among different tasks calling for the same operation or among measures of different operations. Equivalently, for a pair of noncontinuous measures he expects to find no more than a few Ss in the (pass A-fail B) and (fail A-pass B) cells of the fourfold table (if only the latter cell were near-vacant, one would of course have evidence for an A-B sequence). How often have predicted within-period concurrences been found by such methods? In the words of the Pinafore's captain—"hardly ever." Braine (1959) and Lovell (1961) have reported developmental consistencies in the case of certain concrete- and formal-operational skills, respectively, but asynchronisms of all within- and between-operation varieties have been the general rule (e.g., Beard, 1960; Chittenden, 1964; Dodwell, 1960, 1961, 1962, 1963; Kooistra, 1965; Lovell & Ogilvie, 1960, 1961b; Lunzer, 1960b; Mannix, 1960; Nassefat, 1963; Smedslund, 1964a; Swinson, 1966; Uzgiris, 1964; Wohlwill and Katz, 1967). Moreover, as Wohlwill (1963) has noted, a number of these asynchronisms may prove to be instances of invariant sequence.

It should be pointed out, however, that the empirical identification and theoretical interpretation of between-operation concurrences in particular are beset with many of the difficulties previously described in connection with sequences. On the methodological side, for instance, there is the familiar problem of differential test sensitivity. As in the case of se-

quences, this factor could lead us to misdiagnose an asynchronism as a synchronism or, more often perhaps, the converse. There are also questions of interpretation, given an indisputable-looking instance of concurrence. It would be at least conceivable that the two operations in question were unrelated or only very distantly related, despite their simultaneous appearance, for example, temporally coincident way stations on two parallel but independent developmental "tracks." More probably, however, consistent synchronism would suggest some kind of functional connection. It might be that both operations have some of the same mediators in common, or (and) reciprocally mediate each other during their evolution. If the observed concurrence really reflected a high degree of functional interdependence, any experimentally induced developmental progress in one should be accompanied by similar progress in the other, whereas this should not be the case if the two were only coincidentally synchronous.

According to the argument outlined earlier, data on developmental concurrences ought to provide vital evidence for or against Piaget's assumptions about the generality and the structural interrelatedness of cognitive operations, and hence for or against his general view of the nature of intellectual development. If the analysis set forth in the preceding paragraph is basically correct, there is reason to question whether an empirical finding suggesting concurrence in the case of two different operations is *sufficient* evidence for a structural relation between them. The concurrence might, as we have seen, be entirely coincidental. Even if it were not, there might be no plausible structural connection between, say, certain pairs of operations which owe their synchronism only to a common underlying mediator. The much more important point, however, is that it is hard to see why concurrences should be taken to constitute *necessary* conditions for the validity of *either* the generality *or* the structural-interrelatedness assumptions.

The matter of generality vis-à-vis a single operation (or any cognitive item, considered as an isolated entity) has really been dealt with in our previous discussion of developmental diagnosis and sequence. Everything we know about intellectual development continually forces us to distinguish between the potential generality of any cognitive tool and the child's current ability to exploit that potential. Although it is still far from clear just how the developmental lag between early buddings and later blossomings ought to be conceptualized (our competence-performance conception appears only a little less inadequate in this respect than Piaget's original notion of horizontal *décalage*), it is simply a fact that the full evolution of any cognitive item almost invariably looks more like an extended process than a punctate episode. To use developmental concurrences as a criterion for the generality of an operation is really to confuse generality with generalizability—two quite different things in the case of an evolving mind. For a single operation within the concrete-operational period, then, the best statement would seem to be that this period is the segment of childhood *during which,* or *by the end of which,* this particular kind of operation *acquires* much of the generality and stability that it has in adulthood.

There are similar difficulties with the concurrence test as applied to the structural-interrelatedness question. It is perhaps symptomatic of these difficulties that recent treatments of the question have tried to liberalize this criterion. For instance, Pinard and Laurendeau (1969) argue that all the constituent operations of all the concrete-operational groupings should become more or less simultaneously effective within any given conceptual domain (e.g., all the operations underlying conservation, transitivity, measurement, etc., in the domain of weight), but not across all domains at once. In contrast, Wohlwill (1966a; see also Flavell and Wohlwill, 1969) has suggested that only the operations within a given grouping might be expected to emerge concurrently, thus allowing for the possibility of asynchronisms among the different groupings. However, a closer analysis of "structural interrelatedness" and equivalent expressions suggests that this criterion might better be abandoned altogether.

What does it mean to say that cognitive operations X, Y, and Z comprise a cognitive "structure," or are "structurally interrelated" within the child's cognitive system? For most psychologists, it would probably imply several things. First, the theorist-observer is able to characterize the structural relationships among the operations in some formal way,

for example, show that they can be modelled by a mathematical group, as with certain Piagetian structures (see Gyr, Brown, and Cafagna, 1967). Second, the operations do indeed coexist in the child's system, that is, he has acquired these operations. Finally, they do not *merely* coexist but also interact psychologically in some fashion. For instance, one might perhaps expect that the operation of uniting subordinate classes to form a superordinate class "calls to mind"—is associatively linked with—the inverse operation of redifferentiating the superordinate into its subordinate classes for any child whose cognitive system contains the concrete-operational grouping of class addition. Similarly, the engagement of either operation might also be expected to lower the threshold for operations from related groupings such as class multiplication. In other words, the external, logical-mathematical relations among operations should be paralleled by some kind of internal, psychological ones, if we are to claim that they constitute unified structures (*structures d'ensemble*) rather than simply a set of psychologically independent abilities. An important and still unresolved research problem is to find ways to confirm (or disconfirm) the psychological reality of the structures Piaget has described.

What "structural interrelatedness" does *not* seem to imply, however, on either logical or psychological grounds, is that the operations in question have to enter the repertoire synchronously. I assume that my knowledge of developmental psychology is in some sense a cognitive structure rather than a collection of independent pieces of information. However, it would be factually wrong to argue that this structure abruptly emerged at a given point in my adult development—elements, relations, and all—and logically absurd to claim that, since it did not, it could not *now* be a genuine structure. Similarly, no one would want to argue that adult linguistic operations do not constitute a complex structure merely because, as all evidence suggests (e.g., Klima and Bellugi, 1967), the components of this structure are acquired piecemeal rather than all at once. If Piaget's theory is correct, the normal child *comes to* acquire the full set of, say, concrete operations during middle childhood, and these operations *come to be* organized as psychological structures; it is theo-

retically unnecessary and probably empirically
false to claim also that all these developmental events transpire concurrently. Much more,
and much better research evidence will be
needed before the full developmental story
for this or any other period can be told, but
it might have the following general character.
Some sets of operations may regularly begin
their evolutions more or less synchronously,
perhaps because they have underlying mediators in common or perhaps because they tend
to mediate one another. Other sets may emerge
in fixed sequence, as a consequence of mediational connections of a unidirectional sort.
Still other operations may show no invariant
temporal relations at all. Each operation,
whenever and however inaugurated, will require a more or less extended period of consolidation and generalization before it becomes
reliably serviceable to the child across tasks
and content areas. Either during this whole
process or during the latter part of it, the
evolving operations become psychologically
interconnected, this too probably taking place
in a gradual and stepwise manner. Only when
the process is completed (if, in fact, it ever
gets fully completed) will the child's cognitive system present most or all of the features
described in the theorist's idealization of it.
This image of how development proceeds suggests the following, not entirely facetious
proposition: If you really want to study a
Piagetian concrete-operational structure in all
its power and glory, choose an adolescent as
your subject—or better yet, a bright adult!

If the various same-stage acquisitions need
not and probably do not show a really tight
developmental synchronism, it cannot be denied that they do show at least a looser kind.
Although the temporal gap between the evolutions of two concrete operations might be
3 years, for example, it clearly would never
be 10 years. There obviously is some kind of
glue that binds acquisitions together in ontogenetic time, albeit not as closely as we had
once thought necessary, and its ingredients
need to be analyzed. The most likely explanation here seems to be the Piagetian one that
all within-period skills are of the same general
kind, are at the same "level" in some specifiable way. For instance, concrete operations
are conceived as internalized, symbolic actions
(in contrast to sensorimotor actions), which
take external data rather than other operations

as their objects (in contrast to formal operations). Furthermore, each period is regarded
as necessarily prior to the one that follows it,
with successor integrating predecessor (e.g.,
Piaget, 1967b). These conceptions together
with all the preceding ones may thus serve to
explain why a cognitive-developmental period
is not a temporal point, why it is likewise not
synonymous with all of childhood, why it occurs roughly when it does, and—more generally—why its postulation represents a substantive claim about the nature of intellectual
development.

Organismic and Environmental Factors in Concept Development

The concluding section of this chapter will
attempt little more than a summary of the
major questions underlying the search for
organismic and environmental factors in concept development, a rough categorization of
the types of research studies which have been
designed to answer these questions, and the
citation of relevant bibliography. The questions can be divided for exposition's sake into
those focusing primarily on the changing organism itself and those emphasizing its developmental environment or millieu.

On the organismic side, the principal question is essentially the following: what design
features of the immature human organism
make possible the characteristically human
patterns of intellectual growth described in
this and other *Manual* chapters? No such
growth would be imaginable unless the child's
basic "program" contained special processes
or mechanisms that would somehow permit,
if not ensure, significant, nonrandom changes
in that program during childhood. On the environmental side, the questions concern the
contribution of external information and other
sorts of input to developmental change, since
no one believes that these processes and mechanisms operate independently of inflow from
the milieu. We therefore also want to know,
among other things, what kinds of inflow
play what causal role (e.g., constitute necessary and/or sufficient conditions) in the
operation of these processes vis-à-vis what
segments of conceptual growth. Since the effects of environmental factors have been given
a great deal of attention by developmental
psychologists, especially in this country, it is
worth emphasizing that the growth-making

activities of the child himself must remain one of our most fundamental subjects of study. In this connection, our scientific objectives might well include a kind of ethological characterization of the course of human conceptual growth, one emphasizing those underlying processes and surface conceptual outcomes that are species-typical, in the sense of remaining essentially constant over a rather wide range of human environments.

The organismic-environmental distinction can also be applied to the research literature in this area (although not always effortlessly). Some studies show a relative emphasis on the child's own capacities and activities, whereas others pay particular attention to milieu variation and its effects. Cross-cutting this division is a second, more cleanly dichotomous one. Some investigations involve active attempts to engender developmental change, whereas others take it as they find it. The contrast is the familiar one between experiment and study, or between intervention and nonintervention; where the emphasis is upon environmental effects, it could be rephrased as a distinction between programmed and unprogrammed inputs to the child's conceptual growth.

Studies. Noninterventionistic studies have investigated the developmental influence of several organismic variables. Predictably, IQ has been one of them, with most studies finding some positive association between this warhorse factor and, for example, performance on various Piagetian tasks (e.g., Dodwell, 1960; Feigenbaum, 1963; Goodnow and Bethon, 1966; Hood, 1962). A potentially more interesting variable is linguistic ability, since it has long been assumed that language development and conceptual development must interact in some fashion. So far as this writer can discover, no one has yet formulated the possible nature of this interaction in any really clear and precise way, particularly with respect to putative influences of language acquisition on conceptual growth. Furth's (e.g., 1964, 1966) recent studies of cognitive development in the deaf strongly suggest that the acquisition of a linguistic system (defined broadly to include, for instance, a codified gesture language of comparable structural complexity) cannot be a *necessary* condition for the growth of human thinking, at least up to the level of concrete operations. Further

research will be needed to clarify some alternative possibilities that come to mind: that (broadly-defined) linguistic abilities have some weaker, facilitative function up to that level; that they might play a stronger, perhaps even indispensable role in the more abstract realm of formal-operational thought (Pettifor, 1964); and, generally, that they assist the growth and continued operation of some kinds of cognitive activities much more powerfully and directly than they do others. Other recent writings dealing with this murky issue include Brown (1965, Chap. 7), Bruner, Olver, and Greenfield (1966), Farnham-Diggory and Bermon (1967), Inhelder, Bovet, and Sinclair (1967), Lantz and Lenneberg (1966), Piaget (1967a, Chap. 3), Sinclair (1967), and Werner and Kaplan (1963).

There is one interesting individual-difference variable which so far appears to be lacking a research literature. Piaget's theory seems to imply that an otherwise normally endowed child who has a congenital incapacity for manual interaction with the environment (e.g., born without arms) would suffer a gross retardation of intellectual growth, since the theory assigns a very important developmental role to the infant's motor actions vis-à-vis surrounding objects (these actions subsequently becoming internalized as "operations," etc.). One would therefore like to see a case study report on the intellectual attainments of such a child, analogous to Lenneberg's (1962) report on the receptive linguistic abilities of a boy born without the capacity to make speech sounds. The writer's guess is that Piaget's theory would not fare well in this research encounter.

Environmental factors which have been considered include family background (socioeconomic status, religion, etc.), cultural milieu, and schooling. We cite here only the bulk of available references on the effects of schooling-nonschooling (Bruner, Olver, and Greenfield, 1966; Goodnow, 1962; Goodnow and Bethon, 1966; Mermelstein and Shulman, 1967; Price-Williams, 1962) and cultural environment (Bruner, Olver, and Greenfield, 1966; Cowley and Murray, 1962; Goodnow, 1962, 1967; Hyde, 1959; Jahoda, 1956, 1958a, 1958b; Piaget, 1966; Price-Williams, 1961, 1962; Vernon, 1965). The influence of these two factors has generally been found to be quantitatively and qualitatively different from task to task. While really satisfactory explanations for these variable effects are not yet in view, there have at least been some interesting recent attempts (e.g., Bruner, Olver, and Greenfield, 1966; Goodnow, 1967, 1969 Piaget, 1966). One of the major problems with all such research, of course, it the difficulty one has in translating global characterizations of the child's environment (e.g., "has had no schooling," "is growing up in a Wolof village") into specific descriptions of the developmentally relevant life experiences he has undergone. The recent work of Hess and Shipman (1965) is an example of how at least partial translations of this kind can be effected.

Experiments. A complete inventory of investigative efforts to influence the child's intellectual growth would take us deep into the trackless wastes of educational research. We propose instead to consider only a certain group of such experiments, a group that is short on history but rather long on contemporary interest: laboratory or quasi-laboratory attempts to foster the acquisition of Piagetian concepts. The paradigmatic experiment here begins with a pretest diagnosis of the child's initial status vis-à-vis the concept or concepts of interest, proceeds to a brief (e.g., 2 hours), individually administered training experience of some kind, and concludes with one or more repetitions or elaborations of the original diagnostic procedures in order to assess the effects of the training. The implicit assumption in most of these experiments is the following: if a particular developmental change *can* be generated by the essential components of a given training procedure (provision of a certain kind of environmental information, activation of a certain type of organismic process, or whatever), then it is probable that this same change *is* regularly so generated in real life. Although this assumption has a certain plausibility in the case of some of these studies (but not in all), there is of course always the risk for the investigator of mistaking the sufficient but atypical for the necessary or normative.

The number of these Piagetian training studies has increased markedly during the past 5 years. There appears to have been only about a dozen of them completed by 1961–1962 (Flavell, 1963, pp. 370–379). It is doubtful if anyone knows exactly how many have been carried out since (a number of

them are described only in unpublished theses, for instance), but there must be a total of at least five dozen by now. The following list of relevant sources should therefore not be regarded as exhaustive: Anderson (1965), Beilin (1965, 1966), Beilin and Franklin (1962), Beilin, Kagan, and Rabinowitz (1966), Braine and Shanks (1965a, 1965b), Brison (1965), Bruner, Olver, and Greenfield (1966), Carbonneau (1965), Churchill (1958a, 1958b), Feigenbaum and Sulkin (1964), Flavell and Wohlwill (1969), Fleischmann, Gilmore, and Ginsburg (1966), Fournier (1965), Fry (1966), Gagné (1966a, 1966b), Gilmore (1966), Gréco (1959, 1963b), Gruen (1965), Hétu (1966), Inhelder, Bovet, Sinclair, and Smock (1966), Inhelder, Bovet, and Sinclair (1967), Karplus (1964), Kohnstamm (1963, 1965, 1967), Langer (1967), Lasry (1966), Laubengayer (1965), Morf (1959) Northman (1964), Ojemann and Pritchett (1963), Ojemann, Maxey, and Snider (1965a, 1965b), Pascual-Leone and Bovet (1966), Piaget (1964a—see also Piaget's chapter in this book), Pinard and Laurendeau (1969), Pufall (1966), Shantz and Sigel (1967), Sigel, Roeper, and Hooper (1968), Sinclair (1967), Smedslund (1961a, 1961b, 1961c, 1961d, 1961e, 1961f, 1963b, 1963c, 1963e, 1963f, 1964b), Stendler (1967), Suchman (1960), Thier, Powell, and Karplus (1963), Wallach, Wall, and Anderson (1967), Wallach and Sprott (1964), Wohlwill (1964a, 1966a, 1966b), Wohlwill and Lowe (1962), Wynns (1967), and Zimiles (1963).

Our earlier distinction between organismic and environmental research orientations becomes very strained when applied to this group of experiments. The purest example of an organismic variable here would perhaps be Piaget's hypothesized process of equilibration of cognitive actions, since the emphasis is on what the child actually *does* vis-à-vis stimulus input rather than on the particular nature of that input itself or on its manner of delivery. On the other hand, the investigator must also pay very careful attention to these latter factors if he really expects to elicit this supposedly formative, "spontaneous" process in a laboratory setting (Beilin, 1965; Carbonneau, 1965; Fournier, 1965; Gruen, 1965; Inhelder, Bovet, and Sinclair, 1967; Langer, 1967; Smedslund, 1961e, 1961f, 1963e, 1963f,

1964b, 1966a). Conversely, the researcher who is more interested in the nature and mode of presentation of environmental information (e.g., Anderson, 1965) must, it would seem, eventually speculate about the particular kind of machine that could make developmental progress in the course of processing this information.

This Janus-faced character of the training study is also expressed in the multitude of potential scientific uses it may have. Given the right design and unequivocal results, we could variously conceive of it helping us to understand, in the case of the cognitive device (child) as a whole, how this device is constructed at any given developmental level, what it characteristically does with environmental inputs in order to change its current structure, and what type, form, and range of information from the milieu will sustain or elicit this growth-building activity. And in the case of any particular hallmark of that device (e.g., a conservation concept), it could help us understand what its underlying components are, and how these particular components might have entered the system (again, by what organismic processes and vis-à-vis what environmental inputs). Most if not all of these scientific aims find their expression somewhere within the existing literature, and other variations could be mentioned. For instance, training studies might be used for purely diagnostic purposes, with the training being regarded only as a useful procedure for stripping away performance obstacles in order to make manifest the child's underlying competence (in rather the same way that psychotherapy can be thought of as one route to better diagnosis). Recent research by Braine and others (e.g., Braine and Shanks, 1965b) has some features of this approach.

Similarly, it would be worth exploring whether the effectiveness of a given form of training depends, not only upon the child's initial developmental status vis-à-vis the target concept (the familar "readiness" notion), but also upon the general developmental period he is in and, consequently, the general *kind* of skill he is to acquire. Verbal-didactic methods, for example, might prove more effective for teaching formal-operational skills to preadolescents than for teaching concrete-operational skills to preschoolers, because of the basic differences involved in what is to be learned and in what kind of organism does the learning.

In what measure have existing training studies realized the scientific potential we have somewhat optimistically ascribed to them? A vague generalization must suffice in lieu of a properly detailed and documented statement: to a very limited extent only. The basic requirements for a good training study are simple enough in principle: exact specification of initial cognitive status, of final cognitive status, and of intervening inputs and processes. For reasons frequently mentioned in previous sections, however, these requirements are extraordinarily difficult to meet in practice, and even the most careful and sophisticated of the available training experiments (e.g., Fournier, 1965; Inhelder, Bovet, and Sinclair, 1967—each reader of this literature would have his own favorites) raise more questions than they answer. It may seem a trite and lame ending to this chapter to say that much more really good research is needed, and that really good research always seems to be the hardest kind to do. Nonetheless, nothing could be truer of the whole area of concept development at the present time.

References

Aebli, T. *Über die geistige Entwicklung des Kindes.* Stuttgart: Ernst Klett, 1963.

Almy, M., Chittenden, E., and Miller, P. *Young children's thinking: studies of some aspects of Piaget's thinking.* New York: Teachers College Press, 1966.

Ames, L. B. The development of the sense of time in the young child. *J. genet. Psychol.,* 1946, **68,** 97–125.

Anderson, R. C. Can first graders learn an advanced problem-solving skill? *J. educ. Psychol.,* 1965, **56,** 283–294.

Anderson, R. D. Children's ability to formulate mental models to explain their observations of natural phenomena. *Dissert. Abstr.*, 1965, 25(7), 3994.

Annett, M. The classification of instances of four common class concepts by children and adults. *Br. J. educ. Psychol.*, 1959, 29, 223–236.

Anthony, S. A study of the development of the concept of death. *Br. J. educ. Psychol.*, 1939, 9, 276–277.

Apostel, L., Mays, W., Morf, A., and Piaget, J. Les liaisons analytiques et synthétiques dans les comportements du sujet. *Etudes d'épistémologie génétique*, Vol. 4. Paris: Presses Universitaires de France, 1957.

Austin, J. A., Gekoski, W. L., and Zivian, M. T. Clustering in recall as a function of age and list structure. University of Michigan, Develpm. Lang. Functions Program-Project, Report No. 7, 1965.

Ausubel, D. P., and Schiff, H. M. The effect of incidental and experimentally induced experience in the learning of relevant and irrelevant causal relationships by children. *J. genet. Psychol.*, 1954, 84, 109–123.

Babska, Z. The formation of the conception of identity of visual characteristics of objects seen successively. In P. H. Mussen (Ed.), European research in cognitive development. *Monogr. Soc. Res. Child Develpm.*, 1965, 30, No. 2 (Whole No. 100), 112–124.

Baldwin, A. L. A is happy—B is not. *Child Dev.*, 1965, 36, 583–600.

Baldwin, A. L. *Theories of child development.* New York: Wiley, 1967.

Baldwin, C. P., and Baldwin, A. L. Children's judgments of kindness. Paper read at Soc. Res. Child Develpm., New York, March, 1967.

Beard, R. M. The nature and development of concepts. *Educ. Rev.*, 1960, 13, 12–26.

Beard, R. M. The order of concept development; studies in two fields. I. Number concepts in the infant school. *Educ. Rev.*, 1963, 15, 105–117. (a)

Beard, R. M. The order of concept development; studies in two fields. II. Conceptions of conservation of quantity among primary school children. *Educ. Rev.*, 1963, 15, 228–237. (b)

Beilin, H. Perceptual-cognitive conflict in the development of an invariant area concept. *J. exp. Child Psychol.*, 1964, 1, 208–226.

Beilin, H. Learning and operational convergence in logical thought development. *J. exp. Child Psychol.*, 1965, 2, 317–339.

Beilin, H. Feedback and infralogical strategies in invariant area conceptualization. *J. exp. Child Psychol.*, 1966, 3, 267–278.

Beilin, H. Stimulus and cognitive transformation in conservation. In D. Elkind and J. H. Flavell (Eds.), *Studies in cognitive development: essays in honor of Jean Piaget.* New York: Oxford University Press, 1969. Pp. 409–437.

Beilin, H., and Franklin, I. C. Logical operations in area and length measurement: age and training effects. *Child Dev.*, 1962, 33, 607–618.

Beilin, H., Kagan, J., and Rabinowitz, R. Effects of verbal and perceptual training on water level representation. *Child Dev.*, 1966, 37, 317–329.

Bousfield, W. A., Esterson, J., and Whitmarsh, G. A. A study of developmental changes in conceptual and perceptual cognitive clustering. *J. genet. Psychol.*, 1958, 92, 95–102.

Bower, T. G. R. The development of object-permanence: some studies of existence constancy. *Percept. Psychophys.*, 1967, 2, 411–418.

Bradley, N. C. The growth of the knowledge of time in children of school age. *Br. J. Psychol.*, 1947, 38, 67–78.

Braine, M. D. S. The ontogeny of certain logical operations: Piaget's formulation examined by nonverbal methods. *Psychol. Monogr.*, 1959, 73, No. 5 (Whole No. 475).

Braine, M. D. S. Piaget on reasoning: a methodological critique and alternative proposals. In W. Kessen and C. Kuhlman (Eds.), Thought in the young child. *Monogr. Soc. Res. Child Develpm.*, 1962, **27**, No. 2 (Whole No. 83), 41–61.

Braine, M. D. S. Development of a grasp of transitivity of length: a reply to Smedslund. *Child Dev.*, 1964, **35**, 799–810.

Braine, M. D. S., and Shanks, B. L. The development of conservation of size. *J. verb. Learn. verb. Behav.*, 1965, **4**, 227–242. (a)

Braine, M. D. S., and Shanks, B. L. The conservation of a shape property and a proposal about the origin of the conservations. *Can. J. Psychol.*, 1965, **19**, 197–207. (b)

Brison, D. W. Acquisition of conservation of substance in a group situation. Unpublished doctoral dissertation, University of Illinois, 1965.

Brown, R. *Social psychology.* New York: Free Press, 1965.

Bruner, J. S. The course of cognitive growth. *Amer. Psychol.*, 1964, **19**, 1–14.

Bruner, J. S., Goodnow, J. J., and Austin, G. A. *A study of thinking.* New York: Wiley, 1956.

Bruner, J. S., and Olver, R. R. The development of equivalence transformations in children. In J. C. Wright and J. Kagan (Eds.), Basic cognitive processes in children. *Monogr. Soc. Res. Child Develpm.*, 1963, **28**, No. 2 (Whole No. 86), 125–143.

Bruner, J. S., Olver, R. R., and Greenfield, P. M. (with others). *Studies in cognitive growth.* New York: Wiley, 1966.

Carbonneau, M. Apprentissage de la notion de conservation de surfaces. Unpublished thèse de licence, University of Montreal, 1965.

Carroll, J. B. Words, meanings and concepts. *Harvard Educ. Rev.*, 1964, **34**, 178–202.

Case, D., and Collinson, J. M. The development of formal thinking in verbal comprehension. *Br. J. educ. Psychol.*, 1962, **32**, 103–111.

Charlesworth, W. R. The growth of knowledge of the effects of rotation and shaking on the linear order of objects. Unpublished doctoral dissertation, Cornell University, 1962.

Charlesworth, W. R. Development and assessment of cognitive structures. *J. Res. Sci. Teach.*, 1964, **2**, 214–219.

Charlesworth, W. R. Development of the object concept: a methodological study. Paper read at Amer. Psychol. Assoc., New York, September, 1966.

Charlesworth, W. R., and Zahn, C. Reaction time as a measure of the child's comprehension of the effects produced by rotation on the order of objects. *Child Dev.*, 1966, **37**, 253–268.

Chittenden, E. A. The development of certain logical abilities and the child's concepts of substance and weight: an examination of Piaget's theory. Unpublished doctoral dissertation, Columbia University, 1964.

Chomsky, N. *Aspects of the theory of syntax.* Cambridge: M.I.T. Press, 1965.

Churchill, E. The number concepts of the young child: Part 1. *Researches and Studies.* Leeds University, 1958, **17**, 34–39. (a)

Churchill, E. The number concepts of the young child: Part 2. *Researches and Studies.* Leeds University, 1958, **18**, 28–46. (b)

Churchill, E. *Counting and measuring.* Toronto: University of Toronto Press, 1961.

Corah, N. The influence of some stimulus characteristics on color and form perception in nursery-school children. *Child Dev.*, 1966, **37**, 205–211.

Cowan, P. A. Cognitive egocentrism and social interaction in children. Paper read at Amer. Psychol. Assoc., New York, September, 1966.

Cowley, J. J., and Murray, M. Some aspects of the development of spatial concepts in Zulu children. *J. Soc. Res.*, 1962, **13**, 1–18.

Danziger, K. The child's understanding of kinship terms: a study in the development of relational concepts. *J. genet. Psychol.*, 1957, **91**, 213–232.

Danziger, K. Children's earliest conceptions of economic relationships (Australia). *J. Soc. Psychol.*, 1958, **47**, 231–240.

Danziger, K., and Sharp, N. The development of children's explanations of growth and movement. *Aust. J. Psychol.*, 1958, **10**, 196–207.

Davies, C. M. Development of the probability concept in children. *Child Dev.*, 1965, **36**, 779–788.

Davol, S. H., Chittenden, E. L., Plante, M., and Tuzik, J. The conservation of continuous quantity investigated as a scalable developmental concept. *Merrill-Palmer Quart.*, 1967, **13**, 191–199.

Davol, S. H., and Hastings, M. L. Effects of sex, age, reading ability, socio-economic level, and display position on a measure of spatial relations in children. Paper read at East. Psychol. Assoc., New York, April, 1966.

DeVries, R. Conservation of generic identity in the years three to six. Paper read at Soc. Res. Child Develpm., New York, March, 1967.

Dodwell, P. C. Children's understanding of number and related concepts. *Can. J. Psychol.*, 1960, **14**, 191–205.

Dodwell, P. C. Children's understanding of number concepts: characteristics of an individual and of a group test. *Can. J. Psychol.*, 1961, **15**, 29–36.

Dodwell, P. C. Relations between the understanding of the logic of classes and of cardinal number in children. *Can. J. Psychol.*, 1962, **16**, 152–160.

Dodwell, P. C. Children's understanding of spatial concepts. *Can. J. Psychol.*, 1963, **17**, 141–161.

Donaldson, M. *A study of children's thinking.* New York: Humanities, 1964.

Dubin, R., and Dubin, E. R. Children's social perceptions: a review of research. *Child Dev.*, 1965, **36**, 809–838.

Dymond, R. F., Hughes, A. S., and Raabe, V. L. Measurable changes in empathy with age. *J. Consult. Psychol.*, 1952, **16**, 202–206.

Easton, D., and Hess, R. D. The child's political world. *Midwest. J. Polit. Sci.*, 1962, **6**, 229–246.

Elkind, D. The development of quantitative thinking: a systematic replication of Piaget's studies. *J. genet. Psychol.*, 1961, **98**, 37–46. (a)

Elkind, D. Children's discovery of the conservation of mass, weight, and volume: Piaget Replication Study II. *J. genet. Psychol.*, 1961, **98**, 219–227. (b)

Elkind, D. The development of the additive composition of classes in the child: Piaget replication study III. *J. genet. Psychol.*, 1961, **99**, 51–57. (c)

Elkind, D. The child's conception of his religious denomination: I. The Jewish child. *J. genet. Psychol.*, 1961, **99**, 209–225. (d)

Elkind, D. Piaget's conceptions of right and left: Piaget replication study IV. *J. genet. Psychol.*, 1961, **99**, 269–276. (e)

Elkind, D. Quantity conceptions in junior and senior high school students. *Child Dev.*, 1961, **32**, 551–560. (f)

Elkind, D. Children's conceptions of brother and sister: Piaget replication study V. *J. genet. Psychol.*, 1962, **100**, 129–136. (a)

Elkind, D. The child's conception of his religious denomination: II. The Catholic child. *J. genet. Psychol.*, 1962, **101**, 185–193. (b)

Elkind, D. Quantity conceptions in college students. *J. soc. Psychol.*, 1962, **57**, 459–465. (c)

Elkind, D. The child's conception of his religious denomination: III. The Protestant child. *J. genet. Psychol.*, 1963, **103**, 291–304.

Elkind, D. Discrimination, seriation, and numeration of size and dimensional differences in young children: Piaget replication study VI. *J. genet. Psychol.*, 1964, **104**, 275–296. (a)

Elkind, D. The child's conception of his religious identity. *Lumen Vitae*, 1964, **19**, 635–646. (b)

Elkind, D. Conservation across illusory transformations in young children. *Acta Psychol.*, 1966, **25**, 389–400.

Elkind, D. Piaget's conservation problems. *Child Dev.*, 1967, **38**, 15–28. (a)

Elkind, D. Egocentrism in adolescence. Unpublished paper, 1967. (b)

Elkind, D., and Flavell, J. H. (Eds.). *Studies in cognitive development: essays in honor of Jean Piaget.* New York: Oxford University Press, 1969.

Elkind, D., Spilka, B., and Long, D. The child's conception of prayer. Unpublished paper, 1966.

Escalona, S. K. Personal communication, 1966.

Farnham-Diggory, S., and Bermon, M. Verbal compensation, cognitive synthesis and conservation. Paper read at Soc. Res. Child Develpm., New York, March, 1967.

Feffer, M. H. The cognitive implications of role taking behavior. *J. Personality*, 1959, **27**, 152–168.

Feffer, M. H., and Gourevitch, V. Cognitive aspects of role-taking in children. *J. Personality*, 1960, **28**, 383–396.

Feffer, M. H., and Suchotliff, L. Decentering implications of social interaction. *J. pers. Soc. Psychol.*, 1966, **4**, 415–422.

Feifel, H., and Lorge, I. Qualitative differences in the vocabulary responses of children. *J. educ. Psychol.*, 1950, **41**, 1–18.

Feigenbaum, K. D. Task complexity and IQ as variables in Piaget's problem of conservation. *Child Dev.*, 1963, **34**, 423–432.

Feigenbaum, K. D., and Sulkin, H. Piaget's problem of conservation of discontinuous quantities: A teaching experience. *J. genet. Psychol.*, 1964, **105**, 91–97.

Flapan, D. P. Children's understanding of social interaction. *Dissert. Abstr.*, 1965, **26**(4), 2310–2311.

Flavell, J. H. The ontogenetic development of verbal communication skills. Final Progress Report, NIMH Grant M-2268, 1961.

Flavell, J. H. *The developmental psychology of Jean Piaget.* Princeton: Van Nostrand, 1963. (a)

Flavell, J. H. Piaget's contributions to the study of cognitive development. *Merrill-Palmer Quart.*, 1963, **9**, 245–252. (b)

Flavell, J. H. Role-taking and communication skills in children. *Young Children*, 1966, **21**, 164–177. (a)

Flavell, J. H. The development of two related forms of cognition: role-taking and verbal communication. In A. H. Kidd and J. L. Rivoire (Eds.), *Perceptual development in children.* New York: International Universities Press, 1966. Pp. 246–272. (b)

Flavell, J. H. Heinz Werner on the nature of development. In S. Wapner and Kaplan (Eds.), *Heinz Werner, 1890–1964: Papers in memoriam.* Worcester: Clark University Press, 1966. Pp. 25–32. (c)

Flavell, J. H. (in collaboration with Botkin, P. T., Fry, C. L., Wright, J. W., and Jarvis, P. E.). *The development of role-taking and communication skills in children.* New York: Wiley, 1968.

Flavell, J. H., and Wohlwill, J. F. Formal and functional aspects of cognitive development. In D. Elkind and J. H. Flavell (Eds.), *Studies in cognitive development: essays in honor of Jean Piaget.* New York: Oxford University Press, 1969. Pp. 67–120.

Fleischmann, B., Gilmore, S., and Ginsburg, H. The strength of non-conservation. *J. exp. Child Psychol.*, 1966, **4**, 353–368.

Fournier, E. Generalisation intra-notionnelle et inter-notionnelle d'un apprentissage empirique de la notion de conservation des surfaces. Unpublished thèse de licence, University of Montreal, 1965.

Fraisse, P. *The psychology of time.* New York: Harper, 1963.

Friedman, K. C. Time concepts of junior and senior high school pupils and adults. *Sch. Rev.*, 1944, **52**, 233–238. (a)

Friedman, K. C. Time concepts of elementary-school children. *Elem. Sch. J.*, 1944, **44**, 337–342. (b)

Fry, C. L. Training children to communicate to listeners. *Child Dev.*, 1966, **37**, 675–685.

Furth, H. G. Conservation of weight in deaf and hearing children. *Child Dev.*, 1964, **35**, 143–150.

Furth, H. G. *Thinking without language: psychological implications of deafness.* New York: Free Press, 1966.

Gagné, R. M. Elementary science: a new scheme of instruction. *Science*, 1966, **151**, 49–53. (a)

Gagné, R. M. Contributions of learning to human development. Presidential address, Division 1, AAAS, Washington, D.C., December, 1966. (b)

Geis, F. L. Review of F. I. Greenstein, *Children and politics. Contemp. Psychol.*, 1966, **11**, 584–586.

Gellert, E. Children's lateralizations of human figures: analysis of a developmental transition. Unpublished paper, 1966.

Gilmore, S. E. The effect of screening the visual cues in the classic conservation of liquid quantity experiment. Unpublished masters thesis, Cornell University, 1966.

Glucksberg, S., and Krauss, R. M. Studies of the development of interpersonal communication. Paper read at Soc. Res. Child Develpm. Meetings, New York, March, 1967.

Glucksberg, S., Krauss, R. M., and Weisberg, R. Referential communication in nursery school children: Method and some preliminary findings. *J. exp. Child Psychol.*, 1966, **3**, 333–342.

Goldberg, S. Probability judgments by preschool children: task conditions and performance. *Child Dev.*, 1966, **37**, 157–167.

Goldman, A. E., and Levine, M. A developmental study of object sorting. *Child Dev.*, 1963, **34**, 649–666.

Goldman, R. J. The application of Piaget's schema of operational thinking to religious story data by means of the Guttman scalogram. *Br. J. educ. Psychol.*, 1965, **35**, 158–170.

Gollin, E. S. Forming impressions of personality. *J. Personality*, 1954, **23**, 65–76.

Gollin, E. S. Organizational characteristics of social judgment: a developmental investigation. *J. Personality*, 1958, **26**, 139–154.

Goodnow, J. J. A test of milieu effects with some of Piaget's tasks. *Psychol. Monogr.*, 1962, **76**, No. 36 (Whole No. 555).

Goodnow, J. J. Cultural variation in cognitive skills. Paper read at Amer. Psychol. Assoc., Washington, September, 1967.

Goodnow, J. J. Problems in research on culture and thought. In D. Elkind and J. H. Flavell (Eds.), *Studies in cognitive development: essays in honor of Jean Piaget.* New York: Oxford University Press, 1969. Pp. 439–462.

Goodnow, J. J., and Bethon, G. Piaget's tasks: the effects of schooling and intelligence. *Child Dev.*, 1966, **37**, 573–582.

Gouin-Décarie, T. *Intelligence and affectivity in early childhood.* New York: International Universities Press, 1965.

Gréco, P. L'apprentissage dans une situation à structure opératoire concrète: Les inversions successives de l'ordre linéaire par des rotations de 180°. In P. Gréco and J. Piaget, Apprentissage et connaissance. *Etudes d'épistémologie génétique*, Vol. 7. Paris: Presses Universitaires de France, 1959. Pp. 68–182.

Gréco, P. Une recherche sur la commutativité de l'addition. In P. Gréco and A. Morf, Structures numériques élémentaires. *Etudes d'épistémologie génétique,*

Vol. 13. Paris: Presses Universitaires de France, 1962. Pp. 151–227. (a)

Gréco, P. Quantité et quotité. In P. Gréco and A. Morf, Structures numériques élémentaires. *Etudes d'épistémologie génétique*, Vol. 13. Paris: Presses Universitaires de France, 1962. Pp. 1–70. (b)

Gréco, P. Le progrès des inférences itératives et des notions arithmétiques chez l'enfant et l'adolescent. In P. Gréco, B. Inhelder, B. Matalon, and J. Piaget, La formation des raisonnements recurrentielles. *Etudes d'épistémologie génétique*, Vol. 17. Paris: Presses Universitaires de France, 1963. Pp. 143–281. (a)

Gréco, P. Apprentissage et structures intellectuelles. In P. Fraisse and J. Piaget (Eds.), *Traité de psychologie expérimentale: Vol. 7. Intelligence.* Paris: Presses Universitaires de France, 1963. Pp. 157–207. (b)

Gréco, P., Inhelder, B., Matalon, B., and Piaget, J. La formation des raisonnements récurrentielles. *Etudes d'épistémologie génétique*, Vol. 17. Paris: Presses Universitaires de France, 1963.

Greenstein, F. I. More on children's images of the president. *Pub. Opin. Quart.*, 1961, **25**, 648–654.

Greenstein, F. I. *Children and politics*. New Haven: Yale University Press, 1965.

Gruen, G. E. Experiences affecting the development of number conservation in children. *Child Dev.*, 1965, **36**, 963–979.

Gruen, G. E. Note on conservation: methodological and definitional considerations. *Child Dev.*, 1966, **37**, 977–983.

Gunderson, A. G. Thought-patterns of young children in learning multiplication and division. *Elem. Sch. J.*, 1955, **55**, 453–461.

Gyr, J. W., Brown, J. S., and Cafagna, A. C. Quasi-formal models of inductive behavior and their relation to Piaget's theory of cognitive stages. *Psychol. Rev.*, 1967, **74**, 272–289.

Hall, V. C., and Kingsley, R. C. Problems in conservation research. Paper read at Soc. Res. Child Develpm., New York, March, 1967.

Halpern, E. The effects of incompatibility between perception and logic in Piaget's stage of concrete operations. *Child Dev.*, 1965, **36**, 491–497.

Harvey, O. J., Hunt, D. E., and Schroder, H. M. *Conceptual systems and personality organization*. New York: Wiley, 1961.

Heald, J. E., and Marzolf, S. S. Abstract behavior in elementary school children as measured by the Goldstein-Scheerer Stick Test and the Weigl-Goldstein-Scheerer Color Form Sorting Test. *J. clin. Psychol.*, 1954, **9**, 59–62.

Heider, F. *The psychology of interpersonal relations*. New York: Wiley, 1958.

Hess, R. D., and Easton, D. The child's changing image of the president. *Pub. Opin. Quart.*, 1960, **24**, 632–644.

Hess, R. D., and Shipman, V. C. Early experience and the socialization of cognitive modes in children. *Child Dev.*, 1965, **36**, 869–886.

Hétu, J. C. L'apprentissage de l'inclusion logique obtenu par les lectures empiriques et par l'exercice de la multiplication. Unpublished thèse de licence, University of Montreal, 1966.

Hood, H. B. An experimental study of Piaget's theory of the development of number in children. *Br. J. Psychol.*, 1962, **53**, 273–286.

Hunt, E. B. *Concept learning: an information-processing problem*. New York: Wiley, 1962.

Hunt, J. Mc V. *Intelligence and experience*. New York: Ronald, 1961.

Hunt. J. Mc V. Piaget's observations as a source of hypotheses concerning motivation. *Merrill-Palmer Quart.*, 1963, **9**, 263–275.

Huttenlocher, J. Development of formal reasoning on concept formation problems. *Child Dev.*, 1964, **35**, 1233–1242.

Huttenlocher, J. Children's ability to order and orient objects. *Child Dev.*, 1967, **38**, 1169–1176.

Hyde, D. M. An investigation of Piaget's theories of the development of the concept of number. Unpublished doctoral dissertation, University of London, 1959.

Inhelder, B. Some aspects of Piaget's genetic approach to cognition. In W. Kessen and C. Kuhlman (Eds.), Thought in the young child. *Monogr. Soc. Res. Child Develpm.*, 1962, **27**, No. 2 (Whole No. 83), 19–34.

Inhelder, B., Bovet, M., and Sinclair, H. Développement et apprentissage. *Rev. Suisse Psychol.*, 1967, **26**, 1–23.

Inhelder, B., Bovet, M., Sinclair, H., and Smock, C. D. On cognitive development. *Am. Psychol.*, 1966, **21**, 160–164.

Inhelder B., and Piaget, J. *The growth of logical thinking from childhood to adolescence.* New York: Basic Books, 1958.

Inhelder, B., and Piaget, J. De l'itération des actions à la récurrence élémentaire. In P. Gréco, B. Inhelder, B. Matalon, and J. Piaget, Le formation des raisonnements récurrentielles. *Etudes d'épistémologie génétique,* Vol. 17. Paris: Presses Universitaires de France, 1963. Pp. 47–120.

Inhelder, B., and Piaget, J. *The early growth of logic in the child.* New York: Harper & Row, 1964.

Jahoda, G. Assessment of abstract behavior in a non-western culture. *J. abnorm. soc. Psychol.*, 1956, **53**, 237–243.

Jahoda, G. Child animism: I. A critical survey of cross-cultural research. *J. soc. Psychol.*, 1958, **47**, 197–212. (a)

Jahoda, G. Child animism: II. A study in West Africa. *J. soc. Psychol.*, 1958, **47**, 213–222. (b)

Jahoda, G. Development of the perception of social differences in children from 6 to 10. *Br. J. Psychol.*, 1959, **50**, 159–175.

Jahoda, G. Development of Scottish children's ideas and attitudes about other countries. *J. soc. Psychol.*, 1962, **58**, 91–108.

Jahoda, G. Children's concepts of time and history. *Educ. Rev.*, 1963, **15**, 87–104. (a)

Jahoda, G. The development of children's ideas about country and nationality: Part I, the conceptual framework. *Br. J. educ. Psychol.*, 1963, **33**, 47–60. (b)

Jahoda, G. The development of children's ideas about country and nationality: Part II, national symbols and themes. *Br. J. educ. Psychol.*, 1963, **33**, 143–153. (c)

Jahoda, G. Children's concepts of nationality: a critical study of Piaget's stages. *Child Dev.*, 1964, **35**, 1081–1092.

Jenkins, J. J. Meaningfulness and concepts; concepts and meaningfulness. In H. J. Klausmeier and C. W. Harris (Eds.), *Analyses of concept learning.* New York: Academic Press, 1966.

Kagan J., Moss, H. A., and Sigel, I. E. Psychological significance of styles of conceptualization. In J. C. Wright and J. Kagan (Eds.), Basic cognitive processes in children. *Monogr. Soc. Res. Child Develpm.*, 1963, **28**, No. 2 (Whole No. 86), 73–112.

Karplus, R. Relativity of position and motion. Science curriculum improvement study, University of California, 1964.

Keats, J. A. Formal and concrete thought processes. Technical Report, 1955, Princeton University, Contract Nonr 270–20, Department of Psychology.

Kendler, T. S. Concept formation. *Ann. Rev. Psychol.*, 1961, **13**, 447–472.

Kessen, W., and Kuhlman, C. (Eds.), Thought in the young child. *Monogr. Soc. Res. Child Develpm.*, 1962, **27**, No. 2 (Whole No. 83).

King, W. H. The development of scientific concepts in children. *Br. J. educ. Psychol.*, 1963, **33**, 240–252.

Klausmeier, H. J., et al. *Concept learning and problem solving: a bibliography,*

1950–1964. Technical Report No. 1, 1965, University of Wisconsin, Research and Development Center for Learning and Re-education.

Klima, E. S., and Bellugi, U. Syntactic regularities in the speech of children. In J. Lyons and R. J. Wales (Eds.), *Psycholinguistic papers: the proceedings of the 1966 Edinburgh Conference.* Edinburgh: Edinburgh University Press, 1967. Pp. 183–208.

Kofsky, E. Developmental scalogram analysis of classificatory behavior. Unpublished doctoral dissertation, University of Rochester, 1963.

Kofsky, E. A scalogram study of classificatory development. *Child Dev.,* 1966, **37,** 191–204.

Kohlberg, L. Stages in children's conceptions of physical and social objects in the years four to eight. A study of developmental theory. Unpublished manuscript, 1963.

Kohnstamm, G. A. An evaluation of part of Piaget's theory. *Acta Psychol.,* 1963, **21,** 313–356.

Kohnstamm, G. A. Developmental psychology and the teaching of thought operations. *Paedagogica Europaea,* 1965, **1,** 79–99.

Kohnstamm, G. A. *Teaching children to solve a Piagetian problem of class inclusion.* Uitgevers: Mouton, 1967.

Kooistra, W. H. Developmental trends in the attainment of conservation, transitivity, and relativism in the thinking of children: a replication and extension of Piaget's ontogenetic formulations. Dissertation abstract, Center for Cognitive Studies, Wayne State University, 1965.

Krauss, R. M., and Glucksberg, S. Some aspects of verbal communication in children. Paper read at Amer. Psychol. Assoc., Chicago, September, 1965.

Kreezer, G., and Dallenbach, K. M. Learning the relation of opposition. *Am. J. Psychol.,* 1929, **41,** 432–441.

Kreitler, H., and Kreitler, S. Children's concepts of sexuality and birth. *Child Dev.,* 1966, **37,** 363–378.

Kruglov, L. P. Qualitative differences in the vocabulary choices of children as revealed in a multiple-choice test. *J. educ. Psychol.,* 1953, **44,** 229–243.

Langer, J. Disequilibrium as a source of development. Paper read at Soc. Res. Child Develpm., New York, March, 1967.

Langer, S. K. *Philosophy in a new key.* New York: Mentor, 1948.

Lantz, D., and Lenneberg, E. H. Verbal communication and color memory in the deaf and hearing. *Child Dev.,* 1966, **37,** 765–780.

Lasry, J. C. Apprentissage empirico-didactique de la notion d'inclusion. Unpublished thèse de licence, University of Montreal, 1966.

Laubengayer, N. C. The effects of training on the spatial egocentrism of preschoolers. Unpublished masters thesis, University of Minnesota, 1965.

Laurendeau, M., and Pinard, A. *Causal thinking in the child.* New York: International Universities Press, 1962.

Lee, L. C. Concept utilization in preschool children. *Child Dev.,* 1965, **36,** 221–227.

Lenneberg, E. Understanding language without ability to speak: A case report. *J. abnorm. soc. Psychol.,* 1962, **65,** 419–425.

Lord, F. E. A study of spatial orientation of children. *J. educ. Res.,* 1941, **34,** 481–505.

Lovell, K. A follow-up study of some aspects of the work of Piaget and Inhelder on the child's conception of space. *Br. J. educ. Psychol.,* 1959, **29,** 104–117.

Lovell, K. A follow-up study of Inhelder and Piaget's *The growth of logical thinking. Br. J. Psychol.,* 1961, **52,** 143–153.

Lovell, K. *The growth of basic mathematical and scientific concepts in children.* New York: Philosophical Library, 1962.

Lovell, K., Healey, D., and Rowland, A. D. Growth of some geometrical concepts. *Child Dev.*, 1962, 33, 751–767.

Lovell, K., Kellett, V. L., and Moorhouse, E. The growth of the concept of speed: A comparative study. *J. Child Psychol. Psychiat.*, 1962, 3, 101–110.

Lovell, K., Mitchell, B., and Everett, I. R. An experimental study of the growth of some logical structures. *Br. J. Psychol.*, 1962, 53, 175–188.

Lovell, K., and Ogilvie, E. A study of the concept of conservation of substance in the junior school child. *Br. J. educ. Psychol.*, 1960, 30, 109–118.

Lovell, K., and Ogilvie, E. The growth of the concept of volume in junior school children. *J. Child Psychol. Psychiat.*, 1961, 2, 118–126. (a)

Lovell, K., and Ogilvie, E. A study of the conservation of weight in the junior school child. *Br. J. educ. Psychol.*, 1961, 31, 138–144. (b)

Lovell, K., and Slater, A. The growth of the concept of time: a comparative study. *J. Child Psychol. Psychiat.*, 1960, 1, 179–190.

Lunzer, E. A. *Research into Piagetian theory: an annotated bibliography.* London: Nat. Found. Educ. Res. England Wales, 1959.

Lunzer, E. A. *Recent studies in Britian based on the work of Jean Piaget.* London: Nat. Found. Educ. Res. England Wales, 1960. (a)

Lunzer, E. A. Some points of Piagetian theory in the light of experimental criticism. *J. Child Psychol. Psychiat.*, 1960, 1, 191–202. (b)

Lunzer, E. A. Les co-ordinations et les conservations dans le domaine de la géométrie. In Vinh-Bang and E. Lunzer, Conservations spatiales. *Etudes d'épistémologie génétique*, Vol. 19. Paris: Presses Universitaires de France, 1965. Pp. 59–148. (a)

Lunzer, E. A. Problems of formal reasoning in test situations. In P. H. Mussen (Ed.), European research in cognitive development. *Monog. Soc. Res. Child Develpm.*, 1965, 30, No. 2 (Whole No. 100), 19–46. (b)

Maccoby, E. E., and Bee, H. L. Some speculations concerning the lag between perceiving and performing. *Child Dev.*, 1965, 36, 367–378.

Mannix, J. B. The number concepts of a group of E. S. N. Children. *Br. J. educ. Psychol.*, 1960, 30, 180–181.

Matalon, B. Recherches sur le nombre quelconque. In P. Gréco, B. Inhelder, B. Matalon, and J. Piaget, La formation des raisonnements récurrentielles. *Etudes d'épistémologie génétique*, Vol. 17. Paris: Presses Universitaires de France, 1963, Pp. 121–141. (a)

Matalon, B. Etude du raisonnement par récurrence sur un modèle physique. In P. Gréco, B. Inhelder, B. Matalon, and J. Piaget, La formation des raisonnements récurrentielles. *Etudes d'épistémologie génétique*, Vol. 17. Paris: Presses Universitaries de France, 1963. Pp. 283–316. (b)

Mead, G. H. Language and the development of the self. In T. M. Newcomb and E. L. Hartley (Eds.), *Readings in social psychology.* New York: Holt, 1947. Pp. 179–189.

Meltzer, H. Children's social concepts. *Teach. Coll. Contr. Educ.*, 1925, No. 192.

Mermelstein, E., and Shulman, L. S. Lack of formal schooling and the acquisition of conservation. *Child Dev.*, 1967, 38, 39–52.

Meyer, E. Comprehension of spatial relationships in preschool children. *J. genet. Psychol.*, 1940, 57, 119–151.

Milgram, N., and Goodglass, H. Role style versus cognitive maturation in word associations of adults and children. *J. Personality*, 1961, 29, 81–93.

Moore, O. K. Problem solving and the perception of persons. In R. Tagiuri and L. Petrullo (Eds.), *Person perception and interpersonal behavior.* Stanford: Stanford University Press, 1958. Pp. 131–150.

Morf, A. Apprentissage d'une structure logique concrète (inclusion): effets et limites. In A. Morf, J. Smedslund, Vinh-Bang, and J. F. Wohlwill, L'apprentissage des structures logiques. *Etudes d'épistémologie génétique*, Vol. 9. Paris: Presses Universitaires de France, 1959. Pp. 15–83.

Morf, A. Recherches sur l'origine de la connexité de la suite des premiers nombres. In P. Gréco and A. Morf, Structures numériques élémentaires. *Etudes d'épistémologie génétique*, Vol. 13. Paris: Presses Universitaires de France, 1962. Pp. 71–103.

Murray, F. B. Conservation of illusion distorted lengths and areas by primary school children. *J. educ. Psychol.*, 1965, **56**, 62–66.

Murray, F. B. Some factors related to the conservation of illusion-distorted length by primary school children. Unpublished doctoral dissertation, Johns Hopkins University, 1966.

Murray, F. B. Conservation of illusion-distorted length and illusion strength. *Psychon. Sci.*, 1967, **7**, 65–66. (a)

Murray, F. B. Phenomenal-real discrimination and length conservation. Paper read at Soc. Res. Child Develpm., New York, March, 1967. (b)

Muuss, R. F. The transfer effect of a learning program in social causality on an understanding of physical causality. *J. exp. Educ.*, 1961, **29**, 231–247.

Nagy, M. H. The child's theories concerning death. *J. genet. Psychol.*, 1948, **73**, 3–27.

Nagy, M. H. Children's conceptions of some bodily functions. *J. genet. Psychol.*, 1953, **83**, 199–216. (a)

Nagy, M. H. Children's birth theories. *J. genet. Psychol.*, 1953, **83**, 217–226. (b)

Nagy, M. H. The representation of "germs" by children. *J. genet. Psychol.*, 1953, **83**, 227–240. (c)

Nass, M. L. The deaf child's conception of physical causality. *J. abnorm. soc. Psychol.*, 1964, **69**, 669–673.

Nassefat, M. *Etude quantitative sur l'évolution des opérations intellectuelles.* Neuchâtel: Delachaux & Niestlé, 1963.

Natadze, R. G. Studies on thought and speech problems by psychologists of the Georgian S. S. R. In N. O'Connor (Ed.), *Recent Soviet psychology.* New York: Liveright, 1961. Pp. 304–326.

Nielsen, R. F. *Le développement de la sociabilité chez l'enfant.* Neuchâtel: Delachaux & Niestlé, 1951.

Northman, J. E. The effects of training on the concept of quantity conservation. Unpublished study, 1964.

Oakden, E. C., and Sturt, M. The development of the knowledge of time in children. *Br. J. Psychol.*, 1922, **12**, 309–336.

Ojemann, R. H., Maxey, E. J., and Snider, B. C. F. The effect of a program of guided learning experiences in developing probability concepts at the third grade level. *J. exp. Educ.*, 1965, **33**, 321–330. (a)

Ojemann, R. H., Maxey, E. J., and Snider, B. C. F. Effects of guided learning experiences in developing probability concepts at the fifth grade level. *Percept. Mot. Skills*, 1965, **21**, 415–427. (b)

Ojemann, R. H., and Pritchett, K. Piaget and the role of guided experiences in human development. *Percept. Mot. Skills*, 1963, **17**, 927–940.

O'Neill, R. P. The development of political thinking during adolescence. *Dissert. Abstr.*, 1965, **25**(12), 7371–7372.

Ordan, H. *Social concepts and the child mind.* New York: King's Crown Press, 1945.

Pascual-Leone, J., and Bovet, M. C. L'apprentissage de la quantification de l'inclusion et la théorie opératoire. *Acta. Psychol.*, 1966, **25**, 334–356.

Peel, E. A. Experimental examination of some of Piaget's schemata concerning children's perception and thinking, and a discussion of their educational significance. *Br. J. educ. Psychol.*, 1959, **29**, 89–103.

Pettifor, J. L. The role of language in the development of abstract thinking. Dissertation abstract, Center for Cognitive Studies, Wayne State University, 1964.

Pflederer, M. The responses of children to musical tasks embodying Piaget's principle of conservation. *J. Res. Mus. Educ.*, 1964, **12**, 251–268.

Phillips, T., and Feffer, M. The use of an experimental confederate in password interaction: a preliminary report. Unpublished paper, 1966.

Piaget, J. *The language and thought of the child.* New York: Harcourt, Brace, 1926.

Piaget, J. *Judgment and reasoning in the child.* New York: Harcourt, Brace, 1928.

Piaget, J. *The child's conception of the world.* New York: Harcourt, Brace, 1929.

Piaget, J. *The child's conception of physical causality.* London: Kegan Paul, 1930.

Piaget, J. *The moral judgment of the child.* London: Kegan Paul, 1932.

Piaget, J. *Le développement de la notion de temps chez l'enfant.* Paris: Presses Universitaires de France, 1946. (a)

Piaget, J. *Les notions de mouvement et de vitesse chez l'enfant.* Paris: Presses Universitaires de France, 1946. (b)

Piaget, J. *The child's conception of number.* New York: Humanities, 1952.

Piaget, J. *The construction of reality in the child.* New York: Basic Books, 1954.

Piaget, J. Les stades du développement intellectual de l'enfant et de l'adolescent. In P. Osterrieth et al. (Eds.), *Le problème des stades en psychologie de l'enfant.* Paris: Presses Universitaires de France, 1955. Pp. 33–42.

Piaget, J. Transposition du problème de l'analytique en termes génétique. In L. Apostel, W. Mays, A. Morf, and J. Piaget, Les liaisons analytiques et synthétiques dans les comportements du sujet. *Etudes d'épistémologie génétique,* Vol. 4. Paris: Presses Universitaires de France, 1957. Chap. 3.

Piaget, J. Introduction. In P. Gréco, J. B. Grize, S. Papert, and J. Piaget, Problèmes de la construction du nombre. *Etudes d'épistémologie génétique,* Vol. 11. Paris: Presses Universitaires de France, 1960, Pp. 1–68.

Piaget, J. Les travaux de l'année 1959–1960 et le cinquième Symposium du Centre international d'Epistémologie génétique. In P. Gréco, B. Inhelder, B. Matalon, and J. Piaget, La formation des raisonnements récurrentielles. *Etudes d'épistémologie génétique,* Vol. 17. Paris: Presses Universitaires de France, 1963. Pp. 1–46.

Piaget, J. Development and learning. *J Res. Sci. Teach.,* 1964, **2**, 176–186. (a)

Piaget, J. Les travaux de l'année 1960–1961 et le sixième Symposium du Centre international d'Epistémologie génétique. In Vinh-Bang et al., L'epistémologie de l'espace. *Etudes d'epistémologie génétique,* Vol. 18. Paris: Universitaires de France, 1964. Pp. 1–40. (b)

Piaget, J. Nécessité et signification des recherches comparatives en psychologie génétique. *Int. J. Psychol.,* 1966, **1**, 3–13.

Piaget, J. *Six psychological studies.* New York: Random House, 1967. (a)

Piaget, J. *Biologie et connaissance.* Paris: Gallimard, 1967. (b)

Piaget, J., and Inhelder, B. *Le développement des quantités chez l'enfant.* Neuchâtel: Delachaux et Niestlé, 1941.

Piaget, J., and Inhelder, B. *La genèse de l'idée de hazard chez l'enfant.* Paris: Presses Universitaires de France, 1951.

Piaget, J., and Inhelder, B. *The child's conception of space.* London: Routledge and Kegan Paul, 1956.

Piaget, J., and Inhelder, B. Les opérations intellectuelles et leur développement. In P. Fraisse and J. Piaget (Eds.), *Traité de psychologie expérimentale:* Vol. 7. *Intelligence.* Paris: Presses Universitaires de France, 1963. Pp. 109–156.

Piaget, J., and Inhelder, B. *La psychologie de l'enfant.* Paris: Presses Universitaires de France, 1966.

Piaget, J., Inhelder, B., and Szeminska, A. *The child's conception of geometry.* New York: Basic Books, 1960.

Piaget, J., and Weil, A. The development in children of the idea of the homeland and of relations with other countries. *Internat. Soc. Sci. Bull.*, 1951, **3**, 561–578.

Pinard, A., and Laurendeau, M. "Stage" in Piaget's cognitive-developmental theory: Exegesis of a concept. In D. Elkind and J. H. Flavell (Eds.), *Studies in cognitive development: essays in honor of Jean Piaget.* New York: Oxford University Press, 1969. Pp. 121–170.

Pratoomraj, S., and Johnson, R. C. Kinds of questions and types of conservation tasks as related to children's conservation responses. *Child Dev.*, 1966, **37**, 343–354.

Price-Williams, D. R. A study concerning concepts of conservation of quantities among primitive children. *Acta Psychol., Amsterdam*, 1961, **18**, 297–305.

Price-Williams, D. R. Abstract and concrete modes of classification in a primitive society. *Br. J. educ. Psychol.*, 1962, **32**, 50–61.

Pufall, P. B. Acquisition and generalization of spatial order conservation in young children. Unpublished doctoral dissertation, Catholic University, 1966.

Raven, R. J. An investigation into the development of the concept of momentum in primary school children. Unpublished doctoral dissertation, University of California at Berkeley, 1965.

Reichard, S., Schneider, M., and Rapaport, D. The development of concept formation in children. *Am. J. Orthopsychiat.*, 1944, **14**, 156–162.

Ricciuti, H. N. Object grouping and selective ordering behavior in infants 12 to 24 months old. *Merrill-Palmer Quart.*, 1965, **11**, 129–148.

Ricciuti, H. N. Geometric form and detail as determinants of comparative similarity judgments in young children. Unpublished paper, 1966. (a)

Ricciuti, H. N. Selective cue utilization in young children's comparative similarity judgments of pictoral stimuli. Unpublished paper, 1966. (b)

Ricciuti, H. N., and Johnson, L. J. Developmental changes in categorizing behavior from infancy to the early pre-school years. Paper read at Soc. Res. Child Develpm., Minneapolis, March, 1965.

Ripple, R. E., and Rockcastle, V. N. (Eds.). Piaget rediscovered: selected papers from a conference on cognitive studies and curriculum development. *J. Res. Sci. Teach.*, 1964, **2**, No. 3.

Rivoire, J. L. Development of reference systems in children. *Percept. Mot. Skills*, 1962, **15**, 554.

Robinowitz, R. Learning the relation of opposition as related to scores on the Wechsler Intelligence Scale for Children. *J. genet. Psychol.*, 1956, **88**, 25–30.

Ross, B. M. Probability concepts in deaf and hearing children. *Child Dev.*, 1966, **37**, 917–927.

Ross, B. M., and Levy, N. Patterned predictions of chance events by children and adults. *Psychol. Rep.*, 1958, **4**, (Monogr. Suppl. 1), 87–124.

Rossi, E. Development of classificatory behavior. *Child Dev.*, 1964, **35**, 137–142.

Rossi, E., and Rossi, S. I. Concept utilization, serial order and recall in nursery-school children. *Child Dev.*, 1965, **36**, 771–778.

Rothenberg, B. B. Children's ability to comprehend adults' feelings and motives. Paper read at Soc. Res. Child Develpm. Meetings, New York, March, 1967.

Russell, D. H. *Children's thinking.* Boston: Ginn, 1956.

Russell, D. H., and Saadeh, I. Q. Qualitative levels in children's vocabularies. *J. educ. Psychol.*, 1962, **53**, 170–174.

Saarinen, P. Developmental results in a block sorting task. *Repts. Psychol. Institute*, University of Helsinki, 1964.

Safier, G. A study in relationships between the life and death concepts in children. *J. genet. Psychol.*, 1964, **105**, 283–294.

Santa Barbara, J. F., Jr., and Paré, W. P. Information processing in young children. *Psychon. Sci.*, 1965, **2**, 143–144.

Schaffer, H. R., and Emerson, P. E. The development of social attachments in infancy. *Monogr. Soc. Res. Child Develpm.*, 1964, **29**, No. 3 (Whole No. 94).

Schuessler, K. F., and Strauss, A. A study of concept learning by scale analysis. *Am. Soc. Rev.*, 1950, **15**, 752–762.

Scottish Council for Research in Education. *The early development of number concepts.* Bickley, England: University of London Press, 1942.

Shantz, C. V., and Sigel, I. E. Logical operations and concepts of conservation in children: a training study. Final Report, Office of Education Grant No. OEG-3-6-068463-1645, Merrill-Palmer Institute, 1967.

Shantz, C. V., and Smock, C. D. Development of distance conservation and the spatial coordinate system. *Child Dev.*, 1966, **37**, 943–948.

Shure, M. B. A developmental study of the concepts of fairness, generosity, and selfishness. Paper read at Soc. Res. Child Developm., New York, March, 1967.

Sigel, I. E. Developmental trends in the abstraction ability of children. *Child Dev.*, 1953, **24**, 132–144.

Sigel, I. E. The dominance of meaning. *J. genet. Psychol.*, 1954, **85**, 201–207.

Sigel, I. E. The attainment of concepts. In M. L. Hoffman and L. W. Hoffman (Eds.), *Review of child development research.* New York: Russell Sage, 1964.

Sigel, I. E., and Hooper, F. H. *Logical thinking in children: research based on Piaget's theory.* New York: Holt, Rinehart, and Winston, 1968.

Sigel, I. E., and Mermelstein, E. Effects of nonschooling on Piagetian tasks of conservation. Unpublished paper, 1966.

Sigel, I. E., Roeper, A., and Hooper, F. H. A training procedure for acquisition of Piaget's conservation of quantity. In I. E. Sigel and F. H. Hooper (Eds.), *Logical thinking in children: research based on Piaget's theory.* New York: Holt, Rinehart, and Winston, 1968. Pp. 295–308.

Sigel, I. E., Saltz, E., and Roskind, W. Variables determining concept conservation in children. *J. exp. Psychol.*, 1967, **74**, 471–475.

Sinclair, H. *Acquisition du langage et développement de la pensée.* Paris: Dunod, 1967.

Smedslund, J. Transitivity of preference patterns as seen by pre-school children. *Scand. J. Psychol.*, 1960, **1**, 49–54.

Smedslund, J. The acquisition of conservation of substance and weight in children. I. Introduction. *Scand. J. Psychol.*, 1961, **2**, 11–20. (a)

Smedslund, J. The acquisition of conservation of substance and weight in children. II. External reinforcement of conservation of weight and of the operations of addition and subtraction. *Scand. J. Psychol.*, 1961, **2**, 71–84. (b)

Smedslund, J. The acquisition of conservation of substance and weight in children. III. Extinction of conservation of weight acquired "normally" and by means of empirical controls on a balance scale. *Scand. J. Psychol.*, 1961, **2**, 85–87. (c)

Smedslund, J. The acquisition of conservation of substance and weight in children. IV. An attempt at extinction of the visual components of the weight concept. *Scand. J. Psychol.*, 1961, **2**, 153–155. (d)

Smedslund, J. The acquisition of conservation of substance and weight in children. V. Practice in conflict situations without external reinforcement. *Scand. J. Psychol.*, 1961, **2**, 156–160. (e)

Smedslund, J. The acquisition of conservation of substance and weight in children.

VI. Practice on continuous versus discontinuous material in conflict-situations without external reinforcement. *Scand. J. Psychol.*, 1961, **2**, 203–210. (f)

Smedslund, J. The acquisition of conservation of substance and weight in children. VII. Conservation of discontinuous quantity and the operations of adding and taking away. *Scand. J. Psychol.*, 1962, **3**, 69–77.

Smedslund, J. Development of concrete transitivity of length in children. *Child Dev.*, 1963, **34**, 389–405. (a)

Smedslund, J. The effect of observation on children's representation of the spatial orientation of a water surface. *J. genet. Psychol.*, 1963, **102**, 195–201. (b)

Smedslund, J. The acquisition of transitivity of weight in five-to-seven-year-old children. *J. genet. Psychol.*, 1963, **102**, 245–256. (c)

Smedslund, J. The concept of correlation in adults. *Scand. J. Psychol.*, 1963, **4**, 165–173. (d)

Smedslund, J. Patterns of experience and the acquisition of concrete transitivity of weight in eight-year-old children. *Scand. J. Psychol.*, 1963, **4**, 251–256. (e)

Smedslund, J. Patterns of experience and the acquisition of conservation of length. *Scand. J. Psychol.*, 1963, **4**, 257–264. (f)

Smedslund, J. Concrete reasoning: a study of intellectual development. *Monogr. Soc. Res. Child Develpm.*, 1964, **29**, No. 2 (Whole No. 93). (a)

Smedslund, J. Internal necessity and contradiction in children's thinking. *J. Res. Sci. Teach.*, 1964, **2**, 220–221. (b)

Smedslund, J. The development of transitivity of length: a comment on Braine's reply. *Child Dev.*, 1965, **36**, 577–580.

Smedslund, J. Les origines sociales de la décentration. In F. Bresson and M. de Montmollin (Eds.), *Psychologie et épistémologie génétiques: Thèmes piagetiens.* Paris: Dunod, 1966. Pp. 159–168. (a)

Smedslund, J. Performance on measurement and pseudomeasurement tasks by five- to seven-year-old children. *Scand. J. Psychol.*, 1966, **7**, 81–92. (b)

Smedslund, J. Microanalysis of concrete reasoning. I. The difficulty of some combinations of addition and subtraction of one unit. *Scand. J. Psychol.*, 1966, **7**, 145–156. (c)

Smedslund, J. Microanalysis of concrete reasoning. II. The effect of number of transformations and non-redundant elements, and of some variations in procedure. *Scand. J. Psychol.*, 1966, **7**, 157–163. (d)

Smedslund, J. Microanalysis of concrete reasoning. III. Theoretical overview. *Scand. J. Psychol.*, 1966, **7**, 164–167. (e)

Smith, R. F. An analysis and classification of children's explanations of natural phenomena. *Dissert. Abstr.*, 1963, **24**(2), 653.

Spiegel, L. A. The child's concept of beauty: a study in concept formation. *J. genet. Psychol.*, 1950, **77**, 11–23.

Springer, D. Development in young children of an understanding of time and the clock. *J. genet. Psychol.*, 1952, **80**, 83–96.

Steiner, G. L. Children's concepts of life and death: a developmental study. *Dissert. Abstr.*, 1965, **26**(2), 1164.

Stendler, C. B. The transition from the stage of concrete operations to formal thinking. Paper read at Soc. Res. Child Develpm., New York, March, 1967.

Stott, D. H. An empirical approach to motivation based on the behavior of a young child. *J. Child Psychol. Psychiat.*, 1961, **2**, 97–117.

Strauss, A. L. The development and transformation of monetary meanings in the child. *Am. Soc. Rev.*, 1952, **17**, 275–286.

Strauss, A. L., and Schuessler, K. Socialization, logical reasoning, and concept development in the child. *Am. Soc. Rev.*, 1951, **16**, 514–523.

Suchman, J. R. Inquiry training in the elementary school. *Sci. Teacher*, 1960, **27**, 42–47.

Suchman, R. G., and Trabasso, T. Color and form performance in young children. *J. exp. Child Psychol.*, 1966, **3**, 177–187. (a)

Suchman, R. G.,and Trabasso, T. Stimulus preference and cue function in young children's concept attainment. *J. exp. Child Psychol.*, 1966, **3**, 188–198. (b)

Swinson, M. E. The development of cognitive skills and role-taking. *Dissert. Abstr.*, 1966, **26**(27), 4082.

Szeminska, A. The evolution of thought: some applications of research findings to educational practice. In P. H. Mussen (Ed.), European Research in Cognitive Development. *Monogr. Soc. Res. Child. Develpm.*, 1965, **30**, No. 2 (Whole No. 100), 47–57.

Thier, H. D., Powell, C. A., and Karplus, R. A concept of matter for the first grade. *J. Res. Sci. Teach.*, 1963, **1**, 315–318.

Thompson, J. Ability of children of different grade levels to generalize on sorting tests. *J. Psychol.*, 1941, **11**, 119–126.

Uzgiris, I. C. Situational generality of conservation. *Child. Dev.*, 1964, **35**, 831–841.

Uzgiris, I. C., and Hunt, J. McV. Ordinal scales of infant development. Paper read at XVIII Intern. Congr. Psychol., Moscow, August, 1966. (a)

Uzgiris, I. C., and Hunt, J. McV. An instrument for assessing infant psychological development. Unpublished manuscript, 1966. (b)

Vernon, P. E. Environmental handicaps and intellectual development: Part I. *Br. J. educ. Psychol.*, 1965, **35**, 9–20.

Vinacke, W. E. *The psychology of thinking.* New York: McGraw-Hill, 1952.

Vinh-Bang. Intuition géométrique et déduction opératoire. In Vinh-Bang and E. Lunzer, Conservations spatiales. *Etudes d'épistémologie génétique*, Vol. 19. Paris: Presses Universitaires de France, 1965. Pp. 1–38. (a)

Vinh-Bang. De l'intuition géométrique. In Vinh-Bang and E. Lunzer, Conservations spatiales. *Etudes d'épistémologie génétique*, Vol. 19. Paris: Presses Universitaires de France, 1965. Pp. 39–58. (b)

Vygotsky, L. S. *Thought and language.* Cambridge, Massachusetts: M.I.T. Press, 1962.

Wallace, J. G. *Concept growth and the education of the child: a survey of research on conceptualization.* Slough, Eng.: Nat. Found, Educ. Res. England, Wales, 1965.

Wallace, J. G. Some issues raised by a non-verbal test of number concepts. *Educ. Rev.*, 1966, **18**, 122–135.

Wallach, L. On the bases of conservation. In D. Elkind and J. H. Flavell (Eds.), *Studies in cognitive development: essays in honor of Jean Piaget.* New York: Oxford University Press, 1969. Pp. 191–219.

Wallach, L., and Sprott, R. L. Inducing number conservation in children. *Child Dev.*, 1964, **35**, 1057–1071.

Wallach, L., Wall, A. J., and Anderson, L. Number conservation: the role of reversibility, addition-subtraction, and misleading perceptual cues. *Child Dev.*, 1967, **38**, 425–442.

Wallach, M. A. Research on children's thinking. In National Society for the Study of Education, 62nd Yearbook, *Child Psychol.*, Chicago: University of Chicago Press, 1963. Pp. 236–276.

Weigl, E. On the psychology of so-called processes of abstraction. *J. abnorm. soc. Psychol.*, 1941, **36**, 3–33.

Weinstein, E. A. Development of the concept of flag and the sense of national identity. *Child Dev.*, 1957, **28**, 167–174.

Welch, L. The genetic development of the associational structures of abstract thinking. *J. genet. Psychol.*, 1940, **56**, 175–206.

Welch, L., and Long, L. The higher structural phases of concept formation of children. *J. Psychol.*, 1940, **9**, 59–95. (a)

Welch, L., and Long, L. A further investigation of the higher structural phases of concept formation. *J. Psychol.*, 1940, **10**, 211–220. (b)

Werner, H. *Comparative psychology of mental development.* Chicago: Follett, 1948.

Werner, H., and Kaplan, B. *Symbol formation: an organismic-developmental approach to language and the expression of thought.* New York: Wiley, 1963.

Werner, H., and Kaplan, E. The acquisition of word meanings: a developmental study. *Monogr. Soc. Res. Child Develpm.*, 1950, **15**, No. 1 (Whole No. 51).

Whiteman, M. Children's conceptions of psychological causality. *Child Dev.*, 1967, **38**,143–156.

Wohlwill, J. F. A study of the development of the number concept by scalogram analysis. *J. genet. Psychol.*, 1960, **97**, 345–377.

Wohlwill, J. F. Some current problems and issues in the study of cognitive development. Paper read at Soc. Res. Child Develpm., Detroit, March, 1962.

Wohlwill, J. F. Piaget's system as a source of empirical research. *Merrill-Palmer Quart.*, 1963, **9**, 253–262.

Wohlwill, J. F. Cognitive development and the learning of elementary school concepts. *J. Res. Sci. Teach.*, 1964, **2**, 222–226. (a)

Wohlwill, J. F. Review of Aebli, H. *Uber die geistige Entwicklung des Kindes. Contemp. Psychol.*, 1964, **9**, 434–435. (b)

Wohlwill, J. F. Piaget's theory of the development of intelligence in the concrete-operations period. *Am. J. Ment. Defic., Monogr. Suppl.*, 1966, **70**, No. 4. (a)

Wohlwill, J. F. Readiness, transfer of learning, and the development of cognitive structures. Paper read at Canad. Psychol. Assn., Montreal, June, 1966. (b)

Wohlwill, J. F., and Katz, M. Factors in children's responses on class-inclusion problems. Paper read at Soc. Res. Child Develpm., New York, March, 1967.

Wohlwill, J. F., and Lowe, R. C. An experimental analysis of the development of the conservation of number. *Child Dev.*, 1962, **33**, 153–167.

Wolfe, R. The role of conceptual systems in cognitive functioning at varying levels of age and intelligence. *J. Personality*, 1963, **31**, 108–123.

Wolman, R. N., and Barker, E. N. A developmental study of word definitions. *J. genet. Psychol.*, 1965, **107**, 159–166.

Woodward, M. The behavior of idiots interpreted by Piaget's theory of sensori-motor development. *Br. J. educ. Psychol.*, 1959, **29**, 60–71.

Wortman, R. A. Development of a transitive inference in children. Unpublished doctoral dissertation, Western Reserve University, 1964.

Wynns, F. Ability of children to solve a problem requiring the use of a combinatorial system as a function of training. Unpublished masters thesis, University of Rochester, 1967.

Yost, P. A., Siegel, A. E., and Andrews, J. M. Nonverbal probability judgments by young children. *Child Dev.*, 1962, **33**, 769–780.

Youniss, J., and Furth, H. G. The influence of transitivity on learning in hearing and deaf children. *Child Dev.*, 1965, **36**, 533–538.

Youniss, J., and Furth, H. G. Prediction of causal events as a function of transitivity and perceptual congruency in hearing and deaf children. *Child Dev.*, 1966, **37**, 73–82.

Zimiles, H. A note on Piaget's concept of conservation. *Child Dev.*, 1963, **34**, 691–695.

Zimiles, H. The development of conservation and differentiation of number. *Monogr. Soc. Res. Child Develpm.*, 1966, **31**, No. 6 (Whole No. 108).

15. The Development of Language*

DAVID MCNEILL

Like the humors of the mind, the development of a child may be divided conveniently into four parts.

One part is physical maturation. Another is personality development, including the process of socialization. A third is intellectual development. And a fourth is language development. The division is artificial but useful, tolerated because of its advantages for orderly inquiry. However, it should not be allowed to obscure the fact that the four parts intertwine in complex ways to make up a process absolutely unique in the animal kingdom—human growth.

It is clear, for example, that socialization depends on the acquisition of language. Yet it is equally clear that language bears the marks of socialization, as the linguistic differences among social classes attest. The devel-

* The research for this chapter was supported by Grant # 5 PO1 HD 01368-03 from the National Institute for Child Health and Human Development, and by Contract # OEC-3-6-061784-0508 from the U.S. Office of Education, both with The University of Michigan, and by the Advanced Research Project Agency # SD-187, and the National Science Foundation # GS1153, both with Harvard University.

Mrs. Meredith Kimball of The University of Michigan performed stalwartly in preparing bibliographic information; Dr. Kalon Kelley of the Massachusetts Institute of Technology, Dr. Dan I. Slobin of the University of California at Berkeley, and Dr. Ursula Bellugi-Klima of the University of California at San Diego gave the chapter a critical reading; Mr. J. W. MacDonald of Harvard University was helpful on phonological matters; Mrs. Nobuko B. McNeill was helpful on all other matters; and Mrs. Mavis Atamian provided excellent secretarial service.

opment of personality both acts on and reacts to the development of intellect, as evidenced by the cases where both fail in schizophrenia (Inhelder, 1966). Indeed, although the interaction is rarely examined, the network of characteristics we call personality could not develop at all were it not for a child's capacity to represent his world in the particular way that forms the subject matter of cognitive psychology. Yet there are also differences in cognitive style, in the characteristic modes of thought that accompany particular types of personality (Kagan et al., 1963).

This chapter is concerned with two such interactions. One is between the acquisition of language and the growth of intellect. The other is between both of these and the process of maturation. The parts so intertwined may strike the reader as an arbitrary selection. However, the selection is a sensible one, and the interaction among them provides considerable insight into the process whereby a child becomes an adult. But this is the substance of the chapter.

PLAN OF THE CHAPTER

To understand the acquisition of language, it is essential first to understand something of what is acquired. There is, therefore, a Linguistic Appendix. Readers unfamiliar with developments in modern linguistics are urged to begin with it; others may want to refer to the Appendix only as the occasion requires.

The phenomenon of language poses a challenge for psychologists. A grammar is a system of knowledge. It is everywhere complex and at many points abstract. Yet very young children acquire grammars, and they do so in a surprisingly short period of time. For reasons to be discussed in the first section of the chapter, various theories of development cannot account for this achievement. Explanation must follow other lines. One view is that the acquisition of language rests on certain linguistic capacities (which are reflected in language as linguistic universals). These capacities may be innate and may mature with time.

The bulk of the chapter is a survey of language acquisition itself. It is organized under three major headings, one for each of the three main components of a grammar: syntax, phonology, and semantics. A description will be given of the methods typically used in studying the development of each component; then the emergence of the components themselves will be traced, insofar as this is known; finally, there will be a discussion of various theoretical issues in the light of the empirical findings presented. Wherever possible, mention will be made of children exposed to languages other than English, with the chief contrast languages being Russian and Japanese.

A Caveat. There has been no serious attempt to survey the literature on language acquisition in a comprehensive way. This chapter is organized on principles other than inclusion. First, most of the references are recent. McCarthy's review (McCarthy, 1954) should be consulted for the earlier work. Moreover, recent developments in linguistics pose important issues for psychology, and examination of them takes priority within the limits of space over comprehensive citation. The criteria for including studies in this chapter, therefore, have been two: that they have not been covered by earlier editions of this *Manual*, or that they contribute in some way to the clarification, definition, or resolution of theoretical questions raised by the process of linguistic development.

SYNTAX

One major issue can be stated immediately. Normal children, not impaired by deafness, brain damage, or other physical or psychic disorders, begin to babble at about 6 months, utter a first "word" at 10 to 12 months, combine words at 18 to 24 months, and acquire syntax almost completely at 48 to 60 months. All children pass such a sequence of "mile-stones," always at roughly these same ages (Lenneberg, 1967). They do so regardless of the language they acquire, or of the circumstances under which they acquire it. Such massive regularities of development remind one more of the maturation of a physical process, say, walking, than of a process of education, say, reading. One might even say that children cannot help learning a language, whereas they can easily avoid learning to read.

The acquisition of language thus shows some of the characteristics of physical maturation. Yet, at the same time, it is obvious that language is learned. Without certain linguistic experiences children acquire no language at all—as in the case of congenitally deaf or criminally neglected children.

One psychological issue, then, deals with the explanation of this peculiar combination of facts. The regular development of language strongly suggests the operation of a maturational process, as Lenneberg (1967) has argued recently. The complete absence of language in children deprived of all linguistic experience equally suggests a process of learning. Both learning and maturation are necessary conditions for the development of language, but neither is sufficient. To understand such a problem, clearly we must consider both the innate and the acquired aspects of linguistic competence, as well as the way in which they combine.

Nativism and Empiricism in Developmental Psycholinguistics. The question of what is innate and what is acquired in behavior and language is often posed in the same terms one would use in describing the selection of a wife. Except for polygamous societies, a person can have only one mate—either potential wife A or potential wife B must be chosen. Similarly, many wonder if language is innate or acquired. These questions are raised on the assumption that there is some reason to choose between the two alternatives, as if the truth about language acquisition required advancing one view at the expense of the other. In fact such questions are of marginal interest. The promotion of one of these views over the other merely serves the cause of obfuscation, not of truth.

The dichotomy between nature and nurture has been a pernicious one for psychology. It is pernicious because it has mainly polemical value and obscures a far more basic question of the *interaction* of innate abilities with experience. One must suppose that there is a correct view of the latter, although of course it may not yet have been discovered. Whatever this correct view is, however, it is logically independent of the argument over whether language is largely innate or acquired. The two questions are quite distinct. It is misleading to state what children learn in acquiring a language without understanding what is inborn; conversely, it is misleading to state what is innate in language without understanding how it interacts with experience. Only one hypothesis is reasonable, not a pair of rival hypotheses. However, nearly all the debate over the existence of an innate endowment for language acquisition has rested on the dichotomy of innate and acquired aspects of language, and not on the question of how the two interact.

The Problem of "Cognition and Language." Given that the basic problem in explaining language acquisition is to understand how the innate abilities of children interact with their linguistic experience, there remains a need to consider such theories of learning and cognitive development as are currently available, and whether or not they can account for this interaction.

For reasons considered at various points in the Linguistic Appendix and in this section on syntax, theories of learning based on S-R principles are inappropriate to the task. The acquisition of language involves the development of abstract linguistic knowledge, and there appears to be no way without question-begging to apply a theory couched in terms of "S" and "R" to a phenomenon where neither "S" nor "R" can be defined. For a number of strong arguments on this point, see Chomsky (1959); for a defense of S-R theory, see Osgood (1968), Palermo (in press), and Staats (in press).

Theories of cognitive development, such as Piaget's, cannot be dismissed so easily. There are no a priori reasons to doubt the appropriateness of these theories to language acquisition; the problem instead is an empirical one. For each such theory we must ask whether or not the facts of linguistic development can be understood in the terms offered by the theory.

Such an inquiry, when it succeeds, would make a fundamental contribution, for it would explain an aspect of the universal form of human language on the basis of general psychological principles. Let us call this enterprise the problem of "cognition and language" to distinguish it from the exactly opposite question of language influencing thought, which historically has been called the problem of "language and cognition."

The problem of cognition and language has not been widely recognized. There is little or nothing written of it. Moreover, the impression of this reviewer is that little or nothing could be written of it. The most comprehensive theories of cognitive development take the general form of language for granted; they do not regard it as a phenomenon to be explained. Vygotsky (1962) and Bruner (1966), for example, have concentrated on the opposite problem of language and cognition; Piaget (1926; also Sinclair-de Zwart 1967) has dealt with the expression of thought in language—which again is not the problem of "cognition and language."

Although occasional aspects of Piaget's theory may help explain fragments of language acquisition (such as the fusion of early speech with action, which seems to reflect the operation of sensory-motor intelligence), successes are rare and always leave one wondering if a reformulation of the cognitive theory would not lead to a stronger grip on language.

The immediate prospects of explaining the acquisition of language are bleak, but not hopeless. One can reverse the direction of exploration. Can the aspects of linguistic development that lie beyond psychological explanation be construed as matters of cognitive development? And if they can, then how might our theories of cognitive development be enriched to include the new cognitive phenomena? We shall encounter two outstanding examples of such a possibility. One is predication and the other is the set of transformational relations that universally exist between the deep and surface structures of sentences in all languages. Both are prominent in the acquisition of language, and yet neither apparently can be explained in terms of any cognitive theory.

It is important in this context to maintain a distinction between two kinds of linguistic universal. We shall call the two "weak" and "strong" (McNeill, 1969).

Weak. Features that automatically appear in language because of conditions existing outside language, e.g., in cognition or perception.

Strong. Features that appear in language because of peculiarities of the human communication system itself, and so are not caused by general cognitive or perceptual abilities.

There exists no way a priori to tell into which of these categories a particular linguistic universal falls. A linguistic description does not tell us *why* a feature is universal.

The importance of the difference between the two kinds of linguistic universal should not be overlooked. Only weak universals are relevant to the problem of cognition and language; a theory of cognition would be in error if it explained strong universals. Consider predication: well-formed sentences in every language must contain a subject and a predicate, the two being related by predication. *Mary* alone and out of context is not a sentence, whereas *Mary sings* is. In Japanese also, *Mary* alone and out of context is not a sentence, but *Mary-wa utaimasu* is. Languages differ, often radically, in the form taken by predication, but they do not differ in the sense that any language fails to include it. We may wonder, therefore, if predication appears universally in language because it is imposed by a general cognitive ability, or if there is instead a universal linguistic ability to *express* predication. In the second case, linguistic predication belongs to the category of strong universals, and we expect to find examples of "cognitive predication" in the absence of linguistic predication—among animals, for instance, or among very young children. In the first case, however, linguistic predication is a weak universal and therefore should appear when nonlinguistic predication appears and must be included in any attempt to explain the development of language on the basis of the development of cognition.

The problem of cognition and language is not pursued in this chapter. Nonetheless, the reader is invited to bear it in mind as he follows the development of language, as it is set forth in the following pages.

We now turn to the development of syntax.

Methodology and Methodological Issues

There is little in the study of language acquisition that can be called Methodology, with a capital M. The very speed of linguistic development constrains the methods used in studying it. Massive changes in the grammatical status of children take place between 1½ and 3 years. The age at which studies can be conducted is thereby fixed, and it is no one's fault that this age falls at a time for which there is, in general, no well developed methodology. In such circumstances, the simplest methods—for example, turning on a tape recorder—are as good as any, and the bulk of recent observations has been collected in this way.

Recent studies of the development of syntax can be organized in terms of three contrasting strategies:

1. Observers have examined either the production or comprehension of speech.
2. They have attempted either to trace general linguistic advancement or the emergence of particular grammatical systems.
3. They have conducted either experimental studies or made observations of spontaneous linguistic behavior.

Of the eight possible categories of methods formed in this way, only four have been used at all, and most studies have used just two. There have been no studies, for example, of general comprehension. Most have worked with spontaneous linguistic production, following the development of either general linguistic competence or particular linguistic systems. Certain strategies naturally go with others; comprehension, for example, has almost always been studied experimentally. With the exception of Sinclair-de Zwart (1967) there have been no studies seriously attempting to relate linguistic development to intellectual development, which is, perhaps, a fourth strategy, as well as a substantive issue.

Rather than make a list of the extant categories of research methods—a list that may change tomorrow—it seems more profitable to discuss the broader categories of research that present certain methodological issues.

General versus Particular Analyses. The richest details and the deepest insights have so far come from longitudinal collections of observations. Such studies follow general linguistic development as well as the emergence of particular grammatical systems. Very often the same project lends itself to both strategies, so their proper relationship must be understood. But first a word on the studies themselves.

Almost without exception, observational studies have been engaged with the production and not the comprehension of speech. All are descendants of the early diary studies long conducted by newly parental linguists (Stern and Stern, 1907; Leopold, 1939; 1947; 1949a; 1949b), and they differ from the earlier work mainly in the use of other people's children and in the collection of tape-recorded protocols. Braine (1963a), Weir (1962), Brown and Bellugi (1964), Miller and Ervin (1964), McNeill (1966b), and Gruber (1967) have all contributed varying amounts to this literature.

Typically, a small group of children is visited, at home, once or twice a month, where everything the child says and everything said to him, is tape recorded. The recordings are usually supplemented by running commentaries, made on the spot, describing the general situation in which the speech was uttered. The ultimate step in such extralinguistic record-keeping is to place everything on film or television tape, a step recently taken by Bullowa, Jones, and Bever (1964). Longer intervals between visits are possible and, for many purposes, are as useful as the 2- to 4-week intervals customarily used. The reason for these visits is to acquire a corpus of spontaneous utterances from a child. The significant part of the study lies in the analyses made of the corpus so collected.

It is in the treatment of the corpus that the two strategies—the analysis of general linguistic development and the analysis of particular grammatical systems—differ. The decision to conduct one analysis or the other rests in part on certain methodological issues.

One can try to write a grammar that describes a child's complete corpus. The hope in this case is to capture his total linguistic system at the time the corpus was collected, without distortion from adult grammar. It is often done by performing a distributional analysis of the child's speech. The procedure followed is clearly described in Brown and Fraser (1964); Braine (1963a) also provides some helpful comments. Essentially, an investigator searches for words that appear in the same contexts, the assumption being that such words are members of the same grammatical class in the child's grammatical system. Words with different privileges of occurrence are assumed to belong to different grammatical classes.

Suppose, for example, that a corpus collected from a 2-year-old contains the following utterances:

> My cap
> that cap
> a shoe
> that horsie
> other dog
> a daddy
> big shoe
> red sweater

One could conclude that the words on the left all belong to one grammatical class, the words on the right all belong to a different grammatical class, and the child's grammar at this point considers a "sentence" to be any word from the first class followed by any word from the second class.

Words are placed into the same categories in a distributional analysis when there are no systematic differences in their usage relative to other words—they then have identical privileges of occurrence. *My* and *that* belong together because they both appear with *cap*. *Horsie* and *cap* go together because they both follow *that*. *Cap* and *shoe* are semantically similar, or so one assumes, so words that they can follow—*my, that, a,* and *big*—are placed together in the first class, and words that can in turn follow these words—*cap, shoe, horsie,* and *daddy*—fall together into the second class. The similarity of *horsie* and *dog* justifies adding *other* to the first class, as does the similarity of *sweater, cap,* and *shoe,* which justifies adding *red* also to the first class.

As these examples make clear, the independence of distributional analysis from the analyst's own knowledge of language is limited. A distributional analysis does not insist on the co-occurrence of words in strictly identical contexts, but counts appearance in the context of meaningfully related words as co-occurrence also. Moreover, one assumes that nonoccurring combinations—for example, *that sweater* or *big daddy*—are allowed by the child's grammar but are not observed because of sampling limitations.

Having established what seem to be a child's grammatical classes, the rules of his grammar are written to state the manner in which classes are combined—in this case, Class 1 + Class 2. More complex categories demand more complex rules, but in every case the rules merely summarize the patterns of categories observed in a child's corpus. Studies that have prepared distributional analyses in this manner are Braine (1963a), Brown and Fraser (1964), and Miller and Ervin (1964).

An important methodological question is raised by such investigations. An investigator combines individual utterances (*my cap, a shoe,* etc.) into categories through the application of certain principles of combination (shared privileges of occurrence), and then states the regularities observed among the categories so formed (Class 1 + Class 2 is a sentence). But none of this necessarily comprises a statement of a child's linguistic competence, his knowledge of language. It is a summary of his performance, whereas a statement of competence is a *theory* about what a child knows.

Moreover, there is serious question whether or not a theory of competence can ever be developed from manipulations of a corpus. Contemporary linguists deny that it can be done (see Chomsky, 1964, Lees, 1964, for a discussion of such investigations of child language). A corpus is incomplete, unsystematic, and (in the case of adults, at least) insensitive to a number of important grammatical distinctions. Insofar as utterances from children are limited in the same way, a distributional analysis will not lead to a correct description of competence, however neatly it may summarize performance; and there is no way to tell when a corpus is so limited. A distributional analysis at best provides a description of a child's grammatical classes, plus some hints as to his grammatical rules. A theory of competence that explains these classes and rules may well take an entirely different form, a phenomenon that we shall see repeatedly in the pages that follow. The most elaborate general analyses of child grammar go far beyond the distributional evidence of a corpus (e.g., Brown, Cazden, and Bellugi, 1968).

As a description of performance, distributional analysis is but one source of information among many. Other observations, dealing with other aspects of performance, are often

of equal importance; in some cases, they are more easily justified.

Among other sources of information are observations made under the second strategy mentioned above. Rather than attempt to describe the total corpus collected from a child at some point in time, one examines the emergence of a particular grammatical system as it is manifested at different times. Thus one might study the development of negation (Bellugi, 1964), or questions (Klima and Bellugi, 1966), or a host of other grammatical systems. The advantage of this strategy lies in the demands it places on observation, arising from the very fact that it does what a distributional analysis typically strives to avoid—it exploits the fact that adult grammar is the endpoint of linguistic development. A distributional analysis attempts to discover parts of a grammar from a corpus. The second strategy begins with a part of adult grammar and judges if there is sufficient evidence in the corpus to justify ascribing it to a child. The demands on the second strategy are weaker than the demands on the first, for it must only recognize the applicability of a known theory; it does not have to discover an unknown theory.

When an adult analysis cannot be ascribed to a child, one can still describe the sequence of events followed in reaching the adult system. Thus, for example, children first negate by saying *not want,* then *don't want some,* then *don't want none,* and finally, *don't want any* (Bellugi, 1964). At each point, one can say what a child lacks with respect to the adult system: he does not have auxiliary verbs, he does not have negative pronouns, and he does not have indeterminate pronouns, respectively. But one does not attempt to *discover* from these observations the child's grammatical system. That is a separate step—a matter of the investigator's invention, ingenuity, imagination, and good fortune. It is everything, indeed, except a matter of discovery.

The following quotation from Brown, Cazden, and Bellugi (1968) summarizes many of the dangers and opportunities of following either strategy when interpreting a corpus of utterances collected from a child:

We operate on the general assumption that the child's terminal state of knowledge is of the sort represented by current transformational grammars. However, we do not simply attribute to each sentence that the child produces the analysis that would be appropriate to that sentence if it were produced by an adult: if we were to do that the inquiry would be largely vacuous. Insofar as the child's particular sentence—and all related sentences—depart from adult forms the grammar is tailored to the departures. The most informative departures are analogical errors of commission such as *goed* . . . Harder to interpret, but still important, are errors of omission such as the absence of auxiliary *did* . . . Omissions in a sentence are at least easy to detect but omissions in the distributional range of a form are harder to detect and harder to interpret since it is necessary to weigh the probability that an omission is simply a consequence of the size of the sample that has been taken. Finally all the errors that occur must be considered in comparison with conceivable errors that do not occur. Even this full procedure will not render the construction completely determinate in all respects. The indeterminacies are tentatively resolved by assigning the usual adult representation insofar as that representation does not depend on forms that have never appeared in the child's speech (p. 31).

It is possible to carry the second strategy to the level of true experimentation. Instead of observing the spontaneous occurrences of particular grammatical features, one tries to evoke them. For example, Ervin (1964), working with W. Miller, tested children's knowledge of English plurals by presenting free-form figures made of wood, each named with a nonsense syllable. A child is first shown one such figure, perhaps shaped like a salt-cellar and called a *bunge*, and then is presented with a second figure exactly like the first. What does he call the two figures together—*bunge* or *bunges?* The latter would indicate mastery of the rule for the pluralization of English nouns ending in sibilants. The age at which a child demonstrates such mastery can be compared to the age at which he correctly uses such genuine plurals as *oranges*.

A similar method can be used to elicit the past-tense inflection of verbs. The procedure suffers some uncertainty in this case, inas-

much as past time is difficult to exemplify perceptually. A failure to elicit a past-tense inflection may result from a failure of the experimenter to present the appropriate conditions, as well as from a failure of the child to add past-tense inflections when the conditions are right. Nonetheless, one can at least approach the problem by demonstrating a novel gesture, saying at the same time *I'll sib it,* and then asking a child what had been done.

A child's ability to change model sentences into transformationally related sentences—to change, for example, active sentences into passives—has been studied by Brown (1968), working with Anita Olds, by means of the "alligator test." Two adults, each with a puppet, engage in the following dialogue:

Bear: The cat chased the dog.
Alligator: The dog was chased by the cat.

Bear: The zebra pushes the hippo.
Alligator: The hippo is pushed by the zebra.

And so on. The alligator speaks only in passive sentences. After a child has witnessed such exchanges for a time, he is given the alligator and asked to play its part. The method can be extended to many kinds of sentences and to many kinds of relations among sentences. Bellugi (1967) suggests studying negation in this way; questions could be approached through the alligator also.

Bellugi (1967) has described a number of tests of negation, some for comprehension, others for production. All are suitable for use with young children. Since the variety of syntactic forms covered is quite large, only a sampling will be given here.

To test a child's comprehension of negatives affixed to auxiliary verbs, a child can be shown a doll with movable arms, one arm up and the other down. The child is told to make the doll fit either of the sentences, "the boy can put his arms down" or "the boy can't put his arms down."

To test a child's comprehension of negation used in Wh-questions, a child is shown an array of objects—a boy doll, an orange, an apple, a ball, a toy, a tomato, and an ashtray —and is asked "What can the little boy eat?" or "What can't the little boy eat?"

To test a child's comprehension of affirmative pronouns (such as *some*) and negative pronouns (such as *none*), a child is shown a doll and a few blocks and is told to make the doll fit either of the sentences. "The doll can push some of the blocks," or "The doll can push none of the blocks."

To elicit negative indefinite forms (pronouns based on *any*), a child is first shown a doll with a hat on its head and is told "Here is John. He has something on his head." The child is shown a second, hatless doll and is told "Here is Bill. What does he have on his head? He doesn't have_____."

Another technique is to give a child systematically distorted forms, the distortions being designed to bear on points of syntactic interest, and ask the child to correct the errors. For example, "he not touching it," can be corrected by a child who knows that in English negatives must be attached to auxiliaries, but not by a child ignorant of this fact.

The reader can exercise his own ingenuity in devising other tests. It would be well, however, to bear in mind Bellugi's admonition that such techniques serve only to supplement the findings obtained from children's spontaneous speech. Tests of linguistic competence can never be rich enough, subtle enough, or sensible enough to stand on their own.

Perhaps the best known test of children's productive abilities is the test devised by Berko (1958). A comparable test has been independently developed by Bogoyavlenskiy (1957) for use with Russian children (see Slobin, in press). Berko investigated the development of the morphological inflections of English: plural marking of nouns, past-tense marking of verbs, comparative marking of adjectives, plus some others.

The test uses a set of drawings of exotic creatures doing ordinary things, or ordinary creatures doing exotic things. Berko used it with children 4 to 6 years old, although it has been used with children as young as 2 (Lovell, 1968). One drawing, for example, shows a shmoolike creature. It is introduced as a *wug*: "Here is a wug." Then two more are shown, the experimenter saying, "Here are two others, there are two . . . ," his voice trailing off, hoping to elicit a plural inflection. The test includes items presenting each of the conditioning phonemic environments of the plural and past-tense inflections

of English, so by the end, one has collected a complete sample of a child's morphological inflections.

Studies of Comprehension. A second methodological issue involves the comprehension of grammatical forms—how it is to be investigated, and why. Unlike the first methodological issue, which involves the clarification of the proper role of an existing method, this methodological issue involves the clarification of the requirements of a method that does not yet exist.

There are several reasons for studying comprehension. As one of the linguists at The Fourth Conference on Intellective Processes (Bellugi and Brown, 1964) pointed out, in comprehension the investigator knows what the input to the process is—it is the sentence comprehended. Thus when comprehension fails, the source of trouble can be located. The same cannot be said for production. What is the input for, say, *What I can do mommy?*

Moreover, even though the results of production are easy to observe, it is not always obvious what the observations mean. Does the fact that a child systematically excludes auxiliary verbs from his speech signify the absence of Aux from his grammar, or does it, on the contrary, indicate censorship of Aux from his speech in order to meet the constraints of an abbreviated memory span? Although these are matters of production, it is only through the testing of comprehension that such questions can be settled.

We shall now describe the few studies that have attempted to investigate comprehension, point out their limitations, and present some promising new techniques.

Brown (1957) demonstrated that certain of the major grammatical classes have semantic correlates for children. He used a test of comprehension that apparently has not been employed since. A child is shown a drawing of someone performing a strange action with a peculiar substance contained in an odd bowl. The picture thus presents an action, a mass, and a container—three states that would be described in English by a verb, a mass noun, and a count noun, respectively. As the picture is shown, the experimenter says what it is: it shows *how to wug*, or *some wug*, or *a wug*. Whichever the child is told, he is next shown three drawings—one of the action alone, one of the mass alone, and one of the container alone—and is asked to select the one that portrays what was labeled in the first picture. To the degree that a child is sensitive to the referential implications of verbs, mass-nouns, and count-nouns, he will be able to make appropriate choices (but see Braine, in press, for a different interpretation). Brown used this test with nursery-school children, finding them to be sensitive to the implications of each grammatical class. In view of the claim sometimes made (e.g., Slobin, 1966a) that children first construct grammatical classes on a semantic basis, it would be useful to repeat the experiment with younger, say, 2-year-old children.

A second test of the comprehension (as well as the production) of speech appears in an experiment by Fraser, Bellugi, and Brown (1963). Their method has come to be called the ICP Test, for Imitation, Comprehension, and Production. Again a set of drawings is shown to a child, this time in pairs. Each pair presents a referential correlate of some syntactic contrast—for example, subject versus direct object (a boy pushing a girl and a girl pushing a boy). In all, 10 different contrasts are represented. Comprehension is tested by saying to a child, "Here are two pictures, one of a boy pushing a girl, and the other of a girl pushing a boy," care being taken not to show which picture goes with which sentence. The child is then asked to point to the picture that illustrates one of the sentences: "Show me the picture of the girl pushing the boy." The test of production begins in the same way, but instead of asking the child to point to the picture for a sentence, he is asked to give a sentence for a picture. Fraser et al. conducted their study with 3-year-olds. Lovell and Dixon (1965) have done it with 2-year-olds, with much the same results.

Shipley, Smith, and Gleitman (n.d.) have studied comprehension in children as young as 18 months by giving them commands and observing whether or not the command is followed. Bever, Mehler, and Valian (1967) have used a similar method. In the case of Shipley et al., the commands are either well-formed by adult standards (e.g., *throw me the ball*) or are typical child-forms (e.g., *ball; throw ball; Please Johnnie, throw ball*). In addition, a given command might contain only words known to a child (as in the examples above) or it might contain one or more words novel to him (e.g., *gor ball; throw ronta ball; gor ronta ball*). A major difficulty with the method resides in the identification of comprehension. Except when a child performs exactly as instructed, there is no way to tell if he has successfully analyzed a command or merely has responded to a part of the command, for example, to the noun. In commands using novel words, obviously it is impossible for a child to perform exactly as instructed.

Such studies of comprehension, clever though they sometimes are, suffer a common limitation. All use portrayable correlates of various grammatical contrasts and classes. But not every aspect of syntax has a portrayable correlate. Indeed, most of syntax cannot be so represented, as the reader can persuade himself by a glance at the Appendix. It is always possible, of course, that further ingenuity will discover more grammatical forms that can be tested in this way. However, this is of little significance, for as the method is extended further, it must use more and more remote connections between language and portrayable events. The methodological problem is to devise tests of comprehension that make use of the linguistic materials themselves, not the fortuitous correlations between language and the external world.

Two studies that point in this direction are Bellugi's (1965) and Brown's (1966). They searched their longitudinal records for spontaneous dialogues between children and adults, looking at the children's answers to the adults' questions. The aptness of the answer was the index of comprehension. If an adult asks *what did you hit?* and a child answers, *arm*, we can assume that the question was understood. But if the answer is *hit*, we can conclude that the child does not yet know the transformation relating Wh-forms to the underlying object of sentences. Some caution must be exercised in accepting appropriate answers at face value, since it is always possible that extralinguistic factors evoke an utterance that happens to be appropriate. Nonetheless, the method applies to any Wh-question, and has the virtue of involving a spontaneous linguistic performance. But only Wh-questions are within its reach, so it is hardly general, even though it is not limited by language-environment correlations. A third study escapes some of these shortcomings.

Slobin and Welsh (1967) have used the simplest of methods for studying linguistic development—imitation. For reasons discussed later, children usually reformulate sentences given to them for imitation. Adult sentences too long to be retained in immediate memory are invariably altered to fit the child's grammar of the moment, which means that imitation can be used to study children's productive capacities, a fact known and utilized for some time (Menyuk, 1963; Lenneberg, Nichol's and Rosenberger, 1964; Slobin, in press). For example, suppose that a child who is not yet inflecting verbs for the progressive aspect is asked to repeat *Adam's nose is dripping this morning.* If the entire sentence is beyond the child's capacity for immediate recall, the relevant part will tend to be imitated *nose drip,* not *nose dripping.* The model is reduced to the child's current grammar. Beyond the limits of immediate memory, a child produces in imitation only what he produces in spontaneous speech.

However, Slobin and Welsh have used imitation to study comprehension as well as production. In contrast to the use of imitation to study production, where the focus is on verbatim repetition, the focus in comprehension is on nonverbatim repetition combined with the preservation of meaning. When children reformulate a sentence in imitation, they express parts of the underlying structure of the model in a surface structure consistent with their own grammars. But when children fail to comprehend the model, they are unable to recover its deep structure. The imitation will then inevitably express a different meaning, or, more likely, no meaning at all. In this way—by noting whether or not reformulated imitation preserves meaning—comprehension can be studied.

The method can be (and has been) used with very young children, and can be applied to any aspect of the structure of sentences. Children can be induced to repeat what adults say, particularly if they are familiar with the investigator; and the sentences to be imitated are entirely a matter of the investigator's choice, so the method can be used across the complete range of sentence types.

The following are a few of the examples given by Slobin and Welsh (1967). All are imitations by a 2½-year-old child. The first two are meaning-preserving, the last two are meaning-changing:

Adult: Here is a brown brush and here is a comb.
Child: Here's a brown brush an' a comb.
Adult: John who cried came to my party.
Child: John cried and he came to my party.
Adult: The batman got burned and the big shoe is there.
Child: Big shoe is here and big shoe is here.
Adult: The boy the book hit was crying.
Child: Boy the book was crying.

The first two imitations indicate an ability to comprehend but not produce certain grammatical forms, whereas the last two indicate a failure of comprehension. The second example is particularly interesting, since the child decomposed an embedded sentence into the matrix and constituent sentences underlying it. Slobin and Welsh's method deserves exploration, for it appears to have the virtues of generality and naturalness that the other methods for testing comprehension lack. Its main limitation is probably that children have to be well acquainted with the tester for the method to work. Slobin and Welsh's subject was very familiar with her tester, and may have been more willing than most young subjects to repeat incomprehensible sentences.

The Berkeley Cross-Cultural Project. Although not a method itself, except insofar as a program for investigating language acquisition in other cultures may be called a method, a group at the University of California (Berkeley) has compiled a manual of procedures (Slobin, 1967) for use in field studies of children and their language. In addition to the manual, the Project sends workers into remote places, pith helmet in hand, to observe children acquiring exotic languages.

Theories of Language Acquisition and Early Speech

Perhaps the most striking recent development in the study of language acquisition is a resurgence of interest in theory. In an earlier period the explanation of linguistic development was a major goal. Entire books were devoted to the problem; for example, Stern and Stern (1907) and de Laguna (1927). But that was 40 or more years ago. Since then the field has been devoted to description, noteworthy as much for its indifference toward theory as for its sturdy accumulation of facts and figures. The entire literature has been excellently summarized in preceding editions of this *Manual,* and will not be much touched on here. We shall instead concentrate on the recent developments in theory and the empirical work associated with them. The issues posed, both by theory and observation, are significant enough to warrant the devotion of space and attention.

Let us begin with a description of the speech of a 2-year-old. Not everyone has had the privilege of attempting to converse with such a person, at least not recently. The following examples, taken from records collected by Brown and Bellugi (1964), will set the tone. The first sample is from a 27-month-old child, the second from the same child at 35 months, and the third at 38 months. Vivid changes take place from sample to sample; a number of these will be discussed.

Child (28 months)	Adult
What dat . . . somebody pencil	Whose pencils are they?
Floor	Floor?
Where birdie go?	
Birdie	
Birdie up dere	
Birdie	
Read dat?	
Read dat?	Will you read it to me?
What inere?	Is that a hammer, Adam?
Hammer	
Hit hammer, mommy	
No Cromer ——, mommy?	
Hurt	Poor Adam. Did you hurt yourself? What happened, Adam?
Screw (did) happen	Screw happened? You didn't even have a screw.
have screw	
——no down there . . .	
table . . . get broom	Does that one fit?
Yep, it fit	
Yep, it fit	Does it fit?
No . . . fit	
Put suitcase . . . for?	What did you put it in the suitcase for?
What dat?	That's tape. We'll use that one tomorrow.
All right 'morrow	Shall we use it tomorrow?
Yep	
Use morrow, yep	
Sure, use morrow	

Child (35 months)	Adult
What his name?	His name
His name, Ursla?	I know his name
No . . . I don't know his name	
I don't know	
Can't come up, fellah (to a yo-yo)	
Going pick pick up	
Lemme do again	
Don't . . . don't hold with me	
Turning round	Yes, it is turning around
It's stop	It stopped?
What dat . . . feeled . . . like?	
What dat feeled like?	It feels like rubber, I guess.
I . . . going . . . drop my books	
(drops one book)	
An' what happens?	
I going drop it . . . inne dump truck	
No . . . please cry, cracker	What?
Cracker	Please what?
Please cry, cracker.	Please cry?
Yes	How can a cracker cry? Crackers can't talk.
Why not . . . cracker can't talk?	
Romper domper tell me boo	
Romper domper tell me boo	
I got someping show you	
What's dat . . . you have?	
Why me go?	
Why me going?	
D'you want brush him?	
D'you want he walk?	
Where's it?	
Why you rolling up?	
Hey, why . . . why you waking me up?	
What you doing . . . taking out?	
Why you knocking me off?	I'm not knocking you off
Why not?	
I can't . . . couldn't . . . show it . . . to her	You're going to show it to her?
No	
I too big	
Dose are mines	
Dat's mines	

Child (38 months)	Adult
I like a racing car D'you like some? I broke my racing car	Oh, did you used to have one?
Yes Look at dat one	
Like dis part broke Dis part broke, like that It's got a flat tire What is dat? It's a what? He . . . his mouth is open What shall we shall have? Why he going to have some seeds? Why it's not working?	What part broke?
You got some beads?	Yes
Just like me? I got bead 'round myself Hit my knee	Hit *my* knee
Hit your knee What dat teacher will do?	
Why you pull out?	Dust in your hair
Who put my dust on my hair?	Can you tell Ursula what the lesson is . . . on the blackboard?
On the black which board? We going see another one We can read 'bout dis You wanto read? What is dat? What is dat got? It's got a flat tire When it's got flat tire, it's needs to go to the . . . to the station. The station will fix it. Tank come out through what? Really . . . tank come out through . . . here Mommy don't let me buy some	
What is dis?	That's a marble bag
A marble bag for what?	For marbles It would be good to carry tiny cars.
What is dat? Can I keep dem? Why I can keep dem? Now can I keep dem? We don' do some games It's broked?	

At 28 months a child's speech often may seem random; some may uncharitably claim that it is not much improved at 38 months. Words appear to be thrown together haphazardly. The meanings often seem bizarre. But this is not so. Even the earliest word combinations are organized on definite principles; and the content is not bizarre but banal. In the following sections, we shall review the evidence for these claims and some possible explanations of them.

Telegraphic Speech. Brown and Fraser (1963) have called the patterned speech of very young children "telegraphic." The expression aptly captures one characteristic feature of children's first multiple-word utterances: both in telegrams and in child speech, certain words are systematically eliminated. Looking at the sample collected at 28 months, we can see that articles, auxiliary verbs, copular verbs, and inflections of every sort are all missing: *put suitcase . . . for? where birdie go? what innere?* and *yep, it fit.*

The telegraphic analogy is provocative and worth considering. Perhaps child speech is telegraphic for the same reason that real telegrams are—to save on costs. Just as a telegram-writer, in order to save currency, may delete the least informative words of a message while retaining content words and their order, a child may do the same to save space in memory. The fact that identical words, by and large, are eliminated in both situations adds some credence to the argument. But there are two difficulties with this account— one conceptual and one factual.

The factual problem is that children learning Russian also omit inflections from their early speech (Slobin, 1966b). Russian is a case-inflected language, and so conveys a great deal of information through certain inflections. Indeed, some of the information conveyed by word order in English is conveyed by inflections in Russian—the subject of a sentence, for example. Thus, in terms of informational importance, Russian children eliminate what American children retain, though both eliminate inflections. Clearly, it is not informativeness that counts.

The conceptual difficulty is that, although the least informative words of English tend not to appear in child speech, a lack of informativeness is itself a highly implausible explanation of this fact (Weksel, 1965). The only way a child could know whether or not a word is informative without knowing its syntactic role in advance (a possibility excluded in this case) is by keeping records of the speech he has heard from his parents. Equipped with such records, he could discover which words are used with low frequency, and so are informative. But this is a vast actuarial undertaking—implausibly vast for a 2-year-old, whose exposure to speech is necessarily limited, and whose ability to keep unedited records must be small indeed.

Telegraphic speech is the outcome of the process of language acquisition. It is not the process itself. To understand it, we must penetrate more deeply into what children do.

Holophrastic Speech. It is convenient to begin even before the period of telegraphic speech. "Holophrastic speech" refers to the possibility that the first single-word utterances of young children express complex ideas— that *ball* means not simply a spherical object of appropriate size, but that a child wants such an object, or that a child believes he has created such an object, or that someone is expected to look at such an object.

Many investigators of children's language (e.g., de Laguna, 1927; Stern and Stern, 1907; Leopold, 1949; McCarthy, 1954) have said that the single words of holophrastic speech are equivalent to the full sentences of adult grammar. It is true, of course, that adults typically require a full sentence to express the content of children's holophrastic speech. But this is not what is meant by the term "holophrastic." Rather, holophrastic speech means that children are limited phonologically to uttering single words at the beginning of language acquisition, even though they are capable of conceiving of something like full sentences. Let us look into this possibility, for it is central to understanding the course of events in later stages of language acquisition.

In what sense do children have in mind the content of a full sentence while uttering a single word? No one believes that children have detailed and differentiated ideas in the adult manner. On the contrary, everyone who has written on the earliest stages of language acquisition agrees that the conceptual side of holophrastic speech is undifferentiated and global. As Leopold (1949a) puts it, " . . . the word has at first an ill-defined meaning and an ill-defined value: it refers to a nebulous complex, factually and emotionally; only gradually do its factual and emotional components become clearer, resulting in lexical and syntactic discriminations" (p. 5).

A degree of semantic imprecision in holophrastic speech is therefore taken for granted. There remains, however, a question of what it is that children are imprecise about. Several factors seem to be important. Often children's single-word utterances are closely linked with action, sometimes so closely linked that action and speech appear fused. A child speaks both when he acts and when he wants action from others. Leopold's daughter, for example, said *walk* as she got out of a cart to walk, *away* as she pushed something away, and *blow* as she blew her nose (all at 20 months). Leopold (1949) calls these utterances self-imperatives to distinguish them from true imperatives, which are utterances apparently directed toward someone else. Of the true imperatives, *mit* from *komm mit*, *ma* from *come on*, and *away* from *put it away* are examples (also at 20 months). (Leopold's daughters grew up as German-English bilinguals.)

Besides such imperatives and self-imperatives, children's early speech often seems imbued with emotion. Indeed, Leopold believes that the first step in linguistic development occurs when a child attaches emotional significance to sounds produced accidentally while babbling. Meumann (1894) holds a similar view, believing that a child's first words express his "emotional relation" toward the objects and events referred to. This expressive aspect of children's speech maintains its dominating role for some time. According to Stern and Stern (1907; summarized briefly in English by Blumenthal, in press), the first word combinations of children consist of one part interjection and one part statement, the former continuing from the earliest stages of development 6 to 12 months before.

There is some consensus, then, that holophrastic speech is expressive of children's emotional states, as well as fused with action. There is a third characteristic sometimes claimed for holophrastic speech: it rests on an ability to name things. A child expresses his feelings about whatever is labeled in his utterance. The utterance [mam:a], for example, seems to have meant for Leopold's daughter both "delicious!" and "food." The utterance apparently had both an expressive and referential component. (It did not mean "mama" until 6 months later.)

Not every single-word utterance names something, however. Some utterances are purely expressive. Leopold's daughter said [dididi] in a loud voice to indicate disapproval and in a soft voice to indicate comfort. [dididi] was in fact an exclamatory call, much like the calls of apes, and was graded as these calls are from loud to soft; [dididi] was an articulated grunt. (See Marler, 1965, for examples of grading in the calls of rhesus monkeys.)

Examples of all these characteristics of holophrastic speech are included in Table 1, which is a list of the first seven "words" observed in the development of Leopold's daughter. Utterances marked with an asterisk were originally babbled sounds; the rest have recognizable sources in adult speech. The "words" of Table 1 are typical of the early one-word utterances recorded by others (Stern and Stern, 1907).

Various psychologists have at one time or another assumed that the truly linguistic utterances of children begin with labeling: a child learns the name of an object and says the name when the object appears before him (see Brown, 1958). However, it is far

Table 1. The First Seven "Words" in One Child's Linguistic Development.

Utterance	Age (months)	Gloss
ʔəʔ*	8	An interjection. Also demonstrative, "addressed" to persons, distant objects, and "escaped toys"
dididi*	9	(loud) disapproval (soft) comfort
mam:a	10	Refers to food vaguely. Also means "tastes good" and "hungry"
nenene*	10	scolding
tt!*	10	used to call squirrels
pIti	10	Always used with a gesture, and always w h i s p e r e d. Seems to mean "Interested (-ing)"
dɛ:	10	An interjection. Also demonstrative. Used with the same gesture as above

After Leopold, 1949a.

from clear that this interpretation is correct. The single-word utterances of children are ambiguous between naming and predication; no utterance can be both a name and predicate of the same thing. When a 1-year-old says *daddy*, he might be referring to that personage or he might be saying of that personage that he *is a* daddy. He cannot be doing both. We have here a fundamental fact of language acquisition.

Holophrastic Speech as Predication. The expressive and enactive aspects of holophrastic speech are best understood on nonlinguistic grounds; expressiveness is an example of the exclamatory function of primate communication in general (see Marler and Hamilton, 1966); the fusion of speech with action is probably a consequence of the sensorimotor period in general cognitive development (Piaget, 1952). Here we consider a more special question, that holophrastic speech is not nominal, but rather is predicative. It is in this way that holophrastic speech corresponds to full sentences in adult speech.

De Laguna (1927) viewed the single-word utterances of children as predicates, comments made by a child on the situation in which he finds himself. The holophrastic word is the comment; together with the extralinguistic context, the topic of the comment, it forms a rudimentary kind of proposition, and thus amounts to a full sentence conceptually. It is worth quoting de Laguna's peroration in full:

It is precisely because the words of the child are so indefinite in meaning, that they can serve such a variety of uses; and it is also—although this sounds paradoxical—for the same reason, that they are fit to function as complete rudimentary sentences. A child's word does not . . . designate an object *or* a property *or* an act; rather it signifies loosely and vaguely the object together with its interesting properties and the acts with which it is commonly associated in the life of the child. The emphasis may be now on one, now on another, of these aspects, according to the exigencies of the occasion on which it is used. Just because the terms of the child's language are in themselves so indefinite, it is left *to the particular setting and context to determine the specific meaning for each occasion.* In order to understand what the baby is saying you must see what the baby is doing (1927, pp. 90–91, italics in original).

In Table 1 [mam:a] is listed as meaning both "food" and "delicious!" But this is only its apparent meaning if we accept de Laguna's interpretation of early speech. With that interpretation, Leopold's daughter said [mam:a] as a comment (is delicious) on an extralinguistic topic (food). The utterance is nonreferential. Several other "words" in Table 1 can be interpreted in the same way—[ʔəʔ] and [dɛ :], and possibly [pIti], [nenene], and [t t!]. On the other hand, [dididi] was not a comment at all (except in the trivial sense that "ouch!" is a comment on a pin prick), and [nenene] and [pIti] may not have been either.

If we accept de Laguna's interpretation of holophrastic speech, we suppose that purely nominal utterances play a marginal role in early stages of language acquisition. Except for those occasions when children's speech is purely expressive, it is invariably predicative. Children cry, or comment, and sometimes both. This remarkable fact of human communication has effects at every stage of linguistic development. One such stage is the following.

Pivot and Open Classes. The terms "pivot" and "open" are taken from Braine (1963a) and refer to the outcome of a distributional analysis of child speech. When such analyses are conducted of the speech collected from children of 18 months or so, at least two classes of words emerge. One class contains a small number of words, each of them frequently used—the "pivot" class. Words from the pivot class always appear in combination with words from the open class, and the class itself is slow to take in new members. The position of pivot-words in two-word sentences is fixed, first for some pivot classes and second for others, but never both for any particular pivot class. The "open" class contains the words not in the pivot class. There is typically a large number of open-words, which are therefore used infrequently in two-word sentences. The open class is quick to take in new members, and may stand alone in a child's speech. Given a two-word sentence the position of open-words is fixed with respect to the position of pivot-words. Open-words also appear in combination with each other, although not necessarily in fixed relative positions.

Such are the characteristics of the pivot-open distinction. The distinction can be summarized by setting down the combinations in which pivot- and open-words appear—the basic fact supporting the distinction in the first place. Using "P" and "O" for pivot and open, and assuming a child with a full complement of both classes, the following can occur:

$$P + O$$
$$O + P$$
$$O + O$$
$$O$$

The only possibilities that never appear are pivot-words uttered alone or in combinations with each other. Everything else is possible.

Table 2 shows the pivot and open classes of three children studied by Brown and Bellugi (1964), Braine (1963a), and Miller and Er-

vin (1964), respectively. The table itself is from McNeill (1966a). For want of space, only a portion of each open class is represented, but the pivot classes are included in their entirety.

For the children in Table 2, sentences consisted of a word from the list on the left followed by a word from the list on the right—that is, P + O. Thus, *byebye fan, wet sock* and *that doed* all occurred. Not every combination allowed by Table 2 was actually observed, of course. But there are no evident differences between the combinations that did occur and those that did not, so it is assumed that the gaps arise from sampling, not grammatical restrictions.

What is to be made of the pivot-open distinction? Perhaps nothing at all. It is possible that the speech of young children arises through rote memory, as a simplified imitation

Table 2. Pivot and Open Classes from Three Studies of Child Language

Braine		Brown		Ervin	
allgone byebye big more pretty my see night-night hi	boy sock boat fan milk plane shoe vitamins hot Mommy Daddy . . .	my that two a the big green poor wet dirty fresh pretty	Adam Becky boot coat coffee knee man Mommy nut sock stool tinkertoy . .	this that	arm baby dolly's pretty yellow come doed . .
				the a	other baby dolly's pretty yellow . .
				here there	arm baby dolly's pretty yellow . .

of adult speech. If so, it would be a mistake to ascribe grammatical significance to what, in this case, would be an artifact of a distributional analysis. Before proceeding therefore we must first consider the possibility that the pivot and open classes do not mark the beginning of grammar in children.

There are several reasons for rejecting such a possibility. For one thing, if the sentences recorded from children are not produced but reproduced, the fact would reflect an astonishing ability to memorize verbal material. The number of *different* combinations recorded from one of Braine's (1963a) children in successive months was: 14, 24, 54, 89, 350, 1400, 2500+. It is unlikely that the child was echoing 2500+ different combinations already heard.

Not only is it implausible that a great variety of forms in the speech of children could result from imitation, but in some cases it is impossible that their speech could be so derived. Take Braine's subject in Table 2, for example. He said such things as *allgone shoe, allgone vitamins,* and *allgone lettuce*—all apparently inversions of the corresponding adult models: *the shoe is allgone, the vitamins are allgone, the lettuce is allgone.* Similar observations can be made of other children. Ervin's subject said *that doed,* and Brown's, *big a truck.* Children do not hear English even remotely like this from their parents, but these examples correspond to a pivot-open pattern, and their occurrence reinforces a belief that the distinction reflects a genuine division of children's vocabulary into two classes.

The most compelling argument in behalf of the pivot-open distinction is the fact that pivot words never occur alone or in combination with each other. It is impossible to think of such a development as not reflecting a restriction on the use of words—that is, as not reflecting a grammatical system of some kind. In fact, the pivot-open distinction is a reflection of children's most primitive grammar. It is to a description of that grammar that we now turn.

Early Grammatical Rules. The present section relies heavily on the work of Brown and his colleagues (Brown and Fraser, 1963; Bellugi and Brown, 1964; Brown, Cazden, and Bellugi, 1968). They have followed the linguistic development of three children, two girls and a boy, beginning in each case at

roughly 2 years and continuing for one child until age 5. The goal of Brown and his colleagues has been to describe the linguistic competence of these children at different points in development and to express the descriptions in the form of generative grammars. We shall first consider the results of their descriptive efforts, and then turn to a theoretical interpretation of them.

Not amazingly, grammars written for the earliest stages of development are simple in the extreme. The following rules summarize the performance of one child in Brown's study, Adam, at 28 months (after McNeill, 1966a):

$$S \rightarrow (NP)\ (VP) \qquad (1)$$

$$NP \rightarrow (P) \left\{ \begin{matrix} N \\ N\ N \end{matrix} \right\} \qquad (2)$$

$$VP \rightarrow V(NP) \qquad (3)$$

Rules (1), (2), and (3) describe sentences of one to five words, the length depending on the options adopted in each rule. As usual, optional elements are enclosed within parentheses and alternatives within braces. The successive parentheses of Rule (1) mean that at least one element must be included in each sentence. Rules (1) and (2) apply to such sentences as *ball, that ball,* and *Adam ball:* N, PN, and NN. Rules (1), (2), and (3) apply to such sentences as *want ball, want that ball, Adam want ball,* and *want Adam ball:* VN, VPN, NVN, and VNN. Rules (1) and (3) produce such sentences as *want* and *Adam want:* V and NV.

The combinations allowed by Rules (1), (2), and (3) did not occur in Adam's speech with equal frequency. For example, Rule (3) was employed more often than was Rule (2); sentences longer than three words were very rare; and two patterns (NNN and NPN) that should not have occurred at all according to these rules occurred 2% of the time.

All these characteristics and more are set forth in Table 3, which lists every combination of P, V, and N observed to occur in Adam's speech at the earliest stage for which observations exist, along with the frequency of occurrence of each combination. It is of course possible that a larger sample of Adam's speech would contain examples of other combinations; there is no way to judge such a possibility. However, as will be discussed

Table 3. Sentence Patterns that Correspond to Basic Grammatical Relations

Child's Speech		
Pattern	Frequency	Corresponding Grammatical Relations
P + N	23	modifier, head noun
N + N	115	modifier, head noun, subject, predicate
V + N	162	main verb, object
N + V	49	subject, predicate
Sum	**349**	
P + N + N	3	modifier, head noun
N + P + N	1	subject predicate, modifier, head noun
V + P + N	3	main verb, object, modifier, head noun
V + N + N	29	main verb, object, modifier, head noun
P + N + V	1	subject, predicate, modifier, head noun
N + N + V	1	subject, predicate, modifier, head noun
N + V + N	4	main verb, object, subject, predicate
N + N + N	7	subject, predicate, modifier, head noun
Sum	**49**	

From McNeill, 1966a.

later, the combinations that did occur in Adam's speech possess a certain consistency, which the combinations that did not occur lack.

Rules (1), (2), and (3) adhere closely to the superficial details of Adam's speech. They summarize the patterns in Table 3, but they do not necessarily describe Adam's linguistic competence exhaustively, and they may not represent it at all. It appears, for example, that phrases described by Rule (2) can have two different interpretations when a P is chosen for the first position. Sentences of this type strike an adult as being sometimes demonstrative (*that ball*) and sometimes modificational (*little ball*). If Adam was actually honoring such a distinction but not marking it in overt speech, Rule (1) would fail to reflect it. Adam in this case would in truth treat as different two constructions the Rule treats as the same. We shall return to this matter; there are a number of issues involved and it is convenient to discuss them in one place.

Rule (2) defines a particular grammatical constituent: it says that Adam possessed NPs at 28 months and that these consisted of an N, a PN combination, an NN combination, or a PNN combination. Rules (1) and (3) in turn contain NP as a subpart. What justification is there for ascribing such a superordinate constituent as NP to Adam? Could we not instead write several separate rules—one for N, one for PN, one for NN and one for PNN? Doing so would account for the same combinations of grammatical classes in Table 3, but would avoid claiming that Adam was acquainted with the abstract sentence constituent NP. However, there are several lines of evidence pointing toward the "reality" of NP in Adam's grammar, and hence supporting such definitions of NP as Rule (2).

Consider, first of all, some distributional facts. One is that single nouns and developed noun phrases appear in the same environments in children's speech (Brown and Bellugi, 1964). For example,

Positions for Single N

that (flower)
where (ball) go?
Adam write (penguin)
(horsie) stop
put (hat) on

Positions for NP

that (a blue flower)
where (the puzzle) go?
doggie eat (the breakfast)
(a horsie) crying
put (the red hat) on

Apparently, wherever N can go NP can go, presumably because individual Ns are actually NPs.

Another bit of evidence is that pauses in children's speech usually bracket NPs, not Ns. "Put . . . the red hat . . . on" is a likely occurrence, whereas "put the red . . . hat . . . on" is not. Insofar as pauses reflect points of decision in speech (Goldman-Eisler, 1961), such utterances indicate that decisions are made in terms of NP and not N.

Finally, consider the fact that the pronoun *it* is really a pro-noun phrase, since it replaces NP and not N. This is the case in the English of adults, and it is also the case in the English of children, as the following pairs reveal:

Mommy get *ladder*	Mommy get *it*
Mommy get *my ladder*	Mommy get *it*

Adam sometimes combined both the pronoun and the NP the pronoun should have replaced in a single utterance, as in *Mommy get it ladder* and *Mommy get it my ladder*. That NP and N are treated alike, even in this case of deviation from adult English, is further evidence that NP is a genuine constituent.

There are, then, grounds for assuming that NP is a superordinate constituent in children's early grammars. Except for sentences like . . . *get it my ladder*, which were peculiar to Adam, all children provide evidence of the sort summarized above; NPs appear in the life of a child even before measles do.

Rules (1), (2), and (3) describe Adam's sentences when he was 28 months old. At this point, his sentences were slightly less than two morphemes long on the average. Nine months later Adam's sentences have increased only slightly in length—to nearly three morphemes on the average—but his grammar has been much elaborated. Instead of three phrase-structural rules, the grammar now contains 14; instead of there being no transformational rules, the grammar now has two dozen. Table 4 presents the entire phrase-structural component and two rules from the transformational component of the grammar written for Adam's speech at 36 months. The sentences generated by this grammar are like those listed at the beginning of this section, all of which are taken from Adam's protocols at 35 and 38 months.

Table 4. Part of the Grammar of a Child Thirty-Six Months Old

Complete-phrase structure rules

1. $S \rightarrow [(\begin{Bmatrix} Imp \\ Wh \end{Bmatrix})]$ (Neg) Nominal—Predicate

2. Predicate $\rightarrow \begin{Bmatrix} MV \\ Cop \end{Bmatrix}$

3. MV $\rightarrow$ Vb (Comp)

4. Vb $\rightarrow$ (Aux) V (Prt)

5. Aux $\rightarrow \begin{Bmatrix} V^c \\ B + ing \\ Past \end{Bmatrix}$

6. Comp $\rightarrow \begin{Bmatrix} Adverb \\ Nominal \, (Adverb) \end{Bmatrix}$

7. Cop $\rightarrow$ B—Pred

8. B $\rightarrow \begin{Bmatrix} be \\ \beta \end{Bmatrix}$

9. Pred $\rightarrow \begin{Bmatrix} Det \\ Nominal \\ Adverb \end{Bmatrix}$

10. Adverb $\rightarrow \begin{Bmatrix} Locative \\ Adv \\ Prep \, Phrase \end{Bmatrix}$

11. Locative $\rightarrow \begin{Bmatrix} somewhere \\ Adv \\ Prep \, Phrase \end{Bmatrix}$

12. Prep Phrase $\rightarrow$ Preposition $\begin{Bmatrix} Nominal \\ Adv \end{Bmatrix}$

13. Nominal $\rightarrow$ some $\begin{Bmatrix} (one) \\ (thing) \end{Bmatrix}$

14. NP $\rightarrow$ (Det) N

Two transformation rules

T1. Wh incorporation for main-verb sentences

Wh Nominal Verb (Nominal) − some $\triangle \rightarrow$ Wh + some $\triangle$ − Nominal Verb (Nominal)

T2. Affixation of *Past*

X − Past − V − X $\rightarrow$ X − V + Past X

Modified version of two tables in Brown, et al. (1968).

The easiest way to convey an idea of how such sentences are described by the grammar in Table 4 is to provide a few examples; this is done in Figs. 1 to 4. Before considering

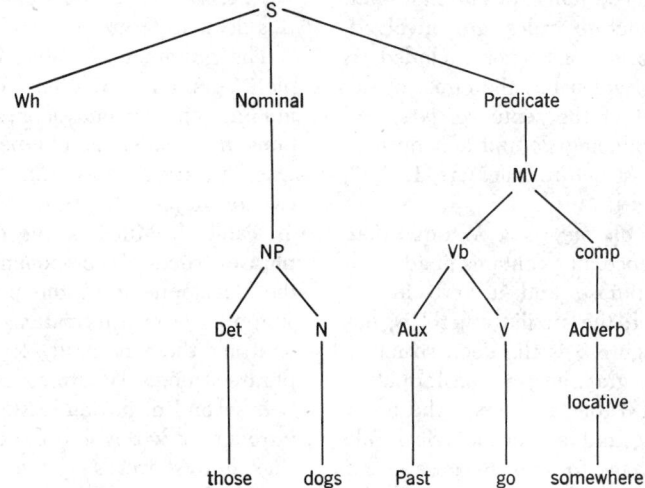

Fig. 1. Deep structure of *where those dogs goed?* (from Brown, et al., 1968).

them, however, it is necessary to introduce certain notational conventions.

Imp and *Wh* are grammatical markers, representing in the first case imperative sentences and in the second case such questions as *what*, *where*, and *who*. *Neg* stands for negation, *MV* for main verb, and *Cop* for copula (e.g., *is* in *the dog is an animal*). V^c is a "catenative" verb—*wanna*, *gonna*, and *hafta*. *Adverb* is a sentence constituent, like NP, whereas *Adv* is the grammatical category of adverbs proper. Because Adam sometimes produced sentences of the form *that my book* and sometimes of the form *that's my book*, a distinction is drawn between *be* and *β*; *be* is a variant of the auxiliary verb, *to be*; *β* represents the same syntactic function but is never expressed in the superficial form of a sentence. *Det* stands for "determiner," a category including such words as *the, a, that, this, these*, and *those*. *Prt* stands for "particle"—the *up* in *look up*, and the *down* in *put down*. The symbol *some* △ in the first transformational rule covers both *somewhere* (from phrase-structure rule 11) and *something* (from phrase-structure rule 13), both of which are grammatical markers, not words. The remaining symbols are defined by the grammar itself.

Consider now some of the sentences the grammar in Table 4 yields. The particular examples are *where those dogs goed, don't throw that ball, who jumping on me*, and *Susan is in the bath*. Four sentences, of course, do not exhaust the variety of grammatical forms

that Adam produced, but together they illustrate the workings of much of his grammar.

Figure 1 shows the deep structure of *where those dogs goed*, a well-formed question for Adam (from Brown et al., 1968). Of the 14 phrase-structure rules in Table 4, 10 are used to generate this phrase marker (rules 1, 2, 3, 4, 5, 6, 10, 11, 13, and 14); the two transformations listed at the bottom of the table relate the phrase marker to the surface structure of the sentence.

Figure 2 shows the deep structure of an

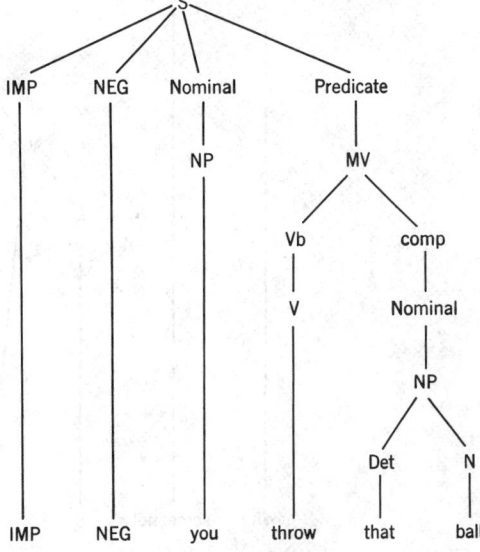

Fig. 2. Deep structure of *don't throw that ball*.

imperative sentence, *don't throw that ball.* Seven phrase-structure rules are involved, plus two transformations (not included in Table 4), one of which has the effect of deleting the subject of the sentence, *you,* and the other of introducing *do* and affixing it to *Neg.* The phrase-structure rules are 1, 2, 3, 4, 6, 13, and 14.

Who jumping on me, is a Wh-question, like the first sentence, but contains in addition a prepositional phrase and a verb in the progressive aspect; the auxiliary verb, *is,* has been omitted. Figure 3 is the deep structure generated by the grammar; a transformation parallel to T2 in Table 4 reverses the order of *ing* and *jump,* and a morphological rule changes *Wh-someone* to *who.* Because β and not *be* is the form of the auxiliary verb, the surface structure omits an auxiliary.

A final example is diagrammed in Fig. 4— the deep structure of *Susan is in the bath.* In this case, *be* is part of a copular not an auxiliary verb, so the affix-verb transformation required for *who jumping on me* does not apply. Phrase-structural rules 1, 2, 7, 8, 9,

10, 11, 12, 13, and 14 are used to generate this deep structure.

The grammar in Table 4 is not the complete grammar written for Adam at 36 months, and its omissions create two distortions the reader should be warned against. One distortion arises from the fact that only two of Adam's transformations are included in Table 4. Much of the complexity in the phrase-structural component, particularly in the development of the predicate, exists to support the transformations not in the table; omitting them naturally leaves a number of phrase-structural features undemonstrated.

A second distortion exists in the manner of introducing words into the deep structure. In Figs. 1 to 4 words—*Susan, on, jump,* etc.— are simply appended to the bottom of the phrase marker. Their relation to the remaining structure of the sentence is left unanalyzed. However, the grammar developed for Adam by Brown et al. goes farther. Each word in Adam's lexicon is represented as a set of syntactic features. The features state, in effect, the contexts each word can occupy,

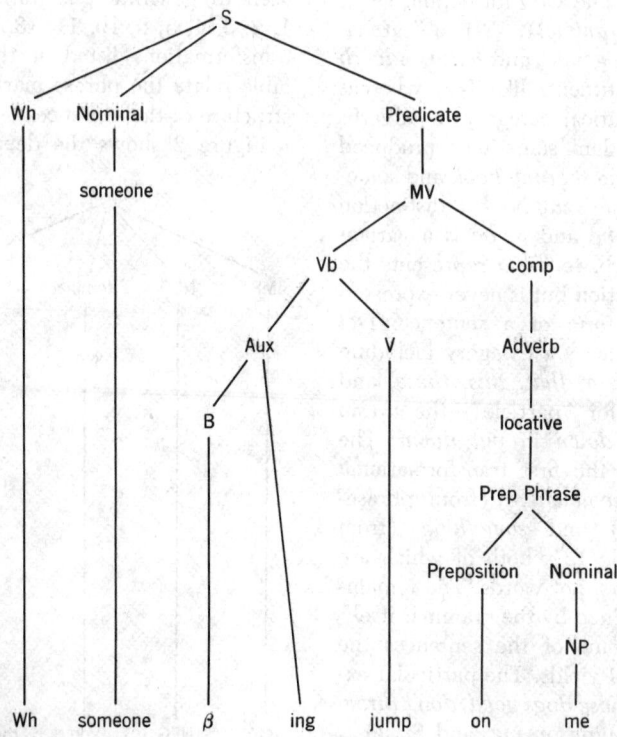

Fig. 3. Deep structure of *who jumping on me?*

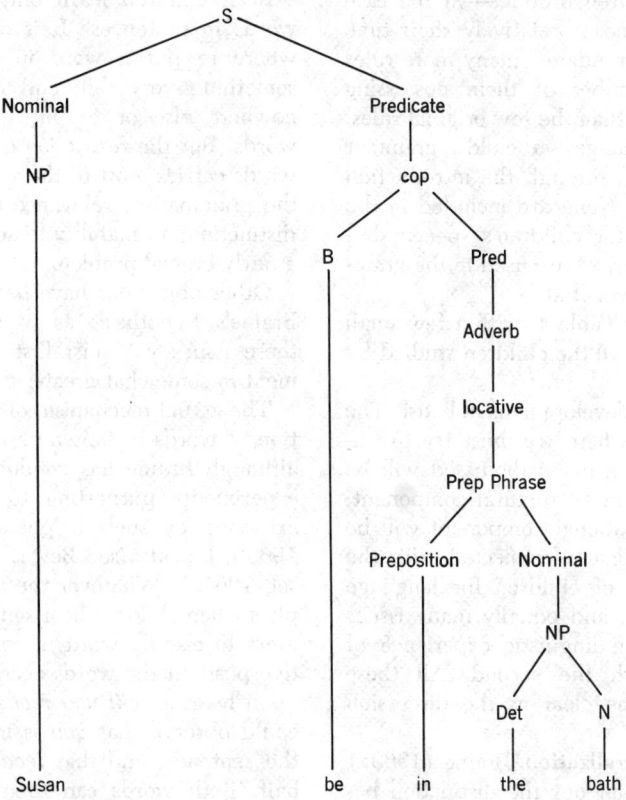

Fig. 4. Deep structure of *Susan is in the bath.*

plus the characteristics of each word as a context for other words. This can be done quite compactly. Take *dog*, for example. For Adam at 36 months, *dog* was a count noun, it could be pluralized, and it could follow determiners. The last feature states a context for *dog*, whereas the first two features state characteristics of *dog* when it is the context of something else. In formal notation, these properties of *dog* can be collected in the form of a lexical entry as follows:

$$\begin{bmatrix} + \text{N} \\ [+ \text{Det}\underline{\quad}] \\ + \text{ct} \\ \pm \text{no} \end{bmatrix} \; dog$$

The + N at the top signifies that *dog* belongs to the category of nouns. The + ct indicates that *dog* belongs to the subcategory of count nouns—that it is a word like *table, man,* and *idea* and unlike *sand, mush,* and *justice. The* ± *no* indicates that *dog* belongs to the subcategory of nouns that can be either singular

or plural, and so is unlike such words as *pants, imagination,* and *John.* Finally, the [+ Det—] means that *dog* can follow determiners.

A rule of the grammar governs the insertion of words into phrase markers by requiring that all such phrase markers present the features specified in the word's lexical entry. Fig. 1, for example, can receive *dog*—there is a slot of the right kind; this is also true for Figs. 2 and 4. But Fig. 3 has no place for *dog* or any other noun, for it accepts only pronouns in the two "nominal" positions.

When a lexicon is completely specified, it is possible to play items off against each other when inserting words into phrase markers. In this way the grammar can avoid describing bizarre combinations—such nonsentences as *Where is in the dog.*

We have sketched briefly the development of the phrase-structural component of child grammar. We have seen that only a few rules are needed in the early stages to summarize the sentences children produce—in the case of Adam, only three. A relatively short time later—9 months for Adam—many more rules are needed, a number of them possessing greater complexity than the few original rules.

Beside these changes, a child's grammar becomes elaborated through the introduction of transformations. None are included in the earliest grammars for children's speech; but 6 to 12 months later, 24 are used in the grammar written by Brown et al.

The grammar in Table 4, with a few small changes, serves for all the children studied by Brown, et al.

What do such developments tell us? The point has arrived where we must try to understand them. First to be discussed will be the rules of the phrase-structural component; then the transformational component will be considered. Many issues connected with the innate endowment of children for language arise with the first, and equally many issues connected with the linguistic experience of children arise with the second. All these matters will become clear as the discussion proceeds.

Contextual Generalization. Braine (1963a) was the first to point out the distinction between pivot and open classes, and we shall begin with his account of the distinction and the view of language acquisition it entails.

Pivot words are so called because to Braine they are the only words for which a child knows the proper temporal location in a sentence—that they occur first, last, etc. Open words are used wherever pivot words are not, which means that in two-word sentences the positions of both pivot and open words are locked in place.

Various characteristics of the pivot-open distinction neatly follow from this simple account. Because at first a child knows the location of few words, pivot words are used with high frequency, and the class itself has few members. The pivot class increases in membership more slowly than the open class, presumably because it is more difficult to learn the positions of words than it is to learn new vocabulary regardless of position.

The main characteristic of the pivot-open distinction not accounted for by Braine's theory is the restriction on the use of pivot words—that they rarely appear alone or with other pivots. Why should such a restriction exist if children learn only the positions of words in sentences? It is one thing to learn where to put a word in a sentence. It is something very different to learn to put it nowhere else or to put it only with open words. But the restriction on the use of pivot words carries most of the weight in justifying the grammatical relevance of the pivot-open distinction; an inability to account for it poses a fairly crucial problem.

Other objections have been leveled against Braine's hypothesis as well, but to present these issues we must first go into his argument in somewhat greater detail.

The actual mechanism of learning the position of words in sentences is left unspecified, although Braine has conducted a number of experiments purporting to demonstrate the existence of such a phenomenon (Braine, 1963b; but also see Bever, Fodor, and Weksel, 1965a). Whatever the mechanism, it applies when children hear sentences and causes them to classify words according to the relative position the words occupy. For example, upon hearing *will you read it to me?* a child could observe that *you* is in the first half of the sentence, and that *read* is in the second half. Both words can then be so classified. Contextual generalization—the process by which this theory is generally known—carries *you* and *read* into new, analogous contexts.

Contextual generalization is not essentially different from ordinary stimulus or response generalization, except that it takes place across temporal positions. Its merit in the present context is that it serves to explain linguistic productivity. Having learned that *you* comes first in some sentences, contextual generalization places it first in other sentences. From *you read,* a child can produce *you come, you want, you sit, you bad,* and even *you all.* In short, *you* has become a pivot.

Two-word sentences grow to three-word sentences and beyond because a child observes the *relative* position of words. Having learned that *you* appears in the first half of some phrases, a child can later discover that these phrases appear in the first half of other more encompassing phrases. A child might learn, for example, that *you* is first in the phrase *you should,* and that this phrase is first in the sentence *you should come.* Contextual generalization again provides flexibility and the child can produce *you can come, you should read,* etc.

More important than an increase in length gained this way, there is also an increase in structural complexity. By learning that a word is first in a phrase, and that a phrase is first in a sentence, a child learns that sentences are hierarchically organized. It is ((*you should*) *come*). Thus positional learning, extended through contextual generalization, leads to the kind of sentence structure conventionally represented by a phrase-structural grammar. It is on this point that a rather loud dispute over Braine's theory has arisen.

The difficulty is that the order and arrangement of words in the surface structure of sentences is not necessarily the same as the order and arrangement of elements in the underlying structure (Bever, Fodor, and Weksel, 1965a, 1965b). Although it is only the underlying structure that contains information represented as a phrase-structure grammar, it is only the surface structure that is available for positional learning. The correct bracketing of the sentence above is (*you* (*should come*)). There is no guarantee that positional learning would arrive at this structure and not ((*you should*) *come*).

There is a dilemma here. The solution adopted by Braine (1965) is to restrict positional learning to simple declarative sentences, where the order of elements in the underlying and superficial structure is more or less the same. But this is to beg the question of syntactic learning. The cases where underlying and superficial structure are the same are among the things that a child must learn in acquiring language. The only way to avoid this difficulty, equally adopted by Braine (1965), is to change the syntactic analysis of sentences, by construing them all as having the same underlying and superficial structures. But this is to avoid the problem of language acquisition altogether (McNeill, 1968a). It is instead to do a novel kind of linguistics, asking what kind of language *could* be acquired through positional learning. Thus when faced with the alternatives of either begging the question of learning a transformational grammar or being irrelevant to it, it is evident that Braine's theory fails in a fundamental way to explain the acquisition of such grammatical systems.

There is a further difficulty. Braine (1963, 1965) considers transformations to be "sublanguages," each a specific way of deforming simple declarative sentences. Passive sentences, negative sentences, and the like, result. However, the resemblance of a sublanguage to a grammatical transformation is entirely superficial, dealing only with the manifest form of sentences. Whereas a transformation in linguistic theory is a relation between a deep and surface structure, a sublanguage is a relation between two surface structures. The difference between these views is discussed by Braine (1965) and Bever et al. (1965a, 1965b; see also McNeill, 1968a, and Weksel, 1965).

If positional learning is not the way children develop knowledge of syntax, what then are we to make of the pivot-open distinction? Is it learned positionally, as Braine argues, only to lead nowhere—a syntactic cul-de-sac? If it is a cul-de-sac, it is one fallen into by virtually all children (according to Slobin, in press, a pivot-open distinction appears in the early stages of learning Russian, Bulgarian, Serbian, French, German, as well as English). This is a possibility. But there is another fact about these early grammatical classes, which suggests they are directly related to later syntactic development, at least for some children.

Differentiation and Generic Classification. Adam, one of Brown and Bellugi's (1964) subjects, developed the grammatical classes of adult English through differentiation. The class differentiated was a pivot class, the same one reproduced in Table 2, and the classes developed from it were articles, demonstrative pronouns, possessive pronouns, adjectives, and determiners. The entire process took place in 5 months, and followed the sequence diagrammed in Fig. 5.

Each step in Fig. 5 is the result of differentiating the pivot class then existing into one or more adult classes plus a new residual pivot class. The essential aspect of such differentiation is that entire adult classes are removed from an ancestral pivot class in one step—separate words do not straggle out at different times.

Zhenya, the son of the Russian linguist Gvozdev (1961), developed a pivot class equivalent to Adam's and formed adult grammatical categories through a comparable process of differentiation.

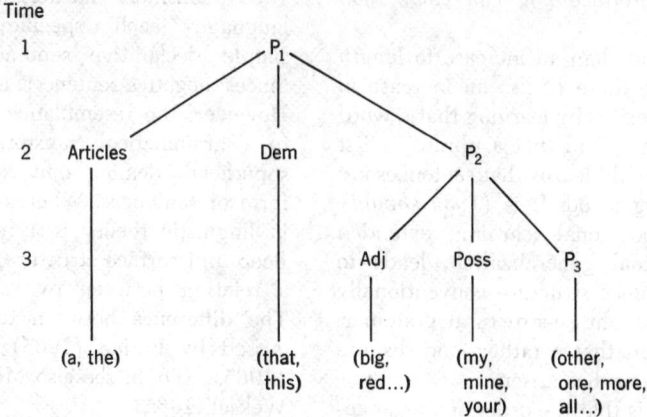

Fig. 5. Differentiation of one child's pivot class (McNeill, 1966a).

It is the phenomenon of differentiation that suggests a direct relation between the pivot-open distinction and later syntactic developments. For differentiation can take place only if the classes differentiated—the pivot class in Adam's case—are *generically appropriate* (McNeill, 1966a).

A generically appropriate pivot class is one that ignores but potentially admits all the relevant distinctions of the adult grammar. Adam, for example, had the two articles in his pivot class at Time 1; he did not have one in the pivot class and one in the open class. Similarly, every adjective then in Adam's vocabulary was in the pivot class; there were none in the open class. In fact, Adam's pivot class contained every available member of several adult grammatical classes, even though none of these classes were themselves recognized in Adam's grammar.

Differentiation always presupposes generic classification—a fact not usually recognized. But generic classification is puzzling. For it means that children classify words (as pivot and open) in a way consistent with more subtle distinctions they are *yet* to draw, when differentiation takes place in the future. What guides children in such apparent teleology? The answer is by no means obvious or settled. Even to consider it, we must cover many of the recent observations made of children learning language.

Linguistic Capacities, Linguistic Universals, and the Problem of Abstraction. According to one traditional view, language is a systematic relation between expression and content (see Appendix). In a transformational grammar such a view is embodied in the distinction between deep and surface structure: the deep structure of a sentence is associated with meaning and the surface structure with sound; deep and surface structures are in general different from each other but stand in a specific relation, which is explicitly described for every possible sentence by the transformations of the language.

One inherent aspect of each sentence therefore is the existence of an abstract deep structure. It is the phenomenon of abstraction, which all children face and overcome, that eliminates stimulus-response theory as a possible explanation of language acquisition. The difficulties with Braine's theory, discussed previously, derive from its commitment to this more general difficulty. The issues have been discussed in many places (Chomsky, 1959; 1965; Katz, 1966; Bever et al., 1965a, 1965b; McNeill 1966a, 1968a), as well as in the Appendix of this chapter, and need not be repeated here.

The phenomenon of linguistic abstraction presents a major theoretical challenge in the explanation of language acquisition. Fluent speakers somehow gain knowledge of the deep structure of sentences. They do so even though they never encounter such information in the form of examples, stimuli, or anything else. Moreover, children make use of information organized as deep structure very early in the acquisition of language. From the first moment of speech, indeed, children have the ability to communicate meaning, and do so in a manner understandable to adults. It is easy to overlook what an astonishing fact this is. But it seems to mean that the most abstract part of language, its propositional content, is the first to develop. Children present evidence of employing something related to the deep structure of sentences *before* grammar is acquired.

Let us put the problem in a semiformal way, to help clarify some of the issues involved. Consider the "language acquisition device" discussed by Chomsky (1957, 1965), which we can call LAD for short (alternatively, a language acquisition system, or LAS —the feminine form). LAD receives a certain corpus of utterances. Some of these utterances are grammatical sentences in the language to which LAD is exposed; but besides grammatical sentences, the corpus also contains blunders, false starts, interruptions, and a certain amount of nonsense. The corpus may be large, but it is not unlimited in size. Assume that it contains the number of utterances overheard by a typical 2-year-old child.

Given such a corpus, LAD is so constructed that it can develop a theory of the regularities that underlie the speech to which it has been exposed. It can exclude the nongrammaticality in the corpus by constructing a theory about the regularities of the language. This theory is LAD's grammatical competence, its knowledge of the language behind the corpus. After developing such a grammatical theory, LAD becomes able to go far beyond the corpus with which it began. LAD can distinguish the infinitely many grammatical sentences in its language from the infinitely many nongrammatical alternatives, and it can judge how far from full grammaticality each of the latter deviates. The situation may be diagrammed as follows:

Corpus → | LAD | → **Grammatical Competence**

Clearly, the problem of understanding how LAD develops grammatical competence given a corpus requires understanding the internal structure of the box labeled LAD.

It seems useful to distinguish two major components of LAD. One is a set of *procedures* for operating on a corpus—for example, conducting a distributional analysis, or looking for transformations of certain kinds. The other is a body of *linguistic information*—for example, that all sentences include noun and verb phrases, or that there *are* sentences, for that matter. It is conceivable that LAD is limited to just one of these components. LAD might contain a set of procedures for discovering a grammar or it might contain a set of assumptions about the form of grammar (McNeill, 1966b), or, of course, it might contain both (Fodor, 1966).

Whatever LAD contains, however, must be universally applicable. For LAD must be able to acquire any language; it cannot be biased toward some languages and away from others for reasons of internal structure. Thus LAD may contain information and procedures bearing on the general form of language but presumably contains nothing bearing on the form of any particular language to the exclusion of others. The following remarks are directed to the possibility that LAD contains universal linguistic information; almost nothing has been written on the possibility that LAD contains universal procedures of analysis.

The description of linguistic universals has already been alluded to. The theory of grammar—as opposed to the grammar of a single language—is a description of the general form of natural language (Chomsky, 1965; Katz, 1966). Its purpose is to state the conditions that grammars describing individual languages must meet. For example, grammars must all be transformational, and the base component must include rules stating the relations that hold among such syntactic categories as NP and N. When the grammar of a particular language represents the linguistic knowledge of the speakers of the language, and also conforms to the theory of grammar, one can claim to have *explained* the grammar of the language (Chomsky, 1965).

The argument becomes clear if we carry it a step further. Let us take the theory of grammar to be a description of LAD's internal structure. Whatever comprises the structure of LAD, is (or will be) described in the theory of grammar. The output of LAD— competence in a language—would then be explained by reference to the theory of grammar. A language has the particular grammar it does because the universal principles embodied in linguistic theory constrain the grammar that accounts for the corpus of sentences LAD has received. We thus have a hypothesis about the internal structure of LAD: it is described in the theory of grammar. It is an empirical question whether or not LAD can be so described.

LAD, of course, is a fiction. Our purpose in considering it is not to design an actual machine. On the contrary, our purpose is to isolate crucial aspects in the acquisition of language by real children, not by abstract ones. The purpose is served because LAD and children present the same problem.

LAD is faced with a corpus of utterances, some of them grammatical sentences and some not. So are children. From such a corpus, LAD develops a grammar on the basis of some kind of internal structure. So do children. Since children and LAD arrive at precisely the same grammar from precisely the same corpus, children and LAD must have precisely the same internal structure, at least within the limits that different children may be said to have the same structure. Accordingly, a hypothesis about LAD is *ipso facto* a hypothesis about children.

The proposed relation between the theory of grammar and children's innate linguistic capacities is simple and straightforward (e.g., McNeill, 1966b). Languages have all necessarily evolved to correspond to children's capacities. No language can evolve to be unlearnable. Because children automatically impose those features of language that reflect their capacities, such features appear universally. The theory of grammar thus becomes possible.

What are the universals mentioned in the theory of grammar, which we now presume to be a reflection of children's innate capacities? Some are phonological. Every language, for example, employs consonant and vowel types, syllabic structure, and not more than 15 distinctive features (Jakobson and Halle, 1956; Halle, 1964a). Other universals may be semantic—universals that are essentially constraints on possible concepts, on what is thinkable (Katz, 1966)—a fascinating possibility, which unfortunately cannot be discussed in these pages.

In the case of syntax, some universals describe characteristics of the deep structure of sentences (Chomsky, 1965). Every language utilizes the same basic syntactic categories, arranged in the same way—such categories as sentences, noun phrases, verb phrases. Every

language utilizes the same basic grammatical relations among these categories—such relations as subject and predicate of a sentence, verb and object of a verb phrase and modification within a noun phrase. Every language can recursively include sentences within sentences. And every language distinguishes deep and surface structure, and so is transformational.

The transformations of a language are mostly, though not exclusively idiosyncratic. However, the *types* of relation that exist between deep and surface structure are universal. For example, English relates the underlying and surface structure of auxiliary verbs by permuting the order of verbs and affixes (see Appendix). This transformation appears in English and French (Ruwet, 1966), and possibly elsewhere, but is not universal. However, the relation of permutation is universal. The transformational idiosyncrasy of each language arises from the way in which a few universal transformational types, such as permutation, are exploited.

We can put these several considerations from linguistic theory together into a hypothesis about language acquisition (McNeill, 1966b). Much of the deep structure of sentences is described by various syntactic universals; most transformations are idiosyncratic uses of universal types of relation. Making the assumption that such linguistic universals exist because of innate abilities, we can say that the abstractions of the deep structure are those universal categories and relations that reflect children's innate capacities, and they are *made* abstract when children discover the transformations of their language.

A language is thus acquired through discovering the relations that exist between the surface structure of its sentences and the universal aspects of the deep structure, the latter being a manifestation of children's own capacities. The interaction between children's innate capacities and their linguistic experience occurs at this point, in the acquisition of transformations—and it is here that parental speech must make its contribution. (A similar argument is given by Schlesinger, in press.)

Predication and the Basic Grammatical Relations. If a language is acquired through discovering the transformations that relate surface structures to the universal aspects of the deep structure of sentences, then these universal aspects must be present in children's earliest speech; at least, they must logically be present before the transformations that depend on them are acquired. An aspect of children's capacities will not appear until it has "matured," but everything in earliest speech that is not transformational should reflect an aspect of children's capacities. The early linguistic constructions of children should therefore be the universal parts of the deep structure of sentences but, in effect, pronounced directly. It is for this reason that children are able to express meaning from the onset of language acquisition.

Recall the phenomenon of holophrastic speech. Such speech consists of single-word utterances that have the conceptual content of full sentences. De Laguna (1927) argued that holophrastic utterances have such content because they are comments on aspects of the situation in which the speech occurs. If we accept de Laguna's argument, the phenomenon of holophrastic speech can be seen as the most primitive manifestation of a basic grammatical relation, predication, and therefore as a very early appearance of what ultimately becomes part of the deep structure of sentences. Children's speech is understandable by adults even in its most primitive form because it makes use of predication, and predication is a fundamental aspect of the deep structure of sentences.

De Laguna believed that two-word sentences emerge when children label the topics of their comments. She was interested in this step because it liberates the interpretability of child speech from an extreme dependence on nonlinguistic context. She was little concerned with the extension of grammar beyond that. Nevertheless it is clear that her views encompass the early phases of patterned speech in general.

The basic grammatical relations correspond to the traditional grammatical functions of subject, predicate, verb, object, modifier, and head. Such relations hold among the syntactic categories of the deep structure; they are universal; and they are honored in the early speech of children.

Table 3, presented in the preceding section, contained every combination of Adam's grammatical classes observed in his speech at 28 months. It was remarked at that point that the combinations of grammatical classes observed in Adam's speech possess a certain consistency that the combinations not observed in his speech lack. We can now see what the consistency is.

The combinations in Table 3 are the patterns of Adam's grammatical classes that result from a mechanical application of the definitions of the basic grammatical relations as contained in linguistic theory (McNeill, 1966a). A predicate, for example, is defined in linguistic theory as a VP directly dominated by S. For Adam, the following combinations are consistent with this definition: VN, NV, VNN, VPN, NVN, NNV, and NPN (the last assuming an absent V—the sentence was *Adam two boot*). The other relations can be defined in a similar way. A subject is an NP immediately dominated by S; a main verb is a V immediately dominated by VP; an object of a verb is an NP immediately dominated by VP; a modifier is a determiner (Det) immediately dominated by NP; and a "head" is an N immediately dominated by NP. Opposite each combination in Table 3 are listed the basic grammatical relations with which it could be consistent. As the reader can see, every combination of grammatical classes Adam did produce is consistent with at least one basic grammatical relation, and most of the combinations Adam did not produce are not consistent with any basic grammatical relation (Kelley, 1967, points out that two combinations, consistent with the basic grammatical relations, did not occur in Adam's speech). With three grammatical classes, there are $(3)^2 = 9$ different patterns two-words long and $(3)^3 = 27$ different patterns three-words long. Five of the two-word patterns and 17 of the three-word patterns do not correspond to the basic grammatical relations; none of them occurred in the sample of utterances collected from Adam at 28 months.

One explanation of Table 3 therefore is that Adam organized utterances in terms of the basic grammatical relations, but he had not yet acquired any of the transformations in English that combine structures or add elements—for example, conjunctions, complements, or embeddings. It is for this reason that patterns such as VVN did not occur in his speech, even though such sentences correspond to common surface structures in the speech of adults—for example, *come and eat lunch*. Indeed, many of the patterns excluded from Adam's speech correspond to patterns available in the surface structure of adult sentences.

We can relate Table 3 to de Laguna's argument about predication. If we search Table 3 for patterns that could express predication, we find that in one way or another every pattern except PN (*another ball*) and PNN (*big Daddy book*) could do so (and even some of these sentences probably are predicative—*that Becky*, for example, or *that Becky ball*). In terms of frequency of occurrence, between 70 and 90% of Adam's utterances express predication (the lower figure excludes all potential modificational combinations, the higher figure includes them). If predication is a primitive form of semantic organization, as de Laguna claimed, most early utterances of children should express it, and such is the case with Adam. In contrast, only four patterns (PN, NN, NNN, and PNN in Table 3) could conceivably be subjects without predicates. All other instances of NP occur in the context of the object or predicate relations.

If now we look in Table 3 for patterns that could be predicates with subjects and patterns that could be predicates without subjects, we find a preponderance of the latter. The patterns that correspond to predicates without subjects are VN (*change diaper*), VPN (*hit my ball*), and VNN (*read Cromer paper*)— none of which was judged to be imperative; there were 194 such utterances at 28 months. The patterns that correspond to predicates with subjects are NN (*Joshua home*—meaning "Joshua is at home"), NV (*daddy go?*), NPN (*Adam two boot*), PNV (*another doggie run*), NNV (*Adam mommy stand*), NVN (*Adam change diaper*), and possibly NNN (*Adam mommy pencil*); there were 178 such utterances at 28 months.

Even though there is a greater variety of predicates with subjects, there is more frequent use of predicates without subjects. The divergence becomes more pronounced when we look for the single most frequent two- and three-word patterns. In both cases they are predicates without subjects—VN and VNN— and they are more frequent by a large margin (Table 3). Such a relation with frequency would result if the sentences with subjects were all recent acquisitions and the sentences

without subjects had existed in Adam's repertoire for some time. Gruber (1967) draws a similar conclusion for the speech of another child. There is therefore some support for de Laguna's contention that children first produce isolated predicates and later add subjects.

Predication, however, is not the only relation evident in the speech of children at this early stage. In addition, children express direct and indirect objects, modification, and possibly other relations. Among Adam's utterances, for example, were *see truck, write paper,* and *dirty paper*—a direct object, an indirect object, and a modificational construction, respectively. He also uttered apparent possessives—for example, *Adam hat*—which is a variety of modification, according to recent views (Chomsky, 1967).

All these examples manifest different grammatical relations, and a question arises concerning their origin. It is impossible to say from Adam's evidence whether or not these relations had equal tenure in his grammar at 28 months. All four conceivably existed at the holophrastic stage. But it is equally possible that originally Adam's utterances expressed only predication, to which was first added modification (including possessives), then direct objects of verbs, then subjects, and finally indirect objects of verbs—this being the order of the frequency of these relations in Adam's speech at 28 months.

Whatever the order of emergence of such relations, however, it is difficult to imagine that they were, in any sense, discovered by Adam. For example, Adam apparently expressed the object of a preposition before he included prepositions in his speech, as in *write paper* and several other examples. It is difficult to see how he could have discovered such a relation from surface structures without also discovering the preposition: the preposition is the only feature on the surface that identifies the relation. It seems rather that Adam used the different basic grammatical relations, as they became available, to organize his other linguistic experiences—for example, acquisition of such prepositional phrases as *write on the paper*.

Other children also manifest these relations. A child studied by Gruber (1967) has already been mentioned. The two other children followed by Brown and his collaborators give parallel evidence. Perhaps more striking is the appearance of these relations in the speech of children exposed to other languages. Evidence for Japanese children has been discussed by McNeill (1966b). Slobin (in press) has reviewed a number of diary studies and found evidence for the early emergence of the basic grammatical relations in Russian, Serbian, French, German, Georgian, Italian, and Bulgarian.

Intrinsic and Extrinsic Predication.[2] Adam's sentences without subjects at 28 months often made reference to himself as the omitted but implied subject. *Change diaper* meant that Adam wanted to change his diaper; *hit my ball* meant that Adam was claiming this act for himself; *read Cromer paper* described something that Adam was doing. His sentences with subjects, on the other hand, almost always had an NP other than *Adam* or *I* as the subject—*Joshua, daddy, another doggie,* etc.

The pattern of omitting *Adam* and *I* from the subject position of sentences reflects a distinction between two types of predicative relation available to children, between what we may call *intrinsic* and *extrinsic* predication. The distinction is widespread. It appears as a conditioning factor for the presence of subjects in children's sentences; it appears as a permanent distinction in the Negro dialect of English (as between *he working* and *he be working;* Labov, Cohen, and Robins, 1965); and it controls two transformations in Japanese.

Adult speakers tend to omit the subjects of sentences when it is clear that the subject will be understood by a listener. To use Vygotsky's (1962) example, one would not say "the bus for which we have been waiting so long is here at last"; one would simply say "at last." Adam apparently believed that sentences involving himself as the subject were clear in this sense, whereas sentences containing other NPs were not.

How did he arrive at such a conclusion? The egocentrism of young children comes to mind as a possible explanation, but in fact it does not provide an answer. For if Adam was egocentric in the sense of Piaget (1926), we must wonder why he ever included subjects in sentences; all subjects would appear to

2 The discussion in this section has been developed jointly with Nobuko B. McNeill.

be "understood" to an egocentric mind. Egocentrism plays a role in Adam's speech, but it is secondary to the more fundamental role of intrinsic and extrinsic predication.

Let us turn to the acquisition of Japanese. It is here that the distinction between extrinsic and intrinsic predication is most clearly revealed; then we can return to the acquisition of English.

Japanese, like many languages, uses postpositions. Two of them are reserved for marking the superficial manifestation of the subject of a sentence. The two postpositions have nearly identical distributions in the surface structure of sentences, in that they can replace one another, but they have different implications for the underlying structure. One postposition, *wa*, is used when the relation between the subject and predicate of a sentence is of an intrinsic type; the other, *ga*, is used when this relation is of an extrinsic type.

The distinction between intrinsic and extrinsic predication may be cognitive in origin (and thus fall in the domain of "cognition and language"), and all languages may therefore exploit it, although in different ways. In Japanese the two types of predication resolve themselves into a distinction between the subject (*ga*) and topic (*wa*) of sentences; this distinction is a special syntactic point and need not concern us here.

Sentences requiring the postposition *wa* in Japanese have predicates that state an intrinsic property of the subject. It is felt intrinsicalness that counts; no difficult ontological insights are required of a Japanese speaker. Habitual activities, for example, are regarded as intrinsic—*daddy works in an office.* So is attribution—*government architecture is grotesque;* membership in a hierarchy—*a collie is a dog;* definition—*that is a collie;* and various truisms such as *all men are mortal.*

Sentences with *ga* have predicates that state extrinsic properties of the subject. Such sentences often take the form of momentary description—*there is a dog in the yard* (when this is not customary). As with an intrinsic predicate, the information contained in an extrinsic predicate is asserted about a subject; but unlike an intrinsic predicate such information is not felt to be an inherent part of the subject.

How are *wa* and *ga* acquired? Both postpositions are introduced into the surface structure of sentences by transformations (Kuroda, 1965) and at first do not appear in the speech of children. At 28 months or so (in the children studied by McNeill, 1966b), *ga* first comes to be used, although not frequently. When used, however, it is used appropriately —always with extrinsic predicates. About 6 months later *wa* first appears, and it too is always used appropriately—with intrinsic predicates. Thus extrinsic predication appears to develop before intrinsic predication.

However, we have only half the story, and the second half reverses the interpretation of the first. It is possible for a native speaker of Japanese to classify children's utterances containing neither *wa* nor *ga* according to the postposition required. McNeill (1968b) found that approximately 90% of Japanese children's sentences are sufficiently clear to be so classified. The results of this procedure are clear: the great majority of children's early sentences consist of intrinsic predicates. Although *ga* is the first postposition to be included in child speech, *wa* is the postposition most often called for.

We have what appears to be a paradox. On the evidence of the postposition first acquired, extrinsic predication is dominant; but on the evidence provided by direct judgments of children's predicates, intrinsic predication is dominant.

The paradox is resolved when we observe the effect of the two types of predication on the inclusion of subject-NPs in sentences. If one looks at whether a child utters an isolated predicate or a predicate with a subject, one finds that subjects are usually included with extrinsic predicates and are usually omitted with intrinsic predicates. The transformation for *wa* cannot be formulated if there is no superficial NP to which the postposition can be·attached. The situation is the opposite with extrinsic predication. Subjects are usually included with such predicates, so the transformation that introduces *ga* can be, and is, formulated early.

The same tendency exists in the speech of English-speaking children. English-speaking children, of course, also do not include *wa* or *ga* in their early speech. They therefore present a situation comparable to the speech of young Japanese children, and a native (but bilingual) speaker of Japanese can also classify their sentences according to whether they "require" *wa* or *ga*. The procedure leads to the same outcome (McNeill, 1968b). There is a strong tendency for the children studied by Brown and his colleagues to include subjects with extrinsic predicates and to omit subjects with intrinsic predicates.

The following are examples of the two types of predication from four children—two English-speaking and two Japanese-speaking:

Eve

(extrinsic)   Mommy sit bottom
              Fraser read Lassie
(intrinsic)   on Wednesday (the stock answer to "When's Cromer coming?")
              on my head (said of a hairband)

Adam

(extrinsic)   Bunny rabbit running
              Cromer right dere
(intrinsic)   pretty, Mommy?
              go dere, Mommy? (said of a puzzle piece)

Izanami

(extrinsic)   Reiko said "no"
              tape goes round and round
(intrinsic)   the same (said of two dresses)
              office (said of her father)

Murasaki

(extrinsic)   the lion's mommy is seated
              a giraffe is eating grass
(intrinsic)   can't eat the rind (said of an orange)
              delicious (said of a cracker)

We can now see why Adam tended to omit mentioning himself as the subject of sentences. The predicates of such sentences were intrinsic. An intrinsic predicate is one that entails its subject; the information contained in the predicate is felt to be inherent in the subject, which therefore need not be mentioned. Possibly Adam egocentrically felt that anything predicated about himself was intrinsically true. Other NPs, when serving as the subjects of sentences, were or were not included precisely according to whether or not the predicate was felt not to be intrinsically true of the NP.

It is possible that holophrastic utterances consist largely if not exclusively of intrinsic predicates. That would be one reason for a limitation of such utterances to single words and for a dependence of holophrastic speech on context. Children would add subjects to predicates, as de Laguna believed, when the predicates become extrinsic. Such an event appears to happen first when children are 18 to 24 months old. It is as if one suddenly realized that he was talking to a blind man when he said "at last" as a bus appeared around a distant corner.

The Differentiation of Grammatical Categories. Figure 5 traced the history of the pivot class of one child, Adam. According to Slobin (in press), Gvodzev's son Zhenya had a pivot class almost identical to Adam's: both children included demonstrative and personal pronouns, various adjectives, and such determiners as *other*. Presumably the two children passed through a similar series of steps in reaching the grammatical classes of their languages.

The interpretation made before of Adam's pivot class can also be made of Zhenya's pivot class: although exposed to a different language, Zhenya as well as Adam arrived at a generically appropriate classification of the words in his vocabulary; indeed, Adam and Zhenya arrived at the same classification. Now, after having reviewed evidence for the existence of children's innate linguistic abilities, in particular the ability to organize sentences according to the basic grammatical relations, we can return to the problem of generic classification.

The reader will recall the problem: a generically appropriate pivot class honors distinctions in adult grammar that children have not yet drawn. Both Adam and Zhenya, for example, placed all adjectives into a pivot class even though adjectives themselves were not yet recognized as a grammatical class. The problem is to explain such apparent teleology.

Two accounts come to mind. Each corresponds to a different conception of grammatical classes in linguistic theory. In the end, we shall find a way to put the two explanations together; but to begin with we shall present them as if they were alternative accounts.

One explanation was proposed by McNeill (1966a). The argument in this case relates the telegraphic sentences of young children to the semigrammatical sentences of adults. A speaker of English will recognize *John plays golf*, for example, as being well-formed. He will also recognize *golf plays John* as being semigrammatical, a deviation from the grammar of English, and *golf plays symmetrical* as being even less grammatical than *golf plays John*. Moreover, speakers of English can interpret semigrammatical sentences: *Golf plays John* is a devastating remark in part because it is deviant and in part because it is analogous with the well-formed *John plays golf*.

There are two salient facts in connection with the phenomenon of semigrammaticality. One is that semigrammatical sentences are ordered according to how far they depart from being well-formed. The other is that fluent speakers have an ability to interpret semigrammatical sentences, even though they are not well-formed.

Chomsky (1961), who raised this problem, gave an explanation of it in terms of a postulated hierarchy of grammatical categories. Such a hierarchy has never actually been established, but one can imagine what some of its properties would be. Every level of the hierarchy would encompass the total lexicon of English. The lowest level would comprise all the grammatical classes of English; the next level would include the same words except that certain distinctions are lost; the level above this would include again the same words except that even more distinctions are lost; and so on until the top-most level, which would consist of one gigantic grammatical class. The actual number of words, of course, is irrelevant. Chomsky's hierarchy could be established within the much smaller vocabulary of children.

A semigrammatical sentence is one that can be represented by the rules of the grammar only at some intermediate level in the hierarchy of categories. Of two semigrammatical sentences, the one that deviates most from being completely well-formed is the one that is represented at a higher level in the hierarchy of categories. *John plays golf* is represented by the rules of the grammar at all levels of the hierarchy, including the most differentiated level at the bottom. However, *golf plays John* can be represented only down to the level where the distinction between animate and inanimate nouns is lost, and *golf plays symmetrical* cannot be represented below the level where the distinction between nouns and adjectives—two major grammatical categories—is lost.

Understanding a semigrammatical sentence depends on noting an analogy with well-formed sentences represented in the same way as the semigrammatical sentence at the appropriate level in the hierarchy. Thus *golf plays John* is perceived as analogous to *John plays golf* because both receive the same representation when the distinction between animate and inanimate nouns is abolished.

McNeill's (1966a) suggestion was that children's sentences are semigrammatical in this technical sense. Like *golf plays John* and *golf plays symmetrical*, the telegraphic sentences of children omit certain grammatical distinctions. Moreover, it was claimed that the differentiation of the grammatical classes shown in Fig. 5 is in fact a record of Adam's progress down the hierarchy of categories Chomsky discussed. Thus early sentences from children honor fewer distinctions than later sentences do, just as semigrammatical sentences honor fewer distinctions than well-formed sentences do, and the distinctions children draw at any time are generically related to the distinctions they draw at later times, just as the category of nouns (for example) is generically related to the categories of animate and inanimate nouns.

Children's sentences are therefore understood by adults as semigrammatical sentences. Since the information is the same, adults understand such infantile utterances as *that a Adam ball* through the same mechanisms they use to understand such semigrammatical sentences as *golf plays John*. In both cases, grammatical distinctions of English are violated, thus placing the sentences on an intermediate level in the hierarchy of categories and the sentences are understood on the basis of analogies with well-formed sentences.

An experiment reported by McNeill (1966a) lends support to this identification of child sentences with semigrammatical sentences. Pairs of sentences recorded from children at different ages were given (in written form) to adults, who had to decide which member of each pair had been uttered by a younger child. Vocabulary and length were matched within pairs; every sentence was grammatically deviant; only the age of recording and, presumably, the degree of grammaticality differed. Adults could accurately pick the earlier sentence 81% of the time (chance being 50%); earlier sentences thus tend to be more deviant when judged against the standards available to adults. Unless adults have special standards for judging child speech, it seems clear that there is a basic similarity between the phenomenon of semigrammaticality in adults and the linguistic development of children.

The suggestion in McNeill (1966a) was that the upper levels of the hierarchy of categories are universal among languages and are a reflection of one aspect of children's innate linguistic abilities. It is certainly difficult to imagine that children learn such generically appropriate categories. There is no class of "modifiers" in English or Russian that corresponds to Adam's and Zhenya's pivot class. However, children may be equipped to notice a general function of modification when it exists in the speech of adults, and to place words together when they serve this function. At some (fairly high) level in Chomsky's hierarchy, articles, demonstrative and personal pronouns, adjectives, and such determiners as *other* are all alike. Adam and Zhenya, if they had available such a level in the hierarchy, would treat these different adult classes as the same, that is, as pivots. Discovery of the adult categories could then proceed, as it did, by differentiation.

Such is one account of children's early syntactic organization. It makes a strong prediction, which can easily be examined. If children initially classify words according to a universal hierarchy of categories, then all primitive grammatical classes must be generically appropriate. Children must never place words from the same adult class into different grammatical classes of their own.

In fact some children do not arrive at a generically appropriate classification of words. One of Miller and Ervin's (1964) subjects, for example, placed adult adjectives in both the pivot and open classes. Izanami, one of McNeill's (1966c) subjects, did the same. The early grammatical classes of these children were not generically appropriate and could not possibly be refined through differentiation.

There is a difficulty then. The problem appears to lie with the original analysis of adult syntactic classification, and not with the extension of such an adult analysis to the syntactic classification of children. On independent grounds, Chomsky (1965) rejected the notion of grammatical categories, replacing it with the concept of syntactic features. The change in theory was made to take into account the cross-classification of words. Consider, for example, the four nouns, *John, elephant, ocean,* and *Egypt.* Two are proper nouns (*John* and *Egypt*) and two are common nouns (*elephant* and *ocean*). One might suppose that English contains these two grammatical categories. But the four words present a second distinction, which cuts across the first. *John* and *elephant* also are animate nouns, and *Egypt* and *ocean* are inanimate nouns. Logically no way exists to make one of these distinctions hierarchically superior to the other. Inanimate nouns, for example, are not all proper nouns, nor are they all common nouns. They may be either, for nouns are cross-classified.

A consideration of such facts led Chomsky to do away with the idea of a grammatical category, and to replace it with the idea of a syntactic feature. Thus *Egypt* has the features [inanimate] and [proper]; *John* has the features [animate] and [proper]; etc.

It is not surprising therefore to find that children also cross-classify grammatical classes. Words in the same adult "class" can have in part different features. Depending on which features a child uses, words from the same "class" may find their way into different categories in the child's grammar. Suppose, for example, that at an early point in development a child classifies words encountered in adult speech according to whether they are [animate] or [inanimate], but in no other way. Then *elephant* and *ocean,* two nouns, would appear in different syntactic categories, as would *Egypt* and *John.* Miller and Ervin's and McNeill's subjects apparently cross-classified adjectives in a way comparable to such cross-classification of nouns.

If we accept the possibility that children classify words according to features, then how can we explain such generically appropriate classification as does occur? What led Adam and Zhenya to treat demonstrative and personal pronouns, articles, determiners, and adjectives alike?

In the view sketched above, generic classification can mean only one thing. At the time Adam's and Zhenya's speech was observed, they were classifying words according to a single feature. The feature must have been one shared by the various words classified together as pivots; these words, as they were encountered in adult speech, were then placed into the pivot "class."

The function played by Adam's and Zhenya's pivot words was modification; indeed, Brown and Bellugi (1964) referred to Adam's pivot class as a modifier class. We therefore might suspect that the pivot class and the feature on which it is based are associated in some way with the basic grammatical relation of modification. As mentioned previously a relation of modification holds between a determiner and a noun when both belong to the same NP. In order for this definition to hold, any word understood to modify a noun must be classified [+ Det] and [+__N]; similarly, any word understood to be modified by a determiner must be classified [+ N] and [Det__]. That is, the grammatical relation of modification automatically imposes two grammatical categories, Det and N, and establishes a contextual relation between them—__N and Det__, respectively. Evidence has already been presented that the basic grammatical relations are reflected in children's earliest linguistic performances. A child able to recognize that two words are related as modifier and modified is also able to classify one as [+ Det, +__N] and the other as [+ N, + Det__]. Doing so is an automatic result of understanding the basic grammatical relation. The second set of features designates a class of nouns. The first set exactly designates the pivot class of Adam and Zhenya.

This argument can be generalized to cover each of the basic grammatical relations. If the reader will visualize a tree-diagram representing the deep structure of a simple declarative sentence (or look at Table 10 in the Appendix), he will see that each of the six following sets of features can be derived from the basic grammatical relations (asterisks will be explained below):

predicate	[+ VP, + NP__]*
subject	[+ NP, +__VP]
main verb	[+ V, +__NP]*
object	[+ NP, + V__]
modifier	[+ Det, +__N]*
head	[+ N, + Det__]

The basic grammatical relation responsible for each set is indicated on the left. (The use of + NP and + VP as features has been proposed for adult grammar by Chomsky, 1967.)

It is important to note that these features are automatically made available whenever a child obtains *any* meaning from adult speech. Not everything in adult speech is necessarily understood, of course, but everything understood is necessarily classified according to the preceding list of features, at least momentarily. That is true by virtue of the definitions of the basic grammatical relations. However, entering such information into a lexicon is a separate step, not guaranteed by these definitions. A child may at first draw on only one relation to develop a lexicon (as with Adam), and he might not make an entry every time he encounters an example of an appropriate relation in adult speech. The fact that a single word never goes into different pivot classes for the same child reflects this restriction—at first, children assume that each word has one and only one classification.

Moreover, there is no assurance that a child understands adult speech correctly. Inappropriate classifications can occur. When they do, however, it is because words are used in the wrong grammatical relations, not because they are used in esoteric relations or in no relation at all. Such are the constraints within which child language exists. Utterances like *allgone shoe* can be understood in this light: Braine's subject either treated *allgone* as a modifier (and so as a word like *big* or

that) or *allgone shoe* as a complete but backward sentence (and so equivalent to the English *the shoe is allgone*).

Some children utter sentences both forward and backward for a time, the two directions expressing the same grammatical relation. It is as if some nouns were (for example) tagged [+ VP__] and others [+ __VP]. Thus we can hear both *ball hit* and *read mommy* as expressions of the subject and predicate relations. Braine (in press) lists several such examples. It is not necessarily the case, as sometimes has been thought (e.g., Slobin, 1966b), that children adhere to a fixed order of words when expressing the basic grammatical relations. It should be noted that contextual features, such as [+__VP], show *logical* relations. They show *ordinal* relations in addition, only via a further principle that logical relations are expressed through the order of words. In languages other than English contextual features often control inflections and the order of words serves an altogether different function, for example, style.

A word classified with just one set of features can be used only in the corresponding relation. Eventually all words are classified in several ways, thus enlarging the distributional range of each word. However, additional features sometimes lead to temporary restrictions of range instead. Two of Brown's subjects, for example, used for a time only animate nouns as the subjects of sentences and only inanimate nouns as the objects of verbs (unpublished materials). Nouns apparently had been tagged in the lexicon as [+ NP, +__ VP, + animate] and [+ NP, + V__, + inanimate]; an enlargement of the feature roster produced a restriction in distributional range.

The question is sometimes raised whether or not children rely on semantic considerations in classifying words syntactically (e.g., Slobin, 1966a). Doing so would presuppose a link between semantic and syntactic information: words alike on a certain semantic feature (say, activity) are all given the same syntactic feature (say, + V). Brown (1958) found evidence that children of three or four are alert to the semantic implications of nonsense words used as mass nouns, count nouns, or verbs. Braine (in press), using a technique like Brown's, concluded that whereas the classification of verbs might be assisted by semantic implications, the classification of nouns probably is not. His observations are interesting and worth reporting in some detail.

Braine taught his 2-year-old daughter two new words, one the name of a kitchen appliance (*niss*) and the other the name of the act of walking with the fingers (*seb*). Niether word was used by an adult in a grammatical context. However, the child used both words appropriately—*niss* as a noun and *seb* as a verb, as in *more niss* and *seb Teddy*. She also used *seb* as a noun, but never used *niss* as a verb. There were sentences like *more seb* and *this seb*, but none like *niss the vegetables*. Evidently there is no requirement that nouns be associated with things, although there is a requirement that verbs be associated with actions. Braine also observed his daughter using newly acquired Hebrew verbs as nouns, but he never observed her using nouns as verbs.

These observations show that although semantic information is helpful in syntactically classifying words, such information is not identical with syntactic classification: *seb* was used as a noun, regardless of its association with action.

The child's productive use of both *seb* and *niss* in sentences, even though the words had been introduced out of context, reflects the degree of freedom of child speech from the circumstances in which examples are encountered—a matter we return to later.

If children develop lexical features from the basic grammatical relations, how then are we to interpret the pivot and open classes? An answer is suggested by a chart prepared by Slobin (in press), which is reproduced here as Table 5. The chart shows examples of pivot words from the early grammars of children exposed to three different languages: English, German, and Russian. The examples have been collected from various diary stud-

Table 5. Pivot Structures in English, German, and Russian

Function of Pivot	Language		
	English	German	Russian
Modify, quality	*pretty*—	*armer [poor]*—	—*bo-bo [hurt]*
	my—	*mein [my]*—	—*khoroshaya [good]*
	allgone—	*alle [allgone]*—	—*tyu-tyu [allgone]*
	all—		
	big—		
	other—		
Locate, name	*there*—	—*da [there]*	—*tam [there]*
	here—	*da-is [there is]*—	
	see—	*gukuk [see]*—	
	it—		
	that—		
	—*on-there*		
	—*up-there*		
Describe act	—*away*	—*bah [away]*	—*tprua [walk]*
	—*on*	—*an [on]*	—*bay-bay [sleep]*
	—*off*	—*auf [on]*	—*upala [fell down]*
	—*it*	—*aus [off]*	—*bukh [fell down]*
	—*do*		
	—*come*		
	I—		
Demand, desire	*more*—	*mehr [more]*—	*eshche [more]*—
	give—	*bitte [please]*—	*day [give]*—
	want—		
Negate	*no*—	*nein [no]*—	*net [no]*—
	don't—	*nicht [not]*—	*ne-nado [don't]*—

From Slobin, in press.

ies. Slobin organized the chart to reflect certain semantic regularities—for example, that some pivots serve to modify meaning (*pretty, mein, bo-bo*), that others locate or name things (*there, da, tam*), that still others describe acts (*away, bah, bukh*). Such distinctions may indeed be important in child speech; it is impressive that a word for *allgone*, for example, is used as a pivot by each child. However, semantic factors do not explain the pivot-open distinction. Even if all children have use for a concept like "allgone," the term representing it could appear as either a pivot or an open word.

In order to understand why the pivot-open distinction appears as it does we must note another regularity running through Table 5. Aside from negation (which is treated below), the pivots of Table 5 involve only certain sets of syntactic features—those marked by an asterisk in the preceding list. It is the case, apparently, that pivot words are never Ns or NPs, whereas open words are always Ns or NPs. Such a restriction would exist if pivot words could express only the basic grammatical relations of modification, predication, and main verb. From this point of view, the distinction between pivot and open classes is a superficial and imperfect reflection of the development of these three relations and its effects on a child's lexicon. The distinction necessarily appears in a distributional analysis because a child's lexicon is derived from the three basic grammatical relations of modification, predication, and main verb, and sentences constructed from this lexicon are limited to two or three words. Each of the observed relations yields N or NP as a contextual feature.

Why are the other basic grammatical relations—subject, object, and "head"—never a source of pivot words? One reason may be the following. Each such relation involves an N or NP in combination with some other category. By *not* establishing N and NP as pivot words a child treats N and NP as unmarked categories and all other categories as marked: every word is either an NP (or N) or a word that appears with an NP (or N). Such a division of the lexicon requires 4 distinct lexical entries—the 3 marked by an asterisk in the list above plus NP (or N). It is the simplest possible lexicon that can be derived from the 6 basic grammatical relations. If the marked-

unmarked distinction is reversed, with NPs (or Ns) as pivots, there are 5 distinct lexical entries, and if it is not established at all, there are 6. Children therefore seem to be guided by a principle of simplicity. Since Ns outnumber all other words in children's vocabulary at this point in development, simplifying nominal entries is the largest single simplification possible that does not lose contact with the basic grammatical relations.

All the distributional and featural characteristics of the pivot-open direction can be thus understood. Pivot words are either modifiers, predicates, or main verbs; open words appear with pivot words in the complementary relations. Open words appear without restriction because they are unmarked; pivot words appear with open words because they are marked. Modifiers, for example, cannot occur alone because they have the obligatory feature $[+\_\_N]$ and cannot occur with each other because they do not have the feature $[+ \text{Det}\_\_]$. Nouns appear alone because they have no contextual feature and appear with pivots because pivots have nouns as a contextual feature. Kelley (1967) has built one of these features—modification—into a computer program that successfully acquires certain aspects of English syntax.

Summary. The basic grammatical relations penetrate deeply into the linguistic powers of children. We now summarize what has been said of them, exposing clearly the line of argument followed.

One basic grammatical relation—predication—appears to be present form the earliest moments of holophrastic speech. Later developments depend on an elaboration of this relation as well as an introduction of the remaining grammatical relations—subject, verb, object, and modification. All such developments produce forms that eventually become the deep structure of sentences.

We have reviewed two lines of change. One is the incorporation of subjects with predicates in children's speech; another is the construction of a lexicon where words are classified according to the grammatical relations they can occupy.

It is important to observe that the basic grammatical relations, combined with the definition of grammatical categories in terms of syntactic features, give children's grammar a certain necessary form. Without exception, children construe everything understood in adult speech according to the basic grammatical relations; equally without exception therefore they identify words encountered in parental speech as possessing such features as $[+ N]$, $[+ Det\_\_]$, $[+\_\_VP]$. Children may or may not *record* such information (a lexicon is not developed instantly), but merely to understand adult speech its vocabulary must at least momentarily be classified according to the features imposed by the basic grammatical relations. Children's own speech is constructed according to the same basic principles—for children presumably understand most of what they say.

Insofar as the basic grammatical relations reflect the innate abilities of children, the type of grammar just outlined will be developed regardless of the language to which a child is exposed. It is a universal child grammar, and it leads to a convergence of child and adult grammar at the level of meaning no matter what language a child happens to be exposed to. Other aspects of grammar also are universal and may be a reflection of children's innate abilities. Syntactic features derived from the basic grammatical relations, such as $[+\_\_VP]$ and $[+ N]$, are what Chomsky (1965) called categorical features; they make such strings as *golf plays symmetrical* grammatically deviant. However, categorical features do not exhaust the information contained in the deep structure of sentences. In addition there are features, called subclassificational by Chomsky, which serve to eliminate such strings as *golf plays John*. Features of the first type specify where a word can appear in a deep structure, for example, in NP but not in V. Features of the second type specify how words coexist in deep structures, for example, *plays* takes only animate subjects and inanimate objects. Subclassificational features cannot be developed from the basic grammatical relations.

The differentiation of Adam's pivot class (Fig. 5) produces a family of such subclassificational features. The pivot class itself is based on the categorical features $[+ Det, +\_\_N]$. It is conceivable that a universal hierarchy of features, much like the universal hierarchy of categories described by Chomsky (1961), is responsible for this differentiation. If such is the case, the arguments developed earlier would again apply. Sentences that vio-

late a subclassificational feature would be understood by adults through reference to a higher level in the hierarchy, and children's linguistic advancement would be the result of progressing from higher to lower levels in the same hierarchy.

The Acquisition of Transformations

The deep structures of sentences are largely a reflection of children's innate linguistic abilities. It is for this reason that such information can be totally abstract in sentences. Deep structures become abstract when children learn the transformations of their language. The interaction between linguistic experience and innate linguistic ability thus occurs here —in the acquisition of transformations—and here is the appropriate place to examine the role of parental speech. Such is our guiding hypothesis.

The present section reviews what is known of this interaction. It can be viewed as a history of the way that children, beginning with a universal child grammar, diverge in the direction of the grammar of their local language. We shall have occasion to trace the emergence of several transformations of English, and to examine the suitability of several psychological proposals—both traditional and otherwise— for the acquisition of language.

The Emergence of Inflections. We begin with the acquisition of certain morphological details. Although inflections are usually not introduced through major formations, they are easily traced features of the surface structure of sentences, and they clearly illustrate some aspects of the way children learn to relate deep and surface structures.

Table 6 lists the order of emergence of several noun and verb inflections in English (Bellugi, 1964). The data are based on observations of two children. Also shown is the relative frequency of the same inflections in the speech of the children's mothers.

There are several matters worth noting. One is that the order of emergence is the same for the two children. Order is the same even though the children's rate of development is radically different, one child taking twice as long to acquire the six inflections of Table 6 as the other. A second point is that forms employing the same phonetic variants do not appear at the same time. Three inflections have the same phonemic realization, *-s*.

Table 6. The Emergence of English Inflections in the Speech of Two Children

Inflection	Age of Appearance (in months)		Combined Rank Order in Mothers Speech
	Adam	Eve	
Present progressive, -ing	28	19½	2
Plural on nouns, -s	33	24	1
Past on regular verbs, -ed	39	24½	4
Possessive on nouns, -s	39½	25½	5
Third person on verbs, -s	41	26	3

From Bellugi, 1964.

These are plural marking of nouns, nouns marked for possession, and third person verbs. The last appears anywhere from 2 to 8 months later than the first, so it is not phonemic development that regulates the acquisition of inflections. Finally, the order in which inflections emerge in the speech of children is weakly correlated with the frequency of the forms in the speech of adults. The most glaring discrepancy involves third-person marking on verbs, which is third most frequent in maternal speech but last to emerge in child speech.

Now consider the equivalent phenomenon in the acquisition of Russian. Here matters are more complex. The language is highly inflected, and for this very reason more interesting. Slobin (in press), after examining a number of reports in the Russian literature, reconstructed the following chronology. The first inflections to appear are the plural and diminutive marking of nouns and the imperative marking of verbs. This happens at 22 months or so. Next to appear are various case, tense, and person markings on verbs—a complex story to which we return shortly. Then appears the conditional marking of verbs, much later than the inflections of case, tense, and person, even though the conditional is structurally simple in Russian. After this, nouns come to be marked for various abstract categories of quality and action, and finally, last by a large margin, appears gender marking of nouns and adjectives.

Slobin argues that three major factors influence the point at which inflections appear in linguistic development. One is the frequency of occurrence of an inflection in adult speech; we see the effects of this factor in Table 6. A second is the superficial complexity of an inflection (e.g., the accusative emerges late in German, where it is relatively complex, and early in Hungarian, where it is simple). The third is something Slobin calls the "semantic content" of an inflection, which probably refers both to the deep structure of sentences and to the sheer intellectual difficulty of the idea represented by an inflection. The relatively late appearance of the Russian conditional, for example, is explained by its difficult semantic content.

Gender in Russian is an ambiguous case. It is by far the most difficult aspect of Russian morphology for children to master: errors typically continue until 7 or 8 years. Slobin attributes the confusion over gender to its difficult semantic content: most nouns are arbitrarily marked; some nouns with real implications of gender are marked in the wrong way; etc. However, the problem may not be the semantic difficulty of gender at all. Gender in adult Russian appears to have little or no semantic content. But for children it may have definite semantic implications. If this is correct, then the difficulty children experience with gender-marking is not a matter of deep complexity but of superficial complexity. If a Russian child reacts to gender-marking at an early age, he will *exclude* these inflections from "inappropriate" words. Thus gender-marking will be slow to develop, for a child must learn a large number of localized and superficial rules.

It is interesting to note in passing that public education in a society seems to be withheld until children have mastered morphology. The morphology of English, which poses relatively few problems, is largely mastered by age 4 or 5. Schooling begins at 5 or 6. The morphology of Russian, which poses many more problems, is not mastered until 7 or 8. Schooling begins at 7. The intellectual readiness of children for school apparently has traditionally been judged by mastery of one of the most peripheral parts of language.

In keeping with the visibility of morphology, it is not surprising that when inflections are overgeneralized, the phenomenon attracts a good deal of attention. All parents know that children regularize strong verbs (*runned, goed, sitted*, etc.) and nouns (*foots, mouses, tooths*, etc.). However, the actual development of such forms is more complex than is usually realized. Tracing their history is instructive on a number of points.

Overgeneralization, Simplification, and the Question of Overt Practice. English has a number of strong verbs, verbs with irregular past tenses. There are also nouns with irregular plurals. Although children long regularize these forms—adding *-ed* to the verbs and *-s* to the nouns—this is not the way they begin (Ervin, 1964). Initially, strong verbs appear in child speech in the correct irregular form —*came* instead of *comed, ran* instead of *runned*, and *did* instead of *doed*. The development of irregular plurals shows the same phenomenon—*feet, mice*, and *teeth* appear in child speech before *foots, mouses*, and *tooths*. Regularization, when it occurs, is a step forward.

The explanation of the early appearance of such correct irregular verbs and nouns has to do with the frequency of these forms in adult speech. Strong verbs are by far the most frequent verbs, and strong nouns occur commonly also. Children are thus given many opportunities to discover the association of the underlying morphemes (past) and (plural) to these words, and they make such discoveries early.

But for many irregular verbs and nouns each word is a case unto itself; no rule covers more than one. For others, only 2 or 3 words are subject to the same rule (*lead-led, read-read*).[3] Because of the limited scope of the strong forms, the weak, or regular, forms remain untouched when the strong forms change. A child who only knows how to say *feet, mice*, or *oxen* may have in mind plurality when he says *two box*, but he cannot express this underlying idea. Should it be *beex, bikes*, or, possibly, *boxen?* Obviously, it is *box*.

It is general rules that children seek; indeed, they seek the simplest such rules possible. The evidence is dramatic. Ervin (1964) searched her records of child speech for the first examples of the regular past-tense and plural inflections. Correct usage of irregular forms was already present. For verbs she first found the regular *-ed* on these same irregular

forms! Overgeneralizations apparently occurred before anything existed in speech to generalize form. Plural inflections on nouns first appeared with weak forms, but very shortly thereafter with the strong forms as well.

The finding with verbs, of course, is an illusion. Strong verbs are frequent in child speech, just as in adult speech. Accordingly, Ervin had a better chance of observing *-ed* on strong than on weak forms. However, the superior frequency of strong verbs does not influence the force of Ervin's observation. Children treat strong and weak verbs alike, and for this reason they encompass strong verbs within the regular past-tense rule as soon as it is formulated. The same is true of plural inflection on nouns. The gap between the first appearance of *-s* and its overgeneralization to irregular forms is brief, usually only a matter of weeks.

Slobin (in press) refers to such encroachments of regularity as "inflectional imperialism." There are no political connotations in the fact that inflectional imperialism is a major factor in the acquisition of Russian; it rather has to do with language. To quote Slobin:

Overregularizations are rampant in the child's learning of Russian morphology—small wonder, what with the great variety of forms within each category, determined on the bases of both phonological and grammatical relations. For example, not only must the child learn an instrumental case ending for masculine, feminine, and neuter nouns and adjectives in singular and plural, but within each of these sub-categories there are several different phonologically conditioned suffixes (not to mention zero-endings, morphologically conditioned suffixes, and other complications). The child's solution is to seize upon one suffix at first and use it for every instance of that particular grammatical category.

In the evolution of the instrumental inflection, Gvozdev's son Zhenya first employed *-om*, the suffix for masculine and neuter nouns in the singular. Zhenya used *-om* on all nouns, including the feminine nouns that were at that time most abundant in his speech. The corresponding feminine form, *-oy*, appeared only some time later, but when it did, *-oy* immediately dominated the original inflection,

[3] I am indebted to Dan I. Slobin for reminding me of these cases.

-om. Much later, *-om* reappeared in Zhenya's speech, this time to be used appropriately. An experiment by Zakharova (1958) found the same sequence of events in a sample of 200 children. Such is inflectional imperialism.

Inflectional imperialism in Russian and English do not seem at first glance to be the same. The English regular verbs often invade a domain where no rule exists at all; the Russian suffix *-oy* invades where a rule is already in force. One appears to fill a vacuum, whereas the other seems truly imperialistic. The difference, however, is more apparent than real, for on closer examination we can see that the two cases demonstrate the same phenomenon.

The phenomenon is that children always strive to formulate the most general rule possible. That is what English-speaking children do in extending regular inflections to irregular forms. Instead of having several ways of expressing (past) or (plural), they have only one for each. Russian children do the same. Both *-om* and *-oy* have multiple uses in adult Russian, but *-om* has fewer (two) than *-oy* (five). Russian children thus first select the suffix with the fewest uses, as Slobin points out.

One reason for making such a choice is that a rule formulated for the morpheme *-om* can be more easily discovered. The morpheme *-om* has fewer exceptional uses than has the morpheme *-oy*. Later, when a child also discovers that gender is a grammatical category, the balance between the two inflections changes. To mark gender as well as to mark the instrumental case, *-oy* is the inflection with greater generality, for it applies to some masculine nouns as well as to the large number of feminine nouns then in a child's vocabulary. The imperialism of *-oy* thus results from Russian children doing with *-oy* what American children do with *-ed,* which is to follow the rule of larger scope.

Russian- and English-speaking children are alike in yet another respect. Inflectional imperialism in the acquisition of morphology clearly shows that overt practice has little influence on linguistic development. When we observe one form imperialistically driving out another, we observe a form that has received little or no overt practice displacing another that has received a great deal of overt practice.

The inflection of regular verbs in the past-tense in English was so rare in the speech of Ervin's children that *-ed* first appeared on the strong verbs. These verbs, in contrast, had been used with their correct irregular inflections for months and in large numbers. Such extensive practice offered no protection against the tendency to express the past tense in a single rule. Since correct irregular forms are *replaced* by incorrect regularizations, it is clear that children actually expressed past time in the original correct forms. The same situation exists in the development of Russian morphology. The masculine suffix *-om* is well practiced but easily and immediately displaced by the feminine suffix *-oy.*

We therefore can draw at least a negative conclusion concerning the role of parental speech in language acquisition. Its role is not to provide children with opportunities to practice. As we shall see later, the acquisition of morphology is not different in this respect from the acquisition of other transformations.

Imitation. One traditional view of language acquisition holds that the process is advanced through imitation. However, there are several reasons to doubt that imitation plays a role in language acquisition, and it is appropriate to consider the question at this point.

But first we must clear up an ambiguity. The word "imitation" is used in two quite different senses; only one of them can be applied to language acquisition. In one sense, "imitation" refers to a process whereby one organism comes to resemble more and more closely another. The trait on which the resemblance develops must necessarily be within broad limits arbitrarily variable—resemblance in height, for example, is not the result of imitation. However, all sorts of other things develop through imitation in this sense; etiquette, driving a car on the left side of the road in England, typing, writing prose in the style of Faulkner—all are included. In this sense, it is also true that children acquire language through imitation.

There is a second, more technical use of the word "imitation": details of behavior—for example, plural inflections on English nouns—are first acquired by copying the behavior of a model. Such a view of language acquisition was presented by Allport (1924), and it has appeared in psychology texts ever since;

but it is the technical sense of "imitation" that is inappropriate for language acquisition.

There is no question that children imitate the speech of adults a good deal. In the records collected by Brown, fully 10% of children's speech at 28 to 35 months is imitative, as, for example, in such exchanges as the following:

Adult	Child
Oh, that's a big one	big one
But he was much bigger than Perro	big a Perro
Salad dressing	salad dressing
That's not a screw	dat not a screw
Are they all there?	all dere?

However, the fact that children imitate the speech of adults does not mean that the process of acquisition is imitation. It is clear from examples given in previous sections that not everything in child grammar originates in such a fashion. *It runned, allgone shoe, a that man,* for instance, have no models in adult speech, but they are grammatical within a child's system.

Nonetheless, it is possible that forms are first introduced into a child's speech through imitation. As long as grammar is not fully developed, a child might produce such utterances as *a that man,* and yet still enrich his grammar through the imitation of well-formed examples. In this case, imitations will be "advanced" grammatically relative to spontaneous speech.

Ervin (1964) looked into this possibility by comparing children's naturally occurring imitations to their free speech. She found that the grammatical organization of the imitations was identical to the organization of the free speech. Only one child in Ervin's sample of five was an exception, and her imitations were more primitive than her spontaneous speech. For all these children therefore imitations were not "grammatically progressive," as Ervin put it.

The result reflects a general characteristic of child speech. There is a strong tendency among children to include nothing in the surface structures of sentences that cannot be related to deep structures—nothing for which the transformational derivation is not known. The principle encompasses imitation as well as spontaneous speech. If a child does not yet include the progressive inflection -ing in his

speech, he also will not imitate -ing in the speech of adults, particularly if the adult model is long relative to his memory span (see Slobin, 1964; McNeill, 1966a). *Adam's nose is dripping* might be imitated *Adam nose drip* but probably not *Adam nose dripping.* It is for this reason that imitation can be used as a test of children's productive capacities, and it is for this reason also that children's early utterances are patterned as deep structures. Slobin and Welsh's (1967) stunning observation of a child imitating a sentence containing a relative clause with two conjoined sentences reflects the same principle. In all cases, children exclude superficial forms when they cannot be related to deep forms.

The resistance of children to new forms sometimes goes to extravagant lengths. Consider, for example, the following exchange between one mother and her child (from McNeill, 1966a):

Child: Nobody don't like me.
Mother: No, say "nobody likes me."
Child: Nobody don't like me.

.

.

.

(eight repetitions of this dialogue)

.

.

Mother: No, now listen carefully; say *"nobody likes me."*

Child: Oh! Nobody don't likes me.

Although children do not ordinarily behave differently when imitating and speaking, it is possible to instruct children to imitate, as Slobin and Welsh (1967) and Fraser, Brown, and Bellugi (1963) have done. Under these circumstances, a child's imitations may depart from his grammar. But instructed imitation is not typical of the ordinary circumstances of child speech, and phenomena observed here cannot be extended to the actual acquisition of grammatical structure.

Rather than serve didactic purposes, imitation often seems to be carried out in play. It therefore is the opposite of instruction, if indeed it has any effect at all: rather than change his grammatical system a child manipulates it, often in fantastic ways. Take as an example one of Brown's subjects, who, starting from an ordinary imitation, elaborated on it in an almost fuguelike manner (mentioned by Slobin, 1964; also McNeill, 1966a):

Adult: That's the tattooed man
Child: Tooman. Tattoo man. Find too tat-
          too man. Tattoo man. Who dat?
          Tattoo. Too man go, mommy? Too
          man. Tattoo man go? Who dat?
          Read dat. Tractor dere. Tattoo
          man.

Weir (1962) found many examples of similar grammatical play in the presleep soliloquies of her 2½-year-old son. The child selected a particular paradigm—sometimes grammatical, sometimes phonological—and then elaborated a stream of examples. The following uses a syntactic paradigm; it might be considered the linguistic equivalent of repeatedly building up and knocking down a tower of blocks.

> go for glasses
> go for them
> go to the top
> go throw
> go for blouse
> pants
> go for shoes

We thus arrive at the same negative conclusion as before: the role of parental speech in language acquisition is not to supply opportunities for children to practice. The practice of forms already in a child's grammar (e.g., *dug*) contributes nothing to the viability of the forms when they come into conflict with a child's changing system; such is the case in inflectional imperialism. The practice of forms not yet in a child's grammar simply does not occur; such is the case with imitation. The dominating factor is a child's own system of rules. The contributions of parental speech are always most severely filtered through this system.

What, then, of adult speech? To see even the beginning of an answer to this question, we must examine more closely the acquisition of transformations. It is here, as noted before, that the interaction of a child's linguistic abilities with his linguistic experience takes place.

Negation in the acquisition of English. The study of how children acquire transformational systems has barely begun. One would like to have detailed observations of a wide range of transformational relations, as it is only through investigations of such scope that our views on the process of acquisition can be evaluated. However, few transformations have been investigated from a developmental point of view, and even here the investigations are incomplete.

Menyuk (1964a, 1964b, 1964c, 1968, in press) has pursued a number of surveys of linguistic development. They possess the desired degree of scope—a large variety of sentence types being examined—but the results are presented in terms of a kind of contrastive analysis, and little can be discovered from it about the actual acquisition of transformations.

More direct analyses of transformations are presented by Klima and Bellugi (1966), Brown, Cazden, and Bellugi (1968), and Bellugi (1967). These studies are so far confined to the acquisition of two transformational systems—negation and questions—by the three Biblically named children in Brown's study, Adam, Eve, and Sarah. We shall first consider the emergence of negation and then of questions.

Brown and his colleagues have organized their longitudinal records into a series of "stages." The stages are not intended to have linguistic or psychological significance, although some of them in fact coincide with true junctures in development. Instead, stages are defined in terms of average utterance length, measured in morphemes, and merely provide a way of comparing children whose rates of development are different. Figure 6, taken from Brown et al. (1968), shows the relation between chronological age and mean utterance length for the three children of Brown's study. Roman numerals indicate the stages into which the analysis has been divided; the following discussion focuses on the first three of these.

At the first stage, coinciding with the appearance of pivot constructions, children utter such negative sentences as the following (Klima and Bellugi, 1966):

> No . . . wipe finger
> More . . . no
> No a boy bed
> Not . . . fit
> No singing song
> No the sun shining

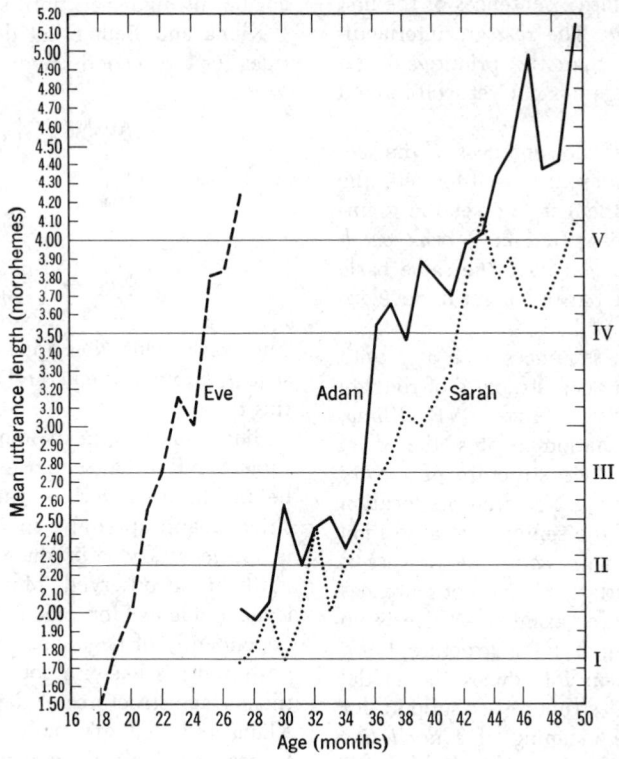

Fig. 6. Mean utterance length as a function of age in three children (Brown et al., 1969).

No play that
Wear mitten no
Not a teddy bear
No fall!

The form of these sentences is fixed, simple, and universal. They all consist of a negative operator (*no* or *not*) plus an otherwise affirmative sentence. The internal structure of the sentence, if any, remains undisturbed by the negation—*the sun shining, play that,* and *a teddy bear,* for example, are all possible affirmative sentences. The earliest schema for negation, then, is Neg + S. Since a negative operator *(no)* sometimes appears after sentences instead of before them, there also is the alternative form, S + *no.*

According to Slobin (1966), Gvozdev's son Zhenya also produced negative sentences in accordance with these schemas. Whereas an adult would say *nyet nikavo* (literally, "not no-one"), Zhenya said *nyet kavo,* reducing the well-formed double negative to the single negative required by the schema Neg + S. French children use *non* or *pas* in an analo-

gous fashion (Grégoire, 1937), and Japanese children do essentially the same thing with *nai* (McNeill and McNeill, 1968).

Some 2 to 4 months later, depending on the child, Klima and Bellugi found a flowering of negative forms. Compared to the two simple forms of negation of the first period, there are now seven distinct types:

I can't catch you
We can't talk
I don't sit on Cromer coffee
I don't like him
No pinch me
No . . . Rusty hat
Touch the snow no
This a radiator no
Don't bite me yet
Don't leave me
That not "O," that blue
There no squirrels
He no bite you
I no want envelope

Certain of these sentences are well-formed in English—*I can't catch you.* Others are identical to the negative sentences of the first stage—*no pinch me*. The rest are intermediate, more complex than the primitive negatives of the first stage but not yet well-formed —*he no bite you*.

Although some of the sentences of the second period are apparently well-formed, the grammar yielding them is not yet the grammar of adult English. In fact, *I can't catch you* and *he no bite you* have the same basic structure for children at this point in development.

In adult English, sentences such as *I can't catch you* possess a deep structure of roughly the form Neg + NP + Aux + VP (Klima, 1964). A transformation relates the deep structure to the surface structure of *I can't catch you* by removing Neg from its location at the beginning of the sentence to a position behind the modal verb *can*. The process is called "Neg-transportation." In other sentences —*I don't like you*, for example—there is no modal verb in the underlying structure, but a second transformation introduces the modal *do* into the surface structure as support for negation. Thus the meaning of *I don't like you* is really the meaning of *I n't like you*, since *do* serves merely to support the negation of the sentence. This process is called "*do*-support."

The only well-formed sentences listed among the child examples given above were sentences of these two types. If children indeed utter well-formed sentences in such cases, transformations for Neg-transportation and *do*-support must be involved. However, there is no indication in the second stage of development that *do*-support exists, although a precursor of Neg-transportation might already be established.

The auxiliaries *can* and *do* appear only in the context of Neg at this stage. There are no affirmative sentences such as *I can do it, can I have it?*, or *do you think so?* Children instead say *I do it, I have it?*, and *you think so?*, all without the modal verbs *do* and *can*. Klima and Bellugi represent the fact that *do* and *can* are restricted to negation by including in the children's grammar a constituent they call the negative auxiliary (Aux^{neg}). Aux^{neg} in turn eventually leads to *don't* and *can't* as two lexical items. Aux^{neg} can be regarded as an undifferentiated amalgam of negation and "auxiliary verbness." Its two components will

not be distinguished until some months later.

Klima and Bellugi set down the following rules for the second stage:

$$\text{Aux}^{neg} \rightarrow \begin{Bmatrix} \text{Neg} \\ \text{V}^{neg} \end{Bmatrix}$$

$$\text{V}^{neg} \rightarrow \begin{Bmatrix} can't \\ don't \end{Bmatrix}$$

$$\text{Neg} \rightarrow \begin{Bmatrix} no \\ not \end{Bmatrix}$$

The constituent Neg appears in *that no fish school, he no bite you,* and other sentences of this type.

Since Aux^{neg} appears immediately after the subject NP of a sentence and immediately before the main verb, negation is already positioned appropriately, so Neg-transportation is not necessary to produce surface structures of the type observed. Moreover, since there is no evidence for modal verbs existing independently of negation, a transformation for *do*-support is likewise not necessary to obtain the surface structures of the second stage. By Klima and Bellugi's analysis, then, such sentences as *I don't like you* and *he no bite you* are fundamentally alike. Neither includes a modal verb, both include the constituent Aux^{neg}, and the transformations for Neg-transportation and *do*-support are not involved. Clearly therefore the well-formedness of *I don't like you* and *I can't catch you* is illusory.

There is another interpretation of sentences like *he no bite you*. Such sentences include internal negation and in this respect differ from the more primitive sentences observed in the first stage of development such as *no the sun shining*. One innovation occurring between the first and second stages of development may therefore be the appearance of Neg-transportation. If we accept this interpretation the consequence for Klima and Bellugi's grammar is merely to reverse the order of elements assumed to underlie negative sentences. Instead of NP + Aux^{neg} + VP, as in Klima and Bellugi, it becomes Aux^{neg} + NP + VP, with the constituent Aux^{neg} being developed as before.

Neg-transportation now applies to every sentence, including *I can't catch you*. One advantage of this interpretation is that it leaves room for the negatives—such as *no pinch me* and *no . . . Rusty hat*—that appeared in the second stage but seem to be relics of the first. In Klima and Bellugi's analysis, they are truly relics, coming from an earlier and unintegrated system. In the alternative analysis they are identical to the underlying form of all negative sentences in the second stage, except that they have no subjects—still a common omission of children's sentences at this time.

Consider, as examples, the three pharse markers below. The first is the deep structure of *I can't catch you,* the second of *he no bite you,* and the third of *no pinch me.*

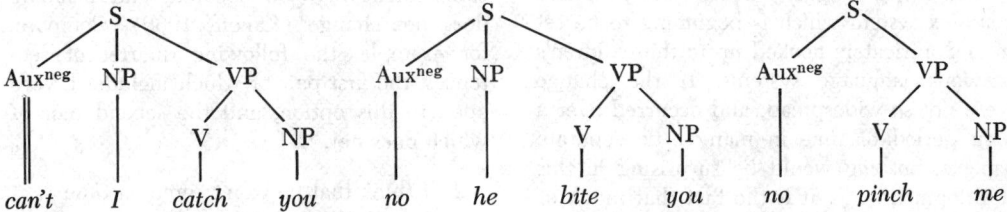

The transformation for *Neg*-transportation at the second stage is

$$Aux^{neg} + NP \rightarrow NP + Aux^{neg}$$

This transformation must apply to the first two phrase markers above, as they meet the condition of the transformation; *I can't catch you* and *he no bite you* result. However, the transformation cannot apply to the third phrase marker, since it has no NP after Aux^{neg}; the sentence remains *no pinch me.* According to the alternative interpretation, therefore, such sentences as *no pinch me* are untransformed deep structures.

Notice that the well-formedness of *I don't like you* and *I can't catch you* is illusory in the alternative analysis as well as in Klima and Bellugi's analysis. The basic kinship of these sentences to *he no bite you* remains undisturbed by assuming the existence of a transformation.

Two to six months later, again depending on the child, sentences of the following types occur:

Paul can't have one
This can't stick
I didn't did it
You don't want some supper
Donna won't let go
No, it isn't
I am not a doctor
This not ice cream
They not hot
I not crying
He not taking the walls down
Don't kick my box
Don't touch the fish
Ask me if I not make mistake
I not hurt him

There are a few new developments in the third stage, though apparently not so many as in the second; however, as is often the case in child language, superficial changes are not a valid guide to changes taking place in a child's underlying system. Grammar can develop "silently." Whereas the five new forms of the second stage resulted from changes (in Klima and Bellugi's analysis) of little scope, the negative sentences of the third stage come from a grammatical system that has been fundamentally altered: there are now auxiliary verbs; a transformation for *do*-support is now present; and, in Klima and Bellugi's analysis as well as in the alternative analysis previously given, there is a transformation for Neg-transportation.

A basic development is the first appearance of the English system of auxiliary verbs. Unlike the second stage, there are now affirmative sentences with modal verbs, as in *I can do it* and *can I have it?* Negation is therefore no longer tied to the auxiliary, as in the second stage, for the constituent Aux^{neg} has been differentiated into its negative and auxiliary components. Since *do* and Neg coexist in the surface structure but are not united in the deep structure, a transformation for *do*-support becomes necessary to derive such sentences as *I don't like you.* The continuity of surface forms between the second and third stages masks a basic discontinuity in the grammar. One indication of the discontinuity is that sentences based on the schema Neg + S no longer appear; the schema has been made abstract by the changes of the third stage.

The development of the auxiliary system is very rapid and pervasive during the third stage. It is as if the auxiliary, once freed from negation, flowed in to fill all the available space in a child's grammar. As Bellugi (1967), who has studied these developments closely, puts it:

> The change suggests a carefully prepared complex system which is beginning to be set in and intricately hooked up to the children's previous language systems. If the change were not so widespread, and occurred over a long period of time in many little separate aspects, nothing would be surprising in this development. . . . It is the fact that much of the apparatus comes in in a relatively short period of time and appears in a variety of structures that surprises us (p. 90).

Table 7 gives some impression of the pace of these changes. In it are shown the number of times that one child, Eve, used modal verbs in several different grammatical contexts in three successive samples of her speech; the samples were collected over a period of 1½ months. Along with a growth in numbers is a growth in variety—more and more modal verbs appear with more and more main verbs, tenses of verbs, subjects, etc.

Negation in English is a complex system. Klima's (1964) analysis, for example, includes almost two dozen phrase-structural and an equal number of transformational rules. The sketch presented here—including as it does only three phrase-structural and two transformational rules—is clearly highly selective and incomplete. Bellugi (1967) goes somewhat farther, but detailed understanding of the entire system is far from being at hand; as already noted, the work has only begun.

Two other aspects of children's negation should be mentioned, however. Both illustrate the autonomous and inventive character of child grammar and its indirect dependence on the speech of adults.

Table 7. **The Use of Modal Verbs by One Child**

	Age (months)		
Context	26.5	27	27.5
Affirmative	8	20	27
Negative	6	12	14
Yes-No question	—	4	12

From Bellugi, 1967.

One has to do with the rather special corner of the English negative system that controls such verbs as *think, believe, anticipate, expect,* and *want.* All have the unique property that when in sentences with embedded object complements, either these verbs or the verb of the complement may be negated, and meaning does not change (Lakoff, 1966). Compare, for example, the following quartet of sentences, the first pair of which includes a verb open to this option, and the second pair of which does not.

1. I think that he won't come on time.
2. I don't think that he will come on time.
3. I know that he won't come on time.
4. I don't know that he will come on time.

Sentences (1) and (2) mean the same thing, whereas (3) and (4) do not.

For the small set of verbs admitting such moveable negation, Bellugi counted the number of times each option was employed in the speech of the parents of Adam and Sarah. (Eve's records contained no example of such embeddings.) The verbs most often used were *think* and *want,* and in all utterances except one, negation fell on the matrix sentence. *I don't think that he will come in time* was more frequent by a large margin than was *I think that he won't come on time.* Such is the linguistic evidence given to Adam and Sarah.

However, in the children's own speech, precisely the opposite arrangement dominated. This was the case even though negation appeared elsewhere in matrix sentences at this stage—as in *I don't know that.* The following is an exhaustive list:

> He thinks he doesn't have nothing
> I think it's not fulled up to the top
> He thinks he doesn't have to finish it
> I think we don't have a top
> I think he don't like us no more
> I think I can't find white
> I think I don't better cut it
> I think I don't know what it is
> I think I don't

The explanation of the difference between what children do and what is presented to them is simple. Verbs such as *think* and *want* are exceptions to the general rules of negation in English. Unexceptionable verbs are not open to the option of moveable negation in this way. Children, if they have worked out the general rules of negation but not yet the exceptions, will treat *think* as any other verb (so that negation of the matrix verb is reserved for the improbable situation where a child is *not* engaged in thought *and* he is talking about it). They will do so even though they are contradicted by the evidence of parental speech. We have again an indication of the inviolability of children's grammar and the strong filtering effect it exerts on the speech of adults.

Another phenomenon in the acquisition of negation similarly reveals the autonomy of grammar, in this case that children's grammar is autonomous when it changes just as when it does not. In English, adults say affirmatively, *I want some supper,* and at an early point in development children do the same (Bellugi, 1964). To negate such utterances, adults may either say *I want no supper* or *I don't want any supper.* Children at first use neither of these forms, but say *I don't want some supper.* After a few months, however, the grammar changes, and denial takes the form of double negation, as in *I don't want no supper.* It is only after many months that children say *I don't want any supper.* Thus the order of appearance of pronouns in negative sentences is *some-no-any.* Other pronouns built on these forms—for example, *something, no one, anybody*—behave in the same way.

Sentences with *some,* such as *I don't want some supper,* occur at the second stage of negation described above, and result from the insertion of *don't* as an Aux[neg] into such affirmative sentences as *I want some supper.* A child receives no examples of this process in the speech of adults; it is an autonomous consequence of his own grammar. The double negatives of the next stage are even more interesting. The middle-class parents of children who say *I don't want no supper* do not themselves use double negatives; indeed, Cazden (1965) found some indication that children exposed to a double-negative dialect differ both from middle-class children and from the dialect to which they are exposed. Middle-class parents, far from providing examples of double negatives, would tend to correct such utterances with one or another of the well-formed forms of denial.

Bellugi (1967) interprets the double negatives of the third stage as "negative coloring" —a kind of emphatic denial—although it is unclear of what negative coloring consists, except a tendency to use double (and sometimes triple) negatives. It is also unclear why there is not "affirmative coloring" in cases of emphatic assertion, if indeed emphasis has anything to do with double negation. Although negative coloring might play a role in the double negatives of the third stage, it seems also that they are a natural development of the form of negation in the second stage; for some speculations along this line, see McNeill (in press).

The exclusive schema for negation in the first stage is Neg + S or S + *no.* In the second stage, sentences adhering to these schemas continue to appear but they are no longer the exclusive means of negation. In the third stage, negation based on these simple schemas disappears completely. As was pointed out earlier, these schemas also appear in the acquisition of French, Russian, and Japanese, at least. It is possible therefore that they are the universal starting points for negation.

Let us propose that a fundamental ability for negation, from which all children build, allows children to deny a proposition by affixing to it something like a minus sign. If this is actually the case, all children would commence their linguistic careers with one or another of the two schemas mentioned before, and all languages would have sentence-external negation as the deep structure of negative sentences. The suggestion is identical to a remark made by Grégoire in 1937 (p. 169, quoted by Braine, in press): "*pas* devance [la phrase] à la façon d'un sign algebrique qui l'annule."

From such a beginning, children develop in two general directions. On the one hand, the semantics of negation evolves from its primitive starting point, whatever that may be, to a level where distinctions are drawn between such different forms of negation as, for example, *no (I don't want it), no (it is untrue),* and *no (it is not here).* On the other hand, children must discover the syntax of negation of their local language—a process traced in part for English in the preceding pages.

Let us briefly consider semantics. Bellugi (1967) reports an impression that the meaning of negation develops quickly. In the first stage of development, negation seemed, diffusely, to mean refusal, rejection, or displeasure. By the second stage, however, a number of examples appeared where a child clearly negated the content of a previous proposition:

Adult: Daddy's getting old, huh?
Child: No, I get old
Adult: That's your valentine
Child: No, Becky valentine

McNeill and McNeill (1968) found a similar sequence in a study of the development of negation in Japanese children. An initial incoherent period, where denial seemed to depend on the absence of an object, was followed within a few months by the emergence of a single semantic contrast between the denial of the truth of propositions and the denial of the existence of objects or events— that is, by the form of negation also observed by Bellugi. McNeill and McNeill (1968) found that negation in the sense of rejection or refusal did not appear until some months later.

When a child says, for example, *no, Becky valentine*, he denies the truth of an intrinsic predicate—that the valentine is Becky's. If, as previously claimed, intrinsic predicates are the first form of predication to appear in child

language, the initial meaning of the "algebraic minus sign" must be the negation of such predicates. Only later, when extrinsic predication also becomes available, will children negate the existence of things or events. The first distinction drawn in the semantics of negation therefore will be between the denial of truth and the denial of existence.

McNeill and McNeill (1968) analyzed the semantic system of Japanese negation into three such contrasts, and then traced the emergence of each. It is conceivable that the same system applies to English negation also, and that children learning English acquire the system in a similar way.

Figure 7 shows the Japanese arrangement. The contrast between "Truth" and Existence" refers to the negation of intrinsic and extrinsic predicates, respectively. The contrast between "Entailment" and "Nonentailment" refers to the difference between, for example, *no, that's an apple, not a pear* and *no, that's not a pear.* Both deny the truth of an intrinsic predicate (as in *that's a pear*), but in *no, that's an apple, not a pear,* the denial of one predicate "entails" the contrasting truth of another (*that's an apple*). The examples above from Bellugi (1967) apparently are of the entailment type. A final contrast, between "Internal" and "External," refers to the difference between denial on internal grounds (e.g., *I*

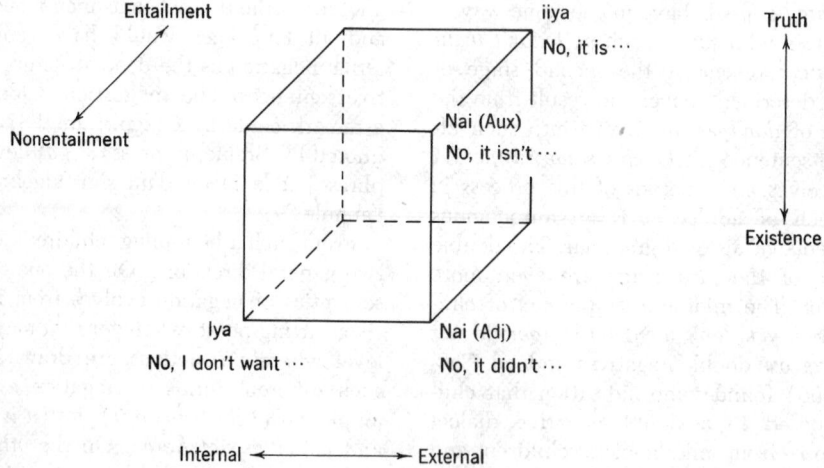

Fig. 7. The organization of negation in Japanese. Negative terms in Japanese and English are located at the appropriate corners. The English examples are merely representative of each contrast: *No, it is a pear (and not an apple),* versus *no, it isn't a pear,* versus *no, it didn't happen that a pear was thrown through the window,* versus *no, I don't want a pear.* (McNeill and McNeill, 1928).

don't want it to happen) and denial on external grounds (e.g., *it didn't happen*).

As already mentioned, the Japanese children studied by McNeill and McNeill (1968) developed first the contrast between Truth and Existence. A few months later, they began to honor also the contrast between Internal and External. Before this time their expression of refusal took weirdly dogmatic form: the Japanese expression for "I don't want" (*iya*) was not used in situations where refusal was evidently intended (as in reply to "Let's do x"), but instead there appeared the expression for "it doesn't exist" (*nai*, an adjective). Thus, exchanges like the following occurred: "Let's give your sister some of your ice cream"—"It doesn't exist." The children expressed a lack of willingness with a term already known to express a lack of existence; clearly, the distinction between Internal and External did not yet matter. Finally, after several more months, the contrast between Entailment and Nonentailment appeared.

The entire structure represented in Fig. 7 emerged within a period of 4 to 6 months. Although it may be true that semantic development is generally slower than is syntactic development, that is not the case with negation. Accepting Bellugi's examples at face value, entailment-nonentailment appears in the language of American children when negation is still fused syntactically with the auxiliary system, and a number of months before the transformations of neg-transportation and do-support make their first appearance.

The Development of Questions. Questions at the outset are simple in the extreme, and in this respect are like negation. Rising intonation, or the use of one of a few Wh-words, is the only interrogative device. Nonetheless, even very young children distinguish between yes-no and Wh-questions—asking, for example, both *see hole?* and *what doing?*

The following account will concentrate on the development of Wh-questions and, within this limit, will concentrate on the second and third stages of development defined by Brown et al. (1968). The first stage comprises essentially the simple system just described.

In the second stage children ask Wh-questions of the following kinds:

Where my mitten?
What me think?
What the dollie have?
Why you smiling?
Why not he eat?
Why not . . . me can't dance?

A clue as to the structure of such questions lies in the fact that in every case except one deleting the Wh-word (or *why not* in the case of negative questions) leaves a "grammatical" sentence as a residue. *My mitten, me think, you smiling, he eat,* and *me can't dance* are all possible declarative sentences in the second stage; the only exception is *the dollie have,* which lacks an NP-object. In general therefore, Wh-questions are formed simply by using a Wh-word to begin a declarative sentence, the sentence otherwise being left undisturbed.

Questions asking *why* and *why not* are not different from other Wh-questions, although the distribution of the former pair is more restricted. *Why not* itself seems to be a single Wh-word possessing negative import, not a construction made up of *why* and negation as separate parts. More significantly, both *why* and *why not* tend to be restricted to discourse exchanges in which the declarative part of the question comes from a previous utterance of an adult and the Wh part comes from the child. Table 8 presents some examples from the speech of Adam and his mother (Brown et al., 1968). The other Wh-words available to children in the second stage of development do not depend on such discourse exchanges. McNeill (1963) found a discourse restriction similar to the restriction of *why* and *why not* in children's use of personal pronouns—in its first occurrences the first-person, pronoun, *I*, always followed adult sentences with *you*.

It is clear from Table 8 that Adam's rule for deciding between *why not* and *why* is to choose the former when his mother's sentence is negative and the latter when it is affirmative. However, it is difficult to say what semantic constraints exist for Adam's *why* and *why not* questions. He wants to know, for example, *why you see seal?*, *why me bend that game?*, and *why not me careful?* Such questions suggest that although Adam probably seeks an explanation when he asks *why* or *why not*, his conception of

Table 8. The Restriction of *Why* and *Why Not* Questions by Discourse

Mother	Adam
He was playing a little tune	Why he play little tune?
I see a seal	Why you see seal?
You bent that game	Why me bent that game?
Well, because she wanted to	Why she want to?
I think it's resting now	Why it's resting now?
I guess I'm not looking in the right place	Why not you looking right place?
Because you weren't careful	Why me not careful?
I don't see any	Why not me can't dance?
You're going to have to buy another one and give it to Ursula because you're breaking that one	Why not me break that one?

From Brown, Cazden, and Bellugi, 1968.

an explanation is remote from an adult's. It would be surprising, of course, if it were otherwise. Piaget (1924) long ago demonstrated that children are unable to conceive of true explanations at Adam's age. Nonetheless, the possibility of explaining things—as opposed to knowing what counts as an explanation—apparently exists early in development.

Wh-questions in the third stage reveal a number of interesting features. Some examples from Klima and Bellugi (1966) are the following:

> Where small trailer he should pull?
> Where the other Joe will drive?
> What he can ride in?
> What did you doed?
> Why he don't know how to pretend?
> Why the kitty can't stand up?
> How he can be a doctor?
> How they can't talk?

The third stage, it will be recalled, is marked by a general emergence of the English auxiliary system, and this development is much in evidence in the Wh-questions children ask. However, children do not use auxiliary verbs in quite the English manner. They ask, for example, *what he can ride in?* or *why he don't know how to pretend?* An adult would put these questions differently: *what can he ride in?* or *why doesn't he know how to pretend?* Both the child and adult versions have a Wh-word in the initial position of the sentence, but the child version does not invert the order of auxiliary verbs and subjects. Children do not invert the order of subject and auxiliary in Wh-questions

even though they do invert these same elements in yes-no questions. Along with *what he can ride in?* children also say *can he ride in it?*

Brown et al. (1968) take the different treatment of Wh- and yes-no questions to mean that children perform just one major transformation per question, even though they have more than one appropriate transformation available. In yes-no questions, only inversion of subject and auxiliary is required, and it is performed. However, in Wh-questions, both inversion and a transformation called "preposing" are required, and children perform only the latter.

Preposing refers to one of the transformations in Klima's (1964) and Katz and Postal's (1964) grammar for Wh-questions. In this analysis, the derivation of a Wh-question begins with a deep structure that contains, in effect, a blank for the constituent being questioned. The deep structure of *what can dinosaurs eat?*, for example, is roughly *dinosaurs can eat* $\triangle$, where $\triangle$ stands for the NP about which information is sought. One relation between the deep structure *dinosaurs can eat* $\triangle$ and the surface structure *what can dinosaurs eat?* is therefore preposing $\triangle$, the result of which is $\triangle$ *dinosaurs can eat;* morphophonemic rules then convert $\triangle$ to *what.* A second relation between the deep and surface structures of *what can dinosaurs eat?* is inversion of *can* and *dinosaurs.*

Since children say *what dinosaurs can eat?* in the third stage of development, it appears that they do not perform the second transformation when they perform the first. *What dinosaurs can eat?* is an example of what

Brown et al. call a "hypothetical intermediate"—a structure defined by the grammar of adult English only at an intermediate stage of derivation.

The account of Brown et al. assumes that the transformations correspond to actual operations in the production of sentences; it is because of such correspondences that psychological complexity is reduced by eliminating transformations. Some might object to this assumption (see Fodor and Garrett, 1966, 1967). Nonetheless, evidence from a number of experiments with adult subjects shows that transformations do indeed contribute to the psychological complexity of some sentences, at least where the transformation is associated with a change in meaning, although it is far from clear how such effects are brought about (e.g., Miller and McKean, 1964; McMahon, 1963; Gough, 1965; Mehler, 1963; Slobin, 1966c; Savin, and Perchonock, 1965). It is possible, though not yet demonstrated, that a similar relation between psychological and linguistic complexity holds for small children.

However, there is a problem of a different kind. Children always eliminate the same transformation. Children never say, for example, *can he ride in what?* or *will the other Joe drive where?*—questions in which subject-auxiliary inversion has occurred but preposing has not. If children actually reduce complexity by eliminating one of two generally available transformations, it would seem that both types of Wh-questions must occur in a large sample of utterances.

One way to explain the presence of *what he can ride in* and the absence of *can he ride in what?* is to assume that the underlying form of the Wh-questions of the third stage is not yet the adult form—in particular, that the vacant constituent △ is not in the object position of sentences. In that case there would be nothing to prepose, and a transformation for preposing would not exist. As in the second stage, Wh-words in the third stage would instead be added to the beginning of sentences and therefore invariably appear there. *What + he can ride in* is a possible question under this arrangement, whereas *can he ride in + what* is not.

However, this suggestion also encounters a difficulty. If different Wh-words are introduced at the beginning of sentences, it is puzzling that such questions are semantically appropriate. The Wh-questions of the third stage are semantically appropriate, however, a fact that demonstrates an association of Wh-words with particular sentence-constituents and (in contrast to the consistent omission of subject-auxiliary inversion) suggests the existence of a preposing transformation. The contradiction only deepens when we recall that the Wh-questions of the *second* stage, when even Brown et al. agree that Wh-words are introduced at the beginning of sentences, also are semantically appropriate.

How could appropriate Wh-questions be derived, if not by preposing? Perhaps the contradictory indications just mentioned can be resolved through a more careful scrutiny of the status children give to questions. Klima and Bellugi (1966) list the following answers of children to Wh-questions asked by adults. All are from the second stage.

Adult: What d'you need?
Child: Need some chocolate

Adult: Who are you peeking at?
Child: Peeking at Ursula

Adult: Who were you playing with?
Child: Robin

Adult: What d'you hear?
Child: Hear a duck

Every question is answered appropriately from a semantic point of view. However, in every example except one, the child's answer is a full VP instead of the NP customary in English. A semantically appropriate reply appears in an unusual syntactic setting, one which makes clear that *what* and *who* are not associated with NP alone.

Let us suppose that *what* has as part of its lexical entry a feature such as [+ common noun], that *who* has [+ proper noun], and that *why* has both [+ common noun] and [+ proper noun] as two options. Whenever one of these Wh-words is heard in an adult question, nouns of the specified type are given in reply. Let us also suppose that each Wh-word is understood as a kind of introductory word for an entire sentence, and not as a replacement of a constituent of a sentence as in adult grammar. Then a child's answer to an adult Wh-question will be a sentence that contains an N of a type specified by the Wh-word; it will not be a noun or verb phrase. Moreover, a child's own Wh-questions will be declarative sentences with Wh-words before them. Children with such a grammar can ask semantically appropriate Wh-questions and not have to prepose Wh-words while doing so.

The facts almost fit this explanation. As expected, a child's own Wh-questions in the second and third stages are generally sentences with Wh-words before them; it is for this reason that subject-auxiliary inversion does not occur in Wh-questions. But the explanation also leads us to expect that a child's answers to adult Wh-questions are sentences, whereas the answers actually given in the second stage are VPs.

However, there is a natural explanation of the VPs of the second stage. A child answers an adult Wh-question with a sentence that includes the material specified by the Wh-word, but he omits the redundant subject of the sentence. Omitting redundant subjects, of course, is a common occurrence in sentences with intrinsic predicates, especially when the subject makes first-person reference. The omitted subjects in the child answers given above are all the pronoun *I*.

In the third stage of development, children answer adult Wh-questions with NPs, as is customary in English (Brown et al., 1968). Doing so, however, contradicts the tendency of children at the same stage to ask Wh-questions by placing a Wh-word before a sentence. There is no process in child speech, corresponding to the omission of subjects, which systematically reduces complete sentences to NPs. However, such contradictions are not peculiar to Wh-questions. As has been widely noted, children often comprehend syntactic forms before they produce them (e.g., Fraser, Bellugi, and Brown, 1963; Lovell and Dixon, 1965), and such apparently is the case here.

The third stage of development is transitional. Children understand Wh-words in the speech of adults as representing particular constituents, but children do not yet produce Wh-questions this way. McNeill (1966a) offers some speculation on the cause of the gap between the production and comprehension of speech—essentially, that the constraints of memory are less in comprehension than in production.

The Role of Adult Speech

One major interaction that takes place between a child's linguistic abilities and his linguistic experiences is localized in the acquisition of transformations. A large part of the problem of understanding language learning is precisely the problem of understanding how this step is taken. In this, the final section on syntax, we shall consider what can be said of the process of transformational development.

Imitation. Imitation has already been mentioned but can be considered again in the present context. There is no reason in principle why imitation cannot be used as a strategy for discovering transformations. By imitating the surface forms of adult sentences, children can pair well-formed surface structures with deep structures of their own devising, and so notice how the two are related. Situational cues might suggest particular deep structures, so the method need not proceed blindly. However, the potential usefulness of imitation is confronted by another principle, which, in actual practice, dominates it. Children systematically convert adult sentences into forms allowed in their own grammatical system. The consequence is that even though deep and surface structures are paired through imitation, the only structures paired in this manner are ones related by rules already known. Apparently children always assimilate adult models into their own grammars; imitation thus plays no role in the acquisition of new transformations.

Expansions and "Prompts." One way to avoid the problem of assimilation is to place the burden of introducing new surface forms on adults. In that case, assimilation to child grammar cannot occur. Brown et al. (1968) discuss two situations that have such an effect, one they call "expansion" and the other "prompting." The effectiveness of the first is open to dispute and the usefulness of the second is so far unknown, but both at least illustrate some of the possibilities that exist.

An expansion is an imitation in reverse. An adult, imitating a child's telegraphic sentence, typically adds to the child's sentence the parts he judges the child to have omitted. The result is an expansion. There is always a number of possibilities available as expansions, and an adult will choose the one that he believes best expresses the child's intended meaning. *That mommy hairband*, for example, could be expanded in many directions—*that's mommy's hairband, that was mommy's hairband until you dismantled it, that looks like mommy's hairband*, etc. Usually one sentence will best fit the extralinguistic situation, and that sentence becomes the expansion.

An expansion that fits both a child's utterance and the extralinguistic situation can reveal one or more transformations. Further, if the child's meaning is correctly guessed from the extralinguistic situation, the expansion presents a surface structure that expresses the deep structure the child has in mind. The expansion is necessarily experienced by the child in contiguity with his intended meaning, and it is effective when the child notices the way the two are related. In this case, there is no intrusion of a child's tendency to assimilate adult speech to his own grammar.

Cazden (1965) looked into the effectiveness of expanding child speech by deliberately increasing the number of expansions given to a group of children. The children were 2½ years old, from working-class homes, spent each weekday in a nursery school, and received in the normal course of events few expansions either at school or at home. In Cazden's experiment every child spent ½ hour a day, 5 days a week, looking at picture books with an adult who systematically expanded everything the child said. At the beginning and at the end of the experiment, 3 months later, the children were given a specially devised test of linguistic performance (covering, for example, NP and VP complexity and the imitation of various syntactic forms).

These expansion children were compared to two other groups of children, taken from the same nursery school, who received in one case what Cazden called "models," and in the other case no special treatment at all. "Modelling" was commenting. Everything said by a child in the modelling group was commented upon rather than improved upon through expansion. If, for example, a child said *doggie bite,* an expansion might be *yes, he's biting,* whereas a model might be *yes, he's very mad.* Children in the modelling

group also spent ½ hour a day, 5 days a week, looking at picture books with an adult.

The results were clear-cut. Relative to the group of children who received no special treatment, there was a modest gain in linguistic performance among the children who received expansions, and a large gain among the children who received models. Cazden interpreted her results by pointing to a difference in the variety of syntactic and lexical forms required for expanding as compared to modelling child speech. In expansion an adult is closely led by a child—he must use the child's words and something like the child's syntax. The opposite is typically true of modelling—he must avoid the child's words and often his syntax. Apparently therefore constraint by a child's own utterances is not beneficial to linguistic development. However, it is this very fact that presumably makes expansion advantageous; clearly, if Cazden is right, the theory of expansion is wrong.

Cazden's experiment shows beyond doubt that modelling benefits linguistic development. However, it is less clear what it shows of the relative benefits of expanding. The rate of expansion of the speech recorded of middle-class children is about 30%. One can ask why this rate is not higher—say 50 or 70%. There must be many reasons why the rate of expansion stabilizes where it does, but one reason is particularly significant: not everything said by a child has an unambiguous meaning in the extralinguistic context, and in such ambiguous circumstances adults tend not to expand.

In Cazden's experiment, on the other hand, the rate of expansion was 100%, by design. Aside from the possibility that young children might not pay attention to many expansions in the face of an avalanche of expansions (Brown et al., 1968), some utterances in Cazden's experiment must have been inappropriately expanded. In such cases a child could formulate a "transformation" that does not belong in English—for example, one that relates the meaning of "that's mommy's hairband" to the surface structure of *that looks like mommy's hairband.* If such misinterpretations took place, the poor showing of expansion in Cazden's experiment is to be expected even on the excessively strong assumption that expansions are decisive in the acquisition of transformations. The question of the effectiveness of expansion therefore remains open.

Brown et al. (1968) have recently looked at the matter in another way, and again obtained negative results. However, once again counterarguments can be offered in defense of expansion. As noted before, Brown et al. calibrate the linguistic development of their subjects against the mean length of utterances, rather than, as usual, against chronological age. When the calibration is done against utterance length, the rate of advancement of the three subjects in Brown's study is (in declining order) Sarah, Adam, and Eve. When the calibration is against chronological age, the order is Eve, Adam, and Sarah. These orders of development can be compared to the order of expansion by the children's parents. In this case it is Adam, Eve, and Sarah. In other words, Sarah, who is most advanced relative to utterance length, received the fewest expansions.

However, one can dispute the choice of baseline by Brown et al. At any given utterance length, the least advanced child, Eve, used fewer modal verbs, inflections, prepositions, articles, and other superficial sentence-forms than did Sarah, the most advanced child. Length for Eve was increased with content words—nouns, verbs, and adjectives. Thus Sarah's speech was syntactically more like adult English at any given length but Eve's was more informative, as Brown et al. point out. Sarah might have said *that's mommy's hairband,* a well-formed sentence five morphemes long, whereas Eve might have said, semigrammatically, but with the same length, *that mommy broken hairband there.*

Cazden (1967) concludes from the differences between Eve and Sarah that Eve's intellectual development was greater than Sarah's. A difference between Eve and Sarah in intellectual level may well exist, and comparisons of children on syntactic complexity relative to mean utterance length is one appropriate way of demonstrating such a fact— at every point, Eve had more to say but Sarah said it better. Such comparisons, however, do not bear on the alleged role of expansions. This role is to facilitate the acquisition of transformations. A child who receives more

expansions has more opportunities to observe relations between deep and surface structure and therefore can formulate relations sooner. An appropriate baseline against which to measure this effect is chronological age. And relative to chronological age Eve's linguistic development is far in advance of Sarah's.

The role, or lack of role, of expansion in linguistic development is thus open to dispute. The one experiment done on the phenomenon has an ambiguous outcome. The evidence of recorded adult and child speech can be interpreted in diametrically opposite ways, depending on the baseline of comparison.

"Prompting" is discussed by Brown et al. as a possible training variable, but its effectiveness is yet to be investigated. As noted earlier, one transformation in the derivation of Wh-questions in English is a preposing of $\triangle$ to the head of a sentence. *Dinosaurs can eat* $\triangle$ becomes $\triangle$ *dinosaurs can eat.* In a "prompt" something very much like preposing is demonstrated to a child.

A prompt begins with a Wh-question from an adult—*what did you eat?* If a child does not answer, the question may be repeated in a different form—*you ate what?* The second version differs from the first in several respects, one being that preposing has not occurred. If a child understands the second question, and so has in mind the deep structure *you eat* $\triangle$, he is in a position to observe the relation of this deep structure to the surface structure of *what did you eat?* The relation is preposing, and for a child who has not formulated the transformation, a "prompt" may provide an occasion to do so. Brown et al. note that children usually answer non-preposed questions, so prompting is at least potentially effective in revealing preposing to a child.

Brown et al. describe a third parent-child exchange, "echoing," which also can be mentioned although it probably does not provide an opportunity for children to learn a transformation. An "echo" begins when a child's utterance is in part unintelligible—for example, *I ate the gowish.* An adult may then echo the child but replace the unintelligible part with a Wh-word—*you ate the what?* The form of the adult question is the same as in prompting. However, even if a child understands the adult question he could not discover preposing, for that relation is nowhere revealed. The only relations available in an echo are, on the one hand, between the deep structure *you ate* △ and the surface structure of *you ate the what?* and, on the other hand, between *you ate* △ and the surface structure of *I ate the gowish*. If a child recovers the deep structure of *you ate the what?*, he already understands that relation; if he notices the relation between *you ate* △ and *I ate the gowish*, he observes the relation of a question to an answer. Echoing might tell a child something about answering questions therefore, but it cannot teach him about preposing. Echoing might also help a child discover what in his own utterance belongs to a single sentence-constituent (Brown et al., 1968); the *what* of *you ate what?*, for example, replaces an NP in the child's sentence; the *where* of *you got it where?* replaces a locative adverbial; etc.

A General Condition for Learning Transformations. Both expansions and prompting have in common an ability to demonstrate transformational relations; echoes, on the other hand, do not have such an ability. There are no doubt other exchanges between parents and children that reveal transformations, and it is helpful in the search for such exchanges to isolate the condition that all must meet. In order for a child to observe a transformational relation not yet part of his linguistic competence, he must have in mind the deep structure of a sentence obtained from the speech of someone else; a structure that can only be in a child's mind must coexist with another structure that can only be in the speech of an adult. Expansions, prompts, and imitation meet this demand, but echoes, talking to oneself, rote practice, and many utterances simply overheard by children do not (McNeill, in press). The effect is to reduce even further the effective size of the corpus on which all language acquisition is based.

Such situations as expansion or imitation, which potentially combine a child's deep structure and an adult's surface structure, may not, of course, result in the discovery of transformations. In the case of imitation discovery is systematically blocked by a contradictory tendency to imitate in terms of a child's own grammar. The usefulness of expansions and prompts, while not systematically blocked, depends on a child actually noticing that both a deep and surface structure are available. Children may not always do this.

Languages differ hugely in their surface structures; they also differ hugely in the transformations that relate surface structures to deep structures. However, there is a small number of universal transformational relations. One transformation discussed in the Appendix permutes the order of verbs and affixes in developing an auxiliary verb. The relation of permutation is universal. Besides permutation, the addition of elements (as in the English passive) and the deletion of elements (as in the English imperative) are universal transformational relations. So is the requirement that deletions from the deep structure be recoverable (forcing, e.g., English relative clauses to be made up of constituent and matrix sentences with identical *NPs*; see Appendix). There may be a few other relations universal in scope; but their total number probably is less than the number of fingers.

Universal transformations may play a crucial role in language acquisition, for it is possible that they describe relations to which young children are innately predisposed. Indeed, that would be at least one reason why they are universal.

If indeed the acquisition of transformations proceeds through the formulation and refinement of hypotheses, the hypotheses apparently take the most general form possible. Children are not cautious theoreticians. They do not, for example, attempt to find an integrating principle that covers two or three local observations, to which they add the results of other small theories devised elsewhere —that is, they do not follow the model of a systems engineer. They are more like theologians in this respect, as their goal is to find hypotheses with the largest possible scope and the fewest possible exceptions. The consequences are visible throughout language acquisition—in inflectional imperialism, in the differentiation of grammatical classes, in negation, and in Wh-questions.

It is possible that the systematization carried out by children can itself be described in terms of a regular principle. The so-called simplicity metric of linguistic theory (e.g., Halle, 1964b; Katz, 1966) is designed to select the simplest grammar that fits both the rest of linguistic theory and the intuitions of native speakers. Children, in extending linguistic hypotheses to cover different cases, may act in a manner described by such a simplicity metric.

It is worth considering the possiblity that children cannot avoid formulating hypotheses about language. Given any kind of linguistic experience, children very quickly develop rules that cover the experience. A few instances of an NP and a VP becoming a sentence may lead to the hypothesis that all sentences are NP-VP constructions. The tremendous generality of children's first grammars suggests the existence of such a phenomenon throughout language acquisition. Generalizations appear immediately. What requires time and further experience is the modification of these generalizations. Language acquisition thus appears to be the opposite of concept formation, where strategies for organizing information lead to the discovery of rules (Bruner, Goodnow, and Austin, 1956). Indeed it is different from most forms of learning studied by psychologists.

The starting-point of grammar is more or less the same for all children; a good deal of space in the preceding pages has been devoted to describing this initial condition. Being universal, child grammar is not the grammar of any language, but is instead something that can become the grammar of any language through a process of formulating and modifying linguistic hypotheses.

In so evolving, language for a child moves from a maximally diffuse to a maximally articulated state. It starts with an intimate and extremely general relation between sound and meaning; it progresses from there to a less intimate and general relation mediated by deep structures; eventually it arrives at the complex and systematic relation between sound and meaning that comprises a transformational grammar. Such is the sequence of events that has been traced in these pages.

The events described in the preceding sections of this chapter take place for the most part before age 4½. At one point it was thought that all of syntax was acquired by this age (McNeill, 1966a; Slobin, 1966a). However, it is now clear that some aspects of syntax are not acquired until much later, and for some speakers certain details of grammar may never be acquired.

C.S. Chomsky (1968) has reported a num-

ber of interesting observations bearing on these questions. She was interested in how children older than 5 understand sentences that depart from what she calls the "minimum distance principle" (MDP). The MDP is a general characteristic of English predicate complements, a type of embedding. *John required Mary to be an enthusiast,* for example, is a predicate complement to which the MDP applies. In such sentences the subject (*Mary*) of the complement (*to be an enthusiast*) is the first *NP* to the left. This rule is the MDP, and it applies to the vast majority of English sentences. However, there are a few exceptions. In *John promised Mary to be an enthusiast,* the MDP does not apply, for the subject of the complement is *John*— the second NP to the left. *Promise* is one of a small number of exceptional English verbs where the MDP is required not to apply. Another such verb is *ask.* Compare *I asked Mary what to do about the enthusiast* to *I told Mary what to do about the enthusiast.* In the second the subject of *do* is *Mary,* as required by the MDP, but in the first it is *I.*

Sentences with *promise* or *ask* are more complex than sentences with *know* or *tell.* To understand them a child must not only be able to recognize that the complement has a hidden subject but also that the subject is— in contradiction to a general rule—the first NP of the main clause. Inasmuch as children strive to formulate general rules we would expect them to apply the MDP before they discover the exceptions to the MDP. When instructed to "ask Mary what to feed the doll" a child who knows the MDP but not that *ask* is an exception should say something like *what are you going to feed the doll?* Similarly, if asked who will do the feeding in *John promised Mary to feed the doll,* a child who knows the MDP but not that *promise* is an exception should say *Mary.* Such confusions are exactly what Chomsky found.

The course of acquisition is interesting. In the case of *promise* all children above 5 know about the MDP. Some as young as 5 also know that *promise* is an exception to the MDP, whereas others as old as 10 do not. There seems to be no age at which all children discover that *promise* requires the MDP to be violated. A similar history exists for *ask.* Again there is no age at which all children acquire full knowledge of how to use the verb. Some as young as 5 never make mistakes, others as old as 10 always make mistakes. The situation with *ask*, however, is more complicated than with *promise*, because at first children interpret *ask* as *tell*. In response to the instruction "ask Mary what to put in the box" a child may tell Mary what to put in the box—a doll, for instance. In this case the MDP is applied, but because the child has interpreted *ask* as *tell* there is no reason it should not apply. Only later do children actually ask a question when instructed in this way, and then it is possible to observe incorrect applications of the MDP —"what are you going to put in the box?"

The scattered acquisition of *promise* and *ask* stands in sharp contrast to the acquisition of a third grammatical feature. In sentences such as *after he got the candy Mickey left* and *Mickey thinks he knows everything*, the pronoun *he* is ambiguous—it could be "Mickey" or it could be someone else. Pronouns generally have ambiguous referents in English sentences. However, when the pronoun appears in a main clause and the main clause precedes a NP there is no ambiguity —the pronoun must refer to some other NP. In *he found out that Mickey won the race*, for instance, he cannot be "Mickey." Chomsky studied the acquisition of this "nonidentity" rule for pronouns (a study of pronominal ambiguity has been carried out by Chai, 1967, who found children of 10 unable to resolve ambiguous usages). Like *promise* and *ask*, the nonidentity rule is an exception to a general case. Unlike the verbs, however, the absence of ambiguity of the pronoun is itself the result of a grammatical rule. *Promise* and *ask* are exceptional words; pronouns in clauses before NPs are parts of exceptional structures. In contrast to the scattered acquisition of *promise* and *ask*, Chomsky found a discontinuity in the acquisition of the nonidentity rule. All children were in possession of it by age 5½, and none were in possession of it before. The difference in acquisition probably has something to do with the difference in the underlying grammatical situation. Rules might be acquired at uniform ages, whereas lexical information is not.

SEMANTICS

Semantic development is at once the most pervasive and the least understood aspect of language acquisition. It is pervasive because the emergence of a semantic component in a child's grammar has repercussions in wide areas of cognition beyond language itself. It is little understood because there has as yet been little guidance from linguistic theory on what to expect. However, theories of semantics are currently under active development, and matters in this quarter may soon improve (see Katz and Fodor, 1963; Katz and Postal, 1964; Katz, 1966; 1967; Weinreich, 1963; 1966).

The level of sophistication in the study of semantic development is not comparable to the level in other aspects of linguistic development. It differs from syntax, where by now several investigations of language acquisition have been carried out under the general, if not the specific influence of contemporary linguistic theory. And it is diametrically opposite from the situation in phonology: in semantics there are huge quantities of data, but no theory to say which are relevant; in phonology there are almost no data, but there is a theory to say what relevant data would be like in the event they should be collected.

The treatment of semantics that follows will concentrate on a few topics—the development of semantic "features," semantic influences on syntax, the association of semantics with action, and the exchange of information among children. The topics have been chosen in part because of their general interest and in part because they bear on certain theoretical issues.

Studies mainly of a statistical or normative nature are not included. Such studies mostly have to do with children's word associations (e.g., diVesta, 1964a; 1964b; Riegal, 1965b; Riegel, and Feldman, 1967; Riegel and Zivian; 1967); and children's ratings on the semantic differential (e.g., diVesta, 1966c; diVesta and Dick, 1966; Rice and diVesta, 1965). Extensive norms of children's free word associations have been published recently by Entwisle (1966), and of children's restricted associations by Riegel (1965a). DiVesta (1966a) has published norms of children's semantic differential ratings.

Also omitted are studies of children's cognitive development, including those that deal with the role of language. The reader should consult other chapters in this book for reviews of this work. See also Bruner, Olver, and Greenfield (1966) for a summary of recent research on the topic.

For summaries of work on vocabulary development and the development of reference, see previous editions of this book, Brown (1958), and, from a special point of view, Werner and Kaplan (1951).

Semantic Features

It is clear that children have some kind of semantic system at a very early point in linguistic development.

Children at first use words holophrastically. One way of viewing this phenomenon is to conceive of the earliest semantic system as consisting of a dictionary in which words are paired with sentence-interpretations. Each interpretation embodies a particular predicative relation; each word is paired with several interpretations. A holophrastic dictionary of this kind is burdensome for a child's memory and susceptible to ambiguity. The ambiguity can be reduced by the creation of a new dictionary in which words are paired with single sentence-interpretations. However, such a one-to-one dictionary is even more burdensome on memory, as each word must be entered several times, and it too must be abandoned. The ultimate solution is a word dictionary. A word dictionary has the same effect as a sentence dictionary, but not the same bulk (Miller, personal communication).

Both these hypothetical transitions effects a reworking of a child's semantic system. Of the two, however, the second is by far the most significant, and it is from the point of the first construction of a word dictionary that we can date the rudiments of a system basically similar to adult semantic competence (see Katz and Fodor, 1963). In changing from a holophrastic to a sentence dictionary, a child continues to store undifferentiated semantic information; the definition of one sentence is not related to the definition of any other. In changing from a sentence dictionary to a word dictionary, on the other hand, a fundamental modification is introduced in the format of the dictionary entries themselves. A child begins to elaborate a system of semantic features, and sentences come to be interrelated through semantic rules for using dictionary entries.

The evidence is that the accretion of se-

mantic information, in contrast to the acquisition of syntactic information, is a slow process not completed until well into school age. It is the development of a word dictionary that is emphasized in this section.

A child's first effort to compile a word dictionary presumably does not occur earlier than his use of base-structure rules in the construction of sentences. It is difficult to conceive of a word dictionary that does not receive input from some sort of syntactic component; without such input, a word dictionary would result in a loss of power to encode sentence meaning. If one cause of the transition to a word dictionary is a need to retain sentence meaning while reducing the load of a sentence dictionary on memory, compilation of a word dictionary ought not to begin before the first sign of a base-structure grammar, at about 18 months. This sets a lower bound on the beginning of a true semantic component of grammar.

Setting an upper bound is more difficult. Children could continue to use a sentence dictionary after becoming able to construct grammatically organized sentences. Each construction would be referred to the dictionary to learn its meaning. However, such an effort must end when the variety of sentences becomes at all large, as when transformation rules come to be used. A sentence dictionary coupled with transformations requires storing the same sentence-meaning in many places, once for each tranformation of the same deep structure. The result would be a large increase in the size of the dictionary. On the other hand, transformations can lead to a reduction in dictionary size if the dictionary is a word dictionary. A word dictionary therefore is favored (in two ways) by the development of transformations; so we can set an upper bound for the first compilation of a word dictionary at the time transformations appear in abundance, at about 28 to 30 months.

We can only guess how the compilation of a word dictionary is carried out. A simple assumption is that semantic features are sequentially added to dictionary entries. Such an assumption is no doubt incorrect in its simplest form. It ignores, for example, the possibility that features are related to one another, and so may enter a dictionary together (Katz, 1966). Nonetheless, a sequential accretion of semantic features is plausible as an initial hypothesis.

Consider a purely hypothetical example. An entry for the word *flower* would have to include at least the following: a syntactic feature [common noun], several semantic features, perhaps (physical object) (living) (small) (plant), plus certain selection restrictions. An adult dictionary contains more than four semantic features for *flower*, but the ones given are a minimum set. The assumption that dictionary entries are built up sequentially means that the semantic features (physical object), (living), (small), (plant) are added one at a time, though not necessarily in the order listed.

The addition of each feature is an event with widespread consequences. By definition, semantic features appear in more than one dictionary entry; in some cases—the feature (small), for example—a feature appears in a great many dictionary entries. Each new semantic feature is a distinction that separates one class of words from another, a fact that may contribute to the apparently slow manner in which such additions to a dictionary take place.

If the compilation of dictionary entries is sequential, words can be part of a child's vocabulary but have semantic properties different from the same words in the vocabulary of an older child or adult. Semantic development in this case consists of completing the dictionary entries of words already acquired, as well as the acquisition of new words. Simple vocabulary counts miss this internal aspect of semantic development entirely, and in this respect give a misleading picture of linguistic advancement.

Semantic Anomaly. One consequence of the sequential enrichment of a word dictionary is that sentences regarded as anomalous by adults and older children will be regarded as acceptable by younger children. Every dictionary entry contains a set of "selection restrictions" (Katz and Fodor, 1963), which set forth information about a word's allowable contexts. The selection restrictions of a word consist of those semantic markers that can appear as context for the word. A semantic marker in one of the senses of *crane*, for example, matches the selection restrictions of *construction;* so we can have *construction crane*. However, none of the semantic markers

of *construction crane* matches the selection restrictions of the predicate *laid an egg;* so we avoid as anomalous *the construction crane laid an egg*, even though we accept *the crane laid an egg*.

A child who lacks knowledge of some semantic features of a word will accept grammatical combinations that an adult, with a fuller dictionary entry, marks as anomalous. A child accepts anomalous combinations when the features and selection restrictions responsible for the anomaly are missing from his dictionary. If we think in terms of distribution classes—that is, in terms of words that can appear in the same contexts—we can say that a child has distribution classes wider in scope than those possible for an adult. The result of adding semantic markers is a narrowing of distribution classes and an increased tendency to reject as anomalous once accepted word-combinations.

Miller and Isard (1963) performed an experiment in which adult subjects listened to three different kinds of verbal strings through a masking noise. The strings were fully grammatical sentences (*the academic lecture attracted a limited audience*), or anomalous sentences (*the academic liquid became an odorless audience*), or scrambled strings (*liquid the an became audience odorless academic*). A subject's task was to shadow the strings as they were heard. Since a masking noise randomly obliterated parts of the acoustic signal, the performance of a subject depended on an ability to fill in the obliterated parts by guessing on the basis of what was actually heard the structure of each string.

At several noise levels, Miller and Isard's subjects shadowed fully grammatical strings most accurately, anomalous strings next most accurately, and scrambled strings least accurately. The difference between grammatical and anomalous strings reflects an ability to exploit the semantic restrictions on word combinations, whereas the difference between anomalous and scrambled strings reflects an ability to exploit syntactic restrictions.

What should we expect of children in this experiment? If a child lacks some semantic features, he will be less able than an adult to guess the words of a fully grammatical sentence partly obliterated by noise. If both a child and an adult heard . . . *ate the cheese*, an adult might guess that the subject of the sentence was *mouse,* but a child might guess *tiger.* What of anomalous sentences? In this case adults and children should not differ, as the presence or absence of semantic features in a dictionary is irrelevant to the reconstruction of sentences where semantic features and selection restrictions do not match in the first place.

Thus, to the degree that a child lacks knowledge of semantic features, performance on fully grammatical and anomalous sentences should be the same. McNeill (1965) repeated Miller and Isard's experiment with children 5, 6, 7, and 8 years old. The procedure was identical to Miller and Isard's in all respects except that McNeill used less exotic vocabulary and that the task was immediate recall. Children of 5 take so long to respond when shadowing that the test was converted automatically into immediate recall.

The results are summarized in Fig. 8, which shows the percent of complete strings correctly recalled by children of different ages. (The percent of content words correctly recalled shows essentially the same result, although the data are less regular.) The conclusion to be drawn from Fig. 8 is clear: 5-year-olds are less able than 8-year-

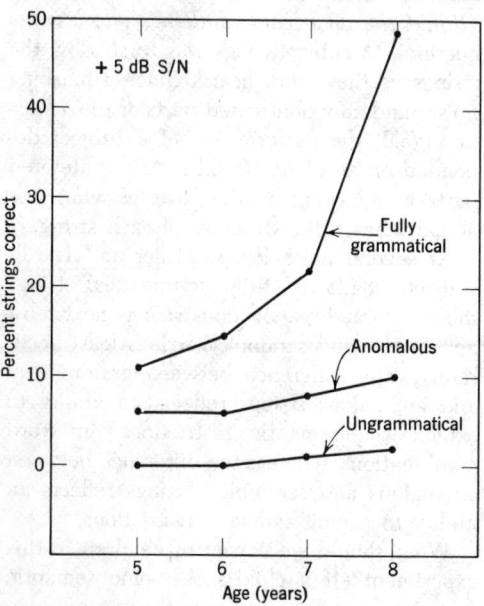

Fig. 8. Percentage of strings correctly recalled by children 5, 6, 7, and 8 years old (McNeill, 1965).

olds to take advantage of semantic consistency in sentences. Accurately guessing the obliterated parts of sentences depends on the sentences being constructed in accordance with semantic principles available to the guesser; 5-year-olds evidently depart from the semantic rules of English. Since a lack of semantic markers does not affect the accuracy of guessing the obliterated parts of anomalous sentences, performance with such sentences changes very little between ages 5 and 8, as can be seen in Fig. 8.

A third curve in Fig. 8 summarizes the performance of children with scrambled strings. Accuracy in this case is parallel to, but always worse than, accuracy with anomalous strings. The difference suggests that the ability of children to exploit the syntactic information contained in anomalous strings does not change between 5 and 8, a fact consistent with the slow development of dictionary entries relative to the rapid development of syntax.

In general, one can conclude from this experiment that children of 5 find fully grammatical sentences only slightly superior to anomalous sentences. It apparently makes little difference whether one says to a child *wild Indians shoot running buffaloes* or *wild elevators shoot ticking restaurants.* The sentences are equally remarkable.

The experiment just described revealed a tendency for children to reconstruct anomalous and fully grammatical sentences in the same (inappropriate) way. Poor performance in this case was presumably a matter of poor perception. Turner and Rommetveit (in press) have in addition observed anomalous sentences in the linguistic productions of children—for instance, *the tractor drives the farmer, the pony rides the girl,* and *the branch carries the bird.* These sentences were not uttered in play or fantasy; they were mistaken but serious descriptions of pictured scenes—a farmer driving a tractor, a girl riding a pony, and a bird resting on a branch.

The word associations of children also show the effects of incomplete dictionary entries. If stimulus and response are regarded as potentially forming a grammatical unit in word association, children's responses often make syntactically possible but semantically anomalous combinations with their stimuli. *Soft-*

wall, bright-rake, and *fast-shout* are adjective-noun combinations given in association by 6- and 7-year-olds, and all are anomalous. Adults rarely if ever respond in this way.

Word associations may be divided into two general categories according to the grammatical relation of the stimulus and response. If the response belongs to a different grammatical class from the stimulus, the association is called "syntagmatic" (Ervin, 1961) or "heterogeneous" (Brown and Berko, 1960). If the response is in the same grammatical class, it is called "paradigmatic" (Ervin, 1961) or "homogeneous" (Brown and Berko, 1960). Both Ervin (1961) and Brown and Berko (1960) noted that young children respond mostly with syntagmatic associations, whereas older children and adults respond mostly with paradigmatic associations. The change from a predominance of one response to a predominance of the other takes place between 6 and 8 years—the same ages at which children come to distinguish anomalous and fully grammatical sentences in the experiment by McNeill (1965).

The coincidence of ages suggests that the shift to paradigmatic responding occurs because of semantic, not syntactic, consolidation. McNeill (1965; 1966d) offered a view of how the shift is accomplished on semantic grounds—essentially, that early "syntagmatic" responses are often actually paradigmatic, but fall outside the grammatical class of the stimulus because of the breadth of the semantic categories available to young children. Entwisle (1966) has found some support for this account in her extensive data on children's word associations. Anderson and Beh (1968), while agreeing that the paradigmatic shift results from some kind of semantic consolidation at 7 or 8, argue instead that syntagmatic associations reflect a basically different and less efficient principle of organization of a child's lexicon than do paradigmatic associations. White (1965) has argued that there is a massive change in the intellectual abilities of children at this age, which affects language and cognition alike.

Why is Semantic Development so Slow? We have reviewed some evidence for the slow, possibly sequential development of dictionary entries. Word association and the recall of sentences both indicate that children continue to compile dictionary entries as late as age 8, at least. Semantic development thus stands in contrast to syntactic development, which appears to be complete in many respects by 4 or 5.

Why is there such a difference? There must be numerous reasons, and we can barely guess at them. Nevertheless, a few possibilities come to mind. One certainly is the complexity of the information that is encoded in a dictionary. Another is that developments in a child's lexicon, far more than developments in syntax, depend on achieving a certain level of intellectual maturity. A child capable of saying of 20 wooden beads, 15 white and 5 green, that white beads outnumber wooden beads is also likely to say *Lassie's not an animal, she's a dog.* Presumably it is with reference to semantic development that Piaget (1967) comments, ". . . [intellectual] operations direct language acquisitions rather than vice versa."

A third reason for the slow course of semantic development must have to do with the abstractness of semantic features. There is *nothing* in the superficial form of sentences capable even of hinting at underlying semantic regularities. Unlike syntactic abstractions, which are systematically related to surface structure by means of transformations, the semantic relations between surface and deep structure are unsystematic. No general relation holds between the phonemic form of *school* or *uncle* or *space ship* and the meaning of these words. It is one measure, perhaps, of how little insight we have into the acquisition of word meaning that it should thus seem impossible.

Occasionally, one hears the hypothesis that children acquire semantic knowledge from explicit definition. A parent may say *the zebra is an animal,* from which a child may acquire the semantic feature (animal). Perhaps the slow advance of semantic development is a result of a dependence on definitions; unlike syntax, adults may have to provide explicit instruction in semantics.

This argument is fallacious and is so for a simple reason. The sentence *the zebra is an animal* may indeed serve to introduce the marker (animal) into a new point in a child's dictionary, but it cannot affect his basic semantic competance. Explicit definitions may work to expand vocabulary, but they are irrelevant to the problem that has been considered in this section—the addition of semantic features to a dictionary. In order for the sentence *the zebra is an animal* to influence the dictionary entry for *zebra,* the feature (animal) must already be in the dictionary entry for the word *animal.* If it were not, the sentence *the zebra is an animal* would be without effect on a child's dictionary. But if *animal* contains the feature (animal), then obviously (animal) is already acquired, and the defining sentence merely locates it in a new entry. Explicit definitions are not the vehicle for enlargement of a child's stock of semantic features.

Not all semantic development is slow. The emergence of various semantic distinctions in negation has already been mentioned. They apparently are fully developed by children of 2½ years. Greenfield (1967) has made a similar analysis of the infant term *dada,* tracing the development of its meaning in the speech of her 11-month old daughter. The relevant semantic distinctions (e.g., male versus female; caretaker versus noncaretaker) had all appeared by the first birthday!

It is clear that only some aspects of semantic organization develop slowly. Negation and the idea of a parent emerge very early. So must many other semantic distinctions. Yet 5-year-olds fail to distinguish anomalous from fully grammatical sentences in McNeill's (1965) experiment and they describe a picture of a girl on a pony as *the pony rides the girl* in Turner and Rommetveit's (in press) experiment. It is a fair measure of our understanding of semantics that we cannot say how the last two examples differ from the first two.

A Method for Discovering Semantic Features. One major obstacle faced in the study of semantic development is a sweeping ignorance of the semantic features of English. Very few features have been isolated, and the procedure for discovering them is difficult and slow (see Katz, 1964, for an example).

Recently Miller (1967) has devised a method, based on word-sorting and cluster-analysis, which yields categories of words not unlike the categories defined by the semantic features of linguistics. The method requires subjects to classify large samples of necessarily written words into self-imposed groups,

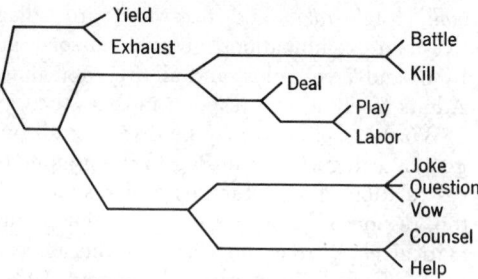

Fig. 9. Cluster analysis of some English nouns; data from adults (Miller, 1967).

and cannot therefore be used with young children. However, the results of the method with adult subjects can be used to organize such observations of children as are available.

For example, Miller (1967) found that as nouns *yield, exhaust, battle, kill, deal, play, labor, joke, question, vow, counsel,* and *help* fall into the clusters pictured in Fig. 9. Each node in the tree represented in Fig. 9 is taken to represent a particular semantic feature: every word beneath a node possesses that feature; words elsewhere do not. Although one cannot obtain such structures from young children, it is possible to see if children honor the distinctions recovered from adults. Do children distinguish, for example, between *the clown told a joke* and *the clown told a battle?* If they do, we infer that children are acquainted at least with the semantic features defining the two large clusters containing *joke* and *battle.* We can also ask about the narrower distinction between *joke* and *help.* Do children distinguish, for example, between *jokes make everybody laugh* and *help makes everybody laugh?* The method is suggestive and deserves exploration.

Semantic Influences on Syntax. Slobin (1963; 1966) performed an experiment with children of 5, 7, 9, and 11 years, in which the truth of sentences was judged against pictured scenes. A picture might show, for example, a dog in pursuit of a cat. A true sentence describing this picture is *the dog chases the cat,* and a false sentence is *the cat chases the dog.* Slobin presented such true and false descriptions in several syntactical forms, using the familiar transformations of negation and passivization to produce variants. For the picture of a dog chasing a cat the following sentences are available:

True	*False*
The dog is chasing the cat	The cat is chasing the dog
The cat is being chased by the dog	The dog is being chased by the cat
The cat is not chasing the dog	The dog is not chasing the cat
The dog is not being chased by the cat	The cat is not being chased by the dog

One variable in the experiment therefore was syntactic—simple declarative sentences were compared to negative sentences, passive sentences, and negative-passive sentences. Another variable was the truth or falsity of the description. A third variable was semantic content.

Actually two semantic factors are involved. One is negation, and it in turn appears in two forms. Each sentence, being a description of a picture, invokes negation in the sense called "Existence" by McNeill and McNeill (1968). Also, a subject in judging the truth or falsity of a sentence must react—affirmatively or negatively—to the dimension called "Truth" by McNeill and McNeill. The two varieties of negation were therefore invoked at different points in the experiment. Slobin found negative sentences to be more difficult than affirmative sentences—a result also found by Wason (1965). Slobin also found judgments of false to be more difficult than judgments of true when sentences were affirmative, but to be easier than judgments of true when sentences were negative. The interaction of affirmation and truth reveals a general difficulty in combining affirmation and denial: Slobin's task was relatively easy both when affirmative judgments of truth (in the sense of McNeill and McNeill) were made of sentences that were affirmative on existence, and when negative judgments of truth were made of sentences that were negative on existence; but the task was difficult whenever affirmation and negation had to be combined, either as an affirmation of truth for a negation of existence, or as a negation of truth for an affirmation of existence.

The second semantic consideration is something Slobin called "reversibility." A picture of a dog chasing a cat is reversible. Cats can chase dogs as well as vice versa. Deciding whether a sentence is true or false with respect to such a picture depends on deciding which word—*cat* or *dog*—is the grammatical subject and which the object, and then matching this grammatical analysis to the episode shown in the picture. The difficulty of the comparison should be increased when the superficial and underlying subject and object are not the same—as in passive sentences. Thus Slobin expected, and found, that judgments of truth or falsity were less accurate and took longer with passive than with active sentences.

The problem of verification is simplified, however, with pictures of a second type, called "nonreversible" by Slobin. An example of a nonreversible picture is a girl on a pony. If a child understands that girl is the underlying object of the passive sentence *the girl is being ridden by the pony*, he can correctly judge that the sentence is false without matching the sentence to the picture. The semantic constraint simplifies verification by making a judgment possible on internal semantic grounds. Slobin found nonreversible passives to be judged as accurately and rapidly as nonreversible actives. This result held true of children at every age studied by Slobin.

Thus two semantic effects—negation and reversibility—influence children's ability to verify sentences. Negation, although less complex syntactically than passivization, retards verification more: it is the semantic and not the syntactic effect of negation that dominates. Nonreversibility has even greater impact than negation, for it removes every vestige of passivization as a source of difficulty in verification.

Turner and Rommetveit (in press) report a similar result with reversible and nonreversible pictures. They required children to describe pictures as well as to judge the truth or falsity of sentences about pictures. In production, as previously noted, children often reverse the order of subject and object—say, *the pony rides the girl*. The gains produced by nonreversibility for comprehension thus do not seem to extend to production at the ages studied (4 to 9 years). Describing a picture of a girl on a pony with the sentence *the pony rides the girl* is equivalent to saying that *the girl is being ridden by the pony* is true. But children who commit the first error do not commit the second in Turner and Rommetveit's experiment.

Recent work by Bever, Mehler, and Valian (1967) clarifies the role played by reversibility in these experiments. Bever, Mehler, and Valian's subjects were very young: 2 to 4 years, compared to 5 to 11 years in Slobin's experiment. The difference in age makes for an important and surprising difference in outcome. Bever et al. found that the semantic constraint of nonreversibility does not help performance at all at 3 years, even though children this young can comprehend some passive sentences more than half the time. By 4 years, however, children's comprehension of reversible passive sentences begins to deteriorate and their comprehension of nonreversible passive sentences correspondingly begins to improve. Children begin at 4 years to perform as in Slobin's and Turner and Rommetveit's experiments. Thus, at first, reversible and nonreversible situations are treated alike when described by passive sentences; later they are treated differently, and children actually retreat from a level of performance previously reached in reversible situations. A similar study by Hayhurst, 1967, also found "young" children not taking advantage of nonreversibility; however, her subjects were older than Bever et al.'s subjects—in fact, the age of Slobin's subjects, 5 years.

Bever et al. argue plausibly that children adopt certain general strategies in understanding sentences—for example, that English sentences are semantically coherent, and that they describe an actor, an action, and an object acted upon. Such semantic strategies depend on a conviction that utterances make sense and on a knowledge of what makes a situation reversible or nonreversible. Information of this kind is distinct from grammatical knowledge—for example, that the underlying relations in a sentence are subject, verb, and object. The semantic strategy is acquired later than knowledge of the grammatical relations among elements, and is derived from a different source—perhaps a statistical predominance in speech of sentences describing actors, actions, and objects acted upon. It is not the same as a syntactic analysis of a sentence. It is, rather, a method, based on semantic coherence, for facilitating a syntactic analysis.

A statement of the strategy, differing slightly (but importantly) from the version described by Bever et al., is as follows:

1. Assume that noun-verb-noun stands for actor-action-object.
2. If this is implausible, assume that noun-verb-noun stands for object-action-actor.

Under the influence of this strategy, reversible passive sentences can be construed as active sentences, even though the transformation of passivization is available. *The cat is being chased by the dog* becomes under the strategy: *cat* (actor) *chase* (action), and *dog* (acted upon). The semantic coherence of a cat chasing a dog leads to a reversal of grammatical subject and object. The same strategy, however, protects a child from a reversal of subject and object in nonreversible situations. *Pony* (actor), *ride* (action), and *girl* (acted upon) must be rejected by a child expecting semantic coherence, so *the pony is being ridden by the girl* is correctly understood as a passive sentence. Young children without a semantic strategy treat reversible and nonreversible situations alike and sentences describing both are open to the same confusions.

The strategy of exploiting nonreversibility is an example of what Jakobson (1960) has called the "metalinguistic" function of language. An expectation that sentences will contain an actor, an action, and an object acted upon is a hypothesis about language. It is comparable to such other hypotheses as, for example, that all words have a rhyme, or that all sentences have a middle. It is different from the linguistic hypotheses considered in the section on Syntax, which comprise the syntactic competence of a child.

The relatively late appearance of a strategy based on semantic coherence probably is related to the insensitivity to semantic anomaly uncovered in McNeill's (1965) experiment; there is, however, a discrepancy in ages.

The Association of Semantics and Action. The strategy mentioned earlier—that sentences contain an actor, an action, and an object acted upon—can take other forms. For example, children following this strategy can use sentences to direct their own activity. They can do so, that is, if the actor in an action and the subject of a sentence directing the action are the same. But if children must performs an action that violates the strategy, performance becomes disrupted. Such is the conclusion reached by Huttenlocher, Eisenberg, and Strauss (1968) and Huttenlocher and Strauss (1968).

The experiments are elegant in their simplicity. In one (Huttenlocher et al., 1968) a child sees before him a "road" consisting of a flat board divided into three spaces. The middle space already contains a toy truck. The child has in hand a second truck, which he is told to place either before or after the fixed truck. It is the way of telling that counts. Assume that the child's truck is painted green and the fixed truck is painted red. Any one of four possible instructions can then be given: (1) the green truck is pulling the red truck; (2) the red truck is pulling the green truck; (3) the red truck is pulled by the green truck; and (4) the green truck is pulled by the red truck. Another four instructions are available with the verb *push*. In every case, the actor is the green truck the child is holding: it is the one that must be moved. Thus in sentences (1) and (3) the actor and the underlying subject of the sentence are the same, whereas in sentences (2) and (4) the actor is the underlying object of the verb *pull*. Sentences (1) and (3) should therefore be more easily followed as instructions than sentences (2) and (4).

Sentences (1) and (2) are active sentences, whereas (3) and (4) are passive. If children treat the superficial instead of the underlying subject of a sentence as an actor, then sentences (1) and (4) ought to be easiest, and (2) and (3) hardest, as *green truck* is the superficial subject in the first pair and the superficial object in the second pair.

Huttenlocher et al. found the amount of time for 9-year-old children to place the moveable truck correctly increased from sentence (1) to sentence (4). Since (1) < (2) and (3) < (4) it is clear that children associate the subject of a sentence with the actor of an action. This is the strategy discussed by Bever et al. (1967). Since (3) < (4) it is also clear that the underlying and not the superficial subject is the one associated with the actor. Finally, since (2) < (3) it is clear that passivization poses problems of its own; the situation in Huttenlocher's experiment was reversible.

Huttenlocher et al. also discovered a systematic difference between the two verbs *push* and *pull*. For all four types of sentence, children's reaction time to *push* was faster than to *pull*. In terms of comprehension, at least, a push is not a backward pull.

An experiment by Huttenlocher and Strauss (1968) produced similar observations of children following instructions of the form, *the red block is on top of the green block* and *the yellow block is under the brown block*. A child in this experiment was faced with a ladder, the middle rung of which contained a block; the instruction told him to place a second block above or below the block already fixed in place, the position depending on the color of the block the child had in hand. The instructions were easiest to follow when the actor (the child's block) was also the subject of the sentence. Since there are no passive forms of the sentences used in this experiment, the association of an actor with the underlying subject of a sentence could not be demonstrated.

Bem (1967) has replicated Huttenlocher and Strauss' results in all particulars, but arrives at a rather different conclusion. In the view of Huttenlocher and Strauss, sentences such as *the red block is on top of the green block*—when a child is holding a green block—are difficult because the sentence must be changed into one where the child's block is the grammatical subject—*the green block is under the red block*. The extra step takes its toll in time. In Bem's view, the problem facing a child is not to perform a linguistic operation, but to imagine a situation in which the sentence as given is a true description. Again the extra step takes its toll in time. Whereas in Huttenlocher and Strauss' view a *sentence* must be transformed, in Bem's view a *situation* must be transformed. In order to distinguish the two interpretations, Bem asked her subjects to describe the tower of blocks they had made. If subjects first had to transform the sentence to make the tower, the transformed sentence ought now to appear as a description. However, 90% of Bem's subjects used the original untransformed sentence, as if nothing had been done to alter its form.

Many psychologists have assumed that language and action in children are closely associated. Although this sometimes has meant that child language is primarily an expression of action (see de Laguna, 1927), the regulative function of language has been more often studied (however, see Clark, in press, for evidence that prepositions are at first expressive of movement). The many experiments of Luria (1961; also see Luria, 1959; Birch, 1966) have traced the development of verbal control—that is, the ability of children to follow verbal instructions. The experiments of Huttenlocher et al., Huttenlocher and Strauss, and Bem bear on the same question. The present chapter is not the place to explore the possibility that the emergence of verbal control in children depends on the emergence of the metalinguistic hypothesis that sentences describe an actor, an action, and an object acted upon. However, the matter deserves investigation. Such an exploration presumably would look into a child's knowledge of grammar in relation to his application of such strategies; it is clear that the two are not the same, and the problem arises as to how they are interrelated.

This problem arises with particular acuteness in the experiments described by Luria (1959, 1961). Working within the general framework established by Vygotsky (1962), Luria and his colleagues have traced the development of what they consider to be voluntary action. In the Vygotskyan scheme of things a basic continuity exists between the control of one's action by others and the voluntary control of one's action by oneself. All control is a matter of following instructions, either external or internal. Self- or internal control depends on the development of inner speech, and inner speech in turn derives from socialized speech. Self-control is therefore preceded genetically by external control.

To very young children, commands are simly occasions for action. The speech of others triggers an action a child is ready to perform. A child who has repeatedly been made to retrieve a coin beneath an inverted cup will still search under the cup when told to find a coin under a nearby glass. The specific property of the instruction—that it contains the word *glass* rather than *cup*—has no effect. The same tendency appears in other situations. Told to press a ball when a light flashes, children younger than 2½ immediately look for the light and press the ball. When the light is subsequently flashed a child looks at it but ignores the ball. A command at this stage initiates two independent acts that are not put together. Children fail to react to the grammatical structure of the command.

Commands possess for young children what Luria (1961) calls an "impulsive quality." If children of 3 are told *not* to press a ball when a light goes on, they press anyway. Moreover, if they are told to say "don't press" when a light goes on, they still press even while saying "don't press." A 3-year-old child's reaction to his own speech is therefore independent of the content of his speech. Speech is more like a metronome. If told to say "I'll press twice" when a light goes on, a child of 3 presses once and maintains pressure for the duration of the sentence. If on the other hand, he is told to say "go! go!" when the light goes on, he presses twice because there are two impulses. It is not until 4½ or 5 that children react to "go! go!", "I'll press twice," and "don't press" in appropriate ways.

One wonders, in line with the preceding remarks, if the change at 4 or 5 results from application of a metalinguistic strategy that relates the grammatical subject, verb, and object in a sentence to the actor, action, and object acted upon in a situation. Because such a strategy is discovered relatively late in development, children before this point react to commands as if they had no internal structure, but are instead merely external signals to act. However, once a strategy is adopted ". . . the regulatory function is steadily transferred from the impulsive side of speech to the analytic system of elective significative connections which are produced by speech" (Luria, 1961, p. 92; italics omitted).

The Exchange of Information among Children. Piaget (1923) long ago devised an experiment in which children instructed other children on the operation of a mechanical device—a syringe, for example. Children less than 6 are not very good at this. They use gestures and such pronouns as *this, that, something, there,* and *here*—even when the child being instructed is, for example blindfolded. For Piaget, the difficulty of communication arises from the egocentrism of children. The instructor takes it for granted that the other child already knows how a syringe works, since he, the instructor, also knows how it works. All that must be done in order to communicate therefore is to make reference to common knowledge.

More recently Glucksberg and Krauss, and various of their collaborators (Glucksberg, Krauss, and Weisberg, 1966; Glucksberg and Krauss, 1967; Krauss and Rotter, n.d.; Krauss and Bricker, 1967; Krauss and Weinheimer, 1964, 1966), have looked at the same phenomenon as a mater of communication efficiency. Viewing an exchange of information as a question of communication efficiency is not, of course, incompatible with explaining poor efficiency by reference to egocentrism.

In a typical experiment two children (or adults) are seated on opposite sides of an opaque screen. One is an encoder and the other is a decoder of messages about a set of unusual visual forms. The forms are chosen in advance as ones without readily available names in English; the experiment therefore differs from Piaget's, where vocabulary existed (in fact, was taught) to describe the object.

In general, the success of children's messages to other children is low. Children use shorter descriptions than adults do, and the descriptions are sometimes highly idiosyncratic. Idiosyncratic messages are not meaningless, however, even though they are poor for communication; when children serve as their own decoders, the level of accuracy is relatively high (Glucksberg et al., 1966). Brevity of description is characteristic of adults when the same form has been described several times previously, and arises because messages about familiar things tend to minimize redundancy (Zipf, 1935; Krauss and Weinheimer, 1964). That young children *begin* with such messages possibly reflects the egocentrism discussed by Piaget. It suggests that children differ from adults in their conception of familiarity, egocentrically assuming that every known thing is a familiar thing.

When children are given messages encoded by adults, communication accuracy soars (Glucksberg et al., 1966). An adult will say of a figure that it looks like an "upside down cup." Children respond to this description much as adults do. But children *say* of the same figure that it looks like "mother's dress," "Ideal" (referring to the trademark of a brand of toys), "digger hold," "a caterpillar," or "a ghost." Children are therefore better at decoding than encoding messages.

Even though children are better decoders than encoders, children as decoders do not treat the communicative messages of adults differently from the noncommunicative messages of other children. All messages are accepted passively and with little comment. Moreover, children as encoders do not modify messages when explicitly requested to do so by adult decoders (Glucksberg and Krauss, in press). In these respects children are sharply different from adults, who request and receive new descriptions when a description seems to them insufficiently precise. One of the children described by Glucksberg and Krauss (1967), when told to pick up "this one," asked the child on the other side of the opaque screen "do you mean that one?"; the reply was "yes." Although children can understand the messages of adults, they act as if they can understand every other message as well.

Symbol Formation. A review of semantic development would not be complete without mention of the work of Werner and Kaplan (1963). They have attempted to explain certain aspects of language acquisition as a consequence of cognitive development, and so, unlike other cognitive theorists, have confronted the problem of cognition and language.

Werner and Kaplan raise a number of fundamental questions. What are symbols? How do they develop in children? How is language intertwined with action? How does the relation between language and action change with development? It is not surprising, perhaps, that Werner and Kaplan do not provide satisfactory answers to these questions. No one does. But it is ironic in their case that a source of difficulty is a commitment to an analysis of symbolization promoted by the very empiricist philosophers whom Werner and Kaplan are at pains to dispute.

Werner and Kaplan regard the problem of learning the meaning of words as a problem in "distancing." A child must distinguish between himself and the objects to which words refer; he must distinguish between himself and words; and he must distinguish between words and objects. At first speech is held to be limited to onomatopoeia. A child tries to imitate the acoustic qualities of objects. Objects are not clearly distinguished from a child's own activity, including the activity of imitating acoustic quality, and imitation clearly is something a child himself does. Word, object, and child are therefore fused. In contrast, the words and meanings of adult languages are arbitrarily related to oneself and to objects. To move from such an onomatopoeic beginning to the arbitrary vocabulary of adults, a child must interpose "distance" between himself, words, and objects.

The first step is to transcend the single sensory modality of hearing. Onomatopoeia is necessarily limited to objects that make a noise. Synesthesia rests on a similarity between sensory modalities, and thus provides a means whereby the visual (or tactual or olfactory) qualities of objects also can be vocally imitated. Werner and Kaplan firmly believe that sounds have physiognomic qualities (of which synesthesia is one special type): it is a physiognomic similarity between acoustic and visual perception that causes "zigzag" to be a bad name for a circle and a good one for a jagged line. Through such synesthetic similarities "distance" is first interposed between words and objects. Continuing in this physiognomic direction, a child eventually arrives at the arbitrariness of adult lexicon; by then all outward similarity between words and referents has been lost.

Fodor (1964) has written a blistering critique of this theory. He finds in it an entire catalogue of philosophical blunders. According to Fodor, the theory is "surprisingly conservative"; it is "circular"; it is "irrefutable"; it is "doctrinaire"; and it is "not scientific." Unlike the classical empiricists, who regarded symbolization as a result of both causation and similarity, and unlike modern learning theorists, who regard it as a result of causation alone, Werner and Kaplan regard symbolization as a result of similarity alone. The key, as noted, is physiognomic similarity.

Sounds and objects are physiognomically similar when they are integrated into similar "postural-dynamic patterns." Since these patterns govern the similarity of words and objects, outwardly the properties of words and objects may differ markedly—and so may appear to be arbitrarily related—but inwardly they are similar. The difficulty with such an argument, as Fodor points out, is

that it is essentially post hoc. The *only* way to find out if a word and an object are physiognomically the same it to find out if the word refers to the object. There is no way in principle to test such a theory.

Fodor's review should be read carefully. It shows the difficulties and hazards of proceeding in the area of semantics. To his critique, perhaps only one thing should be added. As previously noted, Werner and Kaplan are concerned with the problem of cognition and language. Their effort in this direction is unique. However, the relevance of Werner and Kaplan's theory to the problem of cognition and language is quite unknown. Werner and Kaplan take for granted that symbolization is a weak universal—a universal imposed by human cognition. But, for all we know, symbolization is a strong universal—a peculiarity of the human system of communication. There have been no empirical investigations of the distinction.

PHONOLOGY

If semantics is regarded as the basement of syntax, then phonology is the penthouse. It is ironic that so little can be said of the acquisition of this most visible part of language. Little can be said, even though the study of sound has long been a dominant concern of linguistics and an explicit theory of phonemic development has existed for more than a quarter of a century (Jakobson, 1941, 1968). The challenge posed by phonology has never been accepted.

We must distinguish at the outset between phonemic and phonological development. The first refers to the emergence of the sound units of a language; something can be said about phonemic development, and it is here that Jakobson's theory applies. Phonological development on the other hand refers to the emergence of rules for combining sounds into pronounceable sequences in a language and for relating such sequences to the surface structure of sentences. Virtually nothing can be said about this aspect of development.

The Relation of Babbling to Speech. All parents know that children babble during the second 6 months of life. Before that time vocalization is highly limited, and after that time speech proper begins with the appearance of holophrastic utterances. During the babbling period children vocalize an immense variety of sounds in ever more complex combinations. It is possible that the babbling period is a bridge between the limited vocalization of the first 6 months of life and the appearance of communicative speech itself. Such a hypothesis has indeed been proposed. Allport (1924) believed that children develop the phonemic system of their native language by matching speech sounds they hear to sounds they produce in babbling. Staats and Staats (1963) and Mowrer (1952, 1960) hold a similar view. However, it is a view with no basis in fact; there is on the contrary a sharp discontinuity at both ends of the babbling period. Babbling, if it plays a part in the emergence of speech, does so far behind the scenes. It is not a bridge.

The direction of development during the first year of life is from the back to the front of the mouth for consonant-type sounds and from the front to the back of the mouth for vowel-type sounds (Irwin, 1947a, 1947b, 1947c, 1948; McCarthy, 1954; however, see Bever, 1961, for some qualifications). The direction of development during the second year of life is exactly opposite. First to appear as *speech* sounds are front consonants and back vowels. The back consonants and front vowels that were the first uttered in the period of prespeech are among the last organized into a linguistic system.

Children younger than 3 months vocalize such consonantlike sounds as [k], [g], and [x], and such vowel-like sounds as [i] and [u]. That is the beginning. In the babbling period many more sounds are added—sounds necessarily more forward in the case of consonants and more backward in the case of vowels. When linguistically meaningful utterances first occur, however, they consist of a front consonant, /p/ or /m/, and a back vowel, /a/. (Following the usual practice, linguistically significant sounds—phonemes—are enclosed in slant bars and linguistically nonsignificant sounds—phones—are enclosed in square brackets.) Front consonants and and back vowels provide a starting point for speech regardless of the language to which children are exposed: children exposed to English say *tut* before *cut;* children exposed to Swedish say *tata* before *kata;* children exposed to Japanese say *ta* before *ka;* and so on (Jakobson,1941). The early appearance of /m/ and /p/ as speech sounds is no doubt one reason why *mama* and *papa* are among the first words acquired by all children.

The baby talk of adults usually corresponds to this initial phonemic organization. Ferguson (1964) found replacement of velar by dental consonants in the adult speech addressed to children among speakers of Syrian, Marathi, Comanche, English, and Spanish. An English example is *tum on* for *come on* (phonemically, /kum/). The only exceptions among the languages Ferguson reviewed were Arabic and Gilyak, in both of which velar consonants play a particularly large role. Baby talk is conventionalized speech for children. In spite of the large differences among the phonemic systems of Syrian, Marathi, Comanche, English, and Spanish, the conventions for baby talk are the same, presumably because actual child speech in each of these languages is organized in the same way.

The front consonants and back vowels organized by children into an initial linguistic system also occur in babbling. However, many other sounds occur in children's babbling, as well, including the back consonants, [k] and [g], and the front vowels, [i] and [u], which are added to a child's linguistic system only after many months of further development. Rather than continuity there is discontinuity. Children quickly pass from a wealth of vocalization to concentration on a few sounds for communication. It is not a question of selecting some sounds from many; it is rather a question of why the same specific sounds constitute the beginning of every child's phonemic system. Intentional vocalization requires a structure that unintentional vocalization does not. A child who uses only /p/, /m/, and /a/ in speech will at the same time use [k], [g], and many other sounds in nonspeech (Jakobson, 1941). As Jesperson (1925) remarked,

It is strange that among an infant's sounds one can often detect sounds—for instance, k, g, h, and uvular r—which the child will find difficulty in producing afterwards when they occur in real words. . . . The explanation lies probably in the difference between doing a thing in play or without a plan—when it is immaterial which movement (sound) is made —and doing the same thing of fixed intention when this sound, and this sound only, is required . . . (p. 106).

Jakobson's theory of phonemic development is addressed to the sound structure of early speech. However, before discussing his theory, let us look a little more carefully at the period of development before the emergence of speech. Doing so will make more concrete the discontinuity between speech and prespeech.

Prespeech and Neurological Maturation in the First Year of Life. There are in fact two discontinuities during the first year of life— one at 4 months and a second at 11 or 12 months. The two together roughly bracket the babbling period. Bever (1961) reanalyzed the extensive data reported by Irwin and his collaborators (Irwin, 1947a, 1947b, 1947c, 1948) in terms of the rate of change in sound development. Irwin transcribed children's vocalizations in the International Phonetic Alphabet, so his data consist of information on a large number of separate phonetic types; in general the data reveal a steady proliferation of phonetic types with age. Bever focused instead on the rates of change of phonetic types and found discontinuities at 4 and 11 or 12 months.

The two discontinuities mark off three periods. The first period, from birth through the third month, consists of a very rapid rate of change in the frequency and variety of vowel-like sounds and a somewhat lower though still rapid rate of change in the frequency and variety of consonantlike sounds. At 4 months, the rate of change drops abruptly, thus ending the first period and starting the second. The second period is a succession of peaks without large intervening troughs. A peak in the rate of change in the variety of vowel-like sounds occurs between 5 and 6 months; then a peak in the rate of change in the variety of consonantlike sounds at 7 months (affecting dental and labial consonants particularly); finally a large peak in the rate of change in the variety of all consonantlike sounds at 9 or 10 months. Then, total collapse at 11 or 12 months. The collapse at 11 or 12 months is the beginning of

true linguistic development; the events it introduces are discussed in the next section.

Bever points to similar cyclical phenomena elsewhere in development (e.g., in the amount of sleep per day) and argues that the episodic advance of vocalization reflects a series of changes in cerebral maturation, particularly of an unfolding pattern of inhibition and integration during the first year of life. The hypothesis is provocative and worth quoting:

The cycles observed in vocal development are produced by phases of neurological maturation. a) The first cycle is concurrent with and presumably a manifestation of a primary level of neurological organization of vocal behavior. b) The end of the first cycle is a result of the end of the reflex stage of behavior due to cortical inhibition. c) The second vocal developmental cycle occurs as the cortex gradually reorganizes the activity it had inhibited.

The difference in the manifest behavioral characteristics of the first and second cycles in vocal development are due to differences between the lower and higher levels of neurological organization. a) There are two essential features of the first cycle of vocal development, and thus of the primary neurological phase, a concern with tonal activity and the primary differentiation of affective crying. b) The second cycle and thus the second neurological phase is associated with the development of consonant-like activity, and is often referred to as the period of "preparation" for the onset of language-learning proper. The babbling stage is presumably a reflection of the process of integrating vocal activity and cortical organization (Bever, 1961, p. 47).

So much for prespeech and its alleged connection with the nervous system. We now turn to the beginnings of language.

The Differentiation of Distinctive Features. The name of Roman Jakobson is associated with what is, beyond doubt, one of the most useful concepts in contemporary linguistics. This is the notion of a linguistic feature. In phonemics, where Jakobson developed the idea, linguists speak of distinctive features, but essentially the same insight into language has been invaluable in semantics and syntax, and previous sections of this chapter have relied on it heavily.

It is Jakobson also—in a celebrated paper, *Kindersprache, Aphasie, und allgemeine Lautgesetze* (1941)—who first applied the concept of a linguistic feature to questions of language development. In the same paper, moreover, he presented for the first time a modern conception of the relation between linguistic universals and the development of language. (The general importance of universal grammar had been realized centuries before; see Chomsky, 1966.) Developmental psycholinguistics thus owes Jakobson a considerable debt. It is fortunate that *Kindersprache* has at last been translated into English by A. Keiler (Jakobson, 1968). For a brief discussion of the theory, see Jakobson and Halle (1956); for a general discussion of distinctive features, see Jakobson, Fant, and Halle (1963).

It is remarkable that Jakobson's theory has inspired so few empirical investigations. The few studies that have been conducted, however, support the general line of argument, although not every detail (see Velten, 1943; Leopold, 1947).

The development of a phonemic system, according to Jakobson, is the result of filling in the gap between two sounds, /a/ and /p/. The process of development is differentiation. /p/ is a consonant formed at the front of the mouth; it is a stop; it is unvoiced; and it represents a nearly total absence of acoustic energy. /a/ contrasts with /p/ in each of these respects. It is a vowel; it is formed at the back of the mouth; it results from a complete opening of the vocal tract; and it represents a maximization of acoustic energy. One might say that /a/ is an optimal vowel and /p/ is an optimal consonant. Each is an extreme example of its type, and the contrast between them is as large as possible. With this contrast, linguistic development begins on a phonemic level.

However, neither /p/ nor /a/ are phonemes at the outset of development (and thus, strictly speaking, should not be written between slant bars). A phoneme is a meaningless sound used to distinguish meaningful messages. /p/ and /a/ are instead meaningful sounds that distinguish no messages. The consonant always appears with the vowel, and there are only two possible utterances:

pa and (with reduplication) *papa*. The meaning of these words may be highly diffuse, and a child may attempt to communicate more than one message with each word, but there is not yet a phonemic system.

In order to establish a phonemic system, the space between /p/ and /a/ must be differentiated. The first such split occurs on the consonant side and (according to Jakobson's observations) results in a distinction between a labial stop /p/ and a nasalized labial /m/. The distinction therefore is between nasal and oral sounds and it creates two words— *ma* and *pa* or (with reduplication) *mama* and *papa*—distinguished by what are now two phonemes, /m/ and /p/. Velten (1943) found the first consonant distinction to be slightly different: labial stops were first contrasted with continuants (/f/ and /s/), and only later with nasals. The nasal-oral distinction thus appeared second in development rather than first.

The vowel /a/ at this stage merely supports the consonants /m/ and /p/, and itself has no phonemic status. However, the vowel plays a crucial role of a different kind, for together with the consonants /a/ establishes a syllable. Syllabification is present from the outset of speech. It is not obvious why such should be the case. Perhaps there is some basic rhythmicity underlying speech, as Lenneberg (1967) has argued, which takes as its earliest manifestation syllabification and reduplication. Jakobson (1941) believed that children always formed consonant-vowel (or vowel-consonant) syllables in earliest speech, but apparently this is not invariably the case. Weir (1966) observed Chinese children uttering syllables that consisted of vowels only, although Russian- and English-speaking children also included consonants, as expected. Chinese is a language in which syllabification is measured by vowels alone, whereas Russian and English are not. Weir's findings may reflect the existence of language-appropriate syllabification at an extremely early age.

After the consonants have been divided into nasal and oral categories, there appears a division of oral consonants into labial and dental categories. /ta/ comes to be contrasted with /pa/ (Jakobson, 1941). After this there occurs the first division on the vocalic side. Narrow vowels are set off against wide vowels, as in /pi/ versus /pa/. The next step according to Jakobson may be in either of two directions. One alternative is to divide the narrow vowel into a narrow palatal vowel /pi/ and a narrow velar vowel /pu/. The other alternative is to create a high-mid-low vowel series by inserting /e/ between /a/ and /i/, as in /pa/ versus /pe/ versus /pi/.

Jakobson argues that the sequence of phonemic development is invariant and universal among children. All children pass through the same steps, although children may differ from one another in the rate of advancement. Moreover, the phonemic system created by the first two or three steps in phonemic development is universal among the languages of the world. ". . . the child possesses in the beginning only those sounds which are common to the world, while those phonemes which distinguish the mother tongue from the other languages of the world appear only later" (Jakobson, 1968; quotation from the Keiler translation).

There is a striking similarity between phonemic and syntactic development. Both begin with a primitive form that is universal. In both, the starting point is not any particular language, but is so organized that it may become any language through a process of differentiation. Perhaps we should not be surprised at the similarity; the separation of sound and syntax is a scholarly artificiality. In fact, human communication always takes a specific form and it is not surprising that the same basic form appears in all its aspects.

The differentiation of the space between /p/ and /a/ is the result of successively introducing certain distinctive features. Jakobson summarizes the process of development in terms of a series of vowel and consonant triangles (Jakobson, 1941; Jakobson and Halle, 1966).

The first phonemes, /p/ and /t/, together with the optimal vowel /a/, comprise what Jakobson and Halle call the "primary triangle." It defines two distinctive features—

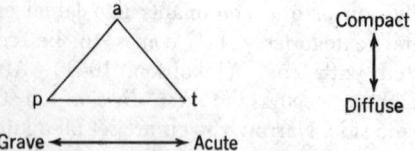

compact-diffuse on the vertical axis and grave-acute on the horizontal.

When the vowel /a/ is in turn differentiated into wide (/a/) and narrow (/i/) vowels, the distinction between compact and diffuse is introduced into the vocalic category. Thus, compact versus diffuse no longer sets vowels off from consonants, and we have instead,

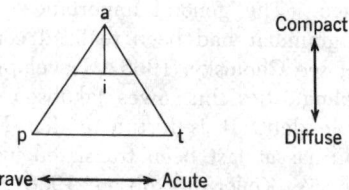

If the narrow vowel /i/, which is also palatal, is next distinguished from the velar vowel /u/, which is also narrow, the distinctive feature grave-acute is likewise introduced into the vocalic category. Grave-acute is therefore the first contrast shared by vowels and consonants. It gives rise to the following triangle:

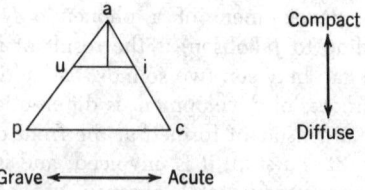

At this point, vowels embody more distinctions than consonants. Balance is restored when the front consonants /p/ and /t/ are distinguished from the back consonant /k/; /p/ and /t/ are diffuse, whereas /k/ is compact. We now have two complete triangles defined by the same features,

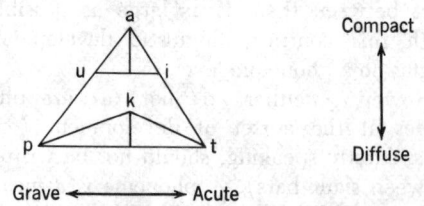

The succession of vowel and consonant triangles explains why the first phonemic contrast that children draw is between /a/ and /p/ and not between /a/ and /k/, or

/i/ and /p/, or some other pair. /a/ is the most compact of all sounds, whereas /p/ (along with /t/) is the most diffuse. It is on the distinctive feature of compact-diffuse that /a/ and /p/ are the optimal vowel and consonant. To utter /a/ the mouth forms a funnel opening forward; to utter /p/ it forms a funnel opening backward. In the case of /a/ a large amount of acoustic energy is concentrated in a narrow band of frequencies; in the case of /p/ a small amount of energy is distributed over a wide band of frequencies. The sound /t/ is as diffuse as /p/ in terms of the distribution of energy, but it differs less from /a/ in the location of closure of the mouth, and for this reason is not chosen first as the consonant to be set off against the new vowel /a/.

The Development of a Phonemic System and the Laws of "Irreversible Solidarity." The laws of irreversible solidarity describe universal asymmetries in the phonemic systems of the languages of the world. For example, no language has back consonants without also having front consonants, but languages exist with front consonants and no back consonants. There is an irreversible "solidarity" between back and front consonants such that the former presuppose the latter but not conversely. The laws of irreversible solidarity describe languages (see Greenberg, 1963, 1966, for a number of examples of universals of this kind). Jakobson's (1941) suggestion is that the same laws describe the development of language by children (as well as the loss of language by aphasics). Thus no child arrives at back consonants without first developing front consonants. /p/ and /m/ always appear before /k/ or /g/, for example. Jakobson gives many examples of such an identity between the order of acquisition and the distribution of phonemes among the languages of the world.

Phonemes that are relatively rare among the languages of the world—for example, the English /θ/ as in "thing"—are the last phonemes acquired by children exposed to languages that contain them. It is as if, when children must push farther and farther from the universal core of language, fewer and fewer languages force them to do so (see discussion of the informal dialect of New York speakers as described in Labov, 1964). In general, rare phonemes embody more distinctions, of a more subtle type, than do phonemes of wider distribution and earlier appearance. If the acquisition of phonemes is the result of differentiation, as Jakobson argues, then phonemes that embody numerous and subtle distinctions are naturally acquired after phonemes that embody less numerous and subtle distinctions. A natural order of acquisition and distribution therefore results from the latent but universal structure of distinctive features. Jacobson (1941) argues that the structure inherent in the set of distinctive features is the result of general perceptual principles, and that the order of appearance of phonemic contrasts corresponds to the order of complication of any complex perception. He thus contends that the laws of irreversible solidarity are weak linguistic universals. As in the case of semantics and syntax, however, there are not yet empirical grounds to support such a conclusion; as usual, the question has not been investigated.

Jakobson and Halle (1956) give the following series, presumably universal, for the successive differentiation of distinctive features. The numbers are analogous to paragraph headings or indentations. Thus 1.0 is

Consonants	dental vs. labial (e.g., /t/ vs. /p/)	1.0
Vowels	narrow vs. wide (e.g., /i/ vs. /a/)	1.1
Narrow vowels	palatal vs. velar (e.g., /i/ vs. /u/)	1.11
Wide vowels	palatal vs. velar	1.111
Narrow palatal vowels	rounded vs. unrounded	1.112
Wide palatal vowels	rounded vs. unrounded	1.1121
Velar vowels	rounded vs. unrounded (e.g., /a/ vs. /a/)	1.113
Consonants	velopalatal vs. labial and dental	1.12
Consonants	palatal vs. velar (e.g., /s/ vs. /k/)	1.121
Consonants	rounded vs. unrounded or pharyngealized vs. nonpharyngealized	1.122
Consonants	palatalized vs. nonpalatalized	1.123

the first contrast to be developed (/t/ versus /p/), 1.1 is the second contrast, etc. Later contrasts occur rarely among the languages of the world; examples in English are given where possible.

Some recent work of Preston, Yeni-Komshian, and Stark (1967) nicely illustrates how such contrasts arise in development. They have studied the distinctive feature of voicing. Among adults the acoustic manifestation of voicing is a particular relation in time between the onset of voicing and the release of a consonant—that is, all consonants, including voiceless consonants, have voicing; voiced and voiceless consonants differ only in when voicing appears. To describe this situation Preston et al. speak of "voice onset time" or VOT, which is the number of milliseconds the release of a consonant appears before voicing. VOT can range from negative values (voicing before release) through zero (release and voicing at the same instant) to positive values (release before voicing).

Consonants with smaller VOTs are perceived as voiced; consonants with higher VOTs are perceived as voiceless. As with all distinctive features, the contrast is a relative one. The VOTs of /b/, /d/, and /g/ in English, for example, are between 0 and +5 msec, whereas the VOTs of /p/, /t/, and /k/ are between +50 and +70 msec. The same voiced-voiceless contrast in Lebanese Arabic takes values of VOT of approximately −70 msec for voiced consonants and +5 to +15 msec for voiceless consonants. That is to say, the VOT of *voiced* consonants in English is the same as the VOT of *voiceless* consonants in Lebanese Arabic, but in both languages voiced consonants have smaller VOTs.

Preston et al. have measured the VOTs of stop consonants uttered by children just at the beginning of linguistic development, at about 12 months. The children lived in either Lebanon or the United States. Because of their ages, the children were expected to be alike; the distinctive feature of voicing had not yet appeared. But because of the difference between Lebanese Arabic and English, development was expected to move in opposite directions. It turns out that Lebanese and American children both utter consonants limited to VOTs in the region common to the two languages—between 0 and +40 msec.

Are these sounds voiced or voiceless? They are neither. Ultimately Lebanese children develop a new group of sounds with VOTs in the negative range and thus make the original sounds voiceless. American children on the other hand develop a new group of sounds with VOTs in the +50 to +70 msec range and thus make the original sounds voiced.

These observations raise an interesting question about the linguistic distinction between marked and unmarked features. Roughly, a marked feature is derived from its unmarked mate through the addition of something—voicing, for example. Marked features are regarded as yoked deviations from the corresponding unmarked features. There are reasons internal to a linguistic analysis for maintaining such a dichotomy, and there are reasons (such as Jakobson's laws of universal solidarity) for supposing that the dichotomy appears in the same form in every language.

But what of the development of language? Ordinarily one would say that voiced phonemes are marked with respect to voiceless phonemes. This could be true of Lebanese Arabic but not of English if marking is the result of adding something. In English the additional phoneme is the voiceless member of each pair. There is a dilemma here for those who want to interpret the distinction between marked and unmarked features in a literal way. Either marking can be defined on internal linguistic grounds, in which case the concept loses contact with the notion of something being added; or marking can be defined as the result of something being added, in which case it leads to different classifications in different languages. It is impressive nonetheless that Lebanese Arabic and English are organized around a common core—a VOT of 0 to +40 msec. The combination of universality and idiosyncracy in this case is quite diabolical.

Lateralization. Among all animals man is the only one with bilateral asymmetry; only man has a systematic preference for one hand over another. Since man is also alone in possessing language, we get a sense of penetrating close to the heart of things when we discover that language, like handedness, is asymmetrically organized in the brain. It has been known for more than a hundred years that the left side of the brain serves a special function in language. Lesions to the left side of the brain produce more damaging aphasia than do lesions to the right side, and they take longer to recover from, if indeed there is any recovery at all.

The emergence of lateralization therefore seems a promising place to look for the physiological underpinnings of language acquisition. Lenneberg (1967) relates it to the existence of a critical period in linguistic development. The ability to recover from damage to the left side of the brain declines with age. A newborn with a damaged left hemisphere develops language normally with the right hemisphere; a 2- or 3-year-old loses language in some degree after damage to the left hemisphere but then quickly recovers with the right; beyond puberty recovery is always limited or nonexistent. The degree of recovery is thus correlated with the degree of lateralization before injury.

Aside from such observations of aphasia in children the development of the lateralization of speech functions has not been studied. It is possible nevertheless to state some consequences of lateralization in normal adults, and so to describe the terminus toward which development points. A series of studies at the Haskins Laboratories (Shankweiler and Studdert-Kennedy, 1966, 1967; Liberman, Cooper, Shankweiler, and Studdert-Kennedy, 1967; Shankweiler, 1968) has revealed a number of surprising effects on the perception of speech of left-hemisphere dominance. Their methodology, first employed by Kimura (1961), is suitable for young children, so developmental studies could easily be carried out along the same lines.

Kimura observed that when an adult hears two digits simultaneously in the two ears— a different digit in each—the right ear is more accurately reported. The left hemisphere therefore dominates the right. The Haskins experiments have used this dichotic task to measure separately hemispheric dominance in listening to consonants and vowels. If one ear receives /pap/ and the other /tap/, the experiment measures sensitivity to consonants; if one ear receives /pap/ and the other /pip/, the experiment measures sensitivity to vowels. In a number of studies, the right ear (left hemisphere) has been shown to be dominant in the perception of consonants, but neither ear (hemisphere) has been

shown to be dominant in the perception of vowels. This difference between consonants and vowels is reminiscent of the difference Kimura (1964) found between digits and melodies: digits were best perceived by the right ear (left hemisphere), but melodies were best perceived by the left ear (right hemisphere). One consequence of lateralization therefore seems to be a migration of consonants but not vowels to the left side of the brain. The part of the brain involved in the perception of the melodic aspects of speech, the vowels, is different from the part involved in the perception of the nonmelodic aspects, the consonants.

Vowels and consonants have been shown to differ in another respect. If small differences in speech sounds are to be discriminated, the discrimination of consonants is "categorical" but the discrimination of vowels is continuous (see Liberman et al., 1967, for a summary of the work on which this conclusion is based; see Lane, 1965, for a critical review). "Categorical" perception means that differences among speech sounds can be detected no more accurately than the sounds can be identified. It is possible to prepare a set of artificial consonants (with the aid of a device called the "pattern playback") that differ from one another by a series of small steps. Each such step is of the same physical magnitude as every other, and the series as a whole ranges from a clear instance of one phoneme (say /g/) to a clear instance of another (say /b/) with a phoneme boundary somewhere in the middle. If the sounds are consonants, successive steps within a single phoneme are poorly discriminated, whereas sounds separated by the same physical distance but belonging to different phonemes are well discriminated. In contrast, if the sounds are vowels, discrimination depends on physical separation alone, not on category membership. One is tempted to relate the findings on categorical perception to the findings on lateral dominance by saying that categorical perception occurs only in the left side of the brain.

In some degree this may be so, but matters are complicated by yet another set of observations. Certain kinds of epilepsy are treated by a complete surgical severance of the two cerebral hemispheres. In effect, the operation leaves a patient with two independent functioning brains within a single skull. In most circumstances the left hemisphere dominates the right, but with a certain amount of contrivance it is possible to force the right hemisphere to reveal itself, even in the comprehension of speech (Gazzaniga and Sperry, 1967). In one study the experimenter speaks a short phrase ("used to tell time") and then exposes to the patient's left visual field a series of written words (one of them "clock"). The phrase reaches both hemispheres, but the series of words is so presented that it reaches only the right. Gazzaniga and Sperry's patients succeeded in matching the phrases to the words—not only does the right hemisphere understand speech but it also reads!

Unfortunately, this experiment is unclear on *what* the right hemisphere understands. Although given a phrase, the correct written word could have been selected from the perception of a single spoken word ("time" in the example given). There is no evidence therefore that the right hemisphere can comprehend syntax, although one might plausibly expect it to do so in view of the fact that language acquisition is underway long before lateralization is complete. It is clear nonetheless that the right hemisphere has access to word meanings and also to the phonemic structure of language. The latter observation tempers any extreme conclusions one might want to draw from the Haskins experiments described above. Lateralization evidently has not gone so far as to segregate completely the manner of perception (categorical or continuous) in the two hemispheres.

Phonological Rules. Beside the phonemic structure of a language there are rules for using this structure. *Sporn* is not a word in English, but it could be a word—perhaps the name of an acne cure. However, *kporn* could never be a word in English, even though the individual phonemes of *kporn* are within the language just as are the phonemes of *sporn*. A phonological rule of English requires initial consonant clusters all to begin with /s/ (/l/ and /r/ follow consonants other than /s/, but /l/ and /r/ are classified as liquids, not as consonants; Halle, 1964b). Other phonological rules determine the intonation patterns of sentences. In *black board* (a kind of board) main stress falls on *board*, but in *blackboard* (a writing surface) it falls on

black. One rule for relating stress to the surface structure of sentences in English requires main stress to fall on the first vowel of an N, but to fall elsewhere in constituents of other kinds (Chomsky, Halle, and Lukoff, 1956). *Blackboard* is an N and so receives main stress on *black*; *black board* is an NP and so receives main stress elsewhere, in this case, on *board*.

There are many such rules; for examples, see Chomsky, Halle, and Lukoff (1956); Halle (1964b); Chomsky and Halle (1966); Chomsky and Halle (1968). It appears from informal observation that children continue working on phonological rules for many years, but there are few actual studies of this aspect of development. The entire question is theoretically ripe but empirically untouched. Certainly, future work should push in this direction.

We can mention the handful of studies that have been conducted on phonological questions. Berko's (1958) well-known work on children's morphology belongs in part in this category. Anisfeld and Tucker (in press) and Anisfeld, Barlow, and Frail (1967) have found evidence for sensitivity to the featural properties of sounds among 6-year-old children. However, Menyuk (1967) finds that 4- and 5-year-old American children are no better at memorizing sound sequences drawn from English than they are at memorizing sequences drawn from other languages, although they are better at repeating English sequences. And Messer (1967) finds children even younger than 4 able to discriminate between English and non-English sequences that differ by no more than one or two distinctive features. Clearly work in this area has barely begun.

LINGUISTIC APPENDIX

Take a sentence of a dozen words, and take twelve men and tell to each one word. Then stand the men in a row or jam them in a bunch, and let each think of his word as intently as he will; nowhere will there be a consciousness of the whole sentence (James, 1893, p. 199).

Thus did William James state one psycholinguistic problem. Consciousness of a whole sentence takes place in a single mind. It is something *done* with the separate words of a sentence, and this something could not be done under the conditions of James' proposed experiment. In this section, we review what is known of the structure underlying the consciousness of sentences.

Propelled by the same revolution of thought that led to behaviorism in psychology, American linguists of the 1920s and 1930s were concerned to describe language in absolutely neutral terms. Descriptions were to reflect data. Linguistics was engaged in the discovery of the structure inherent in samples of speech. The aim was for completely objective, automatic, and rigorous procedures that would, when correctly applied, yield a correct portrayal of these structures. This would be the grammatical analysis, and it was not only to be correct, but also independent of extralinguistic suppositions. Thus Bloomfield (1933) wrote: "We have learned that we can pursue the study of language without reference to any psychological doctrine, and that to do so safeguards our results and makes them more significant to workers in related fields." Although one can question Bloomfield's actual independence from behaviorism, the general tenor of linguistic thought in the 1930s was that linguistics had no concern with psychology. By the same token, psychology had little direct concern with linguistics. It is not surprising therefore that James' problem received little attention.

However, a different approach is possible, and, of late, has been under active development. In this alternative approach, linguistics aims to describe exactly what Bloomfield wanted to avoid—the specialized form of human knowledge brought to bear in the comprehension and production of sentences. Descriptions of knowledge have obvious import for psychology: whatever we know, we know by some psychological process. Thus, under its new development, linguistics makes strong psychological assumptions, with the result that it occupies common ground with psychology. As we shall see, the direction of traffic through this common region has been almost entirely one way. Discoveries in linguistics pose the challenge; psychology attempts to assimilate them. Perhaps, in the future, two-way traffic will become possible. If so, a full answer to James' problem wil be at hand.

We shall then understand the process that leads to a consciousness of a whole sentence. Until that psychological millennium arrives, however, our discussion must be limited to describing the linguistic knowledge that is applied in this process, and it is to this better understood question that we now turn.

Linguists call the systematic characterizations of linguistic knowledge *grammars.* It is important to realize that these grammars are psychological theories. They strive to portray certain facts about the mind, that is, they are supposed to be psychologically correct and they stand or fall accordingly (Katz, 1964). The psychological interest in such grammars is therefore straightforward. However, it is important—even crucial—to understand the limitations placed on this claim of psychological validity. A grammar relates to mental phenomena of a particular kind; it is not an all-purpose psychological theory. In particular, it is not a theory about behavior—the actual encoding and decoding of speech. This brings us to a fundamental distinction.

Competence and Performance. A sharp distinction between competence and performance has been traditional in linguistics since Saussure's *Cours de linguistique générale* (1916) and was first drawn at least as early as the eighteenth century (Chomsky, 1966). One can think about language in either of two ways. There are, first of all, actual acts of speaking and hearing, taking place in time, subject to various distractions, limited by memory and by the general weakness of human flesh. These were called *actes de parole* by Saussure and *performance* by Chomsky (1957). Performance is linguistic behavior, either encoding or decoding speech. A theory of performance would clearly be a psychological theory, a fact that presumably needs no defense. At the present time, there are no theories of linguistic performance. Indeed, there is only the most fragmentary knowledge of the relevant parameters of such a theory, although the problem is one that now inspires considerable interest. A number of recent experimental studies can be regarded as bearing on it (e.g., Miller, 1962; Miller and Isard, 1963, 1964; Mehler, 1963; Slobin, 1966; McMahon, 1963; Gough, 1965; Savin and Perchonock, 1965).

The second aspect of language is the knowledge of syntax, meaning, and sound that makes performance possible. Saussure called such knowledge *langue,* and Chomsky has called it *competence.* A theory of competence is also a psychological theory, although of a type not usually developed by contemporary psychologists. Piaget, perhaps, comes closest in his aim to characterize the structure of logical thought. Because a grammar is concerned with knowledge, not behavior, factors (such as memory limitations, time restrictions) that are important to performance can be disregarded in thinking about competence. Competence is an idealization, an abstraction away from performance (Chomsky, 1965). Theories of performance and competence therefore deal with different aspects of language. A grammar is not a recipe for producing sentences. That recipe is given by a theory of performance. Indeed, the problem for a theory of performance is to explain just how the information represented by a grammar is realized in actual acts of speaking and hearing (Miller, 1962). The linguist's solution will not answer the psychologist's problem.

Perhaps the distinction between competence and performance, and the way they are related, will become clearer if we consider an artificial example. In Table 9 are several strings of letters.[4] In each string there is an *a* or a *b* or both. Some of the strings have been circled. These we shall call "sentences," by which is meant that they have a certain structure in common not shared by the other strings, the "nonsentences." Table 9 is a skeletonized version of the set of all possible strings—all possible combinations of the letters *a* and *b*—and thus is analogous to the output of that hypothetical group of 1,000,000 monkeys set before 1,000,000 dictionaries, who work out the plays of Shakespeare and next week's shopping list, along with every other combination of English words, merely by pointing at random.

Our problem is to discover the structure that makes a string a "sentence" in Table 9. This can be done by the reader if he carefully examines the "sentences" and "nonsentences" listed in the table—the problem is not a difficult one. The reader can then test his discovery by judging the status of new

---

[4] The example is based on a lecture by G. A. Miller in 1964.

Table 9. "Sentences" and "Nonsentences" from a Language Consisting of the Letters *a* and *b* (many strings have been omitted). Circled Strings are "Sentences"

Length 1	*a*
	b
Length 2	*aa*
	ab
	bb
Length 3	*aaa*
	.
	aba
	.
	bbb
Length 4	*aaaa*
	.
	abaa
	.
	.
	aabb
	.
	baba
	bbbb
Length 5	*aaaaa*
	.
	.
	abbba
	.
	.
	bbbab
	.
	.
	bbbbb
Length 6	*aaaaaa*
	.
	.
	aabbaa
	.
	aaabbb
	.
	bbbbbb
	.
	.

examples. Try, for instance, *aaaaabbbb,
aaaaabbbbb, aaaab, bbbbaaaa, aaabbb.* The
second and the last of these are "sentences,"
the rest are not.

Knowledge of the principle that determines
which strings are "sentences" and which are
not is *competence.* It is not performance. Understanding the principle does not automatically lead to a correct judgment. It would
not, for example, in the case of a string that
contained 10,000 *as* followed y 10,001 *bs.*
One must *count* the *as* and *bs* and judge the
result against the principle. Conversely,
counting without knowledge of the principle
will not tell one that *ab* is a "sentence."
Counting is performance, whereas knowledge
of the principle that adjudicates the result
of counting is competence. A grammar is concerned with the latter only. Some further
theory is needed to explain how the principle
is applied to the result of counting, and this
would be a theory of performance. There is,
of course, competence in the counting, but
that is a different domain (Klima, 1966).

The status of a grammar is the same as for
any other scientific theory. It is an empirical
hypothesis that deals with a mental phenomenon. Because it is an empirical hypothesis,
a grammar is either true or false, and observations are made to discover its adequacy
in this respect. Because it is a hypothesis
about a mental phenomenon, the relevant
observations have to do with knowledge of
language. The possibility of describing a
branch of human knowledge in an explicit
way is surely one of the most exciting aspects of contemporary linguistics.

Let us now continue the example of Table
9 and consider several hypotheses that might
account for the reader's understanding of the
structures represented there.

Finite-State Grammars. One method of
representing structure and hence competence
is to construct a *state diagram.* Such a diagram can be thought of as portraying a
machine that can be in any of several states.
The machine is so restricted that when it is
in one state, it can move to other states only
over specified legal routes. The resulting
network of states and transitions will then
embody a structure. Can such a machine,
however construed, talk correctly? In particular, can it produce the "sentences" in Table
9? To make the machine talk at all, we must

provide it with a means of recording its progress as it moves from state to state. We can
do this by having the machine utter the name
of the state it has just left. Since, in Table 9,
the machine must produce strings of *as* and
bs, all the states will be labeled *a* or *b,* and
nothing else.

There is one further requirement to place
on our machine. We want it to be superior
to a mere list. One could, if patient enough,
prepare a list of all the "sentences" made up
from *a* and *b*—writing down *ab, aabb,
aaabbb,* etc. The difficulty with this list is
that it would be endless, because there is no
longest sequence of *as* and *bs.* Thus, to be an
advance over a list, our machine must be
finite, although it may be large. It must have
a finite number of states connected by a
finite number of transitions, and yet be capable of producing an infinite number of correct
sequences of *a* and *b.* Such a machine, if
successful, would provide the *grammar* of the
"sentences" in Table 9. Let us now try to
construct a grammar along these lines.

Figure 10*a* shows a machine of three states
and three transitions, which is able to produce
the "sentence" *ab.* It cannot, however, produce

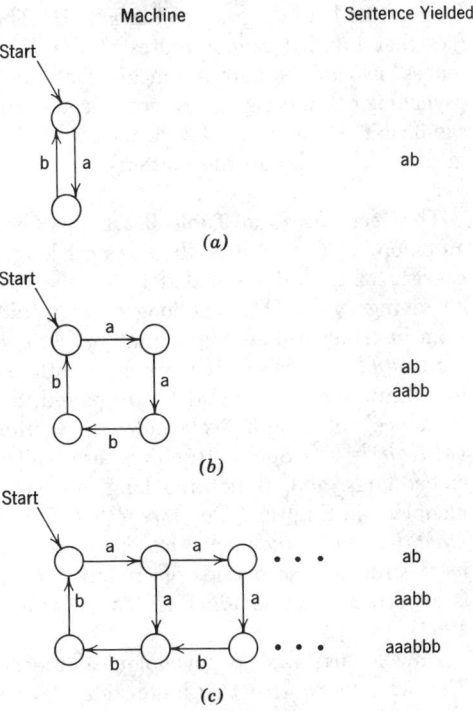

Fig. 10.   Finite-state machines.

"sentences" longer than this. Running the machine twice yields a repetition, not a new "sentence," since we obtain *abab*. In order to produce the next longer "sentence" we must add two new states and three new transitions, as in Fig. 10*b*. This new machine produces *aabb*. as well as *ab*. However, it produces nothing else, and to enrich it we must add two more states and three more transitions, as in Fig. 10*c*. However, this machine is likewise restricted—its longest "sentence" is *aaabbb*. In short, for each additional length of sentence, we must add further states and transitions. Since the list of "sentences" consistent with Table 9 is endless, the addition of states and transitions is endless also. The machine thus fails the last requirement stated above. It is not superior to a mere list, which means that different kinds of grammars are needed.

Before considering these different grammars, however, it should be noted that the "sentences" in Table 9 and the grammars in Fig. 10 are not simply formal exercises. On the contrary, they are directly relevant to the concerns of this chapter. English has sentences of the kind listed in Table 9, and much psychological theorizing accounts for structures of the kind diagrammed in Fig. 10. The fact that Fig. 10 cannot represent the "sentences" in Table 9 therefore means that much psychological theorizing cannot account for significant portions of the structure of English. Let us take up the matter of structure first.

The "sentences" in Table 9 are built like an onion. The shortest is *ab*. The next longer consists of second *ab* sealed inside the first *ab* giving *aabb*. The next longer yet results from inserting still another *ab* into *aabb*, giving *aaabbb* and so on. If we use parentheses to indicate how the *a*s and *b*s are paired, the "sentence" of length six would be written $(a(a(ab)b)b)$. Such structures are called embeddings, and, if not too long, are commonplace in English. (*The race (that the car (that the people sold) won) was held last summer*) stretches the bounds of credulity but it is a perfectly grammatical sentence (Miller, 1962).

Now let us take up psychological theory. The way to construct a finite-state device, clearly, is to link states by transitions. If the device is also a model of a learner, then it must be exposed to each link in the chain so that states will be connected by transitions moving in the correct directions. In the case of Fig. 10*a*, the device must have been exposed first to an *a* and then to a *b*. This requirement is inescapable. As long as the structure to be acquired can be presented in this steplike way, a finite-state device will faithfully reproduce it. Other structures, however, lie beyond its grasp.

This limitation—faithful reproduction of transitions but nothing else—is shared by every stimulus-response theory of learning, from the simple (Skinner's) to the complex (Osgood's). It is inherent in the basic S-R paradigm. Learning occurs when one presents an appropriate stimulus together with the correct response and stamps in a connection between the two through (depending on the theory) reinforcement, repetition, drive reduction, etc. All S-R theories are variations on this basic empiricist theme, and they all lead to the development of a finite-state device. This is the relevance of Table 9. The principles underlying the "sentences" there could not be learned through *any* process consistent with an S-R theory. The reader who understands the structure of these "sentences" is himself a refutation of all consistent S-R models.

This critique might be answered by observing that there is no proof that our knowledge of the "sentences" in Table 9 is anything other than what the diagrams in Fig. 10 claim. The requirement of infinite productivity might be psychologically meaningless, and perhaps an S-R analysis expresses the processes that actually take place.

There are, however, at least three things wrong with this defense. One is simply that it fails to explain how S-R theories are logically superior to the compilation of lists in the case of embedded materials; that is, how S-R theories are actually theories.

A second difficulty is that the diagram in Fig. 10 cannot account for correct judgments about "sentences" never before encountered. If a novel "sentence" goes beyond the current degree of complication of a finite-state device, then it must be rejected as a "nonsentence," unless there is further training. This is the point of the test the reader was asked to take. If the reader had discovered the principle underlying the "sentences" in Table 9, he could correctly judge the sentencehood of novel strings without additional instruction. And if the reader could do this, then what he had learned could not be represented by a finite-state device.

The third difficulty is the opposite side of the coin. If we assume that a speaker's knowledge of English *can* be represented by a finite-state device, then we are forced to hold quite incredible beliefs about the learning ability of children. Take the following sentence: *The people who called and wanted to rent your house when you go away next year are from California* (Miller and Chomsky, 1963). It contains a grammatical connection between the second word (*people*) and the seventeenth word (*are*): changing either but not both of these words to the singular form would produce an ungrammatical sentence. If the connection between *people* and *are* is carried by a finite-state device, then each of us must have learned a unique set of transitions spanning 15 grammatical categories. Making the conservative estimate that an average of four grammatical categories might occur at any point in the development of an English sentence, detecting the connection between *people* and *are* signifies that we have learned at least $4^{15} = 10^9$ different transitions. This is, however, a *reductio ad absurdum*. As Miller and Chomsky point out, "We cannot seriously propose that a child learns the values of 10^9 parameters in a childhood lasting only 10^8 seconds" (1963, p. 430). And even a highly efficient child, one who somehow *could* learn 10 transitions a second, would still miss the dependency when *people* and *are* are separated by 16 words or more.

These three difficulties add up to a single flaw. There is no way for a finite-state device to express the idea of embedding—the insertion of one component inside another component like itself. However, embedding is a psychological fact. It is what the reader grasped in Table 9. It is behind the comprehension of sentences such as *the race that the car that the people sold won was held last summer,* as well as *the people who called and wanted to rent your house when you go away next year are from California.* What is needed therefore is a hypothesis about this mental ability. One is introduced in the next section.

Recursiveness and Linguistic Abstraction. Finite-state devices in general and S-R models in particular can copy only those structures that consist of states and transitions among them. These models will misrepresent anything that possesses some other structure. That was the difficulty with the description of the "sentences" in Table 9 by means of the state diagrams in Fig. 10. If the reader understands the principle underlying these "sentences," he can tell that the part missing from *aab* is a second *b* to go with the first *a*. Similarly, he can tell that the sentence *the car that the people sold was held last summer* is peculiar because there is an incorrect verb for the noun-phrase, *the car.* In both cases, part of what is known about the structure of the sentence is that elements separated from each other actually belong together and not with the material that separates them. What they jointly belong to is an important fact about the sentence, and a correct linguistic representation must somehow portray it. It is on this hidden structural feature that a finite-state device founders.

Consider now the following two grammatical rules. Together, they will produce all and only the "sentences" consistent with Table 9.

$$X \rightarrow aXb$$
$$X \rightarrow ab$$

The arrow ($\rightarrow$) means that the element on the left is rewritten as, or becomes, the elements on the right. By employing a further notational convention—that parentheses in a rule indicate optionality—the possibility of choosing or not choosing an element—the two rules above can be collapsed into one, as follows:

$$X \rightarrow a(X)b$$

One may apply the expanded version of this rule (with the X) indefinitely. Each application lays down an *a* and a *b* with another X in between. The new X calls for application of the rule again, *ad infinitum.* This is embedding. The development of a "sentence" comes to an end when the option of not including X is taken. Figure 11 shows the successive steps taken in producing a "sentence" of length six, *aaabbb.*

The constituent in these "sentences" labeled X is the part to which each *ab* pair belongs, even though they are separated by other *ab* pairs. The existence of X is essential

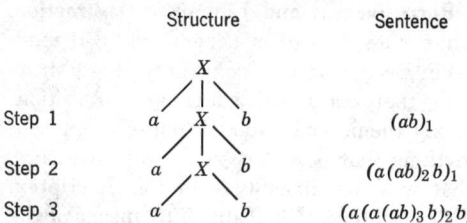

	Structure	Sentence
Step 1	$a \quad X \quad b$	$(ab)_1$
Step 2	$a \quad X \quad b$	$(a(ab)_2 b)_1$
Step 3	$a \qquad b$	$(a(a(ab)_3 b)_2 b)_1$

Fig. 11. Generation of aaabbb by phrase-structural rules.

to the recursiveness of the rule, since its presence on the right is the only feature that requires another application of the rule.

However, note one important thing. The constituent X is *abstract*. It never appears in the final form of a sentence, only in its derivation: aXb is not a "sentence" in Table 9, just as the equivalent in English, *the people Sentence are from California,* is not a sentence. Nonetheless, an abstract constituent is part of the structure of these sentences. It is such an abstraction that the reader gleaned from Table 9 and it is such an abstraction that he discovers in the sentence, *the people who called and wanted to rent your house when you go away next year are from California.* According to this hypothesis, speakers can grasp aspects of sentence structure that are never included in the overt form of a sentence. The question of linguistic abstractions poses a most challenging problem for psychologists. Somehow, linguistic abstractions are developed by children—for just as the reader learned about an invisible X in Table 9, children learn about structural features in English that are never presented to them.

Phrase-Structure Rules. A grammar, we have said, represents linguistic knowledge. A grammatical rule, accordingly, represents a bit of linguistic knowledge. In the case of a rewriting rule such as $X \rightarrow a(X)b$, the knowledge represented is that $a(X)b$ is a species of the genus X. The rule itself is simply a means of expressing this idea.

Many aspects of language take such a form. *The frog caught a mosquito,* for example, *is* a sentence; *the frog* and *the mosquito* both *are* noun phrases, and *caught the mosquito,* in turn, *is* a verb phrase. Knowledge of these elementary facts can be represented naturally by means of rewriting rules.

Table 10 shows how it is done for *the frog caught the mosquito.* Note that each of the examples given above, where one constituent is an instance of something else, is represented in the table by a separate rule. The derivation makes the genus-species relation, as it applies to the sentence, explicit.

It is easy to show that the relations established by the rules in Table 10 correspond to facts that speakers of English know about *the frog caught the mosquito.* First, if a speaker is asked to divide the sentence into two major parts, the split will most likely be made between *the frog* and *caught the mosquito,* that is, between the NP and PredP of the first rule. If he is now asked to divide *caught the mosquito* into two parts, the line will come between *caught* and *the mosquito,* that is, between the V and NP of the second rule. It is very unlikely that a speaker would divide *the frog caught the mosquito* into *the* and *frog caught the mosquito,* or divide *caught the mosquito* into *caught the* and *mosquito.* Speakers honor the rules because the rules reflect information speakers have about the sentence. This correspondence can be revealed in a second way.

Table 10. Rewriting Rules for Producing a Simple Declarative Sentence

1. S $\longrightarrow$ NP PredP

2. PredP $\longrightarrow$ V (NP)

3. NP $\longrightarrow$ Art N

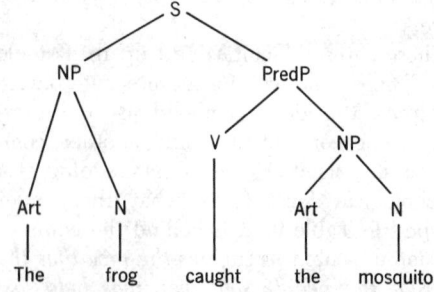

S = sentence. NP = noun phrase. PredP = predicate phrase. Art = article. N = noun. V = verb. Rule 2 covers both transitive and intransitive verbs, and for this reason has *NP* as an optional development. (See Chomsky, 1965, for a more detailed treatment.)

Suppose that we take *the frog caught the mosquito* and try to derive from it another sentence in the following manner (Miller, 1962). We try to find a single word that can replace a *group* of words in the original sentence, without changing the grammatical structure. Our interest lies in seeing which groups of words can be replaced. Replacements exist only for the constituents of the sentence—English has no words that belong to no constituents. A series of these derivations is shown in Table 11, and it can be seen that the replacements obtained in this manner correspond exactly to the derivation obtained through application of the rules in Table 10. We have here hard-core evidence for the validity of the rules in Table 10.

The structures portrayed in Tables 10 and 11 are a part of the phrase structure of English. Accordingly, the rules in Table 10 that produce this structure are called *phrase-structure rules,* and the diagram in the table is called a *phrase marker.* The function of the rules is to define which constituents of sentences are superordinate to which other constituents, to establish the order of constituents, to display the grammatical elements of the sentence (e.g., NP), and to define the so-called basic grammatical relations—subject of a sentence, object of a verb, etc. (See the section on "Predication and the Basic Grammatical Relations" above.) The phrase marker is the structure produced through application of the rules. It can be presented a a diagram, as in Table 10, or by means of labeled brackets.

(((the) (frog)) ((caught) ((the) (mosquito))))
S NP Arat N   VP V   NP Art N

includes exactly the same information as Table 10, and both represent the structure that speakers of English find in *the frog caught the mosquito.*

Note that grammatical rules *represent* linguistic structure. They describe tacit knowledge, not explicit knowledge. No one claims that the rules given in Table 10 are known to speakers of English as rules. If that were actually the case, linguistics could not exist as a science—the field would be as pointless as would a "science" setting out to discover the rules of baseball. The distinction is perhaps obvious, but its importance justifies some elaboration.

One can imagine a series of interpretations

Table 11. The Result of Replacing Groups of Words by Single Words in a Simple Declarative Sentence

A Sentence			
It		acted	
The	frog	acted	
The	frog	caught	it
The	frog	caught	the mosquito

Based on Miller, 1962.

of the rules in Table 10. At the weak end of the series, phrase-structure rules might be regarded as summarizing regularities in behavior. In this case, S → NP PredP means that when English sentences occur, they consist of noun phrases followed by predicate phrases. There is no interest at this end of the series in representing linguistic competence. The relevant observations are the frequency of sentences following the NP PredP format, of PredPs following the V NP format, and so forth. There is no doubt that such observations would falsify the weak interpretation of Table 10. As a count of the sentences appearing in this chapter would reveal, sentences like *the frog caught the mosquito* simply are not common.

At the opposite extreme, the strong end of the series, the claim is that English speakers know the rules in Table 10 in much the form that the rules take when written. Clearly, this claim is false for the vast majority of English speakers.

The midpoint in this series of interpretations is the one intended for Table 10. English speakers do not know the rules in Table 10. But what they do know (it is claimed) is represented by these rules. Observations relevant to the intermediate interpretation have to do with a speaker's intuitions—for instance, that *the mosquito* is a grammatical constituent in English, whereas *caught the* is not. As we have already seen, such observations support this intermediate claim.

Phrase-structure rules, interpreted in the intermediate sense, are said to *generate* sentence structures. A term like "generate" tempts us to think that speakers actually plan sentences along the lines outlined in Table 10—they first decide to utter a sentence, then decide that the sentence will consist of an NP and a PredP, and then, only at the end, decide what vocabulary to use. Such a scheme is one possible, though improbable hypothesis about linguistic performance (Yngve, 1960, 1961; Johnson, 1968). However, this hypothesis is not part of the grammatical analysis in Table 10. A grammar is neutral with respect to hypotheses about performance. The term *generate* is used by grammarians in a logical rather than a mechanical sense. As the linguist Lees once put it, a correct grammar generates all the possible sentences of a language in the same way that a correct zoology generates all possible animals. Both capture the structural relations within their subject matter. The term *generate* is used throughout this chapter in its logical, nonmechanical sense.

The linguistic observations made so far serve a fairly obvious purpose. The parsing of *the frog caught the mosquito* given in Table 10 does not require elaborate defense. The facts are straightforward, and the principal merit in discussing them at all is that they acquaint the reader with some linguistic notation at a point where it is reasonably easy to see what the notation means. However, there are more profound, and psychologically more significant, insights entailed by three other linguistic concepts; and it is to these concepts that we now turn.

Transformations and the Notions of Deep and Surface Structure. In a general way, language can be described as a system whereby sound and meaning are related to each other. That sound and meaning are separate, and so need relating, is evident from paraphrase, where the same meaning is expressed in different patterns of sound (*the man pursued the woman* and *the woman was pursued by the man*), and from ambiguity, where the same pattern of sound has different meanings (*outgoing tuna*). Between sound and meaning stands *syntax*. The relation between sound and meaning is therefore understood to the degree that the syntax of a language is understood. In this section we examine what is known of this relation.

Rationalist philosophers have argued since the eighteenth century that sentences have both an inner and an outer aspect—the first connected with thought and the second with sound (Chomsky, 1966). The kind of evidence that leads to this conclusion, and hence to the phenomenon of concern here, is given in Table 12 (after Miller and McNeill, 1968). The three sentences on the left of Table 12 all have the same superficial form. They start with a pronoun, *they*, followed by *are*, followed by a progressive form, followed by a plural noun. Despite superficial identity, however, there are clear differences in structure among these three sentencs. To understand the differences, we will eventually need the notions of a transformation rule and of deep and surface structure.

Sentence (a) differs from sentences (b) and (c) in several fairly obvious respects. One difference is that the two kinds of sentence accept pauses in different places. With sentence (a), one might say *they—are buying—glasses*, but probably not *they—are—buying glasses*. It is the opposite with sentences (b) and (c). One could say *they—are—drinking companions* or *they—are—drinking glasses*, but not *they—are drinking —companions* or *they—are drinking— glasses*, unless the reference was to cannibalism or suicide. A second difference is in the proper location of articles. We have *they are buying the glasses* but not *they are the buying glasses*. We have *they are the drinking companions* but not *they are drinking the companions*.

The location of pauses in a sentence is fixed by its phrase structure. Pauses tend to go around constituents, not inside them. The location of articles is similarly determined by phrase structure. They go before NPs only. We can thus summarize the differences be-

Table 12.

Sentences	Paraphrases	Nonparaphrases
a. They are buying glasses.	—	—
b. They are drinking glasses.	They are glasses to use for drinking.	They are glasses that drink.
c. They are drinking companions.	They are companions that drink.	They are companions to use for drinking.

tween sentence (a) and sentences (b) and (c) by saying that they have different phrase structures. In particular, the progressive form in sentence (a) is associated with the verb *are*, whereas in sentences (b) and (c), it has moved over to the plural noun. The essential parts of the three phrase markers are as follows: (*they*) (*are buying*) (*glasses*), (*they*) (*are*) (*drinking companions*).

Sentence (a) and sentences (b) and (c) are distinguished in their *surface structure*. The difference, as we have seen, has to do with the distribution of pauses and the location of articles. Surface structure is also intimately connected with stress and intonation. In general, the surface structure of a sentence has to do with phonology—with one of the two aspects of language that need to be related by syntax.

Let us now look more carefully at sentences (b) and (c). They accept pauses in the same way, they take articles at the same places, they are accordingly bracketed in the same way, and, indeed, they have the same surface structure. But it is clear that they are not structurally identical throughout. They differ in a way that is important to meaning, the other aspect of language that is to be related by syntax. That they differ in meaning can be seen in the paraphrases and nonparaphrases of the two sentences in Table 12. Sentence (b) means "they are glasses to use for drinking," and sentence (c) means "they are companions that drink." Exchanging the form of the paraphrase between (b) and (c) leads to a nonparaphrase. Sentence (b) does not mean "they are glasses that drink" any more than sentence (c) means "they are companions to use for drinking." Despite the identity of surface form, (b) and (c) differ importantly in underlying form. We shall say that they differ in *deep structure*, saving until later a more precise definition of what this means. First, however, let us note two implications that follow from the fact that (b) and (c) have the same surface structure but different deep structures.

One is that the *relation* between deep and surface structure must be different in the two sentences. The statement of this relation is assigned a special place in a grammar. It is done by *rules of transformation*, and it is these rules, together with the deep and surface structure of sentences, that embody the

connection between sound and meaning in a language. The reader will have realized, of course, that in a statistical sense, sentences (b) and (c) are freakish. The vast majority of sentences that have different deep structures and different transformations also have different surface structures. Sentences (b) and (c) happen not to, but for this very reason they conveniently illustrate what is true of all sentences. Every sentence, however simple, has some kind of deep structure related to some kind of surface structure by means of certain transformations. The substance of grammar consists of making explicit these three terms.

The second implication of the difference in paraphrase between sentences (b) and (c) is that the deep and surface structures of sentences are not identical. This is evidently true of at least one of these sentences, (b) or (c). In fact, it is true of all sentences. Transformations provide enormous flexibility in developing surface structures from deep structures, and this advantage has been pressed by language in even the most elementary sentence types (an example with simple declaratives is given below). Thus the deep structure of every sentence is abstract in the sense given above. The underlying structure, the part connected with meaning, it not present in the overt form of any sentence. The existence of linguistic abstractions is a universal phenomenon—acquisition of them is a basic fact about the development of language and on its success rests the emergence of all adult grammar. It would be impossible to understand sentences (b) and (c) correctly if this were not so.

All these concepts—deep structure, surface structure, linguistic abstraction, and the way transformations tie them together—can best be seen in an example. The one we shall use is borrowed from Miller and McNeill (1968) and is based on Chomsky (1957). Consider the following sentences:

He walks	(present singular)
They walk	(present plural)
He walked	(past singular)
They walked	(past plural)

These four sentences mark two distinctions: number (singular and plural) and tense (present and past). Number is marked both in the form of the pronoun and in the inflection of the present-tense verb. Tense is marked in the inflection of the verb. Let us focus on the verbs, for it is here that a transformation becomes involved.

There are three verb suffixes: $-s$, $-\phi$ (which means null, but is a suffix all the same), and $-ed$. They encode information of a certain type, namely, the form of the verbal auxiliary, so we might suppose that this information can be expressed by a rewriting rule of the type already discussed. If we label the genus part of the rule C, then we can use the following context-sensitive rule:

$$C \rightarrow \begin{cases} -s \text{ in the context NP}_{sing} \\ -\phi \text{ in the context NP}_{pl} \\ -ed \end{cases}$$

and summarize all four of the sentences above by a single schema NP + V-C.

Let us now complicate the sentences slightly by incorporating an auxiliary verb, *be*, and see what happens to C:

> *He is walking*
> *They are walking*
> *He was walking*
> *They were walking*

The first thing to note is that using a form of *be* adds *-ing* to the following main verb. C, for its part, has moved forward. It is no longer attached to the main verb but to the auxiliary, and we have *be-s* (pronounced *is*), *be- φ* (pronounced *are*), and *be-ed* (pronounced *was* or *were*, number being marked on past-tense verbs in this case—a detail we can ignore). The schema for these sentences therefore is, NP + *be*-C + V-*ing*.

Next, consider the effect of adding a different auxiliary verb, a form of *have*, to the original sentences. In doing so, we obtain:

> *He has walked*
> *They have walked*
> *He had walked*
> *They had walked*

The main verb again takes a suffix, this time, *-ed*, and C again moves forward to the auxiliary. It is the same therefore as when *be* is the auxiliary, except that different pronunciation rules are involved (*have-s* is *has*, *have-φ*

is *have, have-ed* is *had*) and the main-verb suffix is *-ed*, instead of *-ing*. By indicating these changes, we obtain the schema NP + *have*-C + V-*ed*, for the use of *have* as an auxiliary.

The two auxiliaries can be combined, of course, as in these sentences:

> *He has been walking*
> *They have been walking*
> *He had been walking*
> *They had been walking*

Both auxiliaries have the effects already demonstrated. *Be* adds the suffix *-ing* to the following verb and *have* adds a "past" suffix to *be*. (In this case, it is *be-en*, another difference in detail that we can ignore.) C also follows its pattern, for it is still attached to the first auxiliary verb. The schema therefore is NP + *have*-C + *be-en* + V-*ing*.

These sentences can be complicated still further by adding one of the modal auxiliaries. Modals are the words *will, can, may, shall, must*. Let us add *will*:

> *He will have been walking*
> *They will have been walking*
> *He would have been walking*
> *They would have been walking*

C has moved forward again, attached now to the modal. *Have* still adds a "past" inflection to the following *be*, and *be* still adds *-ing* to the following main verb. The schema thus is NP + M-C + *have* + *be-en* + V-*ing*, where M stands for "modal."

It is evident from these examples that C always appears with the first member of an auxiliary construction, no matter how long this construction is. The location of C is a fact known to all speakers of English—*he will had been walking* obviously is not the way to indicate past tense in an auxiliary construction. Part of an English speaker's competence thus has C at the start of a verb phrase. Another part involves the contingency between *have* as an auxiliary and a following "past" inflection, as well as the contingency between *be* as an auxiliary and the following *-ing*. Let us try to represent these facts about competence by constructing a rule that meets the following two conditions: (1) the true order of elements is maintained, and (2) elements contingent on one another are placed together. This will lead to a simple solution.

Meeting the first condition requires placing C first, then M, then *have,* and finally *be.* Since C appears in every sentence, our rule must make it obligatory. The remaining constituents, however, are optional, so we write them with parentheses. Let us call the whole construction "auxiliary," abbreviate it "Aux," and put down the following rule:

Aux → C (M) (*have*) (*be*)

The following main verb V is omitted from this rule because it is introduced along with Aux by the PredP rule, which is now enlarged to read:

PredP → Aux V (NP)

The Aux rule is still incomplete, since it does not yet meet the second condition. The contingencies to be represented are that *have* goes with *-en* (or *-ed*), and *be* goes with *-ing,* so we write these elements together, and thereby produce the following:

Aux → C (M) (*have-en*) (*be-ing*)

after which there will always be a V.

We now have all but one of the rules necessary to generate the examples previously given. The missing one, a transformation, will be provided shortly. However, in order to see the need for the transformation, and to appreciate the role it plays in representing the structure of these sentences, we should first see the result of producing sentences without it. The structural relations to be expressed by the transformation will be those not expressed by the rules already developed. If we have done our job well, the division between the two kinds of rules, the transformation and the phrase-structure rules, will correspond to a real division between two kinds of structural information within sentences.

Figure 12 contains a phrase marker generated by the phrase-structure rules presented in the preceding paragraphs. Note that the order of elements at the bottom of the phrase marker is *they + Past + will + have + en + be + ing + walk.* This string and its associated structure is the deep structure of *they would have been walking.* The surface structure is a specific instance of the last schema given above—*they + will-Past + have + be-en + walk-ing.* The deep structure thus differs from the surface structure in the order of affixes and verbs. Accordingly, it is abstract in the sense used here, since the

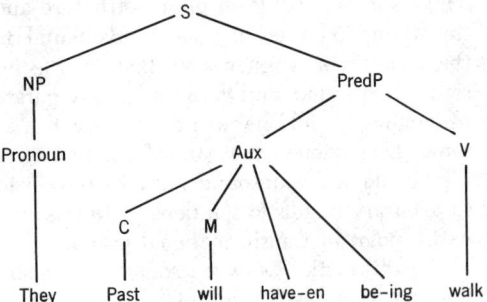

Fig. 12. Deep structure of *they would have been walking.*

deep-structure order never appears overtly. It is important to realize, nonetheless, that the deep structure in Fig. 12 reflects actual linguistic knowledge—the information summarized by C *is* always first in a predicate phrase, *have* and *-en do* always appear together, just as *be* and *-ing* do.

The deep structure therefore must be transformed to obtain the surface structure. The transformation is simple: wherever the sequence affix-verb appears in the deep structure, change the order to verb-affix (Chomsky, 1957). If the reader applies this transformation, he will find the surface structure of *they would have been walking* rolling out quite automatically.

There remains one important point. Note that the linguistic information expressed by the phrase-structure rules in generating *they would have been walking* is fundamentally different from the information expressed by the transformation rule. Which is to say that the distinction between the two is linguistically meaningful. The former rules define such matters as the genus-species relations within the sentence (e.g., *they* is an NP), establish the basic order of elements (e.g., C is first in the PredP), and indicate what the elements are (e.g., *have-en* is an element). Information of this kind is essential for obtaining the meaning of the sentence. The relations just mentioned, among others, are exactly what we understand of *they would have been walking.*

The transformation, in contrast, makes no contribution to meaning. It exists only because sound and meaning are not identical in English (or any language), and its sole purpose is to state the relation between them.

The distinction between phrase-structure and transformation rules is thus fundamental to the analysis of language. Without it, the insight that sound and meaning are separate in language would be lost; and to suggest, as some have done, that transformations are methodologically unsound because they lead to arbitrary linguistic solutions, is to miss the entire point of transformational grammar.

The distinction between sound and meaning is a basic justification of transformational grammar, but the use of transformations in grammatical analysis is supported by other arguments as well. One is economy. If we dispense with transformations and try to generate sentences with phrase-structure rules alone, the result becomes unnecessarily complex. The sentences given above, for example, require eight different and independent phrase-structure rules, one for each combination of auxiliary verb and C, instead of the single phrase-structure rule required when a transformation is allowed. Without the transformation, we would need at least the following rules: $\text{Aux}_1 \rightarrow$ V-C, $\text{Aux}_2 \rightarrow$ *be*-C + V-*ing*, $\text{Aux}_3 \rightarrow$ *have*-C + V-*ed*, $\text{Aux}_4 \rightarrow$ *have*-C + *be-en* + V-*ing*, $\text{Aux}_5 \rightarrow$ M-C + V, $\text{Aux}_6 \rightarrow$ M-C + *be* + V-*ing*, $\text{Aux}_7 \rightarrow$ M-C + *have* + V-*ed*, and $\text{Aux}_8 \rightarrow$ M-C + *have* + *be-en* + V-*ing*. Note that these rules cannot be collapsed onto one another by means of the parentheses notation used before, since there is no way to locate C correctly if optional elements are introduced. The phrase-structure version of the auxiliary therefore not only overlooks valid linguistic generalizations— such as the fact that C always appears first in the auxiliary, or that there *is* an auxiliary, or that -*ing* depends on *be* and not on V—but it is simply cumbersome. Relative economy is always an argument in support of one theoretical interpretation over another, and using it in the present case inclines the balance toward a transformational grammar.

The argument of economy has special significance in the context of language acquisition. We prefer to think of children doing the simpler thing, whatever that might be. In the case of linguistic development, the simpler thing is to acquire a transformational grammar instead of a phrase-structure grammar. Accordingly, it is the former that we suppose is learned.

The affix-transformation used in generating the English auxiliary verb is one rule within a vast and intricate network of transformations making up the language. Passive sentences, negation, questions of various kinds, conjunctions, complements, and many others, all depend on transformations. The technical literature dealing with these rules is large and sophisticated; rather than summarizing it here, a task almost as unnecessary as it is hopeless, the interested reader is encouraged to turn to original sources. A book edited by Fodor and Katz (1964) contains a number of significant papers. In addition, one should look at Chomsky (1957, 1963, 1964, 1965, 1966), Chomsky and Miller (1963), Chomsky and Halle (1966), Fillmore (1965), Katz (1966), Katz and Postal (1964), Miller and Chomsky (1963), Postal (1964), and Bach and Harms (1968). A review of transformational grammar written for psychologists is contained in Miller and McNeill (1968).

There is one set of transformations of special significance, however, and this section will conclude with a discussion of them. Recall the artificial language presented in Table 9. Its "sentences" were built like an onion— such structures as $(a(a(ab)b)b)$. The rule given to generate the "sentences" in Table 9 was $X \rightarrow a(X)b$, in which there is an abstract recursive element, X. This much is phrase structure and it has an exact analogy in English (and all other languages).

In developing the deep structure of any sentence, it is possible to include the element S, thus calling for the insertion of *another* deep structure at that point. That sentence, in turn, may also have an S in it, calling for the insertion of yet another deep structure, and so forth. The result is the same onion-like structure presented in Table 9, and it has the same effect—making unlimited productivity possible through recursion. Figure 13 shows a succession of such deep structures, each with another deep structure embedded within it.

Figure 13 is the result of applying phrase-structure rules alone. It is, in other words, the deep structure of (*the ostrich* (*that was terrified by the zebra* (*that the hunter shot*)) *stuck its head in the sand*), a sentence with two relative clauses. English employs several tranformations to develop this surface structure from the deep structure in Fig. 13. In discussing them, we shall use terminology

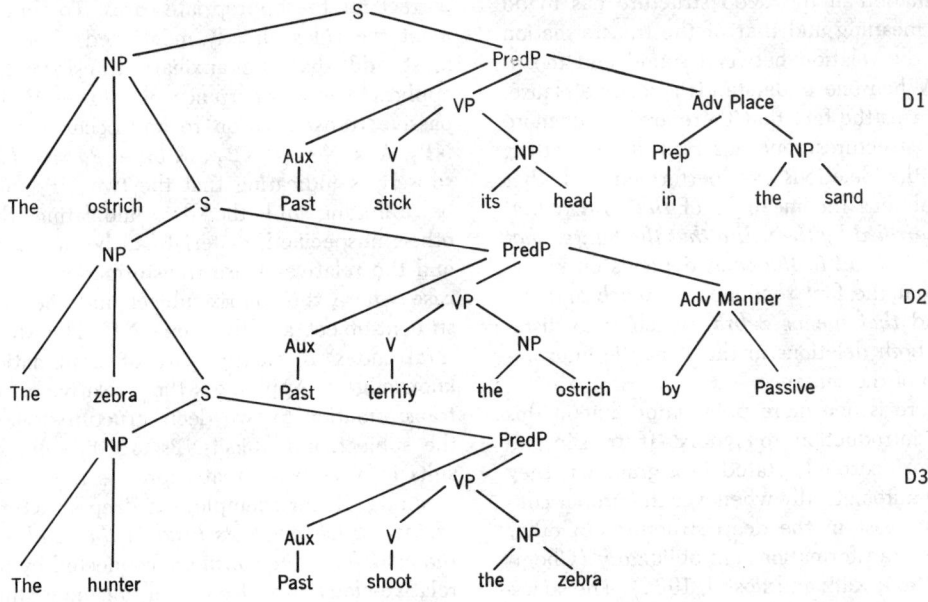

Fig. 13.   Deep structure of *the ostrich that was terrified by the zebra that the hunter shot stuck its head in the sand.*

suggested by Lees (1960) and call the structure containing S the *matrix* and the S contained the *constituent*. Thus D3 in Fig. 13 is the constituent of the matrix D2, and both are the constituent of the matrix D1. In Fig. 13, D3 is only a constituent, D1 is only a matrix, but D2 is both—a matrix for D3 and a constituent (containing D3) for D1.

These three components are complete structures unto themselves. If developed in isolation (ignoring the S in D1 and D2), each would result in a sentence. D1 is the deep structure of *the ostrich stuck its head in the sand;* D2 is the deep structure of a passive sentence, *the ostrich was terrified by the zebra;* and D3 is the deep structure of *the hunter shot the zebra.* It is obvious that more is required in combining these elementary structures than simply applying the transformations that each calls for alone—the auxiliary transformation in every case, and the passive transformation in D2. Doing only this much produces non-English: *the ostrich was terrified by the zebra the hunter shot the zebra stuck its head in the sand.* To avoid a word salad like this, an embedding transformation must delete double occurrences of the same NP. Not every NP repeated in an English sentence need be deleted, of course.

The ostrich stuck its head in the sand and the ostrich ate the worm is grammatical even though redundant or ambiguous. However, in the case of an embedded relative clause, deletion must occur, and the rule is that when the same NP is both a matrix subject and a constituent object, the object-NP is moved to the front of its sentence structure and replaced by the word *that.* Let us call this operation the deletion transformation. In the case of Fig. 13, it produces *the ostrich that the zebra that the hunter Past+shoot Past+ terrify by+Passive Past+stuck its head in the sand.* Applying the auxiliary transformation to this structure wherever called for (e.g., *Past-shoot* becomes *shot*), and the passive transformation to D2, the surface structure, of which Fig. 13 is the deep structure, rolls out. (Actually, such "singulary" transformations are all applied first to the most deeply embedded S, then to the next most deeply embedded S, and so on up to the top, before the embedding transformations are applied. See Chomsky, 1965, for a discussion of such transformational cycles.)

Again, notice that a natural distinction exists between the information contained in the transformation and the information contained in the deep structure. As before, the information in the deep structure has to do with meaning and that of the transformation with the relation between sound and meaning. When one understands a relative clause, he grasps the fact that there are two or more deep structures, one inserted in the other, with the deletions *not* performed. Whether one obtains the meaning of *the ostrich that was terrified by the zebra that the hunter shot stuck its head in the sand* depends on knowing that the first *that* means *ostrich* and the second *that* means *zebra*, which is to disregard both deletions in the semantic interpretation of the sentence.

There is one more point important in this brief introduction to syntax. If transformations are correctly stated in a grammar, they apply automatically whenever the proper conditions exist in the deep structure. In other words, transformations are obligatory (Chomsky, 1965; Katz and Postal, 1964). The specification of the "proper" conditions is done by the *structural index* of a transformation and setting it down is an important part of writing a transformational rule. Should the structural index be wrong, a transformation will inevitably relate wrong deep and surface structures, even though the operations described in the transformation and themselves

correct for the appropriate cases. To supplement the rules already mentioned, then, we must add that the auxiliary transformation applies to any occurrence of *affix* + V, the passive transformation to any occurrence of NP_1, Aux, V, . . . NP_2 . . . *by* + *Passive* (the subscripts indicating that the two NPs must be different and the dots indicating that other, unspecified, material can be inserted), and the relative-clause transformation to any case where the matrix-subject and the constituent-object are the same NP. The structural index is clearly part of grammatical knowledge. Applying the relative-clause transformation to two deep structures where the subject and object-NPs are different results in a sentence that expresses the wrong meaning. If, for example, the deep structures of *the ostrich stuck its head in the sand* and *the ostrich ate the worm* are connected by the relative-clause transformation, meaning shifts and the result becomes something out of Alice in Wonderland—*the ostrich stuck its head in the sand that ate the worm*. Since violation of the structural index of a transformation leads to an inappropriate expression of meaning, it is evident that the structural index is a part of the relation between meaning and sound.

References

Allport, F. H. *Social psychology.* Cambridge, Mass.: Houghton Mifflin, 1924.

Anderson, S. A., and Beh, W. The reorganization of verbal memory in childhood. *J. verb. Learn. verb. Behav.,* 1968, **7**, 1049–1053.

Anisfeld, M., and Tucker, R. G. English pluralization rules of six-year old children. *Child Dev.,* in press.

Anisfeld, M., Barlow, J., and Frail, C. M. Distinctive features in the pluralization rules of English speakers. Unpublished paper, Department of Psychology, Cornell University, 1967.

Bach, E. and Harms, R. T. (Eds.). *Universals in linguistic theory.* New York: Holt, Rinehart, and Winston, 1968.

Bellugi, U. The emergence of inflections and negation systems in the speech of two children. Paper presented at New England Psychological Association, Boston, 1964.

Bellugi, U. The development of interrogative structures in children's speech. In K. Riegel (Ed.), *The development of language functions.* Univ. Mich. Lang. Develpm. Program, Report No. 8, 1965.

Bellugi, U. The acquisition of negation. Unpublished doctoral dissertation, Graduate School of Education, Harvard University, 1967.

Bellugi, U., and Brown, R. (Eds.) *The acquisition of language, Monogr. Soc. Res. Child Dev.,* 1964, **29**, No. 92.

Bem, S. L. The role of comprehension in self-instruction. Unpublished paper, Department of Psychology, University of Michigan, 1967.

Berko, J. The child's learning of English morphology. *Word*, 1958, **14**, 150–177.

Bever, T. G. Pre-linguistic behavior. Unpublished honors thesis, Department of Linguistics, Harvard University, 1961.

Bever, T. G., Mehler, J., and Valian, V. V. Linguistic capacity of very young children. Lecture at Graduate School of Education, Harvard University, 1967.

Bever, T. G., Fodor, J. A., and Weksel, W. On the acquisition of syntax: a critique of "contextual generalization." *Psychol. Rev.*, 1965, **72**, 467–482. (a)

Bever, T. G., Fodor, J. A., and Weksel, W. Is linguistics empirical? *Psychol. Rev.*, 1965, **72**, 493–500. (b)

Birch, D. Verbal control of nonverbal behavior. *J. exp. Child Psychol.*, 1966, **4**, 266–275.

Bloomfield, L. *Language*. New York: Holt, Rinehart, and Winston, 1933.

Blumenthal, A. Early psycholinguistic research: a review. In T. G. Bever and W. Weksel (Eds.), *The structure and psychology of language*. New York: Holt, Rinehart, and Winston, in press.

Bogoyavlenskiy, D. N. *Psikhologiya usvoyeniya orfografii*. Moscow: Akad. Pedag. Nauk RSFSR, 1957.

Braine, M. D. S. The ontogeny of English phrase structure: the first phase. *Language*, 1963, **39**, 1–13. (a)

Braine, M. D. S. On learning the grammatical order of words. *Psychol. Rev.* 1963, **70**, 323–348. (b)

Braine, M. D. S. On the basis of phrase structure: a reply to Bever, Fodor, and Weksel. *Psychol. Rev.*, 1965, **72**, 483–492.

Braine, M. D. S. The acquisition of language in infant and child. In Carroll Reed (Ed.), *The learning of language*. Nat. Council Teachers Engl., in press.

Brown, R. Linguistic determinism and the part of speech. *J. abnorm. soc. Psychol.*, 1957, **55**, 1–5.

Brown, R. *Words and things*. Glencoe, Ill.: Free Press, 1958.

Brown, R. The dialogue in early childhood. Presidential address, Div. 8, Amer. Psychol. Assn., 1966.

Brown, R. Derivational complexity and the order of acquisition in child speech. Carnegie-Mellon Conference on Cognitive Processes, 1968.

Brown, R., and Bellugi, U. Three processes in the child's acquisition of syntax. *Harvard Educ. Rev.*, 1964, **34**, 133–151.

Brown, R., and Berko, J. Word association and the acquisition of grammar. *Child Dev.*, 1960, **31**, 1–14.

Brown, R., Cazden, C., and Bellugi, U. The child's grammar from I to III. In J. P. Hill (Ed.), *Minnesota symposium on child psychology*. Minneapolis: University of Minnesota Press, 1968.

Brown, R., and Fraser, C. The acquisition of syntax. In U. Bellugi and R. Brown (Eds.), *The acquisition of language, Monogr. Soc. Res. Child Dev.*, 1964, **29** (No. 92), 43–78.

Bruner, J. S., Goodnow, J. J., and Austin, G. A. *A study of thinking*. New York: Wiley, 1956.

Bruner, J. S., Olver, R. and Greenfield, P. M. *Studies in cognitive growth*. New York: Wiley, 1966.

Cazden, C. Environmental assistance to the child's acquisition of grammar. Unpublished doctoral dissertation, Graduate School of Education, Harvard University, 1965.

Cazden, C. The acquisition of noun and verb inflections. Unpublished paper, Department of Social Relations, Harvard University, 1967.

Chai, D. T. Communication of pronomial referents in ambiguous English sentences for children and adults. Unpublished doctoral dissertation, Department of Communication Sciences, University of Michigan, 1967.

Chomsky, C. S. The acquisition of syntax in children from 5 to 10. Unpublished Doctoral Dissertation, Department of Linguistics, Harvard University, 1968.

Chomsky, N. A. *Syntactic structures.* The Hague: Mouton, 1957.

Chomsky, N. A. Review of *Verbal Behavior,* by B. F. Skinner. *Language,* 1959, **35**, 26–58.

Chomsky, N. A. Formal properties of grammars. In R. D. Luce, R. R. Bush, and E. Galanter (Eds.), *Handbook of mathematical psychology,* Vol. 2. New York: Wiley, 1963. Pp. 323–418.

Chomsky, N. A. Current issues in linguistic theory. In J. A. Fodor and J. J. Katz (Eds.), *The structure of language: readings in the philosophy of language.* Englewood Cliffs, N. J.: Prentice-Hall, 1964.

Chomsky, N. Discussion of Miller and Ervin's paper. In U. Bellugi and R. Brown (Eds.), *The acquisition of language, Monogr. Soc. Res. Child Dev.,* 1964, **29** (No. 92), 35–39.

Chomsky, N. A. Some methodological remarks on generative grammar. *Word,* 1961, **17**, 219–239. (Reprinted in J. J. Fodor and J. A. Katz (Eds.), *The structure of language.* Englewood Cliffs, N. J.: Prentice-Hall, 1964.)

Chomsky, N. A. *Aspects of the theory of syntax.* Cambridge: M.I.T. Press, 1965.

Chomsky, N. A. *Cartesian linguistics.* New York: Harper & Row, 1966.

Chomsky, N. A. Remarks on nominalization. Unpublished paper. M.I.T. 1967.

Chomsky, N. A., and Halle, M. Some controversial questions in phonological theory. *J. Ling.,* 1965, **2**, 97–138.

Chomsky, N. A., and Halle, M. *The sound pattern of English.* New York: Harper and Row, forthcoming.

Chomsky, N. A., Halle, M., and Lukoff, F. On accent and juncture in English. In M. Halle, H. Lunt, and H. Maclean (Eds.), *For Roman Jakobson.* The Hague: Mouton, 1956.

Chomsky, N. A., and Miller, G. A. Introduction to the formal analysis of natural languages. In R. D. Luce, R. R. Bush, and E. Galanter (Eds.), *Handbook of mathematical psychology,* Vol. 2. New York: Wiley, 1963. Pp. 269–321.

Clark, H. On the use and meaning of prepositions. *J. verb. Learn. verb. Behav.,* in press.

Entwisle, D. R. *The word associations of young children.* Baltimore: Johns Hopkins, 1966.

Ervin, S. Changes with age in the verbal determinants of word-association. *Am. J. Psychol.,* 1961, **74**, 361–372.

Ervin, S. Imitation and structural change in children's language. In E. H. Lenneberg (Ed.), *New directions in the study of language.* Cambridge: M.I.T. Press, 1964.

Ferguson, C. A. Baby talk in six languages. *Am. Anthro.,* 1964, **66**, 103–114.

Fillmore, C. J. *Indirect object transformations in English and the ordering of transformations.* The Hague: Mouton, 1965.

Fodor, J. A. Review of H. Werner, and B. Kaplan, *Symbol formation. Language,* 1964, **4**, 566–578.

Fodor, J. A. How to learn to talk: some simple ways. In F. Smith and G. A. Miller (Eds.), *The genesis of language: a psycholinguistic approach.* Cambridge: M.I.T. Press, 1966.

Fodor, J. A., and Garrett, M. Some reflections on competence and performance. In J. Lyons and R. Wales (Eds.), *Psycholinguistics papers.* Edinburgh: University of Edinburgh Press, 1966.

Fodor, J. A., and Garrett, M. Some syntactic determinants of sentential complexity. *Percept. Psychophys.,* 1967, **2**, 289–296.

Fodor, J. A., and Katz, J. J. *The structure of language: readings in the philosophy of language.* Englewood Cliffs, N. J.: Prentice-Hall, 1964.

Fraser, C., Bellugi, U. and Brown, R. Control of grammar in imitation, comprehension and production. *J. verb. Learn. verb. Behav.*, 1963, **2**, 121–135.

Gazzaniga, M. S., and Sperry, R. W. Language after section of the cerebral commissures. *Brain*, 1967, **90**, 131–148.

Glucksberg, S., and Krauss, R. M. What do people say after they have learned to talk? Studies of the development of referential communication. *Merrill-Palmer Quart.*, 1967, **13**, 309–316.

Glucksberg, S., Krauss, R. M., and Weisberg, R. Referential communication in nursery school children: method and some preliminary findings. *J. exp. Child Psychol.*, 1966, **3**, 333–342.

Goldman-Eisler, F. Hesitation and information in speech. In *Information theory.* Fourth London Symposium. London: Butterworths, 1961.

Gough, P. B. Grammatical transformations and speed of understanding. *J. verb. Learn. verb. Behav.*, 1965, **4**, 107–111.

Greenberg, J. H. Some universals of grammar with particular reference to the order of meaningful elements. In J. H. Greenberg (Ed.), *Universals of language.* Cambridge: M.I.T. Press, 1962.

Greenberg, J. H. Language universals. In T. Sebeok (Ed.), *Current trends in linguistics,* vol. III. The Hague: Mouton, 1966.

Greenfield, P. M. Who is "DADA?" Unpublished paper, Syracuse University, 1967.

Grégoire, A. *L'apprentissage du langage. I. Les deux premières années.* Paris: Droz, 1937.

Gruber, J. Topicalization in child language. *Found. Lang.*, 1967, **3**, 37–65.

Gvozdev, A. N. *Voprosy Izucheniya detskoy rechi,* Moscow: Akad. Pedag. Nauk RSFSR, 1961.

Halle, M. On the basis of phonology. In J. A. Fodor and J. J. Katz (Eds.), *The structure of language.* Englewood Cliffs, N. J.: Prentice-Hall, 1964. (a)

Halle, M. Phonology in generative grammar. In J. J. Fodor and J. A. Katz (Eds.), *The structure of language.* Englewood Cliffs, N. J.: Prentice-Hall, 1964.

Huttenlocher, J., Eisenberg, K., and Strauss, S. Comprehension: relation between perceived actor and logical subject. *J. verb. Learn. verb. Behav.*, in press.

Huttenlocher, J., and Strauss, S. Comprehension and a statement's relation to the situation it describes. *J. verb. Learn. verb. Behav.*, in press.

Inhelder, B. Cognitive development and its contribution to the diagnosis of some phenomena of mental deficiency. *Merrill-Palmer Quart.*, 1966, **12**, 299–319.

Irwin, O. C. Infant speech: variability and the problem of diagnosis. *J. speech hearing disorders*, 1947, **12**, 287–289. (a)

Irwin, O. C. Infant speech: consonantal sounds according to place of articulation. *J. speech hearing disorders*, 1947, **12**, 397–401. (b)

Irwin, O. C. Infant speech: consonant sounds according to manner of articulation. *J. speech hearing disorders*, 1947, **12**, 402–404. (c)

Irwin, O. C. Infant speech: development of vowel sounds. *J. speech hearing disorders*, 1948, **13**, 31–34.

Jakobson, R. *Kindersprache, Aphasie, und allgemeine Lautgesetze.* Uppsala: Almgrist and Weksell, 1941.

Jakobson, R. Concluding statement: linguistics and poetics. In T. A. Sebeok (Ed.), *Style in language.* Cambridge and New York: M.I.T. Press and Wiley, 1960.

Jakobson, R. *Child language, aphasia, and phonological Universals* (trans. by A. Keiler). The Hague: Mouton, 1968.

Jakobson, R., Fant, C. G. M., and Halle, M. *Preliminaries to speech analysis,* Cambridge: M.I.T. Press, 1963.

Jakobson, R., and Halle, M. *Fundamentals of language*. The Hague: Mouton, 1956.

James, W. *Psychology, the briefer course*. New York: Holt, Rinehart, and Winston, 1893.

Jesperson, O. *Language*. New York: Holt, 1925.

Johnson, N. F. Sequential verbal behavior. In T. Dixon and D. Horton (Eds.), *Verbal behavior and general S-R theory*. Englewood Cliffs, N. J.: Prentice-Hall, 1968.

Kagan, J., Moss, H. A., and Sigel, I. E. Psychological significance of styles of conceptualization. In J. C. Wright and J. Kagan (Eds.), *Basic cognitive processes in children, Mongr Soc. Res. Child Dev.*, 1963, **28**, (No. 2), 73–112.

Katz, J. J. Mentalism in linguistics. *Language*, 1964, **40**, 124–137.

Katz, J. J. *The philosophy of language*. New York: Harper & Row, 1966.

Katz, J. J. Recent issues in semantic theory. *Found. Lang.*, 1967, **3**, 124–194.

Katz, J. J., and Fodor, J. A. The structure of semantic theory. *Language*, 1963, **39**, 170–210.

Katz, J. J., and Postal, P. *An integrated theory of linguistic descriptions*. Cambridge: M.I.T. Press, 1964.

Kelley, K. L. Early syntactic acquisition. RAND Corporation Report No. P-3719, 1967.

Kimura, D. Cerebral dominance and the perception of verbal stimuli. *Can. J. Psychol.*, 1961, **15**, 166–171.

Kimura, D. Left-right differences in the perception of melodies. *Quart. J. exptl. Psychol.*, 1964, **14**, 355–358.

Klima, E. S. Negation in English. In J. J. Fodor and J. A. Katz (Eds.), *The structure of language*. Englewood Cliffs, N.J.: Prentice-Hall, 1964.

Klima, E. S. Knowing language and getting to know language. In E. Zale (Ed.), Proceedings of the Conference on Language and Language Behavior. New

Klima, E. S. and Bellugi, U. Syntactic regularities in the speech of children. In York: Appleton-Century, 1968.

J. Lyons and R. Wales (Eds.), *Psycholinguistics Papers*. Edinburgh: University of Edinburgh Press, 1966.

Krauss, R. M., and Bricker, P. D. Effects of transmission delay and access delay on the efficiency of verbal communication. *J. acoust. Soc.*, 1967, **41**, 286–292.

Krauss, R. M., and Rotter, G. S. Communication abilities of children as a function of status and age. Unpublished paper, Princeton University, n.d.

Krauss, R. M., and Weinheimer, S. Changes in reference phrases as a function of frequency of usage in social interaction: a preliminary study. *Psychon. Sci.*, 1964, **1**, 113–114.

Krauss, R. M., and Weinheimer, S. Concurrent feedback, confirmation, and the encoding of referents in verbal communication. *J. pers. soc. Psychol*, 1966, **4**, 343–346.

Kuroda, S.-Y. Generative grammatical studies in Japanese. Unpublished doctoral dissertation, Massachusetts Institute of Technology, 1965.

Labov, W. Social factors in learning standard English. In R. W. Shuy (Ed.), *Social dialects and language learning*. Champaign, Ill.: Nat. Coun. Teach. Engl., 1964.

Labov, W., Cohen, P., and Robins, C. A preliminary study of the structure of English used by Negro and Puerto Rican speakers in New York City. Unpublished paper, Columbia University, 1965.

de Laguna, Grace A. *Speech: its function and development*. Bloomington. Ind.: Univ. Press, 1927.

Lakoff, G. On the nature of syntactic irregularity. Computation laboratory of Harvard University, Report No. NSF-16.

Lane, H. The motor theory of speech perception: a critical review. *Psychol. Rev.*, 1965, **72**, 275–309.

Lee, L. and Ando, K. Language acquisition and language disorder in Japanese. Unpublished paper, Northwestern University, n.d.

Lees, R. B. *The grammar of English nominalizations.* Indiana Univer. Publ. in Anthro. and Ling., Memoir 12, 1960.

Lees, R. B. Discussion of Brown and Fraser's, and Brown, Fraser, and Bellugi's papers. In U. Bellugi and R. Brown (Eds.), *The acquisition of language, Monogr. Soc. Res. Child Dev.*, 1964, **29** (No. 92), (92–97.

Lenneberg, E. H. *Biological foundations of language.* New York: Wiley, 1967.

Lenneberg, E. H., Nichols, I. A., and Rosenberger, E., F. Primitive stages of language development in mongolism. *Proc. Assoc. Res. nerv. ment. Disease*, 1964, **42**, 119–137.

Leopold, W. F. *Speech development of a bilingual child: a linguist's record.* Vol. 1, *Vocabulary growth in the first two years.* Vol. 2, *Sound learning in the first two years.* Vol. 3, *Grammar and general problems in the first two years.* Vol. 4, *Diary from age 2.* Evanston, Ill.: Northwestern University Press, 1939, 1947, 1949 (a), 1949 (b).

Liberman, A. M., Cooper, F. S., Shankweiler, D. P., and Studdert-Kennedy, M. Perception of the speech code. *Psychol. Rev.*, 1967, **74**, 431–461.

Lovell, K. Some recent studies in cognitive and language development. *Merrill-Palmer Quart.*, 1968, **14**, 123–138.

Lovell, K., and Dixon, E. M. The growth of the control of grammar in imitation, comprehension and production. *J. child psychol. Psychiat.*, **5**, 1965.

Luria, A. R. *The role of speech in the regulation of normal and abnormal behavior.* New York: Liveright, 1961.

Luria, A. R. The directive function of speech in development and dissolution. *Word*, 1959, **15**, 351–352. [Reprinted in R. C. Anderson and D. P. Ausubel (Eds.), *Readings in the psychology of cognition.* New York: Holt, 1965.]

Marler, P. Communication in monkeys and apes. In I. De Vore (Ed.), *Primate behavior.* New York: Holt, Rinehart, and Winston, 1965.

Marler, P., and Hamilton, W. J. *Mechanisms of animal behavior.* New York: Wiley, 1966.

McCarthy, D. Language development in children. In L. Carmichael (Ed.), *Manual of child psychology*, 2nd ed. New York: Wiley, 1954.

McMahon, L. E. Grammatical analysis as part of understanding a sentence. Unpublished doctoral dissertation, Harvard University, 1963.

McNeill, D. The psychology of "you" and "I." Paper read at American Psychological Association, 1963.

McNeill, D. Development of the semantic system. Unpublished paper, Center for Cognitive Studies, Harvard University, 1965.

McNeill, D. Developmental psycholinguistics. In F. Smith and G. A. Miller (Eds.), *The genesis of language: a psycholinguistic approach.* Cambridge: M.I.T. Press, 1966. (a)

McNeill, D. The creation of language by children. In J. Lyons and R. Wales (Eds.), *Psycholinguistics papers.* Edinburgh: University of Edinburgh Press, 1966. (b)

McNeill, D. Some universals of language acquisition. In H. Lane and E. Zale (Eds.), *Studies of language and language behavior. Centr. Res. Lang. Lang. Behav.*, Report No. 2, 1966. (c)

McNeill, D. A study of word association. *J. verb. Learn. verb. Behav.*, 1966, **5**, 548–557. (d)

McNeill, D. On theories of language acquisition. In J. Dixon and D. Horton

(Eds.), *Verbal behavior and general S-R theory*. Englewood Cliffs, N. J.: Prentice-Hall, 1968. (a)

McNeill, D. Two problems for cognitive psychologists. Problem I: predication. Center for Cognitive Studies Colloquium, Harvard University, 1968. (b)

McNeill, D. Explaining linguistic universals. Paper presented at XIXth International Congress of Psychology, London, 1969.

McNeill, D. The capacity for grammatical development in children. In D. I. Slobin (Ed.), *The ontogenesis of grammar in children*. New York: Academic Press, in press.

McNeill, D., and McNeill, N. B. What does a child mean when he says "no"? In E. Zale (Ed.), *Proceedings of the conference on language and language behavior*. New York: Appleton-Century, 1968.

Mehler, J. Some effects of grammatical transformations on the recall of English sentences. *J. verb. Learn. verb. Behav.*, 1963, **2**, 346–351.

Menyuk, P. A preliminary evaluation of grammatical capacity in children. *J. verb. Learn. verb. Behav.*, 1963, **2**, 429–439.

Menyuk, P. Alternation of rules in children's grammar. *J. verb. Learn. verb. Behav.*, 1964, **3**, 480–488. (a)

Menyuk, P. Syntactic rules used by children from preschool through first grade. *Child Dev.*, 1964, **35**, 533–546. (b)

Menyuk, P. Comparison of grammar of children with functionally deviant and normal speech. *J. speech hearing disorders*, 1964, **7**, 109–121. (c)

Menyuk, P. Children's learning and recall of grammatical and nongrammatical phonological sequences. Paper read at Society for Research in Child Development, March, 1967.

Menyuk, P. Acquisition of grammar by children. In K. Salzinger (Ed.), *Research in verbal behavior*. New York: Academic Press, 1968.

Menyuk, P. Children's grammatical capacity. In T. G. Bever and W. Weksel (Eds.), *The structure and psychology of language*. New York: Holt, Rinehart and Winston, in press.

Messer, S. Implicit phonology in children. *J. verb. Learn. verb. Behav.*, 1967, **6**, 609–613.

Meumann, E. *Die Sprache des Kindes*. Zurich: Zurcher and Furrer, 1894.

Miller, G. A. Some psychological studies of grammar. *Am. Psychol.*, 1962, **17**, 748–762.

Miller, G. A. Psycholinguistic approaches to the study of communication. In D. L. Arm (Ed.), *Journeys in science: small steps—great strides*. Albuquerque: University of New Mexico Press, 1967.

Miller, G. A., and Chomsky, N. A. Finitary models of language users. In R. D. Luce, R. R. Bush, and E. Galanter (Eds), *Handbook of mathematical psychology*. New York: Wiley, 1963.

Miller, G. A. and Isard, S. Some perceptual consequences of linguistic rules. *J. verb. Learn. verb. Behav.*, 1963, **2**, 217–228.

Miller, G. A., and Isard, S. Free recall of self-embedded English sentences. *Inform. Control*, 1964, **7**, 292–303.

Miller, G. A., and McKean, K. O. A chronometric study of some relations between sentences. *Quart. J. exper. Psychol.*, 1964, **16**, 297–308.

Miller, G. A., and McNeill, D. Psycholinguistics. In G. Lindzey and E. Aaronson (Eds.), *Handbook of social psychology*. Reading, Mass.: Addison-Wesley, 1968.

Miller, W. and Ervin, S. The development of grammar in child language. In U. Bellugi and R. Brown (Eds.), *The acquisition of language, Monogr. Soc. Res. Child Dev.*, 1964, **29** (No. 92), 9–34.

Mowrer, O. H. The psychologist looks at language. *Am. Psychol.*, 1954, **9**, 660–694.

Mowrer, O. H. *Learning theory and the symbolic processes.* New York: Wiley, 1960.

Osgood, C. E. Toward a wedding of insufficiences. In T. R. Dixon, and D. L. Horton, (Eds.), *Verbal behavior and general behavior theory.* Englewood Cliffs, N. J.: Prentice-Hall, 1968.

Palermo, D. S. On learning to talk: are principles derived form the learning laboratory applicable? In D. I. Slobin (Ed.), *The ontogenesis of grammar: facts and theories.* New York: Academic Press, in press.

Piaget J. *The language and thought of the child.* New York: Harcourt, Brace, 1926.

Piaget, J. *The origins of intelligence in children.* New York: International Universities Press, 1952.

Piaget, J. Review of "Studies in cognitive growth" by J. S. Bruner, R. Olver, and P. M. Greenfield. *Contemp. Psychol.*, 1967, **12**, 532–533.

Postal, P. *Constituent structure: A study of contemporary models of syntactic description.* Indiana Univer. Publ. in Anthro. & Ling., Memoir 30, 1964.

Preston, M. S., Yeni-Komshian, G., and Stark, R. E. Voicing in initial stop consonants produced by children in the pre-linguistic period from different language communities. Annual Report Neuro-Communications Laboratory. The Johns Hopkins Univ., 1967.

Riegel, K. F. The Michigan restricted association norms. Univ. Mich. Dept. Psychol. Rep. No. 3, 1965. (a)

Riegel, K. F. Free associative responses to the 200 stimuli of the Michigan restricted association norms. Univ. Mich. Dept. Psychol. Rep. No. 8, 1965. (b)

Riegel, K. F., and Feldman, C. F. The recall of high and low meaningful sentences generated from the Michigan restricted association norms. Univ. Mich. Ling. Develpm. Program, Report No. 37, 1967.

Riegel, K. F., and Zivian, I. W.-M. A study of inter- and intralingual associations in English and German. Univ. Mich. Lang. Develpm. Program., Report No. 15, 1967.

Rice, U. M., and diVesta, F J. A developmental study of semantic and phonetic generalization in paired-associate learning. *Child Dev.*, 1965, **36**, 721–730.

Ruwet, N. Le constituent "auxillaire" en Française moderne. *Langage*, 1966, **4**, 105–122.

de Saussure, F. Cours de linguistique générale. Paris: 1916. (Trans. by W. Baskin, *Course in general linguistics.* New York: Philosophical Library, 1959.)

Savin, H., and Perchonock, E. Grammatical structure and the immediate recall of English sentences. *J. verb. Learn. verb. Behav.*, 1965, **4**, 348–353.

Schlesinger, I. M. Production of utterance and language acquisition. In D. I. Slobin (Ed.), *The ontogenesis of grammar: facts and theories.* New York: Academic Press, in press.

Shankweiler, D. P. Some correlates of performance in dichotic perceptual tasks. Paper presented at a conference on the perception of speech, University of Pittsburgh, 1968.

Shankweiler, D. P., and Studdert-Kennedy, M. Lateral differences in perception of dichotically presented synthetic consonant-vowel syllables and steady-state vowels. *J. acoust. Soc. Amer.*, 1966, **39**, 1256.

Shankweiler, D. P., and Studdert-Kennedy, M. Identification of consonants and vowels presented to left and right ears. *Quart. J. exp. Psychol.*, 1967, **19**, 59–63.

Shipley, E. F., Smith, C. S., and Gleitman, L. R. A study in the acquisition of language: free responses to commands. Tech. Rept. VIII, Eastern Pennsylvania Psychiatric Institute, n.d.

Sinclair-de Zwart, M. *Acquisition de langage et development de la pensee.* Paris: Dunod, 1967.

Slobin, D. I. Grammatical transformations in childhood and adulthood. Unpublished doctoral dissertation, Harvard University, 1963.

Slobin, D. I. Imitation and the acquisition of syntax. Paper presented at Second Research Planning Conference of Project Literacy, 1964.

Slobin, D. I. Grammatical development in Russian-speaking children. In K. Riegel (Ed.), *The development of language functions.* Univ. Mich. Lang. Develpm. Program, Report No. 8, 1965.

Slobin, D. I. Comments on "Developmental psycholinguistics." In F. Smith and G. A. Miller (Eds.), *The genesis of language: a psycholinguistic approach.* Cambridge: M.I.T. Press, 1966. (a)

Slobin, D. I. The acquisition of Russian as a native language. In F. Smith and G. A. Miller (Eds.), *The genesis of language: a psycholinguistic approach.* Cambridge: M.I.T. Press, 1966. (b)

Slobin, D. I. Grammatical transformations and sentence comprehension in childhood and adulthood. *J. verb. Learn. verb. Behav.,* 1966, **5,** 219–227. (c)

Slobin, D. I. (Ed.) A field manual for cross-cultural study of the acquisition of communicative competence. Unpublished paper, University of California (Berkeley), 1967.

Slobin, D. Imitation and grammatical development in children. In N. S. Endler, L. R. Boulter, and H. Osser (Eds.), *Contemporary issues in developmental psychology.* New York: Holt, Rinehart, and Winston, 1968.

Slobin, D. I. Early grammatical development in several languages, with special attention to Soviet research. In W. Weksel and T. Bever (Eds.), *The structure and psychology of language.* New York: Holt, Rinehart, and Winston, in press.

Slobin, D. I., and Welsh, C. A. Elicited imitation as a research tool in developmental psycholinguistics. Unpublished paper, Department of Psychololgy, University of California (Berkeley), 1967.

Staats, A. W. Integrated-functional learning theory and language development. In D. I. Slobin (Ed.), *The ontogenesis of grammar: facts and theories.* New York: Academic Press, in press.

Staats, A. W., and Staats, C. K. *Complex human behavior.* New York: Holt, Rinehart, and Winston, 1963.

Stern, C. and Stern, W. *Die Kindersprache.* Leipzig: Barth, 1907.

Turner, E. A., and Rommetveit, R. The acquisition of sentence voice and reversibility. *Child Dev.,* in press.

Velten, H. V. The growth of phonemic and lexical pattern in infant language. *Language,* 1943, **19,** 281–292.

di Vesta, F. J. The distribution of modifiers used by children in a word association task. *J. verb. Learn. verb. Behav.,* 1964, **3,** 421–427. (a)

di Vesta, F. J. A simple analysis of changes with age in responses to a restricted word-association task. *J. verb. Learn. verb. Behav.,* 1964, **3,** 505–510. (b)

di Vesta, F. J. Norms for modifiers used by children in a restricted word-association task: grades 2 through 6. *Psychol. Reps.,* 1966, **18,** 65–66. (a)

di Vesta, F. J. A normative study of 220 concepts rated on the semantic differential by children in grades 2 through 7. *J. genet. Psychol.,* 1966, **109,** 205–229. (b)

di Vesta, F. J. A developmental study of the semantic structure of children. *J. verb. Learn. verb. Behav.,* 1966, **5,** 249–259. (c) di Vesta, F. J., and Dick, W. The test-retest reliability of children's ratings on the semantic differential. *Educ. Psychol. Meas.,* 1966, **26**, 605–616.

Vygotsky, L. S. *Thought and language.* Cambridge: M.I.T. Press, 1962.

Wason, P. C. The contexts of plausible denial. *J verb. Learn verb. Behav.,* 1965, **4**, 7–11.

Weinreich, U. On the semantic structure of language. In J. H. Greenberg (Ed.), *Universals of language.* Cambridge: M.I.T. Press, 1963.

Weinreich, U. Explorations in semantic theory. In T.A. Sebeok (Ed.), *Current trends in linguistics,* Vol. III. The Hague: Mouton, 1966.

Weir, R. *Language in the crib.* The Hague: Mouton, 1962.

Weir, R. Some questions on the child's learning of phonology. In F. Smith and G. A. Miller (Eds.), *The genesis of language: a psycholinguistic approach.* Cambridge: M.I.T. Press, 1966.

Weksel, W. Review of "The acquisition of language," U. Bellugi and R. Brown (Eds.). *Language,* 1965, **41**, 692–709.

Werner, H., and Kaplan, B. *Symbol formation: an organismic-developmental approach to language and the expression of thought.* New York: Wiley, 1963.

Werner, H. and Kaplan, E. *Development of word meaning through verbal context: an experimental study, Monogr. Soc. Res. Child Dev.,* 1951.

White, S. H. Evidence for a hierarchical arrangement of learning processes. In L. P. Lipsitt and C. C. Spiker (Eds.), *Advances in child development and behavior,* Vol. 2. New York: Academic Press, 1965.

Yngve, V. A model and an hypothesis for language structure. *Proc. Am. Phil. Soc.,* 1960, **104**, 444–466.

Yngve, V. The depth hypothesis. In R. Jakobson (Ed.), *Structure of language and its mathematical aspect. Proc. 12th Symp. in appl. Math.* Providence, R. I.: American Mathematical Society, 1961. Pp. 130–138.

Zakharova, A. V. Usvoyeniye doshkol'nikami padezhnykh form. *Dolk. Akad. Pedag. Nauk RSFSR,* 1958, **2**, (3), 81–84.

Zipf, G. K. *The psycho-biology of language.* Cambridge: Houghton Mifflin, 1935. (Reprinted with an introduction by G. A. Miller, Cambridge, M.I.T. Press, 1965.)

16. Development of Mental Abilities[*]

NANCY BAYLEY

With the 1905 publication by Binet and Simon of the first version of their tests of intelligence, a practical device became available for use in the measurement of mental abilities. These tests, and their successive revisions and adaptations by the original authors and then by others (in the United States, for example, Goddard, 1910; Kuhlmann, 1912, 1939; Terman, 1916; Terman and Merrill, 1937, 1960), inaugurated a new field in psychology and education. The mental test soon became an established tool for use in research, in diagnosis, and in theoretical formulations about intelligence.

In the 60 years since its inception, the mental (or intelligence) test has undergone many changes and refinements, and it has had a profound influence on theories of the nature of mental processes as well as on the methods of investigation into mental abilities.

The early history of mental testing has been ably reviewed a number of times, and need not be repeated here. Reference may be made, for example, to Goodenough (1949, 1954), Jones (1954), Hunt (1961), Anastasi (1961), and Tuddenham (1968).

DEFINITION

In the first 10 or 15 years of the use of tests of intelligence a controversy developed over the definition of "intelligence." Although there was much in common among the vari-

[*] This research was supported in part by Grant MH08135 from the National Institute of Mental Health, United States Public Health Service. I am indebted to John R. Reid for critically revising the manuscript.

ously worded definitions, there were two principal areas of difference. (1) There was disagreement over whether intelligence is a general unitary function on the one hand or a composite of several or many more or less independent abilities on the other. (2) There was disagreement over whether intelligence is innate, and grows in a child in somewhat the same way as he grows in stature, or whether mental abilities are learned and thus increased or decreased in accord with the degree of enrichment or impoverishment of a child's environment. Although the controversy has waxed and waned, it has never been quite resolved. This failure of resolution may be only an indication of our lack of information and the need for further research in this area.

THEORIES OF INTELLIGENCE

The efforts to define intelligence reflect the wide range of interpretations of its nature and causal determinants. They range from strongly genetic orientations: "an inherited capacity of the individual which is manifested through his ability to adapt and to reconstruct the factors of his environment in accordance with his group" (Boynton, 1933), or "by intelligence, the psychologist understands inborn, all-round, intellectual ability" (Burt et al., 1934); through neutral descriptions of mental processes such as Terman's "ability to carry on abstract thinking" (1925), Thorndike's ability "to make good responses from the point of view of truth or fact" (1926), and Wechsler's "the aggregate or global capacity . . . to act purposefully, to think rationally and to deal effectively with [one's] environment" (1958); to emphasis on the role

1163

of the environment, as in Hunt's (1961) "intellectual capacities based on central processes hierarchically arranged within the intrinsic portions of the cerebrum . . . [processes] approximately analogous to the strategies for information processing and action with which electronic computers are programmed. [Therefore,] assumptions that intelligence is fixed and its development is predetermined by the genes are no longer tenable." An even more strongly environmental position is expressed by Hayes (1962), who concludes that "manifest intelligence is nothing more than an accumulation of learned facts and skills: . . . innate intellectual potential consists of tendencies to engage in activities conducive to learning, rather than inherited capacities, as such." What may be the most extreme pro-environmental position has been expressed by Liverant (1960), who holds that "the behavioral realm typically ascribed to intelligence [is] within the confines of modern learning theory, particularly a social learning theory."

A close examination of the views held by the proponents of each of these definitions would reveal that either (1) for those who make the simpler, more general statements, there has been little concern about or exploration into the details of the processes of intellectual function, or (2) among those who do try to understand the detailed processes, incomplete knowledge still forces them to make unverified assumptions. In the second instance there is always the danger of personal bias and preference in the assumptions made and in the consequent conclusions.

With the accumulation of recent empirical data it has become increasingly evident that mental abilities as measured by standard tests are a function of (or the end product of) many determinants. These determinants include, first, the human organism with its basic complement of neurons, sense-perceptors, motor reactors, hormones, enzymes along with their related organizing tendencies for action and reaction to the environment. There is much still unknown about the determinants of individual differences among all these— differences that may be a function of many things, including chromosome patterns, some of which now appear to be sex-linked. They may include complex inherent differences in rates of maturing of the various biological structures and functions, as well as of their ultimate potential.

There is the possibility also of various kinds of prenatal and paranatal "environments" resulting in damage or interfering with the development of optimal function. Postnatally, there is a wide range of environmental factors which may alter differentially the manner and degree, at successive maturational stages, of the organism's utilization of its potential. These aspects of the environment may be classed in several ways, for example: (1) enrichment versus impoverishment of relevant stimuli, (2) the specific relevance or lack of it, in terms of meaningful positive and negative "feedback," for specific behaviors, and (3) the emotional climate, which may be one of pervasive warmth and approval, fostering security, or it may be a climate of disapproval and hostility— conditions that tend to cause anxiety and insecurity, thus interfering with "clear-headed" reasoning, problem-solving, and curiosity, that is, an impetus to explore, to learn and to find answers to questions. On the physical side, (4) mental abilities may be adversely affected, either before or after birth, by nutritional deficiencies, severe infections, or genetically determined blood-group incompatibilities.

Children's mental abilities, as measured by records of their performance, whether on intelligence tests, achievement tests, graded series of learned tasks, or other measures of specific abilities, are always end-products of the total prior complex of interactions among these multiple determinants. It is to be expected that there will be differential effectiveness of these various causal factors, between different children, and at different ages, as well as among the different types of ability. If we keep in mind the preceding list of complexities involved in the development of mental abilities, it becomes clear that those definitions of intelligence that stipulate *either* heredity *or* environment as its primary determiner, patently rest on false assumptions. On the other hand, broad definitions such as Thorndike's and Terman's do little more than orient us to the general class of mental processes under consideration; and those that refer loosely to the interaction of the growing organism with its environment add very little information about the specific determiners of intelligence.

There is, however, an increasing body of knowledge which, when properly integrated, should afford us some understanding of the nature of mental abilities and the processes involved in their development.

DEVELOPMENTAL ASPECTS OF MENTAL ORGANIZATION

In the developing human organism the earliest behaviors are not clearly differentiated, but would seem to be the precursors of sensory, perceptual, and motor processes, and thus basic to developing mental abilities. The first action of the fetus is an independent motor function, the rhythmic heartbeat which occurs at about 3 weeks gestational age (Carmichael, 1954). Simple reflexes involving neural function have been noted first in the fetus at about 8 weeks (Hooker, 1943). By the time the infant is born, at term, he is equipped with some 27 reflexes, which serve to carry on the extrauterine processes of life. These include responses to the various organs of sense, vision, hearing, temperature, taste, equilibrium, touch, and pressure.

The manner in which these earliest neuromuscular structures and functions develop has recently been described by Anokhin (1964), who summarizes a series of studies carried out in Russia and elsewhere, and presents a theory of systemogenesis as the regulator of developing nervous activity. Anokhin points out that for any species, certain adaptive functions must necessarily "be ready at the moment of birth." He goes on to cite experiments that show specific departures from the general rule of the cephalocaudal sequence of development proposed by Coghill (1929): development is most advanced at the head, and the temporal order of development proceeds from the head downward and from the body out to the extremities (hands and feet). Instead, as Anokhin points out, we find superimposed on this general trend another organizing principle. Neural fibers that had previously shown quite independent developmental processes will at a given stage grow rapidly and coordinate to produce a new functional unit. Such combinations occur repeatedly, each one timed to materialize at a particular stage in the developing organism, so that an appropriate (though often immature) reflex is functional at a crucial point in the growth process. For example, the sucking reflex in the newborn involves the facial nerve. At a certain stage in development there is a rapid growth of those fibers that activate cheek muscles to contract in such a way as to permit suction, yet at the same time other facial muscles have not yet reached a comparable maturity of function. Another example is seen in the grasping reflex, which can be detected as early as the fifth prenatal month. In this instance the nerve that innervates the flexor muscles of the fingers matures before other nerves in the forearm.

Necessary for such a functional system is an integrative organization of the various parts, but also necessary are a receptive apparatus, and central as well as peripheral structures, which afford "an afferent feedback about the achieved final adaptive effect." "The functional system as represented in an adult . . . does not appear from the beginning in mature form" but it "begins to play an adjusting role in the life of the newborn long before its complete and definite maturation." Although the studies he cites are primarily of the fetus and newborn, Anokhin (1964) proposes that the principles derived from them might well apply to postnatal development of the brain and its functions.

Certainly there is evidence that the processes of myelinization of nerve fibers continue during the first 3 or 4 postnatal months (McGraw, 1943). During this period the infant's reflexive behaviors mature rapidly, and many of them are soon replaced by voluntary, more complexly adaptive responses. It may well be hypothesized therefore that such processes of neural integration relevant to developing mental abilities may continue to occur in later development, although at a much slower rate. The organizers of later neural integrations would probably be more complex and under different (perhaps enzymatic) controls.

Such a form of continuing neural integrative action, or "systemogenesis," would be congruous with available information on the behavioral aspects of developing mental abilities. That is, increasingly complex abilities with different mental "factors" emerge at successive points in the child's development. As long as these integrative neurological processes play a role in the developing organism, they may play a role in controlling the rates at which mental growth occurs. This role could operate differentially among children with different inherent patterns of maturation. On the other hand, specific training (including practice) might also serve to speed up the processes of higher integration and thus allow the child to function at a more abstract level.

If, by inheritance of mental abilities, we mean that there are inherited individual differences in the facility and degree to which "systemogenesis" takes place, then the findings from studies of learning and of "impoverished" versus "enriched" as well as other types of environments would all fit into a reasonable pattern in which these inherent trends in maturation would be retarded or accelerated by relevant environmental conditions. Information about the relation to age of different kinds of mental ability, or "factors" of intelligence, may indicate the extent and manner in which such inherent neural integrative processes may continue over the life span.

INTELLIGENCE TESTS: THE MEASURING INSTRUMENTS

The assessment of a child's mental abilities is made by means of carefully standardized tests, which are graded in difficulty. The items in these scales may be thought of as problems or tasks; and the solutions or correct responses to these items are samples of the child's capacity to think or to reason—that is, of his intelligence. The first of these scales, the Binet-Simon, was designed to assess ability to do schoolwork. In a general way, the character of the tasks set in those original tests has been maintained on subsequent tests. Problems of arithmetic, of verbal reasoning, of general information, of discriminating complex spatial relations, and the like, as well as vocabulary, are all carefully selected according to several criteria. The tasks must be of such a nature that they are approximately equally familiar (or strange) to all of the children in the population for which they are relevant. They must be reliable (i.e., they must yield stable scores that will be essentially unchanged on repetition of the test after a short interval). Each type of task must contain items ranging from relatively simple to difficult, and the entire scale must show

increasing difficulty as measured by the scores earned by children of successively older ages. The tests must be "valid" measures of the mental functions they purport to test—a criterion that presupposes an agreed upon and consistently applicable definition of the term which designates the mental function in question. The tests must be administered in a standard way so that the problems set will be the same for all children who take them.

Finally, the norms or standards of the test scores must be based on tests given to a large number of persons, selected to represent the ages for which the tests are intended and the populations on which the tests are to be used. This reference population is usually selected to be a representative subsample of a country (say, the United States) in such matters as socioeconomic, demographic, and ethnic distribution. In other words, a standard test is meant to sample mental abilities in such a way that the scores of a given individual state his position relative to the average person the same age, and from the same general population, or else to a specified sample with known limiting characteristics. For an example of a limiting condition, tests may be standardized for use with blind or deaf children.

Mental tests are divided according to the manner of their administration into individual and group tests. The first tests were individual. That is, a test was given to each child separately by an examiner who asked questions and then recorded the child's responses, or supervised his drawings and written responses. This procedure insures the subject's greatest attention to and effort in appropriately carrying out the tasks at hand. It enhances the validity and reliability of the scores. However, it is a very time-consuming and therefore expensive procedure.

In order to obtain scores on large numbers of persons in a short period of time, the tests were adapted for group use. Printed forms and pencils could be distributed to an entire roomful, and the group could then be instructed to mark answers according to a formal set of directions. Group tests are widely used in schools, in military installations, and in other situations where it is important to test large numbers quickly. Group tests work best with testees who can read, who are familiar with the pencil and paper operations required, and who are well motivated to succeed. If the scores obtained are less accurate than those from individual tests, they nevertheless are adequate for assessing relative abilities or averages for groups (e.g., a school population). They also are useful screening devices: the few persons whose scores are very low or very high on a group test can then be tested individually to obtain more accurate evaluations of their capacities.

Individual Tests

Probably the best-known and most-used individual intelligence test in the United States is the Stanford-Binet. This revision of Binet's French tests was first published in 1916 by Lewis M. Terman. It was quickly adopted by psychologists and educators and soon became widely used. This test covered the ages 3 to 18 years; the items were arranged by age, according to their difficulty, with six tests at each year through age 10, after which tests were set at 2-year intervals with eight items at year 12, and six at each of years 14, 16, and 18. Mental ages were calculated on the basis of the number of tests passed, each item weighted according to the number of tests at the age-level. That is, each 6-year item is worth 2 months' credit, a 12-year item counted 4 months, and so on. The total months credited, including the first 3 years and all items passed, became the *mental age*. Mental age (MA) divided by the child's *chronological age* (CA) gave the IQ, or *intelligence quotient*. For persons 16 years and older, 16 years was used as the CA for obtaining the IQ. This general procedure for obtaining scores on the intelligence tests had grown up gradually, from the earlier versions of the scale. Another revision of the Binet Scale was made by Kuhlmann (1912), and for a time it had considerable use, in part because it included tests for infants at 3, 6, 9, 12, 18, and 24 months. However, it soon lost out to the Stanford revision, which was simpler to give and score.

In 1937 Terman and Merrill published an extensively revised Stanford-Binet with two equivalent forms, L and M. This revision covers the ages 2 years to superior adult, although in contrast to the main portion of the scale the standardization was less adequate for the 2- and 3-year tests. Another revision, in 1960, updates some of the materials, and

offers a single form, L-M, which is a selection of the best parts of scales L and M and with improved norms for years 2 and 3.

In this newest revision, the CA/MA ratio was dropped as the method of obtaining the IQ. Instead, deviation IQs were derived from the means and standard deviations of the mental age scores obtained for the standardization sample, at each year in childhood and in the tested sample of adults. In this way the authors followed procedures which had previously been established for tests of adults, whose scores on mental tests change very little with increasing age.

The concept of mental age had grown out of the finding that school-age children's performance on the tests increases at a steady rate in relation to their chronological age. However, at a stage somewhere near 13 to 16 years, the rates of mental growth diminish and the yearly increments in mental ability grow smaller. Clearly a year of mental growth is not the same at all ages. For example, the change from 15 to 16 years is not the equivalent of the change from 9 to 10 years. The use of standard scores based on a person's standing relative to his age-peers yields the most adequate measure of that person's relative intelligence at a given time, and of the stability of his mental growth as measured in tests at different times. It avoids the difficult problem of adjusting for unequal rates of mental growth at different ages.

With increasing use of intelligence tests, not only for children, but also for adults, a number of both individual and group tests were designed for the purpose of testing adults. These tests served two purposes. Their content was specifically appropriate for adults and consequently appealed to them and resulted in good motivation to succeed. Also, in contrast to the earlier scales for children, the new tests were designed to have more "top"— that is, to include more difficult tasks, which tapped the more abstract mental processes. The added levels of difficulty produced a relatively discriminating instrument for identifying highly intelligent adults.

Of the adult individual tests the best known and most widely used are those of David Wechsler. The first version, published in 1939, known as the Wechsler-Bellevue Intelligence Scale (W-B), has norms for ages 10 through 49 years. The W-B is composed of 10 subscales, 5 verbal and 5 performance, plus an eleventh vocabulary subscale. The raw scores on each subscale were converted to scale scores on the basis of the means and SDs (standard deviations) of the total tested population ($n = 1750$), which ranged in age from 7 to 65 years. These scale scores were then summed to give point scores for the 5 verbal, the 5 performance, and the 10 full-scale tests. Vocabulary could be treated as a separate scale or, by prorating the scale scores, included in the verbal scale. IQs were obtained for successive ages by conversion from standard scores based on the means and SDs of point scores at each age interval. The mean point score was assigned an IQ of 100, and each standard deviation from the mean was equated to 15 IQ points. This is in essence the same procedure that has been used for most adult scales, and which (as we have noted) was later used for obtaining IQs in the 1960 Stanford-Binet.

Since the original 1939 scale, Wechsler has published a number of scales of intelligence, all of them along the same general plan, and all tests to be administered individually. Form II of the W-B was published in 1946, for use as an alternate form of the scale for adults. This form of the scale was later extended downward to approximately 5 years and published in 1949 as the Wechsler Intelligence Scale for Children (WISC). The 1955 Wechsler Adult Intelligence Scale (WAIS) is a revision of the original W-B form I. Among other changes, this revision extends the upper levels of the scale to include more difficult items, and thus in comparison with the original version permits more discriminating scores among adults of superior intelligence. This revision also is standardized on a more adequate sample of older people, and includes norms for scoring at ages 16 to 74 years and over. The latest in this series of scales, the Wechsler Preschool and Primary Scale of Intelligence (WPPSI) was published in 1967. Designed for use with young children, this scale has norms for scoring at 11 ages from 4 to 6½ years. Wechsler states (1967) that about 4 years is the youngest age at which one can, as a practical operation, obtain a measure of "global intellectual capacity" by using tasks the same as or similar to those he includes in his scales at later ages. The three most recent of his scales, the WPPSI, the

WISC, and the WAIS, together afford measures of intelligence for most of the life span. The lowest age and score possible are for a 4-year-old with an IQ of 45.

These Wechsler scales differ from the Binet scales in furnishing subscores at all ages for each of 10 or 11 different aspects of intelligence, as well as IQs for verbal and performance subscales and Full Scale (global) scores. The nature of the abilities measured is indicated by the names of the subscales. The Verbal subscales are Information, Comprehension, Arithemetic, Similarities, Digit Span (or Repeated Sentences), Vocabulary, Digit Symbol (or Animal House), Picture Completion, Block Design, Picture Arrangement (or Mazes), and Object Assembly (or Geometric Design). The titles in parentheses are for the WPPSI scales for children 4 to 6 years of age. Although these subscales were not selected to represent statistically determined discrete factors, they lend themselves to factor analysis, and perhaps deceptively (because their reliability as independent scales is low), they offer the possibility of drawing for each person a "profile" showing the more and less advanced aspects of his mental abilities. The tests can be administered with comparative ease and speed, because the examiner moves rapidly from one test series to another, as the testee reaches his capacity on each. For these reasons the scales have caught on rapidly and are widely used. They do not, however, give IQs at the extremes of high and low capacity, and they are not applicable to infants and children under 4 years of age. For these reasons, at least, they cannot entirely replace such tests as the Stanford-Binet.

There are in this country several individual tests of mental abilities for infants. As has been noted, the Kuhlmann-Binet included some tests for infants, starting at 3 months, whereas the Stanford-Binet (1937 and 1960 revisions) starts at 2 years. Among tests specifically designed to assess mental ability in early infancy, Gesell's is the first (1925, 1928) and best known (e.g., *Developmental diagnosis*, 1962). Another, widely used, is Psyche Cattell's Mental Test for Infants and Young Children (1940, 1960). Bayley's California First-Year Mental Scale (1933) and Infant Scale of Motor Development (1936) have been revised and published as the *Bayley Scales of Infant Development*: For babies 2 to

30 months of age (1969). The Griffiths scale, *Abilities of Babies* (1954), is standardized on an English population. Other tests by Charlotte Bühler (1930), by Linfert and Hierholzer (1928), and by Gilliland (1949b) are of historical interest but are not in current use. Graham, Matarratzo, and Caldwell devised a scale for assessing neonates 5 days or younger (1956). On this scale, scores are obtained for Vision, Muscular Tension, Maturation, Pain Threshold, and Irritability. Rosenblith has revised the scale (1961) and is using it in a series of researches.

Infant scales, by the very nature of the young human's level of functioning, must be administered individually. Also, at these early ages, there are inherent problems in subdividing the tests into different mental abilities, as well as in the procedures of testing and scoring.

Gesell's scales were first reported in 1925 and he published a series of books, successively clarifying the details of administering the tests and evaluating the scores, eventuating in the book *Developmental Diagnosis* (latest edition, 1962), which is essentially a manual for their use. The Gesell scales give norms for "key ages" at weeks 4, 16, 28, 40 and months 12, 18, 24, and 36. For each of these key ages behaviors are given, by 4-week intervals, for ages below and above the key for the first 56 weeks, and for 3-month intervals, 15 to 24 months and every 6 months to 42. The behaviors at each age are divided into four categories: Motor, Adaptive, Language, and Personal-Social. The Motor behaviors consist of body control, manual coordination, creeping, walking, balance, and jumping—behaviors which are not ordinarily classed as mental. The Personal-Social items are for the most part scored on the basis of an interview with the mother. They include trained behaviors such as feeding self, toileting, dressing, and communications such as asking for things and comprehending demands. The tested (observed) mental responses are those classed as Adaptive and Language. Adaptive items include: looks at, reaches for, grasps, or manipulates a rattle, ball, or 1-inch cube; builds a tower of two or more blocks, puts blocks in form board, etc. Language items include: "alert expression," coos, polysyllabic vowel sounds, says dada and mama, uses other words, names, and points to objects and pic-

tures. Developmental ages are given by the examiner according to his general impression of the infant's responses and the age-level of response which is most characteristic. The norms are derived from a small longitudinal sample of middle-class New Haven babies, with the number of children tested at any one age varying between 26 and 49 in the first year and between 18 and 60 for the preschool ages.

The Cattell Infant Intelligence Scale utilizes many of the Adaptive and Language items from the Gesell scales. The format of this scale is patterned after the Stanford-Binet, and may be thought of as a downward extension of the 1937 Form L of the Binet. Tests start at 2 months, with five tests at each age, monthly through the first year, bimonthly in the second year, and then at 3-month intervals to 30 months. Between 22 and 30 months items from the Stanford-Binet are intermingled with other items designed by Cattell. These tests are standardized on the infants in the Harvard Growth Study conducted by Dr. Harold Stuart (1939). The subjects were seen at 3-month and then 6-month intervals, the number at any one age ranging between 20 and 67. Because of the interval between tests, the placement of many items was made by interpolation. Mental ages and IQs are determined by the original method of the Stanford-Binet.

The original versions of the Bayley Mental and Motor scales, like the Gesell and Cattell scales, were derived from scores earned in a series of often-repeated testings on a longitudinal sample. This sample of 61 infants was somewhat above the average of the Berkeley, California, population in 1928. The parents' education ranged from 3 to 19 years, with a mean of 13.7. The children were tested monthly from 1 to 15 months with a few absences at most ages. The number tested at any one age ranged from 46 to 61, with a mean N of 54. In the revision of these scales, the preliminary standardization, 1 to 30 months was based on 1700 Mental and Psychomotor tests, for 1500 of which the Infant Behavior Record was also scored. The final standardization is made from tests on a representative U.S. sample, of 1262 children, about one third of which are drawn from the 1500 complete tests of the preliminary standardization. These form a strictly cross-sectional sample.

Many of the test items and materials are similar to those found in other scales. In the revised form practical improvements have been made on the materials (e.g., wherever feasible, more durable and washable plastic has replaced wood), much care has gone into details of placing individual items on a scale of difficulty, and in clarifying the directions for administering and scoring. The materials in the Mental scale were selected to elicit adaptive responses, including such behaviors as attending to visual and auditory stimuli, grasping, manipulating and combining objects, shaking a rattle, ringing a bell, interacting with the examiner by smiling, cooing, babbling, imitating, following directions, relating to toys in meaningful ways (e.g., putting cubes in the cup, banging spoons together), showing memory or awareness of object constancy (e.g., looking for a fallen toy, uncovering a hidden toy), goal-directed persevering tasks such as placements of pegs in pegboard, completing simple form boards, and following directions involving correct use of object names, prepositions, and a concept of "one."

The Motor scale includes such abilities as holding the head up, turning over, sitting, creeping, standing, walking, going up and down stairs and manual skills such as grasping small objects and throwing a ball.

The Mental and Motor scales are scored separately: raw scores composed of the total number of items passed are converted to mental (or motor) ages and to MDIs (Mental Development Index) or PDIs (Psychomotor Development Index). These indices are derived from the means and SDs at each age for the standardization sample.

The Infant Behavior Record is filled in immediately after the mental and psychomotor tests are completed. It is composed of ratings of such general behaviors as responsiveness to persons and toys, happiness, fearfulness, reactivity, endurance, and goal directedness. There are age norms expressed in terms of the most characteristic ratings at each age.

In their revised form, the Bayley scales are based on both a larger and a more representative sample of infants than is true of previous infant scales. Therefore they should form a sound set of current standards for evaluating development in the first 2 years. As of 1969 studies of the development of mental abilities in the first 2 years are, in most instances, dependent for their normative reference points on the earlier scales, whose age-placements are derived from small, selected samples.

Group Tests

Among the first group tests of intelligence are the Army Alpha and Beta tests, which were widely used for testing during World War I. These tests, their revisions, and others derived from them, have continued in use with adults. Among the first group tests for children are the Pintner General Ability Tests (1923) and the Pintner-Cunningham Primary Test (1927). Pintner's earlier work had formed the basis of the Army Alpha and Beta scales, and with colleagues he went on to develop similar scales for use in the schools.

From this start, many group tests were developed. An early one by E. L. Thorndike (Thorndike, 1926; Thorndike, Woodward, and Lorge, 1935) called the CAVD (Completions, Arithmetic, Vocabulary, and Directions), has norms for 3 years to superior adult. The Miller Analogies Test (1960) is designed for testing college students, and Terman's Concept Mastery (Synonym-Antonym and Analogies) Test (1956) is designed for testing superior adults. Thurstone's Primary Mental Abilities Test (1938, 1947, Thurstone and Thurstone, 1943, 1958) pioneered the way in devising group tests on the basis of factors derived from statistical analysis of test contents.

Group tests proliferated and soon became the bases for many statistical studies of mental abilities. Because of the ease with which scores for large samples can be obtained with group tests, they lend themselves well to such analyses. Some representative scales will be referred to later in a discussion of factors of mental abilities.

BASES FOR THEORIES OF INTELLIGENCE

The foregoing "intelligence tests" in their various forms are the available tools for measuring, or it may be more accurate to say sampling the mental abilities of persons at various ages and degrees of maturity. As noted earlier, the processes through which the human organism develops from concrete to increasingly abstract mental functions, as measured by the tests, are clearly a function of the interactions of the organism with his environment. The various theories of the nature of intelligence have grown out of differing interpretations of the relevant characteristics of both the organism and the environment. To a considerable extent the amount and kind of information the theorist has about either or both will determine this theory.

Early theorists such as Galton (1869), G. Stanley Hall (Pruette, 1926), Burt (1934), Terman (1916), and Gesell (1962) most often classed intelligence, along with other characteristics both mental and physical, as being genetically determined. It was noted that not only did the shape of one's ears or the tendency to hemophilia run in families, but so also did a tendency to "genius" or to "feeblemindedness." The evidence adduced for the hereditary nature of mental abilities was at first very crude, and did not take into account many possible influences of the environment.

The findings from intelligence test scores, in their first applications, gave corroborative support to Galton's studies of family resemblances. Outhit (1933), for example, obtained correlations between test scores of children and their parents of .61 to .76 on a sample of 51 families with 257 tested children. Conrad and Jones (1940), who tested an entire Vermont community, obtained parent-child correlations of .49 for an N of 501 parent-child pairs. These correlations are representative of those obtained by other investigators of the relation between parents' and children's intelligence, or between parents' education (as an approximate indicator of ability) and their children's IQs.

Another kind of evidence, from early studies, which favored the hereditary interpretation of intelligence came from studies of retests of children after a lapse of time. In a number of instances children (usually of school age) were retested after several months or a year or longer. The average change from test to retest was about 5 IQ points, a change which could be accounted for by the imperfect reliability of the instruments used. In

these first studies of the constancy of the IQ, there had been no control over such important variables as the age at testing or the time-interval between test and retest.

On the basis of the findings from these early studies, there was a widespread concurrence among educators and psychologists in the belief that intelligence is a general, inherited ability that increases in amount with growth. The growth of intelligence was seen as stable; that is, the IQ was held to be constant. Any changes in a child's score over time were attributed to imperfections in the testing instrument or the manner in which the test was given.

There were, however, some early signs that individual children's scores did not necessarily follow this principle of the constant IQ. Baldwin and Stecher (1922) reported a detailed and careful study of repeated tests on the Stanford-Binet, on 143 children tested once a year at irregular intervals between the ages of 5 and 16 years. They found that the mean IQ increased with age and with repetitions of the test. They noticed, also, that the correlations between first tests and successively later tests became progressively smaller.

Bayley's (1933a) study of mental growth in the first 3 years, by repeating tests on the same children, showed that the infants grew very rapidly in mental abilities but that there were great individual differences in their rates of growth. Tests were given at regular intervals, monthly 1 to 15 months then trimonthly to 3 years. Their scores during the first 6 months were entirely independent of scores at 2 or 3 years, and even at 10 to 12 months the correlation with 3-year intelligence was only .45. Since that time other studies (Honzik, Macfarlane, and Allen, 1948; Hindley, 1960; P. Cattell, 1940) repeatedly show that scores on tests during the first 2 years are correlated very little or not at all with scores earned at 4 years or later. These findings raised a series of questions about the reliability and validity of infant tests and about the nature of the developing mental functions in infancy and early childhood (Stott and Ball, 1965).

In recent years there has been renewed interest in Piaget's theory of the stages of developing intellect and of the possibility of accelerating the rates of progress through these stages. The findings from animal research on the effects of environmental deprivation in infancy (Bennett et al., 1964; Freedman, 1958; Harlow, 1962; Scott, 1958, 1963) led to investigations of deprivation (institutionalism) on human infants (Bowlby, 1952; Brodbeck and Irwin, 1946; Fischer, 1952; Gilliland, 1949a; Goldfarb, 1945, 1955; Levy, 1947; Moore, 1947; Rheingold, 1961; Spitz; 1945 Woodworth, 1941). Factor analyses were made of infant tests in efforts to differentiate early mental processes and to seek out possibly more adequate predictors of later intelligence (Cameron, Livson, and Bayley, 1967; Richards and Nelson, 1939; Stott and Ball, 1965). All of these approaches have resulted in increased knowledge about the processes of early mental development, and their causes: genetic, congenital, and environmental.

There are those (e.g., J. B. Watson and B. F. Skinner) who say that we can only know about an organism's mental processes from his behavior. If this is true, then (it is argued) all we need concern ourselves with is the observed behaviors and the ways they can be controlled and changed by carefully designed experiments. Because the human organism is flexible, and learns readily, experiments designed to produce learned or conditioned responses (Watson) or operant conditioning (Skinner) as a rule yield results in the form of adaptations appropriate to the child's environment. It is an easy next step to conclude that mental abilities are purely a function of learning, and that therefore individual differences in intelligence result entirely from more or less adequate opportunities for the infant and young child to learn.

Hunt's (1961) position, as stated in the definition quoted earlier, is strongly influenced by this kind of thinking. He points to the more advanced behavior of animals and children who have been trained to make appropriately adaptive responses, and he shows that experience is necessary for the child to have learned the more advanced or abstract forms of thinking. That is, a child learns to read, and with this reading ability as a tool he can learn many more things. Hunt's position is developed not only from the effects of specific learning experiments, but to a considerable extent by studies of the damaging and retarding effects of environmental impoverishment, on both animals and humans.

The general consideration of the depressing role of environmental impoverishment has, as its corollary, the importance of enrichment of the environment to secure optimal mental abilities. The questions about the divergent effects of contrasting amounts of stimulation lead to at least two further broad questions that need to be answered if we are to understand the role played by the environment in mental growth. The first of these is a need to identify and understand those aspects of the environment to which infants and children at different ages respond differently or not at all. The second question is whether there are what some have referred to as "critical periods." That is, are there specific ages or stages in the child's development at which certain aspects of his environment are crucially important in determining later mental abilities? Or, from a somewhat different assumption, in order to maximize all children's abilities, is it necessary to insure that each child has, from the very start of life, the best possible environment—if we can know what that is? To what extent can a child recover from earlier impoverishment? And is there somewhere during growth a "point of no return?" That is, what are the conditions that permit recovery? How do they relate to the length of the period of impoverishment, and to its intensity?

To date, few if any definitive experiments have been made that can give us clear answers to these questions. However, there is a considerable body of information about the relation between test scores and various aspects of the environment. From what we now know, it should be possible to construct a rough map of the kinds of stimuli (environmental variables) that are related (perhaps causally) to mental abilities at successive ages. There is also some material that is relevant to the persistence of the effects of earlier experience on later functions.

THE EVIDENCE FROM LONGITUDINAL STUDIES

When the same persons are tested repeatedly over time, it becomes possible to identify those changes that are clearly functions of developmental changes and processes of organization within the individual. It is, furthermore, possible to study individual differences in rates of mental growth, not only of global "intelligence" but also of different types or factors of mental ability. It also affords knowledge of stability and change in mental abilities, and indicates the conditions and limits of predictability over time of the IQ, that is, of relative performance on tests of intelligence..

In interpreting these longitudinally observed processes, however, it is necessary to take cognizance of some limitations which are inherent in the longitudinal method. As a safeguard against possible methodological errors, checks can often be made by posing relevant questions to analyses of cross-sectional data—that is, data collected once from a sample composed of subjects of different ages. The two methods can, in this way, serve to check each other in testing theories that originally derive from either method.

Specifically, the problems arising from the longitudinal method are related to both sampling and practice effects. The sampling difficulties are of several kinds. First, such studies usually must rely on voluntary cooperation of the subjects; thus only those who are interested and willing participate, and such willing samples presumably leave out an important segment of the population. The alternative, a captive audience (as a rule, inmates of an institution), is atypical in a different way. Another problem is sample attrition. Not only does the size of the sample diminish over time, but one must be concerned with the possibility that the attrition is selective in important ways. For example, the more restless migrant subjects may leave, the less healthy may die, and the less able or less educated may more often become reluctant to participate. The investigator must therefore be aware of these limiting conditions, test their relevance to his own materials, and be cautious of generalizing his findings beyond the kinds of sample he is studying. Nevertheless, there are enough differences among longitudinal studies, in the extent to which specific sampling limitations occur, so that often the various studies can be used to cross-validate each other. Furthermore, these problems of sampling errors can often be resolved by comparisons with findings on the same tests from an appropriately selected cross-sectional sample both larger and more representative of the general population.

The same kinds of checks and balances can be applied to study the effects of practice or general familiarity with the tests and testing procedures—conditions that are inevitable in longitudinal samples. For such checks, comparisons can be made with appropriately matched cross-sectional samples composed of subjects who are not familiar with the tests and procedures of the longitudinal program.

STABILITY AND CHANGE IN MENTAL GROWTH RATES

As already noted, starting with the pioneering work of Baldwin and Stecher (1922), a series of studies utilizing repeated tests of the same children over time has gradually eroded the belief in the "constant IQ." In an early report, Furfey and Meuhlenbein (1932) obtained negative correlations between Stanford-Binet IQs at 4 years and scores on the Linfert and Hierholzer test (1928) for groups at ages 6, 9, and 12 months. These rs of −.11, −.34, and −.20 for the three ages were attributed to unreliability or invalidity of the infant tests. Shortly after this Bayley (1933a) reported a detailed analysis of mental tests given to a longitudinal sample of 54 to 61 children at 20 ages, between birth and 36 months. Again, small negative correlations (−.04 and −.09) were found between 1-, 2-, and 3-month tests and tests at 18 to 36 months. A later report (Bayley, 1949) on these same children shows rs with the 4-year test of −.21 for the 1- to 3-month scores. −.16 for the 4- to 6-month scores, .02 with 8-month, .27 with 11-month, .35 with 14-month, and .49 with the 21-month level of tests. The 3- and 4-year tests correlate generally higher with tests at later ages, through 18 years. These latter rs range between .82 and .46, their size depending largely on the elapsed time between tests.

Analyses of Bayley's First-Year Mental Scale show reliabilities to be adequate when equal halves of the scale are correlated and corrected by the Spearman-Brown formula. These correlations average .82 but were lowest in the first 3 months (.51 to .74, with an estimated reliability of the combined scores for months 1, 2, and 3 of .84). For ages 4 to 36 months the single-month, split-half reliabilities range from .75 to .95 (Bayley, 1933a). Similar reliabilities have been reported for other mental test scales, which measure abilities in the first 3 years of life (Werner and Bayley, 1966). Thus the lack of stability in the first 3 years cannot be attributed to poor reliability of the measuring instrument.

The findings of these early studies of mental growth of infants have been repeated sufficiently often so that it is now well-established that test scores earned in the first year or two have relatively little predictive validity (in contrast to tests at school age or later), although they may have high validity as measures of the children's cognitive abilities at the time.

Moreover, a careful look at individuals' growth in intelligence after 4 or 6 years has revealed many instances of changing IQs at all ages. Even though the rates of growth in intelligence, and consequently the IQs, are relatively stable in most persons after 6 years, various investigators have reported widely divergent growth patterns among individual children. There are always in the reports a few children who evidence large shifts in IQ. Among these studies are those of Dearborn and Rothney (1941) on the Harvard Growth

Study; Honzik, Macfarlane, and Allen (1948) on the Berkeley Guidance Study; Sontag, Baker, and Nelson (1958) on the Ohio children of the Fels study; Hilden (1949) on the Denver children studied at the University of Colorado Child Research Council; Freeman and Flory (1937) on Chicago children; Ebert and Simmons (1943) on Cleveland children; and Bayley (1940, 1949) on the Berkeley Growth Study.

Examples of individual growth in intelligence over time are given for the Berkeley Growth Study in Figs. 1 and 2. The scores in these two figures are standard scores, based on the means and SDs of mental ages for this sample. Therefore changes in scores represent changes in ability relative to the other members of a stable, frequently tested population. Cases for whom there are 36-year records have been selected to represent the brightest and dullest of each sex as well as several with intermediate intelligence.

GROWTH IN MENTAL ABILITY AFTER SIXTEEN YEARS

The longitudinal method has also produced new information on age changes in intelli-

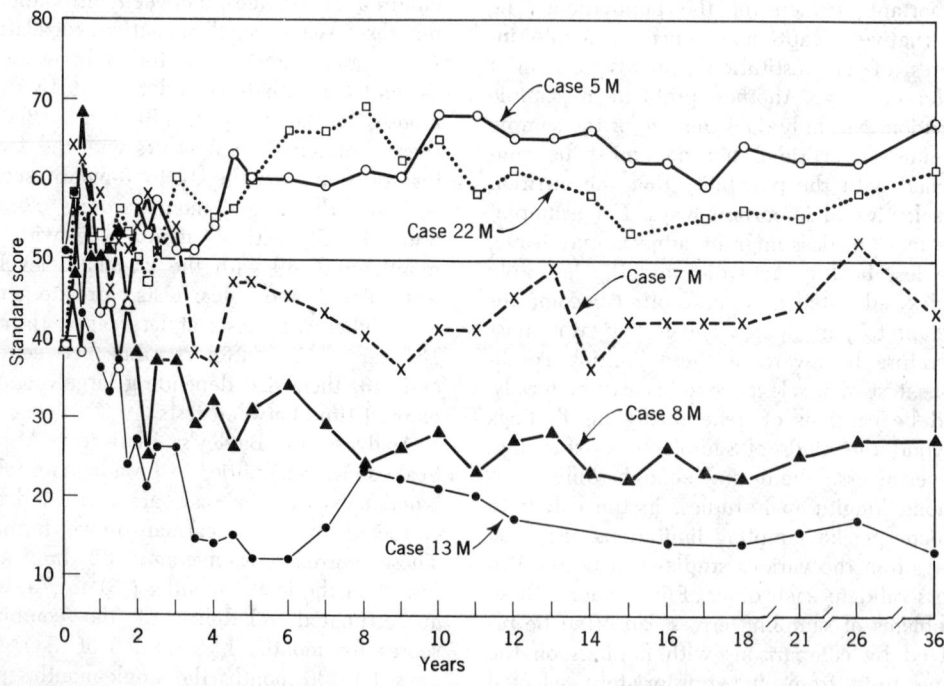

Fig. 1. Individual curves of relative intelligence (standard deviation scores) of five males, birth to 36 years, Berkeley Growth Study cases.

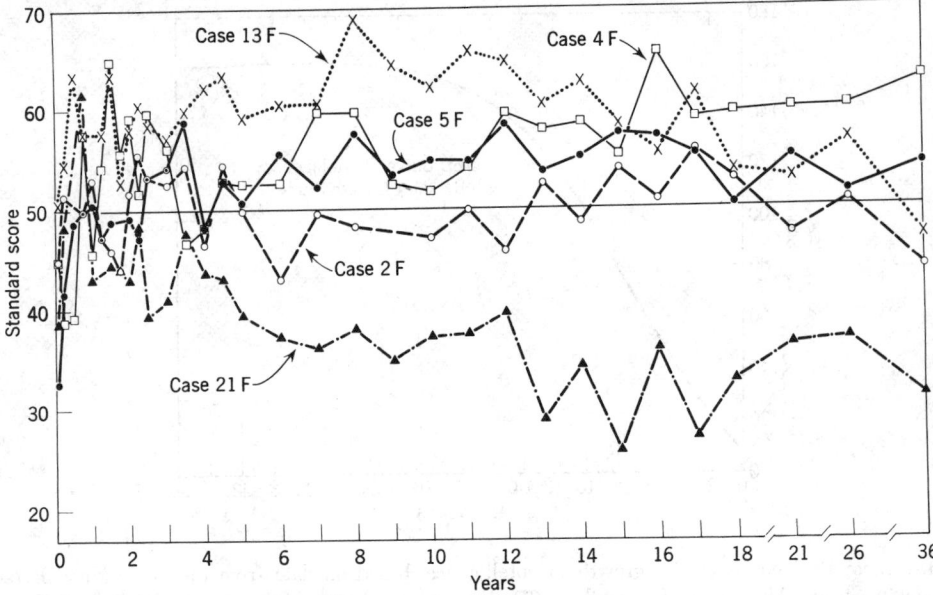

Fig. 2. Individual curves of relative intelligence (standard deviation scores) of five females, birth to 36 years, Berkeley Growth Study cases.

gence of adults, that is, the age at greatest ability (i.e., at which highest test scores are obtained), and the extent to which intelligence levels are maintained during middle and old age. When the mean test scores of a large sample of adults were computed for subsamples of increasingly older ages, such investigators as Miles and Miles (1932), Jones and Conrad (1933), and Wechsler (1944) showed the highest scores occur in the early twenties, decreasing thereafter. In contrast to these reports, the results of recent longitudinal testing of adults (Bayley, 1955, 1957, 1966a; Bayley and Oden, 1955; Freeman and Flory, 1937; Owens, 1953) have challenged this concept that growth in intelligence stops at an early age and then declines. (The ages given for cessation of growth have varied from 13 to 21 and more recently to 30 years; see Miles and Miles, 1932; Jones and Conrad, 1933; Wechsler, 1944, 1958.) However, when the same subjects are retested over age spans extending in some instances to 50 years, the scores have continued to increase, more clearly so for tests of verbal knowledge and information. Freeman and Flory (1937) were among the first to report increased scores through 21 years for a small selected sample of college students whom they

had tested as children. Owens (1953) was able to locate and test 127 50-year-olds on the same Army Alpha Intelligence test they had taken as 19-year-old freshmen at Iowa State College. Their scores at 50 years were significantly higher than their scores at 19. Bayley and Oden (1955) reported on adult tests given 12 years apart on 768 subjects of Terman's "gifted" (IQ 140 to 200) sample and 335 of their spouses. When the samples were divided by age into 5-year samples, it was found that on the retest the scores had increased for all age groups for both sexes and for both the gifted sample and their spouses.

Bayley (1966a, 1968a, 1968b) has recently extended the Berkeley Growth Study growth curves through 36 years. As measured on the Wechsler adult scales (W-B at years 16, 18, 21, and 26; WAIS at 36), the scale scores increase through 26, after which age for the full scale score and total sample, scores level off and remain unchanged through 36 years. When the "absolute scale" growth curve developed for the BGS sample in "16D" units (Bayley, 1955) is now extended to 36 years, the result is the curve shown in Fig. 3. The mean score shows no change after 26 years. However, there are increments after 26 years in the males' scores on the verbal scale. The

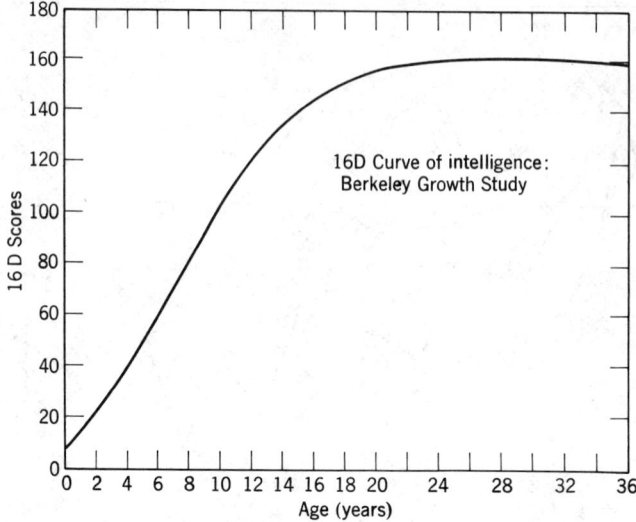

Fig. 3. Theoretical curve of the growth of intelligence, based on data from the longitudinal Berkeley Growth Study. The units of growth (16D scores) are derived from a modification of Thurstone's method of absolute scaling. (See Bayley, 1955.)

female scores either actually drop (Performance scores) or remain unchanged (Verbal scores) between 26 and 36 years.

Birren (1968) reports from studies of elderly men that there was very little deterioration in intelligence scores of those who were in optimal health. However, for some who were found to have subclinical disease, the scores were significantly lower. On a retest 5 years later, some showed no change in scores, whereas others showed considerable change. Precipitant drops in this instance were related to deteriorated health. Birren makes an important observation that the average changes in scores do not represent a general trend for small drops but include some cases that do not change and others who change markedly. That is, the rates of growth and decline in individuals vary with both internal and external factors—in this case with health.

GROWTH RATES AT DIFFERENT LEVELS OF ABILITY

The subjects of the longitudinal studies on which most of the forgoing reports are made were selected, to varying degrees, as above-average or superior in intelligence. However, several investigators have reported increased adult IQs among populations who as children

were classified as average (Charles and James, 1964) and retarded (Charles, 1953; Baller, 1936; and Miller, 1965). Bayley (1968a) found continued increases in scores through 36 years for the lowest-scoring half of the Berkeley Growth Study sample. The increase was found for the lowest-scoring male, whose IQs on the Wechsler scales increased from 64 at 16 years to 80 at 36. McCulloch (1957) found evidence of increased scores on verbal tests through 30 years or longer in mentally retarded institutionalized adults. Thus there is ample evidence that some kinds of intelligence increase well into middle age and perhaps beyond, not only for the bright but also for the "dull." It may be that those whose intelligence does *not* increase after 26 years are for the most part women. Bayley and Oden (1953) in their study of highly intelligent subjects found greater increases in men, through 50 years, and Bayley (1968b) found slight decreases in the Berkeley Growth Study women's scores after 26 years.

AGE CHANGES IN MENTAL ORGANIZATION

The failure in predictive validity from the infant tests has focused attention on the need to learn more about the earliest levels and presumably the more simple processes of mental growth. There is a felt need to know more about the nature of mental processes in infancy, about their determining conditions both genetic and environmental, and the ways in which these determining conditions operate to enhance, retard, and in various ways alter mental development. Investigation of these processes includes not only study of the intelligence tests as such, but also inquiries into the nature of cognition, attention, and learning, and their bearing on general intelligence.

Bayley, in 1933, concluded that "the low correlations between scores made during the first year and those made later force one to the conclusion that superiority in one function does not insure superiority in the subsequent development of more complex functions. . . . There was no evidence for a general factor of intelligence during the first 3 years, but the findings indicate, instead, a series of developing functions, or groups of functions, each growing out of, but not necessarily correlated with, previously matured behavior patterns." Later (1949, 1955), Bayley extended this reasoning to apply to mental development over the whole growth period. She suggested that the lack of consistency over time in mental test scores reflects a series of changes in the nature of mental processes as they progress from simple sensorimotor adjustments to increasingly complex forms of adaptations, generalizations, abstractions, and their accompanying reasoning processes. Piaget's theory of the stages of intellect (1952) similarly represents a developmental pattern of changes in reasoning processes from the concrete to the abstract. Bayley's findings are congruent with Piaget's, and from the theoretical position of either there is no logical necessity that the adequacy of function at the simpler level will predict a child's abilities in the more complex thought processes at a later time.

The fact that after infancy rates of mental growth continue to exhibit variable individual trends calls our attention to a need to consider age changes in mental organization throughout the life span, and to inquire more carefully into the nature of the various mental processes which are classed as "intelligence."

Early efforts to study different kinds of mental ability were made by setting up separate scales each composed of series of tasks which were judged on a priori grounds to tap different intellectual processes. Such scales did show differing rates of growth. For example, Freeman and Flory (1937) obtained separate scores for each of four scales: Vocabulary, Analogies, Completions, and Opposites (VACO). The Vocabulary scale they used was taken unchanged from the 1916 Stanford-Binet test. The other scales were adapted from scales that were available in 1921. For each of the four scales, they developed mental age units based on the performance of their 8- to 18-year sample. Freeman and Flory found, in this longitudinal sample, different rates of growth in scores for each of the four scales. When Conrad, Freeman, and Jones (1944) converted the scores from that study to comparable standard deviation scale units, the growth rates between 10 and 16 years were found to be greatest for Completions, second for Opposites, third for Vocabulary, and least for Analogies. In a like manner, the subscales for the Army Alpha were treated separately by Jones and Conrad (1933), and were found to show different age-trends in their scores. They found that scores in tests of Information and Vocabulary held up better in aging adults than scores on Arithmetic and Reasoning. Clearly, mental growth is a function of the kinds of ability tested, as well as of the age and kind of person.

However, the unreliability of scores on subscales of such tests as the preceding, among them the various forms of the Wechsler adult and children scales, make them of little or no use for evaluating the abilities of any one person.

FACTOR ANALYSIS AS A TOOL FOR STUDYING MENTAL ORGANIZATION

Consequently, investigators concerned with this problem sought a way to build up more reliable measures of the various kinds of mental ability. The statistical method of factor analysis was found most useful for selecting tests which were highly intercorrelated and which therefore might be assumed to measure the same "factor" in intelligence. Spearman (1904, 1927) pioneered much of this work. In an early analysis he derived a large general, or pervasive factor, which he called g, and several smaller or specific factors, which appeared to vary with the specific content of the test involved. These might, for example, be arithmetic, memory span, spatial discrimination, or perhaps even musical ability. L. L. Thurstone (1947) did much to develop the factorial method to identify different mental abilities. He derived a number of independent factors, and he used these to develop scales for measuring more adequately the several factors. From a nucleus of a few similar items, it was possible to select and test additional likely items to build up reliable batteries of tests. Thurstone and Thurstone (1943, 1958), using this procedure, devised and standardized tests of Primary Mental Abilities. Their primary factors are Verbal Comprehension, Word Fluency, Number, Space, Associative Memory, Perceptual Speed, and Induction (or General Reasoning). Others whose work in this field is prominent are Guilford (1956), Tryon (1935), R. B. Cattell (1957), and Vernon (1960).

Each method has proved to be fruitful in identifying factors or clusters of related items which can then be used as criteria for developing scales of the various mental abilities. As these tools became increasingly sophisticated, increasingly adequate scales were developed. These in turn permit the study of growth rates and of individual stability of scores in the various abilities for different samples of subjects and for different environmental conditions. Such factorial scores also make possible the study of age-related changes in the relative contribution of different mental abilities to general intellectual functions.

The Thurstone Primary Mental Abilities tests have been developed for use in the elementary school grades. Both R. B. Cattell (1957) and J. P. Guilford (Guilford, 1956; Christensen and Guilford, 1955–1956; Hertzka and Guilford, 1955) have utilized factorial material in developing mental tests for adults.

One of the earliest factor analyses of infants' mental test scores was done by Richards and Nelson (1939). Using the Gesell scales at ages 6, 12, and 18 months, they derived a general factor and two additional factors which they called Alertness and Motor Ability. Since the items from all four of the Gesell scales were included in the analysis, the result, insofar as they might identify factors of *mental* ability, is of little or no value. For example, such motoric items as "walks alone" and "bowel control" are included as well as

the more usual mental items such as "says three words" and "looks for fallen spoon." None of the factor scores they derived proved to be predictive of later intelligence.

Recently Stott and Ball (1965) made a meticulous analysis of scores from 14 studies utilizing five mental scales applied to samples ranging in age from 3 months (P. Cattell) to 5 years (Stanford-Binet). The other scales included are the Bayley California First-Year Mental Scale, the Gesell Developmental Schedules, and the Merrill-Palmer Scale (Stutsman, 1931). In analyzing these infant scales, Stott and Ball used Guilford's Structure of Intellect (1956, 1957) as a frame of reference. Guilford, through factor analyses of test scores on adults, identified five categories of operations which he conceives as constituting the basic kinds of mental processes, or operations of the intellect. The three "thinking abilities" are: Cognition (the discovery of new and recognition of old information), Production (the use of information to effect certain outcomes), and Evaluation (decisions as to the goodness, accuracy, or suitability of information or products). Production is further divided into Convergent Thinking (where there is one unique answer or conclusion to a problem) and Divergent Thinking (for which multiple answers may be appropriate). The fifth general factor of intellect in this structure is Memory. Each of these general factors can be divided into more specific abilities. Guilford's factorial structure is three-dimensional and he identifies 44 specific factors of a theoretically possible 72. It is interesting to see to what extent the factors derived from infant test scales can be fitted into Guilford's structure.

Stott and Ball (1965) have presented in Table 1 their summary of the infant scale factors at nine ages (3 to 60 months). As we see from this table, which utilizes the Guilford structure of intellect classification as a base, they were able to show loadings at various ages for all five classes of factors plus a few additional ones. Also, at one age or another for at least one test, 31 of Guilford's specific factors are represented. (For identification of these specific factors see Guilford, 1956, 1957.) For the 3- and 6-month tests they found loadings on four of the five classes: Cognitive, Divergent, and Convergent Production, and Evaluation. For one Gesell item at 6 months, but more generally at 12 months,

Table 1. *Summary of Factor Interpretations of Infant Scales Allowing Comparisons of Tests and Age Levels for Interpreted Factor Content According to Guilford's Detailed Diagram of the "Structure of Intellect"*

Intelligence Factor	Cattell		California		Gesell		M-P					S-B(L)			Total
	3	6	6	12	6	12	24	30	36	48	54	36	48	60	
Cognitive:															
CFU	X	X	X						X			X		X	6
CFR				X							X				2
CFS							X	X	X	X					4
CFT								X		X	X			X	4
CFI	X														1
CMU							X								1
CMR										X			X		2
CMS											X				1
CBU			X	X	X										3
															24
Memory:															
MFU													X		1
MFR				X						X					2
MFS									X						1
MSS													X		1
MMU													X		1
MMR				X								X	X		3
MBR				X		X									2
															11
Divergent prod.:															
DFU	X					X									2
DFR			X		X										2
DFT			X												1
DBR						X									1
															6
Convergent prod.:															
NFU			X		X										2
NFR	X				X					X	X				4
NFS								X	X		X				3
NMU						X									1
NMI				X											1
NBR						X		X							2
															13
Evaluation:															
EFU							X								1
EFS					X							X			2
EMR			X												1
EMS			X	X	X										3
EMT													X		1
															8

Table 1. Summary of Factor Interpretations of Infant Scales Allowing Comparisons of Tests and Age Levels for Interpreted Factor Content According to Guilford's Detailed Diagram of the "Structure of Intellect" (Continued)

Intelligence Factor	Intelligence Tests: Age Level (Months)													Total
	Cattell		California		Gesell		M-P					S-B(L)			
	3	6	6	12	6	12	24	30	36	48	54	36	48	60	
Others:															
Hand Dext'y							X	X	X		X				4
Gross Psychom.							X	X							2
Whole Body					X										1
Locomotor					X										1
Reflex					X										1
															9
Total															**71**

Reprinted from Stott and Ball, 1965.

Note. Guilford's factors are listed at the left by sets of three letters. The first refers to the principal five intellectual operations: C = cognitive, M = memory, D = divergent production, N = convergent production and E = evaluation. The second letter in each group refers to four classes of information, or content: F = figural (i.e., concrete perceived materials), S = symbolic (e.g., letters, words, digits), M = semantic content or meaning, and B = behavioral content concerned with interpersonal relations. The third letter refers to outcomes or products of the operations: U = units, C = classes, R = relations, S = systems, T = transformations, and I = implications.

Thus "CFU" refers to a factor which is described or classed as composed by cognitive, figural (perceived through senses) units. Such a factor was found at ages 3, 6, 36 and 60 months in one or more of the tests.

loadings on Memory occur for the first time. The "Other" factors in the Stott and Ball analysis are tests that would ordinarily be classed as motor coordinations. It is clear that the Cattell and the California Mental Scale do not include this type of item. [There is a separate California Infant Scale of Motor Development (Bayley, 1936), which is not included here.] Gesell included motor performance as one of the four parts of his Developmental Schedule. This factor analysis clearly separates the motor factors from the factors of intellect for the tests in which they occur.

Between 12 and 24 months there is a change in the scales used in this analysis. The Divergent Production factor does not appear in the Merrill-Palmer and Stanford-Binet, both of which were given first at 24 months. Starting with the 24-month tests, there is evidence of constricted selection of items in the areas tapped, and therefore of the factors derived. The Merrill-Palmer scale has loadings on four of the main classes with none on Divergent Production, but it also has loadings on Manual

Dexterity. The Stanford-Binet at 3, 4, and 5 years loads on Cognitive, Memory, and Evaluation factors only.

It is clear from the table that the different scales are selective, and the factors obtained are functions of the items included. The Gesell scale has a number of body-control motor factors, but only one Cognitive loading, at 12 months. Otherwise cognitive factors are well represented at all ages. It appears that memory factors cannot be tapped until 6 months or later. Stott and Ball point out that the "rational" division of tests into, for example, verbal and nonverbal tests "is not necessarily discriminative" in infancy. Profiles of types of ability may more appropriately be based on items which are grouped by appropriate factor analysis.

Although the authors do not utilize scores based on the factors they derived in order to predict later mental growth, they do present a basis for differentiating mental abilities in infancy and early childhood. In order, through use of the Guilford Structure, to explore possible continuities of related abilities across ages, it appears from this table that a wider variety of items should be selected with a view to filling as many as possible of the empty cells. Such a procedure should, theoretically, lead to a map that would show whether mental abilities grow from a simple to complex structure with age, or whether traces of the many factors of Guilford's theory can be identified in early infancy.

Another approach to identifying emergent mental abilities has been possible with the materials of the Berkeley Growth Study. Because the children in this study were tested so frequently (monthly 1 to 15 months, trimonthly to 36 months, and biannually to 6 years), it has been possible to use as item-scores age-at-first-passing each item, for all 115 items in the California First-Year Mental Scale (Bayley, 1933b) and 110 of the items of the California Preschool Mental Scale (Jaffa, 1934). The total sample was composed of 35 males and 39 females. Through attrition, the sample was reduced over time. At 6 years 30 of each sex were tested. Intercorrelations (product-moment) using age-at-first-passing were computed between all items within each scale, and a Tryon cluster analysis was carried out for each scale. This procedure made it possible for any item on the entire scale to be included in a factor if it correlated sufficiently with the other items in that cluster. By this procedure six factors were derived for the First-Year Scale, and six for the Preschool Scale.

If a given mental ability is present throughout the first year, or over a considerable portion of the year, and if the test items are available to measure this ability, then items loading on the factor that measures it should be found over the given age-range. Actually there is no evidence in our analysis (Bayley, 1966b, Cameron, Livson, and Bayley, 1967) for such continuity in the first year. The clusters (or factors) tend to be restricted to age-levels or stages. In this regard they are congruent with the earlier interpretations of Bayley (1933a) and those of Piaget (1952).

These factors and the items loading on them at each age are shown in Fig. 4, in their ascending order of difficulty. These factors are relatively discrete. Significant correlations occur between a few which are adjacent in difficulty. These correlations are indicated at

the right in the figure. The one factor which is most clearly correlated with other factors is First-Year Factor VI: Meaningful Objective Relations. It is composed of nine items ranging in difficulty from 10 to 17 months. It correlates .34 with the adjacent Preschool Factor I: Visual Discrimination (18 to 21 months). It correlates .48 with Preschool II: Object Relations (Dexterity), 18 to 35 months; .43 with Preschool III: Memory for Form (21 to 60 months); and .42 with Preschool IV: Verbal Knowledge (Spatial), 25 to 72 months. In addition, the First-Year Factor V, Vocal Communications (8 to 14 months), correlates .45 with Preschool I, Perceptual Discrimination. The thread of relationship which runs through these five intercorrelated factors appears to be perceptual discriminations, as they are utilized in various ways: vocal-verbal and manipulatory.

From this pattern of interrelated factors whose age placements are primarily in the 10- to 60-month range, it may be suggested that in this 1- to 5-year period the child develops and consolidates his ability not only to differentiate but also to classify the objects in his experience. Both perception and language play primary roles in this process.

This kind of ability once developed, however, is not a good indicator of the later ability of these children. Instead, it may be interpreted as characterizing Piaget's stage of concrete thought processes. Such concrete processes are necessary but not sufficient conditions for the later development of abstract thinking.

The two factors, among the 12 in this series, which do correlate with later intelligence scores, are both "verbal": the First-Year Factor V, Vocalizations, is composed of items which are the beginnings of verbal communications; for example, vocalizes eagerness and displeasure, jabbers expressively, says two words. This factor, however, in the Berkeley study predicts later verbal intelligence for the girls through 26 years but for the boys only through 3 years (Bayley, 1968b; Cameron, Livson, and Bayley, 1967). The later-occurring Preschool Factor IV, Verbal Knowledge, predicts later intelligence for both sexes and, more clearly for the boys, for whom the relationship is high with later scores on verbal intelligence (Bayley, 1966b). Since language is a primary

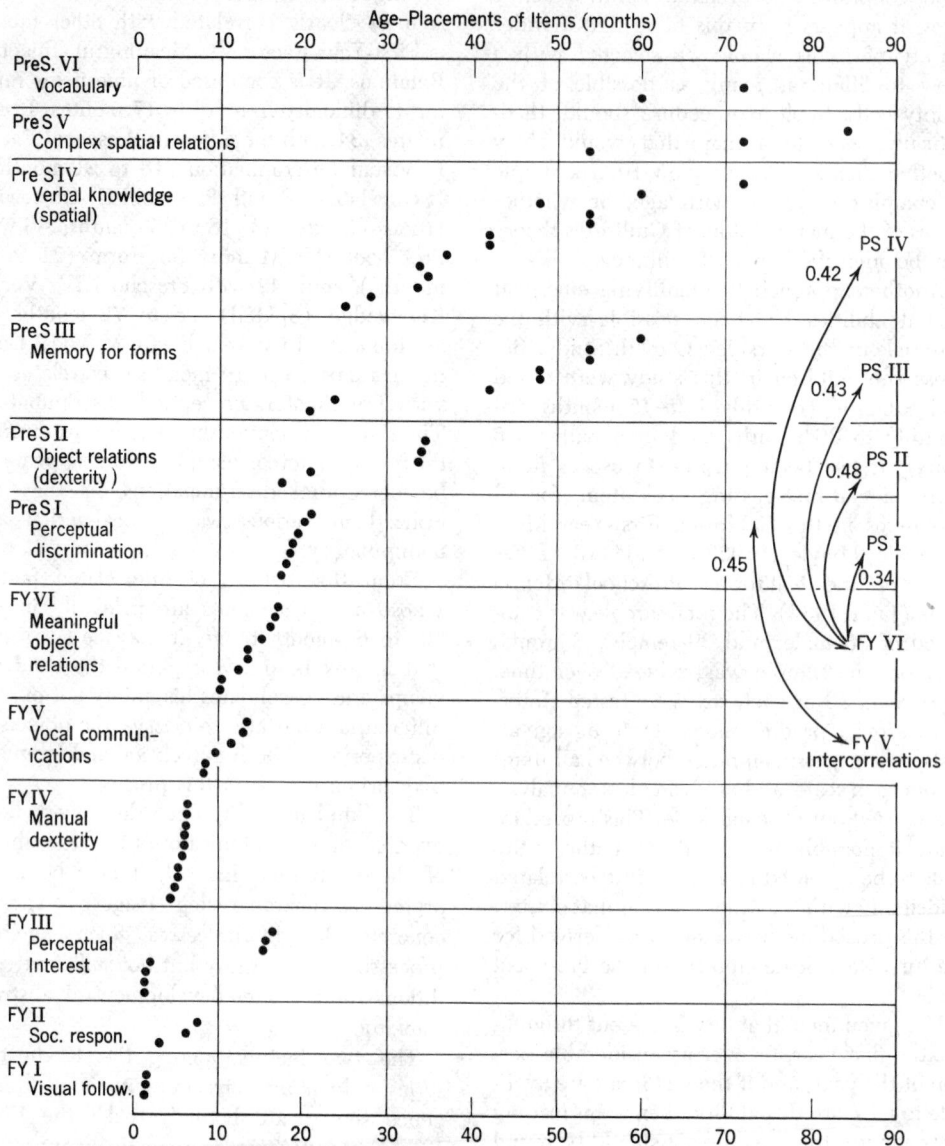

Fig. 4. Age-placement of items in the Berkeley Growth Study precocity factors for the First-Year and Preschool mental scales. Significant correlations between factor scores are indicated at the right.

tool in abstract thinking processes, we may interpret these findings as indicating that not only are verbal abilities necessary for later mental abilities, but they also play an important role in facilitating the development of increasingly abstract thought processes. If this is true, then it may be that the earlier the age at which facility in language is established, the greater the opportunity a child has to realize to the full his intellectual capacities.

In analyzing the later test scores of this same sample of Berkeley children, it was possible, for seven tests covering ages 8 to 17 years, to compute factor scores using McNemar's factors for the 1937 Stanford-Binet (McNemar, 1942). For five ages, 16 to 36 years, Wechsler adult tests were factor analyzed for this sample. In both of these scales (the Stanford-Binet and the Wechsler), the most general first factor is a verbal one, heav-

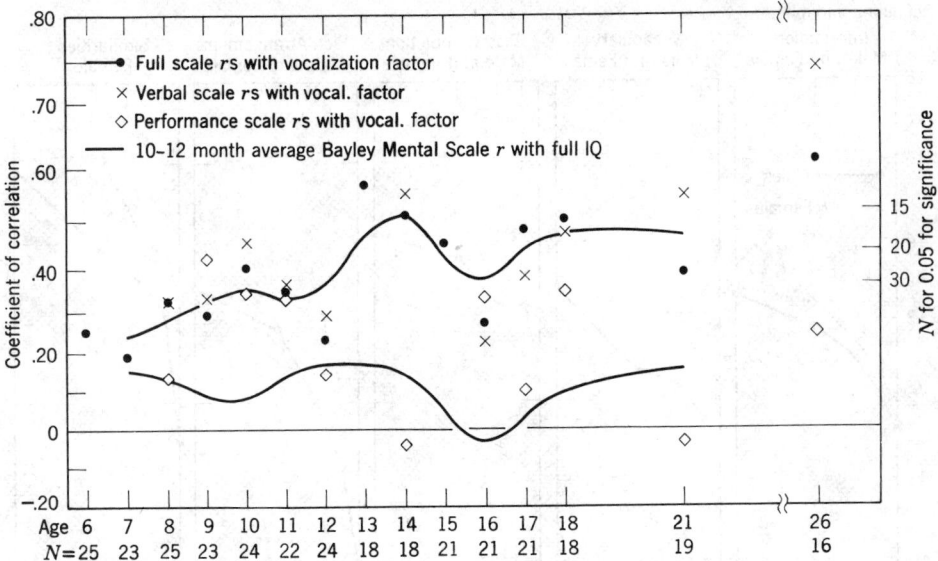

Fig. 5. Girl's Vocalization factor correlations with Verbal, Performance, and Full-Scale intelligence scores at ages 6 through 26 years. (Reprinted from Cameron, Livson, and Bayley, 1967.)

ily weighted with Information, Vocabulary, and Verbal Comprehension. The scores on these verbal factors are the most consistent over time. Further, the First-Year Vocalization factor for the girls and the Preschool Verbal factor for the boys when correlated with the childhood and adult factors are more highly related to the verbal than to the other factors. This relation to the early Vocalization scores for the girls is illustrated in Fig. 5.

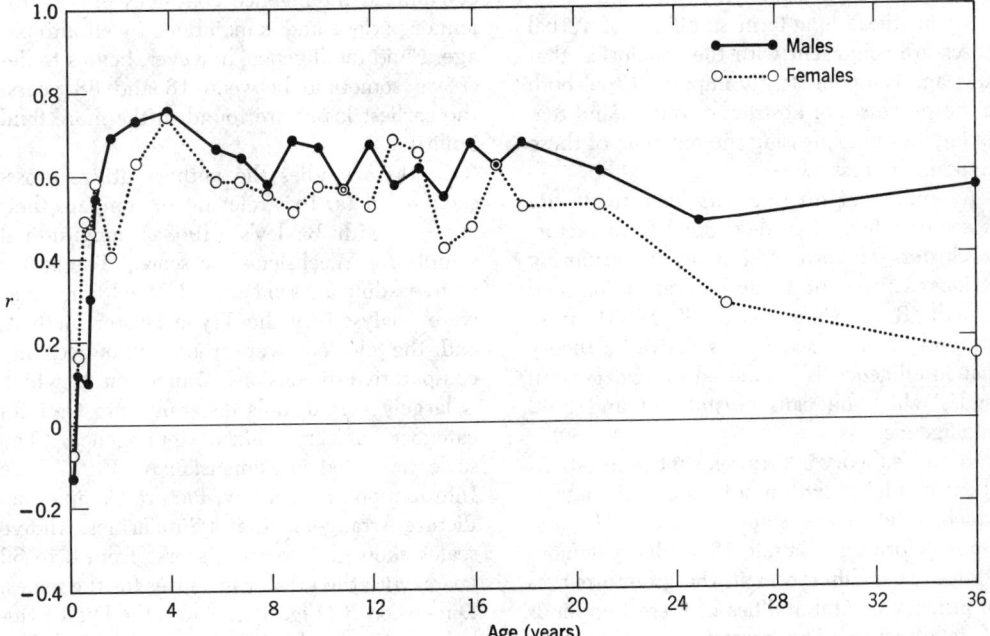

Fig. 6. Correlations of Preschool Verbal Knowledge factor scores (24 to 72 months) with IQs at all ages. (Reprinted from Bayley, 1966b.)

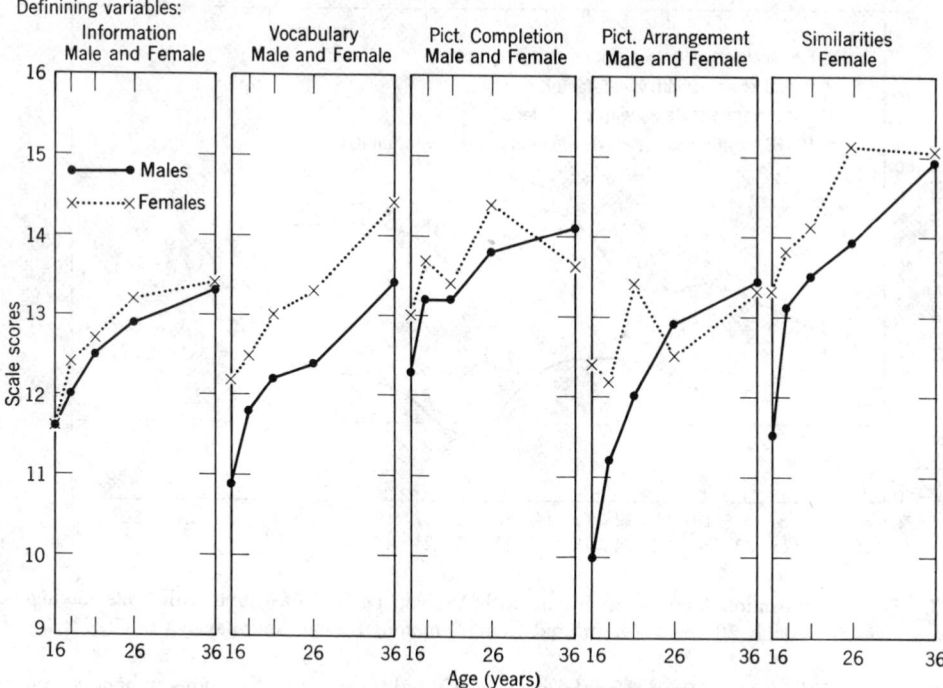

Fig. 7.   Means by age and sex for Wechsler scales in Comparative Dimension A, 16 to 36 years (36-year score adjusted to equate W-B and WAIS). (Reprinted from Bayley, 1968c.)

The correlation with general IQ for the Verbal Knowledge factor is shown in Fig. 6.

Again, these long-term stabilities of verbal scores are congruent with the conclusion that language is a consistently important tool both in the processes of abstract cognition and reasoning and in expressing the outcome of these thinking processes.

A number of investigators have made use of scores which they developed from factors or clusters of correlated items, in exploring various aspects of mental organization and growth. R. B. Cattell (Cattell, 1963), from his work on such scales, has derived a theory that intelligence is composed of two general kinds, which he calls crystallized and fluid intelligence.

Cattell's theory is very relevant to questions about mental growth in adults and the age at which intelligence stops growing. He and Horn (Horn and Cattell, 1966) have demonstrated clear differences in the growth curves of primary mental abilities of these two kinds of intelligence. The crystallized factors are characterized by accumulated and retained knowledge; the fluid factors are processes of

discriminating and reasoning. They find that crystallized intelligence continues growth for longer periods and is maintained well into old age. Fluid intelligence, however, begins to decrease sometime between 18 and 38 years; the earliest losses are found in the more fluid abilities.

In these studies the authors utilize cross-sectional data. It is relevant to compare their findings with Bayley's (1968a) longitudinal sample for Wechsler scale scores. The scores at five adult ages on the 11 Wechsler scales were analysed by the Tryon cluster method, and the clusters were then regrouped into comparative dimensions. Dimension A, which is largely verbal, falls generally into Cattell's category of crystallized intelligence. The scales included in Dimension A (Fig. 7) are Information, Vocabulary, Picture Completion, Picture Arrangement, and Similarities. All five scales showed increasing scores from 6 to 36 years, with the greater increases for the males. Dimension B (Fig. 8) includes the Digit Symbol substitution for both sexes and Block Design for the females only. Other scales not included in either dimension are shown in

Fig. 9. Most of the curves in both Figs. 8 and 9 show decreasing scores for both sexes after 21 or 26 years. These six scales are similar to those classified by Cattell as fluid.

From these studies again we have evidence for multiple mental abilities, which develop in different ways. Some show more continuous growth than others. Some are more consistent over time than others. It appears that one general class of abilities, which may be referred to as verbal facility and knowledge, is not only more stable within individuals throughout growth but also continues to increase in adults to 30 years of age or older. Other abilities appear to be more bound to stages of development, to be less stable over time, and to reach their peak in the twenties. Such fluid abilities include reasoning processes, arithmetic and verbal reasoning, perhaps attention span or short-term memory, and speed.

These broad generalizations, however, leave out of account the many sex differences that become clear when the mental abilities are treated for each sex separately and when their stability over time is explored.

The evidence for continuous age changes in the nature and organization of mental abili-

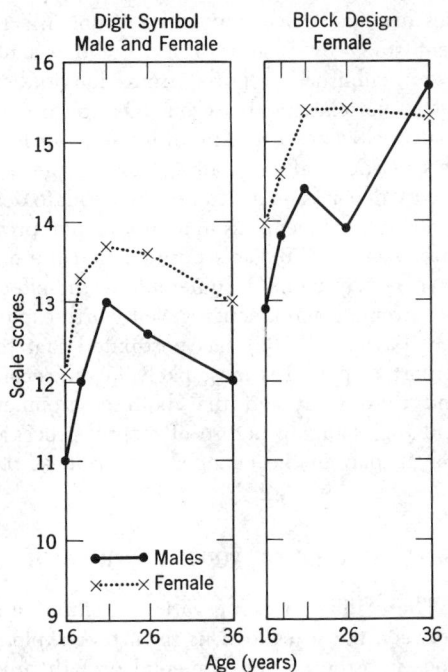

Fig. 8. Means by age and sex for Wechsler scales in Comparative Dimension B, 16 to 36 years (36-year score adjusted). (Reprinted from Bayley, 1968c.)

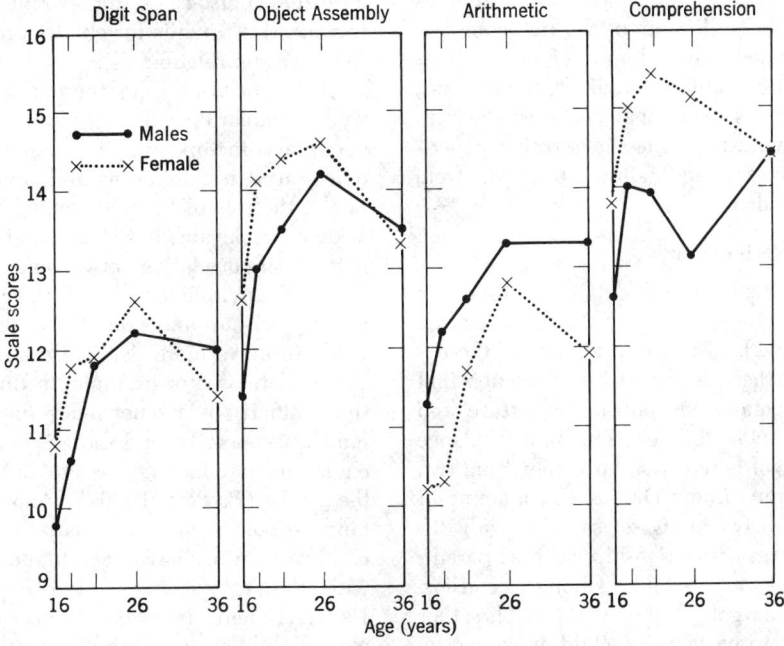

Fig. 9. Means by age and sex for Wechsler scales with low loadings in Dimensions A and B, 16 to 36 years (36-year score adjusted). (Reprinted from Bayley, 1968c.)

ties has not been taken into account in a recent study by Bloom (1964), who has utilized published reports from longitudinal retest correlations between IQs to propose that intelligence is plastic in infancy but loses this plasticity after about 4 years of age. His theory depends on a patently inadequate definition of intelligence as a unitary mental property. However, Bloom's position that the first 4 years may be most vulnerable to the effects of extreme environments is well worth exploring. Bayley (1966c) has postulated that the important period is most likely in the second and third year, and that both environment and the changing nature of mental processes play a part in the changes occurring at this time.

DETERMINERS OF MENTAL GROWTH

These differences in various abilities and between the sexes lead us to further explorations into the nature of mental growth processes, their determiners, or at least their correlates. Differences in mental abilities have been atributed to many things, some of which may be basically hereditary, others primarily environmental, with many gradations between these extremes. The various correlates which have so far been found with mental abilities are impressive indicators of the rich complexity, still largely unexplored, of interactions among such variables as abilities, motivations, attention spans, emotional climates, environmental complexities, specific learning experiences, successes, and failures resulting from effort expended.

The Role of Heredity

Even though children's IQs are found to change over time, and these changes are often correlated with identifiable aspects of the environment, there is also strong evidence that heredity operates to control the nature and level of mental abilities. The best evidence for the role of heredity so far comes from two general comparisons. One is the amount of correlation between IQs of samples with differing degrees of relationship, such as parent-child, grandparent-child, siblings, cousins, twins (monozygotic and dizygotic). The other is the comparison between children reared by their own parents and children reared by unrelated, adoptive (or foster) parents.

Burt, who has long been a strong proponent of heredity as the primary determiner of intelligence, recently (1966) reported an impressive analysis of his long-time studies of correlations between IQs of persons with varying degrees of familial relations and of monozygotic and dizygotic twins reared together and reared apart. His highest correlation is .92 for 95 pairs of monozygotic twins reared together. Next is the r of .87 for 53 pairs of monozygotic twins reared apart. Since such twins should be expected to have identical genetic potential, the differences between these two correlations should reflect the differential effects of growing up in different environments. His correlations of .55 for 71 like-sex and .52 for 56 opposite-sex dizygotic twin pairs reared together is very similar to the r of .53 for the 264 ordinary siblings reared together and a little more than the r of .44 of 151 pairs of siblings reared apart. He found a correlation of .27 for 136 pairs of unrelated children reared together. In other degrees of relationship he reports correlations between children and their parents as adults as .49, with parents as children .56, with grandparents .33, between uncle (or aunt) and nephew (or niece) .34, between first cousins .28, and second cousins .16. Among unrelated persons, foster parent and child correlated .27, while for children reared apart there was no relation.

Burt concludes from these correlations as well as similar ones of other investigators that hereditary factors are of paramount importance in determining mental abilities. Certainly, the role of heredity cannot be brushed aside as irrelevant, but since we do find clear patterns of correlation between measured abilities and environment, it becomes necessary, if we wish to understand the processes at work, to make more detailed examinations of these relations. For example, in Burt's studies the comparisons are not made for males and females separately, and there is evidence that environmental factors operate differently for the sexes (Bayley, 1966a). Another important variable is age. The patterns of parent-child correlations have been found to increase with the age of the child (Bayley 1954, 1966a). There is evidence also that some mental abilities are more affected than others by environments. Osborn and Gregory (1966), for example, studying 33 pairs of monozygotic twins and 12 pairs of like-sexed dizygotic twins concluded that for some of the tests they used, as much as 89% of the within-family variance is hereditary, whereas for others the hereditary contribution was only 15%.

Another approach to the use of twins for determining the role of heredity was made by Freedman and Keller (1963). They studied 20 pairs of like-sexed twins on a monthly basis during their first year. They selected this age because it is "before mental imitation becomes a factor." At the end of the year, by blood group determination 11 pairs were identified as fraternal and 9 as identical. On Mental and Motor scales and on the Infant Behavior Record (Bayley, 1969) within-pair differences were significantly greater for fraternal than for identical pairs. An interesting aspect of this comparison was the application of the behavior rating to filmed behaviors of the infants. Using films of 8 consecutive months of behavior of each child separately, the films of one twin were shown to a group of four professionals who had worked with children, and the films of the other twin were shown to a different, comparable group. These judges rated each child on the Infant Behavior Record, which includes such behaviors as responsiveness to persons and to toys, activity, attention span, goal directedness, fearfulness, and emotional tone. The scores for each child were then averaged. From these independent ratings intrapair differences for the fraternal twins were significantly greater $(p < .005)$. From this study, there is a clear indication that personality, or nonintellective behaviors are also genetically determined. If this is so, then the correlations found at later ages between mental abilities and behaviors may result from genetically determined tendencies to react in characteristic ways to the environment. In other words, genetic determiners of mental abilities may be based not purely on capacities to carry on varying degrees of abstract thinking, but they may operate through inborn response tendencies which are manifested more generally as behaviors which in themselves are not classed as "intelligence."

Mental Abilities and Socioeconomic Background

The socioeconomic level of the children's parents has long been a subject for comparisons with children's intelligence. Figure 10 presents a series of such correlations for the Berkeley Growth Study (Bayley and Schaefer, 1964). This chart may be used to illustrate the socioeconomic variables frequently used in such correlations, as well as to give some representative correlations.

Many studies have reported correlation coefficients in the neighborhood of .50 between school-age children's IQ and parents' education and occupation (e.g., Goodenough, 1927; Kagan and Moss, 1959; Marks and Klahn, 1961). We see that for the BGS sample the relations are highest for the boys with fathers' occupation, and for the girls with both parents' education. In general, income and a social rating show only small relations. The low and even negative correlations between mental scores in infancy and parents' education were reported by Bayley in 1933. Since then similar findings have been reported by Honzik (1963), Hindley (1960), and others. An interesting aspect of the rs in Fig. 10 is that the negative correlations found with the 3- to 7-month tests occur for the boys but not for the girls. These correlations have been attributed, according to the theoretical bias of the interpreter, either to the long-term effects of environment on the child's mental development or, from a genetic basis, to the late appearance of mental abilities which are stable and similar to those evidenced by the adult parents, with a possible sex difference in the age at which the more mature, stable relation appears. There is evidence in favor of the hereditary interpretation in the study of Skodak and Skeels (1949) of parent-child relations of adopted children. In that study, as has been pointed out by Honzik (1957) the correlations between the children's IQs and those of their true mothers increase from zero at 2 years to .44 by 13.5 years, even though they had been separated from their biological mothers in early infancy. What is more, although the children's IQs were much higher than their mothers', evidently as a result of the more favorable environments afforded by their adoptive parents, there was no positive relationship found between the children's IQs and educational level of the adoptive parents.

Aside from this study of Skodak and Skeels there is little available information on children reared by other than their own parents to confirm this change with age in the true (biological) parent-child correlation in mental

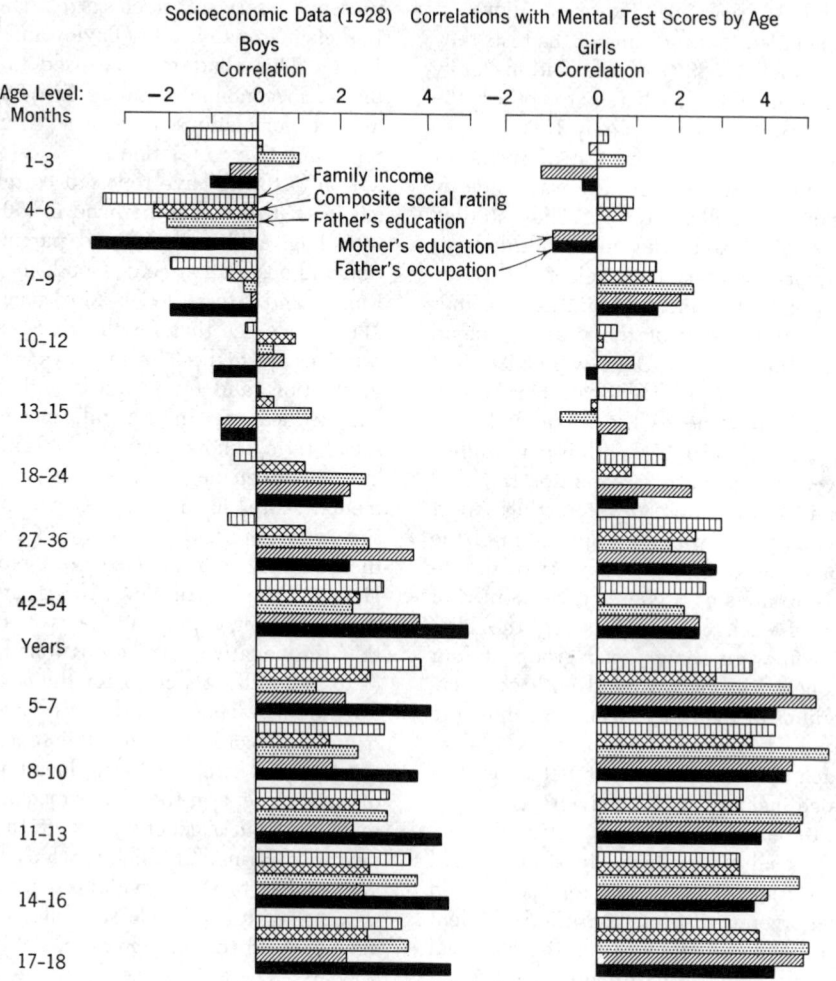

Socioeconomic Data (1928)   Correlations with Mental Test Scores by Age

Boys
Correlation

Girls
Correlation

Age Level:
Months

Family income
Composite social rating
Father's education
Mother's education
Father's occupation

Fig. 10. Correlations of mental test scores by age, birth to 18 years, with five indicators of parents' socioeconomic status at the time the children were born. (Reprinted from Bayley and Schaefer, 1964.)

ability. Bayley (1966b) has utilized the Skodak and Skeels material to compute parent-child correlations by sex of the child. As shown in Fig. 11, the correlations increased with the children's ages, but for the boys the correlations at 2 years were negative(-.34 with true mothers' IQ) and then became moderately positive. The correlations for the girls rose from approximately .20 to *r*s on the order of .50. The pattern holds for education of true mother and father and for IQ of true mother. The correlations with adoptive parents' education are in most instances insignificant, but with some indications of negative correlations with adoptive mothers' education.

Lesser, Fifer, and Clark (1965) have reported some relevant class and ethnic differences in school-age children for different mental abilities. An interesting aspect of this Lesser et al. study is their finding that social class and cultural groups differed not only in general IQ level but also in patterns of ability. The middle-class children were consistently superior to lower-class children, with the greatest class differences in IQ for the Negroes. On Verbal Ability Jewish children scored highest, Negroes second, Chinese third, and Puerto Ricans fourth. On Reasoning, the rank order was Chinese, Jews, Negroes, and Puerto Ricans. On Number Ability, the ranks

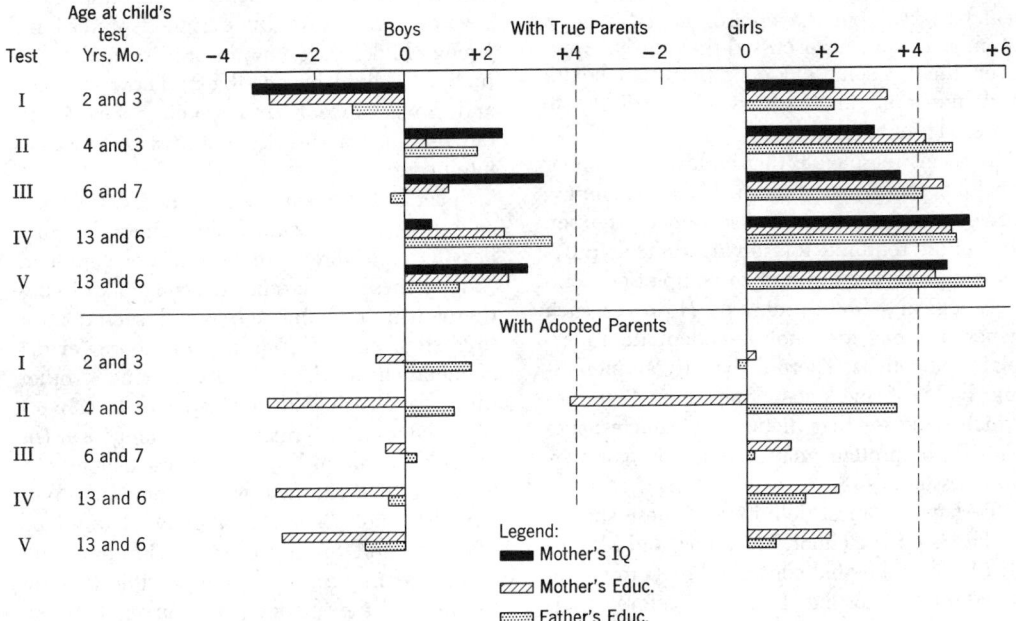

Fig. 11. Correlations of children's IQs with indicators of true parents' and adoptive parents' mental ability (data from Skodak and Skeels, 1949). (Reprinted from Bayley, 1966a.)

were: Jews, Chinese, Puerto Ricans, Negroes. On Space, the order was Chinese, Jews, Puerto Ricans, Negroes. These findings raise the question of the extent to which the ethnic differences result from innate potentials or from differences between the groups of cultural value systems and hence of differential rewards for skills in the mental abilities tested. The lower-class Negroes in this study evidently suffer the most from lack of relevant rewards for intellectual competence.

Effects of Environmental Impoverishment

There is now a general consensus that children growing up in impoverished environments earn low scores on intelligence tests. Among the most impoverished environments to which many young children have been subjected are the orphanages and other institutions in which infants and young children are cared for over protracted periods. The mental and emotional deprivations of such children have been reported in the well-known studies of Spitz (1945), Goldfarb (1945, 1955), Bowlby (1952), and others. The effects of an orphanage environment can perhaps be best illustrated in a pioneer study

at the University of Iowa (Skeels, Updegraff, Wellman, and Williams, 1938). The children were retarded in mental, motor, and social maturity. A significant finding of this study is that a small group of these children who were given training in an enriched preschool program showed marked gains in all three areas. These gains resulted, at least in part, from the children's learning of skills in interacting with adults, and in attending and responding in a relevant way to stimuli which would facilitate adequate measures of intelligence. However, this process of meaningful interaction would in itself promote mental growth; if this is true, then Skeels and his associates are correct in their assertion that the children's intelligence actually increased as a result of their preschool experience.

The Effects of Physical Impoverishment

On the physical side, low socioeconomic status and economically deprived populations are regularly associated with poor nutrition, high incidence of disease, slow growth, and small size. Along with these conditions, we also find diminished mental ability. It is difficult to differentiate the effects of these physical hazards from the environmental aspects of impoverishment discussed previously. However, there is some evidence that poor health and nutrition in themselves contribute to lowered mental abilities.

It seems reasonable that children with poor health or inadequate food will lack the energy, drive, and curiosity for the sustained attention and effort required for solving difficult problems or carrying through to completion complex, logical thought-processes. However, such generalizations may not be adequate to explain the deficits. There is recently an increasing body of evidence from animal studies which indicates that dietary deficiencies, specifically of protein, may actually impair nervous tissues.

Perhaps the most definitive of these studies to date is by Zamenhof, Marthens, and Margolis (1968). They fed controlled diets to young female rats, starting 1 month before pregnancy and continuing throughout gestation. The only differences in the diets were that one group was fed a low protein and the other a high protein diet. The brains of the newborn rats were analyzed. DNA and protein were determined for the litters of the rats on the two differing diets. The results showed significant differences between the dietary groups not only in body and brain weights, but the progeny of the protein-deprived mothers showed a significant reduction in the total number of brain cells. In addition, the amount of protein per cell was lower. Therefor, the authors conclude that: "This quantitative alteration in number as well as the qualitative one (protein per cell) may constitute a basis for the frequently reported impaired behavior of the offspring from protein-deprived mothers."

The results of this and similar studies on animals may be compared with a study by Stoch and Smythe (1963) on two groups of Cape colored children in South Africa. One group had been severely malnourished in the first year of life, the other adequately nourished. At the end of 7 years, the malnourished group was significantly below the other in stature, IQ, and head circumference. It was pointed out that the age at which nutritional deprivation occurred in these children was at a crucial stage for brain development. During the first year the brain is still growing rapidly and is still in the process of myelinization. Several more carefully designed studies on young children are now in process, and eventually it should be possible to know whether and to what extent early protein deficiency in the diet has a directly depressing effect on intelligence.

Several forms of mental retardation are now known to result from genetic anomalies that interfere with normal development. Among these are cretinism (congenital hypothyroidism implying subnormal secretion of thyroxin), phenylketinuria (an inborn "error" of metabolism which results in, among other things, a greatly reduced capacity to convert phenylalanine to tyrosine), and mongolism (or Down's Syndrome), whose cause beyond the evidence of a characteristic chromosome pattern has not been completely determined (Penrose and Smith, 1966). With time and better techniques, it may be possible to identify most of the specific determiners of mental retardation. As this process continues and the hereditary and environmental determiners of mental defects become known, corrective measures for each may become possible.

Effects of Intervention on Mental Abilities

Psychologists and educators were slow to accept the implications of the Iowa studies on the effects of inappropriate living conditions because at that time the concept of the "constant IQ" was thoroughly ingrained in the theoretical formulations about the nature of intelligence. In recent years, with the accumulation of evidence that children's IQs do change, and that these changes often appear to result from environmental conditions, numerous studies designed to assess the effects on mental abilities of various types of interventions have been reported. These interventions may be concerned with improving motivation, or supplying opportunities to learn, or reducing anxiety, or eliminating debilitating diseases and malnutrition.

A good example of an experiment to increase mental abilities in young children is the one at Peabody College, in which the aim is to control the environment through appropriate reinforcements. Gray and Klaus (1965) made an interim report at the end of the third year of this 5-year project to improve the mental abilities of culturally deprived Negro children. From an analysis of the general environments of these children they selected five most probably relevant dimensions of patterns of interaction between the children and adults. These dimensions are (1) total amount of reinforcement of the child's behaviors, (2) the source of reinforcement, (3) the amount of verbal reinforcement, (4) the direction of reinforcement, and (5) the focus of the reinforcement. That is, (1) the culturally deprived mother spends her time *coping with*, rather than *shaping* her child's behavior, (2) those reinforcements the child gets are most often from siblings and peers, (3) very little of the reinforcement is verbal, (4) it is directed toward keeping the child quiet and easy to manage and thus discourages spontaneity and curiosity, and (5) it is vague and general ("you're a bad boy") rather than relevant to specific behaviors.

In a research design involving 87 children, divided into two experimental and two control groups, starting at 3 years all children were given mental tests twice a year for 3 years, with plans for two additional annual follow-up tests. One experimental group was given special nursery school training for 3 summers, the second experimental group, starting at 4 years, had 2 summer school training sessions. In the original tests the average Stanford-Binet IQ of the experimental groups was 88; that of the control groups was 86. At the end of the third year the experimental groups' IQs averaged 95, whereas the control groups' IQs had dropped to 81. The difference is significant at the .05 level of confidence, or better. Similar differences were obtained for the Peabody Picture Vocabulary Test (Dunn, 1959) and the Illinois Test of Psycholinguistic Abilities (McCarthy and Kirk, 1961–1963).

Recently an enrichment program for institutionalized mongoloids (Bayley, 1966c; Bayley, Rhodes, and Gooch, 1966) has shown that intensive training with emphasis on language can increase the mental scores of 4- to 6-year-old mongoloids to levels more in line with the performances of a home-reared matched control sample.

Such increases, as exemplified in the preceding and other studies, at least have the practical effect of increasing the level of the children's mental functioning at the time. A further question that may be asked here is the extent to which the beneficial effect of these training experiments is maintained as the children grow older. Skeels (1966) has shown that the benefits do last for a small sample of 13 institutionalized Iowa children who were mentally retarded as infants. These babies were given enriched experiences that involved individualized love and attention from adult mother-surrogates, and all but two were later placed in adoptive homes. The mean IQ of these children at 18 months when the study started was 64; and on the latest testing at 6 years, their mean IQ was 96, a gain of 30 points. A contrast group from the orphanage had a mean IQ of 87 at 17 months and of 66 at 7 years, a loss of 21 points. In his follow-up study of these two groups as adults Skeels found striking differences between them. For example, the experimental group had a median of twelfth-grade education, the contrast group of third grade. Eleven of the experimental group were married, nine of them had children; only two men of the control group had married, and one had one child. Those in the experimental group were self-supporting or functioning well as housewives; those in the contrast group were either inmates of an institution or unskilled laborers. On the Warner scale of socioeconomic status the experimental group fell in the lower-middle-class category; the contrast group in the lower-lower class. Clearly, the early gains of the experimental group had been maintained.

The extent to which such environments are impoverished in a meaningful way is to some degree a function of the child's stage of mental development. Rheingold (1956) has shown that the enrichment provided by the one-person mothering of 6- to 8-month-old institutionalized infants did not show increased mental growth, although it did increase the baby's social responsiveness. A follow-up on these children a year later (Rheingold and Bayley, 1959) showed no differences between the experimental (mothered) babies in either IQ or social responsiveness, although the mothered babies were perhaps a little more talkative. If these findings are related to the information from the factor analyses of mental organization in the first year, we may tentatively assume that a rather simple bland environment is not depriving until the children are about 8 to 10 months old, and capable of perceptual discriminations in which meaningful relationships among objects and events are recognized, and incipient language communication is present.

The Role of Emotions, Attitudes, and Drives

In recent years there is increasing evidence from several longitudinal studies for the role of the emotional climate in children's mental growth. Moss and Kagan (1958) have found moderate correlations between the children's IQs at 3 years and maternal concern with the child's achievement.

Hill and Sarason (1966) report the effects of test anxiety and defensiveness on abilities in a longitudinal study of school children. In this study increasing anxiety was related to decreasing test performance in one group of children from the first to fifth grade. For another group from fourth to sixth grades, increases in anxiety were also accompanied by lower test scores but more significantly in the boys than in the girls. As Hill and Sarason point out, during the intervals between tests "the child is faced with a number of new, important and varied tasks of a cognitive and interpersonal nature." Anxiety decreases as a child masters the problems he faces and increases as he finds new problems that he does not know how to cope with. The result appears to be an interaction between degree of anxiety and test scores. On the one hand, relief from anxiety comes from successful performance. On the other hand, severe anxiety over new difficulties may interfere with a child's full use of those abilities he does have, in his efforts to find good solutions to these new problems.

Honzik, Macfarlane, and Allen (1948), in a study of mental test performance from 2 to 18 years, show that a number of the children who experienced emotional disturbances during this period of growth maintained relatively stable IQs. On the other hand, where there were instances of marked instability, the fluctuations in IQ paralleled fluctuations in the emotional climate in the home.

One example they give indicates this kind of fluctuation in a boy whose scores were affected by the emotional climate of the home. When first tested at 21 months, his IQ was 106, he was very shy, and the mother, who was uneasy, had been subjected to periods of acute anxiety. This same child, however, at 4 years had an IQ of 140, he was less shy, and the family situation was much improved, the

mother reporting this as the best period in her marriage. At 6 years, when the mother was again acutely disturbed, the child's IQ dropped to 123. After this his test scores gradually rose as the home situation improved until at 12 years his IQ was 163. Two years later, with a recurrence of the mother's mental disturbance, the boy's IQ started dropping, and at the 18-year test, when he was depressed and worried about his heredity, his IQ had fallen further, to 122.

Another approach to the parent-child relations was made by Bayley and Schaefer (1964) for the same Berkeley Growth Study for which the correlates of socioeconomic status are presented in Fig. 10. Ratings of the mother's behavior were made from observational notes written during the testing sessions in the children's first 3 years. A second set of ratings was made from an interview with the mother about 10 years later. Both sets of these ratings may be classed, roughly, into behaviors that are warm, understanding, and loving, as opposed to punitive and harsh, and those that grant autonomy and freedom in contrast to those that are controlling and intrusive.

When the maternal behaviors are arranged in an order of neighboring, based on their intercorrelations, from autonomy through love, control, and hostility, to ignoring, the pattern of their correlations with the children's intelligence scores shows consistent shifts both with age and by sex. These patterns of relation to the early (0 to 3 years) maternal behaviors are illustrated in Fig. 12, 13, and 14. Figure 12 presents, for each sex, the correlations of the maternal behaviors with test scores in the first year. Each bar represents the average of three consecutive tests. There are four of these three-test averages for the first year, and each maternal behavior is correlated with the four levels. In the first year the boy's scores are seen to be negatively correlated with equalitarian, affectionate maternal behaviors but positively correlated with maternal hostile rejecting behaviors. For the girls these correlations are reversed. For both sexes controlling, achievement-demanding maternal behaviors are positively correlated with children's scores. As the children grow older, the pattern shifts. At the preschool ages, shown in Fig. 13, the boys' correlations become more like those for the girls. At school ages (Fig. 14)

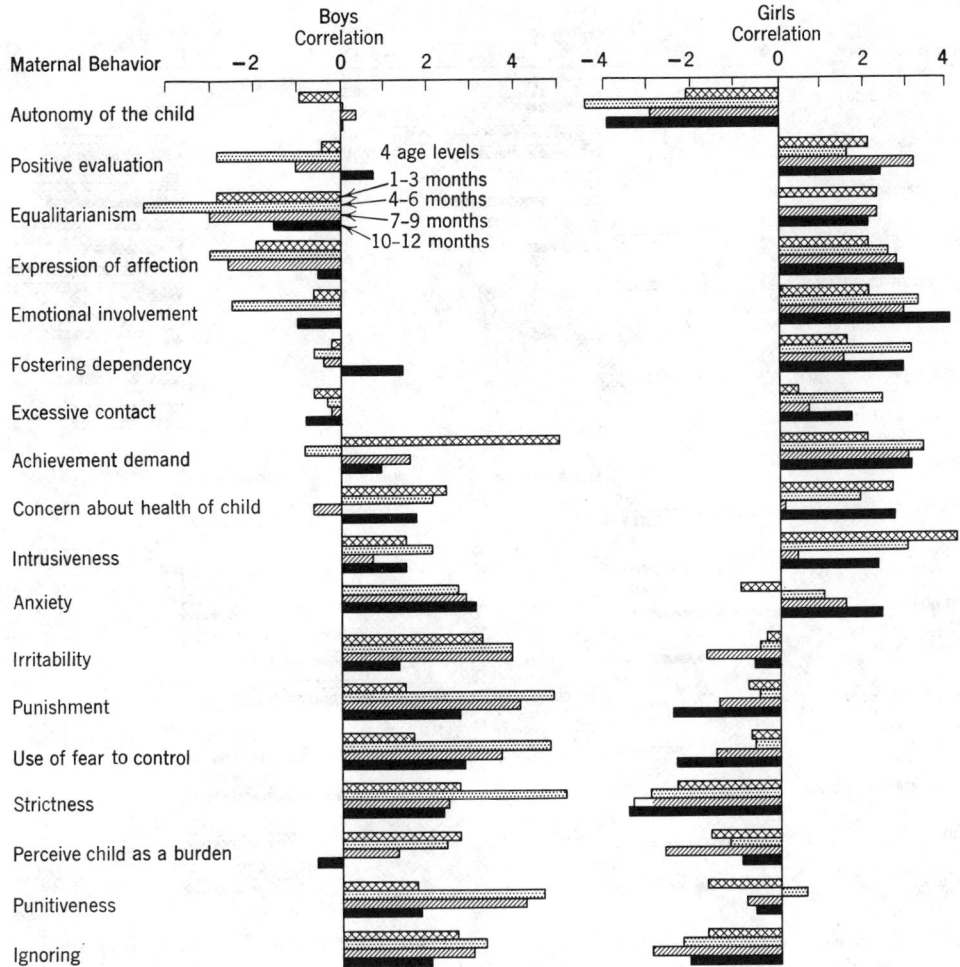

Fig. 12. Correlations between maternal behavior (0 to 3 years) and intelligence at four age-levels, 1 to 12 months. (Reprinted from Bayley and Schaefer, 1964.)

the boys' scores are seen to be clearly related to the early maternal love-hostility dimension, whereas the girls' scores are almost completely independent of these maternal variables. For the boys there is a correlational pattern which may be stated briefly: early maternal love and acceptance goes with slow development at first but later high achievement in mental abilities, with the reverse pattern for boys with punitive rejecting mothers. For the girls, although early maternal love goes with high scores in infancy, its influence diminishes after 3 years and then drops out almost completely.

The later maternal behaviors, when the children's ages were 9 to 13 years, were found to be related to their sons' intelligence in much the same way as were their early behaviors. In contrast, the girls' test scores show little or no relation to their mother's attitudes toward them as preteen-agers. In general it appears that the relatively stable maternal behaviors (which have been classified as love or warmth versus hostility or rejection) were continuously related to the boys' abilities, while the girls' abilities after 3 or 4 years remained relatively free of their mothers' behaviors.

These findings are in many ways in agreement with those from another, similar population, the Berkeley Guidance Study, as recently reported by Honzik. She investigated parent-child relationships of children's intelligence and several aspects of the family en-

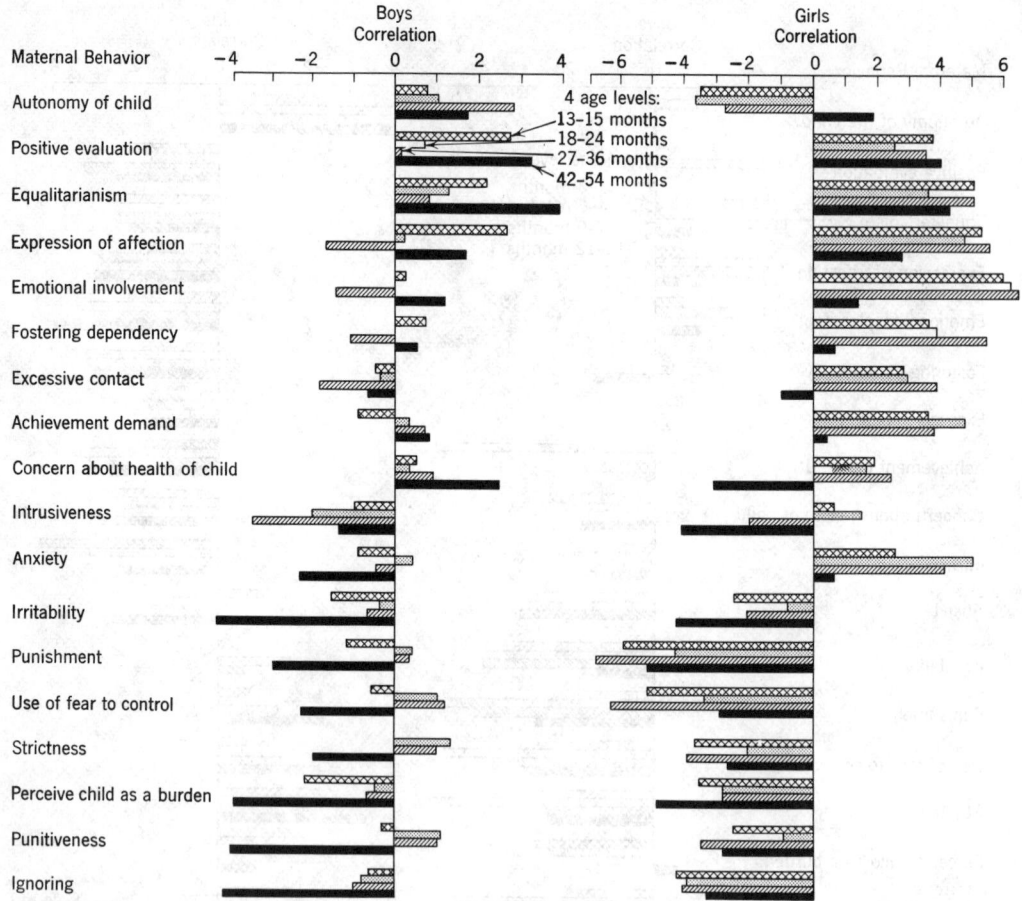

Fig. 13. Correlations between maternal behavior (0 to 3 years) and intelligence at four age-levels, 13 to 54 months. (Reprinted from Bayley and Schaefer, 1964.)

vironment as observed over time, starting when the children were 21 months old. The parental variables were correlated with children's IQs between 21 months and 18 years (1967a) and with their scores on the Wechsler-Bellevue subscales at 18 years (1967b). The importance of this longitudinal study is accentuated by the fact that there is considerable information about the fathers as well as about the mothers. The sample size at each test age varied around 55 for each sex, with a range from 39 to 59 for ages 2 to 18 years. Honzik found that for tests at ages 6 to 18 years there were consistent sex differences in the correlations with IQ. The sons' IQs correlated more highly "with a rating of close mother-son relation and with the father's occupational success and satisfaction." The daughters' IQs were positively correlated with

"father's friendliness to this daughter" and with ratings of parental compatibility. Scores of both sexes correlated positively with parents' concern for their achievement (Honzik, 1967a).

The correlations with the 18-year W-B subscale scores (Honzik, 1967b) are based on a sample of 41 boys and 40 girls. For this sample, findings on the relation between early maternal affection and children's 18-year IQs is very similar to the Bayley and Schaefer (1964) results for similar ages. Boys' Verbal IQs correlated with maternal behaviors described as "close" .56, as "friendly" .34, and as "affectionate" .27. For the "close" and "friendly" variables the mother-daughter correlations were each .29. The highest mother-daughter r was with maternal "concern about health" (.42). The girls' W-B Performance IQ was positively correlated with mothers' irritability. In contrast, the girls' but not the boys' 18-year scores, were correlated with a close affectional relationship between the father and the mother. The parent-child correlations of the early affectional relationships to the subscale scores of the 18-year Wechsler-Bellevue tests are shown in Fig. 15.

In the Berkeley Growth Study, the children's own behaviors, as rated during the tests, were seen to be related to their mental scores (Bayley and Schaefer, 1964). These relations may be summed briefly as follows.

Boy babies who were rated as happy, positively responding, and calm tended to have low scores in the first year or so and high scores by 4 or 5 years and later. If they were active between 10 and 15 months, their scores were high early but low after 4 years; if they were active after 15 months, the pattern of mental scores was reversed, that is, active 2-year-old boys tended to have high IQs at later ages. As for the girls, happy, positive, and calm behaviors correlated with high mental scores early, but the correlations approached zero after 3 or 4 years.

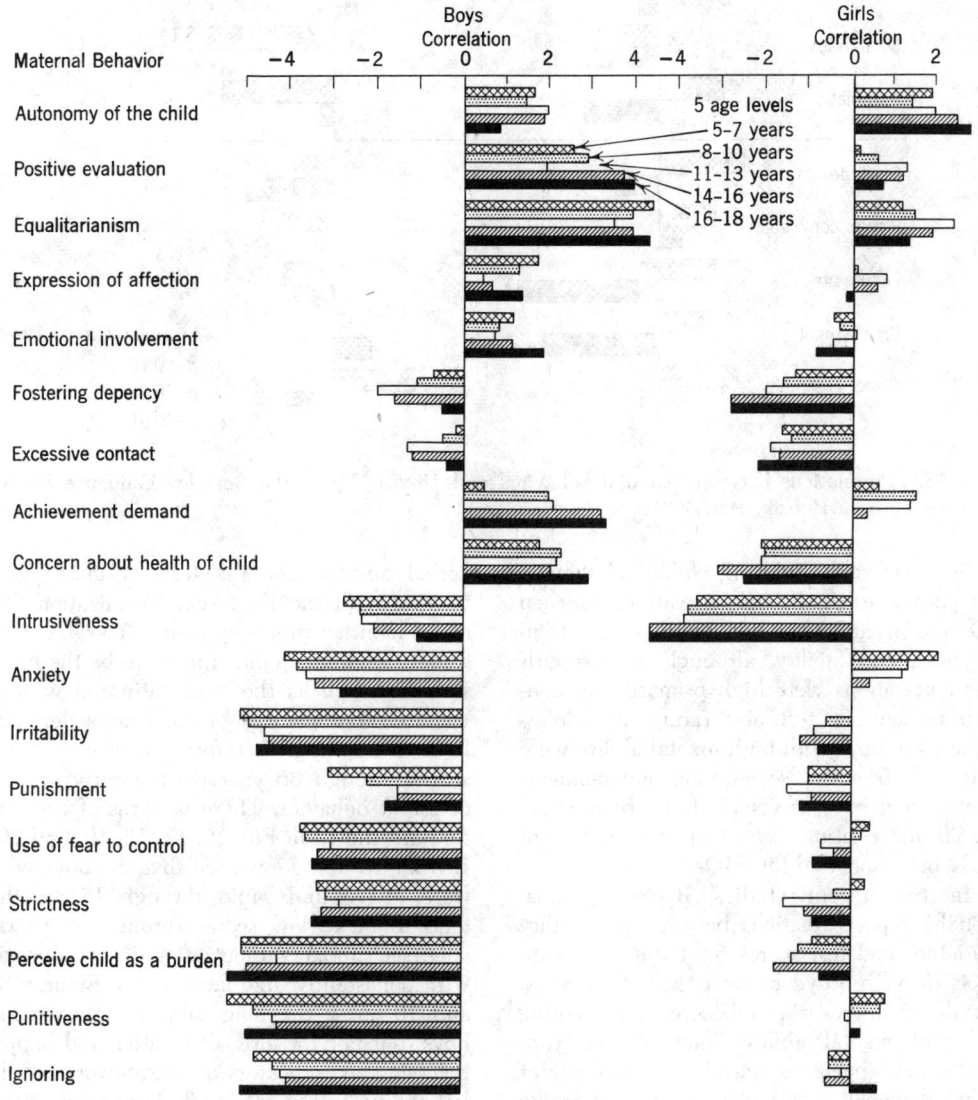

Fig. 14.   Correlations between maternal behavior (0 to 3 years) and intelligence at five age-levels, 5 to 18 years. (Reprinted from Bayley and Schaefer, 1964.)

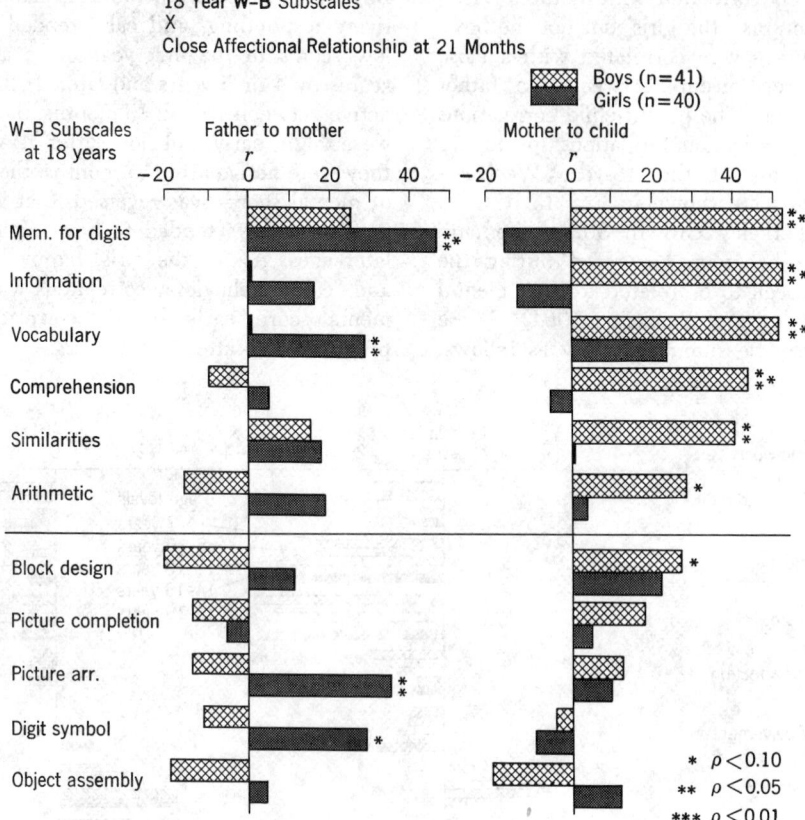

Fig. 15. Correlations between parental behaviors and 18-year IQ in the Berkeley Guidance Study. (Reprinted from Honzik, 1967.)

Series of ratings during childhood showed for both sexes significant correlations between IQ and friendliness, cooperativeness, attentiveness, and facility, although for the girls the correlations were high primarily for concurrent ages at test and rating. At adolescence, the boys with high mental ability were rated as friendly, social, and independent; low-scoring boys as reserved. There were no significant relations between the adolescent girls' behaviors and their IQs.

In two recent studies Bayley (1968a, 1968b) reports relations between personality variables and test scores for these same subjects through 36 years for a total of 54 cases. In these studies the subscores representing different mental ability "factors" and subscales have been compared with two sets of adult personality variables in addition to the earlier behavior ratings.

It has been possible to obtain scores of verbal ability from the tests at most ages, starting with the First-Year Vocalization (8- to 14-month) precocity score. These verbal scores, for this sample, appear to be the most stable as well as the most saturated with g (general intelligence) of the factors derived. It is interesting therefore to relate verbal scores through 36 years to the early ratings of infant behavior. These patterns of correlation are shown in Fig. 16, 17, 18, 19, and 20. In Fig. 16 and 17 we see that the boys who were active and rapid through 15 months tend to make low scores through 36 years, whereas similar ratings after 15 months go with persistently high later scores. Figures 18 and 19 show the long-range persistence for boys, but not for girls, of positive and happy behaviors as indicators of above-average verbal ability. In Fig. 20, we find some indication that girl but not boy babies, who were shy before 2 years are among those who later

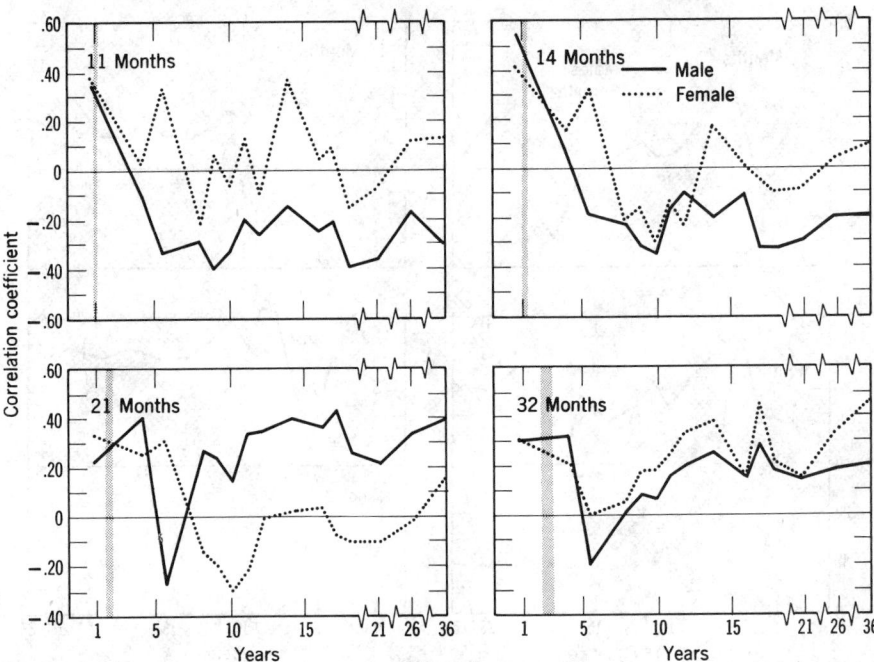

Fig. 16. Correlations between ratings of Activity at ages 10 to 36 months and Verbal scores for all ages 1 to 36. (Reprinted from Bayley, 1968b.)

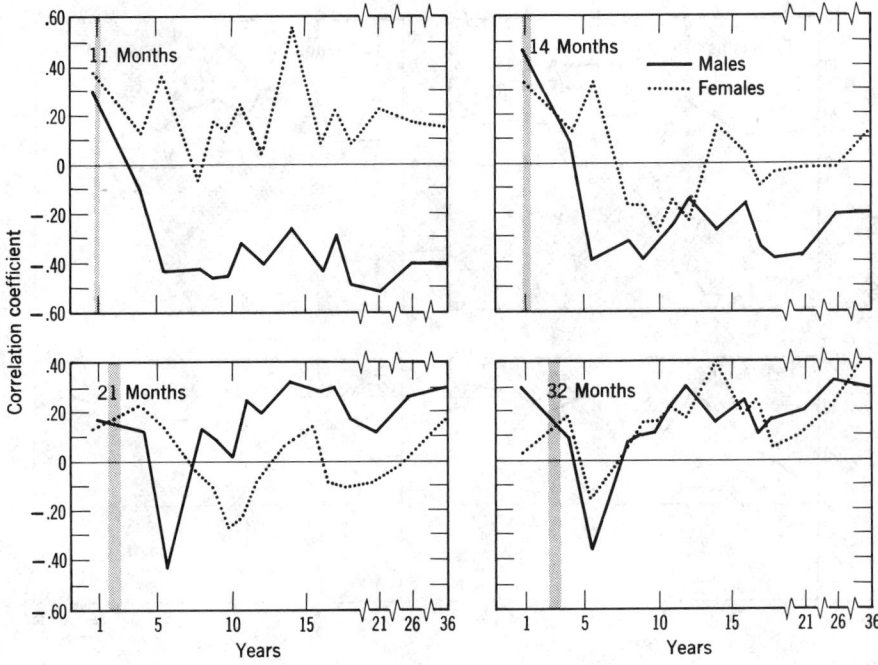

Fig. 17. Correlations between ratings of Rapidity at ages 10 to 36 months and Verbal scores for all ages 1 to 36 years. (Reprinted from Bayley, 1968b.)

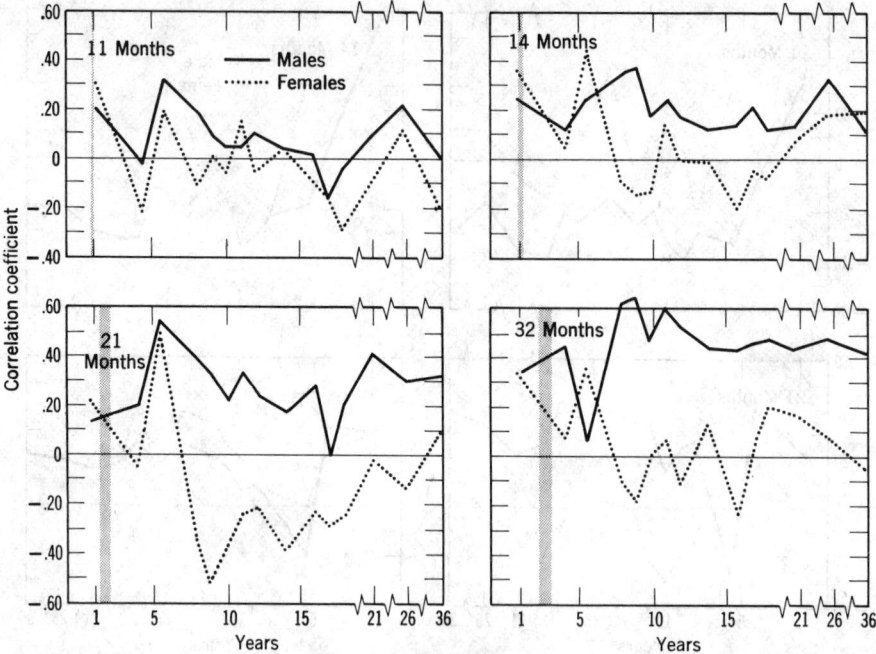

Fig. 18. Correlations between ratings of Positive Behavior at ages 10 to 36 months and Verbal scores for all ages 1 to 36 years. (Reprinted from Bayley, 1968b.)

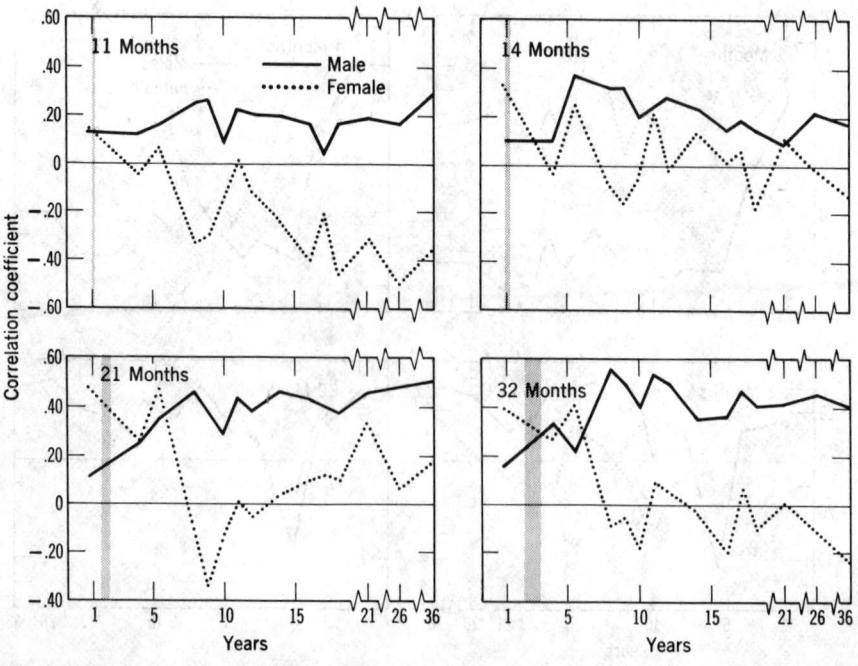

Fig. 19. Correlations between ratings of Happiness at ages 10 to 36 months and Verbal scores for all ages 1 to 36 years. (Reprinted from Bayley, 1968b.)

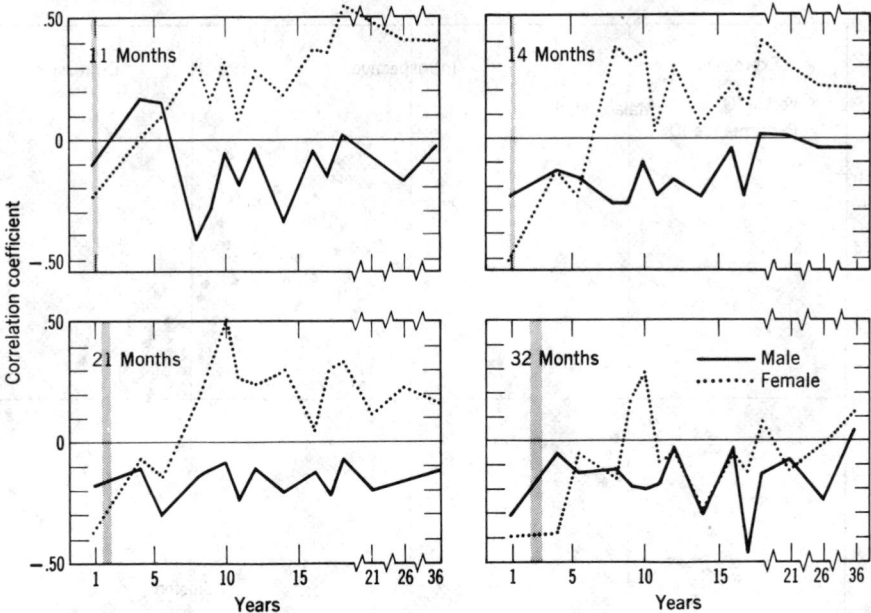

Fig. 20. Correlations between ratings of Shyness at ages 10 to 36 months and Verbal scores for all ages 1 to 36 years. (Reprinted from Bayley, 1968b.)

score high in verbal ability. In general, the scores after 4 years show very different relations to these infant behaviors than do the scores earned at the time.

Another aspect of the relations between mental abilities and attitudes and interests is revealed in the correlations with the Wechsler scale scores at 16 to 36 years. These have been correlated with scores on sets of 70 behaviors based on Q-sorts (with the Block Q set; Block, 1961). The behaviors have been arranged in a Guttman (1954) order of neighboring, or circumplex. The circumplex arrangement places a set of variables in a circular order in such a way that highly intercorrelated items are close together, uncorrelated items are about 90° apart on the circle, and negatively correlated items are on opposite sides of the circle, with the strongest negative correlation 180° apart.

Examples of related behaviors with their angular placements on the circumplex for the males in this sample are such uncontrolled or expressive behaviors as: 18° Expresses hostile feelings directly, 33° Represses anxiety and conflicts, 46° Is self-indulgent, 58° Unable to delay gratification, 69° Irritable, 72° Transfers blame to others. Withdrawn be-

haviors include: 110° Vulnerable to threats, 121° Submissive, 126° Keeps people at a distance, 144° Avoids action. Generally intellectual behaviors are: 232° Socially perceptive, 236° Values intellectual matters, 244° Wide range of interests, 246° High intellectual capacity, 252° Sees to heart of important problems. Expressive adjusted or gregarious behaviors are: 273° Has warmth and capacity for close relationships, 277° Objective, 278° Calm and relaxed, 280° Good-looking, 285° Gets things done, 288° Liked and accepted by others, 312° Satisfied with self.

The circumplex for females is similar to the males', except that the maladjusted half of the circle is better described by the terms conventional and negative. The conventional quadrant includes such items as 11° Fastidious, 16° Conservative, 34° Conventional, 37° Moralistic, 49° Transfers blame to others, 63° Bland. The negative quadrant includes 99° Self-pitying, 102° Subtly negativistic, 109° Persistent and preoccupying thoughts, 111° Irritable, 111° Hostile, 116° Moody, 136° Changeable. The Intellectual and Gregarious behaviors on the adjusted half of the circle are very similar to those of the males.

With this organization of the ratings of

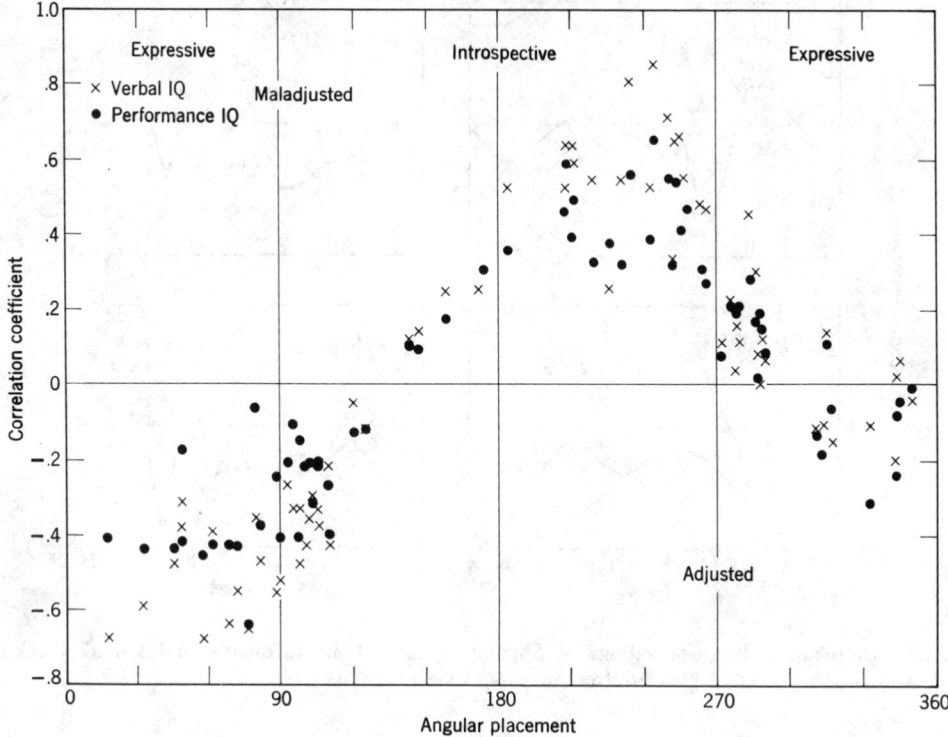

Fig. 21. Circumplex-ordered correlations between 36-year Block Q-set scores and WAIS Verbal and Performance IQs at 36 years for males. (Reprinted from Bayley, 1968b.)

patterns of behaviors, it is possible to compare the relations between behavior tendencies (or personalities) and mental abilities. The pattern of correlations with the Verbal and Performance WAIS scores at 36 years is shown for the males in Fig. 21 and for the females in Fig. 22. The correlations for both parts of the test are high with behaviors which are characterized as introspective-adjusted, that is, High intellectual capacity, Wide interest, Thoughtful, and Fluent, whereas strong negative correlations are found with maladjusted expressive behaviors such as Uncontrolled, Expresses hostile feelings freely, Impatient. The correlations show greater extremes with the verbal than with the nonverbal scale. The correlational pattern for the females (Fig. 22), although it tends to follow the same directions of positive and negative correlations, is much less marked. Other comparisons show that the pattern for the males is as strong with the 16-year Wechsler-Bellevue tests as with that shown in Fig. 21 for 36 years. However, for the

females the relations across time drop out. There are evidences also, for each sex, of somewhat different patterns of correlations between the Q-sort variables and the different subscales of the Wechsler tests. The pattern of correlations is even reversed in the 16-year Information and Arithmetic scales. For example, at 16 years the girls' correlation between scores on Arithmetic and "Warmth" is −.42 and with "Charm" is −.62; positive correlations are found between Arithmetic and "Feels a lack of personal meaning in life" (.48) and "Is subtly negativistic" (.64).

In another study (Bayley, 1968a) these same Wechsler scores have been correlated with the 18 behaviors of the California Psychological Inventory (Gough, 1957), a self-rating instrument. In this study, again, there are patterns of positive and negative correlations with test scores, and marked sex differences. The sexes are most alike in their relations to verbal scores (Fig. 23), whereas the greatest differences are for Digit Span (Fig. 24).

It is evident that the behavioral and emotional correlates of mental abilities are complex, and there is need to explore these differences more thoroughly. From much of the evidence discussed here, there are clear indications that mental abilities of males are more strongly related than the females, both positively and negatively, to emotional aspects of their environment. There are also indications that for the boys, early experiences are likely to have long-lasting effects, even though the nature of these effects may not at first be evident.

SUMMARY

In following the processes of mental growth from birth to some time near 30 years, when growth in most mental test scores finally appears to level off, it becomes clear that mental abilities are complex both in their nature and in their causes. With growth, abilities change in nature as they become increasingly complex and as they move from concrete to abstract processes. Abilities which are characteristic of a given stage of develop-

ment may or may not be predictive of later mental capacities.

In general, mental test scores indicate variable rates of growth in the first 3 or 4 years, but become more stable after that age.

The most stable of the mental abilities which have been differentiated appear to be verbal in nature. Verbal scores stabilize earlier in girls. However, once established, the boys' verbal scores may be more consistent than the girls'.

There is some evidence that during growth mental abilities in females are more independent of emotional climates than is true for males. There are also some indications that for the males early emotional conditions may be more persistent in their effects on later mental growth.

Such characteristics as degrees of drive, perseverance, and attention span, which themselves are in varying degrees genetically determined, may operate to enhance or retard the development of mental abilities.

The complex interaction of genetic potentials and environmental stimulation, in the

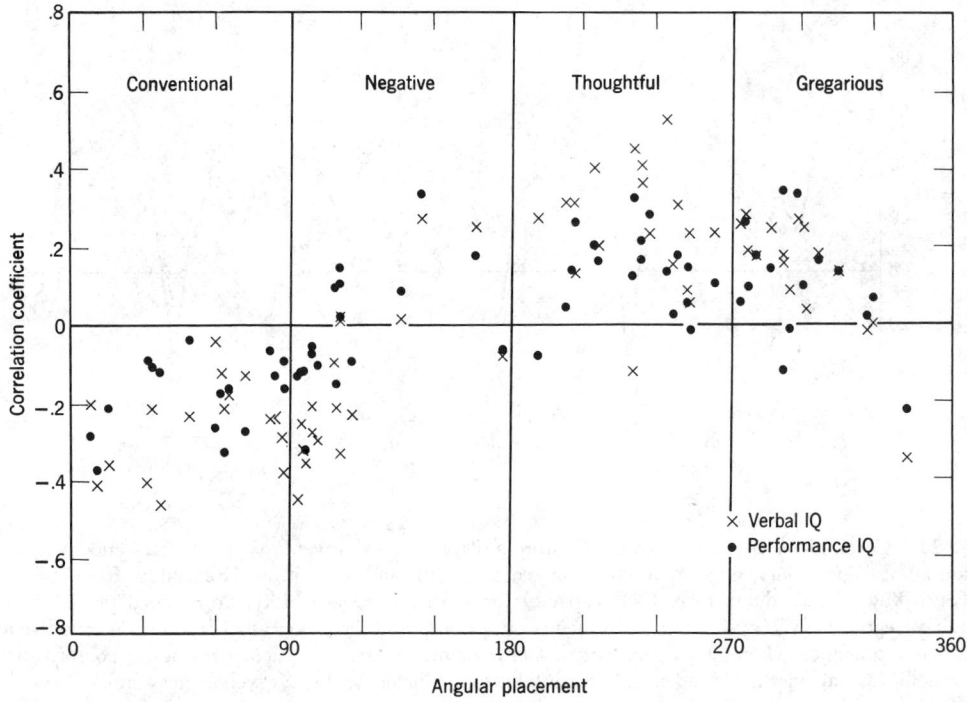

Fig. 22. Circumplex-ordered correlations between 36-year Block Q-set scores and WAIS Verbal and Performance IQs at 36 years for females. (Reprinted from Bayley, 1968b.)

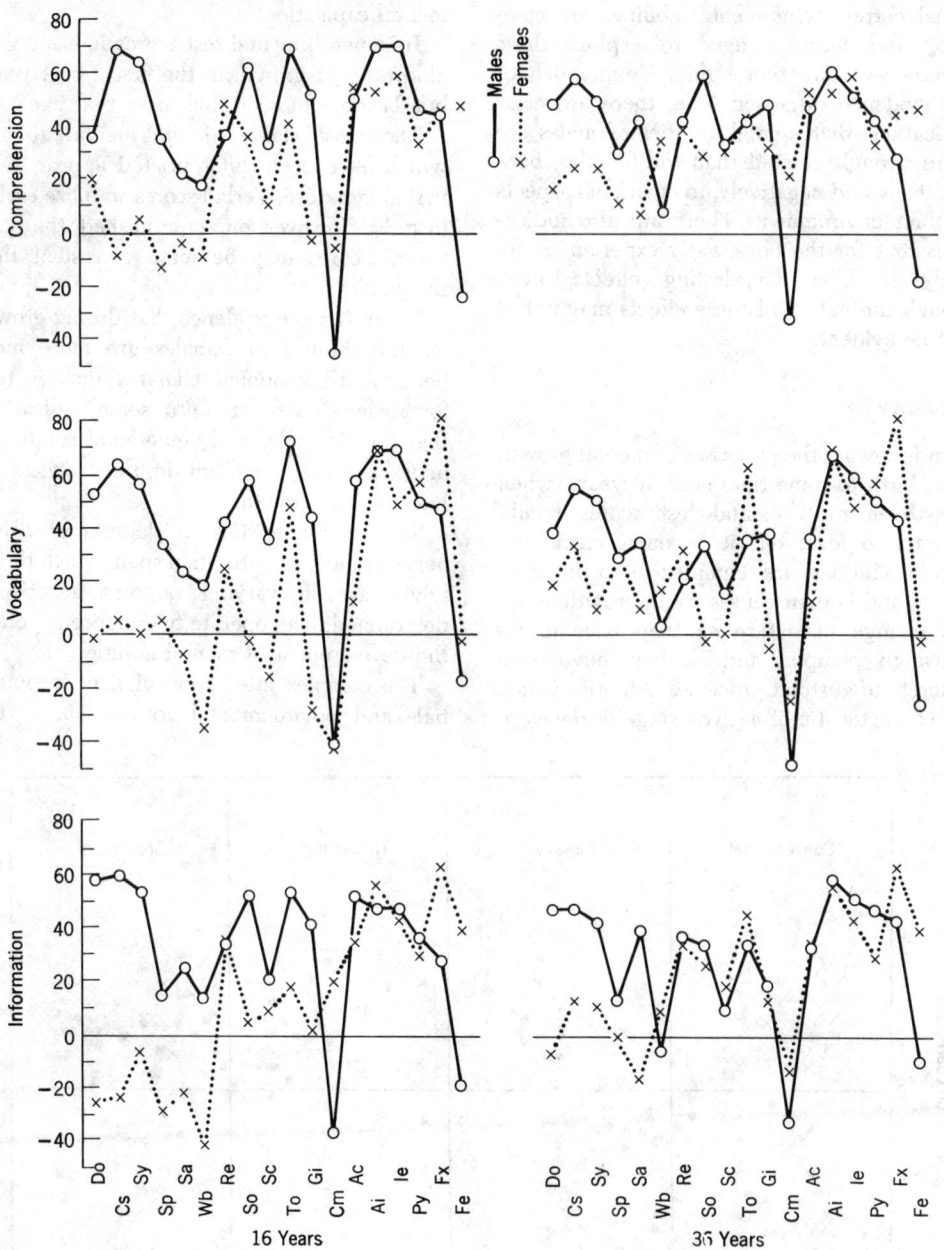

Fig. 23. Correlations by sex between California Psychological Inventory at 36 years and Wechsler Information, Vocabulary, and Comprehension scores at 16 and 36 years. (Reprinted from Bayley, 1968c.) Key: Do = dominance, Cs = capacity for status, Sy = sociability, Sp = social presence, Sa, = self-acceptance, Wb = sense of well-being, Re = responsibility, So = socialization, Sc = self-control, To = tolerance, Gi = good impression, Cm = communality, Ac = achievement via conformance, Ai = achievement via independence, Ie = intellectual efficiency, Py = psychological-mindedness, Fx = flexibility, Fe = femininity.

context of maturing and pliable neural structures, presents a setting in which the exact expression of mental abilities may be impossible to predict. However, we have in this complex process a number of indicators of the best ways to facilitate mental growth.

In essence, given the undamaged genetic potential, mental growth is best facilitated by a supportive, "warm" emotional climate, together with ample opportunities for the positive reinforcement of specific cognitive efforts and successes.

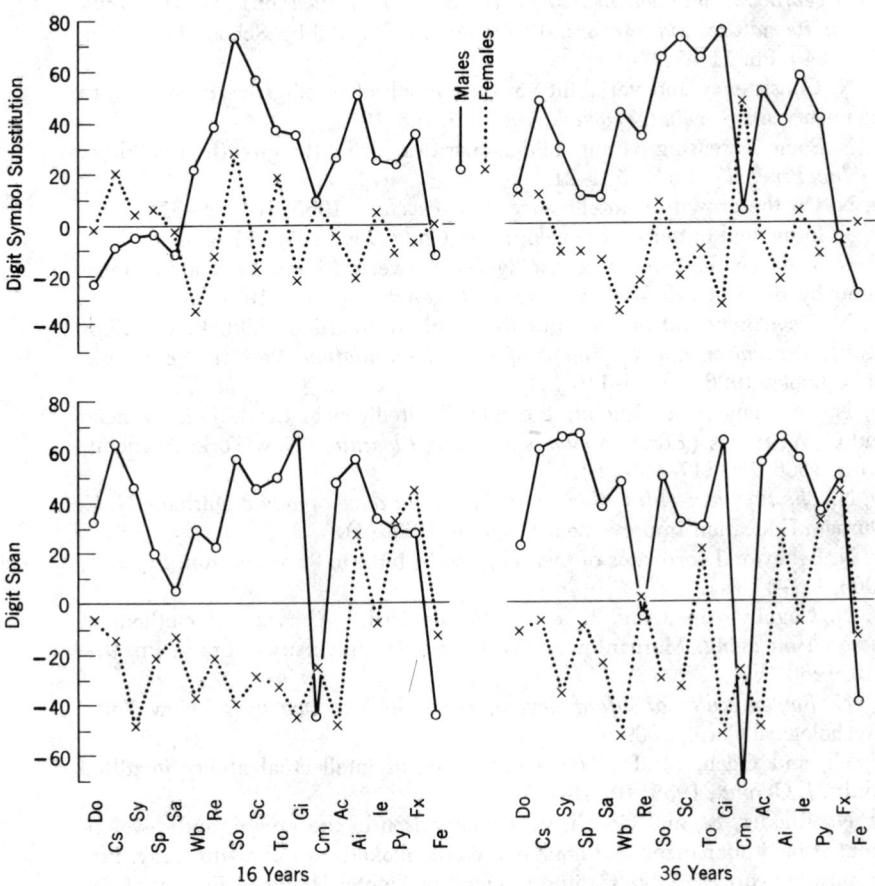

Fig. 24. Correlations by sex between California Psychological Inventory at 36 years and Wechsler Digit Span and Substitution scores at 16 and 36 years. (Reprinted from Bayley, 1968c.) See Fig. 23 for key.

References

Anastasi, A. *Psychological testing.* (2nd ed.) New York: Macmillan, 1961.

Anokhin, P. K. The developing brain. *Prog. Brain Res.*, 1964, 9, 54–86.

Baldwin, B. T., and Stecher, L. I. Additional data from consecutive Stanford-Binet tests. *J. Educ.*, 1922, 13, 556–560.

Baller, W. R. A study of the present social status of a group of adults who, when they were in elementary schools, were classified as mentally deficient. *Genet. Psychol. Monogr.*, 1936, 15, 285–295.

Bayley, N. *The California first-year mental scale*. Berkeley: University of California Press, Syllabus Series No. 243, 1933 (a).

Bayley, N. Mental growth during the first three years. A developmental study of 61 children by repeated tests. *Genet. Psychol. Monogr.*, 1933, **14**, 1–92 (b).

Bayley, N. *The California infant scale of motor development*. Berkeley. University of California Press, Syllabus Series No. 259, 1936.

Bayley, N. Mental growth in young children. In G. M. Whipple (Ed.), *Thirty-ninth yearbook, national Society for the Study of Education*. Part II. *Intelligence: its nature and nurture*. Bloomington, Ill.: Public School Publishing Co., 1940. Pp. 11–47.

Bayley, N. Consistency and variability in the growth of intelligence from birth to eighteen years. *J. genet. Psychol.*, 1949, **75**, 165–196.

Bayley, N. Some increasing parent-child similarities during the growth of children. *J. educ. Psychol.*, 1954, **45**, 1–21.

Bayley, N. On the growth of intelligence. *Am. Psychol.*, 1955, **10**, 805–818.

Bayley, N. Individual patterns of development. *Child Dev.*, 1956, **27**, 45–74.

Bayley, N. Data on the growth of intelligence between 16 and 21 years as measured by the Wechsler-Bellevue Scale. *J. genet. Psychol.*, 1957, **90**, 3–15.

Bayley, N. Developmental problems of the mentally retarded child. In I. Philips (Ed.), *Prevention and treatment of mental retardation*. Part II. New York: Basic Books, 1966. Pp. 85–110 (a).

Bayley, N. Learning in adulthood: the role of intelligence. In H. J. Klausmeier and C. W. Harris (Eds.), *Analyses of concept learning*. New York: Academic Press, 1966. Pp. 117–138 (b).

Bayley, N. *The two-year-old: is this a critical age for development?* Durham, N. C. Durham Education Improvement Program, 1966 (c).

Bayley, N. Behavioral correlates of mental growth: birth to 36 years. *Am. Psychol.*, 1968, **1**, 1–17 (a).

Bayley, N. Cognition in aging. In K. W. Schaie (Ed.), Theory and methods of *research on aging*. Morgantown: West Virginia University Library. Pp. 97–119, 1968 (b).

Bayley, N. *Bayley scales of infant development: birth to two years*. New York: Psychological Corp., 1969.

Bayley, N., and Oden, M. H. The maintenance of intellectual ability in gifted adults. *J. Geront.*, 1955, **10**, 91–107.

Bayley, N., Rhodes, L., and Gooch, B. A comparison of the growth and development of institutionalized and home-reared mongoloids: a follow-up study. Pre-publication copy no. 356, California Dept. of Mental Hygiene, Bureau of Research, 1966.

Bayley, N., and Schaefer, E. S. Correlations of maternal and child behaviors with the development of mental abilities: data from the Berkeley Growth Study. *Monogr. Soc. Res. Child Dev.*, 1964, **29** (6, Whole No. 97).

Bennett, E. L., Diamond, M., Krech, D., and Rosenzweig, M. R. Chemical and anatomical plasticity of the brain. *Science*, 1964, **146**, 610–619.

Birren, J. E. Psychological aspects of aging: intellectual functioning. *The Gerontologist*, 1968, **8**, 16–19.

Block, J. *The Q-sort method in personality assessment and psychiatric research*. Springfield, Ill.: Thomas, 1961.

Bloom, B. S. *Stability and change in human characteristics*. New York. Wiley, 1964.

Bowlby, J. *Maternal care and mental health*. Geneva: World Health Organization, Monograph Series No. 2, 1952.

Boynton, P. *Intelligence: its manifestations and measurement*. New York: Appleton-Century-Crofts, 1933.

Brodbeck, A. J., and Irwin, O. C. The speech behavior of infants without families. *Child Dev.*, 1946, **17**, 145–156.

Bühler, Ch. *The first year of life*. New York: Day, 1930.

Burt, C. The genetic determination of differences in intelligence: a study of monozygotic twins reared together and apart. *Br. J. Psychol.*, 1966, **57**, 1–2; 137–153.

Burt, C., Jones, E., Miller, E., and Moodie, W. *How the mind works*. New York: Appleton-Century-Crofts, 1934.

Cameron, J., Livson, N., and Bayley, N. Infant vocalizations and their relationship to mature intelligence. *Science*, 1967, **157**, 331–333.

Carmichael, L. The onset and early development of behaviors. In L. Carmichael (Ed.), *Manual of child psychology*. (2nd ed.) New York: Wiley, 1954. Pp. 60–185.

Cattell, P. *The measurement of intelligence of infants and young children*. New York: Science Press, 1940; Psychological Corp., 1960.

Cattell, R. B. *The IPAT culture fair intelligence scales*. Champaign, Ill.: Institute for Personality and Ability Testing, 1957.

Cattell, R. B. Theory of fluid and crystallized intelligence: a critical experiment. *J. educ. Psychol.*, 1963. **54**, 1–22.

Charles, D. C. Ability and accomplishment of persons earlier judged mentally deficient. *Genet. Psychol. Monogr.*, 1953, **47**, 3–71.

Charles, D. C., and James, S. The development of average abilities. *J. genet. Psychol.*, 1964, **105**, 105–111.

Christensen, P. R., and Guilford, J. P. *Ship destination test*. Beverly Hills, Cal.: Sheridan Supply Co., 1955–1956.

Coghill, G. E. *Anatomy and the problem of behavior*. New York: Macmillan, 1929.

Conrad, H. S., Freeman, F. N., and Jones, H. E. Differential mental growth. In N. B. Henry (Ed.), *Forty-third yearbook, National Society for the Study of Education*. Part I. *Adolescence*. Chicago: University of Chicago Press, 1944. Pp. 164–184.

Conrad, H. S., and Jones, H. E. A second study of familial resemblance in intelligence: environmental and genetic implications of parent-child and sibling correlations in the total sample. In G. M. Whipple (Ed.), *Thirty-ninth yearbook, National Society for the Study of Education*. Part II. *Intelligence: its nature and nurture*. Chicago: University of Chicago Press, 1940. Pp. 97–141.

Dearborn, W. F., and Rothney, J. *Predicting the child's development*. Cambridge, Mass.: Science-Art Publ., 1941.

Dunn, L. M. *Peabody picture vocabulary test*. Minneapolis, Minn.: American Guidance Service, 1959.

Ebert, E., and Simmons, K. The Brush Foundation study of child growth and development. I. Psychometric tests. *Monogr. Soc. Res. Child Dev.*, 1943, **8** (2, Whole No. 35).

Fischer, L. Hospitalism in six-month-old infants. *Am. J. Orothopsychiat.*, 1952, **22**, 522–533.

Freedman, D. G. Constitutional and environmental interactions in rearing of four breeds of dogs. *Science*, 1958, **127**, 585–586.

Freedman, D. G., and Keller, B. Inheritance of behavior in infants. *Science*, 1963, **140**, 196–198.

Freeman, F. N., and Flory, C. D. Growth in intellectual ability as measured by repeated tests. *Monogr. Soc. Res. Child Dev.*, 1937, **2** (2, Whole No. 9).

Furfey, P. H., and Muehlenbein, J. The validity of infant intelligence tests. *J. genet. Psychol.*, 1932, **40**, 219–223.

Galton, F. *Hereditary genius*. London: Macmillan, 1869.

Gesell, A. *The mental growth of the preschool child*. New York: Macmillan, 1925.

Gesell, A. *Infancy and human growth.* New York: Macmillan, 1928.

Gesell, A., and Amatruda, C. *Developmental diagnosis: normal and abnormal child development, clinical methods and practical applications.* (3rd ed.) New York: Harper, 1962.

Gilliland, A. R. Environmental influences on infant intelligence test scores. *Harvard Educ. Rev.*, 1949, **19**, 142–146 (a).

Gilliland, A. R. *Northwestern intelligence tests for measuring adaptation to the physical and social environment: Test A, ages 4–12 weeks; Test B, ages 13–36 weeks.* Boston: Houghton Mifflin, 1949 (b).

Goddard, H. H. A measuring scale for intelligence. *The Training School*, 1910, **6**, 146–155.

Goldfarb, W. Effects of psychological deprivation in infancy and subsequent stimulation. *Am. J. Psychiat.*, 1945, **102**, 18–33.

Goldfarb, W. Emotional and intellectual consequences of psychologic deprivation in infancy: a revaluation. In P. H. Hoch and J. Zubin (Eds.), *Psychopathology of childhood.* New York: Grune & Stratton, 1955. Pp. 105–119.

Goodenough, F. L. The relation of the intelligence of preschool children to the education of their parents. *School and Society*, 1927, **26**, 1–3.

Goodenough, F. L. *Mental testing.* New York: Rhinehart, 1949.

Goodenough, F. L. The measurement of mental growth in childhood. In L. Carmichael (Ed.), *Manual of child psychology.* (2nd ed.) New York: Wiley, 1954. Pp. 459–491.

Gough, H. G. *Manual for the California psychological inventory.* Palo Alto: Consulting Psychologists Press, 1957.

Graham, F. K., Matarazzo, R. G., and Caldwell, B. M. Behavioral differences between normal and traumatized newborns. II. Standardization, reliability, and validity. *Psychol. Monogr.*, 1956, **70** (21, Whole No. 428).

Gray, S. W., and Klaus, R. A. An experimental preschool program for culturally deprived children. *Child Dev.*, 1965, **36**, 887–898.

Griffiths, R. *The abilities of babies: a study in mental measurement.* New York: McGraw-Hill, 1954.

Guilford, J. P. The structure of intellect. *Psychol. Bull.*, 1956, **53**, 267–293.

Guilford, J. P. A revised structure of intellect. *Reports from the Psychological Laboratory: The University of Southern California, Los Angeles*, 1957, No. 19.

Guttman, L. A new approach to factor analysis: the radex. In P. F. Lazarsfeld (Ed.), *Mathematical thinking in the social sciences.* Glencoe, Ill.: Free Press, 1954. Pp. 258–348.

Harlow, H. The development of learning in the Rhesus monkey. In W. R. Brode (Ed.), *Science in progress: twelfth series.* New Haven, Conn.: Yale University Press, 1962. Pp. 239–269.

Hayes, K. J. Genes, drives, and intellect. *Psychol. Rep.*, 1962, **10**, 299–342.

Hertzka, A. F., and Guilford, J. P. *Logical reasoning.* Beverly Hills, Cal.: Sheridan Supply Co., 1955.

Hilden, A. H. A longitudinal study of intellectual development. *J. Psychol.*, 1949, **28**, 187–214.

Hill, K. T., and Sarason, S. B. The relation of test anxiety and defensiveness to test and school performance over the elementary-school years. *Monogr. Soc. Res. Child Dev.*, 1966, 31 (2, Whole No. 104).

Hindley, C. B. The Griffiths scale of infant development: scores and predictions from 3 to 18 months. *Child Psychol. Psychiat.*, 1960, **1**, 99–112.

Honzik, M. P. Developmental studies of parent-child resemblance in intelligence. *Child Dev.*, 1957, **28**, 215–228.

Honzik, M. P. A sex difference in the age of onset of the parent-child resemblance in intelligence. *J. educ. Psychol.*, 1963, **54**, 231–237.

Honzik, M. P. Environmental correlates of mental growth: predictions from the family setting at 21 months. *Child Dev.*, 1967, 38, 337–364 (a).

Honzik, M. P. Prediction of differential abilities at age 18 from the early family environment. *Proc. 75th Ann. Con., APA*, 1967, 151–152 (b).

Honzik, M. P., Macfarlane, J., and Allen, L. The stability of mental test performance between two and eighteen years. *J. exp. Educ.*, 1948, 4, 309–324.

Hooker, D. Reflex activities in the human fetus. In R. Barker, J. S. Kounin, and H. F. Wright (Eds.), *Child behavior and development.* New York: McGraw-Hill, 1943. Pp. 17–28.

Horn, J. L., and Cattell, R. B. Refinement and test of the theory of fluid and crystallized general intelligences. *J. educ. Psychol.*, 1966, 57, 253–270.

Hunt, J. McV. *Intelligence and experience.* New York: Ronald Press, 1961.

Jaffa, A. S. *The California preschool mental scale, form A.* Berkeley: University of California Press, Syllabus Series No. 251, 1934.

Jones, H. E. The environment and mental development. In L. Carmichael (Ed.), *Manual of child psychology.* (2nd ed.) New York: Wiley, 1954. Pp. 631–696.

Jones, H. E., and Conrad, H. S. The growth and decline of intelligence: a study of a homogeneous group between the ages of ten and sixty. *Genet. Psychol. Monogr.*, 1933, 13, 223–298.

Kagan, J., and Moss, H. A. Parental correlates of child's IQ and height: a cross-validation of the Berkeley Growth Study results. *Child Dev.*, 1959, 30, 325–332.

Kuhlmann, F. A revision of the Binet-Simon system for measuring the intelligence of children. *J. Psycho-Asth., Monogr. Suppl.*, 1912.

Kuhlmann, F. *Tests of mental development. A complete scale for individual examination.* Minneapolis, Minn.: Educational Test Bureau, 1939.

Lesser, G. H., Fifer, G., and Clark, D. H. Mental abilities of children from different social-class and cultural groups. *Monogr. Soc. Res. Child Dev.*, 1965, 30 (4, Whole No. 102).

Levy, R. J. Effects of institutional versus boarding home care on a group of infants. *J. Personality*, 1947, 15, 233–241.

Linfert, H. E., and Hierholzer, H. M. A scale for measuring the mental development of infants during the first year of life. *Stud. Psychol. Psychiat. Cath. Univ. Am.*, 1928, 1(4), 1–33.

Liverant, S. Intelligence: a concept in need of re-examination. *J. Consult. Psychol.*, 1960, 24, 101–110.

Marks, J. B., and Klahn, J. E. Verbal and perceptual components in WISC performance and their relation to social class. *J. Consult. Psychol.*, 1961, 25, 273.

McCarthy, J. J. and Kirk, S. *Illinois test of psycholinguistic abilities, experimental edition.* Urbana: University of Illinois Press, 1961–1963.

McCulloch, T. L. The retarded child grows up: psychological aspects of aging. *Am. J. Ment. Defic.*, 1957, 62, 201–208.

McGraw, M. *The neuromuscular maturation of the human infant.* New York: Columbia University Press, 1943.

McNemar, Q. *The revision of the Stanford-Binet scale: an analysis of the standardization data.* Boston: Houghton Mifflin, 1942.

Miles, C. C., and Miles, W. R. The correlation of intelligence scores and chronological age from early to late maturity. *Am. J. Psychol.*, 1932, 44, 44–78.

Miller, E. L. Ability and social adjustment at midlife of persons earlier judged mentally deficient. *Genet. Psychol. Monogr.*, 1965, 72, 139–198.

Miller, W. S. *Miller analogies test.* New York: Psychological Corp., 1960.

Moore, J. K. Speech content of orphanage and nonorphanage preschool children. *J. exp. Educ.*, 1947, 16, 122–133.

Moss, H. A., and Kagan, J. Maternal influences on early IQ scores. *Psychol. Rep.*, 1958, 4, 655–661.

Osborne, R. T., and Gregory, A. J. The heritability of visualization, perceptual speed and spatial orientation. *Percept. Mot. Skills,* 1966, **23,** 379–390.

Outhit, M. C. A study of the resemblance of parents and children in general intelligence. *Arch. Psychol.,* 1933, No. 149.

Owens, W. A. Age and mental abilities: a longitudinal study. *Genet. Psychol. Monogr.,* 1953, **48,** 3–54.

Penrose, L. S., and Smith, G. F. *Down's anomaly.* Boston: Little-Brown, 1966.

Piaget, J. *Origins of intelligence in children.* New York: International Universities Press, 1952.

Pintner, R. *Pintner general ability tests, verbal series.* Tarrytown-on-Hudson, N.Y.: World Book, 1923.

Pintner, R. The Pintner-Cunningham primary test. *J. Educ. Psychol.,* 1927, **18,** 52–58.

Pruette, L. *G. Stanley Hall: a biography of a mind.* New York: Appleton-Century-Crofts, 1926.

Rheingold, H. L. The modification of social responsiveness in institutional babies. *Monogr. Soc. Res. Child Dev.,* 1956, **21** (2, Whole No. 63).

Rheingold, H. L. The effect of environmental stimulation upon social and exploratory behavior in the human infant. In B. M. Foss (Ed.), *Determinants of infant behavior.* New York: Wiley, 1961. Pp. 143–171.

Rheingold, H. L., and Bayley, N. The later effects of an experimental modification of mothering. *Child Dev.,* 1959, **30,** 363–372.

Richards, T. W., and Nelson, V. L. Abilities of infants during the first eighteen months. *J. genet. Psychol.,* 1939, **55,** 299–318.

Rosenblith, J. F. The modified Graham behavior test for neonates: test-retest reliability, normative data, and hypotheses for future work. *Biologia Neonat.,* 1961, **3,** 174–192.

Scott, J. P. Critical periods in the development of social behavior in puppies. *Psychosom. Med.,* 1958, **20,** 42–54.

Scott, J. P. The process of primary socialization in canine and human infants. *Monogr. Soc. Res. Child Dev.,* 1963, **38** (1, Whole No. 85).

Skeels, H. M. Adult status of children with contrasting early life experiences. *Monogr. Soc. Res. Child Dev.,* 1966, **31** (3, Whole No. 105).

Skeels, H. M., Updegraff, R., Wellman, B. L., and Williams, H. M. A study of environmental stimulation: an orphanage preschool project. *Univ. Iowa Stud. Child Welfare,* 1938, **15**(4), 1–191.

Skinner, B. F. *Science and human behavior.* New York: Macmillan, 1953.

Skodak, M., and Skeels, H. M. A final follow-up study of 100 adopted children. *J. genet. Psychol.,* 1949, **75,** 85–125.

Sontag, L. W., Baker, C. T., and Nelson, V. L. Mental growth and personality development: a longitudinal study. *Monogr. Soc. Res. Child Dev.,* 1958, **23** (2, Whole No. 68).

Spearman, C. "General intelligence" objectively determined and measured. *Am. J. Psychol.,* 1904, **15,** 201–292.

Spearman, C. *The abilities of man.* New York: Macmillan, 1927.

Spitz, R. A. Hospitalism. An inquiry into the genesis of psychiatric conditions in early childhood. *Psychoanal. Study Child,* 1945, **1,** 53–74; 113–117.

Stoch, M. B., and Smythe, P. M. Does undernutrition during infancy inhibit brain growth and subsequent intellectual development? *Archs. Dis. Childhood,* 1963, **38,** 546–552.

Stott, L. H., and Ball, R. S. Infant and preschool mental tests. *Monogr. Soc. Res. Child Dev.,* 1965, **30** (3, Whole No. 101).

Stuart, H. C., and staff. Studies from the Center for Research in Child Health and Development, School of Public Health, Harvard University. I. The Center, the group under observation, sources of information, and studies in progress. *Monogr. Soc. Res. Child Dev.*, 1939, 4 (1, No. 20).

Stutsman, R. *Mental measurement of preschool children with a guide for the administration of the Merrill-Palmer Scale of Mental Tests.* Yonkers-on-Hudson, N.Y.: World Book, 1931.

Terman, L. M. *The measurement of intelligence.* Boston: Houghton Mifflin, 1916.

Terman, L. M. *Genetic studies of genius.* Vol. 1. *The mental and physical traits of a thousand gifted children.* Stanford, Cal.: Stanford University Press, 1925.

Terman, L. M. *Concept mastery test.* New York: Psychological Corp., 1956.

Terman, L. M., and Merrill, M. *Measuring intelligence: a guide to the new revised Stanford-Binet test of intelligence.* Boston: Houghton Mifflin, 1937.

Terman, L. M., and Merrill, M. *Stanford-Binet intelligence scale. Manual for the third revision: Form L-M.* Boston: Houghton Mifflin, 1960.

Thorndike, E. L. *The measurement of intelligence.* New York: Bureau of Publications, Teachers College, Columbia University, 1926.

Thorndike, E. L., Woodyard, E., and Lorge, I. *Intelligence tests: revised.* New York: Institute of Educational Research, Teachers College, Columbia University, 1935.

Thurstone, L. L. Primary mental abilities. *Psychomet. Monogr.*, 1938, No. 1.

Thurstone, L. L. *Multiple factor analysis: a development and expansion of "the vectors of mind."* Chicago: University of Chicago Press, 1947.

Thurstone, L. L., and Thurstone, T. G. *The Chicago tests of primary mental abilities.* Chicago: Science Research Associates, 1943.

Thurstone, L. L., and Thurstone, T. G. *SRA primary mental abilities—ages 5 to 7, ages 7 to 11, ages 11 to 17.* Chicago: Science Research Associates, 1958.

Tryon, R. C. A theory of psychological components—an alternative to "mathematical factors." *Psychol. Rev.*, 1935, 42, 425–454.

Tuddenham, R. D. Intelligence. In R. L. Ebel (Ed.), *Encyclopedia of educational research.* (4th ed.) New York: Macmillan, 1969, in press.

Vernon, P. E. *The structure of human abilities.* (Rev. ed.) London: Methuen, 1960.

Watson, J. B. *Psychological care of infant and child.* New York: Norton, 1928.

Wechsler, D. *Measurement of adult intelligence.* Baltimore, Md.: Williams & Wilkins, 1939 (1st ed.), 1944 (3rd ed.).

Wechsler, D. *Wechsler Bellevue intelligence scale, form II.* New York: Psychological Corp., 1946.

Wechsler, D. *Wechsler intelligence scale for children, manual.* New York: Psychological Corp., 1949.

Wechsler, D. *Wechsler adult intelligence scale, manual.* New York: Psychological Corp., 1955.

Wechsler, D. *The measurement and appraisal of adult intelligence.* (4th ed.) Baltimore, Md.: Williams & Wilkins, 1958.

Wechsler, D. *Wechsler preschool and primary scale of intelligence, manual.* New York: Psychological Corp., 1967.

Werner, E., and Bayley, N. The reliability of Bayley's revised scale of mental and motor development during the first year of life. *Child Dev.*, 1966, 37, 39–50.

Woodworth, R. S. Heredity and environment: a critical survey of recently published material on twins and foster children. *Soc. Sci. Res. Coun. Bull.*, 1941. No. 47.

Zamenhof, S., van Marthens, E., and Margolis, F. L. DNA (cell number) and protein in neonatal brain: alteration by maternal dietary protein restriction. *Science*, 1968, 160, 322–323.

17. Creativity

MICHAEL A. WALLACH

There is no end to the study of creativity, and almost no beginning. Perhaps especially in our culture, with its abiding value emphasis upon excellence or competence by some criterion or another, it is not surprising that a term which can epitomize virtually whatever the society values in its members should be so widely celebrated. There is, however, a danger in this practice: what is called creativity today may simply describe what was called by some other name in the same culture only yesterday. One need not go back too far in time within the circles of child psychology and education to find other terms with denotations suspiciously similar to what is called "creativity" today—such terms as giftedness, insight, discovery, intuition, and, indeed, intelligence.

The range of emphases that can be embraced by the creativity term has been indicated and documented at length in a number of recent reviews (e.g., Stein and Heinze, 1960; Getzels and Jackson, 1962; Barron, 1963; Golann, 1963; Taylor and Barron, 1963; Taylor, 1964a, 1964b; Barron, 1965; and Taylor and Williams, 1966). Faced with such a profusion of material, and especially in a chapter that must take as its frame of reference the study of children, adolescents, and young adults, certain limitations must be imposed upon the task one seeks to accomplish. These limitations of focus will be set forth in this introductory section.

A rough distinction can be made in the creativity literature among studies oriented to products, to persons, and to processes. The first two of these three perspectives have in the nature of the case taken the examination of mature adults as their point of departure.

Thus, for example, an extensive literature has accumulated concerning evaluations of the products of research scientists. The bases for evaluation of products have been varied, including such indices as occupational salary, number of publications, membership in various professional organizations, listing in such sources as *Who's Who in America*, output of patentable inventions, and ratings by peers, supervisors, or panels of informed judges (see, e.g., Knapp and Goodrich, 1952; Taylor, 1959; Taylor, Smith, Ghiselin, and Ellison, 1961; Harmon, 1963; Taylor, 1963; Taylor, Smith, and Ghiselin, 1963; Chambers, 1964; Hoyt, 1965; and Taylor and Ellison, 1967). A provocative conclusion has emerged from some of this work: the worth of scientific contributions seems to be relatively independent of traditional intellective assessment information available as of the college years. Other studies in this field, on the other hand, have found relationships with customary intellective data. Product-centered criteria of these various kinds, however, turn out to be relatively uncorrelated among themselves (e.g., Golann, 1963), so that it is difficult to justify the application of some single term such as creativity to all of them. Furthermore, here one is considering primarily the occupational achievements of mature adults—a task that would easily require a chapter in its own right.

A second perspective in the creativity literature has been concerned with describing the personalities of individuals who have been judged creative by virtue of evaluations of their occupational products. Although, to be sure, this line of endeavor overlaps with the first, a difference can be delineated in terms

1211

of the degree to which the investigator seems more concerned with studying products as criteria of creativity or with studying the persons who become identified through any means as creative. The emphasis has been upon painting a picture of what the person who achieves eminence in the arts or the sciences is like (see, e.g., Roe, 1951a, 1951b, 1953a, 1953b; Cattell and Drevdahl, 1955; Drevdahl and Cattell, 1958; MacKinnon, 1960, 1962a, 1962b). Given, for example, the identification of some architects as more creative than others in terms of the judgments of fellow architects who are recognized as competent to make the evaluations, MacKinnon (1960, 1962a, 1962b) has been interested in depicting, through the use of a wide range of measurement probes, what the creative architect is like. Not surprisingly, he turns out to be a very complicated person: "The successful and effective architect must, with the skill of a juggler, combine, reconcile, and exercise the diverse skills of businessman, lawyer, artist, engineer, and advertising man, as well as those of author and journalist, psychiatrist, educator, and psychologist" (MacKinnon, 1962b, p. 486). Work that is focused upon creative persons requires essentially comments similar to those we offered concerning work that is focused upon creative products. There is, of course, a great variety of relatively disjunctive ways in which the term creativity is applied, yet we find again that the major focus is upon the occupational achievements of mature adults. Thus the literature concerned with creative persons turns out once more to be a vast one that would easily constitute the subject matter for yet another chapter.

We turn, then, to the third perspective that has concerned students of creativity—processes. It is this perspective upon which we propose to concentrate in the present chapter, for it is on processes that research presuming to study creativity in children, adolescents, and young adults has concentrated. To propose that there are in fact psychological processes that can be appropriately assigned to the creativity concept is to argue that these processes cannot be embraced within the ways that are already at hand for understanding thinking, that these processes have some face validity for being described in terms of a disposition for creativity, and that these

processes are necessary, although they need not be sufficient, for the achievement of products that the society would construe as reflecting creativity. Most of the research conducted thus far has dealt with the first two of these points, and hence these are the issues that will mainly concern us. Research is sorely needed concerning the third—an imbalance that hopefully will be redressed by the time the next edition of this book appears.

The early history of the concern with thinking processes that are involved in creativity (e.g., Wallas, 1926; Woodworth and Schlosberg, 1954) tended to make use of concepts drawn from the study of problem-solving. Whether the use of models drawn from general problem-solving can succeed in describing thinking processes that differ from the more mundane ones, which we would not want to call creative, however, is a moot point, and one that will be of continuing concern to us. If problem-solving skill is all that the term creativity can mean at the level of psychological processes, use of the term will gain us nothing. The concept of general intelligence has, after all, been with us for a long time as a descriptive summary for the abilities that contribute to effective problem-solving, and these abilities have been found to cohere in the sense that individuals can be reliably ordered in terms of their overall competence at coping with the problems offered them by their environment. Indeed, the intelligence concept forms the focus of another chapter in this *Manual* (see chapter by Bayley). Are there thinking processes, then, that differ from those that form the basis for the general intelligence concept, and that at the same time possess face validity as signs of creativity? To suggest such processes differ from those associated with intelligence is to ask whether a dimension of individual differences can be located whose content reflects processes that seem appropriately described as a disposition for creativity or as a creative ability trait, but which is still essentially independent of individual differences in general intelligence.

THE INITIAL STIMULUS

Guilford and the Structure-of-Intellect Model

Theoretical Considerations. The major impetus to the search for thinking processes that may be appropriately described as concerned with creativity dates from the work of J. P. Guilford and his associates beginning in the early 1950s. For the last 15 years or so, they have been seeking to evaluate a model of how humans think that involves three basic considerations: processes or thinking operations carried out; contents to which the operations are applied; and products that can result (e.g., Guilford, 1956, 1957, 1959a, 1959b, 1959c, 1963, 1964, 1967a, 1967b). The kinds of process Guilford calls attention to may be roughly grouped into those concerned with raw informational material, those concerned with producing further information from what is already in hand, and the process of making evaluations concerning information that confronts us. Regarding raw material, Guilford distinguishes between *cognition*—the perceiving of data from the outside world—and *memory*—the retention of what has been perceived. Regarding the producing of further information, he distinguishes between *convergent* thinking—zeroing in upon an answer that is rather precisely implied or specified by the nature of the informational givens—and *divergent* thinking—searching for material that is only loosely related to what is already known, so that one's search model has a much more broad-gauged template than in the former case. The fifth process to which Guilford calls attention, *evaluation*, refers in turn to whatever is involved in reaching decisions about the appropriateness, suitability, elegance, or goodness of material that is perceived, remembered, reached by convergent thinking, or reached by divergent thinking.

The further major considerations involved in Guilford's structure-of-intellect model are descriptive in character. They concern possible distinctions that can be drawn among contents to which the forgoing processes can be applied—such as meaningful verbal content, numbers, or material that represents nothing beyond itself; and possible distinctions among the products that can eventuate from applying the processes to one or another kind of content—such as logical arrangements of classification or implication. Our attention quickly returns, therefore, to the cognitive operations that he postulates and, among these, to the concepts of convergent and divergent thinking in particular. Some kind of evaluative process, after all, is implicit in

carrying out any kind of cognitive work; and such work must in the nature of the case begin with the raw materials supplied by the senses and memory. The core of Guilford's analysis of the processes by which thinking is carried out thus consists of his distinguishing between convergent and divergent cognitive operations:

In view of the active nature of creative performances, the production aspects or steps are most conspicuous and probably most crucial. Among the productive-thinking abilities another logical distinction appears. With some productive-thinking factors and the tests that measure them, thinking must at some time converge toward one right answer; the significant type of thinking involved has been called "convergent thinking." With other productive-thinking factors and their tests, thinking need not come out with a unique answer; in fact, going off in different directions contributes to a better score in such tests. This type of thinking and these factors come under the heading of "divergent" thinking. It is in divergent thinking that we find the most obvious indications of creativity. (Guilford, 1957, pp. 111–112).

In order further to characterize what Guilford means by divergent thinking, let us turn to the specific divergent-thinking subprocesses that the Guilford group claims to have isolated by factor-analytic techniques, and briefly describe each (see, e.g., Wilson, Guilford, Christensen, and Lewis, 1954; Guilford, 1956, 1959a, 1959b). They are "word fluency," "associational fluency," "ideational fluency," "expressional fluency," "spontaneous flexibility," "adaptive flexibility," "redefinition," and "originality."

Word fluency refers to the ability to generate words that fulfill particular structural requirements, such as providing as many words as possible that begin with a certain letter or solving anagrams.

Associational fluency refers to the ability to rapidly generate words that meet particular requirements of meaning, such as providing a word which has the same meaning as each of a pair of words that differ in meaning themselves.

Ideational fluency refers to the ability to generate—within a limited time—ideas that will fulfill particular requirements, such as naming uses for bricks, naming problems that are suggested by certain common situations, writing titles for a story plot, or naming the consequences that might be entailed by certain changes.

Expressional fluency concerns the ability to put rapidly into juxtaposition words that meet particular requirements of sentence structure, such as writing alternative four-word sentences when the first letter of each word in the sentence is specified.

Spontaneous flexibility denotes the ability to vary one's ideas over a wide range, even though this is not specifically called for on the test, such as giving many different categories of possible uses for a brick rather than offering uses that all fall within the same general category.

Adaptive flexibility refers to the ability to vary one's ideas widely when the test requires such variety be displayed, for example, solving problems wherein a given number of matchsticks must be removed from a particular array of matchstick triangles in such a way that a certain number of triangles will remain.

Redefinition concerns the ability to relinquish old ways of construing familiar objects in order to make use of them for a new purpose, such as choosing from among five objects one with a part that will serve some function alien to the customary usages of all the objects (called "Gestalt Transformations").

Originality, finally, refers to the making of responses that are statistically unique or unusual, such as the giving of uncommon uses for a brick, the hypothesizing of nonobvious consequences as ones that might follow from a particular event, or the offering of plot titles that are evaluated as clever.

In sum, then, four of these divergent-thinking factors concern some form of fluency, three of them concern some sort of flexibility, and one involves novelty or uniqueness. Convergent thinking, on the other hand, refers to tests that probe such matters as verbal comprehension, verbal reasoning, the size of a person's vocabulary, and the ability to solve mathematics problems. It is evident that such procedures assess what is commonly referred to as the general intelligence concept. Here too, the Guilford group argues that a large number of specific subprocesses are disclosed

by the results of factor analysis. Before turning to the evidence that bears upon the tenability of the Guilford group's distinction between divergent- and convergent-thinking processes, however, several further points require consideration—two issues concerning the face validity of the creativity indicators and one concerning the relationships among individual differences in performance on the various tasks that we have described.

Despite the fact that the Guilford group defines divergent thinking in terms that oppose a search for particular correct answers, they have, as Wallach and Kogan (1965a) point out, embedded their divergent-thinking tasks within an evaluative testing context— hence one that is familiar to the respondents as putting a premium upon the locating of right answers. By the Guilford group's own definition of divergent thinking as thinking which "goes off in different directions," therefore, an ability-testing context with its natural emphasis upon correctness may not be maximally conducive to divergent thinking's display.

In addition to its reliance upon a context of ability testing and partly as a result of this reliance, the Guilford group also has imposed time limits—usually quite stringent ones— upon its divergent-thinking tasks (Wallach and Kogan, 1965a). Again returning to Guilford's own definition of divergent thinking, however, there would seem to be no reason to put a premium upon speed of responding. Rather, the concept of thinking in different directions suggests an emphasis upon freedom and spontaneity that is quite inconsistent with the imposition of brief time limits upon performance. The face validity of the divergent-thinking tasks hence would seem greater were they administered without time limits and in a context that did not carry ability-testing connotations.

Can assessors of divergent and convergent thinking be distinguished in terms of differences that are large enough to be psychologically meaningful in the resultant orderings of the respondents? This is the crucial empirical question that must be asked of the proponents of the structure-of-intellect model. Thorndike (1963a, 1963b) and Wallach and Kogan (1965a) have argued that Guilford's divergent-thinking measures do not correlate with one another more strongly than the degree to which they correlate with measures of convergent thinking. If this is the case, one would have to conclude that the creativity assessors devised by the Guilford group have nothing more in common than their correlation with traditional intelligence measures. The warrant for claiming the separate existence of one or more cognitive dispositions that should be graced with the name of creativity or divergent thinking as distinct from intelligence therefore would be difficult to find. This dimensionality issue, however, must be subjected to closer scrutiny, for it lies at the very heart of the Guilford group's research enterprise.

To put the issue in perspective, we must return briefly to the history of intelligence testing. In the course of that history can be found a controversy between those who emphasized the existence of a single, broadly defined dimension of ability—the G factor—and those interested in demonstrating the existence of a variety of distinguishable "primary mental abilities" (see Thurstone, 1936, 1938; McNemar, 1964; Vernon, 1965). More recently, these positions have become blurred, as, on the one hand, various "specific factors" come to surround G, and, on the other, a factoring of the "primary mental ability" factors is found to yield a single "second-order" factor that accounts for most of the variance in the former (see, e.g., Burt, 1954, 1958). As Thorndike (1963b) puts it:

Although there is a degree of specialization of intellectual functioning, so that tests within a specific region of content or process correlate more highly than those from different regions, still the correlations across regions are appreciably positive. It is these uniformly positive correlations, whether conceptualized as G, or a second-order factor among the primary factors, or as an overlapping of group factors, that give some substance to the general concept of abstract intelligence . . . (pp. 46–47).

An example of the evidence on this point is provided by Kennedy (1960), who isolated for study a group of 40 adolescents from a pool of 5000 applicants on the basis of proficiency in mathematics. Specific selection of this kind in terms of mathematics skill was found to yield a group that was extremely

high on all of a variety of measures of verbal and of performance intelligence. The strongly unitary character of general intelligence in terms of high intercorrelations among different kinds of assessment thus is demonstrated. Similar findings by Wallach and Kogan (1965a) point to high intercorrelations for 151 fifth graders among measures of verbal aptitude, mathematical aptitude, and verbal and quantitative academic achievement. Another instance is provided in a recent study of adolescents by Hoepfner, Nihira, and Guilford (1966). Evidence for a large variety of separate factors within the general intelligence domain is claimed; yet inspection of the test intercorrelations indicates a high order of relationship among the vast majority of pairs of variables.

The result is that a ranking of individuals in terms of one measure of intelligence or convergent thinking will have a high degree of correspondence with the ranking that will result from application of another such measure. Still, there will be some differences, and Guilford would propose that these differences are of predictive significance. Recent articles by McNemar (1964) and Vernon (1965), however, have argued persuasively that no grounds exist in terms of predictive validity for the making of any further ability distinctions beyond a G factor within the general intelligence domain. In terms of predicting outside criteria of almost any practical kind, in other words, a reliable index of general intelligence does just about as well as a measure of any more specific thinking characteristic that lies somewhere within the general intelligence area.

In the absence of clear support for making distinctions among conventional intelligence or convergent thinking abilities, we must ask, then, if there is an empirical warrant for making *any* distinction at all between such abilities and those described in terms of divergent thinking, before turning to the Guilford group's even more extreme claim that a number of divergent-thinking abilities can be usefully distinguished from one another. The ideal state of affairs would exist if one had adequate criteria of creative accomplishments in hand, against which one could then evaluate purported assessors of divergent thinking. Such criteria are hard to come by within the age range bounded by young adulthood; however, studies concerned with thinking processes that may be implicated in creativity have concentrated on this age range. We thus are forced to consider first correlations among the measures of divergent and convergent thinking themselves.

Factor analysis as such, the research tool upon which the Guilford group depends for examining these correlations, does not seem to provide a satisfactory way of answering the dimensionality question. Guilford (e.g., 1956) assumes that any factor emerging from the application of his tests which does not seem to be specific to the tests defining it ought to be included in his psychological model. It is extremely unlikely, however, that the 100 or so factors that can be isolated in this manner represent predictively useful distinctions. To follow Guilford's practice of using the statistical separability of factors as the ground for claiming the psychological distinguishability of traits or dispositions thus does not seem defensible. Distinctions of some kind can, after all, be made almost without end, depending simply upon how refined is the choice of tests administered to the respondents. Thorndike (1963a, 1963b) and Wallach and Kogan (1965a) therefore propose a somewhat different approach to the dimensionality question. They argue that the warrant for claiming an empirically separable divergent-thinking domain depends—once the matter of face validity is taken care of—upon showing that the divergent-thinking tasks share a substantial amount of variance in common, that they share substantially less variance with convergent-thinking tasks than they share with one another, and that the measures of convergent thinking share a substantial amount of variance in common as well.

The formulation just described differs, really, in only one major respect from that advanced by the Guilford group. Both approaches to the dimensionality issue must, after all, be based upon some prior theorizing concerning what cognitive measures to include in one's assessment attempts. They do not therefore differ in this regard. The basic difference is that the stipulations that there be "substantial" amounts of shared variance among measures within both the divergent and the convergent-thinking domains, and of unshared variance between the two domains,

represent a more conservative basis for defining a dimension than does the statistical criterion used in factor analysis of the Guilford variety. The statistical rule in question settles for only a minimal amount of distinguishable variance in common, whereas the alternative formulation asks for considerably more than that. Why does it seem appropriate to require a conservative basis for claiming the separability of divergent thinking as a process or set of processes? Because in the absence of clear external validating criteria for divergent-thinking abilities, our primary empirical ground for defending their separate status rests upon their distinguishability from conventional intelligence measures in terms of the orderings of individuals that are obtained. Recall that little empirical warrant can be mustered for the psychological utility of distinguishing among the small differences in orderings of respondents that result from the application of one or another measure in the general intelligence domain. In the light of that outcome, we must be suspicious indeed when a whole class of thinking operations is proposed, under the name of divergent thinking or creativity, as separable from the processes measured by conventional intelligence tests.

What is the evidence, then, concerning the dimensionality of the factors that Guilford and his associates take as contributing to creative thinking? In the two sections that follow we shall consider studies with young adults and with children that have been carried out by the Guilford group or by others using essentially the same divergent-thinking measures. In exploring this research we shall inquire, first, to what degree the divergent-thinking factors cohere, despite their differences, as a relatively unified dimension and, second, whether this dimension in turn can be distinguished from the factors that have been identified with convergent thinking. We have found that convergent-thinking factors possess sufficient variance in common to justify assigning them to a single dimension of individual differences—that of general intelligence. The creativity domain, on the other hand, may or may not constitute a unitary dimension. If not, then we must consider whatever subparts emerge, and ask for each subpart whether it shows a substantially greater degree of internal consistency than the degree to which it correlates with measures of convergent thinking.

Studies with Young Adults. Thorndike (1963b) has subjected studies by the Guilford group to reanalysis along the lines that we have been considering. His procedure was to take the two tests possessing the strongest loadings on a given factor as representative of that factor, and he has distinguished between divergent- and convergent-thinking factors in accordance with the Guilford group's concepts concerning these abilities. Thorndike compares the magnitudes of the average correlation among tests representing convergent thinking, the average correlation among tests representing divergent thinking, and the average correlation between these two groups of tests. In the first of two studies analyzed in this manner by Thorndike, results by Guilford and Christensen (1956) were considered. From the Guilford and Christensen factor analysis there emerged three factors in the convergent-thinking domain: "verbal comprehension," "general reasoning," and "eduction-verbal correlation." Five other factors that emerged were taken by Guilford and Christensen to refer to divergent thinking: "word fluency," "associational fluency," "ideational fluency," "expressional fluency," and "originality." Taking the two highest-loading tests to stand for each factor, Thorndike found that the average correlation among the convergent-thinking measures was .43, the average correlation among the divergent-thinking measures was .27, and the average of the correlations between these two sets of measures was .24. Thus the divergent-thinking measures have little variance in common apart from the variance that they also share with the convergent-thinking domain.

A comparable analysis was carried out by Thorndike (1963b) of a study by Wilson, Guilford, Christensen, and Lewis (1954). Here the Guilford group found evidence for six factors of convergent thinking and eight factors taken to reflect divergent thinking. The convergent-thinking factors were "verbal," "numerical," "perceptual," "visualizing," "reasoning," and "closure." The divergent-thinking factors were "word fluency," "associational fluency," "ideational fluency," "spontaneous flexibility," "adaptive flexibility," "redefinition," "originality," and "sensitivity to

problems."[1] With the two highest-loading tests again taken to represent each factor, Thorndike found the average correlation among the convergent-thinking tests to be .23, the average correlation among the divergent-thinking tests to be .14, and the average correlation between the two domains to be .12. Thus the divergent-thinking tasks again are found to have little variance in common apart from the degree to which they are also related to the convergent-thinking tasks.

By using a procedure identical to Thorndike's, Ward (1966) reanalyzed the data from yet a third study by the Guilford group and obtained the same results. For a study by Guilford, Frick, Christensen, and Merrifield (1957), the average correlation among the convergent-thinking measures was .24, the average correlation among the divergent-thinking measures was .18, and the average correlation between these domains was .15. All of the studies that we described utilized young adult males as subjects. None of them found correlations among divergent-thinking factors to be appreciably higher than those between divergent- and convergent-thinking factors.

Although divergent thinking as a whole therefore does not seem to be distinguishable from convergent thinking, might some subset of the tasks defining the divergent-thinking domain turn out to be distinguishable in this regard? With this question in mind, let us first return to the evidence already considered, and then go on to further studies. The divergent-thinking factors fall, as noted earlier, into three groupings: four concerned

[1] Strictly speaking, the factor of "sensitivity to problems" is considered an evaluative rather than a divergent-thinking factor by the Guilford group, yet they believe it to be relevant to creativity in thinking. Sensitivity to problems concerns the ability to describe problems or difficulties that may arise in connection with various situations. Its tests are rather similar in fact to some of those used to tap the factor of "ideational fluency." Thus, although all the factors that are taken to reflect divergent thinking are considered by Guilford to be relevant to creativity, an occasional factor defined as outside the divergent-thinking domain also has been discussed by Guilford in relation to creativity. With but an occasional exception such as this, however, Guilford takes the term "creativity" to be roughly synonymous with his set of divergent-thinking factors.

with fluency, three with flexibility, and one with originality. We again take the two highest-loading tests to represent a factor, and draw upon reanalyses of the Guilford group's studies by Thorndike (1963b) and Ward (1966).

Turning first to fluency, recall that Guilford and Christensen (1956) obtained four fluency factors. Their average intercorrelation is .29, whereas the average correlation between the fluency factors and the convergent-thinking domain is found to be .24. Three fluency factors emerged in the study by Wilson et al. (1954). Their average intercorrelation is found to be .23, and their average correlation with convergent thinking, .14. In the study by Guilford et al. (1957), only one fluency factor was found—ideational fluency—and its correlation with the convergent-thinking domain turns out to be .01. Some evidence begins to emerge, then, for the distinguishability of the fluencies from convergent thinking. Thorndike (1963b), furthermore, has pointed out that in both the study by Guilford and Christensen and that by Wilson et al., the word-fluency factor actually correlates more strongly (in the latter study, twice as strongly) with the convergent-thinking domain than with the divergent-thinking domain. Thorndike therefore suggests, although admittedly this is post hoc, that we delete word fluency from the divergent-thinking domain. Following his prescription, the three remaining fluency factors in the Guilford and Christensen study are found to correlate .31 among themselves and .22 with convergent thinking, whereas the two remaining fluency factors in the Wilson et al. study are found to correlate .28 among themselves and .08 with convergent thinking. Perhaps therefore the fluency factors—especially if one deletes word fluency—correlate more strongly among themselves than they do with convergent thinking.

Turning next to flexibility, the studies by Wilson et al. (1954) and by Guilford et al. (1957) each yielded three flexibility factors. In the Wilson group's research, the mean correlation within the set of flexibility factors was .13, while that between the flexibility factors and convergent thinking was .15. In the Guilford study, the corresponding mean correlations were .24 and .20, respectively. Taking both studies together, the flexibility factors thus do not seem more strongly related among

themselves than the degree of their relationship with convergent thinking.

Originality, finally, is defined only by a single factor in Guilford's model. In the three studies that we have been considering, the tests representing this factor are found to possess average correlations with general intelligence of .25 (Guilford and Christensen, 1956), .01 (Wilson et al., 1954), and .19 (Guilford et al., 1957). On balance, then, there do not seem to be clear grounds for considering originality distinguishable from convergent thinking.

The conclusion thus far appears to be that although the divergent-thinking domain in toto is not distinguishable from convergent thinking, one part of that domain—the fluency factors, especially with word fluency deleted—may be distinguishable in some degree. No evidence, in turn, for the distinguishability from intelligence of the flexibility factors or of originality could be claimed. With these tentative generalizations in hand, we proceed to other reports for further clarification.

In a detailed study of the originality domain as Guilford would define it, Barron (1955, 1957, 1963) administered to 100 young male adults eight tasks designed to probe the domain in question. Included, for example, was an unusual-uses procedure scored for infrequency, in the sample under study, of the uses proposed; a consequences procedure in which the subject was to write down what would happen if certain changes were suddenly to occur, with the scoring in terms of how nonobvious were the imagined consequences; and a plot titles instrument in which, for each of two story plots, the subject was to write as many titles as possible, with the titles then scored for cleverness (see Guilford, Wilson, Christensen, and Lewis, 1951; Guilford, Wilson, and Christensen, 1952). The average of the 28 correlations among all possible pairs of originality measures was found to be .19. A composite originality score was constructed by summing the standard scores on all eight measures, and this composite was found to correlate .33 with a general intelligence index—the Terman Concept Mastery Test. Whatever major dimensionality the originality measures possessed therefore was accountable for in terms of the measures' correlation with convergent thinking.

Barron went on, however, to partial out the

effects of intelligence as defined by the Concept Mastery Test from his composite originality score, and then to study the relationships that remained among the composite score and a range of other variables that had been gathered on the sample during the course of a 3-day "living-in" assessment regime. And here an intriguing finding emerged: with the effects of intelligence partialled out, the major cognitive dimension that remained in terms of partial correlations with the originality composite appeared to be best definable as something like ideational fluency. Comprising the dimension were such measures as the number of kinds of idea discerned in sets of varied objects and properties, the number of different determinants made use of in one's Rorschach responses, degree of fluency and motility in acting out a charades task, degree of participation in an improvisation task, and a staff rating provided for fluency of ideas. Part of the tendency to give unusual or original responses, then, seems to arise as a function of greater response fluency or productivity; and this part, along with fluency or productivity itself, seems to be separable from convergent thinking.

Additional evidence along the same lines was reported by Christensen, Guilford, and Wilson (1957); here uncommonness of uses and remoteness of consequences were found to be greater for later than for earlier responses in the sequence produced by the subject. Interestingly enough, cleverness of plot titles was not found to vary with number of responses in this way, suggesting a distinction within the originality domain between forms of originality that are dependent upon fluency of output and forms that are not. Those dependent on fluency of output seem to concern statistical infrequency of content, whereas those not dependent seem more concerned with verbal facility.

A recent study by Garwood (1964) casts further light on the empirical link between ideational fluency and originality of content when they are investigated by similar procedures. With 105 young adult male students as subjects, two measures—the total number of feasible uses offered, and the total number of feasible uses that were fully unique in the sense of their being offered as a use for the given object by only one person in the sample—were strongly correlated in an alternate-

uses task in which the respondent was to list uses other than the primary one for common objects (Wilson, Christensen, Merrifield, and Guilford, 1960). Similarly, two measures correlated strongly in a consequences task where the subject was to list all the consequences he could imagine if each of various proposed changes were to occur (Christensen, Merrifield, and Guilford, 1958); these measures are the total number of relevant consequences offered and the total number of suggested consequences that were remote, that is, temporally or geographically distant. That the measure of unusual responses correlated with the measure of total number of responses within a given procedure of course would be expected on analytic grounds because of the part-whole relationship between the scores. The measure of unusual responses on either procedure, however, also correlated substantially with the measure of total number of responses on the other, thus supporting the view already fostered by the Barron and the Christensen et al. (1957) results that there is an aspect of originality which is in fact tied to fluency of output.

But does Garwood's work provide any evidence on the issue of relationships to convergent thinking abilities? Regrettably, her final creativity measure was a composite which also included scores on other Guilford-type tasks, such as a matchstick procedure designed to assess the factor of adaptive flexibility (Marks, Guilford, and Merrifield, 1959) and a Gestalt transformations procedure in which the respondent had to indicate which of a set of objects could best serve a specified purpose alien to the customary usage of the objects— a measure for assessing the factor of redefinition (Guilford, Wilson, and Christensen, 1952). These flexibility assessors had weak and ambiguous correlations with the fluency and originality indices discussed earlier. With our previously formed suspicion that measures of flexibility factors may not be distinguishable from the convergent-thinking domain, we are not surprised to find that Garwood's composite creativity index showed some degree of relationship to general intelligence indicators. It would be interesting to know, of course, if the relationship with intelligence would disappear in a comparison involving the measures of ideational fluency in particular.

Studies with Children and Adolescents.
Our review continues with studies concerning the Guilford group's tasks as applied to somewhat younger subjects. Where the "adolescent" grouping of this section ends and the "young adult" grouping of the previous section picks up is partly an arbitrary matter; we take this point roughly as corresponding to the student's leaving high school.

Cline, Richards, and Abe (1962) and Cline, Richards, and Needham (1963) administered to high school students of both sexes a battery of tasks designed to tap a range of divergent-thinking factors. The creativity indices, as taken from the Guilford group's work, provided measures of ideational fluency, associational fluency, spontaneous flexibility, adaptive flexibility, redefinition, and originality. California Mental Maturity Inventory scores provided an intelligence measure, and grade point averages also were collected. In the Cline, Richards, and Abe study, the average correlation among the divergent-thinking measures was .21 for males and .22 for females, while the average correlation between the divergent-thinking indices and intelligence was .35 for males and .32 for females. In the Cline, Richards, and Needham study, the comparable correlations were .21 and .24 for males and females, respectively, within the divergent-thinking domain; .35 and .33 for males and females, respectively, between divergent thinking and intelligence. Results were essentially the same if we consider the measures of fluency, flexibility, and originality as separate subgroups. Data on academic achievement were found, in the work by Cline and his collaborators, to behave like intelligence scores: correlations between grade-point average and the creativity tasks are if anything stronger, on the average, than correlations among the divergent-thinking tasks themselves. As would be expected from this outcome, intelligence and grade-point average are in turn quite highly related. In sum, both of these studies, using a broad range of divergent-thinking tasks, did not find the Guilford procedures as a group, nor any relevant subgroup of these procedures, cohering to a degree that suggested their possessing any common psychological meaning apart from what was indicated by their correlating with general intelligence or academic achievement, that is, convergent thinking.

Other studies that tended to yield either negative or ambiguous findings concerning the divergent-thinking-convergent-thinking separation include the following. Iscoe and Pierce-Jones (1964) found, for 267 children of ages 5 to 9, that most of a large number of correlations between a set of intelligence measures on the one hand and measures of ideational fluency and spontaneous flexibility on the other turned out to be significant. Klausmeier, Harris, and Ethnathios (1962) investigated several fluency measures in relation to teacher ratings for the kinds of fluency under consideration, with almost 200 tenth and eleventh graders as subjects. Although moderate positive relationships were obtained between the teacher ratings and the fluency indices, no examination of possible relationships to general intelligence was carried out. Given the possibility of halo effects from intelligence information as an influence upon the teachers' ratings, it could well be that the degree of relationship obtained between fluency ratings by teachers and fluency scores on the tests depended on variance shared by each of these indicators in the present study with intelligence. In another study, Klausmeier and Wiersma (1964) administered a heterogeneous range of divergent thinking tasks to fifth and seventh graders, but they did not investigate the relationships among these tasks or the degree of their relationship to intelligence indicators. Anderson (1966), in an extensive investigation of seventh graders, found a range of convergent-thinking tasks to separate in some degree from a range of divergent-thinking tasks, but he then found individual differences on the convergent-thinking composite score to correlate .51 with individual differences on the divergent-thinking composite score—a very substantial correlation indeed for a sample of 320 children. Compared to a number of other variables that were studied, the most powerful predictor by far of scores on the divergent-thinking composite index turned out to be scores on the convergent-thinking composite index.[2]

A number of reports can be located, however, which suggest the separability from convergent thinking of one part of the divergent-thinking domain as Guilford defined it: once

[2] See also Cropley, 1966.

again, it is ideational fluency this work tends to point toward.

Research by Gewirtz (1948a, 1948b) and by Bereiter (1960, 1961) helps to clarify the detachment of word fluency from the divergent thinking domain and its assignment rather to the general intelligence category. With children of ages 5 to 6½ years, Gewirtz (1948a, 1948b) found measures of the word fluency variety to intercorrelate strongly among themselves and also with a Stanford-Binet measure of intelligence. Other fluency tasks, closer in character to the Guilford group's definition of ideational fluency, on the other hand, have been found in Bereiter's (1961) reanalysis of the Gewirtz data to load heavily on a factor to which the Stanford-Binet measure makes no contribution at all. The tasks found to load heavily on this intelligence-free factor included a measure of the child's naming as many objects as possible and a measure of the number of different words used by the child in describing his house. Such indices would seem to depend in fair degree upon the number of ideational possibilities that the child can conjure up. In a study of over 250 tenth graders, Bereiter (1960) in turn found no clear warrant for viewing verbal and ideational forms of fluency as having much in common psychologically. One therefore begins to glimpse the possibility that not only should word fluency be banished from the divergent thinking category but that the concept of ideational fluency may be paradigmatic for the kind of cognitive performance that is maximally cohesive in itself and maximally distinguishable from convergent thinking.

Using a range of Guilford divergent-thinking tests with a sample of 114 seventh and eighth graders, Piers, Daniels, and Quackenbush (1960) found the average correlation among the divergent-thinking indicators—including measures of both originality and ideational fluency—to be .26, while their average relationship with the Otis Intelligence Test was .19. However, separation of the divergent-thinking tasks into those concerned with originality and those concerned with ideational fluency yielded a different picture. The four measures designed to tap originality exhibited an average correlation of .37 among themselves and an average correlation of .31 with intelligence. The three measures designed to tap ideational fluency, on the other hand, al-

though also showing a satisfactory degree of internal coherence with an average correlation of .36 among themselves, manifested an average correlation of −.03 with intelligence. Thus, whereas the originality indicators correlated to about the same degree with intelligence as they did among themselves, the ideational fluency measures correlated substantially among themselves but not at all with general intelligence.

With a sample of more than 1000 seventh graders, McGuire, Hindsman, King, and Jennings (1961) administered, among other tasks, such "convergent-thinking" indicators as the California Test of Mental Maturity, a Sequential Test of Educational Progress instrument concerned with the comprehension of verbal passages and questions that were read aloud (the STEP "listening" test), and a test concerned with the ability to reason about pictorially presented mechanical situations. Also administered were such presumed "divergent-thinking" indicators as a word fluency task in which the subject was to write words that rhyme with given words, the Gestalt transformations task as a measure of the factor of redefinition, an ideational fluency indicator in which the subject was to list different possible consequences of various proposed changes, and another ideational fluency measure in which the subject was to list possible problems suggested by various common situations (see Frick, Guilford, Christensen, and Merrifield, 1959; Guilford, Wilson, Christensen, and Lewis, 1951; Wilson, Guilford, and Christensen, 1953; and Wilson, Guilford, Christensen, and Lewis, 1954).

Two strong factors that differentiated the preceding measures in a quite intriguing way resulted from analytic rotation to an orthogonal Varimax solution. Following, rounded to the nearest tenth, are the respective loadings on these two factors for the measures just described: California Test of Mental Maturity, .6 and .2; STEP "listening" test, .7 and .2; mechanical reasoning test, .6 and .1; word fluency task, .6 and .3; Gestalt transformations measure of redefinition, .6 and .0; "consequences" measure of ideational fluency, .3 and .6; "common situations" measure of ideational fluency, .2 and .6. Hence we find a clear general intelligence cluster, adhering to which are an indicator of word fluency and an indicator of one of Guilford's flexibility factors, redefinition. There also emerges, however, another factor that is heavily defined by the ideational fluency measures, which, in turn, have minimal loadings on the general intelligence factor. Not only is a strong separation suggested by these results between ideational fluency and convergent thinking therefore, but we also find two other ostensible measures from the divergent-thinking domain —tasks assessing word fluency and one of the flexibilities—cohering strongly with the convergent-thinking cluster.

In a study of almost 200 students in the 11- to 15-year-old range, Clark, Veldman, and Thorpe (1965) utilized a type of originality scoring that, as we indicated in considering Garwood's (1964) study, has been found to correlate quite highly with ideational fluency. Such Guilford tasks as the "consequences" and "common situations" procedures already described were scored for the number of statistically unique yet relevant responses offered by the subject. When individual differences on such a uniqueness measure were correlated for a sample of both sexes with total IQ scores on the California Test of Mental Maturity, the result was an r of only .04. Here is suggestive evidence once again, then, that measures in and around the ideational fluency domain may be relatively independent of convergent thinking. The present study is less than conclusive, however, since, contrary to what we would expect, a reading achievement measure correlated with the uniqueness index rather than with the intelligence index. On the other hand, various Rorschach indicators reflective of the degree to which the respondent gives free rein to imaginative production were found to correlate with the uniqueness index and not with the intelligence index; these indicators included the number of movement responses given and the incidence of signs presumed to reflect anxiety. The perception of movement in Rorschach patterns and scores on measures that have been assumed to indicate "anxiety" will be of interest to us later in the chapter.

A set of 10 measures, designed to tap ideational fluency, spontaneous flexibility, and originality, was utilized in a recent study by May and Metcalf (1965) concerning eighth-grade students. Correlations among these measures were presented, as were their relationships with an intelligence index—a "ver-

bal reasoning test" containing verbal analogy items. Taking first the three ideational fluency measures, correlations among them averaged .60, whereas their average correlation with the intelligence measure was .04. Turning to the three measures of spontaneous flexibility, the average correlation among them was .41, whereas their average correlation with intelligence was .13. The four originality measures, finally, yielded an average correlation of .23 among themselves, and an average correlation of .17 with intelligence. Thus it is the ideational fluency indices therefore that show the strongest coherence among themselves and also show the greatest independence from intelligence.

Feldhusen, Denny, and Condon (1965), in another recent report, utilized an alternate uses task as the basis for assessing spontaneous flexibility, while using a consequences procedure as the basis for assessing both ideational fluency and originality. Seventh and eighth graders were the subjects. Indicators of both intellective aptitude (the School and College Ability Tests) and academic achievement (the Sequential Tests of Educational Progress) were available as convergent-thinking assessors. Ideational fluency was found to be independent of the SCAT and STEP measures for both sexes. Spontaneous flexibility, on the other hand, was found to be related to the SCAT and STEP measures for both sexes. Originality, finally, turned out to be related to the convergent-thinking indicators for the boys but not for the girls. Once again, then, ideational fluency was essentially independent of convergent thinking.

Finally, consider a paper by Orpet and Meyers (1966) concerned with 100 6-year-olds. Within the divergent-thinking domain, only tasks dealing with ideational fluency were administered. Various general intelligence assessors, however, also were included in the battery. From a factor analysis with an orthogonal Varimax rotation there emerged a clear factor whose highest loadings were provided by the four tasks that were taken to represent ideational fluency. At issue in all of these tasks was the number of acceptable ideational responses produced by the child. Loadings for these tasks ranged from .57 to .66 on the factor in question. By contrast, typical intelligence measures have loadings that do not exceed .30 on the ideational fluency factor. Turning to the factor on which the WISC vocabulary and WISC comprehension sub-tests both have their highest loadings (.71 and .69, respectively), the four ideational fluency tasks have loadings that range from .02 to .22. Considerable separation seems to exist here, then, between ideational fluency and typical intelligence measures.

The Evidence in Retrospect. In this part of the chapter we have been considering evidence bearing on Guilford's divergent-thinking formulation where the operations utilized have been taken directly from the Guilford group's work or have stayed very close to the procedures devised by Guilford and his associates. Several generalizations have emerged from passing this evidence in review. Most clearly supported as a dimension of individual differences independent from the convergent-thinking domain but also cohesive in its own right when one measures it in different ways has been what Guilford defines as ideational fluency: the person's ability to generate in plentiful number ideas that are appropriate to a given task constraint. Fluency with respect to words instead of ideas, which Guilford defines as the word-fluency concept, seems to have much more in common with general intelligence than with ideational fluency. One also begins to suspect that insofar as the other two fluency concepts dealt with by the Guilford group—associational and expressional fluency—move closer in particular task materials to tapping facility with words, they will end up more strongly aligned with general intelligence; whereas insofar as particular task contents for those concepts move closer to tapping facility with producing ideas as distinct from specific verbal trappings, the concepts will end up more strongly aligned with ideational fluency. Among the fluencies, in other words, as well as among all the divergent-thinking characteristics that have been proposed, it is the ideational fluency notion that seems to define the kind of cognitive functioning that is most clearly independent of convergent thinking.

Little evidence, in turn, supports the tenability of viewing any of the three flexibility concepts—spontaneous flexibility, adaptive flexibility, and redefinition—as more cohesive in its own right than the degree to which that concept merges with general intelligence. The set-shifting ability that these concepts imply

is more closely identified empirically with the traditional intelligence domain than with some different kind of functioning that might properly be considered an aspect of creativity.

In considering the originality concept, finally, the situation seems more ambiguous. Sometimes the originality indicators seem to be more related to convergent thinking, sometimes less so. We begin to suspect that the originality concept therefore may not have been defined with maximum clarity in its initial formulation by the Guilford group. In fact, the drift of the evidence suggests that originality measures may turn out to be more independent of intelligence to the extent that they correlate with ideational fluency measures, and more related with intelligence to the extent that they are independent of ideational fluency measures.

It may be that originality measures will tend to exhibit independence from intelligence if they depend upon assessing the uniqueness or unusualness of the ideas that a person generates, whereas they will tend to show relationships with intelligence if they depend upon a judgment of cleverness or facility in choice of words for expressing one's ideas. The kind of originality that is independent of intelligence, then, may be the kind that is facilitated by high ideational fluency: unusual or unique ideas are likely to occur later in a sequence of responses to a given task, so that the more plentiful the person's flow of ideas, the more likely he is to hit upon original ones. The giving of unusual uses for a brick, or of remote consequences as possibilities to which a particular event may lead, would be more likely to the extent that the respondent offers a larger number of uses or suggests a larger number of consequences to begin with. The kind of originality that correlates with intelligence, on the other hand, may be the kind that resides in sheer cleverness of verbal expression, which should depend heavily upon vocabulary size. The offering of plot titles that seem more out of the ordinary and hence earn higher "cleverness" scores may constitute an example of this second meaning for originality.

One final point should be emphasized. The vast majority of the studies that we reviewed administered the "divergent-thinking" tasks with relatively brief time limits and in an ability-testing context, that is, group administration in a classroom. As we pointed out earlier, however, emphasis upon speed of response and presence of the implication that there are correct answers would not seem to have an appropriate part in attempting to assess a person's talent for thinking in divergent ways. Were the task contexts less evaluative and the time limits more lenient or even nonexistent, therefore, the evidence for the independence from intelligence of ideational fluency and of forms of originality that are related to such fluency might have been even stronger.

DIRECT DESCENDANTS OF THE GUILFORD TRADITION

Two lines of further research stem directly from the work of the Guilford group, in the sense of leaning heavily upon that group for deriving a number of procedures, and also in the sense of sampling a comparably broad range of cognitive skills as presumably constituting what should be defined as creativity in thinking processes: the program of E. P. Torrance and the work of Getzels and Jackson. Both of these lines of research differ from most of what has already been considered, on the other hand, in that they both devote attention to the developing of further assessment procedures. We turn first to the work of Torrance and of other investigators who have utilized his assessment devices. Then, in the next part of the chapter, we shall consider the work of Getzels and Jackson.

Torrance's Studies and Related Work

Theoretical Considerations. Torrance defines creative thinking as "a process of becoming sensitive to problems, deficiencies, gaps in knowledge, missing elements, disharmonies, and so on: identifying the difficulty; searching for solutions, making guesses, or formulating hypotheses about the deficiencies; testing and retesting these hypotheses and possibily modifying and retesting them; and finally communicating the results" (Torrance, 1966a, p. 6). Thus Torrance considers the entire problem-solving sequence, in its broadest sense—from detecting a problem to communicating one's solution—to be the appropriate referent for the notion of creativity in thinking processes. It is difficult, as a matter

of fact, to detect much clear divergence between the forgoing definition and customary views of what intelligence involves. For example, compare this to Wechsler's definition of general intelligence: "Intelligence is the aggregate or global capacity of the individual to act purposefully, to think rationally and to deal effectively with his environment" (Wechsler, 1952, p. 3). The Torrance definition seems to include everything contained in Wechsler's, but to add explicit references to divergent thinking: "searching for solutions, making guesses, or formulating hypotheses. . . ." Thus what Torrance seems to mean by creativity is a general intelligence concept liberalized by the addition of references to a problem-solution phase in which it is useful for thinking to go off in different directions. If anything, then, Torrance's concept of creativity is even broader than that of Guilford, since Torrance's seems to imply a single basic dimension of which both divergent and convergent thinking would be parts.

What are Torrance's procedures for probing creativity? Some of his assessment devices involve verbal, others figural materials. Although the various tasks are intended to tap somewhat diverse functions, the customary practice of Torrance and his followers is to derive a single overall creativity index score—or, at most, one summary score for the verbal tasks and another for the visual—and to take the index score as signifying the subject's level of creative functioning. The various verbal and figural procedures are, as far as possible, all subjected to the same four types of scoring: for fluency, flexibility, originality, and elaboration (Torrance, 1966a, 1966b, 1966c). The first three of these scoring concepts already are familiar to us from the work of Guilford; regarding the first two, it is ideational fluency and spontaneous flexibility that are meant. Torrance's use of a common set of scoring templates for his tasks contributes further, of course, to the impression that, although he sometimes describes them as dealing with various psychological characteristics, they in fact are treated as functionally equivalent. Thus scores for fluency, flexibility, originality, and elaboration will be summed across all the verbal and/or all the figural tasks, and then these four totals are summed in turn into the single index score.

The administration context for the procedures is similar to that described for the Guilford tasks. The various tasks are timed and given relatively brief time limits. Torrance would have the typical administrator of the procedures be the teacher, so that whatever evaluative connotations are conveyed by her role will be present for the creativity instruments. In the research involving these tasks, furthermore, group administration typically prevails; although Torrance does recommend individual administration from the kindergarten to third-grade levels. Finally, a further feature reminiscent of convergent-thinking situations that even goes beyond the typical instructions for the Guilford tests is to be found in Torrance's instructions: a subtle implication to the respondent that some answers are more correct than others, and that the ones to be preferred are the ones that are more unusual and clever.

Here is an overview of one of two alternate parallel sets of test materials that Torrance (1966b, 1966c) has developed. The battery includes seven verbal tasks—a three-part "ask-and-guess" test, product improvements, unusual uses, unusual questions, and the "just suppose" activity—and three figural tasks—picture construction, incomplete figures, and parallel lines.

In the *ask-and-guess* test, the subject is shown a picture of a clownlike figure viewing his reflection in the water. With 5 minutes to devote to each task, the subject is first to write down all the questions he can think of about the picture; second to list as many possible causes as he can of the situation depicted in the picture; and third to list as many possible consequences of the depicted situation as he can. As to scoring, the number of relevant responses offered defines the fluency variable; the number of spontaneous shifts from one category to another regarding the kinds of questions, causes, and consequences presented defines flexibility; the statistical infrequency of the responses defines originality; and the amount or degree of detail and specificity incorporated into the responses defines elaboration.

For the *product improvement* task, a toy stuffed elephant is shown to the respondent, and he is given a set time period in which to list all the most clever and unusual ways he can think of for changing the toy to make it more fun for children to play with. Here again

and in the remaining procedures as well, except where otherwise noted, scoring is carried out for fluency, flexibility, originality, and elaboration in ways analogous to those described for the ask-and-guess test.

The *unusual uses* procedure requests the respondent to indicate, in a set time, as many interesting and unusual uses as he can imagine for cardboard boxes.

In the *unusual questions* task, the subject is to think of as many intriguing questions as possible that one can raise concerning cardboard boxes. Only fluency and originality are scored for this procedure.

Finally, the *just suppose* activity requires the subject to entertain a particular improbable situation and describe all the events that its occurrence would entail. The situation in question is clouds having strings attached that hang down to earth.

Turning to the figural tasks, the *picture construction* instrument presents the respondent with a piece of green paper in an egg-like shape, which he is to glue wherever he wishes on a blank page, then adding lines so as to incorporate this shape into a picture that will be as clever and imaginative as possible. The product is scored for originality and elaboration.

For the *incomplete figures* procedure, the subject is confronted with different schematic line forms, to each of which he is to sketch additions to represent a picture or object that is as unusual as possible.

The *parallel lines* task is similar to the preceding procedure, except that all the presented line forms that the subject must work from are the same—a pair of parallel straight lines.

In reviewing research that has utilized Torrance's tests, the major question we must address is, once again, the dimensionality issue: Do the Torrance procedures define a dimension of individual differences that is cohesive to a substantially greater degree than the degree to which those procedures correlate with measures of general intelligence?

Relationships with Intelligence and Academic Achievement. Evidence already has been noted to the effect that customary measures of intellective aptitude and of academic achievement seem, at least during the childhood and adolescent years, to be very substantially correlated. To cite examples of still further data to this effect, Edwards and Tyler (1965) found for the 181 ninth graders in a given school system that the correlation between performance on the School and College Ability Tests (a general intelligence measure) and performance on the Sequential Tests of Educational Progress (an academic achievement measure) was .86. They furthermore reported that the children between the intelligence index just cited and the students' grade point average was .66. From such findings we can surmise that studies of the relationship between the Torrance tests and academic achievement will, at least in large measure and perhaps entirely, actually be examining to what extent the Torrance battery is related to general intelligence. For this reason, it seems appropriate to consider work on achievement and on intelligence correlates of the Torrance tests under a common heading.

There is little direct evidence explicitly comparing the magnitudes of relationships among the Torrance measures with the extent of relationship between those measures and intelligence indicators—the type of issue we studied at length in considering Guilford's tasks. This lack seems to derive from the heavy dependence upon use of one or another overall creativity index score by those who have worked with the Torrance tests. Perhaps the most extensive evidence on the issue derives from a study by Cicirelli (1964) of more than 600 sixth graders. If we consider the correlations between all possible pairs of eight summary variables that were derived—fluency, flexibility, originality, and elaboration scores for a verbal and a figural battery—the average r turns out to be .37. This number, however, represents an artifactually inflated value to some degree, because, as we noted earlier in discussing Garwood's study, total number of ideas and number of relatively unique or unusual ideas as derived from the same procedure—the fluency and originality variables—possess a whole-part relationship to each other. As a result, some magnitude of positive correlation is guaranteed between fluency and originality scores. Cicirelli also reported correlations between the creativity indicators and various intelligence and achievement measures, such as the California Mental Maturity IQ index and California Achievement Test scores for reading, arithmetic, and language. All correlations were significant and

tended to fall in the 20s and 30s. If we estimate the effect of removing the spurious inflationary component from the average r of .37 among the creativity scores, the result would be a value quite similar to their degree of correlation with the intelligence and achievement measures.

A number of other studies, although not considering the strength of relationships among the Torrance measures, have reported on relationships between Torrance index scores and intelligence or achievement measures. These relationships, which usually have been substantial, further support the likelihood that the major role of the Torrance tests is to assess conventional forms of intellective aptitude and academic achievement. Thus, for example, Perry (1966) administered to sixth-grade children a verbal battery of the Torrance tests. These children had been continuously enrolled in the same school since kindergarten. Their creativity index scores yielded significant rho correlations of .54 with the kindergarten administration of the Metropolitan Reading Readiness test; .50 with the fifth-grade administration of the Otis Quick-Scoring Mental Ability Tests; .44, .46, and .59 with the sixth-grade administrations of the Reading Comprehension, Arithmetic Reasoning, and Spelling Achievement tests, respectively, from the Stanford Achievement Test battery; and .55 with an overall academic achievement score derived from the sixth-grade administration of the Stanford Achievement Test battery.

Yamamoto (1965) administered a set of verbal and figural creativity tasks and the verbal battery from the Lorge-Thorndike Intelligence Test to one sample of over 450 and another of over 800 fifth graders. Using a single creativity index score, the correlation with intelligence was 33 in the first sample and .39 in the second, both very substantial for such large samples. Since the first sample represented a socioeconomically homogeneous middle-class group, whereas the second represented a group more heterogeneous in socioeconomic status, we find these kinds of background factors to have relatively little effect upon the creativity-intelligence linkage that was obtained. From our earlier discussion of the Cicirelli findings concerning a comparably large sample of sixth graders, the evident implication to be drawn is that the various creativity measures constituting Yamamoto's index most likely are no more highly intercorrelated than the degree of correlation between the creativity index and the intelligence measure.

Among the numerous further studies providing documentation for the existence of comparably substantial relationships between Torrance procedures and intellective aptitude or achievement indices, we may cite the following instances. Yamamoto (1964a) reported a significant correlation of .30 between measures of creativity and intelligence for a high-school sample. With children in grades 4 and 5, Wodtke (1964) found that an index combining verbal and figural creativity tasks correlated .44 with an intelligence composite including verbal and nonverbal parts of the Lorge-Thorndike intelligence test among 100 fourth graders, while the comparable correlation was .45 among 100 fifth graders. In a study of fifth and sixth graders, Long and Henderson (1965) even found a significant positive relationship between a figural creativity task and a verbal academic achievement task.

Although occasional exceptions do occur in which Torrance measures and intelligence or achievement indicators are unrelated (Fleming and Weintraub, 1962; Edwards and Tyler, 1965), these can be accounted for in terms of restriction of range for the intelligence assessment, partialling out of age from the intelligence but not from the creativity index, or unreliablity of creativity measurement. Thus Fleming and Weintraub (1962) utilized a specially selected sample of "gifted children" with a very high mean IQ (approximately 136) and consequent restriction of IQ range. There also is the problem in the Fleming-Weintraub study that an IQ score was used to measure intelligence with a sample that varied widely in age—from 8 to 12½ years. Since an IQ score partials out the effects of age, the implication is that age was partialled out of the intelligence measure but not the creativity measure, with underestimation of their degree of relationship as a necessary consequence. Edwards and Tyler (1965), in turn, summed a single figural and a single verbal creativity task, even though the figural and verbal domains show relatively low coherence (Torrance and Gowan, 1963), and relationships with intelligence or achievement

criteria are stronger for the verbal than for the figural task (Bish, 1964). In sum, it is fair to state that the clear majority of the studies using Torrance's assessors have found substantial linkages between creativity and measures of intellective aptitude or achievement.

Having begun with the fact of strong relationships between aptitude and achievement indicators, we have found that Torrance index scores correlate with these in about the same degree to which we can expect the array of Torrance's measures to correlate with one another. No unitary dimension is defined by these measures therefore, apart from that of general intelligence. Hence there is still no cause for assuming the Torrance measures reflect a cognitive disposition that could be appropriately described in terms of creativity. Somewhat paradoxically, Torrance (e.g., 1962, 1963, 1966a) has ignored this dimensionality issue and bases a large part of the defense of his instruments upon their ability to predict academic achievement criteria—despite the demonstrably high relationship between such criteria and conventional intelligence assessors. His argument—the "threshold of intelligence" concept—is that, above a certain level of intelligence, academic achievement is more strongly related to his creativity measures than to further increments of intelligence. Why the prediction of academic accomplishment should be thought to redound to the credit of a purported assessor of creativity, however, is difficult to understand. After all, memorization of rule systems and the ability to manipulate their terms toward the goal of finding a correct answer—hence convergent thinking—constitute the very core of what is required for earning high scores on academic achievement tests. Be this as it may, what kind of evidence would be needed to support the threshold-of-intelligence concept?

Given the sizable correlations found among Torrance's index scores, traditional intelligence measures, and academic achievement yardsticks, there already is the strong presumption, of course, that most of the ability of the Torrance indicators to predict achievement criteria would depend upon the substantial variance shared by the Torrance and the achievement measures with general intelligence. A small amount of further predictability might be expected from the Torrance instruments, in turn, not because they tap a different cognitive domain from that of general intelligence, but simply because they increase the thoroughness with which convergent thinking abilities are being sampled. To put the matter another way, if a single intelligence measure does a fair job of predicting academic achievement, addition of a second correlated intelligence assessor should increase predictability somewhat just because a more adequate sampling of the abilities that comprise the intelligence domain would thereby be provided. What the threshold-of-intelligence concept requires, on the other hand, is that the predictability of academic achievement be sizably enhanced by adding a creativity assessor when the sample of subjects under study ranges into high levels of intelligence. Let us turn now to some research on this issue.

With more than 600 sixth graders as subjects, Cicirelli (1965) found that most of the ability of the Torrance indices to predict various academic achievement criteria depended on shared variance with intelligence. Thus, of 12 correlations computed between creativity and achievement measures, eight were .2 or better. However, when intelligence was held constant by partialling out IQ scores, only three of the 12 correlations remained .2 or better.

In another study, Yamamoto and Chimbidis (1966) utilized a sample of almost 800 fifth graders, administering the verbal battery of the Lorge-Thorndike Intelligence Test, a battery of verbal and figural creativity instruments from which were derived a single index score, and the Stanford Achievement Test battery. With a mean IQ of 110.3 for the entire sample, a division was made between children with IQ of 121 and above and children with IQ of 120 and below. Relationships between intelligence and achievement scores tended to be substantial for all groups —for the total sample, the lower IQ group, and the higher IQ group—although less strong for this last-mentioned group. When, however, partial correlations were computed between creativity and academic achievement holding intelligence constant, all of the relationships turned out to be near zero. A further indication of how little the creativity scores add to the intelligence scores in predicting

achievement is provided by the following comparison. With correlations combined across a variety of academic achievement areas, we present first the single-order correlation between IQ and achievement, and next the multiple correlation for IQ and creativity as joint predictors of achievement. For the entire sample, the correlation goes up from .56 to .57. For the lower IQ group, the simple and multiple correlations remain the same—.56. For the higher IQ group, the correlation goes up from .22 to .27. On the whole, then, intelligence predicts achievement less well in the high IQ range than elsewhere, but creativity scores do not offer much predictive help anywhere along the IQ continuum.

The relatively small further contribution that is made by the Torrance creativity battery to predicting academic achievement, as distinct from the contribution made by general intelligence, can be given further illustration in the results of a study by Bowers (1966). The subjects, almost 300 ninth-grade pupils approximately equally divided between the sexes received a creativity battery that included five verbal and two figural procedures, from which was derived an overall creativity index. The academic achievement criteria were grade level and scores on the Iowa Tests of Educational Development. The Otis Quick-Scoring Test of Mental Ability provided the intelligence measure. The single-order correlation between the intelligence measure and achievement was about .6 or .7, whereas the multiple correlation in which the creativity index and the intelligence measure serve as joint predictors of achievement typically was only a few hundredths higher.

In extensive studies of the issue, therefore, the threshold-of-intelligence concept has not been supported by the results obtained. Index scores derived from the Torrance tests behave, in relation to academic achievement, as if they constitute an alternative means for assessing the convergent-thinking domain, not as if they predict academic achievement in subjects of superior intelligence. Given the degree—and it will be substantial—to which a particular intelligence assessor predicts academic achievement, addition of the Torrance battery can be expected to increase predictability only marginally—and, indeed, to no greater an extent than would also be afforded by the addition of a second measure of general intelligence. The evidence of the present section supports the conclusion that the type of cognitive ability most clearly measured by the Torrance battery is in fact the conventionally demarcated notion of convergent thinking or general intelligence, rather than a conceptually distinguishable domain for which the term "creative thinking" would be appropriate. Two other major kinds of evidence, however, are invoked by Torrance in further support of his argument that the Torrance instruments measure a characteristic that is suitably described as creativity—studies of evaluations by teachers or other judges and studies of evaluations by the subjects' peers. We shall consider each of these types of work in turn.

Evidence on Evaluations by Judges. Since we have demonstrated that the Torrance instruments coalesce strongly with the general intelligence domain, it will not be surprising to find that teachers or other judges can make cognitive evaluations that relate in some degree to scores on the Torrance tests. What would need to be demonstrated is that the evaluations in question are doing something more than essentially depicting contrasts along the general intelligence continuum. Evidence indicates, however, that even when explicitly instructed to do so, teachers or other judges find it difficult to evaluate elementary and high school students on bases that do not boil down to the familiar arena of convergent thinking. We shall first look at some general documentation of this point and then turn to studies involving the Torrance tests in particular.

In an extensive study of more than 1000 high school seniors who were National Merit Scholarship finalists, Holland (1959) obtained ratings by the students' teachers and principals for the trait of originality. Since National Merit Scholarship finalists will, after all, be a high intelligence group, the opportunity should be particularly present in such a case for judgments of originality to signify something other than the conventional intelligence concept. Yet the evidence clearly indicated that the judges could do little more with reliability in their originality ratings than discriminate individual differences in talent at convergent thinking. Not only did the originality ratings correlate highly with ratings for

such conventional characterizations as intellectual leadership, citizenship, maturity, achievement drive, and dependability, but the originality ratings also exhibited strong correlations with verbal aptitude scores and academic grades.

Similar results are found in work by Wallen and Stevenson (1960) on teacher judgments of the creativity of fifth graders' compositions. After practicing on an initial set of compositions, each of five teachers rated each of three compositions by over 60 fifth graders for creativity, with the concept defined in such terms as the following: "Creativity is the expression of information, ideas and feelings colored by original thoughts and inspired by the inner urge of an individual to express himself" (p. 274). The judges were explicitly instructed that spelling, neatness, vocabulary, and length were not to be considered, nor was poetry as such to be considered more creative than prose. With high agreement among judges and high consistency over stories for a pupil, the creativity ratings turned out to be strongly correlated (approximately .6 or .7) with measures of intellective ability and academic achievement.

In yet other work along the same lines, Rivlin (1959) asked the teachers of students in the tenth and eleventh grades to study such criteria of creativity as "will venture into unfamiliar or new areas," and "demonstrates imaginative and original solutions to problems." The teachers then were to select from each of their classes five students who were not only intelligent but also creative, and five students who were equally intelligent but not creative. With over 100 high school students thus selected, the creative students were found to score significantly higher than the noncreatives on the Pintner measure of intelligence and on the Iowa Tests of Educational Development. Despite the request that they subjectively equate their creative and noncreative nominees for intelligence, therefore, the judges found it difficult to leave that domain out of the picture. Finally, we cite a study by Piers, Daniels, and Quackenbush (1960), where the correlation with intelligence of teacher ratings for creativity was less strong (.20), although still significant at the .05 level for the sample of 114. Here, however, rating agreement among the three teachers who evaluated each student was found to be very low.[3]

All in all, the findings that we have considered put the burden of proof on the investigator if he wishes to use evaluations by judges as evidence for the distinguishability of a creativity dimension from the more familiar concept of general intelligence. Rating reliability for "creativity" judgments seems to be found, by and large, to the degree that the basis for evaluation rests heavily upon the traditional convergent-thinking domain. In most of the research that has been conducted relating scores on the Torrance tests to putative creativity evaluations by judges, however, this crucial consideration has been ignored. Thus, for example, Torrance (1962, 1963), Torrance and Myers (1962), and Yamamoto (1963) have reported investigations in which teachers are asked to nominate pupils who are the highest and the lowest in the class with regard to fluency in production of ideas, flexibility concerning their ideas, originality in thinking, and ability to elaborate ideas. The classes in this work were at or above the fourth-grade level. The general finding is that significant relationships are obtained between teacher ratings in terms of one or another of the criteria just presented and the children's scores on the respective creativity variables from the Torrance tests. Hence there will be a relationship between ratings for fluency and test scores for fluency, between ratings for flexibility and test scores for flexibility, and so on. Such evidence then is cited in support of the construct validity of the Torrance measures (see, e.g., Torrance, 1966a). To do so ignores, however, our knowledge that the Torrance creativity variables tend to be intercorrelated, that ratings in terms of the criteria described tend to be intercorrelated—the well-known "halo-effect"

phenomenon—and that the Torrance measures as well as the kinds of rating designation in question produce results that are substantially correlated with intelligence. These findings clearly can be accounted for in terms of intelligence differences as the common mediating variable: the teacher ratings predict the creativity indices to the extent that the ratings are judgments of general intelligence and the creativity indices share variance with intelligence.

Direct evidence on these points has been provided in a recent study by Lieberman (1965) with a sample of 93 kindergarten children. Utilizing two teachers as independent judges, ratings were obtained for five aspects of playfulness, defined respectively in terms of physical spontaneity, social spontaneity, cognitive spontaneity, manifest joy, and sense of humor. High interrater agreement was found in all cases. These five ratings, however, turned out to be strongly intercorrelated, indicating that a halo existed and hence only one characteristic in effect was being rated. Tasks for assessing ideational fluency, spontaneous flexibility, and originality were adapted from the work of Torrance and Guilford. The Peabody Picture Vocabulary Test served as the index of general intelligence. The findings were quite unequivocal: correlations between intelligence and the playfulness ratings were approximately .3 and significant; correlations between intelligence and the creativity variables were approximately .2 to .3 and significant; and correlations between the playfulness ratings and the creativity variables also were approximately .2 to .3 and significant. Clearly, the relationships of the ratings and of the creativity indicators to intelligence accounted for their relationship to one another. In view of this result, it is difficult to understand how Torrance (1966a) can cite the Lieberman study as an indication that evaluation by judges of creativity-relevant traits lends construct validity to his creativity assessors. Rather, the appropriate conclusion would seem to be that judgmental ratings fail to support the view that Torrance's measures tap a characteristic distinguishable from convergent thinking.

Evidence on Evaluations by the Subjects' Peers. The situation with regard to peer evaluations seems to be similar to that regard-

---

[3] Ironically enough, the teacher ratings also were found to correlate with the originality measures that were used in this study, but not with the ideational fluency measures. As we recall from our earlier discussion of this research, however, it was the ideational fluency measures that were uncorrelated with intelligence, whereas the originality measures were correlated with intelligence. These further results reinforce the conclusion that the judges, when using their definition of creativity, in fact were evaluating intelligence.

ing evaluations by judges. Indeed, such an outcome should not surprise us, since if teachers or other judges find it difficult to evaluate a cognitive trait apart from general intelligence, such should be the case *a fortiori* for age-mates of the subjects. We present first a study that indicates the extent to which one can expect peer ratings for creativity to correlate with intelligence, and then turn to a study indicating findings obtained with Torrance's procedures.

In an investigation by Reid, King, and Wickwire (1959), seventh graders were asked to provide peer nominations in regard to creativity. Each pupil was requested to select three of his classmates who could be most appropriately described as having "good imaginations. They have new ideas and new ways of doing things" (p. 731). When peer nominations were carried out in these terms, the result amounted to very strong differentiation along conventional lines of academic aptitude and achievement. Nominated as more creative were the children who scored higher on such assessors as the California Test of Mental Maturity, the California Achievement Test, the Sequential Tests of Educational Progress, and mechanical and clerical ability tests as well.

Turning now to research relating peer ratings to the Torrance procedures, we fail to find information on general intelligence measures even though, as the Reid et al. study demonstrates, such information would be essential. Thus Yamamoto (1964b) carried out an extensive investigation of more than 400 students in grades 7 to 12. A battery of Torrance procedures was administered near the start of a term, and the students evaluated one another near the term's end by using judgmental criteria that were assumed to represent the types of creativity variable that were derived from the tests. Thus, for example, a fluency judgment was related to fluency scores on the creativity tests, a flexibility judgment to flexibility scores, and so on. Correlations for the entire group between the rating criteria and the test scores were on the order of the low 20s, and hence significant for this sample size. From the evidence already considered on relationships between cognitive ability ratings and intelligence, and on relationships between Torrance test scores and intelligence, it is evident that

the correlations here reported between the judgment criteria and the Torrance variables can be fully accounted for in terms of the extent to which relationships with general intelligence should be present. No information on intelligence was considered in the study. Thus the results are less likely to indicate that a creativity score for fluency correlates with sociometric nominations in terms of a fluency criterion, or that a creativity score for flexibility correlates with sociometric nominations in terms of a flexibility criterion, as Torrance (1966a) proposes, than to indicate that a halo effect is operating so that sociometric nominations by any criterion are tending to reflect general intelligence. The relationships between such nominations and the creativity scores then would be expected because the creativity scores are known to be reflective of general intelligence to a significant degree.

Neither evaluations by peers nor by judges, then, offer evidence for the distinguishability of Torrance's procedures from the convergent-thinking domain. While the major lines of findings regarding the grounds for construct validity of the Torrance instruments have now been reviewed, two further classes of studies involving these tasks will be described briefly: work on training effects and on age effects. Both kinds of research can be said to deal with the modifiability of scores on the Torrance tests as a function of experience.

Effects of Experience. A number of studies have been conducted where effects upon Torrance test performance of various kinds of training have been investigated. The general rule seems to be that enhanced performance can be obtained in this manner. Since, however, we have not been able to find satisfactory evidence indicating that the Torrance scores tap a trait that stands apart from the general domain of convergent-thinking skills, such training effects do not cast light on the construct validity issue.

In some of this research, the training procedures utilized were relatively similar to the Torrance tests themselves, so that what was provided amounted more or less to practice on the criterion. For example, Cartledge and Krauser (1963) provided groups of first graders with five 20-minute training sessions concerning how to improve toys to make them more fun to play with. Not only was intensive instruction provided, but competition was encouraged as well. Various principles for improving toys were taught to the group. By using as pretest and posttest a product improvement task in which the subject was to think of ways to improve a toy dog, the experimental regime just described resulted in a greater score increase than did its absence. With the training involving such specific tutoring in the test skill, however, it would be surprising not to find an effect. Similar points apply regarding a comparable study by Torrance (1961a).

In other studies, while the training experience may be more distant from what is tested for on the creativity instrument, another factor seems free to operate—a factor which, incidentally, could well play a role in the Cartledge-Krauser study—enhanced confidence due to one or another form of greater attention by the teacher and greater acceptance of the individual's responses. For instance, Torrance (1966d) has described research using a battery of his verbal and figural tasks as both pretest and posttest material with approximately 1500 fourth graders. The pretest took place near the start, the posttest near the end of the school term, with the experimental classes receiving a complicated training regime as the treatment. Every 2 weeks a new unit of the materials developed by Cunnington and Torrance (1965) was administered to the classes. Each unit consisted of a recorded dramatization, of say, a great moment in scientific discovery such as the Wright Brothers' inventing of the airplane, exercises designed to serve as a stimulus for the kind of thinking illustrated on the record, and a teacher guide suggesting other related activities in which the teacher may lead the children. One would expect the intensive enrichment represented by such materials, with the greater amounts of attention which the teacher pays thereby to the students, to enhance the students' feelings of confidence and acceptance. The result should be a generalized training effect, so that enhanced performance would be found not just on the Torrance tests but on a range of other tasks as well. This is not to deny, of course, the social desirability of the enrichment here described, but rather to suggest its functional equivalence to other ways in which greater

attention to and acceptance of the pupils might also be provided, and to suggest the generality of the cognitive effects that most likely ensue.

Perhaps the most convincing training research yielding enhanced performance on the Torrance tests is that which has been carried out at the instigation of Crutchfield (see, e.g., Crutchfield and Covington, 1963; Crutchfield, 1964; Olton, 1966), where the materials were relatively distant in character from the Torrance tests and also were self-instructional in nature rather than requiring teacher intervention for their transmission. Fifth- and sixth-grade children who have gone through a series of self-instructional lessons concerning detective stories, which serve as vehicles for teaching certain problem-solving skills, have performed better on certain Torrance tasks than comparable children not so instructed. We have no clear grounds, however, for considering these effects to be evidence of increased creativity rather than of increased convergent-thinking skills.

Turning to research on age differences, the general finding has been an increase with age across the elementary and high school years in performance levels on the Torrance tests (e.g., Torrance, 1961b; Yamamoto, 1962; Lembright and Yamamoto, 1965). Such an increase would seem to reflect the cumulative impact of the various sources of information to which the child in our culture is exposed over time, and to be comparable to age-related increases that we would expect for this reason in other kinds of cognitive performance as well.

The Evidence in Retrospect. In sum, we have not been able to find evidence suggesting that the Torrance instruments cohere among themselves to a degree greater than that to which they correlate with tests of convergent thinking. Nor have investigations concerning the threshold-of-intelligence hypothesis, evaluations by judges, and evaluations by peers, supported the construct validity of the Torrance battery. Given the promising leads that we obtained from research in the Guilford tradition, coupled with the general similarity between Torrance's materials and those of Guilford, why should work using the Torrance tasks lead us to such a disappointing verdict? We can suggest two major reasons.

Recall that our examination of the Guilford procedures suggested that the greatest independence from convergent thinking was found in the case of ideational fluency measures, with originality indicators also tending to exhibit independence from intelligence if they represented a kind of originality that should depend at least partly on the number of ideas emitted by the respondent. Flexibility measures, in turn, seemed to be more appropriately understood as within the convergent-thinking domain rather than as standing apart from it. We have found that the Torrance procedures are scored in terms of four variables: ideational fluency, originality of a kind that should indeed depend upon degree of fluency, spontaneous flexibility, and elaboration. The typical practice has been to construct as the creativity indicator an overall index score—hence a measure in which all four of these variables are reflected—whether restricted to verbal or visual procedures or representing a combination of both. We have already noted that spontaneous flexibility, however, seems to coalesce with general intelligence. Elaboration, in turn, seems on its face to be more appropriately construed as relevant to convergent than to divergent thinking, since it refers to a propensity for interpolating or filling in details. The upshot thus appears to be an index score in which two variables that seem relatively distinguishable from intelligence are confounded with two other variables that are not. An index score concerned only with ideational fluency and with fluency-related forms of originality would, in this view, exhibit considerably greater orthogonality from intelligence than an index score that is concerned with spontaneous flexibility and with elaboration as well.

Even if the prescription just set forth were followed, however, some degree of relationship with intelligence might still be found because of the administration context which surrounds the Torrance tasks. As we noted in considering the Guilford materials, the presence of relatively brief time limits and of a traditional aptitude or achievement testing situation with its evaluative connotations would not seem to be features conducive to the display of forms of thinking that depend upon generating new ideas. Thus some degree of relationship with traditional aptitude and achievement tests may accrue simply as a result of shared method variance; that is, subjects who are proficient at following instructions in evaluational situations which set a premium upon speed should show up relatively well on the Torrance tests. Recent results by Boersma and O'Bryan (1968) in fact support this line of interpretation.

Getzels and Jackson

Theoretical Considerations. In their research on students ranging from the sixth grade to the senior year of high school, Getzels and Jackson (1962) considered, as their basic means of contrasting the subjects, one or another IQ measure and a battery of five presumed creativity indicators. Of the five, one was derived from Guilford and three were original with the authors. What was the kind of cognitive excellence that they were expected to measure? Getzels and Jackson (1962) offer the following discussion of what they mean by creativity:

As it is used in this study, the term "creativity" refers to a fairly specific type of cognitive ability reflected in performance on a series of paper-and-pencil tests. . . . Our tests of creativity involved the ability to deal inventively with verbal and numerical symbol systems and with object-space relations. What most of these tests had in common was that the score depended not on a single predetermined correct response as is most often the case with the common intelligence test, but on the number, novelty, and variety of adaptive responses to a given stimulus task (pp. 16–17).

In short, the authors mean to describe a single ability which their creativity instruments reflect in common—an ability that differs from intelligence along essentially the same lines as does Guilford's concept of divergent thinking. To the terms "number," "novelty," and "variety," as they appear in Getzels and Jackson's definition, we can, of course, coordinate the Guilford terms fluency, originality, and flexibility, respectively. We turn next to the five creativity instruments comprising the Getzels and Jackson battery: word association, uses for things, hidden shapes, fables, and make-up problems.

In the *word association* test, the subject is

presented with 25 words, each of which has multiple meanings—for example, bolt. His task is to set forth as many meanings as he can for each word. Thus "word association test" really is a misnomer. The task would more appropriately have been named the "word definition test." With different meanings required by the instructions, what Guilford would call "adaptive flexibility" is at issue here.

The *uses* test requests the subject to write as many different uses as he can for each of five common objects that are named. Derived from Guilford, the procedure is, however, scored somewhat differently, in that measures of ideational fluency and of originality are combined into a single index: credits for number of responses are added to credits for number of statistically uncommon responses in arriving at a final score.[4]

Turning to the *hidden shapes* task, the respondent is shown, on each of a number of items, a simple geometric figure followed by four complex geometric figures, one of which contains the simple figure as a part. The subject is to choose the complex figure in which the simple figure is embedded. Credited to Cattell (1956), the authors justify its inclusion as a creativity assessor on the grounds that it appears to call for the ability to disregard superfluous detail and perceive essentials quickly in perceptual situations. Presumably, some kind of adaptive flexibility, to use Guilford's term again, would be at issue, in that the person must keep reorganizing his viewing of the complex figures until he finds the simple one.

For the *fables* test, each of several fables with a missing last line is presented, with the subject to supply three alternative endings to the fable—one moralistic, another humorous, and the third sad. The endings are scored in terms of whether they are sufficiently related to the rest of the story and whether they succeed in achieving the particular affective tone called for in a given instance—moralistic, funny, or sad. Something on the order of verbal sensitivity and of adaptive flexibility in shifting affective tone

[4] Since, as noted earlier, this type of originality measure does seem to be strongly correlated with ideational fluency, construction of a single score reflecting uncommonness as well as total output is quite justified.

"upon demand" seem to be tapped in this procedure.

Finally, the *make-up problems* test offers the respondent various sets of numerical information from which he is to devise as many problems as he can. At issue here is the ability to sift carefully through the data offered as raw material for problem construction, and then to shift flexibly among alternative parts and arrangements of this material. A form of adaptive flexibility would again seem to represent at least part of what is tapped by this procedure.

As far as context of administration is concerned, the procedures just described were defined to the respondents as tests and administered to them in the fashion of academic examinations as they sat in their classrooms. That four of the five creativity tasks in the authors' battery seem to concern aspects of flexibility already must sensitize us to the issue of how distinguishable are these creativity assessors from convergent thinking, since, as we recall, our examination of the Guilford procedures suggested that measures of flexibility seemed to be part and parcel of the general intelligence domain. To what extent, then, does the present battery define a dimension that is separable from intelligence?

Relationships with Intelligence and Academic Achievement. For the 292 boys in the Getzels and Jackson sample, all five of the creativity tests correlated beyond the .05 level with IQ, while four of the five did so for the 241 girls in the sample. Given such large samples, however, correlations might be relatively small and still significant, so that we must turn to the question of comparing the magnitude of correlations among the creativity tests with that between the creativity tests and the intelligence index. For the boys, the average correlation was .28 among the five creativity measures, but it was .26 between those measures and IQ. For the girls, the corresponding correlations were .32 and .27. Thus the only ability that the creativity assessors point to as what they jointly measure is the same kind of ability that is indexed by the IQ assessor. IQ was evaluated with different instruments and at different times for various members of this sample, with its extensive grade level spread from the upper elementary years to the end of high school, whereas the creativity battery was administered at one point in time to the entire sample. It is not surprising therefore that the creativity tests would intercorrelate slightly more highly than their degree of correlation with IQ. Were a fresh IQ test to have been administered at the same time as the creativity battery, even this slight difference would, we suspect, have disappeared.

The general point just described has been made in a number of discussions of the Getzels and Jackson work—for example, by Burt (1962), Cronbach (1962), de Mille and Merrifield (1962), Faris (1962), Thorndike (1963b), Marsh (1964), and Wallach and Kogan (1965a). Furthermore, critics have noted that the correlations between the intelligence test and the creativity measures are artifactually depressed because age effects have been removed from the intelligence scores by using the IQ metric, but they have not been removed from the creativity scores.

From the initial sample of more than 500 students, Getzels and Jackson proceeded to concentrate on two very specific subgroups, one containing 26 and the other 28 subjects. "Creativity" was defined as the summation of the individual's performances on the five creativity tests—a practice which should result in a score that, like the IQ measure itself, can only constitute another estimate of general intelligence. The two groups were composed as follows. One, the "high creativity group," contained students scoring within the top 20% of their class and sex grouping on the creativity index but below the top 20% on IQ. The other, the "high intelligence group," contained subjects who scored within the top 20% of their class and sex grouping on the IQ measure but below the top 20% on the creativity index. Given a very high mean IQ —132—for the initial sample as a whole, what we have here are two groups that are both quite high in regard to convergent-thinking ability. Since most of the creativity tests were, at least, not *intended* to measure general intelligence,[5] and since their degree of internal coherence is not strong, the index score that reflects the variance they have in common probably represents a more imperfect

[5] Ironically, the hidden shapes test actually *has* been used in connection with intelligence assessment. For a discussion and some findings, see, e.g., Witkin, Dyk, Faterson, Goodenough, and Karp (1962).

estimate of the convergent-thinking domain than does the IQ score. The IQ was, after all, explicitly fashioned as an intelligence measure, and its component parts are known to have high internal coherence. With the IQ score and the creativity battery functioning therefore as a somewhat better and a somewhat poorer estimate, respectively, of general intelligence, the high creativity group consists of students who have scored a little higher on the poorer intelligence index than they have on the better intelligence index, whereas the high intelligence group is composed of students who have scored a bit higher on the better intelligence index than they have on the poorer intelligence index. The clearest inference one can draw is that the two groups are of comparably high intelligence and not shown by these tests to be different in any other respect. The only further inference that may be valid is that the "real" intelligence level of the high creativity group may—although still high—be lower than that of the high intelligence group, given their relative standings on the poorer and better intelligence indices. It should also be the case, of course, that the group comprised of persons in the top 20% by both criteria should be the most intelligent of all—since, in their case, the two intelligence probes are in full agreement. The authors did not study, however, this last-named group.

If the two groups studied are comparably high on intelligence, and if the creativity index score provides no information with any reliability other than a second estimate of intelligence, then we are left with two groups that are similar rather than different in the authors' fields of interest. If the two groups are found to differ on some other measure, it could be for any number of reasons stemming from the vagaries of sampling, but it cannot be because of a "creativity versus intelligence" contrast. To mention just one of the myriad accidental contrasts that could have arisen between the groups, Cronbach (1962) notes that the ". . . age distributions of the two groups are not reported and perhaps differ" (p. 279). The differences that are reported by Getzels and Jackson between their high creative and high intelligence groups therefore cannot be taken seriously because we cannot know why they arise. The similarities that are found between the groups, on the other hand, can be readily understood on the ground that the two groups are comparable in general intelligence.

Perhaps the major similarity to which the authors call attention is in regard to scholastic achievement. Both the high creative and the high intelligence groups were found to exceed the general sample average regarding school achievement as measured by standardized achievement tests. Since the two groups are of comparably high intelligence, however, and since we know that achievement and aptitude indicators are strongly correlated, we could hardly expect otherwise. What the authors quite inappropriately conclude from this finding, on the other hand, is that high creative students achieve just as well in school as do high intelligence students.

Before reviewing several studies that have used a set of procedures similar to the Getzels and Jackson battery, it is of interest to dissect the authors' battery into its five constituent measures and consider whether their separate relationships with intelligence and academic achievement vary in a manner that we can predict from evidence examined earlier. According to our description of the tasks, four—word association, hidden shapes, fables, and make-up problems—seem to tap aspects of Guilford's adaptive flexibility concept, whereas one—uses for things—represented a combination of ideational fluency and the type of originality index that should covary with such fluency. If we recall our earlier analysis of studies using the Guilford procedures, flexibility measures turned out to be indistinguishable from the convergent-thinking domain, while ideational fluency and the type of originality score that would be dependent upon high ideational output seemed to be maximally distinguishable from convergent thinking. This immediately leads to the hypothesis that the failure of the Getzels and Jackson battery to gain separability from intelligence arises because the majority of its component tests reflect aspects of flexibility. On this interpretation, the uses measure should have a lower correlation with IQ and with scholastic achievement than the other four creativity tasks.

From the relevant data in the Getzels and Jackson book, this hypothesis receives some support. Of all five creativity measures, the uses task has the lowest correlation with ver-

bal scholastic achievement for males and for females, the next to lowest correlation with numerical scholastic achievement for each sex, and the next to lowest correlation with IQ for each sex.[6] To give some magnitudes, uses correlates .19 with verbal achievement for males, whereas the average correlation of the other four creativity tasks with verbal achievement for males is .44. For females, the corresponding correlations are .23 and .47. Turning to numerical achievement for the males, uses correlates .21, while the average r for the other tasks is .29. In the case of the females, .24 and .31 are the corresponding correlations. Regarding IQ, for the males, uses correlates .19, with an average r for the other tasks of .28. For the females on IQ, the corresponding r values are .15 and .30. The other four creativity tasks by the way show an average intercorrelation of .31 for the males and .35 for the females, thus indicating somewhat greater cohesiveness as well as a stronger correlation with IQ when uses is left out of the battery. In sum, although the Getzels and Jackson creativity battery as a whole cannot be separated from the convergent-thinking domain, the only one of its five parts that taps ideational fluency and a fluency-related form of originality does seem to be more distinguishable in this regard. Viewed in relation to the achievement question, what this means, of course, is that to the extent that one finds a creativity measure that does look relatively distinguishable from intelligence, it also will turn out to be relatively unrelated to academic achievement.

In closing this section, we consider three investigations that used a range of procedures closely resembling the Getzels and Jackson creativity battery, although none was identical to it. Ripple and May (1962) found, not surprisingly, that correlations between IQ and creativity task scores will be higher when IQ variability in the sample is greater. They compared samples of seventh graders that were more homogeneous versus more heterogeneous in IQ. Detailed inspection of their results, however, yields a very intriguing further out-

[6] The three tasks that uniformly show the highest correlations with IQ, with verbal achievement, and with numerical achievement—ranging, indeed, into the 50s—are word association, hidden shapes, and make-up problems, all of which have an evident dependence on adaptive flexibility.

come. If we consider their sample that was maximally heterogeneous in IQ—the sample where correlations of IQ with creativity scores were highest—six of the nine creativity measures had correlations with IQ significant beyond the .01 level. Of the remaining three measures, two were unrelated with IQ, whereas the third just passed the .05 level in its degree of relationship. What these three measures had in common was that they all concerned aspects of ideational fluency.

With 110 sixth graders as subjects, Flescher (1963) derived a presumed creativity index from summing the standardized scores on seven procedures, which, if anything, were even broader and more heterogeneous in content range than the Getzels and Jackson battery. Although the average correlation between the creativity measures and IQ scores from the California Test of Mental Maturity was only .04, the average correlation among the creativity scores themselves was a mere .11. The creativity measures thus had little in common with IQ, while they also had little in common with each other. Clearly, there was no warrant for the summing of these creativity measures into a single overall index.

An extensive replication of the Getzels and Jackson work was recently reported by Hasan and Butcher (1966). The subjects were 175 male and female students in their second year of high school, to whom were administered 10 creativity instruments that included all the tasks from the Getzels and Jackson battery except the hidden shapes test. Standard measures of intelligence, verbal achievement, and numerical achievement also were obtained. The results strikingly confirmed our conclusions from the Getzels and Jackson research: the type of creativity battery in question yields essentially the same overall orderings of individuals as provided by measures of intelligence or achievement. If anything, the creativity scores correlated even more strongly with intelligence than they did among themselves. For the total sample, the average correlation of the 10 creativity measures with intelligence was .42, while the average correlation among the creativity indicators themselves was .25. The creativity composite score, intelligence score, verbal achievement index, and numerical achievement index all intercorrelated with sufficient strength—in the 60s, 70s, and 80s—to indicate that they clearly

were functioning as alternative measures of the same dimension. Thus, for example, the correlation between the creativity composite and intelligence was .74.

Hasan and Butcher point out, furthermore, that their sample actually was less variable on intelligence than was the Getzels and Jackson sample. Despite this reduced spread of IQ scores, the results once again indicated that the only characteristic which the kind of creativity battery under consideration can measure with any reliability is none other than general intelligence.

Evidence on Teacher Preferences. Apart from the claim that the high creative and the high intelligence groups both show superior academic achievement, perhaps the other best-known assertion that Getzels and Jackson have made is that, in terms of which students the teacher most enjoys and most prefers to have in class ". . . teachers give better ratings to the high IQ students than to the high creativity students . . ." (1962, p. 32). We shall explore the evidence for this assertion at some length because a replication study by other investigators has included the key comparison group omitted by Getzels and Jackson—students in the upper 20% on both IQ and creativity.

In the Getzels-Jackson study, teachers were asked to evaluate their students by a criterion that emphasized personal liking: the degree to which they preferred having the student in their class. Compared were the high intelligence group, the high creative group, and the remainder of the total sample in the research. The high intelligence group was found to earn significantly higher teacher preference ratings than the remainder of the sample. The high creativity group, in turn, earned teacher preference ratings that also were higher than those for the remainder, but not significantly so. From these findings, the authors conclude that while the "high IQ group stands out as being more desirable than the average student, the high creativity group does not" (1962), p. 30). They quickly lapse, furthermore, into a language which directly compares the two groups, referring in subsequent pages to the high intelligence group as preferred by the teachers over the high creative group.

What do these findings really show? As de Mille and Merrifield (1962) and Wallach and

Kogan (1965a) note, the high intelligence and high creative groups actually do not differ significantly from each other regarding teacher preferences. At best one comes away with the suggestion that the two groups may both be somewhat preferred by their teachers to the remainder of the sample, with the evidence a bit clearer in the case of the high intelligence group. But now we must return to the question of what these groups mean psychologically. As we discussed earlier in considering how the groups were constituted, all we can know is that the two group are of somewhat superior intelligence, with the further possibility that the high intelligence group exceeds the high creativity group regarding intelligence. We hence find complete correspondence between the ordering of the samples in terms of intelligence and in terms of teacher preferences: values on both dimensions are highest for the high intelligence group, lower for the high creativity group, and still lower for the remainder of the sample.

With the creativity composite as well as the IQ measure both providing estimates of general intelligence, we should expect, of course, that the highest teacher preferences of all would be awarded to the students who score within the top 20% by both measures. In this case, as we noted earlier, the two estimates of intelligence agree in placing the student very high on the continuum. Although Getzels and Jackson report no data on such a group, it has been studied in relation to the teacher preference issue by Hasan and Butcher (1966). These authors replicated Getzels and Jackson's findings of stronger teacher preferences for the high intelligence group than the high creativity group, but they found further that the strongest teacher preferences were awarded to the group high on both measures. As implied by our interpretation, then, the results indicate that teacher preferences are maximal for the group high by both criteria, lower for the group high by the IQ measure but not correspondingly high by the creativity index, and lower still for the group high by the creativity index but not correspondingly high by the IQ measure. Hasan and Butcher's evidence thus supports the view that all the creativity score provides is another estimate of general intelligence, and a poorer one at that.

It might be noted that the present material on jointly predicting teacher preferences from an intelligence measure and the Getzels-Jackson type of creativity index is quite analogous in outcome to the work discussed in connection with Torrance on jointly predicting academic achievement from an intelligence measure and the Torrance type of creativity index. In both cases, the IQ score carries the major predictive burden, with addition of the creativity index increasing predictability by about the margin one would expect if that index were functioning as an ancillary estimate of intelligence. In neither case is the purported creativity index doing work that would not be equally well, and perhaps even better, performed by administering a second intelligence test.

Other differences reported in the Getzels-Jackson research program between their high creative and high intelligence groups (see, e.g., Getzels and Jackson, 1960, 1962) are uninterpretable because, as already discussed, responsibility for the differences may rest upon any number of accidental ways in which the two groups are distinguished, and does not in any case rest upon a creativity-intelligence contrast. Since the crucial comparison information on the "high-high" group is never considered, we can gain no clues as to what really may be at issue psychologically. One further study in that program, where a different mode of analysis was employed, gives some instructive findings. Jackson, Getzels, and Xydis (1960) correlated each of the five creativity measures separately with an index presumed to tap "nonpathological fantasy" on a group-administered Rorschach test. The subjects were the ones already described in our consideration of the Getzels-Jackson book, with results examined in the present case for the total sample of 292 males and 241 females. As the Rorschach measure, each of four Rorschach cards was projected on a screen, with the subject to choose from ten multiple-choice responses the three that he considered most appropriate to the picture. Included among each set of ten responses were four considered to be "pathological," most of which involved references to violent aggression, such as "bloody clouds" or "bloody stomach." The smaller the number of such responses included among the subject's choices, the higher his score for nonpathological fantasy.

Given the character of the measure just described, it would seem that something on the order of sensitivity to or interest in making the more socially appropriate selections is at issue here. The measure in question did not correlate with any of the five creativity scores for the boys. In the case of the girls, however, it correlated with three of those creativity scores: the word association test, the hidden shapes test, and the make-up problems test. It will be recalled that these are the very same three creativity tasks that were found to possess the strongest correlations with IQ, verbal achievement, and numerical achievement. And, indeed, the Rorschach measure under consideration is also found to correlate with the females' IQ, verbal achievement, and numerical achievement scores. The positive results obtained for the girls therefore would seem to mean not that creative individuals are more given to nonpathological Rorschach fantasy, but rather that intelligent individuals are more likely to make socially appropriate choices on the Rorschach task.

As an example of the confusion that has been sown among others by the Getzels and Jackson research, consider finally a report by Smith and White (1965). In using the Getzels-Jackson word association procedure as their measure of creativity, a significant correlation (.17) was observed in a sample of 156 young male adults between creativity and a sociometric choice indicator of how witty and amusing the person seems to his peers. Since the word association task in question has been found to measure nothing apart from convergent-thinking ability, what the present finding would seem to indicate is that, not surprisingly, the more intelligent subjects seem more witty to their peers. The authors, however, view their results as suggesting that wittiness is an attribute of the creative person.

The Evidence in Retrospect. As in the case of the Torrance procedures, for the creativity assessment battery developed by Getzels and Jackson we have not found evidence of greater coherence among the tasks in question than the degree to which they correlate with measures of intelligence. The composite score presumed by Getzels and Jackson to reflect a form of cognitive excellence separable from intelligence and appropriately described with the term "creativity" has turned out, rather, to constitute a second—and less reliable—measure of general intelligence. The high intelligence and high creative groups defined

and contrasted by the authors have been found to reflect no intelligence-creativity contrast, but rather to consist in both instances of high intelligence students, with the former group likely to be of somewhat higher intelligence than the latter, and with the two groups differing otherwise in accidental ways. In regard to teacher preferences, it is not the case that—as the authors propose—teachers prefer the high intelligence group over the high creative group, but rather that—as we would already suspect from our earlier review of evidence on evaluations by judges—teacher preference is correlated with general intelligence level.

Our internal analysis of the Getzels-Jackson creativity battery has suggested that an important reason for its failure to yield a measure separable from convergent thinking resides in the battery's emphasis upon assessors of what Guilford would call adaptive flexibility. Of the five tasks in the creativity battery, the three that showed the strongest relationships with intellective aptitude and achievement measures concern a person's ability to give alternative definitions for words, to perceive alternative structures in visual patterns, and to use alternative parts and arrangements of descriptive material in constructing problems. All of our evidence points, however, to the conclusion that set-shifting ability of this type characterizes the high intelligence individual, and thus cannot be separated from the convergent thinking domain. The one task in the battery that reflects ideational fluency and a fluency-dependent kind of rarity or uniqueness of ideas, on the other hand, showed only weak relationships with convergent thinking assessors, thus confirming earlier indications that the characteristics in question may well be distinguishable from intelligence. Since the present work, moreover, once again utilized an assessment context characterized by evaluational stress and time pressure, the degree to which ideational fluency and fluency-related forms of originality are independent of traditional forms of intelligence may well have been underestimated.

A Look Ahead. From all of the research reviewed to this point in the chapter, we can distill a major positive conclusion. There does indeed seem to be a kind of cognitive excellence that both is empirically distinguishable from convergent thinking and also possesses some face validity in connection with the "creativity" term. However, it is much more specific and restricted in character than has been assumed by the investigators considered thus far. The type of cognitive talent in question seems to concern a person's ability to produce a large number of ideas in response to a given task constraint, where the ideational content that is generated is reasonably appropriate to the task at hand and, at least partly by virtue of its quantity, includes a goodly amount of content that is relatively unique or unusual. Procedures reflective of such ideational fluency and of forms of originality that seem dependent upon an extensive flow of ideas have been found to be maximally orthogonal to intelligence. That the ideational content at issue here remains relatively appropriate to the given task rather than ranging into the bizarre can be asserted for a simple reason. Appropriateness has constituted an implicit part of the task instructions, and most of the studies have been conducted with subjects who, either by virtue of membership in the middle class or by virtue of their involvement in a social system with authoritarian overtones—such as the classroom or the military—can be expected to conform reasonably well to the demands set by the experimenter.

Our concern with isolating thinking processes that may be described as creative without doing violence to the term thus has led us to consider what may be called associative fluency and uniqueness: the flow of ideas and the uniqueness of their content. Notice that we use the term "association" in a different sense from that which Getzels and Jackson implied when they designed their word association test, where performance depended upon a person's flexibility in coming up with diverse meanings for a given word. We are referring not to flexibility in shifting from one cognitive category to another, but to fluency in generating cognitive units whatever their category membership. Such fluency is, indeed, considerably more associative in character than the ability to shift set, where a heavy emphasis must be placed upon evaluating whether, for instance, the second definition one offers for a word is sufficiently different from the first. As a matter of fact, it may well be this necessarily heavy emphasis upon evaluational processes—as distinct from the business of generating ideational possibil-

ities as such—that leaves measures of flexibility closely united with convergent-thinking ability (see Wallach, 1967). What may be at the psychological root of associative fluency and uniqueness therefore is one's disposition to produce ideational possibilities under circumstances where evaluational activities are at a minimum. One is referring here to a person's disposition to "ride associative currents," as it were.

Warrant can in fact be found in the introspections of undeniably creative artists, musicians, writers, scientists, and mathematicians, for emphasizing the riding of associative currents when one seeks to formulate a definition of creativity in thinking processes. A volume edited by Ghiselin (1955) contains many relevant quotations along these lines, as does a volume edited by Hadamard (1945). To offer just two examples, Einstein refers to the need for "combinatory play" and "associative play" regarding images and ideas (Ghiselin, 1955, p. 43), and Dryden notes that his writing activities involve the generating of "a confus'd Mass of Thoughts, tumbling over one another in the Dark" (Ghiselin, 1955, p. 80). Implicit in such introspective accounts are a temporary suspension of evaluational processes and an obtaining of innovative possibilities by means of the very abundance of ideational output. Analogous points have been made by McKellar (1957) and by Rugg (1963). Associative fluency and uniqueness as the core of a process definition of creativity thus can be said to possess a modicum of face validity—at least if one accepts such introspections as reasonably veridical.

Work that concentrates on associative processes, then, may move us closer to an understanding of creativity in thinking, and it is to such work that we turn in the sections that follow.

RESTRICTING THE DEFINITION TO ASSOCIATIVE PROCESSES

Three major lines of research can be delineaed whose operational approach has concentrated on associative processes: work by Maltzman and others who have dealt with training in the giving of original associative responses, studies oriented around Mednick's Remote Associates Test, and work by Wallach and Kogan. We shall take up these research paths in their order of historical emergence, turning first to studies on the training of associative originality.

Maltzman and the Training of Associative Uniqueness

Maltzman provided the stimulus for many researchers' efforts to enhance the level of uniqueness of a person's associations when confronted with a particular task request through experimental manipulations that encourage subjects to give unique responses to stimuli. What these training regimes seem oriented toward is the establishment of an attitude on the subject's part conducive to his entertaining diverse associative possibilities in response to a given stimulus—and hence the entertaining of possibilities that are more unique or remote. Thus Maltzman and his collaborators (Maltzman, Bogartz, and Breger, 1958; Maltzman, Brooks, Bogartz, and Summers, 1958; Maltzman, 1960; Maltzman, Simon, Raskin, and Licht, 1960; Maltzman, Belloni, and Fishbein, 1964) were interested in facilitating "original thinking," which they defined as "behavior that occurs relatively infrequently, is uncommon under given conditions, and is relevant to those conditions" (Maltzman et al., 1960, p. 1). In one experiment, Maltzman, Bogartz, and Breger (1958) found that repeated evocation of different associative responses to the same stimuli in a free association task led the undergraduate subjects to provide associative responses of greater uniqueness when offering free associations to a list of stimulus words different from that on which training had occurred. Evidence of transfer from such training to the production of unique uses on Guilford's unusual uses test, however, was equivocal. A more extensive examination of this issue in a subsequent study (Maltzman et al., 1960), on the other hand, found clear evidence of transfer to uniqueness of ideational content on the unusual uses test as well.

Let us consider the latter investigation in greater detail. In all conditions, the experiment began by presenting the undergraduate subjects with a list of 25 stimulus words, for each of which they were to respond with the first word that came to mind. The training regime then presented the subjects with five successive repetitions of this list, requesting that they give a different associative response

than the one used before when a word came up on each successive repetition. The individual thus was forced to search his repertoire for relatively remote associates of a given word. The number of statistically unique uses provided on the unusual uses task was significantly greater after this experience than after various control regimes administered to other subjects, such as giving the same associative response to a particular word when it came up on each of five repetitions of the list, giving an associative response to each of 125 different common stimulus words, giving an associative response to each of 125 different uncommon stimulus words, reading different unique associates on five successive repetitions of the original list of 25 words, or simply having no special training at all. Indeed, the experience of providing the same associate in response to a given word when it occurred on each of its five repetitions was found to eventuate in significantly less productivity of unique uses on the unusual uses task than was the case for the other control conditions.

These findings are by no means obvious, since a sizable conceptual gap intervenes between a task in which the subject responds with an association that occurs to him when presented with a particular word and a task in which the subject describes as many uses as possible for a given object, with the implication that the uses must be of relevance rather than bizarre. What the results suggest is that productivity with respect to unique uses is influenced by experiences that orient the subject toward or away from the utilization of lower likelihood associates of a stimulus. Maximum generation of unique uses is found to follow a situation in which the subject was urged to seek out lower likelihood associates to a stimulus word and to foreswear the common associates; minimum generation of unique uses, on the other hand, is found to follow a situation in which the subject was urged to concentrate his attention on the most likely associate of the stimulus word. One can think of these instructions as influencing the likelihood of emission of more and less probable associates in response to a stimulus: the "lower likelihood" instruction reduces the likelihood of responding with common associates and increases the likelihood of responding with uncommon associates, whereas the "most likely" instruction increases the probability of making common associative responses and reduces the probability of making uncommon associative responses. We know that in general there will be a falling gradient of probability levels for responses to a given stimulus as the responses become decreasingly common associates of that stimulus (see, e.g., Maltzman, Bogartz, and Breger, 1958; Maltzman et al., 1960). With decreasing commonness of response therefore the gradient of response probability starts lower and falls off more gradually as a result of the former instructional regime, whereas it starts higher and falls off more steeply as a result of the latter.

All that the preceding formulation does, of course, is describe the effect of the contrasting instructional conditions upon the likelihood of emitting associative responses of greater and lesser commonness when presented with a stimulus word. That a flattened gradient does in fact emerge from encouragement to give different associates upon subsequent repetitions of a stimulus word is evidenced by Maltzman et al.'s (1960) finding that as the word list receives more repetitions under the instruction in question, the percentage of fully unique associative responses offered by the sample keeps rising—from approximately 10% on the first repetition to approximately 70% on the fifth. What is of particular note, however, is that the present experiment's instructional manipulation of the shallowness or steepness of the probability gradient for making common and uncommon associative responses transfers to influence whether or not the subject comes up with unique uses when subsequently confronted with the unusual uses task. Flatness or steepness of associative gradient thus has been found to be a germane concept for interpreting unusual uses performance.

To argue that the transfer effects regarding uses performance result from manipulations of the subjects' associative gradients depends, of course, not only on the findings for the two conditions that, respectively, maximized and minimized such transfer, but also on the findings for the remaining conditions, where uses performance was uniformly intermediate. The latter conditions, it will be recalled—all of which yielded the same results—included the giving of an associative response to each of a

variety of stimuli, the reading of a variety of unique associates to a given stimulus, and the absence of training altogether. Thus for training to cause positive transfer, the subject had to generate a multitude of associates to a given stimulus, insuring thereby that relatively uncommon associates to that stimulus would result; and the subject had to search his own head for the associates rather than engage in mere observation of unique associates served up by another.[7] The first point means that a flattened gradient had to be produced; the second means that the gradient concept refers to the effects of an active process of generating associates.

In a recent study with undergraduates, Sieber and Lanzetta (1966) investigated another effect of the flattening of associative gradients in response to a stimulus: the implication that a person who is permitted only one task response will be more indecisive in choosing the response to offer if he has been trained in the use of flatter gradients. This outcome was in fact obtained. Whereas the Maltzman group found the flattening of associative gradients to induce greater productivity of unique ideational content, Sieber and Lanzetta have found the flattening of associative gradients to result in greater indecisiveness because of conflict among alternative possible responses. An experiment also has been carried out which provides a direct demonstration of the congruence implied by the aforementioned work between such indecisiveness and the generation of original responses. We would expect, in other words, that if it is appropriate to view the Maltzman et al. and Sieber-Lanzetta lines of work as both concerned with the slope of associative gradients for responses to a stimulus, then indecisiveness among alternative posibilities, as measured in one situation, should be correlated with productivity of unusual ideational associates, as measured in another. In confirmation of this expectation, Worell and Worell (1965) found, with undergraduate subjects, that persons who displayed more indecisiveness in describing aspects of their behavior also exhibited greater uncommonness in the responses they gave to each of a number of stimuli on a word association test. There is a convergence of evidence,

---

[7] A similar finding has been reported by Freedman (1965).

then, supporting the view that the relative originality or unusualness of the ideational content produced in response to one or another kind of task requirement may be usefully conceptualized in terms of the relative flatness of a person's associative gradient.

Although it is clear that experimental induction of flattened associative gradients results in the enhanced production of unique ideas in a given task setting, it is not clear how successful this kind of training will be when the criterion concerns enhanced availability of one particular unusual associate that is defined in advance by the experimenter. Since the latter criterion is much more strict and specific than the former, it is perhaps not surprising that the results would be more equivocal. Thus training in the entertaining of uncommon ideas in response to a given task stimulus was not found to facilitate problem-solving that depended on producing a particular idea that was unusual relative to its context in studies by Anderson and Anderson (1963) with sixth graders, Caron, Unger, and Parloff (1963) with high school students, and Maltzman, Belloni, and Fishbein (1964) with undergraduates. On the other hand, at least partial evidence for this kind of highly specific facilitation as a function of such training was found in studies by Flavell, Cooper, and Loiselle (1958), Maltzman, Brooks, Bogartz, and Summers (1958), Freedman (1965), and Yonge (1966), all conducted with college students. That any positive instances can be located of this kind of facilitation is, of course, quite noteworthy, since various extenuating factors can always account for the negative instances.

To take an example from each group of investigations, consider first the report by Anderson and Anderson (1963). Sixth-grade boys were trained to generate unusual uses for familiar objects through group tutoring sessions in which the experimenter would direct the subject's attention to various properties of a given object and would provide encouragement for offering uncommon usage possibilities. Such training transferred to the production of larger numbers of novel uses for familiar objects that had not been included in the training series, but not to the solution of problems which required that a familar object be used in one specific unusual way in order for success to be attained.

On the other side of the ledger, consider Yonge's (1966) research. With female undergraduate subjects, the solution of interest to the experimenter in a criterion problem required that an electrical switch be given the uncommon function of serving as a weight to be attached to a string so as to form a pendulum.[8] Prior experience utilizing the switch in its customary role as part of an electrical circuit makes it difficult to ascribe to the switch the required use of functioning as a weight. Such negative transfer was overcome, however, in the case of subjects who received prior experience not only with the common function but also with the use of the switch in a variety of uncommon functions—for example, as a straightedge ruler when drawing a design and as a holder for a piece of cardboard—as long as experience with the common function did not precede experience with all the uncommon functions. Involvement in tasks requiring that the switch function in unusual ways thus was found, under certain circumstances, to facilitate solving a problem by using the switch in a particular unusual way that had not been experienced before.

In this section of the chapter, we have brought together some work that bears upon the psychological underpinnings of the unusual uses procedure. It is productivity and uniqueness of ideational content on tasks of this kind, we recall, that were found in earlier sections to define a form of cognitive activity that is maximally independent of convergent thinking. Given the evidence that we have considered regarding how to enhance performance experimentally on the present type of task, it has proven useful to conceive of the person who is able to suggest numerous unusual uses for an object as possessing a flattened associative gradient relative to the person who can suggest only few such uses.

A step has been made, then, toward our understanding the cognitive difference between the person who can suggest many possible—and therefore also many that range into unusual and remote ideas—uses for an object, or consequences of some event, or

[8] The problem—adopted from Maier (1931)—requires the subject to grasp two strings suspended from the ceiling at a greater separation than his arms can span, which he can do if he swings one string with the switch attached as a weight.

problems suggested by certain common situations, or titles for a story plot and the person who can suggest but few. To view this difference in terms of shallow versus steep associative gradients is, of course, only to provide a descriptive model for what we have observed, but one, nevertheless, which seems to possess a fair amount of summary power. The next step is to ask why some people seem to bring flatter associative gradients than others to the cognitive tasks that confront them. In the following part of the chapter, we turn to a line of research from which we can begin to glimpse an answer to this question.

Mednick and the Role of Attention Deployment in the Remote Associates Test

Theoretical Considerations. The starting point for Mednick's approach to creativity is the associative gradient concept to which we were led in our preceding discussion. By basing his view upon the kind of introspective accounts cited earlier, where we noted that outstanding contributors to the arts and sciences emphasized the importance of generating abundant quantities of associative content in arriving at novel principles and products, Mednick (1962) proposed that the creative thinker will be characterized by a relatively flat rather than steep gradient regarding the likelihoods with which different associates will occur to him as he contemplates a task. Given an associative gradient whose downward slope is more gentle, the creative individual will be less fixated upon the common associations to an idea and more capable of reaching the distant, inaccessible associations[9]—those which, in relation to the initial idea, constitute "new combinations which either meet specified requirements or are in some way useful" (p. 221).

How does Mednick measure creativity? Rather than assessing associative productivity and uniqueness directly, he chose to deal with a by-product of the number and uniqueness of the associates that a person is capable of generating: the person's ability to produce a particular associate that is related on a purely associative basis to each of three words with which he is presented. The likelihood of solv-

[9] Emphasis upon the importance of variation among the cognitive elements that are available for use also is present in Campbell's (1960) analysis of creative thinking.

ing this kind of associative problem should depend upon how numerous—and therefore also how unusual—are the associates that the person produces in response to the three words that are offered. The greater this productivity, the easier it will be for the person to hit upon the word that provides an associative "mediating link" to the other three. To give some examples from Mednick's (1962) measuring instrument—the Remote Associates Test (RAT)—one item consists of the words rat, blue, and cottage, while another item presents the words go, poke, and molasses. For still other items the word triads are: sixteen, heart, cookies; surprise, line, birthday; and railroad, girl, class. The respective answers for the five items that have been presented are cheese, slow, sweet, party, and working. By comparing each answer with the triad that is to elicit it, we can see that the items have been constructed in such a manner that the mediating link in all cases is "strictly associative rather than being of a sort that follows elaborate rules of logic, concept formation, or problem solving" (Mednick, 1962, p. 227).

Although the RAT typically is administered as a test with a time limit, the timing is quite lenient—40 minutes for 30 items—so that time pressure should be minimal. However, the fact remains that Mednick's own formulation would seem to imply rather that the procedure be administered without any time limit at all. Some individuals who would otherwise be able to better their scores may be prevented from doing so by even the lenient time limit adopted. Since the RAT is a procedure with a correct answer specified in advance for each item, it has of course in this regard the look of a test of convergent rather than of divergent thinking. Given the dependence of the RAT upon strictly associative processes for solution, however, its resemblance to tests of convergent thinking is only superficial. A potential problem caused by this format nevertheless is that the experimenter's creativity in composing test items limits the degree of creativity that a subject can display. The consequence is that the instrument therefore may not be as sensitive in its upper range as would otherwise be the case. For most purposes this issue would not seem to be a serious one.

The clearest retort to these procedural

questions, however, consists of demonstrating, as Mednick's formulation implies, that productivity and uniqueness of content in generating associates are related to RAT performance. A number of studies have shown this to be the case.

The Bridge from Associative Productivity and Uniqueness to Remote Associates Test Performance. Two kinds of research can be cited to document the assertion that associative productivity and uniqueness, on the one hand, and RAT performance, on the other, constitute equivalent operations: manipulatory and individual difference investigations. Turning to manipulation research first, Freedman (1965) contrasted the effects of three kinds of experience upon subsequently measured RAT performance levels: generating associations to stimulus words, reading the associations produced by others to stimulus words, and defining stimulus words. In more detail, the subjects in the first condition were to associate freely to each of 10 words, with encouragement to respond with whatever words came to mind. Every subject in the second condition was paired with a subject in the first condition, receiving for each word a card to be read containing the associations that the other person had offered for that stimulus. Subjects in the third condition were to provide a definition of each of the same stimulus words used in the other conditions. Neither the stimulus words nor any of their common associates were the answers to any of the RAT items. For all of the undergraduates in the study, the experience prior to taking the RAT was described as a brief warm-up exercise. The results indicated that significantly higher RAT scores were earned by subjects in the first condition than by subjects in either of the other two conditions, which in turn yielded similar RAT levels. Generation of plentiful associates—and hence also of relatively uncommon ones—thus was found to facilitate RAT performance. That passive reading of associates produced by others was not sufficient to facilitate RAT performance indicated that the generating process itself, and not just its cognitive consequences, had to be present. That the providing of definitions for the stimulus words also failed to facilitate RAT performance indicated that the generating process at issue

had to be strictly associative in character.

Whereas the results of the Freedman study were quite clear-cut, an earlier related experiment by Caron, Unger, and Parloff (1963) had failed to obtain facilitation of RAT performance from an associative training condition. Freedman (1965) has pointed out, however, that greater remoteness from the stimulus word most likely was attained in his association condition rather than in that of Caron et al. Unlike the Caron et al. procedure, where the stimulus word was repeated each time a new associate to it was requested, Freedman presented the stimulus word only once, with all of the subject's associations to it then following. The Caron method should keep the associates more closely linked to the stimulus than the Freedman technique, and hence the latter should result in flatter gradients—that is, in the production of associates of greater uniqueness or remoteness relative to the stimulus.[10]

Turning next to individual differences research, Mednick (1962), for example, has reported a correlation of .38 between associative productivity and RAT scores for a sample of 38 college students. The association task, not unlike Freedman's, requested the subjects to write as many associates as they could to each of 20 words, with 1 minute per word.

In a study by Mednick, Mednick, and Jung (1964), male undergraduates were selected from the top, middle, and bottom of a distribution of RAT scores and were requested to provide as many associations as possible to each of various words. A strong positive relationship was found between RAT scores and the number of associates generated. The high and medium RAT groups were comparable in mean intelligence levels, but the low RAT group had a lower intelligence mean. High, medium, and low RAT groups all were significantly differentiated from one another, however, in terms of associative productivity, thus suggesting that the contribution of intel-

[10] The problem just described in connection with the Caron et al. study also applies to a study by Gall and Mendelsohn (1967), where association training once again involved repetition of a stimulus word each time a new associate to it was requested. In the Gall-Mendelsohn investigation, a facilitation effect was found for females but not for males.

ligence to such a relationship most likely was minimal.[11]

Riegel, Riegel, and Levine (1966) also have demonstrated the same kind of relationship. By using extreme-scoring undergraduates on a measure that has been found (Walker, 1962) to correlate highly with standing on the RAT, high scorers exceeded low scorers on number of responses offered in a free association task, number of different responses given to any particular stimulus in that task, and number of different responses offered to each stimulus in various controlled association tasks, that is, tasks where specific classes of associates were requested.

In general, it should be kept in mind that evidence reviewed earlier has suggested that individual differences in quantity and uniqueness of associative output seem to be relatively independent of intelligence, thus rendering it very implausible that intelligence accounts for the obtained relationships between these associative variables and RAT performance.

Given the demonstrated correlation between level of RAT performance and the generation of associative content, is there any evidence on whether the production of unusual associates to a stimulus by high RAT scorers is per se a goal or rather is simply a necessary by-product of generating larger numbers of associates to that stimulus? Research by Houston and Mednick (1963) suggests that it is a goal. Using undergraduates scoring at the high and low extremes of the RAT, these authors found in a word-preference situation that the high RAT group sought out words that entailed novel associates and/or avoided words that entailed common associates, while the reverse was the case for the low RAT group. The greater output of unique associates found in other work to characterize high RAT scorers therefore seems not just to constitute a by-product of their greater productivity but also to re-

flect a preference difference in favor of unique over common associates.

With RAT performance and the generation of plentiful and unique associates thus shown to be congruent operations, our further review of the RAT literature has evident bearing upon fluency and uniqueness of ideational associates as well. Since our consideration of earlier evidence has suggested that productivity and uniqueness of associates are relatively independent of functions concerned with intelligence and academic achievement, we should expect a sizable component of performance ability on the RAT to show the same kind of independence. Research on this issue will concern us next.

Relationships with Intelligence, Academic Achievement, Occupational Achievement, and Research Creativity. The general picture seems to be one of varying relationships, averaging out to somewhere in the vicinity of zero, between RAT performance and assessors of intelligence and achievement—whether the achievement be measured in academic or occupational settings. The correlations with intelligence indices are positive, whereas those with achievement indicators tend to be negative. On the other hand, a strong positive relationship has been found between RAT performance and a criterion of research creativity as distinct from general intellective ability and also as distinct from achievement even in research-oriented occupations. Let us turn first to the findings on achievement and traditionally assessed intelligence.

Regarding correlations with intelligence assessors, M. Mednick (1963) reported a correlation of .41 between RAT performance and Miller Analogies Test scores for a sample of psychology graduate students. For undergraduate subjects, Rainwater (1964) found the RAT to correlate .31 with a vocabulary test; Mendelsohn and Griswold (1966) obtained a correlation of .35 between the RAT and a different vocabulary test; and Laughlin (1967) reported a correlation of .48 between the RAT and Terman's Concept Mastery Test. Shared method variance—the fact that the RAT and the intelligence measures are administered as tests with a time limit—may account for some or all of this positive relationship. In addition, or alternatively, the finding supports the possibility that amount of stored information—for example, size of

---

[11] Level of RAT performance related not only to number of associates produced but also to rate of production, thus suggesting that the associative gradient for high RAT scorers not only has a flatter slope than that for low scorers, as the Mednick view implies, but also—contrary to the Mednick formulation on this point—may involve higher likelihoods for common as well as for uncommon associates.

vocabulary—may play a role in RAT performance.

When we turn from intelligence assessors to academic achievement, the relationships with the RAT, if present at all, are found to be negative rather than positive. Thus a correlation of −.27 was found between RAT scores and the first-2-year grade point averages for 74 undergraduates at an engineering school, while the same correlation of −.27 was found between the RAT and summer grades for a smaller group of 34 summer school students at a liberal arts college (Mednick, 1962; Mednick and Mednick, 1964). The correlation was significant for the first sample, not significant for the second. M. Mednick (1963) reported a nonsignificant correlation of −.11 between the RAT and grade point averages for a sample of psychology graduate students. The obtaining of additional negative correlations between college grades and RAT scores also has been mentioned (Mednick and Mednick, 1964).

The picture for occupational achievement seems to be similar to that for academic achievement. Studying scientist and engineer personnel in research settings, Andrews (1965) found either zero-order or negative correlations between RAT scores and various definitions of achievement on the job, such as number of publications over a 5-year period, or judgments by peers and supervisors of a man's overall usefulness to his organization. No explicit attempts to judge creativity were made. Rather, the performances assessed all were ones to which motivation for achievement against competitional standards of success could make a sizable contribution. Tangible signs of success at competitive achievement, whether in academic or occupational settings, thus are unrelated or even inversely related to RAT scores. The trend toward negative correlations with the achievement indices suggests, indeed, that the kind of thinking reflected in high RAT scores may actually impair the pursuit of achievement success—a matter that will become more understandable later when we explore what seems responsible, apart from general intelligence, for the attainment of high RAT levels.

Two studies can be cited where explicit assessments of research creativity possessing high face validity were related to RAT scores.

In the first (Mednick, 1962), 21 students of architecture were rated for creativity by faculty members who had been supervising the students for at least 1 and in many cases 2 or more years in the development of new designs for buildings. The correlation between creativity ratings and RAT scores was .70, which was quite significant even with this small sample. No appropriate controls for intelligence, however, were reported. A second study (M. Mednick, 1963), on the other hand, obtained analogous results and included appropriate control information as well. Faculty research supervisors of 43 psychology graduate students who had been carrying out independent projects rated the students for research creativity. The definitional basis for the ratings—adapted from Taylor (1963)—concerned the student's ability to develop new research methods and/or to unite disparate areas of theory or of research in useful and original ways. The ratings for research creativity—made without knowledge, of course, of RAT scores—correlated very significantly (.55) with the RAT but did not correlate with Miller Analogies Test scores (−.08) or with grade point average (.06). As already noted, RAT scores in this study correlated moderately with Miller Analogies Test scores but not with grade point average. The variance held in common by the RAT and the creativity ratings, however, clearly is different from the variance which the RAT shared with the Miller scores. We thus have begun to glimpse some evidence of what the RAT relates to apart from general intelligence. The component of the RAT that does not concern general intelligence is what correlates with the creativity ratings.

What is it that high scorers on the RAT may do that, on the one hand, leads to their earning high research creativity ratings but, on the other, actually may depress their average grade level? We have found that, whatever the process is, it has nothing to do with intelligence—although intelligence does make a contribution to RAT scores. A clue to the answer originates in another study concerned with academic grades, but this time from a different perspective. Walker (1962) administered the RAT to a sample of almost 600 high school juniors. Students scoring in the upper or lower 30% of the resulting score distribution were selected for further study and equated for intelligence as indexed by the California Test of Mental Maturity. Greater grade variance—variability from grade to grade earned by the student—was found for the high than for the low scoring boys (but not girls) on the RAT. Perhaps—at least among the boys—the highs are willing to expend a great deal of effort on a course if it interests them—but they are equally willing to let their other courses slide. Presumably therefore the attention of the highs is not automatically invested in academic subject matter but is more likely to wander to topics outside of the curriculum. The highs may be more distractible on the basis of what the environment has to offer by way of varied stimulation, regardless of how relevant or irrelevant the stimulation may be to the pursuit of a narrowly and abstractly defined focus such as earning good grades to gain entrance to college. The mechanism that begins to suggest itself on the basis of this line of interpretation—that highs are more inclined than lows to deploy attention from the center to the periphery of their field of action—has received direct investigation in the research to which we now turn.

Attention Deployment as the Intelligence-Free Mechanism behind the Remote Associates Test. Can the directing of attention, as distinct from the providing of a solution-response, facilitate RAT performance? Our consideration of attention deployment should begin with this question, since an affirmative answer will encourage the attempt to understand individual differences in RAT scores in attentional terms. Maltzman, Belloni, and Fishbein (1964) gave various prompting experiences to different experimental groups of undergraduates prior to solution attempts at each of a number of RAT problems. The general character of all the prompting conditions involved presentation of a dominant associate of the solution-word before the subject tried to solve the given RAT problem. What the conditions that maximized facilitation had in common, in contrast to the other conditions, was that the first conditions directed the subject's attention most specifically to the cognitive domain in which the search for the solution word should be conducted. Such directing of attention was achieved in one case by a single presentation of the dominant associate of the solution word with

instructions to give the first associate that came to mind, and in another by 6 presentations of the dominant associate with instructions to write it down each time it was heard —but without any request to associate to it.

Given the preceding demonstration of attentional processes in RAT performance, we can inquire whether it is a difference in how their attention is directed that underlies the characterization of high RAT scorers as possessing flatter associative gradients than lows. Perhaps a flat gradient arises because attention is more readily deployed to lower likelihood associates: a broader range of stimulus information was searched out regarding these associative possibilities in the first place, and/or a broader range of memory traces regarding this material is subjected to a search process. Such a proposal could be given substance if we found high RAT scorers to display greater sensitivity to the utilizing of incidental cues from their external environment, for then we would have a correlate that is indisputably concerned with attentional scanning. Whether such incidental cue utilization were based upon broader search patterns at the time of registration, in the course of storage, or at both times, we would know that breadth of attention deployment has a bearing upon RAT performance.

Two studies that sought to relate breadth of attention deployment to individual differences in RAT performance obtained positive evidence but failed to include an intelligence control in their design, thus leaving interpretation of their findings ambiguous. Mednick, Mednick, and Mednick (1964), in a variant of the Maltzman et al. (1964) prompting study, found high RAT scorers to show greater facilitation from a presumably irrelevant prompting task than low RAT scorers. High RAT scorers therefore were exhibiting greater incidental cue utilization than the lows.

In the second study, which also lacked an intelligence control, degree of incidental cue utilization of high and low RAT scorers was investigated in a problem-solving context quite removed from the RAT. Mendelsohn and Griswold (1964) explored the performance of 108 undergraduates of varying RAT levels in the following situation. Each subject was given a list of 25 words to try to memorize in 10 minutes (the focal stimuli) while another list of 25 words which the subject was told to ignore was played through 16 times on a tape recorder (the peripheral stimuli). The subject knew he would then have some presumably irrelevant problems to work on, following which there would be a recall test for the focal list. The problem task consisted of 30 anagrams—scrambled letters to be rearranged into a word. Ten of the anagram solutions were words from the focal list, ten were words from the peripheral list, and the remaining ten were from neither. After the period devoted to solving anagrams, the subject then was given 5 minutes to write down all the words he could recall from the list he had tried to memorize before—the focal list. The results were provocative. Mendelsohn and Griswold (1964) found that high RAT scorers exceeded lows in number of anagram solutions attained that were words from the focal list and also in number attained that were words from the peripheral list— both of which constituted, of course, incidental stimuli from the perspective of the anagrams task, with the peripheral stimuli in even more of an incidental role than the focal. The RAT groups did not differ, however, in their ability to recall the 15 words from the focal list that were not anagram solutions—the appropriate recall test since the groups differed in number of anagram solutions attained involving focal list words and thus in degree of experience with those words. Hence memory ability differences could not account for the results.

A more extensive investigation by Mendelsohn and Griswold (1966) with the same materials both replicated the above results and also found that although intelligence had a moderate positive relationship with the RAT, intelligence was unrelated to the utilization of either focal or peripheral incidental cues. That intelligence plays a role in RAT performance thus has nothing to do with the relationship between the RAT and incidental cue utilization. It is, rather, the intelligence-free part of the RAT's variance that accounts for its relationship with the measures of incidental cue utilization.

The interpretation just presented received further confirmation from a study by Laughlin (1967) with yet a different incidental cue utilization procedure, one which, as in the case of Mendelsohn and Griswold, involved a problem-solving task unrelated to the RAT. Laughlin found that RAT scores were strongly related to degree of incidental cue utilization and were also, although less strongly, related to degree of intentional cue utilization. Intelligence scores, on the other hand, while once more related to the RAT, were not at all related to degree of incidental cue utilization or to degree of intentional cue utilization. Once again therefore it is the extent to which RAT performance is independent of intelligence that accounts for greater utilization of incidental cues on the part of higher RAT scorers. In striking corroboration of the Mendelsohn-Griswold (1966) study, Laughlin's work presents further evidence indicating that breadth of attention deployment underlies a sizable component of individual differences in RAT scores, and, indeed, the very component that has nothing to do with intelligence.

The Evidence in Retrospect. The research inspired by the RAT has permitted us to come considerably closer to understanding the source of individual differences in productivity and uniqueness of ideational associates. The flatter associative gradients implied by high levels of these variables may well arise because of a penchant toward more diffuse or extensive deployment of attention in the reception of information, in its retrieval from storage, or in both.

Performance on the RAT has been found to depend in some degree on intelligence and in some degree on breadth of attention deployment. The empirically demonstrated relationship between individual differences in RAT scores and in ideational fluency and uniqueness on associative tasks cannot be mediated by intelligence, since associative fluency and uniqueness seem to be relatively independent of intelligence—a point that will receive further explicit documentation in the next section of the chapter. This leaves the intelligence-free variance of the RAT as the necessary source of its link with associative productivity and uniqueness, and it is specifically the intelligence-free variance of the RAT that has proven to be accountable for in attention deployment terms. This leads to the strong presumption that associative productivity and uniqueness are to be explained on the basis of an attention deployment mechanism.

Not only have we found breadth of attention deployment to constitute the process that accounts for the intelligence-free variance in RAT performance, but we also have found that it is only the intelligence-free variance on the RAT that in turn correlates with a criterion of research creativity. It thus seems likely that at least one important process eventuating in higher judged research creativity is a disposition to deploy one's attention from the center to the periphery of a task context—a greater readiness to utilize incidental cues.

As a final point to be made in this section, we are now in a position to clarify a theoretical issue that goes back to Guilford's initial formulation and which was previously unresolved. Recall that Guilford's concept of divergent thinking included heavy reference to flexibility—the postulation of various abilities to recenter or redirect thought processes as relevant to creativity in thinking. One can, indeed, find many references to one or another kind of flexibility in discursive treatments of what may be involved in creativity (e.g., Mandler and Kessen, 1959). Yet our review of the evidence on Guilford-type measures of flexibility indicated that the concept failed to be distinguishable from the general intelligence domain.

The role of an attention deployment mechanism in accounting for associative productivity and uniqueness, as suggested by our analysis of the RAT literature, permits us to see what kind of psychological meaning seems appropriate to attach to the flexibility notion in relation to creativity, and thus to resolve the apparent paradox just described. What Guilford meant by flexibility was a tendency to shift from one category of meaning to another, or, if you will, from one kind of logically defined entity to another. This kind of shifting concerns the application of rules of concept formation and logic, and hence must give emphasis to a process of judgment or evaluation of cognitive output in the light of such rules. The kind of flexibility to which the concept of attention deployment refers, on the other hand, is quite different. Broad attention deployment is defined as a tendency toward the wandering of attention away from a task focus along routes that have nothing to do with logic or classification but rather are strictly associative in character, whether the attentional wandering takes place in the course

of information registration, information retrieval, or both. Since the path traversed is an associative route, judgment or evaluation is at a minimum. While flexibility in Guilford's sense, then, seems indistinguishable from general intelligence, flexibility in the sense of broad attention deployment seems to have nothing to do with general intelligence and, indeed, seems rather to provide a basis for comprehending associative productivity and uniqueness.

The Research by Wallach and Kogan

Theoretical Considerations. Wallach and Kogan (1965a, 1965b) began with the same conceptual approach to creativity as Mednick, following him in taking their warrant for this approach from introspective accounts by creative persons in the arts and sciences which emphasized the importance of associative flow and the freedom to entertain wide-ranging associative possibilities in a playful manner. Such points led Wallach and Kogan to formulate a definition of the creative process in terms of the following considerations: "first, the production of associative content that is abundant and that is unique; second, the presence in the associator of a playful, permissive task attitude" (1965a, p. 289). The second consideration aimed at describing a psychological state that would maximize the associative production in question, and the definition assumed that some criterion of relevance would have to be met by the associates produced.[12]

Although Wallach and Kogan's assessment procedures originated in Guilford's work, two differences prevailed. First, rather than embracing the range of abilities tapped in the Guilford research—with their varying degrees of independence from convergent thinking—the indicators used were limited to measuring productivity and uniqueness of ideational associates. Second, the procedures were administered in a manner that would maximize the opportunity to generate associates on the subject's part. In contrast to the time limits and testing context prevailing in the work carried out within the Guilford tradition, with their possibly inhibitory implications, the present

[12] Jackson and Messick (1965) also have called attention to cognitive playfulness as a means of predisposing the individual toward generating unusual associative combinations.

procedures were administered without time limits and in a setting structured to convey the impression that the materials were under investigation as potential games rather than constituting tests for evaluating the competence of the subjects.

Both of the differences just described were dictated, of course, by the Mednick formulation: the first, in that associative processes should be the topic of concern; the second, in that maximal opportunity for the detection of the results of a shallow associative gradient should be present. Since, in turn, the Guilford tasks require that the responses offered by the subject must fulfill a criterion of relevance—for example, must be possible uses for a given object or possible similarities between a given pair of objects—the "relevance" or "usefulness" part of Mednick's formulation also was met.

We turn next to a description of the five procedures used by Wallach and Kogan in their assessment of associative processes. Of these, three are concerned with verbally presented and two with visually presented stimulus materials.

Taking the verbal procedures first, the *instances* task requested the subject to generate possible instances of a class concept specified to him by the experimenter, such as round things or things that move on wheels. The *alternate uses* procedure requested the subject to think of as many uses as possible for a verbally specified object, such as a newspaper, a cork, a shoe, and a chair. The third verbal procedure was the *similarities* task, in which the subject was to generate possible similarities between a verbally specified pair of objects, such as a cat and a mouse, or milk and meat.

Moving on to the visual procedures, the *pattern meanings* task presented each of a number of abstract visual designs, with the subject requested to think of as many meanings or interpretations as possible concerning what each design might represent. In the *line meanings* procedure, finally, the same kind of request was made of the subject, with the stimulus materials this time consisting of various nonobjective line forms.

Two variables were derived from each of the five procedures: number and uniqueness of responses. Number of responses refers simply to the total output of ideas offered by a subject for a given item, and thus is a measure

of ideational fluency. Uniqueness of responses, in turn, refers to the number of fully unique ideas provided by a subject in the case of a given item—that is, the number of responses given by only one person in the sample under study to the item in question. Uniqueness thus is an index of the kind of originality or novelty that is defined in terms of statistical infrequency. In accordance with the Mednick formulation, it was assumed that uniqueness would tend to increase with a subject's successive responses to an item, and hence that a subject who produces a larger number of responses also should generate a larger number that are unique.

Relationships with Intelligence and Academic Achievement. In addition to the 10 associative indicators just described—a productivity and a uniqueness measure in the case of each of five procedures—the 70 male and 81 female fifth graders in Wallach and Kogan's work received 10 assessments concerning general intelligence and academic achievement. We turn now to a consideration of the individual-difference relationships among the 10 associative measures, among the 10 indicators of ability or achievement in the convergent thinking area, and between these two sets of variables.

The 10 associative variables, all of which proved to be highly reliable, were found to intercorrelate strongly for the sample as a whole and also for each sex considered separately. The average of the 45 correlations between all pairs of the 10 measures was .41 taking the sample of 151 children as a whole. Correlations were equally strong across verbal and figural procedures as within each of these domains, and the productivity and uniqueness variables correlated strongly both within a given procedure and across different procedures.[13] The evidence was clear that the associative indicators in question defined a unitary dimension, with novel associates emerging as a function of greater response productivity and with consistent levels of performance obtained regardless of the nature of the five procedures used. Having demon-

13 In order to avoid artifactual inflation of correlations through part-whole contamination, the productivity measures that were used in these computations consisted of the total number of responses given by a child to an item minus those of his responses that were unique.

strated such dimensionality, however, the critical question is whether the degree of interrelationship among these 10 variables is appreciably greater than the degree of their relationship with the convergent-thinking domain.

The convergent-thinking assessors consisted of five measures that would be categorized as indicators of academic "aptitude" and five that would be considered indicators of academic "achievement." We have already found that the separation just described is difficult to maintain in practice, in that aptitude and achievement yardsticks turn out to be highly correlated. The 10 assessors covered verbal, quantitative, and performance definitions of intelligence and an array of academic subject matter skills. To what degree do the 10 measures intercorrelate? The results indicate strong intercorrelation for all of the convergent-thinking indicators in the case of the total sample and also for each sex taken separately. Considering the sample as a whole, the average of the 45 correlations between all pairs of these 10 measures was .51. No warrant was found in terms of correlational magnitudes for distinguishing between the ability and achievement indicators or among verbal, performance, and numerical skills.

Although the associative and the convergent-thinking measures thus were found to define strong and cohesive respective dimensions of individual differences, the relationships between the two kinds of assessors turned out to be uniformly low. With 10 measures in each of the two domains, there are 100 correlations between all pairs of the indices in the two groups. The average of these correlations was .09 for the total sample and was comparably low for each sex taken separately. That the measures in the two groups were essentially independent of each other and that each group in turn defined a strong dimension in its own right demonstrated that the associative variables had considerably more in common with one another than the degree of their relationship with intelligence.

The present evidence offers strong support for the Mednick formulation and also confirms the indications from earlier work that ideational fluency and fluency-dependent forms of uniqueness are maximally orthogonal to convergent-thinking skills. It may be that the virtually complete orthogonality demon-

strated in the Wallach-Kogan research depended in some degree on absence of time limitations and reduced evaluative pressure for the associative tasks, since the separation attained between such tasks and the convergent-thinking indicators seems more thoroughgoing than we found to be the case in at least some of the earlier work reviewed. On the other hand, we have noted in our analysis of other studies a substantial degree of separation from intelligence for Guilford-type measures of ideational fluency and fluency-based indicators of originality, even though such measures were administered as tests and with time limits. And the RAT, in turn, has been found to yield a strong, intelligence-free dimension of individual differences despite administration within a time limit—albeit a quite liberal one. Most likely, therefore, at least near-orthogonality between the associative variables and convergent thinking can be attained even when relatively constraining administration conditions prevail for the associative variables, with complete orthogonality perhaps requiring that the conditions of administration be more open.

In a recent study by Ward (1966) of preschool age children who were heterogeneous with respect to socioeconomic background, three associative tasks adapted from the Wallach-Kogan work—two verbal and one visual—were administered together with the Peabody Picture Vocabulary Test as an index of intelligence. Scoring of the associative materials for productivity and uniqueness was carried out. The measures derived from the two verbal procedures cohered substantially and were independent of intelligence, whereas the results for the visual procedure were ambiguous. Ward (1968) also has reported that with a sample of 7- to 8-year-olds using similar procedures, the measures derived from all three associative tasks cohered significantly and were essentially independent of intelligence. Ward's work thus constitutes additional empirical support for the distinguishability from intelligence of the associative dimension that we have been describing.

Are there increases with age in the kinds of associative variable under discussion? It would, of course, be surprising if this were not the case to some degree, since the increase in amount of stored information that takes place with age must have at least some effect upon associative output and number of unique associates. On the other hand, age-related increases have not been invariably obtained. Thus, for example, although Becher (1960) found college seniors to give a larger number of unique responses on a free association task than did college freshmen, Davidon and Longo (1960) found no increase in number of unique responses offered when free associating to various stimuli across an age range extending from fourth graders to college freshmen and sophomores. Davidon and Longo, indeed, were led to conclude from their evidence that "the diversity of associations is not a simple function of the number of different experiences or of developing verbal ability" (1960, p. 91). That any evidence at all can be found running counter to an age-related increase in such associative indices seems noteworthy, since it supports the view that size of storage reservoir is only one determinant of such variables and leads us back rather to the question of how the associates are organized—that is, the issue of gradient slope.

In sum, the evidence seems clear that there is a dimension of considerable generality concerned with associative productivity and uniqueness, and that this dimension stands quite apart from the traditionally demarcated domain of convergent thinking. Much of the work carried out by Wallach and Kogan was concerned with the search for correlates that would distinguish this associative dimension from that of general intelligence. We turn next to one of these correlates.

Evidence on Remoteness of Instances in Categorizing. Having found the associative variables and convergent thinking to define orthogonal dimensions, Wallach and Kogan (1965a, 1965b) proceeded to distribute their sample of children in terms of the subjects' standing on the two dimensions considered jointly. Potential correlates then were investigated concerning such areas as the social behavior and esthetic sensitivity of the children. Males and females were found not to differ in their average levels on the associative and convergent-thinking dimensions. Recall also that orthogonality between the two dimensions had been found to prevail in equal degree for both sexes. Nevertheless, the correlates were investigated separately for the two sexes, and many of the results indicated rather complicated sex differences in correlated behaviors. As an example of the correlates that were studied, we shall consider a domain where the same findings emerged for both sexes. The question studied was how remote from one another are the instances which a child was willing to assign to a common class.

When the nature of a category is specified to a person, the boundaries of that category still will remain ambiguous in many cases. Individuals have been found to show systematic differences, in fact, regarding their preferred "category width" under such circumstances, that is, their inclination to broaden or narrow a specified category to include or exclude, respectively, instances whose membership status is ambiguous. Pettigrew (1958) constructed a series of questions in which the central tendency value of a category would be specified and the subject then requested to estimate, from multiple-choice alternatives, the most deviant instances of that category that might ever be encountered. One item, for example, concerned the typical speed of birds; another, the typical width of windows. In the first case, the boundaries to be specified were the speed of the fastest bird and of the slowest; in the second case, the width of the widest window and of the narrowest. Wallach and Caron (1959) adapted the Pettigrew instrument for use with children and found it to correlate with the child's willingness to assign visually ambiguous instances to an already defined category of geometric forms.

What psychological process is reflected in a person's disposition toward maintaining broad or narrow categories? To say that there is a differential willingness to entertain deviant instances as possibly relevant to a given class domain leaves the matter, after all, at a descriptive level. Necessary for attaining broad categories is some kind of mechanism whereby the focus of a person's concern moves outward from the most frequently encountered exemplars of a class to those that would be met only rarely. We therefore find ourselves looking for the same kind of mechanism that seems needed in order to account for productivity and uniqueness of associates, where again high performance means that the person must fail to stop at common associates to a task stimulus and instead must generate further ideas that bear a more deviant relationship to his starting point. From the evidence considered earlier, we are led to speculate that the mechanism may be attentional in character, with the broad categorizer's attention more likely to wander toward doubtful instances of a class. At any rate, there seems good reason to expect some commonality in terms of process between a person's preferred category width and his levels of associative productivity and uniqueness. The ability to "see" possible relationships between instances of greater diversity—and hence to assign them to the same class—thus should be found in the case of persons more disposed toward a rich associative flow in response to a task request.

In the Wallach-Kogan research, the category width measure used by Wallach and Caron was administered. In addition to items on the speed of birds and the width of windows, other questions concerned such matters as the length of whales, the length of dogs, the speed of cars, and the width of roads. Wallach and Kogan found that in both sexes high associatives exhibited broader categorizing tendencies than low associatives. Intelligence level, on the other hand, was unrelated to category width, and there was no interaction effect between high versus low associative and intelligence levels in relation to category width. While the relationship between a child's standing on the associative dimension and his breadth of categorizing was stronger for females than for males, the obtained linkage was similar for both sexes, as also was the absence of relationship with intelligence or with the interaction between associative level and intelligence. It can therefore be concluded that category width is a correlate of associative level as distinct from intelligence. In somewhat the same way as Houston and Mednick (1963) found higher RAT scorers to demonstrate a greater preference for novel associates, Wallach and Kogan found children who exhibit higher associative output and uniqueness to demonstrate a preference for entertaining unusual or deviant instances for membership in a category. The presence of flatter associative gradients thus seems to describe what is involved in setting broader category limits as well as in showing greater associative productivity and uniqueness. An acceptance of instances of greater remoteness as possibly warranting assignment to the same

category may describe the attitude that permits someone of high associative level to achieve the novel ideational combinations and integrations from which significant insights arise.

The Evidence in Retrospect. As the last three sections of the chapter indicate, restricting the definition of creativity to associative processes has yielded an evolving set of research strands, which all can be ordered in terms of the associative gradient concept. Each of the three traditions of studies that have been under consideration—work centering around Maltzman, Mednick's RAT, and Wallach and Kogan—served to further our understanding of how associative processes enter into thinking. The result has been a formulation which is quite distinguishable from the notion of convergent-thinking ability and which there is some reason to align with a term such as creativity. The formulation did not arise unheralded, of course; it was foreshadowed earlier in the chapter and was in fact found to emerge from what the evidence presented there seemed, upon interpretation, to suggest.

In the light of what we have learned concerning associative phenomena, we are in a position now to draw a tentative conclusion as to their major defining property as far as the creativity issue is concerned. The conclusion—one that has been hinted at in preceding pages—is that the crux of the matter revolves around the process of generating or producing associates without regard to evaluating them for relevance or applicability to a problem or task. Although novel associative content must be useful or relevant to qualify as creative according to such definitions as that presented by Mednick, the evidence we have reviewed suggests that sensitivity to relevance has but a tangential role in the thinking style which in fact leads to ideational content that is both novel and relevant. While a definition such as Mednick's or Maltzman's thus describes the nature of a creative thought product and sets down appropriate guidelines for fashioning operations that will capture such products, relevance sensitivity does not seem to be an important part of the process that eventuates in these products. What matters most is the generating of associates; once produced, the evaluation of their relevance and appropriate action in the light of this judgment seems to pose little difficulty.

The evidence for this conclusion arises from considering the range of associative procedures that have been found to be related to one another—both in terms of individual differences and in terms of experimental manipulation effects. This range runs the gamut from situations where judgments of relevance to a task are of paramount importance for a person's performance level to situations where evaluations of relevance play no part at all. Since the individual who shows up well in the former class of situations also shows up well in the latter, relevance sensitivity cannot play a strong role in a psychological account of what makes for his proficiency. What all the situations demand, on the other hand, is that the person generate associates in accordance with a flat rather than a steep gradient of response likelihoods. Let us recall some of the evidence in question.

In the course of the last three sections of this chapter, we have found, for instance, that training in the emitting of free associations to a stimulus—where virtually no relevance criterion exists for the responses—transfers to enhance a subject's performance on the unusual uses task; this is a situation where it is understood that one's responses must be relevant and not bizarre. So, also, we have found that free association training transfers to facilitate performance on the RAT, where the relevance criterion is so stringent that only one particular response will meet it. Individual differences in productivity of associates under completely free conditions, furthermore, have been found to correlate with RAT performance level. When we examine more closely the nature of what a person who is deficient at unusual uses or RAT performance can and cannot do, the issue of evaluating response relevance immediately is shown to be unimportant. Give a person who cannot suggest unique uses for a newspaper a list of the unique uses suggested by someone else, and that person has no trouble recognizing the relevance of the unique uses in question. Tell a person who cannot provide the solution to a RAT item what the answer is, and he easily sees that the answer-word is relevant to each of the three words constituting the problem. Links do exist across performances ranging from completely free association, where any response to a stimulus is acceptable, to procedures such as the unusual uses test, where responses must meet a minimum relevance criterion, to the RAT, where but a single response is defined as relevant. Generation or production of unique associates by virtue of a relatively flat associative gradient thus is seen to define the attribute of associative phenomena most relevant for creativity, and it is an attribute that possesses substantial independence from convergent-thinking skills. What we have come to is quite consistent, we might note, with the introspective accounts by eminent men in the arts and sciences cited earlier, where the emphasis seemed to be on ease of associative flow as such—evaluational processes being relegated to a later phase of work. Can we locate other correlates of associative output and uniqueness, however, that will permit us to obtain a clearer picture of their degree of behavioral generality? The final two sections of the chapter are addressed to this question.

FANTASY

As the term "fantasy" is used by psychologists, it typically refers to cognitive products having two characteristics: they rest to at least some degree upon associative relationships among their constituent elements, and they possess to at least some degree an integrated or sustained character. Given the utilization of associative material in fantasy, its character should be importantly influenced by the variables of associative productivity and uniqueness that we have been considering, and hence it should help define the implications of these variables. Given the potential significance of linguistic skills in the structure and expression of fantasy, however, it is evident that the role of verbal intelligence will have to be disentangled from a subject's fantasy behavior if we are to understand the part played in fantasy by associative processes. We have touched upon this issue before; here we turn to evidence that permits us to face it directly in the sense of determining as specifically as possible what aspects of fantasy rest upon the associative creativity dimension to which our review has led. First we discuss some research on the TAT by Maddi and his associates.

Research by Maddi and His Collaborators

Novelty of Story Productions on the TAT: Scoring Considerations and Some Findings. We can view the Maddi group's research on fantasy as falling into two phases. In the first phase, three possible definitions of novelty or newness as reflected in TAT stories were explored, and some results were obtained which began to suggest that one of these definitions might tap the same vein as the associative creativity dimension. In the second phase, the definition that had looked most fruitful in this regard was in fact found to fulfill its promise. To begin, then, what were the three approaches to novelty in fantasy that were taken?

Curiosity, desire for novelty and novelty of productions were the labels applied by Maddi and his associates (see, e.g., Maddi, Charlens, Maddi, and Smith, 1962; Maddi and Berne, 1964; Maddi, 1965; Maddi, Propst, and Feldinger, 1965) to the aspects of TAT fantasy that they isolated for study. Scoring for *curiosity* was based upon content in which story characters ask questions, raise problems, or express perplexity, with the implication that new or further information would aid in resolving such puzzles. *Desire for novelty*, in turn, was defined as story content in which characters express interest in the novel and/or dissatisfaction with the familiar. Thus statements indicating concern with what is new, exciting, unusual, or different would earn scores for this category, as also would statements reflecting disenchantment with the status quo. Finally, *novelty of productions* referred to various categories of character treatment and plot that were judged to constitute unusual or infrequent ideational content on the part of members of the subculture in question. The categories of character treatment that earned scores were unusual role designations (e.g., uncommon occupations) and uncommon naming. The categories of plot treatment earning scores were unusual events (e.g., an illegal or catastrophic happening), novel interpretations (e.g., a story based upon paradox), and unexpected endings (an ending that violates an expectation generated by the preceding narrative).

A contrast can immediately be drawn between the last of these three scoring definitions and the other two. Whereas curiosity and desire for novelty both concern the expression of a subject's ideology or values regarding novelty-related behaviors, novelty of productions concerns the actual incidence of statistically infrequent story content—although inferred, to be sure, on the basis of judgmental approximation rather than actual counting. A further distinction should be kept in mind, however, between a person's verbalized values or ideology in relation to novelty and the actual preference behavior that he would exhibit when faced with more and less novel stimuli—the stimuli that he would actually seek to approach or avoid. Demonstrated preferences need not be in line with espoused doctrine. Curiosity and desire for novelty therefore do not concern preference for novelty but rather concern beliefs about how one should act toward various novelty-related issues. In novelty of story productions, then, we have a measure that looks as if it should reflect uniqueness and volume of associative output as defined in the kinds of task with which we are already familiar. In curiosity and desire for novelty, on the other hand, we have measures that stay close to the surface of expressed beliefs, telling us neither about actual incidence of novelty in the subject's story productions nor about actual preference for unusual ideational content.

The strongest finding in the first of the Maddi group's studies (Maddi et al., 1962) was that exposure to a period of monotony led to a decrease in novelty of TAT story productions relative to the results obtained under each of three other experimental conditions, all of which involved either a period spent in free activity or an attempt to provide novel stimulation to the subjects. These three conditions yielded similar outcomes. A contrast between greater and lesser monotony in the environment, then, was found to have a parallel effect on the level of novelty in obtained story content—less monotony eventuating in higher novelty production than greater monotony. If novelty of story productions can be primed by the environment, then the incidence of novelty in story content is behaving in a manner analogous to the incidence of novelty in detached associates as studied by the Maltzman group. When we turn to individual difference relationships, will story novelty be linked with productivity of discrete associates and be relatively independent of intelligence?

In the first of their sets of data that bear upon this question, Maddi et al. (1965) and Maddi (1965) provided some clues suggesting that the answer is affirmative, but the evidence remained ambiguous. Three tasks concerned with productivity regarding discrete associates were given to a sample of 62 male undergraduates. In one, the subject was to write down, during a 5 minute period, single words describing the feelings and sensations that he actually experienced, with number of words produced constituting the measure. In a second, the subject was to spend 5 minutes writing down any thoughts at all that came to him, with number of separate thoughts providing the measure. The final task requested the subject to list all the uses of a brick that he could think of during 5 minutes, with number of uses as the score. The three procedures just described were found to be strongly correlated among themselves but only marginally correlated with an index of verbal intelligence—thus confirming once again the presence of an associative creativity dimension. But what of relationships with novelty of story productions on the TAT? Whereas the novelty of productions measure was only marginally correlated with verbal intelligence, it was somewhat more strongly correlated with two of the three tasks that reflected productivity of discrete associates. To at least some degree, then, novelty of story productions was found to be linked with the associative creativity dimension in a manner that could not be explained away in full on an intelligence basis.

A further provocative lead was obtained from the material just described. Although positively correlated with the measures concerning output of discrete associates, novelty of productions was inversely correlated with what seems best described as a measure of random activity during a sham waiting period. The subjects found to be higher in novelty of story productions were those who waited more quietly—did not carry out as much manipulation of things in the office where they waited. One can interpret this finding as suggesting that the persons who produce a great deal of novel content in their stories are more likely to spend the waiting period immersed in their own imaginings—and hence spend more time in general producing fantasies. As we shall note later, a similar kind of finding has been observed by Singer (1961) with children. Such a relationship again seems consistent with what would be expected if a linkage existed with the associative creativity dimension. Nevertheless, we would like to have firmer evidence of a bridge between associative creativity measures and novelty of story productions.

Novelty of Story Productions, Preference for Novelty, and Associative Uniqueness: The Evidence for a Syndrome. In a report by Maddi and Andrews (1966), 56 naval medical corpsmen trainees, ranging in age from 17 to 27 years and in education from ninth grade to several years of college, wrote stories in response to customary TAT pictures and instructions. Scoring of the stories was carried out for curiosity, desire for novelty, and novelty of productions. An adaptation of Guilford's uses task also was administered. Derived from this task was an index of the statistical infrequency of the uses offered. Correlations with originality of uses were .12 for curiosity, —.09 for desire for novelty, and .62 for novelty of productions. Not only was novelty of productions strongly related to the uses measure, but the other two story indicators were unrelated to the uses task. Correlations with general intelligence, on the other hand, were .27 for curiosity, .15 for desire for novelty, and .01 for novelty of productions. While highly correlated with uses originality, novelty of productions thus was quite independent of general intelligence. Such an outcome is particularly impressive in the case of the present sample, where the wide heterogeneity of educational level meant that chances for a relationship between intelligence and novelty of productions were maximized.

This demonstration was replicated on another sample by Pearson and Maddi (1966), which also explored a measure of preference for novelty. Included in the Pearson-Maddi research were the sample of naval medical corpsmen already described and a new sample of 40 undergraduate volunteers of both sexes. For the second sample, novelty of story productions correlated .42 with originality on the uses task but only .05 with a verbal intelligence indicator, thus repeating the findings described for the corpsmen. A novelty preference measure—the Similes Preference Inventory—was devised and administered to both samples. Each of the items on this instrument presented the beginning of a common simile followed by five alternative endings from which the subject was to select the one he most preferred. Of the five possible endings for each simile, two were designed to be more usual and the other three more unusual. Scoring depended upon the number of similes for which an unusual rather than a usual ending was selected. Note that the present indicator represents a measure not of beliefs or values concerning novelty, but rather of actual preference behavior where a choice must be made which will favor stimuli of greater or lesser novelty. Novelty preference was found in this study to be related both to novelty of story productions and to associative uniqueness, while at the same time also standing independent of intelligence. It was furthermore found that novelty preference did not relate significantly with either of the other two story measures. Not only, then, has the relationship between novelty of productions and associative uniqueness been replicated in the Pearson-Maddi study, but two independent demonstrations of the relationship between each of those variables and preference for novelty have been provided as well. Intelligence—already known to be essentially independent of associative uniqueness—has been shown in two replications to be likewise independent of novelty of story productions and of preference for novelty. Finally, neither of the remaining story indices—curiosity or desire for novelty—showed relationships with associative uniqueness or with novelty preference.

It will be recalled that previous evidence already testified to a connection between associative uniqueness and novelty preference: RAT performance and novelty preference were found to be related. The present findings linking associative uniqueness with novelty preference offer further evidence for this relationship.[14] We are therefore left with

strong evidence in support of the view that the generating of unique associates reflects a preference for unusual ideational content as well as coming about as a necessary consequence of high associative output. Turning to the data on TAT stories, it has become clear that the associative creativity dimension has strong implications for one particular aspect of fantasy—the novelty or unusualness of its actual content. Expression in fantasy of beliefs supportive of curiosity or of the search for novelty is the result, however, of determinants other than the disposition to produce plentiful and unique associates. That associative creativity generalizes to the novelty of a person's TAT productions is of no small importance, of course, since this finding serves to broaden the behavioral arena for which associative productivity and uniqueness have demonstrable consequences. With clear relationships thus shown to obtain among novelty of TAT fantasy productions, preference for novelty, and associative uniqueness, we shall consider next some strands of further research in which assessment of fantasy has played a major part.

Singer's Studies and Related Work

Terms such as "imaginative play" and "daydreaming" refer to forms of fantasy that are spontaneous, in contrast to, for example, TAT stories or Rorschach responses, which represent forms of fantasy that are elicited by an experimenter's request. As types of spontaneous fantasy, the difference between imagina-

---

[14] A study also can be cited in which description of oneself as preferring novelty—although a belief-centered type of index—was found to correlate significantly with ideational fluency and originality scores on the uses task for sixth-grade children (Penney and McCann, 1964). In the

Penney-McCann investigation as well as in a subsequent study by Penney (1965) that was also conducted with children, the self-descriptive measure of novelty preference—the Children's Reactive Curiosity Scale—proved to be independent of intelligence. Of possible relevance in addition is research by Teeter, Rouzer, and Rosen (1964), where third-, sixth-, and ninth-grade children were asked if they would rather look at a list of information that many people know or that only a few people know. Expressions of preference for the novel list—with the expectation that one would then receive the preferred list—were found to be independent of intelligence for both sexes at all grade levels. No relationships with associative measures, however, were investigated. Similarly, expressions of novelty preference and incidence of unusual interpretations of visual figures were found. by Acker and McReynolds (1967) to be related in a college student sample.

tive play and daydreaming would seem to reside in the question of task relevance. If the self-generated fantasy behavior is relevant to some immediate task faced by the person, we tend to consider it imaginative play; if it is irrelevant to the immediate task he faces, on the other hand, we tend to consider it daydreaming.[15]

In the preceding part of the chapter, we discussed some evidence on a type of elicited fantasy—TAT stories. Now we turn to work which concerns spontaneous as well as elicited fantasy.

Incidence of Spontaneous Fantasy, Novelty of Elicited Fantasy, and Associative Creativity: Evidence on Relationships. The link between novelty of elicited fantasy and associative creativity already has been documented —at least for TAT stories—in the work by Maddi and Andrews (1966) and by Pearson and Maddi (1966). But what of spontaneous fantasy? Let us turn first to work relating spontaneous fantasy to novelty of elicited fantasy. A study by Singer and Schonbar (1961) with female graduate students assessed spontaneous fantasy by asking the subjects to indicate the frequency with which they experienced each of a large number of daydreams. This type of daydreaming questionnaire—reported on in more detail by Singer and McCraven (1961) and Singer (1966b)—presents a heterogeneous range of daydream content and has been shown to possess high internal consistency. Singer (1966b) furthermore has noted that high scorers in general subscribe to daydreams that are more fantastic or unlikely of occurrence. Regarding novelty of elicited fantasy, the subjects were asked to write an original story and also to write an account of an actual daydream. These two written products were scored in terms of five criteria—degree of novelty of materials, novelty of character, novelty of time sequences, novelty of spatial sequences, and emotional vividness. A total score was derived. Four of the five scoring considerations—all but emotional vividness—concern the introduction of one or another kind of novel content, and thus seem quite analogous to Maddi's scoring system for novelty of productions. "Creativity in storytelling" as defined by Singer

15 On daydreaming as task-irrelevant spontaneous fantasy, see, e.g., Singer (1966a), Antrobus, Singer, and Greenberg (1966).

and his associates thus appears to represent the same variable as the Maddi group's "novelty of productions" concept, and hence we shall continue to use the latter term. The Singer-Schonbar research yielded a correlation of .48 between novelty of written productions and frequency of daydreaming. Furthermore, independence from verbal intelligence was found in the case of both variables. A clear demonstration has been provided, then, of the linkage between incidence of spontaneous fantasy and novelty of elicited fantasy, and of the independence of both from the intelligence domain.

The same kind of demonstration was presented in a study of children of ages 6 to 9 by Singer (1961). Degree of spontaneous fantasy was defined in terms of the answers to four interview questions, two of which concerned play and the other two daydreaming. The play questions inquired about the child's favorite game and about the games he plays when playing alone. Choice of games requiring imaginative play in contrast to vigorous physical activity earned positive scores. The daydreaming questions asked whether the child ever has pictures in his head and whether he has a make-believe playmate. The spontaneous fantasy measure was found to be independent of intelligence, age, and sex, but was strongly related to novelty of storytelling productions. The interview measure also was found to be related to each of two overt behavioral indicators of the tendency to engage in spontaneous fantasy, thus offering validation for the self-report questions. The overt behavior indices concerned "waiting ability" and were introduced in the context of selecting people for enduring the solitary confinement of space flight. The children able to wait the longest were those who filled the interval with imaginative play—making believe, for example, that they were piloting a rocket ship. A study by Singer and Chipman (1961) provided the same kind of overt behavioral validation for a children's version of the daydreaming questionnaire. Whether spontaneous fantasy is measured in terms of a daydreaming questionnaire as in the Singer-Schonbar study or in terms of the kind of interview questions asked in the Singer (1961) research, such intelligence-free relationships have been obtained with novelty of elicited fantasy productions.

Other evidence supporting a relationship between spontaneous fantasy and novelty of elicited fantasy can be cited as well, and we shall give a few more brief examples. Page (1957), for instance, found that incidence of daydreaming was linked for female undergraduates with the giving of M responses on the Rorschach. With M responses relatively unusual as such, they were rendered even more novel in the Page study by crediting for M only if movement was clearly verbalized in a person's first response to a blot and only if the response was not a popular one. In an investigation by Riess (1957), children exhibiting greater restraint during a waiting period—and hence presumably more make-believe play—were found to offer a greater frequency of M responses on the Rorschach.[16] Preference for toys requiring minimal motor activity and maximal spontaneous fantasy participation—such as a science kit or a fort with toy soldiers in contrast to a basketball or a baseball bat—turned out in a study by Lesser (1962) to characterize children who showed more unusual imaginal content in

[16] We should hasten to emphasize that, notwithstanding relationships such as have just been described, the meaning of M scoring on the Rorschach is far from clear. There have, for example, been considerable variations in scoring criteria and stimulus materials. Thus the fact that Griffin (1958) failed to obtain a relationship between M scores and subjective creativity ratings of undergraduates equated on intelligence may have been due to the use of a set of inkblots—the Legy Movement Blots—specifically designed to elicit M responses. As a consequence, M responses may have been rendered too likely in that study. On the other hand, further results favoring a linkage between one or another definition of plentiful spontaneous fantasy and one or another type of M scoring are contained in Barron (1955), Myden (1959), and Clark, Veldman, and Thorpe (1965). Further, a study by Doris, Sarason, and Berkowitz (1963) linking self-reported anxiety with M responding for second graders may be of relevance on the assumption that the former measure reflects introspective sensitivity. In a recent study, however, Swartz (1965) found just the reverse relationship, with higher M scores earned by the low-anxious children. With this type of elusiveness characterizing the M concept, it is doubtful that the kinds of theoretical promissory notes offered in favor of M by such writers as Stark (1964, 1965a, 1965b, 1966) will soon be cashed in.

their TAT productions and Rorschach responses. Since incidence of reported night dreams constitutes a form of spontaneous fantasy that is known to correlate with frequency of daydreaming behavior (see, e.g., Singer and Schonbar, 1961), we also might note a study by Adelson (1960), where undergraduate females reporting night dreams that contained more unusual content also were found to show greater originality in choice of theme and treatment in creative writing products.

With evidence in hand supporting relationships between spontaneous fantasy and novelty of elicited fantasy as well as between the latter and associative creativity, can the circle be completed with findings showing that spontaneous fantasy and associative creativity are linked? Regrettably, the explicit evidence on this question is relatively meager, although—in the light of the material already reviewed—it would be most surprising if this link were not present. Positive support for the link was provided by Page (1957), who found that frequency of daydreaming among college females was strongly related to the number of ideational responses offered per Rorschach card. The number of different construings by the subject as to what an inkblot suggests is, of course, an index of associative productivity. Interestingly enough, whereas the number of different responses given to a blot stimulus was highly related with incidence of daydreaming, the sheer number of words given per response or per stimulus card was unrelated to the daydreaming index. This is precisely what we would expect on the assumption that number of words reflects verbal intelligence, since it has been demonstrated that daydreaming frequency as well as associative productivity are independent of intelligence.

Apart from Page's results, however, the only other relevant study yielded an ambiguous outcome. Singer and Antrobus (1963) found, with male freshman subjects, only a trend toward relationships between day-dreaming frequency and certain Guilford tasks. However, the array of Guilford procedures—chosen to cover the whole range of factors distinguished by him—all were administered with brief time limits. We have already noted how time pressure can mitigate against attaining high levels of associative creativity. The brief time limits utilized in the Singer-Antrobus research thus may have heavily restricted the range of individual differences concerning productivity and uniqueness of associates on those of Guilford's tasks that tapped these characteristics. In the Page study, no such time pressure was operating.

It seems fair to conclude that the connection between novelty of elicited fantasy and associative creativity can be extended at least tentatively to include incidence of spontaneous fantasy as well. In closing this section, there is a further point that we should like to mention. It is that spontaneous fantasy—especially of the daydreaming variety, where the cognitive activity is task-irrelevant—can be readily interpreted in terms of breadth of attention deployment. Daydreaming represents a form of attentional wandering par excellence. Inclusion of spontaneous fantasy in the correlational network surrounding associative creativity thus provides further support for an attention-deployment interpretation of associative creativity.

The Question of Origins. Since some work has been carried out on the issue of factors influencing the development of fantasy, clues may be at hand for understanding how associative creativity develops also. Most of what can be said, however, remains quite speculative. To begin, there is evidence suggesting that visual experience is particularly likely to form the raw material for fantasy. Thus, for example, Singer and McCraven (1961) found that most of the daydream reports they gathered involved visual imagery. Maupin (1965), in turn, reported that level of involvement in carrying out quiet contemplation or meditation was correlated with the amount of visual imagery obtained in a free association task. The result did not appear to be accountable for in terms of a simple relationship with intelligence. Moreover Singer and Streiner (1966) compared blind and sighted children who were matched for intelligence, sex, and socioeconomic background, with the result that the sighted group substantially exceeded the blind group regarding incidence of spontaneous fantasy and novelty of elicited fantasy productions. It is possible, then, that the availability of varied visual experience is particularly conducive to fantasy development. At the least, it seems

that, contrary to psychoanalytic formulations, fantasy is more likely to reflect a perceptually rich environment than to arise in compensation for the blocked expression of impulses. This is an etiological proposal that has been made by Singer (1966b), who goes on more specifically to suggest that fantasy may constitute the internalization of play.

Drawing on Piaget (1962), White (1959, 1963), and Schachtel (1959), Singer suggests that the child engages in spontaneous play activity when pressing urges are relatively quiescent, utilizing, for this play, raw materials provided by the environment. For the very young infant, phenomena associated with one's own body will suffice—for example, the appearance and disappearance of the baby's hands in his visual field. Subsequently, raw material of a more complex order is needed—thus making important the provision by parents of varied experience, as well as the leisure and privacy to carry on playful commerce with a heterogeneous range of environmental stimulation. Pressures toward cognitive economy then force the progressive internalization of play into thought, since the child becomes increasingly unable to find the time for re-creating games in all their full-blown response characteristics and instead must store their associative content in a form—fantasy—that can be used privately. While such a proposal is influenced by Piaget, its aim is not to characterize the role of play in moving the child toward more sophisticated expressions of general intelligence—which is, as Sutton-Smith (1966) has observed, Piaget's basic orientation—but rather to claim for play a crucial role in fantasy—a type of cognitive activity whose spontaneous incidence and novelty cannot be predicted from level of general intelligence. What kinds of evidence bear upon this proposal?

Singer (1961) found that children showing higher levels of spontaneous fantasy activity differed from those showing lower levels by reporting more interaction with their parents that would involve fantasy, such as games and storytelling, a higher degree of personal, extensive contact in general with a parent, and less involvement with siblings by virtue of being the oldest child, an only child, or having fewer older siblings. These results constitute particularly good evidence since the high and low fantasy groups did not differ regarding intelligence. On the other hand, there is the problem that the kinds of familial situations described here in contrasting high and low fantasy children also are ones that would tend to differentiate higher from lower intelligence children. Abstract thought capacities and the ability to work with language and other formal systems should likewise be enhanced by the family circumstances that have been described as fostering fantasy. Thus consider the following results obtained by Helson (1965, 1966). With a sample of 135 female college seniors, a checklist of childhood activities was administered and a measure was developed concerning the extent to which the subject had derived pleasure from a subset of activities concerned with imaginative play and artistic expression. This measure, however, was found (Helson, 1966) to correlate beyond the .01 level both with verbal Scholastic Aptitude Test scores and also with grade point averages.[17] Helson (1966) points out that the measure of childhood concern with imaginative play and artistic activities that she used in her earlier study (Helson, 1965) was based on fewer items and had weaker relationships to presumed creativity criteria than the measure used in her later study. Ironically, however, the newer measure also has stronger relationships to verbal aptitude than the older measure. An early childhood setting that should promote fantasy involvement, therefore, as reflected in recollections of such activities as solitary play, writing of poems and stories, and creating of complicated imaginary situations, is found to eventuate in higher levels of verbal intelligence and academic achievement.

While a close parental relationship, the carrying on of games and storytelling with parents, and the time and privacy for solitary play activities all can be expected to foster the development of fantasy capacities, they hence can be expected to enhance general intellective functioning as well. Although sub-

[17] Among high scorers on the activities cluster just described, those nominated as creative by their teachers also were found to have significantly higher verbal SAT scores and grade point averages than those who were not so nominated. The teachers' creativity judgments thus were reflecting traditional intellective criteria, just as were the scores on the childhood activities cluster in question.

tle differences may well exist between intelligence- and fantasy-promoting family background characteristics in terms of greater parental tolerance for deviation from reality and hence for error on the child's part as more conducive to development of fantasy, such differences may be difficult to tease out empirically. One comes away with the feeling that a major source of variance concerning individual differences in the novelty of elicited fantasy and the incidence of spontaneous fantasy—and hence, presumably, also in associative creativity—resides in hereditary factors. For example, Scarr (1966) found identical twins to be more similar to each other than fraternal twins in the amount of time spent viewing novel stimuli. Given the environmentalistic bias of our culture, it seems likely that the role of heredity in the present domain is much greater than has been assumed, thus rendering it eminently worthy of investigation.

Finally, we should note that—whether based upon environmental or hereditary considerations or both—there is evidence indicating that the kinds of fantasy and associative indicators that we have been considering are related to self-report scores on manifest anxiety indicators. Such evidence suggests that manifest anxiety indicators may function more as indices of introspective sensitivity than of pathology—at least in grossly normal samples. To begin with, consider that relationships between manifest anxiety scores and intelligence measures are found to be zero or negative, but never positive (see, e.g., Spielberger, 1958; Sarason, Davidson, Lighthall, Waite, and Ruebush, 1960; Ruebush, 1963). This implies that linkages between higher anxiety scores, on the one hand, and higher scores on the fantasy or associative indicators, on the other, cannot be mediated by higher intelligence levels. And linkages of this kind have been obtained in several studies.

Maddi and Andrews (1966) found manifest anxiety scores to be positively correlated with novelty of TAT story productions. So also, both Singer and Schonbar (1961) and Singer and Rowe (1962) found positive relationships between manifest anxiety indicators and frequency of daydreaming. Analogous positive correlations have been obtained between manifest anxiety and another arena of spontaneous fantasy activity—incidence of night-dreaming, as inferred from dream reports (Schonbar, 1959; Singer and Schonbar, 1961; Tart, 1962) or from amount of sleeping time during which periods of rapid eyeball movement occurred (Rechtschaffen and Verdone, 1964). Turning to associative behavior, Davids and Eriksen (1955) reported a positive relationship between manifest anxiety and an index of associative productivity—the number of associates offered in response to each of a variety of stimulus words. Both the anxiety and the associative productivity measures, in turn, were independent of general intelligence and academic achievement for the undergraduates in the study. Wallach and Kogan (1965a, 1965b) found—in the case of boys but not girls—that high associative productivity and uniqueness were linked with intermediate rather than low levels of manifest anxiety. And in a possibly relevant study concerned with preferences for "feminine" versus "masculine" play activities, where the feminine emphasized imaginative fantasy and dramatization, whereas the masculine emphasized forceful physical contact and large-scale motoric involvement, Sutton-Smith and Rosenberg (1960) found that preference for the games involving imaginative play rather than extensive bodily movement was greater among the high-anxiety than the low-anxiety boys. All in all, the results just reviewed seem to argue for greater introspective sensitivity on the part of persons displaying the types of fantasy and associative behaviors with which we have been concerned. However such sensitivity arises, it may well be causally implicated in associative creativity, novelty of elicited fantasy, and incidence of spontaneous fantasy.

In this chapter the question of locating and conceptualizing psychological processes to which the term "creativity" can be justifiably applied has been our main concern. Given the encouraging results of this enterprise, next on the agenda for the psychology of creativity should be the study of how these processes are implicated in the attainment of products judged creative by the society.

References

Acker, M., and McReynolds, P. The "need for novelty": a comparison of six instruments. *Psychol. Rec.*, 1967, **17**, 177–182.

Adelson, J. Creativity and the dream. *Merrill-Palmer Quart.*, 1960, **6**, 92–97.

Anderson, C. C. A cognitive theory of the nonintellective correlates of originality. *Behav. Sci.*, 1966, **11**, 284–294.

Anderson, R. C., and Anderson, R. M. Transfer of originality training. *J. educ. Psychol.*, 1963, **54**, 300–304.

Andrews, F. M. Factors affecting the manifestation of creative ability by scientists. *J. Personality*, 1965, **33**, 140–152.

Antrobus, J. S., Singer, J. L., and Greenberg, S. Studies in the stream of consciousness: experimental enhancement and suppression of spontaneous cognitive processes. *Percept. Mot. Skills*, 1966, **23**, 399–417.

Barron, F. The disposition toward originality. *J. abnorm. soc. Psychol.*, 1955, **51**, 478–485.

―――― Originality in relation to personality and intellect. *J. Personality*, 1957, **25**, 730–742.

―――― *Creativity and psychological health*. Princeton, N. J.: Van Nostrand, 1963.

―――― The psychology of creativity. In *New directions in psychology II*. New York: Holt, Rinehart, and Winston, 1965. Pp. 1–134.

Becher, B. A. A cross-sectional and longitudinal study of the effect of education on free association responses. *J. genet. Psychol.*, 1960, **97**, 23–28.

Bereiter, C. Verbal and ideational fluency in superior tenth grade students. *J. educ. Psychol.*, 1960, **51**, 337–345.

———— Fluency abilities in preschool children. *J. genet. Psychol.*, 1961, **98**, 47–48.

Bish, G. G. A study of the relationships of intelligence, achievement, creativity, anxiety and confidence among intermediate grade pupils in a suburban area elementary school. Doctoral dissertation, George Washington University, Washington, D.C., 1964.

Boersma, F. J., and O'Bryan, K. An investigation of the relationship between creativity and intelligence under two conditions of testing. *J. Personality*, 1968, **36**, 341–348.

Bowers, J. E. A study of the relationships among measures of productive thinking, intelligence, and ninth grade achievement. Doctoral dissertation, University of Minnesota, 1966.

Burt, C. The differentiation of intellectual ability. *Br. J. educ. Psychol.*, 1954, **24**, 76–90.

———— The inheritance of mental ability. *Am. Psychol.*, 1958, **13**, 1–15.

———— The psychology of creative ability. *Br. J. educ. Psychol.*, 1962, **32**, 292–298.

Campbell, D. T. Blind variation and selective retention in creative thought as in other knowledge processes. *Psychol. Rev.*, 1960, **67**, 380–400.

Caron, A. J., Unger, S. M., and Parloff, M. B. A test of Maltzman's theory of originality training. *J. verb. Learn. verb. Behav.*, 1963, **1**, 436–442.

Cartledge, C. J., and Krauser, E. L. Training first-grade children in creative thinking under quantitative and qualitative motivation. *J. educ. Psychol.*, 1963, **54**, 295–299.

Cattell, R. B. *Objective-analytic test battery.* Champaign, Ill.: Institute for Personality and Ability Testing, 1956.

Cattell, R. B., and Drevdahl, J. E. A comparison of the personality profile (16 P. F.) of eminent researchers with that of eminent teachers and administrators, and of the general population. *Br. J. Psychol.*, 1955, **46**, 248–261.

Chambers, J. A. Relating personality and biographical factors to scientific creativity. *Psychol. Monogr.*, 1964, **78**, No. 7 (Whole No. 584).

Christensen, P. R., Guilford, J. P., and Wilson, R. C. Relations of creative responses to working time and instructions. *J. exp. Psychol.*, 1957, **53**, 82–88.

Christensen, P. R., Merrifield, P. R., and Guilford, J. P. *Consequences: manual for administration, scoring, and interpretation.* Beverly Hills, Cal.: Sheridan Supply, 1958.

Cicirelli, V. G. The relationship between measures of creativity, IQ, and academic achievement; interaction and threshold effects. Doctoral dissertation, University of Michigan, 1964.

———— Form of the relationship between creativity, IQ, and academic achievement. *J. educ. Psychol.*, 1965, **56**, 303–308.

Clark, C. M., Veldman, D. J., and Thorpe, J. S. Convergent and divergent thinking abilities of talented adolescents. *J. educ. Psychol.*, 1965, **56**, 157–163.

Cline, V. B., Richards, J. M., Jr., and Abe, C. The validity of a battery of creativity tests in a high school sample. *Educ. psychol. Measur.*, 1962, **22**, 781–785.

Cline, V. B., Richards, J. M., Jr., and Needham, W. E. Creativity tests and achievement in high school science. *J. appl. Psychol.*, 1963, **47**, 184–189.

Cronbach, L. J. Review of J. W. Getzels and P. W. Jackson, *Creativity and intelligence. Am. J. Sociol.*, 1962, **68**, 278–279.

Cropley, A. J. Creativity and intelligence. *Br. J. educ. Psychol.*, 1966, **36**, 259–266.

Crutchfield, R. S. Instructing children in creative thinking. Address delivered at the annual convention of the American Psychological Association, Los Angeles, Cal., September 1964.

Crutchfield, R. S., and Covington, M. V. Facilitation of creative thinking and problem solving in school children. Paper presented in a symposium on Learning Research Pertinent to Educational Improvement, American Association for the Advancement of Science, Cleveland, Ohio, December 1963.

Cunnington, B. F., and Torrance, E. P. *Imagi/Craft productions.* Boston: Ginn, 1965.

Davidon, R. S., and Longo, N. Conceptual development reflected in age differences in associations to names and pictures of objects. *J. genet. Psychol.,* 1960, **96,** 85–92.

Davids, A., and Eriksen, C. S. The relation of manifest anxiety to association productivity and intellectual attainment. *J. consult. Psychol.,* 1955, **19,** 219–222.

de Mille, R., and Merrifield, P. R. Review of J. W. Getzels and P. W. Jackson, *Creativity and intelligence. Educ. psychol. Measur.,* 1962, **22,** 803–808.

Doris, J., Sarason, S. B., and Berkowitz, L. Test anxiety and performance on projective tests. *Child Dev.,* 1963, **34,** 751–766.

Drevdahl, J. E., and Cattell, R. B. Personality and creativity in artists and writers. *J. clin. Psychol.,* 1958, **14,** 107–111.

Edwards, M. P., and Tyler, L. E. Intelligence, creativity, and achievement in a nonselective public junior high school. *J. educ. Psychol.,* 1965, **56,** 96–99.

Faris, R. E. L. Review of J. W. Getzels and P. W. Jackson, *Creativity and intelligence. Am. sociol. Rev.,* 1962, **27,** 558–559.

Feldhusen, J. F., Denny, T., and Condon, C. F. Anxiety, divergent thinking, and achievement. *J. educ. Psychol.,* 1965, **56,** 40–45.

Flavell, J. H., Cooper, A., and Loiselle, R. H. Effect of the number of preutilization functions on functional fixedness in problem solving. *Psychol. Rep.,* 1958, **4,** 343–350.

Fleming, E. S., and Weintraub, S. Attitudinal rigidity as a measure of creativity in gifted children. *J. educ. Psychol.,* 1962, **53,** 81–85.

Flescher, I. Anxiety and achievement of intellectually gifted and creatively gifted children. *J. Psychol.,* 1963, **56,** 251–268.

Freedman, J. L. Increasing creativity by free-association training. *J. exp. Psychol.,* 1965, **69,** 89–91.

Gall, M., and Mendelsohn, G. A. Effects of facilitating techniques and subject-experimenter interaction on creative problem solving. *J. Pers. soc. Psychol.,* 1967, **5,** 211–216.

Garwood, D. Personality factors related to creativity in young scientists. *J. abnorm. soc. Psychol.,* 1964, **68,** 413–419.

Getzels, J. W., and Jackson, P. W. Occupational choice and cognitive functioning: career aspirations of highly intelligent and of highly creative adolescents. *J. abnorm. soc. Psychol.,* 1960, **61,** 119–123.

—— *Creativity and intelligence: explorations with gifted students.* New York: Wiley, 1962.

Gewirtz, J. L. Studies in word fluency. I. Its relation to vocabulary and mental age in young children. *J. genet. Psychol.,* 1948, **72,** 165–176 (a).

—— Studies in word fluency. II. Its relation to eleven items of child behavior. *J. genet. Psychol.,* 1948, **72,** 177–184 (b).

Ghiselin, B. (Ed.) *The creative process.* New York: Mentor, 1955.

Golann, S. E. Psychological study of creativity. *Psychol. Bull.,* 1963, **60,** 548–565.

Griffin, D. P. Movement responses and creativity. *J. consult. Psychol.,* 1958, **22,** 134–136.

Guilford, J. P. The structure of intellect. *Psychol. Bull.,* 1956, **53,** 267–293.

—— Creative abilities in the arts. *Psychol. Rev.,* 1957, **64,** 110–118.

—————— Three faces of intellect. *Am. Psychol.*, 1959, **14**, 469–479 (a).

—————— Traits of creativity. In H. H. Anderson (Ed.), *Creativity and its cultivation*. New York: Harper, 1959. Pp. 142–161 (b).

—————— *Personality*. New York: McGraw-Hill, 1959 (c).

—————— Potentiality for creativity and its measurement. In *Proceedings of the 1962 invitational conference on testing problems*. Princeton, N. J.: Educational Testing Service, 1963. Pp. 31–39.

—————— Some new looks at the nature of creative processes. In N. Frederiksen and H. Gulliksen (Eds.), *Contributions to mathematical psychology*. New York: Holt, Rinehart and Winston, 1964. Pp. 161–176.

—————— Creativity: yesterday, today, and tomorrow. *J. creative Behav.*, 1967, **1**, 3–14 (a).

—————— *The nature of human intelligence*. New York: McGraw-Hill, 1967 (b).

Guilford, J. P., and Christensen, P. R. A factor-analytic study of verbal fluency. *Rep. psychol. Lab.*, 1956, No. 17. Los Angeles: University of Southern California.

Guilford, J. P., Frick, J. W., Christensen, P. R., and Merrifield, P. R. A factor-analytic study of flexibility in thinking. *Rep. psychol. Lab.*, 1957, No. 18. Los Angeles: University of Southern California.

Guilford, J. P., Wilson, R. C., and Christensen, P. R. A factor-analytic study of creative thinking: II. Administration of tests and analysis of results. *Rep. psychol. Lab.*, 1952, No. 8. Los Angeles: University of Southern California.

Guilford, J. P., Wilson, R. C., Christensen, P. R., and Lewis, D. J. A factor-analytic study of creative thinking: I. Hypotheses and description of tests. *Rep. psychol. Lab.*, 1951, No. 3. Los Angeles: University of Southern California.

Hadamard, J. S. *The psychology of invention in the mathematical field*. Princeton, N.J.: Princeton University Press, 1945.

Harmon, L. R. The development of a criterion of scientific competence. In C. W. Taylor and F. Barron (Eds.), *Scientific creativity: its recognition and development*. New York: Wiley, 1963. Pp. 44–52.

Hasan, P., and Butcher, H. J. Creativity and intelligence: a partial replication with Scottish children of Getzels' and Jackson's study. *Br. J. Psychol.*, 1966, **57**, 129–135.

Helson, R. Childhood interest clusters related to creativity in women. *J. consult. Psychol.*, 1965, **29**, 352–361.

—————— Personality of women with imaginative and artistic interests: the role of masculinity, originality, and other characteristics in their creativity. *J. Personality*, 1966, **34**, 1–25.

Hoepfner, R., Nihira, K., and Guilford, J. P. Intellectual abilities of symbolic and semantic judgment. *Psychol. Monogr.*, 1966, **80**, No. 16 (Whole No. 624).

Holland, J. L. Some limitations of teacher ratings as predictors of creativity. *J. educ. Psychol.*, 1959, **50**, 219–223.

Houston, J. P., and Mednick, S. A. Creativity and the need for novelty. *J. abnorm. soc. Psychol.*, 1963, **66**, 137–141.

Hoyt, D. P. The relationship between college grades and adult achievement: a review of the literature. Iowa City, Iowa: American College Testing Program Research Report, 1965 (Whole No. 7).

Iscoe, I., and Pierce-Jones, J. Divergent thinking, age, and intelligence in white and Negro children. *Child Dev.*, 1964, **35**, 785–798.

Jackson, P. W., Getzels, J. W., and Xydis, G. A. Psychological health and cognitive functioning in adolescence: a multivariate analysis. *Child Dev.*, 1960, **31**, 285–298.

Jackson, P. W., and Messick, S. The person, the product, and the response: conceptual problems in the assessment of creativity. *J. Personality*, 1965, **33**, 309–329.

Kennedy, W. A., and the Human Development Clinic Staff. A multidimensional study of mathematically gifted adolescents. *Child Dev.*, 1960, **31**, 655–666.

Klausmeier, H. J., Harris, C. W., and Ethnathios, Z. Relationships between divergent thinking abilities and teacher ratings of high school students. *J. educ. Psychol.*, 1962, **53**, 72–75.

Klausmeier, H. J., and Wiersma, W. Relationship of sex, grade level, and locale to performance of high IQ students on divergent thinking tests. *J. educ. Psychol.*, 1964, **55**, 114–119.

Knapp, R. H., and Goodrich, H. B. *Origins of American scientists.* Chicago: University of Chicago Press, 1952.

Laughlin, P. R. Incidental concept formation as a function of creativity and intelligence. *J. Pers. soc. Psychol.*, 1967, **5**, 115–119.

Lembright, M. L., and Yamamoto, K. Subcultures and creative thinking: an exploratory comparison between Amish and urban American school children. *Merrill-Palmer Quart.*, 1965, **11**, 49–64.

Lesser, L. An experimental study of the drive-reducing function of imagination and fantasy in young children. Doctoral dissertation, New York University, 1962.

Lieberman, J. N. Playfulness and divergent thinking: an investigation of their relationship at the kindergarten level. *J. genet. Psychol.*, 1965, **107**, 219–224.

Long, B. H., and Henderson, E. H. Originality, reading, and arithmetic. *Percept. Mot. Skills*, 1965, **21**, 553–554.

MacKinnon, D. W. The highly effective individual. *Teachers Coll. Rec.*, 1960, **61**, 367–378.

——— The personality correlates of creativity: a study of American architects. In G. S. Nielsen (Ed.), *Proceedings of the XIV International Congress of Applied Psychology, Copenhagen, 1961*, Vol. II. Copenhagen: Munksgaard, 1962. Pp. 11–39 (a).

——— The nature and nurture of creative talent. *Am. Psychol.*, 1962, **17**, 484–495 (b).

Maddi, S. R. Motivational aspects of creativity. *J. Personality*, 1965, **33**, 330–347.

Maddi, S. R., and Andrews, S. L. The need for variety in fantasy and self-description. *J. Personality*, 1966, **34**, 610–625.

Maddi, S. R., and Berne, N. Novelty of productions and desire for novelty as active and passive forms of the need for variety. *J. Personality*, 1964, **32**, 270–277.

Maddi, S. R., Charlens, A. M., Maddi, D.-A., and Smith, A. J. Effects of monotony and novelty on imaginative productions. *J. Personality*, 1962, **30**, 513–527.

Maddi, S. R., Propst, B. S., and Feldinger, I. Three expressions of the need for variety. *J. Personality*, 1965, **33**, 82–98.

Maier, N. R. F. Reasoning in humans. II. The solution of a problem and its appearance in consciousness. *J. comp. Psychol.*, 1931, **12**, 181–194.

Maltzman, I. On the training of originality. *Psychol. Rev.*, 1960, **67**, 229–242.

Maltzman, I., Belloni, M., and Fishbein, M. Experimental studies of associative variables in originality. *Psychol. Monogr.*, 1964, **78**, No. 3 (Whole No. 580).

Maltzman, I., Bogartz, W., and Breger, L. A procedure for increasing word association originality and its transfer effects. *J. exp. Psychol.*, 1958, **56**, 393–398.

Maltzman, I., Brooks, L. O., Bogartz, W., and Summers, S. S. The facilitation of problem solving by prior exposure to uncommon responses. *J. exp. Psychol.*, 1958, **56**, 399–406.

Maltzman, I., Simon, S., Raskin, D., and Licht, L. Experimental studies in the training of originality. *Psychol. Monogr.*, 1960, **74**, No. 6 (Whole No. 493).

Mandler G., and Kessen, W. *The language of psychology.* New York: Wiley, 1959.

Marks, A., Guilford, J. P., and Merrifield, P. R. A study of military leadership in relation to selected intellectual factors. *Rep. psychol. Lab.*, 1959, No. 21. Los Angeles: University of Southern California.

Marsh, R. W. A statistical re-analysis of Getzels and Jackson's data. *Br. J. educ. Psychol.*, 1964, 34, 91–93.

Maupin, E. W. Individual differences in response to a Zen meditation exercise. *J. consult. Psychol.*, 1965, 29, 139–145.

May, F. B., and Metcalf, A. W. A factor-analytic study of spontaneous-flexibility measures. *Educ. psychol. Measur.*, 1965, 25, 1039–1050.

McGuire, C., Hindsman, E., King, F. J., and Jennings, E. Dimensions of talented behavior. *Educ. psychol. Measur.*, 1961, 21, 3–38.

McKellar P. *Imagination and thinking: a psychological analysis.* New York: Basic Books, 1957.

McNemar, Q. Lost: Our intelligence? Why? *Am. Psychol.*, 1964, 19, 871–882.

Mednick, M. T. Research creativity in psychology graduate students. *J. consult. Psychol.*, 1963, 27, 265–266.

Mednick, M. T., Mednick, S. A., and Jung, C. C. Continual association as a function of level of creativity and type of verbal stimulus. *J. abnorm. soc. Psychol.*, 1964, 69, 511–515.

Mednick, M. T., Mednick, S. A., and Mednick, E. V. Incubation of creative performance and specific associative priming. *J. abnorm. soc. Psychol.*, 1964, 69, 84–88.

Mednick, S. A. The associative basis of the creative process. *Psychol. Rev.*, 1962, 69, 220–232.

Mednick, S. A., and Mednick, M. T. An associationistic view of creative thinking. In C. W. Taylor (Ed.), *Widening horizons in creativity.* New York: Wiley, 1964. Pp. 54–68.

Mendelsohn, G. A., and Griswold, B. B. Differential use of incidental stimuli in problem solving as a function of creativity. *J. abnorm. soc. Psychol.*, 1964, 68, 431–436.

Mendelsohn, G. A., and Griswold, B. B. Assessed creative potential, vocabulary level, and sex as predictors of the use of incidental cues in verbal problem solving. *J. Pers. soc. Psychol.*, 1966, 4, 423–431.

Myden, W. Interpretation and evaluation of certain personality characteristics involved in creative production. *Percept. Mot. Skills,* 1959, 9, 139–158.

Olton, R. M. A self-instructional program for the development of productive thinking in fifth and sixth grade children. In F. E. Williams (Ed.), *First seminar in productive thinking in education.* St. Paul, Minn.: Creativity project, Macalester College, 1966. Pp. 54–60.

Orpet, R. E., and Meyers, C. E. Six structure-of-intellect hypotheses in six-year-old children. *J. educ. Psychol.*, 1966, 57, 341–346.

Page, H. A. Studies in fantasy: daydreaming frequency and Rorschach scoring categories. *J. consult. Psychol.*, 1957, 21, 111–114.

Pearson, P. H., and Maddi, S. R. The similes preference inventory: development of a structured measure of the tendency toward variety. *J. consult. Psychol.*, 1966, 30, 301–308.

Penney, R. K. Reactive curiosity and manifest anxiety in children. *Child Dev.,* 1965, 36, 697–702.

Penney, R. K., and McCann, B. The children's reactive curiosity scale. *Psychol. Rep.,* 1964, 15, 323–334.

Perry, J. M. Correlation of teacher prediction for student success six years beyond sixth grade. Doctoral dissertation, University of Illinois, 1966.

Pettigrew, T. F. The measurement and correlates of category width as a cognitive variable. *J. Personality*, 1958, 26, 532–544.

Piaget, J. *Play, dreams and imitation in childhood.* New York: Norton, 1962.

Piers, E. V., Daniels, J. M., and Quackenbush, J. F. The identification of creativity in adolescents. *J. educ. Psychol.,* 1960, **51,** 346–351.

Rainwater, J. M. Effects of set on problem solving in subjects of varying levels of assessed creativity. Doctoral dissertation, University of California, Berkeley, 1964.

Rechtschaffen, A., and Verdone, P. Amount of dreaming: effect of incentive, adaptation to laboratory, and individual differences. *Percept. Mot. Skills,* 1964, **19,** 947–958.

Reid, J. B., King, F. J., and Wickwire, P. Cognitive and other personality characteristics of creative children. *Psychol. Rep.,* 1959, **5,** 729–737.

Riegel, K. F., Riegel, R. M., and Levine, R. S. An analysis of associative behavior and creativity. *J. Pers. soc. Psychol.,* 1966, **4,** 50–56.

Riess, A. A study of some genetic behavioral correlates of human movement responses in children's Rorschach protocols. Doctoral dissertation, New York University, 1957.

Ripple, R. E., and May, F. B. Caution in comparing creativity and IQ. *Psychol. Rep.,* 1962, **10,** 229–230.

Rivlin, L. G. Creativity and the self-attitudes and sociability of high school students. *J. educ. Psychol.,* 1959, **50,** 147–152.

Roe, A. A psychological study of eminent biologists. *Psychol. Monogr.,* 1951, **65,** No. 14 (Whole No. 331) (a).

——— A psychological study of physical scientists. *Genet. psychol. Monogr.,* 1951, **43,** 121–235 (b).

——— *The making of a scientist.* New York: Dodd, Mead, 1953 (a).

——— A psychological study of eminent psychologists and anthropologists, and a comparison with biological and physical scientists. *Psychol. Monogr.,* 1953, **67,** No. 2 (Whole No. 352) (b).

Ruebush, B. K. Anxiety. In H. W. Stevenson (Ed.), *Child psychology: the sixty-second yearbook of the National Society for the Study of Education, part I.* Chicago: University of Chicago Press, 1963. Pp. 460–516.

Rugg, H. *Imagination.* New York: Harper, 1963.

Sarason, S. B., Davidson, K. S., Lighthall, F. F., Waite, R. R., and Ruebush, B. K. *Anxiety in elementary school children: a report of research.* New York: Wiley, 1960.

Scarr, S. Genetic factors in activity motivation. *Child Dev.,* 1966, **37,** 663–673.

Schachtel, E. G. *Metamorphosis: on the development of affect, perception, attention, and memory.* New York: Basic Books, 1959.

Schonbar, R. A. Some manifest characteristics of recallers and nonrecallers of dreams. *J. consult. Psychol.,* 1959, **23,** 414–418.

Sieber, J. E., and Lanzetta, J. T. Some determinants of individual differences in predecision information-processing behavior. *J. Pers. soc. Psychol.,* 1966, **4,** 561–571.

Singer, J. L. Imagination and waiting ability in young children. *J. Personality,* 1961, **29,** 396–413.

——— Daydreaming and planful thought: a note on Professors Stark's conceptual framework. *Percept. Mot. Skills,* 1966, **23,** 113–114 (a).

——— *Daydreaming: an introduction to the experimental study of inner experience.* New York: Random House, 1966 (b).

Singer, J. L., and Antrobus, J. S. A factor-analytic study of daydreaming and conceptually-related cognitive and personality variables. *Percept. Mot. Skills,* 1963, **17,** 187–209.

Singer, J. L., and Chipman, A. The generalization of imaginative learning to delaying capacity in children. Report to the National Institute of Mental Health under grant M-2279, 1961.

Singer, J. L., and McCraven, V. G. Some characteristics of adult daydreaming. *J. Psychol.*, 1961, **51**, 151–164.

Singer, J. L., and Rowe, R. An experimental study of some relationships between daydreaming and anxiety. *J. consult. Psychol.*, 1962, **26**, 446–454.

Singer, J. L., and Schonbar, R. A. Correlates of daydreaming: a dimension of self-awareness. *J. consult. Psychol.*, 1961, **25**, 1–6.

Singer, J. L., and Streiner, B. F. Imaginative content in the dreams and fantasy play of blind and sighted children. *Percept. Mot. Skills*, 1966, **22**, 475–482.

Smith, E. E., and White, H. L. Wit, creativity, and sarcasm. *J. appl. Psychol.*, 1965, **49**, 131–134.

Spielberger, C. D. On the relationship between manifest anxiety and intelligence. *J. consult. Psychol.*, 1958, **22**, 220–224.

Stark, S. Rorschach movement and Bleuler's three kinds of thinking: a contribution to the psychology of creativity. *Percept. Mot. Skills*, 1964, **19**, 959–967.

———— An essay on Romantic genius, Rorschach movement, and the definition of creativity. *Percept. Mot. Skills*, 1965, **20**, 409–418 (a).

———— Toward a psychology of knowledge: hypotheses regarding Rorschach movement and creativity. *Percept. Mot. Skills*, 1965, **21**, 839–859 (b).

———— Rorschach movement, fantastic daydreaming, and Freud's concept of primary process: interpretive commentary. *Percept. Mot. Skills*, 1966, **22**, 523–532.

Stein, M. I., and Heinze, S. J. *Creativity and the individual: summaries of selected literature in psychology and psychiatry.* Glencoe, Ill.: Free Press, 1960.

Sutton-Smith, B. Piaget on play: a critique. *Psychol. Rev.*, 1966, **73**, 104–110.

Sutton-Smith, B., and Rosenberg, B. G. Manifest anxiety and game preferences in children. *Child Dev.*, 1960, **31**, 307–311.

Swartz, J. D. Performance of high- and low-anxious children on the Holtzman inkblot technique. *Child Dev.*, 1965, **36**, 569–575.

Tart, C. T. Frequency of dream recall and some personality measures. *J. consult. Psychol.*, 1962, **26**, 467–470.

Taylor, C. W. (Ed.) *The third (1959) University of Utah research conference on the identification of creative scientific talent.* Salt Lake City: University of Utah Press, 1959.

———— *Creativity: progress and potential.* New York: McGraw-Hill, 1964 (a).

———— *Widening horizons in creativity.* New York: Wiley, 1964 (b).

Taylor, C. W., and Barron, F. (Eds.) *Scientific creativity: its recognition and development.* New York: Wiley, 1963.

Taylor, C. W., and Ellison, R. L. Biographical predictors of scientific performance. *Science*, 1967, **155**, 1075–1080.

Taylor, C. W., Smith, W. R., and Ghiselin, B. The creative and other contributions of one sample of research scientists. In C. W. Taylor and F. Barron (Eds.), *Scientific creativity: its recognition and development.* New York: Wiley, 1963. Pp. 53–76.

Taylor, C. W., Smith, W. R., Ghiselin B. and Ellison R. Explorations in the measurement and prediction of contributions of one sample of scientists. Report ASD-TR-61-96, Aeronautical Systems Division, Personnel Laboratory, Lackland Air Force Base, Texas, 1961.

Taylor, C. W., and Williams, F. E. (Eds.) *Instructional media and creativity.* New York: Wiley, 1966.

Taylor, D. W. Variables related to creativity and productivity among men in two research laboratories. In C. W. Taylor and F. Barron (Eds.), *Scientific cre-*

ativity: its recognition and development. New York: Wiley, 1963. Pp. 228–250.

Teeter, B., Rouzer, D. L., and Rosen, E. Development of a dimension of cognitive motivation: preference for widely known information. *Child Dev.,* 1964, **35,** 1105–1111.

Thorndike, R. L. The measurement of creativity. *Teachers Coll. Rec.,* 1963, **64,** 422–424 (a).

———— Some methodological issues in the study of creativity. In *Proceedings of the 1962 invitational conference on testing problems.* Princeton, N. J.: Educational Testing Service, 1963. Pp. 40–54 (b).

Thurstone, L. L. The factorial isolation of primary abilities. *Psychometrika,* 1936, **1,** 175–182.

———— Primary mental abilities. *Psychomet. Monogr.,* 1938, No. 1. Chicago: University of Chicago Press.

Torrance, E. P. Priming creative thinking in the primary grades. *Elem. Sch. J.,* 1961, **62,** 34–41 (a).

———— Factors affecting creative thinking in children: an interim research report. *Merrill-Palmer Quart.,* 1961, **7,** 171–180 (b).

———— *Guiding creative talent.* Englewood Cliffs, N.J.: Prentice-Hall, 1962.

———— *Education and the creative potential.* Minneapolis: University of Minnesota Press, 1963.

———— *Torrance tests of creative thinking: norms—technical manual.* Princeton, N.J.: Personnel Press, 1966 (a).

———— *Torrance tests of creative thinking: directions manual and scoring guide; verbal test, booklet A, research edition.* Princeton. N.J.: Personnel Press, 1966 (b).

———— *Torrance tests of creative thinking: directions manual and scoring guide; figural test, booklet A, research edition.* Princeton, N.J.: Personnel Press, 1966 (c).

———— Exploring the limits on the automation of guided, planned experiences in creative thinking. In J. S. Roucek (Ed.), *Programmed teaching.* New York: Philosophical Library, 1966. Pp. 57–70 (d).

Torrance, E. P., and Gowan, J. C. The reliability of the Minnesota tests of creative thinking. (Research Memorandum BER-63-4.) Minneapolis: Bureau of Educational Research, University of Minnesota, 1963.

Torrance, E. P., and Myers, R. E. *Teaching gifted elementary pupils how to do research.* Minneapolis: Perceptive Publishing, 1962.

Vernon, P. E. Ability factors and environmental influences. *Am. Psychol.,* 1965, **20,** 723–733.

Walker, H. E. Relationships between predicted school behavior and measures of creative potential. Doctoral dissertation, University of Michigan, 1962.

Wallach, M. A. Creativity and the expression of possibilities. In J. Kagan (Ed.), *Creativity and learning.* Boston: Houghton Mifflin, 1967. Pp. 36–57.

Wallach, M. A., and Caron, A. J. Attribute criteriality and sex-linked conservatism as determinants of psychological similarity. *J. abnorm. soc. Psychol.,* 1959, **59,** 43–50.

Wallach, M. A., and Kogan, N. *Modes of thinking in young children: a study of the creativity-intelligence distinction.* New York: Holt, Rinehart and Winston, 1965 (a).

———— A new look at the creativity-intelligence distinction. *J. Personality,* 1965, **33,** 348–369 (b).

Wallas, G. *The art of thought.* New York: Harcourt, Brace, 1926.

Wallen, N. E., and Stevenson, G. M. Stability and correlates of judged creativity in fifth grade writings. *J. educ. Psychol.,* 1960, **51,** 273–276.

Ward, W. C. Creativity and impulsivity in kindergarten children. Doctoral dissertation, Duke University, Durham, N.C., 1966.

———— Creativity in young children. *Child Dev.*, 1968, **39**, 737–754.

Wechsler, D. *The measurement of adult intelligence.* (3rd ed.) Baltimore: Williams and Wilkins, 1952.

White, R. W. Motivation reconsidered: the concept of competence. *Psychol. Rev.*, 1959, **66**, 297–333.

———— Ego and reality in psychoanalytic theory. *Psychol. Issues*, 1963, **3**, No. 3 (Whole No. 11).

Wilson, R. C., Christensen, P. R., Merrifield, P. R., and Guilford, J. P. *Alternate uses: manual of administration, scoring, and interpretation.* Beverly Hills, Cal.: Sheridan Supply, 1960.

Wilson, R. C., Guilford, J. P., and Christensen, P. R. The measurement of individual differences in originality. *Psychol. Bull.*, 1953, **50**, 362–370.

Wilson, R. C., Guilford, J. P., Christensen, P. R., and Lewis, D. J. A factor-analytic study of creative-thinking abilities. *Psychometrika*, 1954, **19**, 297–311.

Witkin, H. A., Dyk, R. B., Faterson, H. F., Goodenough, D. R., and Karp, S. A. *Psychological differentiation· studies of development.* New York: Wiley, 1962.

Wodtke, K. H. Some data on the reliability and validity of creativity tests at the elementary school level. *Educ. psychol. Measur.*, 1964, **24**, 399–408.

Woodworth, R. S., and Schlosberg, H. *Experimental psychology.* (2nd ed.) New York: Holt, 1954.

Worell, J. and Worell, L. Personality conflict, originality of response, and recall. *J. consult. Psychol.*, 1965, **29**, 55–62.

Yamamoto, K. Development of ability to ask questions under specific testing conditions. *J. genet. Psychol.*, 1962, **101**, 83–90.

———— Relationships between creative thinking abilities of teachers and achievement and adjustment of pupils. *J. exp. Educ.*, 1963, **32**, 3–25.

———— Role of creative thinking and intelligence in high school achievement. *Psychol. Rep.*, 1964, **14**, 783–789 (a).

———— Evaluation of some creativity measures in a high school with peer nominations as criteria. *J. Psychol.*, 1964, **58**, 285–293 (b).

———— Effects of restriction of range and test unreliability on correlation between measures of intelligence and creative thinking. *Br. J. educ. Psychol.*, 1965, **35**, 300–305.

Yamamoto, K., and Chimbidis, M. E. Achievement, intelligence, and creative thinking in fifth-grade children: a correlational study. *Merrill-Palmer Quart.*, 1966, **12**, 233–241.

Yonge, G. D. Structure of experience and functional fixedness. *J. educ. Psychol.*, 1966, **57**, 115–120.

18. *Individual Variation in Cognitive Processes*[1]

JEROME KAGAN and NATHAN KOGAN

with the assistance of Anne L. Bloxom and Regina Yando

The traditional insularity among the complementary processes of thought, motivation, and behavior is being overcome, making it necessary to invent concepts that reflect the new relations among these processes. The introduction of the concepts of field independence, reflection-impulsivity, leveling-sharpening, automatization, and creativity reflects an initial attempt to provide structure to the reliable variability that is characteristic of cognitive functioning among humans. The theoretical substance of these concepts typically implies that a blend of biological and motivational variables is responsible for the public phenomena. The vigorous and systematic study of variability in cognitive products represents a return to an interesting topic rather than a new frontier. Sir Francis Galton and James McKeen Cattell directed much investigative energy to individual differences in quality of cognitive functioning. Cattell, as early as 1890, proposed 10 tests that could be used to evaluate differences among people. The procedures included dynamometer pressure, rate of movement, two-point skin threshold, pressure causing pain, least noticeable difference in weight, reaction time to sound, time for naming colors, bisection of a 50 centimeter line, judgment of 10 seconds time, number of letters remembered on one hearing (Cattell, 1890).

Four of these tests focus on temporal functions and the rest assess sensory acuity or simple motor skills. This early battery mirrors the intellectual prejudices of the nineteenth century. Speed of nerve impulse conduction and psychophysical functions were dominant empirical and theoretical issues, and it was reasonable to conclude that differences in quality of thought were the sequellae of differences in sensitivity of receptor function and central nervous system transmission speeds.

The contrast with today's tests is instructive and encouraging. A modern-day Cattell might select a test battery that included verbal analogies, object sorting tests, memory for digits and sentences, the rod and frame test, embedded figures test, verbal fluency, haptic-visual matching test, Stroop color word test, and matching familiar figures.

The contemporary battery evaluates richness of language, reasoning, classification, and perceptual synthesis and decision processes. The contemporary tests are clearly more cognitive and complex than those devised 80 years earlier. Immediate memory represents the only node of overlap, and its survival attests to its centrality in cognition.

[1] Preparation of this chapter was supported in part by Research Grant MH-8792 from the National Institute of Mental Health, Contract No. 43-65-1009 and Research Grant 1 PO1 HD-01762 from the National Institute of Child Health and Human Development, and a grant from the Carnegie Corporation of New York. Various people contributed to the preparation of this chapter. We are indebted to Laura Carde, Ann King, Katherine Moore, Doris Simpson, and Terry Stagman for their invaluable assistance. This chapter has profited from the comments and criticisms of Walter Emmerich, Roy Shore, William Ward, and Sheldon White, but the authors assume full responsibility for its contents.

The Current Concern with Cognition

A concern with social-class differences in school performance, creativity, and new discoveries in personality research has sparked the contemporary analysis of systematic variability in cognition. The awesome differences between lower- and middle-class children are apparent to even the most inexperienced observer. The lower-class child has a sparser language reservoir and is more impulsive than his middle-class peer. These cognitive characteristics contribute to the lower-class child's poorer performance in school. It is imperative that we inquire into the origins of this deficit and the mechanisms of its development.

The second incentive was born from the concern with creativity and the need to differentiate, among the verbally proficient, those who had fluent, flexible, and novel approaches to problems from those whose hypotheses were normative and stereotyped.

A third force stems from the insights of personality theorists who demonstrated not only that motives and conflicts affected perceptual and problem-solving performance, but also that responses to traditional personality tests—be they projective or objective—were as strongly influenced by cognitive as by motivational forces.

These three diverse historical forces have led to a substantial body of literature, but, equally important, they have provided a fresh perspective to our view of cognition.

The Emphasis on Cognitive Processes. Psychology has returned for the second time to court the problems of mental life. The turnabout of the last decade is appreciated if one compares the last issue of *Child Development* in 1967 with the last issue 10 years earlier. Whereas 20 of the 27 empirical papers in the December 1967 journal were inquiries into cognitive functioning, there were none in the December 1957 issue. The return to internal processes reflects more than a cyclical change in popularity of a topical area. The return is characterized by a realization that psychology is not only the "science of the study of behavior," but also the science of the structure of mental life. We are beginning to acknowledge the potential validity of three important premises.

First, a particular motive, conflict, or expectancy will lead to different behaviors at different ages or in different contexts. The child with a strong motive for social recognition may work hard in the school setting or be mischievous in a recreational setting. He may choose academic success as a route to recognition if he grows up in a middle-class neighborhood; he is likely to choose antisocial aggression if he is reared in a lower-class, urban setting. He may tease his mother at age 3 and compete with his peers at age 15. This principle is analogous to the concept of pleiotropy in genetics, where a particular gene can have different manifest effects (King, 1967).

Second, it is likely that the possible variety in behavior cannot match the potential variety of covert cognitive processes. As a result, a particular behavior must be in the service of many different processes. Consider the relatively simple response of smiling. The smile can reflect an insight, a reaction to a joke, a familiar greeting to a friend, or a hostile feeling. Similarly, the cry can mirror sadness or joy, dependence or fear.

Finally, each response is typically multidetermined—the result of more than one fundamental process. This principle is analogous to the concept of polygeny in genetics, where many genes act in concert to produce a particular manifest character (King, 1967).

These three premises require that psychology be as much concerned with cognitive processes as with behavior. An analogy to our sister sciences may be helpful. Chemistry is defined as the science of the structure of matter, not the science that studies public manifestations of these structures. Contemporary biology is more concerned with the structure of genes and proteins than with the morphological characters that are the final result of the actions of these units. However, 400 years ago each of these natural sciences took the study and explanation of external features as its central mission. All natural sciences begin their inquiries with the public phenomena that they wish to explain. With maturity, however, they turn their attention to the more covert hypothetical processes that must form the basis of their theories. Psychology may be beginning to make the critical turn from preoccupation with interesting external phenomena to the internal processes upon which the public behaviors rest.

One danger to be avoided in this regard is to assume necessarily an isomorphism between the terms in which behavior is conceived and the terms used to describe relevant internal processes. Treisman (1968) has noted:

A Martian arrives on earth and for the first time in his life sees an automobile, something completely new to him. He is puzzled by it. He watches how it performs and finds that automobiles hold the road well or poorly, have high or low maximum speeds, travel downhill better than uphill, prefer smooth roads, and never fly or swim. But when he opens the hood and looks inside, all he sees is bits of metal, various wires, and a tank of smelly fluid. There is nothing that looks like the maximum speed, or the road-holding ability. He concludes that the automobile's behavior cannot be explained in terms of what lies under the hood, and he gives up in despair. . . . Our position is similar when we want to explain the behavior of a human being, in health or disease. . . . We have to try to discover what its structure is and the laws which govern its functioning. Not until we have got these straight can we see how far they explain human behavior (pp. 460–461).

The task is to gain full understanding of the structure of behavior, the structure of cognitive processing, and the mechanisms that join these two domains. It is possible, and indeed likely, that the structure of behavior does not match that of cognition. The heuristic assumption of the 'fifties that internal thought processes be treated as if they were overt responses may have outlived its usefulness.

A Definition of Cognition

The term "cognition" has typically referred to mental activities in the sense of both product and process. In this chapter, cognition stands for those hypothetical psychological processes invoked to explain overt verbal and motor behavior as well as certain physiological reactions. Cognitive process is a superordinate term, subsuming the more familiar titles of imagery, perception, free association, thought, mediation, proliferation of hypotheses, reasoning, reflection, and problem solving. All verbal behavior must be a product of cognitive processes, as are dreams and intelligence

test performances. But skeletal muscle movements or visceral reactions are not necessarily linked to cognition.

At a metatheoretical level, it is possible that the units comprising the essence of cognitive processes may eventually be recognized as the structures currently missing in psychological theory. Contemporary psychology seems to be a science of functions searching for its basic units. The laws of biology, chemistry, and physics consist, in the starkest sense, of collections of functional statements about entities. In biology the cell and the gene are the basic units, and the principles of biochemistry describe their functions. In chemistry the molecule and atom are fundamental units, and the principles of chemistry describe how these units behave. In physics particles and planets, are units, and the laws of particle decay and planetary motion describe the functions of these units. Psychology's units may turn out to be cognitive structures, and laws about cognitive process will describe how these units function.

The Mission of This Chapter

This chapter contains three related sections. The initial theoretical discussion analyzes the historical basis for the interest in individual variation in cognitive functioning. The long section that follows considers some salient sources of individual differences in cognition. It focuses on the dimensions that have come to be called, perhaps unfortunately, cognitive style and presents a detailed review of the concept of field independence. And the final section examines the role of motivational forces on the quality of cognitive functioning.

Lest the reader fear that we have taken too large a responsibility, we list here what is omitted. We shall not dwell on differences that are associated primarily with age, a topic central to several other chapters. Indeed, a developmental description of cognitive functioning is one of the central concerns of this book. Similarly, we shall not be concerned, in any bibliographic detail, with the differences that are associated with social class, mental retardation, or psychopathology. These issues are considered adequately elsewhere in this book. The major goal of the present chapter is to review and summarize some of the contemporary constructs invoked to explain individual differences in cognitive functioning. We trust that a reasonable integration of this material is feasible.

THEORETICAL BACKGROUND

A thorough account of the theoretical-historical background of current research on the cognitive structures of children would be no less than a history of cognitive psychology. Clearly, such a venture is well beyond the scope of this one chapter. We shall not attempt to describe the various theoretical forces that contributed to make the study of cognitive processes the large-scale enterprise that it is today. Excellent historical treatments are available elsewhere (e.g., Dember, 1964; Mandler and Mandler, 1964). Rather, we shall confine our attention to more recent theoretical efforts that bear a relation to current research on the differential cognitive structures of children. The theorists most relevant to "individuality and cognitive performance" in children are the psychoanalytic ego psychologists, and those theorists who have been concerned with problems of psychological differentiation and integration— Lewin and Werner, in particular. Since separate chapters of this book are devoted to each of the foregoing theories, the theoretical discussion offered here will be quite brief. We shall, in addition, consider a number of other, more contemporary positions that borrow from the theories just cited but go off in essentially new directions, for example, the "conceptual systems" approach of Harvey, Hunt, and Schroder and the studies in cognitive growth pursued by Bruner and his associates. Our treatment will be rather narrowly focused on what the various theorists have been able to offer to the study of individuality in cognitive performance. Since a large portion of the research on cognitive controls, styles, and strategies[2] has been conducted within broad, theoretical frameworks, it would seem essential that we discuss these frameworks before the relevant empirical studies are considered.

Psychoanalytic Influences

We begin with a brief comparison of psychoanalytic ego psychology (e.g., Gill,

[2] Definitions and distinctions among these cognitive constructs will be considered later in the chapter.

1959; Hartmann, 1958, Rapaport, 1957) and the orthodox psychoanalytic position (e.g., Fenichel, 1945; Freud, 1936). According to the latter, all cognitive functions rest upon a motivational base. It is only upon the failure of wish-fulfilling behavior ("pleasure principle") in meeting survival needs that the organism becomes cognitively attuned to its environment ("reality principle"). Even when the reality principle is dominant, however, the drives constantly press toward overt or covert expression. Hence cognition remains very much in the service of motivational and affective processes.

In contrast to the passive role assigned the ego in orthodox psychoanalytic theory, the ego psychologists have placed great emphasis upon the autonomous functions of the ego. Rapaport (1959), for example, has distinguished between primary ego structures— those that constitute the "conflict-free sphere" of the ego—and secondary ego structures— which largely comprise the defense mechanisms elucidated by Anna Freud (1946). Contained within this region are the classical cognitive functions of perception, memory, and thinking. These primary ego functions may be linked to the secondary defensive functions, however. Also, the autonomy and independence of the primary functions from drive processes are relative rather than absolute. For although the ego has been freed from dependence on sexual and aggressive instincts, *neutralized* energy from those instincts is viewed as the basic motivational source for ego function. An incisive discussion of the theoretical complexities surrounding these issues is available in R. W. White (1959).

The relation between the ego structures and drive system has been rendered most explicit by Klein (1958). He maintains that cognitive structures intervene between drives and environmental demands. It is because the cognitive structures are conceived to have a steering and modulating function in respect to both drives and situational requirements that Klein has given them the designation of "cognitive control principles." These cognitive controls are viewed as serving an accommodative function in the sense of regulating drive expression to accord with the requirements of the situation.

In sum, we note that the dominant role of

drive in respect to cognition characteristic of orthodox psychoanalytic theory has been modified substantially in the theoretical position formulated by Klein and other ego-oriented analysts. Nevertheless, drives and cognitive structures in psychoanalytic ego psychology continue to be in a close interactive relation with one another. Rather unclear, however, is the issue of whether specific drives evoke particular kinds of cognitive controls. Klein (1958) suggests that there is no fixed relation between *specific* drives and cognitive structures. On the other hand, a close link is proposed between the type of task confronting the individual and the particular cognitive structures engaged by such tasks.

What are the distinguishing features of the research carried out within the foregoing theoretical framework? Its psychoanalytic roots are most evident in two types of study. First, there is the work intended to demonstrate how motivational influences are mediated by cognitive structures. Illustrative is research by Klein (1954), showing how the influence of thirst on perceptual processes is mediated by the cognitive-control principle of "constricted-flexible control." (We shall have more to say about this principle in a later section.) The second type of study (e.g., Holzman and Gardner, 1959) has probed the relations between various cognitive controls and the classical mechanisms of defense. Both of these types of research have a distinctive psychoanalytic flavor.

We shall not describe this research in detail here since none of it has employed children as subjects. This is not to imply that such work has no developmental relevance. It would be of great theoretical interest to know how drive expression is modulated by various cognitive structures as the child grows older. From the perspective of the present chapter, differences between children in the interaction of drive states and cognitive structures would also be of interest. It should be further noted that studies of children could help to clarify questions concerning the direction of causal relations between defensive structures and cognitive controls. Thus a repressive mode of coping with conflict may be shown to contribute to the development of a cognitive control of leveling (as opposed to sharpening) in regard to conflict-free perceptual and re-

call tasks. At the same time, we must recall that Rapaport (1957, 1959) considers certain cognitive structures as *primary,* that is, as outcomes of genetic, constitutional, and early learning factors, occurring prior to the development of the mechanisms of defense. But Rapaport has also asserted that the secondary autonomous ego functions, though drive-based and defensive in origin, constitute forms of cognitive structures in their own right. The empirical specification of these primary and secondary cognitive structures and their possible relations remains a task for the future.

Although the issue of the links between cognitive controls, on the one hand, and drives and defenses, on the other, is of profound theoretical importance, its complexity has necessarily limited the extent of the re-search effort. The major portion of the relevant research (much of it conducted at the Menninger Foundation) has been devoted to the conceptual and empirical delineation of the various cognitive controls and the examination of their relationships and patterning within individuals. The various cognitive controls are alleged to be organized as superordinate structures. Klein (1958) has described them as "cognitive styles."[3] The distinction between "controls" and "styles" has not been strictly maintained, however, for one often finds the terms used interchangeably in the relevant research literature.

As defined by the Menninger group (Gardner, Holzman, Klein, Linton, and Spence, 1959), cognitive controls are stabilized ego structures that serve to coordinate "a class of adaptive intentions and a class of environmental situations." Their level of generality is presumed to be greater than that distinguishing the cognitive functions of perception, judgment, recall, etc., considered separately. Thus the same cognitive control may be manifested in tasks whose adaptive requirements lie in different cognitive domains —perception versus recall, for example. One cannot take issue with the definition of cognitive control principles provided by the Menninger group. Unfortunately, the definition provides little insight into the basis for in-

[3] This approach parallels Piaget's (1957) distinction between operations and combinative structures.

dividual differences in the functioning of the cognitive controls, for the intentions of most subjects in regard to specific experimental tasks should be more alike than different. One must assume that all subjects *intend* to perform as best they can, unless there is independent evidence to suggest otherwise. Hence it is difficult to see how a variable of "intentions" can be useful in explaining how individuals differ in their modes of cognitive functioning.

There is, however, a more basic problem with respect to the approach of the Menninger group. With the increased concentration on the autonomous primary ego functions, the anchorage of cognitive-control research in psychoanalytic theory has been considerably loosened. The extensive program of research by Gardner and his associates into the workings of the cognitive controls alone and in combination (see Gardner, 1962, for a review) may owe a substantial debt to psychoanalytic ego psychology. It is perhaps not surprising, however, that an overarching theoretical superstructure attains limited value when a diverse array of cognitive processes are at issue. One is soon forced to deal with such processes at their own level. At this stage, the psychoanalytically inspired research of Gardner and his associates has been forced into the theoretical marketplace. The resulting conceptual and methodological controversies have been played out at a level quite far removed from general psychoanalytic concerns. This is not intended as a fundamental criticism of the work of Gardner and his colleagues. Gardner's group has been concerned with relations between cognitive controls and mechanisms of defense, a problem admirably suited for study within a psychoanalytic framework; however, they have not hesitated to lean on other theoretical systems to clarify the operation of the various cognitive control principles.

It is beyond the scope of the present chapter to review the published research by Gardner and his colleagues, for it is almost entirely based on adult samples. A large-scale, empirical study of cognitive controls in children has been carried out (Gardner and Moriarty, 1968), but only a highly tentative summary account of those findings was available in published form (Gardner, 1964) at the time this chapter was prepared.

Differentiation and Hierarchic Integration

These two concepts are fundamental to almost all theories of cognitive development. Cognitive structures in the course of development become more differentiated and hierarchically integrated, according to Lewin (e.g., 1935, 1951), Piaget (e.g., 1952, 1954), and Werner (e.g., 1948, 1957). A similar theme can be detected in the work of Harvey, Hunt, and Schroder (1961), Birch and Lefford (1967), and Bruner, Olver, and Greenfield (1966). However, since the concepts in question are embedded within the particular theoretical systems of the authors cited, agreement among them regarding the meaning of differentiation and hierarchic integration may be more apparent than real. As we shall show, differences in conceptualization have led to diversity in the operational definition of the constructs at issue.

The Influence of Kurt Lewin. In the Lewinian formulation, differentiation has two aspects: an increasing "complexity of units" and a decreasing "interdependence of parts." The complexity of units refers to the growing variety of behavior expressed in the domains of skills, emotions, needs, knowledge, etc.; the interdependence of parts is concerned with the trend away from dependence and toward independence of the various parts of the person in the way he functions. The distinction between these two aspects of differentiation is exceedingly important. Lewin actually proposed that they be given different labels. Since increasing variety involved matters of similarity and dissimilarity, he suggested that the kind of differentiation represented by "complexity of units" be designated "specialization" or "individualization," while the term "differentiation" proper be reserved for dependence-independence relations between parts of the person and between the person and the environment. Lewin's labeling recommendations have generally not been followed, however, for the term "differentiation" has until the present time been used to describe both of the processes outlined above. This is somewhat unfortunate, of course, for one tends to expect that identically labeled constructs reflect the same underlying processes. From a developmental perspective, differentiation can naturally be presumed to increase along both of the routes under discussion. From an individual-differences perspective, on the other hand, there is no guarantee that the rate at which differentiation proceeds is the same in both cases, or that the same developmental endpoint is achieved.

It is a tribute to Lewin that the two major traditions of individual-differences research on processes of differentiation can be derived from the distinction under consideration. On the one hand, complexity of units with its implications for issues of similarity-dissimilarity can be considered a theoretical ancestor of Kelly's (1955) psychology of personal constructs and the derivative work on cognitive complexity by Bieri (e.g., 1961). These two authors have applied Lewinian differentiation notions (in the complexity-of-units sense) to the issue of similarity and difference in the perception of people. In Bieri's system, cognitive complexity is defined in terms of the number of dimensions generated or employed by subjects when asked to specify how familiar others (and the self) are similar to and different from each other. Lewin clearly intended, however, that differentiation also apply to the physical world. In that respect, complexity of units can be considered one of several intellectual ancestors of the burgeoning research on the cognition of similarities and differences between objects and concepts in the physical world. Much of this research has been carried out with children (e.g., Bruner, Olver, and Greenfield, 1966; Kagan, Moss, and Sigel, 1963; Wallach and Kogan, 1965), and hence falls within the purview of this chapter.

The other conceptualization of differentiation proposed by Lewin—extent of dependence-independence of parts within the person and between the person and his environment—represents a direct intellectual forbear of the extensive program of research conducted by Witkin and his associates (e.g., Witkin, Dyk, Faterson, Goodenough, and Karp, 1962). The relevance of this research to the Lewinian formulation is highlighted by the initial conceptualization of the dimension later presumed to reflect more versus less differentiated functioning—field independence and field dependence, respectively (Witkin, Lewis, Hertzman, Machover, Meissner, and Wapner, 1954). This dimension was first assessed with a variety of perceptual tasks in which adaptive, accurate performance depended upon the utilization of internal kinesthetic cues and the suppression of conflicting external cues. In other words, field independents had apparently succeeded in differentiating themselves from the external physical environment, whereas field dependents remained strongly susceptible to its distracting influence. Subsequent research by Witkin and his associates offered evidence for the greater internal differentiation of personality and cognitive structure in the case of field independents relative to field dependents. It must be stressed that the foregoing description of Witkin's work represents the briefest of introductions to what is undoubtedly the most massive and thorough empirical examination of a particular cognitive structure in the psychological literature. We shall have much more to say about Witkin's program of research in a subsequent section of the chapter.

In sum, we have shown how the two forms of differentiation distinguished by Lewin are reflected in two quite divergent contemporary research traditions. The exploration of the number of dimensions employed by subjects in discriminating and categorizing their social and physical world—the issue of similarities and differences—has roots in Lewin's "variety" conception of differentiation. Current research on part-whole relations in cognitive functioning—the issue of global-diffuse versus articulated-analytic functioning—can be traced to Lewinian notions of interdependence of parts in the structure of the person and the relation of that structure to the external world.

A blurring of the boundaries between a "variety" and a "part-whole" conceptualization of differentiation is revealed in the theory and research of Bieri and his associates (e.g., Bieri, Atkins, Briar, Leaman, Miller, and Tripodi, 1966). Working within the general theoretical framework of Kelly's (1955) psychology of "personal constructs" and using the Kelly Role Construct Repertory Test, Bieri (1955) derived an index of cognitive complexity representing the number of different dimensions employed by an individual in construing similarities and differences between familiar people in his social environment. The greater the level of cognitive complexity, the more multidimensional is the cognitive structure involved in the perception of other people. In its original form, the index clearly reflected the Lewinian "variety" conceptualization of differentiation. More recently, however, Bieri (1966), in considering possible developmental aspects of cognitive complexity, demonstrated how that construct divides into two separate components. To the extent that individuals construe their environment on the basis of continuous dimensions rather than discrete categories (a reasonable assumption where other people constitute the stimuli), one can distinguish between the *number* of different dimensions used and the extent of gradation *within* each such dimension (the number of categories or intervals that are discriminated along the dimension). Bieri proposes that the label of "differentiation" be reserved for the number of dimensions, while gradation within dimensions be called "articulation." One might initially regret the choice of "articulation," for the part-whole form of differentiation studied by Witkin and his associates is often characterized as "field-articulation" (e.g., Gardner et al., 1959). Yet one must acknowledge that the form of articulation posed by Bieri represents the fractionation of a whole into parts—that is, the conversion of a dichotomy into a more finely graded scale. We cannot conclude that the two forms of articulation are cut from the same cloth, for empirical research directed to that question has not yet been carried out. Bieri (1966) does, however, offer numerous suggestions on how developmental considerations can be brought to bear upon the components of cognitive complexity.

There is one further important respect in which the Bieri group has extended the Lewinian "variety" conception of differentiation. For Lewin, increasing variety in the course of development implied a more highly differentiated cognitive structure and set of behaviors. Bieri et al. (1966) have shown that the ecological characteristics of the social environment can also be described in terms of extent of differentiation. The dimensionality of stimuli and tasks can vary radically. Within such an interactional framework, one can no longer speak in unqualified terms of the greater advantage accruing to a more as opposed to a less differentiated cognitive structure. Rather, the problem becomes one of studying the effects on performance of varying degrees of discrepancy in the dimensionality of the cognitive structure and the stimulus task. As Bieri (1966) has noted, there has been essentially no research of this kind within a developmental framework. Indeed, such investigations are quite infrequent even in the case of adults. The few relevant studies are discussed in the Bieri et al. (1966) volume.

Let us turn now to the matter of hierarchic integration. Lewin recognized that increasing differentiation implied decreasing "unity" of the person. Hence it made good theoretical sense to invoke a construct of hierarchic integration to put the person back together again, figuratively speaking. Lewin proposed that hierarchic integration showed a discrete, steplike increase with development. By imposing such integration upon the continually decreasing "unity" produced by differentiation, Lewin was able to show that the organizational unity of the person was essentially cyclical over the course of development. In other words, the extent of unity at a later time period might be greater or smaller than at an earlier period, for hierarchic integration is presumed to lag behind differentiation during the course of development.

While hierarchic integration is an evident logical counterpart of a "variety" or "part-whole" view of differentiation, it has been difficult to arrive at a conceptual formulation that lends itself to research on the problem in the cognitive domain. Kelly (1955), for example, distinguished superordinate from subordinate constructs in his theory, the superordinate presumably having an organizational and controlling function over the subordinate. But he did not solve the problem of devising independent measures of such higher and lower level constructs. Recent sophisticated attempts to derive independent measures of differentiation and organization are offered by Wyer (1964) and Zajonc (1960). Their efforts were only partially successful, and their procedures have not as yet been adapted for use with children.

As we noted earlier, Bieri's construct of cognitive complexity fits the Lewinian definition of differentiation rather than hierarchic integration. Further, cognitive-complexity research has been tied to the Kelly (1955) REP Test, an instrument too cumbersome for use with children. Clearly, that test will have to be modified or other techniques devised, if the important tradition of research on cognitive complexity is to be given developmental significance. Bieri (1966), taking cognizance of these difficulties, has proposed that developmental studies be directed toward the perceptual-cognitive processes subsumed by cognitive complexity rather than toward the latter construct itself. A first and only attempt to examine cognitive complexity from this point of view is represented by the work of Signell (1966).

Three forms of complexity are distinguished in Signell's work. Two of the three are related to Bieri's distinction between the variety of dimensions employed by a subject and the extent of articulation along a specific dimension. Signell describes the extent of articulation as "complexity of single concepts" and the variety of dimensions as "complexity of cognitive structure." The more complex single concept is alleged to discriminate among objects more efficiently. A dichotomous concept (e.g., nice versus not nice) has little complexity since objects (e.g., people, nations) can be classified only in one of two categories. Where a concept has several gradations, greater complexity is associated with more equal distributions of objects across the set of categories. In Signell's words, "The more complex concept has maximal power to differentiate objects" (p. 519).

Complexity of cognitive structure is derived from the Lewinian "variety" conception of differentiation. Here we are dealing with the number of relatively independent concepts or dimensions available to the individual for differentiating among objects. Signell also introduces the notion of an individual's differentiation among the objects in his environment, for the number of independent objects construed is only partially dependent upon the number of concepts available.

The third type of complexity distinguished by Signell is called "complexity of content." Whereas the two types of complexity previously described are determined on the basis of the internal relation between the elements of an individual's cognitive structure, complexity of content relies on external judgments of the diversity of concepts generated by the child. Signell employs the example of the child whose nation concepts are exclusively geographical, in contrast to the child who uses geographical, economic, and political concepts.

Thirty-six children ranging in age from 9 to 16 participated in the study. The objects of judgment consisted of persons and nations, with half of the children assigned to the former and the remaining half to the latter. Intelligence, sex, and socioeconomic status were comparable across age groups and object content. To insure that the various procedures would be appropriate for children, only objects and concepts provided by the child were employed. These were elicited from the child through direct questioning and through the use of the triads method. Instructions for this method require the child to specify which two of three stimuli are most similar for what reason and in what respect the third stimulus is different. Striking differences in the magnitude of the correlations across the two domains were observed. For "complexity of single concepts," correlations with age were highly significant in the "person" domain, but negligible in the "nation" domain. The reversed pattern was found in regard to "complexity of cognitive structure." For "complexity of content," the correlations were again considerably higher in the "nation" domain. Thus it appears that with increasing age (in the 9 to 16 range) children develop progressively greater cognitive complexity in regard to significant people in their lives by finer differentiation of concepts already in their repertoire, rather than by acquiring a more complex array of concepts. Where nations are concerned, on the other hand, cognitive complexity shows a developmental increase through the acquisition of an array of new concepts for differentiating nations, rather than through the refined articulation of already existing concepts.

Signell accounts for the observed domain differences in terms of the contrast between "experiential" and "didactic" learning. Experiential learning is presumed to be characteristic of the way children learn about the people in their world; didactic learning is alleged to describe the more abstract, formal learning about nations—objects quite remote from the child's personal experience.[4] According to Signell, it is in the child's interests to build workable, efficient concepts with respect to others, for these enable him to cope better with these others. No such need is presumed to underlie the child's learning about nations, with the

[4] It is probably safe to presume that Signell's distinction would not hold for children who have traveled extensively in foreign countries.

consequence that the child assimilates new, undifferentiated concepts offered to him by adults, rather than progressively refining the concepts already in his repertoire.

It is apparent from Signell's work that there are diverse forms of differentiation that can be studied within a "variety" framework. Differentiation in children of the "variety" form appears to be very much influenced by object content. W. A. Scott (1963) and Crockett (1965), in reviewing the evidence for adults, also concluded that cognitive structures vary with event domains. The issue remains highly controversial, however, for evidence in favor of generality of cognitive styles across object domains also exists (e.g., Allard and Carlson, 1963; Glixman, 1965).

Conceptual Differentiation and the Issue of Breadth of Categorization. Another descendant of a "variety" conception of differentiation is the tradition of research concerned with size of groupings in object-sorting performance. In his early work with adults, Gardner (1953) observed that subjects varied in the number of groups generated under instructions to sort common objects. Some individuals formed a large number of piles with relatively few objects in each pile; others preferred a small number of piles with a rather large number of objects in each pile. Initially characterized as the cognitive control of "equivalence range," the variable under study has more recently been designated as "conceptual differentiation" (Gardner and Schoen, 1962). The person with a high level of conceptual differentiation prefers to differentiate an array of objects into a larger number of categories; the person low in conceptual differentiation prefers a smaller number of categories.

There is a certain temptation to equate a high level of conceptual differentiation with high cognitive complexity, on the assumption that both imply the availability of a larger number of dimensions in one's conceptual repertoire. The resemblance is more apparent than real, however. Vannoy (1965) found no relation whatever between conceptual differentiation and cognitive complexity in college students. Of greater importance in the present context, however, is the meaning of conceptual differentiation from a developmental point of view. Olver and Hornsby (in Bruner et al., 1966) have observed a strong disposition in

their youngest subjects (6-year-olds) to form pairs in an object-sorting task. About 61% of their groupings were of the pair form, in contrast to 36% for 8-year-olds and 25% for 11-year-olds. The basis for the pairwise grouping in the youngest children has been clarified by Vurpillot and Zoberman (1965). They have shown how the young child is willing to settle for a judgment of similarity when a single element of two stimuli are in correspondence. In the context of object sorting, the 6-year-old will apparently group a "house" and a "barn" because they are colored red and then ignore other objects of the same color. The remaining red objects will then be grouped pairwise on some other basis. It is quite evident, then, that young children will manifest a high level of conceptual differentiation according to Gardner's criteria.

A measure of conceptual differentiation will probably have different psychological meanings for children of different ages. Of course, Gardner and his associates were not overly concerned with developmental issues in their early work. One study involving children has been published, however (Mercado, Diaz Guerrero, and Gardner, 1963). Third- and fourth-graders of middle-class status in Guadalajara, Mexico, and Topeka, Kansas, were compared with respect to object-sorting performance. The American children manifested a higher level of conceptual differentiation than did the Mexican children. This difference was due largely to the greater willingness of the American children to leave certain objects as "singles" rather than group them with other objects. In the Gardner scoring scheme, such singles were treated as separate groups. It is difficult to justify this procedure in the light of the Messick and Kogan (1963) evidence that the number of groups formed with two or more objects is independent of the number of singles. On the basis of these methodological problems, it would certainly be premature to conclude that American children are more conceptually differentiated than their Mexican counterparts. The empirical datum of fewer singles in the Mexican sample may in fact reflect a more literal compliance to the experimental instructions, which, after all, did request that items be grouped together.

In the research of Gardner and his associates, a relationship has been postulated and empirically confirmed in adults (Gardner and Schoen, 1962) between conceptual differentiation and breadth of categorization. A person who employs few groupings in an object-sorting task is presumed to have broad category boundaries; a person who uses many groupings is alleged to have narrow category boundaries. It is assumed that the subject in an object-sorting task is in some way concerned with the sheer number of instances to accommodate within a category. This may be so, but it is probably more reasonable to assume that the qualitative character of the categories used by those high and low in conceptual differentiation determines the number of items subsumed by them. Gardner and Schoen (1962) have, in fact, demonstrated that the person who forms fewer groupings tends to use more "abstract" categories, when abstraction is defined by an index derived from Rapaport, Gill, and Schafer (1945).

Quite clearly, an object-sorting measure is a very indirect way of assessing breadth of categorization. It can be measured much more directly when a specific category is provided and the subject is required to establish the category boundaries or "band width." Such a procedure has, in fact, been employed in several studies, some conducted with children as subjects. In the research of Wallach and Caron (1959), for example, sixth-grade children participated in a concept-attainment exercise in which they learned that certain geometric figures, distinguished by a particular size of angle, constituted a class called "poggles." This exercise was followed by a task in which a series of geometric figures, identical except for variation in acuteness of angle, were offered for judgment as "poggles" or "nonpoggles." Children displayed considerable variation in their "band width" for "poggles," some admitting many exemplars into the criterial class, others admitting few. This breadth-of-categorization measure yielded significant sex differences, with boys manifesting a broader "poggle" class.

Comparable sex differences have been observed on the Pettigrew (1958) Category Width Test, for which a children's form is available (see Wallach and Kogan, 1965). The Pettigrew instrument consists of a series of items, each of which provides the central-tendency value for a category and a set of multiple-choice alternatives. The subject's task is to choose the most deviant member of the category at each extreme. A broad categorizer would locate the outer boundaries of the category further away from the central-tendency value than would a narrow categorizer. It should be noted that the "band-width" scores derived from the "poggles" and Pettigrew procedures were significantly correlated (rs in the 30s) in the sample of children employed in the Wallach and Caron study.

Still another procedure for assessing category breadth in children is exemplified by the dot-numerosity and line-length judgments employed in the Bruner and Tajfel (1961) work. Stimuli containing a specified number of dots and lines of a particular length were made criterial (i.e., "target" patterns). Subjects were required to judge a series of dot and line patterns on the basis of their membership or lack of membership in the "target" class. Considerable variation among children was observed in the number of patterns judged to fit the criterion. A high rate of pattern acceptance was presumed to reflect a preference for broad categorizing; a high rate of pattern rejection was considered indicative of a preference for narrow categorizing.[5]

The construct of category breadth lends itself very neatly to interpretation in strategic, as opposed to strictly stylistic terms. One can conceptualize broad "band width" as a preference for errors of inclusion over errors of exclusion. The reversed preference would characterize the child showing a narrow "band width." The child designated as favoring broad categorization has chosen to include doubtful or extreme exemplars in a category at the risk of including those that do not

[5] Most of the procedures used in assessing category breadth require the subject to make a judgment in a situation of response uncertainty. Therefore subjects who adopt an impulsive strategy (decide quickly) are likely to form judgments that will be classified as evidence for broad categorization. (See discussion of impulsivity later in chapter.) In addition, Gardner and Schoen (1962) have reinterpreted the Bruner-Tajfel results in terms of an acquiescent response style possibly moderated by the latter's relation to IQ. In response to the Gardner-Schoen criticism, Bruner and Tajfel (1965a) offered a counterargument, which in turn evoked a rejoinder from Gardner and Schoen (1965) and a further rejoinder from Bruner and Tajfel (1965b).

really belong. The child distinguished by narrow categorizing, in contrast, has chosen to reject doubtful or extreme exemplars at the risk of excluding those that really belong. The broad categorizer prefers errors of commission; the narrow categorizer prefers errors of omission. Rejection of an exemplar is generally an assignment to limbo in a "band-width" task where no contrast category is available. In an object-sorting task, on the other hand, rejection of an exemplar for one category or grouping will often imply candidacy for an alternative category or grouping.

On the basis of the sex difference obtained in category breadth—boys favoring broader categories—Wallach and Caron (1959) suggested that broad versus narrow categories might be indicative of cognitive risk taking versus conservatism. Subsequent research (Kogan and Wallach, 1964) into relations between cognitive and more explicit risk measures failed to confirm the Wallach-Caron proposal.

In their study of the intelligence-creativity distinction in children, Wallach and Kogan (1965) examined both of these dimensions in relation to category breadth, assessed by a children's version of Pettigrew's test. In both boys and girls, "band width" was unrelated to intelligence and positively associated with creativity. To the extent that creativity involves a capacity to emit original and unique responses, and since broad "band width" implies a tolerance for deviant instances, the relationship observed is theoretically consistent and supportive of the psychological meaning offered earlier for the construct of category breadth. It should be further noted that conceptual differentiation assessed by object sorting and category breadth assessed by the Pettigrew instrument were uncorrelated in the sample of fifth-grade boys and girls studied by Wallach and Kogan (1965). Conceptual differentiation was also unrelated to those authors' creativity indices. In sum, the kind of category breadth tapped by fineness or coarseness of grouping on an object-sorting task has a quite different meaning from the setting of category boundaries where the category at issue is explicitly provided.

The Influence of Heinz Werner. Let us turn now from the Lewinian conceptualization and the research it inspired to consider the contribution of Heinz Werner. There are

many similarities between these two major figures. Thus Werner's work is based firmly on what he described as developmental psychology's one regulative, orthogenetic principle: "wherever development occurs it proceeds from a state of relative globality and lack of differentiation to a state of increasing differentiation, articulation, and hierarchic integration" (1957, p. 126).[6] Further reading of Werner indicates that it is in the part-whole and the subject-object interdependencies rather than in the sheer variety aspect that the resemblance with Lewin's formulation becomes manifest. Hence it is probably more than accidental that Witkin acknowledges his debt to both Werner and Lewin, whereas Bieri does not cite Werner in his published work.

Although there is much that is similar in Lewin and Werner, there is also much that is different. From the perspective of a "differentiation" construct, Werner is more explicitly committed to a developmental "stage" conception than is Lewin. The various stages are distinguished not only on the basis of part-whole and subject-object differentiation, but also in terms of the particular operations engaged at each stage. Thus development is presumed to span three levels of functioning—sensorimotor, perceptual, and conceptual—each successive level reflecting a higher degree of part-whole articulation and subject-object differentiation. At the sensorimotor level, differentiation between the person and the environment is least advanced, for cognitive functioning consists of direct, motoric commerce with the world of objects. The perceptual level is more differentiated, for the person is not in direct contact with objects but viewing them from afar, so to speak. Differentiation between subject and object is, of course, most advanced at the conceptual level, where the subject is capable of internal manipulation of symbols and abstract representations of the environment.

As Werner has noted, the "orthogenetic law, by its very nature, is an expression of unilinearity of development," (1957, p. 137).

[6] It should be noted that, in essence, the principle is irrefutable. If, as sometimes happens, older children exhibit lesser differentiation than do younger children, this can be attributed to a hierarchic organizing principle present in older and lacking in younger children.

In other words, the developmental sequence from lesser to greater differentiation and hierarchic integration, and from sensorimotor to perceptual to conceptual functioning, is presumed universal. Despite his strict adherence to a unilinearity conception, however, Werner at the same time recognizes that there can be a multiplicity of individual developmental forms. It is necessary, for example, to reconcile a conception of physiognomic perception (e.g., the fusion of perception and feeling, as in a "gloomy landscape") as developmentally primitive and undifferentiated with the capacity for esthetic appreciation and artistic productivity in the mature adult. Evidently, operations that were initially "genetically primordial" can develop in parallel with initially more advanced operations. Werner recognizes that physiognomic perception can grow, "in certain individuals such as artists, to a level not below but on a par with that of 'geometric-technical' perception and logical discourse" (1957, p. 138).

A multilinear view of development implies that the child cannot be so easily assigned to the same developmental stage in regard to all aspects of cognitive functioning. Rather, depending upon the operations demanded by the task, one may find that the child operates at various developmental levels. Werner in fact proposes that differentiation can assume a "vertical" form, that is, individuals can vary in the number of developmentally different operations at their disposal. Associated with this idea of developmental heterogeneity is the degree of flexibility shown by the person in shifting levels in accordance with task requirements. It is noteworthy that, for Werner, shifts to lower developmental levels can be quite adaptive, if not in fact essential, for creative thinking. The more creative person, in Werner's estimation, is the one who can function at various developmental levels—in other words, is capable of progressing and regressing between more developmentally primitive and advanced operations. There is an obvious resemblance between the foregoing view of creativity and the psychoanalytic construct of "regression in the service of the ego" (Kris, 1953; Schafer, 1958). A more extended discussion of these matters is available in the chapter by Wallach in this book.

Werner's theory of multilinear development, though having strong intuitive appeal, has not really generated much work of an empirical character. Most developmental and personality researchers are simply not accustomed to looking at a subject on the basis of his developmental heterogeneity, or the capacity to switch from one level of cognitive functioning to another. There is a strong indication in Werner's conceptualization of a preference for an intraindividual rather than an interindividual analysis of cognitive functioning. Such notions as developmental homogeneity or heterogeneity and the capacity to switch from one developmental level to another do not suggest the kinds of variables that are employed in individual-differences research of the normative type. Rather, Werner's ideas point to the study of cognitive organization within persons and hence suggest the need for ipsative analyses, which have not been particularly popular in the cognitive domain. D. M. Broverman—the psychologist most committed to an ipsative analysis of cognitive phenomena—has shown little interest in Werner's developmental ideas. In ironic contrast, Witkin has acknowledged the strong influence of Werner, but has adhered to standard interindividual analyses of Werner's concepts. It is no surprise, then, that Witkin and his associates have shed little light on Werner's conception of multilinear development.

As in the case of Lewin's conceptualization, hierarchic integration is an essential component of Werner's theory. As the individual progresses through the sensorimotor, perceptual, and conceptual phases of development, each earlier phase is presumed to become reorganized in a way that permits it to become hierarchically integrated within the subsequent, higher phase. No one can quarrel with the preceding formulation, for, quite obviously, the adult functions at all three developmental levels. The problem is, again, one of how to conceptualize hierarchic integration in operational terms. There is nothing in the Werner multilinear theory of development to help one in this regard.

It may prove useful to examine the manner in which Witkin copes with the problem. We should note first that Witkin distinguishes two aspects of integration—complexity and effectiveness. Complexity is considered to be a function of differentiation level, according to Witkin et al. (1962), for "more complex relationships among system components, and between the system and its environment, are possible in a system with many varied components than in a system whose components are few and relatively unspecialized. Psychological development toward greater differentiation must be accompanied by successively more complex reintegrations of the system" (p. 11). Since complexity of integration is contingent upon extent of differentiation, Witkin evidently did not feel it necessary to be further concerned with that aspect of integration. At least, no attempt is made to operationalize complexity of integration in the *Psychological Differentiation* volume, even though Witkin and his associates admit that the preceding construct is only *partially* determined by level of differentiation.[7] This implies that two children whose extent of differentiation is highly comparable can nevertheless vary considerably in complexity of integration. Though Witkin et al. (1962) do not use the term "hierarchic integration," their definition of "complexity of integration" is essentially identical to both Lewin's and Werner's definitions of "hierarchic integration." If Witkin had been able to operationalize the "complexity of integration" variable, he presumably would have done so.

Another aspect of integration—its effectiveness—offers a direct link with adjustment and pathology. These can be assessed without great difficulty, and Witkin (1965) has in fact carried out such assessments. He believes that effectiveness of integration is essentially independent of level of differentiation. Both highly differentiated individuals and those with limited differentiation are presumably capable of either adequate adjustment or pathological breakdown. However, the quality and nature of the adjustment or the pathology varies with the level of differentiation. As one might well expect, impairment in highly differentiated persons takes the form of gross separation of parts and/or complete detachment from the environment; whereas impaired individuals with low levels of differentiation manifest the dissolution of already weak boundaries between subsystems and between the self and the outside world.

[7] As we shall note later, there is considerable controversy over the question of whether Witkin is assessing differentiation in the Werner sense. This issue is side-stepped here for the sake of the theoretical argument.

Discussing disturbances in "normal" children, Witkin et al. (1962, pp. 212–213) have maintained that global (less differentiated) children manifest "impulse control problems, a poorly developed sense of responsibility, and lack of resources and initiative," whereas analytic (more differentiated) children exhibit problems of "too rigid controls, too great emotional distance, too great an investment in intellectualization and intellectual life, sometimes with corresponding circumscription of interpersonal relations." While Witkin's efforts along the lines indicated deserve much praise, it is doubtful whether Lewin and Werner conceived of hierarchic integration exclusively in terms of adjustment and pathology. To view integration in such terms implies, to a considerable extent, a break with the universe of developmental discourse. Conceivably, pathology may be a consequence of faulty hierarchic integration. Ideally, however, we should like to assess differentiation and hierarchic integration within a common systematic framework.

Conceptual Systems. Consider next the developmental theory of "conceptual systems" proposed by Harvey et al. (1961). These authors are fully committed to the proposition that development proceeds from minimal to maximal differentiation and subsequently to hierarchic integration. The consequence of this developmental process is presumed to be variation in individuals' "conceptual systems" along a dimension of "abstractness-concreteness." A conceptual system is broadly defined by Harvey et al. (1961) as "a schema that provides the basis by which the individual relates to the environmental events he experiences" (pp. 244–245). Four levels of abstractness-concreteness are distinguished, ranging from minimal differentiation at one extreme to maximal differentiation and hierarchic integration at the other. Harvey et al. (1961) have also used the term "integrative complexity" to refer to the abstract extreme.

What kind of differentiation do the creators of conceptual systems theory have in mind? The relevant writings (Harvey, 1963, 1966; Harvey, Hunt, and Schroder, 1961; Schroder, Driver, and Streufert, 1967) suggest that it is a "variety" conception in the Lewinian sense. In Harvey's (1966) words, "there seems little doubt that exposure to diversity is probably the most central prerequisite to differentiation and integration, and hence of greater abstractness" (p. 63). One would presume that such exposure would enhance the variety of dimensions available to the person for construing his environment. There are many similarities here with the Bieri conceptualization discussed earlier. However, it will be recalled that Bieri is concerned exclusively with the cognition of other people, whereas the Harvey-Hunt-Schroder conceptualization apparently refers to cognition in general. Another difference is the treatment of hierarchic integration. Bieri's cognitive complexity construct is basically a differentiation index. For the Harvey-Hunt-Schroder team, hierarchic integration is critical to the abstractness-concreteness dimension, as reflected in the frequent use of the term *integrative* complexity in delineating the positive extreme of abstract functioning.

Despite these differences, however, the overall conceptualizations and research strategies have much in common. The most critical similarity is in the emphasis upon the match between cognitive structure and the structure of the environment. We have already mentioned Bieri's efforts to derive objective measures of environmental dimensionality. The research of the "conceptual systems group" in this regard has had the same basic aim but has been less rigorous in execution. It must be stressed, however, that the Harvey-Hunt-Schroder group has placed great stress upon the person's capacity to cope with changing environments. The recent book by Schroder, Driver, and Streufert (1967) is concerned with comparisons between abstract and concrete subjects in their responses to variations in the informational complexity of the environment.

Does conceptual systems theory adhere to a unilinear or multilinear view of development? There appears to be some ambiguity with respect to this point. On the one hand, a conceptual system is described as a highly generalized cognitive structure affecting all areas of transactions with the environment. Hunt (1966) has recently emphasized that a conceptual system has both structural and motivational aspects. At the same time, Harvey et al. (1961) have indicated that a "person need not reach the same level of abstractness of subject-object ties in all areas of development. Individuals vary considerably

in terms of the generality of their stage of functioning" (p. 111). The foregoing statement has much in common with the multilinear developmental conception favored by Werner (1957).

Thus far, we have said little about the specifically developmental aspects of conceptual systems theory. The fundamental developmental postulate in the theory is that the level of differentiation and integration attained is a function of the growing child's interactions with the principal training agents in his environment. In other words, the level of an adult's abstractness-concreteness essentially depends upon the way he was treated by parents, parent surrogates, and teachers. Thus "system I functioning" (the concrete extreme) implies a pattern of training in which the child's efforts at environmental exploration were hindered and deviation from the absolutistic standards of the training agent were not tolerated. In the case of "system II functioning," the child is presumably confronted with "laissez-faire" training practices with the consequence that he experiences more diversity than is optimal. Such persons are described as manifesting rebelliousness against the normative standards of the training agent without any corresponding development of internalized, personally derived standards. "System III functioning" is characterized by a child training pattern of overprotection and overindulgence. Exploration of both the physical and social environment is restricted, so the child presumably learns to manipulate people through dependency in order to gain his ends. Finally, for "system IV functioning" (the abstract extreme), the training pattern is presumed to be optimal in the sense that the child's exploration is not inhibited and he is free to evolve standards based on his own experience and thought.

Consider now the measurement of conceptual systems. The standard instrument has consisted of a series of sentence completion stems incorporating a variety of personal and social content. In Harvey's (1966) version of the instrument, the sentences assume the form: "This I believe about . . . ," followed by such referents as "friendship, the American way of life, guilt, marriage, myself, religion, sin, majority opinion, people, and compromise." Another version, along with a scoring manual, is presented in Schroder et al. (1967).

In the Harvey version, the classification of an individual on the abstractness-concreteness dimension depends on the following criteria: "absolutism of his expressed beliefs, consideration of contingencies or modifying circumstances, dependency on external authorities, especially God and/or religion, frequency of trite and normative statements, degree of ethnocentrism, acceptance of socially approved modes of behavior, concern with interpersonal relationships, and the apparent simplicity-complexity of the interpretations of the world" (p. 47). Evidently, the sentence completion responses are scored for both structure and content, which is consistent with the view that conceptual systems are both cognitive and motivational.

High levels of interjudge reliability are reported in the assignment of sentence completion responses along the abstract-concrete dimension. The fundamental question, however, is the extent to which the mélange of verbal material generated by a sentence-completion device is relevant to differentiation and hierarchic integration as those terms have been employed in this chapter. Both differentiation and hierarchic integration are structural in nature, and one somehow expects to see them assessed with tasks that capture the essence of such structures. Perhaps we are simply talking about "face validity." The sentence completion devices favored by the conceptual systems theorists, unfortunately, use scoring criteria which obscure the manifestation of strictly structural properties under a layer of diverse personal and social content. If conceptual systems theory is relevant to matters of differentiation and integration, the favored measuring instrument seems to be tapping those particular processes in a rather subtle and indirect way. Some of the instruments employed for "construct validation" purposes by the conceptual systems theorists would, in fact, impress many observers as supplying more direct indices of differentiation and integration than do the various sentence completion devices themselves. Of particular interest is the use of person perception procedures (Asch, 1952; Gollin, 1958) to tap the integration component of a conceptual system. Those procedures require that subjects produce brief characterizations of two manifestly different stimulus persons, A and B. The subjects are then informed that A and B are, in reality, the same person. The task now is to integrate the prior, discrepant impressions to form a unified portrayal. Such person-perception techniques appear promising as measures of hierarchic integration tied to a "variety" type of differentiation. Unfortunately, the procedures described do not assess differentiation as such, and hence do not really demonstrate how hierarchic integration operates on previously differentiated material.

There are other shortcomings to conceptual systems theory, some acknowledged by the Harvey, Hunt, and Schroder group. Of primary importance, from the perspective of the present chapter, is the question of whether we are dealing with a theory of adult personality couched in developmental language or with a genuine developmental theory. If the latter applies, one would expect much of the research effort to concentrate on establishing empirical links between child training experiences (even if measured only by recollections of adults) and current conceptual functioning. To the extent that such connections are not demonstrated, the entire theoretical superstructure has a highly tentative quality, at least from a developmental perspective. Harvey (1966) has acknowledged that "attempts at delineating the developmental determinants of the different conceptual systems, although not extensive, have been mainly unsuccessful" (p. 62). A comparable statement may be found in Hunt (1966): "Although considerable construct validity is available on the contemporaneous effect of Conceptual Systems . . . , there is as yet only sparse evidence directly supportive of the developmental model . . ." (pp. 291–292).

A study by Cross (1966) contains one of the few attempts to provide an empirical test of the developmental postulates of the conceptual systems theory. Working with a sample of 377 boys from the eighth to twelfth grades, Cross selected those who scored at the extremes on a sentence-completion measure of conceptual level. The parents of the 33 boys scoring at each extreme were contacted, and an interview was requested. The final sample consisted of 54 families: 27 parents of high conceptual-level boys and 27 parents of low conceptual-level boys. Mothers and fathers were interviewed separately. Seven basic questions were directed to the parents. These concerned matters of discipline, standards, differences of opinion, reaction to criticism from the child, and desired learning experiences for the child. The questions were intended to assess the "unilaterality-interdependence" of the parent-child relation. A five-point scale was employed, with a "one" assigned to the case of complete parental control (high unilaterality) and a "five" assigned where the "parent influences only through dissemination of factual information" (high interdependence). In addition to the interview, a shortened form of the PARI (Schaefer and Bell, 1958) was administered to the parents to provide a measure of parental authoritarianism and warmth.

Both mothers and fathers of high conceptual-level boys were more "interdependent" (less "unilateral") than were the parents of the low conceptual-level boys. With respect to the authoritarianism dimension from the PARI, nonauthoritarian parents (particularly mothers) were linked to boys of high conceptual level. Such boys also had fathers who were more "intrinsically accepting" relative to the fathers of boys of low conceptual level.

The results are supportive of the developmental postulates of the Harvey et al. (1961) theory. Parents who grant greater autonomy to the child, tolerate his point of view, and encourage diversity apparently produce sons who yield high conceptual-level scores on the instruments devised by the Harvey, Hunt, and Schroder group. There is one serious difficulty with the Cross study, however. In the course of interviewing the parents, the interviewer can probably infer the conceptual level of the son, which could well bias the rating assigned to the parents. Since a global judgment of parental unilaterality-interdependence was employed, the danger of such bias is particularly acute. Also disturbing is Cross' failure to specify whether the interviewer was or was not informed of the extreme group to which the son belonged. If such information was in the possession of the interviewer before the session with the parents, the outcomes of the interview portion of the study would be of little scientific value. Of course, Cross' PARI data, which were not susceptible to biasing, tended to be consistent with the interview findings.

With the Cross research as an impetus, we can probably look forward to further empirical research specifically aimed at the developmental propositions of the theory. Unless these propositions can be verified, the developmental aspects of the theory will obviously have to be abandoned or drastically modified.

A promising direction for future developmental research within the conceptual systems framework is contained in a recent contribution by Hunt (1966). Given that conceptual systems are presumed to represent the "precipitates" of past encounters with training agents, Hunt has been attempting to enhance individuals' levels of abstractness by means of planned educational experiences. Research of this type can best be conducted with children, on the presumption that their level of cognitive functioning is still susceptible to change. The success or failure of such experimental interventions will certainly provide further clues concerning the viability of the developmentally relevant, theoretical propositions.

Conceptual Systems and the Piagetian Construct of "Decentering." Ideas drawn from other developmental theorists are woven into the rather complicated (if not cumbersome) conceptual systems fabric. Thus abstractness-concreteness is sometimes characterized in terms highly reminiscent of Piaget's egocentrism-relativism dimension—the disposition to view the environment exclusively from one's own point of view without any awareness of doing so. Whereas egocentrism for Piaget (1926, 1954) is a developmental stage and not a way of characterizing persons, efforts have been made to distinguish among children in their degrees of egocentrism. This is the closest that psychologists have come to the empirical study of individual differences in differentiation within Piaget's system.

The egocentrism-relativism dimension can be subsumed under the more general construct of "decentering"—the ability to shift or decenter from one aspect of a situation to another, an ability that emerges when abstract conceptual thought has gained ascendancy over sensory and perceptual processes in the child's commerce with his environment. The Piagetian notion of coping with one's environment through decentering mechanisms has evoked a responsive chord in investigators assessing conceptual level within the Harvey-Hunt-Schroder framework. Not surprisingly, investigators in this tradition have incorporated Piaget-inspired tasks in their assessment program.

A favored instrument has been the role-taking task (RTT) developed by Feffer (1959). First applied to adults, the RTT is a projective task derived from Schneidman's Make-a-Picture-Story (MAPS). The test materials consist of several background scenes and a variety of human and animal figures. The subject is required to tell a story, based on a particular background scene, that uses at least three of the available figures. Then he is asked to retell the story from the point of view of each of the three figures. In other words, the subject must decenter and adopt the perspective of others while remaining consistent with his previous stories.

Of particular interest is the Feffer and Gourevitch (1960) research on a sample of boys in the 6 to 13 age range. In addition to the RTT, the boys were administered four traditional, Piaget-type cognitive tasks. A correct solution on these tasks required the balanced decentering typical of conceptual thought. Consistent with expectations, the older children performed better than the younger on both RTT and the strictly cognitive tasks. The relation between performance in the two domains was significant, with both age and intelligence controlled. This outcome should have come as no great surprise to Piaget, who has always maintained that the same cognitive principles apply in both the impersonal and personal world of the child. Feffer and Gourevitch suggest that decentering in the child's physical world might precede the ability to take the perspective of others in the social world. Research of a longitudinal character would be required to settle the issue. Note, finally, that Sullivan and Hunt (1967) did not find a relation in 7- to 11-year-olds between Feffer's RTT and a Piaget-type task based on shifting spatial perspectives. Evidently the RTT does not relate to all Piaget-type tasks with decentering properties.

An explicit bridge between Piaget's decentering construct and conceptual systems theory (Harvey et al., 1961) can be found in Wolfe (1963). System III and IV functioning implies a level of differentiation between self and others where one should prove able to adopt the perspective of another person. Accordingly, Wolfe examined the extent of association between a conceptual systems index and Feffer's RTT. Gollin's (1958) Impression Formation Task was also employed. The male subjects of the study ranged from age 10 to 21 and were enrolled in grades 6 to 12.

With age and intelligence held constant, conceptual level was significantly related to role-taking ability. Rather disturbing, however, was the evidence that verbal productivity (number of words) on the RTT was significantly correlated with the RTT score $(r = .61)$. Though it is unlikely that verbal productivity could mediate the relation between the RTT and Piaget-type cognitive tasks, the possibility of such mediation should certainly be examined.

The Research of Bruner and His Associates. We consider, finally, the very important, recent contribution of the Harvard Center for Cognitive Studies (Bruner, Olver, and Greenfield, 1966). Although the examination of individual differences has not been the central focus of the work of Bruner and his associates, the implications of that work for individuality of cognitive functioning are strikingly clear. Such implications were already apparent in the earlier work on concept attainment (Bruner, Goodnow, and Austin, 1956), where young adult subjects were distinguished on the basis of preferred strategies of information seeking and problem solving. This conceptual and methodological orientation has been extended and elaborated in the more recent research with children. There are numerous instances in *Studies in Cognitive Growth* where differences among children at a specific age level are discussed (especially as they relate to the influence of cultural differences). One also finds occasional tests of the children's consistency of cognitive functioning across diverse tasks. There is even a detailed description of an unpublished study (Kuhlman, 1960) in which children were classified on the basis of a theoretically relevant cognitive typology. Note also should be made of the diverse research procedures employed by the Bruner group. Many of these procedures would be admirably suited for the study of individual differences in the cognitive functioning of children.

The developmental sequence of differentiation and hierarchic integration is not so explicitly stated in the research of Bruner and his associates as in the writings of the other developmentalists considered thus far. In fact, references to differentiation as such are quite rare in Bruner et al. (1966)—reflected by the term's absence in the book's index. On the other hand, there is frequent reference to "hierarchical thought structures" throughout the book. As we shall see, however, the research described in *Studies in Cognitive Growth* is highly relevant to both differentiation and hierarchic integration, and, in fact, offers operational indices of both of those constructs within a common frame of reference.

The fundamental developmental theme in Bruner et al. (1966) concerns the changes in the child's favored mode of representation of his world as he grows older. The term "enactive" is used to describe the very young child's dependence upon sensorimotor activity in the representational process. With growth, the emphasis shifts to the "ikonic" mode. The child can now represent the world in the form of an image or schema that is relatively independent of motor action. Cognitive growth culminates with the achievement of the "symbolic" mode. In short, the child acquires conceptual structures that free him from undue dependence upon the way things look and permit the kind of internal manipulation of symbols characteristic of abstract and logical thought. This schematic outline hardly begins to do justice to the richness and complexity of the conceptualization. But, to reiterate, it is not the goal of the present chapter to review the various theories of cognitive development, but rather to consider whatever implications such theories may have for individuality of cognitive functioning in children.

The enactive-ikonic-symbolic sequence parallels the developmental sequence described by both Piaget and Werner. Although *Studies in Cognitive Growth* does not offer an explicit commitment to multilinear development and individuality as propounded by Werner in his 1957 paper, one has the impression that the Bruner group was compelled to accept multilinearity of development on the basis of the empirical outcomes of their cross-cultural studies. The transition from a perceptual to a conceptual mode of cognizing, so typical of children in Western civilization, was discovered to be much less characteristic of chil-

dren from underdeveloped areas of the world who had not been exposed to Western types of schooling. For these children, development often reaches an end product of finely differentiated perception rather than abstract conceptual thinking. Analogous results have been reported with respect to differences between middle-class American children and so-called "culturally deprived" minorities. There is, in other words, more than a single developmental path. The sensorimotor-perceptual-conceptual sequence may well have a biological basis, but cultural influences can evidently bring about substantial variation on the general theme. Once cultural influences are admitted as a determining factor in cognitive development, the path has been thrown open to the study of subcultural and individual differences as well. One finds occasional hints in the recent Bruner et al. work of important individual variations in cognitive functioning outside of the context of basic cultural differences. It is also of particular interest to note that Bruner dissociates himself from any value judgment regarding the superiority of one particular cognitive mode over another. There is the recognition that abstract conceptual thought is not the sole, or even the ideal vehicle for art and poetry.

Let us now return to the issues of differentiation and hierarchic integration. Much of *Studies in Cognitive Growth* concerns the child's apprehension of identity and equivalence—that is, his manner of coping with similarity and difference. Bruner offers much evidence in support of the fundamental proposition that development proceeds from global and diffuse functioning, through differentiation, to an end product of hierarchic integration. Using children varying in age from approximately 4 to 12, the Bruner group has been able to examine the preceding three phases of the developmental process within the framework of a single task. Results obtained with one such task, developed by Olver and Hornsby, will be described in some detail later in this chapter. In contrast to this accomplishment of the Bruner group, we note that hierarchical integration is an important construct in the work of both Witkin and Bieri, yet neither has had much success in operationalizing the construct in a way that represents a higher level of functioning than differentiation. Harvey, Hunt, and Schroder claim that they are able to assess all three developmental levels with the identical instrument, but the relevance of such assessment to cognitive functioning in children at various age levels has not yet been conclusively demonstrated.

Bruner's conceptualization of differentiation can be distinguished from that of Lewin and Werner. For the latter authors, differentiation refers to cognitive and personality processes closely linked to the self system. Bruner's use of this term is confined to words and concepts largely extrinsic to the self. As a result, he views differentiation as characteristic of a relatively primitive level of cognitive functioning. Children at a relatively young age are able to focus on small details in perceptual tasks, to distribute objects across a variety of categories, and to generate numerous hypotheses in information-seeking tasks. Such performance turns out to be less than adaptive, however, for the tasks in question demand the application of hierarchical thought structures for effective performance, and these the younger children do not yet possess.

The contrast between differentiation and hierarchic integration in Bruner et al. (1966) is best illustrated in the chapters on "culture and equivalence" authored by Maccoby and Modiano and by Greenfield, Reich, and Olver. In the former chapter, Mexican children from a village and from a city were compared with one another and with New England children on the Olver and Hornsby (1966) task. This task consisted of a set of items—banana, peach, potato, meat, milk, water, air, germs, stones—presented one at a time with instructions to indicate the way in which each succeeding item was different from and similar to the items that preceded it.

The findings of major relevance here concern the sharp distinction (increasing with age) between the children from a Mexican village and the children from the urban areas of Mexico City and Boston in the capacity to analyze and synthesize, that is, cope with differences and similarities on the Olver-Hornsby task. At the youngest age levels (6 to 8), there were few rural-urban differences. Children of that age were better able to discriminate differences accurately than to synthesize accurately. With development, the urban children made the leap toward adequate synthesizing ability, an advance that eluded the older village child. This village child, in contrast, followed the developmental path of progressively finer, subtler discrimination of differences.

Synthesis, or the recognition of similarities in the Olver-Hornsby procedure, requires that the child go beyond the external, perceptual attributes of objects to a higher-order abstraction. This jump from the perceptual to the conceptual proved much more difficult for the unschooled village child than for the child attending urban schools. It is our view that the accurate discrimination of differences can be considered an index of differentiation; the accurate apprehension of similarities can be considered an index of hierarchic integration. Differentiation requires that the child have reached the perceptual or "ikonic" stage of development; hierarchic integration is achieved only when the child has progressed to the conceptual or symbolic level. Of course, the foregoing operational definitions do not exhaust the possible theoretical meanings of the constructs of differentiation and hierarchic integration.

Research reported in the chapter by Greenfield, Reich, and Olver confirms and extends the findings obtained by Maccoby and Modiano. The former authors studied Eskimo children in Alaska and Wolof children in Senegal. As with the Mexican village children, the Eskimo child is slower than the white urban child in making the transition from the perceptual to the conceptual level, though the older Eskimo child does eventually provide as many superordinate constructs as his urban age peer.

The work of Greenfield et al. in Senegal, employing Wolof children from both the bush and the school as well as French children, demonstrates the manner in which the processes of differentiation and hierarchic integration are linked to the differential usage of superordinate constructs by speakers of the Wolof and French languages. The Wolof language, according to Greenfield et al., is at a single level of generality and hence adequate for differentiating between objects; synthesis depends on superordinate terms, however, and these cannot readily be generated within the structure of the Wolof lexicon. It is not surprising, then, that bilingual Wolof children show considerably more hierarchic integration in equivalence judgments when employing French as opposed to their native Wolof tongue. On the other hand, it must be noted that the use of French and Wolof is confounded with schooling and lack of schooling, so that differences in hierarchic integration could be as much a function of Western-oriented education as of the lexical structure of the French and Wolof tongues.

The evidence for processes akin to differentiation and hierarchic integration is not confined to the study of equivalence in Bruner et al. (1966). The work on strategies of information seeking (the 20-questions game) and on perceptual recognition by Mosher and Hornsby and by Potter, respectively, has yielded results consistent with the data on equivalence. In the information-seeking context of the 20-questions game, younger children emitted a discrete series of unconnected hypotheses. Older children, by contrast, asked questions derived from a hierarchic structure. General constraint-seeking questions preceded more specific hypothesis-testing questions in an orderly, efficient sequence. Comparable effects were observed in the domain of perceptual recognition (a scene, initially out of focus, gradually moving into focus). The youngest children offered an unrelated series of hypotheses as to the nature of the viewed picture. Older children were better able to integrate the stimulus features and their memory store in a cyclical, hypothesis-testing manner. It should be noted, finally, that the primacy of differentiation over hierarchic integration in regard to similarity-difference judgments was also found to prevail in Piaget-type tasks. Bruner and Kenney, reporting on conservation research in Bruner et al. (1966), claim that 41% of their 3-year-olds spontaneously reported a *difference* between two beakers when asked how the two beakers were *alike*. Thus conservation phenomena appear to have much in common with equivalence rules. As Bruner et al. (1966) have asserted: "Learning to recognize the underlying respect in which two quantities are alike (though they appear different) is the same task as learning how a bell and a horn are alike—or a man and an animal" (p. 325).

It should be reiterated that the treatment of both differentiation and hierarchic integration in the research of Bruner and his associates has proceeded within a developmental, not an individual-differences framework. One finds occasional reference, however, to tests of consistency across different kinds of tasks—for example, equivalence versus information seeking. This certainly represents a gesture in the direction of an examination of individual consistency and difference, and it opens up the empirical possibility of placing children of comparable age along one or more dimensions of differentiation and hierarchic integration.

Summary. As can be seen, the same limited set of constructs—differentiation and hierarchic integration—has supplied the framework for a variety of developmental studies of cognition. A major difficulty with these constructs is their conceptual ambiguity: different investigators have used them in profoundly different ways. In addition, most researchers have not provided a truly adequate operational base for these constructs, quite apart from the theoretical meaning attributed to them. As a result, differentiation and hierarchic integration have not been as useful as they might conceivably have been. For this reason, a large portion of the empirical research on individual differences in children's cognition has been conducted outside the framework of a theory of differentiation and hierarchic integration. This will be reflected in the limited application of these constructs in most of the research described in the subsequent sections.

THE PROBLEM-SOLVING PROCESS AS AN APPROACH TO THE STUDY OF INDIVIDUAL DIFFERENCES

There are three ways to structure the discussion of individual differences in cognition —by method, theory, or description. We have chosen the last. More specifically, we shall consider the topic from the point of view of the problem-solving process in a scheme that approximates the chronology of that process. The strategy was derived from two premises —more research has been concerned with directed problem solving than with undirected thought, such as free association or reverie; and tracing the chronology of the problem-solving process seems to have heuristic value. This section shall consider, in sequence, the separate processes of encoding, memory, generation of hypotheses, evaluation, and deduction. There will also be a discussion of public report. In all cases, the text shall focus on sources of individual differences in these functions. The choice of these functions does not imply that they are the only sources of variation in cognition. These domains have been the areas explored most extensively. Nor are these choices to be interpreted as implying a view of cognition as a completely linear chain of events. We hope, however, that the categories suggested above represent a useful way to analyze the fluidity of thought.

Processes of encoding, memory, hypothesis generation, evaluation, and deduction bear some relation to the cognitive controls originally suggested by Gardner et al. (1959) and studied in children by Santostefano (1964a, 1964b) and Santostefano and Paley (1964). Gardner, Santostefano, and their associates postulate a set of cognitive controls whose aim or purpose is to assist the individual's adaptation to the environment. They include focal attention, field articulation, leveling-sharpening, and equivalence range. It is assumed that there are consistent individual differences in each of these dimensions.

Differences in focal attention refer to tendencies to scan an object passively in contrast to an active, vigorous, and more purposive study of the environment. Differences in field articulation refer to selectivity of attention, that is, the ability to attend selectively to the salient or figural aspect of a context. This dimension is related to, but certainly not identical with Witkin's construct of field independence. Differences in leveling-sharpening refer to the ability to hold recent events in memory so that comparisons between current and immediately preceding inputs can be made accurately. Equivalence range refers to the category width preferred by a person— the breadth of the category boundaries for particular classes of events.

There is considerable similarity between the cognitive process of encoding and the controls of focal attention and field articulation; that is, between hypothesis generation and equivalence range. The authors have chosen to structure this section around the more traditional categories for several reasons. First, such a strategy allows easier assimilation of the existing empirical data that are developmental in nature. Second, the construct of

style or control is less independent of value considerations than such processes as encoding, memory, or hypothesis generation. The dimensions of field independence versus dependence, constricted versus flexible control, and complexity versus simplicity leave few doubts regarding the positively valued poles. When these value distinctions are associated with veridical or accurate performance, in contrast to nonveridical or inaccurate performance, the distinction between cognitive style constructs and abilities becomes blurred. This does not necessarily mean that the stylistic dimensions are isomorphic with the "simple and sovereign" IQ. Rather, these dimensions will be selectively related to certain abilities but unrelated to others (Gardner, Jackson, and Messick, 1960). The link between stylistic variables and the traditional separate *abilities* is a delicate and controversial issue to which we shall devote considerable attention.

Finally, the decision to organize the discussion around the more traditional cognitive categories does not require a judgment as to the motivational bases for these cognitive processes. Cognitive controls, as conceived by Gardner and Santostefano, are viewed as instrumental processes serving ego motives and are part of motivational and defensive structures. Although selectivity of attention, memory, and categorization strategies can and do serve motivational forces on occasion, it is not clear whether this is always the case. More important, there is honest disagreement as to the specific motives served. The cognitive controls derive directly from a psychoanalytic conception of motivational structure and there is some profit in examining cognition initially from a motivationally more neutral stance.

We shall now consider the separate processes of encoding, memory, hypothesis generation, evaluation, deduction, and public report. Since a variety of theoretical forces have spawned the relevant empirical investigations, we shall attempt to blend the available ideas and data into a reasonably harmonious form.

Encoding (or Decoding)

The translation of information is the first process in the cognitive sequence. Guilford (1956, 1959) has labeled this process *recognition* in his systematic description of intellectual processes. But encoding is more than merely labeling. Encoding involves selective attention to one event rather than another; and selectivity of attention is partly a function of the individual's adaptation level. The reader is referred to Neisser (1967) for an imaginative summary of research on perceptual processing in adults. The nature of the decoded product depends, first, on the nature of the information and on the availability of cognitive units to process the material. There are dramatic differences among children in available language resources for labeling events (Bernstein, 1961; Hess and Shipman, 1965) and correspondingly dramatic differences in quality of product.

The nature of the encoded event is also a function of the preference for perceptual analysis. Existing data suggest, for example, that girls may be less likely than boys to analyze a geometric design into its component parts (Kagan, Rosman, Day, Albert, and Phillips, 1964; Witkin et al., 1962). Similarly, younger children may be less likely to attend to component parts of an object than older children (Lee, Kagan, and Rabson, 1963). Elkind, Koegler, and Go (1964) showed pictures to 195 children (aged 4 to 9 years) and asked the children to describe the stimuli. There was a regular increase with age in the proportion of children who described both parts and wholes, with the brighter children most likely to describe parts rather than wholes.

A recent study of social class differences in encoding strategies in 10-year-olds revealed that middle-class children were more likely to use descriptive and analytic language when asked to differentiate a design or face from a group of similar stimuli. Specifically, the child was shown an array of five designs (or faces) plus one cue stimulus and asked to describe the cue stimulus so that another child of his age could easily pick it out from the array. Middle-class boys and girls were not only more analytic and descriptive in their encoding of the visual stimuli in contrast to the lower-class children who were global, but they were also better able to decode (understand) the analytic descriptions of their middle-class peers. "The style of encoding in which each class was most successful as decoder was the style used most frequently by

that class in encoding" (Heider, 1968, p. 104).

Although the corpus of research on set and recognition will not be reviewed here, it emphasizes the proposition that the expectations of the adult direct his interpretations of experience (see Blum, 1957; Jones and Bruner, 1954; Petigrew, Allport, and Barnett, 1958; Tajfel, 1957). Recent research with children on the role of set in perception (Maccoby, 1967; Maccoby and Konrad, 1967) demonstrated that preparatory set for auditory stimuli was generally an advantage for children if the signal was given before a stimulus, especially if the information was complex. In these experiments, a child (aged 5 to 14 years) is presented two tape recorded word messages simultaneously, one in a man's voice and one in a woman's voice, played over external speakers. After the speaking has stopped, the child must report the message spoken by one of the voices. The results are relatively clear. With age, the children are better able to report the voice they were requested to report, and they report fewer words spoken by the voice they were instructed to ignore. It is important to determine whether this is a difference in perception or in performance. Is the age difference produced because the young child cannot shut out the unwanted voice or because he cannot inhibit reporting the unwanted information? This issue is still not resolved. As might be expected, the greater the difference in familiarity of the words spoken by the two voices, the better able the child is to report only the instructed voice. Distinctiveness of the signal aids selected recall, and meaning lends distinctiveness to a signal. Maccoby (in press) concludes:

It is not especially useful to think of the deficit in terms of the child's having a more limited information processing capacity or memory storage capacity in the usual meaning of these terms. Rather the problem would seem to be that the capacity the young child does have is not effectively employed. . . . It is the effect of the unwanted material on the perception of the wanted material that is the heart of the problem.

It is possible that the perceptions of the children are accurate, but their report is deficient. During the act of reporting, the young child may be unable to keep the signals separate. Thus interference may occur in the act of reporting and destroy the quality of performance. This hypothesis could be tested by playing simultaneous messages but not asking the child to report what he heard. Rather, the child should be asked to point to pictures that illustrate each of the messages. If the children were accurate in this task, it would be reasonable to conclude that the problem is not in the perceptual but in the reporting phase.

Constricted versus Flexible Control. These terms were used first by Klein (1954) to describe the extent to which subjects were susceptible to distraction and cognitive interference in tasks containing conflicting cues. The Stroop (1935) Color-Word Interference Test has been the favored instrument for assessing constricted versus flexible control.

In the traditional Stroop test, the subject first reads color words to provide an index of reading speed, then names the colors in a series of colored patches to provide an index of speed of naming colors, and finally names the colors of a set of color words printed in incongruous colors (e.g., the word "red" printed in blue) to provide an index of susceptibility to interference. Ratio or difference scores are generally used, and sometimes reading speed and speed of naming colors are regressed out of the interference score. The various scoring formulas are available in an exhaustive review of research with the Stroop test published by Jensen and Rohwer (1966).

Since word reading habits are not well established in young children, Santostefano and Paley (1964) devised a Fruit-Distraction Test as a reasonable equivalent to the Stroop. The test consisted of two cards, one of which contained pictures of fruits appropriately colored. The second card was identical to the first, but, in addition, a variety of food and nonfood objects were drawn adjacent to the relevant fruits. The child's task was to report orally the colors of the fruits on the first and second cards. The difference in performance (reading speed and errors) between the first and second cards provided an index of the degree to which the child was disrupted by the intrusive information on the second card. Also obtained was a measure of the number of intrusive stimuli recalled.

Significant age differences in interference were obtained for reading speed. The oldest children were apparently least distracted by the intrusive stimuli, whereas the youngest children were most distracted. Reading errors did not yield significant age effects. With respect to recall of the intrusive information, significant age differences were found for the number of intrusive food stimuli remembered—the youngest children showed the best recall, the oldest children showed the worst. The data on reading speed and number of intrusive stimuli recalled are consistent, of course. It appears that the younger children are less able than the older to avoid attending to the distracting information.

In sum, younger children are more vulnerable to interference in situations where wanted and unwanted signals—from the experimenter's point of view—are presented simultaneously. The interpretation of these differences is still unclear, however.

Encoding across Sensory Modalities. Birch and his colleagues (Birch and Belmont, 1964, 1965; Birch and Lefford, 1963, 1967) emphasize developmental differences in the interpretation and integration of sensory inputs from various sense modalities. Birch assumes that development is accompanied by (1) hierarchical shifts in the locus of control of actions (e.g., tactile to visual control of a particular motor pattern), (2) integration across sensory modalities, and (3) differentiation within modalities. In a classic study derived from this point of view, 145 children (5 to 11 years of age) had to make judgments about the equivalence of two geometric forms in a situation in which a form presented in one sensory system (the standard) was compared with a form presented in another sensory system (the variable). A *visual* standard was compared with a series of forms presented haptically or kinesthetically; a haptically presented form was compared with a kinesthetically presented variable. The stimuli were eight blocks from the Sequin Form Board, and paired stimuli were presented to each child. The first member of a pair was presented in either the visual or the haptic mode. The second member of the pair was either haptic or kinesthetic if the standard was visual, and kinesthetic if the standard was haptic. Some of the forms were identical with the standard, some were different from the standard. The child had to say whether the comparison form was the *same* as or *different* from the standard.

Errors for all three classes of comparisons decreased with age. The visual-haptic comparison was easiest for all children; the haptic-kinesthetic and visual-kinesthetic comparisons were much more difficult, with the latter being the most difficult. By 8 to 9 years of age most children were performing very well; differential difficulty of the three classes of comparisons was most apparent over the age range 5 to 7 years. The intercorrelations of quality of performance across the three types of comparison were close to zero at 5 years of age, but increased with age, approaching .70 by the time the children were 7 years old. No major sex differences were found.

Birch suggests that visual-haptic integration has its most rapid period of growth during the age span 3 to 4 years, whereas visual-kinesthetic and haptic-kinesthetic integration grow during the period 6 to 8 years of age. The flavor of Birch's discussion emphasizes a biological basis to these changes, and this is a plausible interpretative stance. It is also possible, however, to view these data as studies in decision making. The decrease in error scores over age could be a partial function of longer decision times. The issue of individual differences in decision time—the reflection-impulsivity dimension—will be considered later in the chapter.

Visual-haptic comparisons may be easy because these comparisons are made more often in the environment, and the child has had extensive experience in this integration. If children were reared in an environment in which visual-kinesthetic judgments were frequently required, there might be a reversal of these trends. This supposition finds support in a comparison of American and Nigerian subjects on the Witkin versions of the Rod-and-Frame and Embedded Figures Tests (Wober, 1967). The Nigerian subjects were more field independent than Americans (i.e., had lower error scores) on the Rod-and-Frame Test where attention to proprioceptive cues is critical. Moreover, there was a negligible correlation for the Nigerians between performance on the Rod-and-Frame and on the Embedded Figures Tests ($r = .21$), whereas among Americans the correlations were highly positive, ranging from .5 to .8.

Wober argues effectively that the Nigerian subjects grow up in a culture that emphasizes analysis of proprioceptive cues and minimizes the value of visual analysis. He suggests: "The prevailing patterns of childhood intake and proliferation of information from the various sense modalities differ according to culture" (Wober, 1967, p. 31).

It is therefore not beyond reason to suggest that the relative difficulty of visual-kinesthetic over visual-haptic integration reported by Birch and Lefford might be reversed if American children's life experiences required visual-kinesthetic comparisons. Cognitive functioning appears to be a most plastic enterprise, and generalizations about universalistic hierarchies or stages of development should be tempered until adequate cross-cultural data are examined.

Encoding and Attention. The encoding process touches directly the issue of individual differences in selectivity of attention— selective focusing on one particular aspect of an array or event rather than another; attention that is maintained versus attention that is shortlived. Directed attention refers to selective focusing—the selection of one aspect from the available field over another, and the inhibition of urges to turn from the field of focus. Directed attention is relatively free from interference. One can define selectivity of attention (or focused attention) as the degree to which thresholds are selectively lowered for one class of stimuli relative to others. Attention is focused when the profile of thresholds for an orientation response to classes of stimuli forms a "V," that is, when the threshold for a given stimulus is low, and thresholds for other stimuli are high. Attention is diffuse when the function relating orientation threshold to the envelope of immediate stimuli is horizontal; that is, when the thresholds for orientation for many classes of immediate stimuli are the same.

Broadbent regards selectivity of attention as the result of the action of sets of filters. The central nervous system decides which information arriving at the eyes, ears, or skin is to be admitted through the filters. Only the information that passes is processed (Broadbent, 1958). Broadbent's experiments tend to support this hypothesis, and he has suggested that it is difficult to attend to more than one input channel at a time. It is possible that a major difference between younger and older children is that the younger cannot shift focus of attention rapidly, whereas an adolescent can redirect focus quickly, although the number of channels that can be simultaneously monitored may not change much with age. If this were true it would suggest, albeit at a conjectural level, that the old saw about the "booming, buzzing confusion" of the world of the infant is in error. If the infant does not shift foci quickly and attends to one channel at a time, then he may not hear the television while he is watching his fingers, not see the colored lights on the Christmas tree while he is listening to his mother, not feel the jostling of the crib while he is feeling the discomfort of hunger contractions.

Measurement of Attention in Children. Although this chapter is not primarily concerned with methodology, it is appropriate to consider, if only briefly, procedures for assessing aspects of attentional processes. As indicated earlier, attention refers to the differential selectivity of thresholds to a range of stimuli in the child's life space. As that profile approaches a peaked "V," attention becomes more selective. Under those conditions, respiration becomes more regular and heart rate decreases and becomes less variable (Lacey, 1959, 1967). Moreover, the cardiac changes are not necessarily completely dependent upon changes in respiration (Brener and Hothersall, 1967) and may be concomitants of decreased somatomotor activity (Obrist and Webb, 1967). These variables are some of the indexes one can quantify during periods of sustained and selective attention to an external stimulus.

The state of concentration is accompanied by different patterns. The child who is concentrating is selectively attending to internal images or thoughts, and wishes to insulate himself against external stimulation. The profile of reactions to this class of selected investment of attention includes an increase in cardiac rate and variability, dilation of the pupil, and a decrease in skin resistance (Kahneman, Tursky, Shapiro, and Crider, 1969).

The peripheral responses under selective attention to external stimuli are different from the pattern of responses shown under concentration. It is possible that subtle changes in the profile of muscle tone in various parts

of the body are critical mediators of the differences in autonomic responses described above (see Obrist and Webb, 1967). In any case, the pattern of autonomic responses can be helpful in investigation of these attentional states. Kahneman has demonstrated that the degree of dilation of the pupil covaries, in almost a linear fashion, with the difficulty of the mental task being presented (Kahneman and Beatty, 1966, 1967) and he suggests that the critical psychological variable is attentional commitment (i.e., the degree to which the attentional apparatus is committed to working on the problem at hand). The more difficult the problem, the more imperative it is that the attentional system be totally committed to the problem. It appears that sensitive combination of somatic and autonomic reactions will be useful in monitoring the fragile phenomenon of attention. Fortunately, children do not object to these procedures, and the availability of telemetric devices does away with the necessity of constraining the child in one place.

The Bases for Attention in Infancy. The bases for orientation, selectivity, and maintenance of attention are crucial for understanding cognitive processes. We shall consider briefly these bases for attention as they emerge in the first two years.

The earliest determinant of attention, from an ontogenetic point of view, is high rate of change in the physical parameters of a stimulus. Lights that blink on and off are more likely to capture the newborn's attention than a steady light source. Intermittent tones are more attention getting than continuous ones. Visual events with high black-white contour contrast possess more power to recruit sustained attention than stimuli with minimal contour contrast (Fantz and Nevis, 1967; Salapatek and Kessen, 1966). These conditions are naturally distinctive. They seem to elicit the infant's attention without prior learning. These stimulus conditions dominate the recruitment of attention during the first 10 to 12 weeks.

A second class of conditions that produces distinctiveness is the product of experience and involves the relation between external events and the child's acquired schema for that event. The schema is defined as a hierarchical arrangement of distinctive elements of an event. The schema is not a replica of the event but a schematic or partial representation. Selectivity and maintenance of attention appear to be curvilinearly related to the degree to which the features of an event are a distortion or discrepancy from an established schema. A child gives maximal attention to an event that is a moderate deviation from the distinctive features of his schema. The discrepant stimulus event is to be distinguished from a novel event. A novel stimulus is one that has minimal similarity or relation to any schema the child possesses. Thus the random shape or meaningless design is a novel event to a 6-month-old infant. A picture of a face with only one eye, however, is a discrepant event. A 4-month-old infant will look longer at a photograph of a face—regular or disfigured—than he will at a randomly generated figure with a high degree of black-white contrast (McCall and Kagan, 1967). This difference does not appear to be present at birth (Fantz and Nevis, 1967); the child must develop some primitive schema for a human face before the representations contained in the achromatic faces gain their attention-recruiting power. Moreover, the relation between discrepancy and sustained attention is as valid for older children as it is for infants. School-age children will invest longer periods of sustained attentional involvement with events that are discrepant from schema than to those that are congruent with schema (Charlesworth, 1964).

A third determinant of sustained attention, which begins to assume importance during the last part of the first year, involves the richness or density of available cognitive hypotheses for a particular class of events—that is, the degree to which a transformation of a familiar stimulus activates a nest of hypotheses that might explain the event. The richer the network of such hypotheses, the longer the child will remain attentive to the stimulus that elicited these structures.

For heuristic purposes these three conditions can be viewed as additive. Therefore an event that contains high rate of change is a discrepancy from the existing schema of the viewer; if, in addition, the event engages a rich set of hypotheses, it should hold attention with maximal power. The cartoon probably owes its attractiveness to these principles.

Differences in Sustained Attention after Infancy. An important issue in the develop-

ment of attentional processes hinges on the interpretation of the obvious differences in attentional dynamics between preschool and school-age children. The younger child does not typically invest long periods of attention in many activities, and it is often impossible to test him because of his restlessness and distractibility. The 7-year-old, in contrast, is a tractable subject. He persists with tasks, maintains orientation to test objects, and sits for minutes without getting up from the chair. Are these differences between younger and older children due to the young child's inability to focus attention (i.e., his lack of capacity) or due to interference with his existing capacity for attention (e.g., his unwillingness to invest attention in the task)? Earlier theorizing emphasized the younger child's inability, implying that his central nervous system did not permit long periods of focused attention to an activity or to an interesting stimulus. Recent observations of young children suggest that the typical distractibility of a 2-year-old is more likely to be the result of interfering factors than a defect in capacity.

The newborn will show long periods of fixed gazing (Salapatek and Kessen, 1966), and at any month during the first year it is possible to create stimuli that will hold the attention of the infant for several minutes. An attractive, moving, and colorful mobile can elicit prolonged following and fixed attention for 5 minutes or more in a 4-month-old infant. One of us has watched a 1-year-old boy play for 15 minutes with a rubber quoit that bounced and rolled in a unique way each time he threw it. The child would pick up the quoit, throw it, and follow it visually as it oscillated along the floor. The boy repeated this process perhaps 20 times, a laserlike beam of attention binding him to the quoit.

The 2-year-old is capable of sustained attention and inhibition of inappropriate responses on perceptual analysis tasks such as Embedded Figures. The child is shown a familiar object (a cat) and a larger stimulus in which the familiar object is disguised or embedded. Most 2-year-olds are able to locate the object after search and are capable of inhibiting false starts and maintaining interest in the problem.

One particular boy is instructive. He was 4 weeks premature (weighed under 5 pounds at birth), was cyanotic upon delivery, and was in an incubator for the first week. At 4 months, he was immature in his patterns of fixations to faces, motorically retarded, and not alert. At 8 and 13 months of age, he was hyperactive and showed short attention spans. At 27 months of age, he was placed with his mother in a large room and allowed to play for 30 minutes with a set of attractive toys. Most children settle down with a toy, play with it for a minute, and then repeat this pattern with another toy. This boy was pathologically active, and he exhausted himself in very short attentional epochs with the toys. He presented the classic picture of a premature infant with some central nervous system damage. He was hyperactive, restless, and seemed incapable of prolonged attention and inhibition. When he began the Embedded Figures Test, he pointed at the figures randomly and would not sit down to take the test. He ran to the item, pointed haphazardly at the array, and then ran off. He behaved like this for 6 minutes, until his mother suggested that the boy might perform better if he were sitting on her lap. He was put on his mother's lap; she whispered some encouraging words to him, and for 2 minutes and three test items he behaved like a typical 2-year-old. He attended to the array, inhibited false starts, and showed appropriate selective inhibition. Even this child, for whom a diagnosis of central nervous system damage is likely, was capable of sustained attention and inhibition for a time. His capacity for sustained attention was not destroyed. One might argue that the child was not ordinarily motivated to inhibit motoric behavior and attend to external events. There was no goal he desired that would be forthcoming if he inhibited his task-irrelevant motoricity.

A second possibility is that the child had not learned any responses to the toys and task stimuli. Attention is maintained if the external event releases a set of responses. If the child did not know what responses to make to the tasks, his attention would wander. It is not clear which interpretation is correct, but both imply that the lack of sustained attention was not due to any basic incapacity.

The important role of motivation in the apparent capacity for inhibition is seen in the positive correlation among preschool children between the ability to inhibit motor activity under instruction and quality of intellectual performance, in contrast to the zero-order relation between spontaneous motor activity and IQ (Maccoby, Dowley, Hagen, and Degerman, 1965). The children were asked to draw a line and to walk a line, both as slowly as possible. The children who showed the greatest ability to conform to that instruction had the highest intelligence test scores, despite the relatively restricted range of social class in the sample. Inhibition in the service of a task may be more a reflection of motivation than an inherent defect in inhibitory control.

The motivation to sustain attention on a continuous task is probably one of the most important determinants of quality of performance. Elliott (1964) found that children were much less willing (or able) to sustain attention on an auditory reaction time task than adults. Similarly, Katz and Deutsch (1963) report that grade school boys with reading problems showed much longer reaction times than good readers on trials where the signal to respond was in a modality different from the modality used on the preceding trial (visual to auditory or auditory to visual). Maintenance of a set to respond—which is almost synonymous with sustained attention—may be a central factor in the differential performance of various symptom groups.

The Change in Sustained Attention at Six Years. Developmental scores on selected intellectual tasks show a marked increase in quality between 6 and 7 years of age, in contrast to the less dramatic changes between 5 and 6 years of age. This generalization seems to hold for American children as well as for children in more primitive cultures. S. H. White (1965, 1968) has summarized some of the psychological and biological events that change at this age. They include qualitative differences in transposition learning and reversal shift—nonreversal shift performance; a leveling of the amplitude of the visual evoked potential, which reaches a peak voltage at age six; and a spurt in the growth of neural tissue. The anthropometric literature refers to the growth spurt at age 6 as the juvenile growth spurt. More provocative is Rimland's comment that between 5½ and 6 much of the symptomatology of the autistic child abates (see S. H. White, 1968). If the child develops useful language by 6 years of age, prognosis is good; if he does not, the prognosis is poor. In the case of the genetic disorder phenylketonuria, there is some suggestion that the child must take a prescribed diet until about 6 years of age, but he can be taken off the diet after this age with no serious mental retardation resulting. This result suggests that an important reorganization of brain chemistry may occur somewhere between 5 and 7 years of age. Such a conclusion matches the fact that children suffering convulsive seizures during childhood are commonly given medication until about 6 years of age, for this is the time at which febrile convulsions tend to disappear (Carter, 1964).

Consider a recent set of developmental data gathered on 200 children from 4 to 7 years of age living in small villages in Guatemala, none of whom was attending school (R. Klein and O. Gilbert, personal communication). The children's performance was assessed on the following tests: Embedded Figures Test, Matching Familiar Figures, Haptic Visual Matching Test, Memory for Digits, Memory for Sentences, Incidental Learning, and, finally, Vocabulary. For the first six tests, there was a dramatic increase in performance between 4 and 5 years and 6 and 7 years but minimal change in performance between 5 and 6 years of age. Vocabulary, however, did not show this pattern but rose linearly with age. The tasks that showed this pattern required sustained attention; vocabulary does not require sustained attention. It has been shown that the amplitude of the evoked potential is correlated with the degree to which the organism is attending to the visual stimulus (E. Beck and R. Dustman, personal communication). There is therefore an association between the amplitude of the visual evoked potential and attentional processes as well as an association between tests requiring sustained attention and a dramatic increase in performance between 6 and 7 years of age. One speculative hypothesis states that the central nervous system changes that may be responsible for the dramatic increase in performance between 6 and 7 are affecting primarily the child's capacity for sustained attention. It is clear that an important experiment in the future would be to devise tasks of equal difficulty graded for the degree to which they require the child's sustained attention. The tests that require sustained attention should show the 5 to 7 break; those that do not should not.

Attention and Scanning. The cognitive control of scanning refers to the distribution of attention. Santostefano and Paley (1964) describe focusers as systematic attention deployers and scanners as unsystematic attention deployers. The initial conceptualization of focusing by Schlesinger (1954) was developed in the context of size estimation. When focusers were presented with disks containing distracting cues for size estimation, they narrowed attention to the critical elements of the task, ignored the distraction, and consequently estimated size more accurately. Subsequent to Schlesinger's work, Piaget, Vinh-Bang, and Matalon (1958) published their evidence on centration effects, that is, the tendency for objects in the center of the attentional field to be overestimated in size as a function of length of focus. Thus the focusing of attention on the standard in a size estimation task should produce less accuracy, whereas extensive deployment of attention should be associated with greater accuracy. With the evidence of Piaget et al. (1958) as background, Gardner et al. (1959) suggested that the subjects originally called "focusers" by Schlesinger were in reality individuals who scan or deploy attention widely. Accordingly, in subsequent research (e.g., Gardner and Long, 1962a, 1962b), the term "focusing" was dropped and the control principle was designated by the single label of "scanning," referring to the extensiveness of attention deployment. Thus the focusing-scanning dimension as employed by Santostefano and Paley would be designated as extensive versus limited scanning in current usage. Given the greater descriptive accuracy of the latter labels, we shall recast the Santostefano-Paley work accordingly.

Scanning was assessed with a Circles Test in which a standard and a set of variable circles were compared in a context of size estimation. Accuracy of size estimation improved significantly with age. Such evidence is consistent with the view that older children deploy attention more extensively than do younger children and show longer decision times in perceptual tasks. It is not conclusive evidence, however, for no independent measures of the scanning process were obtained. As Santoste-fano and Paley point out, data on eye movements would have been exceedingly useful as a check on the actual perceptual behavior of the child.

A useful theoretical discussion of conceptions of broad and narrow attention by Wachtel (1967) has been published recently. That author attributes the confusion in the focusing-scanning domain to the presence of two logically distinct dimensions. Using Hernández-Peón's (1964) metaphor of attention as a beam of light with a central, brilliant focus and a less intense fringe, Wachtel distinguishes between the width of the beam (the original meaning of focusing in Schlesinger's work) and the extent to which the beam moves around the field (Gardner's view of scanning). Wachtel cites the case of obsessive personalities, who "show considerable breadth of attention along the scanning dimension but, metaphorically speaking, tend to view with a narrow and sharply focused beam" (p. 418). In other words, the obsessive individual scans the field for a broad sampling of information but is overly concerned with narrow detail and fails to notice the links between the various elements scanned. Wachtel's discussion brings considerable clarity to a murky area. Any further research dealing with the cognitive controls of focusing and scanning in the realm of attention, whether conducted with adults or children, cannot afford to ignore Wachtel's important conceptual distinction.

Memory

The second cognitive process, following decoding, involves memorial functions. Inquiry into memory processes has been accelerated as a result of the recent, controversial distinction between short- and long-term memory, which has been added to the older distinction between registration and retrieval. It had been assumed traditionally that all decoded events were registered initially with equal strength. If a person could not remember an event that was decoded, the fault lay with the retrieval process, and interference theory was called upon to explain the failure of recall. There was no predilection to reject parsimony and assume different laws for different kinds of storage. Recent data argue in favor of a meaningful distinction between short- and long-term memory (Adams, 1967). Short-term memory usually refers to a trace available for a maximum of 30 seconds, typically for a shorter period of time. The distinction between short- and long-term memory implies that, without special control processes, decoded information in short-term memory is not transferred to long-term memory and hence cannot be retrieved at a later time.

The problem of diagnosing the content of long-term memory is complex. A description of the traditional methods of studying memory—recognition, recall, and relearning—clearly falls outside the scope of the present chapter. It should be mentioned, however, that the context in which the memory is retrieved is probably central. Although experiments have not elucidated the exact role of context in recalling information, it is reasonable to assume that the context in which the recall is generated affects the completeness of the recall.

Individual Differences: Available Units and Memory. Individual-difference dimensions could touch memorial processes in several places. Differences in the availability and use of vocabulary units to encode the event appear to be central factors. After a thorough review of developmental and IQ differences in short-term memory, Belmont and Butterfield (1967) conclude that short-term memory is more influenced by encoding processes than by forgetting.

It is hopefully more than coincidence that John (1967), who approaches the explanation of memorial processes from a neurophysiological point of view, comes to a similar conclusion. John suggests that four different processes might account for differences in the effectiveness of storage of a habit as a result of the action of various drugs. First, a larger number of nerve cells engaged in coherent activity would lead to better storage. Second, the density of coherent nerve cells could remain the same, but the total time that this set of cells was active could vary. Third, the rate of circulation of reverberatory activity could vary, with density of cells and total time constant. Fourth, the contribution of each neural event might be enhanced. John eliminates alternatives two and four because he does not consider them to be viable on the basis of existing empirical data. Thus we are left with either the possibility that the number of cells involved in storage or the rate at which they operate is the explanation for differences in quality of memory storage. Electrophysiological data presented by John (1967) suggest that the first hypothesis is, at the moment, the most viable: "Learning may be accelerated by involving more cells in the process. . . . More rapid storage is accomplished by increasing the number or density of neurons involved in coherent representation of the event" (p. 63).

This conclusion resembles the suggestion made by Belmont and Butterfield, who surveyed molar recall data. Registration is increased to the degree that mediational units are engaged or elicited by the external stimulus. Differences in effective registration may stem from the density of mediational units, which in turn may be determined by the number of coherent nerve cells evoked by the stimulus.

Lack of existing cognitive units—primarily, but not exclusively, verbal in nature—appears to be one major cause of poor recall. The implication is that the initial registration was also deficient, because registration of information requires units to which the new information can become attached. This suggestion is completely consonant with the observation that children from language-poor environments exhibit performance deficiencies on memory tasks and do not seem to assimilate new information with the fidelity and extensiveness characteristic of children with richer language resources (Cazden, 1966; Hess and Bear, 1968). Similarly, age differences in memory are compatible with variation in the availability and use of verbal mediators (Flavell, Beach, and Chinsky, 1966).

Attention and Memory. The dimension of attention provides a second point of contact between individual differences and memory. Lack of selective attention leads to imperfect registration of events, even in short-term memory. Fragility of focus of attention could be the result of several factors, but the two most obvious, and probably the most frequent, are interfering responses and distracting stimuli—preoccupation with other thoughts and visceral afferent sensations (Maccoby and Hagen, 1965).

One of the best validated findings is the negative relation between the quality of immediate recall and anxiety (Kaye, Kirschner, and Mandler, 1953; Walker and Spence, 1964). Subjects who are made anxious experimentally show poorer recall than those attempting to store material under less anxiety-provoking circumstances. Similarly, children who tried to solve puzzles under ego-involving instructions recalled fewer incompleted, as compared to completed puzzles than they did under task-oriented instructions. Moreover, they recalled fewer puzzles with anxiety-arousing content as compared to those with more neutral content (Smock, 1957). Messer (1968) assessed quality of recall of a simple story under conditions where children had been threatened and under control conditions. He found poorer recall in threatened children.

The favorite interpretation of this relation between anxiety and quality of retention is that anxiety creates distracting stimulation, visceral as well as ideational, which deflects attention from relevant incoming information, and thus impairs memory. The negative correlation between test anxiety and verbal skills is congruent with this idea. An illustration of this notion is contained in Messer's data. The subjects were third-grade boys matched on age and IQ. The following story was read to each subject, with the instruction to recall it as completely as possible.

The American horse known as Man of War was a very fine horse. He ran in races in the United States, in France, and in Germany. He was brown with a red mane and had very strong legs. Five times a year he was in horse shows in Boston where children came to see him trot and run. After watching him the children were served hot chocolate, biscuits, and fudge.

One group of boys was made anxious just before the reading of the story through experimental creation of failure on an anagrams test. The second group did not have this failure experience, and a third group succeeded on the anagrams test. There are two major differences in the recall of the anxious group, in comparison with the others. First, more of the anxious subjects distorted the phrase, "Man of War," and called him either a "war horse" or a "horse that fought in the war." Second, anxious boys were more likely to substitute colors other than brown or red in describing the horse and to substitute foods other than hot chocolate, biscuits, or fudge. If the anxious children were not completely attentive to the initial reading of the story, the imperfect registration would naturally lead to the kinds of errors described.

Leveling-Sharpening and Memory. A third example of individual differences in memory processes is represented by the cognitive control of leveling-sharpening (e.g., Holzman and Gardner, 1960). This control refers to the degree to which the subject holds in memory an image of gradually changing stimuli presented sequentially. Levelers are so named because they merge new stimuli with previously presented ones. Sharpeners, by contrast, maintain a high degree of separation between the memory of previous stimuli and current information. Thus the memorial image of stimuli presented in sequence remains discrete for sharpeners, whereas it tends to lose its articulation for levelers.

The principal measure of leveling-sharpening employed by the Gardner group—the Schematizing Test—requires subjects to make size judgments of a series of squares of progressively increasing size. The test is administered by first presenting the five smallest squares for judgment, once in ascending and then twice in random order. At this point, the smallest square is removed and replaced by a square slightly larger than any seen before. This procedure is repeated after each series of trials, so that all of the squares are eventually replaced. Individuals, of course, vary in the degree to which their judgments reflect or lag behind the actual shifts in size. This individual variation defines the leveling-sharpening dimension in the research of Gardner and his colleagues.

Given the lengthy and tedious nature of the Schematizing Test, Santostefano (1964a) constructed a leveling-sharpening procedure of greater interest value for children. He devised a Wagon Test in which 8 elements of the wagon could be subtracted or added. A Circles Test using a set of 14 circles of gradually increasing diameter was also employed. The child had to note and indicate when a particular stimulus changed relative to the previous exposure. There were 10 boys and 10 girls from each of three age groups—6, 9, and 12—participating in the study.

Three leveling-sharpening scores were derived for each procedure: (1) the point at which the child detected and reported the first stimulus change; (2) the number of correct changes reported; and (3) a ratio score based on reported relative to actual changes. For all three procedures—Wagon Test (elements subtracted), Wagon Test (elements added), and Circles Test—significant age effects were observed for most of the leveling-sharpening indices. The older children tended toward sharpening; the younger toward leveling. A sex difference in favor of sharpening for boys was obtained, but only in the case of the Wagon Test with elements subtracted. Intercorrelations among the three leveling-sharpening indices were substantial within a single procedure but were low to moderate across procedures. Given the multiplicity of scores, and the variation in the magnitude of the correlations across the two tests, it is not clear whether Santostefano has successfully demonstrated the existence of a generalized leveling-sharpening dimension in children.

Motivation and Memory. A final source of individual differences in memory stems from motivational variables. Is the child motivated to work at recalling material, or does he stop searching after the first layer of information has been retrieved? Retrieval is effortful, and the child who works longer is likely to ferret out more information (Hertzig, Birch, Thomas, and Mendez, 1968). The role of motivational factors is considered in more detail later in the chapter.

In sum, variation in quality of recall in children can stem from differences in available mediational units or their use, anxiety, focused attention, susceptibility to distraction, and motivation. One of the perplexing problems is the fact that it is still not clear whether, or to what degree, recall failure is the result of imperfect registration, deficient rehearsal, or the effect of interference on the recall process.

Generation of Hypotheses

Decoding and storage of information are typically the first two processes in a problem-solving sequence. The third process is the generation of possible solution hypotheses—the production of alternative routes of mentation. Individual differences are operative in full force in this phase of the process. Guilford (1956, 1959) refers to this aspect of problem solving as induction. Most standardized tests of mental ability include items that require the generation of mediational links that connect apparently unrelated elements (as in verbal analogies) or the proliferation of characteristics of objects or events. The generation of hypotheses is a fundamental aspect of the problem-solving process.

The number of hypotheses generated is a function of the number and variety of cognitive units in the child's repertoire and the level of permissiveness-restrictiveness in the child's attitude toward error. A third determinant of hypothesis generation concerns the novelty and variety of the hypotheses available. This quality has been the subject of much investigation under the more attractive titles of functional fixedness, rigidity, flexibility, and most recently creativity (see chapter by Wallach in this book).

Generation of hypotheses is so much at the heart of mental functioning that a variety of forces can influence it directly. Anxiety can lead to distraction and interfering hypotheses; motivation affects persistence of search; strength of particular beliefs might prevent proliferation of associations dissonant to the belief. For example, a child who believed that all animals were dangerous might have difficulty recognizing the similarity between mother and cat, even though he possessed the mediational link "alive" in his repertoire.

There are dramatic age differences in hypothesis generation when the task forces the child to rely almost completely on his acquired supply of interpretations and does not give him much information with which to work. Potter (see Bruner et al., 1966) presented to children and adults (age range 3 to 22 years) photographs of familiar objects in a procedure in which the picture was initially out of focus and gradually (in 12 to 14 steps) became clear and obvious. The subject was allowed to view each step for a total of 10 seconds. The younger children, in contrast to the older children and adults, took much longer to recognize the correct picture. The 4- and 5-year-olds, in addition, repeated the same hypotheses frequently and rarely mentioned details in their descriptions of the picture. School-age children, on the other hand, were more analytic in their descriptions and less likely to repeat hypotheses. The older children were also more cautious, often refusing to guess, indicating that they recognized and took ac-

count of the inadequacy of their hypotheses.

Developmental studies of learning set (Levinson and Reese, 1967) document the dramatic differences betwen preschool and fifth-grade children in the ease with which a discrimination learning set is established. The younger children persist with position hypotheses and specific object preferences, whereas the older subjects have a much stronger faith that there is, indeed, a problem to be solved— not a random walk—and, as a result, are more highly motivated to attend to relevant cues to try to solve the problem.

Hence increased availability of varied hypotheses, greater flexibility in discarding inadequate hypotheses, an appreciation of the formal nature of a problem, and greater anxiety over error are major developmental changes in situations requiring proliferation of hypotheses.

Generation of Hypotheses and Concept-Sorting Tasks. The process of hypothesis generation touches the phenomenon of preferences for particular conceptual groupings. There are developmental and intraindividual differences in the structure and content of conceptual categories produced when the situation is relatively free and allows for a variety of dimensions to be chosen. The bases for regarding a group of objects as alike or as sharing attributes are a function of (1) the stimulus qualities of the objects, (2) the context in which the objects are presented, (3) the child's available categories, and (4) the motivationally based strategies of the conceptualizer.

American research has been overly preoccupied with the content dimensions of form, color, and size (perhaps because of their obviousness), but has neglected equally significant formal categories like symmetry, contrast, movement, or orientation. These latter dimensions are essential, though less static attributes of objects. Unfortunately, too little attention has been paid to categorization of objects or events presented in the auditory, haptic, or olfactory modes.

The child's categorizations can be examined from a formal or content perspective. The formal aspects of a concept or category, which are independent of their specific content, include:

1. Superordinate (or categorical). A categorical term is used which characterizes the

common class membership of the objects as wholes (fruits, animals, men, money).

2. Functional-relational. The bases of similarity involve a thematic relation between or among members of the class (they play together; the match lights the pipe).

3. Functional-locational. The members of the class share a common location (these animals live on a farm).

4. Analytic. The basis for categorization involves similarity in a *manifest* component of the members of the class (these have two arms; these have feathers).

Recent work has revealed lawful developmental trends in the use of these four modes (see Sigel, 1953, 1964). With age, the child is more likely to use superordinate categories and less likely to use functional-relational categories. Children 4 to 6 years of age usually classify visually presented objects or pictures into functional-relational categories (the boy and the dog play together; the paper and the match burn). Older children prefer superordinate and analytic groupings (Kagan, Rosman, Day, Albert, and Phillips, 1964). Among young children, those of lower social-class background are apt to give more functional groupings than middle-class subjects of the same age (see Sigel, Anderson, and Shapiro, 1966).

The Significance of Analytic Concepts. A series of studies has suggested that the production of analytic concepts with visually presented material increases with age (Kagan et al., 1964) and seems to be in the joint service of a reflective attitude and a preference for visual analysis. Trios of pictures were shown to children from 6 to 11 years of age. The child had to select two pictures that were "alike in some way." The pictures were constructed so that analytic, functional-relational, or superordinate groupings were possible. There was a linear increase in number of analytic concepts with age for children in grades one to six. Moreover, the children who produced many analytic concepts obtained higher scores on the Picture Arrangement subtest of the Wechsler Intelligence Scale for Children but were not superior to other children on the Information or Vocabulary subtests.

In one experiment, children were either told to pause and delay before giving their conceptual grouping or urged to respond quickly. The first instruction produced increased analytic responses. This finding was replicated for nonanalytic children, but analytic children did not produce fewer analytic responses when told to respond quickly (Ostfeld and Neimark, 1967). More impressive is the fact that within a group given the same instructional set (to respond quickly or slowly), there was a positive relation between response time to produce a concept and number of analytic concepts. The children with many analytic concepts made fewer errors in match-to-sample tasks and showed longer decision times on these tasks.

The production of analytic concepts to pictorial stimuli with subtle analytic detail seems to be mediated by tendencies to reflect over the validity of the response and to engage in analysis of visual arrays (Lee, Kagan, and Rabson, 1963). Children were taught to associate a nonsense syllable with a series of geometric designs that had figure and ground components. After reaching criterion the child was shown the figure and ground components separately. Fourth-grade boys who produced many analytic concepts were more likely to label the figural component correctly when it was presented alone.

In a similar study, third-grade boys were classified as showing a high versus low disposition to produce analytic concepts on a task in which the child had to group pairs of stimuli from sets of three pictures. These children were then administered a concept-induction task where the child had to induce the concept for visual stimuli that contained two analytic, two relational, and two categorical concepts. Nonsense syllables were used to represent the conceptual categories. The analytic children attained the analytic concepts before the relational or categorical concepts. The relational boys, on the other hand, showed the opposite pattern. Thus when familiar materials are used, an analytic attitude shows some generality (Lee et al., 1963).

Consider now some other characteristics associated with a preference for an analytic mode of categorization. Observation of normal children who were both analytic and reflective, in contrast to those who were nonanalytic as well as impulsive, indicated that the first group was more attentive and less distractible in a normal classroom setting

(Kagan et al., 1964). School-age children who produced analytic concepts were likely to have spent long periods of time in solitary task activities during the first four years of their lives (Kagan et al., 1964). This evidence is concordant with the report that kindergarten boys who produce analytic groupings are rated as more controlled emotionally than boys who produce categorical or relational concepts (Sigel, Jarman, and Hanesian, 1967). In sum, school-age children who produce analytic concepts with familiar, visual material seem to be more reflective, less distractible, and more likely to analyze pictorial arrays.

The Meaning of the Child's Conceptual Response. It is important to note that the data quantified are typically the child's verbal explanations of his conceptual groupings. It is possible that the child was thinking in superordinate terms, but because he did not have the words for a superordinate explanation, he employed a functional basis for categorization. Moreover, the child might have realized that he would have to explain his grouping and, as a result, selected a grouping that he was capable of explaining, rather than one he would have used had he not been under the social pressure to account for his behavior. This is a serious methodological problem that reminds us of the competence-performance distinction in psycholinguistics. Much of our data on preferred conceptual categories may be specific to the artificial laboratory situation in which it is gathered.

A second, controversial issue concerns the relation between developmental trends and the specific nature of the array categorized by the child. Some investigators have suggested that age trends are independent of the specific material being sorted. However, the data question the validity of this view. Lower-class Negro children have much more difficulty categorizing pictorial representations of familiar objects than three-dimensional representations of these objects (Sigel et al., 1966; Sigel and McBane, 1967; Sigel and Olmsted, 1967).

Olver and Hornsby (in Bruner et al., 1966) asked subjects 6 to 19 years of age to state the similarity among groups of words. The child was first read a pair of words, a third word was added to the pair, a fourth was added to the trio, and so on, until eight words had been presented for successive similarity judgments. The use of analytic bases to tie the words together decreased with age, while superordinate categories increased. Another group of subjects (6 to 12 years of age) was presented an array of 42 pictures of familiar objects and asked to select those that were "the same in some way." Analytic concepts were more frequently used with the pictures than they were with the words. However, analytic concepts decreased and functional concepts increased with age. Kagan et al. (1964), on the other hand, who also used pictures of objects as instances to be grouped, found that analytic concepts increased while functional categories decreased with age.

The fact that the use of a preferred mode of categorization depends on the specific test materials presented to the subject is further illustrated in a study by Gilmore (1968). Ten-year-old children were asked to name some familiar adults and to state how these adults were similar. These children also sorted pictures of people into conceptual categories. Reflective girls (girls who showed long response times on tests of uncertainty) produced many analytic concepts when stating the similarity among the five familiar adults (a verbal task), but showed no preferential tendency to produce analytic concepts to the picture-sorting task. Similarly, middle-class, elementary school children produced many more analytic and relational concepts when they were sorting human figures than when they were sorting objects or animals. However, older children produced more analytic responses for all classes of stimuli—people, objects, or animals (Sigel and Olmsted, 1967). Still another investigation (Wallach and Kogan, 1965) found that creative children give more functional concepts than less creative, but equally intelligent children.

On the surface there seems to be little consistency in these diverse sets of data. Some order emerges if one takes into account the nature of the array being sorted. By nature of array we mean the modality in which the information is presented as well as the relative salience versus subtlety of the bases for grouping. Let us consider some assumptions about sorting behavior before proceeding further.

A 3-year-old child has already developed standards concerning quality of concepts and quality of performance. He has begun to learn what are, in his culture, the characteristics of good or appropriate concepts, and, indeed, even the characteristics of esthetically pleasing concepts. Part of his judgment is related to the subtlety of the category as reflected in the amount of work required to detect it. The extraction of pleasure from an event, as evidenced by the nonsocial smile, is likely to occur when the person attains a successful solution following a period of mental effort. The smile is not likely to occur if minimal effort was associated with goal attainment. This generalization is illustrated in several contexts. If one observes a parent watching his child being tested, the parent is most likely to smile when the child succeeds either following a failure experience or after a difficult item where the parent has had a chance to build up some uncertainty about the outcome. If the child succeeds on an easy item, the parent is not likely to smile. The child also is most likely to smile when he succeeds on a test item that follows a long period of search. He is unlikely to smile following success on an item requiring no work. These observations suggest that the child has acquired an association between success on a difficult task, on the one hand, and positive affect, on the other. A child of 5 years seems "to know"—in the sense that he can tell you—which concepts are "good" and which are "bad" on purely formal grounds. The defining criteria depend, in part, on difficulty of detection. An answer to a hard problem is more valuable than an answer to an easy one (see Smith and Wing, 1961). The nature of the array is an important determinant of the concepts chosen by the child. If the array makes functional concepts easy to detect and analytic ones difficult, the older child is more likely than the younger to select the analytic concepts, because he believes them to be better or more elegant. The older child may choose the analytic concept not because he failed to note the relational, but because he preferred the analytic. If the analytic concept were obvious and the relational one subtle, he might do the opposite. Thus Kagan et al. (1964), using pictures that made functional concepts easy to detect, found a decrease in their use over age. On the other hand, using an array for which functional concepts were difficult, Olver and Hornsby (1966) found an increase in their use over age.

As suggested earlier, the mode of presentation is also critical. In the Olver-Hornsby work, where words rather than pictures of objects were used, the functional bases were relatively easy to produce. Analytic concepts are unlikely with older children when words are the events categorized. The child is not likely to produce an analytic conceptual basis to the two words potato and banana, but he might say "both have spots" if he saw them illustrated. There are major interactions between the child's stage of development and the relation between the specific nature of the array and the conceptual categories reported by the child. The power of these interactions should increase with age, for the older child has greater freedom of category selection.

Perhaps the best illustration of the importance of the array on the nature of the dimension selected is contained in Wohlwill's (1963) study of relational versus absolute response to number. Children in grades 1, 3, 5, and 8 were rewarded either for an absolute choice of number 5 (when the number 1, 2, 3, 7, 8, or 9 was paired with the number 5), or they were rewarded for a relational choice, where the child had to pick the smaller number of the pair. One group of subjects was exposed to a perceptual representation of the numbers (e.g., 5 dots versus 7 dots). Other children were exposed to an abstract representation (5 triangles versus 7 crosses). Still others were exposed to pairs of numerals (the numeral 5 versus the numeral 7). Under the perceptual and abstract modes of presentation, the relational discrimination was much easier than the absolute. Under the numeral condition, the absolute choice was much easier. The importance of mode of presentation was clearest among the first-grade children. Under the perceptual condition, learning the relational response was easy; under the numeral condition, the absolute response was easy to attain; under the abstract condition, neither the relational nor the absolute response was easily learned. It is not reasonable to conclude that first-grade subjects are preferentially relational in their thinking about number, or preferentially absolutistic. Their preferences depend intimately on the specific nature of the material being presented. A preferred conceptual response is rarely independent of the materials to be classified (Wohlwill, 1963).

There is a more profound moral contained

in these data and implied by this general discussion. The child learns classification responses to specific sets of events. He classifies events and does not always carry around a generalized conceptual rule for all stimulus contexts. This principle holds as well for Kendler's and Piaget's empirical generalizations as it does for those based on object sorting data. Children of 3 years of age will not show mediational reversal shifts involving the size and color of squares in a typical Kendler laboratory procedure (Kendler and Kendler, 1962). But absence of a reversal shift in this context is not a sufficient data base to declare that a 3-year-old does not mediate when he arranges six sticks in a vertical position, blows at them, and sings "Happy Birthday." A 5-year-old may not classify on two dimensions simultaneously if he is presented with pictures of birds and leaves in a Geneva, Denver, or Cambridge laboratory. But that observation is not sufficient to conclude that 5-year-olds never classify an event on two dimensions simultaneously. Younger children do this each day when they load all the red, square blocks in a wagon and leave the red and blue circular ones.

Psychology is concerned, naturally with generalized laws about responses and cognitive functions. Our theoretical ambitions tempt us to proclaim that cognitive structures displayed in one limited situation can be generalized across varied situations. It would be convenient if children possessed generalized rules rather than specific reactions to specific classes of events. However, much of our data fail to support this wish. Save for a few exceptions (e.g., the syntactic behavior of the young child), there is less transfer than we like to believe. This issue is reminiscent of the old transfer of training controversy in educational psychology. Existing empirical research suggests that a child learns a set of skills to a particular class of problem. Generalization of preferred conceptual categories is limited. Statements about individual differences in categorization strategy must contain a strong statement about the materials manipulated. A child may be analytic with visual stimuli containing subtle analytic cues but superordinate with verbal representations of those objects. The descriptive term "analytic" is not different from the word "prejudiced." In both cases we must know the target of the attitude.

The Role of Evaluation in Problem Solving

Let us focus now on a fourth process in problem solving. The degree to which the child pauses to *evaluate* the quality of his cognitive product acts on the entire spectrum of cognitive processes by influencing the quality of initial decoding, recall, and hypothesis generation. Some children accept and report the first hypothesis that is printed on the screen of awareness and act upon it with only the barest consideration for its appropriateness or validity. Others devote a long period of time to study and reflection and censor many hypotheses. This individual-difference dimension is apparent in children as early as 2 years of age.

The hardiness of this evaluative dimension is beautifully illustrated in a psychophysical study of light intensity. Ten trained adult subjects judged whether a light was on or off in a situation in which light intensities were close to threshold. The adults viewed the lights under three viewing conditions—both eyes, dominant eye, and nondominant eye. Decision time was the variable quantified. Although response times decreased with increasing light intensity and were fastest with use of the dominant eye, as might be expected, there was a subject-by-intensity and a subject-by-viewing condition interaction which was significant at less than .01. Even under these stringent, experimental conditions with trained observers, consistent individual differences in decision time emerged. Some adults make decisions quickly, others slowly (Minucci and Connors, 1964).

The evaluation dimension is relevant to all ages and can be assessed with a variety of instruments. Our discussion focuses on one series of related investigations with children that used the same instruments to index this dimension, called reflection-impulsivity.

The reflection-impulsivity dimension is concerned with the degree to which the subject reflects on the validity of his solution hypotheses in problems that contain response uncertainty. There are many test procedures that would be adequate indexes of this disposition. The specific test used most often is called Matching Familiar Figures. The child is asked to select one stimulus, from six variants, that is identical with the standard. Number of errors and response time to the first hypothesis are the two major variables coded. The is a clear and dramatic decrease in errors and a corresponding increase in response time with age, over the age range 5 to 11 years, in American children. Moreover, at every age there is a negative relation between response time and errors—usually ranging between −.40 and −.65 (Kagan, 1965a, 1965b, 1965c, 1966).

Reliability of Reflection-Impulsivity. The short-term stability of this dimension is illustrated in a study with second-grade children tested for 10 weeks in a row on variations of Matching Familiar Figures in which the number of variants was increased by one each week (Yando, 1968). The first week the child was shown a standard and two variants, the second week a standard and three variants, the third week a standard and four variants, and so on through ten tests, in the last of which the child was shown the standard and twelve variants. Looking at the response-time and error scores for children previously classified as reflective, impulsive, or neither, one finds a remarkable stability of the tendency to be reflective or impulsive. The average correlation for response time across the 10 weeks was .70. There is also good long-term continuity for the reflection-impulsivity classification. In one study, 104 boys and girls were individually administered one version of the MFF when they were in grades three or four and a different version one year later. The correlations between response time on the first and second administrations were high for both sexes and averaged .62. A second study of stability involved a group of 102 children who were given the Matching Familiar Figures Test in the spring of their first year in school and one year later were administered the same test again. The stability correlations for response time were .48 for boys and .52 for girls (Messer, 1968). The stability of response time over a period of 2½ years was .31. In general, the tendency to display fast or slow decision times to this response-uncertainty problem is relatively stable among young children over a short period of time and, as we shall see, generalizes to other tasks.

Generality of Reflection-Impulsivity across Tasks. Evidence for the consistency of this disposition can be seen in the cross-task generality of the tendency to be impulsive or reflective. The correlations between response time on the Matching Familiar Figures task and re-

sponse time on a Haptic-Visual Matching task were consistently high across many samples of children in the first three grades (Kagan, 1965c; Kagan et al., 1964). Correlations for response time on each task ranged from .61 to .87, with a median coefficient of .64. Comparable correlations were found in kindergarten children for two variants of the matching figures task (Ward, 1968b). It is important to note that there is generally a low, usually nonsignificant relation between language skills and this dimension. The correlation between response time and the verbal scale of the Wechsler Intelligence Scale for Children is usually under .20, but it is higher for girls than for boys. The tendency to show long versus short decision times in selection of a hypothesis also generalizes to tasks in which the child must generate his own alternative hypotheses. Inkline drawings of incongruous scenes were presented tachistoscopically to a group of young children in the second and third grades (Kagan, 1965a). The pictures were shown at increasing exposures for a minimum of 18 trials. Each child made a minimum of 108 descriptions across all 6 scenes, and the response latency from exposure of picture to first significant verbalization was recorded. The response time on the tachistoscopic recognition task was positively related to the response time on MFF ($r = .40$, $p < .01$ for 60 boys; $r = .40$, $p < .01$ for 53 girls).

Reflective and impulsive children behave differently in an interview in which they are answering an adult's questions. A group of 56 boys and 52 girls in the fourth and fifth grades were individually interviewed by a female adult about their hobbies, subjects in school, and favorite pastimes. A sample question would be, "What games do you like best to play?" or "What are you poorest at in school?" Most of the questions had some degree of uncertainty. The interview was tape recorded, and the tapes were scored for temporal delay between termination of the interviewer's question and the beginning of the child's reply for a series of 20 questions. The average delay score across the 20 questions was computed for each child, and this score correlated with measures of reflection-impulsivity gathered earlier. Correlations with response time on MFF were .30 for boys and .38 for girls ($p < .05$). In sum, there is some generalized tendency for a child to show long or short decision times across various kinds of problem situations that contain response uncertainty.

Reflection-Impulsivity and Recall. Impulsive children are likely to make errors of commission in a serial-recall task, which reflective children rarely do. In one study, over 200 third-grade children were assessed for their tendency to be reflective or impulsive using the Matching Familiar Figures task. Three months after this session, the children were seen for a serial-learning task in which lists containing 12 familiar words were read, and each child was asked to recall the words on the lists. Each subject was given two trials on each list; the second trial presented the words in an order that was an exact reverse of the first trial. After the first two lists, during which all subjects were treated alike, three different experimental treatments were created. One group, the threat group, was told that the first two lists did not count, and they would have to do very well on the next two lists, which were very difficult. The intent of this communication was to arouse anxiety over possible failure. The children in an adult rejection group were told that their performance was poor, and they would have to do better. The control group was told nothing. Two new lists were read to the children. Children in both anxiety conditions produced more errors of commission than those in the control condition. The impulsive children made many more errors of commission on both prethreat and post-threat lists. The reflective children who were made anxious over possible failure showed a larger increase in errors of commission than reflective children in the control group who showed the smallest increase in errors of commission. Thus anxiety as well as a disposition toward impulsivity lead to substitution of incorrect for correct elements in recall tasks (Kagan, 1966).

Decreases in an impulsive style of responding have been obtained by means of experimental instructions deliberately discouraging guessing under conditions of uncertainty. Gould and Stephenson (1967) read Bartlett's passage, "The War of the Ghosts," (Bartlett, 1932) to 75 adults and obtained recall under three different instructional sets. One group was instructed to "write down the story I've just read to you as exactly as you can." A second group was told to write down "as much as you can remember. Don't set down facts and incidents which were not in the original. Do not invent material to fill the gaps for the sake of being able to tell a complete story; leave blanks." A third group was told to write the story "as best as you can. Take care that each item you set down corresponds with something in the story, not word for word, but fact for fact. If you come to something you can't remember don't fill in to make a story of it; leave a blank. If you have doubt over an item, come down on the side of doubt, don't come down on the side of certainty." Later, each subject was read his own reproduction and was asked to indicate how certain he was of the elements he reproduced. Group one, which was not given any specific warning about inhibiting guesses, produced recalls with the greatest amount of error; there was no difference in error rate between groups two and three. Instructions to inhibit guesses reduced error rate dramatically.

Reflection-Impulsivity and Reading Prose. Reflective children make fewer errors in reading English prose than impulsive children (Kagan, 1965b). First-grade subjects (65 females and 65 males) were assigned to reflective or impulsive groups based on their performance on the Matching Familiar Figures task. They were then shown a card on which five words were printed. The examiner read one word aloud and asked the child to point to the single word on his card that matched the one that had been read. The longer the child delayed before offering a solution hypothesis on the Matching Familiar Figures task, the more accurate his initial recognition of the words spoken by the examiner. Although verbal ability predicted quality of performance, the relation between a reflective orientation and reading errors remained significant even after the influence of verbal skills had been partialled out ($r = .28$ for boys, $r = .28$ for girls; $p < .05$). The multiple correlation, using word errors as the criterion and verbal skills and response time as separate predictors, was .51 for boys and .59 for girls. When the correlations were computed separately for children high or low on verbal ability, the results were more dramatic for the high-verbal children. Among high-verbal children the correlations between response time on MFF and reading-word errors were $-.21$ for boys and

—.44 for girls, while the corresponding correlations for low-verbal children were —.14 for boys and —.21 for girls. The low-verbal children had acquired minimal reading skills, and therefore their delays and errors were less a function of response uncertainty than they were of conceptual deficit. This situation is analogous to asking the authors to write the equation describing the trajectory of Mariner IV. The ensuing delay reflects incompetence, not cautious brooding over a set of alternative answers. When these same children were seen one year later, in the spring of their second year of school, they were asked to read some prose paragraphs. The impulsive children made more errors than the reflective. The most frequent error was one in which the child articulated a word that had some graphemic similarity to the correct word—for example, reading nose for noise or truck for trunk (Kagan, 1965b).

Reflection-Impulsivity and Reasoning. The reflection-impulsivity dimension also influences quality of inductive reasoning. First-grade children previously classified as reflective or impulsive were given tests of inductive reasoning. For example, on one test the child was given three attributes of an object, and he had to guess the object (e.g., What is yellow, melts in the sun, and you eat it? What has doors, wheels, and moves?). In a second procedure, the child was shown three pictures in a fixed order that portrayed the beginning of a story sequence. He was then given four more pictures and asked to select the one picture (from the four) that illustrated the next thing to happen in the story. On both procedures the impulsive children responded more quickly and made more errors than the reflective children (Kagan, Pearson, and Welch, 1966a).

Reflection-Impulsivity and Tracking Patterns. Recent studies of the eye tracking patterns of reflective and impulsive children are consonant with the suggested interpretation of their molar behavior (Drake, 1967). Third-grade children, previously classified as reflective or impulsive under ordinary test conditions, took the Matching Familiar Figures Test while seated at a Mackworth eye camera so that their eye fixation patterns could be recorded on film. During the first 6 seconds of each test item, the reflective children made more homologous comparisons than the impulsive. A homologous comparison is a visual comparison of similar details across the variants (i.e., the dog's tail in variant 1 is compared with the tail in variant 2). If one examines the data during the time prior to the first response (which is longer for reflectives than for impulsives), reflective children covered more details in the pictures and scanned more variants. In effect, the reflective children made a more careful visual search of the standard and all four variants before they were willing to offer a response to the examiner. This molecular scanning behavior is congruent with their response-time and error scores (Drake, 1967).

In similar studies, fourth-grade boys were administered the Matching Familiar Figures Test in the following way. The standard and six variants were placed behind frosted glass compartments. For the child to view the stimuli, he had to press a manipulandum. Quantification of these instrumental responses permitted a rough reconstruction of his probable tracking behavior. The reflective child had longer average durations of looking for each visual opportunity, especially when looking at the variants. More important, however, the reflective children tended to examine all of the variants, whereas the impulsive boys looked at only one or two of them and then offered a solution hypothesis. The reflectives were cautious; the impulsive children adopted a much riskier strategy (Nelson, 1968; Sigelman, 1966).

In general, lower-class Negro children are more impulsive than middle-class Negro children, and lower-class Negro mothers are more impulsive than middle-class Negro mothers (Hess and Shipman, 1965). Several studies have shown a nonsignificant but suggestive trend toward greater impulsiveness for children who are low in intelligence but high on performance on the Wallach and Kogan (1965) creativity test procedures (Ward, 1966, 1968a).

Modification of Reflection-Impulsivity. Several studies indicate that the disposition to be reflective or impulsive can be modified. First-grade children were divided into training and control groups. The training consisted of requiring the children to inhibit a response for 15 seconds. After a few 30-minute training sessions, trained children exhibited longer response times to a strange examiner who did not impose any time constraints. However, error scores were not influenced to any appreciable degree by the training (Kagan, Pearson, and Welch, 1966b).

A training regimen that emphasizes accuracy only and ignores speed of response produces both longer response times and fewer errors in impulsive children (Nelson, 1968). Fourth-grade boys previously classified as reflective or impulsive on the MFF were trained to be more accurate in their selection of the correct variants, using geometric forms rather than pictures of familiar objects. Control subjects were exposed to the training apparatus and stimuli but experienced no training. After training, the impulsive boys showed marked increases in response time and marked decreases in errors, when contrasted with the untrained controls. The trained reflectives showed the same effects, but the differences were not as large.

In another extensive training study, fourth-grade children previously classified as reflective or impulsive were placed into one of three groups: trained to be reflective, trained to be impulsive, or trained to be neither. Reflective subjects trained to be reflective became slower than those trained to be impulsive, whereas impulsive children trained to be impulsive became faster. Each type of child was capable of modifying his preferred speed of responding. Moreover, error scores were affected in the expected direction (Briggs, 1966).

Debus (1968) attempted to modify response time through modeling procedures. A group of 100 third-grade children were assigned to one of four experimental modeling groups or a control group. The model was a sixth-grade child the same sex as the subject. The subject saw the model perform on 10 items of the Matching Familiar Figures Test. One group watched an impulsive model who showed latencies of 7 seconds. The second group watched a reflective model who showed latencies of 30 seconds. A third group watched a model behave impulsively for five items and then behave reflectively for the last five items. A fourth group was exposed to two models—one reflective and one impulsive. The fifth group, a control, watched no model at all.

The subjects were tested immediately following exposure to the model and tested again 2½ weeks later. The largest increase in response time on the immediate test occurred for children who had watched the reflective model (an increase of about 12 seconds). On the delayed test, 2½ weeks later, the boys who had watched a reflective model showed longer response times than all other groups. Among girls, exposure to any reflective model (group 2, 3, or 4) led to increased response times on the delayed test, whereas the controls and the subjects exposed to the impulsive model were markedly faster. Exposure to a reflective model led to slower response times for all subjects, with girls being more influenced than boys by any exposure to a reflective performance. As in earlier studies, errors were not changed, despite the increase in response time (Debus, 1968).

A similar finding in a more naturalistic setting has implications for the educational establishment. Each of 20 first-grade teachers was classified as reflective or impulsive using an adult version of the Matching Familiar Figures Test. A random sample of subjects from each of the 20 classrooms was tested in the early fall and then again in the late spring to determine if exposure to a teacher with a preferred strategy influenced the child's tempo. The children changed in a direction consonant with the teacher's tempo, the effect being most marked for impulsive boys assigned to a classroom with experienced reflective teachers. These boys showed the greatest increase in response time from fall to spring (Yando and Kagan, 1968).

The Dynamics of Reflection-Impulsivity. The tendency to be reflective or impulsive is stable over both time and tasks and is somewhat modifiable. How can we conceptualize the psychological bases for this disposition? As with most behaviors, it is likely that a reflective or impulsive attitude can be in the service of several different forces.

One dynamic could be based on the assumption that a strong motive to appear competent may prompt too rapid a conclusion. Since our culture generally equates speed of thinking with intelligence, a person who required validation of his intellectual competence would be predisposed to produce answers quickly. This tendency should be strongest in those who had some doubt of their ability and, in addition, were anxious over this deviation from a standard. Thus a child who doubted his ability, but wished to deny this doubt, would behave impulsively. A child with a strong fear of failure, and no strong tendency to disguise it, is likely to become reflective. A child with minimal anxiety from either source would be neither extremely reflective nor extremely impulsive. An impulsive or reflective strategy can be the result of anxiety, but the source of anxiety is different in the two types of child. For the reflective, the source of anxiety derives from the expectation that the social environment will regard the person as incompetent because he has made a mistake. For the impulsive, the source of anxiety derives from the expectation that he will be judged incompetent if he responds too slowly. The difference hangs on the behaviors that will be judged negatively.

It is possible that this difference in personal definition of competence and the subsequent differences in strategy have historical links during the preschool years. The child who experienced continual emphasis on avoidance of error (i.e., he was praised for inhibiting asocial behavior) would define adult approval and positive self-evaluation in terms of *inhibition of inappropriate behavior*. The child whose experience emphasized success (i.e., praise for successful walking, climbing, and talking) might define adult approval and competence in terms of success at difficult tasks, that is, in terms of active accomplishment rather than inhibition of the inappropriate. The child who experienced reward for success may set up an unrealistic standard for level of competence required for approval and be pushed constantly to action, often impulsive in nature, in order to attenuate the anxiety over the thought, "I may not be competent."

A simpler dynamic, to which we feel more friendly and for which the evidence is much better, suggests that the greater the fear of making a mistake, the more reflective and cautious the performance. Minimal anxiety over a potentially inaccurate answer is likely to be a primary determinant of an impulsive performance. Reflectives seem to be overly concerned with making a mistake and wish to avoid error at all costs. Impulsives seem minimally apprehensive about error and consequently respond quickly. It will be recalled that impulsive subjects did not scan all the alternatives before offering a solution hypothesis and reported words that they did not hear in a serial recall procedure.

A recent study lends the strongest support to this notion. Third-grade boys initially categorized as reflective or impulsive on the basis of their time and error scores on the Matching Familiar Figures Test were assigned to one of three experimental groups. Those in a "failure" induction group were administered a difficult anagrams test and led to believe they had performed poorly. A "success" group was administered the same anagrams test but was led to believe those in the group had performed well. A control group experienced neither success nor failure. Immediately after the manipulation, each child was administered a new version of the Matching Familiar Figures Test and changes in response time and errors were recorded for each group.

The impulsive and the reflective boys in the success group showed a decreased response time on the posttest; the failure and the control groups showed an increased response time. An independent study revealed that the control group interpreted the second administration of the Matching Familiar Figures Test as indicating that they must have performed poorly on the first administration. Thus the children who were likely to be most anxious over the quality of their intellectual performance showed the largest increases in response time. Moreover, the subjects who showed an increased response time also displayed a decrease in errors on the posttest; the children who did not display an increase in response time made more errors on the posttest (Messer, 1968).

A cross-cultural study of developmental changes in decision times to the Matching Familiar Figures Test furnishes important indirect support for the relevance of anxiety over error. Mayan Indian children (5, 6, and 7 years of age) living in small villages in Guatemala were administered a culturally appropriate version of the Matching Familiar Figures Test along with a battery of other tests (R. Klein and O. Gilbert, personal communication). Although quality of immediate memory, Embedded Figures Test performance, and vocabulary scores all increased with age, there were no significant changes in response time or error scores on the Matching Familiar Figures Test across the age period of 5, 6, and 7 years. Moreover, the mean response times were well under 5 seconds. Comparable data gathered on American children during this age period indicate dramatic increases in response time with age and corresponding decreases in errors. Close observation of these Guatemalan children during testing suggested that they persisted in coping with the task, but they showed minimal signs of disturbance or anxiety in the face of failure. American children tend to become resistant and restless when they fail one or two items on any test and often withdraw from the task after several failures. The Indian children showed neither signs of task withdrawal nor any evidence of distress when they failed. Their relatively fast decision times were accompanied by evidence of little anxiety over error. This minimal anxiety may in fact account for the fast performance in the sample studied.

Similar conclusions can be drawn from a study by Weintraub comparing normal, hyperaggressive, and overly inhibited 11-year-old boys from middle- and lower-class backgrounds (S. Weintraub, personal communication). The effect of type of pathology was more important than social class. The boys with externally directed symptoms (aggression, lying, cheating, delinquency) were dramatically more impulsive on the Matching Familiar Figures Test than the children who showed internalized symptoms (fears, phobias, signs of guilt). The preferred interpretation of the difference between an internalizing or an externalizing symptomatology hinges on the excessive fear and anxiety over adult disapproval characteristic of the internalizing children, contrasted with the minimal fear of violating social norms characteristic of the externalizing children. The fact that the externalizing boys were more impulsive than their internalizing counterparts is persuasive support for our interpretation of the reflection-impulsivity dimension.

Moreover, the developmental increase in a reflective strategy among American children is accompanied by a change in the more general disposition to grow more cautious with age, i.e., to become increasingly concerned with avoiding a mistake. Draguns and Multari (1961) showed children in grades 1, 3, 5, and 7 an ambiguous picture and then gradually added clues which decreased the ambiguity of the stimulus. The younger children offered guesses early, whereas the older children were cautious and inhibited hypotheses until they were more certain of the accuracy of their response. Similar results are reported by Mosher and Hornsby and by Potter (in Bruner et al., 1966) as well as by Westcott (1968).

Is the age-related increase in caution, as reflected in avoiding mistakes and inhibiting hypotheses, also found in risk-taking behavior conceived more generally? Kass (1964) obtained no age differences between 6-, 8-, and 10-year-olds in a "pay to play" gambling situation. Cohen (1960), on the other hand, reported very substantial differences in risk taking between 9-, 12-, and 15-year-olds in a gambling context with candy as the incentive. The decline in risk taking with age in Cohen's work may, however, simply reflect the lesser incentive value of candy for the older children. Sex differences in risk taking (under gambling conditions), in favor of boys, have been observed by Kass (1964) in the 6 to 10 age range and by Slovic (1966) in the 11 to 16 age range. A comprehensive review of age and sex differences in risk taking is available in Kogan and Wallach (1967).

It should be emphasized that test anxiety as conceptualized and measured by Sarason, Davidson, Lighthall, Waite, and Ruebush (1960) is not synonymous with what we have called anxiety over error. Typically, scores on test anxiety questionnaires are not correlated with long decision times or errors in tasks with response uncertainty and do not predict the phenomena that are correlated with a reflective attitude (see Messer, 1968; Palermo, 1961; Phillips, King, and McGuire, 1959).

Review of the literature (Ruebush, 1963) relating test anxiety to intellectual performance suggests consistently negative ($r =$ $-.20$ to $-.30$) correlations between scores on test anxiety questionnaires and verbal IQ tests or tests of verbal ability. The correlation between test anxiety and either intelligence or achievement test performance is fairly low in the primary grades, increasing with grade level (Hill and Sarason, 1966; Sarason, Hill, and Zimbardo, 1964). Typically, there is no consistently reliable relation between test anxiety and scores on tests that minimize the verbal component of performance. Stevenson and Odom (1965) correlated test anxiety scores with children's performance on a variety of learning and problem-solving tasks. There was no relation between test anxiety and ease of discrimination learning, but a negative correlation between test anxiety and performance on such verbal tasks as paired associates and anagrams. The index of reflection-impulsivity does not involve verbal processes, and perhaps that is the reason for the minimal relation between test anxiety scores and the reflection-impulsivity dimension.[8]

Consider, finally, the matter of sex differences and attitude toward error. Sex differences in level of performance on varied intellectual tasks are less common than sex differences in the pattern of relations among performances. Lewis, Rausch, Goldberg, and Dodd (1968), for example, found no sex differences in mean response time or error scores on a test of reflection-impulsivity; but they found errors to be more strongly related to IQ in girls than in boys, and more strongly related to response times in boys than in girls. Maccoby (1966) has prepared a most valuable summary of the literature on sex differences. She proposes an integrative hypothesis in which a personality dimension of inhibition-impulsiveness is presumed to be curvilinearly related to quality of intellectual performance. Boys and girls occupy different positions on this dimension as indicated in Fig. 1 (from Maccoby, 1966). Extremely inhibited girls and extremely impulsive boys give the poorest performance. Girls must become less inhibited and boys more inhibited in order to

[8] Kimble and Posnick's (1967) demonstration of a high positive correlation between the test anxiety score and a score on a comparable scale in which all semantic references to anxiety were deleted highlights the enigma of the anxiety construct.

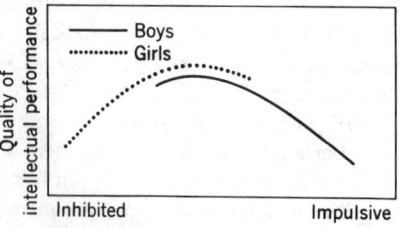

Fig. 1. Relative positions of girls and boys on a hypothesized personality dimension, running from inhibited to impulsive, which is curvilinearly related to quality of intellectual performance.

increase the quality of their performance on most intellectual tests. Existing research generally supports this hypothesis, for one finds that boys are usually more willing to tolerate the risk of error than girls (see Wallach and Caron, 1959). Maccoby's hypothesis implies that when sex differences occur for particular intellectual performances, they may be the result of differences in attitude toward error, rather than differences in decoding, memory capacity, or hypothesis generation. Sex differences in these latter functions, when observed, may in fact be linked to a "cautiousness" vector.

The Role of Evaluation in Decision-Making Tasks. Many experimental tasks and procedures involve evaluation in the sense described previously, although this may not be apparent from the title of the construct cited in the published report (see fn. 5). Age differences in performance on these procedures may, in some instances, be partially influenced by the increase with age in a reflective strategy. This suggestion may help to explain puzzling differences in susceptibility to illusions. Some illusions, like the Ponzo, increase with age; others, like the Poggendorff, decrease with age (Leibowitz and Gwozdecki, 1967; Parrish, Lundy, and Leibowitz, 1968). It is suggested that the nature of the Ponzo illusion is such that the closer you attend to the stimulus, the *greater* the illusory effect. The nature of the Poggendorff illusion is such that the closer you attend to the stimulus materials, the *less* the illusory effect (see Fig. 2).

In a recent study (Parrish, Lundy, and Leibowitz, 1968), adults were hypnotically age regressed to age 5 and were then administered the Ponzo and Poggendorff illusions. These regressed adults performed as children 5 to 10 years typically perform. The authors' preferred interpretation is that the perceptual process was altered by the hypnotic regression. However, it is possible that the regression merely created a set to respond impulsively. In the administration of the Ponzo illusion one vertical line remained fixed at 10.16 centimeters, while the second line (closer to the point of convergence) varied in length from 6.35 to 12.70 centimeters in 0.32-centimeter steps. The subject had to state which line was longer. An impulsive strategy might predispose a subject to alternate his answers from one line to another. Such

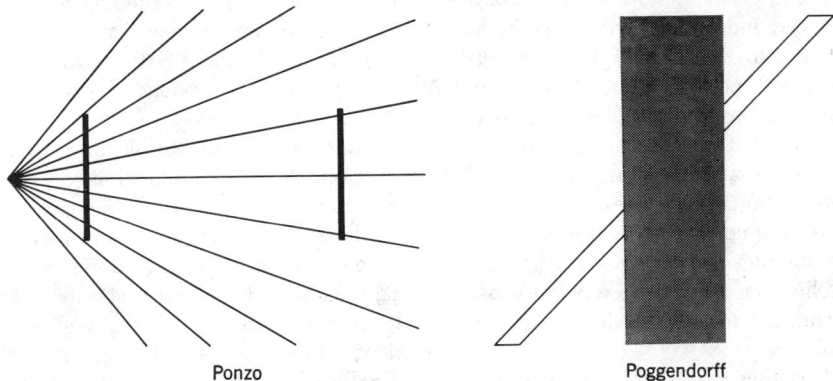

Ponzo   Poggendorff

Fig. 2.   In the Ponzo illusion the vertical lines are equal but appear to be unequal. In the Poggendorff illusion the diagonal portion is physically continuous but appear to be discontinuous.

a strategy would make him appear as if he did not experience the illusion as strongly as a subject who compared each stimulus carefully.

In the Poggendorff illusion the subject was required to adjust a bar so that the right half of the diagonal was in line with the left half. An impulsive person would not check his adjustment carefully, and hence might show an exaggerated illusion. The suggestion that these illusion results might be products of evaluation strategy rather than basic changes in perceptual processing is presented only as a possible interpretation. The intention is to alert the reader to at least consider the potential role of this dimension in all problem-solving contexts where the child must make a decision.

Relation of Reflection-Impulsivity to Early Behaviors. Although anxiety over error is believed to be the primary incentive for a reflective strategy, there is a possibility that other factors can contribute to this disposition. It is of interest, moreover, to inquire into the early history of this disposition. How early can one detect and predict the signs of future reflectivity or impulsivity?

The Matching Familiar Figures Test (or any similar task involving uncertainty) may top two different components: anxiety over error, on the one hand, and a dimension called "tempo of information processing," on the other. Some people appear to process information rapidly; others process information slowly, even in situations where the negative sanctions of public failure are lifted. The fast-

processing individual may actually assimilate more information per unit of time, or it may be that he only *appears* to process faster. He may be processing less minutely, matching to a grosser and less perfect standard, and therefore finishing in less time. One analogy uses the image of an electronic scanner programmed to locate all the combinations AB in a text. It could finish the task faster if it only searched for As rather than ABs and tallied a find each time. The fast rate would be the result of a looser standard of detection. Hence many false positives would be noted.

At the moment, there are not sufficient data to postulate a construct of "tempo of processing," independent of anxiety over error, that influences decision time. Moreover, even if this idea were viable, it is not clear whether the tempo differences are due to faster rates of processing or lower standards of detection. With this apology behind us, let us consider some data suggesting that something like a tempo dimension may exist during infancy and show predictive validity to the reflection-impulsivity dimension tested during the school years.

One argument for the existence of differences in tempo of processing is contained in the dramatic variation in rate of habituation to visual or auditory stimuli. Young infants show differential rates of habituation to visual stimuli such as representations of human faces, randomly generated nonsense designs, and novel mobiles. Rapid habituation to the faces could be the result of a firmer schema of the face. The closer the match of stimulus to schema, the faster should be the habituation. However, individual differences in rate of habituation to the meaningless geometric designs or novel mobiles cannot be explained as a result of differential familiarity. It is unlikely that any of the infants had prior schemata for these novel stimuli. The rapidly habituating infants either established firm schemata for the novel stimuli at a faster rate, or their processing was less analytic (i.e., the internal schemata they created were grosser than the ones created by the slow habituating infants).

These hypotheses resemble those used in discussing the reflection-impulsivity dimension. It was suggested that impulsives either processed faster or had a grosser standard of equivalence. Would it be possible to obtain an early preview of the disposition to be reflective or impulsive at age 3 or 4 years from habituation rates during the first year? Preliminary data lend some tentative support to this idea.

As part of an ongoing longitudinal study by Kagan and his colleagues, 150 infants have been seen at ages 4, 8, 13, and 27 months. At 4 months, the infants viewed 16 presentations of 4 achromatic faces. Some children showed a rapid habituation of fixation time; others showed a more gradual habituation. At 8 months, the boys who had previously been rapid habituators showed a pattern of play with toys that can be characterized as having many short involvements. The slow habituating boys showed fewer, but longer involvements with the same toys. Rate of habituation at 4 months predicted tempo of play at 8 months. Moreover, boys who showed a fast tempo of play with the toys at both 8 and 13 months (many short involvements) were less attentive to visual stimuli at both these ages and more vigorous and excitable at 4 months. This evidence suggests the operation of a tempo factor (manifested in rate of satiation with toys and rate of habituation to visual stimuli) that is stable during the first year of life.

Some of these boys ($N = 52$) have been assessed at 27 months of age. The 27-month assessment variables include tempo of play with toys and decision times to two problem situations that contain response uncertainty (i.e., a specially devised embedded-figures test and a perceptual-conflict procedure).

There were positive intercorrelations (Reppucci, 1968) among decision times on the two response-uncertainty tasks and a slow tempo of play (i.e., long epochs of involvement with the toys).

Moreover, the 2-year-old boys who showed long epochs of attentional involvement in a particular activity, in contrast to those who displayed short-duration involvements, showed a slower tempo of play at 8 months and more rapid habituation to visual stimuli at 4 months. In this analysis, the duration of each attentional involvement with an object at 27 months of age was quantified, and each child's distribution of time scores was cast into a frequency distribution. The seventy-fifth percentile (Q_3) value was chosen as the index of tempo of play. The range of seventy-fifth percentile values was from 30 to 187 seconds. For the total group of 52, there was a positive relation between slow tempo of play at 8 and 27 months ($\chi^2 = 3.8$, $p < .05$). When the 10 boys with the largest Q_3 values were compared with the 10 boys with the smallest Q_3 values (slow versus fast tempo), more of the slow tempo boys had a small number of act changes at 8 months of age ($p < .01$, exact test). The median value was 11 act changes for the slow tempo boys versus 30 act changes for the fast tempo boys at 8 months. More dramatic, however, is the fact that the 10 slow tempo boys showed a shallower habituation function for first fixation to achromatic faces at 4 months than did the fast tempo boys (see Fig. 3). These data give tentative support to the possibility that during the first year of life a tempo dimension is present which remains, at least for boys on the extremes of the dimension, somewhat stable throughout the second year.

The independent work of Pedersen and Wender (1968) is also supportive. Children 2½ years old were observed in a nursery school setting and were evaluated on their tendency to show long periods of attentional involvement with toys. (This variable is very similar to the one coded in the play behavior at 27 months.) Four years later, when these children were about 6½ years of age, each was administered the verbal and performance scales from the Wechsler Intelligence Scale for Children. The children who had shown prolonged periods of involvement with toys in the nursery school setting (i.e., slow tempo)

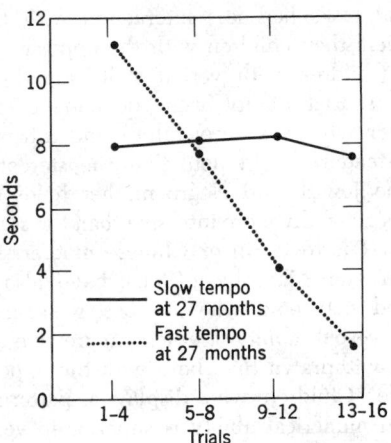

Fig. 3. Differences in habituation of fixation time at 4 months for extreme groups on the tempo dimension at 27 months (boys). (First fixation to achromatic faces at 4 months.)

performed better on the subtests that contained some response uncertainy (e.g., Picture Arrangement, Mazes) than the children who had shown short involvements. However, there were no differences between the two groups on the verbal scales. A slow tempo of play at 2½ years predicted a reflective attitude at age 6. Our longitudinal data suggest a positive relation between slow tempo of play and a reflective attitude at 2 years.

These data are still far from conclusive, but they offer some credibility to the hypothesis that children differ in the tempo of processing. Slow tempo children are more likely to become reflective; fast tempo children are more likely to become impulsive. The early display of these behaviors could be completely the product of differential experience, or it could be the partial product of biological differences among the infants. There is some reason to suspect that the differences in tempo and inhibition may have a genetic basis. For example, among 4-month-old males, the slow habituating infants tend to be larger, fatter, and smile more frequently than fast habituating infants. In addition, both body size and frequency of smiling during the first half year display greater similarity between monozygotic than between dizygotic twins. Further, two behavioral genetic studies implicate a tempo dimension. In one study, monozygotic and dizygotic boys and girls were observed in a free play situation at 8 months of age.

The tendency to show very few or many act changes during the opening 4 minutes of play —which is a partial index of inhibition— showed heritability (C. M. Reppucci, personal communication). In a second study, 61 pairs of identical and fraternal twin girls, aged 6 to 10 years, were observed in two experimental games and were interviewed. One of the critical variables was the time required for the child to decide which toy she wanted to play with after the testing session was over. The tendency to display short or long response times in this uncertain situation showed the best evidence of heritability. An overall rating of apprehensiveness (which was based, in part, on the response times) yielded an intraclass correlation of .88 for the monozygotic twins, but only .28 for the dizygotic twins (Scarr, 1966). Future studies will judge the fruitfulness of the idea that a disposition toward inhibition has a heritable basis. Existing information does not allow us to reject this notion out of hand (Gottesman, 1963).

Implementation of Hypotheses—The Deductive Phase

The complementary processes of "induction" and "deduction" have always been at the heart of cognitive work. Guilford (1959), among others, has emphasized the differential factorial structure of these two components of thought. On the other hand, in the natural sequence of thinking, the induction of similarities and hypotheses and the deduction of conclusions occur in close temporal contiguity, each nurturing the other. The induction that both air and ocean have permanent, spatially located currents, for example, is likely to be followed by the deduction that each flows in a preferred direction, each has turbulence, and each influences the weather. Of course, adequate deductive products also necessarily require a rich knowledge of rules.

A provocative example of individual differences in deductive problem solving is contained in a study of ethnic differences in profile of intellectual skills (Lesser, Fifer, and Clark, 1965). First-grade children from four ethnic groups in New York City (Chinese, Jewish, Negro, and Puerto Rican) were administered four tests: verbal ability, reasoning, number facility, and space conceptualization. Lower-class children in all four ethnic groups had significantly poorer performances on all tasks than the middle-class children, but the profile of scores on the four tests was different for each of the ethnic groups. Although Jewish and Chinese children performed better than Negro and Puerto Rican children on most tests, the ipsative profiles were different. Jewish children gave their best performance on the verbal test and their poorest performance on the test of spatial ability. Chinese children showed the opposite pattern, performing poorly on the verbal test and best on the spatial test. The two less adequate groups—the Puerto Rican and Negro children —also differed from each other. The Negro pattern resembled that of the Jewish children —higher on verbal ability than on the other tests. The Puerto Rican child was lower on verbal ability than on the other skills. It is important to note that the profiles for each ethnic group were similar for both the lower- and middle-class children of that ethnic group, attesting to the importance of the genetic and experiential factors that are linked with ethnicity. This study was replicated in Boston (with Chinese and Negro children) with remarkably similar results.

There are at least two possible environmental interpretations of these provocative and consistent ethnic differences. One interpretation is that the Puerto Rican and Chinese children were exposed to a second language in the home, whereas the Negro and Jewish children were not. The former groups therefore might perform more poorly on verbal tests as a result of the interference produced by the language environment. A second and less likely interpretation assumes, first, that the vocabulary test had less response uncertainty than the reasoning, spatial, and number tests; and, second, that the Negro and Jewish children were temperamentally more impulsive than Chinese or Puerto Ricans. In this case, the pattern of findings could be explained as a result of differences in impulsivity among the ethnic groups.

Role of Family Experiences on Implementation. Some investigators have explored possible familial experiences associated with differential problem-solving abilities on verbal or spatial tasks. Freeberg and Payne (1967) have prepared a review of this literature. Bing (1963) found that fifth-grade children who were much better on spatial than on verbal tasks had less interaction with their mothers than children with the opposite profile. Children with verbal skills superior to their spatial ability were dependent on a mother who was acceleratory and intrusive. The reader should note that the stereotype of the Jewish and Negro mother holds that she is generally more intrusive than the stereotyped Puerto Rican or Chinese mother. Ferguson and Maccoby (1966) have also reported that boys who are better in spatial than verbal ability are less aggressive and more withdrawn than boys with the opposite profile. Children who display a pattern in which numerical ability is superior to verbal or spatial skills tend to be popular and well liked (Ferguson and Maccoby, 1966) and are assertive and self-confident (D'Heurle, Mellinger, and Haggard, 1959). Thus there is some concordance among the few studies that have investigated the relation among family experience, intellectual skills, and personality. It would appear that children who are more highly skilled on spatial than verbal tasks are more withdrawn and less aggressive than their age-mates, whereas those who are more highly skilled on verbal tasks tend to be more dependent than their peers.

Influence of Content and Mode of Presentation of the Problem. Personality factors are likely to influence quality of deductive sequences when the content of the problem has differential motivational relevance for the person. For example, Milton (1957, 1958) has found that college females perform better on deductive problems requiring arithmetic reasoning if the content of the question refers to feminine objects (i.e., deals with gardens and pies rather than guns and planets).

As with generation of hypotheses and concept sorting, the quality of deductive products is likely to be influenced by the mode of presentation of the problem. Since many deductive problems require the child to manipulate several bits of information, it is probable that oral versus written presentation will be an important determinant of quality of answers. Donaldson (1963) administered various deductive problems (e.g., matching, seriation) to children 10 to 14 years of age. An example is the following problem.

Five boys, Jack, Dick, James, Bob, and Tom go to five different schools in the same town. The schools are called North School, South School, East School, West School, and Central School. Jack does not go to North, South, or Central School. Dick goes to West School. Bob does not go to North or Central School. Tom has never been inside Central School. Which school does Jack go to?

The problem was *read* to the child, but he could take notes if he wished. Donaldson analyzed the errors and reports of the children and attempted to diagnose the causes of the mistakes. Some children did not understand the problem; others were impulsive and did not check the validity of their final solution; others had difficulty with the negation in the problem. But the most frequent cause of error was a memory failure—the child had forgotten elements of the problem. If the problem had been presented in written form, it is likely that this cause of failure would have been eliminated.

The importance of mode of presentation has relevance to Piaget's assertion that children under 7 or 8 cannot perform class inclusion or seriation problems (Inhelder and Piaget, 1964). These problems are usually *read* aloud to the child. In order to solve the *simplest* class inclusion problem the child must hold in memory a minimum of *three* elements. It is possible that one basis for immature answers on these problems is memory failure.[9]

The number of bits of information that can be held in immediate memory increases with age over the period 3 to 10 years. It is reasonable to suppose that one of the many determinants of the "inferior" performance of preschool or kindergarten-age children on seriation and class inclusion problems is memory failure. Presentation modes that give the child continuous access to the elements of the problem might yield different results.

[9] One of the authors has collected unpublished data on 6-year-old children in the first grade who were administered the following class inclusion problem: "There are 13 boys and 10 girls in the class. Are there more boys or more children?" When the problem was administered orally, less than 10% gave the answer, "More children." When the problem was presented in written form so that the child had access to all elements of the problem as long as he wished, 70% said, "More children."

We may conclude from this discussion that the answer produced by the child is a resultant of diverse forces. An incorrect answer could be the result of defective encoding of the problem, a failure in memory, generation of an incorrect solution hypothesis, insufficient evaluation of a solution hypothesis, inability to apply the proper deductive rule, or combinations of these failures. The nature of the final report does not typically provide information on its construction. Let us consider, in a bit more detail, the meaning of the "final answer."

The Significance of Public Performance

An answer—spoken, written, drawn, or acted out in gesture—is the datum from which we ordinarily infer cognitive process. The discussion thus far has been concerned primarily with the private mental processes of encoding, memory, generation of hypotheses, evaluation, and deduction. Psychology uses public performance to make wise guesses about these processes. This brief section addresses itself directly to the relation of performance to these cognitive constructs. How faithful is the public response to the inferred cognitive structure? Among the psycholinguists, this issue takes the form of the difference between linguistic competence and language performance. The transformational grammarian is concerned primarily with competence and often seems too little concerned with language behavior. At one extreme, it is acknowledged that absence of a particular performance is always ambiguous as to meaning and cannot be taken as a reflection of the presence or absence of a structure. But once a behavior occurs it is natural to ask what structure it serves or represents. If a child says "sheeps" for "sheep," or "wented" instead of "went," does this error necessarily mean that he could not tell you that "went" is correct and "wented" incorrect?

In many instances, incorrect performance does not signify deficient cognitions. Consider an extreme example. If a child of 4 is asked to draw a man as faithfully as possible, he is likely to draw the man's arms attached to the head. However, if the child is shown a drawing of a well-formed man and a drawing of one with arms emanating from the head and is asked to point to "the man," the child quickly points to the correct representation.

Competence leads performance. At a less obvious level, some psychologists assume that if the child cannot reproduce a nonsense design (e.g., an item from the Bender-Gestalt Test), he must have a perceptual deficit. However, Birch and Lefford (1967) have shown, in elegant fashion, that a child who cannot reproduce a design has no trouble identifying the correct design when it is presented along with a group of similar ones. Maccoby and Bee (1965) have also addressed themselves to this issue.

In the Birch-Lefford work, children 5 to 11 years of age were asked to reproduce triangles and diamonds under five different conditions, ranging from no visual support to considerable visual support. As expected, the quality of these reproductions increased with age. These children were also given a series of purely perceptual tasks, where they had to match a geometric form to a standard (perceptual analysis) or judge the equivalence of a geometric form with a set of its component elements (perceptual synthesis). Performance on both perceptual tasks increased with age. However, the correlations, at any age, between each of the two perceptual performances and quality of reproduction were about .20 or lower. The ability, or inability, to draw a simple geometric form is relatively independent of the ability to discriminate it from a set of similar forms—that is, to perceive it correctly. The goal-directed motor action is not a faithful index of cognitive competence. Of course, when age groups were pooled, a positive association emerged between quality of reproduction and perceptual performance. But these positive correlations are likely to be a derivative of more central growth parameters that produce increases in quality of all performances. This study provides the best empirical demonstration of the fact that perceptual-motor performance or graphic reproduction of events provides a distorted view of cognitive competence, in much the same manner that quality of speech is unfaithful to richness of thought.

Children also differ in their preferred behavioral reaction to difficult problem situations. Some persist, whereas others directly refuse to go on with the tasks, still others become quietly passive and neither speak nor act. A recent study of 3-year-olds compared lower-class Puerto Rican children with middle-class Caucasian children (Hertzig et al., 1968). There were two interesting differences between the groups in their behavioral reaction to intellectual problems. The middle-class children were more likely to work at a problem than the Puerto Rican children. Moreover, when problems became difficult, the middle-class children were more likely to overtly shake their heads, say they couldn't do it, or push the material away. The Puerto Rican children frequently sat passively, saying or doing nothing. These behavioral differences held, even when pairs of children were matched on intellectual ability. Differences in quality or style of public performance, although striking, may be misleading indexes of competence. These isolated examples may be the rule rather than exceptions.

Another category of behavior includes spontaneous responses to external stimuli, sometimes called released behaviors by comparative psychologists. A child hits a ball, grasps a mallet, pounds clay, or smears paint. These behaviors are not untarnished reflections of cognitive structure, for each is fitted specifically to the target stimulus. The hitting of the ball with the full hand, the grasping of the mallet, and the pounding of the clay may be of the same dynamic significance. Each appears different to the observer because the act must be accommodated to the external object. Each behavior is a result of cognitive structure and immediate context. In order to infer the nature of the structure one has to separate and assess these vectors, a task for which psychology does not yet possess sufficiently sensitive procedures.

In sum, the child's drawings, speech, and test responses are under the supervision of many factors. A careless attitude toward a drawing can yield a poor reproduction; an inability to coordinate lines can yield a gross distortion of a public event; immature syntax can destroy effective communication of a well-formed idea. Psychology is forced to remain tied to public behavior as the major data base for inferring cognitive structure. Test performance is the combined result of motivation, language, expectancy of success, preferred strategies for perceptual analysis, and reflection-impulsivity, to name only a few. Without separate controls (statistical or experimental) or independent assessments of these constructs, the final performance is an indeterminate index of each of them, or, in other words, a unique composite of them all.[10] The invention of analytic procedures for separate evaluation of the qualitatively different components of a public performance deserves the highest priority in the future.

Field Dependence-Independence

Although we have referred to the work of the Witkin group in passing, its coherence, influence, and scope warrant detailed treatment. In many respects, Witkin's research can be considered the most serious attempt at construct validation with respect to a dimension of cognitive functioning. The following sections discuss the research in the Witkin tradition with special emphasis upon the criterion measures, developmental changes, relationships with ability indices, body concept, sex differences, personality correlates, social behavior, antecedents in parent-child interaction, and cross-cultural evidence.

Criterion Measures. The Witkin group has relied heavily on three procedures for assessing an individual's level of field independence-dependence, alternatively called field articulation-diffuseness, analytic-global functioning, psychological differentiation.[11] These

[10] This dilemma is inherent in all the empirical sciences. The notion that a physical measurement always invokes the disturbance of the quantity being measured has long been appreciated in physics and found its most classic expression in Heisenberg's law of indeterminacy. However, earlier in the century there was considerable resistance to this idea.

[11] We shall use the various labels interchangeably with the exception of "psychological differentiation," which reflects a particular theoretical conception of the phenomena under investigation, whereas the other constructs are more operationally descriptive and more directly tied to the actual performance of the subjects. Since there is considerable controversy and ambiguity surrounding the construct of differentiation, the acceptance of Witkin's conceptualization would clearly prejudge the issue. It should be further noted that Witkin's research on analytic functioning can be distinguished from that of Kagan (as discussed previously) with regard to both conceptualization and measurement procedures. A critical discussion of these differences can be found in Wallach (1962). Empirical evidence has been obtained on adult subjects, suggesting that Witkin's EFT measure may relate to analytic

three procedures are the Body Adjustment Test (BAT), the Rod-and-Frame Test (RFT), and the Embedded Figures Test (EFT). They constitute the core of Witkin's assessment program. We shall describe them in summary form. Detailed descriptions of the three procedures are available in the two Witkin et al. (1954, 1962) volumes.[12]

In the case of the Body Adjustment Test (BAT), the subject is seated in a tilted chair within a tilted room, and his task is to adjust his chair to the true vertical while the room remains tilted. The deviation of the chair's adjusted position from the true upright constitutes the subject's score.

In the Rod-and-Frame Test (RFT), the subject is seated in a completely darkened room facing a luminous rod suspended within a luminous frame. The subject is required to adjust the rod to the true vertical, when his body is tilted or upright, and when the rod and frame are tilted in the same or opposite directions. The subject's score is the extent of absolute deviation of the rod setting from the true upright.

Finally, the Embedded Figures Test (EFT) consists of a series of complex geometric figures in which a series of simple figures is embedded. The test derives from an earlier instrument (Gottschaldt, 1926), but Witkin has made his test more difficult by superimposing colored patterns over the simpler achromatic Gottschaldt figures. The subject's score on the EFT represents the mean amount of time required to locate each of the simple figures.

Scores derived from the BAT, RFT, and EFT satisfy most psychometric standards for reliability. Split-half reliabilities have ranged in the low 80s to high 90s, and test-retest data over a period of 3 years have produced reliability coefficients ranging from the 60s to the 80s.

A more fundamental question concerns the

functioning in Kagan's sense for those tasks (e.g., conceptual learning) where analytic functioning is required for good performance, but not for those tasks (e.g., sorting) in which it is a stylistic preference (Messick and Fritzky, 1963; Wachtel, 1968).

[12] Sometimes the Figure Drawing Test is treated as a criterial measure, at other times as a correlate. For our purposes, the test will be considered a correlate in the domain of body-image.

relationships among the three indices of field dependence. Recent evidence (Witkin, Goodenough, and Karp, 1967) has indicated a substantial level of consistency for cross-sectional groups (age 8 to 21). The vast number of significantly positive correlations found in this work provides considerable justification for combining the three separate indices into a composite perceptual index. This procedure is typically followed in the work of the Witkin group.

This procedure may not be justifiable in non-Western cultures, however. Wober (1966, 1967) found no relation between EFT and RFT performances in Nigerian men. This result is explained on the basis of American-African differences in "sensotypes." West African cultures place less emphasis upon visual analysis than do Western cultures and concentrate more on the proprioceptive skills involved in dancing and other forms of physical expressiveness. Since the RFT has proprioceptive features, whereas the EFT is strictly visual, the RFT may be a better index of analytic ability in certain West African cultures. In the Wober studies, RFT performance was significantly related to "job efficiency," whereas the EFT was related to educational level. The last relation reflects the test-like properties of the EFT. Consistent with Wober's observations of Nigerians are Gruen's (1955) findings on professional American dancers. For the latter group, RFT measures with a proprioceptive component—that is, with body tilted—were unrelated to EFT scores.

Nevertheless, the measures developed by Witkin and his associates are reliable and cohere with one another in unselected American subjects. This raises the important issue of the psychological basis for the coherence. A series of alternative explanatory constructs has been proposed, with all but one eventually being rejected on empirical grounds. Thus Witkin has offered evidence against interpretations based on "perceptual accuracy" and "body sensitivity." Relevant to the latter, Witkin observed that performance in the BAT when the subject closed his eyes was not significantly related to his performance with eyes open. Obviously, open or closed eyes should make little difference to a body-sensitivity hypothesis. In due course, the current interpretation was accepted—the common element in the three criterial measures is the ability to overcome an embedding context. The BAT, RFT, and EFT all require that something—body, rod, and geometric design, respectively—be separated from the field or context in which it is embedded. Subsequently, Karp (1963) has demonstrated that the critical attribute of the item-field relation is embeddedness rather than distraction. Performance on a series of tasks with distracting contexts generated one factor, whereas a different factor was found to load the three "embedding" tests (BAT, RFT, and EFT). Also congruent with the embedding notion is the indication that subjects in the tilted-room–tilted-chair situation, when asked to adjust the room rather than their bodies to the upright, do not perform consistently in the two tasks. Scores derived from the Room Adjustment Test (RAT)—deviation of the position of the adjusted room from the true vertical—were essentially unrelated to BAT scores and the other indices of differentiation. Witkin et al. (1962) have noted that the task of adjusting the room presents no problem of an item embedded in a field. Rather, the subject has essentially been asked to cope directly with the position of the field itself.

Brief mention might also be made of the fact that RFT scores proved to be most satisfactory as an index when the chair was not tilted (Witkin et al., 1967). The Witkin group traces the difficulty under chair-tilted conditions to Müller's (1916) E-effect, according to which subjects tend to perceive the upright as displaced in the direction opposite to body tilt. It is not very clear, however, why individual differences in the E-effect should stand apart from differences in extent of field dependence.

From the perspective of the present chapter, it is especially important to note that the various procedures described have been employed with children as young as 10 years of age for the EFT and 8 years of age for the BAT and RFT. A children's form of the Embedded Figures Test (CHEF) appropriate for subjects as young as 5 years of age has been developed by Goodenough and Eagle (1963). In this test, meaningful complex figures (e.g., car, man, boat) are substituted for the abstract geometric designs of the standard EFT. Again, the child is expected to locate a simple figure embedded within the whole, where the whole resembles a giant jigsaw puzzle. A knob protrudes from each of the separate pieces of the puzzle, but only the piece corresponding to the correct simple figure is removable when the child pulls the knob. The child's score consists of the number of items on which the correct knob is pulled first.

The reliability of the CHEF in 6- to 9-year-olds ranged from the high 50s to the low 80s. For a sample of 10-year-olds, the CHEF yielded statistically significant correlations of .46, .70, and .63 with the BAT, RFT, and EFT, respectively. Thus the CHEF appears to be a valid index of field dependence at the 10-year age level, although this does not insure, of course, that the same degree of validity applies for younger children. Some support for such validity may be derived from the evidence that CHEF performance significantly improved from age 5 to age 8. Note, finally, that another version of a children's embedded-figures test (CEFT) is available whose psychometric properties are somewhat superior to the Goodenough-Eagle version (see Karp and Konstadt, 1963).

Developmental Change. In the preceding section, high test-retest correlations were offered as evidence for the reliability of the various field-dependence indices. As the time between test and retest increases, the correlations are informative with respect to both the reliability of the instrument and the relative stability of field-dependence level during the course of development. Recently, Witkin et al. (1967) have offered coefficients of stability for two longitudinal groups, one tested at ages 8 and 13, the other tested at ages 10, 14, 17, and 24. For both groups, all of the correlations were significant and substantial, with rs ranging from .48 to .92. Hence a preadolescent child classified as field-dependent or field-independent (or of in between status) has a quite high probability of being identically classified as a young adult.

The foregoing evidence implies that the *relative* position of an individual on Witkin's perceptual dimension remains fairly constant over a time span of as much as 14 years. Is such stability also obtained in regard to an individual's *absolute* level over time? Witkin et al. (1967) explored this question in both cross-sectional and longitudinal samples

of children, adolescents, and young adults. In the case of the cross-sectional data, the developmental curves reveal a progressive improvement in performance with increasing age up to 17, followed by a slight decline through age 21. This increase and subsequent decrease in level of field independence with chronological age was observed for all three indices—BAT, RFT, and EFT. In the case of the longitudinal groups, only the RFT data were considered, since there is evidence for learning effects—knowledge of results being available to subjects—in both the BAT and EFT (see Goldstein and Chance, 1965; Witkin et al., 1954). As in the case of the cross-sectional data, the longitudinal evidence also showed that maximal field independence was achieved at age 17. Unlike the cross-sectional evidence, however, no decline in RFT scores from age 17 to age 24 was found in the longitudinal data. Witkin et al. attribute the difference in separate sets of data to the character of the young adults employed in the cross-sectional studies. Most were students attending a local college and living at home, characteristics presumed to be associated with lower field-independence levels. This interpretation based on selection bias appears to be very reasonable. Though a decline in field independence does seem to occur very late in life—geriatric groups were highly field dependent (Schwartz and Karp, 1967)—it is most unlikely that such a decline would begin in the early 20s.

In considering the implications of their developmental findings, Witkin and his associates noted that both the family and the overall environmental settings of the longitudinal subjects were fairly stable over the 14-year period in which they were studied. Nevertheless, as those authors have also emphasized, the period from age 10 to 24 is characterized by great personal change, including such events as puberty, lessened dependence on the family, choice of occupation, and, sometimes, marriage and the assumption of family responsibilities. Any psychological dimension that manifests so high a level of stability through so turbulent a period of life must surely be ranked as one of the most powerful continuities in the domain of human development, comparable in many respects to the observed stability of the IQ. However, one should not lose sight of the fact that the stability of field independence is basically interindividual, not intraindividual. In other words, the subject maintains his position relative to others. At the same time he is progressively increasing in field independence.

In a critique of Witkin's work, Zigler (1963a, 1963b) has unfavorably contrasted Witkin's emphasis upon continuity and stability with Werner's and Piaget's stress upon developmental change. In actual fact, the disagreement may be more apparent than real, for most of Witkin's research has employed children who have reached the age where many of the fundamental cognitive changes of development have already taken place. Under any circumstances, however, it must be acknowledged that the course of development is distinguished by both continuities and discontinuities. A comprehensive developmental theory should be able to incorporate both the dimensional stability observed by the Witkin group and the changes in cognitive organization observed by Werner and by Piaget. There is no a priori reason why one should be deemed more important than the other.

Relationships with Ability. One of the most controversial aspects of Witkin's research concerns the role played by intelligence with respect to performance on the BAT, RFT, and EFT. Evidence is available (Witkin et al., 1962) for 10- and 12-year-olds of significant correlations between field independence, on the one hand, and the Stanford-Binet and WISC total IQs, on the other. However, in the case of the WISC specifically, the correlations were somewhat higher with the performance scale than with the verbal scale. With the view toward discovering whether the positive link between total IQ and field independence might be "carried by" specific subtests of the WISC, a factor analysis was performed on a variety of cognitive tasks including the WISC subtests and the three indices of field independence (Goodenough and Karp, 1961). Three major factors emerged that were reasonably matched for 10- and 12-year-olds. The pattern of loadings of the various WISC subtests on the three factors corresponded in many respects to the outcomes of a previous factor analysis of the WISC (Cohen, 1959). Factor I was labeled "verbal comprehension" by virtue of the substantial loadings for the Vocabulary, Information, and Comprehension subtests. Factor II was designated "attention-concentration," given the substantial loadings for Digit Span, Arithmetic, and Coding. Finally, Factor III was assigned the label "analytical field approach" on the basis of substantial loadings for Picture Completion, Block Design, and Object Assembly. The RFT, BAT, and EFT also yielded fairly high loadings on Factor III.

Witkin et al. (1962) present a convincing case for commonalities between the three WISC subtests loading Factor III and the three field-independence indices on the basis that all require the overcoming of an embedding context. It is, in fact, the evidence of such correspondences across the intellectual and perceptual domains that prompted the redefinition of the major construct at issue as "analytic versus global field approach." Field dependence-independence is presently considered by the Witkin group as the perceptual component of the more pervasive cognitive style of analytic-global functioning.

Given the evidence that the field-dependence indices are negligibly loaded on the "verbal comprehension" and "attention-concentration" factors, an argument can be made against Zigler's (1963a, 1963b) contention that the significant link between field-dependence measures and *general* intelligence mediates most of the findings reported in *Psychological Differentiation*. It is doubtful whether our understanding would be advanced by reducing the constructs of field independence and analytic functioning to an amorphous "general intelligence" construct which bears no conceptual relationship to any major psychological theory. As long as most intelligence tests are constructed on the basis of intuitive hunch and psychometric item analysis, scores on such tests can hardly serve as the cornerstone of a major theoretical effort. We are not implying, of course, that a g factor of intelligence does not exist. In fact, we sympathize with Zigler's suggestion that g should serve as a control variable when examining relations between field-dependence indices and other variables. The factor-analytic findings obtained by Cohen (1959) do show that the three WISC subtests loaded on Witkin's "analytical field approach" factor are also substantially loaded on g. Hence it would be of considerable interest to know how the impressive array of findings obtained by the Witkin group would be affected by a statistical control for the g factor.

More disturbing than the possible influence of g on analytic functioning is the evidence that such functioning may not be as independent of verbal skills as the Witkin group has claimed. Crandall and Sinkeldam (1964) obtained significant correlations in 10- to 12-year-olds among field independence and the three WISC subtests loading the "verbal comprehension" factor. Comparable results were found for young adults by Wachtel (1968). Note further that the intelligence subtest most closely related to analytic functioning—Block Design—correlates between .27 and .54 with the Vocabulary subtest in normative data presented by Wechsler (1949, 1967). Holtzman (1965) reports similar evidence. Although a case can be made against the partialling out of the g factor on the grounds that some of its components are determined by the analytic dimension (and Witkin has tried to make such a case), no such argument can be applied where verbal skills are at issue. The Witkin group has rejected the possibility of any theoretical bridge between analytic functioning and the WISC verbal cluster. Since field independence is sometimes empirically linked to verbal IQ, however, the control of verbal IQ becomes imperative when field independence is related to other variables.

We conclude our discussion of the ability area with a consideration of relations between mode of field approach and verbal skills considered more generally. Witkin et al. (1962) demonstrated that the child's "verbal expressiveness" as manifested in clinical interviews and TAT story telling bears no significant relationship to mode of field approach. However, "cognitive clarity" indices, which presumably circumvent the dimension of verbal expressiveness, were significantly related to field-independent functioning. "Cognitive clarity" implies nothing more than the ability of the child to make his thoughts and ideas intelligible to the interviewer.

Of particular interest in the present context is the question of whether a verbal task with the property of embeddedness taps the kind of cognitive style represented by Witkin's dimension of analytic-global functioning. Such a task was employed in a study by Podell and Phillips (1959). It made use of an ana-

gram format in which already meaningful words had to be broken up in order to form new words. Performance on the task was not related to spatial decontextualization, a factor quite similar to Witkin's perceptual mode-of-field-approach index. Related to this outcome is the evidence that another verbal-embeddedness task—Camouflaged Words—was not related to the "adaptive-flexibility" factor delineated by Guilford, Frick, Christensen, and Merrifield (1957). This factor includes a variety of perceptual-restructuring tasks of the type used by Duncker (1945) and others. The Gottschaldt test also loads on the factor. Karp (1963) has subsequently shown that Guilford's adaptive-flexibility factor is strongly related to Witkin's field-independence measures.

In sum, verbal tests, even under conditions where they require that an embedding context be overcome, manifest no relation to mode of field approach. It is evident, then, that "embeddedness" tasks with spatial, configural properties are most relevant to the kind of analytic functioning with which Witkin and his associates have been concerned. The implication drawn by the Witkin group from their empirical evidence is that most verbal processes are of little relevance to psychological differentiation. It is this assertion that has provoked the most vigorous dissent from Zigler, who has noted that verbal ability (as reflected in mental age) is a prime indicator of level of differentiation in most developmental theories. The relegation of verbal skills to a secondary role by the Witkin group forms the basis of Zigler's attack on their theoretical conceptualization of the differentiation construct. Zigler argues that the procedures devised by Witkin and his associates reflect "decontextualization," a construct that can be subsumed under differentiation at a considerably lower level of abstraction. We shall return to this point later in our final summary and evaluation of Witkin's contribution.

Body Concept. In our review of the work of the Witkin group thus far, we have focused on procedures that assess the child's capacity to differentiate a field and to differentiate his body from a field. The present section concerns the child's articulation of the body concept itself, as reflected in drawings of the human figure. The cognitive, intellectual aspects of human figure drawing have been recognized for a long time. In 1926, F. L. Goodenough published the Draw-a-Man Scale as a test of nonverbal intelligence. In contrast to this intellective emphasis, the initial use of figure-drawing procedures by Witkin and his associates (Witkin et al., 1954) was strongly influenced by Machover's (1949) approach. Machover viewed figure drawing as a projective test capable of assessing such motivational constructs as anxiety, sexual identification, and self-confidence. In their more recent work, Witkin et al. (1962) have employed the figure-drawing technique exclusively for the purpose of measuring the level of primitivity-sophistication of the child's productions; this is considerably closer to Goodenough's original conception.

Assessment of the sophistication of body concept in Witkin et al. (1962) was based on "the form level of the drawings, the extent of identity and sex differentiation of the figures, and the level of detailing" (pp. 119–121). Judges were required to use the foregoing three categories in making a global rating of sophistication of body concept on a five-point scale. Satisfactory interjudge reliability was obtained ($r = .84$). Highly significant correlations in 10- and 12-year-old boys were found between the sophistication-scale scores and perceptual index scores (a composite of BAT, RFT, and EFT). Sophistication of body concept was also significantly related to the analytic cluster of WISC subtests, but unrelated to the WISC verbal cluster.

In sum, fairly strong evidence exists to support the proposition that children with an analytic field approach have more articulated body drawings than do children with a global field approach. On the other hand, it must be granted that definitive evidence is lacking to support the claim that the child's figure drawings actually reflect his conception of his own body. In fact, the pattern of correlations with mode of field approach did not differ very much when Goodenough's intelligence scale was substituted for Witkin's sophistication-of-body-concept scale. Indeed, the two scales were highly correlated ($r = .74$, $p < .01$). Hence a case can be made that the figure drawings are really tapping a facet of nonverbal intelligence.

Personality and Motivational Correlates. In the earlier phase of their work, Witkin et al. (1954) conceived of an "active, coping" ver-

sus "passive, submissive" relation to the environment as the personality dimension most closely linked to field-independent versus field-dependent functioning, respectively. The more recent book (Witkin et al., 1962) de-emphasizes the importance of a general activity-passivity dimension. Diverse forms of activity are recognized. Some are presumed to be relevant to field independence; others are presumed to be irrelevant. Assigned to the irrelevant category is the type of activity represented by high energy level and/or motoric output. Where activity assumes the hyperkinetic form suggestive of lack of impulse control, Witkin predicts a global field approach. No empirical evidence relevant to this point is offered, however. Where activity assumes the character of striving and assertiveness toward well-formulated goals, a relationship with an analytic field approach is anticipated. A TAT assessment of the preceding type of "active attitude" was carried out in 10-year-old boys. Stories were scored for assertiveness and counteraction (overcoming adversity). For neither variable was a stable relation with field independence obtained.

Witkin and his associates (1962) have also tested the proposition that an active or passive attitude would be expressed in the characteristic posture of the body. One of the samples of 10-year-old boys was photographed, with no special instructions given as to the pose to be assumed. With the face blotted out, the posture of each boy photographed was evaluated on a four-point scale ranging from "active-assertive" stance at one extreme to "passive" stance at the other. These ratings were significantly correlated with the field-independence composite, suggesting that "children with an analytic field approach tend to give evidence of greater 'readiness for action' than children with a global approach" (p. 183).

Although the findings from this (Witkin et al., 1962) study tend to confirm the hypothesized link between activity-passivity and field independence-field dependence, the evidence considered as a whole is unimpressive. It should be emphasized, however, that Witkin and his associates have clearly relinquished any claim to a simple, direct association of activity-passivity in the behavioral sense with mode of field approach. Activity-passivity in overt behavior is multidetermined;

and, further, outwardly similar behaviors will often have quite different psychological meanings. It is hardly surprising, then, that Witkin's earlier (1954) formulation regarding the activity-passivity dimension has not held up well under subsequent empirical examination.

Another attempt to show that modes of field approach reflect deep-seated personality dispositions is found in the evidence concerning defensive structures. Witkin et al. (1962), on the basis of their "differentiation" hypothesis, proposed that children with an analytic field approach would tend to employ "complex, specialized defenses" (e.g., intellectualization, isolation), whereas children inclined toward a global field approach would tend toward the use of simple, primitive defenses (e.g., repression, denial). Particular defenses and modes of field approach are presumed to develop in closely interlocking fashion. Thus highly structured defenses would be expected to contribute toward impulse control, which, in turn, might relate to the kind of attention regulation necessary to perform in an analytic manner. Correspondingly, where primitive denial is a favored mechanism of defense, one might well expect the child to structure his experience in a vague, global manner.

The degree of structure of controls and defenses was evaluated in a sample of 10-year-old boys by means of a blind clinical analysis of protocols from three projective tests—the Rorschach, the TAT, and a figure-drawing procedure. The 23 boys under study were classified on the basis of a five-point scale, ranging from low to high degree of defensive structure. Correlating these ratings against the perceptual-index scores yielded a highly significant r of .61. This finding is supportive of Witkin's hypothesis, but one still must consider the validity question: Do the clinical projective-test ratings actually reflect the child's defensive structure?

Comparable validity problems arise with respect to further tests relating to modes of handling aggression and denial of aggressive stimuli in TAT imagery. According to the Witkin group, field-dependent boys displayed more uncontrolled aggression and at the same time were less likely to perceive salient aggressive stimuli in the TAT cards than their field-independent peers. There is, of course, something of a contradiction in this outcome,

which receives no acknowledgment from the Witkin group. One might argue that denial occurs where the stimuli, though emotionally provocative, are relatively mild, whereas more impelling stimuli make denial impossible and consequently produce a breakdown in control mechanisms. The validity problem arises, however, in the question of whether judges are, in fact, rating the protocols on the basis of maturity or personality integration. The latter characteristics were claimed to be irrelevant to the analytic-global style elsewhere in the Witkin et al. (1962) volume. Yet all of the projective data reported appear to attribute greater psychopathology to the field-dependent than to the field-independent child. Part of the reason for this is the absence of any empirical inquiry into the hypothesized link between analytic functioning and employment of such specialized defenses as intellectualization and isolation.

Social Behavior. Scattered through both of the published volumes by Witkin and his associates are numerous references to studies that have reported differences in the social behavior of field independents and field dependents. The large bulk of this research is based upon adult samples. More recently, however, there have been a few published papers concerned with the social behavior of children in relation to their status on the field-dependence dimension.

Where adults are concerned (Witkin et al., 1954), there is evidence suggesting that field dependence in perception is associated with passive, dependent interpersonal behavior. Crandall and Sinkeldam (1964) have explored this issue in the case of a sample of children in the 6 to 12 age range. Both dependent and achievement behaviors in free-play social situations were assessed. A relation between an achievement orientation and perceptual field independence was anticipated, on the grounds that the EFT measure of perceptual field independence (the measure employed by Crandall and Sinkeldam) was saturated with achievement cues. Hence achievement-oriented children would be expected to perform at a higher level on the EFT than those children less preoccupied with achievement. Three types of social behavior indicative of dependence on adults—instrumental help seeking, affection seeking, and recognition-approval seeking—were examined in relation to EFT performance. Similarly, Crandall and Sinkeldam explored the relation between field independence and four kinds of achievement behavior—concern with motor mastery, time alone on tasks, independent achievement efforts, and task persistence. Since the three indices of dependent behavior and the four indices of achievement behavior yielded two relatively homogeneous clusters (in terms of the pattern of correlations), overall dependency and achievement scores were also derived.

One methodological feature of the Crandall-Sinkeldam study is especially worthy of note. Since IQ was significantly correlated with field independence and with some of the social behavior ratings, the major relationships at issue were examined with IQ controlled by means of partial-correlation procedures. It will be recalled that the Witkin group did not employ such procedures, a fact that served as one of the major criticisms leveled against their work by Zigler. With both age and intelligence controlled, dependent social behavior was only minimally related to perceptual field dependence.[13] The dimension of "affection seeking from adults" yielded a marginally significant correlation with EFT performance. From one point of view, such findings can be considered as damaging the construct validity of the field-dependence construct. On the other hand, Witkin has stressed the multideterminacy of overt social behavior. As Witkin et al. (1962) have noted:

In children recognition-seeking may signify primarily a need for support from others and so be interpreted as socially dependent behavior, or it may signify primarily a strong interest in mastery. In the conceptualization of socially dependent behavior it seems useful to delineate the contributions of extent of sense of separate identity, active-vs-passive attitude,

nature of emotional involvement with others, and kinds of motivation (p. 187).

The achievement behavior variables, in contrast to the variables of dependent behavior, were substantially related to perceptual field independence (with age and IQ statistically controlled). Only the dimension of "time alone on tasks" failed to share in the overall relationship.

Responding to a suggestion by Witkin that the meaning of the testing situation may not be the same for younger and older children, Crandall and Sinkeldam report separate analyses for these groups based on a median age split. It was expected that the testing situation might prove to be difficult for younger children, thereby evoking dependency needs; on the other hand, older children, being more accustomed to testing, might bring an achievement orientation to bear on the task. The results generally did not support Witkin's suggestion. Dependent social behavior was unrelated to field dependence in both age groups, and achievement-oriented behavior was related to field independence in both younger and older children.

As we have indicated, the absence of an association between perceptual field dependence and dependence in free-play social behavior constitutes something of a challenge to Witkin's position. We also observed, however, that the free-play situation may not be an ideal setting for testing the hypothesis at issue, given the multidetermined nature of behavior under such conditions. A study by Konstadt and Forman (1965) has examined the effects of field dependence upon dependency-related behavior in an experimentally controlled setting. Fourth-grade children selected from the extremes of the CEFT score distribution were given a letter cancellation test under conditions of experimenter approval and disapproval. Statements of approval or disapproval were offered orally by the experimenter at frequent intervals during the testing session. The statements had no connection with the subjects' levels of performance on the assigned task. Konstadt and Forman anticipated that the field-dependent children would exceed their field-independent peers in sensitivity to the experimental conditions. It was expected that such differential

---

[13] It can also be argued that field independence affects level of performance on particular subtests of intelligence, and therefore controlling for total IQ is not entirely justified. The Witkin group, of course, would favor such an argument. Within the context of the Crandall-Sinkeldam findings, however, the foregoing issue is not too important, for the overall pattern of results does not change much when IQ is statistically controlled.

sensitivity would be manifested both in level of performance on the task and in the orientation toward peers and experimenters as reflected in looking behavior during task performance.

The results were generally consistent with the preceding hypotheses. There was a significant tendency in the direction of poorer performance from field-dependent children under disapproval relative to approval conditions. No such discrepancy was obtained in the case of the field-independent children. With regard to the number of times subjects gazed at some other person in the room, there was significantly more "looking" behavior for field-dependent than for field-independent children, but only under the condition of experimenter disapproval. A significant interaction effect with condition order was also obtained. Field-dependent children under the disapproval condition looked at others more when they experienced this condition *after* having experienced approval than when the order of the conditions was reversed.

In sum, both the test-taking and the looking behavior of the children suggested that field dependents were more disrupted by an unfavorable emotional climate than were field independents. The dependent group appears to be more externally directed, in the sense that their cognitive-affective behavior is differentially influenced by the positive or negative social cues emitted by others. Thus in order to demonstrate a relationship between field dependence and behavioral dependency it was necessary to create a situation in which social rewards were withdrawn or replaced by punishments. Such circumstances are not ordinarily found in free-play, and this may account, in part, for the differing outcomes of the Crandall-Sinkeldam and Konstadt-Forman studies.

Antecedents. Consider now the evidence offered by Dyk and Witkin (1965) and Witkin et al. (1962) on antecedents of field dependence in parent-child relationships. Interviews were conducted with the mothers of the boys under study. For one of the samples, the boys were 14 years of age when their mothers were interviewed; in the other two samples, the mothers were interviewed when their sons were 10 years old. A variety of indicators

was employed for evaluating the interview data. The characteristics of the mother as a person and the nature of her interaction with her son were among the areas measured. In the former category, the major indicators concerned the mother's sense of self-assurance and self-realization in life. In regard to interaction with the child, the indicators focused on training for independence and training for control of aggressive behavior. Ratings made on the separate indicators were used to make an overall global judgment of the mother as "fostering or inhibiting differentiation"; that is, mothers were placed in one of two groups corresponding to these classifications. Where there were conflicting signs for the separate indicators, the global judgment was based on the "overall impact of the evidence."

Correlations between the sons' perceptual index scores and the global rating of the interview data provided by mothers were statistically significant and very high. The point biserial rs were .85 and .65 in the 10-year-old samples and .82 in the 14-year-old sample. It would thus appear that mothers of field-independent and field-dependent boys interact with their children in a manner that fosters one or the other cognitive orientation. The exceptionally high magnitudes of the correlations, however, arouse suspicion that the relationships noted may have some spurious basis. Zigler has, in fact, offered an interpretation along such lines. Given the fact that the interviewer necessarily had to discuss the son's behavior with the mother, it was highly probable that the interviewer could accurately categorize the child as field dependent or field independent. Such an inference would come naturally to a trained rater or interviewer and could readily have biased the global judgments in a direction consistent with the judgment of the child's status on the field-dependence dimension. Although there is likely to be some relation between the mother's attitudes and behavior, on the one hand, and her child's style of cognitive functioning, on the other, the actual magnitude of such relationships must remain uncertain. It is, of course, no simple matter to remove this type of contamination as long as the interviewer wishes to obtain information from the mother concerning her child-rearing attitudes and methods. A step in the right direction would be a systematic analysis of the individual indicators that comprise the final global judgment.

Witkin and his associates (1962) have indicated some awareness of the difficulties surrounding the use of global impressions and have accordingly employed additional methods to ascertain the influence of the mother on the cognitive functioning of her son. Thus the field-dependence level of mothers was assessed and then examined in relation to that of their own sons. The Witkin group anticipated a positive relationship between the field-dependence scores for mother-son pairs. The basis for such a hypothesis rested on the assumption that field-dependent mothers, by virtue of their attitudes and behavior, would create the kind of home climate likely to inhibit the development of field independence in their sons, whereas mothers who were field independent would foster differentiation in their sons. Confirmation of the hypothesis would be a fact of considerable importance, for, unlike the interview data, there is no possibility of contamination in the present case. However, a positive association would not conclusively establish the role of the family environment as a mediating factor.

One set of mothers was given a shortened form of the EFT and a figure-drawing test approximately 2 to 3 years after their initial interview. The testing took place in the home situation under less-than-ideal conditions. Despite this shortcoming, the EFT and sophistication of body concept were significantly correlated in the sample of mothers.[14] Further, these scores related significantly to the interview classification of mothers as "facilitators or inhibitors of differentiation" in their children. EFT scores did not relate significantly to the interview data, however. The sophistication-scale scores taken from the mothers' figure drawings were also significantly correlated with the various criteria of analytic functioning in the sons. On the other hand, the corresponding correlations for mothers' EFT scores did not achieve statistical significance. Witkin et al. (1962) attribute the low predictive value of the mothers' EFT

[14] Though it is correlated with EFT, one can question the use of figure drawing as an index of analytic functioning if the latter is to be conceptualized as the ability to overcome an embedding context.

performances to the difficulties in test administration. Conceivably, the EFT might be tapping a factor other than mode of field approach when administered under the special conditions that exist in the home. In sum, the hypothesis that the mother's mode of field approach will correspond to that of her son received only partial support. Regrettably, one cannot tell whether the cognitive similarity between mother and son is, in fact, quite weak or whether the link is really quite strong but vitiated by the special assessment conditions that prevailed in Witkin's research.

A fundamental question left unanswered by the work of the Witkin group on parent-child antecedents concerns the role of the father in fostering or inhibiting "differentiation" in the child. Recall further that Witkin's research into the possible family origins of an analytic versus a global field approach has been based exclusively upon boys. Corah (1965) has attempted to fill in the gaps by examining the field-dependence levels of both mothers and fathers in relation to the field-dependence levels of both sons and daughters. Corah selected 30 boys and 30 girls (ranging in age from 8 to 11) from 60 middle-class families. The EFT and figure-drawing procedures were used to assess field dependence in both parents and children. The CEFT (Karp and Konstadt, 1963) rather than the standard EFT was administered to the children. Age and IQ were regressed out of the field-independence indices before the parent-child correlations were computed. The correlational pattern when EFT, or CEFT, and figure drawing were combined into a single index assumed the cross-sex form (i.e., the field-dependence scores of mothers and sons and of fathers and daughters were positively and significantly associated). The same-sex correlations were nonsignificant.

The Corah results are clearly consistent with those reported in Witkin et al., but at the same time they introduce a new complicating element. Why the relation between parent and child in regard to the analytic-global dimension should assume the cross-sex form is not easily explained. Corah has proposed that it is the opposite-sexed parent who attempts to foster the appropriate sexual identification in the child. But independent evidence for such an assertion is lacking, and, furthermore, the theoretical link between an "appropriate sexual identification" and field independence is not at all clear.

Other relevant evidence can be brought to bear on the issue. Bieri (1960) explored the relation between field dependence, on the one hand, and parental identification and acceptance of authority, on the other, in a sample of college men and women. Field dependence was assessed by the EFT; parental identification was assessed by the degree of similarity of self-ratings to mother- and father-ratings on a semantic differential;[15] acceptance of authority was assessed with the Bales-Couch AA scale, which has been shown by Bieri and Lobeck (1959) to correlate highly with the F scale (Adorno, Frenkel-Brunswik, Levinson, and Sanford, 1950).

The findings obtained by Bieri (1960) that are of particular interest concern the simultaneous effects of AA level and parental identification upon field dependence. For males, greater field independence occurred when low AA was combined with *mother* identification. Females, by contrast, manifested the highest level of field independence in the combined presence of low AA and *father* identification. Thus the cross-sex feature of Corah's (1965) results finds some parallel in the outcomes of Bieri's research. Bieri has, in addition, provided some insight into the psychological mechanisms that may mediate the cross-sex, parent-child associations in the domain of field dependence-independence. At the same time, caution should be exercised in interpreting Bieri's results, given the exceedingly small Ns that result when AA and identification variables are treated simultaneously.

In the research described thus far, the large majority of subjects had both parents in the home during the formative years. What would be the effect of the father's absence from the home on level of field dependence? This question was explored in a study conducted by Barclay and Cusumano (1967). These authors proposed that father absence would have a differential effect on the son's overt as opposed to covert masculine identification. It was expected that the boy's sex-role con-

15 It is rather doubtful that such an assessment gets at the essence of the identification concept. Nothing more is implied in the present context than perceived similarity to a parent.

flict produced by growing up in an exclusively matriarchal setting would lead to a compulsive denial of feminine tendencies, with the resultant consequence of no difference between father-absent and father-present boys in extent of overt masculine identification. This expectation was confirmed in a sample of 40 adolescents (with a mean age of 15) divided into 20 father-absent and 20 father-present boys matched on age, grade point average, IQ, and socioeconomic status. In the father-absent group, no real or surrogate father had lived in the subjects' homes after the boys had achieved 5 years of age. No significant differences emerged between the groups on the Gough (1957) Femininity Scale from the *California Psychological Inventory*. Similarly, no significant differences were observed on a semantic differential requiring ratings of self, father, and mother. In sum, extent of overt masculine identification was no less in father-absent than in father-present boys.

The second hypothesis formulated by Barclay and Cusumano asserted that father-absent boys, in contrast to father-present boys, would reveal their sex-role conflicts at a deeper, more basic level in the form of a passive, field-dependent orientation. The RFT was administered to all of the adolescents participating in the study. Comparison of the RFT performance of the father-absent and father-present boys indicated a significantly higher level of field dependence in the father-absent group. It should be further noted that both groups were equally divided into white and Negro adolescents, with Negroes yielding higher levels of field-dependence than whites. Race did not interact significantly with the variable of father presence versus absence.

In sum, the data are highly consistent with the Barclay-Cusumano hypotheses. There is somewhat more incongruity, however, between the outcomes of the Barclay-Cusumano research and the results of studies considered earlier. It will be recalled that the cross-sex identification of the son with the mother under certain conditions was associated with greater field independence. Recall further that field-dependence levels of sons were correlated with those of their mothers, not their fathers. Now, we observe that the absence of the father from the home does have a significantly depressing effect on a male child. It is, of course, also possible that the results can be attributed to the altered character of the mother role in the father's absence. Conceivably, the mother is forced to play a more harshly authoritarian role in the father's absence, a factor which might inhibit the growth of an analytic or a field-independent style in the child. Of great relevance in this regard is the Witkin et al. (1962) evidence indicating that mothers classified as "inhibiting differentiation" claimed that their husbands did not participate in decisions about their sons' raising. Such evidence is also consistent with Seder's (1957) observation that fathers were more likely to be the disciplinarians for field-independent boys, whereas mothers filled the disciplinary role for field-dependent boys.

It is difficult to comprehend why Barclay and Cusumano did not report the correlations between their overt and covert indices. These could be very helpful in understanding the processes at work. For example, did the boys with the greatest hypermasculinity at the level of overt identification also yield the highest levels of field independence? In other words, are the relationships across the covert and overt indices positive, negative, or random? Were the relationships similar or different for the father-present and father-absent groups? Such important questions remain unanswered in the Barclay-Cusumano report.

It is now apparent that the issue of sex differences is closely intertwined with the problem of parent-child antecedents of field-dependent behavior. In the section that follows we shall confront the matter of sex differences directly.

Sex Differences. There now exist several dozen studies which have reported that males perform better than females on the EFT, RFT, and BAT measures of field independence. The relevant studies are cited in Maccoby (1966). The greater field independence of males, though generally achieving statistical significance, is of relatively small magnitude. Within-sex variation in field dependence is very substantial. The consistent small difference observed between males and females has become something of a *cause célèbre* in the personality-cognition area, as various genetic, physiological, learning, and cultural factors have been advanced to account for the apparent sexual inequality. We shall consider these diverse interpretations in due course.

To begin on a cautionary note, it should be stressed that sex differences in field dependence have not been observed in children in the 4 to 8 age range (Goodenough and Eagle, 1963; Maccoby et al., 1965); nor have sex differences been obtained in geriatric groups (Schwartz and Karp, 1967). Occasionally, sex differences have not been obtained in college samples (e.g., Bieri, 1960). Differential sex selectivity—the greater percentage of eligible boys than girls who go on to higher education—would tend to operate against the emergence of a sex difference at the college level. Girls who enter a college or university may be considerably more field independent than their peers who settle for a high school diploma. Thus sex differences are likely to be most pronounced between the upper elementary school grades and the last year of high school. It might be noted that these are the years when sex-role differentiation shows a pronounced increase.

In an effort to reduce within-sex relative to between-sex variance in field-dependence scores, certain investigators have gone beyond the simple, biological sex distinction to an examination of sex-role identification. The availability of masculinity-femininity scales (e.g., Gough, 1957) has naturally fostered this trend. Regrettably, little relevant research has been carried out on samples of children. The most definitive study (Vaught, 1965) is based on college students. Vaught examined RFT performance in males and females as a function of sex-role identification (assessed with Gough, 1952, femininity scale) and ego strength (assessed with the Barron, 1953, ego-strength scale). Vaught hypothesized that the presence of high ego strength—a dimension closely linked to self-esteem—would tend to reinforce associations between masculinity and field independence and between femininity and field dependence.

Although significant main effects were obtained favoring males over females, masculine identifiers over feminine identifiers, and high ego-strength subjects over low ego-strength subjects in level of field independence, the significant triple interaction among these three components is the finding of major interest. For males, low ego strength was associated with field dependence; high ego strength with field independence, regardless of sex-role identification. For females, in contrast, high ego strength was associated with field independence in the presence of low or medium feminine identification; but high ego strength combined with high femininity yielded extremely high field-dependence levels.

Vaught bases his interpretation of his findings on Sarbin and Jones' (1955) contention that ego strength reflects role-taking ability. Feminine males and masculine females are presumed to represent unstable role identities, with the consequence that ego strength becomes the major determiner of mode of field approach. Where biological sex and sex-role identification are consistent, on the other hand, ego strength is presumed to be of lesser importance in regard to field dependence.

It is of interest to compare Vaught's findings with Bieri's (1960) evidence on cross-sex identification with parents in relation to field dependence. The findings are reasonably consistent for female subjects if one can assume that a masculine identification and high ego strength are in some way equivalent to identification with the father and a less authoritarian outlook.[16] Those are the conditions in the respective studies that are associated with field independence in females. The consistency is somewhat less pronounced for male subjects, however. It will be recalled that Bieri found the highest levels of field independence in mother identifiers with a nonauthoritarian orientation. Vaught obtained relatively high field-independence levels in high-femininity males with high ego strength, but the low-femininity males were somewhat more field independent overall. On the whole, the correspondences between the studies are encouraging, for neither sex-role and parental identification, on the one hand, nor ego strength and nonauthoritarianism, on the other, can be treated as equivalents. The fundamental point demonstrated by both the

Bieri and the Vaught studies is that a good part of the variance in field dependence left unexplained by biological sex differences can be accounted for on the basis of psychological variables relevant to sex role. The evidence that cross-sex-typing contributes to field independence in females is quite strong. There is greater ambiguity regarding the advantage of cross-sex-typing for males on field independence, although data can be found in support of such an inference.

The foregoing discussion of sex differences has been based on the presumption that statistically significant differences between the sexes on EFT and RFT, for example, necessarily imply that boys are, indeed, more field independent and analytic, whereas girls are more field dependent and global. In a provocative paper, Sherman (1967) has seriously questioned whether such implications can in fact be drawn. Her argument, in brief, runs as follows. There is considerable evidence to suggest that the RFT and EFT (or the highly similar Gottschaldt figures) are significantly correlated with tests of spatial ability (Gardner, Jackson, and Messick, 1960; Podell and Phillips, 1959; L. L. Thurstone, 1944). Females have been shown to perform more poorly than males on spatial tasks even when there is no embedding context to be overcome. Reviews of this literature are available in Anastasi (1958) and L. E. Tyler (1965). Males are better than females in the spatial area because cultural sex-typing provides the male with more opportunities to practice spatial tasks. With adequate training, girls' spatial ability could be improved, with consequent declines in alleged field dependence and globality. That is the sum and substance of Sherman's case. She offers a strong argument for sex-typed learning as the basis for the observed sex differences.

Sherman's paper is important and hence deserves additional, more critical consideration. It is difficult to dispute the point that spatial ability may be contaminating the measures of analytic-global functioning. If spatial tasks without properties of embeddedness are, nevertheless, substantially correlated with Witkin's dimension, it is impossible to invoke the argument that an analytic style produces a higher level of spatial ability. It will be recalled that the Witkin group, with some

---

[16] The link between ego strength and low authoritarianism finds strong support in the research of Jensen (1957), who has found that "prejudiced, authoritarian persons have less well-developed ego defenses and thus are more exposed and vulnerable to psychological stress . . ." (p. 310).

justification, claimed that an analytic style was responsible for superior performance on WISC subtests highly loaded on the analytic factor. Recent research, in line with Zigler's (1963a, 1963b) criticisms, has controlled for IQ when relating field-dependence indices to other measures (e.g., Barclay and Cusumano, 1967; Crandall and Sinkeldam, 1964). Sherman's observations raise the issue of the possible value of statistically removing the spatial component from the field-dependence measures when they are related to other variables. It would be of great value to know whether the dimension of analytic versus global field approach is inextricably tied to a configural or spatial task format. If the statistical removal of the spatial element should serve to eliminate theoretically anticipated relations between field dependence and other variables, it would be most difficult to defend the overcoming of an embedding context as the critical aspect of the construct at issue. As we previously noted, performance on the criterial measures of field dependence bore no relation to performance on a verbal task with the properties of embeddedness. Hence it has already been demonstrated that the capacity to cope with an embedding context is not a *sine qua non* for analytic functioning as defined by Witkin and his associates.

Consider next the differential-practice argument to account for the female's inferiority in the spatial domain. To quote Sherman (1967): "Boys as a group spend more time in aiming activities and games, model construction, building with blocks and later with other materials. It seems very likely that these activities are involved in the development of spatial skills" (pp. 295-296). Maccoby has challenged such an explanation on the grounds that there is no evidence for it. The following quote from Maccoby (1966) is particularly instructive:

It is true that if one watches nursery school children at play, one is more likely to find boys building with blocks and girls placing doll furniture in a doll house or pretending to cook with beaters and bowls; but it is difficult to see why one of these kinds of object manipulation should lead to greater spatial ability than the other. We know little about what kinds of learning experiences are involved when a child dissects stimuli (as the analyt-

ical, field-independent child does) instead of responding to them globally, but it is difficult to see why sheer quantity of stimulus exposure should make a difference beyond a certain point (pp. 41-42).

In defense of Sherman, it should be noted that sex differences in field dependence are not evident at nursery school age, but rather emerge in the middle years of elementary school. It is not inconceivable that sex-typed activities assume a more spatial character for boys than for girls over time. As Sherman has noted, girls tend not to gravitate toward shop work, car tinkering, model building, and map reading. It is doubtful whether feminine-oriented tasks exist which call upon spatial skills to the same extent, but once again we are in the realm of conjecture.

The most dissonant evidence with respect to the hypothesis of masculine sex-typing of spatial activities derives from a study by Ferguson and Maccoby (1966) on the interpersonal correlates of differential abilities. From a large population of fifth-grade children, these authors selected a sample of boys and girls who showed marked discrepancies among verbal, number, and space abilities on the T. G. Thurstone (1958) Primary Mental Abilities Test. The interpersonal characteristics of these children were assessed by self-report questionnaires and peer ratings. Of special interest in the context of the present discussion is the personality of the boys and girls high in spatial ability but relatively low in number and verbal ability. Such differential spatial ability was associated with cross-sex-typing in both boys and girls. For boys with relatively high spatial relative to verbal ability, the peer ratings pointed to a behavior pattern of low aggression, low masculinity, and low mastery, and a high level of withdrawal. Consonant with the low masculinity ratings was the self-report evidence indicating a low score on the Sex-Role Acceptance Scale. Girls high in spatial ability, in contrast to the boys, scored higher in overt aggressiveness (peer ratings) and were less anxious about expressing aggression (self-report data). These findings are clearly paradoxical. If high spatial ability is a reflection of distinctly masculine sex-typed activities, it is difficult to comprehend why the boys judged least masculine should have the highest scores on spatial ability, while at the same time the high space girls manifest much masculine-oriented behavior. Such outcomes cannot easily be reconciled with Sherman's differential-practice hypothesis, at least as far as boys are concerned.

It will be recalled that some evidence was found to support the idea that identification with the mother might enhance field independence in males (Bieri, 1960). But such processes of identification in college-age men seem quite far removed from the patterns of overt behavior manifested by the preadolescent boys with differentially high spatial ability in the Ferguson-Maccoby investigation. One clue to the puzzle is that the characteristics of the child high in spatial ability may be as much a function of his deficits as of his strength. The high-space children were simultaneously low in number and verbal ability. Conceivably, children who perform well on the EFT and the RFT have high number and/or verbal ability as well as strong spatial capacity. If this could be demonstrated, one would be forced to conclude that an analytic field approach involves more than simple spatial ability.

The most relevant evidence is presented by Bieri, Bradburn, and Galinsky (1958) who obtained substantial and significant correlations between EFT performance and mathematical ability (SAT-M) in college men and women. If such a correlation should also be present in children, it would necessarily have been eliminated in the Ferguson-Maccoby study by virtue of the manner in which the children in their sample were selected. Of considerable interest in this regard is the evidence that boys with differentially high number ability received high masculinity ratings from their peers. To the degree, then, that numerical ability is separated from spatial ability by differential selection procedures, the latter may simply not manifest the kind of close link to Witkin's analytic-global dimension proposed by Sherman (1967).

Another point of contrast between spatial ability and analytic functioning in the Witkin sense can be noted in the sociometric findings of the Iscoe and Carden (1961) study. Among sixth-grade boys, those scoring the highest on the EFT measure of field independence were the most frequently chosen by their peers on affective and work criteria. Ferguson and Maccoby, it will be recalled,

found that their high space boys were low in masculinity and high in social withdrawal. These are hardly the characteristics likely to contribute to a preadolescent male's popularity and influence with his peers. Where sixth-grade girls are concerned, Iscoe and Carden observed a significant sociometric preference for those with a global field approach. Thus, for girls, the data on field dependence and spatial ability are in agreement. Whether a girl is high in field independence or in spatial ability, she is likely to manifest more masculine qualities, and this inappropriate sex-role behavior might be expected to reduce her popularity and influence with same-sexed peers. Iscoe and Carden also found that anxiety level was unrelated to EFT performance in boys, but field-independent girls relative to their field-dependent peers expressed more anxiety symptoms on the Children's Manifest Anxiety Scale (Castaneda, McCandless, and Palermo, 1956). The causal direction of this relation cannot be definitely established, but a reasonable conjecture is that the unpopularity of the more masculine, field-independent girls contributes to the symptoms reflected in the CMAS.

To continue the comparison of spatial and analytical ability, consider the matter of training. The evidence on this point with regard to an analytic field approach has been largely negative (e.g., Elliott and McMichael, 1963; Wolf, 1965). In contrast, spatial visualization has been shown to improve during engineering study (Blade and Watson, 1955) and by means of programmed instructional techniques (Brinkmann, 1966). Such efforts have been quite intensive and prolonged, and their success raises the issue of whether the training failures in analytic, field-independent functioning might have been due to the brevity or inadequacy of the training procedures employed. It would be of interest to observe whether intensive training in spatial visualization would enhance field independence on Witkin's three criterial tasks. Such an outcome would serve to reinforce the view that the spatial component is a critical aspect of Witkin's dimension.

Cross-Cultural Findings. Within the past few years, data relevant to the field-dependence dimension have been collected in a number of primitive non-Western cultures. Witkin (1967) has recently reviewed this cross-cultural evidence. Its importance can hardly be exaggerated, given claims by Witkin and others that certain kinds of family influences and cultural sex-role differences contribute to greater or lesser field dependence. Primitive societies with diverse child-rearing practices and norms of sex-typed behavior constitute a "natural laboratory" for tests of some of Witkin's major hypotheses.

Consider first the research of Dawson (1967a, 1967b) in Sierra Leone (West Africa). As Dawson (1967a) has pointed out, the tribal social organization and child-rearing methods in Sierra Leone "place considerable emphasis on values of conformity, group reliance, maintenance of authority, polygamy and strict discipline" (p. 116). Such values should, in line with Witkin's hypothesis, contribute to high levels of field dependence. Dawson describes the way in which Temne children in Sierra Leone who resist their elders' wishes are accused of being "affected by witchcraft" and are accordingly punished. An additional feature of the Sierra Leone cultural scene is the polygamous family group, which forces the mother to assume a dominant role in raising her children. The adequacy of the father as a role model for the son is limited, given the responsibilities of the father toward other wives and children.

Within the overall pattern of parent-child relations in Sierra Leone, further variations can be distinguished. Thus parents can be expected to show some variation in disciplinary strictness. Dawson (1967a) had his subjects (male skilled workers aged 20-24) rate their mothers and fathers as "very strict," "fairly strict," or "not so strict." These categories of strictness were significantly related to field dependence (assessed with the EFT and Kohs Blocks) for mothers but not for fathers. Thus, consistent with Witkin's hypothesis, those males who felt that they had been subjected to very strict discipline by their mothers (implying a pattern of maternal dominance) were more likely to have higher field-dependence scores.

Further corroborating data for the influence of maternal dominance on field dependence come from a comparison of subjects drawn from the Temne and Mende tribes in Sierra Leone (Dawson, 1967a). In contrast to the Temne mother, for whom extreme dominance and strictness is the norm, the Mende mother is considerably less dominating and more permissive and encouraging of individual initiative in her child. Consistent with expectations, a comparison of young adult males from the Temne and Mende tribes revealed the Temnes to be significantly more field dependent than the Mendes on the EFT. These results clearly strengthen the proposition that field independence in the son will be inhibited or facilitated as a function of the degree to which his mother encourages individual initiative and independence.

In a subsequent paper, Dawson (1967b) factor analyzed the data from his Sierra Leone samples. Of particular interest in the present context is a powerful factor with positive loadings (in the field-independent direction) for EFT, Kohs Blocks, three-dimensional perception of pictures, general intelligence, and educational achievement. Maternal dominance and preference for traditional (as opposed to Western) values yielded substantial negative loadings. The relatively high loadings for intelligence and education are disturbing, and one must regret that these variables were not held constant or regressed out of the field-dependence scores when relations with child-rearing variables were examined.

The variable "three-dimensional perception of pictures" refers to the capacity to attribute depth when viewing two-dimensional pictures. Hudson (1960) reported that many Africans lacked this capacity, possibly as a consequence of lack of exposure to pictorial materials. Dawson included Hudson's materials in his research. These materials consist of a set of pictures containing various objects, where the subjects' task was specifying which of a number of objects was closer in distance to another object. The relation between performance on this test and on the EFT again highlights the role of spatial factors in regard to the field-dependence dimension.

We turn now to a cross-cultural comparison of field dependence in the Temne from Sierra Leone and the Canadian Eskimo (Berry, 1966). The Eskimo offer a sharp contrast to the Temne on a number of ecological and cultural variables. The Temne exist in a physical environment characterized by a diversity of vegetation of variegated color. Farming constitutes the main occupation, hence there is little need to stray from the fixed paths through the bush. By contrast, the

Eskimo inhabit a bleak environment distinguished by minimal variation in color. Given an environment of fairly uniform visual stimulation and a dependence on hunting for subsistence, the Eskimo must, in order to survive, develop certain perceptual skills. They must learn to discriminate very slight variations in their physical environment, and they must develop an articulated view of open space so that they can orient themselves relative to the objects around them. More geometric-spatial terms are available in Eskimo than in Temne language. Further, the Eskimo are noted for their soapstone sculpture, their graphics, and their map-making skills, activities that are quite alien to the Temne. The figure drawings made by Eskimo children actually appear to be more articulated than those produced by a comparison group of American children (Harris, 1963).

The difference in socialization practices between the Temne and the Eskimo is particularly striking. We have already discussed the strong emphasis on severity of discipline and conformity pressures in the case of the Temne. Children in the Eskimo culture, on the other hand, are generally the recipients of unconditional love and approval, are rarely punished (even verbally), and are able to manipulate parents into granting their wishes. The child is encouraged fairly early in life to assume responsibility for his welfare. Given these striking differences between child-rearing practices in the two cultures—differences that appear relevant to Witkin's conceptualization of the forces inhibiting or facilitating differentiation—Berry (1966) predicted higher field-dependence levels in Temne subjects and lower field-dependence levels in Eskimo subjects.

For both the Temne and Eskimo, Berry selected samples living in relatively isolated rural areas (the "traditional" group) and samples living in more urban, Western-type environments (the "transitional" group). Males and females were sampled equally from all four groups. In addition, Berry sampled equally from five age groups: 10 to 15, 16 to 20, 21 to 30, 31 to 40, and over 40. Within the traditional and transitional categories, the Temne and the Eskimo had comparable levels of formal education. For control purposes, two Scottish samples, comprised largely of farmers and manual workers, were also selected for study. Consistent with the traditional-transitional comparison, one sample was drawn from a small farming village, the other from a city.

Four tests of a spatial character—EFT, Kohs Blocks, Morrisby Shapes, and Raven Matrices—were administered to all subjects. Virtually all of the correlations between the four tests in the six samples were statistically significant and substantial. Sherman's (1967) assertions regarding the spatial aspects of Witkin's construct are clearly confirmed in Berry's work. Comparison of the Temne and Eskimo separately for "traditional" and "transitional" samples yielded highly significant differences on all four of the tests described. A great gulf was found between the Temne and the Eskimo, with hardly any overlap in scores between the two groups. The Eskimo clearly exceeded the Temne in field independence and spatial ability; furthermore, they came very close to matching the performance of the Scottish samples.

Although it is hardly surprising that the transitional Temne were more field independent than the traditional Temne, the fact of superior performance in transitional relative to traditional Eskimo is rather puzzling. The ecological requirement of highly articulated space should be considerably less marked for Eskimo who live on a trading post and engage in limited hunting than for those who live in small camps and rely entirely on hunting for a livelihood. The transitional Eskimo, of course, have had more formal education than their traditional counterparts, hence they may well have developed the test-taking attitudes that contribute to better performance. The need for a finely articulated perception of space in conducting one's livelihood obviously contributes to doing well on spatially oriented tests. Nevertheless, tests of any sort do require that the subject sit fairly still for an extended period of time, focusing his attention on the task at hand. Such experience is not entirely foreign to the westernized Eskimo with a few years of schooling. Also contributing to the observed difference between more rural and more urbanized groups, according to Witkin (1967), is the selective migration of relatively field-independent persons to populated areas. Note should be taken, finally, of Vernon's (1965) claim that Eskimo coming from the most isolated Arctic communities performed better on spatial tests than those living in closer contact with whites. Obviously, more research is needed to resolve these discrepancies.

We turn, finally, to the matter of sex difference within the context of culturally prescribed sex-role-typing. Berry has pointed out the sharp contrasts between Temne and Eskimo societies in the way females are treated. Unlike the Temne, who exercise very firm control over wives and children, the Eskimo allow their women and children a considerable degree of autonomy. Consistent with these cultural differences, the Temne males were found to be significantly more field-independent than the Temne females on most of the tests employed. Comparable sex differences were observed in the Scottish groups, but no sex differences of any consequence were obtained from the Eskimo samples. This result was replicated in another sample of Eskimo by MacArthur (1967). In sum, the Berry and the MacArthur data constitute strong evidence for the proposition that sex differences in field dependence may be largely a function of social-role influences.

We conclude the present section with a brief consideration of the nature-nurture issue. The Eskimo have lived in the same environment over a long period of time in relative sexual isolation from other groups. Given the adaptive importance of an articulated mode of functioning in the harsh environment of the Eskimo, differential selection on that attribute may have taken place. No such adaptive selection was ever necessary in the highly articulated Temne environment. It is doubtful, however, whether such evolutionary interpretations will prove theoretically useful in the present context. Of much greater relevance is the evidence of strong associations among the ecological demands of a culture, socialization practices and their consequences for sex-role-typing, and the level of field dependence typical of the culture. On the whole, this cross-cultural evidence is quite congruent with the outcomes of American investigations concerned with the effects of parent-child interaction and sex-role identification upon level of field dependence. It appears that Witkin's twofold classification of mothers as either inhibiting or facilitating differentiation has its analogue at the level of primitive, homogeneous cultures.

It has been shown that field dependence in the Temne has as much adaptive, survival value as field independence in the Eskimo. Each mode of field approach fits the ecological requirements of the particular culture. What are the ecological requirements of the American culture? It is commonly assumed that there is wide heterogeneity in such requirements as a function of a host of demographic variables. Accordingly, can one justify a value bias in favor of field-independent functioning? No conclusive answer to the question is possible, of course, but we shall speculate about it a bit more in the process of a final summing-up of the contribution of Witkin, his co-workers, and other investigators whose work has been inspired by the Witkin group.

Evaluative Summary. To begin with the positive, there is no doubt that the Witkin team has uncovered and empirically exploited an exceedingly important dimension of perceptual-cognitive functioning. Its importance derives in large part from its fertility: the dimension is not confined to perception but impinges upon cognition, intelligence, personality, and social behavior. The boundaries between these various domains—so often treated in isolation from one another in psychology—are shown to be exceedingly permeable in Witkin's research. The analytic-global dimension, in Witkin's hands, has become a major organizing principle around which many aspects of the child's functioning have been shown to cluster. In other words, to describe a child as analytic or field independent as opposed to global or field dependent is to provide a huge amount of information about that child. The constructs developed by the Witkin group have considerable "surplus meaning."

On the negative side, issue can be taken with the decision of the Witkin group to use "differentiation" as their major unifying construct. Zigler (1963a, 1963b) has proposed that the dimension at issue might have been better labeled "spatial decontextualization," after Podell and Phillips (1959). Such a proposal has a great deal of merit, given the evidence that the field-articulation principle is manifested largely on spatial tasks. Certainly, there is nothing in the differentiation concept as formulated by Lewin or Werner to suggest that its field of applicability is limited to the spatial domain. On the other hand, as we have noted, performance on Witkin's spatial tasks does relate to areas of personal functioning that have no relation whatever to spatial decontextualization. Some organizing principle was obviously needed to tie the diverse sets of variables together. The Witkin group chose the differentiation construct to serve this organizing function. Perhaps the link between the wide variety of processes examined and the construct of differentiation was largely metaphorical, as Zigler has claimed. Nevertheless, the preference for differentiation over spatial decontextualization may have some justification, given the limited generality of the latter construct. Still another term might have been superior, but there are as many disadvantages to coining new labels as there are in refurbishing old ones.

The controversy over the differentiation issue between Zigler and the Witkin group can probably be traced to the Witkin group's presumption that all processes relevant to differentiation can be incorporated within their definition of that term. Yet it must be admitted that processes with little or no relationship to Witkin's differentiation cluster are nevertheless subject to Werner's orthogenetic principle. That principle, it will be recalled, simply states that development proceeds from a relatively global state to one of differentiation, articulation, and hierarchic integration. As stated, the principle is sufficiently general to accommodate verbal and numerical as well as spatial-analytic capacities. Thus the evidence that verbal-numerical processes are only weakly related to spatial-analytic ability in the work of Witkin and his associates cannot mean that verbal-numerical processes do not follow Werner's main developmental principle. Rather, such findings must necessarily mean that the Witkin group has examined a particular form of differentiation, perhaps the most important and most highly generalized form, while choosing to ignore other forms.

Paradoxically enough, the data reported by Witkin and his co-workers are consistent with Werner's views on multilinear development, for certain cognitive capacities obviously follow a different route than that taken by spatial decontextualization. One is hardly justified in attacking Witkin for choosing this route, given the enormous payoff in significant findings that ensued. The alternative research strategy of pursuing all possible paths simultaneously is hardly viable.

The dispute over the differentiation issue appears to be partially semantic. On the one hand, differentiation was originally defined by Werner as a heuristic principle that does not lend itself to experimental acceptance or refutation; its value lies in the network of constructs generated by it. For Witkin, on the other hand, differentiation has become an explanatory, higher-order construct capable of tying together a diverse set of lower-level dimensions. The point worth noting amidst all of the heated controversy is that the validity of Witkin's findings would not be diminished if their organizing principle were designated by a term other than differentiation. It is perhaps unfortunate that the Witkin group chose a term that implicates variegated meanings and levels of abstraction. But the ultimate value of Witkin's work will almost certainly rest on the significance of the further research it generates, rather than on the specific explanatory construct in favor at the present time.

Apart from its theoretical implications, Witkin's work is of practical import, particularly to those working in educational fields. There is a strong tendency for teachers in our elementary schools to value verbal and number skills. The Witkin team has pointed to another domain of intellectual functioning, likely to be ignored by the schools, which is nevertheless highly relevant to the child's modes of thinking, feeling, and acting. A recent paper (Witkin, Faterson, Goodenough, and Birnbaum, 1966) has shown some boys deemed mentally retarded to be nevertheless approximately average relative to their age group in field-articulation capabilities, a fact that might be put to valuable educational use. Also instructive is the high level of field independence in Eskimo with minimal levels of formal education. Recall that there were no material differences in field dependence between Eskimo and Scots, despite the educational opportunities open to the latter.

In sum, it would appear that formal schooling tends to develop verbal-numerical capacities, whereas the development of an articulated mode of field approach may be under the influence of early family experience. Witkin (1967) has proposed that programs for the culturally disadvantaged have neglected the issue of the development of field independence and have instead focused on the enhancement of verbal skills. The paradoxical elements in the equation are the fact that cognitive capacities determined by early familial factors would be most difficult to modify; and, furthermore, the more disadvantaged children, on the basis of Witkin's evidence, already manifest the least deficit in the analytic area. Of course, the presence of particular cognitive strengths, as we have seen, does not imply that they will be recognized by the important educational agents in the child's life. Nevertheless, one is faced with the difficult choice of devising programs of educational value that capitalize upon the existent analytic strengths of the child or that attempt to overcome the more glaring deficiencies in the child's repertoire of cognitive skills.

It is in the forgoing problem that one confronts the basic value dilemma inherent in Witkin's system. Can one really claim that field independence from the point of view of ecological requirements and societal needs is more socially relevant and useful than field dependence? Solid evidence exists that field dependents are more alert to social stimuli. They do better than field independents, for example, in tasks that require the incidental memory of social words (Fitzgibbons, Goldberger, and Eagle, 1965) and the memory for faces (Messick and Damarin, 1964). Groups of field-dependent males are able to achieve a unanimous consensus in significantly less time than is required by field-independent groups (Wallach, Kogan, and Burt, 1967). Field dependents are probably more skilled at the art of interpersonal accommodation; field independents are better able to resist the influence of others. When one reflects upon the adaptive requirements of our heterogeneous American culture, it is far from evident that the field-independent orientation is best suited to the needs of the future. In situations where social groups are in conflict over means, goals, and values, a cognitive style that facilitates fine articulation and sensitivity to the social environment may be considerably more helpful than a cognitive style encouraging articulation of the self and of external physical space. Before one begins to train children for field independence, then, the value dilem-

mas described must clearly be spelled out, for the long-term adaptive significance of a field-articulated cognitive orientation has not been definitively established.

Ipsative Analysis of Cognitive Functioning

All of the research discussed in the present chapter thus far has concerned itself with the description and interpretation of *interindividual* differences for various cognitive dimensions. Broverman (e.g., 1960a, 1960b) has favored the ipsative, *intraindividual* analysis of data, that is, individual differences derived from the relative status of different functions within people. Thus when a large battery of tests is administered to a sample of subjects, it is feasible to express a particular individual's score on each test as a deviation from his overall mean score across all of the tests. Such an analysis has the effect of removing something like the intellectual g factor from a set of test data. It is beyond the scope of the present chapter to discuss the relative psychometric merits of ipsative versus normative measurement procedures. Such a discussion is available elsewhere (Broverman, 1962, 1963; MacAndrew and Forgy, 1963; Ross, 1963). An obvious difficulty with an ipsative approach is the fact of noncomparability between Broverman's work and the bulk of the research carried out by others, despite the use of identical cognitive tasks. The fact remains, however, that Broverman's research is of considerable substantive interest, and since some of it is based on adolescents and children, the relevant portions cannot be omitted from any comprehensive account of cognitive styles in children.

A set of 30 tests—some more perceptual-motor, others more conceptual in nature—was administered to a sample of 103 pairs of male and female adolescent twins (Broverman, 1964). The use of twins does not appear to be of any particular significance. A factor analysis of the ipsatized scores yielded two bipolar factors. The first factor was defined positively by the three scores from the Stroop test—speed of reading color words, naming color hues, and reading incongruously colored words (interference)—and by speed of tapping a simple pattern on the L. L. Thurstone (1944) Two Hand Coordination Test. Loaded negatively on the factor were the Gottschaldt Test, the Kohs Blocks, and the

Primary Mental Abilities Space and Reasoning subtests. Broverman has labeled the factor "automatization," given the positive loadings for simple verbal and motoric tasks. The tests that load negatively on the factor are strongly suggestive of Witkin's field articulation dimension.

The second ipsative factor was defined by positive loadings on the Primary Mental Abilities subtests of Verbal Meaning, Word Fluency, and Reasoning. A variety of tapping tasks and telegraph key operations yielded negative loadings on the second factor. The contrast between the conceptual and the perceptual-motor is very distinctly drawn.

The two factors obtained in the adolescent sample were quite comparable to those derived from two adult samples. Thus the two-factor, bipolar pattern reported by Broverman seems to reflect stable contrasts in styles of cognitive functioning. There are, however, ambiguities in the outcomes of Broverman's investigations. Particularly astonishing is the evidence that the kinds of interference represented by the Stroop and the Gottschaldt have opposite effects on individual performance. Broverman (1964) attempts to explain this paradoxical outcome in terms of the role of the conflicting cues in the two tasks. In the Stroop, the correct stimulus attribute (the color in which the color name is printed) is directly perceptible, and the subject must suppress the strong, overlearned habit of reading the color words. In hidden-figures tests of the Gottschaldt type, the correct stimulus element is not directly perceptible, but rather must be discovered and extracted from an embedding context. One must grant that the two tasks at issue do pose quite different problems for subjects, but it is, nevertheless, a surprise to find the tasks located at the opposite extremes of a bipolar factor.

The interpretation of Broverman's automatization factor could be extended along motivational lines. If weak automatization is essentially Witkin's field-independence dimension, it is conceivable that this automatization factor is not a cognitive or motor deficit, but rather a reflection of the field-independent's lack of motivation to work hard at an uninteresting, repetitive task. We already know that field independence is associated with less conformity (e.g., Jackson, 1958; Linton, 1955; Linton and Graham, 1959; Rosner,

1957). Field independents may simply fail to take a repetitive motor task very seriously and hence not put forth their best effort. This interpretation is sheer conjecture, of course. Further research is quite clearly needed.

Broverman (1964) has attempted to relate the automatization factor to life performance in the case of adult samples. Data were available on the occupations of both the subjects (males) and their fathers. These were converted to occupational levels by means of the Hollingshead (1957) scales. Strong automatizers had achieved higher occupational levels than weak automatizers, despite the absence of any difference in years of education and overall intelligence. Further, the strong automatizer's occupational level manifested a sharp rise relative to father's occupational level. No such increase was obtained for weak automatizers. Again, if weak automatizers are truly field independents, Broverman's data stand in sharp contrast with other evidence pointing to a significant, positive link between field independence and achievement motivation (e.g., Crandall and Sinkeldam, 1964). However, one must not lose sight of the fact that comparisons between normatively and ipsatively designed studies are not entirely legitimate.

We conclude our coverage of Broverman's work with a brief discussion of two additional pieces of research based on adolescents and children. In the first (Broverman, Broverman, Vogel, Palmer, and Klaiber, 1964) the automatization style was related to adolescent physical development in a sample of 16-year-old male students. Seventeen body measurements were obtained. No overall height or weight differences between strong and weak automatizers were observed, but the strong automatizers did have significantly shorter necks and legs and significantly wider shoulders than did the weak automatizers. The former group also possessed more body hair and shaved more frequently than the latter group.

Broverman and his associates explain the observed physical differences on the basis of the higher androgen levels in strong automatizers, the consequence of which is a more rapid rate of physical maturing. Furthermore, a higher androgen level is presumed to enhance resistance to muscular fatigue, thereby accounting for the superior performance of the strong automatizers on repetitive motor tasks. Such a physiologically based interpretation stands in obvious contrast to the proposal advanced earlier to the effect that weak automatizers (field-independent individuals) are not concerned about doing well on a tedious motor task.

The attempt to explain cognitive functioning in terms of physiological maturity and androgen level can be considered a precursor of a subsequent effort (Broverman, Klaiber, Kobayashi, and Vogel, 1968) to account for sex differences in cognition on the basis of physiological, hormonal sex differences. A great deal of evidence is offered (some of it from the animal behavior literature) in support of the view that females do better on simple perceptual-motor tasks, whereas males exhibit superior performance on perceptual-restructuring tasks. In the words of Broverman et al. (1968), "We hypothesize that the sex differences in cognitive abilities are reflections of differences in relationships between adrenergic activating and cholinergic inhibitory neural processes, which, in turn, are sensitive to the gonadal steroid 'sex' hormones, androgens and estrogens" (p. 24). Performance on the two tasks at issue—perceptual-motor and perceptual-restructuring—can apparently be manipulated by pharmacological hormonal agents that affect the adrenergic-cholinergic neural balance.

An array of evidence from diverse sources is brought forth by Broverman and his co-workers in support of a physiological basis for sex differences in cognitive functioning. Indeed, one is mildly astonished at so massive an effort in the service of explicating sex differences that are, after all, quite small in magnitude. As we have already demonstrated, sex-role identity may account for as much, if not more, of the variance in analytic functioning than does biological sex as such. It is, of course, feasible that the neural and hormonal processes described by the Broverman group have a direct impact upon sex-role-typing. An examination of such a possibility might be highly informative.

It will be recalled that Broverman et al. (1964) associated strong automatization with physiological characteristics of maleness. In Broverman et al. (1968), the emphasis is placed on male superiority on perceptual-restructuring tasks and female superiority on automatized tasks. The earlier study linked weak automatization (high capacity for perceptual-restructuring) with a slower rate of physiological maturation as reflected, for example, in less hirsuteness. One is reminded here of the Ferguson-Maccoby evidence discussed earlier of lower masculinity in boys of high spatial ability. There are distinct resemblances between the Ferguson-Maccoby method of subject selection and the ipsative approach favored by Broverman. Indeed the first can be considered an ipsative analysis based on extreme groups. It is surely no accident, then, that the outcomes in the two cases at issue are reasonably congruent and different from results obtained in studies using the traditional normative methods.

We turn, finally, to a study of automatization in fourth-grade male children by Blum and Broverman (1967). Automatization was assessed with a variant of the Stroop test (the strong pole) and with various perceptual-restructuring tests (the weak pole). Regrettably, it was merely assumed that the bipolar factor that had been observed in adolescents and adults would emerge in children. Though this might well be so, empirical verification would have been highly desirable. A significant correlation was obtained between the automatization variable and the tendency to persevere with the same response in a test derived from the concept of rigidity or intolerance for ambiguity. This latter test consisted of a set of cards in which a cat was slowly transformed into a dog, and vice versa. Strong automatizers generally persisted with their original verbal report beyond the point in the series where the weak automatizers had shifted. While acknowledging that their results might be suggestive of greater intolerance for ambiguity or rigidity in strong automatizers, Blum and Broverman derive little comfort from such a conclusion. They argue, in fact, that maintenance of an original response during stimulus change may be "evidence of cognitive flexibility, since the individual is then including new and diverse stimulus relations within his original concept" (p. 101). Such an argument is not at all persuasive and merely suggests the need to make the current evidence congruent with earlier results pointing to the adaptive value of strong automatization.

Broverman has maintained that the greater the extent to which routine tasks and activities are automatized, the more energy will be available for coping with tasks of a novel, concentration-demanding type. One can certainly question the usefulness of such an energic conception in the domain of cognitive functioning. Given the inverse relation between strong automatization and field articulation in perceptual structuring, we can only note with amusement that Broverman and Witkin place high value upon distinctly different, if not opposed modes of cognitive functioning.

One firm conclusion can be drawn from the studies cited in the present section. Until investigators begin to analyze their data both normatively and ipsatively (a rather unlikely and not necessarily desirable event), Broverman's work will be exceedingly difficult to articulate with the mainstream of research on cognitive styles.

THE ROLE OF MOTIVES, STANDARDS, EXPECTANCIES, AND ANXIETY

The heart of this chapter has been a description of the dimensions that seem to be helpful in accounting for reliable variation in the interpretation, storage, and transformation of information. This task was the chapter's central mission. However, it is not altogether inappropriate to append a brief discussion of the dynamic forces that initiate and maintain cognitive effort. These forces include, at a most general level, motives, standards, expectancies and anxiety over possible failure.

Earlier generations, wedded closely to Hull, Freud, and the nineteenth-century mechanists, did not wish to conceive of any action or thought without its special antecedent cause. The concepts of drive and need or motive became psychology's translation for *force* and *cause*, respectively. Natural observations of infants and the technically more elegant neurophysiological data have recently forced the important acknowledgment that some psychological and biological systems have their own spontaneous activities whose production does not depend upon deprivation, altered homeostasis, or impingement of external stimulation. There are many aspects of cognitive processing that proceed without a special motive or drive. The infant spontaneously fixates a figure that moves or possesses high contour contrast. He may cry over a discrepancy from

an acquired schema. The infant does not want to behave in this manner; he does not need to do so; he does. Newly hatched ducklings follow the first moving object they see. There seems to be neither practical nor theoretical profit in postulating a motive to follow the imprinting object.

Similarly, the child learns much from his environment without any special motive force catalyzing this learning. The infant learns a schema for his mother's face, he learns to laugh at a clown, to pile blocks into tall piles and to knock them down. The appearance of these responses seems to proceed naturally, requiring only contiguity and attention to relevant events. But the postulation of special motives is required, or at least helpful, if we are to understand why a child learns selected academic and socialization rules—to multiply, to tell the truth, to parse a sentence. Each culture requires its children to acquire many intellectual skills that they might not otherwise master because they would not devote long periods of sustained attention to them. Special motives are catalytic in this enterprise; they create the conditions that facilitate the acquisition of these cognitive competences. Individual differences among children in rate of acquisition of these tasks are typically attributable to differences in the strength of these motives.

Motives

It is a truism to state that a child's attention to events will be enhanced if he is motivated to attend to the events. If the child recognizes that attention to and subsequent mastery of a task are prerequisites for attaining a desired goal, he is likely to make an effort at mastery. How does a goal—or class of goals—acquire desirability or value? There are probably several mechanisms. For expository convenience, we shall discuss these under the rubric of specific motivational states without implying a commitment to a particular theory of the acquisition and content of human motives.

Motive to Maintain Response-Appropriate Contexts. The infant and child are always behaving in the sense of issuing responses to the stimulus context that surrounds them. With time, classes of responses gradually become firmly and selectively attached to specific people, objects, and contexts. The infant or child is often distressed when he is in a context in which he has no response to make. An anecdotal observation is helpful here. If a 2-year-old child is brought to a room containing a variety of toys, he typically plays with the toys with zeal and joy. However, when he has become satiated after 10, 30, or 60 minutes he often whines, "I want to go home." He has no more responses to issue in this context, and he is motivated toward that place in which he has developed a richer repertoire of behaviors. The child develops a motive to preserve familiar contexts and to maintain contact with stimulus situations for which he possesses adaptive and easily issued classes of behavior. Differences in the modal environments to which children are exposed will produce motives for different contexts. A 1-year-old child who has experienced continual contact with his mother has developed a set of reactions toward her. He will have a strong motive for her presence. He announces this motive by crying when she is gone for too long a time, by pulling on her apron, by dragging the lamp from the living room to the kitchen in order to draw the mother into interaction with him.

The 5-year-old has learned a set of responses to particularly favorite toys, to the permanent objects in his home, to other children or siblings. If we place him in a context that does not allow manifestation of these habitual responses and one in which he has no responses to make, he becomes apprehensive and, occasionally, extremely fearful. There is therefore a motive to maintain contact with contexts and objects to which the child has an available set of behaviors and, correlatively, a motive to avoid contexts to which the child has not learned an easy set of behaviors. The motive for maintaining contact with the familiar is congruent with J. P. Scott's (1967) suggestion that puppies develop in the first 12 weeks a motive to maintain contact with a familiar context. The puppy vocalizes in distress if removed from a familiar to an unfamiliar context and stops his distress vocalizations when he is placed back in the familiar locus. It appears that the infant mammal—puppy or human—develops schemata for and responses to the context in which it grows. Encounter with a highly discrepant context elicits distress as an automatic reaction. This principle may be one basis for a child's motive to maintain contact with familiar people and contexts.

Motive for Pleasant Sensations and Reduction of Pain. The infant and child, of course, are motivated to reduce pain, anxiety, and discomfort. They learn to desire contact with those objects and events that have served this purpose in the past. Thus the child's motive to maintain a close relation with the mother or her surrogate rests on two bases— her association with reduction of discomfort and the fact that she is a target object to which the child has developed a set of behaviors. The parent or parental surrogate becomes a valued object and leads the child to develop a more symbolic motive—the desire for signs of positive evaluation of the child.

Motive for Symbolic Signs of Positive Evaluation. When the child begins to acquire language at about 18 months of age, the ground is prepared for the emergence of a desire for symbolic signs of approval and positive evaluation from others. This motive rests on previous learning in which words or phrases that represented good or its synonyms were associated with hedonically pleasant goal states and the availability of the mother as a target for behavior. The child wishes to be regarded as good and interprets positive evaluation from others as a sign of his goodness. If parents and adults who are valued give positive evaluation for mastery of cognitive tasks, the child will be motivated for that mastery.

Motives Characterized by a Wish for Selected Behaviors in Other People (hostility and dominance). The earliest motives in the child are for external events that produce a change in the child's own experience. By 2 to 3 years of age, a new set of motives emerges whose goal is the perception of a particular state in another person. A hostile motive is defined as the desire to see another display signs of pain, worry, fear, or discomfort. The wish is for misfortune and discomfort to befall another, and the gratification is contained in perceiving and/or knowing of that event. If the child thought that attainment of good grades would make a rival peer unhappy, hostility toward that peer could promote motivation to master intellectual tasks. A child who grows up in a peer group milieu in which intellectual competence is valued is more likely to work at school tasks in the service of hostile motivation than one who lives in a peer milieu which places minimal value on intellectual competence.

The motive to dominate has similar roots. It can be defined as the wish to have another assume a submissive posture with respect to the child. During preadolescence, dominance becomes elaborated and gives birth to the motive for power. Motive for power is defined as the desire for signs that enable the child to believe that another will assume a passive, submissive posture in relation to him. The motive to dominate could facilitate cognitive performance if such competence allowed the child to dominate others.

At a general level, desires for recognition, approval, dominance, and power can be distinguished in children. The specific behavioral routes chosen to gratify these motives will depend on the instrumental habits taught by the child's rearing environment. Some environments teach that attainment of athletic skills will lead to power; others teach that intellectual competence will provide the same goal. The specific behaviors the child chooses to gratify his motives are obviously relativistic with respect to the values of the social context in which he spends his formative years.

Identification. The child also develops a desire to maintain and increase his similarity to desired models. This motive is part of the process of identification. Briefly stated, the child perceives certain models in his environment that possess attributes that he would like to attain (dominance, interpersonal competence, receipt of affection from others), and he tries to increase his similarity to these models by adopting their attributes. If intellectual competence is one of the model's central attributes, the child will attempt to increase his mastery in order to increase his similarity to the desired model.

Unfortunately, there has not been systematic empirical research on the relation of the motives for hostility, dominance, approval, or identification to quality of mastery. The greater variability of cognitive performance among boys than girls as well as the consistently poorer relation between social class and level of cognitive performance in boys than girls may be due to the more varied motive spectrum for intellectual competence that exists for boys. A primary motive for girls' performance in school is the desire to maintain symbolic signs of approval from parents and teachers. Upper-middle-class parents are more likely to promote this value with their daugh-

ters than are lower-middle-class parents. As a result, the girls' motivation is likely to covary highly with social class. Although the motive for symbolic signs of approval is operative for boys, motives for hostility, dominance, and identification are more clearly operative for boys than for girls, and these latter motivations do not vary so strongly with social class.

Standards

As implied earlier, a standard is a belief about the desirability and appropriateness of a particular class of cognitions and behaviors. Children attempt to develop and maintain a belief system about the self that is maximally congruent with those attributes they have learned to regard as good, whereas they renounce and avoid the possession of attributes that they regard as bad. The bases for the evaluation of good or bad are culturally derived and for the Western community include the beliefs that one is valued by others, that one is attractive to others, that one possesses the necessary intrumental skills and competence to deal with selected problems, that one possesses the attributes and skills that the primary reference group judges to be appropriate for the biological sex, that one is rational and coherent, that one is independent and responsible, and that one does not engage in behaviors or become preoccupied with thoughts that are prohibited by the primary reference group.

The establishment of stable beliefs about what one should be and about how the world should appear is a universal characteristic of human functioning. The Western middle-class child is convinced he should tell the truth, speak and think coherently, and behave in a way appropriate to his sex role. The learning of standards is not always a simple consequence of reward and punishment. Although most 9-year-old girls have not been punished for being unattractive, they have learned a standard about attractiveness that is relatively stable and well articulated, and they try to maximize their attractiveness. The details on how such standards are learned are not clear, but it is likely that sheer repetition of a standard by someone who adheres to it and whom the child respects and loves can lead to a belief in its validity. The standards learned during the first 10 years of life derive in large measure from those communications about behavior and attributes that are most frequently presented to the child by his family and friends. Parents continually remind their son, "Don't cry, don't cry," several times a day, several days a week for most of the weeks of the year. This repetition eventually has a permanent impact on the child's evaluation of the act of crying. The most significant standards are summary statements about proper thinking, feeling, and behavior; they are the ego-ideal.

The present chapter is concerned with competence and cognitive skills. It seems reasonable to suggest that a standard of intellectual competence will be an important determinant of whether the child will be highly motivated to strive for intellectual mastery. The child is often willing to reveal these standards. For example, children 7 to 17 years of age were asked whether they wanted to read material containing information only a few people knew or information that many people knew. There was a clear increase in preference for the unknown as the child grew older (Teeter, Rouzer, and Rosen, 1964). Similarly, fourth-grade subjects are more likely than second graders to choose a difficult over an easy task. As R. W. White (1959) suggests, the child develops a standard that dictates a desire to seek optimal challenge and to improve cognitive skills. This dynamic is essential to the educational enterprise.

Expectancies

An expectancy is an anticipation of an event. The anticipation can be an image or a thought. Expectancies are probably among the first psychological structures to develop, and they are constantly guiding behavior. One of man's continuing tasks is to create expectancies for the future so that he can reduce uncertainty about events to come. As we shall see, a major cause of anxiety is uncertainty about events in the future—the absence of fixed expectancies about the actions of others, one's own actions, or the vicissitudes of the environment. There are four major classes of expectancies. The first includes anticipations of the behavior of others; these form the essential fabric of social interaction. A second class includes the reactions of inanimate objects. The child learns that a glass will break if he drops it; milk will spill if he tips the cup. A third, more subjective class deals with the

individual's anticipation of the products of his own behavior; whether he will succeed or fail at a task. As a child approaches his third year he becomes more acutely conscious of his ability to complete certain tasks or to solve problems. The child seeks to avoid the unpleasant feelings characterizing failure, so he approaches tasks when he expects to succeed and avoids tasks when he expects to fail. The balance of successes and failures at a particular task accumulates over time and gradually leads to the establishment of a relatively stable expectancy for varied classes of problems. A final set of expectancies includes anticipations of internal feelings—feelings of pleasure, anger, fear, or sadness. The 6-year-old child has learned that if he steals money from his parents he will feel bad. We assign the label anxiety or guilt to this feeling state.

Relation of Motives and Expectancies to Quality of Cognitive Performance

Motives and expectancies are intimately related to each other and to quality of cognitive performance in a complex way. The most important relation ties expectancy of success at an intellectual task with motivation to master that task. If expectancy of success remains low for a long period of time, motive strength should become weak. If expectancy of success is high, motive strength will increase. There are several studies that verify this idea (Irwin, 1953; Jessor and Readio, 1957; MacCorquodale and Meehl, 1953). Some studies, however, have not found a positive relation between motive and expectancy. Rotter (1954) suggests that these constructs are independent. Atkinson (1957, 1964) argues for a negative relation between expectancy and value of outcome in intellectual tasks.

With other conditions equal, the child who has a high expectancy of success will perform better than one whose expectancy of success is low. It has been demonstrated (Rosenthal and Jacobson, 1968) that a child's IQ may rise when the teacher in his classroom is led to believe that the child is brighter than he is. This rise in IQ was probably mediated by an increase in the child's expectancy of success which, in turn, increased the quality of his performance on the intelligence test.

The Crandalls have shown positive correlations between expectancy of success, on the one hand, and motivation and quality of performance on intellectual tests, on the other. For example, 20 boys and 20 girls aged 7 to 9 years were asked to state whether they could solve mazes and memory tasks of varying difficulty (i.e., they were asked to state their expectancy of success). The subjects were later observed in a free-play situation, in which observers coded how long the subjects played with intellectual games and puzzles. There was a positive relation, especially for boys, between high expectancy of success and frequency of approach to the intellectual materials (Crandall, Katkovsky, and Preston, 1962). A related study with 12- and 13-year-old children found a positive correlation, for both sexes, between high expectancy of success and persistence with difficult mathematical problems (Battle, 1965). This relation between expectancy and quality of performance can be manipulated experimentally. Some children were given a high expectancy of success by receiving encouraging remarks from the examiner while they were solving a task. Others were given no such encouragement. Those with high expectancy were more successful in reaching the correct solution of a difficult problem (B. B. Tyler, 1958).

In a series of studies by Crandall and her colleagues on samples ranging in size from 70 to 256 there was a consistent positive correlation between stated expectancy estimates of intellectual competence and quality of report card grades. When the expectancy was specific to the particular area in which the grades were obtained, the correlations were very high (in the 80s). When the expectancy estimates were given for general competence, or in an area different from that in which the grade was obtained, the correlations were lower in the 30s but always positive (V. C. Crandall, in press).

Covariation between stated expectancy and quality of performance has some permanence and is remarkably consistent across populations. Although some prefer to interpret these correlations as indicating that high expectancies cause better quality of performance, it is just as reasonable to conclude that high quality of performance leads to higher expectancies. The subject's expectancy derives partly from his subjective assessment of the quality of his performance. It is most likely that performance and expectancy are wedded continually, each influencing the other, with the simultaneous resolution of these two forces affecting motivation.

Girls' expectancy estimates are consistently lower than those of boys (V. C. Crandall, in press), despite equivalent IQ scores and equivalent experimental feedback. Why do boys state that they will do better on intellectual tasks than girls? There are several possibilities. Boys, in their daily lives, may have actually experienced more positive feedback than girls, or they may have *perceived* more positive feedback. More likely, however, they may feel they should state a higher expectancy for intellectual tasks, since intellectual competence is more appropriate for the male than the female sex role. The sex differences in expectancy seem to persist despite equivalent objective feedback over a year.

In an interesting analysis, the entire entering freshman class at Antioch College in 1963 ($N = 380$) was studied over four academic quarters. At the beginning of each academic quarter the students were asked to list each course they would be taking and the grade they expected to receive. The expected grades stated by the males were always higher than those stated by the females ($p < .01$). However, examination of the actual grades received revealed no sex differences. Moreover, the mean expectancy statements and mean grades remained generally constant over the four quarters. Both males and females overestimated the grades they thought they would obtain, but males' overestimates were larger than those of females. Actual success or failure seems, in the short run, to be relatively unimportant in controlling expectancy statements. The subjects who, in actuality, were doing more poorly in school gave slightly inflated expectancy estimates. Among subjects who were in the middle of a group in actual ability (and therefore had ambiguous feedback), the boys gave slight overestimates, whereas the girls gave slight underestimates.

Crandall has also considered a variable dealing with the child's attribution of responsibility for the quality of his performance. By a questionnaire procedure, the child is asked whether he attributes his good or poor grades to his own efforts or to the vicissitudes of the external environment. Does the child take responsibility for his success and failure, or does he assign this responsibility to chance or actions of the environment? In general, children who obtain better grades and have higher expectancies of success state that they are responsible for both success and failure; children with lower grades and lower expectancies of success attribute the cause of their evaluation to the environment (McGhee and Crandall, 1968). Moreover, there is some suggestion that sons with nurturant mothers are more likely to assume responsibility for their own success or failure than are sons with less nurturant mothers. On the other hand, daughters with nurturant fathers are likely to project responsibility more than are daughters with less nurturant fathers (Katkovsky, Crandall, and Good, 1967).

The relation between motivation to master a task and expectancy of failure is established early in development and can be seen in clear form as early as 2 years of age. Two-year-old children can become very involved in perceptual discrimination tasks. If the initial problems are easy and correct solutions come after a brief expenditure of effort, motivation is maintained and expressions of delight punctuate the child's performance. But after one or two failures there is a sudden, sullen withdrawal, which is difficult to overcome. Children seem to know when they have failed without being told; they know whether answers are correct or incorrect. The child prefers to avoid the pain of possible failure rather than risk the possible joy of success.

It is difficult to explain why expectancy of failure is so strong a force in governing the Western child's behavior. It is not likely that the visceral afferent feedback associated with failure is stronger or more salient than the feelings linked with success. When the child succeeds, he often smiles or laughs and munches his candy reward with gusto. The mosaic of stimulus experience linked with success seems to be as rich in sensory qualities as that accompanying failure. A second possibility is that the anticipation of the unpleasant feelings associated with failure is readily conditioned to a withdrawal response, whereas the anticipation of pleasant stimulation is less easily linked to the act of persistence. An escape habit seems to be more readily acquired than an approach habit. A third interpretation is that the related responses of inhibition and withdrawal are more easily elicited than the more diffuse acts that characterize involvement. Expectancy of failure often

leads to withdrawal, and it may take less incentive to elicit and maintain withdrawal than it does to maintain continued attention and involvement. This hypothesis is closely related to a final possible interpretation to which we feel most friendly. Failure leaves the child with no response to make to the task. The child who has failed is uncertain as to what he should do, so he withdraws. The child feels pressure to behave, but he has no response to make. The habits he has relied on are not appropriate, and he has no others available. If the child has no response to initiate, he will withdraw to a context where he does have an available response. This particular interpretation of the reaction to failure places the burden of the explanation as much on the availability of task-related responses as on the unpleasant-feeling tone of failure or disapproval. In any case, the Western child is driven to avoid failure, and the quality of his performance on any cognitive task is continually influenced by his expectancy of failure.

Anxiety

Anxiety is a label used to designate a class of unpleasant affective states. The reasons for the unpleasantness, which is usually accompanied by particular cognitions, are not easily specified. There is no sharply felt pain, nor does headache or muscle tightness universally accompany this feeling; and there is no fixed set of afferent sensations that characterize anxiety. At times, however, the person perceives a change in afferent stimulation which may result from discharge of the gastrointestinal tract or increases in heart rate, palmar sweating, shivering, flushing, or muscular contractions. The second central characteristic of anxiety is uncertainty about an unwanted event. Thus anxiety is usually defined as "an unpleasant feeling state accompanied by an uncertainty surrounding an undesirable event."[17] To be sure, people sometimes mislabel the source of their feelings. The 8-year-old who is afraid of going to school and feels unpleasant

[17] We do not wish to reify the construct of anxiety. Sarbin (1968) has cogently argued that anxiety was originally invented as a metaphor and, with time, became a myth. He suggests that the phrase "cognitive strain" be used to denote the experience that "arises in connection with solving problems of choice, conflict, interference, interruption, overloading, etc" (p. 418).

because he anticipates failure on an arithmetic test may tell his mother he is sick. He is not lying; he interprets his distress as illness and asks to stay home. Adults currently are often subject to the opposite error. The mass media have so sensitized them to the likelihood that many uncomfortable feelings are psychologically based, they may mislabel the ache of a viral infection as anxiety and take tranquilizers rather than a more appropriate drug.

We consider next the psychologically important relation between expectancy of success (or failure) in a particular problem situation and the experience of anxiety. This relation appears to be curvilinear. A child with low expectancy of success on a particular task is as certain of the outcome as is one who has high expectancy of success. Children at either of these extremes are assumed to experience less anxiety than children who are uncertain of their competence, that is, those who have a moderate expectancy of success or failure.

There is a small set of conflicts and sources of anxiety, in addition to anxiety over failure, that can block quality of cognitive performance. This set includes lack of congruence with sex-role standards, anxiety over competitiveness, anxiety over peer rejection, and anxiety over passivity. Let us consider each briefly.

Lack of Congruence with Sex-Role Standards. As indicated earlier, one of the child's major motives is to adopt behaviors and values that are maximally congruent with sex-role standards. Classification of an activity as masculine or feminine is based on the gender of the person most often associated with it. Schoolwork is usually classified as feminine, because women are normally associated with the monitoring of elementary school activity. Research has shown that girls and boys in the elementary school tend to classify school and school-related objects as more feminine than masculine (Kagan, 1964). The greater number of boys than girls with reading problems in the United States can be attributed, in part, to the fact that boys see the school situation as feminine and therefore not congruent with their sex. This conclusion is supported by the fact that on the island of Hokkaido in Japan, were men do much of the teaching in the elementary grades, there are no more boys than girls with reading problems (K. Miyake, personal communication).

The Role of Anxiety over Hostility. Since the public school classroom often contains a competitive, rank-order atmosphere, children who feel anxiety about outdoing a rival or feel guilt over the hostile motives that are associated with competitive mastery may begin to inhibit effort. It is possible that the girls' lower expectancy of success (V. C. Crandall, 1968) may be due to reluctance to report high estimates of performance, because they may be seen as "boasting" and, by inference, as aggressive and assertive acts.

Anxiety over Peer Rejection. One of the child's major motives is to recruit and maintain peer acceptance. He will inhibit many behaviors that the peer group regards as undesirable. Coleman's (1961) study of adolescent society indicates that children's performance in school tends to be in close accord with the values of the peer group. Thus strong desires for peer acceptance and anxiety over peer rejection can inhibit involvement in the school situation.

Anxiety over Passivity. A final source of conflict, especially relevant in the early school years, concerns the child's anxiety over playing the passive role. Typically, the child is placed in such a passive position in the school situation. He is to sit quietly, listen to the teacher, and conform to her requests. Some children have a conflict over passive submission to adults and are threatened by such a posture. If the anxiety generated by this conflict were high, it could lead to poor performance in the school situation. Boys usually have greater anxiety over passivity than girls, and this may be one more reason why boys' performance in the elementary school years is usually inferior to that of girls.

EPILOGUE

Few systematic conclusions flow easily from this long, yet not exhaustive review. Inquiry into variation in cognitive functioning has not had the beneficial guidance of strong theory and, on occasion, has become empirically barbaric. The movement began in a revolutionary atmosphere and, like many revolutions, has constructed its principles a posteriori, rather than a priori. The subsequent fabric of generalizations has more intuitive appeal than logical coherence or commandingness.

The dividends of the revolution are obvious.

The psychological distance between investigations of perception, language, and thought, on the one hand, and studies of personality dynamics, on the other, has been shortened. This engagement will, we suspect, lead to a more cognitive framework for personality theory. The work of Kelly and Rotter is early evidence of this trend. Study of cognitive performances may put man back together by denying the artificial dissection of his psyche into categories labeled thinking, feeling, and willing. The association between quality of performance on a perceptual decision task (such as rod-and-frame) and patterns of child-rearing lends a concrete vitality to this synthesis. These dividends from the work on cognitive variation are to be applauded. There are, however, several serious faults that deserve solemn concern.

First, there is the possibility that there is more method variance in the existing data than we normally acknowledge. Two of the parents of contemporary psychology—Hull and Freud—have taught their children to look closely at the agent of action (his history and his motives) in order to understand and predict his behavior. Correlatively, psychologists were rarely told to heed the context of the agent's actions. A hungry rat should run fast in any T-maze; a dependent child should ask for help from everybody. This cavalier dismissal of the critical and complementary roles of the social and impersonal environments has, regrettably, been inherited by many of the cognitive-style investigators. It is presumed that a field-independent person is field independent in all situations that require restructuring; an analytic child analyzes all visual material; a "sharpener" articulates sequential experience continually. This is probably the most serious fallacy in the interpretive structures that have been built around the work on cognitive variation.

The research reviewed suggests that the probability of a child analyzing a visual array is seriously dependent on the materials presented. A child can be analytic with one set of words and nonanalytic with another set of words or with pictures. The use of rod-and-frame and embedded-figures tasks, which are masculine in their accoutrements, may be one source of the consistent sex differences in field independence. It is of extreme importance to determine the generalizability of the

Witkin conclusions to test contexts that are less masculine or more feminine (e.g., an embedded-figures task that did not illustrate geometric forms but cooking utensils or flowers). The disregard of specific task materials implies that we may have been studying species of findings rather than genera or families. It is imperative that tasks sample a wide variety of contexts in order to demonstrate the power of the construct. In sum, it is not clear how much variance in test performance is specific to the test and how much is attributable to the hypothetical construct the procedure was designed to serve.

Although the names applied to theoretical constructs for "style" often have an exotic quality, it is possible that the phenomena they serve touch more familiar dynamic themes. Anxiety over error, attention distribution, expectancy of success or failure, and vulnerability to distraction are central to many of the test procedures utilized. The majority of the procedures reviewed present the subject with an "intellectual" task for which he believes there is a correct answer. Thus anxiety over intellectual competence and expectancy of success in the intellectual domain are always relevant variables controlling the final product. The emphasis on evaluative intellectual tasks as indexes of "style" should give us pause, for it does not seem intuitively reasonable that the basic psychological functions of human beings are most sensitively revealed in contexts in which the subjects believe their intellectual competence is being evaluated. Perhaps these procedures continue to be validated because they correlate with other test procedures that involve the same dynamic. Psychology gathers most of its human data (be they projective tests, memory-recall procedures, interviews, or paired-associate learning) from subjects whose behavior is geared to a strange examiner's reaction to or evaluation of their performance. This influence can be so pervasive that behavior in such potentially evaluative contexts may generate apparent construct validity within a diverse set of tasks.

Psychological phenomena possess the dual aspects of form and content. Motives, beliefs, expectancies, and standards are among psychology's central contents, but these contents are manifested in specific forms of behavior.

The operational probes we use to diagnose these contents must acknowledge those forms. Individual cognitive styles are almost always engaged when one attempts to explore a person's motives, expectancies, and standards. If we ignore these variables, our probes will provide noisy information. The small and courageous cadre of scientists who have spent the last decade systematizing these dimensions have done a high service. It is clear that an individual's preferred fashion of interpreting, transforming, and reporting information will have to be a variable in any equation that seeks to explain him.

References

Adams, J. A. *Human memory*. New York: McGraw-Hill, 1967.

Adorno, T. W., Frenkel-Brunswik, E., Levinson, D. J., and Sanford, R. N. *The authoritarian personality*. New York: Harper, 1950.

Allard, M., and Carlson, E. R. The generality of cognitive complexity. *J. soc. Psychol.*, 1963, **59**, 73–75.

Anastasi, A. *Differential psychology: individual and group differences in behavior*. (3rd ed.) New York: Macmillan, 1958.

Asch, S. E. *Social psychology*. Englewood Cliffs, N.J.: Prentice-Hall, 1952.

Atkinson, J. W. Motivational determinants of risk-taking behavior. *Psychol. Rev.*, 1957, **64**, 359–372.

Atkinson, J. W. *An introduction to motivation*. Princeton, N.J.: Van Nostrand, 1964.

Barclay, A., and Cusumano, D. R. Father absence, cross-sex identity, and field-dependent behavior in male adolescents. *Child Dev.*, 1967, **38**, 243–250.

Barron, F. An ego-strength scale which predicts response to psychotherapy. *J. consult. Psychol.*, 1953, **17**, 327–333.

Bartlett, F. C. *Remembering: a study in experimental and social psychology*. London: Cambridge University Press, 1932.

Battle, E. S. Motivational determinants of academic task persistence. *J. pers. soc. Psychol.*, 1965, **2**, 209–218.

Belmont, J. N., and Butterfield, E. C. The relations of short term memory to developmental level and intelligence. Unpublished manuscript, Yale University, 1967.

Bernstein, B. Social structure, language, and learning. *Educ. Res.*, 1961, **3**, 163–176.

Berry, J. W. Temne and Eskimo perceptual skills. *Int. J. Psychol.*, 1966, **1**, 207–229.

Bieri, J. Cognitive complexity-simplicity and predictive behavior. *J. abnorm. soc. Psychol.*, 1955, **51**, 263–268.

Bieri, J. Parental identification, acceptance of authority, and within-sex differences in cognitive behavior. *J. abnorm. soc. Psychol.*, 1960, **60**, 76–79.

Bieri, J. Complexity-simplicity as a personality variable in cognitive and preferential behavior. In D. W. Fiske and S. R. Maddi (Eds.), *Functions of varied experience*. Homewood, Ill.: Dorsey, 1961. Pp. 355–379.

Bieri, J. Cognitive complexity and personality development. In O. J. Harvey (Ed.), *Experience, structure and adaptability*. New York: Springer, 1966. Pp. 13–37.

Bieri, J., Atkins, A. L., Briar, J. S., Leaman, R. L., Miller, H., and Tripodi, T. *Clinical and social judgment: the discrimination of behavorial information*. New York: Wiley, 1966.

Bieri, J., Bradburn, W. M., and Galinsky, M. D. Sex differences in perceptual behavior. *J. Personality*, 1958, **26**, 1–12.

Bieri, J., and Lobek, R. Acceptance of authority and parental identification. *J. Personality*, 1959, **27**, 74–86.

Bing, E. Effect of childrearing practices on development of differential cognitive abilities. *Child Dev.*, 1963, **34**, 631–648.

Birch, H. G., and Belmont, L. Auditory-visual integration in normal and retarded readers. *Am. J. Orthopsychiat.*, 1964, **34**, 852–861.

Birch, H. G., and Belmont, L. Auditory-visual integration, intelligence and reading ability in school children. *Percept. mot. Skills*, 1965, **20**, 295–305.

Birch, H. G., and Lefford, A. Intersensory development in children. *Monogr. Soc. Res. Child Dev.*, 1963, **28**, No. 5 (Serial No. 89).

Birch, H. G., and Lefford, A. Visual differentiation, intersensory integration, and voluntary motor control. *Monogr. Soc. Res. Child Dev.*, 1967, **32**, No. 2 (Serial No. 110).

Blade, M. F., and Watson, W. S. Increase in spatial visualization test scores during engineering study. *Psychol. Monogr.*, 1955, **69** (12, Whole No. 397).

Blum, A. The value factor in children's size perception. *Child Dev.*, 1957, **28**, 3–14.

Blum, A. H., and Broverman, D. M. Children's cognitive style and response modification. *J. genet. Psychol.*, 1967, **110**, 95–103.

Brener, J. M., and Hothersall, D. Paced respiration and heart rate control. *Psychophysiology*, 1967, **4**, 1–6.

Briggs, C. H. An experimental study of reflection-impulsivity in children. Unpublished doctoral dissertation, University of Minnesota, 1966.

Brinkmann, E. H. Programmed instruction as a technique for improving spatial visualization. *J. appl. Psychol.*, 1966, **50**, 179–184.

Broadbent, D. E. *Perception and communication.* New York: Pergamon Press, 1958.

Broverman, D. M. Cognitive style and intra-individual variation in abilities. *J. Personality*, 1960, **28**, 240–256. (a)

Broverman, D. M. Dimensions of cognitive style. *J. Personality*, 1960, **28**, 167–185. (b)

Broverman, D. M. Normative and ipsative measurement in psychology. *Psychol. Rev.*, 1962, **69**, 295–305.

Broverman, D. M. Comments on the note by MacAndrew and Forgy. *Psychol. Rev.*, 1963, **70**, 119–120.

Broverman, D. M. Generality and behavioral correlates of cognitive styles. *J. consult. Psychol.*, 1964, **28**, 487–500.

Broverman, D. M., Broverman, I. K., Vogel, W., Palmer, R. D., and Klaiber, E. L. The automatization cognitive style and physical development. *Child Dev.*, 1964, **35**, 1343–1359.

Broverman, D. M., Klaiber, E. L., Kobayashi, Y., and Vogel, W., Roles of activation and inhibition in sex differences in cognitive abilities. *Psychol. Rev.*, 1968, **75**, 23–50.

Bruner, J. S., Goodnow, J. J., and Austin, G. A. *A study of thinking.* New York: Wiley, 1956.

Bruner, J. S., Olver, R. R., and Greenfield, P. M. *Studies in cognitive growth.* New York: Wiley, 1966.

Bruner, J. S., and Tajfel, H. Cognitive risk and environmental change. *J. abnorm. soc. Psychol.*, 1961, **62**, 231–241.

Bruner, J. S., and Tajfel, H. Width of category and concept differentiation: A note on some comments by Gardner and Schoen. *J. pers. soc. Psychol.*, 1965, **2**, 261–264. (a)

Bruner, J. S., and Tajfel, H. A rejoinder. *J. pers. soc. Psychol.*, 1965, **2**, 267–268. (b)

Carter, S. Diagnosis and treatment: management of the child who has had a convulsion. *Pediatrics*, 1964, **33**, 431–434.

Castaneda, A., McCandless, B. R., and Palermo, D. S. The children's form of the manifest anxiety scale. *Child Dev.*, 1956, **27**, 317–326.

Cattell, J. McK. Mental tests and measurements. *Mind*, 1890, **15**, 373–381.

Cazden, C. B. Subcultural differences in child language: an inter-disciplinary review. *Merrill-Palmer Quart.*, 1966, **12**, 185–219.

Charlesworth, W. R. Instigation and maintenance of curiosity behavior as a function of surprise versus novel and familiar stimuli. *Child Dev.*, 1964, **35**, 1169–1186.

Cohen, J. The factorial structure of the WISC at ages 7–6, 10–6, and 13–6. *J. consult. Psychol.*, 1959, **23**, 285–299.

Cohen, J. *Chance, skill, and luck*. Baltimore: Penguin, 1960.

Coleman, J. C. *The adolescent society*. New York: Free Press, 1961.

Corah, N. L. Differentiation in children and their parents. *J. Personality*, 1964, **33**, 300–308.

Crandall, V. C. Sex differences in expectancy of intellectual and academic reinforcement. In C. P. Smith (Ed.), *The development of achievement related motives and self-esteem in children*. New York: Russell Sage Foundation, in press.

Crandall, V. J., Katkovsky, W., and Preston, A. Motivational and ability determinants of young children's intellectual achievement behaviors. *Child Dev.*, 1962, **33**, 643–661.

Crandall, V. J., and Sinkeldam, C. Children's dependent and achievement behaviors in social situations and their perceptual field dependence. *J. Personality*, 1964, **32**, 1–22.

Crockett, W. H. Cognitive complexity and impression formation. In B. A. Maher (Ed.), *Progress in experimental personality research*, Vol. 2. New York: Academic Press, 1965. Pp. 47–90.

Cross, H. J. The relation of parental training conditions to conceptual level in adolescent boys. *J. Personality*, 1966, **34**, 348–365.

Dawson, J. L. M. Cultural and physiological influences upon spatial-perceptual processes in West Africa. Part I. *Int. J. Psychol.*, 1967, **2**, 115–128. (a)

Dawson, J. L. M. Cultural and physiological influences upon spatial-perceptual processes in West Africa. Part II. *Int. J. Psychol.*, 1967, **2**, 171–185. (b)

Debus, R. L. Effects of brief observation of model behavior on conceptual tempo of impulsive children. Unpublished manuscript, University of Sidney, Australia, 1968.

Dember, W. N. *Visual perception: the nineteenth century*. New York: Wiley, 1964.

D'Heurle, A., Mellinger, J. C., and Haggard, E. A. Personality, intellectual, and achievement patterns in gifted children. *Psychol. Monogr.*, 1959, **73** (13, Whole No. 483).

Donaldson, M. *A study of children's thinking*. London: Tavistock, 1963.

Draguns, J. G., and Multari, G. Recognition of perceptually ambiguous stimuli in grade school children. *Child Dev.*, 1961, **32**, 541–550.

Drake, D. M. Unpublished doctoral dissertation, Harvard University, 1967.

Duncker, K. On problem-solving. *Psychol. Monogr.*, 1945, **58** (5, Whole No. 270).

Dyk, R. B., and Witkin, H. A. Family experiences related to the development of differentiation in children. *Child Dev.*, 1965, **36**, 21–55.

Elkind, D., Koegler, R. R., and Go, E. Studies in perceptual development: II. Part-whole perception. *Child Dev.*, 1964, **35**, 81–90.

Elliott, R. Physiological activity and performance: a comparison of kindergarten children with young adults. *Psychol. Monogr.*, 1964, **78** (10, Whole No. 587).

Elliott, R., and McMichael, R. E. Effects of specific training on frame dependence. *Percept. mot. Skills*, 1963, **17**, 363–367.

Fantz, R. L., and Nevis, S. Pattern preferences and perceptual-cognitive development in early infancy. *Merrill-Palmer Quart.*, 1967, **13**, 77–108.

Feffer, M. H. The cognitive implications of role taking behavior. *J. Personality,* 1959, **27**, 152–168.

Feffer, M. H., and Gourevitch, V. Cognitive aspects of role-taking in children. *J. Personality,* 1960, **28**, 383–396.

Fenichel, O. *The psychoanalytic theory of neurosis.* New York: Norton, 1945.

Ferguson, L. R., and Maccoby, E. E. Interpersonal correlates of differential abilities. *Child Dev.,* 1966, **37**, 549–571.

Fitzgibbons, D., Goldberger, L., and Eagle, M. Field dependence and memory for incidental material. *Percept. mot. Skills,* 1965, **21**, 743–749.

Flavell, J. H., Beach, D. R., and Chinsky, J. M. Spontaneous verbal rehearsal in a memory task as a function of age. *Child Dev.,* 1966, **37**, 283–300.

Freeberg, N. E., and Payne, D. T. Parental influence on cognitive development in early childhood: a review. *Child Dev.,* 1967, **38**, 65–87.

Freud, A. *The ego and the mechanisms of defense.* New York: International Universities Press, 1946.

Freud, S. *Inhibitions, symptoms, and anxiety.* London: Hogarth, 1966.

Gardner, R. W. Cognitive styles in categorizing behavior. *J. Personality,* 1953, **22**, 214–233.

Gardner, R. W. Cognitive controls in adaptation: research and measurement. In S. Messick and J. Ross (Eds.), *Measurement in personality and cognition.* New York: Wiley, 1962. Pp. 183–198.

Gardner, R. W. The development of cognitive structures. In C. Scheerer (Ed.), *Cognition: theory, research, promise.* New York: Harper and Row, 1964. Pp. 147–171.

Gardner, R. W., Holzman, P. S., Klein, G. S., Linton, H. B., and Spence, D. P. Cognitive control: a study of individual consistencies in cognitive behavior. *Psychol. Issues,* 1959, **1**, No. 4 (Monogr. 4).

Gardner, R. W., Jackson, D. N., and Messick, S. J. Personality organization in cognitive controls and intellectual abilities. *Psychol. Issues,* 1960, **2**, No. 4 (Monogr. 8).

Gardner, R. W., and Long, R. I. Control defense and centration effect: a study of scanning behaviour. *Br. J. Psychol.,* 1962, **53**, 129–140. (a)

Gardner, R. W., and Long, R. I. Cognitive controls of attention and inhibition: a study of individual consistencies. *Br. J. Psychol.,* 1962, **53**, 381–388. (b)

Gardner, R. W., and Moriarty, A. E. *Personality development at preadolescence.* Seattle: University of Washington Press, 1968.

Gardner, R. W., and Schoen, R. A. Differentiation and abstraction in concept formation. *Psychol. Monogr.,* 1962, **76** (41, Whole No. 560).

Gardner, R. W., and Schoen, R. A. Reply to the note by Bruner and Tajfel. *J. pers. soc. Psychol.,* 1965, **2**, 264–267.

Gill, M. The present state of psychoanalytic theory. *J. abnorm. soc. Psychol.,* 1959, **58**, 1–8.

Gilmore, M. C. A study of concept formation, reflection-impulsivity, and production of alternate uses in nine- and ten-year-old boys and girls from different social classes. Unpublished honors thesis, Radcliffe College, 1968.

Glixman, A. F. Categorizing behavior as a function of meaning domain. *J. pers. soc. Psychol.,* 1965, **2**, 370–377.

Goldstein, A. G., and Chance, J. E. Effects of practice on sex-related differences in performance on Embedded Figures. *Psychon. Sci.,* 1965, **3**, 361–362.

Gollin, E. S. Organizational characteristics of social judgment: a developmental investigation. *J. Personality,* 1958, **26**, 139–154.

Goodenough, D. R., and Eagle, C. J. A modification of the embedded-figures test for use with young children. *J. genet. Psychol.,* 1963, **103**, 67–74.

Goodenough, D. R., and Karp, S. A. Field dependence and intellectual functioning. *J. abnorm. soc. Psychol.*, 1961, **63**, 241–246.

Goodenough, F. L. *Measurement of intelligence by drawings.* Yonkers, N.Y.: World, 1926.

Gottesman, I. I. Heritability of personality: a demonstration. *Psychol. Monogr.*, 1963, **77** (9, Whole No. 572).

Gottschaldt, K. Über den Einfluss der Erfahrung auf die Wahrnehmung von Figuren, I; Über den Einfluss gehäufter Einprägung von Figuren auf ihre Sichtbarkeit in umfassenden Konfigurationen. *Psychol. Forsch.*, 1926, **8**, 261–317.

Gough, H. G. Identifying psychological femininity. *Educ. psychol. Measmt*, 1952, **12**, 427–439.

Gough, H. G. *Manual for the California Psychological Inventory.* Palo Alto, Cal.: Consulting Psychologists Press, 1957.

Gould, A., and Stephenson, G. M. Some experiments relating to Bartlett's theory of remembering. *Br. J. Psychol.*, 1967, **58**, 39–49.

Gruen, A. Dancing experience and personality in relation to perception. *Psychol. Monogr.*, 1955, **69** (14, Whole No. 399).

Guilford, J. P. The structure of intellect. *Psychol. Bull.*, 1956, **53**, 267–293.

Guilford, J. P. Three faces of intellect. *Am. Psychol.*, 1959, **14**, 469–479.

Guilford, J. P., Frick, J. W., Christensen, P. R., and Merrifield, P. R. A factor-analytic study of flexibility in thinking. *Rep. psychol. Lab.*, 1957, No. 18, Los Angeles, University of Southern California.

Harris, D. B. *Children's drawings as measures of intellectual maturity.* New York: Harcourt, Brace, and World, 1963.

Hartmann, H. *Ego psychology and the problem of adaptation.* New York: International Universities Press, 1958.

Harvey, O. J. Authoritarianism and conceptual functioning in varied conditions. *J. Personality*, 1963, **31**, 462–470.

Harvey, O. J. System structure, flexibility and creativity. In O. J. Harvey (Ed.), *Experience, structure and adaptability.* New York: Springer, 1966. Pp. 39–65.

Harvey, O. J., Hunt, D. E., and Schroder, H. M. *Conceptual systems and personality organization.* New York: Wiley, 1961.

Heider, E. R. Style and effectiveness of children's verbal communications within and between social classes. Unpublished doctoral dissertation, Harvard University, 1968.

Hernández-Peón, R. Psychiatric implications of neurophysiological research. *Bull. Menninger Clin.*, 1964, **28**, 165–185.

Hertzig, M. E., Birch, H. G., Thomas, A., and Mendez, O. A. Class and ethnic differences in the responsiveness of preschool children to cognitive demands. *Monogr. Soc. Res. Child Dev.*, 1968, **33**, No. 1 (Serial No. 117).

Hess, R. D., and Bear, R. M. *Early education: current theory, research, and action.* Chicago: Aldine, 1968.

Hess, R. D., and Shipman, V. C. Early experience and the socialization of cognitive modes in children. *Child Dev.*, 1965, **36**, 869–886.

Hill, K. T., and Sarason, S. B. The relation of test anxiety and defensiveness to test and school performance over the elementary-school years: a further longitudinal study. *Monogr. Soc. Res. Child Dev.*, 1966, **31**, No. 2 (Serial No. 104).

Hollingshead, A. B. *Two factor index of social position.* New Haven, Conn.: Author, 1957.

Holtzman, W. H. Intelligence, cognitive style, and personality: a developmental approach. In *Intelligence: perspectives 1965.* Harcourt, Brace and World, 1966. Pp. 1–32.

Holzman, P. S., and Gardner, R. W. Leveling and repression. *J. abnorm. soc. Psychol.*, 1959, **59**, 151–155.

Holzman, P. S., and Gardner, R. W. Leveling-sharpening and memory organization. *J. abnorm. soc. Psychol.*, 1960, **61**, 176–180.

Hudson, W. Pictorial depth perception in sub-cultural groups in Africa. *J. soc. Psychol.*, 1960, **52**, 183–208.

Hunt, D. E. A conceptual systems change model and its application to education. In O. J. Harvey (Ed.), *Experience, structure and adaptability*. New York: Springer, 1966. Pp. 277–302.

Inhelder, B., and Piaget, J. *The early growth of logic in the child*. New York: Harper and Row, 1964.

Irwin, F. W. Stated expectations as functions of probability and desirability of outcomes. *J. Personality*, 1953, **21**, 329–335.

Iscoe, I., and Carden, J. A. Field dependence, manifest anxiety, and sociometric status in children. *J. consult. Psychol.*, 1961, **25**, 184.

Jackson, D. N. Independence and resistance to perceptual field forces. *J. abnorm. soc. Psychol.*, 1958, **56**, 279–281.

Jensen, A. R. Authoritarian attitudes and personality maladjustment. *J. abnorm. soc. Psychol.*, 1957, **54**, 303–311.

Jensen, A. R., and Rohwer, W. D., Jr. The Stroop Color-Word Test: a review. *Acta psychol.*, 1966, **25**, 36–93.

Jessor, R., and Readio, J. The influence of the value of an event upon the expectancy of its occurrence. *J. genet. Psychol.*, 1957, **56**, 219–228.

John, E. R. *Mechanisms of memory*. New York: Academic Press, 1967.

Jones, E. E., and Bruner, J. S. Expectancy in apparent visual movement. *Br. J. Psychol.*, 1954, **45**, 157–165.

Kagan, J. The child's sex role classification of school objects. *Child Dev.*, 1964, **35**, 1051–1056.

Kagan, J. Individual differences in the resolution of response uncertainty. *J. pers. soc. Psychol.*, 1965, **2**, 154–160. (a)

Kagan, J. Reflection-impulsivity and reading ability in primary grade children. *Child Dev.*, 1965, **36**, 609–628. (b)

Kagan, J. Impulsive and reflective children: significance of conceptual tempo. In J. D. Krumboltz (Ed.), *Learning and the educational process*. Chicago: Rand McNally, 1965. Pp. 133–161. (c)

Kagan, J. Reflection-impulsivity: the generality and dynamics of conceptual tempo. *J. abnorm. Psychol.*, 1966, **71**, 17–24.

Kagan, J., Moss, H. A., and Sigel, I. E. Psychological significance of styles of conceptualization. In J. C. Wright and J. Kagan (Eds.), Basic cognitive processes in children. *Monogr. Soc. Res. Child Dev.*, 1963, **28**, No. 2 (Serial No. 86). Pp. 73–112.

Kagan, J., Pearson, L., and Welch, L. Conceptual impulsivity and inductive reasoning. *Child Dev.*, 1966, **37**, 583–594. (a)

Kagan, J., Pearson, L., and Welch, L. Modifiability of an impulsive tempo. *J. educ. Psychol.*, 1966, **57**, 359–365. (b)

Kagan, J., Rosman, B. L., Day, D., Albert, J., and Phillips, W. Information processing in the child: significance of analytic and reflective attitudes. *Psychol. Monogr.*, 1964, **78** (1, Whole No. 578).

Kahneman, D., and Beatty, J. Pupil diameter and load on memory. *Science*, 1966, **154**, 1583–1585.

Kahneman, D., and Beatty, J. Pupillary responses in a pitch-discrimination task. *Percept. Psychophys.*, 1967, **2**, 101–105.

Kahneman, D., Turskey, B., Shapiro, D., and Crider, A. Pupillary, heart rate, and skin resistance changes during a mental task. *J. exp. Psychol.*, 1969, **79**, 164–167.

Karp, S. A. Field dependence and overcoming embeddedness. *J. consult. Psychol.*, 1963, **27**, 294–302.

Karp, S. A., and Konstadt, N. L. *Manual for the Children's Embedded Figures Test*. Baltimore, Md.: Authors (5900 Greenspring Ave., 21209), 1963.

Kass, N. Risk in decision making as a function of age, sex, and probability preference. *Child Dev.*, 1964, **35**, 577–582.

Katkovsky, W., Crandall, V. C., and Good, S. Parental antecedents of children's beliefs in internal-external control of reinforcements in intellectual achievement situations. *Child Dev.*, 1967, **38**, 765–776.

Katz, P. A., and Deutsch, M. Relation of auditory-visual shifting to reading achievement. *Percept. mot. Skills*, 1963, **17**, 327–332.

Kaye, D., Kirschner, P., and Mandler, G. The effect of test anxiety on memory span in a group test situation. *J. consult. Psychol.*, 1953, **17**, 265–266.

Kelly, G. A. *The psychology of personal constructs*. New York: Norton, 1955.

Kendler, H. H., and Kendler, T. S. Vertical and horizontal processes in problem solving. *Psychol. Rev.*, 1962, **69**, 1–16.

Kimble, G. A., and Posnick, G. M. Anxiety? *J. pers. soc. Psychol.*, 1967, **7**, 108–110.

King, J. A. Behavioral modification of the gene pool. In J. Hirsch (Ed.), *Behavior-genetic analysis*. New York: McGraw-Hill, 1967. Pp. 22–43.

Klein, G. S. Need and regulation. In M. R. Jones (Ed.), *Nebraska symposium on motivation*. Lincoln: University of Nebraska Press, 1954. Pp. 224–274.

Klein, G. S. Cognitive control and motivation. In G. Lindzey (Ed.), *Assessment of human motives*. New York: Rinehart, 1958. Pp. 87–118.

Kogan, N., and Wallach, M. A. *Risk taking: a study in cognition and personality*. New York: Holt, Rinehart and Winston, 1964.

Kogan, N., and Wallach, M. A. Risk taking as a function of the situation, the person, and the group. In *New directions in psychology III*. New York: Holt, Rinehart and Winston, 1967. Pp. 111–278.

Konstadt, N., and Forman, E. Field dependence and external directedness. *J. pers. soc. Psychol.*, 1965, **1**, 490–493.

Kris, E. Psychoanalysis and the study of creative imagination. *Bull. N. Y. Acad. Med.*, 1953, **29**, 334–351.

Kuhlman, C. Visual imagery in children. Unpublished doctoral dissertation, Harvard University, 1960.

Lacey, J. I. Psychophysiological approaches to the evaluation of psychotherapeutic process and outcome. In E. A. Rubinstein and M. B. Parloff (Eds.), *Research in psychotherapy*. Washington, D.C.: American Psychological Association, 1959. Pp. 160–208.

Lacey, J. I. Psychophysiological approaches to the evaluation of psychotherapeutic theory. In M. H. Appley and R. Trumbull (Eds.), *Psychological stress*. New York: Appleton-Century-Crofts, 1967. Pp. 14–42.

Lee, L. C., Kagan, J., and Rabson, A. Influence of a preference for analytic categorization upon concept acquisition. *Child Dev.*, 1963, **34**, 433–442.

Leibowitz, H. W., and Gwozdecki, J. The magnitude of the Poggendorff illusion as a function of age. *Child Dev.*, 1967, **38**, 573–580.

Lesser, G. S., Fifer, G., and Clark, D. H. Mental abilities of children from different social-class and cultural groups. *Monogr. Soc. Res. Child Dev.*, 1965, **30**, No. 4 (Serial No. 102).

Levinson, B., and Reese, H. W. Patterns of discrimination learning set in preschool children, fifth-graders, college freshmen, and the aged. *Monogr. Soc. Res. Child Dev.*, 1967, **32**, No. 7 (Serial No. 115).

Lewin, K. *A dynamic theory of personality.* New York: McGraw-Hill, 1935.

Lewin, K. *Field theory in social science.* New York: Harper and Row, 1951.

Lewis, M., Rausch, M., Goldberg, S., and Dodd, C. Error, response time and IQ: Sex differences in cognitive style of preschool children. *Percept. mot. Skills,* 1968, **26**, 563–568.

Linton, H. B. Dependence on external influence: correlates in perception, attitudes, and judgment. *J. abnorm. soc. Psychol.,* 1955, **51**, 502–507.

Linton, H., and Graham, E. Personality correlates of persuasibility. In I. L. Janis et al., *Personality and persuasibility.* New Haven, Conn.: Yale University Press, 1959. Pp. 69–101.

MacAndrew, C., and Forgy, E. A note on the effects of score transformations in Q and R factor analysis techniques. *Psychol. Rev.,* 1963, **70**, 116–118.

MacArthur, R. S. Sex differences in field dependence for the Eskimo. *Int. J. Psychol.,* 1967, **2**, 139–140.

Maccoby, E. E. Sex differences in intellectual functioning. In E. E. Maccoby (Ed.), *The development of sex differences.* Stanford, Cal.: Stanford University Press, 1966. Pp. 25–55.

Maccoby, E. E. Selective auditory attention in children. In L. P. Lipsitt and C. C. Spiker (Eds.), *Advances in child development and behavior.* Vol. 3. New York: Academic Press, 1967. Pp. 99–124.

Maccoby, E. E. The development of stimulus selection. In *Minnesota symposia on child psychology.* Vol. III. Minneapolis: University of Minnesota Press, in press.

Maccoby, E. E., and Bee, H. L. Some speculations concerning the lag between perceiving and performing. *Child Dev.,* 1965, **36**, 367–377.

Maccoby, E. E., Dowley, E. M., Hagen, J. W., and Degerman, R. Activity level and intellectual functioning in normal preschool children. *Child Dev.,* 1965, **36**, 761–770.

Maccoby, E. E., and Hagen, J. W. Effects of distraction upon central versus incidental recall: developmental trends. *J. exp. child Psychol.,* 1965, **2**, 280–289.

Maccoby, E. E., and Konrad, K. W. The effect of preparatory set on selective listening: developmental trends. *Monogr. Soc. Res. Child Dev.,* 1967, **32**, No. 4 (Serial No. 112).

MacCorquodale, K., and Meehl, P. E. Preliminary suggestions as to a formalization of expectancy theory. *Psychol. Rev.,* 1953, **60**, 55–63.

Machover, K. *Personality projection in the drawing of the human figure.* Springfield, Ill.: Thomas, 1949.

Mandler, J. M., and Mandler, G. *Thinking: from association to Gestalt.* New York: Wiley, 1964.

McCall, R. B., and Kagan, J. Attention in the infant: effects of complexity, contour, perimeter, and familiarity. *Child Dev.,* 1967, **38**, 939–952.

McGhee, P. E., and Crandall, V. C. Beliefs in internal-external control of reinforcements and academic performance. *Child Dev.,* 1968, **39**, 91–102.

Mercado, S. J., Diaz Guerrero, R., and Gardner, R. W. Cognitive control in children of Mexico and the United States. *J. soc. Psychol.,* 1963, **59**, 199–208.

Messer, S. B. The effect of anxiety over intellectual performance on reflective and impulsive children. Unpublished doctoral dissertation, Harvard University, 1968.

Messick, S., and Damarin, F. Cognitive styles and memory for faces. *J. abnorm. soc. Psychol.,* 1964, **69**, 313–318.

Messick, S., and Fritzky, F. J. Dimensions of analytic attitude in cognition and personality. *J. Personality,* 1963, **31**, 346–370.

Messick, S., and Kogan, N. Differentiation and compartmentalization in object-sorting measures of categorizing style. *Percept. mot. Skills,* 1963, **16**, 47–51.

Milton, G. A. The effects of sex-role identification upon problem-solving skill. *J. abnorm. soc. Psychol.*, 1957, **55**, 208–212.

Milton, G. A. Five studies of the relation between sex role identification and achievement in problem solving. Technical Report No. 3, Department of Industrial Administration, Yale University, 1958.

Minucci, P. K., and Connors, M. M. Reaction time under three viewing conditions: binocular, dominant eye, and nondominant eye. *J. exp. Psychol.*, 1964, **67**, 268–275.

Müller, G. E. Über das Aubertsche Phänoman. *Z. Psychol.*, 1916, **49**, 109–244.

Neisser, U. *Cognitive psychology*. New York: Appleton-Century-Crofts, 1967.

Nelson, T. F. The effects of training in attention deployment on observing behavior in reflective and impulsive children. Unpublished doctoral dissertation, University of Minnesota, 1968.

Obrist, P. A., and Webb, R. A. Heart rate during conditioning in dogs: relationship to somatic-motor activity. *Psychophysiol.*, 1967, **4**, 7–34.

Olver, R. R., and Hornsby, J. R. On equivalence. In J. S. Bruner et al. (Eds.), *Studies in cognitive growth*. New York: Wiley, 1966. Pp. 68–85.

Ostfeld, B. M., and Neimark, E. D. Effect of response time restriction upon cognitive style scores. *Proceedings of the 75th annual convention of the American Psychological Association*, 1967. Pp. 169–170.

Palermo, D. S. Relation between anxiety and two measures of speed in a reaction time task. *Child Dev.*, 1961, **32**, 401–408.

Parrish, M., Lundy, R. M., and Leibowitz, H. W. Hypnotic age-regression and magnitudes of the Ponzo and Poggendorff illusions. *Science*, 1968, **159**, 1375–1376.

Pedersen, F. A., and Wender, P. H. Early social correlates of cognitive functioning in six-year-old boys. *Child Dev.*, 1968, **39**, 185–193.

Pettigrew, T. F. The measurement and correlates of category width as a cognitive variable. *J. Personality*, 1958, **26**, 532–544.

Pettigrew, T. F., Allport, G. W., and Barnett, E. O. Binocular resolution and perception of race in South Africa. *Br. J. Psychol.*, 1958, **49**, 265–278.

Phillips, B. N., King, F. J., and McGuire, C. Studies on anxiety: I. Anxiety and performance on psychometric tests varying in complexity. *Child Dev.*, 1959, **30**, 253–259.

Piaget, J. *The language and thought of the child*. London: Routledge & Kegan Paul, 1926.

Piaget, J. *The origins of intelligence in children*. New York: International Universities Press, 1952.

Piaget, J. *The construction of reality in the child*. New York: Basic Books, 1954.

Piaget, J. *Logic and psychology*. New York: Basic Books, 1957.

Piaget, J., Vinh-Bang, and Matalon, B. Note on the law of the temporal maximum of some optico-geometric illusions. *Am. J. Psychol.*, 1958, **71**, 277–282.

Podell, J. E., and Phillips, L. A developmental analysis of cognition as observed in dimensions of Rorschach and objective test performance. *J. Personality*, 1959, **27**, 439–463.

Rapaport, D. Cognitive structures. In *Contemporary approaches to cognition*. Cambridge: Harvard University Press, 1957. Pp. 157–200.

Rapaport, D. The structure of psychoanalytic theory: a systematizing attempt. In S. Koch (Ed.), *Psychology: a study of a science*. Vol. III. *Formulations of the person and the social context*. New York: McGraw-Hill, 1959. Pp. 55–183.

Rapaport, D., Gill, M., and Schafer, R. *Diagnostic psychological testing: the theory, statistical evaluation, and diagnostic application of a battery of tests*. Vol. I. Chicago: Year Book Publishers, 1945.

Reppucci, N. D. Antecedents of conceptual tempo in the two-year-old child. Unpublished doctoral dissertation, Harvard University, 1968.

Rosenthal, R., and Jacobson, L. *Pygmalion in the classroom.* New York: Holt, Rinehart and Winston, 1968.

Rosner, S. Consistency in response to group pressures. *J. abnorm. soc. Psychol.*, 1957, **55**, 145–146.

Ross, J. The relation between test and person factors. *Psychol. Rev.*, 1963, **70**, 432–443.

Rotter, J. B. *Social learning and clinical psychology.* Englewood Cliffs, N.J.: Prentice-Hall, 1954.

Ruebush, B. K. Anxiety. In H. W. Stevenson (Ed.), *Child psychology: the sixty-second yearbook of the National Society for the Study of Education.* Part I. Chicago: University of Chicago Press, 1963. Pp. 460–516.

Salapatek, P., and Kessen, W. Visual scanning of triangles by the human newborn. *J. exp. child Psychol.*, 1966, **3**, 155–167.

Santostefano, S. G. A developmental study of the cognitive control "leveling-sharpening." *Merrill-Palmer Quart.*, 1964, **10**, 343–360. (a)

Santostefano, S. G. Cognitive controls and exceptional states in children. *J. clin. Psychol.*, 1964, **20**, 213–218. (b)

Santostefano, S. G., and Paley, E. Development of cognitive controls in children. *Child Dev.*, 1964, **35**, 939–949.

Sarason, S. B., Davidson, K. S., Lighthall, F. F., Waite, R. R., and Ruebush, B. K. *Anxiety in elementary school children.* New York: Wiley, 1960.

Sarason, S. B., Hill, K. T., and Zimbardo, P. G. A longitudinal study of the relation of test anxiety to performance on intelligence and achievement tests. *Monogr. Soc. Res. Child Dev.*, 1964, **29**, No. 7 (Serial No. 98).

Sarbin, T. R. Ontology recapitulates philology: the mythic nature of anxiety. *Am. Psychol.*, 1968, **23**, 411–418.

Sarbin, T. R., and Jones, D. S. An experimental analysis of role behavior. *J. abnorm. soc. Psychol.*, 1955, **51**, 236–241.

Scarr, S. Genetic factors in activity motivation. *Child Dev.*, 1966, **37**, 663–673.

Schaefer, E. S., and Bell, R. Q. Development of a parental attitude research instrument. *Child Dev.*, 1958, **29**, 339–361.

Schafer, R. Regression in the service of the ego: the relevance of a psychoanalytic concept for personality assessment. In G. Lindzey (Ed.), *Assessment of human motives.* New York: Rinehart, 1958. Pp. 119–148.

Schlesinger, H. J. Cognitive attitudes in relation to susceptibility to interference. *J. Personality*, 1954, **22**, 354–374.

Schroder, H. M., Driver, M. J., and Streufert, S. *Human information processing.* New York: Holt, Rinehart and Winston, 1967.

Schwartz, D. W., and Karp, S. A. Field dependence in a geriatric population. *Percept. mot. Skills*, 1967, **24**, 495–504.

Scott, J. P. The development of social motivation. In D. Levine (Ed.), *Nebraska Symposium on Motivation.* Lincoln: University of Nebraska Press, 1967. Pp. 111–132.

Scott, W. A. Conceptualizing and measuring structural properties of cognition. In O. J. Harvey (Ed.), *Motivation and social interaction.* New York: Ronald, 1963. Pp. 266–288.

Seder, J. A. The origin of differences in extent of independence in children: developmental factors in perceptual field dependence. Unpublished bachelor's thesis, Radcliffe College, 1957.

Sherman, J. A. Problem of sex differences in space perception and aspects of intellectual functioning. *Psychol. Rev.*, 1967, **74**, 290–299.

Sigel, I. E. Developmental trends in the abstraction ability of children. *Child Dev.*, 1953, **24**, 131–144.

Sigel, I. E. The attainment of concepts. In M. L. Hoffman and L. W. Hoffman (Eds.), *Review of child development research.* Vol. I. New York: Russell Sage Foundation, 1964. Pp. 209–248.

Sigel, I. E., Anderson, L. M., and Shapiro, H. Categorization behavior of lower- and middle-class Negro preschool children: differences in dealing with representation of familiar objects. *J. Negro Educ.*, 1966, **35**, 218–229.

Sigel, I. E., Jarman, P., and Hanesian, H. Styles of categorization and their intellectual and personality correlates in young children. *Human Dev.*, 1967, **10**, 1–17.

Sigel, I. E., and McBane, B. Cognitive competence and level of symbolization among five-year-old children. In J. Hellmuth (Ed.), *The disadvantaged child.* Vol. 1. Seattle, Wash.: Special Child Publications, 1967. Pp. 435–453.

Sigel, I. E., and Olmsted, P. Styles of categorization among lower class kindergarten children. Paper presented at the meeting of the American Educational Research Association, 1967.

Sigelman, E. Y. Observing behavior in impulsive and reflective children. Unpublished doctoral dissertation, University of Minnesota, 1966.

Signell, K. A. Cognitive complexity in person perception and nation perception: a developmental approach. *J. Personality*, 1966, **34**, 517–537.

Slovic, P. Risk-taking in children: Age and sex differences. *Child Dev.*, 1966, **37**, 169–176.

Smith, D. C., and Wing, L. Developmental changes in preference for goals difficult to attain. *Child Dev.*, 1961, **32**, 29–36.

Smock, C. D. Recall of interrupted and non-interrupted tasks as a function of experimentally induced anxiety and motivational relevance of the task stimuli. *J. Personality*, 1957, **25**, 589–599.

Stevenson, H. W., and Odom, R. D. The relation of anxiety to children's performance on learning and problem-solving tasks. *Child Dev.*, 1965, **36**, 1003–1012.

Stroop, J. R. Studies in interference in serial verbal reactions. *J. exp. Psychol.*, 1935, **18**, 643–662.

Sullivan, E. V., and Hunt, D. E. Interpersonal and objective decentering as a function of age and social class. *J. genet. Psychol.*, 1967, **110**, 199–210.

Tajfel, H. Value and the perceptual judgment of magnitude. *Psychol. Rev.*, 1957, **64**, 192–204.

Teeter, B., Rouzer, D. L., and Rosen, E. Development of a dimension of cognitive motivation: Preference for widely known information. *Child Dev.*, 1964, **35**, 1105–1111.

Thurstone, L. L. *A factorial study of perception.* Chicago: University of Chicago Press, 1944.

Thurstone, T. G. *SRA primary mental abilities.* Chicago: Science Research Associates, 1958.

Treisman, M. Mind, body, and behavior: control systems and their disturbances. In P. London and D. Rosenhan (Eds.), *Foundations of abnormal psychology.* New York: Holt, Rinehart and Winston, 1968. Pp. 460–518.

Tyler, B. B. Expectancy for eventual success as a factor in problem solving behavior. *J. educ. Psychol.*, 1958, **49**, 166–172.

Tyler, L. E. The psychology of human differences. (3rd ed.) New York: Appleton-Century-Crofts, 1965.

Vannoy, J. S. Generality of cognitive complexity-simplicity as a personality construct. *J. pers. soc. Psychol.*, 1965, **2**, 385–396.

Vaught, G. M. The relationship of role identification and ego strength to sex differences in the rod-and-frame test. *J. Personality*, 1965, **33**, 271–283.

Vernon, P. E. Ability factors and environmental influences. *Am. Psychol.*, 1965, **20**, 723–733.

Vurpillot, E., and Zoberman, N. The role of common and distinctive indices in perceptive differentiation. *Acta psychol.*, 1965, **24**, 49–67.

Wachtel, P. L. Conceptions of broad and narrow attention. *Psychol. Bull.*, 1967, **68**, 417–429.

Wachtel, P. L. Style and capacity in analytic functioning. *J. Personality*, 1968, **36**, 202–212.

Walker, R. E., and Spence, J. T. Relationship between digit span and anxiety. *J. consult. Psychol.*, 1964, **28**, 220–223.

Wallach, M. A. Commentary: active-analytical vs. passive-global cognitive functioning. In S. Messick and J. Ross (Eds.), *Measurement in personality and cognition*. New York: Wiley, 1962. Pp. 199–215.

Wallach, M. A., and Caron, A. J. Attribute criteriality and sex-linked conservatism as determinants of psychological similarity. *J. abnorm. soc. Psychol.*, 1959, **59**, 43–50.

Wallach, M. A., and Kogan, N. *Modes of thinking in young children*. New York: Holt, Rinehart and Winston, 1965.

Wallach, M. A., Kogan, N., and Burt, R. B. Group risk taking and field dependence-independence of group members. *Sociometry*, 1967, **30**, 323–338.

Ward, W. C. Creativity and impulsivity in kindergarten children. (Doctoral dissertation, Duke University.) Ann Arbor, Mich.: University Microfilms, 1966. No. 66–13, 692.

Ward, W. C. Creativity in young children. *Child Dev.*, 1968, **39**, 737–754. (a)

Ward, W. C. Reflection-impulsivity in kindergarten children. *Child Dev.*, 1968, **39**, 867–874. (b)

Wechsler, D. *Wechsler intelligence scale for children*. New York: The Psychological Corporation, 1949.

Wechsler, D. *Manual for the Wechsler preschool and primary scale of intelligence*. New York: The Psychological Corporation, 1967.

Werner, H. *Comparative psychology of mental development*. (Rev. ed.) Chicago: Follett, 1948.

Werner, H. The concept of development from a comparative and organismic point of view. In D. B. Harris (Ed.), *The concept of development: an issue in the study of human behavior*. Minneapolis: University of Minnesota Press, 1957. Pp. 125–148.

Westcott, M. R. *Toward a contemporary psychology of intuition: a historical, theoretical, and empirical inquiry*. New York: Holt, Rinehart and Winston, 1968.

White, R. W. Motivation reconsidered: the concept of competence. *Psychol. Rev.*, 1959, **66**, 297–333.

White, S. H. Evidence for a hierarchical arrangement of learning processes. In L. P. Lipsitt and C. C. Spiker (Eds.), *Advances in child development and behavior*. Vol. 2. New York: Academic Press, 1965. Pp. 187–220.

White, S. H. Changes in learning processes in the late preschool years. Paper presented at the meeting of the American Educational Research Association, Chicago, 1968.

Witkin, H. A. Psychological differentiation and forms of pathology. *J. abnorm. Psychol.*, 1965, **70**, 317–336.

Witkin, H. A. A cognitive-style approach to cross-cultural research. *Int. J. Psychol.*, 1967, **2**, 233–250.

Witkin, H. A., Dyk, R. B., Faterson, H. F., Goodenough, D. R., and Karp, S. A. *Psychological differentiation.* New York: Wiley, 1962.

Witkin, H. A., Faterson, H. F., Goodenough, D. R., and Birnbaum, J. Cognitive patterning in mildly retarded boys. *Child Dev.*, 1966, **37**, 301–316.

Witkin, H. A., Goodenough, D. R., and Karp, S. A. Stability of cognitive style from childhood to young adulthood. *J. pers. soc. Psychol.*, 1967, **7**, 291–300.

Witkin, H. A., Lewis, H. B., Hertzman, M., Machover, K., Meissner, P. B., and Wapner, S. *Personality through perception.* New York: Harper, 1954.

Wober, M. Sensotypes. *J. soc. Psychol.*, 1966, **70**, 181–189.

Wober, M. Adapting Witkin's field independence theory to accommodate new information from Africa. *Br. J. Psychol.*, 1967, **58**, 29–38.

Wohlwill, J. F. The learning of absolute and relational number discriminations by children. *J. genet. Psychol.*, 1963, **101**, 217–228.

Wolf, A. Body rotation and the stability of field dependence. *J. Psychol.*, 1965, **59**, 211–217.

Wolfe, R. The role of conceptual systems in cognitive functioning at varying levels of age and intelligence. *J. Personality*, 1963, **31**, 108–123.

Wyer, R. S., Jr. Assessment and correlates of cognitive differentiation and integration. *J. Personality*, 1964, **32**, 495–509.

Yando, R. Stability of reflection-impulsivity. Unpublished manuscript, Harvard University, 1968.

Yando, R. M., and Kagan, J. The effect of teacher tempo on the child. *Child Dev.*, 1968, **39**, 27–34.

Zajonc, R. B. The process of cognitive tuning in communication. *J. abnorm. soc. Psychol.*, 1960, **61**, 159–167.

Zigler, E. A measure in search of a theory. *Contemp. Psychol.*, 1963, **8**, 133–135. (a)

Zigler, E. Zigler stands firm. *Contemp. Psychol.*, 1963, **8**, 459–461. (b)

Addendum.[1] The Use of Multivariate Procedures in Developmental Psychology[2]

ROBERT B. McCALL

Through much of its history psychology has tended to limit itself to univariate measurement and data analysis. One reason for this tendency resides in the fact that researchers have not been concerned about the possible diverse facets of a concept. For example, some investigators may use stated preference as a dependent variable and the research context does not require that stated preference be broken down into a set of component variates (e.g., interestingness, pleasantness). In these instances, univariate measurement is quite appropriate.

However, the modern *Zeitgeist* increasingly encourages the elementarization of phenomena and the investigation of constructs whose total conceptual implications are not efficiently encompassed by a single measurement. For example, in many contexts "socioeconomic status" is employed as a multivariate concept. Income, although a major component, does not envelop the total meaning of socioeconomic status because some semiskilled workers earn as much or more than highly trained people (e.g., foundry worker versus assistant professor). Education is certainly another facet of this global concept, but again it is not sufficient in itself because many people of only average education hold positions of influence and social prestige (e.g., some politicians). Consequently, by definition socioeconomic status involves a cluster of attributes, and therefore in cases in which the diverse contributions of these components are important, socioeconomic status should be indexed by a corresponding cluster of variables rather than by a single, easily obtained but insufficient measurement.

Alternatively, a construct may be quite unitary at a conceptual level but still benefit from multivariate measurement. For example, suppose that the research question centers upon whether or not an infant can discriminate between two visual arrays. The experimental logic dictates that if the subject consistently behaves differently in the presence of one than the other stimulus *in any way,* then it may be assumed that the infant detects the difference between the two patterns. The research question is not tied to specific responses but rather the search is for any behavioral

[1] This addendum was planned originally as a discussion of a method or technique that is particularly useful in studies of cognitive functioning and cognitive styles. However, as will become obvious to the reader, multivariate analysis is a method of wide applicability in all kinds of investigations of the development of individual differences.—Editor's note.

[2] Portions of this paper were supported by the Research Council, Computation Center, and Institute for Research in Social Science of the University of North Carolina. In addition, Grant MH-8792 from the National Institute of Mental Health and Contract PH-43-65-1009 from the National Institute of Child Health and Human Development provided to Jerome Kagan, Harvard University, supported the empirical work described here. The author was an NSF Postdoctoral Fellow working with Professor Kagan when some of this research was conducted. Gratitude is expressed to Mark Appelbaum and Elliot M. Cramer for their guidance with the statistical analyses and interpretations and to Nancy Cole, Steven Cool, Fred Grote, Marshall Haith, David Jacobowitz, Lyle Jones, Jerome Kagan, and Stanley Mulaik for their helpful comments on earlier drafts of this paper.

difference of plausible psychological relevance. Therefore a multivariate approach may be a more powerful assessment technique since, because of the patterning of response variables (discussed later), it is quite possible to obtain no univariate effects but a significant multivariate difference. In this event, the univariate conclusion of "no evidence supporting discrimination" would be misleading in view of the multivariate result.

A third reason for considering multivariate procedures is to accumulate evidence on the interaction of dependent variables. For example, does the smile an infant displays to a visual stimulus have the same meaning when accompanied by vocalization as it does when it occurs alone? Psychologists often have used the analysis of variance because it offers information on the potential interaction among independent variables, yet the penchant for univariate measurement obviates the possibility of examining the pattern of interaction among dependent as well as independent variables. Even if several response measures have been taken, separate univariate analyses must be interpreted with the tacit assumption that each response occurs independently of every other response. Such a model is often untenable because responses cannot usually be extricated from their behavioral context without denuding them of much of their meaning. A response gathers psychological meaning as the cluster of its relationships and covariances with other independent and dependent variables matures. However, univariate measurement fails to provide a large portion of this information, and therefore the construct validity of our measures continues to be determined largely in an a priori rather than an empirical manner.

Consequently, a multivariate approach to issues in developmental psychology is likely to be profitable if the theoretical constructs would benefit from being broken down into their components, if the research question is so general that it is not tied to specific measures, and/or if the interactions among dependent as well as independent variables is of interest.

The purpose of this paper is to amplify these points by describing a few multivariate methods, illustrating them with sample data, and evaluating their advantages and disadvantages. There is no pretension to cover the entire spectrum of such techniques (indeed, factor analysis will be omitted completely), and no more mathematical and statistical sophistocation will be required than an average acquaintance with correlation and the analysis of variance in its simpler forms. Consequently, the orientation of this paper is not to describe the procedures in such detail that they may be readily assimilated into the reader's methodological arsenal, but rather to sketch their purpose, general procedure, and advantages so that the researcher may acquire a sense for what these methods offer him as research strategies. Should the reader wish to apply these techniques, he is advised to do additional reading (see list of supplementary references) and consult a skilled proponent of these procedures *before* doing the experiment.

CANONICAL CORRELATION

Research Question

In many instances a researcher would like to know the degree of association between two *classes* of variables rather than between two *single* variables. Although the familiar multiple correlation reveals the degree of association between a class of measures and a single variable, the canonical correlation provides a direct extension of the multiple R to the case in which the dependent as well as the independent constructs are both represented by several rather than just one response measure.

For example, in a study of the distribution of attention of 4-month-old infants to a repeatedly presented standard stimulus (habituation phase) followed by a novel stimulus (McCall and Kagan, 1970), it was of interest to ask if there was any association between (1) the pattern of attentional responses during habituation to the standard and (2) the pattern of attentional responses to the change relative to the familiar stimulus. That is, was there any relationship between the pattern of attention during the repeated presentation of a single stimulus and the attentional pattern elicited by the introduction of a novel stimulus? On the independent variable side (habituation phase), the first visual fixation, total fixation, time vocalizing, number of smiles, and habituation rate were measured. The attention variables were summed over several presentations of the standard stimulus, and the habituation score consisted of the per cent decline in first fixation evidenced over repeated showings of the standard. Subjects who responded minimally from the beginning and therefore could not show habituation were not considered in this analysis. On the dependent variable side, the ratio of the attentional response given to the novel stimulus relative to all the stimuli (familiar plus novel) was computed for first fixation, total fixation, vocalization, smiling, and cardiac deceleration (see Graham and Cliften, 1966). The question was whether or not there was any relationship between attentional pattern during habituation and the attentional pattern to novel versus familiar stimuli when several measures of responsiveness both during habituation and during the novel-familiar stimulus presentations are weighted in a linear fashion in order to best reveal that possible. relationship.

Statistical Procedure

The statistical task is to develop a set of weights c_i for the i independent variables and a set of weights k_j for the j dependent variables so that the correlation between

$$c_1X_1 + c_2X_2 + \ldots + c_iX_i$$

and

$$k_1Y_1 + k_2Y_2 + \ldots + k_jY_j$$

is a maximum.

Example. For boys, the results of the canonical analysis for the data just described are presented in Table A1. The bottom of the table indicates that the canonical correlation between attention during habituation and attention to a stimulus change was .97 for boys ($p < .006$) but a negligible .59 for girls ($p < .965$). Although these correlations seem high, recall that the variables of both groups have been linearly weighted in order to produce the maximum possible relationship. Since the sampling distribution employed for significance tests is appropriate to this weighted result, a canonical correlation of .59 may be quite nonsignificant.

Information permitting a more detailed interpretation of this result is provided in Table A1, which contains the matrix of simple correlations and the standardized weights determined by the canonical analysis. Looking at the weightings for independent variables presented in the last column, first fixation (1.55), vocalization (1.28), and habituation (.65) were given high positive values, where-

Table A1. Canonical Correlation between Attention during Habituation and Responsivity to Stimulus Change (Males)

	Univariate Correlation									Standardized Weights
	2	3	4	5	6	7	8	9	10	
Habituation										
First fixation										1.55
Total fixation	.78***									−.74
Vocalization	.50*	.21								1.28
Smiling	.53*	.27	.73***							−1.71
Habituation	.42	.19	.12	−.24						.65
Response to change										
First fixation	.60*	.42	.08	−.08	.55*					.50
Total fixation	.39	.32	−.04	−.02	.33	.82***				−.27
Vocalization	−.05	−.32	−.06	−.07	.48*	.13	.18			.11
Smiling	.07	.03	.48*	−.17	.27	.24	.00	−.14		.57
Deceleration	.45	.10	.58*	.34	.12	.20	−.02	−.38	.45	.42

	Canonical Correlation	Chi Square	df	p
Males	.97	46.31	25	.006
Females	.59	13.79	25	.965

* $p < .05$.
*** $p < .001$.

as smiling and total fixation were assigned negative values. The interpretation of these weightings is quite analogous to the interpretation of beta weights in multiple correlation (for an excellent discussion of this subject, see Darlington, 1968). A high positive weight indicates that variation in such a variable contributed to the multivariate relationship. Thus first fixation, vocalization, and habituation were important variables in the present analysis. A large negative weight may have one of several meanings. First, a negative coefficient may be obtained if the variable is inversely related to the composite score which the analysis computes for that set of variables. In this case such a variable would have negative bivariate correlations with some of the other measures in its set. Second, it is possible for a variable to be positively correlated with the members of its set but still be assigned a negative weight by the analysis. In this event, the interpretation may be that a portion of the variance of the negatively weighted variable is shared with a variable that otherwise makes a positive contribution to the canonical relationship but that this common variance is irrelevant to the multivariate relationship. Within the context of multiple correlation, a predictor assigned a negative weight is called a "suppressor" variable if the variance it shares with another predictor "suppresses" the capability of that measure to predict the criterion.

Consider the two examples of a suppressor-like variable contained in the sample data. First fixation (1.55) is a positive contributor to the canonical relationship while total fixation (−.74) was given a negative weight, yet the two measures correlate .78. This simple correlation is not surprising in view of the fact that total fixation includes first fixation as one of its components. Consider a psychological interpretation to illustrate how the negative weighting given to total rather than first fixation could be interpreted in terms of a suppressor effect.[3] In the experimental situation, there is very little else for the 4-month infant to do except look, and almost nothing else to

[3] Since first fixation is a part of total fixation, the confounding of these measures represents the best explanation for the observed result. However, the psychological explanation is presented to illustrate the potential function and interpretation of a suppressorlike variable.

look at but the experimental stimulus. Therefore a certain amount of baseline or stimulus-irrelevant looking occurs. Of course, some looking is governed by the nature of the stimulus that the experimenter presents. It is likely that first fixation reflects more stimulus-controlled looking because it is the infant's initial glimpse of the newly introduced display, whereas total fixation may be influenced relatively more by the baseline looking tendencies of the infant, which are largely extraneous to the nature of the stimulus. Thus first fixation becomes a more salient contributor to the canonical relationship with responsivity to a change in the quality of stimulation. Further, first fixation is likely to be influenced to a lesser but nonzero extent by the baseline looking tendencies of the subject and the simple correlation between first and total fixation may reflect, in part, that shared variance. Therefore if this variance which first fixation shares with total fixation which is irrelevant to the response to stimulus change is substracted out by weighing total fixation negatively, then the predictive power of first fixation is sharpened.

In a similar situation involving a suppressorlike variable, vocalization (1.28) during the habituation phase was a positive contributor to the canonical relationship, whereas smiling was not (−1.71), even though smiling and vocalization were highly correlated (.73). In this instance, the analysis has suggested that a component of the vocalization response which is related to smiling does not contribute to the canonical correlation. Thus vocalization becomes a better contributor if the irrelevant component it shares with smiling is subtracted from it.

On the other side of the relationship the weightings for dependent variables presented in Table A1 show that in terms of the responsivity to change, smiling, first fixation, and cardiac deceleration are the major variables contributing to the canonical correlation with habituation pattern.

The fact that the canonical relationship was very high for boys (.97) but almost significantly absent for girls (.59, $p < .96$) suggests that these variables play different roles for the two sexes. Since other evidence (McCall and Kagan, 1970) suggests that the girls did indeed respond to the changes, this result implies that boys and girls express their responsivity to stimulus change differently. That is, because the pattern of relationships among these variables differs as a function of sex, a smile or a vocalization during the habituation phase may carry a different message for boys than it does for girls.

To summarize, the canonical analysis suggested that for those subjects whose attentional responses provided an opportunity for habituation to a repetitively presented stimulus to occur, the pattern of habituation was related to responsivity to stimulus change for boys but not for girls. The habituation measures primarily contributing to such a relationship were first fixation, vocalization, and magnitude of habituation, with total fixation and smiling acting in the manner of suppressor variables. The response to a change was reflected in smiling, first fixation, and deceleration. Further, it appears that these variables may carry a different meaning for the two sexes.

Additional Applications

Canonical correlation could be used in longitudinal studies of personality and intellectual ability. For example, do maternal attitudes of protection, restriction, hostility, and acceleration relate to the child's passivity, emotional dependency, withdrawal, etc.? Which of these variables weighs most highly in this relationship? What is the extent and pattern of the possible relationship between maternal attitudes and the child's intellectual abilities as measured by an extensive test battery? What is the nature of the potential relationship between personality and ability measures?

Is it at all possible to predict later behavior from neonatal or infant assessment? In this regard, it may well be that one of the reasons why infant measures have largely failed to correlate with later behavior is that the predominant strategy has been to use univariate techniques. Examination of the pattern of interactions among variates with canonical correlation may prove valuable in this context.

MULTIPLE DISCRIMINANT ANALYSIS

Research Question

If a researcher had two or more distinct groups of subjects with several measures on each subject, it might be of interest to ask whether the groups can be significantly discriminated on the basis of a derived variable composed of a linearly weighted combination of the several dependent variables. A multiple discriminant analysis performs this task.

For example, in the previously described experiment (McCall and Kagan, 1970), subjects were classified into the following groups on the basis of their looking responses to the repetitively presented stimulus during the habituation phase.

1. *Rapid Habituators*—subjects whose first visual fixation to the presentation of a stimulus declined markedly with repeated presentations of that same stimulus.

2. *Slow Habituators*—subjects whose first fixations did not decline over trials.

3. *Short Lookers*—subjects whose first fixations were always of such extremely short duration that they had no opportunity to demonstrate habituation because of their low initial values.

The question was posed as to whether these three groups, selected as a function of their first fixation to the standard stimulus, could be discriminated from one another on the basis of the nonlooking dependent variables of resting heart rate (heart rate taken during the interstimulus interval), the time spent vocalizing during the habituation period, the number of smiles during the habituation period, educational attainment of the infant's parents, and the weight of the subject.

Statistical Procedure

Algebraically, the purpose of the multiple discriminant analysis is to determine the set of weights or coefficients c_i for the several dependent measures X_i which will separate the groups to the maximum extent. For example, if the composite or discriminant function is called Y, and if there are two groups to be discriminated with four dependent variables, the analysis will produce a discriminant function of the form

$$Y = c_1X_1 + c_2X_2 + c_3X_3 + c_4X_4$$

such that the mean values of Y for the two groups will be maximally different. In terms of variance, the analysis selects a set of weights which will maximize the between-group variance relative to the within-group variance in the derived variable Y.

Geometrically, Cooley and Lohnes (1962) diagram the procedure for the case of two

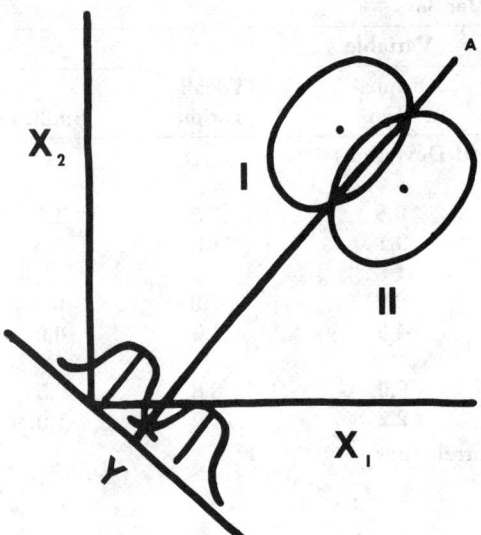

X_2

A

I

II

Y

X_1

Fig. A1. Diagram of a geometric interpretation of a discriminant analysis (see text; from W. W. Cooley, and P. R. Lohnes, *Multivariate procedures for the behavioral sciences*, John Wiley & Sons, Inc., New York, 1962).

groups with two dependent measures in the manner of Fig. A1. The two variables X_1 and X_2 are on the abscissa and ordinate, respectively, and the two groups I and II are represented both by their centroids (points) and by their .90 centours (the ellipse surrounding each centroid, which encloses 90% of the frequencies of each group). If a line A is drawn through the intersection of the two centours and the discriminant dimension Y is drawn perpendicular to this line, then the projections (discriminant scores) of the two groups on the discriminant dimension will be maximally separated (there will be the least possible overlap between the distributions).

In short, the multiple discriminant analysis produces a set of coefficients or weights for the several dependent measures which best separate or discriminate between the groups on this derived dimension. The between-group variance is maximized relative to the within-group variance.

Example. The boys' data from the McCall and Kagan (1970) study described previously were submitted to a multiple discriminant analysis to determine if the three groups (rapid habituators, slow habituators, short lookers) could be discriminated on the basis of a linear combination of five nonlooking variables. The results are given in Table A2,

which presents the means and standard deviations, within-cell correlations (correlations of dependent variables with the effect of the grouping parceled out), the univariate F-tests and associated probabilities corresponding to a one-way analysis of variance on each variable separately, and the discriminant function coefficients (coefficients for each standardized dependent variable, which when multiplied and summed yield the best discriminating composite score).

The first point to note about the results is that not one of the univariate F-tests revealed a significant difference between the three groups, although the heart rate measure reached the .07 level. In contrast, the multiple discriminant function was significant ($F = 2.50$; $df = 10$, 36; $p < .02$), suggesting that the groups could be discriminated on the basis of a linear combination of the dependent measures. It is possible to obtain a significant multivariate discrimination without significant univariate Fs because the multivariate analysis considers the relationship among the dependent variables. A collection of univariate tests does not permit an interpretation in which dependent response measures interact with each other. In contrast, the multivariate analysis permits assessment of the possible pattern of interactions between various facets of behavior. With this method, responses are not artificially extricated from their behavioral context, and although a given manipulation or condition may not be clearly manifested in a single variable, it may be observed in the pattern of several dependent measures considered as a conjunctive display (although the "display" is a function of the variables selected by the experimenter).

To interpret this result in more detail, consider first the standardized discriminant scores in Table A2. Smiling (1.43) and heart rate (.62) were given positive weights. In terms of the means of the groups on these variables, the slow habituation subjects smiled the most while the short lookers had relatively slow resting heart rates. However, vocalization (−1.66), education (−.81), and body weight (−.41) received negative coefficients. Again, a negative weight may imply that the variable acted in the capacity of a suppressor. That is, such a variable correlates with a nondiscriminating component of a positive contributor to the discrimination and thus should be sub-

Table A2. Discriminant Analysis of Habituation Phase for Boys

	Heart Rate	Weight	Education	Vocalization	Smiling
			Variable		
	Means and Standard Deviations				
Slow habituation (N = 9)					
$\overline{X}$	149.4	224.0	6.8	7.3	1.0
s	12.3	86.4	3.1	11.3	1.4
Rapid habituation (N = 4)					
$\overline{X}$	150.4	264.8	6.8	7.6	0.0
s	10.0	25.0	4.3	11.3	0.0
Short fixation (N = 12)					
$\overline{X}$	140.0	240.8	9.0	8.8	.5
s	8.0	18.3	2.2	11.2	1.0
	Within-Cell Correlations				
Weight	− .19				
Education	.08	− .17			
Vocalization	.15	.10	− .49*		
Smiling	.01	.27	− .31	.81***	
	Discriminant Analysis				
Univariate F					
(df = 2,22)	2.95	.79	1.73	.05	1.22
p less than	.07	.46	.20	.96	.31
Standardized discriminant coefficients	.62	− .41	− .81	− 1.66	1.43

* $p < .05$
*** $p < .001$

tracted from the contributor in order to sharpen the discrimination between criterion groups. Consider vocalization and smiling. Smiling is a positive contributor to the discrimination (1.43) but the within-cell correlations in Table A2 show that vocalization correlates .81 with smiling. Since vocalization is given a negative weighting by the analysis, the implication is that the smiling variance shared by vocalization is irrelevant to the discrimination and subtracting it sharpens the separation of the groups. Considered from a psychological point of view, a smile is often observed after an infant looks at a stimulus for a few seconds without any accompanying vocalization. This is sometimes regarded as a response of recognition. However, on other occasions a child will become excited and as a result he will both vocalize and smile in temporal contiguity. These latter smiles, correlated with vocalization, may be irrelevant to the discrimination between groups, and the discriminant analysis may be highlighting this fact.

In summary, although no single univariate test attained significance, the multiple discriminant function did. It would have been misleading to conclude on the basis of the univariate analyses alone that the nonlooking variables were unrelated to the three habituation groups. Further, it would also have been incorrect to conclude that although the univariate F for vocalization was substantially less than 1, that vocalization was unimportant to the discrimination between groups because vocalization did act as a suppressor. This result further punctuates the fact that in many cases dependent measures must not be viewed in isolation but rather in the context in which they occur. A variable extracted and isolated from its behavioral environment loses some of its meaning and power as an index of psychological events.

Additional Applications

Discriminant analysis could find application in the many instances in which the independent variable falls neatly into discrete groups.

For example, the entire area of sex differences could benefit from discriminant analysis. What is the difference between the sexes when ability measures are considered conjointly? What is the nature of the sex difference in personality traits? In what ways do blind and seeing or deaf and hearing children differ in mental abilities or personality traits? What is the pattern of differences between normal and mentally retarded children on ability measures, personality traits, or performance indices?

MULTIVARIATE ANALYSIS OF VARIANCE (MANOVA)

Research Question

Multiple discriminant analysis is directed at outlining how separate groups of subjects could be discriminated. The same general orientation may be taken toward the groups in an analysis of variance design. Indeed, a one-way multivariate analysis of variance is multiple discriminant analysis, but the same procedures may be applied to designs involving more than one independent variable—how to determine how the several dependent variables may be weighted to produce the biggest effect for factor A, for factor B, and for their interaction. Viewed from another orientation, MANOVA is simply the analysis of variance using several rather than just one dependent variable in which these variates are weighted to provide the maximum possible effects.

To illustrate with data from Kagan and McCall (1970), 4-month-old boys and girls viewed a series of four facelike, three-dimensional stimuli (for pictures of the stimuli see Kagan, Henker, Hen-Tov, Levine, and Lewis, 1966). First fixation, total fixation, vocalization, smiling, and cardiac deceleration were summed over all stimuli. Collectively, these measures indexed the gross attentional characteristics of the child. With reference to specific stimuli, some children gave longer first fixations to a faithful representation of a male face, while others locked longer at a scrambled rearrangement of the same features. Was there any difference in terms of gross attentional characteristics between boys and girls and between those subjects who looked longer at the regular face than those who looked longer at the scrambled version? Was there an interaction?

Statistical Procedure

The multivariate analysis of variance computes a set of weights separately for each factor in the analysis of variance design so that after the total variance has been partitioned, the weighted combination of the several dependent variables produces a maximum effect. In this sense a discriminant analysis is a one-way multivariate analysis of variance. In addition to the partition of variance, a two-way MANOVA is composed of three discriminant analyses—one for each of the main effects and one for the interaction.

Example. The MANOVA for the data described above is reported in Table A3. Only the sex effect was significant in the multivariate case ($F=3.59$; $df=6$, 82; $p<.003$). The standardized weights show that cardiac deceleration and smiling contributed most to the sex differences, boys decelerating and smiling more than girls. The F for deceleration was the only univariate test reaching significance ($F=18.22$; $df=1$, 87; $p<.001$), even though smiling as well as deceleration received a positive weighting of some consequence in the multivariate case. Further, although first and total fixation each had univariate Fs that approached significance ($p<.14$), the MANOVA assigned them weights of essentially zero (.09 and .04). This result derives from the fact that the pattern of correlations between fixation times and deceleration (the major contributing variable) and the variability of fixation relative to deceleration are such that deceleration performs the discrimination between sexes more efficiently than fixation times. Therefore when all the dependent measures are considered jointly and the best selection is required, even though fixation times may reflect sex differences in their univariate cases, the MANOVA minimizes their apparent contribution because deceleration and smiling make the same sex discrimination more efficiently. This result points up another advantage of multivariate analyses: the statistical procedures not only compare the several dependent variables being analyzed in terms of their joint contribution to discrimination between groups, but they also determine the most efficient combination of variables for this purpose. Therefore, if one were restricted to a few dependent variables with which to assess sex differences

Table A3. Sex × Regular-Scrambled Face Manova on Gross Attentional Measures

	First Fixation	Total Fixation	Number Fixes	Vocalization	Smiling	Cardiac Deceleration
Means						
Boys						
Regular	78.8	156.6	28.9	18.7	4.6	15.4
Scrambled	75.9	150.2	29.3	25.0	7.1	14.0
Girls						
Regular	54.8	136.8	37.5	20.7	2.3	10.6
Scrambled	70.6	140.0	26.9	17.4	3.7	10.6
MANOVA						
Sex effect ($F = 3.59$; $df = 6, 82$; $p < .003$)						
Standardized weights	.09	.04	.07	.13	.41	.94
Univariate						
$F(df = 1, 87)$	2.27	2.27	.83	.65	1.57	18.22
p less than	.14	.14	.37	.42	.21	.001
Regular-Scrambled ($F = 1.00$; $df = 6, 82$; $p < .43$)						
Sex × Reg. —Scr. ($F = 1.38$; $df = 6, 82$; $p < .23$)						

in this setting, cardiac deceleration and smiling would be the most efficient selection.

Since variables are weighted in multivariate analyses, replication of results is more important here than for univariate procedures. Four-month-old infants also viewed a series of two-dimensional slides composed of a photograph of a male face and a collage of that face (Kagan and McCall, 1967; for stimuli see Kagan et al., 1966). Again, on the basis of their first fixation to the photographs, infants could be classified into those looking longer at the regular versus those looking longer at the scrambled collage of the photographed face. A sex × regular-scrambled MANOVA using the same dependent variables as above produced results that were almost identical with the prior analysis: deceleration (.94) and smiling (.39) again received the highest weightings, indicating that boys decelerated and smiled more than girls. The other variables were assigned weights near zero. Similarly, no other effects were evident.

Additional Applications

If the design has more than one independent variable and several dependent variables, MANOVA may be appropriate. What is the pattern of intellectual abilities in different socioeconomic status groups of several ethnic-racial subcultures? What is the nature of the effects of sex and socioeconomic status upon various facets of language development? In what patterns of personality traits are early and late maturing boys and girls different? What is the cluster of cognitive abilities which distinguishes reflective or impulsive boys and girls? Multivariate techniques may be used with experimentally generated as well as observational data. Not all measures of learning (number correct, trials to criterion, etc.) reflect the same information, and therefore analysis of variance designs of children's learning which employ several dependent measures may find MANOVA profitable.

CRITICISMS OF MULTIVARIATE PROCEDURES

Multivariate techniques are often questioned by researchers who are somewhat unfamiliar with the procedures. A few critical questions are now discussed.

Doesn't weighting several variables to produce the greatest possible correlation or discrimination capitalize upon chance? Yes, it does to some extent. Although the sampling distributions used to test multivariate effects are appropriate for the number of variables involved and also to the weighted statistics being evaluated, multivariate results need experimental replication just as beta weights and *R*s in multiple regression demand replication. Replication may take the form of redoing the experiment and the analyses, or as in the case of multiple regression the obtained weights may be assigned to the dependent variables produced by a second group of subjects (or second half of the total sample) and univariate analyses performed on the resulting derived composite scores. The need for such replication varies somewhat with the level of detail one wishes to highlight in the interpretation of multivariate analyses. It is considerably less risky to emphasize the fact that a canonical relationship or a discrimination was or was not obtained than to focus conceptual and theoretical importance upon minor details, such as whether variable A was assigned a weight of .40 or .50. Thus by placing more confidence in the general results and less in the specific details, one is less likely to build his house on sand. Nevertheless, although sometimes tedious, replication (even splitting the sample into two parts) is always valuable, and the researcher must decide if the advantages of multivariate procedures (discussed later) are sufficient to make replication worthwhile.

Is it not a somewhat circular and biased procedure to determine whether or not a relationship or a discrimination exists by employing methods which are designed to produce the maximum possible effect? The weighting procedure is precisely analogous to that which exists in multiple correlation. The techniques seek to determine whether there exists *any* linear combination of response variables that produce a significant effect. Since there are many possible combinations of these measures, the procedure picks only the weightings that generate a maximum effect, testing the resultant statistic against a known distribution, which reflects the fact that there are many possible combinations of which the maximum has been selected. If the maximum value is not significant, then a relationship or discrimination probably does not exist. Conversely, if the maximized statistic is significant, it is incumbent upon the researcher to make conceptual sense of this fact. This interpretative phase may require a theory or additional empirical work, but it is not fundamentally different from any other research situation—the statistical techniques attach a probability to a given statement but they do not provide a psychological interpretation for the result.

It seems that one has to resort to univariate procedures in order to interpret the results of multivariate analyses, so why perform the multivariate tests in the first place? Although multivariate procedures are direct extentions of their univariate analogues, they pose a somewhat broader research question: Is there any relationship at all between this *class* of variables and another *class?* Can certain groups be distinguished in any way by this *group* of measures rather than by a single variate examined in isolation? Further, since multivariate results reflect the pattern of relationships among the measures, the interpretation made of the meaning and salience of any single variable may be quite different as a result of using multivariate as opposed to univariate analyses. Thus, although it is certainly true that univariate tests help to interpret multivariate results, the two procedures often provide different types of information and even suggest different implications for the same research questions.

Since the results of multivariate procedures are frequently so intricate, qualified, and without convincing psychological interpretation, don't they confuse the issue more than they clarify it? There is no doubt that parsimony is a goal of science, but the law is to be applied only when the choice is between two equally plausible alternatives. It is one thing for the scientist to invoke parsimony in a decision without an alternative basis of selection, but it is quite another to *impose* parsimony a priori. Occasionally, the lack of parsimony exists in nature. Further, there is no question that experimental control is more desirable than statistical control, but in the many cases in which experimental and scientific knowledge are not yet adequate to the task, it appears presumptuous for the scientist to a priori select a single measure or to ignore the interrelationships among the several dependent variables at hand. Finally since responses do not ordinarily occur in behavioral isolation, the simplicity of methods relying upon the unnatural extrication of single measures from their behavioral context may be deluding. Therefore the question should not be one of the facility of interpreting multivariate results but whether or not their complexity appropriately matches the complexity of nature.

Moreover, as psychology investigates increasingly more complicated phenomona it must also accept the responsibility of evaluating them in all their intricacy.

Doesn't the result of a multivariate analysis depend upon the variables selected for inclusion in that analysis? Yes, it does, but the selection of dependent measures is always a major decision which determines the outcome of any experiment. Is the result of a multivariate experiment any more a spurious product of the cluster of dependent measures chosen than the result of an experiment in which an a priori decision restricts the empirical evidence to a single measure?

What if the variables should be combined in a nonlinear rather than linear fashion? Since most researchers do not run a nonlinear measure of correlation (e.g., *Eta*) for every Pearson *r* they calculate, nonlinearity does not appear to be a de facto concern when using other techniques. However, the assumptions of any model require examination, and the question of linearity should be investigated empirically. However, considering the pervasive use of linear models in psychological research, there is little reason to question this assumption more in the context of multivariate procedures than in most univariate methods (e.g., Pearson *r*, the analysis of variance).

ADVANTAGES OF MULTIVARIATE METHODS

A first advantage is that multivariate methods address general questions of relationship and discrimination. If the researcher wishes to know if a relationship exists between two multifaceted concepts or whether or not several groups differ in any way on a set of dependent measures, then multivariate procedures may be appropriate. For example, is there any relationship between maternal behavior and later dependency in the child? Can delinquent boys be discriminated from nondelinquents on the basis of parental disciplinary techniques? Multivariate procedures, because they consider several measures in concert, ask a somewhat broader question than their univariate counterparts.

Second, if several variables possessing some psychological cohesiveness are measured, multivariate procedures are preferred over a proliferation of univariate tests in much the same manner as the analysis of variance is preferred over several t-tests.

Third, most responses should not be viewed in isolation but as a conjunctive display. There are several implications of this proposition. First, the power of the analysis is often increased by using multivariate methods. As has been illustrated, a multivariate result may be significant without obtaining significant univariate *F*s (though the reverse is also possible). Second, the pattern of relationships or interactions among the dependent variables constitutes important psychological information. The relative weightings of variables and the detection of suppressorlike measures contribute another dimension of information. Third, the knowledge thus gained by examining the pattern of several variables adds to the construct validity and interpretation of the dependent measures themselves.

In summary, methods of data analysis provide the researcher with models for the behavior he observes. The major feature of multivariate models is that they make provision for considering the interaction among dependent (as well as independent) variables. As such, they allow for examination of a more global behavioral display rather than artificially excising variables out of their natural context.

References

Cooley, W. W. and Lohnes, P. R. *Multivariate procedures for the behavioral sciences.* New York: Wiley, 1962.

Darlington, R. B. Multiple regression in psychological research and practice. *Psychol. Bull.,* 1968, **69**, 161–182.

Graham, F. K. and Cliften, R. K. Heart-rate change as a component of the orienting response. *Psychol. Bull.,* 1966, **65**, 305–320.

Kagan, J., Henker, B., Hen-Tov, A., Levine, J., and Lewis, M. Infants' differential reactions to familiar and distorted faces. *Child Dev.*, 1966, **37**, 519–532.

Kagan, J. and McCall, R. B. Continuities in psychological development in the first year. Unpublished manuscript, 1967.

McCall, R. B., and Kagan, J. Individual differences in the infant's distribution of attention to stimulus discrepancy. *Developmental Psychology*, 1970, **2**, 90–98.

Supplementary References

General

Anderson, T. W. *An introduction to multivariate statistical analysis.* New York: Wiley, 1958.

Cattell, R. B. (Ed.) *Handbook of multivariate experimental psychology.* Chicago: Rand McNally, 1966.

Cooley, W. W. and Lohnes, P. R. *Multivariate procedures for the behavioral sciences.* New York: Wiley, 1962.

Kendall, M. G. *A course in multivariate analysis.* London: Charles Griffin, 1957.

McKeon, J. J. Canonical analysis: some relations between canonical correlation, factor analysis, discriminant function analysis, and scaling theory. *Psychom. Monogr.*, No. 13.

Morrison, D. F. *Multivariate statistical methods.* New York: McGraw-Hill, 1967.

Canonical Correlation

Horst, P. Generalized canonical correlations and their applications to experimental data. *J. clin. Psychol.* (monograph supplement), No. 14, 1961, 331–347.

Hotelling, H. The most predictable criterion. *J. educ. Psychol.*, 1935, **26**, 139–142.

Hotelling, H. Relations between two sets of variates. *Biometrika*, 1936, **28**, 321–377.

Discriminant Analysis

Anderson, T. W. Classification by multivariate analysis. *Psychometrika*, 1951, **16**, 31–50.

Bryan, J. G. The generalized discriminant function: mathematical foundation and computational routine. *Harvard Educ. Rev.*, 1951, **21**, 90–95.

Rao, C. R. *Advanced statistical methods in biometric research.* New York: Wiley, 1952. Chap. 8.

Rulon, P. J. Distinctions between discriminant and regression analysis and a geometric interpretation of the discriminant function. *Harvard Educ. Rev.*, 1951, **21**, 80–90.

Tatsuoka, M. M. and Tiedeman, D. V. Discriminant analysis. *Rev. educ. Res.*, Washington, D.C.: AERA, 1954.

Multivariate Analysis of Variance

Jones, L. V. Analysis of variance in its multivariate developments. In R. B. Cattell (Ed.), *Handbook of multivariate experimental psychology*, Chicago: Rand McNally, 1966.

19. Cognitive Development and Education

WILLIAM D. ROHWER, JR.

The study of cognitive development and the education of children have much in common. In both, the object of concern is the individual over a considerable portion of the human life span. Although the particular age interval falling within the purview of the two enterprises may differ somewhat, the amount of overlap is still substantial. The ages that fall within the compass of education may be limited to those covered by the median years of formal schooling, say kindergarten through grade 12. Or the education interval may be extended to cover one or two preschool years at the lower end of the age scale and four to eight years of higher education at the upper end. By either definition, the interval does not cover a span of years sufficient to circumscribe the major interests of many psychologists working in the field of cognitive development. The concern of those interested in early periods of life exceeds the lower educational age boundary and the concern of psychologists interested in maturity and aging exceeds the upper educational age boundary. But the concerns of educators themselves often overrun the conventional boundaries of formal education. A number of university departments of education recognize as formal specialties both early childhood education and adult education. Thus the generalization stands that both education and the psychology of cognitive development largely share the same object of concern.

Educators and psychologists interested in problems of cognitive development have more in common than the object of their concern. They also share a principal interest in the same aspects of human functioning—the intellectual aspects. Even though "intellec-tual" is as slippery a term as "cognitive," it does serve to underline a relatively general consensus that the major emphasis both in education and in cognitive development is not upon the social, emotional and physical aspects of human beings. The educator's intent is to institute those conditions that insure the acquisition of intellectual competence across the widest possible range of human beings and the psychologist's is to specify determinants of intellectual competence in all human beings.

With so much substantive overlap between concerns in education and in cognitive development, effective commerce between the two should be guaranteed. This expectation is strengthened by two additional conditions prevailing in education and in the psychology of cognitive development. The schools are beset by problems that obstruct the attainment of the educator's goal of insuring the achievement of intellectual competence by all students. Consequently schoolmen, for the most part, are open to suggested solutions for these problems. On their side, psychologists working on cognitive development have already obtained partial verification of some propositions as to the determinants of intellectual competence through research conducted under laboratory conditions. To complete the task of verification, such research must be extended to more naturalistic conditions, conditions that may be found in more appropriate form in the schools than anywhere else. Such psychologists are also faced with the task of illuminating the very large number of remaining mysteries of cognitive development. Work on this task might well begin with observations made under conditions that explicitly direct the child toward intellectual activity in a relatively regular and orderly manner, that is, under school conditions. Again, it seems warranted to conclude that profitable commerce between education and the psychology of cognitive development is assured.

But *commerce* between the two fields can have a variety of meanings; it can mean a great deal of interpenetration resulting in mutual progress or it can mean little more than conversations of varying degrees of formality with very little consequence. Our consideration of this question will be one-sided: we shall attend principally to the matter of exports from the psychology of cognitive development to education. Within this limitation, the question of commerce may be reduced to two forms: "Does the psychology of cognitive development have relevance for education?"; and "Does the psychology of cognitive development have contributions to make to education?" As we shall see, the relevance of cognitive development for education is easier to establish than the assertion that a substantial contribution to education will result from its study.

If the proposition is accepted that the greater the amount of information about children available to schoolmen, the better the chances of improving educational practice, then the products of the psychological study of cognitive development are of obvious relevance. In the weak sense of the term "relevance," virtually all theory and research qualify, subject only to the restriction that it be valid. Not only teaching, but curriculum design, production of educational materials, and other educational functions could benefit from the information produced by psychologists in the course of their work on problems of cognitive development. Even psychological investigations that are planned, conducted, and completed without regard for educational problems may have relevance for educational practice. But it is a separate question whether such investigations can effectively contribute to education. Establishing educational relevance requires only a modicum of facility in conceiving of relationships between education and cognitive development, whereas a contribution to education requires that the products of psychological theory and research result in alterations of educational practice and of its outcomes. It is

unlikely that such changes can be accomplished without an explicit intention to do so. That is to say, theory may have to be rewritten in educational terms and research may have to be redesigned with an educational context clearly in mind. When theory and research are revised in this manner, their components will have reference to school variables rather than to laboratory conditions, to classroom procedures rather than experimental procedures, to teachers and students rather than experimenters and subjects, and to long- rather than short-term objectives. This does not mean the present form of education must be taken as unchangeable but that the matter of effecting educational change involves more than excellence in the construction of psychological theory and research.

So far, each of the topics relating to the possibility of interplay between education and the psychological study of cognitive development has only been alluded to in general terms. Before proceeding to a discussion of particular aspects of available psychological theory and research that have the potential for making educational contributions, or, at least, for being educationally relevant, these issues of the relationship between the two fields deserve a more detailed treatment.

EDUCATION, PSYCHOLOGY, AND COGNITIVE DEVELOPMENT

Education is plagued by problems. They are widely recognized and publicly proclaimed by both educators and laymen in speeches and in writing, in books and in periodicals, in professional journals and in popular magazines, in reports of governmental agencies and of private foundations. The broad consensus that problems exist begins to dissolve when it comes to specifying the nature of the problems and to recommending possible solutions. Nevertheless, the events that constitute evidence of the existence of problems permit a generalization. There is enormous variation in the outcomes of schooling, whether that variation is measured in an absolute way in terms of failures to reach some agreed upon standard of accomplishment or, in a relative way, in terms of differences among individuals in the extent to which they attain any particular level of accomplishment. Consider, for example, the substantial (although decreasing) proportion of individuals who do not complete a high school education, that is, the widely-publicized drop-out problem. Or, in a more relative vein, consider the striking variations among individuals in performance on a standardized examination of educational-intellectual achievement such as the Armed Forces Qualification Test. In 1966, the proportion of persons who failed (those scoring below the 10th percentile) the so-called mental test for entrance into the Armed Forces was 11.5% (Department of the Army, 1967). Another feature of these variations compounds the problems for the schools within this society; this is the fact that the proportion of failure is not equal across all groups within the culture. For example, 27% of Negroes failed the armed services mental test, whereas the proportion for whites was only 4.3% (Department of the Army, 1967).

Variations of this sort and of this magnitude emerge earlier than at the secondary-school level. Within a single school system, for instance, the average performance of junior high school students on standardized tests of reading, writing, and arithmetic achievement may be above the 95th percentile in a predominantly white school, whereas that of students in a predominantly Negro school may be below the 15th percentile. To continue on down the age scale, the performance of first-grade children on tests designed to assess readiness for initial formal reading instruction results in similar variation in rates of failure across ethnic and socioeconomic (SES) groups. Thus the problem is pushed back further to the point where some are tempted to conclude that eventual drop-outs can be detected at preschool ages (Jensen, 1968). If this is so, then the schools face the task of effectively upsetting these predictions by means of the practices they implement for the education of children. An enormous task it is, given the variation that exists when the children first enter the formal educational system and given that schooling appears to amplify rather than reduce the magnitude of individual differences (Anastasi, 1958).

The response of both educators and interested laymen to these problems has been substantial and varied. Unprecedented amounts of money have been earmarked by governmental agencies and private foundations for experimentation in educational practice in the schools. New techniques of instructional organization have been initiated from team teaching to reduced numbers of students per classroom and from elaborate homogeneous grouping of students to ungraded schools with heterogeneous grouping. New curricula have been developed and introduced in the schools, especially in mathemetics and the sciences. Special services have proliferated and the ranks of those engaged in them have been increased: school psychology, counseling, speech therapy, remedial reading, special teachers of the retarded, and so on. In most of these specialties, practice requires that expertise come into play only after problems emerge in specific children, and there is no paucity of work to be done in any of the fields mentioned. Preventive approaches have been initiated with preschool and early elementary school children, notably in the federally financed Project Headstart.

In some cases, these responses to educational problems are too new for proper evaluation and in other cases specific programs have been successful, some marginally, others impressively so. Still, the general result has been little change in the range of variability in the outcomes of education (Stephens, 1967). The problems still persist and for those directly involved—teachers, parents, students—the problems are more pointed than these summary remarks can make clear. There is no mistaking the dedication of those bending their efforts in the search for solutions, and yet the goal still exceeds the struggle toward it.

Schoolmen, in large numbers, know and admit that the problems exist. As educators, they are eminently receptive to potential solutions. The members of social groups among whose children school failure is disproportionately large insist upon changes in educational practice that will substantially reduce the disparities. Broad press coverage is given to vocal critics of the schools. As a consequence of these and other conditions, schooling is open to innovation and to substantive contributions to educational practice almost without regard for their source. Consider, for example, the adoption by one school district of a technique originally developed for the retraining of mentally retarded children as a part of their program for culturally disadvantaged students. Whatever the merits of the technique in the case of the population for which it was developed, there is little indication that it is even relevant for those children with whom this school district must deal. Nevertheless the practice has been implemented eagerly by those involved.

The situation in education clearly warrants optimism as to the kind of reception relevant psychological theory and research might receive. The present situation also justifies optimism about the prospect that the work of many psychologists will be directed toward educationally relevant problems. Historically it is possible to discern three loosely defined periods since 1900 with respect to the relationship between psychology and education. The first was marked by substantial efforts on the part of psychologists to speak to matters of classroom practice as they directly affected learning (Thorndike, 1931; Dewey, 1916). It was also marked by the beginning of efforts to devise tests to measure the effects on school learning of previous educational experience and of abilities brought to that experience. But the latter movement was only in its infancy during this period, whereas it dominated what may be distinguished as the middle period. During the first period, a truly major figure in the history of experimental psychology, E. L. Thorndike, addressed himself to problems of educational practice and did contribute to changes in practice. By contrast, during the middle period, the major figures among psychologists who contributed to changes in educational practice came from the fields of differential psychology and measurement. Eminent investigators such as Terman and Thurstone along with Wechsler and many others promoted the remarkable growth in the use of aptitude tests in schools.

The alliance between the psychological testing movement and the schools grew strong and commerce between the two was frequent and substantial. Three major functions were served by testing. First, tests permitted objective, systematic evaluation of changes in students as a function of age and/or education. Second, it became possible to detect differences among individuals with respect to educational promise. And, third, it became feasible to reduce the magnitude of variability within classroom units by classify-ing children with respect to what the tests measured and, for the purposes of instruction, grouping them relatively more homogeneously than had previously been possible. The first of these functions prepared the way for the more recent awareness of the magnitude of school failure. The availability of relative achievement data made visible the great extent of variation in educational outcomes. The second function was a necessary prerequisite for the third one, that is, the grouping of children according to tested ability. Of the three functions, it was the third that had the greatest impact on classroom conditions of learning. Even here, however, the impact was indirect: it had minimal reference to procedures used in the classroom. Its influence was on the composition of the membership of classroom units or of subunits within classrooms.

A more advanced potential function was not quickly realized in practice during this middle period and still remains only partially fulfilled. The development of reliable instruments for the classification of children in terms of intellectual ability and achievement, along with the corollary development of grouping practices, permitted the systematic design of different curricula, tailored to accommodate the individual differences revealed by testing programs in the schools. The term curricula as used in this context does not refer to widely divergent educational programs as exemplified by the difference between an academic and a vocational curriculum. Rather, the reference is to cases in which the educational objectives for several different categories of students are virtually identical, but the means for attaining them are varied to take account of the revealed ability and achievement differences between the groups. This is not to say that no curricular variations were introduced by the inception of classificatory techniques and grouping practices within the schools, for these did indeed ensue. But, for the most part, these variations consisted in simply diluting or enriching the content to be mastered. With a few exceptions, say, for the mentally retarded and the neurologically handicapped, minimal variation was introduced into the methods by which schoolmen attempted to forward the progress of students toward common educational objectives.

During the second major historical period

identified by the influential role of psychological testing, experimental psychologists were largely concerned elsewhere, not with problems of educational practice and school learning. For example, the major figures in the field, Hull and Tolman, were almost entirely concerned with laboratory research, phenomena produced in the laboratory, and the building of theories in which laboratory restrictions provided the boundary conditions.

With the onset of the third discernible historical period, the attention of some established figures within experimental psychology gradually began to shift to phenomena observed in school settings and many young psychologists embarked upon their careers with considerable sensitivity to educational phenomena. A few examples will suffice to illustrate the point. Among established psychologists, increasing attention to education is shown in the publication of "The Science of Learning and the Art of Teaching" by B. F. Skinner in 1954, *The Process of Education* by J. S. Bruner in 1960, and *Conditions of Learning* by R. M. Gagné in 1965. Among psychologists whose doctoral degrees were taken after 1950, A. R. Jensen, J. Kagan, and A. W. Staats illustrate the magnitude of interest given to educational problems from a psychological viewpoint. Finally, the growth in membership of the Division of Educational Psychology between 1950 and 1966 substantially exceeded the average of that in the Divisions of General, Experimental, and Developmental Psychology (1431 versus 456).

Despite the impressive evidence that can be marshalled to demonstrate an increasing recognition by both schoolmen and psychologists of the *relevance* of psychological theory and research for education, the possibility that such theory and research will make substantial *contributions* to education is still quite uncertain. There are two general classes of reasons for this uncertainty. The first concerns the character of the educational system itself and the second has to do with the feasibility of reworking what is essentially psychological, not educational theory and research within the framework of the conditions of educational practice. On the latter point there is sharp divergence among psychologists as to the strategies that should be followed in order to permit contributions to be made, as will be documented shortly.

It is possible to single out instances in which particular schools or particular school systems have readily adopted new educational procedures. Nevertheless, behaviors in the classroom on the part of both teachers and students are not easily changed in marked, systematic, and relatively permanent ways. The classroom itself, for example, has persisted as the primary unit of school organization in spite of a complete absence of evidence that it promotes optimum learning and development.

One factor that makes the possibility of substantial change in educational practice seem remote is the decentralization of control in educational systems. To say that educational practice has not changed much in the past 50 years is not to say that it is homogeneous. Variability, not constancy, is the striking characteristic of educational practice, at least on the face of it, when observational comparisons are made across classrooms and across schools. Even in an educational effort that is subject to more centralized control than any other, Project Headstart, there is very little evidence of consistency in practice from classroom to classroom, whether with regard to teacher behavior, student behavior, group organization, or curriculum (Williams and Stewart, 1966; Boyd, 1966; Temp and Anderson, 1966). The implication of such persistent variability is that orderly, systematic, generalized change in educational practice will be very difficult to promote.

Change is difficult but not impossible to effect. The question is: "How can the leverage necessary for change be obtained?" One of the first loci of such leverage that comes to mind is the teacher. It seems that it should be possible to modify teacher training markedly enough to produce dramatic changes in educational practice. But this assumption may be fallacious. For it is probable that since the institutions that train the largest proportion of the nation's teachers are less subject to external pressure for reform, they may be even more resistant to change than the public school systems themselves. Furthermore, as Gagné argues,

The idea that teachers can by themselves bring about the changes required to modernize education is itself part of what needs changing. Teachers cannot possibly do all of the things they are supposed to do, or that they say they are responsible for doing. They do not have the time, not to mention the capabilities, to design curricula, execute curricula, design instruction, execute instruction, guide individual development, measure individual progress, and consult with parents (Gagné, 1966a, p. 49).

If not in the teacher, the leverage for change must be found elsewhere. Whatever the method decided upon, it should permit the incorporation of relevant theory and information regarding cognitive development, insure control over content, procedures, ordering, and organization of instruction, and provide for the evaluation of the outcome of the changes instituted relative to a previously specified set of criteria. Gagné (1966a, p. 52) makes a strong case that these things can be achieved where research itself undertakes to *"design, develop* and *evaluate systems of education."* (For a complete account of recommendations in this vein, the reader is referred to Gagné, 1966a, pp. 52–57). Thus hopeful avenues for effecting change can be delineated, but even this does not obviate all of the obstacles in the way of substantial flow of contributions from research and theory in the psychology of cognitive development to educational systems. The issue in this connection is what the psychology of cognitive development has to offer education presently, and how psychology can go about enhancing theory and research to the point where the offering can be substantially increased.

At least two major strategies have been elucidated whereby psychological theory and research may be able to contribute to educational practice. These strategies are markedly divergent in their content and in their implications for *psychological* practice. Consider the antinomies among the following sets of quotations.

The fact that schooling is regarded as an organic process does not mean that it cannot be improved. . . . True enough, our frantic manipulation of the externals of schooling has produced no such improvement. These efforts have tried to produce improvement while ignoring the humble, basic processes by which schooling proceeds. When we honestly turn to a realistic study of these ancient,

earthy and pervasive forces themselves, who knows what improvement may result? (Stephens, 1967, p. 14).

Under these circumstances, it seems to me the better part of wisdom to find the good school situations— . . . and engage in close observation and intellectual resonance; then try to recreate such situations and make them more abundant and reproducible, no holds barred (Hawkins, 1967, p. 4).

Develop the best pedagogy you can. See how well you can do. Then analyze the nature of what you did that worked. . . . Later on, design hypotheses to determine what you did (Bruner, 1966e, p. 113).

The major thrust of the three positions represented by these quotations is that the strategy recommended for improving educational practice is: find and observe schooling in its "best" present form, attempt to understand it, and by understanding it as it is, increase the capability for improving it.

By way of contrast, consider the following quotations from Gagné (1966a):

. . . [E]ducation needs to be newly designed in a very fundamental way—a way which devotes primary attention to the development of the human individual from early years onward (p. 51).

. . . If we are satisfied with our present system, the application of knowledge about learning can only refine the preparation of textbooks and the nature of teacher procedures; it cannot be expected to demonstrate improvements of great magnitude. In contrast, the full exploitation of learning knowledge is possible in a newly designed system of education which focusses attention upon the individual learner and his continued development (p. 57).

The position implied here is that schooling in its present form, even at its best, is not sufficiently effective to deserve intensive study if the objective is to improve educational practice. Furthermore, this view assumes that knowledge gained in the psychological study of learning and development can contribute to education, whereas the position contained in the former views is that much available psychological theory and research is grossly inappropriate for application to the problems of schooling.

The strategy inherent in the views of Stephens, Hawkins, and Bruner suggests that the path to educational improvement should begin with a theory that accounts for the process and results of present schooling practices. The view enunciated by Gagné and held by many others (see Skinner, 1958; Melton, 1959) suggests that the path begins with a theory that explicates the process of learning itself. The former view asserts that an understanding of the process of schooling will have implications for the practice of educationally relevant psychological research. The latter view implies that what is known about the conditions of learning has application in educational practice, indeed that it dictates a radical reorganization and redesign of educational practice.

This difference of opinion regarding an optimal strategy for relating psychological theory and research to educational practice may be summarized as follows. First, there is little disagreement among psychologists that their craft, in one form or another, has relevance for the solution of educational problems. Second, there is considerable disagreement among psychologists about how to succeed in making positive contributions to educational practice and therefore about whether or not it is even possible. Finally, the dispute indicates that the eventual result of following either strategy is presently unknown and the choice remains, for the time, a matter of personal propensity. From all of these conditions it seems to follow that education and psychology are separated from one another by no more than a membrane but that this membrane may be successfully penetrated only with great effort and care.

The stance that will be assumed here regarding the relevance of a psychology of cognitive development for education and the possibility that contributions will in fact be made to change educational practice differs somewhat from those that have been reviewed thus far. This position is that the question of relevance in its superficial sense should be disposed of quickly. Virtually anything that psychologists do by way of advancing our knowledge of cognitive development will be relevant to education because of the shared concerns of the two fields. If this were the total of what could be said, its substance would be that everything, and therefore nothing, in the psychology of cognitive development would have relevance for education. Fortunately, more can be said.

In our view, the probability that psychological theory and research will have *effective* relevance for education is conditional upon the way in which investigators proceed. The most favorable starting point is marked by the activity of subjecting some educational objective to psychological analysis. As a first step, this activity has two virtues. First, it produces a formulation of the problem in psychological terms, a necessary prerequisite for any kind of fruitful investigation. Second, it insures that the problem investigated will be germane to education. Too much available psychological research lacks effective educational relevance simply for want of an additional condition or two that would have made it isomorphic with some form of school learning.

After the task of formulating a problem in psychological, that is, researchable, terms has been accomplished, the next step is to subdivide it into components that will yield to the methods of basic experimental research. This may sound quite traditional, differing little from the course followed in the past. Nevertheless, it may be suggested that it does differ and that it differs significantly. It is plausible that the relation between psychology and education has suffered not so much from an overabundance of laboratory research and a paucity of field research, but from the fact that laboratory research, since the early part of the century, increasingly has taken as its objective the understanding of phenomena detected in the laboratory itself rather than in more natural settings. Thus the task of generalization to socially occurring tasks has been made formidable by the lack of fit between laboratory phenomena, on the one hand, and the phenomena of the schoolroom, on the other. The point is not to depreciate this strategy for advancing psychological knowledge but to emphasize the availability of an alternative that has potential both for acquiring basic knowledge and for contributing to education.

The results of basic research performed on

component problems yielded by analyses of school phenomena should have effective relevance for education; such results should provide curriculum makers with guiding information as to the necessary components of optimal curricula. For example, suppose the objective is to assemble the components necessary for an effective curriculum in reading. The psychologist can provide for the curriculum maker an analysis of the skills necessary for attaining reading competence, specifications of an optimal sequence for promoting the acquisition of those skills, specifications of conditions for acquiring each skill most efficiently, information about individual differences relevant to the efficacy of such conditions, as well as means of indexing and then providing for these differences. It is here, in the processes of devising curricula, that direct contributions to educational change can most likely be made. But note that the agent of change is not a psychologist as a psychologist, although he may happen to be one, but as a curriculum maker. The contents of curricular materials, the conditions of their administration to students, and the procedures for monitoring their administration to insure proper implementation—these are prime sources of educational change and the psychology of cognitive development is not at the heart of the process. Psychologists, even those whose objective is the understanding of cognitive development, have no special qualifications for constructing curricula. They are well qualified, however, to produce information that can inform those who do make curricula and it is by performing this function that psychologists can contribute substantially, although indirectly, to educational change.

The potential for contributing to education does not end here, with the discovery of basic information relevant to school phenomena. For rarely will a curriculum embody and exploit properly or fully available psychological information in its first version. It would be equally rare for all the basic psychological information to be valid when generalized to the school setting. Revision should be the rule, revision attendant upon trial, evaluation, and additional basic research provoked by trial and evaluation. Thus the psychologist of cognitive development has additional functions relevant to the development of curricula. His expertise and understanding are needed for proper evaluation of the effects of a curriculum upon the cognitive capabilities of the students involved. These qualities are also needed for the solution, probably through additional laboratory research, of puzzles presented by the results of curricular efforts, puzzles relevant to both the advancement of basic psychological theory and the effecting of salutary educational change. For example, the method of learning sets is known to be a powerful procedure for establishing discrimination skills in relation to laboratory tasks. When applied to the acquisition of letter discrimination as a part of early reading training, however, it might prove ineffective. Thus might an explanatory puzzle be posed for psychological theory and a practical obstacle be placed in the way of educational improvement.

Note also that this view of the possible growth of relationships between cognitive development and education requires an alliance among psychologists, curriculum makers, and probably teachers and other schoolmen as well. Such an alliance need not be constant but it is crucial at two points. The first is that at which the curriculum maker attempts to map psychological information into curricular materials and procedures—at this point the effective communication of his work is mainly the psychologist's task. Second, the processes of evaluation and subsequent revision require a well-functioning liaison between these disparate agents, so that the sense of evaluation can be made clear to all concerned and so that the implications of evaluative results can be persuasively explicated.

Thus far in the discussion, "psychology" and "the study of cognitive development" have been used rather indiscriminately, almost as if the referents of the terms were identical. Obviously this is not the case and before proceeding further, it is well to clarify the extent and the limits of the domain with which we are concerned. As we regard education, our concern shall be with psychological theory and research in the area of cognitive development. Consistent with this avowed purpose, little consideration will be given to matters of personality growth and development, physical growth and development, or group processes and organization. We shall admit within our view topics such as learning, problem-solving, concept attainment, cognitive style, individual differences in intellectual behavior, perceptual development, reasoning, psycholinguistics, attention, and even measurement and evaluation. Our principal focus shall be on the changes and constancies in these psychological functions and attributes as the human organism grows and our aim will be to relate this focus to the problems of schooling and the needs of educational practice.

The succeeding discussion is organized in terms of educational needs on the one hand and corresponding resources in the psychology of cognitive development on the other. The educational needs emphasized are those implied by the educational problems already noted. The assumption here is that as solutions to the problems are obtained, the needs will be met.

TOWARD A RATIONALE FOR EDUCATIONAL PRACTICE

At a very general level, schoolmen need a widely acceptable rationale of educational practice. Such a rationale would be comprised of many components, each of which should serve to satisfy relatively more specific educational needs underlying the problems with which schoolmen must deal. Some of these components could be furnished with contributions from the psychological study of cognitive development and it is to these components that we now turn our attention.

A Theory of Educational Development. Even though the term "theory" interpreted in its strict sense may be inappropriate in this context, it will be used to refer to a set of assumptions about the nature of the processes whereby students come to be educated and about the kinds of conditions that affect those processes. Substantial contributions to this component may come from selective revisions of theories of cognitive development that have been made and are being made by psychologists.

Criteria of Successful Education. An adequate rationale of educational practice ought also to specify the objectives or goals of the educational process. The broad goals of education must, of course, be determined by a number of agencies in the society, not by psychologists alone. Nevertheless, the work of psychologists in the area of cognitive develop-

ment can contribute to efforts in this direction by analyzing the criteria into psychological components and by providing behavioral translations of these components. In this connection we are concerned with rather broad capabilities, such as that of intelligent behavior, or creative thinking, rather than with narrower capabilities such as those that might be specified as the proper outcome of the completion of courses in secondary-school mathematics.

Curricula Leading to Criterial Attainment. Once the criteria of a successful education are specified it becomes necessary to consider the means by which students can be guided to them. In educational terms such a specification involves the description of curricula. In psychological terms, this task involves describing the capabilities necessary for the attainment of the criteria and the order of their acquisition or emergence in the developmental course of the student. The task cannot, however, end here, for formal education is interventionist in nature, not observational. Thus the psychologist's role may be larger than that of describing developmental sequences of capabilities. It may include as well the function of specifying the conditions and sequences of learning that are most fruitful at the various developmental statuses. These two functions of the psychologist's role can be brought directly to bear on educational practice in his efforts to collaborate in the construction and revision of curricular materials.

Prerequisites for Curricular Educability. Another major educational need is the need for a specification of the prerequisites a student must have in his possession in order to make successful use of succeeding curricula. Statements of these prerequisites must be made separately for each of the major educational junctures. Perhaps the most important of these junctures is at the very beginning of formal schooling and, fortunately, the resources in the psychology of cognitive development are probably richest with respect to just this juncture. Other junctures can be identified but for the moment it will suffice to think in terms of the succession of grade level interchanges that form the major demarcations of schooling. In each case the question to be answered is: What are the capabilities that are assumed to be in the student's repertory by the curricula that will next be imposed on him? Resources relevant to this question that are presently available in psychological theory and research are of two kinds. First, they consist of descriptions of the capabilities that a child brings to any given educational juncture by virtue of his developmental status. Second, resources are to be found in analytic studies of the tasks that underlie school curricula. The results of such studies yield specifications of capabilities necessary for the successful accomplishment of these tasks. Thus psychological work on cognitive development can provide critical information about the extent to which the capabilities a child brings to a curriculum mesh with the prerequisites dictated by the nature of the curriculum.

Indexing the Possession of Prerequisites. Another component of an adequate educational rationale is the development of means for determining whether or not, or to what degree, a prerequisite is in the repertory of a student. It is one thing to describe the capabilities that are required by immediately succeeding tasks and another to construct means for indexing the student's possession of those capabilities. One of the glaring weaknesses in available methods of assessing intellectual status is their inability to reveal what has been learned in direct relation to (1) curricula completed and to (2) curricula scheduled to follow immediately. Help for this condition is probably not to be found in traditional work on problems of psychological assessment but instead in research on cognitive development. That is to say, the customary approach to the measurement of individual differences assesses the status of an individual by comparing his performance with that of other comparable individuals. So that, for example, a first-grade child may be judged to be progressing adequately if his performance on a reading achievement test is equivalent to the average performance of all other first-grade children. Unfortunately, judgments made in this fashion may be entirely irrelevant to the questions whether the child has learned what was intended in the first grade and whether he possesses the prerequisite capabilities for successful performance in the second grade. Accordingly, a different measurement model is required for application in education, and such a model

may be found in the practice of psychologists who conduct experimental research on cognitive development. In an experiment on learning, for example, a subject's performance is measured by comparing it with a criterion rather than with the performance of other subjects in the experiment. The criterion in these cases is simply a behavioral translation of what the subject was instructed to learn, such as making response A to sentences in the active voice and response B to sentences in the passive. It is precisely this kind of measurement that is necessary for adequate indexing of the possession of curricular prerequisites.

Facilitating the Acquisition or Emergence of Prerequisites. If the need for adequate assessment methods is satisfied, it will still remain to construct procedures for speeding up the processes whereby prerequisites emerge. At one level, the psychology of cognitive development cannot presently supply unequivocal answers to this problem since such would presuppose the resolution of a corresponding issue in psychological theory itself. This issue, of course, is to what extent experience can alter the pace of maturation. But as empirical work continues toward a resolution of this abiding dispute, considerable information is produced. And this information largely concerns methods for facilitating the acquisition of capabilities whose emergence is a function of experience.

Providing for Individual Differences. Inevitably, individuals differ. For educators, the pervasive character of such differences creates an enormously important brace of needs. The first is for reliable and fruitful methods of identifying the nature of these differences in educationally useful terms. The second of the needs is for effective methods of dealing with such differences once they are identified. Although the psychological study of individual differences in intellectual capabilities has a relatively long history, help for education is to be found not so much here as in the field of our present focus. Even though the psychology of cognitive development is comparatively young, it is beginning to produce important ideas about assessing and providing for individual differences that may contribute substantially to fulfilling this signal educational need.

CONTRIBUTIONS TO A THEORY OF EDUCATIONAL DEVELOPMENT

Two rather distinct kinds of efforts to rework psychological theories in the interest of enhancing their relevance for education may be distinguished. The first effort emphasizes maturational processes, drawing heavily upon the work of Piaget (1952). One of the principal versions of this kind of theory has been promulgated by Bruner (1966a, 1966b, 1966c, 1966d). The second effort emphasizes learning over maturational processes; one of its major exponents is Gagné (1965a, 1965b, 1965c, 1966a, 1966b, 1968).

In thinking about theories of cognitive development while keeping educational purposes in mind, it is tempting to set forth alternative conceptions, that is, ones that are opposing and mutually exclusive. An apparent beginning in this direction appears in the present organization of the topic into two separate sections pitting a maturational emphasis against a learning emphasis. Let it be clear, however, that here this adversary approach is more appearance than substance. With regard to educational purposes, the viewpoints are often not at all mutually exclusive. Indeed, at some points they are complementary. And, as we shall see, the two types of theory, even when taken together, leave a number of important gaps for a theory of educational development.

A word is in order about the strategy used here of concentrating attention on single representatives of major theoretical positions. The choice is not based on the mistaken belief that these are the only exemplars available in each category nor upon the judgment that they will necessarily prove to be the most fruitful. Rather, the specific expressions of the two viewpoints were selected because their authors, to a somewhat greater extent than others, have concerned themselves not only with the construction of a theoretical position in the psychological domain but also with drawing implications for and making contributions to educational theory and practice. In consequence these theoretical viewpoints are especially well-suited for examination with respect to their relevance for education.

A Maturational Emphasis

A schoolman may be principally concerned either with what it is a child learns and how well he learns it or with what functions the child will be capable of performing at the end of some learning episode. In fact, the schoolman is properly concerned with both, with the extent to which students master set theory and with the extent to which they can engage in effective mathematical reasoning. Nevertheless, there are two different emphases here and they emerge in parallel fashion when we examine theories of cognitive development. In a theory that partakes more of a maturational than a learning viewpoint, the emphasis is on the relatively longer term and more general functional capabilities of the maturing organism and on the structures that underlie them.

What Bruner (1966c) has called *instrumental conceptualism* is representative of a theoretical viewpoint having a maturational emphasis. Characterizing the theory, he notes:

In brief, it is a view that is organized around two central tenets concerning the nature of knowing. The first is that our knowledge of the world is based on a constructed model of reality, a model that can only partially and intermittently be tested against input. . . . [T]he second is that our models develop as a function of the uses to which they have been put first by the culture and then by any of its members who must bend knowledge to their own uses (pp. 320-321).

In more conventional language, instrumental conceptualism holds that what is known is constrained and determined by characteristics of the organism (from within) and by characteristics of the environment, especially the cultural environment (from without), in which the organism grows. Innate propensities are granted by the theory and, in fact, justify the importance given by it to the tenet that reality is "constructed." For in this view, human beings exhibit far more competence than would be expected on the basis of the experiences they have had. The best known example in this regard is linguistic competence. It can be shown that adults have the capacity to construct an infinite number of different sentences, all of which may be grammatical. Clearly, this capability cannot be accounted for entirely by what an individual hears; some mechanism for generating sentences must be posited. Furthermore, it turns out that any mechanism adequate to account for linguistic competence must have certain properties that cannot be acquired solely from the experiences that human beings have. Accordingly, it is necessary to assume that human beings have a propensity for the development of certain linguistic mechanisms and that the particular one that does develop in an individual depends upon the specific language he hears. Thus the linguistic environment determines which of several inherent mechanisms is activated, but the environment does not account for the formal properties of the mechanism. Similarly, when this view is extended to knowledge acquisition and intellectual capabilities in general, it implies that the organism must build its reality on the basis of relatively little information and such building involves the modification of inherent capacities. The occasions for and the possible forms of modification are both provided and limited by the environment.

Central to this theory of cognitive development is the notion of *representation*. The *media* and *objectives* of representation, indeed, form both the criteria of the extent of development and the major content of what has developed in an organism to any particular point in time.

The concern with representation is a concern with the ways in which the organism's experience with its world are encoded and stored. Three media of representation are distinguished: action (enactive representation), image (ikonic representation), and symbol (symbolic representation). Each one of these media of representation, according to Bruner, can be used in the service of the objectives of symbolic manipulation, image organization, and motor action. Note that each mode of representation is versatile in this sense; it can be recruited in the service of objectives that seem more akin to one of the other modes. Symbolic representation, for example, can be useful in the organization of action, as when a paragraph specifies the steps to be taken and the order in which to take them to accomplish such an objective as finding one's way to the nearest gas station. Despite the each-to-all relationships obtain-

ing between media and objectives of representation, the three media are construed as landmarks of development. Such a construction can be placed upon the media by virtue of the sequence of their inception in the cognitive activities of the child; it is supposed that the enactive mode emerges first, followed by the ikonic, followed, in turn, by the symbolic. It must be noted in this connection that the theory is not a simple one. It does not refer to an enactive stage nor to an ikonic or a representational stage. It does not contend that enactive representation is *replaced by* ikonic representation; each kind of representation can be and is used at all ages after its inception so that an older adolescent in this culture would be expected to exhibit all three kinds of representation. Finally, the theory is not simple in the sense that it assumes the three modes of representation to be universal in terms of the forms in which they develop, that is, constant across cultures. On the contrary, the viewpoint explicitly contains a description of at least one culture in which it appears that some possible uses of the symbolic representational mode never emerge (Bruner, 1966b).

The latter point illustrates the important place assigned to the cultural environment in instrumental conceptualism, especially as regards the determination of the nature of cognitive processes and structures. If the culture does not in some sense require the emergence of some of the forms of a mode of representation, especially in the case of the symbolic mode, those forms are not likely to develop. If the culture does not make available certain conceptual tools, they will not be acquired.

Thus in instrumental conceptualism some of the prime conditions for cognitive development are environmental; these conditions are to be found both in the demands the environment makes and in the opportunities it offers. At least two other sources of developmental propulsion are distinguished in the theory. The first is curiosity and its attendant competence motive, which flourish in the presence of specifiable kinds of environmental stimulation. The second additional source of developmental propulsion is also internal, a kind of equilibrium-disequilibrium mechanism but in a novel form that is well-suited to the representational emphasis of the theory. This source of propulsion is occasioned by conflict between representational media. The contention (Bruner, 1966a, p. 11) is that when one mode of representation contradicts another, cognitive growth ensues, as when "how one must act overtly and how the world appears" are not consistent.

Given this much of the theory, it is possible to infer that development from the viewpoint of instrumental conceptualism will be characterized by plateaus and relatively abrupt changes. These can be seen as such, however, only when close observations are made on the same children over time with regard to their performance on the same task. Discontinuities would not be expected to appear when performances are averaged across children, or when a child's performances are averaged across tasks, since the inception of a representational mode is not tied directly to a particular chronological age for all children, nor does it emerge at the same time in connection with all kinds of intellectual functions. The development of a new mode of representation will permit a child to perform in a way that is markedly different from what he could have done previously on the same task.

Two further features of the theory of instrumental conceptualism need emphasis before we turn to a consideration of its potential for contributing to a theory of educational development. The first is its explicit recognition of the nature of the organism as a determinant of the forms and boundary conditions of cognitive development. This feature of the theory marks its nativistic propensity but as we shall see shortly, the sort of nativism involved is neither naive nor traditional. This characteristic of the theory is illustrated in the following passage.

To sum up our discussion of symbolic representation, symbolic activity stems from some primitive or protosymbolic system that is species-specific to man. This system becomes specialized in expression in various domains of the life of a human being: in language, in tool-using, in various atemporally organized and skilled forms of serial behavior, and in the organization of experience itself. We have suggested some minimum properties of such a symbolic system: categoriality, hierarchy, prediction, causation, and modification. We have suggested that *any* symbolic activity, and especially language, is logically and empirically unthinkable without these properties. . . .

In view of the autonomy of the syntactic sphere from other modes of operating and of its partial disjunction from the semantic sphere, one is strongly tempted to give credence to the insistence of various modern writers on linguistics that language is an innate pattern, based on innate "ideas" that are gradually differentiated into the rules of grammar (McNeill, 1966; Chomsky, 1965; Katz, 1965) (Bruner, 1966b, pp. 47-48).

The material in this quotation represents fairly accurately the role assigned to innate factors in the theory. Further comment, however, is needed to clarify Bruner's conception of the relation between language and other forms of symbolic representation and activity.

In spite of the admission that language constitutes a special case, Bruner nevertheless argues: (1) that it evolves out of the same organismic givens as do other forms of symbolic activity; and (2) that it is, therefore, not the sole determinant of other forms of intellectual activity. On the contrary, the contention is that a necessary precondition for the development of linguistic control of other kinds of activity is the modification of the representational processes originally underlying such activity so that they are isomorphic with the structure of symbolic representation in language. Only after such preparation is complete can control of the activity be shifted to the language system. More must be said about this matter later in reference to its implications for educational practice.

The sort of nativism that characterizes the theory does not have the implication that experience is irrelevant to cognitive development. Indeed a second feature of the theory tempers its nativistic stance. As already noted, considerable importance is assigned to the culture in determining the specific nature of cognitive processing that develops in children. But even more specifically and explicitly, the theory assigns a substantial role in cognitive development to the school and to the tutor-tutee dialogue as represented by relationships between teachers and students and by those between parents and children. This kind of contention takes such a strong form that the theory appears to assert the *necessity* of such dialogues for the development of pervasive use of symbolic forms of representation along with all the intellectual potency they entail.

We turn now from instrumental conceptualism as a psychological theory to consider its implications for educational theory and practice. We will also consider whether these implications can be traced back to the developmental theory to indicate its potential for making contributions to education. In seeking answers to these questions we rely heavily on a book by Bruner (1966d), *Toward a Theory of Instruction*, which is informed with the psychological version of the theory.

For Bruner, "the heart of the educational process consists of providing aids and dialogues for translating experience into more powerful systems of notation and ordering" (Bruner, 1966d, p. 21). Thus the development of the various modes of representation is as central in educational development as in intellectual development in general.

As Bruner notes, a theory of instruction may be distinguished from a theory of learning or a theory of development in that the first is necessarily a "prescriptive" theory, whereas the latter are essentially "descriptive." A theory of instruction, for example, ought to specify not only how learning and development normally proceed but how they can be made optimal. Four features of a theory of instruction are distinguished. The first concerns the specification of conditions that are necessary and sufficient for producing in the child an affection and a propensity for engaging in learning. Second, the theory should specify the optimal way in which what is to be learned ought to be organized relative to the capabilities of the learner. The third feature of a theory of instruction concerns the optimal sequencing of what the child is expected to learn. Fourth, a theory of instruction should contain specifications of the kinds and timing of reinforcements to be delivered to the learner.

The details of these features are of interest since it is in them that we can see the inferences that may be drawn from the theory of instrumental conceptualism for educational theory and practice. First, consider the matter of engendering a positive regard for, and a tendency to engage in learning. Bruner tends to reduce this feature of the theory to the task of activating, maintaining, and directing the exploration of alternatives on the part of the child. *Activation* is equated with the arousal of curiosity. This, it is contended, can best be done by presenting tasks that are characterized by optimal uncertainty. The hand of the instructor is important here in the selection of appropriate tasks. It is important as well for *maintaining* exploration since this depends upon insuring that the activity is more rewarding than punishing. The *direction* of exploration is held to be determined by two things: information about the goal to be achieved; and information about the relevance of one's way of proceeding. Both of these things can be provided by the instructor.

An obvious addition to this list of conditions relevant to exploration is concerned again with activation and maintenance and is suggested directly by instrumental conceptualism. As we noted, the theory holds that one of the main propulsions to problem-solving activity is conflict between two modes of representing the same knowledge. It is an obvious inference that the selection of tasks should be made with such conflict as a criterion and that the maintenance of exploration ought to be aided when the instructor sees to it that the conflict remains salient during the course of the learner's activity. For example, if the aim is to teach Archimedes' principle of flotation, exploration might be maintained by presenting to the student a series of instances of "light" objects that sink in water and "heavy" objects that float.

With regard to the *organization* of knowledge to be acquired, Bruner restates the widely disseminated notion that "Any idea or problem or body of knowledge can be presented in a form simple enough so that any particular learner can understand it in a recognizable form" (Bruner, 1966d, p. 44). Three variables are distinguished to define the form in which knowledge is presented. The first of these, familiar by now, is the mode of representation in which the knowledge is communicated. The other two variables are the economy and the effective power of the organization adopted. The contention is that any sort of knowledge can be represented initially in each of the three representational modes, the one chosen depending upon the child's presenting capabilities, that is, the capabilities already in the child's possession when he begins work in an instructional sequence. Economy of presentation refers to the information load necessary for comprehension of a subject matter: the less the load, the easier the comprehension. A prescription is implied here: find the most economical form consistent with the inherent nature of the material to be learned and present materials in that form. The power of a particular way of organizing knowledge apparently refers to whether or not it permits the learner to make maximal use of knowledge in solving problems as yet unencountered, a form of transfer.

Before considering the problem of sequencing materials, it is important to pause and examine more carefully the notion that any idea can be acquired by any learner at any age. On its face, the assertion seems to give the lie to an interpretation of instrumental conceptualism as a theory having a maturational emphasis. For this contention seems to require the assumption that prior growth is never necessary for the acquisition of any given kind of knowledge. But a more careful examination of the assertion reveals that it is consistent with a maturational view, although not with a passive, *laissez-faire* version of such a view. Notice the conditional phrase, ". . . . knowledge can be presented in a form *simple enough*. . . ." The form of presentation must fit the status of the organism. The theory does not contend that any child of any age can, at that age, be taught any particular knowledge, even in its most complex form, by simply sequencing the material properly. Rather it contends that the instructor can formulate any knowledge in a form consistent with the developmental level of the child, a contention that may leave many an instructor both flattered and disbelieving.

The *sequencing* of materials involves decisions made in accord with criteria that are multiply determined. The ground rule suggested by instrumental conceptualism is that in terms of modes of representation, a task should first be presented, and the learner should first be engaged in the task enactively, then ikonically, and finally symbolically. This inference follows from three properties of the parent theory: first, that this sequence of modes is the ontogenetic sequence for most children; second, that all modes persist after they have initially emerged, thereby providing alternative ways of representing almost any subject matter; and, third, that the earlier modes provide a second line of attack when the symbolic mode, for one reason or another, fails. Another reason for the recommendation that instruction should begin by presenting knowledge enactively, then ikonically, and then presenting it symbolically is partially obscured. It seems to be presumed that the only fruitful route to the symbolic representation of any knowledge is through prior enactive and ikonic representations. If true, this position has important implications for educational practice. It suggests, for example, that verbal modes of presenting material on the part of the instructor and of responding to it on the part of the student are much overemphasized in schooling. Furthermore, it suggests that the concern of many educators and psychologists with the alleged language deficiencies of lower-SES children may be excessive. The excess, however, is not a general one. Bruner would surely agree that a well functioning symbolic system such as language is necessary for symbolic representation. But the possession of such a system is not sufficient. Thus the implication is that lower-SES children need training in enactive and ikonic representation as well as in symbolic representation of the material to be learned.

Despite its interesting implications, however, the assertion that all kinds of knowledge should first be presented to students enactively must be viewed with considerable skepticism. Some kinds of knowledge may not lend themselves to enactive representation. Consider, for example, the difficulty of presenting a concept such as that of an imaginary number enactively. In the case of knowledge of this kind, the principal task of instructional design may involve questions of the optimal sequence of presentation *within* the symbolic mode rather than *across* the three modes of representation. What should be the sequence of presenting subsidiary knowledge symbolically in order to facilitate the student's eventual acquisition of the concept of imaginary numbers? The theory offers little assistance in arriving at answers to this kind of question regarding the problem of sequencing.

The timing and nature of effective reinforcements is judged to be crucial for their success in aiding learning. Optimally, feedback should occur when the learner is judging the product of his activity against the standard of the goal that has been presented to him. The form of reinforcement, taken now to mean informational feedback, must be consistent in representational mode with the mode being used by the learner. Otherwise the learner's task will be made more difficult rather than facilitated by the reinforcement. Furthermore, the reinforcement must itself contain information as to whether or not the learner's activity is advancing him toward his goal.

Clearly, all of these features of a theory of instruction are relevant to the activities of a variety of schoolmen, those concerned with the construction of educational materials, those responsible for curriculum planning, and those directly responsible for instruction, namely, teachers. Indeed, in the theory of instruction that follows from instrumental conceptualism, the role of the teacher is especially crucial in two respects. First, the teacher is a source of knowledge that the student does not possess. In comparison with other sources of knowledge, such as books, for example, the teacher is unique in that he himself represents the student's goal of having acquired the knowledge in question. Secondly, the teacher is crucial insofar as he can modify his activity as a source of knowledge in direct consequence of the student's successes and failures in the course of acquisition. Bruner says, for example, *"Intellectual development depends upon a systematic and contingent interaction between a tutor and a learner*, the tutor already being equipped with a wide range of previously invented techniques that he teaches the child" (Bruner, 1966d, p. 6). Perhaps it is a misconstruction issuing from a too literal reading of this theory that the teacher, as this position is usually understood, occupies a crucial role. For *teacher* can refer to any method for availing the child of knowledge possessed by others, including personal interaction with adults. Nevertheless, there is running throughout Bruner's explication of instrumental conceptualism and of its implications for a theory of instruction a respect for and an acceptance of existing modes of organization of the school. Not so for the existing practices of presenting knowledge to students, however. In this area, innovation, change, experimentation, all are recommended.

The contribution of instrumental conceptualism to a theory of educational development cannot be properly evaluated in the absence of some attention to its specific application in education. Bruner (1966d, pp. 54-72; Bruner and Kenney, 1965) describes an effort to teach quadratics to four 8-year-old children. The account is remarkable in two regards. First, it succeeds in illustrating the four propounded features of an instructional theory. A predisposition for learning was found in the children, further activated through the introduction of novelty, maintained by alterations of the materials and problems presented, and directed in truly ingenious ways by the two teachers. With respect to organization and sequencing of presentation, the practices followed were clearly consistent with the theory. The children were initially engaged in enactive behaviors. For example, they were presented with a square block of wood and were asked to make a succession of larger squares by physically adding other pieces of wood of constant size to the original one. It was assumed that the children represented the outcomes (appearance of the new squares) to themselves ikonically through imagery. Symbolic representation was initiated by encouraging the children to keep a written record of the numbers of pieces of wood added to each square in the course of making the next larger one. The economy of the underlying structure was given in the notation used for record-keeping, a notation provided by the teachers. The power of the structure was demonstrated when the children were encouraged to transfer their newly acquired skills, as well as the attendant notation, for square-building to the task of balancing a beam. Because of the materials used (the squares and the beam balance) reinforcement was contingent upon the child's own actions, came immediately, and was directly available in the child's product rather than being mediated by the teacher. Thus in these ways the theory did make palpable contribution to this limited bit of educational practice, and impressive practice it was.

The second remarkable aspect of this instructional effort is that very little of it seems to be directly and explicitly implied by the theory. This may mean that the educational utility of the theory is severely limited. The point is that this theory of development cannot make substantial contributions to educational practice if it can be used very successfully only by extraordinarily ingenious and gifted schoolmen. Consider, for example, that aspect of quadratics instruction that most clearly reflects the influence of the theory—the sequencing of modes of representation. To be sure, the sequence was initiated in an enactive mode and this was eventually followed by guided transitions to ikonic and symbolic modes. But the particular expressions of these modes appear to be entirely *ad hoc* with respect to theory. Moreover, there are no "instructions to schoolmen" as to procedures for deciding precisely what expression to give to each of the modes in constructing a sequence of instruction.

It might properly be said in response to this reservation about the utility of the theory for education that it is misdirected. After all, the author of the theory explicitly states that it is in the early stages of formation and that considerable work of the sort described in connection with the sequence of quadratics instruction must be done before applicability can be demonstrated one way or another. But the point must still be emphasized that for a theory of cognitive development to effect changes in education, it must contain means for its implementation. To put the matter another way, a theory of instruction must give attention to instructing schoolmen in its use. One of the advantages of a theory is that it makes public and explicit what would ordinarily be relatively private and implicit. One way of accomplishing the aim of implementation is largely to bypass the teacher and to guide the production of self-contained instructional sequences that leave little room for instructor intervention except, perhaps, in matters of administration. But in the theory emanating from instrumental conceptualism this seems an inappropriate strategy since so much is ascribed to the functions of the teacher. Thus even though the goal has not been achieved, it must remain salient, for too much can be lost in the translation of theory into practice when the success of the translation depends critically on the translator and his individual talent.

To sum up this review of a theory of cognitive development that emphasizes maturation, here is an annotated list of educationally relevant positions that emanate from instrumental conceptualism.

1. The heart of intellectual development is the emergence of three major systems of representation, the enactive, the ikonic, and the symbolic. Ontogenetically, these systems emerge in the order given but after their initial apparance all continue to operate concurrently. One or the other system may be especially relevant to a given kind of knowledge and in instruction this fact must be specifically taken into account. In many instructional sequences, the best route starts with the enactive mode and recapitulates ontogenetic development in teaching the subject matter.

2. Relationships among the three modes of representation must be prepared. If, for example, the goal of an instructional sequence is to permit the student to represent material to himself symbolically, the structure of the symbolic representation must be specified. Then the structure of representation in the prerequisite enactive and ikonic modes should be made isomorphic with that envisioned for the symbolic mode. Only after this is accomplished should translation be attempted from one mode to the other. To give an example of an implication following from this position, it would suggest that the culturally disadvantaged child should be led to reorganize his knowledge in existing enactive and ikonic modes *before* any attempt is made to force that knowledge prematurely into a symbolic mode of representation.

3. Readiness is a matter of prior learning and development and need not be awaited. Although the theory is adamant on this point, it is not altogether clear. That is to say, the issue is complicated. The extent to which maturational factors limit what can be learned appears to be determined only by the ingenuity of the schoolman in properly representing the subject matter to the student. Yet it is also suggested in the theory that some growth is required, in addition to instructional experiences before final representations of an area of knowledge can take, say, an optimal symbolic form. In this light it is unclear what educators should do about the notorious problem of readiness.

4. In addition to its emphasis on a few powerful innate and maturational factors, the theory relies heavily on the role of culture as a determinant of the nature of intellectual development. In its praiseworthy dissatisfac-

tion with the simple statement that culture is important, the theory goes on to specify the agency by which culture determines cognitive development: the tutor-tutee relationship. The teacher's role, whether it is performed by a formal teacher or informally by a parent or some other adult, is critical for making available to the child the tools of cognition, for instigating and maintaining learning, for structuring and sequencing knowledge, and for arranging materials and the environment so that they deliver informative reinforcement of appropriate kinds at appropriate times. Thus a crucial implication of the theory is that the preparation of teachers for providing successful instruction is prerequisite for optimal educational development.

5. Individual differences are explicitly expected to emerge in connection with any one of the four functions of the teacher listed. The implication drawn from this is that a variety of means must be found to the same ends, depending on the presenting characteristics of the child. The theory, however, does not discuss at any great length the problems presented for education by individual differences nor does it make sufficient proviso for their solution.

6. Finally, as it stands presently, the theory is stated at such a high level of generality that the implementation of its implications in educational practice is left almost entirely to the ingenuity of the schoolman, whatever his capacity. Presently it can make contact with educational practice only in the hands of brilliant and inventive practitioners. Its relevance for education is well-substantiated; its contribution to education is almost entirely potential; and the likelihood that it will truly effect improvement is indeterminate.

A Learning Emphasis

Any number of theorists among psychologists could be chosen to represent a learning emphasis in connection with the topic of cognitive development and education: Gibson, Jensen, Kendler, Osgood, Skinner, Staats, or Underwood, to name some. Although the views of these psychologists will be referred to later, principal attention will be given here to Gagné's explication of a theory of cognitive development with a learning emphasis (Gagné 1965a, 1965b, 1965c, 1966a, 1967, 1968). The reason for the choice is a simple one;

Gagné (1965a, 1965b, 1965c, 1966a, 1967) has made the most thoroughgoing attempt to translate a learning approach into a view of development that speaks directly to educational issues.

Gagné (1968) distinguishes between learning and development principally in terms of the time span occupied by the changes in capabilities of an organism. Both learning and development are defined as changes in capabilities. Both learning and development are contrasted with growth and maturation as principles for explaining changes over time. While admitting that development must be viewed as a joint function of learning and growth, Gagné's emphasis is clearly upon learning:

If growth is the dominant theme, educational events are designed to wait until the child is ready for learning. In contrast, if learning is a dominant emphasis, the years are to be filled with systematically planned events of learning, and there is virtually no waiting except for the time required to bring about such changes (Gagné, 1968.)

Although Gagné's emphasis is upon learning processes and although it starts with learning conceived in an associationistic framework, his approach departs in crucial ways from a strict connectionist model. The theory is descriptively called a *cumulative learning* model and its major components are the traditional ones of learning, memory, and transfer. It differs from other learning models of development, however, in its identification of what it is that can be learned.

In a traditional model *connections* between specific stimuli and responses are the entire content of learning, regardless of the complexity of the connections required to account for behaviors. But in the cumulative learning model, it is allowed, indeed it is firmly asserted, that much more complex forms of content, such as rules and principles, are learned. This being the case, the question is what distinguishes the cumulative learning model from more cognitively oriented theories such as that of Bruner (1964, 1965, 1966a, 1966b) or Piaget (see Flavell, 1963). The difference is in the detailed specifications of prerequisite learnings that the cumulative model requires for the occurrence of rule or principle learning. Thus cumulative learning theory contends that acquisition processes are hierarchically organized and that the various processes are distinguished from one another in terms of the characteristics of the performances by which each is expressed and in terms of the internal and external conditions necessary for their occurrence.

The most complete exposition of the hierarchical model itself is given in *Conditions of Learning* (Gagné, 1965a). Seven varieties of learning are distinguished: *S-R connections* (motor acts), *motor chains, verbal chains, multiple discriminations, concepts, principles,* and *higher-order principles* or *strategies.*

The simple fact that learning is subdivided in this manner has the consequence of asserting that all learning processes are *not* the same. Each of the varieties of learning is identified in terms of the characteristics of

its attendant *performances,* necessary *internal conditions,* and necessary *external conditions.* Later we shall see how each of these means of identifying a variety of learning has implications for education. But for now examine the following summary of the matter taken from Gagné (1967, p. 301).

Each one of the internal conditions of learning forms a prerequisite capability for learning of the next higher variety. Thus:

1. The possession of *stimulus-response* connections is prerequisite to the learning of . . .

2. *chains,* whether motor or verbal. These (or in the simplest case, S-R connections) are prerequisite to the learning of . . .

3. *multiple discriminations,* which are prerequisite to the learning of . . .

Table 1. Summary of Conditions Considered Necessary for Seven Kinds of Learning

Performance Established by Learning	Internal (learner) Conditions	External Conditions
Specific responding	Certain learned and innate capabilities	Presentation of stimulus under conditions commanding *attention;* occurrence of a response *contiguous* in time; *reinforcement*
Chaining		
Motor	Previously learned individual connections	Presenting a *sequence* of external cues, effecting a sequence of specific responses *contiguous* in time; repetition to achieve selection of response-produced stimuli
Verbal	Previously learned individual connections, including implicit "coding" connections	Presenting a *sequence* of external verbal cues, effecting a sequence of verbal responses *contiguous* in time
Multiple discrimination	Previously learned chains, motor or verbal	Practice providing *contrast of correct and incorrect stimuli*
Classifying	Previously learned multiple discriminations	Reinstating discriminated response chain contiguously with *a variety of stimuli* differing in appearance, but belonging to a single class
Rule using	Previously learned concepts	Using external cues (usually verbal), effecting the recall of previously learned concepts contiguously in a suitable sequence; specific applications of the rule
Problem solving	Previously learned rules	Self-arousal and selection of previously learned rules to effect a novel combination

4. *concepts*, which are prerequisite to the learning of . . .

5. *principles*, which are prerequisite to the learning of . . .

6. *high-order principles* including *strategies*. (Gagné, 1966a, p. 41).

Clearly, learning is conceived to be organized hierarchically so that complex forms of learning are dependent upon prior, simpler forms.

Although it may not be so clear, it is equally a characteristic of this theory that the more complex forms of learning are not simply a collocation of the learning of many, many connections. The learning of a rule like "Alleviation of the conditions of an oppressed social group produces revolutionary behavior in members of that group," is not a matter of learning the connections between the individual words in the rule. But the acquisition of such a rule does presuppose the prior learning of the concepts involved, of the multiple discriminations necessary for the learning of these concepts, of the chains necessary for the learning of the discriminations, and of the connections necessary for the learning of the chains.

An additional specification of the model deserves emphasis. The acquisition of a higher-level capability, such as a rule, depends not only upon the prior acquisition of lower-level capabilities but also upon the retention of those previous learnings. That is to say, even if all of the learnings prerequisite to the learning of a rule can be shown to have been accomplished, this will not suffice unless these previous learnings can be recalled when the rule is to be learned. This assertion fits well with recent evidence concerning the conditions necessary for demonstrating a facilitory effect of mediational conditions in verbal learning tasks (Horton and Wiley, 1967). It has been shown that unless a mediate term in a supposed verbal chain can be recalled at the time the two ends of the chain are being learned, its previous acquisition will not facilitate the new learning. Later we shall examine the pronounced implications that this facet of the cumulative learning model has for educational practice.

With this brief summary of Gagné's explication of the varieties and conditions of learning, let us turn to a discussion of the significance of the term *cumulative* in the learning model. In part, this discussion has already begun because some portion of the meaning of cumulative is given in the specification that the learning of capabilities is hierarchically organized and that earlier learnings must be recalled in order for newer ones to proceed successfully. In this sense learning may be said to be cumulative, but it is also held to be cumulative in another way having to do with transfer and generalization.

Cumulative learning theory needs a transfer component if it is to be at all persuasive. Consider, for example, the inconceivably large number of hierarchies of learning that would have to be specified to outfit a growing human being with all of the principles that most adults have at their disposal. A lifetime would probably not be long enough for each individual to acquire such a vast set of rules if it is held that in the case of every rule capability he must traverse anew the relevant hierarchy from its base to its apex. Without some sort of transfer mechanism, the same property that gives cumulative learning theory its appeal—that is, its intent to specify in detail the conditions necessary for the acquisition of a complex capability,—also limits it to virtual inapplicability to human intellectual development.

Fortunately, the model does contain a transfer component. Indeed, Gagné says, "cumulative learning . . . assumes a built-in capacity for transfer. Transfer occurs because of the occurrence of specific identical (or highly similar) elements within developmental sequences. Of course, 'elements' here means rules, concepts, or any of the other learned capabilities I have described" (1968). Transfer, in other words, can be counted upon to occur by virtue of the fact that many different terminal capabilities share the same lower-level conditions of learning. After one complete cumulative learning sequence has been traversed, the entire journey will not have to be negotiated again. Other related terminal capabilities can be acquired in shorter order since the learning sequence can begin at a higher level, say at that of concepts, rather than at a lower one, say at that of verbal chains.

The conception of transfer in the cumulative model has two advantages. To be sure, it provides a mechanism for rationalizing the enormous number of capabilities of the adult human being, but it also leads to the expectation that transfer will not be automatic from the acquisition of some one specific principle to the acquisition of another related one. Consider an example that emerges in Gagné's discussion of work on the acquisition of principles of conservation in children. He notes (Gagné, 1968) that the completion of a learning sequence culminating in the successful performances "judging equalities and inequalities of volumes of liquids in rectangular containers" would not guarantee that the related principle for matching volumes in cylindrical containers had also been learned. In fact, he says, "Probably not, because he (the child) hasn't yet learned enough about cylinders, volumes of cylinders, and areas of circles" (Gagné, 1968). Thus substantial portions of the hierarchies are the same for the two principles, but the identity is not complete. And, wherever two hierarchies diverge, new capabilities have to be learned before transfer can be complete from one to the other. Accordingly, from the viewpoint of cumulative learning theory, the failure of a number of investigations in their attempts to facilitate the acquisition of conservation in children is attributable to incomplete prerequisite learning rather than to insufficient structural growth in the child.

The transfer mechanism in the cumulative learning model, by itself, is probably not sufficient to account for all of the capabilities the adult can display. In fact, to give such an account, it is likely that the cumulative learning model must be extended beyond learning to thinking. Consider, for example, the case of an individual who has learned a set of principles which are all related to similar human performances. Suppose that the capabilities represented by these principles and the subordinate capabilities acquired along the way contain in themselves all of the components necessary for the possession of an additional principle that has in no sense been directly taught. Remember that this instance would lend itself to a transfer analysis in terms of the model only if it were the case that the additional principle represented the apex of an intact hierarchy or learning sequence. Further, then, suppose that this is not the case, that in order for the additional principle to be possessed by the individual, a self-initiated reorganization of existing capabilities would be necessary, some being taken from one specific hierarchy, some from another. By extending the cumulative learning theory to give an account of this kind of process, the model could presumably cover thinking as well as learning. Gagné admits of this possibility when he remarks:

. . . [I]t is recognized that such generalizations can readily occur when the individual himself initiates the intellectual activity; the new learning does not have to be guided by external instruction. The process of cumulative learning can involve and be contributed to by the operations of inductive and deductive thinking. The cumulative learning model obviously does not provide a theory of thinking; but it suggests the elements with which such a theory might deal (Gagné, 1968).

In terms of the educational implications of the cumulative model, its greatest service in connection with the problem of thinking could probably be done by providing an explicit specification of the conditions necessary for self-initiated intellectual activity. As we have noted, the existence of such processes must be assumed. But for education as well as for psychological theory itself it is important to know the external and internal conditions that determine thinking processes.

The absence of an elaborated theory of thinking is perhaps the most serious inadequacy of the cumulative model. Without such a component the model cannot provide a comprehensive account of cognitive development. But this is not to say that the model could not be augmented to do so. Indeed, it is one of the model's positive attributes that the sources of its inadequacy are so clearly apparent.

Any complete version of the cumulative model, in addition to containing a theory of thinking, would also need to deal with the necessity for assumptions regarding human capacities that make both learning and thinking possible. Although they are not specified at present, the model seems to assume inherent human propensities for the development of learning abilities and for the development of processing or organizational abilities that are commonly referred to as thinking. Some such assumptions are required by the model because it insists upon specifying explicitly the conditions under which particular human intellectual activities can take place. Thus one would expect that in cases where neither external nor internal conditions of learning are sufficient to account for observable capabilities, recourse would have to be taken to inherent human capacities.

In general, cumulative learning theory is a strong theory in the sense that it insists upon detailed accounts of the conditions necessary and sufficient to produce the acquisition of any given capability. These accounts, apart from being detailed, must qualify as testable hypotheses as well. Derivations from the theory are eminently falsifiable. In another regard, however, the position is a weak one. For it shares with all other models having a learning emphasis an ultimate indeterminacy if its predictions are not confirmed. As an illustration consider whether or not it is possible to advance intellectual development in children through specific training so that they can successfully evince conservation behavior before untrained age-mates can do so. Suppose that an analysis of the required terminal capability is made and the conditions necessary and sufficient for its acquisition are specified in accord with the cumulative model. Suppose then that these conditions are fulfilled but it is found that the trained children do not, in fact, perform at a more mature level on conservation tasks than relevant control children. Two very different conclusions may be drawn from this result. The first is that a growth model provides a more adequate account of the conditions of cognitive development than a cumulative learning model. But there is an alternative conclusion: the analysis of the subordinate capabilities necessary for the acquisition of the terminal one was itself not sufficient. This second conclusion has the consequence simply of causing the analysis of subordinate capabilities to be modified and then incorporated in a new training sequence. Theoretically the cycle of analysis-training-evaluation can be repeated indefinitely. That is, there is no criterion built into the theory by which a decision can be made that the cumulative model itself is inadequate.

With this much of the basic theory of cumulative learning in hand, we shall turn to an examination of its potential contribution to the construction of a theory of educational development. In large measure, this task has already been accomplished in its general form as well as in specific applications (Gagné, 1963, 1965a, 1965b, 1965c, 1965d, 1966a, 1967). Obviously, given its hierarchical character and its analytical emphasis, the cumulative learning model would set the starting point of a derived theory of educational development as the statement, in behavioral terms, of the objectives to be attained. Gagné has distinguished six different educational activities to which the cumulative learning model can make contributions:

1. Deriving objectives for portions of the educational process directed toward the goals of education.

2. Describing the various curricula designed to meet the objectives.

3. Designing the process of instruction.

4. Designing a system for guiding individual development.

5. Developing a means to assess student progress in learning.

6. Establishing a method for evaluation of the means chosen to achieve objectives (Gagné, 1966a, p. 5).

Deriving Objectives for Education. The contribution of the cumulative learning model of cognitive development to the task of setting educational objectives is made largely in terms of the requirements it imposes upon the form in which such objectives are stated. For the cumulative learning model to be of maximal value for education, the objectives must be *comprehensive, systematic,* and *behavioral.* Comprehensively stated objectives are to be understood in contrast with fragmented statements. This means the objectives of education should be stated for the entire span of time for which formal education is to be imposed on the student. Thus they will be comprehensive with respect to both the full range of contents in which capabilities are to be acquired and the full range of levels of capability to be attained within each content. The objectives should be stated systematically in the sense that they include explicit reference to the hierarchical relationships obtaining between subordinate and superordinate objectives. Thus considerable effort is demanded both in detailing the components of ultimate objectives and in specifying the priority ordering of the various components. Finally, objectives are to be stated in behavioral terms. The primary justification for such a demand is that if objectives are not stated in behavioral terms it is a matter of guesswork to determine just what it is that the child is to learn. Unless an unambiguous answer can be given to the question "What is to be learned?" there is little hope that the cumulative learning model will make contributions of any substance to education. In addition to this demand for behavioral statements of objectives and the obvious improvement in communication such a practice would entail, other advantages accrue, as Gagné rightly notes:

Unambiguous statements of learning outcomes are necessary to guide the behavior of the teacher. They can be of considerable importance in providing students with immediate goals, and thus in contributing to their motivation. And they are needed as a basis for assessment of the student's progress by means of tests or other measures (Gagné, 1966a, p. 10).

Although the contribution of the cumulative model to the derivation of objectives for education is not a substantive one, it is nevertheless of considerable worth. The implementation of these three requirements—comprehensiveness, systematization, and behavioral definitions—in the formulation of educational objectives would by itself advance educational practice.

Curricular Routes to Educational Objectives. As viewed from the cumulative learning model, curriculum design is a matter of translating behaviorally defined objectives into a designation of capabilities to be acquired. In other words, a curriculum is a statement of terminal capabilities along with the sequence of prerequisite capabilities leading to them. Once the components of a curricular hierarchy are specified, the main task remaining is the determination of the optimal sequence in which the subordinate capabilities should be acquired. The theory of cumulative learning by itself cannot yield unequivocal predictions about such matters. The strategy required is to construct sequences, threat them as hypotheses, and subject these hypotheses to empirical test. The construction of these hy-

potheses is the joint task of subject-matter scholars (mathematicians, historians, philosophers, as the case may demand), curriculum experts, teachers, and psychologists, none of whom can guarantee the superiority of one sequence over another a priori. Examples of the application of this approach have been reviewed by Gagné (1966a).

Stipulating the Conditions of Instruction. By leaning heavily on a learning orientation, the cumulative model draws principally upon research in human learning in specifying its implications for the design of instruction. The kind of information relevant to this task comes from studies that yield reliable conclusions about the conditions external to the learner that yield the most efficient learning, the maximum retention, the widest possible transfer, and the greatest propensity for self-activating intellectual activity. The amount of information available about the first three of these matters is already large and is still growing at a rapid rate. Less is known about the conditions necessary or conducive to self-activating processes.

In his discussion of instructional functions, Gagné (1967) distinguishes seven separate ones. Presumably all of these functions are presently performed by the teacher, but their complexity suggests that a single teacher cannot possibly perform them all adequately in classroom situations. Consequently, Gagné recommends (1967, pp. 309-310) that instruction should be predesigned with regard to the performance of each function so as to reduce to manageable proportions the teacher's task and to insure that the functions are effectively accomplished.

1. Selecting and Presenting Stimuli. Broadly construed, this function is one of the most important in instruction. For the selection and presentation of stimuli must be done with full attention to three considerations: the presenting capabilities of the learner; the fit between the stimuli chosen and the variety of learning to be accomplished; and the extent to which the stimuli are representative of the criterion tasks the learner will be expected to deal with. The task of selecting and presenting stimuli is guided by the cumulative learning model in the following way. A task analysis of the objective of an instructional sequence yields a specification of the subcapabilities and their ordering that are necessary for the attainment of the objective. Each subcapability represents some one of the several varieties of learning that the theory distinguishes. For each variety, external conditions necessary for acquisition would be identified and these conditions would include the relevant properties and manner of presenting stimuli.

Suppose, for example, the objective was to facilitate the performance of pronouncing each of a small set of French words in such a way that native speakers could reliably identify the words uttered. One of the subcapabilities yielded by an analysis of this objective is that of imitating the pronunciation of each of the words immediately after hearing it. If the learner has this capability, then it is appropriate to inaugurate conditions that will assist him in learning to make each of the responses in the absence of the model utterances, that is, given only the presentation of the words in print. Such a task is a multiple discrimination in the terminology of cumulative learning theory and therefore would require the repeated presentation of each of the printed words as stimuli and the evocation of the appropriate responses, probably through a prompting method. Following mastery of the task in this form, prompting would be eliminated and practice would be continued using informative feedback after each response. Thus the stimuli presented in the terminal phase would be identical with those to be used in evoking the terminal performance itself.

2. *Controlling Attention.* Gagné's (1967, p. 305) discussion of this function is limited to an indication of some means for directing the learner's attention to important aspects of the materials presented to him—means such as the use of verbal commands and pointers. The paucity of content on this important topic may reflect a weakness in the theory. Compare this treatment with that reviewed in connection with instrumental conceptualism, where at least a minimally adequate attempt was made to deal with the topic in terms of activating, maintaining, and directing attention. It is interesting to note the contrast between the emphasis in instrumental conceptualism on attentional factors inherent in the stimulus materials themselves and the corresponding emphasis in the cumulative model on extraneous factors.

3. *Informing the Learner of Objectives.* Gagné views the importance of this function in much the same way that Bruner views the importance of setting forth clearly for the learner the "goals" of his activity. Informing the student clearly about the terminal performance expected of him permits the introduction of informative and effective reinforcements along the way to the attainment of the relevant capability.

4. *Stimulating Recall of Subordinate Capabilities.* This function of instruction comes directly from the cumulative learning model. In order for a superordinate capability to be acquired, subordinate capabilities must not only have been previously learned but must also be recalled at the time the new capability is being learned. Thus it is critical for instruction that methods of cueing be employed that will insure the recall of relevant previous learnings. Although it is not explicitly stipulated, the theory presumably also implies that the recall of these capabilities should be ascertained before instruction proceeds further.

5. *Determining a Sequence for Evoking Performance.* The next step in instruction is to stimulate the learner to engage in relevant activity. An initial move toward this goal is made by deciding upon the sequence of performance that is most conducive to efficient acquisition and durable retention. For example, the decision is whether to present materials in parts or in wholes, whether to institute massed or distributed practice, etc. The term sequence in this connection does not refer to the problem of ordering the presentation of materials relevant to the acquisition of the series of subcapabilities in a given hierarchy—that sort of decision has presumably already been made in connection with the construction of curricular routes to objectives. Similarly, concern with the structure of knowledge to be imparted is nowhere evident in this connection as it was in Bruner's account of instructional functions. But once again it must be pointed out that a concern with structure is subsumed elsewhere in the cumulative model, namely, in the tasks of designing hierarchies of objectives and of curricular routes to each of them.

6. *Prompting and Guiding the Learning.* A second move in the effort to evoke desired performance in the learner consists of the introduction of cues or prompts into the learn-

ing situation. One of the key instructor functions is to provide (usually verbal) stimulation in addition to the central stimuli that are intended by themselves to evoke the desired terminal response. This may consist of providing codes for the use of the learner or information as to what direction to take next in a problem-solving effort. It will be recalled that in Bruner's view this function was incorporated in a concern with the timing and nature of informative feedback as it relates to guiding the learner.

7. *Promoting Generalization.* The last function of instruction is to provide conditions that increase the probability that what is learned will be appropriately transferred to contexts other than those of original learning. Often the conditions of initial learning have a bearing on the extent of transfer and Gagné draws upon the research literature to specify some of these.

Guiding Individual Development. The fourth educational activity to which the cumulative model can make contributions is guidance. Guidance here is conceived to have three kinds of relationship to learning. The first is that by providing the developing individual with clear statements of the relationship between learning activities and his long-term goals, positive motivation for continued learning can be maintained. The second relationship between guidance and learning concerns the task of providing the individual predictive information as to the likelihood that his goals can be achieved. But more than this, given an achievable goal, an appreciation of the cumulative nature of learning on the part of the guidance counselor can issue in the establishment of specific sequences of subordinate objectives leading to the attainment of the student's terminal goal. Third, the planful relating of subordinate objectives to terminal ones can itself be a fruitful learning experience, assisting the individual in acquiring the capability for such planning so that he can eventually engage in it without external guidance.

Assessing Student Progress. As Gagné has noted, "the effective management of cumulative learning virtually demands that assessment be undertaken at every step of the way" (Gagné, 1966a, p. 19). Since the cumulative model presumes learning to be hierarchical in its organization, the mastery of

lower-level skills is a necessary prerequisite for the acquisition of higher-level capabilities. Instruction, then, cannot succeed unless techniques are used for reliably determining whether or not a student has learned adequately from a particular segment of instruction. If he has not, other conditions of learning must be instituted to insure that he will. Only when the individual has attained a particular objective should he be permitted to commence work toward the next.

The instruments needed for this form of assessment are not readily available. Most tests currently used in schools, even those that are referred to as "achievement" tests, are constructed to permit comparisons between a given individual and his compeers rather than between the extent of the individual's mastery of a capability and the level of mastery required for further progress. Gagné (1966a, pp. 20–21) specifies four desirable properties of tests for assessing individual progress. The first is that they be criterion-referenced rather than norm-referenced. Tests should be constructed to reveal the degree of the individual's deviation from the performance required rather than from other individuals in his group. Second, items in such tests should be designed and selected in terms of their capacity for unequivocally measuring the attainment of an objective, not in terms of their level of difficulty. Third, the relation of an item to its attendant objective should be clear not only to the persons who construct the item but to the testee, teachers, and parents. Finally, the meaning of a total test score should be clear to all such persons. Tests designed in accord with these strictures would be truly revolutionary in the field of education and an application of the cumulative model to education is virtually impossible without them.

Apart from assessment techniques and the statement of educational objectives in behavioral terms, the cumulative learning model has a third implication which, if implemented, would be revolutionary in educational practice; it concerns the role of individual differences in educational development. With regard to individual differences, the position of the cumulative model accurately reflects the facts of the school situation, namely, that individual differences are pervasive. The position, predictably, is that instruction must be "individualized." If successful learning is predicated upon the mastery by any given learner of all subordinate capabilities necessary for the acquisition of a terminal capability, and if children vary in their possession of these prerequisites, then it follows that instructional events must be scheduled to accommodate the status of the individual.

Admittedly, the schools have already attempted to make provision for individual differences through various within-grade grouping practices frequently called "tracking." But tracking is usually decided in terms of performance on norm- rather than criterion-referenced tests. Children are grouped in accord with estimates of their typical rate of learning or of their "intelligence" rather directly in terms of the relevant capabilities they have acquired. Furthermore, the instructional practice that results from tracking is that of presenting to students assigned to "high" tracks more extensive and intensive curricular materials than those in the other tracks receive. Students assigned to the lowest tracks, especially, receive a much reduced curriculum. The learning sequences planned for children in a tracking system, in other words, are not designed to eventually afford all children the same capabilities but instead provide low-track individuals with a simplified version of the high-track curriculum at each grade level.

An alternative means of dealing with the immense variety of learned capabilities and inherent capacities presented by individuals in the schools is the ungraded school. This practice more nearly conforms to the implications of the cumulative model than does the practice of tracking. For in an ungraded school, children are grouped in accord with the level of relevant learning they have achieved rather than with respect to the rate at which they achieved it or at which they promise to achieve a higher level. Only a radically ungraded school, however, would permit the implementation of the full implications of the cumulative model. Only in such a system could all children with a common set of educational objectives be provided with a complete set of opportunities for achieving them. To be sure, objectives would be achieved at different rates, but they would be achieved. This solution is not altogether as satisfying as it initially seems. Consider a small elementary-level class constituted of children varying in age between 6 and 10 years and in IQ between 80 and 130. Assume that despite the marked variance in chronological age and IQ, all of the children have the same status with respect to measurable capabilities subordinate to the objective of their presence in the class, say, learning to read aloud accurately some specific materials at some specified rate. Clearly, given these characteristics, all children could be provided with the same next set of external learning conditions and learning objectives. It is equally clear, however, that the rate at which those next objectives would be achieved by the members of the class would vary widely. Thus after a short period of time, regrouping would be necessary—in fact, if it were necessary to adhere to some form of homogeneous class composition, regrouping would need to be carried out with great frequency.

Strict homogeneous grouping in this manner would probably prove quite bothersome and virtually unmanageable. The need for it assumes the necessity of teaching children in groups that is, the necessity of group-centered instruction. The cumulative model suggests, to the contrary, that the necessity is for individual-centered instruction where the situation of a single teacher working simultaneously with an entire roomful of children would be atypical rather than commonplace. The operational conditions for individualized instruction are distinguished by Gagné as follows:

1. Beginning at an early age, the student needs to learn the general principle that learning takes place as a result of his own intellectual activity.

2. The materials constituting the stimuli for learning need to be designed for maximum accessibility and ease of use by the student. . . .

3. Each stage of learning needs to begin with a communication that makes the objectives of learning clear to the learner. . . .

4. The student needs to be provided with a means of appraisal of his own performance which bears a direct and obvious relation to the objectives of the learning. . . .

5. Activities designed to insure transfer of learning need to be provided for, in the form of discussions with the teacher or other stu-

dents, and other opportunities for application of the student's acquired knowledge (Gagné, 1966a, pp. 33–34).

It may be inferred from this list that the teacher's function as an interactive figure in the classroom setting is largely confined to the fifth item. His principal functions in such a system have more to do with guiding individual development across instructional segments and arranging for the implementation of the other four items on the list than with being a direct source of knowledge or the primary stimulus to learning in the individual.

To evaluate the educational implications of the cumulative model in more concrete terms, the reader is referred to examples of its implementation with curricular materials. As should be clear by now, the approach required is so detailed that present space is not adequate for describing concrete applications. Some examples of such applications may be found in Gagné and Paradise (1961), Gagné, Mayor, Garstens, and Paradise (1962), Gagné and Bassler (1963).

As a means of summarizing our examination of cumulative learning theory and its potential for contributing to education, let us try to characterize some of the main features of the model as they relate to education and educational practice. First, the model grows out of the tradition of learning theory and research. It emphasizes the importance of learning, retention, and transfer. But, second, it allows for the learning of units much more complex than elementary connections—units such as concepts and rules or principles. Nevertheless, it is third, adamantly behavioristic in its demands for definitions of objectives in terms of observable performance. Fourth, when the model is turned toward education, its implication is that one must begin with the requirements for successful learning in individuals rather than with the present structure and organization of educational practice, which is largely in terms of classrooms. This feature of the approach may be of inestimable importance, for it means that radical change in educational forms may have to be made. It insists, for example, that the individual student is the prime unit of instruction, not the classroom or the grade level. Thus, fifth, individual differences are to be expected and planned for, not remediated. Sixth, it implies

the necessity for a hierarchically organized, comprehensive, and continuous curriculum design that extends across the entire educational lifetime of the student. And, seventh, continual assessment of student progress forms an integral part of the materials and procedures of learning. The instruments of assessment implied by the cumulative approach are not typical of those used in present practice. That is to say, they are concerned with the student's attainment of behaviorally defined, specific capabilities, not with his performance relative to a norm group. Finally, as we have seen, the cumulative model is weakest when the form of intellectual activity to be installed is at its most complex, that is, when it is a matter of self-initiated reorganization or reformulation of what is already known in the interest of reducing what is unknown. Eighth, as was the case with instrumental conceptualism, the capabilities of the student when presenting himself for instruction are crucial in determining the events to which he will be exposed in beginning his journey through the school. But, and again this is surprisingly consonant with Bruner's position, readiness in the traditional sense is dismissed; readiness is important only insofar as it indicates what it is that the individual has yet to learn, not insofar as it implies that growth must be awaited before the onset of instruction.

OBJECTIVES OF EDUCATIONAL DEVELOPMENT

An attempt to set forth the objectives of educational development reveals the enormity of the work remaining to be done in relating cognitive development and education. The magnitude of the task is produced by at least two factors: it is desirable that the human individual acquire a large number of complex capabilities, and investigations of the conditions that determine the development of these capabilities have barely begun.

It would be desirable to list general objectives of educational development, including broadly described skills and intellectual tools along with a variety of kinds of knowledge from particular subject-matter fields. Presently it is not possible to attain this goal. Instead, we shall have to be content with a very short list of objectives, stated at too general a level and with far too little direct connection with the psychology of cognitive development. Thus it is important to emphasize that the gaps in need of spanning are cavernous.

Let us begin by agreeing, at least provisionally, that education has two objectives: to facilitate the development of (1) the most intelligent and (2) the most productive forms of thinking possible in individuals. Alternatively, the terminal objectives of education may be said to be those of maximizing intelligence and creativity. Obviously, neither of these phrasings is satisfactory, for we must go on to say what we mean by intelligence and what we mean by creativity. Considerable effort has gone into attempts to specify the referents of the two objectives and to explicate the relationship between them. Notable contributions have been made by Guilford (1950, 1959), Crutchfield and Covington (1965), Mackinnon (1960), Torrance (1962), and Getzels and Jackson (1962).

The most straightforward and, at the same time, the most unsatisfying referent of the term intelligence is the score obtained on an intelligence test such as the Wechsler or the Binet. With respect to education, a high IQ is unsatisfying as a criterion because the performances required for such an outcome seem not to be representative of the capabilities sought through the process of schooling. The idea of using a criterion such as test performance as an objective of education, however, has a very attractive feature; it is a behaviorally defined objective that is widely understandable. The critical thing is to select the criterion properly and this means thinking in terms of multiple tests rather than a single one.

Guilford (1959, 1967) has constructed a general mode of intelligence that accords with this stipulation. The method followed in building this structure-of-intellect model consists of two major strategies. The first is to apply factor analytic techniques to intercorrelations among scores on a wide variety of measures of intellectual functioning. Such analyses have yielded factors that have been grouped into three principal dimensions. The second strategy is to cull from the psychological literature possible additional factors which, when combined with the original set, form a logically exhaustive list. The resulting model predicts at least 120 separate abilities, each of which is determined by one or more factors of intellect. This rather long list of abilities is yielded by the intersection of the various components arrayed along three dimensions that describe the structure of intellect. The dimensions and their components are as follows:

Operations	Contents	Products
Memory	Behavioral	Units
Cognition	Figural	Classes
Divergent Thinking	Symbolic	Relations
Convergent Thinking	Semantic	Systems
Evaluation		Transformations
		Implications

Theoretically, any one of the operations can be carried out upon any one of the kinds of content and can result in any one of the kinds of products listed, as when the evaluation of symbolic content results in transformations. For example, consider the task of choosing the one of two series of scrambled letters that contains a meaningful English word and then unscrambling the one chosen. In doing so, a subject evaluates symbolic units in making his choice between the two series and transforms the one chosen in order to produce an English word.

Whether or not these 120 capabilities turn out to be accepted goals of education is not of prime importance for our purpose here. Agencies other than or at least in addition to psychological ones will have to be involved in determining whether or not these abilities constitute acceptable educational objectives.

The striking features of the model are that it specifies a large enough number of varieties of intelligence to be comprehensive and it identifies each one in terms of observable performances on concrete tasks.

When one examines these tasks, it is clear that they do not sample adequately in any sense from particular subject-matter areas that usually form the mainstream of school curricula. If capabilities in particular subject-matter areas form the objectives of education, then the structure-of-intellect model is patently insufficient. This conclusion should not be construed as foregone, however, since it is possible to conceive that the primary objective of education may cut across subject-matter specialties and thus fail to represent adequately any one of them. For example, a principal educational objective might be to foster efficient learning of symbolic relations. Such a capability is not specific to any particular subject-matter area but is of clear relevance to a variety of school subjects and might be acquired in the course of learning, say, mathematics, logic, physics, and political science.

In Guilford's view, the structure-of-intellect model includes what we have referred to as creativity or productive thinking as well as what we have called intelligence. Other researchers have pointed out that in its usual sense, that is, performance on an IQ test, intelligence does *not* encompass creative or productive thinking. Getzels and Jackson (1962) evaluated the abilities of secondary-school students on both an intelligence test and a creativity test. The creativity test included items drawn from those mentioned by Guilford (1959) as measures of divergent thinking. One of the results of the investigation was that of the highest 20% of students on creativity tests, 70% did *not* score in the highest 20% on the intelligence test. The conclusion is that since these two forms of intellectual capability are not inextricably tied, neither one, by itself, is a sufficient criterion of intellectual development. Torrance (1960) confirmed the Getzels and Jackson (1958) results for younger children, grades one through six.

A cautionary note must be sounded before proceeding further. Thorndike (1963) has pointed out that the use of the term "creativity" to refer to a single capability as measured by the tests of divergent thinking used in these studies may be unwarranted. His argument turns on the fact that the inter-task correlations among "creativity" tests are relatively low as compared with similar inter-correlations among subtests on standard tests of "intelligence." The point is that for the intelligence tests there is some reason to assume a single underlying ability, whereas several discrete abilities appear to determine performance on creativity tests.

On the basis of their findings, Getzels and Jackson (1962) and Torrance (1960) emphasize that schoolmen should recognize the intellectual validity of creative capabilities and should incorporate this recognition in their efforts to guide the educational development of highly creative students of moderate IQ. A more radical view can be taken, however, as illustrated by the position of Crutchfield and Covington (Covington, 1967a). In brief, their thesis is that productive or creative approaches to a wide variety of intellectual tasks should form the central core of the school curriculum. It follows that particular content areas—mathematics, English, social studies—should simply provide concrete materials in terms of which to permit students to practice and perfect their use of the skills of productive thinking. According to this view, the objectives of education are to promote effective use of a variety of thinking skills across widely differing subject-matter areas. Notice, however, that these objectives are not defined behaviorally, at least not if they are conceived as the goals to be attained by the end of secondary school.

Nevertheless the work of Crutchfield and Covington (1965) has been quite concrete and has produced definite behavioral criteria of productive thinking capabilities. The criterion test battery used by these investigators has included three kinds of tasks. In the first the child is required to solve problems that vary with respect to the amount of constraint inherent in the intial statement of the problem. For example, two of the problems that have been used are: (1) to discover methods by which gigantic ancient statuary might be saved when the valley in which it is located is flooded by the building of a dam; and (2) to explain an apparent change in location of a nearby house during a single night. The second kind of task consists of several tests of divergent thinking that require the child to produce, for example, several consequences of some hypothetical event such as a world-wide increase of 5 inches in sea level. Third, the criterion battery has included inventories designed to index attitudes toward self, intellectual activity, and intellectual tasks. Unfortunately, the research of Crutchfield and Covington has so far been limited to individuals of approximately fifth-grade age. Hence considerable systematic work remains to be done across both later age spans, and probably the prefifth-grade years as well, before it will be possible to give explicit behavioral definitions of terminal educational objectives. Moreover, the work to date has not incorporated content that is germane to customary school subjects, so that it is not possible presently to judge the potential of this approach for replacing the commonly accepted prime purposes of education. Clearly this kind of revolution cannot come about quickly and for the moment it appears the contribution to education of the productive-thinking approach will be auxiliary. Even so, it seems clearly to be a salutary adjunct to the current emphasis on discipline-bound instruction.

After these few examples of educational objectives produced in the course of work by psychologists on problems of intellectual functioning, we still must consider what contributions developmental psychologists can make to the setting of educational objectives. This consideration is not a simple matter. The setting of educational goals is not the task of the psychologist, but he can contribute to both the formulation of goals and the setting of objectives in at least three ways. First, he can broaden the view of educators by carefully isolating and describing the range of intellectual attainments that are within the reach of human beings. Second, he can make concrete, in behavioral terms, the meaning of these attainments, that is, he can inform the schoolman about overt indicators of the possession of such capabilities. Finally, he can provide evidence about the consequences of various kinds of environmental intervention, that is, instructional or educational intervention, for the attainment of these objectives at various points in the development of the individual. The work of psychologists concerned with intelligence and creativity illustrates the first two kinds of contribution. The present status of the work is such that it qualifies only as illustration because it has not been truly comprehensive nor has it been adequately correlated with the requirements of the schools. The third kind of contribution, providing information graded developmentally about the effects on later intellectual functioning likely to result from specific kinds of earlier training, involves an examination of the entire topic of curricular routes to educational objectives.

CURRICULA, CAPABILITIES AND EDUCATIONAL OBJECTIVES

In educational terms, the means for guiding students to the attainment of educational objectives are the curricula that describe the sequence and content of schooling. What are the curricula that will best lead to intelligent and productive behavior by the end of secondary school? In psychological terms the task may be described as that of isolating the subcapabilities or subskills necessary for intelligent and productive behavior, specifying the conditions that promote the acquisition of these capabilities, and discovering the optimal timing and sequence in which to impose these conditions in view of the presenting status of the individual. The last two psychological components of the curricular task will be taken up in subsequent sections of this chapter. Our present concern will be with the matter of isolating and specifying the subskills necessary for intelligent and productive behavior.

When reviewing the work of psychologists relative to the topic of acquiring capabilities, one is struck by the disproportionate distribution of effort at the lower end of the age range. Comparatively, the amount of theory and evidence available for preschool and primary-school children is massive and that for secondary-school age groups is slender indeed. Some of the possible reasons for this state of affairs are worth mentioning. One is that the terminal capabilities expected of the secondary-school graduate are highly complex, involving as they do the structure and contents of a variety of scholarly disciplines. In contrast, the terminal capabilities expected of a third-grade student are simple indeed, although they still defy a completely satisfying account in terms of psychological theory. Since the nature of psychological research is slow and painstaking, it is no surprise that the amount of progress made in describing and understanding the cognitive capabilities necessary for attaining terminal secondary-school objectives is quite small relative to the overall dimensions of the task. A second reason is that the kind of research most often conducted by psychologists, especially experimental psychologists working on problems connected with topics of cognitive development, is most relevant to the kinds of educational capabilities demanded of pre-school and primary-school children. Consider the instance of the experimental psychology of verbal learning (see, e.g., Cofer, 1961; Cofer and Musgrave, 1963; Goss and Nodine, 1965). To be sure, the subjects in verbal learning studies are drawn most often from college-age populations. Nevertheless, the tasks set for the subject and, consequently, the referents of generalizations issuing from the experiments, are more applicable to the learning that occurs in kindergarten and the primary grades than they are to the learning a student is expected to manage in college. The memorization of lists of single items, whether according to a serial, paired-associate, or free-recall paradigm may be characteristic of school tasks in the early grades but not at the college level. For these and other reasons, the consideration that will be given here to potential contributions of psychology to curricula will be heavily concentrated in the preschool and primary-school period. Nevertheless, we shall begin at the other end with a discussion of elementary and secondary curriculum developments to which a psychology of cognitive development can contribute.

Elementary and Secondary Levels

Most of the research activity directed toward constructing curricula for promoting the attainment of terminal educational objectives has been concentrated in mathematics and the sciences. Although it started somewhat later, there is now promise that a similar substantial outpouring of effort will occur in the areas of English and various social studies as well. Our present scope will be limited, including only the topics of mathematics and creativity as they pertain to newly constructed curricula for elementary- and secondary-school children. Other curricular areas could be included as well, but due to the presently minimal contribution of developmental psychologists, they will be omitted. Curricular developments in the areas to be reviewed are, in some cases, relevant for the younger age groups as well. But for now, we follow present educational practice and recognize a major juncture at the interface between primary and later elementary education.

Mathematics. The amount of work in mathematics education is presently quite sub-stantial and well-received in school systems. Numerous projects have developed in which full-scale curricular construction programs have been undertaken. Among those having already received considerable attention from educators are the School Mathematics Study Group (SMSC) (see Begle, 1958; Cahen, 1963; Weaver, 1963), Madison Project (see Davis, 1963, 1966), University of Illinois Arithmetic Project (see Hohn, 1961; Deans, 1963; Page, 1962), Sets and Numbers Project (see Suppes, 1964, 1965; Suppes and Hill, 1963; Suppes and Ginsberg, 1962; Suppes and McKnight, 1961), and the University of Maryland Mathematics Project (see Gagné and staff, 1965). To greater or lesser degrees, these projects have taken the reworking of the entire mathematics curriculum as their task; some pertain to the elementary curricula only and others to junior high school curricula as well. In general the "new math" as represented here marks a shift away from the presentation of commercially relevant arithmetic ideas to an emphasis on central mathematics concepts as conceived by mathematicians.

Relative to these efforts, the questions we shall consider are: What have been the contributions of psychology? And what additional contributions might be made? The answer to the first question is that the contributions of psychologists to the construction of these mathematics curricula have varied from one project to the next. The contributions of Suppes to the Sets and Numbers project and of Gagné to the Maryland Mathematics project have been quite central. Suppes' approach (Suppes, 1964, 1965; Suppes and Hill, 1963; Suppes and Ginsberg, 1962; Suppes and McKnight, 1961) has been notable in several respects. The construction of the materials, the mode of presentation, and methods of practice instituted were informed by a psychological theory, specifically a modified version of stimulus sampling theory; the efficacy of the materials used has been evaluated systematically; and an analytic concern with basic theoretical questions of the nature of concept learning, concept transfer, and generalization has issued in concurrent experimental studies designed to shed light on these issues. For example, some of the early objectives of the Sets and Numbers first-grade curriculum are the acquisition of the notions of sets, identity of sets, equipollence of sets, and ordered sets. These notions are presented in a workbook, frequently by means of figural illustrations, and students respond by answering multiple-choice questions that assess their understanding of the concepts given.

In initially constructing curricular materials of this kind and in seeking to revise and improve them, questions arise regarding the optimal sequencing in instruction of the series of concepts, the stimuli that should be used to present the concepts, and the sorts of responses to require in order to improve transfer and generalization of the concepts learned. Suppes and his colleagues have conducted empirical studies designed to provide answers to these questions. One of the laudable aspects of the studies is that the materials were very similar to those used in the Sets and Numbers curriculum. Suppes and Ginsberg (1962) have summarized the results of such studies with young children (kindergarten and first-grade): learning is more efficient if errors are corrected immediately; incidental learning of concepts cannot be expected; concept transfer is enhanced when the child is required to recognize the presence or absence of a concept in a display rather than simply matching one display with another; and learning of the concepts of identical, equipollent, and ordered sets is quite specific—the learning of one of these does not appear to facilitate the learning of another. Attention has even been given to some developmental questions in terms of an appraisal of how children of different ages respond to a series of questions demanding logical inference (Hill, 1961).

As reported by Gagné and others (1965), the contribution of psychology to the Maryland Mathematics project has also been quite substantial. Predictably, the contribution in this case has been in terms of specifying behavioral objectives, constructing the materials in accord with a hierarchical analysis of the capabilities necessary for acquisition of the terminal skill, and evaluating the effects of previous attainment of subordinate capabilities on the ease of attaining a superordinate capability. In particular, one objective was that of "specifying sets, intersections of sets, and separations of sets, using points, lines and curves." Analysis of the objective yielded a number of subcapabilities (e.g., identifying and drawing a plane, identifying and drawing a curve) and experimental learning programs were constructed to promote the acquisition of these skills. Among five programs, the number and variety of examples used for each subskill were varied. The efficacy of the programs was evaluated by posttests designed to measure performance with respect to both terminal and subordinate capabilities. The results indicated that number and variety of examples were not effective variables and provided confirmation for the notion that the acquisition of a capability depends upon the previous acquisition of subordinate capabilities.

The role of psychological theory and methodology apparently has not been as central in many of the other projects; certainly it has not been as visible.

This brings us to our second question: What psychological contributions might be made to the development of mathematics curricula? At the risk of redundancy, it must be said that there is room and need for collaboration at a number of points in such curricular efforts. In addition to those functions already mentioned, specifying objectives, analyzing the necessary steps to curricular objectives, and sound evaluation, a psychology of cognitive development can contribute substantially in other ways. It can focus concern upon questions regarding the acquisition, retention, generalization, and transfer of concept learning in the case of both simple and complex concepts of the sort involved in mathematics (see Morrisett and Vinsonhaler, 1965, pp. 102-108).

But there is still another kind of contribution that a psychology of cognitive development can make to the development of mathematics curricula. There is an almost entirely unfilled need for assessing the efficacy of curricular materials developmentally both as a function of the age of the students and as a function of their previous relevant learning. An available but quite limited example of this approach is provided in a study reported by Joyce and Joyce (1964). Their aim was to evaluate the ease of acquisition of some of the concepts involved in SMSG curricula by fifth- and sixth-grade children. A preliminary assessment was made of the ability of the subjects to perform both concrete and formal operations so that controls for this ability could be built into the study. The pretest results revealed that the sixth-grade children were superior to the fifth-grade children in their capacity for formal reasoning. Nevertheless, children from both grades derived significant benefit from the SMSG materials. More complete assessments of this kind are needed both with respect to the ease of acquisition of a particular mathematical capability and with respect to the effects of acquiring a given capability at one age rather than another on the acquisition of other capabilities. That is to say, an experimental examination should be made of an interaction between age and particular training contents with respect to the amount of savings produced in the later learning of some transfer task (see Cronbach, 1965; Mussen, 1965). Such curricular involvements on the part of psychologists concerned with cognitive development would facilitate efforts to answer psychological questions as well. Too little is presently known about concept development in the realm of complex, well-structured subject matters and it is precisely from investigations of the sort mentioned that advances are likely to come.

These comments apply equally well to current developments in the area of elementary and secondary science curricula. Brief descriptions of some of the more visible programs in this area may be found in the *Review of Educational Research* (Atkin, 1964; Hurd and Rowe, 1964; Leiderman, 1965).

The observational studies of Piaget (see Flavell, 1963; and chapter by Flavell in this book) have had some influence upon those working in the area of science curricula, as well they might have. Again, the need is for systematic planning and execution of psychological research in the various phases of these projects rather than for additional influential theoretical pronouncements. The presentation of concepts and the attempt to institute conditions that facilitate their acquisition is a principal task of efforts in science curricula programs, a task that encompasses some of the central concerns of psychologists interested in cognitive development. And yet, only in exceptional, scattered cases has the form of collaboration necessary to yield fruitful psychological information and enduring educational contributions been instituted.

The type of supporting research that permits one to assess how well one is succeeding in the management of relevant instructional variables requires a constant and close collaboration of teacher, subject-matter specialist, and psychologist. As intimated earlier, a curriculum should be prepared jointly by the subject matter expert, the teacher, and the psychologist, with due regard for the inherent structure of the material, its sequencing, the psychological pacing of reinforcement, and the building and maintaining of predispositions to problem solving. As the curriculum is being built, it must be tested in detail by close observational and experimental methods to assess not simply whether children are "achieving" but rather what they are making of the material and how they are organizing it. It is on the basis of "testing as you go" that revision is made. It is this procedure that puts the evaluation process at a time when and place where its results can be used for correction while the curriculum is being constructed (Bruner, 1966d, p. 70).

Two additional dicta should be mentioned. The first may simply be a matter of giving greater emphasis to the importance of explicitness in research done in support of curriculum development. Ingenuity and flair are not enough to effect enduring and extensive changes in education, however much virtuosity is involved. Only with painstaking efforts at specifying objectives in terms of the behavior expected of students and at specifying methods, materials, and procedures in terms of the behaviors expected of *teachers,* can full impact be made. The second addition concerns the form of the research to be carried out in connection with curriculum-building. Such research must be designed with the intent of contributing directly to psychological understanding of the basic processes in cognitive development. This means planning studies that conform to the demands of experimental design in order that valid inferences may be drawn.

It also means using designs that will permit the testing of developmental hypotheses—providing, in other words, for an adequate assessment of possible interactions between age, past experience, sequencing, and treatment components. The point is not that psychological training is crucial for the initial creation of curricular materials—it is not. Rather, the point is that a psychological contribution is necessary if we are ever to know anything about the effects of new curricula and if we are ever to learn anything lasting from curricular efforts about the development of the human mind.

Creativity. Research and development related to curricula and creativity are burgeoning activities. At least two different approaches to these problems may be distinguished. One holds that the acquisition of any subject-matter ought to be infused with creativity (Suchman, 1960). The other holds that the cognitive processes involved in creative thinking are themselves worthy objectives of education and therefore ought to be taught (Covington, 1967a). Both approaches arise from the assumption that one of the most important potential outcomes of schooling is the ability to approach both knowledge and the unknown in a self-activated manner with well-developed skills for both the acquisition and the discovery of knowledge. Both approaches have produced curricular materials and programs that follow from their assumptions. And both approaches have achieved a modicum of acceptance for actual school use. Nevertheless, the differences between them are important, since students learn different things from the two forms of training.

The point of those that are committed to the importance of creativity or productivity as a major objective of education is well taken; the specific contents of subject-matter areas are transitory, and education therefore cannot take as its sole objective that of assuring the memorization of existing knowledge which is likely to become obsolete soon after it is acquired.

The argument is persuasive but it is important to note that there are variations on it. One version has it that the crucial thing is to teach children creative habits of inquiry as they acquire the subject-matter that the schools normally provide. A second version starts by noting that creativity or productive thinking cannot occur in the absence of some kind of concrete materials with which the student can be productive or creative. It finishes by arguing that being creative means being creative in one field or another, and creativity in a field can occur only *after* the subject matter of the field has been so over-

learned as to free the individual from the task of comprehension and retention (Eisner, 1963). The third approach takes the view that unless the capabilities for creative thinking are taught as a subject in their own right, they will not be learned well or retained for long since the principal content of learning will inevitably be that of the subject matter at hand (Covington, 1967).

The absence of decisive empirical evidence means that a definitive choice among these variations on the theme of creativity in educational development cannot yet be made. It is also clear that they are not mutually exclusive, except in the sense that limits on educational time and educators' energies may prevent their simultaneous implementation. Few would disagree that for some children, at some ages, with particular backgrounds of experience in connection with some subject matters, learning through discovery (methods through which students are led to arrive at principles by induction after being given examples) is a good thing. Equally few would disagree that despite the danger of early obsolescence there is much benefit to be derived from mastery of a field followed by creative contributions to it (although many would stipulate that excessive focus on mastery precludes originality). Finally, few would disagree that if it is possible to create curricula having the sole objective of installing capabilities for creative thinking, it is worth doing.

Despite all of this potential complementarity among the various conceptions of the place of creativity in education, our focus here will be on only the one associated with the work of Crutchfield and Covington (1965). The conception identified with Suchman (1960), the Inquiry Method (discussed later), when viewed in connection with creativity properly belongs in a more general discussion of the conditions that facilitate educational development. The version associated with Eisner (1965), which holds that mastery of subject matter must precede creativity, represents a distinct position on the issue of fostering creative thinking but hardly seems capable of generating a curriculum directed toward that objective. Thus our focus for the remainder of this section will be upon the third version, that concerned with directly promoting skills of creative thinking through curriculum development.

This approach is well-represented by work done in the Creative Thinking Project under the direction of Crutchfield and Covington (Covington, 1967a, 1968; Covington and Crutchfield, 1965; Crutchfield and Covington, 1965). The objectives of the curricula developed by these investigators are to foster *dispositions* toward engaging in tasks that permit of creative thinking, positive *attitudes* of the student toward himself as a productive thinker and toward intellectual activity, and *cognitive skills* that do, in fact, improve the individual's ability to think productively.

An auto-instructional program was constructed to facilitate the attainment of these objectives.

The program consisted of a series of simplified detective and mystery stories. Such stories were chosen because they interest children, because they effectively combine many of the essentials of the problem-solving process, and because they can deal with a variety of situations which cut across curriculum content areas.

Each lesson posed a single mystery which the child was to solve. The lesson was constructed so that the child, by being given a succession of clues and information, was finally led to discover the solution for himself. At various points in the story sequence, the child was required to restate the problem in his own words, formulate his own questions, and generate ideas to explain the mystery. Feedback to his responses was given on following pages in the form of examples of ideas or questions that he might have thought of in the given situation. These examples were primarily ones which fifth- and sixth-graders would find novel and uncommon, and which would open new lines of investigation or new ways of viewing the problem. It was assumed that the exposure to numerous examples of this type would tend to broaden the child's vision and limits of acceptance as to what constitutes important questions and fruitful ideas.

A story line was maintained throughout the lessons by developing a narrative concerning two school children (named Jim and Lila, brother and sister) as they learn to become detectives by taking lessons from their uncle, a high school science teacher who is a spare-time detective. The novel and uncommon responses given as feedback to the student were presented as Jim's and Lila's ideas. Thus, the student could work on the problem in concert with Jim and Lila—first the student generating his own questions or ideas, then Jim and Lila responding with theirs. This allowed the student to participate in the solution of problems with a pair of curious and imaginative children, one male and one female, who acted as models to be emulated. The models were not meant to be perfect; they make mistakes, but learn by them. From being poor problem solvers at first, they develop their skills progressively to become much better ones. It was hoped that identification with such realistic models would induce in the student a sense of his own progressive improvement in thinking skills as he worked through the program.

These stories were presented primarily by cartoon illustration in a booklet format. It was assumed that such visual presentation would not only increase the student's interest in the material, but would make it easier for him to follow the dialogue and thought sequences of the story characters.

The training program consisted of 13 lessons with an average of 30 pages per lesson. Each lesson was self-administering and self-paced. The program was of a linear type with primary emphasis on constructed responses (Covington and Crutchfield, 1965, p. 3).

The method formulated for achieving these objectives has at least three aspects that are instructive for our concerns here. First, it issued from a sensitivity to conditions of educational practice. That is, the materials that were constructed for fostering creative thinking were designed to be self-administering. This has two obvious advantages: the program is *relatively* less subject to between-classroom variability than those in which the teacher is the crucial source of information; and the materials are in a form that can be adopted by schools without extensive training and indoctrination for teachers who are to use them.

The second notable aspect of the method adopted by the Creative Thinking Project is that the creation of the instructional materials themselves was not stringently guided by psychological theory and research, although in an informal manner there is no doubt that it was influenced by them. Whether or not this is a virtue depends at the present time upon the observer's bias more than upon evidence, since it is yet to be determined whether or not materials generated by deductions from theory produce superior results.

The point to be emphasized is simply that the principal contribution of a psychology of cognitive development to a curricular effort may not be through the initial construction of materials. For example, the construction of one program produced by the project, the General Problem Solving Program, proceeded somewhat as follows. It was decided to create materials for use with fifth- or sixth-grade elementary-school children. A few preliminary lessons were constructed and administered to groups of children in these grades. The lessons contained provisions for the children to respond at various points throughout each one and on the basis of these responses the lessons were revised and extended. Additional lessons were added and subjected to the same sort of preliminary testing and evaluation. The process of pilot work continued until a more or less complete series of lessons had been evaluated in a preliminary way. Then full-scale empirical studies were made of the effectiveness of the materials. Note that at no point did scientific information about the cognitive structures of children in the target age range play a crucial role in the design of the materials, nor did methodological strictures coming from research on programmed instruction, although both kinds of information contributed in a background fashion.

The third aspect of these materials that is worth special attention is concerned again with their self-administering character. This feature of the program permits accommodation to individual differences, at least with respect to the characteristic paces at which students are able to traverse instructional lessons. Admittedly this marks only a first step in taking account of individual differences in curriculum making, but it is at least that.

The question remains: What sort of contribution can a psychology of cognitive development make to a curriculum effort such as that of the Creative Thinking Project? The question must be answered in terms of the unfulfilled needs that such a project has in the absence of such a contribution; needs that

can be clarified by examining the results of the introduction of the program in elementary-school classrooms.

In the best designed of the studies using these materials, they were administered to fifth- and sixth-grade children in classroom settings. Within each classroom, children were assigned to two groups at random; in one the General Problem Solving Program was administered, whereas in the other a placebo program, concerned with state history, was administered. Prior to the onset of training, an extensive battery of pretests was given to all children. These pretests were paralleled by posttests administered at the end of training. A variety of tasks was used for this purpose, including a number drawn from those developed by Torrance (1965), a number of problems to be solved, some created especially for this project, others, such as Duncker's X-ray problem, drawn from the literature on problem-solving. In addition, some other unique problem-solving tasks have been developed to permit an assessment of the child's preference for intellectual as against clerical activity (see Covington, 1967). Finally, the battery includes an inventory designed to assess attitudes toward self, school, and intellectual activity.

At the conclusion of the pretest, the training is begun and administered at the rate of one lesson per day for a total of some 16 school days. Each lesson requires approximately 30 minutes of time for completion, so that it is not excessively disturbing to a school schedule. The contents of the program are fully described by Covington (1968). Suffice it to say here that the child is induced to engage in activities such as generating ideas, evaluating ideas, suspending criticism, forgoing premature fixation on solutions, noticing subtle hints and clues to problem solution, and reformulating information. These activities are tied together through the medium of a story-line presentation of the problems, in which continuing characters engage in activities that are replete with puzzling phenomena and problems to be solved.

The results in a number of replications of variants of this same study consistently show that children who receive the General Problem Solving Program perform significantly and substantially better on criterion tasks, gain more from pretests to posttests, show greater changes toward positive attitudes toward self and school, and show a stronger disposition to formulate problems and engage in their solution than do the control children. In general, greater benefits are derived from the program by fifth- than by sixth-grade children. In sum, the effort to improve capabilities relevant to problem-solving and other related forms of productive thinking has been eminently successful.

We now return to our central concern with what kind of contribution the study of cognitive development can make to an effort such as this one. There are many possible answers to this question. The program described has been successful as judged by performance on criterion tasks but very little is known, so far as can be determined from reports presently available, regarding the reasons for its success. That is to say, the task of isolating the components of the treatment that determine its success has not been accomplished. Until it is, the utility of the approach is limited to the specific materials produced. Similarly, the question of whether or not the training provided by the program facilitates acquisition of other capabilities is entirely indeterminate. The differential effectiveness of the training materials for fifth- and sixth-grade children suggests that a systematic developmental study is needed to reveal the limits of effectiveness of the present form of the materials and to isolate the determinants of these limits. Finally, the kind of information that could be yielded by a psychological analysis of the present program in terms of basic processes in cognitive development promises to permit modifications and additions that would strengthen its effectiveness. These, then, are some of the contributions to this particular form of educational practice that might be made by those interested in research and theory in cognitive development.

In order for a child to profit from the General Problem Solving Program or from any of the other curricular materials that involve the child in obtaining information from printed materials and giving evidence of his possession of the relevant terminal capabilities, he must already possess some lower-order capabilities. One of these, reading, long formed the heart of the primary-school curriculum. Thus we next consider the contributions that

the study of cognitive development can make to the acquisition of this capability.

Primary Level

Present educational practices have changed sufficiently that children are asked to learn more in the primary grades than reading, writing, and arithmetic. Indeed, most of the curricular topics we have considered are taught in primary school as well as at elementary and secondary levels. Nevertheless, the acquisition of the capabilities involved in reading persists in being one of the very major concerns of schoolmen responsible for primary-school education. Not only is reading central in the primary-school curriculum—it is also problematical. For much too large a percentage of children do not learn to read well, or in some cases at all, by the end of the third grade. Furthermore, reading is properly taken up at this point in our discussion because it is prerequisite for much other later learning.

Reading is well worth our attention for another reason. It provides a clear illustration of the point that the relevance of research for educational practice does not guarantee that it will effect changes in practice. The recent book by Chall (1967) provides striking documentation of the plethora of research that has been done on reading and the paucity of effect that it has had. True enough, the results of some studies were not unequivocal. But, even where the results were clear, as in their indication that "code emphasis" methods of promoting beginning reading are superior to "meaning emphasis" methods, their impact on practice has been negligible.

Thus it is appropriate to state again the distinction that has recurred throughout this discussion of the relationship between cognitive development and education. The first step in accomplishing a liaison between the two fields is the growth of research that in one way or another pertains to schooling problems. This is the step that psychologists of cognitive development can themselves accomplish in substantially effective ways. The next step, however, does not follow ineluctably from the momentum generated by the first. The step of effecting change in educational practice requires methods and procedures beyond those required for research and theory construction in cognitive development. It requires the creation of curricular materials suitable for use in schools, well-managed introduction of those materials into the schools and, at least at the beginning, relatively constant monitoring of their use to insure that it continues beyond, let us say, the first week. After this has been accomplished—in fact, while it is being accomplished—the psychologist's methods can make additional contributions to the goal of evaluating the materials constructed, indicating modifications or diversifications of them, and determining the conditions under which their effectiveness is maximal. But these functions are to be distinguished from those necessary for the actual use of the products of research in daily educational practice. The necessary functions must be carried out as well or it seems probable that the best of research in cognitive development will come to very little in terms of the improvement of education.

As we saw to be the case for curriculum developments in mathematics and creativity, research activity in connection with reading has burgeoned. Of all the curricular developments reviewed thus far, however, the contributions of the study of cognitive development are far more exciting in connection with reading than in any other. The talents and concepts of many psychologists interested in cognitive development have turned to the problems of reading and the results of the investigations and speculation that have ensued are fascinating. Those interested in perceptual development, learning, language acquisition, psycholinguistics, sociolinguistics, and even psychophysiology have made provocative contributions to these developments. A perusal of the tables of contents of the various *Project Literacy Reports* reveals the breadth, variety, and intensity of interest that has been generated in research related to the topic. Among the reviews that have recently appeared, those by Williams (1965), and by Kerfoot (1967) provide another index of these developments.

In work related to the problem of reading instruction, the overriding strategy of developmental psychologists has been to analyze the process into its components and to subject these components to experimental and theoretical analysis. These analyses, as we shall see, have not yielded uniform results, nor have empirical investigations yielded uniform

interpretations and speculations, but they do share a concern for specifying the processes that underlie the acquisition of reading skills. In other words, the method of attack has been to ask about the subskills that are prerequisite to the acquisition of the capability of reading. It is important to recognize that the present status of this relatively new work on the components of reading skills has not advanced sufficiently far to have promoted the development of validated instructional materials for the teaching of reading. Thus the remainder of our discussion of this topic anticipates our next concern—the general categories of basic cognitive skills that must be presupposed if any of the kinds of learning that are commonly identified as school learning can go forward.

Much of the current basic research on reading has been conducted by a number of investigators loosely organized into a consortium called Project Literacy. In reviewing studies done within the Project, let us begin with a psychological analysis of reading capabilities, which is notable for its clarity and for the quality of the research it has generated (Gibson, 1965a, 1965b). Gibson divides the acquisition of reading skills into four stages that form a developmental sequence:

(1) Learning speech, in all its aspects such as hearing, comprehending and producing it; (2) learning to differentiate graphic symbols; (3) learning to decode graphic symbols to speech; and (4) progressive utilization of the higher-order constraints and regularities in the system, the system being considered as an intermodal, graphic-phonic set of correlations (Gibson, 1965b, p. 1).

We shall not consider the first stage until we have discussed the more general problem of language development. Gibson's approach to the second stage is of considerable interest. Drawing upon the work of Jakobson and Halle (1956) on distinguishing among phonemes in terms of their unique patterns of distinctive features, Gibson (1965a) has developed a scheme for analyzing letters in a similar fashion. The original list of features includes such things as the directionality of straight lines and open and closed curves, if any, that form the letters. Using this list of features as an index of interletter similarity, a modicum of success was achieved in an attempt to predict the relative confusability of letters. In another study (Yonas and Gibson, 1967) it was found that children as young as those in a second-grade sample could make use of the feature of diagonality in a task requiring discrimination among two sets of letters, the sets being defined by the experimenter.

These two studies, by themselves, do not establish the hypothesis that learning to discriminate letters is a perceptual learning task in which the child makes use of the distinctive features list developed. Accordingly, the implications for education are not direct. Nevertheless, work to date does suggest that it would be worthwhile to develop an instructional sequence for letter discrimination in which heavy reliance would be placed upon techniques for highlighting the distinctive feature properties of letters.

Work on the third stage of reading acquisition began with studies of the effects of learning single-letter to single-sound correspondences. Bishop (1964) showed that transfer of such learning to new words was successful when component correspondences had been learned as individual units but not when learned by a whole-word method. The implication here, of course, is that regular correspondences ought to be taught and that some successful means of instruction should be found. But before this effort is expended, Gibson and her colleagues suggest that a critical prior question must be answered: What is the primary psychological unit of spelling-to-sound correspondence? Their answer, drawing on the work of Hockett (1965) and Venezky and Weir (1966), is that this unit is not the letter; rather it is the relatively invariant set of correspondences between pronunciation and letter *clusters* when the location of the clusters within a word, with respect to both position (initial, medial, final) and environment (context provided by the other letters in word) are specified (e.g., ban, mat versus bane, mate). Thus work on the fourth stage of development, concerning the use of higher order constraints, overlapped into the third stage.

The results of this line of investigation are absorbing. Initially it was established that nonwords formulated in accord with morphophonemic rules of English spelling (letter clusters) so as to be pronounceable (e.g., "nop") are perceived more readily than other nonwords formulated so as to be less pronounceable but matched with the pronounceable ones for identity of letters used (e.g., "onp") (Gibson, Pick, Osser, and Hammond, 1962). That is to say, it was found that Ss as young as first graders were able to make use of such constraints in recognizing the letter composition of nonwords (Gibson, Osser, and Pick, 1963). In more recent work along this line Gibson, Shurcliff, and Yonas (1966) demonstrated that the presence of some sort of morphophonemic structure, over and above learned spelling-to-sound regularities, is responsible for the relative ease with which Ss perceive the pronounceable words.

The import of this line of work for reading instruction concerns the implication that children can take advantage of both the letter-cluster-to-sound relationships and the inherent structural regularities of English spelling in learning to read. Thus the indication is that instruction designed to emphasize these features of printed language should facilitate the acquisition of reading skills.

To this matter as well, Gibson et al. have devoted considerable effort. At the outset, they reasoned as follows. Since skilled readers are able to take advantage of the structure inherent in English spelling, it ought to be possible to discover the means by which this capability is acquired. The importance of the capability is clear: once the structures have been discovered, their transfer value is potentially very high, thus permitting the new reader to master previously unseen printed words without specific instruction. Experimental results strongly indicate the existence of such rules and yet even skilled readers are unable to state them. Thus it was decided to explore the effects of a learning-set paradigm for instruction, a paradigm that should permit induction and use of regularities without requiring a verbal statement of the regularities.

Gibson, Farber, and Shepela (1967) have reported the results of a pilot study using this approach. The study was conducted with kindergarten and first-grade children, the interest being to determine whether or not such children could be led to make the necessary abstractions from sequences of patterned words and pseudowords. A discrimination problem method was used initially but proved too difficult for the Ss, confirming the experience of Silberman (1964) with a similar approach. Finally, resort was made to a sorting task procedure for inducing the children to discriminate whether words fit a given pattern (e.g., lack, muck, deck, sock) or not (e.g., lake, much, derk, soak). Each item was typed on a separate card and the cards were presented individually to the S. When a card was presented, the S's task was to place it in one or the other of two categories, positive or negative. A correction procedure was used and the child was permitted to view the last cards placed in both the positive and negative categories while making his next choice. This method proved superior to a simple discrimination method and at least a few children demonstrated acquisition of the intended learning set. Obviously, this research is not sufficiently far along to permit strong inferences about the nature and development of curricular materials for facilitating the acquisition of reading capabilities. But the approach seems to promise some such implications in the finite future.

A related enterprise, also directed at problems attendant to promoting successful acquisition of reading skills, is that under the direction of Levin (1965). Marchbanks and Levin (1965), for example, found that children discriminate among similar words on the basis of initial letter differences whenever possible and ignore other features of the words. The same effect has been confirmed by Samuels and Jeffrey (1966). This, of course, implies that in any discrimination learning procedure, great care must be taken both to construct alternative sets in ways that induce the child to attend to the word features to be learned and to evaluate what the child has learned at the end of training. In another study related to the problem of word identification, Levin and Watson (see Williams, 1965) found that in children, training in variant grapheme-to-phoneme correspondences (one grapheme to two phoneme responses) facilitated acquisition of similar transfer materials more than training in invariant grapheme-to-phoneme (i.e., letter-to-sound) correspondences (one grapheme to one phoneme). Incorporating these two findings, Levin et al. are exploring the effects of various conditions of discrimination learning

on the acquisition of spelling-to-sound correspondence rules.

In a somewhat different vein, Levin and Turner (1966) have investigated the role of larger-unit language structures on reading performance using as a measure the eye-voice span. The results indicated that the more advanced the reader (whether indexed by his grade level or his reading speed), the greater the tendency to read to the end of major phrase units after illumination is withdrawn. A related study (Weber, 1967) examined oral reading errors made by first-grade children in a classroom setting. Errors were crosstabulated according to the reading-achievement level of the students and their effect on the grammaticality of the sentence being read. The results revealed a substantially greater sensitivity to grammatical constraints among the good than among the poorer readers. That is to say, of the errors made by the good readers, a large proportion maintained the grammatical integrity of the sentence, and of those that violated grammaticality, a large share were subsequently corrected.

To summarize the results of this sampling of Project Literacy studies, the indication clearly seems to be that skillful reading depends upon knowledge of both lower- and higher-order structures inhering in reading materials. The question of whether or not knowledge of these structures is facilitated more by emphasizing reading-to-speech correspondences than by emphasizing the inherent structure of printed materials (including both morphological and syntactic rules) is still open. The data seem to suggest the validity of the position explicated by Bever and Bower (1966) that it is preferable to encourage the acquisition of visual reading skills over auditory reading skills.

Finally, with regard to the matter of the direct implications of these results and hypotheses for the construction of curricular sequences for reading, it is appropriate once again to reiterate the contrast between educational relevance and contribution to educational change. Without question the work emanating from Project Literacy has substantial relevance for schooling in reading skills. Moreover, much of this work has contributed to knowledge in parent disciplines as well, whether psycholinguistics, the psychology of learning, or, more generally, the psychology of cognitive development. As yet, however, these lines of research have not progressed far enough to permit firm recommendations for programmatic changes in educational practice. This step remains to be taken and will probably not be taken, nor should it be, until additional basic research is completed. Nevertheless, the direct attack being made by the psychologists involved in Project Literacy upon the problems of optimal instructional conditions as well as upon the basic nature of psychological processes involved in reading acquisition promises to yield information that can indeed be used in effecting propitious changes in educational practice.

This same mode of attack has, of course, been used by other psychologists of cognitive development whose interests lead them into research relevant to reading. Elkind (Elkind, 1965, 1967a; Elkind, Horn, and Schneider, 1965; Elkind, Larsen, and Van Doorninck, 1965), for example, has reported a number of studies examining the relationship between developmental status (defined in Piagetian terms) and reading proficiency. Perceptual decentration (e.g., the ability to reverse figure and ground in perceptual objects) has been shown to relate to reading achievement in children drawn from grade levels two through six (Elkind, Horn, and Schneider, 1965; Elkind, Larsen, and Van Doorninck, 1965). Such results are interpreted within a strongly maturational framework that draws heavily upon notions introduced by Piaget. It is argued that the acquisition of the capability of letter identification is a matter of perceptual decentration rather than a matter of the discrimination of distinctive features. Perceptual decentration is held to come about when the child engages in an underlying process of logical multiplication of, say, the class of all letters with the class of all sounds, yielding all of the possible combinations of letter-to-sound relationships in English spelling. This product forms the basis of the necessary abilities for reading acquisition. It is this underlying capability—logical multiplication of properties of perceptual objects— that is responsible for the observed relationships between performance on figure-ground tasks and reading achievement. Finally, since it is presumed that initial reading depends upon the attainment of such underlying pro-

cesses, and since it is also assumed that these attainments are more heavily determined by maturation than by learning (Elkind, 1967a), the capability of acquiring reading skills is itself held to be determined in large measure by maturational factors.

A position such as that promulgated by Elkind is in no sense incompatible with the evidence available. Indeed it is consistent with evidence in some striking ways. The puzzling property of this kind of position is that it touches down at so few points. Given the wide expanse of the theory and its complexity in terms of numbers of propositions, it might be expected to be vulnerable to data more frequently than it seems to be. Consider, for example, the matter of categorizing figure-ground discriminations as perceptual decentration and the attendant assertion that this same process is involved in the acquisition of letter discrimination. Empirical demonstrations of both these assertions would make the case considerably more convincing. The problem that arises when more empiricism is demanded of the approach is that its maturational component virtually precludes the possibility of obtaining compelling experimental evidence of the usual sort. That is to say, suppose it were decided to test directly the hypothesis that increased skill in perceptual decentration produces increased skill in reading. The direct test would be to increase experimentally decentration capabilities and to observe the effect on, let us say, letter identification. But if change in decentration skill, that is, the development of logical multiplication, comes about largely as a result of maturation, the essential experimental manipulation would be ineffective; it would not be possible to increase decentration experimentally. Thus an adequate test of the hypothesis could not be made.

Obviously, the difficulties involved in evaluating theories having a maturational emphasis is no reason for rejecting them. In fact, as discussed earlier, learning emphases are subject to a complementary indeterminism precisely with respect to the maturational issue. In the present case the issue revolves around the question of whether the development of perceptual decentration in children can be accelerated through instructional procedures of some kind. The learning theorist would take the position that such a goal could be accomplished, but he is free to conclude that failure to do so is attributable not so much to maturational factors as to insufficient conditions of instruction. On the other hand, success in accomplishing this sort of acceleration would provide evidence inconsistent with the maturational emphasis (see Elkind, 1965; Gibson, 1965b). With regard to education, this sort of dispute can have two fruitful implications. The first is that considerable effort ought to be expended in attempts to facilitate the development of perceptual skills that are presumed necessary for reading competence. The second implication is that methods should be found for presenting reading materials that circumvent the child's maturational deficiency.

Recent work suggests that the initial teaching alphabet (ITA) may provide an instance of this last implication, that is, of accommodating to the child's developmental level by specially designed curricula. Thus before leaving the topic of reading, it is important to consider briefly the relationship between some of the findings and hypotheses emanating from psychological research on basic reading processes and developments in the field of reading instruction per se. Specifically, it is well to be aware of the results of studies comparing the relative efficacy of regularized and traditional orthographies for facilitating the acquisition of reading skills. A review of this issue involving comparative studies of traditional orthography (TO) and ITA has recently been published by Downing (1967).

The ITA was designed to promote the acquisition of beginning reading skills in children who do not have the capability of constructing sets of complete letter-to-sound correspondences. By and large, the characters used were chosen to provide a unique correspondence for each of the component sounds in English speech, and the corollary spelling system was designed to take advantage of this property. Elkind's (1965) position leads to the conclusion that children should be able to read more easily in ITA than in TO because the capability of logical multiplication or perceptual decentration is not required. Since there is a different character for each speech sound, it is not necessary for the child to learn variable relationships between graphemes and phonemes. The evidence appears

to be consistent with this position: in relatively well-controlled studies comparing the effects of TO and ITA (see Downing, 1967), the acquisition of literacy skills does appear to proceed more rapidly when regularized spelling is used. Does this outcome present a problem for the sort of theory outlined by E. J. Gibson (1965a)? The answer depends upon the results of a distinctive feature analysis of the ITA characters rather than, as suggested by Elkind, Larsen, and Van Doorninck (1965), simply upon the fact that more characters must be discriminated in ITA than in TO. It might turn out to be the case that a distinctive feature analysis of ITA characters would show them to be less confusable and therefore more easily discriminated than TO characters.

Relative to the research of Levin and his associates, the comparisons of ITA and TO raise another question. Beside evaluating the relative ease of reading acquisition in groups instructed by ITA and TO *within* whichever orthographic system instruction was conducted, an assessment was made as well of the relative reading achievement of both groups with TO materials exclusively. That is to say, data are available regarding the performance of ITA-trained children on TO materials at variable intervals after the transition in instruction had been made. Recall that Levin and Watson (see Levin, 1965) found performance on variant paired-associate (PA) transfer tasks to be better after variant PA training than after invariant PA training. In contrast, the results of research by Downing and others on the effects of ITA and TO training in initial reading on subsequent reading achievement in TO shows ITA training, that is, relatively invariant training, to be superior. This result holds despite an initial setback in reading achievement among the members of the ITA groups immediately after the transition to TO materials.

This discrepancy in research outcomes is not a simple one to interpret; the conditions of the two experiments differ in complex ways. However, it is worthwhile to note the possibility that even the best planned and conducted programs in basic research may not produce results that can be directly generalized to instruction without further empirical evaluation.

EARLY PREREQUISITE COMPETENCIES

Whether one chooses to follow out the implications of theories of cognitive development having a maturational emphasis or of those having a learning emphasis, he is led very quickly to a consideration of the requisite capabilities for subsequent development or learning at the earliest of the major educational junctures. Both kinds of theories direct attention to the critical importance for educational development of the child's initial status when he enters school; for the instructional experiences the schools provide presuppose considerable prior learning. Thus it is necessary to specify the capabilities prerequisite for additional progress in the kinds of cognitive development demanded in schooling. Consistent with the intensity of present concern among those working in the field of cognitive development, considerable emphasis will be given to capabilities deemed necessary for a successful transition across the boundary separating formal schooling from prior experience. The focus will be upon the capabilities presumed to result from home, preschool, and kindergarten experiences.

The discussion of capabilities pertinent to the transition to formal schooling will be organized in terms of six general areas of competences: attentional, behavioral control, perceptual, linguistic, learning, and conceptual. Our concern will be to draw upon the work of psychologists in an effort to specify the competence necessary within each of these domains for a child at this level of development. Although our primary focus will be upon children in the chronological age range of 4 to 6 years, we shall find it necessary occasionally to extend our discussion beyond this interval. In the case of each of the varieties of competence distinguished, we will proceed by first describing it, then inquiring about individual differences, and last by considering research relevant to augmenting the competency in children.

Attention

Since instruction is the principal aim of education and since instruction is concerned mainly with arranging environmental conditions conducive to cognitive development, the capacity of the individual to attend to relevant environmental events is critical for success. It will be recalled that considerable notice is given to matters of arousing and maintaining attention in both types of theories reviewed here. Each considers attention to be absolutely crucial for school success. Hence there is little argument about its importance.

The meaning of attention is a different matter. What is attention? What are its manifestations? What are its determinants? How does it relate to learning and educational development? Clear and complete answers to these questions cannot yet be given. Indeed, despite its obvious importance in cognitive functioning, the topic of attention as such has been dealt with by psychologists mainly in indirect ways. Frontal assaults on the problem are rare even within psychology, and psychological research on attention that focuses on educational relevance is even harder to come by. Some reasons for the paucity of research devoted to attention may be found in peculiarities of the history of theory construction in psychology (see Maltzman, 1967). Other reasons have to do with the incorporation of attentional factors in work on other psychological topics such as motivation, perception, and discrimination learning. Thus at the very outset, it must be said that the entire problem of attention and educational development is badly in need of both theoretical and research effort.

The importance of attention for education is plain enough, whether one means attentiveness or arousal. In the complete absence of attention it is unlikely that any learning would occur. In the presence of reduced attention, learning that does occur is likely to be incidental and consequently quite inefficient. A visit to schools where student achievement is characteristically low will frequently reveal a number of classrooms in which a major portion of the teacher's time is consumed with the effort to simply gain the attention of the students. Noise levels in such rooms are often high, diverse activities are engaged in by the students, and a common focus on the material being presented for learning is scarcely ever observed.

What is attention? Let us begin by thinking of it in terms of the probability that available stimulation will be registered by the individual. Thus attention is to be thought of in terms of a response of the organism, which may be indexed physiologically in various ways (see Maltzman, 1967). Attention is related to notions of motivation and drive but is not necessarily coincident with them. For example, exceptionally high drive has the consequence of interfering with performance on difficult tasks, whereas heightened attention appears to improve performance on such tasks (Belloni, 1964). Nevertheless, at this point in the development of a psychology of attention, it is well to consider a number of related notions—conflict, arousal, curiosity, orienting reflexes, and observing responses— as they pertain to education.

Perhaps more than any other single psychologist, Berlyne has systematically examined and investigated the importance of arousal for the occurrence of cognitive activities (1960, 1965). As he points out, the sort of arousal that most often eventuates in *epistemic* behavior (knowledge acquisition) is evoked by conceptual conflict, that is, by a discrepancy between expectation and reality in the form of antagonistic or contradictory beliefs. An example of conceptual conflict is provided by the antagonism between the long-held belief that the so-called inert gases are in fact inert and the contradictory observation that under certain conditions they are reactive. The notion is closely related to that of equilibrium-disequilibrium in Piaget (see Flavell, 1963) and to that of conflict between representational modes in Bruner's theory of instrumental conceptualism. Thus conflict between what the child expects to see, hear, or happen—whether it takes the form of stimulus complexity, novelty (Berlyne, 1958), an encounter with an unanswered question (Berlyne, 1954), or an unexpected physical event (Suchman, 1960)—can provoke attending behavior.

At bottom, the attention-producing effects of conflict may partake of the basic processes referred to under the rubric of the orienting reflex (OR). Much of the work on the OR has been carried out in Russia and has been summarized elsewhere (Razran, 1961; Maltzman, 1967). We shall simply note here that the necessary precondition for the OR is stimulus change, that it is respondent in nature, and that heightened ORs can produce better performance on learning tasks. Closely related to the OR is the observing response, an instrumental response, such as a voluntary movement of the eyes, which facilitates stimulus reception. Shortly we shall consider ORs again, along with observing responses in connection with the problem of augmenting attention.

Individual Differences. The comparatively retarded state of theory and research on attention has predictably yielded very little in the way of results and conclusions regarding related individual differences. Maltzman (1967) has reported evidence to the effect that individual differences in OR are related to conditionability, "awareness" of contigencies between CS words and semantically related generalization test words, and paired-associate learning efficiency on both easy and difficult lists of PAs. There are no data, however, concerning the relationship between strength of ORs and variables such as age, IQ, race, or socioeconomic status. Similarly, little is apparently known about the extent and stability of individual differences in observing responses or about the relationship between these and individual differences in other variables. Even though there is little doubt that individual differences do exist in the effects of novelty and complexity upon attention, systematic work on these is only barely underway (see Spitz and Hoats, 1961).

Before leaving the topic of individual differences in attention, it is appropriate to mention the attention theory of Zeaman and House (1967; also see House and Zeaman, 1963). In brief, their position is that the observed relationship between individual differences in IQ and in discrimination learning performance is largely ascribable to an attentional factor rather than to differences in rate of learning per se. The case made is a persuasive one and finds support in the work of White and Plum (1964), but it provides relatively little educationally useful information about the factors controlling attention, being directed rather at an explanation of variations in learning proficiency.

Augmenting Attention. The question of how attention may be elicited in children and maintained or controlled thereafter is also largely unanswered. There are, however, some data available and some relevant speculations as well.

With respect to ORs, the basic condition

for elicitation is stimulus change. It is known that ORs habituate readily, implying that if stimulation is to be attended to it must be varied frequently. This bit of lore does not advance us very far with respect to the educational problem of controlling children's attention, however, for we know little about how to change characteristic individual differences in ORs or, in fact, about how to measure them in any useful way outside the laboratory.

With regard to observing responses and other still higher-level behavioral expressions of attention, the situation is somewhat better. It is common to attack the problem of specifying factors that determine the maintenance of attention by distinguishing between extrinsic and intrinsic reinforcement. Without becoming involved in the definitional tangle that sometimes ensues upon the mention of this distinction, let us specify that by extrinsic reinforcement we shall refer to properties or events that are not inherent in the materials to be learned or attended to, and that by intrinsic reinforcement we mean properties of the materials or stimuli themselves that have the effect of increasing the probability of the behavior in question.

Apparently both kinds of reinforcement can be effective in controlling attention. Fisch and McNamara (1963), for example, have shown that it is possible to control the attention of college students in a perceptual task through the delivery of simple verbal approval. With regard to intrinsic properties of stimulation, the work of Berlyne (1958), Fantz (1961), and Hershenson (1967) shows that properties of visual stimulus materials (although there is still dispute about just what the properties are) control the direction and extent of attention in infants. Comparable research is not available for children of early school age in any substantial quantity. One study reported by Cantor, Cantor, and Ditrichs (1963) indicates that complexity of stimuli controls attention in preschool-age children. Other studies (see Cantor, 1963) suggest that novelty or unfamiliarity as well as complexity exert control over children's attention.

In a different approach to the problem of attention, Hagen (1967) has investigated developmentally the effects of vigilance distractors on both central and incidental perfor-

mance on a memory task. Drawing upon an information-processing model of attention and memory (Maccoby and Hagen, 1965), Hagen hypothesized that older children to a greater degree than younger children would be able to attend to relevant stimulus features in the presence of distraction. The results, however, showed a clear age effect across grades 1, 3, 5, and 7 but, at all ages, attention was poorer with distraction conditions.

Clearly, with regard to education, at least three kinds of developmental information are urgently needed about attentional processes. The first need is for research that isolates the sources and provides a means for measuring individual differences in attention, that is, in intensity of ORs, latency of observing responses, duration of attention, and resistance to distraction. The second sort of data concerns the problem of specifying stimulus properties that gain and control attention, especially across the preschool and primary school age ranges. Third, it is important to construct and evaluate methods for training attentiveness, whether they involve extrinsic or intrinsic means of reinforcement. Without substantial additional work on these problems, the psychology of cognitive development has only minimal contributions to make to education with regard to the truly significant task of gaining and controlling attention.

Behavioral Tempo

In addition to attention competence, a child needs to be capable of modulating his behavior, his overt responses, if he is to maximize his learning. The three different but related kinds of behavioral control important to successful schooling may be distinguished: bringing overt responses under the control of verbal instructions emanating from another person; the capability of controlling behavioral responses by giving verbal instructions to oneself; and the delay of overt responding to provide time for internal scanning and processing of information.

Recent research by psychologists of cognitive development is relevant to each of these areas of behavioral control. Each has been shown to change as a function of age during the early childhood years. Consider first the matter of bringing motor response under external verbal control. A series of experiments reported by Luria (1961) indicates that this capability of subjugating motor responses to the control of outside verbal instructions develops rather slowly in the child between the ages of 1½ and 6 years. About the best kind of external control that was observed in children up to the age of 4½ to 5 years consisted of verbal utterances being effective only as signals, not as directions. Thus the utterance "Press!" (a rubber bulb) is effective in instigating a response in the younger child, but "Don't press!" is not effective in terminating responding. In contrast, children in the older age range are capable of abiding by the semantic instructions contained in verbal utterances. They can, for example, on the basis of prior instructions, withhold responses until the onset of some exteroceptive signal and cease responding in accord with such instructions as well.

Similarly, with regard to the capability of regulating overt responses by the child's own speech, verbal control in terms of its semantic content emerges later than in terms of its initiatory signal properties. Up to age 4½, the child's self-instruction "Press!" is effective in instigating a response, but "Don't press!" is not effective in terminating responding. It is only later that the semantic content of the child's own speech comes to control and direct behavior. In connection with a very different task, discrimination learning, a similar change has been reported in the efficacy of self-originating verbalizations for controlling overt responses (Kendler and Kendler, 1962). The Kendlers report their observation that 4-year-olds frequently utter the verbal label of the correct choice in a discrimination task while simultaneously making the incorrect choice as indexed by their motor responses, whereas by age 7 years the two modes of response are consistent.

Finally, a series of studies under the direction of Kagan (1965) demonstrates a distinct, generalized, developmental trend in the direction of an increased tendency to delay responding in a variety of tasks. This tendency has been shown to be sufficiently general to be identified as a trait dimension, impulsivity-reflectivity, contrasting a propensity for offering responses at the first opportunity with a propensity for withholding responses long enough to permit an adequate evaluation of their validity.

Typically, a child's tendency toward an impulsive or a reflective style is measured in terms of his performance on one or another of several tasks that have in common the property that answers to each of their items must be made in the face of considerable degrees of uncertainty. The major index of impulsivity-reflectivity is response latency. Each of the tests used has been demonstrated to have a moderate degree of reliability across time, or the trait has been shown to have a moderate degree of stability over time ($rs =$ .60, Kagan, 1965). Furthermore, the degree of relationship across tasks has been satisfactorily high. Developmentally, response latencies on such tasks have been shown to increase with age, at least as evaluated by cross-sectional research, from first through eighth-grade levels.

Finally, the dimension of impulsivity-reflectivity has been shown to relate to measures of performance adequacy on the index tasks and on other tasks. That is to say, the tests used to measure response latency also yield error measures. The general result is that latency and errors correlate negatively so that reflectivity seems to be associated with a tendency for the first response to be a correct one. It has also been shown that latency on the defining tests correlates negatively in serial learning tasks with the frequency of extralist intrusions, that is, of overt erroneous responses not contained in the serial list. Furthermore, errors in word recognition among first-graders have been shown to correlate with impulsivity so that relatively reflective children, especially among those having high verbal ability as measured by WISC performance, make fewer reading errors than impulsive children.

The work of Luria and that of Kagan and his associates are of impressive relevance to educational practice, especially as regards the early years of formal schooling. Luria's work shows that a child's ability to be controlled by the verbal utterances of the teacher and to control his own behavior through self-instruction and verbal monitoring cannot be assumed to be intact when he enters the schoolroom for the first time. In terms of present school practice, these abilities are of considerable consequence. Tasks are set for children almost entirely in terms of teachers' verbal instructions. Task persistence, due to the relatively large number of children in classrooms, is less a function of the teacher's continuing verbalizations to individual children than of the child's own ability to extend his efforts over time in response to his own verbal instructions whether they are covert or overt.

The results of both lines of investigation, the development of the regulatory function of speech and the development of conceptual tempo, indicate the necessity for modifying the classification categories used by schoolmen to identify children. In many cases a child's failure in the early school years may be attributable to slower than average development of the abilities to control behavior through verbalization and to withhold responses long enough to assess their validity. At the early stages of schooling, children who are impulsive and who cannot seem to follow instructions or persist on tasks without constant supervision may be classified too readily as less bright and less promising than others. Furthermore, they may be subjected to punishment for their behaviors, resulting in apathy, anxiety, or hostility to schooling and to intellectual activities, rather than being provided with training in these subskills that appear to be necessary for school success.

Despite the fact that a strong case can be made for the urgency of incorporating the information yielded by the theorizing and the research of Kagan and of Luria into early childhood schooling procedures, a clear recommendation to this effect cannot be made. Research information is not yet sufficient, nor are the means for accomplishing incorporation yet available in a form appropriate for school use. In the case of impulsivity-reflectivity, for example, it is not clear to what extent school-related cognitive abilities are *determined* by tendencies toward one or another of these response dispositions, nor are the instruments necessary for locating individual children along the dimension fully enough developed to permit their use as diagnostic tools. By way of examining these qualifications more closely, let us turn to a consideration of the topic of individual differences in connection with behavioral tempo and control.

Individual Differences. The exploration of individual differences in the role of speech as a behavior regulator has barely begun. The investigations reported by Luria indicate

clearly that the efficacy of speech regulation varies substantially as a function of age, and this information is useful for alerting the schoolman to the fact that this capability cannot be assumed in all children of all ages. But the information is minimal since for the purposes of educational practice, it is essential to know how differences in speech regulation relate to other differences among individuals *within* the same chronological age range. For example, it seems likely that ethnic group membership or socioeconomic status might bear substantial relationships to differences in the ability to bring motor behavior under verbal control. Also, we know virtually nothing about the relationship between early childhood differences in the capacity for verbal control and broader intellectual capacities such as intelligence test performance during the same period and at later ages.

Beyond the problems presented by the absence of basic information about such individual differences, another major obstacle to educational use of the notion of verbal control is the lack of a reliable method for classifying children with regard to this capability. The need here is for a measuring instrument that is feasible for in-school use. As we saw to be the case with the orienting reflex, the operations for measuring the extent of development of speech as a mechanism of behavior regulation are appropriate for laboratory use only. It is inconceivable that children could be routinely tested using these methods. Thus a massive job of test construction remains to be done.

The situation with respect to the dimension of impulsivity-reflectivity is somewhat better. The path is shorter from presently available measuring instruments to instruments appropriate for school use than is the case for general verbal control. Kagan and his associates have already demonstrated the existence of reliable individual differences in the disposition for impulsive responding, although a variety of relationships between impulsivity and other subject characteristics remain to be explored. We already know that impulsivity decreases with age, the correlation between impulsivity and verbal ability is relatively low, there are relatively unsystematic sex differences in impulsivity, and the degree of relationship between impulsivity and reading proficiency in young children is negative and moderately high (Kagan, 1965). What we do not know is the nature of relationships between impulsivity-reflectivity and ethnic and socioeconomic differences.

Thus the principal needs are two: one for a single measuring instrument to detect individual differences in impulsivity, which can be used in school settings; and one for additional information about relationships between impulsivity-reflectivity and other subject variables.

Indeed, in general, the means presently available to schoolmen for diagnosing children relative to difficulties in educational development are painfully meager. Psychological research makes it clear that performance on intellectual tasks such as reading is a function of more factors than the IQ and the extent of brain damage (see Kagan, 1965) along with vaguely defined motivational differences. Schoolmen agree that this is the case, but the techniques available to them for classifying children do not permit this belief to exert a systematic effect on practice. Indeed one of the reasons for the strength of anti-testing sentiment, at least as it exists in some quarters, may well be that testing programs are not comprehensive enough rather than that they are too pervasive. The curricular consequences of the narrow range of available diagnostic techniques are that effective programs for dealing with individual differences cannot be developed.

Facilitating the Emergence of Verbal Control and Reflectivity. The task of facilitating the acquisition or emergence of competencies believed to underlie successful school performance is of substantial significance for two purposes. The first, and most obvious, is that the effort to facilitate development coincides precisely with the goal of education. The purpose of instruction, after all, is to promote intellectual development beyond the levels possible in its absence. Discovering means for facilitating the acquisition of basic competencies, then, is central for the educational enterprise in its effort to maximize the positive effects of schooling on individuals. The second reason for dealing with the question of means for effecting facilitation is that when such efforts are successful, a methodology becomes available for ascertaining whether

or not a competency hypothesized to be a determinant of school success does, in fact, contribute to observed variations in school learning. For example, if an effective program were found to install prematurely in children the capability of verbal control of behavior, it could then be ascertained experimentally whether or not such control is related to success in early school tasks.

With regard to verbal control, Luria (1961) has reported an instance of a limited but successful technique for advancing its emergence. The procedure essentially consists of first instituting conditions of nonverbal control over the same behaviors later to be brought under verbal control, and only afterward transferring control to conditions of verbalization. In children of very early ages, 2 to 3 years old, it has been possible to bring bulb-squeezing behavior under at least minimal verbal control by first training them to make overt motor responses in a sequence that is later signalled by the verbalizations. Bruner (1966a) makes much of this technique of sequencing enactive conditions of behavior prior to imposing symbolic or verbal conditions, pointing out that its success is consistence with the tenets of instrumental conceptualism. Clearly, it is a method of facilitation worth more extensive application and evaluation.

Kagan (Kagan, Pearson, and Welch, 1966) has undertaken to explore the possibilities of changing first-grade children's conceptual tempi in the direction of greater reflectivity, that is, longer response latencies. Apart from manipulations, which proved to have little effect, only emphasizing the similarity between the subject and the trainer, the training consisted of three sessions in each of which individual children were asked to work on three different tasks, a haptic-visual matching task, a design matching task, and a test of inductive reasoning. With respect to all of the items on the three tasks, the training simply involved instructing the child not to offer an answer until after a short (10 to 15 second) delay interval had elapsed. Both before and after training, the Matching Familiar Figures (MFF) Test and the Picture Completion Reasoning Test (PCRT) were administered to the children. Each test yielded two scores: response latency and number of errors. The results showed that the experimental treatment effected changes in impulsive children such that their response latencies on MFF items were significantly longer than those of untrained impulsive children and no shorter than untrained reflective children. Comparable results for PCRT items were not significant.

This experiment demonstrates that it is possible to make short-term, specific modifications in impulsivity, that is, to facilitate the emergence of reflectivity. With respect to the question of the status of reflectivity as a determinant of successful performance on intellectual tasks, however, the experiment is inconclusive. That is to say, despite the changes in response latency produced by training, no significant changes were effected in error frequency. This kind of null result cannot be construed as evidence that reflectivity does not determine quality of performance, but neither does it lend support to the assertion that it is such a determinant. Obviously, then, improvements in the efficacy of training procedures must be made in an effort to affect not only response latencies on a single measure but on many related indices and to affect as well the quality of performance on relevant intellectual tasks. For if reflectivity training can serve only to slow behavioral tempo and not to modify other performances, its educational relevance as a means for effecting change would be questionable.

Even given such an unhappy future conclusion, the utility of the reflectivity-impulsivity dimension for classifying children might still be considerable. The detection of basic dimensions of cognitive style is of no small importance for education, even when such dispositional factors are relatively impervious to modification. For the availability of the dimension as a means of classification makes it possible to design educational programs in such a way as to take account of this source of individual differences and to provide methods for reducing the probability that such differences will obstruct educational development.

Perception

The capacity for perceptual achievements, along with those of attention and behavioral control, is a necessary precondition for successful school learning. Of all the perceptual modalities, the visual and the auditory are perhaps the most important for schooling because most instructional information is presented in these modes. Since White noted that "The literature on perception in childhood is scant" (1965, p. 201), the situation has improved somewhat and part of the improvement has been in research relevant to education. We have already discussed much of this in connection with the topic of reading. In that discussion, however, we were concerned more with matters of perceptual learning and perceptual discrimination than with phenomena that are purely perceptual in nature and so it must be here. In terms of schooling processes, the major importance of perception has to do with the capacities for learning and discrimination of materials presented in instructional communications.

Gibson (in press) has made an impressive case for the general implications of perceptual learning for education, very much in the manner that we have reviewed them in connection with the acquisition of reading skills. With regard to the question of what is learned through perceptual processes, Gibson's position is that there are two answers. Early in the process of acquiring reading skills, the distinctive features of letters are differentiated. Later in the process, the content of learning consists of acquiring the invariants of higher order structures such as those yielded by the linguist's analysis of morphophonemic and syntactic rules. One of the implications of this kind of view is that the skills and abilities necessary for successful performance at one stage of reading competence are not the same as at another.

This last implication is consistent with results reported by Elkind (1965) of a factor analytic solution of correlational data relating reading performance to other variables. The results apparently showed that a different factor structure emerges for novice than for skilled readers. Elkind's approach to reading is also a perceptual one, informed, as we noted earlier, by Piagetian theory. The kind of perceptual approach, however, is quite different than that espoused by Gibson. One crucial difference is that Elkind's theory of perceptual development rests on maturational assumptions about the growth of conceptual structures that are prerequisite to successful reading performance. In brief, the necessary structure in question here is the internalization of motor schema and their transformation into operational structures permitting the manipulation of properties of stimuli as is necessary for the carrying out of logical multiplication. Another variant on the schema approach to perception has been provided by Liberman (1957) in an articulation theory of speech perception and discrimination. Roughly, the theory holds that incoming speech signals are identified by matching to articulatory schema built up out of the sequences of movement used in speech production.

Whichever of these major points of view about perceptual development is adopted, they lead to a focus upon the conditions whereby the child becomes capable of identifying and distinguishing among perceptual objects. And it is precisely this capacity that is so important in connection with school learning. The child must be able to, or at least be capable of learning to, identify and distinguish among perceptual events.

A third major theory of how this capability is acquired can be characterized as a response theory. The notion is that perceptual objects or stimuli come to be distinguishable by virtue of the fact that the individual makes differential responses to them. Without entering the controversy over explanations of the "acquired distinctiveness of cues" (Smith and Goss, 1955; Spiker, 1956; Cantor, 1965) it is possible to point out that the learning of verbal responses to perceptual events does seem to facilitate their discrimination (e.g., learning distinctive nonsense-syllable responses to lights of different hue; Reese, 1961).

By way of exploring the implications for education of work in the area of perceptual development let us turn first to a discussion of individual differences and then to the problem of augmenting perceptual development.

Individual Differences. Methods for identifying individual differences in perceptual competence are available. The error scores on the Matching Familiar Figures (MFF) Test (Kagan, 1965) are an appropriate example in the visual mode and, as we have seen, perceptual competence as so defined does increase with age. Kagan (1965) has also reported data indicating a moderately low but statistically reliable relationship between

WISC verbal skills and error scores in visual discrimination in MFF (median $r = -.28$). Covington (1967b), using the Perceptual Discrimination Subtest of the Primary Mental Abilities (PMA) Examination, found upperclass kindergarten children to be significantly superior to lower-class kindergarten children. Both of these measuring instruments, the MFF and the PMA, are, of course, appropriate for school use and could be administered with profit to identify children who are in need of experiences designed to improve their capacity for discriminating among stimulus materials.

With regard to auditory discrimination, much has been made recently of the possibility that lower-class children are considerably disadvantaged in their opportunities for acquiring this capacity (Hunt, 1961; Bloom, Davis, and Hess, 1965; Deutsch et al., 1967). The hypothesis is a simple one. The noise level in low-SES homes is presumed to be exceedingly high, thus providing nonoptimal conditions for perceptual learning. The excessive noise level in such homes is supposed to interfere most severely with the acquisition of capacities for discriminating speech events and for segmenting utterances. These conditions are presumed to contribute to a general language deficiency in low-SES children and to make more difficult the task of learning to read as well as that of learning to register accurately verbal communications from teachers.

In view of the importance attached to auditory discrimination as a correlate of social class differences in more general varieties of intellectual development, it is unfortunate that so few measuring instruments have been developed for investigating the hypothesis.

Perhaps the most used index of capacity for auditory discrimination is the Wepman Auditory Discrimination Test. The test is administered individually and consists of the oral presentation of 40 pairs of words. The Ss task is to indicate for each pair whether they are the same or different. Ten of the pairs are identities and the other 30 are different, differing in either initial or terminal phoneme. The Wepman Test has been given considerable use in a series of studies conducted by Deutsch and his associates (see Deutsch, 1967a; Deutsch, Levinson, Brown, and Peisach, 1967; Katz, 1967; Katz and Deutsch, 1967). The general results of these investigations may be summarized as indicating that there is a relationship between Wepman performance and age, Thorndike-Lorge IQ, and reading ability. The correlation between Wepman performance and reading ability was observed in lower-SES Ss and appeared stronger at earlier (second-grade) than later (sixth-grade) ages. As nearly as can be determined, however, the major component of the hypothesis relating school success to SES through the mediator of auditory discrimination ability was not supported. That is, the correlation between SES and Wepman performance was negligible in both a first- and a fifth-grade sample. Although this evidence goes against the assumption that perceptual capabilities in the auditory mode are deficient in low-SES children, the design may not have been adequate to reveal these. Apparently, a more thoroughgoing study of the issue is now in progress (C. Deutsch, 1967b). Nevertheless, other data already available suggest that the outcome is doubtful. Stern and Rabbitt (1966) administered the Wepman and a variant of it, in which the items were nonsense words, to upper- and lower-status children and obtained equivocal results: no clear and systematic difference was found favoring the upper-status groups. Even when reliable SES differences in Wepman performance have been obtained (see, e.g., Clark and Richards, 1966), the results must be interpreted with caution, for the question remains unanswered whether the inferior performance of low-SES children is due to deficiencies in discrimination or to the meaning such children attach to the response terms "same" and "different." In sum, although auditory discrimination ability does appear to be related to reading task performance, there is no persuasive evidence that it mediates SES differences in reading ability.

Educational needs demand both more research in the area of the development of perceptual abilities relevant to education and the construction of instruments for indexing these abilities reliably in children.

Augmenting Perceptual Development. A variety of attempts to facilitate the development of perceptual abilities has been reported. All of these have relevance for educational practice but all are, at this point, still in the nature of pilot programs, whether they be long- or short-term ones.

We have already covered much of the available research on facilitating perceptual abilities as they relate to reading from the viewpoint of perceptual learning. One other demonstration guided by this theoretical approach should be mentioned, namely, that of J. J. Gibson (Gibson, Kennedy, and Toleno, 1967). The idea was to explore the possibility of leading young children to overcome the bent-stick illusion, that is, the illusion that a straight stick bends at the air-water interface. By an ingenious use of materials and by implementing a key component of perceptual learning theory, some children were indeed induced to discover that the phenomenon of a bent stick, half in and half out of the water, indicates that the stick is in fact straight. As the theory suggests, perceptual learning consists of an appreciation of invariance over transformations and one way of inducing invariance is to view perceptual events from multiple perspectives. This is precisely what Gibson's Ss were led to do, and for at least some of them the procedure was successful.

One of the appealing features of the entire approach of the perceptual learning theorists to problems of perceptual development consists of their emphasis upon experience with the physical world, in contrast, let us say, to experience with symbolic representations of that world, as a major avenue of education. The assumption seems to be that experience with primary objects and events is the basic precondition for the success of later learning about these objects and events. There is in this view no argument against the notion that much of this kind of learning, if it is ever to have utility beyond itself, must eventually be represented symbolically, to permit manipulation by abstract operations of thought. But the implication is that fruitful learning begins with concrete experience. The notion is not unique to Gibsonian theory. It is found as well in the theorizing and in the research of Piaget (see Flavell, 1963; Bruner, 1966b; Gagné, 1965a). Piaget and Bruner, in fact, might argue that learning, if it is to be successful, *must* begin with concrete experience.

In a somewhat different vein, some of the research of Elkind (Elkind, Larsen, and Van Doorninck, 1965) offers an example of the possible benefits of training in advancing perceptual development. These investigators, you will recall, were concerned with perceptual decentration in young children, specifically with the ability of such children to perceive figure-ground reversals in viewing ambiguous drawings. Besides the results already reviewed in connection with their relationship to reading performance, the results of training in the perception of such reversals indicated that significant short-term gains could be brought about by a masking method. The method involved essentially forcing the perception of the nonpreferred figures in a series of ambiguous drawings through the technique of masking the preferred figure by covering it with a template. The success of the training, in fact, provides a real, though minor, contradiction to the notion that the attainment of perceptual decentration as here defined is entirely a matter of maturation.

Longer term efforts that have been designed within a Piagetian framework (Gray, 1966) should eventually provide additional evidence with regard to the maturational issue. More important for educational practice, they will produce evidence about the effects that can be induced in preschool age children through this approach.

Again with regard to competence in visual discrimination, the study of Covington (1967b) mentioned earlier demonstrates the facilitory effect of simple exposure to the materials to be discriminated. Between the pretest and posttest administrations of the PMA items, experimental groups of both upper- and lower-status kindergarten children were exposed daily to each of the stem figures from all the PMA items in the criterion test. Only the stem from each item was exposed and only for a total of 5 seconds a day per item for 14 days. The two control groups received similar treatment except that the content of the training items was not drawn from the PMA subtest. Significant pretest to posttest gains were reported for both the low- and high-status groups but only in the low-status group was the gain due to treatment greater than that observed in the corresponding control group. Furthermore, there was a significant interaction such that the low-status children gained more from exposure to the test items than did the high-status children. The implication of this study is that the task

of augmenting the ability to make specific visual discriminations in lower-status children is in no sense an insurmountable one. Indeed, the results suggest that children deficient in such a capability can be detected and successfully trained within a school situation. The results of the Covington experiment warrant considerable additional research to provide answers to questions regarding the generalization of such training to other tasks as a function of SES and of age and regarding the effect of successful training in visual discrimination among low-SES groups on their performance in other tasks in which the same materials are used.

Clearly in the limited instances reviewed, sufficient success has been achieved in efforts to augment quite specific aspects of perceptual development to suggest that more systematic and more long-term intervention attempts might be worthwhile. Some kinds of perceptual competence appear to yield more readily to facilitory intervention than others [cf. the ease of producing change in the Covington experiment with the difficulties reported by Gibson, Farber, and Shepela (1967) in inducing a discrimination set with respect to readinglike materials]. It is equally clear that research designed to explore factorially the effects on the acquisition of various perceptual skills produced by type of intervention, age of intervention, and individual differences in presenting status is required before clear recommendations can be made for educational practice. Such research is of practical importance, to be sure, but it is of theoretical importance as well. It could be designed to shed light on both the contributions of maturational components and experiential components to the development of competencies in specific skills.

Language

Language competence is believed to figure importantly in school success for a variety of reasons. Three functions may be distinguished that are performed by language in connection with education (see Deutsch, Levinson, Brown, and Peisach, 1967). The first is that linguistic competence at the phonological, syntactic, and semantic levels is necessary so that a child can register and comprehend the communications directed toward him in the process of schooling, whether they are oral or written. Second, a child's success in performing the intellectual tasks set for him by the school is more frequently judged by his written and oral linguistic productions than by any other means. Finally, evidence continues to grow in support of the proposition that language affects extralinguistic cognitive processes such as perceptual discrimination and behavior control, in critical ways (see Ervin-Tripp and Slobin, 1966; Ervin and Miller, 1963) even though it is not a necessary condition for general intellectual competence (Furth, 1964). As the latter function of language has been dealt with in connection with the topics of reading and of perception and will be considered again in relation to learning and conceptual competencies, the present discussion will be confined to the first two functions.

Since the development of linguistic competence with respect to both comprehension and production has been ably discussed both in this book (see chapter by McNeill) and elsewhere (see, e.g., Ervin and Miller, 1963), brief comment will suffice here. In children whose cultural and social backgrounds are consistent with those typically assumed in the present design of schooling, both phonological and syntactic development are reasonably far advanced by the age of school entrance. Thus the areas of language development having the greatest relevance for education are semantic development, individual differences in phonological, syntactic, and semantic development, and means for advancing language development in those children who, for whatever reason, are retarded.

Individual Differences. As in most areas of cognitive functioning, individual differences in rate of language development are pervasive. Apart from cases of exceptional abnormality, however, the final levels of linguistic attainment, in the linguist's sense of underlying competence, are reasonably equivalent across individuals. Rate of development does vary across individuals as revealed by the average length of utterances in small-scale, intensive studies (e.g., Brown and Bellugi, 1964), by larger-scale psychometric studies of the sort carried out with the Illinois Test of Psycholinguistic Abilities (ITPA) (McCarthy and Kirk, 1961, 1963), and by larger-scale studies of speech samples in which measures of type-token ratios and

vocabulary size are obtained (Loban, 1965).

A singular problem is presented by the decision of how to measure or index a child's status with respect to language development. Language is a complex function and there is little doubt that many of its facets are worth assessing across individuals: receptive and productive phonological competence; receptive and productive syntactic competence; and receptive and productive semantic competence. The ITPA represents an attempt to provide an instrument capable of making comprehensive assessments of language development and of permitting selective diagnosis of language deficiencies. Its strength lies in the simple fact that it has been developed, standardized, and used. Nothing else has even this much to offer. There are, however, two limitations inherent in the ITPA.

The first limitation concerns the theory that guided and informed the construction of the test, which was promulgated by Osgood (1963). Saying this is not at all to fault the test or the theory but to point out that of the two major theoretical positions currently available regarding the skills or competencies that are central to language development, the test represents adequately only Osgood's. Even to one only mildly acquainted with modern linguistic theory, an inspection of the nine subtests on the ITPA evokes surprise at the paucity of attention given to strictly linguistic matters. Specifically, what the instrument assesses may be described as verbal vocabulary, pictorial vocabulary, verbal analogies, pictorial similarity, object description, knowledge of the function of objects, knowledge of inflections, digit-span, and memory for the arrangement of visual stimuli. With regard to the second of these major theoretical positions, there is no psychometrically standardized instrument available to assess language development from the point of view of that large body of theorists and investigators who espouse some version of the kind of linguistics so imposingly explicated by Chomsky (1957, 1965). Thus there is need for a test capable of assessing the components of language development from this alternative point of view. The absence of such an instrument from the psychometric scene is not due to a lack of appropriate tasks with which to compose it. Brief reflection yields a number of possibilities, drawn mainly from the literature of experimental research on psycholinguistics (e.g., Berko, 1958; Slobin, 1966; Ammon, 1967).

The second limitation of ITPA with respect to the study of individual differences concerns the overlap of the test with commonly used tests of intelligence. Suppose one wanted to evaluate the relationship between language development and intelligence. The fact is that ITPA would not be a good instrument for achieving the goal since of its nine subtests, six have virtually direct analogues in the Stanford-Binet and/or the WISC. Accordingly, a relationship would almost certainly be detected between language development and intelligence. This problem is not unique to ITPA. Virtually any attempt to answer the IQ-language development question is beset with problems since the most commonly used intelligence tests include a number of scales that measure verbal skills.

Perhaps the most lively topic of individual-differences speculation and research relative to language is that which concerns variance associated with social class or ethnic group membership. Many of those concerned with the poor school performance of children from culturally disadvantaged homes attribute a large measure of observed deficiencies in such children to language differences relative to the dominant culture (Bereiter and Engle-.mann, 1966; Bernstein, 1961, 1962, 1964a, 1964b; Bloom, Davis, and Hess, 1965; Deutsch, 1963, 1967). Available data on this issue are meager; available speculation is plentiful. Bernstein (1961, 1962, 1964a, 1964b) has provided both and has well instructed us in the distinction between restricted and elaborated linguistic codes. The distinction may be understood best from the viewpoint of a listener. If the speaker is using a restricted code, the structure of the message he utters will be characterized by one or another of a small number of syntactic alternatives. Thus from the listener's point of view, the structure of the message is highly predictable. In contrast, the structure of a message uttered by a speaker using an elaborated code is highly unpredictable. In an elaborated code, the number of available syntactic alternatives is large. Because of this property, an elaborated code permits the precise expression of discrete intent solely within the verbal channel. In a restricted code, however, the communication of precise meaning is not

possible. Bernstein's hypothesis is that persons in all social strata have available to them the restricted codes of their social group. But higher-strata members are also capable of using elaborated codes, whereas working-class members, because of their early experience in a restricted linguistic environment, have not acquired the capacity for using such codes. Since elaborated codes are well-fitted for communications related to academic matters and restricted codes are not, working-class children are severely disadvantaged in the face of school-learning tasks.

Loban (1965) has collected extensive data relevant to language development as a function of age, social class, and ethnicity. Although his study was not experimental in design, it provides information of substantive importance, much of which is consistent with Bernstein's contentions. For example, in both low- and middle-SES samples, complexity of speech, as measured by the average number of words per communication, increases with chronological age. But the speech of middle-SES subjects is consistently more complex than that of low-SES subjects and the magnitude of the difference increases with age. Moreover, the speech of middle-SES subjects is more flexible than that of low-SES subjects, as measured by the variety of structures used in nominalization (nouns, pronouns, noun clauses, infinitives, verbals) and by the frequency of use of subordination (dependent clauses, participial and infinitive phrases, gerunds, and appositives). These data support Bernstein's hypothesis regarding deficiencies in the use of elaborated codes by members of the lower socioeconomic classes.

A promising line of research on this problem is that under the direction of Labov (Labov and Cohen, 1967). This mode of attack consists of the elicitation of spontaneous and imitative speech from Negro Ss living in New York City and the subsequent linguistic analysis of these productions in an effort to formulate the phonological and syntactic rules of nonstandard English speech in the populations sampled. Their Ss have been sampled according to a stratified model designed to permit comparisons among males and females, older and younger Ss, middle- and working-class Ss, those raised in the north versus those raised in the south. Although preliminary in nature, their results at this point suggest that observable differences between the "non-standard vernacular of the urban ghettoes" and standard English are "greater on the surface than in the underlying grammatical structure" (Labov and Cohen, 1967, p. 66) and that their Ss are capable of perceiving, understanding, and reproducing the meaning of many standard English utterances even though they themselves cannot produce them.

The work of Labov cannot be construed as contradictory to the contention of Bernstein and others that lower-class deficiencies in the use of elaborated codes impairs intellectual abilities that relate to school performance. This remains a very lively hypothesis. Nevertheless, it still awaits experimental validation.

Facilitation of Language Development. Two instructive attempts to facilitate language development are those of Cazden (1965, 1967) and of Bereiter and Englemann (1966). At its inception, Cazden's work was guided by the hypothesis that grammatical development was assisted by contingencies between children's utterances and adult expansions of these into acceptable standard English form. Brown and Bellugi (1964) observed that mothers frequently imitate the young child's utterances. This imitation, however, is not exact. Indeed, the mother's utterance characteristically expands the child's into standard English (e.g., child: "Throw Daddy." Mother: "Throw it to Daddy."). Brown and Bellugi (1964) noted the possibility that these processes of expansion might facilitate the child's acquisition of syntax. In both an experimental study with children aged 28 to 38 months and in later observational studies, however, Cazden (1967) did not find support for this hypothesis. Instead, the indication seems to be that considerable assistance to language development is provided by the availability to the child of various syntactic components in adult usage, that is, adult "modeling" seems to be of more help to the child than contingent expansions.

The efforts of Bereiter and Englemann (1966) are impressive for their comprehensiveness, their thoroughgoing dedication to the efficacy of overt practice in the performances to be acquired, and in the results achieved. Theirs was a programmatic attempt to improve the intellectual abilities of disadvantaged preschool-age children. In the initial study, 15 children were subjected to a 9-month "academic" preschool program in which they were given direct training in speech, arithmetic, and reading skills. For example, the children were required to repeat in unison the utterances of a teacher until they could use them with considerable facility. The results of the training were an increase in average IQ from 93 to 100, performance on the ITPA at or above grade level, and performance on the reading and arithmetic subtests of the Wide-Range Achievement Test sufficient to place the children in the category of those ready to enter the first grade. These results must be evaluated with respect to the usual status of children drawn from equivalent populations, who at comparable ages are substantially retarded on these measures. Even though an adequate control group was not used in evaluating the success of this program, the method seems promising. Furthermore, the program was conducted in a classroom setting, making the techniques used almost directly available for adoption by schoolmen.

Unfortunately, the absence of a control group and the very comprehensiveness of the program create difficulties in construing the results as evidence relevant to the issue of whether it is, in fact, a language-centered deficiency that determines the poor school performance of lower-class children. This issue is sufficiently important to command experimental verification.

Learning and Conceptual Competencies

The combination of learning and conceptual competence under a single heading deserves brief comment. The division between any pair of topics covered here, language and perception, perception and learning, etc., is somewhat arbitrary but is made for convenience of exposition and in order to follow conventions of demarcation widely shared among psychologists. Learning, however, is something of an anomaly among the other topics since it can be applied to each of them. It is, in fact, common to refer to perceptual learning, conceptual learning, learning of language (although this is presently out of fashion), learning of behavioral self-control. In other sense it is also true that perception, attention, and so on, are prerequisites for some kinds of learning. All of this is to say that there are *varieties* of learning which can be distinguished from one another in various ways (cf. Gagné, 1965a, with Melton, 1964). With regard to educational relevance, some of these varieties can conveniently be discussed together because of their apparent centrality for the attainment of educational objectives. It is to such varieties that we refer here.

Recent developments in research on learning reveal an increasing emphasis on the role of nonrote processes, especially as they contribute to successful or efficient learning. Our discussion of learning will focus upon such processes and our discussion of conceptual processes will likewise center upon those presumed to underlie successful conceptual behavior. First, however, let us sketch briefly some of the known facts about developmental changes in learning and conceptual behaviors.

The general fact about learning proficiency —as measured by performance on laboratory tasks such as those of discrimination learning, serial learning, and paired-associate (PA) learning—when plotted as a function of age, is that it improves. It is of pronounced importance to determine whether this improvement consists of a simple, linear accretion of skills that make for progressively greater efficiency or if it consists in one or more relatively discrete shifts in underlying processes. Before considering this issue and its implications, consider the bare curve of improvement for some selected learning tasks.

Simple discrimination learning improves in children, at least up to ages 5 to 7 years (Stevenson, Iscoe, and McConnell, 1955; Weir and Stevenson, 1959) and, in some cases, even up to age 12 (Katz, 1967). Performance on both serial and PA learning tasks improves considerably across the age range 5 to 14 years, although serial learning performance appears to asymptote earlier than PA performance (Jensen and Rohwer, 1965). With regard to more complex forms of concept learning, Piaget and his associates have found considerable increases in the ability to handle problems of conservation, transitivity, and classification over the age range from 3 or 4 to 11 (see Wallach, 1963).

So much for the basic facts indicating improvement with age. What are some of the component processes that may be presumed to account for the increased facility with which children perform on these varieties of learning tasks? With regard to discrimination learning, the answer is ambiguous. Gibson's position as we have already noted would lead to the presumption that children increasingly are able to differentiate stimuli in terms of their distinctive features. An alternative position is that children come increasingly to attach distinctive responses to individual stimuli, in the main to verbal responses, and these serve to facilitate discrimination (e.g., Reese, 1961).

With respect to this last assertion, it is well to pause at this point for brief comment that is relevant to other similar assertions that follow. The general explanatory notion that will be reiterated in connection with age-related improvements in learning and conceptual behaviors is that children engage more and more in mental manipulations, elaborations, and even reductions of the materials presented for learning or problem-solving. The evidence that children do, in fact, engage in such processing will always remain indirect barring discovery of a direct method for revealing covert events. What can be directly established is that acts presumed to occur covertly facilitate, or, in some cases interfere with, performance when they are made overt. This characteristic of the argument about processes underlying the present forms of cognitive development has an interesting consequence. Research aimed at assessing the facilitating or interfering effects of externally imposed conditions of learning or problem-solving can simultaneously provide evidence relevant to questions on the nature of processes that underlie naturally occurring performance changes. Thus the issue of augmenting learning and conceptual competencies is intimately related to the issue of the determinants of the development of such competencies (see Rohwer, 1967, in press).

The signal work of the Kendlers (Kendler and D'Amato, 1955; Kendler, and Kendler, 1961, 1962; Kendler and Mayzner, 1956; Kendler, 1960, 1963; Kendler and Kendler, 1959; Kendler, Kendler, and Wells, 1960) on reversal shift behavior in young children, ages 4 to 10, has led to the hypothesis that children increasingly respond to stimuli with verbal labels that identify one or another or several of their properties. Although the final interpretation of observed age changes in the ease of making reversal shifts (see House and Zeaman, 1962) is in considerable doubt, the Kendlers (1961) have provided evidence that verbalization can either facilitate or interfere with reversal shift performance depending upon whether the verbalization is relevant or irrelevant.

Both serial and PA task performance can be facilitated in children by inducing them to use relevant verbalizations. Levin and Rohwer (1968) have shown that the learning of a serial list of nouns by fourth- and fifth-grade children is advanced by presenting the nouns in the context of a single, rather long sentence. Jensen and Rohwer (1965) found that PA learning efficiency is increased in second-, fourth-, and sixth-grade children by the instruction to formulate a sentence containing the two nouns of each pair. Kindergarten children seemed to derive no benefit from this instruction, but in a later study Rohwer and Lynch (1968) showed that sentences provided by the experimenter can facilitate PA learning in children as young as kindergarten age.

Verbal elaboration is not the only method whereby PA learning can be made more efficient. Reese (1965) observed that PAs presented to children 3 to 5 years of age in the form of line drawings depicting some interaction of the two items in each pair (e.g., a picture of a CAT carrying an UMBRELLA) improved performance relative to a condition where the two items were presented separately. In a similar study, Rohwer, Lynch, Levin and Suzuki (1967) showed that pictorially represented interactions among PA items facilitated learning in first-, third-, and sixth-grade Ss. Furthermore, it has been shown that third- and sixth-grade children learn PAs more rapidly when they are presented in the form of pictures than when presented as printed words (Rohwer, Lynch, Levin and Suzuki, 1967). In sum, these results are consistent with the assertion that when children augment the materials presented for learning by elaborating verbal or imaginal structures containing those materials, their performance is facilitated. The next step in the argument is to say that the propensity for engaging in these kinds of elaboration increases with age.

At this point it is appropriate to note that results such as those just reviewed have two kinds of implication for education. First, they suggest that conditions under which materials are presented for school learning determine the ease with which mastery will be attained. At least with regard to the forms of school learning that conform to the paradigms of discrimination learning, serial learning, and PA learning, it seems clear that an informed and selective use of pictorial representations and verbal labels and contexts will result in more efficient performance. Second, the results suggest that some school time could be used profitably, especially during the kindergarten and even the pre-kindergarten years, to induce habits of elaboration in children so that when confronted with unelaborated materials, as is so frequently the case in schooling, these tactics for learning can be voluntarily brought to bear. Clearly, however, there is a major limitation on the results of these studies insofar as their educational relevance is concerned: the extent to which the conclusions generalize to the learning of school subjects is entirely unknown. Additional evaluation of the effects of these variables must be conducted using materials that are like, if not identical with those used in education.

With regard to problem-solving processes and other forms of learning that are more conceptual than those mentioned thus far, it again appears to be the case that increasing competence arises from increased use of underlying elaborative and analytical processes. Roughly speaking, an account of the increased ability of the child to handle problems in conservation, classification, and transitivity depends upon the emergence, in Piaget's terms, of concrete operations of thought including the property of reversibility. There remains considerable doubt as to whether or not language or verbalization plays anything like a central role in the acquisition of these capabilities. The performances themselves, however, clearly demand that the child engage in mental manipulations, whatever their character. Following the same inference strategy used in connection with improved learning performances, we may ask: What are the conditions under which conservation and reversibility are and are not observed? Assume now that we are speaking of children who do not display these capabilities at the beginning of training. The problem is to explain how children who do evince the capacity for conservation and reversibility come to be able to do so.

A considerable quantity of research has been reported relevant to these issues and the results have been contradictory. The contradictions in part stem from differences in methodology of investigation (Braine and Shanks, 1965; Davies, 1965) and from differences in definitions of the capability being assessed (Elkind, 1967b). But other contradictions apparently have to do with the educationally relevant matter of the method of training used to facilitate acquisition of the concepts in question. For example, in an experiment comparing two methods of training for number conservation, Wallach, Wall, and Anderson (1967) found training in reversibility to be effective and training in addition and subtraction of relevant objects to be ineffective. Again, a variety of procedures used with the intent of facilitating the acquisition of conservation (Smedslund, 1962, 1961a, 1961b; Wohlwill, 1960; Wohlwill and Lowe, 1962) have failed to produce considerable differences between trained and control children, whereas other procedures that involve masking the results of transformations of materials from the view of Ss (see the discussion of the Frank experiment in Bruner, Olver, and Greenfield, 1966) seem to be successful.

Clearly, the conditions under which numeric and scientific concepts of the sort that appear with great frequency in the work of Piaget and of those who are concerned to validate and extend his findings are of special significance for education. It is equally clear that with regard to instructional implications, there are large gaps in the information presently available with regard to two major questions. The first is whether or not it is possible, and, if so, profitable to facilitate the early emergence of capabilities in children. Piaget apparently thinks that the answer is no (Elkind, 1967a). The second question concerns the possibility of designing instruction so that whatever needs to be taught to children can be presented without requiring unattained capabilities for its acquisition. If this is to be the focal educational strategy, then accurate and reliable means for assessing children's presenting status are an absolute necessity. This brings us to a discussion of

individual differences and of means for assessing them.

Individual Differences. Individual differences in learning and in conceptual behaviors is a bifurcated topic. The assessment of individual differences in conceptual attainments has long been a major effort of psychologists and therefore has a long tradition yielding considerable amounts of data. These data pertain, as we noted at the beginning of the chapter, largely to performance on standard, well-known tests of intelligence. We need not review here the present status of knowledge on these kinds of individual differences as traditionally conceived. Rather, we shall take note of recent developments related to the matters of learning and conceptual behavior just reviewed and related as well to the more traditional conceptions of intelligence.

That there is a need for more kinds of assessment than those provided by the traditional intelligence test is amply testified to by recent theoretical formulations emphasizng the need for positing at least two rather different kinds of intellectual processing in children. The position was explicated at some length by White (1965) in connection with a wide variety of experimental data concerning age changes in performance on a number of different learning and conceptual tasks. The second view that we shall mention was prompted in large measure by another body of evidence, one that contains an internal contradiction, namely, the data showing SES and ethnic differences in intelligence but not in learning efficiency (Jensen, 1969).

White (1965) distinguishes a lower level (associative) and a higher level (cognitive) of mental processes. He marshalls considerable, strikingly varied sources of evidence to the effect that a shift from the dominance of the associative to that of the cognitive processes occurs in the age range of 5 to 7 years. The shift is summarized in terms of four general transitions: (1) from direct responses to available stimuli to responses produced by mediated stimuli; (2) the emergence of the capability of inducing invariants in the face of phenomenal variability; (3) the capacity for organizing past experience to allow inference and prediction; (4) increased sensitivity to information yielded by distance as against near receptors. Obviously, each one of these relatively general changes from lower- to higher-level mental processes is capable of translation into a number of measurable variables, each of which may yield reliable individual differences. Given the developmental nature of the theory, the most interesting kind of individual differences would be those that might emerge as a result of interactions between subject variables, task variables, and age. Thus, for example, one might expect to find that males and females cross the various transitions at different chronological ages or that within one of the four transitions, males would be found superior to females and within another the reverse would be the case.

It is precisely because of observed interactions of this kind that Jensen (1969) has promulgated a similar version of a two-process theory of learning abilities. This version, like White's, posits a lower-level, associative ability and a higher-level, cognitive ability. The lower-level ability is illustrated in terms of the kinds of capability necessary for adequate performance on a task such as that of the simple digit span. The higher-level ability is exemplified in terms of the kinds of processing required by a task such as that of solving the Raven Progressive Matrices problems.

The two-process theory is especially potent with regard to some interesting data that are beginning to be reported regarding SES- and ethnic-related differences in performance on learning and conceptual tasks. It has been shown, for example, that low- and high-strata children of elementary-school age perform equally well on tests of serial learning (Rapier, 1968), PA learning (Rapier, 1968; Rohwer, Lynch, Suzuki, and Levin, 1968), and digit-span (Jensen, 1969). Children drawn from these same populations, however, have repeatedly been found to differ markedly on tests of intelligence (see, e.g., data reported in Deutsch and Associates, 1967; Rohwer, 1967, 1968). These two kinds of data are consistent with an interpretation in terms of two levels of learning ability. The conception is that low- and high-SES children differ in cognitive abilities but not in associative learning abilities.

The data relevant to the issue are by no means complete and an attempt to furnish more adequate evidence is presently underway (Jensen and Rohwer, 1966; Rohwer,

1968). Even at this point, however, the issue is not quite as clear as described thus far. The complication is an interesting one, for it involves a developmental factor. It has been shown that SES differences in learning ability can be detected at early age levels (3 to 5 years) on the same kind of PA task that yields SES equivalence at later ages; the task is sufficiently difficult that a ceiling-effect interpretation cannot be made (Rohwer, 1967; also see Semler and Iscoe, 1963, for a parallel effect with respect to Negro-White comparisons). When the necessary data are obtained, similar convergence may be found for other tasks as well. The important question to be answered by such data is whether or not convergence with age of SES groups obtains for both lower- and higher-level learning abilities or just for the lower-level abilities.

The answer to this question is critical for educational practice. Suppose that Jensen's two-process theory is valid, that is, suppose that substantial numbers of low-SES children are characterized by an enduring deficit in higher-level, cognitive abilities. Also suppose, as Jensen (1969) has suggested, that SES differences in cognitive abilities are largely attributable to genotypic differences between populations. The implication that follows from these suppositions is that instruction must be designed in very different ways for children from upper- and lower-SES populations. For example, if a curriculum were designed for low-SES children, it could not be assumed that the children were capable of self-initiated cognitive activity of the sort needed for the induction of rules from examples. If induction were a necessary component of the subject matter to be learned, it would have to be taught explicitly. In contrast, suppose that variance between upper- and lower-SES children in cognitive level abilities is principally attributable to environmental rather than to genetic variation. In this case the implication is that systematic attempts would be needed to explicitly induce low-SES children to acquire the use of cognitive skills. Presumably, such an attempt would not be particularly successful if it were prosecuted by means of enrichment methods since these are predicated upon the child's possession of inferential cognitive abilities. Instead, the indication is that the conditions for acquiring cognitive skills should be designed to permit the low-SES child to use maximally his associative learning abilities.

On the other hand, suppose that a developmental interpretation of SES differences in associative and cognitive abilities is valid, that is, suppose that with respect to both kinds of learning the abilities of lower- and higher-SES children converge with increasing age so that the convergence of associative abilities occurs at earlier ages than that of cognitive abilities. This supposition suggests two alternative educational strategies. The first assumes that these developmental differences are maturationally determined and simply involves scheduling instruction at later ages for lower- than for higher-SES children. The low-SES child, for example, might not enter kindergarten until age 7 rather than at age 5. Alternatively, SES differences in developmental rate might be assumed to be environmentally determined and therefore susceptible to change through the implementation of specially prepared preschool curricula. This, of course, is the assumption that underlies current efforts such as Project Headstart. Note, however, that the developmental interpretation implies the selection of preschool curricula that involve explicit instruction in the acquisition and use of cognitive skills. The enrichment approach common in many middle-class nursery schools is contraindicated for low-SES children since many of the cognitive skills necessary for the success of such a program are precisely the ones that must be fostered. Instead, the approach should provide for the acquisition of cognitive skills by means of available associative processes.

Most impressive data relevant to these educational implications have been reported by Lesser (Stodolsky and Lesser, 1967; Lesser, Fifer, and Clark, 1965). Specially designed tests of mental abilities (Verbal, Reasoning, Number, and Space) were administered according to a balanced design to samples of first-grade children drawn from each of the eight populations defined by the factorial combination of two variables, social class (middle versus lower) and ethnicity (Chinese versus Jews versus Negroes versus Puerto Ricans). The results were clear and striking. Within every ethnic group, there was a substantial effect associated with social-class membership such that middle-class chil-

dren performed significantly better on each of the four subtests than lower-class children. But the pattern of performance across the ethnic groups was relatively independent of social-class and quite distinctive for each ethnic group. As Fig. 1 reveals, the *pattern* of performance within an ethnic group was virtually the same for both social-class groups but the pattern for one ethnic group differed markedly from that of the others. There were also differences among the various groups with respect to absolute levels of performance on the four subtests, but for the present issue the important result was that marked individual differences associated with ethnic group membership emerged for the mental abilities assessed. These findings are the more impressive because they have been replicated on two entirely independent samples (Stodolsky and Lesser, 1967).

What conclusions and implications for educational practice are to be drawn from these data? It is clear the implications are not simple ones. As Stodolsky and Lesser (1967) argue so persuasively, the goal of identical educational development for all children must give way to the goal of maximal educational development for all children. The most important implication is that psychologists of

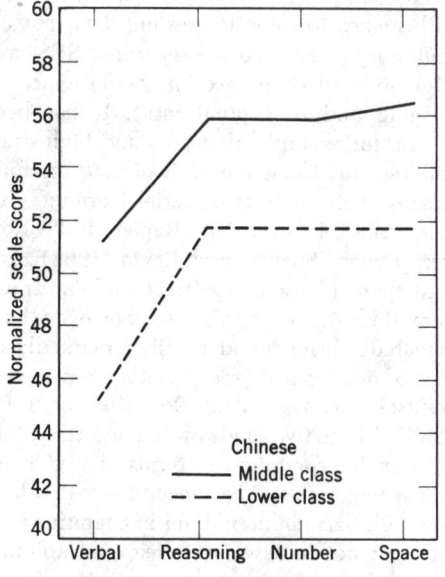

Fig. 1. Patterns of normalized mental-ability scores for middle- and lower-class Chinese children.

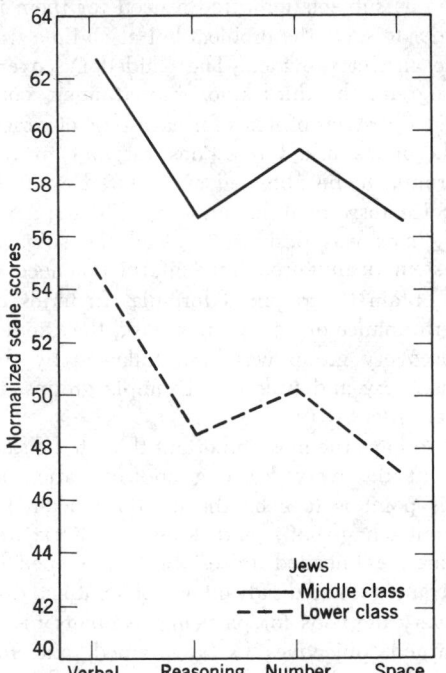

Fig. 2. Patterns of normalized mental-ability scores for middle- and lower-class Jewish children.

cognitive development and educators alike must face up to and begin to make provisions for individual differences. As Hirsch (1967) has so vigorously emphasized, variability among individuals is the basic fact of behavior; it must guide our efforts at educational design and our attempts to enhance educational development.

Finally, with respect to individual differences in learning and conceptual behavior, it should be clear that research must continue to be designed to reveal the sources and the patterns of variation among children. It must be repeated that research of the kind reported by Stodolsky and Lesser (1967), by Jensen (1969) and by Rohwer (1967, 1968) urgently needs to be carried out developmentally, that is, across an age range that at least matches that spanned by the elementary school years. It is important to know, for example, whether or not the ethnic differences in patterns of mental ability reported by Stodolsky and Lesser (1967) for first-grade children endure throughout the educational life-span. Without such information it is impossible for curriculum designers to know at what points it is necessary to provide for such individual differences in order to facilitate educational development.

Augmenting Learning and Conceptual Competencies. We have already noted some procedures that are promising for facilitating the acquisition of specific forms of learning and conceptual competencies as, for instance, in the case of the verbal and visual elaboration of learning materials (Rohwer, 1967; Milgram, 1967) and in the case of reversibility (Wallach, Wall, and Anderson, 1967). There remain developments in five other areas that have more general application to the problem of facilitating educational development. These are discovery methods, programmed instruction, computer-assisted instruction, detailed operant techniques for remediation, and preschool programs. Each of these areas of application has such direct implications for educational practice and is so thoroughly discussed elsewhere that they will be mentioned here only in summary form.

The approach to instruction known as the discovery method has acquired great fashion among some psychologists and among many educators. Many of the new curriculum efforts, in fact, are built largely upon the assumption that learning by discovery has the advantage over the alternatives (see, e.g., Suchman, 1960, 1961; Davis, 1966). The advantages of the discovery method are presumed to be increased motivation, better retention, and wider transfer rather than more efficient initial mastery of presented materials.

Let us consider, for example, the method of inquiry training developed by Suchman (1960). This method has been applied principally to elementary science instruction and is designed for use in groups of about 10 students each. A typical training session begins with the presentation of a silent motion picture depicting some physical event such as the collapse of an empty sealed varnish can with cooling. The students' task is to discover an explanation for the event by asking questions in a form that the teacher can answer either "Yes." or "No." For example, the teacher will answer a question like "Was the can at room temperature to begin with?" but will not answer one like "Why did the can collapse?" Thus the teacher is a source of information but not a source of strategies for gaining information. The intent of the method is for children to learn to frame questions so as to obtain unequivocal information, to sequence the questions so as to establish early in the session the information prerequiite for further progress, and to draw inferences from the information obtained in order to evaluate hypothetical explanations of the event observed. At the end of each inquiry session, a critique period follows in which the children and the teacher discuss the tactics and strategies of inquiry in order to improve the students' competence in the use of the method. Suchman (1960) reports that after 15 1-hour sessions of this kind:

Most of the children who receive training become more productive in their design and use of verification and experimentation. They develop a fairly consistent strategy which they can transfer to new problem situations. They make fewer untested assumptions; they formulate and test more hypotheses; and they perform more controlled vs. uncontrolled experiments in the course of their inquiry (Suchman, 1960, p. 47).

Critical reviews of the literature on discovery methods have appeared (Ausubel, 1961; Gagné, 1966b; Wittrock, 1966) and reveal that, as yet, we have very little systematic evidence about the effects of discovery methods on motivation, retention, and transfer. Evidence that has been collected seems to indicate that unguided discovery is inferior on all measured counts to procedures of guided discovery (Kersh, 1958).

Gagné and Brown (1961), for example, have reported the results of an experiment in which the terminal task presented to ninth- and tenth-grade subjects was that of finding a formula for obtaining the sum of four different kinds of number series. The subjects were divided into three groups according to the kind of pretraining administered. The first kind, Rule and Example, consisted of an expository learning program in which a rule for finding the sum of a particular kind of number series was presented followed by appropriate examples of such series. The second kind of pretraining, Discovery, involved the presentation of a number series with the instruction to find a formula for obtaining the sum of such a series. A series of successive hints was available for presenta-

tion as subjects indicated a need for them in order to solve the problem but at no time was the answer provided. The Guided Discovery program, the third kind of pretraining, contained a series of items for each type of series. The items asked questions relevant to the formula to be obtained and offered multiple choice answers to the questions. The sequence of items was designed to lead the subjects systematically through the information needed to obtain the required formula. In terms of performance on the terminal task, the Guided Discovery group was best, followed by the Discovery and Rule and Example groups, in that order.

Perhaps the most important thing to be said about discovery learning and education at this point is to echo the positions taken by Cronbach (1966) and Kagan (1966): research is needed to establish the specific advantages and disadvantages of identified discovery methods for particular contents to be learned, objectives to be attained, and for specific kinds of learners who are to be instructed. For additional discussion of the topic, the reader is referred to Shulman and Keislar (1966).

Just as discovery methods have enjoyed a certain fashion among educators, so have methods of programmed instruction. Unlike the case of discovery, the topic of programmed instruction is replete with experimental studies of the effects on learning outcomes of component factors such as step size, mode of response, type, frequency and mode of feedback, and sequencing (see Lumsdaine, 1964, for a review). From a currently dominant viewpoint, the educational importance of programmed instruction is not so much that it provides a discrete set of techniques for instruction but that it concretely illustrates the possibility of predesigning instructional materials (see Lange, 1967). Research on programming, then, is useful insofar as it sheds light on the variables that contribute to the success or failure of attempts to map out instructional sequences that are relatively independent of teacher decisions. The argument is a simple one. Teaching virtuosity is and in all probability will continue to be rare and the teacher has much too much to manage already without the burden of making minute-by-minute curricular decisions. The practice of leaving the success of schooling to the teacher cannot be warranted any longer.

To take an example, the line of research reported by Rothkopf (Rothkopf, 1965, 1966; Rothkopf and Coke, 1963, 1966; Rothkopf and Bisbicos, 1967) has considerable relevance for the task of predesigning instruction, even though it is not advertised much as research on programmed instruction. Rothkopf has shown, for instance, that the incorporation of certain kinds of testlike questions within sequences of written material can facilitate learning from such materials. The types of questions asked and the placement of the questions have been shown to affect the success of the method. Moreover, it has been shown that testlike questions can have effects that interfere with performance as well as effects that enhance performance. Developmental studies of these effects on learning are needed to support the investigations already reported, especially insofar as they can extend the age range of the populations sampled down into the elementary-school level. According to Rothkopf (Rothkopf and Bisbicos, 1967) the effect of questions placed immediately after the relevant segments of written material is to increase inspection behaviors on the part of students. Although he is pessimistic about the possibility of installing such behaviors as enduring habits, this potential is worth considerable assessment in its own right.

All of the remarks made thus far about programmed instruction and the predesign of educational materials apply equally to the topic of computer-assisted instruction (CAI). The role of the computer in CAI is manifold. Consider, for example, the system in use at Stanford University in connection with first-grade reading instruction (Atkinson, 1968). Each of 16 children is seated at an individual terminal equipped with presentation devices (projection screen, cathode ray tube, and earphones) and response devices (typewriter keyboard and light pen). A program of instruction is predesigned and stored in the computer which selects items for presentation to the child depending upon his previous record of performance on an initial screening test and on the test items contained within each frame of the program. Materials can be presented on any one or a combination of the display devices in connection with a given frame of instruction. If a child's answer to the question contained within a frame is correct, he is presented with the next frame in the main line of the program. If his answer is incorrect he is presented with the initial frame of an appropriate remedial loop. The child's response with either the light pen or the typewriter input provides the information necessary for the computer to choose between these alternatives. The response is also sufficient to permit the computer to display to the child informative feedback as to whether or not his response was correct. Finally, the system is designed to record automatically the child's performance, providing a history of his progress through the instructional program. At the end of the first year the CAI program was evaluated. The performance of the CAI group on standard tests of reading achievement surpassed that of a comparable control group that had been provided with customary first-grade instruction in reading.

An additional comment must be made about a distinctive feature of computer-assisted instruction precisely because of its signal importance for education. As Suppes (1964) has indicated, the enormous magnitude of individual variation in learning is revealed most clearly by methods of instruction, such as computer-assisted methods, that provide for the accommodation of these differences. The individualization of instruction has been a positively valued goal in American education for many years. But literal provision for individual differences has been minimal for very good reasons, including (1) the extent of individual variation has only been suspected and not dramatically or empirically known; and (2) providing for individual variation is an arduous and perhaps even an impossible task without technological aid, especially given the dominance of classroom modes of organization in the schools. The use of computer methods in education will, hopefully, remove the possibility of ignoring in practice the necessity of individualizing instruction.

Our concern with individual variation has thus far taken us only part of the way out toward the tails of frequency distributions of children's performance on educational tasks. What of children who seem irredeemably fated to fail in school? Recent work informed by a rather strict commitment to the tenets of operant and classical conditioning shows some promise of remediating seemingly irreversible deficits. The work of Lovaas (Lovaas, Freitag, Gold, and Kassorla, 1965; Lovaas, Schaeffer, and Simmons, 1965), although still quite controversial, is impressive for its attempt to modify seemingly intractable behaviors in autistic children. Less bizarre behaviors such as pervasive reading deficiencies have been shown to yield to intervention using operant techniques (Staats and Butterfield, 1965). The characteristic specificity of the operant approach to learning is clearly evident in this effort and apart from its apparent success as a remediation technique, the approach can contribute to educational practice if it succeeds in impressing schoolmen with the fact that learning is a complex undertaking composed of almost innumerable specific acquisitions that are prerequisite to any further progress.

Finally, mention must be made of a very different educational strategy designed to ameliorate individual differences, namely, the burgeoning interest and implementation of programs in preschool education. All manner of such programs are presently in operation, from the sort predicated on the value of traditional nursery school enrichment to those that lean heavily on the presumed efficacy of early training in academic skills. In other connections we have already mentioned the programs under the direction of Deutsch et al. (1967), Gray (1966), and Bereiter and Engelmann (1966). The last of these is notable for its rigid adherence to an academic model of preschool education in marked contrast to the customary nursery school enrichment model. Bereiter and Engelmann (1966) set forth 15 academic objectives as the minimal goals of a preschool education program. These objectives are specific and stated in behavioral terms as illustrated by the following selections:

Ability to use the following prepositions correctly in statements describing arrangements of objects: on, in, under, over, between. "Where is the pencil?" "The pencil is under the book."
Ability to perform simple *if-then* deductions. The child is presented a diagram containing big squares and little squares. All the big squares are red, but the little squares are of various other colors. "If the square is big, what do you know about it." "It's red."
Ability to name the basic colors, plus white, black and brown.
Ability to count aloud to 20 without help and to 100 with help at decade points (30, 40, etc.).
A sight-reading vocabulary of at least four words in addition to proper names, with evidence that the printed word has the same meaning for them as the corresponding spoken word. "What word is this?" "Cat." "Is this a thing that goes 'Woof-woof'?" "No, it goes 'Meow.'" (Bereiter and Engelmann, 1966, pp. 48-49).

The program of instruction instituted to achieve these objectives may be characterized as one of specific, direct teaching. If the objective is the capability of counting objects correctly up to 10, the children are given highly repetitive practice in counting objects up to 10. It is interesting to note that the instructional practices described by Bereiter and Engelmann conform closely with principles of simple, associative learning. The two principles most in evidence throughout are repeated practice of correct responses and reinforcement for correct responses.

The instructional program is designed to fit within a 5-day-a-week, 2-hour-a-day schedule. One hour each day is devoted to intensive teaching and learning directed toward the attainment of the program's objectives. This hour is distributed in three 20-minute segments separated by periods of less structured activity. The three segments are devoted to instruction in language, arithmetic, and reading skills. A different teacher is responsible for each of the three subject-matter areas so that the children are in the charge of three individual teachers.

The results of a preliminary assessment of the Bereiter-Engelmann preschool program suggest that it is a promising method for increasing the rate of educational development in culturally disadvantaged children. Fifteen low-SES children were enrolled in the program for a 9-month period. The average age of the group at the outset was 4½ years and the average IQ was 93. At the end of the period, the average IQ had risen to 100. Moreover, the average performance of the sample on the reading and arithmetic subtests of the Wide-Range Achievement Test was advanced a full year beyond age level. The conclusions that can be drawn from these results are limited by the fact that appropriate control groups were not selected for purposes of comparison.

Massive programs like Project Headstart and related governmental efforts have also been subjected to evaluation (Williams and Stewart, 1966; Boyd, 1966; Temp and Anderson, 1966), but their characteristic inattention to design for evaluation makes it difficult to draw compelling conclusions. That is to say, unless such efforts are planned with evaluation in mind, the amount of information yielded cannot be maximal. In an effort as large and as unsystematically varied as Project Headstart little can be discovered about the relative effectiveness of specific variants of preschool education. At a time when the mood in education and in public agencies responsible for education strongly favors the institution of pre-kindergarten schooling as a matter of routine, it is crucial that hard information be made available about the effects of such practices.

A model piece of research in this regard has recently been reported by Lenrow (1967). The study contrasted the effectiveness of three different preschool programs for assisting children to achieve increased competence in both convergent and divergent modes of thinking and problem-solving. Provision for assessing the effects of the programs on these behaviors was made quite intentionally and no effort was spared to institute the best possible version of each of the kinds of program studied. Apart from demonstrating the advantages of a convergent training or direct teaching program for performance on tests of logical thinking and that such a program had no deleterious effects on divergent thinking abilities the study revealed once again the pervasiveness of individual differences, not only in presenting status but in response to intervention. It was found, for example, that a number of the children given convergent training showed a greater propensity for exploratory activity than children given divergent training, whereas other children given the convergent training showed considerably less. Clearly, these results are not, by themselves, of enormous significance. Both longer-term programs and longer-term effects of such programs need similar evaluation; more attention should be given to the number and variety of dependent measures to be used in indexing the effects of such programs. Nevertheless, Lenrow's effort is remarkable for the care taken to plan for evaluation and the attention given to the possibility that multiple consequences, some of which could be contradictory, might result from a single type of preschool education.

SUMMARY, SPECULATION, AND IMPLICATIONS

Let us conclude by reiterating some of the themes that have appeared and reappeared in these pages. It is important as well to characterize what the reader has been offered here in the name of implications of cognitive development for education, for the present treatment has by no means exhausted all of what the psychology of cognitive development has to offer to education. Intentionally, greater emphasis has been given to what schoolmen need from the scientific study of cognitive development than to what they can now obtain from it. This choice was made in the belief that the current status of theory and research as it relates directly to educational practice is very preliminary indeed. The purpose was to underline the kinds of research that are desperately needed if education is to be improved. The need is desperate because education is presently changing and the changes are, in many cases, being made without recourse to evidence that the direction is favorable for the children who will be involved—thus the recurrent themes.

Two kinds of research are necessary if the psychology of cognitive development is to contribute to educational change. The first is basic research, which starts with psychological phenomena that reveal themselves in schooling, such as the phenomena associated with learning to read. For a developmental psychologist to engage in such research, he must change only his strategy for choosing researchable phenomena. After the choice, the method is that of experimental analysis and, with luck, the results are of both practical and theoretical significance. The second kind of research is ancillary to the first but of equal importance if the first is ever to contribute to educational change. This kind of research involves the psychologist with subject-matter and curriculum specialists in evolving, evaluating, and modifying instructional programs and materials. An emphasis on this kind of research belies an underlying skepticism about the direct applicability of the results of basic research in the schools. Hence, the typical pattern will probably involve modifications as the translation to practice is attempted.

The present character of research in the general area bounded by education, psychology, and cognitive development is that educational research is too infrequently developmental and research in cognitive development too infrequently begins with phenomena that arise in schooling. Despite this, there are hopeful signs. Theoretically, the recent formulations by Bruner and by Gagné indicate a commitment to work toward the satisfaction of the educational needs we have reviewed. Both formulations incorporate attention to phenomena germane to schooling along with a developmental view of the educational process. With regard to research, the various efforts that have come under the umbrella of Project Literacy, for example, promise to result in both evidence and materials that can contribute to educational change. In general, the trend, if one can be perceived, seems to be toward a growing relevance of research and theory in cognitive development for educational problems and toward a growing use of this resource by schoolmen.

A second major theme of the chapter has been the contention that special attention to individual differences is crucial for the success of any enterprises aimed at promoting educational development. It is variability after all that forms the starting point of psychological research, and one of the most legitimate and important aims of such research is surely isolating and describing the sources and determinants of individual differences. There are several topics embedded here. One concerns the development of means for measuring individual differences, for classifying them, and for reliably identifying individuals who belong to the various classes. Another concerns the specification of the measures that are necessary for determining the presenting status of students at any important educational juncture. Still another matter that awaits clarification is the extent

to which individual differences detected at one developmental level persist to and through other levels. Finally, it remains to determine which of the individual differences detected are amenable to modification and which will simply have to be provided for by distinctly different forms of educational practice.

Related to all of these issues of individual variation is the enormous task of designing instruction to be responsive to them. The problems here are not easy to solve. We do not know what learning conditions are most facilitative for impulsive as compared with reflective children, for Chinese as compared with Negro children. But even given this kind of knowledge, we will still be faced with the task of detecting and providing for individual differences in the response of such groups to the instructional programs designed for them.

It is not yet clear how the commanding need for individualization of instruction is to be met. It seems certain that the conception of the classroom must give way to that of the student as the basic unit of educational organization. Indeed, it might be the better strategy to induce schools to shift in the direction of psychological experimentation than to expend effort in determining how to maximize the effectiveness of present school practices. That is to say, for manifesting what and how much an individual has learned, the individually administered task has a distinct advantage over classroom recitation. But such a recommendation cannot be made until we have provided educators with effective means for assessing students and their progress all along the interval of life devoted to formal education, and with respect to the kinds of learnings and development the schools seek to engender. Not that these objectives must be accepted as is. Changes here are probably warranted as well, but until we can provide adequate methods for assessing more than measures of PA learning efficiency or the propensity for making reversal shifts, our suggestions must remain limited. Make no mistake, the capability for making such assessments is important as well, for it is clearly necessary to identify a diverse array of competencies in children including various kinds of learning abilities as well as more general collections of abilities such as intelligence and creativity.

The final theme that deserves emphasis in

closing is the need for explicit, behavioral statements of educational objectives. At a time when an increase in the number of years to be devoted to formal schooling is seriously planned, it is nearly unconscionable to do so for vague and general purposes regardless of the humanitarian and altruistic character of the rhetoric used to describe them. It may require a considerable sacrifice of illusions about educational objectives, but until we demand to know specifically how we can tell a successful education when we see one, we may never be able to help in producing one. Nor can we assist in solving one of the great and continuing problems of instruction—revealing to the instructor whether or not a student has learned whatever it is he was intended to learn.

References

Ammon, P. R. The perception of grammatical relations in sentences: a methodological exploration. *J. verb. Learn. verb. Behav.*, in press.

Anastasi, A. *Differential psychology.* (3rd ed.) New York: Macmillan, 1958.

Atkin, J. M. Science in the elementary school. *Rev. educ. Res.*, 1964, **34**, 263–272.

Atkinson, R. C. The computer is a tutor. *Psychol. Today*, 1968, **1**, 36–39; 57–59.

Ausubel, D. P. Learning by discovery: rationale and mystique. *Bull. Nat. Assoc. sec. sch. Princ.*, 1961, **45**, 18–58.

Begle, E. G. The school mathematics study group. *Math. Teacher*, 1958, **51**, 616–618.

Belloni, M. L. The relationship of the orienting reaction and manifest anxiety to paired-associates learning. Unpublished doctoral dissertation, University of California, Los Angeles, 1964.

Bereiter, C., and Englemann, S. *Teaching disadvantaged children in the preschool.* Englewood Cliffs, N.J.: Prentice-Hall, 1966.

Berko, J. The child's learning of English morphology. *Word*, 1958, **14**, 150–177.

Berlyne, D. E. A theory of human curiosity. *Br. J. Psychol.*, 1954, **45**, 180–191.

Berlyne, D. E. The influence of complexity and novelty in visual figures on orienting responses. *J. exp. Psychol.*, 1958, **55**, 289–296.

Berlyne, D. E. *Conflict, arousal and curiosity.* New York: McGraw-Hill, 1960.

Berlyne, D. E. *Structure and direction in thinking.* New York: Wiley, 1965.

Bernstein, B. Social class and linguistic development: a theory of social learning. In A. H. Halsey, J. Floud, and C. A. Anderson (Eds.), *Education, economy, and society.* New York: Free Press, 1961. Pp. 288–314.

Bernstein, B. Linguistic codes, hesitation phenomena, and intelligence. *Lang. Speech*, 1962, **5**, 31–46.

Bernstein, B. Aspects of language and learning in the genesis of the social process. In D. H. Hymes (Ed.), *Language in culture and society.* New York: Harper & Row, 1964. Pp. 251–263. (a)

Bernstein, B. Elaborated and restricted codes: their social origins and some consequences. In J. J. Gumperz and D. H. Hymes (Eds.), *The ethnography of communication.* Menasha, Wisc.: Amer. Anthrop. Assoc., 1964. Pp. 55–69. (b)

Bever, T., and Bower, T. How to read without listening. Project Literacy Reports No. 6, 1966, **6**, 13–25.

Bishop, C. H. Transfer effects of word and letter training in reading. *J. verb. Learn. verb. Behav.*, 1964, **3**, 215–221.

Bloom, B. S., Davis, A., and Hess, R. *Compensatory education for cultural deprivation.* New York: Holt, Rinehart & Winston, 1965.

Boyd, J. L. Facilities and resources of Head Start centers. Section two of final report by *Educational Testing Service*, Contract No. OEO–1359, 1966.

Braine, M. D. S., and Shanks, B. L. The development of conservation of size. *J. verb. Learn. verb. Behav.*, 1965, **4**, 227–242.

Brown, R. and Bellugi, U. Three processes in the child's acquisition of syntax. *Harv. educ. Rev.*, 1964, **34**, 133–151.

Bruner, J. S. *The process of education.* Cambridge, Mass.: Harvard University Press, 1960.

Bruner, J. S. The course of cognitive growth. *Am. Psychol.*, 1964, **19**, 1–15.

Bruner, J. S. The growth of mind. *Am. Psychol.*, 1965, **20**, 1007–1017.

Bruner, J. S. On cognitive growth: I. In J. S. Bruner, R. R. Olver, and P. M. Greenfield, *Studies in cognitive growth.* New York: Wiley, 1966. (a)

Bruner, J. S. On cognitive growth: II. In J. S. Bruner, R. R. Olver, and P. M. Greenfield, *Studies in cognitive growth.* New York: Wiley, 1966. (b)

Bruner, J. S. An overview. In J. S. Bruner, R. R. Olver, and P. M. Greenfield, *Studies in cognitive growth.* New York: Wiley, 1966. (c)

Bruner, J. S. *Toward a theory of instruction.* Cambridge, Mass.: Harvard University Press, 1966. (d)

Bruner, J. S. Some elements of discovery. In L. S. Shulman, and E. R. Keislar (Eds.), *Learning by discovery: a critical appraisal.* Chicago: Rand McNally, 1966. Pp. 101–113. (e)

Bruner, J. S., and Kenney, H. J. Representation and mathematics learning. *Monogr. soc. res. Child Dev.*, 1965, **30**, 50–59.

Bruner, J. S., and Kenney, H. J. On multiple ordering. In J. S. Bruner, R. R. Olver, and P. M. Greenfield, *Studies in cognitive growth.* New York: Wiley, 1966. (a)

Bruner, J. S., and Kenney, H. J. On relational concepts. In J. S. Bruner, R. R. Olver, and P. M. Greenfield, *Studies in cognitive growth.* New York: Wiley, 1966. (b)

Bruner, J. S., Olver, R. R., and Greenfield, P. M. *Studies in cognitive growth.* New York: Wiley, 1966.

Cahen, L. S. The national longitudinal study of mathematical abilities. *Sci. educ. News.* Miscellaneous Publication No. 63-4. Washington, D.C.: American Association for the Advancement of Science, 1963, 5–6.

Cantor, G. N. Responses of infants and children to complex and novel stimulation. In L. P. Lipsitt and C. C. Spiker (Eds.), *Advances in child development and behavior.* Vol. I. New York: Academic Press, 1963.

Cantor, G. N., Cantor, J. H., and Ditrichs, R. Observing behavior in preschool children as a function of stimulus complexity. *Child Dev.*, 1963, **34**, 683–689.

Cantor, J. H. Transfer of stimulus pretraining to motor paired-associate and discrimination learning tasks. In L. P. Lipsitt and C. C. Spiker (Eds.), *Advances in child development and behavior.* Vol. II. New York: Academic Press, 1965.

Cazden, C. B. Environmental assistance to the child's acquisition of grammar. Unpublished doctoral dissertation, Harvard University, 1965.

Cazden, C. B. The role of parent speech in the acquisition of grammar. Project Literacy Reports No. 8, Ithaca, N.Y.: Cornell University, 1967.

Chall, J. S., *Learning to read: the great debate.* New York: McGraw-Hill, 1967.

Chomsky, N. *Syntactic structures.* The Hague: Mouton, 1957.

Chomsky, N. *Aspects of the theory of syntax.* Cambridge, Mass.: MIT Press, 1965.

Clark, A. D., and Richards, C. J. Auditory discrimination among economically disadvantaged and nondisadvantaged preschool children. *Exceptional Children,* 1966, **33**, 259–262.

Cofer, C. N. (Ed.) *Verbal learning and verbal behavior.* New York: McGraw-Hill, 1961.

Cofer, C. N., and Musgrave, B. (Eds.) *Verbal behavior and learning: problems and processes.* New York: McGraw-Hill, 1963.

Covington, M. V. Productive thinking and a cognitive curriculum. Invited paper presented at Symposium *Studies of the Inquiry Process: Problems of Theory, Description and Teaching.* American Psychological Association Convention, Washington, D.C., 1967. (a)

Covington, M. V. Stimulus discrimination as a function of social-class membership. *Child Dev.,* 1967, **38,** 607–613. (b)

Covington, M. V. Promoting creative thinking in the classroom. In H. J. Klausmeier and G. T. O'Hearn (Eds.), *Research and development toward the improvement of education.* Madison: Dembar Educational Research Services, 1968.

Covington, M. V., and Crutchfield, R. S. Facilitation of creative problem solving. *Programmed Instruction,* 1965, **4,** 3.

Cronbach, L. J. Issues current in educational psychology. *Monogr. soc. res. Child Dev.,* 1965, **30,** 109–125.

Cronbach, L. J. The logic of experiments on discovery. In L. S. Shulman and E. R. Keislar (Eds.), *Learning by discovery: a critical appraisal.* Chicago: Rand McNally, 1966.

Crutchfield, R. S., and Covington, M. V. Programed instruction and creativity. *Programmed Instruction,* 1965, **4,** 1.

Davies, C. M. Development of the probability concept in children. *Child Dev.,* 1965, **36,** 779–788.

Davis, R. B. The evolution of school mathematics. *J. res. Sci. Teach.,* 1963, **1,** 260–264.

Davis, R. B. Discovery in the teaching of mathematics. In L. S. Shulman and E. R. Keislar (Eds.), *Learning by discovery: a critical appraisal.* Chicago: Rand McNally, 1966.

Deans, E. Elementary school mathematics: new directions. U. S. Department of Health, Education, and Welfare, Office of Education, Bulletin No. 13. Washington, D.C.: Government Printing Office, 1963.

Department of the Army, Office of The Surgeon General: Supplement to *Health of the Army,* March, 1967.

Deutsch, C. P. Auditory discrimination and learning: social factors. In M. Deutsch, and Associates. *The disadvantaged child.* New York: Basic Books, 1967. (a)

Deutsch, C. P. The development of auditory discrimination: relationship to reading proficiency and to social class. Project Literacy Reports No. 8, Ithaca, N.Y.: Cornell University, 1967. (b)

Deutsch, M. The disadvantaged child and the learning process. In A. H. Passow, *Education in depressed areas.* New York: Teachers College, 1963. Pp. 163–179.

Deutsch, M. and Associates. *The disadvantaged child.* New York: Basic Books, 1967.

Deutsch, M., Levinson, A., Brown, B. R., and Peisach, E. C. Communication of information in the elementary school classroom. In M. Deutsch and Associates. *The disadvantaged child.* New York: Basic Books, 1967.

Dewey, J. *Democracy and education.* New York: Macmillan, 1916.

Downing, J. Recent developments in i.t.a. *Calif. English J.,* 1967, **3,** 66–73.

Eisner, E. W. Research in creativity: some findings and conceptions. *Childhood Educ.,* 1963, **39,** 371–375.

Elkind, D. How children learn to read. *Science,* 1965, **149,** 1325.

Elkind, D. Piaget and Montessori. *Harv. educ. Rev.,* 1967, **37,** 535–545. (a)

Elkind, D. Piaget's conservation problems. *Child Dev.,* 1967, **38,** 15–28. (b)

Elkind, D., Horn, J., and Schneider, G. Modified word recognition, reading achievement and perceptual de-centration. *J. genet. Psychol.,* 1965, **107,** 235–252.

Elkind, D., Larson, M., and Van Doorninck, W. Perceptual decentration learning and performance in slow and average readers. *J. educ. Psychol.,* 1965, **56,** 50–56.

Ervin, S. M., and Miller, W. R. Language development. *Yearb. nat. Soc. Stud. Educ.*, 1963, **62**, 108–143.

Ervin-Tripp, S. M., and Slobin, D. I. Psycholinguistics. *Ann. Rev. Psychol.*, 1966, **17**, 435–474.

Fantz, R. L. The origin of form perception. *Sci. Am.*, 1961, **204**, 66–72.

Fisch, R. I., and McNamara, H. J. Conditioning of attention as a factor in perceptual learning. *Percept. Mot. Skills*, 1963, **17**, 891–907.

Flavell, J. H. *The developmental psychology of Jean Piaget.* Princeton, N.J.: Van Nostrand, 1963.

Furth, H. G. Research with the deaf: implications for language and cognition. *Psychol. Bull.*, 1964, **62**, 145–164.

Gagné, R. M. Learning and proficiency in mathematics. *Math. Teacher*, 1963, **56**, 620–626.

Gagné, R. M. *The conditions of learning.* New York: Holt, Rinehart & Winston, 1965. (a)

Gagné, R. M. The analysis of instructional objectives for the design of instruction. In R. Glaser (Ed.), *Teaching machines and programed learning II: data and direction.* Washington, D.C.: National Education Association, 1965. Pp. 21–65. (b)

Gagné, R. M. Educational objectives and human performance. In J. D. Krumboltz (Ed.), *Learning and the educational process.* Chicago: Rand McNally, 1965. Pp. 1–24. (c)

Gagné, R. M., and Staff, Univ. of Md. Math. Project. Some factors in learning non-metric geometry. *Monogr. soc. res. Child Dev.*, 1965, **30**, 42–49. (d)

Gagné, R. M. Learning and education. A contribution to the research project "Resources for learning," conducted by the Nuffield Foundation, September 15, 1966. (a)

Gagné, R. M. Varieties of learning and the issue of discovery. In L. S. Shulman and E. R. Keislar (Eds.), *Learning by discovery: a critical appraisal.* Chicago: Rand McNally, 1966. (b)

Gagné, R. M. The learning of principles. In H. J. Klausmeier (Ed.), *Conceptual learning.* New York: Academic Press, 1966. Pp. 81–95. (c)

Gagné, R. M. Curriculum research and the promotion of learning. Invited address to the 50th Annual Meeting, American Educational Research Association, Chicago, February 18, 1966. (d)

Gagné, R. M. Instruction and the conditions of learning. In L. Siegel (Ed.), *Instruction: some contemporary viewpoints.* San Francisco: Chandler, 1967.

Gagné, R. M. Contributions of learning to human development. *Psychol. Rev.*, 1968, **75**, 177–191.

Gagné, R. M., and Bassler, O. C. A study of retention of some topics of elementary non-metric geometry. *J. educ. Psychol.*, 1963, **54**, 123–131.

Gagné, R. M., and Brown, L. T. Some factors in the programming of conceptual learning. *J. exp. Psychol.*, 1961, **62**, 313–321.

Gagné, R. M., Mayor, J. R., Garstens, H. L., and Paradise, N. E. Factors in acquiring knowledge of a mathematical task. *Psychol. Monogr.*, 1962, **76**, No. 7, (Whole No. 526).

Gagné, R. M., and Paradise, N. E. Abilities and learning sets in knowledge acquisition. *Psychol. Monogr.*, 1961, **75**, No. 14 (Whole No. 518).

Getzels, J. W., and Jackson, P. W. The meaning of giftedness—an examination of an expanding concept. *Phi Delta Kappan*, 1958, **40**, 75–77.

Getzels, J. W., and Jackson, P. W. *Creativity and intelligence.* New York: Wiley, 1962.

Gibson, E. J. Learning to read. *Science*, 1965, **148**, 1066–1072. (a)

Gibson, E. J. Experiments on four aspects of reading skill and its attainment. Project Literary Reports No. 5, Ithaca, N.Y.: Cornell University, 1965. (b)

Gibson, E. J. Perceptual learning in educational situations. In R. M. Gagné, and W. J. Gephart, *Learning research and school subjects.* Eighth annual Phi Delta Kappa symposium on Educational Research. Itasca, Ill.: F. E. Peacock, in press.

Gibson, E. J., Farber, J., and Shepela, S. Test of a learning set procedure for the abstraction of spelling patterns. Project Literacy Reports No. 8. Ithaca, N.Y.: Cornell University, 1967.

Gibson, E. J., Osser, H., and Pick, A. D. A study in the development of grapheme-phoneme correspondences. *J. verb. Learn. verb. Behav.,* 1963, **2**, 142–146.

Gibson, E. J., Pick, A. D., Osser, H., and Hammond, M. The role of grapheme-phoneme correspondence in the perception of words. *Am. J. Psychol.,* 1962, **75**, 554–570.

Gibson, E. J., Shurcliff, A., and Yonas, A. The role of pronounceability in perception of pseudo-words by hearing and deaf subjects. Project Literacy Reports No. 7, Ithaca, N.Y., Cornell University, 1966.

Gibson, J. J., Kennedy, J. M., and Toleno, T. L. A study of the stick-in-water illusion with children. Project Literacy Reports No. 8. Ithaca, N.Y.: Cornell University, 1967.

Goss, A. E., and Nodine, C. F. *Paired-associates learning: the role of meaningfulness, similarity, and familiarization.* New York: Academic Press, 1965.

Gray, S. *Before first grade.* New York: Teachers College Press, 1966.

Guilford, J. P. Creativity. *Am. Psychol.,* 1950, **9**, 444–454.

Guilford, J. P. Three faces of intellect. *Am. Psychol.,* 1959, **14**, 469–479.

Guilford, J. P. *The nature of human intelligence.* New York: McGraw-Hill, 1967.

Hagen, J. W. The effect of distraction on selective attention. *Child Dev.,* 1967, **38**, 685–694.

Hawkins, D. Learning the unteachable. In L. S. Shulman and E. R. Keislar (Eds.), *Learning by discovery: a critical appraisal.* Chicago: Rand McNally, 1966.

Hershenson, M. Development of the perception of form. *Psychol. Bull.,* 1967, **67**, 326–336.

Hill, S. A study of the logical abilities of children. Unpublished doctoral dissertation, Stanford University, 1961.

Hirsch, J. Behavior-genetic, or "experimental," analysis: the challenge of science versus the lure of technology. *Am. Psychol.,* 1967, **22**, 118–130.

Hockett, C. F. Relationships between written and spoken English. Project Literacy Reports No. 5, Ithaca, N.Y.: Cornell University, 1965.

Hohn, F. E. Teaching creativity in mathematics. *Arith. Teacher,* 1961, **8**, 102–106.

Horton, D. L., and Wiley, R. E. Mediated association: facilitation and interference. *J. exp. Psychol.,* 1967, **73**, 636–638.

House, B. J., and Zeaman, D. Reversal and nonreversal shifts in discrimination learning of retardates. *J. exp. Psychol.,* 1962, **63**, 444–451.

House, B. J., and Zeaman, D. Miniature experiments in the discrimination learning of retardates. In L. P. Lipsitt and C. C. Spiker (Eds.), *Advances in child development and behavior.* Vol. I. New York: Academic Press, 1963.

Hunt, J. McV. *Intelligence and experience.* New York: Ronald Press, 1961.

Hurd, P. D., and Rowe, M. B. Science in the secondary school. *Rev. educ. Res.,* 1964, **34**, 286–297.

Jakobson, R., and Halle, M. *Fundamentals of language.* The Hague: Mouton, 1956.

Jensen, A. R. Learning ability, intelligence, and educability. In V. Allen (Ed.), *Psychological aspects of poverty.* New York: Free Press, 1969.

Jensen, A. R. Social class and verbal learning. In M. Deutsch, A. R. Jensen, and

I. Katz (Eds.), *Social-class, race, and psychological development.* New York: Holt, Rinehart, & Winston, 1968.

Jensen, A. R., and Rohwer, W. D., Jr. Syntactical mediation of serial and paired-associate learning as a function of age. *Child Dev.,* 1965, **36,** 601–608.

Jensen, A. R., and Rohwer, W. D., Jr. An experimental analysis of learning abilities in culturally disadvantaged children. U. S. Office of Economic Opportunity. Contract No. 2404, 1966.

Joyce, B., and Joyce, E. Studying issues in mathematics instruction. *Arith. Teacher,* 1964, **11,** 303–307.

Kagan, J. Impulsive and reflective children: significance of conceptual tempo. In J. D. Krumboltz (Ed.), *Learning and the educational process.* Chicago: Rand McNally, 1965.

Kagan, J. Learning, attention and the issue of discovery. In L. S. Shulman and E. R. Keislar (Eds.), *Learning by discovery: a critical appraisal.* Chicago: Rand McNally, 1966.

Kagan, J., Pearson, L., and Welch, L. Modifiability of an impulsive tempo. *J. educ. Psychol.,* 1966, **57,** 359–365.

Katz, P. A. Verbal discrimination performance of disadvantaged children: stimulus and subject variables. *Child Dev.,* 1967, **38,** 233–242.

Katz, P. A., and Deutsch, M. The relationship of auditory and visual functioning to reading achievement in disadvantaged children. In M. Deutsch and Associates. *The disadvantaged child.* New York: Basic Books, 1967.

Kendler, H. H., and D'Amato, M. F. A comparison of reversal shifts and non-reversal shifts in human concept formation behavior. *J. exp. Psychol.,* 1955, **49,** 165–174.

Kendler, H. H., and Mayzner, M. S., Jr. Reversal and nonreversal shifts in card-sorting tests with two or four sorting categories. *J. exp. Psychol.,* 1956, **51,** 244–248.

Kendler, H. H. and Kendler, T. S. Effect of verbalization on reversal shifts in children. *Science,* 1961, **134,** 1619–1620.

Kendler, H. H., and Kendler, T. S. Vertical and horizontal processes in problem solving. *Psychol. Rev.,* 1962, **69,** 1–16.

Kendler, T. S. Learning, development, and thinking. *Ann. N.Y. Acad. Sci.,* 1960, **91,** 52–65.

Kendler, T. S. Development of mediating responses in children. In J. C. Wright and J. Kagan (Eds.), Basic cognitive processes in children, *Monogr. soc. res. Child Dev.,* 1963, **28,** No. 2. (Serial No. 86).

Kendler, T. S., and Kendler, H. H. Reversal and nonreversal shifts in kindergarten children. *J. exp. Psychol.,* 1959, **58,** 56–60.

Kendler, T. S., Kendler, H. H., and Wells, D. Reversal and nonreversal shifts in nursery school children. *J. comp. physiol. Psychol.,* 1960, **53,** 83–88.

Kerfoot, J. F. Reading in the elementary school. *Rev. educ. Res.,* 1967, **37,** 120–133.

Kersh, B. Y. The adequacy of "meaning" as an explanation for superiority of learning by independent discovery. *J. educ. Psychol.,* 1958, **49,** 282–292.

Labov, W., and Cohen, P. Systematic relations of standard and non-standard rules in the grammars of Negro speakers. Project Literacy Reports No. 8. Ithaca, N.Y.: Cornell University, 1967.

Lange, P. C. (Ed.) *Programed Instruction.* Sixty-sixth Yearbook of Nat'l Soc. Study Educ., Chicago: University of Chicago Press, 1967.

Leiderman, G. F. Mathematics and science programs for the elementary school years. *Rev. educ. Res.,* 1965, **35,** 154–162.

Lenrow, P. B. Preschool facilitation of convergent and divergent cognitive modes:

What price acceleration? Paper presented at annual meeting of the Society for Research in Child Development, 1967.

Lesser, G. S., Fifer, G., and Clark, D. H. Mental abilities of children from different social-class and cultural groups. *Monogr. soc. res. Child Dev.*, 1965, **30** (No. 4).

Levin, H. Studies of various aspects of reading. Project Literacy Reports No. 5, Ithaca, N.Y.: Cornell University, 1965.

Levin, H., and Turner, E. A. Sentence structure and the eye-voice span. Project Literacy Reports No. 7, Ithaca, N.Y.: Cornell University, 1966.

Levin, J. R., and Rohwer, W. D., Jr. Verbal organization and the facilitation of serial learning. *J. educ. Psychol.*, 1968, **59**, 186–190.

Liberman, A. M. Some results of research on speech perception. *J. Acoust. Soc. Am.*, 1957, **29**, 117–123.

Loban, W. Language proficiency and school learning. In J. D. Krumboltz (Ed.), *Learning and the educational process*. Chicago: Rand McNally, 1965.

Lovaas, O. I., Freitag, G., Gold, V. J., and Kassorla, I. C. Experimental studies in childhood schizophrenia: analysis of self-destructive behavior. *J. exp. child Psychol.*, 1965, **2**, 67–84.

Lovaas, O. I., Schaeffer, B., and Simmons, J. Q. Building social behavior in autistic children by use of electric shock. *J. exp. Res. Pers.*, 1965, **1**, 99–109.

Lumsdaine, A. A. Educational technology, programmed learning, and instructional science. *Yearb. nat. Soc. Stud. Educ.*, 1964, 371–401.

Luria, A. R. *The role of speech in the regulation of normal and abnormal behavior*. New York: Liveright Publ. Co., 1961.

McCarthy, J. J., and Kirk, S. A. The Illinois test of psycholinguistic abilities: an approach to differential diagnosis. *Am. J. ment. Defic.*, 1961, **66**, 399–412.

McCarthy, J. J., and Kirk, S. A. *Illinois test of psycholinguistic abilities*. Urbana: University of Illinois Press, 1963.

McNeill, D. Developmental psycholinguistics. In F. Smith and G. A. Miller, *The genisis of language*. Cambridge, Mass.: The M.I.T. Press, 1966.

Maccoby, E. E., and Hagen, J. W. Effects of distraction upon central versus incidental recall: developmental trends. *J. exp. child Psychol.*, 1965, **2**, 280–289.

MacKinnon, D. W. The highly effective individual. *Teach. Coll. Rec.*, 1960, **61**, 367–378.

Maltzman, I. Individual differences in "attention": the orienting reflex. In R. M. Gagné, *Learning and individual differences*. Columbus, O.: Merrill, 1967.

Marchbanks, G., and Levin, H. Cues by which children recognize words. *J. educ. Psychol.*, 1965, **56**, 57–61.

Melton, A. W. The science of learning and the technology of educational methods. *Harv. educ. Rev.*, 1959, **29**, 96–106.

Melton, A. W. (Ed.) *Categories of human learning*. New York: Academic Press, 1964.

Milgram, N. A. Retention of mediation set in paired-associate learning of normal children and retardates. *J. exp. child Psychol.*, 1967, **5**, 341–349.

Morrisett, L. N., and Vinsonhaler, J. (Eds.) Mathematical learning. *Monogr. soc. res. Child Dev.*, 1965, **30** (No. 1).

Mussen, P. H. Discussion on issues current in educational psychology. *Monogr. soc. res. Child Dev.*, 1965, **30**, 126–129.

Osgood, C. E. On understanding and creating sentences. *Am. Psychol.*, 1963, **18**, 735–751.

Page, D. A. *Maneuvers on lattices: an example of intermediate invention*. Watertown, Mass.: Educ. Services, 1962.

Piaget, J. *The origins of intelligence in children*. (2nd ed.) New York: International Universities Press, 1952.

Rapier, J. L. The learning abilities of normal and retarded children as a function of social class. *J. educ. Psychol.*, 1968, **59**, 102–110.

Razran, G. H. S. The observable unconscious and the inferable conscious in current Soviet psychology: interoceptive conditioning, semantic conditioning, and the orienting reflex. *Psychol. Rev.*, 1961, **54**, 81–147.

Reese, H. W. Level of stimulus pretraining and paired-associate learning. *Child Dev.*, 1961, **32**, 89–94.

Reese, H. W. Imagery in paired-associate learning in children. *J. exp. child Psychol.*, 1965, **2**, 290–296.

Rohwer, W. D., Jr. Social class differences in the role of linguistic structures in paired-associate learning. Final report of U. S. Office of Education Project No. 5-0605, Contract No. OE-6-10-273, 1967.

Rohwer, W. D., Jr. Socioeconomic status, intelligence and learning proficiency in children. Paper presented at the American Psychological Association Convention, San Francisco, 1968.

Rohwer, W. D., J. Mental mnemonics in early learning. *Teach. Coll. Rec.*, 1968, **70**, 214–226.

Rohwer, W. D., Jr., and Lynch, S. Retardation, school strata and learning proficiency. *Am. J. ment. Defic.*, 1968, **73**, 91–96.

Rohwer, W. D., Jr., Lynch, S., Levin, J. R., and Suzuki, N. Pictorial and verbal factors in the efficient learning of paired associates. *J. educ. Psychol.*, 1967, **58**, 278–284.

Rohwer, W. D., Jr., Lynch, S., Levin, J. R. and Suzuki, N. Grade level, school strata and learning efficiency. *J. educ. Psychol.*, 1968, **59**, 26–31.

Rohwer, W. D., Jr., Lynch, S., Suzuki, N., and Levin, J. R. Verbal and pictorial facilitation in paired-associate learning. *J. exp. child Psychol.*, 1967, **5**, 294–302.

Rothkopf, E. Z. Some theoretical and experimental approaches to problems in written instruction. In J. D. Krumboltz (Ed.), *Learning and the educational process*. Chicago: Rand McNally, 1965. Pp. 193–221.

Rothkopf, E. Z. Learning from written materials: an exploration of the control of inspection behavior by test-like events. *Am. educ. Res. J.*, 1966, **3**, 241–249.

Rothkopf, E. Z., and Bisbicos, E. E. Selective facilitative effects of interspersed questions on learning from written materials. *J. educ. Psychol.*, 1967, **58**, 56–61.

Rothkopf, E. Z., and Coke, E. U. Repetition interval and rehearsal method in learning equivalences from written sentences. *J. verb. Learn. verb. Behav.*, 1963, **2**, 406–416.

Rothkopf, E. Z., and Coke, E. U. Variations in phrasing, repetition interval, and the recall of sentence material. *J. verb. Learn. verb. Behav.*, 1966, **5**, 86–91.

Samuels, S. J., and Jeffrey, W. E. Discriminability of words, and letter cues used in learning to read. *J. educ. Psychol.*, 1966, **57**, 337–340.

Semler, I. J., and Iscoe, I. Comparative and developmental study of the learning abilities of Negro and white children under four conditions. *J. educ. Psychol.*, 1963, **54**, 38–54.

Shulman, L. S., and Keislar, E. R. (Eds.) *Learning by discovery: a critical appraisal*. Chicago: Rand McNally, 1966.

Silberman, H. F. Empirical development of a beginning reading skill. Project Literacy Reports No. 4, Ithaca, N.Y.: Cornell University, 1964.

Skinner, B. F. The science of learning and the art of teaching. *Harv. educ. Rev.*, 1954, **24**, 86–97.

Skinner, B. F. Teaching machines. *Science*, 1958, **128**, 969–977.

Slobin, D. I. Grammatical transformations and sentence comprehension in childhood and adulthood. *J. verb. Learn. verb. Behav.*, 1966, **5**, 219–227.

Smedslund, J. The acquisition of conservation of substance and weight in children: IV, Attempt at extinction of the visual components of the weight concept. *Scand. J. Psychol.*, 1961, **2**, 153–155. (a)

Smedslund, J. The acquisition of conservation of substance and weight in children: V, Practice in conflict situations without external reinforcement. *Scand. J. Psychol.*, 1961, **2**, 156–160. (b)

Smedslund, J. The acquisition of conservation of substance and weight in children: VII, Conservation of discontinuous quantity and the operations of adding and taking away. *Scand. J. Psychol.*, 1962, **3**, 69–77.

Smith, S. L., and Goss, A. E. The role of the acquired distinctiveness of cues in the acquisition of a motor skill in children. *J. genet. Psychol.*, 1955, **87**, 11–24.

Spiker, C. C. Experiments with children on the hypotheses of acquired distinctiveness and equivalence of cues. *Child Dev.*, 1956, **27**, 253–263.

Spitz, H. H., and Hoats, D. L. Experiments on perceptual curiosity behavior in mental retardates. Final report, NIMH Grant M-4533, Johnstone Training and Research Center, 1961.

Staats, A. W., and Butterfield, W. H. Treatment of nonreading in a culturally deprived juvenile delinquent: an application of reinforcement principles. *Child Dev.*, 1965, **36**, 925–942.

Stephens, J. M. *The process of schooling: a psychological examination.* New York: Holt, Rinehart, & Winston, 1967.

Stern, C., and Rabbitt, P. Differences in auditory-discrimination ability of young children as a function of socioeconomic status. Paper presented at the California Educational Research Association, Palo Alto, 1966.

Stevenson, H. W., Iscoe, I., and McConnell, C. A developmental study of transposition. *J. exp. Psychol.*, 1955, **49**, 278–280.

Stodolsky, S. S., and Lesser, G. Learning patterns in the disadvantaged. *Harv. educ. Rev.*, 1967, **37**, 546–593.

Suchman, J. R. Inquiry training in the elementary school. *Science Teacher*, 1960, **27**, 42–47.

Suchman, J. R. Inquiry training: building skills for autonomous discovery. *Merrill-Palmer Q. Behav. Dev.*, 1961, **7**, 147–169.

Suppes, P. The ability of elementary-school children to learn the new mathematics. *Theory into Practice*, 1964, **3**, 57–61.

Suppes, P. On the behavioral foundations of mathematical concepts. *Monogr. soc. res. Child Dev.*, 1965, **30**, 60–95.

Suppes, P. and Ginsberg, R. Experimental studies of mathematical concept formation in young children. *Sci. Educ.*, 1962, **46**, 230–240.

Suppes, P., and Hill, S. Set theory in the primary grades. *New York State Math. Teachers J.*, 1963, **13**, 46-53.

Suppes, P., and McKnight, B. A. Sets and numbers in grade one, 1959–60. *Arith. Teacher*, 1961, **8**, 287–290.

Temp, G., and Anderson, S. B. Pupils and programs. Section three of final report by *Educ. Test. Serv.*, Contract No. OEO-1359, 1966.

Thorndike, E. L. *Human learning.* New York: Appleton-Century-Crofts, 1931.

Thorndike, R. L. The measurement of creativity. *Teach. Col. Rec.*, 1963, **64**, 422–424.

Torrance, E. P. Explorations in creative thinking. *Educ.*, 1960, **81**, 216–220.

Torrance, E. P. *Guiding creative talent.* Englewood Cliffs, N.J.: Prentice-Hall, 1962.

Torrance, E. P. *Rewarding creative behavior.* Englewood Cliffs, N.J.: Prentice-Hall, 1965.

Venezky, R. L., and Weir, R. H. A study of selected spelling-to-sound correspondence patterns. Cooperative Research Project No. 3090, Stanford University, 1966.

Wallach, L., Wall, A. J., and Anderson, L. Number conservation: the roles of reversibility, addition-subtraction, and misleading perceptual cues. *Child Dev.,* 1967, **38**, 425–442.

Wallach, M. A. Research on children's thinking. The sixty-second *Yearbook nat. Soc. Stud. Educ.* 1963, **62**, 236–276.

Weaver, J. F. Student achievement in SMSG classes, Grades 4 and 5. *Sch. Math. Study Group Newsletter* 15, 1963, **15**, 3–8.

Weber, R. M. Grammaticality and the self-correction of reading errors. Project Literacy Reports No. 8, Ithaca, N.Y.: Cornell University, 1967. Pp. 53–59.

Weir, M. W., and Stevenson, H. W. The effect of verbalization in children's learning as a function of chronological age. *Child Dev.,* 1959, **30**, 143–149.

White, S. H. Evidence for a hierarchical arrangement of learning processes. In L. P. Lipsitt and C. C. Spiker (Eds.), *Advances in child development and behavior.* Vol. 2. New York: Academic Press, 1965.

White, S. H., and Plum, G. E. Eye movement photography during children's discrimination learning. *J. exp. child. Psychol.,* 1964, **1**, 327–338.

Williams, J. P. Reading research and instruction. *Rev. educ. Res.,* 1965, **35**, 147–153.

Williams, R. H., and Stewart, E. E. Some characteristics of children in the Head Start Program. Section one of final report by *Educ. Test. Serv.,* Contract No. OEO-1359, 1966.

Wittrock, M. C. The learning by discovery hypothesis. In L. S. Shulman and E. R. Keislar (Eds.), *Learning by discovery: a critical appraisal.* Chicago: Rand McNally, 1966.

Wohlwill, J. F. A study of the development of the number concept by Scalogram analysis. *J. genet. Psychol.,* 1960, **97**, 345–377.

Wohlwill, J. F., and Lowe, R. C. An experimental analysis of the development of conservation of number. *Child Dev.,* 1962, **33**, 153–167.

Yonas, A., and Gibson, E. J. A developmental study of feature-processing strategies in letter discrimination. Project Literacy Reports No. 8, Ithaca, N.Y.: Cornell University, 1967.

Zeaman, D., and House, B. J. The relation of IQ and learning. In R. M. Gagné, *Learning and individual differences.* Columbus, O.: Merrill, 1967.

Name Index

928, 1442, 1451
Lovejoy, A. O., 449, 553
Loveland, M., 210, 280
Lovell, K., 958, 977, 991, 995, 997,
   1000, 1007, 1014, 1015, 1018,
   1022, 1027, 1034, 1038, 1051,
   1052, 1068, 1069, 1114, 1157
Lowe, M. J., 582, 642
Lowe, R. C., 1005, 1042, 1059,
   1436, 1454
Löwenfeld, B., 410
Lowrey, G. H., 196-198, 237, 281
Lowrey, L. G., 603, 645
Lu, E. G., 324, 410
Lu, T. W., 457, 560
Lubchenco, L. O., 332, 396
Lubker, B. J., 869, 870, 881, 928,
   935
Lucas, W., 538
Lucas, W. P., 348, 353, 410
Luce, R. D., 1154, 1158
Luchsinger, V. P., 582, 645
Ludwig, G. N., 241, 270
Lukoff, F., 1138, 1154
Lumsdaine, A. A., 408, 666, 695,
   1440, 1451
Lundy, R. M., 1316, 1361
Lunt, H., 1154
Lunzer, E., 1052, 1058
Lunzer, E. A., 958, 977, 991, 1006,
   1007, 1014, 1015, 1018, 1019,
   1034, 1035, 1037, 1038, 1052
Luppova, N. N., 319, 331, 332,
   370
Luppova, V. A., 855, 922
Lupton, A. A., 876, 931
Luria, A. R., 410, 659, 689, 690,
   695, 701, 812, 893, 928, 953,
   954, 976, 977, 979, 980, 1128,
   1157, 1423, 1424, 1426, 1451
Lush, J. L., 48, 73
Lustman, S. L., 292, 318, 321, 322,
   410, 425
Lykken, D. T., 73, 587, 625, 645
Lyman, F. L., 612, 645
Lynch, S., 908, 932, 933, 1435,
   1437, 1452
Lynip, A. W., 410
Lynn, R., 576, 645, 659, 690, 695
Lyons, H. A., 229, 270
Lyons, J., 1051, 1154, 1156, 1157
Lyons, K., 328, 371

Maas, H., 623, 645
Maddi, D. A., 1256, 1267
Maddi, S., 652
Maddi, S. R., 1256-1259, 1262,
   1267, 1268, 1353
Magee, H. E., 170, 256
Magendie, F., 518, 540, 553
Magnus, O., 246, 279
Magnus, R., 410, 460, 479, 524,
   525, 553
Magoun, W., 250, 270, 461, 546
Maher, B. A., 640, 1355
Mahler, M. S., 410
Mahon, R., 410

Mai, H., 245, 270
Maier, H. W., 298, 410
Maier, N. R. F., 940, 963, 964, 978,
   1243, 1267
Mailliot, L., 500, 553
Mainardi, D., 600, 645
Maire, F., 804, 840
Major, D. R., 410
Makkink, G. F., 29, 36
Makoski, E. J., 238, 239, 263
Malacarne, P., 74
Malakhovskaia, D. B., 410
Malan, A. F., 227, 270
Malapert, M., 410
Malebranche, 493
Mali, A., 190, 270
Mall, F. P., 495, 496, 504, 526,
   528, 530, 553
Maloney, J., 177, 178, 254
Malpighi, 460
Malrieu, P., 410
Malter, W. W., 592, 637
Maltzman, I., 666, 673, 695, 1240-
   1243, 1248, 1254, 1256, 1267,
   1421, 1422, 1451
Mandelbrot, B., 979
Mandell, S., 410
Mandler, G., 316, 335, 338, 402,
   658, 695, 1250, 1267, 1276,
   1303, 1359, 1360
Mandler, J. M., 658, 695, 1276,
   1360
Mangham, C. A., 585, 650
Mann, H., 501, 553
Mann, I., 346, 348, 349, 410
Mann, I. C., 530, 553
Manning, A., 56, 74
Mannix, J. B., 1038, 1052
Manolakes, G., 817, 839
Manosevitz, M., 55, 74
Manson, W. A., 187, 255
Marcel, M. P., 206, 270
Marchbanks, G., 1418, 1451
Marcus, C. C., 151
Marden, P. M., 410
Mares, P., 252, 266, 347, 396
Maresh, M. M., 209, 271
Margolis, F. L., 1190, 1209
Margoshes, A., 410
Marild, K., 190, 258
Marinello, M., 491, 544
Marinesco, G., 410, 411
Markowitz, H., 589, 651
Marks, A., 1219, 1268
Marks, J., 168, 170, 263
Marks, J. B., 1187, 1207
Marler, P., 1075, 1076, 1157
Marler, P. R., 536, 553, 594
Marquis, D. G., 677, 694, 952, 976
Marquis, D. P., 295, 296, 310, 316,
   322, 323, 332, 334, 338, 411,
   854, 929
Marr, J. H., 592, 645
Marsden, R. W., 350, 411
Marsh, G., 884, 889, 890, 929
Marsh, M. E., 232, 271, 416
Marsh, R. H., 482, 540

Marsh, R. W., 1235, 1268
Marshall, 99
Marshall, W. A., Dr., 148
Marston, L. R., 411
Martensson, L., 177, 271
Marthens, E. van, 1190, 1209
Marticornena, E., 187, 274
Martin, C. E., 585, 640
Martin, J. G., 908, 929
Marzolf, S. S., 997, 1049
Mason, M. F., 411, 501, 539
Mason, W. A., 596, 645
Massé, G., 291, 383
Massell, B. F., 209, 253
Mast, E. T., 411
Masuoka, J., 291, 376
Matalon, B., 715, 804, 805, 968,
   976, 1005, 1006, 1049, 1050,
   1052, 1054, 1301, 1361
Matarazzo, R. G., 303, 391, 1169,
   1206
Mateer, F., 323, 411, 659, 695,
   849, 929
Matheson, E., 960, 978
Matoth, Y., 173, 271
Matsaniotis, N., 179, 280
Matsuda, G., 173, 271
Matthews, S. A., 458, 554, 594,
   645
Mattingly, R. F., 206, 271
Maudry, M., 411
Maughan, G. B., 227, 280
Maupin, E. W., 1261, 1268
Maurer, K. M., 307, 411, 616, 640
Mautner, H., 411
Mavor, W. O., 127, 154
Mavrinskaya, L. F., 522, 554
Maxey, E. J., 1042, 1053
Maxwell, S. S., 524, 554
May, F. B., 1222, 1236, 1268,
   1269
Mayerhofer, A., 411
Mayor, J. R., 1405, 1448
Mays, W., 1004, 1044, 1054
Mayzner, M. S., Jr., 1434, 1450
MacAndrew, C., 1342, 1360
MacArthur, P., 229, 273
MacArthur, R. S., 1340, 1360
Maccoby, E., 22, 38, 298, 311,
   329, 430, 618, 649, 695
Maccoby, E. E., 675, 697, 821,
   832, 839, 910, 928, 1034, 1052,
   1292, 1295, 1300, 1303, 1316,
   1320, 1322, 1334, 1336, 1337,
   1344, 1356, 1360, 1423, 1451
MacCorquodale, K., 1348, 1360
MacDonald, J. W., 1061
MacDonald, S., 188, 262
MacDowell, C. G., 151
MacDowell, E. C., 151
Macfarlane, J., 1171, 1174, 1192,
   1207
Macfarlane, J. W., 308, 410
Machover, K., 806-808, 842, 846,
   1279, 1323, 1325, 1328, 1329,
   1360, 1365
Macintyre, M. N., 46, 74

Subject Index